TWENTY-SIXTH EDITION

KOVELS'
Antiques &
Collectibles
PRICE LIST

TWENTY-SIXTH EDITION

KOVELS'

Antiques &
Collectibles
PRICE LIST

For the 1994 Market

ILLUSTRATED

CROWN TRADE PAPERBACKS   NEW YORK

Copyright © 1993 by Ralph and Terry Kovel
All rights reserved. No part of this book may be reproduced or transmitted
in any form or by any means, electronic or mechanical, including
photocopying, recording, or by any information storage and retrieval
system, without permission in writing from the publisher.
Published by Crown Publishers, Inc., 201 East 50th Street, New York,
New York 10022. Member of the Crown Publishing Group.
Random House, Inc. New York, Toronto, London, Sydney, Auckland
CROWN TRADE PAPERBACKS and colophon are trademarks of Crown Publishers, Inc.
Manufactured in the United States of America
Library of Congress Catalog Card Number: 83-643618

ISBN: 0-517-88065-2 (pbk.)
10 9 8 7 6 5 4 3 2 1
First Edition

This is a book for the average collector. We check prices all year, visit shops and sales, read our mail, and decide what antiques and collectibles are of most interest. We do not list the top of the market but concentrate on the average pieces in any category. We will often add one or two high-priced pieces in a category so you will realize that some of the rarities are quite valuable. For example, Ohr pottery can sell for $300 to $5,775. Although pieces of furniture, silver, Tiffany, or Art Pottery may sell for more than $50,000, we do not list those examples here. Most pieces we list are less than $10,000. The highest price in this book is $12,500 for a Seeburg Nickelodeon. The lowest price is $.05 for a milk-bottle cap. We even list the weird and wonderful, and this year you can find prices for a Dracula puzzle, Gene Autry galoshes, a belsnickle, and a bathtub. The book is changed slightly each year. Categories are added or omitted to make it easier for you to find your antiques. The book is kept about 800 pages long because it is written to go with you to sales. We try to have a balanced format—not too much glass, pottery, or collectibles, not too many items that sell for more than $5,000. The prices are *from* the American market *for* the American market. Few European sales are reported. We take the editorial privilege of not including any prices that seem to result from "auction fever." The computer-generated index is so complete it amazes us. Use it often. An internal alphabetical index is also included. For example, there is a category for "Celluloid." Most items will be found there, but if there is a toy made of celluloid, it will be listed under "Toy" and also indexed under "Celluloid." All pictures and prices are new every year, except pictures that are pattern examples shown in "Depression Glass" and "Pressed Glass." Pictured antiques are not museum pieces, but items offered for sale. The hints are set in easy-to-notice special type. Leaf through the book and learn how to wash porcelains, store textiles, guard against theft, and much more. Old Kovels' price books should be saved for future reference, tax, and appraisal information.

RECORD PRICES

Record prices still attract the interest of the newspapers and television news broadcasts, although prices do not always reflect the general market for antiques and collectibles. High prices for door handles or duck decoys seem to fascinate the general public, perhaps because each of us secretly hopes that one of grandmother's heirlooms will turn out to be a real treasure. Some unusual collectibles set records this year. One of the strangest seen in many years was the record price for a piece of cheese. A 200-year-old lump of

Tibetan cheese brought $1,523. The Stanley Plane No. 42, patented in 1870, sold for $6,820. A bronze door handle shaped like a female term mounted on a faun, with grapes and a lion mask, brought more than $63,000 at a London auction because it was made by a famous craftsman about 1581. A pocket mirror picturing a police officer, doctor, and bleeding victim was a give-away ad for the Standard Identification System. Made in the early 1900s, it sold this year for $5,940. A Dudley Do-Right metal lunch box with thermos brought $2,200. An Action Comics No. 1 featuring Superman brought $82,500. A 1930s baseball autographed by Josh Gibson of the Negro League's Pittsburgh Crawfords auctioned for $26,400. But a higher price, $363,000 was paid for Lou Gehrig's New York Yankees flannel road uniform worn in the 1927 World Series.

Toys continued to set record prices. The original Monopoly game, handmade by Charles Darrow about 1930, sold for $71,500. A 10¾-inch cast iron Dent Hardware cement mixer, made about 1920, sold for $47,300, and a 3¼-inch Dinky Toy black Triumph 1800 Saloon car sold in London for $9,000. Robots always interest collectors. Robby Space Patrol Robot, which had rubber arms and a clear plastic dome, was in mint condition with box, sold for $24,200. A Ferris Wheel penny toy—at today's prices a misnomer—brought $4,070. A paper and wood lithographed Santa Claus ladder toy made by Bliss, auctioned at $11,500. Top-priced dolls included a pair of 1899 Jumeau dolls dressed as African royalty, which sold at $115,000 for the man, $112,000 for the woman.

Highest priced furniture this year included an American Queen Anne 18th-century Philadelphia walnut marble-top table, for $462,000, a kas cupboard decorated by the Nase family for $132,000, a pair of 18th-century Chippendale-style mirrors for $611,500, and an Art Nouveau two-tier table by Hector Guimard for $187,000.

Pottery and porcelain records included a grotesque stoneware jug made about 1858, probably by the Remmey family of Philadelphia, for $411,800, a Dedham Volcanic glaze vase by Hugh Robertson for $45,100, and a 21-inch-high Kay Finch Stallion for $1,350.

A silver ship made about 1922 by Omar Ramsden set a record at $154,000. A rare George Washington Bicentennial box camera, one of two made in 1932, sold for $28,300, and a daguerreotype, the first portrait of Frederick Douglass dating from 1840, brought $20,000 with the leather case. Carousel figures set a number of records: Bruno, a dog by the Philadelphia Toboggan Company, was $174,900, a goat was $76,850, a Daniel Muller horse with roached mane was $79,500, and a Dentzel lion was $95,400.

Decoys continued to set records. A 110-year-old Canada goose carved by Nathan Cobb, Jr., brought $192,500, while a Canada goose by Charles Schoenheider, Sr., from the 1920s brought $99,000. A small leather-covered mallard's-head duck call made by Kinney and Harlow about 1900 auctioned at $11,000. Glass records this year include a Tiffany spiderweb lamp for

$770,000, and a John Degenhart window paperweight with the silhouettes of George and Martha Washington for $3,575.

Advertising items continue to be strong. A Hood's Sarsaparilla sign, 42 x 28½ inches, sold for $9,075; a Boschee's German Syrup, reverse-on-glass sign, 23½ x 29 inches, was $5,940, and a Hires Mettlach syrup dispenser was $28,050.

The prices in this book are reports of the general antiques market, not the record-setting examples. Each year, every price in the book is new. We do *not* estimate or "update" prices. Prices are the actual asking price, although the buyer may have negotiated to a lower figure. No price is an estimate. We do not ask dealers and writers to estimate prices. Experience has shown that a collector of one type of antique is prejudiced in favor of that item, and prices are usually high or low, but rarely a true report. If a price range is given, it is because at least two identical items were offered for sale at different times. The computer records prices and prints the high and low figures. Price ranges are found only in categories like "Pressed Glass," where identical items can be identified. Some prices in *Kovels' Antiques & Collectibles Price List* may seem high and some may seem low because of regional variations. But each price is one you could have paid for the object.

If you are selling your collection, do not expect to get retail value unless you are a dealer. Wholesale prices for antiques are from 20 to 50 percent less than retail. Remember, the antiques dealer must make a profit or go out of business.

ACKNOWLEDGMENTS

Special thanks should go to those who helped us with pictures and deeds: Alderfer Auction Company, Noel Barrett Antiques & Auctions, Ltd., Frank H. Boos Gallery, Butterfield & Butterfield Auctioneers & Appraisers, Christie's, Cincinnati Art Galleries, Collectors Auction Services, Chuck DeLuca of Maritime Antiques, Douglas Auctioneers, William Doyle Galleries, DuMouchelles Art Galleries Co., Dunning's Auction Service Inc., Dynamite Auctions, Robert C. Eldred Co. Inc., Garth's Auctions, Inc., Robert Gibbins, Robert H. Glass Auctioneers, Morton M. Goldberg Auction Galleries, Leslie Hindman Auctioneers, Michael Ivankovich Antiques, Inc., James D. Julia, Inc., LFK Art & Antiques, Joy Luke Auctions, Mapes Auctioneers & Appraisers, Martone's Gallery, Paul McInnis Inc., McMasters, Gary Metz's Muddy River Trading Co., Miller, Hamilton & Co., Neal Auction Company, Northeast Auctions, Richard Opfer Auctioneering, Inc., Phillips, David Rago, Harmer Rooke Galleries, Skinner, Inc., Sotheby's, Theriault's, Don Treadway Gallery, Inc., Weschler's, Willis Henry Auctions, and Woody Auction. Special help was given by Lee Markley and Pamela Curran.

To the others in the antiques trade who knowingly or unknowingly contributed prices to this book, we say "thank you!" We could not do it without you. Some of you are: Eloise W. Adams, Jack Adamson, Jon Alk, Loretta

Anderson, Norma Angelo, Animal Farm Antiques, Ann Marie's Antique Dolls, Antique Junction, Antique Stove Exchange, Archers Antiques, ARK Antiques, ARKIES, Jeff Baker, Barbara's Dolls, Harold Barker, R. E. Barnett, Frank R. Baron, Scott Benjamin, James L. Bensinger, Roslyn Berlin, Doris Bernard, Bernardine Biske, Block's Box, Roselyn A. Blum, Bobin's Antiques, Dick Bowman, Harrold Boyd, Joe Brisson, Shirley Brodoinski, Carolyn Brooks, William E. Brown, Samantha Burdick, Burnt Mills Antiques, Busby Land & Auction Co., Camera Snapper, Steven Carter, Charisma Antiques, Joan Chestern, Cobb's Doll Auctions, Collector Glass News Auction, Collector's Trading Service, Collector's Wedgwood, Conestoga Auction Company, Inc., Bob & Sallie Connelly, Greg Cooney, Chris & Linda Cooper, Scott Creswick, Anthony Cross, Crystal Reflections, Dancing Cat Antiques, Dee's Antiques, Lila DeLellis, Dial's Antiques, Betty Dierdorf, Dishes Delmar, Dobbin House Antiques, Donna Donnelly, Edward Dowling, Down Home Music, W. Fagan & Co., John Farley, Dave Fazzini, Lavon Fisher, Flo-Blue Shop, Dorothy Foden, David Garcelon, John Gascoyne, David C. Gaydos, Leigh Giarde, Ron Giese, Lynda Givens, R. S. Goldberg, Stan Good, Larry Gottheim, D. M. Govan, Grandma's Attic, Rachel Grimes, Jim Gross, Carl R. Gurley, Inc., Paul F. Hadley, Gloria Hall, Judy & Merrill Ham, L. Harbets, Ron & Donna Haring, Vicki Harman Antiques, Charles Hegedus, Hi-De-Ho Collectibles, Homestead Collectibles, Michael Hovenkamp, Jack & Scottie Imrie, Colleen Jaco, Marguerite Jiamachello, Terry Jones, Don Jordon, Ken Keki, Charlene Kelbley, Jim & Louis Kelsey, Harold Kervolin, Linda Ketterling, David Kingston, Rich Koller, Jame Koval, Mike Kranz, Carolyn Kriner, Ted Kromer, Jack Krumdick, Joanne Landry, Sue Langley, Nancy Leonard, Craig C. Leverenz, Mike Levy, Lewis/Welch Collectors Exchange, Jan Lindenberger, Carl Lobel, Shirlee Long, Howard Lowery, Robert Lynn, Mike & Jan Mansker, Marie-Louis Antiques, Michael Marin, Martin Auction Co., Michael Mastromonica, Matrix Quality Antique Dolls, May's Antiques, Don McBride, Donna McGilvrey, MCL Associates, Charles McSorley, Melton's Antiques, Marilyn Merrell, Shelby Messinger, Midwest Fair Auction, Mike's General Store, Mel Miller, W. R. Miller, Paul M. Mintz, Miscellaneous Man, Dorraine Modesett, Robert Morin, Dan & Sally Mosholder, Mouse Man Ink, Carole Murdock & Valerie Moody, Nana's Dolls, Nelson Inc. Rarities, Mike Neuendorf, Noah's Ark, Philip R. Norman, Ida A. Noser, Oak Tree Antiques, Old Friends Antiques, Old Mercantile Store, Old Storefront Antiques, Once Upon A Time, Ken Oppenlander, Rick Padron, Jean & Don Parrett, Howard Parzow, Paula's, Genevieve Pavlic, Jerry Pearson, Pennpacker-Andrews Auction Centre, Inc., Jim Pietryga, Pine Tree, Plantation Galleries, Political Americana II, Pook & Pook Inc., Betty Price, C. G. Rainey, Tom Ramsey, Anton Reiche, Mickey Reichel Auction Service, Remember When Auctions, Stewart Richardson, Jim & Jan Righeimer, John F. Rinaldi Nautical Antiques, Edward Rivera, RJG Antiques, Rick Ronczka, Roseville Pottery Mart, Nancy Ruepp, Chris Russell, Ted Salveson, Sanctified Cross-Eyed Bear Antiques, Norma Sanders, Mary Sathoff,

Roselle Scheleifman, Schiller Antiques, Ron Schwinnen, Bernard Scott, Beverly Segar, Seven Gables, Showcase Antique Center, Inc., Shuler-Duross, Smith House Toys, Bill Smith, Donna Kirsch Smith, Ruth Smith, Tom Smith, So Rare Galleries, Evan Sommerfeld, Stacy's Sebastian Auction, Steele Ent., Kenny Steenholdt, Stratford Auction Center, Donna Stultz, Sunshine Peddler, Mark Supnick, Suzy Doll House, Frank Sykes, Joseph Szabat, Jenny Tarrant, Team Antiques, Tesseract, Then & Now, Al Thompson, Robert Thompson, Norm & Jan Thran, Time Will Tell, R. Tinsley, Tools 'n Rules, Toy Scouts, Inc., Toy Tree, Trails West Trading Post, Gus & Marty Trowbridge, Billie Nelson Tyrell Dolls, Sondra Vaughn, Victorian House Antiques, Vintage Lill, Larry & Nancy Werner, Robert Wieland, Blanche Williams, Williston Auctions, Carolyn Winkler, R. A. Wool, D. D. Woollard, Jr., Yesterday, Once Again, Pat York, and Monty Young.

MORE ANTIQUE PRICE NEWS

Have you kept up with prices? They change! Last year a Robby Space Patrol Robot sold for $24,200, a Stanley Plane No. 42 was $6,820, and an Art Nouveau table sold for $187,000. How did the owners know these collectibles had such a special value? Prices change with discoveries, auction records, even historic events. Every entry and every picture in this book is new and current, thanks to modern computer technology, making this book a handy overall price guide. But you also need current news about collecting.

Books on your shelf get older each month, and prices do change. Important sales produce new record prices. Rarities are discovered. Fakes appear. You will want to keep up with developments from month to month rather than from year to year. *Kovels on Antiques and Collectibles*, a nationally distributed, illustrated newsletter, includes up-to-date information on the world of collectors. This monthly newsletter reports current prices, collecting trends, landmark auction results for all types of antiques and collectibles, and tax, estate, security, and other pertinent news for collectors.

Additional information and a free sample newsletter are available from the authors at P.O. Box 420420, Palm Coast, FL 32142.

HOW TO USE THIS BOOK

There are a few rules for using this book. Each listing is arranged in the following manner: CATEGORY (such as Pressed Glass or Furniture), OBJECT (such as vase), DESCRIPTION (as much information as possible about size, age, color, and pattern). Some types of glass are exceptions to this rule. These are listed CATEGORY, PATTERN, OBJECT, DESCRIPTION. All items are presumed to be in good condition and undamaged, unless otherwise noted.

Several special categories were formed to make the most sensible listing possible. For instance, "Tool" includes special equipment because the casual collector might not know the proper name for an "adze." Last year we reorganized the glass entries into these categories: "Glass-Art," "Glass-Contemporary," "Glass-Midcentury," and "Glass-Venetian." Major glass factories are still listed under the factory names, and well-known types of glass such as cut, pressed, Carnival, etc., can be found in their own sections. New categories include "barbed wire, ""bottle cap," "Bossons," "garden furnishings," and "plastic." The index can help you locate items.

Several idiosyncrasies of style appear because the book is printed by computer. Everything is listed according to the computer alphabetizing system. This means words such as "Mt." are alphabetized as "M-T," not as "M-O-U-N-T." All numerals fall before all letters, thus "2" comes before "A." A quick glance will make this clear, as it is consistent throughout the book.

We made several editorial decisions. A bowl is a "bowl" and not a "dish" unless it is a special dish, such as a pickle dish. A butter dish is a "butter." A salt dish is called a "salt" to differentiate it from a saltshaker. It is always "sugar and creamer," never "creamer and sugar." Where one dimension is given, it is the height, or if the object is round, the dimension is the diameter. The height of a picture is listed before the width. Glass is clear unless a color is indicated.

Every entry is listed alphabetically, but the problem of language remains. Some antiques terms, such as "Sheffield" or "snow baby," have two meanings. Be sure to read the paragraph headings to know the meaning used. All category headings are based on the language of the average person at an average show, and we use terms like "mud figures" even if not technically correct.

This book does not include price listings of fine art paintings, books, comic books, stamps, coins, and a few other special categories.

All pictures in *Kovels' Antiques & Collectibles Price List* are listed with the prices asked by the seller. "Illus" (illustrated nearby) is part of the description if a picture is shown.

There have been misinformed comments about how this book is written. We *do* use the computer. It alphabetizes, ranges prices, sets type, and does other time-consuming jobs. Because of the computer, the book can be produced quickly. The last entries are added in June, the book is available in October. This is six months earlier than would be possible any other way. But it is human help that finds prices and checks accuracy. We read everything at least twice, sometimes more. We edit from 100,000 entries to the 50,000 entries found here. We correct spelling, remove incorrect data, write category headings, and decide on new categories. We sometimes make errors. Information in the paragraphs is reviewed and updated each year.

Prices are reports from all parts of the United States and Canada (translated to U.S. dollars at the rate of $1.18 U.S. to $1 Canadian) between June 1992 and June 1993. A few prices are from auctions, most are from shops and shows. Every price is checked for accuracy, but we are not responsible for errors.

It is unprofessional for an appraiser to set a value for an unseen item. Because of this, we cannot answer your letters asking for specific price information. But please write if you have any requests for categories to be included in future editions or any corrections to information in the paragraphs.

When you see us at the shows, stop and say hello. Since our television show has been aired in all parts of the country, we find we can no longer be anonymous buyers. It may mean the dealers know us before we ask a price, but it has been wonderful to meet all of you. Don't be surprised if we ask for your suggestions for the next edition of *Kovels' Antiques & Collectibles Price List.* Or you can write us at P.O. Box 22200-K, Beachwood, OH 44122.

RALPH & TERRY KOVEL
Senior Members, American Society of Appraisers
July 1993

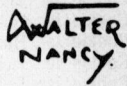

A. WALTER made pate-de-verre glass under contract at the Daum glassworks from 1908 to 1914. He started his own firm in Nancy, France, in 1919. Pieces made before 1914 are signed *Daum, Nancy* with a cross. After 1919 the signature is *A. Walter Nancy.*

Dish, Molded Green Bumble Bee On Rim, Triangular, Signed, 4 3/8 In.	1650.00
Inkwell, Slithering Lizard, Bee Amid Foliage, Berries On Lid, Signed, 4 In.	6050.00
Paperweight, Gray Mouse Nibbling On Nut, Grassy Mound, Signed, 3 3/4 In.	1760.00
Vase, Pillow, Molded Flowers With Leaves, Signed, 5 x 7 In.	950.00

ABC plates, or children's alphabet plates, were most popular from 1780 to 1860, but are still being made. The letters on the plate were meant as teaching aids for children learning to read. The plates were made of pottery, porcelain, metal, or glass. Mugs and other items were also made with alphabet decorations.

Bowl & Pitcher, Animal Figures Between Each Letter, Germany	95.00
Bowl, Kiddieware, Divided, Stangl	40.00
Bowl, Mickey Mouse Playing Piano, Disney, 1932	350.00
Child's Set, Bunnykins, 1980, 3 Piece	35.00
Creamer, Jumbo Playing Tennis, Germany	45.00
Dish, Baby's, Pink, Hot Water Warmed	10.00
Dish, Feeding, Jumbo Playing Tennis, Germany	85.00
Dish, Little Boy Blue	65.00
Eggcup, Old Mother Hubbard, Porcelain	15.00
Plate & Creamer, Cow Jumped Over The Moon, Luster Trim, Germany, 2 Piece	110.00
Plate, 3 Cats, Elderly Man & Child Leading Donkey Over Bridge, 7 1/2 In.	75.00
Plate, Alice In Wonderland	8.00
Plate, Boy & Girl With Dolls, Clowns & Dogs, Bavaria, 1920s	45.00
Plate, Chicks In Basket, Their First Day	55.00
Plate, Children Teaching Dog To Be Polite, Black Transfer, Staffordshire, 5 3/8 In.	45.00
Plate, Clock Face In Center, Glass	65.00
Plate, Clock, Porcelain, 7 In.	25.00
Plate, Clock, Scalloped, Amber Glass	42.50 To 65.00
Plate, Cock Robin, Tin	59.00
Plate, Constant Dripping Wears Away Stones, Little Strokes Fell Great Oaks	95.00
Plate, Couple Working In Fields, Black Transfer, Staffordshire, 5 1/8 In.	55.00
Plate, Donkey, Brown & White, 6 1/2 In.	65.00
Plate, Elephant Design Center, Pressed Glass	75.00
Plate, Fashionably Dressed Rabbits, Blue Transfer, Sign Language, Aynsley & Co.	170.00
Plate, Feeding, Little Bo Peep, Glass	35.00
Plate, Girl On Swing, Tin Lithograph, 3 1/2 In.	55.00
Plate, Going To Market, 3 1/2 In.	125.00
Plate, Grace Drayton, Buffalo Pottery	165.00
Plate, Hi Diddle Diddle, Tin	45.00
Plate, Humphrey's Clock, Ridgway	40.00
Plate, Jumping Through The Hoop, Brown Transfer, Oriental Boy	135.00
Plate, Kittens Playing With Basket of Wool, Tin, 4 1/4 In.	75.00
Plate, Leap Frog, Blue & White Transfer, Raised Letters	40.00
Plate, Mary & Lamb, Tin, 8 In.	85.00
Plate, Pride of The Barnyard, 7 In.	110.00
Plate, Rabbit, Frosted	90.00
Plate, Red Transfer, Children's Tea Party, Blue Rim, Staffordshire, 6 3/8 In.	165.00
Plate, Running Deer, Frosted, Iowa City	85.00
Plate, Whippet In Center, Germany, 5 1/4 In.	75.00
Plate, Who Killed Cock Robin, Tin, 8 In.	65.00 To 85.00
Plate, Wild Animals, Leopard, Staffordshire	75.00

ABINGDON POTTERY was established in 1934 by Raymond E. Bidwell as the Abingdon Sanitary Manufacturing Company. The company made art pottery and other wares. Sixteen varieties of cookie jars are known. The factory ceased production of art pottery in 1950.

Candleholder, Double, Pink	55.00

Cookie Jar, Clock	85.00 To 95.00
Cookie Jar, Clock, Green Trim	150.00
Cookie Jar, Hobby Horse	105.00 To 250.00
Cookie Jar, Humpty Dumpty	225.00 To 300.00
Cookie Jar, Jack–In–The–Box	155.00 To 295.00
Cookie Jar, Jack–O'–Lantern	265.00 To 450.00
Cookie Jar, Little Bopeep	450.00
Cookie Jar, Little Miss Muffet	295.00 To 375.00
Cookie Jar, Little Old Lady, Black	800.00
Cookie Jar, Little Old Lady, Turquoise	200.00
Cookie Jar, Mammy, With Flowers	130.00
Cookie Jar, Money Bag	40.00 To 80.00
Cookie Jar, Rocking Horse	135.00
Cookie Jar, Train	125.00
Cookie Jar, Windmill	175.00 To 225.00
Cookie Jar, Yogi Bear	385.00
Figurine, Goose, Blue, 5 In.	30.00
Flowerpot, Hand Painted	45.00
Match Holder, Pink Pigs	50.00
Planter, Cactus, Mexican Man, Siesta	55.00 To 75.00
Wall Pocket, Butterfly	65.00

ADAMS china was made by William Adams and Sons of Staffordshire, England. The firm was founded in 1769 and is still working. All types of tablewares and useful wares have been made through the years. Other pieces of Adams will be found listed under Flow Blue.

ADAMS
ENGLAND

Bowl, Tokyo, 6 x 3 1/2 In.	40.00
Bowl, Vegetable, Pink, Schenectady On The Mohawk River, 9 3/4 In.	325.00
Plate, Mitchell & Freeman's China & Glass Warehouse, 10 1/4 In.	850.00
Plate, Pink, View Near Conway, New Hampshire, 9 In.	95.00
Platter, Black, Falls of Niagara, 19 1/2 In.	1200.00
Platter, Military School, West Point, N.Y., Red, 17 1/2 In.	900.00

ADVERTISING containers and products sold in the old country store are now all collectibles. These stores, with the crackers in a barrel and a potbellied stove, are a symbol of an earlier, less hectic time. Listed here are many of the advertising items. Other similar pieces may be found under the product name, such as Planters Peanuts. We have tried to list items in the logical places, so large store fixtures will be found under the Architectural category, enameled tin dishes under Graniteware, paper items in the Paper category, etc. Store fixtures, cases, and other items that have no advertising as part of the decoration are listed in the Store category.

Ad, Ronald Reagan For Jeris Hair Tonic, Smiling Reagan, 5 x 14 In.	20.00
Ad, The Boston Sunday Globe, Cardboard, 1895, Fat Man, 7 1/2 In.	93.00
Album, Storyland Stamps, Horlick's Malted Milk, Complete, 1939	35.00
Ashtray, Armstrong Tires, Tire Shape	20.00
Ashtray, Boeing 247 Airline, 1935	150.00
Ashtray, Braniff Airlines, Metal, 4 x 2 1/2 In.	48.50
Ashtray, Cavalier Statue, G. Heileman Brewing Co., Pot Metal, 8 In.	75.00
Ashtray, Century of Progress, Firestone Tire	55.00
Ashtray, Ceresota Flour, 7 In.	6.00
Ashtray, Enamelware, Dow Ale & Stout	8.00
Ashtray, Firestone Tire, Amber Insert	8.00 To 15.00
Ashtray, Golden Rule Gas & Oil	15.00
Ashtray, Goodrich, Silvertone Glass	85.00
Ashtray, Griesdieck Bros. Beer	12.00
Ashtray, Howard Johnson's Motor Lodges	35.00
Ashtray, Kessler Whiskey, Milk Glass, Triangular	15.00
Ashtray, Levy's Real Jewish Rye Bread, c.1970s	330.00
Ashtray, Match Stand, Texaco	110.00
Ashtray, Michelin Man, 3–D Image, 1940s	55.00
Ashtray, Michelin Man, Molded White Plastic, On Black Base, 5 In.	38.00
Ashtray, Peter Pan Peanut Butter, Princess Tiger Lilly, Pirate, 3 In., Pair	35.00

Ashtray, Pfaelzer Bros., Bull, Cast Iron 85.00
Ashtray, Queen Elizabeth Ocean Liner, Bone China, 5 x 4 In. 38.00
Ashtray, Tuborg Beer, Milk Glass, Triangular 15.00
Ashtray, Vulcan Anvil, Man With Anvil & Hammer, Metal, 4 3/4 In. 35.00
Ashtray, Western Holly Gas Ranges, Green, Porcelain 10.00
Bag Holder, Schmitt's Blue Ribbon 100.00
Bag, Aunt Jemima Meal 7.00
Bag, Black Plantation Coffee 3.00
Bag, Corn Meal, No. 5, Sam's Creek Mill, Red & Blue Design 2.50
Bag, Dinner Bell Coffee, Brownwood, 1930s, 1 Lb. 8.50
Bag, Martha White Flour, 18 x 18 In. ....*Illus* 2.00
Banner, Amoco Service Station, Man Driving Car, 1940s, 3 x 3 Ft. 75.00
Banner, Campbell's Soup, Felt, 17 3/4 In. 148.00
Banner, Cold Spring Brewing, Embroidered Gent With Mug, Cloth, 24 In. 137.00
Banner, DeLaval Cream Separator, Cloth, Woman Using Machine, 10 Ft. 330.00
Banner, DeLaval, Oval Insert of Girl & Separator, Cloth, 8 x 3 In. 187.00
Banner, Murphy Hatter, Top Hat, Cloth, 17 3/4 x 26 In. 605.00
Banner, Prince Albert Tobacco, Canvas, 1939, 20 In. 95.00
Banner, RCA, Cloth, Nipper, Victrola, Aqua Green, 48 x 40 In. 72.00
Banner, Slingerland Drums, Gold Embossed, 1930s, 20 In. 85.00
Banner, Winchester, Horse & Shotguns, Cowboy, Rifle, 19 x 31 In. 495.00
Barrel, Whiskey, Private Stock of Carl Hanekers, Wooden Spigot, 2 Gal. 40.00
Beer Tap, Piel, Bakelite 65.00
Bill Holder, Ceresota Flour, Red, Cardboard, With Hook 165.00
Bin & Sift, Cream City Flour, Pat. Nov. 21, 1893, Dark Red Paint 495.00
Bin, Boston Roasted Coffee, Dwinell–Wright Co., 18 In. 90.00
Bin, Express, Pie Shape, 2 x 8 In. 750.00
Bin, Forbes Brothers Tea 60.00
Bin, Golden Grains Coffee, Slant Lid, Tin, 9 1/4 x 8 In. 193.00
Bin, Honest Scrap, Dog & Cat, 12 x 18 x 14 In. 1815.00
Bin, Meadow Cream Toffees, Tin, Slant Top, Orange, Green Logo, 11 x 15 In. 38.00
Bin, Monroe Taylor Baking Soda 185.00
Bin, Reid Murdock Coffee, Wooden, Cardboard, 100 Lb. 325.00
Bin, Sure Shot Tobacco, Indian, Bow, 15 1/4 x 10 1/4 In. .... 605.00 To 750.00
Bin, Sweet Cuba Fine Cut Tobacco, Slant Front, Yellow Paint 185.00
Bin, Sweet Cuba, Tin Box, 12 x 18 x 14 In. 385.00
Bin, Tiger Tobacco, Red, Round 175.00
Bin, Wood's Boston Coffee, Lithograph, Roll Top, 1900s, 20 x 20 In. 450.00
Birdhouse, Nationwide Grocery Store, Clapboard Sides, Asphalt Shingles 440.00
Blackboard, Pabst Beer, Metal 18.00
Blotter, American Fire Insurance, 1891 .... 5.00
Blotter, Black Gold, 1924 Derby Winner 8.00
Blotter, George L. Sands, We Grow All Varieties, Cabbage, 1920, 3 1/2 x 6 In. 7.50
Blotter, Grants Hygienic Health Food, Medical Claims, Pretty Girl, 1920 .... 7.50
Blotter, Morton's Salt 1.00
Blotter, P & D Oregon Roses, Scappoose, Ore., Pink Rose Design, 1910 .... 5.00
Blotter, Smith Brothers, 1920 .... 35.00
Blotter, Sunoco Winter Oil, Goofy, Igloo, Polar Bear, Water Stain, 1939 .... 17.00
Blotter, Underwood Portable Typewriter, 1935, 6 x 3 1/2 .... 6.00
Blotter, Waterman's Fountain Pen, 1917–1918, Used, 3 1/2 x 6 In. 5.00
Blotter, Yosemite Transportation Co., View of Ahwahnee Hotel, 1927 .... 12.50
Books may be included in the Paper category
Booklet, Bunnies In Wheatiesland, General Mills, 16 Full Color Pages 20.00
Booklet, Dr. Seuss, McElligot's Pool, Crest/Prell, 1975 .... 8.00
Booklet, Jackson's Best Chewing Tobacco, Black Advertising, Lithograph 49.00
Booklet, Jell–O Girls Entertain, 1920s 30.00
Booklet, Nursery Rhymes, Libby Food Products, 1893, 10 Pages 15.00
Booklet, Paint, Dutch Boy, 1929 .... 17.00
Booklet, Quaker Oats, Dick Darling Magic 15.00
Bottles are listed in their own category
Bottle Cap, Old Red Eye Soda, 1930–1950 .... .50
Bottle Openers are listed in their own category
Bowl & Mug, Digger Frog, Sugar Smacks Cereal, 1973 .... 20.00

Advertising, Bowl, Japan Airlines,
Rust-Colored Plastic, 3 1/2 In.

◆◆◆◆◆◆◆◆◆◆◆◆◆◆◆◆◆◆◆◆◆◆◆

Some repairs make the sale of
an antique very difficult, if not
impossible. Don't buff pewter.
Don't wash ivory. Don't repaint
old toys. Don't tape old paper.
Don't wash oil paintings.

◆◆◆◆◆◆◆◆◆◆◆◆◆◆◆◆◆◆◆◆◆◆◆

Bowl, Japan Airlines, Rust-Colored Plastic, 3 1/2 In. ....*Illus*   10.00
Box, see also Box category
Box, Adams Tutti-Fruitti, Display 65.00
Box, Banana, Slatted, Small 50.00
Box, Bazooka Gum, With Mays & Gentile Panels, 1963 ....   100.00
Box, Bentwood, Oval, Stenciled Label, Figs, 3 1/2 In. 25.00
Box, Betty Crocker Party Cake Mix 25.00
Box, Bixby's Shoe Polish, Man Having Boots Polished, Paper, 12 x 17 1/2 In. 413.00
Box, Bloomers Club, Ladies, Blacks, Bicycles, Cigar 95.00
Box, Burns Cigar, 4 x 5 In. 5.00
Box, Buster Brown & Tige, Shoe 10.00
Box, Cheerios, Lone Ranger Badge and Flashlight 150.00
Box, Chemcraft Chemistry, Label 22.00
Box, Chex, Super Sugar, Casper 200.00
Box, Chicklets Gum, Glass Lid 125.00
Box, Cigar, Cabin Home, Wooden 295.00
Box, Cigar, Lucke's Stogie, Illustration Inside Cover 25.00
Box, Cigar, Quaker City, Wooden, Packing 60.00
Box, Cigar, Winnie Winkle, Picture On Inside of Cover 25.00
Box, Corn Flakes, Fernando Valenzuela, Flat 18.00
Box, Coverbloom Cheese, Wooden, 2 Lb. 3.80
Box, Crescent Macaroni & Crackers, Wooden, 12 x 21 x 14 In. 18.50
Box, Duke's Cameo Cigarettes, 6 Original Cigarettes, NC Stamp, 1900 ....   275.00
Box, Dupont Explosives, Wooden, Dated 1940s 10.00
Box, E. T. 75.00
Box, Eatmor Cranberries, Label 75.00
Box, Esquire, Shoe Shine, Oak, Dovetailed, Foot Rest 10.00
Box, Firecracker Salute, 1940s 20.00
Box, Freakies, Reeses Pieces Coupon, 1987 ....   20.00
Box, Frosted Flakes, Tony With Stanley Cup 15.00
Box, G.I. Joe Action Stars, T-Shirt Offer, 1985 ....   35.00
Box, Garden Flight Poison, Cardboard, Soldier Picture 5.00
Box, Gillman's Candy, Cardboard 3.00
Box, Gold Dust Twins, Washing Powder, Contents, 9 In. 38.00
Box, Gulf Oil Crayons 10.00
Box, Gurney Shoe Heel Nails, Wooden, Embossed, 11 x 17 In. 12.00
Box, Hat, Mallory, Victorian Man, Large 42.00
Box, Hollingsworth Candy, Memories of Old South, Metal, Hinged, 6 x 4 In. 35.00
Box, Jack & Jill Gelatin Dessert, Lemon & Cherry, Empty, Pair 8.00
Box, Jolly Time Popcorn, Orange, Blue, Folded, 1918, 7 x 10 In. 12.00
Box, Jumbo Brand Cigarette, Unopened 40.00
Box, Kellogg's Rice Krispies, Jumbo Box, 1935 ....   200.00
Box, Kraft American Cheese, Wooden, 2 Lb. 4.25
Box, Lucky Cat Banana, Wooden 22.00
Box, Manderville Seed 65.00
Box, Marlin Razor Blade 9.00

Box, Mason's Blacking, Wooden 75.00
Box, Mel–O–Bit Cheese, A & P, Wooden, 2 Lb. 4.00
Box, Mother Hubbard Energy, Wheat Cereal, 1940s 130.00
Box, Moxie, Dovetailed, 15 x 11 In. 40.00
Box, Old Dutch Klenser, Wooden, Packing 70.00
Box, Packing, Black Pellet Powder, Wooden 50.00
Box, Peters High Velocity Shotgun Shell, 12 Gauge, Contents, Unused 125.00
Box, Pill, Beecham's Laxative Pills, Wooden, Wax Sealed Instructions, 1 1/2 In. 20.00
Box, Pill, Brass, Embossed Grumman, Airplane, 1940s 50.00
Box, Premier Cigarettes, Rust–Colored Plastic, 3 1/4 In. ....*Illus* 10.00
Box, Rice Krispies, Vernon Grant Nursery Rhyme, 1934 .... 150.00
Box, Rice Seed, Display, Large 375.00
Box, Richard Hudnut Powder, 2 Art Deco Women On Top, Unopened 40.00
Box, Shoe Lace Service Station, Tin, Inside Shelves, 11 1/4 In. 990.00
Box, Star Sewing Thread, 12 Spools, Complete 12.00
Box, Sweet Orange Slices, Wooden, Lithographed Label, 12 In. 98.00
Box, Swifts Brookfield Cheese, Wooden, 5 Lb. 4.25
Box, Tasteless Blazers, 1877, 2 x 2 In. ....*Illus* 45.00
Box, Truth Spice Cake, Hinged Front Door, George Washington On Sides 225.00
Box, War Eagle Cheroots Cigar, Pictures Eagle & Civil War Scene 195.00
Box, Wheaties, Bulls, 1991 .... 15.00
Box, Wheaties, Michael Jordan, Left Hand Lay Up 18.00
Box, Wheaties, Penguins, Logo 67.00
Box, Wheaties, Walter Payton Running 20.00
Box, Wishing Stars 100.00
Box, Woman's Hosiery, 1920s 10.00
Box, Woonsocket Rubbers, With Elephant, Wooden, 20 x 18 In. 98.00
Bracelet, Charm, Kelloggs, Gold Metal, 8 In. 39.00
Bracelet, Lucky Strike, Bakelite 250.00
Bumper Sticker, Big Boy 10.00
Butter Tub, Lily Whipped, Red & White Farm Scenes, 10 Lb. 5.00
Button, Harley Davidson, Pinback, Says 100 Miles Per Gallon, 1 1/4 In. 18.00
Cabinet, American Thread Co., Tin, 2 Drawers 85.00
Cabinet, Arrow Collars, Arrow On Front, 14 Collars, Glass & Wood, 4 Ft. 1500.00
Cabinet, Banasch Sewing Supplies, 400 Buttons, 40 Drawers, 24 x 18 In. 250.00
Cabinet, Button, Banasch's Sewing Supplies, 40 Drawers, 24 x 18 In. 250.00
Cabinet, Coleman's Mustard, 3 Shelves, Tin, 16 x 10 In. 73.00
Cabinet, Diamond Dyes, Children With Balloons, Embossed Front, 23 x 30 In. 715.00
Cabinet, Diamond Dyes, Embossed Tin, Mansion, 15 x 24 x 9 In. 440.00
Cabinet, Diamond Dyes, Governess 1800.00
Cabinet, Diamond Dyes, Maypole, 24 x 15 In. 1347.00
Cabinet, Display, Bowes Tire Repair, Tin 45.00
Cabinet, Display, Sapoline Gold Powder, Tin, 19th Century, 20 x 17 In. 99.00
Cabinet, Dr. Calvin Cranes Remedies, 10 x 15 x 15 In. 715.00
Cabinet, Dr. Daniels' Veterinary Medicine, For Horse & Cattle, 30 x 20 In. 950.00
Cabinet, Dr. Lesure's Famous Remedies, Embossed Horse Head, Tin Panel 2475.00

Advertising, Box, Premier Cigarettes, Rust-Colored Plastic, 3 1/4 In.

Advertising, Box, Tasteless Blazers, 1877, 2 X 2 In.

Advertising, Clip, B.F. Goodrich

Cabinet, French Carabon Battery Co., Flashlight, Wooden 400.00
Cabinet, Giblin's Liniment, 2 Doors, Shelves, Wooden Case, 24 In. 825.00
Cabinet, Gillette Razors, Glass Top, Wooden 70.00
Cabinet, Hoosier, Oak, Original Finish, Brass Knobs, Salesman's Sample, 17 In. 245.00
Cabinet, Humid–A–Gar Tobacco, Quarter Sawed Oak, 72 x 94 In. 3200.00
Cabinet, Jones Spring & Wire Co., 7 Drawers, Painted Tin Drawer Fronts, 21 In. ... 88.00
Cabinet, Licking Laundry, Stenciled, Tin, Wooden, Mirror, Small 75.00
Cabinet, Peerless Dyes, Lithographed Tin Insert, Roll Top Opening, Oak, 23 In. 610.00
Cabinet, Pratt's Veterinary Remedies 900.00
Cabinet, Putman Dye, Lithographed Tin, 100 Packets of Dye 450.00
Cabinet, Putnam Fadeless Dyes, Tints, Tin 50.00
Cabinet, Rainbow Dye, Counter Top All Metal, Dye Packets, 14 x 13 In. 145.00
Cabinet, Remington Pocket Knives, 24 Slots, Stained Glass Front, 29 In. 125.00
Cabinet, Royal Garden Tea, Glass Panels, Wooden 425.00
Cabinet, Sanford's Ink, Wooden, Glass Door, 21 1/2 x 36 x 9 1/2 In. 550.00
Cabinet, Schrader Tire Gauges 225.00
Cabinet, Spice, Schotten Spice Litho Label, Oak 695.00
Cabinet, Spool, Belding, Mirrored Front, 1 Lower Drawer 475.00
Cabinet, Spool, Clark's O. N. T., Glass Panels, 6 Drawers 700.00
Cabinet, Spool, Coats & Clark's, Blue Metal, Gold Lettering, 10 x 23 In. 18.00
Cabinet, Spool, Desk, Chadwick, Lift Lid, Gold Leaf On 6 Drawers, Oak, 32 In. 600.00
Cabinet, Spool, Eureka, 10 Solid & Glass Drawers, Mirrored Sides, 25 1/4 In. 853.00
Cabinet, Spool, J & P Coats, Spool Cotton, Molded Drawer Fronts, 22 x 26 In. 468.00
Cabinet, Spool, Lister's, Swivels, Vertical Columns, Glass On 4 Sides 375.00
Cabinet, Spool, Merrick's, Double Cylinders, Curved Glasses, Mirrors 850.00
Cabinet, Spool, Merrick's, Oak, Revolving Interior, Glass, 23 x 23 In. Diam. 495.00
Cabinet, Spool, Willimantic Six Cord Star Thread, 4 Drawers, Refinished 450.00
Calendars may be found in the Calendar category
Can, Gold Dust Twins, Full 30.00
Canisters, see introductory paragraph to Tins in this category
Canister, Beeman's Gum, Mr. Beeman, Sticks of Gum, Tin, 1910 .... 1250.00
Canister, Cameo Cleanser, Insert, Red & Black, 1940s 20.00
Canister, Click's Crispy Fluff's Candy, Green, Red Lettering, 9 x 8 1/2 In. 11.00
Canister, Great American Tea Co., Slip Top, Red, Black Graphics, 4 x 7 In. 165.00
Canister, Queen Quality Salted Peanuts, Lancaster, Pa., 9 3/4 In. 133.00
Canister, St. James Coffee, 5 Lb. 105.00
Canister, Summer Time Tobacco 34.00
Cap, Baseball, Carnation Research Farms 7.50
Cards are listed in their own category
Case, Belding's, Revolving, Glass & Oak, 24 x 28 x 24 In. 550.00
Case, Boye Needles, Metal Inserts, Decals, Wood & Glass, 11 x 12 In. 225.00
Case, Edwin Cigar Co., New York, Pocket 15.00
Case, High Class Biscuits, Reverse Glass, Wooden, Marble Top, 43 In. 770.00
Case, Keen Kutter, Floor Model 875.00
Case, Lorillard Tin Tag Tobacco, Glass Door & Drawer, 34 x 43 In. 1815.00
Case, Men's Shirts, 27 Drawers, Brass Pulls, Glass Top, 1915, 10 Ft. 1500.00
Case, Milk Bottle, Jersey Gold Dairy, Embossed Wire 15.00
Case, Remington Pocket Knife, Slanted Glass Front, 24 Slots, 29 In. 125.00
Case, Schrader Tire Gauge, Tire Gauge Shape, 20 In. 185.00
Chair, Folding, Piedmont Cigarettes 192.00
Chair, RCA Victor, Aluminum Tube, Tan Vinyl Seat & Back, Logo, 1940s, Pair 500.00
Chair, Recruit Cigarettes, Wooden, Folding, 17 x 32 x 20 In. 27.00
Chalkboard, A. & W. Root Beer 100.00
Chalkboard, Five Roses Flour, Cardboard, 20 x 15 In. 325.00
Chalkboard, Sun Spot, Golden Girl 115.00
Change Receiver, see also Tip Tray in this category
Change Receiver, Baby Ruth Gum 95.00
Change Receiver, Calvert Reserve Whiskey, Figural, Bottle, Key Chain 15.00
Change Receiver, Don Digo Cigars, Glass 25.00
Change Receiver, Doral Cigarettes, Glass 10.00
Cigar Cutter & Match Vendor, Yankee, Cast Iron, 8 x 7 x 6 In. 440.00
Cigar Cutter & Tamper, Pharaoh 10 Cent Pebble Cigars, Hand Held 20.00
Cigar Cutter, Bantam Brand Sweet Corn, Ortonville, Minn. 25.00

Cigar Cutter, Country Gentleman, 10 Cent, Chrome Base, Patent 1891	110.00
Cigar Cutter, Griswold	65.00
Cigar Cutter, Havana, Oval Mirror, Cigars Around Frame, 8 1/2 x 8 In.	247.00
Cigar Cutter, Horse Head	350.00
Cigar Cutter, Indian Motorcycle	175.00
Cigar Cutter, Man Slapping Hip	100.00
Cigar Cutter, Rifle	100.00
Clip, B. F. Goodrich ....*Illus*	2.00
Clipboard, Ludlow–Saylor Wire Co., St. Louis, Brass, 75th Anniv., 1931, 6 In.	26.00
Clocks are listed in their own category	
Coaster, Berghoff, 4 In.	20.00
Coaster, Harold's Club, Reno, Nev., Cowboy, 1950s, 3 1/2 In.	4.00
Coffee Grinders are listed in their own category	
Coffeepot, Blankes Drip Coffeepot, White Semiporcelain Body	165.00
Coffeepot, With Cup & Saucer, Nestle, Globe	140.00
Comb, Brush & Mirror Set, Kellogg's, Box, 1984	10.00
Cooler, 7–Up, Metal	37.50
Cooler, Storz Beer, Metal, Blue, Red & White Logo	40.00
Cooler, Water, Red Wing, 49 In.	560.00
Crate, Colgate Mechanics Soap Paste	22.00
Crate, K. C. Baking Powder	25.00
Crate, Kundo 400–Day Clock	25.00
Crate, Monarch Coffee	16.00
Crate, Winner Plug Tobacco, Paper Label, Wooden, 17 In.	220.00
Creamer, Borden's, McCoy	75.00
Crock, Cheese, Summe Brothers Dairy, Stoneware	40.00
Crock, Cheese, Wehr Dairy, Stoneware	35.00
Crock, Fairmont's Cottage Cheese, Stoneware	35.00
Crock, Fenley's Tasty Cream Cheese, Stoneware	40.00
Crock, Meadow Gold Creamed Cottage Cheese, Stoneware	55.00
Cuff Links, Tampa Cigar, 1940s	30.00
Cup & Saucer, Greyhound, International House of Pancakes	45.00
Cup, Capitol Airlines, Holiday, Melmac, 1950s	6.00
Cup, Charlie The Tuna, Plastic	20.00
Cup, Collapsible, McConnell's Irish Whiskey, Brass Case	75.00
Cup, Measuring, Kellogg, Pink Glass	28.00
Cup, Pillsbury, 4 In.	10.00
Cup, Sundae, Hershey's	8.00
Cuspidor, Havana Cigars 5 Cents, Brass	65.00
Cutter, Cake, Swansdown	10.00
Desk, Willimantic Spool, Leather Lift Top, Oak, 6 Drawers, 36 x 16 x 24 In.	275.00
Dinner Set, The Big Payoff, Meyerson, Serving For 6, Plus Serving Pieces	250.00
Dish, Fish Cover, Chicken of The Sea, Ceramic, Holder, 9 In., Set of 4	55.00
Dish, His Master's Voice, Nipper In Relief Interior, Glass	10.00
Dish, Ice Cream, Haagen–Dazs, Ceramic, Tub Type, 1980	5.00
Dispenser, Boyce, Needle Case, Tin Front, Oak, 16 x 16 In.	55.00
Dispenser, Buckeye Root Beer Syrup, Porcelain, 7 1/2 x 17 In.	550.00
Dispenser, Buckeye Root Beer Syrup, White Jar, Cleveland Fruit Juice Co.	565.00
Dispenser, Buttermilk, Beige, Navy Blue Trim, Red Dome, 5 Cent	425.00
Dispenser, Cherry Smash, Bowl, Spigot & Bracket, 16 In.	175.00
Dispenser, Cup, Puritan, Wall Mount, Picture of Ship On Tube, Push Lever	165.00
Dispenser, Dr Pepper Syrup, Lime Green, Nickel–Plated Spigot, 16 In.	88.00
Dispenser, Hires Root Beer Syrup, Hires Pump, 12 1/2 In.	165.00
Dispenser, Hires Syrup, Bright Blue Porcelainized, Steel Tank, Hires Logo, 20 In.	88.00
Dispenser, Hires, Hour Glass, Syrup, Pump, 7 In.	467.00
Dispenser, Howell's Orange Julep, Pump	1650.00
Dispenser, Ice Cream Cones, Mosteller	400.00
Dispenser, Johnston Hot Fudge	125.00
Dispenser, Kemp's Nuts, White, Glass Door, Painted Sheet Metal, 32 In.	49.00
Dispenser, Key Chewing Tobacco, Tin	15.00
Dispenser, Liberty Root Beer, Oaken Barrel, Spigot Front, Decals, 27 x 16 In.	1073.00
Dispenser, Magic Yeast, Gravity Feed, 27 1/4 In.	248.00
Dispenser, Mission Juice, 12 In.	250.00

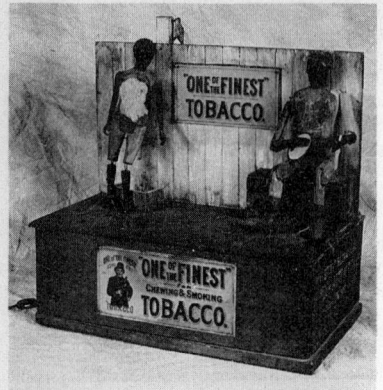

Advertising, Display, One of Finest, Tobacco,

Mechanical, 20 X 20 In.

✦✦✦✦✦✦✦✦✦✦✦✦✦✦✦✦✦✦✦✦✦

If you use a glass shelf to display a paperweight collection, be sure it is strong enough. The ideal size for the shelf is 18 inches long, 4 inches deep, and ¼ inch thick. Paperweights are very heavy, and collectors tend to add "just one more," which overloads the shelf. Remember also, glass will become more fragile with age.

✦✦✦✦✦✦✦✦✦✦✦✦✦✦✦✦✦✦✦✦✦

Dispenser, Mission Orange, Glass, 13 In.	66.00
Dispenser, Nesbitt's Orange, Clamp On Counter, Box	225.00
Dispenser, Nesbitt's Syrup, Glass Bowl, Nickel Plated Base, Wooden Top, 17 In.	155.00
Dispenser, Puritans Cup, Stenciled Green Lettering On Glass, 21 In.	22.00
Dispenser, Richardson's Orangeade, Green Glass	225.00 To 275.00
Dispenser, Rochester Root Beer Syrup, China, Barrel, On Stump	325.00
Dispenser, Rochester Root Beer, Barrel On Stump	450.00
Dispenser, Root Beer, U–Bet	700.00
Dispenser, Straw, Grape Smash, Enameled Advertising Both Sides	300.00
Dispenser, Ward's Lemon Crush	575.00
Dispenser, Ward's Lime Crush, Lime Shape, Replaced Pump, 10 x 9 x 7 In.	880.00
Dispenser, Ward's Orange Crush, Orange Shape, No Pump, 10 In.	330.00
Dispenser, Ward's Orange Crush, Black Lettering, Ceramic	1980.00
Dispenser, Watta Pop, Bulldog Pup, Lollipop	495.00
Dispenser, Welch's Grape Juice, Grapes & Leaves, Slogan	85.00
Dispenser, Wild Cherry, Yours Truly	195.00
Dispenser, Zipp's Cherri–O Syrup, 16 In.	2520.00
Display, Bias Tape, Tin, Red Letters, 1920s, 11 1/2 x 12 1/2 x 4 1/2 In.	45.00
Display, Big Smith Shirts, Cardboard, Standup, World War II Airplane, 1940s	25.00
Display, Box, Noble 5 Cent Cigar, Tin	275.00
Display, Broom, Fresh Bonds Bread, Green, Red Emblem, 41 x 19 In.	412.00
Display, Champion Spark Plug, With Plugs, Tin	400.00
Display, Chase & Sanborn Coffee, Black Comical, 1888	75.00
Display, Chicklets Gum, Monkey, Die–Cut Tin, Easel Back, 1916, 9 x 6 In.	2500.00
Display, Clockwork, Butterfly, Movable Wings, Birthstones, 20 x 15 In.	385.00
Display, Dr. West's Toothbrush & Toothpaste, Mirror Back, 1940s	40.00
Display, Figural, 3–D, Eat–It–All Ice Cream Cone, 21 x 9 In.	60.00
Display, Figural, Buy Rx By The Carton, Cardboard, Standup, 1950s	35.00
Display, Figural, Hickory Children's Garters, Wooden, 2 Kids, 13 x 19 In.	366.00
Display, Figural, Michelin Man, Plastic, 13 In.	55.00
Display, Floralo Incense, Chalkware	125.00
Display, Franklin Mills Flour, Standup, Little Girl, Cardboard, 9 In.	330.00
Display, Goebel Beer, Plaster Chicken, 1948 Bottle	85.00
Display, Hush Puppy, Plastic, Mid–1970s, 16 In.	35.00
Display, Kellogg's Corn Flakes, Girl, Blue Dress, Cardboard, 21 x 45 In.	176.00
Display, Lifesavers Counter, Tin Litho, Fruit, Vine Pattern, Shonk Co., 14 1/2 In.	187.00
Display, Lifesavers, Tin, 3 Racks, 14 x 15 In.	1100.00
Display, Lion Hats, Cardboard, Standup, 1930s, 13 x 22 In.	35.00
Display, Mazda Light Bulb, Round	125.00
Display, One of Finest Tobaccos, Mechanical, 20 x 20 In. ....*Illus*	2695.00

Display, Pez, Clown 160.00
Display, Pharmacy Show Globe, Ornate Metal Base, 1920s, 23 In. 175.00
Display, Primrose Ice Cream, Cardboard, Die Cut, 39 In. 1650.00
Display, Reddy Kilowatt, Standing, On Outlet Cover, 1961, 5 1/2 In. 45.00
Display, Rippled Wheat, Standup, Boxer Jack Dempsey, 6 In. 275.00
Display, Rit Dye, Metal, 32 Boxes, 1950s, 22 x 16 In. 60.00
Display, Sinclair Dinosaur, Green Vinyl, 1960s, 12 In. 75.00
Display, Somoset Chocolates, Plaster, Indian, Canoe, Embossed, 36 x 12 In. 257.00
Display, St. Joseph Aspirin, Counter Top, Tin 78.00
Display, Towle's Log Cabin Syrup, Paper Lithograph, 1915–1920 .... 1400.00
Display, U.S. Rubber Co., Pull–On Boots, 36 In. 450.00
Display, W. Parker Lucky Curve Fountain Pen, Cardboard, Standup, 9 x 7 In. 60.00
Display, White Rock Ginger Ale, Tin, 16 x 11 In. 825.00
Dolls are listed in their own category
Door Knob, Fuller Brush, Brass 10.00
Door Pull, Chesterfield, Tin, Red, Gold, White, 2 x 10 1/2 In. 10.00
Door Push, Canada Dry, Porcelain, 7 x 24 In. 50.00
Door Push, Duke's Mixture, Porcelain 88.00
Door Push, Fleischmann's Yeast, Porcelain 250.00
Door Push, Grapette, Aluminum 145.00
Door Push, Nuyana 5 Cent Cigar, Aluminum 25.00
Door Push, Orange Crush, Porcelain 110.00
Door Push, Perry's Beverages, Tin 35.00
Door Push, Red Rose Tea, Porcelain 295.00
Door Push, Salada Tea, Porcelain .... 65.00 To 85.00
Door Push, Sprig Soda 30.00
Door Push, Vicks, Porcelain, 7 In. 40.00
Door Push, White Rock, Embossed Tin, 14 x 4 In. .... 100.00 To 181.00
Egg Slicer, Rustcraft Greeting Cards, c.1930 .... 10.00
Eggcup, Fanny Farmer, Ceramic 25.00
Emblem, Norge Refrigeration 22.50
Emblem, State Farm Insurance 3.75
Eraser Figure, Yogi, Kellogg's, 1960s, 2 In. 20.00
Fans are listed in their own category
Figure, Bartender, Glass Bottle, Pot Metal Base, 12 1/2 In. 50.00
Figure, Bengal Gin, Roaring Tiger, Yellow, Black, 9 x 6 x 7 In. 77.00
Figure, Blatz, Barmaid, Dancing, Chalkware, Plaster, 9 x 19 In. 192.00
Figure, Blue–Jay Corn Plasters, Grandpa In Rocking Chair, 6 x 3 x 5 In. 130.00
Figure, Boy, Mechanical, Hammer In Hand, Used In Hardware Store, 52 In. 275.00
Figure, Brewery, Tyrolean, Felt Hat, Lederhosen, Stein of Beer, 5 Ft. 4 In. 3575.00
Figure, California Raisin, Playing Drums, In Bag, 5 Piece 30.00
Figure, Casper 45.00
Figure, Clayton's Dog Remedies, Papier–Mache, Brown, Black, 30 In. 1200.00
Figure, Dinosaur, With Bag, Sinclair Gas Co., 1959, 3 x 6 1/2 In., 4 Piece 3.00
Figure, Gerber Kid 15.00
Figure, Goose, Red Goose Shoes, Concrete 65.00
Figure, Horse, Rolling Rock Beer, Plaster, 11 In. 45.00
Figure, Humpty Dumpty, Red Rose Tea 3.00
Figure, Magic Chef, Vinyl, 7 1/2 In. ....*Illus* 22.00
Figure, Man, Carries 7 Flip–Up Fabric Samples, Store Promotional, 7 1/4 In. 20.00
Figure, Man, Tobacco Barrel, Painted, 32 In. 6160.00
Figure, Michelin Man, 14 In. 60.00
Figure, Michelin Man, Molded White Plastic, Yellow & Black Banner, 18 In. 28.00
Figure, Miss Curity, Store Promotional 125.00
Figure, Moxie, Waiter & Waitress, Holding Serving Tray, Pair 325.00
Figure, Mr. Peanut, Cast Iron, 11 1/2 In. 14.00
Figure, Ohio Indian Chief, Reclining, Chalkware, Counter, 24 x 12 x 9 In. 192.00
Figure, Owl, R. M. Bishop & Co., Fine Cigars, Blue & Brown Glaze, 13 In. 3700.00
Figure, Poll Parrot, Bisque 75.00
Figure, Red Goose Shoes, Red Paint 75.00
Figure, Sparkly The Elf, 7–Up, 18 In. 40.00
Figure, St. Bernard, Kentucky Whiskey, Missing Barrel, Plastic, 4 Ft. 600.00
Figure, Tobacconist, Man Leaning On Barrel, 32 In. 6160.00

Advertising, Figure, Magic
Chef, Vinyl, 7 1/2 In.

Advertising, Glass, McDonald's,
Snoopy, 5 7/8 In.
Advertising, Glass, Burger King,
Empire Strikes Back, 6 In.

Figure, William Penn Cigar, Papier-Mache, 65 In.	2750.00
Flag, Nipper, His Master's Voice, Cloth, 4 x 6 Ft.	120.00
Funnel, Coleman Filtering Funnel For Lamps, Stoves	15.00
Gas Globe, Cadillac Dealership	145.00
Glass, 7-Up, Soda Fountain, 5 1/4 In.	10.00
Glass, A & W, Great Root Beer, 6 1/4 In.	7.00
Glass, Arby's, Loony Tunes, Bugs, 1988	34.00
Glass, Bonnie Rye, Script, 2 1/4 In.	15.00
Glass, Burger King, Empire Strikes Back, 6 In. *Illus*	5.00
Glass, Columbus Brewing Co., Christopher Columbus	140.00
Glass, Compliments of Brunn & Co., Portland, Ore., 3 3/4 In.	35.00
Glass, Domino's, Noid, Happy Holidays From Domino's Pizza	14.00
Glass, Dr Pepper, Fountain, Flared Lip, Etched, 1906	3000.00
Glass, Dr Pepper, Kirk	30.00
Glass, Dr Pepper, Spock	30.00
Glass, Falstaff Beer, Billiken	30.00
Glass, Fehr's Beer, Louisville, Ky.	65.00
Glass, Gerst 57, Nashville, Tn.	110.00
Glass, Golden's Pharmacy, Portland, Ore., Measure, 2 5/8 In.	25.00
Glass, Grainbelt Beer	12.00
Glass, Hamm's Smooth & Mellow	115.00
Glass, Jack and Jill, Yellow Orange, 4 5/8 In.	2.00
Glass, Jesse Moore, San Francisco, 2 1/4 In.	25.00
Glass, Jungle Book, Shere Kahn	73.00
Glass, Keeblers, 135th Birthday	4.00
Glass, Kentucky Derby, 1963	28.00
Glass, Lunn & Brooks Capital Drug Store, Salem, Ore., 1 7/8 In.	35.00
Glass, McDonald's, Snoopy, 5 7/8 In. *Illus*	3.00
Glass, Mister Magoo, Where's The Beach, Pink and Blue, 1963	24.00
Glass, Old Mother Hubbard, White, Ribbed, Hazel Atlas, 4 1/8 In.	6.00
Glass, Old Yucca Rye, Wm. Theoblad & Co., St. Paul, Etched, 3 In.	50.00
Glass, Pappy, Al Capp, 1975, 16 Oz.	40.00
Glass, Popeye, 1982	10.00
Glass, Raggedy Ann, Gone Fishin'	6.00
Glass, Rockwell, Country Time Lemonade, Set of 4	12.00
Glass, Southern Airways, 6th Year, 3 In.	55.00
Glass, Southern Brew, Tampa, Fl.	45.00
Glass, Star Trek, Captain Kirk, 1976	20.00
Glass, Super Heroes, Superman, 1978	7.00
Glass, Superman, Fighting The Dragon, Short, 1964	18.00
Glass, Walter's Beer	10.00
Glass, Warner Bros., Tasmanian Devil, White, 1973, 16 Oz.	15.00
Glass, Wendy's, Where's The Beef, 1984	11.00
Glass, Western Springs Distributing Co., Chicago, Etched, 2 1/2 In.	60.00
Glass, Whistle Soda, Picture of Air Ship	20.00
Glass, Wizard of Oz, Dorothy, Fluted	9.00

Glass, Woodward, Clarke & Co. Druggists, Portland, Ore., Measure, 2 5/8 In. 25.00
Glass, Yogi Bear, Hanna Barbera, 1983 .... 36.00
Grater, Fels Naptha Soap 10.00
Hair Net, White House, San Francisco, Pack, 1915 .... 7.00
Hat, Texaco Fire Chief, Speaker & Siren, Early 1960s 45.00
Horseshoe, Take Simmons Liver Regulator, Brass 35.00
Humidor, Twin Oaks Mixture, Pottery, Black Writing Under Glaze, Tan 45.00
Ice Pick, Sebasticook Ice Co., Steel 18.00
Inkwell, Colburns Laundry Blue and Colburn Philada. Mustard 30.00
Jar, Big Top, D–Lux Nuts, Automated, Warm Bulb Revolves Scene, 1950 .... 275.00
Jar, Borden's Malted Milk 350.00
Jar, Borden's Malted Milk Candy, Embossed Metal Top, 5 1/2 In. 110.00
Jar, Carnation Malted Milk, Barrel Shape, 15 Lb. 22.00
Jar, Chamberlain's Tables, Yellow Decal, 2 Sided 49.00
Jar, Glass, Crisco, Embossed, Original Metal Cap 35.00
Jar, Green River Cigars 135.00
Jar, Kis–Me Gum, Glass Lid 100.00
Jar, La Palina Cigars Since 1896, Glass, Lid, Embossed 95.00
Jar, Licorice Lozenges, Embossed, Metal Screw Top, 5 1/2 In. 33.00
Jar, M & M, Mars Inc., Olympiad XXIII, 1983 .... 3.00
Jar, Ramon's Medicines, Tin Litho, Blue On Yellow, Counter, 7 3/4 In. 49.00
Jar, Schlitz, Brown Pottery, Cover, 7 In. 60.00
Jar, Wesson Oil, Beater 55.00
Jigger, Hiram Walker's Ten High, Silver Plate, 1940, 2 In. 16.00
Jug, Green River Tobacco 400.00
Jug, J. Hungerford Smiths Imitation Wild Cherry Fountain Syrup, 1 Gal. 10.00
Jumping Rope, Peter's Weatherbird Shoes Best For Boys & Girls 25.00
Key Chain, Blue Ribbon Gas & Oils, Wichita, Ks. 15.00
Key Chain, Token, Airship Akron, Durallumin 45.00
Key Ring, Chevron 10.00
Kit, Shinola Shoe Shine, 1920s 15.00
Label, A. J. Cassalt Cigars, Image of Railroad President 70.00
Label, Aaron Burr Cigar, Colonial Man, Moonlit Night 40.00
Label, Abraham Lincoln Cigar, Profile of President, End Type 18.00
Label, Big Bear Cigar, Bear On Hind Legs, End Type 3.00
Label, Black River Ale 20.00
Label, Broadway Perfecto Cigars, Knight On Horseback 45.00
Label, Chez Pierre Ginger Ale, Woman, Modern Dance, 1929, 4 x 3 In. 8.50
Label, Crescent Brewing Co., Aurora Lager Beer 75.00
Label, Cupid's Best Cigar, Offering Box To Woman, Inner Lid 25.00
Label, Dana's Jardiniere Canned Tomatoes, 4 x 11 In. 5.00
Label, David Brewster Cigar, Inventor of Kaleidoscope, Inner Lid 10.00
Label, Diamond Crown Cigars, Crown, Queen & 2 Kings 5.00
Label, Dixie Broom, Black Man, Banjo, 1928, 3 1/2 x 5 In. 8.50
Label, Dr. Bonker's Pepsin Stomach Bitters, J. H. Xelowski, 1900, 2 x 5 In. 4.00
Label, Durham Tobacco, Side–Saddled Woman, 10 x 12 1/2 In. 330.00
Label, Export Lager Beer, Black Hills Brewing & Malting, 1898–1900 ....*Illus* 60.00
Label, Garfield Manor Cigars, Cluster of Houses, 1934 .... 25.00
Label, Grand Knight Cigars, Knight Wearing Gold Armor, 1896 .... 14.00
Label, Haven's Tonic Bitters 3.50
Label, J. J. Bagley Tobacco, Lass Peking Through Blossoms, 13 1/2 x 10 In. 550.00
Label, King Solomon Brand Sardines, Playing Card King, 1928, 9 x 4 In. 6.50
Label, Kirk's Summer Bouquet Soap, Red Roses, 1890, 7 x 9 1/2 In. 10.00
Label, Kittie Lee Inn, Bishop, Ca., Fish Design, 1930s, 6 In. 7.00
Label, Lifestaff, Gutsch Brewing Co., 1919–1923 ....*Illus* 55.00
Label, Log Cabin Tobacco, Black Man Front of Log Cabin, 13 1/2 x 8 1/4 In. 880.00
Label, Mammy Oranges, 1930, 8 x 3 In. 10.00
Label, Muenchener Beer, Chicago, c.1905 ....*Illus* 65.00
Label, Old Milwaukee Beer 60.00
Label, Oliver & Robinson Cigars, Victorian Woman, Cherubs, 10 1/2 x 13 In. 220.00
Label, Pacific Beer, Mt. Tacoma Scene, 12 In. 35.00
Label, Portola Brand Sardines, Monterey Bay, Ca., 1916, 9 x 4 In. 6.50
Label, St. Louis Lager Beer, St. Louis, Missouri, c.1885 ....*Illus* 65.00

Label, Superior Lager Beer, I. S. Miller, Macon, Missouri 65.00
Label, Union Sport Cigar, Formal Dressed Man, Yacht, Horse Race, End Type 5.00
Label, Wide Awake Cigar, Eagle & Fleet, 1908, 4 x 4 In. 14.00
Letter Opener, Embalmer Supply Co., Bottle Like Handle 20.00
Letter Opener, Nabisco, Tin, 6 In. 69.00
Letter Opener, Seldlitz Powders, Copper 35.00
Letter Opener, Welsbach Light Company, Litho On Both Sides, 10 In. 66.00
Lunch Boxes are listed in their own category
Match Holder, Ceresota Flour, Tin, 5 1/2 x 2 1/5 In. 250.00
Match Holder, Columbia Mill Co., Tin, 5 1/2 x 2 1/2 In. 935.00
Match Holder, Dutch Boy Paint, Embossed Tin, 6 1/2 x 3 1/2 In. 1100.00
Match Holder, Mother's Worm Syrup, Tin, 7 x 2 1/2 In. 632.00
Match Holder, Old Judson, Tin, 5 x 3 1/2 In. 165.00
Match Holder, Rex Flintkote Roofing, Tin, 5 x 3 1/2 In. 198.00
Matchbook, Coon Chicken Inn 25.00
Menu Board, Arctic Ice Cream 35.00
Menu Board, Kayo, Colorful Kid 90.00
Menu Cover, Miller High Life Beer, Original, 1950s 1.50

Advertising pocket mirrors range in size from 1 1/2 to 5 inches in diameter. Most of these mirrors were given away as advertising promotions.

Mirror, A Friend Loveth At All Times, Lassie, Round, Pocket 25.00
Mirror, ABC Power Washer, Pocket 44.00
Mirror, Aetna Life, Pocket 36.00
Mirror, American Druggist Fire Insurance, Large 40.00
Mirror, Angelus Marshmallows, Cherub, Oval, Pocket 135.00
Mirror, Anheuser–Busch Ginger Ale, Pocket 90.00
Mirror, Arm & Hammer, Frame, 1988, 27 3/4 x 21 1/4 In. 68.00
Mirror, Automobile Invincible Oil, Barrel Shape, Pocket 95.00
Mirror, Bagleys Tobacco, Pocket 45.00

Advertising, Label, Export Lager Beer,

Black Hills Brewing & Malting, 1898-1900

Advertising, Label, Lifestaff,

Gutsch Brewing Co., 1919-1923

Advertising, Label, Muenchener Beer,

Chicago, c.1905

Advertising, Label, St. Louis Lager

Beer, St. Louis, Missouri, c.1885

Mirror, Bee Hive Overalls, Pocket	250.00
Mirror, Beemans Pepsin Gum, Blue, Pocket	185.00
Mirror, Beemans Pepsin Gum, Green, Pocket	200.00
Mirror, Big Joe Flour, Pocket	55.00
Mirror, Binswanger & Co., Glass & Paint Advertising, Memphis	300.00
Mirror, Black Cat Cigarettes, Pocket	175.00
Mirror, C. D. Kenny Co., Tea Cup, Oval, Pocket	350.00
Mirror, Calox Tooth Powder, Oval, Pocket	35.00
Mirror, Campbell Soup, Pocket	65.00
Mirror, Cascarets, Cherub On Chamber Pot, Round, Pocket	55.00
Mirror, Ceresota Flour, 2 In.	75.00
Mirror, Compliments of Oak Cafe, Girl & Flowers, Round, Pocket	125.00
Mirror, Continental Cubes Tobacco, Pocket	390.00
Mirror, Depicts Logo of Soup Can, Pocket, 1 3/4 x 2 3/4 In.	77.00
Mirror, Drink Golden Dome Whiskey, Bottle, Round, Pocket	55.00
Mirror, Duffy's Pure Malt Whiskey, Duffy At Still, Oval, Pocket	145.00
Mirror, Duffy's Pure Malt Whiskey, Duffy At Still, Round, Pocket	55.00
Mirror, Dutch Cleanser, Pocket	25.00
Mirror, Empire Cream Separators, Pocket	195.00
Mirror, Enrico Caruso, Victrola Shape, Round, Pocket	165.00
Mirror, Ford Bedford Peanut Butter, Round, Pocket	185.00
Mirror, Frisco Railroad, 1890s, Pocket	95.00
Mirror, Galli–Curchi, Victrola Record Shape, Round, Pocket	165.00
Mirror, GAR, Gilchrist Company, Medal, With Eagle, Round, Pocket	35.00
Mirror, Garland Stoves & Ranges, Pocket	40.00
Mirror, Garrett's Baker Rye, Near Nude Woman, Pocket	220.00
Mirror, Good Whiskey At Low Prices, New Orleans, Pocket	40.00
Mirror, Herdrich & Boggs, Certified Public Accountants, Pocket	40.00
Mirror, Hood Rubbers, 1913 Calendar, Round, Pocket	75.00
Mirror, Horlick's Milk, Girl With Cow, Pocket	95.00
Mirror, Hyler's Candy, Young Girl, Oval, Pocket	135.00
Mirror, Ideal Day's Lunch, With Mom, Round, Pocket	55.00
Mirror, Kleinerts Dress Shields, Pocket	28.00
Mirror, Lewis Bergdoll Brewing Co., Girl, Oval, 1 3/4 x 2 3/4 In.	94.00
Mirror, Lyken's Cream Topped Lager, Girl, Red Shawl, Oval, Pocket	50.00
Mirror, Maryland Casualty Insurance, 3 1/2 In.	35.00
Mirror, Mascot Crushed Cut Tobacco, Mascot Dog, Round, Pocket	45.00
Mirror, Mascot Tobacco, Celluloid, Pocket	45.00
Mirror, Mennen's Violet Talcum Powder, Oval, Pocket	125.00
Mirror, Michelob Beer, 1972, 16 x 24 In.	35.00
Mirror, Murphy Mills Clothing Co., Nude Woman's Bust, Oval, Pocket	110.00
Mirror, Nashville Show Case, Pocket	60.00
Mirror, New York Plate Glass Insurance Co., Pocket, 3 In.	55.00
Mirror, Northeastern Trust Co., Large	40.00
Mirror, Old Reliable Coffee, Pocket	75.00
Mirror, Oliver Plows, Pocket	175.00
Mirror, Oxford Chocolates, Woman Graduate, Oval, Pocket	110.00
Mirror, Parry Buggy Manufacturing Co., Factory Scene, Oval, Pocket	165.00
Mirror, Queen Quality Shoes, Woman, With Star Tiara, Oval, Pocket	45.00
Mirror, Red Seal Lye, Can of Lye, Round, Pocket	75.00
Mirror, Remington Typewriter, Pocket	45.00
Mirror, Schaefer Beer, World's Fair, Pocket, 1939	65.00
Mirror, Shawmut Rubbers, Pocket	25.00
Mirror, Shoe Wizard, Pocket	34.00
Mirror, Singer, Spanish Writing, Pocket	90.00
Mirror, Star Soap, Pocket	45.00
Mirror, Sterling Range Has No Equal, With Stove, Round, Pocket	110.00
Mirror, Studebaker Vehicle Works, Pocket	155.00
Mirror, T. F. Mercer, Good For 10 Cents, Pocket	100.00
Mirror, True Value Hardware, Pocket	25.00
Mirror, Virginia Dare, Nude Shooting Arrow, Pocket	175.00
Mirror, Watch Case Union, Pocket	36.00
Mirror, Wear Union Stamped Shoes, Shield & Shoe, Oval, Pocket	75.00

Money Clip, Phillips 66	25.00
Mug, Anheuser–Busch, Embossed A & Eagle, Glass, 5 In.	100.00
Mug, Borden's, Elsie, Embossed	75.00
Mug, Budweiser Light, White Ceramic, Gold Rings, 6 1/4 In.	45.00
Mug, Budweiser, Black, Red, Brown, Pottery, 3 3/4 In.	45.00
Mug, Busch–Bavarian, Blue & White, 2 Sides, 6 1/2 In.	55.00
Mug, Cheerios, Black & White Plastic, 1950's	29.00
Mug, Exxon Tiger, Early 1960s	15.00
Mug, Grafts Root Beer	20.00
Mug, Kayo Hot Chocolate	20.00
Mug, Michelob, Red Ribbon, Gold Medallion, Hof–Brau Type, . 05 Liter	35.00
Mug, Piel Bros., New York, November 1954, Glass Bottom	25.00
Mug, Poppin' Fresh, 1979	12.00
Mug, Soup, Campbell's, 4 Piece	15.00
Mug, Twin Kist Root Beer, Fluted	25.00
Mug, Uncle Wiggily, Ovaltine	45.00
Night Light, Mr. Peanut, Glows In The Dark, 8 1/2 In.	75.00
Oil Can, Columbian Steel Tank Co., Kansas City, 20 Gal.	29.00
Oil Can, Hammer & Co., Cast Iron, Dated Sept. 16, 1884	26.00
Opener, Cigar Box, Parker & Gordon's El Roi Tan	12.00
Opener, Jax Beer	10.00
Opener, Old Falstaff Beer	6.00
Opener, White Rock, Figural	10.00
Pack, Baby Gorilla Firecrackers, Checkerboard Crackers, 7/8 x 80's	7.00
Pack, Black Cat Firecrackers, 1 1/2 x 16's	3.00
Pack, Grenade Bomb Firecrackers, 1 1/2 x 16's	6.00
Pack, Peacock Brand Firecrackers, Green & Feather Logo, 1 1/2 x 32's	34.00
Pack, Rocket Brand Firecrackers, 1 1/2 x 20's	5.00
Pail, Armour's Peanut Butter, 1 Lb.	110.00
Pail, Armour's Peanut Butter, 1 Lb.	247.00
Pail, Bagdad Coffee, Tin, 12 x 5 In.	200.00
Pail, Buffalo Peanut Butter	135.00
Pail, Charms Hansel & Gretel, Tin, 5 In.	200.00
Pail, Climax, Peanut Butter, 1 Lb.	198.00
Pail, Dixie, Peanut Butter, 1 Lb.	121.00
Pail, Elsie Borden, With Shovel, Sand	65.00
Pail, FI*NA*ST, Peanut Butter, 1 Lb.	72.00
Pail, Frontenac, Peanut Butter, 12 Oz.	30.00
Pail, Jackie Coogan Peanut Butter, Tin, 3 x 3 In.	200.00 To 350.00
Pail, Jolly Time Popcorn, 10 Oz.	72.00
Pail, Kenny's Maid Coffee, Bail Handle, 5 Lb.	225.00
Pail, Kidd, Peanut Butter, Tin	780.00
Pail, Landers Satin Candies, Wire Handle, Children Flying Kites, 2 1/2 Lb.	55.00
Pail, Louis Brand, Peanut Butter, 4 3/4 In.	165.00
Pail, MacLaren's, Peanut Butter, 13 Oz.	99.00
Pail, Master Guard Stogies, Tin, 6 x 5 In.	350.00
Pail, Mayo Cut Plug, Tin, 4 1/2 x 8 x 3 1/2 In.	53.00
Pail, Merry Christmas & A Happy New Year, Peanut Butter, 1 Lb.	192.00
Pail, MJB Coffee, 4 Lb.	65.00
Pail, Monadnock, Peanut Butter, 1 Lb.	126.00
Pail, Monarch Teenie Weenie, Peanut Butter, Lid Handle, 1920s	195.00
Pail, Monarch Teenie Weenie, Popcorn, 1920s	215.00 To 225.00
Pail, Morris Supreme, Peanut Butter, 12 Oz.	200.00 To 220.00
Pail, Nigger Hair Tobacco, Slip Lid, African Queen Image, 6 3/4 In.	275.00
Pail, Ontario, Peanut Butter, 1 Lb.	166.00
Pail, Parrot, Peanut Butter	550.00
Pail, Patterson's Seal Cut Plug	35.00
Pail, Pickanniny, Peanut Butter	175.00
Pail, Planters, Peanut Butter, 1 Lb.	1210.00
Pail, Red Robin, Peanut Butter, 1 Lb.	3410.00
Pail, Red Seal Brand, Peanut Butter, Cincinnati, Ohio, 1 Lb.	22.00
Pail, Red Tiger Tobacco, Tin, Red, 6 x 8 x 6 1/2 In.	38.00
Pail, Shedd's, Peanut Butter, Circus Lithograph	20.00

Pail, Squirrel, Peanut Butter, 1 Lb. 121.00
Pail, Sultana, Peanut Butter, Early 1900s 175.00
Pail, Sweet Girl, Peanut Butter, 1 Lb. 3300.00
Pail, Teddy Bear, Peanut Butter 550.00
Pail, Toy Land, Peanut Butter, 1 Lb. 132.00
Pail, Uncle Wiggily, Candy 850.00
Pail, Uncle Wiggily, Peanut Butter, 1 Lb. 715.00
Pail, Union Leader Cut Plug, Tin, 4 x 7 x 5 In. 62.00
Pail, Wilson's, Peanut Butter, 12 Oz. 330.00
Paperweight, Kool Cigarettes, Penguin 35.00
Paperweight, Secret Service, Sterling, 3 In. ....*Illus* 5.00
Peanut Warmer, Fisher's Salted In The Shell 250.00
Pendant, Bull Durham, 14K Gold Plated 28.00
Pennant, National Electric Light Association, Logo 35.00
Pin, Big Boy Restaurant, Face Flashes, 3 In. 30.00
Pin, Braniff Airlines, Metal, 2 1/4 In. 22.50
Pin, Happy New Year, The Bulletin, Phila. Newspaper, Celluloid, 1920–1930 .... 30.00
Pin, Kellogg's Pep, Toots, Pinback 12.00
Pin, Lapel, Lincoln–Mercury, Gold, With Ruby, 100 Club 50.00
Pin, Reddy Kilowatt, Enameled 30.00
Pin, Willie & Millie, Kool Cigarettes, Original Card 12.75
Pin, Winnie Winkle, Kellogg's, Multicolored, Tin, 1945–1947, 13/16 In. 10.00
Pitcher, D. G. Wuengling & Son's Porter Beer, Gold Leaf Over White, 9 3/4 In. 82.50
Pitcher, Esso, Tiger In Your Tank 20.00
Pitcher, Orange Crush .... 65.00 To 95.00
Pitcher, Water, Fro–Joy Ice Cream 65.00
Pitcher, White Horse Whiskey 12.00
Plate, Jocko Yo–Yo, Clown, 10 In. 24.00
Platter, Spark's Perfect Health For Kidney & Liver 675.00
Pot Holder, Campbell's Soup, Boy 8.00
Pot Holder, Reddy Kilowatt 5.00
Pouch, Pedro Cut Plug Tobacco, Parchment 2000.00
Premier Cigarettes, Green, Menthol, 3 1/4 In. 10.00
Print, Ask For White Rose Flour, Mounted On Board, Color Litho, 15 In. 33.00
Print, Egyptian Deities Cigarettes, Litho, Wood Frame, Anargyros, 14 x 11 In. 99.00
Puppet, Hand, Pillsbury Dough Boy & Girl, Attached To Can, 1974, 11 In. 65.00
Rack, Prince Albert Tobacco 18.00
Rack, Seed, J. Brown Seed Co., Dark Wood, Floor Model, 3 Shelves, 2 Drawer 325.00
Ring, Olive Oyl, Post Cereal 30.00
Ring, Shadow Blue Coal, Radio Premium 475.00
Ring, Straight Arrow Gold Nugget 35.00
Rolling Pin, Burlington Feed Co., Stoneware, Wildflower 335.00
Rug, Buster Brown Shoes, Store, Buster, Tige, Yellow, Blue, Red, 4 In. 133.00
Ruler, Hector Whips, White, Black Letters, Celluloid, Tri–Fold, Small 9.00
Ruler, Old Hood Ice Cream, Wooden, 12 In. 28.00
Ruler, Pontiac, 1938 .... 10.00

• •

Put a silver spoon in a glass
before pouring in hot water. It
will absorb heat and keep the
glass from cracking.

• •

Advertising, Paperweight,
Secret Service, Sterling, 3 In.

Advertising, Bag, Martha White Flour,
18 X 18 In.

◆◆◆◆◆◆◆◆◆◆◆◆◆◆◆◆◆◆◆◆◆◆◆

Smelly matchcovers can be deodorized. Wipe the front and back and remove any mildew. Put a thin layer of Borax powder or cat litter in a tray, cover with flat matchcovers, and sprinkle on more Borax. The odor will leave in a few days. Or put the matchboxes in a covered box with some unwrapped bars of unscented soap. Turn them over each week. Leave them for a month. This should work for other small paper items.

◆◆◆◆◆◆◆◆◆◆◆◆◆◆◆◆◆◆◆◆◆◆◆

Ruler, Rhodes Preparatory School, Celluloid, Dated 1912, 6 In.	140.00
Salt & Pepper shakers are listed in their own category	
Scales are listed in their own category	
Screwdriver, Indian Motorcycle	35.00
Seat, Shoe Salesman's, Oak, With Mirror	85.00
Secret Writing Manual, Tom Mix, 8 Pages, Ralston, 3 x 5 In.	100.00
Shade, Roller, Dry Goods & Notions, Blue, Gilded Lettering, Hardware Window	125.00
Shaker, Ovaltine, Aluminum, Cover, 16 Oz.	15.00
Sharpener, Cuday's Meat Meal, Big Strong Healthy Hogs, Hogs In Hat	50.00
Sharpener, Fur & Pelt Buyer, Celluloid	46.00
Shot Glass, Borderland Whiskey, Etched	55.00
Sidewalk Marker, Grapette, Brass, Pin In Back, 4 In. Diam.	9.00
Sign, Abbott's Angostura, Man, Informal Dress, Framed, 1899, 50 x 38 In.	4070.00
Sign, Admiration Cigars, Easel Back, Tin Lithograph, 5 1/2 x 7 1/2 In.	182.00
Sign, America's Taste Sensation, Nichol 5 Cent Kola, 1930s, 12 x 36 In.	100.00
Sign, Anheuser–Busch, Dr. Stork, Tin, 1915, 12 x 7 1/2 In.	95.00
Sign, Anheuser–Busch, Girl In Red Dress, Framed, 23 1/2 x 38 1/2 In.	550.00
Sign, Armour's Corn Flakes, Tin, Box, Bowl of Cereal, Roses, 20 x 15 In.	154.00
Sign, Ayer's Ague Cure, Tin, 28 x 14 In.	935.00
Sign, Ayer's Hair Vigor, Nymph Rising From Lily, Paper, 10 3/4 x 13 3/4 In.	1815.00
Sign, Ayer's Sarsaparilla, Multicolored Cardboard, c.1880, 16 x 13 In.	1320.00
Sign, Bakers Cocoa, Tin, 31 In.	440.00
Sign, Barbers Union, Metal, 9 x 7 In.	15.00
Sign, Bartell's Malt Extract, Tin, 13 x 6 In.	175.00 To 225.00
Sign, Beech–Nut Tobacco, Package Shape, Tin, 11 x 14 1/2 In.	65.00
Sign, Best Bicycle On Earth, Screen Printed, Tin, 12 x 36 In.	99.00
Sign, Bogart's Hat Shop, High Hat Shape, Double Sides, 1940, 3 Ft.	375.00
Sign, Borax Is King, Tin Lithograph, Full Color, 30 In.	7.00
Sign, Breyers Ice Cream, Neon, 25 x 22 In.	22.00
Sign, Brownie Chocolate Soda, Cardboard, Framed, 5 Ft.	500.00
Sign, Bulldog Safety Switches, Papier–Mache, 16 In.	1210.00
Sign, Butter–Krust Bread, Comical Boy With Milk Can, Tin, 26 1/2 x 38 1/2 In.	137.00
Sign, C. J. Fell & Brother Spice Co., Paper, 16 x 18 In.	425.00
Sign, Campbell's Tomato Soup, Porcelain, Curved, 15 x 22 1/2 In.	1100.00
Sign, Canada Dry Spur Beverage, Embossed Tin, 12 x 3 1/2 In.	38.00
Sign, Canadian Pacific Express, Rectangular, Single Sided, 20 x 13 In.	385.00
Sign, Carbon's Medicated Gin, Nurse, Bottle, Tin Over Cardboard, 9 x 13 In.	170.00
Sign, Carnation Gum, Self–Framed, Tin, Chew Carnation & Taste The Smell, 13 In.	880.00
Sign, Champion Ginger Ale, Tin Lithograph, Orange & Green Ground, 19 3/4 In.	38.50
Sign, Cherry Smash, Celluloid, Light Up, 14 x 10 In.	330.00

Sign, Cherry Smash, Tin, Curled Edges, 4 x 9 1/2 In. 2200.00
Sign, Chevrolet, Owl Shape, Illuminated, 22 x 34 x 6 In. 770.00
Sign, Cinco Cigar, Porcelain, 14 x 48 In. 125.00
Sign, Cinco Cigars, Tin, 9 x 20 In. 45.00
Sign, Colgate Soaps, 4 Horses Draw Man's Carriage, Paper, 21 x 16 1/2 In. 495.00
Sign, Confectionery Tonic, Ice Cream, Oil On Canvas, 35 x 42 In. 970.00
Sign, Conkey's Y–O Feeds, Bag of Feed Shape, Tin, 29 1/2 x 17 1/2 In. 55.00
Sign, Conoco Greasing Service, Porcelain, 40 x 28 In. 595.00
Sign, Cook's Gold Blume Beer, Tin, 2–Sided, Red, Black, Yellow, 28 x 14 In. 120.00
Sign, Cranford Dairy, Twelve Trees, Cardboard, 4 x 9 In. 12.00
Sign, Crown Quality Ice Cream, Embossed Tin, 19 x 28 In. 93.00
Sign, Dad's Root Beer, Horizontal, Bottle Cap, Tin, 12 x 30 In. 45.00
Sign, Damarin Rooms & Bath, Wood, 2–Sided, 32 x 12 In. 154.00
Sign, Dandelion Stout, Reverse Painting On Glass, 5 x 8 In. 220.00
Sign, David's Prize Soap, Comic Chinese Laundry Man, Paper, 16 x 21 In. 3300.00
Sign, Davis' Pain Killer, Labeled Medicine Bottle, Tin, 24 x 18 In. 5500.00
Sign, DeLaval Cream Separator, Tin Lithograph, 26 In. Diam. 3410.00
Sign, Deppen Beer, Reverse Painted, Elk, Copper Frame, 13 1/4 x 25 In. 880.00
Sign, Devoe Varnish, Cloud Pouring Water On Auto, Cardboard, c.1878, 34 1/2 In. ... 330.00
Sign, Diamond Dyes, Tin, Bessie Gutmann's, Busy Day In Dollville, 25 x 17 In. 2805.00
Sign, Diamond Gloss Starch, Baby In Bonnet, 22 x 17 In. 33.00
Sign, Dixon Crucible Co., Paper, Stove Polish, Pencils, Child, Sailboat, 9 x 20 In. 38.00
Sign, Don't Forget Uneeda Biscuit, Cardboard, Framed, 15 3/4 x 20 3/4 In. 132.00
Sign, Dr Pepper, Good For Life, Porcelain, 1947, 10 1/2 x 26 In. 225.00
Sign, Dr Pepper, Porcelain, 8 x 12 In. 40.00
Sign, Dr. B. J. Kendall's Blackberry Balsam, Cure Cholera, 1880, 25 x 38 In. 110.00
Sign, Dr. Clark's Life Balsam, Paper, Young Lady, Yellow Dress, 9 x 13 In. 467.00
Sign, Dr. Daniels Stock Medicines, Wood, 29 x 12 In. 165.00
Sign, Dr. Hyman Painless Dentist, Figural, Tin Arrow, 19 x 4 In. 160.00
Sign, Dr. Lymas Flavoring Extracts, Blue & White, Cardboard, c.1915, 10 x 14 In. .. 17.50
Sign, Dr. Pierce's Medicinal, Purgative Pallets, Paper, 1872, 21 1/2 x 27 In. 3410.00
Sign, Dr. Russell's Pepsin Calisaya Bitters, Paper, 21 x 15 In. 1925.00
Sign, Dr. Swett's Root Beer, Great Health Beverage, Tin, Square, 14 1/2 In. 550.00
Sign, Drink Moxie, Embossed & Stenciled Tin, White, Yellow, Red Lettering, 31 In. 137.00
Sign, Duchess Trousers, Factory Image, Tin, Frame, 34 1/2 x 24 1/2 In. 110.00
Sign, Dupont Powder, Canvas Lithograph, Wagon Train Scene, 1911, 15 x 18 In. 285.00
Sign, Dutch Boy Paint, Porcelain, 4 x 4 Ft. 250.00
Sign, Dutch Master Cigars, Picture On Canvas, 16 x 24 In. 135.00
Sign, Dyer's Pork & Beans, Tin Lithograph, 11 In. 247.00
Sign, Eastern States Farm Supply, Tin, 71 x 47 In. 30.00
Sign, Eddy Plows, Wood Trade Sign, Mr. Walden Eddy Himself, 5 x 2 In. 523.00
Sign, Egyptian Straights Cigarettes, White Lettering, Red Ground, 15 x 13 In. 198.00
Sign, Eigenbrot Brewery, Corner, Embossed Tin, 14 x 20 In. 605.00
Sign, Electric Luster Starch, 4 Women Showing Product, Paper, 18 x 9 In. 83.00
Sign, Elgin American Compacts, 36 Different, Prices, 1950s, 21 x 16 In. 25.00
Sign, Empire Fire Insurance, Aluminum, Frame, 15 x 21 In. 75.00
Sign, Eshelman Red Rose Dog & Puppy Food, Pointer On Front, Tin, 18 X36 In. 38.50
Sign, Fairy Soap, Little Girl Sitting On "O", 11 x 21 In. 55.00
Sign, Fall River Line, Bristol Steamer, Paper, 13 x 10 1/2 In. 633.00
Sign, Falstaff Beer, Double Sided, Porcelain, 41 x 31 In. 22.50
Sign, Falstaff Beer, Family In Castle, Concave, Tin, Round, 24 In. 125.00
Sign, Firestone, Porcelain, 1930s, 4 x 1 1/2 In. 195.00
Sign, Foyle's Library Cigars, 2–Sided, Porcelain, 20 x 15 In. 49.00
Sign, Frank Fehr Brewing Co., Tin, Self–Framed, 22 1/4 x 28 1/4 In. 550.00
Sign, Fremlins Family Ale & Stout Depot, Saloon Front, Metal, 2–Sided, 45 x 42 In. .. 825.00
Sign, Frostie, Die Cut, Cardboard, Full Color, 13 x 21 In. 45.00
Sign, Frostlene Frosting, Embossed Tin, 27 x 19 In. 1100.00
Sign, G. F. Burkhardt's Lager Beer, Tin Lithograph, 13 1/2 x 16 3/4 In. 600.00
Sign, Genuine Chevy Parts, 2–Sided, Porcelain, 24 x 19 In. 750.00
Sign, Genuine Kickapoo Indian Oil, Paper, c.1890, 21 1/2 x 28 In. 4950.00
Sign, Gettelman Milwaukee Beer, Die Cut Red Letters, Metal, 12 x 8 In. 80.00
Sign, Gillette, Safety Razor, Tin, 2 Sides, Hanging, 13 1/2 x 15 In. 3025.00
Sign, Gold Dust Twins, Uncle Sam, Roosevelt Welcome Twins, 20 x 10 1/2 In. 1375.00

Sign, Gold Tone Razor Blades, Cardboard, 5 x 13 In. 25.00
Sign, Golden Girl Cola, Sundrop, Bottle Shape, Metal, 5 Ft. 150.00
Sign, Golf Ball, Fiberglass, 3 Ft. 350.00
Sign, Gorton's, Puddings, Pies, Peacock Feathered Fans, Paper, 26 x 20 In. 335.00
Sign, Grape–Nuts, Girl, Dog, Tin, Self–Framed, 20 1/2 x 30 1/2 In. ....885.00 To 2200.00
Sign, Great Interstate Fair, Paper, 1896, Trotter, Bicycle Racers, 40 x 37 In. 575.00
Sign, Green River Whiskey, Black Man & Horse, Jug of Whiskey, Tin, 31 x 40 In. 195.00
Sign, Gures Root Beer, Embossed Tin, 27 x 9 In. 148.00
Sign, Harmonica, 3 Ft. 255.00
Sign, Hellmann Brewing Co., Big Horn Sheep, Beer In Paw, Paper, 23 1/2 In. 138.00
Sign, Henrietta Cigar, Man At Desk, Phone & Cigar, Embossed Tin, 13 1/4 In. 275.00
Sign, Hershey's Ice Cream, Chocolate & Vanilla Cone, Easel Back, 23 x 14 In. 40.00
Sign, Hickman & Ebbert Co., Wagon, Tin, 25 x 37 In. 1595.00
Sign, Hires Root Beer, Woman Answering Door, Girl Selling Hires, 14 x 10 In. 715.00
Sign, Hires To Your Health, Boy, Mug, Tin, 19 1/2 x 27 1/2 In. 2970.00
Sign, Hires, Girl, With Glass, Tin, Frame, 13 1/2 x 19 1/2 In. 550.00
Sign, Hires, Pointing Boy Holding Mug, Tin, Frame, 19 x 27 In. 4100.00
Sign, Hoffman House Bouquet Cigars, Paper, 1900, 10 1/2 x 13 1/2 In. 775.00
Sign, Honest Scrap Tobacco, Paperboard, Framed, 22 x 30 In. 995.00
Sign, Hostetter's Bitters, Reverse Painting, St. Anthony, Dragon, 28 1/2 In. 110.00
Sign, Howard Dustless Duster, Paper, Framed, 32 x 22 In. 1200.00
Sign, Hubbard's Fertilizers, Porcelain, 20 x 10 In. 38.50
Sign, Hudepohl Brewing, Vitrolite Curved Corner, 2 Deer, Barrel, 18 x 22 1/2 In. ... 1100.00
Sign, Hudson River Day Line Ferry Boat, Cardboard, 10 x 19 In. 33.00
Sign, Hy–Quality Coffee, Cardboard, Die Cut, 39 In. 1375.00
Sign, I. W. Harper, Dog, Hunting Cabin, Gold, 1909, 18 x 24 In. 1200.00
Sign, I. W. Hopper Whiskey, Hunting Cabin, Game Pelts, 23 1/2 x 17 1/2 In. 550.00
Sign, J. & P. Coats, Fisherman & Friend Using Spools, Paper, 22 x 17 1/2 In. 115.00
Sign, Japps Hair Rejuvenator, Tin, 9 x 13 In. 60.00
Sign, John Deere Hay Loader, Paper, Farm Scene With Equipment, 14 x 10 In. 137.00
Sign, John Deere, Comb Holder Attached To Front, Iron, 13 x 18 In. 275.00
Sign, Jones Body Shop, Porcelain, 36 x 10 In. 70.00
Sign, Just Suits Tobacco, Porcelain, Figural Pipe, 16 x 6 In. 450.00
Sign, Kellogg's Rice Krispies, 1938, 24 x 16 In. 85.00
Sign, Kessler's Whiskey, Depicting Horse Race, Wooden Frame, 14 x 18 In. 11.00
Sign, Key, Independent Lock Co., Double–Sided, Die Cut Tin, 32 Ft. 155.00
Sign, Kingsbury, Easel Back, Die Cast Metal, 10 In. 45.00
Sign, La Belle Chocolatiere, Woman Holding Serving Tray, 44 x 32 In. 495.00
Sign, Lash's Bitters, Pretty Woman, With Horse Head, Wooden, 14 x 20 In. 385.00
Sign, Lavine Soap, Woman Bathing Child, Paper, 1870s, 9 x 12 In. 440.00
Sign, Liberty Tavern, Carved Eagle Holding Shield, Wooden, 58 x 31 In. 2600.00
Sign, Lifebuoy Soap, Tin, 6 x 13 In. 93.00
Sign, Lime Crush, Embossed Tin, 19 x 14 In. 55.00
Sign, Lipton's Instant Cocoa, Tin Lithograph, 13 x 9 In. 495.00
Sign, Lone Jack Tobacco, Different Men, Framed, 1871, 12 1/2 x 10 In. 275.00
Sign, Lone Jack Tobacco, Men Seated Around Table, Paper, 12 x 9 1/2 In. 1100.00
Sign, Lorillard's Tiger Fine Cut, Embossed, Tin, 9 x 13 In. 467.00
Sign, Malcolm Forbes, Horse, One of Ohio's Greatest Sires, 46 x 74 In. 1650.00
Sign, Marlboro, Tin, 16 x 20 In. 12.50
Sign, Maryland Casualty Co., Tin, Black, Red Images, 23 x 11 In. 49.00
Sign, Masury's Pure Colors, Tin, Framed, 19 x 25 In. 550.00
Sign, Mayo Cut Plug, Roly Poly, Tobacco, Tin, 7 In. 715.00
Sign, McCurdy Seeds, Tin, 14 x 21 In. 18.00
Sign, Mecca Cigarettes, T. Earl Christy, Wooden Frame, 18 x 9 In. 110.00
Sign, Mobil Gas, Flying Horse, Die Cut Porcelain Pegasus, 56 x 70 In. 550.00
Sign, Morrison Plows, Tin Lithograph, Factory, Buggies In Front, 19 1/2 In. 60.00
Sign, Moxie, Girl, Horse Mobile, Tin Lithograph, 12 3/4 x 24 In. 385.00
Sign, Moxie, Red, Man, Horse, Car, Tin, 6 1/2 In. 3740.00
Sign, Munsing Wear Cut, Tin, 24 x 16 1/2 In. 1870.00
Sign, Murad Cigarettes, Harem Girl, Frame, c.1918, 9 x 12 In. 20.00
Sign, Murine Eye Remedies, Glass, Blue Chipped Letters, 38 x 6 In. 375.00
Sign, Murine Rests Tired Eyes, Soothes–Brightens, Glass, 10 x 30 In. 425.00
Sign, Nabisco Uneeda Biscuit, Cardboard, 20 x 15 In. 135.00

Sign, Nabisco, Slicker Boy, Cornucopia of Products, 1948, 24 x 20 In. 35.00
Sign, Neversink Distillery, Reverse Glass, Buildings, Frame, 27 1/2 x 20 In. 220.00
Sign, New Home Sewing Machine, Framed, 44 x 30 In. 770.00
Sign, Nichol Kola, Embossed, Tin, Bottle Cap, 14 x 14 In. 44.00
Sign, Nipper Center, 19 Opera Singers Around, Oilcloth, 15 x 34 1/2 In. 400.00
Sign, Nu–Grape, Embossed, Tin, 23 x 11 In. 55.00
Sign, Nu–Grape, Round, 36 In. 185.00
Sign, Old Continental Whiskey, Large Acorns, 25 x 21 In. 2250.00
Sign, Old Mill Cigarette, Cardboard, Original Frame, 26 x 19 In. 1595.00
Sign, Orange Crush, Bottle Cap, 34 In. 165.00
Sign, Orange Crush, Bottle, Tin, 12 x 30 In. 45.00
Sign, Orange Crush, Pictures Ribbed Bottle, Frame, 48 In. 395.00
Sign, Orange Crush, Porcelain, 12 x 9 In. 300.00
Sign, Pabst Brewing Co., Factory, Framed, 40 x 52 In. 1100.00
Sign, Park–Drive For Pleasure, Porcelain, Red & White Lettering, Blue, 20 x 30 In. 71.00
Sign, Paul Jones Whiskey, Tin, Blacks Pictured, Framed, 19 1/2 x 13 1/2 In. 1760.00
Sign, Paul Webb Mountain Boys, Dealers Advertising, 8 x 9 In. 795.00
Sign, Pepsi–Cola, Cardboard, Pepsi Logo, 1950s, 24 x 36 In. 130.00
Sign, Perfection Cigarettes, Color Lithograph, Heavily Wrinkled, 29 x 19 In. 154.00
Sign, Pettijohn's Breakfast Food, Paper Lithograph, Framed, 10 x 13 In. 247.00
Sign, Pfaff's Lager, Match Striker Attached, Porcelain, 4 x 6 In. 75.00
Sign, Pfeiffer's Beer, Jockey, Horse, 1935 Kentucky Derby Winner, Tin, 11 x 14 In. 175.00
Sign, Phillip Morris, Johnny, All Parties Vote For Johnny, Stand–Up, 3 Ft. 4 In. 495.00
Sign, Phoenix Sparkling Drink, Die Cut Tin, 26 1/4 x 19 1/2 In. 220.00
Sign, Piedmont Cigarette, Porcelain, 30 x 46 In. 625.00
Sign, Pilgrim Fathers, Tin, 24 x 18 In. 260.00
Sign, Pillsbury's Best Feed, Red, White & Blue Letters, Tin, 18 x 18 In. 33.00
Sign, Players Navy Cut Cigarette, Tin, 2 x 3 In. 25.00
Sign, Players Navy Cut Tobacco, Tin, Sailor, Yellow Ground, 19 x 29 In. 135.00
Sign, Pocket Knife, Movable Blades, New York Cutlery Co., 1910s, 30 In. 3100.00
Sign, Porosknit Underwear, Reverse Painted, 30 x 20 In. 400.00
Sign, Price, Diamond Shape, Tin, Red, White, 5 & 10 Cents, 1915, 4 1/2 In., Pair ... 15.00
Sign, Prince Albert Indian Chief, Tin, 20 x 24 In. 800.00
Sign, Prince Albert Tobacco, Paper, Framed, 31 x 24 In. 2400.00
Sign, Prince Albert Tobacco, Tin, Framed, 28 x 22 In. 2695.00
Sign, Pure Gold Baby, Figural, Baby Crawling, Cardboard, Stand–Up, 16 In. 577.00
Sign, Purity Pasteurized Ice Cream, Enameled, 27 x 38 In. 195.00
Sign, Quick Lunch, Prescott & Pierce, Wooden, Painted, 8 Ft. 270.00
Sign, Radway's Medicinal, Resolvent & Regulating Pills, Paper, 13 1/2 In. 1017.00
Sign, Railway Express Agency, Porcelain, 3 x 3 Ft. 575.00
Sign, RC Cola, Metal, 18 x 53 In. 85.00
Sign, Red Goose Shoes, Porcelain, Neon, 3 Ft. 1750.00
Sign, Red Goose, Porcelain, Die–Cut, 3 In. 1100.00
Sign, Red Rose Coffee, Tin, 19 x 27 In. 55.00
Sign, Red Star Yeast, Embossed Tin, 6 x 8 In. 440.00
Sign, Red Top Beer, 8 x 20 In. 30.00
Sign, Redditch Patent Razor, Wooden, Red Paint, 52 In. 275.00
Sign, Reddy Kilowatt, Head, Rectangle, 8 1/2 x 20 In. 125.00
Sign, Reddy Kilowatt, Tin, 28 x 8 1/2 In. 45.00
Sign, Rexall Drugs, Welcome, Illuminated, Plastic & Metal, 37 In. 55.00
Sign, Reynolds' North Bridgewater Eagle Seed Sower, Eagle, Shield, 16 x 19 In. 55.00
Sign, Rio Grande District Sales Office, Railroad, 40 x 84 In. 495.00
Sign, Robert Burns Cigar, On Horse, Tin, 24 In. 225.00
Sign, Rockford Watch, Pretty Girl, Tin, 17 x 23 1/4 In. 300.00
Sign, Royal Crown Cola, Embossed Tin, 11 1/2 In. 140.00
Sign, Ruppert Beer & Ale, Reverse On Glass, Grain Painted Frame, 18 1/4 In. 45.00
Sign, Ruud Automatic Hot Water Heater, Cardboard, Girl, 30 In. 40.00
Sign, Salada Tea, Porcelain, 3 x 15 In. 95.00
Sign, Salada Tea, Porcelain, Tin, 2 x 9 In. 195.00
Sign, Sanford's Ginger, Black Boy With Watermelon, Large Bottle, 28 x 21 In. 3575.00
Sign, Satin Face Cream, Frame, 1905, 30 x 4 In. 375.00
Sign, Schenck's Mandrake Pills, Tin, 1880, 28 x 22 In. 990.00
Sign, Schlitz Beer, Oil Cloth, 2 x 5 Ft. 250.00

Sign, Schlitz, Cardboard, Framed, 33 x 45 In. 2420.00
Sign, Shaking Hands, Figural, Carved Pine, Painted, 9 x 23 1/2 In. 2860.00
Sign, Shears, Oversized Wooden Tinsmith's 155.00
Sign, Shenandoah Valley Railroad, Reverse Glass, Framed, 28 x 21 In. 1260.00
Sign, Sherwood Heating Fuel, Porcelain, 7 x 10 In. 95.00
Sign, Shoe Repair, Wooden Boot, Red & White Lettering, 15 In. 165.00
Sign, Singer Sewing Machine, Porcelain, Red S, Woman By Machine, 24 x 36 In. 412.00
Sign, Sitting Bull Durham Tobacco, With Rifle On Pony, Paper, 9 x 12 1/2 In. 1980.00
Sign, Sleepy Eye Flour, Embossed Tin, 19 x 13 In. 1815.00
Sign, Smiling Baker Holding Nabisco Box, Color Lithograph, 1910, 5 1/2 x 7 In. 65.00
Sign, Snowboy Washing Powder, On Canvas, 42 x 28 In. 5610.00
Sign, Southern Dairies Ice Cream, Blue & Gold Glass, 11 x 6 In. 175.00
Sign, Squire's Arlington Hams, Bacon, Sausage, Tin, Seated Pigs, 20 x 24 In. 1045.00
Sign, Squire's Arlington, Pig Picture, Tin, Framed, 20 x 24 In. 1210.00
Sign, St. Jacob's Oil, Monk Holding Bottle of Product, Paper, 18 x 9 1/2 In. 55.00
Sign, Standard Oil Mica Axle Grease, Frame, 15 x 12 In. 295.00
Sign, Standard Oil, Embossed Porcelain, 3 x 7 Ft. 450.00
Sign, Standard Quality Feed, Premixes of Omaha, Barn Shape, 12 x 22 In. 45.00
Sign, Star Soap, Cardboard, Die Cut, 9 x 6 In. 2035.00
Sign, Street, Mile View A. V., Blue, White Letters, Porcelain, 18 1/4 x 4 1/4 In. 30.00
Sign, Studebaker, Red & Blue, Round, 48 In. 300.00
Sign, Sun Insurance Co., Porcelain, Sun, Blue Lettering, 20 x 14 In. 110.00
Sign, Sunny Brook Good Luck Whiskey, Wooden, 9 x 15 In. 125.00
Sign, Surveyor's, Wooden, Sandpaper Ground, 19th Century, 19 x 9 In. 180.00
Sign, Syrup of Figs, Woman, Picking Figs, Paper, 80 1/2 x 52 In. 2750.00
Sign, Taber & Morses, Horse Drawn Steam Farm Equipment, Wooden, 28 x 22 In. 6600.00
Sign, Tavern, Hand Holding Bell, Figural, Wooden, 19th Century, 20 x 15 In. 1430.00
Sign, Tetley Tea, Gentleman, Holding Glass, England, 34 x 26 In. 195.00
Sign, Texaco Farm Lubricants, Porcelain, 30 x 42 In. 145.00
Sign, Texaco Marine Lubricants, Ships, Buoys, Sea Gulls, Tin, 21 x 12 In. 595.00
Sign, Texaco Sky Chief Gasoline, c.1962, 12 x 18 In. 60.00
Sign, Tobacco, Allen & Ginter's, Racing Colors of The World, Women, 18 x 28 In. 5100.00
Sign, Tokio Cigarettes, Paperboard, Framed, 33 x 25 In. 115.00
Sign, Town Crier Flour, Tin Lithograph, Orange Lettering, 18 3/4 In. 33.00
Sign, Traffic Motor Oil, 1930s Model Car, 19 x 38 In. 145.00
Sign, Train, Pabst Beer, Rocks Back & Forth, 16 x 16 1/2 x 10 In. 110.00
Sign, Tru–Test Brushes, Yellow, Dark Blue Letters, Tin, 24 x 5 In. 2.00
Sign, Turkey Red Cigarettes, Paper Litho, Red, Black, White Lettering, 16 x 15 In. 165.00
Sign, Turkish Delight Cigarettes, Bull Dog, Celluloid, Frame, 13 x 18 In. 143.00
Sign, Turkish Trophies Cigarettes, Color Lithographed Poster, 29 x 19 In. 265.00
Sign, U.S. Cartridge Co. Shot & Powder, Reverse Painted, 9 1/4 x 11 1/2 In. 195.00
Sign, UMC Bullet, Paper Lithograph, Board In Frame, 39 x 53 In. 2805.00
Sign, Uncle Daniel Fine Cut Tobacco, Wooden Crate Slat, 29 x 6 In. 35.00
Sign, Uneeda Bakers, Cardboard, NBC Logo, 18 1/2 x 22 In. 40.00
Sign, Union Central Life Insurance, Self–Framed, Tin, 25 1/2 x 37 In. 605.00
Sign, Union Leader Cut Plug, Tin, Embossed, 25 x 21 In. 253.00
Sign, Van Houten's Cocoa, Cardboard, Framed, 33 x 22 In. 385.00
Sign, Veedol Motor Oil, Cardboard, 28 x 59 In. 230.00
Sign, Verner's, Tin, 24 x 60 In. 205.00
Sign, Victor Records, 2 Sides, Porcelain, Bluebird Records Hanging, 20 In. 1150.00
Sign, Virginia Slims, Looks Like Raquel Welsh, Metal, 14 x 9 In. 15.00
Sign, Vitalized Ginger Ale, Girl On Surf Board, Tin, 6 x 9 In. 25.00
Sign, Watch Store, Don W. Gorrecht, Figural Pocket Watch, Iron Frame, 30 In. 465.00
Sign, Waterman's Fountain Pens, Tin, 13 x 9 In. 695.00
Sign, Welcome Soap, Curtis Davis, Paper, Framed, 16 1/2 x 31 1/2 In. 1320.00
Sign, West Hair Nets, Counter, Metal, Square, 1918, 6 In. 150.00
Sign, Western Farms, Milk That Is Milk, 4 x 13 In. 990.00
Sign, Western Union, Enameled, Both Sides, 15 x 30 In. 35.00
Sign, White Rock, King of Hearts, August Hutaf, Tin, 8 x 13 In. 450.00
Sign, White Rock, Psyche, Paper, 1930s, 60 x 42 In. 275.00
Sign, White Rock, Tin, 8 x 22 In. 120.00
Sign, White's Golden Tonic For Horses, Lists Cures, Pictures Horse, 24 x 30 In. 75.00
Sign, Wild Root, Tin, 13 x 39 In. 75.00

Sign, Wills's Gold Flake Cigarettes, Porcelain, 18 In. 99.00
Sign, Winchester, Deer Jumping, Cardboard, 1930s 300.00
Sign, Wooden Key, Gray Paint, 1930s, 7 Ft. 4 In. 625.00
Sign, Wrigley's Gum, Tin Over Cardboard, 9 x 17 In. 33.00
Sign, Wrigley's Spearmint Gum, Cardboard, Trolley Sign, 21 x 11 In. 35.00
Sign, Yale Beer, Reverse Glass, Factory Scene, Frame, 32 x 24 In. 2200.00
Sign, Yuengling's Beer, Reverse Painted, Corner, Trademark Eagle, 20 x 28 In. 4950.00
Skillet, Western Holly Ranges, 5 3/4 In. 22.00
Soap, Fels Naptha 3.00
Soap, Peter Pan, Colgate, Original Wrapper 20.00
Soda Set, Old Kentucky Root Beer, Mugs, 7 Piece 75.00
Spatula, Rumford Baking Powder 12.00
Spice Cabinet, Schotten Spice, Oak, Lithographed Label 695.00
Spoon Hanger, Honeybee, Nabisco, 1950–1960, 2 In. 10.00
Spoon, Baby's, Gerber, Silver Plate 12.00
Spoon, Gibson Refrigerator 10.00
Spoon, Soup, Union Pacific Railroad, Winged Streamliner, International Silver 25.00
Stickpin, John Deere 40.00
Stickpin, Moline Plow Co. 35.00
Stickpin, Pig, Burk Pork Packers, Philadelphia, 1900 .... 30.00
Stickpin, Sharples Cream Separator, Celluloid 25.00
Stone, Sharpening, Raw Furs, Wool–Hides & Pets, E. A. Stephens, Denver, Co. 35.00
Stool, Foot Sizing, Dr. Scholl's Advertising Faces Customer, 29 In. 17.50
Straw Holder, Glass, Faceted, Brass Capped Insert, 5 x 12 In. 165.00
Straw Holder, Red Glass, Metal Lid, 1950s 145.00
Straw Holder, Welch's, Box, 5 x 2 In. 2750.00
Sugar & Creamer, Elsie & Elmer 165.00
Sweater, Anheuser–Busch Michelob Logo, White, USA, Medium–Large 10.00
Swizzle Stick, Jack Dempsey Restaurant, Green & Orange 18.00
Swizzle Stick, Wurlitzer 5.00
Tap Knob, Beverwyck Breweries 29.00
Tap Knob, Eagle Brewing, Utica, N.Y. 39.00
Tap Knob, Rittenhouse Whiskey, 1930 .... 25.00
Tape Measure, Texaco, Cloth, Celluloid 45.00
Teapot, White China, Gold AB In Script & Rim, Small 50.00
Thermometers are listed in their own category
Tie Bar, Taxco 18.00
Tie Clasp, Charlie Tuna 18.00
Tie Clasp, Mobil Flying Red Horse 30.00

Advertising tin cans or canisters were first used commercially in the
United States in 1819 and were called *tins*. The English language is
sometimes confusing. Today the word *tin* is used by most collectors to
describe many types of containers, including food tins, biscuit boxes, roly
poly tobacco containers, gunpowder cans, talcum powder sprinkle–top cans,
cigarette flat–fifty tins, and more. Beer cans are listed in their own
category. Things made of undecorated tin are listed under Tinware.

Tin, 3 Knights, Condoms 100.00
Tin, Ace High Tobacco, Flat, Pocket 3000.00
Tin, All American Cigars, Round, 6 x 2 x 2 In. 40.00
Tin, All Nations Tobacco, Horizontal Box, 4 x 2 x 1 In. 375.00
Tin, Ambino Tobacco, Pocket 2400.00
Tin, Amicus Cigars, Round, 4 x 5 In 210.00
Tin, Apache Trail Cigars, Oval, 6 x 6 x 4 In. 1100.00
Tin, Arabian Coffee, 1 Lb. 385.00
Tin, Armour's Veribest Peanut Butter, Tin Over Cardboard, 13 x 9 In. 275.00
Tin, Atlantic Blasting Cap 100.00
Tin, Atlas Blasting Cap, No. 6 .... 30.00
Tin, Atwood Coffee, 3 Lb. .... 75.00 To 85.00
Tin, Auto Laks, Laxative, Early Car 300.00
Tin, Avon, To A Wild Rose, Talcum Powder, 1950s–1960s 2.50
Tin, Bag Balm, Teat Salve For Cows, 10 Oz. 25.00
Tin, Baker's Delight Baking Powder, 14 1/4 In. 149.00

Advertising, Tin, Mammoth Salted   Advertising, Tin, Sanford's Ink
Nuts, 3 1/2 In.   Eraser, 3 In.

Tin, Bambino Tobacco, Upright Pocket, 4 1/2 x 3 3/4 In.	760.00
Tin, Beaver Typewriter Ribbon	75.00
Tin, Beech-Nut Coffee, Key, Sample	45.00
Tin, Berma Coffee, 1 Lb.	93.00
Tin, Between The Acts, Minnie Hauk, Flat, Pocket	425.00
Tin, Big Horn Coffee, 3 Lb.	250.00
Tin, Bigger Hair Tonic	125.00
Tin, Bird Brand Coffee, 3 Lb.	125.00
Tin, Black Beau Candy, Black Child, 3 In. Diam.	23.00
Tin, Black Cat Stove Cream, Flat Can, Embossed Cat On Lid	35.00
Tin, Blood Orange Pellets, Vertical Box	210.00
Tin, Bond Street, Pocket	6.00
Tin, Boot Jack Plug Tobacco, Square	50.00
Tin, Bouquet Coffee, 1 Lb.	192.00
Tin, Bowl of Roses Pipe Mixture, Gentleman In Recliner, 3 x 3 3 In.	66.00
Tin, Buckingham Tobacco, Pocket	105.00
Tin, Bull Dog Tobacco, Pocket	665.00
Tin, Bunker Hill Coffee, 1 Lb.	145.00
Tin, Bunte Marshmallow, Round	200.00
Tin, Bunte's Chocolate Candy, Lid, 2 Lb.	3.00
Tin, Butternut Coffee, Paxton & Gallagher, 1 Lb.	2.35
Tin, Cadet Cigars, 6 x 4 In.	175.00
Tin, Cafe Du Monde, Cajun Coffee, 1 Lb.	1.00
Tin, Calox Tooth Powder, 3/4 Oz.	3.00
Tin, Cameron's First Grade Tobacco, Flat, Pocket	275.00
Tin, Campbell Coffee, 4 Lb.	495.00
Tin, Campbell's Shag Tobacco, Pocket, 4 x 2 In.	400.00 To 750.00
Tin, Caravan Condoms	95.00
Tin, Carlton Club Tobacco, Pocket	460.00
Tin, Carte Blanche Tobacco, Pocket	135.00
Tin, Casca Royal Pills, 1 1/2 x 2 1/2 In.	15.00
Tin, Cayenne Pepper, Long John, Norwine Coffee Co., 1/4 Lb.	45.00
Tin, Central Market Coffee, Miss Liberty, 4 Lb.	650.00
Tin, Central Union Cut Plug, Pail, 4 x 7 x 4 In.	49.00
Tin, Chariots Condoms	60.00
Tin, Charles Potato Chips, Lid, 1 Lb.	4.75
Tin, Chesapeake Tobacco, Scene, Pocket	1430.00
Tin, Choice Family Tea, Bail Handle, Ginna & Co.	72.00
Tin, Christy's Oysters, Pictures Elvis Presley	200.00
Tin, Cleopatra Rose, Palmolive Talc, 6 1/4 In. *Illus*	28.00
Tin, Cloverine Talc, Oval, Small Top, 4 x 2 In.	225.00
Tin, Colgate Baby Talcum, Baby Holding Tin	90.00
Tin, Columbia Watch Springs, Pictures Miss Liberty	75.00
Tin, Comrade Coffee, 1 Lb.	65.00
Tin, Constitution Cigars, Round, 5 1/2 x 6 x 4 1/4 In.	375.00
Tin, Continental Cubes Tobacco, Curved, Pocket, 3 1/2 x 2 1/2 In.	220.00

Tin, Cupcake, Swansdown, Angel Food 12.00
Tin, Cupcake, Urban Flour 12.00
Tin, Daisy BB 12.00
Tin, Dan Patch Tobacco, Pocket 95.00
Tin, Davis Baking Powder, Sample 60.00
Tin, Derma Medicone Ointment, Round, Sample 2.25
Tin, Dills Tobacco, Pocket, Sample .... 45.00 To 75.00
Tin, Dixie Kid, Black 400.00
Tin, Dr. Johnson's Educator Cracker, 5 1/2 x 6 x 5 In. 33.00
Tin, Dr. Lyons Tooth Powder, Oval, Lid 5.00
Tin, Dr. Nebb's Baby Powder, Baby & Blocks 50.00
Tin, Drako Coffee, 1 Lb. 1760.00
Tin, Duffee's Laxative, Embossed, 13 x 9 In. 55.00
Tin, Dunnsboro Tobacco, Pocket, 7 1/2 In. 1000.00
Tin, Dupont Blasting Cap, No. 5 .... 40.00
Tin, Dupont Gunpowder 20.00
Tin, Dutch Cleanser, Contents, 1940s 18.00
Tin, Eagle Snack Mix, Lid, 32 Oz. 4.00
Tin, Eastman Cartridge, No. 1 .... 25.00
Tin, Educator Crackers 60.00
Tin, Elephant Salted Peanuts, Elephant Pictured, 10 Lb. 75.00
Tin, Epicure Tobacco, Pocket 90.00
Tin, Eskimo Smoking Tobacco, Gold Lettering, Alaskan Malamute, Igloos, 6 In. 83.50
Tin, Folgers Coffee, Key, 1 Lb. 40.00
Tin, Forbes Coffee Co., Allspice 3.25
Tin, Four Roses Tobacco, Green, Pocket 590.00
Tin, Four Roses Tobacco, Silver, Flip Lid 95.00
Tin, Four Roses, Pocket, Striped, 4 x 3 1/2 In. 35.00
Tin, Fra–Bac Tobacco, Pocket 1400.00
Tin, Friends Tobacco, Man & Dog, 5 x 3 In. 35.00
Tin, Game, Fine Cut Tobacco, 5 x 4 In. 535.00
Tin, Glendora Coffee, 5 Lb. 65.00
Tin, Globe Tobacco, Horizontal Box 50.00
Tin, Gold Dust Tobacco, Canada, Pocket 2250.00
Tin, Gold–Pak, Condoms 60.00
Tin, Golden Rod Coffee, Paper Lithographed Over Tin, Warehouse, 1 Lb. 71.50
Tin, Granger Rough Cut Tobacco, 14 Oz. 10.00
Tin, Great American Tea, Store In New York, 2 Lb. 55.00
Tin, Grey Goose Motor Oil, 5 Gal. 50.00
Tin, Guide Tobacco, 4 x 2 In. 150.00
Tin, Hackers Flour, 6 x 5 1/2 In. 267.00
Tin, Half & Half, Red Cover, 14 Oz. 10.00
Tin, Hard–A–Port Tobacco, Pocket 195.00
Tin, Hershey's Cocoa, 10 Lb. 75.00
Tin, Hi Ho Tobacco, Pocket 1475.00
Tin, Hi–Plane Tobacco, 4 Engines, 4 x 2 In. 425.00
Tin, Hi–Plane Tobacco, Pocket, 4 x 3 In. 60.00
Tin, Honeymoon Tobacco, Pocket 120.00
Tin, Honeymoon, Man In Moon, Upright, 3 x 4 1/2 x 1 In. 220.00
Tin, Honeymoon, Pocket, 4 1/2 x 3 In. 104.00
Tin, Hoot–Mon Talcum Powder, Pictures Bagpiper 35.00
Tin, Hostess Coffee, 3 Lb. 125.00
Tin, Huntley & Palmers Biscuits, Lady At Masquerade Ball, 9 x 9 In. 40.00
Tin, Huntley & Palmers Biscuits, Paper Over Tin, 9 x 9 In 30.00
Tin, Huntley & Palmers, Brown Bell 125.00
Tin, Huntley & Palmers, Faux Marble, Panels of Grecian Figures 300.00
Tin, Huntley & Palmers, Oriental Jewelry Box, Raised Dragon 100.00
Tin, Ideal Coffee, Round, 6 x 4 In. 10.00
Tin, International Typewriter, Green, 2 1/2 In. 25.00
Tin, Jam Boy Coffee, 1 Lb. 315.00
Tin, JBL Cleanzing Tonic, 1920s Douche 55.00
Tin, Johnson & Johnson Talcum, Sample 45.00
Tin, Jolly Time Popcorn, Bail Handle, Children Playing, 1927 .... 90.00

Tin, Julie Carr's Choice Tobacco, Railroad Car, Box 300.00
Tin, Jumbo Peanut, 10 Lb. 275.00
Tin, Just Suits Cut Plug, Pail, 4 1/2 x 7 1/2 x 5 In. 77.00
Tin, Kenney Coffee, Mammy, 4 Lb. 245.00
Tin, Kentucky Club, Pocket 4.00
Tin, Kentucky Club, Tobacco, 14 Oz. 12.00
Tin, Kentucky Rifle Gun Powder, Hazard Powder Co., Label 125.00
Tin, King Edward Tobacco, Pocket .... 435.00 To 475.00
Tin, Kleeko Coffee, 1 Lb. 65.00
Tin, Kohrs Crown Lard, Davenport, Iowa, 2 Handles, 50 Lb. 25.00
Tin, Lady Helen Coffee, 1 Lb. 30.00
Tin, LaPreferencia Cigars 100.00
Tin, Laredo Tobacco, 4 x 6 In. 35.00
Tin, Layman's Aspirin, Man Holding Head 25.00
Tin, Lewis Beauty Tobacco, Vertical Square Cornered 1050.00
Tin, Log Cabin Stockade School & Express Office 125.00
Tin, Log Cabin Syrup, Home Sweet Home, 12 Oz. 125.00
Tin, Log Cabin Syrup, Stockade School 100.00
Tin, London Sherbet Tobacco, Pocket 185.00
Tin, Luzianne Coffee, Red, Handle, 1928, 3 Lb. 90.00
Tin, Mammoth Salted Nuts, 3 1/2 In. ....*Illus* 15.00
Tin, Manor Tobacco, Mansion Picture, Pocket 200.00
Tin, Maryland Club Tobacco, Flat Top, Pocket, 7 1/2 In. 300.00
Tin, Maryland Club Tobacco, Roll Top, Pocket, 7 1/2 In. 385.00
Tin, Maxwell House Coffee, 1 Lb. 2.35
Tin, Mentholateum, Fletcher's Castoria, Sample 36.00
Tin, Merry Widow, Condoms 95.00
Tin, Mexo–Rico Cigars 225.00
Tin, Mid–Channel Mixture, Upright Pocket, 2 3/4 x 3 1/2 x 1 In. 600.00
Tin, Mizpah Typewriter Ribbon 12.00
Tin, Mohican Coffee, 1 Lb. 110.00
Tin, Monarch Peanut Butter, 10 Oz. 200.00
Tin, Morning Glow Coffee, 1 Lb. 30.00
Tin, Morning Joy Coffee, 1 Lb. 30.00
Tin, Moses Cough Drops, Insert Picture of Can, 6 x 4 In. 308.00
Tin, Nigger Hair Smoking Tobacco, Man's Head, Brown, 6 1/2 In. 275.00
Tin, Num Num Chips, No. 1 .... 10.00
Tin, Old Colony Tobacco, Concave 250.00
Tin, Old Glory Tobacco, Flat Pocket, 3 x 1 In. 175.00
Tin, Old Judge, 1 Lb. 25.00
Tin, Old Reliable Gold Bond Tobacco, Blue, White Ribbon, Pocket 125.00
Tin, Old Seneca Cigars, Round, 6 x 3 In. 375.00
Tin, Oxford Gems Cigars, Horizontal Box, 6 x 5 x 4 In. 75.00
Tin, Pail, Frontenac, Peanut Butter 25.00
Tin, Paul Jones Tobacco, Red, Pocket, 7 1/2 In. 3300.00
Tin, Peachey Tobacco, Pocket, 4 x 2 1/2 In. 83.00
Tin, Peacock, Condoms .... 25.00 To 60.00
Tin, Pennzoil Co. Insect Spray, 2 In. 19.00
Tin, Peter Pan Peanut Butter, 25 Lb. 145.00
Tin, Peter Pan Peanut Butter, Sample 90.00
Tin, Petit Cafe, Sunshine Biscuits 65.00
Tin, Picopac Tobacco, Pocket 45.00
Tin, Poison, Paris Green, Multicolor Lithograph 35.00
Tin, Porter's Friend, Train Conductor 50.00
Tin, Pride of Colorado Lard, Nickel–Plated, Lithograph of Pig, 5 1/2 In. 25.00
Tin, Prince Albert Tobacco, Pocket, 1907 .... 2.00
Tin, Punch Cigars, Round 10.00
Tin, Quaker Doctor Cigars, Round, 6 x 4 In. 200.00
Tin, Ramses Condoms 70.00
Tin, Rawleigh's Baking Powder, Picture of Muffins 20.00
Tin, Red Turkey Coffee, 1 Lb. .... 165.00 To 295.00
Tin, Resolute Tobacco, Vertical Box, 4 1/2 x 3 x 2 In. 130.00
Tin, Rex Tobacco, 4 x 2 In. 175.00

Advertising, Tin, Cleopatra Rose,
Palmolive Talc, 6 1/4 In.
Advertising, Tin, Talc, Egyptian,
Palmolive, 6 1/4 In.

Tin, Richard Hudnut Dusting Powder, Maytime Jasmine, Art Deco Floral	45.00
Tin, Richmond Belle Tobacco, Square Cornered Box, 4 x 3 x 2 In.	600.00
Tin, Roly Poly, Dutchman, Dixie Queen Tobacco	575.00
Tin, Roly Poly, Mammy, Dixie Queen	350.00
Tin, Roly Poly, Satisfied Customer, Dixie Queen Tobacco	350.00
Tin, Roly Poly, Singing Waiter, Mayo Tobacco	290.00
Tin, Rough Riders Baking Powder, Roosevelt In Uniform On Horse	75.00
Tin, Royal Blend Coffee, 5 Lb.	140.00
Tin, Runkel's Cocoa, Sample	65.00
Tin, Sanford's Ink Eraser, 3 In. ....*Illus*	25.00
Tin, School Boy Peanut Butter, 5 Lb.	150.00
Tin, Silver Dollar Coffee, 3 Lb.	125.00
Tin, Sir Walter Raleigh, Pocket	4.00
Tin, Smith Bros. Cough Drops, Flat Pocket, 3 x 2 In.	200.00
Tin, Snyder's 331 Tobacco, Lithograph, Pocket	750.00
Tin, Soul Kiss Talc	1250.00
Tin, Sozodent Dental, Oval	175.00
Tin, Spice, Empress, Lithographed Front & Back, 3 In.	15.00
Tin, Sure Shot Tobacco, 4 x 10 x 15 In.	478.00
Tin, Sweet Cuba, Hinged Lid, Pictures 5 Cent Pack, Yellow	45.00
Tin, Sweet Tobacco, Round, 1 Lb., 6 1/2 x 5 1/2 In.	150.00
Tin, Talc, Egyptian, Palmolive, 6 1/4 In. ....*Illus*	25.00
Tin, Terriff's Talcum Powder, Round Store Tin	150.00
Tin, Texide Condoms	50.00
Tin, Thomas J. Webb Tea	15.00
Tin, Three Feathers Tobacco, Upright	235.00
Tin, Tiger Chewing Tobacco	35.00
Tin, Trojan Condoms	50.00
Tin, Turtle Food, Hartz Mountain	20.00
Tin, Tuxedo, George M. Cohan	150.00
Tin, U and I, Coffee, Paper Label, 1 Lb.	324.00
Tin, U.S. Marine Tobacco, Pocket	145.00
Tin, Uncle Daniel Fine Cut Tobacco, 2 x 8 In.	75.00
Tin, Union Leader Tobacco, 4 x 6 In.	30.00
Tin, Union Leader Tobacco, Uncle Sam, Yellow, Pocket	50.00
Tin, United Coffee, 1 Lb.	122.00
Tin, Valspar Varnish, Man & Woman, 1/2 Pt.	28.00
Tin, Velvet Night Talcum Powder, Palms & Sailboat	25.00
Tin, Velvet Tobacco, Pocket	2.00
Tin, Violet Talcum Grand Union, Small Oval Top, 4 x 2 In.	90.00

Tin, Virginia Dare Tobacco, 7 1/2 In. 180.00
Tin, Walter Baker & Co., Footed Bombe Cocoa, 5 In. Square 121.00
Tin, White Ash Cigar, Round, 5 Cent 30.00
Tin, White Goose Coffee, 1 Lb. 1430.00
Tin, White Owl Cigars, Round 15.00
Tin, Wild Fruit Tobacco, Pocket 40.00
Tin, Winchester Talcum, Man, Dog & Gun 165.00
Tin, Winner, Cars 275.00
Tin, Yacht Club Coffee, Key Wind 12.00
Tin, Yacht Club Tobacco, Pocket 1430.00
Tin, Yankee Boy Tobacco, Pocket 750.00

Advertising tip trays are decorated metal trays less than 5 inches in diameter. They were placed on the table or counter to hold either the bill or the coins that were left as a tip. Change receivers could be made of glass, plastic, or metal. They were kept on the counter near the cash register and held the money passed back and forth by the cashier. Related items may be listed in the Advertising category under Change Receivers.

Tip Tray, Cardinal Beer, Pretty Girl, Flowers, 4 1/4 In. 143.00
Tip Tray, Cleveland & Buffalo Steamship Line 65.00
Tip Tray, Clysmic Water, Nude 110.00
Tip Tray, DeLaval, Full–Color Lithograph, 4 1/4 In. 88.00
Tip Tray, Fairy Soap, Round 45.00
Tip Tray, Globe–Wernicke, Lithograph, Couple In Living Room, 4 1/4 In. 65.00
Tip Tray, Globe–Wernicke, Sectional Bookcases ....75.00 To 110.00
Tip Tray, Goebel Beer, Dutch Girls 95.00
Tip Tray, Goebel's Malt Extract 100.00
Tip Tray, Harkert Cigar, Davenport 135.00
Tip Tray, Hennis Whiskey 55.00
Tip Tray, Herzberg Bros., Pretty Woman 95.00
Tip Tray, Indianapolis Brewing, Bottle 32.00
Tip Tray, Kansas City Brewing 75.00
Tip Tray, Kings Pure Malt, Woman, With Beer Tray 125.00
Tip Tray, Laxol Castor Oil, Bottle Pictured 35.00
Tip Tray, Maltosia Beer 75.00
Tip Tray, Miller Beer, Carriage, Mansion, People, 1940s 20.00
Tip Tray, Miller Beer, With Black Boy 12.00
Tip Tray, Moxie, Woman Holding Glass, Flowered Ground, 6 In. 175.00
Tip Tray, National Brewing Co., Racing Scene, 4 1/4 In. 440.00
Tip Tray, National Cigar Stands Co. 80.00
Tip Tray, New England Furnace 80.00
Tip Tray, Pfeiffer Brewing Co., Embossed & Labeled Bottle 75.00
Tip Tray, Pippins 5 Cent Cigar, Tin, 3 x 5 In. 357.00
Tip Tray, Pulver's Cocoa, Girl On Container of Cocoa, Cup, 4 1/2 In. 235.00
Tip Tray, Quandt's Famous Beer, Troy, New York 85.00
Tip Tray, Quick Meal Ranges ....60.00 To 75.00
Tip Tray, Rockford Watches 55.00
Tip Tray, Royal Crown Cola 38.00
Tip Tray, Ruhstaller's Lager Beer, Maid, Sacramento, Cal., 4 1/4 In. 247.00
Tip Tray, Seagram's 7 Crown, Tin 20.00
Tip Tray, State Bell Cigars 35.00
Tip Tray, Stegmaier Brewing Co., Factory Scene, 4 1/4 In. ....65.00 To 110.00
Tip Tray, Stollwerck Cocoa, 5 In. Diam. 28.00
Tip Tray, Stollwerck Coffee 35.00
Tip Tray, Union Brewing Co., Peoria 95.00
Tip Tray, Welsbach Lighting 85.00
Tip Tray, White Rock Whiskey, Nymph At Pool Edge 90.00
Tip Tray, Wise Furnaces 80.00
Tobacco Cutter, Battle Ax 225.00
Tobacco Cutter, Country Gentleman, Cast Iron 285.00
Tobacco Cutter, Double Sided, Perecoy & Moore Wholesale Tobacco 65.00
Tobacco Cutter, Spearhead 120.00
Tobacco Cutter, Star, Iron 55.00

Toy Town, Shredded Wheat, Village Card, 30 Different 28.00
Toy, Bear, Maxwell Coffee, Battery Operated 110.00
Toy, Exxon Tiger, Windup, Marx, 1966, 8 In. 50.00
Toy, Kiddles In Case, Braniff Airlines 25.00
Toy, Launcher, Satellite, Quisp–Quake, 1960's, Plastic, 2 In. 39.00
Toy, Milk Wagon, Horse, Borden's Farms, Painted & Stenciled, 14 In. 800.00
Toy, Popping Heads, Archie & Veronica, Post, 1969 .... 35.00
Toy, Puppet, Hand, Glinda, Wizard of Oz, Procter & Gamble Premium 35.00
Toy, Stove, Iron Is Levitamin, Mini 40.00
Toy, Super Hero Set, McDonald's 18.00
Toy, Tiger, Sambo, Stuffed, 1977 .... 10.00
Toy, Tony Tiger, Kellogg 95.00
Toy, Truck, Dan–Dee Skid, Pull Down Ramps, Balloon Tires, Chein, 9 In. 725.00
Toy, Truck, RCA, Plastic, Box 150.00
Tray, Acme Beer, Cowgirl, Aluminum, Red, Blue Enameled, Los Angeles, 8 x 15 In. 95.00
Tray, Anheuser–Busch Beer, Logo Emblem Center, 12 In. 358.00
Tray, Bellmore Whiskey, Lithograph Man In Spectacles, 12 In. 50.00
Tray, Bergdoll, Philadelphia, Etched, Chrome 50.00
Tray, Bethlehem Liquor, Majestic Elk, Square, 13 1/4 In. 115.00
Tray, Beverwyck Beer, Girl Hefting Glass of Lager, 13 In. 165.00
Tray, Broadway Brewing Co., Hand Holding Ax, 12 In. 275.00
Tray, Bucyrus Brewing Co., Lithographed Dutch Girl, A Helping Hand, 13 In. 38.00
Tray, Budweiser, 1920 .... 55.00
Tray, Budweiser, Pilsner Glass 35.00
Tray, Castanea Beer, 3 Dogs, Playing Cards, 16 1/2 x 13 1/2 In. 520.00
Tray, Cleveland & Sandusky Brewing, Factory Insert, 14 In. 165.00
Tray, Conrad Seipp Brewing Co., Chicago 35.00
Tray, Consumer's Brewing, Eagle In Flight 687.50
Tray, Cream of Kentucky Whiskey, Bare Bosoms, 13 1/2 x 16 1/2 In. 3300.00
Tray, Cunningham Ice Cream 110.00
Tray, Daeufer's Beer, Lithograph Pilsner Glass, Gold Border, 12 In. 27.50
Tray, Deer Creek Ice Cream, Elves Eating & Carrying Ice Cream 275.00
Tray, Drink Mo–Ka Coffee, 20 Cents A Pound, Tin 395.00
Tray, East Buffalo Brewing, Porcelain, 13 3/4 x 11 1/4 In. 162.00
Tray, El Cafeto, Arabian Man In Decorated Room, Tin, Round, 15 In. 60.00
Tray, Fitzgerald Ale, Tin 18.00
Tray, Fredericksburg Beer, Hooded Girl & Flowers, 13 In. 275.00
Tray, Geo. Ringler & Co., Tin, 16 1/2 x 13 3/4 In. 467.00
Tray, Grand Rapids Brewery, Victorian Girl, Black Ground 550.00
Tray, Greatest Show On Earth, Entire Cast Under Big Top 75.00
Tray, Green River Whiskey, Black Man With Mule, 12 In. 750.00
Tray, Hagerstown Brewing Co., Chrysanthemum Girl, 1910, 10 1/2 In. 44.00
Tray, Hanley's Ale, White & Blue 345.00
Tray, Heim Brewery, East St. Louis, Woman On Back, Elf Holding Beer Mug 85.00
Tray, Heptol Splits Laxative, Bucking Horse, 1904 .... 150.00
Tray, Hershey Ice Cream 250.00
Tray, Hubner Toldedo Beer, Pretty Girl, Black Ground 280.00
Tray, Indianapolis Brewing Co., Duesseldorfer Beer 35.00
Tray, Iroquois Indian Head Beer, Profile, Blue Lettering, White Ground, 13 1/4 In. 35.00
Tray, J. Widman & Co., Carnation Girl, 13 In. 325.00
Tray, Jersey Creme Soda .... 100.00 To 125.00
Tray, Joseph Hajicek Hutchinson Brewery, Grandpa Story, 13 x 16 In. 2420.00
Tray, Kraft Cheese, Porcelain 40.00
Tray, Lembeck & Betz 450.00
Tray, Louis F. Neuweiler's Sons Beer, Allentown Pa., Pilsner 40.00
Tray, Louis Obert Beer, Founders Portrait, Factory, 12 In. 495.00
Tray, Lusitania Ship, Tin 1600.00
Tray, Meek & Beech Co., Coshocton, Ohio, Remember The Maine 295.00
Tray, Meek & Beech Co., Coshocton, Ohio, Stag & Lake 695.00
Tray, Miller High Life, Girl Sitting On Half Moon 75.00
Tray, Mo–Ka Coffee, Tin, Oval 425.00
Tray, Mo–Ka Coffee, Woman With Horse, Round 325.00
Tray, Moxie, Reverse Painted 275.00

Tray, National Beer, Cowboy On Horse, Prairie, 12 3/4 x 16 1/4 In. 770.00
Tray, National Brewing Co., 2 Cowboys 2090.00
Tray, Neef Bros., Brewing, Denver, 3 Puppies Shredding Playing Cards 400.00
Tray, Nu–Grape Soda, Hand Holding Bottle 85.00
Tray, Nu–Grape, 1920s 90.00
Tray, Nu–Grape, Woman, 1910 .... 150.00
Tray, Oertels Beer, Bottle & Sandwich 50.00
Tray, Orange Crush, Crushy On Side, 1940s 50.00
Tray, Otto Huber Brewery, Bavarian Scene, Oval, 13 3/4 x 16 1/2 In. 660.00
Tray, Pabst Blue Ribbon Beer, Man Pouring Beer Into Glass 85.00
Tray, Pacific Beer, Mt. Tacoma, 1912 .... 70.00
Tray, Players Cigarettes, China, 3 1/2 x 4 1/2 In. 45.00
Tray, Promotion Wine Co., Grapes & Vines, Cerruti Mercantile Co., 1915 .... 85.00
Tray, Purity Ice Cream, 2 Kids, Piles of Ice Cream, Square, 1915, 13 1/4 In. 358.00
Tray, Reingold, Explorer & Ubangi Native 100.00
Tray, Ritz Crackers, Tin Lithograph, Couple Dancing, 15 1/2 In. 19.00
Tray, Schwarzeneach Beer, Jeannette, Girl In Yellow Dress, 13 In. 605.00
Tray, Seipp's Beer, 2 Girls, Rose Garden, 12 In. 27.00
Tray, Session Ice Cream, Kewpie With Ice Cream Sundae On Tray 150.00
Tray, Southern Dairies Sealtest Ice Cream, Emblem, Beige, Rectangular 55.00
Tray, Standard Brewing Co., Hanging of 38 Sioux Indians 695.00
Tray, Tacoma Beer, Persian Cats, Holding Glass of Beer, 13 1/2 In. 605.00
Tray, Thurston & Kingsbury, Beauty Contest, Premium, 12 x 17 In. 50.00
Tray, Tip, see Tip Trays in this category
Tray, Trommer's Evergreen Brewery, Garden Scene, 16 1/2 x 13 3/4 In. 110.00
Tray, Union Pacific Tea, Multiple Images In Border, Girl, Snowman, 8 In. 77.00
Tray, Wendy's, Where's The Beef 14.00
Tumbler, Aunt Fannie's Cabin Restaurant 40.00
Tumbler, Ballantine's Ale, Green & Red, Stemmed, 8 In. 50.00
Tumbler, Bartels Brewing Co., Syracuse, N.Y., Etched, 3 3/4 In. 95.00
Tumbler, Beer, Spuds MacKenzie Bud Light, 1987 .... 15.00
Tumbler, Best Wishes From Wolfe's Busy Store, Wagner, S. D., Christmas 60.00
Tumbler, Dudley Tea, Bicentennial, 16 Oz. 10.00
Tumbler, Dunkin' Donuts, Wizard of Oz 68.00
Tumbler, Elsie, Borden, Soda Fountain 15.00
Tumbler, Gold Label Beer, Walter Brewing Co., Flared, Etched, 4 1/4 In. 65.00
Tumbler, Howard Johnson 15.00
Tumbler, Kaier's Special Beer, Red ACL, Shell Glass, 4 5/8 In. 30.00
Tumbler, Kentucky Fried Chicken, Forest Park Balloon Race 35.00
Tumbler, Lemp's St. Louis, Standard, Pale, Etched, Crown Center, 4 In. 40.00
Tumbler, National Bohemian Beer, Red ACL, 4 1/4 In. 35.00
Tumbler, Nesbitt's Soda Frosted Syrup Line 8.00
Tumbler, Reymann Brewing Co., Parlor Beer, Etched, Gold Rim, 4 In. 65.00
Tumbler, Squirt, Glob–Ball Red & Yellow, 1953, 3 7/8 In. 60.00
Tumbler, Stroh's Beer, Detroit, Mich., Etched, Gold Rim, 3 1/2 In. 75.00
Tumbler, Sunoco Oil Co., Superman, DC Comics, 1971, 32 Oz. 9.00
Tumbler, Wm. Bierbaw Brewing Co., Mankato, Minn., Etched 195.00
Tuna Baker, Fish Shape, Chicken of The Sea, Ceramic 12.00
Wall Pocket, Fleischmann's Yeast, Tin, Black, Yellow Letters, 6 x 8 x 3 In. 44.00
Whistle, C. D. Kenny Co., Iron, Old Car, Boy Kicking Ball, With Dog 75.00
Whistle, Captain Crunch, Bos'n 12.00
Whistle, Drink Whistle Thirsty 15.00
Whistle, Hot Dog, Oscar Mayer, Plastic, 1960, 2 In. 6.00
Whistle, Peanut, Lunkenheimer, Brass, 7 In. 85.00
Whistle, Red Goose Shoes 28.00
Whistle, Sears, Santa Claus, Cardboard, Metal 15.00
Wristwatch, Coca–Cola, 75th Anniversary, Tenn., Xantia Watch Co., 17 Jewel 125.00
Yardstick, Fuller Brush 3.00
Yo–Yo, Dairy Queen 21.00

AGATA glass was made by Joseph Locke of the New England Glass Company of Cambridge, Massachusetts, after 1885. A metallic stain was applied to New England Peachblow and the mottled design characteristic of agata appeared.

Bowl, Ruffled Trim, 5 1/2 In.	286.00
Pitcher, Square Mouth	4500.00
Toothpick, Cactus, Red	175.00
Tumbler	500.00
Tumbler, Allover Mottling, Blue Spots, Rose To Pink, 3 7/8 In.	695.00
Tumbler, Medium Mottling	445.00
Tumbler, Mottled	650.00

AKRO AGATE glass was made in Clarksburg, West Virginia, from 1932 to 1951. Before that time, the firm made children's glass marbles. Most of the glass is marked with a crow flying through the letter *A*.

Ashtray, 4 Shell	5.00
Ashtray, Square, Wooden Holder	18.50
Dishes, Child's, Green, Box, 1940s	125.00
Flowerpot, Ribbed Top, Green & White, 3 1/2 In.	6.00
Flowerpot, Ribbed Top, Orange & White, 2 3/4 In.	8.50
Flowerpot, White	75.00
Match Holder, Blue & White	12.00
Match Holder, Green & White	10.00
Night Lamp, Green, White, Eagle Finial	95.00
Planter, Yellow, 6 In.	7.00
Powder Box, Grand Piano, Crystal	70.00
Powder Box, Lady, Blue & White	65.00
Powder Box, White Scottie	75.00
Powder Jar, Colonial Lady	65.00
Powder Jar, Cover, Southern Belle, Blue	65.00
Tea Set, Child's, 10 Piece	65.00
Tea Set, Child's, Green, 12 Piece	90.00
Tea Set, Child's, Pink, 16 Piece	215.00
Tea Set, Little American Maid, Cobalt Blue, Box, 20 Piece	550.00
Teapot, Stippled Band	22.00
Tumbler, Raised Daisy, Yellow	25.00

ALABASTER is a very soft form of gypsum, a stone that resembles marble. It was often carved into vases or statues in Victorian times. There are alabaster carvings being made even today. Because the alabaster is very porous, it will dissolve if kept in water, so do not use alabaster vases for flowers.

Bust, Beatrice, Marble Base, Bergini, 6 In.	295.00
Bust, Young Woman, Marble Base, 18 In.	605.00
Figurine, Bearded Prophet, Black & Gold Marble Base, c.1920, 21 1/2 In.	200.00
Figurine, Harem Dancer, Italian, Parcel Gilt, 1880s, 41 In.	9350.00
Figurine, Mother & 2 Children, c.1890, 16 1/ 2 In.	825.00
Figurine, Woman Seated By Lantern, Harp At Side, M. Traveli, 30 1/2 In.	8250.00
Lamp, Gilded Finial, Celluloid Ivory Heads, 15 In., Pair	143.00
Pedestal, Columnar Form, 26 In.	88.00
Powder Holder, Enameled, France	81.00
Urn, Head of Bacchus, Scrolling Acanthus Finial, Dragon Handles, 1890s, 73 In.	930.00
Vase, Color Decoration, Late 19th Century, Europe	175.00
Vase, Enameled Neoclassical Design, 1850–1870	400.00
Vase, Islamic Style, Enameled, 19th Century	150.00
Vase, Snow Enameled Scene, Europe, 1870–1895	75.00

ALEXANDRITE is a name with many meanings. It is a form of the mineral chrysoberyl that changes from green to red under artificial light. A man-made version of this mineral is sold in Mexico today. It changes from deep purple to aquamarine blue under artificial light. The Alexandrite listed here is glass made in the late nineteenth and twentieth centuries. Thomas

Webb & Sons sold their transparent glass shaded from yellow to rose to blue under the name Alexandrite. Stevens and Williams had a cased Alexandrite of yellow, rose, and blue. A. Douglas Nash Corporation made an amethyst–colored Alexandrite. Several American glass companies of the 1920s made a glass that changed color under electric lights and this was also called Alexandrite.

Finger Bowl, Fluted, Blue, Rose, 5 In.	650.00
Toothpick, Honeycomb, Square Top, 3 In.	595.00

ALHAMBRA is a pattern of tableware made in Vienna, Austria, in the twentieth century. The geometric designs are in applied gold, red, and dark green. Full sets of dishes can be found in this pattern.

Coffeepot, Gooseneck, 10 In.	200.00
Creamer	10.00
Cup & Saucer	49.00
Pitcher, 8 In.	200.00

ALUMINUM was more expensive than gold or silver until the 1850s. Chemists learned how to refine bauxite to get aluminum. Jewelry and other small objects were made of the valuable metal until 1914, when an inexpensive smelting process was invented. The aluminum collected today dates from the 1930s through 1950s. Hand–hammered pieces are the most popular.

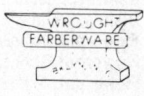

Basket, Harmony House	10.00
Bowl, Pineapple, Lattice Interior, Bruce Box	68.00
Bowl, Platter, Intaglio Design, Hammered, EMPC	18.00
Bread Tray, Handles, Rodney Kent	12.50
Candy Basket, Rodney Kent	12.00
Casserole, Cover, Acorn Finial, Hammered, 3 Piece	24.00
Coffee & Tea Set, Child's, France, 7 Piece	150.00
Condiment Set, Lazy Susan Type, 2 Butter Dishes, 2 Jam Jars, Rodney Kent	35.00
Figurine, Charging Ram, Mahogany, Aluminum Horns, Tail, Base, 7 In.	715.00
Lazy Susan, Ferris Wheel Type, 3 Glass Inserts, Everlast, 11 In.	40.00
Napkin Holder, Hammered, Rodney Kent	18.00
Pitcher, Hand Hammered, Buenilum	12.00
Pitcher, Water, Blue	8.00
Pitcher, Wild Rose, Continental	34.50
Plate, Grape Pattern, Westbend, 8 1/2 In.	12.00
Platter, Gazelles Jumping Around The Center, Floral, Hammered, Large	65.00
Punch Bowl, Wendell August	485.00
Punch Set, Crock Lined Bowl, Tray & Ladle, Hammercraft	35.00
Punch Set, Satellite, Sphere Shaped Bowl, Russel Wright, 8 Cups	990.00
Settee, Swan, Petal Shaped Shell, Fabric Cover, c.1959, 57 In.	1430.00
Sherbet, Colors, Insert, 4 Piece	29.00
Silent Butler, Fruit, Hammered, Rectangular, Cromwell	14.00
Silent Butler, Grape Pattern, Everlast	18.50
Sugar & Creamer, Everlast, Hammered	13.00
Tray, Embossed Flowers, Self Handles, Oval, Lehman, 26 In.	16.00
Tray, Handles, Buenilum, 6 x 18 In.	9.50
Tray, Meat, Bar Handles, Duck On Water Corners, Buenilum, 11 3/4 x 17 In.	12.00
Trivet, Bamboo, Everlast	10.00
Tumbler, Child's, Colored	12.00
Vase, Pine Design, Hammered, Glass Liner, Arthur Armour, 11 1/2 In.	200.00
Warming Dish, Cover, Hammered, Bakelite Handles	35.00
Whiskey, Holder, Celluloid, 6 Different Colors, Airplancs, Monogram, 1930s	55.00

AMBER, see Jewelry category

◆◆

Use one type of furniture polish. If you switch from an oil polish to a wax polish, the surface will appear smudged.

◆◆

AMBER GLASS is the name of any glassware with the proper yellow–brown shading. It was a popular color just after the Civil War and many pressed glass pieces were made of amber glass. Depression glass of the 1930s—1950s was also made in shades of amber glass. All types are being reproduced.

Bell, Hobnail	6.00
Biscuit Jar, Inverted Thumbprint, Brass Rim, Handle & Lid, 7 In.	135.00
Bowl, Crystal Applied Footed & Berry Pontil, 5 x 4 3/4 In.	195.00
Decanter, Embossed Pewter Stopper & Mounted, Bulbous, 10 1/2 In.	295.00
Dish, Cover, Kitchen Stove, Flatiron Finial, 1890, 6 3/4 x 4 1/2 x 4 1/2 In.	300.00
Ewer, Amber, 1870s	275.00
Hat, Crackled, 3 In.	15.00
Hat, Diamond & Button, Little German Band	27.00
Powder Jar, Art Deco	10.00
Punch Set, Gold Edge, 10 Mugs, Cover, Ladle & Tray	795.00

AMBERETTE pieces are listed in the Pressed Glass category under the pattern name Amberette.

AMBERINA is a two–toned glassware made from 1883 to about 1900. It was patented by Joseph Locke of the New England Glass Company, but was also made by other companies. The glass shades from red to amber. Similar pieces of glass may be found in the Baccarat and Plated Amberina categories. Glass shaded from blue to amber is called *Blue Amberina* or *Bluerina.*

Bottle, Cranberry Shaded To Golden Amber, Raised Arches, 11 In.	145.00
Bottle, Wine, Swirl, Cranberry Shaded To Golden Amber, Bubble Stopper, 9 In.	135.00
Bowl, Diamond–Quilted, Deep Ruby–Red, Mt. Washington, 2 x 4 1/2 In.	285.00
Bowl, Mayonnaise, Fuchsia, Applied Feet, Ruffled Top, Signed	650.00
Butter, Cover, Inverted Thumbprint, Tall Finial	235.00
Candy Jar, Cover, Footed, Tall	65.00
Castor Set, Lobed, Pewter Top	4510.00
Celery Vase, Diamond–Quilted, Scalloped Top, 6 1/2 In.	485.00
Celery Vase, New England, Ruffled Top, Fuchsia	575.00
Creamer, Deep Fuchsia Square Top, Honey Amber Body & Handle, 4 1/4 In.	435.00
Creamer, Plated, Squatty	6000.00
Creamer, Square Top, Neck & Shoulder, Amber Handle, 4 1/4 In.	435.00
Cruet, Inverted Thumbprint, Fuchsia Trim, 5 1/2 In.	250.00
Cruet, Inverted Thumbprint, Tricornered Top, Clear Handle, 5 1/2 In.	90.00
Decanter, Swirl, Applied Handle, Bubble Swirl Stopper, 8 3/4 In.	245.00
Decanter, Wine, Swirl, Amber Bubble Stopper, 8 In.	265.00
Dish, Cut, Scalloped, Square, 6 In.	100.00
Dish, Daisy & Button, Oval, 6 In.	70.00
Ice Bucket, Inverted Thumbprint, Tab Handles, 4 3/4 x 6 3/4 In.	705.00
Lamp, Diamond–Quilted, Shell Feet, Diamond Ball Shade, 9 1/2 In.	950.00
Lemonade Set, Ribbed, Amber Handle, Pitcher, 10 In., 5 Piece	425.00
Mug, Lemonade, Raised Swirl Design, Amber Snake Handle, 5 In.	225.00
Pitcher, Amber Shaded To Red, New England Glass, 1883	425.00
Pitcher, Gold Chloride, Reverse Thumbprints, Claw Handle, New England	425.00
Pitcher, Hobnail, Bulbous, 8 In.	139.00
Pitcher, Water, Inverted Coin Spot	275.00
Pitcher, Water, Thumbprint	195.00
Plate, Inverted Thumbprint, New England, 7 In.	145.00
Plate, Ribbed, New England, 8 1/2 In.	300.00
Punch Cup, Venetian Diamond–Quilted, Applied Amber Handle, 3 In.	200.00
Shade, Gas, Diamond–Quilted, Bulbous, 5 1/2 In.	175.00
Slop Bowl, Hobnail, 20–Crimp Ruffled Edge, 5 In.	250.00
Spooner, Swirled Rib, Corset Shape, Polished Pontil	245.00
Tankard, 10 Panels, Applied Amber Reeded Handle, 6 In.	745.00
Toothpick, Daisy & Button	325.00
Toothpick, Inverted Thumbprint, Pedestal Base	185.00
Toothpick, Optic Diamond, Square Mouth	245.00

Toothpick, Tricorn Top	275.00
Toothpick, Venetian Diamond,	165.00
Tumbler, Crackle Glass, 4 1/2 In.	55.00
Tumbler, New England, Diamond–Quilted, 3 3/4 In.	150.00
Tumbler, Water, Swirl, 3 7/8 In.	175.00
Vase, Car, Amberina, 8 In.	85.00
Vase, Lily, Ribbed, 11 3/4 In.	475.00
Vase, Melon Shape, Enameled Flowers, 5 Sides	200.00
Vase, Raised Herring & Serpent	1500.00
Water Set, Swirl, Amber Handle, 7 Piece	375.00
Whiskey, Enameled Yellow & White, 4 Flowers, Green Leaves, 2 3/4 In.	475.00

AMERICAN DINNERWARE is the name used by collectors for ceramic dinnerware made in the United States from the 1930s through the 1950s. Most was made in potteries in southern Ohio, West Virginia, and California. Dishes were sold in gift shops and department stores, or were given away as premiums. Many of these patterns are listed in this book in their own categories, such as Autumn Leaf, Coors, Fiesta, Franciscan, Hall, Harker, Harlequin, Red Wing, Riviera, Russel Wright, Vernon Kilns, and Watt. For more information, see *Kovels' Depression Glass & American Dinnerware Price List.*

Ashtray, Currier & Ives	8.00
Ashtray, Incaware, Advertising, Shenango, 4 1/4 In.	20.00
Ashtray, Native American, Matchbox Holder, Shenango	65.00
Bean Pot, Cover, Poppy Trail, Orange & Brown, Bail Handle, 2 1/2 Qt.	45.00
Bonbon, Chintz, Flat Shell, Blue Ridge	35.00
Bowl, Cover, California Ivy, Metlox	40.00
Bowl, Fruit Pattern, Knowles, 8 In.	20.00
Bowl, Poppy Trail, Fish Shape, Turquoise, Large	27.50
Bowl, Priscilla, Homer Laughlin, Oval, 9 1/2 In.	12.00
Bowl, Vegetable, Pioneer Trails, Oval, Wallace	95.00
Bowl, Vegetable, Poppy Trail, Metlox, 8 1/2 In.	40.00
Bowl, Vegetable, Poppy Trail, Sculptured Grape, Divided, Metlox	75.00
Bowl, Vegetable, Rooster, Brown, Round	7.50
Bowl, Vegetable, Town & Country, Metallic Brown, Zeisel	20.00
Bread Plate, Nautilus, Homer Laughlin	2.00
Bread Plate, Priscilla, Homer Laughlin	3.00
Butter, Cover, Cabbage Rose	55.00
Butter, Cover, Colonial Homestead, Royal	20.00
Butter, Cover, Currier & Ives	20.00
Butter, Cover, Florentine No. 2, Yellow	125.00
Cake Server, Kitchen Kraft	75.00
Candlestick, Bolero, Peach Blossom, W. S. George, Pair	17.00
Casserole, Cover, Bittersweet, Universal	14.00
Casserole, Cover, Fruit Pattern, Knowles, 8 In.	12.00
Casserole, Cover, Kitchen Kraft, Homer Laughlin, 9 In.	20.00
Casserole, Cover, Poppy Trail, Ivy	38.00
Casserole, Figural, Red Rooster, Metlox	120.00
Casserole, Hen On Nest, California Provincial, Poppy Trail, Round	68.00
Chocolate Pot, Chintz, Blue Ridge	158.00
Chop Plate, Chartreuse, Purinton	18.00
Chop Plate, Currier & Ives	15.00
Chop Plate, Some Ha–Meat, Purinton	225.00
Coaster, California Provincial, Poppy Trail	11.00
Coffeepot, Poppy Trail, Metlox	48.00
Cookie Jar, Fruits, Purinton	40.00
Cookie Jar, Humpty Dumpty, Purinton	250.00
Creamer, Apple, Purinton	10.00
Creamer, Currier & Ives, Homer Laughlin	20.00
Creamer, Fruit Pattern, Knowles	7.00
Creamer, Indian Tree, Johnson Bros.	14.00
Creamer, White Rabbit, Alice In Wonderland, Regal China	450.00
Cruet Set, Poppy Trail, Red Rooster, Metlox, 6 Piece	95.00

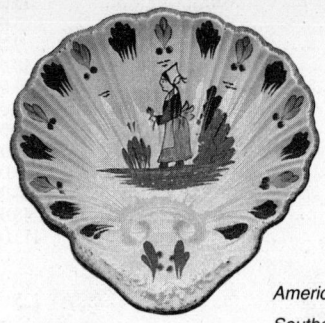

American Dinnerware, Dish,

Southern Potteries, 9 1/4 In.

♦ ♦

To remove the remains of
masking tape and labels from
glass, rub the spot with WD-40
lubricating and penetrating oil.

♦ ♦

Cup & Saucer, Apple, Purinton	18.00 To 20.00
Cup & Saucer, Brittany, Blue Ridge, After Dinner	50.00
Cup & Saucer, California Provincial	12.50
Cup & Saucer, Fruit Pattern, Knowles	20.00
Cup & Saucer, Lu–Ray, Purple	30.00
Cup & Saucer, Maywood, Purinton	5.00
Cup & Saucer, Nautilus, Homer Laughlin	5.00
Cup & Saucer, Poppy Trail, Sculptured Daisy, Metlox	6.00
Cup & Saucer, Queen Anne's Lace, Knowles	12.00
Cup & Saucer, Serenade, Pink	8.00
Cup & Saucer, Virginia Rose, Silver Trim	7.50
Cup & Saucer, White, Blue Trim, Syracuse	18.00
Cup & Saucer, Winchester, Johnson Bros.	8.00
Cup, Poppy Trail, Metlox	5.00
Cup, Red Rooster, Metlox	5.00
Dinner Set, Della Robbia, Metlox, Service For 8	250.00
Dish, Field Daisy, 2 Sections, Blue Ridge	40.00
Dish, Hen On Nest, Poppy Trail, Blue Homestead	38.00
Dish, Southern Potteries, 9 1/4 In. ....*Illus*	12.00
Display, Native American Pottery On All Sides, Pyramid Shape	65.00
Gravy Boat, Amberstone, Homer Laughlin	20.00
Gravy Boat, California Ivy, Metlox	20.00
Gravy Boat, Underplate, Magnolia, Knowles, Large	15.00
Gravy Boat, Virginia Rose, Silver Trim	10.00
Honey Pot, Floral, Purinton	12.00
Jar, Cover, Kitchen Kraft, Large	235.00
Jar, Cover, Kitchen Kraft, Small	250.00
Jug, Calico Fruit, Universal	28.00
Jug, Lu–Ray, Yellow, Flat	35.00
Juice Set, Pitcher, Pt., 9 Piece	200.00
Pink Dogwood Blossoms, Harker, 45 Piece	120.00
Pitcher, Pansy, Blue Ridge, 6 1/2 In.	65.00
Pitcher, Water, Blue Grape, Metlox	16.00
Pitcher, Water, Calico Fruit, Universal	20.00
Place Setting, Colonial Homestead, Royal, 5 Piece	20.00
Place Setting, Currier & Ives, Royal	22.00
Plate, Bluebird, W. S. George	15.00
Plate, California Ivy, Metlox, 9 3/4 In.	8.00
Plate, California Provincial, 10 In.	10.00
Plate, Currier & Ives, Blue	2.00
Plate, Currier & Ives, Gray, 1915, 10 In., 3 Piece	119.00
Plate, Desert, Bluebird, W. S. George	15.00
Plate, Dinner, Magnolia, Knowles	8.00
Plate, Dinner, Priscilla, Homer Laughlin	8.00
Plate, Divided, Lu–Ray, Purple	25.00
Plate, Maywood, Purinton, 9 3/4 In.	7.00

Plate, Native American Potter On Base, Shenango, 12 In. 75.00
Plate, Nautilus, Homer Laughlin, 9 3/4 In. 5.00
Plate, Peach Blossom, Poppy Trail, 10 1/2 In. 9.00
Plate, Queen Anne's Lace, Knowles, 9 3/4 In. 10.00
Plate, Red Rooster, 9 3/4 In. 7.00
Plate, Red Rooster, Poppy Trail, 10 1/2 In. 9.00
Plate, Serenade, Green, 7 In. 4.00
Plate, Serving, French Peasant, Blue Ridge, 3 Sections, Large 235.00
Plate, Town & Country, Rust, Zeisel 5.00
Platter, Blue Grape, Metlox 14.00
Platter, English Hobnail, 20 In. 48.00
Platter, French Peasant, Blue Ridge, 13 In. 115.00
Platter, Petit Point Rose, Blue Ridge 10.00
Platter, Pony Express, Tepco, Oval, 13 In. 78.00
Platter, Rose, Castleton, 15 In. 125.00
Platter, Sculptured Daisy, Poppy Trail, Metlox, 9 1/2 In. 15.00
Platter, Shenango, Western, Oval, 11 1/2 In. 75.00
Range Set, Ivy, Red Flower, Purinton, 3 Piece 40.00
Relish, 3 Sections, Fruits, Wooden Handle, Purinton 30.00
Relish, Town & Country, Rust, Zeisel 10.00
Salt & Pepper, Fruit Design, Knowles 15.00
Salt & Pepper, Maywood, Jug, Purinton 5.00
Salt & Pepper, Peach Blossom, Bolero, W. S. George 10.00
Sculptured Grape, 10 Piece 25.00
Soup, Cream, Rose, Castleton 25.00
Soup, Dish, Magnolia, Knowles, Large 6.00
Soup, Dish, Peach Blossom, Bolero, W. S. George 3.00
Soup, Dish, Priscilla, Homer Laughlin .... 4.00 To 6.00
Soup, Dish, Virginia Rose 5.00
Sugar & Creamer, Apple, Purinton 12.00
Sugar & Creamer, Chintz 125.00
Sugar & Creamer, Colonial Homestead, Royal 18.00
Sugar & Creamer, Intaglio, Purinton 15.00
Sugar & Creamer, Maywood, Purinton 15.00
Sugar & Creamer, Pioneer Trails, Wallace 95.00
Sugar & Creamer, Sculptured Daisy, Poppy Trail, Metlox 10.00
Sugar & Creamer, Sculptured Grape, Metlox 10.00
Sugar, Cover, Apple, Purinton 20.00
Sugar, Cover, Fruit Pattern, Knowles 7.00
Sugar, Cover, Sculptured Daisy, Poppy Trail, Metlox 4.00
Tankard, Milk, Dreamland 225.00
Tea Set, Ivy, Red Flower, Puritan, 3 Piece 50.00
Teapot, Apple, Purinton, 2 Cup 30.00
Teapot, Colonial Homestead, Royal 55.00
Teapot, Colonial, Blue Ridge 110.00
Teapot, Intaglio, Purinton, Large 15.00
Teapot, Jim Ban 32.50
Teapot, Lu–Ray, Cream Color 38.00
Teapot, Old MacDonald, Regal China 275.00
Teapot, Peach Blossom, Bolero, W. S. George 18.00
Teapot, Race Car, Sadler, 1930s 200.00
Tidbit, Darcy, 2 Tiers, Blue Ridge 20.00
Toast Rack, Royal Winton, Yellow, Floral 85.00
Tom & Jerry Set, Bowl, Plate, & 6 Mugs, Homer Laughlin 50.00
Tray, Compartmented, Poppy Trail, Metlox, 15 In. 38.00
Tray, Julie, Oven Ware, Blue Ridge 18.00
Vase, Poppy Trail, Ivy, Cylindrical, 9 In. 55.00

AMERICAN ENCAUSTIC TILING COMPANY was founded in Zanesville, Ohio, in 1875. The company planned to make a variety of tiles to compete with the English tiles that were selling in the United States for use in fireplaces and other architectural designs. The first glazed tiles were made in 1880, embossed tiles in 1881, faience tiles in the 1920s. The firm closed in 1935 and reopened in 1937 as the Shawnee Pottery.

Incense Burner, Kneeling Woman, Celadon Glaze, 7 1/4 In.	165.00
Inkwell	110.00
Plaque, Scene of Sailing Ship, Framed, 12 In., Pair	2860.00
Tile Heater, Open Scroll Design, Mauve, Electric	350.00
Tile, Child	121.00
Tile, Geometric Pattern, Taupe Ground, Marked, 9 1/4 In.	137.00
Tile, President Grant, Framed, 6 In.	303.00
Tile, Tropical, High Glaze, 6 In.	65.00
Tile, Woman Standing, Gentleman With Lyre, 18 x 6 In., Pair	660.00
Tile, Woman's Head, Profile, Blue Glaze, Framed, 7 1/2 In.	82.50

AMETHYST GLASS is any of the many glasswares made in the dark purple color of the gemstone called amethyst. Included in this category are many pieces made in the nineteenth and twentieth centuries. Very dark pieces are called *black amethyst* and are listed under that heading.

Dish, Hen Cover, White Head, Wright	45.00
Pitcher, Blenko, 13 In.	157.00
Pitcher, Enameled Flowers, Large	60.00
Sugar & Creamer, 3 Footed	24.00
Vase, Victorian, Faceted Baluster Form, 1870s, 12 1/4 In., Pair	1540.00

AMPHORA pieces are listed in the Teplitz category.

ANDIRONS and related fireplace items are included in the Fireplace category.

ANIMAL TROPHIES, such as stuffed animals or fish, rugs made of animal skins, and other similar collectibles are listed in this category. Collectors should be aware of the endangered species laws that make it illegal to buy and sell some of these items. Any eagle feathers, many types of cats (such as leopards) and many forms of tortoiseshell can be confiscated if discovered by the government.

Albino Raccoon, On Tree Limb, Pink Eyes	350.00
Baboon, Full	450.00
Buffalo Head	1750.00
Bull Moose Head	797.00
Caribou, Full Shoulder Mounted, Newfoundland, Large, 1963	440.00
Cup, Libation, Carved As Lotus Leaf, Rhinoceros Horn, 2 1/2 In.	4125.00
Cup, Libation, Carved Flowering Prunus, Branches, 17th Century, 3 3/4 In.	4400.00
Greater Kudu, Standing	440.00
Hippopotamus Head	522.00
Hyena, Full, On Wooden Base	440.00
Lion, Black–Maned, Full	990.00
Lion, Reclining, Full	2365.00
Lioness, Full	660.00
Moose, Canadian, Free Standing	4500.00
Python Skin, 11 1/2 In.	115.00
Rug, Bearskin, Black, Green Felt Backing	467.00
Rug, Bearskin, Full Head & Paws, 100 In.	484.00
Rug, Zebra, 7 Ft. 6 In. x 5 Ft. 11 In.	248.00
Wolf's Skin, Pair	150.00
Zebra Head	385.00

ANIMATION ART collectibles include cels that are painted drawings on celluloid needed to make an animated cartoon. Hundreds of cels are made, then photographed in sequence to make a cartoon showing moving figures. Early examples made by the Walt Disney Studios are popular with collectors today. Original sketches used by the artists are also listed here.

Cel, 101 Dalmatians, Cruella De Vil In Roadster, Framed, 1961	2785.00

Cel, Alice In Wonderland, White Rabbit In Costumes, 1951, 5 x 4 In. 1650.00
Cel, Alice In Wonderland, White Rose, Disney, Framed, 6 x 4 1/2 In. 2310.00
Cel, Aristocats, Duchess & O'Malley, 1970, 12 1/2 x 16 In. 2090.00
Cel, Aristocats, Madame Bonfamille Dances, Duchess, 10 x 12 In. 605.00
Cel, Bambi, Mouse Washes Face In Dewdrop, 1942, 8 1/2 x 11 In. 8470.00
Cel, Brave Little Tailor, Mickey and Princess, 5 x 7 In. 1320.00
Cel, Bugs Bunny, Ghostly Hands Lead Bugs, Framed, 1946 .... 3875.00
Cel, Bugs Bunny, Warner Bros., c.1960, 10 1/2 x 12 1/2 In. 1540.00
Cel, Cat In The Hat, Dr. Seuss, Chick Jones, 1971, 10 3/4 x 13 1/2 In. 1100.00
Cel, Charlie Brown's All Stars, 1966, Vinyl On Celluloid, 10 x 35 In. 1760.00
Cel, Cinderella, Duke Tries Slipper, Disney, 1950, 12 1/2 x 16 In. 2750.00
Cel, Cinderella, In Ball Gown, Framed, 1950, 7 1/2 x 4 In. 2540.00
Cel, Daffy Duck, Framed, 1950s 225.00
Cel, Donald Duck Pounces, 1950's, 6 x 9 In. 880.00
Cel, Donald's Dilemma, Golden Voiced Idol, 1947, 7 1/2 x 5 1/2 In. 1850.00
Cel, Donald's Golf Game, Disney, Framed, 1938, 7 1/4 x 11 1/2 In. 3190.00
Cel, Donald's Penguin, Disney, 1939, 6 x 7 3/4 In. 1650.00
Cel, Donald's Penguin, Disney, Framed, 1938, 8 1/2 x 9 In. 3265.00
Cel, Droopy, Yawning, With Wolf, Carrying Tools, 9 x 11 1/2 In. 770.00
Cel, Dumbo, Crows On Telegraph Pole, Disney, 1941, 8 1/4 x 9 1/2 In. 3575.00
Cel, Dumbo, In Stall With Matriarch Elephant, 1941, 9 x 12 In. 6500.00
Cel, Dumbo, Timothy Mouse On Trunk, Disney, 1941, 8 1/2 x 9 5/8 In. 5500.00
Cel, Dumbo, Timothy Mouse, Framed, 1941, 10 x 12 In. 5325.00
Cel, Fantasia, Concept Watercolor, 1940, Devils Dancing Amongst Flames 885.00
Cel, Fantasia, Dance of Hours, Disney, 1940, 10 x 12 In. 1765.00
Cel, Fantasia, Layout Drawing, 1940, 10 x 12 In. 440.00
Cel, Fantasia, Orchid Women Dancers, Framed, 1940 .... 1815.00
Cel, Fox & Hound, 1980 .... 950.00
Cel, Fun & Fancy Free, Jack & Beanstalk Costume, 1947, 5 x 10 1/2 In. 1980.00
Cel, He's Your Dog, Charlie Brown, Bill Melendez, 1968, 10 1/2 x 14 1/4 In. 1775.00
Cel, Horton Hears A Who, Elephant, Dr. Seuss, Framed, 1970 .... 1815.00
Cel, It Was A Short Summer, Charlie Brown, 1969, 11 x 13 In. 995.00
Cel, It's A Mystery, Charlie Brown, Bill Melendez, 1974, 10 1/2 x 14 1/4 In. 2200.00
Cel, It's The Easter Beagle, Charlie Brown, 1974, 10 x 18 In. 2475.00
Cel, It's Your First Kiss, Charlie Brown, Bill Melendez, 1978 .... 2750.00
Cel, Jungle Book, Baloo Has Tiger By Tail, 1967, 8 1/2 x 11 In. 1330.00
Cel, Jungle Book, Baloo, 1967, 8 x 10 In. 935.00
Cel, Jungle Book, Bear, Baloo, 10 x 12 In. 935.00
Cel, Jungle Book, Mowgli, Baby Elephant, Disney, 1967, 8 x 8 In. 1540.00
Cel, Keebler Hollow Tree, Elves, Filled Wheelbarrow, Framed 235.00
Cel, Lady & The Tramp 1800.00
Cel, Lady & The Tramp, Framed, 1955, 7 1/2 x 10 In. 1925.00
Cel, Lady & The Tramp, Full Figure, 1955, 2 1/2 x 2 1/2 In. 385.00
Cel, Lady & The Tramp, Scotty Dog, Framed, 20 1/2 x 15 1/4 In. 220.00
Cel, Lady & The Tramp, Sequestered In Pound, 1955, 12 1/2 x 16 In. 1540.00
Cel, Lady & The Tramp, Smiling Lady, 12 x 16 In. 385.00
Cel, Land Before Time, Great Valley As Spike, 1988, 11 1/2 x 16 In. 1540.00
Cel, Land Before Time, Newborn Duck Rolls From Nest, 1988, 12 x 15 1/2 In. 2200.00
Cel, Little Mermaid, Framed, 6 x 11 In. 2540.00
Cel, Make Mine Music, Alice Bluebonnet & Johnny Fedora, Framed, 8 x 9 1/2 In. 1200.00
Cel, Make Mine Music, Singing Opera, 1946, 8 x 10 1/2 In. 3300.00
Cel, Melody Time, Willie The Giant, 1948, 6 1/2 x 10 In. 1650.00
Cel, Mickey Mouse At Academy Awards, 1988, 5 1/2 x 3 1/2 In. 1200.00
Cel, Mickey Mouse Club, Conductor's Uniform, c.1958, 9 1/2 x 7 3/4 In. 1200.00
Cel, Mickey Mouse, 1950, Gouache On Celluloid, Arms Outstretched, 12 x 15 In. 4400.00
Cel, Mickey's Christmas Carol, Disney, 1983, 11 x 14 3/4 In. 1100.00
Cel, Mickey's Christmas Carol, Mickey As Bob Cratchit, 1983, 9 1/2 x 9 In. 1705.00
Cel, Mighty Mouse Meets Deadeye Dick, 1947, 8 x 6 In. 1450.00
Cel, Mighty Mouse, Terrytoons Studio, c.1955, 10 x 12 In. 825.00
Cel, Mister Magoo, Yellow Tuxedo, Dancing, 1950s, 3 1/2 x 3 In. 825.00
Cel, Mother Goose Goes Hollywood, Oliver Hardy, 1938, 7 1/2 x 7 1/2 In. 1815.00
Cel, Musical Mountaineers, Betty Boop Cartoons, 8 x 11 In. 1540.00
Cel, Peanuts, Linus, Charlie Brown, Woodstock, 1960s, 3 1/2 x 3 In. 1320.00

Cel, Peter & Wolf, 1950s, 6 x 6 In. 605.00
Cel, Peter Pan, Tinker Bell, Disney, 1953, 7 1/2 x 5 1/4 In. 3190.00
Cel, Peter Pan, Wendy's Little Brother, 1953, 7 x 3 In. 875.00
Cel, Pinocchio, 1940, Graphite On Paper, Jiminy Cricket Smiling, 10 x 12 In. 1870.00
Cel, Pinocchio, Centaurette Polishes Nails, Disney, 1940, 4 1/2 x 3 1/4 In. 715.00
Cel, Plausible Impossible, T.V. Show, 1956, 4 1/2 x 5 In. 1870.00
Cel, Popeye & Bluto, Signed 750.00
Cel, Practical Pit, Disney, Framed, 1939, 7 x 5 1/2 In. 885.00
Cel, Professor Ludwig Von Drake Touches His Finger To His Nose, 6 x 9 In. 357.00
Cel, Rabbit Rampage, 1955, 7 1/2 x 4 In. 3995.00
Cel, Reluctant Dragon, 1941, 9 x 11 1/2 & 9 1/2 x 12 1/2 In., Pair 1430.00
Cel, Rescuers, Madame Medusa, 1977, 10 x 7 1/2 In. 385.00
Cel, Robin Hood, Framed, 1973, 9 x 11 In. 3750.00
Cel, Robin Hood, Maid Marion & Prince John, 1973, 8 x 7 In. 1100.00
Cel, Scent–Imental Romeo, Pepe & Mam'Selle Dance, 1951, 8 1/2 x 10 In. 1540.00
Cel, Silly Symphony, Wynken, Blynken & Nod, Framed, 1938, 9 1/2 x 11 In. 2300.00
Cel, Sleeping Beauty, Lover's First Waltz, 1959, 12 1/2 x 17 In. 1300.00
Cel, Sleeping Beauty, Merryweather & Fauna, Gold Label, Framed, 10 x 12 In. 1650.00
Cel, Sleeping Beauty, Prince Phillip & Samson, Framed, 1959, 11 1/2 x 23 In. 9680.00
Cel, Sleeping Beauty, Prince Phillip, Princess Aurora, 1959, 8 1/2 x 10 In. 2650.00
Cel, Sleeping Beauty, Prince Phillip, Princess Aurora, Waltzing, 12 x 17 In. 1350.00
Cel, Snow White & Seven Dwarfs, Dopey Dancing, Framed, 4 1/2 x 4 In. 2300.00
Cel, Snow White & Seven Dwarfs, Dopey Smiling, 1937, 11 1/2 x 12 In. 3575.00
Cel, Snow White & Seven Dwarfs, Forest Scene, 6 1/2 x 9 In. 1225.00
Cel, Song of The South, Brer Rabbit, 1946 .... 3850.00
Cel, Song of The South, Tar Baby, Brer Rabbit, Framed, 10 1/2 x 14 1/2 In. 3005.00
Cel, Superman, 1941, Full Figure, Framed, 11 x 6 1/2 In. 3300.00
Cel, Sword In The Stone, Archimedes Perched On His Cap, 1963, 6 1/2 x 4 In. 935.00
Cel, Sword In The Stone, Disney Sticker 295.00
Cel, Sword In The Stone, Merlin Dances A Jig, 6 x 4 In. 935.00
Cel, Sword In The Stone, Merlin Trudges To Tower, 1963, 10 1/2 x 15 In. 4290.00
Cel, Sword In The Stone, Wart, Merlin & Archimedes, Framed, 1963, 11 x 13 In. ... 2300.00
Cel, Tummy Trouble, Roger Rabbit Holding Baby Herman, 1989, 7 1/2 x 5 In. 1650.00
Cel, Who Framed Roger Rabbit, 1988, 13 x 17 In. 6900.00
Cel, Winnie The Pooh & Friends, Eeyore, Kanga & Roo, 8 1/4 x 11 1/4 In. 1045.00
Cel, Winnie The Pooh & The Blustery Day, 1968, 11 x 13 In. 1210.00
Cel, Winnie The Pooh & The Honey Tree, 1966, 9 1/2 x 5 In. 2035.00
Cel, Winnie The Pooh & The Honey Tree, Framed, 1966, 11 x 14 In. 4840.00
Cel, Winnie The Pooh, Pooh & Eeyore, 1960s, 12 x 10 In. 1760.00
Cel, Yellow Submarine, King Features, 1968, 5 Cels 5500.00
Drawing, Alice, Alice In Wonderland, Pair 770.00
Drawing, Swimming Pegasus, Fantasia, Pastel 1760.00

ANNA POTTERY was started in Anna, Illinois, in 1859 by Cornwall and
Wallace Kirkpatrick. They made many types of utilitarian wares, bricks,
drain tiles, and giftware. The most collectible pieces made by the pottery
are the pig-shaped bottles and jugs with special inscriptions, applied
animals and figures. The pottery closed in 1894.

Anna Pottery

  Pig, A Little Good Old Bourbon In A Hog, Albany Slip 1600.00

APPLE PEELERS are listed in the Kitchen category under Peeler, Apple.

ARC–EN–CIEL is the French word for rainbow. A pottery factory named
Arc-en-ciel was founded in Zanesville, Ohio, in 1903. The company made
art pottery for a short time, then became the Brighton Pottery in 1905.

  Vase, Gold Luster, 10 In. 350.00
  Vase, Molded Floral, Gold Metallic Glaze, Marked, 10 In. 385.00

ARCHITECTURAL antiques include a variety of collectibles, usually very
large, that have been removed from buildings. Hardware, backbars, doors,
paneling, and even old bathtubs are now wanted by collectors. Pieces of
the Victorian, Art Nouveau, and Art Deco styles are in greatest demand.

  Arch, Art Deco, Iron, Allover Vines & Flowers, Swans, 10 Ft. 8250.00

Backbar, Cherry, Beveled Glass Doors, Late 1800s, 7 1 /2 x 9 1/2 Ft. 3000.00
Backbar, Stained Glass, Oak, Marble, 120 x 122 In. 3080.00
Balcony Guards, Geometric, Iron, American, 1920s 375.00
Baluster, Iron, From Chicago Stock Exchange Building, Sullivan, 1884 .... 4000.00
Bathtub, White Paint, Pat. 1891 .... 695.00
Block, Grotesque Face, Ceramic, 13 1/2 x 15 1/4 In., Pair 450.00
Block, Terra–Cotta, Griffins, Polychromed 275.00
Brick, Street, Salt Glaze, Beveled, 1900s, 4 x 4 x 8 1/2 In. .... .80
Column Facade, Roman Style, Mahogany, Painted, Capital, 78 In., Pair 175.00
Corbel, Griffin, Carved Wood, 16th Century, Small, Pair 250.00
Door & Surround, Federal, Green & White Paint, Fan & Side Pillars 1700.00
Door Knocker, Parrot, Metal, Multi–Color, Hand Painted 100.00
Door, Entryway, Beveled Glass, 12–Light, Oak, 86 1/2 x 30 1/4 In., Pair 308.00
Door, Jacobean Type, Beveled Glass, Oak, c.1900, 91 x 27 1/2 In., Pair 600.00
Door, Redwood, Stained Glass Window, Greene & Greene, 88 x 42 In. 1760.00
Door, Revolving, Bronze 5500.00
Door, Revolving, Wooden 2700.00
Doorknob, Brown Marbled, 5 3/4 In. ....*Illus* 25.00
Doorknob, Glass, From Public School, 1860s, 2 Pair 225.00
Down Spout, Boar's Head Shape, Copper 695.00
Drawer Pull Set, Green, Depression Glass, Screws, Large, 10 Piece 65.00
Fan, Federal Style House, Wooden Bars, Green Shades, 4 1/2 x 2 Ft. 1750.00
Fence, Gates & Posts, Arrowhead, Iron, 100 Ft. 1500.00
Fence, Iron Champion Fence Co., Iron, 60 Ft. 1800.00
Fence, Victorian, 2 Gates, Iron Champion Fence Co., Iron, 59 Ft x 38 In. 3000.00
Figure, Cupid, Cast Iron, Life Size, 4 Piece 3960.00
Figure, Sphinx, Cast Stone, 1900s, Pair 7500.00
Finial, Copper, 1880, Pair 5800.00
Finial, Galvanized Sheet Metal, Dark Patina, 34 1/2 In. 302.00
Finial, Sheet Metal, Rusted Patina, 18 In. 247.00
Gate Post, Penguin, Nantucket, Pair 2995.00
Gate, Father Time, Spreading His Wings, American, Iron, 19th Century 1200.00
Gate, Iron, Art Deco, Pair 995.00
Gate, Polychrome Floral Bouquet Center, Iron, Spanish, 77 1/2 In. 1450.00
Gate, Scrolled Top, Iron, 1910, 5 Ft. 65.00
Grating, Lion Mask In Center, Iron, 27 In. 33.00
Head, Liberty's, Molded Zinc, 1875, 18 In. 5200.00
Lamp Post, Cast Iron, 4 Lanterns, 10 Ft. 550.00
Lamp, Street, Gas, Classic Type, 30 In. 395.00
Lamp, Street, Kerosene, Dietz, 1890 .... 200.00
Light Post, Iron, Prairie School, Pair 5500.00
Louver, Putty Color, Fan Shape, Pair 2200.00
Mailbox, Cast Iron, Brass 100.00
Mantel, Baroque Style, Central Cartouche, Classical Figures At Ends, Oak 4675.00
Mantel, Shelf, Irving & Casson 1875.00
Mantel, Sheraton, Mahogany, Cornice, Mirror Has Shelf Sides, 89 x 58 In. 1750.00

♦ ♦

If you live in an earthquake area, a few precautions may help limit damage. Be sure there is a lip on the edge of a shelf that holds dishes and glassware. Use dental wax to stick the objects to the shelf. Keep cabinet doors locked shut so pieces will not fall out.

Architectural, Doorknob, Brown Marbled,
5 3/4 In.

♦ ♦

Mirror, American Empire, Gilt & Black Paint, Reverse Painted, 38 x 18 In. 160.00
Mirror, Fun House, 6 Ft. 100.00
Ornament, Lion, Copper, Fierce Looking, 1900 .... 1550.00
Ornament, Roof, Foo Dog, Blue Glaze, 8 1/2 In., Pair 50.00
Ornament, Stylized Head of A Queen, Wearing Crown, Marble, 35 In. 2200.00
Panel, Door, Etched Urns & Flowers, c.1860, 48 x 22 In., Pair 460.00
Panel, Stained Glass, Adoration of Christ Child, 18 1/8 x 18 In. 165.00
Panel, Stained Glass, Richard The Lion Hearted, 1883, 26 x 21 In. 660.00
Panel, Three Kings Retalbo, Painted Carved Wood, 19 3/4 x 10 1/4 In. 125.00
Plaque, House, Cooper Est. 1863, Horse Ends, Iron 85.00
Post Head, Porch, Wooden, 1880, 14 In., Pair 1850.00
Postmaster's Unit, Sorting, Oak, 60 Pigeonholes 350.00
Shutter, Dark Paint, Canada, 3 Piece 965.00
Sink, Pedestal, Oval, Fluted Base 525.00
Skylight, Frank Lloyd Wright, From Coonley House 2860.00
Stand, Shoe Shine, 2 Oak Chairs, Porcelain Footrests, White Marble 1500.00

AREQUIPA POTTERY was produced from 1911 to 1918 by the patients of
the Arequipa Sanitorium in Marin County Hills, California.

Bowl, Blue, Light Blue Matte, 4 In. 250.00
Bowl, Incised Leaves, High Glaze, Browns, 4 1/2 In. 495.00
Bowl, Peacock & Foliage, Green & Yellow, 10 In. 1980.00
Vase, Grass & Flowers, Curdled Matte Blue Glaze, Bulbous, 7 1/2 In. 522.50
Vessel, Applied Leaves Around Rim, Flambe, Squat, 2 1/2 x 5 In. 330.00

ARGY-ROUSSEAU, see G. Argy-Rousseau category

ART DECO, or Art Moderne, a style started at the Paris Exposition of
1925, is characterized by linear, geometric designs. All types of furniture
and decorative arts, jewelry, book bindings, and even games were designed
in this style. Additional items may be found in the Furniture category or
in various glass categories, etc.

Aquarium, Copper, Brass, Round Sphere On Pedestal 550.00
Ashtray, Horse Head, Black, Green 85.00
Ashtray, Nude, Black Ceramic 40.00
Bowl, Elliptical-Shaped, Applied Fluted Silver Gilt Foot Ring, 3 In. 220.00
Box, Desk, Bronze & Silver, Monogram, Pat. '12, 12 x 8 3/4 In. 110.00
Box, Jewelry, White Pearlized Plastic, Mirror, 3 Swing Out Drawers, 9 x 6 In. 65.00
Box, Tortoiseshell Bakelite, Cover, Diamond Shape, France, 6 In. 30.00
Candleholder, Green, Pair 27.50
Candlestick, Bakelite, Sterling Overlay, Pair 38.00
Cocktail Shaker, Barbell 55.00
Cocktail Shaker, Figural, Penguin, 12 In. 550.00
Coffee Urn, Chrome & Brass, Ball Shape, LaBelle Silver Co. 135.00
Compote, Hammered Aluminum, Fluted Applied Handles, 6 1/3 In. 467.50
Cup, Glazed, Painted, Matisse Style, 5 In. 39.00
Fan, Akro Agate Base 125.00
Figurine, Egyptian Woman, Lying, Outstretched Arms, Black Metal, 15 In. 150.00
Figurine, German Shepherd, Bronze, Signed 195.00
Frame, Picture, Brass, Pine Cones & Leaves 50.00
Knife Rest, Horse, Pottery, Chartreuse, Set of 4 .... 40.00
Mirror, Pink Flamingo, Wall, 1950s 52.00
Planter, Dagwood Bumstead Head 110.00
Powder Box, Triangular, Woman On Top 145.00
Tea Kettle, Ringed Ball Shape, Red Enamelware On Dark Blue Speckled Granite 35.00
Tray, Gilt Brass, Glass Jeweled, Empire Art Gold Co., 10 1/2 x 16 1/2 In. 495.00
Urn, Plaster, Black Paint, 44 1/2 In. 125.00
Vanity Set, Silver Plated, Travel Case, 9 In. 50.00
Vase, 3-Bud, Chase 20.00
Vase, Denby, 19 In. 110.00
Vase, Diamond Deco Motif, Brown-Gray Wash, L. Mairesse, 7 In. 385.00
Vase, Orientalist, 1930, 20 In. 83.00
Wall Pocket, Glamour-Type Woman's Head, Chalkware, A. Backer, 8 In., Pair 48.00

ART GLASS, see Glass–Art

ART NOUVEAU is a style of design that was at its most popular from 1895 to 1905. Famous designers, including Rene Lalique and Emile Galle, produced furniture, glass, silver, metalwork, and buildings in the new style. Ladies with long flowing hair and elongated bodies were among the more easily recognized design elements. Copies of this style are being made today. Many modern pieces of jewelry can be found. Additional Art Nouveau pieces may be found in Furniture or in various glass categories.

Box, Copper & Silver, Wooden Lining, Gorham	1320.00
Box, Jewelry, Mirrored, Mon Image, Delong	35.00
Box, Jewelry, Woman's Face, Unusual Handle, Ormolu, 3 x 3 In.	70.00
Chalice, James Powell & Sons, 12 In.	520.00
Creamer, Iridescent, Silver Plated Handle & Lip	195.00
Figurine, Woman Sitting On The Moon	65.00
Humidor, Stand, Bronze, Glass, Scrolling Pattern, Marshall Field, 33 In.	990.00
Mirror, Hand, Beveled, Figural Cupid Handle	125.00
Platter, Bamboo Tree Decoration, Bronze, 9 In.	165.00
Sconces, 5–Light, Beaded Chain, Wall Bracket, Bronze, 23 In., Pair	825.00
Tray, Lily Pad Shape, Stem As Handle, Male, Female Figures, Bronze, 11 In.	660.00
Vase, 2 Maidens, Stylized Floral Border, Gilt, Enameled, Austria, 12 1/8 In.	1925.00
Vase, Opalescent, Gilt & Black Enameled Design, Green Cast, Blown	250.00
Vase, Oxblood To Cream, Baluster Shape, Metal Mount, Handles, 30 In., Pair	2860.00
Vase, Yellow Flowers, Flared Arm, Swollen, Elongated Neck, 4 1/8 In.	198.00

ART POTTERY was first made in America in Cincinnati, Ohio, during the 1870s. The pieces were hand thrown and hand decorated. The art pottery tradition continued until the 1920s when studio potters began making the more artistic wares. American and English art pottery is listed here. More recent pottery is listed under the name of the maker or in the Pottery category.

Bowl, Bulb, Blue, Fred Johnson	75.00
Bowl, Ming Blue, Flared, Lachenal, 7 1/2 x 4 1/2 In.	137.50
Bowl, Polychrome Fruit Basket, Blue Rim, White Ground, Byrdcliffe, 6 1/2 In.	275.00
Bowl, Wavy Green Glaze, Natzler, 4 5/8 x 8 5/8 In.	1100.00
Centerpiece, Dish, Raised By 3 Putti, Glazed Sapphire Blue, Keramik, 8 1/2 In.	1650.00
Charger, Leaf Pattern, Yellow & Orange Center, H. Albright, 17 1/2 In.	220.00
Flower Frog, Boy, Riding Seashell, Goldfish Peeking Out, Germany, 1800s	120.00
Jardiniere, Standard Glaze, Denver China & Pottery Co., 5 x 6 In.	126.50
Lamp Base, Plant Pod Design, Frothy Glaze, Wheatley, 17 In.	1850.00
Lamp, Egyptian Revival, Cream Crackle Glaze, Figure of Egyptian Maid, 36 In.	305.00
Pitcher, Dog Handle, Vance/Avon, 12 3/4 In.	385.00
Pitcher, Green, Gold & Silver Lead, Swastika, Keramos, 10 In.	205.00
Plaque, King, Multicolored, On Wood, Harris Strong, 10 x 14 In.	525.00
Plate, Mottled Orange Glaze, Flared Rim, Hull House, 10 3/4 In.	137.00
Plate, Polychrome Glazed Finches On Blossoms, Theodore Deck, 11 3/4 In.	975.00
Vase, Allover Dripping Turquoise Glaze, Durant Kilns, 1914, 6 1/2 In.	135.00
Vase, Aztec Design, Green Glaze, Pair	50.00
Vase, Brown Drip Over Green Crystalline Glaze, Prang, 6 In.	230.00
Vase, Bud, Blue & Silver, Scene, Lessell	240.00
Vase, Carved Leaves, Bybee, 1918, 6 In.	55.00
Vase, Center Band of Raised Diamond Design, Emile Decoeur, 8 In.	1760.00
Vase, Crystalline Glaze, Chicago Crucible Co., 8 In.	82.50
Vase, Flattened Flask, Dripping Glaze, Keramic Art Works, 13 1/4 In.	396.00
Vase, Green & Yellow Glaze, Short Rolled Rim, Chicago Crucible, 4 3/4 In.	165.00
Vase, Green Drip, Tan, Paul E. Cox, 3 1/2 In.	375.00
Vase, Green, Gold Trim, Swastika, Keramos, 8 In.	225.00
Vase, Incised Fish, Alexander Lauder, c.1890, 19 1/2 In., Pair	660.00
Vase, Leaf Design Overall, 2 Handles, Markham, 7 In.	360.00
Vase, Limoges–Type, Applied Design, Cincinnati Art Pottery	75.00
Vase, Mythological Scene, Gray & Brown Glaze, Rene Buthaud, 8 1/2 In.	2860.00
Vase, Ribbed Shell Form Sides, Pink, Gold Trim, Bovier	725.00

◆◆◆◆◆◆◆◆◆◆◆◆◆◆◆◆◆◆◆◆◆◆

Candlesticks will melt or even
explode if candles burn too low.
Always support the arm of a
candelabra when putting in the
candles.

◆◆◆◆◆◆◆◆◆◆◆◆◆◆◆◆◆◆◆◆◆◆

Arts & Crafts, Candlestick, Inverted

Semi-Spheres, Brass & Wood, 5 1/2 In.

Vase, Squeeze–Bag & Sgraffito, Vance/Avon, F. Rhead	2500.00
Vase, Strap Handles, Dark Matte Green, Chicago Crucible, 9 1/4 In.	1650.00
Vase, Thick Dark Purple Gloss Glaze, Paper Label, Merrimac, 7 In.	130.00
Vase, Volcanic Blue Glaze, Bulbous, Denver White, 4 1/4 x 7 In.	88.00

ARTHUR OSBORNE collectibles are found in the Ivorex category.

ARTS & CRAFTS was a design style popular in American decorative arts
from 1894 to 1923. In the 1970s collectors began to rediscover Mission
furniture, art pottery, metalwork, linens, and light fixtures from this
period. The interest has continued. Today everything from this era is
collectible, including jewelry, graphics, and silverware. Additional items
may be found in the Furniture category, various glass categories, etc.

Basket, Wall, Woven Flat Silver Strands	85.00
Bowl, Copper, Intricately Worked, Oslund	90.00
Bowl, Sterling Silver, Raised Foot, Arthur J. Stone, 9 1/2 In.	605.00
Box, Peacock Lid, Mahogany Interior, Craftsmen Studio, 2 1/2 x 5 x 4 In.	110.00
Candelabra, 5 Bobeches, Flat Scrolled Base, 6 1/2 x 19 In.	220.00
Candlestick, Brass, Tin Stem, Jarvie–Type, 12 1/4 In., Pair	495.00
Candlestick, Copper, Enameled Flowers, Arts Craft Shop, 16 In.	300.00
Candlestick, Copper, Hammered, Onondaga Metal Shop, 9 1/2 In.	220.00
Candlestick, Inverted Semi–Spheres, Brass & Wood, 5 1/2 In. ....*Illus*	1200.00
Candlestick, Metal, Flower & Lily Pad	165.00
Chandelier, 4–Light, Copper Chains, Hanging Shades, 24 In.	1320.00
Chandelier, Geometric Leaded Glass, Bronze, Chains, 1915, 21 x 19 In.	2200.00
Dish, Chafing, Hammered Copper, Sterling Silver Rivets	445.00
Dish, Nut, Wooden Bowl, Bronze Squirrel Handles, Edith Parsons, 9 In.	35.00
Flask, Liquor, Pewter, Pocket	45.00
Humidor, Hammered Copper, Scrolled Footed, 10 1/2 x 6 1/4 In.	165.00
Jar, Oil, Blue Glaze, Flared Rolled Rim, 22 1/4 x 16 1/2 In., Pair	705.00
Lamp, Ceiling, 1–Light, Brass, Milk Glass Ribbed Open Shade	55.00
Lamp, Floor, Ashtray, 1918	145.00
Lantern, Yellow Slag Glass, Brass Washed Iron, 14 x 7 x 11 In., Pair	209.00
Night–Light, Lotus Blossom From Leaf Shape, E. Burton Type, 9 1/2 In.	385.00
Pen Holder, Fossilized Mastodon Ivory, Copper, Albert Berry, 6 x 10 In.	660.00
Planter, Brass, Hanging	60.00
Planter, Reticulated Leaves, Copper Plated Brass, 8 1/2 x 11 In.	110.00
Plate Warmer, Silk, Reflective Hand Painted Birds & Flowers	30.00
Umbrella Stand, Brass Corner Brackets, Arched Top, 28 In.	165.00

AURENE glass was made by Frederick Carder of New York about 1904. It
is an iridescent gold or blue glass, usually marked *Aurene* or *Steuben.*

AURENE

Bonbon, Ruffled Rim, Blue, Signed, 3 1/2 In.	485.00
Candleholder, No. 686, Blue, Steuben, Pair	1600.00
Candlestick, Blue, Label, 8 1/2 In., Pair	1100.00

Candlestick, Flared Candle Cup, Twisted Stem, 8 In., Pair 2475.00
Compote, Gold, 8 In. 385.00
Cordial Set, Cylindrical Decanter, Conical Glasses, 6 Piece 2850.00
Finger Bowl, Underplate 390.00
Finger Bowl, Underplate, Gold, 2 Piece 995.00
Salt, Calcite, Gold 280.00
Salt, Flare and Scalloped Rim, Signed and Numbered 295.00
Shade, Rib Pattern, Iridescent Gold, Bell Shape, 5 x 4 1/2 x 2 1/8 In. 110.00
Sherbet, Underplate, Signed 285.00
Tazza, Twisted Stem, Gold, 8 In. 660.00
Tumbler, Bronze Highlights, Flared Rim, Signed, 4 1/8 In. 225.00
Vase, Art Glass, Iridescent, Trumpet Shape Base, Scalloped Rim, 9 In. 350.00
Vase, Blue Iridescent, Steuben, 6 In. 775.00
Vase, Blue, 10 1/2 In. 2090.00
Vase, Blue, 6 1/4 In. 525.00
Vase, Flared Pot, Iridescent Surface, 2 5/8 In. 605.00
Vase, Golden Yellow, Signed, 8 In. 500.00
Vase, Iridescent, Flared Ruffled Collar, 1904–1920, 6 1/8 In., Pair 1200.00
Vase, Iridescent, Green Leafage, Floriform, Signed Steuben, 1904–1920, 5 In. 1100.00
Vase, Iridescent, Ovoid, 1904–1920, 2 3/4 In. 660.00
Vase, Jack–In–The–Pulpit, Gold, Signed Steuben, 6 1/2 In. 1500.00
Vase, Ruffled Rim, Blue, 2 1/2 x 2 3/4 In. 525.00
Vase, Stick, Butterfly, Blue, Signed, 7 In. 325.00
Wine, Twist Stem, Signed 200.00

AUSTRIA is a collecting term which covers pieces made by a wide variety of factories. They are listed in this book in categories such as Kauffmann, Royal Dux, or Porcelain.

AUTO parts and accessories are collectors' items today. Gas pump globes and license plates are part of this specialty. Prices are determined by age, rarity, and condition. Signs and packaging related to automobiles may also be found in the Advertising category. Lalique hood ornaments will be listed in the Lalique category.

Bill Hook, Wall, Mobile Oil, Flying Red Horse, Wooden, 1940s 28.00
Blue Book, Volume 4, 1918 .... 10.00
Book, Ford Model A Instructions, 1930, 52 Pages 35.00
Bottle, Battery Oil, Thomas A. Edison 5.00
Bottle, Battery Oil, Union Carbide 5.00
Bottle, Test, Sohio, Glass 25.00
Button, Model A Ford Club of America, Celluloid, Oval, 1930s 12.00
Button, Plymouth Roadking, Celluloid, Attached Ribbon, 1940, 2 1/2 In. 25.00
Card, Registration, California Automobile, Velie 6, Fee $3. 00, License, 35 Cents 6.00
Catalog, Buick Motor Cars, 1922, 48 Pages 37.00
Catalog, Engines & Transmission For The 1959 Fords, 19 Pages 10.00
Clock, Hudson, Super 6 .... 60.00
Gas Gauge, Chevrolet, Key Shape, Brass, 1934 .... 98.00
Gas Pump Globe, Aladdin Gasoline, Milk Glass 175.00
Gas Pump Globe, Apco 75.00
Gas Pump Globe, Ashland Flying Octane 135.00
Gas Pump Globe, Ashland Kerosene 150.00
Gas Pump Globe, Budget, Glass, 13 1/2 In. 325.00
Gas Pump Globe, Canfield 300.00
Gas Pump Globe, Cities Service, Metal Frame, 15 In. 425.00
Gas Pump Globe, Clear Vision Pump Co., Wichita, Kan., Patent 1919 .... 2500.00
Gas Pump Globe, Conocos 200.00
Gas Pump Globe, Dixie Blue 350.00
Gas Pump Globe, Esso Extra, Metal Frame, 15 In. 425.00
Gas Pump Globe, Essolene, 2 Sides, Metal Band, 18 x 21 x 6 In. 127.00
Gas Pump Globe, Federal Super, Metal Frame, 15 In. 400.00
Gas Pump Globe, Flying A Gasoline, Porcelain, Enameled, 11 1/4 In. Diam. 15.00
Gas Pump Globe, Frontier Double Refined, 13 1/2 In. 350.00
Gas Pump Globe, Frontier, With Horse 250.00

Gas Pump Globe, Gulf Coast, Metal Frame, 15 In. 400.00
Gas Pump Globe, Gulf Marine White 125.00
Gas Pump Globe, Gulf, Etched That Good Stuff 650.00
Gas Pump Globe, Gulf, Plastic Front, Aluminum, Round, 18 In. 150.00
Gas Pump Globe, Imperial Refineries, Ethyl Logo, Insert, 13 1/2 In. 300.00
Gas Pump Globe, Indian Gasoline, Porcelain, 2 Sides, 18 x 12 In. 300.00
Gas Pump Globe, Kanotex, Sunflower, Gill Body 500.00
Gas Pump Globe, Kendall Poly Power, 13 1/2 In. 250.00
Gas Pump Globe, Marathon Regular 150.00
Gas Pump Globe, Marathon Super 150.00
Gas Pump Globe, Mobilgas, No Horse, 13 1/2 In. 285.00
Gas Pump Globe, Phillips 66 .... 185.00
Gas Pump Globe, Pioneer Zipper 450.00
Gas Pump Globe, Pure Oil Company, Milk Glass Frame, 2 Side Panels 450.00
Gas Pump Globe, Purol, With Arrow, Metal, Porcelain Body, 15 In. 650.00
Gas Pump Globe, Red Hat Tri-Star Gas, Porcelain, Enameled, 11 1/4 In. Diam. 15.00
Gas Pump Globe, Red x Oil Co., Insert, Red Plastic, 13 1/2 In. 300.00
Gas Pump Globe, Shell 750.00
Gas Pump Globe, Sinclair Dino Gasoline, White Plastic, Red & Green Letters 225.00
Gas Pump Globe, Sinclair Ethyl 400.00
Gas Pump Globe, Sinclair Gasoline, With Ethyl, Red Ground 475.00
Gas Pump Globe, Sinclair H–C 525.00
Gas Pump Globe, Sinclair H–C, Etched 1000.00
Gas Pump Globe, Skelly .... 150.00 To 350.00
Gas Pump Globe, Solite, Crown, Raised Letters, Blue 1200.00
Gas Pump Globe, Standard Gold Crown 300.00
Gas Pump Globe, Standard Oil, Kentucky 500.00
Gas Pump Globe, Standard, Flame 300.00
Gas Pump Globe, Standard, Green Crown 150.00
Gas Pump Globe, Standard, Red Crown 275.00
Gas Pump Globe, Super Mileage 450.00
Gas Pump Globe, Super Shell, Blue 1500.00
Gas Pump Globe, Texaco Diesel Chief, Red 145.00
Gas Pump Globe, Texaco Sky Chief, 1940s .... 300.00 To 400.00
Gas Pump Globe, Texaco, Black T, Glass 325.00
Gas Pump Globe, Top Octane, 12 In. 325.00
Gas Pump Globe, Tydol Ethyl, With Plane, On Gill, 13 1/2 In. 500.00
Gas Pump Globe, Vance Bronze High Octane, 1930s 275.00
Gas Pump Globe, White Eagle 550.00
Gas Pump, Bennett Sunoco, Restored 650.00
Gas Pump, G & B, Visible 500.00
Gas Pump, Phillips, Shield, Black & Orange, 30 In. 200.00
Gas Pump, Quaker State, 1937 .... 125.00
Gas Pump, Shell, Model 17, Restored By Fry Co. 2895.00
Gas Pump, Sunoco, Bennett 650.00
Goggles, Motorist's 25.00
Headlight, Chrysler, Airflow, Battery Operated, Set 1100.00
Headlight, Round Metal Case, Extra Bulbs 25.00
Hood Ornament, Art Deco Nude 65.00
Hood Ornament, Beaver, Auto Club of Canada, Bronze 125.00
Hood Ornament, Bulldog, Mack Truck, Cast Iron 35.00
Hood Ornament, Dancing Couple, Gold Metal, 1940s, 5 In. 20.00
Hood Ornament, Dodge, Long Ram, 1940s 40.00
Hood Ornament, Dodge, Ram 35.00
Hood Ornament, Fish 45.00
Hood Ornament, Five Flags, 1950s 15.00
Hood Ornament, Flying Bitch, Green Celluloid Wings 75.00
Hood Ornament, Hudson, 1936 .... 75.00
Hood Ornament, Nude Woman, Standing, Long Flowing Hair 125.00
Hood Ornament, Nude Woman, Winged Arms, Pontiac 45.00
Hood Ornament, Packard, Goddess of Speed, 1930 .... 65.00
Hood Ornament, Pontiac Chieftan 35.00
Hood Ornament, Rolls–Royce, Spirit of Ecstasy 395.00

Hood Ornament, Super Chief, Box, 1950	145.00
Hood Ornament, Woman's Head, Figural, Brass	50.00
Horn, Brass, Circular Bulb	20.00
Hubcap, La Salle, 1920s	35.00 To 45.00
Hubcap, Packard, Original Envelope, 1956, Set of 4	35.00
Jar, Oil, Standard Oil Co., Ind., Glass	45.00
Key Ring, Oldsmobile, Insignia, 1955	2.00
Knob, Gear Shift, Glass, Orange & Blue Streaks	20.00
Knob, Steering Wheel, Slag Glass	24.00
License Plate, Arizona, 1934, Solid Copper	85.00
License Plate, California, 1956, Pair	24.50
License Plate, Colorado, 1932	10.00
License Plate, Georgia, 1938, Original Wrapper	12.75
License Plate, Georgia, 1938, Pair	25.00
License Plate, Georgia, 1977	3.50
License Plate, Illinois, 1932	35.00
License Plate, Illinois, 1957	35.00
License Plate, Massachusetts, Enameled, 1909	50.00
License Plate, Mississippi, 1932, Wrapper	14.00
License Plate, Mississippi, 1977	3.75
License Plate, Ohio, 1962, Red ....*Illus*	6.00
License Plate, Texas, 1917	20.00
License Plate, Texas, 1967	35.00
License Plate, Washington, D.C., Inauguration, 1977	25.00
Luggage Rack, Model T Ford, Expandable	40.00
Manual, Chrysler, Imperial, 1970	10.00
Manual, Edsel Shop, 1958, Large	33.00
Motor Oil, Amalie Pennsylvania, Oilier Oil, Red & White, Contents	16.00
Motor Oil, C–X Heavy Duty, Cream, Red Ground, Black Letters, Contents	25.00
Motor Oil, Champlin III–VI, Dark Blue, Silver, White & Red Letters, Contents	30.00
Motor Oil, Champlin Transeason, White, Gold Ground, Blue Letters	20.00
Motor Oil, Cities Service Kool, Red Letters, White Ground, Contents	25.00
Motor Oil, Conoco, White, Red Ground, Contents	25.00
Motor Oil, Diamond, D–X Sunray Oil Co., Red Diamond, Paraffin Base, Contents	30.00
Motor Oil, Enco Encolute, Green Ground, White Letters, Contents	25.00
Motor Oil, Gulfpride, White, Blue Letters, Contents	15.00
Motor Oil, Invader, Yellow, Black Band, Contents	35.00
Motor Oil, Penn Drake, Black, White, Red Ground	50.00
Motor Oil, Phillips 66 Aviation, Winged Shield, Blue, Silver Ground, Contents	35.00
Motor Oil, Phillips 66 Heavy Duty Premium, Red Shield, Contents	30.00
Motor Oil, Polorine, Open Touring Car, Wooden Crate, 10 1/2 x 14 1/2 In.	550.00
Motor Oil, Quaker State, White, Green Letters, Contents	15.00
Motor Oil, Sinclair Opaline, Dinosaur, Dark Green, White Ground, Contents	20.00
Motor Oil, Texaco Havoline, White, Navy Ground, Contents	25.00
Motor Oil, Texaco Ursa Super 3, White, Black Stripes, Red Letters, Contents	15.00
Motor Oil, Ursa E. D., White, Red Letters, Contents	25.00

Auto, License Plate, Ohio, 1962, Red

◆◆◆◆◆◆◆◆◆◆◆◆◆◆◆◆◆◆◆◆◆◆◆◆

If you discover a cache of very dirty antiques and you are not dressed in work clothes, make a temporary cover-up from a plastic garbage bag.

◆◆◆◆◆◆◆◆◆◆◆◆◆◆◆◆◆◆◆◆◆◆◆◆

Motor Oil, Wolf's Head, Dark Green & Red Letters, White Ground, Contents 35.00
Oilcan, Cities Service 25.00
Oilcan, Golden Knight, 2 Gal. 85.00
Oilcan, Hyrdrotone, Contents, 1 Qt. 8.00
Oilcan, Kendall Motor, 40s Model Car 20.00
Oilcan, Marathon Endurance Motor Oil, Marathon Man Logo, 2 Gal. 24.00
Oilcan, Mobil, Contents, 1 Qt. 15.00
Oilcan, N. O. S. Penn–Soo, Square, 1/2 Gal. 85.00
Oilcan, Socony, Contents, 1 Qt. 15.00
Plate, Picnic, Ford Model T, White Enameled, Blue Trim, Set of 4 .... 200.00
Radiator Cap, 1929 Buick 195.00
Radiator Cap, Studebaker 165.00
Radiator Cover, Hupmobile, For Winter, 1920s 25.00
Ruler, Gas, Atwater Kent, Model T Ford, Wooden, 1909, 17 In. 15.00
Sign, B. F. Goodrich, Tin, White, Navy Ground, 15 x 7 1/2 In. 15.00
Sign, Chippewa Tires, Dark Blue Letters, Orange Ground, Tin, 15 x 7 1/2 In. 15.00
Sign, Cities Service Oil Co., Citgo, Blue Shield, Red, White Letters, 14 x 7 In. 45.00
Sign, Conoco, Diamond Shape, Green, White Ground, 8 1/2 x 9 1/2 In. 70.00
Sign, Curt's Oil Co., Power Packed Ethyl, Tin, Gold Letters, 12 x 16 In. 175.00
Sign, Dino Gasoline, Green, Black Letters, Porcelain, 21 x 4 In. 45.00
Sign, Dixie Service Station, Dark Blue Letters, Porcelain, 31 x 10 In. 145.00
Sign, Ford Service, Pointed Finger, Tin 395.00
Sign, Good Gulf, Orange Shield, White Ground, 8 1/2 x 11 In. 100.00
Sign, Gulf No–Nox, Orange Shield, White Ground, 11 1/2 x 8 1/2 In. 100.00
Sign, Mobil Regular, Horse, White, Porcelain, 12 x 13 1/2 In. 20.00
Sign, Mobil Tires, Horse, White, Navy Letters, Tin, 22 x 7 1/2 In. 30.00
Sign, Mobilgas, Shield, Horse, Blue Letters, 12 x 12 In. 150.00
Sign, Phillips 66, Shield, Orange, Black Letters, 1930–1940, 30 x 29 In. 250.00
Sign, Pontiac Indian Chief, Neon 1175.00
Sign, Pump, Good Gulf, Porcelain 34.00
Sign, Pump, Gulf Marine White, Logo, Porcelain 125.00
Sign, Pump, Indian Gas 175.00
Sign, Pump, Mobil Gas Special, Porcelain 125.00
Sign, Pump, Pure Premium, Porcelain 65.00
Sign, Pump, Pure Premium, Porcelain 90.00
Sign, Pump, Shamrock Cloud Master 85.00
Sign, Pump, Shamrock Trail Master 85.00
Sign, Pump, Sinclair Dino, Porcelain 55.00
Sign, Pump, Sinclair, Porcelain, 13 1/2 x 12 In. 65.00
Sign, Pump, Texaco Diesel Chief, Green 200.00
Sign, Pump, Texaco Fire Chief, Porcelain 55.00
Sign, Pump, Texaco Supreme, Porcelain 55.00
Sign, Pump, That Good Gulf Gasoline 135.00
Sign, Quaker State Motor Oil, Green, White Letters, Tin, 29 x 26 1/2 In. 125.00
Sign, Shamrock Trail Master Regular, Yellow, Porcelain, 10 x 12 In. 100.00
Sign, Sinclair Cloud Master Premium, Porcelain, 12 1/2 x 10 1/2 In. 65.00
Sign, Sinclair H–C Gasoline, 48 In. Diam. 187.00
Sign, Texaco Fire Chief Gasoline, Red Hat, White Ground, 10 x 15 In. 135.00
Sign, Texaco Sky Chief Gasoline, Green Striped, Red, Black, 1958, 22 x 12 In. 135.00
Sign, Texaco, Red Star, White Ground, Round, 6 Ft. 100.00
Sign, Valvoline, Tin, 28 x 15 In. 150.00
Thermometer, Nash, Wooden 275.00
Tin, Black Joe Axle Grease, 1 Lb. 195.00
Tire Gauge, Model T, 1916 .... 10.00
Tire Gauge, Schraders, Advertising, Bonniwell–Calvin Iron Co., Kansas City, Mo. ... 20.00
Tire Pump, Ford Script On Base, Brass 55.00
Tire Pump, Ford, Missing Hose 27.50

AUTUMN LEAF pattern china was made for the Jewel Tea Company beginning in 1933. Hall China Company of East Liverpool, Ohio, Crooksville China Company of Crooksville, Ohio, Harker Potteries of Chester, West Virginia, and Paden City Pottery, Paden City, West Virginia, made dishes with this design. Autumn Leaf has remained popular

and was made by Hall China Company until 1978. Some other pieces in the Autumn Leaf pattern are still being made. For more information, see *Kovels' Depression Glass & American Dinnerware Price List.*

Ball Jug, Hall	27.50
Ball Jug, Jewel Tea	42.50
Bowl Set, Nested, Jewel Tea, 1 To 3 Qt.	32.50
Bowl, Cereal, 6 In.	5.00
Bowl, Fruit, Jewel Tea, 5 1/2 In.	6.00 To 13.00
Bowl, Vegetable, Hall, Oval, 10 1/2 In.	15.00
Bread Plate, 6 In.	4.00
Butter, Cover, Hall, 1 Lb.	375.00
Cake Stand, Metal Base	110.00 To 150.00
Casserole, Cover, Jewel Tea	25.00
Clock, 9 1/2 In.	550.00
Coaster Set, Jewel Tea, 6 Piece	20.00
Coaster, Jewel Tea, Round, 9 1/2 In.	4.00
Coffeepot, Hall, 9 Cup	37.50
Cookie Jar, Tab Handles, Box	225.00
Creamer, Ruffled	10.00
Cup & Saucer, Jewel Tea	9.00
Dinner Set, Teapot, Shakers, 72 Piece	250.00
Gravy Boat	10.00
Hot Pad, Jewel Tea, Oval, 10 3/4 In.	10.00
Hot Pad, Jewel Tea, Round, 7 1/8 In.	12.00
Jam Jar, Cover, Underplate, Jewel Tea, 3 Piece	70.00
Mixing Bowl, 7 1/2 In.	20.00
Mixing Bowl, 9 In.	15.00
Pie Pan, 9 1/2 In.	14.00
Pitcher, 2 1/2 Pt., 6 In.	15.00
Place Mat, Hall, Box, 8 Piece	320.00
Platter, Jewel Tea, Oval, 11 1/2 In.	10.00
Platter, Jewel Tea, Oval, 13 1/2 In.	22.00
Salada Plate, 7 1/4 In.	6.00
Salt & Pepper, Jewel Tea, Handles	12.50 To 20.00
Serving Bowl, Jewel Tea, Deep	17.50
Sugar & Creamer, Cover, Jewel Tea	20.00 To 25.00
Sugar, Cover, Ruffled	12.00
Tablecloth, Sailcloth, Hall, 54 x 72 In.	40.00
Teapot, Aladdin	28.00 To 40.00
Teapot, Jewel Tea, Square	50.00
Teapot, Newport	150.00

AVON bottles are listed in the Bottle category under Avon.

BACCARAT glass was made in France by La Compagnie des Cristalleries de Baccarat, located 150 miles from Paris. The factory was started in 1765. The firm went bankrupt and began operating again about 1822. Cane and millefiori paperweights were made during the 1860 to 1880 period. The firm is still working near Paris making paperweights and glasswares.

BACCARAT

Box, Amberina, Swirl, Lid, 5 In. Diam.	125.00
Box, Paneled Diamond, Oval, 3 1/4 x 4 3/4 In.	95.00
Candy Jar, Hinged Champleve Enamel Lid, Floral & Scroll, Green Walls, 6 1/2 In.	330.00
Chandelier, 6–Light, Crystal Prisms, 1962, 36 x 23 In.	9350.00
Chandelier, 18–Light, Roping & Drop Prisms, c.1900, 22 In.	2200.00
Dresser Set, Rose Teinte Swirl, Marked, c.1890, 4 Piece	350.00
Figurine, Buffalo, 5 x 8 In.	210.00
Figurine, Chick, Marked 2 1/2 In.	55.00
Figurine, Duck, Crystal, Signed	75.00
Figurine, Polar Bear, 4 1/4 x 7 In.	100.00
Figurine, Porcupine, 3 1/4 x 5 In.	155.00
Goblet, Cut Bowl, Gold Detailing, Various Color Bowls, c.1900, 12 Piece	605.00
Goblet, Water, Perfection, 6 Piece	200.00

Humidor, Green & Red, Chipped Ice Effect, Gold Vermeil, Sterling Cover 950.00
Jam Pot, Amber Cut To Clear, Silver Plated Cover 95.00
Lamp, Fairy, Rose Teinte, Sunburst Pattern, Scalloped Saucer Base, 4 1/8 In. 245.00
Lantern, Hanging, Frosted, Cylindrical Form, Panels, Oriental Scene, 11 In. 1100.00
Paperweight, Anemone, Blue & White, Star Dust Canes, Clear Star Cut, 2 3/8 In. 885.00
Paperweight, Arrow, Whorl, Stardust, Star–Shaped, Pastry Mold Canes, 1848 .... 2700.00
Paperweight, Concentric Millefiori, Roses, Star Canes Rings, 1 3/4 In. 495.00
Paperweight, Crocus, Yellow, White Ground, Signed, 1981, 3 3/16 In. 303.00
Paperweight, Double Clematis, Pink, Clear Star Cut Ground, 2 1/2 In. 1210.00
Paperweight, Dupont, Interlaced Trefoil Garland, Clear, 3 In. 303.00
Paperweight, Eustace Tilley, Sulphide 2750.00
Paperweight, Flower, Star Dust Stamens, Clear Star Cut Ground, 2 7/8 In. 1045.00
Paperweight, Fuchsia, Orange Ladybug, Jasper Ground, 1985, 3 1/8 In. 495.00
Paperweight, Garland Flash Overlay, Canes, Circlet, Red, White, Green, 3 In. 2750.00
Paperweight, Joan of Arc, Clasping Sword, Oak Leaves, Acorns, 3 In. 2090.00
Paperweight, Millefiori, Girdle Birds, Muslin Ground, 2 1/4 In. 1760.00
Paperweight, Open Concentric Millefiori, Star Dust Canes, Blue, Red, 2 1/16 In. 445.00
Paperweight, Pansy, Deep Purple, Bull's–Eye Cane, Clear Star Cut, 3 7/8 In. 468.00
Paperweight, Pompon, White Flower, Clear Star Cut, 2 3/4 In. 2310.00
Paperweight, Primrose, Salmon & White, Red Bull's–Eye Cane, 2 9/16 In. 935.00
Paperweight, Salamander, Green Stripe, Orange Ground, Signed, 1972, 3 In. 385.00
Paperweight, Sand Dunes, Sandy Ground, Green Glass, Mica, 2 9/16 In. 88.00
Paperweight, Snake, Brown, Green Crushed Ground, Signed, 1979, 3 1/8 In. 385.00
Paperweight, Sulphide, Eleanor Roosevelt, Box 55.00
Paperweight, Sulphide, Harry Truman, Box 45.00
Paperweight, Sulphide, James Monroe, Box 45.00
Paperweight, Sulphide, Woodrow Wilson, Box 55.00
Paperweight, Taurus The Bull, Cobalt Blue 160.00
Paperweight, Wallflower, Blue & White, Star Cut Ground, 2 3/4 In. 1430.00
Paperweight, Wheat Flower, Pale Yellow, Black–Spotted Petals, 2 In. 3850.00
Paperweight, Wild Strawberries & Flowers 1600.00
Perfume Bottle, Black Nuit De Noel, 3 In. 59.00
Perfume Bottle, Cranberry, No Atomizer, Signed, 7 In. 75.00
Perfume Bottle, Glass Dome, It's You, Elizabeth Arden 3300.00
Perfume Bottle, Rectangular, Ornate Stopper, 4 1/2 In. 87.50
Perfume Set, Brass Stand, 3 Bottles 295.00
Ring Tree, Rubena 120.00
Salt, Rose Teinte 32.00
Sugar, Cover, Peafowl, 3 Colors 350.00
Toothpick, Cameo, Cranberry Floral Cut To Frosted White, 2 1/4 In. 165.00
Whiskey, Millefiori Canes, Letter B Into Canes 195.00

BADGES have been used since before the Civil War. Collectors search for examples of all types, including law enforcement and company identification badges. Well–known prison or law enforcement badges are most desirable. Most are made of nickel or brass. Many recent reproductions have been made.

Admiral Dewey, Bar Top, Welcome Dewey, Ship Olympia On Back 10.00
Census, 1900 .... 75.00
Chauffeur, Indiana, 1932 .... 20.00
Chauffeur, Michigan, 1909 .... 200.00
Continental Can Co., Employee, Picture, Chrome, Yellow 35.00
Deputy S.S. Marshal, Idaho, 1930s 100.00
Fire Department, Freeland, Pennsylvania 50.00
Fire Department, Marlboro, New Jersey .... 15.00 To 18.00
Fire Department, Rockville, Maryland 65.00
Hunting, Small Game, Michigan, 1930s 48.00
Hunting, Small Game, Pennsylvania, 1943 .... 35.00
Industrial Police 19.00
Marshall Field Toy Center News, Cub Reporter, Pinback 12.00
Metropolitan Police, Inauguration, Franklin D. Roosevelt, Shield Top, White House 1000.00
Patrolman, State of New Mexico 35.00
Police, No. 137, Jersey City, N. J., Dated 1919 .... 30.00

Presentation, Fire Chief's, 10K Gold 250.00
Sheriff's Chaplain, Star, Blackington, 1940s 75.00
Texas Ranger, Silver 110.00
Yellow Cab, 1950s 45.00
Yellow Coach Bus Lines 48.00

BANKS of metal have been made since 1868. There are still banks, mechanical banks, and registering banks (those which show the total money deposited on the face of the bank). Many old iron or tin banks have been reproduced since the 1950s in iron or plastic. Pottery, glass, and plastic banks are also listed here.

Airplane, Spirit of Saving, Aluminum Airplane 550.00
Amish Girl & Boy, On Bench, Cast Iron, Wilton 50.00
Amoco 586, Oil Can 20.00
Aunt Jemima, Cast Iron, 5 1/2 In. 6.85
Auto Coach, With People, Cast Iron 495.00
Auto, Chevrolet Panel, Eastview Pharmacy, Ertl, 1950 .... 75.00
Auto, Chevrolet, 1923, Almond Joy 23.00
Auto, Chevrolet, 1950, Frito Lay 39.00
Auto, Chevrolet, Arm & Hammer, Ertl, 1950 .... 175.00
Auto, Ford, 1905, Bell Telephone of Canada 25.00
Auto, Ford, 1905, Jack Daniels 50.00
Auto, Ford, 1913, Ace Hardware 19.00
Auto, Ford, 1913, Budweiser 185.00
Auto, Ford, 1913, Dr Pepper 29.00
Auto, Ford, 1918, Campbell's Pork & Beans 65.00
Auto, Ford, 1932, Antique Auto Club 30th Anniversary 65.00
Bambam, Figure, Plastic, On Turtle, 10 In. 42.00
Bank Cupola, Cast Iron, Stevens 70.00
Bank, Squirrel, Cast Iron 145.00
Baseball Player, Cast Iron, c.1910, 6 In. 375.00
Baseball, On 3 Bats, Cast Iron, National League, 1914 .... 1200.00
Basketball, Leaf Gum Co., Box 22.00
Battleship Prepared Mustard, Lid, Clear Glass 6.00
Bear, Begging, Gold, Iron, 5 3/8 In. 49.00
Bear, On Hind Legs, Cast Iron 225.00
Bear, Pearl China 195.00
Bear, Stealing Pig, Brass 325.00
Beehive, Cast Iron 185.00
Benjamin Franklin, Full Figure, 11 In. 25.00
Betty Boop, Ceramic 25.00
Big Boy, 10 In. 25.00
Billiken, Stamped C–222, Ceramic, 6 In. 60.00
Black Chef, Roly Poly, Iron, 8 In. 15.00
Black Mammy, Polychrome, Iron, 6 In. 104.00
Blackpool Tower, Cast Iron 200.00
Blue Bonnet Sue 25.00
Bomb, Cast Iron, W. H. Long 27.50
Book, Baby's, With Elephant, Babies In Cloud Box .... 35.00 To 45.00
Book, Key Lock, 1930s 30.00
Boy Scout, Cast Iron, National Supply, Box 125.00
Budweiser Malt 125.00
Buffalo, Cast Iron, Small 135.00
Building, Bank, Cast Iron, 3 In. 30.00
Cabin, Tin Lithograph 335.00
Camel, Cast Iron, A. C. Williams, Large 303.00
Camel, Kneeling, Cast Iron, Kyser & Rex 495.00
Camel, Lying Down, Cast Iron 412.00
Cash Register, Cast Iron, Arcade 65.00
Castle, 4 Towers, Cast Iron 138.00
Cat On Tub, Cast Iron 125.00
Cat With Ball, Cast Iron 360.00
Cat, Felix, Metal, 1959 .... 250.00

Cat, Grapette 50.00
Cat, With Bow, Cast Iron, Hubley .... 150.00 To 300.00
Chicago World's Fair, Transportation Building, Metal, Key 350.00
City Bank, With Teller, Cast Iron, Judd 412.50
Cleveland Indians, Ceramic .... 165.00 To 185.00
Clock, Mantel, Cast Iron 75.00
Clown, Tin Lithograph, Chein .... 60.00 To 100.00
Coffin, Skeletal Hand Grabs Money, Tin, Windup 35.00
Columbia, J. & E. Stevens Company, c.1893, 9 1/2 In. 445.00
Columbia, Kenton, Cast Iron, 8 3/4 x 7 x 7 In. 515.00
Commonwealth, c.1915, 5 In. 135.00
Cottage, 2–Story, Cast Iron 105.00
Cow, Holstein, Cast Iron, Gold, 4 5/8 In. 140.00
Cub Scout, Cast Iron, National Supply, Box 100.00
Cuckoo Clock, Cast Iron, Ideal, Box 12.00
Darth Vader, Star Wars, Ceramic 70.00
Devil, 2 Faces, Cast Iron, 4 1/4 In. 450.00
Devil, 2 Faces, Cast Iron, A. C. Williams 407.00
Do You Know Me, Cast Iron 145.00
Dog, Bulldog, Cast Iron, 4 1/2 In. 60.00
Dog, Bulldog, Cast Iron, 5 In. 70.00
Dog, Bulldog, Seated, Cast Iron, Hubley 97.00
Dog, Cocker Spaniel, Bee On Hindquarters, Cast Iron 20.00
Dog, German Shepherd, Speaking, Painted, Pat. Oct. 20, 1885, 7 1/8 In. 715.00
Dog, Leather, Lock & Key, Split Vertically 60.00
Dog, Nipper, RCA, Glass 70.00
Dog, Scotty, Cast Iron 47.50
Dog, Scotty, Cast Iron, Hubley 119.00
Dog, Scotty, Seated, Cast Iron, Hubley 143.00
Dog, Seated, Gold Paint, Iron, 4 1/4 In. 45.00
Dog, Water Spaniel, With Pack, Cast Iron 70.00
Dog, With Pack, Cast Iron 75.00
Dog, With Pack, Cast Iron, 9 In. 110.00
Donkey, Blue, Iron, 4 1/2 In. 71.00
Donkey, Green, A. C. Williams, Cast Iron, Small 82.50
Doughboy, World War I 350.00
Dutch Boy, On Barrel, Cast Iron, Hubley, Box 385.00
Egyptian Tomb, Cast Iron, 6 1/4 In. 625.00
Electrolux Vacuum Cleaner, Box, 1960s 100.00
Elephant, Brass, 4 1/2 x 8 1/2 In. 500.00
Elephant, Howdah, Gold, Cast Iron, 4 3/4 In. 110.00
Elephant, Jumbo With Howdah, Cast Iron, Old Silver Paint, 4 3/4 In. 55.00
Elephant, Jumbo, Clear Glass Bottle, 1 Pt. 12.00
Elephant, With Trunk, Cast Iron, Arcade 39.00
Elsie The Cow, Head, Metal, 1940s 95.00
Esso, Plastic 15.00
F. D. Roosevelt, Cast Iron, KLT 44.00
Fayette Bank & Trust Co., Stork & Baby Announcement 25.00
Flatiron Skyscraper, Silver & Gold, 5 1/2 In. 121.00
Flintstones, 1961, 11 In. 15.00
Football Player, Cast Iron, 5 7/8 In. 300.00
Foxy Grandpa, Screw, Cast Iron, Hubley 303.00
Fred Flintstone, 1973 .... 10.00
Fred Flintstone, Bubble Gum, 1966 .... 35.00
Frog, Cast Iron 25.00
Fruit Jar, Atlas HA Mason, Clear Glass 12.00
GE Refrigerator, Cast Iron, Hubley 120.00
George Washington, Cast Iron 65.00
Globe Savings Fun, Cast Iron, Kyser & Rex Co. 2100.00
Globe, Hubley 170.00
Graf Zeppelin, 6 1/4 In. 140.00
Graf Zeppelin, Cast Iron, A. C. Williams 176.00
Guessing, Clock Face, Cast Iron, 1882 .... 425.00 To 467.00

H–Dot Stove, Oven Has Coin Slot, Cast Iron, 5 In.	30.00
Hall's Excelsior, Cast Iron	230.00
Hat, Uncle Sam's, Cast Iron	45.00
Haunted House Mystery, Disneyland, 1970's, Box	225.00
Hawkeye, 1931, Allen Organ Company	45.00
Hawkeye, Model 1931, Corona Beer	23.00
Hershey Vending Bar, Box	100.00
Hobo Joe, Restaurant Chain, Dakin, 11 In.	80.00
Horse, Good Luck, Arcade	33.00
Horse, On Wheels, Cast Iron	225.00
Horse, Penny, Bronze Color, 5 In.	50.00
Horse, Prancing, Cast Iron, 4 1/4 In.	45.00 To 50.00
House, 2–Story, Victorian, 1880	110.00
House, Colonial, Porch, Cast Iron, 4 In.	90.00
House, Save Your Money, Tin, George Brown	110.00
House, Tin, Red, Yellow, Black, 3 1/4 In.	104.00
Howard Johnson	22.00
Howdy Doody, Cast Iron	50.00
Huckleberry Hound, Plastic, 9 In.	25.00
Humpty–Dumpty, 90% Paint	396.00
Humpty–Dumpty, Bronzed Cast Iron, 5 3/4 In.	20.00
Indian, Family, Cast Iron, Wilton	230.00
Indian, With Tomahawk, Cast Iron, Hubley	143.00
Indian, Yellowstone, Souvenir, Copper Wash	30.00
Keystone Cop, Cast Iron, Penny, Original Paint	75.00
Keystone Cop, Coin, Cast Iron	30.00
Land–O–Lakes, Wooden	20.00
Liberty Bell, Cast Nickel, Plated Aluminum, 5 1/4 In.	25.00
Liberty Bell, Marigold Glass	25.00
Lincoln National Life Insurance	65.00
Lion, Blue Over Gold, Iron, 5 1/2 In.	33.00
Lion, Green, Large	95.00
Lion, Metal, Harris, 8 In.	22.00
Lion, On Wheels, Spoked, Cast Iron, 4 3/8 In.	180.00
Lion, Tail Right, Cast Iron, A. C. Williams, Large	50.00
Little House, Penny	45.00
Little Lulu, Vinyl	20.00
Little Red Riding Hood, Hull	550.00
Little Sprout, Ceramic, Musical	42.00
Lucky Jumbo, Cast Iron, Lory Industries, Box	27.50
Mailbox, Cast Iron, Stetford Pro, Box	39.00
Mailbox, Eagle, Cast Iron, Kenton	55.00
Mailbox, Standing, Cast Iron, Hubley, Large	143.00
Mailbox, U.S. Mail, 4 1/2 x 3 1/8 In.	20.00
Mailbox, U.S. Mail, Green & Gold, Cast Iron, Lettering, 4 1/4 In.	30.00
Mailbox, U.S. Mail, Hanging, Cast Iron, Black & Gold, Lettering, 5 1/8 In.	60.00
Majolica, Mouse On Top	45.00
Mammy, 8 In.	125.00
Mammy, Red Dress	130.00
Marilyn Monroe, Insert Coin, Dress Blows, Battery Operated, 7 In.	25.00 To 35.00

Mechanical banks were first made about 1870. Any bank with moving
parts is considered mechanical. The metal banks made before World War I
are the most desirable. Copies and new designs of mechanical banks have
been made in metal or plastic since the 1920s.

Mechanical, Acrobat Boy, On Trapeze, Cast Iron	145.00
Mechanical, Acrobat, Cast Iron, 9 1/4 In.	880.00
Mechanical, Acrobats, 7 1/4 In.	4620.00
Mechanical, Addams Family Thing, Black Plastic, Creeping Hand, Poynter, 1965	89.00
Mechanical, Arabian, Box	330.00
Mechanical, Artillery, Union Army Coat, Stevens, Missing Coin Trap, 1892, 8 In.	935.00
Mechanical, Bad Accident, 10 In.	880.00
Mechanical, Baseball Pitcher, Cast Iron, Book of Knowledge	165.00

Bank, Mechanical, Excelsior, Red Roof,
Gray Building, 5 1/8 In.

Bank, Mechanical, Novelty, Gray,
Red & Blue, Stevens, 1873, 4 1/4 In.

Mechanical, Betsy Ross Bicentennial, Cast Iron, 11 x 6 1/4 In. 110.00
Mechanical, Boy Robbing Bird's Nest, J. & E. Stevens Company, c.1906, 8 In. 13200.00
Mechanical, Boy Scout, J. & E. Stevens Company, c.1912, 9 1/2 In. 440.00
Mechanical, Bull, Cast Iron 83.00
Mechanical, Bulldog & Owl, Cast Iron 125.00
Mechanical, Bulldog, Book of Knowledge 225.00
Mechanical, Bulldog, J. & E. Stevens Company, c.1880, 8 In. 1210.00
Mechanical, Cabin, Man Standing In Front 385.00
Mechanical, Cabin, Man Standing In Front, Cast Iron, 3 1/2 In. 605.00
Mechanical, Called Out Bank, J. & E. Stevens, c.1900, 9 In. 8800.00
Mechanical, Cat & Mouse, Cast Iron, 1920s 375.00
Mechanical, Chief Big Moon, J. & E. Stevens, c.1899, 10 In. 6325.00
Mechanical, Clock, Dime Savings Bank, Cast Iron 495.00
Mechanical, Confectionery, Cast Iron, 7 3/4 In. 8000.00
Mechanical, Confectionery, Kyber & Rex Company, c.1881, 8 1/2 In. 6050.00
Mechanical, Creedmoor 1100.00
Mechanical, Darktown Battery, J. & E. Stevens, 9 7/8 In. .... 3080.00 To 4620.00
Mechanical, Dentist, Black Patient In Chair 4750.00
Mechanical, Dentist, Book of Knowledge 325.00
Mechanical, Dinah, Black Woman, Cast Iron, England, 1890s 770.00
Mechanical, Dog, Doghouse, Tin, Put Coin On Tongue & Press 18.00
Mechanical, Eagle and Eaglets, 1883, 5 1/2 x 8 1/4 In. .... 385.00 To 720.00
Mechanical, Elephant, 3 Clowns, Cast Iron, 5 3/4 In. 1870.00
Mechanical, Excelsior, Red Roof, Gray Building, 5 1/8 In. ....*Illus* 165.00
Mechanical, Football Player, Cast Iron, A. C. Williams 440.00
Mechanical, Frog, Cast Iron, Lattice Base, 1872 .... 330.00
Mechanical, Gray, Red & Blue, Stevens, Pat. Oct. 28, 1873, 4 1/4 In. 440.00
Mechanical, Hall's Lilliput, Cast Iron, J. & E. Stevens Company, c.1877, 4 1/2 In. 550.00
Mechanical, Hen & Chicks .... 3400.00 To 3740.00
Mechanical, Hippopotamus, Raises Head & Swallows Coin, Japan, Box, 6 In. 80.00
Mechanical, Hole–In–One, Box 90.00
Mechanical, Horse Race, J. & E. Stevens 5000.00
Mechanical, Horse Race, Paper Label, 1871 .... 2900.00
Mechanical, Humpty–Dumpty 85.00
Mechanical, I Always Did 'Spise A Mule, J. & E. Stevens, Rough Paint 165.00
Mechanical, I Always Did 'Spise A Mule, Stevens, c.1897, 10 In. .... 1000.00 To 1320.00
Mechanical, Independence Hall, Enterprise Mfg. Co., 1870s, 9 In. 220.00
Mechanical, Independence Hall, Multicolor Building 1300.00
Mechanical, Indian & Bear, White Bear, Cast Iron, 10 1/4 In. 2090.00
Mechanical, Jolly Nigger, Aluminum, Polychrome, 6 1/8 In. 231.00

Mechanical, Jonah & The Whale, Cast Iron .... 145.00 To 190.00
Mechanical, Leapfrog, Book of Knowledge 325.00
Mechanical, Leaping Goat & Frog, Cast Iron, Polychrome, 7 1/2 In. 412.00
Mechanical, Liberty Bell, Pat. April 1875, Original Label, 8 In. 412.00
Mechanical, Lion & Monkey 700.00
Mechanical, Little Joe Hi Hat, Cast Iron 310.00
Mechanical, Magician, J. & E. Stevens Company, c.1901, 8 In. 1980.00
Mechanical, Mammy & Child Across Her Lap, 7 5/8 In. 9750.00
Mechanical, Milking Cow, 9 7/8 In. 2310.00
Mechanical, Monkey, Puts Money In Stomach, 7 5/8 In. 330.00
Mechanical, Monkey, Riding Mule, Kicks As Monkey Drops Coin In, Iron, 10 In. 770.00
Mechanical, Mule Entering Barn, Cast Iron 1450.00
Mechanical, New Creedmoor, Cast Iron 908.00
Mechanical, Novelty, Gray, Red & Blue, Stevens, 1873, 4 1/4 In. ....*Illus* 440.00
Mechanical, Organ Bank, Cat & Dog, Kyber & Rex Company, Near Mint, c.1882 ... 2750.00
Mechanical, Organ Grinder & Bear, 5 1/4 In. .... 4500.00 To 4950.00
Mechanical, Organ Grinder, Monkey & Bear, Windup, Bell, 5 1/4 In. 300.00
Mechanical, Organ, Cat & Dog, Cast Iron, Partial Paint, 7 1/4 In. 660.00
Mechanical, Organ, Monkey & Musical Chimes, Cast Iron, 1880s 577.00
Mechanical, Owl, Turns Head, Stevens, Glass Eyes, 1880, 3 7/8 In. .... 305.00 To 450.00
Mechanical, Paddy & The Pig, Cast Iron, Book of Knowledge 150.00
Mechanical, Paddy & The Pig, Cast Iron, c.1882 .... 1400.00 To 1540.00
Mechanical, Paddy & The Pig, J. & E. Stevens, Near Mint, c.1877, 8 1/2 In. 3300.00
Mechanical, Patronize The Blind Man & His Dog, Cast Iron, Stevens, 6 7/8 In. 6650.00
Mechanical, Pelican, J. & E. Stevens Company, c.1878, 8 In. 3575.00
Mechanical, Pig In High Chair, J. & E. Stevens Company, c.1897, 5 1/2 In. 330.00 To 905.00
Mechanical, Popeye Knockout, Tin 660.00
Mechanical, Professor Pug Frog's Great Bicycle Feat, Stevens, c.1892, 10 In. 11000.00
Mechanical, Professor Pug Frog, Cast Iron, A. C. Williams, 3 1/4 In. 450.00
Mechanical, Punch & Judy, Cast Iron, 7 1/2 In. .... 200.00 To 360.00
Mechanical, Punch & Judy, Shepard Hardware Co., Near Mint, c.1884, 7 1/2 In. ... 2310.00
Mechanical, Rabbit In Cabbage, Cast Iron, 4 3/8 In. 330.00
Mechanical, Reclining Chinaman, Cast Iron, 8 3/4 In. 1345.00
Mechanical, Santa Claus, Shepard Hardware Co., Cast Iron, 5 3/4 In. 660.00
Mechanical, Skeleton & Coffin, Tin, Windup 65.00
Mechanical, Speaking Dog, Girl & Dog, Cast Iron, 7 1/8 In. 715.00
Mechanical, Stump Speaker, Pat. June 8, 1886, 10 3/4 In. 1430.00
Mechanical, Tabby, Cast Iron, 4 1/2 In. 275.00
Mechanical, Tammany, J. & E. Stevens, c.1873, 6 In. .... 440.00 To 465.00
Mechanical, Teddy & The Bear, Cast Iron 1430.00
Mechanical, Trick Dog, Yellow & Red Clown Suit, Hubley, Pat. 1888, 8 9/16 In. ... 550.00
Mechanical, Trick Pony, Book of Knowledge 250.00
Mechanical, U.S. & Spain, Cast Iron, Polychrome, 8 1/4 In. 935.00
Mechanical, Uncle Sam, Plastic 27.00
Mechanical, Uncle Sam, Shepard Hardware, Pat. June 8, 1886, 11 1/2 In. 2090.00 To 5225.00
Mechanical, William Tell, J. & E. Stevens, Cast Iron, Pat. 1896, 10 1/2 In. 330.00 To 935.00
Mechanical, World's Fair, Columbus & Indian, Cast Iron, 1892 .... 660.00
Megaphone, College Insignias, Plastic, Japan 27.00
Miller Beer, Can, Red, Green & White 18.00
Mosque, J. I. Judd Company, c.1880, 9 In. 2475.00
Mr. T., Plastic Head, Large 8.00
Mulligan The Cop, Aluminum, 1940s 55.00
Mutt & Jeff, Cast Iron, Gold, 5 1/4 In. 165.00
Nipper, RCA, Metal, Box 385.00
Ocean Spray, Cranberry Sauce, Tin, Can Shape 35.00
Officer, Cadet, Blue Uniform, Gold Trim, Cast Iron, Hubley, 5 3/4 In. 95.00
Old Mother Hubbard, Tin, 2 1/2 x 4 In. 35.00
Oven, Nickel–Plated Top, Green Body, Cast Iron, 3 3/4 In. 90.00
Owl, Franklin Credit Union, Clear Red Plastic, Nebraska 6.00
Owl, Ward's Riverside 65.00
Owl, White Metal 30.00
Peace Sign, Box 48.00
Pepto Bismol, 24–Hour Bug 45.00

Phillips 66	15.00
Picolette, Camera, Ceramic	30.00
Pig, Carnival Glass, Penny	22.00
Pig, Cast Iron, Green Over Gold, 7 In.	39.00
Pig, ESP Gas, White, Gold Trim, Bunting Ware Ceramics ...	45.00
Pig, I Made Chicago Famous, Cast Iron, 1902, 4 In.	150.00
Pig, Invest In Pork, Cast Iron, 6 1/2 In.	220.00
Pig, Pottery	85.00
Pig, Three Little Pigs, Cast Iron, Green, 5 In.	85.00
Pinocchio, Composition, Key	15.00
Pirate On Chest, Metal	35.00
Pizza Hut	18.00
Policeman, Arcade, 5 1/2 In.	90.00
Policeman, Cast Iron, 5 1/2 In.	350.00
Poll Parrot, Shoe Shape, Plastic	20.00
Pot of Gold, Cast Iron, Mattel, Box	27.50
Puppy, Hazel, Aluminum, 5 In.	125.00
Puppy, On Pillow, Cast Iron, Hubley, 1920s, 5 3/4 In.	330.00
Purse, Put Money In Thy Purse, Cast Iron	625.00
R2D2, Star Wars, Ceramic	70.00
Rabbit, Begging, Cast Iron, A. C. Williams	70.00
Rabbit, Cast Iron, 5 5/8 In.	100.00
Rabbit, Cast Iron, Goldtone, 5 1/4 In.	94.00
Rabbit, Oval Base, Cast Iron, White & Green With Red & Gold, 1884, 2 1/4 In.	990.00
Radio, Kenton, 3 Dials, Cast Iron	45.00
Radio, Majestic, Cast Iron, Arcade	82.50
Raggedy Ann, 1976, Pair	45.00
Razor Blade, Listerine Shaving Cream, Donkey Figurine ...	25.00
Red Goose School Shoes, Cast Iron, Arcade	45.00
Register, 5 Coins, Cast Iron, Kingsbury	82.50
Register, Dime, Captain Marvel, 1948	165.00
Register, Dime, Snow White	50.00
Register, Dime, Superman	130.00
Register, Junior Cash Register, Cast Iron, Stevens	82.50
Register, Nickel & Dime, Prudential, 1890, 7 In.	375.00
Register, Tom Thumb, Box	45.00
Register, Uncle Sam, Nickel	20.00
Register, Uncle Sam, Tin, 6 In.	70.00
Remember Pearl Harbor, Cast Iron, Ohio Art	45.00
Rex Water Heaters, Tin	150.00
Rhino, Cast Iron, Arcade	1015.00
Richelieu Coffee	55.00
Rival Dog Food Can, Tin Lithograph, 2 3/4 In.	20.00
Roly Poly, Black Chef, Large	10.00
Ronald McDonald	55.00
Rooster, Cast Iron, Red & Gold, 4 7/8 In.	55.00
Roy Rogers On Trigger, Rearing, Porcelain	245.00
Rudolph The Red–Nosed Reindeer, Cast Iron, E. J. Kayn, Box ...	65.00
Safe, Arabian, Cast Iron, Kyser & Rex	110.00
Safe, Burglar Proof House, Cast Iron, Stevens	145.00
Safe, Cast Iron, Combination	45.00
Safe, Junior Deposit, Combination Lock, Cast Iron, 4 5/8 In. ...	70.00
Safe, National, Key Lock, Cast Iron, 3 3/8 In.	30.00
Safe, Roller, Key Lock, Cast Iron, 3 11/16 In.	65.00
Safe, Treasure Island Savings, H. B. & S. Co., Tin Lithograph, 6 3/4 In.	120.00
Sailor, With Sea Bag, Seaman's Savings, McCoy	47.50
Santa Claus, Seated In Chair, Chalkware	65.00
Schoolhouse, Eagle On Top, Cast Iron	660.00
Seal On Rock, Cast Iron	240.00
Sewing Machine, Singer Trademark	275.00
Sharecropper, 2 Faces, Cast Iron .... 100.00 To	175.00
Ship, Cast Iron, Arcade	250.00
Skyscraper, Cast Iron, A. C. Williams	192.00

Slot Machine, Las Vegas, Metal, 10 Cents, Box	18.00
Smokey The Bear, Ceramic	125.00
Snoopy, On Basketball, Chalkware	25.00
Snoopy, On Doghouse, Ceramic	35.00
Snoopy, On Doghouse, Silver Plate, 1958	28.00
Snoopy, With Woodstock, 40th Anniversary	20.00
Southern Woman, Large Hoop Skirt, Hat, Wooden, Key, 5 x 3 3/4 In.	50.00
St. Bernard, With Pack, Cast Iron, A. C. Williams	88.00
State Savings Bank, Cast Iron, Bankers Thrift Corp.	93.50
Statue of Liberty, Cast Iron, Gold, 6 In.	175.00
Steamboat, Cast Iron, A. C. Williams	410.00
Stove, Figural, Open Door Says Cook With Cash Under Slot, Iron	45.00
Stove, Parlor, Cast Iron & Metal, Key Lock, 6 7/8 In.	210.00
Stove, Roper, Arcade	175.00
Stove, Save The Magic Chef	66.00
Sundial, Cast Iron, Arcade	880.00
Sunmaid Raisins	35.00
Sylvester & Tweety, 1972	25.00
Tally Ho, Horseshoe & Horse With Dog & Fox, Cast Iron	132.00
Tank, Cast Iron, Gold, 4 3/8 In.	94.00
Tanker, Model 1926, Merit Oil Company	75.00
Teddy Bear, Cast Iron, Arcade	120.00
Television, Cast Iron, Kent Merchandise, Box	6.00
Three Wise Monkeys, Cast Iron	150.00
Tiger, Esso, Plastic	30.00
Tom & Jerry, Composition, 1971	125.00
Topo Gigio, Dressed As Nurse	30.00
Treasure Chest, Cast Iron, 3 In.	30.00
Troll, Thomas Dam, 7 In.	40.00
Trolley, Cast Iron, 4 1/2 In.	412.00
Truck, Fire, 1926, Bareville Fire Company	29.00
Truck, Fire, 1926, Hershey Chocolate	29.00
Truck, Model 192, John Deere No. 102	45.00
Truck, Tanker, Mack, Texaco, Ertl, Box	350.00
Turkey, Cast Iron	135.00
Typewriter, Underwood, New York World's Fair, 1939, 11 1/4 In.	50.00 To 150.00
Uncle Sam, Bust, Ceramic, Worn Paint	30.00
United Parcel Service, Model T, Model 3461, Ertl	35.00
Washington Monument, Cast Iron, A. C. Williams	305.00
Watch Your Savings Grow With Esso, Glass, 1939	40.00
White City Puzzle Safe, Cast Iron, Nicol Co.	209.00
Wise Pig, Cast Iron, Hubley	71.50
Wolf's Head Oil, Tin	15.00
Woman, 2 Faces, Cast Iron	180.00
Woolworth Building, Cast Metal, 8 In.	66.00
Work Horse, Cast Iron, Arcade	88.00
World's Fair, City Skyline, Tin Lithograph, American Can Co., 3 1/2 In.	10.00
World's Fair, St. Louis, Cast Iron, 1904	605.00
Yogi Bear, Plastic, Knickerbocker, Bag, 1960, 9 1/2 In.	38.00

BANKO, Korean ware, and Sumida are terms that are often confusing. We use the names in the way most often used by antiques dealers and collectors. Korean ware is now called *Sumida Gawa* or *Sumida* and is listed in this book under that heading. Banko is a group of rustic Japanese wares made in the nineteenth and twentieth centuries. Some pieces are made of mosaics of colored clay, some are fanciful teapots. Redware and other materials were also used.

Cup, Gray	52.00
Teapot, Marbelized White, Blue, Tan, Loose Finial, 4 In.	125.00
Teapot, Monkeys In Relief, Pierced Insert, 4 1/2 In.	220.00

BARBED WIRE was first patented in 1867. Collectors want eighteen–inch samples.

Barber, Chair, Koken, Leather

♦♦♦♦♦♦♦♦♦♦♦♦♦♦♦♦♦♦♦♦♦♦
Aerosol paint strippers are fast but need special precautions. Wear goggles, gloves, and a long-sleeved shirt because the spray will float. With aerosol strippers there is no brushing and they work well on small irregular surfaces such as carvings, but large jobs are better done with conventional brushed-on stripper.
♦♦♦♦♦♦♦♦♦♦♦♦♦♦♦♦♦♦♦♦♦♦

Baker, 3–Line, Barbs On 2 Different Lines, 1883, 18 In.	25.00
Brotherton, Cable Line, 1878, 18 In.	50.00
Brotherton, Flat, Parallel Lines, 1887, 18 In.	50.00
Buffalo Wire, Merrill, 1876, 1/4 In. Diam.	2.00
Champion, Crandal, 1879	1.00
Crowell, Split Square, 1879, 18 In.	300.00
Ford, Splice, Cast Iron Connector, 1875, 18 In.	100.00
French, 2–Point Diamond, Holes At Sides of Barb, 18 In.	200.00
Glidden, 2–Line, Flattened, 1874, 18 In.	20.00
Glidden, Triangle & Round, Barb On Round, 1874, 18 In.	10.00
Greenbriar, Hollner, 1878	1.00
Haish, Loose Loop, 1875, 18 In.	200.00
Kennedy, 2–Line, Extra Large, 18 In.	100.00
Ross, Blunt Point, One Extra Long, 1879, 18 In.	2.00
Snail Barb, Upham, Twisted, Single Oval Line	.50
Track, Underwood, 18 In.	10.00
Two Square Line, Glidden, 1874	.50
U. P. Railroad, Glidden, 1874	.50
Wooden Block, Scutt, Designed To Be Seen By Cattle, 1880	20.00

BARBER collectibles range from the popular red and white striped pole that used to be found in front of every shop to the small scissors and tools of the trade. Barber chairs are wanted, especially the older models with elaborate iron trim.

Backbar, Shop, Koken, 5 Ft. Oak Backbar, Pump Up Leather Chair	5750.00
Cabinet, Oak, Incised Carving	175.00
Chair, Child's, Horse Head, Glass Eyes, Painted Carved Wood, 19 In.	745.00
Chair, Child's, Pedestal	375.00
Chair, Child's, Police Motorcycle, Blue Paint	795.00
Chair, Child's, Wooden Horse's Head, Straddles Barber's Chair	125.00
Chair, Hydraulic, Kokus Barber's Supply, Iron Foot Rest, Red Velvet Upholstery	250.00
Chair, Koken, Leather ....*Illus*	897.00
Chair, Koken, Lion's Head, Footstool, Walnut ....975.00 To	1000.00
Chair, Koken, Round Seat & Back, Hydraulic, Oak	1450.00
Chair, Palda, Red Velvet Covering	350.00
Chair, Porcelain Arms, Original Seat	500.00
Chair, Theo–A–Kochs Co., Refurbished	525.00
Chair, Wood, Partial Leather Upholstery	1650.00
Clippers, Hair, Chrome Handle, Box	10.00
Coat Rack, Art Nouveau Design, Painted Aluminum & Cast Iron, 68 In.	198.00

Hair Trimmer, Durham, Celluloid, 1911	17.00
Pole, Figural Newel Post, Wooden, 74 x 5 1/2 In.	220.00
Pole, Gold Ball At Top & Bottom, Wooden, 29 In.	385.00
Pole, Leaded Glass, Koken, 48 In.	975.00
Pole, Milk Glass Globe, Red, White & Blue	400.00
Pole, Neon, c.1930	7000.00
Pole, Porcelain, Metal Upper & Lower Sections, Glass Enclosed	175.00
Pole, Red, White & Blue, Black Painted Base, Early 19th Century, 8 Ft. 10 In.	2750.00
Pole, Wooden, Painted, 19th Century, 45 In.	250.00
Pole, Wooden, Weathered Blue, Red & White Paint, Gilt Traces, 68 In.	525.00
Razor Kit, Valet Autostrop, Metal Case	17.50
Scissors, Keen Kutter, 7 1/2 Type	15.00
Scissors, Leather Case, Barber Dealers Convention, Dated 1907	110.00
Sign, Barber Shop, Painted Sheet Metal, Round	95.00
Stand, Victorian, Cherry, Carved Floral Panel On Door, Mirror, Eastlake	1210.00

BAROMETERS are used to forecast the weather. Antique barometers with elaborate wooden cases and brass trim are the most desirable. Mercury column barometers are also popular with collectors. It is difficult to find someone to repair a broken one, so be sure your barometer is in working condition.

Banjo, English, Mahogany, 19th Century	245.00
Empire, Giltwood, Shaped & Carved Backplate, France, 1820, 35 x 17 1/2 In.	770.00
English, Bundack	550.00
English, Carved Oak Case, Paper Label, Admiral Fitzroy's Barometer, 48 1/4 In.	295.00
English, Walnut, D.C. & Son, London, 38 In.	300.00
Figural, Father Time, France	2500.00
Hexagonal Shape, Science Trophy Top, Giltwood, Chevallier, 39 In.	8525.00
Louis XVI, Ribbon Crest, Gesso & Giltwood, 1780s, 32 x 22 In.	4620.00
Mahogany, Inlaid, Vanetti & Benzzoni, 38 1/2 In.	770.00
Napoleon III, 2 Gilt Bronze Putti, Winged Busts, 1850s, 3 Ft. 9 In.	3025.00
Nautical, Brass, R. N. Destero, Lisbon, 38 In.	385.00
Rosewood, St. Louis	550.00
Simpson & Hadley	467.00
Stick, Band & Son, Label	2000.00
Stick, Gimbal & Ivory Scales, Thermometer, Bond & Son	37.00
Stick, Maple, Mercury, Removable Top, E. Wilder, 1880, 38 In.	250.00
Stick, Oak, Negretti & Zambra, 19th Century, England, 40 In.	175.00
Stick, Rosewood, England, Early 19th Century, 35 1/2 In.	770.00
Stick, Scotland, Edinburgh	995.00
Stick, Tiger Maple, C. Wilder, Peterboro, N. H.	2400.00
Thermometer, Continental, Giltwood, Voluted Backplate, Matched, 45 In.	3850.00
Thermometer, Dutch Baroque, Crest of Foliate Spray, Burl Walnut, 47 1/2 In.	4950.00
Travel, Andrew Lloyd Co., Boston, England, With Travel Case	175.00 To 200.00
Urn With Thermometer, Wheel-Back, J. Pensa, Inlaid Mahogany, 4 Ft. 9 In.	3025.00
Wall, Hezzanith, Brass, 7 In.	65.00
Walnut, H. A. Clum, Clifton Springs, N.Y.	1500.00
Wheel, George III Style, Mahogany, 19th Century, 42 In.	715.00
Wheel, George III Style, Rosewood, 19th Century, 39 In.	192.50
Wheel, Victorian, Thermometer, Rosewood, 8–In. Dial	440.00

BASEBALL collectibles are in the Sports category, except for baseball cards, which are listed under Baseball in the Card category.

BASKETS of all types are popular with collectors. Indian, Japanese, African, Shaker, and many other kinds of baskets can be found. Of course, baskets are still being made, so the collector must learn to tell the age and style of the basket to determine the value.

African, 2 3/4 In.	49.00
Apple, Splint, Ash Handles, 12 x 21 1/2 In.	44.00
Bentwood, Floral Design, Handle, Inscription Dated 1873, 15 In.	660.00
Berry, Wooden, In Carrying Box, 8 Piece	660.00
Buttocks, Splint, 7 1/2 In.	115.00

Buttocks, Splint, 9 x 8 1/2 In. 115.00
Buttocks, Splint, Bentwood Handle, 10 x 11 In. 220.00
Buttocks, Splint, Bentwood Handle, 2 5/8 In. 155.00
Buttocks, Splint, Bentwood Handle, 8 1/2 In. 110.00
Buttocks, Splint, Bentwood Handle, 8 In. 181.00
Buttocks, Splint, Brown Patina, Bentwood Handle, 10 1/2 x 12 In. 175.00
Buttocks, Splint, Colored Varnish, Bentwood Handle, 3 1/4 In. 85.00
Buttocks, Splint, Old Varnish, 10 1/2 x 11 In. 75.00
Buttocks, Splint, Old Varnish, Bentwood Handle, 3 3/4 In. 95.00
Buttocks, Splint, Painted Floral Design, 5 1/2 In. 25.00
Buttocks, Splint, Red Paint, Bentwood Handle, 5 In. 275.00
Buttocks, Splint, Red Stripe, Bentwood Handle, Rev. Clerke, 13 x 14 In. . 275.00
Cheese, Splint, Old Patina, 12 In. 200.00
Cheese, Splint, Paint Traces, 24 In. 500.00
Gathering, Splint, Herb Drying, Bentwood Handle, 12 1/2 x 14 In. 175.00
Goose Feathers, Attached Lid, Bentwood Handle, 1820s, 8 x 10 In. 350.00
Indian, Cover, McCaw, c.1920, 2 1/2 x 2 In. 65.00
Longaberger, 1982, 8 x 14 x 8 In. 16.00
Market, Willow, Large 65.00
Melon Rib, Light Color, Bentwood Handle, 4 In. 140.00
Nantucket, Cover, Work, Partial Paper Label, 8 1/2 x 9 In. 1210.00
Nantucket, Inscribed Edith Al., Mass., 4 x 4 3/4 In. 605.00
Nantucket, Lightship, Oval, Fred Chadwick, 3 1/2 x 10 In. 468.00
Nantucket, Pocket, Carved Whale Mounted On Cover, 6 1/2 x 9 1/2 In. 330.00
Nantucket, Pocketbook 350.00
Nantucket, Shaped Handle, Zinc & Wooden Base, 9 1/2 x 14 In. 485.00
Nantucket, Swing Handle, David Hall Label, 3 x 6 3/4 In. 315.00
Nantucket, Turned & Incised Wooden Base, 9 x 13 1/2 In. 660.00
Nantucket, Wooden Base, Swing Handle, Small 330.00
Potato Stamp, Salmon & Natural, 15 1/4 x 11 1/4 In. 295.00
Splint, 2–Tone Design, Bentwood End Handles, Rectangular, 10 In. 71.00
Splint, Bentwood Handle, 5 In. 44.00
Splint, Bentwood Handle, 6 In. 93.00
Splint, Bentwood Handle, 7 In. 100.00
Splint, Bentwood Handle, 8 3/4 In. 192.00
Splint, Bentwood Handle, Dark Natural Patina, Green, Yellow, 4 1/4 In. .. 93.00
Splint, Bentwood Handle, Mabel R. McKenzie Tag, 10 x 13 1/2 x 7 1/2 In. . 203.00
Splint, Bentwood Handle, Round, 8 In. 93.00
Splint, Bentwood Handle, Round, 9 In. 192.00
Splint, Bentwood Handle, Square, 14 1/2 x 12 1/2 In. 70.00
Splint, Bentwood Rim Handles, Round, 4 In. 27.00
Splint, Bentwood Swivel Handle, Round, 4 3/4 In. 71.00
Splint, Bentwood Swivel Handle, Round, 8 In. 258.00
Splint, Berry, Round Bottom, 5 In. 11.00
Splint, Cheese, Gray Scrubbed Finish, 8 In. 275.00
Splint, Corseted Square Base, Reddish Brown Paint, Round, 5 1/2 In. 137.00
Splint, Cotton Picking, Blue Paint, Leather Shoulder Strap, 18 In. 302.00
Splint, Cover, Blue, Red, Natural, 11 1/2 In. 55.00
Splint, Gathering, Handled, Old Green Paint, 13 x 19 x 13 In. 110.00
Splint, Green Repaint, Wire Bale, Wooden Handle, Round, 15 1/4 x 9 In. . 125.00
Splint, Handle, 12 x 12 1/2 In. 135.00
Splint, Laundry, Bentwood Handles, Natural, 25 1/2 x 20 1/2 x 10 3/4 In. . 70.00
Splint, Melon Rib, Rim Handholds, 6 In. 99.00
Splint, Mustard Brown Paint, Bentwood Rim Handle, 5 In. 203.00
Splint, Oblong, 2–Tone Design, 5 1/2 x 10 In. 49.00
Splint, Oblong, Bentwood Handle, 9 x 17 1/2 x 10 In. 125.00
Splint, Oblong, Bentwood Handles, 8 3/4 x 9 1/2 In. 50.00
Splint, Oblong, Green Bands, Bentwood Handle, 6 3/4 In. 71.00
Splint, Oblong, Green, Bentwood Handle, 7 In. 45.00
Splint, Oblong, Red, Blue Paint, Yellow, Red Potato Print Flower, 4 1/2 In. . 93.00
Splint, Oval, Bentwood Rim Handles, Short Feet, 11 1/2 In. 95.00
Splint, Painted & Stamped Decoration, 8 3/4 x 10 1/2 In. 40.00
Splint, Pea Picking, Rectangular, Old Red, 10 In. 220.00

Splint, Rectangular, Natural & Red, 9 x 12 x 4 In. 50.00
Splint, Rectangular, Woven Handle, 6 In. 27.00
Splint, Red & Natural Red Dots, Bentwood Handle, 4 1/2 In. 125.00
Splint, Round, 3 In. 60.00
Splint, Round, Bentwood Handle, 6 1/2 In. 71.00
Splint, Round, Bentwood Handle, 7 1/2 In. 75.00
Splint, Round, Bentwood Handle, 8 In. 192.00
Splint, Round, Curlicue Designs, Bentwood Handle, 6 1/2 In. 27.00
Splint, Round, Painted Star Flower Design, Black, Faded Red, 4 1/2 In. 66.00
Splint, Rye Straw Rim, Bentwood Handle, 4 1/2 x 5 x 7 In. 60.00
Splint, Sewing, Curlicue Rim, Attached Pincushion, Needle Cloth, 11 x 13 In. 6.00
Splint, Soft Patina, Mary Thornton, Swivel Handle, 4 1/2 In. 305.00
Splint, Swivel Handle, Bentwood, Round, 8 In. 176.00
Splint, White Paint, Green Trim, 3 3/4 In. 137.00
Splint, Work, Swing Handle, 19th Century, 6 1/2 x 9 In. 154.00
Straw, Rye, 12 x 5 1/2 In. 82.50
Straw, Rye, 4 1/2 In. 33.00
Straw, Rye, Oval, 7 In. 148.00
Straw, Rye, Rim Hanging Loop, 4 In. 137.00
Twig, Wooden Bottom, 7 In. 49.00
Wicker, Green Paint, Handle, 1930, Tall 70.00
Wicker, Rose, Victorian, Metal Ground Spike 95.00
Willow, Deep Color, Handle, Oval, 15 x 16 In. 40.00
Wooden, Flowers, Butterflies, Gold & Blue, Serpentine Rim, 7 1/4 x 9 x 3 In. 135.00
Wooden, Hand Shaped, 6 x 13 x 12 In. 250.00

BATCHELDER products are made from California clay. Ernest Batchelder established a tile studio in Pasadena, California, in 1909 and expanded until in 1916 he built a larger factory with a new partner. The Batchelder–Wilson Company made all types of architectural tiles, garden pots, and bookends. The plant closed in 1932. In 1936 Batchelder opened Batchelder Ceramics, also in Pasadena, and made bowls, vases, and earthenware pots. He retired in 1951 and died in 1957. Pieces are marked *Batchelder Pasadena* or *Batchelder Los Angeles.*

**BATCHELDER
LOS ANGELES**

Bowl, 6–Sided, Advertising 180.00
Bowl, Black, Brown, Iridescent, 6 In. 70.00
Tile, Castle, 6 In. 85.00
Vase, Lime Green, 7 In. 135.00

BATMAN and Robin are characters from a comic strip by Bob Kane that started in 1939. In 1966, the characters became part of a popular television series. There have been radio and movie serials that featured the pair. In 1989 a full–length movie was made.

Batmobile, 1st Issue, Corgi, Box 250.00
Batmobile, Black Plastic, Robin & Batman, Geo. Barris Designed, Simms, 1972 ...... 39.00
Batmobile, Blue, Battery Operated, Tin, ASC, Japan, 1972, 12 In. 280.00
Batmobile, Tin Lithograph, Battery Operated, Box, 1972 .... 325.00
Buckle, Belt, 1960s 10.00
Button, I'm A Batman Crime Fighter, Celluloid 1.50
Cape, 1965 .... 17.50
Car, Tin, 1960s, 11 1/2 In. 135.00
Clock, Alarm, Batman & Robin Wake Up Voices, Box, 1974 .... 95.00 To 120.00
Coin–Operated Machine, Pinball, Back Glass 150.00
Comic Book, No. 27, Penguin, Jerry Robinson Christmas Cover, Feb.–Mar., 1945 ... 330.00
Doll, Mego, 1978, 12 In. 45.00
Doll, Tsukuda, Box, 1989 .... 50.00
Executive Set, Stapler, Pencil Sharpener & Holder, Box, 1977 .... 60.00
Figure, Batman & Working Parachute, CDC, On 11 x 9 In. Card, 1966 .... 39.00
Film, 8 Mm., Adventures of Batman, Columbia, Unused, Box, 1950s 24.00
Game, Batman & Robin, Hasbro, 1965 .... 75.00
Game, Batman Question & Answer, Electronic, Lisbeth Whiting, Box, 1966 .... 98.00
Game, Batman Trace–O–Graph, Emenee, 1966, Box, 19 x 11 x 5 In. 98.00
Game, Board, 1966 .... 42.00

Game, Target Set, Japan, 1960s	575.00
Gun, Escape, On Card, 1966	45.00
License Plate, Over Gotham City, Metal, N. P. P. Inc., 1966	32.00
Lunch Box, Batman & Robin, 1966	70.00
Lunch Box, Blue, Thermos, 1982	10.00
Magic Magnetic Gotham City Play Set, Remco, 1966	900.00
Magic Slate, With Stick, Whitman, 1966	55.00
Model Kit, Batboat, Unassembled, Aurora, Box, 1967	598.00
Model Kit, Batmobile, Aurora, Unpainted, Built, 1966	35.00
Model Kit, Penguin, Unassembled, Aurora, 1967	698.00
Mug, Action Pose Batman, Logo, White, Anchor–Hocking, 1966	12.00
Night–Light, Figural	76.00
Puppet, Hand, Unused, Ideal, 1966, 12 In.	69.00
Puzzle, Frame Tray, 1966	15.00
Puzzle, Tray, Watkins Strathmore, 1966, 11 x 14 In.	29.00
Record, Album, Let's Dance With The Villains, Somerset, 1966	20.00
Sheet, Twin Bed, 1960s	50.00
Tumbler, Pepsi–Cola	8.00
Utility Belt, Remco, Box, 1979	40.00
Wallet, N. P. P. Inc., Unused, 1966	45.00

BATTERSEA enamels, which are enamels painted on copper, were made in the Battersea district of London from about 1750 to 1756. Many similar enamels are mistakenly called *Battersea*.

Box, Mirror, Blue & White, 1700s, 1 x 1 1/8 x 1 1/2 In.	255.00
Plaque, Gilt Frame, 18th Century, 15 x 12 In., Pair	1870.00
Salt, Enamel, 19th Century, 2 1/2 In., Pair	132.00
Salt, Mauve	465.00

BAUER pottery is a California–made ware. J.A. Bauer moved his Kentucky pottery to Los Angeles, California, in 1909. The company made art pottery after 1912 and dinnerwares marked *Bauer* after 1929. The factory went out of business in 1962.

Ashtray, No. 8	250.00
Bowl, Brusche Modern, Chartreuse, 5 In.	5.00
Bowl, Pumpkin, Oval, 8 x 16 In.	16.00
Bowl, Ring, Yellow, No. 12	20.00
Butter, Cover, Orange Ring	75.00
Casserole, Cover, Pastel Green, Brass & Wooden Stand	45.00
Crock, No. 2	55.00
Cup, Elchinco, Deep Blue	35.00
Dish, Pickle, La Linda, Green Handle	35.00
Gravy Boat, Swirl, Jade	30.00
Pie Baker, Cobalt Blue Ring	35.00
Pitcher, Black, 10 In.	70.00
Salt & Pepper, Barrel, Ring, Yellow, Jade	110.00
Salt & Pepper, Ring, Low	20.00
Teapot	8.00
Teapot, Snub Nose	10.00
Tidbit, Brusche Modern, Chartreuse, 3 Piece	25.00
Tidbit, La Linda, 3 Tiers	50.00
Tumbler, Ring, Maroon, 12 Oz.	24.00
Vase, Fan	15.00
Vase, Leaf Form, Turquoise, 13 3/4 x 10 1/4 In., Pair	95.00
Vase, Ring, Green, 6 In.	35.00
Vase, Turquoise, Fred Johnson, 15 In.	275.00
Vase, Venus, White, 11 In.	75.00

BAVARIA is a region in Europe where many types of porcelain were made. In the nineteenth century, the mark often included the word *Bavaria*. After 1871, the words *Bavaria, Germany,* were used. Listed here are pieces that include the name *Bavaria* in some form, but major porcelain makers, such as Rosenthal, are listed in their own categories.

Bread Tray, Center Handle, Woman, Floral, 2 Sections, Signed A. J., 11 x 7 In. 85.00
Figurine, Boy, Geese, Pastel Enameled, Alkakunse, 8 1/2 In. 71.00
Figurine, Girl & Goose, Enameled, Alkakunse, 6 1/2 In. 50.00
Game Plate, Large Pheasant Center, Baby Pheasant Around Edge, 16 In. 105.00
Plate, Quail, Mignon, 7 1/2 In. 25.00
Plate, White Flowers, Green, Phillips, 7 1/2 In. 35.00
Powder Box, Spider Mums, Pinks, Lavender, Green, Shaded Ground, Gold Rim 35.00
Sugar & Creamer, Rose Design, Porcelain, Lid 60.00

BEADED BAGS are included in the Purse category.

BEATLES collectors search for any items picturing the four members of
the famous music group or any of their recordings. Because these items are
so new, the condition is very important and top prices are paid only for
items in mint condition. The Beatles first appeared on American network
television in 1964. The group disbanded in 1971.

Book, Beatles Illustrated Lyrics, Vol. I 76.00
Book, Hard Day's Night, John Burke, 156 Pages, Photos, 1964 .... 30.00
Book, Song, Photographs, 1964, 49 Pages 25.00
Book, The Beatles, Academic Industries, Inc., Pocket Biographies, 1984 .... 12.50
Button, All Beatles Pictured, Large 35.00
Button, Photo, Official Fan Club 2.50
Change Purse, Vinyl 35.00
Comb, Pink 48.00
Doll, Inflatable, Set of 4 .... 100.00
Doll, Paul, With Guitar, Nems, 1964 .... 60.00
Doll, Remco, Set of 4 .... 150.00
Doll, Rooted Hair, 1964, 4 1/2 In., 4 Piece 225.00
Doll, With Drum, Remco 50.00
Figurine, Set of 4 .... 60.00
Game, Flip Your Wig 85.00
Harmonica, Original Blister Display Card, 1964 .... 415.00
Life Magazine, August 28, 1964 .... 35.00
Lobby Card, Help 50.00
Lunch Box, Blue, 1965 .... 325.00
Lunch Box, Yellow Submarine, 1968 ....75.00 To 195.00
Model Kit, Ringo Starr, Drummer, Revell, Box 200.00
Model, Yellow Submarine, Kit, Partially Assembled, Original Box 141.00
Model, Yellow Submarine, Unused, Box 85.00
Nodder, Mascot 495.00
Nodder, Paul McCartney, 1960 .... 120.00
Pass, Backstage 49.00
Pen, Ball–Point, Beatles In Pewter 65.00
Pencil Set, 4 Different 30.00
Pennant, Wool, 1964, 30 In. 25.00
Photograph, Paul McCartney, Autographed, 4 x 6 In. 140.00
Photograph, Paul McCartney, Glossy 7.50
Pin, John Lennon, Printed Upside Down, 1980s, 3 In. Diam. 35.00
Postcard, Group Photo, 1963 .... 1.00
Program, Hard Day's Night, 1964 .... 35.00
Purse, Coin, 1964 .... 5.50
Puzzle, Yellow Submarine, 1968 .... 35.00
Record Case, Green 60.00
Record Player, 1964 .... 1100.00
Record, Eleanor Rigby & Yellow Submarine, Capital 7.50
Record, Hard Day's Night, Capital 11.25
Record, Hey Jude, Apple 1.25
Record, I Saw Her Standing There, Beatles On Cover Sleeve, 45 RPM 15.00
Record, Melodiya, Tribute Album, Paul McCartney, Soviet Label 20.00
Record, She Loves You, Swan 10.00
Sheet, Printed Pinup, Color, Dell, 1964 .... 70.00
Thermometer, Wall, Official Beatles Fan Club, Metal 4.00
Ticket, Concert, 1966 .... 49.00

BEEHIVE, Austria, or Beehive, Vienna, are terms used in English-speaking countries to refer to the many types of decorated porcelain bearing a mark that looks like a beehive. The mark is actually a shield, viewed upside down. It was first used in 1744 by the Royal Porcelain Manufactory of Vienna. The firm made porcelains, called *Royal Vienna* by collectors, until it closed in 1864. Many other German, Austrian, and Japanese factories have reproduced Royal Vienna wares, complete with the original shield or *beehive* mark. This listing includes the expensive, original Royal Vienna porcelains and many other types of beehive porcelain. The Royal Vienna pieces include that name in the description.

Cup & Saucer, Frieze of Figures & Horses, Cobalt Border, 5 1/2 In.	145.00
Ewer, Victorian Scenes, Tulip Handle, Gold Trim, 10 In.	1350.00
Lamp Base, Gilt Handles, Pensive Young Woman, Wrigel, Electrified, 12 1/2 In.	880.00
Painted Centaurs, Cupids, Woman Drinking Wine, Brown Ground, Marked, 8 In.	3500.00
Plate, Entitled Pearl, Blue & Orange Border, c.1840, 9 1/2 In.	250.00
Plate, Festival of Sacrifice, With Aurora & Cephalus Scene, 10 1/2 In., Pair	495.00
Stein, Porcelain, 1 Liter	2000.00
Teapot, Gold Band, Figures of Children At Play, Dolphin Handle, Marked	2200.00
Urn, Cover, Portrait, Cobalt Blue, Raised Gold Design, Brass Handles, 19 In.	335.00
Urn, Portrait Medallion of Ruth, Gold Enamel On Purple, Pink, 14 1/2 In.	695.00
Urn, Portrait Panel, Cavalier & Maiden, Gilt Floral Filigree, Marked, 24 In.	8525.00
Urn, Scene With General George Washington, 24 In.	5325.00
Vase, Ladies & Cupid, Maroon, Cobalt Blue, Geometric Border, 3 1/2 In.	145.00
Vase, Mermaid, Hand Painted, Signed	1025.00
Vase, Semi-Clad Maidens In Pool, Cherubs On Reverse, Signed, 8 3/4 In.	302.50

BEER BOTTLES are listed in the Bottle category under Beer.

BEER CANS are a twentieth-century idea. Beer was sold in kegs or returnable bottles until 1934. The first patent for a can was issued to the American Can Company in September of that year; and Gotfried Kruger Brewing Company, Newark, New Jersey, was the first to use the can. The cone-top can was first made in 1935, the aluminum pop-top in 1962. Collectors should look for cans in good condition, with no dents or rust. Serious collectors prefer cans that have been opened from the bottom.

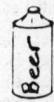

Alta	50.00
Billy Beer	5.00
Exeter, Blue & White Logo, Copper Ground, 12 Oz.	660.00
Old Reading, Reading, Pa., Flat Top	125.00
Sturgis	4.00
Trish Cream Ale	50.00
Union Cream Ale, Flat Top, Wood Graining, Printed Label, 12 Oz.	220.00
Utica Club Bock	195.00
W. F. Tennessee	3.00

BELLS have been made of porcelain, china, or metal through the centuries. All types are collected. Favorites include glass bells, figural bells, school bells, and cowbells. Be careful not to buy a bell made from an old glass goblet.

Country Store, Old Paint, Brass, c.1840	150.00
Cow, Holstein No. 3, Original Paper Label	35.00
Crystal, Swirl Handle, Faceted Ringer, 7 1/2 In.	12.00
Dinner Gong, L. & J. G. Stickley	2200.00
Dinner, Iron, With Bracket	200.00
Dinner, Longhorn Steer	45.00

◆◆◆

The ladies pictured on old cameos often have long thin noses. The cute turned up nose is seen on modern cameos.

◆◆◆

Dinner, On Horseshoe, Brass	25.00
Dog Handle Finial, Sterling Silver	375.00
Hotel Desk, Turtle	400.00
Hotel, Monkey, Lift Leg To Ring, Brass Base, Ball & Claw Feet	105.00
Refrigerator, G. E.	10.00
School, Cast, Mahogany Handle, Mold Hole, 10 In.	145.00
School, Chrome, Hardwood Box	49.00
School, Country, Brass, Wooden, 7 In.	65.00
Sheep's, Strap & Clapper, Brass, 3 In.	37.00
Sleigh, Cast Brass, Graduated, Strap Mounted, Size 3 To 8, 27 Bells	140.00
Sleigh, Leather Strap, 24 Bells	110.00
Sleigh, Leather Strap, Graduated, 22 Bells	250.00
Trolley Car, Brass	135.00

BELLEEK china was made in Ireland, other European countries, and the United States. The glaze is creamy yellow and appears wet. The first Belleek was made in 1857. All pieces listed here are Irish Belleek. The mark changed through the years. The first mark, black, dates from 1863 to 1890. The second mark, black, dates from 1891 to 1926 and includes the words *Co. Fermanagh, Ireland.* The third mark, black, dates from 1926 to 1946 and has the words *Deanta in Eirinn.* The fourth mark, same as the third mark but green, dates from 1946 to 1955. The fifth mark, green, dates from 1955 to 1965 and has an R in a circle added in the upper right. The sixth mark, green, dates after 1965 and the words *Co. Fermanagh* have been omitted. The seventh mark, gold, was used from 1980 to 1993 and omits the words *Deanta in Eirinn.* The eighth mark, introduced in 1993, is similar to the second mark but is printed in blue. The word *Belleek* is now used only on the pieces made in Ireland even though earlier pieces from other countries were sometimes marked *Belleek.* These early pieces are listed by manufacturer, such as Ceramic Art Co., Haviland, Lenox, Ott & Brewer, and Willets.

Basket, Flat Rod, 2nd Mark, Black, 6 In.	2000.00
Basket, Heart Shape, Woven Sides, 2nd Mark, Black, 5 1/4 In.	850.00
Basket, Lily, Twig Handles, Marked, c.1880, 9 1/4 In.	1430.00
Box, Trinket, Acorn, Painted, 3rd Mark, Black, 3 1/2 In.	225.00
Creamer, Lifford, Armorial Crest, 3rd Mark, Black	175.00
Creamer, Lily, Green Trim, 2nd Mark, Black, 3 1/2 In.	50.00
Creamer, Ondine, 3rd Mark, Black, 5 In.	100.00
Cup & Saucer, Harp, Shamrock, 3rd Mark, Black	115.00
Cup & Saucer, Institute, 1st Mark, Black	225.00
Cup & Saucer, Institute, Gilded, 1st Mark, Black	300.00
Cup & Saucer, Shamrocks, 5th Mark, Green	65.00
Dish, 3rd Mark, Black, 2 1/4 x 3 1/2 In.	80.00
Dish, Heart Shape, 6th Mark, Green, 4 In.	35.00
Ewer, Round, 5th Mark, Green	395.00
Figurine, Leprechaun, Pearl, 5 1/2 In.	250.00
Flower Holder, Sea Horse, 1st Mark, Black, 5 In.	675.00
Flowerpot, Cone, 5th Mark, Green, 4 1/4 In.	38.00 To 45.00
Font, Holy Water, 3rd Mark, Black	175.00
Frame, Lily of The Valley, 1st Mark, Black, 6 In.	1850.00
Honey Pot, Shamrock Ware Beehive, 2nd Mark, Black, c.1910, 5 In.	385.00
Honey Pot, Shamrock, 2nd Mark, Black, 6 3/4 In.	450.00
Nautilus Shell, On Coral Base, 1st Mark, Black, c.1875, 8 In.	770.00
Pitcher, Beige, 4 In.	25.00
Pitcher, Figural, Woman, 6th Mark, Green, 4 1/2 In.	55.00
Plate, Shamrocks, 5th Mark, Green, 6 5/8 In.	30.00
Plate, Smiling Bacchus, Yellow Ivy Circles Center, 7 1/2 In.	95.00
Salt, Scalloped Shell, Pink Seaweed, 1st Mark, Black, 3 1/2 In.	135.00
Sugar & Creamer, 4th Mark, Black	125.00
Sugar & Creamer, Beige	85.00
Tea Set, Neptune, Seashell Bodies, Tray, 2nd Mark, Black, c.1900, 3 Piece	1320.00
Tray, Woman Playing Harp, Brown Mark, 6 In.	45.00
Vase, Aberdeen, 3rd Mark, Black, 6 In.	550.00

Vase, Applied Handles, Fish, Yellow Face, Gills, Tail, Marked, 7 In. 95.00
Vase, Centerpiece, Lily On Pads, Molded Flowers, c.1875, 10 In. 1540.00
Vase, Cornucopia, Horse, Green Mark, 5 In. 85.00
Vase, Hoof Tripod, Off–White Luster Trim, 2nd Mark, Black, 13 In. 650.00
Vase, Orchids, Artist, 1903, 13 In. 395.00
Vase, Quiver, Ivory & Gilded, 1st Mark, Black, 7 In. 2400.00
Vase, Sunflower, 3rd Mark, Black, 8 In. 185.00
Vase, Tree Trunk Shaped, Green Mark, Porcelain, 6 1/2 In. 40.00

BENNINGTON ware was the product of two factories working in Bennington, Vermont. Both the Norton Company and the Lyman Fenton Company were out of business by 1896. The wares include brown and yellow mottled pottery, Parian, scroddled ware, stoneware, graniteware, yellowware, and Staffordshire–type vases. The name is also a generic term for mottled brownware of the type made in Bennington.

Bowl, Brown & Tan, 3 1/4 In. 195.00
Candlestick, Flint Enamel Glaze, 7 3/4 In. 198.00
Candlestick, Rockingham Glaze, 8 3/8 In. 368.00
Figurine, Poodle, Flint, Pair 6500.00
Flask, Departed Spirits 725.00
Paperweight, Reclining Spaniel, Marked, 1849 .... 110.00
Pitcher, Tulips, 7 1/2 In. 125.00
Sugar, Domed Cover, Lyman, 1849, 9 In. 875.00
Toby Jug, Fenton, 5 7/8 In. 450.00

BERLIN, a German porcelain factory, was started in 1751 by Wilhelm Kaspar Wegely. In 1763, the factory was taken over by Frederick the Great and became the Royal Berlin Porcelain Manufactory. It is still in operation today. Pieces have been marked in a variety of ways.

Cup & Saucer, 2 Maidens On Front, Snake Form Handle, Marked, c.1830 .... 770.00
Cup & Saucer, Topographical, Trellis Work Border, Marked, 1840 .... 990.00
Plaque, Bust of Young Woman, Long Hair, Easel Frame, Wagner, 3 1/2 In. 320.00
Plaque, Interior Scene, Woman Having Hair Fashioned, Marked, 11 x 9 In. 2090.00
Tureen, Cover, 3 Men In Garden, Figure With Document Other Side, c.1880, 12 In. 1045.00

BESWICK started making earthenware in Staffordshire, England, in 1936. The company is now part of Royal Doulton Tableware, Ltd. Figurines of animals, especially dogs and horses, Beatrix Potter animals, and other wares are still being made.

Figurine, Cat, 5 In. 45.00
Figurine, Chickadee, No. 929 .... 95.00
Figurine, Cymbaler 38.00
Figurine, Dachshund, 9 In. 100.00
Figurine, Family Photograph 50.00
Figurine, Flying Ducks, No. 59 .... 75.00
Figurine, Giraffe, Baby, 4 1/2 In. 40.00
Figurine, Gryphon 80.00
Figurine, Harry Herald 38.00
Figurine, Horse, 9 x 7 In. 55.00
Figurine, Jogger 30.00
Figurine, Mallard, Settling, No. 750 .... 135.00
Figurine, Mr. Bunnybeat 35.00
Figurine, Oompah Bass Drummer 42.00
Figurine, Pecksniff 25.00
Figurine, Pheasant, No. 850 .... 135.00
Figurine, Pony, 7 In. 35.00
Figurine, Queen of Hearts .... 55.00 To 80.00
Figurine, Sheep Family, 4 Piece 60.00
Figurine, Siamese Cat, 6 1/2 In. 48.00
Figurine, St. Bernard 43.00
Figurine, St. Bernard, Large 80.00
Mug, Scrooge 55.00
Pitcher, Blown–Out Palm Tree, Gold Trim, 7 1/2 In. 75.00

Plaque, Figure Scene of King, An Aide & Girl, 12 In. 125.00
Salt & Pepper, Laurel & Hardy .... 65.00 To 75.00

BETTY BOOP, the cartoon figure, first appeared on the screen in 1931. Her face was modeled after the famous singer Helen Kane and her body after Mae West. In 1935, a comic strip was started. Although the Betty Boop cartoons were ended by 1938, there was a revival of interest in the Betty Boop image in the 1980s and new pieces are being made.

Acrobat, Celluloid, Fleischer Studios, Japan, 12 In. Box 1870.00
Button, Bridle 75.00
Button, Pinback, 3 In. 4.00
Cel, Dizzy Red Riding Hood, Colorized, 1930s, 14 3/4 x 12 In. 125.00
Cel, Mask–A–Raid, Betty With Bimbo, Colorized, 14 3/4 x 12 In. 110.00
Christmas Light Bulb 70.00
Clock, Alarm, 1960s .... 25.00 To 55.00
Cookie Jar, California Originals 395.00
Cookie Jar, Head, Vandor .... 75.00 To 125.00
Cookie Jar, Standing, Vandor .... 695.00 To 750.00
Coverlet, Floral, 24 Squares, Embroidered Figural & Face Corners, 88 x 63 In. 195.00
Doll, Composition, Heart Sticker 675.00
Earring Holder 22.50
Figurine, Chalkware, 13 1/2 In. 175.00
Key Fob 7.00
Nodder, Celluloid, Fleischer Studios, Japan, 7 In. Box 1650.00
Stickpin, Cloisonne 12.00

BICYCLES were invented in 1839. The first manufactured bicycle was made in 1861. Special ladies' bicycles were made after 1874. The modern safety bicycle was not produced until 1885. Collectors search for all types of bicycles and tricycles. Bicycle–related items are also listed here.

Acorn, Ice Cream Delivery, Full Size 625.00
Bone Shaker, Painted Pine 3575.00
Bone Shaker, Pope, 1890s 3500.00
Bone Shaker, Wooden Parts 1897.50
Columbia, Boy's, Model 63 .... 400.00
Columbia, Light Roadster, Pope, Hartford, Ct., 1887, 54–In. Diam. Wheel 7500.00
Columbia, Model 65, Shaft Drive, Wooden Rims 410.00
Columbia, Paper Delivery, R–68, 12–Gauge Spokes, 1953 .... 200.00
Columbia, R–19, 3–Star Deluxe, Springer, Boy's, 1953 .... 250.00
Compax The Folding Bike, Westfield Mfg. Co. 115.00
Dayton Huffman, Balloon White Wall Tires, Green, 1937 .... 375.00
Egg–Shaped Rear Wheel, Igo, Adult Size 700.00
Eureka, Girl's, M. W. Grady & Co. 50.00
Gendron "31", Odometer, Patent 1888 .... 85.00
Hawthorne, 3–Speed In Handle Grip, Montgomery Ward, 1967 .... 80.00
High Wheeler, England, 1887, 58 In. 3800.00
High Wheeler, Man, Ark Welded Steel, Figure Is Molded Material, 23 In. 120.00
High Wheeler, Wooden Spokes, Wooden Rims, Metal Frame, 45 In. 990.00
Hopalong Cassidy, Girl's 550.00
J. C. Higgins, Girl's, 1940s 250.00
J. C. Higgins, Girl's, Batwing Double Headlight, c.1950 .... 300.00
J. C. Higgins, Girl's, Deluxe, Early 1950s 800.00
John Deere, Man's, 3–Speed 50.00
Lamp, Carbide, Rowell & Hammer, Brass 100.00
Light, Carbide, Panther, Rowell & Hammer, Chrome 100.00
Man's, Leather Seat, Early 20th Century 220.00
Mead Crusader, Mead Cycle Co., Chicago 82.50
Monarch, Model 410, Super Deluxe Type Frame & Fenders, 1949 .... 250.00
Monarch, Super Deluxe, Boy's, 1947 .... 550.00
Murray, Vanguard, Chrome Fenders, Headlight, Black & White Frame, 68 In. 110.00
Napolean, Cable Operated, 2–Speed, Troxel Seat 110.00
Newsboy, Carrier On Side Car, Telegram & Gazette 225.00
Queen, Chicago, White Frame, Stenciling, Gold Handle Bars 220.00

Rambler, Gormully & Jeffery, c.1897 .... 415.00
Rudge, Roaster, 1880s, 58 In. 4180.00
Schwinn, Black Phantom, Restored 1850.00
Schwinn, Blue Hornet 1000.00
Schwinn, Boy's, Original Paint & Decals, 20 In. 165.00
Schwinn, Mark IV Jaguar, 1960 .... 165.00
Schwinn, Mark IV Jaguar, Middleweight, 1957 .... 245.00
Schwinn, Mark V, Jaguar, Springer Front 550.00
Schwinn, Red Phantom 1250.00
Schwinn, Twin Tandem, 1956 .... 165.00
Schwinn, Whizzer, Rebuilt J Motor, 1949 .... 2500.00
Schwinn, Whizzer, Restored, 1947 .... 3600.00
Shelby, Balloon Tires 205.00
Stearling Mfg., Tandem, Dual Steering, Balloon Tires, 1895 .... 700.00
Tandem, Rambler, Racing, c.1900 .... 1200.00
Tricycle, Child's, Convert–O Built To Last, Anthony Bros., Cast Aluminum 795.00
Tricycle, Ferry, 2 Large Back Wheels, 1890s 600.00
Tricycle, Horse Frame, 1934 .... 275.00
Tricycle, Pony–Byk, Body In Form of Pony .... 1350.00 To 1485.00
Tricycle, Rickshaw, Victory, Leather Passenger Hood, Red, Fenders, Spoke Wheels 550.00
Tricycle, Rubber–Bound Spoke Wheels, c.1920 .... 385.00
Tricycle, Steel, Leather Seat, Wood Hand Grips, 23 In. 247.00
Tricycle, Sunbeam, Waterloo Co., Canada, c.1950 .... 55.00
Troxel Seat, Red Frame, Gendron Wheel Co., c.1910 .... 55.00
Victor Flyer, Overman Wheel Co., c.1893 .... 1760.00
Western Flyer, Fresh Paint & Pin Striping, Rear Carrier, Kick Stand, 1938 .... 550.00
Whizzer, Motorized, c.1953 .... 1000.00 To 1100.00

BING & GRONDAHL is a famous Danish factory making fine porcelains
from 1853 to the present. Underglaze blue decoration was started in 1886.
The annual Christmas plate series was introduced in 1895. Dinnerwares,
stoneware, and figurines are still being made today. The firm has used the
initials B & G and a stylized castle as part of the mark since 1898.

B&G
JØBENHAVN
MADE IN
DENMARK

Bust, Bearded Man, Classical Drapery, 19th Century, 25 In. 440.00
Coffeepot, Seagull 160.00
Figurine, Accordion Player, No. 1001 .... 100.00
Figurine, Boy & Girl Reading Book, No. 1567 .... 90.00
Figurine, Boy Kissing Girl, No. 2162 .... 95.00
Figurine, Boy With Flowerpot, No. 2251 .... 120.00
Figurine, Cellist, Male, No. 2032, 18th Century 600.00
Figurine, Child With Starfish, No. 2265 .... 80.00
Figurine, Fish Seller, No. 1702 .... 300.00
Figurine, Fisher Family, No. 2025 .... 400.00
Figurine, Girl With Cat In Basket, No. 2249 .... 120.00
Figurine, Girl With Flowers, No. 2298 .... 130.00
Figurine, Girl With Little Brother, No. 1568 .... 150.00
Figurine, Hans Christian Andersen, No. 2037 .... 395.00
Figurine, Love Refused, No. 1614 .... 125.00 To 130.00
Figurine, Mason, No. 1786 .... 200.00
Figurine, Milkmaid, No. 2270 .... 295.00
Figurine, Nude Child, White, No. 2230, 6 1/2 In. 55.00
Figurine, Spilt Milk, No. 2246 .... 135.00 To 145.00
Figurine, Woman Feeding Chickens, No. 2220, 9 1/2 In. .... 165.00 To 220.00
Figurine, Woman With Child, No. 1552 .... 400.00
Lamp, Green Spider Web Design Shade, 22 In. 250.00
Plate, Christmas, 1895 .... 1900.00
Plate, Christmas, 1908 .... 93.00
Plate, Christmas, 1911 .... 93.00
Plate, Christmas, 1914 .... 93.00
Plate, Christmas, 1915 .... 126.00
Plate, Christmas, 1919 .... 84.00
Plate, Christmas, 1923 .... 68.00
Plate, Christmas, 1926 .... 67.00

Plate, Christmas, 1927	93.00
Plate, Christmas, 1931	85.00
Plate, Christmas, 1935	72.00
Plate, Christmas, 1938	152.00
Plate, Christmas, 1940	185.00
Plate, Christmas, 1942	178.00
Plate, Christmas, 1945	118.00
Plate, Christmas, 1948	72.00
Plate, Christmas, 1951	93.00
Plate, Christmas, 1953	76.00
Plate, Christmas, 1956	122.00
Plate, Christmas, 1959	122.00
Plate, Christmas, 1962	76.00
Plate, Christmas, 1965	63.00
Plate, Christmas, 1968	45.00
Plate, Christmas, 1970	29.00
Plate, Christmas, 1972	30.00
Plate, Mother's Day, 1969	330.00
Teapot, Loufald	75.00
Vase, Dragonfly, No. 5239	165.00
Vase, Owl On Branch, 8 1/4 In.	140.00

BINOCULARS of all types are wanted by collectors. Those made in the eighteenth and nineteenth centuries are favored by serious collectors. The small, attractive binoculars called *opera glasses* are listed in their own category.

Bardou & Sons, Paris	45.00
Nautical, Leather Case, France, 8 In.	65.00

BIRDCAGES are collected for use as homes for pet birds and as decorative objects of folk art. Elaborate wooden cages of the past centuries can still be found. The brass or wicker cages of the 1930s are popular with bird owners.

Arts & Crafts Style, Low Sloping Roof, Stand	685.00
Bamboo, 16 In.	49.50
Bamboo, 19th Century, 26 In.	55.00
Brass, Hanging, c.1940	65.00
Cello Shape, France, 1920s	2900.00
Hendryx, Brass, 7 x 10 In.	75.00
Hendryx, Brass, Patent, 1906, 9 x 13 In.	110.00
Pagoda Shape, Metal Mesh, Stand, English, 19th Century	1750.00
Parrot, O. Lindemann, N.Y., 1872, 21 x 18 1/2 In.	190.00
Primitive, Built–In Nesting Box, 24 x 12 In.	795.00
Tin, Blue Paint, 20 1/2 In.	192.00
Windsor, Original Paint Design	467.00
Wooden, Parrot, Old Paint, Tole, 13 In.	385.00

BISQUE is an unglazed baked porcelain. Finished bisque has a slightly sandy texture with a dull finish. Some of it may be decorated with various colors. Bisque gained favor during the late Victorian era when thousands of bisque figurines were made. It is still being made. Additional bisque items may be listed under the factory name.

Bust, E.T., Avon, 1983, 2 3/4 In.	20.00
Figurine, Boy Taking Thorn From Foot, Glass Dome	45.00
Figurine, Boy, Curly Hair, Brimmed Hat, Holds Gold Spoon, 9 In.	75.00
Figurine, Boy, Sitting, 5 In.	45.00
Figurine, Father Christmas, Germany, 6 In.	85.00
Figurine, Flower Girl, With Cart, Many Colors, Germany, 6 In.	85.00
Figurine, Girl, With Flower Cart, Colorful, Germany, 10 In.	85.00
Figurine, Nude, Grass Skirt, 5 In.	300.00
Figurine, Rabbit, Sitting, 8 In.	75.00
Figurine, Swan Pulling Girl On Cornucopia, Europe, No. 1815, 8 x 6 In.	45.00

Black, Book, ABC, Cloth, English, 5 X 9 In.

Figurine, Twin Girls, One Holding Spoon, Other Bugle, England, 10 In., Pair	285.00
Figurine, White Dove, Pair	50.00
Figurine, Woman, Holding Apron With Eggs, Man, With Dove, 10 1/2 In., Pair	30.00
Night–Light, Three Faces, Glass Eyes, 3 1/4 In.	395.00
Plate, Cherub Archer, Bow Across Shoulders, Green, Pierced, 5 1/2 In.	45.00

BLACK AMETHYST glass appears black until it is held to the light, then a dark purple can be seen. It has been made in many factories from 1860 to the present.

Ashtray, Match Holder, Adolphus Hotel, Dallas	25.00
Box, Hinged Cover, White & Blue Enameled Flowers, 4 3/8 x 5 1/4 In.	245.00
Dresser Set, Victorian, Gold & White Design, Blown, 3 Piece	80.00
Perfume Bottle, White Enameled Flowers, Tulip Stopper, 9 1/4 In.	100.00
Plate, Cookie	25.00
Vase, Enameled Turquoise Leaves, 10 1/2 In.	55.00
Vase, Fluted Top, 6 In.	25.00
Water Set, 5 Piece	45.00

BLACK memorabilia has become an important area of collecting since the 1970s. The best material dates from past centuries, but many recent items are also of interest. Objects that picture a black person may also be listed in this book under Advertising, Tins; Banks; Bottle Openers; Cookie Jars; Salt & Pepper; Sheet Music; etc.

Ashtray, Boy, Watermelon	48.00
Ashtray, Coon Chicken Inn	35.00
Ashtray, Drummer, Iridescent Trim, Japan, 4 1/2 In.	65.00
Ashtray, Mammy, Breast In Wringer, Oh, My Aching Back, Chalkware	45.00
Badge, Golliwog, Pinback	110.00
Bank, Mammy, Polychrome, 6 In.	138.00
Banner, Aunt Jemima Pancake Jamboree, 15 Ft.	275.00
Bed, Slave, Primitive	275.00
Blotter, Shoeshine Boy, Yea Sah, Star Brand Shoes Are Better, Lithographed	10.00
Book, ABC, Cloth, English, 5 x 9 In.	*Illus*	20.00
Book, History of Slavery, W. O. Bowen, 1859	175.00
Book, Landlord & Tenant On Cotton Plantation, Family On Cover, W. P. A., 1936	125.00
Book, Little Black Sambo, 1931	100.00
Book, Little Black Sambo, 1959	39.00
Book, Nigger Heaven, 1926	10.00
Book, Ole–Mammy Torment, Black Dialect, Dated 1897	110.00
Book, Uncle Remus, Harris, Frost Illustrations, Hard Cover, 1916	35.00
Bowl, Cereal, Aunt Jemima, China	110.00
Box, Anise Babies, Candy, Children	400.00
Box, Candy, Amos 'n' Andy	500.00
Brush, Clothes, Figural Black	68.00
Card, Playing, Old Maid, Sassity Sal & Steppin Sam, 43 Piece	50.00
Clock, Waffle, Aunt Jemima	60.00

Cloth, Golliwog, Appliqued Eyes, Oilcloth & Felt, Dressed, 15 In. 125.00
Clothespin Bag, Mammy, Red Scarf & Dress, Cloth, 16 In. 60.00
Creamer, Butler, Full Figure 85.00
Creamer, Chef, Bisque, Japan, 3 1/2 In. 140.00
Creamer, Mammy, Full Figure 85.00
Creamer, Mammy, Gray Hair, Large Features 140.00
Cup & Saucer, Aunt Jemima, China 125.00
Dish Towel, Mammy Sewing Patch On Boy's Pants 45.00
Display, Porter, Stand–Up, Cardboard, 9 In. 30.00
Doll, Alexis, 2 Rows of Teeth, Glass Eyes, 14 In. 55.00
Doorstop, Mammy, Wooden, Large Features, 1920s 175.00
Fan, Coon Chicken Inn, Cardboard 85.00
Figurine, Alligator, Child, Mouth, Watermelon, Bisque, Germany 55.00
Figurine, Boy & Girl, Bisque, 2 1/2 In., Pair 40.00
Figurine, Boy Holding Chicken, On Wicker, Germany, 4 1/2 In. 145.00
Figurine, Preacher, Women, Children, Signed B. A. M. 1949, 3 To 7 In., 7 Piece 395.00
Glass, Coon Chicken Inn 45.00
Holder, For Potholders, Children Eating Watermelon, Chalkware 20.00
Hose Holder, Man, Figural 110.00
Knife Holder, Girl, Wooden 65.00
Lamp, Man, Chalkware, 1950s 44.00
Marriage Certificate, Colored, John Malone, Dilly Putmand, 3/2/88, 8 x 10 In. 40.00
Marriage License, Former Slave, James Henry Bryan, Eheby Dixon, 1/23/70, 8 In. ... 50.00
Marriage Settlement, Received, Slave & Child, Dated 1845, 7 1/2 x 12 In. 90.00
Matchbook With Matches, Coon Chicken Inn 25.00
Memo Board, I'se Gotta Get, Grocery List, Pegs, Wooden 65.00
Menu, Coon Chicken Inn 110.00
Mug, Mammy, Head 325.00
Mug, Muscles Moe 65.00
Napkin, Paper, Aunt Jemima 35.00
Necklace, Metal, 3 Egyptian Type Woman's Heads 28.00
Pad, Memo, Mammy, Cast Iron 165.00
Pajama Bag, Golliwog, Full Figure 125.00
Paper Towel Holder, Mammy 75.00
Photograph, Chuck & Chuckles Dance & Comedy Team, 8 x 10 In. 50.00
Picture, Portrait of Woman, Stockwell Oil, Signed, Framed, 16 x 19 1/2 In. 189.00
Pie Bird, Chef 85.00
Pie Bird, Chef, Japan 185.00
Pie Plate, Coon Chicken Inn 140.00
Pin, Aunt Jemima, Advertising, 4 In. 45.00
Pin, Aunt Jemima, Breakfast Club, Tin, 3 In. 20.00
Pin, Sailor, Bakelite 275.00
Pincushion, Boy, 1940s 48.00
Planter, Mammy, Plaid 110.00
Planter, Mandy, Girl, Brayton 225.00
Plaque, Boy & Girl, Golliwog Head, Large Red Lips, Pair 35.00
Plate, Coon Chicken Inn, 5 1/2 In. 225.00
Plate, Dinner, Aunt Jemima, Wellesville China 60.00
Plate, Paper, Aunt Jemima, 9 In. 35.00
Plate, Sambo's Restaurant, 9 In. 25.00
Plate, Topsy's Eat With Your Fingers, Girl In Pigtails, Shenango, 7 1/2 In. 380.00
Playbill, Anna Lucasta, Black Cast, N.Y., 1945 .... 21.00
Poster, I Am A Man, Martin L. King, Jr., Memphis Strike, 1968, 22 x 28 In. 55.00
Potholder, Boy & Girl, Chalkware, Hanging 20.00
Purse, Pickaninny 22.00
Recipe Box, Aunt Jemima, Yellow 110.00
Record, Edison Cylinder, Niggers Sure Do Like Possum 40.00
Reel, Viewmaster, Little Black Sambo 35.00
Salt & Pepper, Boy & Girl, Valentine Set 165.00
Salt & Pepper, Chef Holding Bucket, Wooden 50.00
Salt & Pepper, Children In Basket ....75.00 To 100.00
Salt & Pepper, Googly–Eye Young Mammy Holding Salt & Pepper 165.00
Salt & Pepper, Kids Holding Vegetable, Omnibus 35.00

Salt & Pepper, Mammy & Butler, Plaid 110.00
Saltshaker, Aunt Jemima, Plastic, 5 In. 15.00
Saltshaker, Black Face, Yellow Apron, Ceramic, Japan, 4 In. 20.00
Saucer, Coon Chicken Inn .... 135.00 To 160.00
Sewing Kit, Luzianne Mammy 40.00
Shaker, Pepper, Chef, Green, Gold Trim, Ceramic, 5 In. 22.00
Sign, Lime Kiln Club Cigars, Paper Lithograph, 30 x 24 In. 1550.00
Sign, Rest Room, Glass, White–Colored, 1929 .... 225.00
Smoking Stand, Waiter, Sheet Metal & Cast Iron, Red, White, Blue, 35 In. 99.00
Spice Set, Aunt Jemima, F & F 250.00
Spoon, Coon Chicken Inn 35.00
Spoon, Sterling Silver, Figural Boy With Alligator Handle 110.00
Sprinkler, Bottle, Mammy, Ceramic 165.00
String Holder, Aunt Jemima 50.00
String Holder, Black Face, Marked Ty–Me 90.00
String Holder, Mammy, Blue Dress, Pottery, Opening For Scissors 125.00
String Holder, Mammy, Chalkware, Full Bodied, 1947 .... 125.00
String Holder, Mammy, Strawberry, Chalkware 43.00
Sugar & Creamer, Aunt Jemima & Uncle Mose, Green, F & F 250.00
Sugar & Creamer, Tray, Black Figural Pictures, F & F 165.00
Sugar & Creamer, Yellow, F & F 125.00
Syrup, Aunt Jemima, F & F Die Co. 40.00
Table Reserved Sign, Coon Chicken Inn 45.00
Tablecloth, Children Print 70.00
Tea Towel Set, Appliqued Brown Face & Hands, Polka Dot Turban, 7 Piece 60.00
Teapot, Chef 125.00
Teapot, Mammy 35.00
Tin, Nigger Hair Tobacco 200.00
Tin, Pickaninny Salted Peanuts, 10 Lb. 450.00
Toaster Cover, Doll, Orange Floral Dress, Lace Cap & Trim 45.00
Tobacco Jar, Head, Pottery, 5 In. ....*Illus* 95.00
Toothpick, Boy, Cotton Bale, Boy Holding Melon, Pot Metal, 2 3/4 In. 125.00
Toothpick, Brown Face, Ceramic, 2 1/2 In. 110.00
Torchere, Blackamoor, Holding Torch, 6 Ft., Pair 7000.00
Toy, Tip Top The Walking Porter, Pushes Baggage Cart, 1920, Tin, Strauss, 6 In. 1315.00
Tray, Crumb, Mammy 65.00
Tumbler, Coon Chicken Inn 45.00
Wall Pocket, Youth, Japan, 1930s 90.00
Whiskbroom, Bellhop, Figural 58.00

BLOWN GLASS was formed by forcing air through a rod into molten glass. Early glass and some forms of art glass were hand blown. Other types of glass were molded or pressed.

Bottle, Aqua, Club Shape, 24 Swirled Ribs, 8 5/8 In. 159.00
Bottle, Aqua, Flattened Club, 24 Swirled Ribs, Zanesville, 9 In. 60.50
Bottle, Dark Green, Squatty, 18th Century, 7 3/4 In. 66.00

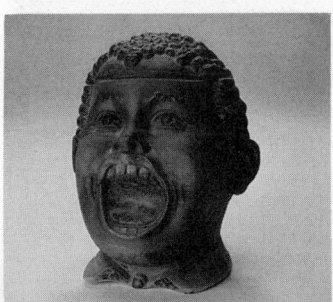

Black, Tobacco Jar, Head, Pottery, 5 In.

Bookends, Man, Full Figure, Brass Plated, 6 In., Pair

Bottle, Grated Cheese, Silver Plated Mount, 19th Century, 6 In. 88.00
Bottle, Ludlow, Olive Green, 7 1/2 In. 104.00
Bottle, Short Neck, Mountain Stag Decoration, Etched, 18th Century, 9 In. 245.00
Bowl, Applied Black Glass Bands, 19th Century, 6 1/2 x 10 1/2 In. 165.00
Bowl, Folded Lip, Aqua, 6 In. 198.00
Bowl, Folded Under Rim, Amber Tint, 9 1/2 In. 104.00
Bowl, Ruffled, Horizontal Ribs, Applied Ruby Rim 55.00
Compote, Cover, Tulip & Sawtooth, 12 1/2 In. 247.00
Cordial, Rounded Funnel Bowl, Air Gauze Core Stem, Footed, 1750, 6 1/8 In. 385.00
Creamer, 3–Mold, Cobalt Rim, 4 Bands of Rings, 3 1/2 In. 1650.00
Creamer, Red Flash, Applied Handle, Clear, 5 1/2 In. 55.00
Cruet, Sapphire Blue, 16 Swirled Ribs, Applied Hollow Handle, 7 In. 2310.00
Cruet, Snail Variant 95.00
Darning Egg, End of Day, Marbelized Pink, Blue, Green, White, 3 x 4 In. 175.00
Decanter, 19th Century, 8 1/2 In., Pair 121.00
Decanter, 3–Mold, Sunburst Stopper, 3 7/8 In. 605.00
Decanter, Baroque Pattern, 3–Mold, Stopper, 8 1/4 In. 49.50
Decanter, Engraved Grapes & Vines, 7 In. 135.00
Decanter, Keene Marlboro St., Keene, New Hampshire, Olive Green, 1825 .... 357.50
Figurine, Monkey, 1 In. 5.00
Figurine, Penguin, 1 In. 5.00
Fish Bowl, Pedestal 275.00
Globe, Hurricane, 23 In., Pair 1000.00
Goblet, Ale, Bell Bowl, 1–Knopped, Spiral Air Twist Stem, 1750, 8 In. 413.00
Goblet, Milk Glass, 2 Blue Bands, 8 x 6 In. 110.00
Jug, Cream, 3–Mold, Midwestern Form, 1840 .... 750.00
Lamp, Clear, Pressed Base, Tin, Cork Burner, 7 3/4 In. 192.00
Milk Pan, Aqua, 1850s, 23 1/2 In. 330.00
Pitcher, Adhesive Design Painted, Powdered Glass Sprinkled Over, 1885 .... 170.00
Pitcher, Applied Band, Tooled Band, Lip, Hollow Applied Handle, 7 5/8 In. 247.00
Pitcher, Clear, Enameled, Fluted, Applied Handle 32.50
Pitcher, Diamond–Quilted, Handle, Amber, 8 In. 5.50
Pitcher, Hobnail & Cleat, South Jersey Type 235.00
Pitcher, Pale Green, Applied Handle, 16 Swirled Ribs, 6 1/4 In. 121.00
Pitcher, Water, Green Opalescent, Green Twisted Handle 225.00
Pitcher, Water, Green, Inverted Rib 70.00
Shade, Hurricane, Folded Lip On Base, 22 In. 275.00
Sherry, 5 1/2 In. 38.00
Smoke Bell, Graduated, Set of 3 .... 375.00
Smoke Bell, Milk Glass, Applied Blue Rim & Handle, 9 In. 77.00
String Holder, Applied Electric Blue Trim, Dome, Ground Bottom, 4 1/2 In. 137.00
Vase, Double Walled Silver, Enameled Design, Uranium Yellow, Crackled 150.00
Vase, Floral Band, Etched, Enamel Decoration, 18th Century, 6 1/2 In. 220.00
Vase, Trumpet, Teardrop Stem, Folded Rim Foot, 9 5/8 In. 71.00
Vase, Wide Foot, Hollow Baluster Stem, Scalloped Rim Bowl, 9 1/8 In. 275.00
Whimsy, Hat, Blue 45.00
Wine, Green, Polished Pontil, 18th Century, Pair 110.00
Wine, Ovoid Bowl, Opaque Twist Stem, Conical Footed, 1750, 5 1/8 In. 385.00
Witch's Ball, Electric Blue, Tear Shape, 5 In. 99.00

BLUE GLASS, see Cobalt Blue category

BLUE ONION, see Onion category

BLUE WILLOW pattern has been made in England since 1780. The pattern
has been copied by factories in many countries, including Germany, Japan,
and the United States. It is still being made. Willow was named for a
pattern that pictures a bridge, birds, willow trees, and a Chinese landscape.

Bowl, Johnson Bros. 5.00
Bowl, Shenango, 5 In. 6.00
Bowl, Vegetable, Cover, Staffordshire 110.00
Bowl, Vegetable, Johnson Bros. 11.00
Cake Plate, With Cake Server, Large 85.00

Carafe & Warmer	150.00
Creamer, Child's, Japan, 2 In.	20.00
Creamer, Ridgway, 3 1/4 In.	35.00
Cup & Saucer, Child's, Japan	12.00
Cup & Saucer, England, Demitasse	23.00
Cup & Saucer, Royal	8.00
Demitasse Set, Occupied Japan, 17 Piece	110.00
Dish, Baking, Moriyama, 7 3/4 In.	40.00
Gravy Boat, Child's, Attached Tray, Japan	50.00
Gravy Boat, Staffordshire	125.00
Grill Plate, Child's	48.00
Grill Plate, Royal	8.00
Jar, Batter, Cover	125.00
Mug, Woods	30.00
Oil Lamp, Johnson Bros.	32.50
Pie Plate, Royal	10.00
Pitcher, Milk, Woods	95.00
Pitcher, Octagonal, Mason's, 11 In. .... 375.00 To 475.00
Pitcher, Ridgway, 5 1/2 In.	70.00
Plate, Child's, Occupied Japan, 3 7/8 In.	20.00
Plate, Royal, 10 In.	3.00
Platter, 18 In.	150.00
Platter, Nesting, Oblong, Ridgway, 11 1/2 In.	65.00
Soap Dish	12.50
Sugar & Creamer, Moriyama	95.00
Sugar, Cover, Child's, Japan, 2 3/8 In.	30.00
Teapot, Child's, Japan, 2 3/4 In.	65.00
Teapot, Rington's Tea Merchant	375.00
Teapot, Staffordshire	125.00
Toaster	1200.00
Tray, Royal, Oval	15.00
Tumbler, Amber Glass .... 7.00 To 12.00
Wall Pocket, Pitcher	39.50
Wall Pocket, Pitcher, Right & Left, Pair	58.50

BOCH FRERES factory was founded in 1841 in La Louviere in eastern Belgium. The wares resemble the work of Villeroy & Boch. The factory is still in business.

Dish, Cover, Red & Yellow Design, Catteau, 4 x 6 1/4 In.	160.00
Vase, Art Deco Floral, Brown, Black & White, Ch. Catteau, 1930, 6 In.	575.00
Vase, Cream & Brown Blossoms On Shoulder, Marked, 11 1/4 In.	440.00

BOEHM is the collector's name for the porcelains of Edward Marshall Boehm. In 1953 the Osso China Company was reorganized as Edward Marshall Boehm, Inc. The company is still working in England and New Jersey. In the early days of the factory, dishes were made, but the elaborate and lifelike bird figurines are the best known ware. Edward Marshall Boehm, the founder, died in 1961, but the firm has continued to design and produce porcelain. Today, the firm makes both limited and unlimited editions of figurines and plates.

Figurine, Angel, Signed, 4 1/2 In.	80.00
Figurine, Baby Chick, Yellow, 1950s	175.00
Figurine, Baby Chickadee, No. 462, 3 1/4 In.	137.00
Figurine, Baby Crested Fly Catcher, No. 458, 5 In.	110.00
Figurine, Baby Robin, No. 437, 3 1/2 In.	110.00
Figurine, Baby Wood Thrush, No. 444, 4 1/2 In.	137.00
Figurine, Ballet Dancer	145.00
Figurine, Cerulean Warblers, Dorothy Doughty, Pair	1100.00
Figurine, Cygnet, 6 1/2 In.	165.00
Figurine, Cygnet, On Lily Pad, 4 1/4 In.	385.00
Figurine, Dappled Gray Mare, Standing, Signed	1800.00
Figurine, Giant Panda Bear, 6 1/2 x 8 1/4 In.	140.00
Figurine, Jockey On Horseback With Attendant, 22 In.	1210.00

Figurine, Little Wren, On Rocks, White Flowers 350.00
Figurine, Rose, Royal Blessing, No. 25066, 7 1/2 In. 330.00
Figurine, St. Maria Goetti, 1953 .... 175.00
Figurine, Thoroughbred Stallion, Adios, Marked 1900.00
Figurine, Tree Sparrow, No. 468F 250.00
Figurine, Vermilion Flycatchers, Dorothy Doughty, Pair 1100.00
Group, Fledgling Western Bluebirds, No. 494/4, 5 1/2 In. 110.00
Paperweight, Baby Buntings, 3 1/2 In. 155.00

BOHEMIAN GLASS is an ornate overlay or flashed glass made during the
Victorian era. It has been reproduced in Bohemia, which is now a part of
the Czech Republic. Glass made from 1875 to 1900 is preferred by
collectors.

Beaker, 3 Handles, Mold Blown, Motto & Seal, Crystal 225.00
Bowl, Garlanded Figure Playing Pipes, 8 Lobes, White Lining, 20 In. 750.00
Bowl, Tea Caddy, Uranium Yellow, Pillar & Miter Cut, Brilliant, 1870s 225.00
Cologne Bottle, Miter & Flute, Brilliant, Uranium Yellow, 1870s 120.00
Compote, Baluster Stem, Red Flashed Morning Glory Designs, Gilding, 7 In. 20.00
Compote, Deer & Castle 190.00
Cordial, Deer & Castle, Ruby Cut To Clear, 3 1/2 In., Pair 35.00
Decanter Set, 7 Piece 135.00
Decanter, Cut Thumbprints At Pinched Neck, c.1890, 17 1/4 In. 440.00
Decanter, Deer & Castle, 10 1/2 In. 75.00
Decanter, Frosted Vintage Between Rows of Thumbprints, Stopper 250.00
Decanter, Hand Painted Flower, White To Peach, 11 1/2 In. 225.00
Decanter, Straight Miter, Pillar & Flute, Uranium Yellow, 1870s 795.00
Goblet, Ruby Cut To Clear, 4 1/2 In. 40.00
Lamp, Fairy, Deer & Castle, Ruby Red, 4 1/2 In. 275.00
Lustres, Ruffled Top, Ruby, 11 In., Pair 600.00
Rose Bowl, Etched Grape, Amber 90.00
Tumbler, Deer & Castle, Blue 35.00
Vase, 6 Panels, Stag & Forest Etching, Red, Gold Trim, 6 In. 175.00
Vase, Amber Overlay, Etched Crystal, Domed Foot, 12 3/4 In. 195.00
Vase, Ruby Flashing, Copper Wheel Engraved Flowers, Vintage, 13 3/8 In. 140.00
Vase, Ruby, Clear & Frosted Design Around Body, 10 1/2 x 3 1/2 In. 45.00
Vase, Ruby, Cut Symmetric Designs, Deer Front, House On Back, 7 1/2 In. 85.00
Wine, Uranium Yellow, 1870s 195.00

BONE DISHES were considered a necessary part of a table setting for the
Victorian table. The crescent-shaped dish was kept at the edge of the
dinner plate so the bones removed from the fish could be stored away
from the uneaten food. Some bone dishes were made in more fanciful
shapes and many resemble fish.

Figural, Fish, Blue Flower Design, China 70.00
Flow Blue, Touraine 22.00
Non Pareil, Flow Blue 75.00
Tea Leaf Ironstone, Meakin 70.00

BOOKENDS have probably been used since books became inexpensive.
Early libraries kept books in cupboards, not on open shelves. By the 1870s
bookends appeared, especially homemade fret-carved wooden examples.
Most bookends listed in this book date from the twentieth century.

Abstracted Repousse Design, Jarvie, Copper, 4 1/2 x 5 1/2 In., Pair 440.00
Angelus, Copper Flashed 35.00
Basket of Flowers, Polychrome, Iron, 5 1/4 In. 27.00
Bison, Cast Iron, 1930 .... 45.00
Boy With Horn, Chalkware 15.00
Classical Lovers Before Garden Wall, Porcelain, German, 6 In. 275.00
Clipper Ship, Full Sail, Brass, Snead & Co. .... 35.00 To 45.00
Clown, Art Deco Style, Molded Lead Figures, Painted Red & Black, 7 1/2 In. 75.00
Dog On Plinth, E. B. Parsons, Bronze 1100.00
Female Nude, Standing, Gilt Metal, Art Deco, 9 3/4 In. 145.00
Fred & Wilma 50.00

Golfer Teeing Off, Brass, c.1920, 10 In. 850.00
Grecian Goddess, Slush Metal Figures, Black Base, 5 In. 88.00
Hammered Copper, Kopper Kraft, San Francisco 128.00
Howdy Doody 38.00
Indian Head, Headdress, Iron, 4 In. 12.00
Knight On Horse, Metal, G. B. Allen 100.00
Knight's Head, Medieval Type, Chalkware 35.00
Knights On Horseback, Cast Iron 20.00
Lincoln & Roosevelt, L. V. Aronson, Bronze, 1921, 5 1/2 x 4 1/2 In. 375.00
Man, Full Figure, Brass Plated, 6 In., Pair ....*Illus* 50.00
Monk, Chalkware, 7 1/2 In. 35.00
Monk, Seated At Bookcase, Metal, Hand Painted, LUA, 1922 .... 35.00
Mutt & Jeff, Cast Iron 650.00
Nude, Verona 65.00
Pelicans, Mouth Open, Drinking At Fountain, Edgar Brandt, 6 3/4 In. 4280.00
Seal, Ceramic, 9 In. 18.00
Ship Design, Billowing Sail, Copper, John J. Brennan 150.00
Swashbucklers, Bronze Finish, Cast Metal, Paul Herzel, 7 1/2 In. 25.00
Totem Poles, Bronze, Cygnus 25.00
Woman's Heads, Art Nouveau, Brass, Table Top Extending 85.00
Wood From Frigate Constitution, Oak, 6 1/2 In. 220.00

BOOKMARKS were originally made of parchment, cloth, or leather. Soon woven silk ribbon, thin cardboard, celluloid, wood, silver, tortoiseshell, and metals were used. Examples made before 1850 are scarce, but there are many to be found dating before 1920.

13 Colonies, George Washington, Columbus Expo, Political, Silk, Advertising 150.00
Chocolate Cocoa, Celluloid, Stollwerck 20.00
Compliments of United States Baking Co., Calendar On Reverse, Little Boy 12.00
Heart Shape, Life Magazine Advertising, Celluloid, Multicolor 18.00
Hoyt's German Cologne, Victorian, Trade Card Type 11.50
Mercury Auto, Silver & Enamel, 1951 .... 16.00
Pictures Jackson Kemper, 1st Missionary Bishop, Silk 65.00
Remember The Maine, Cloth 25.00
Star Spangled Banner, Words & Music, Silk, 12 In. 75.00

BOSSONS character wall masks, plaques, figurines, and other decorative pieces are made by W.H. Bossons, Limited of Congleton, England. The company was founded in 1946 and is still working.

BOSSONS

Figurine, Abdhul 52.00
Figurine, Afghan Dog 80.00
Figurine, Anemones, 6 In. 25.00
Figurine, Birds & Sunflower 400.00
Figurine, Boatman 22.00
Figurine, Briar Rose Fawn 55.00
Figurine, Caspian Man, 1st 135.00
Figurine, Cavalier, Green 250.00
Figurine, Chaka 90.00
Figurine, Cheyenne 53.00
Figurine, Coolie 95.00
Figurine, Corsican 50.00
Figurine, Deccan Hunters 130.00
Figurine, Drummer, Thick 130.00
Figurine, Eagle 155.00
Figurine, Eskimo 30.00
Figurine, Fagin 40.00
Figurine, Fisherman 22.00
Figurine, Golden Puma 285.00
Figurine, Harry Wheatcroft 600.00
Figurine, Highwayman 245.00
Figurine, Jock, With Tooth 60.00
Figurine, Kingfisher 30.00
Figurine, Leichtensteiner 125.00

Figurine, Mexican	450.00
Figurine, Old Timer	35.00
Figurine, Paddy, Red	85.00
Figurine, Pancho	35.00
Figurine, Persian	30.00
Figurine, Pony Girl	490.00
Figurine, Punjabi	35.00
Figurine, Rawhide	35.00
Figurine, Saracen	153.00
Figurine, Serbian	105.00
Figurine, Sikh	33.00
Figurine, Terriers	90.00
Figurine, Uriah Heep	40.00
Figurine, Victorian Fireman	43.00
Plaque, Renault Auto	220.00

BOSTON & SANDWICH CO. pieces may be found in the Lutz and Sandwich Glass categories.

BOTTLE CAP collectors search for the printed cardboard caps used during the past 80 years.

Highland Dairy Chocolate Milk, 2 In.	.10
Littleton's Milk, San Bernardino, Clamp Over, 2 In.	.25
MSC Michigan State Pasteurized Cream, Clamp Over, 2 In.	.50
Quality Dairy, Redlands Fruit Punch, Clamp Over, 2 In.	.10
Quality Dairy, Redlands Whipped Cream, Hood, Paper, 2 1/2 In.	.05
Wauregan Dairy Approved Milk, Clamp Over, Paper, 2 1/2 In.	.10

BOTTLE OPENERS are needed to open many bottles. As soon as the commercial bottle was invented, the opener to be used with the new types of closures became a necessity. Many types of bottle openers can be found, most dating from the twentieth century. Collectors prize advertising and comic openers.

4–Eyed Man, Cast Iron	48.00 To 50.00
4–Eyed Woman, Cast Iron	48.00 To 120.00
Alligator, Head Up, Bronze	125.00
Alligator, Head Up, Cast Iron	45.00 To 110.00
American Sailor, Holding Rifle, World War I, Pot Metal	70.00
Arabian, 1 Dimensional, Original Paint	95.00
Bear, Wall Mount, Cast Iron	65.00
Bishop & Babcock, Cork Screw, Cast Iron, 6 5/8 In.	95.00
Black Man's Face, Cast Iron, Wall Mount	165.00
Black Man's Head, Red Tie, Iron, Painted	75.00
Black Man, Cast Iron, Polychrome Paint, 4 1/4 In.	104.00
Bulldog, Cast Iron	50.00
Cloeter's Corks & Cans, Bakelite, 1940s, 6 In.	7.50
Clown Head, Cast Iron	85.00 To 145.00
Clown, Cast Iron	50.00
Clown, Wall Mount	95.00
Cockatoo On Perch, Polychrome Paint, Iron, 5 1/2 In.	38.00
Cowboy With Guitar, Cast Iron	140.00 To 185.00
Crab, Brass	7.50
Cunard Line, 1940, 3 In.	10.00
Devil, Reclining, Aluminum	240.00
Dog, Brass	15.00
Dog, Dachshund, Collar With Studs, Brass	40.00
Donkey, Cast Iron, 3 3/4 In.	20.00 To 35.00
Drunk At Lamppost, Bourbon Street, Iron	15.00
Drunk In Top Hat & Tails, 5 1/2 In.	65.00
Drunk, Wall Mount	90.00
Drunk, With Palm Tree	50.00
Elephant	30.00
Elephant, Chrome	35.00

False Teeth, Cast Iron	85.00
Goat, Cast Iron	48.00
Gold Crown Beer, Cast Iron	2.00
Golf Club, Brass	20.00
Guitar, Chrome	5.00
Horse's Behind, Cast Iron, Original Paint	75.00
Iron City Beer Bottle Shape, Wooden	40.00
Jayhawk, Kansas, Cast Iron	45.00
John Barleycorn, Wall, Marked Wilton	95.00
Lobster	15.00
Man In Moon, Cast Iron	58.00
Minstrel Holds Banjo	18.00
Nude, Hands Over Head, Brass	20.00
Old Snifter, Corkscrew	35.00
Parrot, Pedestal, Iron	45.00
Parrot, With Corkscrew, Art Deco, Chrome	25.00
Pheasant, Cast Iron	45.00
Pretzel, Cast Iron	65.00 To 90.00
Red Bakelite	24.00
Rooster, Cast Iron, Original Polychrome	94.00
Sailor	33.00
Sea Gull, Cast Iron	40.00 To 45.00
Seahorse, Pewter	35.00
Shark	20.00
Skunk, Cast Iron	160.00
Squirrel, Cast Iron	275.00
Steel Worker, 3 1/4 In.	105.00
Tennis Racket, Cast Iron	20.00
Trout	135.00

BOTTLE collecting has become a major American hobby. There are several general categories of bottles, such as historic flasks, bitters, household, and figural. For more bottle prices, see the book *Kovels' Bottles Price List* by Ralph and Terry Kovel.

Ale, Olive Amber, Blown, Pontil, 1 Qt.	85.00

Avon started in 1886 as the California Perfume Company. It was not until 1929 that the name *Avon* was used. In 1939, it became Avon Products, Inc. Avon has made many figural bottles filled with cosmetic products. Ceramic, plastic, and glass bottles were made in limited editions.

Avon, Bucking Bronco	8.00
Avon, Car, Electric Charger	4.00
Avon, Car, Maxwell, 1923	5.00
Avon, Car, REO Depot Wagon, Box	5.00
Avon, Car, Stanley Steamer	4.00
Avon, Cologne, Angel's Song, With Lyre	3.00
Avon, Cologne, Brisk Spice	3.00
Avon, Cologne, Candleholder, Cape Cod	10.00
Avon, Cologne, Decanter, Spring Song	4.00
Avon, Cologne, Fire Fighter	28.00
Avon, Cologne, Little Red Riding Hood	25.00
Avon, Cologne, Mandolin	3.00
Avon, Cologne, Parisian Garden	2.50
Avon, Cologne, Rapunzel	25.00
Avon, Cologne, Snowflake Bell	3.00
Avon, Cologne, Stein, Indian	28.00
Avon, Cologne, Trazzara	4.00
Avon, Perfume, Gardenia, Box, 1948	35.00
Avon, President Washington	8.00
Avon, Sporting Stein, Miniature, Box, 1983	10.00
Avon, Toilet Water, Apple Blossom	10.00
Avon, Toilet Water, Trailing Arbutus, 1933	15.00
Avon, Tractor, Figural, Brown, 6 In.	20.00

Avon, Viking Horn 5.00
Bar, Pillar Molded, Conical, Midwestern 180.00
Barber, Amber, Metal Stopper, Fostoria 50.00
Barber, Barbasol, 8 Panels, Clear, 1/2 Pt. 3.00
Barber, Figural, Small Boy With Hat, Luster Finish, Germany 140.00
Barber, Florida Water, Engraved, Quilted Neck, Tooled Lip, Clear, 6 In. 25.00
Barber, K. H. Stephens & Sons Hair Oil, Worcester, Mass., Fancy, Clear, 7 In. 12.00
Barber, Parker's Hair Balsam, New York, Olive, Bakelite Cap, Heavy Glass 20.00

Beam bottles were made to hold Kentucky Straight Bourbon, made by the
James B. Beam Distilling Company. The Beam series of ceramic bottles
began in 1953.

Beam, 1907 Thomas Flyer, White 55.00
Beam, 1913 Model T Ford, Black 55.00
Beam, 1914 Stutz Bear Cat, Gray 55.00
Beam, 1929 Ford Phaeton, Green 55.00
Beam, 1930 Model A Ford Fire Engine 75.00
Beam, Antique Trader 12.00
Beam, Camaro Pace Car 44.00
Beam, Casey Jones Locomotive & Tender 59.00
Beam, Corvette, Blue, 1957 .... 425.00
Beam, Decanter, Elephant, 1965 .... 20.00
Beam, Decanter, Father's Day 15.00
Beam, Decanter, Gray Cherub Executive, 1958 .... 150.00
Beam, Decanter, King Kamehameha 15.00
Beam, Decanter, Political, Cowgirl, Bar, 1960, Pair 25.00
Beam, Decanter, Radio Shape 25.00
Beam, Emmett Kelly, 1973 .... 50.00
Beam, Ford Fire Chief, 1934 Roadster 49.50
Beam, Harold's Club, Slot Machine 10.00
Beam, John Henry 50.00
Beam, Liberty Eagle, 6 Coins In Mold, 1970 .... 45.00
Beam, Locomotive, Tender, Boxcar, Tank Car, Caboose, 5 Piece 229.00
Beam, Mortimer Snerd, 1976 .... 50.00
Beam, Pickup Truck 39.50
Beam, St. Louis, 1966 .... 20.00
Beer, Buffalo Brewing, Sacramento, 1 Qt. 20.00
Beer, Eldorado Brewing, Stockton, 1 Pt. 20.00
Beer, John Wieland's Export, San Francisco, 1/2 Pt. 30.00
Beer, Red Wing Brewing Co., Red Wing, Minn., Amber, Picnic 30.00
Beer, Schlitz, Decanter, 125th Anniversary, Ceramarte, 1974 .... 30.00
Beer, Schlitz, Ruby Glass 20.00
Bitters, Angostura, Yellow Olive Green, 6 In. 8.00
Bitters, Arabian, Arnold & Reliable Tonic, Amber, Square, 1870s, 9 5/8 In. 330.00
Bitters, Atwood's Jaundice, Aqua, 12 Panels, 6 1/2 In. 9.00
Bitters, Bavarian, Dark Amber, Square 200.00
Bitters, Carmeliter Stomach, New York, Amber 40.00
Bitters, Carmeliter Stomach, New York, Green, Square 575.00
Bitters, Dingens Napoleon Cocktail, Banjo Shape, Green, 10 1/2 In. 9900.00
Bitters, Dr. Hostetter's, Amber 15.00
Bitters, Dr. A. W. Coleman's Anti Dyspeptic & Tonic, Green, c.1860, 9 In. 4675.00
Bitters, Dr. Caldwell's Herb, Amber 275.00
Bitters, Dr. Carson's, Victoria Wine Canadian West, Aqua 2550.00
Bitters, Dr. Hoofland's German, Aqua, 8 In. 35.00
Bitters, Dr. J. G. B. Siegert & Sons Angostura, Green, 5 In. 10.00
Bitters, Dr. J. Hostetter's Stomach, W. McG & Co., Amber, 8 5/8 In. 15.00
Bitters, Dr. M. M. Fenner's Capital, Light Haze 68.00
Bitters, Dr. Med Koch's Universal Magen, Medium Citron, c.1870 .... 2310.00
Bitters, Dr. Petzold's Genuine German, Amber, 1862 .... 150.00
Bitters, Dr. Stover's, Dark Amber 225.00
Bitters, Dr. Van Deusen's Ague, Springfield, Ill., 8 In. 935.00
Bitters, Dr. Von Hopf's Curacao, Amber, Square 65.00
Bitters, Drake's Plantation, 5 Log, Deep Chocolate Amber 325.00

Bitters, Drake's Plantation, 5 Log, Strawberry Puce 325.00
Bitters, Drake's Plantation, 6 Log, Bright Yellow, Olive 485.00
Bitters, Drake's Plantation, 6 Log, Medium Amber 100.00
Bitters, Drake's Plantation, 6 Log, Medium Puce, Arabesque Type 325.00
Bitters, Drake's Plantation, 6 Log, Red Puce 285.00
Bitters, Drake's Plantation, Olive Green 8865.00
Bitters, Drake's, Plantation, Cabin Shape, Sloping Collar, Golden Amber, 9 7/8 In. 302.50
Bitters, Eagle Angostura Bark, Amber, Globular 60.00
Bitters, Ear of Corn, National, Figural, Amber, 12 1/2 In. 220.00
Bitters, Greeley's Bourbon Whiskey, Plum Puce 330.00
Bitters, Greeley's Bourbon, Olive Green, Barrel Shape, 9 1/4 In. 905.00
Bitters, Hall's, Yellow Amber, Barrel Shape 2450.00
Bitters, Hertrich's Gesundheits, Green, c.1880, 12 In. 4675.00
Bitters, Johnson's Calisaya, Puce, c.1894 .... 2900.00
Bitters, Johnson's Calisaya, Puce, Rectangular, c.1870 .... 3200.00
Bitters, Mishler's Herb, Amber, Square 35.00
Bitters, Old Dr. Townsend's, Magic Stomach, Green 2400.00
Bitters, Old Sachem, Wigwam Tonic, Amethyst, Barrel Shape, 9 5/8 In. 2100.00
Bitters, Pepsin, R. W. Davis, Yellow–Green 90.00
Bitters, Peychaud's American Aromatic, Amber 125.00
Bitters, Reeds, Lady's Leg, Amber, 12 1/2 In. 220.00
Bitters, Russ' St. Domingo, Honey Amber 110.00
Bitters, Severa Stomach, Flask, Amber, 10 In. 50.00
Bitters, W. H. Ware Fish, Fish Shape 145.00
Bitters, Wa Hoo, Indian Label 45.00
Coca–Cola bottles are listed in the Coca–Cola category
Cologne, Base Embossed Ricketts Bristol, c.1880 .... 600.00
Cologne, Portrait, L. Kossuth, Bluish–Aqua 800.00
Cordial, Mrs. E. Kidder Dysentery, Boston, Golden Amber, 1850, 7 3/8 In. 2310.00
Cosmetic, A. I. Mathews Venetian Hair Dye 16.00
Cosmetic, Altenheim Medical Dispensary For The Hair, Cincinnati, Ohio 12.00
Cosmetic, Burma Shave, Ornate, Clear 12.00
Cosmetic, Carnation Pink Sachet, Larkin Soap Company, Box, 1 Oz. 15.00
Cosmetic, Clover Sachet, Larkin Soap Company, Partial Contents, Label, 3 In. 9.00
Cosmetic, Cold Cream, Larkin Soap Company, Milk Glass, Metal Cap, 2 In. 11.00
Cosmetic, Kickapoo Sage Hair Tonic, Cobalt Blue, Tooled Tip 125.00
Cosmetic, Mrs. Allen's World Hair Restorer, Light Honey Amber 25.00
Cosmetic, Retroovey's Turkish Hair Tonic, Philadelphia, Aqua, 1860, 7 In. 20.00
Cosmetic, Safeguard Carbolic Soap, Larkin Soap Company, Fiber Box 15.00
Cosmetic, Smelling Salts, Lavender, Colgate, Green, Contents 15.00
Creamer, Blue Jay Cafe, Blue, Round, 1/2 Oz. 20.00
Creamer, Cloverleaf Dairy, Maroon, 2 Sides, 1 7/8 In. 20.00
Creamer, Dressel–Young Dairy, Granite City, Ill., Orange, 1 7/8 In. 20.00
Creamer, Eastwood Dairy, Syracuse, N.Y., Red, 1 7/8 In. 30.00
Creamer, Raritan Valley Farms, Somerville, N. J., Red, Round, 1/2 Oz. 20.00
Cronenweth Dairy, Orange Pyro, Wide Mouth, 1/2 Gal. 25.00
Decanter, Joel B. Frazier Whiskey, Clear, Bulb Shape, Gold Letters, 9 In. 50.00
Decanter, Keystone Cabinet Whiskey, Seattle Wash., Amethyst, White Letters, 9 In. ... 225.00
Decanter, Pinch, Clear, 4 Channels, Plus Center, Flared, No Stopper, 11 In. 45.00
Decanter, R. H. Parker Whiskey, Amethyst, Enameled Letters, 4 3/4 In. 45.00
Decanter, Silver Overlay, Black Amethyst, Rockwell, 7 In. 302.50
Dr Pepper, Advertising, Good For Life, 6 1/2 Oz. 35.00
Drug, A. C. Tannic, Side Mouth, Stopper, Square, 7 In. 35.00
Drug, Baker's Analyzed Chemicals, Cork, Contents 45.00
Drug, Battle & Co. Chemist, St. Louis, Label, Contents 12.00
Drug, Brown's Iron, Brown Chemical Co., Partial Label, 8 3/4 In. 20.00
Drug, Eli Lilly Sedatussin, 1 Lb. 24.00
Drug, Eli Lilly Wild Cherry Extract 16.00
Drug, Jar, Noxema, Cobalt Blue 2.50
Drug, Jar, Vicks, Cobalt Blue 2.50
Drug, Lightbody's Coughs Colds, Emerald Green, Rochester Label 55.00
Drug, Longley's Panacea, Aqua, Open Pontil 100.00
Drug, Metzger's Catarrh Cure, Aqua 15.00

Bottle, Figural, Shoe, Black Glass,
3 1/2 X 6 In.

♦ ♦ ♦ ♦ ♦ ♦ ♦ ♦ ♦ ♦ ♦ ♦ ♦ ♦ ♦ ♦ ♦ ♦ ♦ ♦

If you want to clean a bottle that has a paper label, try to protect the label. Wrap the bottle tightly in thin plastic wrap. Seal the wrap with tape and rubberbands. Clean the inside carefully, using a mixture of water, automatic dishwasher detergent, and slightly abrasive kitty litter. Fill bottle partway and shake.

♦ ♦

Drug, New York Pharmacal Association, Brilliant Cobalt Blue, 12 In.	195.00
Drug, Nujol, Clear, 1 Qt.	3.00
Drug, Oakland Chemical Company, Amber, 13 In.	30.00
Drug, Owl, Cobalt Blue, 9 In.	2640.00
Eliza Brooks, Decanter, American Legionnaire, Saluting	50.00
Ezra Brooks, Churchill Giving V Sign, 1969	50.00
Ezra Brooks, Decanter, Hunting Dog & Pheasant, 1970	15.00
Ezra Brooks, Kachina No. 1, 1971	110.00
Ezra Brooks, Train, Decanter	10.00
Figural, Black Waiter, Original Paint	450.00
Figural, Bopeep	10.00
Figural, Cigar, Amber	25.00
Figural, Hot Tamale, Ceramic, 6 In.	10.00
Figural, Kummel Bear, Light Olive	60.00
Figural, Lighthouse, Clear	10.00
Figural, Log Cabin, Clear, 1 Pt.	10.00
Figural, Man's Face, Clear	10.00
Figural, Man, Clear, Squatty, 1 Pt.	12.00
Figural, Pot Belly Stove, Clear, 1 Pt.	10.00
Figural, Pumpkin Head, Orange Paint, 1 Pt.	45.00
Figural, Railroad Lantern, Clear	10.00
Figural, Shoe, Black Glass, 3 1/2 x 6 In. ....*Illus*	40.00
Figural, World, Clear, 1 Qt.	12.00
Flask, 12 Diamond, Greenish Aqua, Flattened Egg–Shaped Body, 6 1/2 In.	65.00
Flask, A. H. Powers & Co., Sacramento, Clear, Picnic, 5 1/2 In.	25.00
Flask, Anchor & Eagle, Aqua, Ravenna Glass Works	120.00
Flask, Anchor, Log Cabin, Aqua, Spring Garden Glass Works	75.00
Flask, Anchor, Phoenix, Aqua, Baltimore Glass Works	80.00
Flask, Arch With Agricultural Implements, Eagle, Green, Zanesville	250.00
Flask, Aronson's, Seattle, Wash., Amethyst, Flat, 6 5/8 In.	15.00
Flask, Bellarmine, Heart & Crown Medallion, Mottled Brown, 8 3/4 In.	477.00
Flask, Bellarmine, Medium Brown & Ocher, Glaze Runs, 10 3/4 In.	636.00
Flask, Bellarmine, Mottled Brown & Ocher, Globular, 10 1/2 In.	1293.00
Flask, Bellarmine, Mottled Tiger Glaze, 9 In.	517.00
Flask, Bellarmine, Smiling Mask, Armorial Medallion, Brown, 10 3/4 In.	636.00
Flask, Bellarmine, Smiling Mask, Cobalt Blue Highlights, 7 1/2 In.	1790.00
Flask, Bunch of Grapes, Lion, Vertical Ribbing, Blue, 1 Pt.	165.00
Flask, Celebrated Montezuma Rye Whiskey, Cork, Metal, Copper, 4 1/2 In.	110.00
Flask, Ceramic, Little Nip, Embossed	22.50
Flask, Chestnut, 10 Diamond, Aqua, Zanesville, 1/2 Pt.	800.00
Flask, Chestnut, 10 Diamond, Light Amber, Zanesville, 1/2 Pt.	1200.00
Flask, Double Eagle, Beaded Side, Olive–Amber	9500.00
Flask, Double Eagle, Olive Amber, Cork, 1/2 Pt.	49.50
Flask, Eagle Banner, Calabash, Brilliant Green, Amber Striations, Graphite	145.00
Flask, Eagle, Anchor, Aqua, Ravenna Glass Co., Iron Pontil, 7 7/8 In.	115.00
Flask, Eagle, Blue–Green, Sloping Collar, 1860s, 1 Pt.	357.50

Flask, Eagle, Cornucopia, Historical, 1840s 82.50
Flask, Eagle, Dyottville Glass Works, Medium Puce .... 4600.00 To 5260.00
Flask, Eagle, Yellow, Green Tone, Ravenna Glass Co. 2640.00
Flask, Ear of Corn, Washington Monument, Baltimore Glass Works, Aqua 300.00
Flask, Father of His Country, General Taylor Never Surrenders 95.00
Flask, Franklin, Dyott, Portrait, 1826, 1 Qt. 270.00
Flask, Grandfather, 24 Ribs, Golden Amber, c.1830 .... 1127.50
Flask, Jenny Lind, Ravenna, Aqua, Iron Pontil 135.00
Flask, Masonic Arch On Side, Eagle Over J. K. B. Other Side, Amethyst 5500.00
Flask, Masonic, Olive Amber, 1815–1830, 1/2 Pt. 5170.00
Flask, Men Arguing, Grotesque Heads, 1/2 Pt. 385.00
Flask, Peanut, Embossed & Painted, Screw Lid, 16 x 5 x 6 In. 137.00
Flask, Phoenix, San Francisco, Amber, Coffin, 6 3/4 In. 200.00
Flask, Pictorial, Emerald Green, 1/2 Pt. 1100.00
Flask, Scroll, Aqua, Iron Pontil, 6 7/8 In., 1 Pt. 55.00
Flask, Scroll, Sapphire Blue, Double Collar Mouth 3300.00
Flask, Shield & Clasped Hands, Cannon, Golden Amber, 1 Pt. 220.00
Flask, Sunburst, Olive Green, 1/2 Pt. 210.00
Flask, Tam O'Shanter, Handle, Green, Kingsware Pottery 1491.00
Flask, Washington, Eagle, Portrait, Aqua, 1 Pt. 240.00
Flask, Washington, Ship, Aqua, Albany Glass Works, 1930s 20.00
Flask, Washington, Taylor, Sloping Collar, Lime Yellow, 1 Qt. 495.00
Flask, Western Trade Mark, Aqua, Hutchinson, 6 1/2 In. 30.00
Food, American Oyster Co., 1 Pt. 65.00
Food, B & M Baked Beans, Amber, 1 Pt. 4.00
Food, Borden's Malted Milk, Clear, 1 Pt. 6.00
Food, Bosco, Clear, 1 Pt. 3.00
Food, French's Medford Brand Prepared Mustard, Clear, 1 Pt. 5.00
Food, H. J. Heinz Co. 45.00
Food, Honeycomb Honey, Lake Shore, Clear, 1 Pt. 5.00
Food, Honeymoon Peanut Butter, Dist. By White Stores Co., Clear, 1 Qt. 12.00
Food, Jumbo Apple Butter, Clear, 1 Pt. 10.00
Food, Mrs. Chapin's Mayonnaise, Boston, Mass., Clear, 1 Pt. 6.00
Food, Mustard, Louit Frere Moutarde, Embossed, Cork 25.00
Food, My Own Pickles, Circled By Flowers & Hearts, Clear, 1 Qt. 8.00
Food, My Wife's Salad Dressing, Embossed 35.00
Food, Nestle, Congratulations 25th Anniversary, Clear, 1 Qt. 15.00
Food, Old Judge Coffee, Clear, 1 Qt. 10.00
Food, Orange–Crush, Ornate, Amber, 1 Gal. 50.00
Food, Ovaltine, On Heel of Jar, Amber, 1 Pt. 5.00
Food, Pepper Sauce, Cathedral, Greenish Aqua, 1850s, 8 3/4 In. 132.00
Food, Pickle, Cathedral, Square, Shaded Greens, 8 7/8 In. 715.00
Food, Reed's Patties, Reed's Candy Company, Chicago, Clear, 1/2 Gal. 50.00
Food, Sanitas Nut Food Co., Ltd., Battle Creek, Mich., Aqua, 1 Pt. 10.00
Food, Skippy, Figural, Bear, Clear, 1 Qt. 15.00
Food, Victoria's Yogurt, Orange Script, 1/2 Pt. 12.00
Food, White House Vinegar, Clear, 1 Qt. 15.00
Fruit Jar, Allen, Aqua, Pat. June 1871 .... 150.00
Fruit Jar, Atherholt, Fisher & Co, Aqua, 1 Qt. 200.00
Fruit Jar, Atlas E–Z Seal, Amber, 1 Qt. 40.00
Fruit Jar, Atlas E–Z Seal, Embossed, Wire Bail, Glass Lid, 1 Pt. 4.25
Fruit Jar, Atlas E–Z Seal, Green, 1 Pt. 15.00
Fruit Jar, Atlas Mason's, Patent Nov. 30th, 1858, Olive Green, 1/2 Gal. 35.00
Fruit Jar, Atlas, Four Leaf Clover, Good Luck, Clear, 1 Pt. 12.00
Fruit Jar, Ball Ideal, Wire Bail, Glass Lid, Blue, 1908, 1 Qt. 4.00
Fruit Jar, Ball Mason, Apple Green, 1 Pt. 12.50
Fruit Jar, Ball Mason, Zinc Lid, Aqua, 1858, 1 Qt. 3.50
Fruit Jar, Ball Perfect Mason, 12 Ribs, 1/2 Gal. 4.00
Fruit Jar, Ball, Midget 20.00
Fruit Jar, Battleship Maine Jar, Aqua, 1 Qt. 12.00
Fruit Jar, Beaver, Facing Right, Clear, 1/2 Gal. 85.00
Fruit Jar, Brackett's Perfection, Green–Aqua, 1 Qt. 330.00
Fruit Jar, Brockway Clear Vu Mason, Clear, 1 Qt. 4.00

Fruit Jar, Canadian Sure Seal, Clear, 1 Qt.	6.00
Fruit Jar, Drey Pat'd 1920 Improved Everseal, Clear, 1 Pt.	10.00
Fruit Jar, Foster Sealfast, Wire Bail, Glass Lid, 1 Qt.	6.50
Fruit Jar, Franklin Dexter Fruit Jar, Sky Blue, 1/2 Pt.	50.00
Fruit Jar, Franklin Fruit Jar, Aqua, 1/2 Gal.	150.00
Fruit Jar, Fruit Keeper, Mono, Aqua, 1 Pt.	45.00
Fruit Jar, Galloway's Everlasting, Pat'd Feb. 8th & Pat. App., 1870, Gray, 1/2 Gal.	25.00
Fruit Jar, Garden Queen, Black Glass Co., Baltimore, Md., Clear, 1 Pt.	15.00
Fruit Jar, Gem, Wallaceburg, In Script, Clear, 1 Qt.	7.00
Fruit Jar, Genuine Mason, Aqua, 1 Pt.	15.00
Fruit Jar, Globe, Cover, Amber	50.00
Fruit Jar, Good House Keepers, R In Circle, Clear, 1/2 Pt.	25.00
Fruit Jar, Grandma Wheaton's Old Fashioned Receipts Canning Jar, Green, 1 Pt.	10.00
Fruit Jar, Harvest Mason, Clear, 1 Qt.	15.00
Fruit Jar, Hazel HA Preserve Jar, Clear, 1 Pt.	15.00
Fruit Jar, Hero Improved, Aqua, 1 Qt.	55.00
Fruit Jar, Hollieanna Mason, Clear, 1 Qt.	12.00
Fruit Jar, Honest Mason Jar, Pat. 1858, Clear, 1 Pt.	25.00
Fruit Jar, Improved Gem Made In Canada, Clear, 1 Pt.	5.00
Fruit Jar, Improved King, Clear, 1 Pt.	22.00
Fruit Jar, Improved KO Queen, Widemouth Adjustable, Clear, 1 Qt.	30.00
Fruit Jar, Jay B. Rhodes, Kalamazoo, Mich., Clear, 1 Qt.	25.00
Fruit Jar, Jos Middleby, Jr. Inc., Vertically On Jar, Gray Tint, 1/2 Gal.	18.00
Fruit Jar, Jumbo Apple Butter, Clear, 7 Oz.	12.00
Fruit Jar, Kerr Self–Sealing, Widemouth, Clear, 1/2 Gal.	4.00
Fruit Jar, Lafayette, Profile, Aqua, 1 Qt.	650.00
Fruit Jar, Lightning Clover, English & Chinese Script, San Francisco, 1 Pt.	11.00
Fruit Jar, Mason's Keystone Improved, Aqua	25.00
Fruit Jar, Mason's, Patent Nov. 30th, 1858, Reverse Hero Cross, Aqua	25.00
Fruit Jar, Mason's, Shield, Union, Aqua, 1/2 Gal.	450.00
Fruit Jar, Schram Automatic Sealer, 1 Qt.	8.00
Fruit Jar, Smalley Queen, Glass Lid, 1 Qt.	7.50
Fruit Jar, Trademark Lightning, Dark Smoky Green, 1/2 Gal.	1000.00
Fruit Jar, Wears, In Drape Below Crown Plate, Clear, 1 Pt.	18.00
Fruit Jar, Whitney Mason, Pat. Mason 1858, 1 Dot, Aqua, 1 Qt.	12.00
Gin, J. J. Peters, Hamburg, Light Amber	65.00
Gin, Ruby Sloe, Lady's Leg, Amber	20.00
Hamm's Bear, Tag By Ceramarte, 1972	45.00
Horlick's Malted Milk, Racine, Wis., Light Blue, 1/2 Pt.	15.00
Household, Bakers Extra Strong Bluing, Green, 6 1/2 In.	10.00
Household, Machine Oil, Larkin Soap Company Products, 4 In.	8.00
Household, Stove Polish, Vulcanol	12.00
Ink, 3–Mold, Ring Design, c.1840	2860.00
Ink, Amber, Puce Tinges, Round Burst Top	100.00
Ink, Billings Mauve Ink, Aqua	20.00
Ink, Blue Glass, Cork Stopper, Pair	45.00
Ink, Boat, Deep Cobalt Blue	39.00
Ink, Brass, Domed, 2 Handles, Squatty, c.1850	1540.00
Ink, Estes Metropolitan, Master	3850.00
Ink, Gross & Robinson, American, Writing Fluid, Aqua, Master, 1/2 Gal.	1850.00
Ink, Harrison's Columbian, 12 Sides, Aqua	1750.00
Ink, Harrison's Columbian, Cobalt Blue	2200.00
Ink, Harrison's Columbian, Stoneware, Handle, Master	743.00
Ink, Stoneware, Cork Stopper, Miniature	5.00
Ink, Teakettle, Amethyst	2350.00
Ink, Teakettle, Clear, Green & White Swirl, Hinged Brass Cap	2200.00
Ink, Teakettle, Dense Olive Green, 8 Convex Panels Base, 1830–1860	1350.00
Ink, Teakettle, Green & White Swirls, Hinged Brass Cap, 1830s	2000.00
Ink, Traveling, Wooden, 2 In.	20.00
Ink, Umbrella, Blue	2090.00
Ink, Umbrella, Emerald Green, Open Pontil	85.00
Ink, Waterman, Figural, Screw Metal Cap, 8 x 13 In.	110.00
Ink, Waterman, Filler, Bullet Shape, Wooden, Traveling, Partial Label	45.00

Jar, Aines California Cottage Cheese, Emblem, 12 Oz. 15.00
Jar, Angel City Cheese Co., Superior Brand Dairy Prod., Emblem, 8 Oz. 15.00
Jar, Canning, Pottery, Wax Seal, 6 3/4 In. 45.00
Jar, Dakota Candy, Geometric Colors, 3 Footed, 17 x 8 In. 247.00
Jar, Edwards Pickle, Label, 7 Oz. 65.00
Jar, Embossed Pepper, In Block Label, Milk Glass, 1/2 Pt. 6.00
Jar, Free Blown, Pontil, Rolled Lip, Clear, 1840 .... 14.00
Jar, Gibford's Pure Honey Apiaries, Riverside Calif., Red, 8 Oz. 30.00
Jar, Peerless Oil, Bail, Double Lid, Dated 1914 .... 35.00
Jar, Petal, Bright Yellow–Green, 1/2 Gal. 2200.00
Jumbo Peanut Butter, Elephant Head, 7 1/2 In. 40.00
Lionstone, Blacksmith, Decanter 60.00
McCormick, Decanter, Elvis Presley, Musical, No. 1, With Gold Record List 145.00
McCormick, George Washington Carver 50.00
McCormick, Louis Armstrong 85.00
Medicine, Brain Food, John H. Allen, Chemist, Red Wax Seal 50.00
Medicine, Dr. A. Boschee's German Syrup, 7 In. 7.00
Medicine, Dr. D. J. Whelan, Hutchinson, Blue, c.1880, 6 3/4 In. 6875.00
Medicine, Dr. Jayne's Expectorant, Embossed, Cork Top, Aqua 2.80
Medicine, Dr. Moore's Essence of Life, Aqua, Open Pontil, Flared Lip, 3 1/2 In. 25.00
Medicine, Dr. Phelps, Arcanum, Genuine, Red Amber, Hexagonal, 8 In. 13300.00
Medicine, Dr. Pierce's Favorite Prescription, Aqua, 8 1/2 In. 10.00
Medicine, Dr. Snyder's Death On Worms, Open Pontil 75.00
Medicine, Gargling Oil, Lockport, N.Y., Dark Green, Rectangular, 7 1/2 In. 20.00
Medicine, Holcomb's Blood Purifier, Troy, N.Y., Blue–Green, 9 1/2 In. 175.00
Medicine, Johnson & Johnson, Amber, Square, Pat. 1896, 4 x 7 In. 52.00
Medicine, Purifier, Micklejohn N. O., Olive Green, c.1850, 6 1/2 In. 9625.00
Medicine, Rushton & Aspiwall, Chlorine Tooth Wash, Amber, c.1840, 5 7/8 In. 4400.00
Medicine, Scott's Emulsion With Lime & Soda, 9 1/4 In. 5.00
Medicine, Seminole Indian Medicine Co., Boone, Iowa, Light Amethyst, 8 1/2 In. ... 40.00
Medicine, Tonsiline, Embossed Giraffe 25.00
Medicine, U.S. Marine Hospital Service, 75 Cc. 12.50
Medicine, Warner's Safe Kidney & Liver Cure, Amber, 9 1/2 In. 25.00
Milk, Baby Face, Brookfield, 1/2 Pt. 75.00
Milk, Big Elm Dairy Company, Green, 1 Pt. 188.00
Milk, Borden, Embossed, 1 Qt. 7.25
Milk, Capitol Dairy Co., Chicago, Clear, 1/2 Pt. 40.00
Milk, Cedar Grove Dairy, Memphis, Tenn., Inserted Slug Plate, ISP, Round, 1 Qt. ... 12.50
Milk, Chateaugay Dairy, Blue Pyro, Rectangular, 1/2 Gal. 6.00
Milk, College View Dairy, Northfield, Vt., Horse & Rider, Maroon, Square, 1 Pt. 10.00
Milk, Concord Dairy, Round, 1/2 Pt. 6.50
Milk, Creamer, Purity, Red Oval, Round, 1/2 Oz. 20.00
Milk, Curles Neck Dairy, Baby Face 35.00
Milk, Double Baby Face, 1 Qt. 59.00
Milk, Eureka Dairy, Amethyst, Inserted Slug Plate, Churn Shape, 1 Pt. 20.00
Milk, Excelsior, 50th Anniversary, Blue, Orange Circle, 1915–1965, Square, 1 Qt. 15.00
Milk, Gold Medal, Crown City, Award Ribbon, 1/3 Qt. 20.00
Milk, Golden Arrow, California, Orange Plastic Handle, Square, 1 Gal. 30.00
Milk, Golden Royal Dairy, Amber, 1/2 Gal. 5.00
Milk, Home Dairy, Phoenix Arizona, Shield, With Cow, Orange Pyro, 1/2 Pt. 25.00
Milk, Jersey Farm, 1/2 Pt. 7.50
Milk, Meadow Gold Silver Seal, Embossed, 1 Qt. 5.00
Milk, Metzgers, Baby Face, Embossed, 1 Qt. 75.00
Milk, Midwest Dairy, Cow Head On Side, 1/2 Pt. 2.35
Milk, Miller Dairy, Ione, Calif., Red Pyro, Round, 1 Qt. 30.00
Milk, People's Milk Co., Amber, Inserted Slug Plate, Round, 1 Qt. 60.00
Milk, Portland Damascus Milk Co., Amethyst, Inserted Slug Plate, Round, 1/4 Pt. ... 15.00
Milk, R. Bedford Dairy Co., Brooklyn, N.Y., Tin Top, Bowling Pin, 1 Qt. 100.00
Milk, Reno Model Dairy Inc., 14 Neck Ribs, Inserted Slug Plate, Round, 1/4 Pt. 40.00
Milk, San Bernardino Creamery, Crown Top, Inserted Slug Plate, Round, 1 Pt. 10.00
Milk, Shamrock Dairy, Phone 2542, Cream Top, Inserted Slug Plate, Round, 1 Qt. ... 15.00
Milk, Simple Simon Met A Milkman Going To The Fair, 1950s, 1 Qt. 28.00
Milk, Smalley, Tin Cover, 1890s, 1/2 Gal. 115.00

Milk, Snow's Frame, Conn., Rimmed Neck 12.00
Milk, Somerset Farms Dairy, Middlebush, N. J., Beige, Amber, Square, 1 Qt. 12.00
Milk, Sun Valley Dairy, Highland Park, Ill., Green, Yellow Pyro, 1/2 Gal. 20.00
Milk, Thatcher's Dairy, Embossed Man Milking Cow 250.00
Milk, Thatcher's Dairy, Wire Bail, Porcelain Stopper, 1884, Reproduction, 1 Qt. 6.50
Milk, Universal, 5 Cent, Embossed, 1/2 Pt. 5.00
Milk, Valley Gold, Albuquerque, N. M., Orange In Blue Shield, Square, 1 Qt. 12.00
Milk, Wagner Bros. Dairy, Anacortes, Wash., ISP, Embossed, Round, 1 Qt. 17.50
Milk, Whatcom County Dairymen's Association, Metal Cap, 1 Qt. 25.00
Milk, Windmill Brand Dairy Products, Minden, Nev., Red, Square, 1/2 Pt. 15.00
Mineral Water, Crawford, Hartford, Conn., Mug Base, Brilliant Blue, Graphite 385.00
Mineral Water, E. Roussel's Superior, Philadelphia, Deep Emerald Green 145.00
Mineral Water, Koldrok, Spring Water, Ceramic Lightning Stopper 60.00
Mineral Water, Peerless, Martin & Cherry, New York, Aqua, 1873 .... 20.00
Mineral Water, S. Smith, Auburn, N.Y., Sapphire Blue, Tenpin 345.00
Mineral Water, Sharon Sulfur Water 315.00
Mineral Water, Warwick Tonic Spring, Newark, N. J., Golden Amber, 1 Pt. 605.00
Miniature, Jug, Crown Distilleries, Amber, Cylinder, 5 3/4 In. 20.00
Miniature, Jug, Duffy Malt Whiskey Company, Rochester, N.Y., Amber, 4 In. 25.00
Miniature, Jug, Flanders, Compliments, Tan, Handle, 3 In. 70.00
Miniature, Jug, J. Riegaer & Co., Kansas City, Mo., Clear, 4 1/2 In. 15.00
Nurser, Afro American Insurance Co., Jacksonville, 6 1/2 In. 75.00
Nurser, Avondale Milk, Hygeia Screw Top, Oz. & Cc. Graduations 15.00
Nurser, B & B 7.00
Nurser, Empire, Embossed, Tilted Neck 20.00
Nurser, Golden Arrow, Oz. & Ml. Graduations, Orange, 6 Sides 30.00
Nurser, Good Health For Baby, Taxston Dairy, Red 15.00
Nurser, National Baby's Formula Service, Chicago, Oz. Graduations, Orange Pyro ... 40.00
Oil, Yellow–Green, Long Neck, Bulbous, 9 7/8 In. 15.00
Perfume bottles are listed in their own category
Pickle WauWautosa 145.00
Pickle, Cathedral, Aqua, 1 Pt. 4.00
Pickle, Cathedral, Clear, 13 1/2 In. 75.00
Pickle, E. Gager Manufacturer, Norwalk, Ohio, Aqua, Applied Lip 45.00
Pickle, Goofus, Golden Yellow, Amber Tones, Gardenia Blossoms, 9 3/8 In. 200.00
Pickle, Wine Cured Pickles, In Frame, Clear, 1 Qt. 15.00
Poison, Amber, 3 Sides, Automatic Bottle Machine, Label, 5 In. 15.00
Poison, Amber, Embossed, 4 In. 19.00
Poison, Cobalt Blue, Quilted, Embossed, 3 In. 45.00
Poison, Cobalt Blue, Sharp Pointed Stopper, 4 1/2 In. 60.00
Poison, National Disinfectant, Estey Curtis, Contradictory Paper Label 12.75
Poison, Skull & Crossbones, Amber, Embossed 20.00
Poison, Skull, Cobalt Blue, 2 7/8 In. 935.00
Poison, Tincture of Iodine, Skull & Crossbones, Antidote Formula 9.75
Poison, Vapo Cresolene Co., Aqua, Labels, 5 1/2 In. 35.00
Saki, Green, Blue Glass, Marble Inside, Stopper, Mid–1800s, Japan 36.00
Saki, Green, Marble Stopper To Measure Pouring, Japan, 1900s, 8 In. 28.00
Sarsaparilla, RRR Radway's Sarsaparilla Resolvent, 1860 .... 20.00
Sarsaparilla, Yagers Sarsaparilla, Amber, Label 95.00
Seltzer, Kramers, Atlantic City, New Jersey, Green 19.00
Snuff, 5 Panels, Men, Trees, Scenic, Mountains, Ivory, 4 1/2 In. 190.00
Snuff, Agate, Flattened Rectangular, Mushroom Color, Horse & Bird, China 660.00
Snuff, Agate, Pale Gray, 3 Monkey On Branch, Coral Stopper, Bulbous, China 1045.00
Snuff, Clock Face & Hands On Black & White Disc, Polychrome Porcelain 2800.00
Snuff, Cranberry & Ruby Horses, Double Overlay 3600.00
Snuff, Double, Passion Flower Design 4200.00
Snuff, E. Roome Troy, Olive Amber, Open Bubble, Open Pontil 125.00
Snuff, Figural, Carved Frog & Lizard, Amber, 3 In. 605.00
Snuff, J. J. Mapes, New York, Olive Amber, 4 In. 900.00
Snuff, Jade Green, Lip Top, Scenic View In Lid, 6 In. 75.00
Snuff, Landscape Scene, Blossoms On Reverse, Yixing Slip, Flattened, Coral Stopper 1320.00
Snuff, Moss Agate, Varied Inclusions, 2 1/4 In. 330.00
Snuff, Painted Garden Scene, Man In Boat, Artist, 1875 .... 375.00

Snuff, Painted Interior, Pheasant On Log, Valley & Stream, China, 2 In. 145.00
Snuff, Peking Glass, Yellow, 19th Century, 2 1/2 In. 2970.00
Snuff, Reverse Painted, Jade Top, Peking Glass 250.00
Snuff, Shadow Agate, Standing Duck In Silhouette, 2 1/4 In. 1760.00
Snuff, Wide Beveled Edges, Square, 1820s, 3 3/4 In. 385.00
Snuff, Wooden, Filigree, Stones Around Top & Lid, Late 1800s 175.00
Soda, 7–Up, Anchorage Green, Woman In Bathing Suit 17.00
Soda, C. B. Owens, Cobalt Blue 200.00
Soda, Carpenter & Cobb Knickerbocker, Saratoga Springs, 10 Sides, Blue 335.00
Soda, Chattanooga Glass Co., Anniversary, 1901–1951, Green 45.00
Soda, Chocolate Soldier, Applied Color 8.00
Soda, Christian Schlepegrell, Charleston, South Carolina, Green, Iron Pontil 60.00
Soda, Clawson's Birch Beer, Paper Label 50.00
Soda, Coppahunk, Embossed Indian, Evergreen Trees, Aqua 35.00
Soda, Donald Duck, Applied Color 8.00
Soda, Dr Pepper, Desert Storm, Contents, 1991, 12 Oz. 15.00
Soda, Dr. Belding's Wild Cherry Sarsaparilla, Aqua 65.00
Soda, Dr. Brown, Deep Blue–Green, Iron Pontil, Squatty 89.00
Soda, Essex Root Beer Extract, Box 50.00
Soda, F. Gooseman & Co., Aqua, Paneled 125.00
Soda, Ira Harvey, Tee–Pee 3630.00
Soda, Jeff's Beverage, Applied Color 4.50
Soda, Pacific Soda Works, Portland Oregon 50.00
Soda, Pep–Up, Green, Big Boy Beverages, 8 In. ....*Illus* 11.00
Soda, Portland, Eagle, Blue Aqua, Hutchinson, 6 3/8 In. 35.00
Soda, Root Beer, Aqua Blob Top, 1 Qt. 20.00
Soda, S. J. Esten, Light Green 18.00
Soda, Schweppes Tonic Water, Clear, England 5.00
Soda, Torpedo, Aqua, Blob Top 7.50
Soda, W. Wilke & Co., Aqua, Paneled 125.00
Traveling, Woman's, Silver Tone Covers, England, 1920s 215.00
Wheaton, Eagleton 25.00
Wheaton, F. D. Roosevelt 25.00
Wheaton, J. F. Kennedy 25.00
Wheaton, Jean Harlow 8.00
Wheaton, McGovern 25.00
Whiskey, Atlantic Distilling Co., Sweet Corn Mash, Jug 95.00
Whiskey, Bottled For Clinch & Co., Bubbles, Clear, 11 1/8 In. 665.00
Whiskey, Chestnut Grove, C & W, Handle, Amber 165.00
Whiskey, Crown Distilleries, Crown & Shield, Dark Amber, 11 3/4 In. 20.00

Bottle, Soda, Pep-Up, Green,
Big Boy Beverages, 8 In.

Bottle, Whiskey, Old Cabinet Rye,
Dark Amber, 10 In.

◆ ◆ ◆ ◆ ◆ ◆ ◆ ◆ ◆ ◆ ◆ ◆ ◆ ◆ ◆

To make a quick "photo" of your old bottle, try using a photocopy machine. Put the bottle on the machine, then cover it with white paper or cloth to block out extra light. Lower the cover gently, and take the picture.

◆ ◆ ◆ ◆ ◆ ◆ ◆ ◆ ◆ ◆ ◆ ◆ ◆ ◆ ◆

Whiskey, Davy Crockett Pure Old Bourbon, Amber, 11 7/8 In. 40.00
Whiskey, Duffy Malt Whiskey, Amber, 10 1/2 In. 8.00
Whiskey, E. G. Booz, Paper Label, Amber, 4/5 Qt. 10.00
Whiskey, F. Chevalier & Co., San Francisco, Amber, 4 Mold, 11 7/8 In. 60.00
Whiskey, Glenmore, Jug, Stoneware 18.00
Whiskey, Goldberg Distiller, Amber, 8 Sides, Cylindrical 25.00
Whiskey, H. F. & B. N.Y., Seal, Puce, Melon Shape, Ribbed 975.00
Whiskey, H. L. Nye Bourbon, Inside Threads, San Francisco, Dark Amber, 11 In. ... 20.00
Whiskey, Hawkins Rye, In Circle On Shoulder, 1 Qt. 15.00
Whiskey, I. W. Harper, Amber, Paul Jones Shape, 9 1/2 In. 15.00
Whiskey, J. H. Cutter, Old Bourbon, No. 1 On Back, Amber, 11 7/8 In. 40.00
Whiskey, Jas. Durkin Wines & Liquors, Spokane, Wash., Amber, 11 5/8 In. 20.00
Whiskey, Jesse Moore & Co., Louisville, Ky., Amber, 11 5/8 In. 15.00
Whiskey, Lediards Morning Call 500.00
Whiskey, Licking Valley, Not In The Trust, Cylinder, Clear 15.00
Whiskey, Louis Hunter Pure Rye, Seattle, Wash., Amber, 11 In. 25.00
Whiskey, Louis Taussig & Co., San Francisco, Calif., Smoky Clear, Bubbles, 11 In. 15.00
Whiskey, Old Cabinet Rye, Dark Amber, 10 In. ....*Illus* 25.00
Whiskey, Old Pepper, Jas. E. Pepper & Co., Amber, In Wicker, 5 In. 75.00
Whiskey, Perrine's Pure Barley Malt, Philadelphia, Amber, Triangular Slug Plate 20.00
Whiskey, Pine Tree Cordial, Medium Olive Yellow, 7 In. 225.00
Whiskey, Quaquina Creme De Cafe Coffee Liqueur, Jug, Ceramic, Amber, Miniature 10.00
Whiskey, Remington Liquor Co., Just Right, Light Amber, Swirled Shoulders, 12 In. 65.00
Whiskey, Richardson Brunsing Co., San Francisco, Calif., Amber, 11 1/8 In. 25.00
Whiskey, Rothschild Bros., Philadelphia, 1868, Applied Seal, Orange Amber, Squatty 68.00
Whiskey, Schenley's Old Velvet Rye, Flask, Prohibition, Cork, 1916 .... 15.00
Whiskey, W. J. Van Schuyver & Co., Portland, Ore., Amber, 10 1/4 In., 1 Qt. 12.00
Whiskey, Wright & Taylor Distillers, Louisville, Ky., Amber, 1 Qt. 7.50
Whiskey, Wright & Taylor, Amber, Applied Mouth, 1 Qt. 25.00
Whiskey, Yellowstone, Case 4350.00
Wild Turkey, Gold Miner 450.00
Wild Turkey, No. 1, 1971 .... 165.00
Wild Turkey, No. 6, 1977 .... 35.00
Wild Turkey, No. 7 .... 20.00
Wine, Farue, On Seal, Blown, Olive Green 55.00
Wine, Hock, Dark Amber, Embossed 35.00
Wine, Korean Yi Dynasty, Porcelain, Red Underglaze 2310.00
Wine, Mallet, Bulbous, Black, Dated 1754 .... 1980.00
Wine, Riesling German Wine Cellars, Label, Amber 20.00
Wine, Sol. Bear Native Wines, Wilmington, N. C., Embossed Bear, Holding Grapes 18.00
Wine, Stoneware, Blue & White, Floral, 1880, 14 In. 245.00

BOXES of all kinds are collected. They were made of thin strips of inlaid
wood, metal, tortoiseshell, embroidery, or other material. Additional boxes
may be listed in other sections, such as Advertising, Battersea, Ivory,
Shaker, Tinware, and various Porcelain categories. Tea Caddies are listed
in their own category.

American Eagle Small Arms Ammunition, Wooden 10.00
Apple, Pine, Primitive, 11 1/4 x 12 1/4 In. 132.00
Ballot, Iron Strap Locks, Old Red Paint 68.00
Ballot, Primitive, Slide Top, Red Paint, 10 1/4 x 4 In. 204.00
Band, Wallpaper Covered, America, Oval, 1820, 12 1/2 x 16 1/2 In. 605.00
Bentwood, 1-Finger Base & Lid, Red, Orange, 4 5/8 In. 145.00
Bentwood, 1-Finger Lid, Blue-Gray Paint, 7 In. 195.00
Bentwood, Clown & German Inscription On Cover, Oblong, 6 3/4 In. 225.00
Bentwood, Copper Tack Construction, Round, Green Paint, Yellow Varnish, 4 In. ... 175.00
Bentwood, Cover, Bale Handle, 5 1/2 In. 148.00
Bentwood, Harvard Type, Oval, Varnish Finish, 3 5/8 In. 71.00
Bentwood, Oblong, Spring Latch Cover, Wood-Burned Design, 10 1/4 In. 192.00
Bentwood, Oval, Brownish Finish, 6 1/4 x 9 1/4 In. 44.00
Bentwood, Oval, Carrier, Cover, Handle, Laced Seams, 8 x 12 1/4 In. 380.00
Bentwood, Pine, Green Paint, Oval, Laced Seams, 15 1/4 In. 225.00
Bentwood, Pine, Hardwood, Worn Patina, Laced Seams, Oblong, 16 In. 75.00

Box, Book Shape, Green, Cupid On Cover,

c.1880, 2 3/4 In.

Box, Book Shape, Brown, c.1880, 3 1/2 In.

♦ ♦ ♦ ♦ ♦ ♦ ♦ ♦ ♦ ♦ ♦ ♦ ♦ ♦ ♦ ♦ ♦ ♦ ♦ ♦

If the metal top on your salt-shaker won't unscrew, try this: Turn the saltshaker upside down in a small bowl of white vinegar. Let it soak for about 12 hours. The cap should then be loose. Rub soap on the inside of the cap to keep it from sticking again.

♦ ♦ ♦ ♦ ♦ ♦ ♦ ♦ ♦ ♦ ♦ ♦ ♦ ♦ ♦ ♦ ♦ ♦ ♦ ♦

Bentwood, Pine, Orange Paint, Stylized Floral, Laced Seams, 13 1/4 In.	880.00
Bentwood, Pine, Round, Original Orange Paint, Stylized Design, 6 1/2 In.	250.00
Bentwood, Red Repaint, Floral Band On Cover, 6 In.	214.00
Bentwood, Red, Black Graining, Stenciled Design, Round, 11 3/4 In.	258.00
Bentwood, Round, 2 Birds On Cover, 5 3/4 In.	35.00
Bentwood, Round, Cover, Orange Paint, Wooden Handle, Wire Bale, 6 3/4 In.	375.00
Bentwood, Round, Cover, Wire Bale Handle, Bluish Gray Paint, 11 1/2 In.	66.00
Bentwood, Round, Green Paint, 6 1/2 In.	203.00
Bentwood, Round, Original Dark Green Paint, 6 7/8 In.	115.00
Bentwood, Round, Red Paint, 8 In.	236.00
Bentwood, Round, Red Paint, Black Trim, Stenciled Gold Design, 6 1/2 In.	35.00
Bentwood, Round, Red, 8 3/4 x 4 1/4 In.	380.00
Bentwood, Round, Swivel Handle, 7 1/2 x 5 1/4 In.	355.00
Bentwood, Round, Wire Bale Handle, 6 3/4 In.	247.00
Bentwood, Storage, Round, Brown Patina, 6 1/4 In.	137.00
Bentwood, Stylized Floral Wallpaper Covering, Off–White Ground, Oval, 9 In.	225.00
Bible, Mahogany, Bracket Feet, Dovetailed Case, Strap Hinges, 7 In.	1025.00
Bible, Oak, Carved, 19th Century, 9 x 29 x 16 In.	135.00
Bible, Oak, Dark Finish, Geometric Design, Iron Lock, 17 3/4 In.	605.00
Bible, Oak, Dark Finish, Relief Carved Design, Iron Hinges, Lock, 24 In.	800.00
Bible, Oak, Hinged Slant Front, Pigeon Holes, England, 1600s, 13 x 24 x 18 In.	250.00
Bible, Oak, Stand, 18th Century, 27 In.	300.00
Bible, Softwood, Green, Red, Orange, Iron Strap Hinges & Lock, 10 x 17 x 22 In.	137.00
Bilston, Floral Enameled Sides & Interior Lid, 19th Century, 2 3/4 x 1 x 1 1/2 In.	275.00
Birch Bark, Varnished, Hinge, 3 3/4 x 1 3/4 x 1 1/4 In.	110.00
Book Shape, Brown, c.1880, 3 1/2 In. ....*Illus*	55.00
Book Shape, Green, Cupid On Cover, c.1880, 2 3/4 In. ....*Illus*	50.00
Brass Inlay, Oval, Soapstone, 2 3/8 x 3 1/8 In.	33.00
Bride's, Bentwood, Oval, Couple In Park, German Inscription, 19 1/2 In.	1100.00
Bride's, Bentwood, Oval, Pine, Polychrome Paint, Floral Design, Blue, 20 1/2 In.	1300.00
Bride's, Bentwood, Pine, Floral, Red Ground, German Inscription, Oval, 20 In.	990.00
Bride's, Pine, Floral Design, Black Ground, Scene of Couple Holding Hands, 19 In.	2310.00
Bride's, Pine, Light Blue Paint, Polychrome Floral Design, 15 In.	302.00
Bride's, Pine, Original Paint, Buildings, House, Trees, White Ground, 16 In.	220.00
Burl, Russian Karelian, Imperial Eagle On Lid, 2 In.	75.00
Burnt Wood, Dutch Girl, With Buckets, Goat Carts, Geese, 7 x 5 x 2 In.	26.00
Button & Cuff Link, Adamatine	55.00
Candle, Chippendale, Pierced Heart Over Lid, Gumwood, 18 1/4 In.	1045.00
Candle, Dovetailed, Carved Compass Design In Lid, Painted, 14 1/4 In.	550.00
Candle, Dovetailed, Sliding Lid, Mahogany, Pine Bottom, 9 3/4 In.	247.00
Candle, Hanging, Gumwood	1045.00
Candle, Pine & Poplar, Sliding Lid, 3 Finger Holes, Painted, 19 1/4 In.	180.00
Candle, Pine, Blue Paint, Floral, Pennsylvania, 11 In.	900.00
Candle, Pine, Primitive, Wall Mounted, Red–Washed Finials, Green Paint	330.00
Candle, Pine, Sliding Lid, Orange Paint, 13 3/4 In.	93.00
Candle, Pine, Sliding Lid, Original Red Paint, Black, White, Striping, 14 In.	220.00

Candle, Plain, 18th Century, With Beeswax Candles, Large 495.00
Candle, Sheet Iron 450.00
Candle, Sliding Lid, Original Brown Graining, 14 In. 110.00
Candle, Sliding Lid, Pine, Floral Decoration, 19th Century, 4 3/8 x 9 7/8 x 5 In. ... 500.00
Candle, Sliding Lid, Unpainted, Early Nails, 9 3/8 x 5 7/8 x 5 7/8 In. 180.00
Candle, Sliding Molded Lid, Painted Blue, 6 1/2 x 15 1/2 In. 275.00
Candle, Tin, Footed 495.00
Candy, Die Cut, Cardboard, Blue & Green, Scrap Design, Early 20th Century 35.00
Cash, National, Trolley, Brass & Glass 85.00
Cherry, Sliding Lid, Dovetailed, 9 In. 182.00
Chip Carved, Circles & Stars, Black Ground, Bail Handle, 19 1/2 x 8 1/4 In. 1650.00
Chip Carved, Heart & Hand Design, Small 275.00
Chip Carved, Pine, Wall, Pinwheel Design, Pencil Inscription 715.00
Coin, 4 Velvet–Lined Drawers, Mahogany, Custom Made 225.00
Coquelle Nut, Carved Turk's Head 400.00
Curly Maple, 14 1/2 In. 330.00
Cut–Out Base, Molded Cotter Pin Hinged Lid, Red Paint, 1840s, 9 x 15 1/2 In. 825.00
Cutlery, Dark Green Paint, Lockable Drawer, W. Penna., 19th Century 1295.00
Cutlery, George III, England, Mahogany, c.1790, Pair 3950.00
Cutlery, Pumpkin Interior, Red Exterior, Painted, 19th Century, 5 x 14 7/8 In. 420.00
Decoupage Design, Black, White Engravings, Yellowed Varnish, 12 1/2 In. 165.00
Deed, Yellow Paint, Ohio 165.00
Desk, Georgian, Mahogany, Hinged Slant Top, 19th Century, 7 1/2 x 17 x 14 In. ... 120.00
Desk, Oak, Dovetailed, England, 20 3/4 In. 93.00
Document, Black Paint, Gold Striping, Floral Lid, 19th Century, 11 1/2 In. 115.00
Document, Dovetailed Pine, 6 Boards, Original Red–Brown Finish, Miniature 120.00
Document, Ezra Prescot, Registrar of Deeds, 1827–1840, 5 1/2 x 12 1/2 In. 350.00
Document, Leather, Brass Studded, England, 1830, 6 x 7 3/4 x 14 In. 165.00
Document, Original Paint, Norway, Dated 1882 .... 645.00
Document, Pigskin, Red & Gilt, Chinese, 19th Century, 16 In. 192.50
Document, Punched Leather, 8 In. 300.00
Document, Stand, Scalloped Square Hinged Top, Lacquered Gilt Figures, 16 In. 440.00
Document, William & Mary, Oak, Hinged Cover, Floral, 1700s, 7 x 17 x 11 In. 220.00
Dome Top, Beech, Original Blue Paint, Floral Design, Birds, White, Red, 18 3/4 In. 192.00
Dome Top, Brown Japanning, White Band, Swags & Floral, 10 In. 412.00
Dome Top, Cover, Brass Bale Handle, Lock, Hinges, 15 In. 82.00
Dome Top, Decoupage Flowers, Wooden, 5 In. 30.00
Dome Top, Dovetailed, Black Paint, With Lock, 12 3/4 In. 165.00
Dome Top, Freely Brushed Black Striping & Swirls, Dovetailed, 28 In. 475.00
Dome Top, Pine & Poplar, Smoke Grained Yellow Paint, Iron Lock & Hasp, 24 In. .. 605.00
Dome Top, Pine, Dovetailed, Old Red Graining, 15 In. 110.00
Dome Top, Pine, Poplar, Black Paint, Gold Stenciled Over Red, 15 In. 110.00
Dome Top, Poplar, Black Graining, Red Ground, Iron Locks, 28 In. 630.00
Dome Top, Rosewood, Brass Stripe Inlay, Oval, 3 3/4 x 5 1/2 In. 104.00
Dome Top, Tooled Leather Cover, Iron Lock, Hasp, Handle, 13 In. 55.00
Dough, Cover, Poplar, Country, 27 In. 247.00
Dough, Dovetailed Wood, Free Standing, Large 785.00
Dough, Hepplewhite, Poplar, Worn Red Paint, Striping, Country, 18 x 38 x 30 In. ... 575.00
Dough, Poplar, Splay–Turned Legs 250.00
Duck Caviar, M. S. Kuznetsov, Russia 175.00
Enameled Brass, Ebonized, Egyptian Revival Trim, 8 In. 115.00
Fan, Papier–Mache, Tortoiseshell, With 3 Fans 990.00
Federal, Domed Lid, Twin Carrying Handles, Pine, 10 x 23 1/2 In. 330.00
Glove, Russian, Ivory Paint, Tooled Steel Fittings, 8 1/2 In. 95.00
Gun, Victorian, Brass Handle & Corners, Brass Stand, Fruitwood, 19 1/2 x 36 In. ... 660.00
Hanging, Pine, Poplar, Original Red Paint, Black, White Striping, 15 1/2 In. 2805.00
Hanging, Simulated Oak Paint Design, Dovetailed, Welsh, 1750–1760 .... 695.00
Hardwood Veneer, Pine, Hunters, Man–Eating Dragon On Cover, 12 In. 170.00
Hardwood, Dark Finish, Carved, Paw Feet, 13 3/4 In. 181.00
Hat, Bent Laminated Wood, Lid & Leather Strap, Painted Label, 12 x 16 1/4 In. 65.00
Hat, Cockade & Shako, Tin, Pair 180.00
Hat, Dome Top, Grain Painted, Stenciled, c.1835, 7 x 11 5/8 In. 385.00
Hat, Gray, Blue & White Floral Design, Hand Sewn, 13 3/4 x 10 x 12 In. 245.00

Hat, Lion Hat Co., Red Leaping Lion Picture 15.00
Hat, Military, Tin, Brown Japanning, Brass Label, 15 In. 99.00
Helmschmied Swirl Mold, Frosted Glass, Flowers, Enameled, Hinged, 3 In. 195.00
Hepplewhite, Mahogany, Inlaid, 1 Drawer, Lift Top, England, 15 x 11 3/4 x 27 In. 633.00
Hepplewhite, Walnut, Inlay On Drawer Front, 1 Drawer, Dovetailed Case, 12 In. ... 412.00
High Explosives, Wooden, Hinged Top, Dovetailed Corners 23.00
Index Card, Oak, Double, Brass Hardware 42.00
Instrument, Tin, Black Paint, With Slide Rule & Gravity Bulb, 19th Century 99.00
Jewelry, Brass, Silver Plate Traces, Amethyst Jeweled Cover, 6 3/4 In. 55.00
Jewelry, Case, Block Front, 3 Drawers, Porcelain Pulls, Rosewood, 10 x 12 In. 715.00
Jewelry, Ebony Inlay, Brass Handles, Silk Lined, France, c.1860, 14 1/8 x 9 7/8 In. 2800.00
Jewelry, Marquetry Inlaid, Painted, 8 x 11 1/2 x 7 1/2 In. 330.00
Jewelry, Napoleon III, Gilt Bronze, 19th Century, 7 In. 495.00
Jewelry, Table Shape, Walnut, Turtle-Back Top, Adrienne, 8 3/4 x 12 3/4 In. 225.00
Jewelry, Walnut, Slant Front, Drawers, 19th Century, 12 x 10 3/4 In. 355.00
Knife, Georgian, Mahogany, England, c.1790, 14 1/2 x 8 1/2 In., Pair 3000.00
Knife, Inlaid Eagle & Knife Design 3200.00
Knife, Mahogany, Ebony Line Veneer, Light Wood Inlay, England, 14 1/4 In., Pair 1800.00
Knife, Pine, Dovetailed, Salmon & Brown Paint, 13 In. 115.00
Knife, Pine, Primitive, Worn Black Paint, 10 1/4 x 14 In. 115.00
Knife, Soft Wood, Red, Green Paint, 13 In. 385.00
Knife, Walnut, 1 Drawer, Dovetailed, Pennsylvania 247.00
Lap-Top, Tulips & Pomegranates, A. Bucher, Initials ICH, 8 1/2 x 10 In. 2900.00
Leather, Brass Lock & Hasp, Brass Stud Trim, 12 In. 38.50
Letter, Dish Compartments, Crystal Inkwells, Holder, Walnut, 13 x 8 1/2 In. 190.00
Letter, Oak, 4 Parallel Sections, Leather Covered Bottom, Gustav Stickley, 7 In. 522.50
Lithograph, Jamaica Plains Picture On Cover, Blue-Lined, Moore's, Boston 160.00
Mahogany Veneer, Pine, Maple, Walnut, Inlaid, Ivory Escutcheon, 12 In. 95.00
Mahogany, Ivory Inlay, 8 1/4 In. 27.00
Missionary Collection, Lithographed, Pair 105.00
Open-Fan Shape, 3 Tiers, Gilt Lacquered, Figure, River, 1700s, Japan, 7 1/2 In. 5100.00
Pantry, Blue Paint, Basket of Flowers Cover, 7 1/4 In. 125.00
Pantry, Mustard Paint, 19th Century, 6 3/4 In. 220.00
Patch, Cartier, Hand Painted Courting Scene, Happy Birthday, Blue Enamel 185.00
Pencil, Roll-Up Cover, Wooden, Japan 12.00
Pin, Cat In Baby Bed, Polychrome Enamel, Porcelain, 6 In. 49.00
Pin, Child With Bootjack, Polychrome & Gilt, Porcelain, 4 3/4 In. 60.00
Pine, Dovetailed, Sliding Lid, Worn Blue Green, 7 1/4 In. 225.00
Pine, Green Paint, Cove Molded Base, 2-Section Till, 18 In. 137.00
Pine, Original Black Paint, Orange Striping, 12 3/4 In. 110.00
Pine, Original Brown Stain, Yellow Striping, 16 3/4 In. 302.00
Pine, Original Red Paint, Black & Yellow Striping, 5 3/4 In. 132.00
Pine, Poplar, Brown Finish, Gold Stenciled Design, 10 In. 412.00
Pine, Poplar, Sliding Lid, 8 In. 49.00
Pine, Red, Black Paint, Wire Nail Construction, 13 1/4 In. 35.00
Pipe, Arched Floral Crest, 2 Short Drawers, Painted Gray, 20 In. 2420.00
Pipe, Cresting Centered By Flower Head, Inscribed BB &1723, 12 1/2 In. 1980.00
Pipe, Mahogany, Base Drawer Broken, 19 3/4 In. 1705.00
Pipe, Maple, Scalloped, 1 Drawer, Old Red Paint, New England, 15 1/2 In. 743.00
Pipe, Pine, Arched Top, Tapered Sides, Heart-Pierced Front, 13 3/4 In. 1600.00
Pipe, Pine, Brown Patina, 1 Dovetailed Drawer, Cutout Top Edge, 20 1/2 In. 990.00
Pipe, Recessed Heart & Pierced C Scrolling, 2 Short Drawers, 20 In. 4400.00
Poplar, 1 Drawer, Original Yellow Paint, Black, Olive, Striping, 16 In. 1650.00
Poplar, Brown Flame Graining, Gold Striping, Polychrome Floral Design, 18 1/2 In. 550.00
Poplar, Crest, Brown Varnish, Interior Cast Wax Classical Head, 5 In. 39.00
Poplar, Dovetailed, Sliding Lid, 32 In. 60.00
Poplar, Original Reddish Brown Graining, Iron Lock, 25 In. 203.00
Poplar, Red, Leather Strap Handle, 14 1/4 In. 49.00
Red Velvet Lining, Bird, Foliage, 12 In. 104.00
Salt, Hanging, Lovebirds 225.00
Salt, Hanging, Pine & Poplar, Long Narrow Crest, 35 In. 130.00
Salt, Walnut, 1896 .... 40.00
Sapphire Glass, Gold Floral, White Outlined, Hinged Cover, 4 1/2 x 4 In. 145.00

Scouring, Bentwood Crest, Pine, Worn Patina, 4 3/4 x 18 1/2 In. 135.00
Seashell, Silver Gilt Fittings, 2 3/8 In. 38.00
Shaving, Mahogany, Interior Mirror, England, c.1880 .... 121.00
Sliding Lid, 1 Piece of Pine, 7 In. 148.00
Sliding Lid, Allover Blue–Green Stipple, Bucks County 1100.00
Spanish American War Decoupage, Interior Drawers, 7 3/4 x 8 In. 715.00
Spice, 1 Piece Walnut, Primitive, 8 Sections, Each Has Sliding Lid, Small 375.00
Spice, 6 Drawers, Pyramid–Shape, Mid 19th Century 1095.00
Spice, Bentwood, 7 Matching Interior Canisters, Dark Finish, 8 In. 220.00
Spice, Hanging, Poplar, Dovetailed Case, Divided Interior, Hinged Lid, 12 1/2 In. ... 770.00
Spice, Sliding Lid, 4 Sections, Dovetailed, Cherry, 9 In. 110.00
Spice, Tin, 8 Drawers, 13 3/4 In. 220.00
Spruce Gum, Cross–Hatched 145.00
Storage, Bentwood, Round, Blue Paint, 6 1/2 In. 55.00
Storage, Bentwood, Round, Dark Green Paint, 9 1/2 In. 192.00
Storage, Bentwood, Round, White Repaint, 6 In. 148.00
Storage, Carved, Inlaid, Painted Canoe Applied To Lid, 15 x 6 x 4 In. 110.00
Storage, Sponged Red On Ochre, Miniature 3300.00
Straw, Prisoner of War, Floral, Scenes, Mirror Lid, 1790, 11 x 7 3/4 In. 1270.00
Strong, Bullion Shipping, Wells Fargo 2500.00
Strong, Hinged Coffered Top, Simulated Iron Strapwork, Sweden, 1709, 11 1/2 In. 2300.00
Strong, Iron Mounted, Ring Handles, Hinged Top, Sweden, Dated 1905, 15 1/4 In. ⟩ 1760.00
Strong, Painted Ships, Figures, Country Landscape, Europe, 1680s, 18 x 27 In. 2200.00
Tea, Tin, Lithograph Paper Design, Japan, 23 x 17 x 19 1/2 In. 121.00
Theorem, Hinged Lid, Compartments, Floral, Black Ground, 9 3/4 x 6 1/2 In. 2200.00
Till, Cotter Pin Hinged Lid, Polychrome Paint, New England, 5 x 9 11/16 In. 2200.00
Till, Lift Top, Green Paint, 11 x 11 1/2 x 22 1/2 In. 153.00
Tin, Faux Black Marble, Enameled, Metal Pug On Top, Glass Insert, Square, 2 In. ... 95.00
Tobacco, Engraved Scenes, Farming, Angels, Naked Woman, Canopy Bed, 6 In. 675.00
Tobacco, Oval, Family Life Scenes, Inscribed, Holland, 18th Century, 5 x 2 1/2 In. · 440.00
Tooled Brass, Carved Panels In Lid & 4 Sides, Green Bead Feet, 5 3/4 In. 40.00
Traveling, Cover, Oval, Handles, Brass, 10 1/2 x 13 In. 65.00
Trinket, Dome Top, Pine, Stained Red, America, 5 x 9 In. 66.00
Turtle Top, Jewel–Like Floral Design, Black Enameled, 6 1/2 In. 350.00
Utility, Graduated, Bentwood Pine, Tacks, Painted, Round, 18 1/2 In. Stack, 6 Piece 1100.00
Utility, Graduated, Bentwood Pine, Tacks, Painted, Round, 6 Ft. Stack, 12 Piece 3850.00
Utility, Lift Top, Pine, 6 Boards, Painted Design, America, 35 x 44 x 24 In. 385.00
Utility, Pine, Lace & Floral Design, Blue Ground, Initials M. W., 12 1/8 x 6 In. 1760.00
Utility, Pine, Painted St. Stephen's Park Scene, Yellows, Browns, 5 3/4 x 12 3/4 In. 2090.00
Wall, Original Blue Paint, 19th Century, 17 1/2 x 10 1/2 In. 1100.00
Wall, Painted Design, Double–Arch Top 3600.00
Wall, Pine, Dark Red Brown, Dovetailed Back, 16 In. 325.00
Wallpaper Cover, Leaves, Off–White Ground, 1839 Newspaper Lined, 7 3/4 In. 275.00
Wallpaper, Blue, Leaping Stag & Dog Scene, 17 In. 1800.00
Wallpaper, Horse Pulling Wagon Scene, National Road, Oval, 8 In. 825.00
Walnut Veneer, Fruitwood Star Inlaid, Bird's–Eye Maple Interior, 4 x 10 x 8 In. 352.00
Wooden, Shoe Shape, 19th Century, 4 x 5 In. 176.00
Work, Hinged Lid & Front Panel, Sandalwood Interior, Etched Ivory, 10 1/4 In. 2090.00
Writing, Curly Maple, Walnut Trim, Fitted Interior, 9 1/2 x 15 1/2 In. 82.50
Writing, Dark Wood Veneer, Pewter & Nacre Floral Inlaid, Fitted, 13 3/4 In. 148.00
Writing, Ebony Inlaid, Brass, Fitted Rosewood Interior, France, 10 x 12 1/2 In. 247.00
Writing, Mahogany, Fitted Interior, Brass End Handles, 20 3/8 In. 275.00
Writing, Slanted Lift Top, Jacobean, Carved Rondels On Sides, Oak, 9 x 13 In. 220.00
Writing, Walnut, Brass Bound, Victorian, 17 1/2 x 9 1/2 In. 305.00

BOY SCOUT collectibles include any material related to scouting, including
patches, manuals, and uniforms. The Boy Scout movement in the United
States started in 1910. The first Jamboree was held in 1937. Girl Scout
items are listed under their own heading.

Bank, Figural, Cast Iron, A. C. Williams 105.00
Binoculars, Brass 25.00
Book, Boy Scouts of America, Illustrated 10.00
Book, Boy Scouts of The Air–Lone Stone Patrol 12.00

Book, Boy Scouts Requirements, 1966	3.00
Booklet, Envelope, Colorful, 1921	12.50
Bugle, Embossed, Original Box	165.00
Calendar Top, Boy Scouts, The Right Way, N. Rockwell, 16 1/2 x 21 In.	22.00
Canteen, 1930s	15.00
Catalog, Official Scouting Equipment Catalog, Nov. 1921, 36 Pages, 8 x 10 1/2 In.	75.00
Compass, Bakelite, Taylor, Scout Picture Box, 1930s	40.00
Compass, Taylor, Case, 1930s	60.00
Field Glasses, Brass Trim	45.00
Game, Game of Boy Scouts, Milton Bradley	385.00
Handbook, 1940	10.00
Handbook, 1963	15.00
Hatchet, Steel Handle, True Temper	15.00
Knife, Fairmont Cutlery	20.00
Knife, Pocket, Imperial, 1950s	55.00
Knife, Pocket, Ulster, Box	45.00
Knife, Remington, Fixed Blade, Sheath, 1920s	125.00
Match Safe, Nickel Plated, Cylinder	20.00
Neckerchief, National Jamboree, 1935	125.00
Pin, Official Boy Scout, 1st Class, With Knot, 1917	550.00
Sign, Advertising, Boy Scouts Bicycles, Cycle Trades of America, 10 1/2 x 14 In.	6.50
Signal Set, Twin S. O. S., Box, 1948	45.00
Sun Watch, Patent 1921, Directions	75.00
Tie Rack, Sirocco	50.00

BRADLEY & HUBBARD is a name found on many metal objects. Walter Hubbard and his brother–in–law, Nathaniel Lyman Bradley, started making cast iron clocks, tables, frames, andirons, lamps, chandeliers, sconces, and sewing birds in 1854 in Meriden, Connecticut. The company became Bradley & Hubbard Manufacturing Company in 1875. Charles Parker Company bought the firm in 1940. Their lamps are especially prized by collectors.

Andirons, Dolphin Form, Head At Base, Gilt Brass	1540.00
Andirons, Dolphin, 1850s, 14 In.	425.00
Andirons, Griffins, Snake Feet, 1910, 23 In. ....*Illus*	770.00
Andirons, Sunburst, Figural, Iron, 17 In.	385.00
Blotter & Letter Holder, 2 Piece	50.00
Bookends, Embossed Scotty, Paper Label	75.00
Box, Brush, Slag Glass Inserts	45.00
Candlestick, Triangle Mark	65.00
Inkstand, Two Pointed Glass Wells	75.00
Inkwell, Art Deco, Gold Rim, Hinged Cover, 10 Panels, 5 x 4 3/4 In.	110.00
Inkwell, Attached Pen Tray	55.00
Lamp, Bamboo Trees On Domed Shade, Green Ground, 18 In. Diam.	1100.00
Lamp, Brass, Embossed Base, Glass Shade, Electric Adapter	85.00
Lamp, Floor, Reverse Painted Shade, Bronze	550.00
Lamp, Green Aladdin Shade, 20 In.	375.00
Lamp, Kerosene, Art Nouveau, Pat. 1895	65.00
Lamp, Oil, Onyx Base, c.1880, 37 In.	440.00
Lamp, Rose Paneled Shade, 18 In.	3000.00
Lamp, Store, Pull Down, Brass, Hanging, Smoke Bell, Milk Glass Shade	260.00
Lamp, Table, Dome Shade, 6 Bent Panels, Floral Designs, 24 In.	825.00
Lamp, Table, Leaded Shade, 20 In.	165.00
Lamp, Table, Scroll Base, Yellow Etched Globe	135.00
Stand, Smoking, Brass & Iron	125.00
Teapot, Burner, Stand, Brass, Ornate	150.00

BRASS has been used for decorative pieces and useful tablewares since ancient times. It is an alloy of copper, zinc, and other metals. Additional brass items may be found under Bell, Candlestick, Tool, or Trivet.

Ashtray, Art Deco, Terrier, Bronzed	24.00
Basket, Woven, Porcelain Plaque, Mask & Ring Handles, Oval	198.00
Bed Warmer, Engraved Rooster, Cherry Handle, 44 1/2 In.	440.00

Bed Warmer, Man Smoking Pipe, Hammered Tulips Cover, 18th Century, 44 In. 275.00
Bed Warmer, Raised Ship Design, 1880s, 43 1/2 In. 55.00
Bed Warmer, Tooled Lid With Flowers and Peacock, Wooden Handle, 43 In. 357.00
Bed Warmer, Turned Walnut Handle, Lid Pierced, Engraved Floral Design, 44 In. 300.00
Bookrack, Shakespeare Design, Expandable 59.00
Bowl, Chippendale Scroll Rim, 9 1/2 In. 60.00
Bowl, Square, Incurving Sides, Tapering Or Round, Hammered Finish, 2 3/8 In. 550.00
Box, Jewelry, Gilded, Triangular, Clear Glass Sides & Lid, 10 In. 126.00
Box, Tobacco, Hinged Lid, Colonial Man, 18th Century, 6 1/2 x 3 1/2 In. 660.00
Box, Tobacco, Hunter Shooting Gun, Hinged Lid, 18th Century, 2 3/4 x 2 1/4 In. 190.00
Box, Tobacco, Saxon, Satyr, Eagles, Cavalry On Lid, 19th Century, 6 x 2 In. 330.00
Bucket, Spun, Iron Bale Handle, 9 3/4 x 6 1/2 In. 75.00
Bust, Man, Head Dropped Forward, Hagenauer, 30 In. 3500.00
Bust, Woman, Bands Forming Hair, Hagenauer, 28 3/4 In. 7010.00
Candleholder, Scissor Arm, Wall Mount, 2 3/4 In., Pair 330.00
Candlesnuffer, Stagecoach 35.00
Chamber Stick, Deep Saucer Base, Push-Up, Cast Handle, 5 1/2 In. 150.00
Chamber Stick, Oval Pan, Push-Up, 4 1/2 In. 93.00
Clip, Memo, Frog, Marked, 5 1/4 In. 65.00
Clip, Memo, Owl, 4 1/4 In. 55.00
Coffeepot, Baluster, Scroll Handle, 19th Century, 9 1/2 In. 55.00
Colander, Copper, England, Late 18th Century, 10-In. Diam. 385.00
Compass, Drawing, Eagle, Embossed 3.25
Compote, England, 1820, 10 x 12 3/4 In. 357.00
Cuspidor, Arcade Freeport, Illinois, 7 1/2 In. 250.00
Door Knocker, Eagle, 1830-1840 .... 185.00
Door Pull, Lion, Figural, 4 In. 30.00
Doorbell, Zodiac, 1880s, Large 45.00
Dresser Set, Gilded, Filigree, Rose-Colored Stones, Tray, Mirror, Brush & Perfume 220.00
Figurine, Goat, Standing, Late 19th Century 395.00
Flask, Pistol, Zinc, Relief Design, 1860 .... 45.00
Footman, England, c.1780, 13 x 12 In. 335.00
Girandole, Shape of Basket of Flowers, 17 In. 127.00
Handle, Door, Art Nouveau, Brass, Pair 220.00
Hunting Horn, Steer's Horn, Mid-19th Century 495.00
Incense Ball, Cut-Out Bird & Branch Design 60.00
Jardiniere, In Tripod Stand, Curving Members Ending Ball Finials, Footed, 37 In. 88.00
Jardiniere, Paw Footed, Oval, 9 1/2 x 12 x 6 1/2 In. 148.00
Kettle, Bail Handle, Copper Rivets, 11 In. 70.00
Kettle, Iron Bail Handle, 7 1/4 In. 75.00
Kettle, Iron Bail Handle, American Brass Kettle, Toronto Ohio, 8 3/4 x 12 1/2 In. 35.00
Kettle, Reticulated Top, 7 x 14 x 13 1/2 In. 38.00
Kettle, Wire Bail Handle, Hayden's Pat., 16 3/4 x 11 In. 55.00
Lamp, Bird Finial & Decoration, Domed Shade & Base, Ball Feet, 17 1/2 In. 6135.00
Lock, Box, Keeper, 4 1/4 x 8 In. 375.00
Measure, Victorian, Baluster, England, Mid-19th Century, 5 x 6 In. 137.50

◆ ◆

Small nicks and scratches in iron can be covered with black crayon. Wipe off the excess with paper.

◆ ◆

Bradley & Hubbard, Andirons, Griffins,
Snake Feet, 1910, 23 In.

Mirror, Hand, Winged Cupid On Handle, Victorian, 12 In.	40.00
Padlock, Winchester, Key	100.00
Pan, Jelly, Iron Handle, 9 x 12 In.	70.00
Plaque, Cottage In Woods, Etched, Motto, George Rutledge, 7 1/2 x 6 In.	121.00
Rattle, 2–Piece Top, Wooden Handle, 9 In.	60.00
Samovar, Russia, 19th Century, 14 In.	55.00
Samovar, Teapot, Sugar, Waste Bowl, 2 Trays, Russia, 1898	900.00
Sconce, Candle, Cherub Figure, Ribbon Detail, 21 1/2 x 11 1/2 In., Pair	520.00
Sconce, Candle, Mirrored, 19th Century, 19 x 11 In., Pair	450.00
Sconce, Mirrored, 24 In., Pair	358.00
Scoop, Coffee, Ornate Blue Enameled Handle, Chinese	24.00
Scoop, Ornate Graniteware Handle, Embossed	20.00
Skimmer, Inlaid Heart In Handle, Iron, 9 1/8 In.	467.00
Spoon, Caddy, Imp & Ship, Pair	22.00
Tankard, Shaped Handle, Dome Lid, England, 8 In.	203.00
Tazza, Incised Concentric Design, Spain, 12 3/4 In.	880.00
Teakettle, England, c.1800, 13 1/2 In.	412.00
Teakettle, Engraved, Copper Trim, Chinese, 6 1/2 In.	66.00
Teakettle, Peter Behrens, Ebonized Wooden Finial, Handle, c.1908, 8 1/4 In.	880.00
Teapot, Hammered, Stylized Wheat Sheaves, Rattan Handle, W. M. F., 15 1/4 In.	137.00
Tether, Horse, Dark Patina, 12 1/2 In.	159.00
Tray, 3 Peacocks, Handle, 8 x 24 In.	55.00
Tray, Applied Lobster, Fish & Shells, 10 x 6 In.	60.00
Tray, Beaded Rim, Oval, 8 3/4 In.	38.00
Tray, Maiden's Profile, Nickel Plated, J. Von Schwarz, 18 In.	975.00
Tray, Pin, Art Nouveau, 13 1/4 In.	50.00
Tray, Tooled, 19 3/4 In.	22.00
Vase, Bulbous Base, Flared, Harry Dixon, 5 x 3 1/2 In.	165.00
Vase, Church, Bell & Cross, 3 Handles, Mission Inn, 7 3/4 x 5 3/4 In.	77.00
Vase, Hammered, Cupped Rim, From Shell Casing, Dirk Van Erp, 10 x 4 1/2 In.	1320.00
Vase, Ye Olde Cooper Shoppe, Jauchens, 17 x 7 1/2 In.	275.00
Water Spigot, Figural, Quail	150.00
Watering Can, Polished, England, 12 In.	195.00
Whistle, Victory Songbird, Original Box	28.00

BRASTOFF, see Sascha Brastoff category

BREAD PLATE, see various silver categories, porcelain factories, and pressed glass patterns

BRIDE'S BASKETS OR BRIDE'S BOWLS were usually one–of–a–kind novelties made in American and European glass factories. They were especially popular about 1880 when the decorated basket was often given as a wedding gift. Cut glass baskets were popular after 1890. All bride's baskets lost favor about 1905.

BRIDE'S BASKET, Amber, Enameled Flowers, Fluted, No Stand	150.00
Blue, Gold Plated Holder	825.00
Butterscotch, Gold Mica Cased, Crimped, Fluted, Tufts Silver Plated Holder	245.00
Child's, Roses On Feet, Ruffled Insert, Etched Florals, Tufts	250.00
Dark Cranberry, Enameled, 1 Large Cupid Frame	475.00
Light Blue Glass, Hand Painted, Silver Plated Holder, Handle	395.00
Opal Glass, Polychrome Blossoms, Applied Amber Leaves, Fruits, 11 In.	660.00
Opalescent Cranberry, Pink Ruffled	125.00
Pink Cased, Victorian, Tufts Silver Plated Holder	335.00
Pink To Rose, White Interior, Rope Handles, Oval	900.00
Rose, Birds & Flowers, Ornate Silver Frame With Deer, Notched	350.00
Squirrel, Birds, Silver Plated	45.00
Tortoiseshell, Blue Flowers, Silver Holder, Bird On Top	350.00
BRIDE'S BOWL, Aqua, Pink Interior, 3 Cupids Base, 12 In. ....*Illus*	3100.00
Blue Overlay, Satin Glass, Ruffled, 5 x 10 1/8 In.	245.00
Cream, Yellow Overlay Interior, Brass Ormolu Frame, 9 1/2 In.	235.00
Herringbone Mother-of-Pearl, Meriden Gold Plated Base	1900.00
Hobnail, Cranberry Opalescent, Silver Holder	300.00
Hobnail, Frosted Rubina, Silver Stand, Hobbs	600.00

Pink Overlay, Cream Daisy Type Flowers, Blue Dots, 3 3/8 x 11 3/8 In. 195.00
Pink Overlay, Scalloped, Daisies, 3 3/8 x 11 1/4 In. 175.00
Pink Overlay, Silver Plated Foot, 9 1/2 x 10 In. 295.00
Pink To Lighter Base, Ruffled, Pleated, 7 7/8 In. 115.00
Pink To Rose Interior, Fluted, 10 In. 225.00

BRISTOL glass was made in Bristol, England, after the 1700s. The Bristol
glass most often seen today is a Victorian, lightweight opaque glass that is
often blue. Some of the glass was decorated with enamels.

Biscuit Jar, Allover Enameled, Daisies, Leaves, Brass Rim & Handle, 7 In. 175.00
Bottle, Barber, Ivorene, Sprays of Flowers 75.00
Bottle, Blue, White & Gold Design, 7 In. ....*Illus* 65.00
Charger, St. Bernard, Hand Painted 38.00
Figurine, 2 Cats In Basket, May 11, 1875, 7 1/2 In. 215.00
Figurine, Man Holding Pot, Woman With Basket, c.1775, 4 5/8 In., Pair 6600.00
Jam Jar, Lusterless White, Plated Frame, Handle 65.00
Vase, Bedovin Warrior & Horse, 14 In. 50.00
Vase, Hand Painted Roses, Gold Beading, Scalloped, Frosted White, 8 In., Pair 80.00
Vase, Victorian, Ruffled Top, Enameled Scene, Flowers, Bird, 10 1/2 In. 95.00
Vase, Winter Scenes, Cottages On Front, 13 1/2 In., Pair 225.00

BRITANNIA, see Pewter category

Bride's Bowl, Aqua, Pink Interior,
3 Cupids Base, 12 In.

♦ ♦

If the liquid in a snow dome
gets cloudy or has partially
evaporated, it is very difficult
to replace it. Snow domes with
black plastic bases or brown
pottery bases made in the
1930s and 1940s can be
opened and repaired. The
dome is held by plaster of
paris that can be carefully
chipped away. Domes with
new shiny black plastic bases,
black pottery bases (1940s)
or cobalt blue bases (1920s)
cannot be opened unless they
are one of the few screw-type
examples.

♦ ♦

Bristol, Bottle, Blue, White & Gold
Design, 7 In.

Bronze, Figurine, Bonheur, Cat, With Ball, 4 1/4 In.

To hang copper molds in your kitchen, try this method: Mount a solid brass or wooden curtain rod across the top of the hanging area. Molds can then be hung with hooks over the rod and easily moved when new ones are added.

BRONZE is an alloy of copper, tin, and other metals. It is used to make figurines, lamps, and other decorative objects.

Bowl, Rim Design, Hammered, Craftsman, 16 1/2 x 4 In.	126.00
Box, Woman Cutting Grain, Scythe, Round, Israel, 5 3/4 In.	55.00
Bust, Army Officer, Square Base, c.1918, 13 In.	835.00
Bust, Gruber, Maiden, Art Nouveau, 1900, 5 1/8 In.	1320.00
Bust, Mercury, Messenger of Gods, Winged Helmet, Socle Base, 1880, 10 In.	550.00
Bust, Robert E. Lee, Marble Base, Signed, 9 In.	990.00
Bust, Young Woman, Rouge Marble Pedestal Base, Signed, 19th Century, 20 In.	935.00
Cauldron Gong, Stand, Japanese, Bronze, 1890s, 24 x 15 1/2 In.	2310.00
Desk Set, Jennings Bros., 4 Piece	289.00
Figurine, A. Du Paysage, Traveler On Horseback, Brown Patina, 21 3/4 In.	2090.00
Figurine, A. Dubucand, Hunting Dog, With Pheasant	2090.00
Figurine, Anna D. Hyatt, Cougar On Tree Trunk, 6 In.	1540.00
Figurine, Arnold, Nude Woman, Standing, Holding Scarf, Signed, 25 1/2 In.	990.00
Figurine, Avril, Woman, 2 Lights On Grapevine, 22 In.	295.00
Figurine, B. Bochetti, Marc Anthony, Marble Pedestal, 6 Ft. 1/2 In.	4125.00
Figurine, Barrias, Nature Revealing Herself Before Science	6600.00
Figurine, Barye, Maiden, With Sickle, Art Nouveau, 1896, 23 In.	1475.00
Figurine, Barye, Stag & Doe, Signed	1920.00
Figurine, Barye, Standing Elephant, 8 1/2 In.	1540.00
Figurine, Bennett, Dance	1500.00
Figurine, Bennett, Reflections '82	3200.00
Figurine, Berke, Bear Claw, 1968, 4 1/2 x 3 In.	88.00
Figurine, Bologna, Mercury, Black Stone Base, 35 In.	825.00
Figurine, Bonheur, Cat, With Ball, 4 1/4 In. ....*Illus*	800.00
Figurine, Bulldog, England, 10 1/2 x 7 In.	225.00
Figurine, Claude Colinet, Nude Dancer, Marble Base, 28 7/8 In.	4180.00
Figurine, Clodian, 3 Children, Oval Marble Base, 11 x 11 In.	3500.00
Figurine, Coustou, Horse, Rearing, Man With Sword, 22 x 19 In.	550.00
Figurine, Dana, Boy By Gaslight, 11 5/8 In.	485.00
Figurine, De Lotto, Young Boy, Marble Pedestal, 6 Ft.	5500.00
Figurine, De Tirtoff, Acrobat, Erte, 1980, 15 In.	4400.00
Figurine, De Tirtoff, Firebird, Erte, 1980, 16 1/2 In.	2420.00
Figurine, De Tirtoff, Liberte, Flaming Torch In Hand, 1984, 28 3/8 In.	3850.00
Figurine, Degas Dancer, Base Marked, 7 3/4 In.	71.00
Figurine, Derujinsky, Danseur Adolphe Bohm	2750.00
Figurine, Diana Potter, Dancers, Marble Base, 9 x 19 In.	247.00
Figurine, E. Aizelin, Chastity, Brown Patina, 33 In.	3850.00

Figurine, E. Aizelin, Young Woman, Black Marble Sockle, 16 1/2 In. 770.00
Figurine, Eagle, Shield In Talons, Spread Wings, America, 19 In. 550.00
Figurine, Edouard Drouot, Indian, Brown Patina, 37 In. 2750.00
Figurine, Edris Eckhardt, Unicorn 750.00
Figurine, Elephant, Standing On Ball, Portland Yacht Club Regatta 550.00
Figurine, Elsa Martnus, Boy, Towel Around Waist, 44 In. 4950.00
Figurine, Emile E. Peynot, Young Arab Soldier, Signed, 1883, 26 In. 7150.00
Figurine, Emile Picault, Carolingian Warrior 4125.00
Figurine, English Bulldog, 1 3/4 x 1 1/2 In. 98.00
Figurine, F. Barbedienne, Reclining Classical Woman, 19th Century, 16 x 22 In. 825.00
Figurine, F. Pautrot, Pheasant, 13 In. 550.00
Figurine, Ferdinand Pautrot, Bird On Leafy Perch, c.1870, 7 1/2 In. 695.00
Figurine, Ferdinand Preiss, Aphrodite, Ivory, 8 1/2 In. 2725.00
Figurine, Ferdinand Preiss, Awakening, Carved Black Marble Plinth, 14 In. 2750.00
Figurine, Ferdinand Preiss, Golfer, Ivory, 8 In. 5450.00
Figurine, Ferdinand Preiss, Moth Girl, Ivory, 15 3/4 In. 6620.00
Figurine, Ferdinand Preiss, Oriental Waiter, Ivory, Onyx Base, 6 1/2 In. 975.00
Figurine, Ferdinand Preiss, Our Lady, Ivory Head & Limbs, 11 1/2 In. 2860.00
Figurine, Ferdinand Preiss, Torch Dancer, Ivory, Onyx Plinth, 15 1/4 In. 6815.00
Figurine, Fisher Boy, Holding Rod, Signed, Japan, 16 1/4 In. 605.00
Figurine, Franz Bergman, Arab, Waving Rifle, Rearing Horse, 5 x 4 In. 1000.00
Figurine, Fumiere, Woman, Draped In Robes, c.1850, 7 In. 545.00
Figurine, Girl, Descending Stairs, 7 3/4 In. 104.00
Figurine, Girl, Holding Kitten, Red Marble Base, Signed, 38 In. 8000.00
Figurine, Gladiator, Marble Base, 9 1/2 In. 440.00
Figurine, Goetze, Allegorical Figure, Black–Brown Patina, 32 In. 2310.00
Figurine, Gori, Dancing Girl, Marblehead, Body & Foot, Flowing Dress, 37 In. 5205.00
Figurine, Greek Discus Thrower, 10 In. 247.00
Figurine, Greek Wrestler, 8 1/2 In. 357.00
Figurine, Guiraud–Riviere, Soccer Player, Kicking Ball, Marble Base, 1925, 14 In. ... 2750.00
Figurine, H. Moreau, Chante Des Alouettes, 30 In. 3850.00
Figurine, Hagenauer, Jesus, Wooden Body, Bronze Hands, Head & Feet, 10 In. 685.00
Figurine, Horse, 3 Vultures, Green Patina, 11 In. 275.00
Figurine, Horse, Citation, On Stand, To Calumet Farm By Hialeah Race Course 3200.00
Figurine, Horse, Rearing, Flatly Modeled, Impressed Mark, 13 In. 1870.00
Figurine, I. Bonheur, Mare & Her Foal, 19 1/2 In. 5775.00
Figurine, Iffland, Young Boy, Hands In Pockets, Marble Base, 5 In. 30.00
Figurine, Indian, Dying Horse, Green Patina, 14 1/2 In. 368.00
Figurine, J. De Bologne, Rape of A Sabine, Marble Base, 15 In. 4675.00
Figurine, J. P. Mene, 2 Stallions 1750.00
Figurine, Kauba, Indian Chief On Horse, 1900, 21 In. 2000.00
Figurine, Kossowski, Vide Poche, Reclining Nude, Outspread Arms, 10 1/8 In. 1320.00
Figurine, L. Kottot, Napoleon, Fitted As Lamp, France, 28 In. 1650.00
Figurine, Lion, Sitting, 1920s, 3 Ft., Pair 15000.00
Figurine, Little Girl, Wearing Kimono. c.1890, 8 1/2 In. 395.00
Figurine, Lorenzl, Ballerina, Ivory Head, 1910–1930, 10 7/8 In. 1430.00
Figurine, Lucas Madrassi, Hussar Soldier 2750.00
Figurine, Martel, Accordion Player, Cubist, 11 1/2 In. 2750.00
Figurine, Mathias Schumacher, Die Sturzende, 1964, 22 1/2 In. 1870.00
Figurine, Mathurin Moreau, Allegorical Figure, Golden Patina, 27 1/2 In. 3025.00
Figurine, Mathurin Moreau, Aurora, Stepped Base, 32 In. 4675.00
Figurine, Maurice Bouval, Nude Woman, Marble Base 2200.00
Figurine, Moigniez, Stork 3355.00
Figurine, Mother & Child, Old Gilt Finish, Signed, 27 1/4 In. 1000.00
Figurine, Mountain Man, Cowboy On Horseback, 27 In. 625.00
Figurine, Nude Maiden, Flowing Drape, Marble Base, Signed, 15 1/2 In. 3715.00
Figurine, Nude Woman, Lying On Stomach, Flowing Hair, Reflection '82, 36 x 9 In. ... 3200.00
Figurine, Oliveri, Sleeping Naiad, Reclining In A Open Sea Shell, 18 In. 2200.00
Figurine, Oriental With Staff, Dark Patina, 5 3/4 In. 65.00
Figurine, Ouline, Stalking Panther, Black Marble Base, 1930, 11 3/4 x 28 1/4 In. 1980.00
Figurine, Phillip Martiny, Nude Woman, 46 3/4 In. 3850.00
Figurine, Pierre Tourgueneff, Hunter With Bow & Arrow, Marble Base, 9 In. 1650.00
Figurine, R. Gurbe, Nude Maiden, Sitting, Flowing Drape, Marble Base, 15 In. 3715.00

Figurine, R. Peyre, Maiden, Flowing Hair, Parcel Gilt, 1900, 13 In. 2200.00
Figurine, Rattlesnake, Cowboy On Horseback and Snake, 23 In. 400.00
Figurine, S. Clerc, Seated Woman, Head On Hand, Black Marble Base, 12 In. 880.00
Figurine, Sailor, Splicing Piece of Rope, Handle, 11 1/2 x 12 In. 3100.00
Figurine, Samurai Horseman, 14th Century, 24 In. 8000.00
Figurine, Samurai Warrior 395.00
Figurine, Schott, Ivory Maiden, Rolling Ball, White Onyx Base, 1900, 13 1/2 In. 2750.00
Figurine, Shiva, Seated, Oriental, 19th Century, 5 In. 495.00
Figurine, Simon, Gentleman's Bust, Marble Base, 9 In. 440.00
Figurine, St. George Slaying The Dragon, Russia, 20 In. 2200.00
Figurine, Vidal, Lion, 1874, France, 28 In. 550.00
Figurine, W. Kumm, Roman Hero, Standing, Hand To Pyre, Signed, 20 In. 220.00
Figurine, Waif, Whistling, 16 In. 193.00
Figurine, Winged Victory, Mounted On Marble Base, 26 In. 385.00
Figurine, Woman Dancer On 1 Foot, Marble Base, Signed, 15 In. 1500.00
Figurine, Woman, Arms Outstretched, Ivory Hands & Face, France, 9 3/4 In. 1210.00
Figurine, Woman, Walking Against The Wind, Marble Dish, Austria, 1900, 8 In. 2640.00
Figurine, Young Woman With Umbrella, Signed, 30 In. 1650.00
Figurine, Young Woman, Art Nouveau, 11 In. 250.00
Figurine, Zack, Young Ivory Maiden, On Steed, 1900, Austria, 16 1/2 In. 6600.00
Fountain, D'Orsi, Young Boy, With Basket, Almost Life Size 9500.00
Frame, Photograph, Enameled, Riband Crest, France, 5 x 7 In. 550.00
Garniture, Neo–Classic Style, Black, Starr & Frost, 3 Piece 1300.00
Group, C. L. Pandiani, Barmaid's Craft, 1889, 11 x 17 In. 1430.00
Group, Jean Gutter, Monkey Jockey On Horseback, 5 3/8 In. 990.00
Group, Juan Clara, Little Girl With Puppy, c.1920, 10 1/2 In. 1045.00
Group, Lambert–Rucki, 2 Sleepwalkers, 29 5/8 In. 6600.00
Group, Pandiani, Storyteller, 27 x 15 In. 1540.00
Group, Sandoz, Terrier Seated With A Bee On Its Raised Paw, 6 In. 825.00
Group, Zack, Dancing Couple, 16 1/8 In. 1100.00
Incense Burner, Foo Dog, 1820s 295.00
Jar, Cloisonne Bands, 11 3/4 In. 25.00
Jar, Incense, Cloisonne Band, Oriental, 5 3/8 In. 85.00
Lamp, Figural, P. Higual, Maiden Holding Stem, Lily Shade, 1900, 13 1/2 In. 1320.00
Letter Stand, 3 Tiers, Form of Bouquet of Blossoms, c.1870, 10 In. 145.00
Libation Cup, Cupid & Satyr, Stemmed, 2 Handles 375.00
Mask, Japan, 8 In. 247.00
Mirror, Table, Stylized Female Figure, Framed Oval, Art Nouveau 1210.00
Plaque, Figures & Inscription, Marked P. H. 1940, Oak Frame, 22 In. 110.00
Plaque, Roosevelt, Fraser, 1920 .... 250.00
Plate, Gilded, Red Enameled Cast Rim, 8 1/4 In. 110.00
Rooster, Polychrome Paint, 4 1/8 In. 429.00
Tray, A. Cain, Chanticleer Rooster, On Grape Harvest Basket, 7 x 9 In. 275.00
Tray, Pin, Intaglio Design, Urns, Foliage, 3 1/8 x 8 1/8 In. 5.50
Urn, Cherub Handle, Relief Cast Classical Scene Around Body, 21 In. 385.00
Urn, Empire Style, Gilt, Sienna Marble Base, 9 In., Pair 305.00
Urn, Raised Figure of Greek Warrior, Maiden On Reverse, Bronze, 16 In., Pair 1980.00
Vase, Dragons, Birds, Etc. In High Relief, 9 1/2 In., Pair 130.00
Vase, Flared, Handles On Neck, Mythological Beast, Japan, 12 1/2 In., Pair 352.00
Vase, Gilded Fittings, Red Marble Base, Ormolu Trim, 14 In. 93.00
Wick Holder, Korschann, Art Nouveau Maiden Mask, 1900, 4 5/8 In. 550.00

BROWNIES were first drawn in 1883 by Palmer Cox. They are
characterized by large round eyes, downturned mouths, and skinny legs.
Toys, books, dinnerware, and other objects were made with the Brownies
as part of the design.

Blocks, Puzzle Cubes, Create 6 Scenes, McLoughlin, 1891 .... 852.00
Camera, Box, Palmer Cox 65.00
Candy Container, Popping Out of Shell, Red Shirt, Palmer Cox, 4 In. 225.00
Candy Dish, Turned–Over Sides, 15 Brownies, Script Forget-Me–Not, Silver Plate ... 195.00
Cartoon, St. Nicholas, Brownies At Zoo, Ink On Paper, P. Cox, 1880s, 4 x 5 In. 220.00
Doll, Palmer Cox 125.00
Egg, Papier–Mache, Crepe Paper Lining, Palmer Cox, 12 In. 600.00

Brownies, Game, Brownie 9-Pin Set, McLoughlin, Wooden Cutout

Game, Brownie 9–Pin Set, McLoughlin, Wooden Cutout .... *Illus*	1900.00
Game, New Game of Social Brownies, Horsman, 1894, Board, Box	990.00
Game, Prize Ringtoss, Playing Football, Paper Lithograph On Wood, 13 x 8 In.	143.00
Mug, Palmer Cox	85.00
Paper Doll, Palmer Cox	16.00
Pitcher, Brownies Playing Golf, Tan, 6 In.	300.00
Toothpick, Brownies With Umbrella, Palmer Cox, Silver Plate	450.00
Toy, Ladder, 3 Brownie Figures, Paper Lithograph On Wood, 33 In.	687.00
Tray, 2 Fencing Brownies, Self–Handles, Palmer Cox, 6 1/4 x 4 1/2 In.	75.00

BRUSH Pottery was started in 1925. George Brush first worked in 1901 in Zanesville, Ohio. He started his own pottery in 1907, but it burned to the ground and he joined McCoy in 1909. After a series of name changes, the company became The Brush Pottery. It closed in 1982. Collectors favor the figural cookie jars made by this company.

Bowl, Cherokee, No. 25	850.00
Casserole, Cover, Cherry	35.00
Clock, Heartbeat, Hanging, Pink, No. 33	2000.00
Console Set, King Tut, 10–In. Bowl, 3 Piece	3500.00
Cookie Jar, Bear, Feet Apart	100.00
Cookie Jar, Bear, Feet Together .... 155.00 To	185.00
Cookie Jar, Brown Cow .... 95.00 To	115.00
Cookie Jar, Chocolate Dollop, Yellow, Brown Lid	35.00
Cookie Jar, Cinderella's Pumpkin .... 175.00 To	350.00
Cookie Jar, Circus Horse .... 350.00 To	750.00
Cookie Jar, Clown Bust .... 200.00 To	400.00
Cookie Jar, Covered Wagon .... 675.00 To	750.00
Cookie Jar, Crock, Cat Finial	50.00
Cookie Jar, Crock, Duck Finial, Pink, 1956	30.00
Cookie Jar, Elephant, With Ice Cream Cone, Blue Coat .... 325.00 To	450.00
Cookie Jar, Elephant, With Ice Cream Cone, Burgundy Coat	650.00
Cookie Jar, Formal Pig .... 135.00 To	225.00
Cookie Jar, Granny, With Dots	225.00
Cookie Jar, Happy Squirrel .... 600.00 To	650.00
Cookie Jar, Hen On Nest .... 90.00 To	125.00
Cookie Jar, Hillbilly Frog, Repaired	3700.00
Cookie Jar, Humpty Dumpty, Cowboy Hat .... 175.00 To	285.00
Cookie Jar, Laughing Hippo, Monkey On Back .... 850.00 To	1000.00
Cookie Jar, Little Boy Blue, Large	1100.00
Cookie Jar, Little Boy Blue, Small .... 600.00 To	750.00

Cookie Jar, Little Red Riding Hood, Small 525.00
Cookie Jar, Old Shoe House .... 75.00 To 95.00
Cookie Jar, Panda, Black & Gray 275.00
Cookie Jar, Peter Pan 675.00
Cookie Jar, Pumpkin With Lock On Door 400.00
Cookie Jar, Puppy Police 750.00
Cookie Jar, Purple Cow 1000.00
Cookie Jar, Sheriff Pig 85.00
Cookie Jar, Squirrel On Log, Brown ....90.00 To 120.00
Cookie Jar, Squirrel On Log, Gray 120.00
Cookie Jar, Squirrel With Top Hat 225.00
Cookie Jar, Stylized Owl 325.00
Cookie Jar, Treasure Chest 200.00
Jardiniere, Mushroom Design, Signed 37.50
Jug, Mt. Pele 2750.00
Planter, Boat 45.00
Salt & Pepper, Cherry 16.00
Vase, Florastone, 9 In. 2500.00
Vase, Jetwood, 10 In. 2000.00
Vase, Pond Art, 9 In. 300.00
Wall Pocket, Boxer Dog Shape 95.00

BRUSH McCOY, see McCoy category

BUCK ROGERS was the first American science fiction comic strip. It
started in 1929 and continued until 1965. Buck has also appeared in comic
books, movies, and, in the 1980s, a television series. Any memorabilia
connected with the character Buck Rogers is collectible.

Attack Ship 90.00
Badge, Flight Commander 99.00
Badge, Solar Scout 59.00
Book, Big Little Book, Buck Rogers 25th Century 45.00
Book, Color Illustrated Stories, Kellogg's Advertising 80.00
Comic Strip, Buck Rogers In 25th Century, Ink On Paper, 1948, 24 x 18 In. 550.00
Gun, Disintegrator, Daisy Mfg. Co., Painted Copper & Black Metal, 9 1/2 In. 210.00
Gun, Sonic Ray 70.00
Lunch Box, In The 25th Century, Thermos, 1979 .... 80.00
Map, Solar System, 1930s 750.00
Map, Solar System, Coco Malt Premium, 1933 .... 475.00
Pencil Box, Green, 4 1/2 x 8 1/2 In. 40.00
Pistol, Atomic 75.00
Pistol, Atomic, Daisy, 1946 .... 200.00
Pistol, Atomic, Holster 400.00
Pistol, Atomic, Metal, Daisy, 1930s, 10 In. 222.00
Play Set, H. G. Toys, Sealed 125.00
Pop Gun, Daisy 70.00
Pop Gun, Large Finned, Flash Barrel, 1960s 235.00
Robot, Twiki, Windup, Plastic, Walks, Silver, 7 In., Box 35.00
Space Ranger Kit, Sealed Envelope, 1952 .... 200.00
Spaceship, Plastic Wheels 28.00
Strato–Kite, Instructions, 18 1/2 x 18 1/2 In. 55.00
Watch, Pocket, Ingraham, Lightning–Bolt Hands, Box 2090.00
Watercolor On Paper, Buck's & Wilma's Heads, Calkins, Framed, 12 x 10 In. 825.00

BUFFALO POTTERY was made in Buffalo, New York, after 1902. The
company was established by the Larkin Company, famous manufacturers
of soap. The wares are marked with a picture of a buffalo and the date of
manufacture. Deldare ware is the most famous pottery made at the factory.
It has khaki-colored or green background with hand painted transfer
designs.

BUFFALO POTTERY DELDARE, Ashtray, Fallowfield 225.00
    Bowl, Dr. Syntax, Emerald 950.00
    Bowl, Fallowfield Hunt, Death, Large 1250.00

Bowl, Nut, Ye Lion Inn 695.00
Bowl, Ye Village Tavern, 1908, 9 In. ....*Illus* 250.00
Candlestick, Emerald 695.00
Candlestick, J. Gerhardt, 1909, 9 In. 450.00
Charger, Rouge Ware, Morgan's Road Coach Tavern, 11 1/2 In. 350.00
Charger, Ye Lion Inn, 1909, 12 In ....*Illus* 210.00
Chop Plate, An Evening At Ye Lion Inn, 1908, 14 In. 395.00
Chop Plate, Fallowfield Hunt, The Start, A. Delaney, 14 In. .... 595.00 To 950.00
Chop Plate, Street Scene, 14 In. 650.00
Creamer, Ye Olden Days, Signed J. G., 1909, 3 In. 260.00
Cup & Saucer, Dr. Syntax At Liverpool, Emerald, 1911 .... 650.00
Cup & Saucer, Emerald 495.00
Cup & Saucer, Street Scene 250.00
Cup & Saucer, Ye Olden Days .... 180.00 To 200.00
Hair Receiver, Street Scene 450.00
Humidor, Dr. Syntax, Emerald 1750.00
Mug, Fallowfield Hunt, 4 1/4 In. .... 280.00 To 325.00
Mug, Street Scene, 4 1/2 In. 425.00
Mug, Ye Lion Inn, 4 1/2 In. 250.00
Pitcher, Buffalo Hunt 325.00
Pitcher, Dr. Syntax Stopped By Highwaymen 775.00
Pitcher, Fallowfield Hunt, 6 In. 775.00
Pitcher, Fallowfield Hunt, Octagonal, 8 In. 850.00
Pitcher, Great Controversy, 12 1/2 In. 1150.00
Pitcher, Hunt Supper, 1909, 12 1/2 In. 975.00
Pitcher, Street Scene, 7 In. 595.00
Pitcher, Their Manner of Telling Stories, 1909, 6 In. .... 355.00 To 500.00
Pitcher, To Demand My Annual Rent, 1908, 8 In. ....*Illus* 550.00
Plaque, Breakfast At The Three Pigeons, 12 In. 595.00
Plaque, Fallowfield Hunt, 12 In. 795.00
Plaque, Friday, 12 In. 1575.00

Buffalo Pottery Deldare, Tray, Dancing Ye Minuet, 1909, 9 X 12 In.

Buffalo Pottery Deldare, Charger, Ye Lion Inn, 1909, 12 In.

Buffalo Pottery Deldare, Tankard, Great Controversy, 12 1/2 In.

Buffalo Pottery Deldare, Bowl, Ye Village Tavern, 1908, 9 In.

Buffalo Pottery Deldare, Pitcher, To Demand My Annual Rent, 1908, 8 In.

Plate, Dr. Syntax Losing His Way, Emerald, 1911, 9 1/4 In.	1100.00
Plate, Dr. Syntax, Emerald, 6 In.	750.00
Plate, Fallowfield Hunt, 10 In.	325.00
Plate, Fallowfield Hunt, 11 1/2 In.	225.00
Plate, Fallowfield Hunt, The Death, L. Newman, 1908, 8 1/4 In.	135.00
Plate, Fallowfield Hunt, The Start, H. Ball, 1908, 9 1/2 In.	160.00
Plate, Misfortune At Tulip Hall, Emerald, 8 1/2 In.	585.00
Plate, Street Scene, 8 1/4 In.	175.00
Plate, Village Street, 7 3/8 In.	90.00
Plate, Ye Olden Times, 9 1/4 In.	142.00 To 175.00
Plate, Ye Town Crier, 8 1/2 In.	80.00 To 225.00
Plate, Ye Village Gossip, Signed L. B., 10 In.	90.00
Platter, Ye Evening At Ye Lion Inn, 13 1/2 In.	300.00
Powder Box, Street Scene	550.00
Soup, Dish, Fallowfield Hunt, 9 In.	495.00
Sugar & Creamer, Scenes of Village Life	350.00
Sugar, Cover, Ye Olden Days, L. Newman, 1909, 3 In.	250.00
Tankard, Great Controversy, 12 1/2 In.	*Illus* 700.00
Tankard, Hunt Supper, 1909, 12 1/2 In.	950.00
Tea Set, Village Life, 3 Piece	695.00
Tea Set, Ye Olden Days, 3 Piece	1000.00
Teapot, Breaking Ground	175.00
Teapot, Street Scene	435.00
Teapot, Village Life In Ye Olden Days, 4 1/2 In.	375.00
Tile, Fallowfield Hunt, 1908, 6 In.	295.00
Tile, Traveling In Ye Olden Days, 1908, 6 In.	265.00 To 450.00
Tray, Berdel, Dated 1909, Large	1350.00
Tray, Calling Card, Fallowfield Hunt, 1909, 7 3/4 In.	395.00
Tray, Dancing Ye Minuet, 1909, 9 x 12 In.	*Illus* 350.00
Vase, Signed, 1909, 8 In	850.00
BUFFALO POTTERY, Chamber Pot, Roses On White, 9 x 10 1/4 In.	125.00
Cup & Saucer, Child's, Roosevelt Bears, Marked	225.00
Dish, Feeding, Little Bopeep	14.00
Mug, Abino, Windmill & Boat, 1913, 4 1/4 In.	875.00
Pitcher, Blue Willow	55.00
Pitcher, Calf, Indians Hunting Buffalo, Teal Blue, White Ground, 6 3/8 In.	302.50
Pitcher, George Washington, 1907	200.00
Pitcher, Landing of Roger Williams, c.1906	495.00
Pitcher, Milk, Chrysanthemum, 6 In.	90.00
Pitcher, Robin Hood	325.00
Pitcher, Sailor	500.00
Plate, Campbell Kids	35.00
Plate, Christmas, Dickens Theme, 1955	48.00
Plate, Niagara Falls, 1907	35.00
Platter, Blue Willow, 13 In.	75.00
Platter, Buffalo Hunt, 14 x 11 In.	295.00
Platter, Dancing Ye Minuet, A. Delaney, Rectangular	375.00
Teapot, Argyle	275.00
Tray, Abino, Windmill & Boat, 1911, 8 x 10 3/8 In.	1650.00
Tray, Buffalo Hunt, Rectangular	425.00

BURMESE GLASS was developed by Frederick Shirley at the Mt. Washington Glass Works in New Bedford, Massachusetts, in 1885. It is a two-toned glass, shading from peach to yellow. Some pieces have a pattern mold design. A few Burmese pieces were decorated with pictures or applied glass flowers of colored Burmese glass. Other factories made similar glass also called *Burmese*. Related items may be listed in the Gunderson category, the Fenton category, and under Webb Burmese.

Cruet, Blush, Melon Ribbed, Mushroom Stopper, Mt. Washington, 6 1/2 In.	1065.00
Lampshade, Pleated Ruffled Rim, 4 1/2 In.	225.00
Pitcher, Melon Pink, Pastel Yellow Tankard–Form, Mt. Washington, 9 In.	467.50
Pitcher, Satin, Tightly Pleated Top, 5 1/4 In.	349.00
Pitcher, Yellow Handle, 6 1/2 In.	950.00

Pitcher, Yellow Handle, Pink Shading, Acid Finish, 6 In., 2 Qt. 950.00
Rose Bowl, 3–Footed, 3 1/2 In., Pair 375.00
Rose Bowl, Ruffled 450.00
Salt & Pepper, Ribbed Pillar, Mt. Washington 300.00
Saltshaker, Ribbed, Pair 250.00
Sugar & Creamer, Applied Yellow Handle, 3 3/4 In. 775.00
Sugar & Creamer, Floral, Mt. Washington, 7 In. 1100.00
Sugar & Creamer, Mt. Washington 850.00
Sugar & Creamer, No Design, Creamer–3 3/4 In. 665.00
Sugar Shaker, Chrysanthemums, Melon Ribbed, Mt. Washington, 3 In. 485.00
Toothpick, Berry Sprig, Brown Leaves, Thorny Branch, 3 In. 450.00
Toothpick, Blue/White Daisy Design, Coral Rim, Mt. Washington, 2 7/8 In. 485.00
Toothpick, Diamond–Quilted 350.00
Toothpick, New England, Ball Shape, Hexagonal Rim 475.00
Toothpick, Square Top, Mt. Washington, 2 3/4 In. 485.00
Tumbler, Mt. Washington 295.00
Tumbler, Violets, Mt. Washington 750.00
Vase, Crimped, Mt. Washington, 3 1/2 In. 125.00
Vase, Diamond–Quilted, Thomas Hood Poem, 4 In. 2450.00
Vase, Enameled White Daisies, Tubular, Mt. Washington, 8 1/4 In. 685.00
Vase, Flower Petal Form, 6 Petals, Applied Round Wafer Base, 6 1/2 In. 1050.00
Vase, Fluted Top, Pedestal, Mt. Washington, 10 In., Pair 1150.00
Vase, Jack–In–The–Pulpit, Crimped Rim, Signed, 14 1/2 In. 785.00
Vase, Jack–In–The–Pulpit, Mt. Washington, 14 1/2 In. 985.00
Vase, Jack–In–The–Pulpit, Ruffled 500.00
Vase, Lily, Mt. Washington, 10 In. 375.00
Vase, Opaque Pink To Cream, Floral Transfer, 3 x 3 In. 325.00
Vase, Stick, Queen's Design, Mt. Washington, 9 In. 1500.00
Vase, Trumpet, Yellow Rim, Mt. Washington, 7 In. 335.00

BUSTER BROWN, the comic strip, first appeared in color in 1902. Buster and his dog Tige remained a popular comic and soon became even more famous as the emblem for a shoe company, a textile firm, and others. The strip was discontinued in 1920, but some of the advertising is still in use.

Bank, Buster Brown & Tige, Cast Iron, Traces of Gold, 5 In. .... 127.00 To 145.00
Bank, Counting House, Boy & Dog Tellers, Cast Iron, 6 5/8 In. 150.00
Book, Buster Brown Cameras, How To Make Photographs, 12 Pages, 1917 .... 6.50
Book, Buster Brown Dictionary 30.00
Book, Buster Brown Goes Swimming, 1906 .... 65.00
Book, Coloring 25.00
Book, Comic, No. 29, Lamson's Shoe Dept., Toledo 5.00
Book, Jokes & Jingles 20.00
Box, O How Good Berry's Buster Brown Chocolates, 1906, 5 x 8 In. 25.00
Button, Buster & Tige, Gilt, Club, 7/8 In. 12.00
Card, Playing, Buster & His Dog Tige, Alligator Case, 1909 .... 285.00
Game, Beanbag Toss, Paper Lithograph On Wood, Bliss, 24 x 10 In. 385.00
Game, Buster Brown At Coney Island, Ottman, Board 412.00
Game, Buster Brown At The Circus, Selchow & Righter, Cards, Box, 6 x 8 In. 357.00
Game, Necktie Party, Box, 8 x 10 In. 198.00
Horse, Riding, Pedal 295.00
Nodder, Roly Poly, Papier–Mache, Schoenhut, 9 1/2 In. 880.00
Nodder, Tige, Porcelain, Germany, 3 In. 80.00
Pencil Box, Buster Brown, Tige, Lacquered, Germany 50.00
Pencil, Mechanical, Buster Brown Shoes 20.00
Periscope .... 25.00 To 45.00
Toy, Buster & Happy Hooligan, Tin Lithograph, Spring Lever, 5 x 7 In. 235.00
Toy, Buster & Tige, Lamppost, Tin, Painted, Windup, Guntermann, 4 x 4 x 9 In. 995.00
Toy, Cart, With Tige, Cast Iron 300.00
Toy, Tige, Wool, Airbrush Marked, Button, Steiff, 1915, 9 In. 425.00
Watch, Pocket, Ingersoll, 1928 .... 400.00
Whistle, Tin 22.50
Wristwatch, 1975 .... 125.00 To 150.00

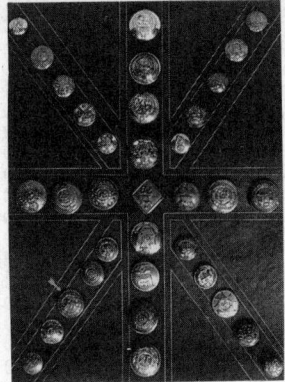

Button, Military, British,
On British Flag Show Card, 34 Piece

BUTTER CHIPS, or butter pats, were small individual dishes for butter. They were in the height of fashion from 1880 to 1910. Earlier as well as later examples are known.

Mimbreno Railroad	45.00

BUTTER MOLDS are listed in the Kitchen category under Mold, Butter.

BUTTONS have been known throughout the centuries, and there are millions of styles. Gold, silver, or precious stones were used for the best buttons, but most were made of natural materials, like bone or shell, or from inexpensive metals. Only a few types are listed for comparison.

Black Glass, 4–Hole Brass Shank, 1 1/8 In., 5 Piece	25.00
Brass, Camel	7.00
Cloak, Jet Black, Silver Overlay, Floral, 2 1/2 In., Pair	35.00
Horse, Glass Eye, Bakelite, Large	55.00
Military, British, On British Flag Show Card, 34 Piece ....*Illus*	60.00
Silver, Woman's Head	10.00
Strawberry, Green Stem Marked, Caramel Bakelite, 5 Piece	28.00
Sulfide, Horse, 7/8 In.	75.00
Sulfide, Spider, 7/8 In.	75.00
Woman's Air Derby, 1929	20.00

BUTTONHOOKS have been a popular collectible in England for many years but only recently have gained the attention of American collectors. The buttonhooks were made to help fasten the many buttons of the old–fashioned high–button shoes and other items of apparel.

Art Nouveau, Embossed Ferrle, Brass, Wire Loop	19.75
Crescent, Box	25.00
Repousse Florals, Sterling Silver	35.00
Sterling Silver, Fancy Handle, 6 1/2 In.	8.00

CALENDARS made to hang on the wall or to be displayed on a desk top have been popular since the last quarter of the nineteenth century. Many were printed with advertising as part of the artwork and were given away as premiums. Calendars with guns, gunpowder, or Coca–Cola advertising are most prized.

1881, January, Russell, Morgan & Co., 9 3/4 x 5 3/8 In. ....*Illus*	4.00

There are many ecologically sound products made for the care and repair of antiques. Look at the product labels. Our ancestors cleaned pewter with wood ashes and oil. Be sure to dispose of paint thinners, harsh chemical cleaners, and other dangerous products in the approved manner. Don't just dump them in the sewer.

1881, March, Russell, Morgan & Co., 9 3/4 x 5 3/8 In. ....*Illus*   4.00
1889, Met Life Insurance Co., Jan. To April, Children, 4 3/4 x 6 In. 8.00
1890, Dubuque Fire & Marine Insurance 75.00
1890, Queen Syrup 120.00
1891, Aetna Insurance Co., Port Scene, Mountain, Frame, 6 1/2 x 9 1/2 In. 28.00
1892, Hood's Sarsaparilla 80.00
1893, John Hancock Ins. Co., Horse Drawn Carriage, 15 3/4 x 12 1/2 In. 50.00
1895, Consumer's Brewing, Woman In Blue Dress, 14 1/2 x 19 In. 440.00
1895, Phoenix Mutual Life Insurance, Little Girls 145.00
1896, Marus Ward, 12 Panels 25.00
1897, Grand Union Tea 125.00
1898, Christian Brecht, Bathing Beauty On Beach, 15 x 22 In. 1100.00
1898, Hood's Sarsaparilla 25.00
1898, Oriental Brewery, Beer Drinking Boaters, 19 1/2 x 27 1/2 In. 1210.00
1898, Prospect Brewing Co. 1210.00
1899, Standard Sewing Machine Co., Admiral Dewey Cover, 3 1/2 x 2 In. 12.00
1900, J. & O. C. Stocker Brewer, Girl Behind Fence, 16 x 22 In. 825.00
1901, Manilla Brewing Co., Girl Draped In Sheet, 26 1/2 x 17 In. 255.00
1901, Singer Sewing Machine, 12–Month Page 95.00
1902, Bergdoll's Beer, Man & Woman Drinking, 22 x 16 1/2 In. 440.00
1902, Fett & Fett Beer, 3 Men Playing Cards, 15 x 22 3/4 In. 495.00
1902, Gallard Hardware & Farm Tools, Movable Arm Points To Dates 35.00
1902, Vermont Mutual Fire Insur., Spread Winged Eagle, 11 1/2 x 16 In. 33.00
1903, John Stocker, Pretty Girl In Gold Chair, 14 1/2 x 19 In. 605.00
1904, David Stevenson Brewing, Uncle Sam, Factory, 19 1/2 x 28 In. 2530.00
1904, Excelsior Stove Co., Gold Medal Award World's Fair 37.50
1904, Heydt Bakery Co., Missouri 95.00
1905, Lauer Brewing Co., Factory, Multiple Products, 27 1/2 In. 715.00
1906, Frank Coe's Fertilizer Company, 9 x 13 In. 38.00
1907, Mathie Brewing, Die Cut Cardboard, 14 1/2 x 15 1/2 In. 1430.00
1907, Meat Market, Schenectady, N.Y., Bull Picture, 10 3/4 x 13 3/4 In. 15.00
1908, California Liquor Distributor, Victorian Woman, Frame 350.00
1908, Rieger & Gretz Brewers & Bottlers, 11 x 21 In. 75.00
1909, Chattanooga Medicine Co., Cardul Weather Chart, 13 x 20 In. 16.00
1910, Oval Insert of Pretty Girl, Roses, 21 1/2 In. 385.00
1912, Lykens Brewing, Frame, 16 1/2 x 23 In. 330.00
1912, Sharples 300.00
1913, Sarasota Flour 150.00
1915, Bowkers Fertilizer, Complete 10.00
1915, Crown Beer, Roll Down, Girl Holding Rose, 34 x 10 In. 358.00

Calendar Paper, 1881, January, Russell,
Morgan & Co., 9 3/4 X 5 3/8 In.
Calendar Paper, 1881, March, Russell,
Morgan & Co., 9 3/4 X 5 3/8 In.

To remove tape or labels from a paperback book or pamphlet, put the book on a flat surface and pour lighter fluid on the tape. Wipe off the fluid after five seconds. Drip a little more fluid on the tape. Pry loose a bit of the label or tape with a letter opener or dull knife and lift up the edge. Continue to pry loose, lift the flap, and pour fluid until the label is off. The fluid dissolves the glue. Go slowly; if the glue is not soft enough you may tear the paper.

1916, Colby College, Leather Bound 13.00
1918, DeLaval, Girl & Horse, Cawker City, Kans., 12 x 17 In. 125.00
1918, Remington Arms 1600.00
1920, Globe Feeds, Children, Chickens, Full Pad 110.00
1920, Remington Firearms 475.00
1921, Theodore Roosevelt, Patriot Design, 52 Weeks, 8 In. 37.50
1923, Blue Star Steamship 165.00
1925, Edison–Mazda Div., Dream Light, Parrish, 15 x 25 In. 633.00
1926, Die Cut Cardboard of Woman, Frame 170.00
1926, Goodrich Tire, Thompson Print 25.00
1926, McCormick Deering, April 125.00
1926, Pretty Woman's Portrait, Yard Long, Frame 300.00
1926, Victorian Woman, Die Cut Flowers, 14 x 21 In. 155.00
1926, Yard Long 300.00
1928, Edison–Mazda, Contentment, Parrish, Frame, Complete 475.00
1929, Edison–Mazda Div. General Electric, Golden Hours, Parrish 176.00
1931, Baby Sitting, Charlotte Becker 25.00
1931, McCormick Deering, December 75.00
1932, Budweiser, Embossed Art Nouveau Border, Reclining Woman, 17 In. 50.00
1932, DeLaval 60.00
1933, Enticing Woman, Orange Bathing Suit, Earl Moran, 10 x 17 In. 65.00
1935, Globe Brewing, Indian Princess, 28 x 14 In. 467.00
1936, Christener Trucking, Die–Cut Stock Truck 100.00
1936, Massachusetts Mutual Life Insurance Co., John Yates, Agent 6.00
1937, DeLaval .... 18.00 To 75.00
1938, DeLaval, Pretty Woman 35.00
1938, Woman In Bathing Suit, DeVorss, 9 x 14 In. 40.00
1939, Pin–Up Type, Woman In Harem, 33 In. 110.00
1940, Little Rascals, Taystee Bread 275.00
1941, Esquire, Vegas, Complete 100.00
1941, Out In Front, Earl Moran, Complete Pad, 11 x 23 In. 80.00
1942, Case Farm Machinery, Picture, 9 x 17 In. 30.00
1942, Cliquot Club 65.00
1942, Texaco 35.00
1943, A Modern Eve, Nude, Earl Moran, Large 20.00
1943, Esquire, Vargas, Full Pad 65.00
1944, A Good Hook–Up, Petty, Full Pad, 15 x 8 In. 60.00
1944, Draped In Silver Fox, Dilly DeVorss, Salesman's Sample, 16 x 33 In. 35.00
1944, St. Joseph's Pharmaceutical 22.00
1944, Vargas Girls 45.00
1945, Donald Duck & Nephews 60.00
1946, Esquire, Vargas, Envelope 75.00
1946, It's A Date, Seattle Jeweler, Rolf Armstrong, 5 1/2 x 7 1/2 In. 25.00
1946, Jeanne, DeVorss, Complete Pad, 16 x 33 In. .... 70.00 To 95.00
1946, Mrs. O'Leary's Cow, Norman Rockwell, Complete, 16 x 33 In. 115.00
1947, Esquire, Vargas 75.00
1947, George Transfer & Rigging Co., 32 In. 70.00
1947, Petty 50.00
1948, Squirt 50.00
1948, Squirt, Pretty Women, 4 Pages, 16 x 23 In. 40.00
1948, Sure Enough, Rolf Armstrong, Complete Pad, 16 x 33 In. 80.00
1949, Mission Orange 50.00
1949, Speedway Gas 25.00
1950, Ford Trucks, Pretty Girl, Black Ground, 16 x 33 In. 55.00
1952, Hopalong Cassidy 225.00
1953, Marilyn Monroe 75.00
1953, Marilyn Monroe In 3 of 6 Poses, Advertising 79.00
1954, Marilyn Monroe, Golden Dreams, 9 x 14 In. 65.00
1954, U.S. Royal Tires, Pinup Girl 20.00
1955, John Deere, Wildlife 35.00
1955, Marilyn Monroe, Nude With Lace Overlay, 16 x 32 In. 175.00
1955, Marilyn Monroe, Nude, 10 x 17 In. 33.00
1956, Marilyn Monroe 75.00

1956, Mining Machine Parts, Cleveland, Ohio, Pinup Girl 35.00
1956, Reddy Kilowatt, Indianapolis Power & Light Co., 4 x 2 1/2 In. 12.50
1957, Mobil 32.50
1957, Nu Grape 65.00
1957, Pennsylvania Railroad 100.00
1958, Boy Scout, Norman Rockwell, 16 x 33 In. 55.00
1958, DuPont 90.00
1958, Everett Ice Cream Co., Baby, Bear, C. Becker, Full Pad, 26 x 14 In. 45.00
1958, Rock Island R.R., 14 x 20 In. 35.00
1958, Studio Sketches, T. N. Thompson, Envelope 15.00
1959, Roy Rogers 195.00
1964, President Kennedy, Before Assassination, Multicolor 30.00
1966, 12 Different Monsters, Don Post, 9 x 12 In. 39.00
1966, Hummel, Each Page Different Figurine, Factory, Large 23.00
1969, Adam, Complete 8.00
1969, All–American Calendar, Presidents Portrait, Nixon Center, Dec. Only 9.00
1974, Penthouse American Dream, Envelope 8.00
1976, Super Heroes 15.00
1978, Sierra Club, Little Creatures Calendar & Almanac 9.00
1980, Rockwell 8.00
1980, St. Louis Cardinals, Budweiser, 15 x 30 In. 25.00
1983, Christie Brinkley Photograph, 12 Pages 15.00
1985, Michael Jackson, With 6 Posters, 15 x 19 In. 35.00

CALENDAR PLATES were very popular in the United States from 1906 to
1929. Since then, plates have been made every year. A calendar and the
name of a store, a picture of flowers, a girl, or a scene were featured on
the plate.

1908, Victorian Woman In Flowered Hat, Dress, Oklahoma 30.00
1910, Queen Louise, R. M. Propp, Shelby, Iowa 25.00
1912, Indian Maiden Center, 8 1/2 In. 35.00
1912, Sporting Equipment & Butterfly Lady With Roses, 8 In. .... 22.50 To 24.75
1915, Panama Canal Map, Flow Blue, Crazed, 8 1/2 In. 30.00
1921, Compliments of A. F. Mahnke Farmersburg, Ia., 9 In. 22.00
1955, Fiesta, Green 20.00

CAMARK POTTERY started in 1924 in Camden, Arkansas. Jack Carnes
founded the firm and made many types of glazes and wares. The company
was bought by Mary Daniel. Production was halted in 1983.

Console, With Butterfly Flower Frog, Pink 35.00
Ewer, Purple Iris, Pale Yellow, 15 In. 115.00
Pitcher, Figural, Medieval Woman 45.00
Vase, 5 In. 24.00
Wall Pocket, Pitcher & Bowl, Yellow 15.00

CAMBRIDGE GLASS Company was founded in 1901 in Cambridge, Ohio.
The company closed in 1954, reopened briefly, and closed again in 1958.
The firm made all types of glass. Their early wares included heavy pressed
glass with the mark *Near Cut.* Later wares included Crown Tuscan, etched
stemware, and clear and colored glass. The firm used a C in a triangle
mark after 1920. Some Cambridge patterns may be included in the
Depression Glass category.

Alpine, Caprice, Bowl, 4 Feet 40.00
Apple Blossom, Bonbon, Handles, 5 1/2 In. 33.00
Apple Blossom, Bucket, Topaz 90.00
Apple Blossom, Candy, Cover, Yellow, 7 In. 175.00
Apple Blossom, Console Set, Pink, 3 Piece 125.00
Apple Blossom, Cup & Saucer, Green 38.50
Apple Blossom, Decanter, Stopper, Crystal, 32 Oz. 225.00
Apple Blossom, Goblet, Water, Crystal 24.00
Apple Blossom, Iced Tea, Yellow 35.00
Apple Blossom, Pitcher, Water, Tubers 200.00
Apple Blossom, Plate, Yellow, 8 1/2 In. 15.00

Apple Blossom, Relish, Center Handle, Amber, 4 Sections	57.00
Apple Blossom, Salt & Pepper, Yellow	90.00
Apple Blossom, Sugar & Creamer, Footed	45.00
Apple Blossom, Tray, Center Handle, Blue, 11 In.	55.00
Apple Blossom, Vase, Green, 10 In.	125.00
Bashful Charlotte, Flower Frog, Green, 6 1/2 In.	145.00
Bashful Charlotte, Flower Frog, Green, 13 In.	225.00
Belfast, Cocktail Shaker, Crystal, 32 Oz.	70.00
Blossom Time, Cake Plate, 2 Handles, 11 In.	55.00
Blossom Time, Compote, Cheese	24.00
Blossom Time, Tumbler, Iced Tea, Footed	25.00
Candlewick, Butter, California	95.00
Candlewick, Cake Stand, Pedestal	50.00
Candlewick, Frame, Eagle	70.00
Caprice, Ashtray, Triangle, Moonlight Blue, 3 In.	12.00
Caprice, Bowl, 4 Sections	55.00
Caprice, Bowl, Blue, 18 In.	165.00
Caprice, Cake Plate, 13 In.	125.00
Caprice, Candlestick, 2–Light, Keyhole, Blue, Pair	130.00
Caprice, Candlestick, 3–Light	55.00
Caprice, Candlestick, 3–Light, Pair	175.00
Caprice, Candlestick, Prisms, Blue, 7 1/2 In., Pair	80.00
Caprice, Candy Dish, Cover, 3–Footed, Blue	110.00
Caprice, Candy Dish, Cover, Moonlight Blue, 6 In.	125.00
Caprice, Console Set, 3–Light Candlesticks, Blue, 3 Piece	130.00
Caprice, Cruet	25.00
Caprice, Cruet, Stopper, 4 Oz.	20.00
Caprice, Cup & Saucer, Blue	45.00
Caprice, Goblet, 9 Oz.	16.00
Caprice, Ice Bucket, Moonlight Blue	225.00
Caprice, Jug, Ball, Alpine, Blue	425.00
Caprice, Mayonnaise Set, Crystal, 3 Piece	47.50
Caprice, Mustard, Moonlight Blue	49.50
Caprice, Pitcher, Crystal	110.00
Caprice, Pitcher, Juice, Pink	1800.00
Caprice, Plate, Blue, 6 In.	15.00
Caprice, Plate, Blue, 12 In.	65.00
Caprice, Plate, Crystal, 7 1/2 In.	7.00
Caprice, Relish, 3 Sections, 8 1/2 In.	40.00
Caprice, Rose Bowl, 4–Footed, 8 In.	145.00
Caprice, Rose Bowl, Frog, Blue	395.00
Caprice, Salt & Pepper, Moonlight Blue	125.00
Caprice, Sherbet, Amethyst	20.00
Caprice, Sugar & Creamer	12.00
Caprice, Sugar, Cover, Moonlight Blue, Miniature	18.75
Caprice, Tumbler, Juice, Footed, Blue, 5 Oz.	40.00
Caprice, Vase, Amber, 4 1/2 In.	85.00
Caprice, Vase, Bowl Shape, Amber, 5 1/2 In.	200.00
Carcassone, Goblet, Sahara, 11 Oz.	35.00
Carcassone, Sherbet, Sahara	25.00
Carmen, Jug, Ball, 80 Oz.	200.00
Cascade, Candy Dish, Cover, Green	80.00
Cascade, Creamer, Crystal	12.00
Cascade, Relish, 3 Sections	25.00
Cascade, Sugar, Cover, Yellow	17.00
Cascade, Tumbler, Juice	4.50
Cascade, Vase, Yellow, 9 1/2 In.	110.00
Chantilly, Candy Dish, Flat, Sterling Lid	85.00
Chantilly, Candy Dish, Sterling Knobbed Cover, 5 1/2 In.	45.00
Chantilly, Decanter, Sterling Silver Base, 12 Oz.	150.00
Chantilly, Goblet, Water, 10 Oz. .... 22.00 To 24.00
Chantilly, Goblet, Water, Stemmed	28.00
Chantilly, Ice Bucket, Chrome Handle	75.00

Chantilly, Lamp, Hurricane, Candlestick, 18 In.	225.00
Charleton, Dish, Shell, Painted	28.00
Cherub, Candlestick, Crystal	225.00
Chintz, Bowl, Footed, Large	425.00
Cleo, Bonbon, 2 Handles, Green, 6 1/4 In.	25.00
Cleo, Bowl, Pink, Oval	65.00
Cleo, Candlestick, Green, Gold Trim, 4 In., Pair	40.00
Cleo, Cup & Saucer, Blue	30.00
Cleo, Cup & Saucer, Green	18.00
Cleo, Goblet, Yellow, 9 Oz.	32.00
Cleo, Ice Bucket, Blue	140.00
Cleo, Ice Bucket, Green	80.00 To 88.00
Cleo, Pitcher, Green	250.00
Cleo, Sugar & Creamer, Pink	49.00
Cleo, Tumbler, Green, 10 Oz.	45.00
Cleo, Vase, Sweet Pea, Amber	110.00
Cobalt Blue, Decanter, Clear Stopper, Chrome Basket	475.00
Colonial, Creamer	20.00
Colonial, Table Set, Child's, 4 Piece	110.00
Colonial, Toothpick, Crystal	30.00
Colonial, Wine	10.00
Crown Tuscan, Bonbon, Cover, 3 Sections, Candlelight	85.00
Crown Tuscan, Bowl, Footed, Chintz, Marked	475.00
Crown Tuscan, Bowl, Handle, 7 1/2 In.	29.50
Crown Tuscan, Candlestick, Dolphin, 3 1/2 In., Pair	250.00
Crown Tuscan, Candlestick, Dolphin, Double	125.00
Crown Tuscan, Candlestick, Fish, Pair	175.00
Crown Tuscan, Candy Dish, Cover, 3 Sections	50.00
Crown Tuscan, Candy Dish, Cover, Candlelight Etch	97.00
Crown Tuscan, Candy Dish, Cover, Footed, 6 In.	55.00
Crown Tuscan, Candy Dish, Ram's Head	250.00
Crown Tuscan, Console Set, Dolphin Candleholder, 3 Piece	150.00
Crown Tuscan, Jug, Ball	475.00
Crown Tuscan, Pitcher, Portia	1650.00
Crown Tuscan, Sherbet, Shell	60.00
Crown Tuscan, Vase, Cornucopia, 3 3/4 In.	19.50
Decagon, Creamer, Flat	12.50
Decagon, Cup, Amethyst	5.50
Decagon, Plate, 6 Piece	50.00
Decagon, Plate, Amber, 6 In.	3.00
Decagon, Plate, Amber, 8 In.	7.00
Decagon, Plate, Pink, 8 In.	10.00
Diane, Bowl, Fluted, 10 In.	65.00
Diane, Cake Plate, Crystal	125.00
Diane, Candlestick, 3–Light	25.00
Diane, Candy Dish, Cover, Gold Tracery	50.00
Diane, Goblet, Stemmed, 9 Oz.	25.00
Diane, Pitcher, Martini	295.00
Diane, Plate, 6 1/2 In.	5.00
Diane, Plate, 8 1/2 In.	10.00 To 12.00
Diane, Relish, 3 Sections, 12 In.	30.00
Diane, Relish, 4 Sections, Crystal, 11 In.	85.00
Diane, Relish, 5 Sections, 12 In.	55.00
Diane, Tray, Center Handle, 11 In.	75.00
Diane, Tray, Round, Crystal, 12 In.	135.00
Draped Lady, Flower Frog, Amber, 8 1/2 In.	195.00

◆◆

Wash aluminum with mild dishwashing soap. Rinse, dry. If needed, use silver polish to add more luster. High temperatures in the dishwasher or oven will dull the shine.

◆◆

Draped Lady, Flower Frog, Crystal, 8 1/2 In.	65.00
Draped Lady, Flower Frog, Dark Amber, 8 1/2 In.	195.00
Draped Lady, Flower Frog, Dark Amber, 13 In.	275.00
Draped Lady, Flower Frog, Green, 8 1/2 In.	125.00
Draped Lady, Flower Frog, Moonlight Blue, 8 1/2 In.	325.00
Draped Lady, Flower Frog, Pink, 13 In.	175.00
Draped Lady, Flower Frog, Yellow, 8 1/2 In.	225.00
Eagle, Bookends, 6 In.	75.00
Elaine, Cordial	65.00
Elaine, Cup & Saucer	22.00
Elaine, Ice Bucket, Handle, Crystal	85.00
Elaine, Ice Tub	110.00
Elaine, Pitcher, 20 Oz.	250.00
Elaine, Pitcher, Martini	250.00
Everglade, Bowl, Swan, Crystal, 14 In.	55.00
Everglade, Candelabra, 2–Light, Pair	90.00
Everglade, Plate, Sandwich, 15 In.	35.00
Everglade, Relish, 3 Sections	28.00
Everglade, Sugar & Creamer, Footed, Amber	75.00
Gadroon, Relish, 3 Sections	30.00
Gadroon, Sugar & Creamer, Pedestal	15.00
Gloria, Bonbon, Green, 5 1/2 In.	35.00
Gloria, Bowl, Blue, 6 In.	55.00
Gloria, Vase, Yellow, 10 In.	225.00
Golf Ball, Ashtray, Green Opaque	15.00
Gyro Optic, Jug, Blue, Ice Lip, 89 Oz.	75.00
Gyro Optic, Pitcher, Blue, Ice Lip, 83 Oz.	60.00
Gyro Optic, Tumbler, Blue, 13 Oz.	9.75
Heirloom, Bowl, Vaseline	48.00
Heliotrope, Candlestick, 8 1/2 In., Pair	135.00
Hunt Scene, Plate, 6 1/4 In.	8.00
Hunt Scene, Plate, 7 In.	10.00
Hunt Scene, Sherbet, 7 1/2 Oz.	42.00
Hunt Scene, Tumbler, 10 Oz.	42.00
Iris, Tumbler, Footed, Carnival, 6 In.	14.00
Japonica, Vase, Carmine, Hand Enameled Design, 1934, 12 1/2 In.	2000.00
Martha, Candlestick, Crystal, 4 In., Pair	35.00
Martha, Console Set, Grape Etch, 3–Light Candlestick, 3 Piece	97.00
Martha, Cup & Saucer, Crystal	15.00
Martha, Plate, Crystal, 10 1/2 In.	35.00
Martha, Sugar & Creamer, Pistachio	28.00
Melody, Plate, Light Green, 8 In.	45.00
Melon Boy, Flower Frog, Pink	250.00
Modern, Celery Tray, Blue, 12 In.	20.00
Modern, Oyster Cocktail	9.50
Modern, Sherbet, Green, Tall	22.00
Modern, Sugar & Creamer, Green, Individual	55.00
Mt. Vernon, Candlestick, Crystal, 4 In., Pair	35.00
Mt. Vernon, Cordial	6.00
Mt. Vernon, Decanter, Amber, 12 In.	30.00
Mt. Vernon, Decanter, Stopper, 40 Oz.	80.00 To 135.00
Mt. Vernon, Decanter, Stopper, Milk Glass	50.00
Mt. Vernon, Goblet, 5 3/4 In.	15.00
Mt. Vernon, Goblet, Wine, Amber	19.50
Mt. Vernon, Pitcher	60.00
Mt. Vernon, Plate, Amber, 8 1/2 In.	6.00
Mt. Vernon, Relish, 5 Sections, 12 In.	30.00
Mt. Vernon, Saucer, Amber	5.00
Mt. Vernon, Vase, 6 1/2 In.	27.50
Mt. Vernon, Vase, Crystal, 7 In.	25.00
Mt. Vernon, Wine, 4 1/2 In.	15.00
Nautilus, Plate, Silver Overlay	125.00
Nude Stem, Ashtray, Amber	325.00

Nude Stem, Ashtray, Crystal	195.00
Nude Stem, Ashtray, Pink	425.00
Nude Stem, Ashtray, Yellow	350.00
Nude Stem, Brandy, Cobalt Blue	125.00
Nude Stem, Claret, Heatherbloom	265.00
Nude Stem, Claret, Red Bowl, 4 1/2 Oz., 8 Piece	1200.00
Nude Stem, Cocktail, Amber	80.00
Nude Stem, Cocktail, Forest Green	85.00
Nude Stem, Cocktail, Light Blue	125.00
Nude Stem, Cocktail, Light Yellow	90.00
Nude Stem, Cocktail, Lime Green	90.00
Nude Stem, Cocktail, Orange	80.00
Nude Stem, Compote, Carmen	200.00
Nude Stem, Compote, Pink, 7 In.	120.00
Nude Stem, Vase, Bud, Amber	750.00
Peacock & Wild Rose, Console Set, Pink	175.00
Portia, Bowl, 11 1/2 In.	65.00
Portia, Celery Dish, Yellow, 12 In.	50.00
Portia, Champagne	14.00
Portia, Cup, Yellow	22.50
Portia, Dish, Mayonnaise, 2 Sections, Ladle	35.00
Portia, Relish, 5 Sections, Crystal	47.50
Portia, Sherry Set, Decanter, 4 Tumblers	275.00
Portia, Vase, 10 In.	130.00
Pristine, Candy Dish, Cover, Box	60.00
Pristine, Condiment Tray, Crystal, 12 In.	30.00
Rondo, Champagne	15.00
Rondo, Cocktail	10.00
Rondo, Goblet	15.00
Rosalie, Candlestick, Blue, Pair	95.00
Rosalie, Candy Dish, Cover, Pink	40.00
Rose Point, Bonbon, 2 Handles, Footed, 8 In.	55.00
Rose Point, Bonbon, Handle, 5 1/4 In.	27.00
Rose Point, Butter, Cover, Round	145.00 To 175.00
Rose Point, Candlestick, 2 1/2 In., Pair	95.00
Rose Point, Candlestick, 3–Light, Etched, Pair	225.00
Rose Point, Candlestick, 3–Light, Keyhole, Pair	145.00
Rose Point, Celery Dish, 11 In.	47.00
Rose Point, Cheese Dish, Crystal	45.00
Rose Point, Cocktail Shaker, Crystal	225.00
Rose Point, Console, Footed, Oval	65.00
Rose Point, Cordial	67.00
Rose Point, Cruet, Stopper, 6 Oz.	115.00 To 125.00
Rose Point, Dish, Cover, 3 Sections, 3 Small Handles	110.00
Rose Point, Goblet, Stemmed, 10 Oz.	30.00
Rose Point, Plate, 10 In.	120.00
Rose Point, Plate, 7 In.	10.00 To 18.00
Rose Point, Plate, 8 In.	24.00
Rose Point, Plate, Cracker, 11 In.	40.00
Rose Point, Plate, Serving, Handle, Piecrust Edge	60.00
Rose Point, Relish, 2 Sections	40.00
Rose Point, Relish, 3 Sections, 12 In.	90.00
Rose Point, Salt & Pepper, Flat, Chrome Lids	65.00
Rose Point, Salt & Pepper, Footed	85.00
Rose Point, Sandwich Tray, Handle, 11 In.	185.00
Rose Point, Serving Bowl, Crystal	80.00
Rose Point, Sherbet, Low	22.00
Rose Point, Sherbet, Tall	35.00
Rose Point, Sugar & Creamer	65.00
Rose Point, Tumbler, Amber, 8 Oz	50.00
Rose Point, Vase, 10 In.	150.00
Seashell, Candlestick, Dolphin, 4 In.	60.00
Swan, Dark Green, 3 1/2 In.	55.00

Swan, Deep Emerald Green, 8 1/2 In.	145.00
Swan, Light Green, 3 1/2 In.	38.00
Swan, Milk Glass, 6 1/2 In.	200.00
Swan, Pink, 3 1/2 In.	30.00
Swan, Pink, 6 1/2 In.	150.00
Swan, Topaz, 3 In.	40.00
Tally–Ho, Champagne, Amethyst	30.00
Tally–Ho, Compote, Divided, 5 In.	95.00
Tally–Ho, Creamer, Amethyst	45.00
Tally–Ho, Goblet, Water, Carmen	35.00
Tally–Ho, Mug, Amber	50.00
Tally–Ho, Mug, Dark Green	22.00
Tally–Ho, Pitcher, Dark Green, Ice Lip	110.00
Tally–Ho, Plate, Asparagus, 8 1/2 In.	17.50
Tally–Ho, Punch Set, Crystal, Red Handle Cups, 12 Piece	175.00
Tally–Ho, Sherbet, Red, Low	18.00
Wildflower, Butter, Cover, Round, 5 In.	110.00
Wildflower, Candy Dish, Red Rose Finial, 3 Footed	260.00
Wildflower, Champagne	28.00
Wildflower, Console Set, 4–Footed Bowl, 3 Piece	70.00
Wildflower, Jug Set, Ball, 6 Piece	325.00
Wildflower, Plate, 6 3/4 In.	30.00
Wildflower, Plate, Sandwich, 11 In.	40.00
Wildflower, Relish, 5 Sections, Round, 10 In.	70.00
Wildflower, Saltshaker, Footed	25.00
Windsor, Candlestick, Blue, Gold Etched, 8 In.	40.00
Windsor, Candlestick, Shell–Footed, Blue, 2 In., Pair	225.00
Ye Old Ivy, Candlestick, 5 1/2 In., Pair	60.00

CAMEO GLASS was made in much the same manner as a cameo in jewelry. Parts of the top layer of glass were cut away to reveal a different colored glass beneath. The most famous cameo glass was made during the nineteenth century. Signed cameo glass pieces are listed under the glasswork's name, such as Daum or Galle.

Bowl, 3 Bats, Outspread Wings, Silvered Bronze, Jouraiz, c.1925, 4 In.	1760.00
Box, Floral, 2 Layers of Glass, Blue Knob	700.00
Inkwell, Dark Amber, Overlaid & Etched, Silver Lid, 4 1/2 In.	1210.00
Jam Jar, White Flower & Leaves, Notched Lid, Blue, England, 5 1/4 In.	1625.00
Perfume Bottle, Duck Bill, England	2800.00
Perfume Bottle, Elongated Teardrop, Turquoise Blue, Silver Rim, 7 In.	1430.00
Perfume Bottle, Yellow Teardrop, Floral Sprays, Hinged Silver Rim, 3 In.	770.00
Rose Bowl, Pink Enameled Cyclamen, Gilt	385.00
Tazza, Chrysanthemums & Peonies, Joseph Brocard, c.1880, 12 7/8 In.	3850.00
Vase, Bud, Mottled Yellow & Green, Turquoise Etched, Pantin, 6 3/4 In.	550.00
Vase, Citron, Florals, Leafy Vine, Gold Ground, 6 1/2 In.	1750.00
Vase, Clematis Flowers, Overlaid & Etched, Ruby Red Ground, 8 In.	1210.00
Vase, Floral, Blue, Orange, 8 3/4 In.	900.00
Vase, Fuchsia, White Florals, England, 8 x 6 In.	1150.00
Vase, Green, Gold, Floral Design, Frosted Ground, 7 In.	193.00
Vase, Long Stem Iris & Butterflies, Brown Shading, La Rochere, 11 In.	985.00
Vase, Man Crossing Bridge Scene, Green, Pink, Arsall, 12 In.	900.00
Vase, Mountains, Trees, La Rochere, 11 1/4 In.	595.00
Vase, Orange Poppies, Mottled Frosted Ground, 16 In.	600.00
Vase, Pastel Blue, Leafy Stems, Buds Below Double Linear Border, 5 In.	770.00
Vase, Purple Flowers & Leaves, Frosted Ground, Signed, 3 1/4 In.	100.00
Vase, Purple Irises, Green Stems, Pink Frost, Arsall, 11 In.	895.00
Vase, Purple Irises, Pink Frost, Arsall, 12 In.	795.00
Vase, Red Layered In White, Trumpet Blossoms, Leafy Stems, 10 In.	1980.00
Vase, Red Sphere, Morning Glory Blossoms, Triple Border Bands, 3 In.	1430.00
Vase, Yellow, Red Berries, France, 3 1/2 In.	400.00

CAMPAIGN memorabilia is listed in the Political category.

CAMPBELL KIDS were first used as part of an advertisement for the Campbell Soup Company in 1906. The kids were created by Grace Drayton, a popular illustrator of the day. The kids were used in magazine and newspaper ads until about 1951. They were presented again in 1966; and in 1983, they were redesigned with a slimmer, more contemporary appearance.

Bank, Cast Iron, 4 1/8 In.	220.00
Bowl, Buffalo Pottery, 7 1/2 In.	60.00
Doll, Boy & Girl, Composition, Colonial Style Clothes, 10 In., Pair	45.00
Doll, Cloth, 10 In.	200.00
Doll, Dressed As Nurse, 8 In.	16.00
Knife, Child's, Picture of Campbell Soup Kid	20.00
Lunch Box, 1975	275.00
Mug, Figural, Plastic	10.00
Mug, Plastic, West Bend	10.00
Mug, Soup, Kids Face, Yellow Plastic, 3 1/4 x 2 3/4 In. ......*Illus*	20.00
Postcard, Campbell's Soup Kids, No. 2, Unused, Writing On Back	45.00
Range Set, Salt & Pepper	15.00
Salt & Pepper	40.00 To 75.00

CANDELABRUM refers to a candleholder with more than one arm to hold many candles; a candlestick is designed to hold one candle. The eccentricity of the English language makes the plural of candelabrum into candelabra.

2–Light, Bronze, Rococo, Wall, Pair	475.00
3–Light, Brass, 15 1/4 In.	49.00
3–Light, Convertible, Sterling Silver, Gorham, 7 1/2 x 12 1/2 In., Pair	385.00
3–Light, Francis I, Reed & Barton, 1952, 7 1/4 In.	2310.00
3–Light, Gardrooned, Sterling Silver, Towle, c.1940, 10 In.	600.00
4–Light, 4 Scrolling Candle Arms, Electrified, Anglo–Irish, 26 In.	2530.00
5–Light, Charles X, Winged Woman, 33 In., Pair	6600.00
5–Light, Cut Glass, Re–Silvered, 18 In.	950.00
5–Light, Empire, Gilt Bronze, Pair	3575.00
5–Light, Figural, Spelter, 13 In.	55.00
5–Light, Gilt Metal, Pottery, Prisms, Victorian, 19 In.	500.00
5–Light, Louis XVI, 25 1/2 In.	2860.00
5–Light, Tin, 18 In., Pair	3750.00
6–Light, Acanthus Clad Arms, Wax Pans, 1870s, 26 In., Pair	2090.00
6–Light, Flame Finials, Silver, J. Charles Eddington, England, 1840, 27 In.	7700.00
7–Light, Neoclassical Style, Patinated Metal, c.1870, 33 In., Pair	990.00
Bronze, Nest of Fledglings, 19th Century, 19 3/4 In., Pair	880.00
Ceramic, Griffen, Shield Base, Blue, White, Gilt, Neuhawenleben, 22 In., Pair	308.00
Reclining Whippets, Marble Base, Bronze, c.1835, 10 1/2 In., Pair	1045.00
Royal Danish, Sterling Silver, International, 13 3/4 In., Pair	385.00
Weighted Base, Kirk Sterling Silver, 6 1/2 In., Pair	145.00

Campbell Kids, Mug, Soup, Kid's Face,
Yellow Plastic, 3 1/4 X 2 3/4 In.

◆ ◆ ◆ ◆ ◆ ◆ ◆ ◆ ◆ ◆ ◆ ◆ ◆ ◆ ◆ ◆ ◆ ◆ ◆

Be careful when cleaning bronze figurines, lamp bases, bowls, etc. Never use steel wool, stiff brushes, or chemicals. They remove the surface patina and lower the value.

◆ ◆ ◆ ◆ ◆ ◆ ◆ ◆ ◆ ◆ ◆ ◆ ◆ ◆ ◆ ◆ ◆ ◆ ◆

CANDLESTICKS were made of brass, pewter, Sandwich glass, sterling silver, plated silver, and all types of pottery and porcelain. The earliest candlesticks, dating from the sixteenth century, held the candle on a pricket (sharp pointed spike). These lost favor because in times of strife the large church candlesticks with prickets became formidable weapons, so the socket was mandated. Candlesticks changed in style through the centuries and designs range from classic to rococo to Art Nouveau to Art Deco.

Amber Glass, Art Deco, 5 1/2 In., Pair	35.00
Bell Metal, Adams Style, c.1790, 11 In., Pair	412.00
Bell Metal, George III, England, 1760, 6 3/4 In., Pair	110.00
Bell Metal, George III, England, 1790, 10 1/4 In., Pair	220.00
Bell Metal, Queen Anne, 7 1/2 x 5 In., Pair	495.00
Black Marble, Corinthian Column, 13 In., Pair	440.00
Brass, 5 3/8 In., Pair	15.00
Brass, 7 In.	38.00
Brass, 9 1/4 In., Pair	176.00
Brass, Ace of Diamonds, 14 In., Pair	1600.00
Brass, Beehive & Diamond Detail, Push Up, 9 7/8 In.	60.00
Brass, Capstan Base, 5 In.	660.00
Brass, Capstan Form, 17th Century, 7 1/2 In.	330.00
Brass, Church, Victorian, 19 1/2 In.	100.00
Brass, Diamond Detail, Victorian, 11 3/4 In., Pair	155.00
Brass, Figural Porcelain Stem, Enameled, 8 3/8 In., Pair	99.00
Brass, Fluted Column, 18th Century, France, Pair	595.00
Brass, George II, England, 1740, 7 3/4 In., Pair	1320.00
Brass, George II, England, 7 1/2 In., Pair	358.00
Brass, George III, Push-Up, Late 18th Century, 12 In., Pair	275.00
Brass, Gimbal, Push-Up & Set Screw, 11 1/2 In.	192.00
Brass, Hog Scraper, Double Wedding Band	395.00
Brass, King of Diamonds, Push-Up, 12 In., Pair	296.00
Brass, Louis XV, Early 18th Century, France, 8 In., Pair	330.00
Brass, Neoclassical Style, Tapering Support, Cavetto Base, 8 In., Pair	77.00
Brass, Octagonal Base, Stem & Socket, 7 3/8 In.	165.00
Brass, Push-Up, 6 3/4 In., Pair	130.00
Brass, Push-Up, Beehive & Diamond-Quilted Detail, Victorian, 8 In.	50.00
Brass, Push-Up, Beehive, Diamond-Quilted Detail, Victorian, 7 In., Pair	66.00
Brass, Push-Up, Oval Base, England, 5 1/2 In.	21.50
Brass, Push-Up, Square Base, England, 6 1/4 In.	71.50
Brass, Push-Up, Victorian, 6 7/8 In., Pair	55.00
Brass, Queen Anne Style, 7 1/2 In., Pair	165.00
Brass, Queen Anne Style, 9 1/4 In., Pair	187.00
Brass, Queen Anne, England, 1760, 8 In., Pair	935.00
Brass, Regency, 1860, 9 In., Pair	200.00
Brass, Square Base, Paw Feet, 6 3/4 In.	247.00
Brass, Square Base, Stamped Initials, 8 In.	220.00
Brass, Victorian, Baluster Turned Support, Octagonal Flat Base, 9 In., Pair	125.00
Brass, Victorian, Knopped Support, Flat Rounded Rectangular Base, 10 In.	77.00
Brass, Victorian, Urn-Shaped Nozzles, Octagonal Flat Base, 9 1/2 In., Pair	132.00
Bronze, Charles X, Fluted Stem, Acanthus Cast Base, 11 1/4 In., Pair	1925.00
Bronze, Cherub Support, Dore & Champ Le Vais, France, 5 1/4 In.	495.00
Bronze, Classically Draped Woman Holding Candle, Italy, 20 In., Pair	2200.00
Bronze, Corseted Bobeches, Jarvie, 13 In., Pair	990.00
Bronze, Empire Style, 3 Swans Around Stem, Leaf Tip Nozzle, 6 In., Pair	1650.00
Bronze, Figural, Dandy & Coquette, c.1880, 13 1/4 In. Pair	245.00
Bronze, Gilded, Peg Lamp Insert, Gold Shade, 12 1/2 In.	247.00
Bronze, Jarvie, Pair	1400.00
Bronze, Verdigris Finish, Green Glass Insert, 22 5/8 In.	770.00
Canary Glass, 1850–1865, Pair	850.00
Canary Glass, Hexagonal, 8 In., Pair	180.00
Canary Glass, Loop & Petal, 7 In., Pair	220.00
Canary Glass, Stepped Base, Fluted Columnar Stem, 9 1/4 In.	71.00
Copper, Jarvie Style, Bulbous Candle Nozzle, Tapering Stem, 14 In., Pr.	550.00

Gilt Bronze, Sconce, 4 Arms, Rococo, Mirrored Back, Pair	2530.00
Glass, Cased White Over Clear, Richardson, 1870s	350.00
Glass, Clear, Flint, Hexagonal, Pewter Insert, Pittsburgh, 9 3/4 In., Pair	420.00
Glass, Dolphin, Clam Broth Base, 1845–1870, 10 1/4 In., Pair	2200.00
Glass, Loop & Petal, 6 7/8 In., Pair	165.00
Glass, Pressed Hexagonal Base, Blown Stem, 8 5/8 In., Pair	352.00
Iron, Hog Scraper, Lip Hanger, Push–Up, 7 1/4 In.	125.00
Iron, Hog Scraper, Push–Up, Brass Ring, 5 3/4 In.	275.00
Iron, Hog Scraper, Push–Up, Iron Ring, 8 1/2 In.	193.00
Iron, Hog Scraper, Push–Up, Lip Hanger, 5 1/2 In.	110.00
Iron, Hog Scraper, Push–Up, Lip Hanger, 6 In.	100.00
Iron, Hog Scraper, Push–Up, Lip Hanger, 7 In.	110.00
Iron, Hog Scraper, Push–Up, Shaw, Birmingham, 7 In.	85.00
Marbelized Glass, Opaque Purple, 5 In., Pair	88.00
Pewter, Beaded Trim, 8 In., Pair	275.00
Pewter, Crowned Rose Touch, 7 In.	275.00
Pewter, Push–Up, 8 5/8 In., Pair	330.00
Pewter, Push–Up, 9 3/4 In., Pair	290.00
Pewter, Reeded Detail, Removable Bobeche, 10 1/4 In., Pair	180.00
Pewter, Ribbed Detail, Removable Bobeche, 9 1/4 In., Pair	210.00
Pewter, Round Base, Scrolled Design, 6 3/8 In.	25.00
Porcelain, Kneeling Figures At Fountain, Bow, c.1765, 10 1/8 In., Pair	1815.00
Porcelain, Trees, Gold & Black Owls, Germany, 7 1/2 In., Pair	245.00
Rock Crystal, Octagonal Drip Pans, Mounted As Lamp, 26 In., Pair	7150.00
Silver Plate, Corinthian Form, 8 In., Pair	121.00
Silver Plate, Raised Floral, 10 In., Pair	175.00
Silver Plate, Regency, Sheffield, 1830, Weighted, 10 1/4 In., Pair	302.00
Silver Plate, Telescopic, Cut Glass, Bolton, 1800, 12 1/4 In., Pair	1540.00
Square Base, Tapered Stem, Drip Pan, Sheffield, 1907, Pair	2230.00
Sterling Silver, Double, Domed Footed, Wooden Base, Cellini Craft, 9 1/8 In., Pr.	2900.00
Sterling Silver, Fluted Stem, Swags, Nozzle, Germany, 10 5/8 In., Pair	2530.00
Sterling Silver, George III, G. Ashforth, England, 1787, 12 1/8 In., 4 Pc.	4950.00
Sterling Silver, George III, Telescoping, Sheffield, 1805, 4 Piece	2640.00
Sterling Silver, Louis XV, Gorham, 1891, 12 1/2 In., 4 Piece	3850.00
Tin, Hog Scraper, Push–Up, Worn Black Paint, 4 1/4 In., Pair	170.00
Wooden, Blue Paint, 8 1/2 In.	27.00

CANDLEWICK items may be listed in the Imperial and Pressed Glass categories.

CANDY CONTAINERS have been popular since the late Victorian era. Collectors have long favored the glass containers; but now all types, including tin and papier-mache, are collected. Probably the earliest glass container sold commercially was the Liberty Bell made in 1876 for sale at the Centennial Exposition. Thousands of designs were made until the cost became too high in the 1960s. By the late 1970s, reproductions were being made and sold without the candy. Containers listed here are glass unless otherwise described.

Airplane, Passenger	325.00
Airplane, Spirit of Goodwill, With Candy	150.00
Airplane, Spirit of St. Louis, Amber	400.00
Amos 'n Andy	525.00
Amos 'n Andy, Original Cover	500.00
Auto Jeep, Willys–Overland, Label	45.00
Auto, Limousine, Glass Wheels	90.00
Auto, Limousine, Westmoreland Speciality Co.	200.00
Auto, Roadster, With Bunny Driver & Passengers, Cardboard, 6 1/2 In.	200.00
Auto, Sedan, 4–Door, Tin Wheels	245.00
Auto, Volkswagon	40.00
Barney Google & Ball	352.00
Baseball Player, With Glove	450.00
Baseball, 3 In.	12.00
Battleship	12.50 To 17.50

Bear, On Circus Tub	325.00
Bird Cage	200.00
Boat, Queen Mary	300.00
Boy & Girl Skater, Porcelain, Germany, 2 1/2 In., Pair	25.00
Bulldog, Red & Green Suit, Blue Cap, 7 In.	75.00
Bunny, Fanny Farmer, Ceramic	16.00
Bus, Greyhound, No. 1	325.00
Camera, Tripod	300.00
Candelabra, Ruby Flashed	95.00
Candlestick, 2–Handles	350.00
Candy Cane, Pink, Mercury Glass, Large	30.00
Cannon, Contents	495.00
Cannon, Tin Closure	600.00
Carriage, Doll, Fanny Farmer	75.00
Cash Register	600.00
Cat, Black, Composition, Removable Head, Germany	155.00 To 180.00
Cat, Papier–Mache, Germany, 1950s, 7 1/2 In.	25.00
Cat, Smiling, Oversize Head, Black Paint, Red, White, Papier–Mache, 4 In.	50.00
Cat, Tabby, Black Stripes, Glass Eyes, Neck Closure, 4 In.	115.00
Cherry Tree Log, With Hatchet, Japan, 1950s, 3 In.	32.00
Chick, In Egg–Shell Auto	350.00
Chick, Papier–Mache, Polka–Dot Clown Suit, 3 1/2 In.	130.00
Chicken, On Oblong Basket	55.00 To 95.00
Chicken, Painted Human Face, Cloth Covering, 7 1/2 In.	220.00
Child, With Candy, Naked	50.00
Church, Steeple, Cross	65.00
Clock, Alarm	275.00
Clock, Mantel, Gold Trim, Paper Dial	185.00
Clock, Round Top	250.00
Cornucopia, Tin Top	45.00
Crystal Palace	375.00
Devil, Papier–Mache, Germany, 1950s, 7 In.	28.00
Dirigible, Los Angeles	95.00
Dog, Circus, Hat, Contents	25.00
Dog, Metal Cap, Red Stripes, Contents	20.00
Dog, Next To Barrel	325.00
Doll Head, Painted Hair, Flowers, Porcelain, Japan, 1950s, 3 In.	14.00
Doll, Bisque Head, Open Mouth, Marked Petite Francais, 12 1/2 In.	475.00
Drum, Eagle On Side, Gold Trim	45.00
Duck, On Rectangular Basket	110.00
Elephant, G. O. P.	175.00
Elephant, With Howdah	55.00
Elf, Cardboard, Glitter Coating, Germany	18.00
Elk's Tooth, Screw–On Cover, Milk Glass	125.00
Express Wagon	300.00
Fat Boy	250.00
Felix, By Barrel, Cover	728.00
Fire Engine, 1914	100.00
Flapper, Paper Mask	75.00
Flower Girl, Blue Dress, Green Blouse, White Apron, 3 1/2 In.	70.00
Football Player, Cotton Clothing, Lifts At Waist, Composition, 8 1/2 In.	330.00
Football, Cardboard, Germany, 2 In.	15.00
Gas Pump	425.00
Girl, In Snowsuit, Papier–Mache & Plaster, Mica Covering, 4 1/4 In.	193.00
Globe	200.00
Globe, World, On Stand	425.00
Gun, Indian Head	500.00
Happifats Boy On Drum	175.00 To 350.00
Helicopter, Single Blade, Label	375.00
Hen, On Nest, 6 In.	40.00
High Hat, Ink Rose, Green Leaves Decal	35.00
Horn, Fanny Farmer, Christmas	48.00
Horn, Trumpet, Clear	95.00

Horse, With Jockey, Metal, Hand Painted, Japan, 2 3/4 In. 12.00
House, Cotton Santa Claus In Front, Cardboard 95.00
Independence Hall 325.00
Jackie Coogan, Contents 1350.00
Jackie Coogan, Pail, Green 350.00
Kettle, 3–Footed 55.00
Kiddie Kar 225.00
Lantern, Glass, Polished Copper Top & Bottom, Pat. 1928 .... 37.00
Lantern, Ribbed Base, Gold Top, Red Reflector, Contents 10.00
Lantern, Signal, Blue–Green Glass 40.00
Liberty Bell, No. 3, Green 55.00
Locomotive, Blue 200.00
Locomotive, Victory Glass, No. 1 .... 85.00
Log Cabin, Tin, Glass Insert 450.00
Mailbox 225.00
Man With Flowers, Glass 25.00
Motorcycle, Driver 500.00
Mule, Pulling Barrel 55.00
Nodder, Indian, Germany, 6 In. 105.00
Nodder, Santa Claus, Holding Christmas, Papier–Mache 85.00
Owl, Candy 225.00
Owl, Glass Eyes, Papier–Mache, 10 In. 95.00
Owl, Wooden Perch, Glass Eyes, Japan, 1950s, 3 1/2 In. 12.00
Palm Tree, Monkey, Coconuts, Japan, 1950s, 8 In. 8.00
Pencils, On Card, Kiddie's Candy 75.00
Peter & Wolf, Scenes From Cartoon, Tin, Belgium, 1940s, 12 x 7 3/4 In. 120.00
PEZ, Bullwinkle 20.00
PEZ, Chicken 10.00
PEZ, Cocoa Marsh Astronaut 85.00
PEZ, Daffy Duck, Big Ears 12.00
PEZ, Doctor 25.00
PEZ, Donald Duck 12.50
PEZ, Giraffe 65.00
PEZ, Green Hornet, 1966 .... 198.00
PEZ, Indian Chief 25.00
PEZ, Mickey Mouse 15.00
PEZ, Mr. Ugly, Green Face 12.00
PEZ, Pluto 30.00
PEZ, Popeye 55.00
PEZ, Roadrunner 4.00
PEZ, Santa Claus 12.00
PEZ, Santa Claus & Snowman, Pair 10.00
PEZ, Skull 9.50
PEZ, Snowman ....6.00 To 10.00
PEZ, Spiderman 10.00
PEZ, Tweety 3.00
PEZ, Witch 28.00
PEZ, Wonder Woman 20.00
PEZ, Yappy Dog, Orange Head 30.00
Phonograph, Glass Horn 475.00
Phonograph, Tin Record 475.00
Piano, Brown Paint 425.00
Pocket Watch, Metal Screw–Off Cover ....110.00 To 175.00
Polar Bear, White, Red Mouth, Fur, 8 In. 165.00
Powder Horn 60.00
Powder Horn, Cambridge 50.00
Pumpkin Man, Composition, Germany 425.00
Pumpkin Man, Papier–Mache, 5 1/2 In. 18.00
Pumpkin, Papier–Mache, 4 In. 18.00
Puppy, Christmas, Brown & White, 4 In. 75.00
Puss In Boots 150.00
Rabbit, Basket On Back, Papier–Mache, 9 In. 45.00
Rabbit, Ears Layed Back, Clear 110.00

Rabbit, Easter, Back Pack, Glass Eyes, Papier–Mache, 11 In. 55.00
Rabbit, Eating Carrot 195.00
Rabbit, Glass Eyes, Removable Head 55.00
Rabbit, Green Hat, Glass Eyes, Felt Suit, Papier–Mache, 11 In. 1500.00
Rabbit, Looking Out Window In Egg 225.00
Rabbit, Papier–Mache, Egg Shape Body, Painted Hands & Feet, 6 1/2 In. 250.00
Rabbit, Papier–Mache, Glass Eyes, White Chalk Finish, 5 1/4 In. 45.00
Rabbit, Paws Together 98.00
Rabbit, Peter, Clear, Signed 20.00
Rabbit, Pink Hat, Green Jacket, Celluloid, 5 In. 145.00
Rabbit, Plain Brown, Papier–Mache, Germany 48.00
Rabbit, Pushing Cart .... 400.00 To 425.00
Rabbit, Running On Log 350.00
Rabbit, Seated, Light Brown, Glass Eyes, Removable, Head, 6 In. 75.00
Rabbit, Standing, Paws Raised, Glass Eyes, Papier–Mache, Germany 225.00
Rabbit, With Apron, Contents 950.00
Rabbit, With Basket On Back, Papier–Mache, 9 In. 45.00
Rabbit, With Clothes, Glass Eyes, Papier–Mache, Removable Head, Germany 245.00
Racer, Driver 200.00
Railroad Lantern, 1 Pt. 10.00
Railroad Signal 12.00
Reindeer, Felt Body, Metal Antlers, Papier–Mache, 10 In. 1000.00
Reindeer, Lead Antlers, Glass Eyes, Composition, 9 In. 465.00
Reindeer, Next To Santa Claus In Wicker Sleigh, 1960s 1250.00
Rocking Horse, Clown Rider, Blue Glass 275.00
Rolling Pin, Handles 250.00
Rooster, Crowing, Green Glass, With Candy 250.00
Safe, Milk Glass 175.00
Santa Claus, Banded Coat 300.00
Santa Claus, Basket, Snow Covered Base, U.S. Zone Germany, 10 1/2 In. 155.00
Santa Claus, Donkey, On Sled, Woolly Trim, 7 In. 375.00
Santa Claus, Felt Suit, Removable Head, Germany, 5 In. 295.00
Santa Claus, Fruit Basket, Celluloid, Irwin, 5 In. 45.00
Santa Claus, Fur Beard, Feather Tree, Neck Closure, Germany, 11 In. 445.00
Santa Claus, Fur Beard, Germany, 9 1/2 In. 425.00
Santa Claus, Fur Beard, Papier–Mache Head & Hands, Germany, 12 1/2 In. 1570.00
Santa Claus, Knapsack, Skiing, Plastic 28.00
Santa Claus, Leaving Chimney 50.00
Santa Claus, Net Body, Celluloid Face 85.00
Santa Claus, Papier–Mache, Cloth, 20th Century, 12 In. 1430.00
Santa Claus, Papier–Mache, Germany, 4 1/2 In. 350.00
Santa Claus, Plastic Head 75.00
Santa Claus, Plastic Head, Label 125.00
Santa Claus, Reindeer, Wicker Sleigh, 1950s 1250.00
Santa Claus, Separates At Waist, Felt Coat, Composition Legs, Germany, 7 In. 450.00
Santa Claus, Sleigh Pulled By Reindeer, Metal Antlers 2900.00
Santa Claus, Victory Glass Co. 195.00
Santa Claus, Wicker Sleigh Drawn By Reindeer, Sponge Trim 1250.00
Santa Head, Painted Composition, 3 1/4 In. 467.00
Schoolhouse, Flag 35.00
Ship, U.S.S. United States, Plastic, Box, 14 x 3 1/2 In. 42.00
Snowball, Cotton Santa Claus On Top, 1930s 110.00
Snowman, Mica–Coated Cardboard, Germany 55.00
Soda Fountain, Red 125.00
Soldier, By Tent 3500.00
Spark Plug, Green Tint 160.00
Stage Coach 125.00
Submarine 400.00
Suitcase, Bears, Milk Glass 225.00
Swan Boat, Original Cover 1000.00
Tank, Driver 45.00
Taxi, 6 Vents 100.00
Telephone, Complete 55.00

Cane, Mother-of-Pearl, Handle, Silver, 9 In.

Telephone, Desk Type, Label	225.00
Telephone, Glass Receiver	95.00
Telephone, Victory Glass, No. 2	225.00
Toonerville Trolley	750.00 To 875.00
Trunk, Clear Glass	135.00
Turkey, Colorful, Papier–Mache, Germany	48.00
Turkey, Metal Feet, Neck Closure, Germany	65.00
Turkey, Papier–Mache, Germany	35.00
Ugly Duckling	125.00
Village Buildings, Tin, Glass Insert	125.00
Wagon, Circus	65.00
Watch, With Fob	325.00
Wheelbarrow	100.00
Wheelbarrow, Yellow & Red, Painted Tin, 3 1/2 In.	77.00
Witch, Cone Shape, Papier–Mache, Germany, 7 1/2 In.	25.00
Witch, Pumpkin Head	650.00 To 850.00

CANES and walking sticks were used by every well–dressed man in the nineteenth century, but by World War I the style had changed. Today canes are used by few but the infirm. Collectors prize old canes made with special features, like hidden swords, whiskey flasks, or risque pictures seen through peepholes. Examples with solid gold heads or made from exotic materials, such as walrus vertebrae, are among the higher priced canes.

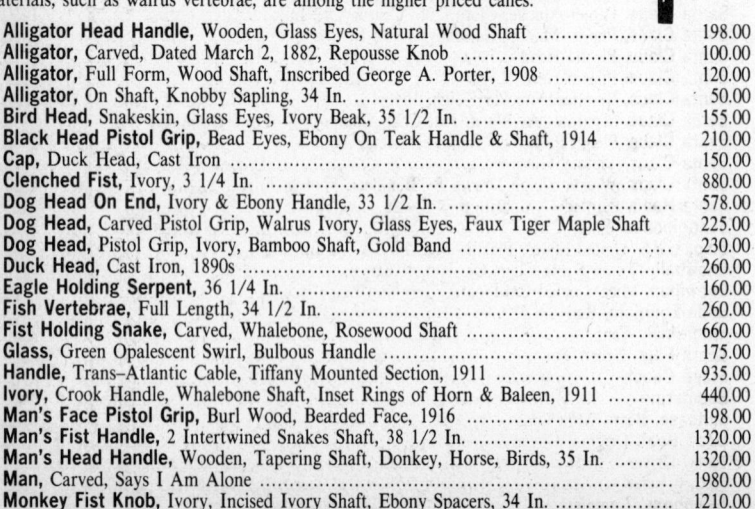

Alligator Head Handle, Wooden, Glass Eyes, Natural Wood Shaft	198.00
Alligator, Carved, Dated March 2, 1882, Repousse Knob	100.00
Alligator, Full Form, Wood Shaft, Inscribed George A. Porter, 1908	120.00
Alligator, On Shaft, Knobby Sapling, 34 In.	50.00
Bird Head, Snakeskin, Glass Eyes, Ivory Beak, 35 1/2 In.	155.00
Black Head Pistol Grip, Bead Eyes, Ebony On Teak Handle & Shaft, 1914	210.00
Cap, Duck Head, Cast Iron	150.00
Clenched Fist, Ivory, 3 1/4 In.	880.00
Dog Head On End, Ivory & Ebony Handle, 33 1/2 In.	578.00
Dog Head, Carved Pistol Grip, Walrus Ivory, Glass Eyes, Faux Tiger Maple Shaft	225.00
Dog Head, Pistol Grip, Ivory, Bamboo Shaft, Gold Band	230.00
Duck Head, Cast Iron, 1890s	260.00
Eagle Holding Serpent, 36 1/4 In.	160.00
Fish Vertebrae, Full Length, 34 1/2 In.	260.00
Fist Holding Snake, Carved, Whalebone, Rosewood Shaft	660.00
Glass, Green Opalescent Swirl, Bulbous Handle	175.00
Handle, Trans–Atlantic Cable, Tiffany Mounted Section, 1911	935.00
Ivory, Crook Handle, Whalebone Shaft, Inset Rings of Horn & Baleen, 1911	440.00
Man's Face Pistol Grip, Burl Wood, Bearded Face, 1916	198.00
Man's Fist Handle, 2 Intertwined Snakes Shaft, 38 1/2 In.	1320.00
Man's Head Handle, Wooden, Tapering Shaft, Donkey, Horse, Birds, 35 In.	1320.00
Man, Carved, Says I Am Alone	1980.00
Monkey Fist Knob, Ivory, Incised Ivory Shaft, Ebony Spacers, 34 In.	1210.00

Monkeys, Carved, Eagle & Flowers, Natural Twist Wood Shaft 125.00
Mother–of–Pearl, Handle, Silver, 9 In. ....*Illus* 65.00
Presentation, Major Mack, Civil War, 14K Gold Top, 1863 .... 850.00
Ram's Head Mount, Ivory Crook Handle, Decoupage Shaft, 1909 .... 308.00
Scrimshaw Handle, Whalebone Shaft, Ivory Knob, Tortoiseshell Inlaid 1430.00
Scrimshaw Handle, Whalebone, Clenched Fist Knob, Initial A 3400.00
Scrimshaw Handle, Whalebone, Rope Carved 715.00
Serpent, Carved, Man's Head, People, Cattle Train, Chicken, Flag, 1905, 34 In. 2310.00
Snake, Full Form, Chip Carved Body, Glass Eyes, 1909 .... 525.00
Sword, Clenched Fist Handle, Ropework Sleeve, Blade–10 In. 522.50
Sword, Ebony Scabbard & Hilt, Bone Inlays, India, 35 1/2 In. 190.00
Sword, Ebony, Brass Lion Head Cap, Carved Bone, 1800s 230.00
Tomahawk Handle, Decal, Souvenir of Wisconsin Dells, 37 1/4 In. 40.00
Walking Stick, 2 Lizards, Bird, Snake, 1926, Two–Tone Brown & Red, 37 In. 94.00
Walking Stick, Alligator Carved Handle, Knobby Shaft, Metallic Eyes, 35 1/2 In. ... 105.00
Walking Stick, Animal Head With Snake, Lizards, Sea Monsters, 36 In. 423.00
Walking Stick, Bald Eagle Head, 6–Pointed Stars, Pine Leaves On Shaft, 37 In. 2750.00
Walking Stick, Bald Eagle Head, Flag & Stars On Shaft, Pine 35.00
Walking Stick, Bird Handle, Detailed Animals, Birds, Flowers, Medallion, 35 In. 385.00
Walking Stick, Carved Designs & Lords Prayer, 35 In. 195.00
Walking Stick, Carved Designs In Bark of People, Animals, Etc., 61 In. 49.00
Walking Stick, Carved, WPA, 1936 .... 50.00
Walking Stick, Chain Link Carved, Knob Head, 34 3/4 In. 80.00
Walking Stick, Curved Handle, Glass Flask Interior, 23 In. 385.00
Walking Stick, Dog Head, Old Paint & Varnish, 35 In. 82.00
Walking Stick, Eagle Form Handle, Carved Eagle Shaft, Wooden, 36 1/2 In. 220.00
Walking Stick, Ebony, Ivory Handle, Carved Shield, Brass Collar, 33 In. 250.00
Walking Stick, Elephant Head Handle, Ivory, Rosewood, Ivory Tip 275.00
Walking Stick, Gambler's, Bamboo, Screw–Off Walnut Knob, Holds Dice, 35 In. 220.00
Walking Stick, Gentleman Bust Handle, Ivory, Rosewood Stick, 36 In. 440.00
Walking Stick, Gold & Rosewood Presentation, Jefferson Davis 7700.00
Walking Stick, Gold Filled Top, Engraved Name, M. W. A. Camp 55.00
Walking Stick, Gold Plated Handle, Flowers, Pine Cone Shaft, Wooden, 34 3/4 In. .. 275.00
Walking Stick, Gold Tip, Senator Farwell's 605.00
Walking Stick, Rabbit Head Handle, Ivory, Ebony Stick, 37 In. 467.00
Walking Stick, Roothead, Carved Mouse Head Handle, 37 3/4 In. 70.00
Walking Stick, Roothead, Carved Shaft, Wenn, N. Bloomfield, O., 1950, 34 In. 70.00
Walking Stick, Silver Dolphins Handle, Ebony Stick, 37 1/ 2 In. 245.00
Walking Stick, Skeletal Figure Over Ebony Shaft, Ivory, Metal Finial, 1880s, 36 In. 440.00
Walking Stick, Snake, Rhinestone Eyes, Ball In Cage, Relief Insignia, 37 In. 220.00
Walking Stick, Snake, White Repaint Over Black, 29 In. 60.00
Walking Stick, Snakes, Lizards, Eagle, Stain, Burned Wood Design, 35 In. 49.00
Walking Stick, Tin, Cast White Metal Knob, McKinley Bust, 1896, 33 In. ... 137.00 To 150.00
Walking Stick, Vine & Leaves, Masonic Emblems, 1920, Inscribed, 35 1/2 In. 330.00
Walking Stick, Willow, Diamond–Like Shapes, 35 In. 55.00
Walking Stick, Woman's, Victorian, Sterling Silver Handle 95.00
Walking Stick, Wooden Pug With Hinged Mouth Handle, Rosewood Stick, 38 In. ... 550.00
Walrus Ivory Handle, Rosewood Shaft 192.50
Walrus Ivory Handle, Tiger & Snake In Combat 247.50
Walrus, Carved, Ivory Handle, Serpent, Inlaid Eyes, Whalebone Shaft, 34 In. 990.00
Whale Ivory Handle, Octagonal Head, Whalebone Ferrule, 37 In. 143.00
Whalebone Handle, Carved, Cylindrical, 36 In. 88.00
Whalebone Handle, Sterling Silver Cap, Last Cane He Carried, Josie, 1909 .... 100.00
Whalebone, Carved, Sailor Going Ashore Type, Ivory Handle, 33 1/2 In. 550.00

CANTON CHINA is blue–and–white ware made near Canton, China, from
about 1785 to 1895. It is hand decorated with Chinese scenes.

Bowl, Scalloped Rim, Blue & White, 4 1/2 In. 750.00
Dish, Cover, 11 x 8 In. 250.00
Dish, Vegetable, Cover, 9 In. 275.00
Fish Tank, Blue & White, With Stand, 26 x 16 In. 6050.00
Garden, Seat, Porcelain 9000.00
Holder, Umbrella 4500.00

Planter, Dark Blue, Oval, Medium	545.00
Plate, Blue & White, 10 In., 6 Piece	99.00
Plate, Hot Water, Blue & White, 10 1/2 In.	110.00
Platter, Blue & White, 10 In.	300.00
Platter, Blue & White, 13 In.	200.00
Platter, Rain Cloud, Medium Blue, 11 1/4 x 9 1/2 In.	295.00
Platter, Scene, Oval	495.00
Shrimp Dish	750.00
Underplate, Leaf Shape	250.00
Vase, Famille Verte, Flower Heads, Tassels, Mounted As Lamp, 19 1/2 In.	3300.00

CAPO–DI–MONTE porcelain was first made in Naples, Italy, from 1743 to 1759. The factory moved near Madrid, Spain, reopened in 1771, and worked to 1834. Since that time, the Doccia factory of Italy acquired the molds and is using the N and crown mark. Societe Richard Ceramica is a modern–day firm often referred to as Ginori or Capo–di–Monte. This company uses the crown and N mark.

Biscuit Box, Barrel Shape, 4 1/2 In.	25.00
Box, Cover, Classical Scenes On Top, Blue Mark, 6 1/4 x 10 In.	660.00
Box, Hinged Lid, 2 3/4 In.	200.00
Bust, Pilgrim Woman, 6 3/4 In.	145.00
Casket, Jewelry, 1820	5500.00
Compote, Multicolor, Signed, 7 In. Diam.	40.00
Cup, 2 Handles	495.00
Figurine, Buccaneer, Signed, 12 In.	225.00
Figurine, Cinderella & Prince	160.00
Figurine, Dear, Belcari	90.00
Jar, Apothecary, Black, Gilt, Ginori, 11 3/4 In., Pair	385.00
Lamp, Floral, Lattice Type Holes Body, Blue, Yellow Floral, No Shade	90.00
Mug, Cover, Lion Finial	550.00
Night Light, China	275.00
Night Light, Owl	225.00 To 325.00
Planter, Seashell, Large	45.00
Plate, Crest & Molded Figures, Marked, 8 3/4 In.	60.00
Plate, Open Handles, Signed, 11 In.	155.00
Tankard, Cover, Cherubs Around Rim, Elephant Head Handle, 13 In.	495.00
Tankard, Lion Top, Elephant Handle	595.00
Tea Set, Pompeiian Scenes, White Ground, Service For 12	1760.00
Tureen, Cupid Design, Cover, Black Crown Mark, Large	550.00
Tureen, Stand, Drunken Cherub Finial, Cavorting Figures, 13 In.	715.00
Urn, Classical Scenes, Dark Blue, Crown Mark, 8 In., Pair	550.00
Urn, Cover, Molded Classical Scene, Blue Crown Mark, 12 In., Pair	885.00
Vase, Applied Roses, Marked, 14 In.	80.00
Vase, Classical Scene, Blue Crown Mark, 6 1/2 In.	495.00

CAPTAIN MARVEL was introduced in February 1940 in Whiz comic books. An orphan named Billy Batson met the wizard Shazam and whenever he said the magic word he was transformed into a superhero. A movie serial was released in 1940. The comic was discontinued in 1954. A second Captain Marvel appeared in 1966, a third in 1967. Only the original was transformed by shouting *Shazam.*

Book, Comic, Captain Marvel, Jr., No. 45	50.00
Book, Comic, Marvel Superheroes, No. 1, King–Size Special, 1966	30.00
Book, Comic, No. 104	19.50
Car, Porsche Audi, Corgi	6.00
Doll, No Cape, Mego, 8 In.	12.00
Game, Shazam	45.00
Wristwatch	250.00
Wristwatch, Original Price Tag & Guarantee, Dated 1948, Box	400.00

CAPTAIN MIDNIGHT began as a radio show in September 1940. The first comic book appeared in July 1941. Captain Midnight was really the aviator Captain Albright, who was to defeat the Nazis. A movie serial was

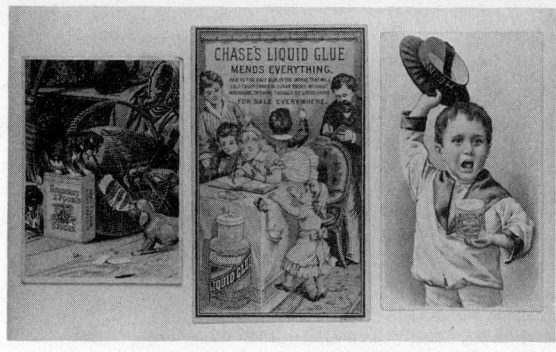

Card, Advertising, Skickney & Poor's Spices, 4 X 3 In.;

Card, Advertising, Chase's Liquid Glue, Mends Everything,

5 1/4 X 3 1/4 In.; Card, Advertising, Heinz Baked Beans

With Tomato Sauce, 5 X 3 In.

made in 1942 and a comic strip was published for a short time. The comic book Captain Midnight ended his career in 1948. The radio premiums are the prized collector memorabilia today.

Airline Map, Flight Patrol, Skelly, 1940–1941, 11 x 17 In.	616.00
Booklet, Skelly Trick & Riddle	40.00
Decoder, 1946	75.00
Decoder, Secret Squadron, 1940	65.00 To 85.00
Flying Cross, Flight Commander	120.00
Manual, Secret Squadron, Ovaltine, 1949, 4 Pages, 4 1/2 x 6 In.	120.00
Medal, Decoder, Plastic	375.00
Mug, Ovaltine	25.00
Ring, Secret Compartment	85.00
Shaker, Ovaltine, 4–Color Decal, 5 In.	85.00
Stamp Album, Air Heroes, Skelly, Unused, 1939, 5 x 6 3/4 In.	125.00
Token, Spinner Membership, Skelly, Brass, Quarter Size, 1940	23.00
Toy, Space Ship, Windup, Tin	357.00
Tumbler, Ovaltine, Red	39.00

CARAMEL SLAG, see Chocolate Glass category

CARDS listed here include advertising cards, greeting cards, baseball cards, playing cards, valentines, and others. Color pictures were rare in the nineteenth century, so companies gave away colorful cards with pictures of children, flowers, products, or related scenes that promoted the company name. These were often collected and stored in albums. Greeting cards are also a nineteenth–century idea that has remained popular. Baseball cards also date from the nineteenth century when they were used by tobacco companies as giveaways. The gum cards were started in 1933, but it was not until after World War II that the bubble gum cards favored today were produced. Today over 1,000 cards are issued each year by the gum companies. Related items may be found in the Postcard category.

Advertising, Adams Chewing Gum, Girl On Front, c.1885	17.50
Advertising, Arm & Hammer, Bird, 120 Piece	75.00
Advertising, Ball's Hip Corsets, Girl On Skates	35.00
Advertising, C. S. Parker, Carriage Maker, 1890, 5 In.	25.00
Advertising, Chase's Liquid Glue, Mends Everything, 5 1/4 x 3 1/4 In. ....*Illus*	6.00
Advertising, Chautauqua Desk & Table of Soap, Larkin Soap Company, 1895	36.00
Advertising, Chiropodist, Corns, Bunions, Ingrown Nails, Chicago, 1895, 2 In.	10.00
Advertising, Chocolate Poulaine, Woman Jockey Within Horseshoe, c.1900	9.00

Advertising, Cleveland's Baking Powder, Old Lady With Biscuits, 1892, 5 1/4 In. ... 15.00
Advertising, Clyde Steamship Co., Moonlight On The St. Johns, 1890s, 4 x 7 In. 37.50
Advertising, Dr. Strong's Tricora Corset, Great Relief, 1880s, 2 1/2 x 5 1/2 In. 20.00
Advertising, Estey Organ Co., Girl With Harp On Front, 1880s, 5 x 3 In. 17.50
Advertising, Estey Pianos, Small Girls With Musical Instruments, c.1890 .... 25.00
Advertising, Fairbank's Tom, Dick & Harry Soap, Black Children, Wagon, c.1885 ... 17.50
Advertising, Foster Kid Gloves, English Rustic Scene, 1870s 12.50
Advertising, French Coffee, Goupy and His Plane In Flight, c.1910 .... 22.50
Advertising, G. R. Hanford & Co., Fan Shape, Owl In Tree, Frog, 1880, 5 x 3 In. 7.50
Advertising, Golden Eagle Hotel, No Chinamen Employed, 1880s, 3 x 4 In. 30.00
Advertising, Greer's California Perfumes, Bothin Mfg., Woman, 1885, 3 x 5 1/2 In. 22.50
Advertising, Hartshorn Shade Roller, Victorian Room, 1880s, 4 1/4 In. 18.00
Advertising, Haskel's Wheat Flakes, Children In Front of Fireplace, c.1890 .... 15.00
Advertising, Heinz Baked Beans With Tomato Sauce, 5 x 3 In. ....*Illus* 8.00
Advertising, Heinz, Pickle Shape, Small Child Catching Can, c.1890, 5 x 1 3/4 In. 35.00
Advertising, Hires Root Beer, All Gone, Small Boy With Empty Glass 22.50
Advertising, Hotel Shelburne, Charter Restaurant, 1961, 2 3/4 x 4 1/4 In. 20.00
Advertising, J & P Coats Thread, Kremlin, Famous Stallion, 1880s 15.00
Advertising, J. A. Lowell, Boston, Ship, New Armory Fair, 3 3/4 x 2 1/4 In. 25.00
Advertising, Kimball's Balsam Cough and Lung Remedy, Man, c.1885 .... 17.50
Advertising, Kosta & Co. Oyster House, Calif., Floral Anchor Design 5.00
Advertising, Larkin Soap Co., Chautauqua Desk Shape, Maidens, 1890s, 7 1/2 In. ... 40.00
Advertising, Larkin Soap Company, Children At Beach, Ocean Series, 5 Piece 27.50
Advertising, Lavine Washing Powder, Cat Shape, 1880s, 4 1/2 In. 12.50
Advertising, Lavine Washing Powder, Owl In Tree, Palette Shape, 1880s, 4 1/2 In. 12.50
Advertising, McLaughlin's Coffee, Military Drummer Boy, Union Army, 1890, 5 In 85.00
Advertising, Mellin's Food, Good Morning, Mamma, Smiling Child, 1892, 3 x 4 In. 10.00
Advertising, Mitchell Bread, Cutout Doll, Hawaii 10.00
Advertising, Monarch Teenie Weenies 10.00
Advertising, Norton's Fine Candies, San Francisco, Cats, 1890s, 5 In. 10.00
Advertising, Orange Flower Cologne, Flint's Pharmacy, Oakland,, 1890, 3 1/2 In. ... 6.00
Advertising, P. P. Mast & Co., Agricultural Implements, Lists Items, 1880s 12.50
Advertising, Parker's Tonic, Builds Up The System Heals The Sick, Child, 1880s 15.00
Advertising, Prang & Son, Hunt's Steam Printing Rooms, Sepia, 1877, 4 1/4 In. 37.50
Advertising, Samuel Hill Co., Typewriters & Sewing Machine, Comic Figure, 1890 27.50
Advertising, Segars, Hotel Brighton, Coney Island 12.00
Advertising, Skickney & Poor's Spices, 4 x 3 In. ....*Illus* 5.00
Advertising, Stonewall Whiskey, Emperor of Germany, 6 x 3 1/2 In. 25.00
Advertising, Vose & Sons Pianos, Angels With Musical Instruments, 1880s 25.00
Advertising, W. W. Coles' Great Circus, Capt. M. V. Bates, 1879, 3 3/4 x 6 1/2 In. 22.00
Advertising, Wings Cigarettes, Aircraft, 7 Piece 18.00
Advertising, Woolson Spice 18.00
Baseball, Babe Ruth, Goudey, 1933 .... 550.00
Baseball, Bill Ripken, Error Face 65.00
Baseball, Carl Yastrzemski, Topps, No. 230 .... 10.00
Baseball, Frank Hogan, Big League Chewing Gum, No. 20, 1934 .... 95.00
Baseball, George Brett, Rookie, Topps, No. 228, 1975 .... 175.00
Baseball, Gil Hodges, 1962 .... 100.00
Baseball, Jackie Robinson, Bowman, 1949 .... 13.85
Baseball, Kirby Puckett, Rookie, Fleer, 1985 .... 50.00
Baseball, Kirby Puckett, Rookie, Topps, 1985 .... 25.00
Baseball, Lou Gehrig, Goudey, 1934 .... 6325.00
Baseball, McGuire, Rookie, Topps, 1985 .... 30.00
Baseball, Mickey Mantle, Bowman, 1954 .... 632.00
Baseball, Mickey Mantle, Bowman, No. 59, 1953 .... 1275.00
Baseball, Mickey Mantle, Topps, No. 95, 1957 .... 475.00
Baseball, Mickey Mantle, Topps, No. 563, 1960 .... 250.00
Baseball, Nolan Ryan & Jerry Koosman, Rookie, Topps 177, 1968 .... 880.00
Baseball, Pete Rose, Topps, No. 430 .... 50.00
Baseball, Reggie Jackson, Topps, No. 500 .... 8.00
Baseball, Ryne Sandberg, Donruss, 1984 .... 30.00
Baseball, Satchel Paige, Topps, 1953 .... 345.00
Baseball, Steve Carlton, Rookie, Topps, No. 477, 1965 .... 425.00

Baseball, Ted Williams, Rookie, Play Ball, 1939 .... 3850.00
Baseball, Willie Mays, Topps, No. 49 .... 15.00
Basketball, Elgin Baylor 27.00
Basketball, Wilt Chamberlain 95.00
Christmas, Mr & Mrs. Lon Chaney, To Jos. DeGrasse & Wife, 1923, 6 1/2 x 5 In. 25.00
Christmas, Scene, Floral, Prang 20.00
Cigarette, Sweet Corporal Little Cigars & Mogul Egyptian, 1890s, Pair 5.00
Fortune Telling, Gypsy Witch, Madame LeNormand 35.00
Fortune Telling, Rameses, Goodall, 1890 .... 40.00
Fortune Telling, U.S. Playing Card Co., Teuila, 1923 .... 25.00
Hockey, Bobby Hull, Topps, 1958–1959 .... 1500.00
Hockey, Bobby Orr, Topps, 1966–1967 .... 1500.00
Hockey, Gordie Howe, Topps, 1954–1955 .... 1100.00
Hockey, Maurice Richard, Parkhurst, 1951–1952 .... 650.00
Hockey, Phil Esposito, Topps, 1966–1967 .... 500.00
Hockey, Wayne Gretzky, O–Pee–Chee, 1979–1980 .... 550.00
Lobby, 42nd Street, Warner Brothers, 1933, 17 x 14 In. 1760.00
Lobby, Babes In Toy Land, Hal Roach, 1934, 11 x 14 In. 770.00
Lobby, Ben–Hur, MGM, Linen Back, 1926, 22 x 14 In. 1430.00
Lobby, Broadway Melody, MGM, 1929, 14 x 22 In. 2750.00
Lobby, Moral Law, Gladys Brockwell, 1923 .... 16.00
Lobby, Tarzan Escapes, Johnny Weissmuller, MGM, 1936, 28 x 22 In. 770.00
Lobby, Wiping The Tears, From Wizard of Oz, 1939 .... 3300.00
New Year, Chinese, U.S. Flags, 2 Languages, Red, White & Blue, 1940 .... 6.50
Playing, 52 Different Golf Cartoon Design, 1950s 22.50
Playing, Bicycle Spotter, 1945, Box 15.00
Playing, Black Cotton Pickers, 53 Piece 45.00
Playing, Delta Airlines, San Francisco On Back 11.00
Playing, Delta, 50th Anniversary 8.00
Playing, Denver & Rio Grand, Box 40.00
Playing, Erie Railroad, Double Deck 50.00
Playing, Florida East Coast, 53 Views, 1910 .... 24.00
Playing, Jerald Sulky Co., Waterloo, Iowa, Double Set, 1950s, Box 25.00
Playing, John Wayne, Unopened, 1950s 20.00
Playing, Las Vegas 5.00
Playing, Marilyn Monroe, Nude, Tom Kelly Photography, 1976 .... 20.00
Playing, Maxfield Parrish, Complete 80.00
Playing, Munsters, Complete 45.00
Playing, Nassau, Dancers & Band, Holder, 52 Piece 40.00
Playing, Pictures Nipper, RCA 20.00
Playing, Rummy, Chocolate Drip Sam, Johnston's 10.00
Playing, Stenciled Courts, John Peter Burgers, Germany, 1800s 225.00
Playing, U.S. Playing Card Co., Cincinnati, Hand Printed & Colored, Pre–1846 .... 750.00
Playing, Win, Lose Or Draw, Sherwin Williams, Earl McPherson, 1944, Gift Box 37.00
Playing, Woman With Dog, Art Deco Design, Red, Gold, White, 1932, Box 30.00
Playing, Yellowstone National Park, Haynes Photographs, Box 35.00
Tarot, Piatnick 15.00
Trade, Burdock Blood Bitters, Louis Paullin 10.00
Trade, Krell Piano Co., Hold To Light, 1893 .... 20.00
Trade, Mrs. President Cleveland, Sulfur Bitters 10.00
Trade, Paducah Ice Co., Kentucky, Window 3.00
Trade, Santa Claus, Star Soap, Schultz & Co., Zanesville, Oh., 5 1/2 x 7 1/2 In. 15.00
Trade, Singer Sewing Machine Co., Women Smoking, c.1890, 3 x 5 1/2 In. 20.00
Valentine, 2 Black Children In Front of Window, Opens To Cupid, Tuck, 1907 ...... 135.00
Valentine, Animated, Beech–Nut Gum, Box 85.00
Valentine, Auto Driven By Cupid, Boy & Girl, Mechanical, c.1910, 6 x 5 1/2 In. 65.00
Valentine, Betty Boop Look Alike, Mechanical 22.00
Valentine, Boy & Girl Kissing, Mechanical, Die–Cut Figures, c.1908, 5 x 2 1/2 In. 22.50
Valentine, Boy & Girl Sitting On Stool, Piano Shape, c.1910, 3 1/2 x 4 In. 42.50
Valentine, Boy Pushing Girl In Wheelbarrow, Mechanical, c.1915, 4 1/2 In. 10.00
Valentine, Child, Sleepware, Mechanical, 2 Heads, Happy & Grouchy, 1926, 6 In. ... 17.50
Valentine, Dove, Cupid, Roses, 3–D 15.00
Valentine, Girl & Dog In Airplane, Mechanical, c.1930, 7 1/4 In. 12.50

Valentine, Girl, Baseball Catcher's Uniform, Mechanical, Germany, 1914, 6 x 4 In. 22.50
Valentine, Golliwog, Full Figure 45.00
Valentine, Little Lulu & Tubby, Stand Up 15.00
Valentine, Mary & Lamb, Die Cut, Mechanical 10.00
Valentine, Quaker, For Sarah Newlin, Chester County, Envelope, 1800 .... 1200.00
Valentine, Sailor, Sailboat, Pull–Down 10.00
Valentine, Snow White, Mechanical, 1938, Set 200.00
Valentine, There's Nothing To "Ball" About, Baseball Design 4.00
Valentine, Wizard of Oz, Good Witch 17.00

CARDER, see Aurene and Steuben categories.

CARLSBAD, Germany, is a mark found on china made by several factories
in Germany. Most of the pieces available today were made after 1891.

Bowl, Portrait, 10 1/2 x 3 1/4 In. 135.00
Box, Malachite, Cover, Frosted Foliate & Bird Design, 4 In. 110.00
Ewer, Enameled Pink Flowers, Bamboo Handle, Marked, 20 In. 685.00
Pitcher, Maroon Peony, Ivory, Gold, Spout, 11 In. 90.00
Plate, Imperial Woman's Portrait, Constance, Handle, 9 3/4 In. 150.00
Plate, Victorian Woman, Green, 10 In. .... 65.00 To 85.00
Platter, Floral Border, Gilded Rim, 17 In. 80.00
Powder Box, Portrait On Cover & Inside Cover, Round 165.00

CARLTON WARE was made at the Carlton Works of Stoke-on-Trent,
England, about 1890. The firm traded as Wiltshaw & Robinson until 1957.
It was renamed Carlton Ware Ltd. in 1958.

Bowl, Rouge Royal, 7 In. 55.00
Dish, Blue Matte, Gold Handles, 8 1/2 In. 20.00
Dish, Embossed Poppies & Daisies, Turquoise, 10 x 5 In. 30.00
Dish, Leaf, Turned Up End Forms Handle, 7 x 5 In. 25.00
Jam Jar, Australian, Raised Flowers, Green 35.00
Mug, Quaker & Verse, 1958 .... 40.00
Sugar & Creamer, Nautilus, Rouge Royal, Pearlized Interior 95.00
Toast Rack, Raised Flowers, Green 35.00
Vase, Flared, Rouge Royale, 6 x 9 In. 65.00

CARNIVAL GLASS was an inexpensive, pressed, iridescent glass made
from about 1907 to about 1925. Over 1,000 different patterns are known.
Carnival glass is currently being reproduced. Additional pieces may be
found in the Northwood category.

Acanthus, Bowl, Green, 8 In. 90.00
Acanthus, Plate, Marigold, 10 In. 180.00
Acorn Burrs & Bark pattern is listed here as Acorn Burrs
Acorn Burrs, Punch Cup, Blue, 6 Piece 450.00
Acorn Burrs, Punch Set, Green, 8 Piece 1200.00
Acorn Burrs, Tumbler, Purple 60.00
Acorn Burrs, Water Set, Marigold, 5 Piece 650.00
Acorn Burrs, Water Set, Purple, 7 Piece 825.00
American Beauty Roses pattern is listed here as Wreath of Roses
Apple Blossom Twigs, Bowl, White 110.00
Apple Blossom Twigs, Plate, Peach Opalescent 400.00
Apple Blossom Twigs, Plate, Ruffled, Lavender, 9 In. 300.00
Apple Blossom Twigs, Plate, White 150.00
Aztec, Pitcher, Marigold 1200.00
Basket, Aqua 600.00
Battenburg Lace No. 1 pattern is listed here as Hearts & Flowers
Battenburg Lace No. 2 pattern is listed here as Captive Rose
Battenburg Lace No. 3 pattern is listed here as Fanciful
Beaded Cable, Rose Bowl, Amber 45.00
Beaded Cable, Rose Bowl, Amethyst 100.00
Beaded Cable, Rose Bowl, Marigold .... 60.00 To 80.00
Beaded Shell, Spooner, Marigold 50.00
Beaded Shell, Tumbler, Amethyst 90.00

Beaded Star & Snail pattern is listed here as Constellation
Big Fish, Bowl, Amethyst, 8 In. 725.00
Birds & Cherries, Bonbon, Blue 85.00
Birds on Bough pattern is listed here as Birds & Cherries
Blackberry & Checkerboard pattern is listed here as Blackberry Block
Blackberry A. pattern is listed here as Blackberry
Blackberry B. pattern is listed here as Blackberry Spray
Blackberry Block, Water Set, Marigold, 7 Piece 700.00
Blackberry Bramble, Compote, Amethyst 32.50
Blackberry Spray, Dish, Hat Shaped, Red 310.00
Blackberry Wreath, Bowl, Green, 8 In. 110.00
Blackberry Wreath, Bowl, Marigold, 7 In. 65.00
Blackberry, Compote, Marigold 85.00
Blossomtime, Compote, Amethyst 325.00
Broken Arches, Punch Set, Purple, 8 Piece 540.00
Bushel Basket pattern is listed here as Basket
Butterfly & Berry, Berry Set, Footed, Marigold, 6 Piece 240.00
Butterfly & Berry, Bowl, Footed, Marigold, 4 3/4 In. 33.00
Butterfly & Berry, Hatpin Holder, Marigold 1600.00
Butterfly & Berry, Pitcher, Marigold 395.00
Butterfly & Berry, Spooner, Marigold 100.00
Butterfly & Berry, Sugar, Cover, Marigold 100.00
Butterfly & Berry, Tumbler, Blue 55.00
Butterfly & Berry, Tumbler, Marigold .... 38.00 To 45.00
Butterfly & Fern, Pitcher, Marigold 280.00
Butterfly & Fern, Tumbler, Purple 45.00
Butterfly & Cable pattern is listed here as Springtime
Butterfly & Grape pattern is listed here as Butterfly & Berry
Butterfly & Plume pattern is listed here as Butterfly & Fern
Butterfly & Stippled Rays pattern is listed here as Butterfly
Butterfly, Bonbon, Amethyst 65.00
Butterfly, Bonbon, Purple 55.00
Butterfly, Bonbon, Ribbed Exterior, Amethyst 250.00
Cactus Leaf Rays pattern is listed here as Leaf Rays
Captive Rose, Bowl, Amethyst 70.00
Captive Rose, Bowl, Blue, 8 3/4 In. 45.00
Captive Rose, Plate, Amethyst, 9 In. 220.00
Captive Rose, Plate, Blue, 9 In. 425.00
Cattails & Fish pattern is listed here as Fisherman's Mug
Cattails & Water Lily pattern is listed here as Water Lily & Cattails
Cherries & Mums pattern is listed here as Mikado
Cherry Chain, Bowl, Ruffled, White, 10 1/2 In. 135.00
Cherry Chain, Plate, Marigold, 6 1/2 In. 60.00
Cherry Wreathed pattern is listed here as Wreathed Cherry
Cherry, Bowl, 4 In. 35.00
Cherry, Bowl, Footed, Marigold, 8 1/2 In. 135.00
Christmas Cactus pattern is listed here as Thistle
Christmas Plate pattern is listed here as Poinsettia
Chrysanthemum, Bowl, Ruffled, Footed, Marigold, 10 In. 80.00
Coin Dot, Bowl, Amethyst, 8 In. 35.00
Coin Dot, Bowl, Green, 8 In. 27.50
Constellation, Compote, White 135.00
Corn, Vase, Ice Green ....*Illus* 400.00
Cosmos Variant, Bowl, Ruffled, Blue, 10 In. 70.00
Cosmos, Bowl, Marigold, 9 1/2 In. 62.00
Daisy & Plume, Compote, Amber 35.00
Daisy & Plume, Compote, Green 49.00
Daisy & Lattice Band pattern is listed here as Lattice & Daisy
Daisy Block, Rowboat, Marigold 125.00
Daisy Squares, Compote, Ruffled, Marigold 350.00
Daisy Wreath, Bowl, Marigold 350.00
Daisy, Bonbon, Blue 250.00

Dandelion Variant pattern is listed here as Panelled Dandelion

Dandelion, Mug, Amethyst	650.00
Dandelion, Mug, Aqua Opalescent	300.00
Dandelion, Mug, Knights Templar, Ice Green	1150.00
Dandelion, Mug, Marigold	375.00
Dandelion, Pin Tray, Amethyst	350.00
Dandelion, Water Set, Purple, 7 Piece	900.00 To 950.00
Diamond Lace, Pitcher, Purple	310.00
Diamond Lace, Tumbler, Purple	45.00
Diamond Lace, Water Set, Purple, 7 Piece	415.00 To 450.00

Dogwood & Marsh Lily pattern is listed here as Two Flowers

Double–Stem Rose, Bowl, Blue	60.00
Double–Stem Rose, Bowl, White	150.00
Dragon & Berry, Bowl, Footed, Marigold	350.00
Dragon & Lotus, Bowl, Blue, 9 In.	105.00 To 165.00
Dragon & Lotus, Bowl, Green, 8 In.	325.00
Dragon & Lotus, Bowl, Marigold, 8 In.	60.00
Dragon & Lotus, Bowl, Marigold, 9 In.	85.00
Dragon's Tongue, Bowl, Ice Cream Shape, Marigold, 10 In.	850.00

Drape & Tie pattern is listed here as Rosalind

Drapery, Vase, Marigold	50.00
Dugan's Cherries, Sauce, Purple	35.00
Eastern Star, Plate, Purple, 9 In.	275.00

Egyptian Band pattern is listed here as Round–Up

Elks, Dish, Ice Cream, Atlantic City, Blue, 1911, 6 3/4 In.	675.00
Elks, Plate, Parkersburg Bell, Blue, 1914, 7 1/4 In.	1050.00
Embroidered Mum, Bowl, Aqua Opalescent	3000.00
English, Dish, Hen Cover, Marigold	90.00

Fan & Arch pattern is listed here as Persian Garden

Fanciful, Plate, Amethyst, 9 In.	270.00
Fanciful, Plate, Ruffled, White, 9 In.	175.00 To 200.00
Fanciful, Plate, Up–Turned Points, White, 8 1/2 In.	160.00
Fanciful, Plate, White, 9 In.	160.00 To 175.00
Fantail, Bowl, Footed, Marigold, 5 In.	70.00
Fashion, Punch Cup, Marigold	12.00
Fashion, Punch Set, Marigold, 12 Piece	200.00
Fashion, Punch Set, Marigold, 13 Piece	275.00
Fashion, Tumbler, Marigold	17.00
Fashion, Water Set, Amethyst, 7 Piece	1550.00
Feather & Heart, Tumbler, Etched Kidda 1911, Marigold	65.00

Carnival Glass, Grape & Cable, Hatpin Holder, Ice Green

Carnival Glass, Corn,

Carnival Glass, Grape & Cable, Hatpin Holder, Aqua

Vase, Ice Green

Carnival Glass, Grape & Cable, Hatpin Holder, White

Feather & Hobstar pattern is listed here as Inverted Feather
Featured Scroll pattern is listed here as Feathered Serpent
Feathered Serpent, Berry Set, Purple, 7 Piece 200.00
Feathered Serpent, Bowl, Amethyst, 10 In. 70.00
Fenton's Arabic pattern is listed here as Illusion
Fenton's Butterfly pattern is listed here as Butterfly
Field Flower, Tumbler, Blue 70.00
File, Spooner, Marigold 70.00
Fine Cut & Roses, Candy Dish, Amethyst 50.00
Fine Cut & Roses, Candy Dish, Green 65.00
Fine Cut & Roses, Candy Dish, White 250.00
Fine Cut & Roses, Rose Bowl, Ice Blue 350.00
Fine Rib, Vase, Cobalt Blue, 10 In. 45.00
Finecut & Star pattern is listed here as Star & File
Fish & Flowers pattern is listed here as Trout & Fly
Fish Net, Epergne, Peach Opalescent 425.00
Fisherman's Mug, Mug, Marigold 375.00
Fisherman's Mug, Mug, Peach Opalescent 1350.00
Fishscale & Beads, Plate, Ruffled, Purple, 7 In. 130.00
Floral & Grape, Pitcher, Amethyst .... 200.00 To 235.00
Floral & Grape, Tumbler, Amethyst 30.00
Floral & Grape, Water Set, Amethyst, 5 Piece 345.00
Floral & Grape, Water Set, Marigold, 7 Piece 195.00
Floral & Wheat, Bonbon, White 135.00
Floral & Diamond Point pattern is listed here as Fine Cut & Roses
Floral & Grapevine pattern is listed here as Floral & Grape
Floral & Wheat Spray pattern is listed here as Floral & Wheat
Florentine, Candlestick, Marigold, Pair 75.00
Florentine, Candlestick, Red, Pair 525.00
Flowering Almonds pattern is listed here as Peacock Tail
Fluffy Bird pattern is listed here as Peacock
Flute, Sugar & Creamer, Purple 125.00
Flute, Sugar, Green 35.00
Flute, Toothpick, Purple 75.00
Four Flowers Variant, Bowl, Ruffled, Purple, 10 In. 180.00
Four Flowers, Plate, Peach, 6 1/2 In. 190.00
Garden Path, Bowl, Ruffled, Marigold, 9 In. 80.00
Good Luck, Bowl, Green, 8 1/2 In. 250.00
Good Luck, Bowl, Marigold, 8 1/2 In. 175.00
Grape & Cable, Berry Set, Purple 400.00
Grape & Cable, Bonbon, Green 110.00
Grape & Cable, Bonbon, Marigold 72.00
Grape & Cable, Bowl, Footed, Green, 8 In. 50.00
Grape & Cable, Butter, Cover, Amethyst 200.00
Grape & Cable, Butter, Cover, Purple 180.00
Grape & Cable, Cracker Jar, Purple 400.00
Grape & Cable, Creamer, Green .... 125.00 To 135.00
Grape & Cable, Dish, Sweetmeat, Cover, Purple 225.00
Grape & Cable, Hatpin Holder, Aqua ....Illus 12000.00
Grape & Cable, Hatpin Holder, Ice Green ....Illus 1700.00
Grape & Cable, Hatpin Holder, Purple 260.00
Grape & Cable, Hatpin Holder, White ....Illus 1800.00
Grape & Cable, Orange Bowl, Green 275.00
Grape & Cable, Orange Bowl, Marigold 170.00
Grape & Cable, Orange Bowl, Persian Medallion Interior, Green 120.00
Grape & Cable, Powder Jar, Amethyst .... 125.00 To 135.00
Grape & Cable, Punch Cup, White 75.00
Grape & Cable, Punch Set, Frosty White, 7 Piece 3500.00
Grape & Cable, Punch Set, Purple, 10 Piece 2100.00
Grape & Cable, Spooner, Amethyst 100.00
Grape & Cable, Spooner, Green 125.00
Grape & Cable, Tankard, Amethyst, 9 1/2 In. .... 495.00 To 600.00
Grape & Cable, Tray, Dresser, Marigold 150.00

Carnival Glass, Hobnail,
Pitcher, Amethyst,

Carnival Glass, Hobstar &
Feather, Punch Bowl, Base,
Amethyst

Carnival Glass, Multi-Fruits &
Flowers, Pitcher, Amethyst,
Millersburg

Carnival Glass, Persian Garden,
Chop Plate, Purple

Carnival Glass, Peacock At The
Fountain, Punch Set, White, 7
Piece

Grape & Cable, Tumbler, Amethyst	45.00
Grape & Cable, Tumbler, Purple	40.00
Grape & Cable, Water Set, Green, 5 Piece	895.00
Grape & Cable, Water Set, Marigold, 6 Piece	595.00
Grape & Cable, Water Set, Purple, 6 Piece	425.00
Grape & Cable, Water Set, Purple, 7 Piece	410.00
Grape Arbor, Tumbler, Marigold	50.00
Grape Arbor, Tumbler, White	200.00
Grape Arbor, Water Set, Ice Blue, 7 Piece	1700.00
Grape Delight pattern is listed here as Vintage	
Grape, Bowl, Nut, Footed, Purple	80.00
Grapevine Diamonds pattern is listed here as Grapevine Lattice	
Grapevine Lattice, Pitcher, Purple	395.00
Grapevine Lattice, Tumbler, Marigold, 7 Piece	120.00

Greek Key, Plate, Green, 9 In. 1100.00
Greek Key, Plate, Marigold, 9 In. 1050.00
Harvest Poppy, Compote, Marigold .... 225.00 To 250.00
Heart & Vine, Bowl, Fluted, Cobalt Blue 135.00
Hearts & Flowers, Compote, Amethyst 525.00
Heavy Grape, Bowl, Ruffled, Amethyst, 10 In. 400.00
Heavy Grape, Chop Plate, Amber, 11 In. 250.00
Heavy Grape, Chop Plate, Marigold, 11 In. 325.00
Heavy Grape, Plate, Green, 8 In. 55.00
Heron & Rushes pattern is listed here as Stork & Rushes
Hobnail pattern is listed in this book as its own category
Hobnail, Butter, Marigold 895.00
Hobnail, Pitcher, Amethyst ....*Illus* 800.00
Hobstar & Feather, Punch Bowl, Base, Amethyst ....*Illus* 3300.00
Holly Spray pattern is listed here as Holly Sprig
Holly Sprig, Bonbon, Issac Benesch Advertising, Marigold 50.00
Holly Sprig, Bowl, Amethyst, 9 In. 50.00
Holly, Bowl, Blue, 8 In. 65.00
Holly, Bowl, Purple 62.50
Holly, Bowl, Red 350.00
Holly, Compote, Marigold 25.00
Holly, Hat, Red 300.00
Holly, Plate, Blue 325.00
Holly, Plate, Marigold 175.00
Honeycomb & Clover, Bonbon, Handles, Marigold 15.00
Honeycomb Collar pattern is listed here as Fishscale & Beads
Horse Medallions pattern is listed here as Horses' Heads
Horses' Heads, Bowl, Marigold, 7 1/2 In. 110.00
Illusion, Bonbon, Blue 75.00
Imperial Grape, Decanter, Stopper, Marigold 85.00
Imperial Grape, Plate, Marigold, 7 1/2 In. 95.00
Imperial Grape, Plate, Ruffled, Clambroth, 9 In. 75.00
Imperial Grape, Plate, Ruffled, Marigold, 8 1/2 In. 45.00
Imperial Grape, Water Bottle, Marigold 80.00
Imperial Grape, Wine Set, Amethyst, 7 Piece 625.00
Intaglio pattern is listed here as Hobstar & Feather
Interior of Cherries & Mums pattern is listed here as Mikado
Inverted Feather, Cracker Jar, Green 300.00
Inverted Strawberry, Cuspidor, Marigold 875.00
Irish Lace pattern is listed here as Louisa
Jack–In–The–Pulpit, Vase, Ribbed, Marigold, 8 1/2 In. 35.00
Kittens, Bowl, Ruffled, Marigold, 6 Piece 200.00
Kittens, Cup, Blue 675.00
Kittens, Cup, Marigold 135.00
Kittens, Plate, Marigold, 4 1/2 In. 135.00
Kittens, Spooner, Marigold 250.00
Labelle Poppy pattern is listed here as Poppy Show
Labelle Rose pattern is listed here as Rose Show
Lattice & Daisy, Tumbler, Blue 50.00
Lattice & Grape, Pitcher, Marigold 150.00
Lattice & Grape, Tumbler, Marigold 32.00
Lattice & Grapevine pattern is listed here as Lattice & Grape
Leaf & Beads, Candy Dish, Amethyst 60.00
Leaf & Beads, Rose Bowl, Amethyst 75.00
Leaf & Beads, Rose Bowl, Marigold 100.00
Leaf Pinwheel & Star Flower pattern is listed here as Whirling Leaves
Leaf Rays, Nappy, Marigold 45.00
Leaf Rays, Nappy, Purple 45.00
Leaf Rays, Nappy, White 50.00
Little Flowers, Berry Set, Blue, 5 Piece .... 200.00 To 240.00
Little Flowers, Bowl, Ruffled, Amber, 10 In. 700.00
Logan, Berry Vase, Amber 400.00
Lotus & Grape, Bonbon, Marigold 45.00

Lotus & Grape, Bowl, Ruffled, Marigold 80.00
Louisa, Bowl, Footed, Purple 75.00
Louisa, Bowl, Ice Green, Footed 47.50
Louisa, Rose Bowl, Amethyst 60.00
Lustre Rose, Water Set, Marigold 130.00
Magnolia & Poinsettia pattern is listed here as Water Lily
Many Fruits, Punch Set, Amethyst, 6 Piece 450.00
Many Fruits, Punch Set, White, 6 Piece 1300.00
Many Stars, Bowl, Green, 9 1/2 In. 425.00
Maple Leaf, Spooner, Blue 70.00
Maple Leaf, Water Set, Amethyst, 7 Piece 325.00
Mary Ann, Loving Cup, Marigold 500.00
Maryland pattern is listed here as Rustic
Melinda pattern is listed here as Wishbone
Memphis, Punch Cup, Green 25.00
Mikado, Compote, Marigold 75.00
Milady, Tumbler, Blue ....80.00 To 100.00
Multi–Fruits & Flowers, Pitcher, Amethyst, Millersburg ....*Illus* 1500.00
Nesting Swan pattern is listed here as Swan, Carnival
Nippon, Bowl, Ice Blue 325.00
Open Rose, Plate, Green, 9 In. 250.00
Open Rose, Plate, Marigold, 9 In. 100.00
Orange Peel, Punch Bowl, Marigold 55.00
Orange Tree, Bowl, Marigold, 6 In. 30.00
Orange Tree, Bowl, White, 8 In. .... 125.00 To 150.00
Orange Tree, Goblet, Light Gold Stem 65.00
Orange Tree, Loving Cup, Blue 200.00
Orange Tree, Mug, Blue 50.00
Orange Tree, Powder Jar, Blue 55.00
Orange Tree, Punch Set, Blue, 5 Piece 325.00
Orange Tree, Punch Set, Blue, 7 Piece 375.00
Orange Tree, Rose Bowl, Green 50.00
Orange Tree, Shaving Mug, Blue 45.00
Orange Tree, Tumbler, Blue 42.00
Oriental Poppy, Pitcher, Marigold 400.00
Oriental Poppy, Tumbler, Marigold 40.00
Palm Beach, Spooner, White 155.00
Paneled Bachelor Buttons pattern is listed here as Milady
Paneled Dandelion, Pitcher, Green 475.00
Paneled Dandelion, Tumbler, Blue 55.00
Pansy, Bowl, Marigold, 8 1/2 In. 40.00
Pansy, Bowl, Marigold, 8 3/4 In. 25.00
Pansy, Dish, Pickle, Amethyst 50.00
Panther, Bowl, Footed, Marigold, 10 In. 160.00
Panther, Bowl, Footed, Marigold, 5 In. 22.00
Peacock & Dahlia, Bowl, Marigold, 7 1/2 In. 50.00
Peacock & Dahlia, Bowl, Scalloped, Amethyst, 7 In. 75.00
Peacock & Grape, Bowl, Amethyst, 7 3/4 In. 75.00
Peacock & Grape, Bowl, Marigold, 7 3/4 In. 65.00
Peacock & Urn, Bowl, Amethyst, 10 In. 325.00
Peacock & Urn, Compote, Ruffled, Blue 85.00
Peacock & Urn, Ice Cream Set, Purple, 7 Piece 700.00
Peacock & Urn, Plate, Amethyst, 11 In. 995.00
Peacock & Urn, Plate, Blue 450.00
Peacock & Urn, Plate, White 350.00
Peacock At The Fountain, Bowl, Fruit, Blue 325.00
Peacock At The Fountain, Butter, Amethyst .... 275.00 To 350.00
Peacock At The Fountain, Orange Bowl, Green 600.00
Peacock At The Fountain, Pitcher, Blue 125.00
Peacock At The Fountain, Punch Cup, Purple 35.00
Peacock At The Fountain, Punch Set, White, 7 Piece ....*Illus* 6000.00
Peacock At The Fountain, Tumbler, Blue 35.00
Peacock At The Fountain, Tumbler, Purple, 5 Piece 185.00

Peacock At The Fountain, Water Set, Purple, 7 Piece 650.00
Peacock on Fence pattern is listed here as Peacocks
Peacock Tail, Bowl, Green, 8 In. 75.00
Peacock Tail, Bowl, Red, 6 In. 1800.00
Peacock, Bowl, Ruffled, Blue, 8 1/2 In. 500.00
Peacock, Plate, Ice Green 475.00
Peacock, Plate, Stippled, Marigold 425.00
Persian Garden, Bowl, White, 11 In. 275.00
Persian Garden, Chop Plate, Purple ....*Illus* 2800.00
Persian Medallion, Bonbon, Amber 65.00
Persian Medallion, Bonbon, Blue 65.00
Persian Medallion, Bonbon, Celeste Blue .... 500.00 To 975.00
Persian Medallion, Bonbon, Red 950.00
Persian Medallion, Bowl, Marigold, 8 3/4 In. 60.00
Persian Medallion, Hair Receiver, Marigold 75.00
Persian Medallion, Orange Bowl, Marigold 170.00
Persian Medallion, Plate, Blue, 9 1/2 In. 300.00
Persian Medallion, Plate, Marigold, 9 In. 750.00
Petal & Fan, Bowl, Ruffled, Peach, 10 In. 150.00
Peter Rabbit, Bowl, Blue 700.00
Pine Cone Wreath pattern is listed here as Pine Cone
Pine Cone, Plate, Blue, 6 1/2 In. 35.00
Plume Panels, Vase, Blue, 12 In. 65.00
Plume Panels, Vase, Red, 11 In. 750.00
Poinsettia & Lattice pattern is listed here as Poinsettia
Poinsettia, Pitcher, Milk, Marigold ....95.00 To 150.00
Poppy Show, Plate, White 450.00
Raspberry, Pitcher, Green 240.00
Raspberry, Pitcher, Milk, Ice Blue 1900.00
Raspberry, Pitcher, Milk, Purple .... 250.00 To 325.00
Raspberry, Tumbler, Amethyst 50.00
Raspberry, Tumbler, Marigold 30.00
Raspberry, Water Set, Purple, 7 Piece 525.00
Ripple, Vase, Amber, 7 1/2 In. 60.00
Ripple, Vase, Marigold, 10 In. 30.00
Rosalind, Bowl, Amethyst, 10 In. 175.00
Rosalind, Compote, Amethyst, 6 In. 500.00
Rose & Ruffles pattern is listed here as Open Rose
Rose Show, Bowl, Marigold 525.00
Rose Show, Plate, Cobalt Blue 800.00
Rose Show, Plate, Ice Blue 2000.00
Rose Show, Plate, White 425.00
Rose Tree, Bowl, Ruffled, Blue, 10 In. 1000.00
Roses & Loops pattern is listed here as Double–Stem Rose
Round–Up, Plate, Blue, 9 In. 350.00
Rustic, Vase, Marigold, 10 In. 30.00
Sailboat & Windmill pattern is listed here as Sailboats
Sailboats, Bowl, Marigold, 6 In. 30.00
Sailboats, Plate, Marigold, 6 1/2 In. 425.00
Scale Band, Pitcher, Green 295.00
Scarab, Hatpin, Deep Amethyst Base, Luster 35.00
Scotch Thistle, Compote, Marigold 35.00
Shell, Bowl, Ruffled, Peach, 8 In. 100.00
Singing Birds, Butter, Amethyst 160.00
Singing Birds, Mug, Blue 200.00
Singing Birds, Mug, Green 300.00
Singing Birds, Mug, Marigold 150.00
Singing Birds, Mug, Purple 100.00
Singing Birds, Pitcher, Amethyst 198.00
Singing Birds, Pitcher, Green 390.00
Singing Birds, Tumbler, Amethyst 55.00
Singing Birds, Tumbler, Marigold 45.00
Singing Birds, Water Set, Green, 7 Piece 800.00

Singing Birds, Water Set, Marigold, 5 Piece 450.00
Ski Star, Sauce, Purple 55.00
Springtime, Bowl, Green, Small 55.00
Springtime, Bowl, Peach, 5 In. 30.00
Springtime, Spooner, Amethyst 300.00
Springtime, Spooner, Purple .... 250.00 To 275.00
Stag & Holly, Bowl, Footed, Marigold, 10 In. 100.00
Stag & Holly, Bowl, Marigold, 9 In. 75.00
Stag & Holly, Bowl, Ruffled, Blue, 11 In. 245.00
Star & File, Tumbler, Amber 60.00
Star Medallion, Pitcher, Milk, Marigold 45.00
Star Spray, Bride's Basket, Smoky 95.00
Starfish, Bonbon, Peach Opalescent 120.00
Stippled Diamond & Flower pattern is listed here as Little Flowers
Stippled Leaf & Beads pattern is listed here as Leaf & Beads
Stippled Posy & Pods pattern is listed here as Four Flowers
Stippled Rays, Bowl, Purple, 8 In. 48.00
Stippled Rays, Compote, Footed, Amethyst 50.00
Stippled Rays, Plate, Marigold 30.00
Stork & Rushes, Cup, Marigold, 4 In. 11.00
Stork & Rushes, Punch Set, Amethyst, 8 Piece 425.00
Stork & Rushes, Tumbler, Blue .... 40.00 To 60.00
Strawberry pattern is listed here as Wild Strawberry
Strawberry Scroll, Tumbler, Blue 60.00
Strutting Peacock, Sugar, Cover, Amethyst 18.00
Sunflower pattern is listed here as Dandelion
Sunflower & Wheat pattern is listed here as Field Flower
Swan, Carnival, Bowl, Marigold, 10 In. 350.00
Swan, Carnival, Bowl, Ruffled, Green, 10 In. 250.00
Thin Rib & Drape, Vase, Bud, 6 In. 16.00
Thistle, Banana Boat, Marigold 300.00
Thistle, Bowl, Amethyst, 7 1/4 In. 95.00
Thistle, Bowl, Amethyst, 8 In. 140.00
Thistle, Bowl, Blue, 8 In. 90.00
Thistle, Bowl, Ruffled, Green, 8 In. 150.00
Thistle, Bowl, Scalloped, Green, 8 1/2 In. 150.00
Thistle, Bowl, Scalloped, Marigold, 8 3/4 In. 90.00
Three Fruits Medallion, Bowl, Meander Reverse, Black Amethyst, 9 In. 750.00
Three Fruits, Bowl, Spatula Footed, Aqua Opalescent 500.00
Three Fruits, Bowl, Stippled Leaves, Basketweave, Marigold 125.00
Three Fruits, Plate, Amethyst 170.00
Three Fruits, Plate, Marigold 115.00
Three-In-One, Plate, Marigold, 6 1/2 In. 65.00
Tree Trunk, Vase, Blue, 11 1/2 In. 60.00
Tree Trunk, Vase, Marigold At Top, Green, 7 1/2 In. 48.00
Trout & Fly, Bowl, Marigold, 8 3/4 In. 525.00
Two Flowers, Bowl, Footed, Marigold, 9 In. 125.00
Two Flowers, Bowl, Ruffled, Amethyst, 9 1/2 In. 150.00
Two Flowers, Bowl, Ruffled, Footed, Red, 10 In. 2000.00
Vintage, Bowl, Blue, 4 1/2 In. 45.00
Vintage, Bowl, Green, 10 In. 85.00
Vintage, Bowl, Green, 6 1/2 In. 30.00
Vintage, Compote, Amethyst .... 35.00 To 45.00
Vintage, Compote, Green, 6 1/2 In. 50.00
Vintage, Rose Bowl, Amethyst 65.00
Vintage, Rose Bowl, White 95.00
Water Lily & Cattails, Tumbler, Marigold 90.00
Water Lily, Bowl, Ball Footed, Marigold, 10 In. 65.00
Water Lily, Bowl, Footed, Marigold, 5 In. 22.50
Whirling Leaves, Bowl, Marigold, 10 In. 80.00
Wide Panel, Vase, Marigold, 6 In. 55.00
Wild Strawberry, Bowl, Basketweave, Marigold, 9 1/2 In. 68.00
Windflower, Bowl, Purple, 8 In. 90.00

Windflower, Bowl, Ruffled, Marigold, 8 In. 40.00
Windmill Medallion pattern is listed here as Windmill
Windmill, Pitcher, Marigold 75.00
Windmill, Water Set, Frosted Amber 240.00
Wishbone & Spades, Plate, Amethyst, 6 In. 165.00
Wishbone, Bowl, Ruffled, Green, 9 3/4 In. 130.00
Wishbone, Plate, Footed, Purple, 9 In. 250.00
Wreath of Roses, Compote, Amethyst 45.00
Wreathed Cherry, Berry Set, White, 6 Piece 485.00

CAROUSEL or merry–go–round figures were first carved in the United
States in 1867 by Gustav Dentzel. Collectors discovered the charm of the
hand–carved figures in the 1970s and they were soon classed as folk art.
Most desirable are the figures other than horses, such as pigs, camels,
lions, or dogs. A jumper is a figure that was made to move up and down
on a pole, a stander was placed in a stationary position.

Antelope, Heyn 4500.00
Camel, 2–Humped, Matthieu, c.1932 .... 2520.00
Cat, Running, Bayol, c.1890 .... 3535.00
Chariot, Illions 3850.00
Chicken, Double Seat, Andersons 2360.00
Cow, Heyn, 1905 .... 4400.00
Derby Racer, Williams 935.00
Derby Racer, Williams, Restored 3025.00
Donkey, Nodding Head, Bayol 8800.00
Giraffe, Matthieu, c.1932 .... 3190.00
Goat, Coquereau 4250.00
Horse, Aluminum, Original Finish 425.00
Horse, Armitage–Herschell 2950.00
Horse, Black Beauty, Painted, Cast Iron 650.00
Horse, Carved In The Round, Military Saddle, Muller, 13 1/2 x 11 In., Pair 3850.00
Horse, Herschell–Spillman, Restored, Stand, 1913 .... 3800.00
Horse, Illions, Park Paint, Seaside Heights 6800.00
Horse, Jumper, Dare, Park Paint 2750.00
Horse, Jumper, Herschell–Spillman 3575.00
Horse, Jumper, Illions 4400.00
Horse, Jumper, Parker, 1914 .... 3670.00
Horse, Jumper, Philadelphia Toboggan Company .... 4675.00 To 6600.00
Horse, Jumper, Second Row, Dentzel, 52 x 52 In. 8250.00
Horse, Jumper, Tiger Skin, Parker 3670.00
Horse, Jumper, Top Knot, Dentzel 7150.00
Horse, Metal, Kiddy's, Allan Herschell 500.00
Horse, Prancer, Cast Iron, c.1890 .... 950.00
Horse, Prancer, Heyn 1925.00
Horse, Stander, Early Primer, Stein & Goldstein 3850.00
Horse, Wooden Body, Metal Head, Legs & Tail, Allan Herschell, 1930 .... 1300.00
Mirror, Distorting, c.1935, Pair 880.00
Ostrich, 2 Seater, Savage 5500.00
Ostrich, Standing, Matthieu, c.1936 .... 2350.00
Pig, Bayol, Park Paint 2200.00
Rabbit, Running, Carrot In Mouth, French, c.1910 .... 4500.00
Reindeer, Raised Front Legs, Gustav Dentzel, c.1895 .... 15400.00
Seat, Single, Charles Looff, 1905 .... 4770.00
St. Bernard Dog, Devos, c.1920 .... 4030.00
Swan Seat 1650.00

CARRIAGE means several things, so this category lists baby carriages,
buggies for adults, horse–drawn sleighs, and even strollers. Doll–sized
carriages are listed in the Toy category.

Baby Buggy, Adjustable Surrey, Wicker, 1880 .... 375.00
Baby Buggy, Gendron, Large 250.00
Baby Buggy, Victorian, Black Leather Upholstery, Fringed Top, Hopkinsville, Ky. ... 770.00
Baby Buggy, Victorian, Woven Rush Sides & Front, Metal Wheels 595.00

Baby Buggy, Vulcan, Brakes	40.00
Baby Buggy, Wicker, Fancy, 4 Large Wheels	700.00
Baby Buggy, Wicker, Mustard Paint Metal Base, Wooden Wheel Spokes	495.00
Baby Buggy, Wicker, Victorian, With Umbrella	605.00
Baby Buggy, Wicker, Wooden Wheels	350.00
Baby Buggy, Wire Wheels, S–Curved Springs, White & Blue Design, 55 1/2 In.	120.00
Buggy, Doctor's, All Original, 1890	8500.00
Cart, Donkey, Brightly Painted, Sicilian, With Harness	2750.00
Cart, Goat, 2 Small Front & 2 Large Rear Iron Wheels, 1875	1850.00
Cart, Pony, Wooden, Steel, Worn Leatherized Cloth Upholstery, Stenciled, 48 In.	75.00
Cart, Red, 2 Large Wheels	325.00
Child's, Leather, 2 Large Wooden Wheels, Early 20th Century, 40 x 25 x 55 In.	975.00
Go–Kart	1200.00
Push Cart, Green & Orange Paint, 19th Century, 19 x 50 In.	440.00
Rickshaw, Convertible Top, Pedal Power, 3 Wheels, Neelam, India	900.00
Sleigh, Designed To Be Pushed, Ironclad Wooden Runners, 19th Century	2600.00
Sleigh, Push, Child's, Light Blue Paint, Red Velvet Upholstered	795.00
Sleigh, Red Striping, Painted White Ground, Gendron Wheel Co., 49 In.	100.00
Sleigh, Red Velvet, Lovejoy Brothers, North Chesterville, Maine, Blankets	605.00
Sleigh, Scout, Hardwood, Green Paint, Wire Tipped Runners, 26 1/2 In.	175.00
Stroller, Wicker, Bangor Bazaar, Folding Legs To Make Bed, Umbrella, 1884	550.00
Wagon, Farm, With Tractor Seat, 2 Wheels	250.00

CASH REGISTERS were invented in 1884 because an eye on the cash was a necessity in stores of the nineteenth century, too. John and James Ritty invented a large model that resembled a clock and kept a record of the dollars and cents exchanged in the store. John Patterson improved the cash register with a paper roll to record the money. By the early 1900s, elaborate brass registers were made. About World War I, the fancy case was exchanged for the more modern types.

McCaskey, 1 Lever	75.00
National, Brass Sign Says Bread, Cake, Pastry, Inlaid Mahogany	550.00
National, Model 30, Nickel Over Brass, 22 x 15 x 8 1/2 In.	1320.00
National, Model 130, Brass Case	875.00
National, Model 216, Brass	1300.00
National, Model 250, Candy Store	550.00
National, Model 300	700.00
National, Model 311, Candy Store	600.00
National, Model 312, Marble Shelf, 1 Drawer, 15 Keys, 50 Cent Maximum, 1914	950.00
National, Model 313, Brass, Restored	900.00 To 950.00
National, Model 313, Candy Store, Embossed Brass, Wooden Base, 16 1/2 In.	550.00
National, Model 317, Candy Store	475.00
National, Model 317, Restored	1250.00
National, Model 324, Brass	1200.00
National, Model 442XX, Brass	650.00 To 675.00
National, Model 451, Brass	140.00
National, Oak Base, Registers To 9. 99, 21 x 19 1/2 x 16 In.	275.00
National, Oak, Nickel Plate Over Brass, 3 Drawers, 1910	900.00

CASTOR SETS holding just salt and pepper castors were used in the seventeenth century. The sugar castor, mustard pot, spice dredger, bottles for vinegar and oil, and other spice holders became popular by the eighteenth century. These sets were usually made of sterling silver. The American Victorian castor set, the type most collected today, was made of silver plated Britannia metal. Colored glass bottles were introduced after the Civil War. The sets were out of fashion by World War I. Be careful when buying sets with colored bottles; many are reproductions. Other castor sets may be listed in various porcelain and glass categories in this book.

5–Bottle, Daisy & Button, Revolving Silver Plate & Holder, Cranberry	650.00
5–Bottle, Daisy & Button, Vaseline, Blue & Amber, Clear Holder	150.00
5–Bottle, Etched Glass, Quadruple Plate Holder	140.00
6–Bottle, Ruby, Silver Plated Holder	125.00

CASTORS for pickles are glass jars about six inches in height, held in special metal holders. They became a popular dinner table accessory about 1890. Each jar had a top that was usually silver or silver plate. The frame, also of a silver metal, had a handle that arched above the jar and a hook that held a pair of tongs. By 1900, the pickle castor was out of fashion. Many examples found today have reproduced glass jars in old holders. Additional pickle castors may be found in the various Glass categories.

Pickle, Cobalt Blue Insert	300.00
Pickle, Cone Pattern, Brooklyn Frame, Ruby, 11 3/4 In.	430.00
Pickle, Coreopsis, Colored Flowers, Frame & Tongs	350.00 To 375.00
Pickle, Cosmos Insert, Footed Frame	495.00
Pickle, Cranberry, Honeycomb, Footed Forbes Frame	325.00
Pickle, Daisy & Button Insert, Silver Holder, Tongs	150.00
Pickle, Fireglow Opalescent Hobnail Insert	375.00
Pickle, Herringbone, Mother-of-Pearl	750.00
Pickle, Loetz Insert, Green Snails, Simpson, Hall, Miller Frame	375.00
Pickle, Optic Honeycomb, White Florals, Green Leaves, Tongs, Frame	295.00
Pickle, Peachblow, Dark Patina Frame, James W. Tufts, Tongs	695.00
Pickle, Rubena, Frosted Design Insert	425.00
Pickle, Shells & Forget-Me-Nots, Scrolls, Fork Holder, Knickerbocker Silver	350.00
Pickle, Vaseline, Button & Cross	225.00
Pickle, Vaseline, Diamond	250.00

CATALOGS are listed in the Paper category.

CAUGHLEY items may be found in the Salopian category.

CAULDON Limited worked in Staffordshire, Great Britain, and went through many name changes. John Ridgway made porcelain at Cauldon Place, Hanley, until 1855. The firm of John Ridgway, Bates and Co. of Cauldon Place worked from 1856 to 1859. It became Bates, Brown-Westhead, Moore and Co. from 1859 to 1862. Brown-Westhead, Moore and Co. worked from 1862 to 1904. About 1890, this firm started using the words *Cauldon* or *Cauldon ware* as part of the mark. Cauldon Ltd. worked from 1905 to 1920, Cauldon Potteries from 1920 to 1962. Related items may be found in the Indian Tree category.

Cup & Saucer, Blue Flowers, Gold Trim	25.00
Plate, Floral Design, 6 In. Pair	10.00
Plate, Gilt & Cobalt Painted Border, White Ground, 10 1/2 In., 12 Piece	660.00
Plate, Multicolored Scroll & Floral Design, 10 1/2 In., 24 Piece	770.00

CELS are listed in this book in the Animation Art category.

CELADON is a Chinese porcelain having a velvet-textured green-gray glaze. Japanese, Korean, and other factories also made a celadon-colored glaze.

Bowl, 6 Sides, Signed, 1800s, 4 In.	48.00
Bowl, Conical Form, Sung Dynasty, 7 In.	33.00
Bowl, Oriental Boat Scene, Teakwood Base, 19th Century, 1 x 3 In.	495.00
Cup, Scalloped, Incised & Inlaid Slip, Floral Design, Korea, 2 1/2 In.	990.00
Dish, Shrimp, Famille Rose, 19th Century, 9 3/4 In.	365.00
Jar, Ginger, Men Amid Swirling Clouds, Ching Dynasty, 12 In.	198.00
Plate, Dragon, 7 3/8 In., Pair	16.00
Teapot, Floral With Gold, Wicker Handle	40.00
Urn, Rose Mandarin Subjects, c.1840, 24 In.	2200.00
Vase, Archaistic Dragons, Elephant Head Handles, Hu-Shape, China, 7 1/2 In.	121.00
Vase, Blue Floral, Applied Foo Dog Handles, 13 In.	300.00
Vase, Diamond Pattern, Cloud Design, Jade Finial, 11 In.	385.00
Wall Pocket, Floral, Late 1800s, 9 In.	90.00
Water Dropper, 1875	125.00 To 175.00

CELLULOID is a trademark for a plastic developed in 1868 by John W. Hyatt. Celluloid Manufacturing Company, the Celluloid Novelty Company, Celluloid Fancy Goods Company, and American Xylonite Company all used Celluloid to make jewelry, games, sewing equipment, false teeth, and piano keys. Eventually, the Hyatt Company became the American Celluloid and Chemical Manufacturing Company, the Celanese Corporation. The name *Celluloid* was often used to identify any similar plastic. Celluloid toys are listed under Toys.

Bookmark, Owl, Advertising	12.00
Box, Comb, Sheep Scene, Victorian	28.00
Box, Dresser, Sections, Rowell & Hammer, Birks	28.50
Card Holder, Golfer, 4 1/2 In., 4 Piece ....*Illus*	75.00
Cat With Ribbon, Painted, 4 In.	11.00
Comb, Brush & Mirror Set, Child's, Floral, Box	68.00
Comb, Leaf Design, Dated 1916	36.00
Doll, Flapper, Painted, Label, Japan, 4 3/4 In.	38.00
Dresser Set, Amber, 15 Piece	59.00
Dresser Set, Embossed Design, Initials, 7 Piece	50.00
Dresser Set, Vanilla, Art Deco, 6 Piece	25.00
Figurine, Elephant, Art Deco, Painted, 4 1/2 In.	16.00
Figurine, Uncle Sam, Painted, 7 In.	77.00
Hair Receiver, Applied Hoofed Legs	25.00
Key Chain, Cowboy, Original Tag	55.00
Picture Frame, 3 x 4 In.	17.50
Pumpkin Head, Holding Owl, Cats, 4 1/2 In.	412.00
Rattle, Clown, Double–Sided, Embossed, 5 1/4 In.	55.00
Rattle, Clown, On Handstand, On Roly Poly Ball, 4 1/2 In.	37.50
Rattle, Elephant Shape, With Whistle	195.00
Rattle, Let Cat Out of Bag, 2 In.	37.50
Rattle, Little Red Riding Hood, Alphabet, Combination Teething Ring & Whistle	225.00
Rattle, Policeman, Big Hand, Painted, Japan, 6 1/2 In.	132.00
Rattle, Rocking Horse Handle	10.00
Santa Claus & Reindeer, Pulling Sled, Windup, 8 In.	145.00
Shaving Set, Mirror, Brush, Mug & Small Clock	50.00
Toothpick, Fancy Sterling Case	18.00
Toy, Aviator, String–Jointed Arms, Painted, Japan, 6 1/4 In.	77.00
Toy, Black Child, Chenille Wrap, String–Jointed Arms, 3 1/2 In.	55.00
Toy, Boy On Ostrich, African, String–Jointed Legs, Painted, 6 1/2 In.	132.00

CERAMIC ART COMPANY of Trenton, New Jersey, was established in 1889 by J. Coxon and W. Lenox and was an early producer of American Belleek porcelain. It became Lenox, Inc. in 1906. Do not confuse this ware with the pottery made by the Ceramic Arts Studio of Madison, Wisconsin.

Chocolate Pot, Hand Painted Grapes	65.00
Compote, Sterling Silver Overlay, 12 1/2 In.	65.00

Celluloid, Card Holder,
Golfer, 4 1/2 In., 4 Piece

♦ ♦ ♦ ♦ ♦ ♦ ♦ ♦ ♦ ♦ ♦ ♦ ♦ ♦ ♦ ♦ ♦ ♦ ♦

Try cleaning 1920s celluloid with a paste of vinegar and flour. Rub, wait a few minutes, then rinse with water and dry. If this doesn't work, try cleaning with a solution of dishwasher detergent and warm water.

♦ ♦ ♦ ♦ ♦ ♦ ♦ ♦ ♦ ♦ ♦ ♦ ♦ ♦ ♦ ♦ ♦ ♦ ♦

CERAMIC ARTS STUDIO was founded in Madison, Wisconsin, by Lawrence Rabbett and Ruben Sand. Their most popular products were expensive molded figurines. The pottery closed in 1955. Do not confuse these products with those of the Ceramic Art Co. of Trenton, New Jersey.

Figurine, Beth & Bruce, Dancers, Pair	60.00
Figurine, Cow & Calf	65.00
Figurine, Dog, Collie & 3 Pups	75.00
Figurine, Kitten, Playing	25.00
Figurine, Michelle & Maurice, Dancers, Pair	65.00
Figurine, Modern Man, Dancer, 10 In.	48.00
Figurine, Peter & Polly, Shelf Sitters, Pair	85.00
Figurine, Russian Boy	20.00
Figurine, Winter Belle, Greens	25.00
Pitcher, Milk, Swiss People, Embossed	30.00
Plaque, Grace & Greg, Dancers, Pair	65.00
Plaque, Shadow Dancers, Pair	75.00
Plaque, Zorina & Zor, Dancers, Pair	65.00
Salt & Pepper, Blackamoor	28.00
Salt & Pepper, Calico Dog & Cat	115.00
Salt & Pepper, Chihuahua & Dog House	115.00
Salt & Pepper, Chinese Boy & Girl, 4 1/2 In.	25.00
Salt & Pepper, Covered Wagon & Long Horn	13.00
Salt & Pepper, Deer & Fawn	50.00
Salt & Pepper, Elephant	35.00
Salt & Pepper, Hansel & Gretel	85.00
Salt & Pepper, Monkey & Baby	75.00
Salt & Pepper, Pigs	75.00
Salt & Pepper, Pixie & Toadstool	115.00
Salt & Pepper, Siamese Cats, Short & Tall	115.00
Salt & Pepper, Southern Belle & Southern Gentleman	90.00
Salt & Pepper, Wee Indians	55.00 To 75.00
Salt & Pepper, Wee Pigs	45.00
Vase, Bud, Oriental, With Drum, 7 In.	40.00
Vase, Bud, Oriental, With Mandolin, 7 In.	40.00

CHALKWARE is really plaster of Paris decorated with watercolors. One type was molded from Staffordshire and other porcelain models and painted and sold as inexpensive decorations in the nineteenth century. Figures of plaster, made from about 1910 to 1940 for use as prizes at carnivals, are also known as chalkware. Kewpie dolls made of chalkware will be found in their own category.

Bank, Basket of Fruit, Original Green, Gold, Yellow Paint, 6 1/2 In.	357.00
Bank, Dog, Seated, 2 Pups, White, Yellow, Red, Black, 6 1/2 In.	25.00
Bank, Dove, Yellow Varnish, Red, Black, Yellow, 11 1/4 In.	100.00
Bank, Santa On Chair, Ringing Bell, 12 In.	45.00
Bust, Mussolini, 1942	125.00
Bust, Young Girl, Reading Book	40.00
Figurine, Angel, Off White Enamel, 19th Century, Pair	395.00
Figurine, Bird, On Base, Original Green, Red, Yellow, Black Paint, 1870s, 5 1/8 In.	330.00
Figurine, Bugs Bunny, 9 1/2 In.	50.00
Figurine, Bulldog, Grinning, With Hat, 10 In.	55.00
Figurine, Bulldog, Sitting, Ears Up	19.00
Figurine, Carousel Horse, Carnival, Pair, 10 In.	28.00
Figurine, Cat, Black and White Striped Paint, Colored Bow, 19th Century, 12 In.	165.00
Figurine, Cat, Black Repaint, Colored Bow, 9 3/4 In.	16.00
Figurine, Cat, Gray, Beige Paint On White, Black Eyes, 7 1/2 In.	38.00
Figurine, Cat, Orange Tiger Stripe, Colored Bow, 12 In.	93.00
Figurine, Cat, Seated, Deep Yellow Paint, With Red & Black, 1870, 9 1/2 In.	990.00
Figurine, Cat, Sleeping, Brown & White Stripe, 19th Century, 12 In.	110.00
Figurine, Clara Bow, Art Deco, 17 In.	85.00
Figurine, Clown, Circus, 17 In., Pair	100.00
Figurine, Dog, Begging	22.00

Figurine, Dog, Black & White 7.00
Figurine, Donald Duck, 14 In. ....60.00 To 165.00
Figurine, Dutch Girl, Gretel, A. Nute, 1938 .... 25.00
Figurine, Girl Reading, 19th Century, 18 1/2 In. 550.00
Figurine, Horse, Tan & Green Paint, 10 1/2 In. 30.00
Figurine, Indian Papoose, Chalk Head, Cloth Body 200.00
Figurine, Indian, Reclining, Ohio Matches 145.00
Figurine, Jiggs, K. F. S., 8 In. 125.00
Figurine, Man & Woman, Victorian, Holding Dog, Borghese, Late 1800's, 9 In., Pair   95.00
Figurine, Nude Flapper, 15 In., Pair 50.00
Figurine, Parrot, Poll-Parrot Children's Shoes, 12 In. 85.00
Figurine, Poodle, Original Polychrome Paint, 19th Century, 7 1/4 In. 285.00
Figurine, Rabbit, Original Black, Yellow Detail, 19th Century, 10 In. 210.00
Figurine, Rooster, Polychrome Paint, 19th Century, 7 1/4 In. 800.00
Figurine, Rooster, Yellow, Red, Green Paint, 5 5/8 In. 687.00
Figurine, Shepherd, Sleeping, Beside Sheep, Staffordshire-Type, 9 x 12 In. 195.00
Figurine, Shoeshine Boy 350.00
Figurine, Spaniel, Seated 160.00
Figurine, Squirrel, 6 1/2 In. 125.00
Figurine, St. Bernard, Life-Size, Advertising 600.00
Figurine, Sweater Girl 58.00
Figurine, Yorkshire Terrier, 14 x 10 1/2 In. 22.50
Garniture, Fruit, Foliage, Black, Green, Yellow, Red Paint, 19th Century, 14 In. 965.00
Garniture, Love Birds Top, 19th Century, 11 1/2 In., Pair 2500.00
Hutch, Watch, Compote of Fruit Form, Polychrome Design, 19th Century, 14 In. 360.00
Nodder, Cat, Dark Gray Patina, Black, Red, Yellow, 19th Century, 8 1/2 In. 200.00
Planter, Frosty The Snowman, Bust, 6 In. 12.00

CHARLIE CHAPLIN, the famous comic and actor, lived from 1889 to 1977. He made his first movie in 1913. He did the movie *The Tramp* in 1915. The character of the Tramp has remained famous and in the 1980s he appeared in a series of television commercials for computers. Dolls, candy containers, and all sorts of memorabilia picture Charlie Chaplin. Pieces are being made even today.

Ad, Old Gold Cigarettes, Photograph 18.00
Button, Picture, Sampeck Triple-Service Suit 85.00
Candy Container, Glass, Painted, George Borgfeldt, 3 3/4 In. ......95.00 To 165.00
Candy Container, Original Cover, Smith 450.00
Card, Comic Event, Color, Uncut, 10 Scenes, c.1915, 14 x 2 1/2 In. 22.50
Card, Lobby, City Lights, United Artists, 1931, 11 x 14 In. 660.00
Card, Lobby, The Gold Rush, United Artists, 1925, 11 x 14 In. 1430.00
Doll, Composition Head, Amberg, 1915, 14 1/2 In. 595.00
Doll, Little Tramp, World Dolls, 19 In. 55.00
Game, Card 12.00
Marionette, Hazells, Box 125.00
Movie Film, Immigrant, 8 Mm 20.00
Pencil Box 30.00
Photograph, Tramp Bust, Signed, Matted, 8 x 9 1/2 In. 160.00
Poster, A Night In The Show, Perfection Pictures, 1915, 41 x 27 In. 6050.00
Poster, Charlie In French, Garcon-Cafe, Himalaya Film, 1920s 3000.00
Poster, Germany, 33 1/2 x 23 1/2 In. 55.00
Toy, Charlie Chaplin Knockoff, Tin, Spinner, Penny Toy, Rico, 1920s 115.00
Toy, Charlie With Walking Stick, Windup Tin, Schuco, Box, 6 1/2 In. 1320.00
Tumbler 12.00

CHARLIE MCCARTHY was the ventriloquist's dummy used by Edgar Bergen from the 1930s. He was famous for his work in radio, movies, and television. The act was retired in the 1970s.

Book, A Day With Charlie McCarthy 20.00
Book, Comic, Edgar Bergen Presents C. McCarthy, Whitman, 1938 .... 81.00
Book, Secrets of Ventriloquism, Edgar Bergen, Charlie On Cover 8.00
Car, Box, 1939 .... 950.00
Crazy Car, Windup, Tin, Marx, 1930s, 7 1/2 In. 300.00

Doll, 1960s	80.00
Doll, Composition, 18 In.	225.00
Doll, Ventriloquist, Dummy	150.00
Game, Questions & Answers	70.00
Puppet, Chase & Sanborn, Cardboard, 18 1/4 x 8 In.	36.00
Puppet, Composition Head & Hands, Cloth Body, Suit, Shoes, 22 In.	75.00
Spoon	10.00
Tumbler, Radio Premium, 1930	40.00

CHELSEA GRAPE pattern was made before 1840. A small bunch of grapes in a raised design, colored with purple or blue luster, is on the border of the white plate. Most of the pieces are unmarked. The pattern is sometimes called *Aynsley* or *Grandmother*. Chelsea sprig is similar but has a sprig of flowers instead of the bunch of grapes. Chelsea thistle has a raised thistle pattern. Do not confuse these Chelsea patterns with Chelsea Keramic Art Works, which can be found in the Dedham category, or with Chelsea porcelain, the next category.

Bowl, 8 In.	10.00
Cup	22.00
Plate, 10 In.	30.00
Saucer	3.00
CHELSEA SPRIG, Cup	25.00
Plate, 8 In.	18.00

CHELSEA PORCELAIN was made in the Chelsea area of London from about 1745 to 1784. Some pieces made from 1770 to 1784 may include the letter *D* for *Derby* in the mark. Ceramic designs were borrowed from the Meissen models of the day. Pieces were made of soft paste. The gold anchor was used as the mark but it has been copied by many other factories. Recent copies of Chelsea have been made from the original molds. Do not confuse Chelsea porcelain with Chelsea Grape, the previous category.

Candlestick, Flowers & Bird, Converted Into Table Lamp, 12 1/2 In., Pair	825.00
Candlestick, Shepherd & Shepherdess Figures, Tree Form, c.1765, 8 1/2 In., Pair	880.00
Clock, Sunflower, Modeled As A Bouquet, Roman Numerals, c.1761, 11 In.	1925.00
Cutlery Set, White Porcelain Silver Mounted Handles, 24 Piece	3080.00
Dish, 2 Insects Amid Sprigs of Fruits, Oval, Marked, c.1759, 10 1/8 In.	1650.00
Dish, Oval, Floral Sprigs, Yellow Ground, Basket Work, c.1752, 10 1/4 In., Pair	3025.00
Figurine, Allegorical, Pride, Maiden Draped In Floral Gown, 7 In.	600.00
Figurine, Boy Playing Flute, Dog At Side, Marked, 3 1/4 In.	220.00
Group, Man & Woman, Tricorn Hats, Flowering Tree, 19th Century, 7 1/4 In.	495.00
Mug, Tall Neck, Floral Spray, Florets, c.1755, 6 In.	1100.00
Perfume Bottle, Plum Design, Molded Leaves, Stem Stopper, c.1756, 2 5/16 In.	550.00
Plate, Floral Sprigs Between Larger Sprig, c.1755, 9 1/4 In., Pair	440.00
Platter, 4 Cornucopia Shaped Cartouches, Oval, 1765, 13 1/4 In.	1540.00
Teapot, Scenic, Flattened Form, Underglaze, 7 In.	1650.00

CHINESE EXPORT porcelain comprises all the many kinds of porcelain made in China for export to America and Europe in the eighteenth and nineteenth centuries. Other pieces may be listed in this book under Canton, Celadon, Nanking, and Rose Medallion.

Bidet, Landscape Design, Blue & White, 19th Century, 23 1/2 In.	44.00
Bowl, Armorial, Arms of Elphinstone, 1780s, 9 7/8 In.	825.00
Bowl, Famille Rose, 3 Woman In Garden, Rings, Mid–1800s, 4 In.	225.00
Bowl, Famille Rose, Hanging, 3 Women In Garden, 4 Rings, 1800s, 6 x 6 In.	275.00
Bowl, Famille Rose, Phoenix Bird Center, Mid–1800s, 8 1/2 In.	165.00
Cache Pot, Rose Mandarin, 19th Century, 4 1/2 In.	575.00
Charger, Famille Rose, Butterflies, Floral, Diapered Edge, 1840s, 12 In.	375.00
Coffeepot, Rose Mandarin, 19th Century, 11 In.	1210.00
Cup & Saucer, Order of Cincinnati, 2 Handled Cup, 1790	6600.00
Cup & Saucer, Pavilion In Garden Landscape	100.00
Cup, Ivory, TK In Shield, 2 1/4 In. ....*Illus*	95.00
Cup, Porcelain, Dragons, Yellow Ground, Daoguang Period, 4 In.	110.00

Chinese Export, Cup, Ivory,
TK In Shield, 2 1/4 In.

Chinese Export, Tureen,
Domed Cover, Blue Floral,
9 1/2 In., Pair

Chinese Export, Water Pot, Cover,
Arms of Smale, 9 1/4 In.

Dish, Hot Water, Cover, American Eagle, Fitzhugh, Green, Oval, 1810–1825 .... 7150.00
Dish, Shrimp, Famille Rose 775.00
Figurine, Elephant, Blanket On Back, 4 In. 155.00
Figurine, Famille Rose, Shou Lao Figure, Holding Staff & Peach, 1880, 10 In. 175.00
Ginger Jar, Famille Verte Figural Design, 19th Century 110.00
Jardiniere, Reserves of Figures & Birds, Flared Square Form, 12 In. 1320.00
Mug, Arms of Penn, Iron, Red & Puce 4400.00
Pitcher, Gilt Star Pattern Border, Enameled Crest, Helmet Form, 4 1/2 In. 250.00
Plaque, Famille Rose, Figures In Garden, 9 x 11 In. 155.00
Plate, Famille Rose, Cabbage Leaf Pattern, Pierced Rim, 1900, 6 In., Pair 77.00
Plate, Gilt Design, 19th Century, 8 1/2 In., Pair 485.00
Plate, Hot Water, Blue & White, Handles, Fitzhugh, 9 5/8 In. 500.00
Plate, Notched Rim, Greek Key Border, Chinoiserie Landscape, 9 In. 110.00
Platter, Flower, Honeycomb Border, 11 1/2 x 13 1/2 In. 990.00
Platter, Porcelain, Shield With Bird, 18th Century, 9 1/2 x 6 1/2 In. 605.00
Punch Bowl, Famille Rose, c.1765, Pair 8800.00
Spoon, Porcelain, Bowl Design, 1780 .... 1650.00
Teapot, Famille Rose, 18th Century 1450.00
Teapot, Famille Rose, Phoenix Bird & Floral, Porcelain, 6 In. .... 225.00 To 325.00
Teapot, Grisaille Landscape, Floral Border, 4 1/2 In. 305.00
Teapot, Mandarin, 6 In. 775.00
Teapot, Mandarin, Strap Handle, Drum Shape 490.00
Tray, Floral Design, Magenta & Gilt, Orange Peel Glaze, 10 1/4 In. 300.00
Tray, Warming, Crest, 18 1/8 In. 1450.00
Tureen, Domed Cover, Blue Floral, 9 1/2 In., Pair ....*Illus* 2750.00
Tureen, Pomegranate Finial, Boar's Head Handles, 14 In. 1100.00
Tureen, Twin Strap Handles, Domed Lid, Fitzhugh, 6 x 7 1/2 In., Pair 1100.00
Umbrella Holder, Famille Rose, Signed, 19 In. 400.00
Vase, Applied Designs On Neck, Blue, 19th Century 220.00
Vase, Bladder Form, 19th Century, 13 1/2 In. 770.00
Vase, Famille Rose, 6 Sides, Late 1800s, 4 1/2 In. 45.00

Vase, Famille Rose, Palace, Bottle Shape, Mid–19th Century 7700.00
Vase, Famille Rose, Raised Bird & Floral, Porcelain, 10 1/2 In. 385.00
Vase, Lamp Mounted, Dignitaries, Cloud Work, 19th Century, 15 1/2 In. 715.00
Vase, Palace, Floral & Figural Design, 25 In., Pair 110.00
Vase, Raised Designs, Birds, Branches, Flowers, Blue Ground, 24 In., Pr. 825.00
Vase, Signing of Declaration of Independence, c.1876 .... 5500.00
Water Pot, Cover, Arms of Smale, 9 1/4 In. ....*Illus* 605.00

CHOCOLATE GLASS, sometimes mistakenly called caramel slag, was made by the Indiana Tumbler and Goblet Company of Greentown, Indiana, from 1900 to 1903. Fenton Art Glass Co. also made chocolate glass from about 1907 to 1915. More recent pieces have been made by Imperial, Heisey, and others.

Berry Set, Dewey, Greentown, 6 Piece 285.00
Butter, Cover, Cactus, Greentown 180.00
Butter, Cover, Leaf Bracket, Greentown ....95.00 To 100.00
Compote, Cactus, Greentown 225.00
Compote, Cactus, Greentown, 8 In. 100.00
Compote, Jelly, Geneva, Footed 125.00
Creamer, 3 In. ....*Illus* 75.00
Cruet, Imperial 35.00
Cruet, Leaf Bracket, Greentown ....225.00 To 235.00
Cup, Cactus, Greentown 85.00
Figurine, Dog, Scotty, Imperial 175.00
Lamp, Wild Rose With Festoon 775.00
Match Holder, 1886, 4 In. 65.00
Mug, Herringbone, Greentown, 5 In. 50.00
Mug, Indoor Drinking Scene, Greentown 140.00
Nappy, Bracket 60.00
Nappy, Left Bracket 65.00
Nappy, Triangular, Handle 135.00
Pitcher, Racing Deer & Doe 570.00
Pitcher, Water, Racing Deer & Doe, Greentown 600.00
Saltshaker, Beaded Triangle 325.00
Shade, Lamp, 8 Panels, Gilt Metal Dome, 3–Light, 18 In. 300.00
Sugar, Cherry 30.00
Sugar, Cover, Leaf Bracket, Greentown ....85.00 To 100.00
Toothpick, Cactus 60.00
Toothpick, Holly 80.00
Tray, Venetian, 10 In. 115.00
Tumbler, Cactus, Greentown ....55.00 To 65.00
Vase, Masonic, 6 In. 250.00
Vase, Scalloped Flange, Greentown, 6 In. ....55.00 To 65.00

Chocolate Glass, Creamer, 3 In.

♦ ♦ ♦ ♦ ♦ ♦ ♦ ♦ ♦ ♦ ♦ ♦ ♦ ♦ ♦ ♦ ♦ ♦ ♦

To remove the remains of sticky glue and tape from antiques, try rubbing peanut butter on the sticky area until the glue is gone. Do not use this method on porous materials, where the oil from the peanut butter could leave a stain.

♦ ♦ ♦ ♦ ♦ ♦ ♦ ♦ ♦ ♦ ♦ ♦ ♦ ♦ ♦ ♦ ♦ ♦ ♦

CHRISTMAS TREES made of feathers and Christmas tree decorations of all types are popular with collectors. The first decorated Christmas tree in America is claimed by many states, including Pennsylvania (1747), Massachusetts (1832), Illinois (1833), Ohio (1838), and Iowa (1845). The first glass ornaments were imported from Germany about 1860. Dresden ornaments were made about 100 years ago of paper and tinsel. Manufacturers in the United States were making ornaments in the early 1870s. Electric lights were first used on a Christmas tree in 1882. Character light bulbs became popular in the 1920s, bubble lights in the 1940s, twinkle bulbs in the 1950s, plastic bulbs by 1955. In this book a Christmas light is a holder for a candle used on the tree. Other forms of lighting include light bulbs.

Aluminum, With Electric Color Wheel, Early 1960s, 7 Ft.	65.00
Battery Operated, Decorations, Star, Trim, Tin Brick Base	35.00
Bottle Brush, With Fruit, 9 In.	10.00
Cellophane, 1950s, 16 In.	35.00
Clip, Candle, Victorian Boy, 1890s	72.00
Feather, Dark Green, Light Green Tips, Germany, 24 In.	165.00
Feather, Germany, 14 In.	120.00
Feather, Germany, 46 In.	300.00
Feather, Stenciled Base, Germany, 28 In.	150.00
Feather, With Candleholders, Germany, 5 Ft.	250.00
Fence, Front Center Gate, Green, 21 x 42 In., 7 Piece	165.00
Fence, Swinging Gate, Wooden, White, Square, 45 In.	175.00
Icicles, Double–Flo Spiral Tinsel, Box	6.00
Light Bulb, Candy Cane	20.00
Light Bulb, Cat, Begging, Purple	35.00
Light Bulb, ClemCo, GE, Box, 7 Piece	35.00
Light Bulb, Kitten	35.00
Light Bulb, Little Red Riding Hood, Oval	50.00
Light Bulb, Mickey Mouse, Noma, Mazda Lamps, Box, 1938	275.00
Light Bulb, Noma, Box, 1939	23.00
Light Bulb, Noma, Celluloid Sockets, 1940, Box	40.00
Light Bulb, Noma, Kristal, Box	39.00
Light Bulb, Pinocchio	65.00
Light Bulb, Santa Claus	75.00
Light Bulb, Santa Claus, 2 Sides, Milk Glass	48.00
Light Bulb, Santa Claus, 8 In., Box	195.00
Light Bulb, Ship	75.00
Light Bulb, Snowman	25.00 To 35.00
Light Bulb, Watch, Girl With Doll, Milk Glass, Cobalt Blue Dogs, 8 Piece	90.00
Light Shade, Popeye, Blue	25.00
Light Shade, Popeye, White	25.00
Light Shade, Sparky & Friend, 5 Piece	60.00
Ornament, Angel, Wax, Spun Glass Wings, Blue Dress, Blond Hair, 4 In.	45.00
Ornament, Ball, Silver Mercury Glass, Swirled Leaf Brass Hanger, 4 In.	75.00
Ornament, Ball, Topped By Lyre, 10 In.	210.00
Ornament, Basket of Flowers, Blown Glass, Silver, Pink, 2 In.	50.00
Ornament, Basket of Flowers, Wire Wrapped	32.50
Ornament, Bear, Brown, Putz, 2 In.	18.00
Ornament, Boy, Papier–Mache, Painted Features, 5 In.	45.00
Ornament, Cane, Silver Mercury Glass, 5 In.	15.00
Ornament, Carrot, Blown Glass, 3 1/2 In.	50.00
Ornament, Cello, Wire Wrapped	55.00
Ornament, Chandelier, Wire Wrapped	70.00
Ornament, Children Caroling, Satin, Hallmark, 1976, Box	30.00
Ornament, Christ On Cross, Glass	88.00
Ornament, Christmas, Cross, Sterling Silver, Reed & Barton, 1974	38.00
Ornament, Church	25.00
Ornament, Clown	10.00
Ornament, Clown On Ball, Red Cap & Shirt, Red Ball, 4 1/2 In.	45.00
Ornament, Cupcake Elf, Hallmark, No. 6	6.00

Ornament, Cupid, Wax 45.00
Ornament, Dirigible, Wire Wrapped, Glass 140.00
Ornament, Donkey, Glass Eyes, Saddle, Germany, 3 1/2 In. 35.00
Ornament, Dracula, Vampire, Dressed In Formal Clothes, 1957, 4 In. 5.00
Ornament, Ear of Corn, Blown Glass, Gold, Germany, 3 1/4 In. 20.00
Ornament, Fish, Blown Glass, Green, Pink, Gold, Germany, 3 1/2 In. 25.00
Ornament, French Hens, Sterling Silver, Towle, 1973 .... 34.00
Ornament, Gondola With Woman & Dove 85.00
Ornament, Grape Cluster, Leaf, Silvered, Pink & Green, 3 1/2 In. 18.00
Ornament, Horse, Saddle, Cotton Batten 120.00
Ornament, Hot Air Balloon, Flag 32.50
Ornament, Icicles, Blown Glass, Silver, Aqua, Frosted Top, Germany 50.00
Ornament, Indian Chief, Mercury Glass 165.00
Ornament, Kite With Ball, Beaded, 7 In. 22.00
Ornament, Kugel, Egg Shape, Cobalt Blue, Embossed Cap, 2 1/2 In. 110.00
Ornament, Kugel, Glass Ball, Red 135.00
Ornament, Kugel, Gold, 9 In. 50.00
Ornament, Kugel, Green Grape Cluster, 4 1/2 In. 60.00
Ornament, Kugel, Red, Embossed Cap, 3 3/4 In. 95.00
Ornament, Kugel, Silvered With Red, Brass Hanger, Vienna, 10 In. 220.00
Ornament, Kugel, Teal Blue–Green, Embossed Cap, 4 1/2 In. 90.00
Ornament, Mandolin, 3–D, Dresden 90.00
Ornament, Moose, Celluloid, 2 In. 5.00
Ornament, Mushroom, Blown Glass, 3 1/4 In. 15.00
Ornament, Parasol, Wire Wrapped 17.50
Ornament, Pear, 2 In. 18.00
Ornament, Pig, Sitting Sideways, Putz, 2 1/2 In. 18.00
Ornament, Pine Cone, Blown Glass, Gold, Frosted, Germany, 2 1/2 In. 20.00
Ornament, Pine Cone, Blown Glass, Silver, 3 1/4 In. 25.00
Ornament, Punch & Judy 45.00
Ornament, Red Horn, Blue Paper Record 250.00
Ornament, Santa Claus Head 18.00
Ornament, Santa Claus In Airplane, Blown Glass, Tinsel Wrapped, 6 3/4 In. 220.00
Ornament, Santa Claus, Cardboard Body, Composition Face, Burlap Bag 135.00
Ornament, Santa Claus, Driving Car, Celluloid, 4 In. 18.00
Ornament, Santa Claus, Paperboard, Green & White Suit, 10 3/4 In. 50.00
Ornament, Santa Claus, Roly Poly, Celluloid 55.00
Ornament, Snake, Metal Spring Body, Green Blown Glass Head, 11 In. 83.00
Ornament, Squirrel, Eating Nut, Cotton, 3 1/2 In. 95.00
Ornament, Swan, Wire Wrapped, Spun Glass Tail, 4 1/2 In. 68.00
Ornament, Teapot 10.00
Ornament, Tree Top, Angel 35.00
Ornament, Tree Top, Glass, Pink & Silver, Gold Frosted, Romania, 16 In., Box 35.00
Ornament, Tree Top, Waterford, Box 75.00
Ornament, Umbrella, Open, Wire Wrapped 35.00
Ornament, Vase, Handles 20.00
Stand, Musical, Revolving, German 300.00
Stand, North Star, Green & Red Steel, Box 8.00

CHRISTMAS collectibles include not only Christmas trees and ornaments
listed above, but also Santa Claus figures, special dishes, and even games
and wrapping paper. A Belsnickle is a nineteenth-century figure of Father
Christmas. A kugel is an early, heavy ornament made of thick blown glass,
lined with zinc or lead, and often covered with colored wax.

Belsnickle, Blue Coat, Gold Mica Covering, Papier–Mache, 5 3/4 In. 155.00
Belsnickle, Chalk, Painted, Black Robe, 7 1/2 In. 275.00
Belsnickle, Mica Coat, Pressed Paper, Feather Tree, 11 In. 176.00
Belsnickle, Red Coat, Black Base, Papier–Mache, 8 3/4 In. 450.00
Belsnickle, Red Coat, Papier–Mache & Plaster, 8 3/4 In. 165.00
Belsnickle, Santa Claus, Gold Coat, Holding Leather Tree, 11 1/2 In. 900.00
Belsnickle, With Fir Tree, Gold Mica, Dark Pink, 8 In. 425.00
Belsnickle, With White Feather Tree, Pink Wash, 7 In. 350.00
Belsnickle, Yellow Coat, Gold Mica, Papier–Mache & Plaster, 9 1/2 In. .....523.00 To 1008.00

Christmas, Sleigh, Santa Claus, Bentwood,

Pulled By Reindeer, 11 In.

♦♦♦♦♦♦♦♦♦♦♦♦♦♦♦♦♦♦♦♦♦♦

A little damage and wear adds
to the charm of old Christmas
ornaments. It indicates an
antique that has seen many
holidays of use.

♦♦♦♦♦♦♦♦♦♦♦♦♦♦♦♦♦♦♦♦♦♦

Candle, St. Peter's, Nuremburg, Box 10.00
Card Holder, Red Metal, Sears & Roebuck, 1950s, 32 In. 45.00
Caroler, Bisque, Painted, Germany, 3 Piece, 2 1/4 In. 44.00
Display, Church, With 6 Figures, Lighted 32.00
Figure, Elf, Plaster, Papier–Mache, 3 3/4 In. 27.00
Figure, Father Christmas, Tree In Arm, Composition, On Cardboard, 4 In. 95.00
Figure, Man, Carved Head & Hands, Silk Faille Clothes, Creche, Italy, 12 In. 165.00
Figure, Santa Claus, Celluloid, Doll Behind Back, Painted, Japan, 7 1/2 In. 176.00
Figure, Santa Claus, Chenille, Bisque Face, Green, Japan, 3 In. 20.00
Figure, Santa Claus, Papier–Mache Face, Hands, Flannel Suit, Pelze Nicol, 13 In. 900.00
Figure, Santa Claus, Papier–Mache Face, Rabbit Fur Beard, Feather Tree, 13 In. 800.00
Figure, Santa Claus, Plaster Face, Felt Clothing, Japan, 9 In. 55.00
Figure, Santa Claus, Plaster Head, Straw Body, Boot Bells, 16 In. 120.00
Figure, Santa Claus, Plastic, Lights Up, 12 In. 27.50
Figure, Santa Claus, Reindeer, Glass Eyes, Rabbit Fur Beard, Feather Tree 450.00
Figure, Santa Claus, Seated, Chalkware, 8 In. 40.00
Figure, Santa Claus, Seated, Plaster Face, Felt Clothing, 6 1/2 In. 110.00
Figure, Santa Claus, Sleigh, 2 Reindeer, Cardboard, Box, 1950s 55.00
Figure, Santa Claus, Sleigh, Papier–Mache, Celluloid Reindeer, Germany, 6 In. 150.00
Figure, Santa Claus, Standing, Composition Face, Felt Clothing, 8 In. 55.00
Figure, Santa Claus, Standing, Papier–Mache, Pelze, 1920s, 13 In. 900.00
Figure, Santa Claus, Standing, Papier–Mache, Rabbit Fur, 1920s, 13 In. 800.00
Figure, Santa Claus, Straw Filled, Silk Suit, Fake Fur Beard, 10 In. 550.00
Figure, Santa Claus, Woven Cloth, Straw Filled, Flannel Coat, 3 3/4 In. 200.00
Lantern, Santa Claus, Blue Hood, Mica, 5 In. 625.00
Mask, Santa Claus, Papier–Mache 140.00
Nativity Set, Snoopy, 7 Piece 45.00
Plates are listed in the Collector Plate category
Print, Santa Claus, Framed, Late 19th Century, 12 x 10 In. 100.00
Santa Claus In Truck, Celluloid, Painted, Red, White & Green, 3 5/8 In. 143.00
Santa Claus, Bisque Face, Chenille, Green, Japan, 3 In. 20.00
Santa Claus, Brown Suit, Geo. Heather Fancy Goods, N.Y., 1882, 13 In. 125.00
Santa Claus, Cloth, Vinyl Face, Rings Bell, Waving Candy Cane, Alps, 7 In. 65.00
Santa Claus, Red Coat, Fur Beard, Papier–Mache, Germany, 16 In. 185.00
Santa Claus, Red Coat, Fur Beard, Squeak, Papier–Mache, 7 In. 55.00
Sleigh, Santa Claus, Bentwood, Pulled By Reindeer, 11 In. ....*Illus* 2090.00
Spoon, Sterling Silver, Santa Claus, Chimney Scene, Merry Christmas Handle 45.00
Stocking, Red Net, Filled, Paper, Tin, 1930, 12 In. 25.00
Toy, Santa Claus Holding Pack, Windup, Rings Bell, Alps, Box 100.00
Toy, Santa Claus On Chimney, Bell, Stand–Up Motion, Battery Operated, 10 In. 405.00
Toy, Santa Claus Rings Bell, Merry Christmas Sign, Celluloid Head, Windup, Japan 65.00
Toy, Santa Claus, On Scooter, Tin, Plastic, Battery Operated, Box 115.00
Toy, Santa Claus, Rings Bell, Holds Candy Cane, Alps, Box 95.00
Toy, Santa Claus, Steiff Tag, 5 1/2 In. 185.00
Toy, Santa Claus, Walks, Rings Bell, Plays Music, Battery Operated, Plastic 35.00
Toy, Santa Claus, Windup, Pull Toy, Occupied Japan, Box, 8 In. 139.00

Toy, Santa Claus, With Bell, Plush Body, Plastic Face, 10 In. 28.00
Tumbler, Merry Christmas, Roses, Enameled 35.00

CHROME items in the Art Deco style became popular in the 1930s.
Collectors are most interested in high–style pieces made by the Connecticut
firms of Chase Brass and Copper Company and Manning Bowman.

Ashtray, Art Deco, Double Bird Center Holder 9.00
Bread Box 35.00
Candy Dish, Art Nouveau, Nude Holding Purple Glass Dish, Farberware 95.00
Candy Dish, Tilted, Bakelite Heart 18.00
Champagne Bucket, Handles, Bacchus & Leaping Goats, Chase, 9 1/4 In. 1045.00
Cigarette Box & Ashtray Set, Copper, White Ball, Chase, 4 Piece, 2 Boxes 325.00
Coaster, Farberware, White & Blue Porcelain Insert 10.00
Cocktail Set, Black, Art Deco, Shaker With 5 Cups, Chase 48.00
Cocktail Set, Skyscraper, Norman Bel Geddes, 8 Piece 1900.00
Cocktail Set, Skyscraper, Stemmed Cordials, Tray, Revere, 8 Piece 2750.00
Cocktail Shaker, 14 In. ....*Illus* 12.00
Cocktail Shaker, Manning Bowman, Farberware 22.00
Cocktail Shaker, Red Bakelite Handle 35.00
Coffee Set, Hammered, Red Lucite Handles, Electric Pot, Belle Oliver Co., 3 Piece 70.00
Coffee Set, Red Lucite Handles, Urn Shape Pot, Plated, 4 Piece 55.00
Coffee Urn, Electric, 1924 .... 30.00
Coffeepot, Ball Shape, Bakelite, Manning–Bowman 100.00
Coffeepot, Sugar & Creamer, Electric, Red Plastic Handles, 3 Piece 50.00
Figurine, Stylized Golfer, Hagenauer, 14 1/ 2 In. 1170.00
Figurine, Stylized Woman, Walking Panther, Silvered Metal, Hagenauer, 10 In. 3500.00
Goblet, Wine, Bacchus, 6 Piece 200.00
Humidor, Art Deco, Holds 14–Oz. Tin 27.50
Ice Bucket, Farberware 20.00
Jigger & Swizzle Set, Art Deco, Top Hat, 4 Golf Clubs For Sticks, Box 90.00
Lamp, Wall Fixture, Dolphin Figure, Electric 300.00
Pitcher, Normandie, Prow of Ocean Liner Form, Revere, c.1935, 12 In. 3300.00
Punch Set, Rim Around Middle Holds 10 Cobalt Blue Cups, Ball Shape 95.00
Rolling Pin, Box 60.00
Server, 3 Tiers, Folding, Chase Brass 22.00
Server, Collapsible, Chase Brass, Triple 65.00
Snack Server, Bakelite Handles, Chase Brass 75.00
Sugar & Creamer, Art Deco, Butterscotch Bakelite 16.00
Sugar & Creamer, Chase Brass 22.00
Sugar & Creamer, Holder, Center Handle 30.00

Chrome, Cocktail Shaker, 14 In.

Don't use old home-canning
jars to preserve food. The jars
with wire bails, glass caps,
zinc porcelain-lined caps, or
metal caps with rubber rings
do not seal as well as the new
two-piece vacuum-cap jars.

Tray, 3 Sections, Standing Nude, Farberware	45.00
Wine Set, Amethyst, Farberware, 6 Piece	60.50

CIGAR STORE FIGURES of carved wood or cast iron were used as advertisements in front of the Victorian cigar store. The carved figures are now collected as folk art. They range in size from counter type, about three feet, to over eight feet high.

Indian Warrior, Hand To Head, White Mahogany	650.00
Indian, Louis J. Lord Co., Cigars Tobacco, 1880s, 68 In.	4950.00
Indian, Painted Pine, Gold Cloak, Boots, Red Fringe, 54 In.	3300.00
Indian, Polychrome Paint, Wooden, 72 In.	925.00
Indian, Squaw, Carved & Polychromed, 1880s, 39 In.	800.00
Indian, Warrior, Solid Wood, Life–Size	2500.00

CINNABAR is a vermilion or red lacquer. Pieces are made with tens to hundreds of thicknesses of the lacquer that is later carved.

Bowl, Floral, Shallow, 2 3/4 x 2 1/2 In.	16.00
Box, 1920s, 4 In.	50.00

CIVIL WAR mementos are important collector's items. Most of the pieces are military items used from 1861 to 1865.

Accounting Sheet, 199th Reg., 1864, 10 x 15 In.	32.00
Bayonet Frog, Confederate Saber	100.00
Belt Buckle, U.S. Militia, GAR, 1854–1870	80.00
Binoculars	66.00
Bowl & Plate, Woman's Relief Corp	55.00
Box, Cartridge, Leather, U.S. Emblem, Shoulder Strap	425.00
Campaign Chair, Folding, c.1863	120.00
Chest, Paymaster	75.00
Cigar Holder, Porcelain, Battlefield Dug, 1860, 1/4 x 2 In.	34.00
Clothing Settlement, Campbell Hospital, 1865, 4 x 7 In.	20.00
Criswell's Confederate & Southern States Currency	37.00
Discharge, Pvt. Henry George, 8th N.Y. Battery Volunteers, May 12, 1862, 2 Pages	55.00
Drum, Stained Red, Stenciled Star Burst, Brass Studs	467.50
Flag, Confederate, Titled Ebb of Confederacy, 4 1/2 x 7 Ft.	5000.00
Glasses, Sharpshooter's, Opaque Amber, Lighter Centers	135.00
Kit, Dressing, Officer's, Rosewood, Mirror Cover, Silver, Ivory, Fitted, France	4675.00
Map, Fort Fisher, Cape Fear River, War Department, 1865	40.00
Medicine Kit, Drugs In Glass Vials	350.00
Mold, Bullet, Brass, . 36 Round Ball & Patch Type	55.00
Order, Prevent Regiments, Holding Extra Horses, Maj. Gen. Wright Signed, 1864	6.00
Powder Flask, Leather, Beaded Brass Spout	45.00
Print, Camp Huntington, Rome, N.Y., Framed, 18 x 24 In.	79.00
Print, Camp Schyler, Herkimer, N.Y., Framed, 28 x 19 In.	55.00
Record, GAR Members, Sarg. Wounded Kettle Run, Discharged In Boston, 1865	10.00
Ribbon, Reunion, 1864 Ohio Volunteers Souvenir, 1905	15.00
Soap Dish, Wooden	65.00
Surgical Knife, Dove, Wooden Handle, 5 In.	45.00
Sword, Dated 1863	200.00
Sword, Dress	245.00
Tax Receipt, 1862, 2 x 4 In.	35.00
Widow's Application For Pension, Confederate Soldier's, Miss., 1862, 8 x 14 In.	48.00

CKAW, see Dedham category

CLAMBROTH glass, popular in the Victorian era, is a grayish color and is somewhat opaque, like clambroth.

Bowl, Wishbone, Footed, 8 1/2 In.	90.00
Candlestick, Columnar, Sandwich Glass, Pair	500.00
Eggcup, Diamond Point	225.00
Epergne, Child's, Flower Bowl Instead of Lily Center	135.00
Plate, Frosted Block, 8 3/4 In.	70.00
Spill, Diamond–Quilted, 3 Bull's–Eye Diamonds, 4 5/8 In.	175.00

CLARICE CLIFF was a designer who worked in several English factories after the 1920s. She died in 1972.

Bone Dish, Blue	10.00
Bowl, Fantasque, Hand Painted Poppies, 9 1/2 In.	495.00
Candlestick, Red Tonquin, Loop Handle	30.00
Cup & Saucer, Bizarre	100.00
Cup & Saucer, Cabbage Flower	650.00
Cup & Saucer, Devonshire	10.00
Jardiniere, Melon, Orange Bands, Ivory Ground, 6 1/4 x 6 1/4 In.	1540.00
Jug, Athens, Melon Design, 6 In.	850.00
Jug, Farmhouse, Landscape Scene On 2 Sides, 9 3/4 x 8 In.	1650.00
Jug, Iris, Summer House Pattern	3000.00
Jug, Lotus, Melon Design	4300.00
Plate, Bizarre, Newport Pottery, 9 In.	75.00
Plate, Devonshire, 10 In.	8.00
Plate, Rural Scenes, Brown Harvest Rim, Ink Mark, 10 In.	27.50
Soup, Dish, Devonshire, Low	10.00
Urn, Geometric Band, 11 3/4 x 10 In.	2200.00
Vase, Blue Chintz, Green, Blue & Pink Flowers, Ivory Ground, 8 x 5 1/2 In.	1200.00
Vase, Budgie, Signed, 8 1/4 x 6 1/4 In.	302.50
Vase, Geometric, Baluster	1600.00
Vase, Inspiration, Metallic Oxide, 7 In.	1800.00
Wall Pocket, Budgie	275.00

CLEWELL ware was made in limited quantities by Charles Walter Clewell of Canton, Ohio, from 1902 to 1955. Pottery was covered with a thin coating of bronze, then treated to make the bronze turn different colors. Pieces covered with copper, brass, or silver were also made. Mr. Clewell's secret formula for blue patinated bronze was burned when he died in 1965.

Bowl, Copper Finish, 3 x 6 1/2 In.	650.00
Bowl, Copper Over Pottery, Brown To Dark Green Patina, Marked, 3 x 6 In.	165.00
Mug, Copper Over Pottery, Riveted Design, Marked, 4 In.	175.00
Vase, Art Nouveau Floral, Copper Over Pottery, 7 In.	495.00
Vase, Copper & Blue–Green Bronze Glaze, Signed, 6 1/2 In.	395.00
Vase, Neoclassical, Brown & Green Patina, Bronze, 2 Handles, 7 x 4 3/4 In.	440.00
Vase, Red To Verdigris Patina, Copper Clad, Marked, 13 1/2 In.	715.00
Vase, Trumpet, Green To Brick Red Patina, Marked, 8 In.	137.00

CLEWS pottery was made by George Clews & Co. of Brownhill Pottery, Tunstall, England, from 1806 to 1861. Additional pieces may be listed in the Flow Blue category.

Plate, B & O Railroad On An Incline, Blue, 9 In.	247.00
Plate, City of Albany, Blue, 10 In.	632.00
Plate, Landing of Lafayette, Blue, 10 3/4 In.	385.00
Plate, Peace & Plenty, Dark Blue, 7 1/2 In.	120.00
Platter, Naval Engagement of Chesapeake & Shannon, 20 In.	1100.00

CLIFTON POTTERY was founded by William Long in Clifton, New Jersey, in 1905. He worked there until 1908 making a line called *Crystal Patina.* Clifton Pottery made art pottery. Another firm, Chesapeake Pottery, sold majolica marked *Clifton ware.*

Humidor, Indian Ware, Geometric, Black	75.00
Mug, Indian, 4 In.	121.00
Teapot, Indian, 1 Cup	65.00
Teapot, Tan, Green Crystal Patina	125.00
Vase, Bud, Crystalline Celadon Glaze, 1905, 5 1/2 x 2 1/4 In.	250.00
Vase, Chrysanthemum, Gray Leaves, Bisque Terra Cotta Ground, 12 x 8 In.	440.00
Vase, Green Glaze, Incised Mark, 1905, 8 3/4 x 5 1/4 In.	220.00

CLOCKS of all types have always been popular with collectors. The eighteenth–century tall case, or grandfather's clock, was designed to house a works with a long pendulum. In 1816, Eli Terry patented a new, smaller

works for a clock, and the case became smaller. The clock could be kept on a shelf instead of on the floor. By 1840, coiled springs were used and even smaller clocks were made. Battery–powered electric clocks were made in the 1870s.

1000–Day, Brass & Glass, 4–Sided, Schatz 250.00
Advertising, 7–Up Your Thirst Away 95.00
Advertising, 7–Up, Green Neon Tubing, 14 1/2 In. 500.00
Advertising, 7–Up, Wooden Frame, Glass Front 165.00
Advertising, AAA Root Beer, Lighted, Hanging 100.00
Advertising, Atlas Tires & Batteries, 1950s 175.00
Advertising, Benson & Hedges, Battery Operated, 4 x 6 In. 12.00
Advertising, Big Smith Work Clothes, Lights Up, 1950s 110.00
Advertising, Brown's Delicious Ice Cream, Light–Up 275.00
Advertising, Budweiser, Reverse Painted At Base, Seth Thomas, 1–Weight, 5 Ft. 900.00
Advertising, Budweiser, Watch Shape 75.00
Advertising, Bulova, Light–Up, Round ....75.00 To 100.00
Advertising, Burger Brau, Tin, Yellow Ground, 19 x 15 In. 143.00
Advertising, Burgermeister, Plastic Front, Metal Frame, Light–Up 75.00
Advertising, Cadillac, Diamond, With V, Light–Up 125.00
Advertising, Canada Dry 160.00
Advertising, Carhart Overhauls, Neon 350.00
Advertising, Charlie The Tuna, Alarm, Original Box 85.00
Advertising, Chesterfield Cigarette, Battery Operated, 8 x 16 In. 17.00
Advertising, Cities Service Petroleum Products, Round, 20 In. 175.00
Advertising, Clapperton Spool Cotton, Figure 8 Shape, Baird 975.00
Advertising, Columbia Built Bicycles Since 1877, America's First Bicycle 330.00
Advertising, Dr Pepper, 1960s 150.00
Advertising, Dr Pepper, Cadillac V, Light–Up, 1950s 125.00
Advertising, Dr Pepper, General Electric, 1940s 225.00
Advertising, Dr Pepper, Good For Life, 1940s 15.00
Advertising, Dr Pepper, Pam, Light Up 140.00
Advertising, Dr Pepper, Regulator, Oak 485.00
Advertising, Drink Sunshine Premium Beer, Electric, Round, 15 In. 105.00
Advertising, El Caza & Honeymoon Cigars, Baird 1200.00
Advertising, Elgin, Wall 75.00
Advertising, Essley Apparel, Round, 1950s, 18 In. 75.00
Advertising, Forestville Hardware & Clock Co., Wall, Chimes, Octagon, 1850s 295.00
Advertising, Four Roses Whiskey, Plastic, Metal Housing, Light–Up, 12 x 13 In. 75.00
Advertising, Gem Razor Blades, Wooden 165.00
Advertising, Gruen Watch Time 125.00
Advertising, Hambone, Battery Operated, Porcelain, Enameled, Wall, 7 In. Diam. ... 25.00
Advertising, Hamm's Beer, Reddish Sunrise & Then Sunset, 1940s 150.00
Advertising, Jolly Tar Past Time Tobacco Bared, 18 1/2 x 31 x 5 In. 825.00
Advertising, Kelvinator Appliances, Neon, 1930s 275.00
Advertising, Kist Beverages, Electric, 1931, 15 1/2 In. 49.00
Advertising, Leon Levi Jewelers & Opticians, Cash – Credit 150.00
Advertising, Lionel Trains Authorized Service Station, Neon 500.00
Advertising, Lucky Strike Tobacco, 15 In. Diameter 495.00
Advertising, Lucky Strike Tobacco, Mahogany Veneer 275.00
Advertising, Mack Trucks, Pictures Bulldog 250.00
Advertising, Marlboro Man 65.00
Advertising, Motorola, Radio For Home & Cars, Neon, With Spinner 850.00
Advertising, None Such Mince Meat, Wall, Pumpkin Shape 450.00
Advertising, Nu–Grape, Plastic 75.00
Advertising, Old Daum Whiskey 95.00
Advertising, Pennsylvania Dutch Beer, Electric, Back–Lit Glass, Metal, 16 x 5 In. ... 192.00
Advertising, Pennsylvania Fire Insurance 100.00
Advertising, Pennzoil, 1960s, 14 x 14 In. 90.00
Advertising, Promix Feeds 100.00
Advertising, RC Cola, Light–Up, 1960s 175.00
Advertising, Red Goose Shoes, Pinwheel, Neon 750.00
Advertising, Red Indian Motor Oil, Neon, Octagonal 895.00

Advertising, Root Beer, Mug Shape 78.00
Advertising, Royal Crown Cola, Light–Up 200.00
Advertising, Sacco Fertilizers, 18 x 18 In. 25.00
Advertising, Sealtest Ice Cream, Light–Up, Square 75.00
Advertising, Simmon's Liver Regulator 225.00
Advertising, Southern Belle Dairy, Square, Girl In Red Dress, 16 In. 65.00
Advertising, Sunkist, Boy & Girl 35.00
Advertising, Tetley Tea 95.00
Advertising, Timer, Purina Poultry Chows, Set For Time On & Off, Plug 30.00
Advertising, Valvoline Motor Oil 130.00
Advertising, Van Camp's Soup 330.00
Advertising, Western Union, Naval Observatory, Battery 150.00
Advertising, Willard Battery, Light–Up, Reversed Glass, 22 In. 467.00
Alarm, Barbie, Talking, Janex, Box 57.50
Alarm, Big Ben, Bakelite 20.00
Alarm, Century of Progress 225.00
Alarm, Cobblers, Animated, Germany, 1880 .... 1250.00
Alarm, Ingersoll, Art Deco, Black On Chrome 30.00
Alarm, Sunbeam, Garfield, Box, 1978 .... 45.00
Alarm, Texaco 70.00
Alarm, Woody Woodpecker, Animated, Illuminated Hands, Columbia, 1959, Box 285.00
Animated, Flying Hummingbird, Shelf, France 4675.00
Ansonia, Black Iron, Gold Scroll Trim, c.1895 .... 425.00
Ansonia, Bronze, 2–Footed Ewers, 3 Piece 495.00
Ansonia, China, Turquoise, La Layon, Outside Escapement, No. 1368, Large 1000.00
Ansonia, Enameled Face, Open Escapement, Hour, Half–Hour Strike, 11 3/4 In. 110.00
Ansonia, Mantel Set, Metal Clock, French Style, Candelabra, 3 Piece 413.00
Ansonia, Mantel, Black, Iron Indian Each Side, Ornate Iron Footed 85.00
Ansonia, Mantel, Cast Iron, Hour & Half–Hour Strike, 12 1/2 In. 125.00
Ansonia, Mantel, Metal Griffins Each Side, Black Case 150.00
Ansonia, Mantel, Royal Bonn Porcelain 275.00
Ansonia, Pink China Case, Open Escapement, c.1900, 13 In. 330.00
Ansonia, Shelf, Alarm, Unusual Winding Hole, 19th Century, 11 x 7 In. 165.00
Arabesque, Skeleton 2750.00
Art Deco, Electric, Cobalt Blue 155.00
Art Deco, Green Onyx, Silvered Brass Face, 8–Day, Switzerland, 8 1/2 In. 60.00
Art Deco, Wall, China, Green & Black, Newark 85.00
Arts & Crafts, Oak, Arabic Numerals, 14 In. 77.00
Arts & Crafts, Shelf, Oak 250.00
Banjo, Bailey, Banks & Biddle, c.1870, 35 In. 675.00
Banjo, Brass Finial, Eagle, 19th Century, 40 1/2 In. 6750.00
Banjo, Chelsea, Ships Bell, Reverse Painted Sailing Ship 1155.00
Banjo, Daniel Monroe & Co., Diamond Top, 38 In. 4000.00
Banjo, Federal, Mahogany, Mass., 1815, 34 1/2 In. 990.00
Banjo, Howard, Brass, Repainted Dial, Reverse Painted, 19th Century, 28 In. 550.00
Banjo, Howard, No. 5 .... 2950.00
Banjo, Mahogany Veneer Case, Brass Works, Painted Metal Face, 33 In. 275.00
Banjo, Mahogany, Eagle Finial, Reverse Painted Throat, 19th Century, 33 In. 688.00
Banjo, Mahogany, Massachusetts, c.1800, 29 In. 495.00
Banjo, Oliver Brackett, Gilded, Cast Brass Eagle Finial, 19th Century, 40 1/2 In. 7425.00
Banjo, Prince of Wales Feather Finial, Mahogany, 19th Century, 40 1/2 In. 688.00
Banjo, Reverse Painted River Scene, Eglomise Throat Glass, 33 In. 990.00
Barnesdale, Victorian, Mahogany, Column, Enamel Dial, 65 x 41 x 13 In. 1325.00
Benjamin Morrill, 8–Day, Reverse Painted Mirror, Time & Strike 6875.00
Benjamin Morrill, New Hampshire, Time & Strike, Signed, Label 6250.00
Birge & Fuller, 8–Day, Hour Strike, Double Reverse Painted Doors, Walnut 725.00
Birge & Fuller, Shelf, Triple Deck 340.00
Bishop & Bradley, Shelf, Reverse Painted Picture of Man With Top Hat 2200.00
Black Forest, Cathedral Form, Turrets, Apostle Appears As Door Opens, 1880 ...... 9000.00
Boston Clock Co., Mantel, White Onyx, Gilded Metal Trim, Enameled Face, 12 In. . 121.00
Bracket, Edwardian, Silvered Dial, Hour & Half–Hour Strike, England, Mahogany 250.00
Bracket, Farrow, Calendar, George III, Fusee Movement, Japanned, 19 In. 3300.00

Clock, Ithaca, Calendar, Ebonized Columns,
Mahogany, 19 X 9 1/2 In.

Clock, Waterbury, Kitchen, Hanging

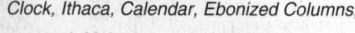

Bracket, Gothic Carved Walnut, Brass Dial, Moon Phase & Calendar Aperture	2250.00
Bracket, Repeating, Silvered Face, Edward & Sons, Glasgow, Oak, 16 1/2 In.	685.00
Brewster & Ingraham, Steeple, 4 Spires	900.00
Brewster & Ingraham, Steeple, Brass Spring	775.00
Carriage, 8–Day Time & Alarm, 19th Century, France, 4 1/4 In.	195.00
Carriage, Alarm, Brass, Enameled Face, Beveled Glass, France, 4 1/2 In.	175.00
Carriage, Bailey, Banks & Biddle, Gold Bronze, c.1850	2200.00
Carriage, Brass, Enamel Face, Beveled Glass Panels, France, 5 1/2 In.	165.00
Carriage, Brass, Repainted Celluloid Ivory Panels, Handle, 7 1/4 In.	28.00
Carriage, Silvered Metal, Enamel Dial, Blue Numerals, c.1900, Miniature	3740.00
Carriage, Sonnerie, Repeat & Alarm, Enamel Dial, Gilt Metal, c.1890	2420.00
Cathedral, Blue Glass Backing, Gothic Design, Bell Tower, Gilt Bonze, 23 In.	2750.00
Charles Fox, Lantern, Pierced Frets, Lion & Unicorn Supports, 1670, 14 1/2 In.	5500.00
Chelsea, Bronze, Griffin Handles, 8 1/4 In.	165.00
Chelsea, Ship, 24–Hour Dial, 8 In.	400.00
Cherub At Top, 3 Cherubs Around Center, Applied Flowers, Sitzendorf	5600.00
Cuckoo, Mantel, Carved Pierced Design, Enamel Face, Wooden, 20 1/4 In.	198.00
Dutch, Starrat Klok, Hooded, Herald Angels & Atlas Figural Top, Pendulum	2495.00
E. Howard, No. 5, Figure Eight	3800.00
E. N. Welch, Steeple, With Music Box, Dresden Figures, Anniversary	400.00
Electric, Dome Shape, Blue Mirror	95.00
Elgin, Desk, Gilt Metal, Onyx Base, Arabic Numerals, Octagonal, 5 1/2 x 4 1/4 In.	25.00
Eli & Samuel Terry, Pillar & Scroll, Reverse Painted Scene, No Key & Weights	2600.00
Eli Terry, Cottage, 30–Hour Time & Alarm, Ladder Movement, 11 In.	225.00
Eli Terry, Pillar & Scroll, Eglomise, Shelf, c.1816	7150.00
Figural, Banjo Player, Painted Black Minstrel, Banjo Contains Clock, 16 In.	825.00
Figural, Blinking Eyes, Black Boy, Standing, Cast Iron, 1880s, 15 1/2 In.	1320.00
Figural, Brass, Crusader, Drawn Sword, Horseback, Porcelain Dial, 18 In.	688.00
Figural, God Bless America, Animated Flags, 1944	130.00
Figural, Kit–Kat, Electric, Eyes Move, Tail Wags, 1950s, 9 In., Box	35.00
Figural, Maiden, Standing Beneath An Arbor, Barrel Shape, Art Nouveau, 15 In.	132.00
Figural, Raggedy Ann, Talks	25.00
Figural, Roosevelt, Helmsman, Electric, 1933	135.00
Figural, Woman, Case With Foliate Design, Green, White, Art Nouveau, 16 In.	385.00
General Electric, Mantel, Bronze Color, Electric, Art Deco Style, Red Dot, 1930s ...	60.00
Gilbert, Mantle, Cast Metal, 14 In.	88.00
Gilbert, Regulator, Wall, Oak	2450.00
Gravity, Gebrauchsweisung Fur Sageht, c.1920	220.00
Gustav Becker, Regulator, Silver Dial, Mullioned Glass Door, 24 3/4 In.	135.00
Howard Miller, George Nelson, Desk, Circular, c.1950	550.00

Ingraham, Grecian, c.1860 .... 425.00
Ithaca, Calendar, Double Dial 715.00
Ithaca, Calendar, Ebonized Columns, Mahogany, 19 x 9 1/2 In. ....*Illus* 5500.00
Jouot & Angouleme, Hanging, Brass Hood, Pendulum, Enameled Face, 18 In. 467.00
Junghans, Bracket, Greek Key Crest, Fluted Columns, Chimes, Oak, 17 1/2 In. 275.00
Junghans, Regulator, Mullioned Door, Silvered Face, Fruitwood, 30 In. 145.00
Kitchen, Porcelain Face, Dutch Children, Windmills, 7–Day, Pendulum, Holland 350.00
Koehn's, Correct Time, Metal Face, Plastic Numbers, Metal Base, 18 1/2 In. 77.00
Krober, Mantel, 8–Day, Iron 200.00
Lantern, Brass, 19th Century, England, 15 In. 475.00
LeCoultre, Art Deco, Brass Frame, Blue & Black Enamel, Collapsible Stand 205.00
LeCoultre, Atmos, 9 1/4 In. 225.00
LeCoultre, Desk, Art Deco, 8–Day, Alarm, Enameled 165.00
LeCoultre, Mantel, Brass Fish & Base, Etched Glass, 7 x 7 In. 275.00
LeCoultre, Shelf, Gilt Metal & Glass, 5 In. 85.00
Louis Philippe, Repeating Cartel, Ormolu, Urn Finial, Key, c.1840, 16 1/2 In. 3415.00
Louis XV, Ormolu Cartel, Circular White Enamel Dial, 22 1/2 In. 7975.00
Lux, Cottage, Green Roof, 8–Day 65.00
Lux, Mantel, Celluloid 45.00
Lux, Wig Wag Cat, Box 275.00
Maison Moderne, Carved Sycamore & Brass, Art Nouveau, 1900, 15 1/4 In. 1980.00
Mantel Set, Art Deco, Marble & Onyx, 8–Day & Striking, France, 3 Piece 645.00
Mantel Set, Empire, White Marble, Gilded Brass, Enameled, France, 3 Piece 550.00
Mantel Set, Victorian, Art Nouveau Woman, France, 3 Piece 1850.00
Mantel, Alexander The Conqueror, 2 Warrior, 19th Century, France 1870.00
Mantel, Apollo's Chariot, Marble Plinth, Lion Paw Feet, Marble Case, 25 In. 6600.00
Mantel, Black & Green Marble, Lion On Top, Germany, 1905 .... 155.00
Mantel, Black, Verde Marble Case, Enamel Face, Open Escapement, Barbaste, 16 In. 390.00
Mantel, Brass Frame, Enameled Porcelain Panels, Dial, 16 In. 495.00
Mantel, Brass, Glass, Automated Musical Bird 2860.00
Mantel, Bronze & Marble, Louis XVI Style, Signed, 15 1/2 In. 495.00
Mantel, Bronze & Marble, Porcelain Face, Black Marble Base, 15 1/2 In. 1760.00
Mantel, Cast Metal, Candelabra, French Style, Rhinestones, 3 Piece 413.00
Mantel, Castle, White Metal, Large 50.00
Mantel, Davies, Brass Face, Mirror, Spelter Figures, Glass Dome, 17 In. 440.00
Mantel, Dewey Manila, Embossed & Gilded Brass, 1898, 9 3/4 In. 50.00
Mantel, Empire, Gilt Metal, Draped Woman, With Lyre, Square Clock, 15 In. 990.00
Mantel, Figural, Brass, Greek Warrior On Top, France, 25 x 16 In. 880.00
Mantel, French Empire Inlaid, 19 In. 468.00
Mantel, Fruitwood & Ivory, Biedermeier, Central Lyre Support, 1820s, 22 In. 3575.00
Mantel, Gilt Bronze, Woman, On Chaise, Raised Birds & Vines, 1850, 14 1/2 In. 330.00
Mantel, Jack & Jill At The Well, Brass & Porcelain, France 475.00
Mantel, Porcelain Dial, Gothic Style Case, France, 19th Century, 17 x 10 x 5 In. 375.00
Mantel, Porcelain, Floral Decoration, Giltwood Base, 19th Century 467.00
Maple & Co., Ltd., Brass Mount, 19th Century, 15 In. 935.00
Maranville, Calendar, Office 1350.00
New Haven, Columbina, 30–Day, Oak 800.00
New Haven, Gallery, Oak Case, 12–In. Dial 125.00
New Haven, Gingerbread, Alarm, Quarter–Hour Strike, Oak, 14 1/2 x 21 1/2 In. 145.00
New Haven, Mantel, Arts & Crafts, Hinged Glazed Door, Oak, 14 In. 175.00
New Haven, Mantel, Statue of Richard The Lion Hearted, Open Escapement 375.00
New Haven, Parlor, 8–Day, Gold Plated Bronze, Painted Garden Scene, c.1885 .... 325.00
New Haven, Parlor, Garden Scene On Porcelain, Gold Plated Bronze, 8–Day, 1885 275.00
Norris North, Pillar & Scroll, Reverse Painted Glass 1550.00
Perpetual Motion, J. Kaiser, Rotating Moon, Sun Face, Dome, 10 1/2 In. 220.00
Peter Max, Wall 95.00
Regulator, Brass Case, 8–Day Time & Strike, 19th Century, 8 1/2 In. 495.00
Regulator, Bronze Dore, France 1750.00
Regulator, Short Drop, 10 Dial, Atkins Clock Co., Rosewood, 24 1/2 In. 195.00
Regulator, Vienna Style, Glass Door, Walnut 425.00
S. Hoadley, 30–Hour Wooden Weight Driven, Grain Painted, c.1810, 85 In. 1320.00
Sawin & Dyer, Banjo, 8–Day, 1822 .... 1870.00
Schmid, Mantel, Pendulum, 8–Day, Key Wind, Japanese Design 95.00

Sessions, 8–Day Brass Works, Maple Case, 38 1/2 x 18 1/8 In. 475.00
Sessions, Bluebird 300.00
Sessions, French Chef, Electric 45.00
Sessions, Kitchen, Windmill, Second Hand Blade On Windmill, Red, 1950s 25.50
Sessions, Mantel, Blond Wood, 1/4 Hour Musical Chimes 50.00
Sessions, Mantel, Ebonized & Incised Metal, c.1880 .... 77.00
Seth Thomas, Crystal Regulator, Brass Top, Hour & Half–Hour Strike, 9 1/2 In. ... 165.00
Seth Thomas, Crystal Regulator, Enameled Face, Hour, Half–Hour Strike, 10 In. ... 140.00
Seth Thomas, Lincoln, Ebony Case 650.00
Seth Thomas, Pillar & Scroll, 30–Hour Wooden Works, Original Glass 1600.00
Seth Thomas, Pillar & Scroll, 8–Day Brass Movement, c.1900 .... 995.00
Seth Thomas, Pillar & Scroll, Eglomise Landscape, Painted Dial, 35 In. 330.00
Seth Thomas, Pillar & Scroll, Mahogany Veneer, 30–Hour Movement, 30 In. 2750.00
Seth Thomas, Pillar & Scroll, Mahogany Veneer, c.1825, 30 1/4 In. 935.00
Seth Thomas, Pillar & Scroll, Shelf, Wooden Weight, Reverse Painted Glass, c.1825 ... 2750.00
Seth Thomas, Pillar & Scroll, Wooden Movement, Rack & Snail Strike, 1820 .... 8800.00
Seth Thomas, Regulator, 1–Weight, G. N. R. Y. On Dial, Oak 1400.00
Seth Thomas, School, Time & Strike, Walnut, 1892 .... 225.00
Seth Thomas, Shelf, Rosewood, Marquetry, Brass Works, 9 7/8 In. 467.00
Seth Thomas, Union Pacific Railroad, Marked 450.00
Seth Thomas, Weight Driven Column, Late 1800s, Reverse Painted 225.00
Shelf, Empire, Triple Decker, Mahogany Veneer, Gold Repaint, Brass Works, 38 In. ... 137.00
Shelf, J. Chadwick, Kidney Dial, Federal Style, 1810s 7500.00
Shelf, Rosewood, Ebony, Marquetry, Brass Trim, Enameled Face, 9 1/2 In. 465.00
Shelf, Wurttemberg, Mahogany, Brass Trim, 9 5/8 In. 80.00
Skeleton, English, Brass Lion Mounts, Marble Base, c.1875, 21 In. 600.00
Skeleton, Fusee Movement, Anchor Escapement, Brass, 19th Century, 17 1/2 In. 885.00
Skeleton, Lion Pillars, Time & Strike, Double Marble Base, English 1950.00
Steeple, Burl Walnut, Fruitwood Inlaid, English Victorian, 8–Day, 1875 .... 2950.00
Tall Case, Bagnall, Tombstone, Waist Door, 8–Day Time & Strike, 1750 .... 605.00
Tall Case, Bernick, Burled Walnut, Veneered 6050.00
Tall Case, Bigelow, Kennard & Co., Mahogany, Engraved Dial, Early 20th Century .. 3740.00
Tall Case, C. Bly, Oak, Chinoiserie Deco, Black, Gold, Brass Works, 86 3/4 In. 2640.00
Tall Case, C. C. Bo'Ness, Mahogany, Silver Moon Phase Dial, 1780, 85 In. 6600.00
Tall Case, Chandler, Cherry, Star Punch On Door, Painted Dial 8250.00
Tall Case, Cherry, Bracket Feet, Arched Hood, Calendar Movement, 79 1/2 In. 4455.00
Tall Case, Cherry, Moon Phase Dial, English Works, Swan Neck Pediment, 87 In. .. 1760.00
Tall Case, Cherry, Polychrome, Gilt Painted Iron Dial, 8–Movement, c.1810, 92 In. .. 3300.00
Tall Case, Chippendale, Mahogany, Fluted Columns, Brass Works, 88 In. 950.00
Tall Case, Chippendale, Swans Neck Crest, Flame Mahogany, Signed No. Joy 6600.00
Tall Case, Christopher Bly, Oak, Chinoiserie, Weights, Pendulum, London, 86 In. ... 2640.00
Tall Case, Cooper & Hedge, 12–Inch Dial, Calendar, Seconds Dial, c.1780, 7 Ft. 1925.00
Tall Case, Double Tombstone Door, Moon Phase, 30–Hour, Mahogany, 91 3/4 In. .. 6750.00
Tall Case, Dutch, Marquetry, Carved Crest, Floral, Early 19th Century, 96 In. 3300.00
Tall Case, Edgar Stennes, Tiger Maple 2300.00
Tall Case, Empire, Molded Cornice, Glazed Hinged Door, Metal Dial, 85 In. 1450.00
Tall Case, Enoch Burnham, Mahogany, Iron Dial, 8–Day, Fretwork Bonnet, 83 In. .. 5115.00
Tall Case, Federal, Cherry, Polychrome, Gilt, 8–Day Movement, 1810, 92 In. 3300.00
Tall Case, Federal, Gilt Painted Iron Dial, Seconds Dial, 8–Day, Cherry, 92 1/4 In. .. 3300.00
Tall Case, Federal, Iron Dial, Calendar, Cherry, Connecticut, c.1800, 93 In. 4125.00
Tall Case, Floral Painted Case, Brass Movement, White Enamel Face, 94 In. 2200.00
Tall Case, Frederick Wingate, Quarter Column Posts, Alligatored, Weights, Key 6325.00
Tall Case, George Hoff, Lancaster, Walnut, Flat Top, Penna., 18th Century, 89 In. .. 6600.00
Tall Case, George II Style, Walnut & Burl Walnut, 66 3/4 In. 825.00
Tall Case, George III, Mahogany, Arched Hood, Ball Finials, 19th Century, 87 In. .. 3300.00
Tall Case, Georgian, Mahogany, Painted Moon Phase Dial, 1760 .... 4650.00
Tall Case, Henry Roi, 30–Hour Movement, Cherry, Hamburg, 1790 .... 2000.00
Tall Case, Hepplewhite, New Jersey, c.1800 .... 1200.00
Tall Case, Herschede, 9–Tube 3750.00
Tall Case, Howard Miller, Oak, Long Glazed Door, Westminster Chimes, 77 1/2 In. .. 440.00
Tall Case, Isaac Reed, 8–Day, Cherry, Mahogany Veneer, 1830, 91 1/2 In. 4500.00
Tall Case, Jacob Cope, Cherry, Inlay, Ebonized Split Columns, 8 Ft. 3 In. 2530.00
Tall Case, Jacob Goodhart, 8–Day, Brass Movement, Painted Face 8800.00

Tall Case, Jacob Gorgas, Chippendale, Mahogany, Bonnet, 18th Century, 89 In. 4950.00
Tall Case, Jacob Krout, Cherry, 8–Day, Moon Phase, Federal Shields, 96 In. 5500.00
Tall Case, Jedediah Weiss, Sheraton, Mahogany, Broken Arch Pediment 7100.00
Tall Case, John Arnold, George III, Mahogany, London, Late 18th Century, 87 In. 3650.00
Tall Case, John Dobie, Scotland, 1780, L84 In. 3800.00
Tall Case, John Eagle, 8–Day Time & Strike, England 6300.00
Tall Case, John Forbes, George III, Roman & Arabic Numerals, Oak, 80 In. 1540.00
Tall Case, Josh. Kerns, Oak, Rope Spiral Molded, Brass Works, England, 84 In. 715.00
Tall Case, Mahogany, Brass Dial, Broken Pediment Crest, 1920s, 6 Ft. 10 In. 300.00
Tall Case, Mahogany, Brass Works, Moon, Calendar, Pendulum, England, 83 In. 550.00
Tall Case, Mahogany, Silver Engraved, Scotland, c.1780, 85 In. 6600.00
Tall Case, New Haven, Regulator, Ornate Carved Walnut 7150.00
Tall Case, Oberholtzer, Moon Phase, 8–Day, Night Alarm, 7 Ft. 8 In. 6500.00
Tall Case, Paulin of Anppegard, French Provincial, Carved Walnut, 1780, 99 In. 2300.00
Tall Case, Phillip Glasco, Mahogany, George III, Ireland 4400.00
Tall Case, Planchon, Mahogany Veneer, Fluted Ionic Column, Early 19th Century 7920.00
Tall Case, Polychrome Dial, 34–Hour Wooden Weight, Red Wash, American, 81 In. 1650.00
Tall Case, Refinished Cherry, Paneled Base, Chamfered Corners, 93 1/2 In. 1100.00
Tall Case, Richard Raymnet, County Clare, c.1710 .... 3000.00
Tall Case, Ruger Stouter, Walnut, Rocking Ship & Angel Movement, 18th Century 8000.00
Tall Case, Samuel Collier Eccles, Alarm, Anchor Escapement, Figured Wood, 5 Ft. 5775.00
Tall Case, Seth Thomas, Painted, Wooden Works By Plymouth, Conn., 83 In. 4600.00
Tall Case, Silas Hoadley, Federal Houses Scene, Masonic Symbols, 86 In. 2100.00
Tall Case, Silas Hoadley, Red, Ocher & Cream Sponge Design, 86 In. 8250.00
Tall Case, Solomon Parke, Chippendale, Sunflowers Hood, 97 1/2 In. 9000.00
Tall Case, Swedish, Glazed Bonnet, Painted, Date & Initials, 1817, 7 Ft. 1 In. 8800.00
Tall Case, Vesper, Mahogany, Brass Ball Finials, Enamel Tin Face, C. 1780, 84 In. 6100.00
Tall Case, Walnut & Figured Walnut Case, 8–Day Moon, Night Alarm, 7 Ft. 8 In. 6500.00
Tall Case, Walnut, Brass Works, Weights, Pendulum, Pennsylvania, 94 1/2 In. 1500.00
Tall Case, Walnut, Ogee Feet, Paneled Base, Floral Designs On Face, 95 In. 5225.00
Tall Case, Westminster & Whittington, Mahogany, Revival, Chimes, Moon Phase 6500.00
Tall Case, William Rout, George III, Strike/Not Strike, Japanned, Green, 7 Ft. 3850.00
Telechron, Art Deco, Allover Design, Glass, Copper & Bakelite, Electric, Round 70.00
Telechron, Moire, Blue Mirror 35.00
Thomas Hunter, Bracket, Musical, Calendar Dial, Seconds Dial, Fusee, 18 1/2 In. 3300.00
Thompson Time Stamp Co., Cast Iron, Brass, 11 1/2 In. 55.00
Thoren, Musical, 2 Gilt Florals At Sides, Walnut, 19th Century, 18 In. 905.00
Tiffany clocks are listed in the Tiffany category
Time Recorder, Rochester, Embossed Cast Iron Case, Oak, 54 In. 385.00
Tortoiseshell, Inlaid Ivory, Arched Frieze, 1830s, 16 1/2 In. 4400.00
Unitec, Swing Dolls 85.00
Vanity, Celluloid, Fancy, Two–Tone 45.00
Wadsworth, Lounsbury & Turner, Pillar & Scroll, Mahogany 3000.00
Wadsworth, Lounsbury & Turner, Shelf, Finials, 1830 .... 2300.00
Wag–On–Wall, Brass Movement, 1790 .... 1195.00
Wall, Louis XVI, Pendant, Tole, Openwork Gilt Hands, Moisy, Round, 15 In. 2300.00
Waterbury, 8–Day Time, Strike and Alarm, 20 In. 120.00
Waterbury, Calendar, Double Dial, Oak Case 895.00
Waterbury, Carriage, Gilded Brass, Beveled Glass, 1891, 4 1/4 In. 105.00
Waterbury, Double Dial Calendar 895.00
Waterbury, Gold Design, Patent 1891, 11 In. 220.00
Waterbury, Kitchen, Hanging ....*Illus* 275.00
Waterbury, Regulator, Jeweler's, Glazed Door, Brass Weight, Pendulum, 80 In. 3300.00
Waterbury, Regulator, Short Drop, Octagonal Wooden Case, 13 1/2 In. 100.00
Waterbury, Regulator, Urn Top, Brass, Glass, Hour, Half–Hour Strike, 18 In. 415.00
Waterbury, Shelf, Carved & Painted, Floral Carving, Front, Sides, 19 In. 1100.00
Waterbury, Wall, Augusta, Oak Case, Early 1800s 1875.00
Waterbury, Wall, Regulator, Carved Oak, 56 In. 743.00
Welch, Regulator, Octagonal, Short Drop Pendulum, Hour Strike, Oak, 19 In. 110.00
Welch, Wall, Ogee, Painted Scene, New Orleans Opera House, c.1850, 26 In. 465.00
Westinghouse, With Radio, Bisque White, Solid State, 1950s 25.00
Willard, Banjo, Federal, Gilt Foliage, Leafy Border, c.1810, 30 In. 3850.00
Willard, Banjo, Federal, Roman Numerals, Flaring Throat, 28 In. 770.00

Willard, Convex Glass Face, 14 In.	110.00
Willard, Jr., Lyre, Reverse Painted Scene	1980.00
Willard, Shelf, Dish Dial, Tiger Maple, Mahogany Frame, Replaced Finial	8250.00
Willard, Shelf, Federal, Brass Finials, Fan Inlay, Mahogany, c.1805, 36 1/4 In.	3300.00
Wm. S. Johnson, Wall, Glass Door, Mahogany	70.00

CLOISONNE enamel was developed during the tenth century. A glass enamel was applied between small ribbons of metal on a metal base. Most cloisonne is Chinese or Japanese. Pieces marked *China* are twentieth-century examples.

Ashtray, Bowl Shape, Floral, Green Ground, Wooden Stand, 7 1/4 In.	16.00
Bowl, Floral Design, Pale Green Ground, Wooden Stand, 6 x 2 1/8 In.	11.00
Bowl, Gilt Wash, Trailing Foliate Band, Ch'ing Dynasty, 6 1/2 In.	495.00
Bowl, Intricate Design, Black Enameled, 8 x 2 3/8 In.	45.00
Bowl, Lions On Outside, Interior Dragons, Center Fish, 12 1/4 In.	187.00
Box, Flower Design, Round, 5 In.	40.00
Box, Foo Lion On Lid, 5 In.	55.00
Box, Multicolored Floral Design, Oriental, 3 In.	35.00
Box, Woman Seated In Garden, 6 Sides, Late 1800s, 4 In.	68.00
Clock, Gilded Brass Trim, Enameled, Portrait Pendulum, 18 3/4 In.	352.00
Compote, Floral Design, Butterflies, Two-Tone Blue, Rust Ground, 6 In.	75.00
Dish, Fruit, Flowers & Bats, 7 1/4 In.	55.00
Figurine, Horse, Early 20th Century, 17 In., Pair	1300.00
Figurine, Rooster, Bright Blue, 1910, Life-Size	2400.00
Jar, Cover, Carved Stone Insert, 3 3/8 In.	30.00
Jar, Cover, Green Scrollwork, Reserves of Florals, 10 In.	120.00
Jar, Flowers, Birds, Dark Blue Ground, Cylindrical, 7 x 9 3/8 In.	93.00
Jar, Ring Handles, Scenes of Soldiers, Flags, 12 In.	95.00
Plate, Birds & Flowers, Turquoise Ground, Japan, 11 7/8 In.	395.00
Plate, Butterflies, Flowers, Early 1900, 9 In.	85.00
Plate, Floral Design, Shades of Green, Wooden Stand, 8 1/4 In.	30.00
Teapot, Design of Birds, Dragons, Enamel, 6 In.	193.00
Teapot, Floral Design, 3 In.	45.00
Toothpick, Pink Flowers, Blue	20.00
Tray, Dragon, Yellow Ground, 19th Century, China, 8 1/2 x 12 In.	130.00
Urn, Cover, Foo Dog Finial, 6 In.	193.00
Vase, Baluster Form, Yellow, 19th Century, 12 In.	105.00
Vase, Bird, Prunus Blossoms, Red Ground, 1930, 7 1/2 In.	125.00
Vase, Crane & Flower, 26 In., Pair	1320.00
Vase, Dragon, Black Ground, Drilled, 19th Century, 12 In.	45.00
Vase, Enameled Design of Dragons, 14 In.	193.00
Vase, Enameled, Flying Eagle Above Rocky Shoreline, Black Ground, 7 In.	330.00
Vase, Fishscale, Pewter Flared Base, 6 In.	60.00
Vase, Floral, Black Ground, Late 1800s, 5 In.	75.00
Vase, Floral, Green, 7 In., Pair	45.00
Vase, Flowers On Dark Green, c.1895, 4 In.	115.00
Vase, Flowers, Dragons, Blue Ground, 9 In.	60.00
Vase, Goldfish, Yellow, Sato	225.00
Vase, Multicolored Foliate, Bulbous Form, Stick Neck, Blue Ground, 6 In.	88.00
Vase, Multicolored Panels, Floral & Butterfly, c.1880, 11 1/4 In.	155.00
Vase, Polychrome Floral Design, Rust Colored Ground, 8 1/4 In.	35.00
Vase, Polychrome Floral, Black Ground, Wooden Base, 7 1/4 In., Pair	49.00
Vase, Polychrome Stylized Floral Medallions, Black Ground, 8 5/8 In.	95.00
Vase, White Mums On Lavender, 6 In.	80.00
Vase, Yellow Dragon, Black Ground, 9 In.	185.00
Vase, Yellow Dragons Below Lotus Leaves Bands, Chinese, 9 1/4 In., Pair	242.00

CLOTHING of all types is listed in this category. Dresses, hats, shoes, underwear and more are found here. Other textiles are to be found in the Coverlet, Quilt, Textile, and World War I and II categories.

Belt, Faux Scarabs, Colorful, Outsize, 1950	75.00
Belt, Woman's, Orange & Amber Bakelite Link	15.00
Bloomer Gym Suit, College Girl's, 1914, 1 Piece	10.00

Bloomers, Black, Long 18.00
Bloomers, Muslin, Knitted Lace Trim, Long 25.00
Blouse, Cutwork, Crocheted, High Neck, Linen, Handmade 125.00
Blouse, Gauze, Black, White Accent Trim, 1880s 22.00
Boa, Feather, Victorian 65.00
Bodice, Red Silk Crepe, Ostrich Trim, Mary E. Rusk, Wife, Sec. Agriculture, 1890 250.00
Bonnet, Amish, Black 22.00
Bonnet, Baby's, Crocheted, Ecru, 1908 .... 10.00
Bonnet, Brown, Ties, Civil War Vintage 140.00
Bonnet, Girl's, Straw, Ribbons 80.00
Bonnet, Woman's, Velvet, Victorian 17.50
Bus Driver's Outfit, Jackie Gleason, Cap, Ticket Puncher, Transfers, 1955, Box 245.00
Cape & Hat, Victorian, Jet Beaded 165.00
Cape, Creme Silk, Fringed, Madam S. Moghabghab, Paris–New York 795.00
Cape, Opera, Chinese Silk, White, Embroidered Dragon, Floral, White Fur Trim 475.00
Cloche, Flapper, Beige Straw 30.00
Coat & Bonnet, Baby's, Silk 35.00
Coat, Arabian Night-Type, Mohair, Gold Sequins, Embroidered 350.00
Coat, Baby's, Double Collar, Pique 38.00
Coat, Baby's, Emblem, 1902, 25 In. Length 75.00
Coat, Black Bear, Extra–Large 500.00
Coat, Child's, Black Wool, Double–Breasted 10.00
Coat, Evening, Flapper, Black Satin, Embroidered Blue & Orange Sleeves 52.00
Coat, Fake Leopard, Green Silk Lined, 1960s, Size 16 .... 30.00
Coat, Hand Embroidered Paisley, 1880s 375.00
Coat, Mohair, Gold Sequins, Embroidered, Arabian Nights Type 350.00
Coat, Raccoon, Large 1355.00
Coat, Raccoon, Long 400.00
Coat, Russian Golden Sable, Portrait Collar, G. Tierney 5500.00
Coat, Shirred Collar & Cuffs, Velvet, Black, Size 10 .... 35.00
Coat, Summer, Dragon Medallions, Rope Sash Cord, Raw Silk, Chinese 55.00
Coat, With Hat, Raccoon, Long 600.00
Coat, Woman's, Black Shantung, Brown Velvet Collar, L. C. Mae, Calif., 1950s 50.00
Coat, Woman's, Black Virgin Wool, Big Collar, Forstmann, 1960s 40.00
Dress Top, Bonnet & Parasol, Emerald Green, Victorian, 3 Piece 295.00
Dress, Allover Jet Beaded, Original Slip, 1920s 275.00
Dress, Amish, Dark Green, 3 Piece 34.00
Dress, Beaded, Blue, Peplum Style, 1930s, Small Size 55.00
Dress, Black Chiffon, 1940s 55.00
Dress, Black Sequins, Worth, 1920s 3200.00
Dress, Butternut Silk, Quaker, c.1830 .... 165.00
Dress, Chiffon, Floral, 1920s 35.00
Dress, Child's, Crocheted 185.00
Dress, Child's, Long Sleeves, Gathers At Yoke & Waist, White Voile 45.00
Dress, Christening, Lace Panels, Tucks, Lace Collar, Cuffs & Hem, 36 In. 85.00
Dress, Christening, Lace Trim At Neck & Waist, White Batiste, 26 1/2 In. 25.00
Dress, Christening, Silk, 19th Century, 30 In. 125.00
Dress, Christening, Valenciennes Lace, Letter of Babies Christened, France, 1870 ..... 350.00
Dress, Cotton, Embroidered, 1900s 80.00
Dress, Crepe, 1940s 70.00
Dress, Dark Green Velvet, Penna. 350.00
Dress, Evening, Beaded, Black, Chemise Style, Paris, 1920s, Large 48.00
Dress, Evening, Flapper, Rhinestones, Gray Beads, 1920s 80.00
Dress, Flapper, Apricot Velvet, Pearl Beaded, Hip, Shoulder Pearl Strands, 1920 ..... 295.00
Dress, Flapper, Bittersweet Silk Pongee, Scalloped Beaded Hem 225.00
Dress, Floral, Green Ground, Lined Silk, Oriental 45.00
Dress, Ivory, Reich Label 275.00
Dress, Jacket, Hat, Wedding Ensemble, Brown Velvet, Fur Trim, 1927, 3 Piece 575.00
Dress, Lace Trim, Leg O' Mutton Sleeves, 2 Piece, 1890s 190.00
Dress, Navy, Lace Collar, 1930s 17.00
Dress, Orange & Cream, Courreges 275.00
Dress, Plastic Mesh, Paco Rabanne, 1967 .... 750.00
Dress, Prairie, Expandable Under–Bodice For Use When Pregnant, c.1880 .... 185.00

Dress, Prom, Pink Bouffant, Slip, Glitzy Strip Says "Prom 1952" 24.00
Dress, Red, Ruffled Neck & Hem, Nina Ricci 600.00
Dress, Rust Brocade, Owl Buttons, 2 Piece 85.00
Dress, Sequins, Chiffon Over Top 150.00
Dress, Silk Velvet, Beaded, 1930s 650.00
Dress, V Neck, Van Dyke Hem Line, Sequins & Beads, Brown 350.00
Dress, Velvet, 1920s 42.50
Dress, Victorian, Baby's, 17 In. 25.00
Dress, Victorian, Blue & White Wool, Little Girl's, 1865 .... 60.50
Dress, Victorian, White Lace 85.00
Dress, Wedding, Duchesse Lace, Organdy Puff Sleeves, 19th Century 2700.00
Dress, Wedding, Hand Crocheted, Pre–World War I 125.00
Dress, Wedding, Long Train, Size 11–12, 1950s 150.00
Dress, Wedding, Off–White Satin, Allover Seed Pearls, Train, 1960s, Size 7–8 .... 190.00
Dress, Wedding, Satin, Lace, Ruching, Train, Leg O' Mutton Sleeves 180.00
Dress, Wedding, Seed Pearls, Long Train, Size 3 .... 500.00
Dress, Wedding, Seeded Pearl Trim, 10–Ft. Train, Unworn 500.00
Dress, White Lace, Edwardian 1000.00
Dress, White Satin, Crystal & Gray Beading 35.00
Dress, White, Applied Flowers, Nina Ricci 2250.00
Dress, Woman's, Jacket, Green, Gold Sequins, NRA Dress Code Auth. Label, 1930s ... 17.00
Epaulets, General, Gilt, America, Pair 193.00
Garters, Man's, Art Deco, Lavender, Paris, Box 48.00
Gloves, Bearskin 75.00
Grass Skirt, Bra & Lei, Child's, Hawaiian, 3 Piece 15.00
Great Coat, Army Air Force 25.00
Hat, Cloche, Brown Ribbon Loops, Amber Beaded, Christine Dior 16.50
Hat, Cloche, Flapper Type, Ribbon & Flower Trim 45.00
Hat, Connoneer's, America, Early 19th Century 44.00
Hat, Derby, Brown Felt, Red Feather, 7 1/2 In. 104.00
Hat, English Bowler, Man's, Black, Size 7 1/8 .... 24.00
Hat, Fedora, Silk Band, Tassel, Stetson, Original Box 121.00
Hat, Girl's, Brown Velvet, 1926 .... 8.00
Hat, Man's, Straw, Black Band 42.50
Hat, Merry Widow Type, Large Brimmed, Black, 1910 .... 80.00
Hat, Russian Golden Sable, G. Tierney 192.00
Hat, Stetson, Prison–Made Horsehair Hat Band, c.1900 .... 250.00
Hat, Straw, Boater, 5 1/2 In. 132.00
Hat, Straw, Wide Brim, Decorated With Flowers, 1910 .... 210.00
Hat, Top, Black Beaver, Box 137.00
Hat, Top, Man's, Box 15.00
Hat, Tyrolean, Mohair Velour, Attached Enamel, Pins, 22–In. Circumference 65.00
Hat, Woman's, Brown Velvet, Gold Metallic Ribbon Trim, 1916 .... 12.00
Hat, Woman's, Feather Covered Crown, Under Net, Tan 55.00
Helmet, Cavalry, U.S., Yellow Horsehair Plume, 12 In. 358.00
Jacket, Bolero, Cutwork, Light Blue 12.50
Jacket, Bonnet & Parasol, Emerald Green, Victorian, 3 Piece 295.00
Jacket, Embroidered Florals, Border of Garden Landscapes, Silk, Chinese 247.00
Jacket, Leather, 1950s 175.00
Jacket, Man's, Air Force, Blue, Medium 12.00
Jacket, Ocelot Fur, Beaver Collar, Wide Turn Back Cuffs, Size 10 .... 265.00
Jacket, Smoking, Chintz & Calico, 1880s 100.00
Jacket, Woman's, Brown Wool, Fitted, Fur Collar, Long, Petite, 1916 .... 22.00
Jacket, Woman's, Crocheted, Rhinestone Buttons, Silk Lining, Irish 750.00
Jacket, Woman's, Tulle, Gold, 1920s 425.00
Jacket–Cape, Evening, Curly Brown Fur, Brown Satin Lined 40.00
Jeans, Man's, Levi 501, Black, Stone Wash 6.00
Jeans, Woman's, Levi 501, Blue, 28–In. Waist 3.50
Kimono, Allover Gold Design, White Silk Lining 20.00
Kimono, Embroidered Butterflies, Black Silk 90.00
Kimono, Satin & Gold Embroidery, Flowers & Leaves, Silk Obi, 63 1/2 In. 330.00
Kimono, Scenic Pattern On Black, Red Silk Lining .... 30.00 To 35.00
Mittens, Woman's, Leather, Wool, Hudson Bay Style, 12 In. 75.00

Moccasins, Woman's, 19th Century	80.00
Muff, Monkey Fur, 1930s, 12 x 14 In.	35.00
Muumuu, Hawaiian, Green, Gold Print	65.00
Nightgown, Lace Tucks, Size 18	35.00
Nightgown, White Lace, 1920s	30.00
Obi, Olive & Blue Design, Silk Brocade, Japan	192.50
Overalls, Man's, Blue, 100 Cotton, 30–In. Waist	4.00
Pajamas, Black Embroidered Silk, Small	25.00
Pajamas, Flannel, Footed, Premier Doll Togs, 1950s, Package	18.00
Pajamas, Lounging, Dynasty Label, Hong Kong	25.00
Pants, Brown & Black Checks, Levi, Marx	37.50
Pants, Gray Pinstripe, Levi, 1920	37.50
Peignoir, White Batiste, French Valenciennes Lace, 1920s	150.00
Petticoat, Victorian, Baby's, 18 In.	18.00
Robe, Beacon	20.00
Robe, Beacon, Geometric Pattern, Twist Rope Trim, 1920s	175.00
Robe, Chinese Emperor's, Blue & Gold, 130 Symbols, c.1820	6200.00
Robe, Man's, Flannel, Geometric Design, Blue Rope Belt, Beacon	95.00
Robe, Metallic Gold Dragons, Blue Clouds & Bats, Brown Silk, 54 In.	1100.00
Robe, Toddler's, Flannel, White Teddy Bears, Blue Cord Belt	45.00
Robe, Woman's, Chenille, Peacock On Back, Black Trim, Cord Belt	75.00
Shawl, Allover Floral, Black Ground, 1 Side Fringed, 1920s	85.00
Shawl, Fern & Flower Scrolls Edge, Wool Challis, c.1870, 64 x 61 In.	225.00
Shawl, Hand Embroidered Pink Roses, Silk, China, Fringed, 54 x 54 In.	175.00
Shawl, Ivory Wool, Embroidered Border	28.50
Shawl, Paisley, Blue Center, 62 x 120 In.	400.00
Shirt Stud, Blue Glass, Set of 4	8.00
Shirt, Camouflage, Winchester, Medium	16.00
Shirt, Hawaiian, Wooden Buttons, Evelyn Margolis, 1970s, Extra Large	50.00
Shoes, Baby's, White Leather, Ankle Straps, Button	95.00
Shoes, Child's, High Top, Two–Tone, Pair	48.00
Shoes, Platform, Alligator, Adrian, 1940s	75.00
Shoes, Woman's, Lucite, Rhinestones, Ankle Strap, High Heels, Size 5 1/2	22.00
Shoes, Woman's, Pumps, Black Satin, Bow, Pointed Toe, Squat Heel, Size 6	18.00
Skirt, Quilted, Glazed Finish Cotton, Velvet Binding, 35 In.	80.00
Slip, Victorian, Ornate	27.50
Slipper, Child's, Victorian	95.00
Smock, Farmer's, Blue Checked, Homespun, Wooden Buttons, 19th Century	300.00
Spats, Black Wool, Button Up	17.00
Stole & Muff, Fox	17.50
Stole, Wool, Large Red Fox Tails	50.00
Suit, Emerald Silk, Pleated Sleeves, Diamante Buttons, Lilli Ann, 1945	325.00
Suit, Groom's, 1895	150.00
Suit, Man's, Button–Fly Pants, 3–Button Coat, 1930s, Size 42, 3 Piece	125.00
Suit, Man's, Double–Breasted, 1920s, 3 Piece	65.00
Suit, Walking, Woman's, Pink Linen, Cream Cluny Lace Panels, 1920s	395.00
Sweater & Hat, University, Navy Blue, Yellow Trim, 1927	50.00
Tam, Rabbit Fur, White	18.00
Teddie, All Lace	150.00
Tie, Silk, Hand Painted, 1940's, 4 Piece	50.00
Top Hat, Austin Reed Bristol, Leather Case	125.00
Top Hat, Beaver, Leather Case	350.00
Top Hat, Man's, Black, Collapsible, Saxon	35.00
Uniform, Camp Fire Girl, Moccasins, Satchel, 1918	200.00
Veil, Wedding, Brussels Bobbin Lace, Appliqued On Net	1500.00
Vest, Bullet Proof, Blue Wool, Dress Suit Style, 7 Buttons, Al Capone, 1925	1210.00
Vest, Man's, Embroidered In Silk, Linen	495.00
Waistcoat, Silk Embroidered, Metallic Threads, Spangles, Late 18th Century	605.00

◆◆

Don't clean coins. Collectors want coins with the patina unchanged.

◆◆

CLUTHRA glass is a two–layered glass with small air pockets that form white spots. The Steuben Glass Works of Corning, New York, made it after 1903. Kimball Glass Company of Vineland, New Jersey, made Cluthra from about 1925. Victor Durand signed some pieces with his name. Related items are listed in the Steuben category.

Vase, Bubbles, Christopher Dresser, Unusual Shape	350.00
Vase, Mottled Green, Horizontal Wide Ribs, 11 In.	795.00
Vase, Pink, Gray & White, 6 In.	295.00

COALPORT ware has been made by the Coalport Porcelain Works of England from 1795 to the present time. Early pieces were unmarked. About 1810—1825 the pieces were marked with the name *Coalport* in various forms. Later pieces also had the name *John Rose* in the mark. The crown mark has been used with variations since 1881. The date 1750 is printed in some marks but it is not the date the factory started.

Bowl, Vegetable, Strange Orchid, Aqua, Oval	80.00
Decanter, Blue & White, 12 In.	35.00
Dinner Set, Strange Orchid, Aqua, 12 Place Setting	85.00
Dish, Serving, Money Tree, Square, 1830s, 8 In.	405.00
Inkstand, Flower Encrusted, Foliate Scrolls, c.1835, 6 1/4 In.	1650.00
Inkstand, White Dots, Panel of Peasants, c.1815, 6 3/8 In.	550.00
Plate, Floral Sprigs, Blue & Gilt Border, Center Gilt Scroll, 10 1/4 In., 12 Piece	585.00
Plate, Regency, 1810–1830	700.00
Plate, Three Finger, Overall Peach & Gilt Floral, 8 1/2 In., Pair	330.00
Platter, Bengal Tiger, Oval, 28 In.	2640.00
Sugar, Domed Cover, Imari, 1840s, 6 1/2 In.	155.00
Tureen, Stand, Bird Finial, Floral Sprays, Swan Feet, 5 1/2 In., Pair	1100.00
Urn, Cover, Lake In Oval Medallion, Jeweled Enamel Dots, 9 1/2 In.	330.00
Vase, Floral Reserves, Cobalt Blue Ground, Gilt Foliage, Made As Lamp, 12 In.	440.00

COBALT BLUE glass was made using oxide of cobalt. The characteristic bright dark blue identifies it for the collector. Most cobalt glass found today was made after the Civil War.

Ashtray, Frying Pan Shape, Small	10.00
Ashtray, Hat, Lowells, Advertising	29.00
Bottle, Painted Gentleman, Pewter Top	425.00
Bowl, Fluted, Rectangular, 4–Footed, 1920s, 12 In.	295.00
Champagne, Saucer Shape, Flutes, Cut Glass	115.00
Creamer, New Jersey, 19th Century, 3 5/8 In.	330.00
Decanter Set, Cruets, Sugar, Tray, Allover Gold Roses, 6 Piece	425.00
Flower Container, Gilt	350.00
Pitcher, New Century	50.00
Rolling Pin, Hand Painted Floral	85.00
Rolling Pin, Sailing Ships Design, 16 In.	100.00
Salt, French Ivory Spoon, Round, 1 x 2 In., Pair	60.00
Salt, Open, Footed, Pair	130.00
Sugar, Faceted Cover, Circular Footed, Octagonal, 1835, 8 3/4 In.	2310.00
Target Ball, Graduated Squares, Flat Center Band	160.00
Vase, Gold Enameled Grapes & Vines, 1850, 12 In., Pair	285.00
Vase, Gold Scalloped Design, White Enameled Flowers, 2 3/4 In., Pair	55.00
Vase, Tapering, Foliate, Round Footed, Silver, America, 7 1/2 In.	250.00

COCA–COLA was first served in 1886 in Atlanta, Georgia. It was advertised through signs, newspaper ads, coupons, bottles, trays, calendars, and even lamps and clocks. Collectors want anything with the word *Coca–Cola,* including a few rare products, like gum wrappers and cigar bands. The famous trademark was patented in 1893, the *Coke* mark in 1945. Many modern items and reproductions are being made.

Ad, Magazine, Delicious–Refreshing–Thirst–Quenching, 5 Cents, 1910	15.00
Ad, Pause That Refreshes & Cools, Soda Jerk Insert, 1937, 7 x 10 In.	8.50
Bank, Dispenser, Lights, Glasses, Battery Operated, Tin, 1950s, 7 x 10 In.	1050.00
Blotter, Shows 1915 Bottles, 1920s	15.00

Bookmark, 1903, Hilda Clark 175.00
Bookmark, 1906, Owl ....930.00 To 1000.00
Bookmark, Heart Shape, Celluloid 650.00
Bottle Cap, Disneyland, 12 Piece 10.00
Bottle Opener, In Bottle, Wall Mount 90.00
Bottle Opener, Pocket, Knife In Handle 7.50
Bottle, 100th Anniversary, Gold Dipped, Velvet Sleeve 200.00
Bottle, Altoona, Pennsylvania, Christmas 15.00
Bottle, Anchorage, Alaska, Embossed 22.00
Bottle, Annie Oakley Day, July 23–28, 1985, Greenville, Ohio 75.00
Bottle, Black Letters 265.00
Bottle, Canton, Ohio, Amber 50.00
Bottle, Coach Bill Chappell, Over 200 Victories, Georgia, 1986 .... 15.00
Bottle, Cumberland, Maryland, Straight Sides, 24 Oz. 150.00
Bottle, Dizzy Dean, Graduate League World Series, Aug. 4–8, Rossville, 1982 .... 15.00
Bottle, Fosler Bottling Works, Amber, Crown Top, Indiana, 6 1/2 Oz. 60.00
Bottle, Georgia Southern University, 1990 Division, 1AA, 1990 .... 8.00
Bottle, Greenwood, South Carolina 45.00
Bottle, Iowa Hawkeyes, Rose Bowl, Big 10 Champions, 1981 .... 6.00
Bottle, Israel, Full 10.00
Bottle, Kentucky Derby 110th Run For The Roses, 1984 .... 7.00
Bottle, Kroger, 100th Anniversary, 1883–1983, 10 Oz. 8.00
Bottle, Montgomery, Alabama 25.00
Bottle, North Carolina State University, Wolf Pack, NCAA Champs, 1983 .... 5.00
Bottle, North Dakota Centennial, 1889–1989, Blue, 1989 .... 8.00
Bottle, Paul Bear Bryant, Alabama Crimson Tide, Tail On Elephant, 1981 .... 20.00
Bottle, Pete Rose, 4192 Hits, September 11, 1985, 1987 .... 85.00
Bottle, Quincy, Florida 30.00
Bottle, Springtime In Atlanta, Christmas In Dixie, Santa Claus, Ga., 1987 .... 35.00
Bottle, Springvale, Maine, Script, 8 Oz. 60.00
Bottle, Square, Embossed Stars 5.00
Bottle, St. Louis Cardinals, 100th Annivesary, 10 Oz. 5.00
Bottle, Syrup, 1960 .... 325.00
Bottle, Texas Fiesta, Contents 4.00
Bottle, University of Florida Gators, 1984 SEC Champs 5.00
Bottle, Washington D.C., 9th Cola Clan Convention, 1983 .... 32.00
Bottle, Winter Olympic, 1980, 8 Piece 45.00
Bowl, Pretzel, 1930 .... 175.00
Button, Drink Coca–Cola Logo, 24 In. 150.00
Calendar, 1918, Store 325.00
Calendar, 1932, 1 Sheet Attached, Framed 325.00
Calendar, 1937, N. C. Wyeth, Matted & Framed 600.00
Calendar, 1941, Thirst Knows No Season 175.00
Calendar, 1943 .... 140.00
Calendar, 1948, Girl With A Bottle 25.00
Calendar, 1950, South America 180.00
Calendar, 1953, Armed Services 65.00
Calendar, 1957, The Pause That Refreshes 110.00
Calendar, 1959, Baseball Game 100.00
Calendar, 1961, Ski Be Really Refreshed 85.00
Calendar, 1962, Enjoy That Refreshing New Feeling 17.50
Calendar, 1968, Coke Has The Taste You Never Get Tired of 65.00
Calendar, 1969, Things Go Better With Coke 35.00
Calendar, 1974, Beautiful Girls 20.00
Card, Playing, 1930s, Unopened 45.00
Card, Playing, 1951 .... 90.00
Card, Playing, 1958, Welcome Friend 85.00
Carrier, 6 Pack, Bentwood, 1940s 38.00
Case, 75th Anniversary Dallas Plant, Presentation 175.00
Case, Wooden, Coca–Cola Bottle, St. Johnsbury, Vt. 37.00
Change Tray, 1917, Elaine 135.00
Chest, 2 Lift Top Doors, Original Paint 685.00
Clock, 1939, Metal Frame 495.00

Clock, 1939, Wooden Frame, Square 175.00
Clock, 1951, Maroon, Round, 17 1/2 In. .... 125.00 To 175.00
Clock, 1960, Things Go Better With Coke, Light–Up, 13 x 16 In. 190.00
Clock, Anniversary, 400–Day, Logo On Face, 1950 .... 2000.00
Clock, Serve Yourself, Light–Up 350.00
Clock, Silhouette Girl, Metal Frame, 1939 .... 595.00
Coin–Operated Machine, Vendo V–39, Original Finish, 10 Cents 1200.00
Cookie Jar, Coke Can, McCoy, 1988–1990, 10 In. 55.00
Cooler, 4 Ft. 120.00
Cooler, Electric, Late 1950s, 6 Ft. 100.00
Cooler, Mexico, Bien Fria, 1940s, 15 x 12 x 8 In. 275.00
Cooler, Picnic, All Original 160.00
Cooler, Vendo 44 .... 3200.00
Dice, Pair 25.00
Dish, Pretzel, Aluminum 150.00
Dispenser, Barrel, Red With Stainless Bands, 2 In. 895.00
Dispenser, Fountain, Vendo 391949 .... 300.00
Display Case, Coca–Cola Chewing Gum, 15 x 10 x 6 3/8 In. 400.00
Display, Santa Claus, With Coke, Cardboard 25.00
Doll, Molly Cola 8.00
Door Handle, Aluminum, 1930s 115.00
Door Pull, Bottle Shape 75.00
Door Push, 1930s 445.00
Door Push, Porcelain, 1950s 150.00
Fan, Cardboard, 1940s 22.50
Fan, Ft. Myers, 1950s 25.00
Figure, Santa Claus, Drinking Coke, Bag of Toys, Papier–Mache, 18 In. 50.00
Game, Checkers, Box 35.00
Game, Checkers, Dragon, Individually Marked 5.00
Game, Chinese Checkers, Wood & Cardboard, 1940s, 16 1/2 x 16 1/2 In. 40.00
Game, Ring Toss, Santa Claus, 1950, 10 In. 10.00
Game, Table Tennis, 1940s 95.00
Glass, Flared Top, Syrup Line 315.00
Glass, Logo, Wizard of Oz, 6 Piece 65.00
Gum Wrapper, Coca–Cola Gum, Pepsin, 1913 .... 200.00
Ice Pick & Bottle Opener 25.00
Jug, Syrup, 1950s, 1 Gal. 15.00
Letter Opener, 1965 .... 10.00
Light Pull, Boy Holding Glass, Bottle Cap On Head, Cardboard, 15 In. 247.00
Lighter, Coca–Cola Bottle 15.00
Lighter, Musical, 1963 .... 150.00
Lighter, Pull Apart, 1950s 15.00
Lionel Train, 1874, Set of 3 .... 900.00
Lunch Box, Vinyl, 1970s 65.00
Marble, Ruby Red Glass, Transparent, Bright Red Print, 15/16 In. 30.00
Menu Board, Wooden, Metal, Attached Gold Bottles, 24 1/4 x 33 In. 250.00
Mirror, Counter, Beveled, Scalloped, Round, 6 In. 175.00
Mirror, Pocket, 1909, The Coca–Cola Girl 655.00
Mirror, Pocket, 1910 .... 90.00
Mirror, Pocket, 1911, Girl, Oval 385.00
Mirror, Pocket, 1916, Elaine, Oval 325.00
Mirror, Pocket, Red, White, Sample No. 22 .... 55.00
Needle Case, Pretty Girl Front, Bottle & Tumbler On Back, 1924 .... 80.00
Night–Light, 1945 .... 5.25
Night–Light, 1950s 15.00
Paper Doll, Girl, Outfits, Color, 1950s, 9 x 12 In., Uncut 3.75
Paper Dolls, Punch Out 7.00
Paperweight, Solid Glass, Coke 25.00
Pencil Sharpener, 1932 .... 25.00
Perfume Bottle, 1930s 55.00
Plate, Porcelain, 1931 .... 200.00
Postcard, 1910 .... 485.00
Poster, Willie Mays, 18 x 24 In. 10.00

Puzzle, 100th Anniversary	30.00
Puzzle, I'D Like To Teach The World To Sing, Unopened	23.00
Radio, Cooler	1000.00
Scale, Computing Scale Co., Weighing To 24 Lb., 30 In.	965.00
Scarf, Kit Carson, 19 x 21 In.	45.00
Sign, A Sign of Good Taste, Bottle, 1960–1963, 12 x 31 1/2 In.	175.00
Sign, Bottle, Christmas, 1929	325.00
Sign, Bottle, Tin, 1953, 20 x 28 In.	250.00
Sign, Bottle, Tin, 3 Ft.	375.00
Sign, Button, Tin, White, 36 In.	350.00
Sign, Button, With Bottle, White, 1950s, 24 In.	240.00
Sign, Coca–Cola Sold Here, Ice Cold, Porcelain, 1948	350.00
Sign, Coca–Cola Sunrise Beverage, Mr. Sun	140.00
Sign, Coke, 6 Pack, Porcelain, Enameled, 8 x 11 In.	25.00
Sign, Cutout, Cardboard, Full Color, 1938, 33 x 14 In.	98.00
Sign, Drink Coca–Cola, Enameled, 2 Sides, Round, 29 In.	250.00
Sign, Drink Coca–Cola, Porcelain, Attached Fountain, 24 x 24 In.	625.00
Sign, Enjoy Coca–Cola, 3 1/2 x 4 1/2 Ft.	50.00
Sign, Enjoy Coke, Red, 12–In. Diam.	17.50
Sign, For Headache & Exhaustion, 5 Cents A Glass, Metal, 20 x 32 In.	4840.00
Sign, Ice Cold Coca–Cola Sold Here, Porcelain, Enameled, 11 1/4–In. Diam.	17.00
Sign, Ice Cold, Yellow, Snow & Ice, Tin, 1948, 11 x 24 In.	150.00
Sign, Lunch, Flanged, Round, 1960	110.00
Sign, Pause Refresh Yourself, Tin, 1950s, 12 x 25 In.	125.00
Sign, Woman In Riding Gear Beside Horse, Cardboard, 1937, 49 x 32 In.	350.00
Sign, Wrap Around, Red, White Letters, 67 x 124 In.	225.00
Tape Measure, Car Tire	3.45
Thermometer, 1964, Round, 12 In.	140.00
Thermometer, Bottle-Shape, Tin, 1958, 17 In.	75.00
Thermometer, Drink Coca–Cola In Bottles, Round, 1950s, 12 In.	175.00
Thermometer, Drink Coca–Cola, 1950	90.00
Thermometer, Drink Coca–Cola, 2 Bottles On Sides	93.00
Thermometer, Drink In Bottles, Glass Front, 1950	115.00 To 140.00
Thermometer, Round, 12 In.	110.00 To 125.00
Tip Tray, 1903, Hilda Clark, 4 In.	1320.00
Tip Tray, 1914, Betty	250.00 To 332.00
Tip Tray, 1917, Elaine	160.00
Toothbrush, Travel Case	3.50
Toy, Popgun, Clown, 1950s	2.00
Toy, Santa Claus, Stuffed, 1980	75.00
Toy, Spinning Top, Merry Christmas	2.00
Toy, Truck, 1972, Corgi, Box	5.00
Toy, Truck, Buddy L, Yellow, 1950s	165.00 To 175.00
Toy, Truck, Marx, Gray, 1960	100.00
Toy, Truck, Plastic	1000.00
Toy, VW Van, 1950s	220.00
Tray, 1905, Juanita, Oval, 13 x 10 7/8 In.	1500.00
Tray, 1909, Coca–Cola Girl	575.00
Tray, 1912, 12 x 14 In.	*Illus* 250.00
Tray, 1916, Elaine	275.00
Tray, 1924, Smiling Girl	385.00
Tray, 1926, Sports Couple	350.00
Tray, 1933, Frances Dee	490.00
Tray, 1938, Girl In The Afternoon	110.00
Tray, 1939, Springboard Girl	125.00
Tray, 1939, Springboard Girl, Canada	145.00
Tray, 1940, Sailor Girl	125.00
Tray, 1941, Girl Ice Skater	95.00 To 195.00
Tray, 1942, Girls At Car	115.00
Tray, 1950, Girl With Menu	70.00
Tray, 1957, Birdhouse	60.00
Tray, 1957, Girl With Umbrella	50.00
Tray, 1958, Captain Cook	45.00

Tray, 1969, Gold Center, Smoked Glass, Sweden	45.00
Tumbler, Bell Shape, Trademark Below Script, 1941–1946, 4 In.	9.00
Tumbler, Christmas, Bell Shape	5.00
Tumbler, Mickey Mouse, Christmas Carol, 6 In., 3 Piece	45.00
Tumbler, Snow White, Peter Pan, McDonald's, 1980s, Set of 4	55.00
Wagon, Coke	27.50
Watch Fob, 1907	125.00
Watch, Bottle Cap, Red & Silver, Issued To Drivers In 1950s	15.00
Watch, Disney World	35.00
Watch, Pocket, Boy Scout, Metal Case	28.00
Wristwatch, 75th Anniversary, Floating Bottle Second Hand, Xantia Co.	150.00

COFFEE GRINDERS of home size were first made about 1894. They lost favor by the 1930s. Large floor–standing or counter–model coffee grinders were used in the nineteenth–century country store. The renewed interest in fresh–ground coffee has produced many modern electric and hand grinders, and reproductions of the old styles are being made.

Arcade Crystal, Wall Mount	129.00
Arcade No. 25, Wall, Glass Jar & Lid	60.00
Brass Keys To Open Top & Drawer	185.00
Charles Parker Co., Red & Gilt Design, Converted To Lamp	93.00
Charles Parker, No. 200, Fancy Wheels, Oval Drawer, Wooden Base, 1897	375.00
Dazey, Child's	125.00
Dovetailed, Cherry, Scalloped Base, Iron Handle, 10 In.	165.00
Elgin National, Counter	145.00
Elgin National, Woodruff & Edwards Mfg. Co., Brass Hopper, 5–Footed	1000.00
Enterprise, Cast Iron, Wooden Base, Black, Gold Trim, Painted Florals, 12 In.	110.00
Enterprise, No. 2, 2 Wheels	525.00
Enterprise, No. 3, Original Paint	450.00
Enterprise, No. 12, Switchboard, Western Electric, 27 x 51 x 34 1/2 In.	250.00
Fairbanks Morse & Co., Red With Painted Acanthus Leaf Patterns, 27 In.	380.00
Gold Paint, Wood & Tin, 11 In.	82.00
Governor	175.00
Guaranteed Forged Grinder, Drawer, Wooden	40.00
Imperial	75.00
Iron, With Drawer, 11 1/2 In.	85.00
Landers, Frary & Clark, Clamp On, Metal	65.00
Landers, Model 24, Wall	60.00
Simmons Koffee Krusher, 2 Wheels	1150.00
Star Mill, 2 Wheels, Original Paint, Dated 1885	375.00

Coca-Cola, Tray, 1912, 12 X 14 In.

◆◆◆◆◆◆◆◆◆◆◆◆◆◆◆◆◆◆◆◆◆◆

Most Coca-Cola trays had green or brown borders in the 1920s, red borders in the 1930s.

◆◆◆◆◆◆◆◆◆◆◆◆◆◆◆◆◆◆◆◆◆◆

◆◆◆◆◆◆◆◆◆◆◆◆◆◆◆◆◆◆◆◆◆◆

If you use plate hangers to display your plates, be sure they are not too tight and the clips are covered with a soft material. Otherwise, the end clips may scratch or chip the plate.

◆◆◆◆◆◆◆◆◆◆◆◆◆◆◆◆◆◆◆◆◆◆

Star Mill, No. 7, 2 Wheels, Original Paint 400.00

COIN SPOT is a glass pattern that was named by the collectors for the spots resembling coins which are part of the glass. Colored, clear, and opalescent glass was made with the spots. Many companies used the design in the 1870–1890 period. It is so popular that reproductions are still being made.

Bowl, Frosted Blue Edging, Mother-of-Pearl, Chartreuse, 8 1/2 In.	695.00
Castor, Pickle, Frame Marked	265.00
Cruet, Crimped Top, Cranberry	200.00
Finger Bowl, Blue Opalescent	35.00
Lemonade Set, White Opalescent Spots, 7 Piece	295.00
Pitcher, Blue Opalescent	150.00
Pitcher, Crimped Top, Cranberry, 8 In.	150.00
Pitcher, Jefferson, Blue	125.00
Saltshaker, Cranberry Opalescent	65.00
Sugar Shaker, Blue Opalescent	175.00
Sugar Shaker, Blue Opalescent, Wide Waist	175.00
Sugar Shaker, Cranberry	75.00
Sugar Shaker, Cranberry Opalescent	350.00
Sugar Shaker, Cranberry To White	245.00
Syrup, Blue Opalescent	150.00
Syrup, Ring Neck	225.00
Syrup, Ring Neck, Blue Opalescent	195.00
Syrup, Ring Neck, White	110.00
Syrup, Spring Lid, Blue Opalescent	145.00
Tumbler, Mother-of-Pearl Satin Glass, 3 3/4 In.	125.00
Tumbler, White	25.00
Water Set, Cranberry Opalescent	450.00
Water Set, Orange To White, Pitcher, 10 1/2 In. 6 Piece	715.00

COIN-OPERATED MACHINES of all types are collected. The vending machine is an ancient invention dating back to 200 B.C. when holy water was dispensed in a coin-operated vase. Smokers in seventeenth-century England could buy tobacco from a coin-operated box. It was not until after the Civil War that the technology made modern coin-operated games and vending machines plentiful. Slot machines, arcade games, and dispensers are all collected.

Candy, Arcade, Exhibit of Chicago, Rotary Type	150.00
Candy, Hershey, 1 Cent	195.00
Cigar, 6 Selection, 5 Cent, Oak Case, Curved Glass	2000.00
Cigar, Elm City, 1890s	2500.00
Cigarette, 7 Brands, From Ralph Capone's Club, Cicero, 1930	1980.00
Cigarette, Silver Comet, 1 Cent, Black, Retains Key	55.00
Condoms, Ramses	80.00
Dart Game, Arachnid, Model 3000	325.00
Dart Game, Arachnid, Model 4500	575.00
Dart Game, Arachnid, Model 5000 .... 650.00 To 775.00
Dice, Bally, Reliance, 5 Cent	5500.00
Dice, Keystone, Winner	620.00
Dice, Shoot'Ems, 5 Cent, Counter Top	300.00
Digger Claw, Floor Model 3	500.00
Duo Scope, 15 Pictures For 1 Coin	450.00
Football, Chester Pollard Amusement Co.	1000.00
Fortune Teller & Gumball, Jennings, Comet	2310.00
Fortune Teller, Grandma, Oak Case	4000.00
Gum, Advance, 1 Cent Gumball, Red, 8 x 6 In.	253.00
Gum, Advance, Model D, 1 Cent Vendor, 1923, 15 In.	60.00
Gum, Bubble, Metal Case, Pays Tokens, 12 1/2 In.	100.00
Gum, Mannequin, Manikin Vending Co.	4700.00
Gum, National Auto Vending Machine Co., Model G, 1 Cent, 17 x 17 In.	248.00
Gum, Northwestern 1 Cent Tab Gum Vendor, 1954, 7 x 19 x 10 In.	22.00
Gum, Oak, 1893	1200.00

Gum, Pulver, Clown, Blue, Restored	950.00
Gum, Pulver, Clown, Yellow, 1 Cent	465.00
Gum, Pulver, Cop Figure, Red, Animated	850.00
Gum, Pulver, Yellow Kid, Clockwork	575.00
Gum, Stollwerck, 1892	1400.00
Gum, Sweepstakes, Horse Race	1400.00
Gum, Wrigley's Stick, 5 Sides, 8 x 14 x 8 In.	110.00
Gum, You Can't Lose	610.00
Gum, Zeno, 1 Cent, 16 1/2 x 10 1/2 In.	660.00
Gumball, Acorn, Oak, 1940s	49.00
Gumball, Advance, Large Globe, Decal, Lock	175.00
Gumball, Atlas Master Deluxe, 1952	55.00
Gumball, Baby Grand, Golden Oak, Restored	65.00 To 70.00
Gumball, Board, Slug Rejecter	225.00
Gumball, E–Z, Decal, Locks	695.00
Gumball, Ford, 1950	50.00 To 55.00
Gumball, Gargoyle Face, Columbus Vending Co., 1929	8500.00
Gumball, Hit The Target, 1 Cent	325.00
Gumball, Northwestern, No. 60	45.00
Gumball, Saturn 2000, Northwestern Co., Red, White & Blue, 4 Ft.	495.00
Gumball, Scoopy	1750.00 To 2000.00
Gumball, Simmons	225.00
Gumball, Spaceship, Key, 6 For 1 Cent	75.00
Gumball, Topper, 1 Cent	65.00
Gumball, Toy & Joy	25.00
Gumball, Victor, Topper, 1 Cent	65.00
Gumball, Yu Chu Co., Glass Top, Nickel Plated Base, 1 Cent	27.50
Helicopter Ride	200.00
Horse Race, Evans, Winterbook, Mirrored Finish	250.00
Horse Race, Games of Nevada, 9 Player, Variable Odds, 44 In.	4400.00
Horse Race, Ju–De–Cours, Counter Top	625.00
Horseshoe, William's Ringer	800.00
Ills Curer, Electric Treatment Machine, 1 Cent	3500.00
Mar–Matic Bingo Bell, Nickel, Deco Styling, Yellow Accents, 25 In.	880.00
Match, Advance, Counter Top, 1 Cent, 9 x 18 In.	357.00
Match, Glass Dome, Cigar Cutter Attachment, Oak, 11 x 18 In.	385.00
Match, Northwestern, Cigar Cutter On Base, 1 Cent, 13 1/2 In.	660.00
Motorcycle Ride	350.00
Peanut, 5 Cent, Cup Holder On Side, Silver Metal	250.00
Peanut, Acorn, Oak, 1950s	49.00
Peanut, Atlas Bantam, Restored, 5 Cent	60.00 To 65.00
Peanut, Black Smilin' Sam	350.00
Peanut, Bluebird, Decal, 1 Cent	495.00
Peanut, Hanse, 1 Cent, Lock & Key	385.00
Peanut, Hilo, Cast Iron, c.1908	1000.00
Peanut, Komet, Counter Top Model, 5 Cent	25.00
Peanut, Lawrence Manufacturing Co., 1 & 5 Cent, 1940, 8 x 19 In.	143.00
Peanut, McGuire, Empire State Building	275.00
Peanut, Northwestern, Cast Iron, c.1933	125.00
Peanut, Northwestern, Frosted Globe	200.00
Peanut, Popcorn Popper, Holcomb & Hoke	2200.00
Peep Show, Cail–O–Scope, Floor Model, Oak & Iron	1500.00
Pinball, Bagatelle, Poosh–Em–Up Rodeo	35.00
Pinball, Bally, Broadway Bingo	325.00
Pinball, Bally, Jumbo Gambling, 5 Cent	605.00
Pinball, Bally, Medusa	625.00
Pinball, Bally, Playboy	850.00
Pinball, Gottlieb, Kingpin	200.00
Pinball, Harlem Globe Trotters	850.00
Pinball, Horse Race	700.00
Pinball, Jennings, Sportsman, No Payout	375.00
Pinball, Rock–Ola, World Series, Baseball	650.00
Pinball, Table Top 10 Cent, Wooden, 16 x 6 x 31 In.	121.00

Pinball, Williams Hayburner	475.00
Poker Hand, 5 Card, Oak	800.00
Poker, 2 Can Play, Metal Art Deco Case	650.00
Punching Bag, Mutoscope, Quarter Sawn Oak	2400.00
Shoe Shine	750.00
Slot, Aristocrat, Espirit, 20 Cent	495.00
Slot, Bally Baby, Play For Cigarettes, 1930, Al Capone	1150.00
Slot, Bally, 3 Line Buy A Pay, 25 Cent	1195.00
Slot, Bally, Draw Bell With Reels, 5 Cent, Floor	550.00
Slot, Bull Durham, Triple Jackpot, Roll Top, 5 Cent	3150.00
Slot, Callie, Ben Hur, 25 Cent	3900.00
Slot, Columbia, Groetchen	800.00
Slot, Fill 'em Up, England	170.00
Slot, Hunt & Co., Baby Bell, 1 Cent	695.00
Slot, Jennings, Chief, Chrome Front, Jackpot, 10 Cent	900.00
Slot, Jennings, Club Chief, 10 Cent	1200.00
Slot, Jennings, Club Chief, 5 Cent, 1949–1964	1695.00
Slot, Jennings, Duchess, 5 Cent	1275.00
Slot, Jennings, Dutch Boy & Girl, 5 Cent	1795.00
Slot, Jennings, Golden Nugget	1795.00
Slot, Jennings, Golf Ball	5000.00
Slot, Jennings, Little Duke, 50 Cent	900.00
Slot, Jennings, Lub Chief, 10 Cent, Stainless Steel, 26 1/2 In.	880.00
Slot, Little Duke, With Gumball Vendor, 1 Cent	2200.00
Slot, Mills, 10 Cent	3630.00
Slot, Mills, Baseball	3500.00
Slot, Mills, Black Cherry, 5 Cent	1400.00 To 1650.00
Slot, Mills, Black Cherry, 50 Cent	1525.00 To 1550.00
Slot, Mills, Castle Front, 25 Cent	1850.00
Slot, Mills, Century Page Boy, Club Bell, 10 Cent	2150.00
Slot, Mills, Futurity, Cheating Mechanism, Side Vendor	3000.00
Slot, Mills, Hi Top, Deuce 2 Wild	1750.00
Slot, Mills, High Hat, Exclusive For Golden Nugget, 25 Cent	2595.00
Slot, Mills, Pace Comet	1050.00
Slot, Mills, Poinsettia	1300.00 To 1495.00
Slot, Mills, Premium Penny Dop	600.00
Slot, Mills, Special Award	1150.00
Slot, Mills, War Eagle	1400.00
Slot, Mills, Watermelon High Top, 25 Cents, 1940s	1430.00 To 1750.00
Slot, Pace Comet, 5 Cent	1495.00
Slot, Pace Deluxe, Chrome Bell, 3–Reel Fruit, 1 Dollar, 1936	2650.00
Slot, Penny Pack, Daval Mfg. Co, Cigarettes, Al Capone, 11 x 8 In.	935.00
Slot, Rol–A–Top, 5 Cent	3150.00
Slot, Rol–A–Top, Bird of Paradise, 10 Cent	3400.00
Slot, Rol–A–Top, Cherry Front, 5 Cent	3300.00
Slot, Rol–A–Top, Diamond Bell Cherry Front, Restored, 5 Cent	4900.00
Slot, Royal Line, Bingo Poker, 25 Cent	400.00
Slot, Watling, Blue Seal	1300.00
Slot, Watling, Jack Pot Treasury, 10 Cent	1550.00
Slot, Watling, Lincoln Deluxe	1700.00
Slot, Watling, Rol–A–Top, 50 Cent, 1930	1700.00
Slot, Watling, Rol–A–Top, Cash Box, Wood Finish, Reel Strips	4500.00
Slot, Watling, Twin Jackpots, 5 Cent	750.00
Stamp, 4 Cent, Hand Crank, Drug Store	42.50
Stamp, Dillion Manufacturing Co., 12 x 11 In.	49.00
Stamp, Four 1 Cent Stamps For 5 Cents, B & S Productions, 1910	2800.00
Stamp, Mills, Patriotic Design, Cast Metal, Oak Case, 1915	2365.00
Stamp, Uncle Sam, Porcelain, Federal Dispenser Corp, 8 x 19 In.	38.00
Strength Tester, 1900s, 7 Ft.	4500.00
Strength Tester, Groetchen	95.00
Strength Tester, Mercury Athletic Scale, 1 Cent	250.00
Tobacco, Mayo Cut Plug, Beveled Mirror	550.00
Trade Stimulator, Cigarette, Marvel, 3 Reel, 8 x 11 x 9 1/2 In.	132.00

Trade Stimulator, Gumball, Dandy, 1 Cent	330.00
Trade Stimulator, Horse Race, A. W. Hoechin, 13 In.	385.00
Trade Stimulator, Merry–Go–Round	450.00
Trade Stimulator, Yankee, 3 Reel	375.00
Vendor, Kotex	35.00
Vendor, Pencil, Parker, Metal Case, 5 Cent, c.1930, 10 x 9 In.	55.00
Vendor, Perfume, 1 Cent Spurts, Lion Headed, 1920s	3500.00

COLLECTOR PLATES are modern plates produced in limited editions. Some may be found listed under the factory name, such as Bing & Grondahl, Royal Copenhagen, Royal Doulton, and Wedgwood.

American Greetings, 1981, Box, 8 In.	25.00
Anri, Father's Day, 1972	23.00
Anri, Mother's Day, 1972	23.00
Avon, 100th Anniversary, 1886–1986, 8 In.	12.00
Rockwell, 4 Seasons, 1974	23.00
Rockwell, 4 Seasons, Boy & Dog, 1971, Set of 4	150.00
Rockwell, Cobbler	50.00
Rockwell, Gay Blades, 1974	23.00
Rockwell, Heritage Music Maker, Box	20.00
Rockwell, Professor, Box	20.00
Rockwell, Scotty Gets His Tree, 1974	150.00
Rockwell, Scotty Plays Santa, Box	20.00
Rockwell, Toymaker	75.00
Rockwell, Triple Self Portrait, Gorham	50.00
Wallace, Indians On Horseback, 9 In.	95.00
Wallace, Westward Ho, Prospector, 6 In.	45.00

COMIC ART, or cartoon art, is a relatively new field of collecting. Original comic strips, magazine covers, and even printed strips are collected. The first daily comic strip was printed in 1907. The paintings on celluloid used for movie cartoons are listed in this book under Animation Art.

Drawing, Blondie, Ink On Paper, Chic Young, 1930, 14 x 17 In.	356.00
Drawing, Blondie, March 27, 1937, Chic Young, Framed, 4 x 19 In.	660.00
Drawing, Fritzi Ritz, Busmiller, Matted, August 11, 1938, 5 x 22 In.	357.00
Drawing, Li'l Abner, Ink On Paper, Al Capp, Framed, 1938, 5 1/2 x 22 1/2 In.	330.00
Drawing, Little Lulu, Roger Armstrong, Ink On Paper, Matted, 1964, 6 x 20 In.	165.00
Drawing, Peanuts, C. M. Schulz, Framed, 1957, 5 1/2 x 27 In.	1980.00
Drawing, Peanuts, Charles Schulz, United Features, Pen & Ink, 5 1/2 x 27 In.	3025.00
Drawing, Terry & The Pirates, Ink On Paper, Framed, 1944, 24 x 19 In.	760.00
Drawing, Terry & The Pirates, Signed Caniff, Sept. 10, 1944	1760.00
Drawing, Toonerville Trolley, Ink Sketch, Fontaine Fox, 10 3/4 x 10 In.	400.00
Page, Marvel Comic Book, Captain America, 1977, 14 1/2 x 10 In.	220.00

COMMEMORATIVE items have been made to honor members of royalty and those of great national fame. World's fairs and important historical events are also remembered with commemorative pieces. Related collectibles are listed in the Coronation and World's Fair categories.

Decanter, Investiture of Prince Charles, Wedgwood, Sealed	125.00
Pin, Queen Victoria, King Louis Philippe, On Coin, 1844, 2 In.	175.00
Spoon, King George & Queen Elizabeth, Silver Plated, 1939	30.00
Stirrup Cup, Princess Anne, Captain Phillips, 1973	28.00
Thimble, China, Princess Diana & Prince William, 1st Birthday, 1983	10.00
Wedding Bell, Prince Andrew & Sarah, Bone China, 1986, Case	25.00

COMPACTS hold face powder. A woman did not powder her face in public until after World War I. By 1920, the beauty parlor, permanent waves, and cosmetics had become acceptable. A few companies sold cake face powder in a box with a mirror and a pad or puff. Soon the compact was being designed by jewelers and made of gold, silver, and precious materials. Cosmetic companies began to sell powder in attractive compacts of less valuable metal or plastic. Collectors today search for Art Deco

designs, commemorative compacts from world's fairs or political events, and unusual examples. Many were made with companion lipsticks and other fittings.

14k Yellow Gold, Radiating Pattern	1030.00
Airplane, Leatherette, Embossed	12.50
American First, Chain	55.00
Art Deco, Lipstick, Chain, Finger Ring, 14K Gold	525.00
Art Deco, Woman's Face	85.00
Basket, Painted Flowers On Lid	45.00
Cara Nome, Art Deco, Silver Plated	28.00
Cara Nome, Box	22.00
Castanet	75.00
Celluloid, Hanger & Tassel	85.00
Celluloid, Raised Rose On Lid, Mirror, Other Side, Lipstick In Handle	15.00
Cloisonne, Octagonal, Sample, 1930	40.00
Comb Case, Mirror, Gray Velvet Case	110.00
Coty, Belt Buckle, Black Enamel, Box	75.00
Coty, Brass Envelope	20.00
Coty, Double, Red Enamel, Gold, Box	85.00
Coty, Lipstick On End, Gold Textured	85.00
Coty, Powder, Lipstick, Textured Gold	20.00
Djer Kiss, Art Nouveau Fairy Design, Silver Overlay, Box	85.00
Djer Kiss, Nymph	150.00
Dorset 5th Avenue, Cluster of Rhinestones On Lid, Brown & Goldtone	50.00
Dressmaker's Bust, Rhinestones & Pearls, Under Lucite, 1940	125.00
Dubury, Tandem Lipstick, Perfume Each Side, Red Rose On Lid	50.00
Eagle Design, Fort Buchanan, Puerto Rico, Brass	25.00
Elgin, Bird–In–Hand	800.00
Elgin, Gold Quilt Floral, Sleeve, Unused, Box	20.00
Elgin, Watch Trunk Shape	150.00
Elgin, White Enamel, Engraved Goldtone Floral, 1946	50.00
Elizabeth Arden, Fabric, 1965, 3 In. *Illus*	25.00
Elizabeth Arden, Rouge, Stars & Dots, Square, 1 1/2 In.	25.00
Enamel, Rouge, Red	7.00 To 8.00
Enamel, Scene, Tree, Ocean & Sunset, Lipstick, Powder & Rouge, France	250.00
Enamel, Suitcase, Travel Stickers, Green, 1930	120.00
Enamel, Woman In Blue, Inlaid Turquoise, France, Sterling Silver, c.1900	895.00
Encrusted Silver Gilt, 60 Sapphires, Rose–Cut Diamonds, Italy	990.00
Evans, Art Deco, Enamel	45.00
Evans, Enamel, Dark Blue, Floral, Pouch, 1948, 3 In. *Illus*	85.00
Evans, Overall Entwining Gold Design, Rhinestone Flower, Cloth Pouch	80.00
Evening In Paris, Enamel, Blue, Silver, Square	55.00
Fordham University, Terra–Cotta Enamel On Chrome	25.00
Gold Plate, Raised Man & Woman Cover, Unused	49.00
Golden Gate International Exposition, Blue Enamel Border, 1939, 3 In.	75.00

Compact, Evans, Enamel, Dark Blue, Floral, Pouch, 1948, 3 In.

Compact, Elizabeth Arden, Fabric, 1965, 3 In.

Houbigant, Powder, 1920s	20.00
Kirk, Sterling Silver	185.00
La Mode, Enamel, Pink, Unused	57.00
Lucite, Blue Mirror, Large, Box	40.00
Marhill, Cigarette Case & Lighter, Rhinestone Covered	110.00
Mary Pickford, Artist Studios	95.00
Metal, Scotty On Top, Wooden Inlay	35.00
Mexican Silver, Chased Design	90.00
Mother–of–Pearl Cover, Heart Shape	45.00
Multicolored Rhinestones, Square, 2 In.	30.00
Musical, Damascene, Gold & Silver Inlay, View of Mt. Fuji	195.00
Norida, Colonial Woman, 1924	35.00
Pocketbook On Chain, Sterling Silver, 2 x 2 1/2 In.	125.00
Prince Matchiabelli, Lipstick, Goldtone & Black Enamel	30.00
Richard Hudnut, Brass, Blue Enamel	25.00
Salvadore Dali, Bird In Hand	800.00
Silver Plated, Rhinestones On Top, Chain	38.00
Silver Tone, Textured, Chain, Round	30.00
Statue of Liberty, 1930s	12.00
Sterling Silver, Engraved Map of India, 7 Rubies, Octagonal, 3 In.	150.00
Sterling Silver, With Coin Purse	45.00
Tortoiseshell	12.50
U.S.N. Insignia, Word Sister In Rhinestones	15.00
Vanity D'Arby	22.00
Volupte, Adam & Eve	125.00
Volupte, Black Enamel, Ford Insignia	55.00
Volupte, Cigarette Case, Purse	145.00
Volupte, Gold Metal, Engraved Rays, Cluster of Rhinestones	38.00
Volupte, Inscribed To You From Mary Pickford & United Artist, Large	300.00
Volupte, Sea Horse	30.00
WAAF, Military Emblems, Black & Gold Tone	28.00
Yardley, Woman & Scene On Lid, Box	50.00
Zell 5th Avenue, Cigarette Case, Maroon, Green & White	85.00
Zell 5th Avenue, Love & Marriage In Rhinestones, Courtship To Marriage	185.00
Zell 5th Avenue, Watch Case Style, Goldtone Engraving Around Cameo	70.00

CONSOLIDATED LAMP AND GLASS COMPANY of Coraopolis, Pennsylvania, was founded in 1894. The company made lamps, tablewares, and art glass. Collectors are particularly interested in the wares made after 1925, including black satin glass, Cosmos (listed in its own category in this book), Martele (which resembled Lalique), and colored glasswares. The company closed for the final time in 1967.

Candy Dish, Cover, Rib Pattern, Frosted, Gold Ormolu Mount, 7 x 6 In.	110.00
Dish, Powder, Lovebirds, Frosted Crystal	65.00
Lamp, Clear Glass, Red Lovebirds	185.00
Lamp, Gone With The Wind, 4 Muses, Mythology, 23 1/2 In.	985.00
Sherbet, Fruit & Leaf, Russet, 8–Footed, Martele	15.00
Snack Set, Green Fruit Design, Ice Cream Cup & Underplate, 9 In.	75.00
Tumbler, Footed, Catalonia, Amethyst, 7 In.	20.00
Tumbler, Footed, Ruba Rombic	125.00
Tumbler, Fruit & Leaf, Russet, Footed, Martele, 5 3/4 In.	24.00
Tumbler, Juice, Barrel, Grape & Leaf, Russet, 4 Oz.	5.00
Vase, Aqua Pine Cones, White Ground, 7 In.	129.00
Vase, Bird of Paradise, 8 In.	125.00
Vase, Catalonia, Amethyst, 3 1/2 In.	45.00
Vase, Dance of Nudes, 12 In.	395.00
Vase, Fan, Dance of The Nudes, 5 In.	125.00
Vase, Red Dogwood, Poppy & Foxglove, Cream Ground, 10 1/2 In.	375.00

CONTEMPORARY GLASS, see Glass–Contemporary

COOKBOOKS are collected for various reasons. Some are wanted for the recipes, some for investment, and some as examples of advertising. Cookbooks and recipe pamphlets are included in this category.

65 Ways To Cook Hamburger, Doyne Nickerson, 189 Pages, 1960	3.50
1000 Ways To Please A Husband, 1917	75.00
1001 Ways To Please A Husband, Hard Cover, 307 Pages, 1958	17.50
Agriculture Dept. & Union Pacific, Recipes For Apple Dishes	25.00
American Woman's, Color, 1942	15.00
Art of Salad Making, Carol Truax, 210 Pages, 1968	3.50
Best of Bake–Off Collection, 1947, 823 Pages	40.00
Better Homes & Gardens, Christmas Time, 216 Pages, 1974	25.00
Better Homes & Gardens, Holiday Cookbook, 1959–1965	3.50
Better Homes & Gardens, Ring Binder, 1962	20.00
Betty Crocker's Cooking Calendar, Illustrated, 1st Edition, 176 Pages, 1962	25.00
Betty Crocker's Picture Cookbook, Illustrated, 1st Edition, 463 Pages, 1950	65.00
Betty Crocker, 1st Edition, Loose Leaf, 440 Pages	45.00
Betty Crocker, Outdoor Cookbook, Soft Cover, 1967	3.00
Bisquick, Movie Stars Pictures, 1935	24.00
Bond Bread, 1934	15.00
Bond Bread, Green Cover, 72 Pages, 1935	5.00
Borden, Elsie	20.00
Borden, Elsie The Cow	28.00
Butterick, 1911	18.00
Campbell's 100 Best Recipes, 157 Family Favorites, Illustrated, 160 Pages	14.95
Carnation Cookbook, Mary Blake, 93 Pages, 1942	3.00
Chiquita Banana, 1950	15.00
Confectionery, Illustrated, 143 Pages, 1910	28.00
Cook It Ahead, Elinore J. Marvel, 1951	3.00
Cook It In A Casserole, Florence Brobeck, 256 Pages, 1955–1958	3.50
Cooking Made Easy, People Gas, Light & Coke Co., Chicago, 1930s	9.00
Dark Shadows, 1970	25.00
Dessert & Fruit, Family Circle, 144 Pages, 1954	3.00
Dorchester 3rd Religious Society, 36 Pages	15.75
Enterprising Housekeeper, 96 Pages, 1906	35.00
Enterprize 1900	25.00
Ford Times Favorite Recipes, Vol. VII, 1979, 137 Pages	8.00
Ford Treasury of Favorite Recipes, Famous Eating Places, Hard Cover, 1955	17.50
Galloping Gourmet, Graham Kerr, Photographs, 286 Pages, 1969	10.00
General Foods Kitchens, First Printing, 436 Pages, 1959	10.00
Golden Rule, Panama Exposition, 1915	22.50
Gone With The Wind	38.00
Good Eating For Health, Battle Creek Sanitarium Foods, 1930s	2.85
Good Housekeeping Complete Basic Cooking, Dorothy Marsh, 1942–1962	8.00
Grace Drayton, 64 Pages	25.00
Granite Ironware, Advertising, 64 Pages, 1880	15.00
Heinz, Book of Salads, 95 Pages, 1925	11.00
Heinz, Lei Lani, Illustrated, Spiral, 1939	9.00
Institute, With War Time Recipes, 1913	10.00
Jell–O, America's Most Famous Dessert, Genessee Pure Food Co., 1920	12.00
Jell–O, Girl At Desk, Color, 14 Pages	14.50
Karo, 47 Pages, 1910	25.00
Karo, Leyendecker, 1910	22.00
Kerr Canning, 1937	8.00
Kickapoo, 31 Pages, 1900	15.00
Kitchen Cabinet Book, Sunset Magazine, 80 Pages, 1931	3.50
Knox Gelatin, 71 Pages, 1933	8.00
Knox Gelatin, Dainty Desserts, 1924	8.00
Land O' Lakes, Tell The Story In Cookies, Holiday Baking Book, 14 Pages, 1973	6.50
Life Picture, 1968	15.00
Low Fat Low Cholesterol Diet, University of California, 1951	3.00
Lucayos, Bahamas, Nassau, From 1859 Manuscript, 58 Pages, 1959	12.50
Magestic, With Catalog, Illustrated, 1913	30.00

Magic Chef Cooking, 17th Edition, 199 Pages, 1938 .... 15.95
Magic Recipes, Ruth Ellen Church, 370 Pages, 1952–1965 .... 3.50
Mahalia Jackson Cooks Soul 18.00
Mayrose Ham, Calendar of Meat Recipes, 1940s 2.00
Modern Encyclopedia of Cooking, Meta Given, Vol. 2, 1502 Pages, 1947–1961 ..... 5.00
Modern Family Cookbook, Hard Cover, 632 Pages, 1961 .... 25.00
Modern Family Cookbook, Meta Given, 1502 Pages, 1942–1961 .... 5.00
N.Y. Times, Jean Hewitt, Large Type 15.00
Natural Healing, 1981 .... 7.50
New England Yankee, 1939 .... 10.00
New England Yankee, Imogene Walcott 15.00
New Way To Eat & Stay Slim, Donald Cooley, 1941–1946 .... 2.00
Old Dixie 48.00
Old Time Pickling & Spicing Recipes, Hard Cover, 126 Pages, 1953 .... 9.50
Out of Alaska's Kitchens 15.00
Peanuts Lunch Bag, Recipes By Jane Dutton, 1974 .... 5.00
Pet Milk, 1953 .... 5.00
Piggly Wiggly 25.00
Pillsbury, 2nd Grand National Prize–Winning Recipes, 1951 .... 15.00
Pillsbury, Illustrated Recipes, 126 Pages, 1913 .... 12.00
Presbyterian Church, Dayton, Ohio, Hard Cover, 1886 .... 20.00
Quaker Oats 20.00
Reynolds Wrap, Outdoor Cooking For Scouts, Hunters & Campers, 1950 .... 1.50
Rock & Roll Celebrity, 106 Pages 20.00
Rock Island Stove Co., Riverside, 64 Pages, 6 x 8 1/2 In. 15.00
Rumford, Fannie M. Farmer, 48 Pages 16.00
Rumford, Little Girls On Cover, 1911 .... 25.00
Salute To Cheese, Betty Wason, 287 Pages, 1966 .... 3.50
Sears Kenmore, American Women's, 1950 .... 23.00
Simca's Cuisine, Simone Beck, Knopf, 1973 .... 6.00
Spark, Lid Top Gas Stove Recipes, 176 Pages, 1926 .... 12.50
Spry Shortening, Aunt Jenny's Recipe, 1930s 2.00
Spry Shortening, What To Cook Today, 1930s 2.00
Western Cookery, Western Drawing, 48 Pages, 1936 .... 12.50
Woman's World, 514 Pages, 1961 .... 3.50
Working Girl Must Eat, 1938 .... 12.00
Wurlitzer 50.00
You Can Be A Better Cook Than Mama Ever Was, Hard Cover, 322 Pages, 1968 ... 17.00

COOKIE JARS with brightly painted designs or amusing figural shapes
became popular in the mid–1930s. Many companies made them and
collectors search for cookie jars either by design or by maker's name.
Listed here are examples by the less common makers. Major factories are
listed under their own names in other categories of the book, such as
Abingdon, Brush, Hull, McCoy, Red Wing, and Shawnee. See also the
Black and Disneyana categories.

Albert Apple, Pittman–Dreitzer, 1942 ....75.00 To 110.00
Alice In Wonderland, Japan 150.00
Amish Oil Man, Pennsbury 65.00
Animal Cookies, Black Stoneware 25.00
Aunt Jemima, Soft Plastic 325.00
Balloon Lady, Pottery Guild 275.00
Barn, Regal China 260.00
Bartender, Tan, Fapco 225.00
Baseball Boy, Treasure Craft 35.00
Baseball Cap, American Bisque 125.00
Basket O' Cookies, American Bisque 90.00
Bear, Avon 40.00
Bear, Brown, Fapco ....50.00 To 65.00
Bear, Climbing 50.00
Bear, Flasher, American Bisque ....350.00 To 375.00
Bear, Girl, American Bisque 80.00
Bear, Kraft Marshmallow 150.00

Bear, On Blocks, Starnes 385.00
Bear, Poppytrail, Blue Sweater, Metlox 75.00
Bear, Ranger, Twin Winton 65.00
Bear, Turnabout, Red & Blue 70.00
Bear, With Cookie, American Bisque 55.00
Bear, With Green Apron, Wisecarver 175.00
Bear, With Skates, Metlox 145.00
Bert & Ernie, Fine Cookies, California Originals .... 325.00 To 495.00
Betsy Ross, California Originals 165.00
Beulah Cow Head, Metlox 295.00
Big Al, Treasure Craft 90.00
Big Bird, California Originals 70.00
Birthday Jar, Walt Disney 135.00
Black Chef, Pearl China .... 325.00 To 595.00
Black Girl, Sears 575.00
Black Potbelly Stove, American Bisque 47.00
Black Scotty Dog, Metlox 135.00
Blackboard Clown, American Bisque 300.00
Blackboard Hobo, American Bisque .... 275.00 To 295.00
Blanket Couple, Little Co. 225.00
Blue Bonnet Sue 25.00
Blue Bonnet Sue, Advertising, Box 35.00
Boots, American Bisque 175.00
Bowling Ball, Treasure Craft 25.00
Boy With Wheelbarrow, Grapes, Cobalt Blue, 2 Handles, Germany, 1910, 10 In. 85.00
Bulls, Twin Winston 50.00
Bunch of Broccoli, Metlox 60.00
Carmen Miranda, Vandor 450.00
Carousel, American Bisque 75.00
Casper, American Bisque 1000.00
Cat & Fish Bowl, Gold Finial, Treasure Craft 55.00
Cat On Pillow, American Bisque 240.00
Cat Tail Finial, American Bisque 275.00
Cat With Straw Hat, Metlox 120.00
Cat's Bust, Metlox 90.00
Cat's Head, Lefton 60.00
Cat, Black, Stafford 75.00
Cheerleaders, Flasher, American Bisque .... 275.00 To 375.00
Chef Head, Maurice of California 125.00
Chef, American Bisque 250.00
Chef, National Silver .... 225.00 To 300.00
Chef, Pearl China 475.00
Chef, USA 40.00
Chef, Westfall 110.00
Chevrolet, Applause, 1957 .... 75.00 To 90.00
Chick, American Bisque .... 55.00 To 70.00
Chicken, Fapco 45.00
Chicks On Nest, Maddox 45.00
Chintzware, Swing Handle 110.00
Christmas House, Cleminson 90.00
Christmas House, Fitz & Floyd 150.00
Chuck Wagon 35.00
Churn Boy, American Bisque .... 220.00 To 250.00
Churn Boy, Regal China 295.00
Churn, American Bisque, Box 125.00
Cinderella, Napco 300.00
Cinderella, Regal China 295.00
Circus Horse, Green, Wisecarver 975.00
Clown On Alphabet Block, American Bisque 80.00
Clown, Black & White, Metlox .... 100.00 To 225.00
Clown, Flasher, Black Curtains, American Bisque 350.00
Clown, Pink, Wisecarver 165.00
Cola, Doranne of California 55.00

Collegiate Owl, Green, Doranne of California 55.00
Cookie Truck, American Bisque .... 55.00 To 85.00
Corn, Stanfordware 100.00
Cow Head, Metlox 180.00
Cow Jumped Over The Moon, Flasher, American Bisque 525.00
Cow Jumped Over The Moon, Green, Doranne of California 295.00
Cow With Suspenders, American Bisque 68.00
Cupcake With Cherry, Doranne of California 35.00
Daisy Mae, Paul Webb 950.00
Dennis The Menace, Sierra Vista 725.00
Derby Dan, Pfaltzgraff 275.00
Desert Rose 75.00
Dino, Flintstones, American Bisque 1175.00
Dinosaurs, Blue, Metlox 150.00
Dog House, Starnes 225.00
Dog In Basket 50.00
Dog On Drum, Sierra Vista 65.00
Dog On Sled, Racing Downhill, Present, Treasure Craft 59.00
Dog, Plaid, Yellow, Brayton Laguna 395.00
Donkey, With Milk Wagon, American Bisque 60.00
Drum, Poppy Trail 60.00
Dutch Boy, American Bisque 70.00
Dutch Boy, Caramel Pants, Pottery Guild 85.00
Dutch Boy, Metlox 165.00
Dutch Girl, American Bisque 125.00
Dutch Girl, Peach Color, Regal China 495.00
Edmund On Vacation, Black Man, Little Co., 19 In. 250.00
Elephant, Sailor, American Bisque 115.00
Elephant, With Cone, Blue, Wisecarver 295.00
Elsie In Barrel 265.00
Elsie The Cow, Pottery Guild 350.00
Elsie, Pottery Guild 265.00
Elves School House, California Originals 55.00
Emmett Kelly, Flambro, Box 350.00
English Cottage 40.00
Entenmann's Chef Head, U.S.A. 575.00
Famous Amos, F & F 75.00
Famous Amos, Treasure Craft 65.00
Feed Bag, American Bisque 85.00
Fifi, Poodle, Regal 525.00
Fire Truck, Twin Winton 110.00
Flintstone, Wilma On Telephone, American Bisque 1850.00
Flintstone, Wilma, American Bisque .... 975.00 To 1700.00
Football, Treasure Craft 25.00
Frango Bag of Cookies 150.00
Fred & Pebbles In Chair, Vandor 175.00
Fred Flintstone & Dino, American Bisque .... 875.00 To 995.00
Fred Flintstone, Hanna Barbera 120.00
Fred Flintstone, Vandor .... 70.00 To 159.00
French Chef, Cardinal 90.00
Friar Tuck, Twin Winton 95.00
Frog, Gray, Yellow, California Originals 77.00
George & Martha Washington, Black, American Bisque 85.00
Girl, Cardinal 45.00
Goldilocks, Regal China .... 125.00 To 350.00
Golf Ball, Treasure Craft, 7 1/2 In. 35.00
Goose, Metlox 40.00
Granny, American Bisque .... 65.00 To 95.00
Granny, Fitz & Floyd 70.00
Green Frog, Sears .... 40.00 To 50.00
Green Giant Sprout .... 29.50 To 40.00
Halo Boy, DeForest of California 825.00
Happy, Cross–Cross Pants, Gold Trim, Pearl China 250.00

Harley Davidson Gas Tank 125.00
Harley Davidson Hog .... 150.00 To 450.00
Harley Hog, Hog Logo, 1984 .... 625.00
Harpo Marx, Regal China 1150.00
Hat Party, F & F 130.00
Hippo Sitting, Doranne of California 95.00
Hobby Horse, Doranne of California 95.00
Hobby Horse, Regal China 255.00
Hobo In Barrel, Down To Last Cookie 50.00
Homestead, Red, Poppy Trail 65.00
House of Webster, Schoolhouse 40.00
Humpty Dumpty 300.00
Humpty Dumpty, California Originals 125.00
Humpty Dumpty, Ceramic 22.00
Humpty Dumpty, With Beanie Wisecarver .... 175.00 To 275.00
Ice Cream Cone, Treasure Craft 49.00
Intaglio, Purinton 65.00
Jack-In-The-Box, American Bisque 75.00
Jack-In-The-Box, Byron Mold 75.00
Jim Beam Association, 1977, Regal, Gold Trim .... 195.00 To 295.00
Jonah On The Whale ....800.00 To 1300.00
Jukebox, Vandor .... 135.00 To 165.00
Katrina, Treasure Craft 1500.00
Keebler Elf, American Bisque 35.00
Keebler Elf, Ernie, F & F 90.00
Keebler Elf, Sitting 75.00
Keebler Tree House ....35.00 To 38.00
Kitten In Basket, American Bisque 50.00
Kitten, On Quilted Base, American Bisque 65.00
Koala Bear, Metlox, 1951 .... 125.00
Koala Bear, Poppy Train 59.00
Lamb, Girl, American Bisque ....38.00 To 95.00
Lighthouse, Treasure Craft ....49.00 To 55.00
Lion, Metlox 180.00
Little Bopeep, Napco 175.00
Little Red Riding Hood, California Originals 225.00
Little Red Riding Hood, Gold Trim, Wisecarver 150.00
Little Red Riding Hood, Napco 250.00
Little Red Riding Hood, Pottery Guild 110.00
Lucy Goose, Metlox 49.00
Ludwig Von Drake, Felt Tongue, American Bisque 1450.00
Majorette, American Bisque .... 255.00 To 450.00
Majorette, Regal China .... 200.00 To 350.00
Mammy & Chef, National Silver, Pair 295.00
Mammy, Blue, Artistic Potteries 475.00
Mammy, Blue, Brayton 995.00
Mammy, Bust, Wisecarver 125.00
Mammy, Happy Face, Brayton Laguna, 1950s 1595.00
Mammy, National Silver Mosaic, 1930s 650.00
Mammy, National Silver, 1930s 450.00
Mammy, Omnibus 375.00
Mammy, Pearl China ....675.00 To 750.00
Mammy, Plaid Apron 550.00
Mammy, Plaid, Basket Handle 950.00
Mammy, Plastic, Dark Face, F & F 425.00
Mammy, Polkadot, Basket Handle 800.00
Mammy, Quilting, Wisecarver 90.00
Mammy, Red Dress, Brayton Laguna 1150.00
Mammy, White, Gilner 2200.00
Mammy, With Churn, Wisecarver 90.00
Mammy, Yellow Polkadots, Metlox 250.00
Mammy, Yellow, Gilner 1900.00
McNutt's, Chicken Coupe, Red 100.00

Midnight Snack, Clay Art	45.00
Milk Bone Dog House, Box	125.00
Mona Lisa, Vendor	50.00
Money Bag, Terrace Ceramics	50.00
Monk, Napco	75.00
Monk, Twin Winton, 1960	75.00
Monkey In Barrel, Doranne of California	65.00
Monkey, Lefton, Sticker	75.00
Mr. Peanut	39.00
Mr. Rabbit, American Bisque	200.00
Mrs. Bunny, Metlox	125.00
Mrs. Rabbit, American Bisque	200.00 To 235.00
Muppets, California Originals, Set of 6	950.00
Mushroom	20.00
Neal The Frog, Sears	59.00
Nerds, Green & Yellow	90.00
Nerds, On Skateboard, Blue & White, Pottery Guild	110.00
Nestle's Toll House Cookies	95.00 To 150.00
Noah's Ark, Treasure Craft	55.00
Nun, DeForest of California	350.00
Octopus On Chest, California Originals	155.00
Old Chef, All White	250.00
Old Granny, Blue, White, Gold Trim, Carol Gifford	275.00
Old Lady In Shoe, Japan	60.00
Old MacDonald's Farm, Barn, Regal China	350.00 To 395.00
Old Saint Nick, Treasure Craft	59.00
Old Woman In Shoe, Pfaltzgraff	175.00
Oriental Girl, Regal China	225.00
Oriental Woman, Regal China	500.00
Oscar, Muppets, California Originals	65.00
Outhouse	95.00
Owl, Doranne of California	110.00
Owl, Gold, Holiday Designs	15.00
Owl, Twin Winton	35.00
Owl, White	25.00
Ozark Hillbilly, Morton Potteries	65.00
Paddington Bear, Toscany	100.00
Pappy, Bust, Wisecarver	90.00
Patchwork Dog, Brayton	625.00
Peek–A–Boo, Regal China	800.00
Penguin, Metlox	55.00 To 85.00
Pennsylvania Dutch Girl, American Bisque	350.00
Peter Peter Pumpkin Eater, Japan	75.00
Peter Pumpkin, Wisecarver	95.00
Peter Rabbit, Sigma	80.00 To 100.00
Pickup Truck, Antique White, Dog Finial, Treasure Craft	55.00
Pig & Three Babies, Fitz & Floyd	85.00
Pig In Poke, American Bisque	40.00
Pig, Boy, American Bisque	75.00
Pig, Diaper Pin, Regal China	385.00
Pig, Pink, Pfaltzgraff	50.00
Pig, With Flowers, Los Angeles Potteries	40.00
Pillsbury Doughboy	39.00
Pillsbury Doughboy Funfetti, Standing By Cupcake, Sprinkles	40.00
Pillsbury Doughboy, 1973	90.00
Pillsbury Doughboy, Bank	15.00
Pine Cone Coffeepot, American Bisque	55.00
Pineapple, Dorrane of California	60.00
Pink Poodle, American Bisque	75.00
Pinky Lee, Blue Hat, American Bisque	595.00
Pinnochio, Dayton Hudson	99.00
Pinocchio, Metlox	425.00
Pirate	90.00

Poodle, Maroon, American Bisque 90.00
Porsche, J. C. Miller 125.00
Pound Puppy, With Cane 90.00
Priest, DeForest of California 150.00
Provincial Woman, Brayton 1395.00
Prunella Pig, Fitz & Floyd 80.00
Pup On Pot, American Bisque 85.00
Purple Cow, Metlox .... 400.00 To 550.00
Puss 'n Boots, Flowers, China, Gold, Regal 385.00
Quaker Oats, Regal China .... 95.00 To 190.00
Rabbit, In Basket, National Silver 50.00
Rabbit, In Hat, American Bisque 75.00
Rabbit, O'Hare, F & F 95.00
Rabbit, On Cabbage, Green, Metlox 195.00
Rabbit, White, Blue & Pink Features 30.00
Raccoon, Bandit, Metlox 145.00
Raccoon, Doranne of California 145.00
Raccoon, Metlox 100.00
Radio, Vandor 59.00
Rag Doll, Starnes 240.00
Rag Doll, White, Treasure Craft 40.00
Raggedy Andy, Metlox .... 75.00 To 150.00
Raggedy Ann & Andy, Twin Winton, Pair 195.00
Ring For Cookies, American Bisque 55.00
Rio Rita, Fitz & Floyd 195.00
Robot 65.00
Rocking Horse, Regal China 250.00
Rooster, Black 55.00
Rooster, Brown 45.00
Rooster, Purinton 200.00
Round House, Sierra Vista 150.00
Round, Deco, Kitchen Kraft, Homer Laughlin 90.00
Rubble's House, American Bisque 1350.00
Saddle Blackboard, Remember, American Bisque 230.00
Santa Christmas Bear, Dayton Hudson 50.00
Santa Claus, Black, Wisecarver 225.00
Santa Claus, Black, Wisecarver, No. 40, 1990 .... 95.00
Santa Claus, California Originals 145.00
Santa Claus, In Airplane, Fitz & Floyd 200.00
Santa Claus, Musical 45.00
Santa Claus, On Motorcycle, Fitz & Floyd .... 295.00 To 300.00
Santa, Old World, F & F 135.00
Says Cookies, Allover Sponged, Stoneware 150.00
Schoolhouse, With Bell, American Bisque 70.00
Scotty, Black, Metlox 200.00
Seal, On Igloo, American Bisque 385.00
Sheriff, Lane Potteries, 1950 .... 1295.00
Shoe, Doranne of California 15.00
Smart Boy, Cardinal 65.00
Smart Cookie, Cardinal 90.00
Smoky The Bear, Napco .... 195.00 To 225.00
Snoopy 150.00
Snoopy, With Woodstock, Willits 50.00
Snow White, California Originals 775.00
Snowman, Doranne of California 165.00
Snowman, Musical 45.00
Spaceship, American Bisque .... 225.00 To 300.00
Spice Rag Doll, Treasure Craft 47.00
Squirrel, Cream, Twin Winton 60.00
Squirrel, Maddox 200.00
Squirrel, On Pine Cone, Metlox .... 60.00 To 65.00
Squirrel, On Stump 50.00
Squirrel, Sierra Vista 185.00

Star Wars, C–3PO, Roman Ceramics, Box	400.00
Star Wars, R2–D2 Reverse To Darth Vader, Sigma	90.00
Stella Strawberry, Pittman–Dreitzer, 1942	75.00
Sundae, Doranne of California	30.00
Superman, California Originals	350.00
Tattle Tale, Helen Hutla, 1940s	1800.00
Telephone, American Bisque	50.00
Telephone, Sierra Vista	85.00
Three Bears, Wisecarver	75.00
Thumper, Terrace Ceramics	75.00
Toby Cookies, Regal China	795.00
Tomato, With Salt & Pepper & Grease, Cover	30.00
Tony The Tiger, Kelloggs	115.00
Toothache Dog, American Bisque	225.00 To 695.00
Top Cat, Hanna Barbera	120.00
Topsy Girl, Yellow, Mettlach	350.00
Topsy, Blue & White Polkadot, Metlox	395.00
Traffic Sign, Race, Metlox	750.00
Train, Japan	40.00
Transformer, Box	55.00
Transformer, Hasbro	200.00
Treasure Chest, American Bisque	125.00
Treasure Chest, Wisecarver	95.00
Trolley, Treasure Craft	55.00
Tugboat	105.00
Tugboat, American Bisque	175.00 To 225.00
Tugboat, Treasure Craft	45.00
Turkey, Morten Potteries	125.00
Umbrella Kids, American Bisque	145.00 To 375.00
Uncle Mistletoe, Peter Pan Co.	595.00
Windmill, Fapco	85.00
Windup Car	250.00
Winnie The Pooh, California Originals	85.00 To 100.00
Witch With Jack-O'-Lantern, Gold Trim, Corl Collection	200.00
Witch, Polkadot, Fitz & Floyd	275.00 To 350.00
Wizard, Clay Art	59.00
Woman & Cat, Animals & Co.	195.00
Wonder Woman, Brown Tones, California Originals	475.00
Wooden Solider, American Bisque	55.00
Woody Woodpecker, California Originals	400.00 To 690.00
Woody Woodpecker, Red, Walter Lantz	975.00
Yarn Doll, American Bisque	100.00 To 110.00
Yogi Bear, Felt Tongue	350.00
You're An Angel	395.00

COORS ware was made by a pottery in Golden, Colorado, owned by the Coors Beverage Company. Dishes and decorative wares were produced from the turn of the century until the pottery was destroyed by fire in the 1930s. The name *Coors* is marked on the back. For more information, see *Kovels' Depression Glass & American Dinnerware Price List.*

COORS
U.S.A.

Bean Pot, Rosebud, Cover	22.00
Bowl, Batter, Rosebud, Blue, Handles	40.00
Bowl, Brown Gloss, Large	30.00
Bowl, Rosebud, 8 In.	38.00
Cake Plate, Rosebud, Yellow, 11 In.	75.00
Cookie Jar, Ivory, Rope Handles	5.00
Creamer, Rosebud	8.00
Lemonade Set, Rosebud, 10 Piece	295.00
Pitcher, Cover, Blue, 8 In.	65.00
Pitcher, Cream, Thermal	17.00
Pitcher, Yellow	17.00
Vase, 7 1/2 In.	40.00
Vase, Bud, Trumpet, Tan, Blue Interior	35.00

Vase, Circle, Glossy Burgundy, 7 1/2 In. 95.00
Vase, Circle, Salmon & Aqua, 7 In. 45.00

COPELAND SPODE appears on some pieces of nineteenth–century English porcelain. Josiah Spode established a pottery at Stoke–on–Trent, England, in 1770. In 1833, the firm was purchased by William Copeland and Thomas Garrett and the mark was changed. In 1847, Copeland became the sole owner and the mark changed again. W. T. Copeland & Sons continued until a 1976 merger when it became Royal Worcester Spode. Pieces are listed in this book under the name that appears in the mark. Copeland Spode, Copeland, and Royal Worcester have separate listings.

Cup & Saucer, Camellia, Blue, White 22.00
Dinner Set, Trade Winds, 60 Piece 650.00
Dish, Sweetmeat, 2 Sections, Self–Handled, Blue, 5 1/4 In. 110.00
Game Bird Set, 1 Platter, 12 Plates, 13 Piece 275.00
Lazy Susan, 4 Inserts, c.1850, 18 In. 495.00
Pitcher, Tower, Blue & White, 7 In. 110.00
Plate, Camellia, 9 In. 18.00
Plate, Tower, 2 Handles, Square, 11 x 9 1/2 In. 60.00
Platter, Diamond Lattice & Dagger Border, 1840s, 17 In. 145.00
Platter, Tower, 12 1/2 x 9 1/2 In. 125.00
Service For 8, Rosebud Chintz, 62 Piece 495.00
Service For 12, Dark Blue Transfer, 54 Piece 633.00
Tea Set, Dancing Classical Ladies, Garlands, Marked, Dark Blue, 5 Piece 245.00
Tea Set, Hunt Scene, Wedgwood Style, 5 Piece 225.00
Tureen, White, Blue Shield Designs, 13 1/2 In. 85.00

COPELAND pieces listed here are those that have a mark used between 1847 and 1976. See also Copeland Spode and Royal Worcester.

Figurine, Dog, St. Bernard, Hand Painted, 1878, 8 In. 200.00
Figurine, Owl With Shrew, 18 In. 550.00
Pitcher, 400th Anniversary Columbus, Atlantic Ocean, 1792–1892, Jasperware 500.00
Soup, Dish, Dark Blue & White, 6 Piece 99.00

COPPER LUSTER items are listed in the Luster category.

COPPER has been used to make utilitarian items, such as teakettles and cooking pans, since the days of the early American colonists. Copper became a popular metal with the Arts & Crafts makers of the early 1900s and decorative pieces, like bookends and desk sets, were made. Other pieces of copper may be found in the Arts & Crafts, Bradley & Hubbard, Kitchen, and Roycroft categories.

Ashtray, Stand, Hammered, Riveted Match Holder, Van Erp, 30 x 8 3/4 In. 550.00
Basket, Hammered, Cutout Handle Riveted To Body, Dirk Van Erp, 11 x 8 In. 467.00
Bed Warmer, Flower Basket Tooled Brass Lid, Turned Wooden Handle, 43 1/2 In. ... 330.00
Bed Warmer, Tooled Floral Lid, Turned Wooden Handle, 43 In. 200.00
Bookends, 3 Semi–Arched Supports, Nickel Plated, Chase, 5 3/4 In. 465.00
Bookends, Cutout Poppies, Dirk Van Erp, 1912, 5 x 6 In. 770.00
Bowl, Hammered Texture, Dirk Van Erp, 1915, 5 3/4 In. 1100.00
Bowl, Hammered, Arts & Crafts Type, Elverhoj Craft Colony, 4 x 8 3/4 In. 250.00
Bowl, Hammered, Scalloped Rim, Flared, Ovoid, M. Zimmermann, 15 x 9 In. 3200.00
Bowl, Hammered, Scalloped, Dirk Van Erp, 13 x 3 In. 192.00
Bowl, Hammered, White–Metal Mounts, Stamped, 4 1/2 In. 595.00
Bowl, Leaf, Hammered, Self–Handled, 5 In. 135.00
Bowl, Silver Lined, Footed, Flower Form, K. Pratt, 1930s, 3 x 6 7/8 In. 550.00
Bowl, Spoon, Shaped Handle, Falick Novick, 6 1/4 In. 695.00
Box, Enameled Medallion Lid, Orange Interior, Society of Arts & Crafts, 5 1/4 In. 725.00
Box, Enameled, Conical Bowl Shape, Domed Cover, RLW Mark, 2 1/2 x 5 In. 550.00
Candelabra, 3–Branch, Hammered, Octagonal Base, Dick Van Erp, 12 x 8 In. 935.00
Candleholder, C–Shaped Arms, Chase, 8 3/8 In., Pair 660.00
Candleholder, Hammered, Riveted Handle, 5 In. 165.00
Candlestick, Hammered, Gustav Stickley, 9 In. 595.00
Candlestick, Hammered, Princess Style, Karl Kipp, Pair 550.00

Charger, Hammered, Scalloped, Harry Dixon, Dated 1927, 14–In. Diam. 165.00
Engraving, Botanical Cabinet, Conrad Loddiges & Sons, c.1817, 6 x 6 3/4 In., Pr. ... 120.00
Ewer, Hand Hammered, Brass Handle, Russian Label, 14 1/2 In. 30.00
Humidor, Hammered, Humidor Corp. 50.00
Jar, Applied Bands, Rivets, Handles, Hammered, 17 1/4 x 21 1/2 In. 1045.00
Jardiniere, Dovetailed Side Seam, Strap Handles, Falick Novick, 9 1/2 In. 1400.00
Jardiniere, Hammered, Arts & Crafts, Dirk Van Erp Style, 12 1/2 In. 770.00
Kettle, Apple Butter 65.00
Kettle, Drilled Bottom For Drainage, 29 1/2 In. 400.00
Molds are listed in the Kitchen category
Mug, Applied Strap Handle, Gailstyn, 4 1/2 In., Pair 65.00
Nut Set, Hammered, Applied Silver Medallions, Benedict Studios, 9 In. Bowl, 7 Pc. 154.00
Ornament, Eagle, Standing, Rockland, Maine, 32 In. 1210.00
Pan, Dovetailed, Turned Wooden Handle, 4 1/2 In. 71.00
Pan, Roasting, Diamond Shape, 19th Century, England, 27 In. 375.00
Pan, Sauce, Iron Handle, 7 1/2 In. 60.00
Pitcher, Brass Handle, Polished, 8 3/8 In 30.00
Pitcher, Dovetailed, Brass Trim, 7 1/2 In. 25.00
Pitcher, Flaring Cylinder, Arched Handle, Chase, 9 5/8 In. 495.00
Planter, Carl Sorenson, Hexagonal 175.00
Sauce Pan, Cast Iron Handle & Cover, E. Thomas & Co., 8 In. 44.00
Sconce, Rectangular, Repousse Peacock Decoration, Glasgow Style, 14 In. 465.00
Sculpture, Woman Triumphant, Bronzed, Cantini, 1958 .... 750.00
Shield, Lion Rampant, Fleur–De–Lis Border, Hand Hammered, 23 x 17 In. 125.00
Stencil, Eagle, Clutching Arrows & Olive Branch, Stripes, 12 1/4 x 14 5/8 In. 330.00
Teakettle, 1875, 4 1/4 x 8 In. 68.00
Teakettle, 2 In. 104.00
Teakettle, Brass Trim, Stamped Mark, Depose, 10 1/2 In. 33.00
Teakettle, Cover, 12 In. 99.00
Teakettle, Gooseneck Spout, Dovetailed, Copper Finial, 10 1/4 In. 95.00
Teakettle, Gooseneck Spout, Dovetailed, Swivel Handle, 6 1/2 In. 49.00
Teakettle, Gooseneck Spout, Dovetailed, Wooden Handle, Oval, 8 In. 104.00
Teakettle, Gooseneck Spout, With Flap, Swivel Handle, 7 3/4 In. 125.00
Teakettle, Gooseneck, C. Moore 700.00
Teakettle, Gooseneck, J. Koch 300.00
Teakettle, Porcelain Trim, America, 1900 .... 65.00
Teakettle, Queen Anne, Gooseneck 850.00
Teapot, Brass Stand, Burner, Teakwood Handle, 1904 .... 235.00
Tray, Hammered, Arts & Crafts, Triangular Medallion, 17–In. Diam. 247.00
Tray, Hammered, Riveted Handles, Gustav Stickley, Oval, 23 x 11 1/4 In. 330.00
Tray, Hammered, Rolled Rim, Riveted Handles, Oval, 20 In. 385.00
Tray, Japanese Scene, Gorham, 8 In. 305.00
Tray, Persian, 20th Century, 31 1/2 In. 25.00
Tray, Serving, Hammered, Onondago Metal Shop 5050.00
Tray, Serving, Hammered, Wide Rim, Riveted Handles, 16 7/8 In. 550.00
Tub, Laundry, Lid 225.00
Vase, Amphora Shaped, Dovetailed, Handles, 16 In. 70.00
Vase, Hammered, Rolled, Gustav Stickley, 10 5/8 In. 165.00
Vase, Hammered, Ruffled, Albert Berry, 4 x 4 In. 165.00
Vase, Leaping Antelope, Inlaid White Metal Design, Signed, 11 3/4 In. 2920.00
Vase, Weed, Flared, Stickley Brothers Label, 29 1/2 x 10 1/4 In. 660.00
Watering Can, 19th Century, 19 In. 198.00

CORALENE glass was made by firing many small colored beads on the
outside of glassware. It was made in many patterns in the United States
and Europe in the 1880s. Reproductions are made today. Coralene-
decorated Japanese pottery is listed in the Japanese Coralene category.

Toothpick, Round Rim, Yellow Design, White 295.00
Vase, Green Coralene Leaves, Beaded, Gold Tracery, Green Ground, 8 1/2 In. 350.00
Vase, Mother–of–Pearl, Diamond–Quilted, Pink Satin, 6 3/4 In. 350.00
Vase, Pastel Flowers, Pierced Handles, Gold Trim, 9 In. 595.00
Vase, Raised Beading, Leaves, Green Ground, 9 In. 350.00
Vase, Red, White, Green Rainbow, White, Gold Seaweed Beaded Design, 5 In. 247.50

CORDEY China Company was founded by Boleslaw Cybis in 1942 in Trenton, New Jersey. The firm produced gift shop items. In 1969 it was acquired by the Lightron Corp. and operated as the Schiller Cordey Co., manufacturers of lamps. About 1950 Boleslaw Cybis began making Cybis porcelains, which are listed in their own category in this book.

Box, 5 In.	27.00
Box, Oval, 6 In.	45.00
Figurine, Bluebird On Stump, No. 6004	95.00
Figurine, Harvester, No. 304, 16 1/2 In.	225.00
Lamp, Man & Woman, 14 In., Pair	175.00
Vase, Chinese Figures, Flowing Robes, Lavender Roses, 9 In.	145.00

CORKSCREWS have been needed since the first bottle was sealed with a cork, probably in the seventeenth century. Today collectors search for the early, unusual patented examples or the figural corkscrews of recent years.

Anheuser–Busch Beer	20.00
Champion, Bar Mount, Iron, 1886	139.00
Gold Cased, Traveling	69.00
Listerine	9.00
Old Snifter, Removable Hat, Dimley	185.00
Parrot, Tail Is Tool, Metal	20.00
Snake Type, Larson P & F., 9 Oz.	45.00
Sterling Silver, Removable Handles	45.00
Used In Vineyards Or Taverns, Brass, Rosewood Handle, c.1870, 22 In.	625.00

CORONATION souvenirs have been made since the 1800s. Pottery, glass, tin, silver, and paper objects with a picture of the monarchs and date have been sold at many coronations. The pieces that mention King Edward VIII, the king who was never crowned, are not rare; collectors should be sure to check values before buying. Related pieces are found in the Commemorative category.

Book, Queen Elizabeth, 100 Pages, 8 1/2 x 11 In.	9.00
Cup & Saucer, Queen Elizabeth, June 1953, Paragon China	25.00
Glass, Elizabeth & George VI, Etched Pictures	32.00
Mirror, Hand, Queen Elizabeth, Celluloid, Picture On Back, Felt Pouch	21.00
Mug, Queen Elizabeth II, Gold, Large	27.00
Paperweight, Queen Elizabeth 25th Anniv., Millefiori, White Friars, 1977	250.00
Plate, Edward VIII, 1937, 10 1/2 In.	75.00
Plate, Queen Elizabeth, With Baby Charles & Anne, Photographer Signed	45.00
Tin, Hinged Lid, Queen 1 Side, Duke Other, 3 x 6 In.	35.00

COSMOS is a pressed milk glass pattern with colored flowers made from 1894 to 1915 by the Consolidated Lamp and Glass Company. Tablewares and lamps were made in this pattern. A few pieces were also made of clear glass with painted decorations. Other glass patterns are listed under Consolidated Lamp and also in various glass categories.

Butter, Cover	175.00
Butter, Cover, Pink Band	195.00
Condiment Set, Glass Base	295.00
Pitcher, Pink Band	250.00
Salt & Pepper, Yellow Flowers	75.00
Spooner, Pink Band	125.00
Syrup, Cranberry	200.00
Water Set, 7 Piece	450.00

COVERLETS were made of linen or wool during the nineteenth century. Most of the coverlets date from 1800 to 1850. Four types were made: the double weave, jacquard, summer and winter, and overshot. Later coverlets were made of a variety of materials. Quilts are listed in this book in their own category.

Appliqued, Multiple Flowers, Fruit & Floral Basket, c.1830, 102 x 103 In.	4400.00
Candlewick, Eagle Design, 1844, 90 x 90 In.	300.00

Double Weave, 9–Patch Pattern, Navy, Red, Natural, Fringe, 74 x 80 In. 302.00
Double Weave, Snow Flakes, Pine Tree Border, Blue, White, 2–Piece, 76 x 86 In. ... 302.00
Double Weave, Wool, Cotton Stars, Flowers, Jacob & Michael Ardner, 1853 .... 745.00
Floral Pattern, Multicolored, 19th Century, 82 x 71 In. 145.00
Floral, Red, White, Zigzags, Single Weave, 71 x 77 In. 125.00
Geometric Pattern, 95 x 83 In. 245.00
Jacquard, 4 Rose Medallions, Bird Borders, Red, Blue, White, 72 x 84 In. 495.00
Jacquard, A. Preston, Quote From General Lafayette, July 4, 1827, 96 x 72 In. 935.00
Jacquard, Bird of Paradise, Navy & White, Double Weave, 2–Piece, 81 x 82 In. 275.00
Jacquard, Birds & Flowers, Navy & White, 2–Piece 275.00
Jacquard, Blue & White, Floral Borders, 2–Piece, 82 x 82 In. 193.00
Jacquard, Blue & White, Floral Medallion, Double Woven, 82 x 86 In. 5000.00
Jacquard, Border of Buildings, Blue & White, Dated 1855, 88 x 80 In. 770.00
Jacquard, Center Blue & White Floral, House Border, 1839, 90 x 74 In. 470.00
Jacquard, Central Floral Medallion, Eagles, Cotton & Wool Yarns, 75 x 78 In. 302.50
Jacquard, Christian & Heathen, Flowers, Blue & White, 2–Piece, 74 x 100 In. 330.00
Jacquard, Double Weave, Star Design, Vining Border, Blue & White, 78 x 88 In. 1375.00
Jacquard, Floral Design, Blue & White, 2–Piece, 78 x 88 In. 192.00
Jacquard, Floral Design, Blue, Olive, Red, White, 2–Piece, 68 x 76 In. 440.00
Jacquard, Floral Design, Double Bird Border, Blue & White, 2–Piece, 66 x 86 In. ... 275.00
Jacquard, Floral Medallion, Bird & Floral Border, Maroon, White, 84 x 90 In. 324.00
Jacquard, Floral Medallion, Eagle Border, E. J. Kernoeban, 1834, 76 x 102 In. 425.00
Jacquard, Floral Medallions, Bird Border, 2–Piece, 86 x 95 In. 440.00
Jacquard, Floral Medallions, Heilbronn, Red, Green, Blue, 1853, 86 x 95 In. 440.00
Jacquard, Floral, Block Border, Teal, Red, Natural, 79 x 90 In. 165.00
Jacquard, Floral, Corners 1848, Greek Key Border, Navy, 70 x 84 In. 495.00
Jacquard, Floral, Eagles, Knox County Oh., 1847, 2–Piece Not Sewn, 66 x 79 In. ... 412.00
Jacquard, Floral, Greek Key Border, Navy, Natural, 2–Piece, 70 x 84 In. 490.00
Jacquard, Floral, Navy Blue, Natural, 2–Piece, 74 x 88 In. 71.00
Jacquard, Floral, Teal, Red, Natural, 79 x 90 In. 165.00
Jacquard, Geometric Floral, Dark Blue, Red & Natural, 1848, 80 x 89 In. 523.00
Jacquard, Geometric Floral, Navy & White, 2–Piece, 82 x 88 In. 231.00
Jacquard, Navy Blue, White, Fruit, Flowers, 2–Piece, 82 x 88 In. 495.00
Jacquard, Patriotic Design, 3 Colors, Wm. Ney, Lebanon Co., Pa., 84 x 90 In. 660.00
Jacquard, Red, White & Blue, George Washington, Dated 1869 .... 330.00
Jacquard, Single Weave, Blue, Natural White, Bird, Eagle, 2–Piece, 66 x 86 In. 495.00
Jacquard, Single Weave, Blue, Natural White, Star Center, 70 x 82 In. 330.00
Jacquard, Single Weave, Blue, Natural, Bird Borders, 66 x 90 In. 578.00
Jacquard, Single Weave, Floral Medallions, 2–Piece, 70 x 88 In. 467.00
Jacquard, Single Weave, Floral Medallions, Bird Borders, 2–Piece, 65 x 69 In. 49.00
Jacquard, Single Weave, Floral, Medallion Center, Red, Navy, 80 x 86 In. 60.00
Jacquard, Snowflake & Pine Tree, Navy & White, 2–Piece, 74 x 82 In. 165.00
Jacquard, Stars, Flowers, Bird Border, Blue–Greeen, John Redick, 1852, 75 x 86 In. 220.00
Jacquard, Wool, Stylized Floral, Navy, Eagle Corner, S.A. McCrillas, 86 x 68 In. ... 220.00
John Redick, Troy Township, Richland County, Ohio, 1853 .... 2375.00
Linen & Wool, Rose & Puce, 1854, 72 x 92 In. 350.00
Linsey Woolsey, Floral Design, 86 x 91 In. 220.00
Linsey Woolsey, Princess Feather, Heart & Flower Quilting, 90 3/4 x 103 In. 4950.00
Linsey Woolsey, Red & Green Striped, Blue Border, Early 19th Century 138.00
Overshot, Blue & White Geometric Pattern, U.S., 19th Century, 92 x 74 In. 110.00
Overshot, Gold, Olive & Natural, 2–Piece, 80 x 96 In. 193.00
Overshot, Navy, Salmon, Natural, 2–Piece, 64 x 92 In. 55.00
Overshot, Twill Weave, Olive, Red & Natural, Fringed, 81 x 88 In. 138.00
Overshot, Woven, Optical Pattern, Blue, Natural, 2–Piece, 72 x 94 In. 137.00
Presidential, 9 Side Portraits, Browns, Green & Red, 86 x 85 In. 400.00
Single Weave, Tan, Natural White, Optical Pattern, Fringe On 3 Sides, 85 x 95 In. .. 275.00
Summer & Winter, Single Weave, Navy, Natural, 2 Sides Not Sewn, 74 x 90 In. 165.00
Woven, Red, Navy Blue, Natural, Plaid Pattern, 2–Piece, 68 x 86 In. 110.00

COWAN POTTERY made art pottery and wares for florists. Guy Cowan made pottery in Rocky River, Ohio, a suburb of Cleveland, from 1913 to 1931. A stylized mark with the word *Cowan* was used on most pieces. A commercial, mass–produced line was marked *Lakeware*. Collectors today search for the Art Deco pieces by Guy Cowan, Viktor Schreckengost, Waylande Gregory, or Thelma Frazier Winter.

Bookends, Elephant Shape, Orange Glaze, 7 In.	110.00
Bowl, Blue Leaf, Open Flower Frog Lid	230.00
Bowl, Blue Luster, 8 In.	12.50
Bowl, Crackled Celadon Glaze, Marked, 7 In.	330.00
Bowl, Diamond Shape, Scroll Footed, Green & Ivory, 11 In.	25.00
Bowl, Lakeware, 3 In.	18.00
Candleholder, Dancing Nude, 9 1/2 In., Pair	290.00
Figurine, Bird On Wave, Blue, Pair	1250.00
Figurine, Dancer, Nude	125.00
Figurine, Elephant, Blue, 4 1/2 In.	185.00
Figurine, Elephant, Postgate	190.00
Figurine, Nude, 12 In.	225.00
Figurine, Radio Woman, Black On Cream, 9 In.	4500.00
Figurine, Ram, 5 In.	48.00
Flower Frog, Mushroom, Ivory	135.00
Flower Frog, Satyr Sitting On Mushroom, 9 In.	385.00
Lamp Base, Art Deco, Peach Crystalline, 10 In.	495.00
Lamp, Art Deco Lines, 23 In.	795.00
Lamp, Chinese Bird, Antique Green	565.00
Lamp, Silver Triangle Parchment Shade, Gunmetal Gray, Caroline Burke, 21 In.	950.00
Soap Dish, Sea Horse At Base	40.00
Soap Dish, White & Pink, 4 x 7 In.	40.00
Trivet, Stylized Goldfish	245.00
Vase, Blue Luster, 11 1/2 In.	85.00
Vase, Blue, 6 In.	48.00
Vase, Fan, Apple Green, Gold Specks, 5 In.	100.00
Vase, Iridescent Purple, Signed, 1920, 6 1/2 In.	55.00
Vase, Orange Luster, 8 In.	42.00
Vase, Sea Horse, Blue Luster, 7 In.	95.00

CRACKER JACK, the molasses–flavored popcorn mixture, was first made in 1896 in Chicago, Illinois. A prize was added to each box in 1912. Collectors search for the old boxes, toys, and advertising materials. Many of the toys are unmarked.

Badge, Police	50.00
Baseball Card, Uncut, Complete Set	14.00
Boat, Wooden	90.00
Book, Birds, 1966, Miniature	20.00
Bookmark, Dog, Tin	30.00
Bookmark, Metal	23.00
Car, 1916 Model Ford, License N.Y. 999	390.00
Car, Tin, 1/2 In.	15.00
Dog, Tin, 3/4 In.	15.00
Doll, Box	72.00
Lion Head	25.00
Pocket Watch	15.00
Police Patrol	30.00
Poster, Cardboard, c.1919, 20 x 15 In.	175.00
Riddle Book	35.00
Sign, Holding Angelus Marshmallows, N. Price, Cardboard, 1919, 15 x 20 In.	45.00
Squirrel, Plastic	8.00
Stand Up Perry	20.00
Tiger Head	25.00
Toy, Car, Mustard, Tin	35.00
Trolley, Tin, 1 In.	20.00
Truck, Red, Tin, 1 3/8 In.	60.00
Uncle Walt, Tin, 2 In.	45.00
Watch, Tin Lithograph, 1940s	75.00
Wheelbarrow, Tin, 2 1/4 In.	30.00

Cranberry Glass, Tankard,

   Cut To Clear, 12 In.

◆ ◆

Decorate with the neighborhood burglar in mind. Large windows can be made less attractive to intruders if you put plants on shelves across the window. Decorative shelves and grills are made for this. Of course, be sure you can open the windows in case of fire.

◆ ◆

Whistle, Plastic	8.00
Whistle, Tin	30.00

CRACKLE GLASS was originally made by the Venetians, but most of the ware found today dates from the 1800s. The glass was heated, cooled, and refired so that many small lines appeared inside the glass. It was made in many factories in the United States and Europe.

Pitcher, Lemonade, Ice Lip, Amber Handle	150.00
Vase, Phoenix Bird, Raised Beading, China, 1875, 10 In.	80.00 To 90.00
Vase, Ruffled & Crimped Top, Clear, Aqua Trim, 8 In.	35.00

CRANBERRY GLASS is an almost transparent yellow–red glass. It resembles the color of cranberry juice. The glass has been made in Europe and America since the Civil War. It is still being made, and reproductions can fool the unwary. Related glass items may be listed in other categories, such as Northwood, Rubena Verde, etc.

Basket, Sugar, Frosted Glass, Sterling Silver, Durgin, 4 In.	125.00
Bell, Clear Handle, 5 1/2 In.	55.00
Biscuit Barrel, Florals, Gold Leaves, Silver Plated Cover, 6 1/2 In.	375.00
Biscuit Jar, White Overshot Craquelle, Brass Bail & Lid, 7 In.	415.00
Bobeches, Raised Diamond–Quilted, 3 1/4–In. Diam., Pair	110.00
Bottle, Cologne, Flattened Ovals On Body, 8 Panels, Facet Stopper, 8 In.	165.00
Box, Peacock, Hinged Lid, 7 In.	375.00
Box, Woman Figure, Hinged Lid, 5 In.	400.00
Castor, Pickle	350.00
Cheese Dish, High Dome, Craquelle, Enameled Cattails, 7 x 8 In.	425.00
Cracker Jar, Thumbprint, Enameled Flowers, Brass Base & Lid	300.00
Creamer, Heart Shape, Clear Reed Handle, White Opalescent, 3 5/8 In.	75.00
Creamer, Optic Pattern, Clear Reeded Applied Handle, 6 1/4 x 3 3/4 In.	79.00
Creamer, Stars & Stripes	260.00
Cruet, Wine, Blown–In Ice Bladder, Bubble Stopper, 12 In.	300.00
Decanter, Bottle, Allover Gold Stars, Clear Cut Bubble Stopper, 10 In.	150.00
Decanter, Clear Applied Handle, 3–Petal Top, Bubble Stopper, 8 3/4 In.	265.00
Goblet, Water, Panel Grape, Clear	22.00
Jar, Apothecary, Diamond–Quilted, Clear Finial	195.00
Jar, Straw, Honeycomb, Clear Knob Finial	325.00
Mug, Name Blanche, 1909	45.00
Ornate Brass Rim, Signed, 6 1/2 In.	185.00
Perfume, Double Muff, Cut In Diamonds, Hinged Center	400.00
Pitcher, Ball, Daisy & Fern, 6 In.	500.00

Pitcher, Blue Flowers, White Branches, Applied Clear Handle, 9 In. 175.00
Pitcher, Child's, Inverted Thumbprint 150.00
Pitcher, Diamond–Quilted, Clear Handle 75.00
Pitcher, Floral Design, Gold Banding, 11 In. 145.00
Pitcher, Fluted Top, Clear Applied Handle, 5 In. 145.00
Pitcher, Inverted Thumbprint, 9 In. 195.00
Pitcher, Inverted Thumbprint, Ruffled Rim, Reeded Handle 185.00
Pitcher, Pleated Rim, White Speckles, Frosted Handle 210.00
Pitcher, Water, Hobnail, Square Mouth, Clear Applied Handle, 8 In. 800.00
Ring Tree, Saucer, Enameled Florals, Clear Stack 195.00
Rose Bowl, Green Applied Feet, Multicolored Design, Leaves, 7 In. 1050.00
Salt, Cut To Clear, Strawberry & Diamond, Notched Rim 95.00
Sauce, Windows, Swirl, Opalescent 45.00
Sugar & Creamer, Clear Applied Handle & Shell Footed, 4 In. 135.00
Sugar Shaker, Leaf Umbrella, Blue 375.00
Sugar Shaker, Windows 395.00
Syrup, Hinged Lid, Daisy, Clear Handle 225.00
Talc Shaker, Victorian, Gold & Enamel Design, 1901 .... 165.00
Tankard, Cut To Clear, 12 In. ....*Illus* 6500.00
Toothpick, Ribbed Lattice 195.00
Tumbler, Crisscross, Stain Finish 135.00
Tumbler, Daisy & Fern, Opalescent 65.00
Tumbler, Inverted Thumbprint 16.00
Tumbler, Opalescent, Hobbs 65.00
Urn, Cover, Crystal Appliqued Flowers, 8 3/4 In. 595.00
Vase, Applied Opaque White Spiral, Ruffled, Clear Footed, 7 3/8 In. 75.00
Vase, Chartreuse & White Opalescent Stripes, Ruffled, Clear Footed, 6 In. 110.00
Vase, Clear Handles, 3 In. 15.00
Vase, Enameled, Ruffled, Cylindrical, 12 In. 145.00
Vase, Fleurette, Fluted, 4 3/4 In., Pair 165.00
Vase, Gold Enameled Daffodil, Stalks & Buds, 7 3/4 In. 65.00
Vase, Gold Enameled Daisy–Type Floral, Scrolls, 5 1/2 In. 55.00
Vase, Gold Scrolls, Trough Shape, Gold Footed, 3 1/2 In. 165.00
Vase, White Enameled Scallops, Ormolu Footed, 5 7/8 In., Pair 265.00
Water Set, Amberina Swirl, 7 Piece 375.00
Water Set, Florentine Cameo, Birds & Floral Enamel, 5 Piece 475.00
Water Set, Thumbprint, 6 Piece 210.00
Whimsy, Honeycomb, Tumbler Turned Into Hat, 3 1/4 x 1 1/2 In. 95.00

CREAMWARE, or queensware, was developed by Josiah Wedgwood about 1765. It is a cream–colored earthenware that has been copied by many factories. Similar wares may be listed under Wedgwood and Pearlware.

Box, Cover, Silver Luster, 6 In. 25.00
Coffeepot, Yellow & Green Stripes, c.1770 .... 1980.00
Dish, Floral Swags, Dated 1807, 5 1/2 In. 165.00
Figurine, Cat, Green & Brown Splashed, Oval Base, 19th Century, 12 In. 2530.00
Mug, Floral Design, Red, Green Enamel, 1 1/2 In. 33.00
Pitcher, Brown & Green Spots, 2 5/8 In. 60.00
Plate, Royal Portraits, Dutch Inscription, Scalloped, 9 3/4 In., 6 Piece 4290.00
Platter, Oriental Decoration, Blue Feather & Drapery Rim, 16 3/8 In. 825.00
Platter, Oval, Reticulated Rim, Molded Foliage Design, 12 1/4 In. 121.00
Sauceboat, Duck Form, 1780s, 6 1/4 In. 165.00
Teapot, Baluster Shape, Flat Sides & Cover, Pierced Rim, c.1775, 4 3/4 In. 575.00
Teapot, Cybele, Seated In Lion–Drawn Carriage, 4 1/2 In. 357.50
Tray, Floral, Reticulated Sides, c.1800 ....*Illus* 325.00
Vase, Blue & Matte Gold Design, Bulbous, Arts & Crafts, 5 In. 65.00
Washbasin, Medallions of Washington, Jefferson, Clinton & Lafayette 1870.00

CREDIT CARDS, credit tokens, metal charge plates, and other similar collectibles are now part of the numismatic collecting hobby.

Gulf Gasoline, 1977 .... 20.00
Machine, Texaco, Red & Green, Embossed .... 45.00 To 75.00
Standard Oil, 1940 Calendar Envelope, 2 1/2 x 3 1/2 In. 5.00

Creamware, Tray, Floral, Reticulated

Sides, c.1800

Don't store foods or beverages in crystal bowls or bottles for long periods of time. Acidic juice, vinegar, and alcoholic beverages will leach out the lead in the glass. It is unhealthy to drink the liquid.

Standard Oil, Paper 65.00

CREIL, France, had a faience factory as early as 1794. The company merged with a factory in Montereau in 1819. They made stoneware, mocha ware, and soft paste porcelain. The name *Creil* appears as part of the mark on many pieces. The Creil factory closed in 1895.

Plate, French Peasants Dancing, 9 In.	140.00
Plate, Le Corbeau, L'Enfant Et Maitre D'Ecole, Yellow Rim, 8 1/4 In., Pair	110.00
Plate, Yellow, Flowers, 10 In.	150.00

CROWN DERBY is the name given to porcelain made in Derby, England, from the 1770s to 1935. Pieces are marked with a crown and the letter *D* or the word *Derby*. The earliest pieces were made by the original Derby factory, while later pieces were made by the King Street Partnerships (1848–1935) or the Derby Crown Porcelain Co. (1876–1890). Derby Crown Porcelain Co. became Royal Crown Derby Co. Ltd. in 1890. It is now part of Royal Doulton Tableware Ltd.

Ewer, Gold Chrysanthemums, Trilobed Top, Twisted Gold Handle, 1890	385.00
Figurine, Cherub, Flowering Tree, Scrolled Base, 19th Century, 8 In., Pair	385.00
Figurine, Cupid Between Youthful & Aged Females, 8 In.	385.00
Pitcher, Quadraplate, Etched, Banded, Footed, 9 In.	95.00

CROWN DUCAL is the name used on some pieces of porcelain made by A. G. Richardson and Co., Ltd., England. The name has been used since 1916.

Bowl & Pitcher, Chinese Lanterns	380.00
Plate, Hunting Scene, Raised, Scalloped, Signed, c.1930, 11 In.	80.00
Platter, Turkey, 21 In.	250.00

CROWN MILANO glass was made by Frederick Shirley at the Mt. Washington Glass Works about 1890. It had a plain biscuit color with a satin finish. It was decorated with flowers and often had large gold scrolls.

Biscuit Barrel, Caramel To Pink, Hand Painted Flowers, 9 1/2 In.	625.00
Biscuit Jar, Florals, Opaque Cream, Blown–Out Crab Cover, Bail, 6 1/2 In.	375.00
Box, Dresser, Young Girl's Portrait On Lid, Signed, 4 3/4 In.	750.00
Castor, Pickle, Forget–Me–Not Design, Peachblow, Pairpoint Holder, Tongs	985.00
Cookie Jar, Raised Panels, Leaves & Jewels, Turtle Finial, Signed	650.00
Cracker Jar, Caramel To Pink, Floral Design, Signed, 9 In.	659.00
Dish, Sweetmeat, Diagonal Pink & White Bands, Gold Mums, Turtle Finial, 7 In.	1025.00
Dish, Sweetmeat, Floral Design, Silver Plated Fittings, 5 1/2 In.	750.00

Dish, Sweetmeat, Starfish Over Molded–In Stars, Bail, 6 x 6 In. 845.00
Lamp, Sprays of Wind–Blown Poppies, Ball–Shaped Shade, 19 3/4 In. 2950.00
Perfume Bottle, Lay Down, 2 3/4 In. 575.00
Pitcher, Acorns & Leaves, Twisted Rope Handle, Signed, 10 In. 2200.00
Rose Bowl, Chrysanthemum Blossoms, 2 3/4 In. 245.00
Salt & Pepper, Pink Floral, Ribbed 195.00
Salt, Molded Swirls, 4–Blossom Collar, Gold Outlined, 1 1/2 x 3 1/4 In. 165.00
Salt, Silver Sterling Edge, Open 180.00
Saltshaker, Vertical Ribs, Blue/White Daisy Design, Mt. Washington, 4 In. 185.00
Sugar & Creamer, Blue Cornflowers, Silver Handles, Lid 1250.00
Tray, Roll–Up Green & Gold Edges, Center Iris, 9 1/2 x 6 3/4 In. 370.00
Tumbler, Gold Garlands of Flowers & Ribbons, Signed, 3 7/8 In. 550.00
Tumbler, Gold Ribbons & Bows, Marked, 3 7/8 In. 550.00
Vase, Allover Gold Flowers, Scalloped, 4 Pinched Sides, Handles, 8 In. 525.00
Vase, Chrysanthemum Blossoms, Shadow Foliage, 11 1/2 In. 485.00
Vase, Enamel Dot Design On Orange Floral & Scroll, 12 1/2 In. 935.00
Vase, Enameled Flamingoes, Spherical, C–Scroll Handles, 9 3/4 In. 2750.00
Vase, Fluted Top, Acorn & Oakleaf Design, Signed, 5 1/4 In. 1210.00
Vase, Multicolored Enamel Dot Design, Floral & Scroll, 12 In. 935.00
Vase, Painted Amber Enamel Orchids, Yellow & Green Leaves 1850.00
Vase, Pansies, Gold Highlights, Triangular Base, Leaf Handle, 8 In. 1875.00
Vase, Raised Fishnet Gold & Flowers, Thorny Handles, 9 1/4 In. 600.00
Vase, Raised Gold, Stylized Florals, Gold Stripes On Top & Base, 8 1/2 In. 985.00
Vase, Snow Geese In Flight, Marked 3500.00
Vase, Swirl Molded Neck, Raised Gold Roses, Reeded Handles 995.00

CROWN TUSCAN pattern is included in the Cambridge category.

CRUETS of glass or porcelain were made to hold vinegar, oil, and other condiments. They were especially popular during Victorian times and have been made in a variety of styles since the eighteenth century. Additional cruets may be found in the Castor Set category and also in various glass categories.

Beveled Star, Green, Not Original Stopper 85.00
Burmese, Scenic 400.00
Cone, Pink Satin, Stopper 165.00
Opalescent Cranberry, Cut 100.00
Porcelain, Pink Roses, Ornate Handle, Stopper, Germany 55.00
Quilted Satin, Blue 110.00
Ribbon 260.00
Vinegar, Reward Pattern 165.00

CT GERMANY was first part of a mark used by a company in Altwasser, Germany, in 1845. The initials stand for C. Tielsch, a partner in the firm. The Hutschenreuther firm took over the company in 1918 and continued to use the *CT.*

C.T.

Bowl, Iris Bouquet Center, Cobalt Blue Scrolled Edge, 13 x 9 In. 125.00
Bowl, Violet Bouquets, Scrolled Edge, Signed, Oblong, 13 x 9 In. 85.00
Plate, Bouquet Center, Gilt, Forest Green Rim, 2 Handles, Tielsh, 11 1/2 In. 85.00
Plate, Bouquet of Flowers, Fruit & Forest Green Edge, Beading, 11 1/2 In. 95.00

CUP PLATES are small glass or china plates that held the cup while a diner of the mid–nineteenth century drank coffee or tea from the saucer. The most famous cup plates were made of glass at the Boston and Sandwich factory located in Sandwich, Massachusetts. There have been many new glass cup plates made in recent years for sale to the gift shops or the limited edition collectors. These are similar to the old plates but can be recognized as new.

Animal Figures Around Edge, Transfer, Leeds 2145.00
Blue Willow, Staffordshire, 4 In. 33.00
Brown, Canova, Staffordshire 35.00
Castle Garden & Battery, Staffordshire 550.00
Double Heart With Arrow, Glass 25.00

Gilpins Mills, Dark Blue, Staffordshire, Impressed Wood, 9 1/4 In.	413.00
Heart Pattern, Sandwich Glass	20.00
Marine Scene Transfer, Shell Border, Staffordshire, Blue, 5 1/4 In.	154.00
Near Philadelphia Scene, Stubbs	350.00
Octagon Church of Boston, Staffordshire	1650.00
Philadelphia Custom House, Staffordshire	2860.00
Scudder's American Museum, Staffordshire	1870.00
United States of America, Prosperity Attend Them, Soft Paste	1760.00
Wistow Hall, Leicestershire, Staffordshire, 8 3/4 In.	50.00

CURRIER & IVES made the famous American lithographs marked with their name from 1857 to 1907. The mark used on the print included the street address in New York City, and it is possible to date the year of the original issue from this information. Earlier prints were made by N. Currier and use that name from 1835 to 1847. Many reprints of the Currier or Currier & Ives prints have been made. Some collectors buy the insurance calendars that were based on the old prints. The words *large, small,* or *medium folio* refer to size. Other prints by Currier & Ives may be listed in the Card category under Advertising and in the Sheet Music category.

2 Souls With But A Single Thought, Comic Black, Porch, Small	345.00
A Night On The Hudson, Thru Daylight, 1864, Large	330.00
American Country Life, Pleasures of Winter, 20 x 26 In.	358.00
American Country Life, Summer, Large	1925.00
American Farm Yard, Evening, Large	1685.00
American Homestead, Summer, 1868, Matted, Framed, 15 3/4 x 19 1/2 In.	220.00
American Homestead, Winter, No. 5, Small	695.00
American Winter Scene, Morning, Skaters, Sleds, Large	6250.00
An Increase of Family, 1863, Gilt Frame, Medium	145.00
Ann Maria, Young Woman, Black Curls, Blue Dress, Norman Currier, Small	89.00
Assassination of Pres. Lincoln At Ford's Theater, April 14, 1865, Small	189.00
Battle of Bull's Run, Va., July 21, 1861, Kellogg, Small	149.00
Battle of Wilderness, Va., May 5–7, 1864, Small	219.00
Between 2 Fires, Hunger On Fence, Irate Farmer, Comic, Small	235.00
Birthplace of Washington At Bridge's Creek, Westmoreland Co., Small	275.00
Brook Trout Fishing, Fisherman Pulling Trout From Stream, Small	275.00
Burning of Clipper Ship, Golden Light, Small	455.00
Camping Out, Some of The Right Sort, Men & Dogs, Large	1320.00 To 2750.00
Canal Scene, Moonlight, Man & Horse On Bank, Small	279.00
Cares of A Family, Large	238.00
Celebrated Clipper Dreadnought, Framed, 11 x 15 1/2 In.	220.00
Celebrated Trotting Mare, Hattie Woodward, Large	1795.00
Celebrated Trotting Stallions, Framed, Large Folio, 25 1/2 x 34 1/2 In.	715.00
Celebrated Trotting Team, Framed, Large Folio, 27 1/4 x 39 1/2 In.	440.00
Celebrated Winning Horses & Jockeys American Turf, Large	176.00
Cliff House, San Francisco, c.1860, 9 1/2 x 13 In.	1887.50
Clipper Ship, 3 Brothers, Small	395.00
Clipper Ship, Great Republic, Under Full Sail, Broadside, Small	375.00
Clipper Ship, Ocean Express, Norman Currier, 1856, Large	2475.00
Day Before Marriage, Brides Jewels, Seated, Small	79.00
Deacon's Mare Getting Word Go, Bad Boy, Sunday Morning, Comic, Small	215.00
Death of Gen. Zach. Taylor, 12th President, 1850, Small	95.00
Death of General Kearney, 12 1/2 x 9 1/2 In.	80.00
Falls of Niagara, From Clifton House, Small	229.00
Fiend of The Road, Framed, 1881, 19 1/2 x 27 1/2 In.	357.50
Flower Basket, Raspberries, Rose, Asters & Bluebells, 1872, Small	129.00 To 139.00
Flushing A Woodcock, 2 Spaniels, Autumn Colors, Small	295.00
Franklin Pierce, 14th President of The United States, Small	169.00
Fruits of The Golden Land, Small	195.00
George B. McClellan, Bust, Large	195.00
German Beauty, Black & Gold Frame, 12 x 16 In.	95.00
Going To The Miller, Boy On Horse, Grain Bags, Medium	465.00
Great Fire At Boston, Nov. 9–10, 1872, Small	395.00

Great West, Train Passing Through Mountain Valley, No, 38, Small 1125.00
Great West, Train Through Mountain Valley, Small 925.00
Grouse, Snip, Woodcock & Duck, F. Palmer, Large 985.00
Hiawatha's Wooing, Deer At Feet of Minnehaha, Poem, Large 465.00
High Bridge At Harlem, N.Y., Horse & Buggy, Viaduct, No. 7, Small 195.00
Home In The Country, Summer, Poem, Large 575.00
Home of The Deer, Large Buck, On Ledge, Medium 575.00
Indian Falls, New York, Autumn Colors, Small 79.00
Indian Lake, Sunset, Large 1475.00
Ivy Bridge, Pen & Ink Presentation, Framed, 12 3/4 x 17 In. 71.00
James K. Polk, 11th Pres. of U.S., Seated, Small 169.00
King of The Turf St. Julian, Large Folio, Framed, 1880, 29 3/4 x 37 3/4 In. 605.00
Lady of The Lake, Scotch Lady, In Boat, 4 Lines of Verse, Small 79.00
Life of A Fireman, The Ruins, Man Your Ropes, Large 1975.00
Life of Fireman, Fire Scene of Men & Equipment, Large 1395.00
Little Brothers & Sisters, Matted & Framed, 19 1/2 x 15 1/2 In. 94.00
Little Brothers, Red Coats 45.00
Little Sisters, 2 Girls Standing By Grape Arbor, Small 75.00
Little White Kittens, Matted, 9 3/4 x 14 In. 150.00
Lookout Mountain, Tenn. & Chattanooga Railroad, Large 7850.00
Maiden's Rock, Mississippi River, Small 425.00
Mammoth Iron Steamship Leviathan, 11500 Tons, Small 289.00
Man In Wagon, Cows, Home, No. 39, Small 365.00
Man That Kept The Bridge, Wagon, Blocking Others Crossing, Small 195.00
March of Miles Standish, Indian Leading Column, Baker, Large 375.00
Moonlight Promenade, 3 Couples On Path, Castle, Small 95.00
Moss Rose, 2 Dusty Pink Roses, Buds, 1847, Round Corners, Small 119.00
My Dear Little Pet, Fluffy White Kitten, Blond Girl, Small 95.00
Night By Campfire, Hunters & Dogs, Medium 495.00
Old Mill In Summer, Men Loading Wagon At Mill, Small 225.00
Old Oaken Bucket, Framed, 12 x 16 In. 148.00
Old Oaken Bucket, Hand Colored, Beveled Frame, 12 x 16 In. 449.00
Our Victorious Fleets In Cuban Waters, Large 1095.00
Outlet of Niagara River, Gorge & River View, Small 229.00
Pacing Horse Billy Boyce of St. Louis, 1868, Large 330.00
Partridge Shooting, Cross Corner Frame, 11 3/4 x 15 3/4 In. 385.00
Perry's Victory On Lake Erie, Fought Sept. 10, 1813, Small 595.00
Pride of The Garden, Vertical Metal Basket, Roses, Asters, Small 109.00
Queen of The Turf Maud, Large Folio, Frame, 29 3/4 x 37 3/4 In. 605.00
Raspberries, Full Plate & In Basket, Small 189.00
Rearing White Horse, Alexander, Held By Arab Handler, Small 185.00
Roadside Mill, Small Folio 154.00
Rosebud & Eglantine, Walnut Frame, 11 x 13 3/4 In. 125.00
Scenery of The Upper Mississippi, Indian Village, Framed, 13 x 17 In. 314.00
She Had So Many Children She Did Not Know What To Do, Dog & Puppies 135.00
Silver Cascade, White Mountains, Stream, 2 Couples, Small 295.00
Summer Evening, Family Watching Workers, Large 1985.00
Summer Evening, Man Driving Cattle Across Bridge, Small 159.00
Summer Night, Couple On Log, Moonlight Scene, Small 159.00
Through To The Pacific, Train Passing Town, Loggers, Small 875.00
Tomb & Shade of Napoleon 125.00
Tomb of Washington, Mt. Vernon, Va., People In Front, Medium 279.00
Trotting Queen Alix, Rubber Tired Sulky, Large 1495.00
U.S. Frigate Independence, New York City, Governors Island, Small 465.00
U.S. M. Steamship Arctic, Collins Line, Small 295.00
View of The Park, Fountain, City Hall, N.Y., 1846, Small 485.00
View On Hudson, Crow's Nest, Man Seated On Rocks, Small 225.00
Village Blacksmith, Man At Forge, Children, F. Palmer, Large 3975.00
William Prince of Orange, Landing At Torbay, Nov. 5, 1688, Small 149.00
Winter Scene, Small Folio, Framed 500.00
Wm. Penn's Treaty, Indians, Province of Penna., 1661, Small 275.00
Woodcock Shooting, 2 Hunters, 3 Dogs, English Style, Small 295.00
Woodlands In Winter, Boy & Girl On Snowy Path, Small 395.00

Young Sailor, Boy In Sailor Suit, Standing, Ship Background, Small 135.00

CUSTARD GLASS is a slightly yellow opaque glass. It was first made in the United States after 1886 at the La Belle Glass Works, Bridgeport, Ohio. It is being reproduced. Additional pieces may be found in the Cambridge, Fenton, Heisey, and Northwood categories.

Agronaut, Toothpick 300.00
Argonaut Shell, Creamer 160.00
Argonaut Shell, Pitcher 475.00
Argonaut Shell, Sauce 59.00
Argonaut Shell, Sugar, Cover 235.00
Beaded Circle, Pitcher 695.00
Beaded Circle, Tumbler 145.00
Bees In A Basket, Toothpick, Amethyst Bees, Gold Trim 60.00
Beggars Hand, Toothpick, Blue 25.00
Cherry Scale, Berry Set, 7 Piece 395.00
Cherry Scale, Spooner 110.00
Chrysanthemum Sprig, Berry Set, 7 Piece 400.00
Chrysanthemum Sprig, Berry Set, Blue, 6 Piece 750.00
Chrysanthemum Sprig, Bowl, Gold Trim, 5 x 11 In. 225.00
Chrysanthemum Sprig, Butter .... 250.00 To 285.00
Chrysanthemum Sprig, Butter, Dome Cover, Blue 1250.00
Chrysanthemum Sprig, Celery 650.00
Chrysanthemum Sprig, Compote 200.00
Chrysanthemum Sprig, Cruet, Gold Design, 7 In. 875.00
Chrysanthemum Sprig, Gold Leaves, Oval, Signed, 11 In. 165.00
Chrysanthemum Sprig, Pitcher, Script Signed 450.00
Chrysanthemum Sprig, Salt & Pepper 275.00
Chrysanthemum Sprig, Salt & Pepper, Blue 375.00
Chrysanthemum Sprig, Salt & Pepper, Cream 275.00
Chrysanthemum Sprig, Spooner 85.00
Chrysanthemum Sprig, Table Set, 4 Piece .... 370.00 To 485.00
Chrysanthemum Sprig, Table Set, Blue, 4 Piece 1450.00
Chrysanthemum Sprig, Toothpick .... 100.00 To 700.00
Chrysanthemum Sprig, Toothpick, Blue 725.00
Chrysanthemum Sprig, Toothpick, Cream 700.00
Chrysanthemum Sprig, Tray, Condiment 500.00
Chrysanthemum Sprig, Water Set, Blue, 5 Piece 1250.00
Circus Etch, Decanter 950.00
Diamond With Peg, Butter, Cover 285.00
Diamond With Peg, Toothpick 75.00
Dish, Fruit, Lake Wilson, Minn., Heisey 35.00
Everglades, Compote 185.00
Everglades, Tumbler 95.00
Fine Cut & Roses, Bowl, Nutmeg Stain 75.00
Fine Cut & Roses, Rose Bowl, Nutmeg Stain 90.00
Geneva, Sugar & Creamer 150.00
Geneva, Syrup, Green & Gold Design 295.00
Geneva, Water Set, Green & Red, 7 Piece 425.00
Georgia Gem, Pitcher, Green 95.00
Georgia Gem, Toothpick, Green 40.00
Georgia Gem, Toothpick, Peach Florals 125.00
Grape & Gothic Arches, Berry Bowl, 3 Small Bowls 265.00
Grape & Gothic Arches, Berry Set, 4 Piece .... 195.00 To 225.00
Grape & Gothic Arches, Tumbler, 4 In. 45.00
Intaglio, Berry Set, Gold Trim, 7 Piece 445.00
Intaglio, Compote .... 90.00 To 215.00
Intaglio, Cruet 315.00
Intaglio, Shaker, Pair 160.00
Intaglio, Sugar, Cover 110.00

Intaglio, Table Set, 4 Piece	425.00
Intaglio, Tumbler, Green	50.00
Inverted Fan & Feather, Berry Set, 5 Nappies, 9-In. Bowl	330.00
Inverted Fan & Feather, Sugar, Cover	225.00
Inverted Fan & Feather, Toothpick	600.00
Ivorina Verde pattern is in this category under Winged Scroll	
Jefferson Optic, Salt	65.00
Little Gem, see Georgia Gem pattern in this category	
Louis XV, Spooner	130.00
Louis XV, Spooner, Raised Flowers, Gold Trim	85.00
Louis XV, Table Set, 4 Piece	395.00
Maize is its own category in this book	
Maple Leaf, Butter, Cover	225.00
Maple Leaf, Butter, Cover, Gold Trim	395.00
Maple Leaf, Salt & Pepper	550.00
Maple Leaf, Spooner	175.00
Maple Leaf, Spooner	110.00
Maple Leaf, Sugar, Cover	185.00
Maple Leaf, Table Set, 4 Piece	650.00
Maple Leaf, Toothpick	900.00
Paperweight, State Hospital For Insane, St. Peters, Minn.	100.00
Peacock & Urn, Bowl, Ice Cream, Nutmeg Stain, 9 3/4 In.	325.00
Punty Band, Toothpick, Beaded Top, Clear	30.00
Punty Band, Toothpick, Gold Beads	75.00
Punty Band, Toothpick, Scalloped Top, Clear	35.00
Rolling Pin, Metal Screw End	365.00
Sowerby, Salt, Basketweave, Handles, 2 x 3 In.	60.00
State of Washington, Toothpick	85.00
Three Fruits, Bowl, Nutmeg Stain, Flared, Sawtooth Rim, 6 3/4 In.	95.00
Vermont, Candlestick, Jeweled	65.00
Wild Bouquet, Toothpick	850.00
Winged Scroll, Cruet	100.00
Winged Scroll, Dresser Set, Complete	2000.00
Winged Scroll, Table Set, Gold Trim, 4 Piece	395.00
Winged Scroll, Toothpick	100.00 To 125.00
Winged Scroll, Toothpick, Heisey	110.00
Wreath & Shell, Cuspidor, Woman's, White	55.00

CUT GLASS has been made since ancient times, but the large majority of the pieces now for sale date from the brilliant period of glass design, 1880 to 1905. These pieces have elaborate geometric designs with a deep miter cut. Modern cut glass with a similar appearance is being made in England, Ireland, and the Czech and Slovak republics. Chips and scratches are often difficult to notice but lower the value dramatically. A signature on the glass adds significantly to the value. Other cut glass pieces are listed under factory names.

Banana Boat, Brilliant, Sawtooth Rim, Hobstars	225.00
Banana Boat, Hunt's Royal, 11 1/2 x 8 In.	550.00
Banana Boat, Hunt, 11 In.	475.00
Banana Boat, Pedestal, Libbey	*Illus* 1700.00
Basket, Crosscut Diamonds, Hobstars, Feather-Filled Arches, 13 x 10 In.	1495.00
Basket, Floral & Rosette, Egginton, 18 In.	1500.00
Basket, Hobstar, Cane, Diamond Point, 6 In.	300.00
Biscuit Jar, Pinwheel Design	500.00
Bonbon Tray, Brilliant, Allover Hobstar Rosettes, Harvard, Sawtooth, 7 1/8 In.	125.00
Bonbon, Flutes, Beading, Intaglio Flowers, Center Handle	165.00
Bonbon, Silver Diamond Pattern, Handle	75.00
Bottle, Bar, Pillar Molded, Conical, 1850-1870	175.00
Bottle, Bitters, St. Louis, Hobstars & Cane, Stiler Stopper	325.00
Bowl, America Pattern, Fry, 8 x 4 In.	345.00
Bowl, Brilliant, 9 x 4 In.	154.00
Bowl, Clark, 4 In.	55.00
Bowl, Drape Pattern, L. Straus & Sons, 7 In.	145.00

Cut Glass, Banana Boat, Pedestal, Libbey   *Cut Glass, Vase, Floral, Turned*

Down Sides, 18 In.

Bowl, Eleanor Pattern, Hoare, 5 In. 185.00
Bowl, Geometric Design, Houndstooth Rim, Flaring Form, 10 1/4 In. 165.00
Bowl, Gilded Brass Filigree Cover, Amethyst To Clear, Stones & Pearls, 8 x 7 In. ... 225.00
Bowl, Hamilton Pattern 350.00
Bowl, Hat Shape, Overturned Rim, Cut Roses & Daisies, 6 x 4 In. 150.00
Bowl, Hobstars & Strawberry Diamonds, Silver Mount, 7 In. 355.00
Bowl, Strawberry, Diamond, 6 In. 275.00
Bowl, Tricolor, 9 In. 1100.00
Box, Puff, Mt. Vernon, Sterling, Floral Repousse, Brilliant 165.00
Bread Tray, Cornucopia, Bergen, 9 x 13 In. 950.00
Bread Tray, Floral, Strawberry–Diamond, Cane, Hoare, 13 In. 385.00
Bread Tray, Hobstars & Buttons, Sloped Ends, 11 x 4 1/4 In. 135.00
Butter, Domed Cover, Hobstars & Hobnails & Fans, 8 In. 435.00
Cake Stand, Intaglio Strawberries & Leaves, Pedestal, Sterling Silver Rim, 14 In. 1765.00
Cake Tray, Leaf Sprays, Daisies, 12 1/2 In. 195.00
Candlestick, Crosscut Diamond Point, Turned–Down Neck, 15 In., Pair 1250.00
Candlestick, Floral Gravic Cut, 9 In., Pair 525.00
Candlestick, Polished Pontil, 10 1/4 In., Pair 248.00
Candy Dish, Cover, Pinwheel, Fan & Crosshatching, Star Base, 5 In. 110.00
Celery Dish, Scalloped Rim, Hobstars, Western Cut Glass Co., 12 In. 330.00
Celery Vase, Roundels, Vertical Grooves, Hourglass, Panels, 1830–1870 .... 350.00
Center Bowl, 2–Part, Flared Punch Bowl Style, Pinwheel, 11 1/2 In. 192.50
Chalice, Flutes, Engraved, Thistle Shape, Pair 175.00
Champagne, Flute, Cut Stem, 1830–1880 .... 75.00
Champagne, Kalana Lily, Dorflinger, 5 1/4 In. 100.00
Champagne, Saucer, Ruby, Flutes, Reverse Baluster Stem 105.00
Champagne, Strawberry–Diamond, Flutes, Beehive Form Stem 250.00
Cheese Dish, Gothic Revival, Opaque White To Clear, 1840s 475.00
Clock, Leaves & Notching Allover, Ansonia, 5 3/4 In. 345.00
Compote Set, Alhambra Pattern, Footed, With 8 Sherbets 190.00
Compote, Alternating Bands of Cane & Hobstars, 6 In. 120.00
Compote, Design No. 17, Rolled–In Rim, Elmira, 6 x 9 1/2 In. 350.00
Compote, Harvard Sides, Scalloped Rim, Intaglio Flowers, Step Cut, 5 In., Pair 295.00
Compote, Marietta, Teardrop Stem, Averbeck, 8 In., Pair 500.00
Compote, Star of David Pattern, Hoare, 4 x 6 In. 55.00
Cruet, Diamond & Fan, Brilliant 50.00
Cruet, Double Circle, Green 125.00
Cruet, Hobs, Zipper, Notched Handle, Deep Step Cut Neck 98.00
Cruet, Zipper Cut Neck, Fan & Hobstars, 24–Point Star Base 60.00
Decanter, American Cut, Silver Plated Spout & Cover, Engraved, 11 1/2 In. 495.00

Decanter, Captain's, Squat Handled Jug, Arched Hobstars, 6 In. 385.00
Decanter, Crystal, Cranberry Flashed, Clear Stopper, 11 1/2 In. 60.00
Decanter, Cylindrical Blank, Flutes Below Crosscut Band, Blown Stopper 175.00
Decanter, Encore, 3 Neck Rings, Straus, 11 1/4 In. 535.00
Decanter, Faceted Stopper, English–Irish, Early 19th Century, 10 1/2 In., Pair 412.00
Decanter, Flattened Ovals, Fans, Cobalt Overlay Cut To Clear, Teardrop Stopper 225.00
Decanter, Flutes Below Silver Diamonds, Diamond Cut Neck, Stopper, Dorflinger ... 450.00
Decanter, Horn of Plenty, Mushroom Stopper, 9 In. 450.00
Decanter, Miters, Fans, Hobstars, Sterling Silver Neck & Rim, 11 In. 185.00
Decanter, Pineapples, Fans, Stars, 14 3/4 In. 195.00
Decanter, Ruby Over Clear, Club Shape, Engraved, New England 600.00
Decanter, Ruby Stain, Cut To Clear, Flute, Engraved, Boston & Sandwich 175.00
Decanter, Ruby To Clear, Curved Miter, Art Nouveau, Brilliant, 19th Century 350.00
Decanter, Santa Maria Pattern, L. Straus, 13 In. 575.00
Decanter, Strawberry–Diamond & Fans, Alternating Roundels, Blazes, Footed 350.00
Decanter, Strawberry–Diamond & Fans, Alternating Vesica & Blazes 325.00
Decanter, Strawberry–Diamond Below Radiating Ray Roundels, Bakewell, 1 Pt. 650.00
Decanter, Teardrop & Hobstar, 12 In. 1195.00
Decanter, Wine, Ireland, 1800, 10 1/2 In., Pair 357.00
Dessert Glass, Syllabub, Flute, Bladed Knop Stem 75.00
Dessert Set, Strawberry, Diamond & Fan, Master Bowl–12 In., 13 Piece 795.00
Dish, Ice Cream, Hobstars & Crosshatch, Sawtooth Rim, 14 1/2 In. 55.00
Dish, Ice Cream, Hobstars, Fans, 11 1/4 In. 125.00
Dish, Pickle, Harvard Sides, Thistles Intaglio Cut In Base, Scalloped Rim, 7 3/4 In. .. 125.00
Dish, Russian, Heart Shape, 7 In. 550.00
Dish, Sweetmeat, Flute, 1830–1850 .... 45.00
Epergne, Cherubs, Playing Porcelain Musical Instruments, England 660.00
Ewer, Grecian Form, Oinochoe, Frosted, England, 1850, Pair 825.00
Ewer, White To Ruby, Stylized Geometrical, W. H. B. Richardson, 1850–1865 .... 650.00
Finger Bowl, Band of Hobstars, Band of Fans, Base Star, Hoare 65.00
Flask, Engraved Rabbits In Woodland, Ovoid, Pewter Screw Lid, 6 1/2 In. 250.00
Flask, Whiskey, Woman's, Lay Down, Sterling Top 415.00
Goblet, Ashburton, Stemmed 120.00
Goblet, Huber Pattern 85.00
Goblet, Myrtle, Rayed Base, Pitkin & Brooks, 1904, 5 In., 8 Piece 295.00
Goblet, Vienna Secessionist, Fluted, Clear, Czechoslovakia, 4 Piece 600.00
Hair Receiver, Hobs, Sterling Silver Lid 98.00
Honey Pot, Underplate, Mt. Washington Pattern, 3 1/2 In. 465.00
Humidor, 2 Large Hobstars, Fans, Hobstar Base, Sterling Silver Lid, 7 In. 465.00
Humidor, Cranberry Cut To Clear, Dorflinger, 9 x 8 In. 6500.00
Ice Bucket, Geometric Design, Houndstooth Rim, 5 1/2 In. 145.00
Ice Bucket, Miter Diamond, 1860–1890 .... 195.00
Jar, Cigar, Harvard, 9 In. 550.00
Jar, Cover, Stars, Miters, Piecrust Rim, Scotland 135.00
Jar, Transparent Red Ribbed Body, Repeating Blossom, Cover, 6 In. 550.00
Jug, Central Diamond Band, Star Cut Base, Irish, 1850s, 5 3/4 In., Pair 325.00
Jug, Florentine Pattern, Sterling Silver Mounted, Bulbous, Dorflinger 950.00
Jug, Water, Brilliant, 7 In. 49.00
Lamp, Dome-Shaped Shade, Beaded Pendants, Circular Base, c.1900, 13 In. 500.00
Lamp, Table, Blossom & Cane, Crystal Prisms & Pedestal Base, 12 In. 880.00
Lamp, Table, Double Star, Hobstar & Fan, Dome Shade, 30 In. 1210.00
Nappy, Heart Shape, Somerset, 5 x 5 In. 95.00
Pitcher & Tumbler, Greek Key, Hobstars & Caning 675.00
Pitcher, Brilliant, Applied Handle, Libbey, 10 In. 185.00
Pitcher, Cover, Etched, Bulbous, 4 Tumblers 60.00
Pitcher, Crosshatched Triangles Below Blazes, Clear, 10 In. 595.00
Pitcher, Daisies & Branches, Hobstar Base, Notch Handle, 1890, 9 In. 220.00
Pitcher, Flutes & Neck Prisms, 10 In. 400.00
Pitcher, Milk, Plymouth, Triple Spout, Hobstar Base, Pitkin & Brooks, 9 1/4 In. 525.00
Pitcher, Triple Miter Cane, Rayed Base, 6 In. 355.00
Plate, Cluster, 10 In. 415.00
Plate, Double Miter Strawberry–Diamond Field, 7 In. 235.00
Plate, Victrola, Floral Center, Hobstar Border, Dorflinger, 10 In. 110.00

Pokal, Clear, Cranberry Flashed, 15 In. 126.00
Powder Dish, Lid, Crosshatching, Fans, 16–Point Star Center Base 85.00
Powder Jar, Amethyst, Czechoslovakia 70.00
Powder Jar, Sterling Floral Repousse Lid, Gorham 170.00
Punch Bowl & Base, Pinwheels, Hobstars, Fans & Crosshatching, 12 In. 750.00
Punch Bowl, Diamond & Fans, Deep Cut Leaves & Flowers, 11 In. 40.00
Punch Bowl, Hobstars, Sawtooth, Zipper, Stand, 12 In. 900.00
Punch Bowl, Ivy, Low Footed, J. D. Bergen Co., 12 In. 2350.00
Punch Bowl, Occidental, Averback 4850.00
Punch Cup, Flutes, Short Stem, Handle 55.00
Punch Cup, Honeycomb, Concave Hexagons 135.00
Rose Bowl, Middlesex, Dorflinger, 7 1/2 x 8 In. 440.00
Salt & Pepper, Notched Prism, Sterling Top, 1 3/4 In. 49.00
Salt, Amethyst, Allover Miter Diamond Pattern 175.00
Salt, Cane & Notched Prism, Sterling Silver Rim, 2 1/4 In. 60.00
Salt, Crosshatching & Fans, Hobstar Base, 3 1/4 In. 85.00
Salt, Individual, 1 1/2 x 3/4 In., 12 Piece 125.00
Salt, Sawtooth, Sterling Silver Rim, 1 3/4 In. 43.00
Spooner, Child's, Allover Hobstars, Buttons & Cross–Hatching, 3 1/2 In. 195.00
Spooner, Notched Vertical Bands, Rim Serration, 4 3/4 In. 100.00
Spooner, Strawberry–Diamond, Demitasse, 3 1/2 In. 95.00
String Holder, Gorham Top, Straus, 2 1/2 In. 250.00
Sugar & Creamer, Clark, 6 1/2 In. 115.00
Sugar & Creamer, Floral, Hoare 220.00
Sugar & Creamer, Pedestal, Hobstar Diamond, 1 Pt. 325.00
Sugar, Waffle & Prism, 1850s 90.00
Syrup, Glenwood, Bergen, 4 3/4 In. 345.00
Tankard, American Brilliant, Cranberry Cut To Clear, 12 In. 6500.00
Toothpick, Fan Design 22.50
Tray, Allover Hobstar Clusters, Vesicas, 12 In. 575.00
Tray, Ice Cream, Allover Strawberry–Diamond, 16 x 9 In. 250.00
Tumbler, Panels, Huber Or Bohemian, 19th Century 55.00
Tumbler, Water, Brilliant, Deep Cut Flowers, Butterfly 75.00
Vase, Allover Hobstars, Buttons, Crosshatching, Notched Rim, 3 1/2 In. 110.00
Vase, Bands of Hobs Midsection, Engraved Floral Top, Hunt, 12 In. 425.00
Vase, Copper Wheel Engraving of Birds & Foliage, Handles, 16 In. 2400.00
Vase, Corset Shape, Hobstar Diamond, 1 Ft. 550.00
Vase, Diamond & Fan, Everted Rim, Cut Flower Petal On Bottom, 13 In. 465.00
Vase, Fans, Hobstars & Prisms, Alternate Triangular Design, Dorflinger, 5 In. 275.00
Vase, Flared Cylindrical Parasol Stand, Alternating Hobstar, 26 In. 5775.00
Vase, Floral, Harvard, 10 In. 65.00
Vase, Floral, Turned Down Sides, 18 In. ....*Illus* 1900.00
Vase, Flower & Harvard, Cosmos Blossoms, Sawtooth Rim, 16 1/4 x 6 3/4 In. 480.00
Vase, Green, Bohemian, 8 1/2 In. 110.00
Vase, Intaglio Cut Florals & Leaves Allover, Blue Base, Clark, 9 3/4 In. 245.00
Vase, Intaglio Cut, Iris Buds & Stems, Scalloped Base, 12 3/4 In. 195.00
Vase, Intaglio Florals & Leaves, Clear, Blue Base, Clark, 9 3/4 In. 110.00
Vase, Pillar & Miter, Baroque Revival, Scalloped Foot, 10 In. 350.00
Vase, Sawtooth, Tapered Down To 3–In. Base, Waterford, 6 x 6 In. 125.00
Vase, Scalloped, Paneled Stem, Star Cut Foot, 14 In. 175.00
Vase, Squat Bowl, Ruffled Crimped Rim, Sapphire Blue, White, 5 1/2 In. 440.00
Vase, Sunflowers & Foliage, Everted Notched Rim, c.1815, 20 In. 715.00
Vase, Trumpet, Sterling Silver Rim, Dorflinger, 10 In. 900.00
Wall Pocket, Green Bottle Glass, 19th Century 200.00
Water Set, Harvard 600.00
Whiskey, Hindoo, Hoare 65.00
Wine, Argus Pattern, 3 Rows of Panels, Faceted Baluster Stem 115.00
Wine, Assyrian, Cranberry To Clear, Bergen, Pair 750.00
Wine, Clear, Copper Wheel Floral Band, Different Color Flashed, 6 3/8 In., 6 Piece 135.00
Wine, Flutes & Horizontal Prismatic Steps, Bladed Knop Stem 85.00
Wine, Honeycomb, Concave Hexagon, Baluster Stem, Dorflinger, 4 Piece 475.00
Wine, Intersecting Rows, Offset Flutes, Faceted French Stem 105.00
Wine, Kalana Lily Etched, Dorflinger, Pair 120.00

Wine, Monarch, Cranberry Cut To Clear, Hoare, Pair 600.00
Wine, Rooster, Dorflinger, Footed 45.00

CYBIS porcelain is a twentieth-century product. Boleslaw Cybis came to
the United States from Poland in 1939. He started making porcelains in
Long Island, New York, in 1940. He moved to Trenton, New Jersey, in
1942 as one of the founders of Cordey China Co. and started his own
Cybis Porcelains about 1950. The firm is still working. (See also Cordey.)

CYBIS

Figurine, Albino Buffalo, Wooden Plinth, 4 In. 135.00
Figurine, Beetle, Pink Flowers 82.50
Figurine, Circus Elephant, 7 In. 220.00
Figurine, Elf On Frog, 6 x 4 In. 220.00
Figurine, Male Jogger, 14 1/2 In. 550.00
Figurine, Squirrel, Bushy Tail 250.00
Figurine, Wood Wren, On Dogwood 500.00

CZECHOSLOVAKIA is a popular term with collectors. The name, first
used as a mark after the country was formed in 1918, appears on glass and
porcelain and other decorative items. The name is still used in some
trademarks.

Ashtray, China Lady By Basket 23.00
Bell, Flower, Red, Green, 3 3/4 In. 55.00
Bowl, Blue & Gold Iridescent, Blown, Ball Footed, 4 1/2 x 9 In. 220.00
Bowl, Pedestal, Black & White Glass 165.00
Box, Cover, Triangular, Erphila, Terra-Cotta, Green, Orange, Blue Enamel 110.00
Bracelet, Enameled Filigree, Topaz Link 40.00
Bracelet, Ruby Glass 35.00
Buckle & Brooch, Enameled Brass, Blue Cabochon 60.00
Candlestick, Multicolor Floral, White, Pottery, Signed 185.00
Canister Set, Luster, 10 Piece 100.00
Cup & Saucer, Sugar, Creamer, White, Gold, Terra-Cotta, P & S, 18 Piece 200.00
Locket, Glass, With Doll Rosary Inside 9.00
Perfume Bottle, Atomizer, Etched Amber, Pyralin Base 68.00
Perfume Bottle, Blue Cut Glass, Fan Stopper, 4 1/4 In. 160.00
Perfume Bottle, Crystal 75.00
Perfume Bottle, Crystal, Prism Stopper, 5 1/2 In. 50.00
Perfume Bottle, Cut Glass, Cut Stopper 150.00
Perfume Bottle, Cut Glass, Feather Cut Stopper, 6 In. 75.00
Perfume Bottle, Green Cut Glass, Clear Stopper, 2 1/4 In. 22.00
Perfume Bottle, Nudes Molded Each Side 660.00
Perfume Bottle, Opaque White, Brown & Beige, Screw Top, 7 1/2 In. 35.00
Perfume Bottle, Orange, Black 110.00
Perfume Bottle, Pink Cut Glass, Stopper, Art Deco, 6 1/4 In. 125.00
Perfume Bottle, Powder Jar, Atomizer, Grecian Lady Stopper, Cut Glass 650.00
Perfume Bottle, Purple Cut Glass, Arrow Stopper 120.00
Tray, Dresser, Pink Roses, Pale Green, 2 Handles, 5 x 12 In. 50.00
Vase, Art Glass, Blue & Pink, Melon Shape, 7 In. ....*Illus* 3900.00
Vase, Aventurine, Green, 6 In. 145.00
Vase, Blue, Black & White Enameling, Red Ground, Signed, 7 In. 265.00
Vase, Cameo, Pink, Red Floral Cutting, 6 In. 850.00
Vase, Fan, Pink & White, Black Rim, Art Glass, 7 1/2 In. 225.00
Vase, Floral, Joseph Fleider, 5 In. 45.00
Vase, Golden Amber Glass, Octagonal Foot, Flared, Signed, 5 3/4 In. 34.00
Vase, Orange & Black, 8 In. 60.00
Vase, Yellow Glass, Black Vertical Lines, 8 1/4 In. 38.00

D'ARGENTAL is a mark used in France by the Compagnie des Cristalleries
de St. Louis. The firm made multilayered, acid-cut cameo glass in the late
nineteenth and twentieth centuries. D'Argental is the French name for the
city of Munzthal, home of the glassworks. Later they made enameled
etched glass.

Lamp, Cameo, Scenic, 17 In. ....*Illus* 4900.00
Lamp, Domed Shade, Wooded Lake Scene, 23 1/2 In. 9900.00

Czechoslovakia, Vase, Art Glass,

Blue & Pink, Melon Shape, 7 In.

Don't use ammonia on glasses
with gold or silver decorations.

Spray a glass flower vase with
nonstick food spray. It will
keep the water from staining
the glass.

Vase, 3 Scenic Panels, Fisherman In Boat, Orange, Green, Frosted, 12 In.	6500.00
Vase, Baluster, Yellow, Tulips, Leaves, Ferns, Signed, Cameo Glass, 12 5/8 In.	1980.00
Vase, Bowl Shape, 4 In.	450.00
Vase, Cameo, Floral, Orange & Green, Pedestal, 6 In.	700.00
Vase, Cameo, Gray, Lemon, Cherry, Scenic, 1915, 9 3/4 In.	1320.00
Vase, Carved Purple Foxgloves, Frosted Ground, 9 1/4 In.	1150.00
Vase, Floral, Orange & Green, Pedestal, 6 In.	700.00
Vase, Purple Floral, White Ground, Signed, 7 In.	750.00

DANIEL BOONE, a pre–revolutionary war folk hero, was a surveyor,
trapper, and frontiersman. A television series, which ran from 1964 to
1970, was based on his life and starred Fess Parker. All types of Daniel
Boone memorabilia is collected.

Book, Comic, 1964	8.00
Book, Opening of The Wilderness, John Mason Brown, Random House, 1952	2.00
Book, Young Hunter & Tracker, Soft Cover, Robert Doremus Pub., 1943	2.00
Lunch Box, Fess Parker, 1965	155.00

D'Argental, Lamp, Cameo, Scenic, 17 In.

Glassware, old or new, requires careful handling. Stand
each piece upright, not touching another. Never nest pieces.
Wash in moderately hot water
and mild detergent. Avoid wiping gold or platinum banded
pieces while glasses are hot.
Never use scouring pads or silver polish on glass. When using
an automatic dishwasher, be
sure the water temperature is
under 180 degrees.

Shoes, Boy's, High Top, Leather, Not Worn, Size 6, Box 90.00

DAUM, a glassworks in Nancy, France, was started by Jean Daum in 1875. The company, now called *Cristalleries de Nancy,* is still working. The *Daum Nancy* mark has been used in many variations. The name of the city and the artist are usually both included.

Bottle, Cachet, Water Lilies, Blue, Gold Trim, Squared Handle Top, 3 In. 2900.00
Bottle, Smelling Salts, Signed 2100.00
Bowl, Crystal, Free–Form, Signed, 14 1/2 x 5 In. 175.00
Bowl, Oak Leaves, Acorns, Insects, 9 In. 7250.00
Bowl, Orange & Purple Mottling, Footed, Signed, 3 1/4 x 5 1/2 In. 265.00
Bowl, Orchids, 4 Colors, 7 In. 1975.00
Bowl, Set In Majorelle, Armature, Foil Inclusions, Marked, 10 1/2 In. 1650.00
Bowl, Summer Scene, 5 x 6 x 7 In. 2900.00
Bowl, Trees & Lake Design, Rectangular 3500.00
Box, Cover, Circular, Grape Vine, Mottled Ground, Cameo Signed, 3 3/4 In. 935.00
Coin Receiver, Lotus Blossoms, Dragonfly Overhead, Signed, c.1900, 7 7/8 In. 9350.00
Compote, Textured Finish, Clear, Circular, Black Base, 11 1/2 In. 460.00
Creamer, Frosted Scene, Gold Trim Top, Signed, 2 7/8 In. 995.00
Creamer, Mottled Gold, Brown Frosted Ground, Signed, 3 1/8 In. 1500.00
Cup & Saucer, Black Ships & Village Scene, Frosted, Demitasse 675.00
Decanter, Corn Flowers & Bees, Frosted Body, Gilt, Stopper, 4 3/4 In. 2420.00
Lamp, Acid–Etched Glass, Domed Shade, Flaring Foot, 17 1/2 In. 7700.00
Lamp, Floriform, Bell Shade, Scrolled Arm, Iron Leaf Base, Signed, 1910, 18 3/4 In. .. 8250.00
Lamp, Lake Shore, Domed Shade, 3–Armed Iron Mount, Signed, 1910, 18 In. 12100.00
Pitcher, Mottled Gold, Frosted Ground, Leaves & Berries, Signed, 3 1/8 In. 1500.00
Scent Bottle, Cameo, Clear, Orange Overlay, Daisies, Silver Mount, 1910, 3 3/4 In. . 498.00
Toothpick, Bleeding Hearts, Green Leaves & Stems, Chipped Ice, Gold Rim 450.00
Toothpick, Cameo Flowers, Gold 550.00
Tumbler, Mistletoe In Cameo, Frosted Blue, White Berries, Gold, 4 3/4 In. 775.00
Tumbler, Water Lilies, Pale Blue, 4 1/2 In. 1200.00
Vase, Balluster, Bulbous Foot, Flaring Neck, Marked, 1898, 18 In. 990.00
Vase, Barrel Shape, Marked, 3 1/4 In. 700.00
Vase, Bell Shape, V Pattern, Topaz, 7 In. 385.00
Vase, Berluze, Red & Pink, Signed, 18 In. 975.00
Vase, Berries, Leaf Clusters, Autumnal Colors, Striated, Cameo, 20 In. 2200.00
Vase, Bleeding Hearts, Gray, Streaked Rose, Orange, Signed, 1915, 11 In. 852.00
Vase, Blown–Out Design of Tear Drops, 12 In. 1540.00
Vase, Bud, Enameled Thistle Blossoms, Bulbous Base, Neck, 1910, 4 1/4 In. 550.00
Vase, Cameo, Cylindrical, Gray, Pale Yellow, Rose, Blossoms, c.1900, 9 In. 1210.00
Vase, Carved Berries & Leaves, Fall Colors, Yellow & Brown, 8 In. 1075.00
Vase, Carved Berries & Leaves, Hammered Ground, 12 In. 7700.00
Vase, Charcoal & Raspberry, Enameled Grape Vines, Cameo, 1900, 4 1/2 In. 1100.00
Vase, Cherry Red Thistle Blossoms, Green Ground, Cameo, Signed, 4 1/2 In. 750.00
Vase, Clematis Vine, Clear Body, Enameled, 12 5/8 In. 1100.00
Vase, Clusters of Grapes, Trailing Vines, Signed, c.1910, 17 1/8 In. 3100.00
Vase, Cut Wildflowers In Reds, Mottled Ground, Silver Foot, 4 3/4 x 5 In. 1950.00
Vase, Enameled Bleeding Hearts, Gray, Cameo, Iron Mount, 1915, 11 1/4 In. 852.00
Vase, Enameled Thistle Blossoms, Green & Fuchsia Stripes, Signed, 18 7/8in. 990.00
Vase, Enameled Winter Forest Scene, Signed, 3 1/4 In. 1320.00
Vase, Enameled Wooded Forest Scene, Mountain Tops, Signed, 3 1/4 In. 825.00
Vase, Etched Freesia, Spiked Leaves, Yellow, Amethyst, Amber, Cameo, 5 1/2 In. ... 1760.00
Vase, Etched Winter Wooded Scene, Yellow Ground, Signed, 11 3/4 In. 1430.00
Vase, Fighting Dragons, Central Band, Black, 6 1/2 In. 825.00
Vase, Floral, Dark Base, Cameo, Footed, 1910 ....*Illus* 4675.00
Vase, Floral, Gold Accents, Cross of Lorraine, Green, 7 In. 950.00
Vase, Floral, Lavender, 5 In. 1200.00
Vase, Geometric, Gray, Gold Foil, Iron Frame, 1925, 4 3/4 In. 1200.00
Vase, Grapes, Cameo, Footed, 1910 ....*Illus* 3080.00
Vase, Harbor, Sunset, Yellow, Orange, Green, Mottled, Cameo, 5 1/2 x 8 1/2 In. 2530.00
Vase, Iris Blossoms, Bee, Silver–Gilt Footed Base, Cameo, 1900, 3 7/8 In. 880.00
Vase, Landscape Scene, Cameo, 1915 ....*Illus* 2750.00
Vase, Landscape, Clear, Green, Olive, Enameled, Rolling Meadow, 1910, 7 In. 1100.00

Daum, Vase, Floral, Dark Base, Cameo, Footed, 1910

Daum, Vase, Grapes, Cameo, Footed, 1910

Daum, Vase, Landscape Scene, Cameo, 1915

Daum, Vase, Summer Scene, Cameo, 10 In.

Vase, Landscape, Green Floral Design, Hammered Ground, 7 In. 2100.00
Vase, Landscape, Meadow, Lime & Olive Green, Cameo, Square, 1910, 6 3/4 In. 1100.00
Vase, Landscape, River, Trees In Foreground, Signed, c.1910, 6 In. 2200.00
Vase, Landscape, Snow Covered Winter, Signed, c.1910, 4 5/8 In. 1320.00
Vase, Landscape, Spring, Bell Form, Signed, c.1910, 5 1/8 In. 2475.00
Vase, Landscape, Stormy Wooded, Rain, Signed, 9 1/8 In. 2230.00
Vase, Landscape, Trees, Boats, Brown & Oranges, 6 In. 1250.00
Vase, Landscape, Trees, Sailboats, Mottled Orange Ground, Signed, 5 1/2 In. 1000.00
Vase, Landscape, Winter Scene, Signed, 5 In. 2400.00
Vase, Landscape, Woodland, Trees In Foreground, Signed, c.1915, 22 1/2 In. 2950.00
Vase, Leaf & Berry, 12 In. 7700.00
Vase, Leaf & Flower Design, Red Cut To Yellow, 23 In. 1450.00
Vase, Mottled Gold, Amethyst & Clear, Cottonwood Limbs & Leaves, 23 In. 8500.00
Vase, Mottled Gold, Wheel Cut Blossoms & Buds, Green, 5 1/4 x 5 In. 4500.00
Vase, Mottled Gray, Footed, Square, Rolled Rim, Cameo, 1910, 4 1/2 In. 1540.00
Vase, Pendent Lilies-of-The-Valley, Grasses, Colored Overlay, Signed, 13 1/8 In. 1980.00
Vase, Rose Hips, Branches, Enameled, Yellow, White, Amethyst, Cameo, 5 In. 1100.00
Vase, Spherical, Clear Glass Sides, Mottled White, Pink, 3 5/8 In. 8250.00
Vase, Summer Scene, 6 x 7 In. 2900.00
Vase, Summer Scene, Cameo, 10 In. ....*Illus* 1600.00
Vase, Thistle Design, Gold Enameled, Diamond Shape, Cameo, 7 1/8 In. 225.00
Vase, Tiger Lilies & Leaves, Cylindrical, Knobbed Base, Signed, c.1910, 19 In. 4675.00
Vase, Trumpet, Acid Washed, Mottled Orange Yellow, Maroon, Green, 8 1/2 In. 660.00
Vase, Twisted Rope Glass, Pedestal, Bowl Shape, 6 x 7 1/4 In. 175.00
Vase, Twisted Rope, Turned Over Rim, Controlled Bubbles At Throat, Signed, 6 In. .. 175.00
Vase, Wildflowers, Leaves & Grasses, Pear Shaped, Signed, c.1910, 14 3/4 In. 2420.00
Vase, Yellow Horizontal Band, Marked, 11 In. 2420.00
Whiskey, Enameled Dragonfly, Moth & Florals 495.00

DAVENPORT pottery and porcelain were made at the Davenport factory in Longport, Staffordshire, England, from 1793 to 1887. Earthenwares, creamwares, porcelains, ironstone, and other ceramics were made. Most of the pieces are marked with a form of the word *Davenport*.

DAVENPORT
LONGPORT
STAFFORDSHIRE

Bulb Pot, Cover, Bridge, Waterfall, Cottage At Sides, 1807, 7 1/2 In.	2475.00
Pitcher, Caneware, Coastal Landscape, Blue Rim & Handle, c.1800, 5 1/4 In.	82.00
Plate, Gilt Geometric & Floral Design, Orange Ground, 9 1/2 In., Pair	245.00
Tureen, Sauce, Pearlware, Twig Handles, Ladle, 1810, 7 x 8 In.	1760.00

DAVY CROCKETT, the American frontiersman, was born in 1786 and died in 1836. He became popular in 1954 with the introduction of a television series about his life. Coonskin caps and buckskins became popular and hundreds of different Davy Crockett items were made.

Alamo Express Fix It Stagecoach & 2 Horses, Original Box	175.00
Bank, Dime, Tin Lithograph, Square, 2 1/2 In.	152.00
Bank, Pony Express Saddlebag, Package	25.00
Bed Sheet, Child's Illustrations of Davy	110.00
Belt, Leather, On Card, 1950s	60.00
Book, Ballad of Davy Crockett Song Book, Fess Parker Cover, 1955	12.00
Bowl	20.00
Bracelet, ID, Alamo, Box	95.00
Cap, Coonskin	25.00
Card, Gum, Fess Parker, Buddy Photographs, 52 Different, 1950s	46.00
Clock, Revolving Lamp, Metal, Davy Figure, Lighted Screen, United, 1950s	454.00
Cookie Jar, Boy, American Bisque	350.00
Cookie Jar, Brush .... 235.00 To	350.00
Cookie Jar, Davy In The Woods, American Bisque .... 795.00 To	1100.00
Cookie Jar, Gold Trim, Regal China .... 385.00 To	550.00
Cookie Jar, McCoy, Box	750.00
Cookie Jar, Shawnee	475.00
Cup	20.00
Cup & Bowl, Milk Glass	20.00
Dispatch Case, Neptune, Plastic, 1950s	39.00
Figure, Remco	65.00
Guitar, Box	200.00
Guitar, Walt Disney Official, Reliable, Box	50.00
Heat Lamp, Cylinder of Pictures of Davy, Indian, Bear, Forest Scene, Iron	250.00
Kit, Mule Team, Box	40.00
Lamp Base, Metal, 11 In.	90.00
Lamp, Cylinder, Forest Scene, Rotate Heat Type, Iron Legs	250.00
Lamp, Figural, Composition, Original Shade	125.00
Lamp, Figural, Copper Metal, Original Shade	125.00
Lamp, Figural, Tree & Bear, Ceramic, Shade, 1950s, 16 In.	182.00
Lamp, Premco, 1955	150.00
Lunch Box, American Thermos, Green Rim, 1955	59.00
Lunch Box, With Kit Carson	250.00
Mug & Bowl, Milk Glass	25.00
Mug, Brush	55.00
Napkin, Official, 5 x 5 In., Box	15.00
Patches, Round	10.00
Pencil Box, Fess Parker	35.00
Pin, Rifle Sharp Shooter, On Card	35.00
Play Suit, Coonskin Hat, Powder Horn, Seneca Mfg., Box	75.00
Projector Gun, 4 Films, Fess Parker Picture, Box	120.00
Puzzle, Davy In Forest Scene, Premium, 1950s	25.00
Puzzle, Set of 3	65.00
Saddle Bag, Pony Express, Package	45.00
Sheet Music, Ballad of Davy Crockett	8.00
Spurs, Pair	195.00
Stool	40.00
Suit, Fringed, Picture, Name	35.00
Sunglasses, 2 Plastic Guns On Rim, Plastic, 1950s	45.00

Target Game, Hand Held, 2 Feather Darts, Box	75.00
Toy, Express Fit It Stagecoach, 2 Horses, Alamo, Box	175.00
Tumbler, 6 1/2 In.	10.00
Tumbler, Indian Fighter, Disney	10.00
Tumbler, Swanky, Crystal, Red, 6 In.	15.00
Wristwatch, Brown Leather Strap, Crystal & Green, WDP, 1950s	85.00
Wristwatch, Davy Face, Powder Horn Mount, Walt Disney	275.00
Wristwatch, Moving Gun, Muros	265.00
Wristwatch, On Card, 1950s	6.00

DE MORGAN art pottery was made in England by William De Morgan from the 1860s to 1907. He is best known for his luster-glazed Moorish-inspired pieces. The pottery used a variety of marks.

Tile, Green & Blue Peacock, High Glazed, Framed, 6 In.	358.00

DE VEZ was a signature used on cameo glass after 1910. E. S. Monot founded the glass company near Paris in 1851. The company changed names many times. Mt. Joye, another glass by this factory, is listed in its own category.

Shade, Cameo, Silk Cords, 16 In.	550.00
Vase, Bird On Pine Branch, Pine Cones At Top, Signed, 7 In.	825.00
Vase, Cameo, Mountain, Gray, Lemon Mottled, Cylindrical, 1920, 10 3/8 In.	1210.00
Vase, Chinese Junks, Scenic, 7 3/4 In.	1400.00
Vase, Flowers Growing Up Sides, 12 In.	750.00
Vase, Mosque & Palm Trees, Pink, Brown & Yellow, 6 3/8 In.	925.00
Vase, Pine Trees, Navy, Pink & Yellow, 6 In.	525.00

DECOYS are carved or turned wooden copies of birds or fish. The decoy was placed in the water or propped on the shore to lure flying birds to the pond for hunters. Some decoys are handmade, some are commercial products. Today there is a group of artists making modern decoys for display, not for use in a pond.

American Brant, Hollow Cedar, Inlet Bill, Original Paint, Cobb Island, 18 In.	715.00
Black Bellied Plover, Elmer Crowell	5225.00
Black Bellied Plover, Glass Eye, Spring Plumage, Mason, 1905	2750.00
Black Duck, A. R. Crowell & Son, 2 1/2 x 3 1/2 In.	495.00
Black Duck, Glass Eye, Original Paint, Mason, 1910	600.00
Black Duck, Hollow, Harry V. Shourds, 1890	3750.00
Black Duck, M. Collins	165.00
Black Duck, Original Paint, A. Elmer Crowell, 1915	3250.00
Black Duck, Original Paint, Joseph Lincoln, 1900	8500.00
Black Duck, Preening, Gus Wilson, 1935	8500.00
Black Duck, Primitive, Original Paint, 20 In.	55.00
Blue Goose, Ben Schmidt, 1920s	1650.00
Blue Wing Teal Hen, Vergle Hodge, Carved Wood	303.00
Blue Wing Teal, John Daddy Holly, Havre De Grace, Maryland, 1880–1890	7150.00
Bluebill Drake & Hen, Glass Eye, Fat Bodied, Mason, 1910, Pair	1350.00
Bluebill Drake, Balsa Body, Glass Eyes, Hinged Lead Weight, 13 In.	49.00
Bluebill Drake, Cork Block & Wooden Head, Original Paint, Glass Eyes, 15 1/2 In.	44.00
Bluebill Drake, Hollow, Lou Barkelow, 1900	750.00
Bluebill Drake, John Mulak	220.00
Bluebill Drake, Repaint, Glass Eyes, Frank Schmidt, 14 1/2 In.	45.00
Bluebill Drake, Thomas Humberstone, Wooden, Cork, Worn, Glass Eyes, 12 1/2 In.	35.00
Bluebill Drake, Working, Repaint, Glass Eyes, 14 In.	99.00
Bluebill Hen, Hollow, Original Paint, Bold Feathering, Mason, 1900	3000.00
Bluebill Hen, Sleeper, Glass Eyes, Chuck Van Heck, 11 1/2 In.	40.00
Bluebill Hen, Working, Original Paint, Glass Eyes	27.00
Bluebill, Swimming, Worn Repaint, Glass Eyes, Nailed Head, 15 1/4 In.	65.00
Bluebill, Working, Repaint, Glass Eyes, 11 1/2 In.	27.00
Brandt, Cork Body, Wooden Head, Glass Eyes, 19 In.	25.00
Broadbill Drake, Madison Mitchell	205.00
Canada Goose, Carved Head, 27 In.	60.00
Canada Goose, Cedar, Lead Weight, Leather Thong, Barnegat Bay, 23 In.	770.00

Canada Goose, Charles Pitman, 1980 .... 1250.00
Canada Goose, Dodge, Repaired, 1890 .... 1950.00
Canada Goose, Prince Edward Island, Canada, Oversized, Original Paint 1100.00
Canada Goose, Stick–Up, Neck In Feeding Position, Solid Construction 357.00
Canada Goose, Stretched Canvas Over Wooden Frame, George Boyd, 1920 .... 6500.00
Canada Goose, Swimming, Cedar, Root Head & Neck 825.00
Canada Goose, Swimming, Glass Eyes, 24 In. 55.00
Canvasback Drake, Balsa & Pine, Snakey Head, Glass Eyes, 15 In. 40.00
Canvasback Drake, Captain Harry Jobes, Maryland 110.00
Canvasback Drake, Factory, Head Nailed, 15 3/4 In. 115.00
Canvasback Drake, Glass Eye, Shot Scars, 18 In. 200.00
Canvasback Drake, Glass Eyes, 16 3/4 In. 15.00
Canvasback Drake, Original Paint, Glass Eyes, 16 In. 55.00
Canvasback Drake, Weathered Paint, Tack Eyes, Canada, 14 In. 35.00
Canvasback Duck, Bob McGaw 3410.00
Canvasback Duck, Dodge 65.00
Canvasback Duck, Schoenheider Jr. 200.00
Canvasback Hen, Glass Eyes, 18 1/2 In. 75.00
Canvasback Hen, Solid Body, Original Paint, Mason, 1900 .... 2350.00
Coot, Matronly Profile, Original Paint, 12 1/2 In. 50.00
Crow, Glass Eye, Original Paint, Mason Wire Mount, 1910 .... 1600.00
Crow, Sculptural, Tack Eyes, Black Paint, 14 1/2 In. 302.00
Crow, Wire Stand, Herter, 1940s 250.00
Duck, Black, Original Paint, Feather Detail, Glass Eyes, 15 In. 104.00
Duck, Flattie–Floaty Black, Set of 3 .... 185.00
Duck, Homemade Soldered Seams, Tin, 17 In. 104.00
Duck, Leather 65.00
Duck, Silhouette, Sheet Iron 95.00
Egret, Courtney Allen N. Truro, Signed Base, 18 1/2 In. 495.00
Fish, Bass, Green Stippled Finish, Jim Rosin, 8 In. 250.00
Fish, Bass, Wood & Copper, 1–Piece Body, Stamped CA, 10 3/4 In. 55.00
Fish, Brook Trout, Mark Brunning, 8 1/2 In. 75.00
Fish, Bufflehead, Hand Carved, Bob White, 10 In. 65.00
Fish, Carved Antler 25.00
Fish, Catfish, Blue, Chuck Meldrum 50.00
Fish, Minnow, Jud DeRay, 6 In. 35.00
Fish, Minnow, Rolf Upjorden, 3 In. 50.00
Fish, Perch, Hedden Bait Co., 5 1/4 In. 150.00
Fish, Pickerel, Wood & Tin, Glass Eyes, Articulated Body, 18 In. 83.00
Fish, Pike, Black Scaled Back, Red & Orange, Ernie Newman, 9 In. 350.00
Fish, Pike, Randall Factory 145.00
Fish, Sucker, Ray Veihl, 6 In. 150.00
Fish, Sucker, Spotted, Bud Stewart, 8 In. 250.00
Fish, Sunfish, Curved Tail, Metal Fins, Glass Eyes, Wooden, 7 1/2 In. 220.00
Fish, Trout, Lloyd Lewis, 7 3/4 In. 125.00
Fish, Trout, Wood & Tin, Glass Eyes, 1–Piece Body, 8 3/4 In. 110.00
Fish, Trout, Wood & Tin, Glass Eyes, 3–Section Articulated Body, 9 In. 155.00
Fish, Walleye, John Fairfield, 12 In. 90.00
Fish, Walleye, Oscar Peterson 2200.00
Fish, Wood & Tin, Original Paint, 7 3/4 In. 33.00
Float of 7 Rustic Ducks, Triangular, Moose Lake, Maine 625.00
Frog, Gliding, Don Hoseney, 4 In. 250.00
Golden Plover, Chief Cuffee, Shinneock, N.Y., 1910, Pair 1850.00
Golden Plover, Shorebird, Elmer Crowell, 1900 .... 9900.00
Golden Plover, Tinny, 1900 .... 175.00
Goldeneye Drake, Mason, 1910 .... 3750.00
Goose, Hank Walker 325.00
Goose, Tin, Wooden Base, Worn Dark Paint, 22 In. 253.00
Great Horned Owl & Crow, Bear Claw Beak, Herter, 1940s 1950.00
Green–Winged Teal Drake, Balsa, Natural, Sperry Co., 1920 .... 475.00
Green–Winged Teal Drake, Paddle Tail, Harold Noland, Ontario, Canada, 1940 ..... 750.00
Green–Winged Teal, Signed, Chas Moore '79, 10 1/2 In. 60.00
Green–Winged Teal, Snakey Head, Taxidermy Eyes, Original Paint, Hollow, c.1905 7500.00

Green-Winged Teal, Stick-Up, Original Paint, Glass Eyes, 18 In.	27.00
Hen, Hand Carved & Painted, Bob White, 13 In.	95.00
Herring Seagull, Hollow, Charles Pitman, 1960	1150.00
Mallard Drake, Brian Mitchell, Half Size	88.00
Mallard Drake, Glass Eyes, Hollow, Lead Weights, 16 3/8 In.	550.00
Mallard Drake, Hollow, Original Paint, Mason, 1910	1750.00
Mallard Drake, Snakey Head, Mason, 1910	2750.00
Mallard Hen, A. Elmer Crowell, Oval Brand, 1915	7000.00
Mallard Hen, Glass Eyes, Hollow, 16 1/2 In.	330.00
Mallard Hen, Slope Breast, Hollow, Original Paint, Mason, 1895	2500.00
Mallard Hen, Wooden Head, Balsa, Glass Eyes, 12 1/2 In.	45.00
Mallard Hen, Wooden, Original Paint, 6 1/2 In.	85.00
Mallard, Balsa, Signed, Pair	135.00
Mallard, Cavanaugh	175.00
Mallard, Pine, Original Paint, 17 1/2 In.	110.00
Maryland Egret	4125.00
Merganser Hen, Brown, White Paint, 14 1/4 In.	275.00
Merganser Hen, Old Repaint, Leather Tail & Crest, 16 In.	171.00
Merganser, Glass Eyes, Carved Bill, 17 1/2 In. ....*Illus*	990.00
Old Squaw Drake, Ben Schmidt, 1945	2500.00
Owl, Papier-Mache, Stick-Up, Original Paint, Glass Eyes, 14 In.	100.00
Perch, Flat Bodied, Carved, Oscar Peterson, 8 In.	2475.00
Pigeon, Original Paint, Pennsylvania Dutch, 1900, Half Size	475.00
Pintail Drake, Amiel Garibaldi, Sacramento, Calif.	1925.00
Pintail Drake, Original Paint, Charles Perdew, 1937	6500.00
Pintail Drake, Textured Feathers, Glass Eyes, 16 3/4 In.	200.00
Pintail Duck, Bob McGaw	3850.00
Quail, Carved, Original Paint, Base Signed, 13 In.	82.00
Red Breasted Merganser Drake, Wooden Comb, Floyd Wallace, 1900, Oversize	400.00
Red Breasted Merganser Hen, Martha's Vineyard, Mass., Original Paint, 1920	750.00
Redhead Drake, Hollow, Original Paint, Mason, 1905	2500.00
Redhead Drake, Hollow, Thomas Chambers, 1920	1750.00
Redhead Drake, Original Paint, Tom Chambers, 1860-1948	895.00
Redhead Drake, Wing & Feather Detail, Glass Eyes, 16 1/4 In.	110.00
Sanderling Peep, Chief Cuffee, 1910	650.00
Turkey, Wooden, 1930s, Pair	650.00
Widgeon Drake, Hollow, Keith Mueller, 1960	775.00
Widgeon Drake, Jobes Family, Maryland	55.00
Widgeon, Bob McGaw	3850.00
Widgeon, Cork Body, Wooden Head, Glass Eyes, 12 1/2 In.	25.00

Decoy, Merganser, Glass Eyes,
Carved Bill, 17 1/2 In.

◆ ◆

Wooden boxes, toys, or decoys should not be kept on the fireplace mantel or nearby floor area when the fire is burning. The heat dries the wood and the paint. Unprotected wooden items on warm TV sets and stereos may also be damaged.

◆ ◆

Willet, Glass Eye, Spring Plumage, Mason, 1905 .... 2500.00
Yellowlegs, Al White 165.00
Yellowlegs, Crowell, Life-Size 3850.00

DEDHAM Pottery was started in 1895. Chelsea Keramic Art Works was established in 1872 in Chelsea, Massachusetts, by members of the Robertson family. The firm used the mark *CKAW*. The factory closed in 1889 and was reorganized as the Chelsea Pottery U.S. in 1891. It became the Dedham Pottery of Dedham, Massachusetts. The factory closed in 1943. It was famous for its crackleware dishes, which picture blue outlines of animals, flowers, and other natural motifs.

Bowl, Grapes, 4 1/2 In. 350.00
Bowl, Rabbits, 12 In 775.00
Candlestick, Elephant, 3 1/2 In. 225.00
Creamer, Rabbits, Tankard Shape 640.00
Cup & Saucer, Rabbits, Demitasse 610.00
Dish, Cover, Rabbits, Ridge, Blue Stamped Mark, 11 In. 495.00
Eggcup, Rabbits 195.00
Ewer, Brown Glaze Dripped, Gray-Green, Long Neck, Bulbous, CKAW, 10 x 5 In. 220.00
Jar, Cover, Elephants, Crackled Ground, Marked, 5 x 4 1/2 In. 520.00
Mug, Rabbits, Tankard Form, Marked, 4 3/4 In. 357.50
Mug, Saucer, Rabbits, 4 1/2 In. 380.00
Paperweight, Rabbits, Set of 3 .... 1100.00
Plate & Pitcher, Milk, Elephants 605.00
Plate, Azaleas, 8 1/2 In. 150.00
Plate, Breakfast, Polar Bear 850.00
Plate, Breakfast, Tapestry Lion Design 1400.00
Plate, Crackleware, Poppy In Center, Bud Border, Blue Over White, 8 1/2 In. 440.00
Plate, Landscape, Center Scene, Corn Crib House Border, 8 1/4 In. 415.00
Plate, Magnolia, 8 1/2 In. 200.00
Plate, Rabbits, 10 In. 190.00
Plate, Rabbits, 6 Piece 550.00
Plate, Rabbits, 7 1/2 In. 225.00
Plate, Rabbits, 8 1/2 In. 245.00
Soup, Dish, Rabbits, 7 1/2 In. 110.00
Teapot, Rabbits, 5 3/4 In. 650.00
Urn, Elephant Head Handles, Blue Crackle, Chelsea Keramic Art, 6 3/4 In. 465.00
Vase, Dragon's Blood, Colored Striations, Marked, 10 In. 1765.00
Vase, Flattened Flask Shape, Applied Handles, Blue Brown Drip Glaze, 13 In. 395.00
Vase, Oxblood, Pitted Tactile Surface, Chelsea Keramic Art, 5 In. 1550.00
Vase, Thick Green Glaze Dipped Over Oatmeal Ground, H. Robertson 1000.00

DEGENHART is the name used by collectors for the products of the Crystal Art Glass Company of Cambridge, Ohio. John and Elizabeth Degenhart started the glassworks in 1947. Quality paperweights and other glass objects were made. John died in 1964 and his wife took over management and production ideas. Over 145 colors of glass were made. In 1978, after the death of Mrs. Degenhart, the molds were sold. The D in a heart trademark was removed, so collectors can easily recognize the true Degenhart piece.

Dish, Lamb Cover, Pearlized 65.00
Hat, Daisy 20.00
Mug, Peacock, Vaseline 38.00
Salt Dip, Bird With Cherry 13.50
Salt Dip, Daisy & Button, Amberina 13.50
Salt Dip, Star & Dew Drop, Vaseline, Opalescent 13.50
Toothpick, Forget-Me-Not, Cambridge Pink 25.00

DEGUE is a signature found acid-etched on pieces of French glass made in the early 1900s. Cameo, mold blown, and smooth glass with contrasting colored rims are the types most often found.

Lamp, Cameo, Brown Cut To White, Twisted Stem, Signed, 16 In. 975.00
Vase, Baluster Shape, Mottled Orange & Purple, 19 3/4 In. 460.00

Vase, Orange To Blue Leaves On Frosted Ground, Signed, 9 In.	595.00
Vase, Stag, Does, Trees, House, Rocks, Signed, 5 1/2 In.	960.00
Vase, Stylized Leaves, Orange To Blue, Frosted, c.1925, 9 In.	750.00

DELATTE glass is a French cameo glass made by Andre Delatte. It was first made in Nancy, France, in 1921. Lighting fixtures and opaque glassware in imitation of Bohemian opaline were made. There were many French cameo glass makers, so be sure to look in other appropriate categories.

Vase, Mottled Yellow & Brown, 23 In.	325.00

DELDARE, see Buffalo Pottery Deldare

DELFT is a tin–glazed pottery that has been made since the seventeenth century. It is decorated with blue on white or with colored decorations. Most of the pieces sold today were made after 1891, and the name *Holland* appears with the Delft factory marks. The word *delft* also appears on pottery from other countries.

Bottle, Figural, Windmill, Blue & White	35.00
Bottle, Water, Blue & White, 18th Century, 8 3/4 In.	660.00
Bowl, Blue & White, England, 10 In.	687.00
Bowl, Blue & White, England, 12 In.	880.00
Bowl, Blue & White, England, 6 x 11 In.	990.00
Bowl, Fluted, 18th Century, 12 In.	1100.00
Bowl, One More & Then, Blue & White, 18th Century, 9 In.	550.00
Bowl, Polychrome Decorated, England, 10 In.	725.00
Brick, Flower, Blue & White, Mid–18th Century, 6 In.	495.00
Bulb Bowl, Blue & White, England, 1750, 8 1/2 In.	1045.00
Charger, Blue & White, England, 18th Century, 13 1/4 In.	385.00
Charger, Gentleman Design, 11 1/2 In.	575.00
Charger, Polychrome, 18th Century, 13 In.	495.00
Creamer, Cow Form, Overall Blue Flowers, c.1920, 6 In.	155.00
Figurine, Cow, With Milkmaid	605.00
Figurine, House, Signed, 4 In.	59.00
Figurine, Shoe, Schoonhoven, 6 1/2 In.	48.00
Garniture Set, Polychrome, Early 19th Century, Europe, 11 In., 5 Piece	4510.00
Pitcher, Sailing Ship, Relief Cartouche, Crossed Sword, 3 1/2 In.	80.00
Planter, Blue & White, 18th Century, 5 3/4 In.	715.00
Plaque, Flemish Gentleman, Signed, Large Frame	880.00
Plaque, Scene, Blue & White, 1800s	1395.00
Plate, Blue, White Floral Design, 8 7/8 In.	159.00
Plate, Central Urn, Orange Plants, Patriotic Design, Marked, 9 In., 5 Piece	550.00
Plate, Merryman, Verse, Half–Griffins, Mask & Crown, 1680s, 7 3/4 In., Pair	1650.00
Plate, Portrait, William & Mary In Crowns, Court Robes, c.1690, 8 1/8 In.	3300.00
Plate, Winged Half–Griffins Surrounded By Crown, 1688, 10 3/8 In.	1200.00
Punch Bowl, Floral, Blue & White, 16 x 8 3/4 In.	4125.00
Punch Bowl, Step Sides, Bristol	697.00
Puzzle Jug, Motto, Blue & White, England	2750.00
Quill Stand, Windmill Design, 18th Century, 5 In.	1045.00
Salt, Form of A Double–Sided Female Figure, Holding Bowls, 7 1/2 In.	99.00
Sugar & Creamer, Windmill Scene	65.00
Tile, Blue & White, 1900, 5 1/4 x 5 1/4 In., 4 Piece	160.00
Vase, Blue & White, 1760, 12 1/2 In.	550.00
Vase, Blue & White, England, Lamp Base, 8 1/2 In.	467.00
Vase, Lamp Mounted, Blue & White, 18th Century, 26 In.	302.00

DENTAL cabinets, chairs, equipment, and other related items are listed here. Other objects may be found in the Medical category.

Cabinet, 9 Drawers, With Models of Teeth	100.00
Cabinet, Mahogany, 6 Drawers, Large Selection of Teeth, 8 x 12 x 12 In.	375.00
Cabinet, Mahogany, Milk Glass Inserts, Tools & Drills, 1920s	3000.00
Cabinet, Oak, 1 Door, Drawers	1500.00
Cabinet, Oak, Ornate, Restored, 1870	5500.00

Cabinet, Walnut, Acanthus Back Splash, Cupboard, 3 Fitted Drawers, 67 x 44 In. ... 2000.00
Cabinet, Walnut, American Cabinet Co., White Marble Top, Drawers, Sterilizer 750.00
Cabinet, Wooden, 2 Shelves, White 45.00
Compressor, Wooden Case, C. M. Sorensen & Co., N.Y., Working 150.00
Elevator, Turned Ebony Handle, Steel Double Claw, 18th Century, 6 In. 110.00
Floss Dispenser, Heavy Glass 15.00
Pliers 9.50
Toothbrush, Ivory, Klenzo Brushes, Rexall, Box, 6 3/8 In. ....*Illus* 5.00

DEPRESSION GLASS was an inexpensive glass manufactured in large
quantities during the 1920s and early 1930s. It was made in many colors
and patterns by dozens of factories in the United States. The name
Depression glass is a modern one. For more descriptions, history, pictures,
and prices of Depression glass, see the book *Kovels' Depression Glass &*
American Dinnerware Price List.

Adam, Bowl, Cover, Green, 9 In. 49.50
Adam, Bowl, Cover, Pink, 9 In. 25.00
Adam, Bowl, Pink, 10 In. 17.00
Adam, Cup & Saucer, Green 25.00
Adam, Grill Plate, Green 12.00
Adam, Grill Plate, Pink 13.00
Adam, Plate, Green, 7 3/4 In. 9.25
Adam, Relish, Divided, Pink 13.00
Adam, Salt & Pepper, Pink 69.75
Adam, Sherbet, Pink 24.00
Adam, Sugar & Creamer, Pink 40.00
Adam, Sugar, Green .... 13.00 To 14.00
Adam, Tumbler, Green, 5 1/2 In. 40.00
Adam, Vase, Pink, 7 1/2 In. 200.00
Alice, Cup & Saucer, Blue & White 9.00
Alice, Cup & Saucer, Jadite .... 4.00 To 6.50
Alice, Plate, Jadite, 8 1/2 In. 15.00
American Pioneer, Cup, Crystal 7.50
American Pioneer, Plate, Crystal, 8 In. 4.00
American Pioneer, Sugar & Creamer, Pink 35.00
American Sweetheart, Bowl, Pink, 6 In. 16.00
American Sweetheart, Creamer, Monax .... 6.50 To 7.00
American Sweetheart, Creamer, Pink 10.00
American Sweetheart, Cup & Saucer, Monax .... 10.50 To 12.50
American Sweetheart, Plate, Monax, 8 In. .... 6.75 To 7.00
American Sweetheart, Plate, Monax, 9 3/4 In. 15.00
American Sweetheart, Plate, Monax, 11 In. 12.00
American Sweetheart, Plate, Red, 8 In. 65.00
American Sweetheart, Plate, Red, 12 In. 125.00
American Sweetheart, Plate, Red, 9 In. .... 65.00 To 75.00
American Sweetheart, Platter, Oval, Monax 50.00

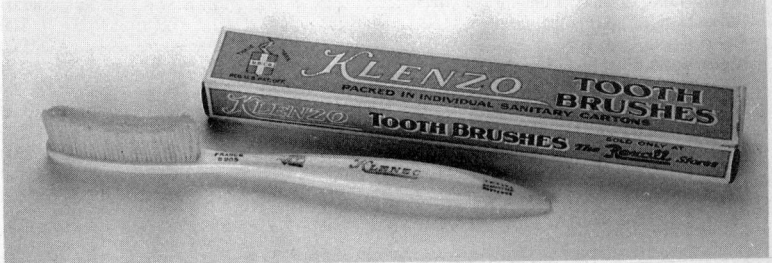

Dental, Toothbrush, Ivory, Klenzo Brushes,

Rexall, Box, 6 3/8 In.

Depression glass,
American Sweetheart

Depression glass, Bubble

Depression glass, Cameo

American Sweetheart, Platter, Oval, Pink	28.00
American Sweetheart, Saltshaker, Monax	115.00
American Sweetheart, Tray, Tidbit, 2 Tiers, Blue	260.00
American Sweetheart, Tray, Tidbit, 2 Tiers, Red	200.00
Anniversary, Cup & Saucer, Iridescent	6.50
Anniversary, Cup, Crystal	3.00
Anniversary, Plate, Iridescent, 9 In.	6.00
Anniversary, Soup, Dish, Iridescent	6.50
Apple Blossom pattern is listed here as Dogwood	
Aunt Polly, Butter, Cover, Blue	175.00 To 200.00
Aunt Polly, Pitcher, Blue	195.00
Aunt Polly, Saucer, Blue	10.00
Aunt Polly, Sherbet, Blue	15.00
Aunt Polly, Tumbler, Water, Blue	23.00
Aurora, Bowl, Cobalt Blue, 5 3/8 In.	11.00
Aurora, Cup, Cobalt Blue	7.00
Aurora, Tumbler, Cobalt Blue	15.00
Avocado, Bowl, Oval, 2 Handles, Green, 8 In.	20.00
Avocado, Plate, Green, 6 3/8 In.	14.00
Avocado, Plate, Green, 8 1/4 In.	17.00
Ballerina pattern is listed here as Cameo	
Banded Rib pattern is listed here as Coronation	
Banded Rings pattern is listed here as Ring	
Baroque, Candlestick, Topaz, 5 1/2 In.	17.00
Baroque, Relish, 3 Sections, Yellow	21.50
Basket pattern is listed here as No. 615	
Block pattern is listed here as Block Optic	
Block Optic, Bowl, Green, 4 1/4 In.	5.00
Block Optic, Bowl, Green, 5 1/4 In.	15.00
Block Optic, Candy Jar, Cover, Yellow, 2 1/4 In.	45.00
Block Optic, Creamer, Cone Shape, Green	12.00
Block Optic, Cup, Footed, Green	5.00
Block Optic, Cup, Pink	5.00
Block Optic, Pitcher, Green, 7 5/8 In.	62.50
Block Optic, Pitcher, Rope Top, Green	45.00
Block Optic, Plate, Green, 6 In.	3.00
Block Optic, Plate, Pink, 6 In.	2.00
Block Optic, Plate, Pink, 8 In.	4.00 To 7.00
Block Optic, Salt & Pepper, Footed, Pink	70.00
Block Optic, Sandwich Server, Green	40.00

✦✦

To remove the brown deposits found in old vinegar cruets fill the
cruets with diluted ammonia for a few hours, then rinse.

✦✦

Block Optic, Saucer, Green .... 6.00 To 7.00
Block Optic, Saucer, Yellow 7.00
Block Optic, Sherbet, Pink, 3 1/4 In. 7.00
Block Optic, Sugar, Cover, Green, 4 1/4 In. ....9.00 To 10.00
Bouquet & Lattice pattern is listed here as Normandie
Bubble, Berry Bowl, Blue, 8 3/8 In. 11.50
Bubble, Berry Bowl, Red, 8 3/8 In. 20.00
Bubble, Bowl, Blue, 5 1/4 In. 12.00
Bubble, Creamer, Blue 30.00
Bubble, Cup & Saucer, Blue .... 3.00 To 4.00
Bubble, Grill Plate, Blue .... 14.50 To 15.00
Bubble, Lamp, Crystal, Pair 35.00
Bubble, Plate, Blue, 6 3/4 In. 3.50
Bubble, Plate, Blue, 9 3/8 In. 5.00
Bubble, Platter, Blue .... 11.00 To 12.00
Bubble, Soup, Dish, Blue ....7.00 To 10.00
Bubble, Tumbler, Iced Tea, Red ....9.00 To 12.00
Bubble, Tumbler, Juice, Red 8.00
Bubble, Tumbler, Lemonade, Red 18.00
Bullseye pattern is listed here as Bubble
Burple, Goblet, Green 7.50
Butterflies & Roses pattern is listed here as Flower Garden with Butterflies
Buttons & Bows pattern is listed here as Holiday
Cabbage Rose pattern is listed here as Sharon
Cameo, Bowl, Vegetable, Oval, Green, 10 In. 30.00
Cameo, Candlestick, Green 38.00
Cameo, Console, 3–Footed, Green 65.00
Cameo, Cookie Jar, Cover, Green 55.00
Cameo, Creamer, Green, 3 1/4 In. 17.00
Cameo, Dish, Mayonnaise, Green ....16.00 To 25.00
Cameo, Goblet, Green, 6 In., 4 Piece 116.00
Cameo, Goblet, Wine, Green, 4 In. 35.00
Cameo, Grill Plate, Green ....5.00 To 7.50
Cameo, Grill Plate, Yellow 10.00
Cameo, Pitcher, Water, Green, 8 1/2 In. 55.00
Cameo, Plate, Luncheon, Green, 8 In. ....5.00 To 6.00
Cameo, Plate, Yellow, 9 1/2 In. 9.00
Cameo, Salt & Pepper, Green 20.00
Cameo, Saucer, Yellow 3.00
Cameo, Soup, Cream, Green 35.00
Cameo, Sugar & Creamer, Green 20.00
Cameo, Tumbler, Green, 5 In. 25.00
Candlewick, Basket, Handle, Round, Crystal 75.00
Candlewick, Candlestick, Crystal, 3 In. 12.00
Candlewick, Celery, Crystal 25.00
Candlewick, Condiment Set, Crystal, 5 Piece 140.00
Candlewick, Cup & Saucer, After Dinner, Crystal 20.00
Candlewick, Ice Tub, Crystal 65.00
Candlewick, Jam Jar, Crystal 40.00
Candlewick, Perfume Set, Crystal, 3 Piece 45.00
Candlewick, Plate, Crystal, 10 In. 24.00
Candlewick, Relish, 3 Sections, Blue 30.00
Candlewick, Relish, 3 Sections, Crystal 25.00
Candlewick, Relish, Round, Crystal 15.00
Candlewick, Salad Set, Crystal, 3 Piece 90.00
Candlewick, Sugar & Creamer, Tray, Crystal, 3 Piece 20.00
Cape Cod, Creamer, Crystal 10.00
Cape Cod, Plate, Crystal, 8 In. 6.00
Cape Cod, Salt & Pepper, Crystal 15.00
Caprice pattern is included in the Cambridge Glass category
Cherry Blossom, Berry Bowl, Pink, 8 1/2 In. ....38.00 To 45.00
Cherry Blossom, Bowl, 2 Handles, Pink, 9 In. 45.00
Cherry Blossom, Bowl, 3–Footed, Pink, 10 1/2 In. 65.00

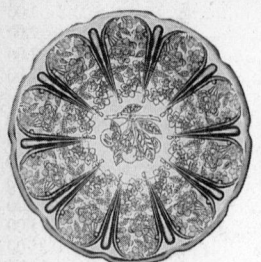

Depression glass,
Cherry Blossom

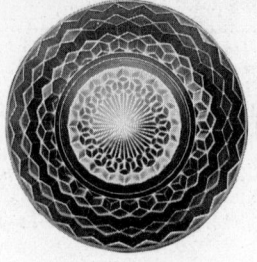

Depression glass, Cubist

Depression glass,
Dogwood

◆ ◆

Don't brag about the value of your collection to strangers. It might
lead to extra interest by the local burglary groups.

◆ ◆

Cherry Blossom, Bowl, Green, 5 3/4 In.	20.00
Cherry Blossom, Bowl, Vegetable, Pink, Oval, 9 In.	40.00
Cherry Blossom, Butter, Cover, Green	50.00 To 89.00
Cherry Blossom, Butter, Cover, Pink	60.00
Cherry Blossom, Creamer, Green	16.00
Cherry Blossom, Cup & Saucer, Pink	22.00
Cherry Blossom, Dinner Set, Child's, Pink, 14 Piece	160.00 To 250.00
Cherry Blossom, Grill Plate, Pink	20.00
Cherry Blossom, Mug, Green	150.00
Cherry Blossom, Pitcher, Footed, Pink, 8 In.	45.00
Cherry Blossom, Pitcher, Pink, 8 In.	55.00
Cherry Blossom, Pitcher, Round Bottom, Pink, 36 Oz.	37.00
Cherry Blossom, Plate, Green, 9 In.	18.50 To 20.00
Cherry Blossom, Sandwich Server, Handles, Pink	22.50 To 32.00
Cherry Blossom, Saucer, Green	3.00
Cherry Blossom, Saucer, Pink	3.00
Cherry Blossom, Sherbet, Green	18.00
Cherry Blossom, Sugar & Creamer, Green	25.00
Cherry Blossom, Sugar, Cover, Green	42.50
Cherry Blossom, Sugar, Cover, Pink	20.00
Chesterfield, Mug, Rose Marie	20.00
Christmas Candy, Cup, Teal	17.50
Christmas Candy, Sugar, Teal	17.50
Circle, Creamer, Green	5.00
Circle, Cup & Saucer, Green	6.00
Circle, Goblet, Water, Green	6.00
Circle, Sherbet, Green, 4 3/4 In.	6.00
Circle, Sugar & Creamer, Green	14.50
Cloverleaf, Creamer, Green	9.50
Cloverleaf, Cup & Saucer, Green	10.00
Cloverleaf, Plate, Black, 8 In.	14.75
Cloverleaf, Plate, Green, 8 In.	4.00 To 6.00
Cloverleaf, Salt & Pepper, Green	30.00
Cloverleaf, Sherbet, Green	8.50
Cloverleaf, Sugar, Cover, Green	8.50
Cloverleaf, Tumbler, Footed, Green, 5 3/4 In.	21.00
Cloverleaf, Tumbler, Footed, Yellow, 5 1/4 In.	20.00
Colonial Block, Sugar, Pink	15.00
Colonial, Bowl, Green, 9 In.	17.75
Colonial, Butter, Cover, Green	35.75 To 38.00

Colonial, Cup & Saucer, Crystal 14.00
Colonial, Cup & Saucer, Green 17.50
Colonial, Pitcher, Green, 7 In. 45.00
Colonial, Pitcher, Pink, 7 In. 55.00
Colonial, Plate, Green, 10 In. 60.00
Colonial, Plate, Pink, 10 In. 60.00
Colonial, Sherbet, Green 7.50
Colonial, Sugar, Cover, Green 30.00
Colonial, Sugar, Green 12.00
Colonial, Whiskey, Pink ....9.50 To 10.00
Colony, Cup & Saucer, Crystal 14.00
Colony, Plate, Crystal, 9 In. 24.00
Colony, Sugar & Creamer, Crystal 32.00
Colony, Tumbler, Footed, Crystal, 4 1/2 In. 14.00
Columbia, Bowl, Crystal, 5 In. .... 10.00 To 12.00
Columbia, Bowl, Crystal, 8 1/2 In. 11.00
Columbia, Butter, Cover, Blue Flashed 19.00
Columbia, Butter, Crystal 4.00
Columbia, Cup & Saucer, Crystal 7.00
Columbia, Cup, Crystal 5.00
Columbia, Plate, Crystal, 6 In. .... 1.50 To 2.00
Coronation, Berry Bowl, Pink, 8 In. 10.00
Coronation, Berry Bowl, Red, 4 1/4 In. 6.00
Cracked Ice, Sherbet, Green 7.50
Craquil, Console Set, Green, 3 Piece 35.00
Cube pattern is listed here as Cubist
Cubist, Bowl, Green, 4 1/2 In. 4.00
Cubist, Candy Jar, Cover, Pink .... 21.00 To 25.00
Cubist, Plate, Green, 8 In. 5.00
Cubist, Salt & Pepper, Green 30.00
Cubist, Saucer, Pink 1.00
Cubist, Sugar & Creamer, Pink 22.50
Cubist, Sugar, Cover, Pink .... 16.00 To 18.00
Cubist, Sugar, Pink, 3 In. 6.00
Daisy pattern is listed here as No. 620
Dancing Girl pattern is listed here as Cameo
Della Robia, Berry Bowl, Crystal, 5 In. 12.00
Della Robia, Candlestick, Crystal, 3 1/2 In., Pair 22.00
Diamond Pattern is listed here as Miss America
Diamond Quilted, Bowl, Blue, 7 In. 14.00
Diamond Quilted, Candlestick, Pink, Pair 22.00
Diamond Quilted, Pitcher, Green 42.00
Diamond Quilted, Plate, Pink, 8 In. 4.00
Diamond Quilted, Sugar, Blue 11.50
Diamond Quilted, Tumbler, Iced Tea, Green 9.00
Diana, Bowl, Crystal, 9 In. 5.00
Diana, Bowl, Pink, 9 In. 16.00
Diana, Bowl, Scalloped, Crystal, 12 In. 12.00
Diana, Candy Dish, Cover, Amber 30.00
Diana, Cocktail Shaker, Crystal, Chrome Top 175.00
Diana, Console, Pink, 11 In. 22.50
Diana, Cup & Saucer, Pink 112.50
Diana, Demitasse Set, Crystal, Gold Rim, Rack, 6 Cups 95.00
Diana, Pitcher, Martini, Crystal 295.00
Diana, Plate, Crystal, 9 1/2 In. .... 4.00 To 5.00
Diana, Platter, Oval, Crystal 5.00
Diana, Sandwich Server, Pink, 11 3/4 In. 20.00
Diana, Soup, Cream, Crystal, 5 1/2 In. 5.00
Dogwood, Cake Plate, Green, 13 In. 75.00
Dogwood, Cake Plate, Pink, 13 In. 70.00
Dogwood, Creamer, Pink 16.00
Dogwood, Cup & Saucer, Pink .... 14.00 To 17.00
Dogwood, Pitcher, Pink 135.00

Depression glass, Floral

Depression glass, Florentine No. 1

Depression glass, Florentine No. 2

Dogwood, Plate, Pink, 6 In.	5.00
Dogwood, Plate, Pink, 8 In.	7.00 To 7.50
Dogwood, Platter, Pink	390.00
Dogwood, Salver, Pink	24.00
Dogwood, Sugar, Pink	14.00
Dogwood, Tumbler, Pink, 4 In.	5.00
Doric & Pansy, Cup, Ultramarine	16.00
Doric & Pansy, Sugar & Creamer, Ultramarine	215.00
Doric, Berry Bowl, Crystal, 4 1/2 In.	7.00
Doric, Berry Bowl, Delphite, 4 1/2 In.	32.00
Doric, Bowl, Pink, 4 1/2 In.	9.00
Doric, Bowl, Pink, 5 1/2 In.	37.75
Doric, Cake Plate, Pink	17.00
Doric, Candy Dish, Cover, 8 In.	33.00
Doric, Creamer, Pink	13.00
Doric, Pitcher, Flat, Pink	30.00
Doric, Plate, Pink, 6 In.	3.50
Doric, Salt & Pepper, Pink	29.00 To 30.00
Doric, Saucer, Pink	3.00
Doric, Sherbet, Green	11.00
Doric, Sherbet, Pink	10.00
Doric, Sugar, Cover, Pink	27.00
Doric, Tray, Green, 2 Handles	11.00
Doric, Tumbler, Footed, Pink, 5 In.	65.00
Double Shield pattern is listed here as Mt. Pleasant	
Dutch Rose pattern is listed here as Rosemary	
Early American Rock Crystal pattern is listed here as Rock Crystal	
English Hobnail, Bowl, Crystal, 4 1/2 In.	5.00
English Hobnail, Candy Dish, Crystal, 15 In.	85.00
English Hobnail, Cologne Bottle, Pink	80.00
English Hobnail, Cup, Crystal	5.00 To 7.00
English Hobnail, Lamp, Electric, Crystal, 8 1/2 In.	25.00
English Hobnail, Plate, 5 1/2 In.	4.00
English Hobnail, Plate, Pink, 8 In.	10.50
English Hobnail, Saltshaker, Green	28.00
English Hobnail, Sugar, Crystal	12.00
Fine Rib pattern is listed here as Homespun	
Fire–King, Measuring Cup, Blue	22.50
Fire–King, Roaster, Cover, Blue, 10 3/8 In.	50.00
First Love, Cup & Saucer, Crystal, After Dinner	22.00

♦ ♦

If you use an old wooden bowl for salad, treat it with edible oil, not a normal wood polish.

♦ ♦

First Love, Goblet, Crystal, 6 3/4 In. 35.00
First Love, Relish, 5 Sections, Crystal 90.00
First Love, Sandwich Server, Crystal, 12 In. 60.00
Flat Diamond pattern is listed here as Diamond Quilted
Floragold, Bowl, Iridescent, 5 1/2 In. 5.00
Floragold, Bowl, Iridescent, 9 1/2 In. ....5.00 To 10.00
Floragold, Butter, Oblong, Iridescent 18.00
Floragold, Candy Dish, Cover, Iridescent 45.00
Floragold, Cup & Saucer, Iridescent 12.00
Floragold, Pitcher, Iridescent 30.00
Floragold, Plate, Iridescent, 8 1/2 In. 28.00
Floragold, Salt & Pepper, Iridescent 30.00
Floragold, Sherbet, Iridescent 12.00
Floragold, Sugar & Creamer, Cover, Iridescent ....18.50 To 19.00
Floragold, Tray, Iridescent, 13 1/2 In. 15.00
Floral & Diamond Band, Berry Bowl, Green, 4 1/2 In. 12.50
Floral & Diamond Band, Berry Bowl, Green, 8 In. 20.00
Floral & Diamond Band, Butter, Cover, Green 125.00
Floral & Diamond Band, Sherbet, Green 8.00
Floral & Diamond Band, Sugar & Creamer, Green 27.50
Floral, Berry Bowl, Green, 4 In. 14.00
Floral, Berry Bowl, Pink, 4 In. 18.00
Floral, Butter, Cover, Pink 60.00
Floral, Candlestick, Green, Pair 70.00
Floral, Candy Jar, Green, Cover 32.00
Floral, Creamer, Green 12.00
Floral, Creamer, Pink 11.00
Floral, Cup & Saucer, Green 19.00
Floral, Cup, Green 10.00
Floral, Pitcher, Green, 8 In. ....30.00 To 32.50
Floral, Plate, Green, 6 In. 6.00
Floral, Plate, Green, 8 In. 9.00
Floral, Plate, Pink, 9 In. 13.00
Floral, Platter, Oval, Pink, 10 3/4 In. 15.00
Floral, Sherbet, Green 15.00
Floral, Sherbet, Pink 12.00
Floral, Sugar, Cover, Pink 22.50
Florentine No. 1, Berry Bowl, Green, 5 In. 10.00
Florentine No. 1, Berry Bowl, Pink, 5 In. ....7.50 To 8.00
Florentine No. 1, Cup & Saucer, Yellow 11.00
Florentine No. 1, Cup, Green 7.50
Florentine No. 1, Salt & Pepper, Green 35.00
Florentine No. 1, Soup, Cream, Pink 9.00
Florentine No. 1, Sugar & Creamer, Green 16.00
Florentine No. 1, Sugar, Pink 8.50
Florentine No. 2, Berry Bowl, 4 1/2 In. 12.00
Florentine No. 2, Creamer, Crystal 4.00
Florentine No. 2, Cup & Saucer, Crystal 7.50
Florentine No. 2, Cup & Saucer, Yellow 10.00
Florentine No. 2, Dinner Set, Service For 6, 47 Piece 225.00
Florentine No. 2, Gravy Boat, Underplate, Yellow 80.00
Florentine No. 2, Parfait, Yellow 55.00
Florentine No. 2, Plate, Green, 6 In. 2.25
Florentine No. 2, Plate, Green, 10 In. 12.00
Florentine No. 2, Plate, Yellow, 6 In. 4.00
Florentine No. 2, Plate, Yellow, 8 1/2 In. ....7.00 To 8.50
Florentine No. 2, Platter, Oval, Yellow, 11 In. ....16.00 To 20.00
Florentine No. 2, Relish, 3 Sections, Yellow, 10 In. 22.00
Florentine No. 2, Salt & Pepper, Green 35.00
Florentine No. 2, Sherbet, Yellow 10.50
Florentine No. 2, Sugar & Creamer, Yellow 55.00
Florentine No. 2, Tumbler, Footed, Yellow, 4 In. 12.00
Florentine No. 2, Tumbler, Green, 5 In. 16.00

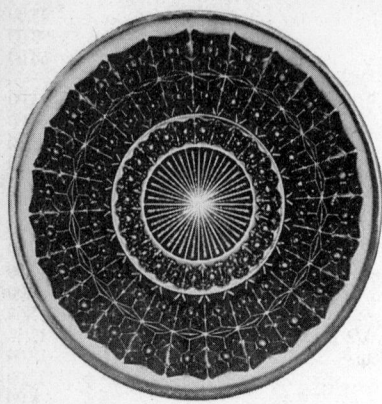

Depression glass, Holiday   Depression glass, Iris, Beaded Edge

Flower & Leaf Band pattern is listed here as Indiana Custard
Flower Garden With Butterflies, Cup & Saucer, Green 60.00
Flower Garden With Butterflies, Plate, Green, 8 In. 16.00
Flower Rim pattern is listed here as Vitrock
Forest Green, Batter Bowl, Spout, Tab Handle, Green 15.00
Forest Green, Bowl, Square, Green, 6 In. 15.00
Forest Green, Mixing Bowl, Green, 6 In. 6.00
Forest Green, Pitcher, Green, 22 Oz. 23.00
Forest Green, Plate, Green, 6 3/4 In. 8.75
Forest Green, Plate, Square, Green, 8 3/8 In. 12.00
Forest Green, Platter, Green 25.00
Forest Green, Punch Cup, Green 3.50
Forest Green, Salt & Pepper, Green, Black Top 10.00
Forest Green, Soup, Dish, Green, 6 In. 9.00
Forest Green, Tumbler, Green, 4 1/2 In. 3.50
Forest Green, Tumbler, Green, 5 In. 4.50
Forest Green, Vase, Ring, Green, 6 3/8 In. 7.00
Forest Green, Vase, Square, Green, 5 x 6 In. 12.50
Forest, Green, Punch Set, Green, 11 Piece 45.00
Fortune, Bowl, Handle, Pink, 4 1/2 In. .... 4.00 To 5.00
Georgian, Berry Bowl, Green, 4 1/2 In. 7.00
Georgian, Butter, Cover, Green 60.00
Georgian, Creamer, Green, 4 In. .... 10.50 To 11.00
Georgian, Cup & Saucer, Green 11.50
Georgian, Hot Plate, Green 45.00
Georgian, Plate, Green, 6 In. 2.75
Georgian, Plate, Green, 8 In. 9.75
Georgian, Saucer, Green 2.00
Georgian, Sherbet, Green 10.00
Georgian, Sugar, Cover, Green, 4 In. 15.00
Hairpin pattern is listed here as Newport
Harp, Cake Stand, Crystal .... 13.50 To 18.00
Harp, Cake Stand, Gold Rim 23.00
Harp, Plate, Crystal, 7 In. 7.00
Harp, Tray, 2 Handles, Crystal 15.00
Heritage, Bowl, Crystal, 10 1/2 In. 12.00
Heritage, Plate, Crystal, 9 1/4 In. 9.00
Hex Optic pattern is listed here as Hexagon Optic
Hexagon Optic, Pitcher, Pink, 9 In. 35.00
Hexagon Optic, Plate, Flower, 8 In. 5.00

Hexagon Optic, Salt & Pepper, Green	25.00
Hobnail, Decanter, Crystal, Red Trim	25.00
Hobnail, Plate, Pink, 6 In.	3.50
Hobnail, Plate, Pink, 8 1/2 In.	5.00
Hobnail, Tumbler, Footed, Crystal, Red Trim, 3 Oz.	5.00
Holiday, Chop Plate, Pink	80.00
Holiday, Creamer, Pink	7.00
Holiday, Cup & Saucer, Pink	8.00
Holiday, Cup, Pink	4.00
Homespun, Plate, Crystal, 6 In.	5.00
Homespun, Sugar, Pink	5.00
Homespun, Tumbler, Flared, Crystal, 4 In.	17.00
Homespun, Tumbler, Pink, Footed, 6 1/4 In.	22.50
Honeycomb pattern is listed here as Hexagon Optic	
Horizontal Ribbed pattern is listed here as Manhattan	
Horseshoe pattern is listed here as No. 612	
Indiana Custard, Sugar & Creamer, Cover, Custard	44.00
Iris & Herringbone pattern is listed here as Iris	
Iris, Bowl, Iridescent, 9 1/2 In.	8.00
Iris, Bowl, Ruffled, Crystal, 11 1/2 In.	8.00
Iris, Bowl, Ruffled, Crystal, 5 In.	7.00
Iris, Bowl, Ruffled, Iridescent, 11 1/2 In.	14.00
Iris, Butter, Cover, Crystal	20.00 To 36.00
Iris, Butter, Cover, Iridescent	25.00 To 38.00
Iris, Candlestick, Iridescent, Pair	37.50
Iris, Creamer, Crystal	8.00
Iris, Goblet, Wine, Crystal, 4 1/4 In.	12.50
Iris, Lamp, Shade, Pink	35.00
Iris, Pitcher, Crystal	30.00 To 33.00
Iris, Plate, Crystal, 8 In.	50.00
Iris, Plate, Crystal, 11 3/4 In.	35.00
Iris, Plate, Iridescent, 5 1/2 In.	7.50
Iris, Sandwich Server, Iridescent	17.50 To 18.00
Iris, Saucer, Crystal	6.50
Iris, Saucer, Iridescent	6.00
Iris, Sherbet, Iridescent	8.00
Iris, Soup, Dish, Iridescent, 7 1/2 In.	55.00
Iris, Sugar & Creamer, Iridescent	30.00
Iris, Sugar, Cover, Crystal	15.00
Iris, Tumbler, Crystal, 6 1/2 In.	22.75
Iris, Tumbler, Crystal, 6 In.	13.00
Iris, Vase, Crystal, 9 In.	18.50
Iris, Vase, Iridescent, 9 In.	22.00
Iris, Vase, Pink, 9 In.	85.00
Jadite, Butter, Cover, Green, 1 Lb.	60.00
Jadite, Custard, Green	7.50
Jadite, Flour Shaker, Green	10.00
Jadite, Measuring Cup, Green, 2 Cup	25.00
Jadite, Pepper Shaker, Green	7.00 To 8.00
Jadite, Reamer, Green	40.00
Jadite, Refrigerator Dish, 4 x 8 In.	20.00
Jane–Ray, Bowl, Jadite, 8 In.	15.00
Jane–Ray, Cup & Saucer, Demitasse, Jadite	22.00
Jane–Ray, Cup & Saucer, Jadite	3.00 To 4.50
Jane–Ray, Plate, Jadite, 9 In.	3.50
Jane–Ray, Plate, Jadite, 9 In.	5.00
Jane–Ray, Platter, Jadite	12.00 To 12.50
Jane–Ray, Sugar & Creamer, Jadite	8.00
Jubilee, Goblet, Yellow, 6 In.	40.00
Jubilee, Sugar & Creamer, Yellow	38.00
Katy Blue pattern is listed here as Laced Edge	
Knife & Fork pattern is listed here as Colonial	
Lace Edge, Bowl, 3–Footed, Pink, 10 1/2 In.	130.00

Lace Edge, Bowl, Pink, 7 3/4 In. 15.00
Lace Edge, Butter, Cover, Pink 50.00
Lace Edge, Compote, Rayed Base, 9 In. 600.00
Lace Edge, Cup & Saucer, Pink 26.00
Lace Edge, Plate, Pink, 10 1/2 In. 25.00
Lace Edge, Platter, Pink, 12 3/4 In. 22.00
Lace Edge, Saucer, Pink 9.00
Laced Edge, Plate, Blue, 12 In. 26.00
Laced Edge, Tumbler, Blue 45.00
Lake Como, Sugar, White 18.00
Laurel, Candlestick, Green, Pair 24.00
Laurel, Creamer, Ivory 9.00
Laurel, Salt & Pepper, Ivory 35.00
Lincoln Inn, Goblet, Wine, Green 27.50
Lorain pattern is listed here as No. 615
Louisa pattern is listed here as Floragold
Lovebirds pattern is listed here as Georgian
Madrid, Butter, Cover, Amber 50.00
Madrid, Butter, Cover, Green 75.00
Madrid, Pitcher, Amber, 5 1/2 In. 30.00
Madrid, Pitcher, Amber, 8 1/2 In. .... 45.00 To 55.00
Madrid, Plate, Amber, 7 1/2 In. 10.00
Madrid, Plate, Amber, 10 1/2 In. 35.00
Madrid, Plate, Green, 8 7/8 In. 9.00
Madrid, Salt & Pepper, Footed, Green 60.00
Madrid, Soup, Cream, Amber 12.00
Madrid, Sugar & Creamer, Amber 5.00
Madrid, Tumbler, Amber, 3 7/8 In. 15.00
Madrid, Tumbler, Amber, 5 1/2 In. .... 12.00 To 15.00
Madrid, Tumbler, Blue, 4 1/4 In. 20.00
Madrid, Tumbler, Footed, Amber, 5 1/2 In. 22.00
Madrid, Tumbler, Footed, Green 38.00
Manhattan, Ashtray, Crystal, Round 6.00
Manhattan, Bowl, Crystal, 4 1/2 In. .... 5.00 To 6.50
Manhattan, Bowl, Handles, Crystal, 8 In. 15.00
Manhattan, Bowl, Handles, Pink, 5 3/8 In. 15.00
Manhattan, Coaster, Crystal 10.00
Manhattan, Compote, Crystal 28.00
Manhattan, Compote, Pink 25.00
Manhattan, Cup & Saucer, Crystal 21.00

Depression glass, Madrid

Depression glass, Mayfair Open Rose

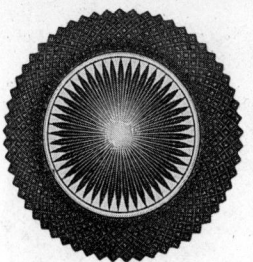

Depression glass,
Miss America

Depression glass,
Moderntone

Depression glass,
Mt. Pleasant

The best cleaner for your cut glass is a perfume-free, softener-free dishwasher detergent. Ammonia is too strong, and scented softeners sometimes leave an oily film.

Manhattan, Fruit Bowl, Pink	45.00
Manhattan, Pitcher, Crystal, 24 Oz.	25.00
Manhattan, Salt & Pepper, Crystal	25.00
Manhattan, Sandwich Server, Crystal, 14 In.	13.00 To 16.00
Manhattan, Sherbet, Crystal	7.00
Manhattan, Tumbler, Footed, Crystal	12.00 To 15.00
Many Windows pattern is listed here as Roulette	
Mayfair Open Rose, Bowl, Fruit, Scalloped, Pink	48.00
Mayfair Open Rose, Bowl, Pink, 5 1/2 In.	20.00
Mayfair Open Rose, Bowl, Vegetable, Pink, Oval	25.50
Mayfair Open Rose, Butter, Cover, Pink	49.50 To 55.00
Mayfair Open Rose, Cake Plate, Pink	24.50 To 45.00
Mayfair Open Rose, Candy Dish, Cover, Pink	35.00 To 50.00
Mayfair Open Rose, Celery Dish, Divided, Blue, 10 In.	50.00
Mayfair Open Rose, Cookie Jar, Cover, Blue	245.00
Mayfair Open Rose, Cup, Blue	45.00
Mayfair Open Rose, Cup, Pink	16.00
Mayfair Open Rose, Decanter, Stopper, Pink	130.00 To 145.00
Mayfair Open Rose, Goblet, Pink, 5 3/4 In.	50.00
Mayfair Open Rose, Pitcher, Pink, 6 In.	45.00 To 48.00
Mayfair Open Rose, Plate, Blue, 8 1/2 In.	40.00
Mayfair Open Rose, Plate, Pink, 9 1/2 In.	45.00
Mayfair Open Rose, Relish, 4 Sections, Pink	28.00
Mayfair Open Rose, Salt & Pepper, Pink	55.00
Mayfair Open Rose, Sandwich Server, Pink	35.00
Mayfair Open Rose, Sherbet, Blue, 2 1/4 In.	95.00
Mayfair Open Rose, Soup, Cream, Pink	38.00
Mayfair Open Rose, Tumbler, Blue, 5 1/4 In.	62.00
Mayfair Open Rose, Tumbler, Pink, 4 1/4 In.	25.00
Mayfair Open Rose, Vase, Blue	85.00
Mayfair Open Rose, Whiskey, Pink	60.00 To 70.00
Miss America, Candy Jar, Cover, Pink	130.00
Miss America, Celery Dish, Pink	25.00
Miss America, Coaster, Pink	20.00
Miss America, Cup, Crystal	8.50
Miss America, Cup, Green	10.00
Miss America, Grill Plate, Pink	18.00
Miss America, Plate, Pink, 8 1/2 In.	18.00
Miss America, Relish, 4 Sections, Pink	18.00 To 20.00
Miss America, Salt & Pepper, Crystal	28.00

Depression glass, No. 612

Depression glass, Normandie

Miss America, Sugar & Creamer, Pink	25.00 To 40.00
Miss America, Water Set, Crystal, 7 Piece	105.00
Moderntone Little Hostess, Cup & Saucer, Green	5.00
Moderntone Little Hostess, Tea Set, Dark, Box, 16 Piece	300.00
Moderntone, Ashtray, Cobalt Blue	130.00
Moderntone, Berry Bowl, Cobalt Blue, 5 In.	22.00
Moderntone, Cup & Saucer, Cobalt Blue	12.00 To 13.00
Moderntone, Plate, Cobalt Blue, 5 7/8 In.	6.00
Moderntone, Plate, Cobalt Blue, 7 3/4 In.	10.00
Moderntone, Plate, Cobalt Blue, 8 7/8 In.	13.00
Moderntone, Salt & Pepper, Cobalt Blue	33.00 To 38.00
Moderntone, Saltshaker, Cobalt Blue	17.50
Moderntone, Sherbet, Cobalt Blue	11.00
Moderntone, Soup, Cream, Cobalt Blue	15.00 To 21.00
Moderntone, Sugar & Creamer, Cover, Cobalt Blue	45.00
Moondrops, Ashtray, Red	30.00
Moondrops, Butter, Cover, Cobalt Blue	400.00
Moondrops, Cocktail Shaker, Cobalt Blue, Metal Handle & Top	65.00
Moondrops, Decanter Set, Amber, 7 Piece	62.00
Moondrops, Decanter Set, Green, 7 Piece	85.00
Moondrops, Decanter Set, Red, 7 Piece	125.00
Moondrops, Plate, Red, 8 1/2 In.	15.00
Moondrops, Sherbet, Red, 2 5/8 In.	16.00
Moondrops, Sugar & Creamer, Red, 2 3/4 In.	31.50
Moondrops, Sugar, Red, 2 3/4 In.	17.50
Moondrops, Tumbler, Amethyst, 2 3/4 In.	10.00
Moonstone, Bowl, Crimped, Handle, 6 1/2 In.	7.50
Moonstone, Bowl, Heart Shape Handle, Crystal	14.00
Moonstone, Candleholder, Crystal, Pair	12.00
Moonstone, Goblet, Crystal	12.00
Moonstone, Powder Box, Cover, Crystal	15.00 To 20.00
Moonstone, Relish, 2 Sections, Crystal	6.50 To 8.00
Moonstone, Sugar & Creamer, Crystal	10.00 To 12.00
Moroccan Amethyst, Candy Dish, Cover, Amethyst	25.00
Mt. Vernon pattern is included in the Cambridge Glass category	
Mt. Pleasant, Dish, Fruit, Square, Footed, Cobalt Blue, 4 In.	15.50
Mt. Pleasant, Dish, Mayonnaise, Footed, Cobalt Blue	20.00
Mt. Pleasant, Plate, Scalloped, Cobalt Blue, 8 In.	14.00
Mt. Pleasant, Saucer, Cobalt Blue	2.00
Mt. Pleasant, Sherbet, Cobalt Blue	14.00 To 15.00

Mt. Pleasant, Sugar & Creamer, Black 34.00
New Century, Butter, Cover, Green 45.00
New Century, Cup & Saucer, Green 9.00
New Century, Pitcher, Cobalt Blue, 8 In. 50.00
New Century, Sugar, Cover, Crystal 14.00
Newport, Cup & Saucer, Amethyst 12.50
Newport, Saucer, Cobalt Blue 4.00
Newport, Sherbet, Cobalt Blue 13.00
Newport, Soup, Cream, Cobalt Blue, 4 3/4 In. 14.00
Newport, Sugar & Creamer, Cobalt Blue .... 27.00 To 27.50
No. 601 pattern is listed here as Avocado
No. 612, Bowl, Round, Green, 8 1/2 In. 16.50
No. 612, Bowl, Yellow, 8 1/2 In. 30.00
No. 612, Cup & Saucer, Green .... 10.00 To 11.00
No. 612, Cup & Saucer, Yellow 11.00
No. 612, Plate, Green, 6 In. 4.00
No. 612, Plate, Green, 8 3/8 In. .... 6.00 To 8.00
No. 612, Plate, Green, 9 3/8 In. .... 12.00 To 18.00
No. 612, Plate, Yellow, 8 3/8 In. 6.50
No. 612, Relish, 3 Sections, Green 15.00
No. 612, Saucer, Green .... 2.50 To 4.00
No. 612, Sherbet, Green 11.50
No. 612, Sugar, Green 12.00
No. 615, Cup, Yellow 14.00
No. 615, Plate, Yellow, 7 3/4 In. 16.00
No. 615, Platter, Yellow 35.00
No. 615, Tumbler, Footed, Yellow, 4 3/4 In. 28.00
No. 618, Plate, Crystal, 9 3/8 In. 15.00
No. 618, Tumbler, Crystal, 4 1/4 In. 35.00
No. 620, Bowl, Vegetable, Oval, Amber, 10 In. 15.00
No. 620, Plate, Amber, 8 3/4 In. 2.75
No. 620, Tumbler, Footed, Amber, 12 Oz. .... 27.00 To 50.00
No. 622 pattern is listed here as Pretzel
Normandie, Bowl, Vegetable, Pink, Oval, 10 In. 45.00
Normandie, Cup & Saucer, Pink 10.00
Normandie, Grill Plate, Iridescent 8.50
Normandie, Grill Plate, Pink 50.00
Normandie, Plate, Iridescent, 6 In. 2.50
Normandie, Plate, Pink, 11 In. 30.00
Normandie, Sherbet, Iridescent 3.50

Depression glass, Princess

Depression glass, Royal Lace

Normandie, Tumbler, Pink, 5 In. 20.00
Old Cafe, Pitcher, Pink, 80 Oz. .... 75.00 To 80.00
Old Cafe, Sherbet, Pink 6.00
Old Florentine pattern is listed here as Florentine No. 1
Open Lace pattern is listed here as Lace Edge
Open Rose pattern is listed here as Mayfair Open Rose
Optic Design pattern is listed here as Raindrops
Parrot pattern is listed here as Sylvan
Patrician, Berry Bowl, Amber, 5 In. 10.00
Patrician, Berry Bowl, Green, 8 1/2 In. 35.00
Patrician, Butter, Cover, Amber 80.00
Patrician, Cookie Jar, Cover, Crystal 80.00
Patrician, Cup & Saucer, Green .... 16.50 To 17.00
Patrician, Cup, Amber 5.50
Patrician, Cup, Crystal 4.25
Patrician, Pitcher, Amber, 8 In. 90.00
Patrician, Pitcher, Green, 8 In. 95.00
Patrician, Plate, Amber, 9 In. 9.00
Patrician, Plate, Amber, 10 1/2 In. .... 4.00 To 5.00
Patrician, Plate, Green, 6 In. 7.00
Patrician, Plate, Green, 9 In. .... 9.00 To 10.00
Patrician, Platter, Oval, Amber 28.00
Patrician, Platter, Oval, Green, 11 1/2 In. 20.00
Patrician, Salt & Pepper, Amber 50.00
Petal Swirl pattern is listed here as Swirl
Petalware, Creamer, Cremax 10.00
Petalware, Cup & Saucer, Cremax, Gold Rim 2.50
Petalware, Cup, Cremax 4.00
Petalware, Cup, Cremax, Pink Bands 8.00
Petalware, Mustard, Cobalt Blue 7.00
Petalware, Plate, Cremax, 6 In. 2.00
Petalware, Plate, Cremax, 9 In. 5.00
Petalware, Plate, Cremax, Gold Rim, 8 In. 2.50
Petalware, Salver, Monax, 11 In. 7.00
Petalware, Saucer, Cremax 1.00
Petalware, Sherbet, Pink, 4 1/2 In. 4.50
Petalware, Soup, Cream, Cremax 9.00
Petalware, Sugar, Monax 5.00
Philbe, Creamer, Blue 130.00
Philbe, Plate, Blue, 8 In. 4.00
Pineapple & Floral pattern is listed here as No. 618
Pinwheel pattern is listed here as Sierra
Poinsettia pattern is listed here as Floral
Poppy No. 1 pattern is listed here as Florentine No. 1
Poppy No. 2 pattern is listed here as Florentine No. 2
Pretzel, Plate, Teal, 9 3/8 In. 5.00
Pretzel, Sugar & Creamer, Crystal 8.00
Princess, Butter, Cover, Green 90.00
Princess, Cake Stand, Green 20.00
Princess, Creamer, Green 10.00
Princess, Cup, Green .... 7.00 To 11.00
Princess, Grill Plate, Topaz 6.00
Princess, Plate, Green, 9 In. 22.00
Princess, Plate, Pink, 8 In. 18.00
Princess, Plate, Pink, 9 In. .... 15.00 To 20.00
Princess, Plate, Yellow, 9 In. 14.00
Princess, Salt & Pepper, Pink 35.00
Princess, Saucer, Green 6.00
Princess, Tumbler, Green, 4 In., 5 Piece 110.00
Provincial pattern is listed here as Bubble
Queen Mary, Berry Bowl, Pink, 5 In. 3.50
Queen Mary, Cup, Crystal 3.75
Queen Mary, Cup, Pink .... 2.50 To 5.50

Queen Mary, Sugar & Creamer 8.00
Radiance, Cup, Red 12.50
Raindrops, Cup & Saucer, Green 5.00
Ribbon, Sherbet, Green 4.00
Ring, Butter Tub, Crystal 24.50
Ring, Creamer, Green 3.75
Ring, Cup, Green 3.00
Ring, Goblet, Green, 7 1/4 In. 14.00
Rock Crystal, Candelabra, 2–Light, Crystal, Pair 65.00
Rock Crystal, Goblet, Champagne, Crystal 14.00
Rock Crystal, Parfait, Crystal 12.00
Rock Crystal, Plate, Red, 7 1/2 In. 14.00
Rock Crystal, Whiskey, Crystal 15.00
Rose Cameo, Sherbet, Green .... 7.00 To 8.00
Rosemary, Berry Bowl, Amber, 5 In. .... 3.00 To 5.00
Rosemary, Cup & Saucer, Amber 8.00
Rosemary, Soup, Cream, Amber 12.00
Rosemary, Sugar & Creamer, Amber 17.00
Rosemary, Sugar, Green 9.00
Roulette, Tumbler, Pink, 4 1/8 In. 17.00
Roulette, Whiskey, Pink 12.00
Round Robin, Berry Bowl, Green, 4 In. 4.00
Roxana, Bowl, Crystal, 4 1/2 In. 10.00
Roxana, Plate, Crystal, 6 In. 5.00
Royal Lace, Bowl, Rolled Rim, Pink, 10 In. 55.00
Royal Lace, Bowl, Ruffled, 3–Footed, Crystal 30.00
Royal Lace, Cookie Jar, Cover, Cobalt Blue 335.00
Royal Lace, Cookie Jar, Cover, Green 75.00
Royal Lace, Creamer, Cobalt Blue 45.00
Royal Lace, Creamer, Pink 15.00
Royal Lace, Cup & Saucer, Pink 16.00
Royal Lace, Hot Toddy Set, Amethyst, Chrome Trim, 7 Piece 245.00
Royal Lace, Hot Toddy Set, Cobalt Blue, Chrome Trim, 9 Piece 275.00
Royal Lace, Pitcher, Cobalt Blue, 8 In. 145.00
Royal Lace, Pitcher, Cobalt Blue, Straight Sides 110.00
Royal Lace, Pitcher, Green, Straight Sides 85.00
Royal Lace, Sherbet, Cobalt Blue 27.00
Royal Lace, Sugar & Creamer, Cover, Cobalt Blue 265.00
Royal Lace, Sugar, Cobalt Blue 30.00
Royal Ruby, Ashtray, Red, 4 1/2 In. 4.00
Royal Ruby, Bowl, Red, 8 1/2 In. 16.00
Royal Ruby, Cup & Saucer, Red 4.00
Royal Ruby, Cup, Red 2.25
Royal Ruby, Pitcher, Tilted, Red, 22 Oz. 30.00
Royal Ruby, Pitcher, Upright, Red, 3 Qt. 35.00
Royal Ruby, Plate, Red, 9 In. .... 7.00 To 9.00
Royal Ruby, Punch Cup, Red 2.00
Royal Ruby, Sherbet, Footed, Red 7.50
Royal Ruby, Sugar & Creamer, Red 10.00
Royal Ruby, Vase, Red, 9 In. 11.00
Sail Boat pattern is listed here as Sportsman Series
Sandwich Anchor Hocking, Bowl, Scalloped, Crystal, 5 1/4 In. 7.00
Sandwich Anchor Hocking, Cookie Jar, Cover, Green 32.00
Sandwich Anchor Hocking, Cup & Saucer, Green 35.00
Sandwich Anchor Hocking, Pitcher, Crystal, 6 In. 53.00
Sandwich Anchor Hocking, Plate, Crystal, 9 In. .... 15.00 To 16.00
Sandwich Indiana, Decanter, Amber 20.00
Saxon pattern is listed here as Coronation
Sharon, Berry Bowl, Amber, 8 1/2 In. .... 3.75 To 7.00
Sharon, Berry Bowl, Pink, 5 In. .... 8.50 To 10.00
Sharon, Bowl, Amber, 10 1/2 In. 10.00
Sharon, Bowl, Pink, 6 In. 15.00
Sharon, Bowl, Pink, 10 1/2 In. 35.00

Depression glass, Sharon   Depression glass, Swirl   Depression glass, Windsor

◆◆

A ground-glass perfume bottle stopper should be turned gently to the right for a snug fit. To remove the stopper, first turn it to the left to "unlock it" before pulling it out.

◆◆

Sharon, Bowl, Vegetable, Pink, 9 1/2 In.	17.50
Sharon, Butter, Cover, Pink	45.00
Sharon, Creamer, Amber	3.00
Sharon, Creamer, Pink	16.00
Sharon, Cup, Amber	7.00
Sharon, Cup, Pink	12.00
Sharon, Pitcher, Ice Lip, Amber	125.00
Sharon, Pitcher, Ice Lip, Pink	115.00
Sharon, Plate, Pink, 9 1/2 In.	16.00
Sharon, Platter, Amber	10.00
Sharon, Salt & Pepper, Amber	30.00
Sharon, Salt & Pepper, Green	55.00
Sharon, Soup, Cream, Pink	36.00 To 75.00
Sharon, Sugar & Creamer, Cover, Green	68.00
Sharon, Sugar & Creamer, Cover, Pink	32.50 To 47.00
Sharon, Sugar, Cover, Amber	55.00
Sharon, Sugar, Cover, Green	43.00
Sharon, Sugar, Cover, Pink	20.00 To 33.00
Sharon, Sugar, Pink	12.00
Sharon, Tumbler, Footed, Pink, 6 1/2 In.	29.50
Sharon, Tumbler, Pink, 4 1/8 In.	37.00
Sharon, Tumbler, Pink, 5 1/4 In.	65.00
Sierra, Berry Bowl, Green, 8 1/2 In.	22.00
Sierra, Plate, Pink, 9 In.	14.00 To 18.00
Sierra, Platter, Oval, Green, 11 In.	37.00
Sierra, Platter, Oval, Pink, 11 In.	25.00 To 30.00
Sierra, Sugar & Creamer, Cover, Pink	46.00
Spoke pattern is listed here as Patrician	
Sportsman Series, Ice Bowl, Fish, Cobalt Blue	24.00
Sportsman Series, Pitcher, Cobalt Blue	40.00 To 50.00
Sportsman Series, Salt & Pepper, Cobalt Blue	7.50
Sportsman Series, Tumbler, Cobalt Blue, 4 7/8 In.	12.00
Sportsman Series, Tumbler, Water, Cobalt Blue, 4 5/8 In.	8.00
Starlight, Saltshaker, Crystal	7.00
Starlight, Sugar & Creamer, Crystal	5.00
Strawberry, Pitcher, Green	140.00
Sunflower, Cake Plate, Green	10.00
Swirl, Bowl, Delphite, 9 In.	20.00
Swirl, Bowl, Handles, Ultramarine, 10 In.	25.00
Swirl, Cup & Saucer, Ultramarine	15.00

Swirl, Pitcher, Footed, Ultramarine, 48 Oz. 1250.00
Swirl, Plate, Pink, 8 In. 3.50
Swirl, Plate, Pink, 9 1/4 In. 6.00
Swirl, Plate, Ultramarine, 7 1/4 In. 10.00
Swirl, Plate, Ultramarine, 9 1/4 In. ....6.00 To 13.00
Swirl, Sugar & Creamer, Delphite 18.50
Swirl, Sugar & Creamer, Ultramarine 25.00
Swirl, Sugar, Delphite 6.00
Swirl, Vase, Ultramarine ....22.00 To 22.50
Sylvan, Butter, Cover, Green 450.00
Sylvan, Dish, Jelly, Amber 22.00
Sylvan, Grill Plate, Green 25.00
Sylvan, Soup, Dish, Green, 7 In. 35.00
Tea Room, Candlestick, Green, Pair 60.00
Tea Room, Creamer, Pink 12.00
Tea Room, Sugar & Creamer, Green, 4 In. 30.00
Tea Room, Sugar, Pink, 3 1/4 In. 15.00
Thistle, Cup & Saucer, Pink 26.00
Thistle, Grill Plate, Pink 18.00
Twisted Optic, Candy Jar, Cover, Green 20.00
Twisted Optic, Sherbet, Pink 6.00
Vertical Ribbed pattern is listed here as Queen Mary
Victory, Bowl, Green, 6 1/2 In. 12.00
Victory, Bowl, Vegetable, Green, 9 In. 35.00
Victory, Cup & Saucer, Green 15.00
Victory, Cup & Saucer, Pink 10.00
Victory, Plate, Green, 8 In. 10.00
Victory, Plate, Green, 9 In. 16.00
Victory, Platter, Green, 12 In. 45.00
Victory, Sugar & Creamer, Green 40.00
Vitrock, Berry Bowl, White, 4 In. 4.00
Vitrock, Bowl, White, 6 In. 5.00
Vitrock, Cup, White 3.00
Vitrock, Soup, Cream, White 14.00
Waffle pattern is listed here as Waterford
Waterford, Butter, Cover, Crystal ....17.50 To 23.00
Waterford, Cake Plate, Pink ....9.00 To 12.00
Waterford, Coaster, Crystal, 4 In. 3.00
Waterford, Creamer, Crystal 3.00
Waterford, Cup & Saucer, Crystal 7.00
Waterford, Plate, Crystal, 9 5/8 In. 7.00
Waterford, Plate, Pink, 9 5/8 In. ....13.00 To 15.00
Waterford, Relish, 5 Sections, Crystal 12.00
Waterford, Salt & Pepper, Crystal 6.50
Waterford, Sandwich Plate, Crystal 7.00
Waterford, Sherbet, Crystal ....2.75 To 3.50
Waterford, Tumbler, Footed, Crystal, 4 7/8 In. 7.50
Waterford, Tumbler, Footed, Pink, 4 7/8 In. ....15.00 To 16.00
White Ship pattern is listed here as Sportsman Series
Wild Rose pattern is listed here as Dogwood
Windmill, Ice Bowl, Tumblers, Cobalt Blue, 7 Piece 45.00
Windmill, Salt & Pepper, Cobalt Blue 9.00
Windsor Diamond pattern is listed here as Windsor
Windsor, Butter, Cover, Crystal ....17.50 To 20.00
Windsor, Butter, Cover, Green 75.00
Windsor, Cake Stand, Pink 9.00
Windsor, Chop Plate, Pink 40.00
Windsor, Creamer, Pink 7.50
Windsor, Cup & Saucer, Green 14.00
Windsor, Cup & Saucer, Pink 10.00
Windsor, Pitcher, Crystal, 4 1/2 In. 14.00
Windsor, Pitcher, Pink, 6 3/4 In. 19.00
Windsor, Plate, Green, 7 In. 15.00

Windsor, Plate, Green, 9 In.	15.00
Windsor, Plate, Pink, 9 In.	10.00
Windsor, Salt & Pepper, Green	45.00
Windsor, Salt & Pepper, Pink	25.00 To 30.00
Windsor, Saucer, Green	3.00
Windsor, Sugar, Cover, Pink	18.00
Windsor, Tumbler, Pink, 4 In.	12.50 To 16.00
X Design, Butter, Cover, Green, 1 Lb.	35.00
X Design, Butter, Pink, 1 Lb.	32.50
X Design, Reamer, Pink	125.00
X Design, Refrigerator Dish, Green, 8 x 8 In.	45.00
Yvonne, Cake Plate, Handle, Yellow, 12 In.	35.00

DERBY has been marked on porcelain made in the city of Derby, England, since about 1748. The original Derby factory closed in 1848, but others opened there and continued to produce quality porcelain. The Crown Derby mark began appearing on Derby wares in the 1770s.

Cup & Saucer, Blue, Gilt Floral Borders, Landscape, 1780–1810	125.00
Cup & Saucer, Landscape Scene, Band Border, Yellow Ground, c.1795	1650.00
Figurine, Allegorical, Britannia, Standing Man In Helmet & Armor, 7 In.	385.00
Figurine, Boy & Girl Seated, White Biscuit, 19th Century, 5 3/4 In., Pair	450.00
Figurine, Discretion, Cupid In Gold Drapery, c.1775, 8 1/4 In.	885.00
Figurine, Dresden Shepherds, Woman & Man, 1760s, 9 1/2 & 9 3/8 In.	1650.00
Figurine, John Wilkes, Putti At Base, White, 1772, 12 1/16 In.	665.00
Figurine, Liberty & Matrimony, c.1765, 8 3/4 & 9 In.	1325.00
Incense Burner, Domed Cover, Border of Flowers, Lion's Paw Feet, c.1820, Pair	2200.00
Platter, Imari Pattern, Bird Among Cherry Blossoms, 14 In.	610.00
Pot-De-Creme, Cover, Black & Gilt Diamond Pattern Border, Marked, 5 In.	220.00
Vase, Cornucopia, Blue, White, Floral Bouquets, Gilt Trimmed, 4 1/4 In., Pair	50.00

DEVILBISS Company has made atomizers of all types since 1888 but no longer makes the perfume bottle tops so popular with collectors. These were made from 1920 to 1968. The glass bottle may be by any of many manufacturers even if the atomizer is marked *DeVilbiss*. More atomizer bottles are listed in the perfume bottle category.

Dresser Set, Cologne, Vase, Hair Receiver, Center Inverted Teardrop	850.00
Perfume Bottle, Atomizer, Gold Design	45.00
Perfume Bottle, Blue Swirl	50.00
Perfume Bottle, Blue, Atomizer, Gold Flamingos, 1950s, 5 In.	40.00
Perfume Bottle, Frosted Satin Glass, Atomizer, Pedestal, 1926, 6 In.	180.00
Perfume Bottle, Green	185.00
Perfume Bottle, Marigold	185.00
Perfume Bottle, Reeded, Art Deco, Made For Imperial	350.00
Perfume Bottle, Sponged Gold Atomizer, Black–Trimmed Window Panes, Pair	550.00

DICK TRACY, the comic strip, started in 1931. Tracy was also the hero of movies from 1937 to 1947 and again in 1990, and starred in a radio series in the 1940s and a television series in the 1950s. Memorabilia from all these activities is collected.

Badge, Crime Stopper, Brass, ID Card, 1940s	10.00
Badge, Dick Tracy Girls Division, Quaker Oats, Goldtone, 1939	52.00
Badge, Junior G Man, 1930s	12.00
Badge, Secret Service Patrol, 1930s	45.00
Badge, Secret Service, Brass, 1939	9.50
Book, Big Little Book, Adventures of Dick Tracy, No. 707, Whitman	135.00
Book, Pop-Up	250.00
Buckle, Suspender, Dick Tracy Crime Stopper, Tracy Picture, Pair	22.00
Cap Gun, Hubley 210	49.50
Cap Gun, Hubley, Box	30.00
Car, Windup, Tin, 11 1/2 In.	150.00
Christmas Bulb	50.00
Comic Book, Pocket Size	35.00
Comic Strip, Crime Stoppers Panel, Ink On Paper, C. Gould, 1956, 18 x 27 In.	935.00

Comic Strip, Dick & Jim Trailer, Ink On Paper, C. Gould, 1936, 6 x 20 In. 2750.00
Crime Stopper Kit, Premium, Flashlight, Whistle, Secret Code, 1961 .... 98.00
Doll, Bonnie Braids, Box 375.00
Doll, Borgfeldt, Pat-Parachute, Composition, Cloth, Box, 1930s, 6 In. 85.00
Flashlight, Secret Service 75.00
Game, Master Detective, S & R, 1961 .... 31.00
Game, Pinball, 1967 .... 75.00
Game, Selchow & Righter 30.00
Game, Target, Darts, Jaru, 1980s 13.00
Gun, G-Man, Windup, On Card 95.00
Gun, Squirt, On Card 30.00
Iron-On Transfer, 8 x 10 In. 4500.00
Jackknife-Whistle, 1940s 75.00
Lunch Box, 1967 ....65.00 To 175.00
Lunch Box, Red, 1990 .... 8.00
Machine Gun, Black, Plastic, Mattel, 1961 .... 85.00
Pinball Game, Marx, 1967 .... 75.00
Pistol, Click, Tracy On Decal, Marx, c.1936 .... 85.00
Pistol, Siren 140.00
Pocketknife 40.00
Police Station, Tin Friction Squad Car, Marx, Box, 7 In. 695.00
Police Station, Tin, Marx ....75.00 To 275.00
Postcard, 1942 .... 10.00
Poster, Dick Tracy Vs. Cueball, 1946, 41 x 27 In. 192.00
Poster, RKO Series, Framed, 1945, 41 x 27 In. 275.00
Poster, Tracy Meets Gruesome, Linen Backed, 1947, 41 x 27 In. 330.00
Puppet, Hand, 1961 ....35.00 To 75.00
Puppet, Hand, Cloth Body, Vinyl Head, 1950s 40.00
Puppet, Hand, With Record, 1961, Box 125.00
Salt & Pepper, Chalkware 17.50
Soaky, Figural, Profile, Trench Coat, Empty, 1960s 89.00
Squad Car, Lights On Top, Battery Operated, Tin ....265.00 To 275.00
Squad Car, Plastic, Playart, 13 In. 38.00
Squad Car, Windup, Tin, Siren, Marx, Key, Box, 11 In. 485.00
Suspenders 48.00
Tommy Gun, Bolt Action, Mattel, On Card 200.00
Wrist Radio, 2-Way, Package 13.00
Wristwatch, Figure Holding Gun On Dial, New Haven, c.1939 .... 600.00
Wristwatch, Madonna On Dial, Timex 65.00
Wristwatch, New Haven, Instructions, Box, 1948 .... 546.00

DICKENS WARE pieces are listed in the Royal Doulton and Weller categories.

DINNERWARE, see American dinnerware

DIONNE QUINTUPLETS were born in Canada on May 28, 1934. The publicity about their birth and their special status as wards of the Canadian government made them famous throughout the world. Visitors could watch the girls play; reporters interviewed the girls and the staff. Thousands of special dolls and souvenirs were made picturing the quints at different ages. Emilie died in 1954, Marie in 1970. Yvonne, Annette, and Cecile still live in Canada.

Ad, Karo Syrup, 11 x 14 In. 18.00
Ad, Palmolive, 1936 .... 8.00
Calendar, 1938 .... 10.00
Calendar, 1953 .... 20.00
Calendar, Fisher, 1963 .... 15.00
Doll, Annette, Composition, Madame Alexander, With Tag, 8 In. 150.00
Doll, Baby, Celluloid, Molded Bottle In Hands, Bibs Have Names, 5 Piece 50.00
Doll, Bisque, Painted, In Cloth Holder, 5 Piece 45.00
Doll, Cecile, Composition, Madame Alexander, With Tag, 8 In. 150.00
Doll, Composition, Madame Alexander, 5 Piece 1000.00

Doll, Cream Crib, Composition, Madame Alexander, 7 In., 5 Piece 522.50
Doll, Madame Alexander, Toddlers, Seated, Hair, Chair, 7 1/2 In. 1200.00
Doll, With Dr. DeFoe, Original Clothes, 7 1/2 In., 6 Piece 2200.00
Fan, Advertising 30.00
Fan, Cardboard, Electrolux Refrigerator, 1935 .... 35.00
Magazine Cover, Liberty, 5th Birthday 19.00
Paper Doll, Complete, Uncut 225.00
Paper Doll, Illustrated, Mailer, Uncut 90.00
Paper Doll, Merrill, 1935, Uncut 175.00
Spoon, Set of 5 .... 75.00

DISNEYANA is a collector's term. Walt Disney and his company introduced many comic characters to the world. Collectors search for examples of the work of the Disney Studios and the many commercial products modeled after his characters, including Mickey Mouse, Donald Duck, and recent films, like *Beauty and the Beast* and *The Little Mermaid*.

Art Stamp Picture Set, Pinocchio, Fulton Specialty, 1939 .... 130.00
Art Stamp Picture Set, Snow White & 7 Dwarfs, Fulton Specialty, 1937 .... 150.00
Award, Mouse Car, To Max Westebbe, 1948, Metal, Plastic, Brass, 8 1/2 In. 1870.00
Band, Wristwatch, Mickey Mouse, Ingersoll, Black Leather, Metal Mickey, 1933 ...... 100.00
Banjo, Mickey Mouse, Cooley Co., 18 x 7 In. 385.00
Bank, Donald Duck, Coffee, Tin, Slit In Top 220.00
Bank, Donald Duck, Nash Relish, Cylinder Jar, Label 75.00
Bank, Epcot Center, Figment, Walt Disney World, 1982 .... 10.00
Bank, Haunted House Mystery Bank, Disneyland, 1970s 225.00
Bank, Mickey Mouse Club, Treasury, Tin Lithograph & Plastic, Box, 1957 .... 185.00
Bank, Mickey Mouse Post Office, Happynak, Tin Lithograph, England, 5 In. 70.00
Bank, Mickey Mouse, Mouseketeers, Knickerbocker 125.00
Bank, Minnie Mouse, Cold Painted, Walt Disney 30.00
Bell, Mickey Mouse As Minuteman, Schmid, Bicentennial, Box, 1976 .... 25.00
Belt Buckle, Mickey Mouse, Brass 195.00
Blotter, Donald Duck, Quick Starting, Nu–Blue Sunoco, 1930s 18.00
Blouse, Clarabell The Cow, Black, Patch, Worn Over Costume, 1930s .... 30.00 To 45.00
Book, Bambi, Little Golden Book, 1948 .... 7.00
Book, Better Little Book, Mickey Mouse On Cave–Man Island, 1944 .... 48.00
Book, Big Little Book, Mickey Mouse & Pluto The Racer, 1936 .... 65.00
Book, Big Little Book, Pinocchio, 1940 .... 25.00
Book, Big Little Book, Snow White & The 7 Dwarfs, 1938 .... 25.00
Book, Coloring, Mickey Mouse Club, 1957 .... 35.00
Book, Coloring, Pinocchio, W. Disney, 1939 .... 45.00
Book, Disneyland Guide, 1957 .... 55.00
Book, Donald Duck In Disneyland, Little Golden Book, 1960 .... 10.00
Book, Donald Duck Prize Driver, Mickey Mouse Club, Little Golden Book, 1956 .... 8.00
Book, Dumbo, Walt Disney, Winkler & Ramen, 1941 .... 48.00
Book, Famous Movie Story of Snow White & 7 Dwarfs, K. K. Pub., 1938 .... 75.00
Book, Fine Art of Walt Disney's Donald Duck, C. Barks, 1981, 13 x 11 In. 990.00
Book, Mickey Mouse Fire Brigade, Whitman, 1936 .... 7.00
Book, Mickey Mouse Goes Christmas Shopping, Little Golden Books, 1953 .... 8.00
Book, Mickey Mouse In King Arthur's Court, Pop–Up, 1933 .... 135.00
Book, Mickey Mouse Stories, No. 2, 1934 .... 95.00
Book, Mickey Mouse, Series No. 1, David McKay, 1931, 48 Pages, 10 In. 125.00
Book, Official Birthday Book, Mickey Mouse 50 Happy Years, Harmony, 1977 .... 25.00
Book, Paint, Ferdinand The Bull, Whitman, 1938 .... 50.00
Book, Pinocchio, Whitman, Cocomalt Giveaway, 1939 .... 20.00
Book, Snow White, Walt Disney Enterprise, 1933 .... 85.00
Book, Wee Little Book, Mickey Mouse Will Not Quit, 1934 .... 27.00
Book, Wee Little Book, Mickey Mouse's Misfortune, 1934 .... 27.00
Boots, Rubber, Mickey Mouse, Red, 1950s 20.00
Bottle, Shoe Polish, Mickey Mouse 30.00
Bowl, Mickey Mouse, Yellow Beetle Ware, 1930s 35.00
Bowling Set, Mickey Mouse 30.00
Box, Mickey Mouse Safety Film, Keystone Mfg. Co., 1930s 60.00
Button, Breakfast With Minnie Mouse, 2 1/2 In. 6.00

Button, Disneyland Tokyo 9th Anniversary, 3 1/4 In. 20.00
Button, Donald Duck, Colorful, 3 In. 1.35
Button, Happy Birthday Mickey, 50th, W. D. W., 1976, 3 1/2 In. 15.00
Button, I Grew Up On Mickey Mouse, 1970s, 1 1/2 In. 12.00
Button, Jungle Book, Mowgli & Baloo On River, 3 In. 6.00
Button, Mickey & Minnie Mouse, Heart Shape, Large 2.25
Button, Mickey Mouse Club Member, Large 2.25
Button, Pooh Bear Stuck In Honey Jar, 2 In. 5.00
Button, Snow White Jingle Club, Pinback, Paper, 1930s 50.00
Calendar, 1977, Mickey Mouse, Glow In The Dark, Clarke Irwin Co. 15.00
Camera, Donald Duck, Box, 1945 .... 155.00
Candy Container, Snow White & 7 Dwarfs, Curtiss, Box 450.00
Candy Container, Snow White & 7 Dwarfs, Germany, Box, 8 Piece 600.00
Candy Container, Snow White & 7 Dwarfs, Papier–Mache, Composition, 8 Piece 695.00
Card, Christmas, 101 Dalmations, Walt Disney Corp., With 1961 Calendar 75.00
Card, Christmas, Lady & The Tramp, Corporate, Castle On Back, 1954 .... 125.00
Card, Christmas, Mickey Mouse As Santa, Corporate, 1947 .... 200.00
Card, Christmas, Mickey Mouse, & Gang, Snow White, Corporate, 1937 .... 400.00
Card, Christmas, Snow White, With Envelopes 15.00
Card, Gum, Mickey Mouse, Series 1, No. 32, 1930s 16.00
Card, Membership, Mickey Mouse Club 14.00
Card, Playing, Silly Symphony, Walt Disney Enterprises 75.00
Card, Season's Greetings, Mickey & Minnie Mouse, Valentine & Sons, 1930s 40.00
Cards, Playing, Dopey, Complete, 1937, Box 60.00
Cartoon, Mickey, Donald & Goofy, Ink On Paper, Gottfredson, 1936, 15 x 10 In. ... 440.00
Catalog, Snow White & 7 Dwarfs, Re–Release Merchandise, 1960s 45.00
Ceiling Fixture, Donald, Pluto, Glass 175.00
Cel, see Animation Art category
Charm, Mickey Mouse, Celluloid, 1930s, 3/4 In. 20.00
Christmas Tree Lights, Mickey, Noma, Mazda Lamp, Original Colorful Box, 1938   275.00
Christmas Tree Ornament, Ball, Mickey, Donald, Minnie, Pluto, Daisy, Goofy 145.00
Clock, Alarm, Mickey Mouse, Bradley 50.00
Clock, Alarm, Mickey Mouse, White, Gold Trim, USA, Tim Ingersoll 415.00
Clock, Alarm, Official Mickey Mouse, Bradley, Plastic Wrapped Box, 1970s 90.00
Clock, Mickey Mouse, Bradley, Alarm, Mickey's Feet Move, Box .... 50.00 To 90.00
Clock, Pinocchio Tell Time 89.00
Colorform Set, Babes In Toyland, 1961 .... 32.00
Comic Strip, Donald Duck, Ink On Paper, Taliaferro, Framed, 1953, 15 x 20 In. 660.00
Cookie Cutter, Cinderella, 2 Mice, Prince Charming, Plastic, 1950s, 4 Piece 35.00
Cookie Jar, Alice In Wonderland, Regal 2500.00
Cookie Jar, Alice, White Cylinder, Disney 95.00
Cookie Jar, Dalmatian Puppy, Roly, Treasure Craft, 13 1/2 In. 55.00
Cookie Jar, Disney Characters, Tin, Chein Co. 65.00
Cookie Jar, Donald Duck & Nephews, Black, American Bisque 90.00
Cookie Jar, Donald Duck, Sitting, Disney 155.00
Cookie Jar, Dumbo, Mouse Finial, Signed Disney, 9 In. .... 85.00 To 135.00
Cookie Jar, Dumbo, Turnabout, Disney 85.00
Cookie Jar, Eeyore 250.00
Cookie Jar, Ludwig Von Drake, Lollipop Jar, Disney 145.00
Cookie Jar, Mickey & Minnie Mouse, Turnabout, 1930s .... 125.00 To 145.00
Cookie Jar, Mickey Mouse's Head, Musical, Disney 145.00
Cookie Jar, Mickey Mouse's Head, White, Disney 165.00
Cookie Jar, Mickey Mouse, Chef Hat, Treasure Craft, 10 1/4 In. .... 85.00 To 110.00
Cookie Jar, Mickey Mouse, Chef, Hoan, Box 79.00
Cookie Jar, Mickey Mouse, On Birthday Cake 825.00
Cookie Jar, Mickey On Drum, California Originals 395.00
Cookie Jar, Tigger, Walt Disney .... 125.00 To 175.00
Cookie Jar, Woody Woodpecker Head, Box 1050.00
Costume, Play Outfit, Mouseketeer, Mickey Mouse Club, Box, 1960s 135.00
Cup & Saucer, Tea, Mickey Mouse, Ohio Art 50.00
Decal, Mickey Mouse, Full Figure, Iron On For T Shirt, Full Figure, 1940s 6.00
Disneyland Express Train, Windup, Casey Jr., Marx 95.00
Doll, 7 Dwarfs, Knickerbocker Toy 1395.00

Doll, Cinderella, Porcelain, Holding Gold Slipper, Ball Gown, Box, 1940s 95.00
Doll, Donald Duck, Knickerbocker, 1930s, 13 In. 450.00
Doll, Goofy, Plastic, Wire Arms, Clothes, Marx, 1960s, 6 1/2 In. 38.00
Doll, Mickey Mouse, Long Nose, Wood Jointed, Cloth Ears 190.00
Doll, Mickey Mouse, Mickey Mouse Club, Knickerbocker, 12 In. 25.00
Doll, Mickey Mouse, Steiff, Complete, 1930s, 8 In. 1000.00
Doll, Mouseketeer, Mickey Mouse Club, Horsman, 1960s 30.00
Doll, Pinocchio, Vinyl, Italy, 1960, 10 In. 85.00
Doll, Sleeping Beauty, Cissette 375.00
Doll, Snow White & 7 Dwarfs, 15 & 9 In., 8 Piece 1300.00
Doll, Winnie The Pooh, Plush, Gund, 1965, 6 In. 35.00
Donald Duck, Sadiron 24.00
Doorstop, Donald Duck, 1971 .... 105.00
Drawing, Comic Art, Huey, Louie & Dewey, Pencil, Carl Barks, 1955, 7 x 9 In. 1100.00
Drawing, Donald Duck, Production, Framed, 1937 .... 495.00
Drum Set, Mickey Mouse 425.00
Drum, Mickey & Minnie, With Pluto, Instruments, Tin, Ohio Art, 1930s, 7 In. 100.00
Drum, Mickey Mouse Band, Stencil, Tin, 5 1/4 In. 100.00
Drum, Mickey Mouse Club, Tin Lithograph 55.00
Eggcup, Mickey Mouse, Sombrero, Japan, 1930s, 3 In. .... 125.00 To 200.00
Figurine Set, 101 Dalmations, Unpainted Plastic, Marx, 1960s, 8 Piece 50.00
Figurine, 3 Little Pigs, Box, 3 1/2 In., 3 Piece 200.00
Figurine, Bambi, Lying, Goebel, Full Bee, 1950s .... 75.00 To 85.00
Figurine, Big Bad Wolf, Bisque, 1930s, 3 1/2 In. 150.00
Figurine, Cinderella, Holding Gold Slipper, Ball Gown, Porcelain, 1940's 95.00
Figurine, Donald Duck, American Pottery, 1950s, 6 In. 200.00
Figurine, Donald Duck, Long Billed, Celluloid, 1930s, 2 3/4 In. 200.00
Figurine, Donald Duck, Seiverling Latex Co., Akron, Ohio 300.00
Figurine, Donald Duck, With Bugle, Bisque, 1930s, 3 In. 85.00
Figurine, Dopey, With Fiddle, Bisque, 1930s, 2 1/2 In. 32.00
Figurine, Dumbo, Sitting, With Bonnet, American Pottery, 1940s, Large 50.00
Figurine, Dumbo, Walt Disney, Goebel 250.00
Figurine, Ferdinand The Bull, Black, Bisque, 1930s, 3 1/4 In. 50.00
Figurine, Ferdinand The Bull, Japan, 1939, 3 1/2 In. 65.00
Figurine, Geppetto, From Movie Pinocchio, Multi Products, 1940 .... 40.00
Figurine, Grumpy, Snow White & 7 Dwarfs, Goebel, Full Bee, 1950s, 2 3/4 In. 85.00
Figurine, Jiminy Cricket, From Movie Pinocchio, Multi Products, 1940 .... 75.00
Figurine, Lady & Tramp, Sitting At Table, Bisque, Ceramic, W. D. P., 1970s 95.00
Figurine, Ludwig Von Drake, Rubber Squeeze, 1960s, 7 1/2 In. 45.00
Figurine, Mickey Mouse & Minnie, Bisque, Painted, Japan, 3 1/4 In. 198.00
Figurine, Mickey Mouse, Bisque, Paper Label, 1930s, 5 1/4 In. 675.00
Figurine, Mickey Mouse, Carved, Whimsical, Large, 1940 .... 2300.00
Figurine, Mickey Mouse, Holding Baseball Bat, Bisque, 1930s, 3 1/4 In. 275.00
Figurine, Mickey Mouse, Hunter, With Rifle, Goebel, Full Bee, 1950s, 5 1/2 In. 450.00
Figurine, Mickey Mouse, Playing French Horn, Bisque, 1930s, 3 1/4 In. 325.00
Figurine, Mickey Mouse, Riding Pluto, Bisque, 1930s, 2 1/4 In. 150.00
Figurine, Mickey Mouse, Seiberling Latex Co., Akron, Ohio 350.00
Figurine, Mickey Mouse, Walking, Celluloid, 1930s, 3 In. 175.00
Figurine, Mickey Mouse, With Rifle, Bisque, 1930s, 3 1/4 In. .... 200.00 To 265.00
Figurine, Mickey Mouse, Wood Balancing, Borgfeldt, 1930s 700.00
Figurine, Minnie Mouse, Bisque, Paper Label, 1930s, 5 1/4 In. 675.00
Figurine, Minnie Mouse, Playing Mandolin, Bisque, Painted, 1930s, 3 3/4 In. 85.00
Figurine, Minnie Mouse, Wooden, Fun–E–Flex, 1930s, 4 In. 175.00
Figurine, Pinocchio, Sitting, Goebel, Full Bee, 1950s, 4 3/4 In. 300.00
Figurine, Pluto, Bisque, Painted, 1930s, 2 1/2 In. 85.00
Figurine, Pluto, Chalkware, 3 In. 25.00
Figurine, Snow White & 7 Dwarfs, American Pottery, Complete, 1940s 1025.00
Figurine, Snow White & 7 Dwarfs, English, Wade, 6 1/2 In. 1800.00
Figurine, Snow White, Wade 150.00
Figurine, Thumper, American Pottery, 1940s, Large 70.00
Game, Cinderella, Parker Bros., 5 Slippers In Bag, 1950s 50.00
Game, Disneyland Monorail, Parker Bros., 1960 .... 40.00
Game, Donald Duck's Party, Donald Piece Only, WDE, 1930s 15.00

Game, Donald Duck's Party, Parker Bros., 1938	145.00
Game, Donald Duck, Card, Whitman, 1941	65.00
Game, Frontierland, Board, Parker Brothers, 1956	39.00
Game, Jungle Book, Board, Solitaire, Ed–U–Cards, 1966	42.00
Game, Mary Poppins Carousel, Parker Bros., 1964	30.00
Game, Mickey Mouse Club, Carnival, Gabriel, 1956	29.00
Game, Mickey Mouse Target, Marks, 1934, Box	270.00
Game, Mickey Mouse, Card, Old Maid, Whitman, 1935	150.00
Game, Pin The Tail, Mickey Mouse, 1930s	155.00
Game, Pinocchio, Card, Whitman, 1950's	10.00
Game, Puzzle, Mickey Mouse, All Wood, W. D. Productions	45.00
Game, Snow White, Board, 1934	50.00
Game, Target, Mickey Mouse, Gun & Darts, Marx	575.00
Game, Target, Snow White & 7 Dwarfs, American Toy Works, 1938	210.00
Game, Who Framed Rodger Rabbit, Milton Bradley, 1987	35.00
Glass, Alice In Wonderland, Eaglet	90.00
Glass, Funny Bunny	80.00
Glass, Goofy	115.00
Gumball Machine, Mickey Mouse, Plastic, Hasbro, Red Base, 1968	18.00
Handkerchief Purse, Mickey & Minnie, 1930's	75.00
Handkerchief, Ferdinand The Bull, Embroidered, Unused, 1938	20.00
Holder, Toothbrush, 3 Little Pigs, Brick Piano, Instruments, 1930s	200.00
Holder, Toothbrush, 3 Little Pigs, Playing Instruments, Bisque, 1930s	150.00
Holder, Toothbrush, Mickey & Minnie Mouse, Pair	475.00
Holder, Toothbrush, Mickey & Minnie, Standing, Bisque, 1930s, 4 1/2 In.	285.00
Holder, Toothbrush, Mickey Mouse & Pluto, Glazed, Large	625.00
Holder, Toothbrush, Mickey Mouse, Figural, Bisque, 1930s, 5 In.	450.00
Holder, Toothbrush, Mickey Mouse, French Horn, Bisque, 1930s, 3 1/4 In.	325.00
Horn, Mickey & Minnie Mouse Party, Marks Bros. Co., Paper, 1930s	175.00
Kaleidoscope, Mickey Mouse, W. D. P., Hong Kong	65.00
Knob, Gear Shift Lever, Mickey Mouse, Walt Disney Prod., 2 1/2 x 1 3/4 In.	49.50
Lamp, Ceiling, Donald Duck & Pluto Chasing Butterflies, Glass Glove, 1940s	195.00
Lamp, Cinderella, Figural, Composition, W. D. E., 1938	195.00
Lamp, Donald Duck, Figural, Standing By Candle, Leeds, 1940s	100.00
Lamp, Mickey Mouse, Metal Base, Shade, Soreng–Manegold Co., 11 In.	385.00
Lamp, Minnie Mouse, Shade, Rielley	150.00
Lamp, Snow White, Figural, Composition, W. D. E., 1938	175.00
Lantern, Donald Duck, Linemar, Box	260.00
Light Cover, Christmas, Mickey Mouse, Noma Decal, 1930s	25.00
Lunch Box, Chitty Chitty Bang Bang, 1968	65.00
Lunch Box, Disney Express, Tin, Aladdin	20.00
Lunch Box, Disneyland Castle, 1957	155.00
Lunch Box, Firefighter, Dome, 1939	50.00
Lunch Box, Fox & Hound, 1982	65.00
Lunch Box, Mickey Mouse Club, Annette, Yellow, 1963	65.00
Lunch Box, Mickey Mouse Club, White Rim, 1967	95.00
Lunch Box, School Bus, Yellow, Dome, 1969	15.00
Lunch Box, Snow White, Ohio Art, 1977	90.00
Lunch Kit, Mickey Mouse, Removable Lunch Tray	2500.00
Magazine, Mickey Mouse Club, Fall, 1956	10.00
Magazine, Walt Disney's Little People, Standard Oil Co., 4 Pages, 1939	125.00
Map, Disneyland, Tinkerbell, Fold Open, 8 1/2 x 12 In.	25.00
Map, Magic Kingdom, Large, 1987	15.00
Map, Mickey Mouse Globetrotter, 1938	125.00
Map, Park Souvenir, Signed By Walt Disney, 8 1/2 x 11 1/2 In.	2780.00
Marionette, Mickey & Minnie, Store Display, Strings, 4 In.	110.00
Mask, Halloween, Donald Duck, Long Billed	55.00
Mask, Mouseketeer, Walt Disney, 1950s	8.00
Mickey & Minnie Mouse, Swinging Exhibition Flights, 1930's, Clockwork, 12 In.	495.00
Mirror, Mickey Mouse, Pocket, Celluloid, Round	2.25
Movie Display, Snow White & 7 Dwarfs, Hand Carved, Wooden, 33 In.	5500.00
Mug, Donald Duck, Dan Brechner Label	45.00
Mug, Donald Duck, Patriot China	50.00

Mural, Lady & The Tramp, 2 x 3 Ft. 85.00
Mural, Many Characters, 6 x 8 Ft. 360.00
Music Box, Dopey, Whistle While You Work 850.00
Music Box, Happy, Heigh–Ho 850.00
Napkin Ring, Mickey Mouse, Porcelain, Black, White, Germany, 1930s, 2 3/4 In. 700.00
Necklace, Mickey Mouse, Sterling, Old Logo 45.00
Nodder, Goofy, Disney World 35.00
Nodder, Mickey Mouse, Green Base 65.00
Ornament, Christmas, Donald Duck, Mickey Mouse, Schmid, 1975, Box 30.00
Ornament, Christmas, Mickey, Minnie, Others, Box, Corning Glass, 6 Piece 145.00
Ornament, Tree Top, Tinker Bell, Plastic, Union Wadding Co., 1970s, 8 In. 100.00
Pail, Mickey Mouse & Minnie Fishing, Tin Lithograph, Handle, Ohio Art, 8 In. 66.00
Pail, Sand, Donald Duck, Tin 88.00
Pail, Sand, Donald, Nephews, Ohio Art, 4 In. 110.00
Pail, Sand, Mickey Mouse, Shovel, Tin Lithograph, Ohio Art, 8 In. 495.00
Paper Doll, Mickey Mouse & Minnie, Saalfield, Cut, 1933 .... 115.00
Paper Doll, Mickey Mouse, Steppin–Out, Giant Size, Whitman, 1977, Uncut 19.00
Paperweight, Donald Duck, Florida Citrus Caverns Coop., Lucite 18.00
Pencil Box, Mickey Mouse, Enterprise 70.00
Pencil Box, Minnie Mouse, Figural, Cardboard, Europe, 8 1/2 In. 385.00
Pencil Holder, Figural, Mickey Mouse, Composition, Painted, 1930s, 6 1/2 In. 400.00
Pencil Sharpener, Joe Carioca, Bakelite, Rectangular, 1940s, 1 1/4 In. 40.00
Pennant, Ice Capades, Snow White & 7 Dwarfs, 1960s 20.00
Pennant, Rescuers, Cloth, Bianca, Bernard, Evinrude, 1970s 10.00
Perfume Bottle, Snow White, Ceramic, 8 1/2 In. 20.00
Phonograph, Snow White & 7 Dwarfs, Drum 100.00
Pin, Cloisonne, Disneyland, 1980s 15.00
Pin, Enameled, Epcot Center, Pie–Eyed Mickey Mouse, Flags, 1980s 8.00
Pin, Mickey Mouse, Cloisonne, Brier Mfg. Co., 1930s 65.00
Pin, Pinocchio, With School Books, Plastic, Brier Mfg. Co., 1940, 2 In. .... 30.00 To 35.00
Pitcher, Cream, Bambi, American Pottery, 1940s, 6 In. 175.00
Pitcher, Milk, Dumbo, Disney, Large 125.00
Planter, Dumbo, Disney 36.00
Planter, Practical Pig, Lusterware, 1930s, 4 In. 35.00
Planter, Snow White, Leeds, 1940s 30.00
Plaque, Mickey Mouse, Figural, Wooden, Wall, Kerk Guild, Inc., 1936, 10 In. 215.00
Plaque, With Thermometer, Goofy, Kemper–Thomas, Ceramic, Square, 1940s 50.00
Plate, 3 Pigs, Divided, Patriot China 75.00
Plate, America On Parade, Donald Duck & Goofy, 1776–1976, Walt Disney World 210.00
Plate, Big Bad Wolf, Huffing & Puffing, Tin, Ohio Art, 4 1/4 In. 25.00
Plate, Christmas, Building A Snowman, Schmid, Box, 1976 .... 35.00
Plate, Christmas, Decorating The Tree, Schmid, Box, 1974 .... 185.00
Plate, Christmas, Mickey & Donald, Grolier, 1985 .... 45.00
Plate, Christmas, Mistletoe Magic, Disney Artists, Box, 1986 .... 50.00
Plate, Disney World 10th Anniversary, Box 175.00
Plate, Fantasia, Pewter Rim & Handles, Vernon Kilns, 1940s, 9 1/2 In. 525.00
Plate, Mickey & Minnie Mouse, Dancing, Tin, Walt Disney, 1930s, 2 In. 12.00
Plate, Mickey Mouse, 50th Birthday, 1978 .... 75.00 To 80.00
Plate, Mickey Mouse, Fireman, 2 Sections, Patriot China, 1930s 300.00
Plate, Mickey's Greatest Moments, 1938 Brave Little Tailor, 1980s, Box, 6 In. 40.00
Plate, Mother's Day, Pluto's Pals, Schmid, Box, 1977 .... 30.00
Porringer, Mickey Mouse, Horse Collar, International Silver, 1930 .... 275.00
Postcard, Donald Duck & Goofy, Valentine & Sons, Unused, 1930s 18.00
Postcard, Grumpy, Real Photograph 20.00
Poster, 101 Dalmatians, Walt Disney 715.00
Poster, Captain EO, Michael Jackson, Disneyland, 1986, 18 1/2 x 28 1/2 In. 50.00
Poster, Donald Duck, In Mathmagic Land, 1961, 27 1/2 x 21 In. 75.00
Poster, Dragon Slayer, Disney & Paramount, 1981, 26 x 41 In. 35.00
Poster, Snow White & 7 Dwarfs, Springbok, 1970s, 28 x 40 In. 12.00
Poster, Snow White, Walt Disney, 1960s, 28 x 41 In. 15.00
Poster, The Three Caballeros, Linen Back, 1944, 36 x 14 In. 495.00
Poster, Trick Or Treat, Movie, Donald Duck, Walt Disney, 1952 .... 1760.00
Print, Bambi Meets His Forest Friends, N.Y. Geographic Soc., 1946, 24 x 27 In. 60.00

Print, Pinocchio, Sitting, Jiminy Cricket, Abrams Art, 1970, 19 x 24 In. 10.00
Print, Tired Bunnies, Snow White, Framed, Courvoisier Gal., 1930s, 13 x 15 In. 325.00
Program, Fantasia, Movie, 1940 .... 38.00
Puppet, Dopey, Composition Head, Hand, Crown, 1938 .... 140.00
Puppet, Mickey Mouse, Push Up, Gabriel, 1978, On Card 25.00
Puppet, Pinocchio, Papier-Mache, Wooden, 10 In. 35.00
Puppet, Zorro, Walt Disney 22.50
Puzzle Block, Snow White & 7 Dwarfs, Box 95.00
Puzzle, Bambi, Jaymar, 2nd Series, 1944, 300 Pieces 32.00
Puzzle, Crossword, Mickey Mouse 20.00
Puzzle, Mickey Mouse, Gang Playing Instruments, Saalfield, Box, 1933 .... 125.00
Puzzle, Tortoise & The Hare, No. 3, Series of 4, Walt Disney 25.00
Puzzle, Zorro, 4 Inlaid Type, Box 95.00
Radio, Mickey Mouse 10.00
Record Player, Mickey Mouse, Mickey's Arm Plays Record, General Electric 75.00
Record, Cinderella, A Dream Is A Wish Your Heart Makes, 78 RPM, 1950s 7.00
Record, I'm No Fool, Jiminy Cricket, 78 RPM, 1950s 6.00
Record, Magic Mirror, Snow White & 7 Dwarfs, Story Book, 78 RPM, 1960 .... 12.00
Record, Talent Round Up & Merry Mouseketeers, 78 RPM, 1950s 6.00
Ring, Mickey Mouse, Sterling Silver, Adjustable 35.00
Rocker, Mickey Mouse, Wooden, Mengel Co., 1935 .... 475.00
Rug, Mickey Mouse, On Donkey, 1949, 21 x 39 In. 85.00
Rug, Pinocchio, Belgium, 55 x 100 In. 75.00
Rug, Snow White & 7 Dwarfs, 1949, 21 x 39 In. 55.00
Rug, Snow White & 7 Dwarfs, Alexander Smith & Co., 45 x 60 In. 440.00
Salt & Pepper, Alice In Wonderland 650.00
Salt & Pepper, Ludwig Von Duck, Dan Brechner, 1961, 5 In. .... 60.00 To 65.00
Salt & Pepper, Mickey & Minnie Mouse, Hoan 19.00
Salt & Pepper, Pluto 30.00
Saltshaker, Ludwig Von Drake 20.00
Saltshaker, Pinocchio, Bisque, Glazed, Japan, 1940s, 5 In. 25.00
Saucer, Tea, Mickey & Minnie Mouse, Tin, Ohio Art, 2 1/2 In. 15.00
School Bag, Minnie Mouse, Canvas 3.50
Sheet Music, Cinderella, Oversized, 1936 .... 10.00
Sheet Music, Ferdinand The Bull, 1938 .... 10.00
Sheet Music, Snow White & 7 Dwarfs, Music & Words, 1937, 14 Pages 25.00
Sheet Music, Snow White, With A Smile & A Song, 1937 .... 10.00
Sheet Music, So Dear To My Heart, Lavender Blue Dilly Dilly, 1948 .... 7.00
Sheet Music, Some Day My Prince Will Come, Snow White 35.00
Sheet Music, Wedding Party of Mickey Mouse, 1936 .... 65.00
Sheet Music, What! No Mickey Mouse?, Irving Caesar Inc., 1932 .... 125.00
Sheet Music, Who's Afraid of The Big Bad Wolf, 1933 .... 15.00
Sled, Flexible Flyer, Mickey & Minnie Mouse, Decals, W. D. Enterprises 240.00
Sled, Myrtle, Mustard Yellow, Allover Painted Line Design, Wooden 675.00
Soaky, Goofy, With Ears 18.00
Soap Set, Snow White & 7 Dwarfs, Figural, Lightfoot Schultz Co., Box, 1938 .... 400.00
Soap, Sleepy, Figural, Castile Soap, Box, 1938 .... 50.00
Spoon, Mickey Mouse, Full-Length Figure, Branford 20.00
Sticker Set, Aristocats Panini, 1980s, 225 Piece 35.00
Tablecloth, Mickey, Pluto, Clarabell Cow, Dennison, 1930s, 5 x 7 Ft. 250.00
Tablecloth, Mickey, Saxophone, Minnie, Paper, Dennison, 1930s, 5 x 7 Ft. 235.00
Tag, Doll's, Pinocchio, Cardboard, Knickerbocker, 1940s 20.00
Tea Set, Mickey Mouse & Minnie Mouse, Chein, 13 Piece 125.00
Tea Set, Snow White & 7 Dwarfs, Marx, Box, 1960s 350.00
Tea Set, Snow White & 7 Dwarfs, Tin Lithograph, Ohio Art, 1937 .... 135.00
Telephone, Mickey Mouse 95.00
Telephone, Mickey Mouse, Figural, WDP, 1976, 15 In. 125.00
Tie Rack, Mickey Mouse & Long-Billed Donald Duck, Wooden, 1936, 9 In. 195.00
Toy, Mouseketeer, Typewriter, Box 175.00
Toy, Airplane, Mickey's Air Mail, No. 44 .... 165.00
Toy, Car, Donald Duck, Crazy, Tin Head, Linemar 1000.00
Toy, Car, Mickey Mouse, Dipsy 185.00
Toy, Cinderella & Prince, Dancing, Walt Disney, Box 195.00

Toy, Cinderella & Prince, Perform The Waltz, Irwin, 1950s, 5 In. 220.00
Toy, Cinderella, Dancing, Windup, Irwin, 1950s, 5 In 220.00
Toy, Danny The Black Lamb, Plush, Ribbon, With Record Album, Book, Disney 100.00
Toy, Disneykins, 34 Characters, Complete, Marx, Display Box, c.1960 .... 323.00
Toy, Disneyland Express Train, Casey, Jr., Windup, Marx 95.00
Toy, Donald Duck Cart, Drum Major, Fisher-Price, 1951, 10 In. .... 195.00 To 200.00
Toy, Donald Duck Choo Choo, Fisher-Price 170.00
Toy, Donald Duck Choo Choo, Wooden, Lithograph, Fisher-Price, 8 1/2 In. 104.00
Toy, Donald Duck Duet, Windup, Marx, 1946 .... 400.00
Toy, Donald Duck, Acrobat, Trapeze, Celluloid, Windup, Linemar, 6 1/2 In. 508.00
Toy, Donald Duck, Acrobat, Windup, On Trapeze, Celluloid, Linemar, 6 1/2 In. 375.00
Toy, Donald Duck, Cart, Battery Operated, 1951 .... 110.00
Toy, Donald Duck, Crazy Car, Tin Head, Linemar 1000.00
Toy, Donald Duck, On Wooden Wheels, Fisher-Price, 1936 .... 200.00
Toy, Donald Duck, Pistol, Water, Figural, Elvin, Package 25.00
Toy, Donald Duck, Plays Drum, Rocks, Windup, Tin, Marx, 10 In. 268.00
Toy, Donald Duck, Pulled By Pluto, Celluloid, Japan, 8 In. 1210.00
Toy, Donald Duck, Ramp Walker, Pulling Wagon, With 3 Nephews 375.00
Toy, Donald Duck, Strutter, 1941 .... 180.00
Toy, Donald Duck, Twirling Tail, Windup, Illustrated Box, Marx 340.00
Toy, Donald Duck, Watering Can, Ohio Art 95.00
Toy, Donald Duck, Xylophone, Fisher-Price, 1946 .... 125.00
Toy, Dumbo, Bouncing, Windup, Marx, 1941 .... 500.00
Toy, Elephant, Elmer, Fisher-Price, Walt Disney, 1936 .... 195.00
Toy, Ferris Wheel, Disneyland, Box 750.00
Toy, Fire Truck, Mickey & Minnie Mouse, Hard Rubber, 1930s 300.00
Toy, Fire Truck, Mickey Mouse, Donald Duck, Red Rubber, 6 1/2 In. 49.00
Toy, Goofy, Scooter, Friction, Marx, Box, 1972 .... 150.00
Toy, Goofy, Windup, Marx, Box 600.00
Toy, Grand Piano, Mickey Mouse, Japan, 9 x 11 x 5 1/2 In. 715.00
Toy, Gun, Mickey Mouse Bubble Buster, Box, 1930s 200.00
Toy, Handcar, Donald Duck & Pluto, Articulated Hands, Lionel, 1930s, 10 In. 605.00
Toy, Handcar, Fantasia, Pride Lines, Box 150.00
Toy, Handcar, Mickey & Minnie, Composition, Clockwork, Steel, Lionel, 8 In. 450.00
Toy, Handcar, Mickey Mouse, Red, Lionel ....825.00 To 1250.00
Toy, Hill Climber Car, Mickey Mouse, Marx, Box 85.00
Toy, Jack-In-The-Box, Mickey Mouse, Musical, Kohner, Box 45.00
Toy, Kitchen Set, Child's, Snow White, 3 Piece 60.00
Toy, Locomotive, Donald Duck, Green, Yellow & Red, Disney, 2 In. 5.00
Toy, Mickey & Minnie Mouse, Donald Duck, Top, Fritz Buesche, 1935, 7 1/2 In. ... 165.00
Toy, Mickey & Minnie Mouse, Wash Tub, Tin Lithograph, Ohio Art, 1930s, 5 In. ... 250.00
Toy, Mickey & Minnie, Tambourine, Pie-Eyed, Red Tin, 1930s, 9-In. Diam. 200.00
Toy, Mickey Mouse & Driver, Windup, Linemar, Box, 6 5/8 In. 825.00
Toy, Mickey Mouse Beating On Drum, Pull Toy, Fisher-Price, 11 x 9 In. 248.00
Toy, Mickey Mouse Cowboy On Pluto, Celluloid, Windup 7500.00
Toy, Mickey Mouse Safety Blocks, Hal-Sam WDE, 1935, Box 357.00
Toy, Mickey Mouse Safety Patrol, Fisher-Price, No. 733 .... 150.00
Toy, Mickey Mouse, Choo Choo, Fisher-Price, No. 485 .... 95.00
Toy, Mickey Mouse, Circus, Trapeze, Painted Wood, Pull Toy, Nifty-Borgfeldt 3850.00
Toy, Mickey Mouse, Drummer, Fisher-Price, 1941 .... 150.00
Toy, Mickey Mouse, Drummer, Jazz, Squeeze Action, Tin 4200.00
Toy, Mickey Mouse, In Locomotive, Pull Toy 18.00
Toy, Mickey Mouse, Jazz Drummer, Squeeze Action, Nifty, 6 1/2 In. 4180.00
Toy, Mickey Mouse, Motorcycle, Travels, Noise, Linemar, 1950s, 3 1/2 In. 601.00
Toy, Mickey Mouse, On High Wheel, Linemar 950.00
Toy, Mickey Mouse, On Rocking Horse, Celluloid, Pie-Eyed, Painted, Japan, 1930s 1540.00
Toy, Mickey Mouse, On Safety Patrol, Fisher-Price 145.00
Toy, Mickey Mouse, Piano, Paper Litho On Wood, Marks Brothers, 10 x 9 x 5 In. 1540.00
Toy, Mickey Mouse, Plastic, Clockwork, Marx, 7 In. 110.00
Toy, Mickey Mouse, Rocking Horse, Windup 26.00
Toy, Mickey Mouse, Roly Poly, Celluloid, Ball Hands & Ears 275.00
Toy, Mickey Mouse, Top, Chein 125.00
Toy, Mickey Mouse, Train, Circus, 3 Cars, Tender, Locomotive, Lionel 15.00

Toy, Mickey Mouse, Train, Circus, Lionel, 1930s 2280.00
Toy, Mickey Mouse, Tricycle, Plastic Figure, Korea, 1960s 175.00
Toy, Mickey Mouse, Truck, Fire Department, Sun Rubber 75.00
Toy, Mickey Mouse, Unicyclist, Tin, Windup, Linemar, 6 In. 2000.00
Toy, Mickey Mouse, Vinyl, Squeeze, Dell, Package, 1950s 35.00
Toy, Mickey Mouse, Wooden, Painted, Barrel-Shaped Torso, c.1935, 5 In. 425.00
Toy, Mickey Mouse, Xylophone, Fisher-Price 375.00
Toy, Mickey The Magician, Battery Operated, Tin 2500.00
Toy, Minnie Mouse, Knitting, Windup, Tin, Linemar, 7 In. ....770.00 To 1025.00
Toy, Paint Set, Donald Duck, Metal, England, 1930s 50.00
Toy, Pluto, Delivery Wagon, Tin, Linemar, 6 In. 650.00
Toy, Pluto, Friction, Plastic, Cragston 125.00
Toy, Pluto, Pop-Up, Fisher-Price 95.00
Toy, Pluto, Pop-Up, Fisher-Price, 440 .... 125.00
Toy, Pluto, Pop-Up, W. D. Ent., 1936 .... 95.00
Toy, Pluto, Rubber, Seiberling, 1930s, 2 In. 100.00
Toy, Pluto, Stuffed, Sits, Character Novelty Co., 11 In. 495.00
Toy, Pluto, The Drum Major, Windup, Linemar, Japan, Box, 6 In 600.00
Toy, Pluto, Unique 350.00
Toy, Pluto, Windup, Plush Over Tin, Linemar, 5 In. 400.00
Toy, Pluto, Windup, Whirling Tail, Plastic, Marx, Box, 1953 .... 200.00
Toy, Projector, Mickey Mouse, Instruction Booklet, Keystone 700.00
Toy, Railcar, Donald Duck, Lionel, 10 x 7 In. 1100.00
Toy, Ramp Walker, Minnie Mouse, Pushing Baby Carriage 45.00
Toy, Rattle, Mickey Mouse Face, Pie-Eye, Celluloid 675.00
Toy, Roller Coaster, Disneyland, Chein 450.00
Toy, Snow White & 7 Dwarfs, Sink, Tin, Disney 75.00
Toy, Tea Set, Mickey Mouse, Blue Luster, Box, 23 Piece 825.00
Toy, Tractor, Mickey Mouse, Donald Duck Sitting, Rubber, Sunruco, Viceroy 55.00
Toy, Train, Mickey Mouse Choo-Choo, Fisher-Price, Red, Blue & Yellow 95.00
Toy, Truck, Delivery, Pinocchio, Marx 850.00
Toy, Watering Can, 3 Pigs, Ohio Art 70.00
Toy, Watering Can, Snow White & 7 Dwarfs, Ohio Art, 1938 .... 145.00
Toy, Xylophone, Disney, Box, 1950s, 7 x 13 In. 75.00
Tray, America On Parade, Tin Lithograph, 1976, 10 3/4 In. 25.00
Tray, Snow White, Ohio Art, 1937 .... 110.00
Tray, Snow White, Squirrels, Deer, Rabbits, W. D. Ent., 9 x 11 In. 80.00
Tray, Tea, Mickey Mouse, Ohio Art 110.00
Tray, Walt Disney World, Tin, Black, 1970s, 10 3/4 In. 10.00
Tumbler, Cinderella, No. 5, 1950, 5 1/4 In. 12.00
Tumbler, Happy Birthday Mickey, 50 Years of Magic 9.00
Tumbler, Juice, Mickey Mouse Club Logo, 1970s, 3 5/8 In. 5.00
Tumbler, Mickey Mouse, Cover, Shefford Process Cheese, 1930s, 3 1/2 In. 75.00
Tumbler, Minnie Mouse, Black, 1930s, 4 3/4 In. 20.00
Tumbler, Pinocchio, Red, 1940s, 4 5/8 In. 12.00
Tumbler, Sleeping Beauty, Touching The Spindle Glass, 1958, 5 In. 20.00
Tumbler, Sleepy, Musical Note, Green, 1937, 4 3/4 In. 45.00
Umbrella, Figural Handle, Mickey Mouse, 1950s 95.00
Umbrella, Red Plaid, Plastic Pluto Handle, F. Hollander & Son, Inc., 1970s 45.00
Valentine Set, Snow White, Mechanical, Moving Arms, 1938 .... 195.00
Viewer, Craftsmen's Guild, Mickey Mouse, 16 Film Strips, 1940s 350.00
Watch, Donald Duck, Happy 50th Birthday, Digital, Box 38.00
Watch, Donald Duck, Pocket, Ingersoll, 1939, 2 In. 800.00
Watch, Mickey Mouse, Child's, Marx 35.00
Watch, Mickey Mouse, Ingersoll, Mid-1930s, Pocket 367.50
Watch, Mickey Mouse, Lapel, Mickey On Back of Case, Ingersoll, 1938 .... 2735.00
Watch, Mickey Mouse, Marx 35.00
Watch, Mickey Mouse, Pocket, Fob, 1934 .... 795.00
Watch, Mickey Mouse, Pocket, Guarantee, 1933, Box 1050.00
Watch, Mickey Mouse, Pocket, Tall Stem, With Fob, 1933 .... 850.00
Wood Burning Set, American Toys & Furniture Co., 1956 .... 75.00
Wristwatch, Alice In Wonderland, U.S. Time, Light Blue Strap, 1950s 50.00
Wristwatch, Daisy Duck, Birthday, Ingersoll, 1947 .... 496.00

Wristwatch, Donald Duck Birthday, Box 95.00
Wristwatch, Mickey Mouse Club, 1960s 55.00
Wristwatch, Mickey Mouse, Ingersoll, 1933, Instructions, Box 1600.00
Wristwatch, Mickey Mouse, Ingersoll, Black Leather Strap, 1933 .... 300.00 To 450.00
Wristwatch, Mickey Mouse, Ingersoll, Box, 1938 .... 1500.00
Wristwatch, Mickey Mouse, Ingersoll, Box, 1948 .... 242.00
Wristwatch, Mickey Mouse, Man's, Pie–Eyed, Quartz, Bradley, 1980s 75.00
Wristwatch, Mickey Mouse, Sport 48.00
Wristwatch, Pluto, Ingersoll, Birthday Series, 1948 .... 200.00
Wristwatch, Snow White, Red Hands, Pink Face 20.00
Wristwatch, Tokyo Disneyland Commemorative 150.00

DOCTOR, see Dental; Medical

DOLL entries are listed by marks printed or incised on the doll, if possible.
If there are no marks, the doll is listed by the name of the subject or
country.

A. B. G., 1352, Toddler, Bisque, Fully Jointed, Composition Body, 1920s, 20 In. 545.00
A. B. G., 1361, Toddler, Chunky Body, 22 In. 775.00
A. B. G., Toddler, Velvet Suit, Bent Limb Body, 26 In. 895.00
A. M., 120, Toddler, Bisque Head, Mohair Wig, Composition, Dressed, 1908, 10 In. 245.00
A. M., 210, Googly, Intaglio Eyes, Campbell Kid Look, 6 1/2 In. 450.00
A. M., 323, Googly, Sleep Side–Glancing Eyes, Toddler Body, 9 In. 950.00
A. M., 340, Brown Fixed Open Eyes, Open Mouth, Jointed Composition Body, 29 In. 220.00
A. M., 351, Baby, Stockinet Body, Brown Sleep Eyes, Wobble Tongue, 20 1/2 In. 350.00
A. M., 352, Happy Boy, Bent Limbs, Dimples, 14 In. 400.00
A. M., 353, Oriental, 5 Piece Composition Body, Oriental–Type Outfit, 7 In. 275.00
A. M., 370, Bisque Head & Arms, Kid Body, Sleep Eyes, Pink Taffeta Dress, 24 In. 375.00
A. M., 390, Bisque Head, Sleep Eyes, Real Lashes, Open Mouth, Peach Outfit, 31 In. 700.00
A. M., 390, Bisque Socket Head, Brown Sleep Eyes, 4 Teeth, Composition, 31 In. 700.00
A. M., 390, Brown Sleep Eyes, Lashes, Ball–Jointed Body, Lace Dress, 30 In. 895.00
A. M., 390, Dutch Girl, Open Mouth, Composition, Complete Dress 155.00
A. M., 410, Bisque Head, Set Blue Eyes, Open Mouth, Kid Body, Blue Dress, 16 In. 60.00
A. M., 990, Character Baby, Original Clothes, 8 1/2 In. 325.00
A. M., 1894, Bisque, Brown Sleep Eyes, 24 In. 795.00
A. M., 1894, Boy, Bisque Head, 4 Teeth, Wood, Composition, Dressed, 18 In. 425.00
A. M., 3200, Kid Body, Old Clothes, Original Wig, 13 In. 195.00
A. M., 3323, Googly, Wig, Shoes & Socks, Old Clothes, 12 1/2 In. 1650.00
A. M., Baby Gloria, Baby, Dimpled, Cloth Body, Composition, Dressed, 21 In. 950.00
A. M., Baby, 5–Piece Composition Body, Sleep Eyes, 21 In. 550.00
A. M., Bisque Head, Sleep Eyes, Fur Eyebrows, Mohair, Composition, 30 In. 275.00
A. M., Boy, Black Suit, Germany, 8 In. 210.00
A. M., Character Baby, Sleep Blue Eyes, Bent Limb, Composition, 22 In. 412.50
A. M., Character Indian, Glass Eyes, Open Mouth, Jointed, Felt Clothes 82.50
A. M., Dream Baby, Blue Sleep Eyes, Closed Mouth, Cloth Body, 17 In. 192.50
A. M., Florodora, Boy, Bisque Socket Head, Open Mouth, Mohair Wig, 16 In. 175.00
A. M., Florodora, Fur Eyebrows, Kid Body, Bisque Hands, Dressed, 23 In. 395.00
A. M., Florodora, Pale Bisque, Sleep Eyes, 18 In. 375.00
A. M., Florodora, Sleep Eyes, Open Mouth, Jointed Composition Body, 27 In. 275.00
A. M., Girl, Sleep Eyes, Pink Dress, 8 In. 175.00
A. M., My Playmate, Tag, 8 1/ 2 In. 395.00
A. M., Queen Louise, Bisque Head, Brown Sleep Eyes, Jointed, 24 In. .... 220.00 To 495.00
A. M., Queen Louise, Socket Head, 1910, 22 In. 450.00
A. M., Rosebud, Sleep Eyes, Kid Body, Bisque Arms, 20 In. 175.00
Advertising, Banana Splits, Stuffed, Cereal Premium 65.00
Advertising, Bunny, Playboy, Stuffed, Bowtie, 24 In. 200.00
Advertising, Burger King, Box 58.00
Advertising, Burger King, Stuffed, 12 In. 12.00
Advertising, C & H, Boy & Girl, Hawaiian 22.00
Advertising, Campbell's Soup Kids, Boy & Girl, Checkered Outfit, 10 In. 95.00
Advertising, Chicken of The Sea, Mermaid, Box, 17 In. 65.00
Advertising, Chicken of The Sea, Mermaid, Stuffed, Acme Premium, 12 In. 18.00

Advertising, Chiquita Banana	12.00
Advertising, Choo–Choo Charlie, Cloth, Vinyl Face, 1972, Hasbro, 10 In.	65.00
Advertising, Coke, Molly Cola, 4 In.	8.00
Advertising, Cream of Wheat, Cloth, Stuffed	75.00
Advertising, Cream of Wheat, Rag, Black	125.00
Advertising, Gerber Baby, Dish, Cup, Bottle, Spoon, Cereal, Sleep, Eyes14 In.	20.00
Advertising, Gerber Baby, Flirty Eyes, 16 In.	25.00
Advertising, Gerber Baby, Sleep Eyes	30.00
Advertising, Kellogg, Johnny Bear, Fabric, Uncut	75.00
Advertising, Kellogg, Little Bopeep, Cloth, Lithograph	125.00
Advertising, Kellogg, Mary Had Little Lamb, Little Miss Muffet Other Side, Stuffed	30.00
Advertising, Kellogg, Papa Bear, Unstuffed	125.00
Advertising, Kellogg, Papa, Mama & Baby Bear & Goldilocks, 4 Piece	100.00
Advertising, Lee, Composition, Buddy Lee	185.00
Advertising, Michelin Man, Seated, Mounting Bracket, 26 In.	125.00
Advertising, Miss Revlon, 18 In.	50.00
Advertising, Morton Salt Girl, Mattel, Box, 1873	135.00
Advertising, Mr. Bib, Michelin Tire Man, White, Vinyl, Hands On Hips, 12 1/2 In.	139.50
Advertising, Nestle's Little Hans, Vinyl	40.00
Advertising, Philco, Eskimo, 1950s	75.00
Advertising, Phillips 66, Composition, Buddy Lee	275.00
Advertising, Pillsbury Doughboy, 1971	8.00
Advertising, Pillsbury Doughgirl, Rubber, 1972, 5 1/2 In.	11.00
Advertising, Pillsbury Poppin' Fresh Girl, Vinyl, Box	25.00
Advertising, Puffy, Pops–Rite Popcorn, 11 In.	30.00
Advertising, RCA, Radiotron, Radio Tube Hat, Painted, Parrish, 15 1/2 In.	110.00
Advertising, Ronald McDonald	30.00
Advertising, Sailor, Holland America Line, 11 In.	65.00
Advertising, Scarecrow Sam, Brach's Candy	9.00
Advertising, Stay Puff Sailor, Vinyl	20.00
Advertising, Stewardess, Continental Trailways, Bus Company, 15 In.	125.00
Advertising, Sugar Bear, Post Sugar Crisp, Cloth, 4 1/2 In.	6.00
Advertising, Texaco, Composition, Buddy Lee	250.00
Advertising, Toni, Comb, Curlers, Wave Lotion, Box, 14 In.	300.00
Advertising, Tyson Chick'N Quick, Stuffed Chicken, Red Running Shoes, 14 In.	65.00
Advertising, Winn–Dixie Supermarket, Baby, Musical, Box	12.00
Alabama Baby, All Original, 14 In.	2000.00
Alexander dolls are listed in this category under Madame Alexander	
Alt, Beck & Gottschalck, Character Baby, Flirty Eyes, Composition, 1920s, 15 In.	385.00
Amberg, Newborn Baby, Bisque Flange Head, Sleep Eyes, Closed Mouth, 12 In.	300.00
American Character, Little Love, Composition, Cloth, 1922, 18 In.	175.00
Annalee, Mr. & Mrs. Claus, Motorized, With Rocking Chair, 1979, Pair	950.00
Archie Andrews, Ventriloquist, Plastic, Peter Brough, England, 14 1/2 In.	195.00
Armand Marseille dolls are listed in this category under A. M.	
Art Fabric Mills, Cloth, Red Hair, Ribbon, Stockings, Laced Boots, 1900, 19 In.	210.00
Automaton, Bubble Blower, Girl, Bisque Head, Lambert, 21 In.	3000.00
Automaton, Cat Quintet, 5 Fur–Covered Cats, Various Instruments, 15 In.	5500.00
Automaton, Girl, Dancing, Bisque Head, Glass Eyes, Original Costume, 6 3/4 In.	195.00
Automaton, Monkey Musicians, 21 In.	7705.00
Automaton, Oriental Tea Server, Lambert, 19 In.	5250.00
Automaton, Phalibois, Tightrope Walker, 21 In.	5250.00
Automaton, Tete Jumeau, Guitar Player, Lambert, 19 In.	5600.00
Automaton, Young Girl With Tambourine, Key Wind, France, c.1885, 20 In.	9000.00
Averill, Bonnie Babe, Bisque & Composition, 1926, 22 In.	1550.00
Baby Bright Eyes, Plaid Cotton Dress, Original Hair, Pin, 18 In.	950.00
Baby Peggy, Child Movie Star of 1920s, 20 1/2 In.	2500.00
Baby Ruth, Cloth, 1930	185.00
Baby Snooks, Fanny Brice, 12 In.	175.00
Baby Stewart, Bisque, Painted Bonnet	600.00
Baby, Bisque, Bent Legs, Arms, Facial Features, Germany, 4 In.	80.00
Baby, Cheerful Tearful, Sad To Happy Face, Mattel, 1961, 13 In.	59.00
Bahr & Proschild, 224, Blond Curls, Stiff Wrist, Tasseled Leather Boots, 20 In.	1250.00
Bahr & Proschild, 244, Indian Girl, Bisque, Original Costume, c.1890, 13 In.	575.00

Bahr & Proschild, 306, Mohair Wig, Threaded Eyes, Composition Body, 16 1/2 In. 525.00
Bahr & Proschild, 320, Child, Bisque Socket Head, Sleep Eyes, Open Mouth, 28 In. 1500.00
Bahr & Proschild, 604, Character Baby, Chubby Bent Limb, Open–Close Mouth 395.00
Bahr & Proschild, 604, Toddler, Ice Skating, Bisque, Open–Close Mouth, 13 1/2 In. 850.00
Bahr & Proschild, 2095, Character, Tommy Tucker's Sister, 28 In. 3500.00
Bahr & Proschild, Bisque Head, Brown Sleep Eyes, Antique Clothes, 23 In. 1795.00
Bahr & Proschild, Character Baby, 5–Piece Body, 19 In. 750.00
Bahr & Proschild, Character Baby, Bisque, Sleep Eyes, Bent Limb, 1920s, 15 In. 247.50
Bahr & Proschild, Character Baby, Bisque, Sleep Eyes, Jointed Bent Limb, 11 In. ... 330.00
Bahr & Proschild, Toddler, Bisque Head, 5–Piece Toddler Body, Long Dress, 24 In. 725.00
Banana Splits, Stuffed, Bowne 45.00
Barbie dolls are listed in this category under Mattel
Barrois, Bisque Arms, Swivel Neck, Pierced Ears, Original Wig, 17 In. 4750.00
Barrois, Fashion, Bisque Head, Sleep Eyes, Antique Fabric Hat & Shoes, 24 In. 4700.00
Beatles, Set of 4, Rooted Hair, 1964 .... 225.00
Bebe, Closed Mouth, Set Eyes, 27 In. 5500.00
Bebe, Phonographe, Sings One French Song, 24 In. 6500.00
Bebe, Socket Head, Gray Paperweight Eyes, Chemise, Box, 20 In. 4800.00
Beecher, Missionary Baby, Stockinet 300.00
Belton, Bisque, Closed Mouth, Straight Wrist, Jointed Body, 14 In. 1595.00
Belton, Paperweight Eyes, Jointed Body, Silk & Lace Costume, 14 In. 1895.00
Belton–Type, Pink Dress, France, 7 1/2 In. 125.00
Bergmann dolls are also in this category under S & H and Simon & Halbig
Bergmann, Bisque, Blue Sleep Eyes, Hair Lashes, Human Hair Wig, Dress, 23 In. ... 795.00
Bergmann, Bisque, Brown Sleep Eyes, Frill Costume, 30 In. 1195.00
Bergmann, Bisque, Sleep Eyes, Open Mouth, Jointed Composition Body, 26 In. 165.00
Bergner, 3–Face, Crying, Sleeping & Smiling, 15 In. 1500.00
Berry, Emmett Kelly, 20 1/2 In. 165.00
Bisque Head, Christmas Tinsel Trim, Stationary Eyes, Brown Wig, Germany 135.00
Bisque, Chubby, 1 Piece, Painted Pajamas, Pug Nose, Germany, 1920, 6 In. 300.00
Bisque, Chubby, Brown Glass Eyes, Wig, Germany, 5 In. 300.00
Bisque, Closed Mouth, Brown Eyes, Kid Body, Wig, Clothes, Germany, 20 In. 1200.00
Bisque, Composition, Germany, 25 In. 750.00
Bisque, Head, Arms & Legs, Blond Hair, Blue Eyes, 8 In. 100.00
Bisque, Head, Wood & Composition Body, Jointed, Blond Wig, Sleep Eyes, 30 In. ... 385.00
Bisque, Head, Wood Arms & Legs, Blond Wig, Sleep Eyes, 7 1/2 In. 176.00
Bisque, Jointed, Glass Eyes, Blond Mohair Wig, Germany, 4 In. 210.00
Bisque, Molded Hair, Blue Stockings & Molded Shoes, 7 1/2 In. 95.00
Bisque, Wavy Blond Hair, Big Eyes, Movable Arms, Japan, 5 1/2 In. 55.00
Black dolls are included in the Black category
Black, Celluloid, Red Dress, Japan, 2 1/2 In. 35.00
Black, Mammy With Button Eyes, Embroidered Mouth, Rag, Worn Dress, Apron ... 27.00
Black, Mammy, Cloth, 1930s, 18 In. 45.00
Black, Minstrel, Cloth, 16 In. 30.00
Black, Provenance, Composition, Can't Break Em, Original Clothes 550.00
Black, Rag, Oil Painted Features, Brown, 18 In. 2250.00
Black, Rag, Printed, Girl, White Dress, 18 In. 137.00
Black, Wooden, Painted Eyes, Lips, Jointed, Flat Black Feet, 1935, 14 In. 300.00
Bonnie Babe, Original Clothes, Sewn–On–Tag, 17 In. 1475.00
Bonnie Braids, On Rocker, 1951 .... 125.00
Boudoir, Molded, Portrait Face, Blond Hair, Pink Lace Dress, 1920s, France, 34 In. 285.00
Boy & Girl, Angel, Cloth, Feather Hair, Felt Wings, 1940, 8 1/4 In., Pair 35.00
Boy & Girl, China, Feather Headdress, Box, 5 In., Pair 75.00
Bozo, Bend Em, Knickerbocker, 8 In. 20.00
Brownie, Lithograph, Googly Eyes, Military Uniform, Cloth, c.1900, 6 In. 1200.00
Bru Jne, Bisque, Paperweight Eyes, Human Hair Wig, Dress, Shoes, 22 In. 8500.00
Bru Jne, Bisque, Silk Antique Dress, Leather Shoes & Gloves, c.1887, 19 In. 5500.00
Bru Jne, Lady In Chariot, Bisque Shoulder Plate, Molded Breasts, 22 x 19 In. 4250.00
Bru Jne, No. 10, Bisque Head, Station Paperweight Eyes, Jointed, 22 In. 1760.00
Bru Jne, Nursing, Bisque Head, Nursing Mechanism, Lace Baby Dress, 18 In. 5200.00
Bru Jne, Nursing, Blue Paperweight Eyes, 17 In. 9500.00
Bru Jne, Walker, 2–Face, Metal Feet, Wire Upper Arms, Windup, Toddles, 11 In. ... 1100.00
Bru Jne, Walker, Bisque Head, Original Clothes, 22 In. 5000.00

Bruckner, Black, Cloth, 13 1/2 In. 850.00
Bruckner, Topsy Turvy, Black & White, Original Tag, 12 In. 695.00
Buschow & Beck, Boy, Celluloid, Intaglio Eyes, Jointed Cloth Body, Clothes, 16 In. 165.00
Bye-Lo, All Bisque, Molded Hair, Label, 4 1/2 In. 375.00
Bye-Lo, Baby, Bisque Head, Sleep Eyes, Frog Legs, Celluloid Hands, 11 In. 350.00
Bye-Lo, Baby, Bisque, Sleep Eyes, Christening Dress, 12 In. 285.00
Bye-Lo, Baby, Blue Sleep Eyes, Closed Mouth, Cloth, Celluloid Hands, 16 In. 275.00
Bye-Lo, Baby, Cloth Body, Celluloid Hands, Baby Dress, 14 In. 350.00
Bye-Lo, Bisque, Chest Label, 4 In. 350.00
Bye-Lo, Bisque, Painted Eyes, Original Clothes, 4 In. 350.00
Bye-Lo, Swivel Head, Sleep Eyes, Jointed Body, Dress, 8 In. 825.00
Bye-Lo, Tiny, Bisque, Incised & Sticker, 4 In. 210.00
C. O. D., 1469, Lady, Bisque, Long Limb Body, Silk Dress, Shoes, 14 In. 3600.00
Cameo, Bandy, Jointed, Wooden, Maxfield Parrish Design 950.00
Captain Action, Extra Flash Gordon Clothes, Box 275.00
Captain Kangaroo, Cloth 45.00
Celluloid, Costume, Original Wig, 9 In. 60.00
Celluloid, Football Player, Straw Stuffed, 8 In. 20.00
Celluloid, Movable Arms, Germany, 1900, 18 In. 150.00
Chad Valley, Highland Lassie, Scarf, Tam & Dress Spats, 16 In. 495.00
Chad Valley, Princess Elizabeth, Painted Blue Eyes, 18 In. 1250.00
Chad Valley, Princess Margaret, Glass Eyes, 16 In. 1750.00
Character Baby, Bisque, Gray Sleep Eyes, Blond Mohair, Christening Dress, 26 In. 750.00
Character Baby, Bisque, Sitting, Long Stockings, 5 In. 110.00
Character Boy, Toddler, Brown Eyes, Molded Hair, Bent Limb Body, 24 In. 2700.00
Character Indian, Painted Bisque, Stationary Eyes, Jointed Composition, 12 In. 385.00
Charlie Chaplin, Hard Rubber, Fabric, Little Tramp, 18 In. 40.00
Chase, Baby, Boy, Oil-Painted Stockinet Head, Hair, Features, Cloth Body, 24 In. 500.00
Chase, Boy, Blond Hair, Sateen Body, White Linen Sailor Suit, 20 In. 550.00
Chase, Girl, Oil Painted Stockinet Head, Painted Hair, Original Clothing, 21 In. 450.00
Chase, Hospital Baby, Oil Painted Stockinet Head, Blond Hair, Diaper, 20 In. 550.00
Chase, Hospital Baby, Stockinet & Cloth, Oil Painted, 21 In. 715.00
Chase, Sateen Body, Stamped On Hip, 23 In. 357.50
Chase, Stockinet, Cotton Sateen Body, Old-Fashioned Child, 20 In. 750.00
China, Head & Limbs, Cloth Body, Original Clothes, Pink Tinted, 9 In. 600.00
China, Head, Black Hair, Brown Eyes, Cloth, Leather Hands, 1850-1860, 21 In. 330.00
China, Head, Blond Molded Hair, Cloth Body, 24 1/2 In. 270.00
China, Head, Cloth, Polka Dot Dress, Shoes, 1860-1870, 23 In. 325.00
China, Head, Molded Bosom, Cloth Body, Wooden Legs, Clothes, 7 1/2 In. 3500.00
China, Ironstone Arms & Legs, Blue Damask Dress, 19 In. 25.00
China, Shoulder Head, Molded Hair, Cloth Body & Limbs, Kid Hands, 24 In. 165.00
Cissette, 865, Jacqueline Kennedy, All Original 500.00
Cloth Mask Face, Painted Eyes, Cloth Body, Jointed At Hips, 14 In. 110.00
Cloth Mask Face, Painted Eyes, Smiling Mouth, Yarn Hair, Red Dress, 14 In. 155.00
Clothespin, Painted Features, Yarn Hair, 9 1/4 In. 22.00
Clown, Character Head, Bisque, Clapping Mechanism, Original, 8 In. 180.00
Cochran, Child, Latex Socket Head, 5-Piece Latex Body, Original Dress, 14 In. 1445.00
Columbia, Bisque Head, Kid Body, Bisque Lower Arms, Floral Dress, 18 1/2 In. 165.00
Composition, Felt Clothing, Germany, 1920s, 4 In. 45.00
Conductor, Black Cloth, Stitched Face, 1900, 20 In. 950.00
Cuno & Otto Dressel, 1912, Bisque Head, 4 Upper Teeth, Striped Dress, 22 In. 285.00
Danny & Daisey, From Romper Room, Pair 90.00
Dennis The Menace, Squeeze, Rubber 25.00
DEP, Bisque Head, Open Mouth, Composition Jointed, Silk Dress & Hat, 17 In. 895.00
DEP, Boy & Girl, Sailor Clothes, Germany, Box, 8 In., Pair 495.00
DEP, Bride, Bisque, Brown Inset Eyes, Jointed Body, Satin Dress, 1894, 23 In. 650.00
DEP, Schoolgirl, Molded Teeth, Ball Jointed Body, Leather & Tweed Outfit, 21 In. 950.00
Dolley Madison, China, Molded Black Bow In Hair, 28 In. 550.00
Door of Hope Mission, Bridegroom, Wooden Head & Hands, 11 1/2 In. 165.00
Dora Petzold, Composition Head, Painted, Muslin Body, Limbs, 1920s, 19 In. 605.00
Dorothy, Wizard of Oz, Judy Garland 70.00
Dressmaker, Molded, Brown Eyes, Germany, 19 In. 850.00
DRGM, Girl, Bisque Head, Sleep Eyes, Open Mouth, Blue Dress, 24 In. 385.00

E. D. Bebe, Bisque Socket Head, Blue Paperweight Eyes, Closed Mouth, 23 In. 2500.00
Effanbee, Abraham Lincoln, 1985, 17 In. 65.00
Effanbee, Alfalfa 59.00
Effanbee, American Child, Barbara Joan 325.00
Effanbee, Amish, Boy & Girl, Toddlers, 8 In., Pair 475.00
Effanbee, Ann Shirley, 5–Piece Composition, 21 In. 245.00
Effanbee, Ann Shirley, Wedding Dress, 18 In. 150.00
Effanbee, Annie Oakley, 1976, 12 In. 75.00
Effanbee, Boy, Button Nose, Original Clothes, 8 In. 95.00
Effanbee, Brownie Scout, Girl, Black, 1965 .... 68.00
Effanbee, Bubbles, 14 In. 175.00
Effanbee, Bubbles, 24 In. 695.00
Effanbee, Button Nose Betty, 1943, 8 In. 200.00
Effanbee, Claudette Colbert, Dressed As Cleopatra 179.00
Effanbee, Dy-Dee, Hard Plastic Head, Rubber Ears & Body, Caracul Wig, 12 In. ... 85.00
Effanbee, Eleanor & Franklin Roosevelt, Pair 175.00
Effanbee, Groucho Marx, 1983, 17 In. 85.00
Effanbee, John Wayne, 1981, 17 In. 95.00
Effanbee, Little Brother, Composition Head, Yarn Hair, Shirt, Pants, Shoes, 16 In. 250.00
Effanbee, Little Sister, Composition Head, Yarn Hair, Cloth Body, Dress, 12 In. 175.00
Effanbee, Lovums, Original Clothes, Large 325.00
Effanbee, Mae Starr, 11 Cylinder Records, 30 In. .... 560.00 To 800.00
Effanbee, Mae West, 1982, 17 In. 75.00
Effanbee, Marionette, Bisque, Kinky Hair, 6 In. 250.00
Effanbee, Marionette, Clippo The Clown, 1936 .... 290.00
Effanbee, Marionette, Emily Ann, Box 150.00
Effanbee, Marionette, Lucifer V. Austin, 14 In. 121.00
Effanbee, Marionette, Lucifer, 1936 .... 375.00
Effanbee, Mary Lee, Composition, 18 In. 150.00
Effanbee, Patsy Ann, 19 In. .... 300.00 To 395.00
Effanbee, Patsy Ann, Metal Trunk, Drawers, Clothes 550.00
Effanbee, Patsy, Swivel Head, Sleep Eyes, Original Clothes & Bonnet, 10 In. 60.00
Effanbee, Patsyette, Bracelet, Tagged Dress, Box, 11 In. 350.00
Effanbee, Skippy, Dressed As World War I Soldier, 13 1/2 In. .... 270.00 To 375.00
Effanbee, Sweetie Pie, Flirty Eyes, 17 In. 175.00
Effanbee, Thomas Jefferson 75.00
Effanbee, W. C. Fields, 1960, 17 In. 125.00
Emma Clear, George & Martha Washington, Signed, 1940, Pair .... 700.00 To 1200.00
F. G., Bisque, Paperweight Eyes, Human Hair Wig, 17 1/2 In. 6500.00
F. G., Chunky Body, Blue Paperweight Eyes, Dress, Shoes, 31 In. 8500.00
F. G., Mechanical, Push Down He Doffs Hat, Silk Costume, 6 1/2 In. 950.00
F. G. . Fashion, Blond Wig, Paperweight Eyes, Dressed, 14 In. 2200.00
Fam-Lee, 3 Interchangeable Heads, Box 400.00
Farrah Fawcett, Box, 1977 .... 34.00
Felix The Cat, Composition, 1930s, 13 In. 150.00
Fisher-Price, Hot Mammy, Box 275.00
Fisher-Price, Joey 25.00
Flapper, Whisk Broom 65.00
Flasher, Character, Man, Trench Coat, Anatomically Correct, Cloth, Label 65.00
Fortune Teller, French, Papier–Mache, 1860s, 25 In. 2500.00
Francois Gaultier, French Fashion, 16 In. 1600.00
Fred Flintstone, Vinyl, 1960, 12 In. 55.00
French Fashion, Bisque Head & Arms, Kid Body, Dress & Hat, 13 In. 2100.00
French Fashion, Blue Paperweight Eyes, Bisque, Original Clothes, 14 1/2 In. 2700.00
French Style, Bisque, Swivel Neck, Brown Glass Eyes, Dress, Yellow Boots, 5 In. ... 500.00
French, Bisque, Fashion, Gray Eyes, Costume, 18 In. 6500.00
French, Bisque, In French Egg, With Trousseau, 5 In. 2500.00
French, Bisque, Paperweight Eyes, Original Clothes, 16 In. 3700.00
French, Mystery Child, Factory Dress, Hat, 19 In. 4200.00
French, Swivel Head, Sleep Eyes, Open Mouth, Teeth, Incised 3, 7 In. 335.00
Freundlich, Baby Sandy, Tin Sleep Eyes, Molded Hair, Composition, 1940s, 17 In. 165.00
Fritz Bartenstein, Wax, 2–Faced, Sleeping & Crying, Glass Eyes, 12 In. 795.00
Frozen Charlotte, Black, 3 7/8 In. 150.00

Fulper, Kid Body, Bisque Head, 22 In. 550.00
Fulper, Kid Body, Bisque Head, Composition Hands, 9 1/2 In. 195.00
G.I. Joe Adventure Team, Black, Hasbro, Box, 1970 .... 225.00
G.I. Joe, Field Pack, 1960s, Package 85.00
G.I. Joe, Footlocker & Accessories 95.00
G.I. Joe, U.S. Navy Life Ring, 1960s 75.00
G.I. Joe, Yellow Flock Hair, Astronaut Suit, Helmet 100.00
Gebruder Heubach dolls are also in this category under Heubach
Gebruder Heubach, 5626, Character Child, Nurse Clothes, 22 In. 2000.00
Gebruder Heubach, 5636, Boy, Laughing, Glass Eyes, Mohair Wig, Teeth, 13 In. ... 2200.00
Gebruder Heubach, 5636, Laughing, Glass Eyes, Cloth Body, 15 In. 875.00
Gebruder Heubach, 5730, Bisque, Sleep Eyes, Human Hair, Costume, 20 In. 2000.00
Gebruder Heubach, 7246, Character Boy, Pouty, 27 In. 5000.00
Gebruder Heubach, 7246, Pouty, Sleep Eyes, 14 In. 2500.00
Gebruder Heubach, 7669, Character, Laughing, Composition, Jointed, 11 In. 650.00
Gebruder Heubach, 7843, Boy, Crying, Squinting Eyes, Crooked Mouth, 17 In. 1650.00
Gebruder Heubach, 8192, Bisque, Dress, Molded Shoes & Socks, 6 In. 850.00
Gebruder Heubach, 9467, Indian Squaw, 1910, 14 In. ....*Illus* 2500.00
Gebruder Heubach, Character Boy, Blond, Knickers, 1910, 19 In. ....*Illus* 6750.00
Gebruder Heubach, Character Boy, Sunday Suit, 1910, 17 In. ....*Illus* 5500.00
Gebruder Heubach, Pouty, Child, Blue Sleep Eyes, 14 In. 2500.00
Gebruder Koch, Mechanical, Clapping Boy, Intaglio Eyes, 7 1/2 In. 395.00
Gebruder Kuhnlenz, 165, Bisque Head, Sleep Eyes, Ball–Jointed Dress, 22 In. 485.00
Gen. MacArthur, Man of Hour, Composition, Army Uniform, Paper Tag, 19 In. 175.00
Georgene, Beloved Belinda 695.00
Georgene, Girl, WPA, Milwaukee, 10 Outfits, 20 In. 450.00
Georgene, Raggedy Ann & Raggedy Andy, 16 In., Pair 185.00
German, Bisque Head, Open Mouth, Peach Satin & Lace Dress, Jointed, 26 In. 1495.00
German, Kid Body, Glass Eyes, Human Hair, Traditional Clothes, 12 1/2 In. 150.00
German, Papier–Mache Head, Kid Body, Bisque Lower Arms, Dressed, 17 In. 245.00
Gilbert, Napoleon Solo, Man From U. N. C. L. E., Gun, Badge, Box, 1965, 12 In. .. 198.00
Golliwog Type, Wooden, Sweden, 5 In. 125.00
Googly, Boy, Girl, Bisque, Molded Shoes & Socks, Jointed, Glass Eyes, 6 In., Pair ... 1100.00
Gotez, Alessandra, Box 299.00
Grace Putman, Bisque Head, Arms, Body, Rolling Eyes, Pink Dress, c.1900, 7 In. .. 445.00
Grace Putman, Bye–Lo, Bisque Head, Cloth Body, Celluloid Hands, Dress, 10 In. .. 350.00
Greiner, Molded Eyelids, Textured Molded Hair, Eye Hollows, 1872, 26 In. 850.00
Gund, Jiminy Cricket, Felt Clothes, Box, 1940s, 13 In. 125.00
Halbig, Blue–Eyed Blond, Ringlets With Bows, Lacey Party Dress, 27 In. 950.00

Doll, Gebruder Heubach, Character Boy,
Blond, Knickers, 1910, 19 In.
Doll, Gebruder Heubach, Character Boy,
Sunday Suit, 1910, 17 In.

Doll, Gebruder Heubach, 9467,
Indian Squaw, 1910, 14 In.

Halbig, Child, Forward Thrust Cheeks, Slant Eyes, Hip Length Curls, 26 In. 795.00
Hamburg, Bisque Head, Sleep Eyes, Human Hair, Jointed, Composition, 23 In. 137.50
Handwerck, 109, Bisque, Human Hair Wig, Blue Sleep Eyes, 25 In. 1100.00
Handwerck, 119, Bisque, Human Hair Wig, Antique Coat & Hat, 27 In. 1295.00
Handwerck, 287, Bisque Head, Glass Sleep Eyes, Open Mouth, Jointed, 21 In. 165.00
Handwerck, 99, Bisque, Blue Sleep Eyes, Original Wig, 28 In. 1350.00
Handwerck, 99, Bisque, Wig, Blue Sleep Eyes, Dress, 28 In. 1350.00
Handwerck, 109, Bisque, Blue Sleep Eyes, Dressed, 29 In. 1550.00
Handwerck, 1099, Bisque Head, Sleep Eyes, Pierced Ears, Marked, 29 1/2 In. 905.00
Handwerck, Bisque Head, Brown Sleep Eyes, Jointed, Composition, 22 In. 165.00
Handwerck, Bisque Head, Kid Body, 14 In. 195.00
Handwerck, Bisque Head, Sleep Eyes, Open Mouth, Jointed Composition, 18 In. 480.00
Handwerck, Bisque Socket Head, Open Mouth, 4 Teeth, Synthetic Wig, 17 In. 315.00
Handwerck, Child, Bisque, Composition, Long Hair, Dressed, 1900, 29 In. 1095.00
Handwerck, Glass Sleep Eyes, Open Mouth, Mohair Wig, Jointed Body, 24 1/2 In. ... 330.00
Handwerck, Kid Body, Blue Sleep Eyes, Human Hair, 24 In. 500.00
Handwerck, Mechanical, Bisque Head, Composition, Cries Mama & Papa, 22 In. 1090.00
Handwerck, Threaded Blue Eyes, Long Curls, Ball–Jointed, Clothes, 20 In. 695.00
Hasbro, Kate Jackson, Charlie's Angels, Package, 1977, 8 1/2 In. 20.00
Heebee, Bisque, O–Shaped Eyes, White Smock, Original Box, Germany, c.1925 ...... 1200.00
Hertel Schwab, 134, Bisque Head, Painted Molded Hair, Composition Body 850.00
Hertel Schwab, 136, Human Hair Curls, Blue Sleep Eyes, 14 In. 450.00
Hertel Schwab, 136, Paperweight Eyes, Human Hair Wig, Old Clothes, 34 In. 750.00
Hertel Schwab, 150, Bisque, Open–Close Mouth, Sleep Eyes, Mohair Wig, 13 In. 650.00
Hertel Schwab, 151, Baby, Stationary Eyes, Bald Dome, 11 In. 550.00
Hertel Schwab, 165, Googly, Blue Sleep Eyes, Pale Bisque, Clothes, 12 In. 3000.00
Hertel Schwab, 165, Googly, Watermelon Mouth, Mohair Wig, 15 1/2 In. 4500.00
Heubach Koppelsdorf, 256, Mohair Wig, Old Clothes, 23 In. 495.00
Heubach Koppelsdorf, 267, Baby, Blue Sleep Eyes, Wig, Old Clothes, 15 In. 425.00
Heubach Koppelsdorf, 320, Baby, Original Clothes, 14 In. 495.00
Heubach Koppelsdorf, 339, Baby, Cloth Body, Jointed At Shoulders, 13 In. 595.00
Heubach Koppelsdorf, 444, Painted Bisque Head, Closed Mouth, Mohair Wig, 7 In. 200.00
Heubach dolls are also in this category under Gebruder Heubach
Heubach, 7602, Pouty, Bisque, Bent Limb Body, 11 In. 650.00
Heubach, Black Character, Bisque, Intaglio Eyes, Cloth Body, Clown Suit, 13 In. 1100.00
Heubach, Clapping Clown, Mechanical 800.00
Heubach, Googly, Blue Sleep Eyes, Original Clothes, 8 In. 3200.00
Heubach, Googly, Toddler, Intaglio Eyes, 7 3/4 In. 395.00
Heubach, Rocking Baby, Mechanical 800.00
Hilda, Solid Dome, Blue Sleep Eyes, Bisque, Old Clothes, 18 In. 4700.00
Horsman, Baby, Composition Head, Cloth Body, Slip, Dress, Bonnet, 21 In. 275.00
Horsman, Billikins, Seated, 12 In. 57.00
Horsman, Bright Star, Composition, Crazed Arms & Legs, 13 In. 175.00
Horsman, Composition Head, Blue Flirty Eyes, Molded & Painted Hair, 21 In. 275.00
Horsman, Dolly Rosebud's Brother, 18 In. 85.00
Horsman, Ella Cinders, Comic Character, Freckled Face, 18 In. 65.00
Horsman, Girl, Pig Tails, Composition, 13 In. 140.00
Horsman, Miss Sunbeam, Original Clothes, 1970 .... 30.00
Horsman, Tessy Talk, Original Dress, Name Written On Front, 1974, 19 In. 45.00
Horsman, Tynie Baby, Bisque, Painted Face, Muslin Body, Antique Costume, 12 In. 750.00
Hoyer, Plastic Head, Skin Wig, 5–Piece Plastic Body, Shirt, Pants & Shoes, 14 In. ... 370.00
Hummel, Wanderbub & Gretl, 1960, 11 In., Pair 175.00
Humpty Dumpty, Celluloid 25.00
Ideal, Betsy McCall, Original Clothes, 8 In. 125.00
Ideal, Betsy McCall, Pink & Black Formal Dress, AC, 14 In. 295.00
Ideal, Betsy Wetsy, 12 In. 30.00
Ideal, Blessed Event, 21 In. 85.00
Ideal, Captain Action, Sgt. Fury Accessories 35.00
Ideal, Composition, Straw–Filled Body, Mexico, 1920 .... 50.00
Ideal, Crissy Velvet, Tote Filled With Clothes, 18 In. 50.00
Ideal, Deanna Durbin, Brown Eyes, Human Hair Wig, Original Dress, 21 In. 695.00
Ideal, Diana Ross, 1960s, Box, 18 In. 650.00
Ideal, Dopey, Composition Cloth, Dressed, 1937 .... 170.00

 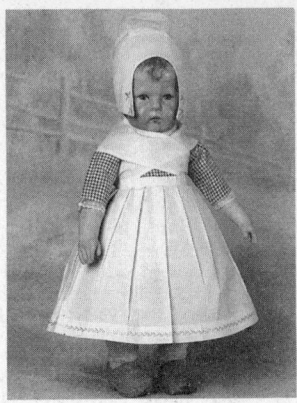

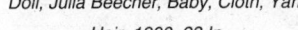

Doll, Julia Beecher, Baby, Cloth, Yarn   *Doll, Kathe Kruse, Cloth, Painted*
Hair, 1900, 23 In.   *Features, 1910, 17 In.*

Ideal, Fanny Brice, Composition	150.00
Ideal, Goody Two Shoes, 18 In.	125.00
Ideal, Kissy, 22 In.	45.00
Ideal, Kissy, Original Clothes, 1961, 22 In.	65.00
Ideal, Little Miss Revlon, Dressed, With Metal Wardrobe, 1950s, 10 1/2 In.	255.00
Ideal, Miss Ideal, Hand–Painted Body, Fully Jointed, Capri Pants, 27 In.	125.00
Ideal, Pinocchio, Composition Head, Wooden	75.00
Ideal, Raggedy Ann & Andy, 1983, Pair	120.00
Ideal, Sauce Walker, Hard Plastic, Original Dress, 23 In.	95.00
Ideal, Snow White & 7 Dwarfs, Muslin, Mohair Wig, Plush Beards, 11 & 15 In.	1600.00
Ideal, Snow White, All Original, 1937	150.00
Ideal, Toni, 14 In.	125.00
Ideal, Toni, 16 In.	185.00
Ideal, Toni, Platinum, 19 In.	325.00
Ideal, Toni, Walker, Jointed Hips & Knees, Rooted Brown Hair, 20 In.	50.00
Indian dolls are listed in the Indian category	
Izannah, Walker, Brush Strokes In Front of Ears, 18 1/2 In.	9500.00
J. D. K. dolls are also listed in this category under Kestner	
J. D. K., 143, Character Child, 18 In.	1050.00
J. D. K., 221, Googly, Blue Sleep Eyes, Toddler Body, Original Clothes, 11 In.	4800.00
J. D. K., 260, Character, Chunky Body, Bisque, Mohair Wig, Clothes, 36 In.	4995.00
J. D. K., Baby, Bisque, Painted Hair, Lower Teeth, Organdy Dress, 12 In.	465.00
J. D. K., Bisque Head, Sleep Eyes, Composition Body, Dressed, c.1910, 26 In.	385.00
J. D. K., Hilda, Blue Sleep Eyes, 1914, 17 In.	4500.00
Jane West Cowgirl, 1964, Marx, 12 In.	139.00
Japanese, Costume, 1900, 44 In.	1000.00
John Travolta, Box, 12 In.	45.00
Julia Beecher, Baby, Cloth, Yarn Hair, 1900, 23 In. ....*Illus*	3700.00
Jumeau, 12, Bisque, Paperweight Eyes, Clothes, Corset, Signed Shoes, 27 In.	6200.00
Jumeau, 1907, Cork Pate, Paperweight Eyes, 19 In.	1600.00
Jumeau, Bisque Head, Open Mouth, Teeth, Ball–Jointed, Lace Clothes, 29 In.	2950.00
Jumeau, Bisque Head, Paperweight Eyes, Lamb's Wool Wig, Clothes, 15 1/2 In.	4675.00
Jumeau, Bisque, Baby, Amber Eyes, Mohair Wig, Antique Costume, 24 In.	4500.00
Jumeau, Bisque, Brown Paperweight Eyes, Applied Ears, Silk Dress, 19 In.	7500.00
Jumeau, Bisque, Child, Brown Eyes, Mohair Wig, Composition Body, 15 In.	3800.00
Jumeau, Bisque, Glass Sleep Eyes, Silk Dress, Underclothes, Shoes, 24 In.	1550.00
Jumeau, Bisque, Paperweight Eyes, Mohair Wig, Open Mouth, 22 In.	2900.00
Jumeau, Blond Hip Length Hair, Cork Pate, Shoes, Socks & Undies, 12 In.	2500.00
Jumeau, Blue Gray Sleep Eyes, Lashes, Jointed Body, 35 In.	2800.00
Jumeau, Closed Mouth, Bisque Head, Blue Paperweight Eyes, Dress, 16 3/4 In.	5500.00

Jumeau, Fashion, Kid Over Wood, Bisque Arms, Clothes, 18 In. 8500.00
Jumeau, Walker, Bisque, Paperweight Sleep Eyes, Curls, c.1899, 22 In. 1495.00
Jump Rope, Wooden Arms & Legs, Lead Feet, Wire Handle, 9 In. 660.00
Jutta, Baby, Bisque, 2 Upper Teeth, Bent Limb Body, Baby Dress, Bonnet, 22 In. ... 675.00
Jutta, Bisque Socket Head, Blue Sleep Eyes, Mohair Wig, Bent Limb Body, 22 In. ... 675.00
Jutta, Boy, Jointed Arms & Legs, 1914, 18 In. 1150.00
K * R, 29, Porcelain Teeth, Almond Eyes, Auburn Hair, Ball-Jointed, 23 In. 1350.00
K * R, 39, Child, 16 In. 600.00
K * R, 73, Blue Sleep Eyes, Curl Wig, Jointed Body, 29 In. 1400.00
K * R, 100, Bisque, Facial Artwork, 28 In. 575.00
K * R, 100, Character Baby, Intaglio Eyes, Open-Close Mouth, Bent Limb, 15 In. ... 220.00
K * R, 100, Old White Dress, 42 In. 3200.00
K * R, 101, Marie, Bisque Socket Head, Closed Pouty Mouth, Mohair Wig, 15 In. ... 3300.00
K * R, 101, Marie, Bisque, Painted Face, Mohair Wig, Ball-Jointed, c.1910, 19 In. ... 5400.00
K * R, 114, Character, Twins, Pouty, 13 In., Pair 5450.00
K * R, 114X, Character Boy, Pouty, 19 In. 7000.00
K * R, 115/A, Bisque, Blue Sleep Eyes, Original Dress, 24 In. 6500.00
K * R, 117n, Flirty Blue Eyes, Braided Mohair, Teen Body, 16 In. 1500.00
K * R, 121, Toddler, Bisque, Fully Jointed, Mohair Wig, Lace Dress, 13 1/2 In. 1695.00
K * R, 121, Toddler, Oily Bisque, Fully Jointed, 25 In. 2250.00
K * R, 122, Baby, Blue Sleep Eyes, Bisque, Gown, 17 1/2 In. 1295.00
K * R, 126, Baby, Bisque Head, Flirty Eyes, Bent Limb Composition, 1920s, 23 In. ... 450.00
K * R, 126, Baby, Bisque Head, Sleep Eyes, Bent Limb Composition, 1914, 15 In. 665.00
K * R, 126, Baby, Blue Sleep Eyes, Wobble Tongue, 14 In. 550.00
K * R, 126, Baby, Flirty Eye, 21 In. 995.00
K * R, 126, Character Baby, Open Mouth, Retractable Tongue, 29 In. 750.00
K * R, 126, Toddler, Ball-Jointed, Brown Sleep Eyes, 19 In. 895.00
K * R, 126, Toddler, Bisque, Brown Sleep Eyes, Human Hair Wig, Jointed, 16 In. ... 1200.00
K * R, 126, Toddler, Blue Flirty Sleep Eyes, 5-Piece Straight Leg, 20 In. 895.00
K * R, 126, Toddler, Blue Sleep Eyes, Bent Limb Body, 22 In. 895.00
K * R, 126, Toddler, Flirty Eyes, Human Hair, Jointed Body, Wobble Tongue, 23 In. ... 1800.00
K * R, 128, Baby, Bisque, Blue Sleep Eyes, Mohair Wig, 16 In. 1500.00
K * R, 131, Googly Toddler, 15 1/2 In. 5750.00
K * R, 402, Bisque, Wire Flirty Sleep Eyes, Ball-Jointed Body, 15 In. 750.00
K * R, 403, Walker, Sleep Eyes, Open Mouth, 25 In. 1200.00
K * R, Baby, Painted Hair, Composition Body & Neck, 14 1/2 In. 605.00
K * R, Baby, Mechanical, Eyes Open & Close, Tongue Goes In & Out, 24 In. 3750.00
K * R, Bisque, Sleep Eyes, Mohair Wig, Bonnet, Papier-Mache Body, Walker, 6 In. ... 625.00
K * R, Child, Bisque, Flirty Eyes, White Work Dress, 33 In. 2995.00
K * R, Girl, Bisque Head, Braids, Composition Jointed, Crocheted Dress, 11 In. 2950.00
K * R, Toddler, Bisque Tongue, Upper & Lower Teeth, Dress, Ruffled Cap, 35 In. ... 2900.00
Karl Hartman, Bisque, Blue Sleep Eyes, Original Wig, Costume, Shoes, 22 In. 695.00
Kathe Kruse, Baby, Cloth, Painted Hair & Eyes, Sand-Weighted Body, 18 In. 4000.00
Kathe Kruse, Boy, Alpine Costume, Stamped 4897, 17 In. 1450.00
Kathe Kruse, Boy, Hard Plastic Head, Closed Mouth, Underwear, Shoes, 14 In. 150.00
Kathe Kruse, Cloth, Painted Features, 1910, 17 In. ....*Illus* 4300.00
Kathe Kruse, Girl, Hard Plastic Head, Closed Mouth, Blue Sailor Dress, 14 In. 125.00
Kathe Kruse, Hampeichen Face, Shoes, 1930s 2200.00
Kathe Kruse, Painted Features, Clothes, Shoes, Signed, 14 In. 1200.00
Kathe Kruse, VII, Dumein, 14 In. 2000.00
Kestner dolls are also in this category under J. D. K.
Kestner, 143, Sleep Eyes, Open Mouth, Mohair Wig, Composition, c.1915, 11 In. 650.00
Kestner, 146, Bisque, Blond Curls, Plaster Pate, Pink Linen Dress, 28 1/2 In. 1200.00
Kestner, 148, Bisque, Mohair Wig, Vintage Clothes, 17 In. 575.00
Kestner, 149, Bisque, Brown Sleep Eyes, Human Hair Wig, 18 In. 1100.00
Kestner, 154, Bisque Arms, Gusseted Leather Body, 22 In. 250.00
Kestner, 154, Bisque Shoulder Head, 4 Upper Teeth, Mohair Wig, 14 1/2 In. 235.00
Kestner, 154, Jointed Kid Body, Ball-Jointed Arms, Tin, Old Clothes, 23 In. 595.00
Kestner, 155, Clothes, Musical Trunk, 7 In. 2250.00
Kestner, 156, Bisque, Brown Sleep Eyes, Platinum Curls, Original Clothes, 25 In. 1600.00
Kestner, 161, Original, Openwork Dress, Undies, Shoes, Bonnet, 23 In. 1400.00
Kestner, 164, Bisque, Blue Sleep Eyes, Old Clothes, Wig, 27 In. 1100.00

Kestner, 167, Bisque, Glass Sleep Eyes, Open Mouth, Jointed Composition, 11 In. ...   485.00
Kestner, 167, Bisque, Mohair Wig, Brown Sleep Eyes, Clothes, 23 In. 1100.00
Kestner, 168, Bisque, Blue Sleep Eyes, Feathered Brows, Ball–Jointed, 26 In. 650.00
Kestner, 168, Sleep Eyes, Brown Hair, Stamped Composition Body, 23 In. 585.00
Kestner, 169, Pouty, Blue Sleep Eyes, Mohair Wig, Embroidered Dress, 16 1/2 In.   2995.00
Kestner, 171, Bisque Head, Sleep Eyes, Mohair Wig, Composition, 18 In. 220.00
Kestner, 171, Bisque Head, Sleep Eyes, Mohair Wig, Jointed, Composition, 29 In. ...   385.00
Kestner, 171, Daisy, Bisque, Ball–Jointed, Redressed, Blue Eyes, 23 In. 800.00
Kestner, 171, Daisy, Bisque, Blue Sleep Eyes, Ball–Jointed, 22 In. .... 895.00 To 995.00
Kestner, 171, Daisy, Bisque, Sleep Eyes, Marked, 31 In. 1795.00
Kestner, 171, Daisy, Jointed Body, Blond Hair, Original Eyelet Dress, 32 In. 1395.00
Kestner, 171, Long Brown Hair, Hazel Sleep Eyes, Factory Clothes, 34 In. 1600.00
Kestner, 172, Gibson Girl, Cloth Body, Bisque Arms & Legs, 10 1/2 In. 1250.00
Kestner, 178, Bisque Arms, Kid Body, Sleep Eyes, Original Clothes, 21 In. 225.00
Kestner, 178, Brown Eyes, Closed Mouth, Dressed, Leather Boots, 11 In. 1800.00
Kestner, 211, Baby, Bisque, Human Hair Wig, Bent Limb Body, Jacket, Hat, 15 In.   525.00
Kestner, 211, Baby, Bisque, Jointed, Glass Eyes, Original Wig, 8 1/2 In. 850.00
Kestner, 211, Baby, Bisque, Jointed, Glass Eyes, Original Wig, 11 1/2 In. 1200.00
Kestner, 211, Baby, Bisque, Open–Close Mouth, Old Dress & Bonnet, 14 In. 900.00
Kestner, 211, Bisque Socket Head, Blue Sleep Eyes, Blond Human Hair Wig, 15 In.   525.00
Kestner, 211, Character Baby, Blond Wig, Jointed, Composition, 13 In. 425.00
Kestner, 211, Sammy, Toddler, Original Wig, Pate and Body, 27 In. 2495.00
Kestner, 211, Toddler Body, Bisque, Jointed, Dressed, Plaster Pate, 15 In. 1695.00
Kestner, 221, Googly, Bisque, Mohair Bobbed Wig, Toddler Body, c.1912, 15 In. 4750.00
Kestner, 221, Googly, Bisque, Original Wig, Old Dress, 16 In. 7500.00
Kestner, 235, Bisque, Sleep Glass Eyes, Open Mouth, Mohair, Kid Body, 13 In. 385.00
Kestner, 235, Toddler, Bisque Shoulder Head, Mohair Wig, Composition, 13 In. 1200.00
Kestner, 257, Baby, Bisque, Sleep Eyes, Side–Glance, Mohair, Cape, Bonnet, 23 In.   1400.00
Kestner, 257, Child, Glass Eyes, Painted Face, Mohair, Bent Limb, 11 In. 750.00
Kestner, 257, Startled Eyes, Period Commercial Clothes, 16 In. 750.00
Kestner, 260, Toddler, Bisque, Glass Eyes, Mohair Wig, Composition, c.1915, 16 In.   850.00
Kestner, Baby, Bisque Head, Sleep Eyes, Antique Baby Dress, 15 In. 675.00
Kestner, Baby, Bisque Head, Sleep Eyes, Mohair, Bent Limb, Composition, 12 In. ...   412.50
Kestner, Baby, Bisque Socket Head, Blue Sleep Eyes, 5–Piece Body, Dress, 15 In. ...   675.00
Kestner, Baby, Bisque, Sleep Eyes, Porcelain Teeth, Mohair Wig, Gown, 26 In. 4100.00
Kestner, Baby, Bisque, Swivel Head, Painted Eyes, Brush–Stroke Hair, 7 In. 895.00
Kestner, Bisque Head, Blue Eyes, Blond Mohair Wig, Jointed, Composition, 19 In.   605.00
Kestner, Bisque, Chubby, Barefoot, Swivel Neck, Sleep Eyes, 7 In. 2600.00
Kestner, Bisque, Swivel Head, Mohair Wig, Jointed, Paper Label, c.1915, 5 In. 475.00
Kestner, Bisque, Swivel Neck, Sleep Eyes, Closed Mouth, 6 In. 1750.00
Kestner, Century Baby, Painted Hair & Face, Muslin Body, Costume, 13 In. 850.00
Kestner, Flirty Eyes, Chubby, Pink Dress, 28 In. 2895.00
Kestner, Gibson Girl, Bisque Head, Up–Lifted Chin, 20 In. 2800.00
Kestner, Girl, Bisque, Gusseted Kid Body, Dress, Underwear, Wool Coat, 18 In. 660.00
Kestner, Girl, Bisque, Sleep Eyes, Red Wig, Dress, 10 1/2 In. 525.00
Kestner, Googly Toddler, Bisque Socket Head, Large Brown Eyes, c.1912, 13 In. 4800.00
Kestner, Hilda, Character Baby, Sleep Eyes, Bent Limb Composition, 15 In. 660.00
Kestner, Open Mouth, Plaster Pate, Closed Mouth, Schmidt Body, 21 In. 1500.00
Kestner, Pouty, Closed Mouth, 23 In. 4750.00
Kestner, Pouty, Long Face, Kid Body, Pinafore Ensemble, 21 In. 1250.00
Kestner, Pouty, Schmitte–Type Body, Antique Clothes, 20 In. 4750.00
Kestner, Siegfried Baby, Brown Sleep Eyes, Cloth Body, Celluloid Hands 2000.00
Kestner, Toddler, Bisque, Glass Eyes, Mohair Wig, Composition, c.1915, 15 In. 800.00
Kestner, Turned Head, Bisque Lower Arms, Pink Ribbon Trimmed Dress, 20 In. 550.00
Kestner, Woman, Bisque, Brown Sleep Eyes, Kid Body, Closed Mouth, 16 In. 895.00
Kewpie dolls are listed in the Kewpie category
Kiddiejoy, Bisque, Baby, Sleep Eyes, Germany, 12 In. 175.00
Kley & Hahn, 166, Character Baby 475.00
Kley & Hahn, 166, Character Baby, Molded Hair, 12 In. 495.00
Kley & Hahn, 250, Bisque, Glass Sleep Eyes, Open Mouth, Jointed Body, 23 In. 165.00
Kley & Hahn, 325, Jointed Composition Body, Sailor Suit, 10 1/2 In. 895.00
Kley & Hahn, Bisque, Intaglio Eyes, Jointed Wood & Composition Body, 12 In. 600.00
Kley & Hahn, Brown Sleep Eyes, Human Hair Curls, White Eyelet Dress, 23 In. 595.00

Kley & Hahn, Father, Solid Dome, Brush–Stroked Hair, Ball–Jointed Body, 16 In. ... 1200.00
Kley & Hahn, Son, Solid Dome, Brush–Stroked Hair, Ball–Jointed Body, 10 1/2 In. 850.00
Kley & Hahn, Walkure, Ball–Jointed, Long Curly Hair, 26 In. 395.00
Kley & Hahn, Walkure, Bisque, Blue Sleep Eyes, Dress, Hat, 28 In. 1100.00
Kling, Child, Bisque Socket Head, 4 Upper Teeth, Jointed, White Clothing, 19 In. 400.00
Knickerbocker, Dwarf, Happy, Tag, 1937, 10 In. 145.00
Knickerbocker, Marionette, Laurel & Hardy, Push Button, 1966, Box, Pair 225.00
Knickerbocker, Mickey Mouse, Cloth, 1930s, 11 In. 515.00
Knickerbocker, Ollie, From Laurel & Hardy, Vinyl Face, Cotton, 1966, 9 In. 54.00
Knickerbocker, Raggedy Andy, Cloth, 1970s, 15 In. 25.00
Konig & Wernicke, Bisque, Toddler, Glass Eyes, Bobbed Wig, c.1912, 22 In. 1550.00
Kuntz, Carnival Knock Down 45.00
Lenci, 109, Blond, Dressed, 1920s, 22 1/2 In. 1850.00
Lenci, Boy, Blond, Painted Features, Felt, Knit Clothes 425.00
Lenci, Boy, Felt Head, Rooted Hair, Felt Shirt, Shorts, Sweater, 16 1/2 In. 600.00
Lenci, Girl, Felt Head, Mohair Wig, Cloth Torso, Felt Arms, Legs, Costume, 17 In. 1000.00
Lenci, Girl, Felt Swivel Head, Cloth Torso, Felt Limbs, Felt Dress & Shoes, 14 In. 250.00
Lenci, Girl, Felt, Blue Eyes, Dressed, 19 In. 150.00
Lenci, Girl, With Ball, Tag On Dress, 14 1/2 In. 1250.00
Lenci, Glinda, Holding Jump Rope, Box, 19 In. 250.00
Lenci, Little Lulu, 14 In. 700.00
Lenci, Mountain Climber, Mascotte, Felt Head, Painted Eyes, Jointed, Cloth, 9 In. 225.00
Lenci, Peasant Girl, Felt Head, Painted Eyes To Side, Felt Peasant Dress, 9 In. 300.00
Lenci, Pierrot, Art Deco, Felt Body, Original Costume, Instrument, c.1925, 23 In. ... 1600.00
Lenci, Russian Cossack, Swivel Head & Waist, Original Outfit, 24 In. 375.00
Lenci, Spanish Girl, Felt Head, Floss Wig, Cloth Torso, Felt Arms, Costume, 13 In. 550.00
Lenci, Tubby Tom, 14 In. 1175.00
Limbach, Bisque Head, Horns, Eskimo Leather Clothes, Germany 375.00
Limoges, Blue Stationary Eyes, Adult Composition 5–Piece Body, 14 In. 850.00
Little Miss Fashion, 4 Outfits, Box, 21 In. 125.00
Liza, Cabaret, In Money Outfit, Jewels By Marilyn, 27 In. 2700.00
Louis Sorenson, Lady, Wax, Glass Eyes, Original, 27 In. 450.00
Louis Wolfe, Paperweight Eyes, Kid Body, Uncut Wig, Clothes, 11 In. 695.00
Madam Hendren, Snookums, 1927, 14 In. 275.00
Madame Alexander, Africa, Bent Knee, All Original, 8 In. 500.00
Madame Alexander, Amy, Little Women, 1951, 14 In. 225.00
Madame Alexander, Amy, Little Women, 1960s, 8 In. 125.00
Madame Alexander, Angel, Pink & Gold Dress & Wings, Green Eyes, 8 In. 550.00
Madame Alexander, Baby McGuffey, Box, 1971, 20 In. 125.00
Madame Alexander, Betsy Ross, 1977, 8 In. 60.00
Madame Alexander, Binnie Walker, Sequin Outfit & Hat, 31 In. 395.00
Madame Alexander, Bride, 1950s, 18 In. 195.00
Madame Alexander, Cinderella, Wrist Tag, Mint In Box, 1950, 20 In. 425.00
Madame Alexander, Cissette Tinkerbell, Wrist Tag 150.00
Madame Alexander, Cissy, Bride, 21 In. 450.00
Madame Alexander, Cissy, Bridesmaid, Fur Coat, Trunk, Extra Clothes 550.00
Madame Alexander, Cissy, Walker, Bride Outfit, 18 In. 250.00
Madame Alexander, Clarabelle, Cloth Body, Tag 350.00
Madame Alexander, Elise, Box, 14 In. 187.00
Madame Alexander, Enchanted Doll, 1981, 8 In. 300.00
Madame Alexander, Fairy Godmother, Box, 1983, 14 In. 150.00
Madame Alexander, First Lady Betty Tyler 65.00
Madame Alexander, Gainsborough, Pink Gown, Lace Overdress, 21 In. 345.00
Madame Alexander, Gody, 1970, 11 In. 700.00
Madame Alexander, Goldilocks, 14 In. 70.00
Madame Alexander, Greek Boy, Bent Knee, 8 In. 250.00
Madame Alexander, India, White Face, 1965, 8 In. 125.00
Madame Alexander, Jackie Kennedy, All Original, 1961, 21 In. 750.00
Madame Alexander, Karen, Ballerina, 15 In. 395.00
Madame Alexander, Kurt, Vinyl Head, Open–Close Mouth, Tagged, 1962, 11 In. ... 435.00
Madame Alexander, Lissy, Amy, Little Women 295.00
Madame Alexander, Lissy, Amy, Little Women, Jointed, Taffeta Dress, 1957, 12 In. 325.00
Madame Alexander, Lissy, Laurie, Little Men 495.00

Madame Alexander, Little Genius, Composition & Cloth, 1946 .... 125.00
Madame Alexander, Little Lord Fauntleroy, 12 In. 70.00
Madame Alexander, Little Women Set, Box, 8 In. 300.00
Madame Alexander, Maggie, Tyrolean, 8 In. 200.00
Madame Alexander, Maggie–Mix–Up, Pants, Shoes & Socks, Box 650.00
Madame Alexander, Manet, 1982–1983, 21 In. 225.00
Madame Alexander, Margaret O'Brien, Composition, 14 In. 575.00
Madame Alexander, Margaret O'Brien, Composition, 21 In. 695.00
Madame Alexander, Margaret Rose, Plastic Head, Body, Sleep Eyes, 17 In. 250.00
Madame Alexander, Marie Antoinette, 1987, 21 In. .... 245.00 To 255.00
Madame Alexander, Mary Martin, Sailor Suit, 14 In. 450.00
Madame Alexander, Mary, Queen of Scots, 1988, 21 In. 245.00
Madame Alexander, Marybel, Vinyl Head, Vinyl Body, Romper, Fitted Case, 15 In. ... 275.00
Madame Alexander, McGuffey Ana, Tagged Clothes, 1937, 15 In. 295.00
Madame Alexander, Meg, Little Women, 1960s, 8 In. 125.00
Madame Alexander, Meg, Little Women, 1969–1982, 12 In. 85.00
Madame Alexander, Mimi, Box, 21 In. 450.00
Madame Alexander, Napoleon, 1982, 12 In. 55.00
Madame Alexander, Nina Ballerina, Original Clothes, 14 In. 325.00
Madame Alexander, Peter Pan Set, Wendy, Peter Pan, Michael, Tinkerbell, 14 In. ... 995.00
Madame Alexander, Piper Laurie, 14 In. 495.00
Madame Alexander, Princess Elizabeth, 13 In. 395.00
Madame Alexander, Princess Elizabeth, 15 In. 585.00
Madame Alexander, Princess Elizabeth, 20 In. 200.00
Madame Alexander, Puddin', Dark Hair, Box 90.00
Madame Alexander, Quiz–Kin, White Batiste Outfit 395.00
Madame Alexander, Rebecca, Wrist Tag, 1972, 14 In. 45.00
Madame Alexander, Renoir, Girl, 1972, 14 In. .... 55.00 To 60.00
Madame Alexander, Renoir, Original Clothes, 1961, 21 In. 375.00
Madame Alexander, Roberta Bride, Wrist Tag, 18 In. 250.00
Madame Alexander, Scarlett O'Hara, Bent Knee, Box, 8 In. 395.00
Madame Alexander, Scarlett O'Hara, Jointed Knees, Print Dress, 1968, 8 In. 295.00
Madame Alexander, Scarlett O'Hara, Original Clothes, 11 In. .... 225.00 To 495.00
Madame Alexander, Scarlett O'Hara, Original Velvet Coat & Hat, 1939, 14 1/2 In. ... 625.00
Madame Alexander, Scarlett O'Hara, White Gown, Lace, 1970, 14 In. 87.00
Madame Alexander, Sergeant, 1984, 14 In. 70.00
Madame Alexander, Shari Lewis, Cissy Dress & Hat, 1959, 21 In. 265.00
Madame Alexander, Sleeping Beauty, Gold Gown 79.00
Madame Alexander, Snow White, Mohair Wig, Composition, Box, 13 In. 1600.00
Madame Alexander, Sonja Henie, Sleep Eyes, Human Hair, Clothes, 1939, 15 In. ... 165.00
Madame Alexander, Southern Belle, 1963, 8 In. 595.00
Madame Alexander, Thailand, Blue & Gold Costume, 8 In. 225.00
Madame Alexander, Tiny Betty, Composition, 1939 .... 35.00
Madame Alexander, Wendy Ann, Sleep Eyes, Closed Mouth, Child Body, 14 In. 350.00
Madame Alexander, Wendy Kins, Bent Knee Walker, Box, 8 1/2 In. 165.00
Madame Alexander, Winnie Walker, Box, 18 In. 275.00
Man & Woman, Southern, Coconut Head, 1880s, Pair 4950.00
Man, Dollhouse, Mustache, Molded Military Cap, Uniform, 5 1/2 In. 300.00
Mannequin, Child, Composition, 28 In. 220.00
Marilyn Monroe, Box, 1983, 18 In. 325.00
Marionette, Black, Civil War Officer, Cloth Body, 1900, 24 1/2 In. 1200.00
Marionette, Clarabelle, Cloth Costume, Peter Puppet Playthings, 14 In. 175.00
Marionette, Cloth & Painted Wood, Balinese, 27 In. 100.00
Marionette, Peter Puppet, Composition, Cloth, 13 In. 264.00
Martha & George Washington, Original Clothes, 1947, 30 In., Pair 1600.00
Martha Thompson, Prince Philip, Military Uniform, Royal Family, 21 In. 800.00
Martha Thompson, Princess Margaret Rose, Royal Family 2000.00
Martha Thompson, Queen Elizabeth II, Royal Family, 21 In. 900.00
Marx, Girl From U. N. C. L. E., 1967 .... 750.00
Mary Hoyer, Composition, Auburn Wig, Knit Skating Outfit, 13 1/4 In. 365.00
Mascotte, Bebe, Bisque Socket Head, Blond Wig, Jointed, French Outfit, 18 In. 4300.00
Mason, Taylor, Paper Waist Band, Pewter Hands, Painted Boots, 11 1/2 In. 475.00
Mattel, Allen, Red Hair, Beach Jacket, 1963 .... 50.00

Doll, Mattel, Francie,
Black, Swimsuit

◆ ◆
Soft vinyl dolls popular in the 1950s often are stained with green, blue, or black marks. These are probably from mold, not from ink or paints. Buy a commercial mold-and-mildew remover that is chlorine-free. Test it in an inconspicuous spot, then wipe it on the entire doll. Wash with warm soapy water, rinse, and dry. Any remaining stain can be bleached.
◆ ◆

Mattel, Barbie, American Girl, Blond, Swimsuit, Bendable Legs	195.00
Mattel, Barbie, Army, Blue Skirt & Jacket, Blond	30.00
Mattel, Barbie, Ballerina, 2nd Issue, 1978	33.00
Mattel, Barbie, Black, Bob Mackie	135.00
Mattel, Barbie, Bob Mackie, Gold Sequined Gown, Display Case	90.00
Mattel, Barbie, Bubble Cut, Original Red & White Striped Swimsuit, 1963 ......45.00 To	150.00
Mattel, Barbie, California Dream, Bikini, Sunglasses	12.50
Mattel, Barbie, Evening Sparkle, Blond, Mini Dress, Turquoise Boa	13.00
Mattel, Barbie, Fantasy, Bob Mackie	160.00
Mattel, Barbie, Fashion Queen, 3 Wigs	80.00
Mattel, Barbie, Gold Greetings, Gold Earrings & Gown, Lace, Box	175.00
Mattel, Barbie, Golden Dream, Quick Curl Hair, Box, 1981	12.50
Mattel, Barbie, Holiday Barbie, USA, 1988	350.00
Mattel, Barbie, Korean	35.00
Mattel, Barbie, Mardi Gras, Blond, Purple Dress, Mask, Stand	50.00
Mattel, Barbie, New Living, Blond, Poseable, Lace Caper	45.00
Mattel, Barbie, No. 1, Box	3500.00
Mattel, Barbie, No. 2, Box	2250.00
Mattel, Barbie, No. 3, Ponytail, Blond, Swimsuit, Glasses, Shoes, Box	450.00
Mattel, Barbie, Olympic Skating Star	55.00
Mattel, Barbie, Patty Sensation	35.00
Mattel, Barbie, Silver Anniversary, Blond, Red Puffy Dress, Box In Spanish, 1988	90.00
Mattel, Barbie, Talking, Blond, Swimsuit & Cover, Bendable Legs	80.00
Mattel, Barbie, Twist 'n Turn, Bendable Knees, 1969	150.00
Mattel, Buffy & Mrs. Beasley, Poseable, 1968	85.00
Mattel, Charmin' Chatty, Original Sailor Dress, Shoes, Socks, Glasses, Talks	180.00
Mattel, Chatty Cathy, Blond, Original Pajamas	30.00
Mattel, Christie, Live Action, Vinyl, Box, 1970	100.00
Mattel, Enzo, Italian Boy	538.00
Mattel, Epstein, Welcome Back Kotter, Box	45.00
Mattel, Francie, Black, Swimsuit ....*Illus*	350.00
Mattel, Ken, Beach Time, Canada, Box, 1984	10.00
Mattel, Ken, Box, 1961	70.00
Mattel, Ken, Flocked Hair, Beach Jacket	15.00
Mattel, Ken, Painted Blond Hair, Sailor Suit	22.00
Mattel, Ken, Painted Hair, Swimsuit & Jacket, 1962 ....50.00 To	55.00
Mattel, Ken, Roller Skating, Black Shorts, 1980	12.50
Mattel, Little Red Riding Hood, 10 In.	12.00
Mattel, Midge, Bendable Legs, Brunette, 1965	95.00
Mattel, Midge, Titian Hair, 1964–1967	45.00

Mattel, Milliner's Model, Slip & Panties, 10 1/2 In. 495.00
Mattel, Mr. Kotter, Welcome Back Kotter 35.00
Mattel, Sanga, Black Girl 536.00
Mattel, Skipper, Black, Homecoming Queen, White Dress 27.00
Mattel, Skipper, Growing Up, Blond, Twist Arms Bust Grows, Box 20.00
Mattel, Skipper, Titian Hair, 1964 .... 25.00
Mattel, Skooter, Brunette Pigtails, 1964 .... 30.00
Mattel, Skooter, Pale Blond Braids, 1964 .... 65.00
Mattel, Skooter, Titian Hair, Freckles, Swimsuit, Box, 1964 .... 105.00
Mattel, Twiggy, 1967, Box 65.00
Max Illfelder, My Sweetheart, Blue Slant Eyes, 24 In. 675.00
Mego, Captain America, 8 In. 15.00
Mego, Dorothy, From Wizard of Oz, 8 In. 15.00
Mego, Mr. Spock, Star Trek, 8 In. 25.00
Mego, Nubia, Wonder Woman's Friend, Jointed, Unused, Box, 1976, 12 In. 79.00
Mego, Sonny & Cher, Box, Pair 85.00
Mego, Spiderman, 8 In. 15.00
Mego, Steve Trevor, Wonder Woman's Uniform, Pilot, 1976, 12 In. 69.00
Midge, Blond Curly Hair, Original 2–Piece Swimsuit, Booklet, Stand, Shoes, Box 110.00
Minerva, Tin Head, 9 1/2 In. 95.00
Minerva, Tin Head, 18 In. 90.00
Mollye, Dutch Boy, Cloth, 14 In. 85.00
Mon Tressor, 7, Bisque Head, 5–Piece Composition Body, 20 In. 300.00
Montanari, Wax, Rooted Hair, Eyebrows, Eyelashes, Clothes, Eng., 1860s, 20 In. 2250.00
Moon Mullins, 3 1/2 In. 35.00
Mork From Ork, Talking 20.00
Mother–To–Be, Cloth, Package, 12 In. 8.00
Nancy Ann, Muffie, Pink Ballerina Clothes 125.00
Nancy Ann, Storybook, Bisque, 12 In. 25.00
Nancy Ann, Storybook, Champagne Lady, Bisque, Box, 1957 .... 175.00
Nancy Ann, Storybook, Mopsey, Little Black Girl, Box 175.00
Nancy, Composition, Brown Sleep Eyes, Open Mouth, Human Hair Wig, 19 In. 150.00
Nippon, Blue Sleep Eyes, Lashes, Ball–Jointed, Human Hair Wig, Clothes, 24 In. 425.00
Paper dolls are listed in their own category
Papier–Mache, Glass Eyes, Antique Clothes, 32 In. 395.00
Papier–Mache, Lady, Original Wig, Blue Glass Eyes, Clothing, 1849, 24 In. 1450.00
Papier–Mache, Painted Pate, Brush Marks Around Face, France, 26 In. 2250.00
Parian, Emma, Scarf Lady, 1940 .... 495.00
Parian, Man, Light Brown Hair, Intaglio, Soldier Clothes, 22 In. 475.00
Parian, Molded Hair, Bisque Hands, 20 1/2 In. 895.00
Paris Bebe, Bisque, Paperweight Eyes, Human Hair Wig, Lilac Silk Dress, 27 In. ... 5500.00
Pat Parachute, Felt, Silk Parachute, 1942 .... 65.00
Patsy, Jointed, Original Dress & Shoes, 9 In. 55.00
Pebbles, Baby, Flintstone, Box 85.00
Pee–Wee Herman, Talking, Box 150.00
Pincushion dolls are listed in their own category
Poor Pitiful Pearl, Box .... 74.00 To 79.00
Porcelain, Bonnet, Sculpted Hair, Muslin Body, Bisque Forearms, c.1885, 13 In. 1200.00
Porcelain, Lady, Sculpted Hair, Muslin Body, Leather Arms, c.1875, 16 In. 1050.00
Porcelain, Lady, Smiling Expression, Muslin Body, Antique Costume, c.1875, 16 In. .. 600.00
Porcelain, Scandinavian Costume, Muslin Body, Leather Arms, c.1870, 11 In. 750.00
Pouty, Antique Clothes, Germany, 24 In. 4000.00
Puppet, Bam–Bam, Flintstone, Knickerbocker 38.00
Puppet, Bruce Lee, Arms Extend & Move, Kung–Fu Type, Hand 30.00
Puppet, Dishonest John, Talking, Mattel, 1962 .... 28.00
Puppet, Dumbo 17.50
Puppet, Dwarf, Steiff, 10 In. 50.00
Puppet, Emmett Kelly, Hand 25.00
Puppet, Fred Flintstone, Push, 1960s 8.00
Puppet, Gumby's Pal Pokey, Hand, Lakeside, 1965 .... 18.00
Puppet, Hazelle Family, Hand, 1950s, 5 Piece 50.00
Puppet, King Friday The 13th, Mister Rogers, Hand, 1950s 19.00
Puppet, Misha, Moscow Olympics Bear, Hand, Dakin, Package, 1980 .... 27.50

Puppet, Mr. Bluster, Original Box 95.00
Puppet, Mr. Do Bee & Happy Jack, Romper Room, Hasbro, 1970, Box, Pair 49.00
Puppet, Rocky, Stallone, Boxer, Hand 18.00
Puppet, Sammy Davis, Jr., Rubber Head, 10 In. 25.00
Puppet, Snap, Crackle & Pop, Rubber Heads, Cloth Bodies 250.00
Puppet, Yogi Bear, Knickerbocker, Hand 33.00
Rag, Blue Calico Dress, Dated 1858 .... 425.00
Rag, Embroidered Face, Black Cloth Hair, Full Skirt With Train, Handmade, 13 In. 60.00
Rapery & Delphieu, Bisque, Human Hair, Closed Mouth, Silk Dress, c.1885, 18 In. 3600.00
Remco, Captain Crook, McDonalds, 1976 .... 30.00
Remco, I Dream of Jeannie, 1977, 6 In. 40.00
Remco, Lily Munster, The Munsters, 1964, 5 In. 198.00
Remco, Lurch, Addams Family, 1965 .... 79.00
Remco, Ronald McDonald, 1976 .... 25.00
Renwal, Baby, Jointed, 2 1/4 In. 15.00
Revalo, Bisque, Sleep Eyes, Chemise, In Revalo Box, 14 In. 1100.00
S & H, 1009, Bisque, Blue Sleep Eyes, Original Dress, 28 In. 2495.00
S & H, 1078, Bisque, Black, Original Wig and Clothes, 16 In. 1400.00
S & H, 1078, Bisque, Human Hair Wig, Antique Dress, 38 In. 2795.00
S & H, 1078, Blue Sleep Eyes, 7 1/2 In. 400.00
S & H, 1079, Brown Sleep Eyes, Ball–Jointed, Human Hair, Clothes, 36 In. 2000.00
S & H, 1079, Brown Sleep Eyes, Human Hair Wig, Silk Dress, 31 In. 1425.00
S & H, 1129, Oriental, 14 In. 3000.00
S & P, Comic Strip Character Nancy, 1954, 15 In. 250.00
S & H dolls are also listed here as Bergmann and Simon & Halbig
S. F. B. J., 60, Bisque, Walker, Kiss Thrower, 12 1/2 In. 1200.00
S. F. B. J., 60, Child, Bisque Head, Paperweight Eyes, Upper Teeth, Dressed, 20 In. 600.00
S. F. B. J., 235, Boy, Molded Hair, Jewel Eyes, Open–Close Mouth, 13 1/2 In. 1250.00
S. F. B. J., 236, Laughing Child, Facial Lines, Straight Leg, Toddler Body, 24 In. 700.00
S. F. B. J., 236, Laughing Girl, Bisque, Sleep Eyes, Old Shoes, 16 1/2 In. 1800.00
S. F. B. J., 236, Laughing Girl, Toddler, Blue Sleep Eyes, Original Wig, 14 In. 1595.00
S. F. B. J., 236, Toddler, Laughing, 23 In. 1750.00
S. F. B. J., 237, Boy, Character, 13 In. 3500.00
S. F. B. J., 252, Pouty, Toddler Body, Human Hair Wig, 23 1/2 In. 9500.00
S. F. B. J., 301, Bisque, Open Mouth, Teeth, Jointed, Clothes, Bonnet, 26 1/2 In. 1595.00
S. F. B. J., 301, Bisque, Sleep Eyes, Fully Jointed Composition Body, 14 1/2 In. 360.00
S. F. B. J., 301, Bisque, Soldier, Fur Mustache, Uniform 450.00
S. F. B. J., 301, Child, Blue Sleep Eyes, Mohair Lashes, Pink Silk Dress, Hat, 26 In. 1695.00
S. F. B. J., Bisque Socket Head, Open–Close Mouth, 27 In. 4950.00
S. F. B. J., Blue Sleep Eyes, Carved Teeth, Wig & Pate, Signed Body, 31 In. 1900.00
S. F. B. J., Embroidered Dress, Purse, 19 In. 750.00
Schoenau & Hoffmeister, 106, Bisque, Sleep Eyes, Mohair Wig, Wool Cape, 32 In. 1400.00
Schoenau & Hoffmeister, 1906, Bisque, Dress, Wool Cape, 32 In. 3400.00
Schoenau & Hoffmeister, 1909, Bisque Head, Blue Sleep Eyes, Mohair, Dressed 285.00
Schoenau & Hoffmeister, Girl, Bisque, Dutch Outfit, Wood & Composition, 27 In. .. 325.00
Schoenau & Hoffmeister, Hanna, Bisque, 29 In. 1695.00
Schoenau & Hoffmeister, Hanna, Character Baby, 25 In. 875.00
Schoenau & Hoffmeister, Princess Elizabeth, Toddler, Bisque, Clothes, 23 In. 2995.00
Schoenhut, 308, Pouty Girl, Intaglio Eyes, 16 In. 685.00
Schoenhut, Boy, Dressed, Hat, Original Pin, 14 In. 850.00
Schoenhut, Boy, Pouty Face, 13 1/2 In. 895.00
Schoenhut, Boy, Wooden Jointed, 1911 .... 800.00
Schoenhut, Carved Hair, Original Clothes, 16 In. 1250.00
Schoenhut, Character Girl, Sober Face, Mohair Wig, 14 In. 412.50
Schoenhut, Clown, 2–Part Head, Tightrope Slots In Shoes, 7 1/2 In. 145.00
Schoenhut, Clown, Bisque Head, Wooden Body, Jointed, c.1910, 9 1/2 In. 500.00
Schoenhut, Clown, Composition Face, Protruding Eyes, 8 1/4 In. 121.00
Schoenhut, Dolly Face, Wooden Head, Spring–Jointed Body, Knit Outfit, 17 In. 375.00
Schoenhut, Girl, 1911, 14 In. 1000.00
Schoenhut, Girl, Sleep Eyes, Blond Wig, Eyelet Dress 775.00
Schoenhut, Molded & Painted, Smiling Face, Dimples, 1920s, 16 In. 220.00
Schoenhut, Pouty, Wooden Head, Jointed Wooden Body, Underclothing, 18 1/2 In. 425.00
Schoenhut, Santa Claus, Roly Poly, 7 1/2 In. 650.00

Schoenhut, Scootles, Roly Poly	650.00
Schoenhut, Toddler, Fauntleroy–Type Outfit, Human Hair Wig, 16 In.	995.00
Schoenhut, Toddler, Walker, Traditional Costume, 18 In.	850.00
Schoenhut, Toddler, Wooden Socket Head, Spring–Jointed, Clown, 16 In. .... 235.00 To	350.00
Schwab, Character Baby, 24 In.	650.00
Serugo, Johnny Appleseed, Rubber, Box, 1954	60.00
Seymour Mann, Scarlett, Porcelain, 16 In.	100.00
Shirley Temple dolls are included in the Shirley Temple category	
Simon & Halbig, 0120, Bisque, Hair Lashes, Original Dress, 19 In.	3900.00
Simon & Halbig, 0428, Bisque, Toddler, Buster Brown–Style Costume, 18 In.	2600.00
Simon & Halbig, 0886, Bisque, High Black Stockings, Clothes, Wicker Trunk, 6 In.	1100.00
Simon & Halbig, 0908, Closed Mouth, Bisque, Mohair, Silk Dress, 16 In.	3700.00
Simon & Halbig, 0939, Bisque, Brown Eyes, Heirloom Gown, 23 In.	1995.00
Simon & Halbig, 1009, Bisque, Blue Sleep Eyes, Human Hair Wig, Dress, 28 In.	2495.00
Simon & Halbig, 1039, Bisque, Teeth, Jointed, Purple Silk Dress, 11 In.	450.00
Simon & Halbig, 1078, Bisque Head, Blue Eyes, Pierced Ears, Ball–Jointed, 22 In.	495.00
Simon & Halbig, 1078, Brown Eyes, Lashes, Human Hair Wig, Jointed Body, 32 In.	1550.00
Simon & Halbig, 1078, Walker, Head Turns Side To Side, 8 In.	450.00
Simon & Halbig, 1079, Ball Jointed Body, Sleep Eyes, Mohair Lashes, 34 In.	1795.00
Simon & Halbig, 1079, Bisque Socket Head, Open Mouth, 4 Teeth, 8 In.	275.00
Simon & Halbig, 1079, Bisque, Brown Sleep Eyes, Human Hair Wig, 31 In.	1600.00
Simon & Halbig, 1079, Bisque, Brown Sleep Eyes, Silk Dress, 30 In.	1500.00
Simon & Halbig, 1079, Blue Sleep Eyes, Mohair Wig, 17 In.	800.00
Simon & Halbig, 1079, Boy, Lord Fauntleroy Outfit, 41 3/4 In.	3400.00
Simon & Halbig, 1159, Bisque, Adult Flapper, Ball–Jointed, Costume, 13 In.	1600.00
Simon & Halbig, 1249, Santa, Bisque, Blue Sleep Eyes, Original Dress, 33 In.	2800.00
Simon & Halbig, 1329, Character, Oriental, Tan Bisque, 18 In.	3250.00
Simon & Halbig, 1468, Lady, Blue Sleep Eyes, Original Wig, 15 In.	3850.00
Simon & Halbig, 1900, Bisque Head, Glass Sleep Eyes, Open Mouth, Jointed, 27 In.	1210.00
Simon & Halbig, Baby Blanche, Bisque, Brown Sleep Eyes, Original Clothes, 23 In.	950.00
Simon & Halbig, Bisque Head, Black, Glass Eyes, Wood Jointed Body, 14 In.	4200.00
Simon & Halbig, Bisque, Blue Sleep Eyes, Wig, Old Clothes, 22 In.	750.00
Simon & Halbig, Bisque, Open Mouth, Ball–Jointed Composition, 17 1/2 In.	660.00
Simon & Halbig, Bisque, Sleep Eyes, Original Dress & Shoes, 31 In.	2800.00
Simon & Halbig, Brown Sleep Eyes, Ball–Jointed, Clothes, Shoes, Box, 30 In.	1300.00
Simon & Halbig, Girl, Brown Bisque Socket Head, Upper Teeth, Dress, 22 In.	3400.00
Simon & Halbig, Girl, Sleep Eyes, Ball–Jointed Body, Dress & Coat, 25 In.	450.00
Simon & Halbig, Oriental Character, Bisque, 18 In.	3250.00
Simon & Halbig, Walker, Bisque Head, Synthetic Wig, Mechanism In Legs, 16 In.	800.00
Simon & Halbig dolls are also listed here under Bergmann and S & H	
Skeezix, Oilcloth, Cotton Stuffed, c.1924, 14 In.	125.00
Skookum, Indian Chief, Squaw, All Original, 16 In., Pair	265.00
Speedy Gonzales, With Tag, 8 In.	75.00
Steiff, Dutch Girl, Glass Eyes, Dressed, 1913, 13 In.	905.00
Steiner, Bisque, Blond, Sleep Eyes, Swivel Head, Jointed, 5 1/2 In.	255.00
Steiner, Bisque, Blue Glass Eyes, Mohair Wig, Silk Dress, c.1885, 15 In.	4400.00
Steiner, Bisque, Blue Paperweight Eyes, French Dressed, A Series, 25 In.	5500.00
Steiner, Bisque, Blue Paperweight Eyes, Straight Wrists, Shoes, 21 In.	6995.00
Steiner, Bisque, French Shoes, Straight Waisted Body, 21 In.	7200.00
Steiner, Bisque, Glass Eyes, Human Hair, Original Dressed, c.1889, 23 In.	4500.00
Steiner, Blue Paperweight Eyes, Original Wig, Bisque, Straight Waisted, 17 In.	6200.00
Steiner, Kicking, Crying, 18 In.	2900.00
Steiner, Le Parisian, Bisque Head, Mohair Wig, French Style Outfit, 10 1/2 In.	2700.00
Steiner, Le Parisian, Bisque, 6 Teeth, Jointed Wood & Composition Body, 22 In.	2900.00
Steiner, Mechanical, Bebe, Crying, Key Wind Body, Dressed, 18 In.	2900.00
Steiner, Woman, Walking, Swivel Head, Key Wind, Original Outfit, 15 In.	4000.00
Steve The Tramp, On Card	35.00
Sunshine, San Diego, Souvenir, 1983	185.00
Sweet Sue, American Beauty, 24 In.	225.00
Sweet Sue, Walker, White & Red Pique Dress, Chignon, Hat, Box	375.00
Terri Lee, Tiny, Plastic Head, 5–Piece Plastic Body, Girl Scout Uniform, 10 In.	95.00
Terri Lee, Tiny, Tagged Clothes, 10 In.	150.00

Tete Jumeau, 8, Blue Paperweight, Original Wig, Clothes, 20 In. 4800.00
Tete Jumeau, 10, Bisque, Paperweight Eyes, French Wig, 23 1/2 In. 2575.00
Tete Jumeau, 15, Bebe, Closed Mouth, 33 In. ...., ... 6500.00
Tete Jumeau, Bisque, Blue Paperweight Eyes, Marked, 23 In. 6000.00
Tete Jumeau, Bisque, Blue Paperweight Eyes, Straight Wrist, 8–Piece Body, 18 In. 5300.00
Tete Jumeau, Bisque, Brown Paperweight Eyes, Cork Pate & Wig, Boxed, 27 In. 6200.00
Tete Jumeau, Bisque, Closed Mouth, Antique Costume, 30 In. 6995.00
Tete Jumeau, Bisque, Mohair Wig, Ball–Jointed Body, Paperweight Eyes, 18 In. 5300.00
Tete Jumeau, Bisque, Paperweight Eyes, Silk Dress, Shoes, Marked, 27 In. 6900.00
Tete Jumeau, Blue Eyes, Teeth, Human Hair, Clothes, 18 In. 2700.00
Tete Jumeau, Blue Paperweight Eyes, Dressed, 16 In. 4300.00
Tete Jumeau, Blue Sleep Eyes, Original Wig, 18 In. 2700.00
Tete Jumeau, Brown Sleep Eyes, Human Wig, Open Mouth, 1880–1890, 17 In. 2100.00
Tete Jumeau, Child, Human Hair, Dark Glass Eyes, Antique Clothes, 27 In. 550.00
Tete Jumeau, Closed Mouth, Human Hair Wig, Clothes, 20 In. 5500.00
Tete Jumeau, Phonograph, Blue Paperweight Eyes, French Style Dress, 24 In. 8500.00
Tete Jumeau, Walker, Mechanical, Bisque, Sleep Eyes, Sailor Dress, Shoes, 21 In. ... 3500.00
Toddler, Ice Skating, Knit Legging Suit, Mittens, Bisque, Open Mouth, 13 In. 850.00
Tootsietoy, Mommy, 19 In. 30.00
Topo Gigio, 8 In. 15.00
Toto, Blue Stationary Eyes, French Body, Limoges, 16 In. 750.00
Troll, 2 Heads, Uneeda, 1965, 3 In. 25.00
Troll, Cow, Dam Thing, 1964, 3 In. 30.00
Troll, Horse, Dam Thing, 1964, 3 In. 30.00
Unis France, 301, Bisque Head, Open Mouth, Teeth, Composition, Dress, 33 In. 2000.00
Unis France, 301, Bisque, Brown Sleep Eyes, Lashes, Human Hair, Clothes, 21 In. 1000.00
Unis France, 301, Bisque, Human Hair Wig, Old Clothes, 29 In. 1100.00
United Features Syndicate, Charlie Brown, Rubber, 7 1/2 In. 22.00
Ventriloquist, Dummy, Composition, Black Tuxedo & Hat, 1930 .... 125.00
Ventriloquist, Dummy, Jerry Mahoney 150.00
Ventriloquist, Dummy, Jerry Mahoney, Suitcase, Juro Celebrity, 1950, 32 In. 354.00
Ventriloquist, Dummy, Laurel & Hardy, 1960s, Pair, Box 250.00
Ventriloquist, Dummy, Laurel & Hardy, 1970s, Large, Box, Pair 250.00
Violin Player, Bisque, Tricorn Hat, Wooden Hands, Violin, Squeeze To Play, 14 In. 798.00
Vogue, Alice In Wonderland, Long Blond Hair, Tagged Dress, Hard Plastic 195.00
Vogue, Brickette, Original Clothes, 16 In. 55.00
Vogue, Ginny, Elastic Strung, Nylon Dress, Gold Shoes, Hard Plastic, 8 In. 160.00
Vogue, Ginny, Hard Plastic, Walker, Molded Eyelashes, Original Clothes 175.00
Vogue, Ginny, Strung, Red Velvet Clothes, Top Snap Shoes 325.00
Vogue, Toodles, Dressed As Nurse, Composition 125.00
Volland, Raggedy Ann & Raggedy Andy, 1917, Pair 250.00
Wax Head, Cloth Body, Composition Limbs, Blue Glass Eyes, 38 In. 800.00
Wax Over Composition, Straw Stuffed Linen Body, Mohair Wig, Dressed, 17 In. 235.00
Wax Over Papier–Mache, Closed Smiling Mouth, Dress, Shawl, Bonnet, 26 In. 700.00
Wax Over Papier–Mache, Mandarin, Paperweight Eyes, Human Hair Wig, 12 In. ... 125.00
Wax Over Papier–Mache, Pupilless Eyes, Cloth Body, Kid Lower Arms, 26 In. 250.00
Wax Over Papier–Mache, Pupilless Eyes, Cloth Body, Wedding Dress, 26 In. 400.00
Wax, 180, Brown Sleep Eyes, Mohair Wig, Signed Montanan, 29 In. 975.00
Wax, Sleep Eyes, Rooted Hair, Fashion Dress, 16 In. 795.00
Wax, Split Head, Clothes, 1830, 21 In. 1750.00
Wiley Coyote, Stuffed, 1971 Tag 25.00
Woman, Dollhouse, Glass Eyes, Wig & Cloths, 5 1/2 In. 350.00
Woman, Lounging Pajamas, Cloche Style Hat With Plume, Holding Cigarette, 14 In. 150.00
Wooden Head, Cloth Body, Cotton & Linen Clothes, c.1845, 21 In. 660.00
Yosemite Sam, Stuffed, 1971 Tag 25.00
Zapf, Melanie, Sleep Brown Eyes, Brown Hair, 21 In. 75.00

DONALD DUCK items are included in the Disneyana category.

DOORSTOPS have been made in all types of designs. The vast majority of the doorstops sold today are cast iron and were made from about 1890 to 1930. Most of them are shaped like people, animals, flowers, or ships. Reproductions and newly designed examples are sold in gift shops.

Airedale, White, Brown Spots, Iron 75.00
Aunt Jemima, Hubley, Cast Iron, 13 In. 385.00
Ballplayer, Yellow & Red, Cast Iron 50.00
Basket of Flowers, Cast Iron, 7 1/2 In. 50.00
Basket of Flowers, Polychrome Paint, Iron, 9 3/4 In. .... 55.00 To 66.00
Basket of Kittens, 10 In. 275.00
Bear, Holding Honey Pot, Standing, 15 In. 575.00
Bell Hop, Black Man, Cast Iron, 7 1/2 In. 90.00
Bulldog, Cast Iron, 10 In. 121.00
Campbell Kids With Dog, Polychrome, Iron, 8 1/2 In. 159.00
Cat With Bow, Black, Iron, 8 In. 71.00
Cat, Cast Iron .... 135.00 To 140.00
Cat, Cast Iron, 7 1/2 In. 55.00
Cat, Full Figure, Black, Yellow Eyes, Cast Iron, 6 3/4 In. 165.00
Cat, Full Figure, Cast Iron, 7 1/2 In. 154.00
Cat, Green Eyes, All White, Hubley 135.00
Cat, Polychrome Paint, 9 In. 85.00
Cat, Ribbon, Polychrome Paint, Iron, 7 3/4 In. 192.00
Cat, Seated, Cast Iron, 7 3/4 In. 115.00
Cat, Seated, Cast Iron, 9 3/4 In. 165.00
Cat, Seated, Cast Iron, Polychrome, 8 1/4 In. 95.00
Cat, Seated, Original Black, With Beige, Green, Blue, Pink, White, 8 In. 247.00
Cat, White Persian, 8 1/2 In. 195.00
Charleston Dancers, Cast Iron, Copyright Fish, 8 7/8 In. 265.00
Child On Knees, Yawning, Cast Iron 220.00
Children Kissing, Cast Iron 125.00
Coach, Cast Iron, Copyright 1930 .... 165.00
Cockatoo, Cast Iron, 8 In. 185.00
Colonial Lawyer, 9 5/8 In. 185.00
Colonial Woman, Cast Iron, 4 5/8 In. 145.00
Conestoga Wagon, Hubley, 8 In. 150.00
Covered Wagon & Oxen, Cast Iron, 6 1/4 In. 165.00
Diana The Hunter, Dog, 7 5/8 In. 66.00
Dog, Boston Terrier, Cast Iron, 8 In. 132.00
Dog, Boxer, Cast Iron, 8 1/2 In. 68.00
Dog, Bulldog, Boston, Full Figure, Black, White, Iron, 9 3/4 In. 27.00
Dog, Bulldog, Cast Iron, 10 In. 110.00
Dog, Bulldog, Full Figure, Black, White, Iron, 9 1/4 In. 60.00
Dog, Bulldog, Full Figure, Original Black, Gray Paint, 4 5/8 In. 93.00
Dog, Bulldog, National Foundry 100.00
Dog, Cairn Terriers, Cast Iron 145.00
Dog, Cocker Spaniel, Red Ribbon, Cast Iron 145.00
Dog, Full Figure, Original Black, Grayish Tan, 7 In. 110.00
Dog, German Shepherd, Bronze, 9 3/4 In. 115.00
Dog, German Shepherd, Cast Iron, Bronze Wash, 9 1/4 In. 175.00
Dog, Greyhound, Full Figure, Red, 12 1/2 In. 148.00
Dog, Pointer, Black, Cast Iron, 8 In. 85.00
Dog, Poodle, Full Figure, White, 8 In. 135.00
Dog, Puppy, Cast Iron, 8 In. 160.00
Dog, Seated, Cast Iron, Glass Eyes, Black, Red, Gold Collar, 13 1/2 In. 125.00
Dog, Setter, Cast Iron, 5 3/4 In. 440.00
Dog, Spaniel, Japan, 9 In. 250.00
Dog, Springer Spaniel, Cast Iron, 6 3/4 In. 187.00
Dog, Wire Hair Terrier, Facing Front, Hubley 170.00
Dolly, Girl Holding Doll, 9 1/2 In. ....*Illus* 375.00
Duck, Full Body, Pants & Top Hat, Cast Iron, 7 3/4 In. 550.00
Eagle, Wings Spread, Cast Iron, 8 In. 130.00
Elephant, By Palm Tree, 13 In. 265.00
Elephant, Cast Iron, 6 1/2 In. 45.00
Elephant, Full Figure, Trunk Up, Cast Iron, 8 1/4 In. 150.00
Fisherman, In Boat, Cast Iron, 6 3/4 In. 165.00
Frog, Cast Iron, Green 12.00
Frog, Iron, Original Paint, 3 1/2 In. 60.00

Galleon, 7 1/2 In.	90.00
Geese, Three, Hubley, 8 In.	385.00
George Washington Crossing Delaware, 8 1/2 In.	65.00
George Washington, Cast Iron, 8 1/2 In.	132.00
George Washington, Full Figure, Cast Iron, 12 1/4 In.	450.00
Girl With Book, Cast Iron	140.00
Gnome, Cast Iron, 13 1/4 In.	600.00
Gnome, Cast Iron, 9 In.	15.00
Gnome, With Keys, Cast Iron, 11 In.	170.00
Golfer, Cast Iron, 8 In.	935.00
Golfer, On Back Swing, Cast Iron, 10 In.	715.00 To 770.00
Grouse, Ring Tail, Green Ground, 7 x 8 In.	125.00
Heron, 7 1/2 In.	135.00
High Button Shoe, Blue, Gray, Iron, 7 In.	55.00
Horse, Black, Cast Iron, Copyright 1949	120.00
Horse, Full Figure, Original Brown, White, Black Paint, 8 In.	214.00
Horse, Hubley, 8 In.	150.00
Indian Brave, Cast Iron	140.00
Indian, End of Trail, Art Deco, Cast Iron	165.00
Jumbo, Elephant, 10 1/4 In.	175.00
Kitten, Hubley, 8 In.	90.00
Lighthouse, Brass, 5 In.	65.00
Lighthouse, Cast Iron, 7 3/4 In.	135.00
Lighthouse, National Foundry, 6 1/4 In.	150.00
Lion, On Hind Legs, Base, 14 1/2 In.	220.00
Little Red Riding Hood, With Wolf, Nuyde, 7 1/2 In.	1350.00
Mail Coach, Cast Iron, 7 1/2 In.	145.00
Mammy, Cast Iron, 6 In.	90.00
Mammy, Hubley, Cast Iron	605.00
Man In Harlequin Coat, Polychrome Paint, 7 1/4 In.	65.00
Mickey Mouse & Minnie Mouse, Cast Iron	55.00
Monkey, Brown, Cast Iron, 8 In.	25.00 To 65.00
Olive Picker, Cast Iron, 7 3/4 In.	475.00
Organ Grinder & Monkey, Cast Iron, 10 In.	395.00
Organ Grinder, Monkey, Cast Iron, 10 In.	467.00
Oriental Child On Pillow, Polychrome, Cast Iron, 5 1/4 In.	25.00
Oriental Girl, Cast Iron, 7 1/2 In.	125.00
Owl, Iron, 6 In.	40.00
Owl, Perched On Rock Formation, 10 In.	190.00
Parrot In Ring, Cast Iron, 13 3/4 In.	100.00 To 185.00
Parrot On Perch, Cast Iron, 8 In.	100.00 To 187.00
Penguin, Full Figure, White, Black, Cast Iron, 10 In.	110.00 To 300.00
Pheasant, Cast Iron, 8 1/2 In.	165.00
Pig, Black & White, Cast Iron, 7 In. .	150.00
Pig, Repainted, 7 1/2 In.	264.00
Plowman, Cast Iron	185.00

◆ ◆ ◆ ◆ ◆ ◆ ◆ ◆ ◆ ◆ ◆ ◆ ◆ ◆ ◆ ◆ ◆ ◆ ◆

Felt dolls are difficult to clean.
Swirl them in corn starch and
leave them in it for a day or
two. Then brush off the corn
starch. This process may help.

◆ ◆

Doorstop, Dolly, Girl
Holding Doll, Iron, 9 1/2 In.

Doorstop, Woman,
Holding Flowers, 8 In.

Polly Parrot, Cast Iron, 8 In.	145.00
Rabbit, Full Figure, White, Cast Iron, 10 3/4 In.	110.00
Ram, Standing, 7 1/4 In.	180.00
Raven, 9 3/4 In.	220.00
Rooster, 13 1/4 In.	2800.00
Rooster, Cast Iron, 6 In.	44.00
Santa Claus, Cast Iron, 10 In.	195.00
Scottish Highlander, Standing, 15 1/2 In.	190.00
Sheep, 9 5/8 In.	275.00
Southern Belle, Cast Iron, 11 1/4 In.	155.00
Squirrel, Cast Iron	90.00
Squirrel, With Nut, Cast Iron, 8 3/8 In.	140.00
Stage Coach, Polychrome Paint, 7 1/2 In.	75.00
Stagecoach, Horse Drawn, Hubley, 11 1/4 In.	125.00
Stork, Cast Iron, 10 In.	65.00
Swan Wedge, England, 8 In.	150.00
Tiger Lily, Hubley	185.00
Tropical Woman, Cast Iron, 12 In.	365.00
Turtle, Cast Iron, 2 In.	75.00
Woman, Holding Flowers, 8 In. ....*Illus*	100.00
Zinnias, Cast Iron, 10 1/2 In.	150.00

DOULTON pottery and porcelain were made by Doulton and Co. of Burslem, England, after 1882. The name *Royal Doulton* appeared on their wares after 1902. Other pottery by Doulton is listed under Royal Doulton.

Ewer, Floral & Berries, Cobalt Blue, Gold Tracery, 1885, 9 1/4 In.	165.00
Jug, Polychrome Floral, 8 1/4 In.	127.00
Pitcher, 2–Tone Applied Tavern Scene, Lambeth, Silver Lip, 1889, 8 In.	132.00
Pitcher, Christopher Columbus Commemorative, 9 In.	225.00
Pitcher, Madras, 7 In.	195.00
Pitcher, Madras, 8 In.	185.00
Pitcher, Victoria, Polychrome, Lambeth, 6 In.	302.50
Pitcher, Victoria, Silver Lip, 2–Tone Glaze, 1896, 5 1/4 In.	235.00
Plate, Alma, 2 Horses & 2 Men, 10 In.	120.00
Vase, 3–Part, Variegated, Rixware, 9 1/2 In. ....*Illus*	850.00
Vase, Frieze of Stags Fleeing Wolves, Hannah Barlow, Lambeth, c.1888, 21 1/2 In.	495.00
Vase, Twin Boys Incised On Front, Brown Rim, Marked, 5 1/2 In.	175.00

DRAGONWARE is a form of moriage pottery. Moriage is a type of decoration on Japanese pottery. Raised white designs are applied to the ware. White dragons are the major raised decorations on the moriage called *dragonware*. The background color is gray and white, orange and lavender, or orange and brown. It is a twentieth–century ware.

Perfume Set, Moriage, Art Deco, 3 Piece	50.00
Teapot, Sugar & Creamer, With 7 1/4 In. Plate, 7 Piece	90.00
Vase, Shoulder Handles, Moriage, 8 3/4 In., Pair	160.00

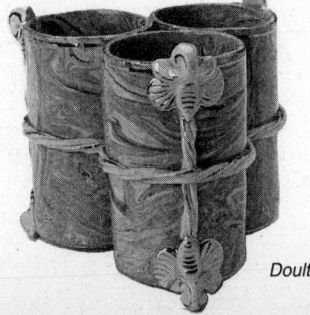

♦ ♦

When moving, remember there is no insurance coverage for breakage if the items are not packed by the shipper.

♦ ♦

Doulton, Vase, 3-Part, Variegated,

Rixware, 9 1/2 In.

DRESDEN china is any china made in the town of Dresden, Germany. The most famous factory in Dresden is the Meissen factory. Figurines of eighteenth–century ladies and gentlemen, animal groups, or cherubs and other mythological subjects were popular. One special type of figurine was made with skirts of porcelain–dipped lace. Do not make the mistake of thinking that all pieces marked *Dresden* are from the Meissen factory. The Meissen pieces usually have crossed swords marks, and are listed under Meissen. Some recent porcelain from Ireland, called *Irish Dresden,* is not included in this book.

Bowl, Applied Flowers, Hand Painted, Boat Shape, Square Feet, 17 In.	350.00
Bowl, Purple Flowers, Handles, Reticulated, Oblong, 9 In.	25.00
Bust, Victorian Young Girl, Pair	200.00
Compote, Hand Painted Flowers, Reticulated, Sticker Attached, 9 In.	375.00
Dish, Condiment, Hand Painted Floral Interior, Leaf Handle, Gold Trim, 10 1/2 In.	515.00
Figurine, Coach, Horse–Drawn	325.00
Figurine, Dancing Lady	40.00
Figurine, Gypsy Girl, With Goat, Marked, 8 x 10 1/2 In.	450.00
Figurine, Lady & Gentleman On Horseback, Dogs, Blue Crown	300.00
Figurine, Lady, Yellow Bonnet, Red Dress, 8 In.	350.00
Figurine, Napoleon & Josephine Scene, Bronze Ormolu Trim, Metal Base, Maxant	370.00
Figurine, Violin Solo, Woman Holding Music Book, Man With Violin, 10 1/2 In.	850.00
Figurine, Woman, Seated In Chariot	450.00
Group, 3 Children, Presenting Bouquets To Seated Woman, 16 x 24 In.	675.00
Group, Monkey Band, Conductor, 3 Musicians, Dated Dec. 1890, 7 In.	445.00
Group, Musical Trio, 7 x 10 In.	495.00
Group, Wedding Procession, 13 In.	495.00
Jar, Rose, Paneled Landscape Scenes, 18th Century People	95.00
Lamp, Applied Pink Flowers, Putti On Base, Marked	235.00
Lamp, Cupids, Multicolored Flowers	235.00
Medallion, Cherub, Oval, Greiner	225.00
Plaque, Expulsion of Hagar & Ishmael, Gilt Frame, 6 1/4 x 4 1/2 In.	605.00
Plaque, Madonna & Child, Virgin In Niche, 6 x 4 1/2 In.	770.00
Plate, Lilies-of-The-Valley, Lavender, Raised Scrolls, Reticulated, 1900, 8 1/2 In.	25.00
Vase, Dutch Girls, White Ground, 11 1/2 In.	485.00
Wall Pocket, Hand Painted Flowers, Applied Cupids, 7 x 9 In., Pair	495.00

DUNCAN & MILLER is a term used by collectors when referring to glass made by the George A. Duncan and Sons Company or the Duncan and Miller Glass Company. These companies worked from 1893 to 1955, when the use of the name *Duncan* was discontinued and the firm became part of the United States Glass Company. Early patterns may be listed under Pressed Glass.

American Ways, Bowl, 4 1/4 x 4 1/2 In.	10.00
Astaire, Cocktail	6.00
Block, Cracker Jar, Cover	55.00
Canterbury, Candy Dish, Cover, Blue, 3 Piece	55.00
Canterbury, Compote, Blue, 5 1/2 x 7 In.	35.00
Canterbury, Pitcher, Martini	126.00
Canterbury, Plate, 9 In.	12.00
Canterbury, Plate, Green, 7 1/2 In.	4.00
Canterbury, Sherbet, Amber	11.50
Canterbury, Sugar, 3 1/4 In.	10.50
Canterbury, Wine	12.00
Caribbean, Bowl, 12 In.	22.00
Caribbean, Cheese Dish, Blue	75.00
Caribbean, Dish, 2 Sections, Red Handle, Crystal	21.00
Caribbean, Dish, Mayonnaise, 2 Sections, Blue	85.00
Caribbean, Goblet, Wine	21.00
Caribbean, Mustard, Cover, Blue	75.00
Caribbean, Nappy, Handle, Blue, 5 In.	35.00
Caribbean, Nappy, Handle, Blue, 10 In.	75.00
Caribbean, Pitcher, Milk, Blue	350.00

Caribbean, Pitcher, Water, Blue 950.00
Caribbean, Punch Set, Blue, 6 Piece 345.00
Caribbean, Relish, 2 Sections, Blue, 6 In. 30.00
Caribbean, Salt & Pepper, Blue, 3 In. 85.00
Caribbean, Syrup, Blue, 8 In. 250.00
Caribbean, Wine, Ball Stem 21.00
Deauville, Champagne 15.00
Deauville, Goblet, Water, 7 7/8 In. 20.00
Diamond, Bowl, 2 Sections, Ladle, Oval, 2 Piece 45.00
Diamond, Jam Jar 50.00
Ellrose, Bowl, Footed, 9 In. 80.00
First Love, Bowl, Flared, 12 In. 56.00
First Love, Bowl, Handles, 6 1/2 In. 42.00
First Love, Candlestick, 2–Light, Pair .... 75.00 To 80.00
First Love, Candlestick, Pair 40.00
First Love, Champagne 30.00
First Love, Cocktail 25.00
First Love, Cornucopia, 3 Feathers, 8 In. 75.00
First Love, Dish, Mayonnaise, 2 Piece 34.00
First Love, Flower Bowl, Flared, 12 In. 90.00
First Love, Goblet, Water 35.00
First Love, Plate, 8 1/2 In. 22.00
First Love, Plate, 12 In. 70.00
First Love, Plate, Sandwich, 12 1/4 In. 60.00
First Love, Relish, 2 Sections, 8 In. 30.00
First Love, Relish, 4 Sections, 9 In. 60.00
First Love, Relish, 5 Sections, 10 1/2 In. 90.00
First Love, Relish, Handle, Crimped 22.00
First Love, Salt & Pepper 45.00
First Love, Vase, 8 In. 60.00
First Love, Vase, Cornucopia 80.00
First Love, Vase, Handles, 7 In. 70.00
Heron, Figurine 58.00
Hobnail, Basket, Pink Opalescent, 10 1/2 In. 150.00
Hobnail, Cruet, Stopper 37.00
Hobnail, Goblet, Water 10.00
Hobnail, Powder Box, Pink 85.00
Hobnail, Salt & Pepper, Glass Top, 2 3/4 In. 25.00
Mardi Gras, Punch Cup .... 9.00 To 10.00
Mardi Gras, Vase, 10 In. 35.00
Murano, Bonbon, 5 1/2 In. 65.00
Murano, Nappy, Ruffled, 6 In. 20.00
Nobility, Cordial, 8 Piece 195.00
Pall Mall, Bowl, Swan Handles, Oval .... 20.00 To 30.00
Plate, Deviled Egg .... 60.00 To 85.00
Plaza, Cocktail 12.00
Plaza, Finger Bowl, Amber 15.00
Radiance, Cup & Saucer, Blue 25.00
Radiance, Plate, Blue, 8 5/8 In. 20.00
Radiance, Punch Set, Crystal, Red Handles, 13 Piece 150.00
Sandwich, Ashtray, 2 1/4 x 3 1/2 In. 12.50
Sandwich, Ashtray, Rectangular 10.00
Sandwich, Basket, Handle, 11 1/2 In. 140.00
Sandwich, Bowl, 6 In. 27.00
Sandwich, Bowl, Flared, 11 1/2 In. 30.00
Sandwich, Butter, Cover, 1/4 Lb. 35.00
Sandwich, Cake Stand, 13 In. 75.00
Sandwich, Candlestick, 4 In., Pair 28.00
Sandwich, Candy Dish, Footed, 8 1/2 In. 65.00
Sandwich, Creamer, Large 18.00
Sandwich, Cup & Saucer 16.00
Sandwich, Dish, Grapefruit 5.00
Sandwich, Goblet, 9 Oz. 10.00

Sandwich, Mayonnaise Set, 3 Piece 32.00
Sandwich, Pitcher, Ice Lip, 64 Oz. 125.00
Sandwich, Plate, 8 1/4 In. 12.00
Sandwich, Plate, 13 In. 50.00
Sandwich, Plate, Torte, Amber, 12 In. 40.00
Sandwich, Relish, 2 Sections, Round Handle, 5 1/2 In. 15.00
Sandwich, Relish, 5 Sections, Round 15.00
Sandwich, Salt & Pepper, 2 1/2 In. 16.00
Sandwich, Sugar & Creamer, Tray .... 35.00 To 40.00
Sandwich, Syrup 50.00
Sandwich, Vase, Footed, 10 In. 70.00
Sandwich, Wine, Footed, 4 1/4 In. 20.00
Sanibel, Plate, Blue Opalescent, 8 1/2 In. 28.00
Sanibel, Plate, Sandwich, 13 In., Pair 85.00
Sanibel, Relish, Pink Opalescent, 3 Sections, 13 In. 45.00
Spiral Flutes, Cup & Saucer, Pink 11.00
Spiral Flutes, Goblet, Green 12.00
Spiral Flutes, Soup, Cream, Footed 25.00
Spiral Flutes, Tumbler, Green, 7 Oz. 12.00
Swan, 10 1/2 In. 85.00
Swan, 10 1/2 In. 45.00
Swan, 10 In. .... 70.00 To 78.00
Swan, 3 1/2 In. 30.00
Swan, 3 x 3 In. 22.00
Swan, 7 1/2 In. 35.00
Swan, 7 In. 40.00
Swan, Green, 7 In. 47.00
Swan, Green, Crystal Neck, 12 1/2 In 95.00
Swan, Ruby, 7 In. 45.00
Swan, Ruby, Crystal Neck, 13 In. 90.00
Swan, Spread Wings, Pink 95.00
Swan, Vaseline, 10 1/2 In. 50.00
Sylvan, Bonbon, Green Handle, 5 1/2 In. 70.00
Sylvan, Candy Dish, 7 x 5 In. 125.00
Sylvan, Relish, 3 Sections, Crystal, Cobalt Blue Handle 40.00
Teardrop, Candy Dish, Heart Shape, 2 Sections 15.00
Teardrop, Cruet, Tray 45.00
Teardrop, Cup & Saucer 7.00
Teardrop, Cup & Saucer, After Dinner 15.00
Teardrop, Jam Jar 24.00
Teardrop, Mustard 25.00
Teardrop, Pitcher, Silver Overlay, 1/2 Gal. 125.00
Teardrop, Pitcher, Water 100.00
Teardrop, Plate, 8 1/2 In. 9.50
Teardrop, Relish, 5 Sections, Round 15.00
Teardrop, Relish, Oval 10.00
Teardrop, Wine, 3 Oz. .... 10.00 To 12.00
Terrace, Plate, 2 Handles, Cobalt Blue, 5 In. 30.00
Terrace, Plate, Square, 6 1/2 In. 7.00
Terrace, Tumbler 20.00
Terrace, Wine 20.00
Three Feathers, Cornucopia, Blue Opalescent, Enameled Leaves, 8 In. 75.00

DURAND glass was made by Victor Durand from 1879 to 1935 at several
factories. Most of the iridescent Durand glass was made by Victor Durand,
Jr., from 1912 to 1924 at the Durand Art Glass Works in Vineland, New
Jersey.

Bowl, Cobalt Blue, White Rim, Footed, 3 In. 175.00
Bowl, Pansy, Gold Aurene, Signed 650.00
Bowl, Trumpet Form, Pink, White Feather Design, 7 3/4 In. 880.00
Bowl, White Rim, Cobalt Blue, Footed, 3 In. 190.00
Cuspidor 150.00
Jar, Cover, Blue Iridescent, Yellow Finial, Signed, 7 In. 1350.00

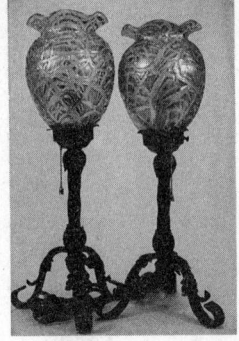

Durand, Lamp, Mantel, Glass Globe, Pair

♦♦♦♦♦♦♦♦♦♦♦♦♦♦♦♦♦♦♦♦♦♦♦♦♦

If it is too good to be true, it usually is! Trust your instincts when buying antiques. Experienced collectors notice many little signs of repair or reproduction, often without realizing it.

♦♦♦♦♦♦♦♦♦♦♦♦♦♦♦♦♦♦♦♦♦♦♦♦♦

Lamp, Boudoir, Iridescent Silver Blue, Swirling Coil Design, 11 1/2 In.	275.00
Lamp, Mantel, Glass Globe, Pair ....*Illus*	1750.00
Lamp, Torch, Crackle Glass, Hipped Elongated Ambergris Glass Shade, 15 1/4 In.	610.00
Vase, Amethyst, Fluted Tapering, Cylindrical, 16 In.	550.00
Vase, Egyptian Crackle, White Feather, 8 3/4 In.	965.00
Vase, Glass Threading, Peacock Blue, 8 In.	2200.00
Vase, Gold Iridescent, 1978, 10 1/4 In.	632.00
Vase, Hearts & Vine, Orange & Green, Pedestal, 8 1/4 In.	1100.00
Vase, Interior Design, Blue & Yellow, 7 1/2 In.	1375.00
Vase, Jar Shape, Blue & White Opalescent, Gold Trim, 6 1/2 In.	725.00
Vase, King Tut, 8 1/8 In. ....825.00 To	1150.00
Vase, King Tut, Blue & Lavender Swirls, Signed	2000.00
Vase, King Tut, Gold Opalescent, Trailing Damascene, 1925, 6 1/4 In.	660.00
Vase, King Tut, Gold Over Pink, Gold Interior, Signed	2600.00
Vase, Peacock Feather, Clear To Cranberry, 14 In.	1250.00
Vase, Pink Feather Design, White, Rose Border, 14 In.	990.00
Vase, Pulled & Trailed Design, Blue Iridescent, Onion Form, Signed, 10 In.	880.00
Vase, Random Threaded, Cobalt Blue Iridescent, 1920, 10 1/4 In.	1100.00
Vase, White Wavy Lines, Silver Blue Ground, 6 1/2 In.	375.00

ELFINWARE is a mark found on Dresden–like porcelain that was sold in dime stores and gift shops. Many pieces were decorated with raised flowers. The mark was registered by Breslauer–Underberg, Inc. of New York City in 1947. Pieces marked *Elfinware Made in Germany* had been sold since 1945 by this importer.

Figurine, Swan	25.00
Teapot, Pink	45.00

ELVIS PRESLEY, the well–known singer, lived from 1935 to 1977. He became famous by 1956. Elvis appeared on television, starred in twenty–seven movies, and performed in Las Vegas. Memorabilia from any of the Presley shows, his records, and even memorials made after his death are collected.

Box, Jewelry	55.00
Box, Music, Blue Hawaii, Decanter, 1977	195.00
Card, Gum, 66 Color Photographs, Donruss, 1978	36.00
Decanter, Musical, McCormick, 1st Edition	225.00
Doll, Glass Eyes, Bisque Head, White Clothes, 36 In.	550.00
Dress, Yellow Knit, Says Elvis 1935, Long Live The King, 1935–1977	25.00
Guitar, Lapin Products, 1984	65.00
Magazine, Photoplay Tribute, Special Collectors Edition, 1977	20.00
Menu, Las Vegas Hilton, 45 Rpm Record Shape, Signed Under Bust Picture	1250.00
Mirror, Elvis & Ed Sullivan, TV Radio, 1956	35.00
Necklace, Heart, Love Me Tender, On Card	175.00
Newspaper, Elvis's Death, Memphis, Dated April 17, 1977, Not Unfolded	25.00
Nodder, Cowboy, Guns, Glancing Eyes, Papier–Mache, 5 1/4 In.	325.00

Perfume Bottle, Teddy Bear, Box, 1957	150.00
Photograph, Leaning Against Fence, Signed, Matted, Framed, 8 x 11 In.	800.00
Poster, Double Trouble	275.00
Record, 25 All–Time Hits, Rock 'n Roll, Vol. 2, Hits From 1960s	7.50
Record, Crying In The Chapel, RCA Victor	6.00
Record, It's Now Or Never, RCA Victor	5.00
Record, Kentucky Rain, RCA Victor	2.00
Record, Return To Sender, RCA Victor	3.00
Sheet Music, Surrender, Autograph	325.00
Ticket, Concert, Asheville, NC, May 30, 1977, Unused	30.00
Wristwatch, Bradley	35.00
Wristwatch, Bradley, Box, 1984	55.00

ENAMELS listed here are made of glass particles and other materials
heated and fused to metal. In the eighteenth and nineteenth centuries,
workmen from Russia, France, England, and other countries made small
boxes and table pieces of enamel on metal. One form of English enamel is
called *Battersea* and is listed under that name. There was a revival of
interest in enameling in the thirties and a new style evolved. Graniteware
is a separate category and enameled metal kitchen pieces may be included
in the Kitchen category.

Ashtray, Red, Pink, White, Claire Wyman, 6 In. ....*Illus*	50.00
Candlestick, Floral, England, 1760, 11 3/4 In., Pair	1650.00
Casket, Jewel, Pietra Dura	1815.00
Cocktail Pick, Enameled Roosters, Fitted Case, France, 6 Piece	175.00
Plate, Four Dancing Figures, Green, Phyllis Sloane, 6 In.	65.00
Pokal, Morning Glories & Butterflies, Egg Shape, Cranberry, England, 13 In., Pr.	1430.00
Portrait, Semi–Nude Portrait, Brass Frame, Oval Opening, France, 6 x 8 In.	595.00
Vase, 2 Girls, Seated On Bench, Allover Painted, Gold Interior, France, 5 In.	425.00
Vase, Multicolored Alternating Patterns, Inverted Bell, E. Winter	275.00
Vase, Stylized Geometric Flower Heads, Copper, Sarlandie–Limoges, 11 In.	3300.00

ERPHILA is a mysterious mark found on 1930s Czechoslovakian pottery
and porcelain. It is thought that the mark was used on items imported by
Eberling & Reuss, Philadelphia, a giftware firm which is still operating in
Pennsylvania. The mark is a combination of the letters *E* and *R* (Eberling
& Reuss) and the first letters of the city, Phila(delphia). Many whimsical
figural pitchers and creamers, figurines, platters, and other giftwares carry
this mark.

Dresser, Doll, Nancy Pert, Germany, 6 In.	60.00
Figurine, Beagle Dog, 9 In.	48.00

Enamel, Ashtray, Red, Pink, White,
   Claire Wyman, 6 In.

◆ ◆

Several types of glue are
needed to repair broken pottery and porcelain. Commercial glues found in a local
hardware store are often satisfactory. Read the labels. Some
types work only with pieces
that are porous, others only
with pieces that are not porous.
Instant glue is difficult to use if
the break is complicated.

◆ ◆

ES GERMANY porcelain was made at the factory of Erdmann
Schlegelmilch from 1861 to 1925 in Suhl, Germany. The porcelain, marked
ES Germany or *ES Suhl,* was sold decorated or undecorated. Other pieces
were made at a factory in Saxony, Prussia, and are marked *ES Prussia.*
Reinhold Schlegelmilch made the famous wares marked *RS Germany.*

Box, Pink Roses On Lid, Marked, 3 x 2 In.	35.00
Cake Plate, Fox Hunter Scene, 10 In.	195.00
Cuspidor, Floral	100.00
Plate, Lady Portrait, 6 Floral Wells, Open Handles, 9 1/2 In.	165.00
Plate, Red & White Roses, 4 Gold Medallions, 11 In.	110.00

ESKIMO artifacts of all types are collected. Carvings of whale or walrus
teeth are listed under Scrimshaw. Baskets are in the Basket category. All
other types of Eskimo art are listed here.

Bowl, Black Pictorial Design On Inside, Wooden, 2 1/4 x 6 1/4 In.	495.00
Cribbage Board, Bisected Walrus Tusk, Engraved Cards, 17 In.	302.50
Cribbage Board, Ivory, Incised Floral, Seals & Ice Floes Reverse, 11 1/2 In.	247.00
Cribbage Board, Walrus Tusk, Seal Heads, People, Birds, 26 In.	880.00
Figurine, Mother & Child, Sealskin Costume, Cottonwood Root, c.1840	2640.00
Figurine, Seal, Soapstone, 19 In.	110.00
Hook, Grappling, Ivory Toggle End of Leather Line, 9 In.	205.00
Mat, Seal Skin, Appliqued Eskimo Scenes, 29 In.	220.00
Pipe, Figural Bowl, Scenes, Ivory, 15 In.	2860.00

FAIENCE refers to tin–glazed earthenware, especially the wares made in
France, Germany, and Scandinavia. It is also correct to say that faience is
the same as majolica or Delft, although usually the term refers only to the
tin–glazed pottery of the three regions mentioned.

Bowl, Matte Black, Turquoise Interior, California, 2 3/4 x 5 3/4 In.	137.00
Candlestick, 2–Light, Portugal, 11 In., Pair	132.00
Match Holder, Figural, Woman, Seated, France, Late 19th Century, 6 In.	137.00
Mug, Blue Stenciled Design, Yellow & Green Stripes, 5 In.	95.00
Plate, Coat of Arms, Scattered Flower Sprigs, Germany, 9 1/2 In.	295.00
Plate, Floral, Blue, Red, Yellow & Green, Underglaze, 11 In.	470.00
Tankard Set, Avon, With Mugs	215.00
Trivet, Cloisonne Blue Peacock, Matte Ocher Ground, California, 5 1/4 In.	110.00
Vase, Deep Blue High Glaze, Closed Rim, Bulbous, 3 1/4 x 3 1/2 In.	77.00
Vase, Trumpet, Mustard Glaze, California, 6 3/4 In.	195.00
Wall Pocket, Bagpipe, France	350.00
Wine Cooler, Foliate Scrolls, St. Clement, 8 In.	302.50

FAIRINGS are small souvenir china boxes and figurines that were sold at
country fairs during the nineteenth century. Most were made in Germany.
Reproductions of fairings are being made, especially of the famous *twelve
months of marriage* series.

Box, Dressing Table, Mirror, Watch, Wax Sealer	85.00
Figurine, Cat, Bed, Mice On Table, Chamber Pot, "Who Said Rats?"	95.00 To 165.00
Figurine, Girl, Peeking Through Bushes At Rabbit	80.00
Figurine, Returning At One O'clock In The Morning, Miniature, 4 x 3 In.	110.00

FAIRYLAND LUSTER pieces are included in the Wedgwood category.

FAMILLE ROSE, see Chinese Export category

FANS have been used for cooling since the days of the ancients. By the
eighteenth century, the fan was an accessory for the lady of fashion and
very elaborate and expensive fans were made. Sticks were made of ivory or
wood, set with jewels or carved. The fans were made of painted silk or
paper. Inexpensive paper fans printed with advertising were giveaways in
the late nineteenth and early twentieth centuries. Electric fans were
introduced in 1882.

Advertising, Darkie Toothpaste, Framed	79.00

Fan, Ivory & Tortoiseshell Sticks,
Trojan War Scene, 1760, 11 1/2 In.

Fan, Silk, Girl & Cherub, Painted Silk,
Mother-of-Pearl, France, 1870, 11 3/4 In.

Fan, Paper, Triple Jewel Design, Lacquered,
Wooden Handle, Korea, 13 In.

Advertising, Hotel Statler	15.00
Advertising, Lititz, Manheim, Lancaster, Pa., Wooden Handle	5.00
Advertising, Newman Electric Co., Asbury, NJ, Christ, Preaching By The Sea	5.00
Advertising, Orange Squeeze	50.00
Advertising, Putnam Dye, Paper	7.00
Black Satin	26.00
Cardboard, Flapper	7.50
Electric, Akro Agate Base	80.00 To 95.00
Electric, Coin-Operated, Brass Blades, Hotel Name & Room Number, 5 Cents	250.00
Electric, Emerson, B & B, 1909, 8 In.	195.00
Electric, Emerson, Rib Base Yoke, B & B, 12 In.	250.00
Electric, GE, Balloon Spider, Oscillating, 1933, 12 In.	85.00
Electric, GE, Green Deco, Oscillating, 12 In.	75.00
Electric, GE, Kidney, Oscillating, 6 Blades, B & B, 1912	395.00
Electric, GE, Oscillating, Gold & Black, Cast Iron & Metal, 1920s, 17 In.	82.00
Electric, GE, Star, Oscillator, B & B, 12 In.	90.00
Electric, GE, Vortlex, Oscillating, Black Aluminum, 16 In.	100.00

Electric, Polar Cub, Akro Agate Base	55.00
Electric, R & M, B & S, 1924, 12 In.	125.00
Electric, Robbins & Myer Co., Oscillating, 1-In. Brass Blades	75.00
Electric, Telechron Clock Housing, 4 In.	150.00
Electric, Westinghouse, No Cage, Brass, 8 In.	185.00
Electric, Whiz, Stationary, 8 In.	80.00
Electric, Winchester, Store	35.00
Feather, Tortoiseshell Handle, Peach Color	75.00
Iron, Luminaire, Floor, Fancy	400.00
Ivory & Tortoiseshell Sticks, Trojan War Scene, 1760, 11 1/2 In. ....*Illus*	300.00
Ivory Oriental Carved Handle, Hand Painted Allegorical Scene	1650.00
Ivory, Hand Painted, Florentine Frame, Gilt, 11 3/4 In.	300.00
Ivory, Skeleton, Pierced Design, Frame, 25 x 16 In.	125.00
Mother-of-Pearl Handle, Hand Painted Allegorical Scene, Gilt	1320.00
Paper, Hand Painted Allegorical Scene, Ivory Handle, 18th Century	825.00
Paper, Hand Painted French Soldier, Ships, Ivory Handle	1100.00
Paper, Pierced Floral, Ivory Handle, Dated 1773	1650.00
Paper, Triple Jewel Design, Lacquered, Wooden Handle, Korea, 13 In. ....*Illus*	495.00
Peacock Feathers, Floral, Painted, Ivory, Frame, 25 In.	75.00
Shabayama, Gold Lacquer, Late 19th Century	2310.00
Silk, Embroidered, Peacocks, Teak Frame, China, c.1810, 21 3/4 In.	440.00
Silk, Girl & Cherub, Painted Silk, Mother-of-Pearl, France, 1870, 11 3/4 In. ....*Illus*	495.00
Silk, Ivory, Scenes From Painting By Goya, Folded-10 1/2 In.	37.00
Silk, Painted, Tooled & Gilded Abalone Shell Ribs, Framed, 16 x 25 In.	440.00
Tortoiseshell Sticks, Silver Sequins, Black Net, 6 x 7 In.	75.00
Vellum, Hand Painted, Bone Handle, France	750.00
Vellum, Hand Painted, Japanned Handle, France	750.00
Vernis-Martin, Hand Painted, Late 18th Century	990.00

FAST FOOD COLLECTIBLES may be included in several categories, such
as Advertising, Coca-Cola, Toy, etc.

FEDERZEICHNUNG is the very strange German name for a pattern of
mother-of-pearl satin glass. The pattern had irregularly shaped sections of
brown glass covered with a pattern of gold squiggle lines. It was first made
in the late nineteenth century.

Vase, Brown, Mother-of-Pearl, White Lining, 8 In.	2200.00
Vase, Browns, Gold Enameling, White Heart, Blue Dots, 6 3/4 In. ....*Illus*	1870.00

FENTON Art Glass Company, founded in Martins Ferry, Ohio, by Frank
L. Fenton, is now located in Williamstown, West Virginia. It is noted for
early carnival glass produced between 1907 and 1920. Many other types of
glass were also made.

Apple Blossom Crest, Candleholder, Pair	85.00
Apple Tree, Compote, Blue Slag Glass, Label, 6 1/2 In.	65.00
Apple Tree, Tumbler, Marigold	105.00

Federzeichnung, Vase, Browns,

Gold Enameling, White Hearts,

Blue Dots, 6 3/4 In.

Aqua Crest, Basket, 8 1/2 In.	55.00
Aqua Crest, Basket, Aqua, 11 In.	85.00
Aqua Crest, Bonbon	20.00
Aqua Crest, Plate, 12 In.	10.00
Aqua Crest, Vase, Triangular, 8 In.	37.50
Bowl & Pitcher Set, Mottled Green, Beige & Blue Glaze, Pat. 1849	2420.00
Burmese, Basket, Rose, 85th Anniversary, Artist	90.00
Burmese, Candy Dish, Cover, Separate Base, Blue	240.00
Burmese, Epergne, 1–Lily, Fuchsia	130.00
Burmese, Hobnail, Vase, Experimental Tag, 11/29/69, 11 In.	175.00
Burmese, Plate, Shiny, 8 1/4 In.	150.00
Burmese, Vase, Jack–In–The–Pulpit, 10 1/2 In.	75.00
Butterfly & Berry, Tumbler	40.00
Buttons & Braids, Tumbler, Green, 6 Piece	95.00
Cherry Blossom, Water Set	325.00
Coin Dot, Basket, 6 1/2 In.	75.00
Coin Dot, Basket, Mulberry, 8 In.	30.00
Coin Dot, Perfume Bottle & Powder Box, Opalescent, 3 Piece	110.00
Coin Dot, Pitcher, 3 Spouts, Cranberry, 6 3/4 In.	125.00
Coin Dot, Pitcher, Mulberry, 32 Oz.	30.00
Coin Dot, Pitcher, Ruffled Top, Blue	95.00
Coin Dot, Vase, Cobalt Blue To Amethyst, 8 1/2 In.	85.00
Coin Dot, Vase, Cranberry, 9 1/2 In.	30.00
Coinspot, Candleholder, Frosted, 4 1/2 In., Pair	80.00
Coinspot, Cruet, Cranberry	100.00
Coinspot, Cruet, Stopper	75.00
Coinspot, Pitcher, Cranberry, 8 In.	110.00
Coinspot, Sugar & Creamer, Cover, Amber	49.00
Colonial, Lamp, Courting, Electric, Amber, 1967	55.00
Colonial, Lamp, Courting, Electric, Blue, 1967	105.00
Colonial, Lamp, Courting, Oil, Green, 1967	70.00
Crystal Crest, Basket, Crystal, Applied Handle	295.00
Crystal Crest, Candlestick, 6 In., Pair	45.00
Crystal Crest, Dish, Heart Shape, Pink Opalescent, Peaches 'n Cream	22.00
Crystal Crest, Plate, Blue, Large	46.00
Crystal Crest, Vase, Melon Rib, 6 1/2 In.	45.00
Crystal Crest, Vase, Tri–Crimp, 6 1/2 In.	65.00
Daisy & Button, Shoe	15.00
Daisy & Fern, Pitcher, Blue, White	110.00
Daisy & Fern, Pitcher, Open Handle	145.00
Dancing Ladies, Vase, Footed	150.00
Diamond Lace, Epergne, 3–Lily, Blue Opalescent, 10 1/2 In.	145.00
Diamond Optic, Shade, Cranberry, 6 1/2 In.	85.00
Diamond Optic, Vase, Mulberry, 11 1/2 In.	40.00
Dot Optic, Pitcher, Amethyst, 70 Oz.	235.00
Drapery, Vase, Cranberry, 7 In.	15.00
Drapery, Water Set, 4 Piece	125.00
Ebony, Candlestick, c.1925, 8 1/2 In., Pair	120.00
Emerald Crest, Flowerpot, Saucer	95.00
Emerald Crest, Plate, 6 1/2 In.	18.00
Emerald Crest, Sugar	17.00
Emerald Crest, Vase, Fan, 4 1/2 In.	15.00
Emerald Crest, Vase, Melon, 5 1/4 In.	18.00
Feather Stitch, Lamp, Dusty Rose Overlay, 17 In.	95.00
Feather Stitch, Pitcher, Cranberry, 70 Oz.	42.50
Feathered Serpent, Bowl, 5 In.	39.00
Georgian, Tumbler, 2 1/2 Oz.	18.00
Georgian, Tumbler, 7 1/2 Oz.	16.00
Hanging Heart, Vase, Custard, Iridescent, Barber, 6 1/2 In.	70.00
Hanging Heart, Vase, Custard, Iridescent, Barber, 9 1/2 In.	90.00
Hanging Heart, Vase, Turquoise, Barber, 4 1/2 In.	50.00
Hanging Heart, Vase, Turquoise, Barber, 9 1/2 In.	95.00
Hanging Vine, Vase, Red, Karnak, 4 In.	1000.00

Hobnail, Banana Stand, Plum Opalescent, Crimped, 12 In.	65.00
Hobnail, Basket, Amber	33.00
Hobnail, Basket, Cranberry Opalescent, 7 In.	45.00
Hobnail, Basket, Cranberry Opalescent, 10 In.	75.00
Hobnail, Basket, French Opalescent	130.00
Hobnail, Basket, Lime Opalescent, Handle, 4 In.	97.00
Hobnail, Bell, Purple Slag	25.00
Hobnail, Bonbon, 5 In.	12.00
Hobnail, Bowl, Milk Glass, Crimped, 10 In.	15.00
Hobnail, Bowl, Topaz, 11 1/2 In.	89.50
Hobnail, Candlestick, Milk Glass, Pair	10.00
Hobnail, Candy Dish, Cover, French Opalescent	47.00
Hobnail, Cookie Jar, White	95.00
Hobnail, Cruet, Cranberry Opalescent, 6 In.	75.00 To 95.00
Hobnail, Fairy Light, Plum Opalescent, 3 Piece	105.00
Hobnail, Jug Set, Ice Lip, Topaz Opalescent, 8 12 Oz. Tumblers, 9 Piece	160.00
Hobnail, Jug, Cranberry Opalescent, Crystal Handle, 5 1/2 In.	40.00
Hobnail, Nappy, French Opalescent	22.00
Hobnail, Pitcher, Cranberry Opalescent, 11 In.	80.00
Hobnail, Powder Jar, Blue Opalescent	38.00
Hobnail, Punch Set, Topaz Opalescent, On Stand, 7 Qt. Bowl, 14 Piece	350.00
Hobnail, Rose Bowl, Plum Opalescent, Crimped, 4 1/2 In.	35.00
Hobnail, Salt & Pepper, Cranberry Opalescent	45.00
Hobnail, Shade, Cranberry Opalescent, 9 1/2 In.	95.00
Hobnail, Slipper, Chocolate Glass	25.00
Hobnail, Sugar & Creamer, Blue	25.00
Hobnail, Sugar & Creamer, Vaseline	55.00
Hobnail, Vase, Fluted, Cranberry	35.00
Hobnail, Vase, French Opalescent, Crimped, 4 In.	20.00
Hobnail, Water Set, Topaz Opalescent, 10–In. Pitcher, 6 4–In. Tumblers, 5 Piece	170.00
Honeycomb & Clover, Tumbler, Blue	85.00
Honeycomb & Clover, Water Set, Green, 7 Piece	675.00
Jacqueline, Bowl, Mulberry, 5 In.	25.00
Jade, Cookie Jar, No Lid, Green Wicker Handle, 1930	70.00
Jade, Jar, Macaroon, Big Cookie, Straw Handle	150.00
Jade, Lamp, Cut, 8 1/2 In., Pair	300.00
Lincoln Inn, Cocktail	15.00
Lincoln Inn, Vase, Jade, 10 In.	175.00
Ming, Console Set, Green, 3 Piece	200.00
Ming, Water Set, Ice Lip Pitcher, 7 Piece	155.00
Mongolian, Vase, Fan, Green, 5 In.	54.00
Moonstone, Bowl, Cupped, Footed, 10 In.	55.00
New World, Bowl, Floater, Cranberry	160.00
Orange Tree, Hatpin Holder	140.00
Paperweight, Neil Armstrong, Crystal, Signed By Fenton	50.00
Paperweight, Pig	12.00
Peach Crest, Basket, 8 1/2 In.	65.00
Peach Crest, Bowl, Peach Blow, 1940s, 6 In.	42.00
Peach Crest, Dresser Box, Melon Shape	40.00
Peach Crest, Perfume Bottle, 7 In.	30.00
Peach Crest, Powder Box, 4 In.	28.00
Perfume Bottle, Blue Ridge, French Opalescent, Pair	60.00
Persian Medallion, Fairy Light, Satin, 3 Piece	55.00
Persian Medallion, Rose Bowl, Blue	80.00
Pineapple, Vase, Crimped Rim, Jacqueline Pattern, 6 x 6 In.	75.00
Plymouth, Goblet, Water, Red	18.00
Plymouth, Wine, Red	14.00
Poppy, Lamp, Gone With The Wind, Lime Sherbet	230.00
Rosalene, Wine, Crystal	12.00
Rose, Lamp, Shell Pink	175.00
September Morn, Nymph Girl, With Base	95.00
Silver Crest, Bowl, 10 1/2 In.	45.00
Silver Crest, Bowl, Heart, Handle	25.00

Silver Crest, Cake Plate	30.00
Silver Crest, Cake Plate, Footed, 13 In.	35.00
Silver Crest, Cake Salver, 13 In.	45.00
Silver Crest, Cake Tray, Footed, 13 In.	45.00
Silver Crest, Candlestick, 5 In., Pair	55.00
Silver Crest, Chip & Dip Set	55.00
Silver Crest, Creamer, 5 1/2 In.	65.00
Silver Crest, Lamp, Hurricane	125.00
Silver Crest, Mayonnaise Set, 3 Piece	50.00
Silver Crest, Plate, 8 In.	18.00
Silver Crest, Relish, Heart Shape, Handle	20.00
Silver Crest, Vase, Oval, 14 In.	110.00
Silver Crest, Vase, Violets & Spanish Lace, Signed, 4 In.	40.00
Spiral Optic, Vase, Cranberry, 11 In.	25.00
Stretch, Bowl, Cupped, Red	110.00
Swirled Feather, Fairy Lamp, White	155.00
Teal Crest, Bell, Milk Glass	45.00
Thumbprint, Basket, Green	37.00
Thumbprint, Sugar & Creamer, Amber	34.00
Tulip, Vase, Cranberry, Opalescent, Sample, 6 1/2 In.	40.00
Vase, Iridescent Blue–Green, No Design, Karnak, 10 1/2 In.	1300.00
Velva Rose, Candy Box, Cover, Dolphin Handle, 75th Anniversary, 9 1/4 In.	25.00
Velva Rose, Epergne Set, 75th Anniversary, 5 Piece	100.00
Violets In The Snow, Top Hat	60.00
Violets In The Snow, Vase, 6 In.	30.00
Wild Rose, Vase, Shiny, 7 1/2 In.	70.00

FIESTA, the colorful dinnerware, was introduced in 1936 by the Homer Laughlin China Co., redesigned in 1969, and withdrawn in 1973. It was reissued again in 1986 in different colors. The simple design was characterized by a band of concentric circles, beginning at the rim. Cups had full–circle handles until 1969, when partial–circle handles were made. Harlequin and Riviera were related wares. For more information and prices of American dinnerware, see the book *Kovels' Depression Glass & American Dinnerware Price List.*

fiesta

Ashtray, Amberstone	18.00
Ashtray, Medium Green	150.00
Bowl, Cobalt Blue, Footed, 11 1/4 In.	375.00
Bowl, Dessert, Red, 6 In.	30.00
Bowl, Dessert, Turquoise, 6 In.	22.00
Bowl, Dessert, Yellow, 6 In.	22.00
Bowl, Medium Green, 5 1/2 In.	60.00
Bowl, Mixing, Light Green, 5 1/2 In.	14.50
Bowl, Mixing, No. 1, Yellow	100.00
Bowl, Mixing, No. 4, Cobalt Blue	65.00
Bowl, Mixing, No. 6, Light Green	85.00
Bowl, Mixing, No. 7, Cobalt Blue	135.00
Bowl, Mixing, No. 7, Light Green	125.00 To 150.00
Bowl, Nesting, Green, Cobalt Blue, Cream & Light Blue, 2 To 6 Qt., 4 Piece	100.00
Bowl, Salad, Medium Green, Individual	32.00
Bowl, Salad, Red	295.00
Bowl, Salad, Red, Individual	100.00
Bowl, Turquoise, 5 1/2 In.	18.00
Bowl, Yellow, 11 3/4 In.	120.00
Bowl, Yellow, 5 1/2 In.	20.00
Cake Plate, Red, Kraft Kitchen, 11 In.	95.00
Cake Server, Light Green, Kraft Kitchen	75.00
Candleholder, Bulb, Light Green, Pair	60.00 To 78.00
Carafe, Cobalt Blue, 3 Pt.	50.00
Carafe, Light Green, 3 Pt.	130.00
Carafe, Red, 3 Pt.	160.00
Carafe, Yellow, 3 Pt.	135.00 To 175.00
Casserole, Cover, Chartreuse	150.00

Casserole, Cover, Cobalt Blue	125.00
Casserole, Cover, Green, Kitchen Kraft	70.00
Casserole, Cover, Yellow	55.00
Casserole, Yellow, French	150.00
Chop Plate, Gray, 13 In.	50.00
Chop Plate, Red, 15 In.	55.00
Coffeepot, Cobalt Blue, After Dinner	200.00
Coffeepot, Ivory, After Dinner	275.00
Coffeepot, Light Green, After Dinner	165.00
Coffeepot, Red	180.00 To 200.00
Coffeepot, Red, After Dinner	265.00
Coffeepot, Rose	300.00
Coffeepot, Turquoise	110.00
Coffeepot, Yellow	75.00 To 100.00
Compote, Jam, Ivory	40.00
Compote, Light Green, 12 In.	85.00
Compote, Sweets, Medium Green, 10 1/4 In.	34.00
Compote, Sweets, Red, 10 1/4 In.	95.00
Compote, Sweets, Turquoise 10 1/4 In.	45.00
Compote, Sweets, Yellow, 10 1/4 In.	30.00
Compote, Yellow, 12 In.	85.00
Creamer, Chartreuse	15.00
Creamer, Ivory	14.00
Creamer, Medium Green	45.00
Creamer, Stick Handle, Red	21.00 To 25.00
Creamer, Yellow, Individual	50.00 To 60.00
Creamer, Yellow, Stick Handle	20.00
Cup & Saucer, Amberstone	5.50
Cup & Saucer, Ivory, After Dinner	50.00
Cup & Saucer, Light Green	20.00
Cup & Saucer, Red, After Dinner	52.00
Cup & Saucer, Tea, Gray	33.00
Cup & Saucer, Turquoise, After Dinner	55.00
Cup & Saucer, Yellow	16.50
Cup & Saucer, Yellow, After Dinner	45.00
Cup, Chartreuse	14.00
Cup, Gray	20.00
Eggcup, Forest Green	85.00
Eggcup, Yellow	34.00
Fork, Cobalt Blue, Kitchen Kraft	80.00
Fork, Green, Kitchen Kraft	70.00
Gravy Boat, Medium Green	175.00
Gravy Boat, Red	35.00
Jam Jar, Turquoise	130.00
Jam Set, Green	125.00
Jar, Cover, Green, Kitchen Kraft	275.00
Jar, Cover, Red, Kitchen Kraft	275.00
Jar, Cover, Yellow, Kitchen Kraft	235.00
Jug, Chartreuse, 2 Pt.	70.00
Jug, Cover, Yellow, Kitchen Kraft	150.00
Jug, Gray, 2 Pt.	80.00
Jug, Turquoise, 2 Pt.	35.00
Mug, Gray	60.00
Mug, Medium Green	70.00 To 75.00
Mug, Tom & Jerry, Chartreuse	60.00
Mug, Tom & Jerry, Red	50.00
Mustard, Cobalt Blue	140.00 To 150.00
Mustard, Red	150.00
Nappy, Chartreuse, 8 1/2 In.	22.00
Nappy, Gray, 8 1/2 In.	28.00 To 36.00
Nappy, Medium Green, 8 1/2 In.	85.00
Nappy, Yellow, 8 1/2 In.	25.00
Nesting Bowl Set, Red, No. 3, 4, 5 & 6, 4 Piece	150.00

Pie Plate, Cobalt Blue, Kitchen Kraft 40.00
Pitcher, Disk, Chartreuse .... 150.00 To 165.00
Pitcher, Disk, Cobalt Blue 95.00
Pitcher, Disk, Gray .... 135.00 To 150.00
Pitcher, Disk, Light Green 95.00
Pitcher, Disk, Medium Green 355.00
Pitcher, Disk, Red 85.00
Pitcher, Disk, Rose 155.00
Pitcher, Ice Lip, Cobalt Blue 55.00
Pitcher, Ice Lip, Red ....95.00 To 150.00
Pitcher, Ice Lip, Turquoise 60.00
Pitcher, Juice, Yellow 30.00
Pitcher, Water, Ivory 60.00
Plate, Chartreuse, 6 In. 4.00
Plate, Cobalt Blue, 6 In. 5.00
Plate, Cobalt Blue, 7 In. 10.00
Plate, Gray, 10 In. 30.00
Plate, Gray, 7 In. 8.00
Plate, Medium Green, 7 In. .... 20.00 To 25.00
Plate, Red, 6 In. 5.00
Plate, Rose, 6 In. 7.00
Plate, Sectioned, Cobalt Blue, 12 In. 35.00
Plate, Yellow, 10 In. .... 15.00 To 20.00
Platter, Chartreuse, Oval 20.00
Platter, Medium Green, Oval 70.00
Platter, Turquoise, Oval 20.00
Platter, Yellow, Oval 95.00
Salt & Pepper, Chartreuse 30.00
Salt & Pepper, Red, Kitchen Kraft 100.00
Sauce Boat, Chartreuse 20.00
Sauce Boat, Dark Green 39.00
Saucer, Chartreuse, After Dinner 45.00
Saucer, Gray, After Dinner 45.00
Soup, Cream, Forest Green 45.00
Soup, Cream, Gray 45.00
Soup, Cream, Yellow 28.00
Soup, Onion, Cover, Green 400.00
Spoon, Red, Kitchen Kraft .... 50.00 To 75.00
Sugar, Cover, Medium Green 80.00
Sugar, Yellow 20.00
Sugar, Yellow, Individual .... 75.00 To 85.00
Syrup, Cobalt Blue 225.00
Syrup, Light Green 200.00
Syrup, Red .... 145.00 To 250.00
Syrup, Turquoise 190.00
Teapot, Cobalt Blue, Large 150.00
Teapot, Green 50.00
Teapot, Medium Green 75.00
Teapot, Turquoise 40.00
Teapot, Yellow 35.00
Tray, Relish, With Inserts, Red 180.00
Tray, Utility, Ivory, Kitchen Kraft 25.00
Tray, Utility, Yellow 20.00
Tumbler, Juice, Gray 100.00
Vase, Bud, Red 65.00
Vase, Green, 12 In. 540.00
Vase, Ivory, 10 In. 450.00
Vase, Ivory, 12 In. 550.00
Vase, Light Green, 8 In. 350.00
Vase, Turquoise, 8 In. 300.00

FINCH, see Kay Finch category

FINDLAY ONYX AND FLORADINE are two similar types of glass made by Dalzell, Gilmore and Leighton Co. of Findlay, Ohio, about 1889. Each piece was made using three layers of glass. Onyx is a patented yellowish white opaque glass with raised silver daisy decorations. A few rare pieces were made of rose, amber, orange, or purple glass. Floradine is made of raspberry or tan colored opaque glass with opalescent white raised floral pattern. The same molds were used for both types of glass.

Bowl, White Platinum Trim, 8 In.	765.00
Celery Vase, White Platinum Trim, 6 1/2 In.	300.00
Creamer, White Platinum Trim	345.00
Sugar Shaker, White Platinum Blossom Design, Brass Lid, 5 3/4 In.	545.00
Syrup, White, Platinum Trim	650.00
Tumbler, Barrel Shape, Platinum Luster Flowers & Leaves, 3 3/4 In.	325.00 To 550.00

FIREFIGHTING equipment of all types is wanted, from fire marks to uniforms to toy fire trucks. It is said that every little boy wanted to be a fireman or a train engineer 75 years ago and the collectors today reflect this interest.

Alarm Box, Gamewell	95.00
Ax, Fireman's, Ace	105.00
Badge, Strasburg, Va., 1900	65.00
Badge, Watertown Fire Dept. No. 1	65.00
Bag, Salvage, Coarse Homespun, Patches, Vermont, 1827, 42 x 20 In.	455.00
Bag, Salvage, Homespun, Patches, Hampton, N. H., 1857, 52 x 19 In.	455.00
Bag, Salvage, Linen, No. 4, Jn. Fox, 1799, 18th, Century, 49 x 27 In.	880.00
Bell, Firehouse, Electric, Double	85.00
Belt, South, Penn, 31, Red Trim, White Letters, Black, 48 In.	75.00
Bucket, Charlestown, Eagle, Thomas Pike, Leather, 1807, 12 In.	1090.00
Bucket, Fire, Leather, Red, Ground, D. C. Ballard, 1811, 13 In.	4620.00
Bucket, John Towne, Salem, 1806 & 1816, With Bag, Pair	7150.00
Bucket, Leather, Europe, Dated 1836, 10 1/2 In.	165.00
Bucket, Samuel Shreve, Enterprise Fire Club	550.00
Extinguisher, American, La France, Wheeled Iron Cylinder, 48-In. Diam.	23.00
Fire Alarm, Station, Birdhouse Type, 11 x 17 In.	43.00
Fire Horn, Brass, Worn Leather Strap, 15 3/4 In.	170.00
Firemark, Eagle, Cast Iron, 11 1/4 x 8 1/2 In.	110.00
Firemark, Tree, Mutual Assurance Co., Philadelphia, 19th Century	275.00
Flyer, Firemen's Annual Ball, 27th, Folded, 1873, 5 x 8 In.	25.00
Gong, Harrington Seabaert	4640.00
Grave Marker, Fireman's, Brass, New York Fire Dept.	100.00
Grenade, Hayward, Hand, Contents, Blue, 6 In.	192.50
Grenade, Imperial, Pair	990.00
Grenade, Universal, Pair	990.00
Grenade, W. D. Allen, Embossed, Crescent Moon, Green, 8 1/8 In.	825.00
Hat, Ceremonial, Crossed Ladders, Inscribed Rescue, 5–In. Shield, 7 In.	4125.00
Hat, Ceremonial, Hand Painted, Initialed J. F., 1790, 7 In.	4400.00
Hat, Chief's, Hallowell, Maine	175.00
Hat, Leather, Irvington, N.Y.	195.00
Helmet, USA No. 5, Leather	1980.00
House Gong, Large	4650.00
Invitation, Firemen's Ball, 1886	15.00
Nozzle, Embossed With Horses & Santa Rosa	30.00
Nozzle, Fire, Brass, 18 In.	20.00
Ribbon, Silk, George Washington, Seattle Fire Dept. Annual Ball, 1886	35.00
Staff, Fire Warden's, 19th Century	500.00
Trumpet, Presentation, 1867	3300.00
Trumpet, Presentation, Rescue Scene, 1860	5250.00
Trumpet, Speaking, Embossed Figure of Woman, Franklin Fire Company	3300.00

FIREPLACES were used to cook and to heat the American home in past centuries. Many types of tools and equipment were used. Andirons held the logs in place, firebacks reflected the heat into the room, and tongs were used to move either fuel or food. Many types of spits and roasting jacks were made and may be listed in the Kitchen category.

Andirons & Screen, Louis XVI Style, Bronze, 35 In.	1540.00
Andirons, Black Butler, Mammy, Arched Stance Figures, 17 In.	950.00
Andirons, Brass Ball & Finial, Hexagonal Plinth, 18th Century, Philadelphia	1800.00
Andirons, Brass Ball & Finial, Penny Foot, Knife Blade, Philadelphia, 21 In.	2530.00
Andirons, Brass Ball Top, Marked R. Wittingham, N.Y.	1260.00
Andirons, Brass Ball Top, Pair	1150.00
Andirons, Brass Raised Foliate Design, 3 Paw Footed, 23 In.	140.00
Andirons, Brass, Urn Top, c.1800, 27 In.	1870.00
Andirons, Brass, Urn Top, Conforming Log Stops, 27 In.	240.00
Andirons, Brass, Victorian, 27 In., Pair	550.00
Andirons, Brass, Washington Memorial Engraved Scenes, 1800–1810	5170.00
Andirons, Bronze, Flame & Urn Finial, Shield & Mask With Gargoyles, 27 In.	1320.00
Andirons, Cherub Figures & Mythical Sea Monsters, Gilt Bronze, With Tools	2530.00
Andirons, Chrome Plated & Cast Iron, Skyscraper Form, 19 1/2 In.	550.00
Andirons, Double Lemon Top, New York, 1800, 17 3/4 In.	875.00
Andirons, Double Lemon-Shaped Finial, Spurred Legs, Brass, 1810, 19 1/2 In.	445.00
Andirons, Eagle Finial, Cast Iron, 12 In. Pair	125.00
Andirons, Empire, Flame Finial, Duck & Lyre Form Shield, Brass, 29 In.	550.00
Andirons, Federal, Ball Top, Turned Shaft, Square Plinth, Snake Foot, 18 1/2 In.	467.00
Andirons, Federal, Brass Ball Top, 1810, 16 1/2 In, Pair	440.00
Andirons, Federal, Brass Urn Top, America, 1800, 19 1/2 In., Pair	522.00
Andirons, Federal, Brass Urn Top, Phila., 1800, 16 In., Pair	600.00
Andirons, Federal, Steeple Top, Brass, America, 1800, 19 1/2 In., Pair	600.00
Andirons, Federal, Steeple Top, Brass, America, 1800, 21 1/4 In.	880.00
Andirons, Iron & Brass, Federal Style, Split Baluster Form, 20 In.	195.00
Andirons, Iron, Hessian Soldier, Red Coats, Eagles On Hats, 1820	895.00
Andirons, Iron, Hessian Striding Cap & Jacket, Late 19th Century	1760.00
Andirons, Iron, Man & Woman, Thomasville Iron Works, 1800s	1500.00
Andirons, Iron, Penny Feet, Gooseneck Finials, 12 In.	85.00
Andirons, Knife Blade, Brass & Wrought Iron, 18 In.	335.00
Andirons, Lion Heads Base, Paw Feet, Swirled Shaft & Ball, 24 In.	395.00
Andirons, Pots of Flowers Finials, Gold Paint, 12 1/2 In.	50.00
Andirons, Sunburst Smiling Face, Arched Base, Black Finish, 16 In., Pair	935.00
Andirons, Urn Top, Pierced Rails With Eagles, Griffith, 23 1/2 In., Pair	650.00
Andirons, Wrought Iron, Basket Top, Spit Holders, Pair	71.50
Andirons, Wrought Iron, Heart Finial, Arched Legs, Penny Footed, 17 x 15 In.	1980.00
Andirons, Wrought Iron, Knife Blade, Penny Feet, Brass Finials, 19 In.	385.00
Andirons, Wrought Iron, Medallions, Griffins' Faces, V-Shaped Base, 23 1/4 In.	770.00
Andirons, Wrought Iron, Penny Feet, Goose Neck Finial, Black Paint, 13 In.	50.00
Andirons, Wrought Iron, Scrolled Finials, Pair	115.00
Andirons, Wrought Iron, Scrolling Top Over Heart On Legs, 1810	770.00
Bellows, Brass Front, Raised Sailing Ship Scene, Restored, 19th Century	185.00
Bellows, Brass Nozzle & Facing, Worn Leather, 15 1/2 In.	70.00
Bellows, Gilt Leafy Design, Painted Wood & Leather, 1850s, 8 In.	550.00
Bellows, Griffin, West Wind On Back, Brass Dolphin Snout, Walnut, 20 1/2 In.	185.00
Bellows, Hand Painted & Hand Carved, Beaver Back	135.00
Bellows, Red & Black, Rosewood Grained, Stenciled Border, Brass Nozzle, 18 In.	248.00
Bellows, Red Paint, Stencil, Brass Nozzle, Worn Leather Handle, 17 In.	71.50
Bellows, Turned Face, Black Paint, Yellow Striping, Tin Nozzle, Leather, 10 In.	71.00
Bellows, Turtleback, Cream Colored Freehand Design, 18 In.	137.00
Bellows, Turtleback, Red, Black Graining, Red Yellow Striping, 17 In.	220.00
Bellows, Turtleback, Stenciled Brown Paint, Brass Nozzle, 18 1/2 In.	82.50
Bellows, Yellow Paint, Floral Design, Red, Black, Brown, Brass Nozzle, 18 In.	192.00
Box, Log, Raised Figural Design, Brass, 1880s, 17 1/2 x 25 In.	165.00
Box, Tinder, Oval Hinged Lid, Hoop Handle, Iron & Brass	110.00
Broiler, Adjustable Lyre, Shaped Rack, Tripod Base, Wrought Iron, 29 1/4 In.	550.00
Clock, Spigot For Turning Cooking Spit, Cast Iron Feet, 7 1/2 x 12 In.	250.00

Coal Hod, Japanned Tin, Orange Poppies 90.00
Coal Hod, Tole, Black Paint, Red & Gold Design, 23 1/2 In. 126.00
Coal Hod, Yellow Enamelware, Nickel Plated Trim, Ornate 210.00
Coal Scuttle, Round Copper Plate, Mac Beth, Brass Lid 25.00
Coal Scuttle, Slanted Hinged Front, Brass Bracket Handle, 13 In. 175.00
Coal Scuttle, Sloping Lid, Original Scupper, Mahogany, c.1870, Pair 195.00
Crane, Iron, 7 In. 45.00
Fender, Brass & Wire, 1800, 10 3/4 x 49 In. 770.00
Fender, Brass, Bowfront, Reticulated, England, 1800, 51 In. 1045.00
Fender, Brass, D Dorm, Pierced, 50 1/2 In. 302.00
Fender, Brass, Paw Feet, Reticulated, England, c.1780, 47 In. 302.00
Fender, Brass, Pierced Engraved Foliage, Animals, Paw Feet, 19th Century, 53 In. ... 600.00
Fender, Brass, Raised Grape & Vintage Design, 54 In. 110.00
Fender, Brass, Reticulated Paw Foot, England, 1780, 47 In. 302.00
Fender, Brass, Serpentine, Reticulated, England, c.1800, 54 In. 467.00
Fender, Bronze, Pierced With Rinceaux & Swans, 51 In. 165.00
Fender, Iron, Posts, Brass Turbin, 19th Century, 42 x 10 In. 100.00
Fender, Iron, Wire Grill, Brass Top Rail, 14 1/4 In. 313.00
Fire Dogs, Brass & Iron, Mid–1800s, 7 x 5 In., Pair 125.00
Fire Dogs, Figure of Sphinx, Bronze, France, c.1870, 9 1/2 x 10 1/4 In. 1430.00
Fire Dogs, Griffins, Gilt Bronze, Late 19th Century, 17 In. 550.00
Fire Dogs, Polished Steel, Engraved Decoration, Scrolled Finials, 12 1/2 In. 372.00
Fire Dogs, Scrolled Leaf Cast Top, Columnar Support, 12 1/2 In., Pair 1650.00
Fire–Starter Bucket, Lid Stick, Brass, Old Mission, Coppercraft, 8 3/4 x 8 In. 220.00
Fireback, Iron, Crown Lion, Unicorn, Virginia, Metal Crafters, 24 x 22 In. 247.00
Footman, Holds Plate Or Kettle, George III, Brass, Mid–18th Century, 12 x 16 In. 412.00
Gate, George III Style, Cast Iron, 1880s, 23 1/2 x 29 1/4 In. 275.00
Hearth, Brass, Neo–Classical Design, Dawson Brothers, 31 x 31 x 12 In. 120.00
Log Holder, Louis XVI Style, Scrolling Openwork, Gilt, Cast Iron, 24 In. 825.00
Mantel, Baroque, Carved Standing Figures Each Side, Floral, 19th Century 4675.00
Peat Bucket, George III, Brass Liner, Bail Handle, Mahogany, 16 In. 4950.00
Screen, Brass, Repousse Landscape Scene On Either Side, 34 x 32 In. 193.00
Screen, Copper Rivets, Wrought Iron Floral Design, Brass, 28 x 40 In. 143.00
Screen, George III, Brass & Wire, England, Late 18th Century, 24 x 37 In. 495.00
Screen, Iron, Sombrero–Figure, Cactus, Calif. Mission, 28 x 52 In. 550.00
Screen, Louis XV Style, Wirework, Cherubs & Vines, Gilt Bronze, 28 3/4 In. 770.00
Screen, Louis XVI Style, Bronze, 28 3/4 x 27 1/2 In. 8000.00
Screen, Mahogany, Salem, 3 Footed, Stand 8000.00
Screen, Needlepoint Insert of Ship, Snake Footed, 1890 .... 345.00
Screen, Painted Peacock, Leather, Art Nouveau 875.00
Screen, Pole, Carved, Scrolling Leaves Frame, Mahogany, England, c.1840, 77 In. ... 1320.00
Screen, Pole, Carved, Standard Cloverleaf Base, 1850s, 7 1/4 In. 410.00
Screen, Pole, Georgian Style, Needlepoint, 57 In. 187.00
Screen, Pole, Needlework, Maiden, Foliage, Hairy Paw Feet, 4 Ft. 3 3/4 In. 3850.00
Screen, Pole, Silkwork Panel, Mahogany Frame, Brass Shaft 410.00
Screen, Pole, Victorian Needlework Cat, Adjustable, Mahogany, 57 In. 495.00
Tongs, Brass Handle, Iron, 26 In. 159.00
Tongs, Georgian, Wrought Iron 22.00
Tongs, Poker & Shovel, Brass, Engraved Flower Design, Benham & Froud, Set 2600.00
Tongs, Shovel With Stand, Brass, Iron, America, 1820, 33 In. 550.00
Tongs, Shovel, Brass, Iron, America, 1800, 32 In., Pair 770.00
Tool Set, Cast Bronze, Figural Pirate Handle, 44 In., 4 Piece 2475.00
Tool Set, Federal, Brass, Lemon Top, America, 1810, 2 Piece 605.00
Tool Set, Wrought Iron, Brass Handle, 23 In., 3 Piece 286.00
Tool Stand, Brass & Iron, Fire, America, c.1820, 33 In. 550.00
Tool Stand, Brass, Marble Base, England, 19th Century, 27 1/2 In. 357.00
Tools & Holder, Polished Steel, Engraved Decoration, Scrolled, 25 In. 1580.00

FISCHER porcelain was made in Herend, Hungary, by Moritz Fischer.
The factory was founded in 1839 and continued working into the twentieth
century. The wares are sometimes referred to as *Herend* porcelain.

MF

Bowl, Birds, Butterflies, Herend, Octagonal, 6 1/4 x 3 3/8 In. 27.50
Bowl, Cover, Leaf Shape, Birds, Flowers & Rose, Vine Handle, Herend, 4 1/2 In. 105.00

Bowl, Scalloped, Basketweave, Relief Band, Birds & Insects, 11 1/2 In. 175.00
Box, Potpourri, Multicolored Florals, Spherical Pierced Form, 2 3/4 In. 120.00
Dish, Scalloped, Shamrocks, Gold Trim, Square, 7 In. 125.00
Group, Leda & Swan, 5 3/8 In. 137.00
Plate, Mayflower, 12 In. 160.00
Vase, Bands of Florals, Ram's Head Terminals With Cloven Feet, 13 1/2 In. 257.00

FISHING reels of brass or nickel were made in the United States by 1810. Bamboo fly rods were sold by 1860, often marked with the maker's name. Metal lures, then wooden and metal lures were made in the nineteenth century. Plastic lures were made by the 1930s. All fishing material is collected today and even equipment of the past thirty years is of interest if in good condition with original box.

Box, Bait, Revolving, Cole's Wisconsin Bob–Bet, Belt Mounted 25.00
Box, Bait, Star Pattern Lid, Handle, England 35.00
Box, Tackle, B. F. Meek 550.00
Box, Tackle, Sherman–Klover, Leather Handle 25.00
Box, Tackle, Sherman–Klover, Leather Handle, Metal 25.00
Bucket, Minnow, Green, Gold & Silver Paint, July 1894 .... 165.00
Case, Tackle, Oak, Leather Covered, England, Fly Fishing, Contents 1760.00
Catalog, Abbey & Imbrie Fishing, Tackle, 1910, 80 Pages 75.00
Creel, Half Moon, Veneered Wood 220.00
Creel, Reversal, Birch Bark 247.50
Creel, Trout, Leather, Willow 550.00
Fly Reel, Humphreys, Model 3a 85.00
Fly Reel, Martin, Auto, 1923 .... 85.00
Fly Reel, Pflueger, Progress No. 1774 .... 85.00
Fly Reel, Shakespeare, Auto, Model HG 65.00
Fly Reel, Shakespeare, Model GE, 1920 .... 85.00
Fly Reel, South Bend, Auto, Model D 65.00
Gaff, Marble Arms Co., Gladstone Mich., 1920s 300.00
Handbook, Bass Bible, 1961 .... 7.00
License, Ohio, 1946 .... 9.00
Lure, Arbogast Hula Poppa 65.00
Lure, Black Sambo 45.00
Lure, Bomber 69.00
Lure, Crazy Crawler, Heddon, Plastic, 2 1/2 In. 20.00
Lure, Deepster, Wooden, 2 1/4 In. 8.00
Lure, Devil Dog, Plastic, 5 1/2 In. 7.00
Lure, Dipsy Doodle, Wooden, 1947, 1 1/2 In. 10.00
Lure, Dowagiac 55.00
Lure, Flying Fluddles, Wooden, 1959, 4 In. 10.00
Lure, Heddon, Basser 115.00
Lure, Heddon, White, Blue 250.00
Lure, Hula Popper, Plastic, 2 In. 3.00
Lure, Jitterbug, Plastic, 1 3/4 In. 7.00
Lure, Lazy Ike, No. 2, Wooden 5.00
Lure, Lazy Ike, No. 3, Wooden 6.00
Lure, Lead, Iron Hooks, Holes For Lines, 6 In., Pair 110.00
Lure, Mity Atom, Wooden, 1947, 1 3/4 In. 10.00
Lure, Paw Paw Lippy Joe, Wooden, 1955, 2 3/4 In. 10.00
Lure, Porter Bait Co. 38.00
Lure, Sambo, Naughty Box 95.00
Lure, Shakespeare, Wooden, 2 1/2 In. 10.00
Lure, Skip Jack, Wooden, 1958, 2 3/4 In. 7.00
Lure, Sputterbug, Wooden, 2 1/8 In. 8.00
Lure, Trout, Long Jointed, Fishing, Hand Made, Tom Schroeder, 5 In. 4950.00
Lure, Wonder Bar, Shakespeare, Plastic, 2 1/2 In. 10.00
Reel, B. F. Meek & Sons, Trout, Louisville, Kentucky 4950.00
Reel, Billinghurst, Trout, 3 1/4 Diameter, 1859 .... 2200.00
Reel, J. C. Higgins, Engraved Fish Design On Case 4.25
Reel, Meek & Milam No. 5 .... 2970.00
Reel, Red River, No. 7345 .... 35.00

Reel, Shakespeare, Model GA, 1920	18.00
Reel, South Bend No. 1150, Spinning, Bakelite	15.00
Reel, Talbot, German, Silver, Box	1000.00
Reel, Ted Williams, Model 53539980, Bakelite & Chrome	20.00
Reel, Winchester, No. 2726, Saltwater	95.00
Rod, Bamboo, Salmon	50.00
Rod, Fly, Murphy, 1862	1100.00
Rod, Fly, Shakespeare Bamboo	55.00
Rod, Fly, Split Bamboo, South Bend	95.00
Rod, Maxwell, 6 1/2 In.	1925.00
Rod, Meddon, Model 20, Featherweight	1760.00
Rod, Payne, Model 201, 8 Ft.	2090.00
Rod, Winchester, Steel, Original Bag	85.00
Trap, Minnow, McSwain, Glass	75.00
Worm Holder, Revolving, Belt Mounted	25.00

FLAGS are included in the Textile category.

FLASH GORDON appeared in the Sunday comics in 1934. The daily strip started in 1940. The hero was also in comic books from 1930 to 1970, in books from 1936, in movies from 1938, on the radio in the 1930s and 1940s, and on television from 1953 to 1954. All sorts of memorabilia are collected, but the ray guns and rocket ships are the most popular.

Book, Big Little Book, Power Men of Mongo, 1930s	45.00
Book, Big Little Book, Red Word Invaders, 1930s	27.00
Book, Big Little Book, Tyrant of Mongo, 1930s	54.00
Book, Comic No. 1, King Comics, 1966	20.00
Book, Pop–Up, Tournament of Death, Alex Raymond, 1935	247.00
Compass, Wrist	40.00
Helmet, Captain Action	23.00
Signal Pistol, Emits Siren Sound, Pressed Steel, Marx, 1935, 7 In.	765.00
Space Rocket, Squadron Set, Display Card, 1952, 5 Piece	130.00
Toy Car, Red & Yellow Paint, Windup	250.00

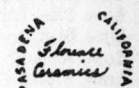

FLORENCE CERAMICS were made in Pasadena, California, from World War II to 1977. Florence Ward created many colorful figurines, boxes, candleholders, and other items for the giftshop trade. Each piece was marked with an ink stamp that included the name *Florence Ceramics Co.* The company was sold in 1964 and although the name remained the same the products were very different. Mugs, cups, and trays were made.

Doll, Laura	100.00
Figurine, Abigail	45.00
Figurine, Ann	90.00
Figurine, Basket Girl	30.00
Figurine, Belle Pink	65.00
Figurine, Birthday Girl, 9 In.	125.00
Figurine, Camille	45.00 To 85.00
Figurine, Child Cowboy, 8 In.	245.00
Figurine, Chinese Boy	30.00
Figurine, Clarissa	65.00 To 85.00
Figurine, David	75.00
Figurine, Delia, Blue	75.00
Figurine, Delia, Green	90.00
Figurine, Douglas	55.00
Figurine, Elaine	30.00 To 75.00
Figurine, Elizabeth, Seated, Green	165.00
Figurine, Grace, Blue, 8 In.	75.00
Figurine, Irene	35.00 To 75.00
Figurine, Jeanette, Green	75.00
Figurine, Jeni & Irene, Gray Clothes, Pair	125.00
Figurine, Jim, Gray	55.00
Figurine, Jim, Peach Suit	65.00
Figurine, Lillian	75.00

Figurine, Linda Lou	50.00
Figurine, Linda Lou, Pink	75.00
Figurine, Madonna, Gold On White	75.00
Figurine, Marie Antoinette, White, 7 In.	60.00
Figurine, Matilda	70.00
Figurine, Musette, 8 1/2 In.	85.00 To 95.00
Figurine, Pamela	45.00
Figurine, Pinky & Blue Boy, 12 In., Pair	595.00
Figurine, Rebecca, Seated, 7 1/2 In.	95.00
Figurine, Rose Marie, Green Dress	135.00
Figurine, Sarah, 8 In.	45.00 To 65.00
Figurine, Scarlett O'Hara	85.00
Figurine, Sue Ellen, 8 In.	65.00 To 75.00
Figurine, Vivian, Parasol, Green, 9 1/2 In.	125.00 To 140.00
Figurine, Yvonne	35.00
Flower Holder, Chinese Girl	16.00
Flower Holder, Rita	25.00
Planter, Chinese Boy & Girl, Black, White, Pair	65.00
Planter, June	40.00
Planter, Lady, Pink, 5 3/4 In.	35.00
Planter, Oriental Girl	42.00
Planter, Vase, Suzette, 6 3/4 In.	55.00
Plaque, Wall, Woman, 10 In.	50.00
Sign, Dealer, Figural Woman	195.00

FLOW BLUE, or flo blue, was made in England about 1830 to 1900. The plates were printed with designs using a cobalt blue coloring. The color flowed from the design to the white plate so that the finished plate has a smeared blue design. The plates were usually made of ironstone china.

Berry Bowl, Marechal Niel, Grindley	45.00
Berry Bowl, Oxford, Johnson Bros., 5 3/8 In.	45.00
Berry Bowl, Touraine, 5 1/4 In.	35.00
Berry Bowl, Touraine, Stanley, 6 1/4 In.	55.00
Biscuit Jar, Seaweed, Gold Trim, Ring Finial, Warwick	195.00
Bone Dish, Bolingbroke, Ridgway	45.00
Bone Dish, Touraine	75.00
Bowl, Amoy, 7 1/4 In.	120.00
Bowl, Argyle, Cove, Grindley, 10 In.	350.00
Bowl, Byzantium, B. W. M. & Co., 6 1/2 In.	75.00
Bowl, Delft, 10 1/2 In.	125.00
Bowl, Delft, 10 In.	125.00
Bowl, Fairy Villas, Cover, 10 In.	595.00
Bowl, Holland, Johnson Bros., 8 1/2 In.	95.00
Bowl, Holland, Oval, 9 1/2 In.	65.00
Bowl, Hudson, Cover, Scalloped Base, Meakin 8 In.	235.00
Bowl, Kyber, 10 In.	175.00
Bowl, La Belle, 5 1/2 In.	90.00
Bowl, Lorne, Cover, Round, 9 In.	55.00
Bowl, Melbourne, Oval, 9 3/4 In.	115.00
Bowl, Nonpareil, 9 In.	150.00
Bowl, Nonpareil, Cover, 9 In.	475.00
Bowl, Olympia, Cover, Grindley	175.00
Bowl, Osborne, Cover, Clover Shape, Ridgway	200.40
Bowl, Potato, California, 9 3/4 In.	95.00
Bowl, Scinde, Alcock, 10 1/2 In.	200.00
Bowl, Shanghai, Shallow, 7 1/2 In.	75.00
Bowl, Touraine, Stanley, 5 1/2 In.	55.00
Bowl, Waldorf, 8 3/4 In.	80.00
Bowl, Watteau, Cover, 9 In.	100.00
Bowl, Watteau, Cover, Malkin, 12 In.	185.00
Butter Chip, Clarence, Grindley	30.00
Butter Chip, Colonial, Meakin, 3 Piece	55.00
Butter Chip, Geneva, New Wharf Pottery	45.00

Butter Chip, Gold Bands, Shell Design, 8 Piece 150.00
Butter Chip, Grace 35.00
Butter Chip, La Belle 45.00
Butter Chip, Nonpareil 55.00
Butter Chip, Osborne, Ridgway 45.00
Butter Chip, Oxford, Johnson Bros. 40.00
Butter Chip, Roseville, Maddock 36.00
Butter Chip, Touraine 35.00
Butter, Cover, Ayr W. & E. Cord 30.00
Butter, Hong Kong, Cover, 4 x 7 In. .... 215.00 To 715.00
Butter, La Belle, Cover 250.00
Butter, Lotus, Cover, Drainer, Grindley 135.00
Butter, Nonpareil, Cover .... 375.00 To 395.00
Butter, Oregon, Underplate, Cover, Johnson Bros. 75.00
Butter, Rose, Cover, Grindley 140.00
Cake Plate, Beauties of China 225.00
Cake Plate, Florida, Grindley 95.00
Cake Plate, Nankin, Ashworth 150.00
Casserole, Seville, Cover, Wood & Son 250.00
Chamber Pot, Glenwood, 8 x 5 In. 170.00
Chamber Pot, Glenwood, Wood & Sons, 8 1/2 In. 170.00
Chamber Pot, Lahore 675.00
Child Set, Old Curiosity Shop 1850.00
Chocolate Pot, La Belle 800.00
Creamer, Amoy 575.00
Creamer, Argyle, Grindley 225.00
Creamer, Chatsworth 120.00
Creamer, Georgia, Johnson Bros. 145.00
Creamer, Indian 475.00
Creamer, Jewel 175.00
Creamer, La Belle 175.00
Creamer, Nonpareil 285.00
Creamer, Savoy 175.00
Creamer, Shell, Challinor 225.00
Creamer, Syrian, Grindley 175.00
Creamer, Willow 110.00
Cup & Saucer, Byzantium, B. W. M. & Co. 45.00
Cup & Saucer, Celtic 95.00
Cup & Saucer, Chapoo 185.00
Cup & Saucer, Dresden 85.00
Cup & Saucer, Fairy Villas 95.00
Cup & Saucer, Hong Kong, Handleless 150.00
Cup & Saucer, Kirkee, Handleless, J. Meir & Son 110.00
Cup & Saucer, Kremlin, Alcock 135.00
Cup & Saucer, Lorne, Grindley, After Dinner 75.00
Cup & Saucer, Lotus, Grindley 30.00
Cup & Saucer, Nonpareil, Burgess & Leigh 95.00
Cup & Saucer, Oriental, Ridgway 40.00
Cup & Saucer, Scinde 85.00
Cup & Saucer, Shell, Handleless, Challinor 165.00
Cup & Saucer, Touraine 105.00
Cup Plate, Amoy, 4 1/4 In. 125.00
Cup Plate, Scinde 125.00
Cup Plate, Tivoli, Furnival, 4 In. 68.00
Dinner Set, Coburg, Service For 12 .... 4140.00
Dinner Set, Monarch, 1890–1894, 39 Piece 1500.00
Dinner Set, Nonpareil, Service For 8 .... 7500.00
Dinner Set, Touraine, Stanley, 103 Piece 7600.00
Dish, Madras, Cover 295.00
Eggcup, Watteau, 6 Piece 550.00
Eggcup, Watteau, Doulton 100.00
Gravy Boat, Albany, Grindley 80.00
Gravy Boat, Clarence 120.00

Gravy Boat, Colonial, Undertray 125.00
Gravy Boat, Dainty, Maddock 80.00
Gravy Boat, Madras, Doulton 55.00
Gravy Boat, Mongolia, Double Spouted, Attached Underplate, Johnson Bros. 165.00
Gravy Boat, Nonpareil .... 150.00 To 175.00
Gravy Boat, Portman, Grindley 95.00
Gravy Boat, Scinde 425.00
Gravy Boat, Shell, Challinor 175.00
Jardiniere, Lotus 295.00
Ladle, Sauce, Clarence, Grindley 175.00
Ladle, Sauce, Nonpareil, B & L 475.00
Pitcher, Beauties of China, 2 Qt. .... 750.00 To 795.00
Pitcher, Corean, Mulberry, 8 1/4 In. 245.00
Pitcher, Cows 195.00
Pitcher, Cream, Kirkee, J. Meir & Son 75.00
Pitcher, Milk, Lily, Gold Handle & Trim, Adderly, 8 In. 135.00
Pitcher, Milk, Touraine, 6 In. 395.00
Pitcher, Nonpareil, 1 Qt. 525.00
Pitcher, Nonpareil, 2 Qt. 595.00
Pitcher, Savoy, S. Ford & Co., c.1900 .... 95.00
Pitcher, Verona, Wood, 2 Qt. 435.00
Pitcher, Whampoa, 1 Qt. 495.00
Plate, Amoy, 8 1/4 In. 95.00
Plate, Amoy, Davenport, 7 1/4 In. 90.00
Plate, Arcadia, 9 3/4 In. 50.00
Plate, Argyle, Grindley, 8 In. 45.00
Plate, Argyle, Johnson Bros., 10 In. 85.00
Plate, Astral, Fruit Center, Grindley, 8 3/4 In. 33.00
Plate, Athena, 9 1/2 In. 50.00
Plate, Byzantium, 10 In. 48.00
Plate, Cambridge, Meakin, 10 In. 80.00
Plate, Carlton, 10 1/2 In. 75.00
Plate, Carlton, Alcock, 8 1/2 In. 100.00
Plate, Carlton, Alcock, 9 1/2 In. 125.00
Plate, Cashmere, 9 1/2 In. 160.00
Plate, Chapoo, 7 3/8 In. 80.00
Plate, Chapoo, 9 1/4 In. 140.00
Plate, Chapoo, Wedgwood, 6 1/4 In. 45.00
Plate, Chapoo, Wedgwood, 7 1/2 In. 55.00
Plate, Chapoo, Wedgwood, 9 In. 65.00
Plate, Chinese, Dimmock, 10 1/2 In. 95.00
Plate, Conway, New Wharf Pottery, 9 In. 55.00
Plate, Dinner, Watteau, 9 Piece 160.00
Plate, Dorothy, 8 1/4 In. 40.00
Plate, Holland, Birds, Bug, Plants 60.00
Plate, Hong Kong, Charles Meigh, 1845, 9 In. 250.00
Plate, Independence Hall, 9 In. 250.00
Plate, Jewel, Johnson Bros., 10 In. 55.00
Plate, Kin Shan, 7 3/4 In. 75.00
Plate, La Belle, 8 3/4 In. 80.00
Plate, La Belle, Wheeling, 11 1/2 In. 135.00
Plate, Leicester 9 In. 85.00
Plate, Lonsdale, Ford 10 1/8 In. 85.00
Plate, Lorne, 10 In. .... 58.00 To 80.00
Plate, Lotus, Grindley & Leigh, 9 3/4 In. 80.00
Plate, Louvre, Meakin, 10 In. 65.00
Plate, Madras, Doulton, 5 5/8 In. 45.00
Plate, Madras, Doulton, 8 5/8 In. 60.00
Plate, Manilla, 8 1/2 In. 95.00
Plate, Manilla, 10 1/2 In. 175.00
Plate, Marechal, 10 1/4 In. 80.00
Plate, Melbourne, 10 In. 85.00
Plate, Nonpareil, 7 3/4 In. .... 45.00 To 55.00

Plate, Nonpareil, 8 3/4 In. .... 65.00 To 70.00
Plate, Nonpareil, 9 3/4 In. .... 95.00 To 105.00
Plate, Nonpareil, Burgess & Leigh, 8 1/2 In., 4 Piece 240.00
Plate, Normandy, 10 In. 70.00
Plate, Normandy, Johnson Bros., 10 In. 85.00
Plate, Oregon, Mayer, 5 In. 100.00
Plate, Oregon, Mayer, 6 1/4 In. 100.00
Plate, Oregon, Mayer, 9 5/8 In. 110.00
Plate, Oriental, Ridgway, 6 3/8 In. 30.00
Plate, Ormonde, Meakin, 14 1/8 In. 180.00
Plate, Oxford, Johnson Bros., 6 1/4 In. 35.00
Plate, Oxford, Johnson Bros., 9 7/8 In. 85.00
Plate, Percy, 10 In. 85.00
Plate, Savory, S. Ford & Co., c.1900, 10 In. 55.00
Plate, Savoy, S. Ford & Co., 1900, 10 In., 4 Piece 220.00
Plate, Scinde, Reticulated, 10 1/2 In. 2227.50
Plate, Shanghai, Adams, 8 3/4 In. 90.00
Plate, Temple, Podmore & Walker, 8 3/4 In. 85.00
Plate, Tonquin, Joseph Heath, 8 1/2 In. 50.00
Plate, Touraine, 6 1/2 In. 40.00
Plate, Touraine, 8 3/4 In. 85.00
Plate, Touraine, Stanley, 7 5/8 In. 40.00
Plate, Touraine, Stanley, 8 3/4 In. 60.00
Plate, Verona, 1890s, 10 In. 85.00
Plate, Vinranka, 10 1/4 In. 45.00
Plate, Vinranka, Soup Dish, 9 1/2 In. 45.00
Plate, Waldorf, New Wharf Pottery, 8 7/8 In. 75.00
Plate, Waldorf, Wood & Son, 10 In. 60.00
Plate, Watteau, Doulton, 9 1/2 In. 50.00
Plate, Watteau, Man Courting Lady, England 20.00
Plate, Watteau, Woman, Musket, Man With Dogs, Doulton, 10 1/4 In. 50.00
Plate, Wild Rose, Geo. Jones, 10 1/2 In. 85.00
Plate, Wild Turkey, 10 In. 90.00
Platter, Amoy, Cobalt 495.00
Platter, Argyle, 15 In. 215.00
Platter, Argyle, 17 In. 235.00
Platter, Argyle, Grindley, 19 In. 350.00
Platter, Argyle, Grindley, Oval, 10 1/2 x 15 In. 160.00
Platter, Carlton, Alcock, 11 x 8 1/2 In. 250.00
Platter, Castle Scenery 25.00
Platter, Chapoo, Wedgwood, 15 3/4 x 12 In. 450.00
Platter, Clytie, Wedgwood, 18 In. 695.00
Platter, Fairy Villas, 15 In. 185.00
Platter, Florida, Johnson Bros., 16 1/2 In. 295.00
Platter, Florida, Johnson Bros., 16 1/2 x 11 In. 250.00
Platter, Formosa, Ridgway, 13 1/2 x 10 1/2 In. 375.00
Platter, Gainsborough, 16 x 12 In. 135.00
Platter, Gainsborough, Scalloped, Ridgway, 16 x 12 In. 235.00
Platter, Gironde, Grindley, 18 In. 185.00
Platter, Haddon, 16 In. 165.00
Platter, Hamilton, 12 1/2 In. 110.00
Platter, Hamilton, 17 In. 150.00
Platter, Hindustan, Maddock, 7 3/4 In. 195.00
Platter, Hindustan, Maddock, 13 1/2 In. 325.00
Platter, Holland, 9 x 12 1/2 In. 128.00
Platter, India, Ashburton, 12 In. 95.00
Platter, Kyber, Adams, 10 1/2 x 7 1/2 In. 50.00
Platter, Lorne, Grindley, 11 1/2 x 16 In. 185.00
Platter, Manilla, 15 3/4 In. 595.00
Platter, Manilla, 15 In. 250.00
Platter, Marechal, 14 3/4 In. 175.00
Platter, Marechal, 16 1/2 In. 195.00
Platter, Mulberry, Corean, Podmore Walker & Co., 1850 .... 215.00

Platter, Nonpareil, 8 1/4 In.	140.00
Platter, Nonpareil, 15 1/2 In.	375.00
Platter, Nonpareil, Burgess & Leigh, 13 3/4 In.	295.00
Platter, Nonpareil, Burgess & Leigh, 15 1/4 In.	350.00
Platter, Ormonde, Meakin, 11 1/8 In.	140.00
Platter, Roseville, Maddock, 14 1/2 In.	175.00
Platter, Scinde, 13 3/4 In.	575.00
Platter, Scinde, 16 1/4 In.	750.00
Platter, Scinde, Alcock 11 In.	395.00
Platter, Scinde, Alcock 13 In.	395.00
Platter, Scinde, Reticulated, J. G. Alcock, 10 1/4 x 10 1/2 In.	2230.00
Platter, Sobraon, 18 In.	595.00
Platter, St. Louis, Johnson Bros., 12 x 16 1/4 In.	275.00
Platter, Tokio, 14 In.	110.00
Platter, Tokio, Johnson Bros., 14 In.	165.00
Platter, Touraine, 12 x 8 1/2 In.	150.00
Platter, Turkey, Cauldon, 19 1/2 x 16 1/4 In.	550.00
Platter, Turkey, Nankin, 18 In.	265.00
Platter, Vinranka, 11 1/4 In.	60.00
Platter, Watteau, 9 x 11 In.	125.00
Platter, Wind Flower, Burgess & Leigh, 18 In.	295.00
Relish, Osborne, Oval, Ridgway, 9 In.	95.00
Relish, Persian, Oval, Johnson Bros., 1902, 8 In.	85.00
Saucer, Byzantium, 6 Piece	65.00
Saucer, Melbourne, 5 3/4 In.	15.00
Saucer, Oregon, Mayer, 1850, 5 1/2 In.	27.00
Soup, Cream, Touraine, Alcock, 7 In.	75.00
Soup, Dish, Argyle, Grindley, 8 3/4 In.	65.00
Soup, Dish, Cambridge, Pair	210.00
Soup, Dish, Fairy Villa	55.00
Soup, Dish, Fruit Basket	125.00
Soup, Dish, Kin Shan, 10 1/2 In.	195.00
Soup, Dish, Manilla	195.00
Soup, Dish, Ning PO	135.00
Soup, Dish, Roma	70.00
Soup, Dish, Scinde, Alcock, 10 1/2 In.	145.00
Soup, Dish, Verona, Wood	75.00
Spooner, Brussels	175.00
Spooner, Chatsworth	110.00
Sugar & Creamer, Abbey	150.00
Sugar & Creamer, Duchess, Grindley	295.00
Sugar & Creamer, Oregon	525.00
Sugar, Belmont, Maddock	160.00
Sugar, Devon, Cover	150.00
Sugar, Melbourne, Cover	225.00
Sugar, Nonpareil, Cover, Burgess & Leigh	295.00
Sugar, Vinranka	100.00
Tea Set, Carlton, Alcock, 30 Piece	5250.00
Tea Set, Child's, Wagon, Wheel, Copper Luster, 20 Piece	850.00
Tea Set, Child's, Wheel, Service For 4, 15 Piece	950.00
Tea Set, Scinde, 4 Piece	1925.00
Teapot, Abbey	280.00
Teapot, Allegheny	495.00
Teapot, Brussels	190.00
Teapot, Cheswick, Ridgway	275.00
Teapot, Hong Kong	1075.00
Teapot, Oregon	1075.00
Toothbrush Holder, Hong Kong, Meigh	895.00
Tray, Togo, Small	100.00
Tureen, Florida, Cover, Grindley	225.00
Tureen, Gainsborough, Cover	295.00
Tureen, Grace, Underplate, Oval	150.00
Tureen, Manila, Tray	1075.00

Tureen, Marie, Cover	295.00
Tureen, Nonpareil, Cover, B. & Go	475.00
Tureen, Sauce, Savoy, Underplate, Grindley	295.00
Tureen, Sauce, Seville, Wood, 4 Piece	495.00
Tureen, Sauce, Tray, Hamilton	225.00
Tureen, Soup, Argyle, Pair	795.00
Tureen, Soup, Baltic, Grindley	425.00
Tureen, Soup, Lichfield	220.00
Tureen, Soup, Nonpareil	695.00
Tureen, Vegetable, Hudson, Cover, Scalloped, Oval, Meakin, 8 x 11 1/2 In.	220.00
Vase, Geneva, Doulton, 5 1/2 In., Pair	350.00
Wash Basin, Lily, Johnson Bros., 16 1/2 In.	350.00
Wash Basin, Scinde	950.00
Wash Set, Etruscan, Myott Family	1700.00
Waste Bowl, Waldorf, New Wharf Pottery	185.00

FLYING PHOENIX, see Phoenix Bird category

FOLK ART is also listed in many categories of this book under the actual name of the object. See categories such as Box, Cigar Store Figure, Weather Vane, Wooden, etc.

Barn, Tin Roof, Wooden, 16 x 18 x 14 In.	485.00
Bird Tree, 3 Small Carved & Painted Birds, 8 1/2 In.	50.00
Birdhouse, 4 Stories, Large Entrance, 1920	385.00
Birdhouse, Airplane Form	650.00
Birdhouse, Copper, Sun Front With Holes For Eyes & Mouth, Wooden	1200.00
Birdhouse, Log Cabin, 1930s	365.00
Birdhouse, Red, Apple Shape	28.00
Box, Carved As Fish, Burled Walnut, 7 3/4 In.	95.00
Box, Carved Ivory, Playing Cards In Middle, Dominoes In Sides, 6 Ft.	2975.00
Box, Carved, Wood, Lion, Trees, Eagle, Star Bursts On Cover, End Handles	5000.00
Box, Cover, Burnt Matches, 7 x 7 x 3 1/2 In. ....*Illus*	45.00
Bust, George Washington, Stone, Dark Gray, Early 19th Century, 6 1/2 In.	350.00
Button Mosaic On Padded Oilcloth, Gilded Gesso Frame, 1920s, 20 x 28 In.	130.00
Candlestick, 2–Light, Figural Angel Wings, Original Paint	950.00
Church, Miniature, Wooden Spire, 41 In.	30.00
Church, Pews & Altar Inside, Matchstick, 17 1/2 In.	195.00
Comb, Cow's Horn, Hand Carved, Massachusetts	12.00
Comb, Horn, Clarified, Hand Carved, Die–Cut Back, Indiana, 1700 To 1800	15.00
Diorama, Workshop, Birdcage Maker, Tools, Workbenches, 25 x 19 x 9 In.	3500.00
Dipper, Coconut Shell, Whalebone & Wood Handle, Shell Inlay, 12 In.	335.00
Doll, Made From Rope Bed Key, Fringed Dress, Crude Carved Face	126.00
Figure, Animated, Horse, Wood, Polychrome Paint, 15 In.	220.00
Figure, Black Man Eating Watermelon, Carved, 16 1/2 In.	2000.00
Figure, Blue Jay, Balsa, Original Paint, Wire Feet, Bead Eyes, Twig Base, 3 3/4 In.	45.00
Figure, Blue Jay, Tin Wings, Original Paint, Wire Legs, 8 3/4 In.	105.00

Folk Art, Box, Cover, Burnt Matches,
   7 X 7 X 3 1/2 In.

◆◆◆◆◆◆◆◆◆◆◆◆◆◆◆◆◆◆◆◆◆◆◆

To remove wrinkles from old paper, set a regular iron for cotton. Iron out the wrinkles from the wrong side of the paper. Be sure to iron quickly so you do not scorch the paper.

◆◆◆◆◆◆◆◆◆◆◆◆◆◆◆◆◆◆◆◆◆◆◆

Folk Art, Mailbox, Uncle Sam,
Holding Box, Wooden, 4 Ft. 9 In.

Figure, Bottle Cap Man, Black	95.00
Figure, Cat, Pouncing, Blue Marble Eyes, Carved, Wood, Zoratti, 1 Ft.	500.00
Figure, Frog, Pine, Inserted Eyes, Attached Legs, 5 In.	115.00
Figure, Giraffe, Carved Wood, 27 In.	450.00
Figure, Indian, Standing, Hand To Ears, Looking, Die Cut, Tin	795.00
Figure, Keystone Kop–Style, Carved, Painted, Almost Life Size	1550.00
Figure, Man, Italian, Yellow Hat, Blue Suit, Carved, Wood, 10 In.	200.00
Figure, Ostrich, Cement, Silvio P. Zoratti, 1956, 4 Ft.	425.00
Figure, Oxen, Yoked, Papier–Mache, Wooden Base, 1920s, 12 In.	185.00
Figure, Peacock, Strutting, Cement, Full Tail, Marble Eyes, Zoratti, 3 Ft.	850.00
Figure, Penguin, Carved Wood, 12 In.	300.00
Figure, Quail, Carved & Painted, 4 1/4 In.	55.00
Figure, Quail, Pine, 8 In.	130.00
Figure, Raccoon, Carved, Painted, 19 In.	357.00
Figure, Rooster, Painted, Carved, 3/8 In.	49.00
Figure, Uncle Sam, Papier–Mache, 20 In.	77.00
Fruit, Stone, Lemon, Orange & Plum, Original Paint, 3 Piece	182.00
Fruit, Stone, Orange & Peach, Original Paint, 2 Piece	120.00
Head, Carved Wood, Dark Varnish, Painted Eyes, 11 3/4 In.	40.00
House, Tin Roof, Brick–Look Exterior, Wooden, 15 x 18 x 11 1/2 In.	385.00
Lamp, Popsicle Stick, 2 Side Compartments, Sequins, 1950s, 13 In.	195.00
Lamp, Popsicle Stick, Hexagonal Base & Shade, Fringe On Shade, 20 In.	155.00
Mailbox, Uncle Sam, Holding Box, Wooden, 4 Ft. 9 In. ....*Illus*	150.00
Mirror, 3–Tombstone Shape, Cutout Hearts & Circles, Frame, Penna.	350.00
Pedestal, Popsicle Stick, Pyramidal Base, Diamond Shape Top, 1930s	165.00
Pencil Box, Slide Top, Chip Carved, Blue Green Paint Traces	715.00
Plaque, Skull Head, 3 Layers of Thin Wood, Brown, Red Stain, White Teeth, 11 In.	27.00
Safe, Wooden, Stenciled, 19th Century	200.00
Shadow Box, Peaceable Kingdom, Polychrome, Carved, Berks County, c.1840	7150.00
Sign, Liberty Tavern, Relief Carved Eagle, 19th Century, 58 x 31 In.	2860.00
Snake, Carved Root, Old Paint, 32 In.	330.00
Stand, Fruit Crates, Lincoln, Washington & Eagle Design, Splayed, 1920–1930	145.00
Stand, Jiggs, Holding Tray, Red Vest, Black Jacket, Top Hat, 28 In.	110.00
Vase, Hanging, Bird Bracket, Wood, Polychrome Paint, 15 In.	225.00
Watch, Hutch, Allover Applied Tree Burls, 1 Drawer, Square Nails, 13 In.	195.00
Whirligig, Bicyclist, 1920s	1420.00
Whirligig, Biplane, Gray, Blue & Red Paint, Wood & Tin, 21 In.	350.00
Whirligig, Black Boy Fishing, Wooden, 28 In.	75.00
Whirligig, Black Crow, American, 19th Century, 25 In.	305.00
Whirligig, Farmer & Wife, Sharpening Wheel, 1930s	825.00

Whirligig, Farmer Milking Cow, 10 1/2 In. 385.00
Whirligig, Indian In Canoe, Polychrome Paint, Wooden 60.00
Whirligig, Indian, Birch Bark Canoe, Carved & Polychromed, 10 x 12 In. 2750.00
Whirligig, Mammy Churning Butter, 12 In. 195.00
Whirligig, Man In Leather Suit, Tin Blades, 1880s, 18 1/2 In. 1210.00
Whirligig, Men Sawing 1210.00
Whirligig, Rooster 285.00
Whirligig, Standing Indian Canoe, Wooden, Leather, 12 In. 1500.00
Whirligig, Uncle Sam Riding Bicycle, Polychrome Paint, 20th Century, 32 In. 997.00
Whirligig, Windmill, Picket Fence, Early 20th Century, 23 In. 93.50

FOOT WARMERS solved the problem of cold feet in past generations.
Some warmers held charcoal, others held hot water. Pottery, tin, and
soapstone were the favored materials to conduct the heat. The warmer was
kept under the feet, then the legs and feet were tucked into a blanket,
providing welcome warmth in a cold carriage or church.

Box Type, Original Paint, America, 10 1/2 x 11 1/2 x 11 In. 385.00
Pierced Heart Pattern, Metal For Coals, Mahogany, Victorian, 10 1/2 In. 440.00
Pierced Tin, Coal Box, Mahogany 275.00
Pottery Handles, Pottery Stopper 95.00
Punched Design, Heart, Tin & Wooden, 5 1/2 In. 200.00
Punched Tin, Circle & Heart Design, Wooden Frame, 6 In. 214.00
Punched Tin, Diamond & Circle Design, Wooden Frame, 8 In. 440.00
Punched Tin, Walnut, With Bellows 104.50
Stoneware, Henderson 110.00

FOOTBALL collectibles may be found in both the Card and the Sports
categories.

FOSTORIA glass was made in Fostoria, Ohio, from 1887 to 1891. The
factory was moved to Moundsville, West Virginia, and most of the glass
seen in shops today is a twentieth-century product. The company was sold
in 1983; new items will be easily identifiable, according to the new owner,
Lancaster Colony Corporation. Additional Fostoria items may be listed in
the Milk Glass category.

Acanthus, Grill Plate, Green, 10 In. 45.00
American, Appetizer, Insert, 4 Piece 30.00
American, Ashtray, 2 1/8 In., Round 16.00
American, Ashtray, 2 7/8 In., Square 6.00
American, Basket, Reed Handle .... 80.00 To 85.00
American, Biscuit Jar, Conversion 750.00
American, Bonbon, 3-Footed 15.00
American, Bonbon, 7 In. 42.00
American, Bowl, 3-Footed, 10 1/2 In. 40.00
American, Bowl, Fruit, 12 In. 130.00
American, Bowl, Oval, 10 1/2 In. 15.00
American, Bowl, Oval, 12 In. 40.00
American, Bowl, Rolled Rim, 12 In. 55.00
American, Bowl, Tricorner, 10 In. 26.00
American, Bowl, Tricorner, 5 In. 10.00
American, Bowl, Vegetable, 2 Sections, 10 In. 32.50
American, Butter, Cover, Round .... 85.00 To 110.00
American, Butter, Dome, 1 Lb. .... 95.00 To 120.00
American, Cake Plate, Handles, 10 In. 45.00
American, Cake Stand Pedestal Square, 10 In. .... 65.00 To 85.00
American, Candlestick, Square, Column, 6 In. 115.00
American, Candlestick, Twin, Footed Pair 58.00
American, Candy Dish, Footed 11.00
American, Celery Dish, 10 In. 10.00
American, Cheese & Cracker Dish 50.00
American, Cigarette Box, Cover, 4 3/4 x 3 1/2 In. 38.00
American, Creamer & Sugar, Tray 18.00
American, Goblet, 5 Oz. 9.00

American, Goblet, 9 Oz.		12.00
American, Ice Bucket, Metal Handle	40.00 To	50.00
American, Mayonnaise Set, 3 Piece		32.00
American, Mustard, Cover		35.00
American, Pitcher, Footed, 1/2 Gal.		60.00
American, Pitcher, Footed, 1/2 Gal., 8 In.		75.00
American, Pitcher, Round, 3 Pt.		78.00
American, Plate, Dinner, 9 1/2 In.		20.00
American, Plate, Sandwich, 10 1/2 In.		17.50
American, Plate, Torte, 18 In.		85.00
American, Platter, Oval, 10 1/2 In.		40.00
American, Platter, Oval, 12 In.		28.00
American, Platter, Oval, 13 1/2 In.		55.00
American, Punch Bowl 18 In.		225.00
American, Punch Set, 14–In. Bowl, 11 Piece		260.00
American, Relish, 4 Sections, 9 In.		45.00
American, Relish, 4 Sections, Square, 11 In.		110.00
American, Salt & Pepper		15.00
American, Salt & Pepper, Nickel Tops		50.00
American, Sandwich Tray, Center Handle, 12 In.		35.00
American, Sherbet, Flared, 4 3/8 In.		9.00
American, Shrimp Boat, 12 In.		350.00
American, Sugar & Creamer, Cover	15.00 To	27.00
American, Syrup, No Drip, 6 1/2 Oz., 5 1/4 In.		45.00
American, Toothpick		32.50
American, Tray, Utility, 10 1/2 In.		28.00
American, Tumbler, Iced Tea, 12 Oz.		6.00
American, Tumbler, Juice, 5 Oz.		8.00
American, Tumbler, Water 9 Oz.		12.00
American, Vase, Flared, 7 In.		65.00
American, Vase, Flared, 9 1/2 In.		50.00
American, Vase, Footed, Square, 7 1/2 In.		60.00
American, Whiskey Set, Rye & Scotch, Locked		325.00
American, Wine, 2 1/2 Oz.		10.00
Arcady, Cordial		35.00
Baroque, Bonbon, Footed, 7 3/8 In.		20.00
Baroque, Bonbon, Topaz, 7 3/8 In.		30.00
Baroque, Bowl, Topaz, 11 In.		45.00
Baroque, Bowl, Topaz, 12 In.		30.00
Baroque, Cake Plate, 10 In.		10.00
Baroque, Cocktail, Footed, Blue, 5 Oz.		20.00
Baroque, Compote, Jelly, Cover, Blue		96.00
Baroque, Compote, Jelly, Cover, Topaz, 7 1/2 In.		58.00
Baroque, Creamer, Footed, Blue, 3 3/4 In.		18.00
Baroque, Cup & Saucer, Topaz		20.00
Baroque, Goblet, Water, 9 Oz.		35.00
Baroque, Mustard, Cover, Topaz		30.00
Baroque, Nappy, Handle, 5 In.	15.00 To	20.00
Baroque, Plate, 7 In.		9.75
Baroque, Plate, 9 In.		12.50
Baroque, Plate, Topaz, 7 In.		7.50
Baroque, Relish, 3 Section, Topaz, 10 In.		30.00
Baroque, Salt & Pepper, Yellow, Individual		100.00
Baroque, Sherbet, 5 Oz.		9.50
Baroque, Sherbet, Blue, 5 Oz.		18.00
Baroque, Sugar & Creamer		12.00
Baroque, Sugar & Creamer, Individual		10.00
Baroque, Tidbit, 3–Footed, 8 1/4 In.		18.00
Beverly, Celery Dish, Green, 11 In.		23.00
Beverly, Pitcher, Green, 7 In.		210.00
Beverly, Plate, Green, 10 1/4 In.		40.00
Bookends, Lyre, 7 In.		75.00
Bookends, Owl, 7 1/2 In.		95.00

Bookends, Seahorse, 8 In. 80.00
Brocade, Plate, Green, 7 In. 45.00
Brocade, Plate, Green, 9 In. 70.00
Buttercup, Bowl, Handle, 10 In. 48.00
Buttercup, Console, Oval, 11 In. 47.50
Buttercup, Cordial 40.00
Buttercup, Creamer, Footed, Crystal, 3 1/4 In. 15.00
Buttercup, Cup & Saucer 17.50
Buttercup, Goblet, Wine, 3 1/2 Oz. 29.50
Buttercup, Iced Tea, 12 Oz. 24.00
Camelia, Plate, 10 1/2 In. 35.00
Camellia, Bowl, 4 1/2 In. 18.00
Camellia, Bowl, Oval, 9 1/2 In. 65.00
Camellia, Sherbet, Tall, 6 In. 16.00
Candelabra, 16 Prisms, 8 1/4 x 10 In., Pair 150.00
Century, Bowl, Rolled Rim, Footed, 11 In. 35.00
Century, Candlestick, 2-Light, 7 In., Pair 45.00
Century, Cup & Saucer 10.00
Century, Goblet, Water, 10 1/2 Oz. 16.00
Century, Pitcher, Milk, 1 Pt. 40.00
Century, Relish, 2 Sections 17.50
Century, Relish, 3 Sections, Etched, 11 In. 25.00
Century, Salt & Pepper, 3 1/4 In. 15.00
Century, Sherbet, 5 1/2 Oz. 8.50
Century, Sugar & Creamer 17.50
Century, Sugar, Individual 20.00
Century, Tray, Oval, 6 1/2 In. 10.00
Century, Tumbler, Juice, 5 Oz. 14.00
Century, Vase, 2 Handles, 7 1/2 In. 60.00
Century, Wine, 3 1/2 Oz. 24.00
Chintz, Cake Plate, 2 Handles, 10 In. 30.00
Chintz, Candlestick, 4 1/2 In., Pair 22.00
Chintz, Compote, 4 3/4 In. 14.00
Chintz, Cordial, 1 Oz. 60.00
Chintz, Cruet, Oil, 3 1/2 Oz. 110.00
Chintz, Cup & Saucer .... 16.00 To 22.00
Chintz, Goblet, Stem, 9 Oz. 26.00
Chintz, Pitcher, 3 Pts. 400.00
Chintz, Plate, 6 In. 7.00
Chintz, Plate, 7 In. .... 10.00 To 15.00
Chintz, Plate, 8 In. 17.00
Chintz, Plate, 9 In. .... 32.00 To 45.00
Chintz, Relish, Handles, 2 Section, 6 In. 30.00
Chintz, Sherbet, Crystal, 6 Oz. 20.00
Chintz, Sugar & Creamer 35.00
Chintz, Tidbit, 3-Footed 20.00
Chintz, Torte Plate, 14 In. 35.00
Chintz, Tumbler, Iced Tea, 13 Oz. 22.50
Chintz, Water Set, 12 Piece 600.00
Coin, Ashtray, Amber, 4 In. 25.00
Coin, Ashtray, Green, Round, 7 1/2 In. 23.00
Coin, Box, Cigarette, Amber 70.00
Coin, Candleholder, Green, 4 1/2 In., Pair 125.00
Coin, Candlestick, Amber, Pair 25.00
Coin, Candy Dish, Amber 30.00
Coin, Candy Dish, Cover, Green 45.00
Coin, Candy Dish, Cover, Olive, Green 50.00
Coin, Candy Dish, Cover, Red 85.00
Coin, Compote, Amber 50.00
Coin, Creamer, Amber .... 14.00 To 35.00
Coin, Lamp, Oil, Coach 200.00
Coin, Pitcher, Green, 1 Qt. 225.00
Coin, Salt & Pepper, Red 25.00

Coin, Vase, Blue, 8 In. 30.00
Colonial–Dame, Sherbet, Green, 6 1/2 Oz. 9.75
Colony, Bonbon, Footed, 4 1/8 In. 22.00
Colony, Bowl, Oval, Footed, 11 In. 40.00
Colony, Cake Plate, Handle, 10 In. 17.00
Colony, Candlestick, 2 Arms, 6 1/4 In., Pair 45.00
Colony, Candy Dish, Cover, Footed, 1/2 Lb. 63.00
Colony, Cup & Saucer 8.50
Colony, Dish, Mayonnaise, 2 Piece 32.50
Colony, Goblet, 9 Oz., 8 Piece 100.00
Colony, Pitcher, Ice Lip, 2 Qt. 85.00
Colony, Plate, 7 In. .... 5.00 To 9.50
Colony, Plate, 9 In. 20.00
Colony, Salt & Pepper 10.00
Colony, Sherbet, 5 Oz. 80.00
Colony, Sugar & Creamer .... 10.00 To 20.00
Colony, Tray, Muffin 35.00
Colony, Tumbler, 12 Oz. 15.00
Colony, Tumbler, 9 Oz. 17.50
Contour, Bowl, Square, 8 1/2 In. 30.00
Contour, Butter, Cover, 1/4 Lb. 25.00
Contour, Candlestick, 4 1/2 In., Pair 18.00
Contour, Relish, 2 Sections 20.00
Coronet, Cup & Saucer 9.75
Coronet, Sugar & Creamer 15.00
Coronet, Sugar, Individual 5.00
Corsage, Bowl, Handles, 9 In. 70.00
Corsage, Relish, 3 Sections, 10 In. 35.50
Corsage, Sugar, Footed, 3 5/8 In. 15.00
Essex, Toothpick 15.00
Fairfax, Baker, Oval, Amber, 9 In. 25.00
Fairfax, Bottle, Salad Dressing, Topaz 125.00
Fairfax, Bouillon, Handle, Amber 10.00
Fairfax, Bouillon, With Liner, Green 12.00
Fairfax, Bowl, Rose, Oval, 9 In. 18.00
Fairfax, Bowl, Topaz, 5 In. 7.00
Fairfax, Bread Plate, Pink, 6 In. 7.00
Fairfax, Canape Plate, Tumbler Insert, Green 38.00
Fairfax, Candlestick, Azure, 3 In., Pair 40.00
Fairfax, Candlestick, Blue, 5 1/2 In., Pair 45.00
Fairfax, Compote, Azure, 7 In. 45.00
Fairfax, Cup & Saucer 5.00
Fairfax, Cup & Saucer, Blue 18.00
Fairfax, Nut Cup, Azure 9.00
Fairfax, Nut Cup, Topaz 8.50
Fairfax, Plate, Green, 7 In. 9.00
Fairfax, Plate, Pink, 7 In. 10.00
Fairfax, Platter, Azure, Oval, 15 In. 78.00
Fairfax, Relish, 3 Sections, Blue 75.00
Fairfax, Sugar & Creamer, Azure, Individual 35.00
Fairfax, Sugar & Creamer, Topaz, Individual 15.00
Fairfax, Sugar, Green 8.00
Fairfax, Tumbler, Topaz, 3 Oz. 15.00
Figurine, Colt, Sitting, 2 1/4 In. 45.00
Figurine, Deer, Standing, 4 In. 40.00
Figurine, Duck Family, Amber, Frosted, 4 Piece 85.00
Figurine, Duck, Mama, Amber 20.00
Figurine, Madonna, 10 In. 12.00
Grape, Candlestick, Green, 3 In. 30.00
Grape, Compote, Green, 7 In. 45.00
Heather, Butter, Cover, Oblong 30.00
Heather, Cake Plate, 2 Handles, 10 In. 24.00
Heather, Candy, Cover, Footed, 7 In. 40.00

Heather, Cup & Saucer	25.00
Heather, Nappy, Handles, 4 1/2 In.	18.00
Heather, Plate, 9 In.	45.00
Heather, Platter, Oval, 12 In.	80.00
Heather, Relish, 2 Sections	27.00
Heather, Salt & Pepper	60.00
Heather, Wine, 4 Oz.	40.00
Heirloom, Epergne, Pink, 9–In. Lily, 14 1/2–In. Bowl	95.00
Heirloom, Vase, Handkerchief, Pink, 6 1/2 x 4 1/2 In.	30.00
Hermitage, Bowl, Oyster Cocktail, 2 Piece	18.50
Hermitage, Goblet, 4 5/8 In.	8.00
Hermitage, Ice Cream Set, Yellow, 3 Piece	25.00
Hermitage, Pitcher, Yellow, 3 Pt.	125.00
Hermitage, Pitcher, Yellow, 7 3/8 In.	125.00
Holly, Champagne, 5 5/8 In.	12.00
Holly, Cocktail, Oyster	12.50 To 17.50
Holly, Cordial, 1 Oz.	45.00
Holly, Goblet, Cocktail	18.00
Holly, Goblet, Water	12.00
Holly, Goblet, Water, 10 In.	30.00
Holly, Plate, Salad, 6 In.	30.00
Holly, Sherbet	14.00
Holly, Sherbet, 4 3/8 In.	30.00
Jamestown, Goblet, Blue, 9 1/2 Oz.	20.00
Jamestown, Goblet, Water, Amber, 10 Oz.	10.00 To 20.00
Jamestown, Iced Tea, Amber, 6 In.	10.00
Jamestown, Pitcher, Green, Pt.	115.00
Jamestown, Sherbet, Amber, 6 1/2 Oz.	7.00
Jamestown, Sherbet, Amber, 6 Oz.	12.00
Jamestown, Sherbet, Blue, 4 1/2 In.	15.00
Jamestown, Tumbler, Amber, 12 Oz.	10.00 To 20.00
Jamestown, Wine, Amber, 4 Oz.	14.50 To 27.50
Jenny Lind, Cologne Bottle, Milk Glass	70.00
June, Bowl, Footed, Rose, 12 In.	95.00
June, Champagne, Topaz, 6 Oz.	25.00
June, Cracker Plate, Topaz	75.00
June, Cup & Saucer, Footed, 5 1/2 In.	23.00
June, Goblet, Topaz, 10 Oz.	27.00
June, Ice Bucket, Topaz	78.00
June, Lemon Dish, Handles, Rose	85.00
June, Pail, Whipped Cream, Azure	195.00
June, Sugar & Creamer, Rose, Individual	225.00
June, Sugar, Topaz, Individual	50.00
June, Tumbler, Iced Tea, Topaz	30.00
June, Tumbler, Topaz, 5 Oz.	75.00
June, Wine, Azure, 3 Oz.	100.00
Kashmir, Cup, After Dinner, Azure	25.00
Kashmir, Plate, Topaz, 10 In.	35.00
Kashmir, Sugar, Azure, Individual	45.00
Kashmir, Tumbler, Azure, 9 Oz.	35.00
Kasmir, Plate, Azure, 7 In.	5.00
Lafayette, Relish, 2 Sections, Topaz	20.00
Lido, Cake Plate, Handle, 10 In.	35.00
Lido, Compoté, 5 1/2 In.	30.00
Lido, Pitcher, 53 Oz.	100.00
Lido, Plate, 7 In.	7.00
Mayfair, Cup & Saucer, Topaz	10.00
Mayfair, Plate, Amber, 7 In.	8.00
Mayfair, Plate, Rose, 7 In.	8.00
Mayfair, Plate, Topaz, 7 In.	7.00
Mayfair, Plate, Topaz, 9 In.	14.00
Mayfair, Sugar & Creamer, Topaz, Individual	25.00
Mayflower, Bowl, Flared, 12 In.	48.00

Mayflower, Candlestick, 4 1/2 In. 22.00
Mayflower, Sherbet, 6 Oz. 25.00
Mayflower, Tumbler, Footed, 5 Oz. 15.00
Mayflower, Tumbler, Iced Tea, 12 Oz. 18.00
Meadow Rose, Bowl, Flared, 12 In. 35.00
Meadow Rose, Cake Plate, 10 In. 38.00
Meadow Rose, Candlestick, 5 In., Pair 45.00
Meadow Rose, Champagne, 6 Oz. 19.50
Meadow Rose, Compote, 5 1/4 In. 22.00
Meadow Rose, Cordial, 3/4 Oz. 45.00
Meadow Rose, Cordial, 8 Piece 350.00
Meadow Rose, Cup & Saucer 25.00
Meadow Rose, Goblet, 10 Oz. .... 25.00 To 40.00
Meadow Rose, Ice Bucket 80.00
Meadow Rose, Plate, 7 In. .... 7.00 To 12.00
Meadow Rose, Plate, Torte, 14 In. 40.00
Meadow Rose, Sherbet, 6 Oz. .... 12.00 To 25.00
Meadow Rose, Sugar & Creamer 15.00
Meadow Rose, Tumbler, 5 Oz. 20.00
Midnight Rose, Bowl, 10 1/2 In. 70.00
Midnight Rose, Celery, 11 1/2 In. 48.00
Midnight Rose, Ice Jug 350.00
Midnight Rose, Relish, 5 Sections, 11 In. 125.00
Midnight Rose, Sugar & Creamer 30.00
Milkweed, Cake Plate, Handle 35.00
Morning Glory, Vase, Crystal, 7 1/2 In. 240.00
Mulberry, Wine 32.50
Navarre, Bowl, 2 Handles, Footed, 10 1/2 In. 60.00
Navarre, Candlestick, 3–Light, 6 In. 40.00
Navarre, Candlestick, 4 In. 50.00
Navarre, Cocktail, 3 1/2 Oz. 25.00
Navarre, Cocktail, Oyster, 4 Oz. 22.50
Navarre, Compote, 4 1/2 In. 40.00
Navarre, Cordial, 3/4 Oz. 55.00
Navarre, Cordial, 8 Piece 350.00
Navarre, Cup & Saucer 25.00
Navarre, Dish, Mayonnaise 50.00
Navarre, Ice Bucket 125.00
Navarre, Oyster Cocktail, 4 Oz. 28.00
Navarre, Plate, 7 In. 15.00
Navarre, Plate, 9 In. 40.00
Navarre, Relish, 3 Sections 45.00
Navarre, Salt & Pepper, Footed 85.00
Navarre, Sherbet, 6 Oz. 12.00
Navarre, Sugar & Creamer 32.50
Navarre, Tumbler, Footed, 10 Oz. 18.00
Navarre, Tumbler, Water, 10 Oz. .... 18.00 To 22.50
Navarre, Vase, 5 In. .... 75.00 To 95.00
Navarre, Wine, 3 1/4 Oz. .... 25.00 To 40.00
Oak Leaf, Console Set, Cornucopia Type, 11 In., 3 Piece 120.00
Oak Leaf, Dish, Lemon, Green 22.00
Pioneer, Ashtray, Green 3.50
Pioneer, Bowl, Amber, 5 1/2 In. 5.00
Pioneer, Plate, Green, 9 In. 10.00
Pitcher, Ice Lip, Footed, 3 Pt. 50.00
Priscilla, Bouillon, Handle, Amber 12.00
Priscilla, Bouillon, Handle, Green 12.00
Priscilla, Plate, Luncheon, Amber, 7 In. 8.00
Priscilla, Snack Set, Cup & Underplate, Green 16.50
Priscilla, Sugar & Creamer, Amber 25.00
Priscilla, Tumbler, Handle, Amber 26.00
Priscilla, Tumbler, Iced Tea, Handle, Green 15.00
Raleigh, Bowl, 13 In. 26.00

Raleigh, Cake Plate, 2 Handles, 10 In. 12.00
Raleigh, Cruet .... 25.00 To 35.00
Raleigh, Cup & Saucer 16.00
Raleigh, Mayonnaise Set, 3 Piece 20.00
Raleigh, Plate, 7 In. 6.00
Raleigh, Sugar, Individual 6.00
Rambler, Pitcher, Footed 118.00
Rambler, Plate, 10 In. 12.00
Rogene, Wine, 2 3/4 Oz. 30.00
Romance, Cocktail, 3 1/2 Oz. 18.00
Romance, Cocktail, Oyster, 4 Oz. 27.75
Romance, Creamer, Footed, 3 1/4 In. 18.00
Romance, Relish, 3 Section 32.00
Romance, Salt & Pepper 45.00
Romance, Server, Sandwich, Center Handle, 11 1/4 In. 35.00
Romance, Sherbet, 6 Oz. 14.00
Romance, Sugar, Footed, 3 1/8 In. .... 15.00 To 17.00
Romance, Tumbler, 9 Oz. 18.00
Romance, Wine, 3 Oz. 29.75
Rose, Goblet, Water, 9 1/2 Oz. 20.00
Rose, Tumbler, Footed, 12 Oz. 18.00
Royal, Server, Center Handle, Green, 11 In. 35.00
Royal, Tumbler, Footed, 9 Oz. 25.00
Royal, Wine, Green 22.00
Seascape, Relish, 2 Sections, Pink 35.50
Seascape, Sugar, Cover, Pink, Individual 22.00
Shirley, Cup & Saucer, Footed 22.00
Shirley, Cup, Footed 17.00
Shirley, Jug, Footed, 53 Oz. 250.00
Sky Flower, Sherbet, 7 1/2 Oz. 8.50
Sylvan, Spooner 15.00
Trojan, Candy Dish, Cover, Topaz, 1/2 Lb. 145.00
Trojan, Creamer, Topaz 15.00
Trojan, Ice Bucket, Topaz 95.00
Trojan, Sugar Pail, Topaz 125.00
Tuxedo, Toothpick 100.00
Vase, Cased White, Multicolor, Signed, 1978, 7 1/2 In. 70.00
Vernon, Plate, Green, 11 In. 45.00
Vernon, Water Set, Green, 5 Piece 375.00
Versailles, Ashtray, Rose 40.00
Versailles, Bowl, Fruit, Blue, 5 In. 25.00
Versailles, Candlestick, Blue, 3 In., Pair 65.00
Versailles, Cocktail, Oyster, Green 32.00
Versailles, Cup & Saucer, Topaz 22.00
Versailles, Goblet, Footed, Topaz, 12 Oz. 25.00
Versailles, Goblet, Topaz, 10 Oz. 45.00
Versailles, Ice Bucket, Blue 150.00
Versailles, Pitcher, Topaz 350.00
Versailles, Plate, Blue, 7 1/2 In. 9.00
Versailles, Server, Sandwich, Center Handle, Blue 95.00
Versailles, Sherbet, Blue, Footed 37.50
Versailles, Sugar Pail, Blue 195.00
Versailles, Whiskey, Green, 2 1/2 Oz. 40.00
Versailles, Wine, Green, 10 Oz. 65.00
Vesper, Bowl, Green, 6 In. 20.00
Vesper, Cake Plate, Amber, 10 1/2 In. 16.00
Vesper, Cake Plate, Green, 10 1/2 In. 32.00
Vesper, Celery Dish, Green 35.00
Vesper, Compote, Twisted Stem, Amber 30.00
Vesper, Cup & Saucer, Green 18.00
Vesper, Goblet, Amber, 11 In. 27.00
Vesper, Plate, Amber, 9 1/2 In. .... 9.00 To 15.00
Vesper, Plate, Green, Center Handle 35.00

Vesper, Tumbler, Footed, Amber, 5 1/2 Oz. 20.00
Victoria, Butter, Cover 110.00
Victoria, Sugar 80.00
Virginia, Toothpick 27.50
Wakefield, Tumbler, 5 Oz. 9.00
Wheat, Cake Plate, 10 In. 24.00
Wheat, Goblet, 10 Oz. 18.00
Willow, Bowl, 12 In. 125.00
Willowmere, Bowl, Whip Cream, 5 In. 18.00
Willowmere, Cup & Saucer .... 12.50 To 20.00
Willowmere, Goblet, 10 Oz. 25.00
Willowmere, Plate, 7 In. 18.00
Willowmere, Relish, 3 Sections 35.00
Willowmere, Sugar & Creamer 27.50
Willowmere, Wine, 3 1/2 Oz. 20.00
Wistar, Sugar & Creamer 30.00

FOVAL, see Fry category

FRAMES are included in the Furniture category under Frame.

FRANCISCAN is a trademark that appears on pottery. Gladding, McBean and Company started in 1875. The company grew and acquired other potteries. They made sewer pipes, floor tiles, dinnerwares, and art pottery with a variety of trademarks. In 1934, dinnerware and art pottery were sold under the name Franciscan Ware. They made china and cream-colored, decorated earthenware. Desert Rose, Apple, El Patio, and Coronado were best sellers. The company became Interpace Corporation and in 1979 was purchased by Josiah Wedgwood & Sons. The plant was closed in 1984 but a few of the patterns are still being made. For more information, see *Kovels' Depression Glass & American Dinnerware Price List.*

Bowl, Coronado, Ivory, 7 3/4 In. 9.00
Bowl, Desert Rose, 5 1/4 In. 6.00
Bowl, Desert Rose, 5 3/4 In. 14.00
Bowl, Salad, Coronado, Coral 30.00
Bowl, Soup, Desert Rose 15.00
Bowl, Vegetable, Desert Rose, Divided 45.00
Bowl, Vegetable, Starburst, Divided .... 15.00 To 20.00
Bread Plate, Desert Rose 35.00
Bread Plate, Ivy 5.00
Chop Plate, Coronado, Aqua, 12 In. .... 12.00 To 15.00
Chop Plate, Desert Rose 45.00
Claret, Renaissance, Gold 28.00
Coffeepot, Autumn, Tall 26.00
Coffeepot, Cover, Ivy 140.00
Coffeepot, Desert Rose .... 65.00 To 110.00
Coffeepot, Starburst 225.00
Compote, Coronado, Coral, 7 1/2 In. 12.00
Cookie Jar, Apple 165.00
Cookie Jar, Nun 300.00
Creamer, Desert Rose .... 5.50 To 7.50
Cup & Saucer, Apple .... 8.00 To 15.00
Cup & Saucer, Desert Rose .... 9.50 To 16.00
Cup & Saucer, Ivy 15.00
Cup & Saucer, Starburst 7.00
Dish, Soup, Apple, 8 In. 15.00
Gravy Boat, Attached Underplate, Coronado, Aqua 16.00
Gravy Boat, Starburst 15.00
Grill Plate, Desert Rose 85.00
Pitcher, California, 1947 Mark, 28 Oz. 95.00
Place Setting, Coronado, 4 Piece 35.00
Place Setting, Desert Rose, 4 Piece 35.00

Place Setting, Duet, 4 Piece 75.00
Plate, Apple, 8 1/2 In. 8.50
Plate, Apple, 10 1/2 In. 12.50
Plate, Coronado, 11 In. 10.00
Plate, Coronado, Ivory, 6 1/4 In. 3.00
Plate, Desert Rose, 6 1/2 In. 10.00
Plate, Desert Rose, 8 In. 6.50
Plate, Starburst, 10 1/2 In. 5.00
Platter, Apple, 12 1/2 In. .... 32.00 To 40.00
Platter, Apple, 14 In. 25.00
Platter, Coronado, Coral, 13 In. 15.00
Platter, Coronado, Ivory, 13 In. 17.00
Platter, Starburst, Oval, 13 In. 40.00
Platter, Starburst, Oval, 15 In. 50.00
Relish, Coronado, Ivory, 9 In. 15.00
Relish, Ivy 20.00
Saucer, Desert Rose 10.00
Sherbet, Desert Rose 18.00
Sugar & Creamer, Apple 35.00
Sugar & Creamer, Ivy .... 22.00 To 22.50
Sugar, Cover, Coronado 10.00
Sugar, Cover, Desert Rose 10.00
Syrup, Coronado, Aqua 20.00
Teapot, Coronado, Coral 35.00
Teapot, Coronado, Yellow 20.00
Teapot, Dark Green Cover, Metropolitan, 1940s 25.00
Tray, 3 Sections, Rose, Round, 11 In. 30.00
Tray, Starburst, 4 Piece 85.00
Tray, Starburst, Loop Handle 25.00
Tumbler, Crystal, Hand Painted 15.00
Tumbler, Water, Renaissance, Gold 22.00
Tureen, Cover, Apple .... 300.00 To 465.00

FRANKART, Inc., New York, New York, mass–produced nude *dancing lady* lamps, ashtrays, and other decorative Art Deco items in the 1920s and 1930s. They were made of white lead composition and spray–painted. *Frankart Inc.* and the patent number and year were stamped on the base.

Ashtray, Nude On Globe, Floor Model .... 345.00 To 595.00
Ashtray, Nude, On Pedestal, Original Insert, 8 1/2 x 5 1/2 In. 500.00
Ashtray, Nude, Sitting .... 200.00 To 275.00
Bookends, Boy, Dog .... 80.00 To 145.00
Bookends, Busts of Women 175.00
Bookends, Deer, Standing, 6 In. 140.00
Bookends, Dog, Scotty .... 65.00 To 145.00
Bookends, Dog, Spaniels 95.00
Bookends, Dutch Boy & Girl 125.00
Bookends, Eagle 65.00
Bookends, Horse Heads, Stylized 120.00
Bookends, Mask–Form 75.00
Bookends, Sailor & Dog 58.00
Bookends, Woman's Bust, Brass Plated 150.00
Lamp, 2 Green Inverted Nude Figures Balance, Pink Crackled Glass Ball, 18 In. 1100.00
Lamp, Elephant Head, With Insert 175.00
Lamp, Flame, Girl 225.00
Lamp, Kneeling Nudes, Face Away, Amber Globe, 10 1/4 x 14 In. 1100.00
Lamp, Nude Seated On Column, Holding Globe On Lap, Signed, 7 1/2 In. 750.00
Lamp, Sailor Boy Next To Lamppost 235.00
Smoke Set, Man Carrying Brick Hod, Pack of Cigarettes On Base 275.00

FRANKOMA POTTERY was originally known as The Frank Potteries when John F. Frank opened shop in 1933. The factory is now working in Sapulpa, Oklahoma. Early wares were made from a light cream–colored

clay, but in 1956 the company switched to a red burning clay. The firm makes dinnerwares, utilitarian and decorative kitchenwares, figurines, flowerpots, and limited edition and commemorative pieces.

Bean Pot, Barrel	35.00
Bookends, Dog, Prairie Green	145.00
Bowl, Green, Brown, 7 1/2 In.	10.00
Carafe, Green, Sticker	25.00
Chocolate Set, Moss Green, 6 Piece	22.50
Dinner Set, Wagon Wheel, Box, 40 Piece	225.00
Figurine, Fan Dancer, Black, Ada Clay	270.00
Figurine, Girl With Bucket, Green, 7 In.	120.00
Figurine, Indian Chief, 8 In.	50.00
Figurine, Indian Chief, Green, 8 In.	40.00 To 70.00
Figurine, Indian Chief, Standing, Black	25.00
Jar, Honey, With Bee, 5 1/2 In.	10.00
Jug Set, Art Deco, Blue, 1935, 4 2-In. Tumblers, 5 Piece	55.00
Mug, Elephant, White, 1968	40.00
Mug, Hamm's	370.00
Pitcher, Cover, Green, Brown, Bulbous, 8 In.	10.00
Pitcher, Wagon Wheel, 2 Qt.	20.00
Pitcher, Wagon Wheel, Green, 2 Qt.	45.00
Planter, Duck, 10 In.	60.00
Plate, Dancing Nymph, 6 1/2 In.	30.00
Plate, Easter, 1972, Oral Roberts, White Satin	75.00
Salt & Pepper, Bull, Sitting	65.00
Sugar & Creamer, Ringed, Marked	100.00
Sugar & Creamer, Wagon Wheel	6.00
Sugar & Creamer, Wagon Wheel, Green	22.00
Teapot, Aztec, Green	52.00
Trivet, Cattle Brand	15.00
Trivet, Cherokee Alphabet	15.00
Trivet, Eagle	9.00
Trivet, Kansas, 1958	3.00
Trivet, Liberty Bell	20.00
Vase, Brown, Ribbed	20.00
Vase, Flying Goose, Clover, Pair	25.00
Vase, Indian Design, Ada Clay	30.00

FRATERNAL objects that are related to the many different fraternal organizations in the United States are listed in this category. The Elks, Masons, Odd Fellows, and others are included. Furniture is listed in the Furniture category. Shaving mugs decorated with fraternal crests are included in the Shaving Mug category.

Eastern Star, Compact, Unusual Clasp, Patented	27.50
Elks, Constitution & Statues, 1919	5.00
Elks, Flask, Figural	55.00
F. O. E., Mirror, Pocket	20.00
Knights of Columbus, Post, Tole & Carved Wood, 5 Ft., Pair	1500.00
Knights of Pythias, Button, Photograph, Ribbon, 51st	60.00
Knights of Pythias, Shaving Mug, Limoges	140.00
Knights of Pythias, Sword, Dress, Ivory Handle, Inscribed, 37 1/2 In.	55.00
Knights of The Golden Eagle & Knights of The Mystic Chain, Mug, Double	150.00
Knights Templar, Sword & Scabbard	125.00
Knights Templar, Watch Fob, Apollo	45.00
Masonic, Apron, White Satin, Blue Ribbon, Framed With History, 22 1/2 x 22 In.	600.00
Masonic, Apron, White Satin, Blue Velvet, Silver Embroidery, Trim, 12 In.	19.00
Masonic, Ashtray, Shriner, Figural Shriner, Chalkware, Seattle, July 1936, 4 3/4 In.	85.00
Masonic, Ashtray, Shriner, Jaffa	10.00
Masonic, Badge, 32 Degree, Gold Blue Ribbon, Joseph E. Skoog On Bar	25.00
Masonic, Black Hole Box	15.00
Masonic, Book, Masonic Lexicon, A. G. Mackey, 14th Edition, 1872	22.50
Masonic, Candleholder, Maple Lodge No. 196, Pewter, 3 In., Pair	25.00

Masonic, Champagne, Shriner, Clear, Amber & Gold Flashed, Louisville, Ky., 1909 ... 65.00
Masonic, Coaster, Shriner 12.00
Masonic, Crown & Scepter, Eastern Star, Rhinestone, 2 Piece 25.00
Masonic, Cuff Links, Gold Filled, Ruby Stones 25.00
Masonic, Door Knocker, Brass, 1800s 87.00
Masonic, Figure, Syria Camel, Hriner 35.00
Masonic, Goblet, Alligators, Pittsburgh, New Orleans, 1910 .... 75.00
Masonic, Goblet, Shriner, St. Paul, Pittsburgh, 1908, 5 In. 85.00
Masonic, Hatpin, Jerusalem Shrine 45.00
Masonic, Lamp, Emblem Inside Bulb 65.00
Masonic, Man, Figural, Iron, Jointed 220.00
Masonic, Medal, 75th Anniversary, 1857–1932, Gold, Diamond 300.00
Masonic, Membership Card, Masonic Temple, New Jersey, 1926 .... 3.00
Masonic, Mug, Shriner, Legion of Honor 30.00
Masonic, Paperweight, Cobalt Blue Glass 40.00
Masonic, Pin 8.00
Masonic, Quilt Top, Pieced Calico, Hope, Faith & Charity, 104 x 92 In. 2640.00
Masonic, Ring, 14K Gold, Small Diamond 75.00
Masonic, Rug, Goethe Lodge, No. 629, F. & A. M., Oriental Type, Heavy Nap 257.00
Masonic, Shaving Mug, Limoges 140.00
Masonic, Sign, 3 Milk Glass Globes, Embossed Emblems, Iron Frame 250.00
Masonic, Sign, Eastern Star, Lighted, Large 25.00
Masonic, Sword, Engraved 129.00
Masonic, Vase, Temple, Portland, Maine 15.00
Masonic, Watch Fob, J. E. King, Rockford, Ill., 1919 .... 22.00
Masonic, Wristwatch, Bulova Accutron, 14K Gold, 4 Emblem 600.00
Odd Fellow, Triptych, Membership, Past Grands From 1833 To 1946, 32 3/4 In. 990.00
Odd Fellows, Badge, Memorial, Rebekah Lodge 25.00
Odd Fellows, Banner, Red, White & Blue, Felt, 1910, 33 x 58 In. 24.00
Odd Fellows, Catalog, Illustrated 20.00
Odd Fellows, Hat 52.00
Odd Fellows, Medal, Grand Lodge Photograph 9.00
Wristwatch, Shriner, 17 Jewel, Pictures Hat & Symbols On Dial, Helbros 125.00

FRY GLASS was made by the H. C. Fry Glass Company of Rochester, Pennsylvania. The company, founded in 1901, first made cut glass and other types of fine glasswares. In 1922, they patented a heat–resistant glass called *Pearl Oven glass.* For two years, 1926—1927, the company made Fry Foval, an opal ware decorated with colored trim. Reproductions of this glass have been made. Depression glass patterns made by Fry may be listed in the Depression Glass category. Some pieces of cut glass may also be included in the cut glass category.

FRY FOVAL, Compote, Delft Blue Stem & Rim 395.00
 Cup & Saucer, Blue Handle 55.00
 Pitcher, Green Handle & Base 295.00
FRY, Baking Set, Child's, 1929, Box 290.00
 Chalice, Venetian Pattern, Loop & Swirl, Pillar Stem & Font, Blue Rim, 1920 ..... 1995.00
 Console Set, Random Reeding, Controlled Bubbles, Blue, 3 Piece 295.00
 Creamer, Fluted Top 30.00
 Grill Plate, 10 1/2 In. 12.50
 Plate, 3 Sections, 10 1/2 In. 16.00
 Vase, Venetian Pattern, Pillar Molded Foot, Stem & Bowl, 1920 .... 1300.00

FULPER is the mark used by the American Pottery Company of Flemington, New Jersey. The art pottery was made from 1910 to 1929. The firm had been making bottles, jugs, and housewares from 1805. Doll heads were made about 1928. The firm became Stangl Pottery in 1929. Fulper art pottery is admired for its attractive glazes and simple shapes.

Bookends, Open Books 300.00
Bookends, Peacock 99.00
Bookends, Rameses, Green, 8 In. 850.00
Bowl, Crystalline Glaze, 8 In. 85.00
Bowl, Famille Rose Glaze, Sectioned Rim, Marked, 15 In. 225.00

Bowl, Flower Frog, Green, Blue, Yellow & Brown Flambe, Shell Shape, 4 x 12 In. ... 248.00
Bowl, Fruit, Crystalline, Yellow & Brown Flambe Interior, 5 x 11 1/4 In. 138.00
Bowl, Green, Flambe Glazed, 4 In. 210.00
Bowl, Lotus, Mottled Green & Gunmetal, Green & Yellow Interior, 4 x 11 In. 137.00
Bowl, Malachite Green, Brown Flambe Glaze, 2 Angular Handles, 3 3/4 x 10 In. 99.00
Bowl, Mottled, Blue–Green, Signed, 2 1/2 x 10 3/4 In. 150.00
Bowl, Petal Design, Blue & Green Mottled, Oval, 15 1/4 In. 100.00
Bowl, Stylized Design, Crystalline Glaze, 13 In. 155.00
Candleholder, Blue Inset Glass, 2 Triangular Yellow Pieces, Marked, 10 1/2 In. 990.00
Candleholder, Crystalline, Blue, Pair 200.00
Candlestick, Browns, 3 In., Pair 95.00
Candlestick, Dark Green To Tan Glaze, 11 In. 135.00
Candlestick, Flaring Bobeche, Brown To Mauve Flambe Glaze, Marked, 15 1/2 In. 355.00
Candlestick, Matte Green Flambe Glaze, Marked, 16 In. 385.00
Chamberstick, Gray, Paper Label 150.00
Cider Set, Black Crystalline Glaze, Vertical Ink Mark, Pitcher, 6 Mugs 445.00
Cup, Blue Flambe 50.00
Decanter, Whiskey, Musical, Pinched 100.00
Ewer, Bleeding Heart, Green, 15 In. 395.00
Flask, Pilgrim, Curled Handles, Gun Metal To Green, 10 x 7 1/2 In. 440.00
Flower Frog, Crystalline Green Flowing Onto Crystalline Brown Base 175.00
Flower Frog, Mushroom 60.00
Flower Frog, Nude, Jonquils, Connecting Turtles 165.00
Jug, Copper Dust Glaze, Upright Handle, 12 1/4 x 7 3/4 In. 2310.00
Lamp Base, 3 Angular Arms, Matte Green Glaze, 10 1/2 x 10 In. 357.00
Lamp, Figural, Bluebird, c.1925 .... 495.00
Lamp, Mushroom Shape, Ceramic & Leaded Glass Shade, c.1910, 18 x 13 In. 9900.00
Lamp, Perfume, Ballerina, Orange 170.00
Lamp, Perfume, Cockatoo 1200.00
Lamp, Perfume, Cytharia, 12 In. ....900.00 To 950.00
Lamp, Perfume, Lady With Snood 1000.00
Lamp, Perfume, Parrot, 12 In. 495.00
Pitcher, Green & Turquoise Flambe, Dark Rose Ground, 4 In. 70.00
Pot, Geometric Design, Matte Brown, 4 1/2 x 6 In. 350.00
Powder Box, Lady Cover, Art Deco Clothing, Plaid Base 125.00
Powder Box, Stylized Deco Woman, Hat, Complete Figure 165.00
Urn, Black To Copper Dust Glaze, 2 Handles, Pedestal, 15 x 7 1/2 In. 385.00
Urn, Green & Gray Leopard Skin Glaze, 3 Handles, Flared Neck, 6 1/2 x 4 3/4 In. 4675.00
Urn, Leopard Skin Glaze, Textured, Handles, 12 1/2 x 11 1/4 In. 1650.00
Vase, 3 Loop Handles At Top, Purple Crystalline Glaze, 6 x 8 In. 210.00
Vase, Beaded Design Around Neck, Feathered Blue Crystalline Glaze, Marked, 7 In. 205.00
Vase, Beige, Brown & Blue Glaze, Drip Effect, 9 7/8 In. 310.00
Vase, Black Mirror Glaze, Paper Label, 17 x 9 In. 715.00
Vase, Black To Pumpkin Cat's Eye Glaze, 13 1/2 x 6 1/4 In. 660.00
Vase, Black, Gray & Brown Flambe Glaze, 4 1/2 x 4 3/4 In. 83.00
Vase, Blue & Silver Glaze, Reticulated Top, Signed, 10 In. 650.00
Vase, Blue Crystalline Glaze, 4 Small Handles, Bulbous, 13 1/2 In. 880.00
Vase, Blue Crystalline, Handles, 5 1/2 In. 480.00
Vase, Blue Flambe, Blue Rim, Hand Incised, 4 1/2 x 4 1/2 In. 130.00
Vase, Blue Flambe, Hammered, Black Crystalline Cap, 2 Handles 550.00
Vase, Blue Glaze, Matte Gray Base, Tall Neck, 15 1/4 x 7 In. 605.00
Vase, Blue To Matte Gray Flambe, Marked, 15 x 7 1/2 In. 1320.00
Vase, Brown Flambe Glaze, Marked, 8 In. 120.00
Vase, Brown Hi–Glaze Drip Over Yellow, 7 Sides, Marked, 9 In. 165.00
Vase, Brown, Gray, Green & Cream Flambe Glaze, Rolled Rim, Label, 17 x 9 In. ... 660.00
Vase, Bubbled Surface, Ridged Wall, Marked, 18 In. 330.00
Vase, Bud, Black, 8 In. 85.00
Vase, Bud, Speckled Blue Hi–Glaze, Marked, 5 In. 175.00
Vase, Cabochons, Arched Handles, Crystalline Glaze, Marked, 11 3/4 In., Pr. 3300.00
Vase, Copper Dust Glaze Over Matte Green, 2 Angular Handles, 9 1/2 In. 445.00
Vase, Crystalline Gold Flambe Glaze, 7 Sides, Marked, 10 1/4 In. 495.00
Vase, Famille Rose Glaze Over Lavender, Marked, 7 In. 100.00
Vase, Feathered Blue–Green Glaze, Ovoid, 6 3/4 In. 110.00

Vase, Gray Gunmetal Flambe Glaze, 3 Handles Under Top Rim, Marked, 7 In. 220.00
Vase, Green Crystalline Glaze, Baluster, 11 1/2 In. 415.00
Vase, Green Crystalline Over Pink Famille Rose, 5 x 9 In. 385.00
Vase, Green Crystalline To Yellow Flambe Glaze, 8 Sides, 7 1/2 x 6 In. 195.00
Vase, Green Drip Over Plum, 3 Handles, Bulbous, 7 In. 250.00
Vase, Green Flambe, 4 Buttressed Handles, 8 In. 330.00
Vase, Green Frog–Skin Glaze, 17 x 9 In. 275.00
Vase, Gunmetal, Brown & Mahogany Flambe, Bulbous, 9 1/2 In. 300.00
Vase, Handles On Flaring Base, Drip Brown Glaze, Signed, 9 1/2 In. 220.00
Vase, Iridescent Green & Purple Glaze, Over Pink, Bulbous, 10 x 8 In. 495.00
Vase, Iridescent Green & Purple Over Rose Base, Ring Handles, 12 1/2 In. 385.00
Vase, Ivory To Chinese Blue Flambe, Flared, 10 1/2 x 6 In. 468.00
Vase, Lavender, Cobalt, Brown & Green Flambe, 9 x 8 3/4 In. 523.00
Vase, Leopard Skin Crystalline Glaze, Box Ink Mark, 13 1/2 In. 303.00
Vase, Leopard Skin, 9 In. 750.00
Vase, Light Green, Crystalline Glaze, 12 In. 825.00
Vase, Mirrored Plum, Bulbous, Sticker, 7 In. 275.00
Vase, Molded Rose, Green Tinged Petals, Blue Ground, Signed, 6 1/2 In. 180.00
Vase, Ochre & Green Flambe Glaze, Mirror Black Base, 13 1/4 x 6 1/2 In. 110.00
Vase, Plum, Green Drip Glaze, 3 Handles, 6 1/4 In. 375.00
Vase, Pumpkin To Black Cat's Eye Flambe, Paper Label, 13 x 5 3/4 In. 715.00
Vase, Thick Green Crystalline Glaze, 2 Handles, Marked, 12 x 11 In. 825.00
Vase, Thorn Apple, Blue, 15 In. 395.00
Vase, Tiger's–Eye Flambe Glaze, 8 Sides, 7 1/2 In. 275.00
Vase, Tiger's–Eye Flambe Glaze, Bottle Shape, 13 1/2 In. 413.00
Vase, Tiger's–Eye Flambe Glaze, Oval Ink Mark, 9 1/2 In. 248.00
Vase, Trumpet, Leopard Skin, Marked, 9 In. 300.00
Vase, Urn Shape, Blue, Handle, Marked, 9 1/2 In. 250.00
Vase, Volcanic Warty Green & Gunmetal Glaze, Ink Mark, 9 1/2 x 5 1/2 In. 385.00
Vase, Yellow, Blue & Purple Flambe, 2 Curved Handles, 9 1/2 In. 495.00
Wall Pocket, Greek Key Pattern, Matte, Brown, 9 In. 225.00

FURNITURE of all types is listed in this category. Examples dating from
the seventeenth century to the 1950s are included. Prices for furniture vary
in different parts of the country. Oak furniture is most expensive in the
West; large pieces over eight feet high are sold for the most money in the
South, where high ceilings are found in the old homes. Condition is very
important when determining prices. These are NOT average prices but
rather reports of unique sales. If the description includes the word *style,*
the piece resembles the old furniture style but was made at a later time. It
is not a period piece.

Armchairs may also be listed under Chair in this category.
Armchair, Aluminum, Bakelite Arms, Flamingo Seat, Back, 1940s, Pr. 595.00
Armchair, Alvar Aalto, Model No. 31, Plywood & Laminated Birch, c.1932 .... 2200.00
Armchair, Beechwood, Carved Shell Top Rail, Caned Seat & Back, Cushion, 1740s 8800.00
Armchair, Beechwood, Horseshoe–Shaped Back, Jugendstil, c.1900 .... 995.00
Armchair, Beechwood, Upholstered Crest, Carved Flower Heads, I. Gourdin, 1748 ... 885.00
Armchair, Belter, Rosalie .... 3400.00 To 4500.00
Armchair, Biedermeier, Walnut, Upholstery, 19th Century, Pair ....*Illus* 6600.00
Armchair, Carved Walnut, Floral Tapestry Upholstery, c.1890, Pair 735.00
Armchair, Child's, Banister Back, Victorian Stencil Over Original Paint, 1770 .... 995.00
Armchair, Child's, Shaker, No. 0, New Lebanon, c.1900 .... 3100.00
Armchair, Chippendale, Cherry, Upholstery, 18th Century, 41 In. 995.00
Armchair, Chippendale, Ladder Back, Arched & Pierced, Mahogany 4950.00
Armchair, Chippendale, Mahogany, Dark Finish, Slip Seat, Green, 44 In. 995.00
Armchair, Chippendale, Mahogany, Library, Needlepoint Upholstery, c.1760 .... 3300.00
Armchair, Chippendale, Oak, Worn Finish, Crest With 1821 & 1844 .... 148.00
Armchair, Chippendale, Pierced Splat, Carved Arms, Walnut, c.1760 .... 7150.00
Armchair, Commode, Turkish Style, Carved & Painted, 42 In. 6600.00
Armchair, Dragon Form Back, Carved & Ebonized, Arms & Legs, China 330.00
Armchair, Dutch Baroque Style, Walnut, Needlepoint Upholstery, Pair 1200.00
Armchair, Federal, Cherry, Striped Upholstery, Conn., 1800, 40 1/2 In. 995.00
Armchair, George I, Vasiform Splat, Black Japanned, Caned Seat 2200.00

Furniture, Armchair, Biedermeier, Walnut,

Upholstery, 19th Century, Pair

Furniture, Armchair, Ottoman, Eames,

Rosewood Veneer, Leather

Armchair, George III, Beechwood, Upholstered Oval Back & Seat, Pair 5500.00
Armchair, George III, Open Back, Cushion, Caned Seat, c.1800, Pair 4950.00
Armchair, Georgian Style, Vasiform Splat, Balloon Seat, Walnut 165.00
Armchair, Georgian, Marlboro Style, Brown Leather Upholstery 4750.00
Armchair, Gustav Stickley, No. 1299a, 2 Horizontal Back Slats, Rush Seat 660.00
Armchair, Gustav Stickley, No. 350–A, 3 Slats, Leather Seat, 38 3/4 x 24 1/2 In. ... 660.00
Armchair, Gustav Stickley, Straight Crest Rail, 3 Slats, Flat Arms, 38 In. 330.00
Armchair, Hardwood, Carved, Silk Upholstery, France, 19th Century, Pair 1000.00
Armchair, Hepplewhite Style, Mahogany, Slip Seat, Arms, Floral Design, 38 In. 195.00
Armchair, Hunzinger, Stamped, 1869 .... 1875.00
Armchair, India, Tree of Life & Star Ivory Inlay, 59 In. 700.00
Armchair, Jeliff Style, Brass Medallion Crest, Man's Head Arm End 1300.00
Armchair, John Jelliff, Renaissance Revival, Walnut, 42 In. 220.00
Armchair, Knoll, Grasshopper, Plywood & Fabric, c.1948 .... 715.00
Armchair, L. & J. G. Stickley, No. 408, Slats, 32 x 27 In. 2535.00
Armchair, Ladder Back, Maple, 5 Arched Slats, Rush Seat, 46 In. 775.00
Armchair, Ladder Back, Slat Seat, Painted, 38 1/2 In. 195.00
Armchair, Limbert, Ladder Back, Saddle Seat, Medium Brown Finish, Branded 192.00
Armchair, Limbert, No. 874, Ebonized 450.00
Armchair, Louis XV Style, Carved Floral Sprays, Damask Upholstery, Beechwood ... 1435.00
Armchair, Louis XVI Style, Acanthus Carved Crest & Arms, Giltwood 1100.00
Armchair, Louis XVI Style, Skirt Framed By Spiral Carved Ribbon, Walnut 245.00
Armchair, Louis XVI, Upholstered Back, Giltwood, Bowfront Seat 3300.00
Armchair, Magazine Rack On Side, Wicker 220.00
Armchair, Mahogany, Gilt Design, Masonic Symbol On Back, Phila., 1815 .... 3575.00
Armchair, Mahogany, Leather Seat, Tooled Leather Back, c.1900 .... 154.00
Armchair, Neoclassical, Ebonized & Gilded Frame, Satin Upholster, 20th Century ... 200.00
Armchair, Neoclassical, Walnut, Italy, c.1800, 33 In., Pair 225.00
Armchair, Ottoman, Eames, Rosewood Veneer, Leather ....*Illus* 2700.00
Armchair, Paul Jallot, Velvet Padded Seat, Arms & Back, Pair 6650.00
Armchair, Prairie School, Maple, Leather Seat & Back, 44 In. 495.00
Armchair, Queen Anne Style, Mahogany, Slip Seat, Upholstery, 28 In. 170.00
Armchair, Queen Anne, Walnut, Cane Back, Upholstered Seat, 1730 .... 2450.00
Armchair, Recliner, Retractable Arms, Walnut, 19th Century 355.00
Armchair, Regency, Mahogany, Ribbon Back, Banded Inlay On Crest Rail 275.00
Armchair, Sausage Turned, Red Paint 770.00
Armchair, Straight Crest Rail, 3 Back Slats, Wide Seat Apron, 35 In. 385.00
Armchair, Swivel, Office, Cordovan Red Leather Upholstery, 41 1/2 In. 225.00
Armchair, Teakwood, Carved Splat, Silk Pad, China, Pair 2200.00
Armchair, Thomas Molesworth, Horsehead On Rounded Back, Leather Seat 2500.00
Armchair, Thonet, Bentwood, Laminated Wood, D–Shaped Seat, Pair 1760.00
Armchair, Thonet, Bentwood, Triangular Cane Seat, 3 Legs, Paper Label 1450.00
Armchair, Victorian, Rose Carving, 44 In. 700.00
Armchair, Wicker, White, Upholstered Cushion 85.00
Armchair, William & Mary Style, High Back, Foliate Carved Arms, Walnut, Pair 245.00
Armchair, Windsor, Fanback, Saddle Seat, Slender Spindle Back, 43 1/4 In. 665.00

Armchair, Wing, Chippendale Style, Padded Back, Cushion Seat, 39 3/4 In. 605.00
Armchair–Bed, Queen Anne, Upholstered Lift Back, Opens To Bed, 1740s 1650.00
Armoire, Bird's–Eye Maple, Mirrored Door, Rosewood Trim, c.1860, 93 In. 3745.00
Armoire, Cherry, Mirrored Door, Bamboo Accents, c.1870, 89 In. 1650.00
Armoire, Cherrywood & Cypress, Brass Hinges, 3 Drawers, 80 In. 5500.00
Armoire, French Provincial Style, Walnut, 2 Drawers, Fabric Lined, 72 In. 3300.00
Armoire, French Provincial, Pine, 2 Paneled Doors, Iron Mounts, 78 1/2 In. 1550.00
Armoire, French Provincial, Pine, Adjustable Shelves, Hand Carved, 72 In. 895.00
Armoire, Fruitwood, Arched Top, Paneled Doors, Cabriole Legs, 94 1/2 In. 2100.00
Armoire, Georgian Style, 2 Doors, 4 Drawers, Walnut & Mahogany, 79 In. 1925.00
Armoire, Louis XIV, Oak, 1700s, Northern France 5500.00
Armoire, Louis XV, Floral Frieze Over Mirror, Walnut, 91 x 53 In. 3300.00
Armoire, Louis XV, Provincial, Arched Top, Paneled Doors, c.1760 .... 2640.00
Armoire, Louis XV, Provincial, Walnut, 2 Arched Doors, France, 1740, 88 In. 9500.00
Armoire, Louis XVI Revival, Walnut, Single Door, Columns, Drawer, 85 x 42 In. ... 1320.00
Armoire, Mahogany, Mirrored Door, Concealed Drawer, c.1850, 86 In. 3080.00
Armoire, Oak, Trophy of Doves & Bouquet Top, c.1800, 100 In. 4950.00
Armoire, Red Paint, 2 Flat Panel Doors, Bracket Brace, Cornice Top, Country 1450.00
Armoire, Renaissance Revival, Walnut, Paneled, 87 x 54 x 19 In. 1155.00
Armoire, Rosewood, Ogee Cornice, 2 Paneled Doors, 3 Interior Drawers, c.1850 ...... 3100.00
Armoire, Scandinavian, Partitioned, Floral Reserves, 1835, 6 Ft. 1 In. 4400.00
Armoire, Teak, Carved Double Doors, Dutch West Indies, 75 In. 1200.00
Armoire, Victorian, 1 Door, Rosewood Trim, Bird's–Eye Maple, c.1860 .... 3745.00
Armoire, Victorian, Eastlake, Carved Mahogany, Molded Top 775.00
Armoire, Victorian, Walnut, Paneled Doors, Drawers, Child's, 55 x 31 In. 775.00
Armoire, Walnut, Beveled Mirror, 1 Drawer, France, 19th Century 2200.00
Armoire, Walnut, Carved Apron, Moldings, Steel Hardware Design, 91 In. 2200.00
Armoire, Walnut, Double Doors, Veneer Columns, Drawers, c.1875, 89 x 55 In. 1265.00
Armoire, Walnut, Oak, Bird's–Eye Maple, 2 Doors, France, Mid–18th Century 3500.00
Bar, Art Deco, Amber Glass Inserts On Doors 80.00
Bed Steps, Commode, Empire, Mahogany, Red Leather, 18 x 22 x 17 In. 700.00
Bed Steps, Middle Step Slides Forward, Storage In Top Step, Mahogany, c.1860 ..... 495.00
Bed Steps, Potty On Top Step, Storage In Middle Step, Mahogany, c.1850 .... 550.00
Bed Steps, Victorian, Leather Treads, Side Handles, Mahogany, 28 In. 2400.00
Bed, Bird's–Eye Maple & Rosewood, Arched Headboard, c.1865, 78 In. 1750.00
Bed, Cannonball, Paneled Headboard, Columns, Ball Finials, Maple, 84 In., Pr. 1350.00
Bed, Cannonball, Poplar, Black Graining, Original Rails, Rope, 45 1/2 In. 275.00
Bed, Cannonball, Poplar, Red, Scrolled Headboard, Rope, 46 In. 190.00
Bed, Cannonball, Rope, Poplar, 40 In. 110.00
Bed, Canopy, Federal, Tall Post, Maple, Child's, 50 x 72 1/4 In. 1650.00
Bed, Canopy, Sheraton, Acanthus Carved Posts 3000.00
Bed, Canopy, Sheraton, Spiral Turned & Acanthus Leaf Posts, Full Size 3300.00
Bed, Curly Maple, Blanket Bar & Crest, Rope, 53 x 69 x 60 In. 1750.00
Bed, Curly Maple, Rope, 1830–1860 .... 2500.00
Bed, Four–Poster, Federal, Cherry, Finials, Solid Headboard, 1820, 81 x 84 In. 1300.00
Bed, Four–Poster, Molded Canopy, Fluted Columns, Painted Pine, 80 In. 1980.00
Bed, Four–Poster, Sheraton, Rope, 1830s, 7 Ft. 2 In. 2250.00
Bed, French Style, Carved Mahogany, N.Y., Child's, 1860 .... 6050.00
Bed, George Nakashima, Walnut, c.1870, Queen Size 2255.00
Bed, Grain–Painted Oyster Pattern Headboard, 1830 .... 2950.00
Bed, Gustav Stickley, Model No. 923, Oak, Tapering Head, 46 x 82 x 40 In. 1925.00
Bed, Gustav Stickley, Woven Rattan Mattress Support, Child's, 1904–1905 .... 4300.00
Bed, Half–Tester, Carved Egg In Ribboned Shell, P. Mallard, Child's, c.1855 .... 2420.00
Bed, Half–Tester, Eastlake, Walnut 1450.00
Bed, Half–Tester, Rococo Revival, Rosewood, New Orleans 4950.00
Bed, Jenny Lind, Spool, 1800s, Full Size 195.00
Bed, Jenny Lind, Walnut, 3/4 Size 260.00
Bed, Mallard, Rosewood, Cartouche Crest, Paneled Back, New Orleans, 1850 .... 4950.00
Bed, Maple & Poplar, New York, 1820–1830, Full Size 1300.00
Bed, Maple, Turned Posts, Scrolled Head & Foot Board, Rope, 53 x 46 In. 550.00
Bed, Murphy, Name Plate, With Brackets 150.00
Bed, Murphy, Oak, Beveled Mirror 510.00
Bed, Nakashima, Sliding Doors Headboard, Walnut, c.1970, 30 In. x 4 Ft. 6 In. 1450.00

Bed, Oak, Floral Crest, Acorn Finials, Upholstered Head & Foot Boards, 58 In. 770.00
Bed, Oak, Ornate Carving, Full Size 995.00
Bed, Plantation, Faceted Posts, Acorn Finials, Cherrywood, c.1840, 100 In. 3550.00
Bed, Poplar, Acorn Finial Posts, High Turned Feet, Early Blue Under Gray, Rope 500.00
Bed, Poplar, Turned Feet, Urn-Like Finials, Rope, 47 1/2 In. 100.00
Bed, Queen Anne, Hired Man, Turned Posts, Duck Feet, Red, 30 x 48 x 70 In. 335.00
Bed, Red & Black Graining, Stenciled Floral, Rope, 49 x 76 x 48 In. 413.00
Bed, Shaker, Lebanon, Maple, Pine, Salmon Ash, 1840, 81 x 36 x 36 In. 4290.00
Bed, Sleigh, Empire, Ormolu Mounts, Mahogany, c.1840, 56 x 74 In. 605.00
Bed, Sleigh, Scroll Ends, Leaf & Floral Carving, c.1845, 42 x 60 In. 2420.00
Bed, Sleigh, Scrolled Head & Foot Boards, Mahogany, c.1830, 77 x 76 In. 825.00
Bed, Sleigh, Striped Round End-Pillows, Child's, 1830s 2900.00
Bed, Tall Post, Arched Tester, Cherry, Child's, c.1800 .... 665.00
Bed, Tall Post, Bird's-Eye & Paneled Poplar Headboard, 85 In. 380.00
Bed, Tall Post, Federal, Maple, Cherry, Child's, 50 x 38 x 72 In. ....*Illus* 1650.00
Bed, Tall Post, Flat Canopy, Painted & Carved Cherry, 1810–1820, 81 x 77 In. 1550.00
Bed, Tester, Federal, Mahogany, Acanthus Posts, Angel, 85 x 52 In. 4400.00
Bed, Tiger Maple, Rope, 1810 .... 1650.00
Bed, Victorian, Draped With Wreaths, Ram Heads Headboard, Cast Iron, 76 In. 1200.00
Bed, Victorian, Walnut, Mattress & Springs, Side Rails, Full Size 3000.00
Bed, Walnut, Baby's, Victorian 235.00
Bedroom Set, Aesthetic Movement, Modern Gothic, Walnut, NYC, 3 Piece 3850.00
Bedroom Set, Berkey & Gay, Renaissance Revival, Walnut, 3 Piece 9000.00
Bedroom Set, Cottage, Brown Grain Painted, Hudson River Valley Scene, 3 Piece 2350.00
Bedroom Set, Cottage, Floral Gold Stripe Design, Late 19th Century, 5 Piece 550.00
Bedroom Set, High-Back Bed, Gentleman's Dresser & Commode, Oak 1700.00
Bedroom Set, Pre-Art Deco, Dark Finish, France, 7 Piece 6500.00
Bedroom Set, Walnut Veneer, 1930s, 3 Piece 400.00
Bench, Bear, Carved Walnut, Iron, Black Forest, 76 In. ....*Illus* 15400.00

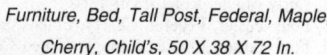

◆◆◆◆◆◆◆◆◆◆◆◆◆◆◆◆◆◆◆◆◆◆

Never scrub threaded coral
beads. The edges of the coral
are so sharp they may cut the
bead string.

◆◆◆◆◆◆◆◆◆◆◆◆◆◆◆◆◆◆◆◆◆◆

Furniture, Bed, Tall Post, Federal, Maple,
Cherry, Child's, 50 X 38 X 72 In.

Furniture, Bench, Bear, Carved Walnut, Iron, Black Forest, 76 In.

Bench, Cherry, Low Back, Rush Seat, 19th Century 38.50
Bench, Chippendale Style, Cabriole Legs, Damask Upholstery, Mahogany, 44 In. 150.00
Bench, Daybed, Clarks Flat Boards, Moose Antler Legs, 1910–1915, 4 Piece 4500.00
Bench, Deacon's, Empire, Maple, 69 In. 440.00
Bench, Deacon's, Federal, Hardwood, 70 In. 495.00
Bench, Deacon's, Heraldic Shield Crest, Carved Female Armrests, Oak, 56 In. 2450.00
Bench, Directoire Style, Upholstery, Parcel Gilt, Fruitwood, 22 In. 220.00
Bench, Dresser, Scroll End With Lion Head, Cast Iron, 24 In. 138.00
Bench, Empire, Claw Footed, Carved Ram's Heads On Arms 410.00
Bench, Fireplace, Columnar Supports, Brass, 62 In. 445.00
Bench, Folding, Slatted, 19th Century, 58 In. 200.00
Bench, Fruits & Flowers On Crest, Shaped Splats, Painted Yellow, 80 In. 550.00
Bench, George III, Upholstered Seat, Marlborough Legs, Mahogany, 18 x 21 In. 335.00
Bench, Georgian, Walnut, Oval Upholstered Seat, Cabriole Legs, 18 x 17 x 12 In. ... 300.00
Bench, Gothic Revival, Hinged Seat, Walnut, 62 1/4 In. 1100.00
Bench, Hardwoods, Brown Finish, White Upholstered Cushions, 76 In. 165.00
Bench, Hickory, Arms 450.00
Bench, Limbert, No. 95, Lift–Up Seat, New Black Leather, 48 x 46 In. 1320.00
Bench, Louis XV Style, Beechwood, Floral Upholstery, 22 In. 275.00
Bench, Louis XVI Style, Caned Sides & Seat, Giltwood, 34 In. 770.00
Bench, Mammy's, Green–Blue Paint, Stenciling 825.00
Bench, Mammy's, Pine, Red & Black Grain Painted, Yellow Stencil, Arms 880.00
Bench, Paneled Back, 3 Marquetry Floral Medallions, Dutch, 71 In. 1760.00
Bench, Piano, Fluted Legs, Walnut 50.00
Bench, Pine, Dark Finish, Bootjack Feet, Mortised Through Top, Country, 18 In. ... 175.00
Bench, Pine, Pencil Post Legs, 17 1/2 x 39 1/2 In. 155.00
Bench, Pine, Wire Nail Construction, 8 1/4 In. 59.00
Bench, Platform, George Nelson 1350.00
Bench, Queen Anne, Walnut, Upholstered Slip Seat, 6 Cabriole Legs, 40 x 17 In. 360.00
Bench, Rocking, Arrow Back Slats, 89 In. 225.00
Bench, Rococo, Out–Turned Arms, Serpentine Seat, Italy, 1750s, 85 In. 1450.00
Bench, Stickley Brothers, Spindles, Cutout Upper Slats, 18 x 13 x 14 In. 195.00
Bench, Streetcar, Reversible Back, Iron & Wood, 30 x 72 1/2 In. 275.00
Bench, Trolley Station, Spindle Back, Hinged Metal Arms That Flip, 7 Ft. 6 In. 545.00
Bench, Venetian, Floral Carved Apron, Painted Wood, 26 In. 1650.00
Bench, Water, Pine, 2 Raised Panel Doors, Tombstone Ends 440.00
Bench, Water, Pine, Poplar, Paneled Doors, 1 Shelf, 45 1/2 In. 2750.00
Bench, Water, Pine, Repaint, Canted Legs, Dovetailed, 12 x 32 In. 270.00
Bench, Water, Poplar, Varnished, Paneled Doors, Open Shelf, 47 1/2 In. 1000.00
Bench, Window, Directoire Style, Gilt Outline, Mahogany, 42 In. 660.00
Bench, Window, Louis XV Style, Walnut, c.1870, 29 In. 550.00
Bench, Window, Scrolled Sides, Caned Seat, Grained Rosewood, c.1820, 4 Ft. 3575.00
Bench, Windsor, Splayed Base, Wide Shaped Seat, Turned Arms Support, 35 In. 5500.00
Bench–Table, Tilt Top, Plank Seat, Frieze Drawer, Maple & Pine, 78 In. 4400.00
Bidet, Louis XV, Carved Back Rest, Carved Seat, Opens To Faience, Pine 1100.00
Bin, Pine, 2 Drawers, Dovetailed, Slant Front, Turned Feet, 38 x 18 x 41 In. 715.00
Bin, Pine, Dark Paint, Angled Sides, 39 In. 71.00
Bonheur Du Jour, Napoleon II, Ormolu Mounted Marquetry Inlaid 2640.00
Book Rack, Stickley Bros., Cutout Handles, 30 3/4 x 33 In. 465.00
Book Trough, Lifetime, No. 260, Tenon Construction, Label, 29 x 14 x 20 In. 705.00
Bookcase, 2 Doors, Arched Top, 3 Carved Rosettes, Walnut, 83 1/2 In. 425.00
Bookcase, 2 Doors, Center Blind Door, Mythological Figures Side Supports 5000.00
Bookcase, 2 Doors, Center Curved Glass Door, Mahogany, c.1910, 69 In. 1650.00
Bookcase, 3 Doors, Frieze of Masks, Side Columns, Mahogany, c.1900 .... 2420.00
Bookcase, Art Nouveau, Oak, Sliding Door, Floral Carved 325.00
Bookcase, Arts & Crafts, 2 Doors With 8 Mullioned Windows, 53 x 46 In. 1100.00
Bookcase, Bronze Mounted, Mahogany, Glazed Vitrine, France, c.1930, 7 Ft. 4400.00
Bookcase, Directoire Style, Glazed Door, 56 x 40 In. 385.00
Bookcase, Drop Front, Texas Cedar, Walnut, Handmade, Mid–1800s 7500.00
Bookcase, Ebonized Oak, c.1870, 110 x 95 In. 6600.00
Bookcase, Georgian, Mahogany, Cupboard Base, Glazed Doors, 86 x 34 In. 1320.00
Bookcase, Georgian, Mahogany, Open Shelf, c.1800, 78 x 49 x 11 In. 550.00
Bookcase, Georgian, Pine, 3 Sections, Lattice Doors, Molded Base, 86 x 102 In. 200.00

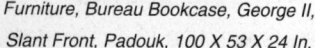

Furniture, Bureau Bookcase, George II,
Slant Front, Padouk, 100 X 53 X 24 In.

Furniture, Bureau, George III, Cylinder Front,
Late 18th Century

Bookcase, Glass & Paneled Doors, 2 Drawers, Shelves, c.1880, 91 x 44 In. 1875.00
Bookcase, Globe Wernicke, Oak, c.1900, 88 In. 550.00
Bookcase, Globe Wernicke, Oak, Stacking, 4 Sections 575.00
Bookcase, Globe Wernicke, Oak, Stacking, Drawer In Base, 3 Sections 565.00
Bookcase, Gustav Stickley, 1 Door, 16 Panes, 54 x 36 In. 4500.00
Bookcase, Gustav Stickley, 2 Doors, Tenon & Key, V–Pulls, 56 x 42 x 13 In. 4400.00
Bookcase, Gustav Stickley, No. 716, 2 Doors 3575.00
Bookcase, Gustav Stickley, No. 717, 2 Doors, Label, 48 x 56 x 13 In. 3300.00
Bookcase, Limbert, 5 Interior & Exterior Shelves, Rectangular Cutouts 8250.00
Bookcase, Louis XV, Oak, 92 x 52 x 21 In. 3500.00
Bookcase, Mahogany, 3 Doors, Curved & Beveled Glass 4675.00
Bookcase, Mahogany, Ogee Frieze Over 3 Drawers, Gothic Fretting, 64 1/4 In. 305.00
Bookcase, Mission, Oak, c.1910, 54 x 39 x 13 In. 400.00
Bookcase, Regency, Mahogany, 2 Glazed Mullion Doors, Lower Doors, 589 In. 9900.00
Bookcase, Regency, Mahogany, Column, Drawer On Bun Feet, 17 x 20 x 6 In. 100.00
Bookcase, Stacking, Drop Front Desk, Pigeon Holes, 4 Drawers, 4 Piece 800.00
Bookcase, Stacking, Harvard, 6 Sections, Bottom Drawer, 86 In. 2145.00
Bookcase, Stacking, Oak, 4 Sections, Leaded Glass Top 750.00
Bookcase, Step Back, Red & Black Grain Painted, 2 Glazed Doors, 80 x 48 In. 6600.00
Bookcase, Stickley Bros., 2 Doors, 3 Mullion Windows Over Large, 52 x 35 In. 880.00
Bookcase, Victorian, Glazed Doors, Molded Base, Cyprus, 98 x 48 In. 1210.00
Bookcase, Victorian, Walnut, Dentil, 2 Sliding Glass Doors, 37 x 22 x 84 In. 440.00
Bracket, Infant Bacchus Atop Eagle In Flight, 1860s, 24 1/2 In. 5775.00
Breakfront, Art Nouveau, Mahogany, Carved, Doors, Shelves, 79 x 22 3/4 In. 1350.00
Breakfront, Lacquered, Mother–of–Pearl, China, 85 x 106 In. 2400.00
Breakfront, Mahogany, Paneled Base Doors, Geometric Mullions, 89 In. 3700.00
Breakfront, Marble Top, Gilt Bronze Mounts, 54 In. 8000.00
Buffet, Louis XV Provincial, Drawers Over Cabinet Doors, Oak, 18th Century 1430.00
Buffet, Mission, Larkin, Beveled Glass Backsplash 200.00
Buffet, Oak, 2 Half Drawers, Full Drawer & Cupboard, Mirrored Back 125.00
Buffet, Oak, 4 Drawers, Leaded Glass Doors, Mirror Back 1600.00
Buffet, Oak, Carved, Brown Marble Serving Area, Curved Top Cabinet, Bonnet 2495.00
Buffet, Southern Pine, Oak Trim, Gallery, 2 Drawers Over 2 Doors 400.00
Bureau Bookcase, George II, Slant Front, Padouk, 100 x 53 x 24 In. ....*Illus* 7150.00
Bureau Bookcase, Mahogany, Mirrored Doors, Candle Slides, 6 Ft. 10 In. 6325.00
Bureau Bookcase, Pilasters, Crackle White Over Blue, Country, 94 In. 7500.00
Bureau Desk, Burled Walnut, Slant Front, Cross Banding, 18th Century, England ... 6600.00
Bureau Desk, Drop Front, Fitted Interior, Mid–19th Century 375.00
Bureau, Chippendale, Cherry, Serpentine, 4 Graduated Drawers, 1770, 42 In. 9350.00
Bureau, Chippendale, Red Paint, 4 Drawers, Country, 38 x 36 x 19 In. 2470.00

Furniture, Bureau, George III, Slant Front,
Mahogany, 18th Century, 42 In.

Furniture, Bureau, William & Mary,
Slant Front, 1690, 37 1/2 X 38 1/2 In.

Bureau, Chippendale, Slant Front, 4 Drawers, Tiger Maple, New England 6600.00
Bureau, George III, Cylinder Front, Late 18th Century ....*Illus* 8250.00
Bureau, George III, Slant Front, Mahogany, 18th Century, 42 In. ....*Illus* 6600.00
Bureau, Grain Painted, New England, 1830, 9 1/2 In. 660.00
Bureau, Hepplewhite, Bow Front, 4 Drawers, Mahogany, String Inlay, 35 In. 2480.00
Bureau, Liberty & Co., Fall Front, Fitted Interior, Oak, 40 3/4 x 38 1/2 In. 1170.00
Bureau, William & Mary, Slant Front, 1690, 37 1/2 x 38 1/2 In. ....*Illus* 8800.00
Cabinet, Apothecary, Grain Painted, 76 1/2 x 60 In. 3300.00
Cabinet, Apothecary, Porcelain Pulls, Grain Varnish Finish, Early 1800s 1500.00
Cabinet, Art Nouveau, Green Glazed Doors, Carved Iris, France, 1900, 4 Ft. 8 In. 1980.00
Cabinet, Bishop's, Red Oak, 16 Small & 12 Large Drawers, 1920, 8 Ft. 9 In. x 8 Ft. 1700.00
Cabinet, Boone Kitchen, Porcelain Top, Bread Box, Cutting Board, Sifter 650.00
Cabinet, Carved Oak, Lotus Pod–Form Handles, Foliage, c.1930, 38 In. 1650.00
Cabinet, China, 2 Glass Doors, 1 Drawer, 1920s 350.00
Cabinet, China, 2 Glass Doors, Full Drawer, 2 Lower Doors, Walnut, 7 Ft. 3 In. ... 750.00
Cabinet, China, 2 Gray Glazed Doors, Glazed Sides, Golden Oak, 59 In. 165.00
Cabinet, China, Arts & Crafts, 2 Doors, Mirror, 3 Shelves, 42 x 64 x 15 In. 1320.00
Cabinet, China, Cherry, Beveled Glass Doors, Hand Carved, 72 x 66 In. 3800.00
Cabinet, China, Glass Doors, Split Drawer Case, Mahogany, 75 1/2 In. .... · 304.00
Cabinet, China, Gray & Baffy Co., Mahogany, Glass Sides & Door, 1900s 1150.00
Cabinet, China, Gustav Stickley, Oak, 2 Doors, 8 Glazed Panels, 1912, 4 Ft. 8 In. 1320.00
Cabinet, China, Hepplewhite Style, Grill Work Over Glass Doors, Mahogany, 81 In. 350.00
Cabinet, China, L. & J. Stickley, No. 746, Mullioned Square Doors, Arched Apron 2860.00
Cabinet, China, Limbert, No. 452, 1 Door, Shelves, 58 x 45 x 16 In. 3630.00
Cabinet, China, Triple Curved Glass, Columns, Claw Feet 1350.00
Cabinet, China, With Butler's Desk, Bowed Door, Victorian 795.00
Cabinet, Chippendale, Mahogany, Carved Base, Lions Head, 45 1/4 In. 995.00
Cabinet, Cincinnati Shop of Crafters, Leaded Roundels 800.00
Cabinet, Corner, Art Deco, Mahogany, Gilt Bronze, France, 35 1/2 In. 2420.00
Cabinet, Corner, Mahogany, Inlaid, Curved Glass Doors, Early 20th Century 550.00
Cabinet, Curio, Chippendale, Mahogany, Mirror Back, Lattice Sides & Fronts 960.00
Cabinet, Curio, Hanging, Ebonized Walnut, Beveled Glass Doors, Mirror, 1880s 205.00
Cabinet, Curio, Louis XV Style, Curved Glass, Couple Painted At Base, 55 1/2 In. 3800.00
Cabinet, Curio, Louis XV, Courting Scene, 77 x 35 x 17 In. ....*Illus* 3250.00
Cabinet, Curio, Mahogany Veneer, Figured Wood, 57 In. 525.00
Cabinet, Curio, Mahogany, 2 Shelves, Claw & Ball Feet, Curved Ends 200.00
Cabinet, Curio, Mahogany, 4 Shelves, Curved Glass 950.00
Cabinet, Curio, Oak, Double Glass Doors, 2 Drawers, c.1900, 70 1/2 x 50 In. 825.00
Cabinet, Display, Glass Door, Shelves, Pine, Miniature 30.00
Cabinet, Display, Ivory Inlaid Winged Lovers, Ebonized, c.1880, 82 1/2 In. ....· 3300.00

Cabinet, Display, Victorian, Oak, Carved, Leaded Glass Door, c.1880, 72 x 38 In. ... 1320.00
Cabinet, Filing, Oak, Tambour Compartments, Shelves, 74 1/2 x 36 In. 465.00
Cabinet, Filing, Stacking, Yawman & Erb, 5 Sections, Oak, 78 1/4 In. 385.00
Cabinet, Framed, Six Drawer, Shaker, 40 1/2 x 26 x 10 In. 1100.00
Cabinet, Hanging, Tiger Maple, Raised Tombstone Panel In Door, 18th Century 3530.00
Cabinet, Hoosier, Frosted Glass Doors, Zinc Work Surface, Oak 900.00
Cabinet, Hoosier, Roll–Up Door, Doors At Top, Porcelain Surface, Oak, 48 In. 700.00
Cabinet, Hoosier, Slag Glass, Porcelain Top, Sliding Door Over Sifter, 1925 .... 975.00
Cabinet, Jelly, 2 Drawers, 3 Board, 50 x 37 x 12 In. 400.00
Cabinet, Jewel, Regency, 1 Drawer, Leopard Head Handles, 4 1/2 x 11 In. 500.00
Cabinet, Kitchen, American Cabinet Co., White Marble Top, Sterilizer Cupboard 750.00
Cabinet, Kitchen, Boone, Sifter, Bread Box, Board, Porcelain Top, Oak 650.00
Cabinet, Kitchen, Oak, Top Doors, Drawers In Base, 9 x 7 Ft. 850.00
Cabinet, Kitchen, Sellers, Porcelain Work Surface 475.00
Cabinet, Lacquered, Japan, 25 x 22 In. 400.00
Cabinet, Liquor, Lifetime, Strap Hinged Door, Copper Pullout Tray, 32 x 24 In. 1650.00
Cabinet, Liquor, Metal, Tray, Overhanging Top, Handles, Green Glass, 35 In. 440.00
Cabinet, Louis XVI Style, Curved Glass Sides, 3 Shelves, Gilt, 1920, 55 In. 935.00
Cabinet, Marie Philipp, Demilune Upper, Marquetry Foliate, Mahogany & Bronze ... 5500.00
Cabinet, Mirrored & Reverse Painted Glass, Doors, Austria, 80 In. 3950.00
Cabinet, Mission Style, Oak, 28 In. 175.00
Cabinet, Music, 1 Glass Door, 4 Shelves, Inlay 100.00
Cabinet, Music, 1 Leaded Glass Door, Adjustable Shelves, Label, c.1907, 46 3/4 In. ... 4400.00
Cabinet, Music, Aesthetic Movement, Ebonized, Inlay, 1880s 445.00
Cabinet, Music, Gustav Stickley, Leaded Glass Doors 4400.00
Cabinet, Music, Oak, Beveled Mirror, Backsplash 275.00
Cabinet, Oak, Rotating, 100 Drawers of Various Sizes, Base, 1890 .... 700.00
Cabinet, Red Leather Book Stack Shape, Stamped Dumas, 17 x 24 x 28 In. 445.00
Cabinet, Regency, 2 Doors, Columns, c.1830 .... 220.00
Cabinet, Satinwood Inlay, Bronze Trim, France, 1900 .... 2400.00
Cabinet, Sewing, Cherry, Lift Top, Needlepoint Footrest, France, Mid–1800s 650.00
Cabinet, Shaving, Mirror Inside Door, Burl Walnut 138.00
Cabinet, Sheet Music, Oak 160.00
Cabinet, Side, Walnut, 2 Doors, Mirror Panel, Shelf, Finials, 50 x 40 x 14 In. 4650.00
Cabinet, Smoker's, Gustav Stickley, Door With Inset Panel, 29 In. 2750.00
Cabinet, Wall, Carved Doors, Open Arch Bottom, 20 x 16 x 7 In. 650.00
Cabinet–On–Stand, Queen Anne, Allover Chinoiseries, Black Japanned, 5 Ft. 5 In. ... 3025.00
Candlestand, Birch Base, Mahogany Top, Spider Legs, 28 3/4 In. 125.00
Candlestand, Birch, Grain Painted Top, Cut Corner, Snake Foot 3500.00
Candlestand, Cherry, 8 Sides, Vase Turned Pedestal, U.S., 16 x 22 In. 465.00

To remove an unpleasant smell from an old chest of drawers, try this: Put the piece outdoors in the shade. Plug in a fan and blow air through the drawers and frame. If that does not work after several days, fill the drawers with baking soda, cat litter, or charcoal chips, which may absorb the odor.

Furniture, Cabinet, Curio, Louis XV,
Courting Scene, 77 X 35 X 17 In.

Candlestand, Cherry, Scimitar Legs, Turned Column, 17 3/4 x 18 x 27 3/4 In. 335.00
Candlestand, Cherry, Tripod Base, Turned Column, 2 Board Top, 28 In. 198.00
Candlestand, Cherry, Tripod, Spider Legs, Matthew Allen, 17 x 18 x 29 In. ....:. 525.00
Candlestand, Chippendale, Cherry, Tripod, Snake Feet, Square Top, Country, 16 In. 435.00
Candlestand, Chippendale, Mahogany, c.1780, 29 In. 880.00
Candlestand, Chippendale, Maple, Tripod, Snake Feet, Country, 16 x 17 In. 550.00
Candlestand, Chippendale, Tilt Top, Maple, 28 1/2 x 17 In. 1430.00
Candlestand, Crotch Walnut, Ball & Claw Feet 6325.00
Candlestand, Curly Maple, Tripod Base, Snake Feet, 28 1/2 In. 1540.00
Candlestand, Cut Corner Top, Tiger Maple Shaft, Cherry Legs, Shaker, 1840 .... 5225.00
Candlestand, Cutout Top, Spade Foot 1800.00
Candlestand, Dish Top, Snake Foot, Red Paint 850.00
Candlestand, Federal, Cherry, Conn., 1800, 19 x 21 x 17 In. 440.00
Candlestand, Federal, Cherry, Conn., 1800, 26 x 17 x 17 In. 990.00
Candlestand, Federal, Cherry, Inlay Top, Rhode Island, Late 18th Century 2250.00
Candlestand, Federal, Cherry, Turned Center, Trifid Base, Rectangular Top, Pair ... 935.00
Candlestand, Federal, Lozenge Form, Tilt Top, Walnut, 26 In. 605.00
Candlestand, Federal, Mahogany, Lift Top, c.1800, 28 x 22 In. 1870.00
Candlestand, Federal, Mahogany, Serpentine Top, Tripod Base, 28 x 21 x 21 In. 4500.00
Candlestand, Federal, Mahogany, Tilt Top, N. H., 1800, 28 x 22 x 16 In. 1870.00
Candlestand, Federal, Tripod, Maple & Cherry, 26 1/2 In. 195.00
Candlestand, Hardwood Base, 1 Board Top, Yellow Pine, 28 1/4 In. 200.00
Candlestand, Hepplewhite, Birch, Oval Top, Spider Legs, 15 x 21 3/4 x 29 1/2 In. 300.00
Candlestand, Hepplewhite, Tripod Base, Spider Legs, 1 Board Top, 29 In. 220.00
Candlestand, Hepplewhite, Tripod Base, Spider Legs, 28 1/2 In. 467.00
Candlestand, Maple, Walnut, Tripod Base, Snake Feet, Round Top, 29 In. 495.00
Candlestand, Poplar, Oak, Round Base, Adjustable Shelf, 32 1/2 In. 415.00
Candlestand, Queen Anne, Snake Feet, Shaped Top 1265.00
Candlestand, Ratchet, Red Paint, Maple, Ash & Poplar, 18th Century, 32 1/2 In. 275.00
Candlestand, Regency, Faceted Top, Elm Wood, 27 In. 605.00
Candlestand, Regency, Tripod Base, Burl Maple, Octagonal, 30 In. 445.00
Candlestand, Scrolled Shelf, Red Paint, 50 1/2 In. 1320.00
Candlestand, Shaker, Cobbler's, New Lebanon 695.00
Candlestand, Tilt Top, Cherry, Refinished, c.1790, 25 1/4 In. 935.00
Candlestand, Tilt Top, Federal, Mahogany, Octagonal, Mass., 1800, 28 x 16 In. 1210.00
Candlestand, Tilt Top, Tripod Base, Walnut, Octagonal Shape, Snake Feet, 29 In. ... 770.00
Candlestand, Tilt Top, Wavy Birch, Saber Leg, Octagonal 1045.00
Candlestand, Tripod Base, 1 Board Top, Turned Column, Walnut, 21 x 31 In. 250.00
Candlestand, Tripod Base, Adjustable Rod, Candle Arm, Iron 220.00
Candlestand, Tripod Base, Curved Legs, Oval Feet, Iron, 53 1/2 In. 1760.00
Candlestand, Tripod Base, Tiger Maple, Snake Feet, New England, 25 1/2 In. 3100.00
Candlestand, Tripod Base, Walnut, Snake Feet, 1 Board Top, 29 In. 550.00
Candlestand, Tripod Base, Walnut, Worn Paint, Snake Feet, Turtle Back, 15 In. 495.00
Candlestand, William & Mary, Walnut, Dish Top, Barley Twist, 20 x 13 In. 275.00
Candlestand, Wooden, Tin Sockets, 30 1/2 In. 300.00
Canterbury, 1 Top Drawer, Rosewood 2425.00
Canterbury, 3–Spindled Sections, Drawer, Bun Feet, Walnut, c.1860, 37 1/4 In. 600.00
Canterbury, Regency, 1 Drawer, Mahogany, Ebony Inlay, Hinged Lid, 20 1/2 In. ... 4125.00
Canterbury, Rosewood, Carved, Early 19th Century, 10 1/2 x 18 1/2 In. 1750.00
Canterbury, Rosewood, Yellow, Marble Top 1000.00
Cart, Flower, 2 Shelves, Wire 450.00
Case, Gun, Leaded Glass Doors, Bottom Drawer, Oak 250.00
Cellarette, Ebony Inlay, Figured Veneer, Rosewood, 10 1/4 x 13 1/4 In. 1450.00
Cellarette, George III, Crossbanded Lid, Divided Interior, Mahogany, 27 In. 4400.00
Cellarette, George III, Oval, Lead–Lined, Brass Feet & Casters, c.1800, 27 1/2 In. 1650.00
Cellarette, Georgian, Brass Bound, Oval, 16 x 22 In. 1750.00
Cellarette, Gustav Stickley, No. 86 .... 3025.00
Cellarette, Walnut, Cherry & Pine, 1840s, 35 In. 4000.00
Cellarette, Walnut, Wild Cherry, Yellow Pine, Southern, 17 In. Wide 4400.00
Cellarette, William IV, Sarcophagus Form, England 2750.00
Chair & Ottoman, Eames, Black Leather Upholstery, Rosewood, Arms :............. 2700.00
Chair Set, Art Nouveau, Carved Floral Designs, Eugene Gaillard, Oak, c.1900, 3 .... 835.00
Chair Set, Asian, Carved Ebony, c.1820, 3 .... 3000.00

Furniture, Chair Set, Biedermeier, Birch, Ebonized, 19th Century

Chair Set, Ballroom, Ivory Glaze, Openwork Back, Upholstered Seat, 12 .... 885.00
Chair Set, Biedermeier, Birch, Ebonized, 19th Century, 4 ....*Illus* 3300.00
Chair Set, Bird's-Eye Maple & Maple, Rush Seat, Double Box Stretcher, 6 .... 600.00
Chair Set, Brown Paint, Decorated Plank Seat, 31 3/4 In., 6 .... 375.00
Chair Set, Chippendale, Carved Mahogany, New England, 1775, 38 In., 8 .... 8250.00
Chair Set, Chippendale, Upholstered Seats, Country, 6 .... 3465.00
Chair Set, Chrome, 1940, 4 .... 485.00
Chair Set, Classical, Splayed Leg, Upholstered Seat, 12 .... 6000.00
Chair Set, Continental, Acanthus & Floral Crest, Projecting Ears, Mahogany, 4 ..... 2200.00
Chair Set, Dining, Cherry, Reticulated Bamboo Back Splat, Upholstered, 12 .... 3300.00
Chair Set, Dining, Chippendale, Carved Mahogany, 8 .... 8250.00
Chair Set, Dining, Empire, Fruitwood, Italy, 6 .... 7150.00
Chair Set, Dining, George II Style, Heart-Shaped Splat, Walnut, 2 Armchairs, 8 ..... 8850.00
Chair Set, Dining, Georgian Style, Mahogany, 8 .... 4950.00
Chair Set, Dining, Hepplewhite, Needlepoint Seat, 1780, 4 .... 900.00
Chair Set, Dining, Jacques Adnet, Limed Oak, Aubusson Tapestry Upholstery, 10 ... 4400.00
Chair Set, Dining, Limbert, Crest Rail, Single Back Slat, Drop Seat, 5 .... 1100.00
Chair Set, Dining, Plywood, Black Aniline Dye, c.1946, 6 .... 4125.00
Chair Set, Dining, Provincial Louis XV, Fruitwood, France, 9 .... 1980.00
Chair Set, Dining, Queen Anne Style, Urn-Shaped Back Splat, Walnut, 6 .... 685.00
Chair Set, Dining, Seignoret, Carved Mahogany, c.1840, 8 .... 4180.00
Chair Set, Dining, Sheraton, Pale Green Paint, Gold Design, Rush Seat, 5 .... 885.00
Chair Set, Dining, Tiger Maple, Rush Seat, 6 .... 3300.00
Chair Set, Dining, William IV, Arched Crest Rail, Upholstered Seat, c.1835, 6 .... 1985.00
Chair Set, Eames, Plywood, Pony Skin Upholstery, c.1946, 4 .... 3100.00
Chair Set, Empire Style, Curved Out Backrest, Ebony Lacquer, France, 8 .... 6655.00
Chair Set, Empire, Black, Gold Striping, Design, Red, Gold, Black, 34 In., 6 .... 429.00
Chair Set, Empire, Fiddle Back, Saber Leg, 12 .... 3245.00
Chair Set, Empire, Flame Grained, Black, Yellow Striped, Rose Stencil, Country, 6 1225.00
Chair Set, Faux Bamboo, Open Back, Caned Seat, 1850s, 4 .... 2200.00
Chair Set, Federal, Paw Foot, Mahogany, 8 .... 1000.00
Chair Set, Federal, Rabbit Ear Stiles, Rush Seat, 1 Armchair, 6 .... 1100.00
Chair Set, Federal, Shield Back, Mahogany, Upholstered Seat, N.Y., 1800, 4 .... 2550.00
Chair Set, Fiddle Back, Caned Seat, Turned Legs, Pennsylvania, 1840-1850, 6 .... 2250.00
Chair Set, George III, Yoked C Above Pierced Splat, Slip Seat, Mahogany, 6 .... 3750.00
Chair Set, Georgian, Carved Mahogany, Drake Feet, 6 .... 7425.00
Chair Set, Georgian, Carved Mahogany, Floral Upholstered Seats, 12 .... 3630.00
Chair Set, Gondola, Mahogany, Upholstered Seats, 12 .... 6050.00
Chair Set, Gothic Revival, Mahogany, Upholstery, 1 Child's Size, 3 .... 1100.00
Chair Set, Gothic Revival, Pointed Arch, Pierced Back, Plank Seat, Oak, 4 .... 2550.00
Chair Set, Gustav Stickley, 3 Back Slats, Tacked Leather Seat, 36 In., 5 .... 1250.00
Chair Set, Gustav Stickley, 3 Slats, Leather Slip Seats, 39 In. 6 .... 2750.00
Chair Set, Half Arrow-Back, Worn Yellow Paint, Green Striping, Stenciled, 6 .... 750.00
Chair Set, Hans Wegner, Molded Plywood Rail & Seat, Ash, c.1950, 6 .... 3575.00
Chair Set, Hitchcock, Rush Seat, Red, Black Grained, Gilt Stenciled, Armchair, 6 ... 3600.00
Chair Set, Hitchcock, Stenciled, Dark Finish, 6 .... 550.00

Chair Set, L. & J. G. Stickley, 6 .... 2600.00
Chair Set, Ladder Back, 4 Slats, Rush Seat, 19th Century, 38 In., 6 .... 770.00
Chair Set, Ladder Back, Reddish Brown, 1 Armchair, 43 In., 5 .... 685.00
Chair Set, Ladder Back, Rush Seat, 2 Armchairs, 8 .... 2475.00
Chair Set, Mahogany, Shield Back, Boston, 4 .... 9500.00
Chair Set, Maple, Pierced Splat, Splayed Legs, 35 In., 6 .... 770.00
Chair Set, Neoclassical, Gilt Stenciled Musical Trophies On Legs, Arms, 4 .... 8800.00
Chair Set, Neoclassical, Outscrolled Backrest, Brass Mounted, Russia, 4 .... 6600.00
Chair Set, Oak, Pressed Back, 5 Spindles, 6 .... 2495.00
Chair Set, Oak, Rectangular Back, Finials, Slats, Upholstered Seat, 4 .... 780.00
Chair Set, Oak, Scrolled Pierced Crest, Double Splat, Rush Seat, Victorian, 8 .... 665.00
Chair Set, Olive Paint, Gold & Black Design, New England, 1800, 2 Armchairs, 8 1750.00
Chair Set, Painted Fruit Stencil, 1875, 6 .... 1400.00
Chair Set, Plank Bottom, Angel Wing Crests, Apple Green Paint, 6 .... 1600.00
Chair Set, Pressed Back & Seat, Oak, Gargoyles, 5 .... 475.00
Chair Set, Pressed Back, Oak, Spool Turned Splats, Cane Seats, 6 .... 375.00
Chair Set, Queen Anne Style, Slip Seat, Brocade Upholstery, Mahogany, 6 .... 1800.00
Chair Set, Regency, Musical Trophies Painted Crest, Caned Back & Seat, Arms, 4 8250.00
Chair Set, Regency, Scrolled Crest, Brass Foliage, Inlay, 1830s, 6 .... 7150.00
Chair Set, Regency, Scrolled Top Rail, Drop-In Upholstered Seat, Ebonized, 6 .... 1550.00
Chair Set, Ribbon Back, Upholstered Seats, 1850, 8 .... 3950.00
Chair Set, Rounded Back & Seat, Ball Feet, Upholstery, Arms, 34 In., 4 .... 1325.00
Chair Set, Salem, Mahogany, Acanthus Splats, Upholstered Seat, 1800, 5 .... 7800.00
Chair Set, Sheraton Style, Mahogany, Shield Form Back, Upholstered Seat, 8 .... 2475.00
Chair Set, Sheraton, Empire, Hand Painted Floral, Grain Design, Rush Seat, 5 .... 550.00
Chair Set, Sheraton, Rush Seat, Stenciled Back, Original Paint, 2 Armchairs, 6 .... 1200.00
Chair Set, Sheraton, Rush Seat, Stenciled, 5 .... 413.00
Chair Set, Slat Back, Woven Seat, 1820, 6 .... 3800.00
Chair Set, Stickley Bros., Rush Seat, 6 .... 2700.00
Chair Set, Thumb Back, Mustard Paint, Stenciled, 6 .... 4800.00
Chair Set, Thumb Back, Yellow Paint, Design, Putty Grained Seats, 6 .... 9350.00
Chair Set, Vase-Shaped Back, Saber Legs, Silk Upholstered Seats, 8 .... 3850.00
Chair Set, Walnut, Cane Seat, c.1890, 7 .... 265.00
Chair Set, Walnut, Demi-Arms, Cane Seats, Victorian, 6 .... 125.00
Chair Set, William & Mary, Carved Gesso & Giltwood, 1740s, 4 .... 4500.00
Chair Set, Windsor, Birdcage, Black Paint, 6 .... 225.00
Chair Set, Windsor, Bow Back, 6 .... 2750.00
Chair Set, Windsor, Hoop Back, New England, 1810, 5 .... 4200.00
Chair Set, Yellow Paint, Fruit Design, Half-Spindle, Plank, 1855, 4 .... 500.00
Chair Set, Yew Wood, England, 34 1/2 In., 8 .... 335.00
Chair Table, Lift-Up Seat, Storage Space Underneath 875.00
Chair Table, Oak, Oval Top, Wood Peg Constructions, Large 6050.00
Chair, Abalone Inlay, Papier-Mache, Victorian, c.1870 .... 520.00
Chair, Airline, Kem Weber, c.1934 .... 8250.00
Chair, Anglo-Portuguese Style, Eagle Splat, Green Stained Mahogany, Pair 600.00
Chair, Arrow-Back, Plank Seat, Worn Finish, 36 In., Pair 90.00
Chair, Arrow-Back, Stenciled Design, Painted, 19th Century 23.00
Chair, Arrow-Back, Thumb Back, Black, Brown & Green Design, Pair 2750.00
Chair, Arrow-Back, Windsor, Bamboo Turnings, Shaped Seats, 35 In., Pair 225.00
Chair, Art Deco, Hardwood, Mahogany Finish, 42 In. 137.00
Chair, Art Nouveau, Crest & Skirt Carved Cartouches, Giltwood, c.1910 .... 1350.00
Chair, Arts & Crafts, Ladder Back, Rush Seats, Jos. McHugh, Pair 495.00
Chair, Balloon Back, Fruit & Leaf Carving, Walnut, Victorian 60.00
Chair, Ballroom, Faux Rosewood Grained, Walnut, c.1860, Pair 132.00
Chair, Banister Back, Black Paint, Arms, 1780s 2550.00
Chair, Banister Back, Black Paint, New England, Arms, c.1710 .... 6800.00
Chair, Banister Back, Black Paint, Shaped Crest, Worn Splint Seat 445.00
Chair, Banister Back, Black Repaint, Yellow Striping, Rush Seat, 43 1/2 In. 100.00
Chair, Banister Back, Dark Stained, Rush Seat, 42 In. 275.00
Chair, Banister Back, Double Dome Crest, Maple, Arms 1600.00
Chair, Banister Back, Maple, Rush Seat, Country, 44 In. 550.00
Chair, Banister Back, Molded Slats, Woven Splint Seat, 39 3/4 In. 115.00
Chair, Baroque, Fruitwood, Cabriole Legs, Leather Seats, Continental, Pair 1595.00

Chair, Belter Style, Rococo, Carved Walnut, 48 x 14 In. 885.00
Chair, Belter, Man's, Laminated Solid Back Rosewood, Heavy Carving, Arms 3500.00
Chair, Belter, Pierced Carved, Padded Back & Seat, Pair 7150.00
Chair, Belter, Pierced Rosewood, 1860–1870, 42 1/2 In. ....*Illus* 4400.00
Chair, Belter, Woman's, Carved Roses, Grapes & Florals 1600.00
Chair, Bentwood, Double Window, John Kone 100.00
Chair, Biedermeier, Crest Rail, Fruitwood, Pair 1980.00
Chair, Biedermeier, Mahogany Frame, Upholstery, 38 In. 1100.00
Chair, Biedermeier, Maple, Natural Finish, Carved Detail, 37 3/4 In. 385.00
Chair, Biedermeier, S–Scrolled Back, Inlay, Fruitwood, c.1820 .... 440.00
Chair, Carved Walnut, Beasts, Cherubs & Gargoyles, Arms, Pair 2300.00
Chair, Carved, Velvet Upholstery, France, Pair 400.00
Chair, Child's, Brown Paint, Black, Red Graining, Floral Design, 21 In. 140.00
Chair, Child's, Classical, Upholstered Seat, 29 1/4 In., Pair 1450.00
Chair, Child's, L. & J. G. Stickley, 7 Spindles, New Leather Upholstery, 33 In. 445.00
Chair, Child's, Ladder Back, Black Repaint, 25 1/4 In. 80.00
Chair, Child's, Ladder Back, Paper Rush Seat, Sapling Posts, 22 1/2 In. 38.00
Chair, Child's, Ladder Back, Splint Seat, Country 28.00
Chair, Child's, Limbert, Arched Front Stretcher, 26 In. 225.00
Chair, Child's, Murphy 190.00
Chair, Child's, Musical, 2 Tunes, Carved Wood, c.1890 .... 1200.00
Chair, Child's, Oak, Removable Baby Guard, Rush Seat, 20 In. 220.00
Chair, Child's, Red Paint, Cane Seat 150.00
Chair, Child's, Rustic, Arms 985.00
Chair, Child's, Stenciled Flowers On Back, Splint Seat 225.00
Chair, Child's, Stenciled, Brown Paint, 1840–1860 .... 365.00
Chair, Child's, Tiger Maple, Rush Seat, Pennsylvania, 1840 .... 1200.00
Chair, Child's, Tilter, 3 Slats, Maple, c.1830 .... 270.00
Chair, Child's, Victorian, Mahogany, Scalloped Crest, c.1850, 31 In. 385.00
Chair, Child's, Westport, H. C. Bunnell, 1905, Pair 5000.00
Chair, Child's, Windsor, Bamboo, Marked Under Seat, 25 1/2 In. 99.00
Chair, Child's, Windsor, Yellow, Green Design, Pair 1400.00
Chair, Chinese Chippendale, Pagoda Back, Needlework Seat, Mahogany, Pair 385.00
Chair, Chippendale Style, Claw & Ball Feet, Open Back, c.1940, Pair 660.00
Chair, Chippendale, Black Paint, Gold Striping, Rush Seat, 35 In. 275.00
Chair, Chippendale, Carved Crest Fail, Upholstered Seat, Philadelphia, 1780, Pair 7200.00
Chair, Chippendale, Cherry, Upholstery, Arms, 41 In. 990.00
Chair, Chippendale, Mahogany, Brocade Upholstery, 39 3/4 In. 495.00
Chair, Chippendale, Mahogany, Fancy Carving, 28 In. 195.00
Chair, Chippendale, Mahogany, Fluted Legs, Slip Seat, 37 1/2 In. 385.00
Chair, Chippendale, Mahogany, Slip Seat, Pierced Splat, 38 1/2 In., Pair 1700.00
Chair, Chippendale, Mahogany, Slip Seat, Upholstery, Green, 37 In., Pair 750.00
Chair, Chippendale, Mahogany, Solid Splat, Cabriole Legs, Ball & Claw Feet, 4 .... 525.00
Chair, Chippendale, Mahogany, Square Legs, Upholstered Seat, 37 In. 605.00
Chair, Chippendale, Mahogany, Upholstered Seat, New England, 1780 .... 990.00
Chair, Chippendale, Mahogany, Velvet Upholstery, 38 In., Pair 1122.00
Chair, Chippendale, Oak, 36 1/4 In. 95.00
Chair, Chippendale, Pierced Interlaced Splat, Mahogany, 1770s, 37 In., Pr. 3300.00
Chair, Chippendale, Rush Seat, Turned Front Stretcher 305.00
Chair, Chippendale, Shell Carved Seat Rail, Acanthus Leaves On Knees 495.00
Chair, Chippendale, Upholstered Seat, Blue, 37 3/4 In. 1320.00
Chair, Chippendale, Walnut, Stretcher, Slip Seat, Gothic Design, 38 In. 935.00
Chair, Club, Black Leather & Chromium Plated Metal, Wolfgang Hoffman, c.1936 ... 2000.00
Chair, Coconut, Upholstery, Herman Miller, c.1955 .... 3575.00
Chair, Cone, Chromium Steel Cage, Pony Skin Upholstery, Verner Panton, c.1959 .... 1875.00
Chair, Continuous Arm, Shaped Back & Arms, Gesso & Giltwood, Pair 4200.00
Chair, Corner, Chippendale Style, Cherry, Elijah Booth, c.1765 .... 9250.00
Chair, Corner, Chippendale, Walnut, Arched Crest, Vase Shaped Pierced Splat, Arms   775.00
Chair, Corner, Chippendale, Walnut, Pennsylvania, 1760, 33 1/2 In. 2200.00
Chair, Corner, Commode, Mahogany, Turned Lid, Upholstered Seat, 30 In. 325.00
Chair, Corner, George III Style, Curved Crest & Arms, Oak Leaf Splats, Mahogany   1325.00
Chair, Corner, Georgian, Oak, Square Legs, c.1780 .... 525.00
Chair, Corner, Pair of Arched Slats, Red Paint, 19th Century, 34 In. 1545.00

Chair, Corner, Queen Anne, Upholstered Seat, Mass., 1760, 33 In. 3300.00
Chair, Corner, Turned Legs, Posts, Arm Rails, Crest, 31 In. 275.00
Chair, Crook Back, Upholstery, Painted, 18th Century, 44 In. 880.00
Chair, Curly Maple, Cane Seat, Concave Stretcher, 1830 .... 165.00
Chair, Curly Maple, Cane Seat, Saber Leg 250.00
Chair, Curved Back, Half Open Arms, Walnut, c.1880 .... 465.00
Chair, Curved Cresting, Inlaid Tablet, Amboyna Wood, Mahogany, c.1790, Pair 9350.00
Chair, Deck, India, Rosewood 400.00
Chair, Deck, Steamer Commonwealth, Cloth Seat, Folding, Arms 187.00
Chair, Deck, Stenciled Commonwealth, Folding 77.00
Chair, Desk, Corner, Walnut, Needlepoint Upholstery, England .... *Illus* 2750.00
Chair, Desk, Swivel, Upholstered, Leather 65.00
Chair, Dining, Low Back, Plank, Spindle Back, Shaker, c.1840, 16 1/2 In. 495.00
Chair, Dining, White Water, Original Blue 800.00
Chair, Eastlake, Carved High Back, Maple, Victorian 110.00
Chair, Eastlake, Tufted Upholstery, Pair 90.00
Chair, Easy, Make–Do, New England, 1810s, 48 In. 605.00
Chair, Easy, Queen Anne, Walnut, Cherry, Loose Cushion, Mid–18th Century 6600.00
Chair, Elastic, Painted, Samuel Gragg 1100.00
Chair, English Regency, Mahogany, Upholstered Seat 325.00
Chair, Eugene Vallin, Arched & Pierced Rail, Mahogany & Leather, c.1900 .... 445.00
Chair, Federal, Shieldback, Mahogany, c.1795, 38 In., Pair .... 2650.00 To 3850.00
Chair, Flemish, Scroll, Dark Finish, Cane Seat, 46 In., Pair 209.00
Chair, Folding, Scandinavian, Walnut, Adjustable Seat, Black, 36 In. 440.00
Chair, Frank Lloyd Wright, Painted Steel, Leather Upholstery, 1904 .... 4675.00
Chair, French Provincial Style, Double Chair Back, Rush Seat, 44 In. 715.00
Chair, George I Style, Burl Walnut Veneer, Cabriole Legs, 39 In. 175.00
Chair, George III, Cluster of Ribbons On Molded Back, Mahogany, c.1780, Pair 2750.00
Chair, George III, Shieldback, Upholstered Seat, Mahogany, 1780s, Pair 665.00
Chair, Gothic Revival, Walnut, Black Tapestry Upholstery, 48 In. 145.00
Chair, Grape Leaves Carved On Crest, Walnut, 1890s 195.00
Chair, Greene & Greene, Mahogany, Crest Rail, Ebony Splines, 39 In. 9900.00
Chair, Gustav Stickley, Adjustable, c.1904, 42 In. .... *Illus* 3850.00
Chair, Gustav Stickley, All Original, Worn Leather Seat, Signed 850.00
Chair, Gustav Stickley, Morris, Adjustable Back, Concave Crest Rail, 31 In. 3850.00
Chair, Gustav Stickley, No. 374, Spindles, Canvas Sling Seat, 46 x 19 x 18 In. 1985.00
Chair, Gustav Stickley, No. 2608, Ladder Back, 4 Slats, 37 x 19 x 17 1/4 In. 450.00
Chair, Half Barrel, Josef Hoffmann, Bowed Front Rail, Upholstery, Bentwood 3850.00
Chair, Half Spindle, Worn Red & Black Graining, Stencil Traces, Pair 150.00
Chair, Hall, Georgian, Mahogany, 1800 .... 150.00
Chair, Hall, Jacobean, Carved Walnut, Plank Seat, Scroll & Mask Back 145.00
Chair, Hardwood, Dark Finish, Carved With Dolphins, Scrolls, 39 In. 85.00
Chair, Hepplewhite, Mahogany, Carved Shield, 40 In. 665.00
Chair, Hepplewhite, Mahogany, Shieldback, Acanthus, Molded Seat Rails 665.00
Chair, Hepplewhite, Shieldback, Mahogany, Salem, 1800, Pair 9800.00
Chair, Heywood–Wakefield, Spindle, Pair 500.00
Chair, Hickory, Indiana, c.1920 .... 285.00
Chair, High Back, 1 Arm, 2 Side, Tapestry Upholstery, Mahogany, 45 1/2 In. 255.00
Chair, High Back, Spindle Splats, Caned Seat, Oak, Pair 70.00
Chair, Hoosier, 1920, Pair 195.00
Chair, Horn, Hide Seat Cover, Arms .... 500.00 To 1000.00
Chair, Horn, Original Oilcloth 1500.00
Chair, Hunzinger, Walnut, Baluster Turned, Upholstered Seat, Arms, 1869 .... 335.00
Chair, Italian Baroque, Carved Giltwood, 18th Century, Pair 2860.00
Chair, Josef Hoffmann, Painted Bentwood & Aluminum, Leather Upholstery, 1901 ... 3300.00
Chair, Knoll, Chrome–Plated Stainless Steel Wire, Purple Wool Upholstery 275.00
Chair, Lacquered, Scalloped Back, Floral Mother–of–Pearl Inlay, Victorian 500.00
Chair, Ladder Back, 3 Arched Slats, Hardwood, Turned Finials, Woven Splint Seat ... 45.00
Chair, Ladder Back, 3 Slats, Green Paint, 37 In. 138.00
Chair, Ladder Back, 3 Slats, Turned Finials, Woven Cane Seat, 37 1/2 In. 49.00
Chair, Ladder Back, 4 Arched Slats, Rush Seat, 38 In. 467.00
Chair, Ladder Back, 4 Slats, Delaware Valley, Ball Feet 415.00
Chair, Ladder Back, 5 Contoured Slats, Rush Seat, Bulbous Stretcher, Pa. 550.00

Chair, Ladder Back, Arched Slats, Turned Finials, Woven Splint Seat, 38 1/4 In. 75.00
Chair, Ladder Back, Reddish Brown, Splint Seat, 3 Slats, 35 1/2 In. 22.00
Chair, Ladder Back, Shaped Arms, Arched Slats, Rush Seat, 44 1/4 In. 440.00
Chair, Ladder Back, Student's, Rush Seat, Oak 88.00
Chair, Ladder Back, Walnut, Rush Seat, Arms, c.1780 .... 605.00
Chair, Ladder Back, White, Yellow Paint, Paper Rush Seat, 34 In. 33.00
Chair, Ladder Back, Woven Rush Seat, 38 In. 60.00
Chair, Library, Mahogany, Padded Arms, Foliate Carved Supports, c.1775 .... 3800.00
Chair, Library, Mahogany, Upholstery, c.1825, 42 In. 1650.00
Chair, Limbert, Oak, Metal & Wood, Inlay, 1905, Pair 7500.00
Chair, Lolling, Federal, Mahogany, Striped Upholstery, Mass., Arms, 1795, 45 In. 825.00
Chair, Louis Majorelle, Mahogany, Upholstered Back Panel 660.00
Chair, Louis XV, Petit Point Oval Insert, Gold Leaf Over Frame, 1850s, 38 In. 450.00
Chair, Louis XVI Style, Carved Fruitwood, Cane Back & Seat, 38 1/2 In. 995.00
Chair, Louis XVI, Gilt Wood, Leaf Carved Back, 41 1/2 In., Pair 265.00
Chair, Lounge, Plywood, Herman Miller, c.1945, 26 3/4 In. 600.00
Chair, Mahogany, Carved Crest Rail, Turned Legs, Tapestry Back Rest & Seat 160.00
Chair, Mahogany, Shell Carved, Serpentine Crest Rail, Slip-In Seat, Philadelphia 1450.00
Chair, Mahogany, Transitional, Pad Feet, Square Set & Pierced Splat 825.00
Chair, Maple, Cane Seat, Spindle Splats, Pressed Back, Leaf Design, Pair 45.00
Chair, Meek, Laminated, New York, Pair 2475.00
Chair, Middle Eastern, Geometric Inlay of Ivory & Fruitwood, 42 1/2 In. 1100.00
Chair, Morris, Arts & Crafts, Slat Sides, 45 x 30 x 39 In. 935.00
Chair, Morris, Gustav Stickley, Adjustable Back, 40 In. 5500.00
Chair, Morris, Gustav Stickley, Slats, 37 1/2 x 29 1/2 x 33 1/2 In. 3100.00
Chair, Morris, Gustav Stickley, Spindle 5775.00
Chair, Morris, Hickory, Arms, 1900s, Pair 2500.00
Chair, Morris, L. & J. G. Stickley, No. 471, Drop-In Spring Seat, 41 x 35 In. 1980.00
Chair, Morris, L. & J. G. Stickley, Slatted Drop Arm 7750.00
Chair, Nursing, Beadwork Upholstery, Walnut Legs, c.1857 .... 300.00
Chair, Oak, Spindle Back, Cane Seat 20.00

Furniture, Chair, Gustav Stickley, Adjustable, c.1904, 42 In.

Furniture, Chair, Belter, Pierced Rosewood, 1860-1870, 42 1/2 In.

Furniture, Chair, Desk, Corner, Walnut, Needlepoint Upholstery, England

Furniture, Chair, Ordway, Ash Splint, Wicker, S-Shaped Arms, 1905

Chair, Oak, Tapered Back, Central Slat, Rush Seat, 40 In., Pair 5575.00
Chair, Office, On Swivel Rocker, Arrow Slats, Cane Seat, Pressed Back, Oak 270.00
Chair, Ordway, Ash Splint, Wicker, S–Shaped Arms, 1905 ....*Illus* 715.00
Chair, Paimio, Laminated Birch & Plywood, Alvar Aalto, c.1929 .... 5500.00
Chair, Polynesian, Chip Carved, Incised Design, Hardwood, 34 1/4 In. 770.00
Chair, Pressed Back, Cane Seat 245.00
Chair, Pressed Back, Dolphin County, 1 Green, 1 Brown, 1900s, Pair 350.00
Chair, Pretzel, George Nelson Design 1300.00
Chair, Queen Anne Style, Scalloped Crest, Mask Inlay, Holland, 44 1/2 In. 385.00
Chair, Queen Anne, Balloon, Walnut, Boston 5500.00
Chair, Queen Anne, Black Paint, Vase Splat, 1 Yoke Crest, Rush Seat, Country 105.00
Chair, Queen Anne, Carved Crest, Slip Seat, Bermuda, Cedar, 1750s, 39 In. 1650.00
Chair, Queen Anne, Cherry, Balloon Seat 3750.00
Chair, Queen Anne, Mahogany, Vase Splat, Balloon Seat, Cabriole Legs 715.00
Chair, Queen Anne, Oak, Needlepoint Seat, Spanish Feet, Black Paint 275.00
Chair, Queen Anne, Various Woods, Spanish Foot, Vase Splat, Rush Seat 1100.00
Chair, Queen Anne, Vase Splat, Slip Seat, Figured Maple, 40 1/4 In. 9900.00
Chair, Queen Anne, Worn Black Gold Striping, Vase Splat, Rush Seat, Country 385.00
Chair, Queen Anne, Yoked Crest Rail, Vase Splat, Walnut, c.1740 .... 3300.00
Chair, Red Lacquer, U–Shaped Back, Folding, Japan, 36 In. 165.00
Chair, Regency, Tub Back, Faux Painted, Fluted Legs, Casters, c.1820, Pair 1550.00
Chair, Rocker, look under Rocker in this category.
Chair, Rococo Carved & Laminated Rosewood, Crewel Work Seat, c.1860 .... 375.00
Chair, Rosewood, Victorian, Carved Seat Rail, c.1850, 34 In., Pair 522.50
Chair, Russel Wright, Slanted Plank Rest, Leather Upholstered, Slip Seat, c.1903 ..... 9350.00
Chair, Shaker, Child's, Tape Seat, Canterbury 775.00
Chair, Shaker, Ladder Back, 3 Arched Slats, Turned Finials, Splint Seat, 38 In. 575.00
Chair, Shaker, Ladder Back, Canterbury, New Hampshire 425.00
Chair, Shaker, Ladder Back, No. 61, 38 1/4 In. 1225.00
Chair, Shaker, Low Back, Enfield 330.00
Chair, Shaker, No. 3, Shawl Bar, Maple, Mount Lebanon, 1880–1920, 32 5/8 In. 192.50
Chair, Shaker, Side, Maple, c.1830, 39 In. 1100.00
Chair, Shaker, Tilter, Tape Seat, 1850 .... 695.00
Chair, Shaker, Tilter, Tape Seat, Pair 1600.00
Chair, Sheraton, Bamboo Turnings, Rush Seat, 38 In. 55.00
Chair, Sheraton, Dark Graining, Gold Striping, Stenciled Design, 33 3/4 In. 85.00
Chair, Slipper, Belter, Fountain Elms 7975.00
Chair, Slipper, Carved Floral, Arms, Upholstery, 1870 .... 550.00
Chair, Slipper, High Back, White & Black Striping, Polychrome Floral, 34 1/2 In. ... 50.00
Chair, Slipper, Ladder Back, 4 Slats, Dark Patina, Worn Splint Seat 40.00
Chair, Slipper, Louis XV, Arched Crest, Upholstered Back, Carved Hand Grips 1650.00
Chair, Slipper, Mother–of–Pearl Inlay, Red Lacquer, Caned Papier–Mache, c.1860 .... 2200.00
Chair, Slipper, Walnut, Tufted Upholstered Back & Seat 160.00
Chair, Spindle Back, Yellow Repaint, Black & Green Striping, Stenciled, Pair 275.00
Chair, Square Tapering Posts, Original Rush Seat, Black Finish, 35 In., Pair 385.00
Chair, Turkey, Velvet Upholstery, c.1885, 33 In., Pair 1100.00
Chair, Wallace Nutting, Imposed Comb, Paper Label 688.00
Chair, Wallace Nutting, Pilgrim 220.00
Chair, Walnut, Bone Inlay, Italy, 37 In., Pair 825.00
Chair, Walnut, Carved, Cabriole Legs, Floral Upholstery, c.1880 .... 450.00
Chair, Walnut, Hip Rest, Needlework Seat, Pair 110.00
Chair, Walnut, Shaped Crest, Cane Seat, Turned Legs, Pair 125.00
Chair, Wicker, Heywood–Wakefield, Pair 340.00
Chair, Wicker, Photographer's Studio 325.00
Chair, William & Mary, Banister Back, Double Arched Crest Rail, 4 Spindles, Maple 8250.00
Chair, William & Mary, Banister Back, Stencil, Grain Paint, Woven Seat 1785.00
Chair, William IV, Tub Form Back, Scrolled Arms, Mahogany 3300.00
Chair, Windsor, Arched Spindle Back, Saddle Seat, England 605.00
Chair, Windsor, Arrow–Back, Bamboo Base, Plank Seat, Country, Pair 425.00
Chair, Windsor, Arrow–Back, Farm Scene Design, Red Paint, 1820 .... 1650.00
Chair, Windsor, Bamboo, Spindle Back, Step–Down Crest, 35 In. 325.00
Chair, Windsor, Bow Back, 7 Spindles, Bamboo Turned Legs, Phila., Pair 660.00
Chair, Windsor, Bow Back, Dark Finish, Bamboo Turnings, 34 In., Pair 250.00

Chair, Windsor, Bow Back, Green Paint, c.1800, 37 In.	4000.00
Chair, Windsor, Bow Back, Oak, Elm, Beech, 19th Century, Pair	1500.00
Chair, Windsor, Bow Back, Red Repaint, 36 3/4 In.	165.00
Chair, Windsor, Bow Back, Saddle Seat, Convoluted Curve Rail, 34 1/4 In.	770.00
Chair, Windsor, Bow Back, Shield Seat, Black Paint, 18th Century, Pair	3700.00
Chair, Windsor, Bow Back, Splayed Base, Bamboo Turnings, H Stretcher, 36 In.	300.00
Chair, Windsor, Bow Back, Splayed Base, Shaped Seat, Black, 37 1/4 In.	700.00
Chair, Windsor, Brace Back, 9 Spindles, Mahogany, Green Paint, 1780	9350.00
Chair, Windsor, Brace Back, H Stretcher, Saddle Seat, Country	400.00
Chair, Windsor, Captain's, Bamboo Turned Legs, Rings, 26 3/4 In.	71.00
Chair, Windsor, Captain's, Low Back, Black Paint, Gold Striping, 29 In.	137.00
Chair, Windsor, Comb Back, Bamboo, Red & Black Graining, Stenciled, 43 In.	300.00
Chair, Windsor, Comb Back, Chamber Pot, Dark Green Paint, 40 In.	1540.00
Chair, Windsor, Comb Back, Saddle Seat, Splayed Base, 48 1/2 In.	1500.00
Chair, Windsor, Comb Back, Saddle Seat, Spoon Arms	1200.00
Chair, Windsor, Comb Back, Scalloped Crest Rail, 7 Spindles, Painted Red	8800.00
Chair, Windsor, Comb Back, Scrolled Ear, Knuckle Arms, Pennsylvania., 1780	7600.00
Chair, Windsor, Comb Back, Writing Arm, Drawer Under Seat	1765.00
Chair, Windsor, Continuous Arm, Old Black Paint, 1800	1250.00
Chair, Windsor, Continuous Knuckle Arm, Varnished Brown Over Green Paint	9800.00
Chair, Windsor, Dark Finish, England, 42 In.	900.00
Chair, Windsor, Fanback, Bamboo Turnings, Yoke Crest, 35 In.	550.00
Chair, Windsor, Fanback, Cherry, 46 1/4 In.	1045.00
Chair, Windsor, Fanback, Dark Red–Brown Paint	385.00
Chair, Windsor, Fanback, H Stretcher, Stamped P. S. Byrn 1708	5700.00
Chair, Windsor, Fanback, Knuckle Arm, Painted, 20th Century	357.00
Chair, Windsor, Fanback, Pine & Hickory, 1765–1780, 41 1/4 In.	495.00
Chair, Windsor, Fanback, Splayed Base, Saddle Seat, 35 In.	360.00
Chair, Windsor, Fanback, Vasiform Legs & Back Posts, c.1800, 36 In.	425.00
Chair, Windsor, Hoop Back, 1820s, Pair	715.00
Chair, Windsor, Hoop Back, 7 Spindles, Red & Black Paint	375.00
Chair, Windsor, Pierced Back Splat, Shaped Arms, Yew, 41 1/2 In.	880.00
Chair, Windsor, Red Over Green Paint, New Hampshire, 1790	1600.00
Chair, Windsor, Sack Back, 7 Spindles, Knuckled Hand Grips, Plank Seat, 41 In.	8250.00
Chair, Windsor, Sack Back, Carved Knuckles, Saddle Seat, Pair	4500.00
Chair, Windsor, Sack Back, Dark Crusty Paint, Arms	1760.00
Chair, Windsor, Sack Back, Original Green Paint, Mass.	2500.00
Chair, Windsor, Sack Back, Spoon Arms, Baluster Legs, Red Paint, Penna.	935.00
Chair, Windsor, Saddle Seat, Drawer Under Seat & Writing Arm, H Stretcher	1600.00
Chair, Windsor, Splayed Base, Bulbous Turnings, Saddle Seat, 38 In.	1375.00
Chair, Windsor, Splayed Base, Saddle Seat, Turned Arm Support, 36 In.	385.00
Chair, Windsor, Splayed Base, Shaped Seat, Step–Down Crest, 34 1/3 In.	330.00
Chair, Windsor, Step–Down, Arms & Headrest, Yellow, 19th Century	1950.00
Chair, Windsor, Step–Down, Old Green Paint, Pair	695.00
Chair, Windsor, Writing, Splayed Base, Bamboo Turnings, 44 In.	2100.00
Chair, Wing Shaped Back, Curved Struts Form Legs, Italy, c.1950, Pair	975.00
Chair, Wing, Chamber Pot, Upholstery, Mahogany, c.1810	4400.00
Chair, Wing, Chippendale, Red Brocade Upholstery	3300.00
Chair, Wing, Federal, Mahogany, Striped Upholstery, U.S., 1795, 44 In.	3410.00
Chair, Wing, Federal, Mahogany, Upholstery, Mass., 1795, 46 In.	7150.00
Chair, Wing, Federal, Mahogany, Upholstery, Stool, Mass., 1820, 46 In.	4675.00
Chair, Wire, Arms, 1950s, Pair	1200.00
Chaise Lounge & Ottoman, Plywood & Rosewood Veneer, Eames	2100.00
Chaise Lounge, Art Deco, Upholstery, Bun Feet, France, c.1925, 72 In.	3300.00
Chaise Lounge, Carved Fruitwood, Gold Damask Upholstery, 33 In.	440.00
Chaise Lounge, George Nakashima, Spindled Back, 30 1/4 In.	1200.00
Chaise Lounge, Grasshopper, Eero Saarinen, c.1940	3850.00
Chaise Lounge, Louis XV Style, Painted Beechwood	1000.00
Chaise Lounge, Rosewood, Caned Seat, Needlepoint Upholstery, 72 In.	715.00
Chaise Lounge, Upholstery, Country, 1855	995.00
Chaise Lounge, Victorian, Finger–Roll	320.00
Chaise Lounge, Victorian, Tufted Upholstered Seat, Carved Supports, 5 Ft. 9 In.	5500.00
Chaise Lounge, Victorian, Upholstery, Mahogany, 72 In.	660.00

Chaise Lounge, Wicker, Plaid Upholstery, 1920 .... 1600.00
Chaise Lounge, Wicker, Shoulder, Upholstery, Hand Woven, Coil Springs, 1920 ..... 1500.00
Chaise Lounge, Wicker, White, Upholstered Cushions 300.00
Chest, 1 Drawer, Pine, Lift Top, Lower Cupboard, Carved Pull, 30 1/2 x 29 In. 200.00
Chest, 1 Hidden Drawer, Hepplewhite, Cherry, Poplar, Kentucky, 1820 .... 3950.00
Chest, 2 Drawers, Dovetailed Case, Iron Strap Hinges, Tulip Design, 50 In. 3850.00
Chest, 2 Drawers, Pine, 5 1/2 x 4 3/8 In. 50.00
Chest, 3 Drawers, Blond Veneer On Pine, 29 In. 400.00
Chest, 3 Drawers, Bombe, Oak, Holland, 1780s, 33 x 34 In. 1750.00
Chest, 3 Drawers, Ebonized Finish, Gilt Trim, France, 34 In. 135.00
Chest, 3 Drawers, Graduated, Cherry, Ogee Bracket Feet 2500.00
Chest, 3 Drawers, Pine, Brown Graining, Scrolled Apron, 10 1/2 In. 687.00
Chest, 3 Drawers, Pine, Brown Vinegar Graining, Pine, 34 In. 935.00
Chest, 3 Drawers, Serpentine Top, Bird Inlay On Feet, Fruitwood, Germany, 13 In. 2200.00
Chest, 3 Drawers, Walnut, Grape Carving, Brass Hardware, 1880, 12 x 12 In. 675.00
Chest, 4 Drawers, Bird's-Eye Maple, Wooden Pulls, Turned Column, 31 x 43 In. 80.00
Chest, 4 Drawers, Cherry, Curly Maple Posts, Walnut Wood, 40 In. 522.00
Chest, 4 Drawers, Cherry, Walnut, Scalloped Apron, 47 3/4 In. 1210.00
Chest, 4 Drawers, Cock-Beaded, Curly Maple, French Feet, 27 In. 770.00
Chest, 4 Drawers, Curly Birch, Ox Bow-Shaped Top, Brown Finish, 38 In. 3080.00
Chest, 4 Drawers, Dovetailed, Cherry, Beaded, Crest, Country, 45 x 20 x 55 3/4 In. 1250.00
Chest, 4 Drawers, Graduated, Pine, Red Wash, Late 18th Century 2860.00
Chest, 4 Drawers, Graduated, Walnut, Serpentine, John Shearer, Dated 1800 .... 8000.00
Chest, 4 Drawers, Over Cabinet Doors, Pierced Brass Designs, Korea, 32 In. 440.00
Chest, 4 Drawers, Overlapping, Cherry, Turned Feet, Refinished, 41 x 21 x 50 In. ... 600.00
Chest, 4 Drawers, Pine, Poplar, Mahogany Veneer Facade, 16 1/2 In. 950.00
Chest, 4 Drawers, Pine, Walnut Pulls, 35 x 38 1/2 x 17 1/2 In. 125.00
Chest, 4 Drawers, Sandwich Glass Pulls, Hairy Paw Feet, Burl Walnut, c.1850 .... 525.00
Chest, 4 Drawers, Trompe l'oeil Design, Italy, 32 x 17 x 35 In. 880.00
Chest, 4 Drawers, Walnut, Applied Beading, 43 1/4 In. 1925.00
Chest, 5 Drawers, Graduated, Maple, 36 In. 3300.00
Chest, 5 Drawers, Mahogany, Marble Top, Ormolu Trim, Brass, France, 33 3/4 In. . 1200.00
Chest, 5 Drawers, Mahogany, Yew Inlay, Bracket Feet, Pair 385.00
Chest, 5 Drawers, Oak, Mirror, Painted 370.00
Chest, 5 Drawers, Pine, Red Stain, Country, 56 In. 1250.00
Chest, 6 Drawers, Carved Mahogany, Carved Anthemion Leaves, 58 3/4 In. 1045.00
Chest, 6 Drawers, Cherry, Poplar, Diamond-Shaped Pewter Inlay, 41 1/2 In. 440.00
Chest, 6 Drawers, Graduated, Tiger Maple, Dark Glossy Finish, 38 x 56 In. 7000.00
Chest, 6 Drawers, Hardwood, Pine, Dark Varnish, 15 1/2 In. 357.00
Chest, 6 Drawers, Walnut, Teardrop Pulls, 4 Ft. 7 In. x 3 Ft. 1 In. 540.00
Chest, American Empire, Walnut, Red Varnish, Curly Maple Drawer, 45 x 67 In. ... 605.00
Chest, Apothecary, 12 Drawers, Walnut 575.00
Chest, Apothecary, Painted Mustard & Salmon, 16 Drawers 605.00
Chest, Apothecary, Wooden Pulls, Mahogany & Painted, England, 36 1/4 In. 1320.00
Chest, Bachelor's, George II Style, 4 Drawer, Walnut Inlay, 19th Century 5775.00
Chest, Blanket, 1 Drawer, Curly Maple, Dovetailed Base, Poplar, 27 1/2 In. 1750.00
Chest, Blanket, 1 Drawer, Lift Top, Pine, Mustard Grain Painted, U.S., 45 In. 358.00
Chest, Blanket, 1 Drawer, Oak, Dark Finish, 2 False Drawers, Lift Top, 33 In. 800.00
Chest, Blanket, 1 Drawer, Old Red Paint, Bootjack End 1400.00
Chest, Blanket, 1 Drawer, Overlapping, Cutout Feet, Staple Hinges, 26 In. 214.00
Chest, Blanket, 1 Drawer, Poplar, Original Brown Graining, 13 In. 2915.00
Chest, Blanket, 2 Drawers, Cherry, Red Crotch Mahogany Veneer, Miniature 365.00
Chest, Blanket, 2 Drawers, Inside, Grain Painted, 31 3/4 x 39 3/4 x 16 1/2 In. 3025.00
Chest, Blanket, 2 Drawers, Lift Top, Maple, Red, 1740s, 47 1/2 x 39 In. 3080.00
Chest, Blanket, 2 Drawers, Poplar, Brown, Green Repaint, 31 In. 330.00
Chest, Blanket, 6 Board, 1 Drawer, Pine, Wooden Pulls, 33 In. 525.00
Chest, Blanket, 6 Board, Pine, 43 x 18 x 34 In. 300.00
Chest, Blanket, 6 Board, Pine, Blue Repaint, 16 1/4 In. 577.00
Chest, Blanket, 6 Board, Pine, Brushed Orange Paint, 22 1/2 In. 302.00
Chest, Blanket, 6 Board, Pine, Cutout Feet, 28 In. 250.00
Chest, Blanket, 6 Board, Pine, Reddish Brown Finish, Cutout Feet, 20 1/2 In. 357.00
Chest, Blanket, 6 Board, Scalloped Sides, Painted Red, 20 1/4 x 44 In. 550.00
Chest, Blanket, Blue, Incised Compass Design, Lancaster County, 1760–1780 .... 3800.00

Chest, Blanket, Brown Over Yellow Vinegar Graining, New England, 1850 .... 370.00
Chest, Blanket, Brown Vinegar Graining, Green Feet, Till With Lid, J. H. Stahl 2950.00
Chest, Blanket, Burled Wood Panels, Sloped Interior 1300.00
Chest, Blanket, Cherry, Dovetailed Case, Reeded Edge Top, 12 3/8 In. 715.00
Chest, Blanket, Chippendale, 2 Drawers, Alligatored Green Repaint, 29 In. 275.00
Chest, Blanket, Chippendale, 2 Drawers, Inlay, Chester Cty., Penn., 1776, 49 In. 7150.00
Chest, Blanket, Chippendale, Walnut, Dark Finish, Country, Ohio, 37 3/4 In. 295.00
Chest, Blanket, Chippendale, Walnut, Dovetailed Case, 52 3/4 x 31 1/2 In. 3575.00
Chest, Blanket, Curly Maple, Paneled Construction, 33 3/4 In. 665.00
Chest, Blanket, Dome Top, Pine, 2 Board, Original Brown Graining, 39 1/2 In. 125.00
Chest, Blanket, Dovetailed Case, Bracket Feet, Stenciled Label, 24 In. 660.00
Chest, Blanket, Dovetailed Case, Strap Hinges & Lock, 22 1/4 In. 412.00
Chest, Blanket, Hepplewhite, 2 Drawers, Pine, Carved Sailing Ships 550.00
Chest, Blanket, Joel Palmer, 1834, Miniature 6500.00
Chest, Blanket, Lift Top, Pine, Notch Work Design, U.S., 29 x 47 x 18 In. 1100.00
Chest, Blanket, Lift Top, Tiger Maple, Paneled, 19th Century, 29 x 49 x 21 In. 176.00
Chest, Blanket, Oak, Green Repaint, Polychrome Angels, Flowers, Stars, 12 In. 137.00
Chest, Blanket, Oak, Octagonal Feet, Hinged, 18 1/2 x 42 x 16 In. 1487.00
Chest, Blanket, Oak, Poplar, Dark Green, Design, Early 20th Century, 12 In. 100.00
Chest, Blanket, Pilgrim, Lower Drawer, Paneled, Oak, c.1700 .... 1200.00
Chest, Blanket, Pine & Oak, Metal Mounts, 20 3/4 x 30 1/4 In. 125.00
Chest, Blanket, Pine, Hinged Lid, Incised Design, Miniature 440.00
Chest, Blanket, Pine, Original Red Graining, French Feet, 25 1/4 In. 665.00
Chest, Blanket, Pine, Original White Paint, Polychrome Floral Design, 7 In. 125.00
Chest, Blanket, Pine, Polychrome Stylized Tulips, Blue Paint, 21 In. 225.00
Chest, Blanket, Pine, Poplar, Dovetailed Case, Bracket Feet, 24 3/4 In. 375.00
Chest, Blanket, Pine, Poplar, Original Black Graining, 18 1/2 In. 385.00
Chest, Blanket, Pine, Poplar, Red Graining, Dovetailed Case, 25 In. 412.00
Chest, Blanket, Pine, Red Graining, Dovetailed Case, 25 1/4 In. 385.00
Chest, Blanket, Pine, Reddish Alligatored Finish, Paneled Sides, 19 In. 935.00
Chest, Blanket, Pine, Turned Feet, Dovetailed Base, 20 1/4 x 24 1/2 In. 495.00
Chest, Blanket, Poplar, Black Repaint Over Blue, 37 x 18 1/4 x 20 In. 550.00
Chest, Blanket, Poplar, Blue Vinegar Graining, 17 1/2 In. 192.00
Chest, Blanket, Poplar, Brown Flame Graining, Green Trim, 25 1/4 In. 715.00
Chest, Blanket, Poplar, Dovetailed Base, Turned Feet, 12 1/2 x 8 x 9 1/2 In. 555.00
Chest, Blanket, Poplar, Red Brown Vinegar Graining, Yellow, 40 x 20 In. 1100.00
Chest, Blanket, Poplar, Red Flame Graining, Dovetailed Case, 23 In. 412.00
Chest, Blanket, Poplar, Red Flame Graining, Turned Feet, Till, 36 3/4 In. 500.00
Chest, Blanket, Poplar, Red Vinegar Graining, Yellow Ground, 24 In. 1815.00
Chest, Blanket, Poplar, Reddish Brown Graining, Dovetailed Case, 20 In. 605.00
Chest, Blanket, Poplar, Yellow, Brown Combed Graining, Till, 47 x 23 x 28 In. 687.00
Chest, Blanket, Queen Anne, Lift Top, Red, Faux Drawers, 45 x 37 x 18 In. 3300.00
Chest, Blanket, Queen Anne, Pine, 1740, 31 x 36 x 17 In. 1980.00
Chest, Blanket, Sailor-Type Carvings, Pine 825.00
Chest, Blanket, Shaker, 1 Drawer, Canterbury 1925.00
Chest, Blanket, Shaker, Pine, Mustard & Red Brown Paint, Snipe Hinges, 1820 .... 1550.00
Chest, Blanket, Sheraton, Walnut, Applied Base, Paneled Sides, 31 In. 605.00
Chest, Blanket, Tulips & Hearts On Corners, Tree Center, Penna., Dated 1817 .... 7500.00
Chest, Blanket, Walnut, Dark Refinishing, Paneled Side & Lid, Country, 52 x 26 In. 325.00
Chest, Bowfront, 4 Drawers, Cherry, French Feet, 38 5/8 In. 4800.00
Chest, Bowfront, Mahogany, Birch, French Feet, Maine 2900.00
Chest, Bowfront, Sheraton, 4 Drawers, Bird's-Eye Maple, Cherry 4400.00
Chest, Bowfront, Sheraton, Mahogany, High Turned Feet, 43 x 45 1/4 In. 995.00
Chest, Bowfront, Sheraton, Mahogany, Salem 2950.00
Chest, Bridle, Pine, Humpback, 1853, 28 x 49 x 24 In. 600.00
Chest, Butler's, Hepplewhite, 4 Drawers, Cherry, Short Post Legs 635.00
Chest, Campaign, 2 Short Over 3 Long Drawers, British Colonial, Mahogany 1540.00
Chest, Carved Fruit & Nut Handles, Side Lock, Walnut, c.1880, 53 1/2 x 46 In. 1550.00
Chest, Cherry, Graduated Drawers, Bracket Feet, 18th Century, 32 x 17 1/2 In. 1980.00
Chest, Cherry, Mustard Paint, Fingerprint Finish, W. Penna., Late 1800s 1250.00
Chest, Child's, Graduated Drawers, Turned Legs, Cherry, c.1830 .... 1285.00
Chest, Chippendale Style, 4 Drawers, Fruitwood Inlay, 19th Century, 30 In. 650.00
Chest, Chippendale, 2 Drawers, Pine, Lift Top, Dovetailed, 39 1/4 x 45 In. 990.00

◆◆◆◆◆◆◆◆◆◆◆◆◆◆◆◆◆◆◆◆◆◆◆

Treat your furniture the same
way you treat your face. Wash
it to remove the dirt. You do
not want to remove the skin.
Don't sand too much or use a
"dip strip."

◆◆◆◆◆◆◆◆◆◆◆◆◆◆◆◆◆◆◆◆◆◆◆

Furniture, Chest, Chippendale, Cherry,

    18th Century, 37 In.

Chest, Chippendale, 3 Drawers, Mahogany, Dovetailed, 35 x 36 1/4 In.	2530.00
Chest, Chippendale, 3 Drawers, Mahogany, Ogee Feet, 27 1/2 In.	50.00
Chest, Chippendale, 3 Over 4 Drawers, Dust Panels, Walnut, c.1780, 68 1/4 In.	7500.00
Chest, Chippendale, 4 Dovetailed Beaded Drawers, Mahogany, Serpentine, 39 In.	6000.00
Chest, Chippendale, 4 Drawers, Block Front, Bracket Feet, 35 In.	1540.00
Chest, Chippendale, 4 Drawers, Cherry, 22 1/2 In.	300.00
Chest, Chippendale, 4 Drawers, Cherry, Bonnet Top, 86 1/2 In.	8800.00
Chest, Chippendale, 4 Drawers, Tiger Maple, 18th Century, 32 x 39 x 19 In.	4400.00
Chest, Chippendale, 4 Drawers, Walnut, Ogee Feet, 35 1/2 In.	2860.00
Chest, Chippendale, 4 Graduated Drawers, Birch, Serpentine, Mass., 1770, 33 In.	900.00
Chest, Chippendale, 4 Graduated Drawers, Cherry, Conn., 1760, 37 x 36 x 18 In.	3300.00
Chest, Chippendale, 4 Graduated Drawers, Walnut, Ogee Bracket Feet, Penna.	1540.00
Chest, Chippendale, 6 Drawers, Poplar, Medium Brown, 55 3/4 In.	1100.00
Chest, Chippendale, 6 Graduated Drawers, Maple, Cutout Feet, Country, 56 In.	4400.00
Chest, Chippendale, 6 Overlapping Drawers, Curly Maple, Cornice, Bale Brasses	7750.00
Chest, Chippendale, 11 Drawers, Mahogany, Sunburst On Top Drawer, 85 In.	4070.00
Chest, Chippendale, Birch, Serpentine, c.1770, 33 1/2 In.	900.00
Chest, Chippendale, Bowfront, Fluted Quarter Columns, c.1765, 44 In.	2310.00
Chest, Chippendale, Cherry, 18th Century, 37 In. ....*Illus*	5500.00
Chest, Chippendale, Graduated Drawers, Bracket Feet, Brass Pulls	2300.00
Chest, Chippendale, Mahogany, Delaware Valley, 1775	3550.00
Chest, Chippendale, Walnut, Serpentine, Blocked Ends, J. Shearer, Va., 1800	8800.00
Chest, Classical, 6 Drawers, Gallery, Signed New Rochelle	1650.00
Chest, Coffer, Oak, Paneled, Relief Carved, Till, England, 40 x 15 x 23 In.	385.00
Chest, Coffer, Oak, Primitive, Crosshatch Carving, Peaked Lid, England, 30 In.	82.00
Chest, Continental, Lacquered, Marble Top	6875.00
Chest, Cottage, 4 Drawers, Basswood Stained Pine, Rabbeted, 1870s	450.00
Chest, Dower, 2 Drawers, Iron Strap Hinges, Till, Painted, 25 x 45 1/4 In.	3850.00
Chest, Dower, 3 Drawers, Yellow Pine, Lift Top, Dovetailed, 19 x 31 In.	1815.00
Chest, Dower, Trees, Heart Corners, Signed Catharina Houser 1817, Penna.	7500.00
Chest, Dower, William & Mary, Lift Top, Drawer Dividers, c.1715, 13 x 12 1/4 In.	4620.00
Chest, Dower, William & Mary, New England, 1710–1725, Miniature	4620.00
Chest, Empire, 1 Serpentine & 3 Graduated Drawers, Maple, 47 x 42 x 12 In.	440.00
Chest, Empire, 3 Drawers, Graduated, Mirror Gallery Lift Off, Stenciled, 39 In.	1320.00
Chest, Empire, 4 Drawers, Dovetailed, Curly Maple, Pilasters, Ebonized Legs, 45 In.	500.00
Chest, Empire, 4 Drawers, Ogee Front Dovetailed, Pine, 35 1/2 In.	350.00
Chest, Empire, 5 Drawers, Cherry & Maple, Pineapple Pilasters, 46 x 49 In.	1265.00
Chest, Empire, 6 Drawers, Graduated, Block Legs, Cherry, 19th Century, 46 1/2 In.	2090.00
Chest, Empire, 7 Drawers, Cherry, Figured Burl Veneer, 51 1/2 In.	1100.00
Chest, Empire, 8 Drawers, Figured Mahogany Veneer, Columnar Pilasters, 48 In.	525.00
Chest, Empire, Tiger Maple Columns, Cherry, Bird's–Eye Veneer, Country	1200.00
Chest, Federal, 4 Drawers, Graduated, Paneled Sides, Turned Front & Back Legs	2800.00
Chest, Federal, 4 Drawers, Maple, Bracket Feet, 43 1/2 x 40 x 20 In.	775.00
Chest, Federal, 4 Drawers, Walnut, Penna., 1790, 33 x 40 x 20 1/2 In.	3550.00
Chest, Federal, 5 Drawers, Cherry, Reeded Stiles, Turned Feet, 43 1/2 In.	825.00
Chest, Federal, 7 Drawers, Mahogany, Figured Veneer, 48 3/4 In.	1045.00

Chest, George III Style, 6 Drawers, Mahogany, Ogee Bracket Feet, 37 In. 995.00
Chest, George III, 2 Short & 3 Long Drawers, Black Japanned, Parcel Gilt, 39 In. 1980.00
Chest, George III, 4 Cock–Beaded Drawers, Serpentine Front, Mahogany, 32 In. 4675.00
Chest, George III, Burl Walnut, Mahogany, Cross Banded Top, 35 In. 715.00
Chest, George IV, Mahogany, Molded Cornice, Inlay Frieze, 79 In. 1430.00
Chest, Georgian, 2 Short Over 3 Long Drawers, Bowfront, Mahogany, 43 In. 1650.00
Chest, Georgian, 5 Drawers, Bowfront, Mahogany, Splay Feet 1925.00
Chest, Georgian, 5 Drawers, Mahogany, Bale Handle, c.1780, 41 x 48 In. 1760.00
Chest, Georgian, 5 Drawers, Oak, c.1780, 43 In. 850.00
Chest, Georgian, Bowfront, Mahogany, Inlay, 43 In. 1500.00
Chest, Gustav Stickley, 3 Long & 6 Short Drawers, Wooden Knobs, Oak, 47 In. 880.00
Chest, Hepplewhite Style, 4 Graduated Drawers, Serpentine, 20th Century 2100.00
Chest, Hepplewhite, 2 Drawers Over 3 Drawers, Cherry 1600.00
Chest, Hepplewhite, 2 Drawers Over 3 Drawers, Walnut, 1795–1805, 42 x 40 In. 4250.00
Chest, Hepplewhite, 4 Drawers, Cock–Beaded, Cherry, c.1800, 36 In. 2700.00
Chest, Hepplewhite, 4 Drawers, Cock–Beaded, Cherry, Ohio, 1820 .... 2400.00
Chest, Hepplewhite, 4 Drawers, Cock–Beaded, Mahogany, 32 x 37 x 20 In. 358.00
Chest, Hepplewhite, 4 Drawers, Curly Maple, French Feet, Scalloped Apron, 22 In. 900.00
Chest, Hepplewhite, 4 Drawers, Curly Maple, Scalloped Apron, 22 1/2 In. 2200.00
Chest, Hepplewhite, 4 Drawers, Curly Walnut, Country, 40 1/2 In. 4000.00
Chest, Hepplewhite, 4 Drawers, Serpentine, Figured Mahogany Veneer, 36 In. 4500.00
Chest, Hepplewhite, 4 Drawers, Walnut, French Feet, 37 x 21 x 38 In. 3630.00
Chest, Hepplewhite, Birch, Mahogany Veneer, NH, 40 x 19 x 41 In. 1430.00
Chest, Hepplewhite, Bowfront, Mahogany, Massachusetts 3800.00
Chest, Hepplewhite, Crotch Mahogany, Pine, Original Pulls, 1800, Miniature 1950.00
Chest, Hepplewhite, Walnut, French Feet, Scalloped Apron, 46 1/2 In. 825.00
Chest, Immigrant's, Pine, Brown Finish, Blue Striping, White Inscription, 26 In. 295.00
Chest, Immigrant's, Pine, Canted Sides, Dovetailed Case, 46 In. 220.00
Chest, Immigrant's, Pine, Green Paint, Black Label, Iron Handles, 41 1/2 In. 125.00
Chest, Immigrant's, Red Pine, Stylized Floral Design, Strap Hinges, 36 In. 715.00
Chest, Jacobean, 2 Drawers, Oak, Hinged Top, Foliate Frieze, 31 x 55 In. 825.00
Chest, L. & J. G. Stickley, No. 77, 5 Drawers, 38 1/2 x 38 x 19 In. 1325.00
Chest, Lingerie, 5 Drawers, Attached Mirror 500.00
Chest, Lingerie, 6 Drawers, Beveled Mirror, Oak 675.00
Chest, Lion, Willow Trees, Eagle Lid, Green, Black, Mustard Top, 22 x 9 x 11 In. 6050.00
Chest, Mahogany, Split Columns, Acanthus Leaves, 41 1/2 In. 245.00
Chest, Mule, 1 Drawer, 2 Board, Yellow Pine, Scrolled Apron, 36 In. 550.00
Chest, Mule, 1 Drawer, Walnut, Lift Top, 39 In. 1100.00
Chest, Mule, 2 Overlapping Drawers, Pine, Dark Repaint, Bootjack Feet, 44 In. 600.00
Chest, Mule, 6 Board, 1 Drawer, Lift Top, Pine, 32 3/4 In. 450.00
Chest, Mule, 6 Board, 1 Drawer, Maple, Cutout Feet, Scalloped Apron, 40 In. 440.00
Chest, Mule, 6 Board, 2 Drawers & 4 False Drawers, Pine, Country, 43 In. 495.00
Chest, Mule, George III, 2 Drawers, Hinged Rectangular Top, Square Legs 550.00
Chest, Mule, Queen Anne, 3 Drawers, Maple, Lift Top, 35 1/2 x 46 1/2 In. 825.00
Chest, Oak, Figured Walnut Veneer Drawers, England, 27 x 39 x 37 In., 2 Piece 1250.00
Chest, Poplar, Reddish Brown Graining, Dovetailed Case, 24 In. 995.00
Chest, Portsmouth Style, 4 Drawers, Mahogany, Swell Front, 37 1/2 In. 1450.00
Chest, Provincial, Oak, Paneled, Lift Top, 18th Century 495.00
Chest, Queen Anne, 4 Top & 3 Base Drawers, Walnut, Mass., 1740s, 62 In. 6600.00
Chest, Queen Anne, 5 Graduated & 3 Base Drawers, Maple, 1760, 76 In. 9900.00
Chest, Queen Anne, 6 Drawers, Cherry, Trifid Feet, Scalloped Apron, 54 In. 1200.00
Chest, Queen Anne, Bartlett, 6 Drawers, Birch, Bandy Feet, N. H., 1815 .... 9500.00
Chest, Queen Anne, Cock–Beaded Surrounds, Maple, 1740–1780, 68 1/2 In. 9350.00
Chest, Queen Anne, Maple, Shell–Carved Drawers, c.1760, 75 In. 9900.00
Chest, Shaker, 3 Drawers, Square Tapering Legs, Pine & Poplar 2300.00
Chest, Sheraton, 4 Drawers, Burl Maple Drawer Fronts, Cherry, c.1810 .... 1100.00
Chest, Sheraton, 4 Drawers, Cock–Beaded, Cherry, Panel Side 525.00
Chest, Sheraton, 4 Drawers, Mahogany, Cornucopia, Scalloped, MacIntire 1700.00
Chest, Sheraton, 4 Drawers, Mahogany, Rope–Turned Posts, Biscuit Corners 800.00
Chest, Sheraton, 7 Drawers, Curly Maple, Scalloped Base, 51 In. 1700.00
Chest, Sheraton, Cherry, Reeded Column 2100.00
Chest, Sheraton, Mahogany, Inlay, Shaped Front 7150.00
Chest, Sheraton, Mahogany, Mirror, Turned Posts, New England, 1825, Small 1350.00

Chest, Sheraton, Mahogany, Rope–Turned Posts 900.00
Chest, Sugar, 2 Bottom Drawers, Pine 325.00
Chest, Sugar, Hepplewhite, Cherry, Breadboard Top, Strap Hinges, 1810–1820 .... 3850.00
Chest, Sugar, Round & Ring–Turned Legs, Walnut, 19th Century, 28 1/2 In. 1760.00
Chest, Tea, Camphorwood, Leather Cover, Brass Binding, 50 x 34 x 18 In. 715.00
Chest, Transitional Style, Mahogany, Crotch Grain, Boston, Turned Feet, 1830 ...... 995.00
Chest, Tulip & Fruitwood, Doors, Drawers, 18th Century, 38 1/2 x 45 In. 4400.00
Chest, Victorian, 1 Drawer, Pine, Cupboard Doors, Bracket Feet, 19th Century 385.00
Chest, Victorian, 3 Drawers, Marble Top 425.00
Chest, Victorian, Hatbox, Gallery Top, Wavy Birch Panels In Door 770.00
Chest, William IV, 4 Drawers, Cock–Beaded, Mahogany, Plinth, 16 x 14 x 9 In. 500.00
Chest–On–Chest, 2 Short Over 4 Long Drawers, Maple, c.1780, 80 1/2 In. 2860.00
Chest–On–Chest, 3 Short Over 3 Long Drawers, Burl Walnut, 1760s, 5 Ft. 9 In. 9350.00
Chest–On–Chest, 6 Drawers, Figural Inlay, Foliage, Walnut, 5 Ft. 8 1/2 In. 8800.00
Chest–On–Chest, Chippendale, 4 Graduated Drawers, Bonnet Top, Cherry, 88 In. 2200.00
Chest–On–Chest, Chippendale, Maple, Replaced Ogee Bracket Feet, New England 4950.00
Chest–On–Chest, Federal, Bowfront, Pine, Grain Painted, 36 x 40 In. 1875.00
Chest–On–Chest, George III, 10 Short Over 6 Drawers, Mahogany, Bracket Feet ... 2750.00
Chest–On–Chest, Georgian, Mahogany, Bracket Feet, c.1780, 72 x 41 In. 3575.00
Chest–On–Frame, Queen Anne, 8 Drawers, Walnut, Cabriole Legs, 62 In. 1815.00
Church Pew, Oak, 11 Ft. 200.00
Clothes Press, Blue Paint, Panel Door & Drawer, Late 18th Century 880.00
Clothes Press, Georgian, Adjustable Board, 1 Drawer & 2 Doors 1100.00
Clothes Press, Georgian, Adjustable Shelf Over 1 Drawer, Oak, c.1760 .... 1210.00
Coffer, Mahogany, Winged Griffins Front, Floral Carving, 64 x 26 x 22 In. 2420.00
Coffer, Paneled Hinged Top Over Fluted Frieze, Stuart Oak, 4 Ft. 4 In. 1870.00
Coffer, Paneled Top, Boxwood & Mahogany Inlay, England, c.1700 .... 3250.00
Commode, 2 Drawers, Burled Walnut, Serpentine, Cross Banded Borders, France 5500.00
Commode, Charles X, 4 Drawers, Marble Top, Burlwood 4400.00
Commode, Directoire Style, 3 Drawers, Fruitwood Inlay, 26 1/2 In. 120.00
Commode, Empire, Chestnut, Lion's Face Handles, c.1820, 45 In. 1650.00
Commode, Fitted Case Over 2 Drawers, Walnut, Sicily, 34 In. 6050.00
Commode, Georgian, Demilune, Figured Mahogany Veneer, 2 Doors 1760.00
Commode, Georgian, Mahogany, 18th Century 1200.00
Commode, Georgian, Mahogany, Tray Top, c.1780, 20 In. 825.00
Commode, Hepplewhite, Mahogany, Lift Top, Country, 17 x 18 In. 135.00
Commode, Inlay, Writing Slide, Walnut, Kingwood Parquetry, Germany, 34 In. 8900.00
Commode, Louis XV Style, 2 Drawers, Serpentine Top, 43 In. 2200.00
Commode, Louis XV, 3 Drawers, Gilt Metal Mount, Marbelized Top, France 5500.00
Commode, Louis XV, Bronze Swags, Marquetry, Walnut, Mahogany, 35 In. 3300.00
Commode, Louis XV, Marble Top, Figures On Drawers, Japanned Pine, 56 In. 5950.00
Commode, Louis XVI, 2 Small & 2 Large Drawers, Variegated Marble Top, 1850 ... 1485.00
Commode, Marble Top, Bird's–Eye Maple & Rosewood, 31 1/2 In. 935.00
Commode, Marble Top, Marquetry Leaf Scrolls, France, c.1920, 33 x 28 In. 995.00
Commode, Marble Top, Tulip & Fruitwood, Round, Floral Inlay, France 6000.00
Commode, Neoclassical, Walnut, 4 Drawers, Fruitwood, Italy, 35 x 50 x 22 In. 8900.00
Commode, Roundabout, Queen Anne, Walnut & Mahogany, 32 In. 1650.00
Commode, Victorian, Marble Inset Top, Mahogany, Pedestal, 1 Door 400.00
Console, Georgian, Gilded Marble Top, Eagle Form 5525.00
Console, Marble Top, Carved Busts, Gilded, France, 1880s 595.00
Console, Marble Top, Stylized Blossoms On Iron Frame, c.1925, 40 5/8 In. 2475.00
Console, Rococo, Marble Top, Painted Iron, France 9460.00
Cradle, Carved Spindle Sides, Rockers 600.00
Cradle, Curly Maple, Canted Sides, Scalloped Step–Down Edges, 41 In. 495.00
Cradle, Cypress Wood, Louisiana, 19th Century ....*Illus* 125.00
Cradle, From Packing Crate, Stenciled, E. Cromwell Drugstore, Blue Paint 350.00
Cradle, Grained, Cast Iron Rockers 525.00
Cradle, Hooded, Paint Design, 30 x 44 In. 330.00
Cradle, Hooded, Pine, Brown Paint, 33 In. 260.00
Cradle, Hooded, Sheet Metal, Red & Blue Paint, 26 1/2 In. 115.00
Cradle, Oak, 19th Century, France, 41 In. 125.00
Cradle, Oak, Slatted 60.00
Cradle, On Stand, Brass 900.00

Cradle, Pine, Maple, Nailed Construction, Side Holes For Handles 250.00
Cradle, Pine, Red Paint, Cutout Rockers, Curved Ends, 44 In. 440.00
Cradle, Rattan Panels, Mahogany 445.00
Cradle, Softwood, Dovetailed, Heart–Shaped Cutouts 185.00
Cradle, Tiger Maple, Rolled Ends 1300.00
Cradle, Valanced Hood, Mahogany, Raised On Tall Rockers, 38 x 41 In. 385.00
Cradle, Victorian, Pressed Oak, Head, Foot & Side Panels Design 650.00
Cradle, Walnut, Dovetailed, Scrolled End, Rockers, 39 In. 275.00
Cradle, William & Mary, Domed Hood, Shaped Rockers, Pine, 40 In. 1760.00
Credenza, William IV, Mahogany, Floral Crest, Shelves, Panel Doors, c.1835 .... 1100.00
Crib, Cast Iron 180.00
Crib, Tiger Maple & Maple, Turned Spindles & Legs, 30 x 30 1/2 In. 880.00
Cupboard, 2 Doors, Old Blue Paint 900.00
Cupboard, 2 Piece, Paneled Doors, Cutout Feet, Shaped Apron, Country, 90 In. 650.00
Cupboard, Bowfront, Reclaimed Pine, Dentil Cornice, England, 96 x 50 In. 8200.00
Cupboard, Child's, Step Back, 2 Blind Doors Over 2 Blind Doors, Green Paint 235.00
Cupboard, Chimney, Amish, Poplar Panels, Oak Frame, Square Nails 365.00
Cupboard, Chimney, Mustard Paint, 1 Door, 1860s 1800.00
Cupboard, Chimney, Original Blue Paint, Open Shelves, 2 Doors 1200.00
Cupboard, Chimney, Pine, Flaky Green Over Red Paint, 2 Doors, Narrow 885.00
Cupboard, Chimney, Pine, H Hinges, Painted, c.1750 .... 1650.00
Cupboard, Chimney, Pine, Poplar, 1 Interior Drawer, Paneled Door, 70 In. 412.00
Cupboard, Chippendale, 2 Piece, Pine, Panel Doors, 3 Drawers, 78 1/2 In. 3025.00
Cupboard, Continental, Walnut, Paneled Ends, Doors, 2 Drawers, 43 1/4 In. 1760.00
Cupboard, Corner, 2 Doors With 6 Panes, Cornice, 80 In. 1250.00
Cupboard, Corner, 2 Glass & 2 Paneled Doors, Oak, 6 Ft. 11 In. x 3 Ft. 7 In. 500.00
Cupboard, Corner, 2 Piece, Pine, Poplar, Bluish Gray Paint, 81 3/4 In. 3025.00
Cupboard, Corner, Arched Glass Door Over 2 Paneled Doors, c.1800, 95 In. 2500.00
Cupboard, Corner, Blind Door, Tennessee 2700.00
Cupboard, Corner, Cherry, 1 Piece, 6 Panes, 77 In. 1870.00
Cupboard, Corner, Cherry, Blue Green Paint, 2 Glass Doors, Cornice, 54 x 93 In. .. 2600.00
Cupboard, Corner, Cherry, Original Finish, 47 x 86 x 31 In. 2850.00
Cupboard, Corner, Cherry, Pie Shelf, Recessed Panels, 2 Piece 2400.00
Cupboard, Corner, Chestnut, Plate Holders, Painted Designs, c.1830 .... 6500.00
Cupboard, Corner, Chippendale, Cherry, 12 Glass Panes Over Door, 1820–1830 ...... 6200.00
Cupboard, Corner, Crown Molding, White Paint, Pine, 7 Ft. 7 1/2 In. 4350.00
Cupboard, Corner, Empire, Poplar, Red Stain, Green Pilasters, 85 In., 2 Piece 2100.00
Cupboard, Corner, Federal, Pine, Molded Cornice, 2 Glazed Doors, 6 Ft. 11 In. 5500.00
Cupboard, Corner, George III, Mullion Glazed Doors, Mahogany, 80 In. 6600.00
Cupboard, Corner, Glazed Doors, Shelf Inside, Cherry, 82 In. 1350.00
Cupboard, Corner, Greek Key Carving, 2 Top & 2 Base Drawers, Lattice, 1840 ...... 6995.00
Cupboard, Corner, Hanging, Pine, 1 Door 1300.00
Cupboard, Corner, Pegged Construction, Cherry, 19th Century 1155.00
Cupboard, Corner, Pine, Butterfly Shelves, 88 3/4 In. 990.00
Cupboard, Corner, Pine, Dentil & Swag, Reeded Panel Doors, 2 Piece 2100.00
Cupboard, Corner, Pine, Dovetailed Case, Raised Panel Door, 33 3/4 In. 577.00

♦ ♦

The general rule about dove-
tailing is the fewer the number
of joints, the older the piece. A
drawer made in the early 18th
century was either joined with
one huge dovetail or was
pegged together.

♦ ♦

Furniture, Cradle, Cypress Wood, Louisiana,
19th Century

Cupboard, Corner, Pine, Green Paint, 72 3/4 In. 8500.00
Cupboard, Corner, Pine, Stripped Finish, Raised Panel Doors, Country, 85 In. 1320.00
Cupboard, Corner, Poplar & Butternut, Pie Shelf, Blue Interior, 2 Piece, 82 In. 1600.00
Cupboard, Corner, Poplar, Dovetailed, Bracket Feet, Crown Molding, 84 In. 800.00
Cupboard, Corner, Provincial, 3 Open Shelves, Paneled Door, Pine, 72 In. 1350.00
Cupboard, Corner, Red Beveled Panel, 18th Century 3295.00
Cupboard, Corner, Rounded Top, 12 Panes, 2 Doors Base, Blue Paint, 8 Ft. 3080.00
Cupboard, Corner, String Inlay, Broken Arch Top, Walnut, 86 In. 2200.00
Cupboard, Corner, Tiger & Maple, Molded Cornice, 2 Glazed Doors, 85 In. 2750.00
Cupboard, Court, Jacobean, Frieze Supported By Turnings, Carved Door, 41 In. 2420.00
Cupboard, Court, Renaissance Revival, Walnut, 20th Century, France, Europe, 104 In. 950.00
Cupboard, Dutch Type, Pine, 3 Drawers, Painted Design, Penna., 1830 .... 3800.00
Cupboard, Dutch, Child's, Grain Painted, 28 1/2 x 15 1/2 In. 1220.00
Cupboard, Federal, Paneled Door, 3 Shelves, Painted Blue, 67 1/4 In. 7150.00
Cupboard, Galleried Plate Rack, 3 Doors, 2 Drawers, France, Walnut, c.1865 .... 3650.00
Cupboard, Geometric Facade Design, Colored Wood, 43 3/4 In. 275.00
Cupboard, Gothic Revival, Floral Carving, 73 In. 660.00
Cupboard, Grain Painted, 2 Glass Doors Over 1 Drawer, Jacob Spitler, 1851 .... 8250.00
Cupboard, Hanging, Blue Paint, Gold Trim, 13 x 16 1/2 In. 520.00
Cupboard, Hanging, Cherry, Dovetailed Drawer, Paneled Door, 13 x 13 x 21 In. 330.00
Cupboard, Hanging, Chippendale, Serpentine Shelves, Painted Red, 26 In. 2420.00
Cupboard, Hanging, George III, Inlaid Door, Stuart Oak, 1890s, 41 In. 1760.00
Cupboard, Hanging, Green, Tan, Porcelain Knobs, 1900, 14 x 24 x 7 In. 265.00
Cupboard, Hanging, Pine, Open Shelves, 2 Drawers, Panel Doors, 28 In. 950.00
Cupboard, Hanging, Pine, Reddish Brown Graining, Blue Interior, 17 3/4 In. 180.00
Cupboard, Hanging, Porcelain Knobs, Green & Tan Paint, 24 1/2 In. 165.00
Cupboard, Hanging, Raised Paneled Door, Grain Painted Pine, c.1790, 34 1/4 In. ... 7400.00
Cupboard, Hanging, Red, 7 Dovetailed Drawers, 3 Doors, 25 x 8 3/4 x 23 In. 2550.00
Cupboard, Hanging, Tiger Maple, 18th Century 3400.00
Cupboard, Hanging, Tombstone Glazed Doors, Late 18th Century, 25 x 21 In. 330.00
Cupboard, Hanging, Yellow Pine, Cornice Moldings, 30 In. 385.00
Cupboard, Hudson Valley, Gray Paint, 1840, 4 Ft. Wide 1650.00
Cupboard, Inside Shelves, Paneled, Cream Designs, Black Striping, Painted, 76 In. ... 1320.00
Cupboard, Jelly, 2 Drawers, Red Wash, Wide Board Back 1650.00
Cupboard, Jelly, Child's, Pine, 1 Drawer, Paneled Doors, 24 1/2 In. 385.00
Cupboard, Jelly, Hepplewhite, Pine, Scrolled Skirt, Original Paint, c.1830 .... 2350.00
Cupboard, Jelly, Orange Design On Green, 73 In. 3190.00
Cupboard, Jelly, Pine, Poplar, Comb Graining Traces, 2 Drawers & Doors, 51 In. ... 600.00
Cupboard, Jelly, Pine, Soft Finish, Turned Feet, Brass Latch, 60 In. 325.00
Cupboard, Jelly, Poplar, Red, 4 Panels, Molded Cornice, 15 x 40 3/4 x 72 In. 1540.00
Cupboard, Jelly, Poplar, Single Board Construction, Dovetailed Case, 65 In. 2640.00
Cupboard, Jelly, Red Paint, Primitive, Poplar, 2 Doors, Gallery 1600.00
Cupboard, Jelly, Tiger Maple Grain Painted, 2 Drawers 950.00
Cupboard, Jelly, Yellow Pine, Geometric Design, Orange, 73 In. 3190.00
Cupboard, Jelly, Yellow Pine, Red Repaint, Geometric Design, 53 1/4 In. 2750.00
Cupboard, Kitchen, 2 Recessed Panel Doors, White Porcelain Knobs, 2 Shelves 3700.00
Cupboard, Kitchen, Pine, 3 Open Shelves Above Paneled Door, 71 x 41 x 16 In. 550.00
Cupboard, Kitchen, Sellers, Work Top, Sliding Door, Yellow 70.00
Cupboard, Louis XVI Style, Cream Paint, Wire Doors, 77 In. 660.00
Cupboard, Mahogany, Ball & Claw Foot, Cabriole Legs, Blind Door 550.00
Cupboard, Mahogany, Inlay, Ormolu Trim, 2 Drawers, Double Doors, 76 In. 880.00
Cupboard, Oak, Blind Door, 2 Drawers, 46 x 86 x 14 In. 2900.00
Cupboard, Oak, Scalloped Base, Paneled Doors, 3 Drawers, 34 In. 1320.00
Cupboard, Pennsylvania Dutch, Pine, 18 Panes, 3 Drawers, 7 Ft., 2 Piece 7500.00
Cupboard, Pennsylvania Dutch, Walnut, 2 Doors & Drawers, 12 Panes Top 3950.00
Cupboard, Pewter, 2 Piece, Open, Paneled Doors, Pine, Red Paint, 75 1/2 In. 1650.00
Cupboard, Pewter, Mustard Paint, Open Top, 6 Ft. 4500.00
Cupboard, Pewter, One Piece, Refinished Pine, Raised Panel Doors, 80 1/2 In. 500.00
Cupboard, Pewter, Pine, Open, Scalloped Edge, 1870 .... 750.00
Cupboard, Pewter, Step Back, Original Red Wash, Ireland, 1840 .... 3950.00
Cupboard, Pine, 1 Piece, Cutout Base, Paneled Doors, 1 Drawer, 86 1/2 In. 3550.00
Cupboard, Pine, 1 Piece, Paneled Doors, 2 Drawers, Tiered Cornice, 44 In. 750.00
Cupboard, Pine, 1 Piece, Paneled Doors, 79 In. 1320.00

Furniture, Daybed, Biedermeier, Walnut, Fruitwood Marquetry, 7 Ft.

Cupboard, Pine, 2 Doors, 5 Shelves, 19th Century, 71 In. 440.00
Cupboard, Pine, Dark Finish, Dovetailed Case, Paneled Doors, 21 3/4 In. 270.00
Cupboard, Pine, Dark Patina, Raised Panel Doors, Crown Molded Cornice, 75 In. 800.00
Cupboard, Pine, Open, Cardboard Back, 10 1/2 In. 77.00
Cupboard, Pine, Paint Traces, Gold Trim, Europe, 55 x 145 x 91 In., 2 Piece 1815.00
Cupboard, Pine, Raised Panel Doors, 3 Drawers, Overhanging Top, 53 In. 687.00
Cupboard, Pine, Red Flame Graining, Paneled Doors, Adjustable Shelves, 24 In. 550.00
Cupboard, Poplar, 2 Piece, Scalloped Base, Paneled Doors, 85 1/2 In. 2700.00
Cupboard, Poplar, 3 Base Drawers, 4 Doors, 6 Panes, Country, 74 In. 1430.00
Cupboard, Shaker Type, Church Vestment & Wine Storage, 3 Sections, 9 x 12 Ft. ... 225.00
Cupboard, Shaker, Hanging, Pine, Original Finish, Yellow Interior, 1 Door, 1840 .... 880.00
Cupboard, Shaker, Hanging, Yellow Interior, Iron & Brass Hardware, c.1840 .... 880.00
Cupboard, Shaker, Pine, Green Paint, 6 Drawers, Panel Doors, 57 In. 4125.00
Cupboard, Shaker, Pine, Raised Panel Door, Canterbury, 1800, 24 In. 440.00
Cupboard, Shaker, Red Wash, Varnished, Mid–19th Century, 84 In. 4675.00
Cupboard, Sheraton, Cherry, Carved Oval Sunbursts, Scrolled Cornice, 72 In. 2970.00
Cupboard, Ship's, Paneled Doors, Burl Walnut & Olive Wood, 77 1/2 In. 2200.00
Cupboard, Spice, Hanging, Mahogany, 19th Century, 24 1/2 In. 160.00
Cupboard, Step Back, 2 Glass Doors Above Pierced Tin Doors, Pie Shelf 1450.00
Cupboard, Step Back, 2 Glass Doors Over Paneled Doors, Cherry, 85 In. 1295.00
Cupboard, Step Back, 3 Shelves, Recessed Door, Red, Green Side, 80 1/4 In. 1875.00
Cupboard, Step Back, 4 Raised Panel Doors, Blue Paint, 65 x 40 In. 4400.00
Cupboard, Step Back, Bracket Base, Yellow Paint, Pie Shelf, Penna., 1820 .... 7400.00
Cupboard, Step Back, Butternut, Original Hardware, 1840, Large 2250.00
Cupboard, Step Back, Cherry, 26 Panes, 2 Doors Over 2 Drawers, W. Penna. 2850.00
Cupboard, Step Back, Chestnut, Butternut Paint, 2 Piece 895.00
Cupboard, Step Back, Dark Yellow Paint, Graining, 4 Doors, 1850, 2 Piece 2150.00
Cupboard, Step Back, Pine, 2 Doors, 2 Drawers, Grain Painted 880.00
Cupboard, Step Back, Poplar, 1 Piece, Weathered Surface, 70 3/4 In. 1100.00
Cupboard, Step Back, Poplar, Blind Doorstop & Base 700.00
Cupboard, Step Back, Wall Mount, Pigeon Holes In Top, Grain Painted, 78 1/2 In. 900.00
Cupboard, Step Back, Walnut, Glazed Doors, Drawers, Spoon Rack, c.1800, 7 Ft. ... 4200.00
Cupboard, Step Back, Walnut, Red Repaint, Country, 49 x 21 x 89 In. 1000.00
Cupboard, Victorian, Oak Grained, 4 Doors & 2 Drawers, 2 Piece 600.00
Cupboard, Walnut, 1 Piece, 3 Drawers, Scalloped Design, 86 1/2 In. 1265.00
Cupboard, Walnut, 2 Piece, Poplar Ends, Scalloped Apron, Paneled Doors, 79 In. ... 1400.00
Cupboard, Walnut, Paneled Doors, Drawers, Cabriole Legs, 43 x 47 x 20 In. 1600.00
Cupboard, Yellow Pine, 10 Drawers, 2 Board Top, Paneled Ends, 33 In. 3190.00
Cupboard, Yellow Pine, Blue Repaint, Paneled Doors, Molded Cornice, 53 In. 1100.00
Cupboard, Yellow Pine, Paneled Spandrels, Arch With Keystones, 96 In. 3520.00

Daybed, Arts & Crafts, Pop–Out, Leather Upholstery, Mission Oak 850.00
Daybed, Biedermeier, Walnut, Fruitwood Marquetry, 7 Ft. ....*Illus* 5500.00
Daybed, Biedermeier, Walnut, Upholstered Head & Foot Boards, 6 Ft. 9 In. 7425.00
Daybed, Cherry, Grayish Blue Ribbed Upholstery, Original Rope Rails, 72 1/2 In. 550.00
Daybed, Curly Maple, Walnut Headboard, Upholstered Cushion, 24 x 77 In. 510.00
Daybed, Empire Style, Rolled Head & Foot Boards, Bronze Mounts, 82 In. 995.00
Daybed, Federal, Horsehair Upholstery, Front Winged Feet, Back Claw Feet 4250.00
Daybed, Green Paint, Pennsylvania 950.00
Daybed, Louis XVI Style, Beechwood, Circular Stop–Fluted Legs 165.00
Daybed, Louis XVI, Carved Beechwood, 1900 .... 2200.00
Daybed, Mahogany, Outward Scrolling Arms, Ogee–Molded Frame, 82 In. 715.00
Daybed, Mahogany, Upholstery, Philadelphia, 1740–1760 .... 3850.00
Daybed, Painted & Parcel Gilt, Upholstered Head & Foot Boards, Sweden 9350.00
Daybed, Quaint, Mission Oak 1050.00
Daybed, Queen Anne, Double Caning Ends, Pillows & Bolsters, Upholstery 585.00
Daybed, Stickley Bros., No. 3236, 3 Vertical Slats Head Board, Green Leather 605.00
Desk Bookcase, Larkin, Drop Front, Oak, Shaped Mirror, Griffins 800.00
Desk, 7 Drawers, Ball & Claw Feet, Mahogany, 45 1/2 x 28 x 31 1/2 In. 500.00
Desk, Apazio, Painted Metal, Cabinet On Side, Olivetti, 29 x 63 In. 935.00
Desk, Art Deco, Rosewood & Mahogany, Inlay, Ebonized, France, 1925, 36 In. 1870.00
Desk, Biedermeier, Fruitwood, Cylinder, Tooled Leather Surface, c.1830, 45 In. 9350.00
Desk, Biedermeier, Mahogany, Cylinder, 19th Century 1980.00
Desk, Block & Slant Front, Curly Maple, Ball & Claw Feet, 42 In. 1980.00
Desk, Boulle, Curved Top, Cabriole Legs, Ormolu Mounted, 1840 .... 400.00
Desk, Butler's, Chippendale, Fall Front, Fitted Interior, Ogee Feet, 49 In. 1100.00
Desk, Butler's, Empire, Fall Front, Flame Mahogany, Mid–1800s 795.00
Desk, Butler's, Sheraton, Fall Front, Mahogany, Fitted, U.S., 32 x 48 In. 1100.00
Desk, Butler's, Tiger Maple Veneer, Mahogany, 1820s ....'. 605.00
Desk, C Roll Top, 7 Drawers, Chair 250.00
Desk, Campaign, Ebony Line Inlay, Mahogany, Brass Corners, 38 In. 995.00
Desk, Campaign, Pine, Lt. Col. Thomas F. Burpee's Property, 1864 .... 995.00
Desk, Captain's, Faux Bamboo, Lacquered, Japan 3960.00
Desk, Carlton House, Fitted, 3 Drawers, Castors, England, 1820 .... 4200.00
Desk, Child's, Roll Top, Center Drawer, 3 Side Drawers, Delphos Label, 1940s 160.00
Desk, Child's, Roll Top, Maple, 5 Pigeonholes, 3 Drawers 125.00
Desk, Chinese Chippendale, Pullout Writing Surface, Cupboard, 37 x 56 In. 330.00
Desk, Chippendale, Fall Front, Walnut, Whale End Shelf, 36 In. 700.00
Desk, Chippendale, Fan–Carved Slant Front, Cherry, Conn., 1780, 36 In. 8500.00
Desk, Chippendale, Slant Front, 4 Drawers, 18th Century 2100.00
Desk, Chippendale, Slant Front, Pine, 4 Dovetailed Drawers, England, 38 x 41 In. ... 3080.00
Desk, Clerk's, Black & Red Grain Painted, 3 Drawers, 1840s 750.00
Desk, Counting House, Slant Front, Spool Frame, c.1860 .... 3000.00
Desk, Cylinder, 3 Drawers, Rosewood Interior, Mahogany, 1830, 49 In. 4000.00
Desk, Cylinder, Pullout Surface, Double Doors, 4 Drawers, Walnut, 65 x 33 In. 3300.00
Desk, Cylinder, Renaissance Revival, Walnut, 8 Burled & 4 Bird's–Eye Drawers 5800.00
Desk, Davenport, England, 1870 .... 1975.00
Desk, Double–Sided, Rectangular, Middle Partition, 1890–1920 .... 395.00
Desk, Empire, Fall Front, Triple Back, Carved Crest, Mahogany, Scotland, 82 In. ... 225.00
Desk, Empire, Slant Front, Mahogany, Carved, Fitted Interior, 44 x 36 In. 1550.00
Desk, Fall Front, A. Toby Furniture Co., Rosewood, Dated 1856 .... 1600.00
Desk, Fall Front, Hinged Opening, Pigeonholes, Oak, Arts & Crafts, 46 x 35 In. 522.00
Desk, Fall Front, Inlaid Birds, Leaf Scrolls, Brass Sabots, Holland, 38 In. 2650.00
Desk, Fall Front, Queen Anne, Gilt Figures, Cabriole Legs, 41 x 29 x 16 In. 825.00
Desk, Fall Front, Tiger Maple, Gallery, Fitted, 19th Century, 39 x 32 x 21 In. 1870.00
Desk, Federal, Mahogany, Cylinder, String Inlay, Baltimore, 1800, 44 In. 6600.00
Desk, Federal, Mahogany, Gothic Mullions, Baize Lined Writing Surface, 1820 .... 2100.00
Desk, Federal, Slant Front, Cherry, 1790 .... 4950.00
Desk, Folding, Myers Chautauqua Industrial Art 125.00
Desk, George III, Mahogany, Rolled Tambour Front, Leather Inset Writing Surface 4400.00
Desk, George III, Slant Front, 4 Graduated Drawers, Yew Wood, 40 In. 4180.00
Desk, Governor Winthrop, Cherry, 4 Graduated Drawers, 36 In. 3905.00
Desk, Governor Winthrop, Tiger Maple 6100.00
Desk, Gustav Stickley, 2 Drawers, Gallery, Paneled Sides, Decal, 35 x 40 In. 1450.00

Desk, Gustav Stickley, No. 720, 4 Drawers, 2 Small In Middle, 38 x 22 x 38 In. 3500.00
Desk, Gustav Stickley, Writing, Gallery Top, Drop Front, 52 In. 1650.00
Desk, H. Miller, Leather Surface, Cubbyholes, Perforated Metal File Basket, 1946 .... 4400.00
Desk, Hepplewhite, Fall Front, 20 Drawers, 3 Secret Drawers, Cherry, 38 In. 5000.00
Desk, Hepplewhite, Slant Front, Butternut, 2 Drawers, Country, 30 x 29 x 36 In. 385.00
Desk, Hepplewhite, Tambour, Cherry, Maple, c.1790, 55 x 42 In. 4000.00
Desk, Hepplewhite, Walnut, Old Varnish, Paneled Ends & Top, Country, 33 In. 425.00
Desk, Jacobean Style, Rope Carved Legs, 9 Drawers, Pullout, Oak, 40 In. 525.00
Desk, Kneehole, 1 Drawer Flanked By 8 Drawers, Mahogany Plywood, 31 x 23 In. 275.00
Desk, Kneehole, George I, Burled Walnut, England, c.1720, 32 x 38 x 21 In. 5000.00
Desk, Kneehole, Marcel Louis Baugnieet, Oak & Beech, c.1935, 4 Ft. 7 In. 1100.00
Desk, L. & J. G. Stickley, Chalet, Shoefoot, Pinned & Doweled, Chair, 1905 .... 2100.00
Desk, Lap, Brass Inlay, France, 19th Century 295.00
Desk, Lap, Child's, Maple, 1880s 235.00
Desk, Lap, Mother-of-Pearl Inlay, Ivory Handles, 22 In. 1875.00
Desk, Lap, Panel of Lovers On Cover, Bronze Female Terms, France, 13 In. 2850.00
Desk, Lap, Victorian, Mahogany, Hinged Top, Late 19th Century, 22 x 17 x 10 In. 415.00
Desk, Lap, Wooden, Blue Paint, Stenciled, Spring Spindle Legs, Golden Rule Line ... 45.00
Desk, Limbert, Drawer, Letter Racks, Cane Center, 35 x 32 x 20 In. 885.00
Desk, Louis XV Style, Bombe, Gilt Bronze Mounted 8250.00
Desk, Mahogany, Oxbow Serpentine, Block & Shell, Mass., 18th Century 9300.00
Desk, Mahogany, Tooled Leather Inserts, Plate Glass, 29 1/2 In. 935.00
Desk, Majorelle, Mahogany Marquetry, Stepped Shelf, Frieze Drawer, 43 In. 5500.00
Desk, Mother-of-Pearl Inlay, Writing Top Lifts To Game Board, Papier-Mache 6600.00
Desk, Partner's, Edwardian, Satinwood, Octagonal Top, 30 x 54 In. 2000.00
Desk, Partner's, George III, Mahogany, 3 Drawers, 30 x 52 x 50 In. ....*Illus* 5225.00
Desk, Partner's, George III, Slant Front, Mahogany, Pine, 1800, 48 x 52 In. 1800.00
Desk, Partner's, Mahogany, Ball & Claw Feet, 32 x 28 x 48 In. 1500.00
Desk, Partner's, Oak, 1 Central Drawer, 3 Short Drawers, 30 1/2 In. 775.00
Desk, Partner's, Walnut, Leather Top, 4 Drawers Each Side, 4 x 6 Ft. 1800.00
Desk, Plantation, Drop Front, Gallery, Walnut 700.00
Desk, Plantation, Fold Down Writing Surface, 2 Drawers, 78 1/2 In. 850.00
Desk, Plantation, Grain Painted, 2 Top Doors, 1 Drawer 1495.00
Desk, Plantation, Slant Front, Setback Cupboard, Walnut, c.1860, 48 1/2 In. 495.00
Desk, Post Office, Lift Top, Mixed Wood, 2 Base Drawers, Mail Slots, 2 Piece 685.00
Desk, Queen Anne, Bandy Leg, On Frame, Early 18th Century, 36 In. 6050.00
Desk, Queen Anne, Fall Front, Walnut, 2 Mirrored Bookcase Doors, 1920s 250.00
Desk, Roll Top, Tambour Door, 3 Drawers Each Side, Mahogany, 41 1/2 x 66 In. 335.00
Desk, Roll Top, Tambour Door, Pedestal, 4 Drawers, J. Fornette & Bros., 50 In. 600.00
Desk, Roll Top, Tambour, Pull-Out Writing Surface, Cherry, 1826 .... 4800.00
Desk, Roll Top, Veneered Still Life, Vases & Swags, Lower Drawers, Walnut, 46 In. 6600.00
Desk, Roll Top, Walnut, Burl Drawer Fronts & Panels, 60 In. 4950.00
Desk, S Roll Top, Quartersawn Oak, 60 In. 3500.00
Desk, S Roll Top, Victorian, Cherry, 60 In. 3750.00
Desk, S Roll Top, Victorian, Oak, Fitted Interior, 50 x 54 x 31 In. 1100.00
Desk, School, Cherry, Victorian, Cast Iron Base 60.00

Furniture, Desk, Partner's, George III,
Mahogany, 3 Drawers, 30 X 52 X 50 In.

♦♦♦♦♦♦♦♦♦♦♦♦♦♦♦♦♦♦♦♦♦♦♦♦

Have you ever pulled a drawer handle and had it fall off the drawer? This problem is not uncommon for very old furniture with bail handles. The best way to get the drawer open is to use a plunger, the plumber's friend. Stick it to the front of the drawer, then pull.

♦♦♦♦♦♦♦♦♦♦♦♦♦♦♦♦♦♦♦♦♦♦♦♦

Desk, School, Child's, Folding, Pine 265.00
Desk, School, Child's, Maple, Original Finish, 1880s 185.00
Desk, School, Hepplewhite, Pine, Reddish Brown Repaint, 30 In. 300.00
Desk, School, Hepplewhite, Pine, Slant Front, 31 In. 125.00
Desk, School, Shaker, Slant Front, Pine, Maple & Ash, Double 725.00
Desk, School, Slant Front, Walnut, Poplar, Varnish, 1 Drawer, 18 x 18 x 29 In. 260.00
Desk, Schoolmaster's, Cherry, Slant Front, 2 Drawers, 31 1/2 In. 522.00
Desk, Schoolmaster's, Lift Top, Pine, Yellow Paint, 42 x 33 x 21 In. 495.00
Desk, Schoolmaster's, North Carolina, 1840 .... 675.00
Desk, Schoolmaster's, Red Paint, Pigeonhole Interior, Beaded Drawer, Maine 165.00
Desk, Schoolmaster's, Slant Top, Apron Drawer, Pine, 1870s, 51 x 33 1/2 In. 1100.00
Desk, Schoolmaster's, Spindle Gallery Top, Fitted Interior, Pine 357.50
Desk, Sewing, Shaker, 4 Dovetailed Drawers, Pullout Slide, 21 x 36 In. 3025.00
Desk, Shaker, Double Slant Front 660.00
Desk, Shaker, Drop Front, Cherry & Butternut 4500.00
Desk, Sheraton, Slant Front, Cherry, Poplar, Gallery, 1 Drawer, 31 x 25 x 32 In. 495.00
Desk, Slant Front, 4 Drawers, 7 Small Drawers, Dovetailed Case, 23 3/4 In. 1350.00
Desk, Slant Front, 4 Drawers, Back Rail, Walnut, 45 x 41 In. 350.00
Desk, Slant Front, 4 Drawers, Fitted Interior, Galley, 41 1/2 x 31 1/2 In. 325.00
Desk, Slant Front, 6 Inside Drawers, Figured Maple, c.1820, 44 1/2 x 44 In. 3400.00
Desk, Slant Front, Birch, Spindly Legs, Pigeonhole, Red Painted Drawers 3850.00
Desk, Slant Front, Cherry, Stepped, Fitted Interior, New Hampshire, 1780 .... 8800.00
Desk, Slant Front, Chippendale, Birch, Pigeonholes, 36 x 43 x 19 1/2 In. 5225.00
Desk, Slant Front, Chippendale, Santo Domingo Mahogany, c.1760, 45 In. 8900.00
Desk, Slant Front, Fitted, 2 Fan Carved Drawers, 18th Century, 42 x 35 In. 3190.00
Desk, Slant Front, Interior Drawers & Cubbyholes, Butternut, 42 1/4 In. 1045.00
Desk, Slant Front, Maple, 3 Dovetailed Drawers & Case, 40 x 43 1/2 In. 1430.00
Desk, Slant Front, Maple, Tiger Maple, Original Hardware, Old Finish 6050.00
Desk, Slant Front, Oak, Carved & Spindle Gallery Top, Fitted Interior, 46 In. 825.00
Desk, Slant Front, Oak, Small Mirror Top 495.00
Desk, Slant Front, Pine, Mahogany Top, 3 Drawers, 10 1/2 In. 200.00
Desk, Slant Front, Queen Anne, Maple, 4 Graduated Drawers, NH 5500.00
Desk, Slant Front, Queen Anne, Red, Mustard Sponging, 18th Century, 36 x 41 In. 3685.00
Desk, Slant Front, Serpentine, Mahogany, Fitted, 7 Interior Drawers, 40 In. 5940.00
Desk, Slant Front, Stand-Up, 4 Graduated Drawers, Pine, 1830s, 49 1/2 In. 770.00
Desk, Slant Front, Stand-Up, Spool Frame, Counting House, Walnut, c.1860 .... 3000.00
Desk, Slant Front, Sycamore, 3 Drawers, 18th Century 6400.00
Desk, Slant Front, Tiger Maple, 3 Graduated Drawers, Rhode Island 5500.00
Desk, Slant Front, Tiger Maple, Refinished, 36 3/4 In. 6875.00
Desk, Slant Front, Walnut, 2 Shell-Carved Drawers, Tombstone Door, Pa., 41 In. ... 2200.00
Desk, Spinet, Carved Chamfered Legs, Mahogany 418.00
Desk, Standing Counter, Red & Black Grain Painted, Lift Top, Pigeonhole Interior 795.00
Desk, Table Top, Writing, Walnut, Slant Front, 1898 Dime Inset, Drawers 195.00
Desk, Tambour, Hepplewhite, Bird's-Eye Oval Inlay, Mahogany, Mass. 4450.00
Desk, Tulipwood, Kidney-Shaped Top, Bronze Parquetry, c.1900, 4 Ft. 9350.00
Desk, Victorian, Railroad, Bookcase Top, Slant Front 525.00
Desk, Walnut, Slant Front, 4 Overlapping Drawers, 44 1/4 In. 1265.00
Desk, Woman's, Kidney Shape, Marquetry 335.00
Desk, Woman's, Slant Front, Painted, R. J. Horner & Co., Ormolu Mounts 995.00
Desk, Woman's, Tambour Shutters, Inlaid Legs, Mahogany, 1880s, 46 In. 1550.00
Dinette Set, Formica, Chrome, 1950s 150.00
Dining Set, Art Deco, Clowns, Self-Storing Leaf, Green Veneer, 1925, 9 Piece 2600.00
Dining Set, Cherry, 2 Corner Cabinets, Signed Virginian, 10 Chairs, 1937, 13 Pc. 3600.00
Dining Set, Child's, Formica Table, Gray Padded Chairs, Chrome Legs, 3 Piece 65.00
Dining Set, Chippendale Style, Mahogany, Acanthus, 1900, 6 Chairs, 10 Piece 6250.00
Dining Set, Chippendale Style, Parquet Fronts, 1920s, 8 Piece 3650.00
Dining Set, Eastlake, Cane Back Chairs, Victorian, 7 Piece 220.00
Dining Set, Jacobean, 3 Leaves, 6 Chairs, Server, c.1910, 10 Piece 5000.00
Dining Set, Lion's Head, Gargoyles & Paw Feet, Round Table, Oak, 8 Piece 8200.00
Dining Set, Needlepoint Seats, Mahogany, 1840s, 7 Piece 4000.00
Dining Set, Robert Irwin, Painted Figural Medallions, 3 Leaves, 9 Piece 1650.00
Dining Set, Walnut, Carved, Claw Footed, England, 1900s, 9 Piece 8900.00
Dresser, 3 Drawers, Bombe, Beveled Mirror, Mahogany, c.1900, 78 x 58 In. 310.00

Dresser, 3 Drawers, Mahogany, Shieldshaped Mirror, Claw Feet, c.1900 .... 750.00
Dresser, 3 Drawers, Wishbone Mirror, Handkerchief Drawer, Walnut 325.00
Dresser, 6 Drawers, Wishbone Mirror, Walnut, 6 Ft. 2 In. x 3 Ft. 2 In. 350.00
Dresser, Eastlake, 3 Drawers, Mirror, Oak 175.00
Dresser, Eastlake, 6 Drawers, Maple, Victorian 250.00
Dresser, Eastlake, 6 Drawers, Oak, Original Hardware, c.1880 .... 895.00
Dresser, Eastlake, 6 Drawers, Victorian 150.00
Dresser, Eastlake, Cherry, Mirror, Stylized Flowers On Drawers 230.00
Dresser, Mahogany & Pine, Mirror, 3 Drawers, Lock & Keys 1800.00
Dresser, Marble Top, Serpentine Front, Acorn Pulls, Swivel Mirror, Burled Walnut 1300.00
Dresser, Mirror, Handkerchief Boxes, Candlestick Holder, Walnut 225.00
Dresser, Renaissance Revival, Carved Walnut, Marble Top, Drop Well, 88 In. 610.00
Dresser, Rococo Revival, Rosewood, New Orleans, 1835 .... 3090.00
Dresser, Serpentine Front, Beveled Oval Mirror, Bird's-Eye Maple 170.00
Dresser, Triple Beveled Mirrors, Oak 825.00
Dresser, Victorian, Arched Mirror, 2 Shelves, Marble Top, Walnut, 56 1/2 In. 885.00
Dresser, Victorian, Mahogany, Marble Top, Swing Mirror, 4 Drawers, c.1850 .... 825.00
Dresser, Victorian, Mirror, 2 Hankie & 3 Drawers, Marble Top, 94 In. x 39 In. 350.00
Dresser, Victorian, Walnut, Brown Marble, Candleholders, 3 Drawers, Mirror 400.00
Dresser, Victorian, Walnut, Shelves, 5 Drawers, Teardrop Pulls, 6 Ft. 6 In. 400.00
Dresser, Victorian, Wishbone Mirror, Porcelain Casters, Leaf Pulls 250.00
Dresser, Walnut, Burlwood, 6 Drawers, Wooden Pulls 300.00
Dresser, Walnut, Contour Marble Top, 3 Drawers, 1 Hidden Drawer, 1870 .... 595.00
Dresser, Walnut, Wishbone Mirror, Carved Pulls, c.1865 .... 645.00
Dresser, Welsh, Oak, 2 Plate Racks, 2 Drawers, 19th Century, 74 In. 1000.00
Dresser, Welsh, Oak, Plate Rack, Drawers, Cupboards, 56 x 80 In. 1430.00
Dresser, Welsh, Pine, 2 Sections, Top With Open Shelves, 19th Century 1320.00
Dresser, White Marble Top, Beveled Mirror, Leaf Pulls 990.00
Dry Sink, 2 Dovetailed Drawers, Shaped Splashboard, Wooden Doors 725.00
Dry Sink, Chestnut, 2 Doors, Pennsylvania, 1910, Small 750.00
Dry Sink, Grain Painted, Raised Shelf Back, 2 Doors 1075.00
Dry Sink, Pine, Blue Repaint Over Gray, Narrow Paneled Doors, 2 Shelves, 33 In. ... 350.00
Dry Sink, Pine, Cutout Feet, Paneled Doors, 2 Dovetailed Drawers, 30 1/4 In. 715.00
Dry Sink, Pine, Raised Panel Doors, Cutout Feet, Drawer, 45 x 21 x 32 In. 875.00
Dry Sink, Poplar, 1 Drawer, Dovetailed, Paneled Doors, 32 3/4 In. 715.00
Dry Sink, Poplar, 2 Doors, New Hampshire, 1850 .... 1450.00
Dry Sink, Poplar, Turned Feet, Paneled Doors, Crest, 34 1/4 In. 440.00
Dry Sink, Recessed Panel, 2 Inside Shelves, Painted Oak & Pine, 57 5/8 In. 825.00
Dumbwaiter, 3 Tiers, 4 Drawers, Leaf-Carved Legs, Mahogany, 4 Ft. 11 In. 4400.00
Dumbwaiter, George III, 3 Tiers, Brass Feet, Casters, Mahogany, 47 1/2 In. 1350.00
Dumbwaiter, George III, 3 Tiers, Cabriole Legs, Mahogany, c.1800, 46 In. 2475.00
Dumbwaiter, Round Top Over Larger Secondary Tier, England, c.1790, 33 In. 2200.00
Dummy Board, Woman, Long Dress, 1900s 725.00
Easel, Bamboo 55.00
Easel, Victorian, Oak, Spool Turnings 180.00
Etagere, 6 Inset Onyx Shelves, 2 Mirrors, Brass, 52 3/4 In. 350.00
Etagere, Carved Face of Columbia Crest, Serpentine Marble Base, Floor 4950.00
Etagere, Emile Guillot, Chromed Tubular Steel, Glass Shelves, 1931, 43 3/4 In. 1540.00
Etagere, Galle, Art Nouveau, 2 Door Top 9460.00
Etagere, Graduated Square Tiers, Scalloped Aprons, Mahogany, 4 Ft. 10 In. 9350.00
Etagere, Pagoda Form, 4 Shelves, Dragons, Ebonized Wood, China, 78 In. 390.00
Etagere, Red & Gold Chinoiserie Design, 55 1/4 In. 135.00
Etagere, Victorian, Cherrywood, Art Nouveau Style, 2 Mirrors, Spindles 1760.00
Etagere, Walnut, Hidden Drawer Base, 5 Galleried Shelves, 1860–1875 .... 650.00
Fainting Couch, Leather Upholstered 225.00
Fainting Couch, Oak, Applied Carving, Green Striped Velvet Upholstery 250.00
Fauteuil, Carved Rosewood, Carved Crest, c.1855 .... 440.00
Footstool, Arts & Crafts, 5 Spindle Sides, Leather Cushion, 17 x 22 x 15 In. 303.00
Footstool, Bronze Paw Feet, Embroidered Upholstery, 10 1/2 x 8 In. 55.00
Footstool, Bulbous Dark Wood Base, Olive Velvet Upholstery, 13 x 13 x 16 In. 465.00
Footstool, Chest, Oak, Pine, Angels & Birds Marquetry, Upholstered Top, 16 In. 330.00
Footstool, Classical Revival, Mahogany, Striped Upholstery 385.00
Footstool, Cow Horn, Needlepoint Upholstery 60.00

Footstool, Embossed Lavender Covering, Spool Legs & Trim Around Frame 80.00
Footstool, Figured Walnut, Dark Finish, Cutout Feet, 8 In. 302.00
Footstool, French Provincial Style, Needlepoint Upholstery, Oak, 21 In. 465.00
Footstool, Gilded, Moss Green Velvet Upholstery, France, 10 x 13 1/2 In. 71.00
Footstool, Hardwood, Pencil Post Legs, Alligatored Finish, 8 1/2 x 13 In. 27.00
Footstool, Iron, Gold Repaint, Upholstered Top, 14 1/2 x 14 1/2 In. 150.00
Footstool, Kittredge & Blake, Scrolled & Carved Base, c.1835, 16 x 21 In. 770.00
Footstool, L. & J. G. Stickley, No. 391, Leather, Straight Stretchers 440.00
Footstool, Lifetime, Drop–In Cushion, Label, 12 x 20 x 14 In. 275.00
Footstool, Mahogany, Adjustable, Red Velvet Cushion, 1880, Extends To 20 In. 185.00
Footstool, Needlepoint Upholstery, Bun Feet, 1880s, 7 x 51 In. 220.00
Footstool, Neoclassical Style, Carved Beechwood 195.00
Footstool, Original Leather Upholstery, Square Legs, 18 x 19 x 14 In. 550.00
Footstool, Oval, Splayed Turned Legs, Black Paint, Upholstery, 12 In. 38.00
Footstool, Paisley Wool Upholstery, France 150.00
Footstool, Pine, Brown Paint, 8 x 24 1/2 x 8 3/4 In. 135.00
Footstool, Pine, Mellow Finish, Wire Nail Construction, 8 3/4 In. 75.00
Footstool, Queen Anne, Needlepoint Upholstery 450.00
Footstool, Shaker, Mt. Lebanon 192.00
Footstool, Stick Construction, Painted Top, Grain Painted 150.00
Footstool, Victorian, Carved Acanthus Handles, Floral Needlepoint Upholstery 120.00
Footstool, Victorian, Cranberry Upholstery, 11 x 19 In. 65.00
Footstool, Victorian, Needlework Upholstery, 19 x 45 In. 880.00
Footstool, Victorian, Ogee Bracket Feet, 15 x 17 x 23 In. 187.00
Footstool, Victorian, Tufted Velvet Upholstery, Clover Shape, 18 x 40 In. 1100.00
Footstool, Victorian, Walnut, Figural Horseshoe, Velvet Upholstery 45.00
Footstool, Walnut, Cutout Splayed Legs, Cutout Initials Top, 12 1/2 In. 71.50
Footstool, Windsor, Alligatored Painted Design, Yellow Striping, 6 3/4 In. 115.00
Frame, Beveled, Original Reddish Brown Flame Graining, 13 x 16 In. 93.00
Frame, Curly Maple, Corner Blocks, Varnished, 7 x 8 3/4 In. 275.00
Frame, Empire, Half Columns, Corner Blocks, Cherry, 16 1/2 In. 423.00
Frame, Gerrit Rietveld, Stained Oak, 1920, 44 1/2 x 32 5/8 In. 7700.00
Frame, Pine, Original Red, Black Graining, Beveled, 17 1/4 In. 137.00
Frame, Tobacco Leaf, Pattern Walnut, W. Va. 247.00
Hall Chair, Renaissance Revival, Charles Baudoine Label, 1865 .... 550.00
Hall Stand, Eastlake, Marble, 1 Drawer Base, C. S. Meininger, 7 Ft. 4500.00
Hall Stand, Limbert, Oak Frame, Slats On Each Side, 7 Copper Hooks, 37 In. 990.00
Hall Stand, Man O' The North Carving, Mirror, Brass Hooks, Lift Seat, Oak 1150.00
Hall Stand, Oak, Beveled Mirror, Lift Seat, 1900s 925.00
Hall Stand, Oak, Mirror, Arms, 19th Century 1995.00
Hall Stand, Tree Trunk Form, Climbing Bear, Umbrella Stand, 5 Ft. 5 In. 3090.00
Hall Stand, Umbrella Holder, Oval Mirror 595.00
Hall Stand, Victorian, Walnut, Beveled Mirror, Umbrella Stand, Drawer 675.00
Hall Stand, Victorian, Walnut, Marble, Mirror 1500.00
Hall Tree, Mahogany, 4 S–Scrolling Arms, Tole Liner, 19th Century, 83 In. 495.00
Hamper, Wicker, Hawkeye, Tall 22.50
High Chair, 2 Slats, Rabbit Ear Post, Worn Rush Seat, Country, 32 In. 99.00
High Chair, 3 Arched Slats, Ball Finials, Splint Seat, Painted Red, 38 3/4 In. 3080.00
High Chair, Banister Back, Scalloped Rail, Painted Black, 36 1/2 In. 2200.00
High Chair, Banister Back, Yoked Crest, Plank Seat, Black, 32 1/4 In. 2640.00
High Chair, Caned Seat & Back, Victorian ....*Illus* 412.00
High Chair, Captain's Chair Back, Striping, 31 In. 185.00
High Chair, Captain's Chair Back, Striping, Stenciled Design, 32 In. 165.00
High Chair, Continuous Bowed Arms, 34 In. 110.00
High Chair, Dutch Children Decal 40.00
High Chair, Green Enameled Tray, Pat. 1928 .... 150.00
High Chair, Ladder Back, 2 Slats, Rabbit Ear Posts, Turned Arms, 31 In. 126.00
High Chair, Ladder Back, Red Stain Traces, Canted, Splayed, 18th Century 935.00
High Chair, Maple, Slat Back, Red Paint 3080.00
High Chair, Oak, Folding 260.00
High Chair, Original Red Paint, New England, 1820 .... 5500.00
High Chair, Sheraton, Hard & Soft Wood, Dark Green Paint, Scrolled Arms, 32 In. . 825.00
High Chair, Turned Legs, Oak, 19th Century 250.00

Furniture, High Chair, Caned

Seat & Back, Victorian

◆◆◆◆◆◆◆◆◆◆◆◆◆◆◆◆◆◆◆◆◆◆◆◆

Wood-boring beetle larvae sometimes find their way into furniture in a house. The adult beetles emerge in July or August and fly to other pieces of furniture. Watch for signs of pinhead-sized holes or sawdust. Spray immediately and treat with appropriate chemicals.

◆◆◆◆◆◆◆◆◆◆◆◆◆◆◆◆◆◆◆◆◆◆◆◆

High Chair, Walnut, Green Paint, 2 Slats, Rush Seat, 36 1/4 In.	715.00
High Chair, Wicker, Natural Finish	120.00
High Chair, Wicker, White Paint	225.00
High Chair, William & Mary, Caned Foliate Carved Back, Spiral Legs, Oak	3300.00
High Chair, Windsor, Bamboo, Black Repaint, 47 1/4 In.	605.00
High Chair, Windsor, Yellow Paint, c.1810, 31 In.	357.50
Highboy, Chippendale, Mahogany, Swan Cornice, Flame Finials, Cabriole Legs	3700.00
Highboy, Chippendale, Walnut, Cross Banded Inlay, 8 Drawers, 64 3/4 In.	6875.00
Highboy, Curly Maple, Shell Carved	9500.00
Highboy, Queen Anne, 8 Drawers, Pad Feet, 65 1/2 x 39 x 25 In.	5500.00
Highboy, Queen Anne, Mahogany, 72 1/2 x 36 1/2 In.	2310.00
Highboy, Queen Anne, Maple, Shell–Carved Drawer	4000.00
Highboy, Queen Anne, Tiger Maple, Fan Carving, 1780–1800	6900.00
Highboy, Victorian, Walnut, Serpentine, Carved Mirror, Original Pulls	770.00
Highboy, William & Mary, 3 Long Under 2 Small Drawers, Walnut, 60 In.	2475.00
Hoosier Cabinet, Bin–Type Drawers, Gallery Back, 6 Small Drawers Across Top	495.00
Hoosier Cabinet, Kitchen, 2 Utility Cabinets, White, Red & Black Design	575.00
Hoosier Cabinet, Porcelain Work Table	300.00
Huntboard, Hepplewhite, Mahogany, Inlay, 3 Dovetailed Drawers, 42 x 22 x 41 In.	5000.00
Huntboard, Yellow Pine, Reddish Black Finish, 3 Drawers, 42 In.	4750.00
Hutch, Oak, 2 Glass & 2 Paneled Doors, Crest	2395.00
Hutch, Walnut, Mahogany Inlay, Flowers, Stars, Diamonds, Drawer, 1860, 17 In.	1850.00
Ice Cream Set, 2 Chairs, Heart Design Backs, Marble Top Table	150.00
Knife Urn, Inlaid Satinwood, 1876, Pair	3400.00
Knife, Holder, Mahogany, England, 1889, 28 In.	1200.00
Ladder, Shaker, 2 Step, 15 In.	413.00
Lectern, Eagle, Pine, c.1880	1875.00
Library Steps, Convert Into Table, 1840s	995.00
Library Steps, Italian Baroque, Walnut, 41 In.	3850.00
Linen Press & Secretary, 1 Piece, Oak, Dark Finish, 3 Drawers, 78 In.	1265.00
Linen Press, 4 Deep Lower Drawers, Walnut & Poplar, c.1790	6800.00
Linen Press, Chippendale, Mahogany, 2 Doors, 3 Base Drawers, Edgerton, 80 In.	7150.00
Linen Press, Feather Painted, New Breman, Ohio, 1850, Large	2175.00
Linen Press, George III, 2 Short & 1 Long Drawer, Mahogany, c.1770, 6 Ft. 4 In.	3300.00
Linen Press, George III, Paneled Doors Opening To Slides, Mahogany, 6 Ft. 3 In.	4400.00
Linen Press, Georgian, 3 Drawer Base, Mahogany, c.1760, 76 x 50 In.	2970.00
Linen Press, Georgian, Bowfront, Oval Inlay, 19th Century	1000.00
Linen Press, Georgian, Mahogany, 1780	2700.00
Linen Press, Hepplewhite, Mahogany Veneer, Inlay, England, 42 x 83 In.	1650.00
Linen Press, Mahogany, 1810–1820	6500.00
Linen Press, Panel Inset Doors, False Drawers, 2 Short Drawers, Oak, 6 Ft. 4 In.	3300.00
Linen Press, Regency, 2 Pairs Figured Doors, Mahogany, 85 x 48 In.	2450.00
Linen Press, Regency, Mahogany, 4 Doors, 1800, 85 x 48 x 23 In.	2200.00
Linen Press, Scalloped Cornice, Inlay, 5 Drawers, 91 x 49 x 24 In.	4100.00
Linen Press, William IV, Gothic Arches Over Doors, Slides, Mahogany, 7 Ft. 3 In.	4400.00
Love Seat, Camelback, Striped Upholstery, c.1890, 60 In.	175.00

Love Seat, Dolphin Carved Arms, 6 Adjustable Positions, Oak 2500.00
Love Seat, Eastlake, Walnut, Floral Carving 280.00
Love Seat, Victorian, Blue–Green Upholstery, Arms, 54 In. 220.00
Love Seat, Victorian, Carved Walnut, Triple Medallion Back, Side Cushions 850.00
Love Seat, Victorian, Walnut, Finger Carved 600.00
Love Seat, Walnut, Grape Carving, Medallion Back, Upholstery, c.1860 .... 750.00
Lowboy, Carved Mahogany, 1 Long Drawer Over 2 Small Drawers, 30 x 42 x 21 In. 445.00
Lowboy, Chippendale, Mahogany, 1 Long & 3 Short Drawers, 31 x 30 x 22 In. 6325.00
Lowboy, Cross Banded Walnut Veneer, Scalloped Apron, 1 Drawer, 28 In. 2800.00
Lowboy, Georgian, Oak, Single Drawer, Crossbands, c.1780, 28 In. 465.00
Lowboy, Queen Anne, Walnut Veneer, 29 In. 742.00
Magazine Rack, Regency, Drawer, Rosewood, 21 x 22 In. 1925.00
Magazine Rack, Roycroft, 5 Shelves, Incised Orb & Leaf Design 2 Sides 5225.00
Magazine Rack, Stickley Bros., Flaring Legs, 36 1/4 x 18 In. 550.00
Mirror, American Empire, Worn Black Paint, Gilt, Reverse Glass, 41 x 19 In. 150.00
Mirror, Beveled Pine Frame, Red Graining, 12 In. 105.00
Mirror, Beveled, Oak, 25 In. x 48 In. 40.00
Mirror, Biedermeier, Gilt Stenciled Waist, 19th Century, 40 1/2 x 17 3/4 In. 330.00
Mirror, Biedermeier, Mahogany, Inlay, c.1830, 39 x 15 In. 335.00
Mirror, Biedermeier, Stepped Cornice, Glazed Panels, Gilted Metal, Cherry, 52 In. ... 3100.00
Mirror, Blooming Flowers & Leaves Pediment, Giltwood & Gesso, 73 x 36 In. 715.00
Mirror, Bull's–Eye, Gold Leaf Finish, Carved Eagle At Top, c.1800, 48 x 30 In. 2500.00
Mirror, Cherry, Turned Columns, Finials, Beveled Glass, 25 3/4 x 39 In. 990.00
Mirror, Cheval, Beveled Plate, Scrollwork Crest, Brass Hands, 68 x 32 In. 495.00
Mirror, Cheval, Candle Arms, Trestle Legs, 6 Ft. 9 1/2 In. 4950.00
Mirror, Cheval, Chippendale, Mahogany, Brass Candle Arms, 71 In. 935.00
Mirror, Cheval, Eastlake, Carved Walnut, 77 In. 715.00
Mirror, Cheval, Federal Style, Mahogany, Inlay, 76 x 28 In. 880.00
Mirror, Cheval, French Provincial Style, 80 In. 330.00
Mirror, Cheval, Gustav Stickley, No. 918, c.1904 .... 9350.00
Mirror, Cheval, Regency, Candle Arms, Brass Bound Mahogany, 5 Ft. 2 In. 5775.00
Mirror, Cheval, Shield Form, Mahogany, Inlay, c.1885, 68 x 31 In. 1545.00
Mirror, Chippendale, Fretwork, Mahogany, Mid–18th Century, 35 In. 605.00
Mirror, Chippendale, Giltwood, Scrolled Frame, 45 x 28 In. 385.00
Mirror, Chippendale, Mahogany & Parcel Gilt, Phoenix Crest, 52 In. 4840.00
Mirror, Chippendale, Mahogany, England, 1760, 56 In. 6650.00
Mirror, Chippendale, Mahogany, Shell Carved, England, c.1780, 31 In. 990.00
Mirror, Chippendale, Parcel Gilt, Eagle Finial, Mahogany, 1760, 47 1/2 In. 4125.00
Mirror, Chippendale, Scroll, Cherry, Molded Frame, Old Glass, 18 In. 525.00
Mirror, Chippendale, Scroll, Mahogany, Molded Frame, Country, 20 x 13 In. 300.00
Mirror, Chippendale, Scroll, Maple, Dark Finish, 19 In. 205.00
Mirror, Chippendale, Scroll, Walnut Veneer On Pine, 28 1/4 In. 90.00
Mirror, Chippendale, Walnut, Applied Gesso Eagle Crest, 26 x 12 In. 440.00
Mirror, Chippendale, Walnut, Scroll, 20 3/4 x 12 3/4 In. 330.00
Mirror, Continental Rococo, Trailing Flowering Vine Border, 4 Ft. 10 In. x 25 In. ... 2200.00
Mirror, Convex, Giltwood, Stippled & Foliate Frame, Crest, 1825, 36 x 27 In. 3800.00
Mirror, Convex, Regency, Giltwood Frame, Eagle, 1830 .... 900.00
Mirror, Courting, 4 Lovebirds Crest, Dry Red Paint, Penna., 1850, 18 x 10 In. 875.00
Mirror, Courting, Queen Anne, Molded Frame, Walnut, 12 5/8 x 7 3/4 In. 440.00
Mirror, Courting, Queen Anne, Reverse–Painted Village, Iron Easel, 13 In. 1800.00
Mirror, Curly Maple, Ivory Inlay, Architectural Frame, 21 In. 605.00
Mirror, Dieppe, Ivory Leaves On Frame, Female Terms, 33 1/2 In. 3300.00
Mirror, Dressing, Brass Frame, On Stand, 59 In. 132.00
Mirror, Dressing, Gibbons Style, Walnut, Scrolled Arms, 4 Paw Feet, 28 x 20 In. 825.00
Mirror, Dressing, Inlaid Seashells, 2 Carved Songbirds At Top, Pine, 52 In. 1200.00
Mirror, Dressing, Louis XVI, Gilt Metal, Latticework Frame, Easel, 24 x 17 In. 253.00
Mirror, Dressing, Silver Plate, Trumpet Columns Support, 2 Branch Holders 1250.00
Mirror, Dressing, Swivel, 4 Drawers, Black Lacquer, China, 32 3/4 In. 1650.00
Mirror, Dressing, Swivel, Cast Iron Frame, Gold Paint 225.00
Mirror, Dressing, Swivel, Oval, Mahogany, 28 In. 275.00
Mirror, Dressing, Victorian, Swivel, Trestle Base, Walnut, 21 x 14 1/2 In. 93.50
Mirror, Eglomise Panel, Thatched Roof House, Half Cluster Column, Tiger Maple ... 2750.00
Mirror, Federal Style, Bull's–Eye, Painted Gold, 36 In. 605.00

Mirror, Federal Style, Convex, Urn of Flowers At Top, 50 x 32 In. 995.00
Mirror, Federal Style, Reverse–Painted Indian Queen, 45 x 23 In. 935.00
Mirror, Federal, Giltwood, Tree Scene, New York, 1810, 46 x 19 In. 1540.00
Mirror, Federal, Mahogany, Reverse–Painted Federal Farmhouse, 41 x 19 In. 385.00
Mirror, Federal, Mahogany, Reverse–Painted Perry's Victory, 37 In. 1650.00
Mirror, Federal, Reverse–Painted Floral Urn, 37 x 22 In., 2 Piece 250.00
Mirror, Federal, Reverse–Painted Panel, Split Column, 31 x 17 In. 335.00
Mirror, Federal, Scrolled Pediment, Moth Inlay, Mahogany, 34 1/2 In. 3850.00
Mirror, Federal, Tabernacle, Giltwood & Reverse Painted, 27 1/2 In. 360.00
Mirror, Federal, Tabernacle, Giltwood, 1810, 42 3/4 x 26 1/2 In. 1350.00
Mirror, Federal, Tiger Maple, Eglomise House Panel, Half Column Sides 2750.00
Mirror, Floral & Foliate Border, Giltwood & Gesso, 42 1/2 x 33 1/2 In. 335.00
Mirror, Foliage Design Frieze, Acorn Drop, Reverse–Painted, 28 1/2 x 17 In. 300.00
Mirror, Foliate Frame, Floral Pediment, Rococo Giltwood, 70 x 44 In. 3300.00
Mirror, Fragment Blue Paint, Tin Corners, Thick Wire Holder 245.00
Mirror, Fun House, Wavy Bent, Green Painted Wooden Frame, c.1950, 72 In. 885.00
Mirror, George II Style, Walnut, Parcel Gilt, 65 x 27 1/2 In. 715.00
Mirror, George III Style, Giltwood, 53 1/4 x 29 1/4 In. 1450.00
Mirror, George III, Carved C–Scrolls On Pierced Frame, 1780s, 30 x 36 In. 1760.00
Mirror, Gilded Gesso, Carved Wood Frame, Acanthus Leaves, Eagle, 32 In. 1650.00
Mirror, Girandole, Convex, England, 19th Century, 36 3/4 In. 1050.00
Mirror, Girandole, Regency, Parcel Gilt, Eagle Crest, England, 1810, 43 In. 4100.00
Mirror, Gold & Black Trim, 13 x 11 In. 852.00
Mirror, Gustav Stickley, 4 Iron Hooks, Chain, 27 3/4 x 35 3/4 In. 2860.00
Mirror, Half Turnings, Worn Original Striping, Gold & Black Trim 775.00
Mirror, Hand Carved, Wooden Frame, Gold Paint, 13 3/8 In. 104.00
Mirror, Herter Brothers, Aesthetic Movement, 8 Ft. 4125.00
Mirror, Louis XIV, Gesso, Gilt, Acanthus, Floral Crest, Al Capone, 10 x 29 In. 330.00
Mirror, Louis XVI, Beaded Carved Giltwood Border, 1880s, 4 Ft. 1 In. x 25 In. 4950.00
Mirror, Mahogany & Gold Leaf Frame, Boston, Mass., Maker Signed, 1780 .... 5500.00
Mirror, Mahogany Veneer, Beveled Frame, Red, Black Repaint, 14 In. 39.00
Mirror, Mahogany Veneer, Spiral Edge Molding, 10 In. 55.00
Mirror, Mantel, Empire, Gilded, 20 x 17 In. 275.00
Mirror, Mantel, Floral Inlays, Profile Center, Masks, 1876, 7 Ft. 11 In. x 6 Ft. 5 In. 4125.00
Mirror, Mantel, Gilt, Crest, Open Work Floral Design, 55 In. 1430.00
Mirror, Napoleon III, Molded Brass Border, 5 Ft. x 38 1/2 In. 3025.00
Mirror, Neoclassical, Giltwood, Eagle, Beveled Glass, Ball Decoration, 37 In. 440.00
Mirror, Octagonal Plate, Surrounded By Mirrored Panels, Giltwood, 4 Ft. 9 In. 5500.00
Mirror, Pier, Empire, Country House, Cove, Giltwood, 19th Century, 39 x 19 In. 825.00
Mirror, Pier, George I Style, Flower Head Frame, 5 Ft. 10 In. x 27 In., Pair 9350.00
Mirror, Pier, Gilded Frame, Spain, 66 x 26 1/4 In. 50.00
Mirror, Pier, Gilded, 2 Part, c.1820, 73 1/2 x 38 1/2 In. ....*Illus* 1870.00
Mirror, Pier, Neo–Classical, Painted & Parcel Gilt, 1840s, 75 1/2 x 33 In. 2420.00
Mirror, Pier, Shelf, Man O' The North Face At Top, Mirrors Each Side, 9 Ft. 825.00
Mirror, Pier, Triple Section, Carved Columns, Painted, 76 x 45 1/2 In. 350.00
Mirror, Pier, Victorian, Beveled Glass, Paw Feet, Brass, 79 x 36 In. 355.00

Furniture, Mirror, Pier, Gilded, 2 Part,
c.1820, 73 1/2 X 38 1/2 In.

Mirror, Pier, Walnut, Open Carved Crest, 94 x 31 In. 495.00
Mirror, Pineapple & Fruit Crest, Bosses Within Scrolls, Oval, c.1850, 70 In. 1210.00
Mirror, Plateau, Beveled Rim, Silver Plate, 13 In. 175.00
Mirror, Plateau, Beveled, Leaf & Scroll Footed, 10 In. 55.00
Mirror, Plateau, Rococo Scroll, Silver–Plated Frame, Depouse, 17 1/2 In. 195.00
Mirror, Queen Anne, Arched Crest, Chinoiserie Design, Lacquered, 56 x 20 In. 825.00
Mirror, Queen Anne, Faux Tortoiseshell, Arched Crest, Beveled, 49 x 26 In. 300.00
Mirror, Queen Anne, Mahogany, England, 37 In. 2200.00
Mirror, Queen Anne, Walnut & Gilt, England, 1750, 48 x 22 In. 2200.00
Mirror, Queen Anne, Walnut Veneer On Pine, Scrolled Crest, England, 11 x 20 In. 550.00
Mirror, Red Graining, Dark Patina, Beveled Frame, 6 3/4 In. 105.00
Mirror, Regency, Carved Giltwood Eagle Top, Convex 2530.00
Mirror, Reverse Etched, Warrior, Woman, Giltwood, 39 1/2 x 21 In., Pair 3300.00
Mirror, Scroll & Acanthus Crest, Flowered Frame, Gesso & Giltwood, 57 x 48 In. ... 3920.00
Mirror, Scroll, Chippendale, Mahogany Veneer, Gilding, 22 1/4 In. 220.00
Mirror, Shaving, Bowfront, Drawer, Line Inlay Mahogany, 16 x 14 In. 220.00
Mirror, Shaving, Chippendale, Mahogany, Block Front, Footed, 25 x 20 x 9 In. 385.00
Mirror, Shaving, Empire Classical Revival, Mahogany, Lyre Crest, 36 x 19 In. 880.00
Mirror, Shaving, Mahogany Veneer, 3 Drawers, Ball Feet, Adjustable, 21 In. 325.00
Mirror, Shaving, Mahogany Veneer, Pine, 1 Drawer, Adjustable Mirror, 17 In. 115.00
Mirror, Shaving, Mahogany Veneer, Pine, Line Inlay, 2 Drawers, 15 x 7 x 20 In. 175.00
Mirror, Shaving, Mahogany, Brass Finial, 15 In. 110.00
Mirror, Shaving, Sheraton, Mahogany, Inlay, 3 Drawers, c.1790, 24 In. 300.00
Mirror, Shaving, Victorian, Mahogany Stand, c.1850, 60 In. 415.00
Mirror, Shaving, Walnut, Cherry, Inlay, 1 Drawer, Country, 17 1/2 x 7 3/4 In. 110.00
Mirror, Shaving, Walnut, Lower Cupboard, Stand 200.00
Mirror, Sheraton, Mirrored Upper Panel, 19th Century, 4 Ft., Pair 2975.00
Mirror, Shield Shape, Shell & Scroll Frame, Giltwood & Gesso, 25 x 16 In. 100.00
Mirror, Tabernacle, Reverse Painted, Giltwood, 1815, 30 x 17 1/2 In. 475.00
Mirror, Urn & Scrolling Pediment, Beveled Glass, Gilt Frame, 66 x 82 In. 1000.00
Mirror, Venetian Glass, Art Deco, 48 x 29 In. 880.00
Mirror, Venetian, Octagonal, Floral Crest, 50 x 29 In. 275.00
Mirror, Victorian, Walnut, Molded Frame, Arched Top, 54 3/4 x 26 1/4 In. 110.00
Mirror, Walnut, Marquetry, Inlay, c.1800, 39 x 33 In. 2400.00
Parlor Set, Carved Walnut, Upholstered Cushions, 3 Piece 1800.00
Parlor Set, Eastlake Style, Walnut, Red Velvet Upholstery, 4 Piece 550.00
Parlor Set, Flemish Baroque Style, Mahogany, Female Masks, c.1870, 3 Piece 2200.00
Parlor Set, Jelliff Style, Warrior Heads, 7 Piece 6500.00
Parlor Set, Jelliff, Walnut, Indian Maiden Heads, Upholstery, 7 Piece 3685.00
Parlor Set, Meeks, Stanton Hall, Laminated Rosewood, 3 Piece 9625.00
Parlor Set, Oak, Gargoyle & Floral Carved, 3 Piece 450.00
Parlor Set, Plail Brothers, Barrel Back, 3 Piece 6600.00
Parlor Set, Rococo Revival, Carved Female Busts, Upholstered Seats, 3 Piece 1750.00
Parlor Set, Rococo Revival, Tufted Back Upholstery, 4 Piece 6750.00
Parlor Set, Rosewood, Upholstery, Europe, 4 Piece 5000.00
Parlor Set, Victorian, Finger Carved Walnut, Velvet Upholstery, 3 Piece 1950.00
Parlor Set, Victorian, Walnut, Balloon Back, Velvet Upholstery, 3 Piece 1000.00
Parlor Set, Walnut, Women's Head Arm Supports, c.1870, 3 Piece 3025.00
Pedestal, Art Deco, Poplar, 19 1/4 In. 90.00
Pedestal, Black Figure Standing On Hands, Supported By Pillow, 34 1/4 In. 4675.00
Pedestal, Burled Walnut, Dark Finish, Marble Insert Top, 43 3/4 In. 250.00
Pedestal, Chippendale, Mahogany, Dark Finish, 37 In., Pair 1045.00
Pedestal, Chippendale, Mahogany, Hexagonal Top, 37 1/4 In., Pair 495.00
Pedestal, Columnar Form, Gilt Bronze Swag, Green Onyx, 43 1/2 In. 715.00
Pedestal, Columnar Form, Rope Turned Standard, Carrara Marble, 42 In. 665.00
Pedestal, Corinthian Capital, Bronze Mount, Green & Rust Veined Onyx, 43 In. 855.00
Pedestal, Florentine Hard Stone, Bacchanalian Figures, Bronze Mounts, 51 In. 1815.00
Pedestal, Neoclassical Style, Animal Paw Feet, Marble, 46 In. 3575.00
Pedestal, Pine, Marbelized Paint, 14 In. 577.00
Pedestal, Porcelain Shaft, Cupids & Lovers In Garden, Signed Quentin, 49 In. 4950.00
Pedestal, Rotating Onyx Top, Bronze Band With Cherubs, Bronze, 43 1/2 In. 885.00
Pedestal, Soft Wood, Orange, Blue Repaint, 30 In. 99.00
Pew, Church, Oak, 4–In. Pink Marble Base, For 2 People 130.00

Furniture, Poudreuse, Louis XV Style,
Walnut, 28 1/2 In.

Furniture, Rocker, Child's, Boston

Pie Safe, 12 Punched Tins, 2 Top Drawers	495.00
Pie Safe, 2 Doors, 1 Base Drawer, 32 In.	950.00
Pie Safe, 2 Glass & Wooden Doors, Cypress, 19th Century, 70 1/2 In.	275.00
Pie Safe, 2 Piece, Poplar, 2 Drawers, 12 Punched Tin Panels, 78 In.	885.00
Pie Safe, Blue Green Paint, 12 Tins, Star Design, Indiana, 1850	1100.00
Pie Safe, Butternut, 12 Punched Tin Panels, Simple Feet, 51 In.	825.00
Pie Safe, Green Paint, 6 Geometric Pierced Tins	450.00
Pie Safe, Hanging, Pine, Punched Tin Panels, Iron Hooks, Dovetailed, 30 In.	350.00
Pie Safe, Mustard & Blue Paint, 4 Long Pierced Tin, Mid–19th Century	5850.00
Pie Safe, On Stand, Pine, Old Green Repaint Over Brown	1400.00
Pie Safe, Pine, 8 Punched Tin Panels, Diamond Design, 60 In.	1550.00
Pie Safe, Pine, Double Doors, 2 Drawers, Gallery Top, 57 In.	500.00
Pie Safe, Pine, Green Paint Over Brown, 8 Punched Tin Panels, On Stand	1400.00
Pie Safe, Poplar, 2 Doors, 3 Punched Tin Panels, 2 Drawers, 50 1/4 x 46 In.	880.00
Pie Safe, Red Painted, Screen Door, 1880	1450.00
Pie Safe, Screen, Original Salmon Paint, Late 1800s	795.00
Pie Safe, Shucked Corn Tins, 1880s	1250.00
Pie Safe, Walnut, Dark Finish, Double Doors, 3 Punched Tin Panels, 50 In.	990.00
Pie Safe, Yellow Pine, 10 Punched Tin Panels, Whirligig, 2 Drawers, Savannah	1900.00
Pie Safe, Yellow Pine, Raised Panel Doors, 2 Drawers, Double Top Doors, 71 In.	2100.00
Planter, 3 Tiers, Basket Form, Wire, 6 In.	445.00
Planter, Louis XVI Style, Giltwood, 42 In.	525.00
Poudreuse, Louis XV Style, Walnut, 28 1/2 In. ....*Illus*	1540.00
Rack, Clothes, Victorian, Folding, Mirror	240.00
Rack, Coat, 8 Wooden Hooks, Faceted Plugs, Charles Rohlf, 64 In.	990.00
Rack, Coat, Elk Horn Hangers	1200.00
Rack, Coat, Extended Hanger Rod, 3 Brackets, Brass Hat Hooks, England, 84 In.	170.00
Rack, Coat, Twisted Black Wrought Iron, Wooden Balls, French, c.1950, 70 In.	1750.00
Rack, Hat, Black Steer Horn, Double	75.00

Furniture, Rocker, Eames,
Molded Fiberglass, Detachable
Leather Upholstery

Furniture, Rocker, Limbert,
Spring Cushion, Branded Mark

Rack, Hat, Brass, c.1900, 69 In.	98.00
Rack, Hat, Victorian, Walnut, Anchor Shape, Diamond Shape Mirror	90.00
Rack, Magazine, Victorian, Hanging, Folds Flat	195.00
Rack, Music, Double Sheet, 3 Legs, Walnut Finish, Black Edge Trim	425.00
Rack, Towel, Mahogany, Chamfered Edge, Mortised, 15 x 17 1/2 x 32 3/4 In.	275.00
Recamier, Classical, Mahogany, Upholstered Back, Carved Dragon Feet, 98 In.	5775.00
Recamier, Empire, Grecian Style, Green & Gold Upholstery	5775.00
Recamier, Empire, Mahogany, Carved, Paw Feet, Upholstery, 67 In.	950.00
Recamier, Victorian, Mahogany, Upholstery, 72 In.	600.00
Rocker, American Flags & Ships Stencil, Black Paint, 2 Scroll Seat, 43 3/4 In.	275.00
Rocker, Arts & Crafts, 5 Slats Under Arm, Tenon Construction, 34 x 32 In.	632.50
Rocker, Arts & Crafts, Caned Back & Seat, 3 Slatted Arms, Grand Rapids	550.00
Rocker, Campeche Form, Leather Upholstery, Arms, c.1830	3520.00
Rocker, Carved, Needlepoint Upholstery, Arms	470.00
Rocker, Child's, Bentwood	75.00
Rocker, Child's, Black Paint, Decal–Decorated Crest, 28 In.	50.00
Rocker, Child's, Boston ....*Illus*	60.00
Rocker, Child's, Gustav Stickley, Back Slats, Leather Seat, Arms, 25 x 18 1/2 In. ...	330.00
Rocker, Child's, Hobby Horse Handles	300.00
Rocker, Child's, Rush Seat, Civil War	135.00
Rocker, Child's, Shaker, No. 0, Decal, Original Finish	2640.00
Rocker, Child's, Shaker, No. 1, Shaped Arms, Tape Seat, Birchwood	3575.00
Rocker, Child's, Swan, Wooden	300.00
Rocker, Child's, Wicker, Brown, Arms	50.00
Rocker, Child's, Wicker, Michigan, 1890s	150.00
Rocker, Child's, Windsor, Bamboo Turnings, Shaped Seat, 28 1/2 In.	250.00
Rocker, Double Comb Back, Rush Seat, Double Box Stretcher, Maple	165.00
Rocker, Eames, Molded Fiberglass, Detachable Leather Upholstery ....*Illus*	605.00
Rocker, Eastlake, Walnut, Upholstered, Arms, 43 In.	165.00
Rocker, Footstool, Cow Horn, Upholstered In Velveteen Crazy Quilt Fragment	2600.00
Rocker, Gustav Stickley, 5 Vertical Slats, Flat Arms, Red Decal, 26 In.	550.00
Rocker, Gustav Stickley, Ladder Back, Upholstered Slip–In Cushion, Oak, 1910	1100.00
Rocker, Gustav Stickley, No. 396	950.00
Rocker, Gustav Stickley, V–Back	500.00
Rocker, Heywood–Wakefield, No. W59D, Willow, Crest Rail Goes Into Arms	225.00
Rocker, Hoop Skirt, Painted, Arms	180.00
Rocker, Hoop Skirt, Rush Seat, Black Finish, 18th Century	150.00
Rocker, L. & J. G. Stickley, No. 803	450.00
Rocker, Ladder Back, 5 Graduated Arched Slats, Turned Finials, Arms, 44 1/2 In.	250.00
Rocker, Ladder Back, Arrow Supports, Saddle Seat, Painted	100.00
Rocker, Ladder Back, Black Repaint, 4 Slats, Spindle Supports, 41 In.	192.00
Rocker, Ladder Back, Green Paint, 5 Arched Slats, Tape Seat, 46 In.	60.00
Rocker, Ladder Back, Rush Seat, Oak & Hickory, 19th Century	72.50
Rocker, Ladder Back, Rush Seat, Painted, U.S.	175.00
Rocker, Ladder Back, Splint Seat, Arms, 6 3/4 In.	49.00
Rocker, Limbert, Cane Back, Signed, Pair	825.00
Rocker, Limbert, High Back, Spring Cushion Seat, 38 In.	330.00
Rocker, Limbert, No. 854, Curved Top	250.00
Rocker, Limbert, Spring Cushion, Branded Mark ....*Illus*	330.00
Rocker, Lincoln, Walnut, Worn Caned Seat & Back	70.00
Rocker, Mahogany, Scroll Arms, Vase Splat, Carved Crest, 36 1/2 In.	125.00
Rocker, Man–In–The–Mountain Carving On Head Rest	190.00
Rocker, Mission Oak, Leather Seat & Back	65.00
Rocker, Oak, Pressed Back	145.00
Rocker, Platform, Eastlake, Porcelain Wheels	110.00
Rocker, Platform, Heywood Bros.–Wakefield, Wicker	595.00
Rocker, Platform, Heywood Bros.–Wakefield, Wicker, Chain Link Pattern Top	595.00
Rocker, Platform, Hunzinger, Mahogany, Twist Supports	715.00
Rocker, Platform, Hunzinger, Upholstery, 40 In.	275.00
Rocker, Platform, Victorian, Wicker, 46 In.	440.00
Rocker, Sewing, 6 Slats, Balls On Top of Back Rail	55.00
Rocker, Sewing, Caned Seat, Walnut Finish, 1930s	35.00
Rocker, Sewing, G. Stickley, No. 307, H–Back, 1910 ....*Illus*	165.00

Rocker, Sewing, Hitchcock, Original Black Finish, Tole Design 160.00
Rocker, Shaker, Arms, Canterbury, Large 935.00
Rocker, Shaker, Dark Finish, Red, Black Taped Seat, Arms, 37 In. 715.00
Rocker, Shaker, Dark Walnut Stain, c.1875 .... 495.00
Rocker, Shaker, Maple, Birch, Ash Stretcher, Armless, 1850, 39 In. 495.00
Rocker, Shaker, Maple, Olive & Blue Tape, Mt. Lebanon ....*Illus* 220.00
Rocker, Shaker, No. 2, Shawl Bar 475.00
Rocker, Shaker, No. 3, Taped Back & Seat, Gold Decal Label 900.00
Rocker, Shaker, No. 3, Taped Seat, Arms 330.00
Rocker, Shaker, No. 4 .... 550.00
Rocker, Shaker, No. 5, Taped Seat, Arms 795.00
Rocker, Shaker, No. 6 .... 1600.00
Rocker, Shaker, No. 6, Mt. Lebanon, c.1875 .... 1675.00
Rocker, Shaker, No. 7, Shawl Rail 550.00
Rocker, Shaker, Web Back, Mt. Lebanon, Maple, 34 In. 220.00
Rocker, Sheet Metal, Tubing, Arms, 33 In. 335.00
Rocker, Spindle Back, Arms, Boston, 19th Century 66.00
Rocker, Spindle Back, Brown Repaint, Stenciled Landscape Design, 38 In. 220.00
Rocker, Spindle Back, Maple, c.1860 .... 55.00
Rocker, Stickley Bros., Oak 100.00
Rocker, Victorian, Walnut, Striped Upholstery, Arms 175.00
Rocker, Walnut, Finger Carved, c.1860 .... 143.00
Rocker, Wicker, Bar Harbor 275.00
Rocker, Wicker, Magazine Rack On Left Arm, White 575.00
Rocker, Windsor, Arrow-Back, Rabbit Ears, America 121.00
Rocker, Windsor, Bow Back, Spindle Supports, Scrolling Arms, Saddle Seat 220.00
Rocker, Windsor, Comb Back, Arms ....*Illus* 3300.00
Rocker, Windsor, Comb Back, Bamboo Turnings, Arrow Slats, Arms, 38 In. 300.00
Rocker, Windsor, Comb Back, Black Paint, Stenciled Crest, Arms, 43 3/4 In. 610.00
Rocker, Windsor, Continuous Arms, Black Paint, c.1810 .... 365.00
Rocker, Windsor, Shaped Arms, Step-Down Crest, Bamboo, 37 1/4 In. 300.00

Furniture, Rocker,
Sewing, G. Stickley,
No.307, H-Back, 1910

Furniture, Rocker,
Shaker, Maple, Olive &
Blue Tape, Mt. Lebanon

Furniture, Rocker, Windsor,
Comb Back, Arms

◆◆◆

If you buy an Art Deco bronze-and-ivory figure, be very careful to
examine the ivory. Even slight cracks or other minor damage
lower the value.

◆◆◆

Furniture, Screen, 4-Panel, Castles, Flowers, 18th Century, 72 X 80 In.

Screen, 2–Panel, Art Deco, Wood & Beveled Glass, Jet Black Paint, 78 x 44 In.	275.00
Screen, 2–Panel, Pierced Floral, Giltwood, 29 1/2 x 63 3/4 In.	775.00
Screen, 3–Panel, Chinoiserie, Figural Design, 30 In.	75.00
Screen, 3–Panel, Decoupage Map of The United States, 20 x 61 In.	495.00
Screen, 3–Panel, Eastlake, Painted Flowers, Mahogany Frame, c.1880	460.00
Screen, 3–Panel, Folding, Needlepoint Flowers, Bird Carved Wooden Frame, 65 In.	750.00
Screen, 3–Panel, Gustav Stickley, Slatted Base	5500.00
Screen, 3–Panel, Louis XVI Style, Embroidered Silk, Giltwood Frame, 56 1/2 In. ...	465.00
Screen, 3–Panel, Lovers In Garden, Landscapes, 15 In.	2200.00
Screen, 3–Panel, Mirrored Panels, Lower Floral Insets, c.1900, 40 In.	550.00
Screen, 3–Panel, Neoclassical, Painted Statuette, Green Ground, 5 Ft. 4 In.	2000.00
Screen, 3–Panel, Pairs of Nude Figures, Caned Panel Over Canvas Panel, 72 In.	1350.00
Screen, 3–Panel, Pierced Heart, Brown Paint, 55 x 23 In.	1650.00
Screen, 3–Panel, River and Village Scene, 68 In.	250.00
Screen, 3–Panel, Urn, Bellflower & Scroll Drapery, Leather, 72 x 20 In.	1985.00
Screen, 3–Panel, Venetian Landscape, America, 20th Century, 6 x 6 Ft.	1850.00
Screen, 3–Panel, Victorian, Decoupage, 1880s, 6 Ft.	4125.00
Screen, 4–Panel, Aubusson, 18th Century, 72 x 80 In.	2750.00
Screen, 4–Panel, Carved Floral Design, Birds, Ivory, 3 3/8 x 10 1/8 In.	305.00
Screen, 4–Panel, Castles, Flowers, 18th Century, 72 x 80 In. ....*Illus*	2750.00
Screen, 4–Panel, Charles X, Grisaille, 85 In.	1430.00
Screen, 4–Panel, Cherry Blossom Trees, River, Gilt Ground, Japan, 35 3/4 In.	225.00
Screen, 4–Panel, Coromandel, Bird & Flower, Figural Design, 72 In.	225.00
Screen, 4–Panel, Figures In Landscape, Gilt Ground, Japan, 67 1/2 In.	247.00
Screen, 4–Panel, Figures In Various Activities, Gilt & Copper, 74 x 68 In.	1540.00
Screen, 4–Panel, Folding, Black Lacquer, Polychrome Painted Design, 18 x 72 In. ...	320.00
Screen, 4–Panel, Hand Colored Lithographs, Wood Panels	7150.00
Screen, 4–Panel, Honeycomb Pierced Design, Oriental	200.00
Screen, 4–Panel, Louis XVI Style, Walnut, Carved Crests, 19th Century	550.00
Screen, 4–Panel, Painted Silk, Sherrill, 72 x 17 In.	80.00
Screen, 4–Panel, Steel, Open Ivy Pattern	340.00
Screen, 4–Panel, Teak, Openwork Carved Floral, Oriental, 18 x 70 1/2 In.	209.00
Screen, 4–Panel, Venetian Scenes, Painted Leather, 76 In.	1430.00
Screen, 6–Panel, Charles Eames, Molded Plywood	4200.00
Screen, 6–Panel, Cranes In Landscape, Japan, 60 x 21 In.	775.00
Screen, 6–Panel, Decoupage Fans, Calligraphy, 48 x 18 In.	250.00
Screen, 6–Panel, Figures In Landscape, Pagodas, Gold Ground, 68 In.	1350.00
Screen, 6–Panel, Flowers & Grasses, Gold Ground, 1740s	4600.00
Screen, 6–Panel, Flowers, Lacquered, 19th Century, China, 91 x 20 In.	4070.00
Screen, 6–Panel, Folding, Scene of Figures, Pagoda, Black Lacquer, 72 1/2 In.	150.00
Screen, 6–Panel, Herman Miller, Plywood, Canvas & Wood, 67 3/4 In.	2420.00
Screen, 6–Panel, Lacquered, Phoenix Birds, 19th Century, China, 106 x 20 In.	2200.00
Screen, 6–Panel, Pine, Bamboo & Flowers, Late Edo Period, 69 In.	2310.00
Screen, 6–Panel, Russel Wright, Mahogany, Cutout Pattern At Top, 1951, 72 In.	6600.00
Screen, 8–Panel, Folding, Teakwood, 21 In.	220.00
Screen, 8–Panel, Huntsmen On Horseback, Painted Canvas, 18th Century, 5 1/2 Ft.	3850.00

Furniture, Secretaire, Biedermeier, Fall

Front, Birch, Early 19th Century

To cover a scratch in a piece of furniture made of dark wood, rub a walnut, Brazil nut, or butternut into the scratch. Eyebrow pencil or shoe polish in a matching shade will also work.

Don't lock furniture with antique locks. If they stick, it is almost impossible to open the door or drawer without damaging the wood.

Screen, 8–Panel, Porcelain Plaques, China, c.1840, 32 1/2 In.	1320.00
Screen, 8–Panel, Tete–De–Negre, Figures, Pavilions, 19th Century, China, 6 1/2 Ft.	3300.00
Screen, Folding, Teakwood, Lacquered Ivory Design of Birds, 76 In.	330.00
Screen, Needlework, Carved Giltwood, c.1880, 53 In.	970.00
Secretaire, Biedermeier, Fall Front, Birch, Early 19th Century *Illus*	7150.00
Secretary, Biedermeier, Fall Front, Birch, Interior Doors, Drawers, 4 Ft. 8 In.	7700.00
Secretary, Cherry, Blind Door, Ogee Bracket Base, 18th Century, 82 x 38 In.	7700.00
Secretary, Child's, Empire, Flame Mahogany Veneer, Raised Panel Doors	3200.00
Secretary, Child's, Empire, Scalloped Top, Raised Doors	2310.00
Secretary, Child's, Victorian, Walnut, 1860s	875.00
Secretary, Continental, Mahogany, Walnut, Floral, 20th Century, 29 x 75 In.	1150.00
Secretary, Curly Maple, Cherry, 1820	3000.00
Secretary, Cylinder, Oak, 3 Base Drawers	1500.00
Secretary, Drop Front, Walnut, c.1880, 8 Ft.	1300.00
Secretary, Empire, Mahogany, Gothic Tracery Arches Over Doors	4400.00
Secretary, Federal, Mahogany, Arched Pediment, Tambour Glazed Doors, 88 In.	2750.00
Secretary, Federal, Mahogany, Inlay, 4 Graduated Drawers, 1810, 53 In.	4400.00
Secretary, Federal, Mahogany, Line Inlay, Gothic Arch Glazed Doors, 68 In.	1650.00
Secretary, Georgian, Slant Front, Mahogany, Flame Grained, Claw Footed, 1920s	600.00
Secretary, Hepplewhite, Bussolini, Tambour, Cherry, 3 Drawers, 48 x 39 In.	2550.00
Secretary, Mahogany Veneer Over Cherry, Drop Front, 1860–1865, Country	2800.00
Secretary, Mahogany Veneer, Paneled Doors, 2 Drawers, Europe, 47 x 17 x 81 In.	385.00
Secretary, Mahogany, Flat Top, Blind Fretwork, 1800	9250.00
Secretary, Oak & Elm, Paneled Doors, Lid, Fitted Interior, 18th Century	4125.00
Secretary, Oak, Fall Front, Swan Neck Pediment, Glazed Doors, England	8800.00
Secretary, Sheraton, Mahogany, 3 Drawers, Double Doors, Pigeonholes, 76 In.	7150.00
Secretary, Sheraton, Pine, Poplar, 3 Drawers, Country, New York, 1840	1850.00
Secretary, Slant Front, Rosewood, Floral Inlay, Bird's–Eye Interior, 36 In.	775.00
Secretary, Slant Front, Walnut, Paneled Doors, Country, 41 x 19 x 79 In.	1000.00
Secretary–Bookcase, Biedermeier Style, Fruitwood, Mirrored Doors, 80 In.	1100.00
Secretary–Bookcase, Federal, Mahogany Inlay	3850.00
Secretary–Bookcase, George III, Mahogany, Mirrored Cupboard Door, 78 In.	5500.00
Secretary–Bookcase, Georgian, Mahogany, 4 Drawers, Stringing Inlay, Borders	6600.00
Secretary–Bookcase, Hepplewhite, Mahogany, Satinwood, Floral & Fruit Inlay	5500.00
Secretary–Bookcase, Mahogany, Bracket Foot, Dated 1780	9500.00
Secretary–Bookcase, Oak, Curved Glass Drop Front, Applied Carving, Crest	885.00
Secretary–Bookcase, Slant Front, Flame–Grained Veneer, Mahogany, 86 1/2 In.	1650.00
Secretary–Bookcase, Slant Front, Side By Side, Curved Glass, 70 x 38 x 14 In.	450.00
Secretary–Bookcase, Walnut, Glazed Doors, 3 Drawers, 1850, 87 x 45 In.	1430.00
Server, Charles Stickley, 2 Drawers, Plate Rail, 32 x 42 x 20 In.	550.00

Furniture, Settee, Aubusson Upholstery, 1850, 58 In.

Server, Empire, Cherry, Paneled Doors, Decorative Scrolled Crest, 33 In. 385.00
Server, Federal, Mahogany, 2 Drop Leaves, 3 Drawers, 44 x 20 x 35 In. 165.00
Server, French Provincial Style, Walnut, Paneled Doors, 42 x 47 In. 550.00
Server, Gustav Stickley, 2 Drawers, Copper Pulls, 1904, 36 x 42 x 18 In. 1875.00
Server, Gustav Stickley, No. 802, 2 Drawers, Hammered Copper Hardware 3000.00
Server, Kittinger, Mahogany, 2 Drawers, Brass Gallery, 2 Slide Out Shelves 625.00
Server, Mahogany, Ebonized, Gold Highlights, Brass Trim, Medallions, 46 In. 375.00
Server, Mahogany, Marble Top, Drawers, Fluted Legs, c.1800, 50 x 44 In. 1650.00
Settee & Armchair, Adirondack, Hickory, 2 Piece 265.00
Settee, Alexander Roux, Carved Birds, Grapes & Leaves, Oval Back, Arms 2000.00
Settee, Aubusson Upholstery, 1850, 58 In. ....*Illus* 2660.00
Settee, Biedermeier, Mahogany, 19th Century, 7 Ft. 5 In. ....*Illus* 4400.00
Settee, Birch, 2 Back Cushions, Center Lion's Head, c.1890, 55 In. 265.00
Settee, Burled Maple Outward Curving Arms, Upholstered, 4 Ft. 7 5/8 In. 6100.00
Settee, Carved Frame, Blond Finish, Gold Needlepoint Upholstery, 49 In. 305.00
Settee, Carved Rosewood, Pineapple Pierced–Carved Crest, 41 x 65 x 36 In. 935.00
Settee, Carved Walnut, Cabriole Legs, c.1860 .... 775.00

Furniture, Settee, Biedermeier, Mahogany, 19th Century, 7 Ft. 5 In.

Settee, Chippendale, Mahogany, High Back, 46 x 62 In. 855.00
Settee, Courting, Wicker, White Paint, 1880s 950.00
Settee, Double Chair Back, Swan Splats, Upholstered Seat, Walnut, 33 In. 1000.00
Settee, Federal, Mahogany, Upholstery, Mass., 1800, 36 3/4 x 79 1/2 In. 3850.00
Settee, French, Art Deco, Upholstery Arched Crest, Melon Form Feet, c.1925, 6 Ft. 1200.00
Settee, Fruitwood, Paneled Back, Stile Legs, 18th Century, 65 In. 300.00
Settee, George III, Mahogany, 4 Paneled Serpentine Back, 6 Ft. 10 In. 4400.00
Settee, George III, Mahogany, Triple Chair Back, Foliage & Scrolls, 5 Ft. 9 In. 3850.00
Settee, George III, Stylized Fretwork Crest, Loose Cushion Seat, 5 Ft. 9 1/2 In. 4950.00
Settee, Georgian Style, Upholstered Back, Rolled Arms, Carved Legs, 88 In. 3960.00
Settee, Hickory, 1930s 495.00
Settee, Hickory, Old Green Paint 450.00
Settee, Josef Hoffmann, Bentwood, Bent Spindles Continuing To Base, c.1905 .... 5500.00
Settee, Larkin, Wicker, Natural, Arms 357.50
Settee, Leaf & Nut Carved Crest Rail, Upholstered Arms & Seat, Tufted Back 385.00
Settee, Louis XVI Style, Giltwood, 27 x 53 In. 360.00
Settee, Louis XVI Style, Guiltwood, Quiver & Torch Crest, 19th Century, 42 In. 1100.00
Settee, Louis XVI, Aubusson Tapestry Upholstery, Giltwood, 58 3/4 In. 6600.00
Settee, Mahogany, Carved Frame, Gilt Panel, Silk Upholstery, c.1825, 90 In. 3750.00
Settee, Mahogany, Triple Chair Back, Serpentine Rail, Leaf Supports, 1860, 50 In. 3300.00
Settee, Mahogany, Upholstered Back & Arms, Loose Cushion, 6 Ft. 5 In. 2000.00
Settee, Mother-of-Pearl Inlay, Scroll Arms, Upholstery 1600.00
Settee, Oak, Curved Back Rail, Maple Spindles, 1920s 455.00
Settee, Oak, Spindles Back & Sides 2400.00
Settee, Regency, Serpentine, Beechwood, 4 Ft. ....*Illus* 3300.00
Settee, Rosewood Dragon, China, Arms 1925.00
Settee, Rosewood, Medallion Back, Carved Fruit & Nuts, c.1860 .... 522.00
Settee, Rosewood, Pierced Carved Frame, Oriental Flowers, c.1855, 64 In. 2750.00
Settee, Sheraton, Mahogany, Camelback, England, 1780, 72 In. 2750.00
Settee, Stickley Bros., Oak, Range of Flat Splats, Cushion, 1915, 5 Ft. 2 In. 1750.00
Settee, Stickley, Wicker, Woven Pillow, 1906, 86 x 31 In. 9750.00
Settee, Victorian, Mahogany, Button-Tufted Triple Chair Back, Arms, 61 In. 400.00
Settee, Windsor, Bamboo-Turned, Plank Seat, Green Paint, 6 Ft. 6 In. 5500.00
Settee, Windsor, Rod Back Crest, 24 Spindles, Brown Paint, 1790-1810, 77 In. 3100.00
Settle, Arched Crest, Wing Arms, Red Paint, 47 1/4 In. 2425.00
Settle, Arrow-Back, Black, Gold Stenciling, 1841 .... 1150.00
Settle, Beige Paint, Black, Gray Striping, Floral Design, 80 In. 775.00
Settle, Child's, Cutout Base, Stencil On Back, 18th Century 1250.00
Settle, Continental, Paneled Back, Upholstered Arms & Seat, Yew Wood, 77 In. 995.00
Settle, Crest Rail, 9 Vertical Back Slats, 3 On Each Side, 32 x 65 x 28 In. 1760.00
Settle, Gustav Stickley, 3-Slat Arms, 8-Slat Back, Oak, Leather Seat, c.1912, 78 In. 6600.00
Settle, Gustav Stickley, No. 70, Wicker, Even Arms 5000.00
Settle, Gustav Stickley, No. 208-H, Broad Slats, 39 x 79 3/4 x 28 1/2 In. 2750.00
Settle, Gustav Stickley, No. 225, Side Slats, Back Board, 29 x 77 x 31 In. 5225.00
Settle, Hood & Arms, Lift Seat, 2 Drawers, Red Paint, 60 x 60 x 20 In. 3000.00
Settle, Molded Crest Rail, 16 Vertical Back Slats, Cushion Seat, 34 In. 3850.00

Furniture, Settee, Regency, Serpentine,
Beechwood, 4 Ft.

Furniture, Stool, Eames, Red, c.1945,
15 X 11 X 8 In.

Settle, Oak, Graining, 2 Base Drawers, Board Back, Arms, England, 72 x 56 In. 1100.00
Settle, Oak, Pewter Inlay, Hinged Seat, Paneled Back, 52 x 54 In. 2416.00
Settle, Original Grayish Yellow Paint, Brown, Black Striping, 80 1/2 In. 1375.00
Settle, Original Red Paint, New England, 1810 .... 3950.00
Settle, Pine, Brown Paint, Curving Sides, Hinged Seat, 55 x 54 x 14 In. 3025.00
Settle, Pine, Cutout Sides, Paneled Back, Folds Out Into A Bed, 48 3/4 In. 700.00
Settle, Pine, Pullout Trundle 975.00
Settle, Pine, Sloping Arms, 5 Molded Square Insert Back, England, 1870, 6 Ft. 1100.00
Settle, Stickley Brothers, 84 In. 4800.00
Settle, Stickley Brothers, No. 3863, Flared Slats, Exposed Tenons, Oak, 62 In. 5280.00
Settle, Windsor, Bamboo, Black Repaint, Arms, 96 In. 660.00
Shelf, 4 Tiers, Painted & Carved, Fox Scene, C. Smyth, 19th Century, 39 x 15 In. ... 385.00
Shelf, Eastlake, Corner, Walnut, Pair 85.00
Shelf, Hanging, Corner, Directoire Style, Pierced Lock Plates, 38 In. 2000.00
Shelf, Hanging, Corner, Poplar, Scalloped Edges, Country, 6 Shelves, 44 In. 225.00
Shelf, Hanging, Pine, Black Painted Sawtooth Edge On Crest, 30 1/2 In. 195.00
Shelf, Hanging, Pine, Dark Finish, Wire Nail Construction, 21 In. 335.00
Shelf, Hanging, Pine, Grayish Green Repaint, 17 3/4 In. 275.00
Shelf, Hanging, Pine, Mortar, Pestle Holder, Spoon Rack, 27 1/4 In. 137.00
Shelf, Hanging, Shaker, Union Village, Walnut, Drawer, 36 x 11 x 6 In. 4300.00
Shelf, Jenny Lind Style, Walnut, 2 Shelves 70.00
Shelf, Mahogany, Whale Sides, 32 x 26 In. 275.00
Shelf, Oak, Corner, Shield Shape, Hunters Drinking, Guns, Deer, 12 In. 165.00
Shelf, Whatnot, Victorian, Walnut, 6 Shelves 325.00
Sideboard, Art Deco, Opens To Desk, Side Doors For Bar, Red Interior, Glass 1800.00
Sideboard, Butler's Desk Center, Mahogany, Columns, Footed, 72 In. 2750.00
Sideboard, Child's, Victorian, With Mirror, 23 In. 225.00
Sideboard, Chippendale, Mahogany, Backsplash, Long Drawer, 40 x 18 In. 525.00
Sideboard, Classical, Mahogany, Ionic Columns, Hairy Paw Feet 3850.00
Sideboard, Crotch Cherry Veneer, Mirror Back, Carved Eagles & Shields, c.1820 .... 2650.00
Sideboard, Eastlake, Walnut, Mirror, 71 In. 137.50
Sideboard, Empire, Backsplash, Drawer, Cupboards, Paw Feet, 55 x 54 In. 775.00
Sideboard, Empire, Mahogany, Gothic Arch Inlays, Doors, Drawers, 72 1/2 In. 1200.00
Sideboard, Empire, Secret Drawer, Harvey Davis, 95 x 25 x 44 In. 1250.00
Sideboard, Federal, Carved Mahogany, Samuel Field McIntire 2800.00
Sideboard, Federal, Mahogany, D Shape, Stringing, Pennsylvania, 44 x 81 x 25 In. .. 7700.00
Sideboard, Federal, Mahogany, Gallery, 5 Short Drawers, 43 x 72 x 24 In. 3685.00
Sideboard, Federal, Mahogany, Inlay, 3 Top Drawers, Mass., 1790, 40 x 42 In. 4950.00
Sideboard, Federal, Serpentine Front, 3 Drawers, Mahogany, 41 x 66 In. 3740.00
Sideboard, French Provincial Style, 2 Drawers, Oak, 77 In. 550.00
Sideboard, George III, String & Bellflower Inlays, Mahogany, 61 In. 8250.00
Sideboard, Gilt Bronze Shells On Doors, Brown & Gold Lacquer, 1940, 6 Ft. 1 In. .. 6600.00
Sideboard, Gustav Stickley, 2 Doors, 3 Drawers, Lower Shelf, 38 3/4 x 54 In. 3750.00
Sideboard, Gustav Stickley, Oak, Open Plate Rack, 3 Central Drawers, 48 In. 2975.00
Sideboard, Hepplewhite, Mahogany, Inlay, Step Back Top, 77 1/2 x 44 In. 1540.00
Sideboard, Hepplewhite, Serpentine, Inlaid Doors, New England, 1790 .... 6875.00
Sideboard, Kimbel & Cabus, Burl Walnut, Inset Tiles On Console Base 7425.00
Sideboard, Mahogany Veneer, Ivory Escutcheons, 3 Drawers, Mass., 1780 .... 4600.00
Sideboard, Mahogany, 3 Short Drawers, Cupboard Doors, 44 1/2 x 49 In. 3100.00
Sideboard, Mahogany, England, 36 1/2 x 36 In. 3900.00
Sideboard, Mahogany, Serpentine, Inlay, 4 Drawers Over 4 Doors 6500.00
Sideboard, Mahogany, Splash Rail, Arched Door, Cabinet Doors, 7 Ft. 2 In. 2310.00
Sideboard, Mahogany, Tambour Doors, Bottle Drawers, J. B. Barry, Phila., 6 Ft. ... 9350.00
Sideboard, Pine, 4 Top Drawers, England, Late 1800s 895.00
Sideboard, Pine, Graining, 3 Graduated Side Drawers, 1 Door 265.00
Sideboard, Plate Rail, Overhanging Top, 4 Central Drawers, 46 In. 2425.00
Sideboard, Queen Anne, Mahogany, Crossbanded Drawers, Kittinger, 77 In. 1450.00
Sideboard, Rectangular Top, 1 Cabinet Door, 4 Drawers, 45 In. 1450.00
Sideboard, Regency, Pedestal, Inlaid Mahogany, 1810, 44 In. 1700.00
Sideboard, Sheraton, Cherry, 4 Doors, 1840 .... 4000.00
Sideboard, Sheraton, Mahogany Inlay, Shaped Gallery, Tapered Legs, 75 In. 1850.00
Sideboard, Sheraton, Mahogany, Serpentine, William Hook, 39 x 62 In. 2750.00
Sideboard, Victorian, Marble Backsplash, 2 Drawers, U.S., 41 In. 330.00

Smoking Stand, Dragon, Lead Insert, Iron, 32 In.	50.00
Sofa, Art Deco, Shaped Rail, Overlapping Flower Heads, France, c.1925, 6 Ft. 7 In.	7700.00
Sofa, Biedermeier, Upholstery, 86 x 22 In.	1265.00
Sofa, Camelback, Needlepoint Upholstery, Arms, England	3850.00
Sofa, Carved Fruit Wood Frame, Ivory Brocade Upholstery, France, 82 In.	65.00
Sofa, Chippendale, Mahogany, Camelback, U.S., Early 20th Century, 73 In.	1200.00
Sofa, Classical Revival, Walnut, Upholstery, 40 x 72 In.	470.00
Sofa, Dali Design, Lip-Shaped, Bright Red Nylon	2310.00
Sofa, Eero Saarinen, Womb, Fabric, Black Steel Frame	2700.00
Sofa, Empire, Mahogany, Rope Back Rail, Cornucopia Arm Supports, 68 In.	775.00
Sofa, Empire, Scroll Arms, Hairy Paw Feet, 96 In.	885.00
Sofa, Federal, Horsehair Upholstery, Squared Tacks, Fruit Carvings	2250.00
Sofa, George Nelson, Marshmallow Back, 1956	8800.00
Sofa, Georgian, Camelback, Upholstery, Block Legs, Baker, 75 In.	1100.00
Sofa, Grecian Style, Mahogany, Brocade, Curved Arms, New England, 1880	8500.00
Sofa, Louis XVI Style, Walnut, Reeded & Ribbon Back & Arms, 86 In.	1100.00
Sofa, Louis XVI, Beechwood, Carved Crest & Arms, High Back, Wings, 78 In.	1210.00
Sofa, Sheraton, Mahogany, Reeded Arms, Fluted Columns, Portsmouth, 80 In.	1050.00
Sofa, Victorian, Carved Walnut, Medallion Back, 44 x 67 In.	715.00
Sofa, Victorian, Floral Upholstered, Curved Arms	550.00
Sofa, Victorian, Medallion Back	385.00
Sofa, Victorian, Walnut, Rose Carving, Upholstery, 7 Ft.	2500.00
Sofa, Wide Cushion Rail, Elongated Corbels, Square Legs, 74 In.	335.00
Sofa, Woven Rattan Seat & Back, Plywood Frame, Edward Durell Stone, 77 In.	770.00
Stand, 1 Drawer, 1 Board Top, Figured Maple, 28 3/4 In.	445.00
Stand, 1 Drawer, 2 Board Top, Cherry, Turned Legs, 29 In.	360.00
Stand, 1 Drawer, 2 Board Top, Clear Lacy Knob, Country, 19 x 21 x 29 In.	250.00
Stand, 1 Drawer, 2 Board Top, Curly Maple, 29 3/4 In.	350.00
Stand, 1 Drawer, Board Top, Pine, Poplar, Red, Turned Legs, Country, 18 x 19 In.	495.00
Stand, 1 Drawer, Bright Green Paint, Square Top	685.00
Stand, 1 Drawer, Empire, Cherry, Scrolled Drop In Apron, 27 1/2 In.	575.00
Stand, 1 Drawer, Empire, Clear Pulls, Flame Grain Veneer, Mahogany, 30 In.	225.00
Stand, 1 Drawer, Hepplewhite, Drop Leaf, Refinished Birch, Square Legs, 28 In.	95.00
Stand, 1 Drawer, Hepplewhite, Walnut, Dovetailed, 24 x 20 x 28 In.	1100.00
Stand, 1 Drawer, Hepplewhite, Walnut, Removable 2 Board Top, 21 x 25 In.	385.00
Stand, 1 Drawer, Pine, Curly Maple, Cherry Finish, Country, 30 In.	325.00
Stand, 1 Drawer, Regency, Burl Veneer, Shelf, England, 1820, 30 x 21 In.	1875.00
Stand, 1 Drawer, Tapered Leg, 28 x 18 In.	885.00
Stand, 2 Drawers, 1 Board Top, Walnut, Poplar, 16 x 19 In.	285.00
Stand, 2 Drawers, 2 Board Top, Cherry, Mahogany Veneer Facade, 30 In.	360.00
Stand, 2 Drawers, Drop Leaf, Cherry, 2 Leaves, 16 3/4 x 22 x 10 In.	350.00
Stand, 2 Drawers, Drop Leaf, Cherry, Bird's-Eye Veneer, 15 x 24 x 27 In.	715.00
Stand, 2 Drawers, Empire, Cherry & Curly Maple, Dovetailed, 22 x 29 1/2 In.	715.00
Stand, 2 Drawers, Empire, Curly Maple, Pine, Cherry, 29 1/2 In.	522.00
Stand, 2 Drawers, Federal, Tripod Base, Brass Castors, 27 3/4 In.	357.00
Stand, 2 Drawers, Hepplewhite, Cherry, Square Legs, 17 1/2 x 28 1/2 In.	440.00
Stand, 2 Drawers, Pine, Poplar, Salmon, Pale Green Striping, 28 1/2 In.	200.00
Stand, 2 Drawers, Sheraton, Curly Maple Inlay	715.00
Stand, 2 Drawers, Sheraton, Original Yellow Paint, Fruit & Leaves	2750.00
Stand, 2 Drawers, Sheraton, Pine, Red Flame Grained, Dovetailed, 17 x 22 In.	1925.00
Stand, 2 Drawers, Victorian, Mahogany, Carved Base & Paw Feet	715.00
Stand, 3 Drawers, Mahogany, Ionic Columns, Carved Paw Feet, 29 In.	350.00
Stand, Barber, Eastlake, Carved Floral Panel On Door	1210.00
Stand, Book, Gustav Stickley, No. 93, Oak, Rectangular, c.1910, 17 1/8 In.	3300.00
Stand, Book, Roycroft, Mission Style	500.00
Stand, Carved Teakwood, Marble Top, 22 In.	171.00
Stand, Cherry, Poplar, Turtle-Shaped Top, Country, 27 3/4 In.	200.00
Stand, Cherry, Tripod Base, 1860–1870	215.00
Stand, Corner, 2 Shelves, Cherry, 19th Century, 33 x 27 In.	305.00
Stand, Demilune, Splayed Hepplewhite Legs	495.00
Stand, Empire, Cherry, 20 1/2 x 22 1/2 x 30 In.	330.00
Stand, Federal, Cherrywood, Line Inlay, Shelf, Demilune Cutout, 31 In.	3300.00
Stand, Floral Inlay Top, Brass Busts Top of Legs, France	445.00

Stand, Graining Simulates Mahogany, New England, 1820, 30 In. 335.00
Stand, Green Onyx Top, Champleve Border, Bronze & Onyx Pedestal, 30 In. 2850.00
Stand, Hepplewhite, Shaped Top, Split Drawer Configuration 1045.00
Stand, Hepplewhite, Walnut, Poplar, Pencil Post Legs, 2 Board Top, 29 In. 75.00
Stand, Louis XV, French Provincial Style, 1 Drawer, 24 In. 135.00
Stand, Lovers, Cherubs On Top, Tripod Bamboo Base, Papier-Mache, 30 In. 415.00
Stand, Magazine, Gustav Stickley, No. 72, 3 Shelves, 42 x 21 In. 1650.00
Stand, Magazine, L. & J. G. Stickley, 4 Shelves, Tapered Sides, 42 x 18 In. 1450.00
Stand, Magazine, Lakeside, 3 Sections, 38 x 14 x 11 In. 665.00
Stand, Marble Top, Gilt Bronze Mounted, Kingwood, Pair 7700.00
Stand, Music, Limbert 700.00
Stand, Music, Lyre Form Stand, Scrolled Feet, Brass, 52 In. 65.00
Stand, Music, Lyre Form, Adjustable, Brass 80.00
Stand, Music, Regency, Musicians In Forest On Tilt Top, Lacquered, 24 In. 275.00
Stand, Pentagonal Top, Carved Frieze Over Apron, 5 Flower Carved Legs, 27 In. 220.00
Stand, Plant, 3 Shelves, Green Paint, Semicircular, 29 x 40 x 24 In. 303.00
Stand, Plant, 3 Sides, 3 Shelves, Dark Paint, 20th Century 550.00
Stand, Plant, Bent Wire, Ornate 575.00
Stand, Plant, Folding, Wire, Oval Top, White Porcelain Casters, 27 In. 181.00
Stand, Plant, French Colonial, Gilt & Ebonized Bamboo, 34 In. 132.00
Stand, Plant, Gustav Stickley, Green Glazed Grueby Tile, 29 3/4 In. 6000.00
Stand, Plant, Gustav Stickley, No. 41, 27 3/4 x 14 3/4 In. 885.00
Stand, Plant, Louis XV Style, Marble Top, Diamond Shaped Stretcher, 22 In., Pr. ... 1325.00
Stand, Plant, Marble Insert, Iron, White Repaint, 19 In. 60.00
Stand, Plant, Oak, Pedestal, 1930s, Pair 85.00
Stand, Plant, Semicircular, 4 Shelves, Bright Blue 345.00
Stand, Plant, Walnut, Turtle Leg 135.00
Stand, Prayer, Shaker, Grain Painted, 32 x 14 x 15 In. 245.00
Stand, Roycroft, Little Journey 415.00
Stand, Rush Light, Iron, Tripod Base, Hooks For Other Lighting, 39 In. 475.00
Stand, Sewing, Lift Top, Compartments, Swing Side Door, Pouch, France, Small 395.00
Stand, Sewing, Marble Top, Rosewood Veneer, Octagonal, 8 x 18 x 14 In. 225.00
Stand, Sewing, Martha Washington Style, Wicker 595.00
Stand, Sewing, Victorian, Bamboo Frame, Woven Grass Mat 125.00
Stand, Sewing, Wicker, Low Shelf 60.00
Stand, Smoking, Bronze, Urn-Shaped, Attached Undertray, 7 In. 275.00
Stand, Smoking, Chromium Plated Metal, Bakelite Top, 24 x 20 1/2 In. 550.00
Stand, Table, Dunbar, Mahogany & Travertine Marble, 21 1/2 In. 65.00
Stand, Teakwood, Marble Top, Oriental, 32 In. 385.00
Stand, Telephone, Arts & Crafts, 21 x 14 1/2 x 14 1/2 In. 192.50
Stand, Tiger Maple, Snake Foot 35.00
Stand, Tilt Top, Walnut, Four Part Feet, Turned Column, 1 Board Top, 26 1/4 In. 200.00
Stand, Tripod Base, Scroll Legs, Rectangular Top, 18 1/2 x 26 1/4 x 27 In. 245.00
Stand, Umbrella, Brass, Raised Figural, Floral, Animal Design, Paw Feet 65.00
Stand, Umbrella, Gustav Stickley, No. 100, Oak 1650.00
Stand, Umbrella, Inlaid, Lyre Form Back, Mahogany, Louis Philippe, 20 1/2 In. 335.00
Stand, Wash, Maple, Back Splash, Lower Drawer, America 80.00
Stand, Wig, Mahogany, 9 1/2 In. 45.00
Stand, Wooden, Blue Paint, 4-Legged, Small 525.00
Stand, Work, American Federal, 1 Short Drawer, Cherry, 19th Century, 28 In. 445.00
Step Ladder, Shaker, 3 Shelves, Canted Sides, Butternut, 23 1/2 In. 3425.00
Stool, Carved Marble, Shaped Pedestal, Red Paint, 4 x 7 1/4 In. 65.00
Stool, Child's, Carved From 1 Log, New England, 11 In. 110.00
Stool, Eames, Red, c.1945, 15 x 11 x 8 In. ....*Illus* 1760.00
Stool, Eastlake, Burl Walnut, Animal Head On Front 550.00
Stool, George III, Needlepoint Upholstery, Raked Legs, 1770s 385.00
Stool, Giltwood, Scrolled & Acanthus Knees, Hoof Feet, Pillow Top, 20 x 20 In. 3960.00
Stool, Giltwood, Upholstered Seat, Intertwining Rope-Like Legs 880.00
Stool, Gout, Jacobean Style, Oak, Turned Legs, 11 x 17 In. 245.00
Stool, Gout, Mahogany, Colonial West Indies, 1820s 750.00
Stool, Jacobean Style, Oak, 1880s, 28 1/2 x 24 1/2 In. 247.50
Stool, Organ, Cast Iron, Horsehair Seat 50.00
Stool, Oval Incised Top, 4 Bamboo Turned Legs, England, 1820, 13 In. 935.00

Stool, Parcel Gilt, Concave Upholstered Seat, Loose Cushion, Venice 4950.00
Stool, Pharmacist's, Leather Seat 100.00
Stool, Piano, Brass & Glass Claw & Ball Feet 100.00
Stool, Piano, Carved Legs, Embroidered Seat 35.00
Stool, Piano, Herter Brothers, Rosewood, Gilded, Original Upholstery 4400.00
Stool, Piano, Mahogany, Acanthus Carved Stem, Animal Paw Legs, c.1825 .... 775.00
Stool, Piano, Regency, Leather Upholstery, Swivel Seat, 19 In., Pair 1100.00
Stool, Piano, Regency, Striped Upholstery Back, 32 In. 885.00
Stool, Piano, Rope Legs, Metal Claw Feet With Glass Balls 115.00
Stool, Shaker, 2 Steps, Varnish Over Orange 1215.00
Stool, Shaker, 3 Steps, Orange Over Mustard 1650.00
Stool, Shaker, Taped Seat, Decal, Ebony Finish, Mt. Lebanon 440.00
Stool, Turned Legs, Brown Finish, Blue, Ecru Woven Taped Seat, 17 1/4 In. 60.00
Stool, Turned Legs, Gold Paint, Twine Top, 5 3/4 In. 22.00
Stool, Victorian, Needlepoint Upholstery, Bamboo–Turned Black Legs, 22 In. 355.00
Stool, Windsor, Green, 24 1/4 In. 104.00
Stool, Windsor, Paint Traces, Branded P. Mitchell, Country, 15 3/4 In. 93.50
Stool, Worn Blue Paint, Primitive 58.00
Swing, Porch, Hickory, Indiana, 1930 .... 425.00
Swing, Porch, Natural Wicker, Large 850.00
Table & Lamp, Red Wicker, Merikord, American Chair Co., 1920s 2875.00
Table Set, Breakfast, Wrought Iron, Glass Top, Stylized Cabriole Legs, 5 Piece 275.00
Table Set, Child's, Enameled Top, Child At Play, Numbers & Alphabet, 2 Piece 125.00
Table Set, Child's, Tubular Chrome Legs, Formica, Gray Padded Chairs, 3 Piece 65.00
Table Set, Wrought Iron, Upholstered, Verdigris Finish, Belgium, 1930s, 7 Piece. 650.00
Table, 2 Board Top, Red Paint, 11 Ft. 795.00
Table, Allover Meandering Foliate, Red Lacquer, 13 1/2 x 47 1/2 In. 9350.00
Table, American Rococo, Rosewood, Shaped Black & Gold Marble Top 7750.00
Table, Arts & Crafts, Oak, Round Top, 29 In. 1100.00
Table, Baker's, Marble Top, Polished Steel, France, 61 In. 2100.00
Table, Baker's, Original Hardware, England, Late 1800s 1100.00

Furniture, Table, Biedermeier, Birch, Ebonized, 42 In.

Furniture, Table, Card, Federal, Mahogany, Maple Inlay, Mass., 1810-1815

Furniture, Table, Walnut, Carved Griffins, 19th Century, 30 X 60 In.

Table, Banquet, Baroque Style, Mahogany, Paw Feet, 75 x 54 In. 605.00
Table, Banquet, Federal, Mahogany, Drop Leaf, 111 x 48 In. 3300.00
Table, Banquet, Federal, Mahogany, Inlay, Baltimore, 1795, 28 x 89 x 48 In. 7150.00
Table, Banquet, Figured Mahogany Veneer, Ogee Apron, 29 1/2 In., Pair 880.00
Table, Banquet, Hepplewhite, Cherry, Inlay, Oval Top 3410.00
Table, Banquet, Mahogany, Veneer On Aprons, 30 In., Pair 495.00
Table, Biedermeier, Birch, Ebonized, 42 In. ....*Illus* 4400.00
Table, Blueprint, 2 Open Compartments, Center Shelf, Oak, 1890s 125.00
Table, Breakfast, Classical Revival, Mahogany, N.Y., 1800, 28 x 36 x 21 In. 2090.00
Table, Breakfast, Federal, Mahogany, Drop Leaf, 1810, 52 In. 3520.00
Table, Breakfast, Hepplewhite, Pine & Chestnut, Painted, c.1850 .... 575.00
Table, Breakfast, Mahogany, Tripod Base, Oval Tilt Top, 1800 .... 1150.00
Table, Breakfast, Regency, Mahogany, 28 3/4 x 36 In. 935.00
Table, Breakfast, Rosewood & Mahogany, Line Inlay, Round, 48 In. 4125.00
Table, Breakfast, Tilt Top, Quatre-Foil Base, Mahogany, 28 x 45 In. 145.00
Table, Breakfast, Tilt Top, Regency, Mahogany, Pedestal Base, Castors, 54 x 39 In. . 1590.00
Table, Breakfast, Tilt Top, William IV, Mahogany, 1835, Square, 45 In. 800.00
Table, Campaign, Folding, Poplar, Ornton & Herne, 25 x 37 In. 350.00
Table, Card, American Empire, Mahogany, Pineapple Pedestal, Swivel Top, 36 In. ... 825.00
Table, Card, Chippendale, Mahogany, 1 Drawer, Carved Apron, 28 In. 1525.00
Table, Card, Chippendale, Mahogany, Folding Top, 15 x 31 1/4 x 27 3/4 In. 1100.00
Table, Card, Chippendale, Mahogany, Serpentine Top, Short Drawer, 1770s 7150.00
Table, Card, Duncan Phyfe, Gilded Acanthus Leaf Carvings On Legs, c.1815 .... 7800.00
Table, Card, Dutch Marquetry, Triangular Hinged Top, Cabriole Pad Feet, 40 In. ... 1650.00
Table, Card, Elliptical Skirt, Tiger Maple Inlay, New England, c.1790 .... 7700.00
Table, Card, Federal, Mahogany, Inlay, Mass., 1800, 30 x 36 In. 2100.00
Table, Card, Federal, Mahogany, Inlay, Pinwheel, Bellflower, 1800, 28 x 36 In. 2975.00
Table, Card, Federal, Mahogany, Maple Inlay, Mass., 1810–1815 ....*Illus* 5225.00
Table, Card, George II, Mahogany, Queen Anne Legs, England, 1750 .... 4500.00
Table, Card, Hepplewhite, Butternut, Swing Leg, 1 Drawer, Leaf, 35 x 14 x 38 In. . 800.00
Table, Card, Hepplewhite, Flame Birch, New Hampshire 650.00
Table, Card, Mahogany & Pine, Lyre Base, Henry Connelly, c.1810 .... 4200.00
Table, Card, Mahogany, 1 Drawer, Gadrooned Apron, Serpentine, Phila., 38 In. 5225.00
Table, Card, Mahogany, Flame Birch, D Shape, Branded N. B. Folsom 9350.00
Table, Card, Mahogany, Gadrooned Edge Apron, Serpentine Front, 38 In. 5225.00
Table, Card, Queen Anne, Mahogany, 1 Drawer, Pad Feet, 28 1/2 In. 770.00
Table, Card, Rosewood & Satinwood, Inlay 3850.00
Table, Card, Serpentine, Rosewood Panels, Satinwood Insert, Massachusetts 4000.00
Table, Card, Sheraton, Mahogany & Mahogany Veneer, c.1830, 30 In. 450.00
Table, Card, Sheraton, Mahogany Veneer, 1/2 Serpentine Ends, 1810, 35 x 17 In. 2600.00
Table, Card, Sheraton, Tapered Rope Legs, Serpentine Top 675.00
Table, Card, Sheraton, Tiger Maple Apron, New York, Pair 4000.00
Table, Carved Rosewood, Marble Top 1650.00
Table, Cast Iron, Cast Aluminum Brackets, Marble Top, 30 1/2 x 54 1/2 In. 375.00
Table, Center, Biedermeier, Birch, Ebonized, Inlay, 19th Century ....*Illus* 9900.00
Table, Center, Biedermeier, Black Walnut, Danhauser, 29 In. ....*Illus* 8800.00
Table, Center, Biedermeier, Walnut, Ebonized, Parcel Gilt, 29 1/2 In. ....*Illus* 9350.00
Table, Center, Mahogany, Ball & Claw Feet, Carved Apron, 29 In. 1127.00
Table, Center, Meeks, Rosewood, Marble Top, 50 In. 3500.00
Table, Center, Pine, Poplar, Red, New York, 1850 .... 425.00
Table, Cherry, Poplar, Round, 3 Turned Legs, 2 Board Top, 24 In. 825.00
Table, Cherrywood, Slate Top, Scalloped Apron, Ball Feet, 28 In. 6000.00
Table, Child's, Hepplewhite, Drop Leaf, Pine, 1880 .... 395.00
Table, Chippendale Pembroke, Mahogany, Rounded Corner Leaves, England 357.00
Table, Chippendale, 3 Drawers, Mortised, Pinned Apron, 29 In. 440.00
Table, Chippendale, Mahogany, Dark Finish, China, 29 In. 302.00
Table, Chippendale, Rosewood, China, 18 x 18 In. 412.00
Table, Chippendale, Tilt Top, Mahogany, Dish-Turned Top, 26 x 28 In. 1200.00
Table, Coffee, Carved Walnut, Rouge Marble Top, c.1875, 19 1/2 x 36 In. 445.00
Table, Coffee, Cherry, White Marble Top, Carved, Oval 230.00
Table, Coffee, Eames, Lacquered Wooden Top, Steel Wire Base, 16 x 34 In. 385.00
Table, Coffee, George Nakashima, Walnut, Uneven Border, 70 1/2 In. 1100.00
Table, Coffee, Kem Weber, Demilune, Black Enameled Wood, 2 Tiers, 22 x 26 In. . 225.00

Furniture, Table, Center, Biedermeier, Birch,
Ebonized, Inlay, 19th Century

Furniture, Table, Center, Biedermeier,
Black Walnut, Danhauser, 29 In.

◆ ◆

Always remove the top drawers from a large chest first. If
you pull out the bottom drawers and then move the chest,
it is likely to tip over.

◆ ◆

Furniture, Table, Center, Biedermeier, Walnut,
Ebonized, Parcel Gilt, 29 1/2 In.

Table, Coffee, Mahogany, 1 Drawer, Carved Top, Zodiac, Flowers, Folk Art, 17 In.	385.00
Table, Coffee, Mahogany, Oval, Plate Glass Top, 18 1/4 In.	110.00
Table, Coffee, Oriental Style, Black Lacquered Coromandel Design, 18 1/2 x 49 In.	300.00
Table, Coffee, Raymond Subes, Marble Top, Wrought Iron Trestle, 1930, 40 In.	7150.00
Table, Conference, Victorian, Walnut, Oval Top	5750.00
Table, Console, Biedermeier, Cherry, 1830s, 33 1/2 x 42 In.	1540.00
Table, Console, French Provincial, Fruitwood, 1 Drawer	2200.00
Table, Console, Limbert, No. 1112, 2 Drawers, c.1906, 29 1/4 x 66 In.	5500.00
Table, Console, William IV, Mahogany, Fantasy Face On Apron, Ireland, 53 In.	1045.00
Table, Corner, Arts & Crafts, Arched Skirt, Lower Shelf, 30 x 21 x 21 In.	440.00
Table, Corner, Majorelle, Carved Mahogany, c.1900, 40 x 24 In.	1500.00
Table, Cricket, George III, Oak, 26 3/4 x 30 In.	357.50
Table, Curly Maple, 1 Dovetailed Drawer, Square Tapered Legs, 29 In.	1155.00
Table, Dark Pine, Tongue In Groove, American, 1800, 6 1/2 In.	1500.00
Table, Dining, Black Lacquered, Ormolu Medallions, 2 Leaves, French, 65 In.	665.00
Table, Dining, Drop Leaf, Plain Frieze, Cherry, 47 3/4 x 28 1/2 In.	165.00
Table, Dining, Federal, Drop Leaf, Tapered Legs, Mahogany, 54 In.	445.00
Table, Dining, Federal, Mahogany, Turned Legs, Mass., 1810, 62 x 46 In.	1100.00
Table, Dining, French Provincial, Scrolled Apron, Cherry, 72 In.	950.00
Table, Dining, Gateleg, Pine, 1 Drawer, Leaves, 18th Century, 40 x 16 In.	495.00
Table, Dining, Gustav Stickley, Arched Cross Stretchers, 30 In.	3400.00
Table, Dining, Gustav Stickley, Overhanging Round Top, 5 Legs, 29 1/2 In.	2425.00
Table, Dining, L. & J. G. Stickley, No. 71B, 4 Leaves, 5 Legs, 29 x 48 In.	2200.00
Table, Dining, Limbert, Circular Top, Octagonal Base, 54 In.	1100.00
Table, Dining, Limbert, Round Top, Base of Octagonal Section, Oak, 54 In.	1100.00
Table, Dining, Mahogany, Vines & Figures, Winged Lions Base, Round	3500.00
Table, Dining, Mission, Oak, c.1825, 120 x 49 x 28 In.	450.00
Table, Dining, Oak, 10 Leaves, 32 Ft. Opened	1300.00
Table, Dining, Oak, Pedestal Base, Round, 45 In.	175.00
Table, Dining, Oak, Rectangular, Chamfered Legs, 29 x 55 x 42 1/2 In.	1859.00
Table, Dining, Oak, Square, Extension, Hexagonal Legs, Platform Shelf	2975.00

Table, Dining, Pedestal, Walnut, Round Top, 29 In. 885.00
Table, Dining, Pembroke Style, Drop Leaf, Red Paint, Nova Scotia Pine, c.1820 ...... 725.00
Table, Dining, Regency, Double Pedestal, Satinwood, Rosewood Band, England 2090.00
Table, Dining, Shaker, Red, Sabbathday Lake, 1850 .... 9500.00
Table, Dining, Victorian, Walnut, Fruit & Leaf Carved, Pedestal, Round, 60 In. 1325.00
Table, Dining, William & Mary, Maple, Gate–Leaf, Oval Leaf, 1740s, 50 1/4 In. 6050.00
Table, Double Pedestal, Boston, 1810 .... 2900.00
Table, Dressing, Bird's–Eye Maple, Wishbone Mirror, Beveled, Drawers 175.00
Table, Dressing, Black & Red Graining, Stenciled, Olive Banding, 1820–1840 .... 6500.00
Table, Dressing, Cherry, Brass Posts, 1 Drawer, Dunbar, 29 1/2 x 32 In. 65.00
Table, Dressing, Chippendale, Walnut, 4 Overlapping Drawers, Phila., 20 x 33 In. ... 3575.00
Table, Dressing, Classical Revival, Mirror, 1810, 39 In. 3300.00
Table, Dressing, Federal, G. & J. Smith, c.1820, 58 In. 3300.00
Table, Dressing, Federal, White Paint, 1 Drawer & 1 Small Top Drawer 7165.00
Table, Dressing, Ivory Inlay, Ebony Veneer, Swivel Mirror, c.1930, 72 x 48 In. 1115.00
Table, Dressing, Ivory Inlay, Oval Mirror, Carved Support, Chinese, 60 x 40 In. 825.00
Table, Dressing, Queen Anne, Cherry, c.1760, 28 In. 8900.00
Table, Dressing, Queen Anne, Cherry, Conn. River Valley, 1760, 35 x 40 x 23 In. ... 7700.00
Table, Dressing, Sheraton, Rosewood, Sandwich Glass Knobs, 19th Century 550.00
Table, Dressing, Step Back, Painted Yellow, c.1830 .... 365.00
Table, Dressing, Victorian, Maple, Bamboo 3000.00
Table, Drop Leaf, Birch, Turned Legs, 42 x 46 In. 345.00
Table, Drop Leaf, Curly Maple, 1 Board Top, Rounded Corner Leaves, 29 In. 1430.00
Table, Drop Leaf, Federal, Mahogany, Pedestal, Brass Paw Feet, 43 x 54 In. 1430.00
Table, Drop Leaf, George III, Oak, 27 1/2 x 42 In. 440.00
Table, Drop Leaf, Georgian, Mahogany, Oval, Pad Feet, c.1750 .... 770.00
Table, Drop Leaf, Gustav Stickley, Shoe Feet, Round, 29 3/4 x 32 In. 1210.00
Table, Drop Leaf, Mahogany, 9 Drawers, Acanthus Carved Stem, 28 In. 528.00
Table, Drop Leaf, Mahogany, Swing Legs Support Top, 27 1/4 In. 160.00
Table, Drop Leaf, Oak, Gateleg, Oval, Drawers, 1680, 42 x 48 In. 550.00
Table, Drop Leaf, Pembroke, Cherry, 1 Drawer, Cross Stretchers, Pa., 30 In. 825.00
Table, Drop Leaf, Pembroke, Sheraton, Cherry & Maple, 18 x 35 1/2 In. 440.00
Table, Drop Leaf, Pembroke, Sheraton, Cherry, 28 3/4 In. 495.00
Table, Drop Leaf, Pembroke, Walnut, 1 Drawer 1100.00
Table, Drop Leaf, Queen Anne, Swing Leg, Maple, Duck Feet, Oval, 29 In. 907.00
Table, Drop Leaf, Queen Anne, Mahogany, Duck Feet, 25 x 38 x 33 In. 1320.00
Table, Drop Leaf, Queen Anne, Maple, Duck Feet, Leaves, 14 1/2 x 17 3/4 x 28 In. . 880.00
Table, Drop Leaf, Queen Anne, Walnut, Scrolled Apron, 27 3/4 In. 900.00
Table, Drop Leaf, Regency, Rosewood, 2 Drawers, Castors, 35 x 28 In. 1750.00
Table, Drop Leaf, Sheraton, Cherry, Birch, 2 Drawers, 28 1/2 In. 650.00
Table, Drop Leaf, Sheraton, Grained Red & Black Paint 175.00
Table, Drop Leaf, Sheraton, Mahogany, 1 Draw In Apron, America, 36 x 46 In. 300.00
Table, Drop Leaf, Sheraton, Walnut, Swing Legs Support Top, 2 Board Top 475.00
Table, Drop Leaf, Tiger Maple, Cross Stretcher, New England, 1800 .... 3800.00
Table, Drop Leaf, Trestle Base, Maple & Pine, 27 x 38 In. 4400.00
Table, Drop Leaf, Walnut, Gate Leg, 60 In. Opened 150.00
Table, Drop Leaf, Walnut, Swing Legs, 2 Board Leaves, 28 x 17 x 41 In. 475.00
Table, Drop Leaf, William & Mary, Cherrywood, Round Top 3500.00
Table, Eames, Surfboard, Black Laminate Top 1980.00
Table, Ebonized, Floral Top, Scroll Paw Footed, Snake Column, Round, 39 x 23 In. . 1320.00
Table, Ebonized, Marble Starburst Inlay, Round Top, 19th Century 2000.00
Table, Ebony, Floral Slate Top, Snake Column, Snake Apron, Round, 23 x 39 In. ... 1320.00
Table, Edwardian, Satinwood, 2 Tiers, 25 1/2 x 31 In. 1430.00
Table, Empire, Mahogany, Hairy Paw Feet, 2 Leaves, Baltimore, 1830 .... 3900.00
Table, Empire, Whimsical Painted Designs, Sailors & Mermaids 3740.00
Table, Farm, French Provincial, Fruitwood, Drawer, Wood Slide 4400.00
Table, Farm, Mixed Wood, Vermilion Paint, 1830–1840 .... 975.00
Table, Figural Marble Base, Glass Top, 17 x 20 In. 225.00
Table, Figured Oak, Walnut, Modern, 28 In. 450.00
Table, French Country, Oak, Parquet Top, Opens To 9 Ft. 995.00
Table, Galle, 2 Tiers, Marquetry, Birds Eating Seeds, c.1900, 22 x 14 In. 935.00
Table, Galle, Fruitwood Marquetry, 2 Tiers, Round, 1900, 21 In. 3025.00

Table, Galle, Fruitwood Marquetry, Frieze Drawer, 1890, 30 x 21 3/4 In. 8800.00
Table, Galle, Mahogany, Marquetry, Rectangular, 28 7/8 x 15 3/4 In. 2750.00
Table, Galle, Marquetry, 2 Tiers, 1900, 29 x 22 x 14 In. 935.00
Table, Galle, Marquetry, 2 Tiers, Flowering Clematis Vines, Butterfly, 30 In. 1325.00
Table, Game, Backgammon & Checkerboard, Red & Black Lacquer, China 1320.00
Table, Game, Checkerboard Top Slides Off To Backgammon Board, Wooden 425.00
Table, Game, Checkerboard, Black & White Squares, Painted Pine, 16 3/4 x 24 In. 360.00
Table, Game, Chess, Pieced Stone Top, Round, Tripod, Casters, 19th Century, 3 Ft. 3000.00
Table, Game, Chessboard, Regency, Penwork & Ebonized 935.00
Table, Game, Chippendale Style, Mahogany, Folding Top, 28 3/4 x 35 In. 1100.00
Table, Game, Chippendale, Mahogany, 1 Drawer, Folding Top, 29 In. 1210.00
Table, Game, George II, Gateleg, Candle Recesses, Chip Wells, Walnut, 29 In. 3300.00
Table, Game, George III, Mahogany, Tapered Legs, 29 1/2 x 34 In. 2090.00
Table, Game, Louis Philippe Style, Rosewood 995.00
Table, Game, Majorelle, Mahogany Marquetry, Leather, Folding, 39 x 19 In. 2750.00
Table, Game, Teakwood, 4 Walnut Chairs, 1850s 3295.00
Table, Game, Triple–Top, Leather Playing Surface, Mahogany 1980.00
Table, Gateleg, Barrel Twist Legs, Oak, 19th Century, 29 1/2 In. 165.00
Table, Gateleg, Oak, England, 19th Century, 7 3/4 x 20 In., 9 1/2–In. Leaves 467.00
Table, Gateleg, Oval Twin Flap Top, Ernest Gimson, Walnut, 31 1/2 x 37 In. 2725.00
Table, Gateleg, Twin–Flap Top, Ernest Gimson, Oak, 41 1/2 x 48 1/2 In. 1655.00
Table, George II, Shell Carved, Rouge Marble Top, Pair 1925.00
Table, Georgian, Mahogany, Circular, Tilt Top, Tripod Base, c.1760, 29 In. 825.00
Table, Georgian, Mahogany, Stringing Inlay 1320.00
Table, Gustav Stickley, Arched Stacked Cross–Stretchers, Apron, 30 In. 885.00
Table, Gustav Stickley, No. 635, Leather Top, Round, 40 In. 6325.00
Table, Hall, Empire, Mahogany, Petticoat, Mirror, Mirrored Base, Burled Top 275.00
Table, Harvest, 7 Narrow Tongue & Groove Boards, Pine, 30 In. 110.00
Table, Harvest, L. & J. G. Stickey, Drop Leaf, Cherry, 72 In. 390.00
Table, Harvest, Pine, Birch Legs, Red Paint, Brass Castors, 22 x 95 x 30 In. 8800.00
Table, Harvest, Pine, Gray Paint, Wide Apron, 2 Board Top, 105 In. 550.00
Table, Hepplewhite, Pine, Square Legs, 2 Board Top, 26 In. 175.00
Table, Hepplewhite, Poplar, Red, 1 Drawer, 25 x 27 In. 195.00
Table, Hepplewhite, Walnut, Scrubbed Finish, Breadboard Top, 26 1/2 In. 415.00
Table, Hexagonal Top, 3 Legs, Elongated Arched Corbels, 26 In. 715.00
Table, Hexagonal, Oak, Dark Finish, 18 3/4 In. 44.00
Table, Heywood–Wakefield, Center, Round Top, Wicker, 31 In. 825.00
Table, Hutch, Pine, Poplar, Brown Paint, Oval Top, Shoe Feet, 27 In. 880.00
Table, Hutch, Pine, Reddish Brown, Blue Paint, 2 Board Top, Lift Top, 27 In. 700.00
Table, Hutch, Pine, Yellow Graining, Shoe Feet, Oval Top, 28 3/4 In. 3300.00
Table, Hutch, Poplar Top, Brown Graining, Hinged Lid Seat, 28 In. 1045.00
Table, Hutch, Poplar, 1 Drawer, 3 Board Top, Shoe Feet, 28 1/4 In. 1045.00
Table, Hutch, Poplar, Cutout Ends, Bench Seat, Country, 33 x 78 x 27 In. 3600.00
Table, Ice Cream, Marble Top, Iron, Wooden Seat Chairs, 3 Piece 585.00
Table, Ice Cream, Wire Base, White Plate–Glass Top, 30 x 36 In. 125.00
Table, Jacob & Joseph Kohn, Circular Brass Banding At Base, c.1908, 28 1/2 In. 3550.00
Table, Jacobean Style, Floral Carved Frieze, Oak, 67 In. 2000.00
Table, Josef Hoffmann, Hourglass, Central X–Form Support, c.1905, 27 1/4 In. 4950.00
Table, Kitchen, Pine, Breadboard Top, 19th Century, H Stretcher, 58 x 38 In. 495.00
Table, L. & J. G. Stickley, No. 87, Drawers, Mirror, 29 1/2 x 44 In. 1450.00
Table, Library, Chamfered Sides & Pegs, Michigan Chair Co., 29 x 44 In. 385.00
Table, Library, Eastlake, Oak 115.00
Table, Library, Empire, Drop Leaf, D Form, Paw Feet, Mahogany, 49 1/2 In. 935.00
Table, Library, Gustav Stickley, Leather Top, Round, Decal, 1902, 48 In. 8500.00
Table, Library, Gustav Stickley, No. 624, 3 Drawers, 30 1/4 x 54 x 32 In. 2310.00
Table, Library, Gustav Stickley, No. 655, 13 Spindles Each End, c.1907, 35 3/4 In. 2310.00
Table, Library, L. & J. G. Stickley, No. 532, Double Drawer, Oak 500.00
Table, Library, Mahogany, 4 Seated Full–Bodied Lion Supports, 6 Ft. 2500.00
Table, Library, Mission, Oak, 1 Drawer 190.00
Table, Library, Onondage, No. 377, Drawer, Pyramidal Wood Pulls, c.1905, 48 In. 665.00
Table, Library, Overhanging Top, 1 Drawer, Copper Hardware, 29 1/2 In. 715.00
Table, Library, Stickley Bros., 2 Drawers, McMurdo Feet, 48 x 30 x 29 In. 825.00
Table, Limbert, No. 135, Open Corbels, 3 Drawers Front, 2 Over 1 Back, 57 In. 1100.00

Table, Limbert, No. 153, Turtle Top, Blind Drawer, c.1906, 29 1/4 x 48 In. 1760.00
Table, Louis XV Revival Style, Painted Stags Inlay, Italy, 28 x 25 In. 335.00
Table, Louis XV, Marquetry Top, Saber Legs, Tulipwood, Kingwood, 29 In. 1540.00
Table, Mahogany, 2 Tiers, c.1900 .... 85.00
Table, Mahogany, Acanthus Leaves On Legs, Brass Paw Feet, New York, 1820 ...... 5300.00
Table, Mahogany, Quarter Veneered Top, c.1925, 24 x 34 In. 6600.00
Table, Marble Top, Black Paint, Stenciled, 37 In. Diam. 3250.00
Table, Marble Top, Brass Apron & Base, Painted Wood, Austria, c.1910, 39 1/4 In. 7150.00
Table, Marble Top, Carved Feathered Masked Legs, Gilt Gesso, 29 In. 7700.00
Table, Marble Top, Carved Frieze, Whorl Feet, Giltwood, 30 x 37 In. 550.00
Table, Nesting, Carved Wood, Dark Finish, Oriental, 14 x 20 x 26 1/2 In., 4 Piece 225.00
Table, Nesting, Drop Leaf, Oak, 4 Piece 595.00
Table, Nesting, Regency, Rosewood, Curved Stretchers, 4 Piece 3575.00
Table, Oak, Carved Cabriole Legs, Scalloped Apron, Europe, 29 1/2 In. 770.00
Table, Oak, Lion Head Base, Claw Feet, Round, 5 Leaves, 59 In. Diam. 1200.00
Table, Oak, Paw Feet, Round, 5 Leaves, 48 In. 600.00
Table, Onyx Top, Frieze of Urns & Scrolls, Caryatid Legs, Bronze, 30 3/4 x 33 In. 935.00
Table, Parlor, Art Nouveau, Rosewood, Hexagonal, Cherub & Griffin Legs 495.00
Table, Parlor, Belter, Rosalie, c.1850, 29 x 42 In. 8250.00
Table, Parlor, Louis XV Style, Inset Onyx Top, Giltwood, 31 x 38 In. 3075.00
Table, Parlor, Mahogany, Shell & Scroll Leaf Design, Oval Top 260.00
Table, Parlor, Oak, Spool Turned Legs, Metal Claw & Glass Ball Feet 250.00
Table, Parlor, Oak, Stick & Ball, Shelf Below 235.00
Table, Parlor, Turtle Top, Victorian Marble, Walnut Base, Carved Legs, 30 x 28 In. 2200.00
Table, Parlor, Victorian, Rococo Revival, Rosewood, Shaped Top 1375.00
Table, Parlor, Victorian, Walnut, Oval, Gilt, 5 Columns, 44 x 32 In. 1100.00
Table, Parlor, Walnut, Marble Top, With Dog 475.00
Table, Parquetry Inlay & Bronze Border, Center Urn With Flame, 29 In. 4400.00
Table, Pembroke, Cherry, Inlaid Reserve, 1 Drawer, c.1790, 31 3/4 In. 4235.00
Table, Pembroke, Cherry, Inlay, Shaped Top, 1 Drawer, c.1790, 28 x 16 In. 4125.00
Table, Pembroke, Cherry, Turned Legs, Leaves, 16 x 36 In., 11 In. Leaves 225.00
Table, Pembroke, Chippendale, Mahogany, Ball & Claw Feet, 28 x 32 1/2 In. 1100.00
Table, Pembroke, Federal, Butternut & Maple, 28 1/2 x 24 In. 770.00
Table, Pembroke, Federal, Mahogany, c.1790 .... 1485.00
Table, Pembroke, Federal, Mahogany, Inlay, N.Y., 1800, 30 x 31 x 36 In. 3190.00
Table, Pembroke, Federal, Tiger Maple, 1800, 28 x 35 In. 5500.00
Table, Pembroke, Geometric Line Inlay, Amboyna Wood & Mahogany, 28 In. 4125.00
Table, Pembroke, George III, Satinwood, Crossbanded Top, Drawer, c.1790 .... 5225.00
Table, Pembroke, Hepplewhite, Mahogany, Inlay, 28 In. 95.00
Table, Pembroke, Hepplewhite, Mahogany, Square Tapered Legs, 28 1/2 In. 1900.00
Table, Pembroke, Pine, Red On Base, Dark Finish On Top, 28 1/2 In. 250.00
Table, Pembroke, Regency, Mahogany, Pedestal, c.1815, 26 1/2 In. 1100.00
Table, Pembroke, Walnut, Reeded Edge, Pierced Cross Stretcher, c.1770 .... 7000.00
Table, Pier, Canted Scrolled Supports, Marble Top, Thomas Robertson, 41 1/2 In. ... 1210.00
Table, Pier, Carved & Gilt Mahogany, Rectangular White Marble Top, Mirror 4125.00
Table, Pier, Classical, Bronze Mounts, Marble Top 4500.00
Table, Pier, Classical, Rosewood, Stencil, Ebonized, Ormolu, Philadelphia, 1825 ...... 8000.00
Table, Pier, Mahogany, Dolphin Sides, c.1890 .... 3300.00
Table, Pier, Mahogany, Marble Top, Drawer On Scrolled Supports, Mirror 1350.00
Table, Pier, Mahogany, Marble Top, Figured Frieze Supports, c.1840, 37 In. 990.00
Table, Pier, Mahogany, Scrolled Support & Feet, c.1840, 34 3/4 In. 880.00
Table, Pier, Pillar & Scroll Mahogany, White Marble Top, 42 In. 825.00
Table, Pier, Rosewood, Stenciled, Mirror, Philadelphia 8800.00
Table, Poplar, Red, Stretcher Base, Button Feet, Removable Top, 29 1/2 In. 350.00
Table, Quaint, Round Overhanging Top, Square Apron, 30 In., Pair 1100.00
Table, Queen Anne, Birch, Original Hinges, 1750–1770 .... 6850.00
Table, Queen Anne, Pine, Button Feet, Splayed Legs, Worn Round Top 3740.00
Table, Refectory, Italian Baroque, Herringbone Inlaid Border, 90 x 32 x 32 In. 550.00
Table, Refectory, Jacobean, Turned Pedestals, Bracket Feet, Walnut, 115 In. 2420.00
Table, Refectory, Jacobean, Walnut, Drawers, Lion Legs, 18th Century 1400.00
Table, Regency Style, Mahogany, Square Leather Inset Top, 1 Drawer, 24 In. 330.00
Table, Regency, Mahogany, 19th Century, 29 x 58 In. 1870.00
Table, Renaissance Revival, Walnut, Philadelphia, 1860 .... 7975.00

Furniture, Table, Rococo Revival, Rosewood,   Furniture, Table, Tilt Top, Stickley

Marble, 1860-1870, 45 In.

Table, Rococo Revival, Rosewood, Marble, 1860–1870, 45 In. ....*Illus*	4400.00
Table, Rosewood, Marble Top, Carved Dolphin Feet	4125.00
Table, Rosewood, Onyx Top, Brass Marquetry & Satinwood	6600.00
Table, Rosewood, Round Marble Top, Gilt Legs	8250.00
Table, Roycroft, No. 73 1/2, Curved Form, Round	4125.00
Table, Sawbuck, Poplar, Mustard Paint, 1 Board Top, 33 3/4 In.	775.00
Table, Sawbuck, Square Nail Construction, 3 Board Top, Pine, 96 In.	1100.00
Table, Scrubbed Top, Red Painted Base, 1790s, 27 x 42 In.	1320.00
Table, Serving, Adams Style, Mahogany, 34 3/4 In.	350.00
Table, Serving, Galle, Oak Marquetry, 3 Tiers, 1890, 43 3/4 x 18 1/4 In.	5775.00
Table, Sewing, 2 Drawer, Canted Corners, Fluted Legs, Brass Pulls, Mahogany	4000.00
Table, Sewing, Bag Slide, c.1800	6800.00
Table, Sewing, Bird's-Eye Maple, Ring-Turned Pedestal, 1825–1835, 28 1/4 In.	1350.00
Table, Sewing, Chippendale, Walnut, Square Legs, 30 1/2 x 41 x 27 1/4 In.	825.00
Table, Sewing, Classical Revival, Mahogany, 2 Drawers, 29 x 18 x 19 In.	935.00
Table, Sewing, Drop Leaf, Mahogany, Pull-Out Bin, 1 Dovetailed Drawer, 28 In.	4125.00
Table, Sewing, Empire, Mahogany, 2 Frieze Drawers, Trestle, Scroll Feet, c.1830	600.00
Table, Sewing, Empire, Mahogany, Lift Top, Octagonal, 29 In.	360.00
Table, Sewing, Federal, 2 Drawers, Mass., 1800, 28 x 18 x 16 In.	1650.00
Table, Sewing, Federal, Bird's-Eye Maple Veneer, c.1810	6555.00
Table, Sewing, Federal, Mahogany, 2 Drawers, Lyre Supports, 1810	8700.00
Table, Sewing, Federal, Mahogany, Mass., 1810, 28 x 19 x 17 1/2 In.	1210.00
Table, Sewing, Gustav Stickley, No. 630, 3 Drawers, Drop Leaf, 1907, 28 In.	2090.00
Table, Sewing, Hepplewhite, 3 Board Top, 30 x 35 x 29 In.	330.00
Table, Sewing, Hepplewhite, Beveled Edge Drawer, 3 Board Top, 31 In.	450.00
Table, Sewing, Hepplewhite, Birch, Serpentine Top, Drawer, 18th Century	650.00
Table, Sewing, Hepplewhite, Pine, Blue & White Paint, 1 Drawer, 29 1/2 In.	300.00
Table, Sewing, Lift Top, Fitted Interior Tray, Carved, Oriental, 30 x 22 x 30 In.	475.00
Table, Sewing, Lift Top, Victorian, Walnut, Marquetry, 27 In.	330.00
Table, Sewing, Lion's Head Pulls, Lyre Base	6600.00
Table, Sewing, Louis Philipe, Brass Inlay, Lift Top, Mirrored Interior, c.1840	375.00
Table, Sewing, Mahogany, Curule Base, 2 Drawers, New York	3300.00
Table, Sewing, Mahogany, Waterleaf Carved Pedestal, Paw Feet, c.1815	3850.00
Table, Sewing, Poplar Base, Tapered Pencil Post Legs, H Stretcher, 26 In.	275.00
Table, Sewing, Poplar, Red, Drawers, Black Legs, 36 x 48 x 28 In.	995.00
Table, Sewing, Rococo Revival	1650.00
Table, Sewing, Sheraton, Inlay, 1 Drawer, 1825	1250.00
Table, Sewing, Sheraton, Square Top, 2 Short Drawers, Cherry, 29 x 19 1/2 In.	355.00
Table, Sewing, Victorian, Mahogany, Lift Top, Mirror, Satin Interior, 28 In.	600.00
Table, Sewing, Walnut, 2 Drawers, Pennsylvania, 1760	5800.00
Table, Sewing, Walnut, Figural Burl Veneer, Fitted Drawer, 15 x 21 x 24 In.	470.00
Table, Sewing, Walnut, Pinned Beaded Apron, 2 Drawers, 2 Board Top, 30 In.	1150.00
Table, Shaker, Trestle Base, 4 Underhung Drawers, 31 x 88 In.	5500.00
Table, Shaker, Trestle, Underslung Drawers, Watervliet	5500.00
Table, Sheraton, 1 Drawer, Green & Red, Floral, Oak Leaf Stenciled, Brass Pulls	1200.00
Table, Sheraton, 2 Drawers, 1810	1100.00

Table, Side, Beechwood, Turned Legs, Ball Feet, England, 15 1/2 x 15 1/2 In. 1430.00
Table, Side, Gilbert Rhode, Herman Miller, 1920s 675.00
Table, Side, Mahogany, Drawer, Round Top 110.00
Table, Side, Majorelle, Mahogany Marquetry, Triangular Top, 1900, 23 In. 6000.00
Table, Side, Marble Top, Brass Gallery, Round, Pair 120.00
Table, Side, Oak, Shelf, Claw & Ball Feet 35.00
Table, Side, Tapered Legs, Drawer, Wooden Knob, 29 1/2 x 20 x 18 In. 1430.00
Table, Tavern, 1 Drawer, Breadboard Top, 27 3/4 In. 330.00
Table, Tavern, Battened Ends, Tapering Splayed Legs, Painted Red, 25 In. 2640.00
Table, Tavern, Block Branded Signature 385.00
Table, Tavern, Breadboard Top, Turned Legs, 18th Century, 26 x 47 x 29 In. 2420.00
Table, Tavern, Chippendale Style, Maple, 26 x 36 1/4 In. 150.00
Table, Tavern, Chippendale, Maple, Drawer, Country, 20 x 29 In. 880.00
Table, Tavern, Curly Maple, 27 x 29 3/4 In. 325.00
Table, Tavern, Hardwood Base, 1 Board Pine Top, Tapered Hickory Legs, 27 In. 495.00
Table, Tavern, Jacobean Style, Carved Apron, Oak, c.1900, 47 1/2 In. 330.00
Table, Tavern, Pine, Maple, Drawer, Breadboard Top, Refinished, 27 x 47 x 29 In. .. 880.00
Table, Tavern, Queen Anne, Cherrywood & Pine, Oval Top, 23 In. 1350.00
Table, Tavern, Queen Anne, Pine, Maple Top, Breadboard Ends, 1760 .... 1300.00
Table, Tavern, Red Base, Curly Maple Top, 27 1/2 In. 295.00
Table, Tavern, Red, Black Graining, 3 Board Pine Top, 28 3/4 In. 440.00
Table, Tavern, Wallace Nutting, 50 x 29 5/8 In. 1750.00
Table, Tavern, Walnut, 2 Drawers, Baluster Turned Legs, 18th Century, 57 In. 1320.00
Table, Tavern, William & Mary, Box Stretcher, Rectangular 3300.00
Table, Tavern, William & Mary, Maple & Pine, Battened End Top, 25 x 27 In. 2420.00
Table, Tea, Arched Cross–Stretchers, Handcraft Decal, 28 1/2 In. 605.00
Table, Tea, Chippendale, Mahogany, Dish Top, c.1780 .... 1600.00
Table, Tea, Duncan Phyfe, Mahogany, Rectangular Top, 29 x 37 x 23 In. 605.00
Table, Tea, Mahogany, Scalloped Edge, c.1890, 30 x 32 In. 357.00
Table, Tea, Majorelle, Fruitwood Marquetry, 2 Tiers, Gilt Bronze, 35 x 21 In. 6050.00
Table, Tea, Queen Anne, 2 Board Oval Top, Drop Leaf, 1750–1760 .... 5800.00
Table, Tea, Queen Anne, Button Feet, Oval Top, Black Paint, Small 3400.00
Table, Tea, Queen Anne, Chestnut, Maple, New England, Country, 1720–1740 .... 2250.00
Table, Tea, Queen Anne, Porringer Top, Curly Maple, Duck Feet, 28 In. 1210.00
Table, Tea, Queen Anne, Porringer Top, Green Painted Base, 27 x 20 x 32 In. 440.00
Table, Tea, Tilt Top, Chippendale, Mahogany, Pie Crust, 30 In. 605.00
Table, Tea, Tilt Top, Chippendale, Mahogany, Turned Column, 29 1/2 In. 990.00
Table, Tea, Tilt Top, Mahogany, Tripod Base, Pie Crust, 28 In. 137.00
Table, Tea, Tilt Top, Tiger Maple, New England, c.1800, 27 1/2 In. 1045.00
Table, Tea, Tilt Top, Venetian Canal Scene, Papier–Mache, 24 In. Diam. 330.00
Table, Tea, Walnut, Tripod Base, Spider Legs, 2 Board Top, Country, 28 3/4 In. 155.00
Table, Telephone, Conforming Chair, Marble Top, 1 Drawer, Wrought Iron 275.00
Table, Tiger Maple, Splay Leg, 1 Dovetailed Drawer, 15 x 15 x 28 1/2 In. 245.00
Table, Tile Top, Shelf, Matte Green Grueby Tiles, 25 3/4 x 24 x 20 1/2 In. 4400.00
Table, Tilt Top, Carved Walnut, 28 In. 330.00
Table, Tilt Top, Chippendale, Curly Maple, Tripod Base, 2 Board Top, 27 In. 1540.00
Table, Tilt Top, Chippendale, Mahogany, Birdcage, New York, 1760, 28 x 34 In. 4500.00
Table, Tilt Top, Chippendale, Mahogany, Tripod Base, 3 Board Top, 28 In. 800.00
Table, Tilt Top, George II, Mahogany, Circular Tripod, 29 In. 445.00
Table, Tilt Top, Georgian, Mahogany, 1760, 36 In. 950.00
Table, Tilt Top, Mahogany, Birdcage, New York, 34 1/4 In. Diam. 4500.00
Table, Tilt Top, Mahogany, Brass Tray Top, 22 x 31 In., Pair 275.00
Table, Tilt Top, Mahogany, Tripod Base, Snake Feet, 1 Board Top, 27 3/4 In. 700.00
Table, Tilt Top, New Hampshire, Red Painted Base, 2 Board Top, 31 x 30 In. 1980.00
Table, Tilt Top, Papier–Mache, Floral Painted, Abalone, Oval Top, 26 x 21 In. 665.00
Table, Tilt Top, Papier–Mache, Mother–of–Pearl & Polychrome Flowers 695.00
Table, Tilt Top, Queen Anne, Cherry, New England, 36 In. Top 4000.00
Table, Tilt Top, Stickley ....*Illus* 1650.00
Table, Tilt Top, Walnut, 3 Legs, 1840 .... 565.00
Table, Tilt Top, Walnut, Curly Maple, Underside Drawer, 28 In. 225.00
Table, Tilt Top, Wood, Papier–Mache, Black, Gold Paint, 27 In. 620.00
Table, Van Der Rohe, Chromium–Plated Tubular Steel, Glass Top, 1933, 33 1/2 In. .. 2200.00
Table, Victorian, Cast Iron, Round Marble Top 885.00

Table, Victorian, Walnut, Fluted Oval Marble Top 850.00
Table, Walnut, Carved Griffins, 19th Century, 30 x 60 In. ....*Illus* 5000.00
Table, Walnut, Veined Rust & Yellow Marble Top, c.1850, 30 x 45 In. 1650.00
Table, Wicker, Ball & Stick Design, 1910 .... 295.00
Table, Wicker, Rotating Bookshelf Under Oak Top 775.00
Table, William & Mary, Oak & Pine, Block & Baluster Supports, 67 3/4 In. 3100.00
Table, Writing, Louis Philippe, Pine, Paneled Apron, 54 1/2 In. 1875.00
Table, Writing, Queen Anne, Mahogany, 2 Drawers, 30 x 45 x 22 In. 357.50
Table, Writing, Regency, Mahogany, Trestle, c.1830 .... 1210.00
Table, Writing, Rosewood, Leaf–Carved Column Supports, c.1845, 4 Ft. 9 In. 4675.00
Table, Writing, William IV, Rosewood, 2 Frieze Drawers, Winged Paw Feet, 54 In. 7795.00
Table, Wrought Iron, Faience Tiles, 22 In., Pair 305.00
Table, Wrought Iron, Round Marble Top, Scroll Legs, France, 31 x 28 In. 990.00
Tabouret, L. & J. G. Stickley, No. 558, Oak, Octagonal Top, 4 Square Legs, 20 In. 1215.00
Tabouret, Octagonal Top, 4–Sided Base, 28 1/2 x 18 In. 990.00
Tabouret, Stickley Bros., Ebonized, Cutouts, Label 500.00
Tea Cart, Lower Shelf, 2 Solid Wheels, Laminated Wood, Finmar, 33 1/8 In. 1850.00
Tray, Butler's, Mahogany, 20 1/2 x 30 3/4 In. 300.00
Tray, Butler's, Mahogany, Folding Stand, Gallery, England, 19 x 31 1/2 In. 335.00
Tray, Mahogany, Gilded Brass Rim, England, Oval, 20 In. 82.00
Tray, Papier–Mache, Chinoiserie Design, Serpent Handles, c.1810, 26 1/2 In. 8800.00
Tray, Papier–Mache, Gilt Figures Flying Kites, Lacquered, China, 17 x 15 In. 385.00
Tray, Papier–Mache, Stand, Victorian, Black Lacquer Parcel Gilt, 30 In. 2750.00
Tray, Queen Anne, Scalloped Rim, Brass Handles, Stand, Mahogany, 23 x 33 In. 825.00
Vanity, Carved Mahogany, Mirror, Signed R. J. Horner, N.Y., c.1890 .... 1495.00
Vanity, Dresser Top, Satin & Velvet Lined, Silver–Plated Panels 190.00
Vanity, Heywood–Wakefield, Blond, Mushroom–Shaped Stool, 2 Piece 525.00
Vanity, L. & J. G. Stickley, 1926 .... 460.00
Vanity, Oval Mirror, Gilded Acanthus Carved Pedestal, 5 Drawers, 38 In. 1215.00
Vitrine, Louis XV Style, Mahogany, Gilt Bronze Mounted Supports, 32 In. 615.00
Vitrine, Louis XVI Style, Brass Ormolu Mounts, Marble Top, 63 In. 1200.00
Vitrine, Louis XVI, Scroll Inlay, Walnut Veneer, Red Velvet Lined 2800.00
Wardrobe, Beveled Mirror Door, 2 Lower Drawers, Carved Oak, 77 x 54 In. 1850.00
Wardrobe, Lilly Reich, Upper Doors, Shelved Interior, Walnut, 1930s, 6 Ft. 5 In. ... 6600.00
Wardrobe, Limbert, Mirrored Door 1045.00
Wardrobe, Pine, Gray Repaint, Short Cutout Feet, 76 In. 352.00
Wardrobe, Victorian, Arched Doors, 2 Drawers, 6 Ft. 5 1/2 In. x 4 Ft. 2 In. 775.00
Wardrobe, Victorian, Walnut, 2 Doors, 73 x 55 In. 650.00
Wardrobe, Walnut, 2 Base Drawers, Spiral Turned Columns, Carved Pulls, 103 In. 1750.00
Wardrobe, Yellow Pine, Bracket Feet, Panel Doors, Country, 77 In. 400.00
Washstand, Cherry, Other Woods, Folk Art, Drawer, Towel Bars, 28 x 14 In. 385.00
Washstand, Cream Paint, Foliage Crest, Gold, Black Striping, 28 1/2 In. 215.00
Washstand, Curly Maple, 1 Drawer, Cutout For Bowl, 31 1/4 In. 550.00
Washstand, Double, Mahogany, 2 Drawers, Bowed Front, 35 1/2 In. 750.00
Washstand, Eastlake, Oak 1775.00
Washstand, Empire, Galleried, Scroll Feet, c.1830 .... 300.00
Washstand, Federal, Bowfront, Mahogany, Corner, Drawer, 1800, 38 In. 2300.00
Washstand, Federal, Convex–Concave Front, High Splashboard 800.00
Washstand, Mahogany, 2 Tiers, Fret–Carved Frieze, Platform Stretcher, 33 1/2 In. 5500.00
Washstand, Mahogany, Corner, Middle Drawer, Bottom Shelf, England, 1840s 275.00
Washstand, Mahogany, Marble Top, Beveled Mirror, 2 Drawers, 71 x 38 In. 1650.00
Washstand, Mahogany, Top Opening, Rim For Wash Bowl, Hinged Door, 34 In. 880.00
Washstand, Oak, 1 Full and 2 Half Drawers, Cupboard 120.00
Washstand, Oak, Small Mirror, Hotel 280.00
Washstand, Pine, 2 Tiers, 1 Short Drawer, 19th Century, 34 x 17 In. 220.00
Washstand, Pine, Towel Bars At Each End, Dovetailed Drawer, 1870 .... 295.00
Washstand, Poplar, Cherry, 1 Drawer, Base Shelf, 27 3/4 In. 350.00
Washstand, Poplar, Original Red Flame Graining, Turned Feet & Posts, 33 In. 250.00
Washstand, Poplar, Reddish Brown Graining, Yellow Ground, 28 In. 137.00
Washstand, Shaker, Maple & Poplar, Red Stained, New York 1100.00
Washstand, Sheraton, 1 Drawer, Stencil, Turned Feet, New England 165.00
Washstand, Sheraton, Cherry, 1 Drawer, Gallery, Country, 19 3/4 x 15 x 29 In. 525.00
Washstand, Tiger Oak, 2 Doors, 1 Drawer, Towel Bar 150.00

Furstenberg, Figurine, Bird, Marked,

5 X 7 In., Pair

◆ ◆

Avoid burglaries. If you are painting your house, do not leave ladders leaning on the building or piled up near the house. Chain and lock the ladders so the casual burglar can't use them. Trim your trees to make access to the roof more difficult.

◆ ◆

Washstand, Victorian, Walnut, 3 Drawers, Marble Top 350.00
Washstand, Walnut, Minton Tile, Marble Top, Cupboard Below, 52 x 42 In. 2200.00
Washstand, Walnut, Mirror, 1880 .... 475.00
Wastebasket, Gustav Stickley, 13 Vertical Slats, Iron Rings, 14 In. 995.00
Window Seat, Classical Revival, Mahogany, Striped Seats, Arms, 42 In., Pair 6325.00
Window Seat, Painted & Parcel Gilt, Upholstered Ends, Baltic, Pair 2200.00
Wine Cooler, George III, Brass Handles, Inlaid Mahogany, Stand, 28 1/2 In. 1650.00

FURSTENBERG Porcelain Works was started in Furstenberg, Germany, in 1747. It is still working. Many of the modern products are made in the old molds.

Figurine, Bird, Marked, 5 x 7 In., Pair ....*Illus* 1750.00
Figurine, Lady, Lace Dress, Pink Slip, Blue Jacket, Marked, 5 1/2 In. 150.00
Group, Man & Woman, Playing Harpsichord & Harp, Marked, 12 1/2 In. 2450.00
Plate, Putto Patting Head of Another, Floral Garlands, 1770, 9 In., Pair 1350.00
Tea Caddy, Painted Bouquets, Floral Sprig Knob, Marked, 4 3/4 In. 770.00

G. ARGY–ROUSSEAU is the impressed mark used on a variety of objects in the Art Deco style. Gabriel Argy–Rousseau, born in 1885, was a French glass artist.

Bowl, Belt of Anemone Blossoms, Signed, 1920, 3 In. 5775.00
Luminaire, Pate–De–Pate, No Mount 6600.00
Pendant, Colored Locust, Green Ground, Black Cord, Signed, 2 1/2 In. 1045.00
Pendant, Curling Blossoms, 1 Green Bead, Tasseled Cord, 2 1/2 In. 995.00
Vase, Base Rows of Dentils, Coiled Fern Leaves At Rim, Signed, 8 1/4 In. 4650.00
Vase, Spider, Signed D. S., 4 1/2 In. ....*Illus* 7150.00

G. Argy-Rousseau, Vase, Spider,

Signed D.S., 4 1/2 In.

Galle, Bowl, Red Flowers & Leaves,

8 X 5 1/2 X 3 In.

Galle, Lamp, Morning Glories, Lobed,
Shallow, 19 1/2 In.

Galle, Vase, Asters, Bulbous

◆◆

Always remove a book from the shelf to dust. All sides need
cleaning.

◆◆

GALLE POTTERY was made by Emile Galle, the famous French designer,
after 1874. The pieces were marked with the initials *E. G.* impressed, *Em.
Galle Faiencerie de Nancy,* or a version of his signature. Galle is best
known for his glass, listed in the next category.

Bowl, Cover, Winter Scene, Off–White Tin Glaze, With Tray, 7 In.	300.00
Figurine, Cat, Seated, Glass Eyes, 13 In.	825.00
Figurine, Hare, Mottled Bronze Glaze, Glass Eyes, Marked, 8 1/4 In.	780.00
Figurine, Owl, Waisted Socle, Brown, Cream & Ocher, 1880, 13 3/8 In.	1100.00
Wall Pocket, Fishing Boat Scene, Signed, 13 In.	1500.00

GALLE was a designer who made glass, pottery, furniture, and other Art
Nouveau items. Emile Galle founded his factory in France in 1874. After
Galle's death in 1904, the firm continued to make glass and furniture until
1931. The name *Galle* was used as a mark, but it was often hidden in the
design of the object. Galle Pottery is listed above and his furniture is listed
in the Furniture category.

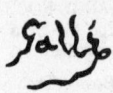

Bottle, Enameled Foliate Design, Warriors On Horseback, Oval Shape, 6 In.	7150.00
Bowl, Enameled Flowers, Pond Scene, Lobed, Shallow, 7 1/2 In.	1450.00
Bowl, Red Flowers & Leaves, 8 x 5 1/2 x 3 In. *Illus*	1900.00
Bowl, Topaz Etched Branches, Leaves, Lily Pads, Signed, 2 1/4 In.	6600.00
Bowl, Vine Leaf, Pink, Blue, Lobed, Shallow, Signed, 13 In.	1900.00
Box, Cover, Floral, Cream Ground, Signed, 2 1/2 In.	600.00
Box, Cover, Flower Blossoms, Blackberries, Cameo, 1900, 5 1/4 In.	1430.00
Box, Domed Cover, Gray, Opalescent Yellow, Purple, Cameo, 1900, 4 1/8 In.	1200.00
Box, Hinged Cover, Fruitwood Marquetry, Lilies of The Valley, 1900, 18 1/2 In.	1200.00
Box, Leafy, Gray, Mottled Yellow, Purple, Signed, 6 In.	1450.00
Box, Yellow, Burnt Orange, Flower Blossoms, Blackberries, Cameo, Signed, 6 In.	1430.00
Chalice, Cameo, Lake Landscape, Opalescent Gray, 1900, 4 7/8 In.	1350.00
Cordial Set, Enameled Flowers, Signed, 3 Piece	1650.00
Creamer, Leaves & Berries, Frosted Peach Ground, Signed, 3 1/4 In.	1500.00
Dish, Enameled Grasshopper Amid Leaves, Lobed, Shallow, Signed, 10 1/2 In.	2200.00
Lamp, Morning Glories, Lobed, Shallow, 19 1/2 In. *Illus*	4000.00
Perfume Bottle, Amber, Raised Leaves, Tapered, Lobed, Shallow, Signed, 3 3/4 In.	600.00
Perfume Burner, Gray, Lemon Yellow, Opalescent, Cherry Red Cut, Signed, 7 In.	1045.00
Shade, Floral, Signed, 13 5/8 In.	4950.00
Toothpick, Orange Water Lilies, Blue Ground, 2 x 2 1/2 In.	875.00
Trivet, Dragonfly & Bug, Faience, Scalloped Border, 1890, Square, 5 In.	380.00
Vase, 3–Color Floral, Amethyst, 6 1/4 In.	1375.00
Vase, Alpine Lake Scene, Frosted Ground, Cameo Signed, 6 3/4 In.	1650.00

Galle, Vase, Floral, Cameo, 1900, 18 5/8 In.
Galle, Vase, Floral, Cameo, Dark Base, 1900,
17 3/4 In.

Vase, Alsatian Landscape, Bubbling Mountain Brook, Signed, c.1900, 12 3/4 In.	4450.00
Vase, Alsatian Landscape, Tranquil Lake, Signed, c.1900, 13 In.	5500.00
Vase, Amber Foliage Landscape, Egg Shape	3750.00
Vase, Amber To Frost, Floral, Enameled, Art Glass, Cameo, 10 In.	1650.00
Vase, Apricot Cut To Frosted White, Floral, Flared, Cameo 10 In.	1750.00
Vase, Asters, Bulbous ....*Illus*	2600.00
Vase, Blossom Cluster, Leafy Boarder, White, Pink, Layered, Cameo, 15 In.	2300.00
Vase, Blossoms, Buds & Leaves Base, White, Yellow & Red–Orange, Cameo, 5 In.	2550.00
Vase, Bud, Rose, Yellow, Umber, Berried Vines, Banjo Form, 1900, 6 1/2 In.	935.00
Vase, Bud, Slender Form, White, Yellow, Blue, Leaf Shape, Cameo, 15 In.	1875.00
Vase, Burgundy Poppies, Cream Ground, Signed, 6 1/2 In.	900.00
Vase, Cherries & Leaves, Frosted Ground, Slender Neck, Cameo, Signed, 6 3/4 In.	850.00
Vase, Cluster Blossoms, Frosted Pink, White & Amethyst, Cameo, 7 1/2 In.	1450.00
Vase, Columbines & Foliage Over Frosted Ground, 3 1/2 In.	950.00
Vase, Cut Leaf & Berry Design, Yellow Ground, 15 In.	6050.00
Vase, Double Overlay, Floral, Dark To Light Green, Frosted, 6 In.	1200.00
Vase, Etched Flowers, Yellow Glass Overlaid In Red, Signed, 2 7/8 In.	385.00
Vase, Exotic Birds In Bamboo, Cream Ground, Signed, 8 1/4 In.	785.00
Vase, Fern Leaves, Green Frosted Ground, Cameo, Signed, 7 In.	1050.00
Vase, Floral Design, Navy Cut To Opaque, Signed, 9 In.	1100.00
Vase, Floral, Amethyst, 6 1/4 In.	1375.00
Vase, Floral, Cameo, 1900, 18 5/8 In. ....*Illus*	2750.00
Vase, Floral, Dark Base, Cameo, 1900, 17 3/4 In. ....*Illus*	7700.00
Vase, Floral, Pedestal Base, Everted Top, 12 In.	7950.00
Vase, Flowering Leafy Stalks, Flattened Base, Signed, c.1900, 18 5/8 In.	2750.00
Vase, Flowering Tulips, Frosted Ground, Cameo, Signed, 3 1/8 In.	825.00
Vase, Foliate Design, Ochre, Light & Dark Brown, Conical Footed, Cameo, 9 In.	1100.00
Vase, Foliate Design, Praying Mantis, Red, Black, Blue, Gold Enamel, 7 In.	2550.00
Vase, Frosted To Pink, 4 1/2 In.	575.00
Vase, Fuchsia Blossoms, Gray, White & Purple Overlay, Cameo, 1903–1910, 12 In.	1200.00
Vase, Gold Poppy Overlay, Signed, 2 1/4 In.	415.00
Vase, Gray To Burnt Orange, Sycamore Pods, Leaves, Bell Shape, Signed, 5 In.	885.00
Vase, Gray, Lime Green, Stalks, Blossoms, Butterflies, Teardrop, 1900, 27 3/8 In. ...	2750.00
Vase, Gray, Pale Pink, Lime Green, Thistle Blossoms, Cameo, 1903–1910, 9 1/4 In.	550.00
Vase, Gray, Pink, Overlaid White, Lavender, Teardrop Shape, 1903, Signed, 15 In.	995.00
Vase, Green, Purple, Cameo, 3 In.	450.00
Vase, Insects In Flight, Signed, c.1890, 3 7/8 In.	5775.00
Vase, Irises & Foliage, White Frosted Ground, Green & Brown, 15 1/2 In.	1985.00
Vase, Large Florals, Charcoal Cut To Opaque White, Signed, 13 In.	1950.00
Vase, Leaf & Berry Design, Frosted Ground, Signed, 5 In.	885.00

Vase, Leafed Plants, Blossom, Mauve Body, Brown Etched, Cameo, 7 In. 2860.00
Vase, Lime Thistle Blossoms & Leaves, Pink, Gray, Pedestal, Cameo, 9 1/2 In. 750.00
Vase, Moth & Floral, Japanese Type, Flattened Circular Body, Cameo 3100.00
Vase, Mountains & Trees, Blue, Purple & White, 6 1/4 In. 1000.00
Vase, Opalescent Gray, Pale Yellow, Spherical, Short Cylindrical Neck, 14 1/2 In. ... 8800.00
Vase, Orchid Blossoms, Trumpet, Yellow, Amber, Yellow & Brown, Cameo, 14 In. 3100.00
Vase, Pendant Clematis Blossoms, Signed, c.1925, 9 1/2 In. 7700.00
Vase, Pendant Fuchsia Blossoms, Flattened Flask Form, 8 1/4 In. 3960.00
Vase, Pendant Gourds, Tendrilled Leaves, Signed, c.1900, 9 5/8 In. 6050.00
Vase, Red Cherries, Orange & Frosted Ground, Banjo Shape, 6 1/2 In. 1850.00
Vase, River Landscape, Trees In Foreground, Signed, c.1900, 13 1/4 In. 7150.00
Vase, Sailing Ships, Moored In Harbor, Signed, c.1900, 10 3/8 In. 3850.00
Vase, Stick, Carved Blossoms, Frosted, Orange, Cameo, 11 3/8 In. 660.00
Vase, Stick, Purple & White, 8 In. 575.00
Vase, Tree & Waterfront Scene, Pink To White To Green, Cameo, 18 1/2 In. 2650.00
Vase, Trumpet, Tray, Enameled Thistle Blossoms, Cameo, 1900, 6 In. 1325.00
Vase, Water Lily Scene, 4 In. 1250.00
Vase, Wild Flowers, Gray, Cameo, Bulbous, 1900, 5 3/4 In. 675.00
Vasecut Blossoms, Lavender, Signed, Cameo, c.1900, 6 In. 600.00

GAME PLATES are plates of any make decorated with pictures of birds, animals, or fish. The game plates usually came in sets consisting of twelve dishes and a serving platter. These sets were most popular during the 1880s.

Pheasant Center, Baby Pheasant Around Edge, Bavaria, 16 In. 105.00
Quail, Gold Rim, Limoges 75.00
GAME SET, 6 Different Game Bird Plates, Platter, 13 Piece 1275.00
Fish, Platter, 25 In., 8 Plates, 8 1/2–In. Plates, 9 Piece 400.00

GAMES of all sorts are collected. Of special interest are any board games or card games. Transogram and other company names are included in the description when known. Other games may be found listed under Card, Toy, or the name of the character or celebrity featured in the game.

10 Little Niggers, Parker Bros., 1893 .... 395.00
12 O'clock High, Ideal, 1965 .... 22.00
12 O'clock High, Milton Bradley, Box, 1965 .... 22.00
3 Cats Lotto, McLoughlin, Box 120.00
3 Good Friends Spelling Slips, McLoughlin 95.00
3 Men On A Horse, Warner Bros., 1936 .... 25.00
5 Wise Birds, Shooting Gallery, Parker Bros., Box, 1950s 95.00
A Voyage Through Clouds, J. W. Spear, Box, 17 x 11 In. 880.00
Addams Family, Card, 1965 .... 40.00
Addams Family, Cartoon, Board, Milton Bradley, 1974 .... 29.00
Addams Family, Ideal, 1964 .... 46.00
Admiral Byrd's South Pole, Microphone Spinners, Parker Bros., 1934 .... 445.00
Alfred Hitchcock's Why, Board, Milton Bradley, 1961 .... 42.00
Ali Baba, Ali Baba Spinner, Selchow & Righter 275.00
All Canadian Sports, Marble, Plastic, Marx, 1972, 12 x 24 In. 22.00
All In The Family, Milton Bradley 15.00
Allee–Oop, Roy–Toy Company, 1937 .... 30.00 To 65.00
Amazing Spider–Man, Milton Bradley, 1967 .... 25.00
American Generals, Instructions, Box 40.00
Annie Oakley, Board, Milton Bradley, 1955 .... 29.00
Archie, Board, Whitman, 1969 .... 69.00
Archie, Whitman, Complete, 1969 .... 15.00
Around The World In 80 Days, From The Movie 15.00
As The World Turns, Board, Parker Bros., 1966 .... 49.00
Auto Bridge, For 1 Or 4 People, 1957 .... 18.00
Automobile Race, McLoughlin, 1904 .... 1320.00
Avilude, Game of Birds, West & Lee, 1873 .... 45.00
Awa–A–A–Y We Go, Jackie Gleason, Board, Transogram, 1956 .... 65.00
Bagatelle, Spring Action, Board, 1889 .... 80.00
Bagatelle, Wooden & Brass, Metal Bell, J. H. Singer, 24 x 11 In. 121.00

Ball Toss, Seated Black Man, Nodding Head, Bull's–Eye Stomach, Germany, 24 In.   3575.00
Barbie, Queen of The Prom, Dress Cards 30.00
Barney Google, 1923 .... 70.00
Barney Miller, TV, Sealed 12.00
Barnum's Animal Cracker, Nabisco Animal Cracker Box 28.00
Baseball, Bambino, Babe Ruth, Wooden Ball & Bat, Mansfield–Zesiger, 1940s 167.00
Baseball, Roger Maris, Spring Loaded Bat Hits Balls, Pressman Toy, 1962, Box 365.00
Bat Masterson, Lithographed Western Town, Lowell, 1958 .... 125.00
Battle Action, Marbles, Tin, Plastic, 10 x 1 x 6 In. 22.00
Battle Cry, Civil War, Milton Bradley, 1962 .... 38.00
Battle Stations, Board, 1940s, McKay 59.00
Battlestar Gallactica, Board, Milton Bradley, 1976 .... 20.00
Beany & Cecil, 1961 .... 25.00
Bear Target, Battery Operated, Tin, Japan, Box, 9 In. 532.00
Beetle Bailey, Board 30.00
Ben Casey Play Hospital, Transogram, 1962 .... 25.00 To 65.00
Beverly Hillbillies, Card, 1963 .... 20.00
Beverly Hillbillies, Standard Toycraft, 1963 .... 15.00
Bewitched, Board 30.00
Bible Rhymes, Card, Goodenough & Woglum Co., 1930s 70.00
Big Bad Wolf, Board 75.00
Big Bluff, Board, Ideal, 1970 .... 20.00
Big Game Hunter, Target, Schoenhut, Metal Gun, Box, 13 x 13 In. 242.00
Black Beauty, Transogram, 1957 .... 20.00
Blackout, Milton Bradley, 1939 .... 40.00
Blondie, Transogram, 1966 .... 28.00
Board, Black & Red Squares, Pine, 15 1/2 x 19 In., With 1 1/8 In. Lip 185.00
Board, Breadboard Ends, Salmon & Black Paint, 13 1/2 x 20 1/4 In. 285.00
Board, Chess, Reverse Painted, Framed 750.00
Board, Cribbage, Bakelite, Box 22.00
Board, Cribbage, Brass, On Oak Stand, England 525.00
Board, Cribbage, Broken Heart Shape, Extra Scoring Spaces, Hand–Crafted 20.00
Board, Cribbage, Inlaid Figures 140.00
Board, Cribbage, Ivory Inlay, 19th Century 47.50
Board, Marbles, Mahogany, c.1900, 11 3/4 In. 170.00
Board, Parcheesi, Multicolored Squares, Black Ground 850.00
Board, Parcheesi, Painted Pine, Molded Edge, 19 1/4 x 19 1/4 In. 1430.00
Board, Parcheesi, Red & Mustard, 24 1/4 x 25 In. 240.00
Board, Red & Black 1 Side, Yellow & Indigo Blue On Other 305.00
Board, Red, Mustard Squares, Wooden, Drawer, In Box, Tan Paint, 17 x 9 x 3 In.   280.00
Bobbing Around The Circle Bookcase, McLoughlin, 7 x 14 In. 357.00
Bobsey Twins On The Farm, Milton Bradley, 1957 .... 20.00
Booby–Trap, Parker Bros., 1965 .... 6.00
Bore Reflector, Winchester, 1892 .... 110.00
Box, Poker Chips, Mahogany, 90 Chips 80.00
Branded, Board, Milton Bradley, 1966 .... 69.00
Break The Bank, Bert Park's, Bettye–B, 1955 .... 49.00
Bringing Up Father, Board, Based On George McManus Comic Strip, 1920 .... 330.00
Buffalo Bill, Parker Brothers, 1910 .... 400.00
Bullwinkle, Electric Quiz, Larami 58.00
Call Me Lucky, Bing Crosby, Board, Parker Bros., 1954 .... 51.00
Calling All Cars, Board, Police, Parker Brothers, 1948 .... 20.00
Calling All Cars, Metal Race Cars, Parker Bros., 1938 .... 50.00
Calling All Cars, Parker Bros., Board, 1930s 28.00
Calling Superman, Transogram, 1954 .... 125.00
Camelot, Knights In Jousting Position, Parker Bros., 1931 .... 28.00
Captain America, Milton Bradley, Board, 1977 .... 12.00
Captain Gallant, Board, Transogram, 1948 .... 98.00
Captain Video, Board, 1950s 139.00
Capture The Cooties, World War I Scene 55.00
Casper The Ghost, Board, Milton Bradley, 1955 .... 18.00
Cats & Mice, McLaughlin, Box .... 350.00 To 385.00
Cavalcade Derby, Tin Horses, Jockey Riders Spin On Base, Wyandotte, c.1930 ...... 87.00

Charlie's Angels, Box, 1977 .... 15.00
Checker Set, Paladin, Have Gun Will Travel, Box 295.00
Checkerboard & Chinese Checkers, Drawer, Wooden Checkers, Clay Marbles 375.00
Checkerboard 1 Side, Different Game On Other, Cue, Instructions, 2 Sides 35.00
Checkerboard, Box, Spruce Gum, Other Wood, Sliding Metal Cover 220.00
Checkerboard, Game On Back, Wooden, 1930 .... 70.00
Checkerboard, Inlaid, Celluloid Ivory Checkers, 16 x 16 In. 45.00
Checkerboard, McCormick's Iron Glue, 1927 .... 95.00
Checkerboard, Oak, Polychrome, Yellow, Green, Black, Brown Ends, 13 x 20 In. ... 368.00
Checkerboard, Pine, Yellow Paint, Black, White, Red, Oak Edge, 24 x 16 In. 155.00
Checkerboard, Red & Black, 15 1/2 x 19 In. 165.00
Checkerboard, Red & Blue Surface, 19th Century, 17 1/2 x 14 1/8 In. 495.00
Checkerboard, Red & Green Paint On Carved Squares, 26 x 16 In. 785.00
Checkerboard, Red, White Paint, Wooden, 17 x 25 In. 275.00
Checkerboard, Tin 35.00
Checkers–Backgammon–Tousel Bookcase Game Set, McLoughlin 38.50
Chess Set, Ivory, Green & White, Turkish, 1820 .... 1800.00
Chess Set, Presidents Up To Kennedy, 1960s 17.50
Chiromagica, Mechanical, McLoughlin, No. 2, 1901, Box, 12 1/4 x 12 1/4 In. 245.00
Chitty Chitty Bang 12.00
Christmas Goose, Box Bottom Board, McLoughlin, 1898, 19 1/2 x 10 1/2 In. 1025.00
Chuck–A–Luck, Wire & Metal Dice Thrower, Bell, 17 1/2 In. 95.00
Cimarron Strip, Board, Ideal, 1967 .... 89.00
Citadel, Wooden Pieces, Parker Bros., 1940 .... 105.00
Civil War, Pictures, The Spy, Lincoln, The Commander, Card 200.00
Coney Island, Technofix, Box 495.00
Consult Elcara, Gypsy Fortune–Teller, Milton Bradley, 1922 .... 27.00
Coon Hunt, Box Bottom Board, Parker Bros., 9 1/2 x 15 In. 905.00
County Fair, Board, Milton Bradley, 1937 .... 42.00
Crazy Clock, Ideal, 1964 .... 85.00 To 98.00
Crazy Traveller, Parker Bros. 70.00
Croquet, Table, Milton Bradley, 1890s 25.00
Cross Up, Lucille Ball, Board 20.00
Crown Red, Parker Bros., 1969 .... 12.00
Dark Shadows, Whitman, 1968 .... 59.00
Dating Game 12.00
Derby Steeple Chase, McLoughlin, 1888 .... 154.00
Dig, Card, Parker Bros., 1940 .... 12.00
Ding Dong, Ottman, 6 x 10 In. 192.00
Doc Holiday, Board, Transogram, 1960 .... 29.00
Dollars & Sense, Sidney Rogers Gitten, 1946 .... 100.00 To 105.00
Dominoes, Budweiser 60.00
Dominoes, Prisoner–of–War, Bone, Sliding Cover, c.1830, 4 1/2 x 2 1/2 In. 193.00
Dominoes, Wooden Box, Miniature 28.00
Down You Go, T.V. Quiz Game, Selchow & Righter, 1954 .... 28.00
Dr. Kildare, Card, Ideal, 1963 .... 29.00

Game, Elmer's Enigma, 9 X 16 In.

Dr. Seuss, Yertyl The Turtle, Revell, 1959 ....98.00 To 118.00
Dragnet, Transogram, 1955 .... 65.00
Dressing The Dandy, Pin The Tail Type, Spear, 8 x 12 In. 176.00
Easy Money, Board, Milton Bradley, 1936 .... 110.00
Ed Wynn, Fire Chief, Selchow & Righter 26.00
Elmer's Enigma, 9 x 16 In. ....*Illus* 10.00
Emmett Kelly, Board, All–Fair, 1953 .... 45.00
English Horse Racing, Wooden Box, Minoru, 8 3/4 x 15 3/4 In. 210.00
F Troop, Ideal, 1965 .... 35.00
Famous Authors, Card, Parker Bros., 1910 .... 70.00
FBI Crime Resistance 25.00
FBI, Board, Transogram, 1963 .... 89.00
Felix The Cat, 1960 .... 60.00
Fibber McGee & Molly, Milton Bradley, 1940 .... 90.00
Fibber McGee & Molly, Wistful Vista Mystery, Milton Bradley, 1940 .... 15.00 To 29.00
Finch, Instructions, Card, 1911 .... 15.00
Fire Alarm, Parker Bros., 1899 ....*Illus* 2750.00
Fireside Football, Board, 1940s 15.00
Fish Pond, Les Plaisers De La Peche, Paris, 1890s 33.00
Fish Pond, Magnetic, McLoughlin, Wooden Box, 1891 .... 385.00
Fish Pond, Milton Bradley, Box 121.00
Fish Pond, National Games Inc., 1950s 75.00
Flinch, Card, Parker Bros. .... 10.00 To 35.00
Flintstone Animal Rummy, Card Tray, Box, 1961 .... 45.00
Flintstone Stone Age, Transogram, 1961 .... 10.00 To 35.00
Flowers, Card, Cincinnatti Game Co., 1899 .... 50.00
Flying G–Men, 1939 .... 250.00
Flying Nun, Board, Milton Bradley, 1968 .... 18.00
Football, Cadaro–Ellis, 1946 .... 65.00
Football, Super Coach, Coleco, Box 30.00
Football, Super Jock, Box, 1976 .... 28.00
Football, Ward Cuff's, Continental Sales Co., 1938 .... 225.00
Fortune–Telling, Card, Box, 1930s 25.00
Fox & Hounds, Board, Parker Bros., 1948 .... 24.00
Fred Flintstone Figural Bowling, 1960s 10.00
Frog Who Would A Wooing Go, Board, United Games Co. 176.00
Fugitive, Board, Ideal, 1964 .... 179.00
Fun Faces, McLoughlin, Wooden Box, 1864 .... 550.00
Gambling Wheel & Table, H. C. Evans, c.1925 .... 7800.00
Game of Bang Round The World, Milton Bradley 85.00
Game of Bugle Horn Or Robin Hood, Cards, Board, McLoughlin 495.00
Game of Detective, 4 Detectives, 4 Assistants, Board, Bliss, 1889 .... 3265.00
Game of Hollywood Stars, Whitman, 1955 .... 10.00
Game of Horror, Great Movie Monsters, Creatures Features, 1975 .... 45.00
Game of Life, Milton Bradley, World War I Reissue 71.50
Game of Nosey, McLoughlin, Papier–Mache Nose, Glasses & Mustache, 1905 .... 302.00
Game of Penny Post, Board, Parker Bros., 1900 .... 715.00
Game of The Crusaders, McLoughlin, 1888 .... 150.00
Game of Travel, Parker Bros., 1894 .... 577.00
Games of Life's Mishaps & Bobbing Round The Circle, McLoughlin, 1891 .... 550.00
Games of Pilgrim's Progress, McLaughlin, Box, 1870s 300.00
Gee–Wiz, Horse Racing, Wolverine, Box 185.00
General Grant, 32 Handmade Swirl Marbles, Board, 10 1/8 In. .... 320.00 To 750.00
General Hospital, Board, Parker Brothers, 1974 .... 20.00
Go For Broke, Selchow & Righter, 1965 .... 15.00
Godfather, In Plastic Violin Case, 1971 .... 45.00
Goldfinger, Board, Milton Bradley, 1966 .... 79.00
Golf, Putting, Box, 1940s 45.00
Goody Two Shoes Spelling, McLoughlin, Wooden Letters, Box, 9 x 12 In. 495.00
Goosey Goosey Gander, Box Bottom Board, McLoughlin, 1890, 14 1/2 x 8 1/2 In. 605.00
Grandma's Geographical, Question Cards, McLoughlin, 3 x 5 In. 550.00
Great American Baseball, 1920s, Box 175.00
Green Ghost, Transogram, 1965 .... 30.00 To 49.00

Gunsmoke, Board, Lowell, 1958 ....89.00 To 125.00
Gypsy Fortune–Telling, Milton Bradley, 1895 .... 220.00
Hand of Fate, Fortune–Telling, McLoughlin, 1901, 14 1/2 x 15 In. 4800.00
Hangman, Vincent Price On Cover 15.00
Happy Days, Board, Parker Bros., Unused, 1976 .... 20.00
Haunted House, Ideal 499.00
Home Baseball, McLaughlin, 1900, Box ....*Illus* 1980.00
Horse Race, Hand Operated, 1900 .... 1500.00
Hot Wheels Wipe Out, 1968 .... 30.00
Hot Wheels, Racing Cars, Mattel, Frame Tray 10.00
Huckleberry Hounds Huckle–Chuck Game, Transogram, 3 Carnival Games, 1961 145.00
Humpty Dumpty, Lowell, 1959 .... 59.00
I Spy, Ideal, 1965, Box ....32.00 To 35.00
Incredible Hulk, Board, 1978, Box .... 11.00 To 20.00
Intrigue, Milton Bradley, Clue–Like Game, 1954 .... 70.00
Jack & Beanstalk, Box Bottom Board, McLoughlin, 1898, 19 3/4 x 10 1/2 In. 1085.00
Jack & Jill, Milton Bradley 25.00
James Bond 007, Milton Bradley, 1964 .... 49.00
James Bond 007, Tarot Cards, 1973 .... 38.00
James Bond, Goldfinger, Board, Milton Bradley, 1966 .... 60.00 To 89.00
Jan Murray, TV Word Game, Lowell, 1973 .... 20.00 To 35.00
Jim Prentice Electric Farmer's Round Up, Electric Game Co., 1950s 45.00
Johnny Ringo, Transogram, 1960, 9 x 18 In. 150.00
Jungo Target, Tin, Wyandotte 45.00
Kentucky Derby, Metal Horses Run Along Track, 1937 .... 95.00
Kentucy Derby, Whitman, 1938 .... 22.00
King Kong, Milton Bradley, 1966 .... 32.00
King Zor, Board, Ideal, 1962 .... 139.00
Kiss–On Tour, Board, Milton Bradley, 1970s 32.00
Knight Rider, Parker Bros., 1983 .... 15.00
Kojack, Board, Ideal, 1977 .... 18.00
Kreskin's ESP, Box, 1966 .... 10.00 To 25.00
Kris Kringle Bean Bag, Board, Cardboard, 17 In. 75.00
Kukla & Ollie, Board, Parker Bros., 1962 .... 59.00
Kukla & Ollie, Board, Parker Bros., 1962, Box 40.00
Land of The Giants, Board, Ideal, 1968 .... 165.00
Land of The Lost, Board, Milton Bradley, 1975 .... 19.00
Laverne & Shirley, Parker Bros., 1977 .... 15.00 To 20.00
Leap Frog Tiddlywinks, Ottman, 22 x 4 In. 143.00
Leap Frog, Cardboard Spinner, McLoughlin, 8 x 10 In., Box, 1900 .... 357.00
Leave It To Beaver, Rocket To The Moon, Hasbro, 1959 .... 30.00
Lee Vs. Meade: Battle of Gettysburg, Strategy, 1974 .... 55.00
Li'l Abner, Parker Bros., 1969 .... 45.00
Lie Detector, Mattel, 1961 .... 65.00 To 79.00
Life of The Party, Figural Donkey Spinner, Octagonal Box, 1935 .... 100.00
Lindy, Parker Brothers, Card, Box, 1927 .... 65.00
Little Beaver, 3 Game Set, Red Ryder, Bilt–Rite, 1956 .... 30.00
Little Black Sambo, Dart, Wyandotte, 14 x 23 In. ....85.00 To 120.00
Little Fireman Game, McLoughlin, 1897 .... 7370.00
Little House On The Prairie, Parker Bros., 1978 .... 30.00
Little Noddy Taxi, Parker Bros. 60.00
Logomachy, McLaughlin, Card 22.00
Long Shot, Parker Bros., 1962 .... 110.00
Loonykins, Hassenfeld Bros. 65.00
Lost In The Woods, Box Bottom Board, McLoughlin, 1895 .... 1330.00
Lucy's Tea Party, Milton Bradley 45.00
M. A. S. H., Milton Bradley, 1981 .... 10.00
Magic Transfer Set, Phantom, Rub On, Hasbro, 1965 .... 59.00
Mah–Jongg Set, Ivory, Wooden Case, 9 In. 192.00
Mah–Jongg, Bone On Bamboo, Rosewood Box, With Racks 250.00
Mah–Jongg, Catalin, Racks & Pieces, Carrying Case, 1920s 125.00
Major League Baseball, Folding Board, Philadelphia Game Mfg., Co. 445.00
Major League Indoor Baseball, Philadelphia Game Mfg. Co., 1912, Box 3080.00

Man From U. N. C. L. E., Board, Ideal, Unused	79.00
Man From U. N. C. L. E., Huskey, 1966	125.00
Mansion of Happiness Or Virtue Rewarded & Vice Pursued, R. L. & J. Whittle	550.00
Mansion of Happiness, Board, Parker Bros., 1894	214.00
Margie, Milton Bradley, 1961	45.00
Meet The Presidents, Board, 1961	39.00
Men In Space, Board, Milton Bradley, 1960	135.00
Merry Go Round, Chaffee & Selchow, 1898, Box, 13 x 13 In.	3300.00
Messenger Boy, McLoughlin Bros.	65.00
Meteor, Marbles, Gilbert, 1916	28.00
Mind Over Matter, Board, Ideal, 1967	15.00
Miss America Pageant, Parker Bros., 1974	12.00
Monopoly, Board, Parker Bros., 1937	65.00 To 70.00
Monopoly, Board, Parker Bros., 1946	30.00 To 45.00
Monopoly, Board, Parker Bros., 1st Edition, 1935	175.00
Monopoly, Darrow, 1934, 20 1/2 x 10 3/4 In.	4840.00
Monopoly, Metal Markers, 1936	25.00
Monster Game, Milton, Bradley, 1965	25.00
Mork & Mindy, Card, Milton Bradley, 1978	15.00 To 18.00
Mother Goose Ball Target, Paper Lithograph On Wood, Reed, 18 In.	797.00
Mr. Magoo, Warren, 1973	48.00
Mr. Ree, Game of Mystery, Selchow & Righter, 1946	30.00
Music Authors, Anagrams, Improved Geographical Cards, Peter G. Thomson	35.00
My Favorite Martian, Board, Transogram, 1963	45.00 To 50.00
My Favorite Martian, Transogram, 1963	39.00
Mystery Date, Milton Bradley, 1965	10.00
Mystic Skull, The Game of Voodoo, Ideal, 1964	35.00
National Derby Horse Race, Whitman, 1938	15.00
National Velvet, Board, Transogram, 1961	39.00
New Bicycle, Parker Bros., 1894	880.00
New Game of Piggies, Box Bottom Board, Selchow & Righter, 1894	665.00
Nuremberg Marble, 6 In. Diam.	467.00
Nuremberg, Board, Soldiers & Sheep, 9 x 9 In.	99.00
Official Drivers Ed, Cadeco, 1973	29.00
Old Maid, 1960	12.00
Old Maid, Box Bottom Board, McLoughlin, 1898, 19 1/2 x 10 1/2 In.	605.00
Ouija Board Mystifying Oracle, Parker Bros., Box	15.00
Owl & The Pussy Cat, Board, Clark & Sowdon, Tokalon Series	220.00
Paines Duplicate Whist, 1898	50.00
Paladin, Have Gun Will Travel, Board, Ideal	65.00
Parcheesi, Instructions, 1920s	20.00
Partridge Family, Board, Milton Bradley, 1971	35.00
Patty Duke, Board, Milton Bradley	30.00
Peg Baseball, Board, Parker Bros., 12 x 11 In.	247.00
Perry Mason, The Case of The Missing Suspect, Board, Transogram, 1956	40.00 To 49.00
Perry Mason, Transogram, 1959	45.00
Peter Pan, Transogram, 1955	32.00
Peter Peter Pumpkin Eater, Parker Bros., 1896	62.00
Peter Rabbit's Race, Beatrix Potter Characters, Frederick Warner	210.00
Petticoat Junction, 1963	32.00
Phantom, Skull Ring, Die–Cut Cardboard Figures of Phantom, Transogram	198.00
Philip Marlowe, Board, Transogram, 1960	25.00
Pick Up Sticks, Lithographed Board, Milton Bradley, 1920	190.00
Pick Up Sticks, Schoenhut, Box, Early 1900s	55.00
Pilgrim's Progress, Tower of Babel, Bookcase Game, McLoughlin, 1875	467.00
Pin The Tail On The Donkey, Box, 1930s	15.00
Pinball, 3 Keys To Treasure, Prizes In Box	155.00
Pinball, Poosh–M–Up, Big 5	30.00 To 40.00
Pinball, Push–Em–Up, 4 In 1	25.00
Pinball, Wingshot, Marx	22.00
Pink Panther, Board, Milton Bradley, 1970	21.00
Pinky Lee, Who Am I, Ed–U–Cards, 1950s, 14 x 18 In., Box	98.00
Planet of The Apes, Milton Bradley, 1974	29.00 To 45.00

Game, Fire Alarm, Parker Bros., 1899

Game, Home Baseball, McLaughlin, 1900, Box; Game, Toy Town Conductor's, Game, Milton Bradley, 1910

Game, Round The World With Nellie Bly, McLoughlin; Game, Wide World & Journey Round It, Parker Bros.,1896

Game, Teddy's Ride From Oyster Bay To Albany, Jesse Crandall, 1899

Plunder Pirate, Milton Bradley, 1939	35.00
Poker Chip Holder, Bakelite Marbelized	75.00
Pop The Bird, Target, Cork Gun, Box	46.00
Prince Valiant Crossbow, Dart Arrows, Target On Back of Box, Parva, 1948	170.00
Prince Valiant, 1950s	38.50
Puss N' Boots, Board, McLoughlin, 1897	143.00
Pussy & The 3 Mice, Box Bottom Board, McLoughlin, 19 1/2 x 10 1/2 In.	665.00
Puzzle, 6 Day War, June 9, 1967, Parker Bros., Unopened	16.00
Puzzle, 8 Is Enough, Family Portrait, Box, 1978	16.00
Puzzle, A Serious Case, Norman Rockwell, 1930s, 12 x 9 In., 294 Piece	20.00
Puzzle, Arithmetic, Multiplication, Holbrook, 1957	6.00
Puzzle, Augie Doggie, Whitman, 1960	20.00
Puzzle, Buffalo, Singer Sewing Machine	85.00
Puzzle, Buy War Bonds, Big Star No. 1010	13.00

Puzzle, Calm of Night, Log Cabin & Mountains, c.1940, 16 x 12 In., 300 Piece 30.00
Puzzle, Captain Kangaroo, Mr. Greenjeans, Dancing Bear, Fairchild, 1956 .... 8.00
Puzzle, Captain Kangaroo, Tray Type, 14 x 10 In., 2 Piece 20.00
Puzzle, Chatty Baby, Frame Tray, Dated 1963 .... 10.00
Puzzle, Cisco Kid & Pancho, Tip–Top Bread, 1955, 7 x 8 In. 67.00
Puzzle, Columbian Exposition, Entire View, Box, 1893 .... 275.00 To 400.00
Puzzle, Cow, McLoughlin Bros., 1898 .... 125.00
Puzzle, Dark Shadows, Barnabas In Cemetery, Whitman, 1968, 200 Piece 79.00
Puzzle, Dark Shadows, Whitman, 1968, 1200 Piece 59.00
Puzzle, Ding Dong School, Miss Frances, 1952 .... 20.00
Puzzle, Donkey, Schelcow & Righter, Late 1800s 20.00
Puzzle, Dr. Seuss, Unopened Box 35.00
Puzzle, Dracula, American Publishing Co., 200 Pieces 22.00
Puzzle, Dudley Do–Right 25.00
Puzzle, Dutch Flower Girls, c.1930, 12 x 16 In., 377 Piece 30.00
Puzzle, Emergency, APC, In Can, 1975 .... 13.00
Puzzle, Evening Devotion, Little Gem, 1930s, 12 x 10 In., 270 Piece 35.00
Puzzle, Folgers Coffee, Unopened 5.00
Puzzle, Fun With Funnies, Tillie The Toiler, KFS, 1942 .... 35.00
Puzzle, Future Home Builders, Norman Rockwell–Style, 3–Ply, 10 x 8 In., 213 Piece 25.00
Puzzle, Gilbert Party, 1952 .... 35.00
Puzzle, Great War, Metal Warships, Havana Harbor Map, George C. Whitney, Box 230.00
Puzzle, Gretchen, Dutch Girl, Wooden Horse, Mahogany, 1905, 8 x 6 In., 79 Piece 25.00
Puzzle, Hood's Sarsaparilla, Box 65.00
Puzzle, Hugh O'Brian As Wyatt Earp, Whitman Jr. 18.00
Puzzle, Humpty Dumpty, Wooden 23.00
Puzzle, Hunting With Roosevelt, Paper & Wood, 7 In. 242.00
Puzzle, Italian City Scene, Rooftop Landscape, 1930s, 6 x 8 In., 165 Piece 15.00
Puzzle, James Bond Thunderball, Milton Bradley, 1965 .... 30.00
Puzzle, Jigsaw, Eveready Flashlight, Is That You Santa Claus? Envelope, 1920s 87.50
Puzzle, Little Bopeep, Horsman, 6 Pictures, 8 x 8 In. 121.00
Puzzle, Little Lulu, 1960 .... 10.00
Puzzle, Lotto, American Indian, Gabriel Sons, 6 Piece 125.00
Puzzle, Maud Humphrey, Parker Bros., 1925, 15 Piece 30.00
Puzzle, Maverick, Frame Tray, Whitman, 1960 .... 30.00
Puzzle, McDonald's, Hamburgler & Mayor McCheese, Wooden, 3 x 3 Ft. 175.00
Puzzle, Model Ship, Sailing, Bradley, Wooden Box, 8 x 7 In. 275.00
Puzzle, Moonbeams Princes, Perfect Picture, No. 356 .... 18.00
Puzzle, Nudi, For Adults, 2 x 3 Ft. 10.00
Puzzle, Old Violinist, Mahogany, c.1910, 11 x 7 In., 116 Piece 25.00
Puzzle, Our Gang, Box 110.00
Puzzle, Outer Limits, Milton Bradley, 1964 .... 633.00
Puzzle, Pan American Clipper, Jaymar 20.00
Puzzle, Prince, Parrish 145.00
Puzzle, Pussy Cat Scroll, McLoughlin Bros. 143.00
Puzzle, Queen Mary, Ship, Wooden 29.00
Puzzle, Rin Tin Tin, Box, 1957 .... 28.00
Puzzle, Rin Tin Tin, Whitman Jr. 12.00
Puzzle, Sheep, Wooden, 16 In. 33.00
Puzzle, Sliced Letters & Sliced Animals, Selchow & Righter, 9 x 8 In., 3 Piece 319.00
Puzzle, Spiderman, Waddington House of Games, Giant, 48 Piece 10.00
Puzzle, Stag, Hardware, Wavy Strips, 1905, 8 x 6 In., 82 Piece 22.00
Puzzle, Star Trek Series II, HG Toys, 1976, 150 Piece 10.00
Puzzle, Star Wars, 1977, 104 Piece 20.00
Puzzle, Statue of Liberty, Fine Arts, No. 2456 .... 7.00
Puzzle, Straight Arrow Indian, Nabisco, 1949, Envelope 145.00
Puzzle, U.S. Map, 2 Sides, Milton Bradley, No. 4202, 14 x 20 In., 62 Piece 25.00
Puzzle, Venice By Moonlight, Push–Fit, c.1920, 8 x 11 In., 149 Piece 25.00
Puzzle, White Squadron Scroll, U.S. Torpedo Boat, McLoughlin, 1892, 22 x 11 In. 357.00
Puzzle, Wizard of Oz, Jaymar, Box, 1940s 75.00
Puzzle, Yellow Kid, McLoughlin, 1896, 12 x 12 In. 935.00
Queer Heads & Odd Bodies, Milton Bradley, 1880 .... 90.00
Quiz Kids Own Game Box, Parker Bros., 1940s 38.00

Race Around The World, McLoughlin, 1891 .... 200.00
Race For The Presidency, Board, W. S. Reed, 1887 .... 330.00
Radio Amateur Hour, Milton Bradley, 1930s 115.00
Raggedy Ann, Board, 1954 .... 25.00
Railroad Game, Parker Bros., 1898 .... 550.00
Ramar of The Jungle, Dexter Wayne, 1950s 80.00
Redskin & Cowboy, Smith Kline & French 187.00
Rin Tin Tin, Nabisco 25.00
Ring Toss, Aunt Sally, Spear, Paper On Wood, Dated Christmas 1904, Box 275.00
Ring Toss, Beany & Cecil, Pressman, 1961 .... 125.00
Ringmaster, 1947 .... 45.00
Ripley's Believe It Or Not, Battery Operated, Box, 1933 .... 95.00
Robin Hood, 3-D Board 22.00
Robot Sam Answer Man 35.00
Rockets Away, Space Game, Amsco, 1952 .... 145.00
Rook, Card, Parker Bros., 1913 .... 32.00
Rootie Kazootie, Card, Box, 1953 .... 40.00
Rough Rider Ten Pins, Paper On Wood, Bliss, Paper-Covered Wooden Box 1650.00
Round The World With Nellie Bly, Board, McLoughlin 154.00
Round The World With Nellie Bly, McLoughlin ....*Illus* 155.00
Route 66, Board, Transogram, 1962 .... 129.00
Run, Sheepie Run, Nu-Deal, 1939 .... 50.00
Safari, Selchow & Righter, 1950 .... 50.00
Sambo Bowling, 5 Pins, Parker Bros., 1921 .... 350.00
Santa Claus, Board, Parker Bros. 522.00
Scoop, Parker Bros. 35.00
Scrabble, 1953 .... 12.00
Sea Lab, Milton Bradley, 1973 .... 15.00
Sgt. Preston, Milton Bradley, 1956 .... 10.00
Shing Gong, Samuel Gabriel & Sons, 1937 .... 115.00
Ships & Amphibious Planes On The Seas, Tin Lithographed, Germany, Set of 5 825.00
Shoot-A-Loop, Marbles, Wolverine 45.00
Sink The Titanic, Strategy, Ideal, 1976 .... 35.00
Sleeping Beauty, McLoughlin 203.00
Sleeping Beauty, Parker Bros. 38.00
Sleeve, Go Bang, Tivoli, Solitaire, Siege & Fox & Geese, McLoughlin, Complete 250.00
Slime Monster, Mattel, Box, 1977 .... 30.00
Smoky The Bear 30.00
Snagglepuss Fun At The Picnic, Box, 1961 .... 25.00
Snake Eyes, Litho Cards, 1920s Characters, Selchow-Righter, c.1925 .... 158.00
Snuffy Smith, Times A Wasting, Milton Bradley, 1963 .... 45.00
Sorry, Board, Parker Bros., 1st Edition, England, 1934 .... 190.00
Sorry, Parker Bros., 1939 .... 155.00
Soupy Sales Old Maid, Sealed 35.00
Space 1999, Board, Box, 1975 .... 29.00
Space Mop, A Game of The Planets, Teaching Concepts, Inc., 1973 .... 28.00
Space Shuttle 101, Planets & Space Stations, 1978 .... 35.00
Space, Captain Video, Box 90.00
Star Reporter, Parker Bros. 55.00
Star Trek Super Phaser II, Target, Mego, Box .... 45.00 To 50.00
Star Trek, Ideal, 1967, Box 169.00
Star Wars, Escape From The Death Star, Kenner, 1977 .... 16.00
Starlight, Box Bottom Board, Wilder, 1931, 10 3/4 x 15 1/2 In. 825.00
Steeple Chase, McLoughlin Bros., 1890 .... 150.00
Steeplechase, French Board, 18 x 28 In. 88.00
Stock Market, Whitman, 1963 .... 19.00
Strategy, Game of Armies, Corey Game Co., 1938 .... 110.00
Street Car, Parker Bros., 1892 .... 250.00
Sugar Bowl, Ice Cream Parlor, Transogram, Box, 1939 .... 45.00
Sunken Treasure, Parker Bros., 1948 .... 55.00
Taking The Fort 125.00
Tales of Wells Fargo, Dale Robertson Picture, Board, Milton Bradley, 1959 .... 55.00
Tandem Party, Cloth, 13 Cut Women Bike Riders, Bike, J. W. Herdler, 36 x 15 In. 412.00

Tantalizer, Northern Signal Co., Box, 1958 .... 50.00
Taragelt, Mother Hen, Box, Japan 5.00
Target, Moose, Shooting Gallery, Cast Iron, 6 1/4 In. 25.00
Target, Ohio Art 75.00
Teddy's Ride From Oyster Bay To Albany, Jesse Crandall, 1899 ....*Illus* 5170.00
Telegraph Boy, Board, McLoughlin, 1888 .... 214.50
Telegraph Office, Wooden Telephone, Toy–Town, Box 48.00
Tell It To The Judge, Eddie Cantor, Board, Box, 1940s 75.00
Ten Pin, Red & Blue Uniformed Military Men, Wood, Ives, No. 1885, 10 In. 2750.00
Terry & The Pirates, Board, Ideal, 1972 .... 18.00
They're Off, Parker Bros., No Instructions, 1920 .... 130.00
This Is Your Life, Board, Lowell, 1955 .... 59.00
Tiger Hunt, Whitman, 1940s 62.00
Time Tunnel, Board 125.00
Tippecanoe, Wooden, 1940s, 13 x 19 In., Box, 1940s 65.00
To The North Pole By Airship, McLoughlin, 1910 .... 550.00
Tony & Jock, Shooting, Circus Design, Parker Bros., 7 x 17 In. 66.00
Tony The Tiger, Astronaut, Kelloggs, 1960s 20.00
Tortoise & The Hare, Russell Mfg. Co., 1922 .... 150.00
Touring, Card, Parker Bros. 2.75
Toy Biscuit Trip, Crispo Biscuits, Board, 1924 .... 22.00
Toy Town Conductor's, Milton Bradley, 1910 ....*Illus* 633.00
Toy Town Post Office, Milton Bradley, 1910 .... 250.00
Trap Shot, Lithographed Paper On Wood, Board, Parker Bros. 165.00
Trip To New York, Peter Caddles 38.00
Twelve O'clock High, Ideal, 1965 .... 79.00
Twiggy, Board, Milton Bradley, 1967 ....26.00 To 49.00
Twister, Milton Bradley, 1st Issue, 1966 .... 15.00
Uncle Sam At War With Spain, Board, Rhode Island Game Co., 1898 .... 660.00
Uncle Sam's Postman, Milton Bradley 80.00
Uncle Wiggily, Milton Bradley, 1920s 35.00
Uncle Wiggily, Milton Bradley, 1954 ....12.00 To 20.00
Undersea World of Jacques Cousteau, TV Show, Parker Bros., 1968 .... 40.00
Untouchables, Board, Transogram 35.00
Van Loons Wide World, 1933 .... 90.00
Vince Lombardi, Box 65.00
Visit of Santa Claus, McLoughlin 2000.00
Visit To Farm, Board, Bliss, 15 3/4 x 7 1/2 In. 605.00
Vox Pop, Milton Bradley, 1938 .... 55.00
Wagon Train, Bell England, 1950s, 14 x 14 In., 24 Piece 65.00
Waterloo, Box Bottom Board, Parker Bros., 1895, 21 x 14 In. 600.00
Watermelon Frolic, Cloth, Horsman, 1900, 35 x 30 In. 302.00
Wells Fargo, Board, Milton Bradley, 1959, Box 49.00
Wendy, Milton Bradley, 1966 .... 59.00
Wide World & Journey Round It, Parker Bros., 1896 ....*Illus* 330.00
Wide World Travel, Parker Bros., 1957 .... 18.00
Wild Bill Hickock, Built–Rite, 1955 .... 79.00
Wildlife, Card, Animal Pictures, E. S. Lowe, 1971 .... 75.00
Winnie The Pooh, 1933 ....55.00 To 80.00
Winnie The Pooh, 1964 .... 20.00
Witch Pitch, Parker Bros., 1970 .... 20.00
Wolfman, Instructions, Board, Box 200.00
Wonderful Game of Oz, Parker Bros., 1921 .... 1980.00
World War, Shooting, Artillery, Cutout Soldiers, U.S. Soldier Co., Box 550.00
Yankee Pedlar, Card, McLoughlin, 1850s, 5 1/2 x 5 3/4 In. 1450.00
Yogi Bear, Milton Bradley, 1971 .... 20.00
Young Folks Geographical Game, Card, McLoughlin 46.00
Zorro, Whitman, 1965 .... 29.00
Zylo–Kart Map, Wm. R. Morris, Dated 1886 .... 495.00

GARDEN FURNISHINGS have been popular for centuries. The stone or metal statues, wire, iron, or rustic furniture, urns and fountains, sundials, and small figurines are included in this category. Many of the metal pieces have been made continuously for years.

Armchair, Fern Pattern, Cast Aluminum, Pair	462.00
Armchair, Fern Pattern, Cast Iron, 19th Century, Pair	935.00
Armchair, Renaissance Revival, Cast Iron, 108, Set of 4	1320.00
Bench, Cast Iron, Arms, White Paint	375.00
Bench, Cast Iron, Fern Design, White Repaint, 43 In.	275.00
Bench, Cast Iron, Rococo Style, Green Paint	795.00
Bench, Cast Iron, White House Rose Garden Type, Pair	2310.00
Bench, Classical Design, Trestle Base, Cast Iron, 36 In.	275.00
Bench, Fern Pattern, Cast Iron, 19th Century, 52 In.	990.00
Bench, Gothic, Cast Iron, 1860	1430.00
Bench, Incised Border Design, Double Pedestal Base, Marble, 45 1/2 In.	330.00
Bench, Iron, Rococo Scroll, White Repaint, Atlanta Stove Works, 37 In.	200.00
Bench, Iron, Spanish Art Nouveau, Green, Marked Sevilla	3600.00
Bench, Marble, Double Pedestal Base, Leaves & Scrolls, 19 1/2 x 55 In.	1350.00
Bench, Pierced, Scroll & Lion Legs, Painted Iron, 24 1/2 In.	88.00
Bench, Tree, Wrought Iron, 3 Sides, 7 Legs, France	1045.00
Bench, White Cast Iron, Arms	3200.00
Chair Set, Wrought Iron, Painted, Curved Rectangular Back, Mesh Seats, 10	250.00
Chair, Cast Iron, 3 Legs, Pair	220.00
Chair, Cast Iron, White Paint, 1920–1930	175.00
Chair, Heavy Wire, Repainted, France, Pair	275.00
Dining Set, Cement, Tree Stump Form, Doincicio Rodriguez, 1920–1930, 5 Piece	8000.00
Fence, Cast Iron, Apple Green	75.00
Figure, Coyote, Zoratti, Cement, 4 Ft.	600.00
Figure, Fawn, Iron, Late 19th Century, 48 In.	3300.00
Figure, Fox, Zoratti, Cement	800.00
Figure, Gnome, Weller	5225.00 To 7500.00
Figure, Ostrich, Zoratti, Cement, 4 Ft.	425.00
Figure, Peasant Boy & Girl, Lead, English, 18th Century, 49 In., Pair	7700.00
Figure, Reindeer, Zoratti, Cement	800.00
Figure, Strutting Peacock, Full Tail, Marble Eyes, Cement, Zoratti, 3 Ft.	850.00
Fountain, 2 Children Under Umbrella On Top, Cast Iron, 5 x 5 Ft.	3410.00
Fountain, Art Pottery, Cupid, Standing, 4 Ft.	6500.00
Fountain, Partially Draped Nude, With Shell, Iron, J. J. Ducell, Pre-1860, 50 In.	6380.00
Fountain, Swan Design, Iron, J. L. Mott Ironworks, 9 Ft. 6 In.	5500.00
Fountain, Tree Trunk, With 2 Shallow Basins, Twig Design, 4 Ft. 4 In.	3250.00
Garden Set, Rustic, Cast Iron, 3 Piece	1540.00
Gate, Cast Iron, Apple Green	125.00
Gate, Father Time, Spreading Wings, Wrought Iron, 19th Century	1200.00
Gate, Iron, Sunflowers & Leaves, James Maginnis, 1976, 60 x 80 In.	2500.00
Gazebo, Thatched Roof, Pierced Gate Work, Slate Floor, 8 Ft. 10 In.	220.00
Gazebo, Victorian, Ornate Cement, Horsehair Plaster, White Paint, Yellow Interior	220.00
Ornament, Armillary Sphere, Astrological Sign Traces, Zinc, 38 x 23 In.	1650.00
Ornament, Birdbath & Sundial, Wrought Iron, 2 Piece	275.00
Ornament, Eagle, Iron, Pedestal	770.00
Ornament, Flagpole, Eagle, Flying, On Ball, Gilt, Fiske, Large	6000.00
Ornament, Frog, Cast Iron, Small	65.00
Ornament, Gnome, Weller, Pair	4750.00
Ornament, Rooster, On Stand, France, 19th Century	3900.00
Ornament, Urn Shape Finial, 19 1/2 In.	330.00
Ornament, Urn, Plinths, Cast Iron, 1880, Pair	850.00
Patio Set, Ivy Pattern, Woodard, Cast Iron, Black, 7 Piece	990.00
Pedestal, Cast Iron, Ornate	875.00
Seat, Elephant Form, Pottery, Polychrome, China, 22 1/2 In.	550.00
Seat, Rose Medallion, 19th Century, 19 In.	1980.00
Set, Steel Frame Table, Glass Top, 4 Matching Chairs, 30 1/2 x 48 In.	225.00
Settee, Vine Back, Cast Iron	685.00
Stool, Butterflies & Chrysanthemums, Gilt Border of Birds, Earthenware, 18 1/2 In.	302.50

Swinging Gate, Posts With 2 Cannonballs, Wooden, 8 Ft. Tall	2950.00
Table, Iron, Rococo Scroll, White Repaint, Atlanta Stove Works, 21 x 18 In.	175.00
Table, Limestone, Gothic Revival, Cluster Column Pedestal, 19th Century, 31 In.	2400.00
Table, Wooden Top, Cast Iron Base, Low, 21 1/2 x 34 In.	175.00
Topiary, Statue of Liberty, Wirework, c.1960, 8 Ft.	2420.00
Urn, Art Nouveau, Iron, White Paint, Large	200.00
Urn, Cast Iron, Small	345.00
Urn, Classical, Plinth Base, Cast Iron, 19th Century, 29 In.	220.00
Urn, Cover, Formed As Woven Wicker Vase, Lead, 27 In.	715.00
Urn, Lion's Head Handles, J. L. Mott, Cast Iron, 1846, 25 In.	340.00
Urn, Tin, Galvanized Metal Insert, Painted, Pair	295.00
Urn, White, Iron, Dated 1845	145.00
Watering Can, Brass Nozzle	42.00

GAUDY DUTCH pottery was made in England for America from about 1810 to 1820. It is a white earthenware with Imari–style decorations of red, blue, green, yellow, and black. Only sixteen patterns of Gaudy Dutch were made: Butterfly, Carnation, Dahlia, Double Rose, Dove, Grape, Leaf, Oyster, Primrose, Single Rose, Strawflower, Sunflower, Urn, War Bonnet, Zinnia, and No Name. Other similar wares are called *Gaudy Ironstone* and *Gaudy Welsh.*

Cup & Saucer, Handleless	275.00
Cup & Saucer, Handleless, Single Rose	330.00
Cup & Saucer, Urn Pattern	400.00
Cup, Dove Pattern, Small	100.00
Pitcher, Grape Pattern, Large	1200.00
Plate, 8 1/4 In.	407.00
Plate, Carnation Pattern	550.00
Plate, Single Rose, 7 1/2 In.	105.00
Plate, War Bonnet Pattern	600.00
Sugar, Dish, Double Rose, 5 1/4 In.	550.00
Sugar, Dish, Oyster, 5 5/8 In.	385.00
Sugar, Single Rose Pattern	600.00
Teapot, Butterfly, Squatty Baluster, 5 In.	1800.00
Teapot, Grape, 6 1/4 In.	550.00
Teapot, Single Rose Pattern	450.00
Teapot, War Bonnet	1900.00
Waste Bowl, Oyster Pattern	100.00
Waste Bowl, Single Rose, 2 1/2 In.	220.00

GAUDY IRONSTONE is the collector's name for the ironstone wares with the bright patterns similar to Gaudy Dutch. It was made in England for the American market. There may be other examples found in the listing for Ironstone or under the name of the ceramic factory.

Biscuit Jar, Replaced Lid, 5 In.	125.00
Bowl, Pitcher Set, Blue Floral Transfer, Polychrome Enameling, 9 In.	247.00
Cup & Saucer, Strawberry	200.00
Cup Plate, Urn, Flowers, 4 1/8 In.	60.00
Dish, Serving, Cover, Urn & Flowers, 7 3/4 In.	770.00
Pitcher, Floral, Staffordshire, 6 In.	99.00
Pitcher, Milk, 19th Century, 6 1/2 In.	143.00
Pitcher, Molded Design, Highlighted In Blue & Luster, 7 7/8 In.	165.00
Plate, Imari, 10 In., 4 Piece	594.00
Plate, Stick Spatter, Floral Rim, Malkin & Co., 8 3/4 In.	30.00
Plate, Urn & Flowers, 9 3/8 In.	165.00
Platter, Floral Rim, Allertons, 14 1/4 In.	25.00
Platter, Floral Rim, Oval, Maastricht, 11 1/2 In.	30.00
Teapot, Floral, 9 In.	275.00

GAUDY WELSH is an Imari–decorated earthenware with red, blue, green, and gold decorations. Most Gaudy Welsh was made in England for the American market. It was made after 1820.

Cup & Saucer, Wagon Wheel	78.00

Pitcher, Paneled, Snake Handle, Mason, 5 3/8 In. 225.00
Pitcher, Underglaze Blue, Red, Green, 7 1/2 In. 440.00

GEISHA GIRL porcelain was made for export in the late nineteenth century in Japan. It was an inexpensive porcelain often sold in dime stores or used as free premiums. Pieces are sometimes marked with the name of a store. Japanese ladies in kimonos are pictured on the dishes. There are over 125 recorded patterns. Borders of red, blue, green, gold, brown, or several of these colors were used. Modern reproductions are being made.

Chocolate Pot, Orange Rim 30.00
Chocolate Set, Parasols, Teahouse, Red Trim, 7 Piece 105.00
Chocolate Set, Signed, 10 In. Pot, 9 Piece .... 125.00 To 135.00
Dinner Set, 24 Piece 125.00
Match Holder, Hanging 20.00
Pitcher, Red 14.00
Vase, Foo Dog Handle, 9 1/2 In. 130.00

GENE AUTRY was born in 1907. He began his career as the *Singing Cowboy* in 1928. His first movie appearance was in 1934, his last in 1958.

Book, Arapaho War Drums, Whitman, 1957 .... 16.00
Book, Comic, Dell, No. 43 .... 13.00
Book, Original Cowboy Songs, M. M. Cole Cover, 88 Songs, 1938 .... 30.00
Book, Songs Gene Autry Sings, 1942, 51 Pages 17.00
Button, Gene Autry Club, Pinback 20.00
Cap Gun, 44 .... 150.00
Cap Gun, Leather Holster & Belt, Leslie Henry 160.00
Cap Gun, Long Barrel, Iron 90.00
Cap Gun, Nickel Plated, Plastic Handles, Henry, 1948, 9 In. 350.00
Cap Gun, Short Barrel, Iron 100.00
Cap Pistol, Dummy, Gray Finish, Plastic Grip, Kenton, 1939, 8 1/2 In. 165.00
Double Holster Set, White Embossed Design, Leather 550.00
Flyer, Movie, Spanish Graphics, 1943 .... 20.00
Galoshes, Brown Shoe Co., Box, 1950s 110.00
Galoshes, Rubber, Brown Shoe Co., Unused, 1950, Box 110.00
Guitar, Emenee, Box 195.00
Gun, Cap, Die Cast, Never Fired 200.00
Lunch Box, Melody Ranch, Thermos 170.00
Lunch Box, Thermos, 1940s 75.00
Paper Doll, At Melody Ranch, 1951, Whitman, Uncut 110.00
Paper Doll, Unpunched, 1950, Whitman 125.00
Photograph, 8 x 10 In. 12.00
Photograph, Autographed 45.00
Pistol, Cap, No. 44 .... 150.00
Puzzle, Framed, Gene & Champion, Whitman, 1950, 9 x 11 In. 50.00
Puzzle, Gene Autry & Horse, Frame Tray, 1950s, 11 x 14 In. 20.00
Record, Frosty The Snowman, Dust Jacket, 78 RPM 35.00
Record, Young Gene Autry, Prairie Justice 71 .... 9.00
Sharpener, Pencil, Pocket 1.85
Sheet Music, Just A Lonely Hobo, Gene's Picture On Cover, Cole, 1932 .... 20.00
Sheet Music, Mail Call Today 15.00
Sheet Music, Red River Valley, 1935 .... 10.00 To 22.00
Sheet Music, Red River Valley, Gene's Picture On Cover, Calumet Publ, 1935 .... 10.00
Sheet Music, You Waited Too Long, Gene's Picture On Cover, Harms Co., 1940 .... 12.00
Sign, Display, Double Mint Gum, Western Belt Frame, Wrigley, c.1950, 12 x 10 In. 87.00
Song Folio 25.00
T–Shirt, Gene On Champion 110.00
Watch, Six–Shooter, Gene On Face, 6–Gun Moves Up, Down, New Haven, 1951 ..... 472.00
Wristwatch, Always Your Pal, Leather Band 240.00
Wristwatch, Autry On Rearing Horse, Wilane, 1948 .... 400.00

GIBSON GIRL black–and–blue decorated plates were made in the early 1900s. Twenty–four different 10 1/2–inch plates were made by the Royal Doulton Pottery at Lambeth, England. These pictured scenes from the

book *A Widow and Her Friends* by Charles Dana Gibson. Another set of
twelve 9-inch plates featuring pictures of the heads of Gibson Girls had
all-blue decoration. Many other items also pictured the famous Gibson
Girl.

Plate, Failing To Find Rest, 10 1/2 In.	100.00
Plate, Miss Babbles The Authoress	125.00
Plate, Mrs. Diggs If Alarmed, 10 1/2 In.	78.00
Plate, Quiet Dinner With Dr. Bottles	100.00
Plate, She Got Into Fancy Dress Ball As Juliet	85.00
Plate, She Looks For Relief, 10 1/2 In.	90.00
Plate, You Furnish The Girl, We Furnish The House, 6 In.	20.00

GILLINDER pressed glass was first made by William T. Gillinder of
Philadelphia in 1863. The company had a working factory on the grounds
at the Centennial and made small, marked pieces of glass for sale as
souvenirs. They made a variety of decorative glass pieces and tablewares.

Sugar Shaker, Blue Design, Melon Shape, Original Cover	165.00

GIRL SCOUT collectors search for anything pertaining to the Girl Scouts,
including uniforms, publications, and old cookie boxes. The Girl Scout
movement started in 1912, two years after the Boy Scouts. It began under
Juliette Gordon Low of Savannah, Georgia. The first Girl Scout cookies
were sold in 1928.

Book, Girl Scouts Triumph	10.00
Booklet, Girl Scouting & The Jewish Girl, 1944	6.00
Camera, Kodak, Official Girl Scout, Folding, 1929	85.00
Catalog, Gifts For All Boys, 1957	10.00
Compass, Official, Box	40.00
Handbook, 1917	75.00
Kit, 1st Aid, Contents	57.00
Lunch Pail	55.00
Pixies, Pair	40.00

GLASS–ART. Art glass means any of the many forms of glassware made
during the late nineteenth or early twentieth century. These wares were
expensive and production was limited. Art glass is not the typical
commercial glass that was made in large quantities, and most of the art
glass was produced by hand methods. Later twentieth-century glass is
listed under Glass–Contemporary, Glass–Midcentury, or Glass–Venetian.
Even more art glass may be found in categories such as Burmese, Cameo
Glass, Tiffany, Venini, and other factory names.

Basket, Enameled Stylized Trees, Gilt Metal Double Dragon Handle, 7 In.	660.00
Basket, Pink Candy Stripe Swirl Overlay, Clear Thorny Handle, 7 1/2 In.	165.00
Bottle, Browns, Tans & Cream, Flat Sides, Ipsen, 1975, 16 3/4 In.	250.00
Bowl, Clear, Footed, Tall Sides, Labino, 1967, 7 1/2 In.	160.00
Bowl, Clear Top, Green Base, Red Stripe, Labino, 1969, 3 1/2 x 6 1/2 In.	575.00
Bowl, Cranberry, Signed, 13 x 10 1/2 In.	335.00
Bowl, Many Colors, Cased, 8 1/2 In.	23.00
Bowl, Mottled Yellow, Blue & Green, Czechoslovakia	85.00
Bowl, Multi–Floral Sunset, 7 1/2 In.	275.00
Bowl, Salad, Underplate, Green, Peacock Feather, Opaque White, Higgins, 12 In.	750.00
Candleholder, Gilt Metal Tripod Frame, Opalescent Bell Shade, Europe, 11 In.	220.00
Candleholder, Nudes Holding 3–Tiered Globe, Homoco	125.00
Celery Vase, Green Opaque, Gold Border, 6 7/8 In.	985.00
Chandelier, Hanging, Bronze Mounts, White, Lavender, 3 Lights, c.1910	550.00
Creamer, Triple Cased Cream, Opalescent Interior, 1875–1885	150.00
Dish, Hen Cover, Deep Blue, 7 1/2 In.	450.00
Dish, Opalescent Swirl, Clear Rigaree, Gold Specks, 3 Footed, 4 In.	20.00
Epergne, 1 Large & 2 Small Lilies, 2 Rope Canes, 2 Baskets	875.00
Figurine, Swan, Atterbury, Black, Large	265.00
Goblet, Clear, Green Knobs On Stem, Base Design, Bontz, 1975, 12 In.	60.00
Inkwell, Clear Green, Labino, 1972, 1 3/4 x 3 In.	125.00

Lemonade Set, Shaded Pink On White, White & Blue Daisies, Mugs, 7 Piece 925.00
Paperweight, King Tut Design, 3 In. 116.00
Pitcher, Heart–Shaped Ruffled Rim, Crystal Handle, 8 3/4 In. 1020.00
Pitcher, Mauve Stained, Gold Scrolls, Floral, Clear Handle, Corset Shape, 5 In. 75.00
Rose Bowl, Applied Pears & Leaves, Clear Blue, Footed, 7 1/2 In. 1395.00
Sculpture, Clear Amber, Sebrean, 12 1/4 In. 25.00
Shade, Hanging, 3–Light, Bird & Vintage Overlay, Degaz, 13 1/2 In. 495.00
Shade, Hanging, Blue Bird & Branch Overlay, Degaz, 13 3/4 In. 715.00
Tumbler, Opaque Red, Labino, 1968, 3 1/4 In. 150.00
Vase, Allover Daisy, Burgundy Ground, 9 1/4 In. 345.00
Vase, Blue & Green Iridescent, Raised Swirl, Early 20th Century, 7 5/8 In. 148.00
Vase, Blue & Purple, Fluted, Tapered, Cylindrical, Leerdam, A. D. Copier, 11 In. ... 770.00
Vase, Blue Enameled Cornflowers, Frosted Pink, 13 1/2 In. 135.00
Vase, Chipped Glass, Blank, Clear Shaded To Blue, Gilding 150.00
Vase, Clear, Olive & Yellow Mottled Spots, Labino, 1970, 4 1/2 x 5 In. 225.00
Vase, Cobalt Blue, Leaf, Vine Design, 11 In. 248.00
Vase, Cranberry To Vaseline, 6 In. 120.00
Vase, Enameled Medieval Knight On Horseback, Borders, 11 In. 880.00
Vase, Enameled Pine Cones, Lithgalin, 7 In., Pair 875.00
Vase, Fan, Pink & White, Czechoslovakia, 7 1/2 In. 225.00
Vase, Free Form, Green, Opalescent Around Top & Side, Littleton, 1963, 8 In. 130.00
Vase, Girl, Covered With Gauze Scarf, Belle Ware, C. V. Helmschmied, 13 In. 385.00
Vase, Gold Ruby Leaf & Vine, 5 1/2 In. 187.00
Vase, Green, Blue Band Top, Mottled Yellow, White Rim, Maurer, 6 In. 25.00
Vase, Lapis Stone, Silver Swirling Overlay, Europe, 7 1/2 In. 440.00
Vase, Misshapen, Pale Brown Pink, Littleton, 1963, 5 1/2 x 10 1/2 In. 525.00
Vase, Pink Pulled Feather, Red Interior, 7 In. 358.00
Vase, Pink, White Floral Leaf & Vine Design, 9 1/2 In. 330.00
Vase, Purple Leaf & Vine, 6 In. 220.00
Vase, Silver Overlay Over Black 20.00
Vase, Smoke Gray, Sabino, 5 In. 22.00
Vase, Spider Web Designed, Iridescent Gold, Lundberg, Signed, 2 3/8 x 2 1/2 In. ... 143.00
Vase, Top & Base Swirled Colors, 8 In. 45.00
Vase, Vine Pattern, Iridescent, Lundberg, Signed, 2 7/8 x 3 In. 143.00
Vase, Yellow & Brown Lines, Purple & Yellow Splotches, Green, Maurer, 6 1/2 In. 60.00
Vase, Yellow, Blue, White & Green Ripples, Clear, Slotchiver, 4 In. 35.00

GLASS–CONTEMPORARY includes pieces by glass artists working after 1975. Many of these pieces are free–form, one–of–a–kind sculptures. Paperweights by contemporary artists are listed in the Paperweight category. Earlier studio glass may be found listed under Glass–Midcentury or Glass–Venetian.

Bottle, Cologne, Stopper, Cobalt, Yellow, Tan, 1976, Ries, 7 In. 130.00
Bowl, Brown Iridescent, Horse Heads On 3 Prunts, Labino, 1981, 3 In. 400.00
Bowl, Cranberry, Opaque White Accents, 1979, Roessler, 4 In. 70.00
Bowl, Red, Opaque Blue, Yellow Swirls, Labino, 1975, 2 x 7 In. 320.00
Candleholder, Cobalt Blue, Applied Relief, Labino, 1983, 2 1/2 In. 100.00
Cologne Bottle, Yellow, Striping, Applied Loops, C. Ries, 1976, 3 In. 50.00
Compote, Clear, Air Twist Stem, Handles, C. Ries, 1976, 8 x 6 In. 110.00
Dresser Set, Crystal, Cobalt Blue Interior, Free Form Design, 3 Piece 275.00
Figurine, Astarte, Fertility, Clear Blue, Labino, 1977, 3 1/2 In. 65.00
Figurine, Bird, Cobalt Blue, Labino, 1980, 1 1/2 x 3 In. 125.00
Figurine, Dolphins, Swarovski 700.00
Figurine, Owl, Sculptured, Yellow, Prof. Cerny, Signed, 5 In. 225.00
Figurine, Rabbit, Floppy Ears, Iridescent Blue, Baker, 1984, 2 In. 250.00
Panel, Vitrana, Broken Sky, Framed, Labino, 1974, 26 x 16 1/2 In. 650.00
Panel, Volcano, Browns, Blue, Green, Vitrana, Labino, 1974, 26 x 16 In. 1300.00
Pitcher, Red Shaded To Gray–Green, Labino, 1970, 6 1/2 In. 300.00
Pitcher, Red, Labino, 1973, 5 x 5 In. 275.00
Rose Bowl, 4 Green Prunts, Red Iridescent, Labino, 1978, 3 1/2 In. 300.00
Rose Bowl, Blue, Air Traps, Labino, 1978, 4 x 4 1/2 In. 575.00
Scent Bottle, Red, Gray Feathered, Stopper, C. Lotton, 1983, 7 In. 230.00
Sculpture, Cobalt Blue, Labino, 1971, 7 1/2 In. 1100.00

Sculpture, Conflagration, Pink, Orange, Red, Clear Case, Labino, 6 In. 3200.00
Sculpture, Crystal, C. Ries, 1980, 5 x 6 In. 450.00
Sculpture, Crystal, C. Ries, 1981, 1 1/2 x 6 In. 300.00
Sculpture, Emergence, Pink, Gold Iridescent, Blue Veil, Labino, 9 In. 4700.00
Sculpture, Emergence, Triangular, Pink, Gold, Clear, Labino, 5 1/2 In. 2400.00
Sculpture, Fountain, Blue, Pink, Gold Veil, Clear, Labino, 1981, 6 In. 2800.00
Sculpture, Solid Base, 2 Formed Pieces, Openings, Littleton, 12 In. 1300.00
Tumbler, Opalescent, Red In Base, Labino, 1970, 3 3/4 In. 200.00
Vase, Amethyst, Random Air Traps, Rolled Rim, C. Ries, 8 In. 80.00
Vase, Blue Iridescent, 4 Swirl Applied Prunts, Labino, 1973, 7 In. 325.00
Vase, Brown Leaves, Amber Opalescent, D. Edler, 1979, 5 1/2 x 6 In. 100.00
Vase, Brown–Olive Iridescent, 4 Pulled Prunts, Labino, 1970, 4 In. 275.00
Vase, Bud, Pulled Feather, Iridescent Red, Footed, Correia, 10 In. 125.00
Vase, Circles & Lines, Blue Ground Inside, Clear Case, Maurer, 5 In. 160.00
Vase, Cobalt, Yellow, Green & Black In Clear, F. Maurer, 1980, 5 In. 100.00
Vase, Dark Alexandrite, Bulbous, Narrow Neck, Labino, 1968, 7 1/2 In. 325.00
Vase, Dark Blue Random Swirls, Orange, Clear, Slotchiver, 4 1/2 In. 55.00
Vase, Dark Iridescent, Green & Gold Design, Roessler, 1979, 5 In. 160.00
Vase, Gold Designs, Clear, C. Ries, 1979, 11 In. 500.00
Vase, Green & White Band, Clear Base & Top, Maurer, 1979, 7 In. 50.00
Vase, Green, Gold Scrolls & Panels, Flowers, 3 In., Pair 55.00
Vase, Horned Satyr Faces, 3 Applied Prunts, Yellow, Labino, 1974, 4 In. 200.00
Vase, Misshapen, Dark Iridescent, Top & Side Opening, Eisch, 13 In. 110.00
Vase, Mottled Olive, Brown & Blue, Narrow Top, Labino, 1971, 8 1/2 In. 150.00
Vase, Olive Opalescent, H. K. Littleton, 1966, 11 In. 400.00
Vase, Olive, Gray & Yellow Design, Clear Case, Maurer, 1980, 6 In. 50.00
Vase, Opalescent, Caramel Pulled Hook, Mark Peiser, 1973, 5 In. 475.00
Vase, Orange, Dark Blue Random Swirls, Slotchiver, 4 x 7 In. 55.00
Vase, Pale Blue, Heavy Base, Labino, 1965, 11 1/2 In. 250.00
Vase, Pale Green To Yellow To Salmon, C. Ries, 1975, 11 In. 110.00
Vase, Pink Case, Gold & White Design, C. Ries, 12 In. 100.00
Vase, Pulled & Pinched Wave–Like Forms, D. Labino, 1972, 7 1/2 In. 495.00
Vase, Pulled Rope Around Center, Lavender & Blue, Labino, 5 1/2 In. 450.00
Vase, Red, Outside Swirls, Labino, 1979, 5 In. 400.00
Vase, White Textured, Multicolored Canes, Ansolo Fuga, 10 5/8 In. 1100.00
Vase, Yellow Cased, Flat, Red Interior, Labino, 1974, 5 x 5 1/2 In. 525.00
Vase, Yellow Opalescent Interior, Clear Case, C. Ries, 1976, 10 1/2 In. 150.00
Vase, Yellow, Orange, Green, White & Cobalt, Labino, 1983, 4 1/2 In. 900.00

GLASS–MIDCENTURY refers to art glass made from the 1950s to the
1980s. Some glass factories, such as Baccarat or Orrefors, are listed under
their own categories. Earlier glass may be listed in the Glass–Art and
Glass–Contemporary categories. Italian glass may be found under Venini
and Glass–Venetian.

Bowl, Blue & Green Overlay, Purple, Higgens, 12 In. 175.00
Compote, Bristol, Blue Opaque, Morgantown 40.00
Compote, Free-Form, Orange & Frosted Ground, Boda, 5 1/2 x 5 1/4 In. 1250.00
Cordial, Chartreuse, Morgantown 35.00
Dish, Dessert, Chartreuse, Morgantown 30.00
Figurine, Dove, Opalescent Blue To Clear Gray, Salviati, 12 In., Pair 825.00
Goblet, Chartreuse, Morgantown 20.00
Pitcher, Cover, Pink, Art Deco, Dunbar 145.00
Pitcher, Juice, Crinkle, Golden Moss, Morgantown 65.00
Sherbet, Rooster Stem, Crystal, Morgantown 15.00
Tumbler, Crinkle, Red, Morgantown, 4 1/4 In. 12.50
Tumbler, Iced Tea, Morgantown, 12 Oz. 18.00
Tumbler, Juice, Golf Ball, Stiegel Green, Morgantown 22.50
Tumbler, Water, Sunrise Medallion, Dancing Girl Stem, Blue, Morgantown 65.00
Vase, Arsall, 12 1/2 In. 875.00
Vase, Gypsy Fire, Morgantown, 3 3/4 In. 25.00
Vase, Jade, Morgantown, 10 In. 75.00
Vase, Man Building Fire, Grazing Cow, Schneckendorf, 2 1/2 In. 575.00
Vase, Pink Opalescent To Clear, Gold Luster, Monet Stumpf, 10 3/4 In. 165.00

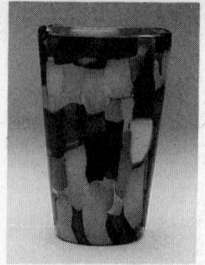

Glass-Venetian, Vase, Red, Blue, Green & Black Pezzato, Murano

Glass-Venetian, Vase, Royal Blue, Applied Blue Rim, 1933, 12 1/2 In.

Vase, Purple Threading, Butterscotch Interior, Pallme Konig, 6 1/2 In. 275.00

GLASS–VENETIAN. Venetian glass has been made near Venice, Italy, since the thirteenth century. Thin, colored glass with applied decoration is favored, although many other types have been made. Collectors have recently become interested in the Art Deco and fifties designs. Glass was made on the Venetian island of Murano from 1291. The output dwindled in the late seventeenth century, but began to flourish again in the 1850s. Some of the old techniques of glassmaking were revived and firms today make traditional designs and original modern glass. Since 1981, the name *Murano* may only be used on glass made on Murano Island. Other pieces of Italian glass may be found in the Glass–Contemporary, Glass–Midcentury, and Venini categories of this book.

Ashtray, Green, White Swirls, Murano, 5 In.	15.00
Ashtray, Red With Silver Cased In White, Murano	45.00
Ashtray, Striped Turquoise & White	25.00
Basket, Kelly Green, White Flowers	55.00
Bottle, Christian Dior, Tartan Design, Barovier, 1969, 9 1/2 In. ....*Illus*	11000.00
Bottle, Liquor, Clown	120.00
Bowl, Amethyst, Crystal, Partial Label, 7 1/2 In.	25.00
Bowl, Amethyst, Crystal, Silver Mica, Label, 5 In.	20.00
Bowl, Cranberry, Clear Nude Cover, Traces of Gilding	295.00
Bowl, Flower, 1920, 10 x 28 In.	300.00
Bowl, Pink, Gold Mica, 5 1/2 In.	25.00
Bowl, Pink, Gold Mica, Murano, 5 1/2 In.	26.00
Bowl, Shell, Latticinio, Blue Swirls, Murano, 6 In.	15.00
Bowl, Shell, Lattino, Blue Swirls, 6 In.	15.00
Candlestick, Blackamoor	65.00
Compote Set, Iridescent Scallop, Sea Animals On Swirled Pedestal, 3 Piece	513.00
Compote, Pale Green, Clear Standard, Silver Speckles, 8 x 8 1/4 In.	132.00
Dish, Leaf, Blue, Gold Mica, 11 In.	25.00
Dresser Set, Art Deco, Several With Covers, Murano, 6 Piece	295.00
Elephant, Latticinio Ears, Brown, Yellow, Trunk Up, Murano, 9 In.	60.00
Figurine, Bird, Blue, Amber, Murano, 10 1/2 In.	40.00
Figurine, Bird, Blue, Amber, Murano, 10 In.	40.00
Figurine, Bird, Red Back, Aqua & Gray Breast, Amber Tail & Crest, 15 In.	125.00
Figurine, Black Dancer, Woman, Applied Face, Hair, Clothes, 9 1/2 In.	220.00
Figurine, Clown As Santa, Clear, Red Buttons & Hat, White Beard, Gloves	385.00
Figurine, Clown, Green Bowtie, Blue Hat, Murano, 8 In.	95.00
Figurine, Clown, Multicolor, Gold Mica, Paperweight, Murano, 5 1/2 In.	95.00
Figurine, Clown, Multicolor, Silver Mica, Murano, 8 1/2 In.	105.00
Figurine, Clown, Paperweight, Multicolor, Gold Mica, Murano, 5 In.	95.00
Figurine, Clown, Striped Body, Hands Behind Back, Murano, 12 In.	295.00
Figurine, Clown, Swirled Color Body, Gold Flecks, Murano, 8 1/2 In.	250.00
Figurine, Duck, Black & Silver, 20 In.	425.00
Figurine, Duck, Blue, Silver Inclusions, Murano, 7 In.	20.00

Figurine, Duck, Cobalt Blue, Silver Mica, Label, 6 1/2 In. 25.00
Figurine, Duck, Cobalt, Crystal, Silver Mica, Label, Murano, 6 In. 25.00
Figurine, Duck, Pink, Bubbles, Murano 225.00
Figurine, Elephant, Trunk Up, Lattino Ears, Brown, Yellow, 9 In. 60.00
Figurine, Fish, Blue, Clear, 22 1/2 In. 330.00
Figurine, Fish, Gold Flecks In Tails & Fins, Cranberry, Pair 175.00
Figurine, Penguin, Latticinio Beak, Black Amethyst, Crystal, Murano, 5 In. 55.00
Figurine, Penguin, Lattino Beak, Black Amethyst, Crystal, 5 1/2 In. 55.00
Figurine, Pheasants, Clear, Yellow Tail, Swirled Base, Murano, 10 In., Pair 110.00
Figurine, Rooster, Multicolor, Gold Mica, 13 In. 55.00
Figurine, Woman, White & Gold Face & Blouse, Latticinio Skirt, 8 1/2 In. 125.00
Goblet, Cushioned Knob With Gold Flakes, Pastoral Scene of Lovers, 8 In. 225.00
Goblet, Dolphin Stem, Gold Mica, Pair 125.00
Goblet, Gold Flecks In Twisted Stem, Red, 7 In. 155.00
Paperweight, Brick, Multicolored Fish, Gold Sand Interior 165.00
Paperweight, Mill, Murano 45.00
Paperweight, Occhi Style 100.00
Plaque, Gondola On Water, Paperweight, 1846, 1 1/4 x 2 In. 2475.00
Sconce, Mirrored, Shield Form, Man & Woman Etched, 22 In., Pair 360.00
Sculpture, Aquarium, Glass Block, Fish, Marine Design, 10 1/2 In. 467.50
Vase, Amethyst, Barovier, c.1957, 14 3/4 In. ....*Illus* 6500.00
Vase, Art Deco, Bud, Ruby, Amber, Clear, Label, 6 In. 45.00
Vase, Barovier, c.1950, 12 In. 880.00
Vase, Chalice Form, Blue Ruffles & Prunts, 12 In., Pair 605.00
Vase, Clear Body, Yellow Rim, Plum Grape, Mosaico, 12 In. ....*Illus* 32500.00
Vase, End–of–Day Pattern, Multicolor Design, Ruffled Neck, Murano, 13 In. 145.00
Vase, Green, Yellow, Black, Clear, Venini, 8 1/4 In. ....*Illus* 7500.00
Vase, Half Amber, Half Amethyst, Murano, Barbini, 9 1/2 In. 302.50
Vase, Handkerchief, Gold Flakes In Base, Murano, White, 5 In. 55.00
Vase, Handkerchief, Murano 400.00
Vase, Handkerchief, Pink, Murano 125.00
Vase, Maroon Scalloped Edge, White, 17 1/2 x 10 In. 50.00
Vase, Orchid, Timo Sarpaneva, 10 1/2 In. 650.00
Vase, Red, Blue, Green & Black Pezzato, Murano ....*Illus* 5500.00
Vase, Royal Blue, Applied Blue Rim, 1933, 12 1/2 In. ....*Illus* 7000.00
Vase, White, Aqua, Murrina, c.1959, 8 1/4 In. ....*Illus* 325.00

GLASSES for the eyes, or spectacles, were mentioned in a manuscript in 1289 and have been used ever since. The first eyeglasses with rigid side pieces were made in London in 1727. Bifocals were invented by Benjamin Franklin in 1785. Lorgnettes were popular in late Victorian times. Opera glasses are listed in their own category.

Gold Filled, Case 5.00
Granny, Sunglasses, Original Case 12.00
Lorgnette, 14K Gold, Woman's Profile 1350.00
Lorgnette, Faceted Amethyst, Scroll Designs, Monogram, 14K Yellow Gold 1575.00

Glass-Venetian, Vase, Green, Yellow, Black, Clear, Venini, 8 1/4 In.; Glass-Venetian, Vase, Amethyst, Barovier, c.1957, 14 3/4 In.; Glass-Venetian, Bottle, Christian Dior, Tartan Design, Barovier, 1969, 9 1/2 In.; Glass-Venetian, Vase, Clear Body, Yellow Rim, Plum Grape, Mosaico, 12 In.; Glass-Venetian, Vase, White, Aqua, Murrina, c.1959, 8 1/4 In.

Lorgnette, Floral Design, Face of Young Woman, 4 Diamonds, 14K Gold, 25 In. ... 4125.00
Lorgnette, Openwork Case, Marcasites, Black Velvet Ribbon 85.00
Lorgnette, Silver Plated, 19th Century 210.00
Lorgnette, Yellow Gold, Foliate Design, Gold Mounts, Art Nouveau 1100.00
Pince–Nez, 14K Gold Chain, Hairpin On Side 600.00

GOEBEL is the mark used by W. Goebel Porzellanfabrik of Oeslau, Germany, now Rodental, Germany. Many types of figurines and dishes have been made. The firm is still working. The pieces marked *Goebel Hummel* are listed under Hummel in this book.

Goebel

Bank, Dog 28.00
Bank, Owl 60.00
Candy Dish, Frosted Glass, Carousel, Marked 35.00
Cinderella, 337 .... 150.00
Condiment Set, Friar Tuck, Stylized Bee 60.00
Cookie Jar, Cat's Head 25.00
Cookie Jar, Friar Tuck .... 250.00 To 295.00
Cookie Jar, Friar Tuck, 1956 .... 850.00
Cookie Jar, Monk 525.00
Cookie Jar, Owl 95.00
Creamer, Cow, Full Bee 50.00
Creamer, Cow, Full Bee, Medium 50.00
Creamer, Cow, Stylized Bee, Large 40.00
Creamer, Friar Tuck, 2 1/2 In. 35.00
Creamer, Friar Tuck, Full Bee 35.00
Cup, Yellow, Blue Cat Handle, Double Crown 85.00
Decanter Set, Monk, Figural, 8 1/2 In. Decanter, 2 1/2 In. Mug, 7 Piece 125.00
Decanter, Friar Tuck, Full Bee 225.00
Decanter, Friar Tuck, Stylized Bee 75.00
Figurine, Bulldog, 1970, 6 1/2 In. 40.00
Figurine, Bulldog, Sitting, No. 569/A 20.00
Figurine, Cinderella, No. 337 .... 150.00
Figurine, Dalmatian, 16 In. 165.00
Figurine, For Father, No. 87, Bee 140.00
Figurine, Irish Setter 40.00
Figurine, Joseph, Bee & V Mark 70.00
Figurine, Madonna With Child, Blue Cloak, No. 151, Bee 700.00
Figurine, Madonna, Full Bee Mark 32.00
Figurine, No. 320, Nurse, 1971, 8 In. 55.00
Figurine, Return Rights, Canary, Feeding Its Young, Artist 85.00
Figurine, Ride Into Christmas, No. 396 .... 150.00 To 260.00
Figurine, Sweet Music, No. 186, Bee 105.00
Figurine, The Mail Is Here, No. 226, Bee 325.00
Flower Frog, Maiden, Carries Water Jar, Porcelain, 6 1/2 In. 200.00
Mug, Friar Tuck, 5 In. 40.00
Mustard Set, Cardinals 495.00
Paperweight, Frosted Grapes, Paper Label 12.50
Pepper Shaker, Friar Tuck, 2 1/2 In. 20.00
Perfume Bottle, Form of Seated Girl, Crown Top 308.00
Pitcher, Friar Tuck 140.00
Pitcher, Milk, Girl Shape, Bee Mark, 6 In. 55.00
Plaque, Display, Steamboat Willie 60.00
Salt & Pepper, Cardinal Tuck, Stylized Bee 65.00
Salt & Pepper, Friar Tuck 35.00
Salt & Pepper, Monk 25.00
Salt, Swan, Clear 25.00
Saltshaker, Friar Tuck, 3 In. 20.00
Sign, Friar Tuck, Merchant's, Last Issue 35.00
Sugar & Creamer, Friar Tuck, With Tray, Stylized Bee 60.00
Sugar, Friar Tuck, Full Bee 30.00
Vinegar & Oil Set 700.00

GOLDSCHEIDER has made porcelains in three places. The family left Vienna in 1938 and started factories in England and in Trenton, New Jersey. The New Jersey factory started in 1940 as Goldscheider–U.S.A. In 1941 it became Goldscheider–Everlast Corporation. From 1947 to 1953 it was Goldcrest Ceramics Corporation. In 1950 the Vienna plant was returned to Mr. Goldscheider and the company continues in business. The Trenton, New Jersey, business, now called *Goldscheider of Vienna,* imports all of the pieces.

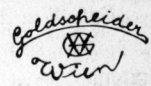

Bust, Madonna, 5 In.	55.00
Figurine, Boy & Girl	185.00
Figurine, Collie, No. 856	120.00
Figurine, Dancing Girl, Holding Skirt Hem, Terra–Cotta, Signed, 14 3/4 In.	875.00
Figurine, Dancing Girl, Holding Skirt Hem, Terra–Cotta, Signed, 19 1/2 In.	1460.00
Figurine, Girl With Umbrella, 11 In.	55.00
Figurine, Juliet W. Doves, 12 1/4 In.	235.00
Figurine, Lady In Plumed Hat & Muff, Marked 802/5/10, 8 1/4 In.	90.00
Figurine, Madonna, Signed P. Fumers	125.00
Figurine, Man, Fancy Cloak, Top Hat, Double Mark, 9 In.	75.00
Figurine, Pierrot, Kissing Companion In Pink Dress, Marked, 18 1/4 In.	1760.00
Figurine, Spaniel, No. 680	105.00
Figurine, Standing Lion, 14 1/4 In.	110.00

GOLF, see Sports category

GONDER Ceramic Arts, Inc., was opened by Lawton Gonder in 1941 in Zanesville, Ohio. Gonder made high–grade pottery decorated with flambe, drip, gold crackle, and Chinese crackle glazes. The factory closed in 1957. From 1946 to 1954, Gonder also operated the Elgee Pottery, which made ceramic lamp bases.

Bank, Sheriff, Yellow	600.00
Bowl, Crescent Shape, Brown Drip, Dark Green, 12 1/2 In.	10.00
Candlestick, Crescent Shape, Blue, 6 1/2 In.	22.00
Ewer, Gold Crackle, Scroll Work At Base, 11 1/4 In.	25.00
Figurine, Coolie, Kneeling, Yellow Marbelized, 3 1/2 In.	25.00
Figurine, Oriental Man & Woman, 14 In., Pair	75.00
Figurine, Panther, Reclining, 19 In.	105.00
Planter, Swan, Golden Crackle, 5 In.	22.00
Planter, Yellow & Pink	25.00
Vase, Doe, Turquoise, 10 In.	75.00
Vase, Double Lip Urn, Dark Green, Brown Splatter, 7 In.	6.00
Vase, Double Lip, Ribbing, Flambe, 6 1/2 In.	13.00
Vase, Drape Form, Rope Cinch, Yellow Mottle, Blue, 9 In.	12.50
Vase, Flower Form, Yellow, 7 1/2 In.	5.00
Vase, Smooth Sphere, Chartreuse With White Drip, 7 In.	10.00
Vase, Violet Blossom, Pink Mottle, Light Blue, 6 1/4 In.	7.50
Wall Pocket, Comedy–Tragedy Masks	18.00

GOOFUS GLASS was made from about 1900 to 1920 by many American factories. It was originally painted gold, red, green, bronze, pink, purple, or other bright colors. Many pieces are found today with flaking paint and this lowers the value.

Bowl, Red Flowers, Gold, 9 In.	17.50
Dish, Roses	18.00
Lamp, Roses In Snow, No Paint	59.00
Powder Jar, Cabbage Rose	65.00
Vase, Statue of Liberty, 12 1/2 In.	75.00
Vase, Statue of Liberty, 13 In.	175.00

GOSS china has been made since 1858. English potter William Henry Goss first made it at the Falcon Pottery in Stoke–on–Trent. The factory name was changed to Goss China Company in 1934 when it was taken

over by Cauldon Potteries. Production ceased in 1940. Goss china resembles Irish Belleek in both body and glaze. The company also made popular souvenir china, usually marked with local crests and names.

Creamer, Sir William Wallace 25.00

GOUDA, Holland, has been a pottery center since the seventeenth century. Two firms, the Zenith pottery, established in the eighteenth century, and the Zuid–Hollandsche pottery, made the brightly colored wares marked *Gouda* from 1880 to about 1940. Many pieces featured Art Nouveau or Art Deco designs.

Pitcher, Arco Royal, High Handle, 9 1/2 In.	165.00
Plaque, Commemorative, Royal Family, 10 1/4 In., Pair	75.00
Plate, Hollard, Florals, Black Outlining, 12 In.	120.00
Platter, Windmill Scene, Round, 10 In., Pair	50.00
Teapot, Windmill Scene, 6 In.	65.00
Tray, Art Nouveau, High Gloss, 10 x 13 In.	350.00
Urn, Cover, Saidjah, 6 In.	55.00
Vase, Art Nouveau, Glossy Regina Black, 14 In.	395.00
Vase, Daisy Pattern, Polychromatic Floral, Marked, 20 1/2 In.	1210.00
Vase, Florals, Windmill Scene, Sailboat In Reserve, Marked, 5 In.	50.00
Vase, Sunburst, Art Deco, Multicolored, 2 1/2 In.	45.00
Vase, Windmill & Peasant With Wheelbarrow, Oval, 4 1/4 In.	65.00

GRANITEWARE is an enameled tinware that has been used in the kitchen from the late nineteenth century to the present. Earlier graniteware was green or turquoise blue, with white spatters. The later ware was gray with white spatters. Reproductions are being made in all colors.

Basin, Blue Swirl, Handles	55.00
Bedpan, Gray, Long Necked	25.00
Berry Bucket, Lid, Bail, Gray, No. 3	65.00
Berry Set, Gray, 6 Piece	145.00
Billy Can, White, Light Blue, Wire Handle	46.00
Bowl, Advertising, Blue	125.00
Bucket, Berry, Gray, Tin Lid, Small	65.00
Bucket, Berry, Tin Lid, Blue & White Large Swirl	165.00
Bucket, Cover, Gray	45.00
Bucket, Cream, Tin Lid, Bail, Gray Swirl, 1/2 Gal.	115.00
Bucket, Water, Deep Cobalt Blue, White Swirl, Large	139.00
Cake Pan, Knudsen's Velvet Cottage Cheese, Blue	26.00
Can, Cream, Gray, 1 Qt	40.00
Can, Cream, Tin Lid, Label, Mottled Gray	100.00
Can, Milk, Blue Swirl, Tin Lid, Wooden Handle	130.00
Can, Milk, Gray, 2 Qt.	50.00
Candleholder, Leaf Shape, Red	55.00
Canister, Cream, Gray, Original Label	100.00
Chamber Pot, Cover, Speckled Light Blue	35.00
Chamber Pot, Gray, Small	50.00
Chamberstick, Beige, Deep	45.00
Child's Set, Green, Children & Bunny Embossed, 3 Piece	125.00
Coffee Boiler, Cobalt Blue Swirl	300.00
Coffee Boiler, Dark Blue, Speckled, Large, Label	38.00
Coffee Boiler, Green, White, 4 Swirl	185.00
Coffee Boiler, Red Swirl	650.00
Coffee Boiler, Solid Blue	35.00
Coffeepot, Blue & White, Wooden Handle	70.00
Coffeepot, Blue Swirl, 9 In.	250.00
Coffeepot, Bluebells Ware	95.00
Coffeepot, Campfire, Cobalt, 8 1/2 x 9 In.	40.00
Coffeepot, Columbian Label, Gray	85.00
Coffeepot, Gray, Bail Handle	40.00
Coffeepot, Gray, Medium Size	30.00
Coffeepot, Gray, Salesman's Sample	25.00

Coffeepot, Green	235.00
Coffeepot, Green, White Specks, Manning Bowman, Tin Top, 1885	90.00
Coffeepot, Hinged Lid, Blue, White Speckled, Magnolia Pattern, 8 In.	35.00
Coffeepot, Hinged Lid, Blue, White Speckled, Magnolia Pattern, 9 1/2 In.	45.00
Coffeepot, Swirled Lid & Handle	200.00
Coffeepot, Tin Lid, Gray	45.00
Colander, Blue & White Swirl Inside & Outside	125.00
Colander, Brown & White Swirl	165.00
Colander, Brown, White	39.00
Colander, Cobalt Blue Swirl	50.00 To 65.00
Colander, Emerald Swirl	150.00
Colander, Gray	25.00
Colander, Iris Swirl	75.00
Colander, Round, Gray	75.00
Cup, Measure, Gray, 2 Qt.	55.00
Cup, Utah Pioneer Jubilee, 1847–1897	245.00
Cuspidor, Blue & White Swirl	225.00
Cuspidor, Hotel, Wooden Handle, Robin's Egg Blue	100.00
Dish, Soap, Cobalt Swirl	110.00
Double Boiler, Bell Shape, Cobalt & White Swirl	295.00
Double Boiler, Gray, Large	49.00
Dough Riser, Gray	80.00
Dripolator, Light Green, Dark Green Trim, 4 Piece	25.00
Dust Pan, Cream & Green	98.00
Eggcup, Cobalt & White Check Trim, Blue, Pair	95.00
Feeding Set, Blue, 3 Piece	45.00
Fish Poacher, Gray, 3 Piece	125.00
Fish Tool, Gray	50.00
Fry Pan, Child's	60.00
Fry Pan, Gray	75.00
Fry Pan, Large Cobalt Blue Swirl, White Interior	550.00
Funnel, Blue–Gray Swirl	14.00
Funnel, Canning, Gray Mottle	40.00
Funnel, Cobalt Blue Swirl, White Interior	260.00
Funnel, Fruit Jar, Gray	40.00
Funnel, White, Black Trim, 4 1/2 In.	26.00
Grater, Brown Speckled, Half Round	70.00
Grater, Flat, Blue	70.00
Grater, Flat, Cream & Green	95.00
Grater, Red, Small	75.00
Grater, Revolving, Gray	75.00
Hot Plate, 2 Burner, Green	85.00
Kettle, Blue, White, 5 Qt.	45.00
Kettle, Cobalt Swirl	85.00
Kettle, Cover, Snow On The Mountain	100.00
Kettle, Fish, Gray	215.00
Kettle, Preserve, Child's	25.00
Kettle, Preserving, Gray	20.00
Ladle, Cobalt Blue Swirl	25.00
Ladle, Cocoa, Tubular Handle, Gray	165.00
Ladle, Gray	20.00
Ladle, Water, Blue & White Swirl	63.00
Ladle, White, Red Trim	5.00
Lunch Box, Cup	195.00
Lunch Box, Cup, Gray, Different Shape	195.00
Lunch Box, Gray	195.00
Lunch Pail, Child's, Gray	125.00
Measure, Dry, Gray	65.00
Measure, Gray, 2 Qt.	55.00
Measure, Gray, Gill	185.00
Melon Mold, Gray	75.00
Mold, Ear of Corn Base, Gray, Fluted	52.00
Mold, Gelatin, Blue & White, White Interior	120.00

Muffin Pan, Blue & White Swirl, 8 Cup 225.00
Muffin Pan, Cobalt Blue Swirl Inside & Outside, 8 Cup 325.00
Muffin Pan, Gray, 12 Cup 50.00
Muffin Pan, Gray, 12 Holes 40.00
Muffin Pan, Gray, 8 Cup 50.00
Pail, White, Red Trim, Small 18.00
Pan, Lady Finger, Gray 295.00
Pan, Lady Finger, Mottled Gray 150.00
Pan, Sauce, Cover, Child's 75.00
Pan, Tube, Gray 45.00
Picnic Set, White Case 125.00
Pie Baker, Turquoise Swirl 30.00
Pie Pan, Blue Marbled 22.50
Pie Pan, Gray 9.00
Pie Plate, Gray 6.00
Pitcher & Basin, Large Blue Swirl 1800.00
Pitcher & Bowl Set, Gray 75.00
Pitcher, Mauve & Green Swirl 275.00
Pitcher, Milk, Marked, Blue 175.00
Pitcher, Molasses, Mottled Gray 120.00
Pitcher, Pink, Green & White, 14 In. 675.00
Pitcher, Snow On The Mountain, 8 In. 50.00
Pitcher, Water, Blue & White, 10 In. 80.00
Platter, Bacon, Brown & White Swirl 295.00
Potty, Painted, Wire Handle 825.00
Reflector, Cobalt, 8 In. 18.00
Rice Ball, Gray 595.00
Rice Ball, White, Small 265.00
Riser, Bread Dough, Cover, Robin's Egg Blue 350.00
Roaster, Cobalt Blue, Oval 30.00
Roaster, Dark Blue Speckled, Oval, 14 3/4 In. 28.00
Roaster, Dark Blue Speckled, Rectangular, 17 1/2 In. 32.00
Roaster, Gray 50.00
Roaster, Robin's Egg Blue, Speckled, Insert, Large 35.00
Salt, Cream, Red, Hanging 65.00
Scoop, Grocer's, Gray .... 40.00 To 85.00
Skimmer, Gray 20.00
Soap Dish, Cobalt Blue Swirl 110.00
Soup, Dish, Cobalt Swirl 140.00
Spoon, Gray 15.00
Spoon, Mixing, Gray 3.50
Spooner, Brown Swirl, White Interior 375.00
Strainer, Soup, Gray 25.00
Strainer, Tea, Fancy Circles, White 28.00
Strainer, Tea, Gray 60.00
Strainer, Tea, Gray 45.00
Strainer, Tea, Star Perforations, Blue 55.00
Strainer, White, Mesh Bottom, Small 20.00
Sugar & Creamer, Blue & White, White Interior 260.00
Sugar, Pewter Trim, Gray Mottled 150.00
Sugar, Tin Lid, Marked L & G, Gray 295.00
Syrup, Brown Onyxware 365.00
Table Set, Child's, Green, Children, Bunny, Red, Yellow, & Blue, 3 Piece 125.00
Teakettle, Gray 125.00
Teapot, Child's, Gray Spatter, Swan Spout, Steelware, 1906 .... 185.00
Teapot, Chrystolite, Gooseneck 625.00
Teapot, Cobalt Blue, Gooseneck 575.00
Teapot, End of Day 395.00
Teapot, Gooseneck Spout, Brown & White Swirl 145.00
Teapot, Gooseneck, Cream & Green, 8 1/2 In. 75.00
Teapot, Gooseneck, Gray 90.00
Teapot, Gray, 1 Cup .... 95.00 To 100.00
Teapot, Hinged Lid, Small Blue Swirl 750.00

Teapot, Mauve Relish Design	225.00
Teapot, Stork In Rushes, Pewter Cover, 10 In.	265.00
Teapot, White, Gooseneck Spout	45.00
Tube Pan, Child's, Gray Mottled	60.00
Tureen, Cobalt Blue	225.00
Utensil Rack, Gray	100.00
Wash Basin, Snow On The Mountain	50.00
Wash Bowl, Salesman's Sample, White	45.00
Wash Pan, Gray, Large	5.00

GREENTOWN glass was made by the Indiana Tumbler and Goblet Company of Greentown, Indiana, from 1894 to 1903. In 1899, the factory name was changed to National Glass Company. A variety of pressed, milk, and chocolate glass was made. Additional pieces may be found in other categories, such as Chocolate Glass, Custard Glass, Holly Amber, Milk Glass, and Pressed Glass.

Berry Set, Cord Drapery, 6 Piece	125.00
Box, Dresser, Aurora	995.00 To 1200.00
Butter, Cover, Leaf Bracket	95.00
Cake Stand, Brazen Shield	55.00
Cake Stand, Herringbone Buttress, Clear	150.00
Compote, Austrian, 8 1/4 In.	65.00
Compote, Pleat & Band, 7 1/2 In.	35.00
Cordial, Shuttle	30.00
Cordial, Shuttle, Pair	42.50
Creamer, Austrian	125.00
Dish, Cover, Amber Hen	135.00
Dish, Cover, Amber Rabbit	135.00
Dish, Cover, Blue Rabbit	135.00
Dish, Rabbit On Nest, Chocolate	285.00
Dish, Sauce, Dewey, Canary	15.00
Goblet, Cord Drapery, Green	150.00
Lamp, Wild Rose & Blow Knot	875.00
Mug, Cactus	80.00
Mug, Elves, Nile Green	95.00
Pitcher, Serenade	995.00
Relish, Cord Drapery, Crystal	25.00
Spooner	75.00
Syrup, Cord Drapery	375.00
Syrup, Inverted Thumbprint	95.00
Table Set, Child's, Austrian No. 200 Pattern, Chocolate Glass, 4 Piece	3575.00
Table Set, Child's, Austrian No. 200 Pattern, Clear, 4 Piece	500.00
Tray, Cod Drapery, Amber, 10 x 6 1/4 In.	88.00
Tumbler, Brazen Shield, Cobalt Blue	55.00
Wheelbarrow, Green	195.00
Wine, No. 11	15.00

GRUEBY Faience Company of Boston, Massachusetts, was incorporated in 1897 by William H. Grueby. Garden statuary, art pottery, and architectural tiles were made until 1920. The company developed a matte green glaze that was so popular it was copied by many other factories making a less expensive type of pottery. This eventually led to the financial problems of the pottery.

Chamberstick, Matte Speckled Dark Blue Glaze, 2 Handles, 2 x 6 In.	247.00
Paperweight, Blue Disk, Carved Spread–Wing Scarab of Mat Yellow, 3 In	247.50
Paperweight, Leather–Green Disk, Spread Wings, Circular Mark, 2 1/2 In.	192.00
Pitcher, Organic Matte Green, Handle, Bulbous, Marked, 6 In.	440.00
Tile, Allegorical, Motifs For Love, Music, Beauty, Industry, 4 x 4 In., Set of 4	467.50
Tile, Brown & Green Trees, Blue Ground, Matte Glaze, Square, 6 In.	1045.00
Tile, Chamberstick, Yellow Candle, Words Grueby Tile, Green, 4 1/2 x 6 In.	990.00
Tile, Cherub With Cornucopia, 2–Color, 6 x 6 In.	650.00
Tile, Colonial Woman Serving Baker's Cocoa, Marked, 6 1/4 x 6 1/4 In.	357.50
Tile, Eros, Red Clay Square Design, Mat Black Background, 6 x 6 In.	165.00

Tile, Ivory Galleon, Green Ground, Square, 6 1/4 In. 935.00
Tile, Landscape, Rolling Hills, Blue & Green, Square, M. R., 6 In. 495.00
Tile, Pond Lily, Red Clay, White Water Lily Blossoms, 6 x 6 In., Set of 3 .... 1100.00
Tile, Sailing Ship, 6–Color, 8 x 8 In. 1250.00
Tile, Seagulls, Over Waves, Cloisonne, Green Ground, Framed, 6 In. 247.00
Tile, Ship, High Waves, Cloisonne, Green Glaze, Ruth Erickson, Framed, 6 In. 495.00
Trivet, Matte Green, Sterling Silver, Monogram MDR, 4 In., Pair 467.00
Vase, 2 Color, Dark Green Mat, 6 Yellow Buds Alternating Leaf Panels, 8 In. 1320.00
Vase, 3 Lobes, Leathery Blue Glaze, Marked, 9 1/2 In. 460.00
Vase, Applied Leaves & Buds, Green Glaze, Flared, 11 x 6 In. 2200.00
Vase, Applied Leaves, Green Matte Glaze, Marie Seaman, 11 1/2 x 8 In. 1540.00
Vase, Bulbous Mat Green, Ridged Body, Organic Leaf Form Arches, 11 In. 1760.00
Vase, Dark Blue Glaze, Flat Shoulder, Circular Mark, 3 3/4 x 3 1/2 In. 110.00
Vase, Everted Pinched Rim, Stems & Blossoms, W. Post, Marked, 10 In. 4185.00
Vase, Flower Blossoms, 9 Broad Leaves, Lavender–Mauve, 8 3/4 In. 3520.00
Vase, Green Matte Glaze, Avocado Shape, Footed, 4 1/2 x 4 1/2 In. 385.00
Vase, Heavy Walled Sphere, 7 Broad Green Leaf Forms, Bottle Top, 8 In. 3190.00
Vase, Jonquil, Star Rim, Green Mat Body, 3 Hand Molded Blossoms, 11 In. 3025.00
Vase, Leaf Design, Dark Green Matte, Paper Label, Marked, 7 In. 305.00
Vase, Leaf–Carved Jardiniere Form, Butterscotch Yellow Mat, 7 In. 4400.00
Vase, Leaves & Floral Buds, Green Glaze, 7 1/4 In. 1045.00
Vase, Leaves Rising From Base, Stems & Buds, Green Glaze, Marked, 11 1/2 In. ... 5500.00
Vase, Leaves, Long–Stemmed Flower Buds, Bulbous, 7 3/4 In. 605.00
Vase, Molded Lotus Leaves, Mottled Green Glaze, c.1905, 10 1/2 In. 1430.00
Vase, Pumpkin, Squat Melon–Ribbed Organic Body, Harvest Glaze, 9 In. 2310.00
Vase, Raised Leaf & Flower, Mottled Green & Yellow, Squat, Bulbous, 4 1/2 In. 1265.00
Vase, Sculpted & Applied Buds & Leaves, Green Matte Glaze, 11 In. 4400.00
Vase, Squat, Ribbed, Matte Yellow Glaze, 6 1/2 x 9 In. 1980.00
Vase, Stylized Stems With Buds & Leaves, Matte Green Glaze, 7 In. 880.00
Vase, Tooled Flaring Leaves, Buds On Tall Stems, Marked, 7 In. 770.00
Vase, Tooled Leaves, Yellow Buds, Squat Bulbous, W. Post, Small 3250.00
Vase, Vertical Leaves, Oval Buds, Green Ground, Egg Shape, Marked, 11 In. 4500.00
Vase, Yellow Buds, Matte Green Glaze, Applied Leaves, 12 x 6 1/4 In. 3850.00
Vase, Yellow Enamel Glaze, Textured Surface, Marked, 8 3/4 In. 880.00
Vessel, Matte Dark Blue Glaze, Gourd Shape, Ruth Erikson, 3 3/4 x 3 1/2 In. 302.50

GUN is the name used for this category, which includes shotguns, pistols, and other antique firearms. Rifles are listed in their own category. Be very careful when buying or selling guns because there are special laws governing the sale and ownership. A collector's gun should be displayed in a safe manner, probably with the barrel filled or a part missing to be sure it cannot be accidentally fired.

BB, Daisey, Model 25 .... 29.00
BB, Daisy No. 118, Targeteer 65.00
BB, Daisy, 1936 .... 95.00
BB, Daisy, Buck Jones 135.00
BB, Daisy, Double Barrel .... 395.00 To 550.00
BB, Daisy, Model 21, Double Barrel, Box 635.00
BB, Daisy, Model 21, Plastic Stock, Double Barrel 375.00
Blunderbuss, Brass Barrel & Fittings, England, Hallmarks, 1813 .... 605.00
Blunderbuss, Converted From Flint, Walnut Stock, France, c.1800 .... 425.00
Carbine, Tripplett & Scott 1160.00
Colt, Frontier, 6 Shooter, 40 Caliber, 6 Shot 742.00
Dueling, Flint Lock, Joseph Manton, London, Bullet Mold, Box 3190.00
Flintlock, Bishop, London, Pair 770.00
Flintlock, Cross Hatched Inlaid Grips, Marked E. L. G., Belgium, Pair 1815.00
Flintlock, Musket, 1776 Tower 850.00
Harpoon, Skeleton Stock, Brass, 37 In. 2785.00
Long, Arab, Octagonal Barrel, Iron Bands, Stepped Butt, 50 In. 190.00
Long, Engraved C. Stark, 1777 .... 1320.00
Long, Parker Bros., 12 Gauge, Double Barrel, Pat. 1878 .... 1450.00
Long, Sharps, Breech Loading, 26 3/4 In. Round Barrel 2000.00
Luger, 9 Mm, World War I, 1917 .... 985.00

Musket, Matchlock, Silver Mounted, Arab, 44 In. 310.00
Musket, Springfield, 1806 .... 775.00
Musket, Trenton, Civil War, 1864 .... 600.00
Nichols Stallion Saddle 300, Box 115.00
Pepperbox, Allen & Thurber 375.00
Pepperbox, Manhattan 2400.00
Pistol, BB, Franklin 35.00
Pistol, Cap & Ball, Hadley–London, 44 Caliber 500.00
Pistol, Colt Army, Model 855, 44 Caliber 1100.00
Pistol, Dimeon North, Safety Lock, Marked 1821, Barrel–10 In. 525.00
Pistol, Dragon, 69 Caliber, England 1400.00
Pistol, Dueling, 45 Caliber, Germany ....⌐...... 950.00
Pistol, Dueling, Carved Wood, France, Pair 2700.00
Pistol, Dueling, Engraved Copper, Mahogany Case, Pair 1870.00
Pistol, Dueling, Flintlock, Joseph Manton, c.1820 .... 3200.00
Pistol, Dueling, Flintlock, Parker Holborn, London, Mahogany Case, Pair 9130.00
Pistol, Dueling, Germany, Pair 1150.00
Pistol, Flare, Mahogany Grip, Brass, New Zealand, World War I, 10 In. 390.00
Pistol, Flintlock, Cannon Barrel, Silver Inlaid Grip & Butt, 12 In. 1210.00
Pistol, Flintlock, Double Barrel, Lepage of Paris, Metal Butt, 12 In. 1430.00
Pistol, Flintlock, Repeating, Adams, 18th Century 9900.00
Pistol, Liberator, 1 Shot, 45 Caliber, 1943, Box 1265.00
Pistol, Luger Mauser, Semi–Automatic, 9 Mm Caliber, Nazi Marked 880.00
Pistol, Militia, Cascd, 60 Caliber, Marked Lewis & Tomes, Case, Pair 3590.00
Pistol, Pepperbox Percussion, Allen's, Engraved 330.00
Pistol, Percussion, A. M. Waters & Co., 1844 .... 245.00
Pistol, Percussion, Screw Barrel, Bag Grip, England 180.00
Pistol, Pin Fire, 32 Caliber, 1890–1900 .... 75.00
Pistol, Rams Horn, Steel, Silver Rondel, Scotland, 11 3/4 In. 1045.00
Pistol, Single Shot, Connecticut Arms & Mfg. Co., 1864 .... 385.00
Remington–Elliott, Pepperbox, 4 Barrel, Pocket Holster, Patent 1860 .... 440.00
Revolver, Colt 45, Lawman Series, Wyatt Earp, Barrel–16 In. 1200.00
Revolver, Colt 45, Single Action 2000.00
Revolver, Colt, 44–40 Bisley 715.00
Revolver, Colt, AR–15M 500.00
Revolver, Colt, Model 1851, Percussion, Navy 4730.00
Revolver, Colt, Model 1862, 36 Caliber, 6 Shot 1100.00
Revolver, Colt, Model SAA, Presentation Case 900.00
Revolver, Colt, Navy, 36 Caliber 2100.00
Revolver, Colt, Percussion, Police, 1862 .... 475.00
Revolver, Colt, Pocket, Steel Grip Strap, Col. Saml Colt, 1849, 4 In. 302.50
Revolver, Colt, Python, 357 Magnum 1430.00
Revolver, Connecticut Valley Arms, Navy, 1961, 36 Caliber 120.00
Revolver, Navy, Prescott, 60 Caliber 450.00
Revolver, Pepperbox, Allen & Thurber, 1860s 680.00
Revolver, Percussion, Tranter, Double Action, 38 Caliber, Fitted Case 1320.00
Revolver, Pin Fire, Le Francheux 300.00
Revolver, Remington, Army, 44 Caliber, 1858 .... 1550.00
Revolver, Smith & Wesson, Schofield, Single Action, c.1876 .... 1100.00
Rifle, Krag, 1889 .... 300.00
Rifle, L. C. Smith, Trap, Double 660.00
Shotgun, Browning, 12 Gauge, Single Selective Trigger 1485.00
Shotgun, Browning, Model A–5 .... 1100.00
Shotgun, Double Barrel, Ithaca, Pre 1920 .... 395.00
Shotgun, Lefever, Model H, Damascus Barrels 375.00
Shotgun, Parker, Dhe–Grade, Double Barrel, 12–Gauge, c.1922, Barrels–32 In. 6500.00
Shotgun, Parker, Dhe–Grade, Double Barrel, 20–Gauge, c.1911, Barrels–26 In. 3000.00
Shotgun, Parker, Dhe–Grade, Double Barrel, 28–Gauge, c.1911, Barrels–28 In. 7500.00
Shotgun, Parker, Vh–Grade, Double Barrel, 12–Gauge, c.1918, Barrels–30 In. 3750.00
Shotgun, Shattuck 1500.00
Shotgun, Shattuck, 8 Gauge 2000.00
Shotgun, Thomas Bladen & Son, Rabbit Eared, Double Barrel 170.00
Shotgun, Winchester, 12–Gauge, Lever Action, 1887 .... 325.00

♦♦♦♦♦♦♦♦♦♦♦♦♦♦♦♦♦♦♦♦♦♦♦♦
Graniteware and other enameled kitchenwares should be cleaned with water and baking soda. If necessary, use chlorine bleach.
♦♦♦♦♦♦♦♦♦♦♦♦♦♦♦♦♦♦♦♦♦♦♦♦

Gustavsberg, Vase, Blue, Silver Crowns,

S. Jonson, 5 1/8 In.

Winchester M53, 25–30 Caliber, Original Tang Sight, SN8885 .... 715.00

GUNDERSON glass was made at the Gunderson–Pairpoint Glass Works of New Bedford, Massachusetts, from 1952 to 1957. Gunderson Peachblow is especially famous.

Compote, Peachblow, White, Pink Trim, 5 1/8 x 6 In. 385.00
Goblet, Acid Finish, Peachblow, 7 1/4 In 245.00
Toothpick, Burmese, 3 In. 75.00

GUSTAVSBERG ceramics factory was founded in 1827 near Stockholm, Sweden. It is best known to collectors for its twentieth–century art wares, especially a green stoneware with silver inlay called *Argenta*.

Gustafsberg

Bowl, Stylized Flowers, Hammered Ground, Marked, 1922, 6 1/2 In. 275.00
Candleholder, Argenta, Pair 165.00
Plate, Floral Design, c.1890, 8 1/2 In. 65.00
Urn, Cigarette, Smokers Bridge Set, Argenta, 5 Piece 65.00
Vase, Argenta, Silver Trefoil Design, Marked, 5 7/8 In. 77.00
Vase, Blue, 10 In. 225.00
Vase, Blue, Silver Crowns, S. Jonson, 5 1/8 In. ....*Illus* 125.00
Vase, Bluebells, Argenta, 9 In. 260.00
Vase, Fish, Green, Argenta, 4 3/4 In. 325.00
Vase, Floral, 5 In. 275.00

GUTTA–PERCHA was one of the first plastic materials. It was made from a mixture of resins from Malaysian trees. It was mold ed and used for daguerreotype cases, toilet articles, and picture frames in the nineteenth century.

Case, Child 78.00
Case, Man & Woman 165.00
Case, Union, Constitution & Laws, 1/6 Case 53.00
Case, Union, Geometric, Floral, Young Man, 1/6 Plate 40.00
Case, Union, Geometric, Scroll, Floral, Ambrotype Man, 1/9 Plate 25.00
Case, Union, Grapes In Oval, 1/6 Plate 60.00
Case, Union, Scroll, Ambrotype Woman, Octagonal, 1/9 Plate 25.00
Case, Union, Scroll, Geometric, Double CDV Size 45.00
Case, Union, Scroll, Geometric, Octagonal, 1/6 Plate 120.00
Case, Union, Scroll, Geometric, Tinted Ambrotype Woman, Octagonal, 1/9 Plate 30.00
Case, Union, Single Pear, Tintype Woman, Octagonal, 1/9 Plate 35.00
Case, Union, Spray of Strawberries, Quadruple 1/6 Plate 45.00
Case, Union, The Bird Bath, Young Man, Octagonal, 1/9 Plate 44.00
Case, Union, Wounded Stag, Ambrotype of 3 Women, 1/4 Plate 150.00
Cigarette Holder, Figural, 1850s 50.00
Match Safe, Red Top Rye, Ferdinand Westheimer & Sons, 1910 .... 65.00

HAEGER Potteries, Inc., Dundee, Illinois, started making commercial art wares in 1914. Early pieces were marked with the name *Haeger* written over an *H*. About 1938, the mark *Royal Haeger* was used. The firm is still making florist wares and lamp bases.

Bowl, Pansy	25.00
Figurine, Cheetah, Pair	230.00
Figurine, Nude, Riding Fish, Green, Large	50.00
Lamp, Art Deco, Deer, Shade	135.00
Planter, Swan, Blue, Mottled	12.00
Vase, Blue Matte, Multicolor Drip, Ribbed, 14 In.	35.00
Vase, Leather–Type Glaze, 15 In.	27.50
Vase, Orange Crackle, 9 1/2 In.	35.00
Vase, Organic, 4 Buttresses, Frosted Green Glaze, 9 In.	250.00
Vase, Smooth Orange Glaze, Crackled, 9 1/2 In., Pair	90.00

HALF–DOLL, see Pincushion Doll category

HALL CHINA Company started in East Liverpool, Ohio, in 1903. The firm made many types of wares. Collectors search for the Hall teapots made from the 1920s to the 1950s. The dinnerwares of the same period, especially Autumn Leaf pattern, are also popular. The Hall China Company is still working. For more information, see *Kovels' Depression Glass & American Dinnerware Price List*. Autumn Leaf pattern dishes are listed in their own category in this book.

Baker, Fluted, 2 Pt.	39.00
Bean Pot, Blue Blossom	195.00
Bowl, Fruit, Crocus	8.00
Bowl, Red Poppy, 6 In.	12.00
Bowl, Red Poppy, 7 In.	14.00
Bowl, Silhouette, 8 In.	24.00
Bowl, Silhouette, 9 In.	30.00
Butter, Cover, Zephyr, Red	65.00
Cake Plate, Poppy	20.00
Casserole, Cover, Westinghouse, Ridged	15.00
Casserole, Dark Brown, Oval, Small	15.00
Casserole, Westinghouse, Yellow	20.00
Coffee Urn, Black, Spigot	195.00
Coffeepot, Autumn Leaf, Electric	275.00
Coffeepot, Blue Bouquet, Banded	80.00
Coffeepot, Colonial	50.00
Coffeepot, Drip, Tulip, Filters, Box	100.00
Coffeepot, Poppy, S Lid	28.00
Coffeepot, Tulip	35.00
Coffeepot, Wildfire	50.00
Cookie Jar, Eva Zeisel	225.00
Cookie Jar, Eva Ziesel	140.00
Cookie Jar, Pretzel Handle, Chinese Red	95.00
Cookie Jar, Sundial, Red	175.00
Cookie Jar, Zeisel, Pink, Gold Trim	50.00
Cup & Saucer, Red Poppy	7.50
Decanter, Whiskey, Jewel Tea	150.00
Frame, Marmiate Chrome, Bakelite Handles, 8 x 10 In.	65.00
French Baker, Flute	20.00
Jar, Leftover, Cover, Dark Maroon, 7 1/2 In.	30.00
Jar, Leftover, Cover, Gray, Square	20.00
Jar, Leftover, Cover, Green, Square, 6 3/4 In.	25.00
Jar, Leftover, Cover, Light Yellow, Square, 8 In.	35.00
Jar, Pretzel, Crocus	130.00
Jug, Apple Green, Loop Handle	25.00
Jug, Ball, Maroon	25.00
Jug, Bow Knot, Red	45.00
Jug, Doughnut, Chinese Red, Large	65.00

Jug, No. 5, Poppy	30.00
Mug, Coffee, City Squire Motor Inn, Pedestal Base	25.00
Mug, Irish Coffee, Autumn Leaf, 4 Piece	380.00
Pepper Shaker, Medallion	15.00
Pitcher & Tankard Set, Monk	360.00
Pitcher, Ball, Autumn Leaf	20.00
Pitcher, Disk, Gray, Ice Lip	27.50
Pitcher, Doughnut	45.00
Pitcher, Rose Parade	25.00
Planter, Madonna	26.00
Plate & Cup, Blue Belle	18.00
Salt & Pepper, Dogwood	12.00
Salt & Pepper, Poppy, Handle	30.00
Soup, Dish, Poppy	20.00
Sugar & Creamer, Boston	45.00
Sugar & Creamer, Cameo Rose	22.00
Sugar & Creamer, Cover, Blue Blossom, Individual	145.00
Sugar, Cover, Poppy	35.00
Tea Set, Twin, Pansy Decal	140.00
Teapot, Airflow	150.00
Teapot, Airflow, Burgundy, 6 Cup	85.00
Teapot, Airflow, Chinese Red, 6 Cup	85.00
Teapot, Airflow, Cobalt Blue	55.00
Teapot, Airflow, Cobalt, Gold Trim, 6 Cup	67.50
Teapot, Aladdin, Cherry Red	95.00
Teapot, Aladdin, Yellow	45.00
Teapot, Albany, Mahogany Stand, Gold Trim, 6 Cup	65.00
Teapot, Albany, Turquoise, Gold Trim	40.00
Teapot, Automobile, Black	850.00
Teapot, Automobile, Blue	425.00
Teapot, Autumn Leaves, Flare	45.00
Teapot, Ball, Blue	55.00
Teapot, Baltimore, Leaf & Vine	225.00
Teapot, Baltimore, Maroon, Gold Trim, Label	52.00
Teapot, Birdcage Bottom, Cobalt Blue & Gold	80.00
Teapot, Birdcage, Maroon	195.00
Teapot, Boston, Maroon, Flower	75.00
Teapot, Boston, Old Rose, Gold Trim, 6 Cup	50.00
Teapot, Bow Knot, Pink	45.00
Teapot, Cameo Rose	35.00 To 55.00
Teapot, Cleveland, Emerald Green, Gold Trim, 6 Cup	45.00
Teapot, Cobalt, Streamline	65.00
Teapot, Doughnut, Cobalt Blue	125.00
Teapot, Doughnut, Maroon	200.00
Teapot, French Monterey, Gold	45.00
Teapot, French, 4 Cup	45.00
Teapot, Globe, No–Drip, Canary	50.00
Teapot, Grape, Black, Rhinestones, 6 Cup	250.00
Teapot, Grape, Ivory, Gold Trim, 6 Cup	65.00
Teapot, Grape, Rhinestones, Black	250.00
Teapot, Grape, Rhinestones, Cobalt	250.00
Teapot, Grape, Rhinestones, Ivory	125.00
Teapot, Gray, Gold Trim	55.00
Teapot, Hook, Cover, Cherry Red	125.00
Teapot, Los Angeles, Blue, Gold Trim, 6 Cup	45.00
Teapot, Los Angeles, Emerald Green, 8 Cup	40.00
Teapot, Los Angeles, Pink, 6 Cup	40.00
Teapot, Matte Black, Gold Rose	55.00
Teapot, McCormick, Maroon, Infuser	30.00
Teapot, Medallion	110.00
Teapot, Melody	200.00
Teapot, Melody, Poppy	185.00
Teapot, Musical, Yellow, Gold	55.00

Teapot, Nautilus, Cobalt, Gold Trim	225.00
Teapot, Nautilus, Turquoise, Gold Trim	165.00
Teapot, New York	55.00
Teapot, New York, Crocus	150.00
Teapot, New York, Yellow	40.00
Teapot, Newport	125.00
Teapot, Newport, Stick, Green	28.00
Teapot, No Drip, Canary	65.00
Teapot, Parade, Canary, Label	35.00
Teapot, Parade, Yellow, 6 Cup	30.00
Teapot, Philadelphia, Turquoise, Gold Trim, 6 Cup	45.00
Teapot, Polka Dot, Gold	40.00
Teapot, Reagan	65.00 To 95.00
Teapot, Red Pert, Cream & Sugar	75.00
Teapot, Rhythm, Ivory	44.00
Teapot, Saf–Handle, Cobalt Blue, Gold	85.00
Teapot, Silhouette, Tavern Banded	50.00
Teapot, Springtime, French	85.00
Teapot, Star, Turquoise, 6 Cup	35.00
Teapot, Streamline	75.00
Teapot, Streamline, Maroon, 6 Cup	85.00
Teapot, Sundial, Cobalt	87.50
Teapot, Sundial, Pink, Gold Trim	90.00
Teapot, Sundial, Red, 6 Cup	95.00
Teapot, Sunshine	225.00
Teapot, Surfside, Green	75.00
Teapot, Tip–Pot, Satin Black, Gold Trim	110.00
Teapot, Twin Spout, Maroon	55.00
Teapot, Windshield	195.00
Teapot, Windshield, Maroon, Gold	34.00 To 50.00
Teapot, Windshield, Polka–Dot	35.00
Teapot, Yellow	29.00
Tile, Tea, Taverne	120.00
Tumbler, Red Poppy	20.00
Water Server, Aristocrat, Tilt Lid, Green	140.00
Water Server, Cover, Blue, 9 In.	40.00
Water Server, Hercules, Cover, Cobalt	100.00
Water Server, Hotpoint, Stopper With Cork	85.00
Water Server, Yellow Lid, General Electric	25.00

HALLOWEEN is an ancient holiday that has been changed in the last 200 years. The jack-o'–lantern, witches on broomsticks, and orange decorations seem to be twentieth–century creations. Collectors started to become serious about collecting Halloween–related items in the late 1970s. The papier–mache decorations, now replaced by plastic, and old costumes are in demand.

Candleholder, Jack–O'–Lantern, Paper Insert, 3 1/4 In.	75.00
Candy Cantina, Witch, Germany, 5 In.	265.00
Candy Container, Black Cat, Molded Cardboard, Coil Neck, W. Germany, 5 In.	30.00
Candy Container, Black Cat, With Horn, Papier–Mache, Wire Neck, 7 In.	28.00
Candy Container, Hide Covered, Wooden Hooves, Pink Muzzle, 5 In.	225.00
Candy Container, Jack–O'–Lantern, Papier–Mache, Tissue Features, 5 In.	45.00
Candy Container, Jack–O'–Lantern, Slanted Eyes, Blue Glass, Bail	150.00
Candy Container, Pumpkin, Orange & Green, Papier–Mache, 6 In.	26.00
Candy Container, Scarecrow, Pumpkin Head, Celluloid	28.00
Candy Container, Witch, Composition, Germany, 4 1/2 In.	265.00
Candy Container, Witch, Red, Black, Papier–Mache, Cone, Germany, 7 1/2 In.	26.00
Carrier, Wire Handle, Cardboard, Orange, 7 In. ....*Illus*	5.00
Clapper, Paper, Lithograph, Tin	30.00
Clicker, 2 Wooden Balls Strike Witch, Cats Candle	45.00
Costume, Batfink, Unused, Collegeville, 1965	59.00
Costume, Bewitched, Flying Broom, 1965, Ben Cooper	49.00
Costume, Bugs Bunny, Ben Cooper, 1950	42.00

Halloween, Carrier, Wire Handle, Cardboard, Orange, 7 In.

Halloween, Mask, Donald Duck Type, Starched Cloth, 11 X 8 In.

Costume, Casper, Ben Cooper, 1963		39.00
Costume, Darth Vader, Ben Cooper		65.00
Costume, Doctor Doom, 1967, Aurora		95.00
Costume, Dr. Jekyll-Mr. Hyde, 2 Face Mask, Ben Cooper, Unused, 1964		98.00
Costume, Evil Knevil, Ben Cooper		50.00
Costume, Flying Nun, Box		145.00
Costume, Fred Flintsone, Ben Cooper, 1962		42.00
Costume, Garrison's Garillas, 1967, Ben Cooper		69.00
Costume, Green Hornet, Ben Cooper, Box		250.00
Costume, Joker, From Batman		250.00
Costume, Jughead, Collegeville, 1960		89.00
Costume, Kung Fu, Face Mask, Illustration On Chest, 1973		17.50
Costume, Marie Osmond, Box		15.00 To 35.00
Costume, Mork, Box		20.00
Costume, Phantom of The Opera, Purple Silk, Collegeville, Box, 1970		59.00
Costume, Rat Patrol, Ben Cooper, 1966		59.00
Costume, Samantha From Bewitched TV Show, Ben Cooper, 1965		49.00
Costume, Secret Agent, Unused, 1965, Box		29.00
Costume, Skeleton, Box		25.00
Costume, Star Wars, Yoda, Ben Cooper, Box		50.00
Costume, Suzy Spy, Unused, Box, 1965		29.00
Costume, T-Shirt, Alien, Bloody Head Coming Out of Front of Shirt		75.00
Costume, T. H. E. Cat, Synthetic Fabric, Black Hood, Collegeville, 1966		59.00
Costume, Tarzan, Ben Cooper, 1967		39.00
Costume, Woody Woodpecker, Collegeville, 1950		39.99
Costume, Wyatt Earp, Box		50.00
Costume, Zorro, Box		48.00
Crepe Paper, Witches, Pumpkins, Girls & Witch Scenes, 1 Yard		15.00
Devil, Papier-Mache, 7 In.		28.00
Figurine, Cat, Black, Pressed Cardboard		17.00
Figurine, Devil, Cat, Pumpkin, Chenille, 3 In., 3 Piece		20.00
Figurine, For Tree, Chalkware, Fruit, Devil On Body, Bisque Head, 6 Piece		110.00
Figurine, Girl, With Jack-O'-Lantern, Bisque, Germany		65.00
Figurine, Witch, Riding Broom, Metal, Double Sided		165.00
Game, Cat & Witch, Whitman, 1940s		50.00
Game, Dumbskull		28.00
Garland, Witches, Bats, Cardboard, 7 In.		95.00
Goblin Head, Cutout Features, Painted Mustache & Eyebrows, Inside Candle		495.00
Hat, Cardboard		8.00
Hat, Derby, Box		42.00
Hat, Party, Orange Cardboard, Black Witch Die-Cut		8.00
Jack-O'-Lantern, Black Face, Wall Decoration, 1930s		75.00
Jack-O'-Lantern, Double Face, Papier-Mache		55.00
Jack-O'-Lantern, Face Insert, Papier-Mache, 1930s		56.00
Jack-O'-Lantern, Metal, Horn Nose, 6 In.		45.00
Jack-O'-Lantern, Painted Eyes & Mouth, Papier-Mache, 3 1/2 In.		58.00

Halloween, Noisemaker, Red, Rounded,

3 1/2 In.; Halloween, Noisemaker, Blue &

White, Flat, 3 1/2 In.

◆◆◆◆◆◆◆◆◆◆◆◆◆◆◆◆◆◆◆◆◆◆

We like this answering machine message we just heard:
"Please leave a message at
the beep. The person now at
home does not speak English."
It is plausible and explains why
the house is occupied yet the
answering machine is on.

◆◆◆◆◆◆◆◆◆◆◆◆◆◆◆◆◆◆◆◆◆◆

Jack-O'-Lantern, Papier-Insert, Germany, 2 1/4 In.	45.00
King Kong, Unused, Ben Cooper, 1965	59.00
Lantern, Black Cat's Head, Germany, 4 In.	165.00
Lantern, Black Cat, Green Insert Eyes, Red Mouth, 3 In.	155.00
Mask, Bashful, Cloth, c.1938	35.00
Mask, Donald Duck Type, Starched Cloth, 11 x 8 In. ....*Illus*	5.00
Mask, Donald Duck, Long Bill	55.00
Mask, Little Black Sambo, 1950s	50.00
Mask, Morticia, 1964	45.00
Mask, Planet of Apes, Molded Hair, Latex, Full Head, 1974	125.00
Mask, Skull, Stiffened Gauze	5.00
Mask, Snow White, 1940s, 10 In., Pair	95.00
Napkins, Paper, 10 Piece	12.00
Noisemaker, Blue & White, Flat, 3 1/2 In. ....*Illus*	18.00
Noisemaker, Jack-O'-Lantern	15.00
Noisemaker, Red, Rounded, 3 1/2 In. ....*Illus*	18.00
Noisemaker, Tin Lithograph	17.50
Ornament, Dracula, c.1939, 4 In.	10.00
Plaque, Black Faced Jack-O'-Lantern, Germany, 1930s	75.00
Pumpkin, Papier-Mache, 6 In.	26.00
Pumpkin, Papier-Mache, Orange	45.00
Rattle, Face, Tin	6.00
Salt & Pepper, Witch & Pumpkin	22.50
Skeleton, Cardboard, Jointed	15.00
Skeleton, Fold-Out, Black & White, H. E. Luhrs, 24 In.	2.00
Sparkler, Witch's Head, Tin	30.00
Tablecloth & Napkins, Paper, 1950	10.00
Tambourine, Black Cat, Orange	22.50
Tambourine, Metal	18.00 To 30.00
Tambourine, Metal, 6 In	25.00
Tambourine, Pumpkin Face, Paper Over Wood Frame, Germany	130.00
Toy, Haunted House, Marx	675.00
Trolley Car, Tin Lithograph, Windup, Scary Things, US Zone, Germany, 4 In.	35.00
Witch, Orange & Black, Tissue Pull-Up Arms, 8 In.	40.00
Witch, Papier-Mache, 7 1/2 In.	26.00

HAMPSHIRE pottery was made in Keene, New Hampshire, between 1871
and 1923. Hampshire developed a line of colored glazed wares as early as
1883, including a Royal Worcester-type pink, olive green, blue, and
mahogany. Pieces are marked with the printed mark or the impressed
name *Hampshire Pottery* or *J.S.T. & Co., Keene, N.H.* Many pieces were
marked with city names and sold as souvenirs.

Bowl, Artichoke, Blue, Signed	140.00
Bowl, Dog Feeding, For My Dog, Rust Glaze	145.00
Bowl, Molded Buds & Leaves, Green Glaze, Marked, 3 x 10 In.	275.00
Candleholder, Hooded, Green, 7 In.	100.00

Handel, Lamp, 9-Sided Slag Glass Shade,
Trifid Base, 27 In.

Handel, Lamp, Hanging, Reverse Painted,
Flowering Branches, 25 In.

Handel, Lamp, Orange
Oriental Poppies

Handel, Lamp, Reverse Painted,
Dutch Landscape, Blue Ground, 23 In.

Handel, Lamp, Reverse Painted,
Ships In Harbor, Tree Trunk, 24 In.

Candleholder, Matte Green, Handle, 6 1/2 In.	175.00
Ewer, Matte Green, 11 In.	130.00
Inkwell, Cover, Matte Green Glaze, 1902, 5 x 5 1/4 In.	302.50
Paperweight, Matte Green	175.00 To 225.00
Pitcher, Art Nouveau, 11 In.	70.00
Pitcher, Feathered Matte Green Glaze, Scroll Handle, 11 3/4 In.	88.00
Pitcher, Green Glaze, Pointy Spout, Marked, 9 1/2 In.	247.00
Sconce, Candle, Hooded	200.00
Tea Set, Gold Letters, Tampa, Florida, Gloss Olive	95.00
Vase, Arts & Crafts, Matte Green, 7 In.	125.00
Vase, Feathered Matte Green Glaze, 3 Handles, Marked, 5 In.	180.00
Vase, Leaves & Buds, 7 In.	302.50
Vase, Leaves & Buds, Matte Green, 8 1/2 x 6 3/4 In.	525.00
Vase, Red To Green Textured Matte Glaze, Marked, 6 In.	195.00

HANDEL glass was made by Philip Handel working in Meriden, Connecticut, from 1885 and in New York City from 1893 to 1933. The firm made art glass and other types of lamps. Handel shades were made not only of leaded glass in a style reminiscent of Tiffany but also of reverse painted glass. Handel also made vases and other glass objects.

Bookends, Arched Formal Doorway, Bronze, Green Patina, 7 1/2 In., Pair	445.00
Bowl, Pink Flowers, Gold Trim, Signed, 8 In.	350.00
Chandelier, Colored Fruits On Apron, Green Mottled Glass, Leaded, 25 1/4 In.	4950.00
Humidor, 7 1/2 In.	660.00
Lamp, 6–Panel, Amber Slag Glass Shade, Repeating Border Design, 23 In.	825.00
Lamp, 8–Paneled Slag Glass Shade, Woven Grillwork, Metal Base, Signed, 20 In.	2310.00
Lamp, 9–Sided Slag Glass Shade, Trifid Base, 27 In. ....*Illus*	3300.00
Lamp, Boudoir, Glass Dome Shade, Painted Landscape, Metal Base, 12 1/2 In.	1100.00
Lamp, Boudoir, Poppy, Domed Teroma Glass Shade, Yellow Interior, 14 In.	3190.00
Lamp, Boudoir, Reverse Painted, Dome Shade	1250.00
Lamp, Boudoir, Scene, Hexagonal	3300.00
Lamp, Desk, Bronze Base, Fold–Down, Cased Shade, Signed	850.00
Lamp, Desk, Curved Cylindrical Shade, Chipped Ice In Dark Green, Zigzag Design	2400.00
Lamp, Desk, Reverse Painted Peacocks	2925.00
Lamp, Desk, Reverse Painted, Landscape Scene, Teroma Finish	1950.00
Lamp, Dragon, Hand Painted, Top Dome Shade, Gold Accents, 16 In.	880.00
Lamp, Greek Key Pattern, Stained Glass	1000.00
Lamp, Hanging, Reverse Painted, Flowering Branches, 25 In. ....*Illus*	2090.00
Lamp, Model 7035a, Reverse Painted & Enameled Glass, 24 3/4 In.	2200.00
Lamp, Mushroom, Floral Frosted Shade, Brass Handled Base, 12 In.	650.00
Lamp, Orange Oriental Poppies ....*Illus*	1350.00
Lamp, Overlay Palm Scene, 16 In.	3600.00
Lamp, Reverse Painted, Dutch Landscape, Blue Ground, 23 In. ....*Illus*	8250.00
Lamp, Reverse Painted, Evergreens	8800.00
Lamp, Reverse Painted, Reading, Bronzed Metal Base, 23 In.	3520.00
Lamp, Reverse Painted, Ships In Harbor, Tree Trunk, 24 In. ....*Illus*	6050.00
Lamp, Reverse Painted, Spring Fields Scene, Fence, Signed	6000.00
Lamp, Reverse Pastel Scenic Shade, Signed	7700.00
Lamp, Reverse–Painted Domed Shade, Woodland Scene, Silver–Metal Base, 24 In. ...	6050.00
Lamp, Reverse–Painted Frosted Shade, River Landscape, Bronzed Metal, 22 In.	775.00
Lamp, Reverse–Painted Shade, Woodland Scene, No. 6754, c.1920, 25 In.	7150.00
Lamp, River Scene, Chipped Ice, Bronze Base, 34 In.	5500.00
Lamp, Snow Scene, Chipped Ice, Signed, 14 In.	3900.00
Lamp, Woodland Scene, Pond, Signed	5800.00
Shade, Hanging, Filigree, Bronze Ornate Crown & Chains, 27 In.	3950.00
Shade, Reverse Painted, Mushroom	1500.00
Table, Reverse–Painted Fall Landscape, Bronzed Metal Vase, Signed, 24 In.	6000.00
Vase, Palm Scene Overlay, Sunset Colors, 16 In.	3500.00
Vase, Scenic, No. 4214, 10 3/4 In.	2900.00
Vase, Teroma, Broggi, 8 In.	1450.00

HARDWARE, see Architectural category.

HARKER Pottery Company of East Liverpool, Ohio, was founded by Benjamin Harker in 1840. The company made many types of pottery but by the Civil War was making quantities of yellowware from native clays. They also made Rockingham–type brown–glazed pottery and whiteware. The plant was moved to Chester, West Virginia, in 1931. Dinnerwares were made and sold nationally. In 1971 the company was sold to Jeanette Glass Company and all operations ceased in 1972. For more information, see *Kovels' Depression Glass & American Dinnerware Price List.*

Bowl, Vegetable, Colonial Lady	22.00
Cake Plate, Cameo Rose, Blue, Square, 3 Individual Plates, 4 Piece	35.00
Cake Plate, Laurelton, Green	5.00
Cake Plate, Petit Point Rose	4.00
Cake Plate, Wild Rose	5.00
Cake Set, Wild Rose, With Server, 7 Piece	20.00

Casserole, Cameo Rose, Blue	28.00
Casserole, Cover, Double, Petit Point Rose	10.00
Dinner Set, Cameoware, Dogwood Blossom, 45 Piece	75.00
Mug, Hound Handle	25.00
Pie Plate, Petit Point Rose	6.00
Pitcher, White Rose, Cover	30.00
Plate, Child's, Cameoware, Sailboats, Pink	4.00
Plate, Petit Point Rose, 8 In.	4.00
Rolling Pin, Basket of Fruits & Flowers	75.00
Rolling Pin, Cameo Rose	65.00
Rolling Pin, Mexican & Burro	68.00
Rolling Pin, Petit Point Rose	88.00
Salad Fork & Spoon, Cameo Rose	20.00
Salt & Pepper, Cameo Rose, Blue	12.00
Serving Set, Amy, Rolling Pin, Scoop, Pie Server, Salad Fork, Knife, 5 Piece.	175.00
Table Set, Cameoware, Yellow Daisy, 5 Piece	20.00

HARLEQUIN dinnerware was produced by the Homer Laughlin Company from 1938 to 1964, and sold without trademark by the F. W. Woolworth Co. It has a concentric ring design like Fiesta, but the rings are separated from the rim by a plain margin. Cup handles are triangular in shape. For more information, see *Kovels' Depression Glass & American Dinnerware Price List.*

Ashtray, Basketweave, Turquoise	20.00
Ashtray, Basketweave, Yellow	25.00
Ashtray, Rose	60.00
Butter, Cover, Spruce Green	95.00
Butter, Cover, Yellow	55.00
Casserole, Rose	85.00
Casserole, Yellow	75.00
Creamer, Novelty, Maroon	20.00
Creamer, Red	10.00
Cup & Saucer, Medium Green	30.00
Cup, Spruce Green	3.50
Eggcup, Cobalt Blue, Double	55.00
Eggcup, Forest Green, Double	30.00
Eggcup, Light Green, Double	37.00
Eggcup, Maroon, Single	15.00
Eggcup, Red, Single	30.00
Eggcup, Turquoise, Double	10.00
Figurine, Cat, Yellow	55.00
Figurine, Duck, Yellow, 1940s	79.50
Figurine, Fish, Green	70.00
Figurine, Lamb, Green	70.00
Figurine, Penguin, Maroon	70.00 To 75.00
Jug, Gray, 22 Oz.	130.00
Nut Dish, Mauve	10.00
Nut Dish, Red	6.00 To 10.00
Pitcher, Ball, Mauve Blue	50.00
Pitcher, Milk, Turquoise	16.00
Pitcher, Tangerine	38.00
Plate, Dark Green, 7 In.	5.00
Sugar, Chartreuse	12.00
Sugar, Red	12.00
Sugar, Turquoise	9.00
Tumbler, Maroon	50.00
Tumbler, Mauve Blue	40.00
Tumbler, Yellow	35.00

HATPIN HOLDERS were needed when hatpins were fashionable from 1860 to 1920. The large, heavy hat required special long–shanked pins to hold it in place. The hatpin holder resembles a large saltshaker, but it often has no opening at the bottom as a shaker does. Hatpin holders were made of all types of ceramics and metal. Look for other pieces under the names of specific manufacturers.

Blue Band At Center, Painted Florals, Dotted Center, c.1875	245.00
Corset Shape, Cobalt Blue Band, Hand Painted Flowers, Sterling Silver Rim	245.00
Ice Green Glass	100.00
Oriental People Scene, Black Satin, England, 4 3/4 In.	65.00
Pottery, Shaded Brown Glaze, G. H. Richards, London, 1890	110.00
Red Glass	90.00
Red Roses, Black Finish, England, 5 In.	55.00
Rose, Victorian, Czechoslovakia	70.00
Roses, Gold & Green, Cobalt Blue, 4 In.	75.00
Scenic, Porcelain	35.00

HATPINS were popular from 1860 to 1920. The long pin, often over four inches, was used to hold the hat in place on the hair. The tops of the pins were made of all materials, from solid gold and real gemstones to ceramics and glass. Be careful to buy original hatpins and not recent pieces made by altering old buttons.

Abalone Shell	30.00
Black Glass	20.00
Black Wooden Ball	5.00
Blue Rhinestones, 8 1/4 In.	15.00
Bulldog Top, Sterling Silver, 2 1/4 In.	75.00
Cattails, Carnival Glass	43.00
Deep Amethyst, Carnival Glass	35.00
Diamond Shape, Victorian, Sparkling Stones	50.00 To 75.00
Escutcheon Head, Lacy Brass Filigree, 9 In.	45.00
Grape & Cable, Amethyst, Northwood	135.00
Indian, Sterling Silver	220.00
Roosters, White, Carnival Glass	65.00
Seashell	20.00
Woman's Head, Art Nouveau, 10K Yellow Gold	235.00
Woman's Profile Relief, Hollow, Sterling Silver	95.00

HAVILAND china has been made in Limoges, France, since 1842. The factory was started by the Haviland Brothers of New York City. Pieces are marked *H & Co., Haviland & Co.,* or *Theodore Haviland.* It is possible to match existing sets of dishes through dealers who specialize in Haviland china. Other factories worked in the town of Limoges making a similar chinaware. These porcelains are listed in this book under Limoges.

HAVILAND & CO.

Box, Dog Shape, 6 1/2 In.	65.00
Butter, Cover, Gold Band	45.00
Butter, Cover, Harrison Rose, Drainer	115.00
Cake Set, Birds & Pink Floral, Scalloped, Gold Rim, 11 Piece	355.00
Chocolate Pot, Flowers, Pink, Green, 9 In.	95.00
Chop Plate, 1910, 13 In.	40.00
Cup & Saucer, Pink Flowers, Green Leaves	25.00
Cup & Saucer, With Dessert Plate, Pink Wild Roses, Gold Trim, 3 Piece	49.00
Dinner Set, Service For 12, Floral Pattern	700.00
Dish, Pudding, White, Gold Trim, 2 Piece	350.00
Gravy Boat, Oval, Blue Flowers, Ribbons	50.00
Hair Receiver, Ranson	125.00
Pitcher, Angels Both Sides, Gold, Oval, 8 In.	125.00
Pitcher, Water, Flowers, Gold Trim, 1860s	85.00
Platter, Fish, Bordeaux Border, 21 In.	110.00
Soup, Dish, Blackberry	25.00
Sugar & Creamer, Multicolored Flowers Sprays, Gold Handles	90.00
Syrup, Anchor Handle	85.00
Teapot, Black Bands, Gold Trim	125.00
Tureen, Cover, Arcade, Birds	110.00
Tureen, Cover, Child's, Colored Flowers, Gold Trim, 8 In.	95.00

*Head Vase, Red Stone Earrings, Brown,
Green, Yellow, 6 1/4 In.*

Vase, Girl's Head Portrait, Limoges–Glaze, Pottery, 12 In. 750.00

HAWKES cut glass was made by T. G. Hawkes & Company of Corning, New York, founded in 1880. The firm cut glass blanks made at other glassworks until 1962. Many pieces are marked with the trademark, a trefoil ring enclosing a fleur–de–lis and two hawks. Cut glass by other manufacturers is listed under either the factory name or in the general Cut Glass category.

Bowl, Chrysanthemum, 12 In.	880.00
Bowl, Grecian, Turned–In Rim, Square, 8 In.	500.00
Bowl, Hat Shape, Gravic Cut, Blackberry Design, 6 In.	95.00
Bowl, Hobstars, 8 In.	110.00
Candy Dish, Cover, Millicent, Sterling Silver Knob, Signed, 10 In.	355.00
Carafe, Strawberry Diamond, Signed	275.00
Compote, English Strawberry Diamond, Signed, 8 In.	170.00
Decanter, Roemer, Handles	1400.00
Decanter, Whiskey, Crystal, Faceted Square Stopper, Flared, 10 In.	165.00
Dish, Hobstar & Cane, 3 Sections, Triangular, 6 In.	225.00
Frame, Picture, Circle of Hobstars On Rim, Oval, 7 x 5 1/4 In.	355.00
Frame, Picture, Cut Glass, Oval, 5 x 7 In.	165.00
Goblet, Iris, Gravic Cut	325.00
Lemonade Set, Engraved Vintage Etching, Optic Panel, Signed, 6 Piece	350.00
Nappy, Clover Shape, Stem of Clover Forms Handle, Signed, 5 x 4 In.	95.00
Nut Cup, Intaglio Flower Basket Design, Set of 6	130.00
Plate, Thistle, Intaglio, Signed, 7 In.	440.00
Powder Box, Hobstar & Fan, 6 In.	325.00
Punch Cup, 7 Panels of Hobstars, Pedestal, Signed	200.00
Tray, 2 Medallions In Diamonds, Birds, Leaves, Oval, Signed, 10 1/2 In.	465.00
Tray, Holland, 13 In.	1300.00
Tray, Ice Cream, Brilliant Cut, 8 x 14 1/2 In.	550.00
Tray, Iris, Signed, 11 In	1000.00
Vase, Bird, Branches & Flowers, Amber, Signed, 8 1/4 In.	250.00
Vase, Brunswick, 8 1/4 In.	120.00
Vase, Engraved Vine & Leaves, Tricorner, Signed, 10 In.	225.00
Vase, Etched Leaves & Vines, Signed, 13 In.	175.00
Vase, Notched Flaring Rim, Horizontal Cuts, Star–Cut Base, 16 In.	285.00
Vase, Pedestal, Signed, 13 1/2 x 10 In.	375.00
Vase, Queen's, 12 In.	750.00
Vase, Queen's, Trumpet Shape, Signed, 10 1/2 In.	360.00
Vase, Trumpet, Brunswick, 14 In.	525.00
Vase, Trumpet, Navarre, Knob & Hobstar Base, Signed, 16 In.	1795.00
Water Set, Iris, 6 Piece	675.00

HEAD VASES, generally showing a woman from the shoulders up, were used by florists primarily in the 1950s and 1960s. Made in a variety of sizes and often decorated with imitation jewelry and other lifelike accessories, the vases were manufactured in Japan and the U.S.A. Less elaborate examples were made as early as the 1930s. Religious themes, babies, and animals are also common subjects.

African Native, Gold Headdress	25.00
Art Deco, 7 1/2 x 7 1/2 In.	49.00
Asian Woman, Gold Skin	55.00
Baby	16.00
Boy, White, Gold Trim, Cole Book	30.00
Girl	19.00
Jean	35.00
Little Girl, Pigtails, Napco	25.00
Madonna	15.00
Nun	20.00
Red Stone Earrings, Brown, Green, Yellow, 6 1/4 In. ....*Illus*	40.00
Sandy	35.00
Sven	80.00
Wall Pocket, Girl With Doll	22.00
Woman, All White, 10 In.	16.00
Woman, Big Hat	24.00
Woman, Blue Hat	25.00
Woman, Hand & Pearl Jewelry	30.00
Woman, Pink Hat	25.00

HEINTZ ART Metal Shop made jewelry, copper, silver, and brass in Buffalo, New York, from 1906 to 1935, when a new company name was taken and the mark became *Silvercrest.* The most popular items with collectors today are the copper desk sets and vases made with applied silver designs.

Bookends, Fir Cone & Needles, Sterling Silver Overlay, Green Bronze	95.00
Compote, Pedestal	345.00
Console Set, Weeds, Thin Leaves, Marked, Bowl 9 1/2 In., 3 Piece	465.00
Desk Set, Original Calendar Insert, 3 Piece	150.00
Frame, Picture, Greek Key	195.00
Humidor, Trophy Design, Handles, Sterling Silver On Bronze, 10 x 8 1/4 In.	165.00
Inkwell, Curled Feet, Brown Patina	195.00
Lamp, Geometric, Secessionist, Silver On Bronze, Mushroom Shape, 9 3/4 In.	467.00
Lamp, Maple Leaves, Helmet Shade, Sterling Silver On Bronze, 15 x 12 In.	770.00
Letter Holder, 2 Sections	95.00
Tray, Match Holder Center, Stylized Lotus, Silver Overlay, 6 3/4 In.	95.00
Vase, Bud, Bronze & Silver, 12 In.	150.00
Vase, Bud, Silver Overlay Design, Arts & Crafts	195.00
Vase, Leaves, Sterling Silver On Bronze, 8 1/2 x 3 In.	250.00
Vase, Montclair Gun Club, Silver On Bronze, Cylindrical	125.00
Vase, Overlaid Weeds, Sterling Silver On Bronze, Bottle Shape, 6 x 3 1/2 In.	250.00
Vase, Peacock On A Branch, Sterling Silver On Bronze, 10 x 3 In.	195.00
Vase, Silver Overlay, Tapered, 10 1/2 In.	250.00
Vase, Silver Overlay, Tapered, 12 In.	300.00
Vase, Sterling Silver Mistletoe Overlay, 12 In.	130.00
Vase, Sterling Silver Pussy Willows, Cylindrical, 10 In.	125.00

HEISEY glass was made from 1896 to 1957 in Newark, Ohio, by A. H. Heisey and Co., Inc. The Imperial Glass Company of Bellaire, Ohio, bought some of the molds and the rights to the trademark. Some Heisey patterns have been made by Imperial since 1960. After 1968, they stopped using the *H* trademark. Heisey used romantic names for colors, such as *Sahara.* Do not confuse color and pattern names. The Custard Glass and Ruby Glass categories may also include some Heisey pieces.

Antarctic, Candlestick, 7 In., Pair	125.00
Arcadia, Goblet, 10 Oz.	20.00
Arch, Tumbler, Cobalt Blue, 8 Oz.	65.00
Aristocrat, Candlestick, 1–Light, Prisms, Bobeche, 16 In.	255.00
Athena, Candlestick, 2–Light, Pair	125.00

Athena, Plate, Sandwich, 14 In.	55.00
Barbara Fritchie, Brandy, 3/4 Oz.	50.00
Barbara Fritchie, Cordial, 1 Oz.	65.00
Barcelonia, Cocktail, 3 Oz.	16.00
Barcelonia, Sherbet, 6 Oz.	15.00
Barcelonia, Tumbler, Footed, 12 Oz.	20.00
Beaded Swag, Butter, Cover, Opalescent	45.00
Beaded Swag, Goblet	22.00
Beaded Swag, Pitcher	65.00
Beaded Swag, Table Set, Gold Trim, 4 Piece	315.00
Beaded Swag, Toothpick, Ruby Flash, Souvenir	55.00
Beaded Swag, Water Set, White Opaque, Floral Design, 7 Piece	395.00
Black, Bowl, Salad, Experimental	1800.00
Bob White, Goblet, Balboa Cut	45.00
Bonnet, Basket, Pedestal, 16 In.	250.00
Cape Cod, Plate, Birthday, 72 Hole	160.00
Carcassone, Goblet, Empress Etch, Sahara, Footed, 11 Oz.	17.50
Carcassone, Goblet, Footed, 9 Oz.	10.00
Cascade, Candlestick, 3–Light, Pair	80.00
Cathedral, Vase, Straight, 9 In.	65.00
Chintz, Plate, Square, 7 In.	20.00
Coarse Rib, Plate, 6 In.	22.50
Coarse Rib, Plate, Flamingo, 4 1/2 In.	35.00
Coarse Rib, Punch Cup	7.00
Coarse Rib, Tankard, 3–Pint	75.00
Cobel, Cocktail Shaker, 1 Qt.	25.00
Cobel, Cocktail Shaker, Motorboat Etch, 2 Qt.	270.00
Colonial Star, Plate, Plate, 8 1/2 In.	25.00
Colonial, Basket, Floral Etched, 7 In.	225.00
Colonial, Basket, Windsor Cut, 8 In.	310.00
Colonial, Butter, Cover	70.00
Colonial, Cocktail, 2 1/2 Oz.	25.00
Colonial, Dish, Ice Cream, Footed	75.00
Colonial, Jam Jar, Etched	50.00
Colonial, Mustard, Marked	40.00
Colonial, Plate, 4 1/2 In.	8.00
Colonial, Plate, 7 In.	18.05
Colonial, Sugar, Hotel	20.00
Colonial, Toothpick	30.00
Colonial, Tumbler, 8 Oz., 4 Piece.	55.00
Console Set, Pink, Silver Overlay	135.00
Continental, Eggcup	7.50
Continental, Sherbet	8.00
Continental, Toothpick	75.00
Country Club, Soda, Winchester Etch, 14 Oz.	95.00
Coventry, Cocktail, 3 Oz.	11.50
Crossed Lined Flute, Vase, 5 In.	35.00
Crystolite, Candlestick, 3–Light, Pair	45.00
Crystolite, Candy Dish, Cover, Round	40.00
Crystolite, Cheese Dish, Footed, 5 1/2 In.	12.00
Crystolite, Cigarette Holder, Round, Footed	20.00 To 25.00
Crystolite, Compote, 5 1/4 In.	15.00
Crystolite, Cordial, 1 Oz.	70.00
Crystolite, Cruet, 3 Oz.	30.00
Crystolite, Cup & Saucer	30.00
Crystolite, Lamp, Globe, Electric	160.00
Crystolite, Mustard, Cover	42.00
Crystolite, Punch Set, Bowl, Ladle, 12 Cups, Undertray–18 In.	325.00
Crystolite, Relish, 3 Sections, 8 In.	12.50
Crystolite, Relish, 3 Sections, Oval, 13 In.	40.00
Crystolite, Relish, 4 Sections, 9 In.	18.00
Crystolite, Relish, 5 Sections	25.00
Crystolite, Sugar & Creamer	40.00

Crystolite, Sugar & Creamer, Tray, Individual	50.00
Crystolite, Vase, Flared, 4 In.	75.00
Cut Block, Creamer, Ruby Stain, Individual	30.00
Danish Princess, Goblet, Cut, 9 Oz.	45.00
Danish Princess, Sherbet, Etched, Cut, 6 Oz.	20.00
Danish Princess, Sugar & Creamer, Cut	85.00
Diamond Optic, Goblet, Flamingo, 5 1/2 In.	12.00
Dolphin Cut, Lamp, Flamingo	225.00
Duck, Flower Frog, 3 1/2 In.	100.00
Duquesne, Champagne, Saucer, Chintz, 5 Oz., 4 Piece	50.00
Duquesne, Cordial, Chintz Etch	40.00
Duquesne, Goblet, Botticelli Cut	85.00
Duquesne, Tumbler, Juice, Tangerine	100.00
Duquesne, Tumbler, Soda, Tangerine	125.00
Eileen, Sugar & Creamer, Floral Cutting	105.00
Elephant, Mug, Amber	650.00
Empire, Candlestick, 3–Light, Center Plug, Pair	495.00
Empress, Ashtray, Cobalt Blue	260.00
Empress, Bowl, Nasturtium, Flamingo, 7 1/2 In.	140.00
Empress, Candlestick, 6 In., Pair	75.00
Empress, Cup & Saucer, Flamingo, Demitasse	48.00
Empress, Ice Bucket, Antarctic Etch	80.00
Empress, Jug, Saraha, 3 Pt.	200.00
Empress, Mustard, Cover, Flamingo	60.00
Empress, Nut Dish, Dolphin, Footed	22.00
Empress, Pitcher, Dolphin Feet, Sahara	300.00
Empress, Plate, Tangerine, 6 In.	85.00
Empress, Relish, Alexandrite, Triplex, 10 In.	220.00
Empress, Relish, Triplex, Orchid Etch, 7 In.	45.00
Empress, Sugar & Creamer, Dolphin Footed	30.00
Empress, Sugar & Creamer, Sahara	40.00
Empress, Sugar & Creamer, Tray	85.00
Enchantress, Goblet, Cut, 10 Oz.	55.00
Essex, Candlestick, 9 In., Pair	260.00
Fairacre, Goblet, Flamingo, 5 Piece	125.00
Fancy Loop, Cocktail	32.00
Fancy Loop, Jar, Potpourri, Covered	275.00
Fancy Loop, Tankard, Silver Plated Lid, 1 1/2 Qt.	145.00
Fancy Loop, Toothpick	60.00
Fancy Loop, Toothpick, Emerald Green	95.00 To 115.00
Fandango, Toothpick	22.00
Figurine, Asiatic Pheasant, 10 1/2 In.	230.00 To 275.00
Figurine, Bull, 4 In.	1095.00
Figurine, Chick, Head Down, 1 In.	75.00
Figurine, Chick, Head Up, 1 In.	75.00
Figurine, Colt, Rearing, 3 3/4 In.	195.00
Figurine, Colt, Standing, 5 In.	95.00
Figurine, Cygnet, 2 1/8 In.	210.00
Figurine, Elephant, 4 1/2 In.	210.00
Figurine, Elephant, 4 In.	160.00
Figurine, Gazelle, 11 In.	1350.00
Figurine, Giraffe, Head Back	135.00
Figurine, Giraffe, Head Back, 11 In.	200.00
Figurine, Giraffe, Head Forward, 11 In.	200.00 To 240.00
Figurine, Goose, Wings Up, 6 1/2 In.	105.00
Figurine, Hen, 4 1/4 In.	475.00
Figurine, Madonna, Frosted	65.00
Figurine, Mallard, Wind Half Up, 5 In.	185.00
Figurine, Mallard, Wings Up, 6 3/4 In.	175.00
Figurine, Pouter Pigeon, 6 1/4 In.	600.00
Figurine, Ringneck Pheasant	115.00
Figurine, Ringneck Pheasant, 4 3/4 In.	125.00
Figurine, Rooster, 5 5/8 In.	495.00

Figurine, Rooster, Fighting, 8 In. 165.00
Figurine, Scotty, 3 1/2 In. ....90.00 To 135.00
Figurine, Sparrow, 2 1/4 In. ....85.00 To 105.00
Figurine, Swan, Crystolite, 7 In. 45.00
Fish, Bookends, 6 5/8 In. 225.00
Fish, Candlestick 160.00
Flame, Candlestick, 2–Light, 9 3/4 In. 60.00
Flamingo, Relish, 3 Sections, 12 In. 35.00
Flamingo, Sugar & Creamer 45.00
Flat Panel, Cigar Jar, Stopper 85.00
Flat Panel, Cruet, 4 Oz. 50.00
Frontenac, Goblet, Stemmed, Marked, 9 Piece 275.00
Gascony, Candlestick, Moongleam 290.00
Gascony, Tumbler, Footed, Tangerine, 10 Oz. 240.00
Gascony, Tumbler, Soda, Footed, Sahara, 5 Oz. 30.00
Gascony, Tumbler, Tangerine, 10 Oz. 200.00
Gascony, Wine, Cobalt Blue, 2 1/2 Oz. 95.00
Gascony, Wine, Tangerine, 2 1/2 Oz. 160.00
Grape Cluster, Candleholder, Pair 300.00
Grecian Border, Ice Tub, Handle, Large 130.00
Grecian Border, Sherbet, Low Foot, 8 Piece 100.00
Greek Key, Compote, Jelly, Handle, 5 In. 52.00
Greek Key, Cruet, Oil, 6 Oz. 100.00
Greek Key, Dish, Chip & Dip 195.00
Greek Key, Punch Bowl & Stand 295.00
Greek Key, Punch Cup, Set of 6 .... 79.00
Greek Key, Sherbet, 4 Oz. 12.50
Greek Key, Tumbler, 3 Footed, 8 Oz. 50.00
Heisey Rose, Cocktail, Oyster, 3 1/2 Oz. 105.00
Horsehead, Bookends 235.00
Horsehead, Cocktail, Sherry 250.00
Ipswich, Bowl, Floral, 11 In. 65.00
Ipswich, Console Set, Prisms & Inserts, 3 Piece, Bowl, 11 1/2 In. 375.00
Ipswich, Goblet, 10 Oz. 24.00
Ipswich, Sugar & Creamer 45.00
Jamestown, Sherry, 1 1/2 Oz. 30.00
Jamestown, Tumbler, Iced Tea, Footed, Barcelona Cut, 12 Oz., 4 Piece 65.00
Jamestown, Wine, 2 Oz. 145.00
Lariat, Ashtray, Coaster, 4 In. 4.50
Lariat, Bowl, Crimped, 12 In. 45.00
Lariat, Bowl, Mayonnaise, Underplate, Loop 10.00
Lariat, Candlestick, 2–Light, Silver Overlay, Pair 70.00
Lariat, Candlestick, 3–Light 35.00
Lariat, Candy Dish, Cover, Etched 95.00
Lariat, Chamberstick, With Globe 50.00
Lariat, Champagne, 4 Oz. 17.50
Lariat, Console Set, Gardenia, Fruit Etch, 3 Piece 50.00
Lariat, Cordial, Moonglo, 1 Oz. 110.00
Lariat, Cup & Saucer 50.00
Lariat, Plate, 14 In. 30.00
Lariat, Plate, Silver Overlay Design, 14 In. 110.00
Lariat, Punch Bowl & Platter 65.00
Lariat, Punch Set, Underplate, 15 Piece ....350.00 To 375.00
Lariat, Relish, 2 Sections, 7 In. 36.00
Lariat, Sugar & Creamer, Tray, Individual 57.50
Lariat, Torte Plate, Hand Painted Flowers, 12 In. 25.00
Lariat, Vase, 7 In. 16.00
Lariat, Wine, 2 1/2 Oz. 8.50
Legionnaire, Goblet, Arcadia Cut 15.00
Locket On Chain, Bowl, Footed, 8 In. 60.00
Locket On Chain, Wine 65.00
Lodestar, Bowl, Mayonnaise, Dawn, 6 1/2 In. 55.00
Mars, Candlestick, 3 1/2 In., Pair 40.00

Mercury, Candlestick, 1–Light, Hawthorne, 3 1/2 In., Pair	95.00
Mercury, Candlestick, 1–Light, Moongleam, 9 In., Pair	425.00
Minuet, Champagne, 4 1/2 Oz.	25.00
Minuet, Champagne, Saucer	45.00
Minuet, Goblet, 9 Oz.	30.00
Minuet, Wine, 2 1/2 Oz.	40.00
Narrow Flute, Celery Tray, 9 In.	20.00
Narrow Flute, Creamer	25.00
Narrow Flute, Mustard, Cover, Spoon	50.00
New Era, Cup & Saucer, Demitasse	65.00
New Era, Goblet, 10 Oz.	18.00
New Era, Sherbet, 2 Oz.	15.00
New Era, Sugar & Creamer	30.00
Octagon, Ice Tub, Flamingo	80.00
Octagon, Ice Tub, Moongleam	75.00
Octagon, Ice Tub, Tongs, Flamingo	65.00
Octagon, Sugar & Creamer, Flamingo, Hotel	50.00
Octagon, Sugar & Creamer, Sahara	60.00
Old Colony, Goblet, Sahara	26.00
Old Colony, Plate, Square, Sahara, 7 In.	18.00
Old Colony, Sugar, Sahara	45.00
Old Dominion, Goblet, Sahara, Tall	30.00
Old Dominion, Tumbler, Iced Tea, Alexandrite, 12 Oz.	65.00
Old Glory, Goblet, Peacock Etch, 9 Oz.	15.00
Old Sandwich, Ashtray, Cobalt Blue, Individual	30.00
Old Sandwich, Ashtray, Moongleam, Square, 2 In.	40.00
Old Sandwich, Bottle, Catsup, Stopper, No 3	40.00 To 60.00
Old Sandwich, Bowl, Floral, Oval, Moongleam, 12 In.	145.00
Old Sandwich, Bowl, Floral, Oval, Sahara, 12 In.	100.00
Old Sandwich, Cocktail, 3 Oz.	55.00
Old Sandwich, Cocktail, Sahara, 3 Oz.	21.00
Old Sandwich, Compote, Footed, 6 In.	50.00
Old Sandwich, Jug, 1/2 Gal.	90.00
Old Sandwich, Tumbler, Footed, 10 Oz., 5 Piece	52.50
Old Sandwich, Wine, Moongleam, 2 1/2 Oz.	22.00
Old Williamsburg, Candelabra, 2–Light	35.00
Old Williamsburg, Candelabra, 2–Light, Sahara	650.00
Old Williamsburg, Candelabra, 5–Light, Cut	775.00
Old Williamsburg, Candlestick, 3–Light	600.00
Old Williamsburg, Candlestick, 9 In., Pair	85.00
Old Williamsburg, Goblet, 9 Oz., 6 Piece	135.00
Old Williamsburg, Jug, Squat, 3 Qt.	160.00
Old Williamsburg, Mustard	28.00
Old Williamsburg, Relish, 5 Sections	42.50
Old Williamsburg, Sherbet, Tall	12.00
Orchi Etch, Ashtray, Square, 3 In.	32.00
Orchid Etch, Ashtray, Individual	20.00
Orchid Etch, Bowl, Mayonnaise, Liner	50.00
Orchid Etch, Candlestick, Double	50.00
Orchid Etch, Cigarette Holder	110.00
Orchid Etch, Compote, Oval, 4 1/2 x 6 1/2 In.	55.00
Orchid Etch, Pitcher, 73 Oz.	450.00
Orchid Etch, Plate, 13 1/2 In.	60.00
Orchid Etch, Plate, 13 1/2 In.	50.00
Orchid Etch, Plate, 8 In.	20.00
Orchid Etch, Relish, 2 Sections, Oval, 11 In.	40.00
Orchid Etch, Sugar & Creamer	45.00
Orchid Etch, Torte Plate, 14 In.	53.00
Orchid Etch, Vase, Fan, 7 In.	75.00
Panelled Cane, Bowl, Flared, 9 In.	35.00
Park Avenue, Cocktail, 3 1/2 Oz.	45.00
Patrician, Candlestick, 9 In.	70.00
Peerless, Compote, 10 In.	150.00

Peerless, Goblet, 8 Oz.	25.00
Peerless, Pitcher, Milk, 3 Pt.	48.00
Petticoat Dolphin, Candlestick, Flamingo, 6 In., Pair	310.00
Pied Piper, Plate, Etch, 8 1/2 In.	15.00
Pillows, Bowl, Crimped, 10 In.	15.00
Pillows, Toothpick, Marked	80.00
Pineapple & Fan, Rose Bowl, 2 1/2 In.	200.00
Pineapple & Fan, Table Set, Emerald Green, Gold Trim, 4 Piece	350.00
Pineapple & Fan, Toothpick	85.00
Pineapple & Fan, Toothpick, Emerald, Gold Trim	105.00 To 135.00
Pineapple & Fan, Tumbler, Ruby Stain, 8 Oz.	30.00
Pinwheel & Fan, Bowl, 8 In.	60.00
Pinwheel & Fan, Nappy, 8 In.	35.00
Pinwheel & Fan, Pitcher, Souvenir, Bruce, Wisc., Custard, 5 In.	67.50
Plain Band, Cake Plate, Footed, 9 In.	65.00
Plain Band, Spooner	30.00
Plantation Tumbler, Ivy Etch, 3 3/4 In.	27.50
Plantation, Bowl, 12 In.	55.00
Plantation, Candleblock, 3 In., Pair	125.00
Plantation, Celery Tray, 13 In.	50.00
Plantation, Claret, Blown, 4 1/2 Oz.	30.00
Plantation, Mayonnaise, Rolled Edge, Footed, Ladle, 4 1/2 In.	65.00
Plantation, Plate, Torte, 11 In.	115.00
Plantation, Punch Set, 9 Piece	750.00
Plantation, Relish, 5 Sections, Oval, 11 In.	75.00
Plantation, Salt & Pepper	55.00
Plantation, Sugar & Creamer	60.00
Plantation, Tumbler, Juice, Footed, 5 Oz.	150.00
Plantation, Tumbler, Water, Blown, 10 Oz.	25.00
Pleat & Panel, Candy Dish, Cover	42.50
Pleat & Panel, Compote, Cover, Moongleam, 6 In.	70.00
Pleat & Panel, Compote, Cover, Pedestal, Flamingo, 5 In.	70.00
Pleat & Panel, Cruet, 3 Oz.	32.00
Pleat & Panel, Cruet, Flamingo, 3 Oz.	75.00
Pleat & Panel, Cruet, Moongleam Stopper, 3 Oz.	22.50
Pleat & Panel, Cruet, Moongleam, 3 Oz.	50.00
Pleat & Panel, Soup, Cream, Moongleam	15.00
Pleat & Panel, Soup, Dish, Liner, Flamingo	35.00
Pleat & Panel, Sugar, Cover, Moongleam	18.00
Portsmouth, Goblet, Moongleam Footed, 9 Oz.	10.00
Prince of Wales Plumes, Toothpick	182.50
Prince of Wales Plumes, Water Set, Gold Trim, 7 Piece	350.00
Priscilla, Toothpick	35.00
Provincial, Bowl, Floral, 12 In.	25.00
Provincial, Butter, Covered	70.00
Provincial, Candlestick, 2–Light, Ball Center, Pair	187.50
Provincial, Candy Jar, Cover, Limelight, 5 1/2 In.	495.00
Provincial, Cocktail, Oyster, 3 1/2 In.	10.00
Provincial, Cruet, Stopper, 4 Oz.	37.50
Provincial, Mayonnaise Set, Limelight, 5 1/4 In.	175.00
Provincial, Sugar	15.00
Provincial, Torte, Plate, 18 In.	30.00
Provincial, Wine, 3 1/2 Oz.	15.00
Punty Band, Bowl, Ruffled, 9 In.	39.00
Punty Band, Creamer, Ruby Stain, Individual	22.50 To 27.50
Punty Band, Spooner	35.00
Puritan, Bottle, Bitters, With Tube, 4 Oz.	55.00
Puritan, Bottle, Cologne, Stopper, 4 Oz.	60.00
Puritan, Compote, 5 1/2 In.	20.00
Puritan, Decanter, Stopper, 24 Oz.	80.00
Puritan, Mustard, Spoon	35.00
Puritan, Nappy, Oval, 6 x 12 In.	50.00
Puritan, Sherbet, 4 1/2 Oz.	10.00

Puritan, Sherbet, Footed, Low, 3 Oz.	22.50
Queen Ann, Berry Set, 5 Piece	125.00
Queen Ann, Bowl, Everglades Cutting, Rolled Top, 13 In.	40.00
Queen Ann, Candelabra, 1–Light, Orchid Etch, 7 1/2 In.	110.00
Queen Ann, Candlestick, Prisms, 8 In., Pair. ....50.00 To	110.00
Queen Ann, Compote, Footed, Oval, 7 In.	25.00
Queen Ann, Goblet	145.00
Queen Ann, Ice Bucket, Tongs	75.00
Queen Ann, Plate, Sandwich, Handle, Orchid Etch, 12 In.	100.00
Queen Ann, Sugar & Creamer	98.00
Quilt, Cigarette Set, Box, Ashtray, 7 Piece	125.00
Recessed Panel, Candy Jar, 1/2 Lb. ....55.00 To	70.00
Recessed Panel, Candy Jar, 1/4 Lb.	75.00
Recessed Panel, Candy Jar, 3 Lb.	225.00
Ridgeleigh, Ashtray, 3 Piece	10.00
Ridgeleigh, Ashtray, Square	5.00
Ridgeleigh, Bowl, Flared Top, 5 In.	25.00
Ridgeleigh, Bowl, Fruit, 12 In.	25.00
Ridgeleigh, Bowl, Marmalade, Cover	35.00
Ridgeleigh, Champagne, 5 Oz.	75.00
Ridgeleigh, Coaster, Limelight	40.00
Ridgeleigh, Cocktail, 4 Oz.	25.00
Ridgeleigh, Cologne Bottle, Stopper, 4 Oz.	95.00
Ridgeleigh, Cup & Saucer	30.00
Ridgeleigh, Nappy, 5 In.	30.00
Ridgeleigh, Relish, 3 Sections	65.00
Ridgeleigh, Relish, 5 Sections, Star	25.00
Ridgeleigh, Tray, Oblong, 10 1/2 In.	30.00
Ring Band, Tumbler, Custard & Gold Design	50.00
Rooster, Cocktail Shaker, Wheat Etching	135.00
Rose Etch, Salt & Pepper	95.00
Rose Etch, Tumbler, Iced Tea	47.50
Rose, Goblet, 9 Oz.	40.00
Rosebud, Syrup, Diamond Cut Rosette	90.00
Saturn Rings, Vase, Ball Feet, 7 In.	12.50
Saturn, Jam Jar, Underplate, Metal Lid	45.00
Sawtooth Band, Sugar, Cover	110.00
Sea Horse, Cocktail	55.00
Souffle, Sherbet, 6 Oz.	20.00
Spanish, Cocktail, Cobalt Blue, 3 1/2 Oz.	90.00
Spanish, Goblet, 10 Oz. ....50.00 To	65.00
Spanish, Wine, 2 1/2 Oz.	32.50
Stanhope, Claret, 3 Oz.	190.00
Stanhope, Cocktail, 3 1/2 Oz.	45.00
Stanhope, Creamer, Black Knob	28.00
Steele, Rose Bowl, Tangerine, 6 1/2 In.	50.00
Sunburst, Jug, 3 Pint	350.00
Sunburst, Pitcher, Marked, 1 Qt.	125.00
Sunburst, Toothpick	125.00
Symphony, Cordial, 3 1/2 Oz.	45.00
Symphony, Goblet, 10 Oz.	45.00
Symphony, Tumbler, Water, Minuet Etch	32.50
Tally–Ho, Cocktail Shaker, 2 Qt.	225.00
Tally–Ho, Tumbler, Etched, 8 Oz.	65.00
Thumbprint & Panel, Candlestick, 2–Light, Cobalt Blue, Pair	260.00
Thumbprint & Panel, Candlestick, 2–Light, Pair	65.00
Tradition, Plate, Birthday, 72 Hole	40.00
Trident, Candlestick, 2–Light, Flamingo	80.00
Trident, Candlestick, 2–Light, Sahara	45.00
Trident, Candlestick, 2–Light, Sahara, Pair	85.00
Trident, Candlestick, Orchid Etch	50.00
Tudor, Cheese Dish, Handle, Moongleam, 6 In.	15.00
Tudor, Compote, Footed, 6 In.	40.00

Tudor, Cruet, 6 Oz. 37.50
Tudor, Jar, Cigarette, Ashtray Cover 75.00
Tudor, Mayonnaise, Moongleam 45.00
Twentieth Century, Tumbler, Cobalt Blue, 9 Oz. 65.00
Twist, Bowl, Nut, Footed, Marigold, 8 In. 85.00
Twist, Butter, Cover, Flamingo 165.00
Twist, Mustard, Covered, Flamingo 50.00
Twist, Mustard, Moongleam 59.00
Twist, Nut Dish, Flamingo 18.00
Twist, Plate, Flamingo, 6 In. 16.00
Twist, Plate, Flamingo, 7 1/2 In. 9.00
Twist, Tray, Pickle, Moongleam, 7 In. 27.50
Tyrolean, Cocktail, Orchid Etch, 3 1/2 Oz. 32.50
Tyrolean, Wine, Orchid Etch, 3 Oz. 75.00
Universal, Cocktail Icer, Liner, Orchid Etch 200.00
Universal, Cordial, 1 Oz. 8.00
Victorian, Plate, 8 In. 18.50
Victorian, Relish, 3 Sections, Oval, 11 In. 75.00
Victorian, Soda, Cut, 12 Oz. 25.00
Victorian, Wine, 2 1/2 Oz. 22.00
Wabash, Goblet, Frontenac Etch, 10 Oz. 15.00
Wabash, Wine, 2 1/2 Oz. 25.00
Wabash, Wine, Moongleam Stem & Foot, Frontenac Etch, 2 1/2 Oz., 5 Piece 140.00
Waldorf–Astoria, Syrup, Cut 100.00
Waldorf–Astoria, Toothpick, Silver Deposit Design, Marked 95.00
Wampum, Candlestick, Pair 35.00
Wampun, Plate, Torte, 13 1/2 In. 30.00
Warwick, Bowl, Floral, Cobalt 465.00
Warwick, Candlestick, 2–Light 60.00
Waverly, Bowl, Crimped, Orchid Etch, 12 In. 65.00
Waverly, Bowl, Crimped, Rose Etch, 12 In. 80.00
Waverly, Bowl, Float, 13 In. 50.00
Waverly, Candlestick, 2–Light, Orchid Etch, Pair 110.00
Waverly, Compote, Oval, Pedestal, Rose Etch 140.00
Waverly, Cruet, Oil, Footed, Rose Etch, 3 Oz. 170.00
Waverly, Plate, 6 1/2 In. 10.00
Waverly, Relish, 3 Sections, Rose Etch, Oval, 11 In. 127.00
Waverly, Relish, 4 Sections, Fern Handles, 9 In. 42.50
Waverly, Relish, 5 Sections, 11 1/2 In. 75.00
Waverly, Salt & Pepper, Footed, Rose Etch 80.00
Waverly, Sugar, Footed, Orchid Etch 25.00
Waverly, Tumbler, Iced Tea, Footed, 7 In. 20.00
Whirlpool, Nappy, Limelight 25.00
Whirlpool, Plate, Limelight, 8 In. 46.00
Whirlpool, Punch Set, Ladle, 15 Piece 275.00
Whirlpool, Sherbet .... 7.50 To 8.50
Windsor, Candlestick, 7 In., Pair 80.00
Winged Scroll, Ring Tree, Emerald, Gold Trim 450.00
Winged Scroll, Tumbler, Custard, Gold Design 100.00
Yeoman, Candy Dish, Center Handle, Bow Tie, Moongleam 55.00
Yeoman, Compote, Moongleam, 5 In. 25.00
Yeoman, Cruet, Moongleam, 2 Oz. 40.00
Yeoman, Cruet, Stopper, Moongleam, 4 Oz. 75.00
Yeoman, Sugar & Creamer, Cover, Flamingo 46.00
Yeoman, Tray, 3 Sections, Ring Handle, Flamingo, 11 In. 40.00
Yeoman, Tray, 3 Sections, Ring Handle, Moongleam, 8 In. 35.00
Zodiac, Champagne, Saucer, 5 Oz., 3 Piece 30.00
Zodiac, Creamer, Footed 22.50

HEREND, see Fischer category

HEUBACH is the collector's name for Gebruder Heubach, a firm working in Lichten, Germany, from 1840 to 1925. It is best known for bisque dolls and doll heads, their principal products. They also manufactured bisque figurines, including piano babies, beginning in the 1880s, and glazed figurines in the 1900s. Piano babies are listed in their own category. Dolls are included in the Doll category under *Gebruder Heubach* and *Heubach.* Another factory, Ernst Heubach, working in Koppelsdorf, Germany, also made porcelain and dolls. These will also be found in the doll category under Heubach Koppelsdorf.

Figurine, Blond Barefoot Girl Praying, 7 1/2 In.	75.00
Figurine, Bubble Blower, 3 1/4 In.	125.00
Figurine, Edwardian Woman, Black, Painted Red Heart, Upswept Hair, 1910, 9 In.	325.00
Figurine, Young Woman, Holding Small Book, 10 1/4 In.	295.00
Plaque, Comic Puppies Chasing Rooster, 9 1/2 In.	150.00
Vase, Bud, With Figural Girl, Bonnet, Playing With Stick & Ring, 5 1/2 In.	95.00

HIGBEE glass was made by the J. B. Higbee Company of Bridgeville, Pennsylvania, about 1900. Tablewares were made and it is possible to assemble a full set of dishes and goblets in some Higbee patterns. Most of the glass was clear, not colored. Additional pieces may be found in the Pressed Glass category by pattern name.

Celery, Diamond Panels Alternating Vertical Grooves, Bryce	55.00
Ladle, Condiment, 6 In.	20.00
Pitcher, Gem Pattern, Bryce, Large	55.00
Plate, Blue Opalescent, Allover Pattern, 7 1/2 In.	38.00
Vase, Hawaiian Lei, 15 3/4 In.	45.00

HISTORIC BLUE, see factory names, such as Adams, Clews, Ridgway, and Staffordshire

HOBNAIL glass is a style of glass with bumps all over. Dozens of hobnail patterns and variants have been made. Clear, colored, and opalescent hobnail have been made and are being reproduced. Other pieces of hobnail may also be listed in the Depression Glass category under Hobnail and in the Fenton and Francisware categories.

Bowl, White, 8 In.	160.00
Cologne Bottle, Opalescent	8.00
Cruet, Cranberry Opalescent	350.00
Cruet, Vaseline	225.00
Goblet, Blue Opalescent	20.00
Lamp, Crystal, Miniature	18.00
Pitcher, Applied Handle, New England Glass Co., Large	185.00
Pitcher, Cranberry Opalescent	325.00
Pitcher, Cranberry Opalescent, 8 3/4 In.	485.00
Pitcher, Water, Cranberry	200.00
Powder Jar, Opalescent, Wooden Cover	10.00
Sugar Shaker, Inverted Thumbprint, Amber, 2 Part Pewter Cover, Hobbs, 5 1/2 In.	250.00
Sugar, Cover, Blue Opalescent	45.00
Toothpick, Vaseline	47.50
Toothpick, White Opalescent	35.00
Toothpick, White Opalescent, Hat	15.00
Top Hat, Blue Opalescent, 2 1/2 In.	22.00
Tumbler, Amber	35.00
Tumbler, Blue	35.00
Tumbler, Blue Opalescent	55.00
Tumbler, Square, White Opalescent	65.00
Vase, Mother-of-Pearl, 5 1/2 In.	450.00
Water Set, Hobnail, Cranberry Opalescent, 7 Piece	965.00

HOCHST, or Hoechst, porcelain was made in Germany from 1746 to 1796. It was marked with a six-spoke wheel. Be careful when buying Hochst; many other firms have used a very similar wheel-shaped mark.

Cup & Saucer, Flowers, 1770	500.00

Figurine, Quail, 8 In. 2100.00
Figurine, Young Boy & Girl, 19th Century, 4 In. 245.00

HOLLY AMBER, or golden agate, glass was made by the Indiana Tumbler and Goblet Company of Greentown, Indiana, from January 1, 1903, to June 13, 1903. It is a pressed glass pattern featuring holly leaves in the amber–shaded glass. The glass was made with shadings that range from creamy opalescent to brown–amber.

Berry Bowl, 4 1/4 In. 335.00
Compote, Cover, 6 In. 900.00
Compote, Jelly, Cover 600.00
Creamer 700.00
Dish, Berry, 4 1/4 In. 275.00
Parfait, Amber Panels of Holly Branch, 6 In. 485.00
Plate, Square 900.00
Sugar & Creamer, Beaded Cover 1550.00
Tumbler 375.00
Vase, Ornate, 2 1/2 x 2 1/2 In. 40.00

HOPALONG CASSIDY was named William Lawrence Boyd when he was born in Cambridge, Ohio, in 1895. His first movie appearance was in 1919, but the first Hopalong Cassidy film was not until 1934. Sixty–six films were made. In 1948, William Boyd purchased the television rights to the movies, then later made fifty–two new programs. In the 1950s, Hopalong Cassidy and his horse, named *Topper,* were seen in comics, records, toys, and other products. Boyd died in 1972.

Ad, America's Favorite Cowboy, Grape Nuts, 1950, 10 x 13 In. 32.50
Badge, Bank Teller, 3 In. 30.00
Badge, Star Shape, 3–D, Silver, Metal, 1950 .... 10.00
Binoculars, Metal, Hoppy Riding Topper, c.1950 .... 80.00
Book, Coloring, Sticker–Stencil, Whitman, 1951 .... 131.00
Book, Pop–Up .... 17.00 To 75.00
Book, Pop–Up, Lends A Helping Hand 35.00
Book, Race, Loose Leaf 95.00
Bottle, Milk, 1/2 Pt. 75.00
Bowl, Cereal 10.00
Box Camera, Box 250.00
Briefcase, Hoppy On Topper Picture 195.00
Bubble Pipe 12.00
Button, Hoppy Savings Club, Teller's, Celluloid, 1950s, 3 1/2 In. 27.00
Camera, Box .... 250.00 To 550.00
Card, Trading, 1950, 10 Piece 60.00
Chair, TV, Folding, Wooden .... 250.00 To 275.00
Chaps, Painted, Box, 1950s 250.00
Charm, Hoppy, Metal, Silver Finish, 1950, 1 1/8 In. 15.00
Chow Set, Stainless Steel, Knife, Fork & Spoon, Raised Figures, Box 250.00
Clothes Hamper, Tin, Blue, Hoppy & Topper, Tin, Large 275.00
Coaster, Spun Honey Sandwich Spread, Hoppy On Horse 10.00
Coin, Metal, Hoppy On Both Sides, 1 1/4 In. 10.00
Container, Ice Cream, White & Yellow, 1 Qt. 65.00
Cookie Jar, Brown 300.00
Costume, 3 Piece, 1950 .... 205.00
Display, Hoppy's Butternut Bread 125.00
Figurine, Hoppy & Topper, Black Hat, Ideal 120.00
Game, Chinese Checkers, Original Box 175.00
Game, Dart Board .... 75.00 To 134.00
Game, Lasso, Hoppy On Topper, 2 Pegs, 3 Lassoes, Box .... 250.00 To 275.00
Game, Milton Bradley, 1950 .... 65.00 To 75.00
Gun & Holster Set, Metal, Hoppy Picture & Signature, c.1950 .... 495.00
Hoppy Western Frontier Set 495.00
Knife, Pocket, Hammer Brand .... 50.00 To 75.00
Lamp, Aladdin, Horsehead, Shade 1500.00
Lamp, Revolving 285.00

Lamp, Revolving, Red Plastic Top & Base, Encolite Corp. 620.00
Lunch Box, Lithograph, 1954 ....225.00 To 350.00
Marble, Black Glass, 1 In. 15.00
Napkins, Hoppy & Topper, Set of 50 .... 65.00
Neckerchief & Metal Longhorn Tie Clasp, c.1950 .... 355.00
Necktie, Cow's Head Slide, Red 80.00
Night–Light, Gun & Holster Shape, Aladdin, 1950, 12 In. 130.00
Night–Light, Spur Honey 25.00
Pen, Hoppy Head Top, Signature, Boxed, Refill, Parker, 1950, 6 In. 133.00
Picture Gun Theater, Metal Film Gun, Stephens, Box 166.00
Plate, Dinner 55.00
Plate, Salad, Milk Glass 65.00
Plate, To My Friend, Hoppy, W. S. George, 9 1/2 In. ....: 35.00
Poster, Bond Bread, Stand–Up, 27 x 21 In. 195.00
Poster, Movie, In Old Mexico 95.00
Projector, Gun, Films, Background Screen Theater, Box 195.00
Puzzle, 3 Pictures, Box 95.00
Puzzle, Jigsaw, TV, Inlaid, Box, 4 Piece 120.00
Radio, Black, With Saddle Back, Initial H/C 650.00
Radio, Hoppy & Topper On Panel, Metal, Arvin, 1950, 5 x 8 In .... 845.00 To 925.00
Record Album, Square Dance Holdup 100.00
Record, Hoppy's Happy Birthday, 78 RPM 45.00
Ring, Hat, Compass 175.00
Rocking Horse, Topper 225.00
Roller Skates 225.00
Rug, Portrait of Topper, Chenille, 35 x 23 In. 135.00
Schoolbag, Hoppy, Handle Wear 60.00
Shooting Gallery, Graphics of Hoppy, Lucky & California, Box, Tin 325.00
Shooting Gallery, Windup Moving Target, Guns Shoot BBs 390.00
Spurs, Box 200.00
Sweater, Hoppy On Front, Topper On Back 200.00
Tin, Potato Chips ....200.00 To 225.00
Tumbler, Milk, Hoppy In 3 Colors 40.00
Watch, Hoppy Face, Saddle Display Box, 1950 .... 345.00
Wristwatch, Saddle Box ....200.00 To 250.00

HOWDY DOODY and Buffalo Bob were the main characters in a children's
series televised from 1947 to 1960. Howdy was a redheaded puppet. The
series became popular with college students in the late 1970s when Buffalo
Bob began to lecture on campuses.

Bank, Shawnee 425.00
Bank, Vandor 45.00
Book, Comic, Vol. 1, No. 23, 1953 .... 32.00
Box, Illustrated Lid, Kagran, 1950 .... 170.00
Bubble Pipe, Box 55.00
Button, It's Howdy Doody Time, Celluloid, Large 1.70
Clock, Time Teacher, 10 x 18 In. 25.00
Cookbook, Welch's, 1952 .... 85.00
Cookie Jar, Cookie–Go–Round, Luce Mfg. 65.00
Cookie Jar, Cookie–Go–Round, Tin ....145.00 To 245.00
Cookie Jar, Purinton 550.00
Cookie Jar, Vandor ....450.00 To 475.00
Cup, Ice Cream, 1950s 20.00
Dinner Set, Children's, 3 Piece 200.00
Display, Welch's, Howdy & Friends On A Picnic, 1955 .... 65.00
Doll, Eyes & Mouth Move, Cloth Body, Bechler Arts, 1950, 8 In. 213.00
Doll, Squeeze 22.00
Doll, Ventriloquist Figure, Original Box, Tee Vee, 1950's 70.00
Doll, Vinyl, Stuffed, Red, White & Blue, 13 In. 60.00
Doll, Wood Jointed, Cameo, 1940s 600.00
Dummy, Ventriloquist 125.00
Dummy, Ventriloquist, 12 In. 30.00
Earmuffs, Clarabelle 65.00

Earmuffs, Figural Face	145.00
Figure, Plastic, 1950s, 5 In.	40.00
Fun Book, Whitman Kagran, 1950s, Unused	22.00
Game, Bowling, Box	145.00
Game, Card	22.00
Game, Hand–Held Puzzle, Howdy On Stage, Bluster & Dilly, 3 Steel Balls	95.00
Game, TV Studio, Board, Box	75.00
Game, Wood Balls Knock Over Howdy, Dilly, Glubadub, Parker, 1950s	40.00
Glass, Jelly, Welsh, 1953	45.00
Handkerchief, Signed Bob Smith, Large, 1949	95.00
Howdy Doody TV Merrimat, Placematters, Plastic, 1955, 10 x 15 In.	55.00
Jack–In–The–Box, Plastic, TeeVee Toys, Box, 1955, 6 In.	161.00
Lamp Shade, Wall	275.00
Lamp, Figural	165.00
Lunch Box, 1955	265.00
Marionette, Flub–A–Dub	275.00
Marionette, Howdy Doody, Peter Puppet, Box, 16 In.	428.00
Marionette, Princess Summerfall Winterspring	80.00 To 250.00
Mug, Vandor	17.00
Neckerchief, Signed Bob Smith, 1949	75.00
Night–Light, Howdy's Face, 3 Dimensional Glass, Leco, 1955, Box, 2 1/4 In.	55.00
Nodder, 6 In.	12.00
Peanut Butter Pail, Children On See–Saw	495.00
Phonodoodle	195.00
Pipe, Bubble	35.00
Place Mat, Vinyl, Howdy Characters, 1955, 10 x 15 In.	61.00
Plate, Taylor & Smith	95.00
Puppet Show, Howdy, Clarabell, Dilly, Princess, Plastic Figures, Package	125.00
Puppet, Dancing, Kagran–Snickers Candy, Cardboard, 1950s, 13 In.	70.00
Puppet, Plastic, Original Card	145.00
Puzzle, 3 Pictures, Box	95.00
Puzzle, Playing Drums, Box	45.00
Puzzle, Whitman, 1952, 14 3/4 x 11 1/2 In.	10.00
Record Player	250.00
Record Set, Circus	45.00
Ring, Flashlight	175.00
Sand Pail, Howdy, Clarabell, Bluster & Flub, Plastic Forms, Shovel, Package	125.00
Sponge, Bath, Ben Hur Industries, Inc., Unused, Bag, 1950s	32.00
Toy, Band, Bob Smith At Piano, Howdy Doody Dancing, Tin Plate, Box	2090.00
Toy, Crazy Jeep, Windup, Cowboy Hat & Horns On Hood	110.00
Toy, Wall Plaque, Electric, Kagran, 1950, Box	200.00
Ukulele, Box	175.00
Wallet, 3 Sections, Pictures Characters, Plastic, Kagran, c.1953, 7 In.	83.00
Watch, 40th Anniversary, Box	50.00
Wristwatch, Girl's, Moving Eyes, Box, 1954	385.00

HULL pottery was made in Crooksville, Ohio, from 1905. Addis E. Hull bought the Acme Pottery Company and started making ceramic wares. In 1917, A. E. Hull Pottery began making art pottery as well as the commercial wares. For a short time, 1921 to 1929, the firm also sold pottery imported from Europe. The dinnerwares of the 1940s, including the Little Red Riding Hood line, the high gloss artwares of the 1950s, and the matte wares of the 1940s, are all popular with collectors. The firm officially closed in March 1986.

Hull
U.S.A.

Ashtray, Ebb Tide, Mermaid, Chartreuse & Wine	100.00
Ashtray, Ebb Tide, Mermaid, Shrimp & Turquoise	85.00
Ashtray, Serenade, Blue, 13 1/2 x 10 1/2 In.	75.00
Ashtray, Swan, White, 4 1/2 x 4 1/2 In.	25.00
Bank, Little Red Riding Hood	430.00 To 575.00
Bank, Piggy, Pink Bow, 7 In.	40.00
Basket, Blossom Flite, Black & Pink, 10 In.	90.00
Basket, Capri, Coral, 6 1/2 In.	37.00
Basket, Magnolia, Matte, 10 1/2 In.	190.00 To 310.00

Basket, Tokay, Moon, No. 11, Pink, 10 1/2 In. 48.00
Basket, Tuscany, Moon, Pink, 10 1/2 In. 95.00
Basket, Water Lily, Tan, Brown, 10 1/2 In. 115.00
Basket, Woodland, Hi–Gloss, 12 In. 60.00
Bowl, Blossom Flite, Boat, Pink, Black, Gold, 10 1/2 In. 60.00
Butter, Cover, Little Red Riding Hood 385.00
Candleholder, Capri, Sea Green, 4 In. 25.00
Candleholder, Open Rose, Dove, Pink, Blue, 6 1/2 In., Pair 225.00
Candleholder, Parchment & Pine, 2 1/4 In. 15.00
Candleholder, Parchment & Pine, 2 1/4 In., Pair 35.00
Canister, Flour, Little Red Riding Hood 650.00
Canister, Salt, Little Red Riding Hood 100.00
Canister, Sugar, Little Red Riding Hood 650.00
Clock, Bluebird, Sessions .... 225.00 To 450.00
Console Set, Blossom Flite, Pink, Black & Gold, 3 Piece 175.00
Console Set, Parchment & Pine, 3 Piece 110.00
Console Set, Serenade, Blue, 3 Piece 110.00
Console Set, Wildflower, Pink & Blue, 3 Piece 250.00
Cookie Jar Set, Little Red Riding Hood, 4 Piece ....*Illus* 550.00
Cookie Jar, Apple, White, 1972 .... 45.00
Cookie Jar, Barefoot Boy 350.00
Cookie Jar, Basket 350.00
Cookie Jar, Duck ....85.00 To 145.00
Cookie Jar, Gingerbread Boy .... 70.00 To 95.00
Cookie Jar, Little Red Riding Hood, Closed Basket .... 265.00 To 325.00
Cookie Jar, Little Red Riding Hood, Open Basket .... 175.00 To 220.00
Cookie Jar, Little Red Riding Hood, Open Basket, Gold Stars Apron 375.00
Cookie Jar, Little Red Riding Hood, Poinsettia .... 750.00 To 995.00
Cornucopia, Blossom Flite, Pink, Black & Gold, 10 1/2 In. 35.00
Cornucopia, Bow Knot, Pink, 7 1/2 In. .... 95.00 To 125.00
Cornucopia, Ebb Tide, Mermaid, Shrimp & Turquoise, 7 1/2 In. 45.00
Cornucopia, Magnolia, Double, Matte, 12 In. 85.00
Cornucopia, Magnolia, Pink Gloss, 8 1/2 In. 49.00
Cornucopia, Sunglow, 8 1/2 In. 20.00
Cornucopia, Tokay, Pink & Green, 6 1/2 In. 50.00
Cornucopia, Wild Flower, Pink & Blue, 7 1/2 In., Pair 150.00
Cornucopia, Woodland, Double, Yellow & Cream, 11 In. .... 105.00 To 195.00
Cornucopia, Woodland, Pink & Blue, 6 1/2 In. 35.00
Cornucopia, Woodland, Pink, Blue, 6 1/2 In. 48.00
Creamer, Blossom Flite, Pink, Black & Gold 25.00
Creamer, Butterfly, Turquoise 25.00
Creamer, House & Garden, Ice Lip 25.00
Creamer, Little Red Riding Hood, Head Pour .... 275.00 To 350.00
Creamer, Little Red Riding Hood, Side Pour 110.00
Creamer, Little Red Riding Hood, Tab Handle .... 225.00 To 275.00
Duck, Planter, Bandana 65.00

Hull, Cookie Jar Set, Little Red Riding Hood, 4 Piece

Ewer, Blossom Flite, Pink, Black & Gold, 9 In. 65.00
Ewer, Bow Knot, Pink, 5 1/2 In. 95.00
Ewer, Butterfly, 13 1/2 In. 125.00
Ewer, Butterfly, 6 In. 25.00
Ewer, Ebb Tide, Shrimp & Turqoise, 11 In. 125.00
Ewer, Magnolia, Pink Gloss, 13 In. 325.00
Ewer, Rosella, Paper Label, 9 1/2 In. 65.00
Ewer, Sueno Tulip, Pink & Blue, 8 In. 140.00
Ewer, Water Lily, Tan & Brown, 5 1/2 In. 45.00
Ewer, Woodland, Blue, 13 1/2 In. 150.00
Figurine, Tuba Player, Swing Band 50.00
Flowerpot, Bow Knot, Saucer, 6 1/2 In. 195.00
Jar, Grease, Little Red Riding Hood 575.00
Jar, Wolf, Ears Up, Yellow 500.00
Jardiniere, Sueno Tulip, Blue, 7 In. 250.00
Jardiniere, Sueno Tulip, Pink, 5 In. .... 35.00 To 90.00
Jardiniere, Water Lily, Tan & Brown, 5 1/2 In. 85.00
Lamp, Little Red Riding Hood 2450.00
Lamp, Rosella, 6 3/4 In. 175.00
Lamp, Teapot 675.00
Lavabo Set, Butterfly, 2 Piece 60.00
Matchbox, Little Red Riding Hood, Wall .... 735.00 To 1200.00
Mustard, Little Red Riding Hood, Spoon 395.00
Pitcher, Batter, Little Red Riding Hood, 6 1/2 In. .... 425.00 To 475.00
Pitcher, Bow Knot, Blue, 5 1/2 In. 150.00
Pitcher, Chanticleer Rooster 40.00
Pitcher, House & Garden, Brown 20.00
Pitcher, Iris, 13 1/2 In. 300.00
Pitcher, Magnolia, 13 1/2 In. 260.00
Pitcher, Milk, Little Red Riding Hood .... 250.00 To 350.00
Pitcher, Serenade, Pink, 13 1/2 In. 275.00
Pitcher, Wildflower, 5 In. .... 20.00 To 30.00
Planter, Dancing Girl .... 36.00 To 45.00
Planter, Geese, Flying 55.00
Planter, Goose & 2 Babies, 8 In. 45.00
Planter, Kitten 14.00
Planter, Lovebirds 20.00
Planter, Open Rose, Hanging 195.00
Planter, Pink Poodle 12.00
Planter, Pink Poodle, Green Foliage, 9 1/2 In. 45.00
Planter, Poodle Head, With Hat 30.00
Planter, Swan, Green, 8 1/2 In. 10.00
Plate, House & Garden, Gingerbread Boy .... 15.00 To 25.00
Salt & Pepper, Little Red Riding Hood, 3 1/2 In. 50.00
Salt & Pepper, Little Red Riding Hood, 5 1/2 In. .... 80.00 To 125.00
Sugar & Creamer, Blue Bell 24.00
Sugar & Creamer, Cover, House & Garden 15.00
Sugar & Creamer, Little Red Riding Hood, Side Pour .... 200.00 To 325.00
Sugar & Creamer, Woodland, Yellow & Cream 85.00
Sugar, Cover, Little Red Riding Hood 400.00
Sugar, Little Red Riding Hood, Crawling .... 225.00 To 250.00
Tea Set, Bow Knot 525.00
Tea Set, Ebb Tide, Shrimp & Turquoise, 3 Piece 165.00
Tea Set, Magnolia, Matte 90.00
Tea Set, Parchment & Pine, 3 Piece .... 85.00 To 250.00
Tea Set, Woodland, Pink Gloss 100.00
Teapot, Blossom Flite, Pink, Black & Gold 65.00
Teapot, Blue Bell 50.00
Teapot, Doughnut, Cobalt 125.00
Teapot, Ebb Tide, Chartreuse & Wine 70.00
Teapot, House & Garden 15.00
Teapot, Little Red Riding Hood .... 195.00 To 325.00
Teapot, Open Rose 300.00

Teapot, Serenade, Pink ....90.00 To 125.00
Vase, Angel Fish, Ebb Tide, 9 1/4 In. 115.00
Vase, Blossom Flite, Pink, Black & Gold, 10 1/2 In. 40.00
Vase, Bow Knot, Blue, 6 1/2 In. 85.00
Vase, Bow Knot, Blue, 6 1/2 In. 100.00
Vase, Bow Knot, Matte, 8 1/2 In. 160.00
Vase, Bow Knot, Pink Gloss, 10 1/2 In. 290.00
Vase, Calla Lily, 9 In. 165.00
Vase, Fan, Magnolia, Matte, 8 1/2 In. 58.00
Vase, Iris, Pink, Blue, 4 3/4 In. 65.00
Vase, Lamp, Open Rose, White, 10 1/2 In. 425.00
Vase, Magnolia, Matte, 15 In. 425.00
Vase, Magnolia, Matte, 6 1/2 In. 42.00
Vase, Magnolia, Matte, 8 1/2 In. 80.00
Vase, Magnolia, Pink Gloss, 12 In. 225.00
Vase, Magnolia, Pink Glossy, 8 1/2 In. 65.00
Vase, Mardi Gras, 9 In. 45.00
Vase, Mardi Gras, Handles, 8 1/2 In. 35.00
Vase, Open Rose, 8 1/2 In. 79.00
Vase, Rosella, Coral, 8 1/2 In. 40.00
Vase, Rosella, Glossy, 5 In. 35.00
Vase, Serenade, Blue, 10 1/2 In. 28.00
Vase, Sueno Tulip, 10 In. 125.00
Vase, Sueno Tulip, 6 In. 45.00
Vase, Sunglow, 8 In. 35.00
Vase, Water Lily, Pink & Blue Matte, 5 1/2 In. 37.50
Vase, Water Lily, Pink & Blue, 6 1/2 In. 50.00
Vase, Wild Flower, Pink & Blue, 10 1/2 In. 90.00
Vase, Wild Flower, Pink & Blue, 8 1/2 In. 65.00
Vase, Wild Flower, Tan & Brown, 6 1/2 In. 60.00
Vase, Woodland, Pink Glossy, 6 1/2 In. 40.00
Vase, Woodland, Yellow & Cream, 8 1/2 In. ....35.00 To 85.00
Wall Pocket, Bow Knot, Cup & Saucer, Blue, 6 In. 165.00
Wall Pocket, Bow Knot, Iron ....185.00 To 195.00
Wall Pocket, Bow Knot, Pitcher 150.00
Wall Pocket, Little Red Riding Hood ....400.00 To 450.00
Wall Pocket, Sunglow, Iron, Gold Trim, 6 In. 45.00
Wall Pocket, Sunglow, Pitcher 28.00
Window Box, Blue & Yellow, 23 2/3 In. 25.00

HUMMEL figurines, based on the drawings of the nun Berta Hummel, are made by the W. Goebel Porzellanfabrik of Oeslau, Germany, now Rodenthal, Germany. They were first made in 1934. The mark has changed through the years. The following are the approximate dates for each of the marks: *Crown* mark, 1935 to 1949; *U.S. Zone, Germany,* 1946 to 1948; *West Germany,* after 1949; *full bee* with variations, 1950 to 1959; *stylized bee,* 1960 to 1972; *three line mark,* 1968 to 1979; *vee over gee,* 1972 to 1979; *new mark, West Germany* 1979 to 1990; *G Mark, Goebel* 1979 to 1991; and the *Goebel, Germany,* mark introduced in 1991. Other decorative items and plates that feature Hummel drawings have been made by Schmid Brothers, Inc., since 1971.

Ashtray, No. 166, Boy With Bird, Stylized Bee 45.00
Bell, Annual, 1978 .... 25.00
Bell, Annual, 1980 .... 18.00
Bell, Annual, 1988 .... 79.00
Bell, Annual, 1989 .... 95.00
Bookend, Bookworm, Boy, 14A, Full Bee 215.00
Candleholder, No. 37, Herald Angels, Full Bee 195.00
Figurine, No. 4, Little Fiddler, Full Bee 221.00
Figurine, No. 5, Strolling Along, Crown Mark 568.00
Figurine, No. 5, Strolling Along, Full Bee ....250.00 To 280.00
Figurine, No. 6/0, Sensitive Hunter, Full Bee 208.00
Figurine, No. 6/0, Sensitive Hunter, Vee Over Gee 112.00

Figurine, No. 6/I, Sensitive Hunter, Crown Mark .... 884.00 To 947.00
Figurine, No. 8, Bookworm, Full Bee 234.00
Figurine, No. 9, Begging His Share, Crown Mark 512.00
Figurine, No. 1, Puppy Love, G Mark 160.00
Figurine, No. 10/I, Flower Madonna, Color, Crown Mark 485.00
Figurine, No. 11/0, Merry Wanderer, Crown Mark 449.00
Figurine, No. 12/I, Chimney Sweep, Full Bee 234.00
Figurine, No. 12/I, Chimney Sweep, Stylized Bee 119.00
Figurine, No. 16/I, Little Hiker, Stylized Bee 100.00
Figurine, No. 20, Prayer Before Battle, Vee Over Gee 90.00
Figurine, No. 21/0, Heavenly Angel, Full Bee 130.00
Figurine, No. 21/0/1/2, Heavenly Angel, Stylized Bee 210.00
Figurine, No. 23/I, Adoration, Crown Mark 900.00
Figurine, No. 23/I, Adoration, Full Bee 185.00
Figurine, No. 23/I, Adoration, Full Bee, ... 390.00
Figurine, No. 28/II, Wayside Devotion, Crown Mark 583.00
Figurine, No. 42/0, Good Shepherd, Full Bee 260.00
Figurine, No. 43, March Winds, Crown Mark 255.00
Figurine, No. 43, March Winds, Crown Mark 28.00
Figurine, No. 43, March Winds, Full Bee 176.00
Figurine, No. 47/3/0, Goose Girl, Stylized Bee 99.00
Figurine, No. 49/0, To Market, Full Bee 293.00
Figurine, No. 51/0, Village Boy, Full Bee 254.00
Figurine, No. 51/2/0, Village Boy, Three Line Mark 45.00
Figurine, No. 51/I, Village Boy, Crown Mark 554.00
Figurine, No. 52/0, Going To Grandma's, Full Bee 299.00
Figurine, No. 52/I, Going To Grandma's, Stylized Bee 600.00
Figurine, No. 56/A, Culprits, Stylized Bee 140.00
Figurine, No. 56/A, Culprits, Vee Over Gee 170.00
Figurine, No. 56/B, Out of Danger, Full Bee 319.00
Figurine, No. 57/0, Chick Girl, Crown Mark 405.00
Figurine, No. 58/0, Playmates, Crown Mark 336.00
Figurine, No. 58/0, Playmates, Full Bee 189.00
Figurine, No. 59, Skier, Full Bee 252.00
Figurine, No. 63, Singing Lesson, Full Bee 85.00
Figurine, No. 66, Farm Boy, Stylized Bee .... 115.00 To 160.00
Figurine, No. 67, Doll Mother, Crown Mark 460.00
Figurine, No. 67, Doll Mother, Full Bee 267.00
Figurine, No. 68, Lost Sheep, Stylized Bee 139.00
Figurine, No. 73, Little Helper, Full Bee 130.00
Figurine, No. 73, Little Helper, Stylized Bee 70.00
Figurine, No. 80, Little Scholar, Full Bee 234.00
Figurine, No. 82/0, Schoolboy, Full Bee 208.00
Figurine, No. 82/2/0, Schoolboy, Crown Mark 322.00
Figurine, No. 84/0, Worship, Full Bee 176.00
Figurine, No. 85/0, Serenade, Full Bee 143.00
Figurine, No. 86, Happiness, Full Bee 143.00
Figurine, No. 87, For Father, Stylized Bee 125.00
Figurine, No. 88/II, Heavenly Protection, Stylized Bee 575.00
Figurine, No. 89/I, Little Cellist, Vee Over Gee 300.00
Figurine, No. 94/3/0, Surprise, Full Bee 169.00
Figurine, No. 97, Trumpet Boy, Full Bee 143.00
Figurine, No. 98, Sister, Crown Mark 350.00
Figurine, No. 98, Sister, Full Bee 230.00
Figurine, No. 111/3/0, Wayside Harmony, Full Bee 163.00
Figurine, No. 111/I, Wayside Harmony, Full Bee 286.00
Figurine, No. 112/3/0, Just Resting, Vee Over Gee 120.00
Figurine, No. 127, Doctor, Full Bee 176.00
Figurine, No. 129, Band Leader, Stylized Bee 110.00
Figurine, No. 131, Street Singer, Full Bee 202.00
Figurine, No. 135, Soloist, Full Bee 142.00
Figurine, No. 136/I, Friends, Three Line Mark 120.00
Figurine, No. 141/I, Apple Tree Girl, Crown Mark 498.00

Figurine, No. 142/I, Apple Tree Boy, Full Bee 293.00
Figurine, No. 142/I, Apple Tree Boy, Stylized Bee 195.00
Figurine, No. 143, Boots, Crown Mark 508.00
Figurine, No. 152/A/II, Umbrella Boy, Stylized Bee 800.00
Figurine, No. 152/B/II, Umbrella Girl, Stylized Bee 800.00
Figurine, No. 169, Bird Duet, Full Bee 210.00
Figurine, No. 172, Festival Harmony, Stylized Bee 425.00
Figurine, No. 174, She Loves Me, She Loves Me Not, Full Bee 275.00
Figurine, No. 175, Mother's Darling, Full Bee 312.00
Figurine, No. 176/I, Happy Birthday, G Mark 150.00
Figurine, No. 178, Photographer, Full Bee 288.00
Figurine, No. 184, Latest News, Stylized Bee 159.00
Figurine, No. 185, Accordion Boy, Full Bee 208.00
Figurine, No. 186, Sweet Music, Full Bee 208.00
Figurine, No. 186, Sweet Music, Striped Slippers, Crown Mark 1740.00
Figurine, No. 186, Sweet Music, Stylized Bee 100.00
Figurine, No. 195/2/0, Barnyard Hero, Full Bee .... 125.00 To 182.00
Figurine, No. 196/0, Telling Her Secret, Full Bee .... 225.00 To 325.00
Figurine, No. 197, Be Patient, Stylized Bee 155.00
Figurine, No. 198/I, Home From Market, Full Bee 234.00
Figurine, No. 199/0, Feeding Time, Full Bee 208.00
Figurine, No. 199/I, Feeding Time, Blond Hair, Full Bee 250.00
Figurine, No. 199/I, Feeding Time, Full Bee 195.00
Figurine, No. 200/I, Little Goat Herder, Vee Over Gee 200.00
Figurine, No. 201/2/0, Retreat To Safety, Full Bee 182.00
Figurine, No. 203/2/0, Signs of Spring, Stylized Bee ....95.00 To 100.00
Figurine, No. 204, Weary Wanderer, Stylized Bee .... 125.00 To 150.00
Figurine, No. 226, The Mail Is Here, Vee Over Gee 375.00
Figurine, No. 300, Bird Watcher, Vee Over Gee 140.00
Figurine, No. 314, Confidentially, Vee Over Gee 160.00
Figurine, No. 317, Not For You, Vee Over Gee 200.00
Figurine, No. 322, Little Pharmacist, Vee Over Gee 175.00
Figurine, No. 334, Homeward Bound, Three Line Mark 375.00
Figurine, No. 344, Feathered Friends, Vee Over Gee 160.00
Figurine, No. 350, On Holiday, Vee Over Gee 95.00
Figurine, No. 363, Big Housecleaning, Vee Over Gee 140.00
Figurine, No. 376, Little Nurse, Vee Over Gee 110.00
Figurine, No. 381, Flower Vendor, Vee Over Gee 100.00
Figurine, No. 385, Chicken Licken, Vee Over Gee 175.00
Figurine, No. 387, Valentine Gift, Three Line Mark 350.00
Figurine, No. 406, Pleasant Journey, New Mark 1100.00
Figurine, No. 415, Thoughtful, G Mark 117.00
Font, No. 35/0, Good Shepherd, Full Bee 77.00
Font, No. 164, Worship, Full Bee 100.00
Font, No. 207, Heavenly Angel, Stylized Bee 45.00
Lamp, No. 228, Good Friends, Three Line Mark 245.00
Music Box, In Tune 275.00
Music Box, Ride Into Christmas 250.00
Music Box, Umbrella Girl .... 300.00 To 375.00
Plaque, No. 106, Merry Wanderer, Crown Mark 4000.00
Plaque, No. 180, Tuneful Good Night 135.00
Plate, Annual, 1971 .... 525.00
Plate, Annual, 1981 .... 43.00
Plate, Annual, 1989 ....85.00 To 110.00
Plate, Annual, 1990 .... 125.00
Plate, Club, 1981 .... 43.00
Plate, Club, 1989 .... 110.00
Plate, Heavenly Angel, 1971 .... 400.00
Powder Box, Chick Girl, 5 In. 100.00
Salt & Pepper, Turkey On Nest, Full Bee 37.50
Sugar & Creamer, Friar Tuck, On 7 In. Tray 69.00
Vase, No. 334, Girl, Stylized Bee 205.00
Wall Vase, No. 360, Boy, Stylized Bee 205.00

Wall Vase, No. 360, Girl, Stylized Bee 205.00

HUTSCHENREUTHER Porcelain Company of Selb, Germany, was established in 1814 and is still working. The company makes fine quality porcelain dinnerwares and figurines. The mark has changed through the years, but the name and the lion insignia appear in most versions.

LORENZ
HUTSCHEN REUTER

GERMANY

Bowl & Flower Frog, Child On Gold Ball, Scalloped Rim	225.00
Cake Stand, 3 Tiers, Blue Onion	185.00
Dish, Blackberries, Blossoms, Boat Shape, Gold Handles, 1912, 12 In.	75.00
Figurine, American Eagle, Outstretched Wings, Signed, 15 In.	695.00
Figurine, Boy On Pony	225.00
Figurine, Bud Vase, Girl, Playing With Stick & Ring, White, Signed, 5 1/2 In.	80.00
Figurine, Cat, Seated, White, Green Eyes, 7 In.	165.00
Figurine, Faust, 7 In.	350.00
Figurine, Girl, Curtseying, Feather In Hat, 7 In.	195.00
Figurine, Horse, White, 9 1/4 x 12 In.	132.00
Figurine, Mercury Riding Reindeer, White, Gold Trim, 9 In.	175.00
Figurine, Shepherd, 6 1/2 x 10 In.	140.00
Group, Children Playing Musical Instruments, 3 1/2 To 4 In., 4 Piece	300.00
Plaque, 3 Women, 12 3/4 x 8 3/4 In. ....*Illus*	3850.00
Plaque, Die Parzen, Marked, 12 3/4 x 8 3/4 In.	3830.00
Plaque, Nude & Lover, Ship, 9 x 11 3/4 In. ....*Illus*	3575.00
Plaque, Portrait of Woman, Signed, 6 x 4 In.	1650.00
Plaque, Woman With Flowers, Signed, 5 3/4 x 8 3/4 In.	1650.00
Plate, Dinner, Gilt Floral Filigree, Cobalt Blue, 20 Piece	1430.00
Plate, Foliate & Scroll Gilt Border, Ivory Ground, 10 3/4 In., 8 Piece	110.00
Plate, Roses of Redoute, 8 Piece	240.00
Plate, Squirrel, Holding Nut On Large Leaf, 3 1/4 In.	55.00
Platter, Kensington, 15 In. ....45.00 To 60.00
Sugar Shaker, Blackberries, Blossoms, Bavaria, 1912	45.00
Tea Set, 22k Gold, Hand Painted, With Tray, Selb, Bavaria	165.00
Tray, Le Roy, Swirl Quatrefoil Shape, Gold Loop Handle, 10 In.	175.00
Vase, Gold Tree Branch Design, Maroon, 10 In.	70.00

ICONS, special, revered pictures of Jesus, Mary, or a saint, are usually Russian or Byzantine. The small icons collected today are made of wood and tin or precious metals. Many modern copies have been made in the old style and are being sold to tourists in Russia and Europe.

12 Holy Days, Russia, Wood Panel	1900.00
Bishop Saint, Silver Riza, Fitted Case, Russia, 5 x 4 In.	250.00

Hutschenreuther, Plaque, 3 Women,
12 3/4 X 8 3/4 In.

Hutschenreuther, Plaque, Nude & Lover,
Ship, 9 X 11 3/4 In.

Christ The Pantocrator, Oil On Panel, Russia, 12 x 9 1/2 In. 137.00
Christ, Gilded Repousse Base, Russia, 19th Century, 12 x 10 1/2 In. 175.00
Christ, Holding Bible, Oil On Velvet Panel, Green, 20th Century, 11 x 8 In. 93.50
Christ, Salvator Mundi, Russia, 12 x 10 In. 440.00
Gabriel With Horn, On Winged Horse, Russia, 1775–1825, 12 In. 795.00
Madonna & Child, Oil On Wood Panel, 18th Century Or Earlier, 12 5/8 x 9 In. 380.00
Madonna & Child, Russia, 12 1/2 x 10 In. 1430.00
Madonna & Child, Russia, 1850–1880 .... 585.00
Madonna & Child, Transfer Design, Tin, Frame, 6 1/2 x 3 3/4 In. 35.00
Many Scenes Around Large Center Scene, Oil On Wood, Russia, 18th Century ... 1375.00
Mary With Child, Oil On Board, Gilded Metal, Velvet Frame, Russia, 17 x 15 In. ... 357.00
Resurrection, Surrounded By Twelve Festivals, Gilt Brass, Russia, 14 x 11 1/2 In. 825.00
Saint, Hand To Heart, Gilt & Enamel Framing, Russia, 19th Century, 8 3/4 x 7 In. 330.00
Saint, Oil On Wood, Russia, Late 18th Century 2200.00
St. George & Dragon, Gold Leaf & Tempera, Greece, 5 1/2 x 5 In. 300.00
St. Gregory, Holding A Cross, Oil On Wood Panel, 12 x 10 1/4 In. 165.00
St. Nicholas, Oil On Panel, Russia, Early 19th Century, 20 x 16 In. 385.00
St. Nicholas, Russia, Late 18th Century, 12 x 9 1/2 In. 495.00
St. Sophia, Wisdom of God, Virgin & John The Baptist, Russia, 10 1/2 In. 715.00
Triumphant Christ of Peace, Enamel On Silver, Frame, Russia, 8 3/4 x 4 3/4 In. .. 3300.00
Virgin Mary & Saint, Cradled Wood, Russia, 14 1/2 In. 275.00
Virgin On Red, Giltwood, Frame, Russia, 10 x 13 In. 1500.00
Visitation, Greece, 15 x 12 In. 495.00
Winged Figure With Sword, Russia, 14 x 10 In. 550.00

IMARI patterns are named for the Japanese ware decorated with orange
and blue stylized flowers. The design on the Japanese ware became so
characteristic that the name *Imari* has come to mean any pattern of this
type. It was copied by the European factories of the eighteenth and early
nineteenth centuries.

Bowl, Blue & White, 4 1/2 In. 104.00
Bowl, Figure In Garden Center, Bluebirds, Iron Red Base, 1860, 7 In. .... 145.00 To 175.00
Bowl, Flared Rim, Marked, 9 3/4 In. 285.00
Bowl, Foliate Medallion, 12 In. 385.00
Bowl, Fruit, Floral & Aquatic Design, 19th Century, 8 1/4 In. 330.00
Bowl, Multicolored Design, 9 3/4 In. 65.00
Bowl, Polychrome & Gilt, Porcelain, 2 3/8 In., Pair 150.00
Bowl, Polychrome, 4 1/2 In. 49.00
Bowl, Polychrome, 5 3/8 In. 11.00
Bowl, Polychrome, Wooden Stand, 7 3/8 In. 85.00
Bowl, Raised Flowers, Butterfly Medallion Center, Blue Rim, 1850, 7 In. 275.00
Bowl, Set, Nested, 5 1/4 To 7 1/2 In., 3 Piece 198.00
Charger, Carp & Iris, Blue, White, Pale Shades of Color, Porcelain, 24 5/8 In. 1975.00
Charger, Dragon Center, 19th Century, 18 In. Diam. 440.00
Charger, Floral & Bird Reserves, Fluted Border, 12 In. 220.00
Charger, Jovial Figures, Iron–Red Ground, Floral & Scroll Border, 16 In. 660.00
Charger, Polychrome Enamel, 21 3/4 In. 120.00
Charger, Scalloped, 12 1/4 In. 275.00
Charger, Warriors, Marked, 10 In. 275.00
Figurine, Parrot, Polychrome, 16 In. 55.00
Figurine, Rabbit, Polychrome, 6 1/2 In., Pair 88.00
Pitcher, Blue Floral & Trees, 1850, 4 1/2 In. .... 85.00 To 125.00
Pitcher, Floral, Trees, Blue, Raised Base Rim, 1800s 90.00
Plate, Fan Shape, 8 1/2 In. .... *Illus* 75.00
Plate, Gaudy Ironstone, 10 In., 4 Piece 594.00
Plate, Landscape Design, Gilt, Blue & White, 8 1/2 In. 33.00
Plate, Wedding, Plum Blossoms, Pine & Bamboo, Signed, c.1840, 8 1/2 In. 220.00
Platter, Floral Design, Red, Blue, Gold Floral Border, Octagonal, 18 x 14 In. 412.50
Punch Bowl, Flower Basket Design, Floral & Bird Panels, 7 x 14 In. 990.00
Ring Tree, Late 1800s 55.00
Stand, Blue, White, 26 In., Pair 440.00
Vase, Blue & White, 3 In., With Wooden Stand 15.00
Vase, Foo Dog Cover, 15 In., Pair .... 1200.00 To 1320.00

Vase, Panels On Brocaded Ground, 24 In.	1320.00
Vase, Storage, Tree & Foliage, 11 In.	525.00
Vase, White Applied Dragon, Red Enameled, Blue Underglaze, 18 1/2 In.	203.00

IMPERIAL GLASS Corporation was founded in Bellaire, Ohio, in 1901. It became a subsidiary of Lenox, Inc., in 1973 and was sold to Arthur R. Lorch in 1981. It was sold again in 1982, went bankrupt that same year, and some of the molds and assets were sold to other companies. The Imperial glass preferred by the collector is stretch glass, art glass, carnival glass, and the top–quality tablewares.

Candlewick, Bottle, Ketchup, 14 Oz.	125.00
Candlewick, Bowl, 10 1/4 In.	22.00
Candlewick, Bowl, 4 In.	18.00
Candlewick, Bowl, Ball Footed, Fluted, 9 x 2 1/2 In.	25.00
Candlewick, Bowl, Cupped, 11 In.	40.00
Candlewick, Bowl, Handles, Divided, 8 1/2 In.	95.00
Candlewick, Bowl, Underplate, Divided, 6 1/2 & 14 In.	40.00
Candlewick, Butter, Cover, 1/4 Lb.	30.00
Candlewick, Cake Stand, Low, 10 In.	45.00
Candlewick, Candy Jar, Beaded Lid	40.00
Candlewick, Candy, Covered	95.00
Candlewick, Compote, 4–Bead, 8 In.	70.00
Candlewick, Creamer	95.00
Candlewick, Cruet	60.00
Candlewick, Cup & Saucer	6.50
Candlewick, Dish, Divided, Aqua	65.00
Candlewick, Mayonnaise Set, 3 Piece	22.00
Candlewick, Mayonnaise Set, Light Blue, 2 Piece	117.00
Candlewick, Perfume Bottle, 4 1/4 In.	75.00
Candlewick, Pitcher, Beaded Handle, 80 Oz.	125.00
Candlewick, Pitcher, Star Cutting, 80 Oz.	150.00
Candlewick, Plate, 10 In.	25.00
Candlewick, Plate, 5 1/2 x 2 In.	12.00
Candlewick, Plate, 7 In.	8.00
Candlewick, Plate, Cut Floral, 7 In.	75.00
Candlewick, Plate, Deviled Egg	100.00 To 105.00
Candlewick, Punch Set, Bowl, Underplate, Ladle, 12 Cups	225.00
Candlewick, Relish, 2 Sections, 6 1/2 In.	20.00
Candlewick, Relish, 3 Sections, Aqua, 7 1/2 In.	48.00
Candlewick, Relish, 4 Sections, 9 1/2 In.	15.00
Candlewick, Relish, Cover, 3 Sections	850.00
Candlewick, Salt & Pepper, Chrome Top, Footed	50.00
Candlewick, Sauce	8.00
Candlewick, Sherbet, Floral Cutting, 6 Oz.	13.00
Candlewick, Spoon & Fork, Salad	20.00
Candlewick, Sugar & Creamer, Tray	22.00

Imari, Plate, Fan Shape, 8 1/2 In.

Turn over reversible rugs once a year. Turn rugs end-to-end in the room at least every three years. If the room is sunny, turn the rug several times a year to even out sun fading.

Candlewick, Sugar, Floral Cutting	15.00
Candlewick, Tray, Lemon, Handle, 5 1/2 In.	35.00
Candlewick, Tray, Oval, 9 In.	32.00
Candlewick, Tray, Wheat, Handle, 9 In.	37.00
Candlewick, Vase, Bud	95.00
Candlewick, Vase, Fan	22.00
Cape Cod, Ashtray, 4 In.	8.00
Cape Cod, Bowl, Vegetable, Oval, 11 In.	65.00
Cape Cod, Butter, Round, Crystal, 5 In.	25.00
Cape Cod, Cake Plate, Birthday	200.00
Cape Cod, Cake Server, Square, 10 In.	75.00
Cape Cod, Claret, 5 Oz.	10.00
Cape Cod, Coaster	6.00
Cape Cod, Cocktail, Wafer Stem	5.00
Cape Cod, Cookie Jar, Wicker Handle	60.00
Cape Cod, Creamer	7.00
Cape Cod, Decanter, Square, 24 Oz.	20.00
Cape Cod, Eggcup	20.00
Cape Cod, Goblet, Water, Amber	45.00
Cape Cod, Jug, Water, Hexagonal Base, Footed	80.00
Cape Cod, Parfait, 6 Oz.	9.00 To 10.00
Cape Cod, Pitcher, Ice Lip, 40 Oz.	60.00 To 85.00
Cape Cod, Plate, 7 In.	5.00
Cape Cod, Plate, 8 In.	3.50
Cape Cod, Punch Set, Underplate & Ladle, Bowl, 15 Piece	230.00
Cape Cod, Relish, 3 Sections, Oval	24.00
Cape Cod, Salt & Pepper, Green	35.00
Cape Cod, Vase, Footed, 11 In.	55.00
Cathay, Bookends, Empress, Frosted, Evans	225.00
Cathay, Candlestick, Figural, Virginia B. Evens, Pair	450.00
Cathay, Vase, Ribbon, Silver Mist	695.00
Free Hand, Vase, Browns, Greens, Handle, 10 x 10 In.	150.00
Free Hand, Vase, Hanging Heart, 4 1/2 In.	450.00
Frosted Peacock, Bowl, Cover	49.00
Grape, Decanter, Stopper, Amethyst Carnival Glass	195.00
Old Williamsburg, Relish, 5 Sections, 13 1/2 x 9 1/2 In.	35.00
Pillar Flute, Bonbon, Crimped, Blue, 7 In.	22.50
Pillar Flute, Bowl, Blue, 6 In.	30.00
Pillar Flute, Celery, Blue, 8 1/2 In.	2.50
Tradition, Cake Plate, 72 Candle	55.00
Twisted Optic, Candy Dish, Cover, Yellow, Footed, 1927–1930	35.00
Vase, Hanging, Heart Shape, 2 Handles, Iridescent Blue, 1920s, 8 1/2 In.	625.00
Vase, Opalescent Drag Loops On Yellow, Orange Lining, 8 1/2 In.	175.00

INDIAN art from North America has attracted the collector for many years. Each tribe has its own distinctive designs and techniques. Baskets, jewelry, pottery, and leatherwork are of greatest collector interest. Eskimo art is listed in another category in this book.

Bag, Crow, Mirror, Beaded Hourglass Design, Fringed	4950.00
Bag, Nez Perce, Corn Husk, Analine Design, Floral On Other Side, 17 1/2 In.	350.00
Bag, Plateau, Beaded, Skunk Design	660.00
Basket, Apache, Burden, 7 x 10 In.	150.00
Basket, Apache, Central Star, Men & Deer, Martynia With Willow, 13 3/8 In.	1200.00
Basket, Apache, Devil's Claw Willow, Dog Figures, Coiled	6600.00
Basket, Apache, Twine, High Flaring Sides, 13 In.	1000.00
Basket, Apache, Twined Weave, Worn Dyed Design, 1900, 15 1/4 x 16 1/4 In.	220.00
Basket, California, Cover, Oblong, 12 1/2 x 3 In.	220.00
Basket, Eastern Woodlands, Blue Bands, Cover	205.00
Basket, Hauasupai, Burden, Forehead Strap	550.00
Basket, Hopi, Brown & Gray Aztec Pattern, 1920s	400.00
Basket, Lillooet, 9 In.	250.00
Basket, Makah, Cover, 1 3/4 x 2 1/2 In.	104.00
Basket, Navajo, Wedding, 22 1/2 In.	950.00

Basket, Navajo, Wedding, c.1930, 14 In. 225.00
Basket, Navajo, Wedding, Willow, Martynia & Suma Root, 14 In. 150.00
Basket, Nootka, Berry Root Dyed, 1890 .... 75.00
Basket, North American Woodlands, 2 Wood Handles, Prince Edward Island, 20 In. 159.00
Basket, Papago, 12 x 10 In. 30.00
Basket, Papago, Cover, 5 In. 60.00
Basket, Papago, Cover, Geometric Design, Martynia & Yucca, 8 In. 85.00
Basket, Papago, Greek Key Design, 8 In. 88.00
Basket, Papago, Pictorial, c.1920, 10 1/4 x 9 In. 135.00
Basket, Penobscot, Baby, Splint, Painted Design, 1900, 31 x 17 1/2 x 16 In. 180.00
Basket, Pima Olla, Ceremonial, Devil's Claw Natural 650.00
Basket, Pima, Coiled, Woven, 2 Steam Engines, Pulling 4 Cars, 4 7/8 In. 5775.00
Basket, Pima, Deep Coiled, 15 In. 715.00
Basket, Plains, Black Dye, 4 Crude Designs, 1860, 9 3/8 x 3 1/2 In. 110.00
Basket, Thompson River, Oval, 8 In. 485.00
Basket, Tlingit, 6 x 11 In. 660.00
Belt, Apache, Concha Shells, Beaded 150.00
Belt, Beadwork, Cloth, 19th Century, 38 In. 88.00
Belt, Navajo, 7 Conchas, Sterling Silver 1450.00
Belt, Navajo, 8 1/2–In. Silver Buckle, Silver Studs, c.1940 .... 550.00
Belt, Navajo, Concha, Silver, Set With Turquoise, Tooled Leather, 1950 .... 1300.00
Belt, Navajo, Conchas, Sterling Silver, 1930s 395.00
Blanket, Banded, Serrated Diamonds, Woman's, 42 x 52 In. 7150.00
Blanket, Chief's, Late–Third Phase, 1910, 52 x 45 In. 350.00
Blanket, Chimayo, Gray Diamond Medallion, Clouds, Arrows, Red, 48 x 88 In. 330.00
Blanket, Crow, Wedding, Striped Snake, 1890 .... 7500.00
Blanket, Mexican, Thunderbird Design, 71 x 44 In. 1050.00
Blanket, Sioux, Saddle, Beaded & Quilled, Hide, Crossed Triangles, 15 1/2 In. 1325.00
Blanket, Sioux, Saddle, Beaded Hide Strips, Hide, 63 x 23 1/2 In. 2300.00
Blanket, Wool, Red, Brown, Orange, Pendleton, Pat. 1926 .... 375.00
Bolo Clasp, Navajo, Buffalo Design, Modern 185.00
Bonnet, Sioux, Baby's, Blue Beads, Red Ground, Early 1900s, 4 1/2 In. 300.00
Boots, Kiowa, Hide Laces, High–Top, Fringed 2640.00
Bowl, Acoma, Floral, White Ground, Pottery, Early 20th Century, 8 1/4 x 10 In. 1045.00
Bowl, Apache, Basketry, Willow, Martynia, Men, Horses, Green Paint Drip, 12 In. 1485.00
Bowl, Apache, Coiled Basketry, Black Devil's Claw, 9 1/2 In. 275.00
Bowl, Apache, Devil's Claw On Willow, Coiled, Oval, 19 1/2 x 13 1/2 In. 825.00
Bowl, Black On Black, Geronimo, 6 1/2 x 8 In. 110.00
Bowl, Black On Black, Rosa Comancho, 5 1/2 x 6 In. 77.00
Bowl, Hopi, Geometric Pattern, Bird Design, 11 In 4300.00
Bowl, Northwest Potlatch, Wolves' Faces, Ivory Teeth, Abalone Eyes 990.00
Bowl, Papago, Basketry, Stepped Polychrome Design, Martynia, Yucca, 10 x 6 In. 325.00
Bowl, Pueblo, Black On Black, Maria, 1990, 4 3/4 x 10 3/8 In. 2500.00
Bowl, Pueblo, San Ildefonso, Black On Black, Pasevalita, 2 1/2 x 6 In. 93.50
Bowl, Santa Clara, Carved Pottery, Flora Naranja, 4 1/2 In. 176.00
Bowl, Zuni, Geometric, Bird & Animal Design, 8 In. 4300.00
Box, Carved, Slide Top, 2 3/4 x 5 In. 165.00
Box, Storage, Parfleche, Beaded Cover 1430.00
Bracelet, Southwestern, Silver & Turquoise 412.50
Bracelet, Zuni, Petit–Point, Blue Gem, Turquoise & Silver, Large 189.00
Breastplate, Bone, Bead, 19th Century 440.00
Breastplate, Sioux, Bone Hair Pipe, Brass Beads, Leather Spacers, Restrung 143.00
Bucket, Algonquin, Sugar, Spruce Root Binding, Birch Bark, 10 In. 450.00
Canoe, Northeast Woodlands, Spruce Root Stitched & Peeled, 2 Paddles, Model 1200.00
Canoe, Northwest, Child's, Carved & Painted Pine, c.1900 .... 1800.00
Canteen, Apache, Parfleche, Red & Yellow Painted, Pre–1900 .... 275.00
Case, Crow, Parfleche, 19th Century 9820.00
Case, Plains, Parfleche, Late 19th Century, 25 In. 1900.00
Check, Seneca Nation of Indians, Brant, N.Y., x Signed On Back, 1897 .... 25.00
Collar, Sioux, Child's .... 500.00 To 550.00
Cradle Board, Algonquin, Bent Face Guard, Laced Construction, 1880s, 34 1/2 In. 250.00
Cradle Board, Apache, c.1880 .... 1100.00
Cradle Board, Apache, Wicker Sunshade, Bentwood Frame, 34 1/2 In. 450.00

♦ ♦ ♦ ♦ ♦ ♦ ♦ ♦ ♦ ♦ ♦ ♦ ♦ ♦ ♦ ♦ ♦ ♦ ♦ ♦

We once pulled off some of the silver plating from a Sheffield candlestick when we removed the cellophane tape that held a Christmas decoration to the candlestick. A friend pulled off some of the glaze from a plate when she removed masking tape from the plate. Don't use anything with a strong glue on an antique surface.

♦ ♦ ♦ ♦ ♦ ♦ ♦ ♦ ♦ ♦ ♦ ♦ ♦ ♦ ♦ ♦ ♦ ♦ ♦ ♦

Indian, Fan, Huron, Turkey Feathers,

Birchbark Shaped Handle, 1880, 15 In.

Cradle Board, Apache, Wicker Sunshade, Cloth Wrap, Beaded Ties, 27 In.	475.00
Cradle, Basketry, 12 x 16 In.	66.00
Dance Stick, Sioux, Ceremonial	852.00
Doll, Hopi, Butterfly Girl, Jimmy Kewanwytewa, c.1955	1850.00
Doll, Hopi, Kachina, Butterfly Girl, Rio Grande, 1920, 8 In.	1100.00
Doll, Hopi, Kachina, Dancer, Painted Carved Wood Costume, Signed, 9 1/4 In.	99.00
Doll, Human Hair, Buckskin Dress, 11 In.	500.00
Doll, Penobscot, Fringed & Beaded Leather Outfit, 12 1/2 In.	110.00
Doll, Seminole, Handmade, 7 1/2 In.	15.00
Dress, Crow, Black Trade Cloth, Red Felt, Beaded, Cowry Shells, 1925	495.00
Dress, Northern Plains, Black Trade Cloth, Ribbon Binding, Beadwork, c.1925	450.00
Dress, Sioux, Girl's, Hide, Beaded, Separate Hide Extender	7500.00
Fan, Huron, Turkey Feathers, Birchbark Shaped Handle, 1880, 15 In. ....*Illus*	385.00
Fetish, Plains, Umbilical, Quilled Lizard, Multicolor Dyed Quills, 7 In.	154.00
Fetish, Sioux, Turtle, Beaded Leather, c.1900, 5 1/2 In. .... 395.00 To	475.00
Gauntlets, Northern Cree, Beaded Deer, Flowers & Trees, 19th Century	1950.00
Gauntlets, Northern Plains, Beaded, Fringed, 1880s	850.00
Gauntlets, Plateau, Beaded, Eagle, With Flag, Star Design, 1880, 15 In., Pair	1500.00
Gloves, Northern Plains, Buckskin, Glass Beaded Columbines	450.00
Headdress, Sioux, Ermine	800.00
Jar, 2–Tone Red, Gray, White, Signed, Pottery, 7 In.	148.00
Jar, Acoma, Bird, Florals, Clay Body, 8 In.	415.00
Jar, Acoma, Pottery, Painted Figures, 19 In.	300.00
Jar, Acoma, Water, Pottery, Designs, White Slip, Concave Base, 1890, 11 1/2 In.	6600.00
Jar, Basketry, California, Bottleneck, 2 1/2 x 4 3/8 In.	415.00
Jar, Hopi, Polychrome, Pottery, Slight Slip, 5 1/4 In.	71.00
Jar, Hopi, Pottery, Contemporary, Mary Tosa Jemmez, 12 In.	550.00
Jar, Hopi, Thunderbird Design, Ear of Corn Symbol Signature, 10 In., Pair	530.00
Jar, Martinez, Pottery, Sityatki Style, 5 1/2 In.	55.00
Jar, San Ildefonso, Pottery, Black On Black, Feather, Marie, Santana, 3 5/8 In.	525.00
Jar, Zia, Water, Design, Creamy Tan Slip, 19th Century, 12 x 9 3/4 In.	1000.00
Jar, Zuni, Bands of Heartline Deer, Birds, White Slip, 19th Century, 12 x 10 In.	3300.00
Knife Case, Plains, Beaded Hide	3960.00
Leggings, Blackfoot, Beaded Strips, Cloth	650.00
Leggings, Blackfoot, Red & Black Trade Blanket, Beaded Strip, 20th Century	275.00
Leggings, Sioux, Beading On Hide, Pair	650.00
Log Bin, Northeast Woodland, Birch Bark, Tomah Joseph, 1903	1870.00
Long Bow, Quiver, Leather Tooled, Fred Bear, 2 Sets of Wooden Arrows	425.00
Mask, Hopi, Kachina, Long–Haired, Painted Hide, 20th Century	3150.00
Moccasin, Seneca, Beaded & Quilled Hide, Ankle Flaps, 9 3/4 In., Single	1875.00

Moccasins, Arapaho, Beaded, 1890 .... 1000.00
Moccasins, Cheyenne, Red, Blue & White, 8 1/2 In. 100.00
Moccasins, Comanche, High Top, Yellow, Green, Silver Concha, Fringe, 1870 .... 5400.00
Moccasins, Crown, Child's 150.00
Moccasins, Great Lakes, Blue Beaded, 1890 .... 1600.00
Moccasins, Iroquois, Beaded Vamps, Black Velvet Cuffs, c.1890, 10 In. 150.00
Moccasins, Minnie Sitting Bull, Rosebud Reservation, Beaded Design, 11 In. 935.00
Moccasins, Minnie Sitting Bull, Rosebud Reservation, Beaded Design, 8 In. 825.00
Moccasins, Navajo, High Top, Concha Closure, 11 1/2 In. 60.00
Moccasins, Northern Plains, Child's, Beaded Star Design, 4 1/2 In. 275.00
Moccasins, Ojibwa, Beaded 242.00
Moccasins, Oto, Child's, Beaded Hide, 1890 .... 3750.00
Moccasins, Sioux, Burial, Overall Beading, Velvet Cuffs, 11 In. 2200.00
Moccasins, Sioux, Man's, Multicolor Beads, Opal White Bead Ground, 1910 .... 550.00
Moccasins, Sioux, Red, Gold & Green Beads, White Beaded Ground, 1890, 11 In. 625.00
Necklace & Earrings, Zuni, Squash Blossom, Petit Point 1800.00
Necklace, Navajo, Turquoise, Silver, 3 Pendant Cabochons 66.00
Necklace, Squash Blossom, Turquoise, Silver, Signed 550.00
Necklace, Zuni, Fetish, Double Strand 250.00
Necklace, Zuni, Graduated Beads, Inlaid Turquoise 205.00
Necklace, Zuni, Squash Blossom, Needlepoint Turquoise, Silver 289.00
Necklace, Zuni, Squash Blossom, Sterling, Blue Stone, Petit Point Setting, VMB 330.00
Olla, Pima/Papago, Step Design, Martynia & Willow, 6 x 7 3/4 In. 375.00
Olla, Zigzag Bands, Human Figures, Quadrupeds 742.50
Papoose Carrier, Double Leather, Wool Designs, Cowl, Carrying Straps, 37 1/2 In. 380.00
Pipe Bag, Blackfoot, Red & Blue Bead Edging, Heart Shaped Ornament, 23 1/2 In. 550.00
Pipe Bag, Ojibwa, Beaded, Fringed, Made For Joseph Cook, 1890s 1500.00
Pipe Bag, Plains, Quilled Hide 3070.00
Pipe Bag, Plains, Tin Cone & Horsehair Drops, Beaded Deerskin 9900.00
Pipe Stem, Plains, Spiral Carved, Red & Green Paint, 1937, 23 3/4 In. 468.00
Pipe Tomahawk, Plains, Lead Bowl, Copper Wire Wrapping, Brass Tacks, 19 In. 2200.00
Pipe, Sioux, Catlinite, Incised Scallop Design, Quill Braid Wrap Stem, 33 7/8 In. 500.00
Pipe, Sioux, Incised Scallop Design, Quill Braid Stem, Mallard Feather Band, 34 In. 550.00
Pitcher, Martinez, Pottery, Brown, Black, 14 In. 50.00
Plate, Pueblo, A'Avanai Design 3850.00
Plate, Pueblo, Feather, Maria, Popovi, 14 In. 550.00
Pot, San Ildefonso, Black On Black, Isabella, 8 In. 150.00
Pot, San Ildefonso, Blue Corn, 2 x 5 In. 150.00
Pot, Santa Clara, Black On Black, Tonita & Juan, 6 x 7 In. 300.00
Pot, Santa Clara, Pottery, Black, Melon Rib, Mela Youngblood, 9/9/77, 4 In. 220.00
Pouch, Apache, Cross Design, Multicolored Beaded Fringe, 10 x 7 1/2 In. 500.00
Pouch, Beaded Leather, Deer Head Design 125.00
Pouch, Micmac, Beaded On Red Wool Trade Cloth, Lined 445.00
Pouch, Northern Plains, Parfleche, Geometric, 20th Century, 26 3/4 x 13 1/2 In. 495.00
Pouch, Seminole, Made From Tanned Crocodile Foot, 8 x 5 1/2 In. 150.00
Pouch, Tanned Leather Backing, Floral Design, Gold, Blue, Pink, Black, 10 1/2 In. 225.00
Pouch, Woodlands, Beaded, Polychrome Floral, Beaded, Velvet, 1890, 6 1/2 x 6 In. 250.00
Pouch, Yakima, Diamond Design, Beaded, 7 1/2 x 7 1/4 In. 192.00
Rattle, Hopi, Gourd, Four Winds Design, Black & Red, 7 1/4 In. 25.00
Rattle, Iroquois, Turtle Shell, False Face Society, 15 1/2 In. 250.00
Rattle, Northeast, Ceremonial, Carved Leaves, 9 1/4 In. 180.00
Rattle, Northwest Coast, Bear, Carved Features, 20th Century, 9 1/2 In. 3100.00
Rattle, Northwest Coast, Head Shape, Painted Features 9350.00
Robe, Puberty, Crown, Calfskin, Beaded 1650.00
Rug, Navajo, 1930s, 3 Ft. 2 In. x 1 Ft. 10 In. 85.00
Rug, Navajo, 3 Black & White Panels, Shaded Red Field, 74 1/2 x 54 1/2 In. 440.00
Rug, Navajo, Airplanes & Swastikas, 1920s, 29 x 49 In. 550.00
Rug, Navajo, Black & White Stepped Geometric, Gray Ground, 92 x 64 In. 1210.00
Rug, Navajo, c.1930, 48 x 72 In. 2000.00
Rug, Navajo, Center Diamond Medallion, Radiating Stripes, 6 Ft. 2 In. x 4 Ft. 4 In. 467.00
Rug, Navajo, Central Green Corn Stalk 3850.00
Rug, Navajo, Cotton, Red, Brown, Gray & Natural Wool, 1900, 4 Ft. x 5 Ft. 5 In. 1325.00
Rug, Navajo, Cross, Red, Tan, Brown, Natural, Hand Carded Yarn, 33 x 53 In. 165.00

Rug, Navajo, Double Diamond Centers, Feather Design, Large	2200.00
Rug, Navajo, Geometric Design, 100 x 68 In.	2750.00
Rug, Navajo, Multiple Rectangles, Brown, Red & White, Border, 36 x 61 In.	170.00
Rug, Navajo, Red & Brown Geometric, Tan Field, 2 Ft. 7 In. x 4 Ft.	220.00
Rug, Navajo, Red, Black & White Geometric, Brown Field, 1920, 62 x 36 In.	275.00
Rug, Navajo, Serrated Diamonds, Natural & Dyed, Mustard Ground, 45 x 40 In.	165.00
Rug, Navajo, Storm Pattern, Hand Carded, 3 Ft. x 4 Ft. 11 In.	400.00
Rug, Navajo, Symbols, Brown, Red, White, Green & Orange, Border, 46 x 66 In.	950.00
Rug, Navajo, Triangular Devices, Ivory Border, Red Ground, 66 x 62 In.	495.00
Rug, Navajo, Two Gray Hills, c.1930, 48 x 72 In.	2000.00
Rug, Navajo, Wool, Orange–Red, Brown, Tan, White, 1915, 4 Ft. 8 In. x 8 Ft.	660.00
Saddle Blanket, Navajo, Black, White, & Gray, Red Diamonds, Double, 32 x 51 In.	250.00
Saddle Blanket, Navajo, White, Double, 27 x 58 In.	150.00
Saddle Throw, Navajo, Expanding Serrated Diamonds, 41 1/2 x 36 In.	300.00
Saddlebag, Navajo, Alternating Dashed Bands, 4 Ft. 2 In. x 2 Ft. 9 In.	143.00
Sash, Eastern Woodlands, Finger Woven, White Beads, Wool, 94 In.	3300.00
Serape, Saltillo, Large Central Diamond, 100 x 51 In.	6600.00
Sheath, Knife, Rain–In–The–Face, Beaded Design, Dated 1916	2500.00
Sheath, Sioux, Knife, White–Heart–Red, Yellow, Green & Blue Beads, 8 3/4 In.	275.00
Sheath, Woodlands, Beaded, 1870	2200.00
Shirt, Athabascan, Beaded Hide	7500.00
Shirt, Blackfoot, Holy, Cutout Diamond Shaped Holes, 37 In.	850.00
Shirt, Plains, Scout, Smoked Tanned Hide, Fringed, Brass Buttons, 31 1/2 In.	1200.00
Sioux, Vest, Beaded Hide, Blue, 2 Pictures of Horses On Back	6500.00
Tool, Woodlands, Roach & Bone Stretcher, Moose Hair	1225.00
Totem Pole, Northwest Coast, Polychrome Surface, 49 In.	3850.00
Toy, Canoe, Carved Chip Wood	70.00
Toy, Sioux, Teepee	3750.00
Tray, Apache, Basketry, Willow, Martynia, 18 Figures, 1920, 20 1/4 x 4 3/4 In.	990.00
Tray, Apache, Dark Arrow Design, Oval, 9 In.	200.00
Tray, Hopi, Coiled Polychrome Basketry, 1890, 14 In.	150.00
Tray, Lacquer Ware, Gold Floral Design, 20 In.	55.00
Tray, Pima, Devil's Claw, Horses & Whorls, 10 1/4 In.	275.00
Trencher, Wooden, Age Cracks, 19 x 20 In.	192.00
Vase, Acoma, Wedding, Pottery, Cream, Brown, 11 In.	75.00
Vase, Lacquer Ware, Floral Design, Brass Lined, 12 In., Pair	44.00
Vase, Qua Paw, Red & White, Mississippi, Spout, 10 In.	605.00
Vase, San Ildefonso, Black On Black, Juanita	137.50
Vase, San Ildefonso, Black On Black, Maria	2750.00
Vest, Sioux, Beaded Hide, Horse Picture, Muslin Lined, Sinew Sewn, Blue Ground	7150.00
Vest, Sioux, Child's, Geometric Beading, Flags, White Ground, 9 x 11 1/2 In.	900.00
Vest, Sioux, Pictorial, Beaded	7150.00
War Club Head, Yemassee, Excavated In Field, 3 1/2 x 6 In.	55.00

INKSTANDS were made to be placed on a desk. They held some type of container for ink, and possibly a sander, a pen tray, a pen, a holder for pounce, and even a candle to melt the sealing wax. Inkstands date to the eighteenth century and have been made of silver, copper, ceramics, and glass. Additional inkstands may be found in these and other related categories.

Baccarat Inkwell Liner, Pierced Urn–Form Wells, Brass, c.1900	285.00
Boat Shape, Sheffield Silver Plate, 1785, 14 In.	1430.00
Boy Pushing Wheelbarrow, Barrel Top Lifts Off, Cast Iron Pot, c.1790, 6 3/4 In.	375.00
Brass Double Well, Letter Holder, Modern	30.00
Brass Dragon, Floral Top, Swirled Glass Wells	145.00
Brass Filigree, Stamp Section, Pat. 1862	60.00
Brass, Cap, Fence Pen Rest, Blown Insert	45.00
Brass, Double Wells, Top Match Base	45.00
Dolphin Handles, Bronze, 14 x 8 In.	350.00
Dolphin Pen Rack, Brass Stand, Glass Well and Top, Square Base	85.00
Embossed Stork, 3 Pen Rests, Cast Iron, 2 Bottles	95.00
Filigree Copper Stand, Porcelain Insert	40.00
George II, Peter Archambo, Silver Sterling, 1932	5500.00

Inkwell, Camels, Cast Metal, Painted, Pair

◆◆◆◆◆◆◆◆◆◆◆◆◆◆◆◆◆◆◆◆◆◆

Jet beads can be washed in mild soapsuds and water. Do not soak the strings. If the jet is carved, you may want to clean it with a wad made from the centers of a few slices of soft white bread. The bread will absorb the dirt and grease, then crumble and fall away.

◆◆◆◆◆◆◆◆◆◆◆◆◆◆◆◆◆◆◆◆◆◆

Gilt Bronze & Marble, Lidded Bell-Shaped Well, Marble Fluted Base, 5 1/2 In.	225.00
Glass, Black Amethyst Stand, Pen Rest, Inserted Bottle, Brass Hinged	85.00
Glass, Swirl & Top, Metal Stand, Double	25.00
Gnomes On Both Sides, Stand	175.00
Gothic Finial On Lid, Cast Stand With Pen Rack, Shaped Well	45.00
Horseshoe Pen Rack, Cast Iron Blown Well	35.00
Leather-Covered Stand, Stamp Box, Quill Pen, Pen Rest	35.00
Metal Base, Glass Well Attached, Brass Pen Rack, 1861	45.00
Napoleon III, 2 Dome Wells, Floral Mounts, c.1855, 9 1/2 In.	185.00
Neoclassical Style, Urn-Form Well, Center Griffins, Silver Plate, c.1900	310.00
Oriental Boy, Hat Is Lid, Sitting On Flat Stand, Pen Groove	80.00
Oval Tray, 2 Pots, Silver, J. Dixon & Sons, England, 1899	660.00
Paperweight Design, Onyx, Glass, Tin Ink Holder	20.00
Paw Feet, Fluted Border, Cut Glass Seal Box, E. Farrell, England, 1813, 11 In.	7425.00
Regency, Mother-of-Pearl Inlay, 2 Wells, Brass Handle, c.1850, 5 x 15 In.	385.00
Silver Plated Stand and Tops, Hinged, 2 Wells	40.00
Snail, Cast Iron Stand, January 14, 1879	160.00
Swirl Glass, Wells & Tray, Hinged Lid, Cast Iron	75.00
Turquoise Glass Base, Pen Rest, Two Clear Wells, Sterling Repousse Top	160.00
Victorian, Brass Hinged Lid and Pen Rack, Clear Well	55.00
White Onyx Base, Ormolu Frame, 2 Crystal Lidded Wells, c.1910, 12 In.	310.00

INKWELLS, of course, held ink. Ready-made ink was first made about 1836 and was sold in bottles. The desk inkwell had a narrow hole so the pen would not slip inside. Inkwells were made of many materials, such as pottery, glass, pewter, silver. Look in these categories for more listings of inkwells.

3-Mold, Blown, Pat. 1861	30.00
Alabaster Paint Design, Double Well Stand	50.00
Amber Cut Glass, Brass Collar Around Hinged Lid, 2 3/8 In.	200.00
Arab, Seated Beside Camel, Austrian, Cold Painted Bronze, 6 1/2 In.	445.00
Art Nouveau, Metal Lid, Porcelain Insert, Glass Well, Loetz-Type	25.00
Artichoke, Matching Loose Lid, Pottery Insert	125.00
Baccarat Style Swirl, Sterling Silver Top, Signed, Whiting	55.00
Bird's Nest, Bird, 3 Eggs, Snake, Coleslaw Coating, Staffordshire	195.00
Birds and Worm, Sand Pottery, Multicolored	45.00
Blacksmith, Bronze, 2 Wells	110.00
Blown Bubble Glass, Silver Plated Lid	115.00
Blue & White Porcelain, Lace Design, China	68.00
Boat, Glass, Anchor Lid	55.00
Brass & Pewter, Glass, c.1861	165.00
Brass Ship, Insert, Victory, England	65.00
Brass Top, Blown, Molded Well	35.00
Brass, Double Porcelain Insert, Stamped, Ges Gesch Austria	70.00
Brass, Glass Insert, Swivel Cover	19.50
Bronze Paint, Hinged Lid, Jennings Bros., Square, 3 1/2 In.	55.00

Bronze, Signed Le Blanc 1500.00
Bronze, Stag Horn Handles, Equestrian Finial, Fox Head & Feet, 5 x 5 In. 605.00
Brown, Yellow Swirl, Brown Glass Chips In Lid, Waylande 95.00
Building, Le Sacre Coeur, Metal 105.00
Bulldog, Silver Plated, Insert 65.00
Camels, Cast Metal, Painted, Pair ....*Illus* 625.00
Capstan, Copper Insert 15.00
Carriage, Porcelain 20.00
Cat, Silver Plated, Green Glass Eyes, Signed JB 410.00
Child, Pulling On Pants, Fairying Conta & Boehms, c.1820 .... 725.00
Concentric Pattern Base & Stopper, Footed, Paperweight, Whitefriars, 6 In. 885.00
Controlled Bubble Glass, Brass Hinged Lid, 2 3/4 In. 250.00
Copper Base and Top, Ceramic Center, Label 15.00
Crab, Insert, Pewter 25.00
Cupid & Floral, Art Nouveau, Silver Plated, Signed 25.00
Curling Stone, Hinged Lid, Tan Marbleized, 2 1/2 In. 75.00
Cut Glass, Billy Goat Relief Top 45.00
Cut Glass, Block Pattern All Sides, Mushroom Shape, 2 1/2 In. 145.00
Cut Glass, Cane, Engraved Sterling Hinged Lid, Gorham, 3 1/2 In. 190.00
Cut Glass, Hand Painted Flower, Brass Hinge 20.00
Cut Glass, Pyramid Shape, Teardrop Insert Well, Silver Plated Lid, 2 3/4 x 3 In. 265.00
Cut Glass, Silver Repose Lid ....65.00 To 125.00
Desk Shape, Soapstone, U.S., 1800, 5 3/4 x 6 In. 192.50
Diamond Shaped, Clear Glass, Repousse Sterling Hinged Top 165.00
Dog's Head, Pewter, Glass Insert 155.00
Dog's Head, Wooden, Glass Eyes, Quill Pen Hole Through Mouth 165.00
Dog, Sitting By Tree Stump, Carved Fruitwood, Glass Eyes 450.00
Dome Top Hinged Lid, Pewter Insert, 5 1/4 In. 95.00
Elephant, Figural 95.00
Floral & Scrolled, Cast Iron Inkwell, Porcelain Insert 25.00
Floral Design, Alabaster Well, Glass Insert 20.00
Form of Monument, Garlands, Gilt Bronze, Napoleon III, 4 1/4 x 7 1/2 In. 355.00
Four-Leaf Clover, Woman's Head, Brass 75.00
Furnace Shape, Iron & Brass, Glass Inserts, Howard Furnace Co., Syracuse, N.Y. ... 230.00
General Supply Co., Danielson. Ct., Green Glass, Clear Molded Top 35.00
Glass Well, Birch Wood Tray 37.00
Glass Well, Faceted Base, Sterling Silver Hinged Top 125.00
Glass, Black, Coventry, 1830 .... 175.00
Glass, Clear Blue, Labino, 1972, 2 x 3 In. 125.00
Glass, Clear, Brass Cork Lid, Double 20.00
Glass, Clear, Hinged Brass Lid 65.00
Glass, Cut Corner, Domed Brass Lid 10.00
Glass, Dark Amethyst Lid, Clear Well, Small 30.00
Glass, Diamond Shape, Blown, Molded, Hinged Pointed Lid 25.00
Glass, Dome Shape, Clear, 16-Point Star On Base, Brass Lid, 2 1/2 In. 95.00
Glass, Dome Shape, Self-Closing 10.00
Glass, Dragonfly, Inlaid Turquoise, Pewter Lid 65.00
Glass, Floral Design, Bristol Type 10.00
Glass, Hunt Scene On Hinged Lid, Square, 2 1/4 In. 150.00
Glass, Octagonal Design, Pointed Lid 35.00
Glass, Painted Overlay Blown, Hinged Lid 10.00
Glass, Sliding Top 25.00
Glass, Wave Crest-Style, Enamel Flowers, Blue 110.00
Golf Ball, Bronze 295.00
Horse Head, Art Nouveau, Brass, Glass Insert, Signed JB 30.00
Iron, Ornate, 1879, Double 185.00
Knight, Cast Iron, Griffin Feet, Porcelain Feet 85.00
Leaf, Cast Iron, Pen Rest, Glass Insert 25.00
Milk Glass Wells, Brass Stand and Covers, Pat. 1897 .... 25.00
Mountain Goat, Glass Eyes, Carved Wood, 4 3/4 In. 195.00
Napoleon III, Bronze, Gilt, Enamel Accents, 19th Century, 5 In. 440.00
Oil Lamp Design, Brass, Small 30.00
Oriental Man, Cap Is Hinged Lid, Marble Base, Bronze, c.1850 .... 100.00

Pen Holder, Cast Iron, 9 In.	45.00
Pewter, Pink Ceramic Insert, 3 1/2 In.	65.00
Pewter, Wide Flat Base, Hinged Lid, Ceramic Insert, 7 3/8 In.	40.00
Pirate's Skeleton Head, Cast Metal, Porcelain Insert	65.00
Polychrome Raised Floral Enameling, Gilded Brass Fittings, 2 1/8 In.	415.00
Porcelain Pot, Black Lacquer Tray, Scrolled Candle Branch, Louis XV, 5 1/8 In. ...	2200.00
Porcelain, Blue & White, Lace Design, Chinese, 1800s	65.00
Porcelain, Floral Design, Hand Painted, France	35.00
Porcelain, French Bronze Mounted, c.1850, 4 1/2 x 5 In.	475.00
Porcelain, Hand Painted, Porcelain Insert	55.00
Porcelain, Olive Green & White, White Porcelain Inserts, 7 In.	50.00
Porcelain, Scalloped Tray, Cherubs In Relief, Gilt Borders, German, 8 1/2 In.	77.00
Porcelain, Transfer Print, Painted Maroon Sections, White Ground, 4 In.	375.00
Porcelain, Yellow, Heart Shaped Base	25.00
Pottery, Blue & White Design, Hinged Pewter Lid, 2 1/2 x 3 In.	75.00
Pressed Glass, Daisy and Button	10.00
Pressed Glass, Daisy and Button, Yellow	65.00
Pug Dog's Head, Chewing Bone, Bronze, Napkin Bib Forms Glass Insert, 1890	235.00
Pyramid, Floral Design, Small	25.00
Quaker City Fire Insurance, Brass	45.00
Rabbit, Painted Metal, Glass Well	135.00
Ship's Keg, Wooden, Original Cork Stopper, Labeled	10.00
Shoe Shaped, Red, Black, With Green, 4 1/2 In.	55.00
Silver Plate Over Copper, Bernard Rices Sons, Scrolled Feet, Silver Plated Top	45.00
Silver Plated Top and Tray, Scrolled Edge, Floral Design	65.00
Square Glass, Leather Lion Crest Design Lid	20.00
Stag Head and Horn Pen Rest, Metal, Blown Well	220.00
Stag's Horn, Brass Lid	45.00
Stag, Cast Metal, Clear Glass, Small	55.00
Starfish, Blown Glass, Cast Iron Lid .... 30.00 To 45.00
Stoneware, Cobalt Blue Design, Miniature	1265.00
Summer House On Pond, Deer, Hinged Roof Lid, Bronze, c.1840, 5 1/4 In.	200.00
Sunburst Design, Pen Rest, Hinged Sterling Top	220.00
Swirl Glass, Pewter Top, Initialed Class 1901	25.00
Swirl Glass, Silver Overlay	35.00
Swirl Glass, Sterling Silver Overlay	750.00
Swivel, Cast Base, Double	25.00
Traveling, Brass, Signed, John Simmons Co., New York	20.00
Traveling, Leather Covered, Label	10.00
Traveling, W. St. and Co., Pair	55.00
Tree Stump, Whippet Dog Attached To Stump, White Metal	125.00
Triple Stairstep Well, Double Inks, Clear Glass	115.00
Umbrella Shape, Glass, Footed, Stopper, Millville, 9 1/4 x 3 1/8 In.	385.00
Weasels, Brass Well, Signed Tiffany, N.Y.	250.00
Well On Attached Square White Porcelain Saucer, Floral Design, Hinged Lid	95.00
Wooden Leaf Well and Cap, Glass Insert	15.00
World Globe, Brass Well	420.00

INSULATORS of glass or pottery have been made for use on telegraph or telephone poles since 1844. Thousands of different styles of insulators have been made. Most common are those of clear or aqua glass; most desirable are the threadless types made from 1850 to 1870.

Brookfield, Apple Green	40.00
Brookfield, No. 38, Olive Green, Amber Swirls	24.00
California, Sage Gray	15.00
Canadian National Railway, Blue	10.00
Canadian Pacific Railway Co., Aqua, Ridges	18.00
Canadian Pacific Railway, Lavender	20.00
Chambers, Aqua, Tiny Bubbles	285.00
Chicago, Rim Embossed, Blue Aqua	35.00
Columbia, Aqua, Smooth Base, Wide Ear	110.00
Columbia, Dark Green	100.00
Diamond, Aqua, Jade Swirls	14.00

Reproductions, Fakes, and Altered Antiques

veryone who collects has been fooled at least once by a fake, a reproduction, or a clever repair or embellishment. Don't be discouraged, as you are in good company. The Metropolitan Museum of Art in New York, the Ford Museum, and the White House have all admitted that they have displayed faked items as originals for years before they learned that they were spurious. Antiques have been copied since the days of the ancient Greeks and Romans, when coin collecting was a popular pastime of the rich and clever craftsmen sold expensive "antique" coins they created to fool the unwary.

Today we look at these and other fakes of the past and wonder how collectors were fooled. Although there were fewer tools to help with detection, that is not the only reason. A collector is often blinded by greed and desire. A great find at a dimly lit flea market or a rare chair in the corner of an old house can seduce the unwary. A quick look, fast decision, and a little rationalizing can result in a sale. The flaws are seen only later when the collector takes a closer look and analyzes the piece with intelligence rather than emotion alone.

There are many types of fakes, concoctions, and reproductions of antiques and collectibles that can confuse the collector. The most difficult to detect are the fakes that have been made deliberately to fool the collector. There are many wholesale giftware suppliers who import porcelain, glass, even furniture items that are all made to closely resemble the old. Some reproductions even have fake marks. For example, the egg-shaped box below (at front right) has a green wreath and star, a mark which was copied from the authentic RS Prussia

Beware! Every piece in this picture is a reproduction. The orange gunpowder tin was made for a museum shop in the 1980s; the other pieces were sold by one firm making reproductions in the 1970s. Although the beige egg-shaped box is marked with a green wreath similar to an RS Prussia mark, the others are unmarked.

Centennial copies of furniture are over 100 years old. In the 1880s this chair was copied from an original 18th-century chair on display at a museum in Dublin. A companion copy was made with arms, an addition designed by the 19th-century craftsman.

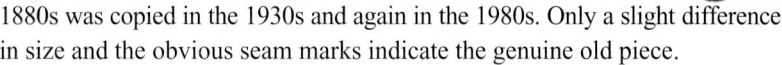

porcelain mark. Other fakes are made from old molds. Iron pieces such as doorstops and many patterns of glass have been reproduced in this manner. Pressed glass reproductions have been made since the 1930s. Oftentimes the details on old and new glass can provide distinguishing clues—such as the position of the arm of the Indian on a Westward Ho goblet. The Good Luck pattern goblet of the 1880s was copied in the 1930s and again in the 1980s. Only a slight difference in size and the obvious seam marks indicate the genuine old piece.

Styles of furniture have also been copied and recopied for centuries. Even today, stores sell new pieces in the styles of the seventeenth through early twentieth centuries. The "new" chairs and tables are made to fill the demand for home furnishings with traditional looks. They are not meant to be sold in antiques shops. They are usually made by modern methods with modern tools and are easily recognized. Authentic reproductions made and sold by museums are usually marked with new marks that are difficult to remove. Some craftsmen still make furniture in the old styles using antique tools and methods. In the 1970s one cabinetmaker, angered by a museum curator's statement that no one working today could duplicate the craftsmanship of the eighteenth century, carefully built a Brewster chair that was slightly different from the known examples made in the seventeenth century. He used old wood, old methods, and old tools. He aged the chair, gave it a fabricated history of ownership, and then waited to see what would happen: The chair was sold to the Ford Museum, where it was featured as a great example of the Brewster-type chair. A year later the cabinetmaker suggested that the chair be X-rayed so it would be seen that the holes had been drilled with modern tools. He proved he could do work as fine as that of the seventeenth century, and he also proved that a good fake can fool anyone, even a museum.

In 1876, at the time of the United States' Centennial, the country looked back at past history and past designs. Many of the seventeenth- , eighteenth- , and early nineteenth-century styles were admired, and handcrafted copies were offered for sale. Today, more than 100 years later, these chairs and chests have worn legs, faded finishes, and cracks and breaks that are some of the signs of

Even experts are confused by pressed glass copies. The Good Luck pattern (also called Horseshoe or Prayer Rug) goblets are almost identical. The reproduction on the left has a visible seam on the base and is ¼ inch higher.

Holt Howard was an importer working in the 1950s and '60s in the United States. The quirky condiment jars with people-head handles were made in 1958. Another company quickly copied the popular jars. The 6-inch-high jar with vertical stripes on the left is by Holt Howard; the jar with horizontal stripes on the right is by an unknown firm.

age. However, careful examination of construction details—late saw marks, use of modern screws and upholstering methods—tell the expert a piece's true age.

Some reproductions are contemporary knockoffs of best-selling items. Lalique, the famous French glass, has been copied by many firms in the nineteenth and twentieth centuries. The Phoenix Glass Company of Phillipsburg, Pennsylvania, for instance, made a line of molded glass vases with raised designs of grasshoppers, rushes, or birds that closely resembled the

The French glass made by Lalique is expensive and popular. In the early 20th century the Phoenix Glassworks of Pennsylvania and a number of other companies made glass that was very similar in design to the pieces being sold by Lalique. The dolphin-handle vase and the large vase on the left are 1930s to 1950s examples of glass works that are similar to Lalique's. In the 1980s a clever forger began to alter some non-Lalique pieces by adding the Lalique name. The low bowl was made by Vallon, a French company. The forger sandblasted the raised letters "R. Lalique" on the back edge of the bowl. A 9-inch Lalique bowl made before 1905 is worth more than $2,000. The forged piece is worth $50.

The large comic bird pitcher was made in Czechoslovakia in the 1930s. It is marked "Erphila." The small creamer was made at the same time but is a copy, marked "Made in Japan." The Erphila piece is worth $175, the Japanese copy about $30.

Lalique pieces. An experienced collector of Lalique would not be fooled by a piece of Phoenix. However, sometimes a fake name is added to a piece that might mislead a novice collector.

Antiques that are damaged and later slightly altered make up another category of "fakes." To eliminate a chip, for instance, the scalloped edge of a vase may be ground down and left smooth. A missing tail on a cow figurine may be replaced with one that has the wrong configuration. That's why you must carefully check any antique for alterations. Alterations lower the value of a piece. For example, if all four of the feet on a piece of furniture are replacements or are missing altogether, there is no way to know how the antique foot looked,

Repairs can also cause problems for a collector. Sometimes a repair, like the replaced tail on this cow, is an accurate copy. At other times the repair alters the look of the piece. The 18th-century cradle originally had a hood that has been removed. Notice the slight variation in the color of the green trim.

With only a quick look at these two 8½-inch-high marriage cups, you might be fooled. The authentic sterling cup has English and Continental hallmarks. The reproduction is made of a heavier white metal that has been silver plated. A thick seam shows on the side of the cup.

and the value of the piece is lowered by 50 percent. If one original foot remains, the value is lowered by only 20 percent.

Most reproductions seen today are modern copies of antiques. Copies of old silver serving pieces, Christmas ornaments, spongeware crocks, and Mission-style furnishings can be found for affordable prices at gift shops. These copies are generally adaptations of old pieces, and there are usually slight variations. The silver serving spoon of the eighteenth century, for example, was made so the tip of the handle bent down toward the table, whereas most modern spoons are made with the tip of the handle bent away from the table top. Chests of drawers are usually made today so they can be lined up against a wall, saving space like built-in units do. Old pieces often had protruding feet or tops that made it impossible to put the sides of two chests flush against each other. Old dinnerware sets copied from antique eighteenth-century patterns sometimes have a few modern serving pieces that were unknown earlier.

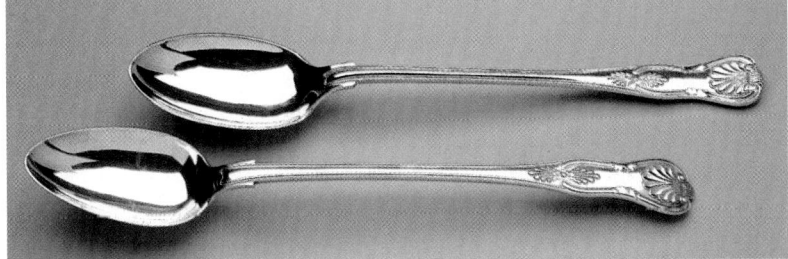

Both of these silver serving spoons are in the traditional Kings pattern. Notice the tip of the handles. The one on the new spoon goes up but the other goes down. Slight changes in silver design, the shape of the spoon bowl, the spacing of the fork tines, and the lines of the handle help to date silverware. The newer spoon is marked E B Rogers. The older one has English hallmarks.

A Picture Dictionary
of Fakes and Finds

Old or new? On the left is an old mustache cup marked "Made in Germany." The center cup is a 1970 left-handed copy marked "JP 1200." The cup on the right is an old shaving mug. Beware of new mustache cups with a blue border, marked "Brandenburg."

The 12-inch rag doll on the left was made in 1992. The white signature of the artist was removed with a black ink stain. Tea-stained fabric was used for the dress. The doll on the right was made about 1940 on a Caribbean island. Notice the steel wool hair. Both dolls might be sold today as "American folk art dolls."

Some reproductions are easy to spot. The tin can on the left was made for gift shops and has a recently reproduced label. The old label on the can on the right has much sharper details and brighter colors.

Recognizing the strangeness in the appearance of photographic copies of old lithographs is easy if examples of the two types of printing are compared. Do not assume the label and the can are the same age. Many old cans have been embellished with labels reproduced in recent years. And many old labels have been pasted on new cans.

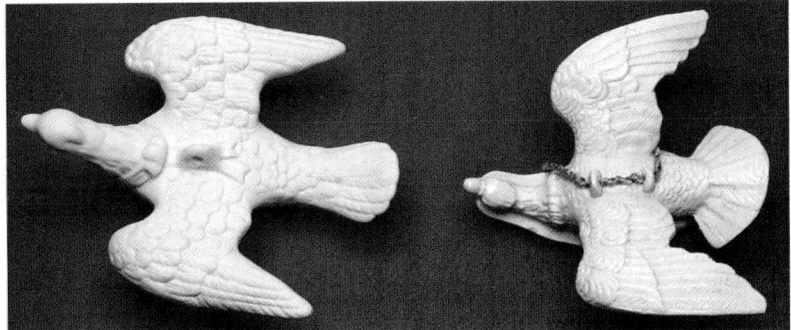

Museum replicas are often confusing. The bottom of the old parian bird on the right shows an American shield with stars and stripes. The string suggests it was used either as a window shade pull or a Christmas tree ornament. It is worth $125. It was probably made in Bennington, Vermont, in the 19th century. The new bird on the left was sold by the Metropolitan Museum of Art store in 1992 for $8.95. It is unmarked. Each is 5 inches long.

These strange 5-inch-long fish dishes were used at dinner parties to hold fish bones. The fish on the left is old. The fish on the right was made in Taiwan and was sold from a mail-order catalog in 1988. Careful examination shows almost no differences. Each has an unglazed bottom, hand-painted cobalt blue decoration, and poor quality porcelain. Buyer beware!

These examples of spongeware were made from local clay in the Midwest. The 4½-inch-high crock is marked "Roseville, 700A," and is currently being made in Ohio; the 17-inch-high, covered crock is old.

Shaving mugs are popular as collectibles and gifts. These early occupational mugs, showing men at work, were hand painted. The copies are often decorated with decals. The mug on the left, showing a tailor, is old. The gold trimmed streetcar-conductor mug, marked 1209, is new.

Onion pattern dishes have been made since the 18th century by the Meissen factory in Germany, and by others in England, Germany, and the United States. The 8½-inch saucer on the left is marked "Blue Danube." It is a recent copy. The 6⅛-inch saucer on the right is marked with the word "Meissen" in an oval, a 19th-century mark used by The C. Teichert factory of Germany from 1882 to 1930. Neither was made by the famous Meissen factory.

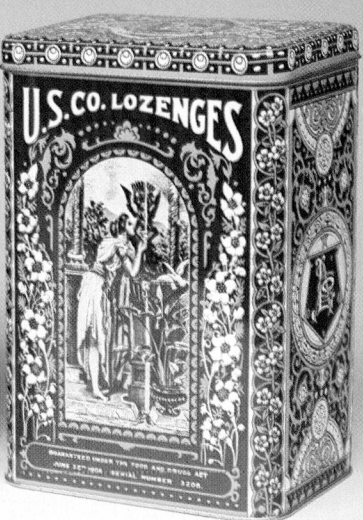

Some old-looking pieces are "concoctions," new products adapted from old ones. The store tin with the glass window on the left was made in England about 1890, to hold lozenges. The new gift shop tin on the right copied the old tin, altered the name, and added a special picture to replace the more expensive glass panel. The shiny finish and quality of the print make the new piece easy to spot as a recent work.

Each of these souvenir toothpick holders is decorated with a date before 1910, yet none are old. They were purchased at a southern Ohio glass company in the 1970s. Because the glass was made using the old molds it is very difficult to spot these fakes.

The numerals 1825 on the brass mortar and pestle are meant to deceive. Although this 1980s copy is now polished, it was originally blackened to look as though it had been left unpolished for years. However, it is much lighter in weight than the authentic 19th-century mortar shown on the right.

Early Staffordshire figurines were unsophisticated, inexpensive pieces made for the average home. The coloring and modeling were less detailed than that of the expensive porcelains of the day. This makes it easy to make modern copies that can fool the unwary. Popular subjects have been copied for years. The Uncle Tom figurine and the bust of Washington have been made in many versions. The Uncle Tom and Little Eva figurine pictured on the left is old and its value over $700. The Washington bust is a 1970s copy found in a London flea market for $50. An old original is worth thousands of dollars.

Fairings are small figurines and trinket boxes that were sold as souvenirs at country fairs. The Twelve Months of Marriage series was first made in the 1870s. The figurine on the left was made in Germany before 1900. The one on the right is a modern copy. Notice the elaborate base on the modern figure. The old ones used a flat base, sometimes with added trim. If you were to turn the figures over you would see a solid bottom on the old piece, a hollow space on the new one. As a general rule, old porcelains are heavier than new ones because of the manufacturing methods.

Parian figurines have been made since the late 18th century. The figurine of a musician was made by the Royal Copenhagen factory of Denmark in the late 1800s. It has the typical blue mark used by the firm. The double-headed hatpin holder is an unmarked "concoction" offered in 1985 through a reproduction dealer. Both may appear to be the same age to the unwary.

No one should be fooled by this pair. The well-detailed 6½-inch-high bronze satyr on the left was made before 1900. It is a small copy of a large Italian bronze figure. A similar small bronze of poor quality was offered for sale as a reproduction in the 1980s.

Many bottles have been reproduced. Some are accurate copies, others are "concoctions." In 1963 Lestoil cleaner was sold in stores in one of three different "historic flasks." One, the amber flask pictured here, has an eagle on one side, the head of Liberty on the other. The new-type flat bottom and the seam up the side and neck are signs that this is a recent bottle. The 9¼-inch-high Hood's Compound Sarsaparilla extract bottle, made in Lowell, Massachusetts, is a c. 1910 original. Many copies of old bottles have been made by the Wheaton-Nuline company, and the name Wheaton is often found on them.

Paperweights are being made today with the same techniques used years ago. The fish weight on the right, 3¾ inches high, is a new weight sold by a reproduction company about 1985. The red and blue weight on the left is American from the early 1900s. Both weights have slight imperfections in the glass and ground pontils.

Sometimes rules don't work. Often an old piece of pottery is used to make a clay mold. But the mold shrinks as it dries, and when a new piece of pottery is cast from the new mold, the finished piece is smaller than the original. The white pitcher called "Viennese Musicians" is described in a 1971 reproduction catalog as a "Salt glaze jug, made from an old mold, $10.50." Poor detail and the modern-style base proclaim that it is a copy. The colored Staffordshire pitcher is an original 19th-century example even though it is smaller than the white pitcher. The copy could not have been made from the mold of this piece. There must also have been a larger 19th-century version.

Nodders are very collectible and sell for high prices. The unmarked 9-inch-high bisque candlestick is one of a pair featuring a black girl or boy with moving hands and heads. It has a hollow bottom. The 5-inch-high, unmarked bisque "oriental nodder" was sold as a reproduction in a 1985 catalog. It is sometimes seen at antiques shops. It has a 20th century–type solid, flat bottom.

If a piece of pottery sells well, it will probably be copied by another manufacturer. The 2½-inch-high Weller clay-wood piece on the left was a popular type of vase in the 1920s. An unknown factory made the similar spider web-decorated pot at the same time. The Weller piece is worth $40, the spider web pot $30.

Serious collectors avoid re-painted ironwork. The Grace Drayton-type girl called "Dolly," made by Hubley, is a 9½-inch-high iron doorstop made in the 1930s. Notice the googly eyes. Value: $350 to $400. The boy is a 1990s copy, made in the Orient, of a 1930s doorstop called "Bobby Blake." Notice the Oriental eyes. Value: $15.

Pressed glass reproductions are always difficult to spot. The train-shaped, 3¼-inch glass candy container on the right was made in the early 1900s. The boxed container on the left was made in Taiwan in the 1970s. Only the box carries the true identification.

The shape of a perfume bottle tells its age. The bulbous glass bottle on the right is from the late 19th century. The sleek bottle with the large stopper on the left is a 1950s example.

This type of souvenir paperweight has been made in England since the 1850s. One of these was purchased in 1975, but it is so much like the old one we had trouble remembering which was the new one. Both have faded leatherlike paper pasted on the back. (The little one is the 1975 purchase.)

The 3-inch-high amethyst inkwell is a recent copy made in the Orient. The labeled bottle was made in the early 1800s. It has the typical rough base with a pontil mark. Notice the different shapes of the tops.

New brass candlesticks can usually be detected by weight, the spinning marks on the bottom, and the patina. The Beehive stick on the left is new. The 19th-century stick on the right weighs about twice as much.

Copper cooking molds have been made since the early 1800s. The large fluted mold on the left is from the 1880s. It is heavy, tin-lined, and has a white metal loop for hanging. The thinner mold on the right was purchased new in 1982 to be used by a cook. It is lined with very shiny tin and has a copper wire hanger. Most molds are unmarked.

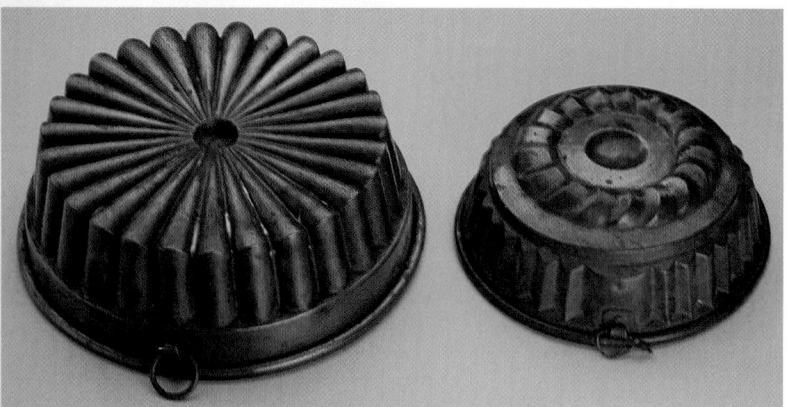

Old toys have become big business. Mr. Dan, a Japanese wind-up toy made in 1992, has a soft plastic head and tin feet. The box has the graphics style of the 1930s, but the toy is new. The clown toy on the left is old.

Diamond, Deep Purple	9.50
Diamond, Royal Purple	15.00
Dominion, No. 42, Honey Amber	39.00
E. L. Co., Aqua	35.00
G. N. W. Tel, Lavender Purple	25.00
H. G. Co., Lime Green, Milky Swirls, 1893	17.00
H. G. Co., Petticoat, Cornflower Blue	125.00
H. G. Co., Petticoat, Medium Yellow Green	40.00
H. G. Co., Petticoat, Teal Blue	45.00
Hemingray, CD162, Dark Cobalt Blue	125.00
Hemingray, Mickey Mouse Eared, Cobalt Blue Carnival Glass	35.00
Hemingray, No. 9, Yellow Green	8.00
Hemingray, No. 19, Sharp Drip Points, Cobalt Blue	82.00
Hemingray, No. 19, Sharp Drip Points, Dark Amber, Orange Cast	25.00
Hemingray, No. 20, Original Carnival	190.00
Hemingray, No. 42, Green	1.00
Hemingray, No. 48, Green	1.00
Hemingray, No. 95, Aqua	50.00
Homer Brookes, Aqua, Rim Embossed	83.00 To 90.00
Isorex, Gingerbread, Black Glass, Small	35.00
Locke, No. 14, Aqua	6.00
Lynchburg, No. 30, Aqua, Black Wisps	5.50
Maydwell, Milk Glass	10.00
Maydwell, No. 20, Pink	8.00
McLaughlin, No. 16, Olive Green	7.00
McLaughlin, No. 20, Emerald Green	8.00
Mickey Mouse Type, Green, 1893	40.00
Montreal Telegraph Co., Light Blue	17.00
N. E. G. M., Flat Rim, Sapphire Blue	75.00
National Corkscrew, Aqua	225.00
Prism, Aqua, 1890	28.00
PRR, Green	6.00
Santa Ana, Yellow Green	35.00
Standard, Royal Purple	30.00
Star, Green Aqua, Amber Shading	14.00
T. & N. O. Railway, White Porcelain	100.00
W. G. M., Sun–Colored Amethyst	22.00
Westinghouse, No. 6, Light Green	275.00
Whitall Tatum Co., No. 1, Light Pink	10.00

IRISH BELLEEK, see Belleek category

IRON is a metal that has been used by man since prehistoric times. It is a popular metal for tools and decorative items like doorstops that need as much weight as possible. Items are listed here or under other appropriate headings, such as Bookends, Doorstop, Kitchen, Match Holder, or Tool. The tool that is used for ironing clothes, an iron, is listed in the Kitchen category under Iron and Sadiron.

Bed Warmer, Brass Pierced Star Cover	300.00
Bill Holder, Wall Mounted, Filigreed, Spike	25.00
Boot Scraper, 4 Faces Around Edge	150.00
Boot Scraper, Curved Ears, 10 1/4 x 17 1/2 In.	115.00
Boot Scraper, Double Scroll Ram's Horn Finials, White Stone Base, 15 In.	385.00
Boot Scraper, Lyre Shape	62.00
Boot Scraper, Lyre Shape, Diamond Base, Green, 12 x 8 In.	149.00
Boot Scraper, Ram's Horn, 13 In.	275.00
Boot Scraper, Scrolled Finials, Single Stake Base, 20 1/2 In.	770.00
Boot Scraper, Turreted, Black Paint, England, 19th Century	330.00
Bootjack, Naughty Nellie	10.00
Bridle, Horse, Rosettes, Bull's–Eye, Round	4.50
Buggy Step, Cutout Heart Design	65.00
Candleholder, Spring Chip, Square Base, 3 Feet, 8 1/2 In.	440.00
Chamberstick, Curved Handle, Matchbox, Drip Pans, Scrolled, 9 In., Pair	370.00

Cigar Cutter, Battle Ax Shape, Roger's Iron Co.	165.00
Corn Planter, Stag Embossed, Lid, Deere Mansur, 1901	15.00
Cuspidor, Turtle, Brown, Red Eyes, Step On Head, Raised Shell Back, 15 x 10 In.	175.00
Door Knocker, Amish Man, Lift Beard Knocker, Eyes Open	40.00
Door Knocker, Flapper	150.00
Door Knocker, Flower Basket	55.00
Door Knocker, Hand Shaped, Black Repaint, 7 In.	94.00
Door Knocker, Rooster	65.00
Figure, Black Boy, J. W. Fiske, Repainted, 19th Century, 45 1/2 In.	550.00
Figure, Frog, Hinged Back, Gold Repaint, 3 1/2 In.	27.00
Figure, Frog, Old Green Paint, 5 1/2 In.	55.00
Figure, Indian, With Tomahawk In Hand, Garden, 20 In.	825.00
Figure, Lion, Regilded, 19th Century, 13 1/2 x 27 In.	715.00
Figure, Whippet, Lying, Front Feet Outstretched, Fiske–Style	1540.00
Frame, For Shaving Mirror, Old Black Paint, Ornate, 20 3/4 In.	200.00
Grill, Interior, Interlacing Scrolling, Edgar Brandt, 1925, 4 Ft. 9 In., Pair	4950.00
Hitching Post, Black Boy Holding Lantern, 42 In.	1300.00
Hitching Post, Black Boy, Weathered Polychrome Paint, 48 In.	750.00
Hitching Post, Black Jockey, Pedestal	600.00
Hitching Post, Horsehead, 15 In.	410.00
Hitching Post, Horsehead, Wavy Mane, 14 In. ....*Illus*	880.00
Hitching Post, Jockey, Red & White Paint	600.00
Hitching Post, Modeled As Black Child, 46 In.	550.00
Holder, For Hand Stamps, Revolving, Fancy, Cast Iron	65.00
Hook, For Hanging Lamp, Ceiling, 11 In.	10.00
Horseshoe, Welcome, With Leaves, Over The Door	32.00
Implement Seat, Jenkin	125.00
Incense Burner, Foo Dog, Removable Head, China, 1800s	95.00
Knuckles, Police	22.00
Ladle, 16 3/8 In.	20.00
Lamp, Street, Gas, Wired For Electricity	1500.00
Lavabo, Shell Design, 19th Century, Pair	700.00
Letter Holder, Desk	18.00
Match Holder, Eagle	140.00
Match Holder, Surround, Columnar Griffins, Grate Holds Spent Matches	125.00
Medallion, Eagle, High Relief, Round, 18 In.	460.00
Mold, Head Cheese, Pig Face	35.00
Pan, Corn Ear, Miniature, Griswold	32.50
Panel, Rectangular, Horses, Houses, Landscape, 17 x 52	855.00
Planter, Tulip Shape, Green, 8 1/2 In	49.00
Pole, Flag, 1900	15.00
Punishment Mask, Hinged, Nasal Bar Gag, Pierced Curved Plate, 18th Century	4550.00
Rushlight Holder, Turned Wooden Base, 10 3/4 In.	577.00
Sconce, Concave Glass, Clear, Sun Design, Wall Bracket, 25 In.	1395.00
Seat, Implement, Dodds	125.00
Shears, Sheep, Wool Wrapped Handles, 10 In.	77.00

Hitching Post, Horsehead,

   Wavy Mane, 14 In.

♦ ♦

Soapstone (steatite) is a very soft mineral. To clean soapstone carvings, wash with soapy water and a soft brush. To improve the sheen, rub with jewelers' rouge. Don't use a harsh abrasive.

♦ ♦

Shield, Heraldic, Orange & Silver Paint, Door Mounted, 1800s, 11 1/8 x 6 3/8 In. ... 130.00
Sign Bracket, Floral Design, Dog, 15 In. ... 247.00
Spike, Climbing, Telephone Lineman, Pair ... 14.00
Striker, Flint, Blacksmith Made, Colonial America, 2 1/2 In. ... 42.50
Urn, Garden, 2 Handles, Washington Iron Works, New York, 36 In. ... 605.00
Urn, Garden, Neoclassic, 2 Handles ... 605.00
Urn, Garden, Sawtooth Rim, White Repaint, 25 1/2 In. ... 192.00
Water Pump, Small ... 39.00
Windmill Weight, Bobtailed Horse, Dempster ... 225.00
Windmill Weight, Boss Bull ... 700.00
Windmill Weight, Buffalo Bill, Stylized Silhouette, 11 1/2 x 16 In. ... 990.00
Windmill Weight, Bull, Black ... 395.00
Windmill Weight, Bull, Fairybury, Nebraska, 24 1/2 In. ... 770.00
Windmill Weight, Chicken, Hummer ... 300.00
Windmill Weight, Crescent Eclipse ... 175.00
Windmill Weight, Horse, In Wooden Stand, 17 x 6 1/2 In. ... 330.00
Windmill Weight, Horse, Short Tail ... 250.00
Windmill Weight, Long Stem, Hummer ... 1000.00
Windmill Weight, Mogul, Base ... 3500.00
Windmill Weight, Rooster, Full–Bodied, Silver Paint, Wooden Base, 12 In. ... 605.00
Windmill Weight, Rooster, Full–Bodied, White Traces, Wooden Base, 20 1/2 In. 900.00
Windmill Weight, Rooster, Hummer ... 225.00
Windmill Weight, Rooster, No Eye, 30 Lb. ... 4000.00
Windmill Weight, Rooster, Standing, Red & White Paint Traces, 19 In. ... 700.00
Windmill Weight, Rooster, Stylized, Molded Feather & Wing, Base, 18 In. ... 3575.00
Windmill Weight, Rooster, Woodmanse, Repainted ... 725.00
Windmill Weight, Squirrel, 35 Lb. ... 3500.00
Windmill Weight, Star, Short Tail Horse With Box ... 300.00
Windmill Weight, Tassel Shape, 8 1/2 In. ... 33.00

IRONSTONE china was first made in 1813. It gained its greatest popularity during the mid–nineteenth century. The heavy, durable, off–white pottery was made in white or was decorated with any of hundreds of patterns. Much flow blue pottery was made of ironstone. Some of the decorations were raised. Many pieces of ironstone are unmarked, but some English and American factories included the word *Ironstone* in their marks. Additional pieces may be listed in other categories, such as Chelsea Grape, Chelsea Sprig, Flow Blue, Gaudy Ironstone, Moss Rose, and Staffordshire, and Tea Leaf Ironstone.

Batter Pail, Cherries, Slip Design, Cowden & Wilcox ... 2750.00
Bowl, Cover, Tapered, Raised Cameo Heads ... 7.50
Chamber Pot, Cover ... 35.00
Cheese Dish, Domed Cover, Blue & White Floral Transfer, 11 1/2 In. ... 275.00
Chop Plate, Pink Vista, Mason's ... 40.00
Coffee & Tea Set, Laurel Wreath, Foster, 4 Piece ... 625.00
Coffeepot, Chippendale, Pink, Johnson Bros. ... 35.00
Coffeepot, White, Emblem Blanke's Coffee ... 48.00
Compote, White, Low Pedestal, Syndenham, John Maddock ... 76.00
Compote, White, Pedestal, Reticulated, Octagonal, Mellor, Venables & Co., 1849 ..... 235.00
Creamer, Blue & White, England ... 12.00
Cup & Saucer, Blue & White ... 8.00
Cup & Saucer, Coaching Scene, Johnson Bros. ... 10.00
Cup & Saucer, Pink Vista ... 13.00
Cup Plate, Blue & White Vintage, 4 In. ... 66.00
Eggcup, Vista Blue ... 12.00
Gravy Boat, Liner, Vista Blue ... 65.00
Gravy Boat, Pink Vista ... 35.00
Gravy Boat, White, England, 1878 ... 150.00
Jam Jar, Cover, Embossed Heads ... 35.00
Jam Jar, White, Walker ... 15.00
Jug, Milk, Brown Castle Scene, Fluted Rim, Mason's ... 35.00
Ladle, Soup, Brown & White ... 45.00
Pitcher & Bowl, Presidents, Edwards, 1856, 13 In. ... 445.00

Pitcher, Brown, Black, Transfer of Dog, 13 1/2 In.	25.00
Pitcher, Mocha Design, Stripes, Blue, White, Molded Leaf Handle, 6 7/8 In.	35.00
Pitcher, Water, Hand Painted Wild Roses, Large	65.00
Pitcher, Woman's Face Handles, White	75.00
Plate, Blue Transfer, Child & Dog, English Registry Mark, 5 3/8 In.	35.00
Plate, Castle Scene, Foliage, Pink, Walley	47.00
Plate, Dessert, Kent 13th Century, Meakin	6.00
Plate, Dinner, Blue & White	7.00
Plate, Dinner, Mason's, 12 Piece	2500.00
Plate, Oriental Blue Transfer, Ashworth, 9 1/4 In.	50.00
Plate, Polychrome Floral Center, Red Striping, Blue Spatter Design Border, 8 In.	75.00
Platter, Black Transfer, 17 3/4 In.	110.00
Platter, Blue Feather Edge, 13 1/2 In.	50.00
Platter, Brown Transfer, Polychrome Enameling, 20 1/4 In.	125.00
Platter, Center Chinoiserie Reserve, Floral Rim, Mason's, 10 1/2 In.	155.00
Platter, Imari Pattern, Lacquered Bamboo Turned Stand, 1860s, 21 In.	605.00
Platter, Light Blue Transfer, Baltimore, 15 7/8 In.	247.00
Platter, Light Blue Transfer, Genoa, Impressed Adams, 15 3/4 In.	165.00
Platter, Mason's, 13 1/2 In.	40.00
Platter, Mason's, 15 1/2 In.	60.00
Platter, Panama Pattern, Challinor, 13 1/2 In.	75.00
Platter, Pink Vista, 13 1/2 In.	40.00
Platter, Red Transfer, Floral Design, Polychrome Enameled, 17 1/4 In.	175.00
Platter, Well & Tree, Imari Pattern, Oval, 1870s, 21 In.	355.00
Salt & Pepper, Mason's	35.00
Salt Box, Hanging, Wooden Lid, Cobalt Blue Design, Rounded Front, Germany	90.00
Sauceboat, Liner, Vista Blue	35.00
Sugar & Creamer, Cover, Meakin	25.00
Sugar, Black Transfer, George Washington, Impressed Label, 8 In.	82.00
Sugar, Cover, Underplate, 8 In.	154.00
Teapot, Mason's	75.00
Teapot, Pink Vista, Mason's	75.00
Tray, Blue, Rectangular, 6 1/2 x 12 1/2 In.	45.00
Tray, Rectangular, 8 3/4 x 11 In., Pair	160.00
Tureen, Acorn Finial, Embossed Leaf Design On Base, Boote, 11 In.	85.00
Tureen, Cover, Blackberry Pattern, Challinor, 11 1/2 x 8 x 6 In.	110.00
Tureen, Gothic, Plateau Underplate, Ladle, Copper Luster Band, 13 1/2 In.	525.00
Tureen, Octagonal, Blue Transfer, Medina, 11 3/4 In.	214.00
Tureen, Octagonal, Bluish Black, Strawberry Design, 7 1/2 In.	65.00
Tureen, Octagonal, Light Blue Transfer, 10 3/4 In.	127.00
Tureen, Soup, Cover, Painted, Oriental Woman & Child, Mason's, 12 3/4 In.	1100.00
Tureen, Vegetable, Cover, Blackberry, Challinor, c.1862, 11 1/2 x 8 In.	110.00
Wash Set, Blue & Gilt Floral Design, 2 Piece	265.00

ISPANKY figurines were designed by Laszlo Ispanky, who began his American career as a designer for Cybis Porcelains. In 1966, he established his own studio in Pennington, New Jersey; since 1976, he has worked for Goebel of North America. He works in stone, wood, or metal, as well as porcelain. The first limited edition figurines were issued in 1966.

Bust, Girl With Ponytail, 8 In.	135.00

IVOREX plaques were made in England by Arthur Osborne in the beginning of the 1900s. The plaques, made of a material he called *sterine wax*, pictured buildings or room interiors modeled in three dimensions. After Osborne's death, his daughter Blanche ran the company. It was closed in 1965, then purchased by W. H. Bossons Ltd. in 1971. Production of the plaques started again in 1980.

"IVOREX"
OSBORNE-COPYRIGHT.
MADE IN ENGLAND.

Plaque, Friendly Call, Osborne	50.00

IVORY from the tusk of an elephant is thought by many to be the only true ivory. To most collectors, the term *ivory* also includes such natural materials as walrus, hippopotamus, or whale teeth or tusks, and some of the vegetable materials that are of similar texture and density. Other ivory

items may be found in the Scrimshaw and Netsuke categories. Collectors should be aware of the recent laws limiting the buying and selling of elephant ivory and scrimshaw.

Basket, Floral Bouquet, Dragon & Pearl Stand, 19th Century, 4 x 9 In.	900.00
Bells, Magic, On Stand, 10 In.	330.00
Billiken, 4 In.	80.00
Bok Choy With Grasshopper, Polychromed, Stand, 6 1/2 In.	350.00
Box, Pearl & Pewter Inlay On Cover, Interior Tray, With 6 Ivory Tools, 7 In.	55.00
Box, Turned Feet & Finial, Embossed Bands In Silver, Gold Colored Metal, 3 In.	35.00
Bracelet, Stylized Flowers, Colored Centers, 1920s	85.00
Brushpot, Incised Scholar At Tea, Landscape, 19th Century, 6 In.	357.50
Candleholder, Double, Wooden Base, 7 In.	248.00
Card Holder, Birds In Landscape, 4 1/2 x 3 In., 2 Piece	770.00
Chess Set, Chinese Warriors On Multilayer Balls	1450.00
Chess Set, Emperor, Empress & Attendants, c.1930, 2 To 4 In.	600.00
Cribbage Board, Carved Dragons With Pegs, 6 1/4 In.	150.00
Cribbage Board, Serpent Design, 8 1/2 In.	45.00
Doctor's Lady, 3 In.	65.00
Dominoes, Bone, 1900, 4 1/2 x 2 3/4 In.	160.00
Figurine, Admiral Nelson, Naval Uniform, Hand In Jacket, 19th Century, 7 1/4 In.	1485.00
Figurine, Buddha, Sitting On Pedestal, 3 Carved Faces, Base, c.1890	750.00
Figurine, Buddha, Sleeping, Signed, 2 1/2 In.	300.00
Figurine, Cupid, Pedestal Base, c.1900, 4 3/4 In.	550.00
Figurine, Doctor's Lady, 3 In.	65.00
Figurine, Elephant, Africa, 3 3/4 In.	250.00
Figurine, Elephant, Carved Ebony, Ivory Tusks & Hooves, Africa, 1951, 8 In.	200.00
Figurine, Elephant, With Lions, Tigers, Monkeys, 3 In.	600.00
Figurine, Emperor & Empress, Stands, Signed, 4 1/2 In., Pair	600.00
Figurine, Farmer, Holding Gourd & Hoe, c.1900, 4 1/4 In.	275.00
Figurine, Horse, Reclining, 1 In.	45.00
Figurine, Horse, Standing, Oriental, 14 x 16 In., Pair	1800.00
Figurine, Immortal, Standing, Holds Staff & Plum, Stand, 12 In.	700.00
Figurine, Man, Africa, 9 3/4 In.	90.00
Figurine, Man, With Abacus, On Fish, 19th Century, 2 1/2 In.	185.00
Figurine, Nudes, Young Boy, With Fish, Girl With Insect, F. Preiss, 7 In., Pair	3100.00
Figurine, Painter, Seated, Carved, Japan, 19th Century, 2 1/2 In.	385.00
Figurine, Peasant Man With Flute, Display Dome & Stand, 8 1/4 In.	470.00
Figurine, Royal Women Attendants, China, 1930s, 7 1/2 In.	295.00 To 395.00
Figurine, Sage, Carrying A Staff, 6 1/2 In.	247.00
Figurine, Samurai, Engraved Clothes, 2 1/4 In.	65.00
Figurine, Sheba, Dark Brown Stain, Teakwood Stand, 18th Century, 5 1/2 x 3 In.	2750.00
Figurine, Shiva, Holding Buddha Aloft, Lotus Carved Base, 20 In.	1760.00
Figurine, Venus, Playing Lyre, 4 3/4 In.	995.00
Figurine, Warrior, Drawing Sword, 16 In.	495.00
Figurine, Warrior, Wooden Base, 6 1/4 In.	60.00
Figurine, Water Buffalo, Cordovan Stained, Natural Ivory Hooves, 6 In.	385.00
Figurine, Woman & Child, Attendants, Carved Wooden Stand, Signed, 10 x 16 In.	2475.00
Figurine, Woman & Child, Stand, 2 1/2 In.	35.00
Figurine, Woman, Nude, 6 In.	227.00
Figurine, Woman, With Sash, Wooden Base, 9 1/4 In.	82.00
Gavel, Wooden Handle, Silver Plated Band, 1906	275.00
Group, Kneeling Warrior, Fealty To Lord, Carved Wooden Base, China, 7 x 8 In.	286.00
Hair Comb, Cut Out Circles & Heart, 5 1/4 In.	38.00
Hairbrush, Carved, 10 1/2 In.	440.00
Lantern, Trellis Pierced, Suspended From Column Next To Scholar, 13 In.	220.00
Medicine Ball, Figural Standard, 20th Century, 10 1/2 In.	275.00
Mirror, Hand, Beveled Glass, Gold, Hand Painted Portrait, Apollo, 13 In.	135.00
Needle Case, Fist-Form Cover, 4 In.	110.00
Pagoda, People, Trees, Animal, Intricate Design, 10 In.	165.00
Pillbox, 1 1/2 In.	75.00
Stretcher, Glove	25.00
Toothpick, Flowers, Triangular	325.00

Triptych, Adoration of The Magi, Ivory Floral Scrolls, Germany, 7 3/4 x 11 In.	990.00
Triptych, Moses With Scroll, 11 1/2 In.	305.00
Tusk, Cigar Cutter	100.00
Vase, Eagle Design, Japan, 19th Century, 4 In.	660.00

JACK ARMSTRONG, the all–American boy, was the hero of a radio serial from 1933 to 1951. Premiums were offered to the listeners until the mid–1940s. Jack Armstrong's best–known endorsement is for Wheaties.

Bombsight	75.00
Book, Comic, 1949	12.00
Flashlight, Torpedo, Black	50.00
Magic Answer Box	50.00
Pedometer	25.00
Ring, Dragon's Eye, Radio Premium	475.00
Ring, Whistle, Egyptian ....80.00 To 125.00
Telescope, Explorers	35.00

JACK–IN–THE–PULPIT vases, oddly shaped like trumpets, resemble the wild plant called jack–in–the–pulpit. The design originated in the late Victorian years. Vases in the jack–in–the–pulpit shape were made of ceramic or glass and the complete list of page references can be found in the index.

Epergne, White, Opalescent, American Hobnail, Fluted	225.00
Vase, Amethyst, Carnival Glass, Ribbed, 7 1/2 In.	60.00
Vase, Burmese, Crimped Rim, 14 1/2 In.	785.00
Vase, Cased Glass, 10 In.	28.50
Vase, Diamond–Quilted, 7 1/2 In.	1750.00
Vase, Multicolored, Flared, Late 1800s, 8 In.	25.00
Vase, White Cased, Maroon Ruffles	110.00

JACKFIELD ware was originally a black glazed pottery made in Jackfield, England, from 1750 to 1775. A yellow glazed ware has also been called Jackfield ware. Most of the pieces referred to as *Jackfield* today are black–glazed, red–clay wares made at the Jackfield Pottery in Shropshire, England, in Victorian times.

Bowl, Silver Trim, 6 In.	200.00
Creamer, Cow, c.1800	295.00

JADE is the name for two different minerals, nephrite and jadeite. Nephrite is the mineral used for most early Oriental carvings. Jade is a very tough stone that is found in many colors from dark green to pale lavender. Jade carvings are still being made in the old styles, so collectors must be careful not to be fooled by recent pieces. Jade jewelry is found in this book under Jewelry.

Belt Hook, Carved Arched & Cut With Cloud Design, 5 In.	275.00
Figurine, Birds, China, 3 x 7 1/2 In.	110.00
Figurine, Elephant, Teak Stand, 2 x 3 In.	440.00
Figurine, Goat, Hardwood Base, China, 19th Century, 4 In.	550.00
Figurine, Man, Holding Beard & Cup, Oriental, Green, Teakwood Base, 3 x 3 In. ...	495.00
Flask, Pale Green, Lion Handles, Carved Wooden Base, China, 10 In.	242.00
Medallion, Carved Bird & Calligraphy, China, 2 1/4 In.	200.00
Medallion, Man With Stringed Instrument, Black, Metal Mount, 2 x 2 1/4 In.	275.00
Salt, Carved, Round	100.00
Snuff Bottle, Carved, Lapis Ball Finial, Teakwood Base, 19th Century, 3 x 2 3/4 In.	550.00
Urn, Cover, Foo Dog, Ring Handles, Bird Finial, 8 1/2 In.	375.00
Urn, Cover, Foo Lion Finial, Stand, White, Oriental, 2 In.	355.00

JAPANESE CORALENE is a ceramic decorated with small raised beads and dots. It was first made in the nineteenth century. Later wares made to imitate coralene had dots of enamel. There is also another type of coralene that is made with small glass beads on glass containers.

Vase, Green, 9 1/4 In.	625.00
Vase, Patent Mark, 7 In.	535.00

Vase, Pink To Orange, 4 1/2 In. 300.00
Vase, Quarter Moon Shape, 5 In. 375.00

JAPANESE WOODBLOCK PRINTS are listed in this book in the Print category under Japanese.

JASPERWARE can be made in different ways. Some pieces are made from a solid colored clay with applied raised designs of a contrasting colored clay. Other pieces are made entirely of one color clay with raised decorations that are glazed with a contrasting color. Additional pieces of jasperware may also be listed in the Wedgwood category or under various art potteries.

Barrel, Biscuit, Blue 135.00
Biscuit Jar, 3 Colors 825.00
Burner, Pastille, Dark Blue 1045.00
Cup & Saucer, Chocolate, Cover, 3 Colors 1760.00
Plaque, Fisherman & His Girl, Blue & White, Germany, 6 3/8 x 8 In. 125.00
Plaque, Lohengrin, Swan Prince & Fair Elaine, Germany, 5 3/4 In. 95.00
Urn, Blue, Dancing Maidens, Garlands, Acanthus, Wedgwood, 14 In., Pair 1115.00

JEWELRY, whether made from gold and precious gems or plastic and colored glass, is popular with collectors. Values are determined by the intrinsic value of the stones and metal and by the skill of the craftsmen and designers. Victorian and older jewelry has been collected since the 1950s. More recent interests are Art Deco and Edwardian styles, Mexican and Danish silver jewelry, and beads of all kinds. Copies of almost all styles are being made. Indian jewelry is listed in the Indian category.

Band, Wedding, Platinum, 28 Full–Cut Diamonds 330.00
Barrette, Baguette & Round Diamonds, Platinum, 14K White Gold 1100.00
Beads, Venetian Glass, Butterscotch, Applied Flowers, Gold Rigaree 45.00
Belt, Claw Set Rhinestones, Christian Dior, 23 In. 275.00
Bracelet & Earrings, Gold Washed, Norway 95.00
Bracelet, 10 Charms, Set With Small Diamonds, Rubies & Sapphires, Platinum 3850.00
Bracelet, 100 Diamonds, 1 Center Diamond, Platinum 9900.00
Bracelet, 4 Colored Agates, 3 Silver Plaques, Scotland, c.1920 .... 195.00
Bracelet, 5 Rows of Curb Link Chains, 18K Gold, 7 1/2 In. 725.00
Bracelet, 6 Faceted Oval Amethysts, Seed Pearl Border, 14K Gold Mounting 725.00
Bracelet, 8 Ivory Sections, Each With Hand Painted Persian Scene, Silver Gilt, 8 In. 60.00
Bracelet, Amethyst Stones, Pearls, Gold Link, Schiaparelli 185.00
Bracelet, Bakelite, Green & Cream Polka Dot, Pair 550.00
Bracelet, Bakelite, Red Cherry 175.00
Bracelet, Bangle, 18K Gold 715.00
Bracelet, Bangle, 5 Large Pearls, 14K Gold, Clasp 990.00
Bracelet, Bangle, Bakelite, Red, Carved, 5/8 In. 40.00
Bracelet, Bangle, Black Onyx & Enamel, Hinged, 14K Pink Gold 390.00
Bracelet, Bangle, Diamond Flower In Center, Yellow Gold 355.00
Bracelet, Bangle, Hammered, Silver, Gaylord Craft 55.00
Bracelet, Bangle, Red Flower, Bakelite 150.00
Bracelet, Bangle, Red, Bakelite, 1 In. 40.00
Bracelet, Barrel Shape, Coral, Turquoise & Semiprecious Stones, Silver 192.50
Bracelet, Bowtie, Bakelite 1000.00
Bracelet, Carved Butterscotch Bakelite, Hinged 65.00
Bracelet, Central Scroll Rosette, 6 Turquoise Domes Flexible Link, 18K Gold 198.00
Bracelet, Child's, 10K Gold, Box, 1915 .... 74.00
Bracelet, Emerald & Diamond, Square & Rose Cut, 14K Gold, c.1920 .... 715.00
Bracelet, Emerald–Cut Sapphire, 27 Round Diamonds, 14K Gold, 7 1/4 In. 990.00
Bracelet, Filigree, Diamond & Platinum, Edwardian 4500.00
Bracelet, Flower Design, 14 Full–Cut Diamonds, 14K Gold Filigree, 1920s 1650.00
Bracelet, Flower Design, Sterling Silver, Canecraft 65.00
Bracelet, Geometric, Textured Floral Sections, Safety Clasp, 18K Gold, 1/14 In. 1175.00
Bracelet, Gold Filled, Black Enamel, Victorian 82.00
Bracelet, Gold Plated Rope, Double Horseshoe Shaped Watch Fob, Goldstone 20.00
Bracelet, Gold, Emerald & Diamond Center, Victorian, Russia 3500.00

Jewelry, Chatelaine, 5 Chains, Silver

Jewelry, Pendant, Masks, Silver, Rebajes

Bracelet, Hard Stone Cameo & Diamonds, France 1810.00
Bracelet, Hinged, Renoir 20.00
Bracelet, Identification, 3 Small Diamonds, 14K Yellow Gold 165.00
Bracelet, Lapis & Sterling, Vintage Design, Georg Jensen, c.1938 .... 605.00
Bracelet, Lapis, Double Link 410.00
Bracelet, Link, 18K Yellow Gold 2090.00
Bracelet, Mesh, Flexible, Blue Enamel, Buckle Clasp, 14K Yellow Gold 825.00
Bracelet, Mesh, Flexible, Pearls & Turquoise Beads, Slide Clasp, 12K Gold 550.00
Bracelet, Mesh, Silver Tone, Whiting & Davis 38.00
Bracelet, Music Box, Brass, Germany 35.00
Bracelet, Nugget Design, Identification Plate, 14K Yellow Gold, 8 1/4 In. 990.00
Bracelet, Pearl, 2 Strands, Large Pearl & Jeweled Clasp, Haskell 100.00
Bracelet, Rhinestone, Ciner 75.00
Bracelet, Silver, Hinged, Miriam Haskell 35.00
Bracelet, Single Diamond Set In Black Onyx, Gold Links 770.00
Bracelet, Slide, Diamond & Turquoise, 14K Gold 1430.00
Bracelet, Slide, Half–Pearls, 2 Gold Tassels, 14K Yellow Gold 1630.00
Bracelet, Snake, Whiting & Davis, Box 125.00
Bracelet, Snake, Yellow Metal, Blue & Green Enamel, Opal, James Cromer Watt 5918.00
Bracelet, Sterling Silver, Spratling, 1920–1930 .... 350.00
Bracelet, Tennis, 22 Cut Citrines, 14K Gold 125.00
Bracelet, Textured Links, Rubies & Diamonds, Ball & Chain Clasp, 15K Gold 575.00
Bracelet, Woven Hair, Gold Clasp, 1800s 175.00
Bracelet, Woven Mesh Link, 18K Yellow Gold, 8 1/2 In. 905.00
Bracelet, Yellow Gold Stretch, Cartier, c.1950 .... 2180.00
Buckle, Belt, Gold, Chased Design, 18th Century, 2 1/4 In. 350.00
Buckle, Double Curved Apple, Bakelite, 4 x 2 In. 98.00
Buckle, Scarab, Sterling Silver, Unger 255.00
Buckle, Sterling Silver, Enamel, Foliage, Openwork, Liberty & Co., 1902 .... 1487.00
Card Case, 14K White, Rose & Yellow Gold Basketweave, Van Cleef & Arpels 385.00
Chain, Platinum & Gold Links, Victorian, 26 In. 845.00
Chain, Turquoise, 14K Yellow Gold Links, 7 Turquoise, Victorian, 50 In. 325.00
Chain, Watch, Alternating Links of Ivory & Ebony 195.00
Charm, Chevrolet, 14K Gold, 1967 .... 75.00
Chatelaine, Chains, Silver ....*Illus* 785.00
Chatelaine, Complete, Sterling Silver, Gorham 1575.00
Chatelaine, Leaf Form, 5 Necessaires, Sterling Silver, 8 In. 330.00
Chatelaine, Vinaigrette, Coin Ball, Compact, Sterling Silver, R & B, c.1900 .... 295.00
Cigar Cutter, Solid Gold 85.00
Cigarette Case, Dog Pictures, 1900, James Blake Sterling 225.00

Clasp, Cloak, Circular, White Metal, Repousse Design	670.00
Clasp, Foliate Design, Seed Pearls, Silver, Liberty & Co. 1905	483.00
Clip, Brown Carved Bakelite Acorn, Pair	85.00
Clip, Cameo, 18K Yellow Gold	165.00
Clip, Fur, Art Deco, Eisenberg	125.00
Clip, Fur, Rhinestone, Trifari, Double Prong	50.00
Clip, Pineapple, Citrine, Gold Filled, Eisenberg	250.00
Clip, Scarf, White & Black Enamel, Red Coral, Cartier	1430.00
Cross, Gold Plated Beaded Chain, 14K Gold, Victorian, 1866	330.00
Cross, Rose–Cut Diamond, Filigree, 18K Gold, 1 1/2 In.	150.00
Cuff Links, Bulldog, Green Enamel, 1930s	50.00
Cuff Links, Center Sapphire, Blue & Gold Enamel, Mother–of–Pearl, France	600.00
Cuff Links, Center Sapphire, Flanked By Diamonds, 14K Gold Cross Bars	905.00
Cuff Links, Coin, Silver, Ancient Greek Head	750.00
Cuff Links, Comedy Mask, 14K Yellow Gold	230.00
Cuff Links, Dragons, Mine–Cut Diamonds, 18K Yellow Gold, Art Nouveau	395.00
Cuff Links, Gold, Hand Hammered, Oval	2200.00
Cuff Links, Intaglio Eagle, 14K Gold Mounts, Victorian	575.00
Cuff Links, Japanese Scenes, Shakudo, Mixed Metals, 1 In.	365.00
Cuff Links, Opal Doublet, 14K Yellow Gold	88.00
Cuff Links, Oval Cameo, Hard Stone, 18K Gold	665.00
Cuff Links, Profile of Warrior, 15K Yellow Gold, Leather Box	605.00
Cuff Links, Reverse Crystal Intaglio, Labrador Retriever, Gold Rim	1500.00
Cuff Links, Sapphires & Synthetic Rubies, 14K Yellow Gold	250.00
Cuff Links, Silver Sterling, Agate, Danish	95.00
Cuff Links, Tie Bar, Intaglio Floral Ovals, Georg Jensen	200.00
Cuff Links, Viking Warriors, Shields, Sterling Silver, Allan Adler	525.00
Dress Clip, Grapes, Bakelite	45.00
Ear Clips, 2 Interlocking Links, 18K Yellow Gold, Turi	365.00
Ear Clips, Coiled Rope Twist Chain, Gold Tassels, 14K Yellow Gold	425.00
Ear Cuffs, Rhinestone, Boucher	45.00
Earrings & Pendant, Seed Pearls, Turquoise Moon & Stars Design, Victorian	295.00
Earrings, Angelfish, Tricolored Metal, Taxco Sterling, Signed Los Castillo	100.00
Earrings, Baroque Pearl, Gold Ear Wires	425.00
Earrings, Brown Swirl Glass, Miriam Haskell	25.00
Earrings, Clip, Yellow Bakelite, Fancy Gold Tone Dangles	55.00
Earrings, Cluster of Cultured Pearls, Diamond Centers, 14K White Gold	545.00
Earrings, Cluster of Mine–Cut Diamonds, 14K Gold Mounting	3000.00
Earrings, Comedy, Tragedy Mask, Copper, Signed Renoir	35.00
Earrings, Coral, 18K Yellow Gold	175.00
Earrings, Diamond & Platinum, Floral Design	7590.00
Earrings, Gold, Ball, Matte Finish, Victorian	1950.00
Earrings, Hoop, Rhinestone, KJL	20.00
Earrings, Hoop, Square Rubies & Brilliant–Cut Diamonds, 18K Yellow Mounting	2100.00
Earrings, Hoop, Square–Cut Rubies At Center, Diamonds, 18K Gold	1200.00
Earrings, Hoop, Textured Gold Leaves, Accent Diamonds, 14K Yellow Gold	600.00
Earrings, Insect Shape, Gold Wings, Citrine Head, Sapphire Body, Tiffany & Co.	1200.00
Earrings, Lucite, Original Card, 1950s	15.00
Earrings, Oval Amber Stones, Whiting Davis	10.00
Earrings, Rhinestone, Bogoff	15.00
Earrings, Rose–Cut Diamond, Silver Mounts, Gold Wire Frames, 7/8 In.	300.00
Earrings, Square–Cut Emeralds, Diamonds, 18K Yellow Gold	850.00
Earrings, Thistle, Gold, Buccellati	3000.00
Hair Comb, Sterling Silver, Filigree, Large	80.00
Hatpins are listed in this book in the Hatpin category	
Lavaliere, Center Red Stone, 12 Seed Pearls, 10K Gold Chain	70.00
Lavaliere, Victorian, Center Red Stone, Seed Pearls, 10K Gold Chain	165.00
Lavaliere, Victorian, Diamond & Seed Pearls, 14K Gold	225.00
Locket & Necklace, Heart, Pave Pearl, Edwardian	1250.00
Locket, Chased Frame, Lock of Hair Within, 18K Gold, 1830	137.50
Locket, Gold Filled, White Stones, Victorian	115.00
Locket, Gold, Bird & Leaf Decoration, Pearl & Diamond, Ruby Eye, Victorian	2200.00
Locket, Heart Shape, Diamond Leaf, 14K Gold, c.1920, 11 In.	250.00

Locket, Heart, Pave Diamond, Gold & Platinum, Edwardian 9800.00
Locket, Heart, Round Mine–Cut Diamond, Rubies, 18K Gold, Victorian 825.00
Locket, Hinged Heart, Diamond Leaf, c.1920, 1 In. 275.00
Locket, Profile of Classical Male, Diamond Wreath, Sardonyx Mount, 14K Gold 300.00
Locket, Seed Pearls, Woven Chain, 14K Gold, Victorian 225.00
Locket, Sterling Silver, Handmade 3–Section Chain, 1840 .... 235.00
Locket, White Sapphires, Horseshoe Shape, Gold Filled, Victorian 45.00
Money Clip, Man's, Dog Design, 14K Yellow Gold 154.00
Necklace & Bracelet, Cherry, Bakelite 250.00
Necklace & Bracelet, European & Mine–Cut Diamonds, Leaf Form, Georgian Style 6500.00
Necklace & Bracelet, Steel Cut Marcasite 75.00
Necklace & Earrings Set, Green Rhinestones, Coro 50.00
Necklace & Earrings, Blue Rhinestone, Sarah Coventry 20.00
Necklace & Earrings, Blue Rhinestones, Sarah Coventry 25.00
Necklace & Earrings, Gold With Pearls, Trifari 35.00
Necklace & Earrings, Triangular Shape, Gold Mesh, Whiting & Davis 125.00
Necklace, 14 Blue Sapphires, 31 White Sapphires, Gold Plated Sterling Silver 95.00
Necklace, 18K Yellow Gold, Gubelin 3850.00
Necklace, 20 Quartz Discs On Celluloid Link Chain, Bakelite 90.00
Necklace, 3 Teardrops, Center On With Diamond, 18K Yellow Gold 630.00
Necklace, Bakelite Pendant, Givenchy 25.00
Necklace, Bakelite, Reversed Carved Flower, 2–In. Pendant, Celluloid Chain 110.00
Necklace, Bi–Color Gold & Diamond, Chaumet 6600.00
Necklace, Bracelet, Earrings, Garnet, Mounted In Silver Filigree, 14K Gold. c.1880 850.00
Necklace, Center Emerald, 40 Round Diamonds, 18K Yellow Gold, 19 In. 3100.00
Necklace, Chalcedony, Intaglio Warrior, Bar Clasp, 18K Gold 2300.00
Necklace, Cherry Amber, Faceted Beads, 26 1/2 In. 175.00
Necklace, Choker, Baroque Pearls, Medallion, Pearl Drop, Miriam Haskell 50.00
Necklace, Chunky Silver Metal, Large Rhinestones, Schiaparelli 145.00
Necklace, Claw Set Rhinestones, Baguette Bow Fastener, Dior, 18 In. 45.00
Necklace, Coral & Clear Glass Beads, 6 Strand, Flower Clasp, Haskell 450.00
Necklace, Coral, 10K Gold Beads Between, Mother–of–Pearl, 24 In. 58.00
Necklace, Coral, Yellow Gold, Turquoise Slide Clasp 187.00
Necklace, Crucifix, 14K Yellow Gold, c.1900 .... 300.00
Necklace, Drop Pendant, Openwork Gold, Female Portrait, 14K Gold, 24 In. 990.00
Necklace, Freshwater Pearls, Colored Beads, 5 Strands, Miriam Haskell 150.00
Necklace, Hand Painted Porcelain Pendants, Vertu, Victorian 4500.00
Necklace, Hand Wrought Silver, Pearl, Gold, Murrle Bennett 1125.00
Necklace, Holland–Cut Garnets, Clusters of Round & Pear–Shaped Garnets, 15 In. 425.00
Necklace, Jade, Graduated Beads, Gold & Diamond Clasp, 20 In. 465.00
Necklace, Jet, 5 Strands, Hobe 200.00
Necklace, Large Faceted Chrysophases, Marcasites In Silver Clasp 185.00
Necklace, Majorca Pearls, Silver Clasp, 28 In. 35.00
Necklace, Moonstone, Trifari 145.00
Necklace, Mourning, Woven Hair, Pendant 165.00
Necklace, Multicolor Bakelite Circles, Celluloid Chain 325.00
Necklace, Peacock Enameled, Charles Horner 325.00
Necklace, Pearl, 7 Mm Double A, Pink Color, 14K Gold Clasp, 28 In. 795.00
Necklace, Pearl, Silver & Gold, Murrle, Bennett & Co. 1350.00
Necklace, Pearls, Pink Sheen, La Tosca, Metal Hinged Box, 27 In. 150.00
Necklace, Red Coral, Victorian, 27 In. 85.00
Necklace, Rose Gold Plated Sterling Silver, Sixteen Garnets 55.00
Necklace, Silver, Moonstones, Leaf, Blossom, Georg Jensen, 16 1/2 In. 885.00
Necklace, Slide, Inset Pearls, Black & Enamel Tracery, c.1900, 60 In. 355.00
Necklace, Sports, Bakelite 450.00
Necklace, Swag Style, Silver & Enamel Elements, Murrle, Bennett & Co. 975.00
Ornament, Feather & Brass, Jeweled Mounts, Lucite Case, African, 17 In. 220.00
Pendant & Earrings, Seed Pearls, Turquoise, Moon & Stars Design, Victorian 295.00
Pendant, 14K White Gold, Jadeite, Diamond 7150.00
Pendant, Anchor & Fish, Chain, Carnegie 65.00
Pendant, Aquamarine, Pearls, Diamonds, Openwork, Gold Chain, 16K 852.00
Pendant, Art Deco, White, Blue Stones, Silver Finish, McClelland Barclay 325.00
Pendant, Cameo, Pink Coral, 10K Yellow Gold, c.1900 .... 500.00

Pendant, Carved Carnelian, Classical Male Figure, 14K Gold Frame, Cameo 357.00
Pendant, Carved Jade, Rose–Cut Diamonds, 9K White Gold 605.00
Pendant, Center Oval Ruby, Surrounded By 13 Diamonds, Platinum Chain, 16 In. 1450.00
Pendant, Circle, Cobalt, Green & White Swirls, Clear Glass Cased, Labino, 2 In. 60.00
Pendant, Egyptian Gold, Beaded Necklace, Haskell 100.00
Pendant, Emeralds & Diamonds Suspended From 14K Gold Chain, 24 In. 905.00
Pendant, Enameled Bumblebee Design, 14K Yellow Gold, Emerald, Link Chain 247.00
Pendant, Etched Sage, China, 2 In. 44.00
Pendant, Fish, Baroque Pearl Head, Coral Drop, Sterling Chain, Albert Wehde 2250.00
Pendant, Fish, Enamel, Signed Margot 175.00
Pendant, Fish, White Metal, Openwork, Opals, Link Chain, Edgar Simpson 2800.00
Pendant, Gold Flower Design, 3 Rubies, 14K 70.00
Pendant, Green Stone Surround By Clear Rhinestone Leaves, Sarah Coventry 22.00
Pendant, Heart Shape, 26 Diamonds, White Gold Chain, 14K White Gold 940.00
Pendant, Leda & Swan, Sterling Silver, Salvador Dali, 1 7/8 In. 330.00
Pendant, Masks, Silver, Rebajes ....*Illus* 138.00
Pendant, Opal & Diamond, Pear Shape, Yellow Gold, 14K 2200.00
Pendant, Open Heart, Sapphires, Diamonds, Rubies, 14K Yellow Gold 135.00
Pendant, Orchid, Pearl & Amethyst, Art Nouveau, 14K Gold, Brassler Co., 20 In. 360.00
Pendant, Pearl, Carved Tourmaline, Emerald, Classical Design, Mid–19th C. 200.00
Pendant, Silhouette Woman In Hoop Skirt, Garden, Rosenthal, 1920–1930 .... 125.00
Pendant, Silver Tone, Enameled, Pink Crystal Center, Diamond Shape, 2 In. 25.00
Pill Box, Hinged Cover, Silver Sterling, Gold Vermeil Interior, R. Blackington 55.00
Pin & Bracelet, Colored Stones, Schreiner 285.00
Pin & Earrings, Butterfly, Marvella 25.00
Pin & Earrings, Flower On Stem, Sterling Silver, Les Bernard 110.00
Pin & Earrings, Form of Plume, Cartier, 14K Gold 550.00
Pin & Earrings, White Rhinestones, Larel 45.00
Pin Set, Rose–Cut Diamonds, Pearl, Scrollwork, Silver, Gold, Victorian 825.00
Pin, 2–Leaf Cluster, Silver & Amethyst, Mexico, Frederick Davis, 3 1/4 In. 225.00
Pin, 4 Stippled Flowers, Diamond Center, 14K Gold, c.1900 .... 515.00
Pin, 5 Carrots, Green Leaves, Dangles From Amber Branch, Bakelite 1200.00
Pin, Air Force, 20 Year, Sterling 25.00
Pin, Air Force, Officer, Gold 450.00
Pin, American Flag, Red, White, Blue Stones, 6 In. 30.00
Pin, Aviator's Wings, Sterling Silver 35.00
Pin, Bakelite, Cut Log Cherry 100.00
Pin, Bakelite, Horsehead 150.00
Pin, Bar, 7 Amethysts Alternating 12 Single Cut Diamonds, Platinum Mount 660.00
Pin, Bar, 7 Swallows, Pearl, Sapphire & Diamond Eyes, Edwardian 3000.00
Pin, Bar, Black, Red & Silver Enameled, Rhinestones, Art Deco 30.00
Pin, Bar, Champleve, Enameled Roses 25.00
Pin, Bar, Filigree, Sterling Silver, Blue Stone 22.00
Pin, Bar, Georg Jensen, Art Nouveau, 3 In. 225.00
Pin, Bar, Peridot, Gold Filigree, Allsopp & Boub, Art Nouveau 650.00
Pin, Bee, Plique–A–Jour Wings, Single–Cut Diamonds, 18K Gold 1695.00
Pin, Beetle, Labradorite, Diamond & Gold, Victorian 2200.00
Pin, Bird & Heart, Sterling Silver, Georg Jensen 150.00
Pin, Bird In Flight, Diamond In Mouth, Cobalt Blue Body, 14K Gold 485.00
Pin, Bird, Gold & Silver, Eisenberg 125.00
Pin, Black Onyx, Sterling Silver, Los Castillo 40.00
Pin, Black Warrior, Shield & Arrow, Salvador 38.00
Pin, Blanket, Police Horse, Metal, 4 3/4 In. 60.00
Pin, Bouquet of Flowers, Gold Wash, Hobe 135.00
Pin, Bow, Center Diamond, Diamonds, Surround, Platinum On Gold, Tiffany 3750.00
Pin, Bow, Double Row of Seed Pears, Edwardian Chatelaine, 14K Gold 550.00
Pin, Bow, Pave Diamond, Platinum, Art Deco 3750.00
Pin, Bow, Rhinestones, Sterling Silver, Trifari 100.00
Pin, Bowtie, Rhinestone, Baroque Pearls, Haskell 150.00
Pin, Brown Scotty, Bakelite 25.00
Pin, Butterflies, Flowers, Circular Frame, Signed Georg Jensen 440.00
Pin, Butterfly, 152 Diamonds, Silver & Gold Mounting ....*Illus* 7560.00
Pin, Calla Lily, Enamel, Diamond & Gold In Flower, Art Nouveau 1850.00

Jewelry, Pin, Butterfly, 152 Diamonds,

Silver & Gold Mounting

Pin, Cameo, Aurora, Gold Shell, Victorian 750.00
Pin, Cameo, Black & White, Victorian, Gilded Mounting, 1 7/16 In. 60.00
Pin, Cameo, Coral, Gold Frame, Victorian 750.00
Pin, Cameo, Cottage Scene, Gold–Filled Fitting, Oval, 1 3/4 In. 60.50
Pin, Cameo, Diamond Necklace, 14K White Gold Frame, 1920, 2 1/4 In. 450.00
Pin, Cameo, Floral Shell, Sterling Mounting 35.00
Pin, Cameo, Full View of Woman, Diamond Border, 15K Yellow Gold Frame 845.00
Pin, Cameo, Male Figure, Carved Shell, Beaded 18K Gold Frame, 2 1/4 In. 785.00
Pin, Cameo, Shell, Mythological Scene, 18K Gold Frame 545.00
Pin, Cameo, Shell, White To Tan Scene, Centaurs & Maiden, Lander 1200.00
Pin, Cameo, Young Woman, Gold–Filled Fitting, Oval, 2 3/8 In. 60.00
Pin, Center Moonstone Cabochon, 14K Gold, William Bramley 695.00
Pin, Center Oblong Blister Pearl, Sterling Silver Pierced Frame 522.50
Pin, Cherries, Cream Bakelite 200.00
Pin, Circle, 4 Overlapping Ribbons of Textured Gold, 18K Gold, Signed Cartier 825.00
Pin, Circle, Colored Scottish Agates, Gold Frame 545.00
Pin, Circle, Flower, Blue Stone, Sterling Silver, Van Dell 15.00
Pin, Circle, Leaf Wreath, Clusters of Green Cabochons, Georg Jensen, 1 3/4 In. 412.50
Pin, Circle, Platinum, Single–Cut Diamonds, Scrolled Floral Piece 2200.00
Pin, Circular Open Work Design, Diamond, Platinum 1210.00
Pin, Clown, Silver Face, Sterling Silver, Erik Mageusseri 425.00
Pin, Cluster of Blue & White Enameled Flowers, Center Diamond 545.00
Pin, Crown, Sterling Silver, Trifari 100.00
Pin, Crown, Trifari 150.00
Pin, Czechoslovakian Crystal, Miriam Haskell 475.00
Pin, Dancing Maiden, Rectangular, White Metal, Enamel Ground, Signed, 1909 .... 835.00
Pin, Diamond, Gold, Circle Design, Victorian 3500.00
Pin, Dog, Red Bakelite, Large 145.00
Pin, Dolphin, Pearl In Mouth, 14K Gold, Rikers 330.00
Pin, Dolphins, Georg Jensen 85.00
Pin, Eagle, Gold, Diamond Held In Feet 950.00
Pin, Emerald, 22 Full–Cut Diamonds, 14K Yellow Gold 935.00
Pin, Enameled Flower, Weiss 28.00
Pin, Enameled Sailboat, Marcasite 55.00
Pin, Equestrian, Carved Ivory, Gold Plated Accents 220.00
Pin, Exotic Flower, Beads, Enameled, Sterling Silver, Nettie Rosenstein, 3 In. 110.00
Pin, Fish, Rhinestone, Capri 15.00
Pin, Flag, American, Enamel & Gold 350.00
Pin, Floral Cornucopia, Amethyst, 14K White Gold Pin Stem, Art Deco 5175.00
Pin, Floral Spray, Sterling Silver, Coro 30.00
Pin, Floral, Moonstone, Sterling Silver, Georg Jensen 295.00
Pin, Floral, Rhinestones, Sterling Silver, Rosenstein 295.00
Pin, Flower Basket, Zircons & Colorless Stones, Textured Leaf, 14K Gold 300.00
Pin, Flower, Gold, Ruby & Diamond Center 1250.00
Pin, Flower, Orchid, Cultured Pearl Center, 18K Gold 110.00
Pin, Flower, Pink Rhinestone Studded Petals, Crystal Centers, Lilly Dache 325.00

Pin, Form of Cross, Flowers & Dove, Micro Mosaic, Victorian 180.00
Pin, Frog, Gold, Cabochon–Cut Ruby Eyes 1250.00
Pin, Frog, Mine–Cut Diamonds, Emerald Eyes, Silver & 15K Gold 5445.00
Pin, Garnet, Pearls, 14K Gold 250.00
Pin, Gilded Setting, China, Box, Pair 99.00
Pin, Gold Branches Hold Diamonds, Set With Opals, 14K Gold 495.00
Pin, Gold, Mountaineering Tools Tied In Center 650.00
Pin, Golfer, Multistone, 18K Yellow Gold 247.00
Pin, Headdress, Mexico, Cecillio Tono, Sterling Silver 95.00
Pin, Heart Shape, 66 Mine Cut Diamonds, Reverse Glazed Compartment 4235.00
Pin, Heart, With Dangles, Black Bakelite 225.00
Pin, Horse, Cantering, Synthetic Ruby Eye, 14K Gold 325.00
Pin, Horse, Pave Diamond, Platinum 3500.00
Pin, Horsehead, With Dangles, Bakelite 175.00
Pin, Key, Gold, Amethyst Stone, Haskell, 3 1/2 In. 115.00
Pin, Kilt, Scottish Agate, Faceted Citrines, 14K Gold, Scotland 425.00
Pin, Kneeling Mystic, Glass Ball, Silver Finish, Thief of Baghdad, Korda, 2 1/2 In. 195.00
Pin, Large Bow Shape, Clear & Topaz Stones, Gold Metal, Eisenberg 125.00
Pin, Leaf, Danecraft 18.00
Pin, Leaf, Rhinestone, Reja 65.00
Pin, Leaf, Sapphire & Diamonds, 14K Gold Mounting 1450.00
Pin, Leaf, Sterling Silver, Danecraft 19.00
Pin, Lily Pads, Clear Cabochon Center, Sterling Silver, Mary Gage, 3 In. 300.00
Pin, Lizard, Demantoid Garnet, Diamonds, Gold Feet, Edwardian 5500.00
Pin, Lobster, Hattie Carnegie 125.00
Pin, Medusa, Ivory Face, Blue–Green Enamel, Pendent Pearls, George Hunt 5920.00
Pin, Mexican, With Poncho, Bakelite 450.00
Pin, Micro Mosaic, Birds & Flowers, Set In Black Onyx, 10K Gold 75.00
Pin, Oriental Man, Sterling Silver, Blue Stones, Coro 100.00
Pin, Pansy, Enamel, Yellow, Pearl Center, Gold Rim, Art Nouveau 1500.00
Pin, Pansy, Gold Pedals, Diamond Center, Art Nouveau 1350.00
Pin, Pansy, Polychrome Enamel, A. J. Hedges, c.1900 .... 1025.00
Pin, Peacock, Silver, Enamel, Abalone, G of H Ltd., London, 1907 .... 2788.00
Pin, Pearl Pansy, Black, Enamel, 14K Gold Mount, c.1900 .... 515.00
Pin, Pine Cones, Butterfly, Openwork, Sterling Silver, 2 1/4 In. 60.00
Pin, Pink & Red, Lilly Dache 250.00
Pin, Poinsettia, 3–Color Enamel, San Francisco, 1915, 1 3/4 In. 25.00
Pin, Poodle, Aqua Glass Center, Sterling Silver, Trifari 200.00
Pin, Profile of Woman, Cultured Pearl Border, 14K Gold Frame 300.00
Pin, Raised Floral, Silver Finish, Round, Joseff of Hollywood, 2 1/4 In. 225.00
Pin, Reverse Carved Leaf, Bakelite 43.00
Pin, Ribbon Bow, Central Knot of Sapphires, Diamonds, 14K Gold 715.00
Pin, Ruby, Diamond, 14K Yellow & Rose Gold 440.00
Pin, Saber, Sterling Silver, Pearls, Blue Stone, Coro 40.00
Pin, Sailboat, Colored Stones 45.00
Pin, Scarecrow, Sterling Silver, Trifari 75.00
Pin, Scarf, Bezel–Set, Gray Baroque Pearl, 18K Yellow Gold, c.1900 .... 440.00
Pin, Scorpio, Metal, Trifari 5.00
Pin, Scotty, Red Celluloid 40.00
Pin, Scotty, With Golf Bag, Celluloid 95.00
Pin, Scrolled Leaf, Tendril, Set With Moonstone, Arts & Crafts, Signed 247.00
Pin, Scrollwork, Cut Diamonds, Central Pearl, Victorian 825.00
Pin, Siam Dancers, Sterling Silver 22.00
Pin, Smokey Quartz Bezel, Pearls & Garnet, Leaves, 14K Gold, Edward E. Oakes ... 2900.00
Pin, Snowflake, Coventry, 2 1/2 In. 29.00
Pin, Soldier, Plastic, Jointed, Original Card, 1940s 40.00
Pin, Spider, Sapphire Body, Ruby Eyes, Diamond Legs, Silver & Gold 2100.00
Pin, Squirrel, Diamond Chip Eye, Ruby Claws, Bushy Tail of Gold Pins 2200.00
Pin, Star Burst, Center European–Cut Diamond, Small Diamonds Around 3625.00
Pin, Starfish, Blue, Weiss 25.00
Pin, Sterling Silver, Cutwork Name Lizzie 25.00
Pin, Sterling Silver, Gemstones, Cutout H & D, With 25, Marion R. Ward, 1929 ..... 225.00
Pin, Stylized Bird In Flight, Sapphire, Turquoise & Ruby Body, Pearl Tail 1350.00

Pin, Sword, Sterling Silver, Colored Stones, Coro, 3 In.	39.00
Pin, Tiger Face, Enamel, Diamond, Ruby, Cartier	9500.00
Pin, Turtle, 18K Yellow Gold, Tiffany	665.00
Pin, Uncle Sam, Bakelite	1000.00
Pin, Victorian, Onyx Plaque, Morning Glories, Pietra Dura, 2 1/4 x 3/4 In.	250.00
Pin, Violin, Sterling Silver, Nettie Rosenstein	125.00
Pin, Winged Insect, White Metal, Opal Body	1394.00
Ring, 1 Brilliant–Cut Diamond, 14K Gold	6600.00
Ring, 2 Seed Pearls, Emeralds, 14K Pink Gold, Victorian	85.00
Ring, 50 Rose–Cut Garnets, 10K Gold	140.00
Ring, Alexandrite, Filigree, 14K Gold	95.00
Ring, Aquamarine, 4 Small Diamonds, Gold	175.00
Ring, Art Deco, Rose Diamond, Filigree, 18K Gold	135.00
Ring, Aurora Borealis, Sarah Coventry	20.00
Ring, Braided Hair Inset, 14K Gold, Size 7	200.00
Ring, Cameo, Carved Green, White Stone, 18K Yellow Gold	115.00
Ring, Cameo, Coral, 10K Gold.	55.00
Ring, Cameo, Coral, Sapphire, 14K Gold	40.00
Ring, Cameo, White, Gray, Marquis Design, Wedgwood, 1900	175.00
Ring, Canary Diamond, 35 Point, Tiffany Mounted	390.00
Ring, Carnelian, Carved Coat of Arms, 14K Yellow Gold Mounting	545.00
Ring, Carved Onyx, Depicting King & Queen, 14K Yellow Gold	330.00
Ring, Dinner, Cut Diamonds, Round Ruby, 6 Baguettes, 14K White Gold	550.00
Ring, Dinner, White Gold, Central Diamond, Circle of Diamonds	1210.00
Ring, Dome, 50 Bohemian Garnets, 14K Gold, c.1900	295.00
Ring, Earrings, Cameo, Intaglio Cut Crystal, Silver Filigree, Whiting & Davis	135.00
Ring, Figural Animal, Diamonds, Rubies, 18K Yellow & White Gold, Signed	302.00
Ring, Filigree Basket, Center Ruby, 1910, 18K Washed Gold, Size 6 3/4	175.00
Ring, Garnet & Seed Pearls, 14K Pink Gold, Victorian	58.00
Ring, Garnet, 10K Yellow Gold, Stamped Germany	145.00
Ring, Garnet, 2 Seed Pearls, 14K Pink Gold	65.00
Ring, Large Amethysts, 14K Pink Gold, Victorian	120.00
Ring, Man's, Gypsy Design, Diamond, 14K Yellow Gold	75.00
Ring, Man's, Lapis, Art Modern, c.1950–1960	150.00
Ring, Man's, Onyx Cameo Stone, 14K Yellow Gold	100.00
Ring, Man's, Star Sapphire & Diamond, 14K White Gold	410.00
Ring, Mexican Opal, Leaves & Beads, Sterling Silver, Petterson Studio	550.00
Ring, Onyx, Diamond Center, Platinum, Art Deco, Tiffany & Co.	4500.00
Ring, Opal, Surrounded By Rubies, 14K Yellow Gold	180.00
Ring, Open Heart, 14K Yellow Gold, Sapphires, Diamonds, Filigree Shank	85.00
Ring, Panther Head, Sterling, Ruby & Emerald Eyes	100.00
Ring, Pear–Shaped Cubic Zircon & 2 Green Stones	20.00
Ring, Pink Tourmaline & Diamond, c.1988	1200.00
Ring, Rattlesnake	18.00
Ring, Sapphire & Diamond, Tiffany, White Gold	2000.00
Ring, Sapphire & Pearls, Crisscrossing Openwork, Margaret Rogers, 18K Gold	4500.00
Ring, Sapphire Surrounded By 12 Small Full Cut Diamonds, 14K Yellow Gold	330.00
Ring, Sapphire, Ruby & Diamond, 16K Yellow Gold	415.00
Ring, Snake, Diamond Eyes, 14K Pink Gold	68.00
Ring, Star Sapphire, Victorian Setting	3500.00
Ring, Wedding, 18K Gold, 1912	60.00
Ring, Wedding, Pink Gold, Victorian, Size 3 1/2	45.00
Stickpin, Deer On Plow, John Deere	45.00
Stickpin, Fleur–De–Lis, Seed Pearls	55.00
Stickpin, French Knot, Seed Pearl, 14K Gold	55.00
Stickpin, Gold, Question Mark Design, 8 Diamonds, 1 Pearl, Tiffany	165.00
Stickpin, Horseshoe, 4 Diamonds & 3 Sapphires, 15K Yellow Gold	165.00
Stickpin, Lover's Knot, Diamond	75.00
Stickpin, Lozenge Shaped Green Tourmaline, 14K Gold, William Bramley	595.00
Stickpin, Man In The Moon, 14K Gold	55.00
Stickpin, Owl, Gold	350.00
Stickpin, Pearl, Emerald, Monet	45.00
Stickpin, Rooster, Brass Shell, 1900s	15.00

Stickpin, Ship's Wheel, Hurricane Lamp, Emerald Center, 14K Gold, Tiffany Co. 485.00
Stickpin, Silver Monkey, Gold Top Hat & Skates 650.00
Stickpin, Turtle, Haskell 75.00
Tie Clasp, Boy Scouts of America 20.00
Tie Clasp, Saddle, Gold Color 20.00
Tie Clasp, Santa Fe, 1969, Zero In On Safety 25.00
Tie Tack, Dictaphone Family, Copper, Blue Enameled 15.00
Watches are listed in their own category
Watch Chain, Edwardian, Curb Links, 18K Yellow Gold, 86 In. 665.00
Watch Fob, Art Nouveau, 2 Female Faces, Suspending Medallion, Sterling Silver 300.00
Watch, Pin, Woman's, Gold Filled, Pearls .... 80.00 To 85.00
Wristwatches are listed in their own category

JOHN ROGERS statues were made from 1859 to 1892. The originals were bronze, but the thousands of copies made by the Rogers factory were of painted plaster. Eighty different figures were created. Similar painted plaster figures were produced by some other factories. Rights to the figures were sold in 1893 and they were manufactured for several more years by the Rogers Statuette Co. Never repaint a Rogers figure because this lowers the value to collectors.

Group, Civil War Soldiers, Wounded To The Rear, 1 More Shot 495.00
Group, Watch On The Santa Maria 475.00

JUDAICA is any memorabilia that refers to the Jews or the Jewish religion. Interests range from newspaper clippings that mention eighteenth- and nineteenth-century Jewish Americans to religious objects, such as menorahs or spice boxes. Age, condition, and the intrinsic value of the material, as well as the historic and artistic importance, determine the value.

Box, Charity, Palestine, Tin, Aid To Charities, 3 In. 100.00
Candlestick, Sabbath, Austria, Marked JK, c.1894, 16 In., Pair 1395.00
Cookbook, How To Cook In Palestine, Text In English, German & Hebrew, 1925 ... 715.00
Cover, Matzo, Embroidered Silk, 1911 .... 45.00
Etrog Container, Polish Silver, c.1930 .... 3520.00
Goblet, Kiddush, Engraved Foliage, Silver, Poland, c.1890, 5 5/8 In. 385.00
Haggadah, Passover, Hebrew & Yiddish Text, 1785 .... 330.00
Haggadah, Printed In Europe During Holocaust, Hungary, 1944 .... 275.00
Hanukah Lamp, Removable Tray, 8 Oil Pans, Servant Light, Pewter, 15 In. 415.00
Hanukah Lamp, Stamped High Priest Kindling Menorah, Brass, c.1920, 10 3/4 In. 995.00
Ketubah, Marriage Contract, Peacocks, Lions, Foliate, Persian, 1865, Frame 600.00
Kiddush Cup, Silver Sterling, Embossed Fruits 60.00
Kiddush Cup, Silver Sterling, With Heart Stones 60.00
Megillat, Esther, Scroll, Waxed Paper, c.1945, Miniature 135.00
Menorah, 7-Light, Adjustable Arm, Brass, Benzimger Bros., 1898, 19 In. 2000.00
Plate, Passover, Biblical Quotes, Eagle Center, Pewter, c.1800, 16 1/2 In. 44.00
Prayer Book, Dutch, Silver Latticework Binding, 1791 .... 2640.00
Prayer Book, Woman's, Italian Manuscript, 1744 .... 990.00
Spice Container, Fish Form, Hinged Head, Red Stone Eyes, Dutch, 1898, 5 In. 330.00
Spice Tower, 2 Filigree Sections, German Silver, 1850s, 11 In. 522.00
Spice Tower, Filigree, Silver, Germany, 19th Century 330.00

JUGTOWN Pottery refers to pottery made in North Carolina as far back as the 1750s. In 1915, Juliana and Jacques Busbee set up a training and sales organization for what they named *Jugtown Pottery*. In 1921, they built a shop at Jugtown, North Carolina, and hired Ben Owen as a potter in 1923. The Busbees moved the village store where the pottery was sold to New York City. Juliana Busbee sold the New York store in 1926 and moved into a log cabin near the Jugtown Pottery. The pottery closed in 1958. It reopened and is still working near Seagrove, North Carolina.

Bowl, Chinese Blue Glaze, Turquoise Interior, Circular Mark, 4 x 7 In. 335.00
Bowl, Light Gray Mottled Glaze, Flared, 4 3/4 x 11 In. 165.00
Eggcup, Cobalt 25.00
Sugar, Orange 15.00

Jukebox, Regina, Model 32, Mahogany,

20 3/4 In.

If your home has just been robbed, don't immediately give the police a list of the stolen items and damage. Sit down later and make a detailed list. This police copy is the one your insurance company will use to settle any claims. Take photographs of the damage as soon as possible.

Urn, Chinese, White, 4 In.	85.00
Vase, 3 Handles, Gray, 8 In.	285.00
Vase, Alligatored Chinese Blue, 2 Handles, Circular Mark, 6 x 5 In.	275.00
Vase, Chinese Blue Glaze, Handles, 8 1/4 x 7 3/4 In.	470.00
Vase, Chinese Blue, Closed–In Neck, Circular Mark, 7 1/4 x 4 3/4 In.	335.00
Vase, Chinese White Drip Glaze, 3 3/4 In.	90.00
Vase, Cobalt Blue Glaze, Closed–In Neck, 5 x 4 In.	165.00
Vase, Frog–Skin Glaze, 4 Handles, Circular, 8 x 6 1/2 In.	165.00
Vase, Mottled Deep Red Glaze, 9 x 6 1/2 In.	935.00
Vase, Oriental Blue, 10 In.	200.00
Vase, Red Splashed Glaze, Chinese Blue, Egg Shape, 4 1/2 In.	195.00
Vase, White Crackle Ware Glaze Over Bisque Body, Ovoid, 6 1/2 x 5 In.	165.00

JUKEBOXES play records. The first coin–operated phonograph was demonstrated in 1889. In 1906 the *Automatic Entertainer* appeared, the first coin–operated phonograph to offer several different selections of music. The first electrically powered jukebox was introduced in 1927. Collectors search for jukeboxes of all ages, especially those with flashing lights and unusual design and graphics.

Aerion, Model 1207a, Art Deco Neon Lighted Front, Wooden Case	500.00
AMI, Model B, 1940s	1995.00
AMI, Rowe, MM3, 1969	700.00
AMI, Rowe, MMIA, Vue Attachment, Film, Dollar Bill, 1967	1400.00
Mills Model 801, With Records, 1927	4750.00
Packard Manhattan, 78 RPM Records, 1946	4200.00
Regina, Model 32, Mahogany, 20 3/4 In. ....*Illus*	15400.00
Rock–Ola, Counter Top, 1939	2950.00
Rock–Ola, Light–Up, 1940 .... 1800.00 To	2000.00
Rock–Ola, Model 1426, Restored	5500.00
Rock–Ola, Model 404, 1963	750.00
Rock–Ola, Model 424, 1964	650.00
Rock–Ola, Model 429, 1965	600.00
Rock–Ola, Model 432, 1966	600.00
Scopitone, Video, 36 Films	1800.00
Seeburg, 1954	2500.00
Seeburg, Blue Mirrored Panels, 1947	2200.00
Seeburg, Model 222, 1959	1400.00
Seeburg, Model 480, 1964	700.00
Seeburg, Model A, Plays 33 1/3 Albums	2850.00
Seeburg, Model AY, 1961	900.00

Seeburg, Model C	1900.00
Seeburg, Model C, 1952	3500.00
Seeburg, Model DS, 1962	850.00
Seeburg, Model KD200	1750.00
Seeburg, Model KD200, T–Bird Style, Taillights Mounted In Front Grill	2200.00
Seeburg, Model LPCI, 1963	700.00
Seeburg, Model LS2, 1969	700.00
Seeburg, Model Q, 1960	900.00
Seeburg, Model SS160, 1967	700.00
Seeburg, Model V20	2500.00
Seeburg, Selectomatic 200, 78 RPM, Blond Wooden Case	375.00
Seeburg, Selectophone, Green & Gold Paint, 1932	2500.00
Wurlitzer, 1st Stereo Model, 1959	1900.00
Wurlitzer, Centennial Model, 200 Selections, 55 In.	660.00
Wurlitzer, Model 600, 1938 .... 2500.00 To	3000.00
Wurlitzer, Model 1015, 1945	7000.00
Wurlitzer, Model 1015, Restored	9500.00
Wurlitzer, Model 1050, Art Deco Curved Case, Neon Lighted Front	3250.00
Wurlitzer, Model 1100, c.1948	3600.00
Wurlitzer, Model 1800, 1955	2600.00
Wurlitzer, Model 2304	1000.00
Wurlitzer, Model 3100, 1966	500.00
Wurlitzer, Model 3300, 1969	500.00
Wurlitzer, Model 3400, 1970	500.00
Wurlitzer, Model P–12, Walnut, 1936	900.00
Wurlitzer, Nickelodeon, Keyboard Style, 1912	7500.00
Wurlitzer, Simplex Model 616, Wood Deco Case, 3 Coin Slot	1500.00

KATE GREENAWAY, who was a famous illustrator of children's books, drew pictures of children in high–waisted Empire dresses. She lived from 1846 to 1901. Her designs appear on china, glass, and other pieces. Figural napkin rings depicting the Greenaway children may also be found in the Napkin Ring category under Figural.

Card Receiver, Bird, Flowers, Dragonfly, Pewter Girl, James W. Tufts	325.00
Tea Set, Child's, Roosters, Hens & Baby Chicks, 18 Piece	225.00

KAUFFMANN refers to porcelain wares decorated with scenes based on the works of Angelica Kauffmann (1741–1807), a Swiss–born painter who was a decorative artist for Adam Brothers, English furniture manufacturers, between 1766 and 1781. She designed small–scale pictorial subjects in the neoclassic manner and painted portraits as well as historical and classical pictures that were later reproduced on chinaware made across Europe. Most porcelains signed *Kauffmann* were made in the late 1800s. She did not do the artwork on the porcelain pieces signed with her name.

Candlestick, Classical Scene, Gold Design, Beehive, 5 1/2 In., Pair	550.00
Humidor, 2 Women, Cherub, Pewter Lid With Pipe, Green Base, Signed	285.00
Humidor, 2 Women, Hand Painted, Pewter Lid, Green, Signed	165.00
Plate, 4 Women & Baby, Signed	85.00

KAY FINCH Ceramics were made in Corona Del Mar, California, from 1935 to 1963. The hand–decorated pieces often depicted whimsical animals and people. Pastel colors were used.

Figurine, Angel	35.00
Figurine, Baby Elephant	49.50
Figurine, Elephant, 7 In.	145.00
Figurine, Elephant, Pink, 4 In.	30.00
Figurine, Monkey, Green Pants, Marked, 9 1/2 In. ....*Illus*	85.00
Figurine, Owl, Set of 3	145.00
Figurine, Pheasant, 17 In.	250.00
Figurine, Yorkshire Puppy	95.00

KAYSERZINN, see Pewter category

Kay Finch, Figurine, Monkey, Green Pants,

Marked, 9 1/2 In.

◆◆◆◆◆◆◆◆◆◆◆◆◆◆◆◆◆◆◆◆◆

Leave a small air space between the wall and the back
of a painting to allow air to
flow. "Bumpers" to put on the
back of pictures are available
at frame shops.

◆◆◆◆◆◆◆◆◆◆◆◆◆◆◆◆◆◆◆◆◆

KELVA glassware was made by the C. F. Monroe Company of Meriden, Connecticut, about 1904. It is a pale, pastel–painted glass decorated with flowers, designs, or scenes. Kelva resembles Nakara and Wave Crest, two other glasswares made by the same company.

KELVA

Box, Daisy Blossoms On Lid & Front, Fuchsia Ground, Signed, 8 In.	650.00
Box, Floral Design, c.1904, 3 3/4 In.	385.00
Box, Floral, Beaded, Green Hinge, 5 1/2 In.	675.00
Box, Hinged Cover, Hand Painted Orchids, Brass Banded, Signed, 5 In.	425.00
Box, Hinged Cover, Rose Hand Painted Orchids, Ornate Brass Band, Signed, 5 In.	425.00
Powder Box, Blown–Out Rose Blossoms, Peach, Yellow & White, C. F. Monroe	685.00
Powder Box, Marbelized, Rose Opaque, Off–White Lilies	520.00
Vase, Mottled Green, Pink, White Fancy Flowers, Signed, 14 In.	850.00
Vase, Pink & White Floral, Mottled Green, Handles, Signed, 14 1/2 In.	850.00

KEW BLAS is the name used by the Union Glass Company of Somerville, Massachusetts. The name refers to an iridescent golden glass made from the 1890s to 1924. The iridescent glass was reminiscent of the Tiffany glass of the period.

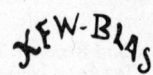

Vase, Cylinder Shape, Carved Bees, Scalloped Rim, Gold, 9 In.	715.00
Vase, Green & White Pulled Feather, 5 In.	660.00

KEWPIES, designed by Rose O'Neill, were first pictured in the *Ladies' Home Journal.* The figures, which are similar to pixies, were a success, and Kewpie dolls started appearing in 1911. Kewpie pictures and other items soon followed. Collectors search for all items that picture the little winged people.

Baby Set, Bisque, Ivory, Rose O'Neill, Box, Sticker, 4 In.	250.00
Book, Biography of A Boy, Rose O'Neill, Illustrated, 1910	45.00
Chocolate Mold, 4 Molds, 1900, 4 In.	265.00
Clock, Jasperware, Rose O'Neill, 6 x 5 1/2 In.	495.00
Cup & Saucer, Rudolstadt	225.00
Doll, Arms Move, Rose O'Neill, 4 1/4 In.	125.00
Doll, Bisque Head, Closed Watermelon Mouth, Rose O'Neill, 13 In.	4600.00
Doll, Bisque, Crepe Paper Clothes, Rose O'Neill, 4 In., Pair	220.00
Doll, Bisque, Movable Arms, Rose O'Neill, 7 In.	250.00
Doll, Bisque, Rose O'Neill, 5 In.	90.00
Doll, Boy & Girl, Original Clothing, Cameo, 1950s, 27 In., Pair	675.00
Doll, Celluloid, Occupied Japan, 7 In., Pair	35.00
Doll, Celluloid, Rose O'Neill, Sticker, 5 In.	90.00
Doll, Composition, Jointed, 12 In.	250.00
Doll, Composition, Original Clothes, Heart, 11 In.	195.00
Doll, Cuddle, Boy & Girl, 20 In., Pair	85.00
Doll, Doctor, 12 In.	22.00
Doll, Kottontail, Bunny Outfit, Standup Ears, 16 In.	35.00
Doll, Kottontail, Bunny Outfit, Standup Ears, 8 In.	15.00

Kewpie, Doll, Reclining, Doodledog On
Back, 1912, 3 In.

Kewpie, Doll, Sailor, Seated,
Bisque, 3 In.

Doll, Reclining, Doodledog On Back, 1912, 3 In. ....*Illus*	4300.00
Doll, Rose O'Neill, Label Front & Back, 4 1/2 In.	145.00
Doll, Sailor, Seated, Bisque, 3 In. ....*Illus*	2250.00
Doll, Sailor, Smock, Jointed Arms, Signed, 6 1/2 In.	750.00
Doll, Scootles, Composition, Original Suit, Rose O'Neill, 1925, 16 In.	360.00
Doll, Thinker, Cameo, Vinyl, Rose O'Neill, 4 In.	35.00
Doll, Traveler, Blue Wings, Umbrella & Suitcase, Signed Rose O'Neill, 3 1/2 In.	185.00
Hair Receiver, Jennie Mae, St. Louis, Bavarai	45.00
Light Bulb, Christmas, In Stocking	45.00
Ornament, Cake Top, Musical Base	350.00
Ornament, Wedding Cake, Musical Base, c.1930	275.00
Place Marker, Kewpie With Rose, Sitting	235.00
Plate, Christmas, 1973	15.00
Plate, Playing Leapfrog, Rose O'Neill, Rudolstadt	100.00
Plate, Rose O'Neill, Rudolstadt, 6 1/4 In.	100.00
Salt & Pepper, Huggers, 2 1/2 In.	195.00
Salt & Pepper, Sterling Silver	95.00
Salt Spoon, Sterling Silver	42.00
Soap, Figural	45.00
Talcum, Figurine, Rose O'Neill, Box	225.00
Tin, Candy, 2 Kewpies On Cover, Round	75.00
Toothpick, Borgfeldt	100.00

KIMBALL, see Cluthra category

KING'S ROSE, see Soft Paste category

KITCHEN utensils of all types, from eggbeaters to bowls, are collected
today. Handmade wooden and metal items, like ladles and apple peelers,
were made in the early nineteenth century. Mass–produced pieces, like iron
apple peelers and graniteware, were made in the nineteenth century. Other
kitchen wares are listed under manufacturers' names or under Advertising,
Iron, Tool, or Wooden.

Apple Corer, Hand Soldered	10.00
Apple Roaster, New England, 1850	625.00
Bacon Fryer, Removable Drip Pan, Fireplace	450.00
Basket, Potato Gathering, Heavy Wire	45.00
Basket, Wire, Bail Handle, 7 x 9 1/2 In.	25.00
Beater, Handi–Whip, Chicago Electric, Jadite Bottom	55.00
Bird Spit, Fireplace, Adjustable Iron, 18th Century, 33 In.	300.00
Bird Spit, Fireplace, Wrought Iron, American	523.00
Blender, Hamilton Beach, Soda Fountain	240.00
Blender, Pastry, Bakelite, Andock, 1929	12.50
Bottle, Sprinkler, Dutch Girl	65.00
Bowl, Burl Figure, Ash, Matching Lid, Scrubbed Finish, 5 3/4 In.	3520.00
Bowl, Butter, Wood, Carved Edge, 10 In.	95.00

Bowl, Chopping, Wood, Red Paint, Black Trim, Large 550.00
Bowl, Chopping, Wood, Yellow Paint, 19th Century, 19 In. 275.00
Bowl, Salad, Turned Wood, 25 1/2 In. 66.00
Bowl, Wood, Exterior Red Paint, 4 1/2 In. 137.00
Box, Recipe, Recipe Cards, 1906 .... 40.00
Bread Box, Art Deco, White Enameled 60.00
Bread Box, White Enamel, Blue Trim, Oval 85.00
Bread Box, White Enamel, Brass Hinges & Latch, Oblong 85.00
Broiler, Rotary, Scrolled Detail, Iron, 32 In. 154.00
Broiler, Whirling, Iron 412.00
Bucket, Egg, Wire Mesh 22.50
Butter Mold, look under Mold, Butter in the Kitchen category
Butter Paddle, Bird's Head Handle, Hook End, 10 In. 495.00
Butter Paddle, Burl, Color & Figure, 8 In. 220.00
Butter Paddle, Lollipop, Carved Star Flower, Gray Scrubbed Finish, 6 In. 302.00
Butter Paddle, Maple, Curl & Hook Handle, 11 In. 70.00
Butter Scoop, Wooden, Large Blade, Curved Handle, 11 1/2 In. 585.00
Butter Stamp, Cow, 1–Piece Turned Handle, 4 1/2 In. 330.00
Butter Stamp, Cow, Tree, Flower, 1–Piece Turned Handle, Scrubbed White, 5 In. ... 148.00
Butter Stamp, Eagle, Shield, 1–Piece Turned Handle, Dark Finish, 3 7/8 In. 137.00
Butter Stamp, Floral, Green Glass 125.00
Butter Stamp, Leaf Shaped, Long Handle, 4 1/4 In. 60.00
Butter Stamp, Lollipop 450.00
Butter Stamp, Lollipop, Heart & Leaf Design, 6 1/2 In. 165.00
Butter Stamp, Lollipop, Star Flower Design, Side Handle, 8 3/4 In. 550.00
Butter Stamp, Pine Tree, Stylized, Hand Carved, 3 1/2 In. 35.00
Butter Stamp, Sailboat, Wooden, Small 10.00
Butter Stamp, Sheaf of Wheat, Long Handle, 1 Piece 45.00
Butter Stamp, Sheaf, Rectangular, Chunky Hand Grip Back, 3 1/2 x 4 1/2 In. 99.00
Butter Stamp, Star Flower, Round, 4 5/8 In. 55.00
Butter Stamp, Star Flower, Round, Wooden, Inserted Turned Handle, 4 In. 121.00
Butter Stamp, Strawberry, Foliage, Flower, 1–Piece Whittled Handle, Round, 4 In. 165.00
Butter Stamp, Stylized Flower, Boat Shaped, 8 3/4 In. 159.00
Butter Stamp, Thistle, Round, Inserted Turned Handle, 4 7/8 In. 49.00
Butter Stamp, Tulip & Heart Design, Round, Walnut, Scrubbed Finish, 4 1/2 In. ... 115.00
Butter Stamp, Tulip, Sturdy Handle, Scrubbed Soft Finish, 4 1/2 In. 357.00
Butter Wheel, Handle, Acorn, Foliage, 5 1/2 In. 49.00
Cabinet, Cake & Bread, Home Comfort 75.00
Cake Decorations, Superman, Figure, Building, Marked, 6 Piece 2.25
Cake Griddle, Mrs. Sheffield's, Patent 1880 .... 125.00
Cake Maker, Universal, Crank, Pat. 1896 .... 50.00
Cake Pan, Angel Food, Star of David Shape, Tin 30.00
Cake Pan, Angel Food, Tin 8.75
Cake Pan, Danish, Griswold, Unusual Handle 150.00
Cake Pan, Tube, Swansdown 10.00
Can Opener, Pet Milk, Logo 12.50
Case, Knife, Wooden, Primitive, Handle 25.00
Cheese Press, Wooden, Cow Pattern 200.00
Cherry Pitter, Enterprise, Cast Iron, Hand Crank, Table Mount 20.00
Cherry Pitter, Goodell, Cast Iron 35.00
Cherry Pitter, New Standard 55.00
Cherry Pitter, New Standard No. 50, Iron 37.50
Cherry Pitter, New Standard, No. 50S 30.00
Cherry Pitter, Rollman 35.00
Chopper, Food, Curved Blade, Wooden Handle, Blade Marked S, 7 In. 25.00
Chopper, Food, Traveler, Ring Turned Wooden Handle, 7 In. 45.00
Chopper, Meat, Enterprise, No. 12 .... 45.00
Chopper, Meat, Wooden 725.00
Churn, Barrel Shaped, Metal Bands, Turned Lid, 26 In. 225.00
Churn, Crank Type, Iron Loop Handle 75.00
Churn, Dazey, 2 Qt. 75.00
Churn, Dazey, Blue, Square 175.00
Churn, Dazey, No. 10, Square, 1 Qt. 795.00

Churn, Drain Tap At Back, Shaped Paddles, Pierced, Wooden Body	315.00
Churn, Electric, Jim Dandy, Cow On Jar	45.00
Churn, Glass, Barrel Shape, Qt.	100.00
Churn, Lightning, 1 Qt.	345.00
Churn, Oak, Old Blue Paint, Industrial Type	165.00
Churn, Tin, Floral Decal, Wood Dasher, 19 In.	55.00
Churn, Wooden, Old Red Paint Traces, Tall	275.00
Clothes Grippers, Aunt Lucy's, Wooden, Box	22.50
Clothes Sprinkler, Cat, Marble Eyes	50.00
Clothes Sprinkler, Elephant, Ceramic, Gray, Pink	25.00 To 35.00
Clothespin Bag, Child's Dress	12.00
Coffee Grinders are listed in their own category	
Coffeepot, Coleman Lamp & Stove Co., Electric, 1950, 8 1/2 In. ....*Illus*	85.00
Coffeepot, Drip-O-Later, Shenango, Cream & Gray	55.00
Cooker, Conservo	20.00
Cookie Board, 14 Animals, 20 x 5 In.	355.00
Cookie Board, 2 Carved Designs, 3 1/2 x 11 3/4 In.	35.00
Cookie Board, Bunches of Grapes, 4, 19 1/4 x 3 1/2 In.	410.00
Cookie Board, Fish, Birds, 12 Hand Carved Blocks, 5 1/2 x 8 1/2 In.	150.00
Cookie Board, Laminated Pine, 16 1/4 x 32 In.	30.00
Cookie Board, Poplar, Round, Cut Out Handle, 19 x 23 In.	160.00
Cookie Board, Print, Springerle, 10 Carvings, Wooden, 3 1/4 x 4 1/2 In.	110.00
Cookie Board, Rectangular, 9 Carved Designs, 6 3/4 x 5 1/4 In.	245.00
Cookie Board, Round, Handle, Poplar, 25 1/2 In.	205.00
Cookie Board, Sea Horse, Wooden, 8 x 12 1/2 In.	45.00
Cookie Cutter, Bird, Long Neck, Tin, 5 In.	40.00
Cookie Cutter, Bird, Tin, 6 In.	70.00
Cookie Cutter, Candy Cane, Red Plastic	2.00
Cookie Cutter, Christmas Tree, Green Plastic, Outline	2.25
Cookie Cutter, Christmas, Aunt Chicks, McBees, Box, 4 Piece	25.00
Cookie Cutter, Complete Alphabet, Germany, Tin	325.00
Cookie Cutter, Holly Hobbie, 7 Piece	95.00
Cookie Cutter, Horse, Tin, 6 1/2 In.	170.00
Cookie Cutter, Horse, Tin, 7 3/4 In.	105.00
Cookie Cutter, Jack-O'-Lantern, Orange Plastic	5.00
Cookie Cutter, Lamb, Davis Baking Powder	12.00
Cookie Cutter, Pilgrim Boy, Orange Plastic	3.25
Cookie Cutter, Raggedy Ann & Andy, Red & Blue Plastic, Hallmark, Pair	24.00
Cookie Cutter, Rose, Plunger Type, Round Wooden	60.00
Cookie Cutter, Santa Claus, Full Figure, Green Plastic	4.00
Cookie Cutter, Santa's Head, Red Plastic, 1974	5.00
Cookie Cutter, Snoopy On Doghouse, Red Plastic, Hallmark, 8 In.	10.00
Cookie Cutter, Snowman, White Plastic, Outline	2.25
Cookie Cutter, Stag, Tin, 8 1/4 In.	340.00
Cookie Cutter, Tin, Circular, Multiple, 6 In.	94.00
Cup, Collapsible, Nickeled, Rayment, Leather Case	30.00

◆ ◆

An iron frying pan should be washed with steel wool and soap. Food will stick and the pan will rust if you use detergent, not soap.

◆ ◆

Kitchen, Coffeepot, Coleman

Lamp & Stove Co., Electric,

1950, 8 1/2 In.

Kitchen, Egg Separator, Sherman's White Rose Pastry Flour, 3 1/4 In.
Kitchen, Egg Separator, Edwards, Menado Coffee, Tin, 3 1/4 In.

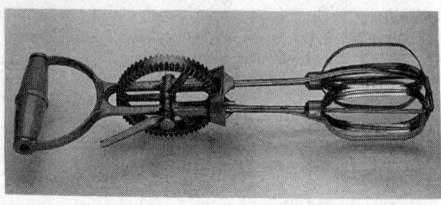

Kitchen, Eggbeater, Superwhirl, Green Wooden Handle, 11 1/2 In.

Cup, Measuring, Jadite	40.00
Cutter, Cabbage, With Box, 3 Ft.	45.00
Cutter, Doughnut, Tin	8.00
Cutter, Marmalade, Table Clamp	48.00
Dipper, Cast Aluminum, Wagner, 12 1/2 In.	18.00
Dipper, Maple, Curled Handle, 9 1/4 In.	104.00
Dough Box, Painted Grain Design, 9 1/2 x 29 x 15 In.	275.00
Dough Box, Scalloped Hinged Top, Walnut, France, 38 x 57 In.	1980.00
Dough Scraper, Cast Iron	50.00
Drinkmaster, Hamilton Beach, Black Porcelain	95.00
Dutch Oven, Griswold, No. 12	125.00
Dutch Oven, Griswold, No. 8, Tite Top	45.00
Dutch Oven, Wagnerware, No. 9	40.00 To 45.00
Dutch Oven, With Trivet, Griswold No. 7	135.00
Egg Case, Farmer's, Folding, Slats	14.00
Egg Lifter, Wire, 1 Piece	13.75
Egg Separator, Clambroth	55.00
Egg Separator, Edwards, Menado Coffee, Tin, 3 1/4 In. *Illus*	3.00
Egg Separator, Sherman's White Rose Pastry Flour, 3 1/4 In. *Illus*	3.00
Egg Timer, Black Chef	110.00
Eggbeater, Cast Iron, Bulb Wood Handle, Black, A & J	4.25
Eggbeater, Child's, Betty Taplin, Glass Bottom	85.00
Eggbeater, Coiled Wire Knob	18.50
Eggbeater, Cyclone	125.00
Eggbeater, Electric, Motor Top, Green	45.00
Eggbeater, Holt, Dated	35.00
Eggbeater, Ladd Royalties, Ball Bearings	23.00
Eggbeater, Red Wooden Handle, 1930s	6.00
Eggbeater, Superwhirl, Green Wooden Handle, 11 1/2 In. *Illus*	28.00
Eggbeater, Swirl Chrome Handle, Push Propelled	16.00
Eggbeater, Taplin, Angled Handle, Iron	45.00
Eggbeater, Taplin, Brass, 15 In.	35.00
Eggcup, Deep Olive Glass, Egg–Shaped Cover, New England, 1850	1420.00
Eyelet Press, Challenge, Cast Iron, Wood Block Mounted, 1907	55.00
Flue Cover, Angelus, 8 1/2 In.	35.00
Flue Cover, Cows, Dairy Maid	8.00
Fork, Heart Design, Iron	412.00
Fork, Shaped Handle, Iron, 7 1/4 In.	302.00
Fork, Toasting, Iron, 1830	145.00
Fryer, Deep Fat, Fryrite	12.00

Kitchen, Hanger, Pants, Grim's Presgard,
Wooden, Green, 1903, 6 3/4 In.

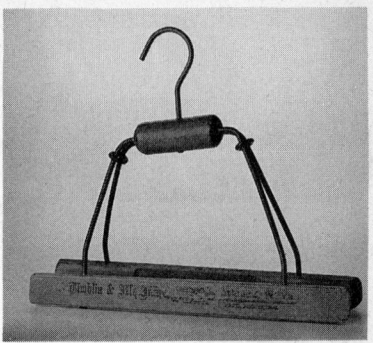

Kitchen, Hanger, Pants, Timblin &
McIntire Men's, Wooden, 8 In.

Funnel, Aluminum, Sinclair, Large	35.00
Grater, Carrot, Colors Butter, Box	210.00
Grater, Cheese, Climax, Clamp, Wooden Insert	48.00
Grater, Climax, Cast Iron, Tin, Large	35.00
Grater, Mouli, Hand Held, Crank, Wooden Handle	28.00
Grater, Nutmeg, Flip Top	10.00
Grater, Nutmeg, Iron, Tin, Germany	18.00
Grater, Nutmeg, Mouli	7.00
Grater, Nutmeg, Tin, Wooden	32.00
Grater, Punched Tin, Pine Back, Cutout Handle, 13 1/2 In.	140.00
Grater, Revolving, Flora Duplex, Ornate Gilt, Hand Painted	25.00
Griddle, Erie, With Bail, Round, Griswold No. 14	60.00 To 125.00
Griddle, Ribbed Handle, Heart, Iron, 10 1/2 In.	93.00
Grinder, Food, Crank Operated, England	17.50
Grinder, Food, Hand Crank, Wood Handle, Foley	2.45
Grinder, Food, Keen Kutter No. 122, Commercial, Large	95.00
Grinder, Food, Keen Kutter, No. 11, 4 Blades	15.00
Grinder, Food, Larkin, 4 Blades	25.00
Grinder, Meat, Griswold, 3 Blades	54.00
Grinder, Meat, Merwin, 1902	15.00
Grinder, Poppy Seed	55.00
Grinder, Sausage, Tin & Copper	25.00
Hanger, Pants, Grim's Presgard, Wooden, Green, 1903, 6 3/4 In. ....*Illus*	14.00
Hanger, Pants, Timblin & McIntire Men's, Wooden, 8 In. ....*Illus*	18.00
Holder, Baking Soda, Frosty The Snowman, HK, 1960s, Box	15.00
Holder, Paper, Double, Keen Kutter	150.00
Ice Cream Freezer, White Mountain, Salesman Sample	375.00
Ice Crusher, Daisy, Rocket Shape	25.00
Ice Pick, Pevely Dairy, Metal	12.00
Ice Pick, Piggly Wiggly, Metal	15.00
Icebox, 2 Doors, Premier, Oak	425.00
Icebox, 4 Doors, Original Brass Hardware, Oak	800.00
Icebox, Oak, 1920	400.00
Icebox, Paneled Doors, Brass Hardware, 46 x 34 In.	300.00
Icebox, White Mountain, Oak, Carved	700.00
Iron, American Beauty, Red Handle	26.00
Iron, Charcoal, Controlling Vents At Rear, Curved Chimney	75.00
Iron, Curling, On, Marcel	6.00
Iron, Curling, Torrid, Red, Box	8.00
Iron, Edison, 3 Settings, 15 Lb.	60.00

Kitchen, Jar Opener, Edlund Co.,
Inc., Chrome, Plastic

Kitchen, Mayonnaise Maker, Silver
Mfg., Glass, Tin, 10 1/2 In.

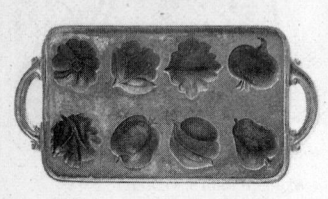

Kitchen, Pan, Muffin, Fruits &
Vegetables, Iron, 13 X 8 In.

Kitchen, Spoon Set, Measuring, Multicolor Plastic, Federsal Housewares, 4
Sizes

Iron, Enterprise, Detachable Handle	22.00
Iron, Flat, Star, Cast Iron, 1911	50.00
Iron, Gad–A–Bout, Travel, KM, Art Deco Bakelite Handle	14.00
Iron, Gas, Blue Enameled	40.00
Iron, Gas, Montgomery Ward, 1936	35.00
Iron, General Electric, Box Marked Demonstrator, Not For Sale, c.1940	35.00
Iron, General Electric, Dial The Fabric, Box	15.00
Iron, General Electric, World Wide, Electric	15.00
Iron, Goffering, Iron, Brass, 12 3/4 In.	110.00
Iron, Turned Wooden Handle, Engraved Designs, 5 3/4 In.	170.00
Ironing Board, Sleeve Size, Portable	17.00
Jar Opener, Edlund Co., Inc., Chrome, Plastic ....*Illus*	8.00
Jar Opener, Speedo, Mechanical	15.00
Juicer, Arcade, Spout, Cast Iron	38.00
Juicer, Enterprise No. 21, Cast Iron, Hand Crank, Table Mount	27.50
Kettle Tilter, Curved Handle, Hook Holds Kettle, Iron, Copper, 23 In.	225.00
Kettle, Apple Butter, Brass, Rat's Tail Bail, c.1840, 16 1/4 In.	190.00
Kettle, Gypsy, Wire Bail Handle, 9 In.	33.00
Kettle, Jelly, Copper, Amish, Fits Under Cap of Wood Stove, 5 1/2 x 11 In.	85.00
Kettle, Rounded Bottom, Enameled Inside & Out, Bail Handle, 3 Legs	40.00
Kettle, Stand, Steel, Circular, Scrolled Legs, Pad Feet, Stamped	260.00
Ladle, Glass Cup, Wood Turned Handle, Marbury Pat. 4/21/96, 9 In.	90.00
Ladle, Iron, Large	160.00
Lazy Susan, Marble, Silver Base & Top Handle	135.00
Lemon Squeezer, Cast Iron, 4 Part, 1800s, 9 In.	55.00
Lemon Squeezer, Iron, Glass Insert, Williams	45.00
Lemon Squeezer, Tinned Iron, Grip Style	12.50
Malt Mixer, Horlich	60.00
Match Safes can be found in their own category	
Mayonnaise Maker, Silver Mfg., Glass, Tin, 10 1/2 In. ....*Illus*	30.00
Meat Tenderizer, Wooden	2.00
Milk Shake Machine, Arnold	50.00
Milk Shake Machine, Hamilton Beach, Stainless Mixing Cup, 1950s	150.00
Mixer, Ice Cream, 3 Sections, Hamilton Beach, Large	275.00
Molds may also be found in the Pewter and Tinware categories	
Mold, Butter, Acorn, 3 1/2 In.	125.00
Mold, Butter, Cow, Clear Glass, 1 Lb.	35.00
Mold, Butter, Cow, Round, With Pointed Legs, 2 Piece	125.00
Mold, Butter, Cow, Round, Wooden	40.00
Mold, Butter, Oak Leaf, Acorn, Wooden, 1 Lb.	325.00

Mold, Butter, Pineapple, 1866, 3 In. 90.00
Mold, Butter, Rose Design, 5 x 8 In. 71.00
Mold, Butter, Sheaf of Wheat, 2 3/4 In. 95.00
Mold, Butter, Strawberry, Square, 3 In. 35.00
Mold, Butter, Swan, Driftwood & Cork Penguin, Wooden, 8 In. 50.00
Mold, Butter, Swan, Round, 5 In. 104.00
Mold, Butter, Swan, Wooden, 2 Piece 125.00
Mold, Butter, Swan, Wooden, 4 1/8 In. 350.00
Mold, Butter, Tulip Stylized, Rectangular, 5 1/2 x 3 1/2 In. 105.00
Mold, Cake, Lamb, Griswold .... 100.00 To 130.00
Mold, Cake, Lamb, Griswold No. 866, Box, Recipe Book, Cast Iron, 7 1/2 In. 165.00
Mold, Cake, Rabbit, Griswold .... 250.00 To 275.00
Mold, Cake, Rudolph Red Nose Reindeer, Box, 1939 .... 65.00
Mold, Cake, Santa Claus, Griswold, Cast Iron .... 385.00 To 550.00
Mold, Candle, see Tinware category
Mold, Candy, Maple Sugar, Wooden 35.00
Mold, Chocolate, 28 Design Candies, Cast Steel, 6 x 12 In. 50.00
Mold, Chocolate, 4 Roosters In A Row 75.00
Mold, Chocolate, 5 Eggs, Hinged 55.00
Mold, Chocolate, Chick, Hatching 80.00
Mold, Chocolate, Dog, Begging 80.00
Mold, Chocolate, Easter Egg, Tin, 6 1/2 In. 70.00
Mold, Chocolate, Hen, On Nest, Tin, 6 In. 75.00
Mold, Chocolate, Hen, Sitting On Basket of Eggs 75.00
Mold, Chocolate, Little Chick, With Top Hat, Tin, 1960s 55.00
Mold, Chocolate, Rabbit, Driving Car 100.00
Mold, Chocolate, Rabbit, Sitting On Stool, Playing Saxophone 100.00
Mold, Chocolate, Rabbit, Sitting, 8 1/2 In. 35.00
Mold, Chocolate, Rabbit, Standing, Basket On Back, 16 In. 110.00
Mold, Chocolate, Rabbit, Tin, 1960s 195.00
Mold, Chocolate, Rabbit, With Egg 55.00
Mold, Chocolate, Rooster, Free Standing, 2 Piece, c.1880 .... 60.00
Mold, Chocolate, Squirrel, Tin, Large 25.00
Mold, Chocolate, Swan, Tin, 2 Piece 30.00
Mold, Chocolate, Turkey, Tin, 9 In. 185.00
Mold, Chocolate, Zeppelin 110.00
Mold, Food, Ear of Corn, Tin, Copper, 4 x 6 In. 105.00
Mold, Food, Flutes & Fruit Design, Pewter, Cylindrical, 6 In. 71.00
Mold, Food, Pear, Tin, 3 1/2 x 5 1/4 In. 70.00
Mold, Food, Sheaf, Tin & Copper, 4 1/2 x 6 In. 95.00
Mold, Food, Swirl, Copper, 6 5/8 In. 80.00
Mold, Ice Cream, see Pewter category
Mold, Jell-O, Beige & Green Graniteware, Cream City 45.00
Mold, Jell-O, Tufglas, Green 35.00
Mold, Patty, Griswold 22.50
Mold, Santa Claus, Griswold, Recipe Book 375.00
Mold, Tulip, Wooden, Pennsylvania, A On Handle 250.00
Noodle Maker, Cast Iron, 3 Different Cutting Rollers, Hand Crank 100.00
Paddle, Curly Maple, 8 3/4 In. 25.00
Pail, Copper Riveted, Iron Hoop Handle, England, 19th Century 55.00
Pan, Corn Bread, Griswold .... 12.50 To 20.00
Pan, Corn Stick, Griswold, No. 273 .... 35.00 To 75.00
Pan, Corn Stick, Griswold, No. 79, 7 Molds 35.00
Pan, Frying, Griswold, No. 8 .... 22.50
Pan, Golf Ball, Wagner, No. 1328, 12 Holes 65.00
Pan, Krusty Korn Kobs, Iron, Wagner Ware, Pat. July 6, 1920, Tea Size 65.00
Pan, Little Slam, Bridge, Hearts, Diamonds, Clubs, Spades, Wagner 155.00
Pan, Muffin, Cast Iron, 8 Bears In 4 Different Poses 65.00
Pan, Muffin, Fruits & Vegetables, Iron, 13 x 8 In. ....*Illus* 175.00
Pan, Muffin, Griswold 45.00
Pan, Popover, Griswold, No. 10, Cast Iron 30.00
Pan, Roasting, Cover, Wagner Ware Magnalite 30.00
Pan, Roll, Waterman, Iron, Pat. Apr. 5, 1859 .... 36.00

Peeler, Apple, 1877 .... 50.00
Peeler, Apple, Bonanza 110.00
Peeler, Apple, Double Swan, Wooden, 11 x 25 In. 1200.00
Peeler, Apple, Goodell Co., 1898 .... 80.00
Peeler, Apple, Hudson .... 55.00 To 95.00
Peeler, Apple, Keen Kutter, Iron 95.00
Peeler, Apple, Little Star, Cast Iron 40.00
Peeler, Apple, Lockey & Hawland, Mechanical, Clamp–On, Cast Iron 85.00
Peeler, Apple, Sinclair Scott, Cast Iron 65.00
Peeler, Apple, Turntable, Goodell, 1898 .... 75.00
Peeler, Apple, Wooden, Geared Wheel, 15 1/4 x 6 3/8 In. 375.00
Peeler, Ram's Horn Handle, 53 In. 220.00
Pepper Mill & Salt, Ball Shape, Winchester 125.00
Percolator, Gold Deer, Electric 65.00
Percolator, Manning–Bowman, No. 391 .... 45.00
Pie Bird, Benny The Baker, Pottery 45.00
Pie Bird, Black Bird 32.00
Pie Bird, Black Chef, Blue Clothing 120.00
Pie Bird, Black Chef, Yellow Clothing 95.00
Pie Bird, Black Crow 20.00
Pie Bird, Green Dragon, 4 1/2 In. 50.00
Pie Bird, Humpty–Dumpty, Yellow Egg On Green Base 50.00
Pie Bird, Mother Cat, Wearing Apron, 4 1/4 In. 52.00
Pie Bird, Pelican On Stump 47.00
Pie Bird, Rooster, Cleminson 28.00
Pie Crimper, Brass 38.00
Pie Crimper, Whalebone & Ebony, Bird Form, 5 1/4 In. 93.00
Pie Lifter, Cast Iron & Wire, 1900s 30.00
Plunger, Wash Day, Patterned Tin, 1890s 15.00
Popcorn Popper, Electric, Chrome, Wood Handles 25.00
Popcorn Popper, Mazola, Karo 30.00
Pot Holder, Reddy Kilowatt .... 5.00 To 12.00
Pot Scraper, King Midas Flour, Picture of Little Girl, Tin 225.00
Pot Scraper, Sharples 155.00
Rack, Drying, 2 Part, Folding, Walnut, Mortised & Pinned Construction, 61 In. 11.00
Rack, Herb, 4 Racks Extend From Center, 4 Ft. 185.00
Rack, Spoon, Pine, Original Rose Malled Design, 15 1/4 In. 110.00
Raisin Seeder, Hand Crank, Enterprise, No. 36, 1860s 47.50
Reamers are listed in their own category
Refrigerator Set, Red Lids, Kitchen Kraft 150.00
Refrigerator, General Electric, Top Motor, 1930s, 64 In. 400.00
Ricer, Metal Cone, Stand, Wood Tamper 15.00
Roaster, 8 Hooks, Tin, 11 3/4 x 9 1/2 In. 185.00
Roaster, Chestnut, W. C. Googins, No. 3, March 14, 1863, 11 x 10 1/2 x 8 In. 215.00
Roaster, Coffee Or Chestnut, Wilcox & Co., Berlin, Conn. Pat. Apr. 17, 1849 .... 450.00
Rolling Pin, Amy, Harker 95.00
Rolling Pin, Bird's–Eye Maple 350.00
Rolling Pin, Blue Glass, Gem, Wooden Handle, Early 1900s 375.00
Rolling Pin, Columbus Flour, Milk Glass, Wooden Handles 80.00
Rolling Pin, Crystal Glass, Cobalt Blue Handles 165.00
Rolling Pin, Curly Maple, 15 1/4 In. 50.00
Rolling Pin, Curly Maple, 21 In. 150.00
Rolling Pin, Glass, Cobalt Blue 12.50
Rolling Pin, Glass, Green, Gilded Tulips, Marked I Wish You Well 90.00
Rolling Pin, Glass, Red & White Looped, 17 In. 495.00
Rolling Pin, Golden Grain Bread, Stoneware 85.00
Rolling Pin, Maple, 17 In. 28.00
Rolling Pin, Mariane Design, Blue Glass 175.00
Rolling Pin, San Antonio, Texas, Stoneware 350.00
Rolling Pin, Springerle, 20 Hand Carved Blocks, Primitive 150.00
Rolling Pin, Wooden, 11–In. Circumference, 27 In. 24.00
Rug Beater, Bentwood, Label, 43 In. 60.00
Rug Beater, Braided Wire Loop 20.00

Rug Beater, Wicker	20.00
Rug Beater, Wicker, Victorian	48.00
Sadiron, Asbestos, Removable Handle, Marked Pat'd. 1900, 6 In.	55.00
Sadiron, Child's, Swan Shape, Yellow Paint, 2 1/2 In.	77.00
Sadiron, Wagner, Square, 11 1/4 In.	150.00
Sadiron, Wapak	15.00
Salt & Pepper Shakers are listed in their own category	
Salt Box, Wall, Wooden, Shaped, Country	110.00
Scoop, Burl, 36 In.	1760.00
Scoop, Butter, Curly Maple, Horsehead Handle, 10 1/4 In.	390.00
Scoop, Cranberry, Cape Cod, Late 19th Century, 20 x 20 In.	248.00
Scoop, Cranberry, Pine, Marked L. H., 8 x 14 In.	303.00
Scoop, Cranberry, Wooden	75.00
Scoop, Flour, Airy Fairy Cake Flour	20.00
Scoop, Ice Cream Sandwich, Wooden Handle, Nickel Plated, 12 In.	55.00
Scoop, Ice Cream, Arnold, No. 50	25.00
Scoop, Ice Cream, Banana Split	700.00
Scoop, Ice Cream, Banana Split, United Products	385.00
Scoop, Ice Cream, Bohlig, 1908	1950.00
Scoop, Ice Cream, Brass, 1920s	22.50
Scoop, Ice Cream, Cone Type, Progressus	20.00
Scoop, Ice Cream, Cone Type, Turn Small Key At End	24.00
Scoop, Ice Cream, Erie Specialty Co.	350.00
Scoop, Ice Cream, Geer	200.00
Scoop, Ice Cream, Gilchrist, No. 31	30.00 To 63.00
Scoop, Ice Cream, Gilchrist, No. 8	85.00
Scoop, Ice Cream, Glad's Disher	35.00
Scoop, Ice Cream, Hamilton Beach, Model 60, Wooden Handle, Thumb Press	25.00
Scoop, Ice Cream, Indestructo, No. 4	27.00 To 45.00
Scoop, Ice Cream, Jiffy, Patent Feb. 25, Curved Bar	225.00
Scoop, Ice Cream, New Gem	100.00
Scoop, Ice Cream, Wooden Handle	23.00
Scoop, Maple Syrup, Carved Wood, 18 1/2 In.	95.00
Scoop, Maple, Hooked Handle, Dustpan Size	235.00
Scoop, Melon Ball, Tin, Wooden Handle, Green	3.00
Scoop, Potato, Heavy Wire, Country Store	30.00
Shelf, Woman's Friend, Iron, Fits Around Stove Pipe, Warms Pots, Pat., 1870	195.00
Sieve, Bentwood, Galvanized Hardware, Cloth, 16 In.	25.00
Sifter, Flour, Androck	12.50
Sifter, Flour, Bromwells, Hand Crank, Tin, 5 Cup	2.25
Sifter, Flour, Magic, Instructions	25.00
Sifter, Flour, Yellow, With Daisies, Androck	15.00
Skillet, Cornbread, Divided Wedges, Cast Iron	11.50
Skillet, Favorite, No. 1	90.00
Skillet, Favorite, No. 12	65.00
Skillet, Griswold, Erie No. 12	35.00
Skillet, Griswold, No. 0	75.00
Skillet, Griswold, No. 6	15.00
Skillet, Griswold, No. 8	19.00
Skillet, Griswold, No. 11	6.00
Skillet, Griswold, No. 12	89.00
Skillet, Griswold, No. 768, Square	45.00
Skillet, Hardware Hank, Cast Iron, Pour Spouts, 3 In.	55.00
Skillet, Indian Head Logo, Cast Iron	100.00 To 125.00
Skillet, Wrought Iron, Footed, 19th Century	60.00
Skimmer, Lard, Iron, Long Handle	3.50
Skimmer, Wrought Iron, Brass, Tooled Handle, 17 In.	236.00
Slicer, Green Bean, Iron	42.00
Slicer, Vegetable, Wooden, Pat. 1898	55.00
Spatula, Christy Knife Co., 1910	1.50
Spice Box, Forget–Me–Nots On Lid, Japanned, 6 Interior Canisters	35.00
Spice Rack, Carved Top, Porcelain Pulls, Walnut	560.00
Spoon Set, Measuring, Multicolor Plastic, Federsal Housewares, 4 Sizes ......*Illus*	2.00

Spoon, Cast Aluminum, Wagner, 10 1/2 In. 15.00
Spoon, Cream Top 7.00
Stocking Stretcher, Wooden 24.00
Strainer, Milk, Tin, Brass Strainer, 8 1/2 In. 8.00
String Holder, Dutch Girl, Chalkware 25.00
String Holder, Frederickburg Porter 275.00
String Holder, Mammy, Green & Brown Dress 115.00
String Holder, Mammy, National Silver Co. .... 135.00 To 160.00
String Holder, Mammy, Orange Bandanna, Teeth, Plaster 270.00
String Holder, O. I. O. Soap, Tin, Hanging 325.00
String Holder, Spanish Man's Head, Plaster 60.00
String Holder, Suchafine Biscuit, Triangle 2100.00
String Holder, Woman's Head, Ceramic 60.00
Swizzle Stick, Bottoms Up, Box, 6 Piece 20.00
Swizzle Stick, Caribe, Cuba, Glass, 5 Piece 30.00
Swizzle Stick, Frosted Shell Top, 6 Piece 20.00
Tea Cozy, Rag Doll 50.00
Tea Safe, Creamer, Art Deco, Tin 15.00
Teakettle, 9 1/2 In. 75.00
Teakettle, Iron, Wrought Iron Bail Handle, 8 In. 115.00
Teapot, Gooseneck, Violets, Pewter Trim 295.00
Teapot, Iron, No. 7 Top 23.00
Teapot, Twist Handle, Aluminum Whistler Spout, Glassbake 40.00
Thermometer, Maple Sugar, Buro's, Copper, Cardboard Cylinder 55.00
Timer, Tillie The Timer, Cast Iron, Pilgrim, Box 20.00
Toaster, 4 Sides, Tin 18.00
Toaster, General Mills, Bakelite Base 25.00
Toaster, Iron, 12 In. 192.00
Toaster, Iron, Twisted Iron & Wood Handle, 14 In. 60.00
Toaster, Kenmore, Chrome, Bakelite Handle 35.00
Toaster, Porcelain Base, Patent 1909 .... 295.00
Toaster, Rotary, Wrought Iron, Twisted & Scroll Design, 26 In. 352.00
Toaster, Sun Chief, Box 45.00
Toaster, Sunbeam, 1920s 40.00
Toaster, Sunbeam, Etched, Pat. 1923 .... 25.00
Toaster, Sunbeam, Model T-9 .... 50.00 To 95.00
Toaster, Toastolater, Bread Moves On Conveyor Belt 150.00
Toaster, Westinghouse, Art Deco Style 24.00
Toaster, Wrought Iron, Twisted & Scroll Design, 12 x 22 In. 192.00
Toasting Rack, Heart, Pierced Wrought Iron, 17 In., Pair 2090.00
Utensil Rack, Tooled Bar & Finials, Wrought Iron, Marked, 12 1/2 In. ... 385.00
Wafer Iron, Cast Iron, Floral Design, Pat. June 28, 1880, 5 1/2 In. 70.00
Wafer Iron, Wooden Handle, America, 27 In. 165.00
Waffle Iron, 5 Hearts, Alfred & Resen Co. 90.00
Waffle Iron, 5 Hearts, Pre-1850, Large 100.00
Waffle Iron, Art Deco, Chrome Top, Flowered Enamel Base 40.00
Waffle Iron, Cast Iron, Wagner, Stand, 1910, Miniature 28.00
Waffle Iron, Child's, Arcade, Rectangular 100.00
Waffle Iron, Double Handles, Iron, 22 In. 38.00
Waffle Iron, Double, Manning Bowman, Electric, Chrome 50.00
Waffle Iron, E. C. Simmons, Keen Kutter Logo 100.00
Waffle Iron, Griswold, No. 8 .... 95.00
Waffle Iron, Heart Shape, Western Importing Co. 175.00
Waffle Iron, Heart Star, Griswold, No. 18 .... 150.00
Waffle Iron, Heart, Griswold, No. 3 .... 50.00
Waffle Iron, Keen Kutter Logo 125.00
Waffle Iron, Landers, Frary & Clark 38.00
Waffle Iron, Long Iron Handles, 30 In. 60.00
Waffle Iron, Pedestal, Ceramic Cover, Tulips 60.00
Waffle Iron, Round, Dominion 10.00
Waffle Iron, Spider Web Design, Griswold, No. 8 .... 900.00
Waffle Iron, Stover, Cast Iron 25.00
Waffle Iron, Universal, Pedestal 25.00

Waffle Iron, Wagner, Dated 1925 .... 45.00
Waffle Iron, Wrought Iron Handles, Lyre Design, 26 In. 77.00
Wash Stick, 2–Prong, Eagle & Flag 1 Side, 3–Masted Schooner Other 137.50
Washboard, Blue Enameled, Griswold 62.00
Washboard, Columbus Washboard Co., Yellow Stoneware, Cobalt Blue Glaze 750.00
Washboard, Cradle Shape, Hand–Hewed, Bleached White, 25 x 11 In. 175.00
Washboard, Enamel King, Dark Blue Graniteware 45.00
Washboard, Glass Scrubber, Cupels Co. 22.00
Washboard, Maid–Rite, Brass 18.00
Washboard, Mother Hubbard 145.00
Washboard, National, Tin, Blue Enamel, Dovetailed Top 75.00
Washboard, Scrubbed Patina, 7 1/4 x 26 1/2 In. 110.00
Washboard, Tin, 10 In. 20.00
Washboard, Top Knotch The Glass King 35.00
Washboard, Wooden, 26 1/2 x 7 1/4 In. 110.00
Washboard, Zing King, Lingerie 16.00
Washing Machine, Wringer, Busy Betty, Green Glass Tub, Hoge Mfg. Co. 430.00
Whisk, Metal, 30 Soldered Wires 15.00
Wringer, Primitive, Rollers & Cogs, Mounted On Pine Board, Dated 1873 .... 90.00

KNIFE collectors usually specialize in a single type. In the 1960s, the
United States government passed a law that required knife manufacturers
to mark their knives with the country of origin. This seemed to encourage
the collectors, and knife collecting became an interest of a large group of
people. All types of knives are collected, from top quality twentieth–
century examples to old bone– or pearl–handled knives in excellent
condition.

Belknap, Anniversary, 3 Blades, Canoe Shape, Oak Box 75.00
Belt, Iron D–Guard, Wooden Grip, Civil War, Confederate 330.00
Bolo, Filipino, 1890 .... 45.00
Boot, Woman's, Victorian ....75.00 To 100.00
Bouka, 1 Piece Ebony Grip, Swedan, 4 3/4 In. 90.00
Bowie, Alfred Field & Co., Bone Haft, Brass Guard, 6 In. 180.00
Bowie, California, Westenholm & Son, Horn Grip, Engraved Hunting Scene 605.00
Bowie, Embossed Leather Hilt, Civil War, 6 1/8 In. 240.00
Bowie, Hand Forged Iron Blade, Wooden Handle, Leather Sheath 1210.00
Bowie, Iron Cap, Carved Rosewood Haft, Double Edge, CSA Stamp, 10 In. 280.00
Bowie, Spanish Colonial, 2 Piece Guard, c.1800, 9 In. 185.00
Bowie, Stag Handle, Utica Razor & Utlery Co., 1920s 62.50
Buck, Folding Hunter, Model 110, Leather Carrying Case 15.00
Buffalo Skinner, Stag Handle, Marbles 225.00
Buffalo, Case XX, 1970 .... 125.00
Case XX, Interchangeable Hatchet 325.00
Ceremonial, Burmese, Iron, Tiger Handle 1500.00
Chamfer, Cooper 45.00
Cheese, Pearl Handle, Sterling Silver 16.00
Commando, British, Stamped NATO & 1976, Sheath & Guard, Sheffield 42.00
Dagger Shape, Pearl–Like Handle, Sheath, 4 In. 12.00
Dagger, Nubian, Ivory & Horn Segments, Ebony Grip, 6 1/2 In. 85.00
Draw, Keen Kutter, 8 In. 35.00
Draw, Pexto, Folding Handles, 8 In. 15.00
Electrician's, Crescent Wrench In The End 35.00
Fish, Marble 175.00
Fruit Set, Brass, 1900s, Austria 50.00
Fruit, Officer's, Cutlery Form, Silver Scale Grips, Folding, 3 1/2 In. 60.00
Fruit, Sterling Silver, R. Blackinton 80.00
Gaucho, Encircling Snake Belt Hook, 19th Century, 7 1/2 In. 210.00
Hamm's, Signature On Reverse, 3 Blades, Leather Case 60.00
Hay, Farmer's, Iron 6.85
Hunting, Kabar–Union, Leather Sheath, 1940 .... 100.00
Hunting, Remington, No. 1306 ....95.00 To 125.00
Jack, Robeson, 2 Blades, Brass Lined, Stag Handle 65.00
Jack, Solingen, 2 Blades 35.00

Jack, Sunshine Biscuits, 2 Blades, Brass Line, Imperial, Providence, R.I., 3 1/4 In.	35.00
Lady's Leg Shape, Sterling Silver	45.00
Oaxaca, Sword Size	77.00
Orange, Pistol Handle, Sheffield, Sterling Silver, 1938	45.00
Pearlized Handles, Steamship Europa	50.00
Pen, 2 Blades, Tortoise Grips, Victorian, Folding, 3 In.	30.00
Pen, Mother–of–Pearl Grip, Victorian, Folding, 2 In.	40.00
Pocket, 14K Yellow Gold, Stainless Steel	77.00
Pocket, 2 Blades, Bier Soil Service, Hannibal, Mo.	3.45
Pocket, Anheuser–Busch Brewing Assn., Leather Case	340.00
Pocket, B. S.A., Remington, Official, Papers, Box	45.00
Pocket, Enameled Silver, Egypt	95.00
Pocket, Jeffrey's Beer, Bottle Opener End	42.00
Pocket, Kahar	35.00
Pocket, Keen Kutte,	18.00
Pocket, Marilyn Monroe	15.00
Pocket, Marilyn Monroe, Nude Pose, 1950s	3.00
Pocket, Mother–of–Pearl, Cattaraugus	40.00
Pocket, Old Crow	18.00
Pocket, Star Brand Shoes	40.00
Pocket, Torrey	35.00
Pocket, Winchester Store	85.00
Race, Folding Leg, John Smith	143.00
Race, John Smith, 18th Century, Large	225.00
Race, T. Symond, Dated 1771	375.00
Race, W. Symond, Papier–Mache Case, Spare Blades	350.00
Remington, Dupont, RH–4	65.00
Sailor's, Scabbard, Finland, 11 In.	130.00
Sailor's, Silver & Leather Haft, Sheath, Janefel, Finland, 1800s, 7 1/ 2 In.	110.00
Skinning, Case XX, Sheath	32.00
Skinning, Green River Type, I. Wilson Sheer Steel, Wooden Grip, 6 1/2 In. Blade	40.00
Spear, Tapered Leather Haft, Leather Wrist Strap, 1920s	55.00
Spear, Thrusting, Aullu, Rattan Wrap, c.1870, 56 In.	95.00
Steak, Butterscotch Handle, 4 Piece	17.00
Stiletto, Triangular Blade, Brass Cross Guard, Horn Grip, c.1850, 5 1/2 In.	140.00
Switchblade, Double–Sided Button, Shapleigh Hardware	150.00
Tobacco	18.00
Trench, Scabbard, Austria	70.00
With Bottle Opener, Signal Oil	25.00

KNOWLES, TAYLOR & KNOWLES items may be found in the KTK and
Lotus Ware categories.

KOCH is the name signed on the front of a series of plates decorated with
fruits, vegetables, animals, or birds. The dishes date from the 1910 to 1930
period and were probably decorated in Germany.

KOCH

Bowl, Apples, Pears, 8 In.	144.00
Mug, Grapes	45.00
Plate, Grapes, Purple, Green Leaves, 10 In.	50.00

KOREAN WARE, see Sumida

KOSTA, the oldest Swedish glass factory, was founded in 1742. During the
1920s through the 1950s, many pieces of original design were made at the
factory. The firm is still working.

KOSTA

Bowl, Cased Green Over Clear, Fish Design, Frosted Ground, 5 x 6 In.	1450.00
Paperweight, Owl	125.00
Paperweight, Seaweed	120.00
Perfume Bottle, Apple, Crystal, 2 In.	50.00
Vase, Butterfly, Green To Clear, 2 1/2 In.	77.00
Vase, Cased Emerald Green, Trapped Bubble Paperweight Bottom, Signed, 8 In.	350.00
Vase, Clear, Signed Lindstrom, 6 In.	135.00
Vase, Etched Nude, Kneeling, Clear, Paperweight Base, Signed, 5 In.	85.00

Vase, Flattened Oval, Submerged Black Spiraled, White Layer, 5 In. 302.50
Vase, Nude Child On Cloud, 6 Sides, Signed, 5 1/2 In. 295.00
Vase, Turquoise Teardrop, Red Stripes, Signed, 9 1/2 In. 350.00

KPM refers to Berlin porcelain, but the same initials were used alone and
in combination with other symbols by several German porcelain makers.
They include the Konigliche Porzellan Manufaktur of Berlin, initials used
in mark, 1823–1847; Meissen, 1723–1724 only; Krister Porzellan
Manufaktur in Waldenburg, after 1831; Kranichfelder Porzellan
Manufaktur in Kranichfeld, after 1903; and the Kister Porzellan
Manufaktur in Scheibe, after 1838.

KPM

K.P.M

Bowl, Pierced & Raised Border, Cobalt & Gilt, 9 1/4 In., 8 Piece 225.00
Bust, Boy & Girl, Porcelain, Pair 175.00
Charger, Scene of Italian Ruins, 16 In. 715.00
Coffeepot, Red Flower, Gold Swirled Ground, 9 In. 150.00
Dinner Set, Field Flower, 7–Piece Setting, Service For 8 .... 1600.00
Dish, 3 Sections, Floral, Gold Scrolls, Butterflies Around Rim, Marked, 5 In. 145.00
Figurine, Man & Woman, With Musical Horns, Marked, 10 In. 195.00
Figurine, Man, Standing, Basket of Grapes, 5 1/2 In. 275.00
Figurine, Peasant Girl, Holding Basket of Greens, Cup of Milk, Marked, 9 In. 550.00
Group, 2 Children, Seated, Playing Instruments, 5 1/2 In. 357.00
Lamp Base, Scrolled Floriform Handles, White, Marked, 28 3/8 In. 935.00
Lamp, Lithophane, 5 Panels With Children Scenes 750.00
Lithophane, see also Lithophane category
Plaque, Charme Mach Asti, 10 1/8 x 7 1/2 In. 6050.00
Plaque, Classically Draped Maiden On Parapet 3740.00
Plaque, Esther, Marked, 9 1/4 x 6 1/2 In. 4675.00
Plaque, Gypsy Woman, Frame, Signed, 16 x 10 In. 8250.00
Plaque, Interior Scene, Lady & Gentleman, Signed, 9 1/2 x 6 1/8 In. 5775.00
Plaque, Jesus The Boy, Frame, Porcelain, 5 x 7 In. 1800.00
Plaque, Madonna & Child, Berlin, 13 1/2 x 11 1/4 In. 1980.00
Plaque, Madonna & Child, Giltwood Frame, 1880s, 11 x 9 In. 1980.00
Plaque, Mermaid Kissing Young Man, Signed, Gilt Frame, 9 x 7 In. 5775.00
Plaque, Mother & Children, In Kitchen, Tasting Bread, 9 1/2 x 7 1/2 In. 2420.00
Plaque, Nymph, Paper Title, Berlin, 9 1/2 x 6 1/2 In. 2750.00
Plaque, Portrait of Young Woman, Flowing Red Hair, Marked, 12 1/2 In. 550.00
Plaque, Reclining Lady Reading Book 2750.00
Plaque, Ruth, Berlin, 13 x 8 In. 2200.00
Plaque, Satin Wearing Colorful Robes, Marked, 10 In. 935.00
Plaque, Woman Portrait, Oval, Signed Wagner, 8 1/2 x 10 1/2 In. 5500.00
Plaque, Woman, Signed Bayerlein 1100.00
Plaque, Woman, Standing, Frame, 16 x 10 In. ....*Illus* 8250.00
Plaque, Young Woman With Roses, Marked, c.1900, 9 x 6 1/4 In. 2860.00
Shaving Mug 95.00
Vase, Fan, Romantic Couple Both Sides, 2 Children On Pillows At Base, 15 In. 2400.00

KTK are the initials of the Knowles, Taylor & Knowles Company of East
Liverpool, Ohio, founded by Isaac W. Knowles in 1853. The company
made many types of utilitarian wares, hotel china, and dinnerwares. They
made the fine bone china known as Lotus Ware from 1891 to 1896. The
company merged with American Ceramic Corporation in 1928. It closed in
1934. Lotus Ware is listed in its own category in this book.

K.T.&K.
CHINA

Creamer, Fruit Pattern 10.00
Jardiniere, Yellow Roses, Scrolled Edge, Gilt Trim, White, 1870, 7 1/4 In. 85.00
Pitcher, Milk, Blue, White, 7 In. 85.00
Plate, Wizard of Oz, Box, Certificate, Edwin M. Knowles, 8 Piece 360.00
Plate, Yorktowne, Cream, 6 In. 5.00
Plate, Yorktowne, Yellow, 9 In. 8.00
Salt & Pepper, Fruit Pattern 25.00
Sugar, Cover, Fruit Pattern 10.00
Water Server, Fruit Pattern 30.00

KU KLUX KLAN items are now collected because of their historic importance. Literature, robes, and memorabilia are available. The Klan is still in existence, so new material is found.

Book, Strange Society of Blood & Death, 1920s, 6 x 9 In.	10.00
Buckle, Belt, Brass, Fine Details	45.00
Knife, Pocket, Emblem, Brass Handle	15.00
Poster, Vote For Dewey, Kill The Klan, Hearst	600.00
Sheet Music, The Bright Fiery Cross, 1913	45.00

KUTANI ware is a Japanese porcelain made after the mid–seventeenth century. Most of the pieces found today are nineteenth–century. Collectors often use the term *kutani* to refer to just the later, colorful pieces decorated with red, gold, and black pictures of warriors, animals, and birds.

Bowl, Cover, Trees, Boats, Houses, Late 1800s, 5 x 4 In.	55.00
Bowl, Late 19th Century, 12 In.	495.00
Box, Bowknot Lid, Overall Multicolored Florals, 5 Sides, 20th Century	35.00
Cup, Cover, 100 Nobles & Ladies, Poem Interior, 4 In.	550.00
Dish, Central Rondel, Border of Figures, 8 1/2 In., 12 Piece	715.00
Plate, Figural Design, 8 1/2 In., 6 Piece	66.00
Tea Set, Geisha Lithophane Cup Bottom, Service For 6	385.00
Tray, Raised Figures, Floral, Red & Gold, Signed, 19th Century, 9 1/2 In.	125.00
Vase, Bottle Form, Checkered Design, Enamels, 11 In.	3850.00
Vase, Elephant Trunk Handle, Small	48.00
Vase, Figures & Flowers, Stand, 3 1/2 In.	95.00
Vase, Floral & Figural Design, Tapering, Cylindrical, 19th Century, 14 1/4 In.	305.00
Vase, Floral, 19th Century, Signed, 5 In.	135.00
Vase, Hundred Head Design, Signed, 7 In.	175.00
Vase, Multifloral, Signed, Early 19th Century, 5 In.	125.00
Vase, Silver Rim, Spherical Shape, Gold Design On Orange, Teak Stand, 5 In.	330.00

LACQUER is a type of varnish. Collectors are most interested in the Chinese and Japanese lacquer wares made from the Japanese varnish tree. Lacquer wares are made from wood with many coats of lacquer. Sometimes the piece is carved or decorated with ivory or metal inlay.

Bowl, Black Floral Band, Red Ground, Japan, 4 In.	40.00
Bowl, Salad, Black, Art Deco, Sterling Silver Base, 1950s, 6 Piece	40.00
Box, Cake, 2 Sections, Black, Red & Gold, Insert In Cover Holds 4 Plates	30.00
Box, Cover, Polychrome Flowers & Insects, 19th Century, 11 In.	550.00

KPM, Plaque, Woman, Standing, Frame,
16 X 10 In.

♦ ♦ ♦ ♦ ♦ ♦ ♦ ♦ ♦ ♦ ♦ ♦ ♦ ♦ ♦ ♦ ♦ ♦ ♦ ♦

Tips on framing paper documents and prints: No glue, scotch tape, or rubber cement. No scissors—don't trim anything. No pencils or pens, and don't try to rewrite an autograph. No staples or clips. No extremes of temperature or humidity. No direct sunlight—it fades the ink.

♦ ♦ ♦ ♦ ♦ ♦ ♦ ♦ ♦ ♦ ♦ ♦ ♦ ♦ ♦ ♦ ♦ ♦ ♦ ♦

Box, Cover, White Eggshell, Geometric Design, Jean Dunand, 3 In. 1750.00
Box, Inlaid Enamel & Mother-of-Pearl, Dragon Design, 8 x 12 1/2 In. 358.00
Box, Robe, Red, Late 1800s, Japan, 14 x 10 x 10 In. 235.00
Case, Cigar, Side-Wheeler, Empire of Troy, 2 5/8 x 5 1/2 In. 660.00
Tray, Kimono, Gold Vines, Bronze Rim, Square, 22 In. 935.00

LADY HEAD VASE, see Head Vase

LALIQUE glass was made by Rene Lalique in Paris, France, between the
1890s and his death in 1945. The glass was molded, pressed, and engraved
in Art Nouveau and Art Deco styles. Pieces were marked with the
signature *R. Lalique*. Lalique glass is still being made. Pieces made after
1945 bear the mark *Lalique*.

LaLique

Ashtray, Feuilles, Oval, Signed, 6 7/8 In. 770.00
Ashtray, Frosted Daisies Rim, Square, Signed, 5 In. 195.00
Ashtray, Sailing Ship 225.00
Ashtray, Sculpted Bird In Center 95.00
Ashtray, Ship Design 60.00
Bookends, Tete-De-Aigle, Head of Eagle, 1928, 5 1/4 In. 3300.00
Bowl, 3 Monkey Faces, Opalescent White-Blue, 4 3/4 In. 6875.00
Bowl, Coupe Verone, Frosted Birds On Branches, 11 x 8 In. 1875.00
Bowl, Dahlias Pattern, Wide Leaves, Clear Frosted Opalescent, Signed, 9 1/4 In. 550.00
Bowl, Frosted Tulips, Signed, 4 In. 160.00
Bowl, Ondines, With Underplate, Sterling Silver Rims, Signed 3250.00
Bowl, Plumes De Paon, Peacock Feathers, Bulging Eyes, Signed, 9 1/4 In. 660.00
Bowl, Roses, 9 3/4 In. 525.00
Bowl, Roses, Square, 9 3/4 In. 525.00
Bowl, Sunflower, Molded Round Dish, Raised Interior Design, Gray, 4 In. 715.00
Bowl, Vagues, No. 1, Wavy Pattern, Everted Rim, Signed, 11 3/4 In. 330.00
Bowl, Venise, 6 1/2 x 8 1/2 In. 65.00
Bowl, Zigzag Pattern, Clear, Signed, 9 1/4 In. 120.00
Box, Cover, Deux Sirenes, 2 Sea Nymphs, Clear Base, Signed, 10 1/4 In. 3850.00
Box, Cover, Grapes & Vine, Circular, Topaz, 5 1/2 In. 310.00
Box, Cover, L'Enfants, Clear, 4 1/4 x 3 In. 220.00
Box, Cover, Raised Florets, Top Floret Handle, Frosted Glass, Signed, 6 1/4 In. 850.00
Box, Domed Cover, Nippon Pattern, Round Spheres, Signed, 5 1/2 In. 467.00
Box, L'Origan, 2 Embracing Women On Cover, Brown Patina, 3 1/2 In. 462.00
Box, Raised Flowers, Opalescent, Light Blue Cast, 8 1/2 x 2 In. 1000.00
Candlestick, Raised Flower Heads, Clear, Ormolu Mounted, Signed, Pair 396.00
Champagne, Bunches of Cherries On Sides, Flat Stem, 4 1/2 In. 85.00
Chandelier, Champs-Elysees 3575.00
Charger, Nude Maiden Amid Surf, Blue Patina, Marked, 14 1/2 In. 3100.00
Clock, Inseparables, Lovebirds Each Side, Square, Signed, 4 1/2 In. 1980.00
Decanter, Body of Spiral Pattern, Ovoid Form, Signed, 10 1/2 In. 302.50
Decanter, Molded Ovals, Worker Shoveling Coal, 4 Sides, Signed, 10 3/4 In. 275.00
Decanter, Triangular Frosted & Clear Pattern, Signed, 9 1/2 In. 330.00
Decanter, Vine Band At Neck, Cone Shape, 11 3/4 In. 1045.00
Figurine, Bird, Paper Label 115.00
Figurine, Bison .... 235.00 To 238.00
Figurine, Cat, Frosted, 8 1/4 In. 550.00
Figurine, Frosted Molded Swan, Raised Head, Polished Feathers, 9 In. 1870.00
Figurine, Madonna, Onyx Base, 14 In. 900.00
Figurine, Nude, Woman, Arcing Over Wave, Signed, Paper Label, 9 1/2 In. 245.00
Figurine, Nude, Woman, With Deer 175.00
Figurine, Sparrow, 3 1/4 In., Pair 195.00
Figurine, Vierge A L'Enfant, Rectangular Block Form, Signed, 13 1/4 In. 247.00
Figurine, Virgin Mary, Clear & Frosted, Signed, 9 3/4 In. 350.00
Goblet, Art Deco Stem, Signed, 8 In. .... 112.00 To 125.00
Hood Ornament, Perch 230.00
Hood Ornament, Woman's Head, Streaming Hair, Stepped Plinth, Marked, 9 In. 9900.00
Lamp, Statuette, Fiery Amber Nude Woman, Center of Base, Metal Base, 9 In. 2860.00
Lemonade Set, Swirling Leaves, Yellow, 5 Tumblers, 8 5/8 In. 990.00
Lighter, Lion's Head 175.00

Liquor Set, Scrolls, Clear & Frosted, Frosted Stopper, 7 3/4 In. Carafe, 5 Piece 1000.00
Paperweight, Blossoms & Leaves, Frosted, Round, Dome Shape, Signed, 2 In. 350.00
Paperweight, Daim, Young Fawn, c.1950, 3 In. 450.00
Paperweight, Fish, 3 3/4 In. 75.00
Paperweight, Frosted Intaglio Thistle, Clear Ground, Signed, 3 1/2 x 2 1/2 In. 135.00
Paperweight, Raised Blossoms & Leaves, Frosted Glass, Dome Shape, 2 x 1 1/2 In. 350.00
Paperweight, Turkey, Frosted 90.00
Pendant, Frolicking Frogs, Open Form, Blue Silk Cord, Signed, 2 In. 1760.00
Pendant, Green Dragonflies, Silk Cord, c.1900 .... 1600.00
Perfume Bottle, 2 Doves Stopper, 4 In. 75.00
Perfume Bottle, Baluster Body, Swirling Lines, Doves As Stopper, 12 3/8 In. 1100.00
Perfume Bottle, Cactus 45.00
Perfume Bottle, Cigalia, Winged Locust At Corners, Wooden Box, 5 1/4 In. 7700.00
Perfume Bottle, Coeur Joie, Heart Shape, For Nina Ricci, 4 In. 220.00
Perfume Bottle, Epines, Brown Wash, 4 1/2 In. 950.00
Perfume Bottle, Fern Frond Ridges, Signed, c.1905, 5 In. 305.00
Perfume Bottle, Flattened Sphere, Ribbed Stopper, Turquoise, 3 1/4 In. 250.00
Perfume Bottle, Frosted Roses Around Bust of Figure, Signed, Labels, 6 In. 315.00
Perfume Bottle, L'Air Du Temps, Box 49.00
Perfume Bottle, La Belle Saison, Houbigant, Box & Outer Box 2750.00
Perfume Bottle, Maidens At Corners, Tapered, Black, Stopper, 5 1/4 In. 1980.00
Perfume Bottle, Molded Fish Body, Frosted, 5 1/2 In. 770.00
Perfume Bottle, Nudes, Pop-Up Atomizer 650.00
Perfume Bottle, Scalloped Heart Shape, Nina Ricci, 5 3/4 In. 400.00
Perfume Bottle, Serie Toilette, For Coty 100.00
Pin, Deux Aigles, 2 Birds, Facing, Green Foil Reflection, 1911, 3 3/4 In. 2200.00
Pin, Satyr's Head, Brass Mount, Quatrefoil, Marked, 1 3/4 In. 2860.00
Plaque, St. Christopher, Signed, 4 In. 490.00
Plate, Jaffa. No. 4, Frosted, Amber, Signed, 8 3/4 In. 495.00
Plate, Swirl Design, Clearl & Opalescent, Signed, 10 1/2 In. 550.00
Plate, Verneuil, 7 3/4 In., 8 Piece 245.00
Powder Box, Emiliane, Frosted & Clear, D'Orsay, 1932 .... 460.00
Seated Eagle, Frosted, Square Base, 3 1/2 In. 1650.00
Toothpick, Cupids & Grapes, 1 1/2 In. 75.00
Toothpick, Frosted Panels, Figure Designs 80.00
Tray, Bahia, Frosted Leaves On Rim, Signed, 18 In. 950.00
Tumbler, Hesperides, Curling Fern Fronds, Signed, 4 1/4 In. 100.00
Vase, 4 Female Masks Between Grape Branches, Conical Form, Signed, 5 1/2 In. 550.00
Vase, Archers Pattern, Large Birds, Frosted, Marked, 10 1/2 In. 5050.00
Vase, Avallon, Birds & Berries, Signed, 6 In. 1980.00
Vase, Bacchantes, Frosted 6050.00
Vase, Bellis, Stylized Leaves, 5 1/4 In. 418.00
Vase, Berry Clusters, Cross Stem Configurations, Molded Sphere, 7 In. 1320.00
Vase, Birds Swirl Around Body, 4 3/4 In. 350.00
Vase, Blown-Out Blossoms, Raised Branches, Frosted, Signed, 6 1/4 In. 525.00
Vase, Bresse, Amber, Art Deco Cutback Design 2310.00
Vase, Chevaux, Horses Before Leafy Stalks, Signed, 7 1/2 In. 1430.00
Vase, Cut Oval Geometric Details, Signed, 15 In. 990.00
Vase, Dahlias, Blossoms, Enameled Stamens, Signed, 5 In. 1650.00
Vase, Dancing Nudes, 9 3/4 In. 1700.00
Vase, Deer, Trees, Clear, Frosted, Late 1940s, 6 1/2 In. 700.00
Vase, Deux A Deux, Pairs of Blooming Flowers, Short Stems, Signed, 7 1/4 In. 1100.00
Vase, Domremy, Amber, 1928, 8 1/4 In. 5000.00
Vase, Domremy, Thistle Blossom, Charcoal Gray, Frosted, 8 1/2 x 7 1/2 In. 1485.00
Vase, Ducks, Molded Spiral Rows, Frosted Oval, 5 In. 990.00
Vase, Ducks, Spiraling, Bulbous Body, Everted Rim, Signed, 5 1/2 In. 1650.00
Vase, Eucalyptus, Leaves Radiating From Berried Base, Signed, 6 3/8 In. 1650.00
Vase, Fish, Frosted Molded Sphere, 4 Rows of Blown-Out Fish, Blue Wash, 5 In. ... 1650.00
Vase, Fish, Painted Fins & Scales, Frosted, Signed, 5 In. 795.00
Vase, Fish, Swimming In Rows, Everted Rim, Signed, 10 3/4 In. 6600.00
Vase, Frosted Sphere, 3 Rows of Lappet Designs, 6 5/8 In. 715.00
Vase, Gui, Opalescent, White, Signed, 7 In. 1495.00
Vase, Gui, Tangled Leaves, Berries, Brown Patina, Signed, 6 1/2 In. 385.00

Vase, Leaf Design, Stylized, Molded Ribbed Oval, Vertical Panels, 4 3/4 In. 660.00
Vase, Leaves, In Row On Bottom, Brown Recessed Areas, Signed, 14 In. 4620.00
Vase, Leaves, Protruding Bands, Frosted, Signed, c.1925, 9 1/4 In. 410.00
Vase, Lucie, 6 In. 175.00
Vase, Mistletoe Berries, Leafy Stems, Broad Oval Form, Molded Surface, ... 770.00
Vase, Mossi, Bubble–Like Protrusions, 6 Alternating Rows, Signed, 8 1/2 In. 330.00
Vase, Orleans, Flowers & Leafy Stems, Blue, Signed, 8 In. 5575.00
Vase, Palissy, Escargots, Signed, 7 In. 465.00
Vase, Perruches, Pairs of Budgies In Flowering Branches, Signed, 10 In. 3850.00
Vase, Piriac, Fish, Swimming Over Waves, Blue Patina, Signed, 7 1/4 In. 1100.00
Vase, Pivoines, Large Flower Buds, Short Stems, Signed, 6 3/4 In. 550.00
Vase, Prunes, Plums & Leaves, Opalescent, Signed, 7 In. 4090.00
Vase, Saint–Marc, 3 Sparrows Each End, Bands, Signed, 6 11/16 In. 990.00
Vase, Swallow, 10 In. 750.00
Vase, Thistle Blossoms, Spiked Leaves, Double Rows, Oval Form, 8 1/2 In. 1540.00
Vase, Thorn Branches, Oviform, Opalescent, 9 1/4 In. 990.00
Vase, Tourbillons, Amber, Signed, 1926, 7 7/8 In. 5500.00
Vase, Tournesols, Floral Ground, c.1927, 4 1/2 In. 1430.00

LAMPS of every type, from the early oil–burning Betty and Phoebe lamps
to the recent electric lamps with glass or beaded shades, interest collectors.
Fuels used in lamps changed through the years; whale oil (1800–1840),
camphene (1828), Argand (1830), lard (1833–1863), turpentine and alcohol
(1840s), gas (1850–1879), kerosene (1860), and electricity (1879) are the
most common. Other lamps are listed by manufacturer or type of material.

Aladdin, B–60, Short Lincoln Drape, Ivory Alacite, 1939 .... 425.00
Aladdin, B–62, Short Lincoln Drape, Ruby 425.00
Aladdin, B–70, Solitaire, White Moonstone, 1938 .... 1375.00
Aladdin, B–76, Tall Lincoln Drape, Cobalt Blue Crystal Art Glass, 1940 .... 850.00
Aladdin, B–88, Vertique, Yellow Moonstone Art Glass, 1938 .... 465.00
Aladdin, B–93, Vertique, White Moonstone Art Glass, 1938 .... 625.00
Aladdin, B–102, Corinthian, Green Beta Crystal, 1935 .... 40.00
Aladdin, B–112, Cathedral, Rose Moonstone, 1935 .... 220.00
Aladdin, Beehive, Oil, Green, 1937–1938 .... 95.00
Aladdin, Caboose, Aluminum Font, Parchment Shade, Spring Wall Bracket 100.00
Aladdin, Caboose, Parchment Shade 230.00
Aladdin, Electric, Silk Shade, Signed, 14 In. 95.00
Aladdin, G–16, Figurine, Alacite, Ivory 3600.00
Aladdin, G–355C, Hopalong Cassidy Holster 250.00
Aladdin, No. 5, Kerosene Mantle 20.00
Aladdin, No. 6, Brass, Opalescent Glass Shade, Electric Adapter 85.00
Aladdin, No. 11, Kerosene Mantle 20.00
Aladdin, No. 12, Hand Painted Shade, Nickel 160.00
Aladdin, No. G–30, Boudoir, Alacite 70.00
Aladdin, No. G–352, Alacite, Electric, Hang–Up 85.00
Alcohol, Blue Spherical Font, March 14th, 1893, 6 In. 27.00
Alcohol, Lampeberger, Pressed Glass, Miniature 55.00
Alcohol, Simplex, Warm Vapor Inhaler, Pierced Tin Holder, 1905, Box, 7 In. 45.00
Argand, Pine Cone Finial, Converted To Kerosene, c.1835, 16 In. 1320.00
Arts & Crafts, Copper, Wicker Shade, New Silk Lining, 16 x 11 In. 440.00
Arts & Crafts, Hammered Copper, Cylindrical Mica Base, Pyramid Top, 14 x 6 In. .. 413.00
Arts & Crafts, Multicolor Slag Glass Shade, Bradley & Hubbard Base, 1908, 19 In. .. 850.00
Astral, Cut & Frosted Shade, Electrified, Table 825.00
Astral, Fluted Standard On Square Marble Base, Etched Shade, Brass, c.1835, 23 In. .. 825.00
Astral, Victorian 470.00
Banquet, Kerosene, Pewter & Brass, Cherubs On Font, Electrified, Pair 240.00
Banquet, Oil, Blown Milk Glass, Floral 85.00
Banquet, Sandwich Glass, Cobalt Blue Cut To Clear, 20 In. 9900.00
Betty, Chicken Finial On Font Cover, Heart Finial On Arm, Twisted Hanger, 7 In. ... 375.00
Betty, Iron Fan Intricately Shaped, Belgium Area 625.00
Betty, Iron, 5 1/2 In. 38.00
Betty, Iron, Hanger, 4 In. 135.00
Betty, Iron, Twisted Hanger, 4 1/2 In. 105.00

◆ ◆ ◆ ◆ ◆ ◆ ◆ ◆ ◆ ◆ ◆ ◆ ◆ ◆ ◆ ◆ ◆ ◆ ◆

Parchment lamp shades can be cleaned with a cloth soaked in milk. Then wipe dry with a clean cloth.

◆ ◆ ◆ ◆ ◆ ◆ ◆ ◆ ◆ ◆ ◆ ◆ ◆ ◆ ◆ ◆ ◆ ◆ ◆

Lamp, Electric, Bronze Base,

Burmese Lamp Shade

Betty, Kerosene, Honeycomb & Panel, Harvest Scene Decal	65.00
Betty, Twisted Hanger, 7 1/4 In.	330.00
Bicycle, Badger Brass Mfg. Co., Nickel Plated, 7 In.	40.00
Bouillotte, Black Paint, Early 19th Century, 19 1/4 In.	770.00
Bradley & Hubbard lamps are included in the Bradley & Hubbard category	
Carbide, Red & Green Light, Badger Man Co.	75.00
Chandelier, 4 Lantern, Gustav Stickley, Wrought Iron	5000.00
Chandelier, 4–Light, Baluster, Turned Shaft, Tin & Iron, Painted Red, 10 x 18 In.	1540.00
Chandelier, 5–Light, Floral Design, Crystal Drops, Wrought Iron, 21 x 16 1/2 In.	45.00
Chandelier, 6–Light, Brass, England, 19th Century, 17 In.	935.00
Chandelier, 6–Light, Brass, Holland, 19th Century, 17 1/4 In., Pair	4500.00
Chandelier, 6–Light, Candle Arms Hung With Crystal Swags, 1770s, 36 1/2 In.	4125.00
Chandelier, 6–Light, Electric Candles, Mid–Eastern, 19 1/2 In.	375.00
Chandelier, 6–Light, Empire, Brass, Lyre Form, Domed Glass Shade, 51 In.	660.00
Chandelier, 6–Light, Gilded Brass, Chain, 14 In.	65.00
Chandelier, 6–Light, Louis XVI–Style, Glass Prisms & Beads, 3 Ft. 2 In.	6325.00
Chandelier, 6–Light, Neoclassical, Copper Mounted, Pine Cone Finial, Chain, 22 In.	4400.00
Chandelier, 6–Light, Serpentine, Tin, 21 x 24 In.	2425.00
Chandelier, 6–Light, Tin, 20th Century, 21 In.	192.50
Chandelier, 8–Light, Brass, Clear Cut Drops, Spires, Pressed Stars, Electric, 40 In.	1550.00
Chandelier, 8–Light, Gilbert Poillerat, Wrought Iron, c.1930, 5 Ft. 6 In.	7150.00
Chandelier, 8–Light, Shell, C Scroll Arms, Napoleon III, Bronze Dore, 22 x 43 In.	880.00
Chandelier, 12–Light, Crimped Drip Pans, Turned Wooden Center, 29 In.	3400.00
Chandelier, 21–Light, 2 Tiers, Georgian, Pewter Tone, Ball Column, 41 In.	400.00
Chandelier, Candle, Scrolling Branch Arms, Crystal Swags, Electrified, 31 In.	495.00
Chandelier, Curtain Swag Design, 5 Tiers of Crystal Drops, Gilt Bronze, 24 In.	385.00
Chandelier, Deskey, Glass, Chrome, Prisms, Hanging Balls, 1930, Pair	1760.00
Chandelier, Domed Shade, Bronze Arms Foliage, Alabaster, Karl Hulstrom, 41 In.	9735.00
Chandelier, Empire Style, Painted, Gilt Metal	5225.00
Chandelier, Hanging, Center Puffy Shade, 4 Smaller Shades, Grapes, Lattice Work	1400.00
Chandelier, Kerosene, Hobnail, Ruby Glass, Hanging, Converted To Electricity	1250.00
Chandelier, Leaf–Tip Font With Female Masks & Swan's Head, 23 In.	2200.00
Copper Base, Silver Inlay, 15 3/4 In.	330.00
Crusie, Double, Alabama	185.00
Crusie, Iron, Double, Twisted Handle, 7 In.	100.00
Desk, Favrile, Glass, Bronze, Irregular Form, Rows of Aztec Designs	4510.00
Desk, Gilt Metal Shade, Ivory Bakelite Arm & Base, 13 1/2 In.	175.00
Electric, 4–Light, Brass, Glass Shade, Chase	190.00
Electric, 6–Light, Louis XVI–Style, Lion Masks, Bronze & Marble, 33 In., Pair	3025.00
Electric, Amber Glass, Wrought Iron, Gustav Stickley, c.1910	5500.00
Electric, Amber Slag Glass Framed In Oak, Mission Style, 18 In.	2200.00
Electric, Art Deco, Peacock, Metal, 16 In.	415.00
Electric, Bakelite, Butterscotch, Small	30.00
Electric, Bent Panel, Floral Decorated Metal Shade, Amber Slag Glass, 24 In.	715.00
Electric, Blackamoor, Man & Woman, Pink & Black, Trimmed Shades, 24 In., Pair	75.00
Electric, Blackamoor, Man & Woman, Seated Figures, Red, Gold Trim, Red Shade	200.00

Electric, Blue, Green Rippled Glass Segments, Decorated Base, 22 In. 770.00
Electric, Boudoir, Dance De Luminaire, Pink Satin 990.00
Electric, Boudoir, Diamond & Button Shade, Clear Glass 25.00
Electric, Brass, Figural, Cut & Pressed Glass Globe, 29 In., Pair 330.00
Electric, Brass, Wall, Opalescent Tulip Shade, Black Trim, 1930s, 18 In. 85.00
Electric, Bronze Base, Burmese Lamp Shade ....*Illus* 2900.00
Electric, Bronze, Bridge, Leaded Glass Shade, Applied Glass Flowers, Opal, 53 In. 795.00
Electric, Bronze, Gilded, Gold Pulled Feather Shade, 18 In. 245.00
Electric, Bronze, Polychrome Floral Design, Deep Amber Ground, 17 1/2 In. 770.00
Electric, Bronze, Slag Glass Shade, With Beaded Fringe 200.00
Electric, Champleve, 29 In. 330.00
Electric, Champleve, Brass, Elephant With Pagoda, China, 65 In. 525.00
Electric, Child's, 3 Bears, 1930s 110.00
Electric, Chrome, Rectangular Frosted Shade, 63 1/2 In. 25.00
Electric, Classique, Reverse Painted Sunset Landscape, Signed 2700.00
Electric, Classique, Reverse Painted, Farm Scene, 18 In. 1850.00
Electric, Classique, Reverse Painted, Trees, Lake, 18 In. 1950.00
Electric, Colonna, Art Nouveau, Lotus Leaves, Gilt Bronze, Fabric Shade, 18 In. 5500.00
Electric, Covered Wagon, Western Graphics 18.00
Electric, Cut Glass, Hobstar & Finecut, Dome Shade, Matching Base, 15 In. 295.00
Electric, Desk, Brass, 3-Way Light With Fan Center, Rewired, 1940s, 22 x 16 In. ... 400.00
Electric, Desk, Domed Copper Shade, Chrome Plated Circular Base, 1930, 15 In. 550.00
Electric, Dirk Van Erp, 2-Light, 20 In. 9500.00
Electric, Dirk Van Erp, 4-Light, Copper, Mica Shade, c.1909, 19 1/2 In. 4400.00
Electric, Dolly Toy Co., Ceramic Children, Plastic Hot Air Balloon, 1970 .... 28.00
Electric, Dolly Toy Co., Winnie The Pooh, 1977 .... 20.00
Electric, Dome Shade, White-Amber Glass Segments, Bronze Base, 20 In. 3080.00
Electric, Double Candlestick, Tole Shade, France 935.00
Electric, Draped Women, Glass Cherries At Base, Bergman, c.1920, 18 In. 4550.00
Electric, Duffner & Kimberly, Floral Design 3740.00
Electric, Duffner, Floral Leaf & Geometric Design, Dichroic Glass, 20 In. 45.00
Electric, Durand, Mantel, Pair 1750.00
Electric, Elevator, J. L. Hudson Store, Brass, Glass Needs Replacement 100.00
Electric, Emeralite, Mushroom Shade, Cased, Pinwheel Design, Signed 495.00
Electric, Floor, Adjustable, Modern Design, Artelluce 715.00
Electric, Gilt Brass Column, Tole Shade, 29 In., Pair 770.00
Electric, Gustav Stickley, Hammered Copper, Original Wicker Shade, 1909 .... 5000.00
Electric, Hammered, Riveted Base, Paneled Copper, Mica Shade, Art Deco, 21 In. 907.00
Electric, Hampshire, Bigelow & Kennard, Emerald Green, Dome Shade, 1900 .... 4750.00
Electric, Heart Shape, Pink, U.S. Glass, 1930s, Pair 500.00
Electric, Indian, Figural, Bobbin Head 18.00
Electric, Ives, Spider, Ives Design Shade, 10 In. 450.00
Electric, Jefferson, Cottage Landscape, 2-Socket Baluster Form Metal Base, 21 In. ... 1540.00
Electric, Jefferson, Reverse Painted, Landscape Scene, Glass Base, 18 In. 1975.00
Electric, Jefferson, Reverse Painted, Scene, Striated Greens, 16 In. 1575.00
Electric, Johnnie Walker, Metal, 20 In. 225.00
Electric, Kopperkraft, Copper & Mica, Mission Type, 1920, 16 In. 3300.00
Electric, L. & J. G. Stickley, Vanity, 1926 .... 460.00
Electric, Leaded Floral Shade, Tiffany Style, 21 In. 385.00
Electric, Leaded Glass Shade, Wicker Metal Base 247.00
Electric, Leviton, Plastic Motion, Flying Ducks, Water, Trees 450.00
Electric, Louis XV, Brass, Putti, On Tree Column, 6 Candle Arms, 29 In., Pair 200.00
Electric, Louis XVI Style, Gilt Bronze, Urn Form, 3 Scrolled Candle Arms, 26 In. 187.00
Electric, Miller, Parlor, Embossed Ornate Base 85.00
Electric, Miller, Reverse Painted, Bridge Scene, Bronze, 16 In. Shade 550.00
Electric, Miller, Reverse Painted, Signed 1800.00
Electric, Miller, Slag Panel, Caramel Shade & Base 475.00
Electric, Mission Oak, Square Post, Hammered Brass Green Slag Panels, 19 In. ......
Electric, Mission, Oak, Central Square Post, Green Slag Glass Panels, 19 1/2 In. 440.00
Electric, Moe Bridges, Boudoir, Floral 400.00
Electric, Moe Bridges, Boudoir, Reverse Painted 1600.00
Electric, Moe Bridges, Dressing Table, Birds of Paradise On Shade, Pair 650.00

Electric, Moe Bridges, Reverse Painted Scene, 15 1/2 In.	1750.00
Electric, Multicolored Slag, 9 Panels, 2–Light, 22 In.	500.00
Electric, Musica, Cigarette Holder Shape	40.00
Electric, Napoleon, Marble Base, France, 14 In.	495.00
Electric, Neoclassical, Candelabra Form, Black Paint, Ormolu Mounted, 38 In., Pair	300.00
Electric, Newel Post, Figural, Art Nouveau	675.00
Electric, Niagara Falls, Revolving	45.00
Electric, Oriental, Blue, White, Porcelain, Modern, 26 In., Pair	363.00
Electric, Pagoda, Chinese Brass, Glass & Porcelain, 21 1/2 In.	45.00
Electric, Painted China, Man & Woman, Victorian, Pair	30.00
Electric, Paneled Slag Glass & Brass, Flared Shade, Green, White Glass, 25 In.	495.00
Electric, Parker, Barley Twist Base	225.00
Electric, Parrot, Figural, Copper	225.00
Electric, Parrot, Figural, Glass	175.00
Electric, Parrot, Figural, U.S. Glass Co.	450.00
Electric, Pool Table, Budweiser, Fluorescent, Chains, 4 Colors, c.1950	175.00
Electric, Porcelain, Female Nude, On Rock Pedestal, 32 In.	300.00
Electric, Prairie Style, Leaded Glass Shade, Box Shape, Architectural Design	825.00
Electric, R.I. Arsenal, Golf Bag	65.00
Electric, Raggedy Ann, Chalkware, Dated 1973	40.00
Electric, Rayo, Brass, Milk Glass Shade	195.00
Electric, Reverse Painted, Art Nouveau Peacock, Original Shade, 1900s	550.00
Electric, Reverse Painted, Pansies, 16 In.	825.00
Electric, Robot, Light Bulb On Top, Eyes Light Up, 1960, 11 In.	275.00
Electric, Rocking Horse, Wooden	20.00
Electric, Ronson, Black Girl Sitting, Cast Metal, Original Shade, 1919	850.00
Electric, Scotty, Figural, Milk Glass, 1930s	120.00
Electric, Shade, Hanging, Blown Out, Fruit, 24 In.	1475.00
Electric, Ship With Lighthouse, Art Deco, Chrome, Lighthouse Lights	45.00
Electric, Silver Plated, Barrel, Branch Type Footed, Miniature	125.00
Electric, Square Base, Cut Wooden Finial, Antique Needlework Shade, 26 In.	44.00
Electric, Student, Brass, Double, White Milk Glass Shades, 27 x 29 In.	770.00
Electric, Student, Brass, Double, Yellow Glass Shade, Pierced, 23 1/2 In.	523.00
Electric, Student, Brass, Green Cased Shade, Original Bulb	275.00
Electric, Student, Brass, Pea Green Ribbed Glass Shade, 18 In.	264.00
Electric, Student, E. G. Ripley, Double, Clear Match Holder	650.00
Electric, Student, Favrile, Glass, Bronze, Brown/Green Patinated Stand, Tulip Shade	7150.00
Electric, Tulip Blossom Design Border, Acanthus Leaf Motif, 25 In.	2420.00
Electric, TV, Black Panther, 1953	30.00
Electric, TV, Jack Be Nimble, With Candlestick, Ceramic	55.00
Electric, TV, Stagecoach, Black & Gold	25.00
Electric, U.S. Glass, Santa Claus, 1904	995.00
Electric, Urn Shaped Base, Stained Glass Dragonfly Shade, 29 In.	302.00
Electric, Victorian Couple, Occupied Japan	100.00
Electric, Wicker, 5 Ft. 9 In.	675.00
Electric, Wicker, Mushroom Shade, White	150.00
Electric, Wilkinson, Leaded Glass, Repeating Blossom & Lattice	4125.00
Electric, Winged Lion Feet, G. Galbiati, Bronze, 38 In.	440.00
Fairy, Blue Satin Glass, Opalescent, 6 Leaf Feet, 3 3/4 In.	350.00
Fairy, Burmese, Design, Fenton	140.00
Fairy, Burmese, Pottery Base, Taylor Tunnicliffe & Co.	225.00
Fairy, Citron, White Loopings, Piecrust Crimp Rim, Dome Shaped Shade, 5 3/4 In.	845.00
Fairy, Owl's Head Both Sides, Enameled Red Eyes, 4 1/2 In.	145.00
Fairy, Pink & White Cased, Pair	180.00
Fairy, Pyramid, Clarke Insert, Ironstone, c.1880, 3 1/4 In.	85.00
Fairy, Pyramid, Pink Swirls, Clarke Base, 4 1/4 In.	175.00
Fluid, Cut Grape & Leaf Design On Font, Blown, 1830s, 8 3/4 In.	440.00
Fluid, J. G. Webb, Brass, Electrified, 20 In.	495.00
Fluid, Pewter, 8 3/4 In.	412.00
Gasoline, Coleman, Brass, Shade	120.00
Gasoline, H. Dana, Bronze, Boy Leaning Against Gaslight, 11 5/8 In.	485.00
Gasoline, Spelter, 6–Arm, Starr, Fellows & Co., 1855, Pair	1760.00
Girandole, 1–Light, Bristol & Cut Glass, Cobalt Glass Standard, Gilt–Bronze, 12 In.	1870.00

Girandole, 1–Light, Wedgwood & Cut Glass, 12 3/4 In., Pair 2200.00
Gone With The Wind, Cherub Face, Ruby Flash Base, 1890s 500.00
Gone With The Wind, Enameled Pansies, Oversized 800.00
Gone With The Wind, Floral Design, 28 In. 300.00
Gone With The Wind, Floral Design, All Original 600.00
Gone With The Wind, Frosted Satin Glass, Grape Pattern 300.00
Gone With The Wind, Pink Flowers, Green Leaves, All Yellow, Electrified, 20 In. ... 450.00
Gone With The Wind, Red Satin Glass 575.00
Gone With The Wind, Ruby, Painted Flowers, Electric Converted 3100.00
Handel lamps are included in the Handel category
Hanging, Glass, 10 Panels, 23 In. 130.00
Hanging, Hall, Brass Counterweights, England 1650.00
Hanging, Hall, Teardrop Form, Stylized Floral Motif, Leaded Glass, 12 In. 770.00
Hanging, Painted Islamic Men, Women & Architecture, Early 20th Century 350.00
Jefferson Scenic, Cottage Landscape, 2–Socket, 21 In. 1450.00
Kerosene, Banquet, Pink Shell Designed Font, Corinthian Column, 31 In. 188.00
Kerosene, Black Stone Base, Brass Stem, White To Clear Overlay Font, 8 In. 60.00
Kerosene, Brass, Alabaster Stem, Cranberry Font, 11 1/4 In. 125.00
Kerosene, Bristol Font, Columbus & Ships, Matching Shade 412.50
Kerosene, Brown & White Flowers, Victorian 500.00
Kerosene, Carriage, Brass, Bull's–Eye Back 65.00
Kerosene, Clear Glass Flint, Sawtooth & Bull's–Eye Font, Brass Collar, 11 1/4 In. ... 255.00
Kerosene, Coach, Glass Engraved, Monogram & Bird, 19th Century, 7 In., Pair 220.00
Kerosene, Cranberry Glass, Cut Panels, 15 In. 495.00
Kerosene, Cranberry Glass, Thumbprint Ball Shades, Enameled, Pair 800.00
Kerosene, Enameled Robins & Floral, Sapphire Blue, Gold 1600.00
Kerosene, Finger, Aquarius 125.00
Kerosene, Finger, Coolidge Drape, Purple 175.00
Kerosene, Finger, Diamond Sunburst, Amber 140.00
Kerosene, Finger, Peanut, Green 140.00
Kerosene, Finger, Princess Feather, 1894, 5 1/4 In. 57.50
Kerosene, Finger, Sheldon Swirl, Opalescent Blue 150.00
Kerosene, Fostoria, No. 1592, Cobalt Blue Font, Clear Footed, Large 500.00
Kerosene, Juno, Urn, Brass, Hand Painted Floral Globe 82.50
Kerosene, Lion & Baboon, Swirl Chimney 350.00
Kerosene, Lomax Vienna, Composite, Dated 9/20/1870 .... 65.00
Kerosene, Mission Style, Milk Glass, c.1914, 6 1/2 In. 95.00
Kerosene, Monot Stumpf, Banquet, Satin Glass, Pink Opalescent, Pink Shade, 22 In. 695.00
Kerosene, Nickel, Faux Marble, Blue Font, France, 10 1/2 In. 105.00
Kerosene, Pressed Glass, Lion & Baboon 285.00
Kerosene, Ripley, Marriage, Blue, Clambroth, Match Holder Lid, Marble, 11 In. 1210.00
Kerosene, Spelter, Partial Nude, Seated, Boston Sandwich Font 525.00
Kerosene, Street, Ham's Patent 1888 .... 275.00
Kerosene, Student, Brass, Cylindrical Reservoir, Green Glass Shade 143.00
Kerosene, Student, Nickel Plate, Cylindrical Reservoir, Green Glass Shade 110.00
Kerosene, Student, Nickel Plated, Manhattan, Floral Glass Globe, 10 In. 1018.00
Kerosene, Triple Flute & Bar, Clambroth Base, 1860s, 13 1/2 In. 1500.00
Kerosene, Tureen, Brass, 8 5/8 In. 159.00
Kerosene, Vaseline Opalescent, Sheldon Swirl, Chimney & Burner 375.00
Kerosene, Victorian, Brown & White Flowers, Shade 500.00
Kerosene, Wall Mount, Milk Glass Shade, Electrified, 10 In. 100.00
Lard, Finger Loop, Fill Cover, Pieced Tin 65.00
Lucerne, Brass, Accessories, 25 In. 130.00
Miner's, Baldwin, Carbide, Cap 125.00
Miner's, Carbide, Auto–Lite, 4 In. 25.00
Miner's, Carbide, Copper 20.00
Miner's, Carbide, Justrite, Hand Held, 8–In. Reflector 45.00
Miner's, Hook, Brass Lid, Pat. 1872, Small 65.00
Miner's, Kohler Safety 75.00
Miner's, Safety, Fancy Trim, 7 In. 750.00
Miner's, Thomas & Williams, Brass, 10 1/4 In., Pair 100.00
Miner's, Tole, Pennsylvania Dutch, Long Spout, Chain & Hook 175.00
Night, Tole, Oval Back Plate, Shade, Red, Laurel Leaves, Electrified, 11 In., Pair 1430.00

Oil, 2–Button Knops, Double Burner, Dish Foot, 1830, 7 1/2 In. 880.00
Oil, Acid–Etched Bird, Brass Collar, Marble Base, 13 1/4 In. 357.50
Oil, American Victorian, Figural Standard, Bronze & Gilt Metal, 34 In. 220.00
Oil, Banquet, 2 Cherubs, Red Satin Glass Glove 350.00
Oil, Blown & Molded Glass, Hand Painted Globular Shade, 16 1/2 In. 132.00
Oil, Brass, Persian Design, Filigree Shade, Tripod Base, Claw–Footed 495.00
Oil, Cast Iron Base, Tin Stem, Pewter Collar, Marked, 8 1/2 In. 192.00
Oil, Cathedral, Opalescent Amber, Butterscotch, Green, Blue, 48 x 22 x 25 In. 2400.00
Oil, Cherubs & Floral Swags, Gilded Removable Brass Font & Burner, 15 3/4 In. 27.00
Oil, Clambroth Base, Gilding, Clear Honeycomb Font, Brass Collar, Connector, 10 In. 71.00
Oil, Cobalt Blue, Swag Pattern 140.00
Oil, Cranberry & Opalescent Dot 950.00
Oil, Cranberry Glass, Fluted, 19th Century, 8 1/4 In. 330.00
Oil, Cranberry Swirl Font, Clear Pedestal, 8 In. 410.00
Oil, Cut Cobalt Blue To Clear, Stepped Marble Base, Engraved Band, 14 1/2 In. 300.00
Oil, Eclipse, Green Pressed Glass 175.00
Oil, Egyptian, Frog Form, Wheat Sheaves & Feathers On Back, 400 B. C., 3 In. 190.00
Oil, F. Porter, Pewter, Acorn Font 175.00
Oil, Flint, Hexagonal Base, Sawtooth Font, Brass Collar, 10 1/2 In. 165.00
Oil, Flint, Round Foot, Hexagonal Stem, Star & Punty Font, Brass Collar, 9 3/4 In. 105.00
Oil, Glass & Brass, Sawtooth Pattern, Original Double Burner, Pair 495.00
Oil, Glass, Flower Decorated Base 20.00
Oil, Glass, Wall Mount, Amber, Double Wick, c.1885 .... 295.00
Oil, Gone With The Wind, Floral, Bluebirds, Large 175.00
Oil, Hanging, Arts & Crafts Shade 100.00
Oil, Hanging, Glass Font, Smoke Deflector, Cast Iron 250.00
Oil, Hanging, Pull Down, Apple Blossom Shape 375.00
Oil, Hurricane, Queen Anne Style, Clear & Etched Shade, Silver Plated Base, 15 In. 55.00
Oil, Inecto, Miniature 35.00
Oil, Large Frosted Glass Base, 4 Molded Lion's Heads, Electrified 30.00
Oil, Little Beauty 85.00
Oil, Little Gem 125.00
Oil, Marble, Gilded Brass, Clear Cut Prisms, Electrified, No Shade, 12 1/2 In. 71.50
Oil, Marble, Glass & Brass, 8 3/4 In., Pair 187.00
Oil, Mercury Glass Reflector, Metal Base 65.00
Oil, Milk Glass, Floral Painted Ball Shade, Electrified 45.00
Oil, Millefiori, Matching Shade, 16 1/2 In. 1400.00
Oil, Miller, Gilded, White Marble Base, 19th Century 145.00
Oil, Moon & Stars, Blue Base, Amber Font 350.00
Oil, Nellie Blye, Miniature, With Shade 225.00
Oil, Opalescent Base, Thumb Print Font, Brass Connector & Collar, 9 3/4 In. 49.00
Oil, Pewter, Brass Label, Bracket For Shade, 8 1/4 In. 150.00
Oil, Pewter, Bull's–Eye, 1830–1840 .... 950.00
Oil, Pewter, Rampant Lion, Marble Base, France, 30 In., Pair 715.00
Oil, Pierced Frame, Stepped Plinth, Putti & Female Masks, Electrified, 22 In., Pair 4125.00
Oil, Rayo, Chimney & Shade, Pat. Nov. 20, 1894 .... 50.00
Oil, Roman Key & Rib, Fancy Base, Large 85.00
Oil, Santa Claus & House, 9 In. 10.00
Oil, Satin Glass Font, Metal & Porcelain Base 25.00
Oil, Snowflake, Cranberry Opalescent, 11 In. 350.00
Oil, Stepped Marble Base, Gilded Brass Column, Clear Pressed Glass Font, 11 In. 105.00
Oil, Stepped Marble, Brass Base, Engraved Vine Font, Brass Collar, Stem, 10 In. 38.00
Oil, Veronica, All Glass 125.00
Oil, White Cut To Clear, Circle Pattern, Spherical Font, Brass, Marble Base, 8 In. ... 77.00
Pairpoint lamps are in the Pairpoint category
Peg, Frosted Rubena Shade, St. Louis On Brass Standard, Pair 950.00
Perfume, Clear To Ruby Red, Swirled Top, 7 1/4 In. 395.00
Sconce, 1–Light, Raised Edge, Incised Rays, Tin, 9 In., Pair 1650.00
Sconce, 2–Light, Carved Giltwood & Faux Marble, 30 In., Pair 395.00
Sconce, 2–Light, Cast As Tasseled Cord, Silvered Bronze, 27 In., Pair 440.00
Sconce, 2–Light, Engraved Gondolier, Venetian Glass Frame, 17 In., Pair 330.00
Sconce, 3–Light, Flaming Urn On Backplate, Leaf Swags, 19th Century, 19 In., Pr. 6050.00

Sconce, 3–Light, Foliate Plate, Gilt Bonze, 19 In., Pair 1760.00
Sconce, 3–Light, Lion & Unicorn Design, Birmingham, 12 In., Pair 355.00
Sconce, 3–Light, Silver Plated, Sheffield, Late 18th Century, 12 1/4 In. 550.00
Sconce, 3–Light, Steel, France, 1930, Pair 2675.00
Sconce, 4–Light, Carved Wooden Sockets, Iron, 18 1/2 In. 140.00
Sconce, 5–Light, Curving Arms, Giltwood 75.00
Sconce, 7–Light, Electric, Louis XVI, Overall Crystal Drops & Swags, 22 In., Pair 1320.00
Sconce, Beveled Mirror Reflector, Brass, 22 In. 49.50
Sconce, Candle, Oval, Crimped Edge Reflectors, Tin, 14 In., Pair 700.00
Sconce, Candle, Tin, Diamond Shape, Crimped, 10 1/2 In. 425.00
Sconce, Chromium Plated Metal, Tubular Glass Cylinder, 21 1/4 In., Pair 242.00
Sconce, Double Circle Design, Birds, Blue, Moravian Tile Co., 4 x 11 In., Pair 385.00
Sconce, Embossed Ships At Sea, Hammered Copper, Arts & Crafts, 11 3/4 In., Pair 305.00
Sconce, Florentine, Mirrored, Portraits, 2 Candle Arms, 18th Century, Pair 2200.00
Sconce, Georgian, Acorn Finial, Bell Form Glass Shade, Brass, 25 In., Pair 1100.00
Sconce, Gothic Design, Archer, Waraner & Minsky, Bronze, c.1845 .... 825.00
Sconce, Prairie School, Wall, Iron, Square, 10 x 5 In. 770.00
Sconce, Prism Hung, Grapevines On Arms, Wax Pan, Gilt Brass, c.1870, Pair 310.00
Sconce, Reverse Painted Glass, Floral, Pair 450.00
Sconce, Scrolling Branch Arms, Crystal Swags, Drops, Bronze, 20 x 21 In., 4 Piece 1870.00
Sconce, Wrought Iron, Frosted Glass, Cylindrical Shade, 18 1/4 In., 6 Piece 2200.00
Skater's, Clear Globe, Tin, 7 1/4 In. 82.00
Skater's, Tin, Clear Globe, 7 In. 71.00
Solar, Cut & Etched Globe, Fluted Column, Patinated Brass, c.1840, 33 In. 385.00
Solar, Cut & Etched Shade, Bulbous Standard, Marble Base, c.1850, 22 1/2 In 500.00
Tallow, 17th Century 185.00
Tiffany lamps are listed in the Tiffany category
Torchere, 2–Light, Gothic, Rope Turned Standard, 19th Century, Iron, 64 In., Pair 195.00
Torchere, 4–Light, Gothic Style, Marble Base, 19th Century, Iron, 75 1/2 In. 110.00
Torchere, Art Deco, Satin, Chrome Base, Pair 40.00
Torchere, Blackamoor, Polychromed Wood, Electrified, 89 In., Pair 3630.00
Torchere, Corinthian Columns, Clear Glass Shade, 6 Ft., Pair 650.00
Torchere, French Style, Crystal Drops & Swags, Gilt Wood, 74 In., Pair 355.00
Torchere, George I, Squared Standard, Giltwood & Gesso, c.1720, 42 1/2 In. 4950.00
Torchere, Iron, Triangular 3 Straps Support, No Glass, France, 1925, 62 In. 990.00
Torchere, Spiral Fluted Baluster, Lion's Masks & Swags, Parcel Gilt, 5 Ft., Pair 5500.00
Whale Oil Burner, Sparking, Loop Pattern, Pewter Collar, 3 In. 155.00
Whale Oil, Free–Blown, Clear, Applied Handle, Circular Dished Base, 5 In. 83.00
Whale Oil, Marine Blue, White Slag Glass Base, 1850s 785.00
Whale Oil, Petticoat, Tin, 3 Spout, Dark Brown Japanning, 5 1/2 In. 66.00
Whale Oil, Pewter, Roswell Gleason 375.00
Whale Oil, Silver Over Copper, Wickpick Burner 215.00

LANTERNS are a special type of lighting device. They have a light source,
usually a candle, totally hidden inside the walls of the lantern. Light is
seen through holes or glass categories.

Barn, Pine Case, Hinged Door, Bluish Paint, 3 Panes, Wire Handle, 13 In. 400.00
Barn, Wire Handle, Tin Vent, Mortised Pine Frame, 18 In. 500.00
Barn, Wooden Frame, Chamfered Posts, Wire Bale Handle, Glass Door, 11 In. 520.00
Brass, Tubular Red Globe, Round, 7 In. 70.00
Candle, Collapsible, Turkey, 1880s 100.00
Candle, Hardwood, Mortised & Pinned, Tin Hood, Wire Bale, Glass Door, 12 In. ... 400.00
Candle, Pierced Pyramidal Top, Glass Sides, Wire Guards, Black Paint, 11 In. 302.00
Candle, Pierced Tin, Paul Revere Type, Cone Top 125.00
Candle, Punched Tin, Paul Revere Type, Conical Top Extra Candle Socket, 12 In. 181.00
Candle, Tin, Hexagonal, Turned Finials, Silver, Red & Gold Paint, Pole, 78 In. 138.00
Candle, Tin, Hexagonal, Wooden Pole, 21 1/2 x 63 In. 110.00
Candle, Tin, Pierced Conical Vent Top, Horn Glazed, 6 In. 236.00
Darkroom, 1882 .... 345.00
Dietz King, Nickel Plated, 15 In. 150.00
Dietz, Comet, Box 35.00
Dietz, Fire Department, Nickel Plated Brass 225.00
Dietz, Little Wizard, Blue Globe, Dated 1918 .... 35.00

Dietz, Little Wizard, Red Globe, Unused	65.00
Dietz, Skater's, Scout, Red Globe	250.00
George III, Etched Glass, Hanging	550.00
Gleason & Bailey	742.00 To 855.00
Gustav Stickley, Heart Cutouts, Chain & Ceiling Mount	1200.00
Hanging, Hall, Bell Shape, Matching Soot Cover, Cobalt Blue, 20 In.	770.00
Hanging, Strap Handle, Round Glass Over Star–Punched Base, 17 In.	715.00
Kerosene, Adams & Westlake Co., Wall, Brass	65.00
Kerosene, Carbutt's Dry Plate, Pat. April 25, 1882, Sheet Metal, Red Glass	345.00
Kerosene, Dietz, No. 2	12.00
Kerosene, Hamm's Mfg.	225.00
Kerosene, Tin, Brass Trim, Clear Glass Globe, 12 1/2 In.	126.00
Nics Freres, 4 Glass Panels, Iron Shaped Oriental Yoke Support, 1925, 30 3/4 In.	4950.00
Oil, Barn, Red Glass Chimney	45.00
Oil, Vortex, Brass, Tank Inserts From Base, 11 In.	149.00
Pierced Tin, Conical Top, Ring Hanger, Gild Traces, 16 In.	1100.00
Policeman's, Cincinnati	200.00
Prairie School, Geometric Reticulated Iron, Pink & Green Slag Glass, 10 In.	275.00
Pumpkin Head, Original Goldenrod, Black, 7 In.	440.00
Punched Brass, Paul Revere Type, 3 3/8 In.	440.00
Punched Tin, Paul Revere Type, 5 3/4 In.	93.00
Shrine, Earthenware, Dark Green Glaze, Japan, 45 In.	330.00
Skating, Child's, 6 1/2 In.	20.00
Tin & Horn, Green & Orange Paint, 19th Century, 18 In.	412.50
Tin, 3 Glass Windows, 3 Vent Hoods, Plus Ring Handle, 12 In.	93.00
Tin, Cobalt Glass 4 Sides, Square, Blue Paint	115.00
Tin, Hexagonal, Glazed Sides, Stepped Pierced Top, 18 1/2 In.	2640.00
Tin, Paul Revere Type, Green Paint, Ring Handle, 13 In.	175.00
Tin, Pierced Circular Chimney, Ring Handle, Painted Red, 16 In.	550.00
Tin, Red, Blue & Green Glass 3 Sides, Door Is 4th, Ring Handle, 10 In.	71.50
Tin, Red, Cobalt Blue Glass, Black Paint, 11 1/2 In.	115.00
Whale Oil, Tin, Brown Japanning, Pierced Star, Diamond, Ring Handle, 13 1/2 In.	192.00

LE VERRE FRANCAIS is one of the many types of cameo glass made in France. The glass was made by the C. Schneider factory in Epinay–sur–Seine from 1920 to 1933. It is a mottled glass, usually decorated with floral designs, and bears the incised signature *Le Verre Francais.*

Bowl, Etched Stems, Blossoms, Orange, Burgundy, Signed, 10 In.	1325.00
Box, Domed Cover, Ball Handle, Thistle, 1925, 7 In.	1200.00
Lamp, Gray, Stylized Blossoms, Wrought Iron, 1925, 14 1/4 In.	3300.00
Pitcher, Deco Design, Signed, 10 In.	1425.00
Vase, Bellflowers, 11 1/2 In.	650.00
Vase, Blue, Orange & Yellow, 15 1/2 In.	900.00
Vase, Etched Floral Garlands, Mottled White, Signed, 15 In.	1650.00
Vase, Gray, Mottled Orange To Cobalt, Pine Cones, 1925, 17 In.	1325.00
Vase, Mottled Pumpkin, Ruby, Etched, Egg Shape, 15 In.	3795.00
Vase, Orange & Yellow, 15 1/2 In.	900.00
Vase, Papillon, Flying Butterflies, White To Aqua, Orange, 12 1/4 In.	1430.00
Vase, Roses, 11 In.	500.00
Vase, Stylized Floral, Yellow, Orange, Blue, Flared, 16 1/2 In.	935.00

LEATHER is tanned animal hide and it has been used to make decorative and useful objects for centuries. Leather objects must be carefully preserved with proper humidity and oiling or the leather will deteriorate and crack. This damage cannot be repaired.

Album, Autograph, 1876 Centennial Graduating Class, Scroll Inscriptions	60.00
Billfold, Tennessee Centennial, 1897	30.00
Bowl, Laced Seam, Primitive, Dark Patina, 16 1/2 x 9 1/4 In.	130.00
Box, Collar, Victorian	25.00
Case, Cylindrical, Attached Brass U.S. Letters, 12 In.	33.00
Case, Prudential Insurance Co., Embossed, Snap Lock, 1932	50.00
Chaps, Batwing, Card Suits, Miles City Saddlery, Montana, c.1925	2300.00
Chaps, Batwing, Parade, Sterling Silver Conches, 1940s	3000.00

Chaps, Black, 40 Silver Conchas, Bohlin, Hollywood 2750.00
Cigarette Case, Alligator Skin, 1920s 40.00
Flask, Chrome Cap 16.00
Gloves, Black Buffalo Hide, 1890 .... 75.00
Holder, Night Stick, Military 4.50
Holster & Cartridge Belt, Moran Brothers, Miles City, Mont., 1880s 9000.00
Holster, White Tooled, Jeweled 38.00
Jacket, Flying Tiger, Words Painted On Front, World War II 1500.00
Jacket, Police, Chicago 275.00
Mailbag, Adirondack, 1900s, Pair 79.00
Pitcher, Blackened, 18th Century 242.00
Riding Crop, Victorian, Sterling Silver Handle 95.00
Saddle, B. F. Grey, Pendleton, Ore., Ridden By Jim Bowler, Deadwood, 1870 .... 3500.00
Saddle, Bonner–Allen, Studded, Tapederos 250.00
Saddle, Hamley, c.1925 .... 450.00
Saddle, Hand Tooled Floral Pattern 302.00
Saddle, Mother Hubbard Style, 1880s 3100.00
Saddle, Silver Studded, Jeweled Headstall 550.00
Tankard, Blackened, 18th Century 143.00

LEEDS pottery was made at Leeds, Yorkshire, England, from 1774 to 1878. Most Leeds ware was not marked. Early Leeds pieces had distinctive twisted handles with a greenish glaze on part of the creamy ware. Later ware often had blue borders on the creamy pottery.

LEEDS POTTERY.

Mug, Geometric Floral Design, 5 Colors, 4 7/8 In. 550.00
Pitcher, Dumbo, 8 In. 175.00
Pitcher, Rainbow, 5 Colors, 9 In. 3600.00
Plate, 4 Colors, Green Shell Edge, 7 In. 650.00
Plate, American Eagle, Green Scalloped Border, 19th Century, 7 In. 467.50
Plate, Blue Feather Edge, Eagle, 4 Colors, 8 In. 825.00
Plate, Blue Feather Edge, Eagle, 5 Colors, 6 3/4 In. 385.00
Plate, Blue Feather Edge, Leeds Backward–Looking Bird, 5 Colors, 8 In. 550.00
Plate, Chinoiserie, Blue & White 275.00
Plate, Eagle, Blue Feather Edge, 4 Colors 750.00
Plate, Peafowl, Green Spatter Ground, Blue Feather Rim, 8 1/2 In. 300.00
Plate, Peafowl, Green Spatter, Green Rim, 9 In. 750.00
Sauceboat, Creamware, Twist Handle, White, c.1785 .... 440.00
Sugar, Gaudy Floral Design, 5 1/4 In. 154.00
Teapot, Gaudy Floral Design, Blue, Green, Yellow, Leaf Handle, 7 In. 203.00
Toddy Plate, American Eagle, Blue Shell Edge 90.00

LEFTON is a mark found on many pieces. The Geo. Zoltan Lefton Company has imported porcelains to be sold in America since 1940. The firm is still in business. The company mark has changed through the years; but because marks have been used for long periods of time, they are of little help in dating an object.

Lefton China
Hand painted
MADE IN JAPAN

Cookie Jar, Baby's Face In Bunny Suit 150.00
Cookie Jar, Bear, Label, 1984 .... 40.00
Figurine, Bride & Groom, Box 20.00
Figurine, Fox, No. 6970 .... 12.00
Figurine, Fox, Standing 15.00
Sugar & Creamer, Pink Flowers, Gold Handles 40.00
Teapot, Sugar & Creamer, Stacked 45.00

LEGRAS was founded in 1864 by Auguste Legras at St. Denis, France. It is best known for cameo glass and enamel–decorated glass with Art Nouveau designs. Legras merged with Pantin in 1920 and became the Verreries et Cristalleries de St. Denis et de Pantin Reunies.

Legras

Bowl, Winter Scene, Forest, 4 In. 325.00
Vase, Cameo, Art Deco, 12 1/2 In. 550.00
Vase, Cameo, Gray, Berry Branches, Gourd Form, 1925, 25 1/2 In. 1320.00
Vase, Cameo, Mountainous Riverside Scene, Colorless Cylinder, 8 In. 412.50
Vase, Cameo, Trumpet Vine, Signed 1940.00

Vase, Dark Plum Fruit & Leaves, Signed, 7 1/4 In.	695.00
Vase, Enameled Snow Scene, Sunset Colored Ground, 15 3/4 In.	990.00
Vase, Hand Painted, Enamel, Trees, Mountains, 11 In.	495.00
Vase, Overlaid Vine & Leaf Design, Signed, 9 In.	550.00
Vase, Ruby Coloring, Enameled Daisies, 8 In.	2450.00
Vase, Trees, Birds, Blossoms On Frost Ground, 14 In.	250.00
Vase, Underwater Scene, 8 In.	1800.00
Vase, Winter Scene, Figure of Woman, Signed, 16 In.	895.00

LENOX is the name of a porcelain maker. Walter Scott Lenox and Jonathan Cox founded the Ceramic Art Company in Trenton, New Jersey, in 1889. In 1906, Lenox left and started his own company called *Lenox*. The company makes a porcelain that is similar to Irish Belleek. The marks used by the firm have changed through the years and collectors prefer the earlier examples. Related pieces may also be listed in the Ceramic Art Co. category.

Bookend, Trojan Horse, White, 7 In.	175.00
Box, Cover, Gray, Gold Leaf, 5 x 3 1/2 In.	50.00
Box, Cover, Raised Floral, Green Mark, 2 1/2 x 5 In.	65.00
Box, Pink, Raised Floral Design, White Ground, Cover, 2 x 5 In.	55.00
Bust, Woman, Art Deco, Side View, White, 4 In., Pair	200.00
Bust, Woman, Cascading Hair, White, Green Mark, 8 1/2 In.	275.00
Cake Plate, Flowers, Handles	65.00
Cup & Saucer, Weatherly	35.00
Dinner Set, Golden Wreath, Gilt, Swan Dish, Service For 8, 55 Piece	330.00
Dinner Set, Lotus Garden, 42 Piece	275.00
Dinner Set, Tuxedo, Gold Banding, Service For 8, 32 Piece	550.00
Figurine, Baby's Head, White, Green Mark	195.00
Figurine, Belle of Ball	87.50
Figurine, Governor's Garden Party	87.50
Figurine, Swan, Cream, Small	30.00
Head, Man & Woman, Cylinder Base, Art Deco, Green Wreath, 9 In.	550.00
Lamp, Diana The Huntress, Silver Plated Fittings, 31 In.	600.00
Pitcher, Orange Peel Body, Face Under Lip, Green Mark	225.00
Pitcher, Stylized Bird of Paradise, Blue Mark, 7 In.	34.00
Place Setting, Autumn, Service For 8, 40 Piece	795.00
Place Setting, Ming, 6 Piece	125.00
Place Setting, Tudor, 5 Piece	175.00
Plate, Holly Pattern, 13 In.	135.00
Punch Set, Cream & Coral, 9 Piece	300.00
Salt & Pepper, Figural, Nipper, RCA Victor Dog	50.00
Salt & Pepper, Snail, Gold Trim	15.00
Stein, Golfer	2400.00
Sugar & Creamer, Belvedere, Gold Mark	55.00
Sugar & Creamer, Sterling Silver Overlay, Brown, Black Mark, 4 In.	85.00
Sugar, Red Rooster Crowing Good Morning, Verse On Back, Marked	165.00
Tea Set, Architect's, Green Mark, 28 Piece	695.00
Toby, William Penn, Indian Handle	190.00
Vase, Embossed Leaf Design, 8 1/2 In.	35.00
Vase, Flowers, Bulbous, 8 x 3 1/2 In.	20.00
Vase, Green Ground, White Roman Columns, Stair Step Canopy Roof, Trees, 10 In.	165.00
Vase, Silver Overlay In Art Nouveau Design, 9 3/4 In.	633.00

LETTER OPENERS have been used since the eighteenth century. Ivory and silver were favored by the well-to-do. In the late nineteenth century, the letter opener was popular as an advertising giveaway and many were made of metal or celluloid. Brass openers with figural handles were also popular.

3-Layer Handle, Ivory, Mother-of-Pearl Inserts	125.00
Acorn, Jensen	115.00
Amish Man's Head, Iron	10.00
Armour, Celluloid, Fancy Rooster Head, Large	55.00
Brass, Napoleon Handle	26.00

Brass, Stylized Design, Acid Etched, Carence Crafters, 7 3/4 In. 250.00
Brass, Tooled Blade, Cast Handle, Silver, Gilt Inlay, Oriental, 12 3/8 In. 150.00
Burrough, Pinned Brass Plates 14.25
Celluloid, Painted Details, Pair 65.00
Copper, Stylized Rose, Acid Etched, Carence Crafters, 7 3/4 In. 250.00
Fuller Brush Man, With Suitcase, Red Plastic, 1940s, 7 1/4 In. .... 12.50 To 15.00
German Silver, Stylized Long–Tailed Lizard, Pierced, Carence Crafters, 8 In. 250.00
Golf, Art Deco 70.00
Gregor's Ice Cream, Celluloid Handle 22.00
Gulf Oil 10.00
Hercules Powder, Dupont Explosives 65.00
Indian, Wooden 23.00
Ivory, 3–Layer Handle, Mother–of–Pearl Inserts 125.00
Ivory, Filigree Handle 125.00
Jester, Brass 70.00
Lady's Leg & High Heeled Shoes, Ivory Handle 175.00
Owl, Brass 20.00
San Felice Cigar, Hammer Attached 18.00
Sarcophagus Shape, Nude Woman On Handle 550.00
Stanhope, Ivory 60.00
Texas Centennial 12.00
Todd Shipyards, Brass, Embossed Plaque 15.00
Trowel Shape, To Cement Our Business Together, Salesman's Sample 45.00

LIBBEY Glass Company has made many types of glass since 1888, including the cut glass and tablewares that are collected today. The stemwares of the 1930s and 1940s are once again in style. The Toledo, Ohio, firm was purchased by Owens–Illinois in 1935 and is still working under the name *Libbey* as a division of that company. Additional pieces may be listed under Amberina, Cut Glass, and Maize.

Libbey

Bowl, Blue Net–Like Design, Oval, Signed, 8 x 11 1/2 In. 400.00
Bowl, Cherries & Flowers, Cut Glass 150.00
Bowl, Corinthian Pattern, Turned In Rim, Signed, 7 1/2 In. 88.00
Bowl, Kimberly, Square, 9 In. 400.00
Bowl, Love Birds On Branch, Leaves, Floral, Signed, 8 In., Pair 1760.00
Bowl, Puritana, Square, 7 In. 400.00
Bowl, Stratford, Turned In Rim, Square, 9 In. 550.00
Carafe, Emerald Green To Clear, Cut Glass 1500.00
Carafe, Sterling Silver Neck, 8 1/2 In. 550.00
Celery Dish, Allover Diamonds & Hobstars, 11 In. 125.00
Compote, Engraved Allover, Leaves & Berries, Braided Stem, Signed, 5 1/2 In. 135.00
Compote, Engraved Florals, Bulbous Stem, Signed, 6 1/4 x 5 1/4 In. 125.00
Compote, Optic Thumbprint, Paper Label, 4 1/8 x 6 In. 985.00
Cuspidor, Woman's, Cut Glass, Signed 600.00
Decanter, Floral, Intaglio, Signed 375.00
Goblet, Wedgemere 850.00
Golden Foliage, Dinner Set, 1950s, 31 Piece 60.00
Pitcher, Cider 925.00
Plate, Cut Leaf Design, Signed, 8 1/2 In., 8 Piece 295.00
Relish, Brilliant Period, Signed, 7 1/2 In. 95.00
Relish, Columbia, Turned In Sides, 12 x 6 In. 1400.00
Toothpick, Cut Glass, Brilliant Period, Signed 165.00
Toothpick, Cut Glass, Satin, Ribbed Enameled Design 100.00
Vase, Allover Engraved Leaves & Berries, Twisted Stem, Signed, 5 1/2 x 7 In. 275.00
Vase, Flower Holder, Signed, 1889 .... 9500.00
Vase, Hollow Blown Stem, Engraved Florals, Signed, 6 1/4 In. 110.00
Vase, Optic Swirl Rib, Fuchsia To Amber, Signed, 9 In. 450.00
Water Set, Cable & Grape, 6 Piece 850.00
Water Set, Signed, 9 Piece 300.00
Whipped Cream Set, Wedgemere 1100.00

LIGHTERS for cigarettes and cigars are collectible. Cigarettes became popular in the late nineteenth century, and with the cigarette came matches and cigarette lighters. All types of lighters are collected, from solid gold to the first of the recent disposable lighters. Most examples found were made after 1940.

Aladdin's Lamp, Art Deco	15.00
Aladdin's Lamp, Brass Fittings	25.00
Alaska Scene Base, Chrome, 2 1/2 In.	38.00
Alligator, Tin, Flask Shape	25.00
Ashtray, Roosters, Richard Ginori	275.00
Black 8–Ball	30.00
Bottle, Figural	15.00
Bowling Pin	25.00
Camel Cigarettes, Pack Shape	12.00
Camera On Tripod, Occupied Japan	25.00
Candle, Flintlock Pistol	25.00
Cartier, 18K Gold	700.00
Cigar, Counter, Battery Operated, 16 x 9 x 7 In.	650.00
Cigar, Fiathens Rexamer & Co., Coffee & Tea Merchants, 5 x 12 In.	60.00
Cigar, Jump Spark	385.00
Cigarette, Table, Anheuser–Busch, 3 1/2 In.	45.00
Continental, Gold Color, 1 1/4 In. ....*Illus*	10.00
Coronet, Multicolor, Enamel, Striped, 2 5/8 x 1 3/4 In. ....*Illus*	15.00
Dog, Ronson, Striker	62.00
Dog, Whippet	20.00
Dunhill, Gold–Filled	35.00
Dunhill, Nude Woman, Silent Flame, Box	57.00
Electric, Green Glass, Domed, Ball Footed, Automatic On & Off	35.00
Evans, 2 Ashtrays	40.00
Evans, Combination Cigarette Case	110.00
Evans, Egg Shape, Table Model, Enameled Flower, Gold Trim	55.00
Evans, With Compact	15.00
Felix, 1930s, 2 In.	247.00
Floor Lamp Form	60.00
Foremost Milk, Pocket	15.00
Foxhole, Instructions, Box	32.00
Fram Filters, Have A Light, Tip To Light	300.00
Gambling Roulette Wheel	55.00
Golf Club, Chrome, Table	25.00
Golfer, Art Deco	385.00
Hand Grenade .... 22.00 To 65.00	
Horse Head, Japan, Table	95.00
Johnnie Walker, Lucite	20.00
K. S. Sze & Sons, Ltd., Enameled, 2 1/2 In. ....*Illus*	12.00
Kelly Tire	10.00

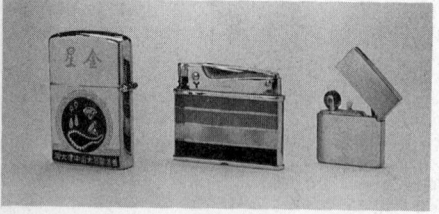

Lighter, K.S. Sze & Sons, Ltd., Enameled,
2 1/2 In.; Lighter, Coronet, Multicolor,
Enameled, Striped, 2 5/8 X 1 3/4 In.;
Lighter, Continental, Gold Color, 1 1/4 In.

Lighter, Tobacco Advertising,
Musical, Japan, 11 1/2 In.

Kent	8.00
Lead Pencil	15.00
Metropolitan Life Insurance	15.00
Moss Rose, Japan	8.00
Newark Shoe Co.	35.00
Old Charlie, Royal Doulton	190.00
Parker Flaminaire	65.00
Penguin, Kools Cigarettes, Metal	195.00
Pistol, Flintlock, Chrome, Inset Design	35.00
Rearing Horse, Figural, Brushed Chrome	37.00
Regens, Side Press, Quilted Pattern, Silver Plate	15.00
Ritepoint Liter, Red & Chrome, Box	9.50
Ronson, Chrome, Set In Heavy Glass, Table	25.00
Ronson, Johnnie Walker	18.00
Ronson, Pen–Lite, Gold Filled	35.00
Ronson, Queen Anne	8.00
Ronson, Touch–Tip, Streamlined Locomotive Form, Chrome & Enameled, 3 3/4 In.	220.00
Ronson, Touch–Tip, With Cigarette Dispenser	250.00
Ronson, Viking, Red Flame, Black & Chrome, Box	85.00
Roulette Wheel, Pocket	55.00
Scripto, Advertising Squirt, Box .... 10.00 To 20.00
Smokey Bear	35.00
Space Needle, Chrome	65.00
Sulky With Jockey & Horse	20.00
Tiffany Silver, Table	400.00
Tobacco Advertising, Musical, Japan, 11 1/2 In. ....*Illus*	195.00
Tripod Camera, Occupied Japan, 3 In.	48.00
Van Cleef & Arpell, Gold Accents, Blue Stones	302.50
Windsor, Coin On Chain	18.00
Zippo, Cartier, 18K Gold	800.00
Zippo, Sterling Silver, Oriental Engraved	75.00
Zippo, Windproof, Caterpillar Advertising, Box	12.00

LIGHTNING ROD BALLS are collected for their variety of shape and color. These glass balls were at the center of the rod that was attached to the roof of a house or barn to avoid lightning damage.

Ball, Mercury, Set of 4	375.00
Blue & White Balls, Green Glass In Directional Arrow	65.00
Blue & White Balls, Red Glass In Directional Arrow .... 50.00 To 85.00
Blue Globe, With Weathervane	125.00
Copper, White Glass Ball	30.00
Milk Glass Ball	35.00
Pig, c.1900	450.00

LIMOGES porcelain has been made in Limoges, France, since the mid–nineteenth century. Fine porcelains were made by many factories, including Haviland, Ahrenfeldt, Guerin, Pouyat, Elite, and others. Modern porcelains are being made at Limoges and the word *Limoges* as part of the mark is not an indication of age. Haviland, Limoges is listed as a separate category in this book.

Ashtray, Fleur–De–Lis, Elongated Oval, 6 In.	15.00
Ashtray, For Bridge Table, Triangular, Monaco, 4 Piece	25.00
Bowl, Cherries In & Out, Gold Rococo Rim & Base, C. C. Hulme, 1912, 9 1/2 In.	165.00
Bowl, Flowers Interior & Exterior, Pedestal, M & Co., 4 x 9 1/2 In.	125.00
Bowl, Pedestal, Bouquets, Signed, 9 1/2 x 4 In.	85.00
Bowl, Underplate, Rose Azalea Type, Scalloped, Elite Mark, 8 In.	115.00
Cake Set, Multicolored Floral, Gilt, Ivory Ground, 12 Piece	100.00
Chocolate Set, Sweetheart Roses, Gold, Signed, 11 Piece	185.00
Cracker Jar, Coral, Yellow & White Flowers On Gold & White, 7 1/2 In.	175.00
Cream Pot, Cover, Floral Tray, 9 Piece	225.00
Cup & Saucer, Silver Overlay	75.00
Cup, Lemonade, Painted Grape Design, Gold Trim, Set of 4	56.00
Decanter, Clown, Pierrot Type, Holding Bottle Cointreau Liqueur	75.00

Dinner Set, Lavender Flowers, Service For 12 .... 400.00
Dish, Peach To White, Man & Woman Scene, Divided, 4 1/2 x 8 1/4 In. 150.00
Dresser Jar, Cover, Purple Pansies, Light Green Ground 85.00
Dresser Set, Flowers, Monogrammed Medallion, Tray, 11 1/2 x 7 1/2 In., 6 Piece 495.00
Dresser Set, Pink Flowers On White, Gold Trim, Tray, 11 1/4 x 9 In., 7 Piece 395.00
Ewer, Hand Painted Roses, Gold Spout & Handle, Squatty, 5 x 7 1/2 In. 195.00
Fish Plate, Jumping Fish, Red & Gold Rim, 9 In., 6 Piece 110.00
Game Plate, Scenes of Man & Woman Riders, Dogs Chasing Stag, 13 3/4 In., Pair 770.00
Jam Jar, Cover, Underplate, Holly Pattern 150.00
Mustache Cup, Saucer, Lavender Floral, Ruffled, Gold Handle, 1908 .... 65.00
Oyster Plate, Roses, Gold Trim 35.00
Oyster Set, Sea Life In Shells, 5–9 In. Plates, Platter, 24 In. 395.00
Pitcher, Cider, Design of Monks Drinking Wine, 13 1/2 In. 385.00
Pitcher, Cider, Hand Painted Cherries, Gold Handle & Trim, Signed, 5 1/2 In. 165.00
Plaque, Bewigged Young Man, Kisses Hand of Woman, Signed, 5 1/4 x 3 1/2 In. ... 467.00
Plaque, Forest Scene, Trees, Lakes, Gold Rim, 12 3/4 In., Pair 400.00
Plaque, Frolicking Water Nymphs, Gilt & Gesso Frame, 1915, 18 In. 1320.00
Plaque, Full Nude Woman, Awash In Ocean Wave, 1890 .... 2200.00
Plaque, Game Birds, Gold Scalloped Border, Marked, 11 In. 125.00
Plaque, Grape and Pear Design, Gilded Border, Signed, 11 1/2 In. 50.00
Plaque, Indian Corn, Shaded Browns, Green Ground, Pierced, 13 In. 150.00
Plaque, Lovers In Garden, Rococo Rim, Signed, 12 In. 225.00
Plaque, Oriental Poppies, Gold Rococo Border, 12 1/4 In. 250.00
Plaque, Portrait, Girl In Jacket, Feathered Hat, Necklace, 1863, 15 In. 450.00
Plaque, Scenic, Ladies and Gentlemen At Tea Table, Gilded Border, 12 1/4 In. 80.00
Plaque, Woman, Enamel, Signed, 9 1/2 In., Pair 825.00
Plate, Birds, Gold Rococo Rim, Pierced For Hanging, 12 In. 295.00
Plate, Boars In Snow, Signed, 10 In. 155.00
Plate, Cave Paintings, Signed, 9 1/2 In. 125.00
Plate, Coronet, Mallard Duck, 10 In. 80.00
Plate, Dessert, Deep Rose Border, F. Pierce Presidential Service, Pair 3300.00
Plate, Dinner, Lily, Yellow Border, U. S. Grant's Presidential Service 2475.00
Plate, Fish, Flying Ducks, Signed, 9 In. 90.00
Plate, Flying Ducks, Signed, 10 In. 135.00
Plate, French Landscape Scene, Irregular Roman Gold Rim, 13 3/8 In., Pair 395.00
Plate, Hummingbird, 10 1/2 In. 225.00
Plate, Indian, Maiden, J. P. I., 1900 .... 450.00
Plate, Lilies, Signed 35.00
Plate, Pastoral Scene, Gold Scalloped Rim, Marked, 10 1/4 In. 145.00
Plate, Peaches & Blueberries Painted 27.50
Plate, Royal Game, Tufted Crest Bird, Signed, 10 In. 140.00
Plate, Tiger Lily, Gold Trim, 6 Sides, T & V 35.00
Platter, Pink Fuchsias, Gold Bows, 18 x 12 1/2 In. 150.00
Punch Bowl, Grapes & Leaves, T & V, 1880s 500.00
Punch Bowl, Strawberries, Signed LeRoy, 9 In. 850.00
Service For 12, Oriental Pattern, 80 Piece 165.00
Smoking Set, Transfer of Man, Mustache, Smoking Cigar, 4 Piece 385.00
Teapot, Bug, 3 Piece, Signed, 1870 .... 295.00
Tray, Feathery Flowers, Salmon To Pale Green, Gold Scalloped Rim, 13 x 8 1/2 In. 65.00
Tray, Hand Painted Floral, 12 x 16 In. 110.00
Vase, Floral, Applied Branch & Flower Handles, Canteen Shape, Redon, 9 In. 225.00
Vase, Maiden On Swing, Soaring Infants, Gilt Handles, Oct. 6, '96, 8 In. 295.00
Vase, Purple Flowers 1 Side, White Other, 2 Handles, Raised Footed, M. R. 185.00
Vase, Violet, White, Flowers, Canteen Shape, Gilt Handles & Feet, 9 In. 300.00

LINDBERGH was a national hero. In 1927, Charles Lindbergh, the aviator, became the first man to make a nonstop solo flight across the Atlantic Ocean. In 1932, his son was kidnapped and murdered, and Lindbergh was again the center of public interest. He died in 1974. All types of Lindbergh memorabilia are collected.

Bank, Lindy, Cast Iron, Grannis & Tolton 165.00
Bookends, Face, Iron, Bronze Color 85.00
Box, Pencil, Lindy & Plane, Metal 38.00

Pin, Spirit of St. Louis, New York To Paris, 3–D, Celluloid	95.00
Plate, Flight, 1927, 20 In.	150.00
Poster, Pacific Electric Railway, Appearance In Los Angeles, 1929	70.00
Tapestry, New York To Paris, 1929	300.00

LITHOPHANES are porcelain pictures made by casting clay in layers of various thicknesses. When a piece is held to the light, a picture of light and shadow is seen through it. Most lithophanes date from the 1825–1875 period. A few are still being made. Many lithophanes sold today were originally panels for lampshades.

Candleholder, 3 Pastoral Scenes, 3 1/2 In.	330.00
Cup, Germany	48.00
KPM, Shade, 54 1/2 x 6 In. Panels, Signed & Numbered	600.00
Lamp, Boudoir, Gold & White, Signed Jefferson	195.00
Lamp, Fairy, Boy With Dog, Boys Climbing Fence, 4 3/4 In.	595.00
Lamp, Oil, Mountainous Landscape On Shade, 4 x 5 In.	450.00
Nicholas & Alexandra Portrait, On Stand	2650.00
Stein, Porcelain & Pewter, Germany, Dated 1899	200.00

LIVERPOOL, England, was the site of several pottery and porcelain factories from 1716 to 1785. Some earthenware was made with transfer decorations. Sadler and Green made print–decorated wares from 1756. Many of the pieces were made for the American market and feature patriotic emblems, such as eagles, flags, and other special–interest motifs.

Bowl, 3 Masted War Ship, Success To Lady Washington, 11 3/4 In.	3950.00
Jug, Gilt & Transfer, 8 1/2 In.	7700.00
Jug, Matrimony Scene, Handle	675.00
Jug, Transfer Print, Masonic, Creamware	1750.00
Jug, Washington, Lafayette, 1824	1250.00
Pitcher, 3–Masted Ship Above MAC, Washington Under Spout, 9 In.	1650.00
Pitcher, 3–Masted Ship, Farmers Arms, American Eagle, 19th Century, 8 In.	2650.00
Pitcher, 3–Masted Ship, Success To Trade, Jefferson On Back, 8 1/2 In.	7700.00
Pitcher, American Eagle Transfer	1350.00
Pitcher, Apotheosis of Washington	2300.00
Pitcher, Farmers Arms Transfer, Peacock Other Side, 8 In.	385.00
Pitcher, Map of Ireland	1250.00
Pitcher, Peace Plenty & Independence U.S., Ship & Seal of U.S., 11 In.	2500.00
Pitcher, Samuel Adams & John Hancock, Ship On Reverse, 1802, 7 5/8 In.	2750.00
Pitcher, Seal of U.S. With Ring of States, 6 1/4 In.	2250.00
Pitcher, Ship Carpenter, Washington On Reverse, 10 1/2 In.	1870.00
Pitcher, Spread–Wing Eagle & U.S. Ship, 7 3/4 In.	2200.00
Pitcher, Transfer, Boston Fusilier, Red, Yellow, Blue, United We Stand, 11 In.	5225.00
Pitcher, Washington In Glory, Cordwainers Arms Under Spout, 8 7/8 In.	1100.00
Pitcher, Washington, Peace, Plenty & Independence, 7 In.	1850.00
Pitcher, Water, Trade & Commerce, 19th Century	700.00
Plaque, Portrait Medallion, George Washington, 5 x 4 In.	1980.00

LLADRO is a Spanish porcelain. Juan, Jose, and Vicente Lladro opened a ceramics workshop in Almacera in 1951. They soon began making figurines in a distinctive, elongated style. In 1958 the factory moved to Tabernes Blanques, Spain. The company makes stoneware and porcelain vases and figurines in limited and unlimited editions.

LLADRÓ

Bell, Christmas, 1987	50.00
Figurine, A Lady of Taste, No. 1495	600.00
Figurine, A Ride In The Park	3675.00
Figurine, A Rockside Ride	1300.00
Figurine, A Stitch In Time, No. 5344	415.00
Figurine, Ballet Trio, No. 5235	855.00
Figurine, Beagle Puppy, Sitting	293.00
Figurine, Best Friend	195.00
Figurine, Boy Meets Girl	375.00
Figurine, Boy, Soccer Player	700.00
Figurine, Can I Play	325.00 To 400.00

Figurine, Carnival Couple, No. 4882, 9 1/2 In. 200.00
Figurine, Carnival Time, No. 5423 .... 2120.00
Figurine, Cymbalist Angel 140.00
Figurine, Dancing Partner 338.00
Figurine, Dawn 1200.00
Figurine, Dentist, No. 4762. 3 .... 400.00
Figurine, Don Quixote & Windmill, No. 1497 .... 1200.00
Figurine, Elephants, No. 1150, 15 In. 450.00
Figurine, Fallas Queen 420.00
Figurine, Flirtatious Jester 890.00
Figurine, Flower Song 395.00
Figurine, Full Moon, No. 1438 .... 575.00
Figurine, Garden Classic 295.00
Figurine, Garden Song .... 225.00 To 295.00
Figurine, Girl, With Bonnet 275.00
Figurine, Girl, With Brush 338.00
Figurine, Girl, With Milk Jugs 425.00
Figurine, Girl, With Mother's Shoe 338.00
Figurine, Girl, With Wagon 275.00
Figurine, Graceful Offering, No. 5773 .... 515.00
Figurine, Heavenly Harpist 135.00
Figurine, Honey Lickers 525.00
Figurine, Jazz Duo 795.00
Figurine, Jazz Sax 295.00
Figurine, Kitakami Cruise 7000.00
Figurine, Little League On The Bench 600.00
Figurine, Little Pals .... 2100.00 To 2500.00
Figurine, Little Traveler .... 1200.00 To 1500.00
Figurine, Lover's Paradise, No. 5779 .... 1365.00
Figurine, Loving Family 950.00
Figurine, Moonlight, No. 1437 .... 375.00
Figurine, Motoring In Style, No. 5884 .... 2090.00
Figurine, Musical Partners, No. 5763 .... 375.00
Figurine, My Buddy .... 275.00 To 280.00
Figurine, Nativity Scene, 8 1/2 x 5 1/2 In. 155.00
Figurine, Nude With Rose, Bisque 600.00
Figurine, Nymph, Sleeping 875.00
Figurine, Pekingese, No. 4641g 375.00
Figurine, Princess & The Unicorn, No. 1755 .... 1300.00 To 1360.00
Figurine, Reverie, No. 1398 .... 485.00
Figurine, School Days .... 395.00 To 560.00
Figurine, Season 305.00
Figurine, Serene Valenciana 365.00
Figurine, Sewing A Trousseau 938.00
Figurine, Shepherd Boy 235.00
Figurine, Shepherd Girl 155.00
Figurine, Spring Bouquet .... 495.00 To 850.00
Figurine, Springtime In Japan, No. 1445 .... 1000.00
Figurine, Story Time, No. 5229 .... 550.00
Figurine, Summer Stroll .... 165.00 To 350.00
Figurine, Suzy & Her Doll 825.00
Figurine, Swan, Wings Spread 325.00
Figurine, Swans Take Flight 2850.00
Figurine, Sweet Harmonies 2035.00
Figurine, Tennis Player, Man 260.00
Figurine, Thai Dance, No. 2069, 17 1/4 In. 400.00
Figurine, Thoroughbred Horse 985.00
Figurine, Tinkerbell, Disney 925.00
Figurine, Trimming The Tree 900.00
Figurine, Valencian Boy, No. 5395 .... 320.00
Figurine, Veterinarian, No. 4825m .... 425.00 To 975.00
Figurine, Victorian Girl On Swing 1250.00
Figurine, Violinist & Girl 1275.00

Figurine, Voyage of Columbus	875.00 To 2750.00
Figurine, Will You Marry Me?, No. 5447	675.00
Figurine, Wishing On A Star	400.00
Figurine, Woman In The Wind	225.00
Figurine, Wounded Monkey, 5 1/2 In.	115.00
Ornament Set, Angel	60.00
Ornament, Ball, 1989	45.00
Ornament, Snowman	50.00
Plate, Christmas, 1972	263.00
Plate, Mothers' Day Plate, 1972	263.00

LOCKE ART is a trademark found on glass of the early twentieth century. Joseph Locke worked at many English and American firms. He designed and etched his own glass in Pittsburgh, Pennsylvania, starting in the 1880s. Some pieces were marked *Joe Locke,* but most were marked with the words *Locke Art.* The mark is hidden in the pattern on the glass.

Bowl, Openwork Top, Leafy Design, Signed, c.1895, 8 In.	395.00
Bowl, Salad, Servers, Foliate Design, Plated Rim & Tools, c.1895	165.00
Muffineer, Leafy Pattern, Silver Plate Top, Signed, c.1895, 6 1/4 In.	195.00
Pitcher, Grapes & Vines, Corset Shape, Signed, 8 1/2 In.	685.00
Sherbet, Poppy Design, 4 Piece	350.00
Sugar, Cover, Poppy	160.00

LOETZ glass was made in many varities. Johann Loetz bought a glassworks in Austria in 1840. He died in 1848 and his widow ran the company; then in 1879, his grandson took over. Most collectors recognize the iridescent gold glass similar to Tiffany, but many other types were made. The firm closed during World War II.

Loetz Austria

Basket, Berry Prunts, Green Iridescent, Clear Handle, 13 1/2 In.	450.00
Basket, Green Iridescent, Crystal, Clear Handle, 9 1/2 x 17 1/2 In.	385.00
Bowl, Crimped Edge, Gold & Purple Oil Spots,, 4 x 10 In.	250.00
Bowl, Crimped Rim, Rain Drops, Red & Green, 10 1/2 In.	325.00
Bowl, Green Iridescent, Flared, Signed, 4 x 7 1/2 In.	265.00
Bowl, Scalloped Rim, Green, Yellow & Blue Swirls, White Interior, 7 1/2 In.	250.00
Cologne Bottle, Signed, 6 In.	295.00
Cracker Jar, Iridescent Colors, Random Threaded, White Metal Fittings, Signed	495.00
Figurine, Stork, Iridescent, Textured Base, Signed, c.1904, 19 1/4 In.	825.00
Figurine, Stork, Yellow Body, Purple Beak & Wings, Glass Base, Signed, 19 1/4 In.	1430.00
Hair Receiver, 2 3/4 In.	55.00
Inkwell, Drape Pattern, Bird On Brass Cover, Green	95.00
Lamp, Ascending Bronze Poppies, Fringed Shade, Bronze Base, 24 1/2 In.	1300.00
Pitcher, Spiraled Body, Spurred Handle, Baluster Form, 4 1/2 In.	300.00
Rose Bowl, Basketweave Pattern, Scalloped Rim	135.00
Shade, Mushroom, On Pairpoint Base	3025.00
Sweetmeat Jar, Irregular Thread, Silver Plated Top & Handle, Green, 4 1/2 In.	295.00
Vase, Amber Iridescent, Applied Tailing Design, Conical, 1900, 7 3/4 In.	550.00
Vase, Ambergris, Free-Form, c.1900	1500.00
Vase, Art Glass, Silver Overlay, Bulbous, 3 In.	400.00
Vase, Blue, Ribbed, 12 In.	250.00
Vase, Bronze Mounted, Yellow, Pink Spotting, 1900, 9 In.	660.00
Vase, Cased Orange To Clear, Silvered Blue & Green Between, Silver Layered, 5 In.	1325.00
Vase, Clear, Pale Yellow Iridescent Design, Blue, Pink Amber, 1900, 8 In.	885.00
Vase, Double Conical Shape, Ruby Red, Yellow Looping Design, Blue, 1900, 3 In.	1045.00
Vase, Emerald, 3 Gold Iridescent Oil Spot Handles, Jardiniere Form, 5 1/2 x 7 In.	550.00
Vase, Enameled Flowers & Butterfly, 6 In.	225.00
Vase, Enameled Iris, Green, 6 3/4 In.	192.50
Vase, Fan, Blue, Purple & Yellow Oil Spots, Crimped, 10 In.	135.00
Vase, Fan, Ruffled Rim, Silver-Blue Iridescence, 8 1/4 In.	1100.00
Vase, Flared Rim, Hipped Form, White Glass, Striped In Black, 9 1/2 In.	1100.00
Vase, Flaring Lip, Mottled Green & Yellow, 13 3/4 In.	165.00
Vase, Floral Overlay, Quatrefoil Rim, Blue, 6 1/4 In.	885.00
Vase, Flowering Clematis, Opalescent, Textured Body, Purple Overlay, 12 1/4 In.	885.00
Vase, Frosted Green To Cranberry, Ornate Brass Rim, Signed, 6 1/2 In.	185.00

Vase, Frosted Green, Flared, 5 Side Indentations, Ribbed, 7 In. 185.00
Vase, Gold Iridescent, Denticulated Rim, Applied Thorns, 5 1/2 In. 330.00
Vase, Gold Iridescent, Flared, Signed, 4 1/2 In. 185.00
Vase, Gold Iridescent, Scrolled Silver Overlay Carnation Blossoms, 2 3/4 In. 522.50
Vase, Gold–Blue Iridescent, Oil-Spot Finish, Ruffled Rim, 3 1/8 In. 275.00
Vase, Green Iridescent, Dimpled Base, Pinched Neck, Signed, 6 1/2 In. 145.00
Vase, Green Iridescent, Pinched Base, Ribbed, 9 3/4 In. 295.00
Vase, Green Iridescent, Pulled Feather, Draped, Flared, Signed 350.00
Vase, Jack–In–The–Pulpit Top, Gooseneck, Gold Iridescence, 9 In., Pair 1500.00
Vase, Looped & Trailed Design, Gilt Leaf Forms At Rim, 3 3/4i N. 110.00
Vase, Marbelized Pull-Ups, 4–Lobed Top, 11 In. 900.00
Vase, Maroon Swirled Inclusions, Enameled, Ruffled, Silver Deposits, 7 In. 495.00
Vase, Maroon, 4 Silver Pulled Feather Design, Oval Body, 6 In. 715.00
Vase, Octopus, Gilt Fleur–De–Lis, Air–Trapped Scrolling, Signed, c.1890, 11 1/2 In. 2200.00
Vase, Olive Green Washed With Gold & Pink, 1899, 13 3/4 In. 2200.00
Vase, Papillon, Green, Amber Oil Spots, Green Bulb Shape, Iridescent, 7 In. 550.00
Vase, Pulled Feather Design On Lower Section, Everted Rim, Signed;5 3/4 In. 2100.00
Vase, Pulled Loop, Pink Interior, Austrian Holder, 12 In. .... 1600.00 To 1750.00
Vase, Pulled Oil Spots, Ruffled Rim, Yellow, Cream & Pink, 9 1/2 In. 495.00
Vase, Purple & Blue Oil Spots, 7 In. 395.00
Vase, Purple, Gold Papillon Deep Green, Red, White, 4 Lobes Top, 11 In. 900.00
Vase, Red Glass, Looping Silvery Yellow, Blue, Iridescent, Pinched, c.1900, 7 In. 1045.00
Vase, Red Oil Spot, Platinum Design, Polished Pontil, 10 In. 1400.00
Vase, Ribbed, Iridescent Blues, Greens & Gold, Dimpled Base, 9 3/4 In. 350.00
Vase, Ruby, Loopings, Trailings, Pinched Bulbous, Iridescent, 1900, 7 1/8 In. 1045.00
Vase, Ruffled, Gold Oil Spot, Polished, 8 In. 450.00
Vase, Scalloped Lip, 7 Openings, Conical Body, 8 In. 990.00
Vase, Scrolling Flared Design, Silver Overlaid, Red, Bulbous, 4 1/2 In. 605.00
Vase, Ship's Decanter Type, 10 In. 8250.00
Vase, Silver & Green Pulled Leaves, Sterling Silver Overlay 4250.00
Vase, Spider Web, Iridescent Green, 16 In. 275.00
Vase, Squared, Pinched Walls, Orange, Silver, Amber, Iridescent, c.1900, 6 3/4 In. 1760.00
Vase, Stylized Iris Blossoms, Leaves, Silver Overlay, Signed, c.1900, 7 3/4 In. 2750.00
Vase, Trailing Design, Clear, Amber To Pink Highlights, Iridescent, c.1900, 7 In. 550.00
Vase, Yellow Iridescent, Pulled Feathers, Egg Shape, 1900, 8 1/4 In. 880.00
Vase, Yellow, Purple Iridescent, Wavy Lines, Pewter Mounts, Handles, 6 3/4 In. 1765.00

LONE RANGER, a fictional character, was introduced on the radio in 1932. Over three thousand shows were produced before the series ended in 1954. In 1938, the first Lone Ranger movie was made. Television shows were started in 1949 and are still seen on some stations. The Lone Ranger appears on many products and was even the name of a restaurant chain for several years.

Badge, Club, Brass, Horseshoe Shape, 1930s 20.00
Badge, Deputy 10.00
Badge, Deputy, On Card, 3 Piece 85.00
Badge, Safety Scout 15.00
Bandanna 39.00
Belt, Glow In The Dark, Instructions .... 185.00 To 210.00
Belt, Jail Key, Badge, Bullet Key Chain, Mask, 1950's 145.00
Belt, Keys, Badge, Mask, On Display Card, 1950s 145.00
Blotter, Colorful 15.00
Book, Comic, Cheerios 15.00
Book, Desert Storm, Hard Cover, Whitman, 1957 .... 65.00
Book, Lone Ranger Gold Robbery, 1939 .... 10.00
Book, Outlaw Stronghold, 1939 .... 10.00
Book, Paint, Whitman, Used, 1938, 14 x 15 In. 10.00
Box, First Aid Kit, No Contents 50.00
Bread Card, Silver Cup Bread, 1938, 4 x 6 1/2 In. 9.00
Brush, Decal 60.00
Calendar, Safety Club, Merita Abread, 1953 .... 1200.00
Cap Gun, Die Cast Copper Plated 275.00
Case, Pencil 75.00

Chuck Wagon Lantern, Dietz	40.00
Comic Book, Lone Ranger In Milk For Big Mike, American Dairy Assoc., 1955	9.00
Costume, Never Used, Box	165.00
Costume, With Lariat, Box	400.00
Dart Board, Metal, 1939	75.00
Display, Calendar, Lone Ranger Safety Club, With Blanks, 1948, 16 x 25 In.	1569.00
Doll, Tonto, Gabriel, Box	25.00
Figurine, Old Chalk, 8 In.	75.00
Flashlight Ring, Instructions	110.00
Flashlight, Signal Siren, Usalite, 1950s	71.00
Game, Board, Hi–Yo Silver, Parker Brothers, 1950's	10.00
Game, Hi–Yo Silver	95.00
Game, New Lone Ranger, Board, Guns Are Spinners, Parker Bros., 1956	237.00
Game, Parker Brothers, 1956	225.00
Game, Target, Tin, Marx, Dated 1938	75.00
Guitar, Pictures Tonto	125.00
Gun, Plastic, Mounted On Metal Bands Ring	60.00
Harmonica	25.00
Hi–Yo Silver, Pencil Box, Contents, 1934	55.00
Holster Set, Double, Mask, Silver Bullet, Mattel, 1965	275.00
Knife, Pocket	175.00
Knife, Silver Bullet	65.00
Lunch Box, 1954	285.00
Lunch Box, Legend, Aladdin, Metal, Thermos	31.00
Lunch Pail	26.00
Pen, Writing, 1950s	32.00
Pistol, Click, Jewel Stud Side, Decal, Metal, Marx, c.1936	85.00
Puzzle, 1951	12.00
Puzzle, Glass, No. 7	45.00
Puzzle, Sealed Box, 1978, 2 x 3 Ft.	20.00
Record Player, Wooden	200.00
Record, No. 3, 1951	22.00
Ring, Atom Bomb .... 60.00 To 75.00	
Ring, Six Gun	75.00
Shaker Maker, Box	65.00
Sign, Merita, 1953	550.00
Signal Siren Fight Light, Ranger & Tonto, 1950s, Usalite	77.00
Snow Dome, Lone Ranger Lassoing Cow, Original Decal	120.00
Soap, Figural	75.00
Target, 2–Sided	65.00
Target, Tin, 1938, 27 x 16 In. .... 75.00 To 95.00	
Tent, Box	250.00
Tonto Play Suit, Pla–Master, 1950's	110.00
Toothbrush Holder, 1938	65.00
Toy, Silver, Complete	105.00
Tumbler, 1938	35.00
View–Master, Story Booklet, 3 Reels, 1956	18.00
Viewer & Film, Action Scenes, Pathe, 1939	185.00
Wallet, 1940s	40.00

LONGWY Workshop of Longwy, France, first made ceramic wares in 1798. The workshop is still in business. Most of the ceramic pieces found today are glazed with many colors to resemble cloisonne or other enameled metal. The factory used a variety of marks.

Bowl, Cubist Style Vine, Blue Exterior, Marked, 14 3/4 In.	528.00
Pitcher, Cloisonne Pattern, 5 In.	255.00
Plaque, Parrot, Spread Wings, Blossoms, Blue Ground, Cloisonne, 9 In.	275.00
Urn, Floral & Dragon Design, Brass Snake Handles, Beaded Rim, 16 x 26 In.	2600.00
Vase, Enameled Flowers, Tubular Shape, 9 In.	325.00
Vase, Low Band of Flowers & Fruits, Ribbed To Rim, Marked, 13 3/8 In.	935.00
Vase, Nude Woman On Waterside, Vegetation, Marked, 11 1/2 In.	2650.00
Vase, Orange & Red On Yellow Body, 7 1/4 In.	175.00
Vase, Turquoise, Multicolor Design	325.00

LONHUDA Pottery Company of Steubenville, Ohio, was organized in 1892 by William Long, W. H. Hunter, and Alfred Day. Brown underglaze slip-decorated pottery was made. The firm closed in 1896. The company used many marks; the earliest included the letters *LPCO*.

LONHUDA

Ewer, Blackberries & Yellow Floral, Folded Over Circular Handle, 10 In.	310.00
Mug, Zinnias, 1st Mark, 6 In.	250.00
Napkin Ring, Brown Glaze	250.00
Pitcher, Molded Waves At Bottom, Fish Handle, 10 In.	215.00
Vase, Blueberries, Deep To Pale Green To Pink Shading, 5 In.	230.00
Vase, Peach & White Carnations, Leaves, Claude Leffler, 9 In.	495.00

LOTUS WARE was made by the Knowles, Taylor & Knowles Company of East Liverpool, Ohio, from 1890 to 1900. Lotus Ware, a thin porcelain which resembles Belleek, was sometimes decorated outside the factory. Other types of ceramics that were made by the Knowles, Taylor & Knowles Company are listed under KTK.

Bowl, Gold Design, 4 In.	143.00
Ewer, Deep Green, Handle	1000.00
Ewer, White Reticulated Ribbon	4000.00
Vase, Enameled Floral Panel In Fishnet Pattern, Cylindrical, Shaped Foot	600.00
Vase, Light Green, Tapered, Bulbous, 10 In.	950.00
Vase, Royal Blue, Tapered, Signed Multi-Flora, 8 In.	500.00
Vase, Stick, Deep Green, Bulbous, Pair, 9 In.	1800.00
Vase, White Reticulated Ribbon, Signed Multi-Flora, 8 In.	500.00

LOW art tiles were made by the J. and J. G. Low Art Tile Works of Chelsea, Massachusetts, from 1877 to 1902. A variety of art and other tiles were made. Some of the tiles were made by a process called *natural,* some were hand modeled, and some were made mechanically.

J.&J.G.LOW

Tile, Arab Gentleman With Beard, A. Osborne, 12 1/4 x 9 1/2 In.	1540.00
Tile, Benjamin Franklin, Frame, 1881, 12 x 12 In.	245.00
Tile, Birds In Flight, Dark Blue, 8 In.	75.00
Tile, Praying Monk, Ave Maria, A. Osborne, 17 1/4 x 6 3/4 In.	990.00

LOWESTOFT was a factory in Suffolk, England, which from 1757 to 1802 made many commemorative gift pieces and small, dated, inscribed pieces of soft paste porcelain. Related items may be found in the Chinese Export category.

Plate, Bird On Branch, Floral Scalloped Border, 18th Century, 9 In.	605.00
Platter, Crest of Abraham Elton, Floral Rim, c.1760, 12 x 8 In.	4125.00
Teapot, Floral Spray, Ball Knop, Loop Handle, 1785, 5 7/8 In.	880.00
Vase, Miniature, Teardrop Shape, Floral Spray, C. 1785, 4 1/2 In.	1320.00

LOY-NEL-ART, see McCoy category

LUNCH BOXES and lunch pails have been used to carry lunches to school or work since the nineteenth century. Today, most collectors want either early tobacco advertising boxes or children's lunch boxes made since the 1930s. Boxes listed here include the original Thermos bottle inside the box unless otherwise indicated. Movie, television, and cartoon characters may be found in their own categories.

LUNCH BOX, A-Team, 1985	8.00
Addams Family, 1974	55.00 To 85.00
Americana, 1958	155.00
Astronaut, Space Dome, 1960	135.00 To 145.00
Bach's, Pittsburgh Music Co., Vinyl	225.00
Barbie & Midge, Vinyl, 1964	135.00
Barbie, Vinyl, 1962	50.00
Battlestar Galactica, 1978	19.00
Beany & Cecil, Tan Vinyl, 1963	425.00
Beany & Cecil, Vinyl, 1962	275.00
Bee Gees, Metal, Maurice, 1978	20.00

Bonanza, Brown Rim, 1965	55.00
Boston Bruins, 1973	450.00
Boston Red Sox, Vinyl, Unused	48.00
Brave Eagle, Blue Band, 1957	75.00
Buccaneer, Dome, Label, 1957	345.00
Bullwinkle and Rocky, Vinyl, Yellow, 1962	350.00 To 475.00
Bullwinkle, Vinyl, 1962	145.00
Captain Astro, 1966	125.00
Care Bears, Metal, 1983	8.00
Charlie's Angels, Aladdin, 1978	15.00
Chuck Wagon, Dome, Label, 1958	185.00
Close Encounters of The Third Kind, 1977	30.00
Colonial Bread Van, Plastic, 1984	80.00
Country Club Tobacco	550.00
Cowboy In Africa, 1968	110.00
Daffy Diner, Vinyl, Zipper Closure, 1950s	1650.00
Debutante, 1958	85.00
Disneyland Castle, 1957	70.00
Donnie & Marie Osmond, Vinyl, 1977–1978	125.00
Early West, Ohio Art, 1982	65.00
Emergency, Dome, 1973	95.00
Empire Strikes Back, 1981	10.00 To 21.00
Evel Knievel, 1974	30.00
Fashion Cut Plug Tobacco, Tin, 7 3/4 x 4 1/2 x 5 1/4 In.	165.00
Fireball XL-5, Steel Thermos, King Seeley, 1963	129.00
Flintstones, Yellow, 1964	150.00
Flying Nun, 1968	95.00 To 110.00
Funtastic World, Flintstones, Hanna–Barbera, 1977	68.00
G.I. Joe, 1982	35.00
Get Smart, 1966	60.00 To 120.00
Globetrotter, Dome, 1959	65.00 To 115.00
Gomer Pyle U.S.M.C., 1966	95.00
Green Hornet, 1967	125.00
Green Turtle Cigars	350.00
Grizzly Adams, 1977	40.00 To 75.00
Gunsmoke, Matt Dillon, 1959	55.00 To 75.00
Gunsmoke, Red Rim, 1962	110.00
Happy Days, 1977	30.00
Hee Haw, 1970	60.00
Hogan's Heroes, Dome, 1966	125.00
Hot Wheels, 1969	18.00
How The West Was Won, 1979	27.00
Huckleberry Hound, Aladdin, 1961	35.00
James Bond, 1966	70.00
Jetsons, Dome, 1963	750.00 To 1200.00
Joe Palooka, 2 Handles, 1948	90.00
Julia, 1969	55.00 To 75.00
Junior Miss, 3 Girls & Duck, 1970	80.00
Junior Miss, Basset Hound, 1978	65.00
Kellogg's Cereals, 1969	150.00
Kiss, 1977	65.00
Knight Rider, 1981–1984	10.00 To 29.00
Kung Fu, 1974	39.00 To 75.00
Land of The Giants, 1968	70.00
Lawman, 1961	55.00
Looney Tunes, 1959	125.00
Lorillard's Tobacco	45.00
Lost In Space, Dome, 1967	850.00
Love Brunch Bag, 1972	95.00
Magic of Lassie, 1979	25.00
Man From U. N. C. L. E., 1966	135.00 To 200.00
Miner's, Nickel Over Brass, Salesman's Sample	500.00
Miss America, 1972	150.00

Monkees, 1967 .... 180.00 To 350.00
Mr. Merlin, 1981 .... 18.00
Munsters, 1964 .... 189.00
Muppet Show, 1978 .... 18.00
Muppet, Fozzie Bear, Plastic, 1976 .... 15.00
N. F. L., Football, 1978 .... 18.00 To 35.00
N. F. L., Football, Universal, 1962 .... 225.00
National Airlines, 1968 .... 75.00
New Kids On The Block, Orange, 1990 .... 5.00
Orbit, 1963 .... 185.00
Osmonds, 1973 .... 17.50
Patterson Seal Tobacco 18.00
Peanuts, Yellow, 1980 .... 5.00
Pebbles & Bamm Bamm, 1971 .... 25.00 To 35.00
Pedro Tobacco 70.00
Pete's Dragon, 1978 .... 37.00
Peter Pan Peanut Butter Sandwich, 1940s 125.00
Peter Pan, 1969 .... 17.00
Rat Patrol, 1967 .... 95.00 To 135.00
Red Indian Tobacco, Red 950.00
Return of The Jedi, Plastic Thermos, 1983 .... 20.00
Road Runner, 1970 .... 25.00 To 55.00
Robin Hood, 1956 .... 120.00
Robin Hood, 1974 .... 47.00
Ronald McDonald, Sheriff, 1983 .... 20.00
Rough Rider, 1972 .... 16.00
Saddlebag, 1977 .... 125.00
Satellite, 1958 .... 115.00
School Bus, Dome, 1960s 15.00
Sesame Street, 1980 .... 28.00
Six Million Dollar Man, 1974 .... 22.00
Smurf, 1983 .... 25.00
Snoopy, Dome, 1968 .... 45.00
Snow White & Seven Dwarfs, Swing Handles, Square, 1930s 395.00
Soupy Sales, Vinyl, 1965 .... 700.00
Star Trek, Dome, 1967 .... 350.00
Star Trek, Next Generation, 1980s 15.00
Strawberry Shortcake, 1985 .... 6.00
Tarzan, 1966 .... 88.00
Thundercats, 1985 .... 10.00
Tiger Chewing Tobacco, Red, Tin 65.00
U.S. Mail, Vinyl, 1971 .... 180.00
Union Commander Cut Plug, Tobacco 475.00
Union Leader Cut Plug, Tobacco .... 25.00 To 70.00
Volkswagen, Dome, 1960 .... 375.00
Wagon Train, 1964 .... 125.00
Welcome Back Kotter, 1977 .... 31.00
Wild Wild West, 1969 .... 149.00 To 200.00
Winner Cut Plug, Tobacco 130.00
Woody Woodpecker, 1972 .... 45.00
World of Barbie, Blue, Vinyl, 1971 .... 60.00
Yellow Submarine, Beatles 550.00
Zorro, Aladdin, Tin, 1958 .... 137.50
LUNCH PAIL, Dixie Queen, Tin 275.00
Graniteware, Blue & White, Rectangular 137.00
Joe Palooka, 1948 .... 95.00
Sunbonnet Sue, Tin Lithograph, Germany 220.00

LUNEVILLE, a French faience factory, was established about 1730 by Jacques Chambrette. It is best known for its fine biscuit figures and groups and for large faience dogs and lions. The early pieces were unmarked. The firm was acquired by Keller and Guerin and is still working.

Jar, Apothecary, Finial Cover, 10 1/4 In., Pair 297.00

Jar, Apothecary, Polychromed, Finial Lid, 10 1/4 In., Pair 297.00
Vase, Cameo, Pink Asters, Muller Freres ....*Illus* 2500.00
Vase, Cameo, Roses, Muller Freres, 7 1/4 x 9 In. ....*Illus* 3200.00
Vase, Clover Spray, Iridescent, K & G., 1895, 8 7/8 In. 880.00

LUSTER glaze was meant to resemble copper, silver, or gold. It has been used since the sixteenth century. Most of the luster found today was made during the nineteenth century. The metallic glazes are applied on pottery. The finished color depends on the combination of the clay color and the glaze. Tea Leaf pieces have their own category.

Copper, Pink, House Design, Ribbed, 5 1/2 In. 66.00
Copper, Pitcher, Dancing Figures, 7 3/4 In. 20.00
Copper, Pitcher, Dancing Girls, 6 In. 40.00
Copper, Pitcher, Golden–Ochre Band, Black Transfer, 6 3/4 In. 2915.00
Copper, Pitcher, House & Landscape Banding, 5 In. 88.00
Copper, Pitcher, House Design, Pink Banding, 6 In. 99.00
Copper, Pitcher, House, Orange–Yellow Bands, 19th Century, 7 In. 88.00
Copper, Pitcher, Milk, 2 Blue Bands, 19th Century, 7 1/2 In. 99.00
Copper, Pitcher, Milk, 2 Medallions, Game of Shuttlecock, Canary Band, 7 In. 303.00
Copper, Pitcher, Our Country's Hope, Black Transfer, Golden–Ocher Band 2650.00
Copper, Pitcher, Pink Luster House Band, 5 7/8 In. 94.00
Copper, Pitcher, Polychrome Decorated, Mask, England, c.1810, 6 In. 412.00
Copper, Pitcher, Portrait Medallions, Lafayette, Cornwallis, Military Mcn, 4 In. 467.50
Copper, Pitcher, Sunderland Luster Band, 4 3/4 In. 60.00
Copper, Sugar & Creamer, Sandland Ware, Leaf Design, England 55.00
Copper, Tea Set, Allerton 295.00
Fairyland luster is included in the Wedgwood category
Pink, Creamer, Floral 125.00
Pink, Creamer, House 150.00
Pink, Cup, Handleless, Small, Pair 35.00
Pink, Feeder, Invalid, Embossed Design 95.00
Pink, Figurine, Cats, Seated, Staffordshire, 19th Century, 7 In., Pair 467.00
Pink, Pitcher, House Design, 7 In. 192.00
Pink, Plaque, Thou God Seest Me, 9 x 8 In. 150.00
Pink, Plate, Floral, 7 3/4 In. 150.00
Pink, Platter, House & Flowers, 18 In. 220.00
Pink, Tea Set, Child's, Circus Animals, Marked Leuchtenburg, 12 Piece 375.00
Pink, Tea Set, Child's, Kittens Transfer, 17 Piece 285.00
Pink, Tea Set, Doll's, Germany, Box, 23 Piece 150.00
Pink, Toothpick, 2 Handles, Germany 42.00
Pink, William Banbridge & Stephen Decatur, Copper Band 935.00
Silver, Jug, Floral, Yellow Ground, 4 3/4 In. 65.00
Silver, Pitcher, Cider, Bird & Flower, Resist 185.00
Silver, Pitcher, Mask, Polychrome, England, 1810, 6 1/4 In. 412.00
Silver, Plate, Center Hummingbird & Flowers, Germany, 10 In. 45.00
Silver, Tea Set, 9 Piece 275.00

Luneville, Vase, Cameo,
Pink Asters, Muller Freres

Luneville, Vase, Cameo, Roses,
Muller Freres, 7 1/4 X 9 In.

Silver, Wall Pocket, 9 In. 225.00
Sunderland luster pieces are in the Sunderland category
Tea Leaf luster pieces are listed in the Tea Leaf Ironstone category

LUSTRE ART GLASS Company was founded in Long Island, New York, in 1920 by Conrad Vahlsing and Paul Frank. The company made lampshades and globes that are almost indistinguishable from those made by Quezal. Most of the shades made by the company were unmarked.

Shade, Feather On Gold, Scalloped, 5 In. 125.00
Shade, Green Pulled Feather, 8 In. 185.00

LUSTRES are mantel decorations or pedestal vases with many hanging glass prisms. The name really refers to the prisms, and it is proper to refer to a single glass prism as a lustre. Either spelling, luster or lustre, is correct.

1 Row of Prisms, Floral, Ruby, 14 In., Pair 745.00
Cobalt Blue, Pair 200.00
Engraved Glass Globes, Oval Medallion, France, Crystal, 21 In., Pair 220.00
Pink, Enameled, Clear Cut Prisms, 12 1/4 In., Pair 319.00
Ruby, Cut To Clear, Bohemian Glass, 12 In., Pair 495.00
Ruby, Enameled, Clear Cut Prisms, 14 1/2 In., Pair 255.00

LUTZ glass was made by Nicolas Lutz working at the Boston and Sandwich Glass Company from 1869 to 1888. He made delicate and intricate threaded glass of several colors. Other similar wares made by other makers are now known by the generic name *Lutz.*

Bowl, White, Blue, Gold Stripes, 5 In. 90.00
Cup & Saucer, Pink, Gold, White Stripes, Handle 135.00

MAASTRICHT, Holland, was the city where Petrus Regout established the De Sphinx pottery in 1836. The firm was noted for its transfer–printed earthenware. Many factories in Maastricht are still making ceramics.

Bowl, Oriental Design, Signed Regout, 6 In. 55.00
Plate, Oriental Scene, 8 In. 32.00
Tray, Gaudy Florals, 11 1/2 In. 30.00

MAIZE glass was made by W. L. Libbey & Son Company of Toledo, Ohio, after 1889. The glass resembled an ear of corn. The leaves were usually green, but some pieces were made with blue or red leaves. The kernels of corn were light yellow, white, or light green.

Celery Vase, Clear, Amber, 6 1/2 In. 175.00
Celery Vase, Green Leaves On White 145.00
Finger Bowl, Yellow Leaves, Outlined In Gold 165.00
Pitcher, Green Handles, White 95.00
Saltshaker 125.00
Sugar Shaker 395.00
Water Set, 4 Piece 800.00

MAJOLICA is a general term for any pottery glazed with an opaque tin enamel that conceals the color of the clay body. It has been made since the fourteenth century. Today's collector is most likely to find Victorian majolica. The heavy, colorful ware is rarely marked. Some famous makers include Wedgwood; Minton; Griffen, Smith and Hill (marked *Etruscan*); and Chesapeake Pottery (marked *Avalon* or *Clifton*).

Ashtray, Koala Bears 195.00
Asparagus Server, Cover, Leaves & Berries, KSK, c.1890, 12 In. 467.50
Asparagus Set, Platter & 5 Matching Plates, France, Platter–14 3/4 x 9 In. 775.00
Berry Set, Basketweave Boarder, Ribbons, Wedgwood, c.1879, 6 Piece 825.00
Bowl, Basketweave & Floral, 8 1/4 In. 90.00
Bowl, Birds & Fan, Footed, Wedgwood, 1870s, 10 In., Pair 850.00
Bowl, Cabbage Leaf 75.00
Bowl, Fleur–De–Lis Knob Lid, Mottled Green, Brown, 8 In. 85.00
Bowl, Grape Leaf, Wedgwood, 9 x 12 In. 375.00

Bowl, Hand Painted Flowers, Handles, Oval 80.00
Bowl, Scrolled Form, Mask Handles, Painted Landscape, Lion Paw Feet, 20 In. 1870.00
Bowl, Shell & Seaweed, 8 In. 300.00
Bowl, Shell Shape, 3 Feet, Blue, 10 In. 300.00
Box, Sardine, Attached Tray, Fence & Floral Design, Fish Handle, 8 x 7 In. 880.00
Box, Sardine, Cobalt Blue 880.00
Box, Tobacco, Pipe On Cover 60.00
Breakfast Set, Black Forest, 3 Piece 60.00
Butter Chip, Fan Shape 65.00
Butter Chip, Leaf 18.00
Butter Chip, Leaf, Etruscan 35.00
Butter Chip, Maple Leaf, 2 In. 40.00
Butter Chip, Portrait 70.00
Butter Chip, Shell & Seaweed, Etruscan 195.00
Butter, Cover, Bamboo, Etruscan 250.00
Butter, Cover, Butterfly & Floral, Brown, 4 1/4 x 8 1/4 In. 305.00
Butter, Cover, Butterfly Finial On Cover, 4 x 8 In. 550.00
Butter, Cover, Seaweed 605.00
Butter, Cover, Shell & Seaweed, Fish Finial, Insert, 3 1/2 x 7 3/4 In. 605.00
Butter, Shell Pattern, Yellow & Pink Rim, Blue Ground 140.00
Cache, Pot, Square, 4 In. 295.00
Cake Plate, Ducks & Turtle, Footed 35.00
Cake Stand, Eureka, With Bird, 9 In. 375.00
Cake Stand, Fruit, 9 In. 250.00
Cake Stand, Leaf, Overlapping Green Leaves, Gold Trim, 5 x 10 In. 195.00
Cake Stand, Overlapping Begonia Leaf, 5 1/2 x 9 1/4 In. ....82.50 To 165.00
Candlestick, Amaryllis, 9 In., Pair 375.00
Candlestick, Triton, Figure Holding Coiled Torch, c.1864, 10 1/4 In. 412.50
Card Holder, Pickle 175.00
Centerpiece, Gold Pheasants, Purple & Green, Czechoslovakia 185.00
Charger, Biblical Scene, Italy, 19th Century, 18 In. 440.00
Charger, Raised Figures, Casa Pirota Mark, 14 In. 500.00
Charger, Reptiles & Insects, Grassy Ground, Marked, Palissy, 13 In. 880.00
Charger, Reptiles & Insects, Leafy, Grassy Ground, Marked, Palissy, 15 In. ......*Illus* 825.00
Cheese Bell, Dogwood, White Ground 1210.00
Cheese Bell, George Jones 275.00
Cheese Keeper, Basket & Dogwood, Twig Handle, Turquoise, 12 In. 2750.00
Cigarette & Match Holder, Boot Maker Lighting Cigarette, Striker, 8 1/2 In. 170.00
Cigarette & Match Holder, Kangaroo, Striker, 5 1/4 In. 85.00
Cigarette & Match Holder, Man On Donkey, 7 1/2 In. 165.00

Majolica, Charger, Reptiles & Insects, Leafy,
Grassy Ground, Marked, Palissy, 15 In.

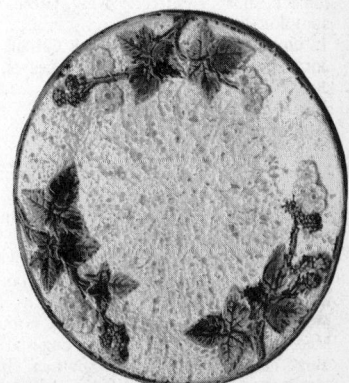

Majolica, Plate, Ivory Ground, Green Leaves,
Clifton Pottery, 8 In.

Cigarette & Match Holder, Pig, Striker, 5 1/2 In.	170.00
Clock, Dresser, Scrolls & Gold Embossing, Pink Flowers, 5 3/4 x 4 1/2 In.	265.00
Clock, Mantel, Cobalt Blue, Yellow Case, 19th Century, 13 x 13 In.	440.00
Coffeepot, Cabbage Form, Snake Handle & Spout, Palissy, 9 3/4 In.	1760.00
Coffeepot, Floral Design, White Fence Ground, 8 In.	65.00
Coffeepot, Shell & Seaweed, Etruscan	950.00
Compote, Daisy, Cobalt Blue, Etruscan	135.00
Creamer, American Indian, 3 In.	45.00
Creamer, Cabbage, Etruscan, Small	325.00
Creamer, Corn, Etruscan	200.00
Creamer, Foliage On Basketweave, Morley & Co., Wellsville, Ohio, 3 x 4 1/4 In.	350.00
Creamer, Shell & Seaweed, Etruscan	250.00
Creamer, Stork In Water, Fan, 5 In.	115.00
Crock, Salt, Corn, 5 3/4 x 5 3/4 In.	330.00
Cup & Saucer, Blackberry, Yellow Basket Weave	110.00
Cup & Saucer, Rose & Rope	275.00
Cup & Saucer, Shell & Seaweed, Etruscan	210.00
Cuspidor, Berry & Leaf	175.00
Cuspidor, Shell & Seaweed, 6 1/4 In.	1100.00
Dish, Banana Leaf	65.00
Dish, Begonia Leaf, Etruscan, 9 In.	145.00
Dish, Cheese, Dome Cover, Brown Cow On Top, Blue, Green & Yellow	2000.00
Dish, Condiment, Leaf, Twig Handle, Multicolor, 9 x 8 In.	187.50
Dish, Pickle, Begonia Leaf, Etruscan, 9 In.	75.00
Dish, Strawberry, Center Well, 7 In.	100.00
Ewer, Classical Scene, Dragon Handle, Cobalt Blue, 6 1/4 In.	65.00
Ewer, Stand, Putto Astride Dolphin, Cupid & Companion, Minton, 1871, 21 5/8 In.	3100.00
Figurine, Black Boy, Seated On Bale, Huge Watermelon, 2 Baskets	245.00
Figurine, Blackamoor, Italy, 39 1/2 In.	2200.00
Figurine, Bull, Cream Body, Chocolate Markings, Wedgwood, 1876, 17 1/8 In.	2475.00
Figurine, Cat, On Roof, Glass Eyes, Clay Body, Ward Off Evil Spirits, 24 In.	550.00
Figurine, Foo Dog, Seated, Italian, 24 In.	1320.00
Figurine, Moore, Long Tunic, Holding Baskets. 41 In.	665.00
Figurine, Two Men In Vineyard, Minton, 17 x 20 In.	385.00
Figurine, Woman, Standing, Hollow Tree, Footed, 12 In.	165.00
Garden Seat, Green Fern & Leaf, Yellow Floral, Pierced Ovals, c.1870, 20 1/4 In.	1430.00
Humidor & Match Holder, Grass Hut, Striker, 6 3/4 In.	77.00
Humidor, Arab, White Headdress	52.50
Humidor, Mother Goose	195.00
Humidor, Pipe Finial, 5 1/2 In.	55.00
Ink Stand, Yellow Enameled Floral, Brown, 4 Gold Paws, 10 1/2 x 5 In.	265.00
Inkwell, Lion's Head Hinged Lid, Green, Gesetzlich Geschutzt	137.00
Jam Jar, Parrot	85.00
Jardiniere, Picket Fence, Fern & Cattail, Blue Bands, Ring Handle, 10 In.	385.00
Jardiniere, White Flowers, Green Leaves, Blue Ground	110.00
Jug, Fish, England	225.00
Jug, Wine, Reptiles, Insects & Leaves, Vine Handles, Palissy, 11 In.	275.00
Match Holder, Black Boy	250.00
Match Holder, Black Man	125.00
Match Holder, Double, Black Boy, Playing Concertina, 5 x 5 In.	125.00
Match Holder, Indian Man With Turban, Riding Elephant, 7 3/4 In.	460.00
Match Holder, Man Singing, Striker, 5 In.	137.50
Match Holder, Oriental Girl	75.00
Match Holder, Shoe, Comical Man, Striker	115.00
Match Holder, Striker, Seated Black Man	82.50
Mug, Acorn, Pink Interior, Etruscan	22.00
Mug, Green & Basket Weave, White Ground	65.00
Mug, Sunflower, White Ground, English	260.00
Mug, Yellow Trimmed Top & Bottom, Green Vine, Pink Blossoms	27.50
Mustache Cup & Saucer, Seaweed Pattern, Etruscan	300.00
Mustache Cup, Water Lily	400.00
Oyster Dish, 4 Tiers, Revolving	4950.00
Oyster Plate, 9 In.	75.00

Oyster Plate, Brown, Green & Yellow, Minton, 10 In. 425.00
Oyster Plate, Turquoise Shell, Shell Feet, 8 Piece 2500.00
Pitcher, Applied Flowers, Cherub Handle, Deep Blue, 1870s, 14 In. 450.00
Pitcher, Baseketweave & Strawberry, Cobalt 375.00
Pitcher, Basketweave, 3 Leaf, Turquoise 170.00
Pitcher, Bird & Pond Lily, 9 In. 165.00
Pitcher, Bird's Nest, Creamware, Pewter Top 77.00
Pitcher, Blackberry, Gray Leaves, Red Flowers, Wedgwood, 6 In. 165.00
Pitcher, Butterfly Lip, 4 1/2 In. 49.50
Pitcher, Corn, 7 In. 45.00
Pitcher, Duck, Beak Forms Spout, Shades of Blue, 10 In. 65.00
Pitcher, Duck, Figural, 8 In. 140.00
Pitcher, Elephant, Running, Palm Tree, Lavender Interior, 7 1/2 In. 465.00
Pitcher, Fish, 8 In. 235.00
Pitcher, Floral, 6 In. 65.00
Pitcher, Floral, Bark Handle, 7 In. 135.00
Pitcher, Floral, Cat Handle, 8 3/4 In. 1100.00
Pitcher, Floral, Etruscan, 4 1/2 In. 65.00
Pitcher, Flower & Leaf, 8 In. 135.00
Pitcher, Flying Crane, 9 1/2 In. 220.00
Pitcher, Heron & Flying Fish, 9 In. 495.00
Pitcher, Heron, Flying Fish, Bamboo Base, Blue Handle, Turquoise, 9 In. 495.00
Pitcher, Lincoln, Washington Centennial, Wedgwood, c.1876, 8 1/4 In. 935.00
Pitcher, Marine Life, Polychrome Glazes, c.1875, 9 1/8 In. 1540.00
Pitcher, Milk, Fish & Shell, Dark Blue Ground, 7 1/2 In. 220.00
Pitcher, Owl, Bamboo-Like Handle, c.1880, 10 1/2 In. 605.00
Pitcher, Parrot, Figural, 8 In. 140.00
Pitcher, Picket Fence & Berry, 6 1/2 In. 135.00
Pitcher, Pig Chef 425.00
Pitcher, Pink & Yellow Flowers In Relief, 6 In. 120.00
Pitcher, Pink Flower, Green Leaves, Bark, Brown, 6 In. 95.00
Pitcher, Pink Flowers, Bark, Etruscan, Hawthorne, 5 In. 120.00
Pitcher, Pug Dog, 5 In. 495.00
Pitcher, Relief Molded Sporting Scenes, Baseball, Soccer, 8 In. 880.00
Pitcher, Robin, Multicolored, 7 1/2 In. 135.00
Pitcher, Rose Decoration, Green Stripe, 5 1/2 In. 80.00
Pitcher, Sheaves of Wheat 95.00
Pitcher, Stork In Rushes, 6 1/4 In. 55.00
Pitcher, Stork In Rushes, Bamboo Handle, 7 1/2 In. 100.00
Pitcher, Tree Bark & Leaf Design, America, 8 1/2 In. 145.00
Pitcher, Turquoise & Basketweave, 3 Leaf, 8 In. 170.00
Pitcher, Wild Rose, Blue Ground, Etruscan, 7 1/2 In. 185.00
Pitcher, Wild Roses, 6 In. 115.00
Planter, Busts of Winged Women, Humanized Rams, 11 1/2 x 13 1/2 In. 495.00
Planter, Satyr Handles, Jenny Lind Type Faces, 4 Paw Feet, 10 x 8 In. 350.00
Plaque, Baby Jesus Center, Fruit Border 35.00
Plaque, Triumph of Madonna & Child, 11 x 7 3/4 In. 440.00
Plate, 3 Fans Whirling, Vines, Pebbled Blue Ground, America, 10 In. 75.00
Plate, Allover Green Glaze, Molded Leaves, Wardle, c.1900, 8 3/4 In., 6 Piece 220.00
Plate, Begonia Leaf Shape, 9 In. 140.00
Plate, Berry & Leaf, 10 1/4 In. 65.00
Plate, Bird & Branch, Eureka Pottery, 8 1/4 In. 88.00
Plate, Blackberry, 8 In. 100.00
Plate, Blue Fans, 8 In. 150.00
Plate, Blue Flowers, Cream Ground, Handles, Germany, 8 In. 95.00
Plate, Boy On Bike, 8 In. 175.00
Plate, Cabbage Leaf, 8 1/2 In. 25.00
Plate, Cauliflower, Etruscan, 9 1/4 In. 88.00
Plate, Elf, Green Center, Pink Border, 11 1/2 In. 55.00
Plate, Fish, Grassy Ground, Marked, 10 1/2 In. 525.00
Plate, Geranium Leaf, Wedgwood, 8 In. 110.00
Plate, Grape Leaf, 9 In. 135.00
Plate, Insect & Fan Shape, 9 1/4 In. 140.00

Plate, Ivory Ground, Green Leaves, Clifton Pottery, 8 In. ....*Illus* 50.00
Plate, Leaf Design, 8 In. 35.00
Plate, Leaf, Blackberry, Wild Rose, 8 In. 75.00
Plate, Leaf, Blue Border, 9 In. 45.00
Plate, Loaf, Turquoise & Green Chestnut, George Jones 325.00
Plate, Maple Leaf, Green & Pink Leaves, Yellow, 10 1/4 In. 85.00
Plate, Red Rose Center, Olive, Turquoise, 8 3/4 In. 80.00
Plate, Reptiles & Insects, Grassy Ground, Marked, Palissy, 11 1/4 In. 745.00
Plate, Reptiles & Insects, Grassy Ground, Palissy, 7 3/4 In. 385.00
Plate, Reptiles & Insects, Multicolored Ground, Palissy, 9 1/4 In. 65.00
Plate, Rose Leaf Tobacco, 3 Dimensional Wild Rose, Chew Rose Leaf, 9 In. 237.00
Plate, Yellow Flower, Green Leaves, Salmon, 9 3/4 In. 85.00
Platter, Begonia Leaf, Marked, 11 1/2 x 8 3/4 In. .... 195.00'
Platter, Deep, Fish Design, 6 Raised Feet, 15 x 8 In. 250.00
Platter, Fox With Goose In Mouth, Ivy Design, 12 1/2 x 13 In. 275.00
Platter, Reptiles & Crustaceans, Leafy Ground, Palissy, 15 In. ....*Illus* 1000.00
Platter, Reptiles & Crustaceans, Leafy Ground, Palissy, 16 In. ....*Illus* 1100.00
Platter, Stag & Dog, 11 In. 135.00
Platter, Thomas Turner, 14 In. 300.00
Platter, Toby, Yellow Center, Pink Border, 11 In. 93.50
Sauceboat, Underplate, Conch Shell 110.00
Smoking Set, Monk Figure, 3 Compartments, 1 With Cover, Striker, 8 In. 285.00
Spoon Warmer, Nautilus Shell Form, Copeland, 5 In. 357.50
Spoon Warmer, Shell Form, Coral Branched Feet, Minton, c.1875, 4 3/4 In. 775.00
Sugar & Creamer, Corn 120.00
Sugar, Cover, Bird & Fan 95.00
Syrup, Bamboo 380.00
Syrup, Bamboo, Etruscan, 8 In. 385.00
Syrup, Bird & Fan, 6 1/2 In. ....85.00 To 95.00
Syrup, Sunflower, Blue, Etruscan 750.00
Syrup, Sunflower, Etruscan 500.00
Syrup, Sunflower, Pink Ground 550.00
Syrup, Sunflower, White, Blue Trim, Etruscan 550.00
Syrup, Wild Rose, Handle, 7 In. 295.00
Tazza, Figural, Molded Top, Pedestal, 3 Ibis, 9 x 10 1/2 In. 275.00
Tea Set, Child's, Robin Red Breast, 3 Piece 300.00
Tea Set, Fence & Floral Design, Cobalt Blue, 3 Piece 1045.00
Teapot, Apple 825.00
Teapot, Basket & Dogwood, George Jones, 6 1/4 In. 742.00
Teapot, Bird Finial, Yellow Apple, Insect & Twig Handle 770.00
Teapot, Cauliflower 355.00
Teapot, Cauliflower, Etruscan 357.00
Teapot, Chinaman Climbing Aboard A Coconut 2570.00
Teapot, Deep Pinks & Greens, Etruscan Shell, 1880 .... 700.00
Teapot, Figural, Dog 125.00
Teapot, Fish Swallowing Fish 745.00

◆ ◆

Mayonnaise can be used to remove old masking tape, stickers, or labels from glass and china.

◆ ◆

Majolica, Platter, Reptiles & Crustaceans,
Leafy Ground, Palissy, 15 In.
Majolica, Platter, Reptiles & Crustaceans,
Leafy Ground, Palissy, 16 In.

Teapot, Flying Crane	220.00
Teapot, Shell & Seaweed, Etruscan	375.00
Tile, Bird & Dragon, Fly In Wire Holder, Square, 6 In.	45.00
Tray, 3 Tiles, Floral, Oak Frame, Signed, 8 x 22 In.	110.00
Tray, Bird & Fan, 13 3/4 In.	495.00
Tray, Bird & Fan, Wedgwood, 1865, 13 3/4 In.	545.00
Tray, Bird, Insect & Floral Design, 16 x 11 In.	110.00
Tray, Figural, Fish, 10 x 7 1/2 In.	110.00
Umbrella Holder, Full–Figure Turkey, Marked, 30 In.	2700.00
Umbrella Stand, Colored Design, 23 In.	450.00
Umbrella Stand, Fruit Design, 24 In.	275.00
Vase, Figural, Grecian Boy, Pan Flute, Grecian Maid, Water Jug, 13 In., Pair	335.00
Vase, Figural, Iris, Unfurled Petals Form Handles, 12 3/4 In.	125.00
Vase, Flowers & Scrolls In Relief, Handles, Block & Co., c.1890, 12 1/2 In.	250.00
Vase, Flowers & Scrolls, Cobalt & Light Blue, Germany, c.1890, 12 1/2 In.	295.00
Vase, Girl Holding Basket, Boy Holding Box, Germany, 11 In., Pair	375.00
Vase, Happy Hooligan, 6 In.	75.00
Vase, Heron & Flower, J. Holdcroft, 14 3/4 In.	1550.00
Vase, Iris, Art Nouveau, 6 In.	98.00
Vase, Man In Period Dress, Throwing Kiss, White Flowers, 18 In.	395.00
Vase, Stork, Flower, J. Holdcroft, 14 1/2 In.	1320.00
Vase, Yellow & Green Decorations, Footed, 15 In.	415.00
Water Set, Bark Pattern, Green Leaves, Golden Acorns, c.1910, 5 Piece	700.00

MAPS of all types have been collected for centuries. The earliest known printed maps were made in 1478. The first printed street map showed London in 1559. The first road maps for use by drivers of automobiles were made in 1901. Collectors buy maps that were pages of old books, as well as the multifolded road maps popular in this century.

Alabama, Hand Colored, Colton, Matted, 1855, 12 x 16 In.	72.50
Alaska Highway, Western Canada, Color, 1943, 21 x 32 In.	4.00
Alaska Territory, Govt. Printing Office, Washington, Folded, 1904, 2 x 4 Ft.	60.00
Alaska, Colorado, U.S. Geological Report, 1898	85.00
Alaska, Rand McNally, 1930, Folded, 18 x 25 In.	30.00
America & The New World, Woodcut, Munster, 14 1/2 x 19 1/2 In.	4500.00
American Republic, Indian Territory, Mitchell's, Roll–Up, 1844, 41 x 49 In.	137.00
Amerique Septeutrional Avex Les Routs, John Mitchell	4125.00
Atlas, 1864	84.00
Atlas, Bristol County, Massachusetts, F. W. Beers Publisher, 1871	270.00
Atlas, Howard Johnson's Restaurants, Motor Lodges, Canada, Mexico, 1956, 112 Pgs.	20.00
Atlas, Rand McNally, Havoline Oil, 34 Pages, World War I	15.00
Atlas, Rock Island County Farm	55.00
Atlas, State of Massachusetts, Walling & Grey, 1871	200.00
Atlas, World, 1944	20.00
Auto & Cycling Routes of New England States, 1905	55.00
Book, World Atlas, Dated 1892	85.00
Boston Market To Burlington Meeting House, Frame, 1816, 53 1/4 x 14 In.	535.00
Cape Cod, By W. P. A., Hand Colored, 1935, 49 x 43 In.	55.00
Cape Cod, Coulton Waugh, Frame, 15 1/2 x 19 In.	22.00
Civil War, United States, Union & Confederate Divisions & Departments, 1865	40.00
Delaware Bay & River, Engraved, Paris, 1777, 20 x 29 In.	450.00
Florida, Hand Colored, Colton, Matted, 1855, 12 x 16 In.	72.50
Geological Survey of York Co., Pa., Color, 40 x 52 In.	17.50
Globe, Celestial & Terrestrial, Newton, Rosewood Plinth, Walnut Standard, Pair	8250.00
Globe, Celestial & Terrestrial, Table, Loring, Dated 1833, Pair	5500.00
Globe, Celestial, Compass Stretcher, Tripod Mahogany Stand, 12 In.	2000.00
Globe, Mars	2180.00
Globe, Moon, Lunar Landing Areas, 1963	45.00
Globe, Terrestrial, Collapsible Umbrella Type	695.00
Globe, Terrestrial, Empire Style	175.00
Globe, Terrestrial, W. & A. K. Johnston, 1893, 18 In.	3500.00
Globe, Terrestrial, With Orrery, Boston, 1850, 9 In. ....*Illus*	1815.00

Map, Globe, Terrestrial, With Orrery, Boston, 1850, 9 In.

Globe, World, Light–Up, 1950s	65.00
Hartfordshire, Hand Colored, Frame, 22 x 26 1/2 In.	82.50
Holland, Belgium & Low Lands, Blue, 17th Century, 17 x 21 In.	987.50
Illinois, Highway 66	20.00
India, Aaron Arrowsmith, Dissected, Hand Tinted, Linen, Square, 8 Ft.	375.00
Island of Luzon, 1899, 24 x 32 In.	18.00
Los Angeles, Calif., Shell, License Plates, 1933, 14 Pages, 4 x 9 In.	25.00
Mexico, California & Texas, Before Statehood, Tullis, 13 x 10 In.	888.00
Minnesota, Railroad Commissioner's, 1917	85.00
Narragansett Bay, Steamship Lines, Blue, 28 x 21 In.	20.00
North & South America, California As An Island, Mallet, 1681, 6 x 4 In.	687.50
North East United States, Richmond Bros. Advertising, 1928	10.00
Northeast Scotland, 1928	10.00
Nuremberg, Homann, Palestine Divided Among The Tribes of Israel, 1707	1870.00
Ohio Counties, Framed, 1840	50.00
Oklahoma, Midwest Map Co., Aurora, Mo., 1930s, 16 x 21 In.	10.00
Oregon Territory, Hand Colored, 1828	18.00
Oregon, Highway, AAA, 1920s	18.00
Pacific Northwest, AAA, 1920s	18.00
Pennsylvania, Sinclair Oil Co., 1957	4.00
Pictorial Atlas of World, Hammond, 1910	30.00
Plain Between San Joaquin & Kings Rivers, Calif., Railroad, 1853, 11 x 14 In.	287.50
Railroad, New York, Jersey City, Hoboken, 1901–1902, Roll–Up, 42 x 48 In.	137.00
Roxbury, Maine, Surveyed By S. Thorla In 1807, Dated 1838, 22 x 29 In.	165.00
Shires of England, Stone Lithograph, 1830, 8 x 10 In.	37.50
Territory of Hawaii, Inset of Midway Island, 1900, 3 1/4 x 3 3/4 In.	45.00
Thomson's General Atlas, Eastern & Western Hemispheres, 1815, 21 x 22 In.	335.00
Topographical St. John & King's County, Canada, Walling, 1862	265.00
U.S. Coastal Survey of San Francisco & Harbor, 1853, 28 x 31 In.	685.00
War Planes, Air Planes, World War II	12.00
World Atlas, Mobil Oil, Mailer, 1942	40.00
Wyoming Highway, Color Illustrated, 1953, 18 x 28 In.	5.00

MARBLE CARVINGS, such as large or small figurines, groups of people or animals, and architectural decorations, have been a special art form since the time of the ancient Greeks. Reproductions, especially of large Victorian groups, are being made of a mixture using marble dust. These are very difficult to detect and collectors should be careful. Other carvings are listed under Alabaster.

Allegorical Figure, Marble Pedestal, P. Barzanti, 6 Ft. 9 1/4 In.	6600.00
Bench, Garden, Arms, Glens Falls, N.Y.	3250.00
Bokhisattva, Seated In Lalitasana, Ruyi Scepter, 39 In.	665.00
Bookends, Eagle, c.1900	325.00
Bust, Child, Curly Hair, 1820s, 17 In.	4125.00
Bust, Louis XIV, Lace Collar, Fur Mantle, Crosses, 27 In.	4400.00
Bust, Man, Christopher Prosperi, 1800, 38 In.	7700.00

◆◆◆◆◆◆◆◆◆◆◆◆◆◆◆◆◆◆◆◆◆◆

A good way to remove rings and stains from a white marble top is to mix TSP (trisodiumphosphate, found in paint stores), water, and scouring powder. Rub on the spots. Too much rubbing may remove some of the polish, so be careful.

◆◆◆◆◆◆◆◆◆◆◆◆◆◆◆◆◆◆◆◆◆◆

Marble Carving, Obelisk, Gray, 21 1/2 In.

Bust, President Woodrow Wilson, Signed, 24 In.	660.00
Bust, Roman Patrician, Marble Socle, White, 18th Century, 22 In.	2200.00
Bust, Woman, F. Saul, c.1900, 23 In.	1430.00
Bust, Young Woman, Purete, c.1900, 19 In.	1760.00
Cherub, 4 Ft., 4 Piece	6000.00
Cherub, Seated, Writing On Tablet, Canova, 19th Century, 16 In.	770.00
Cleopatra, Seated, Gaston Leroux, 30 x 14 In.	6700.00
Cross, Salvador Dali, Metal Rays, Glass Pendants, 13 3/4 In.	825.00
General Napoleon Bonaparte, Tricorn, Arms Crossed, 39 In.	825.00
Jardiniere, Continuous Scroll Design, 3 Cherubs Support, 21 In.	2200.00
Monk, Off–White, 8 x 11 In.	150.00
Mythological Nude, Sitting, Henri Chapu, 32 In.	3850.00
Obelisk, Gray, 21 1/2 In. ....*Illus*	350.00
Obelisk, Louis XVI, Hung With Chains, 1780s, 17 1/2 In., Pair	4675.00
Obelisk, Swan Finial, Turtle Supports, Bronze Mounted, 25 In.	1550.00
Paperweight, St. Peter's Church, Rome, Micro–Mosaic	500.00
Partially Draped Female, Looking To The Side	1375.00
Pedestal, Louis XVI, Musical Instruments, Wooden Base, 3 Ft. 5 In., Pair	3850.00
Plaque, Basilica, Micro–Mosaic, 6 1/4 x 4 1/4 In.	1350.00
Standing Woman, Holding Lyre, Prof. Bastiani, 33 In.	885.00
Tile, Incised, Filled Red Grout, 1880s, 11 1/2 x 12 In.	165.00
Urn, Gadrooned Body, Entwined Serpent Handles, 21 x 26 In., Pair	8900.00
Urn, Louis XVI Style, Neoclassical Frieze, Marble Plinth, 11 1/2 In., Pair.	1760.00
Urn, Pedestal	1250.00
Urn, Stepped Dome Top, Square Plinth, 11 In., Pair	3575.00
Vase, Cover, Curved Leaf Handles, Ormolu Mounted, White, 17 In., Pair	9350.00
Woman, Art Deco, Alabaster Base, 25 In.	2000.00

MARBLES has been a popular game since the days of the ancient Romans. American children were able to buy marbles by the mid–eighteenth century. Dutch glazed clay marbles were least expensive. Glazed pottery marbles, attributed to the Bennington potteries in Vermont, were of a better quality. Marbles made of pink marble were also available by the 1830s. Glass marbles seem to have been made later. By 1880, Samuel C. Dyke of South Akron, Ohio, was making clay marbles and The National Onyx Marble Company was making marbles of onyx. The Navarre Glass Marble Company of Navarre, Ohio, and M. B. Mishler of Ravenna, Ohio, made the glass marbles. Ohio remained the center of the marble industry, and the Akron–made Akro Agate brand became nationally known. Sulphides are glass marbles with frosted white figures in the center.

Aventurine	8.00
Banded Opaque, Red Bands, Creamy Orange Base, 11/16 In.	450.00
Bennington, Boy Stick Figure, Blue & Green, 1 1/2 In.	45.00
Brick, M. F. Christensen & Son Co., 5/8 In.	70.00
Cat's–Eye, Blue, 1 1/4 In., 500 Piece	95.00
Clambroth, Pine Lines, White Opaque, 11/16 In.	140.00
Clambroth, Turquoise, Green, Pink Lines, White Base, 5/8 In.	225.00
Clambroth, White With Red Lines, Evenly Spaced, 9/16 In.	125.00
Comic, Kayo, Black Band, White, 11/16 In.	120.00
Coreless, Amber, White Lines, 11/16 In.	45.00
Corkscrew, Multicolor, 1 In.	12.00
Corkscrew, Popeye, 5/8 In.	45.00
Dispersed Cloud, 21/32 In.	155.00
Divided Core, Red, White & Blue Bands, Yellow Lines, 3/4 In.	40.00
Divided Ribbon, Turquoise, Red, White, Yellow Lines Around, 7/8 In.	75.00
End of Day, Cloud Mica, Clear, 3/4 In.	125.00
End of Day, Joseph's Coat, 1 In.	210.00
End of Day, Joseph's Coat, 5/8 In., Pair	170.00
End of Day, Onionskin, 2 In.	170.00
End of Day, Onionskin, Mica, 1 3/8 In.	250.00
Green, White Net Core, Outer Bands, 13/16 In.	40.00
Guinea, Christensen Agate Co., 5/8 In.	380.00
Indian Swirl, Colorful, 11/16 In.	150.00
Indian Swirl, Gray Lines, Black Opaque, Red, 11 1/6 In.	95.00
Joseph Swirl, White Lines, Black Opaque Base, 9/16 In.	125.00
Latticinio Swirl, 1 In.	35.00
Latticinio Swirl, White, 17/32 In.	375.00
Latticinio, Core Swirl, White, 1 1/2 In.	90.00
Latticinio, Swirl, Blue, Yellow Core, Ribbons, Orange, White, Green, Red, 7/8 In.	125.00
Limeade, Semi–Transparent, 1/2 In.	35.00
Lobed Core, White, Blue, Green & Pink Bands, Yellow Lines, 1 In.	45.00
Lutz, Banded Semi–Opaque, 5/8 In., Pair	575.00
Lutz, Black Glass, Opaque	175.00
Lutz, Black Opaque, Red Bands, 7/8 In.	150.00
Lutz, Cobalt Blue Transparent, White Bands, 11/16 In.	350.00
Lutz, Dark Violet Core, 5/8 In.	475.00
Lutz, Green Glass Ribbon, 29/32 In.	500.00
Lutz, Green Opaque, Blue Bands, 11/16 In.	200.00
Lutz, Green, 5/8 In.	450.00
Lutz, Indian Swirl, Gold Flakes, Yellow & Blue–Green, 13/16 In.	845.00
Lutz, Indian, 3/4 In., Pair	1710.00
Lutz, Indian, 5/8 In.	425.00
Lutz, Onionskin, Green, White, Bands, 1/2 In.	125.00
Lutz, Ribbon, Mustard Ribbon, 3/4 In.	175.00
Lutz, Sapphire, 3/4 In.	215.00
Lutz, Violet Lines, Clear, 11/16 In.	85.00
Mica, Blue, 7/8 In.	45.00
Mica, Green, 15/16 In.	85.00
Mineral, Snowflake Obsidian, 2 In.	240.00
Moon Mullins, Petier Glass Co.	70.00
Onionskin, 1 7/8 In.	325.00
Onionskin, Blue, 2 In.	400.00
Onionskin, Left Twist, Turquoise, Red, Yellow, Cobalt Blue, White Base, 1 In.	120.00
Onionskin, Mica, Pink & White Lines, 5/8 In.	75.00
Onionskin, Paneled, 1 3/4 In.	355.00
Onionskin, Pink, Yellow, Blue & White Lines, 3/4 In.	65.00
Onionskin, Swirl, 3/4 In.	45.00
Opaque, Black, 1/2 In.	25.00
Peppermint Swirl, 3 Red Lines, Large Blue Bands Each Side, 9/16 In.	145.00
Peppermint Swirl, Blue & Pine Lines, White Opaque, 11 1/6 In.	145.00
Slag, Akro Agate, 7/8 In., 6 Piece	85.00
Slag, Christensen Agate Co., Butterscotch Yellow, 7/8 In.	45.00
Slag, Electric Orange, Christensen Agate Co., 5/8 In.	125.00

Slag, Flame 5.00
Slag, Florescent Blue–Green Translucent 25.00
Sulphide, 2 Fish, Swimming, 1 5/16 In. 450.00
Sulphide, Bear, 1 3/4 In. 135.00
Sulphide, Bear, Standing, 1 1/2 In. .... 125.00 To 160.00
Sulphide, Bear, Walking, 1 15/16 In. 120.00
Sulphide, Bison, 1 1/2 In. 20.00
Sulphide, Bust of Columbus, 2 In. 785.00
Sulphide, Camel, 1 1/2 In. 180.00
Sulphide, Dog, Barking, 1 5/8 In. 150.00
Sulphide, Dog, RCA, 1 1/2 In. 110.00
Sulphide, Dog, Running, 1 5/9 In. 165.00
Sulphide, Dog, Sitting, 1 15/16 In. 185.00
Sulphide, Dog, Springing, 1 5/9 In. 160.00
Sulphide, Donkey, 1 1/2 In. 165.00
Sulphide, Eagle, Spread Wing, 1 15/16 In. 350.00
Sulphide, Fish, 1 3/4 In. 250.00
Sulphide, Fish, Swirl 180.00
Sulphide, Fox, 1 1/2 In. 180.00
Sulphide, Girl, Seated, Washing Hair, 1 1/2 In. 300.00
Sulphide, Horse 375.00
Sulphide, Kneeling Figure Praying, 1 3/4 In. 600.00
Sulphide, Lamb, Standing, 1 1/2 In. 130.00
Sulphide, Lamp, Reclining, 1 3/8 In. 115.00
Sulphide, Lion, 1 13/16 In. 185.00
Sulphide, Lion, Standing, 2 In. 270.00
Sulphide, Mark Twain, Seated Man, 1 1/2 In. 400.00
Sulphide, Monkey, Standing On All Fours 140.00
Sulphide, Number 9, 1 5/8 In. 500.00
Sulphide, Owl, Sitting, 1 1/2 In. 180.00
Sulphide, Papoose, 2 In. 350.00
Sulphide, Peasant Boy, Seated, 1 7/8 In. 320.00
Sulphide, Pig, 2 3/16 In. 225.00
Sulphide, Rabbit, Running, 1 13/16 In. 180.00
Sulphide, Rabbit, Sitting, 1 3/4 In. 180.00
Sulphide, Ram, Standing, 1 13/16 In. 180.00
Sulphide, Ram, Standing, 1 3/4 In. 200.00
Sulphide, Rooster, 1 7/8 In. 180.00
Sulphide, Rooster, Aqua, Seed Bubbles, Stand, 1880s 145.00
Sulphide, Sheep, 1 1/2 In. 110.00
Sulphide, Sheep, Detailed, Matrix Bubbles Resemble Snow, 1 3/4 In. .. 150.00
Sulphide, Sheep, Grazing, 2 1/4 In. 250.00
Sulphide, Squirrel, Eating Nut, 1 13/16 In. 180.00
Sulphide, Squirrel, Eating Nut, 2 In. 140.00
Sulphide, Woman In Dress, Standing, 1 1/2 In. 500.00
Sulphide, Woman, Standing With Dog & Basket, 1 3/4 In. 1100.00
Swirl, Black Solid Core, Ribbons In Yellow & Red, White & Purple, 5/8 In. 45.00
Swirl, Contemporary, Jelly–Like Threads & Ribbons, Cranberry, 1 3/4 In. 20.00
Swirl, Divided Core Surrounded By White Ribbons, 2 In. 115.00
Swirl, Divided Core, 2 In. 145.00
Swirl, Indian, Opaque Green Base, 3/4 In. 390.00
Swirl, Ribbon Core, 1 3/4 In. 260.00
Swirl, Solid Core, Triple Layer, 2 In. 150.00
Swirl, Solid Multicolored Core, 1 1/4 In. 95.00
Swirl, Solid White Core, 1 1/2 In. 95.00
Swirl, Solid Yellow Core, 1 1/2 In. 95.00
Uranium Swirl 5.00
Vaseline Opalescent, Uranium 10.00
White Lined Net Core, Blue & Green Bands, 5/8 In. 25.00
Yellow Net Core, Red Lines, Green Bands, 3/4 In. 35.00

MARBLEHEAD Pottery was founded in 1905 by Dr. J. Hall as a rehabilitative program for the patients of a Marblehead, Massachusetts, sanitarium. Two years later it was separated from the sanitarium and it continued operations until 1936. Many of the pieces were decorated with marine motifs.

Bowl, Feathered Matte Ocher Glaze, Marked, 3 1/4 x 5 In.	275.00
Bowl, Flower Frog, Dark Blue Glaze, Paper Label, 1 3/4 x 3 1/4 In.	220.00
Bowl, Pink Semi–Glossy, 4 In.	120.00
Bowl, Purple Matte Glaze, 2 x 4 In.	170.00 To 195.00
Candlestick, Medium Blue, 4 1/4 In., Pair	250.00
Chamberstick, Matte Yellow, Marked, Label	205.00
Cup, Cider, Dark Green Band, Dark Blue, 4 In.	185.00
Pitcher, Matte Green Body, Black Handle, Inscribed Mark, 8 1/4 In.	247.50
Plaque, Copse of Trees, Oak Frame, Marked, 9 1/4 x 6 1/8 In.	2400.00
Tile, Sailing Ship, Blue & White	375.00
Vase, 4 Gray Trees, Black Outlined, Marked, c.1908, 7 In.	3000.00
Vase, 5 Conventionalized Tree Clusters, Green, Brown, Gray, 9 3/4 In.	5500.00
Vase, Blue Exterior, Sky–Blue Interior, Bottle Shape, D. L., 5 3/4 x 3 1/4 In.	220.00
Vase, Blue Oval, 5 Black Outlined Stylized Trees, Green Leaves, 7 In.	1100.00
Vase, Brown Obloid, 3 In.	260.00
Vase, Bud, Green, 3 1/4 In.	210.00
Vase, Dark Blue Glaze, Closed–In Top, Flared, 7 x 4 In.	445.00
Vase, Fan Shape, Ruffled, Paper Label, Marked, 6 x 7 In.	475.00
Vase, Flared, Blue, Pale Blue Interior, 3 1/2 In.	300.00
Vase, Gray Glaze, Blue Interior, Cylindrical, 7 1/2 x 3 1/4 In.	247.00
Vase, Gray Matte, Blue & Gray Floral, 7 In.	900.00
Vase, Gray, 5 In.	265.00
Vase, Green Leaves, Red Berries, Green Top Rim, Marked, 5 1/ 2 In.	665.00
Vase, Matte Blue Glaze, Bulbous, 5 1/2 x 4 1/4 In.	192.50
Vase, Matte Dark Blue Speckled Glaze, Cylindrical, 9 1/2 x 5 1/4 In.	615.00
Vase, Matte Gray Glaze, Blue Interior, Squatty, 4 x 5 1/2 In.	165.00
Vase, Matte Green, Gray Speckles, Swollen Form, 5 x 3 In.	225.00
Vase, Matte Lavender Glaze, Bulbous, Squatty, 5 x 4 In.	358.00
Vase, Speckled Dark Blue Glaze, 7 Z 4 In.	357.50
Vase, Speckled Matte Mustard Glaze, 3 1/2 x 2 1/2 In.	335.00
Vase, Stylized Flowers, Cylindrical, 9 In.	1700.00
Vase, Tapering Base, Deep Blue Matte Glaze, Marked, 6 3/4 In.	135.00
Vase, Yellow, Turquoise Interior, Leaf Design, 6 In.	500.00

MARTIN BROTHERS of Middlesex, England, made martinware, a salt–glazed stoneware, between 1873 and 1915. Many figural jugs and vases were made by the three brothers. Of special interest are the fanciful birds, usually made with removable heads.

Martin Bro?
London

Bird, Stoneware, Wooden Base	6250.00
Pitcher, Arabesque Line Drawing, Snake Handle, Signed, 4 3/4 In.	275.00
Pitcher, Old Man of The Mountain, Foliage, 9 In.	3500.00
Vase, Bud, Expressive Faces, Blue With Beige Ground, 6 3/4 x 3 1/4 In.	775.00
Vase, Green Bushes, Blue Vertical Ridges, Gray Ground, Handles, 8 x 6 In.	775.00
Vase, Grotesque Fish, 7 x 5 1/4 In.	2200.00

MARY GREGORY is the name used for a type of glass that is easily identified. White figures were painted on clear or colored glass as the decoration. The figures chosen were usually children at play. The first glass known as Mary Gregory was made about 1870. Similar glass is made even today. The traditional story has been that the glass was made at the Sandwich Glass works in Boston by a woman named Mary Gregory. Recent research suggests that it is possible that none was made at Sandwich. In general, all–white figures were used in the United States, tinted faces were probably used in Bohemia, France, Italy, Germany, Switzerland, and England. Children standing, not playing, were pictured after the 1950s.

Bottle, Emerald Green, Young Man, Net In Hand, Foliage, 7 In.	150.00

Box, Boy, Carrying Floral Spray, Golden Amber, Hinged, 3 1/2 x 3 3/4 In. 275.00
Box, Hinged Lid, Young Child, Sitting On Fence, Brass Feet, Amber, 4 1/2 In. 395.00
Creamer, Boy & Butterfly, 5 In. 110.00
Cruet, Boy In Knickers, Smelling Flower, Sapphire Blue, 8 In. 385.00
Cup, Girl With Butterfly, Clear Handle, Blue, 3 1/4 In. 75.00
Ewer, Little Girl In Garden, Holding Roses, Gold Trim, Cobalt Blue, 6 In. 195.00
Mug, Girl Carrying Floral Spray, Handle, Lime Green, 4 In. 55.00
Patch Box, Boy With Hoop, Sandwich, Emerald Green, 2 1/4 In. 350.00
Pendant, Black Onyx, White Girl, Filigree Mounting, Silver Chain, 2 In. 245.00
Perfume Bottle, Girl Standing In Foliage, Gold Trim, 5 3/4 In. 175.00
Perfume Bottle, Lay Down, 5 3/4 In. 170.00
Pitcher, 3 Dancing Figures, Green, Applied Handle 80.00
Stein, Beer, Figure of Boy, Blue, Pewter Lid 195.00
Syrup, White Enameled Girl 175.00
Tumbler, Barrel Shape, Young Girl, White Enameled, 4 In. 55.00
Tumbler, Girl Carrying Basket, Amber, 5 In. 55.00
Vase, Bottle Shape, Boy On 1, Girl On 1, Cranberry, 9 In., Pair 375.00
Vase, Boy Holding Cane, Sapphire Blue, 4 In. 95.00
Vase, Boy Holding Flowers, Amber, 4 1/4 In. 85.00
Vase, Boy With Large Flower, Black Amethyst, 9 1/4 In. 160.00
Vase, Bud, Raspberry, White Interior, Applied Clear Base, 4 1/2 In. 135.00
Vase, Girl Picking Flowers, Cranberry, 4 In. 110.00
Vase, Girl Ringing Bell, Clear Shell Trim On Sides, Green, 11 1/2 In. ...., 225.00
Vase, Girl Standing In Foliage, Feeding Swallows, Blue–Gray, 7 1/2 In. 195.00
Vase, Girl With Flowers, Fluted, Blue, 5 In. 85.00
Vase, Girl With Rake, Cranberry, 6 1/2 In. 275.00
Vase, Young Girl With Balloon, Scalloped Top, Amber, 10 1/4 In. 225.00
Vase, Young Girl, Flowers, Deep Amethyst, Stork Design Stand, 4 1/2 In. 750.00
Vase, Young Lass, Sprays, Storks Joined By Leaves, Amethyst, 7 3/4 In. 750.00
Vase, Young Man, Standing In Foliage, Mauve, 7 In. 195.00

MASONIC, see Fraternal

MASSIER, a French art pottery, was made by brothers Jerome, Delphin, and Clement Massier in Vallauris and Golfe–Juan, France, in the late nineteenth and early twentieth centuries. It has an iridescent metallic luster glaze that resembles the Weller Sicard pottery glaze. Most pieces are marked *J. Massier.*

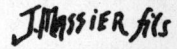

Vase, Hand Painted Autumn Wooded Scene, Narbon D'Honre, 7 In., Pair 550.00
Vase, Iridescent, Leaves, 6 In. 400.00

MATCH HOLDERS were made to hold the large wooden matches that were used in the nineteenth and twentieth centuries for a variety of purposes. The kitchen stove and the fireplace or furnace had to be lit regularly. One type of match holder was made to hang on the wall, another was designed to be kept on a tabletop. Of special interest today are match holders that have advertisements as part of the design.

2 Heads, 1 Black & 1 White 45.00
Adriance Farm Machinery 400.00
Amish Man, Cast Iron, 6 In. 15.00
Bacchus, Cast Iron .... 45.00 To 65.00
Bisque, Victorian Style, 5 In. 28.00
Black Boy, Watermelon Between Legs, Chalkware 55.00
Black Cat & Urn, Striker 15.00
Boy, Holding Cup At Well, Bisque, Victorian 75.00
Bulldog Head, Cast Iron, 2 7/8 In. 65.00
Burntwood, Dutch Boy & Girl, Marked Willow Springs, Missouri, Wall Mount 6.00
Bust of Indian Warrior, Pottery, Hanging, 6 x 4 In. 65.00
Carmel Slag, Challinor, Taylor & Co., 1886, 4 In. 45.00
Ceresota Flour, Tin .... 175.00 To 300.00
Colonial Shoe, On Stand, Iron 10.00
Coon Chicken Inn, Metal .... 150.00 To 250.00
Double, Scalloped, Tin, Pocket 20.00

Dr Pepper, Green, Clock Marked 10–2–4 ....85.00 To 125.00
Dr. Shoop's Health Coffee .... 145.00 To 150.00
Dr. Shoop's Laxets 90.00
Eveready, Hammered Tin 18.00
German Shepherd & Urn, Striker 15.00
Henry Bruner Co. 30.00
Juicy Fruit 145.00
Kate Greenaway Children, Umbrella, Bisque 50.00
L. A. Pressed Brick, Build With Brick, Green Glaze, 3 x 4 x 3 In. 99.00
Leather, St. Louis Exposition, 1904, Wall 45.00
Mammy, Laundry Basket, Chalkware 60.00
Man, With Pipe, Pearl Luster, Bisque, France, 1900 .... 55.00
Match Plucker, Bird Grabs Match, Metal 115.00
McCormick Deering 100.00
Michigan Stove Co., Cast Iron 25.00
Milwaukee Binders 150.00
Moxie, Tin 350.00
Nu–Grape, Tin 80.00
Old Car, Blue Glass, Running Board Is Striker, 1800s .... 125.00 To 135.00
Old Hickory Wagons, Tin 500.00
Old Judson Whiskey, Wall .... 175.00 To 185.00
Parrot On Perch, Silver, Tuft 95.00
Pewter, Battleship Maine, Pewter 35.00
Pig, Brass 95.00
R. B. Grover, Emerson Shoes, Sterling Silver 95.00
Reclining Indian, Chalkware, Ohio Match, 24 In. 145.00
Scotty, Wooden 15.00
Sharples, Tin 175.00
Tole, Black Paint, Red & Yellow Design, 7 3/8 In. 60.00
Woman's Shoe, Green, Depression Glass, Daisy & Diamond Pattern 20.00
Woman, Victorian, Bisque, 6 In. 45.00

MATCH SAFES were designed to be carried in the pocket. Early matches
were made with phosphorus and could ignite unexpectedly. The matches
were safely stored in the tightly closed container. Match safes were made
in sterling silver, plated silver, or other metals. The English call these *vesta
boxes.*

Anheuser–Busch St. Louis, Brass Color 90.00
Anheuser–Busch, Silver Plate 100.00
Bergner & Ensel Brewing Co., Celluloid Cover Tin, 1 1/2 x 2 3/4 In. 66.00
Book Shape, Gutta–Percha, France 75.00
Cigar Cutter On Bottom, Girl, Drink In Hand, L. Kilsheimer & Co. 30.00
Embossed Nouveau Design, Secret Compartment, Sterling Silver 110.00
Enterprise Brewing Co., San Francisco, 1 1/2 x 2 3/4 In. 127.00
Fifth Mass. Regiment, Copper, Hinged, Says Hold Your Ground, 1880s 65.00
Fleur–De–Lis, Silver Plate 16.00
Frisco Line, Telephone Shape, Logo 345.00
Gatley Clothing, Nymphs, Celluloid 80.00
Guilloche, Sterling Silver, Enameled, Bun Footed 100.00
Holder Cream Separators, Mother & Child, With Cow Scene, 2 x 7 In. 110.00
Indianapolis Brewing Co., Winged Girl On Wheel Logo, 1 1/2 x 2 3/4 In. 38.00
John Hauck Brewing Co., King Logo, Globe, 1 1/2 x 2 3/4 In. 143.00
Marbles, Hunters, Pocket, 1900 .... 39.00
Monon Route, Alligator 235.00
Overall Engraved Floral, Sterling Silver 65.00
Pair of Pants, Figural, 1886 .... 100.00
Phoenix Brewery, Trademark Both Sides, Nickel Plated Brass, 2 3/4 In. 72.00
Schlitz Beer, Leather Wrap 95.00
Spaniel Finial, Casket Form, Superior Foundry, Cleveland, Ohio 85.00
Sterling Silver, Sliding, 1935, 2 x 1 1/2 In. 55.00
Walkrite Shoes, Rubber 60.00
Woman On Bicycle, Hand Painted Bisque, 19th Century, 6 In. 148.50

MATSU–NO–KE was a type of applied decoration for glass patented by Frederick Carder in 1922. There is clear evidence that pieces were made before that date at the Steuben glassworks. Stevens & Williams of England also made an applied decoration by the same name.

Bowl, Ruffled, Flowers, Yellow Ovary, Marked, 3 1/4 x 4 In. 425.00

MCCOY pottery was made in Roseville, Ohio. The J. W. McCoy Pottery was founded in 1899. It became the Brush McCoy Pottery Company in 1911. The name changed to the Brush Pottery in 1925. The word *Brush* was usually included in the mark on their pieces. The Nelson McCoy Sanitary and Stoneware Company, a different firm, was founded in Roseville, Ohio, in 1910. The firm made art pottery after 1926. In 1933 it became the Nelson McCoy Pottery. Pieces marked *McCoy* were made by the Nelson McCoy Company. Cookie jars were made from the 1930s until December 1990 when the McCoy factory closed. In 1990 the McCoy mark was put back on pottery by a firm unrelated to the original company.

Coffeepot, El Rancho	60.00 To 95.00
Cookie Jar, American Eagle	30.00
Cookie Jar, Apollo, Spaceship	525.00
Cookie Jar, Apple Red	40.00
Cookie Jar, Apple, Yellow	35.00
Cookie Jar, Bananas	125.00
Cookie Jar, Barn	400.00
Cookie Jar, Barnum's Animal Cracker, Nabisco	265.00
Cookie Jar, Bear & Beehive, 1983	45.00
Cookie Jar, Betsy Baker	135.00 To 150.00
Cookie Jar, Black, With Rose, Concave	22.00
Cookie Jar, Bobby The Baker, 1974–1979	50.00
Cookie Jar, Boy On Baseball	225.00
Cookie Jar, Boy On Football	195.00
Cookie Jar, Bugs Bunny	98.00
Cookie Jar, Burlap Bag	25.00
Cookie Jar, Cat On Coal Bucket	225.00
Cookie Jar, Chairman of The Board	625.00 To 900.00
Cookie Jar, Chef's Head	80.00 To 120.00
Cookie Jar, Chipmunk	85.00 To 98.00
Cookie Jar, Churn, 3 Bands	175.00 To 200.00
Cookie Jar, Circus Horse	115.00 To 175.00
Cookie Jar, Clown In Barrel, Blue	95.00
Cookie Jar, Coalby Cat	255.00 To 425.00
Cookie Jar, Coca–Cola Can	45.00 To 50.00
Cookie Jar, Coffee Mug, 1963	40.00 To 45.00
Cookie Jar, Colonial Fireplace	90.00 To 110.00
Cookie Jar, Cookie Bank, Cabin	78.00 To 195.00
Cookie Jar, Cookie Bell, Red Orange Lettering, 1963–1966	60.00
Cookie Jar, Cookie Jug	25.00
Cookie Jar, Cookie Log, Squirrel Finial, 1965	30.00
Cookie Jar, Covered Wagon, 1960–1961	90.00
Cookie Jar, Cylinder, Yellow, Poppies, Black Lid	75.00
Cookie Jar, Dalmatians, In Rocking Chair	250.00 To 425.00
Cookie Jar, Davy Crockett	600.00
Cookie Jar, Doghouse, Bluebird Finial	350.00
Cookie Jar, Duck, 1964	80.00
Cookie Jar, Dutch Boy	30.00
Cookie Jar, Engine, Black	160.00
Cookie Jar, Friendship 7, 1962	100.00 To 165.00
Cookie Jar, Fruit In Basket, 1961	75.00
Cookie Jar, Grandma	85.00 To 150.00
Cookie Jar, Grandma, Gold Glasses	95.00
Cookie Jar, Hamm's Bear	185.00 To 350.00
Cookie Jar, Happy Face	22.00 To 30.00
Cookie Jar, Hen On Nest	50.00 To 110.00

Cookie Jar, Hidden Valley	20.00
Cookie Jar, Hobnail Pattern, Heart Shape	175.00
Cookie Jar, Honey Bear, Yellow	195.00
Cookie Jar, Indian Head	210.00 To 475.00
Cookie Jar, Jack–O'–Lantern	475.00 To 950.00
Cookie Jar, Jewel Box	105.00
Cookie Jar, Kangaroo, Blue	180.00 To 225.00
Cookie Jar, Keebler Tree House	48.00 To 60.00
Cookie Jar, Kettle, Black, 1961	35.00
Cookie Jar, Kissing Penguins	45.00 To 50.00
Cookie Jar, Lemon	45.00
Cookie Jar, Leprechaun, Red	2300.00 To 3000.00
Cookie Jar, Little Boy Blue	65.00
Cookie Jar, Little Red Riding Hood, Closed Basket, 1956	325.00
Cookie Jar, Lunch Box, 1978	30.00 To 75.00
Cookie Jar, Mac Dog	30.00 To 89.00
Cookie Jar, Mammy	100.00 To 675.00
Cookie Jar, Mammy With Cauliflowers	1000.00 To 1200.00
Cookie Jar, Milk Can, Fruit Decal, Large, 1975	35.00
Cookie Jar, Milk Can, Liberty Bell Front, 1972	35.00
Cookie Jar, Monkey On Stump, 1970	50.00
Cookie Jar, Mr. & Mrs. Owl	85.00 To 115.00
Cookie Jar, Nabisco	110.00
Cookie Jar, Orange	100.00
Cookie Jar, Owl	30.00 To 60.00
Cookie Jar, Penguin	230.00
Cookie Jar, Picnic Basket	50.00
Cookie Jar, Pineapple, 1955	35.00
Cookie Jar, Pink Pig, Bank	95.00
Cookie Jar, Popeye	85.00
Cookie Jar, Pot Belly Stove	10.00
Cookie Jar, Puppy With Sign	95.00
Cookie Jar, Raggedy Ann	65.00 To 125.00
Cookie Jar, Rooster, White With Black Spry	115.00 To 125.00
Cookie Jar, Snoopy On Doghouse	195.00 To 250.00
Cookie Jar, Squirrel, With Acorn	95.00
Cookie Jar, Stagecoach	1000.00
Cookie Jar, Tea Kettle, Bronze, Movable Bail	45.00 To 55.00
Cookie Jar, Teapot, Bronze	18.00
Cookie Jar, Teepee, Slant Top	200.00 To 450.00
Cookie Jar, Teepee, Straight Top	235.00 To 395.00
Cookie Jar, Thinking Puppy	18.00 To 28.00
Cookie Jar, Time For Cookies, Mouse On Clock	40.00 To 50.00
Cookie Jar, Tomato, 1964	75.00
Cookie Jar, Touring Car	75.00 To 120.00
Cookie Jar, Turkey	145.00
Cookie Jar, Upside–Down Panda Bear	50.00
Cookie Jar, W. C. Fields	125.00 To 200.00
Cookie Jar, Wedding Jar, 1961	45.00
Cookie Jar, Winking Pig	550.00 To 650.00
Cookie Jar, Wishing Well	18.00
Cookie Jar, Wishing Well, 1961	40.00
Cookie Jar, Woodsy Owl	85.00 To 200.00
Cookie Jar, World Globe	265.00 To 350.00
Cookie Jar, Wren House	115.00
Cookie Jar, Yosemite Sam	120.00
Jar, Oil, Blue, 16 In.	45.00
Jardiniere, Florastone, 10 In.	95.00
Jardiniere, Green Leaves, Blue Grapes Emblem, 7 x 7 1/2 In.	60.00
Lamp, Boots, Brown, Shade	63.00
Lamp, Loy–Nel, Yellow & Orange Tulip, Brown Glaze, 10 In.	132.00
Match Holder, Blue & White	37.50
Mug, Olympia, Knights	85.00

Pitcher, Buccaneer	55.00
Planter, Gondola	26.00
Planter, Leaf Design, Rectangular, Flat	10.00
Planter, Locomotive	38.00
Planter, Shrimp Boat, Orange & Brown	17.50
Planter, Squirrel	15.00
Planter, Steam Boat, Black	42.00
Planter, Uncle Sam	37.00
Sugar & Creamer, Elsie & Elmer	95.00 To 125.00
Tea Set, High Luster, 3 Piece	125.00
Tea Set, Pine Cone, 3 Piece	40.00
Teapot, Evergreen Cover	20.00
Tureen, Cover, Covered Wagon, El Rancho	130.00
Tureen, El Rancho	45.00
Vase, Loy–Nel, Standard Glaze, Twist, 14 1/2 In.	66.00
Vase, Tulip, Yellow	8.00
Wall Pocket, 3 Brown Owls, Yellow Ground	25.00
Water Cooler, El Rancho	150.00 To 225.00

MCKEE is a name associated with various glass enterprises in the United States since 1836, including J. & F. McKee (1850), Bryce, McKee & Co. (1850 to 1854), McKee and Brothers (1865), and National Glass Co. (1899). In 1903, the McKee Glass Company was formed in Jeannette, Pennsylvania. It became McKee Division of the Thatcher Glass Co. in 1951 and was bought out by the Jeannette Corporation in 1961. Pressed glass, kitchenwares, and tablewares were produced. Jeannette Corporation closed in the early 1980s. Additional pieces may be included in the Custard Glass category.

PRESCUT

Bowl, Jade, 11 1/2 In.	10.00
Bowl, Seville, 4 1/4 In.	8.00
Butter, Seville, 1/4 Lb.	50.00
Canister, Coffee, Delphite	195.00
Canister, Cover, Custard Glass, Round, 10 Oz.	25.00
Cheese Dish, Cover, Laurel	65.00
Clock, Tabour, Day, Cobalt Blue	55.00
Dish, Refrigerator, Cover, Custard Glass, 4 x 4 In.	25.00
Dish, Refrigerator, Seville, 4 x 5 In.	10.00
Goblet, Rock Crystal, Emerald Green	20.00
Jug, Cream, Steadman's Stalagmite Pattern, 1860s	60.00
Lamp, Pink Satin Glass, Danse DeLumiere, 1927	850.00
Measuring Cup, Seville, Footed, Handle, 4 Cup	55.00
Parfait, Rock Crystal	17.00
Percolator, Multicolored Concentric Bands, 1944	48.00 To 65.00
Pitcher, Measuring, Custard Glass, 2 Cup	25.00
Punch Set, Aztec, Stand, 12 Cups	120.00
Reamer, Delphite Blue	200.00
Reamer, Jade	15.00
Salt & Pepper, Seville	12.00
Saltshaker, Kitchen, Black Glass, 4 1/2 In.	8.00
Sherbet, Garland, Crystal, Footed	10.00
Toothpick, Colonial	20.00
Water Bottle, Light Green	22.00
Wine, Rock Crystal, 3 7/8 In.	15.00

MECHANICAL BANKS are listed in the Bank category.

MEDICAL office furniture, operating tools, microscopes, thermometers, and other paraphernalia used by doctors are included in this category. Medicine bottles are listed in the Bottle category. There are related collectibles listed under Dental.

Apothecary, Faceted Stopper, 22 x 12 In.	193.00
Bedpan, Man's, Brown Ceramic	45.00
Bleeder, 3 Blades, Folding, Rogers Cutler To Her Majesty, Cow Hide Scales	75.00

Bleeder, Brass, 1 Blade 200.00
Bleeder, Brass, Jean Metle 98.00
Bleeder, Civil War 75.00
Bleeder, Madeira, Spring Form, Brass 295.00
Blood–Cell Calculator, Dr. Marbel, 16 Readout Digits, Pat. 1922 .... 495.00
Book, Complete Dose, Standard Medicine, Lloyd Bros., 1921 .... 16.00
Book, Hopper's Medical Dictionary, 1825 .... 25.00
Bottle, Apothecary, Amber, Enameled, Stopper 45.00
Bottle, Apothecary, Brown, Large 12.00
Cabinet, Apothecary, Dr. Frost Remedies, Drawers, Shelves, 1880s, 19 x 13 In. 1210.00
Cabinet, Apothecary, Empire, Mahogany, 1 Long Over 15 Small Drawers, 20 In. 1045.00
Cabinet, Apothecary, Oak, 18 Drawers, Wooden Pulls, 22 x 15 x 10 1/2 In. 245.00
Cabinet, Dr. Frost's, Tin Front Lists Cures, 19 x 13 1/2 In. 605.00
Cabinet, Oak, Window In Door, Drawers 1500.00
Card, Trade, American Physician & Surgeon, Wines & Liquors, 2 1/2 x 4 In. 10.00
Chest, Apothecary, 150 Drawers, Oriental 1700.00
Chest, Apothecary, Pine, Poplar, 30 Dovetailed Drawers, 36 x 38 x 40 In. 4180.00
Crutch, Child's 35.00
Drill Set, Bone, Brass, Black Case, Collin & Cie, Paris, 8 x 4 1/2 In. 950.00
Drill Set, Skull, Surgeon's, Wooden Box 100.00
Eyecup, Applied Green, Stemmed, Blown, 2 7/8 In. 120.00
Eyecup, Blue, W. T. Co. 18.00
Eyecup, Clear, Bulbous Fish Bowl, Marked Q6, 2 1/4 In. 17.50
Eyecup, Clear, Squatty, Japan 10.00
Eyecup, Cobalt Blue, On Pedestal .... 18.00 To 20.00
Eyecup, Cobalt Blue, Paneled 20.00
Eyecup, Deep Cobalt Blue, Pedestal, Blown, Wide Foot, 2 1/3 In. 125.00
Eyecup, John Bull, Clear .... 20.00 To 25.00
Eyecup, John Bull, Cobalt Blue 30.00
Eyecup, John Bull, Green, 1918 ....75.00 To 110.00
Eyecup, Milk Glass, Paneled Pedestal, 2 1/4 In. 16.00
Eyecup, Paneled Pedestal, Marked 12, 2 1/4 In. 16.00
Eyecup, Pedestal, Wyeth, Cobalt Blue 10.00
Globe, Apothecary, Leaded Glass, Multicolored, Hanging, 11 x 16 In. 1430.00
Hammer, Percussion, Ebony, Metal Ball, Rubber Heads, France, 7 1/2 In. 395.00
Hot Water Bottle, Child's, This Little Piggy Went To Market 30.00
Hot Water Bottle, Child's, This Little Piggy Went To Market, Rubber 85.00
Hot Water Bottle, Embossed Nursery Rhymes, Pictures 18.00
Hot Water Bottle, Sore Throat, Box 20.00
Jar, Apothecary, Maple, Block Stenciled, 19th Century, 6 In. 78.00
Jar, B & B Corrosive Sublimate Gauge Moist, Sealed Contents, Label, 1910 .... 25.00
Jar, Pharmacy, Arabic Gum, 1790 .... 195.00
Kit, First Aid, Bell Telephone 20.00
Kit, First Aid, Mobil Flying Red Horse 35.00
Kit, Last Rites, Candelabra, Crucifix, Holy Water Font, Oak Box, Homan Silver Co. 200.00
Kit, Quack, Energez, Case 40.00
Kit, Surgeon's, H. G. Kern, Lift–Out Tray, 15 Tools, Civil War 1700.00
Kit, Surgeon's, Tightening Screw For Tourniquet, Tiemann & Co., Tools 1045.00
Kit, Ultraviolet Ray Treatment 35.00
Lancet, Ebony Handle, Millef Bros., U.S.A., Civil War 65.00
Machine, Quack, 1875 .... 100.00
Model, Eye, Black Enameled Brass, Early 20th Century, 3 1/4 In. 185.00
Mortar & Pestle, Brass, Schering Drug, Commemorative, Coricidin, 1975 ...... 55.00
Mortar & Pestle, Burl, 6 3/4 In. 385.00
Mortar & Pestle, Stoneware 10.00
Mortar & Pestle, Turned Wood, 19th Century, 6 1/2 In. 77.00
Mortar & Pestle, Wooden, c.1870 .... 225.00
Ophthalmoscope, Brass Tube, Hawksley, London, Late 19th Century, 11 To 14 In. 1950.00
Ophthalmoscope, Brass, Ivory Handle, Liebreich, 1870, 3 3/4 In. 195.00
Ophthalmoscope, Collapsible, Black Brass, Folding Handle, France, 1900, 5 In. 280.00
Otoscope, Brunton, Plated Brass, Maison L. Mathieu, Late 19th Century, 4 1/2 In. 275.00
Pill Counter, Cobalt Blue, Emerson Drug, Baltimore, 4 1/2 In. 45.00
Renulife, Violet Ray Machine, Fitted Case, Literature, May, 22, 1922 .... 320.00

Saw, Surgeon's, Civil War 125.00
Scalpel, Double, Folding, Bone Handle, 18th Century 135.00
Scarificator, Brass, Steel Blade, Snowden, 19th Century, Case, 1 3/4 In. 250.00
Sign, Apothecary, Wood, Shape of Mortar & Pestle, 23 x 30 In. 88.00
Sign, Pharmacy, Mortar & Pestle, Convex Glass, Reverse Painted RX, 36 In. 330.00
Sprayer, Nasal, Cobalt Blue 45.00
Suppository Maker, Wooden 45.00
Surgical Set, Ivory Handles, Case, Tiemann, 1865, Complete 8500.00
Syringe, Baby's, Goodrich, Box, 1940s 10.00
Urology Set, Charriere, France, Late 19th Century, 18 3/4-In. Case 3950.00
Vaporizer, Milk Glass, 1920s, Box 25.00
Wheelchair, Reclining, Cane Back & Seat, Oak, 1880s 895.00

MEERSCHAUM pipes and other pieces of carved meerschaum, a soft mineral, date from the nineteenth century to the present.

Figurine, Bearded, Gruff Man, Hanging Sash On Back of Hat 50.00
Pipe, Bearded Sultan 40.00
Pipe, Cottage & Horse, 1810 .... 125.00
Pipe, Duck's Head, Frog In Mouth, Glass Eyes, 2 1/4 x 4 1/2 In. 295.00
Pipe, Lion, Carved, Case 375.00
Pipe, Lion, Case, 1 1/2 x 4 3/4 In. 155.00
Pipe, Man's Head, Glass Cigarette, Case, 1 1/2 x 4 In. 260.00
Pipe, Seaman, Carved, Amber Stem, 10 In. 125.00

MEISSEN is a town in Germany where porcelain has been made since 1710. Any china made in the town can be called Meissen, although the famous Meissen factory made the finest porcelains of the area. The crossed swords mark of the great Meissen factory has been copied by many other firms in Germany and other parts of the world. Pieces of Meissen dinnerware in the Onion pattern are listed in their own category in this book.

Basket, Bird In Flight Interior, Oriental Plants, Rope Rim, c.1740, 7 In. 1650.00
Basket, White, Molded, Wickerwork Handles, Oval, c.1740, 7 In. 550.00
Beaker, Garden Scene, Oriental Figures, 2 Handles, 1725, 3 1/8 In. 995.00
Bottle, Gelber Lowe Pattern, Mallet Shaped Body, Painted, c.1740, 2 3/8 In. 1200.00
Bowl, Figural, Reclining Man & Woman, Rococo Costumes, 12 1/2 In., Pair 1650.00
Bowl, Footed, Looped Handles, White, Oval, c.1775, 12 7/8 In. 440.00
Bowl, Kakiemon Pattern, Center Crest, 8 1/2 In. 6275.00
Bowl, Multicolored Flowers, Gold Enameled Leaf Design, 11 In. .... 495.00 To 595.00
Bowl, Painted Garden Flowers, Center Rose, Marked, 8 3/4 In. 55.00
Bowl, Quatrefoil, Turquoise Ground, Gilt Edge, c.1740, Marked, 8 In. 5500.00
Candlestick, Cherub-Form Support, Flower Strewn Base, 9 In., Pair 445.00
Charger, Blue & White, Incised Flower, Crossed Swords, 13 In. 375.00
Charger, Gilt Foliage, White, Crossed Swords, 1700s, 11 1/2 In. 175.00
Charger, Hand Painted Flowers, Blue & White, 11 3/4 In., Pair 895.00
Charger, Incised Flowers, Blue & White, Marked, 13 In. 375.00
Charger, Raised Foliage, Gilt Trim, Crossed Swords, 1700s, 11 1/4 In. 300.00
Coffeepot, Celadon Ground, Cover, c.1735, 7 3/4 In. 2750.00
Coffeepot, Pear Shape, White, Raised Grapevine Pattern, Cover, C. 1745, 9 In. 665.00
Cup & Saucer, Figures & River Landscape, Turquoise, c.1740 .... 1925.00
Cup & Saucer, Portrait Medallion, Paw Feet, Scroll Handle, 19th Century, 2 Sets ... 660.00
Cup & Saucer, Suitors In Garden, c.1750 .... 465.00
Dish, Fliegender Hund Pattern, Blue & White, Stand, 2 1/4 In. 1650.00
Dish, Floral, Gilt, Reticulated Rim, Dresden, 8 x 10 3/4 In. 135.00
Dish, Floral, Gilt, Reticulated Rim, Oval, Dresden, 6 x 9 In. 50.00
Dish, Flying Birds, Shell Shape, 1735, 9 3/16 In. 2475.00
Dish, Leaf Shaped, Eichlornchen Pattern, c.1740, 12 1/4 In. 7150.00
Dish, Pickle, Leaf Shaped, White, Stem Handle, C. 1725, 4 In. 770.00
Feeder, Invalid 250.00
Figurine, Allegorical, Discord, Draped Maiden With Parrot, 10 In. 1210.00
Figurine, Athena, 19th Century, 14 1/2 In. 1550.00
Figurine, Bagpiper Walking, Wearing Hat & Cape, c.1745, 9 1/8 In. 3575.00
Figurine, Boy, Seated & Barefoot, Eating Grapes, Crossed Swords 365.00

Meissen, Figurine, Neptune, On Horse, 6 3/4 In.

♦ ♦

Lusterware requires special handling because if it is improperly washed it can wear away. The ware should be washed in warm water with a mild soap or detergent. Do not rub too hard or you will remove the luster glaze.

♦ ♦

Meissen, Plate, Multicolored, Floral, Handle, c.1790, 9 In.

Meissen, Urn, Allegorical Scenes, 2 Handles, 11 1/2 In., Pair

Figurine, Cherbus, Oval Base, Crossed Swords, 4 3/4 In., Pair	1090.00
Figurine, Chinese Trade Girl, Carrying Parasol, c.1750, 4 3/4 In.	990.00
Figurine, Cobbler Holding Shoes, Dancing, c.1765, 8 1/2 In.	1650.00
Figurine, Cobbler, Brown Coat, White Waistcoat, c.1750, 8 1/2 In.	3575.00
Figurine, Cupid, Caught In Trap, 7 1/4 In.	995.00
Figurine, Cupid, Hammering A Heart, c.1870, 7 1/2 In.	795.00
Figurine, Dog, Sitting, Brown & White	1425.00
Figurine, Elegant Woman, Seated At Dressing Table, Marked, 5 3/4 In.	1325.00
Figurine, Fall Season, 1890, Crossed Swords, 5 In.	550.00
Figurine, Fish Seller, Arm Raised Fish At Feet, 1750s, 6 In.	935.00
Figurine, Fish Seller, Woman Holding Fish In Apron, 1750s, 5 1/2 In.	1325.00
Figurine, Gardener, Digging With Spade, C. 1750, 4 9/16 In.	1210.00
Figurine, Harlequin, Playing Bagpipes, 1737–1749, 4 1/2 In.	3575.00
Figurine, Hercules, Supporting Globe, 1755–1765, 6 1/4 In.	1980.00
Figurine, Maiden, Holding Fan, c.1745, 5 1/2 In.	520.00
Figurine, Man, Chopping Wood, 5 In.	715.00
Figurine, Monkey Holding Apple, c.1740, 1 9/16 In.	770.00
Figurine, Neptune, On Horse, 6 3/4 In. *Illus*	550.00
Figurine, Poultry Seller, Holding Rooster, 1750s, 5 In.	2640.00
Figurine, Sportsman, Carrying Gray Goose, c.1755, . 6 In.	1320.00
Figurine, Turkish Dancer, Woman In Floral Dress, Peaked Hat, 6 In.	775.00
Figurine, Woman & Gentleman, 18th Century Clothes, Marked, 19 In., Pair	4840.00
Figurine, Woman, 18th Century Clothes, Lacy	1800.00
Figurine, Woman, Feeding Chicks, Blue Crossed Swords, 4 3/4 In.	495.00
Figurine, Young Man & Woman Collecting Fire Wood, Marked, 5 1/2 x 5 In.	1045.00
Group, 2 Children, Classical Drapery, Blue Crossed Swords, 5 In.	600.00
Group, Cottage With Thatched Roof, Animals & Figures, c.1775, 4 3/4 x 7 In.	3025.00
Group, Europa & Bull, Seated On Bull, Marked, 9 In.	2750.00
Group, Lovers, Musicians, Cherubs, Rocky Landscape, Marked, 14 In.	4075.00

Group, Peasant Harvester & Minstrel, 6 1/4 x 4 1/2 In. 990.00
Group, Sun God In Chariot, 4 Horses, Cupid, Marked, 12 x 18 In. 1985.00
Jug, Milk, Painted Scene, Scrollwork Rim, Pear Shape, c.1740, 5 3/4 In. 335.00
Jug, Milk, Quay Scene 1 Side, River Landscape, Yellow Ground, c.1740, 6 In. 4950.00
Mustard, Bow Knotted Spray of Flowers, Butterfly, Scroll Handle, 1740s, 4 In. 885.00
Pitcher, Creamer, Balloon, Hand Painted 95.00
Pitcher, Panels of Scenes of Man & Woman, Gold Trim, Marked, 3 In. 110.00
Plate, Center Floral Pattern, Gilt & Blue Border, Marked, 12 1/4 In. 335.00
Plate, Gilt Foliate Rim, Floral & Fruit Clusters, c.1760, 10 In. 440.00
Plate, Jolly Monk, Gold Design Border, White Beading, Marked, 9 1/2 In. 395.00
Plate, Multicolored, Floral, Handle, c.1790, 9 In. ....*Illus* 450.00
Plate, Scalloped, Multicolored Flowers, c.1875, 9 In. 395.00
Platter, Fish, Flower Design, 22 In. 130.00
Platter, Fish, Hand Painted Floral Design, Molded Rim, White, 11 1/2 x 24 In. 247.00
Platter, Fish, Marked, 11 x 23 In. 400.00
Sauceboat, Floral Branches & Birds, Oval, c.1755, 9 In. 1650.00
Saucer, Chinoiserie, Man Watching Child Carrying Rabbit, 1725–1730, 5 1/8 In. 1430.00
Sconce, Signed, 1860, Pair 4200.00
Sugar, Cover, Grapevine Mold, Yellow Ground, c.1770, 4 In. 660.00
Sugar, Cover, Landscape Scene, Turquoise Ground, c.1740 .... 4400.00
Sugar, Cover, Painted, River Landscape, Oval, c.1730, 4 11/16 In. 8250.00
Sugar, Cover, White, Raised Floral Branches, Pear Shape, c.1745, 4 In. 440.00
Tea Bowl, 4 Merchants, 2 Ships, Insects, c.1725, 2 7/8 In. 995.00
Tea Caddy, Figure On Horseback, Port Scene, c.1755, 5 1/2 In. 750.00
Tea Caddy, Floral Bouquet, Sprigs, Floral Sprig Knop, Marked, 5 1/16 In. 1210.00
Tea Set, Lobed Panels, Gold Trim, 19 Piece 1650.00
Tea Set, Multicolored Florals, Dragon's Head Spout, 3 Piece 595.00
Teapot, Fels Und Vogel Pattern, 1730–1735, 4 3/8 In. 5775.00
Teapot, Flowering Plant, Turquoise Ground, Bull Shape, c.1735 .... 2200.00
Teapot, Globular Form, 19th Century, 6 In. 250.00
Teapot, Raised Chrysanthemum Design, White, c.1730, 4 1/8 In. 1980.00
Tray, Reticulated Rim, Underglaze Blue & Gilt, Oval, 9 1/2 In. 137.00
Urn, Allegorical Scenes, 2 Handles, 11 1/2 In., Pair ....*Illus* 12100.00
Urn, Cover, Floral, Vine, Landscape Medallions, Metal Base, Marked, 12 In., Pair ... 1450.00
Urn, Roses, Ornate Rope Handles, Crossed Swords, 18 In. 1500.00
Vase, Baluster, Double Snake Handles, Yellow Ground, 10 1/2 In. 302.50
Vase, Baluster, Painted Floral Design, c.1750, 8 In., Pair 7700.00
Vase, Gilt Design, Entwined Serpent Handles, White Ground, 10 3/4 In. 330.00

MERCURY GLASS, or silvered glass, was first made in the 1850s. It lost
favor for a while but became popular again about 1910. It looks like a
piece of silver.

Candle Lamp, Twist Stem, Aqua Shades, 18 In., Pair 325.00
Candlestick, 10 In., Pair 65.00
Candlestick, Painted Floral & Leaf Design, Pair 275.00
Ornament, Bird, Wading, Crested Head, Hand Blown, Germany Label, 7 In. 48.00
Pitcher, Crimped Handle, 1855–1870, 6 1/2 In. 137.50
Reflector, Waffle Pattern 60.00
Salt, Design, Master 40.00
Salt, Footed 30.00
Tieback, Copper Wheel Engraved Design, 2 5/8 In., Pair 30.00
Tieback, Curtain 15.00
Tieback, Molded Floral Design, 3 In., Pair 50.00
Wine, Footed, 8 Piece 75.00
Witch Ball, Black Base 30.00

MERRIMAC POTTERY Company was founded by Thomas Nickerson in
Newburyport, Massachusetts, in 1902. The company made art pottery,
garden pottery, and reproductions of Roman pottery. The pottery burned
to the ground in 1908.

Mug, Half–Round Handle, Impressed Mark, Label, 5 3/4 In. 220.00
Vase, White Streaks On Mat, Gray–Brown Glaze, Red Clay, 7 In. 330.00

METTLACH, Germany, is a city where the Villeroy and Boch factories worked. Steins from the firm are known as Mettlach steins. They date from about 1842. *PUG* means painted under glaze. The steins can be dated from the marks on the bottom, which include a date–number code. Other pieces may be listed in the Villeroy & Boch category.

Charger, Classical Maiden, Seated In Forest, Initialed H. S., 15 1/2 In.	550.00
Charger, Nuremberg Castle, 1900s	450.00
Charger, Woman In The Woods, Purple Irises, Floral Border, Matte, 15 3/4 In.	880.00
Cookie Jar, Chef Pierre	90.00
Jar, Tobacco, No. 3026, Elf & King	450.00
Mug, No. 3095, Hires, Boy Wearing Dress & Bib, 4 1/2 In.	88.00 To 185.00
Pitcher, No. 2210, Bowling Scene, Gargoyle Pouring Lid, 12 In.	303.00
Pitcher, No. 2210, Pewter Lid, Beer Garden Scene, Mask Spout, 13 In., Pair	500.00
Pitcher, No. 2332-1031, Dwarfs Drinking From Steins, 3 Liter, 9 1/4 In.	198.00
Plaque, Lady Head, Green Ground, 7 1/2 x 8 3/4 In.	495.00
Plaque, No. 1044, Tavern Scene, 17 In.	150.00
Plaque, No. 2187, Knight On Horse, 16 In.	1650.00
Plaque, No. 2361, Castle & Mountain Scene, 17 In.	440.00
Plaque, No. 2622, Cavalier Holding Pipe & Drink, Marked, 7 In.	295.00
Plaque, No. 2625, Cavalier Playing Mandolin, 7 In.	295.00
Plaque, No. 7032, Woman's Head, Green Ground, Marked, 7 1/2 x 8 1/2 In.	495.00
Pokal, No. 168	550.00
Punch Bowl, No. 2814, Art Nouveau Design, 7 Liter	3520.00
Punch Bowl, No. 2814, Art Nouveau Design, Underplate, 7 Liter	3520.00
Punch Bowl, Underplate, No. 2807	440.00
Stein, 1/2 Liter, Singing Group, Blue Ground, Dated 1888	75.00
Stein, No. 485, 1/2 Liter, Children, Musicians, Light Green	275.00 To 357.00
Stein, No. 1028, 3 Liter, Amorous Couple In Medallion, Brown Tree Trunk	125.00
Stein, No. 1184, 3/10 Liter, Scrolls In Relief, Wedgwood Type, Dated 1885	150.00
Stein, No. 1403, 1/2 Liter, Bowling Scene	465.00
Stein, No. 1467, 1/2 Liter, People Picking Fruit, 5 3/4 In.	295.00
Stein, No. 1562, 5 Liter, Cavalier, Knight Near Handle	1600.00
Stein, No. 1725, 1/2 Liter, Cupid In Shield, Cherub Thumb Lift	275.00
Stein, No. 1822, 3 Liter, Floral, Pitcher Type	385.00
Stein, No. 1916, 2 Liter, Cavalier Scene, Inlaid Lid, Pedestal, Pitcher Type	925.00
Stein, No. 1940, 3 Liter, Keeper of Wine Cellar, Pitcher Type	1500.00
Stein, No. 2049, 1/2 Liter, Chess, 3 Crowns Lid	3960.00
Stein, No. 2054, 1/2 Liter, Cavalier Leaning On Barrel, Pewter Thumb Rests, 8 In.	385.00
Stein, No. 2126, 5 Liter, Symphonia, Masters of Music	6875.00
Stein, No. 2182, 1/2 Liter, Bowling & Drinking Scene, 6 1/2 In.	385.00
Stein, No. 2211, 3/10 Liter, Bowlers, Blue Ground, 1895	130.00
Stein, No. 2249, 1/4 Liter, Men Drinking Beer	275.00
Stein, No. 2271, 1/2 Liter, Maidens Serving Soldiers	275.00
Stein, No. 2382, 1/2 Liter, Barmaid, Thirsty Rider Drinking, Pewter Lid, 9 1/8 In.	110.00
Stein, No. 2430, 3 Liter, Cavalier Drinking, Hunter, c.1900, 16 In.	495.00
Stein, No. 2917, 1/2 Liter, Munich, Lion & Shield Lid	2860.00
Stein, No. 2936, 1/2 Liter, Elks Club, Art Nouveau Style	495.00
Stein, No. 2936, 1/2 Liter, Elks Club, Art Nouveau Style, c.1900	125.00
Stein, No. 3202, 1 Liter, Automobile, Man & Woman	3080.00
Stein, No. 3202, 1/2 Liter, Automobile, Man & Woman	3080.00
Stein, No. 3251, 1/2 Liter, 2 Men & Barmaid, Holding Steins Aloft, Etched Lid	345.00
Stein, No. 3329, 1/2 Liter, Gamblers, Card Player	2530.00
Tile, Ducks	30.00
Vase, No. 1409, Beige Tapestry Ground, Dragon Handles, 11 1/4 In.	460.00
Vase, Red & Gold Flowers, Flowing Stems, Blue & Ivory Ground, 15 In., Pair	1550.00

MILK GLASS was named for its milky white color. It was first made in England during the 1700s. The height of its popularity in the United States was from 1870 to 1880. It is now correct to refer to some colored glass as blue milk glass, black milk glass, etc. Reproductions of milk glass are being made and sold in many stores. Related pieces may be listed in the Cosmos and Vallerysthal categories.

Appetizer Set, Paneled Grape, 3 Piece 55.00
Ashtray, Select Beer, Great Falls 12.00
Basket, Hobnail, Ruffled Rim, Handle, 11 In. 55.00
Basket, Paneled Grape, Handle, Westmoreland, 8 In. 85.00
Basket, Paneled Hobnail, 9 1/2 In. 25.00
Bowl, Old Quilt, 8 In. 32.50
Bowl, Paneled Grape, 10 1/2 In. 65.00
Bowl, Paneled Grape, Lipped, 9 In. 45.00
Box, Candy Dish, Heart, 3 Sections, 1950s 45.00
Butter, Cover, Beaded Swag 145.00
Butter, Lacy Dewdrop 35.00
Candleholder, Daisy & Button, 2 1/2 In., Pair 15.00
Candlestick, Spiral, 7 In., Pair 30.00
Candy Dish, Cover, Argonaut Shell 38.00
Candy Dish, Cover, Paneled Grape, 7 In. 32.00
Candy Dish, Stagecoach, Cover, 5 In. 324.50
Compote, Atlas 33.00
Cracker Jar, Cover, Forget-Me-Not 200.00
Cracker Jar, Water Lilies & Cattails, Chartreuse, 9 In. 150.00
Creamer, Cover, Lacy Dewdrop 40.00
Cup & Saucer, Paneled Grape 15.50
Dish, Cat & Lion Cover 90.00
Dish, Cat On Nest, Cover, Atterbury, Pat. 1889 .... 200.00
Dish, Chick On Eggs, Cover, Atterbury, Pat. 1889 .... 165.00
Dish, Embossed Dancing Children, Sowerby 55.00
Dish, Entwined Fish Cover, Lace Base, Atterbury, Pat. 1889 .... 165.00
Dish, Fox Cover, Pat. 1889 .... 150.00
Dish, Hand & Dove Cover, Signed 150.00
Dish, Hand & Dove, Atterbury, Pat. 1889 .... 110.00
Dish, Hen Cover, Blue Ribbed Base 500.00
Dish, Lovebirds Cover, Blue 55.00
Dish, Owl Cover 125.00
Dish, Owl's Head Cover, Split Rib Base 250.00
Dish, Rooster Cover, Basketweave Base, Atterbury 80.00
Dish, Squirrel & Fox Cover 85.00
Dish, Standing Rooster Cover, Blue 38.00
Egg, 1900 .... 12.50
Figurine, Gondola 100.00
Figurine, Scotty Dog, Red Collar, 4 In. 20.00
Goblet, Blackberry, 10 Piece 350.00
Goblet, Old Quilt 20.00
Goblet, Paneled Grape 14.00
Goblet, Paneled Grape, Westmoreland 15.50
Jar, Eagle Cover, Old Abe 120.00
Jar, Owl Cover, Blue, Atterbury 150.00
Match Holder, Black Boy, Striker 198.00
Match Holder, Indian Head, Divided, 3 1/2 In. 65.00
Match Holder, Satchel Shape 60.00
Mug, Atterbury 45.00
Mug, Child's, Henny & Penny, Hazel Atlas 10.00
Mug, Child's, Ranger Joe, Hazel Atlas 10.00
Pitcher 125.00
Pitcher, Beaded Circle, 10 In. 67.50
Pitcher, Curtain, Gold Rim & Handle 225.00
Pitcher, Enameled Flowers 38.50
Pitcher, Milk, Rose Sprig, Blue 95.00
Pitcher, Milk, Scroll, 5 In. 10.00
Pitcher, Old Quilt, 1 Pt. 35.00
Pitcher, Old Quilt, 1 Qt. 42.00
Pitcher, Water, Jenny Lind 90.00
Plate, 3 Bears .... 35.00 To 38.00
Plate, Anchor & Belaying Pin 30.00
Plate, Cupid & Psyche 20.00

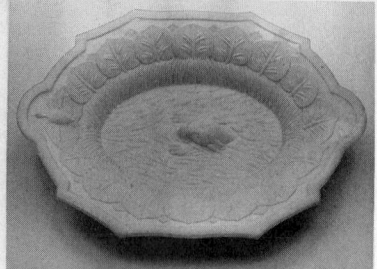

Milk Glass, Platter, Fox Head Center,

Leaf Border, 13 In.

◆◆◆◆◆◆◆◆◆◆◆◆◆◆◆◆◆◆◆◆◆◆◆

Old milk glass is slightly
opalescent at the edge when
held up to a strong light. New
glass is not.

◆◆◆◆◆◆◆◆◆◆◆◆◆◆◆◆◆◆◆◆◆◆◆

Plate, Lattice, Large		45.00
Plate, Paneled Grape, Westmoreland, 8 1/2 In.		18.50
Platter, Fox Head Center, Leaf Border, 13 In.	*Illus*	85.00
Platter, Rock of Ages		160.00
Rolling Pin, Wooden Handles		75.00
Rose Bowl, Embossed Leaves, Scrollwork, Gold Trim, Blue		60.00
Salt, Berry Leaf Shape, Berry Shaped Foot		15.00
Saltshaker, Chick		12.00
Sauce, Blackberry		15.00
Stein Set, Child's, Master, 5 Piece		125.00
Sugar & Creamer, Georgia Gem, Green		85.00 To 95.00
Syrup, Blue		200.00
Syrup, Hand Painted Wild Flowers, Victorian		125.00
Syrup, Tin Top, Allover Flower Pattern		98.00
Table Set, Lacy Dewdrop, 3 Piece		70.00
Table Set, Versailles, Pink Rose, 4 Piece		125.00
Toothpick, Fleur–De–Lis		27.50 To 40.00
Toothpick, Swan		10.00
Toothpick, Tramp's Shoe		35.00
Tray, Dresser, Floral Handles, 9 In.		22.00
Tray, Multinomah Hotel, Portland, Ore., Souvenir, 9 In.		40.00
Tray, Scroll, Triangular, 5 In.		10.00
Tumbler, Della Robbia		9.00
Tumbler, Iced Tea, Paneled Grape		18.00
Tumbler, Louisiana Purchase		35.00 To 45.00
Tumbler, Tulip, Blue, Westmoreland Glass		75.00
Vase, Ear of Corn, Fire Painted, Atturbury, 4 1/4 In.		35.00
Vase, Fan, Blue, Piecrust Edge, 4 1/2 In.		15.00
Vase, Fan, Quilted, Westmoreland, 8 In.		15.00
Vase, Paneled Grape, 12 In.		35.00
Vase, Slant, Blue, Morgantown, 5 3/8 In.		25.00

MILLEFIORI means, literally, a thousand flowers. It is a type of glasswork
popular in paperweights. Many small pieces of glass resembling flowers are
grouped together to form a design.

Coffeepot, White Flowers, Yellow Centers, Blue Handle, Spout, 5 3/4 In.	225.00
Cup & Saucer, Blue	85.00
Dish, Pedestal, Signed, Late 1800s	45.00
Vase, Bottle Shape, Ianlong Mark, 18th Century, 8 In.	375.00

MINTON china has been made in the Staffordshire region of England from
1793 to the present. The firm became part of the Royal Doulton
Tableware Group in 1968, but the wares continued to be marked *Minton.*
Many marks have been used. The one shown dates from about 1873 to
1891, when the word *England* was added.

Basket, Cherub, Celadon & White, 8 1/2 In.	210.00

Demitasse Set, Bird of Paradise, Signed, 1863, 15 Piece .... 300.00 To 350.00
Dinner Service, Floral Pattern, 106 Piece 1800.00
Figurine, Dorothea, Seated, Satchel At Feet, Parian, c.1873, 13 3/4 In. 360.00
Figurine, Lady Repairing Fish Net, 10 In. 310.00
Figurine, Leda & The Swan, Parian Bisque, c.1850, 21 In. 935.00
Mug, Coronation, Edward III 30.00
Plate, Gilt Swag Design, Apple Green Border, 11 In., 12 Piece 525.00
Tile, Boston State House, Blue, White, Square, 6 In. 39.00
Tile, Cows, Brown & Pale Blue Transfer, Framed, Square, 10 1/2 In. 60.00
Tile, Hunter & Horses, Blue & White, 6 x 8 In. 110.00
Vase, White Relief Figures, Deep Blue–Green, 18 In., Pair 9000.00

MIRRORS are listed in the Furniture category under Mirror.

MOCHA pottery is an English–made product that was sold in America during the early 1800s. It is a heavy pottery with pale coffee–and–cream coloring. Designs of blue, brown, green, orange, black, or white were added to the pottery and given fanciful names, such as *Tree, Snail Trail,* or *Moss.*

Bowl, Blue Double Spiral Earthworm, Brown, Tan, White, 7 1/4 x 3 3/4 In. 415.00
Bowl, Cats–Eye & Earthworm, Brown & Blue Bands, 9 3/4 x 4 3/8 In. 775.00
Bowl, Earthworm Band, 6 In. 605.00
Bowl, Earthworm, Orange–Tan Band, Green Strip, 7 x 3 1/2 In. 165.00
Bowl, Green Seaweed, Yellow, 11 In. 490.00
Castor, Worm Wide Band, Early 19th Century, 5 1/4 & 4 1/2 In., Pair 1100.00
Chamber Pot 285.00
Creamer, Wide Brown & Blue Bands, England, 19th Century, 4 In. 125.00
Jar, Waste, Cover, Seaweed 450.00
Mug, Blue, Brown Bands, Earthworm Design, Tan, White, Brown, 4 7/8 In. 165.00
Mug, Buff & 2 Wide Brown Bands, England, 19th Century, 5 In. 165.00
Mug, Earthworm Band, 19th Century, 6 1/4 In. 785.00
Mug, Embossed Bands, Stripes, Leaf Handle, 6 In. 225.00
Mug, Embossed Stripes, Green, White, Tan, Brown, Leaf Handle, 4 7/8 In. 165.00
Mug, Gray Bands, Black & Blue Dots, Stripes, Embossed Blue Band, 5 5/8 In. 410.00
Mug, Seaweed, 5 In. .... 195.00 To 225.00
Mug, Stripes, Bands, Foliage Design, Brown, Blue, White, Leaf Handle, 5 In. 225.00
Mug, Stripes, Olive Green, Blue, Brown, White, Leaf Handle, 4 5/8 In. 225.00
Mug, White Geometric Band, Tan Stripes, Green, Black, Leaf Handle, 5 In. 165.00
Mug, White Stripes, Brown Band, Tan, 3 1/2 In. 145.00
Mustard Pot, Green Band, Stripes Of Orange, Leaf Handle, 3 In. 467.00
Mustard Pot, Tooled Designs, Black & Tan, 2 3/4 In. 65.00
Pitcher, Black Stripes, Bands, Leaves, 7 In. 165.00
Pitcher, Brown & Blue Band, White Swirls & Dots, 7 In. 175.00
Pitcher, Brown Earthworm, Blue Band, Green Stripe, Leaf Handle, 8 In. 335.00
Pitcher, Earthworm Design, Blue Stripes, Tan, Blue, Black, 6 3/4 In. 385.00
Pitcher, Earthworm, Striped 665.00
Pitcher, Grayish Blue Band, Brown Cat's Eyes, Brown Stripes, Leaf Handle, 7 In. ... 215.00
Pitcher, Milk, Cat's–Eye & Earthworm, 6 1/2 In. 1500.00
Pitcher, Milk, Cat's–Eye & Earthworm, 8 In. 880.00
Pitcher, Ochre & Brown Design 335.00
Pitcher, Stripes, Blue, Orange, Black, White, Embossed Green, Leaf Handle, 8 In. ... 195.00
Pitcher, Tree Design, Wide Central Blue Band, Brown Bands, 6 1/2 In. 165.00
Pitcher, Yellow Enameled Floral Design, Metallic Glaze, Leaf Handle, 5 In. 110.00
Salt, Blue–Brown Swirl 385.00

MONMOUTH Pottery Company started working in Monmouth, Illinois, in 1892. The pottery made a variety of utilitarian wares. It became part of Western Stoneware Company in 1906. The maple leaf mark was used until 1930. If *Co.* appears as part of the mark, the piece was made before 1906.

Flowerpot, Blue 45.00
Vase, Cream Leaf Design Border, Blue Ground, 17 3/4 In. 220.00

MONT JOYE, see Mt. Joye

MOORCROFT pottery was first made in Burslem, England, in 1913. William Moorcroft had managed the art pottery department for James MacIntyre & Company of England from 1898 to 1913. The Moorcroft pottery continues today although William Moorcroft died in 1945. The earlier wares are similar to the modern ones, but color and marking will help indicate the age.

Ashtray, Red Hibiscus, Blue, 6 1/4 x 3 1/2 In.	68.00
Bottle, Spring Flower Design, Stopper	550.00
Bowl, Coral Hibiscus, Green, Artist, 6 In.	245.00
Bowl, Eventide, 9 In.	2750.00
Bowl, Florian Ware, Silver Overlay	2310.00
Bowl, Green, Coral Hibiscus, Signed, 6 In.	245.00
Bowl, Mauve Poppies, Cobalt Blue, 3 1/2 In.	65.00
Box, Cover, Floral, Dark Blue, Signed	225.00
Candlestick, Berries On Vine, Green Bands, Cream Glaze, 8 In.	95.00
Candlestick, Blue Landscape, c.1925, 8 1/4 In.	325.00
Cup & Saucer, Pansies, Signed, 1913–1916	375.00
Jar, Cover, Poppy, Deep Blue Mottled Ground, Dated 1927, 14 In.	2750.00
Jar, Flat Cover, Pomegranate Band, Cobalt Blue, Cobridge Ware, 1930, 16 In.	3575.00
Lamp Base, Poppy, Blossoms & Foliage, Cobalt Blue Ground, 14 1/2 x 6 1/2 In.	825.00
Lamp, Flambe Fruit & Leaves, 1934, 10 1/2 In.	1250.00
Lamp, Orchids On Cobalt Blue, Label, 14 1/2 In.	1150.00
Pitcher, Grape Color, Luster, England	60.00
Plaque, Display	85.00
Plate, Floral, Label, 12 In.	165.00
Sugar & Creamer, Raised Blue Flowers, Green Leaves, Poppies	750.00
Tea Set, Pomegranate, Sheffield Silver Trim, 3 Piece	795.00
Vase, Anemone, 5 1/2 In.	400.00
Vase, Anemone, Blue Ground, Marked, 5 In.	192.50
Vase, Black Tulip, Signed, 11 1/2 In.	350.00
Vase, Bramble Pattern, 8 x 6 In.	330.00
Vase, Dragon, Cobalt Blue, 7 In.	300.00
Vase, Flamminian Ware, Mottled Green On Rust, Foliate Rondels, 12 1/2 In.	1350.00
Vase, Floral Garlands, White Ground, MacIntyre, c.1913, 3 1/8 In.	365.00
Vase, Floral, Raised Design, Multicolored, 1918–1929	675.00
Vase, Hibiscus, Blue, 5 In.	110.00
Vase, Landscape of Trees & Hills, Label, Marked, 12 In.	2450.00
Vase, Lemons, Blossoms, Bluebird, 1970, 7 In.	115.00
Vase, Mushroom Design, Dark Blue Interior, 7 In.	2950.00
Vase, Plum & Grape Design, Dark Blue, Tapered, Cylindrical, 1916, 10 1/2 In.	385.00
Vase, Pomegranate, 9 1/2 In.	975.00
Vase, Pomegranate, Mottled Yellow & Green Ground, 1912, 5 In., Pair	1650.00
Vase, Purple Flowers, Green Ground, 5 In.	165.00
Vase, Tulips, Florian, Green & Gold, Macintyre, 1903, 8 3/4 In.	1450.00
Vase, Wisteria, 12 In.	1650.00
Vase, Wisteria, Green, Signed, 6 In.	195.00
Vase, Yellow & Pink Pansies, Boat Shape, 8 In.	125.00

MORIAGE is a special type of raised decoration used on some Japanese pottery. Sometimes pieces of clay were shaped by hand and applied to the item; sometimes the clay was squeezed from a tube in the way we apply cake frosting. One type of moriage is called *Dragonware* and is listed under that name.

Bowl, Gold Dragons, Raised White, 6 In.	135.00
Bowl, Red Flowers, Leaves, Green Wreath Mark, 8 In.	125.00
Cake Plate, Woodland Scene, Handles, 12 In.	115.00
Cup & Saucer, Floral Medallions, Green, Ivory Slip, Footed	92.00
Cup & Saucer, Flowers, Gold, Raised White	50.00
Fernery	195.00
Nippon, Console, House In Woods Scene, Green Wreath, 10 In.	250.00
Plaque, Moose, Pine Cones, 8 In.	85.00
Stein, Overall Florals, Gold Moriage, Beaded	575.00

Sugar, Cover, Greek Key, Butterflies, Gold, Blues 125.00
Sugar, Melon Ribbed, 4 Medallions With Roses, 3 Curved Feet 80.00
Tankard, Edelweiss Flowers, Cobalt Blue, 15 3/4 In. 850.00
Urn, Green, Fuchsia Roses, Handles, Cover, 10 In. 175.00
Vase, Beaded, Double Handles, Footed, Squatty, Royal Nippon, 8 In. 200.00
Vase, Flying Geese, Green Maple Leaf, Nippon, 8 1/2 In. 195.00
Vase, Gold Leaf, Double Handles, Hand Painted, Floral, Morimura Bros., 13 In. 425.00
Vase, Green, Flowers, Raised White, 10 In. 265.00

MOSAIC TILE Company of Zanesville, Ohio, was started by Karl Langerbeck and Herman Mueller in 1894. Many types of plain and ornamental tiles were made until 1959. The company closed in 1967. The company also made some ashtrays, bookends, and related giftwares. Most pieces are marked with the entwined *MTC* monogram.

Box, Pencil, Dog On Lid, Turquoise Glaze, Marked, 4 x 8 In. 225.00
Bust, Marshall, Vice Pres. To Woodrow Wilson, Blue, Dated 1916 .... 45.00
Cookie Jar, Mammy .... 475.00 To 540.00
Cookie Jar, Mammy, Yellow 475.00
Figurine, Elephant, White Tusks, Orange Glaze, 6 1/2 x 10 1/2 In. 220.00
Figurine, German Shepherd, Lying Down, Tan, 10 In. 100.00
Paperweight, Abraham Lincoln 45.00

MOSER glass is made by Ludwig Moser und Sohne, a Bohemian glasshouse founded in 1857. Art Nouveau–type glassware and iridescent glassware were made. The most famous Moser glass is decorated with heavy enameling in gold and bright colors. The firm is still working in Czechoslovakia. Few pieces of Moser glass are marked.

Bowl, Acorn Decoration, 4 Feet, 10 x 7 In. 1200.00
Bowl, Chalice, Cranberry, Hollow Stem, Gold Enameled, 6 In. 200.00
Bowl, Cut Back Design of Fruit & Foliage, Amethyst, Signed, 8 In. 795.00
Bowl, Intaglio Flower & Leaf Design, Amethyst To Clear, 8 1/2 In. 385.00
Bowl, Scalloped Rim, Gold Enamel Floral & Scroll, Signed, 6 x 11 In. 745.00
Bowl, Scrolled Enamel Border, Jewels Under Gold Band, Signed, 7 1/2 In. 1100.00
Bowl, Strawberry, Signed 495.00
Box, Cover, Florals & Foliage, Smoke Gray, Signed 1595.00
Candlestick, Gold Band of Warriors, Signed, 10 In. 350.00
Castor, Pickle, Gold Band of Embossed Warriors 350.00
Cologne Bottle, Amber, Heavy Enameled, Signed, 6 1/2 In. 75.00
Cologne Bottle, Applied Enameled Eel, Clear, Signed, 5 1/2 In. 35.00
Compote, Gold, Enameled, 9 1/2 In. 375.00
Cruet, Clear To Cranberry, Signed, 6 1/2 In., Pair 235.00
Decanter Set, Blue, Florals, Butterfly, Bug, 9 x 12 In. Stand, Tumblers, 15 Piece 1250.00
Decanter Set, Carved Butterflies, Gold Flowers, Signed, 10 In. 225.00
Decanter Set, Cranberry, Crystal Stopper, 4 Gold Trimmed Cordials 275.00
Decanter, Enameled Flowers, Everted Spout, Bulbous Stopper, 8 1/2 In., Pair 1260.00
Decanter, Green, Clear Faceted Stopper, Floral Transfers, Applied Handle, 12 In. ... 165.00
Decanter, Hand Painted Florals, Ruby, Clear Faceted Stopper, Handle, 10 In. 185.00
Dish, Trinket, Polar Bears 85.00
Ewer, Cranberry, Signed 290.00
Ewer, Intaglio Cut, Gold Enameled, 11 In. 550.00
Finger Bowl, Underplate, Amber, Gold & Enameled, Signed 550.00
Goblet, Deer Scene, Clear Pedestal, Cobalt Blue, Clear Frosted, 6 1/2 In. 375.00
Holder, Card, Intaglio, Orange, Pink, Blue & Amethyst, 2 1/2 In., 10 Piece 195.00
Humidor, Purple, White, Yellow & Blue Enameled, Silver Plated Lid 425.00
Perfume Bottle, Finger, Citron, Blue Florals, Hearts, Chain, Teardrop Shape, 2 In. . 235.00
Perfume Bottle, Purple, Warrior Band, Atomizer 260.00
Pitcher, Cranberry, Enameled, 11 In. 350.00
Pitcher, Enameled Flowers, Applied Lizard, Tail Handle 2800.00
Pitcher, Enameled Flowers, Fluted Top, Cranberry, 8 In. 350.00
Pitcher, Peacock, Gold, Silver & Copper Blossoms, Clear, 15 1/4 In. 885.00
Pitcher, Salamander Handle 2450.00
Punch Set, Cranberry, Lace Pewter Base, 5-In. Goblet, 5 Piece 850.00
Rose Bowl, Cranberry, Clear Rigaree, Signed, 4 In. 45.00

Sugar Shaker, Raised Cranberry Panels, Gold Outlined, Allover Traced Florals 265.00
Tray, Enameled, Gold, Oval, 14 In. 1600.00
Tray, Grasses, Florals & Fauna, Crackle Back, 3 Grasshoppers, 10 In. 495.00
Tumbler, Blue, Enameled, Signed, 3 1/2 In. 20.00
Tumbler, Cranberry, Raised Design, Signed, 6 Piece 100.00
Vase, 2 Encircling Crystal Snakes, One Forms Handle, Cranberry, 14 In. 3500.00
Vase, 6 Nude Women, Grapes & Leaves, Malachite, Signed, 5 In., Pair 450.00
Vase, Alexandrite, Stemmed, Signed, 9 In. 150.00
Vase, Amber, Raised Design, Metal Base, 6 1/2 In., Pair 100.00
Vase, Amber, Reverse Thumbprint, Florals, Signed, 6 1/2 In. 45.00
Vase, Amethyst, Intaglio, Signed, Miniature 295.00
Vase, Applied Bees, Cranberry, 9 In. 375.00
Vase, Applied Bees, Gold & Enameled Design, Cranberry, Signed, 7 In. 775.00
Vase, Applied Bronze Bees, Cranberry Glass, Scalloped, Signed, 14 In. 875.00
Vase, Applied Eagle, Enameled, Gold, 9 1/2 x 5 In. ....*Illus* 3200.00
Vase, Bird & Floral Design, Leaf Form Feet, Signed, c.1900, 8 1/4 In. 825.00
Vase, Blue Forget-Me-Nots, Paperweight, Cone Shape, 4 3/4 In. 150.00
Vase, Circular Medallion, Portrait of Woman, Gilt Leaf Scrolls, 7 1/2 In., Pair. 605.00
Vase, Coralene Peacock, Queen Ann's Lace On Reverse, Cranberry, 8 In. 435.00
Vase, Crane Wading Through Reeds & Plants, Smoky, Signed, 8 1/4 In. 247.00
Vase, Enameled Bird & Floral, Opaque Sky Blue, 1880, 12 In. 750.00
Vase, Enameled Cranes, Marshy Swamp, Raspberry Cut To Frosted Clear, 13 In. 660.00
Vase, Enameled Flowers & Birds, Gold Scrolls, Applied Glass Buds, Green, 10 In. 765.00
Vase, Enameled Vines & Poppy, Etched Bugs & Bees, 14 In. 5400.00
Vase, Enameled White & Pink Flowers, Gold Outlined, Rubena Verde, 11 1/2 In. ... 395.00
Vase, Fan, Enameled Cranberry To Clear, Signed, 7 1/2 x 11 In. 35.00
Vase, Fish & Seaweed, Crackle Glass, Amber, Clear, Flared, 7 1/2 In. 210.00
Vase, Flowers Outlined In Gold, Ribbed, 11 1/2 In 495.00
Vase, Forget-Me-Nots, Gold Branches, White Dots, Cranberry, 3 1/2 In. 150.00
Vase, Frosted White, Portrait, Pedestal, Signed, 4 In. 85.00
Vase, Gold Enameled Scrolls, Colored Jewels, Bowl Shape, 7 1/2 x 8 3/4 In. 1100.00
Vase, Gold Floral Design, Cranberry, Gold Rim, Signed, 9 1/2 In. 265.00
Vase, Intaglio, Amethyst, Signed, 3 In. 385.00
Vase, Lions In Jungle Cameo, 3 Layers, Gold, Acid Cut, 7 In. 665.00
Vase, Portrait, Green, Gold Pedestal, Signed, 6 In. 40.00
Vase, Radon, 4 Handles, 9 1/2 x 6 In. 950.00
Vase, Red, Blue & White Jeweled, Enameled, Cranberry, Label, 12 In. 450.00
Vase, Ruby Cut Medallions, Etched Flowers & Birds, Gold Trim, 10 In. 225.00
Vase, Stylized Flowering Design, Elongated Neck, Blue & Green, 7 7/8 In. 445.00
Vase, Trophy, Raised Gold Design, 3 Applied Handles, Signed, 7 x 5 In. 275.00
Vase, Underwater Scene, 2 Applied Fish, Blue Walls, Glass Beading, 9 In. 335.00
Wine, Alexandrite, Signed 65.00
Wine, Green, Signed, 7 In. 30.00
Wine, Sunburst Cut, Cranberry Cup, Clear Stem, Signed, 8 In., 6 Piece 350.00

Moser, Vase, Applied Eagle, Enameled,
Gold, 9 1/2 X 5 In.

◆◆◆◆◆◆◆◆◆◆◆◆◆◆◆◆◆◆◆◆◆◆

The word "trademark" was
used on English wares after
1855, but most of the pieces
with the letters "LTD," the
abbreviation for "Limited,"
were made after 1880.

◆◆◆◆◆◆◆◆◆◆◆◆◆◆◆◆◆◆◆◆◆◆

MOSS ROSE china was made by many firms from 1808 to 1900. It has a typical moss rose pictured as the design. The plant is not as popular now as it was in Victorian gardens, so the fuzz–covered bud is unfamiliar to most collectors. The dishes were usually decorated with pink and green flowers.

Butter Chip	15.00
Cup & Saucer	25.00
Eggcup, 4 Piece	15.00
Pitcher, Gold Trim, Haviland, 9 In.	90.00
Plate, 8 1/2 In.	20.00
Plate, Dinner	24.00
Platter, Meakin, 10 In.	35.00

MOTHER–OF–PEARL GLASS, or pearl satin glass, was first made in the 1850s in England and in Massachusetts. It was a special type of mold–blown satin glass with air bubbles in the glass, giving it a pearlized color. It has been reproduced. Mother–of–pearl shell objects are listed under Pearl.

Bottle, Peacock Eye, Silver Plated Cover, 3 3/4 In.	635.00
Bowl, Pink Diamond–Quilted, Yellow Seaweed, Signed, 6 1/2 In.	785.00
Creamer, Raindrop, White Lining, Blue Handle, 4 1/2 In.	225.00
Cruet, Apricot To White Diamond Quilted, Knobby Stopper	1450.00
Cruet, Purple	350.00
Cruet, Purple, Frosted Handle & Stopper	200.00
Dresser Set, Diamond–Quilted, Bluebird On Flowered Branches, 3 Piece	925.00
Finger Bowl, Diamond–Quilted, Shaded Yellow, Pleated Rim	85.00
Finger Bowl, Rainbow, White Lining, Ruffled Rim, 4 7/8 In.	795.00
Holder, Calling Card, Diamond–Quilted Pattern, 1900s	37.50
Pitcher, Yellow Interior, Applied Reeded Frosted Handle, 7 In.	770.00
Rose Bowl, Rivulet Pattern, White Lining, 2 3/4 In.	225.00
Scent Bottle, White Peacock, Bridal, Silver Plated Lid, 3 3/4 In.	635.00
Sugar & Creamer, Diamond, Quilted, Blue, Clear Frosted Handle, 3 In.	525.00
Vase, Celestial Blue, Herringbone, Threading, Gourd Shape, 8 x 5 In.	450.00
Vase, Coralene Seaweed, 6 1/2 In.	495.00
Vase, Diamond Point, Yellow, Ruffled	110.00
Vase, Herringbone, Amber Applied Handles, White Lining, 9 1/2 In., Pair	595.00
Vase, Raindrop Pattern, Misty Pink Shaded To White	325.00
Vase, Rivulet Pattern, 4–Petal Top, White Lining, 5 1/4 x 4 In.	235.00
Vase, Stick, Herringbone Pattern, Gourd Shape, Light Blue, 8 In.	450.00
Vase, Wave Pattern, Ruffled, White Lining, 6 1/4 In.	225.00

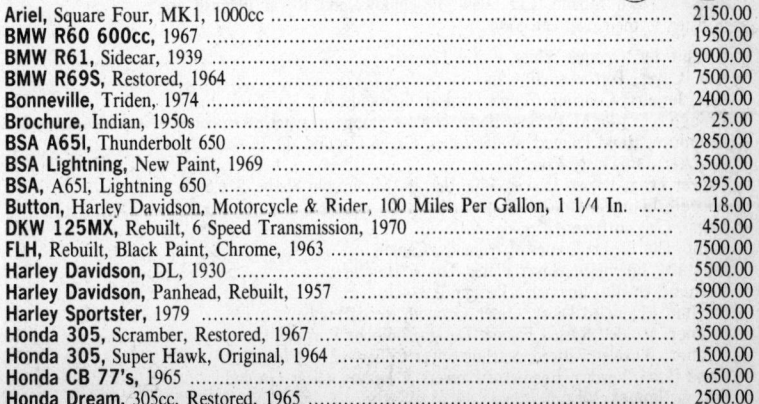

MOTORCYCLES of all types are being collected today. Examples can be found that date back to the early years of the twentieth century.

Ariel, Square Four, MK1, 1000cc	2150.00
BMW R60 600cc, 1967	1950.00
BMW R61, Sidecar, 1939	9000.00
BMW R69S, Restored, 1964	7500.00
Bonneville, Triden, 1974	2400.00
Brochure, Indian, 1950s	25.00
BSA A65l, Thunderbolt 650	2850.00
BSA Lightning, New Paint, 1969	3500.00
BSA, A65l, Lightning 650	3295.00
Button, Harley Davidson, Motorcycle & Rider, 100 Miles Per Gallon, 1 1/4 In.	18.00
DKW 125MX, Rebuilt, 6 Speed Transmission, 1970	450.00
FLH, Rebuilt, Black Paint, Chrome, 1963	7500.00
Harley Davidson, DL, 1930	5500.00
Harley Davidson, Panhead, Rebuilt, 1957	5900.00
Harley Sportster, 1979	3500.00
Honda 305, Scramber, Restored, 1967	3500.00
Honda 305, Super Hawk, Original, 1964	1500.00
Honda CB 77's, 1965	650.00
Honda Dream, 305cc, Restored, 1965	2500.00

Hummer, 1948	1500.00
Matchless G15CSR, 650 Twin	2400.00
Moto Guzzi 1000, LeMans, CX–100	3650.00
Moto Guzzi Ambassador, 1970	1800.00
Motor, Panhead, Standard Bore, Bonneville Left Case, 1955	1200.00
Mustang Stallion, Restored, 1959	5900.00
Ner–A–Car, Restored, Original Leather Seat, 1923	7500.00
Norton 750, Hi Rider	2650.00
Norton 750, Roadster	3295.00
Norton 850, Roadster, 1974	3500.00
Norton Commando 850, Black Roadster, 1975	3950.00
Norton Hi Rider, Metal Flake Gold Paint, 1971	4000.00
Rocket, Gold Star, Spitfire Scrambler, Rebuilt, 1963	9450.00
Royal Enfield, Continental, GT 250	2995.00
Royal Enfield, Indian 500cc, Twin	1850.00
Schwinn, Whizzer	1650.00
Sidecar, Steib S501, Convertible Top, Aluminum Trim, Cobra Lenses	5500.00
Sunbeam S7 Deluxe, 1952	6000.00
Thor, R747, Single Cylinder Engine, Aurora Aut. Machy Co., 1910	1200.00
Triumph 750cc, Bonneville, 1979	3500.00
Triumph T100c, 1971	2400.00
Triumph T100r, Daytona 500	2250.00
Triumph T140v, Bonneville	2650.00
Triumph TSS, 8 Valve	8500.00
Ural M63, Sidecar, 1966	6500.00
Zundapp Bella 200, Electric Start, Blue Metallic Paint, 1957	1500.00

MOUNT WASHINGTON, see Mt. Washington

MT. JOYE is an enameled cameo glass made in the late nineteenth and the twentieth centuries by Saint–Hilaire Touvier de Varraux and Co. of Pantin, France. This same company made De Vez glass. Pieces were usually decorated with enameling. Most pieces are not marked.

Vase, Flowering Plant, Leaves, Green, Gilt, Gourd Shape, Signed, 19 In.	825.00
Vase, Gold Florals Cut To Frosted Amethyst, Bucket, 2 Handles, Signed, 4 3/4 In.	385.00
Vase, Heavy Enameled Floral, Red Ground, 11 In.	285.00
Vase, Intaglio Cut Flowers, Gold Green & Clear, Gourd Shape, 8 In.	225.00
Vase, Intaglio Cut Flowers, Green, Clear & Gold, Square, 10 In.	230.00
Vase, Large Pink Flower, Gold Tracery, 12 In.	250.00 To 350.00

MT. WASHINGTON Glass Works started in 1837 in South Boston, Massachusetts. In 1870 the company moved to New Bedford, Massachusetts. Many types of art glass were made there until 1894, when the company merged with Pairpoint Manufacturing Co. Amberina, Burmese, Crown Milano, Cut Glass, Peachblow, and Royal Flemish are each listed in their own category.

Biscuit Jar, Opaque White, Floral Transfer	135.00
Box, Cover, Tortoiseshell, 6 In.	440.00
Box, Jewelry, Courting Couple On Lid, Garlands, 4 x 3 x 3 In.	235.00
Cologne, Bottle, Mushroom Body, Hollow Stopper, Lusterless	245.00
Compote, Hand Painted, Water Lilies, Green Ground, 11 In.	467.50
Cracker Jar, Dusty Rose	350.00
Flower Frog, Brown Leaves, Blue Berries, Mushroom Shape, 3 x 5 In.	195.00
Inkwell, Ebony & Crystal, Paper Label	85.00
Lamp, Cherub Base	625.00
Lamp, Oil, Desert Scenes of Nomads, Camels	225.00
Mustard, Enameled, Silver Plated Top & Handle	125.00
Perfume Bottle, Enameled Design, 2 3/4 In.	575.00
Pitcher, Enameled Daisy, Green Ground, Reed Handle	210.00
Pitcher, Molded Raised Fishnet Design, Bulbous Form, 8 In.	1100.00
Pitcher, Wheeler Pattern, Sterling Silver Collar, 12 1/2 In.	275.00
Rose Bowl, Verona, Enameled Flowers & Leaves, Clear Ground	195.00
Salt & Pepper, Melon	140.00

Saltshaker, Tomato	55.00
Sugar Shaker, Bouquets of Forget–Me–Nots, Pink Stripes, Pewter Top	595.00
Sugar Shaker, Egg, White To Pink, Enameled Spider Daisies	195.00
Sugar Shaker, Salt & Pepper, Maidenhair Fern	365.00
Sugar Shaker, Single Petaled Chrysanthemums, 3 In.	485.00
Table Set, Dusty Rose	650.00
Toothpick, Pink Shaded, Bulbous Bottom, Flaring Neck, 1 7/8 In.	485.00
Toothpick, Spider Web	450.00
Vase, 8 Pulled–Up Ribs, Gold Enameled Petit Point, Red Leaves, 16 In.	875.00
Vase, Dotted Swiss, Mother–of–Pearl Glass, Alice Blue, 9 1/2 In.	425.00
Vase, Lava Glass, Black, Green, Blue, Pink, White, Gray, Accents, 6 In.	2250.00
Vase, Lava, Gold Tracing, Curlicue Handles, 5 5/8 In.	2250.00
Vase, Lily, Forget–Me–Nots, Coral Stripe Base, 8 In.	975.00
Vase, Pumpkin Shaded To Pink, Diamond–Quilted, Crimped Top, 1885	800.00

MUD FIGURES are small Chinese pottery figures made in the twentieth century. The figures usually represent workers, scholars, farmers, or merchants. Other pieces are trees, houses, and similar parts of the landscape. The figures have unglazed faces and hands but glazed clothing. They were originally made for fish tanks or planters. Mud figures were of little interest and brought low prices until the 1980s. When the prices rose, reproductions appeared.

2 Men Talking, 1 In., Pair	30.00
Elder, Seated, 3 In.	45.00
Elder, Standing, 4 1/2 In.	45.00
Man, With Yoke	65.00
Old Man, Woman Holding Mirror, 14 3/4 In., Pair	357.00

MULBERRY ware was made in the Staffordshire district of England from about 1850 to 1860. The dishes were decorated with a reddish brown transfer design, now called *mulberry.* Many of the patterns are similar to those used for flow blue and other Staffordshire transfer wares.

Bowl, Vegetable, Pelew	275.00
Chamber Pot, Vincennes, Alcock	250.00
Creamer, Corean	285.00
Creamer, Ning PO	245.00
Cup & Saucer, Udina	65.00
Cup Plate, Cyprus	50.00
Cup Plate, Vincennes, Alcock	60.00
Cup, Handleless, Jeddo	25.00
Gravy Boat, Sower, Staffordshire	55.00
Pitcher, Corea, 6 In.	55.00
Pitcher, Washington	375.00
Plate, Acadia University, Centennial, 10 1/2 In.	80.00
Plate, Cypress, 8 1/2 In.	65.00
Plate, Jeddo, Adams & Sons, 10 In.	35.00
Plate, Neva, 8 1/2 In.	50.00
Plate, Rhone Scenery, 8 3/4 In.	45.00
Plate, Rhone Scenery, 9 1/2 In.	50.00
Plate, Singan, T. Goodfellow, 1850, 9 1/2 In.	45.00
Plate, Tonquin, Heath, 8 1/2 In.	45.00
Plate, Washington, 9 1/2 In.	80.00
Platter, Beauties of China, 10 x 8 In.	145.00 To 165.00
Platter, Corean, Podmore & Walker, 16 x 12 In.	250.00
Platter, Rose, 14 x 11 In.	285.00
Platter, Tavoy, 15 In.	255.00
Sugar, Cover, Coberg	195.00
Teapot, Calcutta	325.00
Teapot, Corean, Clementson	300.00
Teapot, Pumpkin	575.00
Teapot, Udina	395.00
Tureen, Sauce, Corean	375.00
Tureen, Sauce, Cover, Pelew Flow	265.00

Muller Freres, Vase, Cameo, Floral, 1900; Muller Freres, Vase, Japanese

Landscape, Spherical Form, Signed, c.1920, 10 15/16 In.;

Muller Freres, Vase, Couple Scene, Cameo, 1920

MULLER FRERES, French for Muller Brothers, made cameo and other glass from the early 1900s to the late 1930s. Their factory was first located in Luneville, then in nearby Croismaire, France. Pieces were usually marked with the company name.

Chandelier, 3–Light, Globe, Bronze Dore Arms, Signed, 17 In.	990.00
Chandelier, 4–Light, Gray, Bell Form Shades, Wrought Iron, 1925, 40 In.	2200.00
Chandelier, 6–Light, Frosted Glass, Wrought Iron, 1925, 34 1/2 In.	247.00
Ewer, Cameo, Yellow Mottled, Orange Floral, 13 1/2 In.	600.00
Lamp, Boudoir, Shade, Mottled Orange & Green, Gilt Metal Base, 12 In.	385.00
Lamp, Mantel, Metal Reticulated Stick Torchere, Glass Shades, 15 In., Pair	1325.00
Lamp, Red Domed Shade, Boat Scene, Tree–Lined River, Signed, 20 In.	7150.00
Rose Bowl, Cameo, Floral	900.00
Sconce, Scalloped Lip Shade, Orange & Brown, Signed, 3 Piece	2090.00
Shade, Deco Style, Molded Design, Peach, Signed, 10 x 12 In.	595.00
Tumbler, Multicolored Forest Scene, Blackbirds, 5 In.	4500.00
Vase, Alsatian Landscape, Conifers, Signed, c.1920, 7 3/4 In.	4950.00
Vase, Apricot Opalescent, Spherical, Signed, c.1920, 12 In.	8800.00
Vase, Berried Branches, Gray, Lemon Yellow, Pumpkin, Cameo, 1915, 12 In.	1980.00
Vase, Cameo, Deep Pink Asters, 14 1/2 In.	2500.00
Vase, Cameo, Floral, 1900 ....*Illus*	3025.00
Vase, Cameo, Pink Asters, 14 1/2 In.	2500.00
Vase, Cameo, Red Roses, 11 In.	2700.00
Vase, Cameo, Roses, 7 1/4 x 9 In.	3200.00
Vase, Cameo, Roses, Bulbous, 12 In.	3200.00
Vase, Couple Scene, Cameo, 1920 ....*Illus*	4950.00
Vase, Dahlia, Gray, Yellow, Rose, Blue, Cameo, c.1925, 15 In.	6050.00
Vase, Foliage & Blossoms, Frosted Pink & White Ground, Signed, 13 1/2 In.	2860.00
Vase, Gray, Dahlia Blossoms, Gray, Egg Shape, 1925, 15 3/4 In.	6050.00
Vase, Japanese Landscape, Spherical Form, Signed, c.1920, 10 15/16 In. ....*Illus*	4950.00
Vase, Mottled Orange & Blue, Everted Cylinder, Signed, 11 In.	440.00
Vase, Red Roses, 11 In.	2700.00
Vase, Silver Foil Inclusions, Pattern of Dots, Scalloped, Signed, 1 1/2 In.	264.00

MUNCIE Clay Products Company was established by Charles Benham in Muncie, Indiana, in 1922. The company made pottery for the florist and giftshop trade. The company closed by 1939. Pieces are marked with the name *Muncie* or just with a system of numbers and letters, like *1A*.

Lamp, Dancing Nudes, Nude Finial	475.00
Lamp, Lovebirds, Yellow, 22 In.	180.00

Sugar, Ruba Rhombie 95.00
Vase, Pillow, Purple & Green, 9 In. 70.00

MURANO, see Glass–Venetian

MUSIC boxes and musical instruments are listed here. Phonograph records, jukeboxes, phonographs, and sheet music are listed in other categories in this book.

Accordion, 21 Keys, Pearl & Brass, Pine Case, France, 12 3/8 In. 150.00
Accordion, Hohner, Mother–of–Pearl 500.00
Accordion, Monarch, Ornate, 1880s 100.00
Accordion, Tanzbar, Player ....750.00 To 1100.00
Automaton, Singing Birds, Floral Setting, Striking Clock, Bontems, 25 In. 7000.00
Banjo, A. C. Fairbands, 5–String, c.1900 .... 2750.00
Banjo, Bacon, Bakelite 3500.00
Banjo, Celluloid Head & Resonator 3500.00
Banjo, Derry Mfg. 1650.00
Banjo, Epiphone, 4–String, Case 195.00
Banjo, Regal Music Co., 4–String 125.00
Banjo, William Tilton, 5–String Fretless, 10 Brackets, Fruitwood Neck, 1870 .... 330.00
Box, Baker–Troll, Sublime Harmony, 10 Tunes, Oak, 26 In. 1650.00
Box, Bird, Geisbaum, Brass Filigree, Germany, 1920 .... 2800.00
Box, Bird, Silver Plated, Miniature 2500.00
Box, Birdcage, 2 Birds, Heads Turn, Caille, 5 Cent 8500.00
Box, Birdcage, Automated, Tin Bird, France, 14 In. 245.00
Box, Brass Roll, 12 Pins, Owned By Alex Templeton, 1800s 2500.00
Box, Callie, Puck, Floor Model, Coin–Opeerated 8800.00
Box, Capital, Oak, 18 Cylinders 2090.00
Box, Criterion, Carved Oak Case, 10 Discs 2900.00
Box, Cylinder, Mahogany, 8 Tunes, Single Comb, 5 In. 550.00
Box, Cylinder, Rosewood, 25 In. 770.00
Box, Cylinder, Rosewood, Inlaid, 8 Tunes, 10 1/2 In. 1600.00
Box, Cylinder, Swiss, Burled & Inlaid Case, 24 x 6 1/2 x 10 In. 605.00
Box, Empress, Mahogany, 30 Discs 8000.00
Box, Euphonia, 15–In. Disc 4000.00
Box, Express, Mahogany, 30 Discs, Storage Cabinet, 14 x 25 x 19 In 8800.00
Box, France, Mahogany Marquetry, Cylinder, 20 1/2 In. 1265.00
Box, Harmonia, 10 Metal Discs, 16 x 12 x 6 In. 5000.00
Box, Hexaphone, Model 104 .... 8000.00
Box, Inlaid Rosewood, Chime Bells 1870.00
Box, Kalliope, 6 Bells, Single Comb, Disc Box 1800.00
Box, Liberace, Figural 50.00
Box, Lynaphon, No. 3, Cupid Transfer Cover, 5 Discs 600.00
Box, Music, Smoking Stand, Nipper, His Master's Voice, 12 x 8 In. 1000.00
Box, Myra, Floor Model, 15 1/2 In. Discs 5250.00
Box, Nickelodeon, Regina, Oak Case, Records 4000.00
Box, Orphenion, 10–In. Disc Box, 10 Discs 1400.00
Box, Paillard, 8 Bells, Tune Booklet, Inlaid Mother–of–Pearl, Burled Walnut Case ... 8500.00
Box, Paillard, Interchangeable Cylinder, 3 Cylinders 6500.00
Box, Polyphon, 19 5/8 In. 7000.00
Box, Polyphon, Upright, 19 5/8 In. 6800.00
Box, Regina, 12 Discs, Oak Case, c.1895, 14 x 13 In. 1650.00
Box, Regina, 50 Discs, Mahogany Case, 9 1/2 x 22 x 18 In. 3025.00
Box, Regina, Coin Slot, Double Comb, 12 Metal Discs, Instructions 2930.00
Box, Regina, Mahogany, Crank, 11–In. Discs 1760.00
Box, Regina, Single Comb, Mahogany, 15 1/2 In. 3400.00
Box, Regina, Table, Oak Case, Coin–Operated, 15 1/2–In. Disc 2500.00
Box, Reginaphone, Lion's Head Style, Double Comb, Metal Discs & Records 9000.00
Box, Schmid, Little Lulu 25.00
Box, Stella, Carved Front, Disc Storage Drawer, 17 1/4–In Disc 4750.00
Box, Stella, Console, Mahogany, 17 1/4 –In. Disc 7000.00
Box, Stella, Double Comb, 17 In.–Disc, Ahogany Case 1695.00
Box, Stella, Mahogany, 15 1/2–In. Disc 3900.00

Box, Stella, Mahogany, Single Comb, 9 1/2–In. Disc. 963.00
Box, Swiss, Bells, Castanet & Drum, Inlaid Mahogany, Cylinder, 10 3/4 In. 715.00
Box, Swiss, Danseurs No. 1780, Dolls Twirl Around, Swiss, 1962, 15 x 10 In. 600.00
Box, Swiss, Key Wind, 8 Tunes, Inlaid Lid, 19th Century, Bremond 2000.00
Box, Swiss, Painted Design, 8 Tune Selection 770.00
Box, Swiss, Rosewood, With Bells, 12 Tunes 1870.00
Box, Symphonion, 7 11/16–In. Disc 700.00
Box, Symphonion, Clock In Top Gallery, Double Comb, Coin–Operated 7500.00
Box, Symphonion, Double Comb, Floor Model, 13 5/8 In. Disc 8500.00
Box, Thorens, 4 1/2 In. 160.00
Box, Victorian, Ebonized, Burlwood, With Stand, Late 19th Century 7750.00
Box, Walnut, Inter–Change, Four 6–Tune Cylinders, 22 1/2 In. 4265.00
Case, Violin, Allover Marquetry 950.00
Cimbalom, Hungary, Mid–1800s 1500.00
Clavichord, 2 1/2 Octaves, Blond Wood, 1780s, 2 1/2 Ft. 2800.00
Concertina, Weidlichs Royal 37.00
Cornet, Henry Poureelle, Paris, Brass, Case 77.00
Drum, American Infantry, Green & Yellow Design, Stars, 18th Century, 25 x 27 In. 660.00
Drum, Bentwood, Brass, Hide Heads, Rope Lacing, Red, Black Graining, 19 In. 1250.00
Drum, Ipuheke, Hawaiian 90.00
Drum, Snare, Ludwig, 1930s 45.00
Drum, U.S. Army–Navy Regulation, Boston Drum Factory, Howe, 19th Century 450.00
Dulcimer, North Carolina, c.1890 .... 850.00
Flute, H. Bettoney, Cocuswood, Silver Plate Keys, 26 13/16 In. 195.00
Graphophone, Columbia, Model AG, Horn & Stand 1500.00
Guitar, C. F. Martin Co., Rosewood Back, Inlay & Rosette, Cedar Neck, Case, 1867 1210.00
Guitar, Electric, Epiphone Inc., Zephyr, Maple Body, Celluloid Binding, 1956 .... 665.00
Guitar, Electric, Gibson, Maple Back & Top, Rosewood Fingerboard, Pearl Eyes 545.00
Guitar, Gibson, Arch Top, c.1939 .... 2750.00
Guitar, Gibson, Light Yellow, Les Paul Anniversary Model 2000.00
Guitar, Gibson, No. ES345TD, Electric, Case 1500.00
Guitar, Gretsch, Anniversary Model G118 .... 1000.00
Guitar, National, Style O, 1930 .... 2035.00
Guitar, Red, White & Blue Painted, U.S. Star Type, Folk Art, 1960s 650.00
Harmonica, Auto–Valve–Harp, Instructions, Box, 4 1/2 In. 65.00
Harmonica, Chromatic, 3 Full Octaves 35.00
Harmonica, Comet 10.00
Harmonica, Contester, Box 12.50
Harmonica, Echo Harp, Box, 6 3/4 In. 95.00
Harmonica, Herb Shriner, Box 45.00
Harmonica, Hohner Echo, Double–Sided 20.00
Harmonica, Hohner Marine Band, Plastic, 1950s, 24 1/2 x 6 1/2 In. 37.00
Harmonica, Hohner, Melodica, Keys 30.00
Harmonica, Marine Band, Germany 15.00
Harmonica, Rolmonica, Bakelite, c.1920 .... 200.00
Harp, Lyon & Healy, Single Action, Gold Leaf, Maple, c.1920 .... 1975.00
Harp, Wurlitzer, No. 821, Starke Model, 67 1/2 In. 3000.00
Hexaphone, Regina, 6 Tunes, Floor Model, Oak Case, 64 x 27 In. 6600.00
Mandola, Vega Co., 1–Piece Rosewood Back, Ebony Fingerboard, Pearl Eyes, 1925 665.00
Mandolin, Case, 1930s 400.00
Mandolin, Gibson, Style F–4, Broad Curl Back, Rosewood Fingerboard, 1921 .... 2055.00
Melodeon, Child & Bishop, Rosewood, 1847, 31 x 22 In. 750.00
Melodeon, Ivory Keys, Trestle Base, Rosewood, c.1860, 30 x 29 x 16 In. 660.00
Melodeon, Jeweled Cartouches, Pierced Rack, Rosewood, c.1850 .... 385.00
Nickelodeon, 27 Violin Pipes, Tiger Oak Case, A Rolls 7500.00
Nickelodeon, Ellingon Piano Co., Stained Glass Panels, Oak, 52 1/4 In. 2200.00
Nickelodeon, National, Horse Race, Grand Rapids, Mich. 2500.00
Nickelodeon, Peerless, Cabinet Style 5500.00
Nickelodeon, Seeburg, Model E 12500.00
Nickelodeon, Seeburg, Model L 10500.00
Nickelodeon, Seeburg, Style B, Leaded Glass 1350.00
Organ, Adler, Parlor, Oak, Louisville, Ky., Restored, 1890 .... 1200.00
Organ, Aeolian, Duo Art Orchestrelle, 200 Rolls 4000.00

Organ, Aeolian, Player, Oak, Rolls, 1898 .... 2500.00
Organ, Austin, Pipe, Chimes Set, Dark Oak, 10 Ft. Pipe, 1922 .... 2500.00
Organ, Concert Roller, Pat. 1885 .... 375.00
Organ, D. W. Karn, Chapel, Oak, Finished Back, 1850 .... 8500.00
Organ, Estey, Parlor Pump, Nine Stops, 48 In. 750.00
Organ, Estey, Pipe, Walnut, 1890s 2500.00
Organ, Estey, Reed, Folding, c.1920 .... 300.00
Organ, Gem, Roller, Tabletop, Hand Crank, 15 Cob Rolls, 1885 .... 2500.00
Organ, Kilgen, Pipe, 32 Bass Pedals, 2 Manuals, Rolltop Console 9000.00
Organ, Magnus, Electric, Bakelite, Salesman Sample 250.00
Organ, Malcomb Love & Co., Parlor, Walnut, 14 Stops, c.1885 .... 1000.00
Organ, McTommany, Paper Rolls, c.1890 .... 495.00
Organ, Mechanical Organette Co., Roller, Stenciled Case, 1 Roll, Walnut 270.00
Organ, Molinari, Monkey 8500.00
Organ, Monkey, 25 Keys, 58 Wood Pipes, 9 Tunes, Crate, 24 x 24 x 14 In. 8500.00
Organ, Monkey, Reed Type 4500.00
Organ, Organina Cabinette 1500.00
Organ, Polyphon, Bells, 22 1/2 In. 6900.00
Organ, Polyphon, Upright, 19 5/8 In. 5500.00
Organ, Pump, Victorian, Bench, Electrified, Walnut, c.1880 .... 285.00
Organ, Stickley Brothers 5225.00
Organ, Street, 34 Keys, 7 Books of Music, Belgium, 1950s 7500.00
Organ, Street, Dutch, Perleof Amsterdam 1000.00
Organ, Street, World's Famous Folding, Bilhorn, Suit Case Type 500.00
Organ, Waterloo Organ Co., Pump 400.00
Organ, Wilcox–White, Rolls 3000.00
Organette, Celestina, Bells, Oak Case, Floor Model, From Penny Arcade 5500.00
Organette, Clariona, Resonator 400.00
Piano, Alpheus Babcock, Brass Inlay Over Mahogany, 5 1/2 Octaves, 67 3/8 In. 3750.00
Piano, Astor Co., Forte, Ebony Inlay, 3 Drawers, Mahogany, c.1820, 67 1/2 In. 1100.00
Piano, Cable–Nelson, Baby Grand, Bench, Mahogany 2850.00
Piano, Chickering, Ampico B, 1394 .... 8500.00
Piano, Chickering, Grand, Ampico, 5 Ft. 8 In. 1600.00
Piano, E. N. Scherr, Empire, Mahogany Veneer, Turned Legs, Square 137.00
Piano, Emil Ascherberg, Upright, Germany, 1865–1870 .... 420.00
Piano, G. Rodgers & Son, London, Baby Grand, Mahogany, c.1900 .... 1650.00
Piano, Grand, Beethoven Concert, Upright, Rosewood 3500.00
Piano, Grand, Forte, Rosewood Veneer, 51 x 95 In. 2000.00
Piano, Hallet & Davis, Grand, Rosewood, Square, 1850s 8500.00
Piano, Hammond–Straube, Player 650.00
Piano, John Broadwood & Sons, Grand, Oyster Walnut Veneer, c.1870 .... 3400.00
Piano, Kurtzmann, Player, With Piano Rolls, 1920 .... 495.00
Piano, Marshall & Wendell, Ampico B, William & Mary Art Case 4500.00
Piano, Mathushek, Orchestral, Brazilian Rosewood, c.1871 .... 1850.00
Piano, P. A. Starck, Player, Electrified, With 1 Roll, Bench 1540.00
Piano, Player, 25 Cents, Plays Large 12–Song Roll 2950.00
Piano, Player, Coin–Operated, Pizza Parlor, Paint & Glass 3500.00
Piano, Price & Teeple, Player, Quartered Oak, Refinished, Rolls, 1916 .... 2500.00
Piano, Regency, Spinet, Mahogany, Ebony Line Inlay, Fluted Legs, 19th Century 450.00
Piano, Remington, Player, Bench, Roll Cabinet, 64 Rolls 3000.00
Piano, River & Pond, Baby Grand, Painted Design, Mahogany, 1916, 5 Ft. 3 In. 990.00
Piano, Samick, Baby Grand 3200.00
Piano, Selectra, Western Electric, Mandolin, Xylophone, Coin–Operated 7500.00
Piano, Steinway, Model F, Upright, Ebony 5800.00
Piano, Steinway, Style I, Carved Legs, C. 1877, 6 Ft. 10 In. 1600.00
Piano, Steinway, Upright, Ebony 3200.00
Piano, Street, Barrel Shape, Louis Caspli, Gaston Fritch, 10 x 24 In. Barrel 700.00
Piano, Stroud, Duo–Art Grand, c.1933, 5 Ft. 4 In. 3900.00
Piano, Weber, Grand, Natural Mahogany, Refinished, 1904, 5 Ft. 6 In. 5000.00
Piano, Wurlitzer Apollo, Reproducing, Upright, Electric, 60 Rolls 800.00
Piano, Wurlitzer, No. 165387, Butterfly, Bench, Walnut, c.1937 .... 990.00
Piano, Wurlitzer, Player, 3 Art Glass Panels, 5–Tune Roll, Oak, 4 Ft. 10 In. 7700.00
Piccolo, Gemeinhardt 100.00

Piccolo, Klemm, Boxwood Body, 1–Keyed, Ivory Mounts, Brass Key, 14 13/16 In.	365.00
Recorder, Wollensak, 4 & 8 Track, With 2 Speakers, Wooden, 1960	1000.00
Rolmonica, 9 Rolls	135.00
Trombone, Frank Holton Co., Case	100.00
Ukelin, Manufacturer's Advertising Co., Half Ukulele & Mandolin, 1912	120.00
Ukulele, Tenor, Gibson, Mahogany Body, Celluloid Binding, Pearl Inlay, 1920s	210.00
Violin, Handmade, Antonio Guadagnini, 1851	3000.00

MUSTACHE CUPS were popular from 1850 to 1900 when the large, flowing mustache was in style. A ledge of china or silver held the hair out of the liquid in the cup. This kept the mustache tidy and also kept the mustache wax from melting. Left–handed mustache cups are rare but are being reproduced.

Butterfly Handle, Nippon	25.00
Floral, Saucer	48.00
Indian Cameo, Decal, Brandenburg, Prussia Type	100.00
Papa, Floral, Gold, Germany	45.00
Ruffled Rim & Base, Gold, Floral, Saucer, Limoges, c.1908	65.00

MZ AUSTRIA is the wording on a mark used by Moritz Zdekauer on porcelains made at his works from about 1900. The firm was established in the town of Alt–Rohlau, Austria, in 1884 and was nationalized in 1945. The pieces were decorated with lavish floral patterns and overglaze gold decoration. Full sets of dishes were made as well as vases, toilet sets, and other wares.

Mz Austria

Chocolate Set, Yellow Roses, Blue, Brown Ground, Scalloped, Gold Band	275.00
Hair Receiver, Pink Roses	50.00

NAILSEA glass was made in the Bristol district in England from 1788 to 1873. It was made by many different factories, not just the Nailsea Glass House. Many pieces were made with loopings of either white or colored glass as decoration.

Bowl, Folded Rim, Red Loopings, Aqua Stem & Foot, 1850s, 5 1/4 In.	880.00
Ewer, Crimson Loopings, Crystal Handle, 5 1/2 In.	100.00
Flask, Flattened Shape, Red & White, Opaque, 7 In.	165.00
Flask, White Loopings, 7 1/4 In.	125.00
Lamp, Fairy, 4 Piece	550.00
Nut Dish, Clear, Orange, Pedestal, 2 x 3 In., 5 Piece	60.00
Paperweight, Thistle, Sulphide, Cameo, Green Glass, 2 3/4 In.	440.00
Paperweight, Veiled Bubble Flower In Pot, Green Bottle, 3 3/16 In.	121.00
Rolling Pin, Pink & White, Clear Loops, 11 In.	235.00

NAKARA is a trade name for a white glassware made about 1900 by the C. F. Monroe Company of Meriden, Connecticut. It was decorated in pastel colors. The glass was very similar to another glass made by the company called *Wave Crest.* The company closed in 1916. Boxes for use on a dressing table are the most commonly found Nakara pieces. The mark is not found on every piece.

NAKARA

Box, 2 Angels, Harp, Raised Enamel Dots, Signed, 3 3/4 In.	400.00
Box, Blown–Out Rococo, Beaded Flowers At Sides & Top, 8 In.	1150.00
Box, Collars & Cuffs, 8 In.	975.00
Box, Cover, 2 Angels With Harp, Raised Enameled Dots, Signed, 3 3/4 In	400.00
Box, Hinged Lid, Bishop Hat Shape, Dots Outline Feathery Design, Marked, 4 In.	335.00
Box, Hinged, Round, Floral Design, Blue, 4 1/2 In.	190.00
Humidor, Tobacco, Word Tobacco Across Front, Floral, Signed, 7 x 7 In.	595.00

NANKING is a type of blue–and–white porcelain made in Canton, China, since the late eighteenth century. It is very similar to Canton, which is listed under its own name in this book. Both Nanking and Canton are part of a larger group now called *Chinese Export* porcelain. Nanking has a spear–and–post border and may have gold decoration.

Coaster, Wine Bottle, Lion Head Handles, Silver, 1760	4800.00
Mug, Chicken Skin, Early 19th Century	715.00

Tureen, Sauce, Knopped Dome Cover, Handles, 1750–1770 .... 1975.00

NAPKIN RINGS were in fashion from 1869 to about 1900. They were made of silver, porcelain, wood, and other materials. They are still being made today. The most popular rings with collectors are the silver–plated figural examples. Small, realistic figures were made to hold the ring. Good and poor reproductions of the more expensive rings are now being made and collectors must be very careful.

Figural, 2 Boys In Caps, Earmuffs, Rectangular Base, Middletown Silver Plate	235.00
Figural, 2 Dogs, 4 Feet, Silver Plate	275.00
Figural, 2 Foxes Sitting, Ring On Back, Simpson Hall–Miller	55.00
Figural, 2 Squirrels Munching Nut, Log Type Ring, Silver Plate	95.00
Figural, Angry Cat, Etched Ring	210.00
Figural, Bird With Chain, Silver Plate	160.00
Figural, Bird, Leaf Bottom, Silver Plate	160.00
Figural, Bird, Queen City Silver, 2 1/2 x 2 3/4 In. ....*Illus*	85.00
Figural, Boy Standing In Front of Scrolled Edge, 6–Sided Ring, Silver Plate	275.00
Figural, Boy With Hat, Pushing Cart, Silver Plate	250.00
Figural, Camel In Front of Ring, Meriden	185.00
Figural, Cherub Pulling Sled, Holds Scrolled Napkin, Silver Plate	275.00
Figural, Cherub With Wings, Watching Bird On Oblong Base, Silver Plate	55.00
Figural, Child, Riding Watermelon, Metal, 5 x 5 1/2 In. ....*Illus*	110.00
Figural, Dog Pulling Open Salt, Movable Wheels, Silver Plate	375.00
Figural, Eagle, Astride Rectangular Base, Ring On Wings, Meriden	120.00
Figural, Fox With Grapes, Silver Plate	75.00
Figural, Girl, Pigtail, Pushing Ring, Meriden	150.00
Figural, Goat Pulling Cart, Wheels Turn, Meriden	250.00
Figural, Horse Pulling Wheeled Cart, Meriden	325.00
Figural, Kittens, Standing On Hind Legs, Silver Plate	175.00
Figural, Navy Man, Standing On U.S. Shield	175.00
Figural, Palm Tree, Shading Giraffe, Ring On Other Side	400.00
Figural, Parakeet On Branch, Leafy Base	100.00
Figural, Penguin, Bakelite	45.00
Figural, Small Bird, Looking Into Nest, Eggs On Top Ring, Tree Branch	100.00
Figural, Stork Standing On Leaf Base, Ring On Back, Simpson Hall–Miller	250.00
Figural, Turtle, Head Up, Ring On His Back, Silver Plate	30.00
Figural, Wolf Baying At Moon, Free–Form Base, Ball Feet	225.00
Figural, Wolverine Pulling Cart, Wheels Move, Triple Plate, Rogers Bros.	300.00
Tartan Ware, 7 Piece	200.00

NASH glass was made in Corona, New York, from about 1928 to 1931. A. Douglas Nash bought the Corona glassworks from Louis C. Tiffany in 1928 and founded the A. Douglas Nash Corporation with support from his father, Arthur J. Nash. Arthur had worked at the Webb factory in England and for the Tiffany Glassworks in Corona.

NASH

Compote, Chintz, Green Zigzag, Blue, Pedestal Base, Scallop Edge, 4 In. 95.00

Napkin Ring, Figural, Bird, Queen City Silver, 2 1/2 X 2 3/4 In.; Napkin Ring, Figural, Child, Riding Watermelon, Metal, 5 X 5 1/2 In.

Nautical, Chest, Sea, Pine, Brown Stain,
17 1/2 X 43 X 18 In.

Nautical, Figurehead, Woman's Bust,
Late 19th Century, 32 In.

Platter, Chintz, Alternating Green Bands & Blue Stripes, Raised Edge, 8 1/4 In.	90.00
Vase, Green–Blue Luster Chintz, Silvery Stripes, Pedestal Foot, Signed, 9 1/2 In.	500.00

NAUTICAL antiques are listed in this category. Any of the many objects that were made or used by the seafaring trade, including ship parts, models, and tools, are included. Other pieces may be found listed under Scrimshaw.

Anchor, Presentation, Eurydice 1878, Bronze, Oak, 10 x 6 In.	390.00
Ashtray, Newport News Shipbuilding & Dry Docks Co., Bronze, Footed	75.00
Bag, Sailor's, Ship Portrait, Sailcloth, Drawstring Top, 1855, 36 x 20 In.	2485.00
Bell, Ship's, Brass, Mimosa Liverpool 1853, Ropework Base, 8 3/4 In.	1590.00
Bottle, Wine, Sea Captain's, Leather	12.50
Box, Shipbuilder's, Grand Rapids, Wooden, Green Stain, 25 x 40 In.	245.00
Candleholder, Brass, Dolphin Bracket, Clear Shade, England, 1850, 10 1/2 In.	395.00
Canoe, Paddles, Wooden, Old Town, Miniature	605.00
Chart, Coast of Maine From Spurwick River To Moose Point, 1776, 31 x 21 In.	335.00
Chart, Coast of Nova Scotia, New England, New Jersey, 1780, 33 x 48 In.	275.00
Chart, Ipswich Bay & Salem Harbor, 1776, 2 Pages, 32 1/2 x 24 In.	445.00
Chart, Nova Scotia, 3 Folio Pages, 1775, 52 1/2 x 32 In.	358.00
Chest, Canted, Painted Clipper Ship Interior of Lid, 41 x 15 x 15 In.	1100.00
Chest, Lift–Top, Inset Brass Hardware & Hinges, Camphorwood, 21 x 42 In.	1045.00
Chest, Medical, Bottles, Captain's, Mahogany Case, 9 1/2 x 10 In.	248.00
Chest, Painted Ship Inside Lid, Green Paint, Rope Beckets, 1863	445.00
Chest, Sea, Lift Top, Brown Stain, Pine, 17 1/2 x 43 In.	440.00
Chest, Sea, Painted Green, New England, Pine, c.1820	785.00
Chest, Sea, Pine, Brown Stain, 17 1/2 x 43 x 18 In. ....*Illus*	440.00
Chest, Sea, Wooden Buckets, Painting Inside of Lid, 17 x 35 x 16 In.	665.00
Chest, Seaman's, Oak, Hinged Top, Brass Plaque, 1883, England, 18 x 33 x 21 In.	475.00
Chest, Solid Brass Hardware, Reddish Paint, 18th Century, 19 1/2 x 27 In.	450.00
Chest, Surgeon's, Mortar & Pestle, Bottles, Botanicals, Blades, 1840	1650.00
Chronometer, Double Case, Hamilton Watch Co., 4 1/2–In. Dial	120.00
Chronometer, Double Case, Thomas Mercer Ltd., England, Carrying Case	1540.00
Chronometer, Ed. Ott, No. 1040, 2–Day, 2–Tier Mahogany Box, Key, c.1860	3300.00
Chronometer, Ulysse Nardin, Locle & Generve, 2–Day, Mahogany Box, 1950	2475.00
Chronometer, W. E. Ehrlich, No. 454, 56 Hour, Mahogany Box, c.1880	3300.00
Clock & Barometer Set, Chelsea, Claremont Model, Brass, 1944, 8 x 14 In.	1290.00
Clock, Chelsea, Ship's Bell, 1940s, 6 In.	600.00
Clock, Chelsea, Ship's Bell, Bronze, 13 x 14 In.	853.00
Clock, Chelsea, Ship's, Admiral, Black Wood Base, 1941, 14 In.	2675.00
Clock, Howard, Brass, Inscribed Enterprise, Spring Driven, Stand, 10 In.	462.00

Nautical, Sextant, W. Gerrard, Brass;

Nautical, Quadrant, Spencer, Browning

& Rust, Ebony, Ivory

♦ ♦

Look through the wrong end of a telescope you plan to buy. If it can be focused, all of the parts are there.

♦ ♦

Clock, Seth Thomas, Boat, Teak, Second Hand, Hinged Face, Early 20th Century	340.00
Clock, Seth Thomas, Ship's Bell, Brass, Outside Gong, 6 1/2 In.	358.00
Clock, Steam Gauge & Valve Mfg. Co., Steel Dial, Key Wind, 13 In.	715.00
Compass, 14K Yellow Gold, With Barometer, Pocket, 1 1/4 In.	605.00
Compass, Gen. C. A. Baker, New York, Wooden Case, 6 In.	120.00
Compass, Stoptani	85.00
Compass, Tell-Tale, J. Bruce & Sons, Liverpool, 1870, 6 In. Diam.	1275.00
Deck-Watch, Waltham, Mahogany, Brass, U.S. Navy, 8-Day, WW I, 2 3/4 In.	895.00
Desk, Tambour Top, Camphorwood, Compartments, China Trade, 1840, 21 In.	2075.00
Diorama, Dockyard, Ships, Buildings, Glass Case, 38 x 24 1/2 x 18 1/2 In.	1980.00
Ditty Bag, With Implements, Canvas, 19th Century	540.00
Ditty Box, Baleen, Whaling Ship Scene, Bird's-Eye Maple, 7 1/2 x 3 In.	1375.00
Ditty Box, Whalebone, Pierced Design, Note & Documents, 1869, 8 3/4 x 7 In.	4250.00
Divider, Chart, Single Handed, Brass, Steel, England, Early 19th Century, 6 In.	295.00
Divider, Chart, Single Handed, Cut Steel, Europe, 1700, 6 1/2 In.	475.00
Figurehead, Captain David Cook, 19th Century	5000.00
Figurehead, Sea Captain, Holding Telescope In Hand, 19th Century, 5 Ft. 6 In.	5500.00
Figurehead, Woman's Bust, Late 19th Century, 32 In. ....*Illus*	5280.00
Figurehead, Woman, Flowing Dress, Thick Paint, 1850, 45 In.	11500.00
Fin, Wooden, 22 In.	40.00
Float, Nova Scotia, Glass	52.00
Fog Horn, Brass Chain, Brass, 13 In.	115.00
Fog Horn, Brass, Hand Operated	375.00
Fog Horn, Lothrop, Inscribed S.S. Nantucket, 13 x 9 x 18 1/2 In.	55.00
Games Box, Prisoner of War, Bone, Sliding Lid, Paintings, 1790, 6 1/2 In.	1575.00
Gas Pump Globe, D-X Marine, Boats	500.00
Gun, Harpoon, Brass, 19th Century	2530.00
Gun, Harpoon, Steel, 19th Century	1045.00
Harpoon, Toggle, Iron, 13 1/2 In.	253.00
Harpoon, Whaling, Wooden Shaft, Rope, Provincetown, Cape Cod, 1850, 32 In.	895.00
Hat, Sailor's, Pensacola	110.00
Helmet, Diving, Chinese, Brass	495.00
Insurance Policy, Neptune Ins. Co., Whale & Sperm Oil, & Whale Bone, $6, 000 ...	40.00
Lamp, Perko, Anchor, Brass, 17 In.	295.00
Lamp, Ship's, Brass, No Burner, 12 In.	165.00
Lamp, Ship's, Port, No Burner, 14 In.	125.00
Lamp, Ship's, Russell & Watson, Starboard, c.1870	425.00
Lantern, 3 Candleholders Inside, Wavy Glass, Wood	302.50
Lantern, Cabinet, Gimbaled, Brass, 9 In., Pair	193.00
Lantern, Davey & Co., Brass, London, Clear Glass Glove, 14 1/2 x 9 1/2 In.	195.00
Leg Irons, Harvard Lock Co., Civil War Style, Key, 14 1/2 In.	220.00
Light, Barge, Red Glass	50.00
Light, Joseph Walton, 360 Degree, Red Lens, Copper, 17 In.	132.00
Light, Ship's, Red Globe, Large	225.00
Liquor Set, Captain's, Oak Case, 12 Bottles, Gilt-Designed Funnel	770.00
Log, Schooner Melinda, Ports of Call, 1885-1893	225.00

Long Glass, Captain's, Brass Draw Tube, June, 1879 .... 1900.00
Menu, Normandie, Diner De Gala, 14 Mars, 1937 .... 12.00
Model, 3–Masted Ship 770.00
Model, Atlantic, Racing Yacht, Planked Deck, Case, 29 x 22 1/2 In. 2100.00
Model, Cabin Cruiser, 3 Decks, Furnished Interior, Stand, Wood, Metal, 25 1/2 In. 65.00
Model, Caledonia, Sail, Steam Brig, Figurehead, Brass Fitting, 32 x 13 x 23 In. 4125.00
Model, Glory of The Seas, Clipper Ship, Case, 53 x 14 x 37 In. 3500.00
Model, Guide Boat, Adirondack, White Cedar, David Kavner, 24 In. 875.00
Model, Half, Schooner, Hustler, Thomas Conlon, 1889, 9 1/2 x 46 In. 303.00
Model, La Ville De Dieppe, France, Boxwood & Baleen, Case, 12 1/2 In. 3850.00
Model, Lobster Smack, Muscongus Bay, Mahogany Deck, 42 1/2 x 40 1/2 In. 1800.00
Model, Monterey Fishing Boat, Wooden, Mid–1950s, 5 Ft. 700.00
Model, New Bedford Whaling Sea Fox, Glass Case, Kjeld Jensen, 34 In. 2750.00
Model, Ocean Liner, Illuminated Interior, 5 Ft. 825.00
Model, Paddlewheel, Cantin Lake, Mi. Model, Hand Made, Working Parts, 1930s 850.00
Model, Paddlewheel, Martha's Vineyard, Working Paddles, Wood Brackets, 23 In. ... 465.00
Model, Paddlewheel, Paddles Turn, Metal Railing, Oak Display Case, 20 In. 2310.00
Model, Paddlewheel, Wood, Timey, 19th Century, 24 In. 4400.00
Model, Riverboat, Chris Argum, Wood & Tin, 50 In. 1650.00
Model, Sailing Boat, Wooden, Mid–1950s, 3 1/2 Ft. 4500.00
Model, Sequin, American Steam Tugboat, Cherry & Basswood, 39 x 8 x 25 In. 1500.00
Model, Side Paddle, Baltimore Prisoner Made, 1860s, 24 In. 4840.00
Model, Tugboat, Haight, Wood, 1892, 3 Ft. 3200.00
Octant, Spencer Barrett & Co., Cased Ebony, Keystone Case, 1860, 13 In. 525.00
Octant, Spencer Browning & Co., Ebony, Brass, 1843, 13 In. Index Arm 625.00
Oil Can, Outboard Marine, Standard Oil, 1 Qt. 40.00
Oil Can, Outboard Marine, Sunoco, With Speedboat, 1 Qt. 45.00
Passenger List, Cabin, S. S. Hamburg, New York To Hamburg, June 22, 1912 ...... 15.00
Photograph, Coast Guard Station, Provincetown, 10 1/2 x 13 1/2 In. 60.00
Picture, Sailing Ship, Oil On Canvas, Wm. Howard Yorke, 1873, 24 x 36 In. 2675.00
Plotting Rule & Protractor, Ivory, c.1840 .... 160.00
Program, Farewell Party, S. S. Normandie, French Line, 1937 .... 35.00
Protractor, Charting, Troughton & Simms, London, Brass, 8 In. Diam. 475.00
Protractor, Cole Course, Brass, Oct. 1907, 22–In. Mahogany Case 180.00
Quadrant, Brass Arm, Engraved Globe, Navigator's Tools, Ivory Dial, Rosewood 1760.00
Quadrant, Dark Rosewood Frame, Brass, Engraved Arm, 1790, 18 In. 1450.00
Quadrant, Spencer, Browning & Rust, Ebony, Ivory ....*Illus* 413.00
Rule, Charting, J. & H. M. Pool, Easton, Mass. 750.00
Rule, Gunter's, Kutz, New York, Boxwood, 19th Century, 24 In. 450.00
Rule, Navigational, B. Donn, Boxwood, 24 In. 695.00
Sailor's Valentine, Shellwork, Frame 605.00
Sailor's Valentine, Shellwork, Octagonal, Frame, 14 x 13 1/2 In. 665.00
Salt & Pepper, Europa 38.00
Schedule, Southern Pacific Co., New York–New Orleans Line, 1908, 5 1/2 In 6.00
Sector, Cook & Bargon, Ivory, c.1920s 121.00
Sector, Elliott & C. Harding, Signed Twice, Ivory 235.00
Sextant, Ivory Bound, Mounted As Lamp 300.00
Sextant, Louis Weule Co., Brass, Black Metal, Fitted Case 220.00
Sextant, Silver Scale, Small Telescope, Leather Case 660.00
Sextant, Spencer Barrett & Co., Ivory Scale & Name Plate, Brass & Ebony 440.00
Sextant, Troughton & Simms, Brass, Mahogany Box, 1825, 4 3/4 In. 2400.00
Sextant, W. Gerrard, Brass ....*Illus* 468.00
Ship In Bottle, Fine Old Pale Sherry, Towed Tug, Holyhead, Stand, 12 x 3 In. 335.00
Ship In Bottle, Florrie, Village, Green Tinted Glass, Teak Base, 1890, 11 x 3 In. 595.00
Ship In Bottle, Ornate Stand, 1900, 9 x 5 1/2 x 10 In. 890.00
Ship Model, 3 Masted, American Flag, Ivory Figurehead, Glass Case, 24 x 29 In. ... 1980.00
Ship Model, Bounty, 1940s 1650.00
Ship Model, British Frigate, Great Harry, Fitted For Electricity, 28 x 14 In. 775.00
Ship Model, Charles W. Morgan, Whale Ship, Case, 31 x 10 In. 2100.00
Ship Model, Charles W. Morgan, Whaler, Longboats, Deadeyes, 44 In. 990.00
Ship Model, City of Holyoke, Glass Case, 32 In. 355.00
Ship Model, Clipper Ship, Black, Red Hull, Early 20th Century, 2 1/2 x 2 Ft. 65.00
Ship Model, Coastal Steamer, American, Wooden, 13 1/4 x 33 In. 385.00

Ship Model, Cutty Sark, Movable Rudder, Brass, Copper Mounted, 48 In. 5850.00
Ship Model, Danish Royal Yacht, Dannebrog, 2 Decks, Case, 46 In. 4400.00
Ship Model, Destroyer, World War II, Wood, Mid–1950s, 7 Ft. 3700.00
Ship Model, English Frigate, Prisoner of War, Bone, 14 Cannons, Elm Base, 21 In. 5225.00
Ship Model, Ester, Chesapeake Bay Skip Ack 137.50
Ship Model, Fishing Schooner, America, 60 In. 2420.00
Ship Model, Flying Cloud American Clipper Ship, Case, 27 1/2 x 40 In. 1760.00
Ship Model, Flying Cloud, of Boston, Wood, Fully Rigged, 29 x 91 In. 3190.00
Ship Model, Gaspe Trade, 5–Masted Schooner, Wooden Stand, c.1930, 35 x 53 In. 1650.00
Ship Model, Grain Rigger, The Matilda, Glass Vitrine, 1910, England, 54 In. 1540.00
Ship Model, H. M. S. Medea, 46–Gun Frigate, Bone, Case, France, 10 1/2 In. 4840.00
Ship Model, Queen Mary, 11 1/4 x 26 In. 88.00
Ship Model, Rig, 12 Guns, Wooden, c.1840, 46 In. 220.00
Ship Model, Sovereign of The Seas, Cased, America, Fully Rigged, 29 x 11 x 20 In. 935.00
Ship Model, Tacoma, West Coast Passenger Steamer, Case, 16 x 8 x 9 In. 1600.00
Ship Model, Two Brothers, Whale Ship, Cased, America, 58 x 78 In. 14300.00
Ship Model, USS Boston, Sloop of War, Oak Case, 20th Century, 40 x 56 In. 5500.00
Ship Model, USS Constitution, Wood, 63 x 74 In. 2425.00
Ship Model, USS Maine, 4 Ft. 550.00
Ship Model, Venetian Sailing Ship, La Pinta, Miniature Lamps, 33 x 26 x 9 In. 550.00
Ship Model, Whaler, Charles W. Morgan, Moored At Mystic Seaport 1760.00
Ship Model, World War II Destroyer, Handbuilt, Wooden, 7 Ft. 3700.00
Signal Horn, Fire Boat 1200.00
Spyglass, Brass, A. Frank Optician, Manchester, Leather Tube, 1881, 30 In. 550.00
Spyglass, Brass, Leather, 5 Pulls, E. Vion, 1800s, 48 In. 695.00
Spyglass, Brass, Leather, E. A. Upton, U.S.N., 1880, Extends To 44 1/2 In. 495.00
Spyglass, Green Braided Canvas Cover, Brass, 1830–1840, Extends To 47 In. 540.00
Spyglass, Tapered Barrel, Leather, Dollond, London, 1820–1830, 25 1/2 In. 550.00
Stove, Coal Burning, Yates Haywood & Co., Colorful Tiles, 36 In. 750.00
Surgeon's Field Kit, Bone Instruments & Tools, Stainless Steel, Box, 10 x 6 In. 1250.00
Swordfish Bill, Painted Ship & Mermaids, Carved Fish, 23 1/2 In. 210.00
Telegram, Ship's, Bon Voyage From Scotland, Gold Envelope, May 19, 1938 .... 15.00
Telephone, Russell & Watson, Captain's, Engine Room, Brass, c.1870, 26 In. 175.00
Telescope, 4 Drawers, Brass, Extends To 27 In. 88.00
Telescope, Leather Barrel, 3 Drawers, Brass, 17 In. 100.00
Telescope, Mahogany, F. Watkins Charing Cross, 1770, Extends To 58 In. 1950.00
Telescope, Victorian, Adjustable Eyepiece, Ebonized Tripod, Brass, 44 1/2 In. 1980.00
Tide Computer, Marescope, France, Plastic, Mid–20th Century, 6 1/4 Diam. 240.00
Trumpet, Speaking, Captain's Whaling Type, 18 1/2 In. 400.00
Wheel, Brass Hub, Walnut & Other Woods, 43 In. 440.00
Wheel, Brass Hub, Walnut & Other Woods, 49 In. 2530.00
Wheel, Ships, John Hastie & Co., Mahogany, 36 In. 248.00
Wooden Leg, Original Leather Strap 550.00

NETSUKES are small ivory, wood, metal, or porcelain pieces used as
toggles on the end of the cord that held a Japanese money pouch. The
earliest date from the sixteenth century. Many are miniature, carved works
of art.

Bone, Faces of The Gods 95.00
Bronze, Samurai On Horseback, 19th Century, 2 1/4 In. 247.50
Horn & Hippopotamus Tooth, Bird Feeder 295.00
Horn, Frog On Stump 65.00
Horn, Snail On Mushroom 150.00
Horn, Swan, Insct Eycs 145.00
Ironwood, Hotai With Fan 75.00
Ivory, 2 Mushrooms, Ryoshu, 1 1/2 In. 220.00
Ivory, Chick Bursting Out of Ivory Shell 675.00
Ivory, Dog With Ball, Inset Eyes 375.00
Ivory, Double Snake, Inset Eyes 195.00
Ivory, Fisherman Holding Net, Boy At His Side, 5 In. 220.00
Ivory, Girl Reading, 1 3/4 In. 220.00
Ivory, Group, Multiple Figures, Tea Part, 3 1/2 In. 440.00
Ivory, Horse With Rider, 3 1/4 In. 120.00

Ivory, Man Chasing A Bat With A Broom, 6 In.	385.00
Ivory, Man With Drum, 1 1/8 In.	45.00
Ivory, Man With Fan, 6 In.	110.00
Ivory, Man With Hat & Stick, 1 7/8 In.	45.00
Ivory, Man With Platform Shoe In Hand, 2 1/4 In.	55.00
Ivory, Man, Child Wearing A Kabuki Mask, 6 In.	220.00
Ivory, Mouse In Basket With Vegetables	48.00
Ivory, Rat With Carrot	350.00
Ivory, Samurai Warrior On Horseback, Vanquished Foe, 4 In.	440.00
Ivory, Samurai, Engraved Clothes, 1 1/4 In.	65.00
Ivory, Seated Dog, Insects & Rat, Signed, 2 3/8 In.	155.00
Ivory, Sleeping Rat, Horaku, 1 1/4 In.	165.00
Ivory, Woman In Kimono, 7 In.	220.00
Ivory, Woman In Kimono, Inset Jewels, 4 1/2 In.	165.00
Ivory, Woman With Gourd, 1 3/4 In.	190.00
Ivory, Woman, Child, Dog, 5 In.	220.00
Tagua Nut, Baby Seal	75.00
Tagua Nut, Hotai Face	75.00
Tagua Nut, Rabbit	85.00
Wood, Boy With Lion Mask, Seated On Drum, Miwa, 1 1/4 In.	660.00
Wood, Samurai, Engraved Clothes, 2 1/4 In.	65.00
Wood, Woman With Fan, Seated, With Writing Brush, 1 1/4 In.	220.00

NEW MARTINSVILLE Glass Manufacturing Company was established in 1901 in New Martinsville, West Virginia. It was bought and renamed the Viking Glass Company in 1944 and is still producing fine glasswares.

Basket, Janice, Crystal, 13 x 10 In.	60.00
Bookends, Hunter	70.00
Bookends, Sailboat	49.75
Bowl, Prelude, 11 In.	45.00
Bowl, Radiance, Amber, 12 In.	40.00
Bride's Bowl, White, Pink, Fluted, 10 1/2 In.	165.00
Butter, Cover, Carnation	65.00
Cake Salver, Prelude, Footed, 11 In.	32.00
Cake Stand, Princess	15.00
Cocktail Shaker, Cobalt Blue, Silver Bands, Deco Style Stem	200.00
Compote, Radiance, Metal Pedestal, Oval, Red, 9 In.	35.00
Console Set, Prelude, Ruffled Bowl, 2–Light Candlestick, 3 Piece	60.00
Decanter Set, Poppy, Fan Stopper, Tray, 6 Piece	125.00
Decanter, Cordial, Hunt Scene, Crystal, Sterling Silver, 7 1/2 In.	60.00
Figurine, Baby Bear	50.00
Figurine, Rooster, Crystal	145.00
Figurine, Russian Wolfhound	60.00
Figurine, Seal, With Ball, 7 1/2 In.	95.00
Figurine, Squirrel, Flat	60.00
Figurine, Swan, Cobalt Blue, Crystal Neck	55.00
Figurine, Tiger, Pair	300.00
Flower Frog, Woman Dancer, Shawl, Pink	375.00
Goblet, Cocktail, Prelude	12.00
Radiance, Compote, Metal Pedestal, Oval, Red	35.00
Radiance, Relish, 3 Sections, Red	60.00
Relish, 3 Sections, Etched, 12 In.	45.00
Relish, 3 Sections, Moondrops, Red	60.00
Relish, Divided, Etched, 13 In.	12.00
Relish, Radiance, 3 Sections, Red	22.50
Server, Center Handle, Prelude, 10 1/2 In.	57.00
Shot Glass, Moondrops, Red	10.00
Sugar & Creamer, Moondrops, Red, Miniature	35.00
Sugar & Creamer, Tray, Radiance	65.00
Sugar & Creamer, Tray, Radiance, Crystal	50.00

NEWCOMB Pottery was founded by Ellsworth and William Woodward at Sophie Newcomb College, New Orleans, Louisiana, in 1895. The work continued through the 1940s. Pieces of this art pottery are marked with the printed letters *NC* and often have the incised initials of the artist as well. Most pieces have a matte glaze and incised decoration.

Bowl, Floral, Matte Blues, Fannie Simpson, 1912, 9 1/2 In.	675.00
Bowl, Landscape, Live Oak Trees, Spanish Moss, C. Longhohn, 6 1/2 x 8 1/4 In.	3410.00
Bowl, Pink Flowers, Deep Blue Ground, 4 x 8 In.	605.00
Honey Pot, Incised Concentric Circles, Blue High Glaze To White, 1930s, 4 In.	308.00
Match Holder, Narcissus Blossoms, Blue Ground, S. Irvine, 1916, 2 1/2 In.	715.00
Mug, Bell Shaped, Blue–Green Trees, Yellow–Ivory Ground, 4 1/4 In.	1540.00
Tile, Floral, L. Nicholson, Square, 4 In.	550.00
Vase, Apple Blossoms, 5 x 6 1/2 In.	1250.00
Vase, Band of Roses, Blue Ground, Henrietta Bailey, 1927, 6 1/4 x 6 3/4 In.	2310.00
Vase, Blue Blossoms, Green Foliage, Blue Ground, Matte, H. Bailey, 1926, 11 In.	1650.00
Vase, Blue, Green, Gray Ethereal Landscape, 3 Pines, 6 In.	880.00
Vase, Blue–Green Speckled Glaze, 11 x 6 1/2 In.	1540.00
Vase, Cylinder Design, Green, Blue, White Iris Blossoms, 12 1/2 In.	3850.00
Vase, Floral Band, Carved, Raspberry Body, Sadie Irvine, 1926, 4 1/4 In.	1100.00
Vase, Floral, Matte, Pink, Yellow, Sadie Irvine, 12 In.	1000.00
Vase, Green & Turquoise Glaze, Dripping Over Red Clay, Dimpled, Marked, 7 In.	140.00
Vase, Incised Design, Ball Shape, Blue, Signed, 3 In.	500.00
Vase, Incised Foliage, Marked, 11 In.	935.00
Vase, Landscape, Tree & Moss, Anna Simpson, 3 3/4 In.	1155.00
Vase, Matte Blue, 1932, 2 1/2 In.	295.00
Vase, Matte Glaze, A. Mason, 1910, 4 x 7 In.	2200.00
Vase, Metallic, Mottled, Copper Rim, Leona Nicholson, c.1900, 5 7/8 In.	1300.00
Vase, Oak Tree & Spanish Moss Scene, Moon, S. Irvine, 6 x 5 In.	2300.00
Vase, Palm Trees, Blue Matte Glaze, Joseph Meyer, c.1912, 15 1/2 In.	3080.00
Vase, Pine Cones & Needles, Blue Matte Ground, A. F. Simpson, 10 1/2 x 6 In.	3960.00
Vase, Sadie Irvine, 3 1/2 x 4 In.	1050.00
Vase, Sculpted To Form Stalks of Iris, Joseph F. Meyer, 1913, 9 /4 In.	1540.00
Vase, Tapering Globular Shape, White Narcissus, Foliage, J. Meyer, 1913, 6 In.	1980.00
Vase, Vertical Leaf, Sectioned, Low Relief, Henrietta Bailey, c.1930s, 3 3/4 In.	1100.00
Vase, White & Yellow Gardenia Band, Blue Ground, Sadie Irvine, 1931, 6 3/4 In.	1045.00
Vase, White Narcissus, Leaves, Blue Ground, A. F. Simpson, 8 x 5 1/2 In.	6600.00
Vase, Yellow & Blue Daffodils, Blue Ground, 7 In.	750.00

NILOAK Pottery (Kaolin spelled backward) was made at the Hyten Brothers Pottery in Benton, Arkansas, between 1909 and 1946. Although the factory did make cast and molded wares, collectors are most interested in the marbelized art pottery line made of colored swirls of clay. It was called *Mission Ware*.

Candlestick, Earth Tone Scroddled, 9 In., Pair	275.00
Candy Jar, Cover, Marbelized, Hand Thrown, Paper Label, 8 1/2 In.	2550.00
Lamp Base, Marbelized, Vase Shape, 9 3/4 In.	350.00
Pitcher, Batter	20.00
Planter, Deer & Fawn	32.00
Planter, Woman, With Bonnet	20.00
Toothpick, Marbelized	92.50
Vase, 3–Color, Marbelized, 5 In.	45.00
Vase, Blue, 5 Holes, 7 1/2 In.	20.00
Vase, Marbelized, 12 In.	290.00
Vase, Marbelized, 7 In.	120.00
Vase, Marbelized, 8 1/2 In.	66.00
Vase, Marbelized, 8 In.	165.00
Vase, Marbelized, 9 3/4 In.	250.00
Vase, Marbelized, Blue, 6 1/2 In.	135.00
Vase, Marbelized, Cone Shape, 9 In.	200.00
Vase, Raised Flower, Pink, Footed, Sticker, 5 In.	20.00
Vase, Swirls, Light Tan, 6 In.	85.00

NIPPON porcelain was made in Japan from 1891 to 1921. *Nippon* is the Japanese word for *Japan*. A few firms continued to use the word *Nippon* on ceramics after 1921 as a part of the company name more than as an identification of the country of origin. More pieces marked Nippon will be found in the Dragonware, Moriage, and Noritake categories.

Ashtray, Scenic, Jeweled, Green Wreath Mark	85.00
Basket, White & Red Roses, Gold Leaf Handle, 5 x 5 In.	95.00
Biscuit Jar, Cover, Dragon Design	450.00
Biscuit Jar, Floral, Greens, Gold Trim, Footed, Blue Maple Leaf, 7 In.	135.00
Biscuit Jar, Floral, Pale & Dark Greens, Gold Trim, Footed, Blue Maple Leaf, 7 In.	165.00
Biscuit Jar, House & Hills Scene, Green Base, Beaded, Wreath	185.00
Biscuit Jar, House Scene, Green Base, Beaded, Wreath	175.00
Bowl, Floral, Browns, Yellows, Crimped, Green Wreath, 8 1/2 In.	80.00
Bowl, Floral, Gold Rim, Footed, Green Mark, 6 Sides, 7 x 5 1/2 In.	65.00
Bowl, Fruit, Chestnuts, 9 In.	145.00
Bowl, Fruit, Trees, Cottage, Lake, 10 1/2 In.	395.00
Bowl, Hibiscus, Avocado Ground, Scalloped Rim, Jeweled, Beaded, Marked, 10 In.	275.00
Bowl, Nut, Butternuts, Beaded Scroll Handles, Green Wreath, 7 x 5 In.	45.00
Bowl, Peanuts, Footed, 7 In.	120.00
Bowl, Wedgwood Type, Open Handles, 10 x 2 In.	98.00
Box, Beaded Lid, Pink Flowers, Green Wreath, Square, 4 In.	65.00
Celery Dish, Snow Scene, Birds In Flight, Handle, Mark 109, 9 In.	45.00
Celery Set, Pink Floral Beaded Rim, Gold Trim, 12-In. Dish, 6 Piece	140.00
Cheese & Cracker, Floral Design	65.00
Chocolate Pot, Colored Blossoms, Buds & Leaves, Green Ground	275.00
Compote, Swan Scene, Gold Trim, Bisque, Marked, 6 1/2 In.	115.00
Compote, Swan Scene, Marked, 6 1/2 In.	95.00
Cracker Jar, Raised Gold Beading, Green Borders, Green M Mark	190.00
Cracker Jar, Scenic, Rising Sun	100.00
Creamer, Egret, Blue Sky, Gold Trim	65.00
Creamer, Liberty Bell Pattern	75.00
Cup & Saucer, Floral, Blue	10.00
Dresser Set, Gold Beaded, 5 Piece	350.00
Ewer, Roses, Gold Flowers, Beaded, Cobalt Blue, 21 In	695.00
Fernery, 3 Sphinxes, Stormy Seascape, Jewels, Beaded, Frame, Marked, 8 In.	450.00
Fernery, Moose & Acorn Branch	120.00
Fernery, Pink Roses, Gold Trim, Green Mark	85.00
Fernery, Pink Roses, Red & Green Geometrics, Gold, 6 1/2 x 6 1/2 In.	109.00
Hair Receiver, White, Profuse Gold ....65.00 To	125.00
Hatpin Holder, Pink Roses	60.00
Humidor, Cigar Top, Molded Relief Cards, Signed, 6 In.	595.00
Humidor, Painted Car On Sides, Brass Lid, Marked, 6 In.	275.00
Humidor, Poppies, Red Ground, Fern Base, Gold Tracery, 6 1/2 In.	165.00
Lamp, Candle, White Paneled Scenes, Geisha Girl, Flowers, Black, Pull Chain	750.00
Lamp, Lake, Mountains, 14 In.	265.00
Lazy Susan, House, Tree, Box	77.00
Loving Cup, Windmill .... 115.00 To	135.00
Mug, Black Silhouette of 2 Riders	95.00
Nut Dish, Gold Beaded, 4 Piece	100.00
Nut Set, Floral, Berries, Footed, Master Bowl, 5 Piece	125.00
Pitcher, Milk, Raised Gold Beading, Green Borders, Green M Mark	185.00
Pitcher, Tankard, Green Stain Ground, Roses, Foliage, Gold Handle, 11 In.	245.00
Plaque, 2 Dogs, Blown Out, 10 In.	595.00
Plaque, American Indian, Horseback, Signed, 10 1/2 In.	695.00
Plaque, Dog, Blue Border With Raised Green Moriage Trim, 8 1/2 In.	450.00
Plaque, Egyptian Symbols & Animals, Signed, 6 In.	125.00
Plaque, Indian Carrying Rifle, Riding Horse, Blown Out, Marked, 10 3/4 In.	595.00
Plaque, Lions, Blown Out, 10 1/2 In.	650.00
Plaque, Venetian Scene, 10 In.	155.00
Plaque, Windmill, Black, 10 In.	260.00
Plate, Apple Blossom, Gold Open Handles, Blue Trim, Rising Sun Mark, 7 1/2 In.	75.00
Plate, Swans, Cobalt Blue, 9 In.	200.00

Powder Box, Oriental Rural Scene, Beaded Base & Lid, 4 x 7 In. 195.00
Powder Box, White, Gold 99.00
Relish, Metallic Butterflies, 3 Sections, 8 1/2 In. 68.00
Sauce Set, Roses, Gold, 3 Piece 89.00
Server, Pancake, Gold, White 75.00
Stickpin Holder, Floral Design 135.00
Sugar & Creamer, Floral, Beaded, Footed, Green Wreath, 6 x 4 1/2 In. 65.00
Sugar & Creamer, Gold Birds, Blue, Maroons 70.00
Sugar & Creamer, Hand Painted, Gold & Pastel Florals, Signed, 3 1/2 & 3 In. 225.00
Sugar Shaker, Raised Gold Beading, Gold Handle 125.00
Tankard, Painted Roses, Gold Trim, 18 In. 137.50
Tea Set, Gold Dragons, 3 Piece 550.00
Tea Set, House Scene, Black & Gold 225.00
Teapot, White, Gold Beaded 125.00
Tile, Pink Azaleas, Green Ground, Maple Leaf Mark 60.00
Toast Rack, Pink Flowers, White & Black 85.00
Toothpick, Desert Scene, 3 Feet, 3 Handles 300.00
Tray, White, Gold Trim, 10 In. 70.00
Vase, 3 White Orchids, Gold Trim, Handles, 11 1/2 In. 200.00
Vase, Blown Out, 2 Dogs, Chasing Stag, 8 In. 795.00
Vase, Cottage & Trees, Orange Sky, Double Handles, Marked, 5 1/2 In. 165.00
Vase, Country Scene, Cottages, Trees, Lake, Marked, 8 1/2 In. 245.00
Vase, Desert Scene, Ornate Handles, Cobalt Blue, 9 In. 695.00
Vase, Farmhouse, Trees, Lake, Key Handles, 16 In. 750.00
Vase, Floral Medallions Overall, Gold Beaded, 8 In. 150.00
Vase, Floral, Gilded Leaves, Handles, 11 1/4 In. 40.00
Vase, Hawk On Scenic Ground, Raised Dots, Enameled Jewels, 12 1/2 In. 425.00
Vase, Multicolored Flowers, Black Ground, 4 Sides, Marked, 7 1/2 In. 75.00
Vase, Painted Camel, Hexagonal Top, 9 In. 450.00
Vase, Pillow Shape, Rose, Gold Overlay, 9 In. 275.00
Vase, Pink & Yellow Roses, Gilded Beadwork, Handles, 8 In. 70.00
Vase, Pink Florals, Misty Trees On Ground, Gold Beads, 7 In. 325.00

NODDERS, also called nodding figures or pagods, are porcelain figures
with heads and hands that are attached to wires. Any slight movement
causes the parts to move up and down. They were made in many countries
during the eighteenth, nineteenth, and twentieth centuries. A few Art Deco
designs are also known. Copies are being made. A more recent type of
nodder is made of papier–mache or plastic. These often represent sports
figures or comic characters.

Salt & Pepper, Walking Pigs 135.00
Banana & Apple, Bank 45.00
Bank, Black Child 40.00
Bank, Donald Duck 400.00
Bank, Pinocchio, Wooden 30.00
Baseball, Baltimore, Green Base, Decal 130.00
Baseball, Boy, Anaheim, Paper Cover 115.00
Baseball, Boy, Angels, White Base, Decal 85.00
Baseball, Boy, Boston, Gold Base, Decal 45.00
Baseball, Boy, Chicago Cubs, White Base, Embossed 260.00
Baseball, Boy, Chicago White Sox, White Base, Embossed 185.00
Baseball, Boy, L. A. Dodgers, White Base, Embossed 105.00
Baseball, Cincinnati, Gold Base, Decal 100.00
Baseball, Cleveland Indians, White Base, Embossed 395.00
Baseball, Cleveland Indians, Yellow Uniform, Gold Base, Decal 80.00
Baseball, Dodgers, Composition 75.00
Baseball, N.Y. Yankees, Green Base, 1964 .... 120.00
Baseball, Portland Trailblazers 25.00
Bear, Painted Gray Body, Lithographed Tin Head, Meier, 3 1/4 In. 357.00
Bladensburg, Papier–Mache 15.00
Boston Terrier 12.00
Bowler, Composition, Box, 1960s 20.00
Boy & Girl With Umbrella, Celluloid 55.00

Boy, Bisque, 5 In.	7.50
Campbell Kids	825.00
Cat, Chalkware, With Goat's Body, Original Red, Yellow, Black Paint, 8 In.	165.00
Charlie Brown	40.00
Col. Sanders	75.00
Daddy Warbucks	175.00
Delong Jones, Comic, Bisque, Germany	90.00
Dog	8.00
Donald Duck, Bobbin Head	120.00
Donkey, Celluloid, Painted, Occupied Japan, 6 1/2 In.	55.00
Donkey, Celluloid, String–Jointed Ears, Painted, 6 In.	44.00
Double Skullson White Tombstone, Gold Trim, Porcelain, Japan	45.00
Elephant, Composite	50.00
Elephant, Windup, Celluloid	85.00
Falls City Beer	400.00
Foxy Grandpa, Papier–Mache, 6 In.	75.00
Girl, Singing, Bisque, 5 In.	8.00
Gold Digger, Blond Woman, 6 In. ....*Illus*	12.00
Golf, Box	75.00
Hank Aaron, Box ....95.00 To 120.00	
Hula Girl	30.00
Hula Girl Playing Ukulele, 10 In.	95.00
Hula Girl, Magnet	18.00
Hula Girl, With Ukulele, 6 1/2 In.	175.00
Inkwell, Cupid	45.00
Jackie Cooper, Bisque, 6 In.	75.00
Japanese Children, Papier–Mache, Pair	45.00
Let's Kiss, Magnets In Lips, Pair	35.00
Lucy, Bobbin Head, 5 1/2 In.	55.00
Mama Katzenjammer, Papier–Mache, 6 In.	75.00
Mammy, Ceramic	165.00
Man & Woman, Germany, Pair	128.00
Mechanical, Moving Cigarette	4500.00
Oriental Ching Chow, Bisque, Germany	100.00
Oriental Woman, Seated, Bisque, 8 In.	385.00
Owl, Celluloid, 3 1/4 In.	55.00
Paul Bunyan, Bobbin Head	120.00
Pig, Chalkware, Original Black, Red Paint, 7 1/2 In.	770.00
Pincushion, Turtle, Florenza	55.00
Portland Beavers, 1950s	85.00
Rabbit, Chalkware, Original Yellow, Red, Black Paint, 6 1/4 In.	1100.00
Salt & Pepper, Walking Pigs	65.00
Santa Claus, Bisque, Comic ....150.00 To 225.00	
Santa Claus, Dashboard, Hard Plastic	6.50
Santa Claus, Holding Feather Tree, Bisque, Germany	110.00
Skippy, Jointed Arms, Bisque, 6 In.	125.00

Nodder, Gold Digger, Blond Woman, 6 In.

♦ ♦ ♦ ♦ ♦ ♦ ♦ ♦ ♦ ♦ ♦ ♦ ♦ ♦ ♦ ♦ ♦ ♦

Worried about where to hang a picture? Put some toothpaste on the top corners of the frame and press it against the wall so the toothpaste leaves a mark. If the postion looks okay, then pound in the hook and wipe off the toothpaste.

♦ ♦

Toy, Rubber Neck, Cast Iron	500.00
Winnie The Pooh, Green Base	65.00

NORITAKE porcelain was made in Japan after 1904 by Nippon Toki Kaisha. The best-known Noritake pieces are marked with the M in a wreath for the Morimura Brothers, a New York City distributing company. This mark was used until 1941. Another famous Noritake china was made for the Larkin Soap Company from 1916 through the 1930s. This dinnerware, decorated with azaleas, was sold or given away as a premium. There may be some helpful price information in the Nippon category, since prices are comparable.

Basket, Miniature, Gold	27.00
Bowl, Black & Yellow Flowers, Luster	24.00
Bowl, Nut, Leaf Pattern, Raised Brazil Nuts	65.00
Bowl, Sandhurst, 8 In.	14.00
Butter, Cover, Avril	75.00
Cake Plate, Exotic Birds, Flowers, Luster, 10 1/2 In.	85.00
Candlestick, Tree In Meadow	45.00
Card Holder, Clown Lute Player, Footed, 4 x 3 1/2 In.	400.00
Card Holder, Fan Lady, Footed, 4 x 3 1/2 In.	350.00
Celery Dish, Chanturo Pattern, M In Wreath	18.00
Compote, Blown Out, Fruit & Nuts, 8 1/4 In.	110.00
Condiment Set, Phoenix Bird, Fruits, Clover-Shape Holder, 4 Piece	110.00
Creamer, Avril	25.00
Dinner Set, Cordova, Art Nouveau Design, Gold Trim, Service For 8, 48 Piece	850.00
Dish, Art Deco Woman, Handle, 5 In.	65.00
Dresser Set, Geometrics, Turquoise & Gold, Tray, Candlesticks, Jar, Pin Tray	165.00
Hatpin Holder, House Scene	73.00
Humidor, Blown-Out Owl	285.00
Humidor, Brown & Black Scene	265.00
Jug, Milk, Azalea	120.00
Mayonnaise Set, White & Gold, 3 Piece	60.00
Planter, Camel	45.00
Plate, Avril, 6 1/2 In.	15.00
Plate, Avril, 10 In.	20.00
Platter, Avril, 16 In.	100.00
Sugar & Creamer, Azalea	110.00
Sugar & Creamer, Tree In Meadow	25.00
Sugar, Cover, Avril	35.00
Toothpick, Azalea	90.00
Tray, Art Deco, Harem Woman, Baird, 6 3/4 In.	135.00
Vase, Azalea, Bulbous	995.00
Vase, Enameled Butterflies, Blue Luster, Bulbous	95.00
Vase, Outlined Pink Roses, Gold Trim, Gold Rain Beads, 9 In.	450.00
Vase, Pink Blossoms, Wide Leaves, 4 Gold-Top Handles, 11 In.	450.00
Vase, Shaded Daisies, Horizontal & Vertical Bands, 4 Handles, 12 In.	475.00
Wall Pocket, Camels, Pyramids, Palm Trees	165.00
Wall Pocket, Floral, Orange & Gold Luster Ground, Wreath Mark, 8 In.	75.00
Wall Pocket, Large Pink Rose, Orange Luster, Red Mark, 9 In.	65.00
Wall Pocket, Pink Rose, Orange Luster, Porcelain, 9 In.	50.00

NORSE Pottery Company started in Edgerton, Wisconsin, in 1903. In 1904 the company moved to Rockford, Illinois. The company made a black pottery, which resembled early bronze relics of the Scandinavian countries. The firm went out of business in 1913.

Bowl, Bronze Ware, Geometric Design At Shoulder, Zigzag Design, 7 In.	190.00

NORTH DAKOTA SCHOOL OF MINES was established in 1892 at the University of North Dakota. A ceramic course was included and pieces were made from the clays found in the region. Students at the university made pieces from 1909 to 1949. Although very early pieces were marked *U.N.D.*, most pieces were stamped with the full name of the university.

Bookend Planter, Cable	105.00

Bowl, Blue, Huck, 4 In.	210.00
Bowl, Brown, J. Mattson, 4 In.	225.00
Bowl, Red River Ox Cart, Green Leathery Glaze, Marked, 10 In.	525.00
Bowl, Shaded Blue, Huck, 5 In.	210.00
Flower Frog, Deer, Lightfoot	155.00
Flower Frog, Deer, M. Cable, Lightfoot	165.00
Ginger Jar, Cover, Burgundy, Middleton, 5 In.	70.00
Ginger Jar, Cover, Oriental Design, 8 In.	1400.00
Paperweight, Lightfoot, Cable	400.00
Pitcher, Floral, 6 In.	265.00
Pot, Band of Wheat, Green, Cream, Huckfield, 3 1/4 In.	175.00
Pot, Thrown, Signed Laura Taylor, Early 1930s	4500.00
Pot, Whale Design, 5 In.	185.00
Teapot, Brown	60.00
Tray, Leaf Shape, Blues & Green, Signed, 6 In.	170.00
Vase, Brown & Cream, Hovelson, 11 In.	190.00
Vase, Brown, Hovelson, 11 In.	195.00
Vase, Browns	200.00
Vase, Cactus, Huck, 5 1/2 In.	550.00
Vase, Carved Leaves, Mattson, 3 In.	350.00
Vase, Cream Glazed Coyotes On Rim, Ocher, 3 1/2 In.	525.00
Vase, Floral, Julie Mattson, 9 In.	595.00
Vase, Huck, Green, 3 x 4 In.	95.00
Vase, Olive & Gray, Pachi, 9 In,	175.00
Vase, Pink Floral Band, Foliage, 1930, 2 3/4 x 4 In.	495.00
Vase, Stylized Tulips, Apple–Green, E. Bradley, 1933, 9 In.	330.00
Vase, Swimming Fish, Gun Metal Ground, Marie, 8 1/2 x 7 In.	1430.00
Vase, Viking Ships, Brown Ground, 5 1/4 x 4 In.	660.00
Vase, Wheat Shafts, 5 In.	245.00

NORTHWOOD Glass Company was founded by Harry Northwood, a glassmaker who worked for Hobbs, Brockunier and Company, La Belle Glass Company, and Buckeye Glass Company before founding his own firm. He opened one factory in Indiana, Pennsylvania, in 1896, and another in Wheeling, West Virginia, in 1902. Northwood closed when Mr. Northwood died in 1923. Many types of glass were made, including carnival, custard, goofus, and pressed. The underlined N mark was used on some pieces.

Berry Set, Grape & Cable, Green, 5 Piece	170.00
Berry Set, Grape & Cable, Purple, Carnival Glass	400.00
Bowl, 3 Fruits, Ruffled, White, 9 In.	275.00
Bowl, Centerpiece, Grape & Cable, Ice Green	750.00
Bowl, Ice Cream, Grape & Cable, Ice Green	1200.00
Bowl, Ice Cream, Trout & Fly, Green	950.00
Bowl, Jolly Bear, Opalescent	75.00
Bowl, Plum & Cherry, 9 In.	45.00
Bowl, Rose Show, Purple, Carnival Glass	725.00
Butter, Cover, Jewel & Flower	65.00
Butter, Cover, Memphis, Green, Gold Trim	105.00
Butter, Cover, Springtime, Purple	385.00
Celery Vase, Regal, Blue	165.00
Cracker Jar, Grape & Cable, Purple, Carnival Glass	400.00
Creamer, Fan, Cobalt Blue	55.00
Creamer, Leaf Mold, Cranberry	160.00
Creamer, Springtime, Purple	225.00
Dish, Ice Cream, Peacock & Urn, Amethyst, 5 1/2 In.	65.00
Pitcher, Apple Blossom	300.00
Pitcher, Leaf Umbrella, Cranberry, c.1905, 9 In.	395.00
Pitcher, Water, Springtime, Purple, Large	750.00
Plate, Apple Blossom Twig, Peach Opalescent	400.00
Plate, Good Luck, Purple, Carnival Glass	600.00
Punch Set, Grape & Cable, White, Carnival Glass, 7 Piece	3500.00
Rose Bowl, Leaf Umbrella, Cranberry	145.00

Rose Bowl, Pull–Up Saating Glass, Green & Yellow, Thorny Footed, Crimped, 3 In	265.00
Salt & Pepper, Paneled Sprig, Amethyst	60.00
Salt & Pepper, Quilted Phlox, Blue	85.00
Spooner, Regent, Amethyst With Gold	50.00
Sugar & Creamer, Butter, Footed Scrolls, Blue Opalescent, 3 Piece	195.00
Sugar Shaker, Leaf Umbrella, Mauve, 5 In.	350.00
Sugar, Memphis, Green, Gold Trim	105.00
Tumbler, Oriental Poppy, Green, Gold Trim	45.00
Tumbler, Regal, Blue Opalescent	55.00
Vase, Blue & Yellow Pull–Up Design, Off–White Ground, 4 1/2 In.	175.00
Vase, Corn, Marigold, Carnival Glass	800.00
Vase, Drapery, White, 7 1/2 In.	160.00
Vase, Fluted Scroll, Opalescent, Enameled Daisy	650.00
Vase, Pull–Up Feather, Cream Satin, Scalloped, Flared, 4 1/4 In.	695.00
Vase, Pull–Up Overlay, Yellow Ground, 3–Petal Top, 3 1/4 In.	325.00
Vase, Tornado, Green, Carnival Glass	500.00
Vase, Town Pump, Purple, Carnival Glass	775.00
Water Set, Gold Rose, Green & Gold	250.00
Water Set, Leaf Umbrella, Cranberry, 3 Piece	325.00
Water Set, Peach, Green & Gold	350.00

NU–ART was a trademark registered by the Imperial Glass Company of
Bellaire, Ohio, about 1920.

Ashtray, Horse	65.00
Ashtray, Rearing Horse	38.00 To 40.00
Ashtray, Seated Scotty	45.00
Bookends, Dogs, Scotties	45.00
Bookends, Pierrot Clown	95.00
Lamp, 2 Nudes, Arms Stretched To Frosted Paneled Shade, Signed	660.00
Lamp, Nude Seated On Bench, Ball Shade	255.00
Lamp, Pearl Gray Nude Sits On Column, Gazing At End of Day, Shade	235.00
Pitcher, Milk, Raspberry, Ice Blue	1900.00
Plate, Chrysanthemum, White	600.00
Plate, Homestead, Amber	900.00
Plate, Homestead, Blue, Signed	5250.00
Shade, Marigold, Signed	37.50

NUTCRACKERS of many types have been used through the centuries. At
first the nutcracker was probably strong teeth or a hammer. But by the
nineteenth century, many elaborate and ingenious types were made. Levers,
screws, and hammer adaptations were the most popular. Because
nutcrackers are still useful, they are still being made, some in the old
styles.

Parrot, Green Paint, Orange & Gold Highlights	250.00
Alligator, Brass	12.00
Clara, Erzgebirge	20.00
Dazey	12.00
Dog, c.1900	165.00
Nickel Plated, Headlight Stoves & Ranges	225.00
Recorder, Erzgebirge	20.00
Rooster, Brass	22.00 To 35.00
Rooster, Pliers, Brass	23.00
Sailor, Her Majesty's Service	25.00
Santa Claus Head, Hand Carved Wood	250.00
Santa Claus, Cast Iron, RD No. 776837, 7 1/4 In.	225.00
Squirrel, Cast Iron	45.00
Table Mount, Cast Iron	18.00
Turkish Soldier	280.00

NYMPHENBURG, see Royal Nymphenburg

OCCUPIED JAPAN was printed on pottery, porcelain, toys, and other goods made during the American occupation of Japan after World War II, from 1945 to 1952. Collectors now search for these pieces. The items were made for export.

Box, Lady In Swing, Man In Garden, Oval, 7 1/2 In.	120.00
Cup & Saucer, Marked SGK, Medium	15.00
Doll, Football Player, Celluloid Head, Cloth Body	35.00
Figure, House, For Aquarium	15.00
Figurine, Children Eating Lunch On Sofa, Painted China	22.50
Figurine, Colonial Man, Seated	10.00
Figurine, Coolie, Green & Yellow, 5 1/2 In.	20.00
Figurine, Cupid Playing Banjo, 5 1/2 In.	30.00
Lamp, Andrea, Shepherd & Shepherdess, 14 In.	70.00
Lamp, Colonial Couple, 7 In.	20.00
Night-Light, Indian Child, Full Figure, 1940s	45.00
Oriental Warrior, Multicolored, 8 1/4 In.	75.00
Planter, Panda Bear Climbing Tree, 3 1/2 In.	12.00
Planter, Pixie, 4 x 4 In.	30.00
Planter, Pixie, 4 x 5 In.	30.00
Plaque, Colonial Lady, Chase	18.00
Plaque, Wall, Oriental Woman Carrying Baskets, Yamaka, 6 1/8 In.	14.00
Salt & Pepper, Floral Coffee Cup Holder	24.00
Saltshaker, Humpty Dumpty, Ardalt	18.00
Stein, 3 Musketeers, Navy Blue & White, 7 1/2 In.	20.00
Strainer, Tray, Original Box, Marked Mioj	22.00
Tea Set, Child's, Blue & Red Flowers, Box, 6 Place Settings	35.00
Tea Strainer, Saucer, Metal	13.00
Toby Jug, 5 In.	20.00
Tray & Nut Set, Lazy Susan, Lacquer Ware, 16 In., 8 Piece	85.00
Trunk, Dome Top, Silver Color, Metal Embossed, 2 1/8 x 3 x 2 3/8 In.	35.00

OHR pottery was made in Biloxi, Mississippi, from 1883 to 1918 by George E. Ohr, a true eccentric. The pottery was made of very thin clay that was twisted, folded, and dented into odd, graceful shapes. Some pieces were lifelike models of hats, animal heads, or even a potato. Others were decorated with folded clay *snakes*. Reproductions and reworked pieces are appearing on the market. These have been reglazed, or snakes and other embellishments have been added.

Bowl, Folded & Collapsed Walls, Dripping Green, Gun Metal Glaze, 4 x 9 In.	2200.00
Bowl, Pinched & Pulled Top, Bisque Finish, Marked, 3 x 5 In.	715.00
Bowl, Rolled Rim, Corseted, Sponged Pattern, Marked, 3 1/4 x 3 1/4 In.	495.00
Bowl, Yellow Glaze, Green Drips, Orange Clay Ground, Dimpled, 3 x 4 1/2 In.	825.00
Chamber Pot, Clear Yellow & Green Glaze, Firing Stilt, 2 1/2 x 3 1/4 In.	303.00
Cup, Iridescent Peacock Blue, Pigeon Feather Glaze, Flared Base, 5 1/2 x 5 In.	705.00
Inkwell, Cabin, Brown Glaze, c.1885, 2 1/2 In.	1100.00 To 1210.00
Jug, Smooth Brown, Gunmetal Glaze, 4 1/2 x 3 1/2 In.	935.00
Mug, Brown Glaze, Gunmetal Speckled, Script, 4 1/4 x 5 In.	467.00
Pitcher, Oval, Waisted, Mottled Raspberry & Green Overglaze, 3 x 5 1/2 In.	1760.00
Teapot, Cover, Pigeon Feathered, Green Over Orange Clay Body, 5 3/4 x 8 1/2 In.	1540.00
Vase, Black, Biloxi, 3 3/4 x 4 In.	550.00
Vase, Brown Glaze Speckled, Gun Metal, Bulbous, Folded Rim, 3 1/4 x 3 In.	275.00
Vase, Bud, Yellow Speckles, Round Base, 4 In.	210.00
Vase, Burnt Red Oxidized, 4 1/2 In.	495.00
Vase, Chalice Shape, Iridescent Brick Red, 4 1/4 x 3 1/4 In.	715.00
Vase, Feathered Green & Black Glaze, Bulbous, Folded Neck, 4 x 2 1/2 In.	770.00
Vase, Folded Rim, Blue-Green Band, Pink Ground, Speckled Interior, 6 1/2 x 5 In.	4950.00
Vase, Gunmetal Glaze, Bulbous, Small	210.00
Vase, Mottled Blue Glaze, Folded Neck	5250.00
Vase, Orange To Brown, Bisque Finish, Marked, 3 In.	250.00
Vase, Speckled Carmel Glaze, Folded, Small	2700.00
Vase, Speckled Green & Beige Glaze, Dimpled, Marked, 3 3/4 x 3 3/4 In.	660.00
Vase, Twisted Neck, Twice-Folded Pendant Rim, 4 3/4 In.	3850.00

OLD IVORY china was made by Hermann Ohme in Silesia, Germany, at the end of the nineteenth century. The ivory–colored dishes have flowers, fruit, or acorns as decoration and are often marked with a crown and the word *Silesia*. Some pieces are also marked with the words *Old Ivory*. The pattern numbers appear on the base of each piece.

OLD IVORY 84

Toothpick, No. 459	20.00
Basket, No. 201, Silesia, 8 1/2 In.	250.00
Berry Bowl, No. 84, 9 In.	95.00
Berry Set, Signed & Numbered, 7 Piece	200.00
Biscuit Jar, No. 16	270.00
Bowl, No. 4, 5 1/2 In., 6 Piece	150.00
Bowl, No. 16, 9 1/2 In.	90.00
Bowl, No. 16, Silesia, 9 1/2 In.	99.00
Bowl, No. 78, 9 1/2 In.	135.00
Bowl, Thistle, 10 In.	50.00
Bowl, Vegetable, No. 22, 9 1/2 In.	225.00
Bowl, Vegetable, Oval, 9 1/4 In.	85.00
Bowl, Waste, No. 16	150.00
Butter Chip, No. 84	135.00 To 180.00
Cake Plate, No. 16, Open Handles, 11 In.	125.00
Cake Plate, Pierced Handles, 11 In.	135.00
Charger, No. 16, 13 In.	150.00 To 325.00
Chocolate Set, No. 16, 7 Piece	650.00 To 825.00
Cup & Saucer	65.00 To 85.00
Cup & Saucer, Coffee, No. 15	75.00
Cup & Saucer, No. 84, Straight Sided	40.00
Cup & Saucer, No. 15, Set of 4	180.00
Cup & Saucer, No. 15, Signed, Large	75.00
Jam Jar, Cover, No. 200	295.00
Luncheon Set, 5 Piece	130.00
Mustard, No. 28	285.00
Nappy, No. 202, Clover Shape, Signed, 6 x 5 1/2 In.	95.00
Plate, 6 1/4 In.	22.50
Plate, 11 In.	135.00
Plate, No. 3 In.	35.00
Plate, No. 16, 7 1/2 In.	35.00 To 50.00
Plate, No. 16, 8 1/2 In.	47.50
Plate, No. A73, Tulips & Forget–Me–Nots, Signed, 7 1/2 In.	85.00
Plate, Tea, No. 11, 6 1/4 In.	45.00
Salt & Pepper, No. 75	135.00
Salt & Pepper, No. 84	110.00 To 185.00
Sauceboat, No. 200, Underplate, Self–Handled	150.00
Shaving Mug, No. 15, Soap Shelf	425.00
Soup, Dish, Silesia, 9 1/2 In.	85.00
Spoon Rest, No. 200, 8 1/2 x 5 In.	110.00 To 195.00
Spoon Rest, No. 200, Cut–Out For Hanging	55.00
Spooner, Scalloped, Handle Signed	450.00
Sugar & Creamer, Cover, No. 16	175.00
Sugar & Creamer, No. 16	135.00 To 155.00
Sugar Shaker, No. 84	395.00
Tile, Tea, No. 84	225.00
Toothpick, No. 16	250.00
Tray, No. 15, Self–Handled, Oval, Signed, 11 1/2 x 8 In.	210.00
Tray, No. 90, Silesia, Yellow Roses, 11 1/2 x 8 1/4 In.	165.00

OLD PARIS, see Paris

OLD SLEEPY EYE, see Sleepy Eye

Onion, Plate, Crossed Swords, 8 1/2 In.

ONION PATTERN, originally named *bulb pattern,* is a white ware decorated with cobalt blue or pink. Although it is commonly associated with Meissen, other companies made the pattern in the late nineteenth and the twentieth centuries. A rare type is called *red bud* because there are added red accents on the blue-and-white dishes.

Butter	75.00
Canister, Rice, Sugar, Turned Tops, 6 1/2 In., Pair.	75.00
Colander	195.00
Compote, Meissen, 8 In.	360.00
Dish, Warming, Metal Cover	135.00
Egg Whipper, Hanging	145.00
Gravy Boat, Meissen, 1880, Large	195.00
Meat Tenderizer, Hanging	145.00
Pestle, Hanging	145.00
Plate, Crossed Swords, 8 1/2 In. ....*Illus*	75.00
Plate, Red Enameled, Gilt, Reticulated, Crossed Swords, 9 1/2 In.	20.00
Platter, Meissen, Marked, 18 x 13 1/2 In.	245.00
Rolling Pin, Meissen	165.00
Soup, Dish, Meissen, 1860	75.00
Spatula, Hanging	165.00
Tea Set, Gilt Trim, Meissen, Late 1800s, 3 Piece	350.00

OPALESCENT GLASS is translucent glass that has the tones of the opal gemstone. It originated in England in the 1870s and is often found in pressed glassware made in Victorian times. Opalescent glass was first made in America in 1897 at the Northwood glassworks in Indiana, Pennsylvania. Some dealers use the terms *opaline* and *opalescent* for any of these translucent wares. More opalescent pieces may be listed in Northwood, Pressed Glass, Spanish Lace, and other glass categories.

Basket, Green, Clear-Reeded Thorn Handle, Shell Footed, Ruffled, 9 1/2 In.	275.00
Basket, Old Man Winter, Handle, Vaseline, 7 3/4 In.	145.00
Berry Bowl, Jewel & Flower, Blue	150.00
Berry Bowl, Petals & Fan, Peach, Master, 10 In.	250.00
Berry Bowl, Tokyo, Master, Green	50.00
Berry Set, Idyll, Blue, 7 Piece	395.00
Berry Set, Scroll With Acanthus, White, 7 Piece	175.00
Bowl, Diamond With Hobnail, Ruffled, Blue, 12 In.	50.00
Bowl, Dugan, Peach, 6 Petals	85.00
Bowl, Fruit, Swirl, Top Band Is Reverse Bars, Blue, 9 In.	75.00
Bowl, Jewel & Heart, White, 10 In.	35.00
Bowl, Poinsettia, Ruffled, Blue, 8 In.	40.00
Bowl, Reflecting Diamonds, Crimped, 2 Sides Turn Up, Green, 9 In.	35.00
Bowl, Ribbed Spiral, Blue, 7 1/2 In.	37.00
Bowl, Spokes & Wheels, Green, 8 In.	27.50
Bowl, Wishbone & Spades, Peach, 5 In.	80.00

Butter, Cover, Alaska, Blue 375.00
Butter, Cover, Fluted Scrolls, Vaseline 165.00
Butter, Cover, Iris With Meander, Green 125.00
Butter, Cover, Michigan, Maiden's Blush 175.00
Butter, Cover, Paneled Holly, Blue, Gold Trim 375.00
Butter, Spooner, Sugar & Creamer, Wreath & Shell, Blue, Enameled, 4 Piece 340.00
Celery Dish, Baby Coin, Blue 38.00
Celery Dish, Buckeye Lattice, Canary 110.00
Celery Dish, Vaseline 125.00
Celery Dish, Wreath & Shell 155.00
Compote, Diamond Spearhead, Yellow 260.00
Compote, Hearts & Flowers, Aqua, Northwood 600.00
Compote, Jelly, Flora, Blue 85.00
Compote, Jelly, Rayed Heart, Green 85.00
Compote, Jelly, Swag & Brackets, Green 75.00
Compote, Pink, Diamond–Quilted, Ruffled, Metal Footed, 7 3/4 x 11 1/2 In. 225.00
Creamer, Child's, Twist, Blue 95.00
Creamer, Diamond Spearhead, Cobalt Blue 175.00
Creamer, Intaglio, Blue 85.00
Creamer, Reverse Swirl, Speckled, Cranberry 195.00
Cruet, Daisy & Fern, Apple Blossom Mold, White 95.00
Cruet, Daisy & Fern, Blue .... 110.00 To 145.00
Cruet, Empress, Green, Gold Trim 350.00
Cruet, Fluted Scroll, Blue 175.00
Cruet, Herringbone, Blue 160.00
Cruet, Herringbone, White 125.00
Cruet, Jackson, Blue 100.00
Cuspidor, Piasa Bird, Footed, Blue 45.00
Dish, Spokes & Wheels, Tricorner, Green, 8 In. 27.50
Finger Bowl, Seaweed, Cranberry 60.00
Gravy Boat, Lacy, Ribbed, Toy, 1840s 165.00
Lamp, Finger, Beaded Swirl, Reeded Handle, Green 350.00
Lamp, Oil, Christmas Snowflake, Cranberry, 1890s 950.00
Lamp, Snowflake, Glass Sleeve On Stem, White, Square Font, 9 1/2 In. 235.00
Lamp, Snowflake, White Base, Cranberry 395.00
Mug, Child's, Stump, Blue 65.00
Mustard, Hinged Lid, Chrysanthemum, Reverse Swirl, Blue 125.00
Nappy, Holly, Handle, Peach 65.00
Nappy, Sea Spray, Green, Tricorner 18.00
Pitcher, Alaska, Blue, 7 Piece 800.00
Pitcher, Alaska, Vaseline 395.00
Pitcher, Blue & White Spatter, Reeded Handle, 8 1/4 In. 155.00
Pitcher, Blue, Swirl, Applied Reeded Handle, 4 1/2 In. 79.00
Pitcher, Buttons & Braids, Blue 195.00
Pitcher, Circled Scroll, Green 160.00
Pitcher, Croesus, Green, Gold Trim 350.00
Pitcher, Daisy & Crisscross, 1 Tumbler, White, c.1885 .... 635.00
Pitcher, Diamond Spearhead, Yellow 275.00
Pitcher, Fluted Scroll, Blue .... 225.00 To 250.00
Pitcher, Fluted Scroll, Vaseline 195.00
Pitcher, Idyll, Green 350.00
Pitcher, Intaglio, Blue 80.00
Pitcher, Iris With Meander, Blue 350.00
Pitcher, Jefferson, Blue 150.00
Pitcher, Jeweled Heart, Blue 350.00
Pitcher, Poinsettia, Blue 275.00
Pitcher, Polkadot, Cranberry 800.00
Pitcher, Seaweed, Square Mouth, Cranberry 110.00
Pitcher, Stripe, Vaseline 175.00
Pitcher, Swirl, Bulbous Mouth, Enameled Flowers, Gold Leaves, 8 In. 165.00
Pitcher, Threaded, Footed, Clear 300.00
Pitcher, Water, Blue, ... 40.00
Pitcher, Water, Reverse Swirl, Blue 225.00

Pitcher, Water, Tokyo, Green 85.00
Plate, Iris With Meander, Blue, 7 In. 38.00
Rose Bowl, Beaded Cable, Aqua 350.00
Rose Bowl, Bushel Basket, Aqua 550.00
Salt & Pepper, Jewel & Flower, Vaseline 250.00
Salt & Pepper, Windows, Cranberry 225.00
Saltshaker, Alaska, Vaseline 75.00
Saltshaker, Beaded Dahlia, Pink 70.00
Saltshaker, Blue, Reverse Swirl 60.00
Saltshaker, Diamond Spearhead 65.00
Saltshaker, Ribbed Lattice, Cranberry 95.00
Sauce, Bubble Lattice, Blue 28.00
Shade, Etched Flower Design, Ruffled Rim, Base Opening, 8 x 5 In. 140.00
Spooner, Diamond Spearhead, Green 190.00
Spooner, Drapery, Blue 80.00
Spooner, Jewel & Flower, White 75.00
Spooner, Jeweled Heart, Green 60.00
Spooner, Michigan, Maiden's Blush 125.00
Sugar & Creamer, Palm Beach, Blue .... 250.00 To 350.00
Sugar Shaker, Beatty Rib, Blue 195.00
Sugar Shaker, Grape & Leaf, Green 245.00
Sugar Shaker, Lattice, Ribbed, Cranberry 235.00
Sugar Shaker, Poinsettia, Blue 235.00
Sugar Shaker, Ribbed Lattice, Cranberry .... 195.00 To 295.00
Sugar Shaker, Ribbed Lattice, Turquoise 295.00
Sugar, Cover, Alaska, Blue 245.00
Sugar, Cover, Regal, White 75.00
Sugar, Creamer & Spooner, Cover, Tokyo, Blue, 3 Piece 295.00
Sugar, Fan, Blue 275.00
Sugar, Fluted Scroll, Blue 125.00
Sugar, Michigan, Cover, Maiden's Blush 150.00
Sugar, Wild Bouquet, Green 265.00
Syrup, Daisy & Fern, White 150.00
Syrup, Petticoat 250.00
Syrup, Ribbed Lattice, Spring Lid, Blue 195.00
Table Set, Alaska, Vaseline, 4 Piece 650.00
Table Set, Beveled Diamond & Star, Ruby Stained, 4 Piece 375.00
Table Set, Everglades, Blue, 4 Piece 550.00
Table Set, Flora, Blue 325.00
Table Set, Flora, White, 3 Piece 225.00
Table Set, Fluted Scroll, Blue, 4 Piece 475.00
Table Set, Fluted Scroll, Vaseline, 4 Piece 475.00
Table Set, Framed Jewel, Enamel Design, Ruby Stained, 4 Piece 400.00
Table Set, Regal, Green, 4 Piece 495.00
Table Set, Swag With Bracket, Vaseline, 4 Piece 450.00
Table Set, Tokyo, Blue, 3 Piece 295.00
Table Set, Wreath & Shell, Vaseline, 4 Piece 595.00
Tea Set, Coin Dot, Cranberry, C. 1950, 7 Piece 650.00
Tieback, Floral Design, Fiery, No Post, 4 3/8 In., Pair 100.00
Toothpicks are listed in the Toothpick category.
Tray, Diamond Spearhead, Vaseline, 7 x 3 5/8 In. 35.00
Tray, Muffin, Sanibel, Yellow 75.00
Tumble–Up, 12 Loops On Tumbler 165.00
Tumbler, Circled Scroll, Blue .... 65.00 To 85.00
Tumbler, Daffodil, Green 65.00
Tumbler, Everglades, Vaseline 85.00
Tumbler, Fern, Blue 30.00
Tumbler, Flora, Vaseline 85.00
Tumbler, Jewel & Flower, Vaseline 85.00
Tumbler, Jewel & Flower, White 45.00
Tumbler, Jeweled Heart, Green 30.00
Tumbler, Lattice & Daisy, Blue 45.00
Tumbler, Lattice & Grape, Blue 40.00

Tumbler, Seaweed, Cranberry	115.00
Tumbler, Shell, Blue	85.00
Tumbler, Swag With Brackets, Vaseline	55.00
Tumbler, Wreath & Shell, Blue	65.00
Vase, Beads & Bark, Blue, 6 In.	55.00
Vase, Fan Shape, Yellow, Green, James Powell, 8 1/2 x 9 /12 In.	850.00
Vase, Pink, Clear Ruffled Foot, 5 5/8 In.	88.00
Wall Pocket, Tree Trunk & Shell, 6 3/4 x 4 In.	110.00
Water Set, Alaska, Blue, 7 Piece	695.00
Water Set, Alaska, Vaseline, 6 Piece	675.00
Water Set, Arabian Knights, White, 5 Piece	1100.00 To 1500.00
Water Set, Diamond Spearhead, Vaseline, 7 Piece	1000.00
Water Set, Everglades, Vaseline, 7 Piece	695.00
Water Set, Iris With Meander, Blue, 6 Piece	650.00
Water Set, Jackson, Goofus Trim, 7 Piece	650.00
Water Set, Jeweled Heart, Green, 7 Piece	550.00
Water Set, Regal, Blue, 7 Piece	595.00
Water Set, Wreath & Shell, Blue, 7 Piece	600.00

OPALINE, or opal glass, was made in white, green, and other colors. The glass had a matte surface and a lack of transparency. It was often gilded or painted. It was a popular mid–nineteenth–century European glassware.

Candelabra, Green, Prisms, 1855, Pair	3150.00
Cider Barrel, Ladle, Gilt, France, 2 Piece	275.00
Dresser Set, Pink, 2 Cologne Bottles, Powder Jar, Enameled Design	225.00
Epergne, Applied Cherries, Flowers, Smoky, Art Glass ....*Illus*	850.00
Lamp, Oil, Pink, Baluster, Electric, England, 21 In., Pair	110.00
Powder Jar, Blue, France	85.00
Vase, Enameled Impressionistic Parrot, 1870–1880	170.00
Vase, Geometric Gilt, England	120.00

OPERA GLASSES are needed because the stage is a long way from some of the seats at a play or an opera. Mother–of–pearl was a popular decoration.

Brass, Abalone Cover, Lamier, Paris	175.00
Dore Brass, Mother–of–Pearl, Lemaire, Paris	55.00
Gold Plated, Extended Lorgnette Handle, Silver Designs, Blue Jewels, Bag	395.00
Mother–of–Pearl, Brass, Folding Handle, Le Maire, Paris	125.00
Mother–of–Pearl, Le Maire, Paris	75.00 To 95.00
Mother–of–Pearl, Theodore B. Starr, New York, Case	100.00
Mother–of–Pearl, With Holder	60.00
Mother–of–Pearl, With Lorgnette Handle	225.00
Painted Black Brass, Leather, Audemair	50.00
Pearlized, France	95.00

♦ ♦ ♦ ♦ ♦ ♦ ♦ ♦ ♦ ♦ ♦ ♦ ♦ ♦ ♦ ♦ ♦ ♦ ♦ ♦

Modern bleach can damage 18th-century and some 19th-century dishes. To clean old dishes, try hydrogen peroxide or bicarbonate of soda. Each removes a different type of stain.

♦ ♦ ♦ ♦ ♦ ♦ ♦ ♦ ♦ ♦ ♦ ♦ ♦ ♦ ♦ ♦ ♦ ♦ ♦ ♦

Opaline, Epergne, Applied Cherries,
Flowers, Smoky, Art Glass

ORPHAN ANNIE first appeared in the comics in 1924. The redheaded girl and her friends have been on the radio and are still on the comic pages. A Broadway musical show and a movie in the 1980s made Annie popular again and many toys, dishes, and other memorabilia are being made.

Biscuit Box	375.00
Book, About Dogs, 1936	35.00
Book, Big Big Book, 1934	90.00
Book, Big Little Book	20.00
Book, Big Little Book, Little Orphan Annie & Mysterious Shoemaker, 1938	14.00
Book, Big Little Book, Orphan Annie & The Chizzler	25.00
Book, Coloring, Junior Commandos, 1943	35.00
Comic Strip, Annie & Sandy, Ink On Paper, Matted, H. Gray, 1967, 6 x 19 In.	550.00
Comic Strip, Ink On Paper, Harold Gray, Signed, Matted, 1956, 6 x 19 In.	300.00
Comic Strip, Ink On Paper, Signed, Frame, Harold Gray, 1963, 6 x 20 In.	770.00
Decoder, 1935	30.00 To 32.00
Decoder, Star Design, Radio Premium, 1938	28.00
Dish Set, Plastic, Box	13.00
Doll, Celluloid, Jointed, 1930s, 8 In.	175.00
Doll, Composition Head, Painted Hair, Cloth Body, Famous Artist, 15 In.	180.00
Doll, Little Orphan Annie, Extra Party Dress, Slippers, 10 1/2 In.	27.00
Doll, Sandy, Cloth, Knickerbocker	60.00
Figure, 1973, Box, 7 In.	18.00
Knife, Pocket, Straight Shoots	49.00
Lunch Box	30.00
Mug, Ovaltine, Plastic, 3 In.	35.00 To 45.00
Paper Doll, Book, 6 Pages of Clothes, Saalfield, 1943, Uncut	95.00
Plate, Annie & Sandy, Japanese Luster, 1920s, 4 In.	28.00
Shaker, Dome Cover, Beetleware	42.00
Stove	65.00 To 85.00
Stove, Green & Cream, 1930s	60.00
Telescope, With Bird Call	55.00
Toothbrush Holder, With Sandy	75.00
Toy, Orphan Annie Skipping Rope, Windup, Tin, With Key	605.00
Toy, Sandy, With Suitcase, Windup, Tin	137.00
Wristwatch, Rectangular Face, Leather Band, New Haven, Box, 1935	150.00 To 275.00

ORREFORS Glassworks, located in the Swedish province of Smaaland, was established in 1898. The company is still making glass for use on the table or as decorations. There is renewed interest in the glass made in the modern styles of the 1940s and 1950s. Most vases and decorative pieces are signed with the etched name.

Orrefors

Bowl, Etched Male Nudes, Signed, 5 In.	285.00
Bowl, Geometric Cut Design, 7 1/4 In.	110.00
Bowl, Woman & Child, 5 In.	330.00
Decanter, Engraved Sailor Looking Out To Sea, Signed, c.1940	225.00

Ott & Brewer, Dish, Cover, Underplate, Dark Blue, Gold Trim, 7 In.

◆◆◆◆◆◆◆◆◆◆◆◆◆◆◆◆◆◆◆◆◆◆◆

Don't store dishes for long periods of time in old newspaper wrappings. The ink can make indelible stains on china.

◆◆◆◆◆◆◆◆◆◆◆◆◆◆◆◆◆◆◆◆◆◆◆

Dish, Cranberry, Signed, 1950s, 6 In. 130.00
Vase, Bottle, Pink To White Interior, Dedication On Bottom, Signed, 1951, 11 In. ... 850.00
Vase, Nudes Swimming, 10 7/8 In. 935.00
Vase, Smoky Black, Signed, 12 In. 95.00

OTT & BREWER Company operated the Etruria Pottery at Trenton, New
Jersey, from 1863 to 1893. They started making belleek in 1882. The firm
used a variety of marks that incorporated the initials *O & B.*

Creamer, Florals, Gold Trim 140.00
Dish, Cover, Underplate, Dark Blue, Gold Trim, 7 In. ....*Illus* 275.00
Egg Frame, Pedestal, Dolphin Finial, Gold Pastel Florals 950.00
Saucer, Shell Shape 25.00

OVERBECK pottery was made by four sisters named Overbeck at a pottery
in Cambridge City, Indiana. They started in 1911. They made all types of
vases, each one-of-a-kind. Small, hand-modeled figurines are the most
popular pieces with today's collectors. The factory continued until 1955
when the last of the four sisters died.

Figurine, Dog, Standing, 3 1/2 x 4 1/2 In. 425.00
Figurine, Man, Standing, 5 In. 295.00
Vase, 2 Colors 1320.00

OWENS Pottery was made in Zanesville, Ohio, from 1891 to 1928. The
first art pottery was made after 1896. Utopian Ware, Cyrano, Navarre,
Feroza, and Henri Deux were made. Pieces were usually marked with a
form of the name *Owens.* About 1907, the firm began to make tile and
discontinued the art pottery wares.

Coffeepot, Jade Green, Signed, 9 1/2 In. 145.00
Ewer, Enameled Pansy Spray, Dark Ground, Handle, High Glaze, Larzelere, 7 In. ... 140.00
Ewer, Pansies, Signed, 6 In. 155.00
Jardiniere, Henri Deux 355.00
Jardiniere, Leaf Design, Footed, Marked, 6 x 7 In. 245.00
Lamp Base, Utopian, Pansies 175.00
Mug, Utopian, Cherries, Brown, Signed, 4 1/2 In. 150.00
Mug, Utopian, Leaves & Berries, 1908 .... 95.00
Pitcher, Utopian, Peach & Brown Grapes, 12 In. 175.00
Tankard, Utopian, 12 1/2 In. 400.00
Tankard, Utopian, Grapes, A. Haubrich, 1901, 12 In. 250.00
Tile, Raised Tulip Bud, Egyptian Revival Style, Rose Against Green, 6 In. 44.00
Vase, Enameled Rose Spray, Pastel Ground, Bisque, Tot Steele, 8 In. 250.00
Vase, Floral, 6 In. 160.00
Vase, Floral, Twisted, 5 In. 95.00
Vase, Floral, Twisted, Matted, 4 In. 75.00
Vase, Gold Floral, Pink, Green & Brown, 5 In. 325.00
Vase, Jonquils, Standard Glaze, Floor, 15 In. 250.00
Vase, Pala Mission, Cylindrical, C. Hoty, 11 In. 200.00
Vase, Pillow, Utopian, Indian Portrait, 10 In. 1400.00
Vase, Pink & Purple Floral, Green To White Ground, Pink Interior, 10 In. 360.00
Vase, Stork Design, Gray To Pink Ground, Allover Crazed, High Glaze, 9 In. 290.00
Vase, Twist, Standard Glaze, Crazed, 4 1/2 In. 71.50
Vase, Utopian, 3 Sides, Standard Glaze, 6 1/2 In. 110.00
Vase, Utopian, Bust Portrait of Spaniel, c.1900, 15 1/2 In. 825.00
Vase, Utopian, Clover, 5 In. 120.00
Vase, Utopian, Clover, Delores Harvey, 7 In. 235.00
Vase, Utopian, Floral Marked, 8 1/ 2 In. 165.00
Vase, Utopian, Indian Portrait, Headdress, 11 x 12 In. 1540.00
Vase, Utopian, Lily of The Valley, Brown Glaze, T. Steele, 13 In. 415.00
Vase, Utopian, Pansies, Paneled, Signed, 4 x 4 In. 190.00
Vase, Utopian, Pinched, Signed, 3 1/2 In. 100.00
Vase, Utopian, Triangular Pinched Sides, Green Shaded Leaves, 4 In., Pair 195.00
Vase, Utopian, Twisted, Signed, 5 In. 150.00
Vase, Utopian, Yellow Tulip, Brown Glaze, T. Steele, 14 In. 410.00

OYSTER PLATES were popular from the 1880s. Each course at dinner was served in a special dish. The oyster plate had indentations shaped like oysters. Usually six oysters were held on a plate. There is no greater value to a plate with more oysters although that myth continues to haunt antiques dealers. There are other plates for shellfish, including cockle plates and whelk plates. The appropriately shaped indentations are part of the design of these dishes.

Hand–Painted Brown & Pink Leaves, 8 In.	55.00
Leaf Design, Haviland, 9 In., 12 Piece	550.00
Pink Roses, Gold Trim, Limoges	100.00
Scalloped Borders, Weimar, Germany, 8 1/4 In., 6 Piece	275.00

PADEN CITY Glass Manufacturing Company was established in 1916 at Paden City, West Virginia. It is best known for glasswares but also produced a pottery line. The firm closed in 1951.

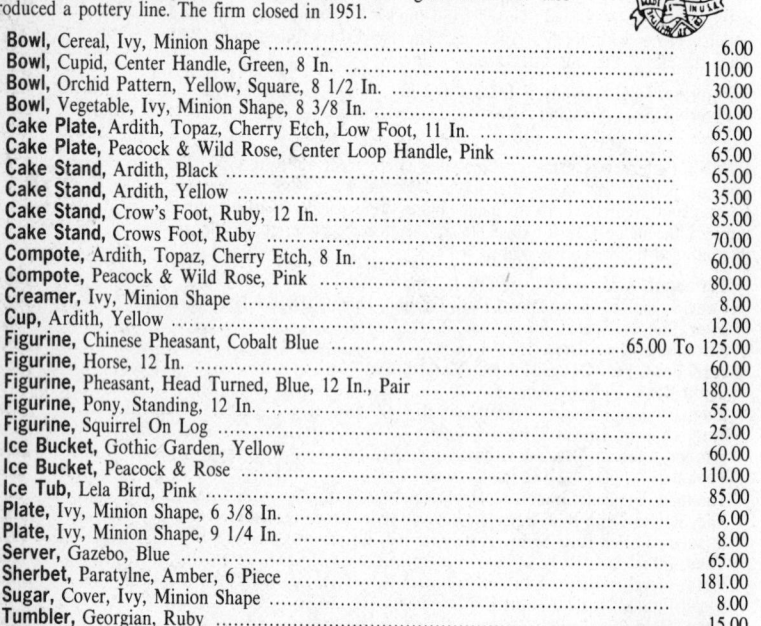

Bowl, Cereal, Ivy, Minion Shape	6.00
Bowl, Cupid, Center Handle, Green, 8 In.	110.00
Bowl, Orchid Pattern, Yellow, Square, 8 1/2 In.	30.00
Bowl, Vegetable, Ivy, Minion Shape, 8 3/8 In.	10.00
Cake Plate, Ardith, Topaz, Cherry Etch, Low Foot, 11 In.	65.00
Cake Plate, Peacock & Wild Rose, Center Loop Handle, Pink	65.00
Cake Stand, Ardith, Black	65.00
Cake Stand, Ardith, Yellow	35.00
Cake Stand, Crow's Foot, Ruby, 12 In.	85.00
Cake Stand, Crows Foot, Ruby	70.00
Compote, Ardith, Topaz, Cherry Etch, 8 In.	60.00
Compote, Peacock & Wild Rose, Pink	80.00
Creamer, Ivy, Minion Shape	8.00
Cup, Ardith, Yellow	12.00
Figurine, Chinese Pheasant, Cobalt Blue	65.00 To 125.00
Figurine, Horse, 12 In.	60.00
Figurine, Pheasant, Head Turned, Blue, 12 In., Pair	180.00
Figurine, Pony, Standing, 12 In.	55.00
Figurine, Squirrel On Log	25.00
Ice Bucket, Gothic Garden, Yellow	60.00
Ice Bucket, Peacock & Rose	110.00
Ice Tub, Lela Bird, Pink	85.00
Plate, Ivy, Minion Shape, 6 3/8 In.	6.00
Plate, Ivy, Minion Shape, 9 1/4 In.	8.00
Server, Gazebo, Blue	65.00
Sherbet, Paratylne, Amber, 6 Piece	181.00
Sugar, Cover, Ivy, Minion Shape	8.00
Tumbler, Georgian, Ruby	15.00

PAINTINGS listed in this book are not works by major artists but rather decorative paintings on ivory, board, or glass that would be of interest to the average collector. To learn the value of an oil painting by a listed artist you must contact an expert in that area.

Oil On Board, 4 Sailing Ships, British Flag, Burl Veneer Frame, 13 In.	415.00
Oil On Board, Fishing Boats At Sea, 11 x 16 In.	2200.00
Oil On Board, Girl With Whip, 20 1/2 x 15 1/2 In.	950.00
Oil On Board, Landscape, Mountains, Water, Gilt Frame, 16 1/2 In.	71.00
Oil On Board, Louisiana Rain, Edgar Malin Craven, 18 x 23 3/4 In.	775.00
Oil On Board, Primitive Landscape With Church, Frame, 11 x 16 In.	50.00
Oil On Canvas, 3 Chicks Eating Oyster, Gilt Frame, 17 In.	185.00
Oil On Canvas, 3 Children Wearing Jewelry, Gilt Frame, 31 x 35 In.	2100.00
Oil On Canvas, American Flag, Schoolhouse, Cross–Corner Frame, 17 1/2 In.	385.00
Oil On Canvas, Amherst, Judgment of Paris, 26 x 36 In.	55.00
Oil On Canvas, Barnyard Scene, Cat, Chicks, Bird, Strip Frame, 15 In.	1100.00
Oil On Canvas, Black Family, Man Shooting Turkeys Out of Tree, 20 x 28 In.	3050.00
Oil On Canvas, Boy & Dog, Doghouse, 19th Century, 8 x 12 In.	445.00
Oil On Canvas, Case & Mummy, Matted, Frame, 28 3/4 In.	550.00

Oil On Canvas, Dog Head, Modern Frame, 11 In. 467.00
Oil On Canvas, Early Farmhouse, Interior, Signed, 8 1/2 x 12 1/2 In. 495.00
Oil On Canvas, Farmers Threshing Wheat, 10 x 14 In. .: 110.00
Oil On Canvas, Gentleman, Black Frock Coat, Rolled Paper, Frame, 32 In. 1210.00
Oil On Canvas, George Washington Portrait, Gilt Frame, 25 3/4 x 22 3/4 In. 900.00
Oil On Canvas, Girl Portrait, Leaves, America, Frame, 19th Century, 23 x 19 In. 825.00
Oil On Canvas, Girl Portrait, Plaid Dress, Gilt Frame, America, 35 x 30 In. 1045.00
Oil On Canvas, Giunta, Cabanas, 52 x 44 In. 3410.00
Oil On Canvas, Holy Family & Cherubs, Florentine Frame, 66 1/2 x 77 In. 1150.00
Oil On Canvas, John The Baptist, Jesus, Children, Lamb, Cherubs, 54 x 61 3/4 In. .. 1600.00
Oil On Canvas, Landscape of Cows, Gilt Frame, 13 1/2 x 23 1/2 In. 633.00
Oil On Canvas, Landscape, Fishing Boats, Frame, 20 In. x 28 In. 150.00
Oil On Canvas, Landscape, Hunting Camp, Frame, 16 1/2 In. 88.00
Oil On Canvas, Landscape, Mountains, Water, Villa, Gilt Frame, 36 In. 330.00
Oil On Canvas, Leopard Devouring A Flamingo, Hermes, 1939, 38 1/2 x 71 1/2 In. .. 110.00
Oil On Canvas, Major Grafton, Frame, 36 x 29 In. 685.00
Oil On Canvas, Man Wearing Gold Frame Glasses, Frame, 22 1/2 In. 27.00
Oil On Canvas, Mrs. Lloyd of Charleston, Frame, Late 18th Century, 30 x 20 In. ... 770.00
Oil On Canvas, Native American Spear Fishing, Frame, 30 x 48 In. 825.00
Oil On Canvas, November Afternoon, Milton, Massachusetts, 8 x 10 In. 4400.00
Oil On Canvas, October In Washington Valley, Frame, 10 x 18 In. 550.00
Oil On Canvas, Old Man With Goatee, Painted Frame, 30 In. 71.00
Oil On Canvas, Portrait of A Young Woman, America, 1840, 26 x 21 In. 1250.00
Oil On Canvas, Portrait of An Engineer, Signed, 1863, 36 x 27 In. 440.00
Oil On Canvas, Portrait of Woman, White Collar, Pink Bow, Gilt Frame, 26 In. 330.00
Oil On Canvas, River Landscape, Alligatored, Gilt Frame, 24 x 32 In. 275.00
Oil On Canvas, Sailboats, Motor Boats, Small Marina, Frame, 20 In. 27.00
Oil On Canvas, Scene of Paris & Pantheon, Frame, 29 In. 100.00
Oil On Canvas, Seascape With Rocks, Gold Repaint, Frame, 25 In. 77.00
Oil On Canvas, Seascape, Gilt Frame, 18 1/2 In. 82.00
Oil On Canvas, Stag, Waterfall Background, Hunter, Frame, 24 x 32 In. 240.00
Oil On Canvas, Still Life With Apples, Ornate Gilt Frame, 20 In. 126.00
Oil On Canvas, The Hitch Hiker, 40 x 30 In. 165.00
Oil On Canvas, View of The Tiber Bridge In Venice, Gilded Frame, 33 x 53 In. 3850.00
Oil On Canvas, Winter Landscape, Tella Kitchen, Frame, 16 x 20 In. 2600.00
Oil On Canvas, Woman In Black, Gilt Frame, 35 3/4 In. 150.00
Oil On Canvas, Woman In Chair, Marked, Framed, 9 1/2 In. 143.00
Oil On Canvas, Woman, Black Dress, White Collar, Brooch, Frame, 38 In. 850.00
Oil On Canvas, Woodland Scene, Hunter, New Hampshire, Frame, 17 x 11 In. 935.00
Oil On Canvas, Young Man, Pine Ogee Frame, 38 3/4 In. 660.00
Oil On Panel, 3 Perch & 1 Salmon, Trophy, Mustard Ground, Frame, 9 x 21 In. 190.00
Oil On Panel, American Military Officer, 19th Century, Frame, 30 x 25 In. 1430.00
Oil On Panel, Peasant Girl, Soldier, Horseback, Alligatored, Frame, 13 x 15 In. 71.00
Oil On Panel, Portrait of Benjamin Stanton, Gold Frame, 32 1/4 In. 2035.00
On Board, Mountain Scene, Hudson River Style, 9 1/4 x 12 1/4 In. 260.00
On Board, Watermelon Party, Frame, 12 3/4 In. 247.00
On Board, Young Boy Portrait, Watercolor, Frame, 1819, 7 1/2 x 5 3/4 In. 880.00
On Ivory, Colonel John Cox, Brass & Leather Frame, 1790s, 3 x 2 3/4 In. 715.00
On Ivory, Man, Portrait, Brass Oval Frame, 3 3/4 In. 265.00
On Ivory, Man, Portrait, Gold–Colored Case, Oval, 1842, Miniature 248.00
On Ivory, Mary Queen of Scots, Ivory Frame, 4 x 3 3/8 In. 105.00
On Ivory, Master Thomas Brodhead Portrait, Naval Uniform, Miniature 850.00
On Ivory, Mirror, Hand, Woman Miniature, Elegant Gown, Gold Ormolu, 15 In. 285.00
On Ivory, Mother & Child, c.1820 .... 875.00
On Ivory, Napoleon & 18th Century Woman, Continental, 2 1/2 x 3 1/2 In., Pair ... 523.00
On Ivory, Portrait, Onyx Frame, 2 1/8 x 1 3/4 In. 495.00
On Ivory, Woman In Plumed Hat, Gilt Oval Frame 210.00
On Ivory, Woman Portrait, Blue Dress, Watercolor, Framed, 5 3/4 x 5 In. 195.00
On Panel, Woman, Coral Necklace, Brown Dress, Balloon Sleeves, 8 1/2 In. 1485.00
On Paper, 2 Children, Straw Hat, Gilt Frame, England, 15 x 12 1/2 In. 82.00
On Paper, 2 Colorful Birds, Stylized Trees, Watercolor, Frame, 6 1/2 In. 181.00
On Paper, Bird On Branch, Watercolor, Child's, 19th Century, Frame, 5 x 6 In. 195.00
On Paper, Child Portrait, Rose, Watercolor, Black Lacquered Frame, 6 3/4 x 5 In. .. 165.00

On Paper, Gentleman Portrait, Pencil & Ink, Gilt Frame, 5 3/8 x 4 1/2 In.	247.00
On Paper, Horse, England, Watercolor, 19th Century, 10 x 14 In., Pair	550.00
On Paper, Man, Black Hair, Black Coat, Watercolor, Pencil, Frame, 5 In.	275.00
On Paper, Morning of The Nile, Signed, Watercolor, Frame, 11 x 18 In.	330.00
On Paper, On The Nile, Near Cairo, Watercolor, Frame, 11 1/2 x 18 1/2 In.	110.00
On Paper, Portrait of Woman, Watercolor, Frame, 18 x 25 In.	495.00
On Paper, Spring Landscape, Sheep, Watercolor, Matted, Frame, 24 1/2 In.	110.00
On Paper, Stylized Tulip, Red, Green, Blue, Yellow, Watercolor, Ink, 8 In.	93.00
On Paper, Venice Canal Scene, Matted, Frame, Watercolor, 1976, 23 x 29 In.	55.00
On Paper, Woman, Brown Hair, Green Dress, Balloon Sleeves, Frame, 6 In.	247.00
On Paper, Woman, Navy & White Plaid Dress, Seated, Rosewood Frame, 9 In.	385.00
On Paper, Young Woman, Watercolor, Gutta–Percha Frame, 5 1/2 x 6 1/2 In.	50.00
On Porcelain, Landscape, Signed, Gilt Frame, 9 1/4 x 7 1/4 In.	150.00
On Porcelain, Napoleon, Gold Epaulets, Oval Brass Frame, c.1890, 3 x 2 1/2 In	175.00
On Porcelain, Plaque, Dancing Greek Maidens, Frame, W. G. & Co., France, 8 In.	325.00
On Porcelain, Portrait of Ruth, 19th Century	880.00
On Porcelain, Woman, Feathered Bonnet, Limoges, Brass Frame	1925.00
On Silk, Emperor & Empress, On Throne, Frame, Qing Dynasty, 54 x 29 In., Pair	1100.00
On Silk, Mourning, Needlework & Water Color, 2 3/4 x 10 1/2 In.	600.00
On Silk, Warrior & Woman, Gouache, Bamboo Frame, Japan, 15 x 18 In., Pair.	99.00
On Silk, Warriors On Horseback, Gouache, Frame, Japan, 16 1/2 x 19 In., Pair	125.00
On Tin, Retablos, Our Lady of Refuge, Mexico	195.00
On Tin, Retablos, Our Lady of Sorrows, Mexico	175.00
On Tin, Still Life, Basket of Tulips, Oil, Black Molded Frame, 14 x 18 In.	80.00
On Velvet, Parrot On Moss Rose Branch, Gilt Frame, 26 1/2 x 22 In.	100.00
On Velvet, Winter In The Country, Oil, 1945	5.00
Reverse On Glass, Abraham Lincoln Portrait, Frame, 18 1/4 x 17 1/4 In.	150.00
Reverse On Glass, Bearded Man & Young Woman, 19th Century, 19 x 13 In.	440.00
Reverse On Glass, Beta, Polychrome, 2–Tone Brown Ground, Frame, 12 In.	330.00
Reverse On Glass, Boy, Bow & Arrow, Gold Leaf Frame, 3 1/2 x 2 3/4 In.	825.00
Reverse On Glass, Figures In Pavilion, Frame, 20 x 14 In., Pair	1650.00
Reverse On Glass, Morro Castle, Ornate Oak Frame, 30 1/2 x 26 1/2 In.	125.00
Reverse On Glass, Oriental Woman, Blue Kimono, Carved Frame, 19 x 15 1/2 In.	440.00
Reverse On Glass, Portrait of Gentleman, Blue Jacket, 13 1/2 x 9 1/2 In.	1210.00
Reverse On Glass, Rosinia, Polychrome, Dark Green Ground, Frame, 9 1/8 In.	412.00
Reverse On Glass, St. Mark With Lion, 13 1/2 x 9 1/2 In.	45.00
Reverse On Glass, Westminster Abbey, London, Frame, 33 x 20 In.	175.00
Reverse On Glass, Woman, Rose In Bodice, Victorian, Frame, 21 1/2 x 17 In.	825.00

PAIRPOINT Manufacturing Company started in 1880 in New Bedford, Massachusetts. It soon joined with the glassworks nearby and made glass, silver–plated pieces, and lamps. Reverse-painted glass shades and molded shades known as *puffies* were part of the production until the 1930s. The company reorganized and changed its name several times but is still working today. Items listed here are glass or glass and metal. Silver–plated pieces are listed under Silver Plate.

Biscuit Barrel, Delft Design, Silver Plated Collar & Ring Handle, 6 In.	350.00
Bowl, Basket Holder, Turned–Down Ruffled Rim, Cranberry Swirl, 9 x 6 1/2 In.	325.00
Bowl, Center, Art Nouveau, Handle, 13 x 16 In.	175.00
Box, Dresser, Nevada, Sterling Silver Top, 3 x 4 1/2 In	185.00
Candlestick, Cobalt Blue, 4 In.	80.00
Candlestick, Colonial, Red Amber, 16 In., Pair	2500.00
Candlestick, Venetti, Bell Bottom, White Spirals, 10 In., Pair	1500.00
Chalice, Adelaide Pattern, 12 In.	880.00
Coffeepot, Gourd of Vines, Spider Webs, Cranes	165.00
Compote, Silver Over Metal, Gold Wash, Cobalt Glass Insert, Bubble Shape, 9 In.	135.00
Cracker Jar, Melon Shape	700.00
Cup Plate, Grandfather Frog	75.00
Cup Plate, Hooty Owl	130.00
Cup Plate, Jimmy Skunk	45.00
Cup Plate, National Quilting Assoc.	27.50
Cup Plate, Paddy Beaver	60.00
Cup Plate, Reddy Fox	145.00

Dish, Serving, Silver Leaf Pattern 550.00
Lamp, Blown–Out Papillon, Reverse Painted Butterflies, 1907, 19 In. 6325.00
Lamp, Boudoir, Painted Garden Scene, Wooden Metal Base, 12 In. 605.00
Lamp, Camels & Pyramids, Signed, 20 In. 4200.00
Lamp, David The Shepherd, Signed, 21 In. 8750.00
Lamp, Directoire With Cornova Design, Signed, 1920s 1050.00
Lamp, Farm Scene, Exeter, Signed, 18 In. 3250.00
Lamp, Fleur–De–Lis White Enameled Shade & Base, Tapestry, 14 In. 3850.00
Lamp, Hummingbird & Roses, Puffy, Silver Plated, 2 Socket Base, 21 1/2 In. 3575.00
Lamp, Puffy, Floral Shade, 2 Handles 4730.00
Lamp, Puffy, Hummingbird & Roses 6875.00
Lamp, Puffy, Red, Blue, Yellow & Green Bonnet Style, Silver Base 4950.00
Lamp, Reverse Painted Carlisle Shade, Ships In Harbor, 16 In. 3200.00
Lamp, Reverse Painted Landscape, Flock of Sheep, Signed Ona. M., 17 1/2 In. 2200.00
Lamp, Reverse Painted Shade, 4 Exotic Birds, Leaves On Base, c.1915, 21 1/2 In. ... 4400.00
Lamp, Reverse Painted Shade, Blown Poppies, Birds & Leaves, Marked, 14 In. 4180.00
Lamp, Reverse Painted, Floral Border Shade, Urn Base, 16 In. 1950.00
Lamp, Reverse Painted, Repeating Design, 3 Arms, Gilt Metal Base, 22 In. 1430.00
Lamp, Sailing Ships 3400.00
Lamp, Table, Floral Panels, Green Ground, Gold Tracery, Signed 5500.00
Lamp, Table, Reverse Painted Carlisle Shade, Farm Scene 2750.00
Lamp, Table, Reverse Painted White Vertical Stripes, 4 Landscapes, 17 In. 1650.00
Lamp, Table, Ribbed Torino Shade 5000.00
Lamp, Tulip Venice 4500.00
Lamp, Windmills On Base & Globe, Miniature 675.00
Paperweight, Controlled Bubbles, Cranberry, 1920s 85.00
Paperweight, Swirl, Tornado Shape, Red & White Twists, 3 In. 385.00
Parfait, Canary Yellow, Fluted, Etched Grape, 6 Piece 375.00
Perfume Bottle, Controlled Bubbles, Paperweight, Clear Stopper, Label 125.00
Plate, Art Nouveau, 1904 .... 365.00
Powder Box, Victorian Lady Cover, Glass Insert, 1800s, Signed 55.00
Powder Box, Victorian Woman On Cover, Metal, Glass Insert, 1800s, Signed 90.00
Salt, Open, Boy Riding Dolphin, On Shell, 5 1/2 In. 350.00
Shade, Reverse–Painted Landscape, Signed, Bronze Base, 17 In. Diam. 3025.00
Tray, Strawberry, Diamond & Cane With Hobstars, Rows of Beading, 14 x 8 In. 775.00
Tumbler, Tavern, Galleon Under Full Sail, Black Enamel, 1910s 235.00
Vase, Bubble Stem, Apple Green, 8 x 8 In. 115.00
Vase, Cranberry Glass, Signed, 5 In. 89.00
Vase, Dolphin Finial, Pot Metal Adornments, Green, 6 In. 145.00
Vase, Etched Grapes, Lavender, 8 In. 325.00
Vase, Green, Dolphins Form Handle, Pot Metal Top & Bottom, 6 In. 195.00
Vase, Hand Painted, Enamel, Merchants, Camel, Flamingos, 14 In. 1650.00

PALMER COX, BROWNIES, see Brownies

PAPER DOLLS were probably inspired by the pantins, or jumping jacks, made in eighteenth–century Europe. By the 1880s, sheets of printed paper dolls and clothes were being made. The first paper doll books were made in the 1920s. Collectors prefer uncut sheets or books or boxed sets of paper dolls. Prices are about half as much if the pages have been cut.

Air Hostess, Saalfield, Uncut, 1947 .... 29.50
Alice Faye, Merrill, 1941, Cut 45.00
American Airline Stewardess, Wooden Doll, 1942, Uncut 40.00
American Beauties, Merville, Uncut 32.00
American Beauties, Uncut 85.00
Baby Brother & Sister, Whitman, 1958, Uncut 30.00
Baby Sisters, Merrill, 1938, Cut 10.00
Baby Sparkle Plenty, Saalfield, No. 1510, 1948 .... 60.00
Baby, Samuel Lowe, Uncut, 1944 .... 15.00
Barbie & Ken Cut–Out Set, Whitman, 1962 .... 85.00
Barbie & Ken, 1984 .... 10.00
Barbie Magic Doll, Box 15.00
Barbie, Bubble Cut, Suitcase, Whitman, Cut 20.00

Barbie, Mattel, Box, 1969	30.00
Betsy & Carol, 1950s, Cut	11.50
Betty & Bill, Black Children, Cut	20.00
Bewitched, Samantha, 1965, Box	70.00
Big Cutout Book, 1941, Uncut	35.00
Blondie, 1944	35.00
Blue Feather & Silver Cloud, 1940s, Cut	22.00
Boots & Her Buddies, Saalfield, Cut	45.00
Bryn Mawr Advertising	12.00
Buffy, Book, 1968	35.00
Caroline Kennedy, Box	15.00
David Cassidy, Box, Unopened	25.00
Deanna Durbin, 1941, Uncut	195.00
Diane & Daphne, The Round About Dolls, McLoughlin Bros., Uncut	45.00
Dolly Dingle, Around The World & Opera Series, 7 Sheets, 1917–1921, Uncut	45.00
Dolly Dingle, Uncut Framed Sheet	30.00
Doris Day, Uncut	15.00
Dotty Double, Saalfield, 1933, Cut	35.00
Double Wedding, 1939, Cut	25.00
Dress Up For New York World's Fair, 1964, Uncut	45.00
Drowsy, Box, 1975	9.00
Elizabeth Taylor, Uncut	15.00
Family Affair, Box, 1968	50.00
Finnigan's Rainbow, 1968 Movie, Box, Unopened	25.00
First Ladies, Presidents Inaugural Ball, Washington, Roosevelt, 4 Dolls	35.00
Flying Nun, Punch Out, 1968	55.00
Fonzie, Box, Unopened	25.00
Francie & Casey, Cut	25.00
Gilda Radner, Book	35.00
Gone With The Wind, 1939, Cut	120.00
Gone With The Wind, 1940, Uncut	300.00
Grace Kelly, Uncut	195.00
Green Acres, 1968, Box	65.00
Gulliver's Travels, Saalfield, 1939, Cut	35.00
Gulliver's Travels, Uncut	150.00
Gulliver's Travels, Walt Disney, 1940s, Uncut	135.00
Hollywood Fashion, 1939, Cut	20.00
Indians, Leather Costumes, Dennison, Pair, Cut	140.00
Jane Arden, Saalfield, 1942, Cut	30.00
Julia, Book, 1970s	40.00
Laraine Day, Uncut	75.00
Lindy Lou & Cindy Lou, Merville, Uncut	40.00
Little Lulu & Tubby, 1974	35.00
Little Red Riding Hood, Cut	22.50
Lucille Ball, Desi Arnez, 1953, Whitman, Uncut	75.00
Mr. Kotter, Welcome Back Kotter, 1976, Uncut	18.00
Mrs. Beasley, Book, 1970	35.00
My Fair Lady, 1960s, Box	40.00
My Twin Babies, Book, 1940, Uncut	35.00
Old Lady Who Lived In The Shoe, 1940, Uncut	55.00
Our Nurse Nancy, Stand–Up, Clothes, Box, 1943, Uncut	25.00
Our Nurse Nancy, Whitman, 1943, Uncut	30.00
Paper Dolls On Parade, Saalfield, 1940, Cut	15.00
Partridge Family, Book, 1971	40.00
Pinocchio, Whitman, 1939, Uncut	275.00
Pitti Sing, 4 Dolls On Sheet, 1892, Uncut	85.00
Prince Valiant & Princess Aleta, Saalfield, 1954, Uncut	192.50
Ranchland, Box, 1952, Uncut	25.00
Reagan Family, Partially Cut, 1981	25.00
Rhonda Fleming, With Coloring Book, Uncut, 1954	45.00 To 60.00
Ricky Nelson, Whitman, 1959	45.00
Rock Hudson, Whitman, 1957, Uncut	70.00
Snow White & 7 Dwarfs, 1939, Uncut	200.00 To 275.00

Snow White & 7 Dwarfs, Cottage, 1940s, Cut	35.00
Sonja Henie, Merrill, 1939, Cut	37.50
Sonja Henie, Merrill, 1940, Cut	45.00
Sonja Henie, Merrill, 1940, Uncut	275.00
Sonja Henie, Merrill, 1941, Cut	40.00
Statuette, 1950s, Uncut	10.00
Tricia Nixon, Uncut	45.00
Tuesday Weld, 1960, Box	50.00
Twin Babies, Book, 1942, Uncut	30.00
Twins, Book, Queen Holden, Uncut	40.00
Walking Paper Doll Family, Saalfield, 1934, Cut	30.00
World's Fair, 1964, Uncut	32.00

PAPER collectibles, including almanacs, catalogs, children's books, stock
certificates, and other paper ephemera, are listed here. Paper calendars are
listed separately in the Calendar Paper category.

Almanac, Ayers American, 1892	2.00
Almanac, Dr. Miles New Weather, 1931	2.00
Almanac, Farmer's, 1859	6.00
Almanac, Medical, Dr. Jaynes, 1888	2.00
Atlas, Scotts Emulsion Co., Pocket Size, 1899	20.00
Bill of Sale, Bicycle Repair Shop, 1890	6.00
Book, Big Big Book, The Story of Mickey Mouse, 1930s	66.00
Book, Big Little Book, Houdini's Book of Magic, 1933	35.00
Book, Big Little Book, Houdini's Magic, Cocomalt, 200 Pages, 1927	25.00
Book, Big Little Book, King of Royal Mounted, Zane Grey, 1936 .... 25.00 To 27.50
Book, Big Little Book, Lassie, Old One Eye, 1975	2.00
Book, Big Little Book, Little Women	30.00
Book, Big Little Book, Lone Ranger & His Horse Silver, 1935	30.00
Book, Big Little Book, Story of Johnny Weissmuller, 1934	35.00
Book, Coloring, American Red Cross Safety, Dick Tracy, Peanuts, Archie, 1970	15.00
Book, Coloring, Raggedy Ann & Raggedy Andy, Uncolored, 1944, 11 x 14 In.	30.00
Book, Coloring, Rin Tin Tin, Unused	35.00
Book, Pop–Up, Jolly Jumpups Vacation Trip	55.00
Book, Pop–Up, Minnie Mouse	60.00
Book, Pop–Up, Santa's Circus Party	57.00
Book, Pop–Up, Santa's Workshop	47.00
Book, Pop–Up, Star Wars, 1978	20.00
Caligraphy, Bird On Nest, Spencerian, Oct. 26th, 1888, Frame, 16 3/4 x 13 3/4 In.	45.00
Catalog, 1933 Chevrolet, Leads Parade of Progress, Small	18.00
Catalog, Alden, 1946 Christmas, 1970 Pages	45.00
Catalog, Bauer & Black Medical Supplies, Color Illustrations, 1929, 95 Pages	48.00
Catalog, Bonwit Teller, 1928, Park Avenue Fashions, 8 1/2 x 12 In.	47.50
Catalog, Butlers Brothers, 1917, Santa Claus Edition, 682 Pages	100.00
Catalog, Cast Iron Toy, 1910, Dent Toy Co.	45.00
Catalog, Chicago Magic Co., 1919, Magical Apparatus, 160 Pages	60.00
Catalog, E. D. Simmons, No. U, c.1930, 2090 Pages	250.00
Catalog, Eastman Kodak Supply, 1916, 64 Pages	30.00
Catalog, Eugene Berninghaus Barber Supply	165.00
Catalog, Foote–Bros. Gear & Machine Corp., Illustrated Parts	3.50
Catalog, Gold Bond Stamps, 1952	2.25
Catalog, H–O Co., 1900, Easy To Get Prizes, Illustrations, 3 x 3 1/4 In.	12.50
Catalog, Home Builders, 1927, Hardware, Homes, Color Plates, 1200 Pages	35.00
Catalog, J. C. Penny, 1963, Christmas	100.00
Catalog, Johnson Smith & Co., 1950s, Novelties, 96 Pages	5.00
Catalog, Lane Bryant Fashion, 1946, Mid–Summer, 36 Pages	17.50
Catalog, Lane Bryant, 1947	10.00
Catalog, Lufkin Small Tool, 1922	7.00
Catalog, Montgomery Ward Groceries, 1911, May–June, 65 Pages	32.00
Catalog, Montgomery Ward, 1907, No. 76	75.00
Catalog, Montgomery Ward, 1918, No. 88	75.00
Catalog, Montgomery Ward, 1920, Spring & Summer	95.00
Catalog, Montgomery Ward, 1926	25.00

Catalog, Montgomery Ward, 1935, Spring & Summer, 478 Pages 18.00
Catalog, Montgomery Ward, 1946, Christmas 75.00
Catalog, Montgomery Ward, 1946, Photographic, 126 Pages 5.00
Catalog, Montgomery Ward, 1968, Christmas 45.00
Catalog, Montgomery Ward, 1973, 352 Pages 30.00
Catalog, National Magic Co., 1957, 335 Pages 75.00
Catalog, Philip Morris Christmas, 1946, For Sportsmen, 32 Pages 18.00
Catalog, Pike Company, 1922, Sharpening Stones, Razor Strops 7.00
Catalog, Radio Corp. of America, 1920, 22 Pages 15.00
Catalog, Roseville, Photographs, History of Pottery, 24 Pages, Copyright 1931 .... 180.00
Catalog, Sears, 1915, Baby Book, Dolls, Carriages, 68 Pages 48.00
Catalog, Sears, 1922, Summer, Seattle Wash., 122 Pages 50.00
Catalog, Sears, 1936, Golden Jubilee, Economy Specials 17.00
Catalog, Sears, 1950, Christmas 25.00
Catalog, Sears, 1961, Diamond Jubilee, 1460 Pages 80.00
Catalog, Sears, Roebuck, 1902 .... 42.00
Catalog, Sears, Wallpaper Samples, 1943, 86 Patterns 12.50
Catalog, Seneca Falls Machine Co., 1940, Metal Lathes 4.00
Catalog, Shapleigh's General Hardware, No. 350, c.1929, 2354 Pages 250.00
Catalog, Spiegel, 1930, New Year, 50 Pages 12.00
Catalog, Spiegel, 1946, Christmas 75.00
Catalog, Spiegel, 1954, Christmas 75.00
Catalog, Spiegel, 1964 .... 10.00
Catalog, Stove, 1910, 44 Page, 11 x 8 1/2 In. 35.00
Catalog, Wallace Nutting Furniture, 1927–1928, 7th Edition 120.00
Catalog, Wright & Co. Boys, Chicago, 1910, Fabric Samples 35.00
Catalog, Wurlitzer Musical Instruments, No. 98 .... 55.00
Fraktur, Angel, Northampton County, Handmade, Dated 1793, 8 x 12 1/2 In. 4290.00
Fraktur, Bird, Wullimann Family From 1840–1877, Frame, 15 x 13 In. 440.00
Fraktur, Birth, Frederick Krebs, Part Printed, Freehand Birds & Flowers, 1803 .... 1700.00
Fraktur, Birth, Geburts & Taufshein, Berks County, Frame, 1773, 11 1/2 Xin. 375.00
Fraktur, Birth, Geburts Und Taufschein 1835, Frame, 17 1/2 x 14 1/2 In. 121.00
Fraktur, Birth, Geburts Und Taufschein, 1825, Frame, 19 x 16 In. 116.00
Fraktur, Birth, Geburts Und Taufschein, 1844, Pine Frame, 19 In. 93.00
Fraktur, Bookplate, Jacob Yotder, For Magdalena Kaufman, 1831, 4 x 6 1/2 In. 200.00
Fraktur, Certificate of Birth & Baptism, 1846, 22 1/2 x 18 1/2 In. 165.00
Fraktur, Christ In Garden, Religious Verse, Pen & Ink 247.00
Fraktur, Folk Style Family Tree, Watercolor On Paper, Pennsylvania, c.1850 .... 425.00
Fraktur, Man & Woman, Watercolor, Pinprick Art 575.00
Fraktur, Path To Heaven & Hell, German Script, Frame, 19th Century, 19 x 15 In. 250.00
Fraktur, Penn. German, Stylized Tulip, Flowers, Red, Blue, Frame, 11 x 9 In. 1375.00
Fraktur, Taufschein For Thomas Brill, Virginia, 1800, 7 1/2 x 12 1/2 In. 3500.00
Fraktur, Tulip & Bird, Verse, 1831, 8 x 6 In. 375.00
Fraktur, Tulips, Hearts & Pomegranates, Martin Brechall 5000.00
Fraktur, Watercolor On Paper, Phebe Beamer, Born 1815, Frame, 10 x 15 In. 2100.00
Manual, McCormick–Deering Owner's, 1920s, 1930s, 1940s 85.00
Manual, Tinsmith's Patterns, Hard Cover, 1901 .... 20.00
Menu, Windsor Hotel, Christmas Dinner, Bill of Fare, Toronto 5.00
Program, Buffalo Bill Wild West Show, 1898 .... 175.00
Program, Cody Wild West Show, 1893 .... 127.00
Program, Gone With The Wind 100.00
Program, National Automobile Show, 1956, 82 Pages 30.00
Program, Robbins Bros. Circus, Hoot Gibson, 1930s 45.00
Program, Shipstads & Johnson Ice Follies of 1951 .... 12.00
Program, Sonja Henie, Red Flocked Cover, Gold Skater, 1948 .... 15.00
Program, Theater, Follow The Girls, 1944, Jackie Gleason, 16 Pages 12.00
Program, Theater, Gone With The Wind, Original, 1939 .... 25.00
Stock Certificate, Alabama Gold & Copper Co., Jarilla, N. M., Garrett Signed 1500.00
Stock Certificate, Bandle Arms Company, Ohio, 1890 .... 110.00
Stock Certificate, Camden & Philadelphia Steamboat Ferry Co., 1873 .... 80.00
Stock Certificate, Cieneguita Consolidated Mines Co., N. Y, State of Ariz., 1915 .... 6.00
Stock Certificate, Denver & Rio Grande Railroad Co., Colorado, 1886 .... 115.00
Stock Certificate, Denver & Rio Grande Railroad Co., Royal Gorge Scene, 1910s ... 85.00

Stock Certificate, Dominion Stores, Brown, Lion, Wilderness, Canceled, 1930s	6.50
Stock Certificate, Goldfield Midnight–Pawnee Mining Co., 1906, 6 1/2 x 9 In.	125.00
Stock Certificate, Houston & Texas Central Railway, Gold Bond, Train Scene, 1873	135.00
Stock Certificate, Ishpeming Livery Co., Ishpeming, Mich., Unissued, 1905	5.00
Stock Certificate, Jumbo Mining Co., Goldfield, Nev., Territory of Arizona, 1915 ...	15.00
Stock Certificate, Mining, Missouri, 1891	150.00
Stock Certificate, Oakland Traction Co., Orange, Trolley Car Scene, 1910s	35.00
Stock Certificate, Palmer Union Oil Co., Santa Barbara, Calif., 1928, 7 x 11 In.	12.50
Stock Certificate, Stewart Mining Co., State of Idaho, Miner Picture, 1914	10.00
Stock Certificate, White Horse Mining Co., 1901	60.00
Warranty Deed, Commonwealth of Mass., Worcester Dist., 4 Pages, 1901	15.00

PAPERWEIGHTS must have first appeared along with paper in ancient Egypt. Today's collectors search for every type, from the very expensive French weights of the nineteenth century to the modern artist weights or advertising pieces. The glass tops of the paperweights sometimes have been nicked or scratched and this type of damage can be removed by polishing. Some serious collectors think this type of repair is an alteration and will not buy a repolished weight; others think it is an acceptable technique of restoration that does not change the value. Baccarat paperweights are listed separately under Baccarat.

Advertising, AMR Insurance, Newark, 100 Anniversary, 1946	8.00
Advertising, Bell, Figural, Cobalt, Bell System, New York	65.00
Advertising, Borden's, Elsie & Milk Carton, Figural	22.00
Advertising, Crawford Shoes, Boston, Steamer Ship, 2 1/2 x 4 In.	30.00
Advertising, Crawford Shoes, Boston, Steamer Ship, 4 In.	30.00
Advertising, Dameron, Pieson Office Supplies, New Orleans, 4 1/2 In.	30.00
Advertising, Dempster Frog, Cast Iron	39.50
Advertising, Dictagraph Corp., President's Award, Wooden, Bronze	65.00
Advertising, Dumbbell, Iron, Scott–Baron, 3 1/4 In.	50.00
Advertising, Fairbanks Scale	85.00
Advertising, First Pig Iron, 1943	20.00
Advertising, General Motors, Commemorative	40.00
Advertising, International Harvester, Cadet, Cast Iron	25.00
Advertising, Laces & Curtains, New York City, Buildings, 1890s	40.00
Advertising, Lumber Co., Figural, Log	25.00
Advertising, Northwestern National Life Ins. Building, 1920	22.00
Advertising, Ort & Co. Dealer In Onions, Churubusco, Ind.	60.00
Advertising, Robinson Canning Co., New Orleans, Shrimp Inside Lucite	8.00
Advertising, Tice & Jacobs, New York, Ground Glass In Mold Cut	75.00
Ayotte, Butterfly, Flowers, Purple, Clear Ground, Signed, 1987	1210.00
Ayotte, Redbird, Branch, White Flowers, Signed, 1984, 1 7/8 In.	550.00
Baker, Blue & Green Interior, Air Traps, Clear Casing, 1980, 3 1/2 In.	45.00
Banford, Pear, Golden, 2 9/16 In.	330.00
Banford, Striped Snake On Pebbled Ground, 3 In.	400.00
Barker, Flower, Orange Blossom, Light Blue Ground, Signed, 2 1/8 In.	165.00
Blue Poinsettia, Swirling White Latticinio, America, 2 13/16 In.	550.00
Blue Rabbit Silhouette, Cane, 4–Leaf Flowers, c.1850, 2 x 3 In.	395.00
Bohemian, Austro–Hungarian Empire, Souvenir, Faceted, 3 3/16 In.	468.00
Bohemian, Concentric Millefiori, 2 Rows of Canes, Rose Center, 2 1/2 In.	550.00
Bohemian, Engraved Swan, Swimming, Amber Flash Ground, 2 1/4 In.	495.00
Bohemian, Mushroom, 24 Rose Canes, Pink, White, Green, 3 In.	3025.00
Bohemian, Open Concentric Millefiori, Latticinio Ground, 2 7/16 In.	121.00
Bohemian, St. Alexandrine, Sulphide, Ringed Outer Edge, 3 3/16 In.	825.00
Bohemian, Sulphide, Franz Josef, Cameo, Yellow Canes, Faceted, 3 3/16 In.	198.00
Botanical, Pine Barren, Blue Blossoms, Seeds, 5 1/2 In.	4950.00
Cameo, Marble, Lady's Profile, White, Purple Ground, 2 x 2 In.	27.00
Charles Wright, Clear, Veils, Brown, Orange & White Ribbons	125.00
Choko, Lizard, Brown Striped, Yellow Ground, Signed, 2 11/16 In.	440.00
Citation, Presentation, Arlington Park Hall of Fame, Etched Glass	475.00
Clear Floral Weight In Top, Porcelain, Crown Mark	35.00
Clichy, Central Pink, Green Rose, Turquoise, White Ground, 2 In.	3025.00
Clichy, Chequer, 2 Pink, Green Roses, Canes, 3 In.	3575.00

Clichy, Chequer, Rose, Edelweiss Canes, Latticinio Strips, 3 3/16 In. 2200.00
Clichy, Concentric Millefiori, Clear Ground, 2 3/8 In. 550.00
Clichy, Garland, Pastry Mold Canes, White, Red, Green, 3 1/8 In. 6050.00
Clichy, Millefiori, Edelweiss Canes, Star-Shaped Canes, Red Ground, 3 In. 3300.00
Clichy, Pansy, Violet, Cream, Clear, 2 5/8 In. 440.00
Clichy, Quatrefoil Garland, Chain of Roses, Pink & Green 6050.00
Clichy, Rose, Pink & Green, Swirl 3025.00
Clichy, Trefoil Garland, Cog Canes, Central Ruby, 2 In. 2750.00
Clichy, Whole & Broken Canes, Florets, 2 7/8 In. 990.00
Columbian Exposition, Molded Glass 45.00
D'Albret, Prince Charles, Sulphide, Blue Overlay, Clear Ground, 1970, 3 In. 99.00
D'Albret, Sitting Bull, Sulphide, Clear, Star-Cut Base, Signed, 1973, 2 7/8 In. 825.00
Dahlia, 5 Layers of Ridged Pink Petals, Central Cog Cane, 3 In. 5225.00
Dameron, Pierson Office Supplies, New Orleans, Building, 4 1/4 In. 30.00
Degenhart, Yellow & Orange Lily, Crystal Cube, Bubble, 3 x 2 1/4 In. 715.00
Dorflinger, Green & Red Lily, Bubbles, 3 5/16 In. 440.00
Egyptian, Art Deco, Bronze 38.00
Elephant, Metal, Small 4.00
Floral, Cube Shape, Cut Corners, Sterling Silver Overlay, Dated 1886 .... 145.00
Garfield Memorial, Mirror 20.00
Gentile, Snake, Green, Ladybug, White & Green Ground, 3 1/2 In. 770.00
Gillinder, Turtle, Moving Appendages, Green Ground, Faceted, 3 1/16 In. 248.00
Hansen, Fruit, Miniature, Pear, Cherry, Blue Ground, Facets, Signed 176.00
John F. Kennedy Profile, Azure Blue 78.00
Kain, Primrose, Orange & White, Cobalt Blue Ground, Signed, 2 1/8 In. 248.00
Kaziun, Bouquet, Roses, Amethyst Ground, 1 13/16 In. 550.00
Kaziun, Rose, Red, Pedestal Base, Height, 3 1/4 In. 825.00
Kaziun, Spider Lily, Pedestal, Signed 395.00
Kaziun, Spider Lily, Yellow & Orange, Lavender Ground, Pedestal, 1 3/4 In. 495.00
Labino, 4-Leaf Clover, Green In Reflected Light, Red, 1973, 1 1/2 x 2 1/2 In. 150.00
Labino, Brown Suspended Center, White Opalescent Canes, 1975, 1 3/4 In. 100.00
Labino, Light Green, Air Traps, 1968, 2 1/2 In. 150.00
Labino, Multicolor Feather, Light Blue Interior, Clear, 1978, 1 1/2 x 3 In. 140.00
Labino, Multicolor Festoons, Blue Interior, Clear, 1975, 2 x 3 In. 185.00
Labino, Snake Form, Blue Iridescent, Yellow Case, 1975, 2 In. 120.00
Labino, Swirl Top, Dark Cobalt Blue Interior, 1975, 1 1/4 x 3 In. 80.00
Littleton, Amber, Flat Sided Arch Form, 1972, 5 In. 400.00
Lundberg, Angelfish, Yellow, Iridescent Blue Ground, Lines, 1974, 3 In. 176.00
Lundberg, Dove, Red, Encircled By Blue Waves, Stars, 1979, 2 3/4 In. 143.00
Lundberg, Pink Jonquils 275.00
Millefiori, Animal Canes, Ribbon-Divided Pillow, 2 7/8 In. 8250.00
Millefiori, Central Silhouette, Dancing Woman, Salmon, Pistachio, 3 In. 4400.00
Millefiori, Swirling White Latticinio, 2 5/16 In. 468.00
Millville, White Sailing Ship, Crushed Blue Glass, Bubbles, 4 In. 1320.00
New England Glass, 5 Pears, 4 Cherries, Latticinio Basket, 2 1/4 In. 770.00
New England Glass, Concentric Millefiori, Rabbit Rings, 2 15/16 In. 275.00
New England Glass, Leaf Spray, Swirling Latticinio, 2 5/8 In. 770.00
New England Glass, Nosegay, White Latticinio, 2 1/2 In. 495.00
New England Glass, Open Concentric Millefiori, Clear, 2 3/16 In. 605.00
New England Glass, Pears & Plums, White Lattice Ground 850.00
New England Glass, Poinsettia, Latticino Ground, 1850 .... 555.00
New England Glass, Red Poinsettia, Bud, Swirling Latticinio, 3 1/8 In. 495.00
New England Glass, Scrambled, Latticinio Strips, Twists, 2 7 1/6 In. 209.00
Pear, Heavy Glass, Gold Wash Leaves 27.50
Perthshire, Aquarium, Fish, Seahorse, Crab, Facets, 1981, 3 7/16 In. 523.00
Perthshire, Bouquet, 3 Flower, Black Ground, Cane Centers, 1978, 3 In. 275.00
Perthshire, Dragonfly, Pink Body, Lace Wings, Facets, 2 1/8 In. 248.00
Perthshire, Hummingbird, Blue Flowers, Clear Ground, 1987, 2 7/8 In. 385.00
Puppy, Cast Iron 75.00
Red Poinsettia, Lutz Rose Cane, 2 7/8 In. 605.00
Ries, Blue, Gold Iridescent Air Traps, 1977, 1 1/4 x 4 In. 90.00
Ries, Opaque White Center Ball, Gold Around, 1977, 2 x 3 1/2 In. 100.00
Ries, Yellow, Red & White Swirls, Clear Glass, Air Trap Center, 1977, 3 In. 70.00

Roman Head, Bronze	30.00
Rosenfeld, Bouquet, Multicolored, Clear Ground, Signed, 1987, 3 1/4 In.	440.00
Snoopy, Seated, & Bird, Schultz, 1958–1966, U. F. S.	65.00
Snow Dome, Astrodome, Ballplayers On Teeter–Totter, Hong Kong	95.00
Snow Dome, Brown Bear	45.00
Snow Dome, Dancers, Musical	15.00
Snow Dome, Halloween, Musical	15.00
Snow Dome, Leaning Tower of Pisa On Chalkware, Seashells	35.00
Snow Dome, New York City	22.00
Snow Dome, St. Francis, Bisque	25.00
Snow Dome, Tree With Candles, Glass, Austria, 6 In.	32.50
Somerville Glass, Aqua Poinsettia, Yellow Stamens, Clear, 3 1/8 In.	550.00
St. Clair, Bird	25.00
St. Clair, Blown Owl, Peppermint Twist, Murano, 5 In.	350.00
St. Clair, Flowers, Orange, Maude & Bob	20.00
St. Louis, Amber Pear, Yellow Stem, Clear Ground, 2 In.	880.00
St. Louis, Clematis, Nosegay, Cane Centers, White Ground, 1971, 3 1/4 In.	303.00
St. Louis, Cornflower, Blue, Clear, Star–Cut Ground, Signed, 1979, 3 1/8 In.	358.00
St. Louis, Dahlia, Pink, Central Cog Cane	5225.00
St. Louis, Flat Bouquet, 4 Cane, Honeycomb Faceting	1320.00
St. Louis, Green & White Alternating Jasper Spokes, 3 In.	715.00
St. Louis, Millefiori, Blue & White Jasper Ground, 1 11/16 In.	275.00
St. Louis, Millefiori, Jasper, 5 Amber Canes Around Salmon Cane, 2 1/4 In.	220.00
St. Louis, Millefiori, Star Shaped Canes Ringed, 2 11/16 In.	1100.00
St. Louis, Millefiori, Woman Dancing, Silhouette, Signed	4400.00
St. Louis, Mushroom, 6 Rows of Canes, Central Star Cane, 3 1/8 In.	3850.00
St. Louis, Pelargonium, Pink Petals, Black Lines, Latticinio, 2 11/16 In.	2400.00
St. Louis, Strawberries, White Latticinio Doily, Signed, 1982, 3 In.	523.00
St. Louis, Strawberry, White & Yellow Flowers, Latticinio Ground, 2 15/16 In.	1100.00
Stankard, Forget–Me–Not, Opaque White Ground, 1973, 2 3/8 In.	605.00
Stankard, Poinsettia, Red Petals, 1973, 2 7/16 In.	1210.00
Stankard, Spider Orchid, Orange & Black, Clear Ground, 3 In.	1100.00
Stankard, Violet, White Buds, Translucent Blue Ground, 1980, 3 1/8 In.	1320.00
Sulphide, Czechoslovakia, Lion, Ruby Cushion, Faceted, 3 3/8 In.	356.00
Sulphide, Czechoslovakia, Sheep, Blue Ground, 3 1/2 In.	165.00
Sulphide, D'Albret, John & Jacqueline Kennedy, 3 In.	413.00
Sulphide, Diana & Charles	95.00
Sulphide, Kewpie, Joe St. Clair	95.00
Tarsitano, Snake, Green & Brown, Grass & Rock Ground, Signed, 4 In.	1540.00
U.S. Shield, Eagle, Twin Flags, Stippled Ground, Book Shape, Marble, 1803	200.00
Union Terminal Tower, Cleveland, Ohio	14.00
Weed Flower, Pansy, Clear, 2 13/16 In.	770.00
White Florals Interior, 3 1/2 In.	30.00
Whitefriars, Close Concentric Millefiori, Red, White & Blue, 4 In.	413.00
Whitefriars, Close Concentric Millefiori, Red, White, Green, Blue, 2 15/16 In.	330.00
Whittemore, Nosegay, Pink, Canes On Stalk, White Ground, 2 11/15 In.	440.00
Whittemore, Red Cherry, Branch, White Ground, Signed, 2 3/8 In.	330.00
Ysart, Butterfly, Multicolored, Green Ground, Garland, 2 15/16 In.	1210.00
Ysart, Clematis, White & Blue, Opaque Black Ground, Canes, 2 7/8 In.	715.00
Ysart, Dragonfly, Red & White Jasper Ground, 2 15/16 In.	440.00

PAPIER–MACHE is made from paper mixed with glue, chalk, and other ingredients, then molded and baked. It becomes very hard and can be painted. Boxes, trays, and furniture were made of papier–mache. Some of the nineteenth–century pieces were decorated with mother–of–pearl. Furniture made of papier–mache is listed in the Furniture category.

Bottle, Man In Top Hat, Monocle Cork	8.00
Box, File, Polychrome Floral, Black Paint, 6 1/4 In.	105.00
Box, Snuff, Comic Hand Colored Print On Lid, 2 7/8 In.	45.00
Candy Container, Rooster, Standing, 10 x 12 In.	825.00
Candy Container, Turkey, 5 1/2 In.	40.00
Cat, Seated, Glass Eyes, 8 In.	19.00
Cow, Black, White Paint, Folksy Detail, 45 In.	165.00

♦ ♦ ♦ ♦ ♦ ♦ ♦ ♦ ♦ ♦ ♦ ♦ ♦ ♦ ♦ ♦ ♦ ♦ ♦ ♦

If you go away on a driving trip, be sure to cover the window in your garage door, so the missing car won't be noticed. New doors usually have no window at all for security reasons.

♦ ♦

Paris, Perfume Bottle, Country

Folk, c.1840, 9 1/2 In., Pair

Dog, Polychrome, White, Black, Flocked Coat, Bellows Squeak, Dated 1899, 5 In. ...	319.00
Easter Rabbit, Nodding Spring Head, 9 3/4 In.	55.00
Grasshopper, Glass Eyes, 7 In.	260.00
Mask, Clown Head	60.50
Mummy, Female, Carnival, Nelson Supply House, 1930s, 4 1/2 Ft.	400.00
Snuff Box, Painted Design of Boy, 3 1/8 In.	145.00
Snuff Box, Shoe Shape, Black Lacquer, Delicate Pewter, Abalone Inlay, 3 In.	135.00
Tiger, From Amusement Park, 1920s	550.00
Tray, Mother-of-Pearl Inlay, Painted, Jennings & Betridge, 17 x 13 In.	525.00
Tray, Reds & Golds, Japan, 8 x 22 In.	30.00
Tray, Scalloped Rim, On Stand, 19th Century	880.00
Uncle Sam, Head, Painted, 22 In.	66.00
Urn, Birds Building Nests, Parrots, Swimming Fish, Indian, 39 In., Pair	715.00

PARASOL, see Umbrella

PARIAN is a fine-grained, hard-paste porcelain named for the marble it resembles. It was first made in England in 1846 and gained in favor in the United States about 1860. Figures, tea sets, vases, and other items were made of Parian at many English and American factories.

Bust, Bearded Gentleman, Wooden Base, 19th Century, 11 1/2 In.	88.00
Bust, Dryden, L & R Boote, 8 In.	60.00
Bust, Lord Clyde, Curly Hair, Socle Base, 11 In	170.00
Bust, Roman Statesman, Sockle Base, J. E. King, c.1850, 18 1/2 In.	500.00
Bust, Scott, 5 In.	62.00
Bust, Ulysses Grant, c.1870, 7 1/2 In.	95.00
Figurine, Classical Maiden, Grape Basket & Amphoras, Brass Stand, 16 In., Pair	358.00
Figurine, Dutch Girl Holding Baskets, 16 In.	120.00
Figurine, Maiden, Standing, Sleeveless Gown, Classical Style, 16 In.	495.00
Figurine, Man, Little Girl Sitting On Fence, 6 In.	45.00
Figurine, Mary, Standing, Detachable Forearms, 15 1/2 In.	55.00
Figurine, Matchmaking, Owls On Branch, Marked, 7 In.	245.00
Figurine, Moses, Basket In The Bulrushes, Signed, 21 x 15 In.	715.00
Figurine, Peasant Girl, Holding Basket of Flowers, England, 11 In. ...95.00 To	125.00
Figurine, Roman Senator, Standing, Scroll In Hand, 10 In.	165.00
Figurine, Whippet, On Pillow, Polychrome Enameled, 5 1/4 In.	135.00
Figurine, Young Augustus, 8 In.	240.00
Figurine, Youth & Maiden, 14 In., Pair	250.00
Pitcher, Cupid & Psyche, 9 1/4 In.	195.00
Vase, Blue Trim, 10 In.	69.00

Vase, Vintage Pattern, Flared, Bulbous Bottom, 5 In. 75.00

PARIS, Vieux Paris, or Old Paris, is porcelain ware that is known to have been made in Paris in the eighteenth or early nineteenth century. These porcelains have no identifying mark but can be recognized by the whiteness of the porcelain and the lines and decorations. Gold decoration is often used.

Bowl, Floral, Cobalt Blue, Vine Border, Hard Paste, 1830, 8 Piece 1000.00
Bowl, Trimmed With 24K Gold, R. Charlotte, 8 x 14 In. 1525.00
Clock, Mantel, Porcelain 935.00
Figurine, Turkish Pasha & Odalisque, Pair 3080.00
Inkwell, Gold, Blue & Pink, 6–Footed, 2 Wells, 10 1/2 x 4 In. 175.00
Perfume Bottle, Country Folk, c.1840, 9 1/2 In., Pair ....*Illus* 578.00
Pot De Creme Set, Serving Stand 185.00
Stand, Center Gilt Flower, Bead & Reel Rim, Gold Arrows, c.1810, 13 3/4 In. 1210.00
Teapot, Mandarin–Form, Caddy, Flowers, c.1850, 6 3/4 In. 1550.00
Vase, Continuous Figural Scene, Baluster, 19th Century, 16 In. 440.00
Vase, Dancing Chinaman, Floral, Amphora, Handles, 1830, 11 In. 198.00
Vase, Flowers, Gold Leaf Trim, c.1920, 6 1/4 In., Pair 95.00
Vase, Gilt Scrollwork Borders, Floral Bouquets, c.1850, 8 1/2 In. 370.00
Vase, Hand–Painted Flowers, Gold Leaf Trim, c.1920, 6 1/2 In. 145.00
Vase, Japanesque, 2 Handles, Prudent Mallard Label 825.00
Vase, L'Ete, Gold Banding, Reserves of Maidens In Garden, 12 1/2 In. 1100.00
Vase, Leaf Body, Jewels, Gold Trim, 7 1/4 In. 125.00
Vase, Overall Scrolling Flowers & Vines, Removable Insert, 1880s, 13 1/4 In. 8250.00
Vase, Romantic Scenes, 1870s, 24 In., Pair 1045.00

PATE–DE–VERRE is an ancient technique in which glass is made by blending and refining powdered glass of different colors into molds. The process was revived by French glassmakers, especially Galle, around the end of the nineteenth century.

Figurine, Seal, Rock Pedestal, Gray–Green Glass, Almaric, 6 1/4 In. 1870.00
Pendant, Red–Brown Beetle, On Gold Oval Medallion, Henri Berge, 2 1/4 In. 660.00

PATE–SUR–PATE means paste on paste. The design was made by painting layers of slip on the ceramic piece until a relief decoration was formed. The method was developed at the Sevres factory in France about 1850. It became even more famous at the English Minton factory about 1870. It has since been used by many potters to make both pottery and porcelain wares.

Pate-Sur-Pate, Plaque, White, Blue Ground, Doat, Frame, 5 5/8 X 8 In.

Plaque, White, Blue Ground, Doat, Frame, 5 5/8 x 8 In. ....*Illus*   450.00
Plaque, William E. Gladstone, 1898, 8 1/2 x 6 In. 440.00
Vase, Nymph, Rosenthal, 12 In. 1500.00

PAUL REVERE POTTERY was made at several locations in and around Boston, Massachusetts, between 1906 and 1942. The pottery was operated as a settlement house program for teenage girls. Many pieces were signed *S.E.G.* for Saturday Evening Girls. The artists concentrated on children's dishes and tiles. Decorations were outlined in black and filled with color.

Bowl, Blue Band, Yellow, SEG, 4 In. 45.00
Bowl, Steel Blue, Band Design, 12 In. 900.00
Candlestick, Blue Glaze, Paper Label, Pair 120.00
Creamer, Ducks 350.00
Creamer, Landscape, SEG 145.00
Dark Gray Hi–Glaze, Marked, 5 In. 95.00
Jar, Cover, Arts & Crafts Border, 1911, 4 1/2 x 5 In. 1540.00
Mug, Viking Ships Band, SEG 550.00
Mug, Viking Ships, Black Outlined Mountains, SEG, 5 In. 605.00
Plate, 3–Color Floral, SEG, 6 1/4 In. 165.00
Plate, Colored Bands, 7 1/2 In. 35.00
Plate, Ducks Around Border, SEG, 1911 ....   275.00
Plate, Steel Blue, Band Design, Large 800.00
Saucer, Steel Blue, Band Design 250.00
Tea Bowl & Plate, SEG, 6 3/8 In. 247.50
Teapot, Outlined Crocus Border, SEG, 1912, 5 In. 192.50
Vase, 2–Tone Yellow Glaze, SEG, 6 In. 85.00
Vase, Band of White Lotus Blossoms, SEG, 1914, 4 1/2 In. 770.00
Vase, Border of Tree Clusters, Black Outlined, SEG, 9 3/4 In. 825.00
Vase, Brown Greek Key, Black Outline, 2–Tone Yellow, SEG, 8 In. 275.00
Vase, Cobalt Blue, 4 1/2 In. 100.00
Vase, Dark Blue Dipping Over Gray, 4 In. 200.00
Vase, Pink Flowers Band, Cream Ground, EG, 3 3/4 x 4 3/4 In. 275.00
Vase, SEG, 11 In. 1320.00

PEACHBLOW glass originated about 1883 at Hobbs, Brockunier and Company of Wheeling, West Virginia. It shades from yellow to peach and is lined with white glass. New England peachblow is a one–layer glass shading from red to white. Mt. Washington peachblow shades from pink to blue. Reproductions of all types of peachblow have been made. Some are poor and easy to identify as copies, others are very accurate reproductions and could fool the unwary. Related pieces may be listed under Gunderson and Webb Peachblow.

Creamer, Ribbed Satin Finish, World's Fair 1893, 2 1/2 In. 475.00
Creamer, Wheeling, Drape, Square Mouth, Clear Handle, 4 1/2 In. 795.00
Mustard, Gold Prunts, 2 1/2 In. 395.00
Pitcher, Glossy Finish, Applied White Handle, 3 In. 385.00
Rose Bowl, Pale To Deep Pink, Pinched, 4 1/2 In. Diam. 45.00
Salt & Pepper, Wheeling, Squatty Bulbous Shape, 2 3/4 In. 1085.00
Sugar Shaker, Enameled Forget–Me–Nots, Egg Shape 225.00
Toothpick, New England, Square Top 350.00
Toothpick, Square Mouth 245.00
Tumbler, Wheeling, Satin Finish 485.00
Urn, Applied Fruit & Flowers, 17 In., Pair 2900.00
Vase, Amber Shading, Dark Fuchsia Top, White Within, 10 1/2 In. 1085.00
Vase, Crimped Extended Rim, Oval Body, Mt. Washington, 4 1/4 In. 3300.00
Vase, Lily, Trumpet Form, Raspberry Pink, Applied Disk Foot, 18 In. 1980.00
Vase, New England, Flared Piecrust Crimped Mouth, 4 3/4 In. 635.00
Vase, New England, White Pedestal & Ruffled Top, 17 In. 750.00
Vase, Stevens & Williams, 13 1/4 In. 725.00
Vase, Wheeling, Lily, Forget–Me–Nots, Randomly Placed, 8 In. 975.00

PEARL items listed here are made of the natural mother-of-pearl from shells. Such natural pearl has been used to decorate furniture and small utilitarian objects for centuries. The glassware known as mother-of-pearl is listed by that name. Opera glasses made with natural pearl shell are listed under Opera Glasses.

Game Token, Fish Shape	10.00
Knife, Silver Blade, Set of 12	125.00
Manicure Set, Metal, Box	14.00
Rattle & Teether, Sterling Silver	95.00
Rosary	25.00

PEARLWARE is an earthenware made by Josiah Wedgwood in 1779. It was copied by other potters in England. Pearlware is only slightly different in color from creamware and for many years collectors have confused the terms.

Pearl

Chamber Pot, Black Transfer, Comic Verse, Polychrome Floral, 10 In.	440.00
Coffeepot, Floral Design, England, 19th Century, 10 In.	770.00
Creamer, Blue & White Designs, Molded, 3 1/4 In.	385.00
Creamer, Blue Feather Band, 2 5/8 In.	35.00
Creamer, Floral Decoration, Blue Band, Brown Ground, 4 3/8 In.	115.00
Creamer, Pineapple Decoration, Blue Rim, 3 7/8 In.	330.00
Cup & Saucer, Black Transfer of Cottage, Pink Luster Trim	60.00
Cup & Saucer, Handleless, Floral Design, Blue, White	105.00
Cup & Saucer, Handleless, Mother & Children, Medium Blue Transfer	82.50
Figure, Blue Glaze Chinoiserie, Landscape, Leaf Border, Leeds, 8 In., 5 Piece	175.00
Figurine, Dog, Green, Brown & Blue Enameled, Staffordshire, 3 In.	240.00
Figurine, Rooster, Enameled, Staffordshire	225.00
Jug, Old Women Ground, Change To Young, Transfer, Handle, Liverpool	935.00
Mug, Floral Decoration, 4 Colors	160.00
Mug, Hound Handle, Hunt Scene, Green, Mahogany Red Enameling, 4 In.	215.00
Pitcher, Blue & White Floral Decoration, Lid, 3 1/2 In.	70.00
Pitcher, Blue Floral Transfer, Polychrome Enameling, 6 In.	94.00
Pitcher, Blue, White Gaudy Floral Design, Leaf Handle, 8 1/2 In.	715.00
Pitcher, Floral Design, 5 Colors, Sheaf, Farm Implements, Landscape, 9 In.	2175.00
Pitcher, Floral Design, Blue, Orange, Leaf Handle, 6 1/8 In.	330.00
Pitcher, Keg Shape, Gaudy Blue Floral, Leaf Handle, 5 7/8 In.	82.50
Pitcher, Milk, England, 1820, 6 In., Pair	275.00
Pitcher, Napoleonic Battle Scene, Black Transfer, Pedestal, 9 1/4 In.	193.00
Plate, Blue & White Oriental Decoration, Embossed Rim, 4 3/4 In.	165.00
Plate, Floral Design, 4 Colors, Brown Rim Stripe, 8 1/4 In.	115.00
Platter, Green Feather Edge, 16 3/8 In.	220.00
Saucer, Floral Decoration, 5 Colors, 5 3/8 In.	95.00
Saucer, Gaudy Floral Design, Blue, Green, Brown, Orange, 4 1/4 In.	82.00
Sugar, Gaudy Floral Design, Blue, Green, Yellow, 4 1/2 In.	330.00
Sugar, Gaudy Floral Design, Blue, White, 5 1/4 In.	165.00
Sugar, Tulip, Yellow, Green, Brown, Orange, 4 3/4 In.	412.00
Tea Caddy, Divided Interior, Floral Design, Green, Brown, Yellow, 5 1/4 In.	1017.00
Tea Set, Child's, Maroon Bands, Blue Flowers, Maroon Buds, 8 Piece	250.00
Teapot, Gaudy Floral Design, Blue, Yellow, Orangish Tan, 7 5/8 In.	385.00
Teapot, Japan, Early 1800s	80.00 To 125.00
Teapot, Rose Decoration, Enamel, 5 7/8 In.	250.00

PEKING GLASS is a Chinese cameo glass first made popular in the eighteenth century. The Chinese have continued to make this layered glass in the old manner, and many new pieces are now available that could confuse the average buyer.

Bowl, 3 Bats, Floral, Longevity Symbols, Cobalt On White, 5 In.	500.00
Bowl, Carved Figural Scene, Red, 6 In., Pair	770.00
Bowl, Carved Floral Design, Qianlong Mark, 18th Century, 6 In.	1760.00
Bowl, Hydras, Purple On White, 6 In.	160.00
Ginger Jar, 19th Century, 9 In.	470.00
Jar, Cover, Red & Yellow, 5 1/2 In., Pair	3520.00

Snuff Bottle, Floral Design, Carved 1980.00
Snuff Bottle, Traveling Lord & Lady, 2 3/4 In. 880.00
Vase, Butterflies & Flowers, Opaque Yellow, 8 1/4 In. 375.00
Vase, Flaring Rim, Yellow, Late 19th Century, 3 In. 305.00
Vase, Lotus & Butterflies, Yellow, 9 In. 325.00
Vase, Red & White, 7 1/2 In. 500.00
Vase, Stick, 2 Squirrels, Leaves & Limbs, Opaque Yellow 350.00

PELOTON glass is a European glass with small threads of colored glass rolled onto the surface of clear or colored glass. It is sometimes called spaghetti, or shredded coconut, glass. Most pieces found today were made in the nineteenth century.

Rose Bowl, Coconut Strings, Shell Feet, Crystal Edging, Opaque White, 4 In. 300.00
Rose Bowl, Opaque White Ground, Coconut Applied Strings, Footed, 3 7/8 In. 295.00
Vase, Stick, White Cased, Blue Coconut Threading, 6 3/4 In. 145.00

PENS replaced hand-cut quills as writing instruments in 1780 when the first steel pen point was made in England. But it was 100 years before the commercial pen was a common item. The fountain pen was invented in the 1830s but was not made in quantity until the 1880s. All types of old pens are collected.

PEN & PENCIL, Parker 51 .... 25.00
Parker 51, Case 65.00
Parker 51, Olive Green, Gold, Box 125.00
Parker, Gold Bands, Original Display Case, 1940s 45.00
Parker, Green & Black Mottling, Wide Barrel, 3 Gold Rings, 5 1/4 In. 275.00
Parker, Horizontal Swirl, Box 45.00
Parker, Lucky Curve, Woman's, Blue, Box, 4 1/2 In. 600.00
Peter Pan 42.50
Sheaffer, Snorkel, 14K Gold 22.00
Sheaffer, Triumph Crest 80.00
Sheaffer, White Dot, Black, Arrow, 14K Point, Calendar 75.00
Wahl, 1920s 50.00
Wahl, Black 85.00
PEN, Ailzum, Giveaway 10.00
Arnold, Celluloid 12.00
Burlington Northern 6.00
Cavalier, Lever, 14K Gold Plate, Blotchy Black & White Marble 55.00
Chilton, Wing-Flow, Gold Inlay Pattern, Black 475.00
Conklin, Black, Gold Trim, Gold Crescent Filler, 4 1/4 In. 310.00
Conklin, Senior Endura, Blue 475.00
Conklin, Woman's, Interlace With Silver 350.00
Cross, Century, CBS Eye Logo Top of Clip 14.00
Diamond, Fountain, Diamond Point Fill-EEz, Red, 5 1/4 In. 50.00
Epenco, Brown, Gold Stars, Moons, Lever 25.00
Esterbrook, Fountain 6.00
Esterbrook, Marbelized Green 29.00
Eversharp, Pearl, Black, Gold Seal, 4 3/4 In. 55.00
Eversharp, Skyline, Lever 40.00
Faber, Permapoint, Iridium Nib, Lever 18.00
Gold Bond, Tortoiseshell, Gold, 1936 .... 325.00
Green Stripes, Celluloid 15.00
Grieshaber, Umpire, Gold Band, 5 1/4 In. 95.00
Holder, Syroco, 3-Masted Sailing Ship 25.00
Jinx Ink, Fountain 24.00
Lady Parker, Duo-Fold 85.00
Lifetime, White Dot, Fountain, 1934, Oversized 145.00
Moore, Black Hard Rubber, 14K Gold Nib 55.00
Moore, Fountain, Woman's, Black Chased 75.00
Morrison, Union Pen, Gold Over Silver 55.00
Parker 21 .... 17.00
Parker 61, 12K Gold Filled 195.00
Parker, Duofold Jr., Green Marbelized 110.00

Parker, Duofold Jr., Red 68.00
Parker, Duofold, Black, Blue & Gray Stripe 65.00
Parker, Duofold, Black, Early 1900s 45.00
Parker, Duofold, Fountain, Woman's, Red 60.00
Parker, Duofold, Lucky Curve, Fountain, Scrambled Green To White, 4 1/2 In. 75.00
Parker, Duofold, Lucky Curve, Woman's 75.00
Parker, Lucky Curve, Woman's, Red 175.00
Parker, Lucky Curve, Yellow 150.00
Parker, Senior, Red 200.00
Parker, Woman's, Lucky Curve, Red, 4 1/4 In. 75.00
Parkette, Burgundy, 1936 .... 22.00
Peter Pan Dux, Box 76.00
Quill, Retracting Tip, Patent Perry, London, Ivory 58.00
Remington, 14K Durium Tip, See Through, Gray, Burgundy Barrel 25.00
Sheaffer, Bullet Nose 25.00
Sheaffer, Craftsman, Blue 30.00
Sheaffer, Dot 25.00
Sheaffer, Dot, Desk, 14K Gold Point 35.00
Sheaffer, Feather Touch, Vertical Gold Striping 35.00
Sheaffer, Fineline, Green 15.00
Sheaffer, Lifetime, No. 1000, Gold Tip 20.00
Sheaffer, Lifetime, White Dot, Fountain, Box 65.00
Sheaffer, Man's, Mottled 50.00
Sheaffer, No. 46, Green Jade 100.00
Sheaffer, Snorkel 25.00
Sheaffer, White Dot, Burgundy, Wide Gold Band 30.00
Sheaffer, Woman's, Green Mottled 50.00
Swallow Visofil, 4 In. 10.00
Tiffany, Peretti, String Pouch, Marked 65.00
Tiffany, Sterling Silver, String Pouch, Marked, Signed 65.00
Wahl, No. 2, Black Design, Fountain, 5 1/4 In. 75.00
Wahl, No. 2, Gold Filled, 1925 .... 105.00
Wahl, No. 2, Woman's, Black Design, 4 In. 50.00
Wahl–Eversharp, Gold Seal, Green, Bronze, Fountain, Oversized, 1930 .... 175.00
Waterman, 100 Years 125.00
Waterman, Ideal, Black, 5 1/2 In. 25.00
Waterman, Ideal, Fountain, Woman's 95.00
Waterman, No. 544, Gold Filigree 1800.00
Waterman, Patrician, Rountain, Onyx 600.00
Waterman, Sterling Silver Overlay 825.00
Webster, Lady K, Black 50.00

PENCILS were invented, so it is said, in 1565. The eraser was not added to the pencil until 1858. The automatic pencil was invented in 1863. Collectors today want advertising pencils or automatic pencils of unusual design. Boxes and sharpeners for pencils are also collected.

PENCIL SHARPENER, Airplane, Bakelite 30.00
  Alarm Clock, Metal, Germany 25.00
  Annie Oakley 10.00
  Army Tank, Bakelite 25.00
  Baker's Chocolate Lady, Metal 25.00
  Baseball, Boy Holding Bat At Side, Ceramic, 4 In. 60.00
  Bullet, Tom Mix 27.50
  Charlie McCarthy, Yellow Plastic 30.00
  Chick, Bakelite 16.00
  Globe, Figural, Sterling, Small, 1950 .... 35.00
  Globe, Germany, 1 1/2 In. 25.00
  Ideal, Double Blades, Pocket 22.00
  Joe Carioca, Bakelite 55.00
  Lantern, Cast Iron 12.00
  Little Shaver, Decal 265.00
  Mickey Mouse 75.00
  Quick Draw McGraw 12.00

Red Devil, Commonwealth Plastics, 1960s 75.00
Rocking Chair, Cast Iron 12.00
Spanky, Bakelite 55.00
Stay Puft, Ghost Buster 20.00
Stove, Cast Iron 12.00
View Camera Shape, Metal, 2 x 1/2 In. 3.00
Wizard, Cast Iron 35.00
PENCIL, Box, A. W. Faber, Sesquicentennial, 1911, Germany 25.00
Box, Billy Club Shape, Wooden, 1930s, 10 1/2 In. 40.00
Box, Felix The Cat, 1930s 50.00
Box, Felix The Cat, 1937 .... 95.00
Box, Tin, Red Goose, Jack's Shoe Store 60.00
Box, Wooden, Slides Open, Swings Around, 1930s 35.00
Bullet, Minneapolis Advertising 15.00
Butternut Bread, Pair 3.00
Case, Scotty 24.00
Case, Zorro, Contents, Disney 85.00
Doric, Gold Seal 45.00
Enamel, Retractable, Sterling Silver, France 75.00
Epenco, Mechanical, Brass Filigree Band, Marbelized Green & Black 15.00
Eversharp, Grecian Design 20.00
Eversharp, Skyline, 14K Gold 175.00
Holder, Andy & Min, Figural, Ceramic, 1930s, F. A. S. Japan, 5 In. 95.00
Hoover For President, 1928 .... 20.00
IAM & AW Union, Aerospace, Button Clip 8.00
Mechanical, Carnelian Seal End, Rolled Gold 65.00
Mechanical, Chevrolet Dealers, Christmas Premium 25.00
Mechanical, Epenco 12.00
Mechanical, Filene, 14K Gold Filled 12.00
Mechanical, Gulf Pride, Oil Floats Inside 25.00
Mechanical, Hol–Guernsey Dairy 18.00
Mechanical, Holsum Bread, Box 16.00
Mechanical, Ink O Graph 125.00
Mechanical, Louisville Slugger, Miniature Bat 45.00
Mechanical, Marbelized Bakelite, Harrison Dispatch 112.00
Mechanical, Mr. Peanut, Figure In Floating Liquid 40.00
Mechanical, Popeye, Box 100.00
Mechanical, Santa Fe R.R. 20.00
Mechanical, Scotty Dog Holder 75.00
Mechanical, Wahl–Eversharp, Box, 1920s 85.00
Mechanical, Wayne Gas Pump 40.00
Parker, Green To White, Gold Top & Bottom, 5 In. 75.00
Slat, 1876 Centennial, American Flag, 5 1/2 In. 5.00
University Club, Kansas City, Mo. 3.00

PENNSBURY Pottery worked in Morrisville, Pennsylvania, from 1950 to 1971. Full sets of dinnerware as well as many decorative items were made. Pieces are marked with the name of the factory.

Pennsbury Pottery

Ashtray, Doylestown Trust .... 15.00 To 25.00
Ashtray, Outen The Light .... 15.00 To 25.00
Ashtray, Such Schmootzers 15.00
Ashtray, What Giffs .... 15.00 To 25.00
Bowl, 11 1/2 In. 15.00
Bowl, Pretzel, Eagle, 8 x 11 In. 85.00
Bowl, Pretzel, Quartet, 8 x 11 In. 100.00
Bowl, Pretzel, Sweet Adeline 45.00
Bowl, Vegetable, Red Rooster, Divided 49.00
Cake Stand, Black Rooster 65.00
Canister, Tea, Red Rooster 100.00
Casserole, Cover, Black Rooster 20.00
Coaster, Schultz 25.00
Cookie Jar, Amish Family 90.00
Cookie Jar, Amish Man 65.00

Creamer, Amish Lady Head, 2 In.	22.00
Creamer, Amish Man At Fence, 2 In.	18.00
Creamer, Rooster	22.00
Cruet, Figural, Pair	90.00
Cup & Saucer, Black Rooster	20.00
Cup & Saucer, Red Rooster	25.00
Figurine, Rooster, Green, White, 12 In.	225.00
Lamp, Wall, Rooster	150.00
Mug, Adeline	25.00
Mug, Beer, Amish People	18.00 To 30.00
Mug, Sweet Adeline	21.00 To 35.00
Pie Plate	125.00
Pitcher, Eagle, 6 1/4 In.	48.00
Pitcher, Red Rooster, 4 In.	45.00
Plaque, Amish Farm Scene, Round, 6 In.	35.00
Plaque, What Giffs, 4 In.	32.00
Plate, Annual, Christmas, Angel, 1972, 8 In.	20.00
Plate, Black Rooster, 10 In.	13.00 To 22.00
Plate, Dinner, Hexagonal, 10 In.	33.00
Plate, Divided, Red Rooster	35.00
Plate, Harvest, 11 In.	95.00
Plate, Hexagonal, 10 In.	20.00
Plate, Hexagonal, 8 In.	30.00
Plate, Mother's Day, 1972	15.00
Plate, Red Rooster, 10 In.	30.00
Plate, United States Steel, Red	35.00
Plate, Yuletide, 1970	15.00
Salt & Pepper, Amish Heads	55.00 To 90.00
Tureen, Ladle, Stand, Black Rooster	150.00
Wall Pocket, Bellows	70.00

PEPSI–COLA, the drink and the name, was invented in 1898 but was not trademarked until 1903. The logo was changed from an elaborate script to the modern block letters on the 1970 Pepsi label. All types of advertising memorabilia are collected, and reproductions are being made.

Bag Rack	85.00
Bank, Vending Machine, Marx, 1940s	120.00
Blotter, Pepsi & Pete, 1930s	75.00
Bottle Carrier, Buy Pepsi–Cola, Wooden, 1930	115.00
Bottle Protector, 1932	3.00
Bottle Tapper, Musical	235.00
Bottle, Desert Storm, Long Neck, Contents, 12 Oz.	15.00
Bottle, Paper Label, 1950s, 1 Qt.	145.00
Bottle, Purple Glass, c.1905	175.00
Bottle, Script Embossed, Savanna, Georgia, Aqua	40.00
Bottle, Syrup, Contents, 12 Oz.	45.00
Cake Carrier, Tin	95.00
Cake Cover, 1960s	55.00
Calendar, 1911, Woman, Pepsi–Cola Glass, 8 1/2 In. ....*Illus*	1760.00
Calendar, 1945	65.00
Carrier, Heavy Paper Bag, 1940s	30.00
Carton, Red, White & Blue, Unopened, 1950s	15.00
Case, Wooden, Marked Salina, Kansas	5.00
Chair, Folding, 1954	200.00
Chalkboard	95.00
Clock, Gilbert, Regulator, Logo, 1910	750.00
Clock, Glass Front, Numbers On Back, Light–Up, Square, 16 In.	80.00
Clock, Neon, 3–Color, 26 In.	850.00
Clock, New Haven, Pendulum, Advertising	750.00
Clock, Round, Light–Up	325.00
Clock, Square, Bottle Cap, 1940s	850.00
Cooler, Blue & White, 1940s	85.00
Cooler, Polished Aluminum	70.00

Pepsi-Cola, Calendar, 1911,
Woman, Pepsi-Cola Glass,
8 1/2 In.

Pepsi-Cola, Dispenser, Napkin, Red,
White & Blue, Logo, 1940s

Pepsi-Cola, Dispenser,
Syrup, Cures
Indigestion, 7 1/2 In.

Pepsi-Cola, Poster,
The American Beverage,
Framed, 15 1/2 X 24 In.

Pepsi-Cola, Sign, Girl On
Beach, Easel Back,
28 1/2 X 40 In.

Dispenser, Napkin, Red, White & Blue, Logo, 1940s	*Illus*	605.00
Dispenser, Syrup, Cures Indigestion, 7 1/2 In.	*Illus*	7150.00
Door Push, 1940		1250.00
Door Push, 1960s		55.00
Door Push, Iron, 1960s		95.00
Door Push, Wire Ends		100.00
Drum, Syrup, 1930s, 5 Gal.		125.00
Fan, Cardboard, Pepsi and Pete, 1940		105.00
Glass, Color Cap, 1962		35.00
Hat, Knit, Dark Blue, Red & White Trim, White Pepsi Logo		10.00
Jacket, Logo Patch On Chest & Back, Quilted Liner, Zipper Front, Large		25.00
Jug, Syrup, Red & White, 1940s, 5 Gal.		50.00
Key Chain, Magnifying Glass		3.45
Lunch Box, Pepsi-Puffy, Vinyl		50.00

Machine, Coin–Operated, 1958 .... 395.00
Menu Board, Pepsi-Cola Goes Great With A Sandwich, 1930s, 12 x 24 In. 525.00
Mirror, Lillian Russell Type Figure, Pocket, 2 3/4 In. 3355.00
Pen, Fountain, 1930s ....60.00 To 125.00
Pen, Jumbo, Ball Point 2.50
Pencil, Mechanical, Bottle Top 32.00
Pennant, White Script Logo, Dark Blue Felt, 27 1/2 In. 4.50
Plate, 85th Anniversary, Picturing 1909 Gibson Girl, Lenox, No. 588 .... 100.00
Poster, Diet Pepsi #1 In Oregon, Cardboard, 18 x 31 In. 15.00
Poster, The American Beverage, Framed, 15 1/2 x 24 In. ....*Illus* 9350.00
Rack, Drink, Die Cut Bottle, 2 Sides, Iron, 1930s, 27 x 47 In. 1870.00
Radio, Bottle Shape, Decal, 1940s, 12 Oz. 360.00
Radio, Transistor, Vending Machine, Leather Carrying Case 255.00
Receipt, Bottling Co., Flat River, Mo., Dated 1947 .... 9.00
Salt & Pepper Mill, 75th Anniversary, Box 55.00
Salt & Pepper, Miniature, Souvenir of Cleveland, Ohio, 1940s 210.00
Shirt, Uniform 35.00
Sign, Celluloid, 1951, 9 In. 150.00
Sign, Crossing Guard 1950.00
Sign, Embossed Bottle, Die Cut, 1940s, 45 In. 440.00
Sign, French Porcelain, 12 x 29 In. 125.00
Sign, Girl On Beach, Easel Back, 28 1/2 x 40 In. ....*Illus* 3630.00
Sign, Ice Cold Sold Here, Celluloid, 1940s, 9 In. 285.00
Sign, Lightup, Changes Colors, 1970s 375.00
Sign, Mirror, Have A Pepsi, The Light Refreshment 45.00
Sign, More Bounce To The Ounce, Tin, 17 x 48 In. 242.00
Sign, Pepsi & Pete, Girl, Under Sun Umbrella, Cardboard, 28 1/2 x 40 In. 3630.00
Sign, Pepsi Bottle, Porcelain, Enameled, 5 7/8 x 21 In. 17.00
Sign, Pepsi Cap, Porcelain, Enameled, 8 In. Diam. 13.00
Sign, Pepsi Logo, Cardboard, Metal Frame, 1950s, 24 x 36 In. 130.00
Sign, Rack, 1936 .... 100.00
Sign, Red, Green & White Logo, Tin, 10 x 4 In. 250.00
Sign, Reverse On Glass, Lightup, 1950s 350.00
Sign, Round, 1950, 9 In. 15.00
Sign, School Crossing, Boy Holding Slow Sign, Tin 350.00
Snack Holder 50.00
Straw Holder, Metal, 1940s 190.00
Straw Holder, Tin, Lithograph, Gibson Girl, 3 x 3 x 6 In. 8250.00
Sweatshirt, Eagle Head & Logo, White, Medium 23.00
Thermometer, 18 In. 75.00
Thermometer, Embossed Bottle Cap On Bottom, Yellow, Tin 50.00
Thermometer, Embossed Bottle Cap, 1950s 165.00
Thermometer, Girl Drinking From Straw, Paper Face Decal, 1930s 325.00
Thermometer, More Bounce To Ounce 100.00
Tip Tray, Blue & White Logo, Round, 6 In. 2970.00
Tip Tray, Gibson Girl, Soda Fountain, 1909 .... 880.00
Tip Tray, Logo, Black Ground, Oval, 1906, 9 1/4 In. 1265.00
Toy, Truck, The Light Refreshment, Tin, Friction, Lithograph, 6 1/2 In. 550.00
Tray, Coney Island 60.00
Tray, Enjoy Pepsi-Cola Hits The Spot, 1940 .... 100.00
Tumbler, 12 Days of Christmas, 12 Piece 65.00
Tumbler, 1776–1976, 200 Years Feeling Free 5.00
Tumbler, Big Baby Huey, Action, 5 In. 5.00
Tumbler, Flash, 1971 .... 12.00
Tumbler, Hot Stuff, 16 Oz. 10.00
Tumbler, Lady & The Tramp 10.00
Tumbler, Pepsi Syrup Line 10.00
Tumbler, Pizza Hut, Friend Bear 8.00
Tumbler, Pizza Hut, Good Luck Bear 10.00
Tumbler, Popeye, 10th Anniversary, 1982 .... 10.00
Tumbler, Rescuer's, Bianca, 1977, 6 1/4 In. 5.00
Tumbler, Rescuer's, Orville, 1977, 6 1/4 In. 5.00
Tumbler, Rockey, Brown, 16 Oz. 11.00

Tumbler, Simon Bar Sinister, 16 Oz.	8.00
Tumbler, Snidely Whiplash, Green, 16 Oz.	13.00
Tumbler, Superman, 1976	10.00
Tumbler, Taste The Right One, Cello Wrapped, Plastic, 6 Piece	2.50
Tumbler, Underdog, Blue Letters, 16 Oz.	20.00
Tumbler, Woody Woodpecker	8.00
Vending Machine, Pullout, Square Top Bottle	125.00
Visor, Paper, Unused, 1950s	22.00
Whiskey, Blue Script Logo, Happy New Year, 1989	6.75
Whiskey, Red Script & Bottle Cap Logo, Happy New Year, 1988	7.00
Whistle, Shaped As 2 Bottles, Plastic, 1950s	75.00

PERFUME BOTTLES are made of cut glass, pressed glass, art glass, silver, metal, enamel, and even plastic or porcelain. Although the small bottle to hold perfume was first made before the time of ancient Egypt, it is the nineteenth– and twentieth–century examples that interest today's collector. Examples with the atomizer top marked *DeVilbiss* are listed under that name. Glass or porcelain examples will be found under the appropriate name such as Lalique, Czechoslovakia, etc.

Amethyst, Blown Mold, 19th Century, 7 1/2 In.	413.00
Art Deco, Blown, Ground Stopper, Flowers	85.00
Art Deco, Gilt Brass, Jewels, Empire Art Gold Co., 7 1/2 In.	465.00
Aurene, Tapered, Steuben	625.00
Bendor Pour Franck, Cameo, Atomizer, 8 In.	300.00
Black Amethyst	125.00
Blown, Flowers, Art Deco, Ground Stopper	85.00
Blue Waltz, Drop Stopper, 3 In.	20.00
Bristol Glass, Allover Gold Dot & Asterisk Design, 4 1/2 In.	95.00
Bristol Glass, Turquoise Blue, White Flowers, Matching Stopper, 8 1/4 In.	118.00
Bristol Glass, White Frosted, Blue Flowers, Gold Trim, Tulip Stopper, 11 In.	110.00
Butterfly, Iridescent Glass, Gold Head Stopper & Antennae, 3 In.	22.00
Candle, Spice By Churchill, N.Y., Red Flame Stopper, Metal Holder, 4 In.	20.00
Caron, Bellodgia	38.00
Carved Ivory, Hammered Brass, Inset Stones, 5 In.	220.00
Ciro, Danger, Spray, Box	20.00
Cologne, Hob Diamond, Pressed Glass, Lapidary Cut Stopper, James B. Lyon	55.00
Coty, Emerald, 2 1/2 In.	26.00
Coty, L'Aimant, 2 1/2 In.	14.00
Coty, Silver Case	15.00
Cut Flying Goose Over Reeds, Faceted Stopper, Cranberry, 6 1/4 In.	140.00
Cut Glass, Purse, Allover Star Cut, Sterling Hinged Lid, 2 1/4 In.	150.00
Donald Duck	35.00
English Hobnail, Cologne, Crystal, Stopper	20.00
Etched Stopper, Amber, 8 In.	89.00
Evening In Paris, Box, 3 Piece	58.00
Evening In Paris, Cobalt Blue, Label	15.00
Evening In Paris, Cobalt Blue, Tassel, Vial	15.00
Faberge, Tigress Cologne, Tiger–Striped Stopper, Box, 4 In.	15.00
Fern & Bamboo Leaves, Green, Gold & Maroon, Ivory Ground, 3 3/4 In.	355.00
Fired On Pink, Clear, Enameled Beaded Design, Hollow Stopper, 11 In.	20.00
Flask, Lay Down	120.00
Flask, Repousse, Sterling Silver, Gorham	425.00
French Cameo, Glass, Mauve Flowers In Basket, Signed, 1920s	385.00
Geisha Joy, Larberry of Paris, Lucite Stopper of Bogota, 5 Oz.	45.00
Gilded Latticework & Floral Tracery, Porcelain, France, c.1880, 4 3/4 In.	145.00
Gilt Design, Treasure Trunk Case, 3 Piece	385.00
Gold Aurene, Steuben, 8 In.	605.00
Gold Iridescent, Tear Drop Stopper, Aurene, Steuben, 7 1/4 In.	385.00
Grandfather Clock, Stuart Co., St. Paul, Minn., 5 In.	25.00
Green, Victorian, Enameled Floral, Atomizer	60.00
Guerlain, Chamade, Ribbed, Teardrop Stopper, Gold Letters, 3 In.	15.00
Helena Rubenstein, Slumber Song, Box	660.00
Kitten, Clear, 4 1/2 In.	18.00

Kneeling Nude, Frosted, Isadora, 3 In.	250.00
Knight, Occupied Japan	125.00
L. Kossuth, Fancy Portrait, Blue–Aqua	880.00
Laura Ashley, Eau De Parfum, Enameled Flower	35.00
Lay Down, Wheel Shape, Cobalt Blue & Orange, Ricksecker, 2 x 2 1/4 In.	75.00
Matchabelli, Frosted Crown	65.00
Max Factor, Le Jardin, Flower Top, 1 Oz.	10.00
May Flower, Matchabelli	22.00
Melon Ribbed, Pink, Long Stopper, Steuben, 5 In.	525.00
Nippon, Bow Stopper, Box, 1/4 Oz.	25.00
Nuit De Noel, Black Amethyst, Flask, Box	37.50
Orange, Gold Foliage, Blue Daisies, Ribbed, Clear Bubble Stopper, 9 In.	100.00
Orchid Paperweight Stopper, Crystal, 6 In.	102.00
Pink Glass, Spray Type, Cambridge, 6 In.	36.00
Pompadour, Needlepoint Fish, Austria	65.00
Portrait, L. Kossuth, Bluish Aqua	880.00
Puppy, 3 1/2 In.	20.00
Purse, Arpege, Gold Cased, Woman Trademark, Gold Purse, Chain, 2 1/2 In.	24.00
Purse, Brass, Glass Bottle & Funnel	15.00
Purse, Evening In Paris, Cobalt Blue, Tube, Tassel, Label, 3 In.	24.00
Red Crystal, Sterling Overlay, Engraved, Stopper, Bulbous Base	435.00
Sandwich Type, Olive Green, Paneled, Ricketts Bristol, 1880	660.00
Schiaparelli, Shocking	165.00
Teddy Bear, Schuco	1100.00
Threaded, Amethyst, Steuben, 4 In.	247.50
Vial, Aurene Iridescent, Bell Form, Knopped Stopper, Steuben, 5 1/8 In.	2640.00
Vial, Aurene Iridescent, Gourd Form, Waist, Steuben, 1905–1920, 3 1/2 In.	2310.00
Virginia Reel Old South Colognes, 3 Decanters, 1941, 3 Piece	49.00
White Shoulders Cologne & Splash, Pink Silk–Lined Box, 1950s, Unused	48.00

PETERS & REED Pottery Company of Zanesville, Ohio, was founded by John D. Peters and Adam Reed in 1897. Chromal, Landsun, Montene, Pereco, and Persian are some of the art lines that were made. The company, which became Zane Pottery in 1920 and Gonder Pottery in 1941, closed in 1957. Peters & Reed pottery was unmarked.

Bowl, Mistletoe, Copper Dust Glaze, 9 In.	55.00
Bowl, Mistletoe, Dark Blue, 4 x 8 In.	85.00
Doorstop, Cat, Black, 11 In.	280.00
Doorstop, Cat, Yellow	375.00
Jug, Applied Flowers, Cavalier Bust, Brown Glaze, 6 In.	85.00
Jug, Standard Glaze, 6 In.	89.00
Jug, Wine, Brownware, Embossed Grapes, 6 In.	70.00
Tankard, Grapes, 16 In.	275.00
Vase, Chromal, Lake, Mountains & Trees, 10 In.	230.00
Vase, Chromal, Scene, 9 x 6 1/2 In.	165.00
Vase, Chromal, Scenic, 14 In.	185.00
Vase, Chromal, Scenic, Trees, Bridge, 9 1/2 In.	395.00
Vase, Flowers, High Gloss Glaze, 4 In.	25.00
Vase, Moss Agate, Grapes, 12 In.	55.00
Vase, Moss Aztec, Leaves, Berries, 7 1/2 In.	45.00
Vase, Mt. Fuji, Abstract Trees Around Base, Drill Hole, 13 In.	355.00
Vase, Olive Jar Style, Matte Green Glaze, 22 3/4 In.	495.00

PETRUS REGOUT, see Maastricht

PEWABIC POTTERY was founded by Mary Chase Perry Stratton in 1903 in Detroit, Michigan. The company made many types of art pottery including pieces with matte green glaze and an iridescent crystalline glaze. The company continued working until the death of Mary Stratton in 1961. It was reactivated by Michigan State University in 1968.

Bowl, Blue, Iridescent Interior, 6 In.	50.00
Bowl, Hammered Iridescent Mauve, Orange & Gold Glaze, 2 1/2 x 4 1/4 In.	195.00
Lamp, Table, Silver Iridescent, Blue Cratered Glaze, Vellum Shade	825.00

Pewter, Centerpiece, Cut Glass Liner,

c.1900, Germany, 7 In.

◆◆◆◆◆◆◆◆◆◆◆◆◆◆◆◆◆◆◆◆◆◆◆

Don't clean badly tarnished
pewter with lye unless you are
aware of the physical dangers
involved. The pewter won't be
hurt, but you might be.

◆◆◆◆◆◆◆◆◆◆◆◆◆◆◆◆◆◆◆◆◆◆◆

Vase, Blue Semigloss Glaze, Pink Highlights, Marked, 7 In. 660.00
Vase, Bud, Turquoise, Iridescent, Silver Glaze, Round Mark, 5 In. 300.00
Vase, Incised Geometric Design, Yellow & Brown Glaze, Marked, 4 In. 470.00
Vase, Iridescent Blue & Turquoise Glaze, Bulbous, 3 x 4 In. 220.00
Vase, Iridescent Blue, Swollen Form, Circular Mark, 6 3/4 x 3 1/4 In. 330.00
Vase, Iridescent, Blue Drippings, Marked, 2 1/2 In. 250.00
Vase, Mottled Beige To Red Iridescent Glaze, Corseted Top, 5 1/2 x 6 1/4 In. 770.00
Vase, Mottled Iridescent Blue Glaze, Marked, 10 3/4 In. 770.00
Vase, Rolled Arm, Cylindrical Neck, Metallic, Iridescent Glaze, 15 In. 1050.00
Vase, Shouldered Vasiform, Black Gloss Glaze, 13 1/4 In. 715.00

PEWTER is a metal alloy of tin and lead. Some of the pewter made after
1840 has a slightly different composition and is called *Britannia metal.*
This later type of pewter was worked by machine; the earlier pieces were
made by hand. In the 1920s pewter came back into fashion and pieces
were often marked *Genuine Pewter.* Eighteenth–, nineteenth–, and
twentieth–century examples are listed here.

Basin, O. Williams, Buffalo, N.Y., 1 Gal. 3300.00
Basin, Steven Barnes 700.00
Basin, Thomas Danforth II, c.1810, 12 In. 825.00
Basin, U.S., 6 x 2 In. 275.00
Beaker, Kayserzinn, Poppy Design, c.1900, 4 1/2 In. 125.00
Beaker, William & Mary, Wriggle Work King & Queen, c.1690, 5 1/2 In., Pair 3520.00
Bowl, Cover, Potter Studio, Blossom Form Finial 295.00
Bowl, Floral Designs, Footed, 5 7/8 In. 35.00
Bowl, Kayserzinn, Art Nouveau, Cartouche Design, Scroll Legs & Handle, 16 In. 375.00
Bowl, Kayserzinn, Flowers & Leaves, Open Handles, Oval, 13 In. 145.00
Bowl, R. Cauman, Pierced Tree Design Handles, Cover, Red Glass Finial, 3 x 5 In. .. 950.00
Bowl, Rampant Lion Danforth Touch, Shallow, 13 1/4 In. 275.00
Bowl, Shallow, London, 1 5/8 In. 100.00
Box, B & W, Hammered, Faux Riveting, Stylized Flowers, 3 x 6 1/2 In. 193.00
Box, Hanging, Salt, Woman's Head At Hole, 7 3/8 In. 27.00
Box, Liberty Tudric, Sailboat At Sunset Insert Lid, Cedar Lined, Square 650.00
Box, Potter Studio, Hinged & Domed Lid, Cedar Lined, 3 x 7 1/4 x 3 5/8 In. 495.00
Box, Thomas Stanford, Tobacco, Cast Eagle Feet, Engraved Label, 1838, 4 3/8 In. ... 115.00
Candle Holder, Flagg & Homan, 2 Arms, 3 7/8 In. 25.00
Candlestick, Beaded Detail, Pushup, 8 In., Pair 330.00
Candlestick, Georgian, Stepped Flaring Drip Pan, 18th Century, 10 In., Pair 2420.00
Candlestick, Pushup, 8 In., Pair ....220.00 To 330.00
Candlestick, Pushup, America, 10 1/8 In., Pair 275.00

◆◆◆

For a pollution-free rug cleaner, use cornstarch. Sprinkle on rugs
or carpet, then vacuum.

◆◆◆

Candlestick, Sellew & Co., 8 In., Pair	700.00
Centerpiece, Cut Glass Liner, c.1900, Germany, 7 In. ....*Illus*	495.00
Chalice, America, 1840, 5 1/2 In.	220.00
Chalice, Communion, 9 1/4 In.	65.00
Chamber Pot, 10 In.	85.00
Charger, 13 1/2 In.	170.00
Charger, 14 3/4 In.	190.00
Charger, 15 In.	135.00
Charger, 18th Century, N. D., England, 14 In.	165.00
Charger, Art Nouveau, Center Woman, Embossed Daisies, Marked, 20 In.	665.00
Charger, Continental, Engraved Design On Back, 1772, 13 1/2 In.	154.00
Charger, Crowned Rose Touch, 16 3/4 In.	220.00
Charger, Frederick Vassett, 16 1/2 In.	2000.00
Charger, John Raymond, Triple Reeded Rim, c.1690, 17 In.	750.00
Charger, Robert Porteous, London, 1770, 16 1/2 In.	365.00
Charger, Stynt Duncumb, Single Reeded Rim, c.1739, 20 In.	940.00
Coffee Set, Kayserzinn, Flowering Roses, Organic Forms, 3 Piece	1560.00
Coffeepot, 10 1/2 In.	44.00
Coffeepot, 10 7/8 In.	25.00
Coffeepot, Dixon	250.00
Coffeepot, Fruit Finial, 10 1/4 In.	115.00
Coffeepot, George Richardson, Lighthouse Type, 1830, 10 In.	275.00
Coffeepot, H. B. Ward, Lighthouse, 11 In.	245.00
Coffeepot, Israel Trask, Lighthouse, c.1825, 12 1/4 In.	605.00
Coffeepot, Josiah Danforth	110.00
Coffeepot, Paneled, Wooden Handle, Finial, Medallion, American Flag, 14 In.	250.00
Coffeepot, Roswell Gleason, Dorchester, Mass., 12 1/4 In.	245.00
Coffeepot, Smith L & Co. 10 In.	330.00
Condiment Set, Enameled Tray, China, 4 Piece	577.00
Creamer, Ear Handle, 5 5/8 In.	175.00
Creamer, Pedestal Stepped Base, Individual	45.00
Creamer, Sellew & Co., Cincinnati, 6 In.	148.00
Dish, Cover, Kayserzinn, Sunflower	90.00
Dish, Cover, Tapered Feet, Sculpted Foliate Design, 4 1/2 In.	412.50
Flagon, Domed Lid, Acorn Finial, Erect Thumbpiece, c.1730. 8 In.	1360.00
Flagon, Double Domed Lid, Georgian, Fishtail Handle, Marked R. S., c.1720, 7 In.	2100.00
Flagon, I. Trask, 10 1/2 In.	300.00
Flagon, Joseph Anton, Germany, Engraved Boot, c.1717	1450.00
Flagon, Kayserzinn, Squirrel Figurine On Top, Acorn & Leaf Design, 13 In.	445.00
Flagon, Potbellied, Domed Lid, Erect Thumbpiece, Scotland, c.1700, 10 In.	5900.00
Flagon, Reed & Barton, 14 1/2 In., Pair	253.00
Funnel, 4 1/2 In.	25.00
Hot Plate, Peg Legs, Round, 6 In.	18.00
Hot Water Bottle, Ring Handles, Screw Cap, 10 12 In.	16.00
Lamp, Chamber, Brass, 4 In.	203.00
Lamp, Fluid, Single	200.00
Lamp, Sparking	95.00
Lamp, Whale Oil, A. Porter, 8 3/8 In.	715.00
Lamp, Whale Oil, America, 9 1/2 In.	44.00
Lamp, Whale Oil, Roswell Gleason, Pedestal, Cylinder Font, 8 In.	275.00
Lamp, Whale Oil, Rufus Dunham, 5 5/8 In.	330.00
Measure, C. Stephens Side Spout, Caste Tavern, 1 Pt.	11.00
Measure, Randell Moring, Double Volute Thumbpiece, c.1780, 1 Pt.	620.00
Measure, William Scott, Flat Lid, Embryo Shell Thumbpiece, c.1826, 1 Pt.	560.00
Mirror, Table, Rectangular Frame, Bracket Feet, Hinged Strut, 21 In.	1205.00
Mold, Ice Cream, Cow	20.00
Mold, Ice Cream, Engagement Ring, E. & Co., Pewter	45.00
Mold, Ice Cream, Flying Stork With Baby	30.00 To 40.00
Mold, Ice Cream, Golf Ball, 2 In.	180.00
Mold, Ice Cream, Pumpkin	28.00
Mold, Ice Cream, Trumpet Lily	40.00
Mold, Ice Cream, Wedding Bell, With Cupid	32.50
Mug, James Yates, George V	375.00

Mug, Presented To Mr. & Mrs. Desi Arnaz, June 16, 1967, 4 In. 250.00
Mug, Samuel Danforth, 1 Qt. 4495.00
Pitcher, Angel Touch, Continental, Swirl Design, Hinged Lid, 6 1/2 In. 71.00
Pitcher, Art Nouveau Floral, Satyr Face, Germany, 12 1/2 In. 145.00
Pitcher, Boardman, Hinged Lid, 7 3/4 In. 400.00
Pitcher, F. Porter, Westbrook, 6 3/4 In. 400.00
Pitcher, Hinged Lid, Ear Handle, 6 1/4 In. 200.00
Pitcher, Insulating Ceramic Liner, Floral Engraving, Figural Handle, Frog, 13 In. ... 100.00
Pitcher, R. Dunham, Hinged Lid, 10 7/8 In. 145.00
Pitcher, Rufus Dunham, 2 Qt. 360.00
Plate, Angel Touch, 9 1/4 In. 99.00
Plate, Boardman, 11 In. 660.00
Plate, Boardman, Eagle In Oval, 9 3/8 In. 440.00
Plate, Boardman, Lion, 8 7/8 In. 248.00
Plate, Chippendale, Dated 1790, 9 In., Pair 75.00
Plate, Communion, Boardman, Marked With 2 Eagles, 12 3/4 In. 770.00
Plate, Continental, Angel Touch, Rim Engraved Initials, 8 3/8 In. 82.00
Plate, Engraved Rim, 10 3/8 In. 65.00
Plate, George Lowes, England, Reeded Raised Rim, c.1750, 9 1/2 In. 430.00
Plate, J. Dolbeare, 9 1/2 In. 145.00
Plate, James Dixon & Sons, Gadrooned Rim, 9 3/8 In. 75.00
Plate, John Will, N.Y., 1766, 8 1/2 In. 1250.00
Plate, Samuel Ellis, 7 3/4 In. 75.00
Plate, Scale, Birchfield, 13 1/2 In. 80.00
Plate, Scalloped Tim, 11 1/2 In. 113.00
Plate, Townsend & Compton, 7 3/4 In. 65.00
Plate, Townsend & Compton, 8 5/8 In. 65.00
Plate, W. Billings, 8 1/4 In. 143.00
Platter, Reed & Barton, 18 In. 130.00
Porringer, America, Crown Handle, 5 1/2 In. 209.00
Porringer, Cast Flowered Handle, 5 1/2 In. 203.00
Porringer, Continental, 5 In. 93.00
Porringer, Crown Handle, Marked IC, 4 1/2 In. 190.00
Porringer, Europe, 2 Solid Cast Handles, 5 3/4 In. 85.00
Pot, Calder, Tall, 11 In. 357.00
Pot, Cover, Tapering Form, Open Handle, 10 In. 88.00
Pot, Homan & Co., Tall, Copper Bottom, 10 1/2 In. 55.00
Salt, Footed, 3 In., Pair 55.00
Sauce Boat, Engraved Lions, 6 5/8 In. 165.00
Soup, Dish, Francis Piggot, London, 9 1/2 In. 150.00
Tankard Set, Graduated, 1/4 Gill To 1 Gal., Strap Handle, Bulbous, 2 To 10 In. 2200.00
Tankard, Side Spout, England, 1 Qt., 6 In. 88.00
Tea Set, Child's, Britannia, Box 145.00
Tea Set, T. B. M. Co., Melon Ribbed, Wooden Finials, 4 Piece 450.00
Tea Set, Wm. Haseler, For Liberty & Co., English Tudric, 1910 .... 575.00
Teapot, 7 1/4 In. 105.00
Teapot, 7 5/8 In. 295.00
Teapot, America, Hinged Cover, 6 5/8 In. 137.00
Teapot, Bellied, 8 1/4 In. 95.00
Teapot, Dome Hinged Lid, Replaced Tin Handle, 6 1/4 In. 590.00
Teapot, F. Porter, Westbrook 165.00
Teapot, Freeman Porter, 1840s 460.00
Teapot, George Richardson, Inverted Mold, 7 In. 330.00
Teapot, McQuilkin, Philadelphia 125.00
Teapot, Morey & Ober, Boston Touch, 6 5/8 In. 214.00
Teapot, Morey & Ober, c.1855, 7 1/4 In. 180.00
Teapot, Oriental, Engraved Design, Copper Bottom, 11 1/2 In. 38.00
Teapot, S. Simpson, 7 3/4 In. 385.00
Teapot, Smith L & Co., 8 In. 176.00
Teapot, Thomas Derby 350.00
Urn, Wooden Feet, Handle & Finials, 11 In. 45.00
Vase, Orivi, Art Nouveau, 5 3/4 In. 75.00
Vase, Tudric, Bullet, 7 1/2 In. 275.00

Vase, Tudric, Hearts At Top, Bulbous Bottom, 5 1/2 In. 225.00

PHOENIX BIRD, or Flying Phoenix, is the name given to a blue–and–white kitchenware popular between 1900 and World War II. A variant is known as Flying Turkey. Most of this dinnerware was made in Japan for sale in the dime stores in America. It is still being made.

Bowl, Shallow	30.00
Cup & Saucer	8.00
Cup & Saucer, Check Floral	12.00
Vase, Etched	65.00

PHOENIX GLASS Company was founded in 1880 in Pennsylvania. The firm made commercial products, such as lampshades, bottles, and glassware. Collectors today are interested in the sculptured glassware made by the company from the 1930s until the mid–1950s. The company is still working.

Bowl, Tiger Lily, Red Cameo	165.00
Box, Powder, Cover, Lovebird Design, Opaque Satin White, 4 In.	125.00
Console, Lily, Blue	230.00
Figurine, Madonna, Green	115.00
Lamp, Blueberries, Orange Leaves, 15 In.	95.00
Lamp, Reverse Painted Bridge Scene Shade, 1910–1920, 18 In.	1650.00
Lamp, Table, Reverse Painted Domed Shade, Daffodils, Pink To Cranberry	935.00
Vase, Cosmos, White Pearl	65.00
Vase, Dancing Nymphs, Brown	295.00
Vase, Dancing Nymphs, Frosted, Sticker, 12 In. .... 325.00 To	395.00
Vase, Dancing Nymphs, White Gloss, 11 1/2 In.	375.00
Vase, Flying Geese, Blue On White Ground, 10 In.	225.00
Vase, Katydid, Orchid Glaze Over Crystal	200.00
Vase, Lovebirds, Pink Flowers, Green Leaves, Custard Ground, 6 In.	100.00
Vase, Madonna, Blue, White Ground, 14 In. .... 115.00 To	160.00
Vase, Madonna, White Iridescent Head, 10 1/2 In.	195.00
Vase, Pillow, Wild Geese Around, Raspberry, Wilson	290.00
Vase, Primrose, Brown	195.00
Vase, Umbrella, Thistle, White Opalescent, 18 In.	450.00
Vase, Wild Geese, White Pearl	85.00
Vase, Wild Geese, Yellow, White Ground	195.00
Vase, Wild Rose, Brown	65.00

PHONOGRAPH NEEDLE CASES of tin are collected today by music and phonograph enthusiasts and advertising addicts. The tins are very small, about 2 inches across, and often have attractive graphic designs lithographed on the top and sides.

Tin, Boyes, With Needles	125.00
Tin, Verona, Nude Woman	35.00

PHONOGRAPHS, invented by Thomas Edison in the 1880s, have been made by many firms. This category also includes other items associated with the phonograph. Jukeboxes and records are listed in their own categories.

Amberola, Fireside, Model B, Cygnet Horn, Cylinder	975.00
Aretino, 3–In. Center Spindle, Green Morning Glory Horn, 1902	750.00
Belknap, Windup, 1900, 45 RPM	1875.00
Brunswick, 1923	50.00
Burns–Pollock, Lamp, Electric, Fringed ....*Illus*	2000.00
Columbia, Console Model, Windup	375.00
Columbia, Grand Type AG, 56 In. Brass Horn, Tripod Stand	1150.00
Columbia, Graphonophone Type, BF, Long Mandrel, 1905	925.00
Columbia, Language, Nickel 21–In. Morning Glory Horn	850.00
Columbia, Model 200	50.00
Columbia, Model BF, Peerless, 25–In. Brass Horn, 1906	425.00
Doll, Westinghouse, Saranade, Extra Batteries	125.00
Edison, Amberola, Cylinder	400.00

Edison, Amberola, Model 30, 165 Cylinders 1000.00
Edison, Cabinet Model Disc Records 950.00
Edison, Carved Footed 220.00
Edison, Cylinder, With Horn, Oak 302.50
Edison, Diamond Disc, Crank, Upright, 33 1/3 RPM, 51 1/2 In. 285.00
Edison, Fireside, Flowered Morning Glory Horn 1250.00
Edison, Home Cylinder, Morning Glory Horn, Winged C Reproducer 425.00
Edison, Home, 30-In. Flowered Horn 775.00
Edison, Model A, Cylinder, Latch Case & Cover, Original Horn, 1900 .... 325.00
Edison, Morron Gem, 2 & 4 Minute Records, 20-In. Horn 975.00
Edison, Opera, Mahogany 4500.00
Edison, Pooley 165.00
Edison, Standard, 85 Cylinders 395.00
Edison, Standard, Brass Horn, Oak, 12 Cylinder Records 675.00
Edison, Standard, Model E, Cylinder, Cygnet Horn 750.00
Edison, Triumph, 11 Petal Cygnet Horn 1500.00
Gem, Edison Keywind 650.00
Heywood-Wakefield, Brown Wicker, Perfektone Mechanism 1475.00
Oxford Jr., Cast Iron 550.00
Pathe Actwelle, 12 In.-Cone Reproducer, 78 RPM, Art Deco Cabinet, 48 In. 1800.00
Polyphone, Bells, 22 1/2 In. 6900.00
Polyphone, Upright, 19 5/8 In. 5500.00
Portable, Birch, Instructions, 78 RPM 175.00
Primaphone, Brass Morning Glory Horn 700.00
RCA Victor, Suitcase 35.00
Seeburg, Symphonola, Coin-Operated 2850.00
Standard, Talking Machine, Model A, Red Morning Glory Horn .... 450.00 To 525.00
Standard-X, Disc Player 575.00
Victor II, Brass Horn, 1902 .... 1175.00
Victor III, Black Morning Glory Horn, 1906 .... 1200.00
Victor, Electrola, Model 9-18X 1000.00
Victor, Model III, Oak Outside Horn, Disc .... 1600.00 To 2200.00
Victor, Model IV, Black Morning Glory Horn, Mahogany 1450.00
Victor, Model IV, Spruce Horn 2995.00
Victor, Oak, Table Model 55.00
Victor, Orthophonic, Credenza 535.00
Victor, School House 2850.00
Victor, Talking Machine, Floor Model, VV-XI 707454 .... 105.00
Victrola, Crank, 1915 .... 275.00
Victrola, Floor Model, Mahogany 120.00
Victrola, Model V, Morning Glory Horn 1650.00
Victrola, Model VV-100 .... 285.00
Victrola, Model VV-V1, Mahogany 195.00
Zenith, Radio, Table Model, 120 Records, 1947 .... 100.00
Zonophone, Brass Horn, Tone Bar, Labels, 1900 .... 1250.00

Phonograph, Burns-Pollock, Lamp,
Electric, Fringed

♦ ♦ ♦ ♦ ♦ ♦ ♦ ♦ ♦ ♦ ♦ ♦ ♦ ♦ ♦ ♦ ♦ ♦ ♦ ♦

White rings on furniture can
sometimes be removed with
liquid metal polish or auto
paint cleaner. Apply the
cleaner to a soft cloth and rub
until the ring is gone. Then
repolish the surface with furniture polish.

♦ ♦ ♦ ♦ ♦ ♦ ♦ ♦ ♦ ♦ ♦ ♦ ♦ ♦ ♦ ♦ ♦ ♦ ♦ ♦

PHOTOGRAPHY items are listed here. The first photograph was a view from a window in France taken in 1826. The commercially successful photograph started with the daguerreotype introduced in 1839. Today all sorts of photographs and photographic equipment are collected. Albums were popular in Victorian times. Cartes de visite, popular after 1854, were mounted on 2 1/2–by–4–inch cardboard. Cabinet cards were introduced in 1866. These were mounted on 4 1/4–by–6 1/2–inch cards. Stereo views are listed under Stereo Card.

Albumen, 2 Ballplayers, Stylized A On Uniform, 1920, 4 x 2 1/2 In.	55.00
Albumen, Alamo View, Unmounted, 1900, 4 x 5 1/2 In.	20.00
Albumen, Cowboy, Sitting In Cave, 1880, 3 1/4 x 4 1/2 In.	25.00
Albumen, Quail Hunters, Rifles, Dogs, Game Suspended, 7 1/2 x 9 3/4 In.	160.00
Ambrotype, Artist At Work, Woman With Jug At Wall, 1/4 Plate	182.00
Ambrotype, Boy On Wicker Chair, Holding Velvet Hat, 1/9 Plate	55.00
Ambrotype, Dentist With Instruments, Union Case, 3 1/4 x 4 1/4 In.	1320.00
Ambrotype, Departed Rose, Post Mortem, Holding Bouquet, 1/6 Plate	137.00
Ambrotype, Fireman, Sideways In Chair, Pioneer On Belt, 1/6 Plate	148.00
Ambrotype, German Couple, Green Velvet Case, Silk Pad, 1/4 Plate	40.00
Ambrotype, Girl On Chair, Button Boots, Thermoplastic Case	65.00
Ambrotype, Kimono, Bonsai Plant, Wooden Case, Japan	1650.00
Ambrotype, Man In Kimono, Plant On Table, Case, Japan, 1/4 Plate	165.00
Ambrotype, Man, Silvery Ground, Kimball, Oval Mat, 1/6 Plate	82.50
Ambrotype, Man, Writing, Cheeks Slightly Tinted, Oval Mat, 1/4 Plate	49.00
Ambrotype, Military Headquarters, Civil War, Case, 1/6 Plate	165.00
Ambrotype, Stephen Douglas, Union Case, 6th Plate	1430.00
Ambrotype, Woman, Seated, Oval Mat, Schoonmaker's, Troy, N.Y., 1/6 Plate	30.00
Ambrotype, Woman, St. Louis, Dobyns & Spaulding, 1/4 Plate	65.00
Cabinet Card, Black Man, Masonic, Arcade Studios, Springfield, Oh., 1890, 6 In.	25.00
Cabinet Card, Black Policeman, No. 3 On Hat, Chicago Studio, 1890, 6 1/2 In.	35.00
Cabinet Card, Count & Countess Magri, Baron Magri, Midget, Swords Bros.	30.00
Cabinet Card, Fat Woman, Charles Eisenmann, 1885	97.50
Cabinet Card, Girl, High Button Shoes, Ornate Stool, Sarony, N.Y., 1880s, 6 In.	15.00
Cabinet Card, Great Republic, Sailboat, Gloucester, Mass., Andrew's Studio	24.00
Cabinet Card, J. M. Fuller, U.S. Naval Academy, M. D., Uniform, Sword, 1880	15.00
Cabinet Card, Man & Woman, Bustle Dress, Ornate Stool, 1880s, 6 1/2 x 4 In.	15.00
Cabinet Card, Man, Standing, Draped Chair, Chicago Studio, 1880s, 6 1/2 In.	11.00
Cabinet Card, Militia Soldier, Gray Uniform, Sword, 1880	20.00
Cabinet Card, Mourning, Smiling Angels Over Headstones, c.1880, 6 1/4 In.	12.00
Cabinet Card, Mourning, Woman Looking Down On Coffin, Girl, Serrated Edge	72.00
Cabinet Card, Peaches, In Glass Bowl, Coles, Pekin, Ill., Penned Verse	110.00
Cabinet Card, President Hayes Home	20.00
Cabinet Card, Teen Boy, Sailor Suit, Monroe Avenue, Detroit, Mi., 1880s, 6 x 4 In.	10.00
Cabinet Card, Wedding Party, Signed Charles & Lavinia Stratton, Brady, 1863	75.00
Cabinet Card, Woman, Long Dress, Bustle, Draped Chair, 1880s, 6 1/2 x 4 In.	10.00
Cabinet Card, Young Man In White, Graduation, Rensselaer, 1880s	10.00
Camera, Accuraflex, Semiautomatic Lens, Box	75.00
Camera, Agfa Plenax, Folding	15.00
Camera, Argus, Color, Case	95.00
Camera, Brownie, Hawkeye, Flash, Box	20.00
Camera, Brownie, Model F 120, No. 2, Red	45.00
Camera, Canon P, Meter, Case, 5 Black Lenses	800.00
Camera, Donald Duck, Herbert George Co.	50.00
Camera, Eastman View, Model 2d, 8 x 10 In.	250.00
Camera, Kassin, Small	22.50
Camera, Kodak, Autographical	36.00
Camera, Kodak, Box, 1888–1889	3700.00
Camera, Kodak, Hawkeye, Leather Case, 1940s	20.00
Camera, Kodak, Medalist II, Flash Supermatic Shutter	145.00
Camera, Kodak, No. 2, Hawkeye Special	35.00
Camera, Kodak, No. 2a, Brownie	25.00
Camera, Kodak, No. 2c, Autographic Junior	25.00
Camera, Kodak, No. 6–16, Chrome Design On Brown Enamel	85.00

Camera, Kodak, No. 135, Pony	10.00
Camera, Kodak, Pony II, Leather Case, 1949	20.00
Camera, Kodak, Rainbow, 50th Anniversary, Red	25.00
Camera, Kodak, Vest Pocket, Patent 1913, Leather Case, 5 In.	60.00
Camera, Leica, Model 4, 3 Lenses, Case, Accessories	1400.00
Camera, Minolta, Miniature	25.00
Camera, Movie, Bell & Howell, 8 Mm., Leather Case	30.00
Camera, Movie, Bell & Howell, Case, 1920s	55.00
Camera, Movie, Bell & Howell, Cinemachinery, Leather Case	350.00
Camera, Novar, Wrinkled Bellows, No Wind Key	65.00
Camera, Pony Premo, No. 6, Rochester Optical Co., Bellows Style	82.00
Camera, Putnam Marvel, Horizontal Folding, Wooden Case, 5 x 8 In.	149.00
Camera, Rand Binocular, 80 Mm. Telephoto Lens, Case	65.00
Camera, Rocca TLR, Steinheil No. 80, Case	300.00
Camera, Societe Francaise, Sept., Paris, Andre Debrie, Carrying Case	214.00
Camera, Stewart Warner, Hollywood Model	23.00
Camera, Stoddard & Kendall, Folding Hub, Dame, Bellows Style	55.00
Camera, Welta, Compurlens, Plate 4 x 6 In.	100.00
Camera, Welta, Weltix, Cassar 50	65.00
Camera, Zorki–R, Case	90.00
Carte De Visite, A. Lincoln Center, Surrounded By Seward, Chase, Stanton	35.00
Carte De Visite, Abraham Lincoln	30.00
Carte De Visite, Abraham Lincoln, Civil War Era	35.00
Carte De Visite, Andrew Johnson	18.00
Carte De Visite, Bearded Infantry Officer, Hardee Hat On Table, B. P. Paige	66.00
Carte De Visite, Cheyenne Squaw, Mrs. Romeo	100.00
Carte De Visite, Chief Tahargustahongon, Tinted Feathers, Pipe, Pease Bros.	57.00
Carte De Visite, Child, Standing, Indian Headband & Feather, J. Kirk	35.00
Carte De Visite, Com. Nutt & Minnie Warren, Queen Victoria Meeting, 1865	15.00
Carte De Visite, Dalles of The St. Croix, Hat & Cloak, Tree, Whitney's Gallery	33.00
Carte De Visite, Dog With Basket, J. H. Aylsworth	35.00
Carte De Visite, Drummer Boy, Zouave Jacket, Star On Fez	110.00
Carte De Visite, Early Washington Policeman, Striped Pants	50.00
Carte De Visite, Marriage of General Tom Thumb	82.50
Carte De Visite, Millie & Christine, Black Siamese Twins	110.00
Carte De Visite, Rutherford B. Hayes	25.00
Carte De Visite, Saluma Agra, The Star of The East, 1860s	20.00
Carte De Visite, Small Dancer, Beside Chair, Topaze, Paris	25.00
Carte De Visite, Soldier With Rifle, Bayonet, Revenues Stamp	50.00
Carte De Visite, Teodore Tilton, Journalist, Long Curly Hair, Name Imprinted	10.00
Cyanotype, Gentleman With Bicycle, 1890, 4 x 4 3/4 In.	15.00
Daguerreotype, 3/4 Portrait Civil War Soldier, Sword, 19th Century	305.00
Daguerreotype, Cemetery, Encampment, Civil War, Case, 6 x 4 3/4 In.	2700.00
Daguerreotype, Family, St. Paul, Signed Upton, 1/2 Plate	75.00
Daguerreotype, Man, At Table, Lace Tablecloth, Scovill, 1/6 Plate	50.00
Daguerreotype, Sisters, Same Eyes & Hair, 1/6 Plate	60.00
Daguerreotype, Soldier, Seated, Musket, Civil War	425.00
Daguerreotype, Woman, Floral Dress, Unusual Short Hair, 1/6 Plate	66.00
Daguerreotype, Young Girl, Sweet, Full Case, 1/6 Plate	35.00
Home Balopticon, 3 Slide Trays, Black Case, Bausch & Lomb, 21 x 16 In.	100.00
Lantern, Dark Room, 1882	345.00
Lantern, Kodak, Dark Room, Candle Type	62.00
Lantern, Kodak, Dark Room, Kerosene	45.00
Magic Lantern, E. P. Germany, 48 Slides, Wooden Slides, 40 Admitting Tickets	375.00
Magic, Lantern, Box, Small	50.00
Mirroscope, Red, Double Vents, Cleveland, Oh.	35.00
Photo Booth, International Mutoscope Co.	950.00
Photograph, 2 Medical Students, Dissecting Cadaver, 1920, 5 3/4 x 3 1/2 In.	37.50
Photograph, Blackfoot War Bonnet, Edward Curtis, 8 x 6 1/2 In.	220.00
Photograph, Bridgeport, Conn. Mayor, Police Dept., 1864, Framed, 26 x 30 In.	880.00
Photograph, Camp McQuade, Saratoga Springs, N.Y., 1857, 9 x 15 In.	117.00
Photograph, Chuck & Chuckles, Black Dance & Comedy Team, 8 x 10 In.	50.00
Photograph, Dancing Shoes, Nude Before Window, 9 x 6 In.	135.00

Photograph, Evening In Old New Orleans, W. Whitesell, 10 x 13 In. 187.00
Photograph, Exhibition of Latest Dancing Steps, Black Boys 28.00
Photograph, G. Sommers & Co. Marching Band, Black, White, 1916, 33 x 12 In. ... 35.00
Photograph, Gentleman Portrait, Crazed, Oil Tinted, Frame, 30 x 25 In. 120.00
Photograph, George Bernard Shaw, Yosuf Karsh, 1943 .... 4400.00
Photograph, George Burns, Gracie Allen, NBC Mike, 1939, 8 x 10 In. 25.00
Photograph, Golden Gate, From San Francisco Bay, Sepia, 4 1/2 x 7 3/4 In. 82.00
Photograph, Hawaiians & Outriggers, Waikiki, 1912, 4 1/2 x 6 3/4 In. 100.00
Photograph, Interior Store, National Biscuit & Sunshine Products 15.00
Photograph, Jerusalem, Mt. of Olives 13.00
Photograph, Large Indian Woman, Sepia, 1910–1920, 5 x 3 In. 20.00
Photograph, Little Boy, Roly Poly Toy, 1915, 4 x 6 In. 7.50
Photograph, Man, With Harley Davidson, Pennants, 1915, 3 x 2 1/2 In. 15.00
Photograph, Mass. Volunteers At Camp Rogers, March 12, 1863, Frame 110.00
Photograph, Middle Aged Woman, On Motorcycle, Sepia, 1920s, 5 x 7 In. 35.00
Photograph, Military Camp, Mt. of Lane, Brothers, Tents, 1892, 4 1/2 x 7 In. 25.00
Photograph, New York City, G. W. Pach, Broadway & Long Branch 38.00
Photograph, Poultry Butter & Egg Truck, Warehouse, Eclipse Studio, 9 3/4 In. 25.00
Photograph, Robert Young, Sepia, 1930s Pose, 5 x 7 In. 40.00
Photograph, Salvation Army, 3 Women & Man, Uniform, 1880, Oval, 5 In. 15.00
Photograph, Sarah Bernhardt, Role As Photine, c.1892 .... 137.00
Photograph, Savings–Empire Trust Co., 4 Pictures, Chicago, 1931, 8 x 10 In. 8.00
Photograph, Shoshone Falls, T. H. O'Sullivan, Wheeler Expedition, 1874 .... 45.00
Photograph, Showroom, Salesmen, Woman Playing Piano, 6 x 8 1/2 In. 45.00
Photograph, Smokehouse, Cigar Store Indian, Shoeshine Chair, 4 x 5 1/2 In. 160.00
Photograph, Steamer De Grasse, San Francisco, 1930s, 6 x 9 In. 12.50
Photograph, Tambourine Girl, Sepia, 6 x 4 In. 50.00
Photograph, Veteran Fire Assn., Hand Pumper, 19th Century, 17 x 21 In. 495.00
Photograph, Watkin's Pacific Coast, 3 Views, Yosemite Falls 24.00
Photograph, We Love Our Country, Women, American Flag, Sepia, 6 x 8 In. 74.00
Photograph, Winter At Gregg House, Children On Sleds, 1895, 34 x 26 1/2 In. 110.00
Photograph, Winter Sunrise, Sierra, Nevada, Ansel Adams, 15 1/2 x 19 1/4 In. 9350.00
Photograph, Woman, Fancy Casket, Floral Displays, 1900, 8 x 10 In. 35.00
Photograph, Woman, Well Dressed, Black Carriage Driver, 1900, 9 x 12 In. 85.00
Photograph, Wreck of The Jason, Following Storm, 26 Died, 1893 .... 70.00
Photograph, Wrecked Engines At M. P. Round House, Kansas City, 1903 .... 20.00
Photogravure, Launching The Whale Boat, Frame, 12 x 16 In. 550.00
Projector, Bell & Howell, No. 173, Silent 16 Mm. Case 69.00
Projector, Bell & Howell, No. 307, Movie, 16 Mm. 349.00
Projector, Bell & Howell, No. 385, Filmosound, Movie, 16 Mm. 125.00
Projector, Bell & Howell, No. 399, Specialis, Movie, 16 Mm 249.00
Projector, Keystone, Bellows Slide, 18 x 6 x 10 In. 95.00
Projector, Keystone, Model E–743, Hand Crank, Electric, 16 Mm. 50.00
Projector, N. Power Company, Movie, Pat. Apr. 1906, Celluloid Film, 5 x 4 1/2 In. .. 6500.00
Projector, Slide, Kerosene, Tin 70.00
Projector, Viewmaster Entertainer, Blue Plastic 85.00
Splicer, Film, Griswold, 1926 .... 75.00
Timer, Kodak 45.00
Tintype, 3 Baseball Players & Manager, 4 1/4 x 3 In. 120.00
Tintype, Child, Pacifier, Lace Dress 42.00
Tintype, Clarinet Player, Uncased 33.00
Tintype, Dwarf, Wagon, Horse 48.00
Tintype, Fireman, Cross In Wreath On Cap, 1/6 Plate 40.00
Tintype, Girl & Boy, With Black & White Cat, Large Frame 80.00
Tintype, Memorial, Child Portrait, Framed With Floral Wreath, 1850s 467.50
Tintype, Mother, With Baby On Lap, Tinted Faces, A. J. Russell 25.00
Tintype, Plasterers, Work Clothes, Holding Mixing Box, Uncased 55.00
Tintype, Policeman, Seated, Large Star 36.00
Tintype, Soldier, Otto Borberg, Leatherette Case, July 28, 1863 .... 95.00
Tintype, Soldier, Pistol & Saber, Frame 425.00
Tintype, Soldier, With Pistol & Saber, Civil War, 5 5/8 x 4 1/4 In. 467.00
Tintype, Union Soldier, Carrying Rifle–Musket, 1/6 Plate 250.00

Pickard, Hatpin Holder,
Yellow Flowers, Beutlich, 5 In.; Pickard,
Hatpin Holder, Violets, Artist M.P., 5 In.

Pickard, Pitcher,
Lemonade, Stylized
Chrysanthemums, Reau, 7 In.

Tintype, Union Soldier, Holding Musket, 2 3/4 x 3 1/4 In.	305.00
Tintype, Woman With Child, 1850s	45.00
Tintype, Woman, 1850s	35.00
Tintype, Woman, Standing By Gate, A. B. Chapman, 1/6 Plate	550.00
Tintype, Women At Parlor Organ, Uncased	27.00
Trimming Board, Kodak	16.00
Tripod, Eastman Kodak, Brass, Wooden, Folding	30.00
Tripod, Studio, Wooden, Center Post, 7 x 9 In. Camera Bed, Early 1900s	58.00
View–Opticon, Motor Driven Carousel, Black Case, Larsen Bros. & Holmes	225.00

PIANO BABY is a collector's term. About 1880, the well–decorated home had a shawl on the piano. Bisque figures of babies were designed to help hold the shawl in place. They range in size from 6 to 18 inches. Most of the figures were made in Germany. Reproductions are being made. Other piano babies may be listed under manufacturers' names.

Child, Sitting On Feet, Blue Intaglio Eyes, Gebruder Heubach, 10 In.	950.00
Figurine, Bisque, 6 In., Pair	175.00
On Stomach, Hand To Mouth, Bisque, 10 In.	155.00

PICKARD China Company was started in 1898 by Wilder Pickard. Hand–painted designs were used on china purchased from other sources. In the 1930s, the company began to make its own china wares in Chicago, Illinois. The company now makes many types of porcelains, including a successful line of limited edition collector plates.

After Dinner Set, Etched, 23K Gold, 1915, 15 Piece	4500.00
Bonbon, Scenic	195.00
Bowl, Floral, Scalloped, 2 Handles, 9 In.	595.00
Bowl, Modern Conventional, Hessler, 9 1/4 In.	285.00
Bowl, Nut, Painted Hazel Nuts, Footed, 1898, 8 1/2 In	175.00
Bowl, Strawberries, Gold Trim, Artist, 9 3/4 In.	195.00
Bowl, Strawberries, Handle, Yeschek	110.00
Bread Plate, Grandeur, 6 1/2 In.	20.00
Cake Plate, Italian Garden Scene, Marked, 11 In.	255.00
Cake Plate, Open Handle, Artist, 10 In.	180.00
Candleholder, Gold, Low, Pair	110.00
Candy Dish, Cover, Crystal, Embossed Gold Overlay Design, Finial, Signed	55.00
Charger, Poppies, 2–Tone Gold, Signed, 12 In.	425.00
Chocolate Pot, Grapes Over Pastels & Greens, Reds, Purples, 1898	435.00
Claret Set, Deserted Garden, Marked, 7 Piece	2000.00
Compote, Lemon Trees, Gold Bands, Marked, 7 In.	165.00

Pickard, Tankard, Falstaff,
Gilded Rim & Handle,
Gasper, 15 In.

Pickard, Vase, Woman,
Flowers, 2 Handles,
Signed 12 In.

Creamer, Aura Argenta Linear, Marked, 3 3/4 In.	65.00
Creamer, Scenic, Signed	125.00
Cup & Saucer, Bouillon, 12 Sets	400.00
Cup & Saucer, Daffodil Pattern, Challinor, Demitasse	85.00
Hatpin Holder, Violets, Artist M. P., 5 In. ....*Illus*	300.00
Hatpin Holder, Yellow Flowers, Beutlich, 5 In. ....*Illus*	250.00
Mayonnaise Set, Deserted Gardens, Ladle, 3 Piece	385.00
Mug, Venetian Canal Scene, Iridescent Luster, Comyn	900.00
Pitcher, Cider, Acorns, Gold Dotted Caps, Gold Beading, Marked	395.00
Pitcher, Forest Scene, Signed, 2 3/4 In.	135.00
Pitcher, Lemonade, Florals, Dark Ground	250.00
Pitcher, Lemonade, Peaches, Leaves	725.00
Pitcher, Lemonade, Stylized Chrysanthemums, Reau, 7 In. ....*Illus*	450.00
Pitcher, Lemons & Blossoms, Schoner	725.00
Pitcher, Red Currants, Leaves, Reau	250.00
Pitcher, Tankard, Chrysanthemum, Reau	550.00
Pitcher, Tankard, Falstaff, Holding Jug, P. Gasper	1400.00
Pitcher, Tankard, Friar, Peeling Turnips, Gasper	800.00
Pitcher, Tankard, Jovial Friar, Holding 2 Steins, Gasper	1800.00
Pitcher, Water Lilies, Roots Down In Water, Leroy, 1905, 7 1/2 In.	595.00
Plate, Floral Design, White–Gold, 8 3/4 In.	90.00
Plate, Flowers	45.00
Plate, Fruit & Flowers, Square, 10 In.	195.00
Plate, Gold, Platinum & Orange Flowers, 9 1/4 In.	50.00
Plate, Gooseberries, Artist	65.00
Plate, Pastel Lilies, Luster, Gold Trim, Yeschek, 9 In.	165.00
Plate, Pink Carnations, Gold, Rene, 8 1/4 In.	140.00
Plate, Poppies, Signed, 1905, 8 1/2 In.	185.00
Plate, Spencer Story Time	30.00
Relish, Floral Design, 1910, 9 1/2 In. ....75.00 To 85.00	
Sauce, Attached Underplate, Pink & Maroon Floral, Gold Handle, 1910, 6 1/2 In.	225.00
Sugar & Creamer, Gold Etched	55.00
Sugar & Creamer, Lily Type Flowers, Boat Shape	125.00
Sugar & Creamer, Plums & Grapes, Marked	175.00
Sugar & Creamer, Tray, Art Deco Design, Gold & Blue, Black Ground, Marked	175.00
Tankard, Falstaff, Gilded Rim & Handle, Gasper, 15 In. ....*Illus*	1400.00
Tea Set, Apple Blossoms, Signed, 3 Piece	625.00
Vase, Art Deco, Gold & Floral Design, 6 1/2 In.	175.00
Vase, Chrysanthemums, Stems, Buds, Neck, 3 Gold Shoulder Handles, 5 1/2 In.	405.00
Vase, Columbines, Colorado Mountains, Signed, 9 In.	375.00

Vase, Deserted Garden, Egg Shape, Marked, Large 1350.00
Vase, Hollyhocks, Challinor 625.00
Vase, Nude, Flowing Blond Hair, With Raven, 2 Handles, Grane, 19 3/4 In. 3400.00
Vase, Poinsettias & Daisies, Gold Band Top, Free–Form Rim, 1905, 12 In. 325.00
Vase, Signed F. Vobor, 14 In. 300.00
Vase, Stag & Mountain Scene, A. Rhodes, 14 In. 1300.00
Vase, Triple Tulip, Double Handled, Signed, 7 In. 325.00
Vase, Tulip, C. Hahn 725.00
Vase, Water Lilies, Eggplant Shape, Signed, 7 In. 275.00
Vase, Woman, Flowers, 2 Handles, Signed, 12 In. ....*Illus* 850.00
Vase, Woman, Flowing Robes, Grane, 9 1/4 In. 2200.00

PICTURE FRAMES are listed in this book in the Furniture category under
Frame.

PICTURES, silhouettes, and other small decorative objects framed to hang
on the wall are listed here. Some other types of pictures are listed in the
Print and Painting categories.

Caligraphy, Spencerian, Bird, Flag & Branch, 4 Colors, Frame, 9 3/4 x 11 3/4 In.   75.00
Calligraphy, St. Nick, Merry Christmas, Signed Wilkins, 11 x 14 In. 75.00
Calligraphy, Woman, Driving 2 Horse Chariot, 19th Century, 18 In. 220.00
Chalk, Girl, Bird On Hand, Early 19th Century, Ogee Frame, 9 1/2 x 13 In.   275.00
Charcoal On Paper, Aftermath, Scharh, Frame, 18 1/2 x 26 In. 27.50
Charcoal On Paper, Sun & Clipper Extra, Newsboy, J. Sanford, 1872, 11 x 7 In. 78.00
Charcoal On Sandpaper, Primitive Landscape, Frame, 13 x 16 1/2 In. 65.00
Cork Work, Windsor Castle, Frame, 18 1/2 x 21 In. 137.50
Crewel, Man On Horse, Dogs, Fanciful Landscape, Frame, 17 1/4 In. 225.00
Crewel, Oversize Flowers, Bird, Squirrel, Wool On Cotton, Frame, 27 1/4 In. 165.00
Embroidered On Silk, Water Fowl, Floral, Frame, Oriental, 20 x 22 In. 35.00
Embroidered, On Laid Finish Paper, Floral Spray, Frame, 11 1/2 x 9 1/2 In. 55.00
Hair, Flowers, Pre–Civil War, Frame 300.00
Ink Wash, 4 People On Hillside, Steamboats On River, 19th Century, 16 x 21 In. 220.00
Needlepoint, 3 Kittens, Partially Completed, Adjustable Wooden Frame, 33 In. 473.00
Needlepoint, Couples With Dog Outside Cottage, Oak Frame, Victorian, 53 x 43 In.   605.00
Needlepoint, Skating On Lake Scene, Bird's Eye Maple Frame, c.1850, 25 x 30 In.   935.00
Needlework, Basket of Flowers, Framed, Round 165.00
Needlework, Bird In Tree, Frame, 12 x 10 In. 440.00
Pencil, On Paper, Pennsylvania Farm Derby Co., Dated 1835, 9 x 12 In. 198.00
Pinprick & Watercolor On Paper, Woman & Child, Frame, 11 5/8 x 7 7/8 In. 300.00
Retablos, Jesus Cristo, Franciscan Style, Tin, 4 x 6 In. 495.00
Reverse Decoupage On Glass, Spring–Summer, Frame, London, 12 x 16 1/4 In. ...   250.00
Reverse Decoupage On Glass, Wise Men, Frame, London, 16 x 12 1/2 In. 55.00
Reverse On Glass, Floral Design, Black Ground, Gilt Frame, 13 1/2 x 13 1/4 In.   110.00
Scissor Cut, Multicolored Design, 1821, Framed, Penna. German, 8 x 11 In. 385.00
Silhouette, Andrew Jackson, Ink & Watercolor, Frame, c.1850, 3 1/8 x 4 1/2 In. ...   270.00
Silhouette, Child & Bird, Full Figure, Black Paper, White Highlights, 8 x 6 In. 50.00
Silhouette, Man & Woman, Ink & Watercolor, Brass Frame, 5 x 4 1/2 In., Pair 715.00
Silhouette, Man Smoking & Woman Playing Piano, Rectangular, 4 x 5 In., Pair 17.50
Silhouette, Man With Book, Full Figure, Brushed Highlights, Frame, 12 x 10 In. 95.00
Silhouette, Man With Top Hat, Full Figure, Frame, 11 3/4 x 9 5/8 In. 145.00
Silhouette, Man, August Pietrsch Aus Altenauard, 1840, Frame, 13 x 18 In. 200.00
Silhouette, Man, Checkered Pants, Full Figure, Ink & Gouache, 10 3/4 x 8 3/4 In.   205.00
Silhouette, Man, Full Figure, Allied Razaar Coliseum, 1917 ....   25.00
Silhouette, Man, Full Figure, Gilt Highlights, Frame, 13 x 6 3/4 In. 275.00
Silhouette, Man, Hollow Cut, Inland Frame, 4 1/8 x 3 1/2 In. 181.00
Silhouette, Man, Top Hat, Full Length, Framed, 12 3/4 x 7 1/4 In. 192.00
Silhouette, Man, Woman, Hollow Cut, Black Cloth Backing, 5 3/4 x 4 3/4 In. 250.00
Silhouette, Man, Woman, Hollow Cut, White Ground Paper, Frame, 8 In., Pair 165.00
Silhouette, Needlework, Napoleon, Velvet, Alice VanLeer Carnick, Frame, 9 x 8 In.   247.00
Silhouette, Sisters, Hollow Cut, Watercolor, Frame, 4 x 3 In., Pair 4800.00
Silhouette, Swordsman, Black Watercolor On Paper, Frame, 5 x 7 1/4 In. 230.00
Silhouette, Woman, Holding Umbrella, White Ground, Frame, 1852, 8 x 4 In. 200.00

Silhouette, Woman, Hollow Cut, Pen & Ink, Frame, 5 In. 320.00
Silhouette, Woman, Seated, Watercolor Ground, 5 3/4 x 7 3/4 In. 120.00
Silhouette, Woman, Shawl, Bonnet, Opaque White, Ink, Black Wooden Frame, 8 In. 170.00
Silhouette, Young Man, Hollow Cut, Gutta Percha Frame, Boston, 1850 .... 190.00
Silhouette, Young Woman, Black Cloth Backing, Gilt Frame, 5 1/4 x 4 In. 60.00
Silhouette, Young Woman, Hollow Cut, Glued To Black Paper, c.1840 .... 130.00
Silhouette, Young Woman, Pen & Ink, Eglomise Glass, Frame, 5 3/4 x 5 In. 55.00
Theorem, Basket of Fruit, Velvet, Frame, 7 x 9 In. 275.00
Theorem, Basket, Summer Fruit & Berries, Stenciled, Frame, 12 x 16 3/4 In. 3850.00
Theorem, Birds, Blue, Black & White, Silk, 19th Century, 13 1/2 x 11 1/2 In. 220.00
Theorem, Bouquet of Flowers, Velvet, Oval, Gilt Frame, 14 x 12 In. 100.00
Theorem, Floral Bouquet, Watercolor, Mahogany Frame, 19 1/2 x 23 3/4 In. 1100.00
Theorem, Fruit, Velvet, Gilt Frame, 9 1/4 x 11 1/2 In., Pair 880.00
Theorem, Still Life With Fruit, Velvet, 1824, 9 1/2 x 7 1/2 In. 450.00
Tinsel, Indian In Canoe, Full Moon, Black Ground, Frame, 9 x 13 In. 55.00

PIGEON FORGE Pottery was started in Pigeon Forge, Tennessee, in 1946.
Red clay found near the pottery was used to make the pieces. Molded or
thrown pottery with matte glaze and slip decoration was made. The
pottery is still working.

Bowl, Turquoise, 6 In. 10.00
Group, Bear & 2 Cubs, Gunmetal Black, 6 In., Bear 125.00

PILKINGTON Tile and Pottery Company was established in 1892 in
England. The company made small pottery wares, like buttons and hatpins,
but soon started decorating vases purchased from other potteries. By 1903,
the company had discovered an opalescent glaze that became popular on
the Lancastrian pottery line. The manufacture of pottery ended in 1937 but
decorating continued until 1948.

Tile, Apache Dancers, 3 Sets 130.00
Tile, Princess Kneeling, Floral Ground, Framed, 11 1/2 x 5 1/2 In. 470.00
Vase, Art Deco Design, Matte Finish, 6 1/2 x 6 1/2 In. 275.00
Vase, Arts & Crafts, 7 In. 165.00
Vase, Bud, Prussian Blue, 5 In. 175.00
Vase, Fish & Seaweed, Blue & Green Luster, 1919, 7 In. 335.00
Vase, Glidden, Sage, 10 In. 35.00

PINCUSHION DOLLS are not really dolls and often were not even
pincushions. Some collectors use the term *half-doll*. The top half of each
doll was made of porcelain. The edge of the half-doll was made with
several small holes for thread, and the doll was stitched to a fabric body
with a voluminous skirt. The finished figure was used to cover a hot pot of
tea, powder box, pincushion, whisk broom, or lamp. They were made in
sizes from less than an inch to over 9 inches high. Most date from the
early 1900s to the 1950s. Collectors often find just the porcelain doll
without the fabric skirt.

Arms Away, Bisque, Wire Base, Bald, 2 In. 85.00
Arms Away, China, Box, 3 In. 150.00
Arms Away, Hands To Body, Powder Box, Germany, No. 506 .... 75.00
Arms Away, Pensive Look, 5 In. 395.00
Arms To Body, Clothes Brush, Japan 35.00
Child, Purple Hat, Dressel & Kister, 5 In. 225.00
Cloche Hat, Germany, 2 In. 30.00
Court Lady, 4 In. 195.00
Dancer, Arms Away, Earrings, Necklace, Eye Shadow, Germany, 4 In. 65.00
Flapper, Outstretched Arms, 6 1/2 In. 225.00
Girl, Dutch Hat, 3 In. 50.00
Girl, Pink Riding Outfit, 3 In. 95.00
Jenny Lind, 3 In. 150.00
Little Girl, Green Hat, Yellow Flower, 2 In. 95.00
Marie Antoinette, 5 In. 195.00
Pierrot's Head, 2 In. 50.00
Pierrot, Ruffled Collar, Dressel & Kister, 5 In. 95.00

PINK SLAG pieces are listed in this book in the Slag category.

PIPES have been popular since tobacco was introduced to Europe by Sir Walter Raleigh. Meerschaum pipes are listed under Meerschaum.

Briar, Bakelite & Silver Sterling Stem	10.00
Cigarette, Lady's Head, c.1915	35.00
Commemorating Napoleon's Defeat, Sterling Silver, 1813	247.50
Henry Clay Type, Portrait, Not Clay, Cream, Austria	95.00
Human & Animal Heads, Coiled Pottery, 18th Century	450.00
Mermaid's Bust, Leather Case	48.00
Opium, Applied Silver Wire Design, Silver Over Tin, 1800s, 13 1/4 In., Pair	375.00
Opium, Pink & White Flowers On Blue, Cloisonne, China	195.00
Rack, Carved Smiling Man Leaning From Cabin Window, 20 In.	55.00
Stand, Smoker's Set, 2 Drawers, Tobacco Jar, Pipe Rack, Oak, England, 10 x 12 In.	225.00
Trader's, Clay, 2 Bone Stems	10.00

PISGAH FOREST pottery was made in North Carolina beginning in 1926. The pottery was started by Walter R. Stephen in 1914, and after his death in 1941, the pottery continued in operation. The most famous kinds of Pisgah Forest ware are the cameo type with designs made of raised glaze and the turquoise crackle glaze wares.

Beaker, Turquoise & Pink, 1936, 6 In.	50.00
Bowl, Blue & Purple, 4 In.	40.00
Bowl, Blue, Low, 1940, 7 In.	45.00
Bowl, Turquoise Crackle, 3 In.	42.00
Bowl, With Underplate, Date, 5 1/2 In.	62.00
Coaster, Incised Design, 6 Piece	35.00
Creamer, Hillbilly & His Dog, Cabin, Mountains, Cameo	350.00
Lamp, Indian Encampment Scene, Cameo, 10 In.	1815.00
Mug, Cameo	295.00
Pitcher, Aqua, 3 In.	15.00
Pitcher, Pioneering Scene, Wedgwood Blue, Cameo, 1953, 3 1/2 x 5 In.	247.00
Pitcher, White Jasper Covered Wagon, Glossy Aqua Border, Cameo, 5 In.	192.50
Sugar & Creamer, Maroon, Large	40.00
Sugar, White Jasper Covered Wagon	295.00
Tea Set, White, Pink Interior, Dated, 11 Piece	275.00
Vase, Blue, 5 In.	50.00
Vase, Crystalline Glaze, Blue & Green, 5 In.	250.00
Vase, Crystalline Glaze, Cobalt Blue & Gold, Dated 1938, 10 1/4 x 5 In.	1100.00
Vase, Green Swirl Glaze, 1921, 4 In.	55.00
Vase, Pioneer Scene, Ox–Pulled Wagon, Cameo, Marked, 5 1/2 In.	770.00
Vase, Pioneer Scene, Periwinkle Crystalline Base, Dated 1939, 13 1/4 In.	1430.00
Vase, Striated Cream To Brown, Dated 1941, Marked, 7 In.	65.00
Vase, Tiger's Eye Flambe, Rose–Pink Interior, Raised Mark, 10 x 4 3/4 In.	220.00
Vase, Turquoise Crackle, Pink Interior, c.1934, 3 1/2 In.	65.00
Vase, Turquoise Crystal Glaze, 1936, 8 1/2 In.	175.00

PLANTERS PEANUTS memorabilia is collected. Planters Nut and Chocolate Company was started in Wilkes–Barre, Pennsylvania, in 1906. The Mr. Peanut figure was adopted as a trademark in 1916. National advertising for Planters Peanuts started in 1918. The company was acquired by Standard Brands, Inc., in 1961. Standard Brands merged with Nabisco in 1981. Some of the Mr. Peanut jars and other memorabilia have been reproduced and, of course, new items are being made.

Ashtray, Figural	50.00
Ashtray, Mr. Peanut Beside Half Shell Which Is Ashtray, 4 1/2 x 3 In.	132.00
Bank, Mr. Peanut, Blue	8.00 To 20.00
Book, Guide To Tennis	10.00
Book, President's Paint Book, 1953	45.00
Booklet, Personal Story of Mr. Peanut, Comic Book, 16 Pages, 1956	25.00
Card, Magic Spooky, 1940s	2.00
Chopper, Nut	15.00

Clock, Alarm	22.50
Coloring Book, 1950	10.00
Cookie Jar, Mr. Peanut	29.50
Cookie Jar, Mr. Peanut, Box	39.00
Dish, Nut, Mr. Peanut, Metal	30.00
Dish, Serving, Mr. Peanut, Logo	24.00
Doll, Mr. Peanut, Cloth, 20 x In.	20.00
Doll, Mr. Peanut, Decal Features, Wooden Hat, Arms & Legs, 9 In.	190.00
Holder, Nut Shape, Cardboard, 11 In. ....*Illus*	35.00
Jar, 75th Anniversary, Peanut Man Picture, Clear, 1 Qt.	5.00
Jar, Clipper, Peanut	80.00
Jar, Cover, Glass, Embossed Name & Peanut Finial, 7 In.	60.00
Jar, Cover, Mr. Peanut Running, Losing Hat, 12 x 8 1/2 In.	248.00
Jar, Figural Lid, Running Peanut, Barrel Shape, 12 In.	225.00
Jar, Grocery Counter Shape, Tin Cover, Clear, 1/2 Gal.	15.00
Jar, Leap Year	62.50
Jar, Lid, Round Glass, Embossed Name, 7 In.	60.00
Jar, Mr. Peanut Leap Year	75.00
Jar, Peanut Handled Lid, Football Shape, 8 1/2 x 8 1/2 In.	242.00
Jar, Running Peanut Man, Pink ....175.00 To 255.00	
Knife, Fork & Spoon, Plastic, Blue	50.00
Letter Opener, Figural, Mr. Peanut Handle	75.00
Mug, Mr. Peanut, Figural, Plastic	10.00
Nut Set, Gold Metal, Mr. Peanut, Box, 5 Piece	75.00
Paint Book, Mr. Peanut, 1950	12.00
Peanut Butter Maker, Mr. Peanut, Box, 1970s ....25.00 To 35.00	
Pencil, Mechanical, Mr. Peanut, Box	24.00
Punchboard, 5 Cents	95.00
Radio, Mr. Peanut, Figural, AM, Battery & Carrying Strap, Box	50.00
Range Set, Mr. Peanut	12.50
Salt & Pepper, Mr. Peanut	15.00
Salt & Pepper, Mr. Peanut, Silver	15.00
Sign, Mr. Peanut, 5 Cents A Bag, Wooden	700.00
Tin, High Hat, Peanut Oil, 1 Qt.	95.00
Tumbler, Circus, Book	150.00
Watch, Presentational, Battery Operated	45.00

PLASTIC objects of all types are being collected. Some pieces are listed in other categories; gutta–percha cases are listed in photography, celluloid in its own category.

Blotter, Black, Bakelite	25.00
Cake Breaker–Server, Butterscotch, Bakelite	8.00
Manicure Set, Art Deco, Bakelite	25.00
Manicure Set, Red, Bakelite, 4 Piece	17.50
Napkin Ring, Bird, Green Bakelite	25.00
Sugar & Creamer, Pink, Royalon Inc. ....*Illus*	15.00

Planters Peanuts, Holder, Nut Shape, Cardboard, 11 In.

♦ ♦

For your health and the well-being of your collection, do not smoke. The nicotine will stain fabrics, pictures, and wood.

♦ ♦

PLATED AMBERINA was patented June 15, 1886, by Joseph Locke and made by the New England Glass Company. It is similar in color to amberina, but is characterized by a cream colored or chartreuse lining (never white) and small ridges or ribs on the outside.

Punch Cup, 9–Paneled, Amber Handle 2300.00

PLIQUE–A–JOUR is an enameling process. The enamel is laid between thin raised metal lines and heated. The finished piece has transparent enamel held between the thin metal wires. It is different from cloisonne because it is transparent.

Bowl, Open Work Sides, 2 1/2 x 4 In. 70.00
Plate, 9 1/8 In. 90.00

POLITICAL memorabilia of all types, from buttons to banners, is collected. Items related to presidential candidates are the most popular, but collectors also search for material related to state and local offices. Many reproductions have been made. A jugate is a button with photographs of both the presidential and vice presidential candidates.

Album, Photograph, J. F. Kennedy, Funeral, Memorial Card, 8 x 10 In., 19 Piece. ...	250.00
Ashtray, Churchill, Face Picture, China	50.00
Ashtray, Republican Convention, 1960	8.00
Badge, Grant, Paper Photo, Frame Hangs From Eagle, Original Pin, 1870s	450.00
Badge, Procession, McKinley For President, Brass, 6 3/4 x 5 In.	150.00
Balloon, Truman For President	28.00
Bandanna, Alton B. Parker, Davis, 1904	350.00
Bandanna, Cleveland & Thurman, Red, White & Blue, 18 1/2 x 21 In.	175.00
Bandanna, Harrison & Morton, Red, White & Blue, 22 x 25 In.	200.00
Bandanna, James G. Blaine & Logan, 1884	200.00
Bandanna, Parker & Davis, Red, White & Blue, 23 x 25 In.	325.00
Bandanna, Stand By The President 1992, Stars and Stripes, 22 x 22 In.	4.50
Bandanna, Theodore Roosevelt, Fairbanks, 23 x 25 In.	285.00
Bandanna, Winfield Scott Standing Beside Horse	3200.00
Bank, Al Smith, Celluloid, 1928	150.00
Bank, Donkey, Democrat, Ceramic	15.00
Bank, Humphrey & Muskie, '68, Metal	35.00
Banner, 1932 Roosevelt, 40 x 60 In.	400.00
Banner, A Gallant Leader Roosevelt, Portrait, Red White & Blue, 37 x 57 In.	450.00
Banner, Anti–Buchanan, 1856 Election, 37 x 40 In.	4800.00
Banner, Franklin Delano Roosevelt, Bust of Roosevelt, Miniature	90.00
Banner, McClellan, Pendleton, Frame	400.00
Banner, Teddy Roosevelt, Gold Lettering & Fringe, 1905, 54 x 66 In.	75.00
Book, Nixon Presidential Inaugural	35.00
Bookends, Teddy Roosevelt, Bronze, Signed, Gregory Allen	400.00
Bookmark, Christmas Greetings From President & Mrs. Truman, 1940	20.00
Bottle Opener, Carter, Caricature, 7 In.	12.00

Plastic, Sugar & Creamer, Pink, Royalon Inc.

Bottle Stopper, Churchill, Caricature	80.00
Bottle Stopper, Eisenhower, Caricature	75.00
Bottle Stopper, Truman, Caricature	100.00
Bottle, Bust of Grover Cleveland, Name On Front Base, Frosted, 10 In.	250.00
Box, Cigar, Garfield & Arthur Portraits, 1880	395.00
Box, Eisenhower, Presidential Portrait	16.00
Button, 60 Million People Working, Why Change, Truman	10000.00
Button, America Needs Kennedy–Johnson, Jugate, 3 1/2 In.	20.00
Button, America Wants Willkie	15.00
Button, Another Republican For McGovern, Words Only, 1 1/4 In.	6.00
Button, Arizona Says Bush For President In 1988, 5/8 In.	3.00
Button, Arkansas' Favorite Son, Elect Clinton For President	15.00
Button, B. Harrison, Rep., Photograph, Flag, Red, White & Blue Ribbon	100.00
Button, Barry Goldwater, President, 1964	3.50
Button, Black Dignity, Nixon's The One!, Black & White, 1968, 2 1/4 In.	20.00
Button, Bryan, Sewell Victory, Jugate, 1896	230.00
Button, Bull Moose, Progressive, Blue Ground, 1912, 7/8 In.	7.00
Button, Bush & Quayle, Picture of Each, 1 1/2 In.	1.25
Button, Bush Picture, Flags Around Rim, 2 1/4 In.	1.25
Button, Bush, In Front of Microphone, 3 In.	2.00
Button, Calvin Coolidge, Keep Coolidge, 1/2 In.	18.00
Button, Campaign '72, McGovern Staff Headquarters, Red and White	6.00
Button, Carry On With Roosevelt, Picture	20.00
Button, Carter & Mondale, Jugate	3.00
Button, Carter & Mondale, President, 1976	1.50
Button, Charles Hughes, My First Vote For President, 1916, 1 In.	3000.00
Button, Come Home America, McGovern & Eagleton	4.00
Button, Cooper For Governor, Ohio, 1900, 5/8 In.	5.00
Button, Davis, Democratic, Sepia, Picture, 1 1/4 In.	110.00
Button, Debs, Seidel, Jugate, Ribbon	3800.00
Button, Democrats For Nixon, Lodge, 1/2 In.	2.50
Button, Dewey & Bricker, Do We, We Do, Trust Faith Hope, 1944	385.00
Button, Dewey, Plastic Elephant, Stud Back	12.00
Button, Dewey, Ribbon, 1944–1948	50.00
Button, Elephant, Figural, Stud, Metal	4.00
Button, F. D. Roosevelt, Picture, 3 1/2 In.	22.00
Button, Flasher, Furcolo, Governor	25.00
Button, For President Henry A. Wallace, Picture	12.00
Button, For President Richard M. Nixon	1.50
Button, For President Willkie, Picture, Pinback	22.00
Button, For The Leadership We Need, President, Kennedy Picture	8.00
Button, Franklin D. Roosevelt, Celluloid	85.00
Button, Goldwater In '64, Celluloid	4.00
Button, Governor Higgins, Lt. Governor Bruce, New York, 1904	6.50
Button, Grover Cleveland, Campaign	22.00
Button, Harry Davis For Governor, Ohio, 1924, 5/8 In.	6.50
Button, Henry Wallace, Vice President, 1968	3.50
Button, Hoover, Red White & Blue, Celluloid	10.00
Button, Hubert Humphrey For President, Staff, Rectangular	330.00
Button, Humphrey & Mondale, Pictured, 1 In.	5.00
Button, I Like Ike, Picture	15.00
Button, I Like Ike, Red, White & Blue, 7/8 In.	8.00
Button, I Sponsored Goldwater Tea Party, 1964	350.00
Button, I Want Roosevelt Again, Stripes & Stars Rim	25.00
Button, I Want Ross Perot For President '92, Uncle Sam Pointing	1.50
Button, I'm On The Rockefeller Team, Red, White & Blue	2.00
Button, Ike & Dick Junior Club, 2 Pictures	48.00
Button, J. F. K. Picture, Says Students For Kennedy, 1 1/4 In.	10.00
Button, J. F. Kennedy, Pinback	10.00
Button, Jesse Jackson, Rainbow Ground, 1984	3.50
Button, John F. Kennedy, 1960	7.00
Button, John F. Kennedy, President, 1960	7.00
Button, Kennedy & Johnson, Jugate, 3 1/2 In.	20.00

Button, Kennedy & Johnson, Leaders of Our Country, Jugate, 3 1/2 In. 30.00
Button, Kiss Me I'm For Bill Clinton For President, Lips 1.25
Button, Lady Bird For First Lady, Picture, Red & White, 2 1/4 In. 35.00
Button, Landon & Knox, Felt Sunflower 10.00
Button, Let's Back Ike–Dick, Pinback 18.00
Button, Let's Back Ronald Reagan For Governor 45.00
Button, Lyndon B. Johnson, President, 1964 .... 3.50
Button, Man of The Hour, Eisenhower, Bust 14.00
Button, McGovern & Shriver, 1972 .... 78.00
Button, McGovern For President In '72 .... 2.50
Button, McGovern For Senator, Picture 45.00
Button, McGovern, Eagleton, President, 1972 .... 4.00
Button, McKinley & Protection, Stud Back 55.00
Button, McKinley & Teddy Roosevelt, 1900 .... 40.00 To 95.00
Button, McKinley, Roosevelt, Ribbon Design, Gold Ground, Jugate, 1 3/4 In. 50.00
Button, Nelson Rockefeller, Rocky Puts It Together, 1960–1970, 1 3/8 In. 7.00
Button, Nix–On Dick, Brown & White, 3/4 In. 3.00
Button, Nixon & Lodge, Jugate .... 16.00 To 18.00
Button, Nixon Eviction, Phase I, Oct. 25–29, Blue On Orange, 1 1/2 In. 23.00
Button, Nixon, 1960 .... 5.00
Button, Not For Sale, Elect Nixon, White House Picture, 3 In. 250.00
Button, Our 35th President, John F. Kennedy 8.00
Button, Parker, 1904 .... 80.00
Button, Peace and Prosperity With Eisenhower, Picture, Ribbon 4.00
Button, Please Vote Dry For Me, Prohibition 17.00
Button, Proud To Be A Republican, Elephant Silhouette, Red White & Blue 1.50
Button, Re–Elect Carter, The President, 6 In. 6.50
Button, Reagan For Ex–Governor, Black & Green, 1/2 In. 9.00
Button, Reagan, Bush, President, 1984 .... 2.00
Button, Reagan, Let's Make America Great Again, White On Blue 5.00
Button, Richard M. Nixon, President, 1960 .... 5.00
Button, Robert Kennedy For A Better America, Flasher 14.00
Button, Ronald Reagan, Quaker Puff, Pinback 30.00
Button, Roosevelt For Humanity 15.00
Button, Stick With Dick 7.00
Button, There Is A Difference, Vote McGovern, Toddlers Looking In Diapers 4.00
Button, This Bush Is For You, Beer Can Shape 1.50
Button, Tsongas Makes Tsense In 92, 1 1/2 In. 1.25
Button, Vote Democratic, Straight Ticket, McGovern & Shriver Face 2.50
Button, Vote For Wilson, Figure 8 With Portraits, 1 In. 8500.00
Button, Vote Hoover For President, Celluloid 35.00
Button, Vote Truman For President, Portrait, White Ground, 9 In. 950.00
Button, Wallace For President 10.00
Button, We Don't Want Eleanor Either, 1930s 10.00
Button, Wilson & Marshall, Jugate, 7/8 In. 1068.00
Button, Win With Taft, Pinback 5.00
Button, Wings For America Willkie, Plane Picture 17.00
Button, Woodrow Wilson, Stand By Wilson The Man On The Job, 7/8 In. 20.00
Button, You Can Be Sure With Ford, Picture of Gerald Ford 3.50
Card, Trade, Campaign 1884, Pair 35.00
Charm, Nixon, N Center, Surrounded By Simulated Pearls 10.00
Clock, Presentation, Reagan, Presidential Seal, Brass, Velvet Bag 50.00
Clock, Re–Elect Bush, 5 Colors 28.50
Comic Book, Forward With Eisenhower–Nixon, 1956 .... 10.00
Compact, Willkie 40.00
Corkscrew, Key Shape, Metal, Man of The Hour, 1933 .... 110.00
Ferrotype, Lincoln & Hamlin, Campaign, Double Sided, 1 In. 935.00
Figure, Barry Goldwater, Rubber & Plastic, Remco, Box, 1964, 5 In. 30.00
Flag, Campaign, Grover Cleveland Inset In Star Area, Silk 700.00
Flag, Clay & Frelinchuysen, Stars & Stripes, Clay's Portrait 6950.00
Flag, Hoover, Red, White & Blue, 8 x 11 In. 28.00
Flag, Our Choice Lincoln, Johnson, Stars & Stripes, Cloth, 1864, 13 In. 5500.00
Frisbee, Reagan For President, Red, White & Blue, 1980 .... 5.00

Game, Richard Nixon Nose Ring Toss, Wooden Board, 12 x 12 In.	25.00
Game, The Kennedy's, 1962	40.00
Gavel, Sam Rayburn, Envelope	35.00
Guitar Pick, Guitarists Pick Bush In 1992	5.00
Handkerchief, Cleveland, Hendricks Picture, Silk, Floral Border	110.00
Handkerchief, Cleveland, Truman Portraits, Silk	85.00
Handkerchief, Eisenhower, 25 x 25 In.	58.00
Handkerchief, Roosevelt & Fairbanks, Flags, Embroidered, Linen	60.00
Hat, Campaign, Benjamin Harrison & Whitelaw Reid	137.50
Hat, He's Alright, Harrison, Glass	155.00
Hat, Parker & Davis, Parade	325.00
Hat, Roosevelt & Wallace, Star & 2 Donkeys, Felt	50.00
Hat, Willkie & McNary, Eagle & 2 Elephants, Felt	50.00
Invitation, Inaugural, President Lyndon Johnson, Frame	24.00
Jug, Grant & Colfax, Stoneware, 1868, 6 Gal.	1950.00
Key Chain, Elect Ford, Dole In '76	7.50
Key Chain, Gerald Ford Picture	10.00
Key Chain, I Like Ike, Flasher	30.00
Key Chain, Jimmy Carter, Smiling Peanut	15.00
Key Chain, Peace & Prosperity, Dwight 'Ike' Eisenhower, 1960	15.00
Key Charm, Match Box Shape, Independent Safety Match Co.	20.00
Kit, Nixon & Agnew Convention, Canvas, Florida, 3 Tickets, Book, Program, 1968	48.00
Knife, Carter & Mondale For 1980, Picture of Each, Black, Blue & White	15.00
Knife, Pen, Reagan, Bush '80, Large	14.00
Knife, Watergate, Caricatures of Men Involved, Blue & White	20.00
Lantern, Accordion, Grant Portrait, Blue, Grant & Colfax On Reverse, Paper	495.00
Lantern, Accordion, Lincoln & Johnson, Leaf Design, Paper	1250.00
Lantern, Bucket, Dinner, Pierced Tin, McKinley & Roosevelt, 8 1/2 In.	1250.00
Letter, Benjamin Franklin, Signed, 1744	2695.00
License Attachment, LBJ For The USA, Pennsylvania	5.00
License Plate, Let's Go Roosevelt, Red White & Blue	110.00
License Plate, Nixon, Agnew, Blue Letters, White Ground	20.00
Lighter, Lite The Light For Goldwater, Picture of Goldwater & Logo	45.00
Lighter, Lyndon Johnson Presidential, With Seal	50.00
Match Holder, Horace Greeley, Cast Iron, 1872	250.00
Matches, Veterans For Nixon	8.00
Medal, Harry S Truman, Inaugural	150.00
Medal, Woodrow Wilson, Inaugural	150.00
Medallion, John Fitzgerald Kennedy Inauguration, Bronze, 2 3/4 In.	15.00
Mirror, Eisenhower Picture, Flags, Perkins & Son, Artesia, NM, 12 x 22 In.	55.00
Mug, Inscribed Cleveland, Silver Plate, 1890s	200.00
Mug, Shaving, U. S. Grant, Portrait, Civil War	550.00
Mug, The New Deal, Roosevelt, Barrel Shape	25.00
Mug, Toby, Roosevelt, Lennox, Edward Penfield, 1909	2500.00
Mug, William H. Taft	105.00
Necktie, I Like Ike	25.00
Necktie, Our Choice Wm. H. Taft, Portrait, Red White & Blue, Black Border	250.00
Newspaper, Headline, Dewey Elected, Gallup Says	200.00
Pamphlet, Oscar Underwood President Hopeful, Picture	17.00
Paperweight, Willkie, Hope of Our Country, Glass, Face Picture	175.00
Pennant, Franklin Delano Roosevelt, Inauguration, White & Blue, 1937, 28 In.	35.00
Pennant, Landon, Yellow & Brown, 11 1/2 In.	40.00
Pennant, Stevenson, Yellow & Brown, 25 In.	22.00
Photograph, Harry S Truman, Sepia, At Desk, Autographed, 12 x 8 1/2 In.	140.00
Pin, Dewey, Anti-Truman 8-Ball, 1948	1150.00
Pin, Elephant, Nixon, Gold Wash, Rhinestones, Pago, 1969, 2 1/2 In.	22.50
Pin, J. F. Kennedy, PT109, Boat Shape, 1960	18.00 To 45.00
Pin, Jack Kennedy, Campaign, Die Cut Name In Script, 1960	20.00
Pin, Kennedy In Rhinestones	22.00
Pin, Landon & Know, On Felt Sunflower, 3/4 In.	4.00
Pin, Lyndon B. Johnson, Donkey	19.00
Pin, McGovern & Eagleton, Come Home America, Jugate, 1 3/4 In.	20.00
Pin, McGovern & Shriver, Come Home America, Jugate, 3 1/2 In.	25.00

Pin, McKinley, Hobart	25.00
Pin, Nixon, Now More Than Ever, Picture, 3 In.	6.00
Pin, Stick, Rooster, Red White & Blue	45.00
Pin, Taft, Sepia Tone	25.00
Pin, Tintype, Abraham Lincoln, Square Frame	1100.00
Pin, Willkie, Elephant Shape	18.00
Plaque, Al Smith, Embossed Copper, 1928	140.00
Plate, American Eagle, Used By Pres. Kennedy On Yacht, Shenango, 1963	770.00
Plate, Franklin D. Roosevelt, President, Pink & Gold Trim, 11 In.	25.00
Plate, John F. Kennedy, 1962	20.00
Plate, McKinley, Purple & Gold Rim, 8 In.	35.00
Plate, McKinley, Weller Pottery	165.00
Plate, Nixon, Agnew Inaugural, Sterling Silver, 1973	165.00
Plate, Pres. Eisenhower's Head, Blue Pressed Glass, 1953, 8 In.	15.00
Plate, President Garfield, Memorial, Scalloped, 10 In.	55.00
Plate, White House, Capital Building & Congressional Building, Silesia, 3 Piece	125.00
Plate, William Howard Taft, Portrait, 1908, 8 1/2 In.	25.00
Platter, Nixon, Agnew, Frankoma	50.00
Portrait, Warren G. Harding, Bust, Sepia, Signature, 7 x 11 In.	695.00
Postcard, Harding, Portrait, San Francisco Trip	32.50
Postcard, Hayes For Senator, 1954	3.00
Postcard, Kennedy & Johnson, Pictures Over White House	6.50
Postcard, Mechanical, Wm. Taft & J. Sherman, Who Is Going To Win The Race	20.00
Postcard, Nixon & Dirksen, Only Names, Red, White & Blue	6.00
Postcard, Vote For Jimmy Carter Democrat, For President	3.00
Poster, General Franklin Pierce, On Horseback, Military Scene, 13 x 17 In.	175.00
Poster, Herbert Hoover, 1928, 24 x 16 In.	38.00
Poster, Hull For Senator, Cardboard, 1936	3.00
Poster, It Takes Courage! Wallace Has It, Cardboard, 14 x 22 In.	6.50
Poster, J. Kennedy, King, R. Kennedy, 3 Faces In Peace Symbol, 21 x 29 In.	45.00
Poster, Kennedy For President, Leadership For The 60s, Plastic, 18 x 24 In.	65.00
Poster, LBJ For The USA, Plastic, Red, White & Blue, 18 x 24 In.	3.50
Poster, Mamie Eisenhower, Frame, Personalized Autograph, 18 x 22 In.	125.00
Poster, McGovern, Shriver, Picture, Natural Colors, 1972, 14 x 21 In.	6.50
Poster, Nixon For Governor, Picture, Blue, Yellow, White, Cardboard, 14 x 22 In.	125.00
Poster, Nixon's The One, Bust, Photograph, 15 x 24 In.	12.00
Poster, Robert Kennedy, Picture, White, Blue, Black, 12 x 19 In.	15.00
Poster, Vote Humphrey & Muskie, Portrait, Paper, Red, White & Blue, 17 x 22 In.	12.50
Poster, Votes For Women, Red, Black, Green, 1914, 11 x 15 In.	45.00
Poster, Wendell L. Willkie For President, Cardboard, 14 x 17 In.	85.00
Print, Democratic Candidates & Party Chieftains, Grover Cleveland, 1884	110.00
Print, Pres. Franklin D. Roosevelt, Green Bay, Aug. 9, 1934, 6 x 7 1/2 In.	10.00
Program, Inaugural, Eisenhower, Rockwell	13.00
Program, Republican National Convention, Chicago, 1960	7.00
Record, Goldwater's Acceptance Speech, Convention, Long–Play, 1964	20.00
Record, Nixon Now Rally Song, Mike Curb Congregation, MGM, 45 RPM, 1972	22.50
Ribbon, Eugene Debs, Socialist Party, 1920	1500.00
Ribbon, Franklin Delano Roosevelt, Picture, Celluloid Donkey Attached	25.00
Ribbon, Garfield & Arthur, Garfield Picture, 1880	150.00
Ribbon, Governor James of Pennsylvania, Elephant Pendant, Picture	22.50
Ribbon, Grover Cleveland, Photograph Inset, 9 x 4 In.	75.00
Ribbon, Republican State Convention, Columbus, Ohio, 1896	11.00
Ribbon, Vandenberg, Bell Tolled Two, Red & White	20.00
Ribbon, Willkie, Celluloid Elephant Attached	16.00
Scarf, John F. Kennedy's Colored Picture, Silk, Flag Border, 1960s, 32 In.	10.00
Sheet Music, Funeral March, James Garfield, 1881	25.00
Sheet Music, Jimmy Carter, Dedicated To 39th Pres. of The U.S., Shaffner	400.00
Sheet Music, March, McKinley, 1896	20.00
Sheet Music, We Are With "R", Theodore Roosevelt, Pictured On Cover	35.00
Sticker, Window, Howlett For Gov., Il., Red White & Blue, 1976, 8 In.	3.00
Sticker, Window, Roosevelt, Red, White & Blue	8.00
Textile, Harrison & Morton, Silk, Portraits, Capitol Dome, 1889–1893, 19 In.	75.00
Thimble, Reagan, Bush, 1984	1.00

Ticket, Admission, Impeachment Hearing of President Andrew Johnson, 1868 .... 330.00
Ticket, Wisc. Pres. Franklin D. Roosevelt Day, Reserved Seat, 8/9/34 .... 8.00
Tie Clasp, J. F. K., Flasher Picture, Says Man For The 60's 10.00
Toy, Yo–Yo, I Like Ike 18.00
Tray, John F. Kennedy, Portrait, Memorial 25.00
Tray, McKinley In Oval Center, Tin, 16 In. 100.00
Tray, W. J. Bryan, Bust Portrait, 16 1/4 In. 100.00
Tumbler, John F. Kennedy, Memorial 12.00
Vase, Abraham Lincoln, Bust, Bearded, Blue Ground, Civil War, 8 1/2 In. 350.00
Watch Fob, Taft & Sherman, Our Choice, Bust of Each, Copper 65.00
Wristwatch, George Wallace, The Fighting Judge, Bill Dinken Time, 1970 ......50.00 To 100.00

POMONA glass is a clear glass with a soft amber border decorated with pale blue or rose–colored flowers and leaves. The colors are very, very pale. The background of the glass is covered with a network of fine lines. It was made from 1885 to 1888 by the New England Glass Company. First grind was made from April 1885 to June 1886. It was made by cutting a wax surface on the glass, then dipping it in acid. Second grind was a less expensive method of acid etching that was developed later.

Butter, Cover, Acanthus Leaf, Curled Handle, 1st Grind, 8 In. 540.00
Celery Vase, Cornflower, Ruffled Rim, 1st Grind, 6 1/4 In. 370.00
Finger Bowl, Cornflower, Ruffled Top, Blue, Amber Edge, 5 1/2 In. 155.00
Finger Bowl, Ruffled, 1st Grind, 1 3/4 x 5 1/2 In. 220.00
Goblet, Amber Rim, 2nd Grind 100.00
Lemonade Set, Cornflower, With Sugar, 6 Piece 1000.00
Pitcher, Inverted Diamond, 2nd Grind, 7 In. 95.00
Punch Cup, 1st Grind 75.00
Punch Cup, Cornflower, Amber Leaves, 1st Grind, 2 3/4 In. 195.00
Punch Cup, Cornflower, Blue, 1st Grind 100.00
Punch Set, Scallop Design, 1st Grind, Tankard & 6 Cups 1045.00
Rose Bowl, Cornflower, Blue, 2nd Grind, 5 1/2 In. 495.00
Sugar & Creamer, Ruffled, Amber Stain On Handles, 1st Grind 585.00
Tankard Set, Scallop Design, 1st Grind, 9 1/4 In., 7 Piece 1045.00
Toothpick, 1st Grind 165.00
Tumbler, Blueberries, Gold Leaves, Stippled Ground, 2nd Grind, 3 3/4 In. 175.00
Tumbler, Enameled Flowers, Green, 2nd Grind 95.00
Tumbler, Juice, Cornflower, Blue, 2nd Grind 100.00

PONTYPOOL, see Tole

POPEYE was introduced to the Thimble Theater comic strip in 1929. The character became a favorite of readers. In 1932, an animated cartoon featuring Popeye was made by Paramount Studios. The cartoon series continued and became even more popular when they were used on television starting in the 1950s. The full–length movie with Robin Williams as Popeye was made in 1980.

Bank, Figural, Alan Jay, 1959, 9 In. 72.00
Bank, Mechanical, Popeye & Brutus, King Features 330.00
Belt, Magnet 38.00
Box, Crayon, Popeye On Lid, Tin 12.00
Can, Spinach 17.00
Candy Container, Pez 20.00
Car, Paddle Wagon, Die Cast, Corgi, 5 In. 165.00
Cartoon, Popeye Sketched On Restaurant Menu, Segar Autograph 850.00
Chalk Crayons, Box 10.00
Clock, Alarm, Windup, Lithograph, Signed, 1932, 4 1/4 In. 1200.00
Comic Strip, Popeye, Olive, Brutus, Wimpy, Ink, Paper, Sagendorf, 1960, 18 In. 660.00
Comic Strip, Popeye, Sappo, Ink, Paper, Bela Zaboly, Frame, 1940, 24 x 19 In. 825.00
Cookie Jar, Olive Oyl, American Bisque 1400.00
Cookie Jar, Popeye In Spinach Can 400.00
Cookie Jar, Popeye, American Bisque ....725.00 To 1250.00
Cookie Jar, Popeye, In Can of Spinach, Napco 145.00
Cookie Jar, Popeye, No Pipe 950.00

◆◆◆◆◆◆◆◆◆◆◆◆◆◆◆◆◆◆◆◆◆◆

Old metal toy trucks were made of iron or tin, not brass or aluminum, which are the metals favored by some reproductions.

◆◆◆◆◆◆◆◆◆◆◆◆◆◆◆◆◆◆◆◆◆◆

Popeye, Toy, Popeye & Olive Oyl

 Handcar, 1935

Cookie Jar, Swee' Pea, American Bisque	4000.00
Doll, Brutus, 22 In.	45.00
Doll, Cloth, Rubber, 1950, 21 In.	125.00
Doll, Equestrian, With Parrots, Painted, Marx	137.50
Doll, Sawdust Filled	185.00
Doll, Uneeda, Box, 1979	33.00
Doll, Wimpy, With Hamburger, 18 In.	35.00
Figurine, Popeye & Wimpy, Chalkware, 9 In., Pair	75.00
Figurine, Popeye, Celluloid, Jointed, Large	250.00
Figurine, Popeye, Chalkware, 1930s	100.00
Game, Adventure of Popeye, Board, Transogram, 17 In.	77.00
Game, Ball & Pipe, 1929	75.00
Game, Ball, Popeye The Juggler, Tin Lithograph, 1929	50.00
Game, Juggler	59.00
Game, Pipe Toss, Box	50.00
Game, Popeye The Juggler, Ball & Pipe	60.00
Game, Ring Toss	75.00
Game, Where's My Pipe, Pin The Pipe On Popeye, Box, 1937	95.00
Guitar, Plastic, Mattel, Box	80.00
Kazoo, 3 In.	175.00
Lamp, Popeye Figure Base, Shade, King Features, 1937, 14 1/2 In.	440.00
Lunch Box, 1964	45.00 To 150.00
Lunch Box, Aladdin, 1980	31.00 To 60.00
Lunch Bucket	25.00
Mug, Olive Oyl, Vandor	25.00
Night–Light, Arrow, Plastic, 3 1/4 In.	32.00
Paint Set, Popeye Paints, American Crayon, 1933	15.00 To 18.00
Paint Set, Tin, 1965	35.00
Pen, Fountain, Popeye & Olive Oyl, Decal, Green Plastic Barrel	350.00
Pencil Box, Blue, KFS, 1929, 5 1/2 x 9 In.	45.00
Puppet, Brutus, Gund	58.00
Puppet, Olive Oyl, 1957	75.00
Puppet, Popeye, 1957	75.00
Puzzle, Jaymar, 1940s	25.00
Record Player, Emerson	65.00
Ring, Olive Oyl, Post Cereal	30.00
Ring, Post Toasties, Metal, Original Package, 1949	32.50
Ring, Swee' Pea, Post Cereal	25.00
Salt & Pepper, Vandor	35.00
Soap, Figural, 1940s, 4 In.	19.50
Tin, Popcorn, Yellow, 1949	55.00
Toy, Airplane, Marx	350.00
Toy, Boxing Popeye, Windup, Tin, Celluloid, Chein	850.00
Toy, Dumper, Celluloid & Tin Lithographed, Box, 9 x 3 x 7 In.	2425.00
Toy, Express, Windup	695.00
Toy, Handcar, Windup, Rubber Figures, Louis Marx, 1935, Box, 6 1/2 In.	4400.00

Toy, Marble Shooter, Original Bag & Box, Akro Agate Co., 1929, 7 x 3 1/2 In. 500.00
Toy, On Roof Top, Marx 675.00
Toy, Overhead Puncher, J. Chein & Co., 1932, 9 1/2 x 4 1/4 In. 3025.00
Toy, Pipe, Bubble 2.00
Toy, Pipe, Card 35.00
Toy, Popeye & Olive Oyl Handcar, 1935 ....*Illus* 4400.00
Toy, Popeye Heavy Hitter, Metal, Lithograph, Windup, Chein, Box 9000.00
Toy, Popeye In Barrel, Windup, Tin, King Features, 1932 .... 300.00 To 700.00
Toy, Popeye In Rowboat, Battery Operated, Linemar, 10 x 4 In. 4400.00
Toy, Popeye The Jolly Sailor, Musical, Clockwork, Woolikin, 15 In. 154.00
Toy, Popeye The Pilot, Lithographed Tin, Windup, Marx, 1930s, 8 1/2 In. 154.00
Toy, Popeye The Pilot, Tin, Windup, Marx, 1940, 7 In. .... 630.00 To 925.00
Toy, Popeye The Sailor, Hoge 2200.00
Toy, Ramp Walker, Hands On Sides, 1930's, 6 In. 150.00
Toy, Ramp Walker, Pushing Can of Spinach, Late 1950s .... 40.00 To 59.00
Toy, Ramp Walker, Wimpy, Hamburger In Hand, 1935, 6 In. 185.00
Toy, Tank, Clockwork, Multicolored Lithographed Tin, Linemar, 3 3/4 In. 255.00
Toy, Turnover Tank, Tin, Windup, Linemar, 4 In. 415.00
Toy, Windup, Tin, Marx, 9 In. 525.00
Tray, Serving, TV, Folding Legs 14.00
Tugboat, Corgi Jr., No Decal 9.00

PORCELAIN factories that are well known are listed in this book under the factory name. This category lists pieces made by the less well-known factories.

Biscuit Jar, Roses, Floral, Children With Tops, Japan, 1875 .... 135.00
Blanc De Chine, Figurine, Man Holding Staff, Hat Over Back, Signed, 8 In. 65.00
Bowl, Applied Flowers & 4 Cupids, Sitzendorf, c.1887, 12 1/2 In. 550.00
Bowl, Black & White Blossoms, Red Ground, Oriental, 10 In. 95.00
Bowl, Blue, White, Shallow, China, 4 1/4 In. 25.00
Bowl, Centerpiece, Applied Flowers, Continental, Blue Mark, 6 1/2 In. 440.00
Bowl, Crackle Glaze, Gray, Rose-Pink Spirals, J. Constantinidis, 7 1/4 In. 555.00
Bowl, Flower, Scenes of Lovers, Panels of Flowers, Germany, 3 x 8 1/2 In. 88.00
Bowl, Hand Painted Yellow Roses, Pearlized Ground, Imperial 45.00
Bowl, Lace Sides, Blue & White, Early 1800s, China 135.00
Bowl, Polychrome Floral Design, Birds, Red Ground, Oriental, 4 3/8 In. 85.00
Bowl, Polychrome Floral Enameled, Lion of Judea Center, 4 1/2 In. 165.00
Bowl, Putti Supporting Scalloped Form, Floral Interior, Sitzendorf, 13 3/4 In. 450.00
Bowl, Shape of Viking Ship, Norway, 5 In. 83.00
Box, Dresser, Cover, Ornate Florals, Beige 10.00
Box, Jewelry, Hinged Lid, Victorian Man & Woman Transfer, Kalk Co., 1875 .... 115.00
Box, Polychrome Floral, Gilded Brass Fittings, 2 3/8 In. 65.00
Box, Portrait Transfer, Opaque White, 4 1/2 In. 20.00
Cache Pot, Transfer, Portrait, French Noblewoman, 8 In., Pair 385.00
Cat, White, Black Splotches, Fornasetti, Italy, 4 3/4 In. ....*Illus* 275.00
Centerpiece, Openwork Basket, Satyr Faces, Blue Mark, 14 In. 358.00

Porcelain, Cat, White, Black Splotches,
Fornasetti, Italy, 4 3/4 In.

Porcelain, Dish, Bird Shape, Ivory,
Turquoise, Holt Howard, 1959, 8 In.

Charger, Center Bird In Flight, Daises, Garden, Blue & White, c.1740, 15 1/2 In. ... 770.00
Charger, Ming Style Scrolling Flowers, Blue & White, 15 1/2 In. 600.00
Coffeepot, Baluster Form, Camel's Head Spout 187.00
Compote, Man & Woman, Basket of Flowers, Sitzendorf 825.00
Compote, Man Leaning On Tree–Trunk Standard, Floral & Vine Design, 8 In. 220.00
Crocus Pot, Hexagonal, Blue & White, China 82.50
Cup, Man & Woman, Separated By Sayings, Bell Shape, 1830, China 55.00
Dachshund, Sitting, Pieffer, Germany, 6 1/2 x 7 In. 85.00
Dish, Bird Shape, Ivory, Turquoise, Holt Howard, 1959, 8 In. ....*Illus* 35.00
Dish, Pickle, Leaf Shape, Floral Spray, Longton Hall, c.1755, 4 3/8 In., Pair 2200.00
Dish, Sweetmeat, Triple–Shell, Blue & White, Bow, c.1765, 7 1/4 In. 880.00
Ewer, Victorian Portrait, Gold Trim, E. S. Prov. Saxe, 18 3/4 In., Pair ....*Illus* 2300.00
Figurine, 3 Gamblers, Ludwigsburg, c.1766, 2 3/4 In. 3575.00
Figurine, Cat, Cream Colored, Brown Streaks, Foley Pottery, c.1790 .... 1295.00
Figurine, Cherubs, Oval Base, Crossed Swords Mark, 4 3/4 In., Pair 1090.00
Figurine, Dancer, Young Man, Ludwigsburg, 1760–1765, 5 1/2 In, ... 2750.00
Figurine, Dancing Couple, Floral Coats, Girl, Tambourine, Sitzendorf, 10 In. 695.00
Figurine, Fernery, Boy, Dog On Lap, 9 x 19 In. 303.00
Figurine, Foo Dog, Blue, 1800s, 5 1/2 In., Pair 90.00
Figurine, God, Bow, c.1780, 9 In. ....*Illus* 1650.00
Figurine, Great Dane, Sitting, No. 1128, Dahl Jensen 175.00
Figurine, Kneeling Ballerina Looking Into Mirror, Dahl Jensen, No. 1224 .... 550.00
Figurine, Little Boy Pushing Wheelbarrow, Flowers, Sitzendorf, 7 In. 125.00
Figurine, Man, Dragon's Phoenix Birds On Blue Robe, Late 1800s, China, 17 In. 400.00
Figurine, Mermaid, Emerging From Pond, Bucket On Shoulder, Wahliss, 7 1/2 In. 550.00
Figurine, Monkey Band, Sitzendorf, 9 Piece 1495.00
Figurine, Pheasant, Perched On Tree Stump, Bow, c.1760, 6 1/4 In. 3025.00
Figurine, Rabbit, At Rest, Pastel Enameled, 3 1/4 In. 40.00
Figurine, Swan, White, Pink & Blue Flowers, Von Schierholz, 8 1/4 In. 115.00
Figurine, The Idyllic Musicians, Man & Woman, Bow, c.1765, 8 1/2 In. Pair 1210.00
Figurine, Victorian Woman, Basket In Hand, Red Jacket, Hat, Germany, 11 In. 135.00
Figurine, Woman, Classical Costume, Holding Staff, Marked, 16 In. 300.00
Figurine, Woman, Flowing Gown, Gold Shoes, Schaubach–Kunst, 9 1/2 In. 375.00
Figurine, Woman, Standing, Red & Green Robe, China, Late 1800s 125.00
Flowerpot, Colored Floral Arrangement, Bow, c.1765, 8 3/8 In. 550.00
Fruit Basket, Pedestal, Tucker 3750.00
Ginger Jar, Battle Scene, Enamel, Cobalt Border, Cover, 9 In. 690.00
Group, Old Friends, Musical Recital, Sitzendorf, A. Voight 2900.00
Jar, Apothecary, Gilt Design, c.1830, 12 In., Pair 825.00
Jar, Cover, Blue, White, 13 1/2 In. 385.00
Jar, Deep Blue & White, Wooden Cover, Khang–Shi, 1810, 9 1/4 In. 525.00
Jar, Flowers, White Reserves, Figures, Flowers, Birds, Gold Design, 31 In., Pair 148.00
Jar, Ginger, Exotic Birds, Pendant Foliage, Kurt Wendler, c.1920, 12 1/4 In. 1300.00
Jar, Polychrome Enameled, Oriental, 14 1/4 In. 75.00
Jar, Water, Black Lacquer Cover, Shishi & Floral Design, 6 1/2 In. 3575.00
Jardiniere, Blue & White, Oriental, 11 1/4 x 7 3/4 In. 93.00

Porcelain, Ewer, Victorian Portrait, Gold
Trim, E.S. Prov. Saxe, 18 3/4 In., Pair

Porcelain, Figurine, God,
Bow, c.1780, 9 In.

Porcelain, Plaque, Apollo, Feiger,
7 1/2 X 15 In.

Porcelain, Plate, Leaf, Caughley,
1790, 14 1/2 In.

◆ ◆

Figurines are often damaged.
Examine the fingers, toes, and
other protruding parts for damage or signs of repair.

◆ ◆

Jewel Box, Hinged Lid, Victorian Man & Woman Transfer Lid, Kalk Co., 1875	75.00
Mirror, Sitzendorf, 16 In.	500.00
Mug, Beer, Man Reading Newspaper, Cobalt Blue, Germany, 1800s, 4 1/2 In.	55.00
Mustard, Cover, Gilt Metal Mounted, Floral Sprays, 8 In.	275.00
Pitcher, Walker Shape, Gilt Design, Tucker, 1828	2000.00
Planter, Figural, Artist Holding Palette, Ch. Levy & Co., 1876	245.00
Plaque, Apollo, Feiger, 7 1/2 x 15 In. ....*Illus*	2750.00
Plaque, Girl, Barefoot, Birds On Branch, Frame, Gaumet, 6 1/2 x 9 1/2 In.	485.00
Plaque, Polychrome Enameled, Children At Play, 14 3/4 In.	22.00
Plaque, Woodlands Spirits, Dancing With Veil, E. Furot, 10 x 10 In.	275.00
Plaque, Young Gypsy Woman, Holding Mandolin, Frame, Oval, 8 In.	275.00
Plate, 8 Classical Scenes, Rose Border, Vienna Style, 10 1/2 In., 8 Piece	605.00
Plate, Couple & Child, Sitting On A Rock, Gold Ground, 1825–1830, 9 1/8 In.	3575.00
Plate, Couple Dancing, Tan Ground, Gilt Bands, 1825–1830, 9 In.	5225.00
Plate, Hand Painted Portraits, Louis Bonaparte, Caroline, France, 9 7/8 In., Pair	150.00
Plate, Leaf, Caughley, 1790, 14 1/2 In. ....*Illus*	300.00
Plate, Poppy Design, Red, 12 3/4 In.	35.00
Plate, Strawberry Leaf, Floral Bouquet, Longton Hall, c.1755, 9 1/8 In.	440.00
Platter, Peonies & Bamboo, Floral Border, China, 1860s, 13 3/4 x 10 1/2 In.	210.00
Salt Box, Wooden Lid, Peasant Couple Dancing, Germany	50.00
Spoon, Floral, White, Oriental, 1880s	6.00
Sugar Shaker, Metal Top, W & W Co., 6 In.	20.00
Sugar, Center Gilt Patera Pattern, Orange & Yellow Banding, England	120.00

♦ ♦

Don't put china with gold
designs in the dishwasher. The
gold will wash off.

♦ ♦

Porcelain, Vase, Woman, Swallows, Gold
Trim, 7 1/4 In.; Porcelain, Vase, Woman, With
Peacock, E.S. Prov. Saxe, 8 1/4 In.

Tankard, Blue Wildflower Design, England	209.00
Tea Bowl & Saucer, Floral Spray, Continental, 3 In.	275.00
Tray, Woman, Carrying Basket, Lozenge Shape, Ludwigsburg, c.1770, 13 3/4 In.	4400.00
Umbrella Stand, Hundred Treasure Design, Turquoise Ground, China, 24 In.	770.00
Urn, Classical Transfer Design, Continental, 12 In., Pair	385.00
Urn, Cover, Figures & Encrusted Flowers, Sitzendorf, 27 In., Pair	1750.00
Urn, Floral Design, Green & Gold, Pair, 7 In.	550.00
Urn, Hand Painted, Floral Design, Continental, 13 In.	468.00
Urn, Palace, Lake Scene 1 Side, Pond & Mill Other, Pelican Handles, 41 In.	1870.00
Vase, Scrolling Flowers, Chinese Blue & White, 19th Century, 16 In., Pair	275.00
Vase, 3 Winged Cherubs, Eggs On Backs, Sitzendorf, 7 1/4 In.	275.00
Vase, Amphora Form, Landscape & Vignettes of Lovers, 11 In., Pair	187.00
Vase, Applied Flowers & Leaves, 40 In., Pair	7500.00
Vase, Bottle Shape, Household Objects, Stylized Bands, Blue & White, 12 In.	825.00
Vase, Bud, Blue Flower & Vines, Lemon Ground, Rope Handles, China, 3 3/4 In.	110.00
Vase, Fish & Seaweed, Green Ground, Oriental, 21 1/2 In.	38.00
Vase, Man & Woman Playing Musical Instruments, Sitzendorf, 12 In.	225.00
Vase, Polychrome Floral Design, Foo Dogs, Butterflies, Gilt, 6 5/8 In., Pair	170.00
Vase, Potpourri, Flower Encrusted, Longton Hall, c.1755, 12 1/4 In.	2200.00
Vase, Satyr Head Mounts, Classical Transfer Scenes, 10 1/2 In., Pair	385.00
Vase, Scene of Victorian Life, Floral Panel, 9 In., Pair	192.00
Vase, Spherical Form, White Crystalline Glaze, Circular Footed Base, 5 In.	5500.00
Vase, Warrior Reliefs, Floral, Ruffled, China, 24 In.	110.00
Vase, Woman, Swallows, Gold Rim, 7 1/4 In. ....*Illus*	750.00
Vase, Woman, With Peacock, E. S. Prov Saxe, 8 1/4 In. ....*Illus*	525.00
Wig Stand, Incised Scenes of Sages Examining Scroll, China, 11 1/4 In.	145.00
Window Box, Maiden & Cupid, Art Nouveau, Incised 1006, France, 12 In.	800.00

POSTCARDS were first legally permitted in Austria on October 1, 1869.
The United States passed postal regulations allowing the card in 1872.
Most of the picture postcards collected today date after 1910. The amount
of postage can help to date a card. The rates are: 1872 (1 cent), 1917 (2
cents), 1919 (1 cent), 1925 (2 cents), 1928 (1 cent), 1952 (2 cents), 1959 (3
cents), 1963 (4 cents), 1968 (5 cents), 1973 (8 cents), 1975 (7 cents), 1976
(9 cents), 1978 (10 cents), 1981 (12 cents), 1981 (13 cents), 1985 (14
cents), 1988 (15 cents), 1991 (19 cents).

Airship Meet At Ashbury Park, Wilbur Wright & Walter Brookins	50.00
Aviation Meet, Chicago, Planes Over Lakefront, 1911, 7 3/4 x 20 3/4 In.	200.00
Balloon Races At Speedway, Indianapolis, 1920s, Majestic Set, No. 90	15.00
Bank of London, Carriage In Front With Heinz 57 Advertising, Color, c.1910	5.00
Baseball Scene, Arrived Safely, Eric Ericson	6.00
Baseball, Mickey Mantle, Black & White, 1956	25.00
Beauty In Hammock, Art Nouveau	12.00
Belief Me, Jewish Theme, Unused, 1906	25.00
Best Wishes For A Joyful Thanksgiving, Postmarked, 1918	10.00
Blackfeet Burning The Crow Buffalo Range, Signed C. M. Russell	30.00

Blacks, Picking Onions, 1913	9.00
Bonzo, Googly Eyes, 1930s	28.00
Bourbon School, Beech Grove, Indiana, 1909	12.50
Cape Cod Cranberry Industry, Scooper & Scoop, 1911	60.00
Champion Basketball Team, Parkersburg, W. Virginia, 1907	16.00
Christmas, Signed Enrico Caruso, 1915	350.00
Christmas, Squeaks, Amer. National Red Cross Sticker, 1908	75.00
Colorado, I Can't Bear To Leave, Berthold, Leather, Bear Fur, 1907	15.00
Columbian Expo, The Woman's Building, Colored, Unused	20.00
Comic, Black Man, Pulling Another's Tooth With Pulley, 1906	27.50
Comic, Black Man, Strapped To Chair, Having Tooth Pulled, 1910	22.50
Comic, Ceaseless Jaw of Mother-In-Law, Fur Muff, Animal Head, 1907	20.00
Comic, Man, Exaggerated Thick Lips, Drunk, With Bottle, Unused, 1906	27.50
Confectionery Parlor Interior, Los Angeles, Calif., Color, 1915	5.00
Cunard White Star, Leaving N.Y. Harbor, K. Shoesmith Painting, 1937	7.50
Darkies Kissing, Mailed To Indian Territory, Leather, 1907	25.00
Dutch Children Within A Heart, Silk	20.00
Eastern, Silversleeper, Relaxation Aloft, Black & White	20.00
Enrico Caruso, Memorial	15.00
Everything Comes To Him Who Waits, Leather, 1907	3.00
Fat Albert, Freak, Fat Man, Weighs 872 Lb., Autograph, 1970s	10.00
Fort Sutter, Sacramento, Calif., Leather, Unused, 1907	5.50
Golf, Hobo To Hit Golf Ball, Hobo Series No. 2, Leather, Unused, 1908	10.00
Grangeville Idaho, Main Street Scene, Photograph, 1908	15.00
Greetings From Punxsutawney, Penna., Home of The Ground-Hog	35.00
Gui De Paris, Signed Raphael Kirchner, Unused	55.00
Halloween, Cauldron, John Winsch, 1914	40.00
Halloween, Woman, Red Dress, 1911	55.00
Hamburg-Amerika Line, Statue of Liberty Ground, 1906	25.00
His Master's Voice, Maarek Weber, Phonograph Dealer, Danish	50.00
Hochschild, Kohn & Co., Baltimore's Best Store, 1908	35.00
Hold To Light, Brooklyn & Williamsburg Bridges	25.00
Hold To Light, Die Cut, Santa Beside Fire With Children, Trim & Fire Light Up	150.00
Hold To Light, New Year, Stars & Year 1909	30.00
Hold To Light, Santa Claus, Children Around Christmas Tree	75.00
Hold To Light, Shooting The Chutes, Coney Island, N.Y.	30.00
Hold To Light, South Station, Boston, Mass.	40.00
Honolulu Harbor, Panoramic View, Folder Type, Postmark 1908	40.00
Honor of Roosevelt As Peace Maker In Russo-Japanese War, France	145.00
Indy Speedway, Track With Trees In Infield, Aerial View, 1935	10.00
International Dog Expo, Stuttgart, Germany, 1896	50.00
Jamestown Exposition, 1907, 27 Piece	135.00
Jewish New Year, 21 Piece	200.00
Josephine Baker, Photograph, Studio Maz, Paris	125.00
Kazenjammer Kids, 1906, 3 Piece	45.00
Kilaurea Crater, Lava Flow, Postmarked Aug. 19, 1904	60.00
Kokomo, Ind. Flood, Photograph, Postmarked 1908	7.00
Lady, With A Pen, Art Nouveau, A. Mucha	125.00
Larkin Soap Company Factory, Postmarked 1911	13.00
Leap Year, 'Tis Sweet To Think, 'Tis Nine-Ten Twelve, Unused, 1911	10.00
Lister Park, Bradford, England, Woven Silk	40.00
Little Boy, Fireman's Costume, Twelve Trees, c.1920	10.00
Lumberjacks, Next To Felled Tree, Northern Mich., Black & White, Feb. 1909	6.00
Lusitania, Dining Salon, Photograph, 1913	35.00
Main Street Bridge, Beech Grove, Indiana	12.50
Main Street, Kewanna, Indiana	35.00
Main Street, Kouts, Indiana	6.50
Man, In Uniform, Arms, Draped Flag, Earl Chambers, 1917-1918	17.50
Marilyn Monroe In Bus Stop, French Version	15.00
Marilyn Monroe, 1950s	4.00
Marilyn Monroe, Bathing Beauty, Color	1.00
Mechanical, Best Wishes, Rotate Wheel, Girl's Bouquet & Arms Move	65.00
Mechanical, Turn Dials & Feather Colors Change, Unused	25.00

Mermaid With Seahorse, Samuel Schmucker, Detroit Publishing Co., 1907 .... 150.00
Metal Filing Cabinet, S. M. Silver, San Francisco, 1920s, 4 1/2 x 7 In. 5.00
Miami Biltmore Hotel & Golf Course, Coral Gables, Fl., Leather, 1933 .... 5.00
Mishawaka, Ind., Flood, Photograph, Postmarked 1908 .... 10.00
Monkees Fan Club, Group Photograph, 1966, 5 1/2 x 8 In. 5.00
Moxie Horsemobile, Horse & Man In Car, Copyright 1916 .... 137.50
My Valentine Think of Me, Boy Watching Girls With Letter, Image On Silver 18.00
Nations, State & City Welcome The Wright Brothers, Dayton, 1909 .... 75.00
Oculist, Boy, Getting Glasses, Norman Rockwell, 1956 .... 18.00
Ornate Entrance To Riverside Park, Nebraska, Photograph, Neligh, 1908 .... 15.00
Ostende Tennis Courts, Sepia, Leather, Unused, 1914 .... 7.50
Our President, Franklin D. Roosevelt, 1933 .... 25.00
Overland Auto Works, Toledo., Ohio, Bird's-Eye View, 1917 .... 12.00
Paper Doll, Fairy Tale Outfit, 1913 .... 125.00
Pasadena Tournament of Roses, Foldout, 1929 .... 25.00
Pres. Roosevelt, Dedication of Great Smoky Mountain Natl. Park 12.00
Puzzle Series No. 2, The Dachshund, Unused, 4 Piece 175.00
Queen Mary, Year It Arrived In Long Beach, Calif., Color, 1970 .... 2.50
Ringling Bros., Florida, Foldout, 1942 .... 12.00
Ringling Bros., Performing Elephants, Photograph 22.00
Sachsenhausen Concentration Camp, Censor Marks 75.00
Santa Claus, In Biplane, Dropping Toys 4.00
Santa Claus, Red Robe, With Toys 15.00
Seattle, Sunset On Puget Sound, Leather, 1909 .... 5.50
Smiling Black Boy, Picking Cotton, Surrounded By White Cotton, 1950 .... 3.50
Southern Negro Cabin, Beaumont, Texas, 1916 .... 22.50
Speedy Alka-Seltzer 10.00
SS Aleutian, Photograph, 1930, Unused 20.00
SS Starr, Photograph, Dated May 4, 1929, Unused 25.00
Street Scene, Pine Bluff, Arkansas, Many Automobiles, Black & White, 1908 .... 8.50
Swift & Co., 4 Horse Team, Chicago, 1902 .... 20.00
The Golliwog, In Overalls, With Paintbrush 40.00
Tournament of Roses Parade, Padadena, Ohio Presidents Float, Leather, 1908 ...... 11.00
Tournament of Roses, Shirley Temple As Grand Marshall, Foldout, 1939, ... 8.00
Tours of The World By Woman's Home Journal, Early 1900s, Set of 50 .... 30.00
Train Depot, Monroe, Mich., Photograph, 1910 .... 12.00
Uncle Sam Thanksgiving Greetings, Uncle Sam, Turkey, Embossed, Color, 1911 ... 18.00
United Nations Day, Special Stamps, Vienna Cancels, 1957 .... 25.00
US Lines, SS Manhattan, Photograph, Sea View, Unused, 1948-1950 .... 5.00
Valentine, To My Darling, Germany, 1907, Unused 5.50
Washington, Taking Oath of Office, First President, Postmarked 1909 .... 7.50
Winter Cruise, Gripsholms, Swedish Ship, Mailed On Board Post Office, 1932 .... 30.00
Winter Sports, Sun Valley, Idaho, Challenger Inn, 1938, 3 1/2 In. 7.50
Woman, Holding Golf Bag & Club, Schlesinger Bros., Leather, 1911 .... 11.00
Zeppelin, Flying Over City Hall Park, New York City 10.00

POSTERS have informed the public about news and entertainment events
since ancient times. Nineteenth-century advertising or theatrical posters
and twentieth-century movie and war posters are of special interest today.
The price is determined by the artist, the condition, and the rarity. Other
posters may be listed under Political and World War I and II.

7-Up, George Brett, 19 x 25 In. 10.00
A Connecticut Yankee, Mark Twin Fantasy Film, Will Rogers, 1931, 41 x 28 In. ... 990.00
A Night In Casablanca, Marx Brothers, 1946, 27 In. Each, 3 Sheets 1540.00
A Sainted Devil, Rudolph Valentino, Paramount, Linen Backed, 1924, 41 x 27 In. ... 8250.00
All American Girl Is Home-Maker, Roy Williams, 1924, 28 x 17 In. 50.00
An Ace & A Joker, Silent Animated Cartoon, 1919, 41 & 27 In. 4840.00
Angel & The Badman, John Wayne, Color, Dated 1959, 41 x 27 In. 40.00
Back Em Up! Buy Extra Bonds, Official U.S. Treasury, 20 x 27 In. 50.00
Barbie Doll Sewing Pattern, Mattel, 1961 .... 25.00
Barnum & Bailey, Madison Square Garden Circus, The Sisters LaRague, 36 x 25 In. 1760.00
Beau Geste, Paramount, Linen Backed, 1939, 41 x 27 In. 3850.00
Beau Hunks, Laurel & Hardy, 1923 .... 9900.00

Black Panther Firecrackers 25.00
Blond Venus, Marlene Dietrich, Paramount, 1932, 41 x 27 In. 2750.00
Bobino–Josephine, Ventouillac, c.1960, 31 x 46 In. 200.00
Bottoms Up, Fox, Linen Backed, 41 x 27 In. 550.00
Bruce Springsteen, 1970s, 23 x 36 In. 35.00
Buffalo Bill's Wild West, Sells Floto Circus, 41 x 27 In. 2090.00
Bus Stop, Movie, Marilyn Monroe, 27 In. 275.00
Cabin In The Sky, MGM, 1943, 41 x 27 In. 3850.00
Calcium, Phosphorus & Vitamin D For Strong Bones, Sunblon, 1940, 24 x 22 In. 35.00
Camp Dog, Cartoon Movie, Pluto & Coyotes, 1950, 41 x 27 In. 660.00
Carrie, Stephen King Movie, 1976, 27 x 41 In. 20.00
Carter The Great, 1935, 14 x 22 In. 95.00
Charlie Chan's Courage, Warner Oland, 20th Century Fox, 1934, 41 x 27 In. 1100.00
Circus Girl, Movie, 1956, 27 In. 45.00
Circus, Christy Bros. Wild Animal Show, 42 x 28 In. 495.00
Clausen Beer, Tutonian King Drinking Flagon of Beer, 22 x 17 3/4 In. 220.00
Corn Is Green, Bette Davis, 1945, 41 x 27 In. 137.50
Crocko–Greatest Freak Alive, Crocodile Body, Girl's Head, 1940s, 22 In. 250.00
Dr. Jekyll & Mr. Hyde, Fredric March, 1913, 27 In. 7700.00
Fleets In, Movie, Clara Bow, Paramount, 1928, 36 x 14 In. 935.00
Flossie De Vere and Her Parisian Flappers, Theater, Burlesques, 27 x 36 In. 38.00
Giant, James Dean Image, Re–Release of Film, 1982, 41 x 27 In. 25.00
Gondoliers, Gilbert & Sullivan, c.1917, 30 x 20 In. 75.00
Gone With The Wind, Movie, Clark Gable, Vivien Leigh, Folded, 1961 .... 275.00
Guion Line, Fastest Steamer Afloat, Paper, 31 x 21 In. 110.00
Happy Thought Tobacco, 27 In. 500.00
Harley–Davidson, Man On Motorcycle, 1940, 27 In. 495.00
Harper's February, Edward Penfield, 1900, Frame, 27 In. 302.00
Health Habits, National Child Welfare Assn., Roy Williams, 1920, 28 x 17 In. 24.00
Iron Mask, Douglas Fairbanks, United Artists, 36 x 14 In. 1100.00
It Came From Outer Space, Ray Bradbury, 1953, 36 x 14 In. 165.00
Jim Thorpe All American, Movie, 27 In. 165.00
Juarez, Warner Brothers, Linen Backed, 1939, 41 x 27 In. 1320.00
Jules Levy Cornet Performance, Paper, 21 x 36 In. 242.00
Last of The Mohicans, Reliance, 1936, 41 x 27 In. 550.00
Little Rascals, Factory Folds, 41 x 27 In. 45.00
Littlest Rebel, Fox, 1935, 41 x 27 In. 3850.00
Maine State Fair, Scene of Fair, 14 Trotting & Pacing Races, 1909 .... 1400.00
Maltese Falcon, Movie, Humphrey Bogart, 1941 .... 6050.00
Mikado, Gilbert & Sullivan, 20 x 30 In. 280.00
Mississippi, Bing Crosby, Paramount, 1935, 41 x 27 In. 2750.00
Moon Over Miami, Don Ameche, Betty Grable, 1941, 27 In. 7975.00
Mother & The Law, D. W. Griffith, 1919, Linen Backed, 41 x 27 In. 4400.00
Mummy Exhibit, Hazel Ferris Muffled Body, 1958, 12 x 18 In. 37.50
My Little Chickadee, Universal Studios, 1939, 41 x 27 In. 4125.00
Mysterians, Color, Monsters & Robots, RKO, Dated 1959, 27 In. 65.00
Nanook of The North, Pathe, Linen Backed, 1921, 41 x 27 In. 6050.00
Napoleon Solo, Man From U. N. C. L. E., Photograph, 1965, 24 x 36 In. 25.00
New York, Movie, Paramount, Linen Backed, 1927, 41 x 27 In. 1100.00
Niagara, Movie, Marilyn Monroe, 1953, 27 In. 1045.00
Office of War Information, UN Nations Fight For Freedom, 21 x 28 In. 25.00
Outlaw, Howard Hughes, 1942, 41 x 27 In. 8800.00
P. T. Barnum's, Various People & Circus Animals, 21 1/2 x 14 1/2 In. 120.00
Parker's Famous Military Band Organ, 27 1/2 x 20 1/2 In. 247.00
Peak of Health Means Beauty, Strength, Success, Woman, 1926, 14 x 23 In. 35.00
Peter's, Victor Shotgun Shells, Die Cut Cardboard, 26 x 20 In. 330.00
Phantom of The Opera, Universal, 1925, 11 x 14 In. 1540.00
Pirates of Penzance, Gilbert & Sullivan, 20 x 30 In. 316.00
Popy Bicycle Works, Connecticut, 53 x 29 In. 1760.00
Radio City Revels, RKO, Musical, 1938 .... 440.00
Randy Rides Again, Lone Star Productions, 1934, 41 x 27 In. 3575.00
Roberta, Irene Dunne, RKO, Linen Backed, 1935, 22 x 28 In. 1760.00
Rocky Horror Show, Original United States Stage Production, 1974, 22 x 14 In. 95.00

Pottery, Bowl, Cream Volcanic Glaze, Natzler,
6 1/2 In.; Pottery, Bowl, Cobalt To Blue
Green, Beatrice Wood, 5 1/4 X 8 3/4 In.;

Rolling Stones American Tour, 1972, 38 x 25 In.	75.00
Romane & Riches, Cary Grant, Grand National, 1937, 41 x 27 In.	660.00
Sarah Bernhardt, Mucha, Frame, 1897, 23 x 68 In.	8750.00
Searchers, Movie, John Wayne	690.00
Seven Year Itch, Movie, Marilyn Monroe, 1955, 22 In.	935.00
Some Like It Hot, United Artists, 1959, 41 x 27 In.	880.00
Sunset Boulevard, Paramount, 1950, Linen Backed, 22 x 28 In.	990.00
Swiss Family Robinson, Movie, Terrytoon Mighty Mouse, 1947, 41 x 27 In.	715.00
Tarzan & His Mate, Johnny Weissmuller, 1934, 27 In.	6050.00
Thundercloud, In Ghost Riders of The West, Robert Kent, Dated 1954, 41 x 27 In.	40.00
Till We Meet Again, 1942, 14 x 22 In.	17.50
Twinkle Toes, Colleen Moore, First National Picture, 1926, 41 x 27 In.	495.00
U.S. Department of Justice, Wanted, Bonnie & Clyde, John Dillinger, 1934	395.00
United States Marines, Lyendecker	75.00
Virginian, 1929	9450.00
Virginian, Paramount, Gary Cooper, Linen Backed, 1929, 41 x 27 In.	9350.00
Wings, Movie, Paramount, 1927, 41 x 27 In.	4950.00
Yellow Kid, George B. Luk, Matted, 1897, 18 x 12 In.	770.00
Yellow Kid, R. F. Outcault, Frame, 1896, 19 x 14 In.	3850.00
Yeoman of The Guard, Gilbert & Sullivan, 20 x 30 In.	350.00

POTTERY and porcelain are different. Pottery is opaque; you can't see through it. Porcelain is translucent. If you hold a porcelain dish in front of a strong light you will see the light through the dish. Porcelain is colder to the touch. Pottery is softer and easier to break and will stain more easily because it is porous. Porcelain is thinner, lighter, and more durable. Majolica, faience, and stoneware are all pottery. Additional pieces of pottery are listed in this book in the Art Pottery category and under the factory name.

Ashtray, Cowboy Hat, Dickota	15.00
Bookends, Frog, Catalina Pottery	2000.00
Bookends, Monk, Catalina Pottery	1000.00
Bowl, Buff Colored Fish, Red Clay, Scheier, 5 3/4 x 5 In.	440.00
Bowl, Cobalt To Blue Green, Beatrice Wood, 5 1/4 x 8 3/4 In. ....*Illus*	2400.00
Bowl, Cream Volcanic Glaze, Natzler, 6 1/2 In. ....*Illus*	1650.00
Bowl, Fish, Black Stylized Fish, Blue Ground, Brown Interior, 4 1/4 In.	385.00
Bowl, Green & Brown Drip Glaze, Merritt Island, 6 1/2 In.	115.00
Bowl, Nested, Pastel, Metlox, 4 Piece	75.00
Bowl, Polished Red, Worn Design, Open Rope Twist Handles, 4 In.	33.00
Bowl, Turquoise Blue, Flared, Glazed, Round, Incised Mark, 2 1/2 In.	440.00

Pottery, Figurine, Boy & Girl,
T. Winter, 5 1/2 In.

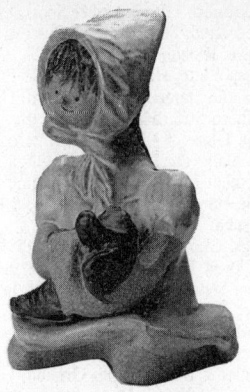

Pottery, Figurine, Poppy,
Poppytails, 6 1/2 In.

Pottery, Pitcher, Bird
Shape, Green, Stewart
McCullock, 6 1/4 In.

Box, Cover, Japanese Beetle, Hand Painted	70.00
Box, Cubist Design, Red, Yellow & Blue, Susie Cooper	875.00
Bust, George Washington, England, 19th Century, 8 In.	660.00
Charger, Central Geometric Panels, Glazed Mauve, Brown, 14 1/2 In.	880.00
Churn, Wooden Lid, Red Clay, Green Ash Glaze, 16 1/2 In.	60.00
Console Set, Oriental Figure, Double Candlesticks, Heidi Schoop, 3 Piece	150.00
Crock, Red Clay, Greenish Glaze, Amber Spots, Brown Flecks, 11 1/4 In.	150.00
Cuspidor, Brown, Bennington Style, Glazed	10.00
Decanter, Robj, Scotsman, 11 In.	350.00
Desk Set, Blue & White	20.00
Figurine, Boxer, Mortens Studio, 6 1/2 x 7 In.	65.00
Figurine, Boy & Girl, T. Winter, 5 1/2 In. ....*Illus*	550.00
Figurine, Crap Shooter, Black, Brayton Laguna	65.00
Figurine, Dutch Boy, Holding Duck, Dated 1895, Joncery, 15 1/2 In.	350.00
Figurine, Goat, Dickota	60.00
Figurine, Jazz Band, Brayton Laguna, 4 Piece	1250.00
Figurine, Jazz Combo Drummer, Black, West Coast Pottery	140.00
Figurine, Lion, Standing, Mortens Studio, 12 In.	165.00
Figurine, Man & Woman, In Bed Clothes, Brayton Laguna, 9 In.	45.00
Figurine, Mary & Her Little Lamb, Glossy White, WPA, 7 In.	200.00
Figurine, Oriental Figures, Pair	195.00
Figurine, Owl, Brayton Laguna, Pair	48.00
Figurine, Peter Peter Pumpkin Eater, WPA	400.00
Figurine, Polar Bear, WPA	250.00
Figurine, Poppy, Poppytails, 6 1/2 In. ....*Illus*	45.00
Figurine, Victoria Girl, Orchid Trim, Modelini, California	25.00
Figurine, White, Gold & Green, Hedi Schoop, 12 In., Pair	100.00
Figurine, Wolf, WPA	190.00
Flower Holder, Blue Girl, Nancy & Walter Wilson, 10 In.	25.00
Flower Holder, Dutch Girl, Heidi Schoop, 10 1/2 In.	35.00
Flowerpot, Saucer, 2 Tone Brown, Finger Crimp Lip, Unglazed, 4 7/8 In.	190.00
Flowerpot, Yellow & Green Design, 5 1/2 In.	579.00
Foot Warmer, Carriage, Brown Glazed	150.00
Humidor, Dog, Brown Glass Eyes, Ashtray, Match Holder, Rottmeir, 1900, 3 Piece	95.00
Incense Burner, Dickota	50.00
Jar, Dark Brown, 1 Pt.	12.00
Jar, Gray, 1/2 Gal.	10.00
Jar, Olive, Yellow Glazed Interior, 29 In.	412.50
Jar, Red Clay, Greenish Glaze, Amber Spots, 6 3/4 In.	205.00
Jar, Red Clay, Greenish Glaze, Amber Spots, Brown Flecks, Wooden Stopper, 6 In.	50.00

Jar, Reddish Bluff Clay, Greenish Glaze, Amber Spots, 8 In. 130.00
Jug, Brown Glazed, Tooled Band, Strap Handle, Boscowin, 10 In. 71.00
Jug, Brown, White, Buckeye, Ribbon Stamp 175.00
Jug, Dark Ash Glaze, Blue, White, Highlights, Double Ear Handles, 18 In. 88.00
Jug, Green Ash Glaze, Handle Stamped JHL, Craford, Ga., 14 In. 85.00
Jug, Green Ash Glaze, Ribbed Strap Handle, 10 1/2 In. 94.00
Jug, Grotesque, Green Ash Glaze, 8 3/4 In. ....880.00 To 1045.00
Jug, Weeks Co., Akron, 1 Gall. 20.00
Keg, Banet, On Stand, German Man & Monk, Drinking, Barrel, Signed, 11 1/2 In. 125.00
Mug, Erotica, Barrel, Nude Handles In Various Poses, 5 Piece 48.00
Mug, Indian, Goodwin, Usona 75.00
Ornament, Roof, Foo Dogs, Glazed, Wooden Stand, 15 1/2 In., Pair 165.00
Pitcher, Beehive, Bee & Clover, Dallas Pottery, Japan 35.00
Pitcher, Bird Shape, Green, Stewart McCullock, 6 1/4 In. ....*Illus* 20.00
Pitcher, Multicolored Blue, T. S. Famester, England 45.00
Pitcher, Pilgrim Jug, Brown Transfer, Polychrome Enameling, 9 1/2 In. 115.00
Pitcher, The Source, Picasso, 11 In. 9900.00
Plaque, Child's Head, Leaves & Berries, Gold Ground, Germany, 11 In., Pair 495.00
Plaque, Jester, Multicolored, On Wood, Harris Strong, 10 x 14 In. 525.00
Plate, Catskill Moss, Fairmount Gardens, Ridgways, 9 1/4 In. 94.00
Plate, French Peasant, Blue Ridge 55.00
Plate, San Juan Mission, Catalina Pottery, 9 In. 25.00
Plate, Undersea Garden, Catalina Pottery, 14 In. 2000.00
Platter, Rooster, Catalina Pottery, 16 x 12 In. 60.00
Sandwich Set, Calla Lilies, Yellow, Orange, Green Border, Susie Cooper 1200.00
Sugar & Creamer, WPA 40.00
Sugar, Cover, Floral, Carter Stable Adams Ltd., Poole 525.00
Tankard Set, Grapes & Leaf Design, Glazed, 5 Piece 70.00
Tankard Set, Indian Portrait, Brown Glaze, Goodwin Pottery, 5 Piece 850.00
Tea Set, Lupine Pattern, Yellow & Orange Flowers, Susie Cooper, 5 Piece 775.00
Teapot, Basalt, Reeded Design, Scrolling Handle, 18th Century, 9 1/4 In. 110.00
Teapot, K'Ang Hsi, Ceramic, 1662-1732 .... 950.00
Teapot, Katrina, Treasure Craft 35.00
Teapot, Tomato, Red Pantry Pride 37.00
Teapot, Trivet, Chintz, Royal Winton 295.00
Umbrella Stand, Yellow, Flower Design Rim, Early 20th Century 50.00
Vase, Handles, Graduated, Mottled Matte Green Glaze, Quaker Road, 7 1/4 x 5 In. 27.50
Vase, Lobular, Light Orange Glaze, Meric Art Ware 20.00
Vase, 4 Nudes, Blue, Pillin, 8 In. 595.00
Vase, Blue, Zark, 7 1/2 In. 325.00
Vase, Chinese Men, Brown, Signed K, Japan 75.00
Vase, Dutch Scene, Frank Beardmore & Co., Sutherland Art Ware, 12 In. 400.00
Vase, Floral, Carter Stabler Adams Ltd., Poole 220.00
Vase, Flow, Ruffled, Blue Ridge, Tall 67.00
Vase, Foliage, Gray Mushroom, Speckled, St. Ives, B. Leach, 7 In. 1485.00
Vase, Half-Man Half-Fish Figures, Brown Over Blue, Scheier, 8 3/4 In. 550.00
Vase, Iridescent Pink & Purple Crackle, 3 Handles, Merrimac, 3 1/2 In. 385.00
Vase, Iron-Brown Glaze Under Gray-Blue, St. Ives, T. Matsubayashi, 3 3/4 In. 165.00
Vase, Large Multi-Colored Flowers, Handle, Blue Ridge 68.00
Vase, Matte Blue Glaze, Flared, 2 Handles, Catalina, 15 1/2 x 10 In. 193.00
Vase, Matte Golden Green, Tony Lang, Rushmore, 6 1/2 In. 120.00
Vase, Meandering Squeeze Bag Ornament, Brown, Squatty, Vance Faience Co. 265.00
Vase, Moon, John Lewis, 6 In. 850.00
Vase, Nude, Carl Romanelli 95.00
Vase, Ohio Statehood, Gunmetal, 2 Handles, Footed, 1903, Florentine Pottery 75.00
Vase, Orange Glaze, Fluted, Catalina, 13 1/2 x 9 3/4 In. 330.00
Vase, Orange, Brown, Cylindrical, Natzler, 6 1/2 x 3 1/2 In. 1200.00
Vase, Orange, Brown, Natzler, 6 1/2 In. 1200.00
Vase, Pitted Glaze, Cream-White, Mottled, Dame Lucie Rie, C. 1960, 5 1/4 In. 930.00
Vase, Sgraffito Designs, Foliage, Birds, Grayish Clay, White Slip, 13 In. 150.00
Vase, Stylized Black & White, California Original Label 32.00
Vase, Swastika, Gold, White & Green Coralene, Flask Shape, Keramos, 12 In. 130.00
Vase, Yellow Squeeze Bag Line Design, Rust Brown, Vance Avon, 5 In. 290.00

Pressed glass,   Pressed glass,   Pressed glass,   Pressed glass,
     Actress   Amberette   Ashburton   Artichoke, frosted

Vase, Yellow–Green Thick Matte Glaze, Rolled Rim, Speckles, St. Ives, 13 1/2 In.   2790.00
Wall Pocket, Gray Swirl, West Coast Pottery, Large 10.00

POWDER FLASKS AND POWDER HORNS were made to hold the
gunpowder used in antique firearms. The early examples were made of
horn or wood; later ones were of copper or brass.

POWDER FLASK, Indian Rifle, Tin, 1800s, Original Label 25.00
  Running Rabbit, Brass 32.00
  Shell Design, Brass, Antique Yellow 35.00
POWDER HORN, Carved, 1749, Abner Whitcome 1100.00
  Eagle & Shield, Carved, Engraved, 8 In. 135.00
  Engraved Dove, A. A. Clark, & Other Is Liberty, 18th Century, 18 In., Pair 248.00
  Engraved Pictures, Verse, Mottoes, Dated April 2nd 1829, 15 In. 275.00
  Engraved, Lt. Oscar Wyche, 12th Infantry, 1847 ....   247.00
  Fort Hampton & Sloop Independence, D. St. John, 1813–1814 ....   880.00
  Lieut. Michah Holt, Brookline Fort, Sept. 7, 1775, 13 In. 7700.00
  Map, Towns & Forts, Lake Champlain To New York, 1755, 12 1/2 In. 5280.00
  Steer, Carved Comfort Johnson, 1775, Roxbury, Massachusetts 2200.00

PRATT ware means two different things. It was an early Staffordshire
pottery, cream–colored with colored decorations, made by Felix Pratt   **PRATT**
during the late eighteenth century. There was also Pratt ware made with   **FENTON**
transfer designs during the mid–nineteenth century in Fenton, England.
Reproductions of the transfer–printed Pratt are being made.

  Bowl, Cornucopia Shape, Man's Face On Spout, Soft Paste 715.00
  Jar, Polychrome Design Lid, Fallen Soldier & Horse, 4 In. 137.50
  Jug, Hunting Scene, Mask Handle, Dated 1856, 6 1/2 In. 145.00
  Mug, Figural, Satyr Head, Vintage, Polychrome Enamel, 4 1/8 In. 193.00
  Mug, Imari Pattern, Bracket Handles, 1850s, 5 In. 88.00
  Pitcher, Fox Hunting Scene 175.00
  Sauceboat, Dolphin Form, Green Glazed Scales, c.1790, 6 1/4 In. 770.00
  Sauceboat, Fox & Swan, Swan's Neck Handle, Fox's Head Spout, 6 1/2 In., Pair ...   1210.00
  Toby Mug, Green & Yellow Figure, Holding Mug 374.00

PRESSED GLASS was first made in the United States in the 1820s after
the invention of glass pressing machines. Hundreds of patterns of pressed
glass were made in complete table settings. Although the Boston and
Sandwich Works was the most famous of the pressed glass factories, there
were about sixteen other factories making pressed glass from 1830 to 1850,
and still more from 1850 to 1900, when pressed glass reached its greatest
popularity. It is now being widely reproduced. The pattern names used in
this listing are based on the information in the book *Pressed Glass in
America* by John and Elizabeth Welker. There may be pieces of pressed
glass listed in this book in other categories, such as Lamp, Ruby,
Sandwich, and Souvenir.

  1000–Eye pattern is listed here as Thousand Eye

Acorn, Creamer 60.00
Acorn, Salt & Pepper, Pink & White 65.00
Actress, Bread Tray 70.00
Actress, Cake Stand, Frosted Base 125.00
Actress, Compote, 6 In. 100.00
Actress, Compote, Cover, 8 In. .... 135.00 To 150.00
Actress, Creamer 50.00
Actress, Goblet, Frosted 75.00
Actress, Jam Jar, Cover ....95.00 To 135.00
Actress, Relish 20.00
Actress, Sugar & Creamer 135.00
Admiral Dewey pattern is listed here as Spanish American
Akron Block, Goblet 15.00
Alabama, Cake Stand 95.00
Alaska, Saltshaker, Blue Opalescent 85.00
Alaska, Sugar, Blue 245.00
Alaska, Sugar, Cover, Vaseline .... 225.00 To 245.00
Albany, Butter, Cover, Ruby Stained 145.00
Amazon, Cake Stand, 10 In. 45.00
Amazon, Pitcher, Leaf Etching 65.00
Amazon, Pitcher, Sawtooth Band Base, Bryce, 1880s 85.00
Amazon, Wine 15.00
Amberette, Creamer 66.00
Amberette, Spooner 77.00
Amberette, Toothpick 135.00
Amberette, Tumbler 150.00
America, Creamer, Etched 25.00
Anthemion, Pitcher, Milk 28.00
Apollo, Compote, Cover, 6 In. 37.50
Apollo, Creamer, Etched 57.50
Apollo, Goblet, Frosted ....45.00 To 47.50
Aquarium, Pitcher, Water 275.00
Arch, Sugar, Cover 55.00
Arched Ovals, Bowl, Oval, 5 1/2 x 8 In. 24.50
Arched Ovals, Mug, Boston, Mass., Ruby Stained 25.00
Argonaut Shell, Bonbon, Anchor, Frosted 35.00
Argonaut Shell, Marmalade, Cover, Frosted Blue, Spoon 110.00
Argonaut Shell, Plate, Handle, Blue, 6 In. 30.00
Argus, Sugar, Cover, 6 1/2 In. 33.00
Arrowhead in Oval pattern is listed here as Style
Art Novo, Table Set, Ruby Stained, 4 Piece 395.00
Art, Cake Stand 65.00
Art, Pitcher, 9 1/2 In. 150.00
Art, Sugar, Cover 48.00
Artichoke, Butter, Cover 20.00
Artichoke, Goblet, Frosted 35.00
Artichoke, Pitcher 195.00
Artichoke, Sugar, Cover 45.00
Artichoke, Syrup 165.00
Ashburton, Goblet, Etched 110.00
Ashburton, Vase, Hexagonal Base & Standard, 11 5/8 In. 1100.00
Ashburton, Whiskey, Flint 125.00
Ashburton, Wine, Fluted Stem, 8 Piece 640.00
Ashman, Butter, Cover 65.00
Ashman, Cake Stand 50.00
Atlanta, Cake Stand, Square, 9 In. 110.00
Atlanta, Sauce, Square 25.00
Atlas, Cake Stand, Crystal, 1890 .... 35.00
Austrian, Goblet 40.00
Baby Face, Compote, High Standard 225.00
Baby Thumbprint pattern is listed here as Dakota
Balder pattern is listed here as Pennsylvania
Balky Mule pattern is listed here as Currier & Ives

Pressed glass,	Pressed glass,	Pressed glass,	Pressed glass,
Atlas	Austrian	Barberry	Beaded Grape Medallion

Baltimore Pear, Compote, 6 1/2 In.	30.00
Baltimore Pear, Creamer	25.00
Baltimore Pear, Sugar	30.00
Baltimore Pear, Tray	20.00
Banded Portland, Wine	27.00
Banded patterns may also be listed under the name of the basic pattern: e. g., Banded Honeycomb is called Honeycomb, Banded	
Banquet, Celery Vase	18.00
Bar & Diamond pattern is listed here as Kokomo	
Barberry, Cake Stand, 1890	95.00
Barberry, Compote, Shell Finial	40.00
Barley & Oats pattern is listed here as Wheat & Barley	
Barley & Wheat pattern is listed here as Wheat & Barley	
Barred Forget–Me–Not, Bowl, Handle, 9 In.	27.50
Barred Forget–Me–Not, Compote	20.00
Barred Forget–Me–Not, Goblet	35.00
Barred Hobnail, Creamer	45.00
Barred Oval, Cruet	42.50
Barred Oval, Goblet	40.00
Barred Oval, Pitcher, 9 In.	150.00
Barrel Ashburton, Creamer, 6 1/2 In.	88.00
Barreled Block pattern is listed here as Red Block	
Basket Weave, Water Set, 5 Piece	175.00
Beaded Band, Creamer	35.00
Beaded Band, Goblet	37.50
Beaded Bull's–Eye & Drape pattern is listed here as Alabama	
Beaded Circle, Table Set, Green, 4 Piece	375.00
Beaded Dewdrop pattern is listed here as Wisconsin	
Beaded Frog's Eye, Goblet	30.00
Beaded Grape Medallion, Cake Stand, Green	85.00
Beaded Grape Medallion, Sugar & Creamer, 7 In.	55.00
Beaded Loop, Toothpick	60.00
Beaded Panel & Sunburst, Toothpick	75.00
Beaded Tulip, Goblet	28.00
Bearded Head pattern is listed here as Viking	
Bearded Man pattern is listed here as Queen Anne	
Beatty Rib, Toothpick, Opalescent	30.00
Beautiful Lady, Banana Stand	65.00
Bellflower, Castor Set, 4 Bottles, Pewter Frame	395.00
Bellflower, Champagne, Knob Stem, Flint	165.00
Bellflower, Compote, Low Standard, Flint, 7 In.	85.00
Bellflower, Eggcup, Banded, Flint	72.00
Bellflower, Goblet, Barrel Shape, Knob Stem	45.00
Bellflower, Sugar, Cover, 9 In.	55.00
Bellflower, Whiskey, Flint, 3 In.	100.00
Bent Buckle pattern is listed here as New Hampshire	

Berry Cluster, Spooner 20.00
Bethlehem Star, Creamer 22.00
Bethlehem Star, Goblet 28.00
Beveled Diamond & Star pattern is listed here as Albany
Beveled Star, Cake Stand, Green 125.00
Beveled Star, Pitcher, Green, 10 In. 185.00
Beveled Star, Toothpick 60.00
Beveled Star, Toothpick, Green 150.00
Big Block pattern is listed here as Henrietta
Birch Leaf, Spooner, Flint 55.00
Bird & Strawberry, Cake Stand, 9 In. 35.00
Bird & Strawberry, Creamer 125.00
Bird & Strawberry, Pitcher, Cream 95.00
Bird & Strawberry, Sauce, Footed, 4 In. 25.00
Bird & Strawberry, Table Set, 4 Piece 210.00
Bird & Strawberry, Tumbler .... 30.00 To 55.00
Bird & Strawberry, Wine 30.00
Bird & Strawbery, Cake Stand, 9 In. 70.00
Birds At Fountain, Goblet 42.00
Blackberry Band, Bowl, Ruffled, 10 In. 65.00
Blazing Cornucopia, Toothpick, Lavender Dots 35.00
Bleeding Heart, Cake Stand, 9 1/4 In. 80.00
Bleeding Heart, Compote, Cover, 8 In. 175.00
Bleeding Heart, Creamer 45.00
Bleeding Heart, Goblet .... 20.00 To 28.00
Bleeding Heart, Mug 65.00
Bleeding Heart, Spooner 30.00
Bleeding Heart, Sugar, Cover 85.00
Bleeding Heart, Tumbler, Pair 125.00
Bleeding Heart, Wine 115.00
Block & Fan, Cake Stand, 10 In. 65.00
Block & Fan, Compote, 8 In. 49.50
Block & Fan pattern is listed here as Romeo
Block & Star pattern is listed here as Valencia Waffle
Bluebird pattern is listed here as Bird & Strawberry
Bordered Ellipse, Mug, Ruby Stained 35.00
Bowtie, Compote, Large 190.00
Bowtie, Jam Jar .... 35.00 To 38.50
Box–In–Box, Toothpick, Ruby Stained 47.50
Branched Tree, Pitcher 50.00

Pressed glass, Bellflower

Pressed glass, Bird & Strawberry

Bringing Home The Cows, Pitcher 350.00
Britannic, Sugar, Cover, Amber Stained 65.00
Broken Column, Banana Stand 90.00
Broken Column, Celery Vase 55.00
Broken Column, Compote, 7 1/2 In. 65.00
Broken Column, Compote, Cover, Square, 5 In. 50.00
Broken Column, Compote, Flared, 7 In. 45.00
Broken Column, Spooner 36.00
Broken Column, Water Set, 7 Piece 285.00
Broughton pattern is listed here as Pattee Cross
Bryce pattern is listed here as Ribbon Candy
Bucket pattern is listed here as Oaken Bucket
Buckle, Compote, High Standard 38.00
Buckle, Pitcher 650.00
Bulging Loops, Mustard, Cover, Pink Cased 135.00
Bulging Loops, Toothpick, Blue 95.00
Bull's–Eye & Daisy, Butter, Cover 25.00
Bull's–Eye & Daisy, Goblet 11.00
Bull's–Eye & Fan, Toothpick 28.00
Bull's–Eye & Fleur–De–Lis, Goblet 85.00
Bull's–Eye & Wishbone, Goblet, Flint 75.00
Bull's–Eye Band, Bowl, Ruffled, 8 In. 75.00
Bull's–Eye Band, Compote, Jelly 40.00
Bull's–Eye, Eggcup, Flint 35.00
Bullet Emblem, Butter, Cover 275.00
Bullet Emblem, Sugar, Cover, Red White & Blue Shield 137.50
Bullet, Sugar & Creamer 295.00
Button Arches, Punch Cup 12.00
Button Arches, Toothpick 22.50
Button Arches, Toothpick, Ruby & Gold 35.00
Button Panel, Creamer 30.00
Button Panel, Spooner .... 30.00 To 48.00
Button Panel, Sugar, Cover 60.00
Buzz Saw, Toothpick 20.00
Buzz Star, Creamer, Child's 15.00
Buzz Star, Cup, Child's 7.00
Buzz Star, Punch Bowl 50.00
Buzz Star, Toothpick .... 18.00 To 20.00
Cabbage Rose, Champagne 95.00
Cabbage Rose, Tumbler 55.00
Cable With Ring, Sugar, Cover, 7 3/4 In. 77.00
Cable, Compote, Flint, 8 1/4 In. 50.00
Cable, Eggcup 65.00
Cable, Eggcup, Opaque Blue, 1850s, 4 In. 470.00
Camel Caravan, Pitcher 135.00
Canadian, Creamer 50.00
Canadian, Pitcher 60.00
Canadian, Pitcher, Water 65.00
Candlewick as a pressed glass pattern is properly named *Banded Raindrop.* There is also a pattern called *Candlewick,* which has been made by Imperial Glass Corporation since 1936. It is listed in this book in the Imperial category.
Candy Ribbon pattern is listed here as Ribbon Candy
Cane & Star Medallion, Sauce 9.00
Capitol Building, Goblet 29.50
Cardinal pattern is listed here as Cardinal Bird
Cardinal Bird, Butter, Cover .... 100.00 To 110.00
Cardinal Bird, Creamer .... 25.00 To 35.00
Cardinal Bird, Sugar, Cover 16.00
Carnation, Berry Set, Ruby Stained, Gold Trim, 7 Piece 145.00
Carnation, Pitcher, Ruby Stained, Gold Trim 265.00
Carnation, Toothpick 25.00
Carolina, Sugar, Enameled Flowers 25.00
Cat & Dog, Pitcher .... 450.00 To 495.00

Pressed glass, Bleeding Heart   *Pressed glass, Broken Column*   *Pressed glass, Buckle*

Cathedral, Sugar, Ruby Stained 28.50
Cathedral, Wine, Vaseline 50.00
Chain With Diamonds pattern is listed here as Washington Centennial
Chain With Star, Compote, Cover, Bryce Brothers, 1880s 70.00
Champion, Toothpick, Green, Gold Trim 40.00
Chandelier, Spooner 45.00
Cherry, Goblet 25.00
Cherry, Pitcher 30.00
Chrysanthemum Leaf, Toothpick, Gold Trim 65.00
Church Windows, Butter, Cover, Maiden's Blush 30.00
Circle, Champagne, Frosted 48.00
Classic, Bread Plate, Warriors 220.00
Classic, Creamer 125.00
Classic, Creamer, Log Feet 175.00
Classic, Goblet 250.00
Classic, Pitcher, Log Feet .... 285.00 To 450.00
Classic, Plate, Warrior, Jacobus 185.00
Classic, Sugar & Creamer, Log Feet 225.00
Clover, Toothpick 27.50
Coin Spot pattern is listed in this book in its own category
Colonial, Eggcup, Flint 45.00
Colorado, Berry Set, Green, Gold Trim, 6 Piece 140.00
Colorado, Butter, Cover, Green, Gold Trim 125.00
Colorado, Cheese Dish, Blue, Gold Trim 70.00
Colorado, Mug, Atlantic City, 2 1/2 In. 20.00
Colorado, Spooner, Green, Gold Trim 70.00
Colorado, Sugar, Cover, Green, Gold Trim 85.00
Colorado, Table Set, Green, Gold Trim, 4 Piece 300.00
Colorado, Toothpick, Blue 30.00
Colorado, Toothpick, Green, Gold Trim 35.00
Columbia, Water Set, 7 Piece 245.00
Columbian Coin, Compote 60.00
Comet, Goblet .... 100.00 To 115.00
Compact pattern is listed here as Snail
Connecticut, Toothpick 110.00
Cord Drapery, Berry Set, 6 Piece 100.00
Cord Drapery, Pitcher 65.00
Cordova, Toothpick 45.00
Cordova, Toothpick, Ruby Stained 30.00
Coreopsis, Syrup 225.00
Cornucopia, Pitcher, Water 80.00
Corona, Toothpick, Ruby Stained 40.00
Cosmos pattern is listed in this book as its own category
Cottage, Cake Stand 16.00
Crane pattern is listed here as Stork
Croesus, Berry Set, Purple, Gold Trim, 7 Piece 395.00

Croesus, Bowl, Footed, Green, Gold Trim, 7 In. 35.00
Croesus, Compote, Jelly, Purple, Gold 265.00
Croesus, Cruet, Green 130.00
Croesus, Pitcher, Green, Gold Trim 325.00
Croesus, Salt & Pepper, Purple 225.00
Croesus, Spooner, Green, Gold Trim 85.00
Croesus, Sugar, Spooner & Creamer, 6 In. 240.00
Croesus, Toothpick, Green, Gold Trim 85.00
Croesus, Water Set, Green, 7 Piece 480.00
Croeseus, Water Set, Purple, 7 Piece 800.00
Crowfoot, Cake Stand 38.00
Crowfoot, Creamer 15.00
Crowfoot, Goblet 35.00
Crown Jewels is a name used for two different patterns listed here as Chandelier or
Queen's Necklace
Crystal Wedding, Butter, Cover, Frosted 110.00
Crystal Wedding, Butter, Cover, Ruby Stained 125.00
Crystal Wedding, Honey Dish, Square, 7 In. 45.00
Crystal Wedding, Lamp, Frosted, 9 In. 145.00
Crystal Wedding, Pitcher 125.00
Crystal Wedding, Pitcher, Etched 165.00
Cube with Fan pattern is listed here as Pineapple & Fan
Cupid & Venus, Jam Jar 33.00
Cupid & Venus, Pitcher, 8 In. .... 65.00 To 95.00
Cupid & Venus, Plate, Handles, 10 1/2 In. 42.50
Cupid & Psyche pattern is listed here as Psyche & Cupid
Currant, Cake Stand, 10 In. 110.00
Currant, Goblet 50.00
Currant, Sugar, Cover 40.00
Currier & Ives, Pitcher, Amber 145.00
Currier & Ives, Syrup, Amber 160.00
Currier & Ives, Tray, Mule, Blue, 12 In. 140.00
Curtain Tieback, Goblet 25.00
Cut Block, Toothpick, Red Stained 100.00
Cut Log, Saltshaker 45.00
Cut Log, Tankard 59.00
Cut Log, Tumbler 39.00
Daisies in Oval Panels pattern is listed here as Bull's-Eye & Fan
Daisy & Button With Crossbar, Pitcher 60.00
Daisy & Button With Crossbar, Pitcher, Amber .... 55.00 To 60.00
Daisy & Button With Crossbar, Sugar Cover, Blue 65.00
Daisy & Button With Prisms, Creamer 25.00
Daisy & Button With Thumbprint Panels, Tumbler, Blue 35.00
Daisy & Button With V–Ornament, Toothpick 18.00
Daisy & Button With V–Ornament, Toothpick 40.00
Daisy & Button With V–Ornament, Toothpick, Amber 35.00
Daisy & Fan, Goblet, Scalloped, Emerald Green 28.50
Dakota, Cake Stand 185.00
Dakota, Compote, Etched, 6 In. .... 30.00 To 45.00
Dakota, Compote, Etched, 8 In. 40.00
Dakota, Goblet, Etched .... 15.00 To 26.00
Dakota, Spooner, Etched 15.00
Dakota, Wine 45.00
Dakota, Wine, Etched 28.00
Deer & Doe, Goblet 220.00
Deer & Dog, Butter, Cover, Frosted Dog Finial, Etched 82.50
Deer & Dog, Creamer, Etched .... 100.00 To 110.00
Deer & Dog, Jelly Jar, Frosted Dog Finial 500.00
Deer & Dog, Pitcher, Etched 192.50
Deer & Dog, Pitcher, Water 125.00
Deer & Dog, Spooner, Etched .... 100.00 To 110.00
Deer & Dog, Sugar, Cover, Frosted Dog Finial, Etched 192.50
Deer & Oak Tree, Pitcher .... 100.00 To 190.00

Pressed glass, Bull's-Eye

Pressed glass, Bull's-Eye & Fan

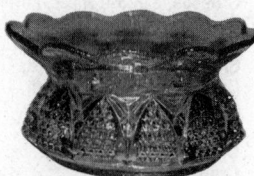

Pressed glass, Button Arches

Pressed glass, Cabbage Rose

Pressed glass, Cable

Pressed glass, Cable with Ring

Deer & Oak Tree, Pitcher, Water	110.00
Deer & Pine Tree, Butter, Cover	105.00
Deer & Pine Tree, Cake Stand	110.00
Deer & Pine Tree, Goblet	55.00 To 70.00
Deer & Pine Tree, Mug, Child's, Blue	45.00
Deer & Pine Tree, Sauce	10.00
Deer & Pine Tree, Sugar, Cover	62.50
Delaware, Banana Boat, Green, Gold Trim	75.00
Delaware, Banana Boat, Rose, Gold Trim	95.00
Delaware, Berry Set, Green, Gold Trim, 6 Piece	145.00
Delaware, Bride's Basket, Silver Frame, Miniature	200.00
Delaware, Cruet, Green, Stopper	295.00
Delaware, Pitcher, Green	175.00
Delaware, Pitcher, Green, Gold Trim	90.00

Pressed glass, Canadian

Pressed glass, Cardinal Bird

Pressed glass, Cathedral

Pressed glass, Classic   *Pressed glass, Columbian Coin*   *Pressed glass, Curtain*

Delaware, Tankard, Green, Gold Trim, 8 1/2 In.	145.00
Delaware, Toothpick, Green, Gold Trim	95.00
Delaware, Toothpick, Rose, Gold Trim	95.00
Delaware, Tumbler, Green	24.00
Delaware, Tumbler, Green, Gold Trim	40.00
Delaware, Water Set, Cranberry, Gold Trim, 5 Piece	275.00
Delaware, Water Set, Green, 7 Piece	400.00 To 500.00
Dewdrop & Raindrop, Tumbler	15.00
Dewdrop With Sheaf of Wheat, Bread Plate	30.00
Dewdrop With Star, Dish, 7 1/4 x 1 1/4 In.	12.00
Dewey, see also the related pattern Spanish American	
Dewey, Butter, Cover, Green	75.00
Dewey, Relish, Amber	42.50
Dewey, Sugar & Creamer, Canary, Small	60.00
Diagonal Band, Celery Vase	30.00
Diamond & Sunburst, Tumbler, Ruby Stained	42.50
Diamond Bridges, Sugar & Creamer, Frosted Panels	275.00
Diamond Medallion pattern is listed here as Grand	
Diamond Point, Champagne, 5 1/4 In.	150.00
Diamond Point, Compote, Pedestal, 7 1/2 In.	175.00
Diamond Point, Cordial, 3 1/4 In.	195.00
Diamond Point, Decanter, Faceted Stopper, 9 1/2 In.	95.00
Diamond Point, Decanter, Flint	125.00 To 225.00
Diamond Point, Eggcup, 3 5/8 In.	55.00
Diamond Point, Eggcup, Flint	60.00
Diamond Point, Honey Dish, 3 1/2 In.	15.00
Diamond Point, Pitcher, Flint	120.00
Diamond Point, Sauce, 4 1/4 In.	20.00
Diamond Point, Whiskey, Handle, 3 In.	175.00
Diamond Point, Whiskey, Handle, Flint	85.00
Diamond Point, Wine, Vaseline	40.00
Diamond Ridge, Syrup	20.00
Diamond Spearhead, Toothpick, River View, Chicago, Ruby Flashed, 1911	55.00
Diamond Spearhead, Toothpick, Vaseline	42.50
Diamond Thumbprint, Compote, Flint, 10 In.	165.00
Diamond Thumbprint, Sugar & Creamer, 7 3/4 In.	88.00
Diamond, Syrup, Anchor Hocking, Dated Lid 1915	55.00
Diamonds & Clubs, Vase, Green, 8 In.	40.00
Dolphin, Compote, 7 In.	65.00
Dolphin, Creamer	125.00
Dolphin, Salt, Dolphin Feet, Frosted, Master	125.00
Doric pattern is listed here as Feather	
Double Arch, Cake Stand, 9 In.	55.00
Double Arch, Compote	20.00
Double Leaf & Dart, Goblet	20.00
Double Loop pattern is listed here as Ribbon Candy	

Pressed glass, Daisy &
Button with Crossbar

Pressed glass, Daisy &
Button with Thumbprint

Pressed glass,
Delaware

Pressed glass,
Diagonal Band

Double Loop & Dart, Goblet	22.00
Drapery, Creamer	35.00
Drum, Table Set, Miniature, 4 Piece	195.00
Duchess, Toothpick, Gold Trim	170.00
Eagle, Compote, Cover, High Stand, 8 In.	275.00
Eagle, Jar, Cover, Emblem	275.00
Eagle, Jelly Jar, Frosted	275.00
Eagle, Sugar, Cover, Frosted	65.00
Earl pattern is listed here as Spirea Band	
Egg In Sand, Bread Plate	22.50
Egg In Sand, Goblet	32.00
Egyptian, Bread Tray	44.00 To 85.00
Egyptian, Compote, Cover, 8 In.	185.00
Egyptian, Creamer	60.00
Egyptian, Pitcher, Water	175.00 To 192.50
Egyptian, Spooner	35.00 To 40.00
Elaine, Bread Tray, Swan Border	82.50
Elephant Toes, Berry Set, Cranberry Flashed, 6 Piece	165.00
Elephant Toes, Tumbler	20.00
Ellipse, Toothpick	105.00
Empress, Cruet, Gold Trim	125.00
Empress, Pitcher, Water, Green, Gold Trim	350.00
Empress, Salt & Pepper, Green, Gold Trim	195.00
Empress, Toothpick, Green, Gold Trim	225.00
Esther, Berry Set, Green, Gold Trim, 6 Piece	215.00
Esther, Butter, Cover, Amber Stained	125.00
Esther, Celery Dish, Amber Stained	125.00
Esther, Creamer, Gold Trim	65.00
Esther, Goblet, Amber	95.00

Pressed glass,
Diamond Thumbprint

Pressed glass,
Egg in Sand

Pressed glass,
Egyptian

Pressed glass,
Frosted Dolphin

Esther, Jelly Jar, Green, Gold Trim .... 35.00 To 65.00
Esther, Pitcher, Amber 180.00
Esther, Spooner 32.50
Esther, Toothpick, Green 110.00
Esther, Toothpick, Green, Gold Trim 80.00
Etched Dakota pattern is listed here as Dakota
Everglades, Sugar & Spooner, Cover, Blue Opalescent, Gold Trim 225.00
Eyewinker, Banana Boat .... 30.00 To 40.00
Eyewinker, Saltshaker 35.00
Eyewinker, Toothpick 85.00
Falmouth Strawberry, Goblet 55.00
Fancy Arches, Tumbler, Green 25.00
Fancy Loop, Toothpick 40.00
Fancy Loop, Toothpick, Green, Gold Trim .... 105.00 To 110.00
Feather Band, Pitcher 20.00
Feather, Bowl, Oval, 8 1/2 In. 16.00
Feather, Cake Stand, 8 In. .... 30.00 To 35.00
Feather, Cake Stand, Green 120.00
Feather, Creamer 35.00
Feather, Cruet .... 25.00 To 28.00
Feather, Goblet 50.00
Feather, Pitcher, Footed, 7 1/2 In. 75.00
Feather, Pitcher, Milk 45.00
Feather, Plate 20.00
Feather, Plate, 9 1/2 In. 12.00
Feather, Spooner 25.00
Feather, Sugar, Cover 55.00
Fern Garland, Claret 15.00
Fern Garland, Tumbler 35.00
Festoon & Grape pattern is listed here as Grape & Festoon
Festoon, Berry Bowl, 9 In. 25.00
Festoon, Mug, Handle 60.00
Festoon, Pitcher 55.00
Festoon, Plate, 9 In. 35.00
Festoon, Tray 15.00
Festoon, Tumbler 22.00
Fine Cut & Panel, Sugar & Creamer 55.00
Fine Cut & Panel, Tray, Water 30.00
Fine Cut & Feather pattern is listed here as Feather
Fine Cut, Cake Stand, Square, Blue 110.00
Fishscale, Plate, 8 In. 32.00
Fishscale, Tumbler 95.00
Flamingo Habitat, Butter, Cover 65.00
Flamingo Habitat, Celery Vase, Etched 55.00
Flamingo Habitat, Creamer 50.00
Flamingo Habitat, Goblet 55.00
Flamingo Habitat, Sugar, Cover 68.00
Flamingo Habitat, Wine 25.00
Flat Diamond & Sunburst, Tumbler 10.00
Flat Diamond, Decanter Set, Tray, 10 Piece 75.00
Flat Diamond, Lamp, Pewter Collar, Double Burner, 1845, 7 In. 110.00
Flat Diamond, Punch Set, Tray, 10 Piece 95.00
Flat Diamond, Wine 20.00
Fleur-De-Lis, Mug, Ruby Stained 36.00
Fleur-De-Lis, Toothpick 10.00
Flora, Butter, Cover, Green, Gold Trim 125.00
Florette, Cracker Jar 225.00
Florette, Syrup, Pink 195.00
Florette, Toothpick, Pink Cased 80.00
Florida Palm, Compote 20.00
Flower & Pleat, Water Set, Ruby Stained, 5 Piece 195.00
Flower Band, Frosted, Creamer 35.00
Flower Band, Goblet, Frosted 155.00

Pressed glass,
Frosted Circle

Pressed glass,
Frosted Eagle

Pressed glass,
Garfield Drape

Pressed glass, Grape
& Festoon with Shield

Flower Flange pattern is listed here as Dewey

Flute, Eggcup, Flint	20.00
Flute, Toothpick	25.00
Flute, Water Set, 12 Piece	115.00

Flying Robin pattern is listed here as Hummingbird

Forget–Me–Not, Toothpick, Turquoise	60.00
Four Petal, Creamer, 6 1/2 In.	44.00
Fox & Crow, Pitcher, Water	250.00 To 275.00
Framed Ovals, Sugar, Cover, Flint, Amber Wash	185.00
Frosted Artichoke, Syrup, Pewter Hinged Lid	115.00
Frosted Circle, Creamer	45.00
Frosted Circle, Sugar, Cover	65.00
Frosted Eagle, Butter, Cover	185.00
Frosted Eagle, Jam Jar	302.50
Frosted Eagle, Sugar, Cover	71.50 To 165.00

Frosted Flower Band pattern is listed here as Flower Band, Frosted

Frosted Fruits, Pitcher	145.00
Frosted Leaf, Eggcup, Flint	100.00
Frosted Leaf, Goblet, Flint	125.00
Frosted Leaf, Sauce	25.00
Frosted Leaf, Sugar, Cover	100.00

Frosted Roman Key pattern is listed here as Roman Key, Frosted

Frosted Stork, Jam Jar	286.00
Frosted Stork, Pitcher, Water	275.00

Frosted patterns may also be listed under name of main pattern

Fuchsia, Creamer	55.00
Fuchsia, Spooner	32.00
Galloway, Pitcher	65.00
Garden Fruits, Goblet, Etched	50.00

Garden of Eden, see also the related pattern Lotus & Serpent

Garden of Eden, Butter, Cover	75.00
Garden, Creamer	30.00
Garden, Sugar, Cover	9.00
Garfield Drape, Creamer	28.00 To 29.00
Garfield Drape, Goblet	30.00
Garfield Drape, Pitcher	95.00 To 120.00
Geneva, Toothpick, Green	135.00
Giant Bull's–Eye, Butter, Cover	45.00
Giant Bull's–Eye, Decanter	400.00
Giant Bull's–Eye, Tankard	85.00
Giant Bull's–Eye, Toothpick	35.00
Gibson Girl, Creamer	45.00
Goat's Head, Pitcher, Frosted	550.00 To 605.00
Goat's Head, Spooner, Frosted	85.00
Golden Rule, Bread Plate	95.00
Gonterman Swirl, Toothpick, Frosted Base, Amber	245.00

Gonterman Swirl, Toothpick, Opalescent 185.00
Good Luck pattern is listed here as Horseshoe
Goose Boy, Cake Stand 150.00
Gooseberry, Cake Stand 55.00
Gothic, Spooner, Flint 65.00
Grand, Cake Stand, 9 In. 37.50
Grape & Festoon, Creamer 30.00
Grape & Festoon, Mug, With Shield 35.00
Grape & Festoon, Salt, Master 20.00
Grape Band, Creamer, Applied Handle 22.00
Grape Band, Goblet 15.00
Grape, see also the related patterns Beaded Grape Medallion, Magnet & Grape, and
Paneled Grape Band
Grape, Bread Plate, It Is Pleasant To Labor For Those We Love 49.00
Grasshopper, Butter 55.00
Grasshopper, Jam Jar, Etched 143.00
Greek Key, Decanter 250.00
Hairpin, Eggcup, Flint 35.00
Hairpin, Salt, 3 In. 121.00
Hamilton With Clear Leaf pattern is listed here as Hamilton With Leaf
Hamilton With Leaf, Lamp, Kerosene, Ruffled Chimney 265.00
Hamilton, Compote, Flint, 8 In. 65.00
Hamilton, Goblet 45.00
Hamilton, Spooner 38.00
Harvard Yard, Toothpick 20.00
Hawaiian Lei, Bowl, 8 1/2 In. 35.00
Hawaiian Lei, Sugar, Cover 25.00
Hawaiian Lei, Wine 22.00
Heart Band, Toothpick 20.00
Heart Plume, Pitcher, 8 1/2 In. 150.00
Heart With Thumbprint, Cruet, Stopper, Pair 135.00
Heart With Thumbprint, Ice Bucket 65.00
Heart With Thumbprint, Tray, 4 In. 30.00
Heart With Thumbprint, Wine 32.00
Henrietta, Sugar, Cover 45.00
Hero, Salt & Pepper, Etched, Ruby Stained 85.00
Heron & Peacock, Mug, Fiery Opalescent 110.00
Hexagon Block, Spooner, Amber 35.00
Hobnail pattern is in this book as its own category
Hobnail & Bars pattern is listed here as Barred Hobnail
Hobnail With Thumbprint Base, Creamer, Blue 35.00
Holly, Butter, Cover, Blue 375.00
Holly, Cake Stand .... 155.00 To 165.00
Holly, Creamer, Cord & Tassel Base 125.00
Honeycomb, Mug, Flint 28.00
Honeycomb, Vase, 10 In., Pair 121.00

Pressed glass, Hairpin
with Rayed Base

Pressed glass,
Hamilton

Pressed glass,
Holly

Pressed glass,
Honeycomb

Pressed glass,
Horseshoe

Pressed glass,
Jacob's Ladder

Pressed glass,
Jeweled Heart

Pressed glass,
Jumbo

Horizontal Oval Frames, Goblet	100.00
Horn of Plenty, Compote, 7 In.	99.00
Horn of Plenty, Eggcup, Flint	30.00 To 42.00
Horn of Plenty, Goblet	70.00
Horn of Plenty, Saucer	40.00
Horn of Plenty, Sugar, Cover, 7 1/4 In.	88.00
Horn of Plenty, Tumbler	75.00
Horse, Cat & Rabbit, Goblet	500.00
Horseshoe, Bread Plate, 12 In.	65.00
Horseshoe, Cake Stand, 9 In.	50.00
Horseshoe, Creamer	20.00 To 22.00
Horseshoe, Cup & Saucer	15.00
Horseshoe, Goblet	25.00
Horseshoe, Jam Jar	165.00
Horseshoe, Wine	275.00
Huber, Compote, Etched, Flint, 8 In.	140.00
Hummingbird, Pitcher	100.00
Hummingbird, Pitcher, Amber	125.00
Hummingbird, Wine	40.00
Ida pattern is listed here as Sheraton	
Idyll, Butter, Green, Gold Trim	85.00
Idyll, Saltshaker, Blue	55.00
Idyll, Toothpick, Blue, Gold Trim	145.00
Illinois, Butter, Cover	75.00
Illinois, Celery Vase	37.50
Illinois, Sugar, Cover	16.00
Illinois, Toothpick	15.00
Indiana Swirl pattern is listed here as Feather	
Intaglio Sunflower, Toothpick	24.00
Intaglio, Sunflower, Tumbler, Green	35.00
Iowa, Pitcher, Gilded	95.00
Iris With Meander, Toothpick, Amethyst, Gold Trim	65.00
Iris With Meander, Toothpick, Opalescent	25.00
Ivy In Snow, Spooner	27.50
Jacob's Ladder, Celery Vase	45.00
Jacob's Ladder, Goblet	50.00
Jacob's Ladder, Pitcher	225.00
Jefferson Optic, Toothpick	64.00
Jenny Lind, Compote	110.00
Jewel & Dewdrop, Bread Plate	26.00 To 42.50
Jewel & Dewdrop, Cake Stand	48.00
Jewel & Dewdrop, Goblet, Amethyst Jewel, Gold Trim	85.00
Jewel & Dewdrop, Toothpick	65.00
Jewel & Dewdrop, Wine	40.00
Jewel & Festoon pattern is listed here as Loop & Jewel	
Jeweled Heart, Cruet, Blue	200.00

Jeweled Heart, Tumbler, Green 38.00
Jeweled Moon & Star pattern is listed here as Moon & Star
Job's Tears pattern is listed here as Art
Jumbo, Butter, Cover 282.00
Jumbo, Butter, Cover, Knife Rest 350.00
Jumbo, Compote, 7 In. 302.50
Jumbo, Compote, Cover, 5 3/4 In. .... 425.00 To 467.50
Jumbo, Compote, Cover, Oval, Elephant Finial 950.00
Jumbo, Creamer 385.00
Jumbo, Goblet, 3 Elephants 650.00
Jumbo, Jam Jar .... 450.00 To 495.00
Jumbo, Pitcher, Flat Sides, Amber 525.00
Jumbo, Spooner .... 385.00 To 750.00
Jumbo, Sugar, Cover 220.00
Kamoni pattern is listed here as Pennsylvania
Kansas pattern is listed here as Jewel & Dewdrop
King Arthur, Tumbler 14.50
King's 500, Punch Cup, Cobalt Blue, Gold Trim 18.00
King's 500, Rose Bowl, Cobalt Blue, Gold Trim 50.00
King's 500, Spooner 85.00
King's 500, Sugar, Cover 50.00
King's Crown, see also the related pattern Ruby Thumbprint
King's Crown, Bowl, Flared, Ruby Flashed, 12 1/2 x 3 In. 65.00
King's Crown, Cake Stand, Ruby Flashed, 12 1/4 In. 75.00
King's Crown, Compote, Cover, 8 In. 56.50
King's Crown, Compote, Pedestal, Ruby Flashed, 7 x 7 In. 55.00
King's Crown, Compote, Scalloped Rim 65.00
King's Crown, Creamer, Ruby Flashed, Individual 22.00
King's Crown, Cup & Saucer, Ruby Flashed 40.00
King's Crown, Goblet, Ruby Stained 50.00
King's Crown, Plate, Ruby Flashed, 8 1/4 In. 15.00
King's Crown, Punch Cup, Ruby Flashed 20.00
King's Crown, Saltshaker 32.50
King's Crown, Toothpick 20.00
King's Crown, Water Set, Ruby Stained, 5 Piece 200.00
King's Crown, Wine 25.00
King's Crown, Wine, Ruby Flashed 20.00
King's Crown, Wine, Souvenir, Chilton, Wisconsin, Cobalt Blue 165.00
King's Curtain, Goblet 12.00
Klondike pattern is listed here as Amberette
Knights of Labor, Mug 45.00
Knights of Pythias, Wine, Green 100.00
Kokomo, Goblet 26.00
Kokomo, Wine 15.00
Lacy Floral, Wine 25.00
Ladders, Spooner, Gold Trim 13.00
Lamb, Table Set, Child's, 4 Piece .... 175.00 To 350.00
Late Butterfly, Tankard, Milk 75.00
Leaf & Dart, Celery Vase .... 32.00 To 35.00
Leaf & Dart, Goblet 23.00
Leaf & Dart, Pitcher, Water 125.00
Leaf & Dart, Sugar, Cover 65.00
Leaf & Dart, Tumbler, Footed .... 30.00 To 35.00
Leaf & Flower, Bowl, Amber, Frosted, 10 In. 135.00
Leaf & Flower, Pitcher, Amber Leaves 195.00
Leaf & Flower, Saltshaker, Amber Stained 85.00
Leaf & Flower, Sugar & Creamer, Amber, Frosted 165.00
Leaf Medallion, Creamer, Cobalt Blue 70.00
Leaf Medallion, Cruet, Amethyst 325.00
Leaf Medallion, Water Set, Amethyst, 3 Piece 275.00
Leaf Umbrella, Pitcher, Blue 450.00
Leafy Scroll, Syrup 85.00
Liberty Bell, Creamer .... 75.00 To 125.00

Liberty Bell, Spooner .... 20.00 To 55.00
Lincoln Drape With Tassel, Goblet, Flint 150.00
Lincoln Drape, Lamp, Burner, Chimney 40.00
Lincoln Drape, Sugar, Cover, Flint 165.00
Lined Smocking, Sugar, Cover, Flint 85.00
Lion With Cable, Compote, Cover, Frosted, 7 x 12 1/2 In. 130.00
Lion's Leg pattern is listed here as Alaska
Lion, Compote, Cover, Rampant Lion Finial, Oval, Frosted, 5 1/2 x 9 In. 120.00
Lion, Compote, Oval, Cover, 8 In. 55.00
Lion, Creamer, Frosted .... 45.00 To 48.00
Lion, Eggcup 30.00
Lion, Goblet, Frosted .... 80.00 To 110.00
Lion, Pitcher, Frosted .... 250.00 To 325.00
Lion, Salt Dip 35.00
Lion, Sugar, Cover, Miniature 110.00
Lippman pattern is listed here as Flat Diamond
Little River, Pickle, Insert 35.00
Locket On Chain, Wine 85.00
Log Cabin, Butter, Cover 210.00
Log Cabin, Spooner 25.00
Loop & Dart With Round Ornaments, Creamer 40.00
Loop & Dart With Round Ornaments, Pitcher, Flint 125.00
Loop & Dart, Compote, Cover, 8 In. 55.00
Loop & Jewel, Butter, Cover 60.00
Loop & Petal, Bowl, 11 1/2 x 3 In. 105.00
Loop & Petal, Candlestick, Canary Yellow, 7 In., Pair .... 132.00 To 138.00
Loop With Dewdrop, Creamer 50.00
Loop with Stippled Panels pattern is listed here as Texas
Loop, see also the related pattern Seneca Loop
Loop, Bowl, Canary Yellow, 8 1/2 In. 495.00
Loop, Celery Vase 35.00

Pressed glass,
Leaf & Dart

Pressed glass,
Liberty Bell

Pressed glass,
Lincoln Drape

Pressed glass,
Magnet & Grape with
Stippled Leaf

Pressed glass,
Maine

Pressed glass,
Moon & Star

Loop, Celery Vase, Flint, Pair 345.00
Loop, Compote, 9 1/2 In. 99.00
Loop, Eggcup 18.00
Loop, Goblet 11.00
Loop, Lamp, Brass Collar, Marble Base, 1840s, 10 1/8 In. 275.00
Loop, Lamp, Pedestal Base, 12 In. 440.00
Loop, Salt Dish, Hexagonal, Canary Yellow, 1850s, 2 In. 100.00
Loop, Sugar, Cover, 9 In. 55.00
Loops & Drops pattern is listed here as New Jersey
Lotus & Serpent, Butter, Cover 68.00
Lotus & Serpent, Mug 100.00
Lucere, Table Set, 4 Piece ....95.00 To 100.00
Magnet & Grape, Tumbler 85.00
Maine, Compote 28.00
Maine, Syrup, Spring Lid 125.00
Majestic, Relish, Green 36.00
Manhattan, Butter, Cover, Rose Flashed, Gold Trim 110.00
Manhattan, Punch Set, 14 Piece 290.00
Maple Leaf, Compote, Cover, Frosted, Clear Foot, 8 In. 175.00
Mardi Gras, Goblet 22.50
Mardi Gras, Vase, Amber, 8 In. 125.00
Maryland, Goblet 25.00
Maryland, Wine, Knob Stem, Flint 75.00
Mascotte, Cake Stand, 10 1/2 In. 75.00
Massachusetts, Mug, Gold Trim 25.00
Massachusetts, Relish, Oval 15.00
McKinley Memorial, Bread Tray, It Is God's Way 40.00
Melon & Leaf, Spooner 100.00
Melrose, Wine 15.00
Memphis, Creamer 50.00
Memphis, Punch Cup 30.00
Memphis, Spooner, Green, Gold Trim 60.00
Memphis, Table Set, Green, Gold Trim, 4 Piece .... 250.00 To 300.00
Memphis, Tumbler, Green, Gold Trim 35.00
Memphis, Water Set, Green, Gold Trim, 7 Piece 295.00
Menagerie, Pitcher, Owl, Amber, 3 3/4 In. 143.00
Menagerie, Pitcher, Owl, Milk Glass, 3 3/4 In. 50.00
Menagerie, Spooner, Fish, Amber 55.00
Michigan, Pitcher, Silver Plated Collar, 11 1/2 In. 85.00
Michigan, Water Set, 7 Piece 195.00
Mikado Fan, Pitcher 28.00
Minerva, Bread Plate, Portrait Center, Motto 70.00
Minerva, Compote, Cover, 8 In. 225.00
Minerva, Goblet 110.00
Minerva, Sugar 25.00
Mirror & Fan, Tumbler 15.00
Mirror, Compote, Flint, 7 In. 60.00
Mirror, Creamer, Flint 125.00
Mirror, Sugar, Cover, Flint 125.00
Missouri, Tumbler, Green 30.00
Mitered Diamond, Pitcher, Amber 45.00
Mitered Diamond, Wine, Yellow 25.00
Monkey Climber, Goblet 150.00
Moon & Star, Butter, Cover ....70.00 To 77.00
Moon & Star, Cake Stand ....125.00 To 137.50
Moon & Star, Creamer 60.50
Moon & Star, Goblet 45.00
Moon & Star, Pitcher, 10 In. 175.00
Moon & Star, Spooner .... 40.00 To 44.00
Moon & Star, Sugar, Cover 66.00
Moon & Star, Tumbler, Enameled Design, Frosted 67.50
Moon & Star, Water Set, Pink, Miniature, 5 Piece 25.00
Morning Glory, Sugar, Cover 190.00

Pressed glass,
Parrot & Fan

Pressed glass,
Pennsylvania

Pressed glass,
New England Pineapple

Nail, Creamer, Etched	35.00
Nail, Goblet	40.00
Nail, Goblet, Etched	50.00
Nail, Saucer, 4 Footed	40.00
Nail, Sugar, Cover, Etched	40.00
Nailhead, Cake Stand, 9 1/2 In.	30.00
Narcissus Spray, Water Set, Amethyst & Gilt Design, 5 Piece	148.00
Narrow Swirl, Creamer	15.00
Nestlings, Compote, Etched, 8 In.	235.00
Nestor, Butter, Cover, Blue, White & Gold Trim	150.00
Nestor, Spooner, Blue, Gold White Trim	35.00
Nestor, Table Set, Blue, 4 Piece	295.00
Nevada, Water Set, Gold Trim, 5 Piece	95.00
New England Centennial, Goblet	325.00
New England Pineapple, Compote, 7 1/2 In.	77.00
New England Pineapple, Spooner	40.00
New England Pineapple, Sugar, Cover, 8 In.	77.00
New Hampshire, Mug	18.50
New Hampshire, Mug, Pink Stained, 4 1/2 In.	35.00
New Hampshire, Spooner	16.00
New Hampshire, Sugar, Cover, Pink Stained	22.00
New Hampshire, Water Set, Bottom Half Clear, Pink Stained Top, 7 Piece	225.00
New Jersey, Syrup, Jug Shape, Pewter Lid	95.00
New Jersey, Toothpick, Gold Trim	75.00
New York Honeycomb, Goblet	14.00
Nursery Tales, Berry Set, Child's, 4 Piece	150.00
Nursery Tales, Water Set, Child's, 7 Piece	175.00
O'Hara's Diamond, Bowl, Cover, 8 In.	125.00
Oaken Bucket, Pitcher	90.00
Odd Fellows, Goblet	25.00
Old Abe pattern is listed here as Frosted Eagle	
One–Hundred, Celery Vase	60.00
One–Hundred, Toothpick, Pink	60.00
One–Thousand Eye pattern is listed here as Thousand Eye	
Oregon, see also the related pattern Beaded Loop	
Oregon, Compote	24.00
Orion pattern is listed here as Cathedral	
Oval Star, Spooner, Child's	20.00
Owl & Possum, Goblet	85.00 To 150.00
Owl & Pussycat, Cheese Dish	385.00
Owl in Fan pattern is listed here as Parrot	
Paddlewheel, Toothpick, Gold Trim	45.00
Palm Leaf Fan, Bowl, Scalloped Rim, 7 1/2 x 10 In.	30.00
Palm Leaf Fan, Tumbler	35.00
Palmette, Bread Plate, Amber	35.00
Panama, Butter, Cover	40.00

Paneled 44, Toothpick, Platinum Stain	95.00
Paneled Cane, Toothpick	55.00
Paneled Daisy, Plate, Square, 9 1/4 In.	20.00
Paneled Dewdrop, Sugar, Cover	40.00
Paneled Diamond Block, Toothpick	20.00
Paneled Flowers, Butter, Royal Blue, Round	78.00
Paneled Heather, Sugar & Creamer	30.00
Paneled Holly, Butter, Cover, Blue Opalescent, Gold Trim	375.00
Paneled Jewels, Wine, Blue	18.50
Paneled Sprig, Pitcher	225.00
Pansy, Toothpick, Pink	40.00
Parrot, Goblet	25.00 To 32.00
Pattee Cross, Pitcher	48.00
Pavonia, Celery Vase	35.00
Pavonia, Spooner, Etched	39.00
Pavonia, Tumbler, Maple Leaf, Etched	35.00
Pavonia, Water Set, Fern, Etched, Ruby Stained, 7 Piece	335.00
Peacock Feathers, Lamp, Finger, Footed	65.00
Peacock Feathers, Mug, Child's	45.00
Peacock Feathers, Mug, Georgia	40.00
Peacock Feathers, Sugar	25.00
Peacock's Eye pattern is listed here as Peacock Feathers	
Peacocks Feathers, Plate, 7 In.	72.00
Pennsylvania, Creamer, Green, Gold Trim	45.00
Pennsylvania, Goblet, Gold Trim	20.00
Pennsylvania, Plate	20.00
Pennsylvania, Syrup	55.00
Pennsylvania, Wine	9.00
Petal & Loop, Candlestick, Blue Prisms, 7 In., Pair	132.00
Petalled Medallion, Compote	29.00
Petticoat, Table Set, Vaseline, 4 Piece	395.00
Petticoat, Toothpick, Gold Trim	50.00
Picket Fence, Creamer	37.50
Picket Fence, Sugar, Cover	25.00
Pillar & Bull's-Eye pattern is listed here as Thistle	
Pillar, Pitcher, 8 Ribs	350.00 To 395.00
Pillow & Sunburst, Toothpick	55.00
Pillow Encircled, Creamer, Frosted, Enameled Flowers	35.00
Pillow Encircled, Tumbler	20.00
Pinafore pattern is listed here as Actress	
Pineapple & Fan, Toothpick, Gold Trim	125.00
Pineapple & Fan, Toothpick, Green, Gold Trim	135.00
Pineapple, Compote	20.00
Pineapple, Salt & Pepper, Blue	50.00
Pittsburg, Tumbler, Etched	35.00
Placid, Toothpick	18.00
Plain Smocking pattern is listed here as Smocking	
Pleat & Panel, Bowl, Footed, 9 In.	35.00
Pleating, Creamer, Ruby Stained	45.00
Plume, Cruet, Plume Stopper	95.00
Plume, Goblet	32.50
Polar Bear, Goblet, Frosted	40.00 To 44.00
Polar Bear, Pitcher, Frosted	425.00 To 467.00
Popcorn, Goblet	25.00
Portland with Diamond Point Band pattern is listed here as Banded Portland	
Portland, Toothpick	30.00
Portland, Wine	18.00
Powder & Shot, Butter, Cover, Flint	145.00
Powder & Shot, Castor	55.00
Powder & Shot, Goblet	40.00 To 60.00
Powder & Shot, Spooner, Flint	45.00
Prayer Rug pattern is listed here as Horseshoe	
Pressed Diamond, Cake Stand, Blue, 9 In.	55.00

Pressed glass, Queen Anne

Pressed glass,
Ribbon Candy

Pressed Leaf, Eggcup, Flint	30.00
Pressed Leaf, Wine, Flint	48.00
Priscilla, Butter, Cover	50.00
Priscilla, Cake Stand, 10 In.	65.00
Priscilla, Toothpick, Silver Overlay	50.00
Prism & Flute, Goblet, Engraved, Knob Stem	50.00
Prize, Banana Stand	95.00
Prize, Pitcher, Metal Spout	135.00
Prize, Salt, Ruby	50.00
Prize, Tankard, Metal Spout	150.00
Psyche & Cupid, Creamer	40.00 To 43.00
Psyche & Cupid, Jam Jar	77.00
Psyche & Cupid, Mug, Child's	35.00
Queen Anne, Butter	15.00
Queen Anne, Creamer, c.1879	65.00
Queen's Necklace, Toothpick	62.50 To 67.50
Racing Deer, Pitcher	145.00
Raindrop, Cake Stand	38.00
Ramsay Grape, Goblet	45.00
Red Block, Butter, Cover	68.00
Red Block, Sugar, Cover	60.00
Red Block, Water Set, 5 Piece	200.00
Red Block, Wine	30.00

Pressed glass, Roman Rosette

Pressed glass, Rose in Snow

Pressed glass, Rose Sprig   *Pressed glass, Ruby Thumbprint*   *Pressed glass, Sawtooth*

Regent pattern is listed here as Leaf Medallion
Reverse Swirl, Pitcher 225.00
Reverse Swirl, Toothpick, Canary Yellow 70.00
Reverse Torpedo pattern is listed here as Bull's–Eye Band
Reward, Toothpick 47.50
Rexford, Pitcher 37.00
Rexford, Wine 9.00
Rib & Bead, Toothpick 10.00
Ribbed Acorn, Sauce, Flint 22.00
Ribbed Opal pattern is listed here as Beatty Rib
Ribbed Palm, Champagne, Flint 125.00
Ribbed Palm, Compote, Low, Flint, 8 In. 90.00
Ribbed Palm, Eggcup, Flint 45.00
Ribbon Candy, Cake Stand, 9 1/4 In. 45.00
Ribbon Candy, Cake Stand, Child's 50.00
Ribbon Candy, Goblet 85.00
Rising Sun, Celery Vase, Green Trim 145.00
Riverside's Victoria, Sugar, Cover, Amber Stained 85.00
Rock of Ages, Bread Tray 220.00
Roman Key, Frosted, Champagne, Flint 125.00
Roman Key, Frosted, Decanter, Stopper 265.00
Roman Rosette, Bread Plate 16.00
Roman Rosette, Creamer 40.00
Romeo, Ice Bucket 20.00
Rooster, Butter, Cover, Child's 125.00
Rooster, Creamer, Child's 75.00
Rooster, Spooner, Child's 65.00
Rose In Snow, Mug, Applied Handle 80.00
Rose In Snow, Mug, Blue, Applied Handle 120.00
Rose In Snow, Plate, 5 In. 35.00
Rose Sprig, Goblet, Amber 55.00
Rose Sprig, Goblet, Canary Yellow 60.00
Rose Sprig, Sauce, Footed, Amber 18.50
Rosette With Pinwheels, Pitcher 39.00
Royal Ivy, Berry Bowl, Master 250.00
Royal Ivy, Butter, Cover, Pink To Clear 150.00
Royal Ivy, Saltshaker, Ruby, Etched 65.00
Royal Ivy, Spooner 55.00
Royal Ivy, Toothpick, Frosted 125.00
Royal Ivy, Toothpick, Rainbow Cracquelle 235.00
Royal Ivy, Toothpick, Rubena 125.00
Royal Oak, Sugar Shaker, Frosted 110.00
Royal Oak, Toothpick, Rubena 100.00
Ruby Rosette pattern is listed here as Hero
Ruby Thumbprint, see also the related pattern King's Crown
Ruby Thumbprint, Celery Vase 110.00

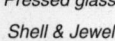

Pressed glass,   Pressed glass,   Pressed glass,   Pressed glass,
Shell & Jewel   Shell & Tassel   Squirrel   Thistle

Ruby Thumbprint, Spooner, Etched 55.00
Ruby Thumbprint, Toothpick 30.00
Rustic, Pitcher, Bulbous 50.00
S–Repeat, Condiment Set, Green, 8 In., 4 Piece 195.00
S–Repeat, Toothpick, Blue 60.00
S–Repeat, Wine, Blue 20.00
S–Repeat, Wine, Blue, Gold Trim 57.50
Sandwich Star, Spill, 5 1/2 In., Pair 77.00
Sawtooth Band pattern is listed here as Amazon
Sawtooth, Compote, Low Stem, Blue, 8 In. 250.00
Scalloped Prism, Spooner 18.00
Scalloped Six–Points, Champagne, Saucer 25.00
Scalloped Six–Points, Claret 25.00
Scalloped Six–Points, Cordial 25.00
Scalloped Six–Points, Wine, Gold Trim 15.00
Scroll With Cane Band, Butter, Cover, Amber 80.00
Seed Pod, Sugar, Cover, Blue 155.00
Seneca Loop, Salt, Master, Flint 20.00
Sheaf & Block, Pitcher, Milk, Ruby Stained 125.00
Sheaf & Block, Spooner, Ruby Stained 40.00
Sheaf of Wheat, Platter, 11 3/4 In. 65.00
Shell & Jewel, Compote, 7 In. 95.00
Shell & Jewel, Pitcher, Green 95.00
Shell & Jewel, Tumbler, Green 45.00
Shell & Jewel, Water Set, Sapphire, 7 Piece 175.00
Shell & Tassel, Bowl, Oval, 9 In. 55.00
Shell & Tassel, Butter, Cover, Dog Finial 265.00
Shell & Tassel, Cake Stand, 6 1/2 In. 155.00
Sheraton, Bread Plate 35.00
Sheraton, Creamer, Blue 42.00
Sheraton, Pitcher, Milk, 7 In. 30.00
Sheraton, Relish, Handle 20.00
Shoshone pattern is listed here as Victor
Shrine, Mug, Handle 65.00
Shrine, Pitcher 65.00
Smocking, Sugar, Cover 100.00
Snail, Butter, Cover 120.00
Snail, Celery Vase, Etched 65.00
Snail, Compote, 9 x 8 In. 50.00
Snail, Creamer, Ruby Stained 60.00
Snail, Salt & Pepper 120.00
Snake Drape, Goblet 18.00
Spanish American, Pitcher, Lemonade 100.00
Spanish American, Tumbler, Etched 48.00
Spanish Coin pattern is listed here as Columbian Coin
Spirea Band, Wine, Blue 25.00

Sprig, Butter, Cover	65.00
Sprig, Cake Stand, 8 In.	40.00
Sprig, Compote, Cover, 6 In.	95.00
Sprig, Goblet	25.00 To 30.00
Sprig, Wine	18.00
Square Fuchsia, Cake Stand, 9 1/2 In.	75.00
Square Fuchsia, Champagne	75.00
Square Fuchsia, Creamer	30.00
Square Fuchsia, Mug, Amber	75.00
Square Fuchsia, Mug, Green	75.00
Square Fuchsia, Plate, 10 In.	40.00
Square Fuchsia, Sugar, Cover, Vaseline	65.00
Squirrel With Nut, Pitcher, Water	110.00
Squirrel, Pitcher	245.00
Stag, Goblet, Etched	95.00
Star & Bar, Saltshaker, Pewter Top, Blue	28.00
Star & Bar, Sugar & Creamer, Amber, Child's	40.00
Star & File, Pitcher	18.00
Star & Punty pattern is listed here as Moon & Star	
Star In Bull's–Eye, Wine	15.00
Starred Cosmos, Water Set, 6 Piece	95.00
States pattern is listed here as The States	
Stippled Dahlia pattern is listed here as Square Fuchsia	
Stippled Forget–Me–Not, Cake Stand, 9 In.	90.00
Stippled Fuchsia, Dish, Cover	22.00
Stippled Grape & Festoon, Creamer	40.00
Stippled Paneled Flower pattern is listed here as Maine	
Stippled Vine & Beads pattern is listed here as Vine & Beads	
Stork & Rushes, Pitcher, Water	250.00
Stork & Rushes, Tray, Water, Frosted	125.00
Stork, Bowl, Frosted, 6 In.	44.00
Stork, Goblet	55.00 To 65.00
Stork, Jam Jar, Cover	75.00
Stork, Platter, Lowa City, Frosted	137.50
Strawberry, Dish, Cover	18.00
Strawberry, Goblet	30.00
Style, Cruet	25.00
Sunbeam, Toothpick, Blue, Gold Trim	125.00
Sunbeam, Toothpick, Green	45.00
Sunburst, Toothpick	75.00
Sunk Daisy, Toothpick, Gold Trim	25.00
Sunk Diamond & Lattice, Pitcher, Water, 1885	371.50
Sunrise pattern is listed here as Rising Sun	
Swan, Cheese Dish, Cover, Etched	250.00
Swan, Goblet, Etched	62.50
Swan, Jam Jar	247.50
Swan, Mug, Sapphire Blue	45.00
Swinger, Toothpick	30.00
Tacoma, Pitcher, Ruby Flashed	120.00
Tacoma, Sugar, Amber Stained	60.00
Teardrop & Tassel, Butter, Opaque Cover	125.00
Teardrop & Tassel, Tumbler, Blue	55.00
Tepee, Toothpick	50.00
Texas, Plate, Centennial, 1936	25.00
Texas, Toothpick, Gold Trim	25.00
The States, Goblet	18.00
The States, Toothpick	15.00
The States, Tumbler	20.00
Thistle, Butter, Handle	10.00
Thistle, Cake Stand, 9 In.	75.00
Thistle, Goblet	40.00
Thistle, Goblet, Flint	85.00
Thistle, Pitcher, Cobalt Blue	185.00

Pressed glass, Three Face   *Pressed glass, Thumbprint*   *Pressed glass, Tree of Life*

Thistle, Spooner	20.00
Thistle, Tumbler	55.00
Thousand Eye, Goblet, Water, 8 Oz.	10.00
Thousand Eye, Mug, Amber, Knob On Handle	40.00
Thousand Eye, Saucer	8.00
Thousand Eye, Spooner, Green	45.00
Thousand Eye, Tumbler, Ale, Mephistopheles, Gold Rim, Flint	95.00
Three Face, Compote, Cover, 6 In.	100.00
Three Face, Compote, Pedestal, 5 1/2 In.	150.00 To 165.00
Three Face, Creamer, Frosted	150.00
Three Face, Goblet, Etched	175.00
Three Face, Spooner, Engraved	100.00
Three Panel, Celery Vase, Ruffled, Vaseline	65.00
Three Panel, Goblet, Amber	25.00
Three Presidents, Bread Plate	75.00
Three Presidents, Goblet	400.00
Three Sisters pattern is listed here as Three Face	
Thumbprint, Creamer, Ruby	55.00
Thumbprint, Cup & Saucer, Ruby, Etched	65.00
Thumbprint, Goblet, Flint	45.00
Thumbprint, Pitcher, Ruby, 8 1/2 In.	125.00
Thumbprint, Saltshaker, Ruby	25.00
Thumbprint, Toothpick, Ruby	30.00
Thumbprint, Wine, Ruby	25.00
Tidy pattern is listed here as Rustic	
Tiny Lion, Jam Jar	143.00
Tiny Lion, Pitcher, Water	82.50
Toltec, Toothpick	40.00
Torpedo, Compote, Jelly, Flared Rim, 5 In.	50.00
Torpedo, Goblet	38.00
Torpedo, Pitcher, Milk	95.00
Torpedo, Sugar, Cover	95.00
Torpedo, Tankard, 12 In.	75.00
Tree of Life Portland, Goblet	95.00
Tree of Life Portland, Tray, Ice Cream	48.00
Tree of Life With Hand, Compote, Cover	29.00 To 42.50
Tree of Life With Hand, Sugar, Cover	135.00
Tree of Life, Butter, Cover, Hand Holding Ball Finial	155.00
Tree of Life, Champagne	85.00
Tree of Life, Champagne, Knob Stem, Flint	60.00
Tree of Life, Compote, Clear Hand Stem, 8 In.	55.00
Tree of Life, Creamer, Silver–Plated Holder, Blue	165.00
Tree of Life, Epergne, With Infant Samuel	285.00
Tree of Life, Ice Cream Set, 7 Piece	95.00
Tree of Life, Table Set, Silver–Plated Holder, 3 Piece	150.00
Trilby, Pitcher	235.00

Truncated Cube, Wine 25.00
Tulip & Honeycomb, Punch Set, Child's, 6 Piece 90.00
Tulip & Honeycomb, Spooner, Child's 20.00
Tulip Petals, Toothpick, Pink Stained 70.00
Tulip With Sawtooth, Champagne 110.00
Twin Teardrops, Cake Stand 50.00
Two Band, Creamer 28.00
Two Panel, Bowl, Green, Oval, 9 In. 35.00
Two Panel, Goblet, Green 38.00
Two Panel, Saltshaker 27.00
Two Panel, Wine, Green 40.00
U.S. Coin, Bread Tray 275.00
U.S. Coin, Compote, 8 In. 300.00
U.S. Coin, Goblet, 1892 .... 165.00
U.S. Coin, Toothpick, 1892 .... 125.00
U.S. Peacock, Goblet 9.00
U.S. Peacock, Punch Cup 6.00
U.S. Rib, Butter, Cover, Green, Gold Trim 95.00
U.S. Rib, Toothpick 40.00
Valencia Waffle, Bowl, Dome Feet, Square, 7 In. 30.00
Valencia Waffle, Compote, Cover, 8 In. 125.00
Valencia Waffle, Goblet 16.00
Vermont, Goblet 50.00
Vermont, Goblet, Green 55.00
Vermont, Toothpick, Amber 20.00
Vermont, Tumbler 50.00
Victor, Cruet 60.00
Victoria, Compote, Cover, Flint, 8 3/8 x 13 In. 82.50
Viking, Bowl, Crystal, Boat Shape 125.00
Viking, Compote, Cover, 9 In. 110.00
Viking, Creamer 50.00
Viking, Dish, Cover, Frosted Base & Finial 90.00
Viking, Eggcup 65.00
Viking, Mug 60.00
Viking, Pitcher 110.00
Viking, Spooner 25.00
Viking, Sugar, Cover 85.00
Viking, Table Set, 4 Piece 185.00
Vine & Beads, Spooner, Child's 35.00
Wading Heron, Pitcher .... 175.00 To 192.50
Waffle & Thumbprint, Celery, Flint 145.00
Waffle & Thumbprint, Decanter, Stopper 325.00
Waffle & Thumbprint, Eggcup, Flint 65.00
Waffle, Eggcup 25.00
Waffle, Tumbler 50.00
Washboard, Creamer 50.00
Washington Centennial, Celery 45.00
Washington Centennial, Wine 65.00
Wedding Bells, Toothpick 115.00
Wee Branches, Creamer 40.00
Wee Branches, Mug, Child's, Cobalt Blue 30.00
Wee Branches, Spooner 40.00
Wee Branches, Sugar Cover 60.00
Westward Ho, Butter, Cover 150.00
Westward Ho, Compote, Cover, 6 In. 120.00
Westward Ho, Compote, Cover, 8 In. .... 300.00 To 330.00
Westward Ho, Creamer 90.00
Westward Ho, Goblet 60.00
Westward Ho, Jam Jar .... 275.00 To 302.50
Westward Ho, Mug, Opalescent, 2 1/2 In. 250.00
Westward Ho, Pitcher .... 195.00 To 412.50
Westward Ho, Saucer 25.00
Westward Ho, Spooner 125.00

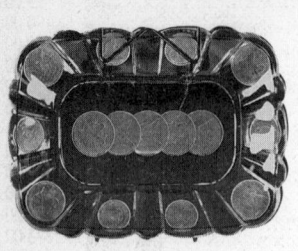

Pressed glass,
Washington Centennial

Pressed glass,
U.S. Coin

Pressed glass,
Waffle & Thumbprint

Pressed glass,
Westward Ho

Pressed glass,
Sheaf of Wheat

Pressed glass,
Wildflower

Westward Ho, Sugar & Creamer	185.00
Wheat & Barley, Creamer	18.00
Wheat & Barley, Plate, Handle, Amber, 9 In.	27.50
Wheat & Barley, Saltshaker, Blue	30.00
Whirligig pattern is listed here as Buzz Star	
Wild Bouquet, Sugar, Spooner & Creamer, Blue Opalescent, 3 Piece	350.00
Wild Rose With Bowknot, Creamer, Child's, Frosted	65.00
Wildflower, Creamer	17.50
Wildflower, Goblet, Blue	38.00
Wildflower, Pitcher	40.00
Wildflower, Spooner, Vaseline	22.50
Wildflower, Tray, Water, Blue	75.00 To 85.00
Willow Oak, Bowl, 7 1/4 In.	42.50
Willow Oak, Bowl, Cover, 8 In.	65.00
Willow Oak, Pitcher, Amber	65.00
Willow Oak, Plate, 9 In.	45.00
Willow Oak, Plate, Amber, 9 In.	36.00
Willow Oak, Tumbler	55.00
Windflower, Pitcher	65.00
Windflower, Salt, Master	20.00
Winged Scrolls, Toothpick, Green, Gold Trim	450.00
Winona pattern is listed here as Barred Hobnail	
Wisconsin, Cup & Saucer	55.00 To 60.00
Wisconsin, Pitcher	90.00
Wisconsin, Plate, Square, 6 3/4 In.	30.00
Wisconsin, Sugar Shaker	100.00
Wisconsin, Wine	75.00
Wooden Pail pattern is listed here as Oaken Bucket	
Worcester, Punch Cup	65.00
Wreath & Shell, Sugar, Cover, Vaseline	125.00
Wreath & Shell, Toothpick, Opalescent	125.00

Wyoming, Cake Stand 45.00
Wyoming, Relish 28.00
X–Ray, Berry Set, 5 Piece 40.00
X–Ray, Berry Set, Green, Gold Trim, 5 Piece 85.00
X–Ray, Butter, Cover, Green, Gold Trim 75.00
X–Ray, Creamer, Green, Gold Trim 45.00
X–Ray, Spooner, Green, Gold Trim 35.00
X–Ray, Sugar & Creamer, Green, Gold Trim, Small 75.00
Yale pattern is listed here as Crowfoot
York Herringbone, Tumbler, Etched, Ruby Stained 49.00
Zipper, Toothpick, St. Joseph, Mich., Ruby Stained 38.00

PRINT, in this listing, means any of many printed images produced on paper by one of the more common methods, such as lithography. The prints listed here are of interest primarily to the antiques collector, not the fine arts collector. Many of these prints were originally part of books. Other prints will be found in the Advertising, Currier & Ives, and Poster categories.

A. F. Tait, Cares of A Family, Quail Family, With Chicks, No. 44, Large 3285.00
Ackermann, Niagara Falls, London, 1833, 23 x 19 1/2 In. 495.00
Alken, Chase of The Roebuck, 1834, 16 1/3 x 22 In. 987.50
Allison, William McKinley, Bust, Large 89.00
Allom, City of Amoy, 1848, 5 1/2 x 7 In. 147.50
Armstrong, Nude, Water Scene, Signed, 11 x 14 In. 350.00
Armstrong, Venus, Full Figure Nude, 1934, 10 3/4 x 13 1/4 In. 22.00

Audubon bird prints were originally issued as part of books printed from 1826 to 1854. They were issued in two sizes, 26 1/2 inches by 39 1/2 inches and 11 inches by 7 inches. The quadrupeds were issued in 28-by-22-inch prints. Later editions of the Audubon books were done in many sizes, and reprints of the books in the original size were also made. The bird pictures have been so popular they have been copied in myriad sizes by both old and new printing methods. This list includes originals and later copies because Audubon prints of all ages are sold in antiques shops.

J.W.Audubon

Audubon, Acyllium Vulturina, 19 x 15 In. 632.00
Audubon, Black–Winged Hawk, 32 x 22 In. 1200.00
Audubon, Canada Goose, 38 x 25 1/2 In. 330.00
Audubon, Cock of The Plains, 24 1/2 x 3 In. 2860.00
Audubon, Common American Crow, 1848, 8 x 11 In. 127.50
Audubon, Fox Squirrel, 1848, 7 x 9 In. 87.50
Audubon, Ivory–Billed Woodpecker, 37 7/8 x 25 1/4 In. 5500.00
Audubon, King Eider Ducks 1650.00
Audubon, Passenger Pigeon, 25 3/4 x 20 1/2 In. 4400.00
Audubon, Pine Grosbeak, 1858, 27 1/2 x 19 1/2 In. 987.50
Audubon, Red–Shouldered Hawk, 37 3/4 x 25 3/4 In. 300.00
Audubon, Red–Tailed Squirrel, Plate #LV, No. 11, 21 1/2 x 27 In. 1500.00
Audubon, Yellow–Crested Heron, 37 3/4 x 25 In. 3080.00
Baaker, March of Miles Standish, Indian Leading, Poem, Small 375.00
Baillie, Battle of Resaca De La Palma, Capt. May's Capture of LaVega, Small 149.00
Barin, Lone Wolf, Chicago, 1905, Frame, 13 1/2 x 17 1/2 In. 22.50
Beauchamp, Twister, 8 1/2 x 11 1/2 In. 75.00
Bellows, Matinicus, Black & White, Matted, Frame, Signed, 19 1/2 x 25 1/4 In. 700.00
Besler, Poma Amoris, Tomato, 17 x 24 In. 4000.00
Besler, Tulip, 16 x 20 In. 5000.00
Biddle, Chippewa Squaw & Child, Frame, 1836, 25 1/4 x 19 1/4 In. 225.00
Biddle, Hunting The Buffalo, 1837, Frame, 11 1/2 x 16 In. 303.00
Biddle, Okee–Maakee–Quid, A Chippewa Chief, Frame, 1836, 25 1/4 x 19 1/4 In. ... 275.00
Biddle, Open Door, Indian, Philadelphia, Matted & Framed, 21 1/2 x 17 1/2 In. 250.00
Blampied, Centenarian 475.00
Blampied, Work In The Fields 425.00
Bochling, Lone Wolf, 16 x 10 In. 70.00
Brown & Bigelow, Beautiful America, 4 Summer Scenes, 1936 To 1942, 4 Piece 590.00
Brown & Bigelow, Winter Scenes, Sunrise, Frame, 1955 .... 225.00

Burton, View of Boston, 1848, Black & White, 23 x 46 1/2 In. 145.00
Cassells, English Poultry, 1870, 10 x 12 In. 127.50
Curtis, Silver, Indian Girl, Leaning Against Tree, Innocence, 5 x 7 In. 577.00
Davidson, Stone Arch, 8 1/2 x 12 1/2 In. 35.00
DeLongpre, Roses & Bees, Frame, 1905 .... 35.00
DeLongpre, String of Pansies, Woolson Spice Co., Frame, 1895, 23 x 8 In. 50.00
Edna Longest, Woman Golfer, Swing Position, 1910, 9 x 7 In. 40.00
Elvgren, Nude, Full Figure, 16 x 11 In. 28.00
Endicot, Douglas & Stanen Hospitals, Washington, D.C., 1862, Medium 195.00
Etching, Fighting Northern Pike, Palenske, 5 x 7 In. 275.00
Fangel, All Tuckered Out, Salesman's Sample, 7 1/2 x 5 3/4 In. 15.00
Fangel, Baby In High Chair, Sleeping, Matted, 15 x 20 In. 25.00
Farrell, Summer On The Hudson, People & Children, Large 225.00
Fisher Harrison, Danger, Framed, 1908 .... 125.00
Fisher Harrison, In Her Black Bonnet, 1912, 8 x 12 In. 35.00
Fox, Cabin Path, 20 x 14 In. 75.00
Fox, English Cottage, 14 x 18 In. 120.00
Fox, Fallen Monarch, Frame 100.00
Fox, Flowers On Verandah, Sky & Water Background, Signed, 20 x 30 In. 225.00
Fox, Good Ship Adventure, 13 x 10 In. 65.00
Fox, Indian Summer, Frame, 20 1/2 x 32 1/2 In. 150.00
Fox, Love's Paradise, Frame, 8 x 14 In. 65.00
Fox, Moonlight & Roses, Frame, 14 x 18 In. 90.00
Fox, Nature's Best, 18 1/2 x 12 In. 85.00
Fox, Tom & Jerry, 9 x 12 In. 40.00
Fox, Urgelles, Love's Paradise, 1925, 18 x 10 In. 295.00
Fox, Where Giants Wrought, Frame, 17 x 13 In. 125.00
Franklin At The Court of France, Colored, William Jay, 30 x 41 In. 165.00
Garrett, An Old Sweetheart of Mine, Framed, 8 x 10 In. 50.00
Gaul, The Pickett, Solitary Soldier Standing Guard, Gesso Frame, 9 1/2 x 15 In. 85.00
Gould & Richter, Anser Albifrons & Anser Segutun, Frame, 25 x 30 In., Pair 450.00
Gutmann, Double Blessing, Original Frame 125.00
Gutmann, First Love, Dated 1907 .... 80.00
Gutmann, Friendly Enemies 85.00
Gutmann, Little Bit of Heaven, 11 x 14 In. 35.00
Gutmann, Message of Roses, Frame, 13 1/2 x 17 3/4 In. 195.00
Gutmann, Miss Flirt, 11 x 14 In. .... 35.00 To 50.00
Gutmann, On Dreamland's Border, Frame 70.00
Gutmann, Seeing, Black & White, 14 x 11 In. 50.00
Gutmann, Thank You God 95.00
Haskell & Allen, Cork River & Blackrock Castle, Ireland, Sailboats On River, Small ... 89.00
Hess, Indian Lake, Sunset, New York Lake, Large 1495.00
Hill, Giant Bell Flower, 11 x 17 1/2 In. 887.50
Huffam, Fox Hunting, The Find, 21 x 29 In. 99.00
Icart, Angry Steed, 1917, 10 1/2 x 16 1/2 In. 2000.00
Icart, Coursing II, Etching & Drypoint, Signed, c.1929, 15 1/2 x 25 In. 5500.00
Icart, Coursing II, Frame, 1929, 15 1/4 x 25 1/4 In. 3450.00
Icart, Coursing II, Signed, Frame, 1929, 15 1/4 x 25 1/4 In. 3300.00
Icart, La Lettre, 1938, 18 x 22 In. 95.00
Icart, Lassitude, Signed, Frame, 1923, 9 x 11 3/4 In., ... 880.00
Icart, Little Kittens, 10 1/4 x 9 1/2 In. 825.00
Icart, Milkmaid La Laitiere, Frame, 1926, 12 1/2 x 19 1/2 In. 1395.00
Icart, Mockery, 1928, 26 1/2 x 23 In. 1500.00
Icart, Rainbow, Etching & Drypoint, Signed, 1930, 24 3/4 x 17 In. 3300.00
Icart, Smoke Fumes, Frame, 1933, 16 1/2 x 22 In. 2495.00
Icart, Thais, Signed, Frame, 1927, 16 x 20 3/8 In. 2640.00
Icart, Woman Picking Lemons, Signed, 17 1/4 x 11 1/2 In. 1210.00
Jackson & De Witt Clinton, Black & White, Frame, 12 x 10 In., Pair 490.00
Jacoulet, Paul, Chinese Poet 3500.00
Jacoulet, Paul, Le Nautilus 3600.00

Japanese woodblock prints are listed as follows: Print, Japanese, name of artist, title or description, type, and size. Dealers use the following terms: Tate–e is a vertical composition. Yoko–e is a horizontal composition. The words Aiban (13 by 9 inches), Chuban (10 by 7 1/2 inches), Hosoban (12 by 6 inches), Oban (15 by 10 inches), and Koban (7 by 4 inches) denote size. Modern versions of some of these prints have been made.

Japanese, 2 Actors, Kunisada, From Triptych, 14 x 10 In.	85.00
Japanese, 4 Actors, 2–Color, Kunisada, From Triptych, 14 x 10 In.	85.00
Japanese, Bird's–Eye View of Tokyo, 1880, 27 x 12 In.	2487.50
Japanese, Hasui, Moon In Magume, 14 1/2 x 9 In.	132.00
Japanese, Hiroshi Yoshida, Fuji From Hoshida, Signed, 1928, 9 1/2 x 14 1/2 In.	550.00
Japanese, Hiroshi Yoshida, Grand Canyon, Signed, 1925, 9 1/2 x 14 1/2 In.	525.00
Japanese, Hiroshige, Figures Passing Through Landscape, Color, 9 x 13 1/2 In.	154.00
Japanese, Hoshida, Hiroshi, Victoria Memorial, Signed, 9 1/2 x 14 1/2 In.	440.00
Japanese, Iris & Frog, Frame, 15 x 7 1/2 In.	33.00
Japanese, Kunisada, Seated Man With Rice Bowl & Chop Sticks, 15 1/2 x 10 In.	88.00
Japanese, Kuniyoshi, Utagawa, Seven Immortals, 28 1/4 x 9 3/4 In.	45.00
Japanese, Nude With Fish, 1917, 10 1/2 x 10 3/4 In.	165.00
Japanese, Travelers Encountering Spirits On Road, c.1800, 4 1/2 x 7 In.	387.50
Japanese, Woman & Child, Both With Halos, Frame, 22 1/4 x 19 1/2 In.	2405.00
Japanese, Woman In Garden, Matted & Framed, 22 3/4 In.	88.00
Japanese, Yoshitora, Gentleman & Lady In New Western Dress, c.1870, 9 x 14 In.	987.50
Kellogg & Comstock, Twelve Miles An Hour Including Stoppages	33.00
Kellogg, Lucy, Curly Maple Frame, 11 3/4 x 10 In.	105.00
Kellogg, My Highland Girl, Scots Clothes, 1/2 Length, Small	55.00
Kelly, My Favorite & My Playmate, Framed, Pair	330.00
Klapka, Precious Awake, Glazed, Framed	45.00
Kurz & Allison, Battle of Atlanta, Gen. McPherson Killed In Battle, 1864, Large	195.00
Kurz & Allison, Battle of Bull Run, Fought July 21, 1861, 17 1/2 x 25 In. ... 235.00 To	265.00
Kurz & Allison, Battle of Bull Run, Gen. McDowell, Gen. Beauregard, 1861, Large	225.00
Kurz & Allison, Battle of Five Forks, Va., Gen. Sheridan's Cavalry Charge, Large	265.00
Kurz & Allison, Battle of Kenesaw Mountain, Gen. Sherman, Gen. Johnston, Large	265.00
Kurz & Allison, Battle of Monmouth, 25 x 21 In.	49.00
Kurz & Allison, Battle of New Orleans, Gen. Jackson & Pakenham, Large	249.00
Kurz & Allison, Battle of Tippecanoe, Harrison, Tecumseh's Indians, 17 x 25 In.	235.00
Kurz & Allison, Battle of Williamsburg, Va., Gen. McClellan, L7 1/2 x 25 In.	265.00
Kurz & Allison, Declaration of Independence, Large	198.00
Kurz & Allison, DeSoto's Discovery of The Mississippi, Soldiers Erect Cross, Large	235.00
Kurz & Allison, Fall of Petersburg, Va., Gen. Grant Vs. Gen. Lee, Large	235.00
Kurz & Allison, Great Connemaugh Valley Disaster, Johnstown Flood, 17 x 25 In.	325.00
Lampied, Come On Boys	375.00
Lithograph, Kellogg & Comstock, Vase of Fruit, Frame, 18 x 14 In.	95.00
Lizar, Crested Cockatoo, 1840, 4 x 6 In.	67.50
Lizar, Lion, Animals of The World, 1838, 6 x 8 In.	87.50
Max, Peter, Pique Dame, Lady, Huge Hat, Signed, No. 49/280	425.00
McKenny & Hall, Ahyouwaighs, John Brant, Iroquois Chief, 1838	195.00
McKenny & Hall, Bear Dance, Small	725.00
McKenny & Hall, Chippawa Squaw & Child, 1836	465.00
McKenny & Hall, Chippewa Squaw & Child, 1836	325.00
McKenny & Hall, Commnosaqua, Pottawatomi Chief, 1827	275.00
McKenny & Hall, Julcee Mathla, Seminole Chief, 1843	325.00
McKenny & Hall, Keeshewaa, Sauk & Fox Chief, 1843	275.00
McKenny & Hall, Le Soldat DuChene, Osage Chief, 1843	375.00
McKenny & Hall, Little Crow, Sioux Chief, 1838	179.00
McKenny & Hall, Major Ridge, Cherokee Chief, 1838	198.00
McKenny & Hall, Major Ridge, Cherokee, 1838	198.00
McKenny & Hall, Meeta Koosega, Chippewa, 1837	179.00
McKenny & Hall, Monkaushka, Sioux Chief, 1837	395.00
McKenny & Hall, Opothle Yoholo, Creek Chief, 1837	385.00
McKenny & Hall, Peechekir, Chippewa Chief, 1843	275.00
McKenny & Hall, Red Jacket, Seneca Chief, Biddle, 1837	495.00
McKenny & Hall, Wa Kaun Ha Ka, Winnebago Chief, Biddle, 1841	325.00

McKenny & Hall, Wakechai, Crouching Eagle, Sauk & Fox Chief, 1838 .... 375.00
McKenny & Hall, Wanatu, The Charger, Sioux Chief, Biddle, 1837 .... 395.00
Moore, Man & Woman, Black & Green, 9 x 13 In. 1320.00
Moran, Grand Canyon National Park, 1912, Frame, 25 1/4 x 34 2/3 In. 1210.00
Moran, Nude Woman, Blond Seated At Table, Black Frame, 10 x 12 In. 200.00
Morris, Golden Eagle, 1840, 8 1/2 x 5 1/2 In. 87.50
Mucha, Reverie Du Soir, 40 x 15 In. 3890.00
Munnings, Brown Jack, Horse, Frame, Frost & Reed of Bristol & London, 1935 ..... 700.00
Nast, Another Such Victory, 1876, 9 1/2 x 14 In. 127.50

Nutting prints are now popular with collectors. Wallace Nutting is known
for his pictures, furniture, and books. Nutting *prints* are actually hand
colored photographs issued from 1900 to 1941. There are over 10,000
different titles.

Nutting, 2 Indian Maidens By Water, 10 x 12 In. 575.00
Nutting, An Old Parlor Idyll, Uncle Sam & Granny, 14 x 16 In. 225.00
Nutting, Announcing The Engagement, 3 Girls Chat At Table, 14 x 17 In. 200.00
Nutting, Baking Day, Girl Puts Pie In Oven, 14 x 17 In. 250.00
Nutting, Bit of Sewing, Girl Sews By Fire, 11 x 14 In. 65.00
Nutting, Canal Road, Windmill, Canal, 11 x 14 In. 160.00
Nutting, Cold Day, Girl Cores Apples By Fireplace, 14 x 17 In. 120.00
Nutting, Comfort & The Cat, Cat Sleeps In Basket, 14 x 17 In. 130.00
Nutting, Corner Cupboard, Girl Reached In Cupboard, 13 x 22 In. 210.00
Nutting, Cottage Scene, 3 x 4 In. 75.00
Nutting, Cup That Cheers, Interior Scene, Frame, 14 x 11 In. 155.00
Nutting, Fair Weather Today, Woman On Porch, 9 x 15 In. 75.00
Nutting, Fleck of Sunshine, 11 x 15 In. 310.00
Nutting, Garden of Larkspur, 4 3/4 x 6 1/2 In. 35.00
Nutting, Hollyhock Cottage, Thatch–Roofed Cottage, 14 x 17 In. 160.00
Nutting, Joy Path, 10 x 12 In. 45.00
Nutting, LaJolla, Seascape, 16 x 20 In. 250.00
Nutting, Leaf Strewn Brook, Fall Colored Leaves By Stream, 13 x 16 In. 90.00
Nutting, Mother's Cottage, Country Cottage, 10 x 12 In. 170.00
Nutting, Nest, Thatch–Roofed Home By Country Lane, 14 x 17 In. 45.00
Nutting, Newton Autumn, Fall Trees, 15 x 16 1/2 In. 135.00
Nutting, On The Shores of The Zuyder Zee, People Dressed In Dutch Attire ....*Illus* 2970.00
Nutting, Orchard Heights, Original Frame, 15 x 18 In. 65.00
Nutting, Our Martyred Presidents, 16 x 20 In. 20.00
Nutting, Patti's Favorite Walk, 9 3/8 x 7 5/8 In. 135.00
Nutting, Proud As Peacocks, 2 Girls Inspect Bonnet, 14 x 17 In. 180.00

Print, Nutting, On The Shores of The Zuyder Zee,
People Dressed In Dutch Attire

Nutting, Quilting, Frame, 12 x 16 In. 215.00
Nutting, Returning From A Walk, Girl Walks Up Stairway, 14 x 17 In. 65.00
Nutting, Sea Ledges, Frame, 14 x 17 In. 325.00
Nutting, Stitch In Time, Girl Sews By Fire, 10 x 13 In. 95.00
Nutting, Swimming Pool, Trees Reflect In Blue Stream, 26 x 30 In. 60.00
Nutting, Very Satisfactory, 11 x 14 In. 310.00
Nutting, Winter Welcome Home, Friends Greet Each Other In Snow, 10 x 16 In. 1500.00
Ottterna, Magnolias, 16 x 20 In. 45.00
Owen, Commercial Traveler, Frame, 23 x 35 In. 400.00
Parkinson, Cupid Awake, Cupid Asleep, Signed, 1897, 13 1/2 x 17 1/2 In. 450.00

Parrish prints are wanted by collectors. Maxfield Frederick Parrish was an
illustrator who lived from 1870 to 1966. He is best known as a designer of
magazine covers, posters, calendars, and advertisements.

Parrish, Air Castles, Frame, 12 1/2 x 16 1/2 In. 175.00
Parrish, Cleopatra, Frame, 1917, 12 1/2 x 13 1/2 In. 135.00
Parrish, Daybreak, 6 x 10 In. 75.00
Parrish, Daybreak, 18 x 30 In. 75.00
Parrish, Daybreak, Frame, 27 1/2 x 13 1/2 In. 125.00
Parrish, Daybreak, Original Frame, 20 x 14 In. 125.00
Parrish, Dinkey Bird, 1904, 21 3/4 x 15 1/2 In. 185.00
Parrish, Garden of Allah, 15 1/4 x 30 In. 275.00
Parrish, Humpty Dumpty, 13 1/2 x 10 1/2 In. 22.00
Parrish, Old Glen Mill, Frame, 12 x 16 In. 231.00
Parrish, Sheltering Oaks, Matted, 8 x 10 In. 35.00
Parrish, Sing A Song of Six Pence, 7 x 16 1/2 In. 45.00
Parrish, Sunlight, Frame, 1958, 8 1/2 x 11 In. 100.00
Parrish, Under Summer Skies, 16 x 19 In. 55.00
Parrish, Woman Scaling Steep Rock, Small 220.00
Pass, Pepper & Insects, 1810, 10 1/2 x 8 In. 227.50
Passmore, Dept. of Agriculture Yearbook, American Apples Group, 26 x 26 In. 587.50
Portrait of Girl In Red, White & Blue Flag Dress, Salt Print, 1860s, 18 X13 In. 825.00
Prang, Battle of Antietam, 15 x 21 1/2 In. 75.00
Prang, Battle of Kenesaw Mountain, 15 x 21 1/2 In. 75.00
Prang, Sheridan's Final Charge At Winchester, 15 x 21 1/2 In. .... 149.00 To 169.00
Reeves, Twilight of Army, Maj. Gen. P. R. Cleburne & Division, 1864, 19 x 24 In. .. 185.00
Reinthal & Newman, Rubaiyat, Matted, 1917, 8 1/2 x 12 1/4 In. 195.00
Remington, Cowboys of Arizona, 1882, 10 x 14 In. 487.50
Rice, Sierra Snow Bank, Wood Block, Matted, Signed, 9 x 7 In. 770.00
Rockwell, Norman, Triple Self–Portrait, Signed, 20 x 25 In. 1000.00
Rosenthal, Raising The Flag, May, 1861, Toned, 25 1/2 x 33 In. 358.00
Rowlandson, Interior of St. Paul's, London, 1810, 7 1/2 x 10 1/2 In. 387.50
Rubaiyat, Loaf of Bread, Flask of Wine, Original Frame, 15 x 37 In. 440.00
Schultz, Payne Peach, U.S. Dept. of Agriculture Yearbook, 1910, 5 1/2 x 8 1/2 In. .. 87.50
Seeks, Black Couple Out For A Stroll, 26 x 18 In. 110.00
Smith, Jessie Wilcox, Little Red Riding Hood, Wolf, Oak Frame 65.00
Stobart, Maiden Lane, New York In 1880 .... 1485.00
Stobart, South Street, New York In 1880 .... 2640.00
Trew, Maple, 16 1/2 x 9 1/8 In. 887.50
Trout Fishing, American, 1860, 7 x 9 In. 187.50
Trubble In De Church, Black Minister, Matted, 16 1/2 x 14 In. 132.00
Turpin, Artichant, Paris, 1810, 5 x 8 In. 187.50
Van Houtten, Corn, Belgium, 14 x 10 In. 485.00
Walker, Indian Love Song, Fame, 14 x 20 In. 85.00
Winter Scene, Evening, 1956 .... 150.00
Wolstenholme, Essex Hunt, 1831, 30 x 35 In., Pair 950.00
Worth, Thos. A Wildcat Train, No Stop–Overs, Small 325.00
Wren, St. Paul's Cathedral, 1715, 15 x 10 In. 887.50
Yard Long, Flowers 32.50
Yard Long, Resort, French Lick, Ind., Color, Frame 22.50
Yard Long, Sweet Peas, Painted Frame, Grace Barton Allen, 34 x 7 1/2 In. 120.00
Yard Long, Violets, White Frame, Mary Hart, 24 x 8 In. 90.00

PURSES have been recognizable since the eighteenth century, when leather and needlework purses were preferred. Beaded purses became popular in the nineteenth century, went out of style, but are again in use. Mesh purses date from the 1880s and are still being made. How to carry a handkerchief and lipstick is a problem today for every woman, including the Queen of England.

Alligator, Baby Alligator Head, Cuba	40.00
Bakelite, White, Elegant	28.00
Beaded & Embroidered Silk, Clutch, 1930s	20.00
Beaded, Blue & Black, 7 x 9 In.	55.00
Beaded, Blue Steel Beads, Blue Long Tassels, Civil War Era	55.00
Beaded, Butterflies, 1910, Large	175.00
Beaded, Carnival Glass	75.00
Beaded, Copper, Diamond Shape, Fringed	130.00
Beaded, Drawstring Closure, 1835, 6 3/8 x 7 3/4 In.	295.00
Beaded, Envelope Style, Chain Handle	39.00
Beaded, Geometrical Pattern	75.00
Beaded, Reticule, Roses, Church & Trees, Homespun Lining, 1800s	85.00
Beaded, Reticule, Scenic, Floral Cornucopias, Homespun Lining, 1800s, Large	95.00
Beaded, Shoulder Bag, Gaudy Multicolored Beads, Fringed	8.00
Beaded, Steel, Hand Crocheted, Civil War Era	55.00
Beads, Wooden, Gray, Japan	12.00
Black Satin, Clutch, Celluloid Medallion, Nettie Rosenstein	95.00
Brass, Copper, Lined, Chain Handle, Pillow Shape	35.00
Brass, Copper, Pillow Shape, Chain Handle	25.00
Brocade, Jade–Type Clasp, Oriental	50.00
Canvas Work, Carnation Pattern, Irish Stitch, Crewel, 18th Century, 5 1/2 x 4 In.	275.00
Celluloid, Pink Marbelized, Long Chain	38.00
Ceramic Jewels, Metal Handle, Clasp & Hinges, Germany, Pre–1945	145.00
Chain Handle, Art Nouveau, Ornate Silver Plated Top	45.00
Cloisonne Lid, Birds, Powder, Rouge, Evans, 1920s	85.00
Cloisonne Lid, Flowers, Powder, Rouge, Mirror, Carrying Chain, Silvered Case	90.00
Cobra, Leather Lined, Adjustable Strap	25.00
Drawstring, 5 Rows of Beaded Fringe, Kelly Green	55.00
Embroidered, Gold Metallic Thread, Colored Stones, India	50.00
Flamestitch, 3 Pointed Top, Square	880.00
Flamestitch, Joseph England, 1761	800.00
Flamestitch, Strawberry Harlequin Pattern	797.00
Floral, Dresden, Sapphire Closure, Whiting & Davis	85.00
Gold Mesh, Eyeglass Case, Whiting Davis	22.00
Leather, Clutch, Brass Closure, Metal Corners	55.00
Leather, Hand Tooled, Man On Mule, Cactus	48.00
Leather, Small, 1915	26.00
Linen, Homespun, Stylized Floral Embroidery, Green, Gold, Yellow, 9 x 9 1/2 In.	82.00
Lucite, Mother–of–Pearl	15.00
Lucite, Rhinestones	12.00
Lucite, Seashells On Lid	38.00
Lucite, Seashells On Top	45.00
Lucite, Tyrolean, 1950s	90.00
Mesh, 1 Old Cut Diamond, 2 Rose Cut Diamonds, 4 Oval Sapphires, 14K Gold	550.00
Mesh, Beaded, Art Deco, Multicolored, Inverted Pyramid, 9 x 4 In.	150.00
Mesh, Black, Silver, Geometric Enameled, Amethyst On Handle, Fringe, 4 x 6 In.	250.00
Mesh, Cathedral Frame, Tassel, 7 In.	85.00
Mesh, Chain Bag, Gold Flowers, 18K Gold Frame, Diamonds & Rubies	825.00
Mesh, Gold, Shoulder Bag, 1950s	15.00
Mesh, Mandalian	250.00
Mesh, Mandalian, Enameled Birds of Paradise, Box, 8 1/2 In.	125.00
Mesh, Metal, 1920s	20.00
Mesh, Silver, 7 Garnets Set On Frame, Matching Coin Purse	400.00
Mesh, Silver, Whiting & Davis, 7 x 12 In.	250.00
Needlepoint, Dated 1767, 8 In.	907.00

Peti–Pak, Compact, Lipstick & Comb, Gold Checkered Design, Zell 5th Avenue 50.00
Petit Point Embroidered, Steel Beaded Trim 62.00
Rhinestones & Sequins, Poodle, 1950s 42.00
Satin, Silver Sequins, Beads, Metallic Rolled Handles, Evening, 1950s 35.00
Seed Pearl, Evening Bag 15.00
Silver & Celluloid, Germany 45.00
Silver Open Work, Gold Trim, Vanglo, 4 1/2 x 6 1/4 In. 42.00
Silver, Coin, Molded & Engraved 47.50
Snakeskin, Pouch Style, Chain Handle, 1950s 35.00
Tin, Child's, Green, Sausage Shape 40.00
Tortoiseshell Top & Bottom, Box Style, Brass Sides, Lucite, Clear Handle 30.00
Velvet, Metallic Thread Embroidery, Pearl Type Ovals 72.00
Velvet, Silver Frame With Blister Pearls, Garnets, Faux Diamonds 270.00
Velvet, Silver Plated Repousse Frame, Chain Handle, Medallion Clip 125.00

QUEZAL glass was made from 1901 to 1920 by Martin Bach, Sr., in Brooklyn, New York. Other glassware by other firms, such as Loetz, Steuben, and Tiffany, resembles this gold-colored iridescent glass. After Martin Bach's death in 1920, his son continued the manufacture of a similar glass under the name *Lustre Art Glass.*

Quezal

Bowl, Pulled Gold Crisscross Design, Gold Aurene Inside, 11 1/4 In. 1250.00
Bowl, Rainbow Colors, Pedestal, Iridescent, Signed, 4 1/2 x 8 1/4 In. 400.00
Lamp, Gooseneck, Brass Base, Green & Gold Pulled Leaf, Gold Lining, Signed 1350.00
Lamp, Lily, 4–Light, Adjustable, 27 In. 3750.00
Lamp, Table, Pulled Feather, Bell Shape Shade, Iridescent, 17 1/2 In. 1045.00
Salt, Ribbed, Gold Iridescent, Signed, 2 1/2 In. 192.50
Saucer, Gold Iridescent, Signed, 5 1/2 In. 85.00
Shade, Flared Rim, Gold Pulled & Trailed Design, Gold Interior, Signed, 5 In. 82.50
Shade, Floriform, Ribbed & Swirl Pattern, Signed, 11 Piece 1430.00
Shade, Wave Design, Gold Ground, Ruffled Rim, Signed, 5 In. 165.00
Vase, Amber Iridescent, Wintergreen Striated Leafage, Onion Shape, 6 1/2 In. 990.00
Vase, Blue & Gold Hearts, Gold Throat, Signed, 8 1/2 In. 800.00
Vase, Double Pulled Feather, Green, Gold, Yellow & White, 10 In. 2530.00
Vase, Elongated Slender Body, Orange–Gold Iridescent Glass, 11 In. 467.50
Vase, Emerald Iridescent Ground, Silvery Amber Bands, 1920, 4 In. 1320.00
Vase, Flower Form, Pulled Feather, Ruffled Top, 8 1/4 In. 1155.00
Vase, Gold & Green Pulled Feather, Gilt Rim, 12 3/4 In. 990.00
Vase, Jack–In–The–Pulpit, Amber Iridescent Feathering, 11 7/8 In. 3300.00
Vase, Jack–In–The–Pulpit, Gold Iridescent, 8 3/4 In. 2420.00
Vase, King Tut, Pedestal, 6 1/8 In. 825.00
Vase, Opal Baluster Body, Yellow–Gold Coiled Design, 6 3/4 In. 715.00
Vase, Orange–Gold Iridized, Flared Conical Form, 6 In. 330.00
Vase, Pull–Up Design, Gold, Purple & Greens, Brass Holder, Signed, 8 1/4 In. 350.00
Vase, Purple Pulled Threading, Gold Aurene, 13 In. 1750.00
Vase, Ruffled Top, Signed, 3 3/4 In. 850.00
Vase, Silver Pulled Feathers, Blue & Green, 6 x 5 In. 3850.00
Vase, Silver–Blue Iridescent Body, Coiled Design, 10 In. 1320.00
Vase, Swirl Decoration, Ruffled Rim, Iridescent, 4 1/2 In. 375.00
Vase, Trumpet, Pulled Feather, Amber Iridescent Interior, 1920, 7 7/8 In. 1210.00

QUILTS have been made since the seventeenth century. Early textiles were very precious and every scrap was saved to be reused. A quilt is a combination of fabrics joined to a filler and a backing by small stitched designs known as quilting. An appliqued quilt has pieces stitched to the top of a large piece of background fabric. A patchwork, or pieced, quilt is made of many small pieces stitched together. Embroidery can be added to either type.

Amish, Lone Star, Black Ground, Contemporary, 41 x 41 In. 115.00
Amish, Patchwork, 9 Patch, Red & Blue, Black Ground, 22 1/2 x 29 In. 185.00
Amish, Patchwork, Center Diamond, Feather & Diamond Quilting, 75 x 73 In. 3025.00
Amish, Patchwork, Diamond In The Square, Plum, Navy & Forest, 80 x 82 In. 7150.00
Amish, Patchwork, Diamond Square, Blue & Brown, 77 x 77 In. 100.00
Amish, Patchwork, Monkey Pattern, Green, Blue, Maroon, 106 x 119 In. 220.00

◆◆◆◆◆◆◆◆◆◆◆◆◆◆◆◆◆◆◆◆◆

Most oriental rugs can be washed. There are many books in the library that give detailed instructions. Don't do it yourself if the rug is silk or if a test shows the colors will run. Don't worry if the rug becomes stiff when soaked in water. It will soften when dry.

◆◆◆◆◆◆◆◆◆◆◆◆◆◆◆◆◆◆◆◆◆

Quilt, Appliqued, Lemon Tree & Tulip,
38 X 35 In.

Amish, Patchwork, Red Center Square, Green Border, Blue Ground, 45 x 45 In.	95.00
Amish, Patchwork, Rocky Road To California, 1940s, 68 x 78 In.	400.00
Amish, Patchwork, Star of The East, Late 19th Century, 69 x 42 1/2 In.	550.00
Amish, Patchwork, Star Pattern, Magenta, Black Grid, Blue Ground, 31 x 31 In.	45.00
Amish, Stripes, 3 Quilting Patterns, 85 x 87 In.	1290.00
Appliqued, 3 Headed Tulips, Green, Brown, Gray, Yellow Calico, 78 x 102 In.	275.00
Appliqued, 4 Flower Ring, Red, Green & Orange, White Ground, 1927, 85 x 85 In.	875.00
Appliqued, 4 Oak Leaf Medallions, Red, Ecru, Quilted Wreaths, 77 x 83 In.	275.00
Appliqued, 4 Scalloped Edge Flowers, Border Fans, Beige, 84 x 84 In.	660.00
Appliqued, 4 Stylized Urns, Fan–Like Shapes, Stripe Along Edges, 74 x 82 In	175.00
Appliqued, 8 Pointed Star, Pink, Blue & Green, 1910, 82 x 82 In.	375.00
Appliqued, 9 Floral Patterns, Vine & Berry Border, 19th Century, 90 x 92 In.	775.00
Appliqued, 9 Large Stars, Green, Red, Pink Calico, Vining Border, 90 x 96 In.	1705.00
Appliqued, 12 Stylized Floral Medallions, Red, Yellow, Green Calico, 76 x 98 In. ...	495.00
Appliqued, 25 Stylized Flowers, Red, Green, Goldenrod, Pink Calico, 92 x 92 In.	385.00
Appliqued, Birds of Paradise, Baskets of Flowers, 19th Century, 86 x 86 In.	715.00
Appliqued, Bright Morning Star, Square, 88 In.	2300.00
Appliqued, Dresden Plate, 85 1/2 x 66 In.	35.00
Appliqued, Embroidered Flowers, Dark Colors, Crib Size	160.00
Appliqued, Floral Design, Green, Red, Yellow, Maroon, Pink, Calico, 86 x 102 In.	2970.00
Appliqued, Floral Medallion, Red, Green Calico, Frame, Crib Size	687.00
Appliqued, Floral, 12 Oversized Blocks, Border, 74 x 97 In.	770.00
Appliqued, Flying Gccsc, Alternating Green & Yellow Calico, 41 x 42 In.	440.00
Appliqued, Green, Yellow, Red Print, White Ground, Floral Pattern, 90 x 92 In.	775.00
Appliqued, Lemon Tree & Tulip, 38 x 35 In. ....*Illus*	2900.00
Appliqued, Log Cabin Medallion, 70 x 71 In.	275.00
Appliqued, Log Cabin, Velvet, Early 20th Century, 80 x 68 In.	220.00
Appliqued, Missouri Rose, Catherine Jane McPeak Stults, 1858, 91 x 72 In.	770.00
Appliqued, Oak Leaf & Reel, Bird Border, Eleanor A. Robison, 1843, 77 x 94 In. ...	2750.00
Appliqued, Poinsettias, Tulips, Red, Green Solids, Yellow Calico, 84 x 86 In.	1402.00
Appliqued, Presentation, Embroidered, R. F. P. Monogram, 1905–1906, 36 x 43 In.	3630.00
Appliqued, Princess Feather, Red & Green, White, 2 Stitches Per Inch, 98 x 95 In.	1200.00
Appliqued, Red & Green Foliate, Mid–19th Century, Square, 106 In.	1650.00
Appliqued, Red & Green Oak Leaf Medallions, Red Sawtooth Border, 82 x 82 In. ...	522.00
Appliqued, Red & Green Stylized Floral Medallion, White, Scalloped, 84 x 101 In.	440.00
Appliqued, Royal Hawaiian Insignia, 4 Union Jacks, S. Kahalew, 69 x 53 In.	4400.00
Appliqued, Sailing Ship Center, President's Wreaths, White Cotton, 72 x 72 In.	4400.00
Appliqued, Star of Bethlehem, Late 19th Century, 86 x 86 In.	3300.00
Appliqued, Star Pattern, Blue and White, Embroidery, Queen Size	100.00
Appliqued, Star, Red & Green, Crib Size	300.00

Appliqued, State House Steps, Log Cabin, Square, 76 In. 450.00
Appliqued, Stylized Floral Design, Tulips, Oak Leaves, Green, Red, 80 x 80 In. 440.00
Appliqued, Stylized Floral Design, Vining Border, Red, Beige Print, 94 x 94 In. 104.00
Appliqued, Stylized Floral Medallions, Teal Green, Red, Goldenrod, 67 x 76 In. 440.00
Appliqued, Stylized Floral, Calico, Scalloped Border, 78 x 78 In. 350.00
Appliqued, Stylized Floral, Red, Yellow, Pink, Calico, Puffed Flowers, 81 x 82 In. ... 550.00
Appliqued, Stylized Roses, Vining Border, Green Calico, Solid Red, 96 x 96 In. 495.00
Appliqued, Stylized Tulip Medallion, Goldenrod, Purple, Brown, Red, 34 x 34 In. ... 285.00
Appliqued, Stylized Tulips, Solid Red, Green, Yellow Calico, 96 x 98 In. 990.00
Appliqued, Tulip Pattern, Heart, Leaf & Flowerhead Quilting, 1858, 91 x 72 In. 770.00
Appliqued, Tulip Pattern, Yellow, Green, Red Patches, 1855, 87 x 71 In. 770.00
Appliqued, Vining Floral Design, Swag, Bud Border, Green, Pink, Red, 84 x 84 In. 1560.00
Crazy, Patchwork, Embroidered Silk & Velvet, Dated 1885, 78 X74 In. 330.00
Crazy, Patchwork, Satin, Sateen & Velvet, Embroidered, 56 x 58 In. 165.00
Crazy, Patchwork, Silk Blocks, Embroidered Velvet Border, 68 x 68 In. 220.00
Embroidered, Center Flowerpot, Blooms, 110 x 108 In. 9900.00
Mennonite, Patchwork, Single Star of Multicolored Solids, 36 x 36 In. 300.00
Mennonite, Patchwork, Sunshine & Shadow, Bar Pattern Back, 82 x 86 In. 550.00
Mennonite, Star Pattern, Crib Size 300.00
Patchwork Applique, American Flag, Flour Sack Back, 1920, 84 x 72 In. 4400.00
Patchwork, 4 Patch In Blue, White & Beige Calico, 67 x 76 In. 85.00
Patchwork, 4 Patch, Calico, Chintz, Border, 34 x 38 1/2 In. 225.00
Patchwork, 8 Point Stars, Calico, Mennonite, 82 x 92 In. 475.00
Patchwork, 8 Point Stars, Red, Blue, Yellow Calico, 70 x 78 In. 715.00
Patchwork, 9 Patch, Multi-Colored Prints, Yellow Sawtooth Border, 78 x 98 In. 93.00
Patchwork, 9 Patch, Prints, Calico, 36 x 36 In. 150.00
Patchwork, 25 Patch, Multi-Colored Calico, Gray Print Ground, 67 x 80 In. 137.00
Patchwork, 30 Stars, Navy Blue, 1 Row In Blue & Red Prints, 70 x 82 In. 192.00
Patchwork, 4 Points, 77 x 70 In. 210.00
Patchwork, 48 Album Squares, Silk & Velvet, 59 x 90 In. 3300.00
Patchwork, 72 Stylized Flowers, Red, Teal Blue Print, 95 x 100 In. 660.00
Patchwork, 8-Pointed Star, Pink, Blue, & Green, c.1910, 82 x 82 In. 375.00
Patchwork, 9-Piece Pattern, Amish, c.1930, 72 x 80 In. 660.00
Patchwork, America's Cup, Puritan & Genesia, 77 x 79 In. 550.00
Patchwork, Autograph, Diamond-Quilted, Dated 1887, 77 x 88 In. 395.00
Patchwork, Basket, Red & White, 66 x 80 In. 176.00
Patchwork, Basket, Teal Blue, White, 75 x 75 In. 116.00
Patchwork, Baskets of Flowers, Green, Pink Calico, 82 x 82 In. 412.00
Patchwork, Bird In Center, Embroidered Borders, Square, 80 In. 1700.00
Patchwork, Bow Tie, Full Size 200.00
Patchwork, Broken Dishes, Pink & White Calico, Doll's, 24 x 28 In. 330.00
Patchwork, Brown & Rose Stars Alternating Trapunto Grape Clusters, 101 x 90 In. 55.00
Patchwork, Calico, Schoolhouse, Printed & Solid Patches, c.1930, 84 x 61 In. 1980.00
Patchwork, Cathedral Windows, 84 x 76 In. 495.00
Patchwork, Cherry Trees, 13 Appliqued Yellow Birds, 93 x 74 In. 355.00
Patchwork, Colored Prints, Yellow Calico Ground, Red Calico Border, 83 x 90 In. ... 130.00
Patchwork, Dahlia, Stuffed Petals, 76 x 90 In. 200.00
Patchwork, Diamond, Pieced Hexagons, Colored Print, 72 x 88 In. 400.00
Patchwork, Dresden Plates, Multicolored Plates, White Ground, 96 x 80 In. 325.00
Patchwork, Dutchman's Britches, 65 x 79 In. 150.00
Patchwork, Flower Garden, 90 x 100 In. 285.00
Patchwork, Flying Geese Border, Red, White, Irish Chain, 78 x 79 In. 170.00
Patchwork, Friendship, Multicolored Calico, White Ground, Pink Grid, 78 x 87 In. 220.00
Patchwork, Goldenrod Print Stars, White Ground, 80 x 81 In. 247.00
Patchwork, Goose Track, Square, 66 In. 145.00
Patchwork, Irish Chain, Blue & White, Large Stitches, Border, 69 x 83 In. 115.00
Patchwork, Jacob's Ladder, Red & Navy Blue, 83 x 96 In. 350.00
Patchwork, Log Cabin Variant, Radiating Diamond, 63 x 79 In. 330.00
Patchwork, Log Cabin Variant, Silk, 19th Century, 62 1/2 x 60 In. 154.00
Patchwork, Log Cabin, Barn Raising Pattern, American, c.1935, 89 x 86 In. 2750.00
Patchwork, Log Cabin, Navy, Red & White, 75 x 64 In. 440.00
Patchwork, Lone Star, c.1930, 77 x 84 In. 895.00
Patchwork, Lone Star, Multicolored Prints, Hot Pink Ground, 84 x 87 In. 165.00

Patchwork, Lone Star, Pale Blue Calico, Red Binding, 76 x 74 In. 1100.00
Patchwork, Maple Leaf, Orange, Tan, 78 x 90 In. 325.00
Patchwork, Monkey Wrench, Calico, Sky Blue Printed Border, 75 x 80 In. 357.00
Patchwork, Multicolored Prints, Beige Ground, Homespun Backing, 32 x 34 1/2 In. 230.00
Patchwork, North Carolina Lily, 80 x 65 In. 255.00
Patchwork, Ocean Waves, Blue, 73 x 88 In. 300.00
Patchwork, Orange, White, Optical Pattern, 74 x 86 In. 220.00
Patchwork, Pine Tree, Green Calico, White Ground, 92 x 110 In. 715.00
Patchwork, Pink Calico Stars, Sawtooth Border, White Ground, 72 x 77 In. 440.00
Patchwork, Pink, Green, Yellow Calico, With White, 75 x 86 In. 82.00
Patchwork, Princess Feather, Green & Red Calico, 90 x 90 In. 3250.00
Patchwork, Printed Cotton Centennial Fabrics, U.S., 96 x 94 In. 880.00
Patchwork, Prints In Navy Blue & Pink Calico, 70 x 80 In. 440.00
Patchwork, Red & White Grid, Scalloped Borders, 74 x 88 In. 300.00
Patchwork, Schoolhouses, Red, Blue Sashing, 77 x 92 In. 300.00
Patchwork, Star & Heart, Tulips Around Hearts, Square, 1840s, 99 In. 3025.00
Patchwork, Star Design, Red Calicos, Pinwheel Designs, 92 x 93 In. 275.00
Patchwork, Star In A Star, Peach, Hot Pink, Medium Blue, On White, 83 x 83 In. .. 143.00
Patchwork, Star of Bethlehem, Printed Chintz, Late 19th Century, 104 x 102 In. ... 665.00
Patchwork, Star of Bethlehem, Red, Yellow & Green Calico, 112 x 107 In. 7150.00
Patchwork, Star, 2 Shades of Blue On White, 75 x 75 In. 170.00
Patchwork, Star, 4 Shades of Goldenrod, Orange, White Ground, 77 x 90 In. 192.00
Patchwork, Star, Black Ground, Blue Border, 1860s, 34 x 44 In. 375.00
Patchwork, Star, Medium Blue Calico On White, 78 x 90 In. 82.00
Patchwork, Star, Pink Calico, Multicolored Prints & White, 86 x 88 In. 195.00
Patchwork, Star, Sawtooth Border, Quilted Trapunto Work, 70 x 82 In. 275.00
Patchwork, Star, Worsted Wool, 19th Century, 90 x 106 In. 545.00
Patchwork, Stylized Leaf Design, Multicolored, 72 x 84 In. 135.00
Patchwork, Stylized Tulip, Multicolored, Brown, Green, White, 72 x 86 In. 400.00
Patchwork, Texas Star, Multicolored, Yellow Calico Ground, 77 x 83 In. 357.00
Patchwork, Tobacco Label, 1910, 64 x 74 In. 250.00
Patchwork, Top, Goldenrod, Medium Blue, 78 x 94 In. 165.00
Patchwork, Top, House Design, Maroon, Goldenrod, Green, 83 x 88 In. 302.00
Patchwork, Triangle Pattern, Machine Sewn, 1900, 32 x 34 In. 115.00
Patchwork, Triple Irish Chain, Lavender, Green On White, 76 x 96 In. 165.00
Patchwork, Tumbling Block, Colorful Silks, Satins, Velvets, 62 x 82 In. 475.00
Patchwork, Tumbling Block, Multicolored Prints, 65 x 72 In. 400.00
Patchwork, Turkey Tracks, Multicolored Prints, 78 x 92 In. 170.00
Patchwork, Variation of Log Cabin, Cotton Patches, Child's, 40 x 34 In. 385.00
Patchwork, Wool Block, Victorian, 80 x 78 In. 66.00
Patchwork, Yo–Yo, 64 x 86 In. 120.00

QUIMPER pottery has a long history. Tin-glazed, hand–painted pottery
has been made in Quimper, France, since the late seventeenth century. The
earliest firm, founded in 1685 by Jean Baptiste Bousquet, was known as
HB Quimper. Another firm, founded in 1772 by Francois Eloury, was
known as Porquier. The third firm, founded by Guillaume Dumaine in
1778, was known as HR or Henriot Quimper. All three firms made similar
pottery decorated with designs of Breton peasants and sea and flower
motifs. The Eloury (Porquier) and Dumaine (Henriot) firms merged in
1913. Bousquet (HB) merged with the others in 1968. The group was sold
to a United States family in 1984. The American holding company is
Quimper Faience Inc., located in Stonington, Connecticut. The French firm
has been called Societe Nouvelle des Faienceries de Quimper HB Henriot
since March 1984.

Bowl, Man Figure, Blue Sponged Handles, 7 1/2 In. 65.00
Candleholder, Breton Hat Shape, 5 In. 60.00
Chamberstick, Green, Blue & Orange, Henriot 295.00
Charger, Woman Peasant, Ferns, Closed Ring Handles, 12 In. 300.00
Cruet, Vinegar, Cover, 6 In. 75.00
Dish, 3 Bowl Type, Armorial Crest, 1890 .... 475.00
Figurine, 2 Sailors & Overturned Boat, Sevellec 495.00
Gravy Boat, Side Handles, Transparent Blue Glaze 295.00

Inkwell, Round, Marked	65.00
Man & Woman, 3 1/4 In.	18.00
Pitcher, Art Deco	175.00
Pitcher, Woman's Head, Gold & Black Trim, Signed, 6 1/2 In.	225.00
Plate, Beton Crest, Lambrequin Border, Marked, c.1890, 9 1/2 In.	345.00
Plate, Peasant Woman, Yellow Ground, 9 5/8 In.	65.00
Sugar Castor, Peasant Woman, Yellow, Marked Elite Maude	75.00
Tray, Hors D'Oeuvre, 11 x 11 In.	400.00
Vase, Man With Horn, Flowers, Henriot, 7 1/4 In.	295.00
Wall Pocket, Peasant Figure, 10 In.	120.00
Wall Pocket, Peasant Man	110.00

RADIO broadcast receiving sets were first sold in New York City in 1910. They were used to pick up the experimental broadcasts of the day. The first commercial radios were made by Westinghouse Company for listeners of the experimental shows on KDKA Pittsburgh in 1920. Collectors today are interested in all early radios, especially those made of Bakelite plastic or decorated with blue mirrors.

Addison, Catalin, Red, Cream Overlay	500.00
Airline, Wards, Model 62, Wooden, Table Model	60.00
Amoco Gasoline, Figural, Box	30.00 To 50.00
Atwater Kent, Model 10, Bread Board	895.00
Atwater Kent, Model 20, Speaker	395.00
Atwater Kent, Model 35	50.00
Atwater Kent, Model 76, Console	350.00
Atwater Kent, Model 660, Console	295.00
Bendix, Green Bakelite, Art Deco, Table Model	425.00
Bendix, Model 526MC, Catalin	750.00
Blaupunkt, Removable, Transportable, 1950s	360.00
Bremer Tully, Battery Operated, Counterphase	95.00
Campbell's Soup Can, Box	135.00
Catalin, Model A526MC	700.00
Charlie The Tuna, Transistor	28.00
Cheese Burger, Transistor	55.00
Crosley, Black Case, Fancy Gold Dial, Working	50.00
Crosley, Bulls–Eye	125.00
Crosley, Model 48, Wigit, Repwood	330.00
Crosley, Model 642	175.00
Crosley, Super Trindyn, 3 Tube	100.00
Crosley, Top Mounted Speaker Horn	70.00
Crystal, 3 Head Sets	125.00
Dahlberg, Model 4130, Hotel Type, Plastic, With Pillow Speaker, Coin–Operated	395.00
Delco, Short Wave, Wooden, 1930s, Table Model	75.00
DeWald B–512, Catalin, Slide Rule Dial, Center Clock, 5 Knobs, BC, AC	1500.00
Dodger's Baseball Shape, Los Angeles Station KABC Promotion	41.25
Emerson, Bakelite	1085.00
Emerson, Explorer, Floating Red Arrow Dial, Aqua, Leather Case	70.00
Emerson, Green & Yellow	395.00
Emerson, Green, Table Model	25.00
Emerson, Mexican Decals, 20th Century, 7 1/2 x 10 1/2 In.	82.50
Emerson, Mickey Mouse, Model 411, Syroco Wood, 1933	2500.00
Emerson, Model 520, Catalin	300.00 To 350.00
Emerson, Model 580, Catalin	675.00
Emerson, Snow White, Model Q236, Painted Figures, 1938	3000.00
Emerson, Tomato Red, 1936	9350.00
Emerson, Tramp Art Case, Floor Model	3450.00
Erla Electrical Research Lab, Table Model	100.00
Fada, Bullet, Butterscotch	695.00
Fada, Bullet, Catlin, Butterscotch	700.00
Fada, Bullet, Model 115, Bullet, Green, Yellow Trim	925.00
Fada, Bullet, Yellow	850.00
Fada, Green Body, Orange Trim	1350.00
Fada, Model 652	775.00

Fada, Model 652, Red, Yellow Insert Grill 1650.00
Fada, Model. 1001, Catalin, Butterscotch 750.00
Fada, Streamliner, Burgundy Bakelite, Bullet Shaped Box, c.1941, 7 In. 935.00
Fada, Temple 495.00
Garod, Commander, Red Case 1700.00
General Electric, Burgundy Bakelite 20.00
General Electric, CD Markings, Pocket 20.00
General Electric, Dial Beam, Plastic, 1950s 45.00
General Electric, Model 622, Tortoiseshell Plastic, 1941 .... 1400.00
General Electric, Model M65, Console, Wooden 27.50
General Electric, Musaphonic 25.00
General Electric, Tackle Box, Bakelite 40.00
Globe, Black 1150.00
Grebe, Synchrophase, Model MU–1, Receiver Type, Batter Box Below 250.00
Grundig Majestic, Model 7063 .... 295.00
Hallicrafters, Model S40B 50.00
Hallicrafters, Receiver, Model SX–28–A 500.00
Hallicrafters, Short–Wave, Model 5–120, 1959 .... 20.00
Hawaiian Punch Punchy 50.00
Heinz Ketchup 40.00
Imperial, Simplex Tire & Rubber Co. 90.00
John Wayne Commemorative, AM 27.50
Lady Bug, Box 25.00
Lumitone Bakelite, With Lamp, Rocket Shape, 1940s 160.00
Monarch, Beehive 125.00
Motorola, Circle, Grill, Yellow 2200.00
Motorola, Portable, Model 56L4, Aqua 85.00
Philco, Boomerang .... 385.00 To 395.00
Philco, Model 46–350, Portable 30.00
Philco, Model 53–656, Green Plastic 85.00
Philco, Phonograph For 33 & 45 Records, Mahogany, Floor Model 265.00
Pollee–Royal, c.1924 .... 140.00
Radiobar, Montgomery Ward, 1962, Floor Model 1300.00
RCA Radiola, Model 20, Battery Powered 66.00
RCA Victor, Levermatic, With AM Clock, Beige, 1950s 50.00
RCA Victor, Model 96T1, Table 52.00
RCA, Aluminum & Bakelite, Portable, 1940s 85.00
Remco, Crystal Set, Box 40.00
Robot AM, Westminster, Box 65.00
Scott, 24 Tube 450.00
Sentinel, Art Deco, Bakelite 350.00
Sentinel, Model 284, Red, Yellow Trim, Case 925.00
Sparton, 5 Chrome Bands, Blue Mirror, c.1936 . ...Illus 1540.00
Sparton, Blue Mirror, Chromium Plated Metal & Wood ....Illus 2650.00
Sparton, Bluebird .... 2500.00 To 2750.00
Sparton, Model 558, Art Deco, Blue Mirror Top & Front, Chrome 2950.00

Radio, Sparton, Blue Mirror, Chromium
Plated Metal & Wood; Radio, Sparton, 5
Chrome Bands, Blue Mirror, c.1936

Spica, Transistor, Bakelite, Leather Case 45.00
Spiderman, AM/FM, Separate Speakers 85.00
Steinite, Table Model 192.50
Stewart Warner, Model B61T2 .... 60.00
Stewart Warner, Model PB520, Porto Baradio, Original Bar Glassware, Plastic 265.00
Telechron, Clock, Bakelite, 1930s 85.00
Tony The Tiger, Transistor 42.50
Universal, Transistor, Box, Accessories 20.00
Zenith, AM/FM, Plastic & Wood, 1950s 45.00
Zenith, Console, 1930s 160.00
Zenith, Noise Transmitter, 8 1/4 In. 1650.00
Zenith, Transoceanic, 1960 ....75.00 To 125.00
Zenith, Transoceanic, Short–Wave, Model 8g005, Black, Gold Knobs 75.00

RAILROAD enthusiasts collect any train memorabilia. Everything is wanted, from oilcans to whole train cars. The Chessie system has a store that sells many reproductions of their old dinnerware and uniforms.

Ashtray, CN, Glass 25.00
Bell, Great Western Railway, No. 8, Bronze, 6 x 6 1/4 In. 165.00
Bell, With Yoke & Cradle, Bronze, 12 In. 695.00
Blueprint, First Locomotive To Be Built In N. J., Seth Bowdoin, 24 x 32 In. 88.00
Book, New York Central System, Rules of Operating Dept., Oct. 28, 1956 .... 6.00
Bowl, Canadian National Railroad 40.00
Bowl, Dessert, B & O RR., Handles, 5 Piece 75.00
Bowl, Pullman, Oval, 6 In. 32.00
Bowl, Southern Railway Systems, Peaches & Leaves Pattern, Buffalo China 14.00
Bowl, Union Pacific 35.00
Box, First Aid, Southern Pacific, Black & Gold Enameled, No Pockets 75.00
Brochure, Route of Streamlined North Coast Limited, SP. Railway, 24 Pages 10.00
Butter Chip, Flora of South, Atlantic Coast Line 84.00
Butter Chip, Keystone, PRR 75.00
Butter Chip, Purple, Laurel, PRR ....65.00 To 68.00
Calendar, 1940, Pennsylvania Railroad, Complete 100.00
Calendar, 1942, Pennsylvania Railroad, Complete 140.00
Calendar, 1958, Rock Island, Jet Rocket Loco, 14 x 20 In. 35.00
Calendar, 1969, Union Pacific Railroad Centennial, 19 x 24 In. 18.00
Cap, Porter's, Missouri Pacific 150.00
Card, Playing, Soo Line Railroad, Box 22.50
Chronometer, Howard, Series 11 .... 365.00
Coaster, Mo–Pac Route of Dome Liners, Cardboard, 40 Piece 25.00
Coffeepot, Union Pacific, Reed & Barton, 16 Oz. 50.00
Creamer, Baltimore & Ohio 35.00
Crossing Light, Dressel 120.00
Cup & Saucer, Baltimore & Ohio 75.00
Cup & Saucer, Wabash, Flag 250.00
Cuspidor, Baltimore & Ohio, Brass 70.00
Cuspidor, Pullman, Nickeled 75.00
Cuspidor, Union Pacific, Train On Both Sides 75.00
Dish, B & O Railroad, Shenango, 6 1/2 In. 25.00
Flag Case, NYHN & H RR 50.00
Head Lamp, Locomotive, Sunbeam 425.00
Holder, Stamp, 2 Tiers, Black, Gold Trim, Cast Iron 25.00
Holder, Stamp, 2 Tiers, PRR, PC & WM, W. Pennsylvania, Cast Iron, With Stamps ... 70.00
Jar, Crock, Pullman Deodorizer, Chatham Station 290.00
Knife, 1 Blade, Cotton Belt, 2 1/2 In. 68.00
Lamp, Aladdin, Caboose, Aluminum Font, Parchment Shade 100.00
Lamp, Bracket, Brass, Cylinder, Double Gallery, Pushup, Wells Fargo, San Francisco .. 95.00
Lamp, Caboose, NYC, Wall, Sheet Steel, Tin 75.00
Lamp, Semaphore Signal, Adlake, Amber Lens 85.00
Lamp, Switch, Adlake, BR 140.00
Lantern, CUTco., 1923 .... 50.00
Lantern, CV RY, Defiance Lantern Co., Twisted Wire Construction 200.00
Lantern, Detroit United, Tail Marker, Red Etched Globe 150.00

Lantern, Dietz, Monarch, Red Globe, Art Deco Stylized Vine Frame 45.00
Lantern, Dietz, Vesta, New York Railroad, Weighted 55.00
Lantern, Grand Trunk, Amber Globe, Bell Bottom, Tall 750.00
Lantern, Hand, Pennsylvania RR, High Globe 60.00
Lantern, Kerosene, Atcheson, Topeka & Santa Fe, Red Globe 68.00
Lantern, Kerosene, Wabash Veta, Pear Shape, Clear, Red Painted Frame 64.00
Lantern, MP–PAC, Red Globe 125.00
Lantern, Pennsylvania RR, Casey, Clear Globe 60.00
Lantern, Rock Island Lines, Clear Globe 60.00
Lantern, Sheboygan Electric Railway, Clear Etched Globe 175.00
Lantern, Switch, Kerosene, AT & SF, Red Globe, Raised Letters 68.00
Lantern, Watchman, Birmingham, Bull's-Eye Lens, Copper 75.00
Lock, 6 Lever, Brass, Push, American Locomotive Co. 250.00
Lock, GR & L RY, Brass 140.00
Map, Los Angeles RY, 4 Pages, 1938–1940 .... 22.50
Map, Ohio Railway, Oilcloth Type, 1902 .... 100.00
Menu, Missouri Pacific Railroad, Steamer Plate & State Flowers Cover, 1933 .... 55.00
Oil Can, Erie Railroad 30.00
Oil Can, New York Central, Filler 20.00
Oil Can, NYC Railroad, Long Spout 33.00
Pass, Employee For Year, Santa Fe Pacific, Southern Calif. Railway, 1899 .... 5.00
Photograph, Railroad Workers, 50 Men, Station, Matted, 1920s, 11 x 13 In. 20.00
Plate, Baltimore & Ohio, 1978, 9 1/2 In. 185.00
Plate, C & O, Buffalo China 95.00
Plate, Dinner, B & O, Set of 4 .... 185.00
Plate, McKinley, Alaska Railroad, Small 300.00
Plate, Missouri Pacific Eagle, China 50.00
Plate, Mt. Laurel, Pennsylvania RR, 7 1/4 In. 25.00
Plate, Mt. Laurel, Pennsylvania RR, 9 1/2 In. 48.00
Plate, NYC Railroad, Veterans, Diesel Engine, 1951 .... 29.00
Platter, Union Pacific 95.00
Postcard, Burlington Route 6.00
Postcard, Union Pacific Railroad, 2 Cent, 20 Piece 8.00
Poster, Union Pacific Railroad, 30 x 10 In. 38.00
Print, Elevation of Passenger & Freight Engine, B & O RR, 1857, 12 x 28 In. 275.00
Print, Empress Passenger Locomotive, Midland Railway, 19 x 35 In. 44.00
Print, Locomotive For Passengers, Lowell Machine Shop, 1852, 21 1/2 x 32 In. 248.00
Safe, Great Northern Railway, 46 x 34 x 30 In 350.00
Seal, Lion's Head, Kinniconick & Freestone Railroad Co., Iron 75.00
Sign, Clinchfield Railroad, Central West & Southeast, White Ground 45.00
Sign, D & H Lackawanna Anthracite, Porcelain, Orange & Black, 12 In. 400.00
Sign, L & N, Rest Room, Glass, White Color 125.00
Sign, R x R Crossing, Yellow & Black Letters, Aluminum, Round, 36 In. .... 25.00 To 55.00
Step, Interior Stove, Pullman 125.00
Switch Key, Illinois Central RR 18.00
Switch Key, New York Central RR 18.00
Switch Lamp, Glass Chimney, Unused 165.00
Syrup, D & RG RR, Silver, Currecanti, Logo, Reed & Barton 450.00
Teapot, Scammells, Baltimore & Ohio, 1827–1927 .... 175.00
Tie Nail, 1926 .... 2.00
Tie Nail, 1934 .... 1.75
Tie Nail, 1947 .... 1.50
Timetable, Boston, Maine, 1938 .... 12.00
Timetable, Canadian Pacific, 1922 .... 12.00
Timetable, Santa Fe, 1934 .... 12.00
Tin, First Aid, CMSP, Colorful 20.00
Tongs, Sugar, Rock Island 45.00
Tool Box, Metal, Marked Gn26229, Operator's Manual 99.00
Tumbler, Penna. RR 4902 .... 10.00
Wax Sealer, American Railway Express, Adams, N. D., Brass 80.00
Wax Sealer, Railway Express, Hershey, Nebr. 60.00
Wax Sealer, Railway Express, Knightsen, Calif., Brass Top 80.00
Whistle, Caboose, Brass 30.00

Whistle, Steam, Bronze, 1877	695.00

RAZORS were used in ancient Egypt and subsequently wherever shaving was in fashion. The metal razor used in America until about 1870 was made in Sheffield, England. After 1870, machine–made hollow–ground razors were made in Germany or America. Plastic or bone handles were popular. The razor was often sold in a set of seven, one for each day of the week. The set was often kept by the barber who shaved the well–to–do man each day in the shop.

Black Demon, Straight, Sterling Devil On Celluloid Handle	18.00
Blade Safe, Gillette, 1920s	20.00
Blade Sharpener, Kriss Kross, Mechanical	45.00
Blade Sharpener, Twinplex	10.00 To 17.50
Blade Sharpener, Twinplex, Chrome Case	55.00
Blade Sharpener, Twinplex, Double Edge	38.00
Blade, Keen Kutter, On Folder, Sample	15.00
Blade, Keen Kutter, Package	40.00
Blade, Marlin	2.00
Collins Safety, Windup, Silver Plated, Case & Blades, 1915	75.00
Durham Dorset, Safety, Blades, Box	12.50
Gem Jr., Art Nouveau, Box	27.50
Gillette, Safety, 6 Piece	24.50
Imperial, Straight, Germany	8.00
Kampfe Bros., Star Safety, Pat. 1901, In Tin	85.00
Keen Kutter, Straight, Etched Eagle Blade, Horn Handle	95.00
Larkin Soap Company, Straight, Black Handle	13.00
Maize, Straight	75.00
My Favorite, Straight, Bakelite Handle, Box, England	23.00
Nude Handle	50.00
Rolls, Viscount Model, Box	30.00
Safety, Brass, Display Type, 8 x 16 x 5 In.	605.00
Safety, Dime, Tin Tube, 1907	50.00
Schick, Repeater Type, Brass	20.00
Schick, Repeater, Brass	20.00
Schick, Safety, Brass, Dated 6–18–26	10.00
Spike, Straight, Celluloid	25.00
Straight, Double Duck, Mother–of–Pearl	45.00
Strop, Box	25.00
Strop, Criss Cross, Box	15.00
Strop, Keen Kutter	95.00
Strop, Keen Kutter, K–80	20.00
Strop, Leather	20.00
Tonsorial Gem, Straight, Germany	8.00
Uncle Sam, Straight, Pyralin Floral Design, Germany, 1890s, 9 1/2 In.	37.50
Wade & Butcher, Solingen, Torrey, 4 Piece	50.00
Wade & Butcher, Straight, Wade	8.00
West Point, No. 7, Straight, Black Handle	30.00
Winchester, Safety	65.00
Winchester, Straight	75.00

REAMERS, or juice squeezers, have been known since 1767, although most of those collected today date from the twentieth century. Figural reamers are among the most prized.

Baby's, Plastic, Pink, Flower Decal, 2 Piece	30.00
Baby, Kitten & Puppy Under Umbrella, Blue	85.00
Boat	65.00
Chalaine	99.00
Cottage	75.00
Fleur–De–Lis, Milk Glass	55.00
Fluted Sides, Fry	30.00
Indiana, Green	20.00
Lemon, Glass Insert, Ideal, No. 12, Cast Iron	29.50
Pink Glass, Crisscross, Hazel Atlas, 2 Piece	175.00

Sunkist, Apple Green	45.00
Sunkist, California Fruit Growers	35.00
Sunkist, Chalaine, Large	225.00
Sunkist, Dark Jadite, Embossed	150.00 To 185.00
Sunkist, Green	35.00
Sunkist, Jadite Opalescent	175.00
Sunkist, Jadite, USA	50.00
Sunkist, Milk Glass	18.00
Sunkist, White	15.00
Sunkist, Yellow	70.00
White, Opalescent	65.00
White, Tab Handle	15.00
Wooden Faucet	25.00

RECORDS have changed size and shape through the years. The cylinder–shaped phonograph record for use with the early Edison models was made about 1889. Disc records were first made by 1894, the double–sided disc by 1904. High–fidelity records were first issued in 1944, the first vinyl disc in 1946, the first stereo record in 1958. The 78 RPM became the standard in 1926 but was discontinued in 1957. In 1932, the first 33 1/3 RPM was made but was not sold commercially until 1948. In 1949, the 45 RPM was introduced. Compact discs became available in the U.S. in 1982 and many companies began phasing out the production of phonograph records.

Album, Bozo The Clown, With Story, 4 Different	80.00
Album, Goldfinger, James Bond, With John Barry, United Artists, 1963	15.00
Album, Hogan's Heroes, Best Songs of World War II, Sunset, 1965	24.00
Album, Mission Impossible, Original TV Soundtrack, Dot, 1967	10.00
Album, Music From Peter Gunn TV Show, Craig Stevens Photo, Lion, 1960	10.00
Album, Pinocchio, Decca, 3 Piece, 1950	25.00
Americano, Flute Nightmare, Xavier Cugat	3.50
Amos 'n Andy, With Sleeve, 1950s, 45 RPM	30.00
As Tears Go By, Gloria, Marianne Faithful	3.00
Autumn Leaves, Roger Williams, Kapp	2.00
Autumn of My Life, Bobby Goldsboro, United Artists	2.50
Best of Aretha Franklin, Atlantic, 12 Classics	6.00
Best of George Jones, Columbia, 1970s	8.50
Bird Dog, Devoted To You, Everly Brothers	3.25
Breathless, Jerry Lee Lewis, Picture, 10 Songs	7.00
Call of The Wildest, Louis Prima, Jasmine	9.50
Casablanca, Lost Love, Pete Fountain	3.50
Chico & The Man, Legend In My Time, Sammy Davis Jr.	1.00
Chipmunk Song, Almost Good, Chipmunks, Liberty	6.00
Christmas With Mahalia, Mahalia Jackson, Columbia	4.50
Count Your Blessings, Cara Mia, Gordon MacRae	2.50
Crystal Clear & Muddy Waters, Sonny & Cher, 45 RPM, 1972	20.00
Da Doo Ron Ron, Holiday, Shaun Cassidy	2.00
Dark Shadows, Philips, 1969, Album, With Poster	45.00
Do You Know The Way To San Jose, Dionne Warwick, Eric	3.25
Don't Just Stand There, Everything But Love, Patty Duke	5.00
Downtown, Kiss Me Good–Bye, Petula Clark	3.25
Early Sacred Harmony, Blue Sky Boys, 20 Religious Songs From 1930s & 1940s	6.50
Enrico Caruso, 78 RPM	20.00
Folsom Prison Blues, Johnny Cash, Columbia	15.00
Funny Girl, Barbara Streisand, Columbia	2.50
Gone With The Wind, Sarah Vaughan, Mercury, 33 Rpm	5.00
Good Hearted Woman, Willie Nelson, RCA, Pair	5.50
Happy Days, Connie Boswell, 1935–1936	7.50
Happy Days, Shoulder To Shoulder, Roy Clark	2.99
Havin' Fun With Nat King Cole, Official 12003	9.50
Heartache Just Walked In, Conway Twitty, Decca	3.00
Honky Tonky Train Blues, Ain't She Sweet, Les Elgart	4.00
Horn Meets The Hornet, Al Hirt, LP, 1966	38.00
Hostess With The Mostess, Dinah Shore, RCA	6.00

How Deep Is Your Love, Bee Gees, 45 Rpm, RSO, 1976 .... 10.00
How High The Moon, Ferrante & Teicher, ABCP 2.00
Hungry Eyes, California Blues, Merle Haggard 1.00
I Cried For You, Woody Herman, MGM 1.25
I'll Shed No Tears, Charlie Rich, UKLP, 1966 Session 10.00
I'm A Little Teapot, With Sheet Music, Sealed 10.00
It Ain't Necessarily So, All Blues, Miles Davis 6.00
Jackie Gleason Plays Romantic Jazz, Capitol, 1959 .... 7.00
Jazz Party, Live In Paris, Duke Ellington, Affinity, 1969 .... 6.50
Jet Flight, No. 707, Pan Am Airlines, Album, Capitol 18.00
Jumpin Jack Flash, Rolling Stones, 45 RPM, Picture Cover 40.00
Little Black Sambo, 78 RPM 20.00
Little Drummer Boy, I'll Remember You, Johnny Cash 6.00
Lord's Prayer, Amos & Andy, 78 RPM 25.00
Love Like Ours, Never My Love, Fifth Dimension 3.00
Lyin' Eyes, Take It To The Limit, Eagles 3.25
Man On The Moon, Apollo 11 Mission, Walter Cronkite, CBS, 1969 .... 30.00
Merry Christmas, Bing Crosby, MCA 5.00
Midnight Cowboy, Henry Mancini, RCA 3.75
Midnight Sunshine, I'm Takin' No Chances, Dave Antrell 4.00
Money's Hard To Get, Temptations, Gordy 2.50
Mr. Sandman, I Don't Wanna See You Crying, Chordettes 3.50
My Melancholy Baby, Some Sweet Tomorrow, Kay Starr 2.50
Original Big Band Recordings, Sammy Kaye, Hindsight, 1941–1944 .... 8.50
Party Lights, Peaceful Living, Nat King Cole 2.00
Rainbow Isle Medley, Waikiki Hawaiian Orchestra, Disc, 78 RPM, Edison, 1925 .... 20.00
Rainy Night In Georgia, Where Do I Go From, Brook Benton 4.50
Ramblin' Rose, Christmas Song, Nat King Cole 4.00
Red Skelton, Pledge of Allegiance, Burger King, 1969 .... 15.00
Rinka Tinka Man, Charleston Parisian, Guy Lombardo 4.00
Roamin' In The Gloamin', Annie Laurie, Guy Lombardo 3.00
Robert The Robot, 1950s 25.00
Rock & Roll Music, Beach Boys, 45 RPM, Brother Records 25.00
Rock 'n Roll Party Live, Chuck Berry, 1977 .... 6.50
Rockabilly Reunion, Live In London, Rose Maddox, Glen Glenn, Magnum Force ... 13.50
Shut Down, Surfin' USA, Beach Boys 3.50
Sing, Sing, Sing, Benny Goodman, RCA 2.50
Smokey The Bear 10.00
Snoopy's Christmas, 1970 .... 9.00
Songs of The Home & Heart, Ferlin Husky, Stetson HAT 9.50
Study In Blue, Album, Vogue 150.00
Sweet Georgia Brown, Harlem Globetrotters–Abe Saperstein Liner 15.00
Venus, I'm Broke, Frankie Avalon 6.00
Very Best of Connie, Vol. 2, Connie Francis, Polydor, Early 1960s Hits 4.00
Wake Up Little Susie, Maybe Tomorrow, Everly Brothers 9.00
Walkin' My Baby Back Home, Johnnie Ray, Columbia 3.00
When I Was Young, Kingston Trio, Capital 4.00
Whistling Tree, Dinah Shore, RCA 8.00
Without You, Like A Criminal, David Bowie 2.00
You Always Hurt The One You Love, Mills Brothers, Dot 4.00
You Light Up My Life, Hasta Manana, Debby Boone 2.50

RED WING Pottery of Red Wing, Minnesota, was a firm started in 1878.
The company first made utilitarian pottery. In the 1920s art pottery was
made. Many dinner sets and vases were made before the company closed
in 1967. Rumrill pottery was made for George Rumrill by the Red Wing
Pottery and other firms. It was sold in the 1930s. For more information,
see *Kovels' Depression Glass & American Dinnerware Price List.*

Bank, Bear, Hamm's, Land of Sky Blue Water 350.00
Bean Pot & Individual Casserole, 5 Piece 50.00
Bean Pot, Advertising 60.00
Bean Pot, Gray & Brown 100.00
Beater Bowl, Bail Handle 40.00

Beater Jar, Advertising, Dated 1925 .... 140.00
Beater Jar, Spongeware 195.00
Bowl, Batter, Spongeband, Large 1250.00
Bowl, Batter, Spongeband, Small 325.00
Bowl, Bobwhite, 12 In. 45.00
Bowl, Merry Christmas From Weigold Nord, Marked, 8 In. 190.00
Bowl, Saffron, Blue Band, Signed, 7 In. 70.00
Bowl, Salad, Hamm's Beer, Large 270.00
Bowl, Spongeware, Cap, 5 In. 165.00
Bowl, Spongeware, Iowa Advertising, Saffron, 7 In. 125.00
Bowl, Swastika, 5 In. 60.00
Bowl, Vegetable, Bobwhite, Divided .... 22.00 To 25.00
Bread Tray, Country Garden 48.00
Butter, Cover, Lute Song 40.00
Butter, Cover, Spongeband No. 3, Compliments of A. H. Peterson 300.00
Cake Stand, Tampico 30.00
Casserole, Cover, Bobwhite, Stick Handles, 3 Qt. 23.50
Casserole, Cover, Stand, Spongeband 325.00
Casserole, Spongeware 92.50
Centerpiece, Flamingo, 9 In. 125.00
Chafing Dish, Roundup .... 295.00 To 350.00
Churn, 5 Gal. 130.00
Churn, Birch Leaf, 5 Gal. 725.00
Clock, Mammy .... 245.00 To 295.00
Coffee Server, Lute Song 60.00
Coffeepot, Blue Shadows 35.00
Cookie Jar, Barrel Shape, Green 55.00
Cookie Jar, Bobwhite 135.00
Cookie Jar, Chef, Ivory 35.00
Cookie Jar, Chef, Yellow .... 65.00 To 75.00
Cookie Jar, Dutch Girl 95.00
Cookie Jar, Dutch Girl, Blue .... 65.00 To 75.00
Cookie Jar, Dutch Girl, Yellow 30.00
Cookie Jar, Dutch People, Gray 65.00
Cookie Jar, Jack Frost .... 310.00 To 395.00
Cookie Jar, King of Tarts .... 600.00 To 700.00
Cookie Jar, Monk, Yellow .... 50.00 To 125.00
Cookie Jar, Saffron 100.00
Cookie Jar, Spongeware 700.00
Crock, 1 Gal. .... 325.00 To 550.00
Crock, Birch Leaves, Gold Smith Advertising, 40 Gal. 3000.00
Crock, Butter, Gray Line 175.00
Crock, Handwritten Blue 40, Birch Leaves, Black Union Oval, 40 Gal. 320.00
Crock, Koverwate, 10 Gal. 110.00
Crock, Large Wing, 1 Gal. 300.00
Crock, Mason, 2 Qt. 3000.00
Crock, Red Wing–Union Stoneware Co., 2 Gal. 30.00
Crock, Stieren Jerman Co., 1 Gal. 450.00
Cruet, Oil, Cover, Bobwhite 50.00
Cup & Saucer, Bobwhite 12.00
Cup & Saucer, Pepe 10.00
Cup & Saucer, Random Harvest 8.50
Custard Cup, Marked Made In Red Wing 200.00
Custard Cup, Spongeware 180.00
Dinner Set, Capistrano 90.00
Figurine, Cow & Calf, Brown 700.00
Figurine, Man & Woman, Flamenco, 10 In. 175.00
Figurine, Pig 45.00
Hors D'Oeuvres, Bobwhite 25.00
Jar, Butter, Bailed, No. 3 .... 200.00
Jar, Canning, Blue Lettering, 1 Gal. 350.00
Jar, Mason, 1 Qt. 1150.00
Jar, Pantry, 3 Gal. 600.00

Jar, Pantry, Cover, 1 Lb. .... 425.00 To 450.00
Jar, Refrigerator, 4 3/4 In. 175.00
Jar, Refrigerator, Blue, White, Bailed, No. 5 .... 200.00
Jar, Refrigerator, Cover, Spongeband 500.00
Jar, Refrigerator, Small 135.00
Jug, Advertising, Wallace & Gregory Bros., Echo City, Ken., Miniature. 285.00
Jug, Advertising, Chas. Petri, Milwaukee, Black Print 160.00
Jug, Advertising, Extra Quality Catsup, Minn. Stoneware Co., Bail Handle, 1 Gal. ... 575.00
Jug, Advertising, N. E. Jesmer, Princeton, Minn., Black Print 180.00
Jug, Advertising. L. W. Harper, Nelson Co., Kentucky, Black Print 190.00
Jug, Beehive, Large Wing, 4 Gal. 595.00
Jug, Beehive, Salt Glaze, Butterfly Design, Turkey Droppings, 5 Gal. 650.00
Jug, Beehive, Stieren Jerman Co., 3 Gal. 600.00
Jug, North Star, 1 Qt. 210.00
Jug, Threshing, Salt Glaze, 6 Gal. 625.00
Jug, Threshing, Salt Glaze, Cobalt Design, Slug Bung, Double Handle, 10 Gal. 110.00
Jug, Who Will Win, Michigan–Minnesota Football, Miniature 195.00
Lamp, Brush Ware, Large 210.00
Mug, Bobwhite .... 25.00 To 40.00
Mug, Bratwurst Haus, Signed 60.00
Pie Baker, Blue & White, 10 In. 75.00
Pitcher, Advertising, Sundberg Bros., Spongeware 110.00
Pitcher, Advertsising, Manitowoc Marine Grocery, 6 In. 115.00
Pitcher, Bobwhite, 12 In. .... 16.00 To 35.00
Pitcher, Cherry Band 170.00
Pitcher, Cream, Bobwhite, Tall ` 18.00
Pitcher, Hall Boy, Mottled Blue, 1/4 Gal. 550.00
Pitcher, Indian Head, War Bonnet, Blue & White, 8 In. 300.00
Pitcher, Orleans, 8 In. 68.00
Pitcher, Rust & Green, Spongeware, 5 In. 80.00
Pitcher, Transportation, Cream Color, 8 In. 180.00
Planter, Deer, Large 35.00
Plate, Bobwhite, 11 In. 11.00
Plate, Capistrano, 11 In. 8.00
Plate, Dinner, Pepe 8.00
Plate, Fantasy, Concord Shape, Pink Ground, Aster, 1947 .... 25.00
Plate, Salad, Bobwhite 7.50
Plate, Salad, Pepe 6.00
Plate, Village Green, 8 In. 4.00
Platter, Bobwhite, 13 1/2 In. 25.00
Platter, Bobwhite, 20 In. 70.00
Platter, Capistrano 55.00
Platter, Lotus 16.00
Platter, Smart Set, Stand, Stamped, 20 In. 30.00
Pretzel Set, Hand Painted Lake, Pine Tree & Deer, Hamm's, 12–In. Bowl, 5 Piece. 575.00
Relish, Divided, Bobwhite 18.00
Rolling Pin, Blue & White Wildflower Design, Compliments of O'Hearn Co. 475.00
Salt & Pepper, Alice In Wonderland 150.00
Salt & Pepper, Bobwhite .... 25.00 To 35.00
Salt & Pepper, Pepe, Tall 12.00
Salt & Pepper, Spongeware 850.00
Shoe, High Button, Green, Marked, 9 In. 80.00
Sugar & Creamer, Bobwhite 60.00
Sugar & Creamer, Pepe 20.00
Sugar, Cover, Bobwhite 20.00
Syrup, Green & Rust Sponge 595.00
Teapot, Bobwhite 48.00
Toothpick, Gopher On Log, Marked 575.00
Tray, Bobwhite, Sugar & Creamer 25.00
Trivet, Minnesota Centennial 35.00
Umbrella Stand, Red & Blue, Spongeware .... 1300.00 To 1475.00
Vase, Advertising, Hans Rosacker, Blue Bands, Handle, 1838, 10 In. 850.00
Vase, Art Deco, Shape 413, 14 In. 55.00

Vase, Grecian, 12 In. 80.00
Vase, Yellow Paneled, 12 In. 110.00
Wall Pocket, Violin, Pink 21.00
Water Cooler, 4–In. Wing, 4 Gal. 500.00
Water Cooler, Cover, 3 Gal. 475.00
Water Cooler, Cover, 5 Gal. 200.00
Water Cooler, Cover, Bar Handle, 4 Gal. 375.00
Water Cooler, Cover, Bobwhite, Metal Spigot 275.00
Water Cooler, Cover, Spigot, RWUSCO 260.00
Water Cooler, From Drug Store Soda Fountain 250.00
Water Cooler, Union Stoneware, Lid, 2 Gal. 2000.00
Water Cooler, Village Green, 2 Gal. 85.00

REDWARE is a hard, red stoneware that originated in the late 1600s and
continues to be made. The term is also used to describe any common clay
pottery that is reddish in color.

Bank, Barrel, Red Paint, 3 1/2 In. 95.00
Bank, Chickens 375.00
Bank, Hen & Chicks, In Basket, 3 1/4 In. 190.00
Bank, Jug, Red Paint, 5 In. 120.00
Bottle Warmer, Baby's, 7 In. 440.00
Bottle, Green Glaze, Incised Label, Made By I. S. Stahl, 11–1–1939, 5 3/4 In. 55.00
Bowl, Black Manganese Splash Design, Honeybrook Pottery, Deep 38.50
Bowl, Milk, Amber Glaze, Brown Flecks, Brown Daubs, 10 1/2 x 3 3/4 In. 60.00
Bowl, Moravian, 12 In. 190.00
Bowl, Pale Yellow, Thin Glaze, c.1840, 11 3/4 In. 190.00
Bowl, Shallow, Slip Design, Brown, White, Green, 2 In. 1430.00
Bowl, Slip Design, 8 5/8 x 1 5/8 In. 180.00
Bowl, Slip Painted, Moravian, 3 1/4 In. 195.00
Bowl, Sponged Glaze, Brown, 10 x 4 In. 95.00
Butcher's Pig, Coin–Slot Top, 19th Century, England, 15 In. 2600.00
Charger, Coggled Edge, Yellow Slip Design, 14 1/2 In. 286.00
Charger, Slip Design, Sgraffito, Farm Scene, 15 1/2 In. 137.00
Charger, Slip Design, Sgraffito, Man & Woman On Horseback, 13 In., Pair 187.00
Cooler, Egg Shape, Dark Brown Glaze, Applied Shoulder Handle, 11 1/2 In. 65.00
Creamer, 3 3/4 In. 49.00
Crock, Albany Slip Glazed, Incised Tree–Type Design, Oval, Large 365.00
Crock, John Bell, Waynesboro, c.1850, 5 1/2 In. 357.50
Cup, Brown Glaze, 5 x 3 In. 83.00
Cuspidor, Woman's, Applied Tooled Floral Design, 2 In. 45.00
Dish, Baking, Slip Design, 2 Sections, 12 1/4 x 10 1/4 In. 240.00
Dish, Brown Spotted Glaze, Oblong, 7 7/8 x 10 7/8 In. 71.00
Dish, Comb Design, 11 1/2 In. 385.00
Dish, Comb Design, 13 1/2 In. 495.00
Dish, Deep Green Glaze, Orange Spots, Oblong, 11 1/2 In. 275.00
Dish, Shenandoah, Rope Handles, White Slip, Green, Brown, 8 In. 2310.00
Figurine, Dog, Seated, Brown, 19th Century, 12 1/2 In. 165.00
Figurine, Recumbent Lion, With Lamb, 12 1/2 In. 6600.00
Flask, Pilgrim Shape, Embossed Eagle, Serpent In Beak, Handle, Black Glaze 475.00
Flowerpot, Ruffled, 6 x 7 In. 85.00
Flowerpot, Speckled, Cinnamon Ground Glaze, Large 950.00
Flowerpot, Tobacco Split Glaze 325.00
Jar, Apple Butter, Interior Glaze, 5 3/4 In. 27.00
Jar, Applied Shoulder Handles, Orange–Tan Glaze, 9 1/4 In. 25.00
Jar, Black, Brown, Amber Mottled Glaze, 5 1/2 In. 60.00
Jar, Brownish–Red Glaze, White Slip, 8 In. 45.00
Jar, Cover, Dark Brown Glaze, Egg Shape, 6 In. 35.00
Jar, Dark Brown Mottled Glaze, 8 3/4 In. 27.00
Jar, Dark Brownish Glaze, Egg Shape, 5 3/8 In. 25.00
Jar, Dark Red Glaze, Brown Splotches, Egg Shape, 5 1/2 In. 55.00
Jar, Egg Shape, Glazed Interior, 8 In. 65.00
Jar, Greenish Glaze, Amber Spots, Galena, 10 3/4 In. 150.00
Jar, Interior Glaze, Handle, 4 3/8 In. 45.00

Jar, Preserving, Dark Brown Shiny Glaze, Impressed Label, 6 3/4 In. 165.00
Jar, Preserving, Yellow Glaze, 7 In. 45.00
Jar, Ribbed Strap Handle, Shiny Glaze, Dark Amber, Brown Splotches, 6 In. 49.00
Jar, Simple Incised Design, Brown Glaze, 10 3/4 In. 55.00
Jar, Tooled Bands, Impressed Stamp Designs, Border, 10 In. 1300.00
Jug, Brown Splotches, Strap Handle, 7 In. 93.00
Jug, Green Glaze, Flecks, Brown Splotches, Applied Strap Handle, 4 1/8 In. 82.00
Jug, Green Speckled Glaze, Egg Shape, 5 1/2 In. 105.00
Jug, Greenish Amber Glaze, Orange Spots, 9 1/2 In. 190.00
Jug, Grotesque, Face, Lizard On Forehead, Incised Chester Hewell, 10 In. 300.00
Jug, Grotesque, Green Ash Glaze, Lizard On Forehead, 10 In. 336.00
Jug, Puzzle, Dated 1789, 7 1/2 In. 330.00
Jug, Puzzle, Slip Design, Dated 1810, Inscription, England, 19th Century, 5 In. 357.00
Jug, Rust Glaze, Egg Shape, 6 1/2 In. 125.00
Jug, White, Gray Spiral Glaze, Blue Eyes, Grotesque, 12 1/2 In. 385.00
Loaf Pan, Coggled Rim, Yellow Slip Design, 14 1/4 In. 625.00
Loaf Pan, Coggled, Yellow Slip Design, 14 In. 425.00
Loaf Pan, Yellow Slip Design, England, 10 1/2 x 13 1/4 x 2 1/2 In. 125.00
Mold, Dark Tone, Hand Shaped, Bundt Pan Style, 10 1/4 x 4 In. 130.00
Mold, Food, Turk's Head, Geometric Design, Olive Amber Glaze, 8 In. 38.00
Mold, Turk's Head, Green Glazed, Applied Handle, 10 In. 60.00
Mold, Turk's Head, Scalloped Rim, 5 3/4 In. 45.00
Mold, Turk's Head, Swirl, Green Glazed, Crimped Rim, Applied Handle, 11 In. 82.50
Muffin Pan, Green Glaze, 12 x 15 1/2 In. 27.00
Mug, Brown Speckled Glaze, Handmade, 5 3/4 In. 25.00
Mug, Shaped Vessel, Pouring Spout, Dark Brown Glaze, 3 1/2 In. 82.00
Pie Plate, Coggled Rim, 3–Line Yellow Slip Design, 9 3/4 In. 478.00
Pie Plate, Coggled Rim, 3–Line Yellow Slip Design, 9 In. .... 150.00 To 375.00
Pie Plate, Coggled Rim, 3–Line Yellow Slip Design, Brown Glaze, 8 In. 220.00
Pie Plate, Coggled Rim, 3–Line Yellow Slip, 10 3/4 In. 247.00
Pie Plate, Coggled Rim, 3–Line Yellow Slip, 9 5/8 In. 385.00
Pie Plate, Coggled Rim, 4–Line Yellow Slip Design, 9 1/2 In. 220.00
Pie Plate, Coggled Rim, Amber Glaze, Brown, Green Slip Design, 8 1/2 In. 1200.00
Pie Plate, Coggled Rim, Yellow Slip Design, 10 1/4 In. 385.00
Pie Plate, Coggled Rim, Yellow Slip, 7 1/2 In. 150.00
Pie Plate, Dark Brown Fleck Glaze, 7 7/8 In. 71.00
Pie Plate, Orange Color, 8 1/4 In. 27.00
Pie Plate, Plaid Design, White Slip, Green, Brown, 8 In. 577.00
Pie Plate, Slip Design, Bird Perched, Branches, Squiggles, Crimped, 11 In. 3300.00
Pie Plate, Slip Design, Crimped, Brown Splotches, 14 3/4 In. 3850.00
Pie Plate, Slip Design, Green Back, Crimped, 10 In. 5500.00
Pie Plate, Yellow Slip Design, 10 1/2 In. 49.00
Pie Plate, Yellow Slip Spots, Green Ground, 8 1/4 In. 110.00
Pitcher, Allover Seashells 18.00
Pitcher, Black Shiny Glaze, 7 In. 22.00
Pitcher, Copper Luster, Stylized Snakes, Black Ground, 6 In. 375.00
Pitcher, Green Glaze, Orange Spots, Brown Flecks, 6 1/4 In. 75.00
Pitcher, Green Slip Decoration, Strap Handle, 7 3/4 In. 225.00
Pitcher, Greenish Glaze, Orange Spots, 4 7/8 In. 82.00
Pitcher, Light Green Slip, Brown Splotches, Strap Handle, Egg Shape, 7 3/4 In. 247.00
Pitcher, Mottled Dark Brown Metallic Glaze, 6 1/8 In. 55.00
Pitcher, Stylized Floral Detail, Cherub Heads, Dark Brown Glaze, 8 In. 192.00
Pitcher, Stylized Snakes Among Vegetation, Black Ground, Copper Luster, 6 In. 450.00
Pitcher, Toby, Flared Mouth, 6 1/2 In. 525.00
Pitcher, Tooling, White Slip With Green & Brown, 4 3/4 In. 130.00
Plate, Coggeled Edge, 6 1/4 In. 137.00
Plate, Distle Fink With Flowers, Dark Amber Glaze, 10 1/2 In. 192.00
Plate, Green & Brown Glaze, 7 In. 450.00
Plate, Slip Design, Lines & Dots, 10 In. 575.00
Plate, Slip Design, Money Wanted, 1974, 12 1/2 In. 49.00
Plate, White Slip, Brown Decoration, 8 1/4 In. 385.00
Plate, Yellow & Green Draping At Notched Rim, Center Flower, 10 In. 1540.00
Plate, Yellow Slip Design, Piecrust, Saying, 1844, 10 1/4 In. ....*Illus* 3960.00

Plate, Yellow Slip, Green Wavy–Line Rim, Brown Polka Dots, 7 3/4 In. 193.00
Tea Set, Doll's, Green & Tan Glaze, Tray, 10 Piece 135.00
Teapot, Black Metallic Glaze, 4 3/4 In. 35.00
Toby, Flared Mouth, Molded Handle, 6 1/2 In. 400.00
Tray, Word Turkey Center, Slip Beaded, 11 1/4 x 15 1/2 In. 385.00
Trencher, Slip Design, Money Wanted, Glazed, Angular, 14 1/2 x 10 1/2 In. 7150.00
Vase, Green & Black Manganese Over Incised Design, Applied Handles 66.00
Whistle, Bird Shaped, Child's 55.00

REGOUT, see Maastricht

RICHARD was the mark used on acid–etched cameo glass vases, bowls, night–lights, and lamps made in Lorraine, France, during the 1920s. The pieces were very similar to the other French cameo glasswares made by Daum, Galle, and others.

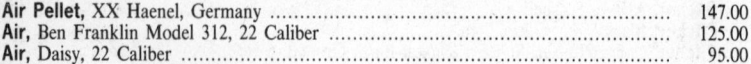

Perfume Bottle, Mauve Floral, Chipped Ice Ground, Signed, c.1920 .... 450.00
Vase, Blue Floral, Orange, 7 1/2 In. 400.00
Vase, Etched Foliate Design, Orange Ground, Signed, 12 In. 825.00

RIDGWAY pottery has been made in the Staffordshire district in England since 1808 by a series of companies with the name Ridgway. The transfer–design dinner sets are the most widely known product. They are still being made. Other pieces of Ridgway are listed under Flow Blue.

Butter, Cover, Liner, Oriental 225.00
Creamer, Coaching Days, Henry VII, Abbey of Reading, Brown, Signed .... 45.00 To 65.00
Drinking Set, Coaching Days, Quart Tankard, 6 1/2 Pint Mugs, c.1906 .... 395.00
Fruit Stand, Gold & White Leaves At Rim, Lozenge Shape, 1745, 12 1/4 In., Pair 2970.00
Mug, Coaching Days, Broken Trade, Brown, Signed 50.00
Mug, Coaching Days, Coach, Horses, Brown, Signed 80.00
Mug, Coaching Days, Horses, Silver Edge, Pair 75.00
Plate, Columbian Star, Gray, Green, 10 1/4 In. 195.00
Plate, Kennel Scene, 10 In. 18.00
Plate, New York City Hall, 10 In. 225.00
Plate, Valley of Shenandoah, Jefferson's Rock, 7 In. 95.00
Plate, View From Ruggles House, 10 1/4 In. 165.00
Platter, Oriental, Burgundy, 11 In. 50.00
Platter, Washington, Capitol, 20 1/2 In. 2400.00
Soup, Plate, Church, Octagonal 375.00
Tankard, Mr. Pickwick 175.00
Tureen, Tray, Oriental Pattern, Blue & White, 1830, Miniature 250.00

RIFLE is a firearm that has a rifled bore and that is intended to be fired from the shoulder. Other firearms are listed under Gun.

Air Pellet, XX Haenel, Germany 147.00
Air, Ben Franklin Model 312, 22 Caliber 125.00
Air, Daisy, 22 Caliber 95.00

Redware, Plate, Yellow Slip Design, Piecrust,
Saying, 1844, 10 1/4 In.

♦ ♦

A quilt that is not in use should be aired each year. Open it up and put it flat on the floor for a few days. A quilt that is used on a bed or hung should be taken down and rested every six months.

♦ ♦

Air, Daisy, Buffalo Bill, Carbine, Model 3030, Box	200.00
Air, Daisy, Carbine, Model 1894, Box	120.00
Air, Daisy, Model 40, Military Style, Sling, 1916	200.00
Air, Daisy, Model 40, Spike Bayonet & Sling, Pat. 1915	550.00
Black Powder, Brass Pod, De Charleville, 18th Century, 52 In.	660.00
Breech Loading, Percussion, Marked Jas. Golcher	200.00
Browning, Semi–Automatic	935.00
Flintlock, A. W. Spies Mechanism, Curly Maple Stock, Octagonal Barrel, 46 In.	675.00
Flintlock, Afghan, Silver Overlaid Foliage On Breech & Muzzle, 34 In.	375.00
Flintlock, Blunderbuss, 18th Century	1485.00
Flintlock, Model 1814, Percussion Conversion	1850.00
H. Pratt, No. 62, 54 Caliber.	1825.00
Kentucky, Curly Maple Half Stock, 50 In.	231.00
Kentucky, Curly Maple Half Stock, Percussion Lock, 55 In.	1100.00
Kentucky, Full Curly Maple, Percussion Lock, 57 In.	412.00
Kentucky, Walnut Full Stock, Front Sight, 50 Caliber	375.00
Lightning Pump, Colt, 38–40 Caliber	500.00
Matchlock Musket, Indo–Persian, Bronze Trigger, Engraved Flowers, 46 In.	475.00
Mauser, M–96	1160.00
Percussion, E. Whitney, New Haven, 1851	1210.00
Pocket, Stevens Pet	450.00
Remington, Percussion, Model, 1863, Zouave, 1862–1865	522.50
Shotgun, Winchester, Model 12, 12 Gauge	6600.00
Springfield, Bayonet Attached, Civil War Type	275.00
Springfield, Trapdoor, Eagle, Breech Block, 1873	330.00
Springfield, Trapdoor, Model 1888, Eagle, Breech Block, 1884	275.00
Swiss 41, Rim Fire, 1880	110.00
U.S. Model 1816, Marked E. Buel, Marlborough	1675.00
Winchester, 38–40 Caliber, Single Shot	700.00
Winchester, Lever Action, 12 Gauge	400.00
Winchester, Lever Action, 44 Caliber	1600.00
Winchester, Model 1873, 44 WCF, 26–In. Octagon Barrel	1850.00
Winchester, Model 1873, 44–40, Lever Action, 29 1/2–In. Octagon Barrel	900.00
Winchester, Model 1876, 40–60 Lever Action, Octagon Barrel	1500.00
Winchester, Model 1890	1650.00
Winchester, Model 1900, Single Shot, Shot–Bolt Action, Boy's	2145.00
Winchester, Model 93, 12 Gauge	400.00

RIVIERA dinnerware was made by the Homer Laughlin Co. of Newell, West Virginia, from 1938 to 1950. The pattern was similar in coloring and in mood to Fiesta and Harlequin. The Riviera plates and cup handles were square. For more information, see *Kovels' Depression Glass & American Dinnerware Price List.*

COLONIAL

Batter Set, Complete, Yellow	260.00
Butter, Red, 1/4 Lb.	90.00
Casserole, Cover, Mauve	35.00
Casserole, Green	65.00
Mug, Orange	45.00
Pitcher, Juice, Yellow	70.00 To 75.00
Sugar & Creamer, Light Green	55.00
Tumbler, Mauve	45.00

ROCKINGHAM, in the United States, is a pottery with a brown glaze that resembles tortoiseshell. It was made from 1840 to 1900 by many American potteries. Mottled brown Rockingham wares were first made in England at the Rockingham factory. Other types of ceramics were also made by the English firm. Related pieces may be listed in the Bennington category.

Bedpan, 16 In.	10.00
Bottle, Molded Urn, Flowers On Both Sides, 10 3/8 In.	352.00
Bottle, Queen Victoria I, 8 7/8 In.	125.00
Bottle, Shoe Form, Anne Reid, 1859, 6 In.	247.00
Bottle, Shoe Form, Sole Has Gold Paint, 9 In.	60.00
Bowl, Green Running Band, 4 3/4 In.	45.00

Bowl, Shallow, 10 1/2 x 2 3/4 In.	83.00
Bowl, Shallow, 3 1/4 In.	93.00
Creamer, Bowl, Cover	400.00
Cuspidor, 19th Century, Octagonal, 6 x 10 1/2 In.	165.00
Cuspidor, Portrait Medallion, 6 1/2 In.	33.00
Dish, 7 3/8 x 2 1/8 In.	44.00
Dish, Leaf Shape, 9 In.	11.00
Dish, Soap, Oval, 4 7/8 In.	50.00
Dish, Soap, Round, 5 1/2 In.	25.00
Figurine, Calf	375.00
Figurine, Dog, Seated, 10 In.	165.00
Figurine, Dog, Seated, Green & Brown Running Glaze, 9 3/4 In.	330.00
Figurine, Owl, RM Bishop & Co., Fine Cigars, Cinci., Blue & Brown Glaze	3700.00
Flask, Pistol Shape, 11 In.	71.00
Furniture Lift, Classic Female Heads, Glazed, 4 Piece	950.00
Jar, Batter, Tin Lid & Spout Caps, Wooden Handle, 8 1/4 In.	45.00
Lamp, Finger, Log Cabin, Original Burner & Cover	575.00
Mold, Turk's Head	145.00
Mug, Shaped Cuspidor, 3 1/2 In.	80.00
Pan, Milk, Glazed, 12 In.	82.50
Pepper Pot, Figural, Toby	330.00
Pie Plate, 9 3/8 In.	71.00
Pie Plate, 9 In.	72.00
Pitcher, 7 7/8 In.	55.00
Pitcher, Hound Handle, 3 1/8 In.	280.00
Pitcher, Hound Handle, Eagle, Boar, Stag, 10 In.	99.00
Pitcher, Hunting Scenes	135.00
Pitcher, Molded Hunt Scene, 9 7/8 In.	115.00
Pitcher, Molded Peacock, 8 1/2 In.	71.00
Pitcher, Swan, 3 In.	137.00
Plaque, Silhouette Bust, Gentleman, Applied Brown Glaze, 9 In.	385.00
Teapot, Molded Leaf Designs, 8 In.	38.00
Teapot, Rebecca At The Well, 9 1/2 In.	275.00
Tray, Dessert, Green Border, Gilt Foliate Design, Square, 9 1/4 In., Pair	187.00
Vase, Floral Sprays, Blue Ground, 8 1/2 In.	150.00

ROGERS, see John Rogers

ROOKWOOD pottery was made in Cincinnati, Ohio, from 1880 to 1960. All of this art pottery is marked, most with the famous flame mark. The R is reversed and placed back to back with the letter P. Flames surround the letters. After 1900, a Roman numeral was added to the mark to indicate the year. The name and some of the molds were purchased in 1984. A few new pieces were made, but these were glazed in colors not used by the original company.

Ashtray, Fox, Figural, Brown Glaze Drip, 1955, 6 1/4 In.	145.00
Ashtray, Frog	150.00
Ashtray, Nude	125.00
Ashtray, Nude, 1959	125.00
Ashtray, Rook, 1950	175.00
Birdbath, Curved In Triangular Base, Foliate Design, Mottled Green, 30 1/2 In.	550.00
Bookends, Basset Hound, White Matte	350.00
Bookends, Bear, K. Shirayamadani, White, 1934, 4 In.	550.00
Bookends, Children Reading Books, Blue, 1921	230.00
Bookends, Crow, Mauve, William McDonald's Design, 6 1/2 In.	412.50
Bookends, Dutch Boy & Girl, 1942	165.00
Bookends, Elephant, Blue, 1926, Single	95.00
Bookends, Elephant, Dark Green, Shape No. 2444	500.00
Bookends, Elephant, Trunk Down, William McDonald, 1935, 4 3/4 In.	350.00
Bookends, Elephant, White, 1928, 5 In.	245.00 To 350.00
Bookends, Fish	69.00
Bookends, Mexican Village, Light Brown, 1954	125.00
Bookends, Molded Floral Design, Green High Glaze, 1945, 4 x 6 In.	410.00

Bookends, Nude Reader 375.00
Bookends, Oak Tree Form, Matte Yellow & Brown, WMC .... 295.00 To 325.00
Bookends, Owl, Brown 225.00
Bookends, Reclining Panthers, Matte Blue Glaze, 1924, 5 1/2 x 5 1/2 In. ... 600.00 To 850.00
Bookends, Rook, Dark Blue, 1927 .... 365.00 To 525.00
Bookends, Rook, Green Matte, William McDonald, 1927, 5 1/2 In. 300.00
Bookends, Trees, Yellow & Green, William McDonald, 1929, 5 1/2 In. 450.00
Bookends, Water Lilies, Celadon, 1950, 6 1/2 In. 125.00
Bookends, Women With Fans 190.00
Bowl, Arts & Crafts, Panel Design, Crystalline Glaze, 2 x 4 In. 90.00
Bowl, Blue Matte, 1926, 11 In. 275.00
Bowl, Blue, Molded Matte, 127, 6 1/2 In. 165.00
Bowl, Cobalt Blue Body, Celadon Interior, 1927, 6 In. 100.00
Bowl, Green & Yellow, 1923, 6 1/2 x 10 In. 160.00
Bowl, Honeycomb With Bees, Brown Glaze At Base, Laura Fry, 1887, 6 In. 1760.00
Bowl, Pink, Matte With Green, 1916, 5 In. 80.00
Bowl, Rook & Animals Band, Blue, 7 1/2 In. 125.00
Bowl, Stylized Flowers, Footed, Matte Glaze, Louise Abel, 1923, 4 1/2 In. 850.00
Box, Floral Design On Lid, White Matte Glaze, 1944, 2 x 9 In. 45.00
Box, Nuts In Script, Peanut Finial, Green, 1949 .... 150.00
Bust, Woman, Porcelain, Blue–White Glaze, 1954, 8 x 7 1/2 In. 247.00
Candlestick, Lotus Blossom, Mauve, Shape 1067, 5 In. 45.00
Candlestick, Raised Tulips On Each Side, Maroon 65.00
Candy Dish, Frog Figure Center, Peacock–Green Glaze, 1922, 4 x 7 In. 330.00
Castor, Pickle, Reverse Thumbprint, Cranberry 300.00
Chamberstick, Green Speckled Glaze, Anna Valentien, 5 In. 330.00
Charger, Galleon, Blue Ground, Wareham, 1905, 12 1/2 In. 1430.00
Coffeepot, Cover, Teal Blue Blossoms, 9 In. 522.00
Console Set, White, Turquoise, 3 Piece 165.00
Creamer, Leaves, Red Berries, Tricorner Top, Sara Sax, 4 1/4 In. 355.00
Creamer, Sailing Ships 50.00
Cup & Saucer, Sailing Ships 55.00
Dish, Nut, Half Shell, 1887 .... 175.00
Ewer, Berries & Leaves, J. Zeitel, 1893, 7 In. 440.00
Ewer, Dark Brown Glaze, Floral Design, Handle, 9 In. 303.00
Ewer, Gold & Green Honeysuckle Flowers, Brown Ground, 7 1/2 x 5 In. 440.00
Ewer, Incised Grape Vines, Gray Ground, 1882, 11 3/4 In. 355.00
Figurine, Bird, Pale Green, Glaze With Blue Highlights, 7 1/4 In. 49.00
Figurine, Collie 395.00
Figurine, Frog, Dancing, Comical, Green Ground, A. Daly, 1889 .... 1200.00
Figurine, Rook, Dark Red, Green & Brown, 5 1/4 In. 150.00
Flower Frog, Satyr, 1922, 7 In. 195.00
Font, Holy Water, 1947, 9 In. 95.00
Font, Holy Water, St. Francis, Clotilda Zanetta, 1947, 9 In. .... 120.00 To 135.00
Fruit Bowl, Sailing Ships, 5 1/2 In. 45.00
Humidor, Carved, McDonald, 1923, 10 In. 350.00
Jar, Cover, Embossed Lilac Blossoms, Green Feathered Wash, 1917, 4 x 6 In. 195.00
Jar, Glazed Berries & Leaves On Cover, Slate Blue Ground, 7 In. 465.00
Jar, Potpourri, Blue, 1823, 4 In. 135.00
Jardiniere, Protruding Curled Leaves, Matte Green, 1906, 11 1/2 In. 715.00
Jug, Corn, Glaze With 4 Ears of Corn, Stopper Cork Insert, 13 In. 1215.00
Jug, Grape Design, Stopper 412.00
Lamp Base, Incised Ferns, Shades of Green, 1905, 12 1/2 In. 9000.00
Lamp, Oil, Ocean Scene, Gray & Brown, Smear Glaze, W. McDonald, 11 In. 770.00
Letter Holder, Blue, 1956 .... 250.00
Mug, Arts & Crafts, Cobalt Blue, 3 Handles, 1931 .... 290.00
Mug, Band of Half Circles Around Top, 1906, 5 1/4 In. 125.00
Mug, Floral, Toohey, 1898 .... 350.00
Mug, Matte Glaze, Sallie Coyne, 1895, 6 In. 295.00
Mug, Profile of Monk Sipping Wine, Horsfall 1550.00
Mug, School of Fish, Herihy, 1903 .... 1750.00
Mug, Story Series, Frightened Man In Tree, K. Shirayamadani, 1891, 4 1/2 In. 935.00
Paperweight, Cocker Spaniel 32.00

Paperweight, Duck 24.00
Paperweight, Elephant, Green Drip, Brown, 1928, 3 In. 245.00
Paperweight, Elephant, Showroom Label, 1930, ... 250.00
Paperweight, Embossed Bull On Top, 1949, 3 1/4 x 3 3/4 In. 175.00
Paperweight, Goat, White, 1934 .... 145.00
Paperweight, Honey Bear 32.00
Paperweight, Ivory Goat, Abel, 6 1/2 In. 235.00
Paperweight, Lamb, 1945 .... 25.00
Paperweight, Monkey, Turquoise, 1929 .... 185.00
Paperweight, Nude, 1936 .... 225.00
Paperweight, Turtle 26.00
Pitcher, Clover & Leaves, Brown To Orange, A. D. Sehon, 1898, 5 1/2 In. 360.00
Pitcher, Incised Geometric Design, Tricorner, 1904, 4 In. 100.00
Pitcher, Lotus Blossom, Carmel Ground, Handles, Valentine, 1898, 14 1/2 In. 880.00
Pitcher, Stylized Flowers, Blue Interior, J. Jensen, 1959, 7 1/2 In. 630.00
Planter, Swan, 1929 .... 125.00
Plaque, Broken Clouds, Ed Diers 990.00
Plaque, Scenic, Vellum, Lenore Ashbury, 1896 .... 7750.00
Plaque, Scenic, Vellum, Lorinda Epply, 1914 .... 2500.00 To 2750.00
Plaque, The Top of The Hill, Snow Covered Landscape, Frame, 13 x 15 In. 4100.00
Plate, Sailing Ships, 6 1/2 In. 35.00
Sugar & Creamer, Breakfast, Blue Sailing Ships, Hexagonal, 1896, 2 1/2 In. 175.00
Sugar, Cover, Insect Finial, Japanese, Celadon Floral, H. Wenderoth, C, 1884 .... 135.00
Sugar, Cover, Sailing Ships 45.00
Tankard, Beer, Cincinnati Cooperage 850.00
Tea Set, Breakfast, Sailing Ships, 3 Piece 375.00
Teapot, Autumnal Tones, E. T. H. Minor, c.1890 .... 1100.00
Teapot, Butterfly Top & Handle, Turquoise 400.00
Teapot, Sailing Ships 65.00
Tile, Cupid Figure, Blue & Yellow Flowers, Oval, 13 3/4 x 23 1/2 In. 880.00
Tile, Floral, Amber & Violet Blue, Art Deco, 6 x 9 In. 110.00
Tile, Leaf & Grape Design, 8 x 8 In. 1995.00
Tile, Man With Hat, Frame, 1897, 8 3/4 x 7 In. 1650.00
Tile, Mountain Landscape In Relief, Frieze, 8 Piece 3250.00
Tile, Ships, 12 Sides, Blue, 1886 .... 225.00
Tile, Stylized Blossoms, Purple, Turquoise & Pink, Frame, 5 3/4 In. 220.00
Tile, Victorian Woman, 1930 .... 185.00
Trivet, Pelican, 1921, 5 1/2 In. 210.00
Trivet, Rose & Blue, 1915, 4 In. 150.00
Trivet, White Birds, Foliage, Water 275.00
Vase, 2 Bluebirds On Branches, Light Brown Ground, McLaughlin, 1918, 9 In. 1350.00
Vase, 3 Elongated Figures of Medieval Saint, 1921, 12 1/4 In. 465.00
Vase, 3 Fish Swimming In Translucent Waters, E. T. Hurley, 9 In. 2700.00
Vase, 3 Gold Flowers, Brown Ground, Leona Van Briggle, 1903, 6 1/2 In. 750.00
Vase, 3 Woman In Relief, No. 2221, Brown Drip Glaze, 12 In. 400.00
Vase, 5-Paneled Landscape of Mountains, Lake, Sunset Sky, 1917, 10 In. 1650.00
Vase, 13 Colored Flamingos, Black Beaks, John D. Wareham, 1904 .... 6000.00
Vase, Apple Blossoms, Wax Matte, D. Workum, 1929, 7 x 6 In. 615.00
Vase, Autumn Leaf Design, Coyne, 1902, 8 In. 695.00
Vase, Band of Cherry Blossoms On White, Pink Ground, Vellum, 6 1/4 In. 495.00
Vase, Band of Incised Dolphins At Shoulder, 1912, 13 1/4 In. 1850.00
Vase, Band of Oak Leaves & Acorns, Blue Matte, 9 In. 585.00
Vase, Band of Stylized Flowers, Matte Glaze, C. Klinger, 1925, 7 In. 475.00
Vase, Bird Scene, Waterfront, 4 White Birds, Vellum, 11 1/2 In. 2200.00
Vase, Black-Eyed Susans, Dark Reddish Brown, 1899, 17 In. 3000.00
Vase, Blossoms, Blue To Pink Ground, Vellum, 8 x 5 3/4 In. 1540.00
Vase, Blue & Green Design Upper Half, Lorinda Epply, 1921, 8 3/4 In. 825.00
Vase, Blue & Green Floral, Katherine Jones, 1927, 9 1/2 In. 975.00
Vase, Blue & Yellow Flowers, Raspberry Pink Ground, Vera Tishler, 1924, 5 In. 385.00
Vase, Blue Blossoms, Blue Bisque Ground, Marie Bookprinter, 1887, 11 In. 445.00
Vase, Blue Floral, Forest Green, Wax Matte, Louise Abel, 8 In 675.00
Vase, Blue Fruit, White Leaves, Mauve Ground, Jeweled, 7 1/2 In. 525.00
Vase, Blue Fruit, White Leaves, Mauve Ground, Jeweled, Jens Jensen, 7 x 3 In. 525.00

Vase, Blue Grapes, Green Leaves, Peach Ground, Vellum, Asbury, 7 3/4 In. 665.00
Vase, Blue–Green Meadow Scene, Peach Sky, Wareham, 1905, 11 In. 3575.00
Vase, Blue–Green Poplar Leaves, Sea Green, Bottle Shape, Artus Van Briggle 1600.00
Vase, Blueberries & Leaves, Golden To Dark Brown Ground, 1890, 10 1/4 In. 4250.00
Vase, Branches & Blossoms, Brown Ground, Edith R. Felton, 1903, 2 1/2 In. 300.00
Vase, Bud, Tan Gloss, 1948 .... 70.00
Vase, Bulging Middle, Sprigs of Lilies of The Valley, E. Lincoln, 1902, 5 1/2 In. 415.00
Vase, Butterfly Handle, 3 Geese In Flight, Blue–Green Areas, 6 1/2 In. 825.00
Vase, Carl Schmidt, 1923, 7 1/4 In. 1760.00
Vase, Carved Branches At Top, Crow At Bottom, Blue Drip, 1923, 4 3/4 In. 235.00
Vase, Carved Rooks Around Top, Yellow Matte Glaze, 1915 .... 225.00
Vase, Celadon, 1954, 3 1/2 x 5 In. 55.00
Vase, Cherry Blossoms & Bird, Brown Ground, A. Conant, 1921, 5 1/2 In. 995.00
Vase, Cheshire Cat, Winged Griffin, Shirayamadani, 9 In. 1100.00
Vase, Chocolate & Amber, Sally Toohey, 1896 .... 1975.00
Vase, Chrysanthemums On Long Stems, Lorinda Epply, 1908, 7 1/2 In. 550.00
Vase, Chrysanthemums, Blue Ground, John W. Pullman, 1929, 10 In. 885.00
Vase, Clover, Iris Glazed, F. Rothenbush, 1900, 10 In. 900.00
Vase, Coramundel, Red, 6 In. 350.00
Vase, Cover, Green & Yellow Dragons, Clouds, Shirayamadani, 1888 .... 3250.00
Vase, Diers, Vellum, 1907, 9 In. 1600.00
Vase, Dragonflies, 1904, 9 In. 700.00
Vase, E. T. Hurley, 1913, 8 1/2 In. 1350.00
Vase, Fighting Fish, E. T. Hurley, 1901, 6 1/8 In. 6600.00
Vase, Floral On Green Matte, Helen McDonald, 1927, 8 In. 395.00
Vase, Floral Vellum of Water Lilies, Lorinda Epply, c.1903, 5 3/4 In. 585.00
Vase, Floral, Artist K. S, 1943, 7 In. 950.00
Vase, Floral, W. Hentschel, 10 In. 825.00
Vase, Flowers & Fish, Jens Jensen, 1945, 8 3/4 In. 1500.00
Vase, Flowers Around Top, Glaze, Squatty, Handles, V. B. Demarest, 3 x 4 In. 137.00
Vase, Flowers, Arts & Crafts, E. Lincoln, 1920, 7 1/2 In. 435.00
Vase, Flowers, Caramel Color, 1929, 5 In. 125.00
Vase, Flowers, Chartreuse High Glaze, 1952, 4 x 4 1/2 In. 65.00
Vase, Flowers, Signed M. N., 1893, 5 1/2 In. 375.00
Vase, Forest Scene, Sallie E. Coyne, Vellum, 1915, 5 7/8 In. 1450.00
Vase, Fruit Design At Rim, Lavender To Pink, 1927, 5 In. 110.00
Vase, Geometric Arts & Crafts Design Top, 1904, 11 In. 395.00
Vase, Glaze, E. T. Hurley, Vellum, 1927, 8 In. 660.00
Vase, Glossy Black, Handles, 1929, 8 In. 195.00
Vase, Gray–Green Trees, Soft Yellow Sky, Vellum, E. T. Hurley, 1908, 9 In. 2310.00
Vase, Green Flower Design, 8 3/4 In. 195.00
Vase, Green Leaves, Red Berries, Bowling–Pin Shape, Brown Ground, 6 In. 350.00
Vase, Green To Teal, L. N. Lincoln, 5 In. 650.00
Vase, Green, Yellow, Footed, 1954, 6 3/4 In. 55.00
Vase, Indian Portrait, Bronze Rim Band, Sturgis Lawrence, 1930, 10 In. 3100.00
Vase, Iris Glaze, Apple Blossom Sprigs, R. Fecheimer, 1903, 8 1/4 In. 1100.00
Vase, Iris Glaze, Lindeman, 1903, 7 In. 950.00
Vase, Iris Glaze, Sara Sax, 12 In. 2950.00
Vase, Iris Glaze, White Flower, Gray–Green Leaves, Wareham, 1902, 17 In. 7700.00
Vase, Iris, 2 Fish In Swirling Waves, E. T. Hurley, 1899, 6 In. 2700.00
Vase, Iris, Banded Design of Peacock Feathers, Schmidt, 1907, 10 In. 4500.00
Vase, Jack–In–The–Pulpit, Speckled Brown On Tan, Trumpet, 1922, 14 1/2 In. 475.00
Vase, Lake Scene Around Top, Brown Banded Rim, L. Ashbury, 1915, 8 In. 1210.00
Vase, Lake Scene, Blues, Green, Vellum, Bulbous, Lorinda Epply, 1918, 9 1/4 In. ... 775.00
Vase, Lake Scene, L. Asbury, 1915, 8 In. 1100.00
Vase, Leaf Design, Green Matte, 1928, 10 In. 300.00
Vase, Lincoln, Floral, Matte, 13 In. 1500.00
Vase, Matte Blue, Cream Interior, Bulbous, 1927, 10 In. 250.00
Vase, Medium Blue To Cobalt, Ferns Over Hills, Wm. Henschell, 1926, 7 1/4 In ... 985.00
Vase, Milkweed Seed Pods, Pink Top, Frederick Rothenbush, 1902, 8 1/2 In. 1650.00
Vase, Molded Leaf & Berry Design, Yellow & Green Matte, 1916, 5 In. 110.00
Vase, Molded Leaves & Flowers, Blue, 5 1/2 In. 65.00
Vase, Molded Village Scene, People & Animals, Label, 1938, 11 In. 335.00

Vase, Narrow Neck, Wide Bottom, John Wareham, 1895, 6 In. 295.00
Vase, Nudes, Jens Jensen, 9 1/4 In., Pair. 8800.00
Vase, Oak Leaf, Signed, 1901, 7 In. 750.00
Vase, Orange & Yellow Berries, Green Leaves, Sara Sax, 1898, 3 x 5 In. 310.00
Vase, Orange Poppies, Dark Ground, C. Schmidt, 1897, 5 In. 445.00
Vase, Oxblood Glaze, 1928, 8 In. 415.00
Vase, Painted Iris, Sea Green, Mary Nourse, 10 1/2 In. 7150.00
Vase, Painted Irises, Carl Schmidt, 1903, 11 1/4 In. 8800.00
Vase, Painted Lilies of The Valley, Gray To Peach Ground, c.1905, 7 In. 665.00
Vase, Panels of Flowers, Rose Glaze, Green, 6 3/8 In. 335.00
Vase, Peaches, Leaves, Green To Brown Ground, Leona Van Briggle, 1903, 7 In. 750.00
Vase, Peacock, Blue Floral, Katherine Jones, 1927, 9 In. 950.00
Vase, Pink & White Cherry Blossoms, Gray To Pink Ground, Vellum, 6 3/4 In. 495.00
Vase, Pink Apple Blossoms, White Ground, E. T. Hurley, 1912, 8 3/4 In. 660.00
Vase, Pink Bleeding Hearts, White Ground, Lorinda Epply, 1920, 6 1/2 In. 850.00
Vase, Pink Cherry Blossoms, Pink, Vellum, E. T. Hurley, 1921, 6 1/4 x 4 1/2 In. ... 495.00
Vase, Pink Flowers, Green Leaf, Navy Blue, W. E. Hentschel, 1916, 9 In. 715.00
Vase, Pink Roses, Celadon Base, Bands, Vellum, 1909, 10 3/4 In. 880.00
Vase, Pink, Light Green, 6 In. 125.00
Vase, Puffy Fish, Swimming, Brown Outline, Jens Jensen, 1934, 5 In. 2250.00
Vase, Scene, Yellow Roses, E. Diers, Vellum, 1907, 9 In. 850.00
Vase, Silver Plated Copper Overlay, Shirayamadani, Globular, 1901 .... 3250.00
Vase, Snow–Covered Ground, Fred Rothenbush, Vellum, c.1905, 9 1/4 In. 2685.00
Vase, Spiders Coming Down From Top, Wm. E. Henschell, 1913, 7 In. 850.00
Vase, Stylized Flower Border, Lorinda Epply, 1918, 6 1/2 In. 695.00
Vase, Stylized Flowers, Blue–Green Ground, C. S. Todd, 1918, 9 1/2 In. 445.00
Vase, Stylized Grape Clusters, Maroon Ground, C. S. Todd, Squatty, 1912, 8 In. 445.00
Vase, Swallow In Flight, Grasses, Gilded Rim, A. M. Bookprinter, 6 1/4 In. 450.00
Vase, Trumpet, Jeweled, Blue, Turquoise Ground, Lorinda Epply, 1921, 6 1/2 In. 600.00
Vase, Tulip, Molded Band of Tulips, Celadon & Blue Glaze, 1940, 6 1/4 In. 245.00
Vase, Turquoise, 1931, 5 1/4 In. 85.00
Vase, Vasiform Shape, Blue–Green Pastoral Scene, 12 In. 2425.00
Vase, Venetian Harbor Scene, Vellum Glaze, Carl Schmidt, 1924 .... 7700.00
Vase, Wax Matte, K. Jones, 5 1/2 In. 415.00
Vase, Wax Matte, L. Abel, 9 In. 850.00
Vase, White & Yellow Honeysuckle, Shirayamadani, 13 In. 6500.00
Vase, Yellow Flowers & Foliage, Olive Green & Yellow Ground, 1902, 8 In. 605.00
Vase, Yellow Roses, Buds, Yellow To Blue Ground, Ed Diers, 1907, 9 In. 935.00
Wall Pocket, Light Blue, Incised 1920–2008 .... 110.00
Water Set, Leaves, Green Ground, 3 Side, 3 Spout Pitcher, S. Coyne, 1905 .... 935.00

ROSALINE, see Steuben category

ROSE BOWLS were popular during the 1880s. Rose petals were kept in
the open bowl to add fragrance to a room, a popular idea in a time of
limited personal hygiene. The glass bowls were made with crimped tops,
which kept the petals inside. Many types of Victorian art glass were made
into rose bowls.

Applied Flowers, Amber Handle, Cream Opaque, 7 5/8 In. 195.00
Blue Herringbone, Mother–of–Pearl, White Lining, 3 1/2 In. 145.00
Blue Ribbon Mother–of–Pearl, Satin Glass, White Lining, 3 Crimp, 3 1/4 In. 165.00
Gold Prunus & Butterfly, Shaded Brown Webb, 8 Crimp, 2 1/2 In. 295.00
Green Overlay, Cut Crystal, Oval, 5 1/4 In. 33.00
Mother–of–Pearl, Diamond–Quilted, Blue, White, Thomas Webb, 2 1/2 x 4 3/4 In. 575.00
Mother–of–Pearl, Diamond–Quilted, Satin Glass, 5 In. 375.00
Opaque White To Pink, Pinched, 4 In. 60.00
Pink Overlay, Satin Glass, Footed, White Lining, 8 Crimp, 5 In. 135.00
Satin Glass, Diamond–Quilted, Green, White Lining, Egg Shape, 4 1/8 x 3 In. 175.00
White Ribbon Mother–of–Pearl, Satin Glass, Frosted Wafer Foot, 2 1/4 In. 195.00

ROSE CANTON china is similar to Rose Medallion, except no people are
pictured in the decoration. It was made in China during the nineteenth
and twentieth centuries in greens, pinks, and other colors.

Dish, Cover, Oblong, 10 1/2 In.	400.00
Punch Bowl, Butterfly Border, Carved Teakwood Stand	3000.00

ROSE MEDALLION china was made in China during the nineteenth and twentieth centuries. It is a distinctive design picturing people, flowers, birds, and butterflies. Pieces are colored in greens, pinks, and other colors. It is similar to Rose Canton.

Bough Pot, Mandarin, Stand, Pair	4500.00
Bowl, 1850, 16 In.	3800.00
Bowl, Hardwood Stand, 11 In.	330.00
Box, Cover, Round, 2 Sizes, 2 & 3 x 2 3/4 In.	143.00
Box, Cover, Square, 5 1/2 In.	450.00
Brush Pot	395.00
Brush Pot, 4 1/4 In.	190.00
Candlestick, Applied Dragon, Pair	935.00
Charger, 14 1/4 In.	200.00
Creamer, Hog Nose, 1800	175.00
Cup & Saucer, 8 Sides	60.00
Dish, Cover, Panels of Bees, Butterflies & Fruit Inside & Out, Oblong	325.00
Dish, Curry, Lozenge Form, Raised Foot, 1900, 9 In.	210.00
Dish, Domed Lid, Gilt Pine Cone Finial, 9 1/2 In., Pair	605.00
Dish, Hot Water, Cover, 19th Century, 10 In.	665.00
Dish, Vegetable, Cover, 8 1/4 In.	176.00
Garden Seat, Large	2200.00
Jar, Temple, Foo Dog Finial, 19th Century, 16 3/4 In.	1870.00
Plate, 11 1/2 In.	88.00
Plate, 1910–1930, 10 In.	85.00
Plate, Bird, People & Floral Panels, 1862, 8 In.	55.00
Plate, Mandarin, Pre–1840	70.00
Plate, Scalloped, Fluted Rim, 9 1/2 In.	50.00
Platter, 16 1/2 In.	198.00
Platter, Butterfly & Peony Border	1875.00
Platter, Oval, 12 In.	77.00
Punch Bowl, 14 In.	2600.00
Punch Bowl, 19th Century, 12 5/8 In.	743.00
Punch Bowl, Figural & Floral Panels Interior & Exterior, 14 1/2 In.	1320.00
Punch Bowl, Figures In Pavilions, Birds, Insects, 16 In.	1540.00
Rice Bowl, Cover, Set of 4	300.00
Sugar & Creamer, Cover, Flowers, Butterfly, 5 1/2 In.	150.00
Sugar, Cover, Handles	58.00
Teapot, Bullet Design, 4 1/2 In.	60.00
Teapot, Cadogan, 19th Century, 5 1/2 In.	575.00
Teapot, Figural Bird & Insect Design, 4 1/4 In.	140.00
Teapot, Wicker Handle, Hinged Basket Case, With Handleless Cup, 1862	275.00
Tureen, Domed Lid, Underplate, Floral	1050.00
Tureen, Sauce, Cover, 19th Century	1760.00
Tureen, Sauce, Cover, 19th Century, 15 In.	1935.00
Umbrella Stand, Vertically Ribbed, Floral Panels, 24 In.	1650.00
Vase, Baluster, 9 1/2 In.	220.00
Vase, Baluster, 12 1/2 In.	275.00
Vase, Figural & Floral, Stand, 37 In., Pair	1210.00

ROSE O'NEILL, see Kewpie category

ROSE TAPESTRY porcelain was made by the Royal Bayreuth factory of Tettau, Germany, during the late nineteenth century. The surface of the porcelain was pressed against a coarse fabric while it was still damp, and the impressions remained on the finished porcelain. It looks and feels like a textured cloth. Very skillful reproductions are being made that even include a variation of the Royal Bayreuth mark, so be careful when buying.

Basket, Braided Handle & Rim, Blue Mark, 3 1/2 In.	375.00
Bell, Pink Roses, White Ground, Wooden Clapper, Gold Handle	3395.00

Bell, Shadow Leaves, Cluster of Roses, Raised Beading, Gold Handle	550.00
Bowl, Woman Portrait, Blue Mark, 5 1/2 In.	145.00
Box, Covered, Violets, Green Mark	425.00
Cake Plate, Free–Form Rim, Gold Beading, 9 1/2 In.	365.00
Chocolate Pot, Turkey Herder	1000.00
Creamer, Pink Roses, 2 1/2 In.	210.00
Dish, Pickle, Scalloped	450.00
Dish, Pin, Gold Rim, Blue Mark, 4 1/2 In.	250.00
Hair Receiver, 3 Gold Feet, Blue Mark	350.00
Hair Receiver, Colonial Couple Cover, Rainbow Bottom, Blue Mark	550.00
Hatpin Holder, Scroll Base, 4 3/4 In.	450.00
Match Holder, Hanging, Scene of Men Drinking, Blue Mark	145.00
Match Holder, Wall, 3–Color Roses, Blue Mark	325.00
Muffineer, Portrait, 5 In.	625.00
Pitcher, Pinched Spout, 4 1/4 In.	295.00
Pitcher, Pink & Yellow Roses, Pinched Spout, 3 3/4 In.	225.00
Pitcher, Pink Roses, 5 3/4 In.	420.00
Pitcher, Tuxedo Spout, 3 3/8 In.	395.00
Planter, 2 3/4 x 3 1/4 In.	280.00
Plate, 6 In.	180.00
Plate, 7 3/4 In.	225.00
Plate, Peacock	1250.00
Plate, Peacock, Blue Mark, 9 In.	950.00 To 1200.00
Powder Box, 3 Feet, 4 1/4 In.	400.00
Rose Bowl, 3–Color Roses, 4 In.	360.00
Salt & Pepper, Blue Mark	550.00
Sugar & Creamer	400.00
Teapot, 4 In.	358.00
Tray, 7 7/8 x 11 1/4 In.	525.00
Tray, Dresser, Courting Couple, Oval, 7 x 4 In.	265.00
Tray, Dresser, Pink Roses, 7 3/4 x 11 In.	385.00
Vase, 2 Columns Each of Pink & Yellow Roses, 4 1/4 In.	325.00
Vase, 5 In.	250.00
Vase, Bulbous, 5 3/8 In.	350.00
Wall Pocket, Woman Feeding Chickens Scene, 9 x 5 1/2 In.	695.00

ROSEMEADE Pottery of Wahpeton, North Dakota, worked from 1940 to 1961. The pottery was operated by Laura A. Taylor and her husband, R.I. Hughes. The company was also known as the Wahpeton Pottery Company. Art pottery and commercial wares were made.

Rosemeade

Ashtray, Deer, Small	60.00
Ashtray, Forest Green, Lettered On Top	30.00
Ashtray, Standing Chicken	125.00
Ashtray, Washington	20.00
Basket, Turquoise Matte, 4 1/2 In.	26.00
Bell, Peacock, 4 3/4 In.	175.00
Cup & Saucer, Pink	20.00
Figurine, Bear, Miniature	10.00
Figurine, Bear, Pair	35.00
Figurine, Buffalo, Turned Head	300.00
Figurine, Coyote	275.00
Figurine, Dove	400.00
Figurine, Elephant, Italian Blue	35.00
Figurine, Elephant, Pink	50.00
Figurine, Horse, Pink	45.00
Figurine, Mice, Pair	35.00
Figurine, Monkey, 3 Piece	500.00
Figurine, Mountain Goat	200.00
Figurine, Pheasant, 10 In.	150.00 To 175.00
Figurine, Pheasant, Miniature	40.00
Flower Frog, Fish Shape	28.00
Flower Frog, Pheasant	25.00
Lamp, T.V., Panther	350.00

Paperweight, Elephant, Glossy Blue, 2 1/4 x 2 3/4 In. 150.00
Planter, Elephant 65.00
Plaque, Trout 130.00
Salt & Pepper, Bears .... 28.50 To 40.00
Salt & Pepper, Bloodhound Dog Heads 35.00
Salt & Pepper, Bobwhites 25.00
Salt & Pepper, Buffalo 75.00
Salt & Pepper, Chickens 40.00
Salt & Pepper, Dogs, Setters, Brown & White 10.00
Salt & Pepper, Dolphins 30.00
Salt & Pepper, Donkey 45.00
Salt & Pepper, Ducks 45.00
Salt & Pepper, Flamingos .... 50.00 To 75.00
Salt & Pepper, Frogs 225.00
Salt & Pepper, Golden Pheasant 125.00
Salt & Pepper, Greyhounds .... 20.00 To 30.00
Salt & Pepper, Mallards .... 35.00 To 60.00
Salt & Pepper, Mice 10.00
Salt & Pepper, Pheasant & Rooster 95.00
Salt & Pepper, Pheasants .... 20.00 To 30.00
Salt & Pepper, Pheasants, Tail Down 60.00
Salt & Pepper, Pheasants, Tail Up 30.00
Salt & Pepper, Pigs 50.00
Salt & Pepper, Ponies, Pink 30.00
Salt & Pepper, Prairie Dogs 40.00
Salt & Pepper, Quails 35.00
Salt & Pepper, Rabbit 75.00
Salt & Pepper, Raccoons .... 75.00 To 105.00
Salt & Pepper, Skunks .... 15.00 To 25.00
Salt & Pepper, Spaniels 22.00
Salt & Pepper, Turkeys .... 28.50 To 60.00
Salt & Pepper, White Chickens 37.00
Salt & Pepper, Windmills 200.00
Saltshaker, Skunk 25.00
Spooner, Pheasant 50.00
Sugar & Creamer, Label 30.00
Sugar, Cover, Bank Advertising 20.00
Vase, Swan, Bronze Metallic Glaze 50.00
Wall Pocket, Acorn Shape, 4 In 37.00
Wall Pocket, Fawns 32.00

ROSENTHAL porcelain was made at the factory established in Selb, Bavaria, in 1880. The factory is still making fine-quality tablewares and figurines. A series of Christmas plates was made from 1910. Other limited edition plates have been made since 1971.

Bowl, Scroll Design, Silver Overlay, Oval, 14 In. 185.00
Charger, Woman With Birds, Black & Gold, Signed, 14 In. 75.00
Compote, Crystal, Studio–Line, 6 In. 20.00
Cup & Saucer, Gladmere 47.00
Figurine, 3 Birds On Tree Trunk, 11 1/2 In. 650.00
Figurine, Ballerina, 12 In. 500.00
Figurine, Crouching Figure, 12 In. 385.00
Figurine, Dachshund, 7 x 7 In. .... 225.00 To 295.00
Figurine, Dog, Borzoi, Sitting, Black & White, 10 1/2 In. 450.00
Figurine, Fox, Signed, 12 In. 425.00
Figurine, German Shepherds, Sitting, 11 3/8 In. 495.00
Figurine, Penguin, Signed, 3 1/2 In. 95.00
Pendant, Garden Woman Scene, Colorful 125.00
Plate, Butterflies, 9 1/2 In. 15.00
Plate, Rheinstein Castle, 10 1/2 In. 135.00
Platter, White Velvet, Platinum Trim, 13 In. 30.00
Platter, White Velvet, Platinum Trim, 15 In. 37.00
Teapot, Freesia, Blue 200.00

Tureen, Sauce, Attached Underplate, White, Gold Trim 95.00

ROSEVILLE Pottery Company was organized in Roseville, Ohio, in 1890. Another plant was opened in Zanesville, Ohio, in 1898. Many types of pottery were made until 1954. Early wares include Sgraffito, Olympic, and Rozane. Later lines were often made with molded decorations, especially flowers and fruit. Pieces are marked *Roseville*.

Roseville U.S.A.

Ashtray, Donatello, 3–Footed	95.00
Ashtray, Hyde Park	10.00
Ashtray, Ming Tree, White	80.00
Ashtray, Pine Cone, Green	75.00
Ashtray, Snowberry, Green	35.00
Bank, Eagle, Teal Sponge	225.00
Bank, Pig	140.00
Basket, Apple Blossom, Green	125.00
Basket, Apple Blossom, Pink, 10 In.	185.00
Basket, Bittersweet, Green	106.00
Basket, Bushberry, Brown, 8 In.	125.00
Basket, Clematis, Brown, 10 In.	125.00
Basket, Columbine, Blue, 12 In.	250.00
Basket, Donatello, Pointed Handle, 6 x 12 In.	230.00
Basket, Foxglove, Blue, 12 In.	225.00
Basket, Freesia, 8 In.	60.00
Basket, Fuchsia, Blue, 8 In.	375.00
Basket, Hanging, Bittersweet, Yellow	175.00
Basket, Hanging, Bleeding Heart, Green	200.00
Basket, Hanging, Bushberry, Blue	325.00
Basket, Hanging, Bushberry, Brown	225.00
Basket, Hanging, Clematis, Brown, Chains	110.00
Basket, Hanging, Columbine, Blue	175.00
Basket, Hanging, Columbine, Pink	195.00
Basket, Hanging, Egypto	125.00
Basket, Hanging, Freesia, Green, 8 In.	95.00
Basket, Hanging, Iris, Brown	195.00
Basket, Hanging, Jonquil	485.00
Basket, Hanging, Magnolia, Green, 8 In.	105.00
Basket, Hanging, Peony, Pink	170.00
Basket, Hanging, Pine Cone, Brown	295.00
Basket, Hanging, Snowberry, Green, Chains, 6 In.	140.00
Basket, Hanging, White Rose, Blue	145.00
Basket, Hanging, Zephyr Lily, Green	95.00
Basket, Magnolia, Brown, 7 In.	68.00
Basket, Magnolia, Brown, 8 In.	75.00
Basket, Ming Tree, White, 8 In.	130.00
Basket, Monticello, Tan, 5 In.	165.00
Basket, Pine Cone, Blue, 10 In. .... 305.00 To	425.00
Basket, Pine Cone, Tan, 10 In.	275.99
Basket, Silhouette, Rose, 8 In.	220.00
Basket, Snowberry, Blue, 12 In.	145.00
Basket, Vista, 12 In.	325.00
Basket, Water Lily, Blue, 12 In.	175.00
Basket, White Rose, Blue, 10 In.	175.00
Basket, White Rose, Green, 10 In.	135.00
Basket, Wincraft, Blue, 8 In.	95.00
Basket, Zephyr Lily, Green, 7 1/2 In.	137.00
Bookends, Freesia, Blue	80.00
Bookends, Magnolia, Blue	135.00
Bookends, Magnolia, Brown	125.00
Bookends, Ming Tree .... 48.00 To	55.00
Bookends, Pine Cone, Blue .... 225.00 To	275.00
Bookends, Pine Cone, Brown	145.00
Bookends, Snowberry, Green .... 175.00 To	210.00
Bookends, Snowberry, Pink	90.00

Bookends, Thorn Apple 175.00
Bookends, Water Lily, Blue 95.00
Bookends, White Rose, Blue 165.00
Bookends, Wincraft, Green .... 80.00 To 95.00
Bookends, Zephyr Lily, Brown 150.00
Bowl, Bittersweet, Gray & Rose, 10 1/2 In. 75.00
Bowl, Clematis, Aqua, 10 In. 65.00
Bowl, Dogwood II, Flower Frog, 6 In. 145.00
Bowl, Donatello, 9 1/2 In. 60.00
Bowl, Ferella, Blue & Yellow Paper Label, 9 In. 330.00
Bowl, Ferella, Flower Frog, Red, Reticulated, Flared 4 1/4 x 9 1/4 In. 275.00
Bowl, Foxglove, Blue, 10 In. 110.00
Bowl, Fuchsia, Brown, 4 In. 65.00
Bowl, Ivory II, Savona Shape, 10 In. 85.00
Bowl, Jonquil, 2 Handles, 4 In. 85.00
Bowl, Jonquil, Attached Flower Frog, 10 In. 225.00
Bowl, Jonquil, Handle, 5 1/2 In. 80.00
Bowl, Magnolia, Green, 8 In. 75.00
Bowl, Morning Glory, Green, 10 In. 275.00
Bowl, Peony, Yellow, 4 In. 40.00
Bowl, Pine Cone, Blue, 6 In. .... 125.00 To 190.00
Bowl, Pine Cone, Blue, 8 In. 125.00
Bowl, Pine Cone, Blue, 9 In. 185.00
Bowl, Pine Cone, Blue, Handles, 12 In. 195.00
Bowl, Poppy, Pink, 5 In. 75.00
Bowl, Raymor, 12 In. 38.00
Bowl, Silhouette, Aqua, 6 In. 225.00
Bowl, Topeo, Blue, 13 In. 325.00
Bowl, Topeo, Red, 9 x 2 1/2 In. 165.00
Bowl, Tourist, 7 1/2 In. 1800.00
Bowl, Velmoss Scroll, 2 1/2 x 9 1/2 In. 65.00
Bowl, Volpato, Paper Label, c.1918, 6 In. 80.00
Bowl, Wisteria, Brown, 4 In. 375.00
Bowl, Zephyr Lily, Brown & Green, 4 In. 50.00
Box, Ming Tree 95.00
Candlestick, Bleeding Hearts, Green, Pair 40.00
Candlestick, Carnelian I, Green, 2 1/2 In., Pair 55.00
Candlestick, Carnelian II, Pair 125.00
Candlestick, Clematis, Brown, 5 In. 65.00
Candlestick, Cremona, Aqua, 4 1/2 In. 87.50
Candlestick, Cremona, Green, 4 In., Pair 100.00
Candlestick, Donatello, 1915, 8 1/2 In. 245.00
Candlestick, Florentine 28.00
Candlestick, Florentine, 8 In. 75.00
Candlestick, Freesia, 2 In., Pair 75.00
Candlestick, Gardenia, Green, Pair 67.50
Candlestick, Morning Glory, White 165.00
Candlestick, Moss, Pink, Aqua, Pair 77.50
Candlestick, Orian, Tan, Aqua, Pair 115.00
Candlestick, Panel, Green, Pair 64.00
Candy Dish, Pine Cone, Blue, 6 In. 165.00
Chamber Pot, Autumn, Open, 10 In. Diam. 195.00
Chamber Set, Dutch, 10 Piece 715.00
Chocolate Set, Dutch, 3 Piece 192.50
Compote, Egypto, Rozane Ware, 1905, 9 In. 650.00
Console Set, Carnelian II, Label, 3 Piece 400.00
Console Set, Ferella, Reticulated, Feathered Red, White & Green, 3 Piece 522.50
Console Set, Topeo, Double Candleholder, Blue, 3 Piece 650.00
Console Set, Tuscany, Pink, 3 Piece 147.50
Console Set, Zephyr Lily, Green, 3 Piece 108.00
Console, Baneda, 8 In. 235.00
Console, Dogwood I, 8 In. 165.00
Console, Foxglove, Blue 100.00

Console, Freesia 59.00
Console, Laurel, Green, 9 x 13 In. 225.00
Cookie Jar, Clematis, Brown 225.00
Cookie Jar, Freesia, Blue 195.00
Cookie Jar, Water Lily, Brown, 8 In. 325.00
Cornucopia, Apple Blossom, Blue, 8 In. 75.00
Cornucopia, Bleeding Heart, Aqua 132.50
Cornucopia, Bushberry, Brown, 6 In. 50.00
Cornucopia, Bushberry, Green, 6 In. 60.00
Cornucopia, Freesia, Brown, 7 In. 50.00
Cornucopia, Magnolia, Green, 8 In. 90.00
Cornucopia, Mock Orange, Yellow, 6 In. 67.50
Cornucopia, Pine Cone, Blue 135.00
Cornucopia, Wincraft, Blue 57.00
Cornucopia, Zephyr Lily, Blue, 6 In. 10.00
Creamer, Child's, Duck 95.00
Creamer, Child's, Rabbits 90.00
Creamer, Medallion .... 60.00 To 80.00
Crocus Pot, Jonquil, 7 In. 335.00
Cup & Saucer, Child's, Rabbit 180.00
Cuspidor, Mostique 225.00
Dish, Feeding, Little Jack Horner 145.00
Dish, Feeding, Rabbits, Sitting 125.00
Dish, Feeding, Standing Rabbit .... 70.00 To 110.00
Ewer, Bleeding Heart, Pink, 10 In. 225.00
Ewer, Clemana, Blue, 10 In. 130.00
Ewer, Clematis, Green, 10 In. 70.00
Ewer, Foxglove, Pink, 10 In. 175.00
Ewer, Freesia, Blue, 15 In. 350.00
Ewer, Freesia, Brown, 15 In. 290.00
Ewer, Fuchsia, Green, 10 In. 225.00
Ewer, Magnolia, Blue, 15 In. 350.00
Ewer, Magnolia, Green, 15 In. 245.00
Ewer, Ming Tree, Blue, 10 In. 125.00
Ewer, Mock Orange, Pink, 16 In. 290.00
Ewer, Pine Cone, Blue, 18 In. 1350.00
Ewer, Poppy, Pink, 10 In. 175.00
Ewer, Rozane, Signed, c.1900, 10 In. 193.00
Ewer, Snowberry, Green, 15 In. 250.00
Ewer, Snowberry, Pink, 10 In. 150.00
Ewer, Water Lily, Brown, 15 In. 215.00
Ewer, White Rose, Pink, 10 In. 235.00
Ewer, Zephyr Lily, Green, 15 In. 350.00
Flower Frog, Carnelian I, Blue Drip Over Rose .... 45.00 To 60.00
Flower Frog, Fuchsia, Blue 110.00
Flower Frog, Peony, Brown, 4 In. 40.00
Flower Frog, Tuscany, Blue–Green, 5 In. 35.00
Flower Frog, Water Lily, Pink, Green 50.00
Flower Frog, White Rose, Pink 65.00
Flowerpot, Florane, 6 In. 75.00
Flowerpot, Iris 50.00
Flowerpot, Magnolia, Blue, Saucer 65.00
Flowerpot, Pine Cone, Blue, Saucer 350.00
Flowerpot, Zephyr Lily, Brown & Green, Saucer 145.00
Hatpin Holder, Mongol, Silver Overlay 400.00
Jar, Cover, Panel, Brown, Orange Dandelions, 10 x 6 In. 220.00
Jardiniere, Apple Blossom, Blue, 6 In. 100.00
Jardiniere, Baneda, 7 In. 475.00
Jardiniere, Blackberry, 12 1/4 x 16 1/2 In. 1760.00
Jardiniere, Blackberry, 4 In. 225.00
Jardiniere, Blueberry, Pink 68.00
Jardiniere, Clematis, Brown, 4 In. 37.50
Jardiniere, Corinthian, 5 In. 65.00

Jardiniere, Corinthian, 8 In. 175.00
Jardiniere, Dahlrose, 4 In. 85.00
Jardiniere, Donatello, 8 In. 110.00
Jardiniere, Donatello, 10 In. 520.00
Jardiniere, Donatello, Pedestal, 27 1/2 In. 975.00
Jardiniere, Florentine, Pedestal, 10 In. 65.00
Jardiniere, Forest, 4 1/2 In. 65.00
Jardiniere, Freesia, Blue, Pedestal, 25 In. 825.00
Jardiniere, Freesia, Brown, 4 In. 60.00
Jardiniere, Fuchsia, Brown, 7 In. 250.00
Jardiniere, Fuchsia, Pedestal, Blue, 24 In. 950.00
Jardiniere, Futura, Tan, 7 x 10 In. 425.00
Jardiniere, Iris, Pink, 4 In. 87.50
Jardiniere, Jonquil, 5 In. 80.00
Jardiniere, Luffa, Brown, 4 In. 70.00
Jardiniere, Magnolia, Green, 24 In. 395.00
Jardiniere, Monticello, Brown, 5 In. 200.00
Jardiniere, Peony, Brown, 4 In. 45.00
Jardiniere, Peony, Yellow, Pedestal, 24 In. 450.00
Jardiniere, Persian, Lavender, Green, 8 1/2 In. 230.00
Jardiniere, Persian, Lavender, Green, 9 x 11 In. 350.00
Jardiniere, Tourist, 9 In. 3300.00
Jardiniere, Water Lily, Brown, Pedestal, 8 In. 575.00
Jardiniere, White Rose, Brown, 5 In. 85.00
Jardiniere, Zephyr Lily, 4 In. 45.00
Jug, Landscape, Pre-1916 .... 250.00
Lamp, Baneda, Green, 25 In. 650.00
Lamp, Cherry Blossom 795.00
Lamp, Oil, Egypto, Seal 425.00
Lamp, Sunflower, Original Fixtures, Metal 650.00
Lamp, Vista, Green & Purple, 10 In. 330.00
Mug, Child's, Chicks 100.00
Mug, Eagle 120.00
Mug, Elk 120.00
Mug, Indian, Dated 1916 .... 175.00
Mug, Knights of Pythias, 4 Piece 690.00
Mug, Moose 120.00
Mug, Pine Cone, Brown 150.00
Pedestal, Fuchsia, Green 650.00
Pedestal, Jonquil, 18 In. 325.00
Pitcher, Bleeding Heart, Pink 220.00
Pitcher, Blended, 7 In. 90.00
Pitcher, Cider, Bushberry, Green 145.00
Pitcher, Cider, Pine Cone, Brown 360.00
Pitcher, Clematis, Yellow Flower, Orange & Brown, 15 In. 165.00
Pitcher, Cornelian, 7 In. 65.00
Pitcher, Cow, 7 1/2 In. 160.00
Pitcher, Freesia, Blue, 10 In. .... 110.00 To 135.00
Pitcher, Freesia, Brown, 10 In. 165.00
Pitcher, Fuchsia, Blue, Ice Lip, 8 In. 395.00
Pitcher, Fuchsia, Handle, Rust, 6 In. 85.00
Pitcher, Mayfair, Green, 6 In. 45.00
Pitcher, Pine Cone, Brown 225.00
Pitcher, Pine Cone, Brown, Ice Lip, 8 In. 600.00
Pitcher, Rozane, Monk Portrait .... 750.00 To 775.00
Planter Bookends, Foxglove, Pink 195.00
Planter, Apple Blossom, Lime Green, 4 x 12 1/4 In. 40.00
Planter, Artwood, Green, Gold Trim 45.00
Planter, Bittersweet, Gray, Rose 48.00
Planter, Bittersweet, Yellow 50.00
Planter, Blackberry, Hexagonal, 10 In. 325.00
Planter, Earlam, 10 In. 195.00
Planter, Medallion, 3-Footed .... 60.00 To 78.00

Planter, Mock Orange, Green, 12 In.	125.00
Planter, Mock Orange, Pink, 5 In.	35.00
Planter, Morning Glory, Green, 13 In.	1900.00
Planter, Panel, Orange & Brown Floral, Dark Brown, 11 x 6 In.	225.00
Planter, Silhouette, Aqua	45.00
Planter, Tourist	5000.00
Plaque, Donatello, c.1915–1925, 8 In.	365.00
Plate, Foxglove, Blue, 10 In.	100.00
Plate, Raymor, Gray, 7 In.	12.00
Plate, Rosecraft, Blue, 5 In.	10.00
Smoking Set, Indian, 3 Piece	467.50
Tankard, Holland, 9 1/2 In.	115.00
Tankard, Holland, 11 1/2 In.	155.00
Tea & Coffee Set, Persian, Purple & Green Arabesques, White Body, 4 Piece	550.00
Tea Set, Dutch, 3 Piece	82.50 To 180.00
Tea Set, Magnolia, 3 Piece	350.00
Tea Set, Persian, Blue Floral, White Ground, 3 Piece	302.50
Teapot, Della Robbia, Rooster & Owl Decoration, Dark Green, 6 x 7 In.	450.00
Teapot, Della Robbia, Sgraffito, Stylized Roses, Rozane, 5 1/4 x 8 1/2 In.	605.00
Teapot, Freesia	195.00
Teapot, Freesia, Brown	125.00
Teapot, Mayfair, Brown	50.00
Teapot, Wincraft, Blue	85.00
Toothbrush Holder, Colonial	62.50
Tray, Dresser, Creamware, 10 In.	165.00
Tray, Pine Cone, Green 12 In.	295.00
Umbrella Stand, Art Nouveau Floral, Matte Green, Scalloped, 22 x 12 In.	302.50
Umbrella Stand, Blended 609, Green, Yellow	85.00
Umbrella Stand, Blended 710, Green, Yellow	140.00
Umbrella Stand, Primrose, Pink, 21 In.	750.00
Umbrella Stand, Vista	450.00
Urn, Cherry Blossom, Brown, 5 x 5 In.	135.00
Urn, Cherry Blossom, Pink, 8 x 8 In.	395.00
Urn, Cherry Blossom, Pink, 8 x 9 In.	495.00
Urn, Clemana, Blue, 7 In.	350.00
Urn, Laurel, Gold, 6 1/2 In.	145.00
Urn, Laurel, Yellow, 10 x 7 In.	495.00
Urn, Morning Glory, White, 2 Handles, Silver Label, 11 3/4 In.	440.00
Urn, Silhouette, Turquoise, 8 In., Pair	500.00
Urn, Tuscany, Gray, 5 In.	75.00
Urn, Velmoss II, Pink, 6 x 7 In.	95.00
Urn, Wisteria, Blue, 5 In.	270.00
Urn, Wisteria, Brown, 5 In.	250.00
Vase, Apple Blossom, Pink, 10 In.	125.00
Vase, Artwood, Plum, Gray, 8 In.	20.00
Vase, Aztec, 6 1/4 In.	375.00
Vase, Aztec, 10 In.	295.00
Vase, Aztec, 11 In.	220.00 To 275.00
Vase, Aztec, 12 In.	190.00
Vase, Baneda, Green, 6 In.	250.00
Vase, Baneda, Green, 7 In.	300.00
Vase, Baneda, Pink, 4 1/2 x 6 In.	350.00
Vase, Baneda, Pink, 8 In.	335.00
Vase, Baneda, Pink, 12 In.	395.00 To 585.00
Vase, Baneda, Pink, 15 In.	1100.00
Vase, Bittersweet, Orange, 8 In.	125.00
Vase, Blackberry, 4 In.	185.00
Vase, Blackberry, 5 In.	250.00
Vase, Blackberry, 6 In.	295.00
Vase, Blackberry, 7 In.	225.00
Vase, Blackberry, 8 In.	265.00
Vase, Bleeding Heart, Blue, 8 In.	165.00
Vase, Bud, Dahlrose, Triple	85.00

Vase, Bushberry, Brown, 4 In. 40.00
Vase, Bushberry, Green, 4 In. 25.00
Vase, Carnelian II, 7 In. 75.00
Vase, Carnelian II, 8 In. 275.00
Vase, Cherry Blossom, 5 In. 230.00
Vase, Cherry Blossom, 7 In. .... 295.00 To 375.00
Vase, Cherry Blossom, 10 In. 425.00
Vase, Chloron, Engraved Silver On Grapes & Leaves, Crackle Glaze, 8 In. 8500.00
Vase, Clematis, Blue, 6 In. 45.00
Vase, Clematis, Blue-Green, 7 In. 60.00
Vase, Columbine, Blue, 8 In. 98.00
Vase, Columbine, Pink, 4 In. 67.50
Vase, Columbine, Pink, 16 In. .... 325.00 To 350.00
Vase, Cosmos, Blue, 8 In, Pair 190.00
Vase, Cosmos, Blue, 12 In. 200.00
Vase, Cosmos, Blue, Bud, 4 In. 65.00
Vase, Cosmos, Tan, 10 In. 165.00
Vase, Cremona, Green, 8 In. 65.00
Vase, Dahlrose, 6 In. 85.00
Vase, Dahlrose, 8 In. 175.00
Vase, Dawn, Beige, 6 In. 80.00
Vase, Dawn, Green, 8 In. 185.00
Vase, Dogwood, Green, 1918, 12 In. 145.00
Vase, Donatello, Green, Double 65.00
Vase, Elk, Fred Steele, 21 In. 3995.00
Vase, Falline, Blue, 6 1/2 In. 355.00
Vase, Falline, Brown, 7 x 6 1/2 In. 380.00
Vase, Fan, Carnelian I, Turquoise & Aqua, 6 In. 68.00
Vase, Fan, Cremona, Blue, 5 In. .:. 30.00
Vase, Ferella, Pink, 4 In. 225.00
Vase, Ferella, Pink, 9 1/2 In. 485.00
Vase, Florentine, 4 1/2 In. 68.50
Vase, Florentine, 6 In. 50.00
Vase, Foxglove, Green, 16 In. 350.00
Vase, Foxglove, Pink, 4 In. .... 38.00 To 50.00
Vase, Freesia, Brown, 2 Handles, 8 In. 45.00
Vase, Fuchsia, Blue, 7 1/2 In. 225.00
Vase, Fuchsia, Blue, 15 In. 450.00
Vase, Fuchsia, Brown, 6 In. .... 125.00 To 155.00
Vase, Fuchsia, Brown, 8 In. 195.00
Vase, Fuchsia, Green, Label, 6 In. 195.00
Vase, Futura, Brown, Blue & Green, 8 In. 485.00
Vase, Futura, Orange & Brown, 4 Sides, 12 1/4 In. 467.50
Vase, Futura, Orange & Green, Stacked Neck, Angular Handles, Triangular, 9 In. ... 850.00
Vase, Gardenia, Green, 2 Handles, 8 In. 65.00
Vase, Imperial I, Handles, 1916, 8 1/2 x 10 In. 165.00
Vase, Imperial II, 4 In. 295.00
Vase, Imperial II, 5 1/2 In. 125.00
Vase, Imperial II, 7 1/4 In. 165.00
Vase, Imperial II, 10 In. 275.00
Vase, Ixia, Green, 10 In. 80.00
Vase, Ixia, Pink, 8 In. .... 85.00 To 90.00
Vase, Ixia, Yellow, 8 1/2 In. 67.50
Vase, Jonquil, Handles, 1931, 3 x 7 In. 154.00
Vase, Jonquil, Label, 8 In. 200.00
Vase, Jonquil, Tapered, Handle, 4 In. 95.00
Vase, Laurel, Gold Trim, 9 1/4 In. 395.00
Vase, Laurel, Red, 9 In. 225.00
Vase, Lily-of-The-Valley, White, Olive Ground, 2 Handles, 8 x 4 In. 550.00
Vase, Lombardy, Blue, 5 In. 85.00
Vase, Magnolia, Blue, 6 In. 10.00
Vase, Magnolia, Blue, 8 In. 115.00

Vase, Magnolia, Blue, Bud, 7 In. 60.00
Vase, Magnolia, Brown, 9 In. .... 75.00 To 95.00
Vase, Magnolia, Green, 8 In. 135.00
Vase, Magnolia, Green, 15 In. 325.00
Vase, Mongol, Bulbous Base, Tapered To Pinch, Rounded Opening, 7 In. 525.00
Vase, Monticello, Aqua, 4 In. 245.00
Vase, Monticello, Aqua, 5 In. 175.00
Vase, Monticello, Blue, 6 In. 175.00
Vase, Monticello, Blue, 8 1/2 In. 185.00
Vase, Monticello, Brown, 5 In. 195.00
Vase, Monticello, Brown, 7 In. 225.00
Vase, Morning Glory, Green, 4 In. 245.00
Vase, Morning Glory, Green, 7 In. 335.00
Vase, Morning Glory, Green, 8 1/2 In. 425.00
Vase, Morning Glory, Green, 14 1/2 In. 850.00
Vase, Morning Glory, White, 8 1/4 In. 250.00
Vase, Morning Glory, White, Gold Label, 8 1/2 In. 850.00
Vase, Moss, Aqua, Tan, Urn Type, 8 In. 135.00
Vase, Moss, Pink, 10 In. .... 295.00 To 325.00
Vase, Moss, Pink, Brown, 12 In. 375.00
Vase, Moss, Pink, Tan, Brown, 14 1/2 In. 475.00
Vase, Mostique, Glossy Flower, Brown Line Design, 10 In. 585.00
Vase, Mostique, Gray, 8 In. 50.00
Vase, Mostique, Gray, 9 In. 45.00
Vase, Orian, Beige & Aqua, 10 1/2 In. 215.00
Vase, Orian, Tan, Blue, 8 1/2 In. 95.00
Vase, Panel, Nudes, Fan Shape, 6 In. 275.00
Vase, Pauleo, Blue & Pink Irises, Pale Blue Ground, 18 In. .... 2500.00 To 2750.00
Vase, Pauleo, Lavender & Beige Top, 15 In. 660.00
Vase, Pauleo, Purple & Blue Glaze, Marked, 9 In. 525.00
Vase, Peony, Brown, 7 In. 55.00
Vase, Peony, Gold, 4 1/2 In. 65.50
Vase, Peony, Green, 4 In. 22.00
Vase, Pillow, Iris, Blue, 8 In. 145.00
Vase, Pillow, Pine Cone, Gold, Brown, 8 In. 225.00
Vase, Pillow, White Rose, Pink, 8 In. 145.00
Vase, Pillow, Zephyr Lily, Green, 7 In. 75.00
Vase, Pine Cone, Blue, Paper Label, 8 In. 250.00
Vase, Pine Cone, Brown, 6 In. 125.00
Vase, Pine Cone, Brown, 7 In. 70.00
Vase, Pine Cone, Brown, 8 In. 155.00
Vase, Pine Cone, Green, 8 1/2 In. 125.00
Vase, Pine Cone, Twig Handles, Brown, 10 In. 225.00
Vase, Poppy, Pink, 6 1/2 In. 78.00
Vase, Poppy, Pink, 7 In. 110.00
Vase, Rosecraft Vintage, 5 In. 70.00
Vase, Rosecraft, Black, 6 In. 65.00
Vase, Rosecraft, Black, 8 1/2 In. 58.00
Vase, Rosecraft, Blue, 3 3/4 In. 90.00
Vase, Rozane Crystalis, Light & Dark Green Crystalline, 3 Footed, 8 x 6 In. 1210.00
Vase, Rozane Egypto, Raised Banded Design, Marked, 12 In. 310.00
Vase, Rozane Fudji, 10 In. 1450.00
Vase, Rozane Mongol, Cylindrical, Burgundy To Black, Marked, 15 In. 605.00
Vase, Rozane Woodland, 11 In. 945.00
Vase, Rozane Woodland, 17 In. 2000.00
Vase, Rozane Woodland, 4 Sides, Brown & Orange, 10 x 3 1/2 In. 220.00
Vase, Rozane Woodland, Art Nouveau, Tan Bisque Finish, Orange Interior, 17 In. .. 2200.00
Vase, Rozane, Blue, W. M., No. 924, 4 In. 285.00
Vase, Rozane, Brown, Coral, 8 1/2 In. 50.00
Vase, Rozane, Elk, 21 In. 3995.00
Vase, Rozane, Floral Design, Brown, 5 1/4 In. 190.00
Vase, Rozane, Floral Design, White, Signed, 7 1/2 In. 575.00
Vase, Rozane, Thistle Decoration, Dark Blue Ground, 17 In. 1200.00

Vase, Russco, Aqua, 7 In. 140.00
Vase, Russco, Gold Crystalline, Footed, 2 Buttressed Handles, 8 1/4 In. 110.00
Vase, Russco, Pink, 10 In. 125.00
Vase, Russco, Tan, Interior Bronze, 8 In. 65.00
Vase, Silhouette, Nude, Green, 6 In. 180.00
Vase, Snowberry, Green, 6 In. 40.00
Vase, Snowberry, Red, 9 In. 67.50
Vase, Sunflower, 5 In. .... 225.00 To 250.00
Vase, Sunflower, 6 In. 225.00
Vase, Sunflower, 9 In. 575.00
Vase, Thorn Apple, Brown, 6 In. 60.00
Vase, Thorn Apple, Brown, 8 In. 87.50
Vase, Thorn Apple, Pink, 6 In. .... 62.50 To 75.00
Vase, Topeo, Blue, Bulbous, 7 1/2 In. 340.00
Vase, Tuscany, Pink, 5 1/4 x 7 1/2 In. 67.50
Vase, Velmoss II, Aqua, 7 1/2 In. 87.00
Vase, Velmoss II, Blue, 7 In. 125.00
Vase, Victorian Art, Yellow & Brown Band, Stylized Design, 10 In. 240.00
Vase, Vista, 10 In. 325.00
Vase, Water Lily, Brown, 18 In. 495.00
Vase, Water Lily, Greens & Blues, 8 In. 85.00
Vase, White Rose, Blue, 6 In. 65.00
Vase, White Rose, Pink & Green, 7 In. 65.00
Vase, White Rose, Pink, 12 In. 175.00
Vase, Wincraft, Brown Pine Cone, 8 In. 85.00
Vase, Wincraft, Tan, 12 In. 95.00
Vase, Wisteria, 5 In. 195.00
Vase, Wisteria, 12 In. 1085.00
Vase, Wisteria, 2 Triangular Handles At Top, Bulbous, 7 x 8 In. 385.00
Vase, Woodland, Blossoms, Twisted 4–Sided, Marked, 10 1/2 In. 660.00
Vase, Zephyr Lily, Brown & Green, 8 1/2 In. 80.00
Vase, Zephyr Lily, Brown & Green, 10 In. 115.00
Vase, Zephyr Lily, Green, 12 In. 140.00
Wall Pocket, Apple Blossom, Blue, 8 1/2 In. 155.00
Wall Pocket, Apple Blossom, Red, 8 In. 125.00
Wall Pocket, Baneda, Pink 1200.00
Wall Pocket, Blackberry 625.00
Wall Pocket, Burmese, Green 175.00
Wall Pocket, Cherry Blossom 600.00
Wall Pocket, Clematis, Brown 175.00
Wall Pocket, Columbine, Brown 275.00
Wall Pocket, Corinthian 125.00
Wall Pocket, Cosmos, Green, 8 In. 295.00
Wall Pocket, Dahlrose, 10 In. .... 155.00 To 165.00
Wall Pocket, Donatello .... 125.00 To 155.00
Wall Pocket, Donatello, 11 1/2 In. 150.00
Wall Pocket, Earlam 150.00
Wall Pocket, Florane, 10 In. 95.00
Wall Pocket, Foxglove, Blue 275.00
Wall Pocket, Freesia, Blue 125.00
Wall Pocket, Freesia, Green 250.00
Wall Pocket, Fuchsia, Green, 8 1/2 In. 305.00
Wall Pocket, Futura, Blue 295.00
Wall Pocket, Futura, Tan, 8 In. 380.00
Wall Pocket, Ivory, 12 In. 135.00
Wall Pocket, Jonquil 395.00
Wall Pocket, Lombardy, Blue 295.00
Wall Pocket, Lotus, Green .... 175.00 To 185.00
Wall Pocket, Magnolia, Green 155.00
Wall Pocket, Mayfair, Corner, Brown 115.00
Wall Pocket, Ming Tree, Aqua 200.00
Wall Pocket, Ming Tree, Blue 195.00
Wall Pocket, Ming Tree, Green 345.00

Wall Pocket, Mock Orange, Green	40.00
Wall Pocket, Monticello, Brown, 5 In.	160.00
Wall Pocket, Moss, Blue	395.00
Wall Pocket, Mostique, 12 In.	175.00
Wall Pocket, Orian, Yellow	595.00
Wall Pocket, Panel, Brown, Orange	165.00
Wall Pocket, Panel, Nude, Green	475.00
Wall Pocket, Panel, Nude, Green Matte Glaze, Marked, 7 In.	270.00
Wall Pocket, Pine Cone, Brown, 8 1/2 In.	300.00
Wall Pocket, Pine Cone, Brown, Double	350.00
Wall Pocket, Pine Cone, Green, Double	295.00
Wall Pocket, Pine Cone, Triple, Brown	395.00
Wall Pocket, Primrose, Pink	395.00
Wall Pocket, Sunflower	495.00 To 595.00
Wall Pocket, Thorn Apple, Blue	350.00
Wall Pocket, Tuscany, Pink	165.00 To 185.00
Wall Pocket, White Rose, Pink	270.00
Wall Pocket, Zephyr Lily, Blue	135.00
Wall Pocket, Zephyr Lily, Tan, 8 In.	165.00
Wall, Shelf, Pine Cone, Brown	295.00
Water Set, Pine Cone, Green, 5 Tumblers	925.00
Window Box, Magnolia, Brown	70.00
Window Box, Pine Cone, Green, 15 In.	225.00
Window Box, Silhouette, Blue	80.00
Window Box, Sunflower	650.00
Window Box, Tourist	5000.00

ROWLAND & MARSELLUS Company is part of a mark that appears on historical Staffordshire dating from the late nineteenth and early twentieth centuries. Rowland & Marsellus is believed to be the mark used by the British Anchor Pottery Co. of Longton, England, for some pieces made for export to a New York firm. Many American views were made. Of special interest to collectors are the blue and white plates with rolled edges.

Plate, Niagara Falls	50.00
Plate, Panama Pacific, Rolled Rim, 1915, 10 1/2 In.	125.00 To 135.00
Plate, Philadelphia	50.00
Plate, Washington's Headquarters, 10 In.	65.00

ROY ROGERS was born in 1911 in Cincinnati, Ohio. In the 1930s, he made a living as a singer; in 1935, his group started work at a Los Angeles radio station. He appeared in his first movie in 1937. From 1952 to 1957, he made 101 television shows. Roy Rogers memorabilia is collected, including items from the Roy Rogers restaurants.

Album, Cowboy Songs, 1941	46.00
Bandanna, Roy & Trigger, Red	35.00
Bank, Book, Metal	70.00
Bank, Roy & Trigger, Ceramic	125.00 To 250.00
Bedspread, Roy & Trigger, 7 1/2 x 7 In.	120.00
Book, Annual, 1954	25.00
Book, Roy Rogers & The Gopher Creek Gunman, D. Middleton, 1945	10.00
Book, Whitman, 1956, 9 x 12 In.	27.00
Boot Cover, For Shoes	75.00
Box, Gun	100.00
Box, Stopwatch, Roy Rogers & Trigger, Bradley, 1959	350.00
Button, Pinback	15.00
Camera, 620 Snapshot, Herbert George Co.	75.00
Cap Gun, Brown Plastic Grip, 10 In.	65.00
Cap Gun, Leslie Henry	130.00
Card Set, 3–D, Cereal Premium, 1950s	28.00
Card, Cereal, Trigger Says His Prayers, Unopened	4.00
Card, Playing	12.00
Chuck Wagon & Jeep, Fix–It, Horses, Figures, Box, Ideal, 15 In.	180.00
Clock, Alarm, Animated	150.00 To 195.00

Coin, Lucky	10.00
Complete Horseshoe Set	125.00
Cowboy Outfit, Felt Cowboy Hat, Shirt & Pants, Yankiboy, 1950	176.00
Cufflinks & Tie Bar Set, On Card	32.00 To 35.00
Dale Evans Official Necklace, On Card	18.50
Dale Evans, Wristwatch, Ingraham, 1951	165.00
Deputy, Copper, Star Shape	9.00
Dog, Realistic Figure, Neck Tag, Hartland, 6 In.	147.00
Fix It Chuck Wagon, With Nellie Belle Jeep, Roy, Dale & Pat Brady Figures, Box	245.00
Flashlight, Box, Decoder Instructions	95.00 To 120.00
Game, Rodeo	135.00
Guitar, Carrying Case	47.00 To 110.00
Gun & Holster, Twin	575.00
Gun, Tuck–A–Way, On Card, 2 3/4 In.	95.00
Harmonica	30.00 To 40.00
Harmonica, On Card	95.00
Hat, Quick Shooter, Ideal, Box	235.00
Hat, Ribbon, No Lining	25.00
Holder, Card, Club	10.00
Horseshoe Set, Ohio Art	125.00
Jacket, Jean, 2 Patches	175.00
Jacket, Suede	300.00
Knife, 2 Blades, Chain, Trigger	90.00
Lamp, Roy On Rearing Trigger, Composition, Signed Roy & Trigger	195.00
Lamp, Trigger, Shade, Signed Plaito	50.00
Lantern, Ranch, Box	200.00 To 250.00
Letter, Fan Club	10.00
Lunch Box, Blue Cowhide, 1955	55.00
Lunch Box, Chow Wagon, Dome, 1955	160.00
Lunch Box, Dale Driving Chow Wagon, American Thermos, 1958	122.00
Lunch Box, Red Shirt, 1957	77.00 To 200.00
Lunch Box, Roy & Dale, Red Band, 1954	140.00
Lunch Box, RR Bar Ranch, Metal	115.00
Lunch Box, Saddlebag, Vinyl, King Seeley, 1960	186.00
Lunch Box, Thermos, Tall, 1953	155.00
Marble, Roy & Trigger, 2 Piece	10.00
Mug, Boot	20.00
Mug, Roy's Head With Hat, Plastic, F & F	24.00 To 45.00
Necklace, Dale Evans, On Card	25.00
Necktie	55.00
Nodder, Figural, Bobbin Head	225.00 To 250.00
Paint Set, Paint By Number, Dale & Roy, 1950's	125.00
Paper Dolls, Roy Rogers & Dale Evans, Whitman, 1950, Uncut	100.00
Pencil	5.00
Phone, Wall, Crank	75.00
Plate, Chuck Wagon, Granite, 3 Piece	28.00
Plate, Salad	65.00
Play Set, Ranch, Complete, Marx, #3979	275.00
Pocketknife	125.00
Postcard, Roy, Dale Evans, Gabby Hayes, Trigger, Eat Quaker Oats, 1949	25.00
Pull Toy, On Trigger, Wooden, Lithographed	295.00
Puzzle, Roy & Dale Evans	16.50
Ranch, Punch Out, Post	85.00
Record, In Another Lifetime, Capital	10.75
Record, These Are The Good Old Days, Capital	2.50
Rifle, Cap, Plastic	70.00
Ring, Branding Iron	110.00
Ring, Microscope	55.00 To 75.00
Rodeo Lariat, Card	175.00
Roy Windup Wild West Stagecoach Pulling Cars, Tin, Set of 3	120.00
Scarf, Pink	70.00
Shooting' Iron, Double Action, Kilgore, Box	350.00
Stagecoach Wagon Train, Tin, Windup, Marx, Box, 14 In.	300.00

Stagecoach, 2 Horses & Roy, Ideal, 1955, 15 1/4 In.	75.00
Sweater, Pullover	150.00
Tablet	10.00
Telephone, Plastic, Wall	55.00
Tent	125.00
Tie Slide, Bolo, Metal	37.50
Tumbler, Roy Rogers & Trigger, Gold, Frosted Ground, 5 1/2 In.	20.00 To 65.00
Viewer, 3–D, Post Sugar Crisp	3.00
Wristwatch, Dales Evans and Buttercup Picture, Display Box, Bradley, 1950	323.00
Wristwatch, Ingraham, 1951	100.00 To 150.00

ROYAL BAYREUTH is the name of a factory that was founded in Tettau, Bavaria, in 1794. It has continued to modern times. The marks have changed through the years. A stylized crest, the name *Royal Bayreuth,* and the word *Bavaria* appear in slightly different forms from 1870 to about 1919. Later dishes may include the words *U.S. Zone,* the year of the issue, or the word *Germany* instead of *Bavaria.* Related pieces may be found listed in the Rose Tapestry, Sand Babies, Snow Babies, and Sunbonnet Babies categories.

Ashtray, & Match Holder, Swan, Red Poppy	950.00
Ashtray, Devil Head, Red	450.00
Ashtray, Turkey, Blue	390.00
Berry Set, Flowers, Gold Bands, Blue Mark, 7 Piece	360.00
Bowl & Underplate, Mayonnaise, Red Poppy	500.00
Bowl, Lavender Floors, 10 1/2 In.	30.00
Bowl, Mayonnaise, Poppy, Red	525.00
Bowl, Multicolored Roses, Shadow Leaves, Blue Mark, 10 1/2 In.	125.00
Bowl, Poppy, 6 In.	80.00
Bowl, Tomato, 8 In.	395.00
Bowl, Tomato, Signed, 4 1/2 In.	50.00
Box, Musicians Sitting On Bench Cover, Oval, 1 3/8 x 4 3/8 In.	40.00
Candleholder, Boy With Donkey	225.00
Candleholder, Jack & Beanstalk, Blue Mark	495.00
Candleholder, Jack & Jill, 4 1/4 In.	135.00
Candleholder, Red Clown, Blue Mark	425.00
Candleholder, Woman On Horse, Dogs	225.00
Chamberstick, Musicians, Shield Back	195.00
Chamberstick, Pastoral Scene, Handle, 5 1/2 In.	220.00
Creamer, Apple	120.00
Creamer, Bell Ringer, Blue Mark	295.00
Creamer, Black Crow, Blue Mark	145.00
Creamer, Black Poodle	210.00
Creamer, Butterfly, Blue Mark	500.00
Creamer, Cable, Blue Mark	325.00
Creamer, Cattle Standing In Water	175.00
Creamer, Cockatoo, Marked	550.00
Creamer, Corinthian, Black, Multicolor	55.00
Creamer, Crow, Black, Red Beak, Blue Mark	250.00
Creamer, Crow, Black, Yellow Beak, Blue Mark	300.00
Creamer, Duck	150.00
Creamer, Eagle	135.00 To 195.00
Creamer, Fish Head, Marked	250.00
Creamer, Frog, Green & Yellow	120.00
Creamer, Gray Poodle, Blue Mark	225.00 To 325.00
Creamer, Lamplighter	185.00
Creamer, Lemon	175.00
Creamer, Lemon, Marked	350.00
Creamer, Man Lighting Pipe, Blue Mark, 3 3/4 In.	75.00
Creamer, Monkey, Green, Blue Mark	550.00
Creamer, Mountain Goat, Blue Mark	400.00
Creamer, Parrot	325.00
Creamer, Pear, Marked	475.00
Creamer, Poodle, Black	195.00

Creamer, Poodle, Gray, Blue Mark 225.00
Creamer, Red Devil, Blue Mark 350.00
Creamer, Red Pig 850.00
Creamer, Red Poppy, 4 In. 160.00
Creamer, Robin, Marked 275.00
Creamer, Rooster, Blue Mark 800.00
Creamer, Shell, Murex, Blue Mark 300.00
Creamer, Strawberry 175.00
Creamer, Tomato, 2 1/4 In. 95.00
Creamer, Tomato, 3 In. 95.00
Creamer, Trout, Blue Mark 450.00
Creamer, Water Buffalo, Marked 300.00
Cup & Saucer, Corinthian, Green Mark 45.00
Cup & Saucer, Gold, Miniature 35.00
Cup, Devil & Dice, After Dinner 60.00
Desk Set, Cows In The Field, Blue Mark, 5 Piece 600.00
Dish, Candy, Devil & Cards 250.00
Dish, Pin, Turtle, Black Mark 500.00
Hair Receiver, Hunt Scene, 3 1/4 x 3 1/4 In. 110.00
Hatpin Holder, Boy With Turkey, Blue Mark 375.00
Hatpin Holder, Dachshund, 4 3/4 In. 800.00
Hatpin Holder, Elk, Mountain Scene, Pierced Base 495.00
Hatpin Holder, Goose Girl .... 325.00 To 495.00
Hatpin Holder, Man Tending Turkeys, Blue Mark 250.00
Hatpin Holder, Owl, Gray, Blue Mark 650.00
Hatpin Holder, Reticulated Rim & Handles, Saucer Base, Blue Mark 275.00
Humidor, Chimpanzee, Blue Mark, 6 1/2 In. .... 1700.00 To 1995.00
Humidor, Clown 1700.00
Humidor, Fox Hunt Scene, Blue Mark, 8 In. 300.00
Humidor, Man In A Canoe, Tapestry, Blue Mark 1000.00
Match Holder, Clown, Black Mark 475.00
Match Holder, Fox Hunting Scene, Dogs, Horse 85.00
Match Holder, Hanging, Formally Dressed Horseman With Dogs, Marked 165.00
Match Holder, Horseman With Dogs, Striker On Rim, Ball Shape, 2 1/2 x 3 In. 110.00
Match Holder, Man Working, 2 Horses, Cottage Background, Blue Mark 150.00
Mug, Arabs On Horseback, Mosque, 8 In. 325.00
Mug, Beer, Devil & Cards, Blue Mark, 8 In. 500.00
Mug, Beer, Elk, Blue Mark 475.00
Mustard, Cover, Friar Tuck 55.00
Mustard, Tomato .... 65.00 To 85.00
Nappy, Little Jack Horner, Spade Shape, Handle, Blue Mark 135.00
Pin Dish, Cover, Lobster, 4 x 3 3/4 In. 40.00
Pin Tray, Little Bopeep, Spade Shape, Marked 125.00
Pitcher, Babes In Woods, Blue, 5 In. 495.00
Pitcher, Cavaliers, Blue Mark, 7 1/2 In. 175.00
Pitcher, Coachman, Blue Mark, 7 In. 650.00
Pitcher, Corinthian, Blue Mark, 7 1/8 In. 135.00
Pitcher, Devil & Cards, 7 1/2 In. .... 495.00 To 500.00
Pitcher, Devil & Cards, Blue Mark, 5 In. .... 300.00 To 375.00
Pitcher, Devil, 7 x 5 In. 398.00
Pitcher, Elk, Blue Mark, 7 In. 495.00
Pitcher, Goat, 4 In. 75.00
Pitcher, Goose Girl, Pinched Spout 75.00
Pitcher, Lemon, Blue Mark, 4 In. 395.00
Pitcher, Lobster, 7 In. 575.00
Pitcher, Lobster, Blue Mark, 5 1/2 In. .... 250.00 To 395.00
Pitcher, Never Say Die–Up Man and Try, Blue, 7 In. 375.00
Pitcher, Oak Leaf, Blue Mark, 5 In. 295.00
Pitcher, Pearlized Oak Leaf, 5 In. 625.00
Pitcher, Poppy, 7 In. 795.00
Pitcher, Santa Claus, 5 1/4 In. ....*Illus* 3500.00
Pitcher, St. Bernard 395.00
Pitcher, St. Bernard, 7 In. 400.00

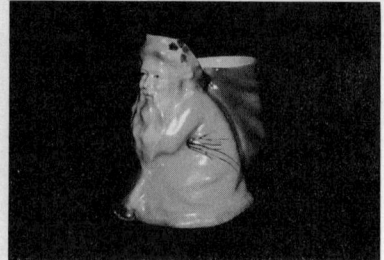

Royal Bayreuth, Pitcher,

Santa Claus, 5 1/4 In.

If you store paper ephemera like trade cards or labels in notebooks or photo albums, be sure to open the albums several times a year to let the air circulate.

Pitcher, Tomato, Marked, 4 3/4 In.	295.00
Plate, Little Bopeep, Child's, Marked	125.00 To 135.00
Plate, Little Boy Blue, Marked	125.00
Plate, Little Miss Muffet, Blue Mark	160.00
Plate, Pansy, Purple, Green Mark, 7 1/2 In.	225.00
Plate, Portrait, 18th Century Woman, 11 In.	58.00
Plate, Tomato, 5 1/2 In.	40.00
Plate, Tomato, 8 1/2 In.	65.00
Salt & Pepper, Cherries	460.00
Salt & Pepper, Purple Grape	90.00 To 125.00
Salt & Pepper, Radish	175.00
Salt & Pepper, Tomato	45.00
Salt, Lobster, Signed	95.00
Salt, Poppy, Leaf Base, 2 In.	150.00
Saltshaker, Floral	25.00
Sauceboat, Underplate, Pearlized Poppy, Blue Mark	150.00
String Holder, Rooster, Blue Mark	225.00
Sugar & Creamer, Corinthian, Blue & White	75.00
Sugar & Creamer, Goose Girl	250.00
Sugar & Creamer, Poppy, Pearlized, Marked	575.00
Sugar & Creamer, Purple Grape	160.00
Sugar & Creamer, Salt & Pepper, Grape, Signed Raines	325.00
Sugar & Creamer, Tomato	125.00
Sugar, Cover, Devil & Cards, Blue Mark	650.00
Sugar, Cover, Purple Grape, Black Mark	85.00
Sugar, Lobster	42.00
Tea Set, Child's, Nursery Rhymes, Each Piece Different, 7 Piece	295.00
Tea Set, Gold Design, Signed, 3 Piece	145.00
Tea Strainer, Red Poppy	300.00
Teapot, Boy & Donkey Scene, 4 In.	100.00
Teapot, Tomato	125.00
Toothpick, 2 Men In Boat Fishing, Boat Shape, Blue Mark, 3 In.	150.00
Toothpick, Coal Hod, Corinthian, Blue & White	250.00
Toothpick, Dice Shape, Table Tennis Scene, 2 1/2 In.	950.00
Toothpick, Elk, Blue Mark	200.00
Toothpick, Girl Tending Geese, 3 Handles, Blue Mark	145.00
Toothpick, Goose Girl	125.00
Toothpick, Man Riding To Hunt, Blue Mark, 3 Handles	78.00
Toothpick, Moose & Dog, 3 Handles	300.00
Tray, Bun, Dice Throwers	1200.00
Tray, Dresser, Devil & Cards	475.00
Tray, Dresser, Elk, Round, Blue Mark, 11 In.	1900.00
Tray, Lettuce, Green, 6 In.	85.00
Tray, Pin, Hunt Scene, Marked, 5 In.	50.00
Vase, 3 Arabs Scene, Handle, 3 1/4 x 2 1/2 In.	30.00
Vase, Children Ice Skating, Blue, Blue Mark, 4 1/2 In.	95.00

Vase, Corinthian, Green, Blue Mark, 3 1/4 In. 25.00
Wall Pocket, Poppy 350.00

ROYAL BONN is the nineteenth– and twentieth–century trade name for the Bonn China Manufactory. It was established in 1755 in Bonn, Germany. A general line of porcelain was made. Many marks were used, most including the name *Bonn,* the initials *FM,* and a crown.

Bowl, Multicolor, Marked, 8 x 12 In. 90.00
Box, Sardine, Floral, Sardine Shaped Handle 75.00
Charger, Portrait of Richard Wagner, Blue & White, Signed, 19 1/2 In. 480.00
Clock, Mantel, Ansonia, Porcelain Case 275.00
Vase, Garden Scene, Tapestry, 7 x 7 In. 445.00
Vase, Gilt Dragon, Men Observing Artist, Gilt Scroll Feet, 27 In. 1980.00
Vase, Knotted Cord Around Neck, Wild Roses, Gilt Scroll Feet, Signed, 50 In. 3300.00
Vase, Orchids, Gilt Trim, Blue Band,, Green Ground, 8 1/2 In. 150.00
Vase, Portrait, Floral Design, Yellow To Dark Green, Signed, 10 In. 395.00
Vase, Woman Portrait, Handles, G. Muller, 10 3/8 In., ... 495.00

ROYAL COPENHAGEN porcelain and pottery have been made in Denmark since 1772. The Christmas plate series started in 1908. The figurines with pale blue and gray glazes have remained popular in this century and are still being made. Many other old and new style porcelains are made today.

Basket, Flora Danica, Oval, Floral Vines, Twig Handles, 10 In. 2475.00
Coffeepot, Flora Danica, Rose Sprig Knob, Marked, 7 In. 2090.00
Creamer, Full Lace 75.00
Figurine, Bird, Sitting On Pedestal, Brown Glaze, 1 3/4 In., Pair 15.00
Figurine, Boy & Girl Reading, No. 1567 .... 80.00
Figurine, Boy At Lunch, No. 865 .... 175.00
Figurine, Boy On Barrel, No. 3647 .... 110.00
Figurine, Boy With Beach Ball, No. 3542 .... 165.00 To 230.00
Figurine, Chinese Youth Smokes Pipe, White, 6 In. 75.00
Figurine, Faun, Pipes, Owl, No. 2107 .... 200.00
Figurine, Girl Seated With Doll, No. 1938 .... 150.00
Figurine, Girl With Calf, No. 799 .... 275.00
Figurine, Girl With Doll, No. 3539 .... 95.00
Figurine, Goat Lady, No. 694 .... 350.00
Figurine, Goose Girl, No. 527 .... 250.00 To 350.00
Figurine, Goose Girl, No. 528 .... 250.00
Figurine, Gossips, No. 1319 .... 400.00
Figurine, Greenland Girl, No. 12415 .... 595.00
Figurine, Hunter, Seated With Dog, 8 1/2 In. 265.00
Figurine, Kitten, Playing With Tail, Gray, White, No. 727 .... 47.00
Figurine, Koala Bear Seated In Tree, 6 3/4 In. 88.00
Figurine, Man With 2 Calves, No. 1858 .... 375.00
Figurine, Moose, 8 1/2 x 10 In. 330.00
Figurine, Nude On Rock, No. 4027 .... 140.00
Figurine, Pan On Leaf, Frog On Knee, No. 1713 .... 175.00
Figurine, Polar Bears, 5 1/2 In. 135.00
Figurine, Sandman, No. 1145 .... 165.00
Figurine, Seal, No. 1441 .... 118.00 To 140.00
Figurine, Sunshine Over Greenland, 1958 .... 100.00
Figurine, Woman Knitting, No. 1317 .... 275.00
Figurine, Woman, Seated With Bouquet Flowers, 4 In. 360.00
Group, Erotic, Satyr & Nymph, 11 In. 605.00
Plate, Christmas Rose & Cat, 1970 .... 25.00
Plate, Christmas, 1908 .... 5500.00
Plate, Christmas, 1910 .... 215.00
Plate, Christmas, 1916 .... 150.00
Plate, Christmas, 1919 .... 130.00
Plate, Christmas, 1922 .... 105.00
Plate, Christmas, 1925 .... 120.00
Plate, Christmas, 1928 .... 120.00

Plate, Christmas, 1931	150.00
Plate, Christmas, 1934	195.00
Plate, Christmas, 1937	225.00
Plate, Christmas, 1940	540.00
Plate, Christmas, 1943	610.00
Plate, Christmas, 1946	230.00
Plate, Christmas, 1949	275.00
Plate, Christmas, 1952	170.00
Plate, Christmas, 1955	240.00
Plate, Christmas, 1958	105.00
Plate, Christmas, 1959	185.00
Plate, Christmas, 1960	100.00
Plate, Christmas, 1962	115.00 To 160.00
Plate, Christmas, 1963	50.00
Plate, Christmas, 1965	115.00
Plate, Christmas, 1966	18.00
Plate, Christmas, 1968	52.00
Plate, Christmas, 1970	67.00
Plate, Flora Danica, Gold Rim, Signed, 5 1/2 In.	450.00
Platter, Flora Danica, Oval, Mallow Plant, 18 1/8 In.	1925.00
Platter, Flora Danica, Wild Rose Branch Center, Marked, 13 1/8 In.	1650.00
Tray, Flora Danica, Rectangular, Buttercup Plant, 11 11/16 In.	1650.00
Tureen, Flora Danica, Oval, Cover, 13 1/2 In.	6050.00
Vase, No. 191, Rundskuedag, 1923	125.00

ROYAL COPLEY china was made by the Spaulding China Company of
Sebring, Ohio, from 1939 to 1960. The figural planters and the small
figurines, especially those with Art Deco designs, are of great collector
interest.

Bank, Pig	22.00
Figurine, Cat With Cello	40.00
Figurine, Dancing Lady	35.00 To 38.00
Figurine, Lamb On Sled	38.50
Figurine, Parrot, Label, 9 In., Pair	58.00
Figurine, Peter Rabbit	30.00
Figurine, Priolo Duck	50.00
Figurine, Rooster	20.00
Planter, Balinese Girl	14.00
Planter, Cat & Tub	15.00
Planter, Oriental Boy, Bamboo	30.00
Planter, Teddy Bear	18.00
Planter, White Cockatoo	22.00
Salt & Pepper, Hen & Rooster, Plymouth Barred Rock	12.00
Vase, Black Head, 7 In.	35.00
Vase, Green & White, 7 In., Pair	15.00
Vase, Head, 8 1/2 In., Pair	59.00
Wall Pocket, Oriental Girl	20.00
Wall Portrait, Pirate, 8 x 7 In.	28.00

ROYAL CROWN DERBY Company, Ltd., was established in England in
1890. There is a complex family tree that includes the Derby, Crown
Derby, and Royal Crown Derby porcelains. The Royal Crown Derby mark
includes the name and a crown. The words *Made in England* were used
after 1921. The company is now a part of Royal Doulton Tableware Ltd.

Figurine, Falcon, Perched On Rocky Base, c.1957, 10 In.	357.50
Fruit Set, White Porcelain, Blue & Gold Design, Knife & Fork, 8 Piece	85.00
Plate, Traditional Imari, 10 1/2 In., 18 Piece	1545.00
Soup, Dish, Traditional Imari, 8 1/2 In., 14 Piece	935.00

♦♦

Worcestershire sauce is a good brass polish.

♦♦

ROYAL DOULTON is the name used on Doulton and Company pottery made from 1902 to the present. Doulton and Company of England was founded in 1853. Pieces made before 1902 are listed in this book under Doulton. Royal Doulton collectors search for the out–of–production figurines, character jugs, and series wares.

Animal, Bulldog, HN 1074	130.00
Animal, Dog of Fo, Flambe, 4 3/4 In.	150.00
Animal, Dog, Airedale, HN 996	750.00
Animal, Dog, Bulldog, HN 1043	325.00
Animal, Dog, Bulldog, HN 1045	550.00
Animal, Dog, Cocker Spaniel, HN 1000	400.00
Animal, Dog, Dachshund, HN 1139	450.00
Animal, Dog, Pup In Basket, HN 2587	145.00
Animal, Dog, Springer Spaniel, HN 2516	250.00
Animal, Dog, Springer Spaniel, HN 2517	225.00
Animal, Dragon, HN 2085, Flambé	850.00
Animal, Horse, Gude Grey Mare & Foal, HN 2519	425.00
Animal, Horse, Merely A Minor, Gray, HN 2531	750.00 To 850.00
Animal, Horse, Pride of The Shires, HN 2534	750.00
Animal, Merely A Minor, Gray, HN 2567	295.00
Ash Bowl, Auld Mac	140.00
Ash Bowl, Parson Brown	140.00
Ash Bowl, Sairey Gamp	140.00
Ashtray, Barleycorn, A Mark	140.00
Ashtray, Dick Turpin, A Mark	140.00
Ashtray, Parson Brown	90.00 To 95.00
Bottle, Chivas Regal Coat of Arms, Green	35.00
Bottle, Zorro, Sandeman, Pair	38.50
Bowl, Bunnykins, Rabbits Golfing, Barbara Vernon, 1930s	65.00
Bowl, Country Scenes, 9 In.	125.00
Bowl, Golfer, Motto, c.1911, 9 In.	525.00
Bowl, Romeo, 9 In.	125.00

Royal Doulton character jugs depict the head and shoulders of the subject. They are made in four sizes: large, 5 1/4 to 7 inches; small, 3 1/4 to 4 inches; miniature, 2 1/4 to 2 1/2 inches; and tiny, 1 1/4 inches. Toby jugs portray a seated, full figure.

Character Jug, 'Ard of 'Earing, Large	950.00
Character Jug, 'Ard of 'Earing, Miniature	895.00
Character Jug, 'Arriet, Miniature	60.00
Character Jug, 'Arry, A Mark, Miniature	60.00
Character Jug, 'Arry, Large	170.00
Character Jug, 'Arry, Tiny	240.00
Character Jug, Annie Oakley, Medium	105.00
Character Jug, Antony & Cleopatra, Large	65.00 To 70.00
Character Jug, Apothecary, Miniature	40.00
Character Jug, Athos, Large	75.00
Character Jug, Auld Mac, Miniature	30.00
Character Jug, Bacchus, Small	40.00
Character Jug, Beefeater, A Mark, Miniature	45.00
Character Jug, Beefeater, Miniature	25.00 To 45.00
Character Jug, Beefeater, Small	35.00 To 78.00
Character Jug, Benjamin Franklin, Small	55.00 To 60.00
Character Jug, Blacksmith, Miniature	40.00
Character Jug, Blacksmith, Small	55.00
Character Jug, Bookmaker, Miniature	40.00
Character Jug, Buz Fuz, Small	85.00
Character Jug, Cap'n Cuttle, A Mark, Small	125.00
Character Jug, Cap'n Cuttle, Small	95.00
Character Jug, Captain Henry Morgan, Large	95.00
Character Jug, Captain Hook, Miniature	365.00
Character Jug, Catherine of Aragon, Large	100.00

Character Jug, Catherine Parr, Large 100.00
Character Jug, Cavalier, Small, ... 85.00
Character Jug, Clown, Red Hair, Large 3000.00
Character Jug, Clown, White Hair, Large 900.00
Character Jug, Dick Turpin, Small 55.00
Character Jug, Dick Whittington, Large 85.00
Character Jug, Don Quixote, Large 50.00
Character Jug, Drake, Large .... 120.00 To 125.00
Character Jug, Falstaff, Large 85.00
Character Jug, Farmer John, Large 135.00
Character Jug, Farmer John, Small 70.00
Character Jug, Fat Boy, A Mark, Miniature 50.00
Character Jug, Fat Boy, A Mark, Small 110.00
Character Jug, Fat Boy, Miniature 60.00
Character Jug, Fortune Teller, Miniature 300.00
Character Jug, Gardener, Large .... 155.00 To 175.00
Character Jug, Gardener, Miniature 50.00
Character Jug, Gladiator, Large 525.00
Character Jug, Golfer, Large .... 60.00 To 110.00
Character Jug, Golfer, Sinclaire, Large 110.00
Character Jug, Golfer, Small .... 30.00 To 35.00
Character Jug, Gondolier, Small 360.00
Character Jug, Gone Away, Large 95.00
Character Jug, Gone Away, Small 35.00
Character Jug, Granny, Large 80.00
Character Jug, Grant & Lee, Large 225.00
Character Jug, Groucho Marx, Large .... 90.00 To 95.00
Character Jug, Guardsman, Large .... 65.00 To 75.00
Character Jug, Guardsman, Miniature 40.00
Character Jug, Gunsmith, Miniature 40.00
Character Jug, Henry Morgan, Miniature 30.00
Character Jug, Henry Morgan, Small 50.00
Character Jug, Henry VIII, Large 120.00
Character Jug, Jane Seymour, Large 100.00
Character Jug, Jarge, Small 225.00
Character Jug, Jester, A Mark, Small 95.00
Character Jug, John Barleycorn, A Mark, Large 175.00
Character Jug, John Barleycorn, Miniature 65.00
Character Jug, John Barleycorn, Small .... 60.00 To 65.00
Character Jug, John Doulton, Small 85.00
Character Jug, John Peel, A Mark, Large 125.00
Character Jug, John Peel, A Mark, Small 50.00
Character Jug, John Peel, Miniature 45.00
Character Jug, Johnny Appleseed, Large 275.00
Character Jug, Lobster Man, Small .... 30.00 To 35.00
Character Jug, Long John Silver, Small .... 27.50 To 55.00
Character Jug, Lord Nelson, Large 295.00
Character Jug, Louis Armstrong, Large 95.00
Character Jug, Lumberjack, Large 75.00
Character Jug, Lumberjack, Small .... 40.00 To 60.00
Character Jug, Mad Hatter, Small .... 75.00 To 110.00
Character Jug, Mae West, Large .... 90.00 To 95.00
Character Jug, Mephistopheles, Large 2200.00
Character Jug, Mephistopheles, Small 1025.00
Character Jug, Mephistopheles, Verse, Large 1210.00
Character Jug, Michael Doulton, Small .... 45.00 To 50.00
Character Jug, Mikado, Miniature 300.00
Character Jug, Mine Host, Miniature 30.00
Character Jug, Mine Host, Small 40.00
Character Jug, Mr. Micawber, Miniature 40.00
Character Jug, Mr. Pickwick, Miniature .... 45.00 To 50.00
Character Jug, Mr. Pickwick, Small 155.00
Character Jug, Mr. Pickwick, Tiny .... 250.00 To 275.00

Character Jug, Napoleon & Josephine, Large 100.00
Character Jug, Neptune, Small 45.00
Character Jug, Night Watchman, Miniature 45.00
Character Jug, Old Charley, A Mark, Miniature 40.00
Character Jug, Old Charley, Miniature 30.00
Character Jug, Old Charley, Small 120.00
Character Jug, Old Charley, Tiny 80.00
Character Jug, Old King Cole, A Mark, Small 95.00
Character Jug, Old King Cole, Large 250.00
Character Jug, Paddy, A Mark, Miniature .... 35.00 To 60.00
Character Jug, Paddy, Small 50.00
Character Jug, Paddy, Tiny 95.00
Character Jug, Parson Brown, Large 135.00
Character Jug, Parson Brown, Small .... 40.00 To 55.00
Character Jug, Pied Piper, Large 80.00
Character Jug, Porthos, Large 95.00
Character Jug, Punch & Judy Man, Large 525.00
Character Jug, Punch & Judy Man, Small 375.00
Character Jug, Regency Beau, Small 525.00
Character Jug, Rip Van Winkle, Large ....75.00 To 100.00
Character Jug, Rip Van Winkle, Large, Special Edition 150.00
Character Jug, Robin Hood, Large .... 118.00 To 175.00
Character Jug, Robin Hood, Miniature 20.00
Character Jug, Robinson Crusoe, Miniature 45.00
Character Jug, Robinson Crusoe, Small 45.00
Character Jug, Sairey Gamp, A Mark, Miniature 45.00
Character Jug, Sairey Gamp, Tiny 95.00
Character Jug, Sairy Gamp, Tiny 80.00
Character Jug, Sam Weller, A Mark, Miniature 40.00
Character Jug, Sam Weller, A Mark, Small 56.00
Character Jug, Sam Weller, Large .... 150.00 To 275.00
Character Jug, Sam Weller, Miniature 50.00
Character Jug, Sam Weller, Special Size 155.00
Character Jug, Sam Weller, Tiny 110.00
Character Jug, Samuel Johnson, A Mark, Small 175.00
Character Jug, Samuel Johnson, Small .... 145.00 To 225.00
Character Jug, Sancho Panza, Large 80.00
Character Jug, Santa Claus, Doll Handle, Large ....90.00 To 100.00
Character Jug, Simon The Cellarer, Large 125.00
Character Jug, Sleuth, Miniature 40.00
Character Jug, Tam O'Shanter, Large 135.00
Character Jug, Tam O'Shanter, Small 58.00
Character Jug, Toby Philpots, A Mark, Large 135.00
Character Jug, Toby Philpots, A Mark, Miniature 35.00
Character Jug, Toby Philpots, Large 125.00
Character Jug, Toby Philpots, Miniature 45.00
Character Jug, Toby Philpots, Small 70.00
Character Jug, Tony Weller, A Mark, Large 125.00
Character Jug, Tony Weller, Miniature .... 45.00 To 55.00
Character Jug, Touchstone, A Mark, Large 325.00
Character Jug, Town Crier, Large 195.00
Character Jug, Trapper, Large 100.00
Character Jug, Trapper, Small 50.00
Character Jug, Ugly Duchess, Small 275.00
Character Jug, Veteran Motorist, Large ....75.00 To 95.00
Character Jug, Vicar of Bray, A Mark, Large .... 175.00 To 300.00
Character Jug, Viking, Large .... 165.00 To 225.00
Character Jug, Walrus & Carpenter, Large .... 100.00 To 155.00
Character Jug, William Shakespeare, Large 70.00
Character Jug, Yachtsman, Large ....60.00 To 90.00
Charger, Jackson of Rheims, 13 In. 175.00
Chop Plate, Dr. Johnson At Cheshire Cheese Shop, 13 1/4 In. 245.00
Creamer, John Barleycorn, A Mark, 3 In. 58.00

Creamer, Town Crier, Red Vest, Black, 4 In. 48.00
Cup & Saucer, Bunnykins 20.00
Cuspidor, Woman's, Design, Green, Gold, 7 In. 230.00
Figurine, Abdullah, HN 2104 .... 500.00
Figurine, Adrienne, HN 2152 .... 149.00
Figurine, Alchemist, HN 1282 .... 1195.00
Figurine, Antoinette, HN 2326 .... 100.00
Figurine, At Ease, HN 2473 .... 140.00
Figurine, Auctioneer, HN 2988 .... 175.00 To 230.00
Figurine, Autumn Breezes, HN 1913 .... 1433.00
Figurine, Autumn Breezes, HN 2147 .... 325.00
Figurine, Babie, HN 1679 .... 75.00
Figurine, Ballerina, HN 2116 .... 250.00 To 295.00
Figurine, Balloon Man, HN 1954 .... 195.00 To 200.00
Figurine, Balloon Seller, HN 583 .... 395.00
Figurine, Bather, HN 687 .... 385.00
Figurine, Bedtime, HN 1978 .... 60.00
Figurine, Betsy, HN 2111 .... 360.00
Figurine, Biddy Penny Farthing, HN 1843 .... 175.00 To 200.00
Figurine, Blithe Morning, HN 2021 .... 350.00
Figurine, Blithe Morning, HN 2065 .... 179.00
Figurine, Bluebeard, HN 2105 .... 385.00
Figurine, Bon Appetit, HN 2444 .... 175.00
Figurine, Bonnie Lassie, HN 1626 .... 425.00
Figurine, Boy From Williamsburg, HN 2183 .... 145.00
Figurine, Bride, HN 2166 .... 210.00
Figurine, Bridesmaid, HN 2196 .... 105.00
Figurine, Bridget, HN 2070 .... 250.00
Figurine, Broken Lance, HN 2041 .... 375.00 To 385.00
Figurine, Buttercup, HN 2309 .... 150.00
Figurine, Butterfly, HN 1456 .... 850.00 To 1195.00
Figurine, Butterfly, HN 719 .... 955.00
Figurine, Cavalier, HN 2716 .... 225.00
Figurine, Cellist, HN 2226 .... 230.00 To 325.00
Figurine, Choice, HN 1960 .... 850.00
Figurine, Christmas Morn, HN 1992 .... 150.00
Figurine, Christmas Time, HN 2110 .... 315.00 To 385.00
Figurine, Circe, HN 1249 .... 770.00
Figurine, Claribel, HN 1951 .... 500.00
Figurine, Clarinda, HN 2724 .... 150.00 To 160.00
Figurine, Clockmaker, HN 2279 .... 225.00 To 240.00
Figurine, Coachman, HN 2282 .... 400.00
Figurine, Coralie, HN 2307 .... 185.00
Figurine, Country Lass, HN 1991 .... 100.00
Figurine, Courtship, HN 3525 .... 295.00
Figurine, Curly Locks, HN 2049 .... 325.00
Figurine, Daffy Down Dilly, HN 1712 .... 250.00
Figurine, Dancing Years, HN 2235 .... 250.00
Figurine, Darling, HN 1319 .... 95.00
Figurine, Darling, HN 1985 .... 35.00
Figurine, Daydreams, HN 1731 .... 110.00
Figurine, Debutante, HN 2210 .... 249.00 To 275.00
Figurine, Deidre, HN 2020 .... 300.00 To 325.00
Figurine, Detective, HN 2359 .... 250.00 To 275.00
Figurine, Dulcinea, HN 1419 .... 850.00
Figurine, Elegance, HN 2264 .... 150.00
Figurine, Eliza, HN 2543 .... 185.00
Figurine, Elsie Maynard, HN 2902 .... 400.00
Figurine, Enchantment, HN 2178 .... 125.00
Figurine, Ermine Coat, HN 1981 .... 164.00
Figurine, Esmeralda, HN 2168 .... 350.00
Figurine, Fair Maiden, HN 2211 .... 125.00
Figurine, Falstaff, HN 2054 .... 140.00

Figurine, Farmer's Wife, HN 2069 .... 350.00
Figurine, Fat Boy, HN 530 .... 80.00
Figurine, Flower Seller's Children, HN 1342 .... 385.00
Figurine, Foaming Quart, HN 2162 .... 260.00
Figurine, Forty Theives, HN 499 .... 950.00
Figurine, Forty Winks, HN 1974 .... 195.00 To 215.00
Figurine, French Peasant, HN 2075 .... 700.00
Figurine, Geisha, HN 1234 .... 185.00
Figurine, Genevieve, HN 1962 .... 350.00
Figurine, Georgina, HN 2377 .... 70.00
Figurine, Giselle, Forest Glade, HN 2140 .... 395.00
Figurine, Giselle, HN 2139 .... 345.00
Figurine, Good King Wensceslas, HN 2118 .... 225.00
Figurine, Grand Manor, HN 2723 .... 145.00
Figurine, Griselda, HN 1993 .... 295.00
Figurine, Gypsy Dance, HN 2230 .... 200.00
Figurine, He Loves Me, HN 2046 .... 135.00
Figurine, Heart To Heart, HN 2276 .... 145.00
Figurine, Henrietta Maria, HN 2005 .... 500.00
Figurine, Innocence, HN 2842 .... 135.00
Figurine, Invitation, HN 2170 .... 90.00
Figurine, Isadora, HN 2938 .... 155.00 To 160.00
Figurine, Ivy, HN 1768 .... 60.00 To 120.00
Figurine, Janice, HN 2165 .... 350.00
Figurine, Jean, HN 2032 .... 250.00
Figurine, Jester, HN 1702 .... 550.00
Figurine, Jester, HN 2016 .... 265.00
Figurine, Jolly Sailor, HN 2172 .... 585.00
Figurine, Jovial Monk, HN 2144 .... 190.00
Figurine, Judge, HN 2443 .... 140.00
Figurine, Julia, HN 2705 .... 110.00
Figurine, Kate, HN 2789 .... 100.00
Figurine, King Charles, HN 404 .... 1540.00
Figurine, Ko–Ko, HN 2898 .... 500.00
Figurine, Lady April, HN 1958 .... 235.00
Figurine, Lady Charmian, HN 1949 .... 195.00 To 230.00
Figurine, Lady Jester, HN 1285 .... 895.00
Figurine, Lambing Time, HN 1890 .... 115.00 To 175.00
Figurine, Last Waltz, HN 2315 .... 110.00 To 250.00
Figurine, Laura, HN 2960 .... 135.00
Figurine, Lavina, HN 1955 .... 135.00
Figurine, Legolas, HN 2917 .... 59.00
Figurine, Lesley, HN 2410 .... 115.00
Figurine, Lily, HN 1798 .... 95.00 To 110.00
Figurine, Lion On Rock, HN 2641 .... 1610.00
Figurine, Lisa, HN 2310 .... 125.00
Figurine, Little Boy Blue, HN 2062 .... 77.00 To 190.00
Figurine, Little Bridesmaid, HN 1433 .... 129.00
Figurine, Love Letter, HN 2149 .... 395.00
Figurine, Lydia, HN 1908 .... 99.00
Figurine, Marie, HN 1370 .... 125.00
Figurine, Marjorie, HN 2788 .... 225.00
Figurine, Mary Had A Little Lamb, HN 2048 .... 140.00
Figurine, Mask, HN 656 .... 430.00
Figurine, Mayor, HN 2280 .... 450.00
Figurine, Maytime, HN 2113 .... 275.00
Figurine, Memories, HN 2030 .... 275.00
Figurine, Midinette, HN 2090 .... 210.00
Figurine, Midsummer Noon, HN 2033 .... 595.00
Figurine, Miss Muffet, HN 1936 .... 140.00 To 225.00
Figurine, Miss Muffet, HN 1937 .... 200.00
Figurine, Miss Winsome, HN 1666 .... 730.00
Figurine, Modena, HN 1846 .... 700.00

Figurine, Mr. Micawber, HN 532. .... 75.00
Figurine, Mr. Pickwick, HN 1894 .... 195.00
Figurine, Mr. Pickwick, M 41 .... 40.00 To 70.00
Figurine, Mrs. Fitzherbert, HN 2007 .... 725.00
Figurine, Nanny, HN 2221 .... 165.00
Figurine, Nell, HN 3014 .... 115.00
Figurine, Newsvendor, HN 2891 .... 125.00
Figurine, Ninette, HN 2379 .... 175.00
Figurine, Noelle, HN 2179 .... 365.00
Figurine, Old Balloon Seller, HN 1315 .... 195.00
Figurine, Old Meg, HN 2494 .... 165.00
Figurine, Orange Lady, HN 1759 .... 250.00
Figurine, Orange Lady, HN 1953 .... 225.00
Figurine, Orange Vendor, HN 1966 .... 800.00
Figurine, Paisley Shawl, HN 1391 .... 485.00
Figurine, Pearly Boy, HN 1482 .... 275.00 To 500.00
Figurine, Penelope, HN 1901 .... 295.00 To 385.00
Figurine, Pied Piper, HN 2102 .... 275.00
Figurine, Poacher, HN 2043 .... 225.00
Figurine, Polka, HN 2156 .... 200.00 To 260.00
Figurine, Polly Peachum, HN 550 .... 310.00
Figurine, Potter, HN 1493 .... 247.00 To 299.00
Figurine, Premiere, HN 2343 .... 195.00
Figurine, Pride & Joy, HN 2945 .... 209.00 To 250.00
Figurine, Prince of Wales, HN 1217 .... 1000.00
Figurine, Prized Possessions, HN 2942 .... 475.00
Figurine, Proposal, HN 715 .... 795.00
Figurine, Puppetmaker, HN 2253 .... 325.00
Figurine, Reverie, HN 2306 .... 250.00
Figurine, Rose, HN 1368 .... 70.00
Figurine, Royal Governor's Cook, HN 2233 .... 395.00 To 450.00
Figurine, Sairey Gamp, HN 2100 .... 275.00
Figurine, Sairey Gamp, HN 533 .... 75.00
Figurine, Schoolmarm, HN 2223 .... 245.00
Figurine, Sea Sprite, HN 1261 .... 400.00
Figurine, Shadowplay, HN 3526 .... 65.00
Figurine, Silks & Ribbons, HN 2017 .... 95.00 To 145.00
Figurine, Skater, HN 2117 .... 350.00
Figurine, Spring Morning, HN 1922 .... 175.00 To 199.00
Figurine, St. George, HN 2067 .... 880.00 To 2100.00
Figurine, Stop Press, HN 2683 .... 122.00 To 150.00
Figurine, Summer's Day, HN 2181 .... 220.00
Figurine, Summer, HN 2086 .... 350.00
Figurine, Summertime, HN 3137 .... 140.00
Figurine, Suzette, HN 2026 .... 500.00
Figurine, Sweet & Twenty, HN 1589 .... 450.00
Figurine, Thanksgiving, HN 2446 .... 250.00
Figurine, This Little Pig, HN 1793 .... 75.00
Figurine, Tinkle Bell, HN 1677 .... 70.00 To 125.00
Figurine, Tom Tom The Piper's Son, HN 3032 .... 59.00
Figurine, Tony Weller, HN 544 .... 75.00
Figurine, Tony Weller, M47 .... 65.00
Figurine, Tootles, HN 1680 .... 115.00 To 135.00
Figurine, Top O' The Hill, HN 1833 .... 175.00
Figurine, Top O' The Hill, HN 1834 .... 110.00 To 175.00
Figurine, Tuppence A Bag, HN 2320 .... 160.00
Figurine, Uriah Heep, HN 545 .... 75.00
Figurine, Valerie, HN 2107 .... 110.00
Figurine, Veronica, HN 1517 .... 450.00
Figurine, Victorian Lady, HN 728 .... 295.00
Figurine, Vivienne, HN 2073 .... 2225.00
Figurine, Wardrobe Mistress, HN 2145 .... 360.00
Figurine, Wigmaker, St. Williamsburg, HN 2239 .... 129.00

Figurine, Winter, HN 2088	335.00
Figurine, Yum Yum, HN 2899	700.00
Hatpin Holder, Hunt Scene, 1910	150.00
Holder, Calendar, 1911, Mr. Micawber, 4 1/2 x 11 In.	250.00
Humidor, Dickens Ware	265.00
Jug, Green Leaves, Blue Flowers, Lambeth, c.1922, Pair	575.00
Lighter, Buz Fuz	85.00
Lighter, Long John Silver	207.00 To 225.00
Pitcher, Cream, Spiked Seashell, Green Mark	55.00
Pitcher, Mr. Pickwick, Kingsware, Sterling Silver Rim, 2 3/4 In.	148.00
Pitcher, Sleuth, 3 In.	350.00
Pitcher, Winston Churchill, 9 In.	125.00
Place Setting, Mayfair, 5 Piece, Service For 12	260.00
Plate, Cavaliers, Signed	85.00
Plate, Cries of London, Milkmaid, c.1896, 9 1/2 In.	55.00
Plate, Doctor, Head Rack, 10 1/2 In.	65.00
Plate, Gibson Girl, She Goes To The Fancy Dress Ball As Juliet	75.00
Plate, Izaak Walton, 11 In.	70.00
Plate, Jackdaw of Rheims, 10 1/2 In. .	15.00
Plate, Jester, 10 1/2 In.	40.00
Plate, Mayor, 10 1/2 In.	65.00 To 85.00
Plate, Niagara Falls	40.00
Plate, Parson, 10 1/2 In.	65.00
Plate, Provence	75.00
Plate, Rustic England, 10 In.	29.00
Plate, Shakespeare, Burns	39.00
Plate, Shylock & Portia, Floral Rim, Marked, 10 1/2 In.	85.00
Plate, Squire, 10 1/2 In.	65.00
Platter, Burgundy, 13 In.	45.00
Powder Box, Mr. Pickwick, Dickens Ware	120.00
Salt & Pepper, Purple Grape, Blue Mark	75.00
Saltshaker, Blue Tulip, Blue & Green, 2 3/4 In.	125.00
Service For 8, Cadence, 60 Piece	450.00
Sugar & Creamer, Dark Brown Glaze Top, Dull Beige Base, Applied Design	110.00
Sugar & Creamer, Purple Grape, Black Mark	135.00
Sugar & Creamer, Stagecoach Scenes	60.00
Sugar, Cover, Grentham	8.00
Teapot, Old Balloon Seller	110.00
Teapot, Old Charley, Dated 1941	13.50
Teapot, Sairey Gamp, Dated 1941	13.50
Teapot, Windmills, Blue	95.00
Toby Jug, Cliff Cornell, Blue, 9 In.	295.00
Toby Jug, Falstaff, 5 1/4 In.	50.00
Toby Jug, Falstaff, 8 1/2 In.	95.00
Toby Jug, Happy John, 5 1/2 In.	50.00
Toby Jug, Happy John, 9 In.	95.00
Toby Jug, Honest Measure, 4 1/2 In.	40.00
Toby Jug, Old Charley, 8 3/4 In.	170.00
Toby Jug, Sairey Gamp, 4 1/2 In.	165.00
Toby Jug, Sir Winston Churchill, 9 In.	80.00 To 95.00
Vase, Painted Flowers & Birds, Textured, Baluster Form, c.1880, 20 In.	715.00
Vase, Bud, Slater, 7 In.	150.00
Vase, Deep Blue, Gold Enameled, 16 1/2 In.	550.00
Vase, Flambe, Red & Blue Glaze, 6 3/4 In.	90.00
Vase, Flambe, Sung, Signed, Noke, 6 In.	350.00
Vase, Horse Plowing Scene, 2 Handles, Pedestal, 6 In.	50.00
Vase, Red Flambe, Veined, 10 In.	325.00
Vase, Veined Flambe, Red Top, Dark Blue, 9 1/2 In. ....*Illus*	225.00

ROYAL DUX is the more common name for the Duxer
Porzellanmanufaktur which was founded by E. Eichler in Dux, Bohemia,
in 1860. By the turn of the century, the firm specialized in porcelain

statuary and busts of Art Nouveau–style maidens, large porcelain figures, and ornate vases with three–dimensional figures climbing on the sides. The firm is still in business.

Bust, Victorian Woman, Lacey Hat & Dress, Pastel, 16 In.	550.00
Figurine, Arab With Water Bag, 15 In.	300.00
Figurine, Elephant, 8 In.	55.00
Figurine, Elephant, Trunk Up, 15 x 10 In.	225.00
Figurine, Man & Woman, Peasant Type, Earth Tones, Purple Triangle, 15 In.	775.00
Figurine, Nude, Seated On Rocky Ledge, 21 1/2 In.	885.00
Figurine, Owl, Standing, White, 10 In.	100.00
Figurine, Rebecca At Well, Marked, 21 In.	850.00
Figurine, Spanish Dancer, Holding Out Skirt, Bolero Hat, Cobalt, Gold, 15 In.	375.00
Figurine, Spanish Dancer, With Fan, 1930s, 8 In.	275.00
Figurine, Spanish Dancer, With Tambourine, 1930s, 8 In.	275.00
Figurine, Spanish Woman Dancer, Pink Triangle, 9 In.	260.00
Figurine, Woman Sitting By A Pond	525.00
Figurine, Woman Sitting On Sea Shell, Another At The Side, 17 1/2 In.	500.00
Figurine, Woman, Pastel Clothes, Basket On Stool, Red Triangle, 10 In.	298.00
Figurine, Woman, Seated On Rock, Reading Book, 14 In.	330.00
Figurine, Young Boy & Teacher, Flute & Tambourine, Pink Triangle, 20 In.	400.00
Figurines, Greek Man & Woman Holding A Gathering Basket, 15 In., Pair	550.00
Group, Boy & Girl, Binding Wheat Sheaves	625.00
Lamp, Figural, Courting Couple, Cobalt Blue, 2 Arms, Aurene Steuben Shades	650.00
Vase, Enameled Leaf & Berry, Mottled, Signed Fanus, 14 In., Pair	325.00
Vase, Figural, Young Girl Playing Flute, 14 1/2 In.	650.00
Vase, Floral & Dragonfly, Gold, Pedestal, Blue Satin, 17 3/4 In.	425.00
Vase, Lady With Violin, Writing Music Notes On Wall, c.1895, 15 In.	1895.00
Vase, Young Woman Figure, No. 1626, 16 1/2 In.	150.00

ROYAL FLEMISH glass was made during the late 1880s in New Bedford, Massachusetts, by the Mt. Washington Glass Works. It is a colored satin glass decorated with dark colors and raised gold designs. The glass was patented in 1894. It was supposed to resemble stained glass windows.

Ewer, Flowers & Circles Over Floral On Neck, Gold Scrolls, Signed, 15 In.	4250.00
Ewer, Mythical Creatures, Twisted Rope Handle, 10 1/2 x 8 In.	4950.00
Ewer, Stopper, Twisted Steppes, Signed, 8 1/2 In.	6050.00
Ewer, Youth Thrusting Spear Into Mythical Creature, 10 1/2 In.	4950.00
Pitcher, Enameled Marine Scene, Multicolored, Gilt, 1890, 8 5/8 In.	5775.00
Vase, Multicolored Pansies, Outlined In Gold, Leaf Handles, 5 3/4 In.	1700.00
Vase, Pastel Pansies, Rayed Suns, Gold Tracery, 7 1/2 In.	1385.00 To 1950.00
Vase, Venetian Boat Scene, Handles, 14 In.	9625.00

ROYAL HAEGER, see Haeger category

Royal Doulton, Vase, Veined Flambe,
Red Top, Dark Blue, 9 1/2 In.

♦ ♦

Royal Doulton collectors can easily identify character jugs and figurines made before 1984. That year the words "hand made" and "hand decorated" were added above the lion and crown mark, in the shape of an arch.

♦ ♦

ROYAL IVY pieces are listed in the Pressed Glass category by that pattern name.

ROYAL OAK pieces are listed in the Pressed Glass category by that pattern name.

ROYAL RUDOLSTADT, see Rudolstadt

ROYAL VIENNA, see Beehive category

ROYAL WORCESTER is a name used by collectors. Worcester porcelains were made in Worcester, England, from about 1751. The firm went through many different periods and name changes. It became the Worcester Royal Porcelain Company, Ltd., in 1862. Today collectors call the porcelains made after 1862 *Royal Worcester.* In 1976, the firm merged with W. T. Copeland to become Royal Worcester Spode. Some early products of the factory are listed under Worcester.

Candelabra, 3–Light, Queen Anne, Boy & Girl At Base, c.1887. 11 1/2 In.	220.00
Candlestick, Spiral, Marked, c.1884, 10 1/2 In., Pair	550.00
Cavalier, No. 2062, c.1953, 7 1/2 In	165.00
Coffee Set, White, Green Top, Flowers, Demitasse, 3 Piece	125.00
Cup & Saucer, Dunrobin	22.00
Cup & Saucer, Mallard, 3 3/4 In.	22.00
Dish, Dessert, Fruit & Flower Cluster, Blue, H. Martin, 18 Piece	2079.00
Dish, Nautilus Shell Form, Coral Support, 1867, 6 In., Pair	660.00
Dish, Sweet Meat, Thistle, Swirl Molded	345.00
Ewer, Raised Floral, Seahorse Handle, Ivory, Flared Base, 8 In.	300.00
Figurine, August, No. 3441	295.00
Figurine, Bather Surprised, T. Brock, 1868, 26 1/2 In.	1100.00
Figurine, Blue Angel Fish, No. 462, Van Ruyckevelt, c.1956, 12 In.	302.50
Figurine, Bob–White Quail, Van Ruyckevelt, c.1969, 6 1/2 In.	275.00
Figurine, Bringaree Indian, No. 1243, 9 In., Pair	695.00
Figurine, Cactus Wrens & Prickly Pear, D. Doughty, 10 1/4 In., Pair	550.00
Figurine, Cairo Water Carrier, Male, 9 In.	150.00
Figurine, Child, Holding An Urn, Marked, c.1901, 4 1/2 In.	220.00
Figurine, February, No. 3453	295.00
Figurine, Girl, Holding Small Keg, Marked, c.1893, 8 In.	220.00
Figurine, Handy Man, Boer War Soldier, No. 2110, c.1899, 7 1/8 In.	220.00
Figurine, Hummingbirds & Fuchsia, D. Doughty, 9 1/4 In., Pair	935.00
Figurine, Irishman, Shamrocks On Vest, Marked, c.1895, 6 3/4 In.	220.00
Figurine, Kingfisher & Autumn Beech, D. Doughty, 11 1/2 In.	330.00
Figurine, Kingfisher, On Stump	95.00
Figurine, Lisette, No. 3642	750.00
Figurine, Marlin, Leaping	700.00
Figurine, Parakeet, Luster Yellow & Green, Dorothy Doughty, 7 In.	55.00
Figurine, Quarter Horse, Doris Lindner, 1962	2500.00
Figurine, Red Cardinals, Doughty, C. 1950, 9 1/2 In., Pair	495.00
Figurine, Robin, Doughty, c.1964, 6 1/2 In.	220.00
Figurine, Scarlet Tanagers, White Oak, D. Doughty, 11 1/2 In., Pair	330.00
Figurine, Three Foxes, No. 3131	375.00
Figurine, Vermilion Flycatcher, Male & Female, Doughty, 1963, Pair	495.00
Figurine, Water Carrier, c.1891, Pair	400.00
Figurine, Yankee, No. 836, c.1902, 6 3/4 In.	165.00
Figurine, Yellow Headed Blackbirds, Doughty, c.1953, 11 In.	275.00
Flask, Pilgrim, Roses & Leaves, Gold Handles, 10 In.	275.00
Ice Jug, Tusk, Multicolored Flowers, c.1890, 8 3/4 In.	285.00
Jardiniere, Raised Leaves, Bisque Glaze, 10 In.	250.00
Jug, Bird Within Foliage, Mask Spout, Foliate Handle, c.1889, 10 In.	520.00
Jug, No. 1094, 6 1/2 In.	138.00
Lamp, Oil, Glass Shade, Gilt Foliage, Electrified, c.1889, 22 1/2 In.	440.00
Pitcher, Classic Floral, Cream Ground, Gold Handle, 1891, 5 1/4 In.	135.00
Pitcher, Cream & Gold Ring Design, Cat Handle, 1912	145.00

Pitcher, Flat Back, Classic Floral Design, Handle, 1891, 5 In.	135.00
Pitcher, Floral Design, Flat Back, Cream Ground, Gold Handle, c.1891	135.00
Pitcher, Tusk Shape, 7 In.	160.00
Pitcher, Wildflowers & Butterflies, Everted Spout, Marked, 9 3/4 In.	165.00
Plate, Floral Cluster, Yellow Border, 10 In., 12 Piece	440.00
Plate, Queen Victoria 1887 Jubilee, Blue, 10 1/2 In.	65.00
Plate, Tewkesbury Village, Marked, 10 3/4 In.	225.00
Plate, Thatched Cottage Scene, Signed, 11 In.	150.00
Tea Set, Black Banded Border, Pink Ground, 24 Piece	550.00
Teapot, Japanese Style, Gilt & Iron–Red Leaf & Stalk, 6 In.	245.00
Vase, Applied Twigs & Leaves, Beige & Green, c.1888, 7 In.	175.00
Vase, Bottle Form, Birds & Fruit, Enameled Leaves, c.1877, 12 In.	440.00
Vase, Crown Ware, Paneled Landscape Scenes, Marked, c.1922, 5 In.	165.00
Vase, Double Draped, Allover Mottled Glaze, Pierced Neck, c.1870, 8 1/2 In.	665.00
Vase, Double Pilgrim, Gold Foliage, Red Ground, c.1877, 5 1/2 In.	412.50
Vase, Enamel Design, Winged Dragon Handles, 16 In.	660.00
Vase, Floral Design, Gold Loop Handles, 14 In.	850.00
Vase, Florals, Phoenix Handles, c.1893, 13 3/4 In.	385.00
Vase, Gilt Elephant Handles, c.1881, 9 In.	220.00
Vase, Nautilus Shell, Gold Trim, c.1888, 8 1/2 In.	395.00
Vase, Pilgrim, Japanese, Marked, c.1876, 10 3/4 In.	357.50
Vase, Sabrina Ware, Cylinder, Cobalt & Blue, Fish, 5 1/4 In.	165.00
Vase, Scrolled Finial, Wild Flowers, Gilt & Silver, Signed, c.1880, 23 In.	2200.00
Vase, Seven Bamboo Sections, Cherry Blossom, 1880, 5 In.	137.50
Vase, Tree Trunk, Coiled Snake Attacking Frog, c.1897,, 4 1/4 In.	605.00

ROYCROFT products were made by the Roycrofter community of East Aurora, New York, in the late nineteenth and early twentieth centuries. The community was founded by Elbert Hubbard, famous philosopher, writer, and artist. The workshops owned by the community made furniture, metalware, leatherwork, embroidery, and jewelry. A printshop produced many signs, books, and the magazines that promoted the sayings of Elbert Hubbard. Furniture by the Roycroft community is listed in the furniture category.

Ashtray, Copper, Mahogany, Orb Mark, 29 x 11 In.	247.00
Book Stand, 2 Shelves, 4 Parallel Side Supports, Oak, 26 1/2 x 26 In.	495.00
Bookcase, Thirty–Third Degree, 1 Door, 16 Panes, Mahogany	4000.00
Bookends, Hammered Copper, Square With Rings, Riveted Bands, 5 x 4 In.	250.00
Bookends, Stylized Peacock, Marked, Brown Patina	190.00
Bookends, Tooled Floral, Copper, 3 1/2 x 2 In.	165.00
Bookstand, Little Adventures, Signed	485.00
Bowl, Hammered, Curly Edge, Orb Mark, 2 1/2 x 4 1/2 In.	198.00
Candlestick, Barley Twist, c.1915, Pair	785.00
Candlestick, Candle Nozzle, Drop Pan, Double Spindle Stem, 7 In., Pair	385.00
Candlestick, Hammered, Princess, Orb Mark, 7 3/4 In., Pair	523.00
Candlestick, Princess, Marked, Pair	250.00

♦ ♦

An unglazed rim on the bottom
of a plate usually indicates it
was made before 1850.

♦ ♦

Roycroft, Vase, Copper, Riveted Base, 11 In.

Roycroft, Vase, Copper, Stylized Floral,

10 1/2 In.

Chamberstick, Hammered Copper, Marked, 3 x 5 In. 195.00
Desk Set, Hammered, Stylized Floral, 14 x 21–In. Blotter Pad, 5 Piece 495.00
Dresser, No. 108, 2 Over 2·Drawers, Beveled Mirror, Copper Hardware, Signed 2900.00
Holder, Letter, Hammered, Poppies, Orb Mark, 4 x 5 3/4 In. 330.00
Lamp, Hammered Brass, Steuben Gold Shade, Marked, 14 In. 880.00
Lamp, Hammered Wood Grained Copper, Mica, Orb Mark, 15 x 8 In. 1210.00
Magazine Pedestal, No. 080 .... 5225.00
Mirror, Ash, Hanging Chain From Board, Restored Finish, 32 x 29 In. 555.00
Stand, Little Journeys, Tenon & Keyed Shelves, Metal Tag, 26 x 26 x 14 In. 523.00
Tray, Hammered Copper, 2 Attached Handles, Orb Mark, 15 In. Diam. 385.00
Tray, Hammered, Stylized Flowers, Orb Mark, 22 1/2 x 9 1/4 In. 600.00
Vase, Copper, Flared Neck, Marked, c.1910, 16 In. 900.00
Vase, Copper, Riveted Base, 11 In. ....*Illus* 1650.00
Vase, Copper, Stylized Floral, 10 1/2 In. ....*Illus* 1320.00
Vase, German Nickel, Silver Overlay, Hammered, 6 1/4 In. 715.00
Vase, Hammered Copper, Applied Silver Squares, Karl Kipp, 8 x 4 1/4 In. 2970.00
Vase, Hammered, 4 Handles, Nickel Plated Studs 2200.00
Vase, Hammered, American Beauty, Orb Mark, 7 x 3 1/4 In. 415.00
Vase, Hammered, Bell Shaped Blossoms, Orb Mark, 9 1/2 x 3 1/2 In. 605.00
Vase, Hammered, Flared, Orb Mark, 8 1/2 x 3 3/4 In. 550.00
Vase, Hammered, Silver Band 1400.00
Vase, Trumpet Neck, Squatty, Orb Mark, 15 1/2 x 9 In. 1045.00

ROZANE, see Roseville category

ROZENBURG worked at The Hague, Holland, from 1890 to 1914. The
most important pieces were earthenware made in the early twentieth
century with pale–colored Art Nouveau designs.

Vase, Art Nouveau, Browns, Blues, Yellows, Ben Haag, 13 In. 1600.00

RRP is the mark used by the firm of Robinson–Ransbottom. It is not a
mark of the more famous Roseville Pottery. The Ransbottom brothers
started a pottery in 1900 in Ironspot, Ohio. In 1920, they merged with the
Robinson Clay Product Company of Akron, Ohio, to become Robinson–
Ransbottom. The factory is still working.

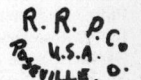

Cookie Jar, Ball Shape, Peaches, Limb Handles 30.00
Cookie Jar, Chef 125.00
Cookie Jar, Cow Jumped Over Moon 150.00
Cookie Jar, Dutch Boy, Gold Trim 395.00
Cookie Jar, Hi Diddle Diddle 275.00
Cookie Jar, Hi Diddle Diddle, Gold Trim 225.00
Cookie Jar, Hootie Owl 100.00
Cookie Jar, Jack The Sailor 250.00
Cookie Jar, Jocko Monkey 265.00
Cookie Jar, Mickey Mouse, Leather Ears 395.00
Cookie Jar, Old King Cole .... 265.00 To 350.00
Cookie Jar, Oscar .... 115.00 To 150.00
Cookie Jar, Peter Peter Pumpkin Eater 90.00
Cookie Jar, Peter Peter Pumpkin Eater, Gold Trim 350.00
Cookie Jar, Sheriff Pig, Gold Trim 165.00
Cookie Jar, Sheriff Pig, Green Hat 90.00
Cookie Jar, Sheriff Pig, Yellow Hat 90.00
Cookie Jar, Snowman 825.00
Cookie Jar, U.S. Airmail Cookie Tin 30.00
Cookie Jar, Whale 950.00
Cookie Jar, Wise Bird 75.00
Cookie Jar, World War I, With Sailor Hat 125.00

RS GERMANY is part of the wording in marks used by the Tillowitz,
Germany, factory of Reinhold Schlegelmilch from about 1869 until about
1956. The porcelain was sold decorated and undecorated. The
Schlegelmilch families made porcelains marked in many ways. See also ES
Germany, RS Poland, RS Prussia, RS Silesia, RS Suhl, and RS Tillowitz.

RS Prussia, Bowl, Lebrun
Portrait, Daisy Mold

RS Prussia, Bowl, Recamier Portrait,
Scenic Medallions, 10 3/4 In.

Berry Bowl, Violets, Green Ground, 6 Piece	95.00
Bowl, Green Cabbage Mold, Rose Design, 9 1/2 In.	225.00
Cake Plate, Snowballs, Marked, 10 In.	80.00
Cake Set, Yellow Daffodil	65.00
Figurine, Troika, Driver, Napoleon & Passenger, Crossed Sword, 15 In.	475.00
Hatpin Holder, Floral, Gold, Hexagonal, 6–Footed	210.00
Pitcher, Child's, Face Ice Lip, Flared Base, Multicolored, Red Wreath, 5 In.	135.00
Plate, Dogwood, Gold Trim, 2 Handles, 9 In.	45.00
Plate, Rose Design, Mustard	100.00
Server, Cheese & Cracker, Floral	67.50
Shaker, Cottage Pattern, Signed	35.00
Teapot, Pink Roses, Small	15.00
Toothpick, Gold Metallic Leaves & Trim, Pink Roses	75.00
Toothpick, Hand Painted Violets, 3 Handles	145.00

RS POLAND (German) is a mark used by the Reinhold Schlegelmilch factory at Tillowitz from about 1946 to 1949, although the factory continued production until 1956. This is one of many of the RS marks used. See also ES Germany, RS Germany, RS Prussia, RS Silesia, RS Suhl, and RS Tillowitz.

Jardiniere, Pheasant, 7 3/4 In.	875.00
Vase, Cottage Scene, Woman With Sheep, Gold Rim, 10 In.	640.00

RS PRUSSIA appears in several marks used on porcelain before 1915. Reinhold Schlegelmilch started his porcelain works in Tillowitz, Germany, in 1869. See also ES Germany, RS Germany, RS Poland, RS Silesia, RS Suhl, and RS Tillowitz.

Berry Set, 5 Panels, Roses, Nut & Leaves, 7 Piece	575.00
Berry Set, Castle Scene, Brown, 10 In.	600.00
Berry Set, Lily Mold, Floral, Gold, 4 Piece	425.00
Berry Set, Old Man In The Mountain	725.00
Berry Set, Old Man In The Mountain, 7 Piece	725.00
Berry Set, Purple, Lavender & White Lilacs, Green Mark, 7 Piece	175.00
Berry Set, Winter Season Center, 6 Portraits On Side, 5 Piece	2400.00
Berry Set, Winter Season Portrait Center, 6 Portraits Around, 5 Piece	2400.00
Biscuit Jar, Hydrangeas, Shaded Green Ground	225.00
Bowl, 3 Swans & Temple, 10 In.	400.00
Bowl, 3 Swans On Lake, Garden Scene, Pearl Luster, Red Mark, 12 1/4 x 6 In.	495.00
Bowl, Blown–Out Carnation Mold, 14 1/2 In.	600.00
Bowl, Castle Scene, Green & Browns, 9 In.	525.00

Bowl, Centerpiece, Carnation Mold, Floral, 14 1/2 In. 600.00
Bowl, Diana The Huntress, 10 In. 1005.00
Bowl, Easter Lily Design, Plume Mold, 10 In. 225.00
Bowl, Floral Center, Beaded Rim, Oval, 12 1/2 x 8 In. 450.00
Bowl, Floral, 3 Lebrun Medallions 650.00
Bowl, Floral, Black Border, 10 In. 400.00
Bowl, French Portraits, Roses 700.00
Bowl, Grapes, Fall Leaves In Reserve, Iris Mold, 10 1/2 In. 275.00
Bowl, Iris Mold, Spring Season, 10 1/2 In. 2100.00
Bowl, Iris Mold, Winter Season, 10 In. 2800.00
Bowl, Iris, 6 In. 235.00
Bowl, Lebrun Portrait, Daisy Mold ....*Illus* 1450.00
Bowl, Lettuce, Red Mark 550.00
Bowl, Masted Schooner Scene, Oval, Marked 915.00
Bowl, Melon Eaters, Point & Clover Mold, 10 In. 1150.00
Bowl, Mill Scene, 10 In. 575.00
Bowl, Multicolored Florals, Scalloped, Deep Greens, Red Mark, 11 In. 225.00
Bowl, Pink & White Dogwood, Holly Berries, Gold Rim, c.1931, 11 In. 120.00
Bowl, Pink & White Roses, Light Blue Scalloped, 10 In. 85.00
Bowl, Portrait, Countess Catherine Litta, Shell Mold, 9 In. 165.00
Bowl, Purple Berries & Leaves, Mold 96, 10 In. 199.00
Bowl, Recamier Portrait, Scenic Medallions, 10 3/4 In. ....*Illus* 1400.00
Bowl, Reflecting Flowers, Cobalt Blue, Red Mark 200.00
Bowl, Reflecting Water Lilies, Bluebirds, 5 Medallions, Marked, 10 7/8 In. 695.00
Bowl, Roses, Jeweled, 11 In. 325.00
Bowl, Roses, Lily Mold, 10 1/2 In. 370.00
Bowl, Roses, Pedestal, 9 In. 250.00
Bowl, Swans, Evergreen, Tassel Mold, 10 1/2 In. 495.00
Bowl, Turkey 500.00
Bowl, Water Lilies 330.00
Box, Cover, Pedestal, Gold Circles With Water Lilies, Scalloped 275.00
Box, Dresser, Mill Scene, Red Mark, 5 x 3 1/2 In. 495.00
Box, Water Lilies On Lid, Scalloped Base, 5 In. 295.00
Butter Pat, Green & White Luster, Dogwood Blossoms, Gold Branches 25.00
Butter Pat, Rim of Tiny Scallops, Hexagonal 25.00
Cake Bowl, Circle Mold, Lily Mold, Green Ground, Gold On Lily, 11 In. 1095.00
Cake Plate, Autumn Portrait, Keyhole Frame, 9 1/2 In. 1300.00
Cake Plate, Barnyard With Swallows, Chickens & Ducks, Marked, 9 3/4 In. 1005.00
Cake Plate, Cobalt Blue, Open Handle, 11 In. 450.00
Cake Plate, Embossed Floral Mold, Lebrun, 8 In. 400.00
Cake Plate, Fall Season, Iris Mold, Open Handle, 10 In. 3000.00
Cake Plate, Garlands of Pink Roses On White, Rippled Ribbon Rim, Green 150.00
Cake Plate, Hummingbird, Open Handle, Brown, 10 In. 2500.00
Cake Plate, Melon Eaters, Open Handle 950.00
Cake Plate, Pink Roses, Ecru To Muted Tan Ground 185.00
Cake Plate, Poppies In Icicle Mold, Open Handles, Red Mark 135.00
Cake Plate, Snowbirds, Open Handles 1700.00
Cake Plate, Spring Season, Keyhole, Maroon, Gold 950.00
Cake Plate, Summer Season, Open Handle, Poppy Mold, 11 In. 1700.00
Cake Plate, White Calla Lilies, 3–Leaf Clovers, Red Mark, 10 1/4 In. 165.00
Centerpiece, Carnation Mold Floral, 14 1/2 In. 600.00
Chocolate Pot, Hummingbird, Brown Tones, 9 1/2 In. 2750.00
Chocolate Pot, Ostrich, Brown Tones 3900.00
Chocolate Set, Carnation Mold, 5 Cups & Saucers 1900.00
Chocolate Set, Chain of Roses, Footed Cups, 13 Piece 2400.00
Chocolate Set, Floral, 11 Piece 600.00
Chocolate Set, Floral, Gold Design, Leaves & Trim, 6 Piece 975.00
Chocolate Set, Hanging Basket, 4 Cups & Saucers 800.00
Chocolate Set, Swan & Pine Trees, 13 Piece 2425.00
Chocolate Set, Teapot, 5 Cups & Saucers 675.00
Chocolate Set, White Flowers, Satin Finish, 11 Piece 525.00
Cookie Jar, Flowers & Leaves, On Gold Branches, Red Mark 125.00
Cracker Jar, 4 Swans & Temple, Lid 600.00

Cracker Jar, Floral	275.00
Creamer, Cottage Scene, 3 1/2 In.	175.00
Creamer, Cottage Scene, Red Mark, 3 1/2 In.	175.00
Creamer, Roses, Lily-of-The-Valley, Ribbon Handle, Footed	55.00
Creamer, Sheepherder, Bluebirds	350.00
Creamer, Swan Design	375.00
Creamer, Swan, Satin, Red Mark	175.00
Creamer, Swans & Chickens	550.00
Cup & Saucer, Flowers, 4 Footed	43.00
Cup & Saucer, Flowers, 4 Tiny Feet, Demitasse	43.00
Cup & Saucer, Pink Roses, Fancy Handle, Fluted, Demitasse	60.00
Cup & Saucer, White & Green Floral, Scalloped, 6 Sides, Demitasse	50.00
Dish, Mint, Flying Swallows, Scalloped Rim, Gold Trim, Triangular, 6 In.	175.00
Dresser Tray, Fall Season	1700.00
Dresser Tray, Old Man In The Mountain	1250.00
Hair Receiver, Pagoda Shape, Pink & White Roses, Green Ground	105.00
Hatpin Holder, Swan, Satin Finish, 2 Handles	500.00
Mustard Pot, 3 Floral Panels, Red Roses, Gold	300.00
Mustard Pot, Duck	425.00
Pitcher, Cider, Poppy Mold	575.00
Pitcher, Dogwood, Red Mark, 6 3/4 In.	235.00
Pitcher, Lemonade, Grapevine & Floral	325.00
Pitcher, Lemonade, Hidden Images	400.00
Pitcher, Lemonade, Swans	500.00
Pitcher, Morning Glory	250.00
Pitcher, Pink & Red Roses, Green Ground, Gold Handle, 5 In.	95.00
Plate, Castle Scene, Green, 9 1/2 In.	185.00
Plate, Cockatoo, Open Handle, 11 In.	750.00
Plate, Hidden Images, Embossed Flowers, Open Handles, 12 In.	1500.00
Plate, Le Brun, White Hat, 9 In.	595.00
Plate, Melon Eaters, Jeweled, 8 1/2 In.	850.00
Plate, Mold No. 330, Small, Red Mark	125.00
Plate, Molded Flower Border, Pink Roses, Green To Gold, Marked, 11 In.	275.00
Plate, Old Man In The Mountain, Open Handle	700.00
Plate, Pink Flowers, Gold Carnations, 8 1/2 In.	125.00
Plate, Pink Poppies, Gilded & Scalloped Rim, 8 1/2 In.	140.00
Plate, Portrait, Le Brun, White Hat, 9 In.	595.00
Plate, Portrait, Le Brun, White Hat, 9 In.	596.00
Plate, Quiet Cover, Medallion Mold, 8 3/4 In.	495.00
Plate, Snowbird Winter Scene, 8 1/2 In.	1750.00
Plate, Spring Season, Keyhole, Teal Trim, 8 1/2 In.	1500.00
Plate, Summer Season, Keyhole, Pink Trim, 8 1/2 In.	1300.00
Plate, Summer Season, Keyhole, Pink Trim, Marked, 8 1/2 In.	1300.00
Plate, Swan, 9 In.	150.00
Plate, Swan, Red Mark, 10 In.	250.00
Plate, Swans & Bluebirds	425.00
Plate, Turkey & Evergreens, Gold Stencil, 8 1/2 In.	700.00
Plate, Violets, Green Ground, Red Mark, 10 1/2 In.	129.00
Plate, Winter Scene, Red & Gold, Keyhole	1750.00
Relish, Blown Out Poppies, Satin Roses	425.00
Relish, Peacock & Evergreens, Icicle Mold, Handles, 9 1/2 x 4 1/2 In.	395.00
Shaving Mug, Poppies, Beveled Mirror	250.00
Smoke Set, Pipe & Cigarette Holder, Striker, Shadow Flowers, 9 x 4 1/2 In.	325.00
Sugar & Creamer, Floral, Lavender Ground, Blown Out	95.00
Sugar & Creamer, Hanging Basket, Red Mark	185.00
Sugar & Creamer, Melon Eaters	800.00
Sugar & Creamer, Mold No. 603, Red Mark	165.00
Sugar & Creamer, Old Man In The Mountain	500.00
Sugar & Creamer, Red Flowers, Gold Scalloped Top	100.00
Sugar & Creamer, Scalloped Top, Allover Roses	150.00
Sugar & Creamer, Shaded Pink, White, Ribbed, Mold 502	210.00
Sugar & Creamer, Stipple Mold	187.00
Sugar & Creamer, Yellow Roses	140.00

RS Prussia, Tankard,

Winter Season, Keyhole,

Gold Iridescent Trim, 14 In.

RS Prussia, Urn, Finial

Cover, Melon Eaters,

2 Handles, 12 1/2 In.

RS Prussia, Vase, Hummingbirds,

Satin Ground, 12 In.; RS Prussia,

Vase, Ostriches, Satin Ground, 12 In.

Tankard, Carnation Mold, Summer Season	6500.00
Tankard, Dice Players, Point & Clover Mold	8000.00
Tankard, Floral Mold, 8 Ball Beet, 14 1/4 In.	750.00
Tankard, Pansy & Poppy, Fall Season	2500.00
Tankard, Pink On Ivory, Roses, Round Gold Feet, Red Mark, 14 In.	995.00
Tankard, Plume Mold, Magnolia, 13 1/2 In.	500.00
Tankard, Stippled Floral, Red Mark, 13 1/2 In.	795.00
Tankard, Winter Season, 18 In.	8500.00
Tankard, Winter Season, Keyhole, Gold Iridescent Trim, 14 In. ....*Illus*	3750.00
Tea Set, Child's, Bluebirds & Roses, 15 Piece	695.00
Tea Set, Child's, Snowbird Scene, 11 Piece	2950.00
Tea Set, Floral Pattern, Pedestal, 3 Piece	225.00
Teapot, 4 Matching Cups, Lily-of-The-Valley, Gold, Green Mark	175.00
Teapot, Roses, Red Mark	300.00
Toothpick, 3 Handles	260.00
Toothpick, Floral	350.00
Toothpick, Floral, 3 Handles	500.00
Toothpick, Handles, 6 Little Feet, Red Mark	95.00
Toothpick, White Lily, Double Handle, Red Mark	125.00
Tray, Bun, Castle Scene, Brown	400.00
Tray, Bun, Ripple Mold, Snowball & Roses Design, 14 In.	225.00
Tray, Dresser, Carnation Mold, Open Handles, Gold Trim, 11 x 7 1/2 In.	280.00
Tray, Dresser, Castle Scene, Yellow & Brown	550.00
Tray, Dresser, Diana The Huntress, 11 3/8 x 7 1n.	895.00
Tray, Dresser, Mill Scene	500.00
Tray, Dresser, Quiet Cove, Medallion Mold, Red Mark	895.00
Tray, Dresser, Roses, Reticulated Handles	220.00
Tray, Medallion Mold, Man In The Mountain Decoration, 11 1/2 In.	825.00
Tray, Swan, Icicle Mold, Red Mark, 11 1/2 x 7 In.	450.00
Tray, White & Pink Roses, Dark Blue Ground, 2 Handles, 12 In.	150.00
Urn, Finial Cover, Melon Eaters, 2 Handles, 12 1/2 In. ....*Illus*	1600.00
Vase, Colonial Courting Couple, Dark Green, Gold Trim, Marked, 1/2 In.	325.00
Vase, Cottage Scene, Art Nouveau, Ornate, 6 1/2 In.	595.00
Vase, Hummingbirds, Satin Ground, 12 In. ....*Illus*	4500.00
Vase, Lion, Handles, Brown, 12 In.	5000.00
Vase, Melon Eaters, Jeweled, 6 In.	1000.00
Vase, Old Man of Mountain, Swans, 6 1/4 In.	550.00
Vase, Ostriches, Satin Ground, 12 In. ....*Illus*	4100.00
Vase, Portrait, Summer Season, Pink & Green, 9 In.	650.00
Vase, Swan & Pines, Handles, 9 1/2 In.	550.00

Vase, Tiger, Handles, Brown, 12 In. 5750.00

RS SILESIA appears on porcelain made at the Reinhold Schlegelmilch factory in Tillowitz, Germany, during the 1930s. The Schlegelmilch families made porcelains marked in many ways. See also ES Germany, RS Germany, RS Poland, RS Prussia, RS Suhl, and RS Tillowitz.

Bowl, Pink Roses, Gold, 9 In. 200.00
Tray, Roses In Vase, Handles, 7 x 12 In. 120.00

RS SUHL is a mark used by the Erdmann Schlegelmilch factory in Suhl, Germany, before 1917. The Schlegelmilch families made porcelains in many places. See also ES Germany, RS Germany, RS Poland, RS Prussia, RS Silesia, and RS Tillowitz.

Tankard, Winter Season, 18 In. ....*Illus* 8500.00
Tea Set, Dogwood, 3 Piece 310.00
Vase, Dancing Women, 12 In., Pair ....*Illus* 2400.00

RS TILLOWITZ was marked on porcelain by the Reinhold Schlegelmilch factory at Tillowitz in the 1930s and 1940s. Table services and ornamental pieces were made. See also ES Germany, RS Germany, RS Poland, RS Prussia, RS Silesia, and RS Suhl.

Cake Plate, Open Handles, Silesia 55.00
Relish, White Azaleas 40.00

RUBENA VERDE is a Victorian glassware that was shaded from red to green. It was first made by Hobbs, Brockunier and Company of Wheeling, West Virginia, about 1890.

Dish, Cheese, Inverted Thumbprint, Vaseline Daisy & Button Base 250.00
Tumbler, 10 Row Hobnail 97.00

RUBENA is a glassware that shades from red to clear. It was first made by George Duncan and Sons of Pittsburgh, Pennsylvania, about 1885. This coloring was used on many types of glassware. The pressed glass patterns of Royal Ivy and Royal Oak are listed under Pressed Glass.

Bowl, Basket, Diamond–Quilted, Half Watermelon Shape, Tab Handles, 5 x 11 In. ... 245.00
Bride's Bowl, Cranberry To Clear Opalescent, Ruffled, Thistles, 11 5/8 In. 245.00
Pitcher, Hobnail, Satin Finish, 7 x 6 1/2 In. 375.00
Pitcher, Inverted Thumbprint, 8 In. 125.00
Pitcher, Milk, Satin Finish, 7 In. 375.00
Pitcher, Opalescent 220.00

RS Suhl, Vase, Dancing Women, 12 In., Pair
RS Suhl, Tankard, Winter Season, 18 In.

♦ ♦

We had a friend whose pet cougar liked to chew on the legs of her 18th-century American chairs. Not good for the chairs. Don't even let your dogs or cats near valuable old furniture.

♦ ♦

Pitcher, Opalescent Swirl	250.00
Pitcher, Syrup, Nickel–Plated Handle, Lid, Collar, 8 3/4 In.	185.00
Pitcher, Water, Inverted Coin Spot	165.00
Pitcher, Water, Verde Hobnail, 8 In.	375.00
Sugar Shaker, Inverted Thumbprint, Tapered, Pewter Cover, 5 1/2 In.	250.00
Wine Set, Hinged Lid, Pewter Mounts, 5 Piece	525.00

RUBY GLASS is the dark red color of the precious gemstone known as a *ruby*. It was a popular Victorian color that never went completely out of style. The glass was shaped by many different processes to make many different types of ruby glass. There was a revival of interest in the 1940s when modern–shaped ruby table glassware became fashionable. Sometimes the red color is added to clear glass by a process called flashing or staining. Flashed glass is clear glass dipped in a colored glass, then pressed or cut. Stained glass has color painted on a clear glass. Then it is refired so the stain fuses with the glass. Pieces of glass colored in this way are indicated by the word *stained* in the description. Related items may be found in other categories, such as Cranberry Glass, Pressed Glass, and Souvenir.

Box, Flower Sprays, Couple Scene Hinged Cover, Brass Rings & Footed, 5 In.	235.00
Candlestick, Morgantown	125.00
Candlestick, Rococo Revival Scrolls, White & Gilt, Europe	105.00
Celery Vase, Double Daisy	85.00
Champagne, Yale Stem, Morgantown	50.00
Cocktail, Golf Ball, Morgantown	25.00
Cocktail, Morgantown	18.00
Cocktail, Yale Stem, Morgantown	48.00
Console, Ruby, Rolled Edge, Morgantown	110.00
Cracker Jar, Florette, Satin	350.00
Creamer, Bulging Loop	150.00
Goblet, Radiant, Ruby, Morgantown	22.00
Ice Bucket, Metal Handle	38.00
Ivy Boat, Ruby, Morgantown	48.00
Pitcher, Water, Swirl	35.00
Salt & Pepper, Snail, Clear	120.00
Sugar & Creamer, Starred Loop, Clear	250.00
Table Set, Double Daisy, Clear	450.00
Vase, Cornucopia Shape, Ends In Ram's Head, Marble Base, 8 x 6 In., Pair	385.00

RUDOLSTADT was a faience factory in the Thuringia region of Germany from 1720 to about 1791. In 1854, Ernst Bohne began working in the area. From about 1887 to 1918, the New York and Rudolstadt Pottery made decorated porcelain marked with the RW and crown familiar to collectors. This porcelain was imported by Lewis Straus and Sons of New York, which later became Nathan Straus and Sons. The word *Royal* was included in their import mark. Collectors often call it *Royal Rudolstadt*. Most pieces found today were made in the late nineteenth or early twentieth century. Additional pieces may be listed in the Kewpie category.

Butter Pat, Gold & Colors, Flower Shape, 11 Piece	60.00
Chocolate Pot, Yellow Roses Front & Back, Marked, 9 1/2 In.	88.00
Powder Bowl, Bluebirds	45.00
Sugar & Creamer, Hand Painted Red Roses & Mums	95.00
Sugar & Creamer, White Mums, Pink Roses	55.00
Tea Set, Happy Fats, Red Trim, 20 Piece	350.00

RUGS have been used in the American home since the seventeenth century. The Oriental rug of that time was often used on a table, not on the floor. Rag rugs, hooked rugs, and braided rugs were made by housewives from scraps of material.

3 Stripes of Pennsylvania Woven Rag Carpet, Blue, Gold, White, 8 Ft. x 11 Ft.	50.00
Afshar, c.1880, 5 Ft. 8 In. x 3 Ft. 9 In.	6000.00
Afshar, Oval Lattice, Flowering Plants, Floral Border, Navy Field, 7 Ft. x 5 1/2 Ft.	3325.00
Afshar, Stepped Diamond Medallions, Red Field, Flowerhead Border, 69 x 48 In.	660.00

Agra, 9 Ft. 7 In. x 12 Ft. 990.00
Agra, Floral Medallion, Magenta Egyptian Border, Avocado, 10 Ft. 10 In. x 9 Ft. ... 4950.00
Alpen Kuba, Geometric, Black Brown Field, 19th Century, 5 Ft. 10 In. x 3 Ft. 4 In. 3300.00
Anatolian Kazak, 3 Ft. 2 In. x 5 Ft. 10 In. 170.00
Anatolian Kilim, Blue & Ivory Hooked Design, Red Field, 8 Ft. 6 In. x 3 Ft. 4 In. 247.00
Anatolian Kilim, Radiating Feathered Design, Ivory Field, 1800, 116 x 66 In. 2640.00
Aubusson, Center Bouquet Medallion, c.1875, 6 Ft. 5 In. x 5 Ft. 4 In. 6600.00
Aubusson, Charles X, Floral Bud Medallion, Apricot, Green, 1820, 8 Ft. x 8 Ft. 9900.00
Aubusson, Floral & Scrollwork Medallion, 1880s, 6 Ft. 6 In. x 4 Ft. 3850.00
Aubusson, Rose Tracery Floral Medallion, c.1900, 14 Ft. 6 In. x 12 Ft. 8 In. 8800.00
Aubusson, Runner, Art Deco Geometric, Ivory Ground, 1930, 13 Ft. x 2 Ft. 6 In. 3300.00
Aubusson, Scattered Floral Sprigs, c.1825, 8 Ft. 2 In. x 3 Ft. 3 In. 3025.00
Bahktiari, 10 x 14 Ft. 505.00
Bahktiari, Allover Floral, Tan Field, Border, 6 Ft. 10 In. x 4 Ft. 6 In. 880.00
Baku, Allover Afshan Design, Walnut Field, Red Border, 6 Ft. 9 In. x 3 Ft. 7 In. ... 3300.00
Baluchi Pattern, Handmade, Wool, 3 Ft. 9 In. x 7 Ft. 9 In. 203.00
Belgium, Floral Design, 8 x 11 In. 500.00
Belouch, Late 19th Century, 5 Ft. 8 In. x 3 Ft. 3 In. 2310.00
Belouch, Red Boteh, Midnight Blue Field, Triangle Border, 58 x 34 In. 1210.00
Belouch, Rows of Boteh, Camel Field, Flowerhead Border, 4 Ft. x 2 Ft. 7 In. 1090.00
Belouch, Tree of Life Design, Camel Field, Geometric Border, 51 x 31 In. 1210.00
Belouchistan Pattern, 3 Ft. 8 In. x 6 Ft. 5 In. 220.00
Bergama, Directional Medallion, Octagons, Gold Border, 4 Ft. 11 In. x 6 Ft. 11 In. 5500.00
Bergama, Ram's Horn In Square Grid, T Motif Border, 3 Ft. 6 In. x 3 Ft 4 In. 1815.00
Bezaalel, Floral Medallion, Rose Field, Floral Border, 7 Ft. 3 In. x 3 Ft. 1 In. 2310.00
Bijar Pattern, Blue Background, 5 Ft. 10 In. x 7 Ft. 10 In. 200.00
Bijar Pattern, Shades of Brown & Ivory, 8 Ft. 3 In. x 8 Ft. 3 In. 225.00
Bijar Wagirch, Allover, Garrus Design, Deep Indigo Field, 7 Ft. 10 x 5 Ft. 2 In. 5500.00
Bijar, 1920s, 8 Ft. 4 In. x 11 Ft. 8 In. 3850.00
Bijar, 2 Portraits, Floral Motifs, Spandrels, Vine Border, 3 Ft. 7 In. x 2 Ft. 5 In. 1030.00
Bijar, 7 Ft. 6 In. x 11 Ft. 9 In. 5700.00
Bijar, Herati Design, Blossoming Vine Border, 20th Century, 64 x 45 In. 1695.00
Bijar, Made For Asini, 10 x 7 Ft. 8800.00
Bokara, Oriental, Geometric Pattern, Red Ground, 7 Ft. 3 In. x 9 Ft. 3025.00
Bokhara Pattern, Salmon Colored Ground, 2 Ft. 7 In. x 4 Ft. 6 In. 85.00
Bokhara, Central Rectangular Medallions, Burgundy Field, 4 Ft. 9 In. x 3 Ft. 5 In. 302.00
Bokhara, Geometric Design Overall, Brown & Navy, 2 Ft. 10 In. x 4 Ft. 11 In. 165.00
Bokhara, Multiple Rows of Guls, Geometric Border, 9 Ft. 4 In. x 10 Ft. 10 In. 3520.00
Bokhara, Oriental, Princess, 4 x 6 Ft. 525.00
Bokhara, Stylized Medallions, Red Ground, 8 Ft. 9 In. x 6 Ft. 2 In. 605.00
Cabistan, 8 Diamond Latch Hook, Blue Field, 3 Ft. 6 In. x 7 Ft. 2310.00
Caucasian, Geometric Designs, Blue Camel & Red Ground, 4 Ft. 2 In. x 7 Ft. 9 In. 990.00
Caucasian, Geometric, Camel Central Ground, Reds, Yellows, 4 Ft. 3 In. x 8 Ft. 660.00
Caucasian, Red Stepped Cartouche, Blue Lattice Field, 1920, 66 x 105 In. 1265.00
ChiChi, Allover Polychrome Palmettes, Cream Field, 4 Ft. 4 In. x 3 Ft. 3 In. 9350.00
ChiChi, Camel & Purple–Brown Latched, Border, Blue–Black Field, 78 x 48 In. 5500.00
Chinese, Circular Medallions, Tan Field, Leaf & Vine Border, 13 Ft. 6 In. x 10 Ft. 1450.00
Chinese, Flowering Branches & Butterflies, Rose Field, 11 Ft. 6 In. x 8 Ft. 10 In. ... 3025.00
Chinese, Medallions, Floral Spray, Vine & Cartouche Border, 12 Ft. 7 In. x L0 Ft. 2180.00
Chinese, Pagoda, Branch & Leaf, Mustard Field, 1925, 11 Ft. 8 In. x 8 Ft. 11 In. ... 1650.00
Chinese, Runner, Floral, Ivory Border, Medium Blue Ground, 3 x 11 Ft. 6 In. 220.00
Chinese, Shou Ideogram, Cloud Field, T–Fretwork Border, 10 Ft. x 7 Ft. 8 In. 1575.00
Chinese, Vases, Border, Cream Field, 1900, 11 Ft. 11 In. x 9 Ft. 8 In. 8800.00
Cuenca, Stylized Floral Cartouches, Yellow Field, 17th Century, 11 Ft. x 8 Ft. 2 In. 2750.00
Daghestan, Lattice Plants, Ivory Field, Interrupted Vine Border, 5 Ft. x 4 Ft. 3630.00
Drugget, Gustav Stickley, Double Honeycomb Pattern, Gray, White, 7 x 10 Ft. 550.00
Drugget, Ivory Ground, Diamond Pattern, Red & Greek Key Border, 139 x 109 In. 192.50
Drugget, Natural Ground, Orange, Black, Repeating Step Design, 119 x 98 In. 137.50
Ersari, Quartered Garden, Plants, Star–In–Hexagon Border, 5 Ft. x 4 Ft. 10 In. 2180.00
Ersari, Red Columns, White Flowers, Dots, 4 Ft. 4 In. x 7 Ft. 9 In. 1210.00
European, Flat Weave, Olive Ground, Red, Gray Bands, Floral Design, 148 x 98 In. 330.00
Fereghan, Herati Design, Floral Scallop, Diamond Motif Border, 6 Ft. x 4 Ft. 8 In. 1935.00
Fereghan, Herati Diamond Medallion, Vines, Floral Border, 2 Ft. 4 In. x 2 Ft. 785.00

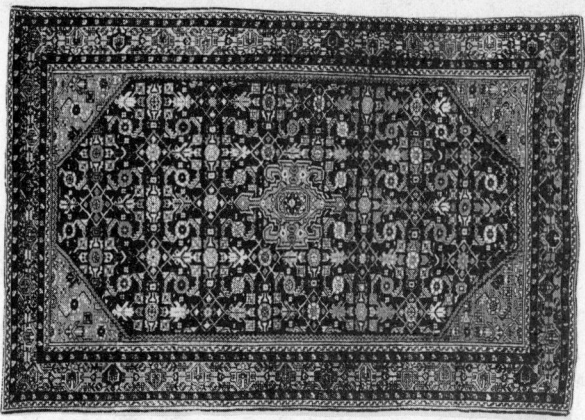

Rug, Hamadan, Blue, Navy, Red, Turtle Border, 7 Ft. X 4 Ft. 9 in.

Fereghan, Overall Floral & Foliate Design, Cranberry Ground, 4 Ft. x 5 Ft. 8 In. ...   1320.00
Gendje, Indigo Latched Diamonds, Deep Indigo Field, 7 Ft. 9 In. x 4 Ft. 8 In. 3300.00
Gendje, Open Boteh, Red Field, Flowerhead-In-Octagon Border, 5 Ft. 9 In. x 4 Ft.   3025.00
Geometric Floral, Camel Center, 3 Ft. 6 1/2 In. x 6 Ft. 9 In. 550.00
Geometric, Central Diamonds, 3 Borders, 3 Ft. 3 In. x 12 Ft. 5 In. 375.00
Golden Afghan, Machine Woven, 9 Ft. x 12 Ft. 137.00
Granule, Eskimo Hunter, Dog, 24 x 38 In. 275.00
Hamadan, Allover Rosette & Serrated Leaf, Sepia Border, 1920, 6 Ft. x 3 Ft. 5 In.   187.00
Hamadan, Allover Stylized Floral, Navy Field, Sky Blue Border, 44 x 32 In. 176.00
Hamadan, Blue, Navy, Red, Turtle Border, 7 Ft. x 4 Ft. 9 In. ....*Illus*   907.00
Hamadan, Heriz, ,Central Navy Blue Medallion, 4 Ft. 6 In. x 6 Ft. 6 In. 440.00
Hamadan, Lobed Medallion With Pendants, Blue Field, 7 Ft. 8 In. x 5 Ft. 2 In. 935.00
Heriz, Allover Ruddy Pattern, Early 20th Century, 9 x 12 Ft. 4125.00
Heriz, Center Medallion, c.1890, 7 Ft. 3 In. x 11 Ft. 8800.00
Heriz, Center Medallion, Ivory Spandrels, Rus Ft. T Field, 20th Century, 15t. 8 ......   4950.00
Heriz, Center Medallion, Rust Field, Blue Serrated Border, 12 x 8 Ft. 6 In. 2090.00
Heriz, Indigo Medallion, Floral, New Fringe, 20th Century, 13 Ft. 7 In. x 10 Ft. 7700.00
Heriz, Red, Ivory, Navy, 1900, 5 Ft. 11 In. x 5 Ft. 8800.00
Heriz, Tomato Red & Ivory, c.1930, 9 x 12 In. 5280.00
Hooked Rag, House & Trees, 18 x 36 In. 130.00
Hooked Rag, Scrolls, Squirrel, Scalloped Black Felt Border, 21 x 37 In. 148.50
Hooked Yarn, Concentric Rectangles, Happy, Pink & Green Shades, 16 x 27 In. 275.00
Hooked Yarn, Covered Bridge In Winter, 23 x 35 In. 70.00
Hooked, 2 Lions In Jungle, Burlap Frame, Dated 1924, 34 1/2 x 63 1/2 In. 700.00
Hooked, 2 Prancing Horses, Cable Design Border, 20th Century, 38 x 27 In. 665.00
Hooked, 2 Prancing Horses, House Center, New England, 40 x 60 3/4 In. 3575.00
Hooked, 3 Rabbits, Purple & Pink Stylized Tulips Ground, 23 x 36 In. 248.00
Hooked, Amish, Stylized Train & Trees, Braided Border, Beige & Brown, 6 x 8 Ft.   850.00
Hooked, Appropriate Games-For Boys-For Girls, Figures, 1930, 33 x 49 In. 4400.00
Hooked, Bennington, Hearth, Floral, 1890-1910 ....   4200.00
Hooked, Black, Pink, Blue & Green, 11 x 26 In. 300.00
Hooked, Blue Grid Stripes, Purple Outlined White Diamonds, 35 x 57 In. 85.00
Hooked, Center Rooster, c.1930, 20 x 24 In. 165.00
Hooked, Center Stylized Flowers, Leaves & Buds, New York, 35 1/2 x 70 In. 880.00
Hooked, Central Floral, Vines Around Edges, Mid-19th Century, 42 x 74 1/2 In. ...   4950.00
Hooked, Farmyard, Ducks, Rooster, Black Man, Woman, B. E. Merry, 47 x 34 In.   2200.00
Hooked, Field of Blossoms, Floral Swags, Shaded Stripe Borders, c.1900, 12 x 9 Ft.   1650.00
Hooked, Floral Center, 31 1/2 x 50 In. 80.00
Hooked, Floral, Red, Blue & Green, Scalloped Rose Blossom Border, 49 x 62 In. 7425.00

Hooked, Floral, Stylized Oak Leaves, Beige & Gold Ground, 44 1/2 x 80 In. 2750.00
Hooked, Folk Art Design, Bird, Hearts & Vining Border, On Stretcher, 29 x 41 In. 660.00
Hooked, Folksy Landscape, Bright Colors, 30 x 46 In. 205.00
Hooked, Gray Donkey, 3 x 2 Ft. 230.00
Hooked, Green & Pink Floral, Black Ground, 6 x 9 Ft. 150.00
Hooked, Horse & Sleigh, 3 x 6 Ft. 425.00
Hooked, House Scene, Blues, Pinks, 36 x 20 1/2 In. 225.00
Hooked, House, Red Roof, Flowers, 35 x 19 In. 375.00
Hooked, Inscribed Welcome, Variegated Field, Frame, 1910, 19 1/2 x 30 In. 575.00
Hooked, Many Maritime Scenes, 28 x 41 In. 385.00
Hooked, Mill Scene, 24 x 49 1/2 In. 45.00
Hooked, Nautical, Sail At Wheel, Colorful, 84 x 50 In. 3300.00
Hooked, Pastel Floral Design, Ivory Ground, 5 Ft. 8 In. x 8 Ft. 6 In. 85.00
Hooked, Pastel Floral Design, Pink Border, Ivory Ground, 6 x 9 Ft. 95.00
Hooked, Patriotic, American, 1880s, 20 x 34 In. 1100.00
Hooked, Pecking Rooster, 15 1/2 x 37 In. 192.50
Hooked, Pictorial, Compote of Flowers, Inscription Elle Stearns, 35 x 64 In. 660.00
Hooked, Pictorial, Figures In Landscape, Floral Border, 36 x 50 In. 385.00
Hooked, Pictorial, Lion, Gray Field, 1880s, 29 x 46 In. 605.00
Hooked, Pictorial, Seated Cat, Floral Border, 19th Century, 20 x 38 In. 330.00
Hooked, Pictorial, Spray of Flowers, Beige Field, Scroll Border, 35 x 64 In. 302.50
Hooked, Pink Roses, Yellow Floral, Black, Odd Fellows Chain Ends, 17 x 36 In. 77.00
Hooked, Rag, Basket of Flowers, Multicolored, Teal Green, Black, 22 x 32 In. 175.00
Hooked, Rag, Blacksmith Shop, Child, Wagon, Dog, Foreground, 32 x 34 In. 291.00
Hooked, Rag, Bowl of Flowers, Lavender Ground, Black Border, 23 x 35 In. 38.00
Hooked, Rag, Cat, 2 Kittens, Yellow Tiger Stripes, Beige Ground, 27 x 51 In. 550.00
Hooked, Rag, Center Diamond, Gray, Purple, Gold, Olive, Red, 23 x 36 In. 40.00
Hooked, Rag, Concentric Rectangles, On Black Cloth, 23 x 38 In. 110.00
Hooked, Rag, Dog In Black, Gray, Brown, Beige Stripe Ground, 21 x 38 In. 357.00
Hooked, Rag, Floral Wreath, Pink, Red, Bluish Gray, Black Border, 24 x 41 In. 93.00
Hooked, Rag, Flower Center, White, Stripes of Pale Green, Pink, 3 Ft. x 15 Ft. 285.00
Hooked, Rag, Flying Geese, Green, Brown, Black, 26 x 41 In. 150.00
Hooked, Rag, Folk Art, Beaver, Tree, Butterfly, Blue, Pink, Red, 20 x 39 In. 49.00
Hooked, Rag, Geometric Design, Stripes, Red Squares, Black Border, 26 x 38 In. 175.00
Hooked, Rag, Geometric Floral Design, Red, Blue, Black, Beige, 28 x 48 1/2 In. 75.00
Hooked, Rag, Geometric Pattern, Earth Tones, Olive, Red, Maroon, 25 1/2 x 34 In. 160.00
Hooked, Rag, Multicolor Abstract, Center Design, Gray Border, 22 x 38 In. 15.00
Hooked, Rag, Purple Moose, Beige Oval, Black Border, 23 x 29 In. 85.00
Hooked, Rag, Semicircular, Floral Design, Brown, Orange, Green, Pink, 25 x 34 In. 70.00
Hooked, Rag, Stylized Evergreen Tree, Gold, Orange, Blue, 18 x 28 In. 60.00
Hooked, Rag, Tumbling Block Pattern, Brown, Blue, Gray, Etc., 26 x 70 In. 220.00
Hooked, Rag, Wool, Pastel Floral Design, Two–Tone Gray Ground, 31 x 49 In. 20.00
Hooked, Rag, Wool, Stylized Leaves, Beige Ground, 19 x 35 In. 10.00
Hooked, Rooster & Chicken, Barnyard, Multicolored Wool, 1800s, 24 1/2 x 33 In. 240.00
Hooked, Rose–Filled Medallions, American, 1920s, 7 Ft. 4 In. x 3 Ft. 10 In. 275.00
Hooked, Sculpted Floral, Early 20th Century, 30 x 60 In. 495.00
Hooked, Squares & Stripes, 23 x 42 In. 200.00
Hooked, Stairway Runner, Multicolored Wool, Burlap Edge, 17 1/2 x 11 1/2 Ft. 345.00
Hooked, Stylized Floral Design, 9 Ft. x 12 Ft. 137.00
Hooked, Tan With Red, Orange and Green, 1800s, 38 1/2 x 79 In. 210.00
Hooked, Tree of Life, Butterfly & Squirrel In Vine Border, c.1940, 61 x 88 In. 1935.00
Hooked, Village, Locomotive & Men Scene, Barbara Merry, 52 x 37 In. 2750.00
Indian, Central Medallion, Floral, Birds, Ivory Vinery Field, 21 Ft. x 14 Ft. 4 In. 6325.00
Indo–Kashan Pattern, Oriental, 3 Ft. x 5 Ft. 125.00
Indo–Kashan, Allover Scrolling Acanthus, Ivory Field, 10 Ft. 3 In. x 2 Ft. 5 In. 247.00
Isphahan, Lobed Arabesque Floral Medallion, Floral Border, Silk, 7 1/2 Ft. x 5 Ft. 5500.00
Isphahan, Palmette, Cloud Band, Floral, Madder Field, Repairs, 9 x 5 Ft. 4 In. 4950.00
Joshogan, Floral Branches, Madder Spandrels, Indigo Field, 19 Ft. 6 In. x 14 Ft. 8800.00
Jules Leleu, Knotted Wool, Central Gray Geometric Maze, 45 x 29 In. 2475.00
Karabagh, 2 Sunburst Medallions, Crab Border, 1880s, 6 x 5 Ft. 1540.00
Karabagh, Central Latch Hook, Navy Blue Field, Crab Border, 3 Ft. 5 In. x 5 Ft. 770.00
Karabagh, Hexagon Medallions, Red & Blue, Large Botech, 6 Ft. 9 In. x 4 Ft. 2180.00

Karabagh, Medallions, Cloud Band Design, Ivory Serrated Leaf Border, 9 x 4 Ft. 990.00
Karabagh, Runner, Anchored Medallions, Ebony Field, 15 Ft. 5 In. x 3 Ft. 4 In. 3300.00
Karabagh, Sunburst Medallions, Crab Border, 6 Ft. 2 In. x 4 Ft. 7 In. 4235.00
Karachopt Kazak, Ivory Medallion, Green Field, 19th Century, 7 Ft. 4 In. x 5 Ft ... 6050.00
Karadja, Center Medallion On Rust Cartouche, Ivory Spandrels, 9 Ft. 2 In. x 12 Ft. 2860.00
Karistan In Kirman Pattern, Oriental, 10 Ft. 6 In. x 16 Ft. 750.00
Kashan Pattern, Runner, 2 Ft. 5 In. x 8 Ft. 10 In. 165.00
Kashan, Birds In Blossoming Tree, Ivory Field, 4 Ft. 9 In. x 2 Ft. 2 In. 357.50
Kashan, Floral Design, Multiple Floral Borders, Red Field, 9 x 12 Ft. 7700.00
Kashan, Scalloped Medallion With Pendants, Red Field, 6 Ft. 8 In. x 4 Ft. 4 In. 660.00
Kashan, Village Landscape Cartouche, Floral Border, Silk, 1925, 2 Ft. 7 In. x 3 Ft. 1100.00
Kazak, 7 Diamond Medallions, Rosette Border, Red Field, 1892, 9 Ft. x 4 Ft. 2 In. 4235.00
Kazak, Blue–Green Tree Design, Animals, Madder Field, 1875, 8 Ft. 3 In. x 4 Ft. ... 4950.00
Kazak, Feathered Hexagonal Medallions, Indigo Field, 3 Ft. 11 In. x 3 Ft. 9 In. 7425.00
Kazak, Lesghi Stars On Rust–Red Field, 7 Ft. 8 In. x 5 Ft. 5 In. 1430.00
Kazak, Prayer, Diamond Medallions, Leaf Border, Red Field, 4 Ft. x 3 Ft. 5 In. 1695.00
Kazak, Prayer, Ivory Latch Hook Medallion, Red Field, 4 Ft. 7 In. x 3 Ft. 3 In. 1640.00
Kazak, Prayer, Latched Polygon Design, Chalice Border, 3 Ft. 4 x 3 Ft. 4 In. 3575.00
Kazak, Prayer, Serrated Diamonds, Ivory Border, Red Field, 2 Ft. 8 In. x 5 Ft. 1650.00
Kazak, Square Medallion, Running Dog Border, Red Field, 1905, 4 Ft. 8 In. x 4 Ft. 4475.00
Kazvin, Center Floral Medallion, Ivory Ground, c.1960, 19 Ft. 5 In. x 9 Ft. 9 In. 5295.00
Kilim, Bag, Allover Geometric, Blue, Orange, Red & Black, 3 Ft. x 1 Ft. 6 In. 77.00
Kilim, Overall Floral Sprays, c.1900, 10 Ft. 6 In. x 7 Ft. 1 In. 5775.00
Kilim, Rows of Floral Sprays Overall, c.1900, 8 Ft. 6 In. x 5 Ft. 1 In. 1320.00
Kilim, Teal, Rust & Gold, 4 x 14 Ft. 1200.00
Kirman, Bird of Paradise, 7 Ft. 11 In. x 4 Ft. 9 In. 500.00
Kirman, Floral Pattern, Ivory Ground, Blue Border, 4 Ft. 5 Ft. 10 In. 440.00
Kirman, Florals, Multicolored Scrolling, Ivory Ground, 9 Ft. 9 In. x 14 Ft. 3 In. 6325.00
Kirman, Runner, Traditional Floral Pattern, 4 x 11 1/2 Ft. 1200.00
Konya Kilim, Allover X–Forms, Ivory Field, Madder Arrow Border, 4 Ft. 9 x 3 Ft. 1980.00
Kuba, Flowering Shrub, Geometric Spandrels, Shobokli Border, 5 1/2 Ft. x 4 Ft. 725.00
Kuba, Hexagonal Lattice, Blossoming Plants, Palmette Border, 6 Ft. x 3 Ft. 10 In. ... 4235.00
Kula, Indigo Shield Palmette, Madder Floral Vinery Field, 1800, 10 Ft. 4 In. x 4 Ft. 1650.00
Kurd Bijar, Blue Floral Design, 9 x 12 Ft. 9625.00
Kurd, Diamond Lattice, Flowering Plants, Leaf Border, Navy Field, 114 x 43 In. 970.00
Kurd, Long, Staggered Rows of Flowering Plants, Floral Borders, 11 Ft. x 4 Ft. 522.00
Kurd, Rows of Flowering Plants, Floral Border, 11 Ft. x 4 Ft. 3 In. 522.50
Lilihan, Flowering Urn, Claret Ground, 7 Ft. x 5 Ft. 8 In. 1840.00
Lillihan, 3 Geometric Medallions, Navy Field, Blue Border, 3 Ft. 8 In. x 2 Ft. 7 In. 176.00
Lillihan, Allover Palmette, Rosette, 1920, 11 Ft. 10 In. x 7 Ft. 11 In. 2420.00
Lillihan, Allover Rosette & Floral, 1920, 4 Ft. 6 In. x 3 Ft. 8 In. 440.00
Lillihan, Pendant Floral Sprays, Serrated Leaves, Burgundy Field, 6 Ft. x 5 Ft. 1 In. 1650.00
Lillihan, Runner, Floral & Rosette Medallions, Navy Field, 1910, 117 x 31 In. 550.00
Mahal, Allover Angular Floral Vinery Lattice, Ivory Field, 11 Ft. 7 In. x 8 Ft. 7 In. 7700.00
Mahal, Overall Herati Deign, Blue Field, Rosette Border, 13 Ft. 2 In. x 10 Ft. 6 In. 1650.00
Mahal, Overall Herati Design, Red Field, Turtle Border, 12 Ft. 9 In. x 9 Ft. 8 In. ... 3025.00
Mahal, Palmettes & Allover Floral Vines, Ivory Field, Brick, 10 Ft. 5 In. x 9 Ft. 5500.00
Mahal, Terra–Cotta Red Field, Vine Border, 11 Ft. 6 In. x 9 Ft. 1650.00
Malayer, Indigo Floral Medallion, Ivory Floral Vinery Field, 78 x 55 In. 4400.00
Mat, Hamadan, Geometric & Floral Design, Navy Blue Field, 32 x 45 In. 120.00
Mat, Hooked, Rag, Multi–Colored Ring Design, 15 x 15 1/2 In. 82.00
Mat, Hooked, Sailboat, White Sails, Black Hull, Color In Sea & Sky, 14 In. 125.00
Mat, Kashan, 2 Ft. x 3 Ft. 9 In. 44.00
Mughal, Animal, Red Field, Early 17th Century, 6 Ft. 4 In. x 4 Ft. 6050.00
Navaho, Cross Design In Red, Brown, Orange, Gray, Black, Natural, 46 x 70 In. ... 170.00
Navaho, Kagetoh Diamond Central Design, Red, Black, Gray, Brown, 39 x 68 In. ... 275.00
Navaho, Serrated Diamond, Red, Brown, Natural, Black, Beige, 52 x 74 1/2 In. 385.00
Navaho, Step Terrace Diamond, White, Orange, Gray, Black, Red, 29 x 50 In. 99.00
Needlepoint, Floral Wreath With Birds, England, 4 Ft. 11 In. x 4 Ft. 8 In. 5500.00
Oriental, Floral On Cream Ground, Machine Made, 8 x 10 Ft. 1925.00
Oriental, Floral, Geometrical, 3 White Diamonds, Blue Ground, 5 Ft. 7 In. x 8 Ft. 1700.00
Oriental, Geometric Caucasian, 3 Diamonds, Red Ground, 3 Ft. 3 In. x 5 Ft. 357.00
Oriental, Geometric Floral, Red & Midnight Grounds, 6 Ft. 11 x 9 Ft. 9 In. 935.00

Oushak, Foliate Border, Red Field, 6 x 12 Ft. 1540.00
Penny, Appliqued, Wool Circles, Red, Blue, Gray, White Cotton, 35 x 66 In. 110.00
Penny, Circular Wool Appliques, Solid Colors With Red, 26 x 36 In. 33.00
Persian, Cruciform Medallions, Blue Field, Crab Border, 6 Ft. 2 In. x 4 Ft. 2420.00
Persian, Floral, 13 Ft. x 8 In. x 11 Ft. 10 In. 500.00
Persian, Ivory Field, Floral Spandrels, Flower & Leaf Border, 6 Ft. x 4 Ft. 10 In. ... 5750.00
Persian, Serebend Center, 3 Ft. 5 In. x 4 Ft. 10 In. 385.00
Princess Booker, Oriental, 3 Ft. 4 In. x 3 Ft. 10 In. 350.00
Qasha'L, 3 Medallions, Navy Field, Allover Boteh Variant, 3 Ft. 11 x 7 Ft. 3 In. 935.00
Qashquai, Connected Hooked Medallions, Birds, Animals, 8 Ft. 10 In. x 5 Ft. 8 In. 715.00
Qashquai, Diamonds, Navy Field, Red Boteh Spandrels, Vine Border, 7 x 4 Ft 4235.00
Qashquai, Floral Boteh, Spandrels, Navy Field, Leaf Border, 6 Ft. 8 In. x 5 Ft. 2180.00
Qashquai, Herati Design, Bird Spandrels, Vine Border, 7 Ft. 8 In. x 5 Ft. 3 In. 4535.00
Qashquai, Multicolored Square Grid, Stars, Geometric Border, 7 Ft. 6 In. x 5 Ft. 1330.00
Quom, Oriental, Persian, 3 Ft. 2 In. x 5 Ft. 2 In. 800.00
Rag, Horizontal Stripes, Olive, Blue, Red, Brown & Beige, 22 Ft. x 33 In. 385.00
Rag, White & Colorful Stripes, Center Seam, 69 x 87 In. 75.00
Runner, Hooked, Yarn, Beige, Lavender, White, 11 1/2 x 69 In. 71.00
Runner, Serebend Pattern, Handmade, Wool, 3 Ft. x 10 Ft. 11 In. 445.00
Sarkisla, Staggered Rows of Concentric Hooked Diamonds, 5 Ft. 9 In. x 4 Ft. 2 In. 665.00
Sarouk, Central Open Medallion, Burgundy Field, 1910, 6 Ft. 6 In. x 5 Ft. 2 In. 1760.00
Sarouk, Columns of Rosettes, Vases of Blossoms, Burgundy, 11 Ft. 8 In. x 8 Ft. 5390.00
Sarouk, Diamond Medallion, Flowering Shrubs, Scalloped Spandrels, 5 Ft. x 3 Ft. ... 1210.00
Sarouk, Floral Design, Red Ground, Fine Weave, 6 Ft. 5 In. x 4 Ft. 2 In. 2475.00
Sarouk, Floral Sprays, Ivory Field, Palmette, Vine Border, 11 Ft. 9 In. x 8 Ft. 8 In. 4840.00
Sarouk, Floral Sprays, Wine Field, Central Persia, 2 Ft. 9 In. x 1 Ft. 11 In. 302.00
Sarouk, Open Medallion, Palmettes, Buds, Red Field, 1915, 20 In. x 11 Ft. 9 In. 8800.00
Sarouk, Overall Floral Design, Red Ground, 4 x 7 Ft. 3300.00
Sarouk, Overall Floral, Blue Field, 6 Ft. 3 In. x 4 Ft. 1 In. 385.00
Sarouk, Red Field, Blue Border, 6 Ft. 6 In. x 2 Ft. 7 In. 575.00
Savonnerie, Center Roundel, Acanthus Leaves, c.1900, 6 Ft. 8 In. x 4 Ft. 6 In. 5500.00
Senneh, Continuous Boteh, Multiple Borders, Plum Field, 10 Ft. 4 In. x 4 Ft. 9 In. 1045.00
Senneh, Saddle Cover, Geometric & Floral, Light Brown Field, 3 Ft. 3 In. x 3 Ft. 300.00
Serab, Hexagonal & Diamond Designs, Camel Field, 13 Ft. 4 In. x 2 Ft. 4 In. 880.00
Serab, Interlocking Medallions, Enclosing Rosettes, c.1900, 5 Ft. 6 In. x 3 Ft. 7 In. 885.00
Serebend Pattern, Oriental, 4 Ft. 8 In. x 6 Ft. 9 In. 275.00
Serebend Pattern, Shades of Brown & Ivory, 2 Ft. 3 In. x 4 Ft. 7 In. 125.00
Shiraz, Double Medallion Design, Blue Field, 6 Ft. x 6 Ft. 6 In. 330.00
Shirvan, 4 Lesghi Stars, Geometric Motifs, Kufic Border, 5 Ft. 10 In. x 3 Ft. 9 In. 3325.00
Shirvan, Afshan Design, Kufic Border, Midnight Blue Field, 11 Ft. x 5 Ft. 8 In. 6655.00
Shirvan, Allover Trellis, Stepped Diamonds, Deep Indigo Field, 5 Ft. 4 x 3 Ft. 9 In. 2750.00
Shirvan, Horizontal & Reciprocal Bands, Hexagons, 10 Ft. 2 In. x 4 Ft. 7 In. 725.00
Shirvan, Narrow & Wide Bands, Inset Polygons, Red, Navy, Gold, 11 Ft. x 5 Ft. 1815.00
Shirvan, Prayer, Ivory Mihrab, Serrated Lattice, Floral Border, 4 Ft. 10 In. x 3 Ft. 3750.00
Shirvan, Staggered Hexagons, Polygon Border, Blue Field, 9 Ft. 10 In. x 5 Ft. 1815.00
Sili Sultan, Red, Border, 19th Century, 6 Ft. 11 In. x 4 Ft. 2 In. 8525.00
Soumak, Allover Geometric Design, Cranberry Ground, 4 Ft. 10 In. x 6 Ft. 8 In. ... 3200.00
Southwest Persian, Hooked Diamonds, Blue Field, 1900, 5 Ft. 6 In. x 4 Ft. 1750.00
Strips of Pennsylvania Rag Carpet, Brown, Gray, Black, 13 Ft. 6 In. x 15 Ft. 250.00
Sultanabad, Field of Palmettes & Leaves, Navy Border, 11 Ft. 6 In. x 14 Ft. 10 In. 6600.00
Tabriz, Allover Vases, Floral Vinery, Cream Field, Border, 11 Ft. 2 In. x 8 Ft. 3 In. 7150.00
Tabriz, Arabesque Vines, Blossoms, Tan Field, Northwest Persia, 140 x 102 In. 1100.00
Tabriz, Center Lozenge, Acanthus & Palmette, Animals, 1910, 12 Ft. 8 In. x 9 Ft. 4400.00
Tabriz, Staggered Rows, Boteh On Gold Field, Boteh Border, 6 Ft. x 4 Ft. 5 In. 1210.00
Tabriz, Tree of Life, Blue Ground, Silk, 6 Ft. 2 In. x 4 Ft. 4 In. 8800.00
Tekke Torba, 3 Rows of Tekke Guls, Brown–Red Field, 1 Ft. 5 In. x 4 Ft. 2 In. 1650.00
Tekke Turkoman, 1900, 3 Ft. 7 In. x 3 Ft. 495.00
Tekke, 8 Colored Panels, Flowerhead Border, 1880s, 5 Ft. 8 In. x 3 Ft. 4 In. 880.00
Tibetan, Tiger Pelt Design, Stripe Motifs, Gold Field, 4 Ft. 10 In. x 2 Ft. 6 In. 1335.00
Transylvania, Prayer, Ivory Floral Center, 18th Century, 5 Ft. 8 In. x 3 Ft. 10 In. 3190.00
Turkish, Wool, 4 Geometric Medallions, Red Ground, 12 Ft. 9 In. x 3 Ft. 5 In. 385.00
Turkoman, Geometric & Latch Hook Design, Red Field, 3 Ft. 3 In. x 5 Ft. 1 In. ... 220.00
Turkoman, Overall Geometric Design, Brown Ground, 2 Ft. 5 In. x 4 Ft. 1 In. 4400.00

Uzbek, Vertical Stripes, Wide & Narrow, Orange Rust & Blue, 8 Ft. x 2 Ft. 4 In. ...	1050.00
Uzbekistan, Embroidered, Diamond Reserves, Trellis, Brown Ground, 3 Ft. x 2 Ft.	2650.00
Wool, Repeating Clamshell Design, Green, Art Deco, 143 x 109 In.	1100.00
Woven, Amish, Felt, Fringed Edge, 28 x 65 In.	165.00
Yei, Figural Design, Red Ground, 3 Ft. 3 In. x 4 Ft. 5 In.	880.00
Yomud, Tauk Nuska Guls, Mahogany Field, Mid–19th Century, 7 Ft. 11 In. x 5 Ft.	4400.00

RUMRILL Pottery was designed by George Rumrill of Little Rock, Arkansas. From 1933 to 1938, it was produced by the Red Wing Pottery of Red Wing, Minnesota. In 1938, production was transferred to the Shawnee Pottery in Zanesville, Ohio. Production ceased in the 1940s.

RumRill

Bust, Head, Art Deco, White Matte, 14 In.	125.00
Urn, Cover, Turquoise	45.00
Vase, Art Deco, Nude Handles, 12 In.	275.00

RUSKIN is a British art pottery of the twentieth century. The Ruskin Pottery was started by William Howson Taylor and his name was used as the mark until about 1899. The factory, at West Smethwick, Birmingham, England, stopped making new pieces in 1933 but continued to glaze and sell the remaining wares until 1935. The art pottery is noted for its exceptional glazes.

RUSKIN POTTERY WEST SMETHWK

Vase, Swollen Cylindrical Body, Gray Ground, Mottled, 23 1/2 In.	2600.00
Vase, Tapered Form, Bulbous Foot, White Ground, Speckled, 4 In.	550.00

RUSSEL WRIGHT designed dinnerwares in modern shapes for many companies. Iroquois China Company, Harker China Company, Steubenville Pottery, and Justin Tharaud and Sons made dishes marked *Russel Wright.* The Steubenville wares, first made in 1938, are the most common today. Wright was a designer of domestic and industrial wares, including furniture, aluminum, radios, interiors, and glassware. Dinnerwares and other pieces by Wright are listed here. For more information, see *Kovels' Depression Glass & American Dinnerware Price List.*

Russel Wright MFG. BY STEUBENVILLE

Bowl, American Modern, Gray, 5 1/4 In.	9.00
Bowl, Divided, American Modern, Gray	75.00
Bowl, Iroquois, Nutmeg, 5 In.	8.00
Bowl, Salad, American Modern, Blue L	95.00
Bowl, Salad, American Modern, Gray, 11 In.	65.00
Bowl, Vegetable, Cover, American Modern, Coral	40.00
Bowl, Vegetable, Residential, Divided, Salmon	10.00
Butter, Iroquois, Pink	50.00
Casserole, Cover, American Modern, Seafoam	40.00
Casserole, Seafoam	45.00
Celery Dish, American Modern, Seafoam	22.00
Clock, Wall	60.00
Cocktail Set, Brushed Aluminum, Sheet Cork Covered, C. 1935, 8 Pc.	1100.00
Coffeepot, American Modern, Coral	90.00
Cordial, Themes Formal	300.00
Creamer, Iroquois	9.00
Cup & Saucer, American Modern, Chartreuse	10.00
Cup & Saucer, American Modern, Gray .... 12.00 To 25.00
Cup & Saucer, Maxi–Cana	26.00
Dish, Soup, American Modern, Lug, Chartreuse	10.00
Gravy Boat, Cover, Gray, Pink Stand, Redesigned	75.00
Gravy Boat, Maxi–Cana	45.00
Pitcher, American Modern, Chartreuse	70.00
Pitcher, American Modern, Seafoam, 10 1/2 In. .... 60.00 To 70.00
Plate, American Modern, Cantaloupe, 8 In.	16.00
Plate, American Modern, Chartreuse, 6 In.	4.00
Plate, American Modern, Chartreuse, 8 In.	10.00
Plate, Cedar, 8 In.	12.00
Plate, Gray, 8 In.	10.00
Plate, Iroquois, Light Green, 10 In.	5.00
Plate, White Clover, Green, 10 In.	10.00

Plate, White Clover, Green, 9 In.	8.00
Platter, American Modern, Blue	50.00
Platter, Iroquois, Avocado, 14 In.	17.00
Platter, Residential, Turquoise	8.00
Relish, Steubenville, Handle	95.00
Salt & Pepper, American Modern, Gray	10.00
Salt & Pepper, White Clover	18.00
Sugar, American Modern, Blue	21.00
Sugar, American Modern, Cover, Chartreuse	10.00
Sugar, American Modern, Cover, Gray	16.00
Teapot, American Modern, Coral	45.00
Teapot, Chutney, White	110.00
Vase, Cinnamon, 5 In.	275.00
Vase, Moroccan Amethyst	27.00

SABINO glass was made in the 1920s and 1930s in Paris, France. Founded by Marius–Ernest Sabino (1878–1961), the firm was noted for Art Deco lamps, vases, figurines, and animals in clear, colored, and opalescent glass. Production stopped during World War II but resumed in the 1960s with the manufacture of nude figurines and small opalescent glass animals. The new pieces are a slightly different color and can be recognized.

Sabino France

Creamer, Elsit, Blue Flowers	60.00
Figurine, Bird, Opalescent, Marked, 2 7/8 In.	45.00
Figurine, Butterfly, Frosted & Opalescent, Signed, 5 3/4 In.	385.00
Figurine, Draped Maiden, Raised Right Arm, Marked, 7 3/4 In.	880.00
Figurine, Fish, 4 1/2 In.	125.00
Figurine, Rabbit, 1 x 2 In.	55.00
Jardiniere, Bird of Paradise In Flight, Paper Label	700.00
Sconce, Gray, Frosted Glass, Silvered Bronze, Ribbed, 1925, 16 In., Pair	1870.00
Vase, Abundance, Opalescent, Pale Blue, 6 3/4 In.	825.00
Vase, Nymphs, Opalescent Blue, Signed, 7 1/2 In.	995.00

SALOPIAN ware was made by the Caughley factory of England during the eighteenth century. The early pieces were blue and white with some colored decorations. Another ware referred to as *Salopian* is a late nineteenth–century tableware decorated with color transfers.

Salopian

Creamer, Milkmaid, Cow, Blue, Green, Black	200.00
Jug, Pear Shape, Floral Spray, Mask Molded Spout, C. 1795, 7 5/16 In.	550.00
Mug, Bird On Branch	150.00
Plate, Women, Children, House, Turquoise, 8 In.	100.00

SALT AND PEPPER SHAKERS in matched sets were first used in the nineteenth century. Collectors are primarily interested in figural examples made after World War I. *Huggers* are pairs of shakers which appear to embrace each other. Many salt and pepper shakers are listed in other categories and can be located through the index at the back of this book.

Salt & Pepper, Typewriter & Desk, Pottery,
2 X 3 3/4 In. & 1 3/4 In.

♦ ♦ ♦ ♦ ♦ ♦ ♦ ♦ ♦ ♦ ♦ ♦ ♦ ♦ ♦ ♦ ♦ ♦ ♦

A monogram can be removed from an old piece of silver by a competent jeweler or silversmith. But it is easier to tell friends that the strange initials on the platter are those of a great-great aunt.

♦ ♦ ♦ ♦ ♦ ♦ ♦ ♦ ♦ ♦ ♦ ♦ ♦ ♦ ♦ ♦ ♦ ♦ ♦

7–Up, Box 105.00
Alcatraz 8.00
Aunt Jemima & Uncle Mose, Ceramic, 5 3/4 In. 55.00
Aunt Jemima & Uncle Mose, F & F, Small 35.00
Aunt Jemima & Uncle Mose, F & F, Large .... 34.00 To 50.00
Aunt Jemima, Small 30.00
Barney Google 30.00
Baseball & Glove 5.50
Bear, Huggers, Green 20.00
Bear, Huggers, Pink, Van Tellingen 24.00
Bears, Huggers, Van Tellingen, Pink 25.00
Bellhop, Carrying 2 Bags 18.00
Bendel, Huggies 130.00
Big Boy, Figural 90.00
Birds On Branch 39.00
Black Babies In Basket 70.00
Black Calico Cat 15.00
Black Cat, 5 In. 25.00
Black Chef & Cook, Range, 7 In. 200.00
Black Girl & Boy, Valentine 165.00
Black Man Holding Watermelon Slice 45.00
Black Mother Holding Baby 50.00
Black Native, Bobbing Heads, Wooden, 4 In. 45.00
Black Porter, Ceramic, Japan, 3 1/2 In. 65.00
Blatz Beer, Logos 25.00
Boy On Potty, Ceramic, Japan, 6 In. 65.00
Brown Bakelite 6.00
Budman 15.00
Bunny, Huggers, Van Tellingen, Green 16.00
Butler & Mammy, 4 1/2 In. 115.00
Charlie Brown & Lucy, On Sofa 20.00
Chicago Silver, Lackritz 175.00
Chickens, Big Eyes, Japan 12.00
Clown, Ceramic, Green Pants, Hat, Japan, 3 1/2 In. 45.00
Cow & Pig, Porcelain 8.00
Cowboy & Cowgirl, On Wheel–Shaped Tray 25.00
Cowboy Boots 10.00
Cowboy, Saddle Tramp, 10 In. 12.00
Cut Glass, Lay Down, Cornucopia Shape, Sterling Top 295.00
Dad's Root Beer, Bottle Hangers 20.00
Dahlia, Green Beaded 35.00
Dennis The Menace 12.50
Devil, Jack–O'–Lantern 25.00
Dog & Cat, Brayton 35.00
Dog & Cat, Ken–L–Ration 16.00
Dorothy With Scarecrow & Tin Man With Lion .... 20.00 To 30.00
Dutch Boy & Girl, Van Tellingen 20.00
Dutch Girl, Regal China 20.00
DX Gas Pump 125.00
Elsie & Elmer, Figural .... 75.00 To 85.00
Fifi & Fido, F & F 15.00
French Peasant, Blue Ridge 150.00
Goetz Beer 10.00
Good Witch, Bad Witch 18.00
Gravestones, Stoneware 35.00
Green Giant Sprout .... 12.00 To 25.00
Hat Boxes, Brown Derby, Hollywood, California 45.00
Huggers, Black Boy With Dog, Van Tellingen 65.00
Huggers, Girl With Lamb, Van Tellingen 50.00
Humpty–Dumpty, Regal China .... 110.00 To 195.00
Ice Cream Cones, Large 10.00
Indian Head 12.00
Indian, Nodding Heads On Drum 75.00

Indian, Teepee	16.00
Ivory Plastic, Red Top, F & F	5.00
J. F. K. & Mrs. Kennedy, Decal	45.00
Jemima, F & F, Small	30.00
John F. Kennedy	28.00 To 60.00
Kayo	25.00
Kewpie, Huggers, O'Neill, Germany	140.00
Kitchen Prayer	15.00
Laurel & Hardy	125.00
Light Bulb, Harper's Ferry, Cobalt Glass	25.00
Lincoln, Ill.	24.00
Lone Ranger Jr.	15.00
Mad Hatter, Dormouse	14.00
Maggie & Jiggs	95.00
Maid & Bellhop	12.00
Mammy & Chef, Blue, Metlox	185.00
Mammy & Chef, Brayton	70.00
Mammy & Chef, Japan	150.00
Mammy, Luzianne, Green, F & F	195.00
Mandy, OCI	45.00
Megaphone	20.00
Mermaid & Sailor, Huggers, Van Tellingen	120.00
Mice, Figural, China, 4 1/2 In.	65.00
Mill & Willy, F & F	15.00
Miss Prayer Girl	15.00
Mixer, Box	12.00
Moon Mullins	25.00
Mouse & Cheese	5.50
Mugsey, Large	75.00
Mugsey, Small	45.00
Paint & Paint Brush	6.50
Peanuts	25.00
Peek–A–Boo, Van Tellingen, Range Top	160.00
Philgas, Gas Can	10.00
Phillips 66, Philgas, Box	65.00
Phillips Gas, Plastic, Blayloc & Reed Oil Co.	27.50
Pillsbury Doughboy & Girl	15.00
Pistol, Metal, 4 In.	15.00
Pop–Up Toaster, Box	10.00
Rabbits, Huggers, White, Pink Dots, Van Tellingen	25.00
Rastus & Liza, Wooden, 3 In.	30.00
RCA Victor	50.00
Red Dutch Couple, Czechoslavakia	15.00
Restaurant Hot Plate & Coffeepot	10.00
Sailor & Mermaid, Van Tellingen	120.00
Salty & Peppy, Pearl, 4 1/2 In.	120.00
Salty & Peppy, Pearl, 8 In.	240.00
Smiley & Winnie, Small	40.00
Smokey The Bear	15.00 To 25.00
Snuffy Smith, Chalkware	30.00
Stacked Animals, Clay Art	16.00
Toaster & Waffle Iron	11.50
Tomato, Red Pantry Pride, 2 In.	14.00
Turkey	15.00
Typewriter & Desk, Pottery, 2 x 3 3/4 In. & 1 3/4 In. ....*Illus*	16.00
Watermelon Slice, Ceramic	12.00
Willie & Millie, Kool Penguins, F & F, Box	12.00 To 20.00
Witch & Pumpkin, Ceramic	25.00
Wizard of Oz Witches	20.00
Zebra, Head Is Salt & Rear Is Pepper, 1 Piece	35.00

SALT GLAZE has a grayish white surface with a texture like an orange peel. It is a method of decoration that has been used since the eighteenth century. Salt-glazed pieces are still being made.

Basket, Handle, 2 7/16 In.	3575.00
Bean Pot, Boston Baked	385.00
Crock, Blue, 4 Gal.	225.00
Crock, Butterfly, 20 Gal.	360.00
Crock, E. B. Taylor, Richmond, Virginia, 11 In.	138.00
Crock, Ice Water, Snowflake On Daisy, Blue & White	165.00
Gravy Boat, Molded Grape Leaf Body, Loop Handle, c.1760, 5 1/4 In.	335.00
Jug, Beehive, 5 Gal.	200.00
Jug, Beehive, Initials & Bee Sting, 3 Gal.	410.00
Jug, Beehive, Lazy Eight Design, 3 Gal.	330.00
Jug, Bellarmine, Strap Handle, Bearded Mask & Beaded Roundel, 14 In.	550.00
Mug, Pear Shape, c.1760	2200.00
Mug, Slanted Sides	5500.00
Pepper Caster, Pear Shaped Body, Molded Seed Pattern, c.1760, 5 1/8 In.	445.00
Pitcher, Avenue of Trees, 10 In.	285.00
Pitcher, Bacchus, 11 In.	475.00
Pitcher, Beer, Armorial & Figural Design, German, 12 In., Pair	445.00
Pitcher, Blue Design, Pewter Lid, 13 1/4 In.	27.50
Pitcher, Doe & Fawn, 10 In.	265.00
Pitcher, Prince Albert Death, 1861, 10 In.	475.00
Pitcher, Raised Vignettes Design, Depicting Evils of Drinking, Tan	165.00
Puzzle Jug, Pierced Date 1761, England, 12 In.	775.00
Salt Crock, Snowflake On Daisy	60.00
Spoon Tray, 6 1/6 In.	3850.00
Teapot, King of Prussia	1875.00
Teapot, White Ribbed, Blue Band, Stripes, Silver Plated Handle, England, 7 In.	27.50
Water Set, Incised Floral, Cobalt Blue, 4 Piece	125.00

SAMPLERS were made in America from the early 1700s. The best examples were made from 1790 to 1840. Long, narrow samplers are usually older than square ones. Early samplers just had stitching or alphabets. The later examples had numerals, borders, and pictorial decorations. Those with mottoes are mid-Victorian. A revival of interest in the 1930s produced simpler samplers, usually with mottoes.

ABCDE

2-Story House, Elizabeth A. Smith, Frame, 19th Century, 14 1/2 x 17 In.	270.00
Alphabet Rows & Numbers, Silk On Linen Homespun, Frame, 6 1/8 x 7 5/8 In.	215.00
Alphabet, 2 Dogs, Vining Strawberry Border, Homespun, 19 In.	385.00
Alphabet, Acorn Border, Flowers, Building, Birds, Homespun, Frame, 13 x 13 In.	742.00
Alphabet, Ann Browne, Age 8, Frame, 1822, 11 x 15 In. ....*Illus*	1400.00
Alphabet, Crows, Trees, Birds, Numerals, Homespun, Frame, 13 In.	1100.00
Alphabet, Flowers, Bird, Basket of Fruit, Homespun, 16 In.	440.00
Alphabet, Flowers, Trees, Homespun, Bird's Eye Frame, 17 1/2 In.	385.00
Alphabet, Green Floss, Mary Bell, 8 Years, Linen, 1831, 3 1/4 x 3 1/2 In.	660.00
Alphabet, House & Flowers, Eleanor Walker, Age 12 Years, Frame, 20 x 17 In.	1875.00
Alphabet, Mary Ann Fennell, Verse, Floral, 1794, England, 15 x 14 In.	358.00
Alphabet, Numbers, Flowers, Deer, Wreath, Homespun, Pine Frame	475.00
Alphabet, Numbers, Pots of Flowers, Dog, Homespun, 16 In.	550.00
Alphabet, Numbers, Silk On Cotton, Olive Brown, Blue, Homespun, 8 x 8 In.	159.00
Alphabet, Numbers, Silk, Linen, Floral Border, Homespun, 21 1/2 In.	990.00
Alphabet, Silk On Linen, Verse, Flowers, Homespun, Frame, 13 3/4 In.	605.00
Alphabet, Silk, Dark Linen, Geometric Design, Homespun, Frame, 18 In.	990.00
Alphabet, Stylized Flowers, Buildings, Animals, Homespun, 9 1/2 In.	379.00
Alphabet, Trees, Dogs, Teapots, Beige, Olive, Blue, Black, Homespun, Frame	300.00
Alphabet, Verse, 1794, Molly Preston Moseley, Frame, 15 3/4 x 7 3/4 In.	445.00
Alphabet, Verse, 1820, Mary Jane Nash, Frame, 17 x 10 1/2 In.	495.00
Alphabet, Vining Border, Flowers, Verse, Matted, Frame, 16 3/4 In.	275.00
Alphabet, Vining Strawberries, Numbers, Homespun, Frame, 18 5/8 In.	330.00
Alphabet, Wilson Family, Flag, Wooden Frame, Dated 1782 To 1900, 24 x 24 In.	950.00
Alphabets, Birds, G. M., Frame, 1890, 16 x 13 In.	75.00

Sampler, Alphabet, Ann Browne, Age 8,
Frame, 1822, 11 X 15 In.

Sampler, Tree, Alphabet, Frame,
1832, 12 X 11 In.

Alphabets, House, Jane D. Baillie, Miss McCallum's School, Homespun, 1834 .... 1050.00
Alphabets, Sarah Hunt, Age 15, May 1827, Homespun, 23 1/2 x 17 In. 1100.00
Alphabets, Stylized Flowers, Animals, People, Homespun, Frame, 21 In. 330.00
Alphabets, Verse, Emma Ann Gould, Age 8, 1842, Homespun, 15 1/4 x 10 1/2 In. ... 605.00
Birds, Animals, Ship, Laurna Weavor, Her Work, Age 13, Frame, 1820, 12 x 16 In. 525.00
Christian Sayings, Elizabeth Rawson, England, 1830, Frame, 23 x 31 In. 1430.00
Consider The Lilies, Punched Paper, Walnut Frame, 9 x 21 In. 140.00
Cow Center, Shepherd & Lady, Linen, Mid–19th Century, Frame, 17 x 17 In. 2310.00
Dark Green, Course Homespun, Mary Goodhue, Gilt Frame, 9 x 10 1/4 In. 345.00
Dec. 1812, Ann Wild, Age 9 Years, Silk, Linen Homespun, Frame, 18 x 13 In. 302.00
Federal Home, Cedar Trees Row, Matilda Parsons, Nov. 4, Aged 9 Years, 1808 ..... 4500.00
Floral Border, Verse, Harriet Adams, March 1860, Homespun, 17 1/2 x 15 In. 465.00
Floral Borders, Angel, Birds, Moon, Sun, Homespun, Frame, 19 1/4 In. 357.00
Floral, Sarah Ann Locock, Age 9 Years, Frame, 17 x 15 In. 895.00
Glaora Goodale, Deering, Born March 16, 1806, Blue & White 1200.00
Heart In Reverse, Hannah P. Tasker, 11 Yrs., 11 Mos., Frame, 1824, 10 x 15 In. .. 545.00
Intricate Stylized Borders, Flowers, Pastel Colors, Homespun, 21 1/2 In. 495.00
Irregular Letters, Mary Elisabeth, Linen, Frame, c.1820, 4 3/8 x 7 In. 325.00
Jette Gerson Maerz, Frame, 1859, Square, 12 1/4 In. 175.00
Linen, 2 Stylized Floral Banners, Blues, Greens, Homespun, Frame, 25 In. 82.00
Linen, Rose Garland Border, Flowers, Lovebirds, Homespun, 25 x 29 3/4 In. 665.00
Lydia Horton, Made In Eleventh Year of Age, Silk Yarns, 1784, Frame, 8 x 6 In. ... 357.50
Needlepoint, Tomb, Angels, Sophia Lucad, Age 75, 1886, Frame, 31 1/2 x 32 In. ... 775.00
Psalm 23, Floral Border, Sarah Barnett, George II, 16 x 11 1/2 In. 385.00
Tree, Alphabet, Frame, 1832, 12 x 11 In. ....*Illus* 1100.00
Urn of Flowers, Rhoda Wilcox, Age 9 Years, New Hampshire, 1807, 12 x 13 In. 525.00
Verse, House, Sarah E. H. Moore's, New York 1834, Maple Frame, 16 x 16 1/2 In. ... 1500.00
Verse, Strawberry Border, Elisa Chapman, Age 9, May 1788, 18 1/2 x 14 1/2 In. ... 465.00
Vining Border, Cottage, Farm, Wild Animals, Homespun, Frame, 12 3/4 In. 1595.00
Vintage, Birds, Flowers, Landscape, Houses, Windmill, Homespun, 22 In. 3300.00

SAMSON and Company, a French firm specializing in the reproduction of
collectible wares of many countries and periods, was founded in Paris in
the early nineteenth century. Chelsea, Meissen, Famille Verte, and Chinese
Export porcelain are some of the wares that have been reproduced by the
company. The firm uses a variety of marks on the reproductions. It is still
in operation.

Jar, Cover, Scrolled Reserves of Birds & Insects, Octagonal, 13 In. 1100.00
Lamp, Famille–Verte, Chrysanthemums, Scrolled Ground, 19 1/2 In., Pair 3850.00

Lamp, Oriental Figures, Scrolling Candle Arms, Gilt–Bronze Mount, 22 In. 7150.00
Lamp, Vase, Cover, Famille Verte, Ribbon Twists, Flower Heads, 16 In. 4400.00
Platter, Octagonal, Chinese Export Style, 15 In. 165.00
Vase, Panels of Birds & Flowers, Rose Ground, Rococo Bronze Mounts, 22 In. 6600.00

SAND BABIES were used as decorations on a line of children's dishes
made by the Royal Bayreuth China Company. The children are playing at
the seaside. Collectors use the names *Sand Babies* and *Beach Babies*
interchangeably.

Planter, Handleless, Blue Mark 95.00
Plate, 4 1/4 In. 125.00

SANDWICH GLASS is any of the myriad types of glass made by the
Boston and Sandwich Glass Works in Sandwich, Massachusetts, between
1825 and 1888. It is often very difficult to be sure whether a piece was
really made at the Sandwich factory because so many types were made
there and similar pieces were made at other glass factories. Additional
pieces may be listed under Pressed Glass and in related categories.

Bowl, Loop, Pedestal, Canary Yellow, Large 6000.00
Candlestick, Amethyst, Toy, 1850s 445.00
Candlestick, Dolphin, Canary, 2–Step, Pair 950.00
Candlestick, Lacy, Waterfall Base, Crystal, Pair 650.00
Candy Dish, Electric Blue, Hollow–Blown Lid, Boston, c.1870 .... 225.00
Compote, Loop, Wafer Scalloped Rim, Hexagonal Base, 10 In. 125.00
Cup & Saucer, Lacy, Toy 220.00
Cup Plate, Log Cabin, Harrison Presidential Campaign, 1840 .... 95.00
Epergne, Cranberry, 5 Flowers 1400.00
Ewer & Basin, Lacy, Scalloped, Toy 495.00
Jar, Pomade, Bear Shape, 19th Century, 4 In. 135.00
Lamp, Blue Font, Leaf Pattern, Marble Base, Ormolu Collar, 11 In., Pair 825.00
Lamp, Fluid, Canary Yellow, Circle & Ellipse Pattern, 10 1/8 In. 358.00
Lamp, Green Font, Brass & Marble Base, 19th Century, 11 1/2 In. 445.00
Lamp, Whale Oil, Bull's–Eye & Fleur–De–Lis, Brass Burner, Pair 795.00
Paperweight, Poinsettia, Purple Ground 850.00
Pitcher, Champagne, Overshot 495.00
Pitcher, Enameled Floral, Fluted Top, Threaded Handle, Blue 390.00
Pitcher, Overshot, Honey Amber, 5 1/2 In. 82.50
Powder Jar, Snake Finial, Gold Rim, Green 350.00
Salt, Open, Clear 1300.00
Sugar, Cover, Gothic, Lacy .... 140.00 To 155.00
Sugar, Loop Pattern, 9 In. 72.00
Syrup, Star & Buckle 110.00
Tie Back, Curtain, Opalescent, 8 Piece 600.00
Vase, Swirl Pattern, Dimpled Sides, Flared Rim, Yellow, 7 1/2 In. 135.00
Vase, Tulip, Canary Yellow, 16 3/4 In. 440.00

SARREGUEMINES is the name of a French town that is used as part of a
china mark. Utzschneider and Company, a porcelain factory, made
ceramics in Sarreguemines, Lorraine, France, from about 1775. Transfer-
printed wares and majolica were made in the nineteenth century. The
nineteenth–century pieces, most often found today, usually have colorful
transfer–printed decorations showing peasants in local costumes.

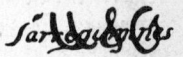

Bowl, Floral, 8 In. 50.00
Butter, Cover, Strawberry 170.00
Chamber Pot, Blue & Red Flowers, Inside Eye, White Ground 95.00
Character Jug 30.00
Humidor, Cover, Figures, Forest Scene Around Body, 7 1/2 In. 125.00
Jar, Cigarette, Organ Grinder & Monkey, 9 1/4 In. 550.00
Plate, French Song, 7 1/2 In. .... 35.00 To 38.00
Tray, Scenic, Peasants 32.00

SASCHA BRASTOFF made decorative accessories, ceramics, enamels on copper, and plastics of his own design. He headed a factory, Sascha Brastoff of California, Inc., in West Los Angeles, from 1953 until about 1973. He died in 1993.

Sascha Brastoff

Ashtray, Abstract Enameling On Copper, 4 In.	22.00
Ashtray, Gold, Silver & White, Glass	10.00
Ashtray, Orange Flowers, Green, Round, Signed, 7 In.	40.00
Bowl, Bird of Paradise, Handle, 15 In.	50.00
Bowl, Star Steed Design, Oblong, 5 1/4 x 10 In.	40.00
Lighter & Cigarette Holder, Abstract Floral, Turquoise	45.00
Tray, Ballet Dancer, 6 1/4 In.	30.00
Tray, Ballet Dancer, 6 3/4 In.	30.00
Tray, Circus Elephant, Gray Mottled Ground, Square, 8 In.	45.00
Tray, Snowflakes, Enamel On Copper, 12 In.	55.00
Vase, Grape Design, Blue Resin, 10 In.	85.00
Vase, Hand Painted, Signed, 5 5/8 In.	67.00

SATIN GLASS is a late nineteenth–century art glass. It has a dull finish that is caused by hydrofluoric acid vapor treatment. Satin glass was made in many colors and sometimes has applied decorations. Satin glass is also listed by factory name, such as Webb, or in the Mother-of-Pearl category in this book.

Basket, Apple Green, Clear Frosted Handle, Fluted, 7 x 8 1/4 In.	175.00
Biscuit Jar, Beaded Drape, Red	175.00
Bowl, Opal White, Swirled Red–Amber Pulled Feather, Design, 4 In.	330.00
Cake Stand, Pink Iridescent	20.00
Candy Dish, Elephant, Green	25.00
Cracker Jar, Floral	245.00
Creamer, Blue Raindrop Mother–of–Pearl, Blue Handle, 4 1/2 In.	225.00
Ewer, Birds & Flowers, Peach Overlay, White Lining, Melon, 12 3/4 In.	245.00
Ewer, Vertically Lobed, Floral, Pale Green, 8 In.	75.00
Pitcher, Pink, 7 1/2 In.	195.00
Rose Bowl, Cut Velvet, White Lining, 4–Crimp Top, 3 3/8 In.	165.00
Rose Bowl, Mother–of–Pearl, Pink, Herringbone, White Lining, 4 Crimp, 3 In.	165.00
Tray, Pink, Blue, Nude	125.00
Tumbler, Diamond–Quilted, Red & White, 4 In.	148.00
Vase, Dragonfly Design, Gold & Floral, Blue, 17 3/4 In.	425.00
Vase, Herringbone, Mother–of–Pearl Overlay, Pink, White Lining, 7 1/4 In., Pair	450.00
Vase, Melon Ribbed, Applied Handles, Bird, Branch, Flowers, 11 In., Pair	385.00
Vase, Mother–of–Pearl, Diamond–Quilted, 6 3/4 In.	350.00
Vase, Oak Leaf & Acorn, Florentine, Yellow & Brown, England, 8 1/2 In.	245.00
Vase, Pink Overlay, White Lining, Ruffled, 9 1/2 In., Pair	185.00
Vase, Pink, Enameled Butterflies, Camphor Handles, 7 In.	185.00
Vase, White Flowers, Green To Salmon Overlay, Dimpled, Square, 11 In.	495.00
Vase, Yellow Swirl	125.00
Vase, Yellow, Quilted, Pear Shape	225.00

SATSUMA is a Japanese pottery with a distinctive creamy beige crackled glaze. Most of the pieces were decorated with blue, red, green, orange, or gold. Almost all Satsuma found today was made after 1860. During World War I, Americans could not buy undecorated European porcelains. Women who liked to make hand painted porcelains at home began to decorate plain Satsuma. These pieces are known today as *American Satsuma*.

Bowl, Interior Water Scene, Water Fowl, Panels of Birds, Signed, 6 In.	665.00
Box, Domed Cover, Overall Figures In Reserves, Gilt Ground, 5 In.	495.00
Box, Musicians & Dancing Geisha On Cover, Yoshigawa, 4 1/4 In.	1650.00
Box, Samurai & Children On Lid, Interior Design, Enameled & Gilt, 4 3/8 In.	605.00
Charger, Figures In 3 Shaped Medallions, 8 3/4 In.	550.00
Charger, Maidens & Cherry Blossoms, Geometric Border, 12 In., Pair	525.00
Console Set, Oval Bowl, Dragon Effigies, 3 Piece	125.00
Creamer, Floral, White Beaded, Blue, Red, 1840, Signed, 3 1/2 In.	50.00
Dish, Warrior Figures, 10 1/2 In.	75.00

Satsuma, Koro, Reserves
On Chrysanthemum Ground,
19th Century, 4 1/2 In.

Satsuma, Tea Bowl, Chrysanthemums,
Butterflies Interior, Shizan, 3 In.

Satsuma, Vase, Allover Rakan,
Satsuma Mon & Seal, Baluster, 18 In.

Satsuma, Vase, Yabu Meizair,
Square, c. 1900, 3 In.

Ewer, Cover, Dragon Handle, Syokuzan, 9 1/2 In. 605.00
Ewer, Red, Yellow & White Enameled Mums, c.1870, 5 1/2 In. 75.00
Ice Bucket, Foo Dog Finial 125.00
Incense Burner, Immortals On Black & White, Lion Handles, 11 In. 445.00
Jar, Cover, Floral Finial, Immortals & Attendants, Gilt Dots, 11 1/4 In. 825.00
Jar, Cover, Interlocking Green & Gold Ring Design, 8 x 8 1/2 In. 1540.00
Jardiniere, Polychrome With Gilt, 11 1/4 In. 71.50
Koro, Reserves On Chrysanthemum Ground, 19th Century, 4 1/2 In. ....*Illus* 2090.00
Pitcher, Cream, Blue & Red Floral, Raised White Beading, Signed, 3 1/2 In. 65.00
Plate, Flying Cranes, Green & Red Floral Scalloped Edge, 1840, 7 In. 125.00
Tea Bowl, Chrysanthemums, Butterflies Interior, Shizan, 3 In. ....*Illus* 1980.00
Tea Set, Bamboo Shape, Birds In Flight, Stoneware, Green, Cream, 1885, 3 Piece ... 158.00
Tea Set, Chrysanthemums, Cream Ground, 15 Piece 385.00
Tea Set, Green & Cream Ground, Hand & Spout Bamboo Shape, Bird, 1885 .... 156.00
Toothpick, Thousand Eye, 2 In., Pair 60.00
Urn, Fan & Shaped Panels, Baluster, 25 In., Pair 125.00
Vase, 2 Panels, Samurai Warriors, Geisha Flute Player, Signed, 12 In. 1450.00
Vase, Allover Rakan, Satsuma Mon & Seal, Baluster, 18 In. ....*Illus* 1540.00
Vase, Applied Slipware, Flowers, Bird of Paradise, Flared Top, 16 In. 485.00
Vase, Dignitaries, Phoenix Borders, Gilded, 19th Century, 29 1/2 In. 360.00
Vase, Enameled & Gilded, Woman & Children, Seascape, Signed, 8 1/2 In. 885.00
Vase, Enameled Florals & Carriage, Signed, 1930, 6 In. 125.00
Vase, Haloes Arhats, Dragon, Cobalt Blue, Gold, 12 1/2 In. 250.00
Vase, Man & Woman, Cobalt Blue, Late 1800s, 6 In. .... 55.00 To 60.00
Vase, Overall Floral & Figural Panel Design, Hexagonal Panel Form, 5 1/4 In. 100.00
Vase, Polychrome Enameled, Gilded Design, Soldiers, 12 1/4 In. 45.00
Vase, Polychrome Floral Design, Birds, Red & Gilt Trim, 11 3/4 In. 175.00
Vase, Samurai Procession, Poetry Reading, Chrysanthemums, 9 1/2 In. 665.00
Vase, Slipware, 1 Side Flowers, Other Bird of Paradise Reserve, Domed Lid, 16 In. .. 485.00
Vase, Small Boys Playing Amid Flowers & Butterflies, Signed, 7 In. 110.00
Vase, Yabu Meizair, Square, C. 1900, 3 In. ....*Illus* 9350.00

SATURDAY EVENING GIRLS, see Paul Revere Pottery

SCALES have been made to weigh everything from babies to gold. Collectors search for all types. Most popular are small gold dust scales and special grocery scales.

2 Outside Balance Pans, Nickel–Plated, Oak & Beveled Case	135.00
Balance, All Wood, Vermont, 18th Century	375.00
Balance, Brass, Mahogany Base, To Weight One Pound, 23 3/4 In.	120.00
Balance, Brass, Swan's Head Finial, Fish Balance Beam, Graduated Weights, 23 In.	265.00
Balance, Cast Iron, Battered Pans, P. Rogers & Co., 27 In.	150.00
Balance, Cast Iron, Brass Trim, Enameled Pan, 17 1/2 In.	65.00
Balance, Chatillon, No. 2, Pan & Chains, Brass, 1892	25.00
Balance, Einer & Amend, 19 1/2 x 16 In.	137.00
Balance, Pharmacist's, Flip Top Lid, Marble Platform, 15 Weights, Oak Box, 13 In.	230.00
Balance, Wooden	415.00
Caille, Washington, Wooden, Iron Trim, 1 Cent, 76 x 28 In.	2450.00
Candy, Pelouze, Pan, Brass Face, 4 Lbs.	85.00
Chatillon, Dairy, Brass Dial, 150 Lb., 8 In.	43.00
Chemist's, Brass & Steel, Becker's Sons, Rotterdam, Drawers, Oak Box, 16 x 17 In.	245.00
Christian Decker, Glass & Mahogany Case, 14 1/4 x 15 1/2 In.	65.00
Computing Scale Co., Grocery, Movable Bar, Weights, Patent Date 1898	265.00
Computing, Flower & Vine Pattern, , Beveled Glass, Cast Iron, 28 1/2 In.	60.00
Computing, Palmer's, 1843, 8 1/2 In. Diam	85.00
Confectionery, O'Hare, 1 Oz.	95.00
Country, Copper Weight Bar, 5 Weights, 1 To 10 Lb.	295.00
Crab, C. Kurtz, Wrought Iron, Brass, 2 Hooks	125.00
Diamond, DeGrave & Son, London, Steel Balance Beam, Mahogany Case	295.00
Doyle Log, Lufkin No. 514, ZZ Style	30.00
Druggist, Weights, Glass 4 Sides	225.00
Egg, Green, Yellow Bar	27.50
Egg, Jiffy Way	15.00
Fairbanks, For Testing Gold & Silver Coins	150.00
Ferd. Russ, Wien, Brass, Twist Column, 2 Brass Bowls, Austria, 49 In.	330.00
Hanging, Balance, Brass Spring, Salter	17.50
Hardware, Jacobs, Brooklyn, Scoop Type, Pan, Suspension Chains, 20 Lb., 8 In.	47.00
Lowell, Dickson's Tea Store	65.00
Mills, Ornate Cast Iron, Porcelain Face, Platform, 1 Cent, 26 x 69 x 24 In.	990.00
Mills, White Porcelain, Lollipop Style, Large	1495.00
National Novelty, Porcelain Dial, Iron Body, Your Weight Indicates Your Health	665.00
Postal, Green Metal, Small, 1940s	15.00
Railroad Depot, Platform	125.00
Simmons Hardware Co., Table, Painted & Stenciled, Pat. 1906, 24 Lb.	30.00
Store, Battery Operated, Lights Up, Miniature	110.00
Store, Howe	28.00
Toledo, Candy, Fan Shape	145.00
Toledo, Model 405A, Brass, 2 Lb.	165.00
Toledo, Parcel Post	140.00
U.S. Postal, Tin, Chrome, W. M. Pelouze, Pat. 1897, Small	22.00
Watling, Penny, Your Weight & Fortune, Porcelain, Red & White Trim, 49 In.	143.00

SCHAFER & VATER, makers of small ceramic items, are best known for their amusing figurals. The factory was located in Volkstedt–Rudolstadt, Germany, from 1890 to 1962. Some pieces are marked with the crown and R mark, but many are unmarked.

Ash Pot, Miner's Bust, Holes In Cap For Matches, Miner's Light, 3 5/8 In.	185.00
Box, Cover, Turtle, Victorian Woman	195.00
Creamer, Cow	190.00
Creamer, Devil, Germany	185.00
Creamer, Kewpie	190.00
Creamer, Mother Goose	75.00
Figurine, Mr. Tenor, Black Tuxedo, Red Stockings, Bug–Eyes, 7 5/8 In.	185.00
Figurine, Nipper	125.00

Flask, His Master's Breath 95.00
Hatpin Holder, Wall, Cameo 350.00
Mug, Blown Out Stag's Head Each Side, Marked, 3 1/4 In. 75.00
Pitcher, Classical Figure, Blue, White, 5 In. 65.00
Pitcher, Girl, White Apron, Holds Jug Which Is Spout, 3 7/8 In. 125.00
Pitcher, Maid With Jug & Keys, 3 1/2 In. 98.00
Pitcher, Maid With Jug & Purse, 4 1/2 In. 98.00
Powder Box, Face On Lid, Pink Jasper, Gold Trim 85.00
Teapot, Smiling Apple, 1 Cup 105.00
Toothpick, Laughing Man, Holes In Tongue 98.00
Vase, Geisha Girl In Front of Open Fan, Blue & White, 4 1/4 In. 145.00
Vase, Leda & Swan, Jasperware, Marked, 8 In. 150.00
Wall Pocket, Blown–Out White Roses, Marked, 5 1/2 x 4 In. 135.00
Whiskey Set, Flask, Skeleton, 6 Skull Whiskey Glasses .... 175.00 To 295.00

SCHNEIDER Glassworks was founded in 1903 at Epinay–sur–Seine, France, by Charles and Ernest Schneider. Art glass was made between 1903 and 1930. The company still produces clear crystal glass.

Bowl, Irregular Bubbles, Amethyst, Turquoise, Colorless, Cluthra, 3 x 5 1/2 In. 469.50
Bowl, Underplate, Mottled Red, Burnt Umber, Clear, Art Glass, 4 1/2 x 7 1/4 In. 535.00
Finger Bowl, Underplate, Incised Mark, 7 1/2 In. 135.00
Globe, Fixture, Teardrop, Hanging, Floral, Mottled Orange, 10 1/4 In. 885.00
Tazza, Orange & Purple, Stemmed Base, 4 1/2 In. 435.00
Vase, Acid Cut Design, Violet, Bronze Base, 13 In. 995.00
Vase, Art Deco, Random Splotches, Raised Rim, Marked, 13 x 12 In. 885.00
Vase, Gray Mottled With Orange, Yellow, Trumpet, 1925, 19 3/8 In. 635.00
Vase, Icicle, Gray & Amber, 6 1/4 In. 295.00
Vase, Inverted Cone Shape, Clear Handles, Mounted As Lamp, 17 1/2 In. 1400.00
Vase, Mottled Gold, Brown & Purple Ground, Flared Rim, 8 In. 335.00
Vase, Opaque Yellow, Deep Brown Irregular Design Base, Signed, 7 In. 245.00
Vase, Turned–Down Rim, Mottled Orange & Yellow To Dark Red, 12 1/2 In. 1195.00
Vase, Yellow & Pink Ground, Crimped Orange Handles, Signed, 7 In. 445.00

SCIENTIFIC INSTRUMENTS of all kinds are included in this category. Other categories such as Barometer, Binoculars, Dental, Nautical, Medical, and Thermometer may also price scientific apparatus.

Adding Machine, Pascal Type, 7 Readout Windows, Box 110.00
Bank Alarm System, Maple, Electric Protection Co., Minneapolis, Minn. 500.00
Barometer & Cyclonometer, Typhoon, Schmidt & Ziegler, 8 In. 4950.00
Binocular Microscope, John Browning, London, 1860 .... 1700.00
Block Set, Johannsen Standard, Steel, Zeiss, Case, 88 Piece 350.00
Bridge, Decade, General Radio Co., America, 1930, 10 x 16 1/2 In. 195.00
Captain's, Spencer Browning & Co., 1840–1850, 5 In. 1975.00
Check Writer, Hedman 25.00
Compass Microscope, Compound Optics, 18th Century, 6 1/2 In. 1350.00
Compass Transit, Surveyor's, Brass, 1889 .... 600.00
Compass, New Bedford, J. Kehew, Box, 1850, 4 In. 480.00
Compass, Steinbrenner 375.00
Compass, Surveying, S. Thaxter, Boston, Brass, 1822, 14 In. 895.00
Compass, Suyden, Oost, West, Fleur–De–Lis, 17th Century 4950.00
Compass, Zeelandia, Azimuth, Oak Box, Brass Bowl, 15 In. 9500.00
Compendium, Drafting, Brass, France, 1900, 4 In. 450.00
Compendium, Geomagnetic, Mahogany, Silvered Brass, 8 1/2 In. 6500.00
Credit Card Machine, Texaco, Metal 65.00
Dividers, 8–Sided Brass Head, Iron Tips, Continental, 4 1/2 In. 875.00
Equinoctial Dial, Brass, Watkins & Hill, London, Fitted Case 935.00
Globe, Rotating Sun & Moon, Joslin's Globe, Boston, 1854 .... 1400.00
Graphoscope, Zebra Wood, England, 19th Century, 16 In. 330.00
Intercom, School, Western Electric, Brass, Bakelite 95.00
Lathe, Belt Driven, Steel, Iron, Late 19th Century, 11 In. 295.00
Magnifier, Double Lens, E. A. Thompson, 1917, Box, 5 In. 190.00
Magnifier, Metal, Floral Patterns, Victorian, 3 In. 150.00

Manometer, Test, Williams, Brown & Earle, Portable, 3 x 8 In.	140.00
Micrometer Slide, C. Reichert, Wien, Early 20th Century	125.00
Microscope, Brass, Original Dovetailed Case, 10 In.	275.00
Microscope, Drum, Mahogany, Lacquered Brass, 1820, 8 3/4 In.	425.00
Microscope, Electric, Science Craft	65.00
Microscope, Portable Field, Brass, Germany, 5 1/2 In.	280.00
Microscopeoptical, Wooden Box	145.00
Monocular, Silver Plate, Gilbert, London, 1780, 2 5/8 In. Closed	475.00
Octant, Cole, Mahogany, Brass Index Arm, Ivory Scale, 1770	3450.00
Octant, Ebony, Hughes, London, Oak Case, Early 19th Century	495.00
Orrery, Joslin's Six–Inch Terrestrial Globe, Boston, 1860, 9 In.	1980.00
Quadrant, Gunter, Boxwood, England, 17th Century, 7 In. Radius	2250.00
Refractometer, Zeiss, Oak Case, 1800s	250.00
Rule, Architect's, Boxwood, France, 19th Century, 10 In.	21.00
Rule, Musketry, Model 17, Range Yards, Mils, Etc., 5 In.	195.00
Rule, Sector, Ivory, Silver, Thomas Heath, 1730, Opens To 12 In.	1450.00
Sextant, Ebony, SBR, Ivory Scale, Late 18th Century, 14 In.	2650.00
Sextant, Ramsden Type, Brass, England, 1780, Walnut Case	3800.00
Sextant, Troughton & Simms, Brass, Mid–19th Century, 13 In.	2850.00
Slide Compressor, Brass, England, Late 19th Century, 3 1/4 In.	120.00
Steam Boiler, 2 Engines, Black, Brass, Scratch–Built, Late 1940s	850.00
Sterilizing Burner, Adjustable, L. Pelleray, Paris, Brass, 2 1/2 In.	120.00
Sundial, Brass, Floral, Folding Gnomon, Ring, Pocket, 1900, 2 In.	395.00
Sundial, Wood Block, Chapter Ring, 19th Century, 9 In.	350.00
Surveying, Neuhoff & Sohn, Vienna, 1900	595.00
Telegraph Key, GNRR, Western Electric	65.00
Telescope, Astronomical, Tripod, Japan, 3 Ft.	125.00
Telescope, Brass, 1880s, Extension, 21 In.	55.00
Telescope, Brass, Lenoir, Micrometrical, Opens To 24 In.	2850.00
Telescope, Brass, Wooden Barrel Mount, Oak Tripod, 18 Power	650.00
Telescope, Pasteboard, Vellum, 18th Century, 10 To 25 1/2 In.	1350.00
Telescope, Ramsden, Variable Power, Pocket, England, 4 1/2 In.	1150.00
Telescope, Sighting Scope, Optics, Floor, 44 In.	2000.00
Telescope, Tripod, Milben	95.00
Telescope, W. C. Cox, 9–Draw, Leather Bound Tube, 6 To 31 In.	895.00
Transit With Compass, K & E, Brass Bound Box, 1940 Model	400.00
Transit, Kuebler & Seelhorst, Phila., 1870, 10 In. Telescope	875.00
Transit, Surveyor's, Atchison, Topeka & Santa Fe, 1879	3900.00
Weather Forecaster, Man In Black, Sunshine Girl, Wooden(Folk Art)	10.00

SCRIMSHAW is bone or ivory or whale's teeth carved by sailors and others for entertainment during the sailing–ship days. Some scrimshaw was carved as early as 1800. There are modern scrimshanders making pieces today on bone, ivory, or plastic. Other pieces may be found in the Ivory and Nautical categories.

Bone, Crochet Hooks, Pair	8.00
Box, Whalebone, Engraved Eagles, Horse & Rider, Oval, 4 x 8 In.	385.00
Busk, 3 Panels, Flower Basket, Sailor, Woman, Whalebone, 1850, 18 3/4 In.	895.00
Busk, Whalebone, Portrait, Virginia, Remember Me, 10 3/4 In.	360.00
Carving, Eskimo Man, 8 In.	85.00
Carving, Shorebird, Eskimo, 5 x 6 In.	95.00
Charm, Sailor's, Heart, Cat, Rose Drawing, To Gail, Love Theo, Verse	28.00
Compass, Allover Carved, Germany, 1870, Round, 2 1/8 In.	245.00
Cribbage Board, Carved Walrus Tusk, Engraved Caribou, Seals, 1901, 19 In.	198.00
Cribbage Board, Walrus Tusk, Seal Heads, Sleds, People & Birds, Eskimo	800.00
Dipper, Coconut Shell Bowl, Early 19th Century	665.00
Eagle's Head Form, Whale Tooth, Wooden Base, 6 In.	523.00
Figurine, Walrus, Polar Bear's Head, 2 1/2 In.	99.00
Needle, Knitting, Whalebone, 13 In., Pair	303.00
Pendant, Carved Fist Joined To Whale's Tooth, Drilled To Hand, Chain, 3 1/2 In.	440.00
Pie Crimper, Whale, Pierced Star Center, 1850, 7 x 1 3/4 In.	1100.00
Pie Crimper, Whalebone, 3–Tined Fork, 1830–1840, 8 x 2 In.	390.00
Pulley, Whalebone, Brass Rivets, 5 In.	264.00

Rolling Pin, Whalebone, Turned Wood, 12 In. 230.00
Ships, Lighthouse, Whalebone, 3 1/2 x 1/2 x 5/8 In., Pair 95.00
Swift, Whalebone, Polychrome Design Traces 1045.00
Swift, Whalebone, Wooden Base, 17 In. 523.00
Tooth, Whale's, American Ship & Flag, Sailor, 1800s, 6 1/2 In. 4125.00
Tooth, Whale's, American Ship, 1850, 6 x 2 1/2 In. 1985.00
Tooth, Whale's, Desk Set, Ivory Inkwell, Whaling Scenes, 3 Piece 550.00
Tooth, Whale's, Engraved Woman 2420.00
Tooth, Whale's, Full–Length Sailor, Black Iron Base, 1850, 5 1/4 x 2 1/4 In. 690.00
Tooth, Whale's, Maidens Bathing, Monks Watching, Geometric Base, 7 In. 1100.00
Tooth, Whale's, Polychrome Figure of Woman, 5 3/4 In. 495.00
Tooth, Whale's, Ship's Portrait, Whaling Scene, In Color, Pair 3850.00
Tooth, Whale's, Ship, Eagle & Flags, L. Boder, 1848, Pair 3850.00
Tooth, Whale's, View of Washington, D.C., Capital 1870.00
Tooth, Whale's, Woman Portrait, Black Iron Base, 1850, 6 In. 975.00
Tusk, English Coat–of–Arms, Various Mottoes, England, c.1870 .... 495.00
Watch Holder, Ivory & Wood, 3–Tier Form, 11 1/2 In. 825.00

SEBASTIAN MINIATURES were first made by Prescott W. Baston in 1938 in Marblehead, Massachusetts. More than 400 different designs have been made and collectors search for the out–of–production models. The mark may say *Copr. P. W. Baston U.S.A.,* or *P. W. Baston, U.S.A.,* or *Prescott W. Baston.* Sometimes a paper label was used.

Abe Lincoln 125.00
America Remembers Family Sing 200.00
Amish Man 30.00
Aunt Betsy Trotwood 80.00
Ben Franklin 125.00
Benjamin Franklin 32.50
Bluebird Girl 525.00
Bob Cratchit 15.00
Bob Cratchit & Tiny Tim 80.00
Boston Tea Party 175.00
Building Days, Girl 33.00
Campfire Girl 750.00
Chiquita 512.00
Cleopatra 225.00
Colonial Glassblower .... 115.00 To 125.00
Colonial Kitchen 40.00
Cowhand .... 35.00 To 90.00
David Copperfield 25.00
Deborah Franklin .... 115.00 To 125.00
Doctor 275.00
Evangeline 138.00
Family Sing 105.00
Fat Man, Jell–O 580.00
Fisherman 150.00
Gabriel 150.00
George Washington 115.00
George Washington, Magnets 75.00
George Washington, With Cannon 25.00
Godey Couple, Marble Head 45.00
Holgrave Daguerreotypist 240.00
Huckleberry Finn .... 25.00 To 42.00
Indian Maiden 132.50
Indian Warrior 126.00
Jack & Jill 65.00
Jack & Jill, 1949 .... 38.00
Jesus 280.00
John & Priscilla Alden, Blue Label 40.00
John Hancock, Small Base 175.00
John Smith & Pocahontas 140.00
Johnny Appleseed 32.00

Judge Thatcher	85.00
Katrina Van Tassel	35.00 To 80.00
Lincoln, Seated	45.00
Martha Washington	90.00
Martha, Cherry Pie	425.00
Mary Lynn, Black	175.00
Mrs. Cratchit	75.00
Mrs. D. Boone	99.00
Mrs. Cratchit	80.00
Mrs. Rittenhouse Square	40.00
Nathaniel Hawthorne	160.00 To 175.00
Nell & Grandfather	85.00
Obocell	150.00
Old Salt	35.00
Parade Rest, Drummer Boy, Sticker, Box	35.00
Paul Revere	65.00
Peggotty	80.00
Pen Stand, Mayflower, Clouds, Marblehead Label	225.00
Phoebe, House of 7 Gables	175.00
Pieman	325.00
Pilgrims	105.00 To 115.00
Pioneer Couple	25.00
Pioneer Couple, Blue Label	45.00
Plaque, Christmas Series, 1985	40.00
Pope John 23rd	288.00
Pray Hands	435.00
Romeo & Juliet	90.00
Sailing Days, Boy	28.00
Sarah Henry	55.00
Scrooge	25.00 To 95.00
Scuba Diver	451.00
Self–Portrait	35.00 To 37.00
Shipbuilder	15.00
Songs At Cratchit	95.00
Swan Boat	68.00
Testing The Recipe	94.00
The Thinker	198.00
Tiny Tim	15.00
Toll House Crier	90.00
Tom Sawyer, Blue Label, 1979	40.00
Town Crier	85.00 To 90.00
Uncle Mistletoe	230.00
Williamsburg Lady	30.00
Yankee Sea Captain	15.00

SEG, see Paul Revere Pottery category

SEVRES porcelain has been made in Sevres, France, since 1769. Many copies of the famous ware have been made. The name originally referred to the works of the Royal Porcelain factory. The name now includes any of the wares made in the town of Sevres, France. The entwined lines with a center letter used as the mark is one of the most forged marks in antiques. Be very careful to identify Sevres by quality, not just by mark.

Bowl, Cameo, Chrysanthemum Blossoms, Silver–Gilt Mounted, 1900, 9 1/4 In.	885.00
Cup & Saucer, Orange Gilt Bands	75.00
Ewer, Cameo, Blossoms, Leaves, Handle, Hinged Cover, Silver Mounted, 11 3/4 In.	2550.00
Figurine, Dancing Couple, Floral Dress, Green Trousers, 11 x 12 In.	1650.00
Group, Hounds Attacking Boar, Stepped Base, 1898 Mark, 18 3/8 x 13 In.	550.00
Jardiniere, Ormolu Frame, Oval, Royal Blue, c.1870, 8 x 15 In.	880.00
Plaque, Woman & Man Courting By Well, Ormolu Square Frame, c.1895, 11 In.	495.00
Plate, Border of Trailing Roses, Central Pansies, 9 In.	385.00
Plate, Bouquets & Scattered Flower Sprays, c.1750, 4 Piece	895.00
Plate, Boy & Girl In Garden, Scalloped Rim, Signed, 9 1/2 In.	95.00

Plate, Gilt Banded Border, Entwined Garland Around Cornflower, 9 1/2 In. 440.00
Plate, Jeweled Cobalt Border, Reserve of Passage Su Rhin, 9 1/2 In. 410.00
Plate, Pate–Sur–Pate, Monkey Medicine Show, Multicolored, J. Celos, 1875, 9 In. 950.00
Plate, Pink & White Peony, Green Ground, Artist Phillip, 7 1/2 In. 85.00
Plate, Service, Scenes, 19th Century, 7 Piece ....*Illus* 2750.00
Plate, Service, Woman Scene, 19th Century, 6 Piece ....*Illus* 3300.00
Tea Set, Breakfast Tray, Children At Play Scenes, Blue Celeste Glaze 2500.00
Teapot, Deep Blue, Ornate Gold Trim, 4 Cup 50.00
Tray, Birds Perched In A Tree, Pink Ground, Gilt Edge, 18th Century, 9 1/2 In. 1100.00
Tray, Center Putti With Bails of Wheat, Scrolled & Rocaille Handles, Oval, 16 In. ... 650.00
Tray, Dutch Couple Dancing, Trellis Pattern Ground, c.1760, 5 13/16 In. 3025.00
Urn, 1st Empire, 2 Handles, 1804–1814, 23 In. ....*Illus* 3250.00
Urn, Cover, Azure Blue, 2 Handles, 19th Century, C. R. Maglin, Pair 3900.00
Urn, Cover, Female Busts, Panel By Luce, Landscape Reverse, 22 In. 7150.00
Urn, Cover, Semi–Clad Woman, Flowing Hair, Gilt Irises & Leaves, Marked, 30 In. 5170.00
Urn, Gilt Bronze Neck & Base, c.1910, 15 1/2 In., Pair 1925.00
Vase, Cameo, Turquoise, Blossoms, Silver–Plated Metal Mount, 1900, 6 3/4 In. 1650.00
Vase, Cover, Napoleonic, Eagle Within Oak Leaves, Signed, 1809, 38 In. 8250.00
Vase, Cover, Pastoral Lovers, Musical Instruments, Scrolled Handles, 16 1/2 In. 495.00
Vase, Cover, Woman & Cupid In Garden, Ormolu Mounts, Signed, 15 In. 495.00
Vase, Portrait of Woman & Cupid In Garden, Galy, 15 In. 550.00
Vase, Silver Splatter, Red Ground, 5 In. 150.00
Vase, Stylized Floral Clusters, White Ground, Bulbous, Lasserre, 1921, 7 1/4 In. 880.00

SEWER TILE figures were made by workers at the sewer tile and pipe factories in the Ohio area during the late nineteenth and early twentieth centuries. Figurines, small vases, and cemetery vases were favored. Often the finished vase was a piece of the original pipe with added decorations and markings. All types of sewer tile work are now considered folk art by collectors.

Crane, Polychrome Paint, 6 1/4 x 11 In. 126.00
Desk Organizer, 3 Stump, On Boat Shape Base, 10 In. 27.50
Desk Set, Fireplace Shape, 8 1/4 x 5 In. 71.50
Dog, Molded, Tooled Detail, Open Feet, Flat Head, Mournful Expression, 13 In. 1100.00
Dog, Seated, Molded, Tooled Detail, Flat Head, Mournful Expression, 11 In. 775.00
Horse Head, Square Base, Incised Inscription, 5 1/2 In. 225.00
Lion, 14 In. 275.00
Lion, 5 In. 450.00
Lion, Recumbent, Incised Mane & Paws, Glazed, 5 3/4 x 9 In. 495.00
Planter, Tree Trunk, 4 Openings, Large 595.00

Sevres, Plate, Service, Woman Scene, 19th Century, 6 Piece

Sevres, Plate, Service, Scenes, 19th Century, 7 Piece

Sevres, Urn, 1st Empire, 2 Handles, 1804-1814, 23 In.

Sewing, Needle Book, Fidelity Life Insurance Co., 3 1/4 X 2 In.

Sewing, Needle Book, Army & Navy Needle Book, 4 5/8 X 2 5/8 In.

Sewing, Needle Book, Warner's Corsets, 3 1/4 X 2 1/2 In.

Sardine Can, 7 1/4 In.	605.00
Stand, Umbrella, Bird & Floral Design, 1920	100.00

SEWING equipment of all types is collected, from sewing birds that held the cloth to old wooden spools.

Awl, Carved Mother-of-Pearl Handle, 4 In.	28.00
Basket, Braided Raffia Woven On Caning, Puffed Inside Cover, 9 x 9 x 4 3/4 In.	27.50
Basket, Lenci-Type Doll Cover	65.00
Basket, Peking Glass Beads & Coins, Chinese, 1915, 12 x 5 In.	35.00
Basket, White Wicker, Legs	37.50
Basket, Woven Over Splint, Old Green Paint	18.00
Bird, Double Cushions	165.00
Bird, Metal, Box	220.00
Bird, Steel, Plain	125.00
Book, Patterns, Doll's Clothes, Mary Francis	80.00
Book, Singer Library, No. 3, How To Make Children's Clothes, 1931, 66 Pages	8.00
Box, Burl Walnut, Inlaid Mother-of-Pearl, Lining, Tools, England, 12 x 8 x 5 In.	1200.00
Box, Classical, Red Leather, Brass Findings, England, 1820, 5 x 7 x 5 In.	715.00
Box, Figural Woman's Shoes, Pincushion Top, Victorian	185.00
Box, Inlaid, Carved, Mirror & Inserts, Paw Feet, 18th Century	425.00
Box, Mahogany Veneer, Fitted Lift Out Tray, 14 1/2 In.	65.00
Box, Mahogany, Black Alligatored Varnish, 1 Drawer, Pincushion, 7 In.	95.00
Box, Mother-of-Pearl Roses On Lid, Compartment, Papier-Mache, 10 x 13 In.	225.00
Box, Musical, Man & Woman Scene, Biedermeier, Ebony & Fruitwood, c.1830	2010.00
Box, Napoleon III, Burl Walnut, 19th Century, 4 1/2 x 10 In.	165.00
Box, Onion Shape Top, 8 Hinged Lids, Compartment Interior, Stand, 44 In.	9900.00
Box, Regency, Ivory, Armorial Crest, Removable Tray, 1810	1200.00
Box, Rosewood, Mother-of-Pearl Tools, Silk Spools, England, 1850, 10 x 6 x 4 In.	795.00
Box, Turned Feet, 1 Drawer, Pincushion Top, Holes For Spool Pins, 7 1/2 In.	40.00
Box, Wood Reed & Woven Braided Straw, Oval, 7 1/2 In.	90.00
Cabinet, Pyrography, Pictures In Drawer Bottoms, 1902	425.00
Cabinet, Spool, see Advertising category under Cabinet, Spool	
Case, Tooled Leather, Woman's Companion, England	185.00
Chest, 3 Front Drawers, 2 Side Drawers, 1910	250.00
Chest, Spool, 4 Drawers, Walnut With Maple Inlay, 23 1/2 x 14 1/4 x 17 1/2 In.	495.00
Darner, Cased Clear & White Glass, Czechoslovakia	165.00
Darner, Clear & Pink Glass, Czechoslovakia	135.00
Darning Egg, Black, Fancy Sterling Silver Handle	42.50
Darning Kit, Leather Folder, Dog Cover	12.00
Dressmaker's Bust, Rhinestones & Pearls Under Lucite, c.1940	125.00

Emery, Tartan Ware 62.00
Gauge, Hem, Holly Berry, Sterling Silver 125.00
Guard, Knitting Needle, Pig's Trotters, Black Hooves, With Hide, England 135.00
Hem Line Marker, Singer, Bulb & Chalk Dust On Frame 15.00
Kit, Felt Covered Box, Contents, Round, 4 In. 12.50
Knitting Sheath, Goosewing 195.00
Knitting Sheath, Inlaid Initials, Early 19th Century, England 225.00
Machine, Davis, Cover, Treadle Stand 12.50
Machine, Portable, Occupied Japan 100.00
Machine, Red Head Singer, Electric 375.00
Machine, Singer Featherweight, Model 221, Attachments, Instructions, Case 240.00
Machine, Singer, Blond Cabinet 7.50
Machine, Singer, Domed Wooden Portable Case 75.00
Machine, Singer, Featherweight, No. 221, Case 250.00
Machine, Singer, Featherweight, No. 221, Case 275.00
Machine, Singer, Model 221, Featherweight, Black, Case, Attachments .... 285.00 To 350.00
Machine, Singer, Portable, Black & Gold Lettering, Great Britain, Wooden Case 45.00
Machine, Singer, Treadle .... 45.00 To 60.00
Machine, Wilcox & Gibbs, Portable, Electric, 1880s 275.00
Mending Kit, Royal Nevada, Home of Dancing Waiters, Logo, 1960s, 3 1/2 In. 7.50
Needle Book 38.00
Needle Book, Army & Navy Needle Book, 4 5/8 x 2 5/8 In. ....*Illus* 15.00
Needle Book, Empire State, Navy Zeppelin, Plane, Ship, New York Ground 12.00
Needle Book, Fidelity Life Insurance Co., 3 1/4 x 2 In. ....*Illus* 8.00
Needle Book, Warner's Corsets, 3 1/4 x 2 1/2 In. ....*Illus* 12.00
Needle Case, Boye, Wood & Glass, c.1910 .... 250.00
Needle Case, Butterfly, Victorian, Brass 550.00
Needle Case, Sterling Silver, 2 1/4 In. 55.00
Needle Kit, Grand Union Supermarkets 12.00
Needle Threader, Prudential Insurance, Tin 6.50
Needle, Book, Bromo Seltzer 15.00
Pattern, Belks, McCalls & Simplicity, Boys, Dated 1930s, 4 Piece 15.00
Pattern, Devil's Costume, Butterick, 1923 .... 20.00
Pattern, Pickaninny Rag Dolls, Simplicity, 1947 .... 28.00
Pincushion & Tape Measure, Red Corduroy Dog On Ball, 4 In. 49.00
Pincushion dolls are listed in their own category
Pincushion, Book, Beaded Flowers & B. E. 1836, 2 1/4 x 2 3/4 In. 50.00
Pincushion, Dachshund, Porcelain 30.00
Pincushion, High–Buttoned Shoes On Either Side, Gilded Wood 110.00
Pincushion, High–Heel Shoe, Metal Roses On Front, Signed SCC, 4 In. 35.00
Pincushion, Mammy's Head 5.00
Pincushion, Man's Leg Shape, Crazy Quilt Pattern 125.00
Pincushion, Nude Bathing Beauty 225.00
Pincushion, Victorian Woman's Leg Shape, Pair 135.00
Pincushion, Woman, Closed Arm Holding Fan & Flowers 48.00
Pinking Machine, Cast Iron 50.00
Press, Eyelet, Patent 1902 .... 50.00
Shears, Tailor's, Left Handed, Steel, America 33.00
Shuttle, Boye, Improved, 1923 ....8.50 To 25.00
Shuttle, Tatting, Silver Over Brass 25.00
Sock Darner, Wooden 9.00
Spool cabinets are in the Advertising category under Cabinet, Spool
Spool, Holder, Horseshoe Shape, Painted, 1890 .... 265.00
Stand, Lift Top, Divided Sections, Tripod Base, Chain Carved Swags 1200.00
Stand, Spool Holder, Painted, Octagonal 1295.00
Table, Simplicity, Measuring Fabric, Folding, 36–Inch Guide, 1884 .... 70.00
Tape Measure, Dutchess Mfg. Co., Poughkeepsie, N.Y. 4.00
Tape Measure, Edison Mazda, Celluloid, Color Graphics 55.00
Tape Measure, Egg With Fly, Celluloid 35.00
Tape Measure, Elephant 39.00
Tape Measure, Flowered Pig, Celluloid, Occupied Japan 35.00
Tape Measure, Hoover Vacuum Cleaner ....22.00 To 75.00
Tape Measure, Minnesota Motor Company 20.00

Tape Measure, Orange Crush	100.00
Tape Measure, Orange Crush, Celluloid	72.00
Tape Measure, Pig, Hand Painted, Celluloid	32.00
Tape Measure, Sailing Ship, Red, Celluloid	35.00
Tape Measure, Santa Claus Pull	30.00
Tape Measure, Ship	30.00
Tape Measure, Woman In Babushka	37.00
Thimble Case, Tartan Ware, With Thimble	165.00
Thimble, 14K Gold, Box	85.00
Thimble, Bass Utilitarian, B Mark On Band, Size 7	40.00
Thimble, Cherub, Pearlized China	5.00
Thimble, Cloisonne, On Brass, Royal Blue, Pastel Flowers & Butterfly	10.00
Thimble, Grapes, Leaves & Vines, Beaded Rim, Size 6	50.00
Thimble, Great Smokey Mt. National Park, 50 Years, AFB Corp.	8.00
Thimble, Holder, Mushroom Shape, Vegetable Ivory, With Ivory Thimble	85.00
Thimble, Pewter, Busch Gardens, Williamsburg, Va.	4.00
Thimble, Pewter, Cinderella, Grimms Fairy Tale Series, Franklin Mint	10.00
Thimble, Pierce Pennant Gasoline & Oils, Aluminum	15.00
Thimble, Plastic, Sinclair Oils, Green Dinosaur, B & B	5.00
Thimble, Porcelain, 4 Gold Angel Faces Around White Band, Gold Top, Spode	30.00
Thimble, Ship, Norman Court, 1869, Sanford Co., Newall Red Rose	9.00
Thimble, Silver, Anchor Mark On Lighthouse	30.00
Thimble, Silver, E. J. Bass	20.00
Thimble, Silver, Enameled Flowers, James Swann, England	35.00
Thimble, Silver, Feather Border, Goldsmith Stern Co.	25.00
Thimble, Silver, Ornate, Mexico	20.00
Thimble, Silver, Waite Thresher, Row of Anchors On Wide Band	35.00
Thimble, Silver, Weinberg, SPNS	10.00
Thimble, Sterling Silver, Allover Pinwheels, Size 9	35.00
Thimble, Sterling Silver, Birmingham, The Spa, 1931	55.00
Thimble, Sterling Silver, Rembrandt Scene, Thorvald Greif	70.00
Thimble, Sterling Silver, Simons, Paneled	20.00
Thimble, Tailor's, Sandalwood, India, 2 Birds Encircling Band	4.00
Thread Cutter, Movable, & Needle Threader, Marked M. T.	15.00
Thread Holder, Magnolia Petroleum Co.	15.00
Thread Holder, Wall, Walnut, 3 Tiers, 1880	45.00
Threader, Lydia Pinkham, Celluloid	20.00
Tracer, Pattern, Parallel Adjustable Width Wheels	35.00
Yarn Winder, Mixed Woods, N. Lindsay, Reading, 24-In. Reel, 30 In.	93.50

SHAKER items are characterized by simplicity, functionalism, and orderliness. There were many Shaker communities in America from the eighteenth century to the present day. The religious order made furniture, small wooden pieces, and packaged medicines, herbs, and jellies to sell to *outsiders*. Other useful objects were made for use by members of the community. Shaker furniture is listed in this book in the Furniture category.

Apple Peeler & Slicer, Mechanical	275.00
Apple Peeler, Stamped J. S.	688.00
Basket, Kitten Head	230.00
Basket, Splint, Carved Handle, 8 1/2 In.	295.00
Bonnet, Quilted, Sugar Glaze, Floral Pattern, Brown	155.00
Box, 3-Finger, Natural, 11 1/2 In.	475.00
Box, 3-Finger, Old Green Paint, Oval	1600.00
Box, 4-Finger, Natural, 13 In.	925.00
Box, 5-Finger, Swing Handle, Oval, 11 3/8 x 4 1/4 In.	660.00
Box, 9-Finger, Natural, 20 In.	1300.00
Box, Bentwood, Oval, Harvard Type, Original Blue, Gray Paint, 5 7/8 In.	440.00
Box, Bentwood, Oval, Single Fingers On Lid, Base, Green Repaint, 6 3/8 In.	385.00
Box, Bentwood, Shaker, Stenciled Lid, Copper Tacks, 9 In.	260.00
Box, Blanket, Bootjack End, Painted, 22 x 38 1/2 x 16 In.	825.00
Box, Candle, Deep Blue, 9 1/2 x 14 1/2 In.	1350.00
Box, Copper Tacks, Lid Branded E. L. H., Harvard, 5 3/8 In.	150.00

Box, Document, Inscription From Father Job Bishop, Canterbury, 1798 .... 5225.00
Box, Document, Painted, Black and Gold Sponge Design, 23 1/4 x 6 1/2 x 8 In. 165.00
Box, Harvard Style Laps, Oval, 4 5/8 In. 90.00
Box, Harvard Style, Iron Tacks, Single Finger, Oval, 5 1/2 In. 150.00
Box, Harvard Style, Pincushion Top 390.00
Box, Hinged Lid, Lower Drawer, Maple, 7 1/2 x 11 1/2 In. 210.00
Box, Maple, Pine, Amber Stain, Paper Labels, Silk Cord, Oval, 1840 .... 2310.00
Box, Natural Patina, Harvard Maine, Fingers Typical, 1/2 x 5 1/4 In. 110.00
Box, Oval, Single Finger Construction, Iron Tacks, Original Green Paint, 7 7/8 In. 415.00
Box, Paper Labels, Silk Cord, Maple & Pine, c.1840 .... 2300.00
Box, Pincushion, Harvard 395.00
Box, Sewing, 4–Finger, Oval, Swing Handle 750.00
Box, Single Finger, Oval, Bentwood, Original Blue Paint, 9 1/4 In. 775.00
Box, Stave Constructed, Wooden Bands, Brown Paint, B. F. Wood, 13 x 6 1/2 In. ... 900.00
Box, Steam–Bent Ash, Kerfed Interior Corners, Finger, Rectangular 2200.00
Box, Thread, 8 Shaker Made Spools of Silk Thread 398.00
Carrier, 4 Compartments, Lids, Cherry, Footed 1200.00
Carrier, Pine, Sabbathday Lake, Oval, 9 1/4 In. 275.00
Carrier, Sewing, Sabbathday Lake, 1920s, 9 In. 275.00
Carrier, Sewing, Swing Handle, Maple, 4 Fingers, Silk Lined, 10 1/2 In. 385.00
Chair, Ladder Back, 3 Slats, Turned Finials, Splint Seat, 36 1/2 In. 85.00
Churn, Butter, Wig–Wag 165.00
Cloak Hanger, 48 In. 220.00
Cloak, Dorothy, Canterbury 795.00
Coat Hanger 95.00
Container, Double Ear Handles, Pouring Spout, Tin, 6 In. 77.00
Corn Husker, 10 1/2 x 2 1/2 In. 132.00
Grinder, Herb, Hinged Chute, Punched Tin Reel, Dovetailed Stretchers, c.1840 .... 935.00
Grinder, Herb, Poplar, Iron, Brown Paint, Hinged Chute, Punched Tin Reel, 1840 ... 935.00
Lemon Squeezer, 11 In. 115.00
Needle Case, Wooden, 3 1/2 In. 30.00
Niddy–Noddy 60.00
Pail, Staved, Alternating Light & Dark Wood Bands, Bail Handle, 7 1/4 In. 385.00
Pill Case, Wooden, Inlaid 135.00
Pill Maker, Wood & Brass 247.00
Pincushion, Poplar Ware 60.00
Rain Barrel, Wood Banded, Tapered 247.00
Rolling Pin, Maple, 19th Century, L5 1/4 In. 60.00
Rug Beater 71.50
Rug, Confetti, Hand Sewn, 23 x 52 In. 413.00
Rug, Silk, Concentric Rings of Color From Brown Center, Round 1400.00
Rush Wringer, Sabbathday Lake 82.00
Sampler, 4 Alphabet Styles, Basket of Flowers, Cotton, Blue & Brown Wool, 1847 4400.00
Saucepan, Cover, Red Paint, Tin, 6 x 8 1/2 In. 88.00
Seed Box, 23 x 3 1/4 x 12 In. 565.00
Sewing Box, Poplar Ware, Stamped Goods, Alfred, Maine, 5 1/2 In. 121.00
Sewing Carrier, Base Stamped Sabbathday Lake Shakers Maine, 9 In. 275.00
Sieve, Horsehair, 19th Century, 9 3/4 In. 137.50
Sieve, Pigment, Oval, 6 3/4 In. 385.00
Spool Holder, With Pincushion, 5 1/2 In. 247.00
Stove, Cast of The Ford Foundry of Concord, c.1870 .... 220.00
Swift, Hancock, Mass., 25 In. 275.00
Tray, Cutlery 140.00
Tub, Stave Constructed, Wooden Bands, Worn Patina, Round, 18 x 6 3/4 In. 275.00
Yardstick, Tailor's, Maple, Nut Brown Patina, 36 In. 715.00

SHAVING MUGS were popular from 1860 to 1900. Many types were
made, including occupational mugs featuring pictures of men's jobs. There
were scuttle mugs, silver–plated mugs, glass–lined mugs, and others.

Beach North of Jetty, Scuttle 75.00
Buff Clay, Ribbed Strap Handle, Mottled Brownish Glaze, Pottery, 3 1/2 In. 49.00
Church, Mountains, Lake, 7 Colors 285.00
Cowboys, 4 At Campfire, No Name 175.00

Elmer Olson, Flowers, Gold, Fancy 100.00
Ferns & Calla Lilies, R. H. Lindsay, Black Ground, Limoges 95.00
Fraternal, F. O. E., Flying Eagle 175.00
Fraternal, Knights of Columbus, Picture & Name 125.00
Fraternal, Knights of Golden Eagle, Knights of Mystic Chain, Gold Name 150.00
Fraternal, Knights of Pythias 160.00
Fraternal, Mason, Hammer & Trowel, M. Schann, 3 1/2 In. 110.00
Fraternal, Shield With Letters KGEFVH, Cross & Crown 27.50
General Store, Pinkleman & Barry Co. 1650.00
H. Sykes, Koken, Limoges 68.00
Horse–Drawn Carriage 575.00
Lions 62.00
Majolica, With Brush 47.50
Occupational, 19th Field Artillery, Henry A. Spies, Intl. Royal China, 3 1/2 In. 330.00
Occupational, 3 Blacksmiths, Chas. Abbott, 3 1/2 In. 55.00
Occupational, A. B. Shutz, Baker, Oven, Heckle Bros., Kansas City, 3 3/4 In. 468.00
Occupational, A. H. Hartmann, Beer Mug, 3 1/2 In. 137.00
Occupational, Automobile Dealer, 1901 Model Oldsmobile 500.00
Occupational, Baker & Oven, Germany, 3 3/4 In. 137.00
Occupational, Baker, Loaves of Bread, A. D. Attlerback, 3 1/2 In. 247.00
Occupational, Baker, Ovens, E. R. Allen, Chicago, Ill., 3 1/2 In. 357.00
Occupational, Bakery, R. L. Neuman 2500.00
Occupational, Bartender & 2 Men Drinking At Bar, 4 3/4 In. 100.00
Occupational, Bartender, 2 Men In Saloon, Remeritt, 4 In. 193.00
Occupational, Bartender, 5 People In Scene 500.00
Occupational, Bartender, Gentlemen, Otto K. W. Bartusch, 3 1/2 In. 357.00
Occupational, Bartender, Limoges 350.00
Occupational, Bartender, Saloon Bar, A. Siefert, 4 In. 220.00
Occupational, Baseball Catcher, Mask, Pads & Glove, 3 1/2 In. 413.00
Occupational, Beer Wagon Driver 500.00
Occupational, Blacksmith, At Forge 425.00
Occupational, Blacksmith, Smithy Shop, Joe Shear, 4 In. 100.00
Occupational, Brewery 350.00
Occupational, Butcher, Cow Head & Tools 250.00
Occupational, Butcher, Reinhardt, Koken, St. Louis, Limoges, 4 In. 110.00
Occupational, Butcher, Steer & Tools 195.00
Occupational, Butcher, Steer, Knife & Sharpener, C. A. Karlin, Koken, 3 3/4 In. ... 330.00
Occupational, Carpenter, Work Bench 350.00
Occupational, Chariot, L. B. Garvin, Marked T. N. V. Leadses, 3 3/4 In. 770.00
Occupational, Clockmaker, Name Cambell 1650.00
Occupational, Conductor, Trolley, J. R. Voidan, 3 3/4 In. 220.00
Occupational, Dance Instructor, Limoges 850.00
Occupational, Doctor 20.00
Occupational, Engineer, Train & Car 300.00
Occupational, Farmer, Plow & Horses, Frank Gunt, Germany, 3 3/4 In. 440.00
Occupational, Firefighter, Hook & Ladder Truck, 5 Firemen 1550.00
Occupational, Fireman, Hat, Ax, Ladder, Lantern & Picks 1050.00
Occupational, Fireman, Reel Horse Cart 800.00
Occupational, Gambler, Horseshoe & Clover 250.00
Occupational, General Store, Daniel G. Barry, 4 In. 1650.00
Occupational, Gilt Pocket Watch, Geo. F. S. Beck, 3 1/2 In. 165.00
Occupational, Grocer Wagon, Horse–Drawn, G. D. Pottle, 3 3/4 In. 330.00
Occupational, Grocer, Man Diving Covered Wagon, Maroon Ground 195.00
Occupational, Gymnast, Horizontal Chin–Up, Jim Bradley 2350.00
Occupational, Haberdasher, Men's Clothing, A. H. Mesem, 3 1/2 In. 110.00
Occupational, Hand Holding Quill Pen, D.C. Greer, 3 1/2 In. 770.00
Occupational, Horned Cow, John Keller On Banner, 4 In. 193.00
Occupational, Horse Breeder, J. M. Walters, Limoges, 3 1/2 In. 303.00
Occupational, Hunter, Bird Dog, Henry H. Kerchner, Limoges, 3 3/4 In. 192.50
Occupational, Hunter, Gun & Dog 185.00
Occupational, Hunter, Shooting Dogs, J. A. Irick, 3 3/4 In. 385.00
Occupational, Jockey, Racehorse Scene, Grandstand 1350.00
Occupational, Lathe Operator, Man Working At Lathe, Name In Gold 425.00

Occupational, Lawyer	135.00
Occupational, Machinist, Steam Engine, Henry A. Greenup, 3 1/2 In.	385.00
Occupational, Man Riding Motorcycle	1320.00
Occupational, Meat Cutter	195.00
Occupational, Men Laying Water Pipes	800.00
Occupational, Men Working Printing Press	1100.00
Occupational, Painter	375.00
Occupational, Pair of Handcuffs	630.00
Occupational, Preacher, Cross & Crown	95.00
Occupational, Race Car Driver, J. N. Woodhull, Track In Woodhull, N.Y.	6250.00
Occupational, Salesman Selling Leather Boots, O. Stoner, 3 3/4 In.	413.00
Occupational, Steam Locomotive, Tender, W. M. Hilton, 3 3/4 In.	137.00
Occupational, Store, Clocks, Watches, 3 3/4 In.	1650.00
Occupational, Tailor	575.00
Occupational, Telegraph, C. G. Albright, 3 3/4 In.	275.00
Occupational, Telegraph, Ordie L. Cobb, Soft Paste	450.00
Occupational, Tinsmith, Working On Roof	750.00
Occupational, Train Engineer, F. J. Luther, Mid–19th Century, 3 1/2 In.	137.00
Occupational, Train Engineer, Locomotive, Mid–19th Century, 3 1/2 In.	165.00
Occupational, Trolley Operator	300.00
Occupational, Undertaker, Hearse, Curtains Open, Wooden Casket	1550.00
Occupational, Wagon Marked Livery, Horse–Drawn Vehicle	575.00
Occupational, Watchmaker, With Watch, 3 1/2 In.	247.00
Occupational, Wire Installer, Electric Trolley, D. H. Sarver, 1901	4500.00
Occupational, Writer, Hand With Pen On Paper	325.00
Occupational, Yacht Builder, Captain Wm. Babcock	5400.00
Old Spice, Hull	22.00
Tea Leaf Ironstone, 12 Sides, Leaf Design Handle, Shaw	225.00
Tea Leaf Ironstone, Tall, Meakin, 3 1/4 x 3 1/2 In.	225.00
Viking, Milk Glass, 1867	75.00

SHAWNEE POTTERY was started in Zanesville, Ohio, in 1937. The company made vases, novelty ware, flowerpots, planters, lamps, and cookie jars. Three dinnerware lines were made: Corn, Lobster Ware, and Valencia (a solid color line). White Corn pattern utility pieces were made in 1945. Corn King was made from 1946 to 1954; Corn Queen, with darker green leaves and lighter colored corn, from 1954 to 1961. Shawnee produced pottery for George Rumrill during the late 1930s. The company closed in 1961.

Bowl, Cereal, Corn King, 6 1/2 In.	25.00
Butter, Corn King	45.00
Butter, Corn Queen	40.00
Casserole, Corn King, No. 74	55.00
Casserole, Lobster, Small	20.00
Coffeepot, Sunflower	98.00
Cookie Jar, Basket	80.00
Cookie Jar, Corn King	120.00 To 195.00
Cookie Jar, Drummer Boy, Gold Trim	450.00
Cookie Jar, Dutch Boy	100.00 To 120.00
Cookie Jar, Dutch Boy, Great Northern	350.00
Cookie Jar, Dutch Boy, Patches, Gold Trim	350.00
Cookie Jar, Dutch Girl, Blond	150.00
Cookie Jar, Dutch Girl, Tulip	85.00
Cookie Jar, Elephant	110.00
Cookie Jar, Elephant, Pink	125.00
Cookie Jar, Jo Jo Clown With Seal	200.00 To 300.00
Cookie Jar, Little Chef, Green	195.00
Cookie Jar, Mugsey	350.00 To 375.00
Cookie Jar, Mugsey, Gold, Decals	675.00 To 895.00
Cookie Jar, Owl, Gold	300.00 To 350.00
Cookie Jar, Puss In Boots	140.00 To 200.00
Cookie Jar, Puss In Boots, Gold, Flowers	425.00
Cookie Jar, Queen Corn	120.00

Cookie Jar, Smiley Pig, Red Scarf 75.00
Cookie Jar, Smiley Pig, Shamrocks .... 130.00 To 145.00
Cookie Jar, Smiley Pig, Shamrocks, Gold .... 375.00 To 395.00
Cookie Jar, Smiley Pig, Shamrocks, Gold, Label 495.00
Cookie Jar, Smiley Pig, Tulips 395.00
Cookie Jar, Smiley Pig, Yellow Scarf .... 200.00 To 295.00
Cookie Jar, Winking Owl 125.00
Cookie Jar, Winking Owl, Gold 450.00
Cookie Jar, Winnie Pig, Bank 495.00
Cookie Jar, Winnie Pig, Gold & Red Collar, Blue Flowers 525.00
Cookie Jar, Winnie Pig, Green, Shamrocks 150.00
Creamer, Cat 40.00
Creamer, Corn King 22.00
Creamer, Elephant .... 20.00 To 24.00
Creamer, Puss In Boots .... 22.00 To 48.00
Creamer, Tulip 30.00
Creamer, Watering Can 30.00
Cup & Saucer, Corn King 40.00
Cup & Saucer, Corn Queen 35.00
Fruit Dish, Corn King, 6 In. 24.00
Mixing Bowl, Corn King, 5 In. .... 20.00 To 30.00
Mixing Bowl, Corn King, 6 1/2 In. 25.00
Mixing Bowl, Corn King, 8 In. .... 35.00 To 45.00
Pie Bird .... 25.00 To 28.00
Pitcher, Bo Peep .... 62.00 To 95.00
Pitcher, Bo Peep, Boy Blue 150.00
Pitcher, Chanticleer Rooster .... 50.00 To 65.00
Pitcher, Fruit 40.00
Pitcher, Little Boy Blue 67.00
Pitcher, No. 40, Flower, Gold Trim 15.00
Pitcher, Smiley Pig, Red Flower ....85.00 To 150.00
Planter, Butterfly 7.00
Planter, Canopy Bed .... 40.00 To 65.00
Planter, Covered Wagon 18.00
Planter, Covered Wagon, Green 20.00
Planter, Deer 13.00
Planter, Donkey With Basket 18.00
Planter, Dove 18.00
Planter, Elephant 15.00
Planter, Elf Shoe, White, Gold Trim .... 10.00 To 16.00
Planter, Fawn .... 12.00 To 15.00
Planter, Flower 8.00
Planter, Flower, White, Gray, Gold, Square, 8 In. 20.00
Planter, Girl 18.00
Planter, Hound With Jug 10.00
Planter, Shoe, Pup, Ivory 17.00
Planter, Squirrel ....9.00 To 12.50
Planter, Standing Deer With Fawn, Yellow, Red Base 16.00
Planter, Train Set, 4 Piece 125.00
Planter, Wishing Well, Dutch Boy & Girl, Brown 24.00
Planter, Wishing Well, Dutch Boy & Girl, Green 25.00
Plate, Corn King, 10 In. 35.00
Platter, Corn Queen, 12 In. .... 30.00 To 49.00
Range Set, Lobster Ware, 4 Piece 45.00
Relish, Corn Queen 28.00
Salt & Pepper, Bo Peep & Sailor Boy 15.00
Salt & Pepper, Bo Peep & Sailor Boy, Blond Hair 35.00
Salt & Pepper, Chanticleer, Large 35.00
Salt & Pepper, Chanticleer, Small 20.00
Salt & Pepper, Corn King, 3 1/4 In. .... 18.00 To 24.00
Salt & Pepper, Corn King, 5 1/4 In. .... 22.00 To 25.00
Salt & Pepper, Dutch Boy & Girl, Gold Trim 38.00
Salt & Pepper, Dutch Boy & Girl, Large .... 40.00 To 45.00

Salt & Pepper, Farmer Pig	20.00
Salt & Pepper, Fruit, Large	15.00 To 25.00
Salt & Pepper, Jug, Hearts & Flowers, Pennsylvania Dutch Line, Large	30.00
Salt & Pepper, Muggsy, Small	30.00
Salt & Pepper, Owl	20.00
Salt & Pepper, Owl, Gold	20.00
Salt & Pepper, Puss In Boots	12.00
Salt & Pepper, Smiley Pig & Winnie Pig, Small	40.00
Saltshaker, Corn Queen, Large	12.00
Saucer, Corn King	10.00
Saucer, Corn Queen	15.00
Sugar & Creamer, Corn King	50.00
Sugar, Cover, Clover Flower	20.00
Sugar, Cover, Corn King	25.00 To 28.00
Sugar, Cover, Corn Queen	25.00
Teapot, Corn King, Large	59.00 To 85.00
Teapot, Corn King, Small	100.00 To 145.00
Teapot, Elephant, Yellow	100.00
Teapot, Granny Ann	80.00 To 120.00
Teapot, Hearts & Flowers, Pennsylvania Dutch Line	45.00 To 65.00
Teapot, Tom Tom The Piper's Son	75.00 To 125.00
Vase, Bowknot, Green	9.00
Vase, Swan, Miniature	10.00
Wall Pocket, Clock, Tall Case	20.00
Wall Pocket, Little Jack Horner	18.00

SHEARWATER pottery is a family business started by Mr. and Mrs. G. W. Anderson, Sr., and their three sons. The local Ocean Springs, Mississippi, clays were used to make the wares in the 1930s. The company is still in business.

Bowl, Iridescent Green Glaze, Marked, 1945, 10 1/2 In.	44.00
Figurine, Pirate	60.00
Pitcher, 6 In.	85.00
Syrup, 5 1/2 In.	37.50
Vase, Blue–Green, 8 In.	275.00
Vase, Brown, Blue, Mottled, 7 In.	75.00

SHEET MUSIC from the past centuries is now collected. The favorites are examples with covers featuring artistic or historic pictures. Early sheet music covers were lithographed, but by the 1900s photographic reproductions were used. The early music was larger than more recent sheets and you must watch out for examples that were trimmed to fit in a twentieth–century piano bench.

Ac–Cent–Tchu–Ate The Positive, Bing Crosby	5.00
Affair To Remember, Cary Grant, Deborah Kerr Cover, 1957	20.00
Alexander Don't You Love Your Baby No More, 1904	15.00
All Aboard For Home Sweet Home, Courtney Sisters Cover, 1918	15.00
Alone, From A Night At The Opera, Marx Bros., A. Jones & K. Carlisle, 1935	20.00
Amos 'n Andy	50.00
Atchison, Topeka & Santa Fe, Judy Garland	6.25 To 10.00
Babes On Broadway, Mickey Rooney & Judy Garland Cover	25.00
Ballad of Davy Crockett, Fess Parker Cover, 1954	25.00
Black Sambo, Story Sleeve, 78 Rpm	115.00
Bouquet of Roses, Eddie Arnold	8.00
Broadway Is My Home Sweet Home	10.00
Buy A Kiss After Tonight, Constance Bennett Cover, 1933	2.00
Candy, King Sisters Cover, 1944	10.00
Chant of The Jungle, Untamed, Joan Crawford, 1929	6.00
College Songs, Abridged Academy Songbook, 1899, 298 Pages	15.00
Cotton Time, 1910	10.00
Darn That Dream, Swingin' The Dream, Benny Goodman, 1939	17.50
Dashing Cavaliers, E. T. Paul, 1911	25.00
Don't Be A Baby, Bay, Mills Brothers Cover, 1946	17.50

Don't Fence Me In, Hollywood Canteen, 1944	16.00
Dream, Pied Pipers Cover, 1945	12.50
Dreamer's Holiday, Perry Como Cover, 1949	1.25
Fine Romance, Ginger Rogers & Fred Astaire	5.00
For Me & My Gal, Judy Garland	10.00
Friend of Yours, Movie, The Great John L., L. Darnell & G. McClure Cover	9.00
Funeral March, James Garfield, 1881	20.00
Gentle Annie, Stephen Foster, 5 Pages, 1856	10.00
Gentlemen Prefer Blondes, Marilyn Monroe Cover	33.00
Goodnight My Love	10.00
Hand Me Down My Walkin' Cane, Ken Houchins, Calumet Music, 1935	12.00
Hidden, Phantom Rider, Buck Jones, 1936	25.00
I Need You Now, Eddie Fisher Cover, 1953	1.75
I'm Gettin' Sentimental Over You, Movie, Ship Ahoy, World War II	8.00
Impecunious Davis, Black Caricature, Kerry Mills, 1899, 11 x 14 In.	¹100.00
Just A Little Lovin', Eddie Arnold	8.00
Klondike Gold, W. R. Hearst, Sunday Supplement, Sunday Examiner, 1898	27.50
Kodak Girl, Dedicated To Eastman Kodak, Rochester, N.Y.	12.00
Labor Union Parade, F. Opper Drawing Cover, 1904	20.00
Liberace Theme, Liberace At Piano, 1955	10.00
Little Ford Rambled Right Along, 1914	13.00
Little French Mother, Good Bye, 1918, Norman Rockwell Cover	15.00
Little White Cloud That Cried, Johnny Ray, Carlyle Music, 1951	5.00
Lullaby, Louis Meyer, Babe In Cradle, With Mother, 1877	10.00
MacArthur's Park, Richard Harris	5.00
McKinley March, Political, 1896	20.00
Melancholy Serenade, Gleason	22.00
Moonlight Bay, Doris Day	8.00
My Heart Reminds Me, Della Reese Cover, 1957	15.00
My Man, Fannie Brice, 1921	24.00
My Ohio Home, 1928	7.50
Night At The Opera, Marx Brothers	35.00
Ocean Telegraph March, Commemorating Laying of Atlantic Cable, 1858	30.00
Oh Dem Golden Slippers, Calumet Publishing, 1935	10.00
Old Folks At Home, Eclipse Publishing, Black Couple In Front of Fireplace	15.00
One–Zy Two–Zy I Love You–Zy, 1946	1.25
Only A Rose, Harrison Fisher	25.00
Over The Rainbow, Wizard of Oz, Cast Members, 1939	25.00
Over Yonder Where The Lilies Grown, 1918, Norman Rockwell Cover	12.00
Pain, Minneapolis, Don Aakhus & Duke Butler, 1931	11.00
Paper Doll, Mills Brothers, 1943	15.00
Political, John Davis March To The White House, 1924	15.00
Poor Little Fool, Ricky Nelson, 1958	15.00
Possum The Latest Craze, Stereotype Black Illustration, 1909	25.00
Prisoner's Song, Only Lettering, 1914	9.00
Put Your Arms Around Me Honey, Betty Grable, Dolly Sisters	4.00 To 8.00
Red Wing, Framed, Kerry Mills	60.00
Rememb'Ring, Topsy & Eva, Duncan Sisters, 1923	10.00
Roaring Volcano, E. T. Paul, 1903	25.00
Saint Louis Blues, W. C. Handy, St. Louis Blues Cover, 1931	25.00
Salvation Lassie, 1919	12.00
Say It, Buck Benny Rides Again, Jack Benny, 1940	22.50
Sentimental Me, Ames Brothers Cover, 1950	12.50
Shortnin' Bread	8.00
Show Boat, Florenz Ziegfeld, Hammerstein & Kern, 1925, 6 Piece	22.00
Sinatra, Strangers In The Night	7.00
Singin' In The Rain	8.00
Smoke, Smoke, Smoke That Cigarette, Tex Williams, American Music, 1936	9.00
Smoky Mokes, 1899	10.00
Snow White, Disney, 1950s	25.00
Some Sunday Morning, E. Flynn, A. Smith Dancing On Cover, 1945	20.00
Somethin' Stupid, Frank Sinatra	6.00
Sooner Or Later, Disney Animal Characters Cover, 1946	17.50

Spike Jones, Favorite Souvenir Song Folio, 48 Pages 30.00
Stormy Weather, Lena Horne 5.00
Strangers In The Night, Frank Sinatra 7.00
Teddy Bears, A March For Little Folks, 1925 .... 15.00
Thanks For The Buggy Ride 20.00
That Silver Haired Daddy of Mine, Cole Publishing, 1932 .... 10.00
There Ain't No Land Like Dixieland To Me, Black Aviator, Parachute, 1917 .... 37.50
There's No One But You, Rita Hayworth Cover 20.00
Those Were The Days, Mary Hopkins 10.00
To The White House, John Davis March, Political, 1924 .... 15.00
To You Roosevelt, Ed. Bamber, Singer Lora Sonderson, 1934 .... 27.00
Trolley Song, Judy Garland, Meet Me In St. Louis .... 5.00 To 10.00
Tumbling Tumbleweeds, Sons of The Pioneers, Photo Cover, 1934 .... 3.00
Untamed, Joan Crawford 8.00
Utah Trail, Outdoor Scene, 1928 .... 9.00
We Did It Before, Eddie Cantor 5.00
We're All Going Calling On The Kaiser, World War I 15.00
We've Only Just Begun, Karen & Richard Carpenter 5.00
What Have They Got On You, Mr. Congressman, 1920 .... 15.00 To 25.00
When You Wish Upon A Star, Pinocchio 15.00
White Lies, Ethel Merman, 1930 .... 6.00
Will You Remember, Jeannette McDonald, Nelson Eddy 12.00
Witches Flight, Picture, 1875 .... 20.00
You'll Always Be The One I Love, Sinatra Cover, 1946 .... 12.00 To 15.00
You'll Never Know, Alice Faye, John Payne Cover, 1943 .... 15.00

SHEFFIELD items are listed in the Silver–English and Silver Plate categories.

SHELLEY first appeared on English ceramics about 1912. The Foley China Works started in England in 1860. Joseph Ball Shelley joined the company in 1862 and became a partner in 1872. Percy Shelley joined the firm in 1881. The company went through a series of name changes and in 1910 the then Foley China Company became Shelley China. In 1929 it became Shelley Potteries. The company was acquired in 1966 by Allied English Potteries, then merged with the Doulton group in 1971. The name *Shelley* was put into use again in 1980.

Ashtray, Star Burst, Blue & Green, 4 In. 20.00
Butter, Cover, Blue Rock 90.00
Chocolate Pot, Dainty Blue 95.00
Coffeepot, Begonia, 8 Cup 240.00
Condiment Set, Rose Spray, 4 Piece 375.00
Cup & Saucer, Begonia, 6 Flutes 24.00
Cup & Saucer, Bridal Rose .... 35.00 To 60.00
Cup & Saucer, Celandine 35.00
Cup & Saucer, Crochet 40.00
Cup & Saucer, Daffodil Time 59.00
Cup & Saucer, Dainty Blue 60.00
Cup & Saucer, Foval, Green Handle 70.00
Cup & Saucer, Harebell, Blue 38.00
Cup & Saucer, Hibiscus 38.00
Cup & Saucer, Pink, Gold Handle 42.00
Cup & Saucer, Plate, Flute, Blue Rock, 3 Piece 78.00
Cup & Saucer, Plate, Heather, 3 Piece 78.00
Cup & Saucer, Plate, Woodland, 3 Piece 78.00
Cup & Saucer, Primrose 28.00
Cup & Saucer, Regency 30.00
Cup & Saucer, Tea, Daffodil Time 45.00
Cup & Saucer, Various Flowers, Blue Rim 35.00
Cup & Saucer, Wild Anemone, 6 Flute 55.00
Cup & Saucer, Wild Anemone, Yellow, Pink Roses, Gold Trim 84.00
Cup & Saucer, Woodland, Demitasse .... 35.00 To 42.00
Cup, 6 Flutes, Blue Rock 20.00

Dinner Set, Regency, Serving Pieces, 95 Piece	1650.00
Dish, Baby's Feeding, 3 Bears	115.00
Eggcup, Blue Rock	48.00
Eggcup, Blue Rock, Double	55.00
Eggcup, Lilac	48.00
Eggcup, Rosecrest, Double	70.00
Place Setting, Dainty Blue, 4 Piece	125.00
Plate, Bridal Wreath, 6 In.	20.00
Plate, Pink, 6 In.	22.00
Saucer, Thistle	12.00
Sugar & Creamer, Begonia	60.00
Sugar & Creamer, Bridal Rose	90.00
Tray, Pink & Blue Flowers, Handles, 14 x 15 In.	135.00
Tray, Yellow Roses, Green Leaves, Handles, 14 x 5 1/4 In.	135.00
Vase, Black, 5 In.	42.50

SHIRLEY TEMPLE, the famous movie star, was born in 1928. She made her first movie in 1932. Thousands of items picturing Shirley have been and still are being made. Shirley Temple dolls were first made in 1934 by Ideal Toy Company. Millions of Shirley Temple cobalt blue glass dishes were made by Hazel Atlas Glass Company and U.S. Glass Company from 1934 to 1942. They were given away as premiums for Wheaties and Bisquick. A bowl, mug, and pitcher were made as a breakfast set. Some pieces were decorated with the picture of a very young Shirley, others used a picture of Shirley in her 1936 *Captain January* costume. Although collectors refer to a cobalt creamer, it is actually the 4 1/2-inch-high milk pitcher from the breakfast set. Many of these items are being reproduced today.

Badge, Police	20.00
Book, Just A Little Girl, 1936	30.00
Book, Susannah of The Mounties, 1936	25.00 To 30.00
Cards, Playing, Shirley Wearing Bonnet, Box	50.00
Carriage, Wicker	825.00
Doll, All Original, 1950s, 19 In.	325.00
Doll, American Legion Clothes, Box, 27 In.	1200.00
Doll, Arms Outstretched, 1930s, 18 In.	650.00
Doll, Baby Takes A Bow, Composition, Redressed, 27 In.	850.00
Doll, Bisque, Jointed, Japan, Molded Curls, 1930s, 8 In.	225.00
Doll, Composition Socket Head, Ideal, 1935	1000.00
Doll, Composition, Blue & White Dress, Crazed, 13 In.	500.00
Doll, Composition, Buttons, 1930s, Ideal, 18 In.	335.00
Doll, Composition, Original Red & White Dress, Underwear, NRA Tag, 13 In.	350.00
Doll, Cowgirl, Jointed Composition, All Original	850.00
Doll, Flirty Eyes, Tagged Dress, Ideal, 27 In.	1100.00
Doll, Flirty Sleep Eyes, Jointed, Open Mouth, Ideal, 26 In.	357.50
Doll, Hawaiian, Composition, Leis, 18 In.	900.00
Doll, Heidi, Ideal, 1982, 8 In.	59.00
Doll, Little Colonel, Composition, Madame Alexander	400.00
Doll, Little Colonel, Trunk & Extra Clothing, 13 In.	950.00
Doll, Original Clothes, Purse, 1950s, 12 In.	135.00 To 200.00
Doll, Original Dress, Box, 13 In.	300.00
Doll, Original Wig, Copy of Original Clothes, 20 In.	725.00
Doll, Ranger, 11 In.	900.00
Doll, Shirley Trunk, 3 Original Outfits, 2 Pictures, 16 In.	1400.00
Doll, Sleep Eyes, Composition Body, Little Colonel Dress, Ideal, 13 In.	950.00
Doll, Tin Eyes, Pink, Combed Hair, Original Clothes, Marked S. T. 11, 12 In.	650.00
Doll, Vinyl, 17 In.	150.00
Doll, Vinyl, Red Polka-Dot Dress, Ideal, 1972, 16 In.	225.00
Figurine, Captain January, Porcelain, Certificate, 6 1/2 In.	65.00
Mirror, Round, Pocket	25.00
Movie, Glad Rags To Riches, 8 Mm	15.00
Paper Doll, 1937, Uncut	275.00
Paper Doll, 1942, Uncut	250.00

Paper Doll, Box, 1976, Unopened 25.00
Paper Doll, Saalfield, 1934, Cut 95.00
Paper Doll, Whitman, 13 Uncut Outfits, 1959, 2–3 Ft. 40.00
Photograph, Saying Merry Christmas 50.00
Photograph, Shirley As Teenager, Sepia Tone 5.00
Pitcher, Cobalt Blue .... 20.00 To 65.00
Saltshaker, Figural 50.00
Sheet Music, An Old Straw Hat, Rebecca of Sunnybrook Farm 15.00
Sheet Music, On The Good Ship Lollipop, 1934 .... 40.00
Sheet Music, The Toy Trumpet, Rebecca of Sunnybrook Farm 15.00
Tea Set, 9 Piece 125.00
Trunk, For Large Doll, Stickers 275.00

SHRINER, see Fraternal category

SILVER DEPOSIT glass was made during the late nineteenth and early twentieth centuries. Solid sterling silver was applied to the glass by a chemical method so that a cutout design of silver metal appeared against a clear or colored glass. It is sometimes called silver overlay.

Bowl, Early 20th Century, 10 In. 255.00
Vase, Green Satin, Art Nouveau, Hawkes 375.00
Water Set, Amethyst, 7 Piece 140.00

SILVER FLATWARE includes many of the current and out–of–production silver and silver–plated flatware patterns made in the past eighty years. Other silver is listed under Silver–American, Silver–English, etc. Most silver flatware sets that are missing a few pieces can be completed through the help of one of the many silver matching services listed in *Kovels' Guide to Selling Your Antiques & Collectibles.*

SILVER FLATWARE PLATED, Alhambra, Bouillon Spoon, Gorham 12.00
Alhambra, Butter Spreader, Individual, Gorham 12.00
Alhambra, Cold Meat Fork, Gorham 25.00
Alhambra, Dinner Fork, Gorham 12.00
Alhambra, Fruit Spoon, Gorham 12.00
Alhambra, Pastry Fork, Gorham, 7 In. 15.00
Assyrian Head, Butter Spreader, Individual, Rogers & Bros. 15.00
Assyrian Head, Pickle Fork, Long Handle, Rogers & Bros. 30.00
Berkshire, Dinner Fork, Rogers 12.00
Berkshire, Gravy Ladle, Rogers 25.00
Berkshire, Gumbo Spoon, Rogers 12.00
Berkshire, Sugar Spoon, Rogers 12.00
Camille, Tablespoon, Pierced, International 12.00
Cardinal, Soup Ladle, Wallace 39.00
Daffodil I, Cold Meat Fork, Rogers Bros. 22.00
Daffodil I, Gravy Boat, Rogers 250.00
Daffodil II, Grill Fork, Rogers Bros. 8.00
Danish Princess, Gravy Ladle, Holmes & Edwards 30.00
Danish Princess, Gumbo Soup Spoon, Holmes & Edwards 8.00
Evening Star, Cream Soup Spoon, Community 8.00
Evening Star, Dinner Knife, Community 8.00
Evening Star, Gumbo Soup Spoon, Community 8.00
Evening Star, Salad Fork, Community 8.00
First Love, Dessert Spoon, Oneida 17.00
First Love, Dessert Spoon, Rogers 8.00
First Love, Grill Fork, Rogers 8.00
Formality, Dessert Spoon, State House, Oneida 15.00
Grape, Master Butter, Rogers 18.00
Heritage, Cold Meat Fork, Rogers Bros. 19.00
Heritage, Pastry Server, Piercedrogers Bros. 19.00
Juliet, Soup Spoon, Wallace 13.00
Lady Hamilton, Salad Fork, Community, 6 1/4 In. 8.00
Laurel, Carving Set, Wallace, 3 Piece 165.00
LaVigne, Cold Meat Fork, Rogers 38.00

LaVigne, Gravy Ladle, Rogers 45.00
LaVigne, Service For 6, Oak Chest, Rogers 475.00
LaVigne, Sugar Spoon, Rogers 18.00
Mayflower, Dessert Spoon, Frank Smith 14.00
Richmond, Dessert Spoon, Alvin 15.00
Siren, Soup Ladle, Wallace 43.00
Spring Bouquet, Soup Spoon, International 14.00
Vintage, Dinner Fork, Rogers, 4 Piece 15.00
Vintage, Knife, Hollow Handle, Rogers, 6 Piece 40.00
Vintage, Salad Fork, Rogers, 6 Piece 40.00
Vogue, Dessert Spoon, Manchester 16.00
Wildflower, Dessert Spoon, Royal Crest 14.00
SILVER FLATWARE STERLING, Abbotsford, Jelly Knife, International 95.00
Acorn, Service For 12, Georg Jensen, 100 Piece 7000.00
Adam, Place Setting, Service For 8, Lunt 695.00
Alexandra, Bouillon Spoon, Dominick & Haff 60.00
American Beauty, Iced Tea Spoon, Manchester 20.00
American Beauty, Luncheon Fork, Manchester 19.00
American Beauty, Sardine Fork, Shiebler 85.00
American Directoire, Master Butter, Lunt 12.00
American Directoire, Sugar Spoon, Lunt 13.00
Angelique, Butter Knife, Hollow Handle, International 12.00
Angelique, Place Setting, International 60.00
Anslo, Jelly Ladle, Arthur J. Stone 99.00
Antique Lily, Teaspoon, Whiting 15.00
Antique, Service For 12, Monogram, Wallace, 70 Piece 605.00
Arabesque, Soup Ladle, Whiting 325.00
Armor, Pie Server, Engraved Blade, Whiting 95.00
Baroque, Service For 8, Serving Pieces, Wallace, 76 Piece 1540.00
Belvedere, Luncheon, Place Setting, Lunt 75.00
Bird, Soup Ladle, Wendt 450.00
Bittersweet, Salad Set, Jensen 575.00
Bittersweet, Teaspoon, Jensen 35.00
Bixler, Pudding Server, Gorham, 9 1/2 In. 275.00
Blithe Spirit, Place Setting, Gorham, 4 Piece 74.00
Blithe Spirit, Salad Fork, Gorham 20.00
Blithe Spirit, Sugar Spoon, Gorham 16.00
Blossom Time, Dessert Spoon, International 16.00
Blossom Time, Salad Fork, International 20.00
Botticelli, Dinner Knife, Whiting 45.00
Breton Rose, Sugar Spoon, International 14.00
Bridal Bouquet, Berry Spoon, Alvin 92.00
Bridal Bouquet, Dinner Fork, Alvin, 7 3/4 In. 32.00
Bridal Bouquet, Dinner Knife, Alvin 25.00
Bridal Rose, Cucumber Server, Alvin 135.00
Bridal Rose, Preserve Spoon, Gold Wash, Alvin 95.00
Bridal Rose, Teaspoon, Alvin .... 14.00 To 22.00
Brocade, Cream Soup Spoon, International 28.00
Buckingham, Service For 6, Gorham, 77 Piece 660.00
Buttercup, Bouillon Spoon, Gorham 19.00
Buttercup, Coffee Spoon, Gorham 16.00
Buttercup, Ice Cream Fork, Gorham 50.00
Buttercup, Tomato Server, Gorham 125.00
Cactus, Dessert Knife, Jensen 88.00
Cairo, Berry Spoon, Wallace, 7 5/8 In. .... 25.00 To 35.00
Cambridge, Berry Spoon, International 38.00
Cambridge, Cheese Scoop, Gorham, 5 1/8 In. 55.00
Cambridge, Demitasse Spoon, Gorham, 1899, 6 Piece 50.00
Cambridge, Serving Fork, International, 8 5/8 In. 25.00
Carmel, Sugar Tongs, Wallace 22.00
Cattails, Lemon Fork, Durgin 75.00
Cattails, Pickle Fork, Durgin 75.00
Celeste, Sugar Spoon, Gorham 16.00

Celeste, Teaspoon, Gorham 13.00
Chantilly, Asparagus Tongs, Gorham .... 137.00 To 180.00
Chantilly, Chocolate Muddler, Gorham 70.00
Chantilly, Olive Spoon, Gorham 95.00
Chantilly, Pickle Fork, Gorham .... 16.00 To 28.00
Chantilly, Punch Ladle, Gorham 180.00
Chantilly, Sardine Fork, Gorham 70.00
Chantilly, Service For 8, Gorham, 108 Piece 1250.00
Chantilly, Sugar Sifter, Gold Wash Bowl, Gorham 140.00
Chantilly, Teaspoon, Gorham, 6 Piece 55.00
Chantilly, Youth Set, Gorham, 3 Piece 95.00
Chased Romantique, Cream Soup Spoon, Alvin 15.00
Chateau Rose, Butter Fork, Alvin 13.00
Chateau Rose, Gravy Ladle, Alvin 38.00
Chateau Rose, Jelly Spoon, Alvin 16.00
Chateau, Baked Potato Server, Lunt 22.00
Chateau, Citrus Spoon, Lunt 16.00
Chateau, Gumbo Soup Spoon, Lunt 13.00
Chateau, Luncheon Fork, Lunt 24.00
Chateau, Luncheon Setting, Lunt, 3 Piece 40.00
Chateau, Seafood Fork, Lunt 17.00
Chateau, Sugar Tongs, Lunt 25.00
Chateau, Sugar, Cover, Lunt 22.00
Chatelaine, Berry Spoon, Lunt 75.00
Chatelaine, Oyster Ladle, Lunt 90.00
Chatham, Baked Potato Server, Durgin 21.00
Chatham, Cocktail Fork, Durgin 13.00
Chelsea Manor, Teaspoon, Gorham 13.00
Cheryl, Knife, Kirk, 9 1/8 In. 20.00
Chesterfield, Bouillon Spoon, Gorham, 12 Piece 176.00
Chesterfield, Gravy Ladle, Gorham 48.00
Chippendale, Citrus Spoon, Gorham 13.00
Chippendale, Dessert Spoon, Gorham, 7 3/8 In. 12.00
Chippendale, Lemon Fork, Lunt 14.00
Chippendale, Sugar Tongs, Lunt 26.00
Chrysanthemum, Berry Spoon, Gold Wash Bowl, Durgin 400.00
Chrysanthemum, Bouillon Spoon, Durgin 25.00
Chrysanthemum, Lettuce Fork, Durgin 230.00
Chrysanthemum, Tablespoon, Gorham 26.00
Chrysanthemum, Teaspoon, Gorham 8.00
Cinderella, Teaspoon, Gorham 6.00
Classique, Lemon Fork, Gorham 10.00
Classique, Place Setting, Gorham, 3 Piece 53.00
Classique, Serving Spoon, Pierced, Gorham 40.00
Clinton, Butter Knife, Stieff 15.00
Clinton, Dinner Fork, Stieff 29.00
Clinton, Knife, Stieff, 8 3/4 In. 9.00
Clinton, Sugar Spoon, Stieff 7.00
Cluny, Fish Slice, Gorham 350.00
Cluny, Ice Cream Knife, Gorham 375.00
Cluny, Toast Fork, Gorham 175.00
Colfax, Citrus Spoon, Durgin 16.00
Colfax, Gumbo Soup Spoon, Durgin 21.00
Colonial Bead, Knife, Weidlich, 9 1/2 In. 15.00
Colonial Rose, Cream Soup Spoon, Amston 13.00
Colonial Rose, Salad Fork, Amston 16.00
Colonial Theme, Iced Tea Spoon, Lunt 19.00
Colonial Theme, Serving Spoon, Lunt 39.00
Colonial, Ice Cream Spoon, Gorham 25.00
Colonial, Lettuce Fork, Towle 150.00
Colonial, Serving Spoon, Pierced, Gorham 21.00
Colonial, Soup Ladle, Gorham 165.00
Colonnade, Dinner Setting, Manchester 45.00

Concord, Butter Fork, Concord Silversmiths	12.00
Concord, Cocktail Fork, Concord Silversmiths	13.00
Contour, Citrus Spoon, Towle	18.00
Contour, Ice Cream Fork, Towle	18.00
Contour, Ice Cream Spoon, Towle	16.00
Copenhagen, Baked Potato Server, Manchester	26.00
Copenhagen, Cocktail Fork, Manchester	13.00
Corinthian, Salad Set, Gorham	265.00
Coronet, Teaspoon, Knowles	7.00
Corsage, Coffee Spoon, Monogram, Stieff	9.00
Corsage, Lettuce Fork, Kirk–Stieff	85.00
Corsage, Sugar Spoon, Monogram, Stieff	18.00
Country Manor, Salad Fork, Towle	20.00
Country Manor, Teaspoon, Towle	15.00
Cromwell, Bouillon Spoon, Gorham	22.00
Cromwell, Ice Cream Fork, Gorham	25.00
Cupid, Master Butter, Dominick & Haff	45.00
Cupid, Sugar Shell, Dominick & Haff	35.00
Cupid, Sugar Tongs, Dominick & Haff	40.00
D'Orleans, Tomato Server, Towle	65.00
Damask Rose, Baked Potato Server, Oneida	27.00
Damask Rose, Iced Tea Spoon, Oneida	20.00
Damask Rose, Place Setting, Oneida	55.00
Deerfield, Olive Spoon, International	14.00
Dorothy Vernon, Beef Fork, Whiting	75.00
Douvain, Demitasse Spoon Set, Unger, 12 Piece	500.00
Dresden Scroll, Place Setting, Luncheon, Lunt	75.00
Dresden, Berry Spoon, Whiting	115.00
Dresden, Sardine Fork, Whiting	65.00
Duke of York, Berry Spoon, Whiting	75.00
Duke of York, Cold Meat Fork, Whiting	55.00
Duke of York, Pea Spoon, Pierced, Whiting	125.00
Egyptian, Serving Spoon, Whiting	45.00
Empire, Seafood Fork, Whiting	13.00
Empire, Sugar Sifter, Towle	30.00
Empress, Iced Tea Spoon, Knowles	6.00
Empress, Tablespoon, Knowles	22.00
Enchantress, Place Setting, International	55.00
Enchantress, Tablespoon, International	34.00
Etruscan, Luncheon Fork, Gorham	19.00
Fairfax, Bouillon Spoon, Durgin	9.00
Fairfax, Dinner Knife, Durgin	17.00
Fairfax, Gumbo Soup Spoon	17.00
Fairfax, Service For 8, Gorham, 136 Piece	2090.00
Fairfax, Teaspoon, Durgin	9.00
Federal Cotillion, Salad Fork, Frank W. Smith	32.50
Festival, Teaspoon, Lunt, 6 In.	6.00
Firelight, Butter Knife, Gorham	11.00
Firelight, Carving Set, Gorham	28.00
Firelight, Dessert Spoon, Gorham	24.00
First Frost, Butter Knife, Oneida	6.00
First Frost, Iced Tea Spoon, Oneida	16.00
First Frost, Luncheon Setting, Service For 6, Oneida	32.00
First Frost, Salad Fork, Oneida	20.00
First Frost, Soup Spoon, Oneida	17.00
First Frost, Tablespoon, Oneida	36.00
First Frost, Teaspoon, Oneida	14.00
Fleury, Gumbo Soup Spoon, Gorham	13.00
Fleury, Teaspoon, Gorham, 5 3/4 In.	8.00
Floral Lace, Cocktail Fork, Lunt	15.00
Floral Lace, Sugar Spoon, Lunt	10.00
Florentine Scroll, Butter Knife, Lunt	12.00
Florentine Scroll, Place Setting, Lunt, 4 Piece	84.00

Florentine Scroll, Teaspoon, Lunt	15.00
Florentine, Teaspoon, Kirk	14.00
Flower Lane, Fork, Oneida, 7 3/8 In.	15.00
Fontaine, Sugar Spoon, Knowles	10.00
Fontainebleau, Sugar Tongs, Gorham, 5 In.	75.00
Formality, Gravy Ladle, State House, Oneida	17.00
Formality, Grill Fork, State House, Oneida	9.00
Formality, Grill Knife, State House, Oneida	13.00
Formality, Grill Setting, Service For 12, State House, Oneida	42.00
Formality, Napkin Clip, State House, Oneida	9.00
Foxhall, Butter Fork, Watson	14.00
Foxhall, Fork, Watson, 7 In.	16.00
Foxhall, Knife, Watson, 9 1/8 In.	9.00
Foxhall, Salad Fork, Watson	9.00
Francis I, Asparagus Server, Reed & Barton	180.00
Francis I, Cheese Scoop, Reed & Barton	55.00
Francis I, Fish Serving Knife, Reed & Barton	175.00
Francis I, Mustard Spoon, Alvin	45.00
Francis I, Punch Ladle, Reed & Barton	300.00
Francis I, Soup Ladle, Reed & Barton	250.00
Francis I, Tomato Fork, Alvin	65.00
French Regency, Cold Meat Fork, Wallace	75.00
French Regency, Salad Fork, Wallace	25.00
French Renaissance, Place Setting, Reed & Barton	70.00
Frontenac, Cocktail Fork, International	25.00
Frontenac, Salad Fork, International	64.00
Gadroon, Cocktail Fork, International	14.00
Gadroon, Cream Soup Spoon, International	23.00
Gadroonette, Cream Soup Spoon, Manchester	10.00
Gadroonette, Fork, Manchester, 9 5/8 In.	14.00
Gadroonette, Knife, Manchester, 8 7/8 In.	15.00
Gadroonette, Potato Server, Manchester	24.00
Gadroonette, Service For 8, Manchester, 53 Piece	850.00
George & Martha, Luncheon Fork, Wallace	13.00
George II, Luncheon Setting, Watson, 4 Piece	91.00
George II, Salad Fork, Watson	29.00
George II, Teaspoon, Watson, 5 7/8 In.	16.00
George III, Meat Skewer, Whiting, 1816, 12 1/2 In.	60.00
George III, Oyster Server, Whiting	75.00
Georgian, Sugar Sifter, Towle, 1898	50.00
Golden Scroll, 4–Piece Setting, Gorham	175.00
Golden Scroll, Gravy Spoon, Gorham	140.00
Golden Scroll, Sauce Ladle, Gorham	125.00
Golden Scroll, Spoon, Gorham	50.00
Golden Scroll, Sugar, Gorham	50.00
Golden Scroll, Tablespoon, Pierced, Gorham	140.00
Grand Baroque, Service For 12, Wallace, 101 Pc. ....*Illus*	5000.00
Grand Colonial, Luncheon, Setting, Wallace	68.00
Grand Colonial, Service For 12, Wallace, 84 Piece	1400.00
Grand Regency, Cheese Server, International	35.00
Grand Regency, Sugar Spoon, International	35.00
Grand Regency, Teaspoon, International	30.00
Grande Renaissance, Place Setting, Reed & Barton	70.00
Greenbrier, Service For 8, Gorham, 82 Picce	605.00
Greenfield, Lettuce Fork, Knowles	40.00
Hanover, Ice Cream Slice, Gorham	250.00
Hanover, Pea Spoon, Gorham	250.00
Helen, Citrus Spoon, Easterling	16.00
Helen, Ice Cream Spoon, Easterling	14.00
Hepplewhite, Stuffing Spoon, Reed & Barton	150.00
Heraldic, Punch Ladle, Watson	395.00
Heraldic, Serving Spoon, Whiting	121.00
Homewood, Butter Knife, Stieff	16.00

♦♦♦♦♦♦♦♦♦♦♦♦♦♦♦♦♦♦♦♦♦♦♦

Flatware that is used regularly should be polished just once or twice a year.

♦♦♦♦♦♦♦♦♦♦♦♦♦♦♦♦♦♦♦♦♦♦♦

♦♦♦♦♦♦♦♦♦♦♦♦♦♦♦♦♦♦♦♦♦♦♦

Never put silverware and stainless-steel flatware in the dishwasher basket together. The stainless can damage the silver.

♦♦♦♦♦♦♦♦♦♦♦♦♦♦♦♦♦♦♦♦♦♦♦

Silver Flatware Sterling, Grand Baroque,

Service For 12, Wallace, 101 Pc.

Homewood, Fork, Stieff, 7 3/8 In.	29.00
Horizon, Baked Potato Serving Fork, Easterling	29.00
Horizon, Citrus Spoon, Easterling	16.00
Hunt Club, Butter Spreader, Gorham	7.00
Hunt Club, Demitasse Spoon, Gorham	7.00
Hunt Club, Ice Cream Spoon, Gorham	16.00
Hyperion, Berry Spoon, Whiting	95.00
Hyperion, Gravy Ladle, Whiting	75.00
Ice Cream Fork, Gorham	17.00
Imperial Chrysanthemum, Tablespoon, Gorham	5.00
Imperial Queen, Asparagus Fork, Whiting	350.00
Imperial Queen, Bonbon Spoon, Whiting	28.00
Imperial Queen, Cheese Scoop, Whiting	125.00
Imperial Queen, Lettuce Fork, Whiting	195.00
Imperial Queen, Serving Set, Whiting, 2 Piece	198.00
Imperial Queen, Tablespoon, Whiting	30.00
Imperial, Luncheon Fork, Gorham	22.00
Inaugural, Cream Soup Spoon, State House, Oneida	12.00
Inaugural, Grapefruit Spoon, State House, Oneida	13.00
Inaugural, Soup Spoon, State House, Oneida	15.00
Intermezzo, Butter Knife, National	39.00
Intermezzo, Citrus Spoon, National	15.00
Irian, Soup Spoon, Wallace	45.00
Irian, Tablespoon, Wallace	55.00
Jefferson, Cocktail Fork, Lunt	10.00
Jefferson, Knife, Lunt, 9 5/8 In.	14.00
Jefferson, Serving Spoon, Pierced, Lunt	32.00
Joan of Arc, Citrus Spoon, International	14.00
Joan of Arc, Salt Spoon, International	11.00
John & Priscilla, Gravy Ladle, Westmoreland	32.00
John & Priscilla, Teaspoon, Westmoreland	12.00
Joy, Citrus Spoon, International	18.00
Juliana, Salad Fork, Watson	14.00
Juliana, Teaspoon, Watson, 6 In.	8.00
Juliet, Serving Spoon, Wallace	10.00
Kenmore, Bouillon Spoon, Alvin	7.00
Kenmore, Cocktail Fork, Alvin	10.00
Kenmore, Gumbo Soup Spoon, Alvin	11.00
King Albert, Baked Potato Server, Whiting	25.00
King Albert, Fork, Whiting, 7 1/4 In.	13.00

King Albert, Ice Cream Fork, Whiting 18.00
King Cedric, Baked Potato Server, Oneida 25.00
King Cedric, Cold Meat Fork, Oneida 28.00
King Christian, Cream Soup Spoon, Wallace 14.00
King Edward, Bouillon Spoon, Whiting 25.00
King Edward, Dinner Knife, Whiting 50.00
King Edward, Fish Fork, Whiting 75.00
King Edward, Teaspoon, Gorham 16.00
King Edward, Teaspoon, Whiting 25.00
King George, Sauce Ladle, Gorham 60.00
King George, Sugar Tongs, Gorham 48.00
King's Court, Cream Soup Spoon, Whiting 16.00
King, Cocktail Fork, Kirk 16.00
King, Salad Fork, Dominick & Haff 90.00
L'Elegante, Gumbo Soup Spoon, Reed & Barton 25.00
La Parisienne, Sugar Sifter, Reed & Barton 47.00
La Reine, Iced Tea Spoon, Wallace 16.00
La Scala, Ice Cream Fork, Gorham 22.00
La Strada, Citrus Spoon, International 20.00
Lady Diana, Baked Potato Fork, Towle 22.00
Lady Diana, Bread Knife, Towle 18.00
Lancaster, Asparagus Fork, Gorham 225.00
Lancaster, Berry Spoon, Gorham 68.00
Lancaster, Bouillon Spoon, Gorham 25.00
Langdon, Salad Fork, Fessenden 8.00
Lansdowne, Butter Spreader, Gorham 19.00
Lansdowne, Iced Tea Spoon, Gorham 29.00
Lansdowne, Serving Spoon, Gorham 33.00
Lastrada, Salad Fork, International 18.00
Lenore, Baked Potato Server, Manchester 28.00
Les Six Fleurs, Fish Server, Reed & Barton 303.00
Les Six Fleurs, Salad Fork & Spoon, Reed & Barton 405.00
Lily of The Valley, Demitasse Spoon, Whiting 15.00
Lily of The Valley, Demitasse Spoon, Whiting, 12 Piece, Case 176.00
Lily of The Valley, Dessert Spoon, Whiting 48.00
Lily of The Valley, Luncheon Fork, Whiting 32.00
Lily, Cake Knife, Whiting 45.00
Lily, Creamer, Whiting 48.00
Lily, Punch Ladle, Whiting .... 245.00 To 300.00
Linden, English Server, Saart 19.00
Linden, Teaspoon, Saart 6.00
Livingston, Berry Spoon, Whiting 70.00
Lorna Doone, Berry Spoon, Alvin, 9 In. 34.00
Louis XIV, Dinner Knife, Towle 18.00
Louis XIV, Salt Spoon, Gorham, 1870, 3 1/2 In. .... 15.00 To 18.00
Louis XV, Bouillon Spoon, Whiting, 12 Piece 25.00
Louis XV, Chocolate Spoon, Whiting 25.00
Louis XV, Cocktail Fork, Durgin 19.00
Louis XV, Cracker Scoop, Whiting 195.00
Louis XV, Ice Cream Slice, Whiting 135.00
Louis XV, Oyster Server, Gorham, 9 1/2 In. 295.00
Louis XV, Punch Ladle, Whiting 350.00
Louis XV, Salad Fork, Whiting 45.00
Louis XVI, Dinner Fork, Gorham 45.00
Louvre, Asparagus Server, Shiebler 250.00
Louvre, Berry Spoon, Wood & Hughes 125.00
Louvre, Cold Meat Fork, Wallace 75.00
Louvre, Luncheon Fork, Wood & Hughes 35.00
Louvre, Preserve Spoon, Wood & Hughes 45.00
Louvre, Sauce Ladle, Shiebler 50.00
Love Disarmed, Ice Cream Slice, Whiting 235.00
Love Disarmed, Toast Server, Whiting 275.00
Lucerne, Berry Spoon, Wallace 95.00

Lucerne, Butter Pick, Wallace	75.00
Lucerne, Fish Slice, Wallace, 11 1/2 In.	225.00
Lucerne, Sugar Tongs, Wallace	35.00
Luxembourg, Cheese Scoop, Gorham, 8 1/4 In.	110.00
Lyric, Berry Spoon, Gorham	100.00
Lyric, Demitasse Spoon, Gorham	7.00
Madame Jumel, Salad Fork, 3 Tines, Whiting	15.75
Madame Jumel, Sugar Tongs, Whiting	35.00
Majestic, Chocolate Spoon, Alvin	30.00
Majestic, Dinner Knife, Alvin	40.00
Manchester, Butter Knife, Manchester	9.00
Manchester, Demitasse Spoon, Manchester	8.00
Mary Chilton, Olive Spoon, Towle	25.00
Maryland, Fruit Spoon, Alvin	12.00
Masterpiece, Teaspoon, International	17.00
Mazarin, Fried Egg Server, Dominick & Haff, 8 In.	75.00
Meadow, Dinner Fork, Whiting	20.00
Melrose, Dessert Fork, Alvin	25.00
Melrose, Service For 12, Serving Pieces, Gorham, 82 Piece	1430.00
Milburn Rose, Luncheon Fork, Westmoreland	15.00
Minuet, Jelly Server, International	12.00
Molly Stark, Butter Knife, Alvin	13.00
Monticello, Teaspoon, Lunt, 12 Piece	55.00
Mount Vernon, Baby Set, Lunt	50.00
Mount Vernon, Food Pusher, Lunt	45.00
Mount Vernon, Lemon Fork, Lunt	20.00
Mount Vernon, Strawberry Fork, Lunt	25.00
Mythologique, Demitasse Spoon, Gorham	35.00
Mythologique, Dinner Fork, Gorham	25.00
Narcissus, Tablespoon, Unger	60.00
Narcissus, Teaspoon, Unger, 6 Piece	210.00
New Art, Berry Spoon, Dominick & Haff	325.00
New Kings, Dessert Spoon, Dominick & Haff	40.00
New Standish, Ice Cream Fork, Durgin	16.00
Nocturne, Service For 12, Serving Pieces, Gorham, 108 Piece	935.00
Nuremburg, Cracker Scoop, Alvin	250.00
Nuremburg, Fork, Alvin	30.00
Nuremburg, Salad Fork, Alvin	42.00
Old Baronial, Luncheon Fork, Gorham	23.00
Old Baronial, Salad Fork, Gorham	30.00
Old Baronial, Teaspoon, Gorham	25.00
Old Charleston, Iced Tea Spoon, International	15.00
Old Colonial, Dinner Fork, Towle	4.00
Old Colonial, Tablespoon, Towle	60.00
Old Colonial, Wedding Cake Knife, Towle	27.00
Old English, Salad Fork, Towle	28.00
Old Newbury, Cream Ladle, Towle	30.00
Old Newbury, Luncheon Fork, Towle	15.00
Old Newbury, Parfait Spoon, Towle	15.00
Old Newbury, Tablespoon, Towle	22.00
Onslow, Iced Tea Spoon, Tuttle	40.00
Orange Blossom, Asparagus Fork, Alvin	650.00
Orange Blossom, Berry Spoon, Alvin	150.00
Orange Blossom, Butter Pick, Alvin	125.00
Orange Blossom, Cold Meat Fork, Alvin	245.00
Orange Blossom, Fish Slice, Alvin	345.00
Orange Blossom, Gumbo Soup Spoon, Alvin	65.00
Orange Blossom, Lettuce Fork, Alvin	185.00
Orange Blossom, Luncheon Fork, Alvin	35.00
Orange Blossom, Luncheon Knife, Alvin	24.00
Orient, Berry Spoon, Alvin	85.00
Orient, Sugar Spoon, Alvin	35.00
Phoebe, Almond Scoop, Watson Newell	90.00

Pine Spray, Teaspoon, International	16.00
Plymouth, Pastry Fork, Gorham, 6 Piece	180.00
Pompadour, Cake Server, Whiting	135.00
Pompadour, Cheese Scoop, Whiting	95.00
Pompadour, Cold Meat Fork, Whiting	40.00
Pompadour, Oyster Ladle, Whiting	195.00
Pompadour, Sauce Ladle, Whiting	33.00
Poppy, Ladle, Gorham, 13 1/2 In.	357.50
Prince Eugene, Dinner Fork, Alvin	25.00
Prince Eugene, Luncheon Fork, Alvin	23.00
Prince Eugene, Teaspoon, Alvin	23.00
Princess Mary, Cold Meat Fork, Wallace	36.00
Princess Mary, Pickle Fork, Wallace	14.00
Princess, Gravy Ladle, Watson	40.00
Psyche, Teaspoon, Watson Newell	50.00
Raindrop, Cold Meat Fork, Lunt	36.00
Raleigh, Food Pusher, Alvin	45.00
Rambler Rose, Berry Spoon, Towle, Large	95.00
Rambler Rose, Dinner Service, Towle, 46 Piece	900.00
Renaissance Scroll, Place Setting, Reed & Barton, 4 Piece	75.00
Repousse, Bacon Fork, Gorham	65.00
Repousse, Bacon Fork, Kirk	85.00
Repousse, Butter Knife, Kirk	15.00 To 18.00
Repousse, Cream Soup Spoon, Kirk	22.00
Repousse, Ice Cream Server, Kirk	125.00
Repousse, Ice Tongs, Gorham	85.00
Repousse, Iced Tea Spoon, Kirk	26.00
Repousse, Pie Server, Kirk–Stieff	65.00
Repousse, Punch Ladle, Gorham	300.00
Repousse, Salad Set, Gorham	170.00
Repousse, Serving Fork, Kirk–Stieff	165.00
Repousse, Teaspoon, Kirk	12.00
Repousse, Tomato Server, Kirk	62.00 To 65.00
Rhapsody, Knife, International	17.00
Rhapsody, Serving Spoon, International	42.00
Richmond, Luncheon Fork, Alvin	18.00
Richmond, Luncheon Knife, Alvin	15.00
Romantique, Teaspoon, Alvin	16.00
Rose, Butter Knife, Kirk	16.00 To 18.00
Rose, Demitasse Spoon, Kirk	13.00
Rose, Fork, Wallace, 7 In.	25.00
Rose, Knife, Kirk	23.00
Rose, Salad Fork, Kirk	28.00
Rose, Serving Fork, Kirk	29.00
Rose, Strawberry Spoon, Kirk	95.00
Rose, Tablespoon, Kirk	42.00
Rose, Teaspoon, Kirk	15.00
Royal Danish, Cream Spoon, International	22.00
Royal Danish, Gravy Ladle, International	48.00
Royal Danish, Luncheon Setting, International	85.00
Serenity, Service For 8, International, 48 Piece	340.00
Signet, Demitasse Spoon, Kirk	7.00
Southern Colonial, Butter Knife, Master, International	20.00
Southern Colonial, Cream Soup Spoon, International	18.00
Spring Glory, Serving Fork, International	19.00
St. Dunstan, Fork, Gorham, 7 3/4 In.	35.00
St. Dunstan, Knife, Gorham, 9 1/2 In.	35.00
Stanton Hall, Dinner Setting, Oneida	75.00
Strasbourg, Fish Fork, Gorham	55.00
Strasbourg, Salad Set, Gorham	165.00
Stratford, Cold Meat Fork, International	35.00
Stratford, Gravy Ladle, International	83.00
Strawberry, Pastry Server, Durgin	140.00

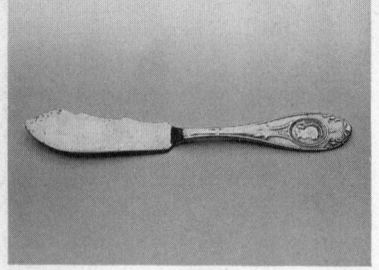

When buying silver with bright cut design, avoid worn pieces. Best prices are paid for silver with clear, crisp designs.

Silver Plate, Butter Knife, Medallion

Head, 7 1/4 In.

Trianon, Cocktail Fork, International	10.00
Trianon, Serving Fork, International	75.00
Versailles, Gravy Ladle, Gorham, Large	455.00
Versailles, Gravy Ladle, Gorham, Small	105.00
Versailles, Sugar Sifter, Gold Wash, Gorham	250.00
Victoria, Carving Set, Whiting, 2 Piece	50.00
Victoria, Dinner Knife, Watson	30.00
Victoria, Teaspoon, Wood & Hughes	17.00
Violet, Luncheon Fork, Wallace	15.00
Violet, Luncheon Fork, Whiting	32.00
Violet, Luncheon Knife, Wallace	27.00
Violet, Olive Fork, Whiting	48.00
Violet, Service For 8, Wallace	525.00
Violet, Teaspoon, Wallace	12.00
Virginia, Dinner Fork, Gorham, 12 Piece	248.00
Wellesley, Salad Fork, International	30.00
Wild Rose, Cream Soup Spoon, International	18.00
Wild Rose, Dinner Fork, International	24.00
William & Mary, Place Setting, Lunt	50.00
William & Mary, Salad Set, Lunt	140.00
Windsor, Fish Slice, Towle, 11 1/4 In.	100.00

SILVER PLATE is not solid silver. It is a ware made of a metal, such as nickel or copper, that is covered with a thin coating of silver. The letters *EPNS* are often found on American and English silver–plated wares. Sheffield silver is a type of silver plate.   Ⓔ Ⓟ Ⓝ Ⓢ

Basket, Bonbon, Vintage Pattern, Grape Clusters On Handle, 7 1/2 In.	275.00
Basket, Cake, Handle, Pairpoint	52.00
Basket, Fruit Pattern, Pairpoint	55.00
Basket, Ruffled Rim, Birds, Worms, Butterflies, Tufts, 19th Century, 10 In.	165.00
Basket, Square, Handle, Pairpoint	120.00
Bell, Wallace, 1972	300.00
Biscuit Warmer, Victorian, 9 In.	770.00
Bowl, Nut, Oak Leaves, Squirrels, Rockford Quadruple Plate, 4 x 7 In.	150.00
Bowl, Vegetable, On Copper, Vintage Rim, Oval, Sheffield, 11 1/4 In.	22.00
Box, Cigar, Victorian, Birds, Dogs & Foliage Design, Rockford Silver Co.	700.00
Box, Dresser, Art Nouveau, Woman Filial, 6 x 7 In.	195.00
Box, Jewelry, Cherub On Globe, Simpson, Hall, Miller	325.00
Box, Jewelry, Pincushion Beaded Scalloped Cover, Embossed Floral, Derby	85.00
Buffeteria, Bakelite Handles In Tray	975.00
Bun Warmer, Victorian, Pierced Liner, Ball & Claw Feet	248.00
Butter Knife, Medallion Head, 7 1/4 In. ....*Illus*	6.00
Butter, Chain & Ball, Pull To Open	550.00
Butter, Resting Cow On Lid, Insert & Knife Rest, 1880s	125.00
Butter, Revolving Top	170.00
Butter, Revolving, Simpson, Hall, Miller	350.00

Silver Plate, Inkstand, Boat Shape, Sheffield, 1785, 14 In.; Silver Plate,

Coffeepot, Rococo, Pear Shape, John Winter, 1765, 12 In.; Silver Plate,

Candlestick, Telescopic, Cut Glass, M. Boulton, 1800, 12 1/4 In., Pair.

Candlestick, Telescopic, Cut Glass, M. Boulton, 1800, 12 1/4 In., Pair ....*Illus*	1540.00
Chamberstick & Snuffer, George III, Sheffield, Early 19th Century, 5 1/2 In.	165.00
Coaster, Bottle, Sheffield, Early 19th Century, 6 1/2 In., Pair	220.00
Cocktail Shaker, Golf Ball Finial, Golf Bag Shape	515.00
Cocktail Shaker, Milk Can Shape	44.00
Coffee Urn, Lion Mounts, Gadroon Edge, Sheffield, 19th Century, 17 In.	825.00
Coffeepot, Angular Spout, Ebonized Side Handle, France, 8 1/8 In.	880.00
Coffeepot, Burner, Chased Florals Allover, Ivory Handle, Hartford Silver Co.	350.00
Coffeepot, Engraved With Foliate Design, Pinecone Finial	88.00
Coffeepot, George III, Early 19th Century, Sheffield, 8 3/4 In.	200.00
Coffeepot, Rococo, Pear Shape, John Winter, 1765, 12 In. ....*Illus*	2970.00
Coffeepot, Triangular Handle, Finial Lid, Reed & Barton, 9 In.	110.00
Compote, Boat Shape, Tooled & Soldier Head Handles, 5 In.	45.00
Cruet, Egg, 6 Holes, Circular Tripod, Center Stem, Elkington & Co., 1878	200.00
Cup, Baby's, Engraved Word Baby	30.00
Dish, Cross, Sheffield, Early 19th Century, 12 1/2 In.	300.00
Dish, Ring, Figural, Cat, Embossed	35.00
Dish, Serving, 2 Part Handles, Repousse Shell, Foliate Design	88.00
Dish, Serving, Cover, Warming Compartment, England	120.00
Dish, Serving, Cover, Wirework Handle, Oval	520.00
Dish, Serving, Disappearing Domed Cover, Oval, 14 In.	205.00
Dish, Serving, George IV, Lion Mask & Ring Handles, Lion Paw Feet	300.00
Dish, Vegetable, Cover, Oval, 11 In.	15.00
Dresser Set, Victorian, 3 Brushes, Mirror	100.00
Epergne, Cherub, 3 Hinged Hoops, Reed & Barton, 19th Century, 9 x 8 In.	2500.00
Flask, Hip, Molded Face of Bacchus, Godinger 1983	70.00
Food Warmer, Domed Base & Handle, Adjustable Arms, Wilcox	110.00
Game Dome, Engraved Crest, Arched Handle, Matthew Bolton, 19 In.	1100.00
Ice Bucket, 9 3/4 In.	55.00
Inkstand, Boat Shape, Sheffield, 1785, 14 In. ....*Illus*	1430.00
Kettle, On Stand, Repousse Plum Tree, Rogers Smith & Co., 19 In.	605.00
Kettle, On Stand, Sheffield, Early 19th Century, 10 3/4 In.	330.00
Knife Rest, Animal Or Bird, Gallia, Box, 3 3/4 In., 12 Piece	4620.00
Ladle, Assyrian Head, Rogers, 11 In.	30.00
Ladle, Marked W. H. & S. B. P., 12 3/4 In.	27.00
Lazy Susan, 8 Eggcups, 8 x 9 In.	135.00
Mirror & Brush, Art Nouveau, Cherub, 2 Piece	95.00
Mirror, Dressing, Double Candlearms, Oval, 19th Century, 27 In.	770.00
Mirror, Dressing, Floral Design, Rectangular, c.1880, 20 x 18 1/2 In.	1700.00
Mirror, Hand, Art Nouveau, Beveled, Figural Cupid Handle	125.00

Mug, Art Nouveau, Engraved Lettie, Rogers, Smith & Co., 1881	90.00
Napkin rings are listed in their own category	
Pitcher, Gorham, 4 1/2 Pt.	85.00
Pitcher, Water, Engraved Inscription, Feb. 24, 1881, Reed & Barton, Fancy	750.00
Pitcher, Water, Monogrammed, Meriden Britannia, 7 In.	225.00
Platter, King Francis, Gravy Well, Reed & Barton, 22 In.	120.00
Punch Bowl, Glass Etched Panels, Double Handle, Floral, 17 In.	1045.00
Punch Cup, Gorham	12.00
Punch Set, 8 Pedestal Cups, Ladle, 10 Piece	925.00
Punch Set, Scrolled & Acanthus Chased, Lion Ring Handles, England, 19 Piece	550.00
Relish Tray, Glass Insert, 1847 Rogers	65.00
Salt & Pepper, Jug Shape, Handle, Engraved	35.00
Salt, Double Wolf, Master	100.00
Salver, Scalloped & Gadrooned Border, Shell Design, American, 18 In.	90.00
Salver, Zeus In Chariot, Putti, Tritons Border, Mappin Bros., 26 1/2 In.	2400.00
Spoon Holder, Figure of Draped Child Handle, Simpson, Hall, Miller	125.00
Spoon Holder, Victorian Woman, Holding Umbrella, Holder For 12 Spoons	285.00
Spoon, souvenir, see Souvenir category	
Spooner, Handle, Ornate Base, 16 In.	75.00
Stand, Flower, Grapevines, Conical Form, c.1820, 26 1/2 In.	310.00
Sugar & Creamer, Engraved Banding & Medallion, Scroll Handles	175.00
Sugar, Holder, Bird Finial, Patent 1923, For 12 Spoons	95.00
Syrup, Nappin & Webb, 1913	165.00
Syrup, Woman's Head Finial Lid & Handle, Meriden	195.00
Tazza, Frosted Bowl, Indians Hunting Buffalo On Base, Reed & Barton, c.1870	192.00
Tea Infuser, Tee–Kugel, Hans Pryzrembel, Wishbone Shape Handle, 6 In.	880.00
Tea Set, Art Nouveau, Flowers, Leaves, Fishscale Handles, Wilcox Co., 5 Piece	475.00
Tea Set, Eternally Yours, With Tray, 4 Piece	425.00
Tea Set, Flair, 1847 Rogers, 4 Piece	350.00
Tea Set, Winthrop Pattern, Reed & Barton, 7 Piece	1430.00
Tea Strainer, Spoon Handle, F. Co., 1911	20.00
Tea Urn, Egyptian Revival, Sphinx Finial, Greek Key Banding, c.1840, 17 In.	660.00
Teapot, Bamboo Shaped Spout & Handle, Raised Figures & Trees	95.00
Teapot, Floral Design, Leaf Spout, Sheffield, 19th Century, 8 1/2 In.	935.00
Teapot, Laurence B. Smith, 1900	200.00
Toast Rack, 6 Sections, Center Handle, Four Bun Feet, Hukin & Heath, 1881	560.00
Toast Rack, Art Deco	27.50
Toothpick, Pair of Boots Shape, Aurora	110.00
Toothpick, Take Your Pick, Handle	20.00
Tray, Allover Bands of Fanciful Animals & Florals, Persian, 25 x 21 In.	165.00
Tray, Assyrian Head, Meriden	225.00
Tray, C–Scroll & Acanthus, Gadroon Handles & Rim, Crescent, 25 1/2 In.	330.00
Tray, Coat of Arms, Gadrooned Rim, Sheffield, 30 x 19 In.	495.00
Tray, Floral & C–Scroll Border & Handles, Walker & Hall, 25 In.	165.00
Tray, Floral Engraving, Reticulated Gallery, Wooden Handles, Oblong, 21 3/4 In.	85.00
Tray, Footed, Sheffield, 18th Century, 14 1/4 In.	192.00
Tray, Grape Pattern, Presentation, 1854, 26 1/2 x 18 In.	1000.00
Tray, Molded Grapevine Border, 2 Handles, Rectangular, 20 In.	150.00
Tray, Profile Medallions, Engraved Design, Reed & Barton, 31 3/4 x 19 1/2 In.	110.00
Tray, Tea, Scroll–Cast Handles, Reeded Rim, Rectangular, 24 x 18 In.	310.00
Tray, Tea, Victorian Border, 35 In.	850.00
Tray, Warming, Double, 2 Covered Inserts, 4 Paw Feet, 9 x 24 x 14 In.	300.00
Tureen, Georgian, Scrolled Handles, 5 1/2 x 9 In., Pair	440.00
Tureen, Revolving, Scrolling Design, Hoof Feet, 14 In.	210.00
Urn, Tea, William IV, Inverted Floral Finial, Scroll Handles, c.1840, 17 1/2 In.	220.00
Urn, Water, Sheffield, 19th Century, 13 In.	192.00
Vase, Gold Wash, Lace White Porcelain Insert, Wm. Rogers, 1922, 16 In.	115.00
Vase, Raised Grape & Vine Design, Monogrammed, Hexagonal, 27 3/4 In.	105.00
Vegetable, Cover, Monogrammed, Lid Has Removable Handle, Oblong, 11 1/2 In.	25.00
Wine Cooler, Grape & Vine Rim, Lion Mask & Ring Handles, Sheffield, 6 1/2 In.	120.00
Wine Cooler, Grape Design, Meriden, 1893	125.00
Wine Cooler, Half Gadroon Body, Lion Head Handles, Sheffield, 6 In., Pair	1540.00
Wine Cooler, Reeded Campagna Form, 19th Century, 8 In., Pair	1430.00

SILVER, SHEFFIELD, see Silver Plate; Silver–English

SILVER–AMERICAN. American silver is listed here. Most of the sterling silver listed in this book is subdivided by country. There are also other pieces of silver and silver plate listed under special categories, such as Napkin Ring, Silver Plate, Silver Flatware, Silver–Sterling, and Tiffany Silver.

SILVER–AMERICAN, Basket, Engraved Scroll Design, Gorham, 18 1/2 In.	1430.00
Basket, Fruit, Pierced Bulbous Body, Woodside Sterling Co., 11 1/2 In.	770.00
Basket, Serpentine Oval Form, Howard, c.1904, 11 1/2 In.	440.00
Beaker, Basett & Waxford, Albany	330.00
Beaker, Molded Foot & Rim, S. Kirk, c.1824, 3 1/2 In.	935.00
Bell, Owl Form, Erik Magnussen, 4 1/2 In.	1850.00
Bill Holder, Imperial Queen, Whiting	95.00
Bonbon, Iris, Shiebler	75.00
Bonbon, Pierced, Pantheon, International	45.00
Bowl, 4 Lobes, Kalo, 1 3/4 x 5 In.	165.00
Bowl, Center, Enameled Cherry Blossoms, Brass Cover, Galt & Bro., 18 In.	605.00
Bowl, Center, Plated Inset Grille, Engraved With Garlands, c.1925	154.00
Bowl, Chased Dragon & Exotic Flowers, Gorham, 9 1/4 In.	715.00
Bowl, Chased Stylized Flowers, Vines, Fluted Body, Gorham, 10 1/2 In.	4950.00
Bowl, Circular Form, Notched Rim, Pedestal Foot, Monteith, 6 1/4 In.	440.00
Bowl, Daisies On Edge, Victorian, William B. Kerr & Co.	775.00
Bowl, Engraved Wheat Design Flange, Porter Blanchard, 10 In.	950.00
Bowl, Floral Relief Border, Square, Whiting, 9 In.	660.00
Bowl, Floriform, Interior Poppy Design, Wallace, 10 In.	265.00
Bowl, Flowers Within Scrolling Panels, Martele, Gorham, c.1905, 9 5/8 In.	3850.00
Bowl, Fluted Rim Holds Glasses For Icing, Kirk & Son	3400.00
Bowl, Fluted, Beaded & Floral Long Handle	155.00
Bowl, Footed, Inscription, Jarvie, Chicago, 1915, 4 1/2 x 8 1/2 In.	550.00
Bowl, Footed, Kidney & Johnson, 19th Century	495.00
Bowl, Francis I, Reed & Barton, 11 1/2 x 15 1/4 In.	550.00
Bowl, Ice, No. 125, Rocky Outcrop Hung With Icicles, Gorham, 1870, 11 In.	4400.00
Bowl, La Paglia, Pierced Standard of Balls & Loops, International, 10 In.	495.00
Bowl, Leamington, Gorham, 9 1/2 In.	220.00
Bowl, Lobed Rim, Pedestal Foot, Monogrammed F. G. R., 6 3/4 x 11 In.	1100.00
Bowl, Myer Myers, 6 In.	2200.00
Bowl, Ovoid Domed Lid, Ivory Knob, Kalo Shop, 11 5/8 x 7 3/4 In.	3800.00
Bowl, Petal Design, Hammered Surface, Kalo, 1919, 7 1/4 In.	355.00
Bowl, Poppy & Oak Leaf Design, Handles, c.1880, Dominick & Haff, 9 In.	1310.00
Bowl, Reed & Barton, 11 1/4 x 8 1/2 In.	265.00
Bowl, Repousse, Scalloped, Whiting, 10 1/2 In.	1650.00
Bowl, Rolled Rim, Pedestal Foot, Lebolt & Co., c.1910, 10 In.	550.00
Bowl, Salad, Francis I	625.00
Bowl, Salem Pattern, Dominick & Haff, 12 In.	440.00
Bowl, Serving, Foliate Design, Raised, Shaped Edge, 14 In.	396.00
Bowl, Serving, Prelude, International, 9 3/4 In.	99.00
Bowl, Shells & Seaweed, Crabs On Sides, Whiting, c.1885, 8 3/4 In.	4620.00
Bowl, Side & Rim Form Leaf–Type Sections, Cellini Craft, 10 In.	595.00
Bowl, Sunburst Design Base, Enameled Turquoise, Mary C. Knight, 4 In.	1200.00
Bowl, Tapering Circular Form, Karl F. Leinonen, 3 3/4 In.	45.00
Bowl, Underplate, Enamel & Turquoise Leaves Band, Mary C. Knight, 5 In.	2200.00
Bowl, Windsor, Scalloped, Reed & Barton, 15 x 10 1/2 In.	355.00
Box, Cigarette, Black, Starr, Frost–Gorham, 7 1/4 x 4 x 1 1/8 In.	193.00
Box, Handwrought, Concave Top, Unger Brothers, 3 x 5 In.	110.00
Box, Pill, Floral Design, S. Kirk, 1 1/2 x 1 In.	77.00
Bread Tray, Royal Danish, International	410.00
Bride's Basket, Pierced, Engraved, Boat Shape, Whiting, 1916, 13 1/2 In.	825.00
Bun Dish, Acorns & Leaves On Rim, Woodside Sterling Co., 2 1/2 x 10 In.	600.00
Butter Chip, Repousse, Kirk	38.00
Butter, Pierced Top, Chased Florals, Monogram, Jacobi & Jenkins, 7 1/4 In.	412.50
Cake Basket, Egg–and–Dart Rim, Gregg & Hayden, 1851, 15 3/4 In.	2860.00

Cake Plate, Monogrammed CBL, Gorham	417.00
Cake Plate, Scandinavian Design, Charter Co.	440.00
Candlestick, Louis XV, Gorham, c.1891, 12 1/2 In., 4 Piece	3850.00
Cann, Double Struck, John Parsons, 5 1/4 In.	2200.00
Cann, Engraved Arms, Samuel Vernon, c.1720, 4 3/4 In.	3850.00
Card Case, Scrolled Edge, Hinged Lid, Birmingham, 1852, 3 3/4 x 2 3/4 In.	225.00
Carving Set, Floral, Jenkins & Jenkins, Baltimore, 1910	165.00
Caster, Slip–On Domed Cover, Samuel Edwards, 1740s, 4 1/2 In.	1540.00
Cigarette Case, Art Deco, Evans	77.00
Cigarette Case, Dog Picture, James Blake, 1900	225.00
Cocktail Shaker, Reed & Barton, 8 In.	145.00
Coffee Set, Green Malachite Finials, Outward Flutes, Cartier, 3 Piece	3500.00
Coffee Set, Repousse Design of Fruit Clusters, Gorham, 4 Piece	2750.00
Coffeepot, Acanthus Fluted Spout, Isaac Cookson, 1744, 9 In.	7150.00
Coffeepot, Deer 1 Side, Hunter Other, Kirk, c.1860, 15 In.	3850.00
Coffeepot, Flared Collar, Putto Finial, Gorham, 1870s, 10 1/2 In.	990.00
Coffeepot, Repousse Floral, Cooper & Fisher, 1850, 11 1/2 In.	854.00
Coffeepot, Scroll & Rocaille Cartouche, S. Kirk, 1840s, 11 1/4 In.	1430.00
Coffeepot, Tapering, Oval, Hinged Lid, Carved Wood Handle, Gorham, 7 In.	165.00
Compote, Berry, Blackberries & Leaves At Base, E. Lownes, c.1815	1250.00
Compote, Cake, Acanthus Leaf Scrolling, Galt & Bro., c.1910, 10 1/2 In.	665.00
Compote, Cake, Beaded Edge, Arthur J. Stone, c.1927, 4 x 8 In., Pair	605.00
Compote, Candy, Hand–Chased Garlands, Galt & Bro., c.1920, 7 1/2 In., Pair	675.00
Compote, Ovoid Top, Buds & Cascading Beads, Cellini Craft, 7 x 6 In.	1100.00
Compote, Raised Oval Medallion Center, Wood & Hughes, 7 1/2 In.	880.00
Compote, Reeded Rim, Howard, 5 1/2 In.	495.00
Compote, Vintage, Georg Jensen, c.1936, 5 In.	825.00
Creamer, Bandy–Legged, Joseph Richardson	3860.00
Creamer, Coin, Floral Chased, Monogrammed, 18th Century, 5 3/4 In.	275.00
Creamer, Cooper & Fisher	412.00
Creamer, Floral Chasing, 5 3/4 In.	275.00
Creamer, Nathaniel Burt	3250.00
Creamer, Punch Work Border, Scrolling Spout, Zachariah Brigden, 4 1/2 In.	1045.00
Creamer, Repousse, Durgin, 3 1/2 In.	200.00
Crumber, Gorham	200.00
Cup, 3 Handles, Applied Floral Border, Gorham, 5 In.	385.00
Cup, Beaker Form, Scroll Strap Handle, Andrew Tyler, 1721, 4 1/2 In.	8800.00
Cup, Presentation, 1842, Savannah Rifle Club, Rectangular, 3 1/2 In.	660.00
Cup, Presentation, 1844, Savannah Volunteer Guards, 3 1/2 In.	990.00
Cup, Waisted Shape, Hammered Interior, Edward H. Breese, 2 3/4 In., 6 Pc.	750.00
Dessert Stand, Circular, Pedestal, Dominick & Haff, 1912, 2 1/2 In.	200.00
Dish, 3 Joined Scallop Shells, Black, Starr, Frost–Gorham	135.00
Dish, Monogrammed A. B. C., Duhme Jewelry Co., Oval, 12 In.	45.00
Dish, Pierced, Handcraft Guild of Minneapolis, Arts & Crafts, 6 1/8 In.	187.00
Dish, Waterfall Texture Flange, William Waldo Dodge, 7 3/4 In.	395.00
Dresser Set, Levitt & Gold, c.1920, 12 Piece	495.00
Ewer, Beaded & Greek Key Borders, Jones, Shreve & Brown, 11 In.	412.50
Ewer, Frolicking Cherubs, Acanthus Leaves On Base, Kirk, 1880, 11 1/2 In.	3000.00
Figurine, Bulldog, Rectangular Platform, Gorham, c.1930, 5 3/4 In.	4125.00
Finger Bowl, Coin Silver, Monogrammed, Late 18th Century, 4 1/8 In.	825.00
Fish Slice, Fiddle Thread, Albert Coles, c.1840, 12 1/2 In.	265.00
Flask, Camel Picture, Blackinton, 1900	125.00
Flask, Cover, Basketweave Top, Removable Cup Case, Gorham, 7 1/2 In.	600.00
Fork, Dinner, Hall & Hewson, 1830s, 12 Piece	1800.00
Fork, Dinner, Louis XIV, Coin Silver, 6 Piece	240.00
Fork, King's Pattern, Bailley & Kitchen, 11 Piece	1650.00
Fork, Tipped Pattern, James Conning, c.1842, 9 Piece	1430.00
Francis I, 11 In.	1000.00
Fruit Bowl, Floral & Scroll Design, Black, Starr & Frost, 8 1/4 In.	440.00
Goblet, Light Hammer Marks, Initial S, Kalo Shop, 6 5/8 In., 10 Piece	4000.00
Inkwell, Camel Form, Cover On Back, Glass Inkpot, F. H. Clark, c.1904, 8 In.	1980.00
Jardiniere, Late 19th Century, S. Kirk & Son	1650.00
Jug, Cream, Wavy Rim, Engraved Initials, John Waite, c.1775, 2 3/4 In.	1210.00

Jug, Leather & Copper, Gorham, 1890s	950.00
Kettle, Hot Water, Stand, George III Style, Gorham	415.00
Kettle, Stand, Rococo Style, Warrin & Co., 19th Century	520.00
Ladle, Flower Design, Enameled Turquoise, Mary C. Knight, 4 3/4 In.	525.00
Ladle, Mustard, Basket of Flowers, H. B. Myers, c.1825	95.00
Ladle, Oyster, Olive, Coin Silver, 12 In.	200.00
Ladle, Punch, Oriental Pattern, Hyde & Goodrich, 1850, 13 In.	770.00
Ladle, Rattail Handle, Monogrammed, Shreve, Crimp & Low, 12 In.	192.00
Ladle, Soup, Allen Armstrong	360.00
Ladle, Soup, Fiddle, R & A Campbell, c.1845, 13 1/4 In.	275.00
Ladle, Soup, H. I. Sawyer, Hartford	245.00
Loving Cup, Presentation, Louis XIV, Shreve & Co., 13 1/2 In.	2750.00
Mug, Bowl & Plate, Child's, Nursery Rhyme Scenes, William B. Kerr & Co.	798.00
Mug, Presentation, Allyn Goodwin, Hartford	1870.00
Napkin Clip, French Scroll, Alvin	12.00
Napkin Clip, Horizon, Easterling	10.00
Napkin Clip, Hunt Club, Gorham	10.00
Napkin Clip, Joy, International	12.00
Nut Pick, J. Polhemus, c.1850, 9 Piece	300.00
Nut Pick, Louis XIV, Coin Silver, 6 Piece	200.00
Pie Server, Curled Handle, Leaf & Bead Form, Cellini Craft, 8 3/4 In.	375.00
Pin Tray, Ribs & Veins, R. Blackinton, 5 x 4 In.	50.00
Pitcher, Champagne, Art Nouveau, Black, Starr & Frost, 15 1/2 In.	4670.00
Pitcher, Champagne, Poppies, Art Nouveau, Black, Starr & Frost, 1900	4675.00
Pitcher, Clam & Oyster Shells On Body, Gilt Seaweed, Whiting, 1885	7700.00
Pitcher, Colonial Style, Gorham, 8 1/8 In.	495.00
Pitcher, Duhme, 8 In.	258.00
Pitcher, Fluted Oval Body, Scrolled Handles, Reed & Barton, 9 1/2 In.	495.00
Pitcher, Foliate Scrolls, Hexagonal Finial, Bennett & Caldwell, c.1845	4620.00
Pitcher, Footed, Gorham, 8 5/8 In.	357.00
Pitcher, Hand Chased, S. Kirk & Son	4950.00
Pitcher, Mask Handle, Engraved Bands, Gorham, c.1871	2500.00
Pitcher, Mulholland Brothers, Arts & Crafts,, c.1905, 9 1/2 In.	1210.00
Pitcher, Vintage Pattern, Ohio State Board of Agriculture, Coin Silver	975.00
Pitcher, Water, Art Nouveau, Martele	8250.00
Plate, Dessert, Fenestrated, Floral Urn, 1910–1915, A. J. Gannon, 12 In.	385.00
Plate, J. E. Caldwell, Reticulated Border, 12 In., 8 Piece	6050.00
Plate, Rococo Pierced Rim, Reticulated	330.00
Platter, C–Scrolling Shell & Floral Design, Gorham, c.1902, 12 x 16 3/4 In.	185.00
Platter, Meat, Plymouth Pattern, Gorham, Oval, 19 In.	550.00
Platter, Octagonal, Engraved Crests & Designs, Dimes, 13 In.	305.00
Platter, Repousse Floral Border, Oval, S. Kirk, 17 1/2 In.	1100.00
Porringer, Bailey & Chapman	770.00
Porringer, Celtic Interlace Handle, Karl F. Leinonen, 5 In.	695.00
Porringer, Pierced Handle, George C. Gebelein, 4 7/8 In.	525.00
Punch Bowl, Grapevine Feet & Rim, Gorham, 1897, 16 1/2 In.	4950.00
Punch Bowl, Revere Bowl Shape, Gorham, 14 1/2 In.	1320.00
Punch Cup, Floral, Jacobi & Jenkins, 1894–1908	137.50
Relish, 3 Glass Sections, Pierced Frame, Watson, 10 3/4 x 8 1/4 In.	330.00
Salt & Pepper, 4 Supports, Dominick & Haff	121.00
Salt, Master, Shell Bowl, Fiddle, P. O'Daniel, c.1840	25.00
Salver, Cast Floral Handle, Reed & Barton, 8 In.	82.00
Sandwich Tongs, Allan Adler	310.00
Sauceboat, Ebenezer Chittenden, Connecticut	1650.00
Server, Pie, Marshall, c.1860	130.00
Spoon & Fork, Serving, Fish & Net Pattern, Whiting	605.00
Spoon, Benjamin Burt	495.00
Spoon, Coin Silver, Engraved N. B. R., I. Vogler, 6 In.	137.00
Spoon, Dessert, Fiddle Shell, W. Roe, c.1820	40.00
Spoon, Jones, Lows & Ball, Monogrammed, 8 3/8 In., Pair	20.00
Spoon, Samuel Vernon	630.00
Spoon, Serving, King's Pattern, Frederick Marquand	1200.00
Spoon, Serving, Mulford & Wendell	1500.00

Spoon, T. J. Meeghar, 3 In., Pair 60.00
Spurs, Inlaid, Heart Pattern, G. S. Garcia, 1910, Pair 3600.00
Sugar & Creamer, Chased Scenes, Kirk, c.1860 .... 1980.00
Sugar & Creamer, Prelude, International 85.00
Sugar & Creamer, Scrolling Grapevines, C. L. Boehme, c.1805, 8 3/8 In. 2200.00
Sugar Sifter, Tuscan, W. Gale, Coin Silver, 7 3/4 In. 150.00
Sugar Tongs, Sheaf of Wheat, H. E. Hoyt, c.1825, 6 1/2 In. 135.00
Sugar, Cover, Grapevine Apron, Floral Swags, Fletcher & Bennet, 1850 .... 1430.00
Tablespoon, Fiddle Thread, Jaccard, St. Louis 240.00
Tablespoon, Fiddle Thread, Melville & Co., 6 Piece 245.00
Tablespoon, Fiddle, Coin Silver, Sayre & Richards, 5 Piece 300.00
Tablespoon, Fiddle, Sayre & Richards, 1810 .... 65.00
Tablespoon, Knot Pattern, Hyde & Goodrich, Pair 100.00
Tankard, Tutorial, Stepped Cover, Benjamin Hiller, c.1717, 7 1/4 In. 2860.00
Tazza, Sweetmeat, Floral Reticulated Rim, Wallace, 6 7/8 x 3 1/4 In. 66.00
Tea & Coffee Set, Classical Bust Medallion, Ball, Black & Co., 5 Piece 2975.00
Tea & Coffee Set, Hampton Court, Monogrammed, Reed & Barton, 4 Piece 1430.00
Tea & Coffee Set, Hanover, Kettle On Stand, Reed & Barton 2420.00
Tea & Coffee Set, Octagonal Baluster Form, R. & W. Wilson, 5 Piece 3080.00
Tea & Coffee Set, Oval Tray, Poole, 5 Piece 1650.00
Tea & Coffee Set, Rococo Revival, Wood & Hughes, 1840 .... 4950.00
Tea & Coffee Set, Russian Style, Gorham, 6 Piece 6600.00
Tea & Coffee Set, Thomas Evans, c.1850, 4 Piece 2800.00
Tea & Coffee Set, Victorian, Reed & Barton, c.1880, 8 Piece 2500.00
Tea Ball, Teapot Shape, Attleboro 65.00
Tea Set, Beaded Bands Overall, Joseph Lownes, c.1795, 11 1/2 In., 3 Piece 4400.00
Tea Set, C–Scrolls, N. A. Freeman, 3 Piece 1870.00
Tea Set, Charters, Cann & Dunn, 1850, 4 Piece 1870.00
Tea Set, Dominick & Haff, c.1930, 3 Piece 550.00
Tea Set, Federal, S. Kirk & Sons, 3 Piece 1800.00
Tea Set, Hampton Court, Reed & Barton, 6 Piece 5000.00
Tea Set, Inverted Pear Shape, Acanthus Border, George Welles, 3 Piece 990.00
Tea Set, Ivy, Punched Ground, Coin Silver, H. B. Stanwood, 3 Piece 4750.00
Tea Set, Johnson & Reat, c.1804, 3 Piece 4400.00
Tea Set, Jones, Lows & Ball, Dated 1840, 3 Piece 1450.00
Tea Set, Oval Tray, A. Stone, c.1936, 4 Piece 1430.00
Tea Set, Repousse Floral, S. Kirk & Son, Monogrammed, 9 Piece 7980.00
Tea Set, Stand With Burner, Whiting, c.1930, 3 Piece 600.00
Tea Strainer, Floral Garland, J. M. Merrill, c.1895, 7 In. 250.00
Tea Strainer, Monogrammed, Coin Silver, 7 In. 60.00
Teapot, Acanthus Leaves, Bellflower Border, Ball, Black & Co. 2500.00
Teapot, Animal Head Spout, Basch & Co., c.1820, 8 3/4 In. 2090.00
Teapot, Barrel Shape, Shreve, Stanwood & Co., 19th Century, 5 In. 445.00
Teaspoon, Coin Silver, Engraved A. E. W. D. & D. Kinsey, 5 3/4 In., 5 Piece 225.00
Teaspoon, Coin Silver, Engraved J. B. S., King & Brother, 8 1/2 In., 4 Piece 60.00
Teaspoon, Dutchess, Coin Silver, J. Polhemus, 4 Piece 60.00
Teaspoon, Fiddle Thread, Melville & Co., 1849, 6 Piece 200.00
Teaspoon, Fiddle, Sayre & Richards, c.1810 .... 25.00
Teaspoon, Fiddle, T. Emery, c.1810 .... 25.00
Thermos Bottle, Mercury Glass, Hammered, Lebolt & Co., 13 1/4 In. 1450.00
Tongs, Asparagus, Josephine, Coin Silver, H. Hebbard, 11 3/4 In. 550.00
Tongs, Bright Cut, Coin Silver, Kidney & Johnson, 10 1/2 In. 500.00
Tongs, E. Benjamin, New Haven, Conn., c.1840 .... 50.00
Tray, Circular Gadrooned Rim 360.00
Tray, Francis I, Oval, Reed & Barton, 1929, 21 1/2 In. 1980.00
Tray, Francis I, Reed & Barton, 30 In. 2000.00
Tray, Golden Wheat Pattern, Parcel Gilt, Gorham, 22 x 15 1/2 In. 1100.00
Tray, Herbert A. Taylor, Oval, Dated 1939, 18 1/8 In. 550.00
Tray, Lord Robert, International Silver Co., 22 In. 825.00
Tray, Maintenon, Oval, Gorham, c.1925, 29 In. 3300.00
Tray, Molded Rim, Kirk, 14 In. 330.00
Tray, Monogram Within Band of Flowers, Gorham, 1910, 32 1/4 In. 4125.00

Tray, Presentation, Chippendale Style, Open Handles, Gorham, 29 1/2 In.	1100.00
Tray, Round, Tuttle, 12 In.	550.00
Tray, Scroll Handles, Bright Cut, William Gale, 1858, 25 3/4 In.	2100.00
Tray, Square, Monogrammed, International, 9 1/2 In.	88.00
Tray, Tooled Edge, Marked Theodore B. Starr 925, 18 1/4 x 22 1/4 In.	700.00
Tray, Tooled Flange, Round, Mary C. Knight, 12 3/4 In.	1650.00
Tray, Undulating Wavy Flange, George C. Gebelein, 11 1/4 In.	1800.00
Urn, Sugar, Band of Leaves, Paneled, Mulford & Wendell, c.1845	330.00
Urn, Sugar, Pierced Gallery, Vase Shape Finial, J. McFee, c.1800, 9 1/2 In.	3300.00
Urn, Sugar, Presentation Inscriptions, Lincoln & Reed, 1845, 8 1/2 In.	247.50
Urn, Tea, Grapevine Rims, Engraved Eliza Bruse, R. & W. Wilson, c.1840	6600.00
Vase, Art Nouveau, Raised Flowers, Gorham, 8 In.	650.00
Vase, Bud, Chrysanthemum, J. E. Caldwell, 12 In.	195.00
Vase, Swirling Art Nouveau Lines, Boyden–Minuth Co., 6 1/2 In.	400.00
Wine Cooler, Fruit Swags, Dolphin Handles, Gorham, 1906, 12 1/8 In.	7150.00
Wine Cup, Bell Form, Wallace, 12 Piece	155.00
SILVER–AUSTRIAN, Chalice, Geometric, Medallion Pattern, Trumpet Base, 7 7/8 In.	192.50
Snuffbox, Center Hunter On Horseback, Pierced Overlay, c.1870	715.00
SILVER–BELGIAN, Sauceboat, Openwork Handles, Goose Or Duck Mark, 1765, 7 In.	7150.00
SILVER–CHINESE, Box, Storage, Dragons & Clouds, Late 19th Century, 4 3/4 x 18 In.	6600.00
Tea Set, Luen Wo, Early 20th Century, 3 Piece	1045.00
SILVER–CONTINENTAL, Candlestick, 19th Century, Repousse, 14 In., Pair	600.00
Container, Spice, Fish Form, Red Stone Eyes, Chain, 3 3/4 In.	300.00
Creamer, Cow Form, Hinged Chased Lid, 19th Century, 5 1/2 In.	1100.00
Dish, Sabbath, Circular Beaded Rim, 19th C., 8 1/4 In.	250.00
Figurine, Street Musician, Glass Jewels, 4 1/2 In., 4 Piece	1155.00
SILVER–DANISH, Bowl, Blossom, Openwork Blossoms On Foot, Georg Jensen, 11 In.	4400.00
Bowl, Grapes, Band of Grapes & Vines, Oval, Georg Jensen, 1945, 14 1/4 In.	9900.00
Bowl, Leaf & Berry Design, Curved Handles, Georg Jensen, 15 1/2 In.	5450.00
Box, Art Nouveau Design On Cover, Unger Bros., 6 In.	275.00
Box, Concave Finial On Lid, Georg Jensen, 3 1/2 In.	1070.00
Box, Cover, Blossom Pattern, Ovoid, Georg Jensen	1100.00
Box, Pill, Floral Top, Georg Jensen	120.00
Carving Set, Cactus, Georg Jensen	400.00
Chocolate Pot, Hourglass Form, Ivory Finial, Carl M. Cohr, 1955, 8 In.	1925.00
Cocktail Shaker, Berry & Leaf Finial, Georg Jensen, 12 In.	3115.00
Coffeepot, Acorn Finial, Ebony Handle, Georg Jensen, 9 1/2 In.	1650.00
Compote, Grape Clusters & Vines, 1968	5225.00
Condiment Set, Scrolled Openwork, Pineapple Finials, G. Jensen, 6 Pc.	2900.00
Cup, Cover, Circular Striped Base, Openwork, 1945, Georg Jensen, 6 In.	1200.00
Dish, Vegetable, Georg Jensen, c.1940	4125.00
Dress Clip, Art Nouveau Design, Georg Jensen	245.00
Fish Set, Acorn, 12 Knives–8 1/4 In., 12 Forks–6 1/2 In., Georg Jensen	1875.00
Frame, Picture, Chased Foliate Border, Unger Bros., 6 x 4 1/2 In.	145.00
Pitcher, Baluster, Rope Work, Leather C–Scroll Handle, Georg Jensen, 9 In.	1980.00
Pitcher, Egg Shape, Georg Jensen, 1922, 9 In.	2000.00
Platter, Meat, Raised Border, Rayed & Beads, Georg Jensen, 18 1/4 In.	2475.00
Sauceboat, Fluted Ivory Handles, Georg Jensen, 1945, 6 1/2 In.	2650.00
Service For 8, Pyramid Serving Pieces, Georg Jensen, 124 Piece	7700.00
Serving Spoon & Fork, Georg Jensen	935.00
Sugar Tongs, Acorn, Georg Jensen	200.00
Sugar Tongs, Blossom, Georg Jensen	250.00
Tea & Coffee Set, Disc Design, Georg Jensen, 1933 Mark, 4 Piece	4475.00
Tea & Coffee Set, Tray, Johan Rohde, 1915–1932, 5 Piece	9350.00
Teapot, Acorn Finial, Ebony Handle, Georg Jensen, 6 In.	1500.00
Tray, Tea, Blossom Pattern, Georg Jensen, 25 1/2 In.	6600.00
Tureen, Hans Hansen, Stepped Disk Cover, Leaf Form Handles, 1933, 6 In.	1650.00
Wine Cooler, Bombe Form, Bail Handles, Hans Hansen, 1931, 10 5/8 In.	7975.00
SILVER–DUTCH, Beaker, Engraved Strap Collar, Dordrecht, 1640s, 4 3/8 In., Pair	4950.00
Box, Tobacco, Engraved, Harbor With Sailing Boats, c.1840, 5 x 2 In.	885.00
Dessert Basket, Interlaced Ribbon Work, Beaded Border, 1786, 14 1/2 In.	7150.00
Pillbox, Landscape On Hinged Lid, 1932, 2 1/4 In.	55.00

Silver-English, Candlestick, George III, George Ashforth, 1781, 12 1/8 In.,

4 Pc.; Silver-English, Cruet Set, George III, Wakelien & Taylor, 1772, 12 In.;

Silver-English, Cruet Set, Scroll Handle, Samuel Wood, 1755, 6 3/4 In.

Snuffbox, c.1870	195.00
Teapot, Apple Shape, Strapwork Collar, 1784, 5 3/8 In.	1870.00

SILVER–ENGLISH. English silver is marked with a series of four or five small hallmarks. The standing lion mark is the most commonly seen sterling quality mark. The other marks indicate the city of origin, the maker, and the year of manufacture. These dates can be verified in many good books on silver.

SILVER–ENGLISH, Asparagus Server, George III, Hawk & Branch, William Kingdon, 9 1/2 In.	330.00
Bowl, Crest, 3 Gryphon Feet, J. Wakely & F. C. Wheeler, c.1890, 8 In., Pair	4125.00
Bowl, Fruit, Repousse Floral, Monogrammed L. L. H., England, 13 In.	605.00
Bowl, George II, Tread Edge, 3 1/4 x 2 In.	210.00
Bowl, Oval, George III, Beaded Border, Wakelin & W. Taylor, 1777, 16 In.	6600.00
Bowl, Vegetable, Georgian, Richard Crosley, 11 x 8 1/2 In., Pair	1875.00
Box, Cigarette, Engraved Arms, Stripes, Cedar Lined, Wakely & Wheeler, Pr.	2200.00
Box, Dresser, Inlaid Tortoiseshell Lid, Adie Bros., 1932, 3 1/2 x 4 In.	220.00
Box, Pierced & Raised Floral, W. Comyns & Sons, 1909, 5 In.	220.00
Buckle & Button, Lad's, Case, Birmingham, 1909, Set	325.00
Butter Chip, Engraved Crest, Hoof Feet, P. Archambo, 1747, 4 1/8 In., Pr.	2200.00
Cake Basket, Scroll & Floral Rim, Swing Handle, E. Aldridge, 1746, 14 3/8 In.	8800.00
Candlestick, George III, George Ashforth, 1781, 12 1/8 In., 4 Pc. ....*Illus*	950.00
Candlestick, George V, Column Form, D & M/D, 1913, 5 In., Pair	140.00

When storing silver in an attic, remember that a temperature of 97° F. or more will melt the filler in some candlesticks; also, heat speeds corrosion.

Silver-English, Champagne Cooler, Sheffield,

1830, 12 In., Pair

Silver-English, Frame, Clover Corners,
c.1900, 4 3/8 X 3 1/4 In.

◆◆◆◆◆◆◆◆◆◆◆◆◆◆◆◆◆◆◆◆◆◆◆◆

If you put camphor (mothballs)
in with the silver to prevent tarnish, don't let it touch the silver. Put the camphor in a
waxed paper cup.

◆◆◆◆◆◆◆◆◆◆◆◆◆◆◆◆◆◆◆◆◆◆◆◆

Chalice, Laurel Wreath Reserve, Robert & Samuel Hennel, c.1807, 9 In.	660.00
Champagne Cooler, Liners, Sheffield, c.1800, 9 1/4 In., Pair	3575.00
Champagne Cooler, Sheffield, 1830, 12 In., Pair *Illus*	2500.00
Cheese Server, Sheffield, Ornate, 1849, 8 In.	40.00
Chocolate Pot, Domed Cover, Wooden Scroll Handle, London, 9 In.	6325.00
Cigarette Case, Enameled St. Andrews, Golfing Insignia On Cover, 1930	95.00
Coffeepot, Banded Dome Cover, William Fawdrey, 1710, 9 1/4 In.	7150.00
Coffeepot, George III, Handle, Acorn Finial, Crest, John Emes, 7 1/2 In.	550.00
Coffeepot, Swan–Neck Spout, Ayme Videau, 1742, 8 1/4 In.	3850.00
Creamer, Helmet Shape, Engraved Crest & Motto, T. Heming, 1774, 5 5/8 In.	1650.00
Cruet Set, George III, Wakelien & Taylor, 1772, 12 In. *Illus*	2200.00
Cruet Set, Scroll Handle, Samuel Wood, 1755, 6 3/4 In. *Illus*	1760.00
Cup, George III, Overall Scrolling Rosette Repousse, Hester Bateman, 1779	385.00
Dish, George III Style, Pierced, G. Fox, 1897, 5 x 9 1/2 In., Pair	1320.00
Dish, Serving, John Emes, c.1799, 11 1/2 In.	650.00
Dish, Sweetmeat, George III, Cut Crystal Bowl, Scrolling Handles, 12 1/2 In.	4850.00
Ewer, Wine, Wood Handle, Beaded Lip, Sheffield, 19th Century, 14 In.	385.00
Frame, Clover Corners, c.1900, 4 3/8 x 3 1/4 In. *Illus*	110.00
Frame, Floral Design, Rectangular, Blue–Green Enamel Detail, 1904	2045.00
Grape Shears, Grape & Vine Handles, Charles Rawlings, 1822, 6 1/2 In.	715.00
Gravy Boat, George IV, Bird With Olive Branch, William Bateman, 5 x 3 In.	825.00
Honey Pot, Cover, Stand, Beehive Form, Bee Finial, John Robins, 1799, 4 1/8 In.	9250.00
Inkstand, George III, Paw Feet, W. Burwash, 1817, 11 1/4 In. *Illus*	3850.00

Silver-English, Inkstand, George III,
Paw Feet, W. Burwash, 1817, 11 1/4 In.

Silver-English, Jug, Hot Water, Stand,
Paul Storr, 1814, 11 In.

Jug, Claret, Thistle Finial, Clover, Thistle & Rose, Daniels, 1807, 15 1/2 In. 2420.00
Jug, Hot Water, Francis Butty & Nicholas Dumee, 1771, 12 3/4 In. 1320.20
Jug, Hot Water, Stand, Paul Storr, 1814, 11 In. ....*Illus* 8800.00
Kettle, Stand, George II, Swing Handle, R. Bayley, 1736, 12 1/2 In. 4675.00
Kettle, Warming Stand, Ivory Handle, Henning & Co., 12 1/2 In. 935.00
Ladle, George III, Thread & Shell, Joseph Coles, 1817, 7 In. 110.00
Ladle, Punch, Shell, William Chawnor, 1825, 12 1/2 In. 300.00
Ladle, Shell, George III, Hanoverian Tip, 7 In. 2475.00
Meat Fork, Anchor At End, Ann & Peter Bateman, 1817, 11 1/2 In. 330.00
Menu Holder, Repousse Sailing Galleon, Ramsben & Car, 1917, Pair 560.00
Mirror, Plateau, Removable Mirrors, Oval, c.1860, 41 x 28 1/2 In. 1210.00
Mustard Pot, Blue Liner, Birmingham, 1909 .... 185.00
Mustard Pot, George III, Reeded Form, Cobalt Liner, Spoon, 1800 .... 220.00
Nutmeg Grinder, George III, Samuel Meriton, C. 1795 .... 300.00
Pap Boat, George II, George Smith & Thomas Hayer 385.00
Pitcher, Molded Girdle, Scroll Handle, William Cripps, 1760, 6 1/4 In. 995.00
Plate, Charles Martin, 1730s, 9 3/4 In., 12 Piece 4000.00
Plate, Charles Martin, Chased Crest On Rim, 1737, 9 3/4 In., 11 Piece 4400.00
Plate, George III, Crest On Rim, William Sumner, 1819, 9 5/8 In., 11 Piece 8250.00
Plate, William IV, Paul Storr, Scalloped Edge, Crest, 11 In., Pair 2475.00
Salt & Pepper, Urn Finial, Crichton Bros., 4 Sets 520.00
Salt, Figural, Suburban Couple & Rustic Couple, Silver Gilt, Set of 4 .... 6000.00
Salt, George III, 3 Hoof Feet, D. Mowden, 1764, Pair 225.00
Salt, Scalloped Rim, Pad Feet, Henry Corry, 1761, 2 1/2 In. 220.00
Salver, Bellflower Rim, Robert Makepeace & Richard Carter, 1777, 12 3/4 In. 2750.00
Salver, George II, Shell & Scroll Rim, Coat of Arms, 1760, 13 1/2 In. 2750.00
Salver, George III, Shell Border, William Peaston, 1747, 12 In. 1450.00
Salver, George III, Shell Border, Thomas Hannam & John Crouch 887.00
Salver, George V, Scrolled Molded Rim, H. H. Plante, 1930 .... 275.00
Salver, George Wickes, 1729–1730, 10 In. ....*Illus* 2500.00
Salver, Shell & Scroll Border, J. Parker & E. Wakelin, 1767, 11 In. 990.00
Sauceboat, George III, Beaded Rim, Hester Bateman, 7 In., Pair 825.00
Scoop, Marrow, Crest On Bowl, William Frisbee, 1719, 8 1/4 In. 305.00
Scoop, Marrow, George III, Hester Bateman, 18th Century, 9 In. 275.00
Snuffer Tray, George III, Falcon With Leaf, John Emes, 10 In. 495.00
Spoon, Jam, Turquoise Setting, Engraved Loma, 1904 .... 280.00
Spoon, Serving, George III, Onslow, Hester Bateman, c.1778, Pair 495.00
Spoon, Serving, Kings, Paul Storr, 9 In., Pair 465.00
Spoon, Stuffing, George III, Armorial Crest, 15 1/2 In. 330.00
Spoon, Stuffing, George III, William Eley, William Fearn & W. Chawner, 12 In. 170.00
Sugar & Creamer, Bird & Floral Design, John Fry II, 1828, 5 In. 550.00
Sugar Box, Engraved Strapwork, Stepped Dome, A. Courtauld, 1735, 5 In. 9350.00
Sugar Tongs, George III, Hester Bateman, 6 In. 275.00
Tea Set, Buckingshire, Monogrammed L. L. S., Sheffield, 6 Piece 850.00
Tea Set, Crest & Monogram, Serpent Handles, Paul Storr, 4 Piece 8250.00
Tea Set, George V, Atkin Brothers, 1917 .... 440.00

Silver polish can be made at home from a cup of cigar ashes, two tablespoons of bicarbonate of soda, and enough water to make a paste. The only problem is finding a cigar smoker.

Silver-English, Salver, George Wickes, 1729-1730, 10 In.

Silver-French, Compote, Louis XVI, Plated,

Bointaburet, 1893, 10 1/4 In., Pair

Don't send out your antique white linen or cotton items to be dry cleaned. The chemicals will yellow the fabric. Hand wash them in soap, nonchlorine bleach, and tepid water. Be sure to rinse until all soap is removed.

Tea Set, Roberts & Slater, 1850s, 4 Piece	1300.00
Teapot, George III, Oval, Reeded Sides, Wm. Plummer, 1809, 5 In.	825.00
Toast Rack, George III, Rebecca Emes & John Barnard, 6 x 5 x 3 1/2 In.	825.00
Toast Rack, Incised Shell, Scroll & Foliate Design, Mappin & Webb, 8 1/2 In.	75.00
Tray, Gadroon Edge, Handles, Monogrammed L. L. S., Sheffield, 17 x 27 In.	125.00
Tray, George III, Handles Rise From Leaves, Marked WB, 1804, 27 5/8 In.	7975.00
Tray, Noble Crest Center, Vine Handles, John Bridge, 1830, 29 x 18 1/2 In.	8250.00
Urn, George III, Handles, Chased Decoration, 1808, J. Robins	1980.00
Urn, Hot Water, George III Style, T. Bradbury, 1899	990.00
Waiter, Gadrooned Border, John Angell, 1824, 28 In.	2860.00
Wine Cistern, Oval, c.1893	8800.00
SILVER–FRENCH, Asparagus Set, Tongs, Slatted Tray, Christofle	205.00
Bowl, Coat of Arms, c.1900, 12 1/2 In.	495.00
Box, Marked Bointaburet, Paris, 2 7/8 x 1 1/4 In.	65.00
Chocolate Pot, Undulating Tulips, Monogram, Cardeilhac, 1900, 9 5/8 In.	4950.00
Coffeepot, Bud Finial, Lion Mask Spout, Marked DG, 11 3/4 In.	1875.00
Coffeepot, Grapevine, Fruit Finial, M. Lebrun, c.1830, 11 3/8 In.	4125.00
Compote, Louis XVI, Plated, Bointaburet, 1893, 10 1/4 In., Pair ....*Illus*	2310.00
Dressing Table Set, Concentric Circles, J. Puiforcat, 1930–1940, 6 Piece	3850.00
Ewer, Basin, Pear Shape Ewer, Female Caryatid Handle, c.1865	5225.00
Frame, Initial G, Cartier, Double, 6 1/4 x 4 1/4 In.	125.00
Inkstand, Classical, Cartouche Footed, E. Hugo, 1860, 16 In. ....*Illus*	2310.00
Pillbox, Portrait On Lid, Beveled Mirror Under Lid, 1 3/8 In.	137.50

Silver-French, Inkstand, Classical, Cartouche Footed, E. Hugo, 1860, 16 In.

Protractor, Butterfield A Paris, 1700, 2 5/8 In. 395.00
Salt & Pepper, Classical Style, Cartier, 4 1/4 In. 300.00
Tray, Chased Poppy & Tendrils, Foliate Handles, Cardeilhac, 1900, 26 3/4 In. 9350.00
Tray, Foliage Rim, Cartier, 14–In. Diam. 412.00
Tureen, Lobster On Cover, Stand, Shell & Scroll Base, 1880s, 14 1/2 In. 6875.00
Vase, Inscribed As Golf Trophy, A. Aucoc, c.1907, 7 In. 330.00
SILVER—GERMAN, Bun Warmer, Berry Finial, Repousse Design, 3 Sections, 10 In. 1350.00
Coffeepot, Shell Thumbpiece, Fruit Finial, J. W. Kolb, 1770, 7 1/2 In. 4675.00
Cup & Saucer, Porcelain Liner, 6 Sets 125.00
Cup, Stirrup, Deer's–Head Form, 1864, 4 1/4 In. 2310.00
Dish, Chased Hydrangea Plants, 3 Scroll Feet, Late 19th Century, 23 In. 2750.00
Grape Shears, c.1890 .... 220.00
Ladle, Punch, Fiddle Tip, c.1880 .... 155.00
Mirror, Dressing Table, Rococo Border, Playful Putti, Easel, 21 1/4 In. 3025.00
Salt, Pedestal Base, Rococo, J. S. Beckensteiner, 18th Century 140.00
Spoon, Baby Feeding, The Cow Jumped Over The Moon 85.00
Sugar Box, Hinged Cover, Border of Running Leaves, c.1820, 7 1/4 In. 1350.00
Tea & Coffee Set, Dome Covers, Ivory Finials, Wollenweber, 5 Piece 3850.00
SILVER—GUATEMALAN, Butter, Cover, Threaded Shaped Rim, Pair 330.00
SILVER—HUNGARIAN, Platter, Lobed, Reeded Rim, Recessed Center, 19 x 13 In. 385.00
Spice Box, Tiered Tower, Gilt Bell, Gilt Pennants, c.1820, 11 1/4 In. 1450.00
SILVER—INDIAN, Tea & Coffee Set, Repousse With Scrolling Vines, 6 Piece 1650.00
SILVER—IRISH, Bowl, Open, William Townsend, c.1750, 5 1/4 x 2 In. 400.00
Cake Basket, Georgian Style, T. Jones, 1783 .... 1100.00
Cake Basket, Pierced Arches & Lattice, Swing Handle, 1776, 14 1/4 In. 2860.00
Creamer, Richard Whitford, c.1815, 4 3/4 In. 350.00
Gravy Spoon, Turned–Down Tip, Divided Bowl, John Pittar, 13 3/4 In. 385.00
Sauceboat, George III, Reeded Body, 1808 .... 165.00
Teaspoon, Michael Keating, c.1790 .... 75.00
SILVER—ITALIAN, Ewer, Helmet Form, Relief Vine Design, 9 1/4 In. 1045.00
Lamp, Oil, Spiraled Stem, Shade & Extinguisher, 18th Century, 8 1/2 In. 3400.00
Spoon, Demitasse, Symbols of Italian Cities On Tips, 13 Piece 110.00
Tray, Foliate Engraving, Rectangular, 22 In. 1100.00
Tray, Oval Molded Rim, Buccellati, 20th Century, 21 1/2 In. 1320.00
SILVER—JAPANESE, Teapot, Chased Floral Design, Paneled, Swing Handle, 5 1/8 In. 137.50
SILVER—MEXICAN, Bell, Dinner, Magnolia Blossom, F. Ramirez 80.00
Bowl, Fluted, Viguerras, 13 In. 137.00
Bracelet & Earrings, Filigree, Green, Oval Mineral Dome 38.50
Bracelet & Earrings, Link, Heart–Shaped Earrings 27.00
Bracelet, Hinged Silver Links, Impressed JJC, Taxco Circular Mark, 7 In. 110.00
Brooch, Blossom Form, Leaf–Form Back, 4 In. 60.00
Dish, Swan Shape, 14 1/4 In. 209.00
Figurine, Fighting Cock, Jeweled Eyes, Ruffled Feathers, 15 In., Pair 1750.00
Gravy Boat, Oval Underplate, Serpentine Rim 155.00
Pitcher, Floral Terminals, Fluted, Open Rope Handle, 9 1/2 In. 330.00
Pitcher, Shell & Scrollwork Band, Scroll Handle, 10 In. 330.00
Platter, Serpentine Rim, 1930s, Round, 14 In. 305.00
Tea Set, Fluted Sides, Ball Finial, 1920s, 5 Piece 935.00
Tea Set, Melon Form, Foliate Feet, 4 Piece 495.00
Tray, Scalloped Gallery, Round, 17 In. 550.00
SILVER—PERSIAN, Coffee & Tea Set, Hunting Scenes, Stylized Florals, 15 –In. Tray 825.00
Dish, Caviar, Engraved Landscape, Fish Bird On Handle, 6 In. 525.00
SILVER—PERUVIAN, Figurine, Rooster, Stamped Alpaca, Pair 330.00
Holder, Place Card, Figural, Llama, 8 Piece 280.00
SILVER—PORTUGUESE, Tray, Everted Arch Gallery, Handles, Vidal, c.1800, 25 In. 3410.00

SILVER—RUSSIAN. Russian silver is marked with the Cyrillic, or Russian, alphabet. The numbers 84, 88, or 91 indicate the silver content. Russian silver may be higher or lower than sterling standard. Other marks indicate maker, assayer, or city of manufacture. Many pieces of silver made in Russia are decorated with enamel. Faberge pieces are listed in their own category.

SILVER—RUSSIAN, Beaker, Niello, 1902 .... 115.00

Box, Tobacco, Gratchev	900.00
Box, Tobacco, Hinged Lid, Scrolled Vines, Niello, 3 1/2 In.	440.00
Candlestick, Gilt & Enamel, 19th Century, 5 1/2 In., Pair	1870.00
Menorah, Vase Shaped Lamps, Palm Trees At Ends, 1883, 8 5/8 In.	2750.00
Plaque, Double–Headed Eagle, Enameled Corners, 1830, 10 1/2 x 9 In.	665.00
Snuffbox, Equestrian Statue of Peter The Great, 1815, 3 1/2 In.	450.00
Sugar Spoon, Enameled, Marked SA88	150.00
Tray, With Stand, Handles, Dated 1857, Marked AM, 28 In.	9450.00
Vase, Turquoise Enamel, Gilt, Gustav Klingert, 1893, 5 1/2 In.	550.00
Wine Cooler, Alexander I, 1806	6050.00
SILVER–SCOTTISH, Cup, Presentation, George IV, Robert Gray, 1820, 9 1/4 In. *Illus*	1320.00
Ladle, Soup, George IV, 1823	600.00
Spoon, Dessert, George IV, 12 Piece	1800.00
Spoon, Stuffing, George IV, 12 In.	500.00
SILVER–SOUTH AMERICAN, Candlestick, Baluster–Turned, Scrolled Feet, 17 In., Pr.	450.00
Dish, Ragout, Hammered, Waved Rim, Bail Handles, 16 1/2 In.	2750.00

SILVER–STERLING. Sterling silver is made with 925 parts silver out of 1,000 parts of metal. The word *sterling* is a quality guarantee used in the United States after about 1860. The word was used much earlier in England and Ireland. Pieces listed here are not identified by country. Other pieces of sterling quality silver are listed under Silver–American, Silver–English, etc.

Belt Buckle, Dinkelstein Cord	345.00
Bowl, Footed, Monogrammed, 2 3/4 In.	25.00
Bowl, Footed, Rococo Rim, 7 In.	990.00
Bowl, Turned–In Rim, Seth Ek, 3 7/8 In.	295.00
Bowl, Vegetable, Pierced Scrollwork, Shell Rim, Fluted Sides, 2 x 10 In.	198.00
Box, Hinged, Peacock Enameled, Bun Feet, 3 1/2 x 2 3/8 In.	990.00
Box, Spice, Rectangular, Sliding Cover, Divided Interior, 2 3/4 In.	1875.00
Bread Basket, Square, Pierced Lattice, Central Floral, Swing Handle, 12 In.	1325.00
Butter, Cover, Oval, Beaded Borders, Cow Finial, 7 1/2 In.	3100.00
Cake Plate, Floral Scrollwork, Playful Putti, c.1910	77.00
Cake Server, Mother–of–Pearl Handle	48.00
Candlestick, Louis XV, Gorham, 1891, 12 1/2 In., 4 Pc. ....*Illus*	3850.00
Card Case, Applied & Engraved Crest, Blue Enamel Lines	154.00
Cigarette Case, Pig Form, Cabochon Clasp, c.1910, 4 x 2 3/4 In.	605.00
Cigarette Holder, Art Deco, Eastern Europe	35.00
Coaster, Fluted Rim, Stylized Flower Chased From Back, 3 5/8 In.	180.00
Cocktail Shaker, c.1936, 3 Pint, 9 1/2 In.	220.00
Cocktail Shaker, Matching Spoon, Cartier	495.00
Coffeepot, Tapering, Oval, Hinged Lid, Wood Handle, 1895, 7 In.	185.00
Compote, Flared Rim, Shallow Bowl, Foliate Stem, Impressed Mark, 5 In.	495.00
Creamer, Handmade, Hammered Finish, 4 1/4 In.	40.00
Cup, George II, Bell–Shaped Body, Engraved, 2 Scroll Handles, 10 1/2 In.	6875.00

Silver-Scottish, Cup, Presentation,
George IV, Robert Gray, 1820, 9 1/4 In.

Silver-Sterling, Candlestick, Louis XV,
Gorham, 1891, 12 1/2 In., 4 Pc.

◆◆◆◆◆◆◆◆◆◆◆◆◆◆◆◆◆◆◆◆◆◆◆

Gold or silver lace may tarnish.
Sometimes it can be cleaned
by rubbing it with a brush
dipped in warm white wine.

◆◆◆◆◆◆◆◆◆◆◆◆◆◆◆◆◆◆◆◆◆◆◆

Silver-Sterling, Tea Set, Johnson & Reat,

   Richmond, Va., 1804-1813, 3 Pc.

Dish, Lobed Scalloped Sides, Volund Shop, 1910s, 11 7/8 In.	2100.00
Dish, Oval, Paw Feet, 5 3/4 In.	50.00
Dish, Scrolled Rim, 4 3/4 In.	26.00
Dresser Set, Hand–Hammered Design, Mirror, Art Deco	385.00
Epergne, Grape Holder, With Grape Shears	775.00
Frame, Double, Initial G, Cartier, 6 1/4 x 4 1/2 In.	125.00
Goblet, George III, Circular Bowl, Square Flat Base, 7 1/4 In.	145.00
Goblet, Pedestal, Engraved L	170.00
Hunting Horn, Bee Mark, Jacquor A. Nancy, Early 1800s, 9 1/2 In.	235.00
Ladle, Leaf Handle, Engraved B, 6 In.	44.00
Mirror, Hand, Carved Green Jade, Velvet Back, Edward I. Farmer, 14 1/2 In.	1950.00
Mug, Traveling, Cover, Alcohol Burner, 6 1/2 In.	121.00
Mustard Pot, Hinged Cover, Footed, Cranberry Glass Container, 2 1/2 In.	215.00
Pitcher, Classic Bulbous Form, Porter Blanchard, 8 3/8 In.	1750.00
Pitcher, Engraved Floral Band, Garlands On Sides, c.1910, 8 In.	165.00
Pitcher, Sleek Lines, Porter Blanchard, Post–1930, 6 1/4 In.	750.00
Pitcher, Water, Lightly Hammered, Engraved FEF, 1900s, 8 1/4 In.	1750.00
Pitcher, Water, Tray, Dunstan Pattern, Art Deco Monogram, 8–In. Pitcher	2475.00
Plate, Cinderella Pattern, Gorham, 1929, 10 7/8 In., 6 Piece	550.00
Plate, Corn & Cornflower Enameled, Gorham, 1871, 10 1/2 In.	715.00
Plate, Fluted Rim, 10 1/2 In.	105.00
Plate, Rising Sides, Square, George C. Erickson, 9 1/8 In.	425.00
Rattle, Clown's Face, 4 Bells & Whistle	250.00
Rattle, Twisted Stem, Crossbars, Heart, Whistle, 2 Bells	15.00
Relish, Repousse Rococo Rim, Monogrammed H, 8 x 13 3/4 In.	192.00
Rosary	95.00
Salt & Pepper, Lighthouse Shape, Bead Finial, F. Walter Lawrence, 2 3/4 In.	450.00
Salt, Chinese Coolie Pulling Rickshaw	125.00
Salt, Swan, Gemstone Ruby Eyes, Spoon	200.00
Saltcellar, Hammered Surface, George Friedell, 1 1/4 x 2 1/2 In.	125.00
Salver, Cast Floral Handles, 9 3/8 In., Pair	374.00
Sauceboat, Lion's Head, Feet, Floral Tooling, 4 1/2 In.	150.00
Sauceboat, Monogrammed, 4 3/4 In.	105.00
Serving Spoon, Pierced Fleur–De–Lis Bowl, Erickson	44.00
Spoon, Feeding, Baby's, Cow Jumped Over The Moon	85.00
Spoon, Jack of Clubs Handle, Pierced Bowl, 4 1/2 In.	60.00
Spoon, Souvenir, see Souvenir category	
Stamp Box, Inset Zircons, c.1936	935.00
Stand, Sugar Cube, Handmade, Blossom Handles	66.00
Tea & Coffee Set, Miniature, 5 Piece	170.00
Tea Set, Johnson & Reat, Richmond, Va., 1804–1813, 3 Pc. *Illus*	4000.00
Tea Set, Monogrammed C. W. A., 3 Piece	300.00
Tea Set, Paneled, Beaded, Monogrammed, 5 Piece	715.00
Tray, Oblong, Tooled Rim, 11 3/4 In.	50.00
Tray, Tea, Oval, 2 Chased Handles, Chased Border, 4–Footed, 26 3/8 In.	4125.00
Tureen, Cover, George III, Thomas Robin, 1811	8250.00

Tweezers, Art Nouveau, Wide	28.00
Vase, Bud, Hammered, Monogrammed, Glass Liner, Friedel, 8 In.	110.00
Vase, Scroll & Acanthus Design, Ruffled Flared Rim, 14 In.	330.00
Vase, Trumpet, Blossom–Form Rim, Tapering Body, 11 In.	77.00
Vase, Trumpet, Stiff Leaves, Star–Burst Foot, Marked ME, 12 1/4 In.	1100.00
SILVER–SWEDISH, Ladle, Punch, Turned Fruitwood Handle, Lundstrom, 18th C.	385.00
SILVER–SWISS, Coffeepot, Collar of Foliage, Flowers & Shells, c.1835, 8 3/4 In.	1760.00

SINCLAIRE cut glass was made by H. P. Sinclaire and Company of Corning, New York, between 1905 and 1929. He cut glass made at other factories until 1920. Pieces were made of crystal as well as amber, blue, green, or ruby glass. Only a small percentage of Sinclaire glass is marked with the S in a wreath.

Bowl, Nature Pattern, Silver Threads, Signed, 9 3/4 x 4 1/2 In.	55.00
Candlestick, Daisies & Leaf, 12 In., Pair	250.00
Cookie Jar, Medallion & Diamond, 8 1/2 In.	1150.00
Dish, Mint, Snowflake & Holly	700.00
Dish, Nut, Snowflake & Holly	700.00
Goblet, Flute & Festoon	50.00
Pitcher, Intaglio, Bulbous	350.00
Platter, Snowflake & Holly, Oval, Signed	1300.00
Teapot, Cut & Etched, 5 In.	1705.00
Tray, Empire Pattern, 8 Sides, Signed, 10 1/4 In.	170.00
Tray, Serving, Adelphia, 12 x 8 3/8 In.	950.00
Vase, Acid Etched, Clearl, 13 In.	145.00

SKIING, see Sports category

SLAG GLASS resembles a marble cake. It can be streaked with different colors. There were many types made from about 1880. Pink slag was an American Victorian product of unknown origin. Purple and blue slag were made in American and English factories. Red slag is a very late Victorian and twentieth–century glass. Other colors are known but are of less importance to the collector. New versions of chocolate glass and colored slag glass are being made.

Caramel slag is listed in the Chocolate Glass category

Green, Box, Cover, Rooster	135.00
Orange, Dish, Rabbit Cover	40.00
Pink, Sauce, Inverted Fan & Feather, Footed, 6 Piece ....995.00 To 1200.00
Pink, Tumbler, Inverted Fan & Feather, 4 In. .... 295.00 To 325.00
Purple, Compote, Cover, Imperial	110.00
Purple, Compote, Design, Pedestal, 5 In.	70.00
Purple, Compote, Spool Pattern, 6 In.	48.00
Purple, Creamer, Sunflower	68.00
Purple, Dish, 3 Ducks Cover	100.00
Purple, Dish, Duck, Hen & Turtle Cover	50.00
Purple, Dish, Lion Cover, Imperial	110.00
Purple, Dish, Rabbit Cover	45.00
Purple, Jar, Cover, Dolphin	100.00
Purple, Match Holder, Square, 4 In.	40.00
Purple, Vase, Square, Footed, 3 3/4 In.	60.00
Red, Vase, Dancing Lady, Imperial, 8 1/2 In.	98.00

SLEEPY EYE collectors look for anything bearing the image of the nineteenth–century Indian chief with the drooping eyelid. The Sleepy Eye Milling Co., Sleepy Eye, Minnesota, used his portrait in advertising from 1883 to 1921. It offered many premiums, including stoneware and pottery steins, crocks, bowls, mugs, and pitchers, all decorated with the famous profile of the Indian. The popular pottery was made by Western Stoneware and other companies long after the flour mill went out of business in 1921. Reproductions of the pitchers are being made today. The original pitchers

came in only five sizes: 4 inches, 5 1/4 inches, 6 1/2 inches, 8 inches, and 9 inches. The Sleepy Eye image was also used by companies unrelated to the flour mill.

Barrel, Grapevine Band	1250.00
Cookbook	7.50
Decanter, Rye Whiskey	655.00
Flour Sack	275.00
Flour Sack, Paper	65.00
Mug, 1977, Collector's Convention	85.00
Mug, Blue & White	185.00 To 200.00
Paddle, Canoe	180.00
Pitcher Set, No. 1 Through 5, 5 Piece	1600.00
Pitcher, No. 1, Blue & Gray	160.00
Pitcher, No. 1, Blue & White	95.00
Pitcher, No. 2, Blue & White	125.00
Pitcher, No. 3, Blue & Gray	175.00 To 395.00
Pitcher, No. 4, Blue Rim	225.00
Pitcher, No. 5, Blue & White	230.00
Pitcher, No. 5, Blue Rim	290.00
Pitcher, Standing Indian, 8 In.	800.00
Salt Crock, Blue & Gray	425.00
Sign, Flour, Metal	210.00
Sign, Tin, Yellow Ground, Large	1525.00
Stein, All Blue	725.00
Stein, All Brown	260.00
Stein, Brown & Yellow	695.00
Vase, Indian & Cattails, 8 1/2 In.	275.00
Vase, Indian & Cattails, Flemish	295.00 To 375.00

SLIPWARE is named for *slip,* a thin mixture of clay and water, about the consistency of sour cream, which is applied to pottery for decoration. It is a very old method of making pottery and is still in use.

Canister Set, 3 Apples & Pear, Tea, Sugar & Flower, Purinton, 3 Piece	58.00
Dish, Coggled Rim, England, 18th Century, 15 In.	1800.00
Jug, Initial TK, England, 1780, 6 In.	425.00

SLOT MACHINES are included in the Coin–Operated Machine category.

SMITH BROTHERS glass was made after 1878. Alfred and Harry Smith had worked for the Mt. Washington Glass Company in New Bedford, Massachusetts, for seven years before going into their own shop. They made many pieces with enamel decoration.

Smith Bros. Co.

Biscuit Barrel, Rampant Lion On Base, Daises, Silver Plated Cover	375.00
Bowl, Yellow Flowers, Blue Scroll, Ribbed, Red Lion, 3 1/2 In.	235.00
Lamp, Signed, Miniature	525.00
Powder Jar, Cover, Floral, Melon Ribbed	250.00
Rose Bowl, Daisies, Yellow Shaded Centers, Beaded Rim, 4 1/2 In.	195.00
Salt, Open, Floral	85.00
Sugar & Creamer, Gold & Jeweled Design, Melon Ribbed, Signed	585.00
Syrup, 4 3/4 In.	685.00
Syrup, Melon Ribbed, Enameled Daisies	650.00
Vase, Bird On Branch, Red Berries, Leaves, Double Ring Bands, 5 7/8 In.	75.00
Vase, Leaves, Cream, 5 In.	300.00
Vase, Wisteria Blossoms On Vine, Cream Ground, Gold Borders, 8 1/2 In.	845.00

SNOW BABIES, made from bisque and spattered with glitter sand, were first manufactured in 1864 by Hertwig and Company of Thuringia. Other German and Japanese companies copied the Hertwig designs. Originally, Snow Babies were made of candy and used as Christmas decorations. There are also Snow Babies tablewares made by Royal Bayreuth. Copies of the small Snow Babies figurines are being made today and can easily confuse the collector.

Chamberstick, Shield, Blue Mark 250.00
Figurine, On Red Sled 155.00
Figurine, On Skis 158.00
Figurine, Riding Polar Bear 185.00
Figurine, Sitting, Outstretched Arms, Germany, 1 1/4 In. 118.00
Planter, Double Handle, Porcelain Liner, 2 3/4 In. 165.00
Plate, Royal Bayreuth, 6 In. 95.00

SNUFF BOTTLES are listed in the Bottle category.

SNUFFBOXES held snuff. Taking snuff was popular long before cigarettes became available. The gentleman or lady would take a small pinch of the ground tobacco or snuff in the fingers, then sniff it and sneeze. Snuffboxes were made of many materials, including gold, silver, enameled metal, and wood. Most snuffboxes date from the late eighteenth or early nineteenth centuries.

Almond–Shaped Horn, Design With Flowers, Man, Woman In Woods, 3 In. 150.00
Animal Horn, Gray, Carved, England 65.00
Argylite, Chinese Man, Riding Mythical Animal, c.1930, 4 In. 125.00
Birchbark, Tooled Sunburst Design 27.00
Black Lacquer, Gold Trim 90.00
Bone Segments, Hinged Bone Cover, Colonial American, 2 7/8 In. 110.00
Burl, Tortoiseshell Lining, People Dancing, General Revelry, Small Town, 4 In. 165.00
Continental Silver, Tavern Scene 100.00
Figural Shoe, Multiple Compartments, 1 With Combination Lock, 1773 .... 6400.00
Gutta Percha, Plays 2 Japanese Tunes 1000.00
Ivory, Gourd With Flowers, c.1930, 3 1/4 In. 195.00
Leather, High Button Shoe, Inlaid Mother–of–Pearl Hinged Lid 175.00
Medieval Woman On Lid, c.1850, 3 5/8 x 2 In. 45.00
Olive Woods Scene, 3 1/2 In. 50.00
Papier–Mache, Presentation of Dowry, Tortoiseshell Lined, French, 3 In. 935.00
Shoe, Pewter Lid 595.00
Tortoiseshell, Gilt Metal Lid, Profile of Napoleon & Josephine, 3 1/4 In. 165.00
Tortoiseshell, Inlaid Gold & Silver, Paris, 1756 .... 410.00
Wooden, Hand Painted Castle, Germany, c.1890 .... 150.00
Yellow Glazed Porcelain, Chinoiserie Design, Round, French 395.00

SOAPSTONE is a mineral that was used for foot warmers or griddles because of its heat–retaining properties. Soapstone was carved into figurines and bowls in many countries in the nineteenth and twentieth centuries. Most of the soapstone seen today is from China or Japan. It is still being carved in the old styles.

Bookends, Demons, 4 3/4 In. 35.00
Figurine, 3 Monkeys, See No Evil, Speak No Evil & Hear No Evil, 3 Piece 36.00
Figurine, Bird, With Flowers 75.00
Figurine, Bison & Children, Wood Stand, 11 1/2 x 15 In. 330.00
Figurine, Bride & Groom, 1920s 75.00
Figurine, Elephant, Dragon Dog, Elephant With Howdah, 7 1/2 In., 3 Piece 82.00
Figurine, Oriental Wise Man, 13 1/2 In. 230.00
Figurine, Rearing Horse, Flying Mane, Hooves Raised, 12 x 9 In. 150.00
Figurine, Sage & Foo Dog, 19th Century, 4 1/2 In. 220.00
Figurine, Woman, Rose Color, Late 1800s, 5 In. 55.00
Incense Burner, Elephant & Foo Dog 65.00
Planter, 4 Pockets, Floral, Vines, Late 1800s, 12 In. 76.00
Plaque, Bird, Trees, Flowers & Rocks, Stand, 9 1/2 In. 120.00
Toothpick, Three Monkeys 15.00

SOFT PASTE is a name for a type of pottery. Although it looks very much like porcelain, it is a chemically different material. Most of the soft-paste wares were made in the early nineteenth century. Other pieces may be listed under Gaudy Dutch or Leeds.

Basket, Fruit, Blue & White Canton–Type Design, Staffordshire, 5 1/2 In. 297.00
Cup & Saucer, 12 Varying Scenes, Gold Clover Border, c.1820, 6 Sets 330.00

Cup, Child's, Sarah 310.00
Mug, Child's, Girl With Donkey & Goat, Black & Pink 65.00
Mug, Child's, Market Lady With Hares, 2 5/16 In. 210.00
Pitcher, Bagpiper, Pig At Feet, 6 1/2 In. 115.00
Pitcher, Child's, Adelaide 295.00
Pitcher, Old Women Ground, Young Woman Transfer, 5 3/4 In. 35.00
Plate, Eagle & Flag Transfer, Union Forever, Centennial & E Pluribus Unum 395.00
Plate, King's Rose, Solid Border, 8 1/4 In. 95.00
Plate, Leaf Design, Feather Rim, Leeds, 6 3/4 In. 450.00

SOUVENIRS of a trip—what could be more fun? Our ancestors enjoyed the same thing and souvenirs were made for almost every location. Most of the souvenir pottery and porcelain pieces of the nineteenth century were made in England or Germany, even if the picture showed a North American scene. In the twentieth century, the souvenir china business seems to have gone to the manufacturers in Japan, Taiwan, Hong Kong, England, and America. Another popular souvenir item is the souvenir spoon, made of sterling or silver plate. These are usually made in the country pictured on the spoon. Related pieces may be found in the Coronation and World's Fair categories.

Apron, $64, 000 Question, Original Paper Tag 36.00
Ashtray, Ceramic, Account of Moon Landing, With Headlines, 8 In. 15.00
Ashtray, Ceramic, Nat King Cole 125.00
Ashtray, Copper, Chrysler Exhibit, Box, 1933 .... 15.00
Ashtray, Sterling Silver, Horseshoe, Worn By Whirlaway The Horse 2200.00
Beer Mug, Kentucky State University, Cranberry, Large 5.00
Belt, Coney Island, Leather, Indian Style Beading, 1940 .... 47.50
Bowl, Illinois Soldiers & Sailors Home, Blue, Carnival Glass 1000.00
Button, John Glenn, Well Done, Col. Glenn, First American In Orbit, 1962, 2 In. ... 18.50
Card, Coney Island, Colored, Packet, 1920, 20 Piece 15.00
Card, Tournament of Roses, 16 Views, Foldout, 1932 .... 35.00
Champagne, Brass, Santa Anita Ball, 1938, Miniature, 3 Piece 300.00
Cigarette Dispenser, Donkey, Tin, Paradise Valley, El Dorado Creek 225.00
Clothes Sprinkler, Iron Shape, Ceramic, Six Flags 18.00
Coloring Book, Amy Carter's White House 8.00
Cup & Saucer, United Nations, Bone China, Demitasse 10.00
Cup, Colorado, Tin, Dog Tag, 1903 .... 75.00
Dish, Canadian National Exhibition, Metal, 1949 .... 17.00
Figurine, Statue of Liberty, Cast Metal, Oak Base, 12 In. 25.00
Hat, Graduation, Felt, University of Illinois, Dated 1914, Autographed 30.00
Hot Water Bottle, Jayne Mansfield, 1957 .... 55.00
Hot Water Bottle, Marilyn Monroe 125.00
Key, Convention Hall, Atlantic City, Box 15.00
Loving Cup, Cat Show, Sterling Silver, 1919 .... 50.00
Mug, Jackson Court House, Kansas City, Mo. 10.00
Mug, St. Louis Exposition, Ruby Stained, Button Arches, 1904 .... 45.00
Pennant, Cisco Kid & Pancho Rodeo, Felt, 1950s, 26 In. 45.00
Placemat, Indy 500, 1964, 4 Piece 20.00
Planter, Louis Armstrong, Ceramic 145.00
Plate, Carnegie Library, Chickasha, Ok., Wheelock, 7 In. 12.00
Plate, Court House, Hamilton, Oh., 6 In. 12.00
Plate, Fairbury, Neb., 5 1/2 In. 10.00
Plate, Old City Gate, St. Augustine, Fla., France Depose, 1910, 8 In. 25.00
Plate, Summer Olympics, 1980 .... 50.00
Ribbon, Columbian Expo, 400th Anniversary, Landing of Columbus, 2 x 7 In. 80.00
Spoon, Silver Plate, Columbian Expo, Columbus Handle, Demitasse 10.00
Spoon, Silver Plate, Hawaii, NASA 5.00
Spoon, Silver Plate, J. F. Kennedy 15.00
Spoon, Silver Plate, Liberty Bell 12.00
Spoon, Silver Plate, Minnesota 9.00
Spoon, Silver Plate, Ohio 9.00
Spoon, Sterling Silver, Alaska, Enameled Fish 25.00
Spoon, Sterling Silver, Anheuser–Busch, Exposition, 1967 .... 10.00

Spoon, Sterling Silver, Battle Monument, Baltimore, Cutout Indian Handle 30.00
Spoon, Sterling Silver, Boston Tea Party, Standing Indian 175.00
Spoon, Sterling Silver, Brooklyn Bridge, New York Handle, 5 1/4 In. 35.00
Spoon, Sterling Silver, Brooklyn Bridge, Statue of Liberty 120.00
Spoon, Sterling Silver, Brooklyn, N.Y., Demitasse, 1905 .... 20.00
Spoon, Sterling Silver, Burlington, Iowa, Civil War Soldier 65.00
Spoon, Sterling Silver, Charleston, S. C. 12.00
Spoon, Sterling Silver, Deer Hunting In Colorado 75.00
Spoon, Sterling Silver, Denver, Mule, Gold Miner On Handle 30.00
Spoon, Sterling Silver, Fayette, N. C. 12.00
Spoon, Sterling Silver, Florida 12.00
Spoon, Sterling Silver, Georgia, State Capitol, Eagle & Flag, Emblem Bowl 12.00
Spoon, Sterling Silver, Hiawatha, Kansas 20.00
Spoon, Sterling Silver, Indianapolis 12.00
Spoon, Sterling Silver, July, Commemorative 30.00
Spoon, Sterling Silver, Log Cabin, Towle 5.00
Spoon, Sterling Silver, Longfellow's Home, Figural Bust At Handle 195.00
Spoon, Sterling Silver, Los Angeles, Lady With Wings Figural Cutout Handle 45.00
Spoon, Sterling Silver, Manchester, Iowa 14.00
Spoon, Sterling Silver, Mary Baker Eddy 47.50
Spoon, Sterling Silver, McCook, Nebr. 14.00
Spoon, Sterling Silver, Minnehaha Falls, Canoe, Teepee, Indian Tools 12.00
Spoon, Sterling Silver, New Orleans 12.00
Spoon, Sterling Silver, Oakland, Calif., Fish Handle 30.00
Spoon, Sterling Silver, Oakland, Calif., Indian, Lake Merritt Bowl 40.00
Spoon, Sterling Silver, Old Indian House, Deerfield, Mass., 1704 .... 40.00
Spoon, Sterling Silver, Old South Meeting House, Standing Indian 150.00
Spoon, Sterling Silver, Park School, Rutherford, New Jersey 30.00
Spoon, Sterling Silver, Salem, Witch Handle, Cat Bowl 135.00
Spoon, Sterling Silver, San Francisco, Sailboat, Setting Sun, Emblem Bowl 15.00
Spoon, Sterling Silver, Seattle, Indian Chief, Mt. Ranier Bowl 30.00
Spoon, Sterling Silver, Seven Falls, Color., Emblem Bowl 12.00
Spoon, Sterling Silver, Stone Mill, Newport, Seal of Rhode Island, 4 3/4 In. 110.00
Spoon, Sterling Silver, Texas, Sam Houston Bust 35.00
Spoon, Sterling Silver, Thousand Islands, Side Wheel, Coastline Engraved 35.00
Spoon, Sterling Silver, Township High School, Joliet, Ill. 35.00
Spoon, Sterling Silver, Vandalia, Ill. 20.00
Spoon, Sterling Silver, Washington Elm, Cambridge, 5 In. 95.00
Spoon, Sterling Silver, White House, U.S. Seal 150.00
Spoon, Sterling Silver, Youngstown, Ohio 25.00
Stickpin, American Exposition, Frying Pan, Embossed Buffalo Head, 1901 .... 33.00
Swizzle Stick, Penthouse Strippers, 8 Piece 15.00
Teapot, Views of Niagara Falls, Copper Luster Neck Band, 7 1/2 In. 50.00
Tie, Man's, Marilyn Monroe Front 24.00
Toothpick, Cuttyhunk Lifesaving Station 35.00
Tray, Alaska–Yukon Pacific Exposition, Gold Trim, Signed, 7 In. 90.00
Tray, New York City, Metal, Occupied Japan 8.00
Tumbler, Blue Glass, Goshen, Ind. 27.00
Tumbler, Frankenstein, Anchor Hocking, 1963 .... 89.00
Tumbler, Green, Gold Flashed, Nappanee, Ind. 23.00
Tumbler, New York Giants, Super Bowl XXI, Jan. 15, 1987 .... 15.00
Tumbler, Saratoga, 1907 .... 25.00
Vase, Blue Glass, Gold Flashed, Valparaiso, Ind. 24.00
Vase, Custard Glass, Ellsworth, Wis. 38.00
White House, Metal 24.00

SPANGLE GLASS is multicolored glass made from odds and ends of
colored glass rods. It includes metallic flakes of mica covered with gold,
silver, nickel, or copper. Spangle glass is usually cased with a thin layer of
clear glass over the multicolored layer. Similar glass is listed in the Vasa
Murrhina category.

Basket, Emerald Green Swirl, Allover Mica, Clear Twisted Handle, 6 1/2 In. 100.00
Ewer, Silver On White, Crystal Cased, Crimped Handle, 9 1/2 In. 155.00

Tumbler, Pink, Amber & Silver Flakes	95.00
Vase, Green, Mica, Enameled Art Nouveau Design	310.00

SPANISH LACE is a type of Victorian glass that has a white lace design. Blue, yellow, cranberry, or clear glass was made with this distinctive white pattern. It was made in England and the United States after 1885. Copies are being made.

Bowl, Upturned Edge, Vaseline	95.00
Lamp, Oil, Miniature	195.00
Pitcher, Cranberry	850.00
Pitcher, Pleated Top, Cranberry	650.00
Pitcher, Star-Shaped Rim, Blue	395.00
Rose Bowl, Cranberry Edge, Ruffled	75.00
Spooner, Ruffled, Blue	85.00
Spooner, Vaseline	80.00
Sugar Shaker, Blue	175.00
Vase, Cranberry, Peach, Rippled Rim	400.00

SPATTER GLASS is a multicolored glass made from many small pieces of different colored glass. It is sometimes called *End-of-Day* glass. It is still being made.

Basket, Mottled Maroon, Pink, Aqua, White Lining, Clear Thorn Handle, 7 In.	165.00
Basket, White Lining, Clear Thorny Handle, Ruffled, 6 x 4 3/4 In.	165.00
Basket, Yellow, White, Clear Twisted Handle, Square, 5 3/4 In.	95.00
Lamp Base, Swirl, Cranberry, Miniature	185.00
Pitcher, Blue Tones, 19th Century	250.00
Rose Bowl, Crimped	60.00
Salt, Open, Oval	210.00
Vase, 10 In.	20.00
Vase, 11 In.	275.00
Vase, Fan, Blue, 8 In.	300.00
Vase, Green, White, 3-Ringed Neck, Ruffled, 8 1/2 In.	30.00
Vase, White & Mica Flakes, Aventurine	195.00

SPATTERWARE is the creamware or soft paste dinnerware decorated with colored spatter designs. The earliest pieces were made in the late eighteenth century, but most of the spatterware found today was made from about 1800 to 1850, or it is a form of kitchen crockery with added spatter designs, made in the late nineteenth and twentieth centuries. The early spatterware was made in the Staffordshire district of England for sale in America. The later kitchen type is an American product.

Bowl & Pitcher, Red, Peafowl, Green, Blue, Black, 11 In.	632.00
Creamer, Cow, Black & Orange, Green Base, 5 In.	400.00
Creamer, Cow, Black, Orange, Green Base, Impressed Label, 5 In.	440.00
Creamer, Rainbow, 3 3/8 In.	100.00
Creamer, Red & Green	285.00
Cup & Saucer, 4-Part Flower, Brown, Handleless, Blue, Black, Red	468.00
Cup & Saucer, Handleless, Purple	258.00
Cup & Saucer, Red & Green, 6 Piece	660.00
Cup & Saucer, Tic-Tac-Toe Design, 6 Sets	660.00
Pitcher, Blue, Fort Scene, 5 1/2 In.	1200.00
Pitcher, Chinoiserie Panel, Transfer Printed, 10 In.	247.50
Pitcher, Diagonal Lines, 5 Colors	880.00
Pitcher, Milk, Rainbow, 9 In.	3600.00
Pitcher, Milk, Red, Acorns & Oak Leaves, 9 In.	3200.00
Pitcher, Rainbow	525.00
Pitcher, Straight Lines	700.00
Plate, Acorn, Oak Leaf, 2 Shades of Green, Black, Yellow, 8 1/4 In.	660.00
Plate, Adam's Rose, Blue With Red, Green & Black, 7 1/2 In.	330.00
Plate, Bull's-Eye Center, Rainbow, Black, Purple, 8 In.	280.00
Plate, Dahlia, Blue, Green & Black, Yellow Ground	925.00
Plate, Dahlia, Yellow, Blue, Green, Black, 8 3/4 In.	1018.00
Plate, Eagle Center, Blue	135.00

Plate, Floral Design, Blue & Green, Polychrome, 8 3/8 In. 358.00
Plate, Gaudy Floral, Blue & Green, 8 3/8 In. 325.00
Plate, Horses, Pink, Blue 120.00
Plate, Oriental Blue Transfer, 9 1/2 In. 45.00
Plate, Peafowl In Blue, Yellow, Green, Black, Red, 8 1/4 In. 248.00
Plate, Peafowl, Red 225.00
Plate, Peafowl, Red, Yellow, Black, 8 1/2 In. 110.00
Plate, Star Center In Red, Green, Yellow, Blue, 8 1/4 In. 600.00
Plate, Tulip, Purple Spatter Border, 8 1/4 In. 275.00
Platter, Rainbow, Red, Blue, Green With White Center, 17 1/2 In. 369.00
Platter, Rainbow, White Center, Adams, 17 1/2 In. 335.00
Platter, Rose In Red, Black, Green, Rose, 13 1/2 In. 220.00
Soup, Dish, Cowboys, Blue, Ted Transfer, 11 In. 50.00
Soup, Dish, Tulip, Purple, Red, Blue, Green, Black, 10 1/2 In. 220.00
Sugar, Blue, Drape In Red, Blue, 5 In. 330.00
Sugar, Green, 4 1/2 In. 155.00
Sugar, Peafowl In Purple, Green, Red, Black, 4 1/2 In. 116.00
Sugar, Peafowl, Blue, 4 1/4 In. 145.00
Sugar, Vining Floral, Black, Red & Green, Purple, 5 3/4 In. 55.00
Teapot, Green, 4 1/4 In. 380.00
Teapot, Holly Berry Design, Blue, Green, Black, 9 In. 275.00
Teapot, Red & Green Rainbow, 7 In. 220.00
Teapot, Rooster, Blue With Red, Blue, Yellow & Black, 5 3/4 In. 275.00
Teapot, With Rose, Red, Green, 6 1/4 In. 275.00
Waste Bowl, Eagle & Shield, Blue, 6 1/2 In. 121.00

SPELTER is a synonym for a zinc alloy. Figurines, candlesticks, and other
pieces were made of spelter and given a bronze or painted finish. The
metal has been used since about the 1860s to make statues, tablewares, and
lamps that resemble bronze. Spelter is soft and breaks easily. To test for
spelter, scratch the base of the piece. Bronze is solid; spelter will show a
silvery scratch.

Figurine, Dad's Pipe, Boy, 7 In. 110.00
Figurine, Girl In Wind, Onyx Pedestal, Melo, 14 1/2 In. 275.00
Figurine, Industrie, Lady Holding Wreath & Hammer, 16 3/4 In. 60.00
Figurine, Little Girls Standing On Chair, Holding Shoe, 13 1/4 In. 120.00
Figurine, Nubian, Standing, Gold Painted, 9 1/4 In. 100.00
Figurine, Youth, Communing With Bird, Marble & Onyx Base 175.00
Figurine, Youthful Shepherd, Staff & Horn, c.1890, 13 x 18 In. 230.00
Garniture Set, 5–Light Candelabras, Mythological Figures, c.1860, 3 Piece 600.00
Lamp, Figural, Art Nouveau, Pair 210.00
Lamp, Woman, Sitting On Piano Singing 135.00
Pipe Rest, Rearing Horse, Art Deco 30.00

SPINNING WHEELS in the corner have been symbols of earlier times for
the past 100 years. Although spinning wheels date back to medieval days,
the ones found today are rarely more than 200 years old. Because the style
of the spinning wheel changed very little, it is often impossible to place an
exact date on a wheel.

Carved, Handmade, Old Red Paint Traces, Rectangular, 33 x 21 In. 325.00
Saxony–Type, Distaff & Arms 375.00

SPODE pottery, porcelain, and bone china were made by the Stoke–on–
Trent factory of England founded by Josiah Spode about 1770. The firm
became Copeland and Garrett from 1833 to 1847, then W. T. Copeland or
W. T. Copeland and Sons until 1976. It then became Royal Worcester
Spode Ltd. The word *Spode* appears on many pieces made by the factories.
Most collectors include all the wares under the more familiar name of
Spode. Porcelains are listed in this book by the name that appears on the
piece. Related pieces are listed under Copeland and Copeland Spode.

Bowl, Chelsea, Oval, 8 In. 50.00
Bowl, Underplate, Famille Rose, Blue & Red Border, Reticulated 1450.00
Cup & Saucer, Imari Pattern, Cobalt Ground, 1830s 275.00

Dish, Serving, Blue & Gilt Basketweave Border, Oval, Pair	585.00
Gravy Boat, Wickerlane	50.00
Plate, Bird, 12 Piece	300.00
Plate, Christmas, 1970	25.00
Relish, Italian, Blue	48.00
Teakettle, Christmas Tree, Large	275.00
Teapot, Buttercup	65.00
Toby Jug, Sir Winston Churchill, 8 1/2 In.	55.00
Tureen, Cover, Stand, Ship's Pattern Border, 1805–1825	850.00

SPONGEWARE is very similar to spatterware in appearance. The designs were applied to the ceramics by daubing the color on with a sponge or cloth. Many collectors do not differentiate between spongeware and spatterware and use the names interchangeably. Modern pottery is being made to resemble the old spongeware, but careful examination will show it is new.

Bowl & Pitcher Set, Rose Decal, Blue & White	225.00
Bowl, Cover, Blue	190.00
Bowl, Mix With Us, Farmers Grain & Mercantile, Minn., 9 3/4 In.	250.00
Chamber Pot, Open Rose, Blue & White	85.00
Cooler, Water, Blue	325.00
Cruet, Spiral Ribbing	250.00
Cup & Saucer, Plate, Stick, 3 Piece	155.00
Pitcher, Barrel, Green & Brown	85.00
Pitcher, Brown–Green On Cream, 5 1/2 In.	45.00
Pitcher, Doe & Fawn, Blue, White	185.00
Pitcher, Thumbgrip Handle	195.00
Syrup Jug	395.00
Tea Set, Child's, Blue, 16 Piece	265.00
Teapot, Blue & White, 1870–1890	2995.00
Water Cooler, Drip Catcher, Cobalt Blue Sponge	595.00

SPORTS equipment, sporting goods, brochures, and related items are listed here. Other categories of interest are Bicycle, Card, Fishing, Gun, Rifle, Sword, and Toy.

Auto Racing, Badge, Pit, Indy 500, 1964	48.00
Auto Racing, Badge, Pit, Indy 500, 1967	85.00
Auto Racing, Bumper Sticker, H–G McLaren Team, 1976 Indy Winner, 3 x 5 In.	2.50
Auto Racing, Glass, Indianapolis 500, Race Car Picture, 1966, Tall	40.00
Auto Racing, Glass, Indianapolis Motor Speedway, 1966	12.00
Auto Racing, Glass, Indianapolis Motor Speedway, Tony Hulman, 1970	12.00
Auto Racing, Glass, Indy 500	25.00
Baseball, Ad, Bob Feller, General Electric TV Show, 1952, 9 x 6 In.	10.00
Baseball, Ad, For Gloves, Stan Musial, Matted	22.00
Baseball, Ad, Phil Rizutto, Shortstop New York Yankees, 1953, 11 x 14 In.	25.00
Baseball, Ball, Autographed, Babe Ruth	1650.00 To 2530.00
Baseball, Ball, Autographed, Honus Wagner, To Freddie, Lucite Case, 1940	1450.00
Baseball, Ball, Autographed, Joe DiMaggio	300.00
Baseball, Ball, Autographed, Pete Rose	30.00
Baseball, Ball, Autographed, Stan Musial	50.00 To 125.00
Baseball, Ball, Autographed, Ted Williams	100.00
Baseball, Ball, Autographed, Tris Speaker, American League, Signed	8250.00
Baseball, Ball, Autographed, World Champion Yankee Team, 1939	247.50
Baseball, Ball, Brooklyn Dodgers, 27 Signatures, World Series, 1952	335.00
Baseball, Ball, Pirates, Roberto Clemente, 1963	360.00
Baseball, Bat Rack, Holds Glove, Aero Bat, Orange–Brown Patina	35.00
Baseball, Bat, Leaguer H & B, Signed, Mickey Mantle	500.00
Baseball, Bat, Louisville Slugger, Chicago Cubs Hall of Fame, Ernie Banks	6600.00
Baseball, Bat, Ted Williams Signed	650.00
Baseball, Bat, Warm–Up, Roy Campanella, Lead Weighted	220.00
Baseball, Bat, Yankees Championship, 1950	500.00
Baseball, Bobbin Head, Willie Mays, 1962	225.00

Baseball, Book, How To Pitch By Bob Feller, 1948 .... 15.00
Baseball, Book, Lucky To Be A Yankee, Joe DiMaggio 15.00
Baseball, Button, Babe Ruth Club Member, Photo, Large 2.50
Baseball, Button, Official American League Ball, Baseball Scene, 1896, 1 In. 95.00
Baseball, Button, Roberto Clemente, Pinback 12.00
Baseball, Cartoon, Dodger & Yankees, Willard Mullin, Signed, 1940, 17 x 14 In. 2035.00
Baseball, Figurine, Player, Celluloid, Painted, Japan, 5 5/8 In. 55.00
Baseball, Fountain Pen, Babe Ruth, Baseball Top 750.00
Baseball, Glove, Billy Martin ....:.......... 300.00
Baseball, Glove, Catfish Hunter 9.00
Baseball, Glove, George Sisler 175.00
Baseball, Glove, George Snuffy Stirnweiss 85.00
Baseball, Glove, Johnny Logan, Fielder's, Reach Co., c.1940 .... 40.00
Baseball, Glove, Mickey Mantle, Full Size 85.00
Baseball, Glove, Peewee Reese, Little League 40.00
Baseball, Glove, Phil Rizzuto 110.00
Baseball, Glove, Ray Jablonski, Box 85.00
Baseball, Guide, Spaldings Official, 1882, 4 x 6 In. 500.00
Baseball, Hat, Pete Rose Autograph 400.00
Baseball, Jersey, Pawtucket Red Sox, Wade Boggs Signed, 1977 .... 700.00
Baseball, Mitt, 1st Baseman's, U.S. Navy, Wilson Sporting Goods, 1930s 95.00
Baseball, Mug, Casey Stengel, Pewter, 1963 .... 22.00
Baseball, Official League Baseball, Don Larsen, In Photograph Box 40.00
Baseball, Pen, New York Mets, Louisville Slugger, Bat Shape, 1970s, Card 7.00
Baseball, Pencil, Mechanical, Louisville Slugger, Blue Plastic Bat, Joe DiMaggio 95.00
Baseball, Pennant, Baltimore Orioles Championship 12.00
Baseball, Pennant, Carl Yastrzemski, 1970s, 29 In. 12.00
Baseball, Pennant, Cubs & Cardinals, Felt, 1960s 15.00
Baseball, Photograph, Chicago Cardinals, Marshall Goldbert, 9 x 7 In. 6.00
Baseball, Press Pin, Chicago Cubs, All-Star Game, 1962, Box 400.00
Baseball, Program, Milwaukee Braves Vs. New York Yankees, 1957 .... 125.00
Baseball, Program, Milwaukee Brewers, 1976 .... 25.00
Baseball, Program, Opening Day, Yankee Stadium, 1923 .... 1870.00
Baseball, Program, Ted Williams' Autograph, 1939 .... 250.00
Baseball, Scorecard, Milwaukee Braves, 1962 .... 25.00
Baseball, Tray Set, Beer, Gil Hodges, Mets Uniform, Tin, 4 Coasters 45.00
Baseball, Tumbler, 1971 World Champion Pirates, Pepsi–Cola 82.00
Baseball, Tumbler, Pirates, Arby's, 1976, 16 Oz. 7.00
Baseball, Tumbler, World Champion, St. Louis Cardinals, Signed, Libbey, 1964 ...... 65.00
Baseball, Tumbler, Yankees & Blue Jays 7.00
Baseball, Uniform, Red Sox, Carl Yastrzemski, 1972 .... 2400.00
Baseball, Wristwatch, Babe Ruth 385.00
Basketball, Ball, Autographed Larry Bird, Celtic 1100.00
Basketball, Jersey, Autographed Larry Bird 200.00
Basketball, Jersey, Autographed Larry Bird, Olympic 375.00
Basketball, Jersey, Autographed Magic Johnson, Olympic 375.00
Basketball, Jersey, Autographed Michael Jordon, Olympic 375.00
Basketball, Jersey, Magic Johnson 275.00
Basketball, Jersey, Michael Jordan 275.00
Basketball, Program, NBA Playoff, Bucks & Lakers, April 14, 1972 .... 25.00
Basketball, Trophy, Sterling Silver, N.Y.U., Free Throw, 1953, International, 3 In. 50.00
Bicycle Racing, Pin, 1898 .... 85.00
Billiards, Book, Collender's Standard American Billiard Tables, 1861, 36 Pages 175.00
Billiards, Table, Brunswick–Balke–Collender, Inlay, Original Felt 9900.00
Billiards, Table, U.S. Standard, Inlay 3900.00
Bowling, Figurine, Man, Plastic, 4 In. ....*Illus* 3.00
Bowling, Figurine, Woman, Plastic, Hong Kong, 4 1/2 In. ....*Illus* 3.00
Boxing, Button, Joe Louis, The Brown Bomber, 1914–1984, 3 1/2 In. 7.50
Boxing, Gloves, Jack Dempsey, Leather, Everlast 65.00
Boxing, Gloves, Soft, Small 45.00
Boxing, Menu, Autographed Jack Dempsey, 50th Street–8th Ave., New York City ... 125.00
Boxing, Program, Ali–Foreman, Heavyweight Championship 25.00
Boxing, Program, Golden Gloves, Fort Worth, 1951 .... 5.00

Sports, Bowling, Figurine, Woman, Plastic,

Hong Kong, 4 1/2 In.; Sports, Bowling,

Figurine, Man, Plastic, 4 In.

Boxing, Ticket Stub, Dempsey–Tunney, 1927 .... 30.00
Boxing, Tin, Joe Lewis, Jack Dempsey 150.00
Canoe, Old Town, Green Paint, Decals, Cane Seats, Salesman's Sample, 50 In. 7700.00
Canoe, Old Town, Wooden, Canvas, 20 Ft. 825.00
Clay Pigeon Thrower, Olin–Western, Hand 15.00
Deep–Sea Diving, Helmet, Mark V, Copper & Brass, 1941 .... 2600.00
Fencing, Program, Naval, 1903 .... 20.00
Fishing, Box, Reel, Pflueger 10.00
Football, Button, Buckeyes Say Let A Winner Lead The Way, Hayes, 1979, 3 In. 18.00
Football, Coca–Cola Bottle, Lions, NFL, 3 Blue Stripes, Bell Shape 3.00
Football, Hat, Florida Citrus Bowl, BYU Vs. Ohio State, White, 1985 .... 15.00
Football, Helmet, Leather, 1920s .... 45.00 To 85.00
Football, Mug, Bally Grand Super Bowl, 23rd 15.00
Football, Mug, Figural, Football Player, Notre Dame 95.00
Football, Mug, Pittsburgh Steelers, Slim Jim, Logo On Helmet, Pepsi–Cola, 32 Oz. 9.00
Football, Mug, Slim Jim, Jets 15.00
Football, Program, Cleveland Browns, 1950s 185.00
Football, Program, Colby Vs. Maine, Nov. 2, 1940 .... 18.00
Football, Program, NFL, Bulldogs Vs. Panthers, Continental Football League 20.00
Football, Program, NFL, Eagles Vs. Cowboys, Nov. 26, 1961, Philadelphia 25.00
Football, Shoulder Pads, 1916 .... 37.00
Football, Ticket Stub, Yale–Princeton, 1924 .... 10.00
Football, Ticket, Army–Navy, 1926 .... 25.00
Football, Tumbler Set, Steeler Hall of Fame, 1991 .... 20.00
Football, Tumbler, Denver Broncos, Alzado 5.00
Football, Tumbler, Houston Oilers, Luv Ya Blue 5.00
Football, Tumbler, Mel Blount, Pittsburgh Steelers, Pepsi–Cola 7.00
Football, Tumbler, NFL Western Division, Team Names, Welch's, 1978 .... 45.00
Football, Tumbler, NFL, Falcons, Burger Chef, 1979 .... 4.00
Football, Tumbler, Rocky Bleir, Pittsburgh Steelers, Pepsi–Cola 7.00
Golf, Award, Women's Golf Association, Silver Plated, Glass Insert, 1940s 60.00
Golf, Book, How To Play Golf, Harry Vardon, Scotland 150.00
Golf, Book, How To Play Golf, Lardner, 1927, 64 Pages 17.50
Golf, Booklet, Union 76, Lloyd Mangrum, 1958 .... 25.00
Golf, Cap, Autographed Arnold Palmer 40.00
Golf, Club, 4–Wood, Louis Suggs 35.00
Golf, Club, Armor, Green Shaft, Putter 35.00
Golf, Club, Armor, IM5, Putter 150.00
Golf, Club, Golfcraft Continental, Wedge 20.00
Golf, Club, Hogan Apex II, Wood 250.00
Golf, Club, Hogan LH, Special, Wedge 35.00
Golf, Club, Iron, Cleveland Classic, 60–Degree Wedge 45.00
Golf, Club, Iron, Nicklaus, 3–PW, 1967 .... 750.00
Golf, Club, Mac Muirfield 20th, Irons, 2–PW, 6–9, 5 .... 280.00
Golf, Club, Medallion Copper Bust, Wedge 35.00

Golf, Club, Nicklaus, Graphite Shaft, Iron 60.00
Golf, Club, Nicklaus, Muirfield, Iron 50.00
Golf, Club, Palmer, Model C, Putter 30.00
Golf, Club, Ping, Echo, Karten Co., Putter 75.00
Golf, Club, Ping, K–I, Double Stamped, Wedge 45.00
Golf, Club, Ping, Kushin Scottsdale, Putter 170.00
Golf, Club, Putter, Aluminum Mallet Head, J. M. Barnes, 1920 .... 3750.00
Golf, Club, Putter, Ambi, Wooden Shaft 50.00
Golf, Club, Putter, Amby Dex, 1910 .... 550.00
Golf, Club, Putter, Anser, Kar Co., 10 1/2 In. 600.00
Golf, Club, Putter, Burke Sav-A-Shot, Brass 40.00
Golf, Club, Putter, Crawford–MacGregor, Popular Putter, Wooden Shaft, 10X 25.00
Golf, Club, Putter, Grip–Rite, Golf Pride 20.00
Golf, Club, Putter, Hickory Shaft 20.00
Golf, Club, Putter, Spalding, TPM 1 .... 50.00
Golf, Club, Putter, Wilson, Willie Hoare, Brown Shaft 30.00
Golf, Club, Set, Palmer The Axion, 2–SW 200.00
Golf, Club, Staff A76, 3–PW 135.00
Golf, Club, Taylor No. 1, Wood 40.00
Golf, Club, Toney Penna Original, G–9 .... 40.00
Golf, Club, Wedge, Mac Murfield 20th, SW 45.00
Golf, Driver, Walter Hagen 2600.00
Golf, Figurine, Golfer, Dunlop Golf Ball, Die Cast, Knickers, Ball–Headed, Painted . 450.00
Golf, Medal, Hole–In–One 95.00
Golf, Pin, Bob Hope Golf Classic, Face On Ball, Gold & Silver Color 110.00
Golf, Ribbon, Silk, c.1925 .... 20.00
Hockey, Tumbler, Wisconsin Hockey, Mountain Dew, 1981–1982 .... 13.00
Horse Racing, Book, Kentucky Derby Jubilee, 1949 .... 38.00
Horse Racing, Glass, Golden Horse Restaurant, Louisville, Ky. 12.00
Horse Racing, Glass, Kentucky Derby, 1940 .... 110.00
Horse Racing, Glass, Kentucky Derby, 1945 .... 375.00
Horse Racing, Glass, Kentucky Derby, 1955 .... 58.00 To 80.00
Horse Racing, Glass, Kentucky Derby, 1957 .... 55.00
Horse Racing, Glass, Kentucky Derby, 1964 .... 33.00 To 50.00
Horse Racing, Glass, Kentucky Derby, 1964, Pair 58.00
Horse Racing, Glass, Kentucky Derby, 1965 .... 38.00
Horse Racing, Glass, Kentucky Derby, 1966, 8 Piece 150.00
Horse Racing, Glass, Kentucky Derby, 1967 .... 38.00
Horse Racing, Glass, Kentucky Derby, 1983–1992, 8 Piece 20.00
Horse Racing, Pinback, Kentucky Derby, Celluloid, 2 1/2 In. 15.00
Horse Racing, Program, Maryland Hunt Cup, Pencil Notations, 1948 .... 6.00
Horse Racing, Tray, 1974 .... 42.00
Hunting, Duck Call, Bill Riming 1250.00
Hunting, Duck Call, Brass Band, Royal 55.00
Hunting, Duck Call, Broadbill 40.00
Hunting, Duck Call, Marked E. D. Dennison, Tenn. 135.00
Hunting, Duck Call, Olt B–4 Slider 250.00
Hunting, Fox Horn, Brass 60.00
Hunting, Launcher, Clay Pigeon, Remington Arms Expert Trap, c.1880 .... 210.00
Hunting, License, Nationwide Male Wolf Hunting, 1945–1946 .... 23.00
Hunting, Moose Call, Adirondack, Birchbark, Copper Rivets 37.00
Lacrosse, Crosse, Hardwood, Rawhide, Primitive, Pair 77.00
Pool Table, Brunswick, Poplar, Rosewood, Maple Inlaid, 1890, 4 x 8 Ft. 8000.00
Pool Table, J. F. Come, Slat Top, Oak, c.1890, 9 Ft. 975.00
Pool Table, Jefferson, Tubular Ball Return, Mother–of–Pearl, 1923, 9 Ft. 6000.00
Pool Table, Mikado, Mahogany, 1913, 4 1/2 x 9 Ft. 4500.00
Pool Table, Slate Top, Leather Bags, Marquetry, Wall Rack, Cues, 1800s, Full Size . 5500.00
Pool Table, St. Bernard, Mission, Quarter–Sawn Oak, 1924, 4 x 8 Ft. 5500.00
Powder Keg, Hazzard, Wooden, 25 Lb. 245.00
Skating, Program, Ice Follies, 1965 .... 15.00
Skating, Program, U.S. Figure Skating Championship, Starbuck, 1968 .... 12.00
Skating, Skates, Ice, Winchester 25.00
Skating, Skates, Roller, Speed King, 1959, Key ....*Illus* 20.00

♦ ♦ ♦ ♦ ♦ ♦ ♦ ♦ ♦ ♦ ♦ ♦ ♦ ♦ ♦ ♦ ♦ ♦ ♦ ♦

August is the peak month for residential burglaries. April has the fewest home break-ins. Most home burglaries occur in the daytime. The average break-in lasts 17 minutes.

♦ ♦ ♦ ♦ ♦ ♦ ♦ ♦ ♦ ♦ ♦ ♦ ♦ ♦ ♦ ♦ ♦ ♦ ♦ ♦

Sports, Skating, Skates, Roller, Speed

King, 1959, Key

Skiing, Leather Bindings, Wooden	50.00
Snow Shoes, Bear Paw Style, Laconia, New Hampshire, 1944	50.00
Target Ball, Agnew & Brown, Pittsburgh, P. A., Amber	4700.00
Target Ball, Amber, Bogardus, 1877	200.00
Target Ball, Bo't of Jas. Brown & Son, Dealers In Firearms, Amber	2850.00
Target Ball, Bogardus Glass Ball, Medium Olive Green, 1877	625.00
Target Ball, Hobnail, Yellow Amber Glass, Patent Applied For	2310.00
Tennis, Ball, Chris Evert	6.00
Tennis, Program, USLTA Championship, 52nd Annual Men's, 51st Women's, 1951	15.00
Tennis, Program, USLTA Indoor Championships, New York City, Feb. 1955	15.00
Tennis, Racket, Spalding, Bancroft Frame	40.00
Tennis, Racket, Wooden Handle, Wire Strings, Dayton	25.00
Tennis, Racket, Wright & Ditson	28.00
Tennis, Tin, Ball, Pancho Gonzales Picture	40.00
Trophy, Rug, Polar Bear, With Kaminski Ice Scrapers, 1940s, 8 Ft.	1210.00
Trophy, Sailfish, Stuffed, Mounted, Plaque, Caught By Al Capone, 1929, 88 In.	5720.00
Weight Lifting, Indian Clubs, Dumbbells, For Commercial Gym, Spaulding, 1920s	1500.00
Wristwatch, Babe Ruth, Face Picture In Baseball Diamond, c.1949	1490.00
Wristwatch, Gruen, Dallas Eagles, Dixie Series Champions, Printed On Face, 1953	600.00

STAFFORDSHIRE, England, has been a district making pottery and porcelain since the 1700s. Hundreds of kilns are still working in the area. Thousands of types of pottery and porcelain have been made in the many factories that worked and still work in the area. Some of the most famous factories have been listed separately, such as Adams, Davenport, Ridgway, Rowland & Marsellus, Royal Doulton, Royal Worcester, Spode, Wedgwood, and others. Some Staffordshire pieces are listed under categories like Fairing, Flow Blue, Mulberry, Shaving Mug, etc.

Ashtray, Players Cigarettes	20.00
Bank, Spaniel, Penny, 4 In.	220.00
Biscuit Jar, Raised Link Pattern & Floral Top, Loop Handle, 1880	95.00
Bowl, Garden Scene, Blue, Excelsior, 1850, 10 In.	90.00
Bowl, Landing of Lafayette, Clews, 10 In.	1350.00
Box, Cover, After David Cox's The Shrimpers, 19th Century, 2 1/4 x 4 1/4 In.	60.00
Box, Pearlized Wicker, Holding 6 Bottles of Champagne	125.00
Box, Trinket, Tray, Railway Transfer, Crazed Lid, 5 3/4 In.	195.00
Carpet Ball, Red Stick Spatter, 3 1/4 In.	258.00
Cheese Keeper, Gaudy	275.00
Cheese Keeper, Petunias	110.00
Chimney Ornament, Hound Chasing Rabbit	875.00
Chimney Piece, Burns & His Mary, Gilt, 12 3/8 In.	137.00
Coffeepot, Lafayette At Franklin's Tomb, Enoch Wood, 11 1/2 In.	1450.00
Cooler, Applied George Washington, Eagles, Liberty, Stoneware, 5 Gal.	3080.00
Creamer, Black, The Captive, 5 3/8 In.	35.00
Creamer, Cow, Gray & Blue	1750.00
Creamer, Cow, Gray With Black Spots, 1880s, 7 x 4 1/ 2 In.	302.00

Creamer, Hoboken 605.00
Creamer, State House, Floral Border, Stubbs, 5 1/2 In. 125.00
Creamer, Wadsworth Tower, Enoch Wood 875.00
Cup & Saucer, American Eagle 440.00
Cup & Saucer, Blue Ridge Parkway, Flowers, Adderly 65.00
Cup & Saucer, Handleless, Adam's Rose 165.00
Cup & Saucer, Handleless, Cabbage Rose 145.00
Cup & Saucer, Handleless, Corinthian, Red, Challinor 50.00
Cup & Saucer, Handleless, Dark Blue Floral Transfer, Impressed Adams 159.00
Cup & Saucer, Handleless, Red, Green & Blue, Miniature 100.00
Cup & Saucer, Lafayette At Franklin's Tomb, Enoch Wood 375.00
Cup & Saucer, MacDonough's Victory, Enoch Wood 575.00
Cup & Saucer, Young Girl At Well, Dog, Blue, Clews, 5 3/4 In. 175.00
Desk Set, Black, Gold Chinoiserie, 9 1/2 In. 137.00
Dish, Brown, Classical Scenes, 9 3/4 x 11 1/4 In. 49.00
Dish, Creamware, Oval, Glazed, Goose, 3 Sprigs of Parsley, 1780, 4 1/2 In. 660.00
Dish, Hen On Nest Cover, 7 1/2 x 5 1/2 In. .... 275.00 To 375.00
Dish, Hen On Nest Cover, Polychrome, 7 1/2 In. .... 286.00 To 302.00
Dish, Sweetmeat, Central Pommel, Blue & White, Footed 425.00
Dish, Vegetable, Underplate, Reticulated, Blue, Fruit Pattern, 8 x 11 In. Bowl 605.00
Dog, Seated, Open Front Legs, Red, White, Polychrome, 5 1/2 In. 154.00
Dog, Seated, White, Glass Eyes, Black, Red Enameled Detail, 12 In., Pair 220.00
Figurine, Admiral Napier 480.00
Figurine, Baby In A Cradle, Pearlware, c.1800, 4 13/16 In. 165.00
Figurine, Benjamin Franklin, 19th Century, 10 In. 1100.00
Figurine, Boy & Girl By Fence 340.00
Figurine, Britannia Triumphant, c.1820 .... 635.00
Figurine, Burns & His Mary, 12 In. 200.00
Figurine, Cat, Pair 209.00
Figurine, Cat, Seated, Polychrome, 6 1/4 In. 55.00
Figurine, Child On Dog, 6 In. 250.00
Figurine, Child On Goat, Twisted Horns, Design On Body, 1845, 5 In. 175.00
Figurine, Cock–A–Too, J. T. Jones, 1900s, Pair 750.00
Figurine, Cow, Calf & Farmer's Wife 2250.00
Figurine, Darby & Joan, Pink Trim, 11 In. 345.00
Figurine, Dog With Basket, White, Polychrome Trim, 4 1/4 In. 93.00
Figurine, Dog, 8 In. 70.00
Figurine, Dog, Black Spots, 9 In., Pair .... 280.00 To 310.00
Figurine, Dog, Dappled Brown, 7 1/2 In., Pair 198.00
Figurine, Dog, Gold Luster, White, 9 3/4 In., Pair 275.00
Figurine, Dog, Red & White, 2 7/8 In., Pair 165.00
Figurine, Dog, Red & White, 5 5/8 In. 214.00
Figurine, Dog, Seated, Brown, Black & White, 5 7/8 In. 27.00
Figurine, Dog, Spaniel, Black Spots, Gold Chain, 13 In., Pair 455.00
Figurine, Dogs, 19th Century, 10 In., Pair 495.00
Figurine, Duck On Nest, 3 x 2 3/4 In. 75.00
Figurine, General Napoleon, 5 In. 350.00
Figurine, George Washington 950.00
Figurine, Gladstone 480.00
Figurine, Good Night, Miniature Group, 3 1/2 x 4 In. 75.00
Figurine, Greyhound, 5 1/2 In. 285.00
Figurine, Greyhound, 11 1/2 In. .... 225.00 To 250.00
Figurine, Greyhound, Standing, Hare In His Mouth, 12 In. 286.00
Figurine, Hen On Nest, Polychrome Enamel 109.00
Figurine, Hen On Nest, Polychrome, 3 3/4 In. 137.00
Figurine, House, Clock, Eagle, Late 19th Century, 8 In. 132.00
Figurine, John Wesley 1250.00
Figurine, Judge & Vicar, 19th Century, 9 1/2 In. 495.00
Figurine, Lamb, Tree, Polychrome Enamel, Sanded Coat, 5 1/4 In. 105.00
Figurine, Lamb, White, Sanded Coat, Polychrome, 3 3/8 In. 192.00
Figurine, Lamp, Sanded Coat, 2 1/2 In. 104.00
Figurine, Lion, Mantel, Glass Eyes, Gray & Black, Pair 175.00
Figurine, Lion, Polychrome Enamel, Porcelain, 2 3/8 In. 80.00

Figurine, Lion, Reclining, 6 In.	325.00
Figurine, Man With Whip, 5 1/4 In.	104.00
Figurine, Monarch Seated, 2 Sections, Storage Container, 10 In.	175.00
Figurine, Naval Officer, Polychrome, 6 1/4 In.	125.00
Figurine, Parrot	2090.00
Figurine, Polar Bear, Earthenware, Inscribed, 1830, 17 1/4 In.	6050.00
Figurine, Poodle With Basket, Coleslaw Coat, 3 1/4 In.	130.00
Figurine, Poodle, 7 In.	100.00
Figurine, Poodle, Standing, Yellowware, 19th Century, 16 1/4 x 15 3/4 In.	660.00
Figurine, Poodle, White, Sanded Coat, Yellow, Black, 3 1/4 In.	105.00
Figurine, Prince of Wales	605.00
Figurine, Princess Royal, On Dog	825.00
Figurine, Queen Victoria	385.00
Figurine, Ram, Sanded Coat, Pastel Enameled Trim, 3 1/8 In.	165.00
Figurine, Richard The Lion Slayer, 16 In.	220.00
Figurine, Rooster, Pearlware, 3 1/4 In.	250.00
Figurine, Sailor's Departure & Sailor's Return, Pair	1400.00
Figurine, Scotsman, 1840, 12 In.	110.00
Figurine, Scottish Couple, 11 In., Pair	250.00
Figurine, Shepherd & Shepherdess, Sleeping, Pair	390.00
Figurine, Spaniels, 12 1/2 In., Pair	253.00
Figurine, Whippet, Pair	137.50
Figurine, Widow of Zarepeth	525.00
Figurine, Widow, 1800	525.00
Figurine, Woman On Horseback, 3 5/8 In.	85.00
Figurine, Woman On Horseback, Duchess, 8 3/4 In.	137.00
Figurine, Zebra, Standing, Rocky Oval Base, c.1870, 8 1/4 In.	495.00
Group, Cows, c.1800, 8 x 9 In., Pair	1430.00
Group, Lad & Lassie, Crazed, 12 3/4 In.	247.00
Group, Lovers Sitting Under A Bird's Nest, Parrot	165.00
Group, Man & Woman Sitting Under Shrubbery, 14 1/4 In.	135.00
Group, Maternal Love, 16 1/4 In.	440.00
Group, Milkmaid & Cow, Blue Willow	1000.00
Group, Scottish Hunter, Setter Dog Near Tree Form, 16 1/2 In.	220.00
Group, Vicar & Moses, 18th Century, 9 In.	550.00
Group, Victoria & Albert, Polychrome, 4 3/8 In.	65.00
Inkwell, Lord Nelson, 4 1/2 In.	110.00
Inkwell, Spaniel Reclining On Cobalt Base, 5 In.	155.00
Inkwell, Whippet, Tan & Black, Blue Base, Marked, 3 3/4 In.	150.00
Loving Cup, Farmer's Arms	125.00
Match Holder, Man On Stump	65.00
Mold, Jelly, Queen Victoria Shape, 2 Piece	495.00
Mug, Black Transfer, Polychrome Enameling, 3 7/8 In.	121.00
Mug, Creditors Have Better Memories Than Debtors, Purple, 2 In.	192.00
Mug, Polychrome Enameling, Blue, 4 In.	93.00
Mug, Woman, Children, Black, Polychrome Enameling, 3 In.	110.00
Pepper Pot, Figural, c.1810	190.00
Pepper Pot, Figural, c.1850	125.00
Pitcher & Bowl, Ontario Lake Scenery, Blue & White	350.00
Pitcher, Blue Ridge Parkway, Virginia	95.00
Pitcher, Cow, Gaudy, c.1900	650.00
Pitcher, Denton Park, Yorkshire, Medium Blue, Riley, 7 In.	247.00
Pitcher, Floral Design, 4 Colors, 7 In.	175.00
Pitcher, Floral Design, 8 In.	130.00
Pitcher, Good Samaritan, Red, 10 1/2 In.	413.00
Pitcher, Milk, Washington Vase, Purple, 5 1/2 In.	98.00
Pitcher, New York City Hall & New York Insane Hospital, Clews	1275.00
Pitcher, Oriental Garden Scene, Man, Woman & Servant, Blue, 9 1/2 In.	495.00
Plate, Adam's Rose, 7 7/8 In.	85.00
Plate, Adam's Rose, 9 3/8 In.	110.00
Plate, Adam's Rose, Impressed Adam's, 9 1/2 In.	95.00
Plate, Alphabet, Civil War General, 4 Piece	1540.00
Plate, America and Independence, Blue, 10 In.	297.00

Plate, Andalusia, Red, 5 3/4 In. 20.00
Plate, Arms of Maryland, Mayer 2200.00
Plate, Arms of New York, Mayer, 10 In. 850.00
Plate, Arms of Rhode Island, Mayer, 8 1/2 In. 795.00
Plate, Arms of South Carolina, Mayer, 7 1/2 In. 750.00
Plate, Baltimore & Ohio Railroad 880.00
Plate, Boston State House, Blue 195.00
Plate, Boston State House, Enoch Wood, 10 In. 265.00
Plate, Boston State House, Openwork, Rogers, 8 1/4 In. 950.00
Plate, Capitol At Washington, Dark Blue, 7 5/8 In. 55.00
Plate, Castle Garden & Battery 660.00
Plate, City Hall, New York, Black, 10 1/2 In. 110.00
Plate, Clyde Scenery, Purple, 9 In. 38.00
Plate, Dam At The Philadelphia Waterworks 800.00
Plate, Dog, Medium Blue, 8 1/2 In. 110.00
Plate, Dr. Manette, 4 1/2 In. 23.00
Plate, Elm At Cambridge, Mass., Washington, Blue, 10 In. 85.00
Plate, English Cathedral, Dark Blue, Impressed Clews, 10 In. 83.00
Plate, English Cities, Liverpool, Black, 9 1/4 In. 27.00
Plate, Erie Canal, Inscription, Enoch Wood, 6 1/2 In. 650.00
Plate, Exchange Baltimore, Blue, 9 3/4 In. 357.00
Plate, Fairmount, Near Philadelphia, Stubbs, 10 In. 295.00
Plate, Farm, Dora, Light Blue, 5 5/8 In. 10.00
Plate, Floral Design, Red, Green, Black, Gaudy, 8 3/4 In. 20.00
Plate, Floral Rim, Gaudy, Alcock, 9 3/8 In., 8 Piece 240.00
Plate, Harvard Hall, Pink, Jackson, 7 In. 165.00
Plate, Hoboken, Stubbs, 7 3/4 In. 325.00
Plate, Hop Mill, Catskill, Wood & Sons 3300.00
Plate, Hunters & Dogs, Dark Blue, 9 In. 125.00
Plate, La Vellita, History of San Antonio, W. Hunter, 1951, 9 1/2 In. 95.00
Plate, Landing of Fathers At Plymouth, Impressed Enoch Wood, 7 In. 77.00
Plate, Landing of Gen. Lafayette, Blue, 8 7/8 In. 83.00
Plate, Landing of Lafayette, Clews, 8 3/4 In. 295.00
Plate, Landing of Lafayette, Dark Blue, Impressed Clews, 10 In. 358.00
Plate, Marine Hospital In Louisville 275.00
Plate, Medallion Series, 10 In. 2750.00
Plate, Millennium, Dark Brown, 10 1/2 In. 68.00
Plate, Near Fishkill, City Series, Clews, 7 3/4 In. 450.00
Plate, Niagara Falls, Fancy Border, Swinnerton, 7 In. 22.00
Plate, Palestine, Red, Green Transfer, 8 1/2 In. 60.00
Plate, Park Theater, Acorn Border, Blue, White, 10 In. 264.00
Plate, Peace & Plenty, Clews, 8 7/8 In. 325.00
Plate, Pittsfield Elm, Blue, Clews, 10 In. 425.00
Plate, Scudder's Museum 1870.00
Plate, Southampton Hampshire, Enoch Wood, 7 1/2 In. 295.00
Plate, States Building, Sheep On Lawn, Clews, 8 3/4 In. 325.00
Plate, Table Rock Niagara, Enoch Wood, 10 In. 422.50
Plate, Toddy, Girl With Goat, Brown, 5 In. 82.00
Plate, Toddy, Queen's Rose, Pair 165.00
Plate, Toddy, Woman At Upright Piano, Blue, Gargen, 5 In. 137.00
Plate, Trenton Falls, Enoch Wood, 7 1/2 In. 350.00
Plate, Upper Ferry Bridge, Stubbs, 8 3/4 In. 295.00
Plate, View of Liverpool, Seashell Border, Blue & White, 9 7/8 In. 245.00
Plate, Villa In The Regents Park, London, Dark Blue, 10 In. 115.00
Plate, Virginia, Black, 10 3/4 In. 55.00
Plate, Washington & Lafayette, Small 1100.00
Plate, Waterworks Philadelphia, Brown, Jackson, 9 1/4 In. 175.00
Plate, Waterworks, Philadelphia, Black, 9 1/8 In. 75.00
Plate, Welcome Lafayette, Small 825.00
Plate, William Penn's Treaty, Brown, Thomas Green 190.00
Platter, Alms House 550.00
Platter, America & Independence, Blue, Clews, 14 3/4 In. 750.00
Platter, America & Independence, Dark Blue, 9 1/2 In. 425.00

Platter, American Eagles, Bird Border, Brown, 19 1/2 In. 180.00
Platter, Arms of Georgia, Octagonal 3960.00
Platter, Cape Coast Castle, Africa, Enoch Wood, 16 1/2 In. 1650.00
Platter, Catskills On Hudson River 2420.00
Platter, Compton Verney, Warwickshire, Blue, 11 In. 192.00
Platter, Conway Castle, Carnavonshire, Wales, Blue, 15 In. 467.00
Platter, Dark Blue Transfer, Sandusky, 16 3/4 In. 3960.00
Platter, Delivery Boy 1540.00
Platter, English Countryside Scene, 18 3/4 x 14 In. 385.00
Platter, Fonthill Abbey, Blue, Large 575.00
Platter, Fruit & Flower Design, Blue, White, 16 In. 468.00
Platter, Hunt Party Outside Tavern, Dark Blue, 16 1/2 In. 250.00
Platter, Italian Scenery, 12 1/2 In. 110.00
Platter, Kenmount House, Blue, White, 19th Century, 16 1/2 In. 385.00
Platter, Medium Blue Transfer, Ship, Seashell Border, 18 In. 797.00
Platter, Near Hudson River, Black, Clews, 9 3/4 In. 250.00
Platter, Niagara From The American Side, Enoch Wood, 14 3/4 In. 1900.00
Platter, Oriental Scene, Green, 15 In. 192.00
Platter, Palestine, Red, 15 In. 181.00
Platter, Pantheon, Green, Border, 13 x 10 3/4 In. 150.00
Platter, Pickett's Charge At Gettysburg 880.00
Platter, Polar Bear, Large 1760.00
Platter, Rabbit Hunters, Medium Blue Transfer, 13 1/2 In. 225.00
Platter, Sandusky Ohio, Clews, 16 1/2 In. 4500.00
Platter, Strawberry & Rose, Red, Green & Black, 14 3/4 In. 225.00
Platter, Upper Ferry Bridge Over The River Schuylkill, 19 In. 303.00
Platter, Well & Tree, Landscape Design, Blue, White, 19th Century, 16 In. 101.00
Platter, Willow, 13 In. 60.00
Relish, Tyrol Pattern, Alcock, Light Blue, Shell Shape, c.1840 .... 68.00
Sauce, Underplate, Cover, Charleston Exchange, Savannah Bank Scenes 1650.00
Soup, Dish, Beach At Brighton, Dark Blue 340.00
Soup, Dish, Belzoni, Light Blue, 10 1/2 In. 71.00
Soup, Dish, Deer, Medium Light Blue, 10 In. 85.00
Soup, Dish, Fair Mount Near Philadelphia, Dark Blue, 9 7/8 In. 275.00
Soup, Dish, Floral Design, Maroon, Green, Blue, Black, 9 1/4 In. 45.00
Soup, Dish, Palestine, Blue, 10 3/8 In. 33.00
Soup, Dish, Palestine, Medium Blue, 10 1/4 In. 38.00
Soup, Dish, Picturesque Views On Fishkill, Hudson River, Black, 10 In. 55.00
Soup, Dish, Ruins, Medium Light Blue, 9 3/4 In. 35.00
Soup, Dish, Temples, Purple, 10 5/8 In. 49.00
Soup, Dish, View Near Philadelphia, Table Rim 375.00
Soup, Dish, View of Liverpool, Dark Blue, 8 3/8 In. 275.00
Stirrup Cup, Fox Head, Sterling Coaster 88.00
Sugar, Landing of Lafayette 850.00
Sugar, Polychrome Floral Design, 5 In. 30.00
Tea Set, Apostles Pattern, 1840s, 4 Piece 1500.00
Tea Set, Child's, Boy With Dog, 23 Piece 500.00
Tea Set, Child's, Tree, Light Blue, 10 Piece 302.00
Tea Set, Commodore MacDonnough's Victory, Wood & Son, 4 Piece 2860.00
Teapot, Brown Seaweed, Pewter Lid, 5 1/2 In. 148.00
Teapot, Cupids, Dark Blue Floral, 6 1/2 In. 275.00
Teapot, Figures In Wooded Landscape, Adams, 6 1/2 In. 385.00
Teapot, Garden Scene, Children, Pink, Diamond Mark, 6 1/2 x 10 In. 185.00
Teapot, Garden Scene, Pink, 6 1/2 x 10 In. 155.00
Teapot, MacDonnough's Victory, Enoch Wood 1475.00
Teapot, Palestine, Red, 7 1/2 In. 60.00
Teapot, Quatrefoil 6820.00
Teapot, Salt Glaze 3080.00
Toby Jugs are listed in their own category
Toddy Plate, Palestine, Red, Green, 6 In. 33.00
Tray, Castle Fleurs, Roxburonheshire, Scotland, Adams, 16 In. 385.00
Tray, Sauce Tureen, Killin, Blue, Impressed Clews, 6 x 9 In. 247.00
Tureen, Base, English Country Scene, Blue, 14 In. 132.00

Tureen, European Castle Scenes, Lid Handle, Blue, 13 In.	220.00
Tureen, Sauce, Cover, Landscape Design, Blue, White, Under, Ladle, 8 In.	445.00
Tureen, Soup, Cover, Rural Scenery, Ladle & Under, 1850s, 11 1/2 In.	1650.00
Underplate, Hope Mill, Catskill Creek	3300.00
Undertray, Blue Oriental, Clews, 6 1/2 In.	71.50
Vase, Cow, Calf & Milkmaid, 11 1/2 In.	375.00
Vase, Dog, Chimney Piece, Polychrome Enameling, Gilt, 6 1/2 In.	225.00
Vase, Spill, 2 Children	550.00
Vase, Spill, Dog, Pair	750.00
Vase, Spill, Sheep	253.00
Vase, White Floral, Gold Leaf, 3 In., Pair	20.00
Waste Bowl, American Eagle & Shield, Dark Blue, 3 1/2 In.	885.00
Waste Bowl, American Eagle & Shield, Dark Blue, 6 1/4 In.	500.00
Waste Bowl, Birds & Flowers, Medium Blue, 3 1/2 In.	115.00
Waste Bowl, Rose Design, Gaudy, 5 1/2 In.	135.00
Waste Bowl, Salt Glaze Enameled, Long–Tailed Bird On Rock, Flowers, 6 In.	2475.00
Watch Holder, 2 Figures, No Color, Gold Trim	185.00

STANGL Pottery traces its history back to the Fulper Pottery of New Jersey. In 1910, Johann Martin Stangl started working at Fulper. He bought into the firm in 1913, became president in 1926, and in 1929 changed the company name to Stangl Pottery. The pottery made dinnerwares and a line of limited–edition bird figurines. The company went out of business in 1978.

Ashtray, Ducks	12.00
Ashtray, Flying Goose	35.00
Ashtray, Pheasant	45.00
Ashtray, Sailfish	45.00
Bird, 2 Bluebirds, No. 3276D	125.00
Bird, Bird of Paradise, No. 3408	110.00 To 135.00
Bird, Blue Headed Vireo, No. 3448	70.00
Bird, Bobolink, No. 3595	135.00
Bird, Broadtail Hummingbird, No. 3626	190.00
Bird, Cardinal, No. 3444, 6 1/2 In.	85.00
Bird, Cerulean Warbler, No. 3456	97.00
Bird, Cock Pheasant, No. 3492	160.00
Bird, Cockatoo, No. 3405S, 7 In.	45.00 To 85.00
Bird, Cocker Spaniel	495.00
Bird, Flying Duck, No. 3443	395.00
Bird, Gray Cardinal, No. 3596	60.00
Bird, Gray Cardinal, No. 3596	62.00
Bird, Group of Chickadees, No. 3581	175.00 To 245.00
Bird, Hen Pheasant, No. 3491	180.00
Bird, Key West Quail Dover, No. 3454	200.00
Bird, Kingfisher, No. 3406S	105.00
Bird, Magnolia Warbler, No. 3925	400.00
Bird, Parakeets, No. 3582D	185.00 To 225.00
Bird, Redstarts, No. 3490D	165.00
Bird, Rufous Hummingbird, No. 3585	73.00 To 75.00
Bird, Titmouse, No. 3592	73.00
Bird, Western Bluebird, No. 3815	160.00
Bird, Yellow Hen, No. 3446	125.00
Bird, Yellow Warbler, No. 3447	110.00
Bowl, Amber Glo, 10 In.	25.00
Bowl, Amber Glo, 8 In.	20.00
Bowl, Blueberry, 5 1/2 In.	12.00
Bowl, Cereal, Fruit	12.00
Bowl, Fruit, Country Harvest	25.00
Bowl, Golden Harvest, 10 In.	15.00
Bowl, Golden Harvest, Large	15.00
Bowl, Thistle, Crimped, 4 In.	7.00
Bowl, Vegetable, Fruit, Divided, Oval	25.00
Bowl, Vegetable, Golden Blossom, Divided	15.00

Box, Cigarette, Terra Rose 20.00
Bread Tray, Amber Glo 25.00
Candy Dish, Cover, Terra Rose 20.00
Charger, Fruit & Flowers, Ruffled Blue Rim, 14 In. 35.00
Chop Plate, Blue Daisy, 11 In. 12.00
Chop Plate, Golden Blossom 20.00
Creamer, Bittersweet .... 7.00 To 8.00
Cup & Saucer, Amber Glo 10.00
Cup & Saucer, Fruit 12.00
Cup & Saucer, Golden Blossom 12.00
Cup, Kittyware 55.00
Dish, Nut, 3-Flower Shape 16.00
Figurine, Cockatoos, No. 3405D .... 115.00 To 225.00
Figurine, Elephant, White 95.00
Figurine, Giraffe 325.00
Gravy Boat, Bittersweet 15.00
Mug, Puppy 40.00
Pitcher, Golden Blossom 20.00
Pitcher, Golden Harvest .... 15.00 To 20.00
Pitcher, Terra Rose 15.00
Planter, Gold Swan 9.00
Plate, Colonial, Blue, 10 In. 10.00
Plate, Dinner, Amber Glo 10.00
Plate, Dinner, Fruit 12.00
Plate, Dinner, Newport, Ships 25.00
Plate, Orchard Song, 8 In. 7.00
Plate, Salad, Fruit 8.00
Plate, Thistle, 12 In. 7.50
Platter, Amber Glo, Curved 25.00
Platter, Magnolia 45.00
Rooster, Yellow, 10 In. 150.00
Salt & Pepper, Hen & Rooster, Marked 125.00
Saucer, Apple Delight 2.00
Saucer, Blueberry 3.00
Sherbet, Green Leaf, Yellow Trim 12.00
Soup, Dish, Orchard Song, Large 9.00
Sugar & Creamer, Bittersweet .... 8.00 To 12.00
Sugar & Creamer, Cover, Fruit 30.00
Sugar, Bittersweet 10.00
Sugar, Colonial, Blue 12.00
Teapot, Golden Harvest .... 12.00 To 25.00
Teapot, Magnolia 65.00
Tray, Fruit, Handle 15.00
Tray, Fruit, Rectangular, 15 In. 18.00
Vase, Urn, No. 2041 .... 20.00
Wig Stand 150.00
Wig Stand, Pair 325.00

STEINS have been used by beer and ale drinkers for over 500 years. They
have been made of ivory, porcelain, stoneware, faience, silver, pewter,
wood, or glass in sizes up to nine gallons. Although some were made by
Mettlach, Meissen, Capo–di–Monte, and other famous factories, most were
made by less important German potteries. The words *Geschutz* or
Musterschutz on a stein are the German words for *patented* or *registered
design,* not company names. Steins are still being made in the old styles.
Lithophane steins may be found in the Lithophane category.

18th Century, Norway, Carved Wood 1815.00
Anheuser–Busch, Ceramarte, Christmas, 1981 .... 190.00
Anheuser–Busch, Decal, Red, Yellow 85.00
Anheuser–Busch, St. Louis, Mo., Dark Brown, Thin Handle 198.00
Bicycle Rider, Pottery, Domed Cover 770.00
Budweiser, Etched Clydesdale Hitch, Clear Glass 30.00
Budweiser, Holiday, Christmas Series, 1981 .... 275.00

Budweiser, L. A. Olympics, Ceramarte, 1984 .... 75.00
Character, Bearded Man Raising Goblet, Enameled, Germany, Ironstone, 5 1/2 In. 85.00
Character, Gentleman Dog, Figural 2640.00
Character, Golfer, Lenox 2420.00
Character, Golfer, Weller 2420.00
Character, Nun, Lithophane of Men & Woman Drinking In Base, 7 1/2 In. 295.00
Character, Potato Head 2090.00
Fairmont Brewing Co., Fairmont, W. Va., Sepia Tone, Tan, Woman On Horse 165.00
Falstaff, Music Box 140.00
Finial Cover, Middle–1700s, Faience 495.00
Frankenmuth, Pewter Lid, W. Germany 20.00
Goetz Beer, Miniature, Green 3.00
Hamm's Octoberfest, Ceramarte, 1977 .... 30.00
Lithophane, Nude, Military, Porcelain, Germany, 1950 .... 75.00
Mettlach steins are listed in the Mettlach category.
Miller Beer, Wright Brothers, Kitty Hawk, 1986 .... 65.00
Miller, Frederick Miller Portrait, Thewalt Limited Edition, No. 612 .... 30.00
Molded Design, Blue & Gray Salt Glaze, Germany, 7 3/8 In. 55.00
Raised Figures, Hunters, Deer, Dog & Woman, Pewter Top, Germany, 9 1/2 In. ... 65.00
Raised Frankfurt Buildings, Cobalt Blue Base, Pewter Top, 8 1/2 In. 85.00
Stoneware, Richard Riemerschmid 880.00
Venator, Antique Color, Horse With Rider Scene, Ceramarte, 8 In. 100.00

STEREO CARDS that were made for stereoscope viewers became popular after 1840. Two almost identical pictures were mounted on a stiff cardboard backing so that, when viewed through a stereoscope, a three–dimensional picture could be seen. Value is determined by maker and by subject. These cards were made in quantity through the 1930s.

Allopathy Vs. Cupidity, When Doctors Disagree, Woman On Sofa 15.00
Army Scene, Box 30.00
Far East Views, India, Ceylon, Japan, 6 Views 46.00
Fort Hamilton, Near Fortress Monroe 75.00
H. I. H. Prince Napoleon & Suite 220.00
Hawaii, 5 Different Views, Keystone View Co., 5 Piece 200.00
Jack Johnson, Champion of World, Chicago Home, Sepia 185.00
Late Captain Harrison, Posed On Deck 110.00
Late Mr. Brunel, Posed On Deck, Holding Top Hat, Cane 330.00
Louisiana Purchase, T. W. Ingersoll, 1904, 100 Piece .... 100.00 To 200.00
Nation's Chief & Head of Navy Dept., Oyster Bay, Teddy Roosevelt, On Deck 15.00
Native Cane Grinders In Sunny Florida, Blacks Harvesting, 1900 .... 25.00
Negro Cabin, Southern Scenes, 8 Kids, Washtub 50.00
Not Worried With Cares of Life, Puppies, In Box 12.00
Scalding Hogs Preparatory To Scraping, Swift K & Co. 30.00
Scenes In Washoe Range, Squaws & Children, A. A. Hart 240.00
Scenes of Humboldt River, Shoshone Indians 165.00
Smith's Barn, Near Keedysville, Used As Hospital, 1862 .... 145.00
Trip Through Sears Roebuck & Co., Box, 50 Piece 195.00
Various Florida Towns, Beach Scenes, 1900, 20 Piece 160.00
Yosemite Views, Horses, People, 5 Views 21.00

STEREOSCOPES were used for viewing stereo cards. The hand viewer was invented by Oliver Wendell Holmes, although more complicated table models were used before his was produced in 1859. Do not confuse the stereoscope with the stereopticon, a magic lantern that used glass slides.

Bates, Viewer 45.00
Corte Scope, Metal, Folding, Box 75.00
Counter Top, 12 Card, Coin–Operated, Oak Case 1850.00
Graphoscope, Viewer, Pat. 1883, Wooden, With Cards 50.00
Keystone Eye Comfort, Viewer, Crinkled Brown Metal, Wooden, 12 Cards 75.00
Keystone, Eye Trainer Viewer Set 60.00
Rosewood, Inscribed Alex. Beckers, Patent April 7, 1857 .... 468.00
Underwood, Wooden, 70 Cards, Box 225.00

STERLING SILVER, see Silver–Sterling category

STEUBEN glass was made at the Steuben Glass Works of Corning, New York. The factory, founded by Frederick Carder and T. C. Hawkes, Sr., was purchased by the Corning Glass Company. They continued to make glass called *Steuben.* Many types of art glass were made at Steuben. The firm is still making exceptional quality glass but it is clear, modern–style glass. Additional pieces may be found in the Aurene and Cluthra categories.

Bowl, Acid Cut Floral Design, Plum Jade, 9 In.	3300.00
Bowl, Aurene On Calcite, Footed, 3 x 5 In.	185.00
Bowl, Calcite & Gold Aurene, Signed Carder, 13 1/2 In.	990.00
Bowl, Covered, Ram's Horn Finial, Crystal, Signed, 5 1/2 x 5 In.	410.00
Bowl, Diamond Quilted, Blue Silverina, Signed, 10 In.	1200.00
Bowl, Fluted, Pink & Yellow Straw, c.1907	395.00
Bowl, Grotesque, 4 Pulled & Crimped Sides, Signed, 12 In.	275.00
Bowl, Grotesque, Clear, Signed, 11 1/2 x 6 3/4 In.	375.00
Bowl, Grotesque, Ivrene, 12 In.	395.00
Bowl, Handkerchief, Clear, 4–Cornered	80.00
Bowl, Inward Turned Lip, 3 Feet, Gold Aurene, 1910s, 10 1/2 In.	275.00
Bowl, Millefiori, Aurene, White, Green & Gold, 4 In.	1155.00
Bowl, Optic Rib, Copper Wheel Cut, Acid Etched, Signed, c.1920	425.00
Box, Cover, Rosaline, F. Carder, 5 x 6 In.	825.00
Cameo, Pate–De–Verre, Roman Senator Bust, Gray, F. Carder, Oval, 1920, 4 In.	1100.00
Candlestick, Double Twist Stem, Light Amber, Signed, 10 In., Pair	550.00
Candlestick, Green Crystal, White Wafers, Signed, 12 1/2 In. Pair	825.00
Candlestick, Knopped Body, Internal Teardrop, Flared Base, Signed, 8 3/4 In., Pair	440.00
Candlestick, Rosaline, Alabaster Stem, Pair	1200.00
Candlestick, Verre De Soie, 8 In., Pair	350.00
Center Bowl, Flared Gold Iridescent, White Calcite Exterior, 3 In.	175.00
Cologne Bottle, Alabaster Floral, Sterling Silver Enamel Stopper, 5 In.	1100.00
Cologne Bottle, Celeste Blue Threading, Stopper, Mark On Base, 4 In.	300.00
Cologne Bottle, Cobalt Blue, Alabaster Teardrop Stopper, 5 1/2 In.	885.00
Cologne Bottle, Flared Bell Form, Turquoise Blue Jade, Glass Stopper, 4 In.	1050.00
Cologne Bottle, Melon Ribbed Form, Alabaster Stopper, Green Jade, 4 In.	550.00
Compote, Diamond Pattern, Green Pedestal, Ribbon Threading, Topaz, 5 x 7 In.	195.00
Compote, Peach Pedestal, Clear Intaglio Cut, Signed, 4 3/4 In.	90.00
Compote, Ribbed Top & Foot, Folded Rim, Twisted Stem, 7 x 7 In.	250.00
Console, Light Green, 16 1/2 In.	1295.00
Cup & Saucer, Rosalene, Alabaster Ring Handle, 1 7/8 In. Cup, 3 1/4 In. Saucer	125.00
Decanter, Teardrop Stopper, Donald Pollard Designer	550.00
Figurine, Baby Bird, Clear, Signed	250.00
Figurine, Duck, Clear, Signed, 4 1/2 In.	355.00
Figurine, Frog, Signed	135.00
Figurine, Gazelle, No. 7399, Pair	460.00
Figurine, Great Koala, No. 5006, 8 In.	1500.00
Figurine, Jumping Porpoise, Clear, 7 1/4 x 12 In.	677.00
Finger Bowl, Rosaline, Alabaster, 10 Piece	1600.00
Goblet, Bicentennial, Fitted Case, 8 In.	175.00
Goblet, Green Ribbed, Clear Stem, 6 In.	65.00
Goblet, Pink Rosaline, Alabaster Pedestal	150.00
Hatpin Holder, Rosaline Top, Alabaster Bottom	695.00
Jar, Green Threading, Lid, 5 x 4 In.	150.00
Jar, Rosaline Cover, Alabaster Finial & Footed, 9 1/2 x 4 5/8 In.	225.00
Lamp, Gooseneck, Climbing Vine On Neck, Brass Base, Gold Aurene Shade	1000.00
Liqueur Set, 7 1/2 In.–Decanter, 5 Piece	175.00
Martini, Teardrop, Initialed, Signed, 4 In., 9 Piece	715.00
Paperweight, Clear Teardrop, Swirled White Cane Center	285.00
Pitcher, Sunflower Intaglio Design, 5 In.	195.00
Powder Jar, Squat Round Holder, Conforming Cover, 3 3/4 In.	302.50
Punch Cup, Yellow, Signed	145.00
Salt, Green Jade, Footed	158.00

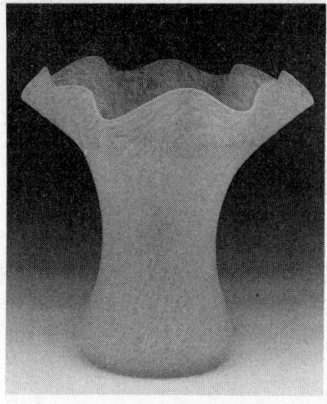

Steuben, Vase, Robin's Egg Blue,

  Cintra, Flared, 8 In.

Salt, Light Topaz, Signed	250.00
Sculpture, Presentation, Geometric Free Form, Red Leather Case	715.00
Sugar & Creamer, John Dreves Designer	357.00
Vase, Air–Trap Diamond Pattern, Mica Flecks, Signed, 10 In.	660.00
Vase, Alabaster Body, Dragon Motif, Green Jade, Glossy Background, 9 In.	1760.00
Vase, Cintra, Footed, 5 1/2 In.	975.00
Vase, Cornucopia, Blown, Signed, 5 1/2 In.	126.00
Vase, Cornucopia, Clear, Signed, 5 1/2 In.	126.00
Vase, Cut–Back Design of Dragon, Jade & Alabaster, 9 1/2 In.	1540.00
Vase, Diagonal Swirl, Pomona Green, Signed, 7 x 7 In.	165.00
Vase, Diamond Pattern, Green Stem & Foot, Amber, 11 In.	250.00
Vase, Embossed Ribs, Jade, 5 5/8 In.	195.00
Vase, Flared & Ruffled Blossom Rim, Robin's Egg Blue, 8 In.	2420.00
Vase, Flemish Blue Threading, 6 In.	150.00
Vase, Florentia	5500.00
Vase, Flower Form, Pedestal, Gold, 6 In.	880.00
Vase, Gold On White Calcite, 10 In.	375.00
Vase, Grotesque, Blue To Clear, Signed	475.00
Vase, Heavy Baluster, Gold Iridescent, 10 3/4 In.	1320.00
Vase, Horn of Plenty, Pair	220.00
Vase, Ivrene, Signed, 4 In.	225.00
Vase, Jade Glass, Lavender Handles, Baluster Form, 10 In., Pair	2530.00
Vase, Jade Opalescent, Sparrows In Prunus Branches, 1925, 9 7/8 In.	1320.00
Vase, Light Green To Green, Heart & Vine Pattern, Inverted Baluster, 11 In., Pair	2200.00
Vase, Millefiori, Flared Goblet–Form, Green Leaf & Vine Design, 11 In.	2860.00
Vase, Optic Fan, Jade & Alabaster, 10 In.	595.00
Vase, Optic, Bristol Yellow, 12 In.	350.00
Vase, Oriental Poppy, 8 In.	1100.00
Vase, Plum Jade, 12 In., Pair	7425.00
Vase, Ribbed, Jade, Signed, 7 x 7 In.	250.00
Vase, Robin's Egg Blue, Cintra, Flared, 8 In. ....*Illus*	2420.00
Vase, Spanish Galleon, Hexagonal Cut Base, Amethyst, 15 1/2 In.	4500.00
Vase, Stump, Blue, 7 In.	770.00
Vase, Stump, Green Jade	1000.00
Vase, Topaz, Diamond Pattern, Green Glass Threaded With Black	450.00
Vase, Tree Trunk, 3–Prong, Emerald Green, Signed, 6 1/2 In.	225.00
Vase, Vertically Lobed & Fluted, Green Calcite, Carder, 9 In.	1100.00
Vase, Yellow Jade, Blue Aurene Overlay, Drilled For Lamp, 1920, 11 1/4 In.	1925.00
Vase, York Pattern, Jade & Alabaster, 7 In.	875.00
Wine, Gold Calcite	250.00

STEVENGRAPHS are woven pictures made like fancy ribbons. They were manufactured by Thomas Stevens of Coventry, England, and became popular in 1862. Most are marked *Woven in silk by Thomas Stevens* or were mounted on a cardboard that tells the story of the Stevengraph. Other similar ribbon pictures have been made in England and Germany.

Pan–American Expo, Elephants, Camel, Balloon, Eastlake Frame, 1901 .... 185.00

STEVENS & WILLIAMS of Stourbridge, England, made many types of glass, including layered, etched, cameo, and art glass, between the 1830s and 1930s. Some pieces are signed *S & W*. Many pieces are decorated with flowers, leaves, and other designs based on nature.

Biscuit Jar, Blue Swirls, Ribbed Crystal Exterior, Metal Lid	420.00
Biscuit Jar, Melon Ribbed, 20 Clear Zipper Ribs	225.00
Bowl, Bubbly Yellow Glass, Late 19th Century	225.00
Box, Intaglio Cut, Pink Cased, Round, 4 1/2 x 5 In.	295.00
Creamer, Blue Flower, Green Leaves, Amber Handle, 3 In.	295.00
Perfume Bottle, Dolce Relievo, Sterling Top, Cameo Flowers & Leaves	1800.00
Rose Bowl, Applied Rigaree, Pink Flower	80.00
Rose Bowl, Pleated Top, Blue Opalescent, Striped, 4 1/2 In.	145.00
Rose Bowl, Turquoise & White Swirl, Satin, Pleated, 4 1/4 In.	195.00
Salt, Open, Applied Rigaree	120.00
Sherbet, Intaglio Cut, Matching Plate, 4 7/8 In.	325.00
Vase, Applied Cherries, Flower, White To Blue, 5 1/2 In.	295.00
Vase, Cameo, Flowers, White Opaque Ground, Flared, 5 3/4 In.	2500.00
Vase, Emerald Green Threading, Clear, 8 In.	345.00
Vase, Fan Shape, Ruffled, Opalescent Swirl, Blue, 6 1/4 In.	165.00
Vase, Floral & Panel Cut, Vaseline, Ruby, 13 1/4 In.	425.00
Vase, Flowers, Amber & Green Leaves, 9 3/4 In.	795.00
Vase, Fluted, Black Flowers & Leaves, 5 3/4 In.	2500.00
Vase, Irregular Emerald Green Threading, Marked, 8 1/4 In.	345.00
Vase, Jonquil Bud & Blossom, Spiked Leaves, Marked, 4 1/4 In.	825.00
Vase, Mother–of–Pearl Satin Glass, Cream Lining, 5 1/8 In.	895.00
Vase, Mother–of–Pearl, Green To Red Swirl, Cream Lining, 5 1/8 In.	895.00
Vase, Opaque Pink, Applied Clear Leaves, 7 In.	135.00
Vase, Optic Rib, Multicolored Flowers, Rigaree Sides, 1890s, 12 In.	230.00
Vase, Pink Flowers, Amber Centers, Leaves, 4 1/4 In., Pair	265.00
Vase, Ruffled Pink Top, Amber Rim, Amber Branches & Leaves, 5 3/4 In.	235.00
Vase, Ruffled Rim, Stylized Floral Design, 10 In., Pair	247.00
Vase, Ruffled Top, Triple Cased, Pulled Design, Pink Inside, 13 In.	695.00
Vase, Ruffled Top, Yellow & White Floral, 5 3/4 In.	577.50
Vase, Ruffled Top, Zipper Air Traps, Vaseline, 4 1/2 x 5 In.	225.00
Vase, Ruffled, Loop Feet, Foil Layered Into Amber, 5 1/2 In.	275.00
Vase, Ruffled, Pink, White & Clear Swirled Stripes, 10 1/4 In.	195.00
Vase, Swirls Alternate With Air Trap Swirls, Blue Lining, 18 In.	1195.00
Vase, White, Blue Interior, Amber Applied Leaves, Flower Handle, 5 1/2 In.	115.00
Vase, White, Crimped Amber Rim, Applied Amber Petals, 8 In.	175.00

STIEGEL type glass is listed here. It is almost impossible to be sure a piece was actually made by Stiegel, so the knowing collector refers to this glass as *Stiegel type*. Henry William Stiegel, a colorful immigrant to the colonies, started his first factory in Pennsylvania in 1763. He remained in business until 1774. Glassware was made in a style popular in Europe at that time and was similar to the glass of many other makers. It was made of clear or colored glass and was decorated with enamel colors, mold blown designs, or etching.

Flip, 3 Mold, Engraved, 6 In. 250.00

STONEWARE is a coarse, glazed, and fired potter's ceramic that is used to make crocks, jugs, bowls, etc. It is often decorated with cobalt blue decorations. Stoneware is still being made.

Bank, Grayish Amber Salt Glaze, 4 1/4 In. 71.00

Bank, Hobo	75.00
Batter Jar, Cobalt Floral Design, Evan B. Jones, Pittston, Pa., 1 1/2 Gal.	600.00
Batter Jar, Floral & Leaf, 1 Gal.	235.00
Batter Jar, Florals Front & Back & At Spout, Handle & Ears, Sipe, Nichols & Co.	605.00
Beater Jar, Blue & White, Advertising	65.00
Birdhouse, Cobalt Blue Design	5100.00
Bottle, Beer, Solid Blue Top, Hancock & Melvin	120.00
Bottle, Fish, Embossed Details, Tan Glaze, 7 1/4 In.	259.00
Bottle, Return Me To My Owner, C. R. M. Wall	65.00
Bowl & Pitcher, Rose Trellis, Blue & White	395.00
Bowl, Apricot, Blue & White	65.00
Bowl, Apricot, Wire Bail Handle, Blue & White, 10 1/4 In.	125.00
Bowl, Daisy & Waffle, Blue & White, 9 1/2 In.	100.00
Bowl, Daisy, Blue & White, With Bail, Large	65.00
Bowl, Deep Well, Flared Sides, Khaki & Amber Glaze, M. Casson, 20 1/4 In.	555.00
Bowl, Lug Handles, Half-Spherical Form, S. Blair, 1 Gal.	495.00
Bowl, Mottled Green–Gray Glaze, K. Pleydell-Bouverie, 7 1/2 In.	500.00
Bowl, Sponged Blue, Rust & Cream, 7 In.	65.00
Bowl, Spongeware, Blue Band, Western, 5 In.	150.00
Bowl, Tea, Floral Brushwork, Mushroom Glaze, Kanjiro Kawai, 2 3/4 In.	100.00
Bust, Buddha Head, Gray, 11 In.	550.00
Butter, Cover, Apricot, Blue & White	195.00
Butter, Cover, Draped Windows, Blue & Tan	135.00
Butter, Cover, Draped Windows, Blue & White	145.00
Butter, Wooden Lid, Apricot, Blue & White	95.00
Butter, Wooden Lid, Daisy, Blue & White	95.00
Carrier, Water, Floral, Ring Type, Rope For Shoulder, Europe, 1800s, 8 In.	180.00
Chamber Pot, Open Rose, Blue & White	85.00
Cheese Strainer, Albany Slip Glaze	110.00
Cheese Strainer, No. 12, Albany Slip, Large	230.00
Churn, Brown Over White, 5 Gal.	32.50
Churn, Brushed Cobalt Blue, Applied Handles, Impressed, Lid, 15 1/4 In.	330.00
Churn, Brushed Cobalt Blue, Stylized Floral Design, 18 In.	220.00
Churn, Cobalt Blue, Prancing Lion, Hubbel & Chesebro, 5 Gal.	3800.00
Churn, Fish, W. Hart, 6 Gal.	2420.00
Churn, Gray Slat, Craquelle Finish, 5 1/2 In.	50.00
Churn, Hubbell & Chesebro, Lion, 5 Gal.	4180.00
Churn, Incised 10, 21 3/4 In.	60.00
Churn, J. White, Utica, Cobalt Blue Floral, 2 Gal.	220.00
Churn, Pulaski River Salmon Fish, W. Hart, 6 Gal.	2200.00
Churn, R. T. Williams, Stenciled & Freehand Design, 3 Gal.	275.00
Churn, Red Clay, Orange–Green Glaze, 19 3/4 In.	83.00
Churn, Red Clay, Orange–Green Glaze, Handles, Incised 6	75.00
Churn, Shenandoah Type, Cobalt Blue No. 3 Design	75.00
Churn, Table, Floral Design, T. Brewer, Havana, N.Y., 2 Gal.	1025.00
Churn, Tabletop, Blue Floral, Havana, Dasher	1125.00
Churn, Vivid Dotted Floral Spray, E. & L. P. Norton, 4 Gal.	1595.00
Coffee Set, Sage–Green Glaze, Matte Finish, 9 Piece	520.00
Coffeepot, Faust	500.00
Cooler, 4 Blue Bands In Front, 3 Gal.	145.00
Cooler, Brass Spigot, Attached Drinking Fountain Bowl, Hart Mfg., 5 Gal.	300.00
Cooler, Cyrus Felten, c.1830	7200.00
Cooler, Cyrus Felten, Cobalt Blue Flowers, 2 Handles, 8 Gal.	5250.00
Cooler, P. A. & G. B. W., Blue Slip, Floral, 2 Ear Handles, Egg Shape, 18 In.	550.00
Cooler, Portraits of George Washington, Blue–Gray Slip	3080.00
Cooler, Ruckels, 2 Gal.	135.00
Cooler, Running Horse Outlined In Blue, Pedestal, 2 Piece	440.00
Crock, Apple Butter, Blue–Gray, Cobalt Blue Flowers	145.00
Crock, Bird On Log, Egg Shape, 1 Gal.	500.00
Crock, Bird, Roberts, Binghamton, 2 Gal.	495.00
Crock, Blue Chicken, Whites, Utica, 1870s, 4 Gal.	247.50
Crock, Blue Eagle, Upson Bros., Southington, Ct., 3 Gal.	425.00
Crock, Blue Floral Design, 2 Gal.	93.50

Crock, Blue Flower, Williamsport, Pa., 5 In. 470.00
Crock, Blue Man Holding Gun, Woman, W. Penna., 2 Gal. 6000.00
Crock, Bold Leafy Flower, A. O. Whittemore, 1 Gal. 198.00
Crock, Bold Triple Dotted Flowers, C. Hart, 2 Gal. 210.00
Crock, Boyers & Harden, Palatine, W. Va., Design, 1 Gal. 385.00
Crock, Butter, Applied Side Handles, Stylized Bird, Cobalt Blue, 5 In. 798.00
Crock, Butter, Cobalt Blue Design, 19th Century, 5 1/2 x 11 1/2 In. 385.00
Crock, Butter, Cover, Cobalt Blue Decoration, 12 x 7 1/2 In. 485.00
Crock, Butter, Flowered, 1/2 Gal. 175.00
Crock, Cake, Cover, Leaf Design 1050.00
Crock, Cake, Revolving Tulips & Leaves, 1 Gal. 575.00
Crock, Chicken Pecking On Dotted Ground, Ottman Bros. & Co., 3 Gal. 155.00
Crock, Cobalt Blue Brushed Vintage Design, 13 In. 66.00
Crock, Cobalt Blue Floral Design, 6 1/4 In. 25.00
Crock, Cobalt Blue Floral, Cowden & Wilcox, 6 Gal. 365.00
Crock, Cobalt Blue Stencil, Freehand Design, 12 Gal. 1600.00
Crock, Cobalt Blue Stenciled Label, E. S. & B. New Brighton, Pa., 10 In. 70.00
Crock, Cobalt Foliage, 2 Gal. 145.00
Crock, Cover, Armstrong & Wentworth, 11 1/4 In. 137.50
Crock, Cross Bros., Sterling, Pa., Cobalt Blue Flower, No. 2, 9 1/2 In. 148.00
Crock, Daisy–Type Flower, 6 Gal. 120.00
Crock, Dotted Bird On Long Vine, Bangor Stoneware Co., 3 Gal. 135.00
Crock, Eagle, Williams & Reppet, 20 Gal. 2975.00
Crock, Emma In Blue Script, C. Hart & Son, 2 Gal. 185.00
Crock, Fantail Bird On Branch, White, Utica, 4 Gal. 375.00
Crock, Fantail Song Bird, Haxstun & Co., 2 Gal. 330.00
Crock, Floral, Blue 2, H. Nash, Egg Shape, 2 Gal. 110.00
Crock, Fluted Sides, Brushed Blue, Applied Handles, 12 1/2 In. 95.00
Crock, Fort Edward Stoneware, Crossed Flags, 1883, 6 Gal. 8000.00
Crock, Fowl, T. F. Connolly, 2 Gal. 742.50
Crock, Fredricktown, Cobalt Blue Eagle, 2 Gal. 1300.00
Crock, Hearts Design, Ear, 16 Gal. 2300.00
Crock, Iced Tea, Maxwell House 150.00
Crock, Impressed 4, Bluish–Black Stenciled Eagle, 11 1/2 In. 50.00
Crock, J. Burger, Rochester, N.Y., Cobalt Blue Quillwork, No. 2, 9 In. 40.00
Crock, James Hamilton & Co., Greensboro, Pa., Cobalt Design, 6 Gal. 413.00
Crock, John Johnston 2000.00
Crock, Knickerbocker Cater Co., Genuine Boston Baked Beans, 1 Qt. 450.00
Crock, Lambright, Newport, Ohio, Cobalt Blue Incised, Handle, 8 Gal. 700.00
Crock, Long–Tailed Bird On Leafy Branch, N. A. White & Co., 3 Gal. 145.00
Crock, McNees & Co., Girty, Pa., Ears, 5 Gal. 1350.00
Crock, N. White & Co., Binghamton, Cobalt Blue Design, 2 Gal. 165.00
Crock, No. 3 & Flourish, Cobalt Blue Quill Work, 11 1/4 In. 71.00
Crock, Ottman Bros., 1876 Centennial, Fort Edward, N.Y. 695.00
Crock, Paddle Tail Bird, N. A. White & Son, 2 Gal. .... 350.00 To 467.50
Crock, Pheasant, No. 10 .... 2200.00
Crock, Polka–Dot Design, Cobalt Blue, Applied Side Handles, 15 In. 110.00
Crock, Ribbed Flower & Leaves, J. Burger, Jr., 4 Gal. 187.00
Crock, Running Bird, Cobalt, 1 1/2 Gal. 150.00
Crock, Salt, Blue, White, Hanging Crest, Wooden Hinged Lid, 6 In. 49.00
Crock, Scene of Standing Stag Between Trees, W. A. Lewis, 4 Gal. 3080.00
Crock, Star Burst & Face, Harrington, 3 Gal. 2090.00
Crock, Stylized Flower, No. 3 Cobalt Blue, 11 1/4 In. 93.00
Crock, Sunflower, Harrington, Cover, 2 Gal. 412.50
Crock, Williams & Ruppert, Greensboro, Pa., Blue Design, Ear Handles, 3 Gal. 82.50
Crock, Wooden Lid, Dasher, Cobalt Blue Quill Work, 16 1/2 In. 110.00
Cuspidor, Blue & White 195.00
Cuspidor, Grape Pattern, Green .... 35.00 To 45.00
Cuspidor, Mottled Rockingham Glaze, 12 In. 101.00
Dog, Oval Base, Mottled Tan, White Glaze, 4 1/4 In. 104.00
Dutch Oven, Cover, Blue, 2 Qt. 35.00
Figurine, Dog, Seated, White With Clear Glaze, Green Spots, 6 1/4 In. 770.00
Figurine, Gazelle, Dark Brown Glaze, 1800s, Pair 65.00

Flask, Shot, Bird On Branch, Bouquet On Other Side, 3 1/4 x 2 1/2 In. 95.00
Fountain, Water, Bird, White Glaze, 5 1/2 In. 137.00
Jar, Abstract Floral Design, Cortland, N.Y., 1 1/2 Gal. 460.00
Jar, Applied Handles, Cobalt Blue Floral Design, 12 In. 302.00
Jar, Applied Handles, Cobalt Blue Foliage Designs, 15 3/4 In. 302.00
Jar, Applied Handles, Egg Shape, Stylized Floral Design, Cobalt Blue, 13 In. 71.00
Jar, Applied Shoulder Handles, 14 In. 49.00
Jar, Applied Shoulder Handles, Cobalt Blue Tulip, 13 1/4 In. 55.00
Jar, Blue Cobalt Design Around Ears, Egg Shape, 6 Gal. 220.00
Jar, Bold Leafy Double Flower, Lyons, 1 Gal. 660.00
Jar, Brushed Cobalt Blue Floral, Egg Shape, 12 1/2 In. 165.00
Jar, Canning, 2–Tone Brown 12.00
Jar, Canning, A. P. Donaghho, Parkersburg, W. V., Cobalt Blue, 8 In. 55.00
Jar, Canning, Barrel Shape, Blue Molded Bands, 8 In. 275.00
Jar, Canning, Cobalt Blue Design, 7 In. 150.00
Jar, Canning, Cobalt Blue Floral Design, 11 In. 45.00
Jar, Canning, Cobalt Blue Lines, Stenciled Label, 9 1/4 In. 255.00
Jar, Canning, Cobalt Blue Shoulder Design, 10 In. 115.00
Jar, Canning, Cobalt Blue, Stenciled Label, Floral Design, 12 In. 75.00
Jar, Canning, Cobalt Blue, Stenciled Label, Rose, 10 In. 225.00
Jar, Canning, Floral, Cobalt Blue, 11 1/4 In. 85.00
Jar, Canning, Stenciled & Freehand Label, Hamilton & Jones, 10 In. 140.00
Jar, Canning, Wax Seal, Brown, 6 3/4 In. 45.00
Jar, Charlestown, Egg Shape, 1790–1810, 2 Gal. 275.00
Jar, Cobalt Blue Beehive Design, 10 Gal. 90.00
Jar, Cobalt Blue Brushed Floral Design, 11 1/2 In. 154.00
Jar, Cobalt Blue Design, Gray Salt Glaze, 8 3/4 In. 160.00
Jar, Cobalt Blue Floral, Ovoid, Impressed, Norton & Fenton, 12 3/4 In. 385.00
Jar, Cobalt Floral, Pennsylvania, 2 Gal. 360.00
Jar, Cobalt Slip, 6 3/4 In. 104.00
Jar, Cover, Cobalt Blue Bird On Branch, Salt Glaze, 10 In. 350.00
Jar, Cover, Cobalt Design, Double Handles, 5 In. 3600.00
Jar, Cover, Meadow Sweet Cheese, 3 In. 10.00
Jar, Double Ribbed Leaves, John Burger, 2 Gal. 120.00
Jar, Face In Center of Star Burst, T. Harrington, 3 Gal. 1900.00
Jar, Faint Blue House & Tree Design, 2 Qt. 2750.00
Jar, Fat Bird On Leafy Branch, White & Wood, 2 Gal. 250.00
Jar, Floral Design, F. Woodworth, 2 Gal. 110.00
Jar, Gray Salt Glaze, Blue Paint, 11 In, ... 93.00
Jar, Grayish Amber Salt Glaze, Albany Slip Interior, 13 1/4 In. 40.00
Jar, House & Tree Scene 2750.00
Jar, Impressed Boston 1804, Gray & Brown Glaze, 9 1/2 In. 1210.00
Jar, Impressed Label, Cobalt Blue Design, Blue At Handles, 11 In. 250.00
Jar, Impressed Label, Floral Design, Cobalt Blue Slip, 12 3/4 In. 742.00
Jar, Impressed Label, Pickles, Shoulder Dots, Cobalt Blue, Egg Shape, 9 3/4 In. 247.00
Jar, Incised Lines, Applied Handles, Cobalt Blue Floral Design, 14 In. 150.00
Jar, J. & E. Norton, Bennington, Vt., Crossed Peacocks In Tree, 4 Gal. 3000.00
Jar, Leafy Tulip, Burger & Lang, 2 Gal. 275.00
Jar, Medium Brown Glaze, Greenish Highlights, Applied Handles, 3 1/2 In. 33.00
Jar, Oyster, Brown & White, E. Swasey, 1/2 Pt. 165.00
Jar, R. T. Williams, New Geneva, Pa., Eagle, 12 Gal. 1450.00
Jar, Raised Blue Horse Head, Whites, Utica 175.00
Jar, Reddish Brown Albany Slip, Impressed Label, 7 1/2 In. 55.00
Jar, Ribbed Leaf & Flower Design, F. Stetzenmeyer & G. Goetzman, 1 Gal. 245.00
Jar, Stenciled Blue Label, 9 1/4 In. 110.00
Jar, Tan Salt Glaze, Brushed Blue Tulip, 7 1/2 In. 220.00
Jar, White Clam Lid, Bail, 1 Gal. 35.00
Jug, 2 With Blue Lines, Hart Sherburne, 2 Gal. 65.00
Jug, Adolf Goldhammer Wholesale Wines & Liquors, Denver, Col., 1/2 Gal. 90.00
Jug, Allover Blue Sponge, 1 Gal. 300.00
Jug, Bird & Nest of 3 Eggs Design, Handle, 5 Gal 5600.00
Jug, Bird On Flowered Branch, Whites, Utica, 3 Gal. 205.00
Jug, Blue Bands Top & Bottom, Stenciled Design, Greensboro, Pa., 1 Gal. 247.00

Jug, Blue Bird, Stetzenmeyer, 2 Gal. 5940.00
Jug, Brown Albany Slip, Sgraffito Label, 3 3/8 In. 71.00
Jug, Brown Albany Slip, Strap Handle, 4 In. 22.00
Jug, Brown Top, Bottom Marked M. S. W. Co., 1/4 Pt. 350.00
Jug, C. Crolius, New York, 13 1/2 In. 325.00
Jug, Cluster of 5 Flowers, E. A. Montell, 4 Gal. 520.00
Jug, Cobalt Blue, No. 2, Lines, Egg Shape, 13 3/4 In. 85.00
Jug, Cobalt On Handle, Salt Glaze, 1 Gal. 25.00
Jug, Cream Spots, Galena 395.00
Jug, Dark Brown Albany Slip, Wire Bale Handle, 10 In. 27.00
Jug, Dotted Floral Spray, J. & E. Norton, 3 Gal. 495.00
Jug, Dotted Floral Spray, Roberts, 3 Gal. 165.00
Jug, Dotted Floral, Ottman Bros. & Co., 1 Gal. 130.00
Jug, Dotted Ribbed Flower, Lyons Cooperative, 4 Gal. 245.00
Jug, Double Birds With Centennial In Script, H. T. Parker & Co., 3 Gal. 330.00
Jug, Double Flower, Ottman Bros. & Co., 1 Gal. 175.00
Jug, Double Flowers, Lehman & Riedinger, Egg Shape, 3 Gal. 395.00
Jug, E. A. Buck Co., Cobalt Blue Floral, 18 In. 176.00
Jug, E. Norton & Co., No. 2, Cobalt Blue, Egg Shape, 12 In. 220.00
Jug, Egg Shape, No. 2 In Cobalt Blue, 13 1/4 In. 237.00
Jug, Face, Applied Features, Greenish Ash Glaze, 4 In. 5170.00
Jug, Floral Design, Cobalt Blue, 13 1/2 In. 126.00
Jug, Floral Design, Impressed Label, Cobalt Blue Slip, 12 3/4 In. 370.00
Jug, Floral Design, Impressed Label, Cobalt Blue, 13 In. 275.00
Jug, Floral Design, Impressed Label, Cobalt Blue, 4 In. 242.00
Jug, Floral Design, Nichols & Boynton, 1 Gal. 88.00
Jug, Floral Spray, Hornets Nests, Cowden & Wilcox, 2 Gal. 1100.00
Jug, Floral, S. S. Perry & Co., Egg Shape, 2 Gal. 175.00
Jug, Gray Salt Glaze, Amber Highlights, Brown Tulip, 13 3/4 In. 185.00
Jug, Gray Salt Glaze, Brown Albany Slip At Neck, Shoulders, 12 3/4 In. 27.00
Jug, Gray Salt Glaze, Brown Highlights, Strap Handle, 3 3/8 In. 38.00
Jug, Gray Salt Glaze, Daubs of Blue, Applied Handle, High Neck, 4 1/2 In. 357.00
Jug, Gray, Dustman Pottery, Cobalt Blue Stenciled Dome Top, Center Handle 180.00
Jug, H. Pudry No. 2, Cobalt Blue Flower, Egg Shape, 13 1/2 In. 522.00
Jug, Incised Bird, C. Boynton, Egg Shape, 3 Gal. 1600.00
Jug, Incised Fish, Gray Salt Glaze, Brown Highlights, 10 In. 300.00
Jug, Ink, Harrison's Patent Columbian, Handle 675.00
Jug, Man In The Moon, Cobalt Blue, Cowden & Wilcox, 2 Gal. 4000.00
Jug, Man In The Moon, Cowden & Wilcox, 2 Gal. 4400.00
Jug, Molded Lady's Leg Handle, 8 1/4 In. 247.00
Jug, No. 2, Bird On Branch, Dark Cobalt Blue Quill, 13 1/4 In. 450.00
Jug, No. 2, Cobalt Blue Design, S. Hart Fulton, Egg Shape, 13 In. 125.00
Jug, No. 3, Cobalt Blue Floral Design, 15 1/4 In. 275.00
Jug, Oyster, E. Swazey & Co., Small 120.00
Jug, Paddle Tail Bird, Flowered Branch, N. A. White & Son, 4 Gal. 660.00
Jug, Poland Mineral Spring Water, Cobalt Lettering 95.00
Jug, Prendergast Bros. & Russ Wholesale Liquors & Cigars, 1 Gal. 100.00
Jug, R. H. Parker, Louisville, Ky., Bail, Miniature 40.00
Jug, R. T. Williams, New Geneva, Pa., Eagle Grasping Arrows, 5 Gal. 1210.00
Jug, Rose Design In Cobalt Blue, Impressed Label, 27 In. 192.00
Jug, Sapiro Wines & Liquors of All Kinds, Denver, Col., 1 Gal. 100.00
Jug, Satterlee & Mory, 3 Gal. 425.00
Jug, Slip Bird, Roberts, Binghamton, New York, 2 Gal. 495.00
Jug, Stenciled Snowflake, F. H. Cowden, 2 Gal. 120.00
Jug, Stylized Floral Design, Cobalt Blue, Impressed Label, 18 In. 495.00
Jug, W. A. Hover & Co. Wholesale Druggists, Denver, Col., 1/2 Gal. 90.00
Jug, W. E. Welding, Cobalt Blue Design, Impressed, Brantford 3, 16 1/4 In. 385.00
Jug, W. Rooker, Easton, Pa., Cobalt Floral, Salt Glaze, 3 Gal. 150.00
Jug, White Rose Rye Whiskey, Blue & Gray, 6 In. 200.00
Jug, Winchell Davis Whiskey, 1/2 Pt., Pair 40.00
Jug, Ye Olden Time, With Pipe 50.00
Loving Cup, Tavern Scene, 3 Hound Handles, Doulton Lambeth, 5 1/2 In. 155.00
Milk Pan, Floral, S. Blair, Cortland, N.Y. 450.00

Mold, Turk's Head, Solomon Bell, Mottled, 10 3/4 In. 1695.00
Mug, Golfing, Blue 200.00
Mug, Pluto Spring Water 125.00
Pail, Butter, Bellflower Design, Tin Lid, Spout, 1 Gal. 550.00
Pie Plate, Black Glaze Interior 20.00
Pitcher, Applied Design, Tan & Cream, 6 3/4 In. 22.00
Pitcher, Apricot, Brown 85.00
Pitcher, Avenue of Trees, Blue & White, 8 In. .... 225.00 To 325.00
Pitcher, Batter, Cobalt Floral Design, 1 Gal. 635.00
Pitcher, Batter, Dark Brown Albany Slip, Wire Handle, 9 1/4 In. 82.00
Pitcher, Batter, Floral Decoration, Signed, 9 1/2 In. 300.00
Pitcher, Bear Paw, Blue & White, Tall 220.00
Pitcher, Blue, White, Tree Bark, Leaves, King Gambrinus, Cobalt Blue, 7 In. 165.00
Pitcher, Brownish Tan Glaze, Tooled Applied Leaves, Handle, 11 In. 110.00
Pitcher, Buttermilk, Dutch Children, Blue & White 145.00
Pitcher, Cattail, 10 In. 155.00
Pitcher, Cherries & Leaves, Salt Glaze, 10 In. 160.00
Pitcher, Cobalt Blue Design, 10 1/4 In. 2750.00
Pitcher, Cow, Blue & White, 8 In. 150.00
Pitcher, Dragonfly, Blue & White 125.00
Pitcher, Dutch Children & Windmill, Small 130.00
Pitcher, Dutch Children Kissing, Blue & White 145.00
Pitcher, Dutch Farm, Blue & White, 7 In. 195.00
Pitcher, Fishscale & Rose, Cobalt Blue & White 95.00
Pitcher, Flemish Figures, Cobalt Blue & Gray 265.00
Pitcher, Floral Design, Cobalt Blue, 10 1/2 In. 660.00
Pitcher, Floral Design, Impressed 2, Cobalt Blue, 13 In. 765.00
Pitcher, Flowers, Cobalt Blue, 14 In. 900.00
Pitcher, Grape On Waffle, Blue & White, 9 In. 175.00
Pitcher, Grapes & Shield, Green & Cream 125.00
Pitcher, Gray Salt Glaze With Blue, 2 5/8 In. 544.00
Pitcher, Impressed Label, Brown Albany Slip, 11 1/4 In. 275.00
Pitcher, Indian Head & Crosshatch, Gray & Blue 60.00
Pitcher, Indian War Bonnet, Blue & White 80.00
Pitcher, Leaf, Cobalt Blue, Egg Shape, 10 In. 385.00
Pitcher, Leafy Dotted Poppy, Whites, Utica, 1 Gal. 355.00
Pitcher, Paneled, Brown Albany Slip, Molded Figures, 6 In. 28.00
Pitcher, Peacock, Blue & White, 10 In. 410.00
Pitcher, Rose On Trellis, 10 In. 120.00
Pitcher, Stag & Pine Trees, 9 In. 200.00
Pitcher, Vintage Rim, Bust of Woman, Hat, White Glaze, 9 1/4 In. 82.00
Pitcher, Wash, Feather & Swirl 250.00
Pitcher, Windmill & Bush, Blue & White, 10 In. .... 150.00 To 225.00
Pot, Tulip-Like Design, Egg Shape, Maxfield–Milwaukee, 6 Gal. 675.00
Ring Jug, Keystone Pottery, Charles Decker, Gray, Cobalt Dots, 1886 .... 2650.00
Salt Box, Butterfly, Blue & White, Wooden Cover 120.00
Salt Box, Daisy On Snowflake, Wooden Lid 77.00
Salt Box, Dutch Scene, Blue Design, Lid, 7 In. 95.00
Tankard, Milk, Dreamland, Loughlin 225.00
Teapot, Banquet Tea, Wonderful Flavor Iced Or Hot, 9 1/2 x 10 In. 155.00
Teapot, Loop Handle, Speckled Olive–Green Glaze, T. Bell–Hughes, 5 1/2 In. 110.00
Tenderizer, Wooden Handle, Pat. Dec. 25, 1877 .... 70.00
Toothbrush Holder, Fishscale & Wild Roses 40.00
Umbrella Stand, Sponged Blue Glaze, Incised A. L. Barber 800.00
Vase, Crackled Glaze, White, Fitted As Lamp, Chinese, 20 In. 880.00
Washstand Set, Rose & Trellis, 5 Piece 500.00
Water Carrier, Floral, Shoulder Carrying Rope, Early 1800s, Europe, 8 In. 225.00
Whistle, Night Owl, Brown Glaze, 1890, 5 1/2 In. 3300.00

STORE fixtures, cases, cutters, and other items that have no advertising as part of the decoration are listed here. Most items found in an old store are listed in the Advertising category in this book.

Backbar, Eastlake Type, Oak, Swivel Mirror, Shelves, No Base, 1890, 7 Ft x 4 Ft. ... 725.00

Basket, Fish, Wooden Lid, Bail, Marked Lake Herring 45.00
Beer Tap, Brass, Tavern, Primitive, Large, 2 1/2 Lbs. 17.00
Bin, Grain, Gray–Green Paint, Battle Creek, Mich. 775.00
Bin, Meal, Square Nails, Unusual Turned Legs 395.00
Brush, Shaving, Made Rite, Badger Hair, No. 649 .... 12.50
Cabinet, Apothecary, Mahogany Front, Labels, Glass Knobs, England, 35 x 122 In. 715.00
Cabinet, Printer's, Hamilton, Oak, 23 Trays 250.00
Cabinet, Screw, 99 Pie–Shaped Drawers, Cast Iron 750.00
Cabinet, Spool, Oak, 6 Drawers, With Legs 650.00
Cabinet, Watchmaker's, Robin's Egg Blue Paint 475.00
Case, Display, Mahogany, Mortised, 6 Sides Glass, Brass Hasp, 19 x 13 x 10 In. 525.00
Case, Display, Oak & Glass, 24 x 13 1/2 In. 468.00
Case, Display, Pine, Glass Window, Scalloped Edge, Lift Lid, 8 x 11 3/4 x 13 In. ... 190.00
Chest, Apothecary, Painted Cranberry & Green, 12 Drawers 1250.00
Chest, Apothecary, Walnut, Marble Center Insert, 1850, 85 x 40 x 20 In. 4350.00
Counter & Grain Bin, 4 Curved Glass Bins, Raised Panel Oak Counter, 90 In. 990.00
Counter, Backbar, Candy & Ice Cream Store, Large 2000.00
Display Case, Counter Top, Curved Glass Front, Open Center, Oak, c.1900, 72 In. 880.00
Display, Corset Form, Simple Corset Attached, 30 x 8 In. 138.00
Display, Early Times, Man In 1902 Ford, Chalkware, 13 1/2 x 12 1/4 In. 40.00
Door Knocker, Cherub's Head, Acorn Finial, Cast Iron, 8 1/4 In. 100.00
Egg, Carrier, Queen City, Bangor, Maine, 15 x 13 x 16 In. 40.00
Faucet Valve, Beer, Chromed Brass 15.00
Mannequin, Tess, Waxed Head, Glass Eyes, Teeth, Wooden Arms, 1909, Full Size 1500.00
Mirror, Ice Cream Parlor, Mahogany, Free Standing, 1910, Large .... 500.00 To 600.00
Mirror, Pretzel–Shaped Frame 160.00
Paper Holder, Keen Kutter 175.00
Seed Bin, Kentucky, 1890s 1895.00
Soda Fountain, Pharmacy, Marble, Cherrywood, 5 Stools, Mass., 1900s, 10 Ft. 6000.00
Straw Holder, Diamond Designed Removable Bottom 325.00
Teller's Cage, General Store, For Gold & Silver Buying, Oak, Raised Panels 1500.00
Teller's Cage, Old West, To Buy Gold & Silver, Golden Oak, Raised Panels 1200.00
Tobacco Cutter, Figural, Eve Holding Apple, Iron, Laminated Handle, 13 In. 385.00
Tobacco, Cutter, Indian Head, Bronze, 5 5/8 In. 210.00

STOVES have been used in America for heating since the eighteenth century and for cooking since the nineteenth century. Most types of wood, coal, gas, kerosene, and even some electric stoves are collected.

Camp, Over Brazier, Revolutionary War 660.00
Charter Oak, Cookstove, With Warming Oven, For Wood 400.00
Child's, Cast Iron, Gold Trim, 13 x 12 x 7 In. 295.00
Cook, Crawford 450.00
Cook, Konwich 80.00
Famous Brand, No. 02–18, White Glossy Finish, Top Bun Warmer 425.00
Griswold No. 3, Classic Parlor 1000.00
Magic Ideal, Wood Or Coal, 6 Lids, Water Jacket 300.00
Parlor, Art Laurel, No. 14, Nickel Plated 1700.00
Parlor, Coral, No. 3, Complete 175.00
Parlor, Florence 800.00
Parlor, Palace, A. Bradley & Co., Cast Iron, Finial, Pat. 1873, 46 In. 325.00
Parlor, Premium Oak, Chrome, 5 1/2 Ft. 1550.00
Parlor, Radiant Estate, Model 515 F, Nickel Plated 3000.00
Starlight, Cast Iron 395.00
Tabletop, Brick Red 325.00
Tabletop, Oil, 1 Burner, Gray & White Mottled Enamel, 2 Qt. Pan, With Cover 275.00
Tabletop, Oil, 3 Burners, Red, With Coffee Boiler 375.00
Wehrle, Range, Blue 700.00
Wincroft, Wood & Coal, 6 Lids 300.00
Wood Burning, Scandinavian, 19th Century 675.00

STRAWBERRY, see Soft Paste category

STRETCH GLASS is named for the strange stretch marks in the glass. It was made by many glass companies in the United States from about 1900 to the 1920s. It is iridescent. Most American stretch glass is molded; most European pieces are blown and may have a pontil mark.

Plate, Decagon, Pair	20.00
Vase, Pink, 6 In.	25.00

SUMIDA, or Sumida Gawa, is a Japanese pottery. The pieces collected by that name today were made about 1895 to 1970. There has been much confusion about the name of this ware, and it is often called *Korean Pottery.* Most pieces have a very heavy orange–red, blue, or green glaze, with raised three–dimensional figures as decorations.

Bottle, Egg Shaped, White Glaze, Yi Dynasty, 9 In.	55.00
Mug, Applied Sea Creature, Black & White Drip Glaze, Signed	115.00
Vase, Child On Limb, Egg & Bird	145.00
Vase, Raised Figures, 1875, 9 1/2 In.	145.00

SUNBONNET BABIES were first introduced in 1902 in the *Sunbonnet Babies Primer.* The stories were by Eulalie Osgood Grover, illustrated by Bertha Corbett. The children's faces were completely hidden by the sunbonnets. The children had been pictured in black and white before this time, but the color pictures in the book were immediately successful. The Royal Bayreuth China Company made a full line of children's dishes decorated with the Sunbonnet Babies. Some Sunbonnet Babies plates have been reproduced, but are clearly marked.

Album, Autograph, Ullman, 1906	45.00
Bell, Cleaning, Royal Bayreuth	450.00
Bell, Cleaning, Wooden Clapper	295.00
Bowl, Mending, Footed, 6 In.	175.00
Candleholder, Sweeping, Shield, 5 In.	700.00
Candlestick, Mending	100.00
Creamer, Cleaning, Blue Mark, 4 In.	185.00
Creamer, Sewing, Royal Bayreuth	175.00
Jug, Cleaning, Gold Handle, Blue Mark, Miniature	245.00
Mug, Cleaning, Blue Mark	195.00
Mug, Ironing, Royal Bayreuth, 2 In.	110.00
Mug, Sweeping, Royal Bayreuth	395.00
Pitcher, Milk, Sweeping, Pinch Spout, Blue Mark, 5 In.	350.00
Pitcher, Washing, Ironing, Gold Handle, Blue Mark, 4 In.	195.00
Plate, Carnation, 7 In.	35.00
Plate, Days of Week, Royal Bayreuth, 7 In., 7 Piece	1500.00
Postcard, Days of Week, 7 Piece	89.00
Postcard, Mechanical, Hold To Light	25.00
Sugar & Creamer, Laundry	450.00
Teapot, Cleaning, Royal Bayreuth	450.00
Teapot, Fishing, 3 1/2 In.	500.00
Toothpick, Cleaning	800.00

SUNDERLAND luster is a name given to a special type of pink luster made by Leeds, Newcastle, and other English firms during the nineteenth century. The luster glaze is metallic and glossy and appears to have bubbles in it. Other pieces of luster are listed in the Luster category.

Bowl, Ship Caroline, 4 x 10 In.	110.00
Creamer, Ship, 3 In.	85.00
Cup & Saucer, Staffordshire	72.00
Jug, Cider, Cast Iron Bridge View, Make–Do Sterling Spout, Large	650.00
Mug, British Ship, 4 In.	45.00
Pitcher, American Ship, 7 1/2 In.	65.00
Pitcher, British Ship, 5 In.	65.00
Plaque, Black Transfer, Polychrome Enameling, 7 7/8 x 8 1/2 In.	255.00
Plate, 6 3/4 In.	55.00
Tumbler, Cloud Pattern	45.00

SUPERMAN was created by two seventeen–year–olds in 1938. The first issue of *Action* comics had the strip. Superman remains popular and became the hero of a radio show in 1940, cartoons in the 1940s, a television series, and several major movies.

Animation Cell, Hand Painted, From TV	195.00
Bank, Dime Register, Tin	150.00
Billfold	18.00
Book, Paint By Number, 1966	55.00
Box, Gum Card, George Reeves Photograph, 1965	129.00
Candy, Cigarettes, Original Pack	45.00
Card, Valentine, 1966	12.00
Carton, Orange Drink, Unused, 1972	15.00
Comic Book, No. 1, Summer, 1930	6490.00
Comic Book, No. 11, July–Aug. 1941, Frederic Ray Cover	440.00
Comic Book, No. 36	47.00
Comic Book, Superboy, No. 1, National Comic Pub., 1949	990.00
Cookie Jar, Brown, Robinson Ransbottom	375.00
Cookie Jar, Superman, In Phone Booth, California Originals	485.00
Costume, Vinyl Cape, Plastic Mask, Ben Cooper, 1970	35.00
Display, 12 Billfolds On Card	180.00
Doll, Mego, 12 In.	35.00 To 40.00
Doll, Plush, Vinyl Head, Commonwealth Toys, 1966, 18 In.	75.00
Drawing, Profile, Bust, Pencil, Joe Shuster, 8 1/2 x 5 1/2 In.	880.00
Figure, Chalkware, 1930s, 14 In.	500.00
Figure, Knickerbocker, Box, 24 In.	40.00
Game, Calling Superman, Transogram, 1954, 8 x 15 In.	100.00 To 109.00
Game, Card, Whitman, 1966	38.00
Game, Superman II, Milton Bradley, Based On Movie, 1981	35.00
Game, Superman Speed, Board, Milton Bradley, 1940	239.00
Game, Superman–Superboy, 2–Sided Board, Milton Bradley, 1967	39.00
Greeting Card Set, 1978, 12 Piece	20.00
Hood Ornament, Auto, Chrome, 1940s	3000.00
Kit, Paint By Number, Hasbro, 1965, Box	125.00
Kite, 1964, Unopened	45.00
Krypto–Ray Gun, Metal, 5 Filmstrips, Daisy, Box, 1940, 7 In.	806.00
Lunch Box, 1967	69.00 To 175.00
Model Kit, Unassembled, Aurora, 1963	298.00
Pogo Stick	35.00
Puppet, Switches From Clark Kent To Superman, Synergistics, 1979	21.00
Puzzle, Slide Tile, Roalex, 1966, Unused	98.00
Puzzle, Superman Surrounded By Brainiacs, Whitman, 1964, Box	29.00
Record Album & Book, The Magic Ring, Musette Records, 1947	49.00
Record Album & Comic Book, 33 1/3 RPM Record Set, Golden Records, 1966	59.00
Ring, Crusader, 1940	225.00
Ring, Goldtone Band, Superman Symbol Center, Nestles, 1976	20.00 To 27.00
Thermos, 1967	60.00 To 65.00
Thermos, 1978	10.00
Toy, Supermobile, Superman Junior, Corgi, England	2.00
Tumbler, 1979, Large	25.00
Wrapper, Bubble Gum Card, Bowman, Early 1940s, 6 x 4 1/2 In.	275.00
Wristwatch	375.00

SWANKYSWIGS are small drinking glasses. In 1933, the Kraft Food Company began to market cheese spreads in these decorated, reusable glass tumblers. They were discontinued from 1941 to 1946, then made again from 1947 to 1958. Then plain glasses were used for most of the cheese, although a few special decorated Swankyswigs have been made since that time. A complete list of prices can be found in *Kovels' Price Guide to Depression Glass & American Dinnerware*.

Checkerboard, Dark Blue	25.00
Jonquil, Yellow, 4 1/2 In.	12.00
Sailboat, Red	20.00

Tulip, No. 2, 6 Gold Bands 20.00

SWORDS of all types that are of interest to collectors are listed here. The military dress sword with elaborate handle is probably the most wanted. Be sure to display swords in a safe way, out of reach of children.

2-Handles, Japan, 1890 .... 325.00
Artillery, Ames Mfg. Co., Leather Scabbard, Belt & Brass Knuckle, Short 770.00
Austrian Cavalry Trooper, Semibowl Guard, Leather Grip, 34 1/4 In. 130.00
Bayonet, Bowie, Plug 1250.00
Bayonet, Side Knife, Pierced Brass Grip, Spain, 1790s 115.00
Bayonet, United States, Springfield, 1873 .... 40.00
Brass Hilt, Triple Brass Guard, Wire Wrapped Grip, Steel Scabbard 120.00
British Infantry, Brass Heart-Shaped Guard, Urn Pommel, 29 1/2 In. 525.00
Cavalry Officer's, 3 Bar Hilt, Etched Blade, c.1850, 32 1/2 In. 250.00
Cavalry Officer's, Silver Hilt, Silver Wire-Wrapped Leather, Austria, 1760, 33 In. ... 2250.00
Cavalry, Ames Mfg. Co., Wire-Wrapped Leather Grip, Civil War, 1858 .... 715.00
Confederate, D-Guard, RaBone Brothers & Co., Civil War 330.00
Cutlass, Navy, Brass Hilt, America, 19th Century, 27 In. 396.00
Cutlass, Navy, Brass Hilt, Fullered Blade, c.1880, 22 1/2 In. 225.00
Cutlass, Navy, Ribbed Grip, England, 1804, 28 3/4 In. 245.00
Dirk, English Naval Officer's, Brass Mounts, Dolphin Head Quillon, c.1790, 15 In. ... 315.00
Eagle Pommel, Wire-Wrapped Ivory Grip 225.00
French Infantry, Curved Blade, c.1820, 29 1/2 In. 170.00
General Officer's, War of 1812, Engraved Eagle & Design On Scabbard, America ... 475.00
Halberd, Hand Hewn Oak Haft, c.1775, 7 Ft. 650.00
Head Hunter's, Naga, Copper Base Hilt, c.1800, 21 In. 110.00
Katana Samurai, Signed Blade, Japan 795.00
Lance, Cane Haft, Leather-Covered Base Shoe, c.1800, 6 Ft. 135.00
Marine, Dress, Ivory Hilt, Engraved Blade, Silver Plated & Brass Scabbard, 35 In. ... 605.00
Naval Officer's, Presentation, Model 1852 .... 575.00
Naval Officer's, U.S. Navy, Boston Regalia Co., 1852, 37 In. 220.00
Naval Officer's, U.S. Navy, Gilt Wire Wrap, 29 1/2 In. 165.00
Naval Presentation, Inscribed, 1890s 300.00
Officer's, Emmerson & Silver, Trenton, New Jersey, Split Brass Guard, 1863 .... 330.00
Officer's, U.S. Eagle, Leather-Covered Finger Grip, Scabbard 140.00
Pirate's, Brass Hilt, Carved Flower Clusters Bone Grip, Malay, c.1800, 20 In. 145.00
Rapier, Double Shell Cup Hilt, Braided Wire On Wooden Haft, 17th Century, 45 In. ... 385.00
Rapier, Straight Guard, Expanded Terminals, c.1600, 41 1/2 In. 2150.00
Saber, Ames Mfg., Chicopee, Mass., Brass Pommel & Basket, 1861, 31 1/2 In. 357.50
Saber, Azande, 2-Step Section Blade, Brass- & Iron-Wrapped Grip, 34 In. 240.00
Saber, Dragoon, Sold By C. & I. D. Wolfe, New York, 1810 .... 110.00
Saber, Hussar, Brass Hilt, Wire-Wrapped Horn Grip, Napoleonic, 31 In. 450.00
Saber, Iron Guards, Wooden Hilt, Metal Scabbard, War of 1812, 33 1/2 In. 220.00
Saber, Iron Hilt, Double Ring Guard, Bronze Monster Head Pommel, c.1650, 28 In. 1350.00
Saber, Leather Scabbard, Single Brass Guard, Leather Grip, Mid-19th Century 95.00
Saber, Navy, Ames, Marked USN 1862, 26-In. Blade 550.00
Scottish Court, Brass Hilt, c.1770, 29 3/4 In. 325.00
Short, Bone Grip, Star Stamp Both Sides, 18th Century 303.00
Side Arm, Brass Mount, Scabbard, Belt, Revolutionary War, 28 3/4 In. 325.00
U.S. Staff & Field, Model 1850, Etched Soldiers, Liberty Figure Holding Flag 6875.00

SYRACUSE is a trademark used by the Onondaga Pottery of Syracuse, New York. The company was established in 1871. It is still working. The name became the Syracuse China Company in 1966. It is known for fine dinnerware and restaurant china.

Bowl, Lady Mary 20.00
Bowl, Lady Mary, Oval, 10 1/2 In. 15.00
Bowl, Vegetable, Celeste, Oval, 10 In. 25.00
Dish, Fruit, Royal Court 27.00
Feeding Set, Child's, Mary & Her Lamb, 3 Piece 35.00
Gravy Boat, Bracelet 25.00
Gravy, Portland 22.00
Place Setting, Bracelet, 4 Piece 65.00

Plate, Lady Mary, 9 In. 10.00
Platter, Lady Mary, 14 In. 25.00
Soup, Dish, Royal Court 35.00

TAPESTRY, PORCELAIN, see Rose Tapestry category

TEA CADDY is the name for a small box made to hold tea leaves. In the eighteenth century, tea was very expensive and it was stored under lock and key. The first tea caddies were made with locks. By the nineteenth century, tea was more plentiful and the tea caddy was larger. Often there were two sections, one for green tea, one for black tea.

Black Lacquer, Sliding Lids, Silver Foil Checkerboard Design, 8 In.	104.00
Burled Walnut & Satinwood, 2 Side Sections, c.1820	550.00
Dark Brown Japanning, Stylized Floral Design, Red, Yellow, Tole, 4 1/4 In.	110.00
Detachable Knobbed Lid, Wiggle Work of Tulips, Dutch, 1740s, 5 1/2 In.	670.00
Dragons In High Relief, Metal	45.00
Floral Design, 2 Sections, Bombe Sides, Tortoiseshell Mounted, 6 1/4 In.	715.00
George III, Ivory Panels On Lid, Pewter, 1830s, 4 In.	2200.00
George III, Mahogany & Rolled Paper, Hexagonal, 18th Century, 4 1/2 In.	470.00
George III, Mahogany, Bombe Case, Bail Handle, Foliate Escutcheon, 6 1/2 In.	825.00
George III, Mahogany, Brass Bail Handle, Sections, 5 1/2 x 8 1/2 In.	247.50
George III, Paper Scrolled, Mother-of-Pearl, Quillwork Cameo, 5 1/4 In.	2300.00
George III, Satinwood, Inlay, c.1800, 13 In.	1760.00
Georgian, Mahogany, Complete Interior, Bowl	300.00
Georgian, Mahogany, Satinwood Banded Top, 2 Sections, 5 x 10 In.	385.00
Inlaid Mother-of-Pearl, Brass, Ebony, France	1420.00
Inlaid Ships & Village, Carrying Handles, Bun Feet, 13 x 7 x 7 In.	1975.00
Mahogany Veneer, Interior Lids, Replaced Ivory Escutcheon, England, 8 In.	170.00
Mahogany, 19th Century, 13 1/2 In.	330.00
Mahogany, Brass Loop Handles, Ball Feet, Rectangular, 7 1/2 In.	467.50
Mahogany, Edge Line Inlay, Ivory Escutcheon & Brass Paw Feet, 11 In.	225.00
Mahogany, Fitted Interior, Rectangular, 19th Century, 12 x 6 x 6 In.	115.00
Mahogany, Original Glass Insert	225.00
Mahogany, Rosewood, Inlaid, Fitted Interior, England, 12 3/4 In.	275.00
Milk Glass, Woven Panel, Blue	40.00
Neoclassical Figural Reserves, Green Ground, Beehive, 6 In.	305.00
Neoclassical, Ribbing, Engraved Band, Silver Plate, Bone Finial, 6 3/4 In.	145.00
Oval, Bright Cut, Silver, England, William Vincent, 1777, 4 1/2 In.	1320.00
Partridge, Wood	420.00
Regency, Fruitwood, 12 x 5 3/4 In.	385.00
Regency, Mahogany, Satinwood Stringing, Sections, 5 x 7 1/2 In.	355.00
Regency, Mahogany, Tripod, Lion's Head Pull On Inner Lid, Brass Inlay, c.1820	5775.00
Regency, Rosewood, 12 In.	275.00
Regency, Tortoiseshell Mounted, 1840s, 6 1/2 In.	1540.00
Regency, Tortoiseshell, Ivory Trim, 2 Lidded Sections, 10 1/4 In.	3300.00
Rosewood Veneer, Inlaid Pearl, 2 Lids Interior, Bowl, England, 11 3/4 In.	247.00
Rosewood, Sarcophagus, 2 Sections, 5 1/2 x 8 x 4 1/2 In.	200.00
Silver On Copper, Tooled Rose Design, Sheffield, 5 In.	115.00
Silver, Pineapple Finial, England, c.1791, 5 3/4 x 6 1/2 In.	1875.00
String Inlaid, Sarcophagus Form, Ormolu Brass Paw Feet, Ring Handles	440.00
Tiger Maple, Inlaid, Handled Lid, England	675.00
Tin, Black Paint, Brass Bale Handle, 3 Sections, Oval, 8 In.	28.00
Tole, Bronze Powder Design, Dark Ground, Lift Out Tray, 2 Sections, 8 1/4 In.	195.00
Tole, Floral, Worn Black Paint, Red Lid, Oval, 4 1/2 In.	165.00
Tole, Red	900.00
Tortoiseshell	1100.00
Tortoiseshell & Ivory, Serpentine Form, Fitted Interior, 4 1/2 In.	935.00
Tortoiseshell, 6 In.	850.00
Tortoiseshell, 7 In.	800.00
Tortoiseshell, Bombe Form, Ivory Handles & Bun Feet, Hinged Stepped Lid	3025.00
Tortoiseshell, Foil-Lined Interior, Hinged Top, 3 1/2 x 4 1/2 In.	715.00
Walnut & Brass, Domed, Victorian, 8 1/2 In.	330.00
Walnut, Dome Top, 9 1/4 In.	135.00

William IV, Rosewood, Brass Carrying Handle, Brass Ball Feet, 7 3/4 In. 440.00

TEA LEAF IRONSTONE dishes are named for their decorations. There was a superstition that it was lucky if a whole tea leaf unfolded at the bottom of your cup. This idea was translated into the pattern of dishes known as *tea leaf.* By 1850, at least twelve English factories were making this pattern, and by the 1870s, it was a popular pattern in many countries. The tea leaf was always a luster glaze on early wares, although now some pieces are made with a brown tea leaf.

Bone Dish	95.00
Bone Dish, Meakin	125.00
Bone Dish, Scalloped, Meakin	65.00
Bone Dish, Scalloped, Wilkinson	65.00
Bowl, Adams, Round, 6 1/2 In.	10.00
Bowl, Adams, Round, 9 1/2 In.	18.00
Bowl, Chamber, Meakin, 14 3/4 In.	235.00
Bowl, Cover, Pedestal, 8 x 10 In.	395.00
Bowl, Crimped Edge, Square, Wilkinson, 9 1/2 In.	65.00
Bowl, Deep, Square, 9 1/2 x 7 x 2 1/2 In.	40.00
Bowl, Meakin	100.00
Bowl, Oblong, 8 x 10 In.	45.00
Bowl, Square, Meakin, 8 x 8 In.	30.00
Bowl, Vegetable, Cane Handles	70.00
Bowl, Vegetable, Cover, Bud Finial, A. Shaw, 11 1/2 x 7 1/2 In.	225.00
Bowl, Vegetable, Cover, Cable, Burgess	245.00
Bowl, Vegetable, Cover, Fishhook, Bracket Feet, Meakin, 11 x 7 In.	165.00
Bowl, Vegetable, Cover, Meakin, 10 In.	125.00
Bowl, Vegetable, Cover, Medallion Finial, Mellor, Taylor & Co.	135.00
Bowl, Vegetable, Cover, Mellor, Taylor & Co., 10 In.	125.00
Bowl, Vegetable, Cover, Octagonal Ribbed Pagoda, Wedgwood	165.00
Bowl, Vegetable, Cover, Pagoda Handle, Ridged, Wedgwood	165.00
Bread Plate, 6 3/4 In.	60.00
Bread Plate, Square, Meakin, 8 1/4 In.	17.00
Bread Tray, Oval, 12 In.	55.00
Butter Chip ....5.00 To 12.00	
Butter Chip, Meakin	12.00
Butter Chip, Meakin, Round, 3 1/4 In.	15.00
Butter Chip, Square Ribbed Corners, Meakin, 2 3/4 In.	12.50
Butter, Cover, Drainer	75.00
Butter, Cover, Fishhook, Drain, Meakin .... 120.00 To 165.00	
Butter, Cover, Square Drain, Wedgwood, 5 1/2 In.	165.00
Coffeepot, Bamboo, Meakin, 9 In. .... 95.00 To 225.00	
Creamer, Adams, 3 In.	55.00
Creamer, Fishhook, Meakin, 5 1/4 In.	135.00
Creamer, Morning Glory, Elsmore & Forster	265.00
Creamer, Plain, Round, Meakin, 5 3/4 In.	135.00
Cup & Saucer	40.00
Cup & Saucer, Adams	48.00
Cup & Saucer, Chelsea Type, Johnson Bros.	85.00
Cup & Saucer, Handleless, A. Shaw	75.00
Cup & Saucer, Handleless, Clementson	145.00
Cup & Saucer, Handleless, Meakin	95.00
Cup & Saucer, Handleless, Teaberry Shape, New York	85.00
Cup & Saucer, Johnson Bros.	15.00
Cup & Saucer, Lily of The Valley, A. Shaw	135.00
Cup & Saucer, Meakin .... 50.00 To 70.00	
Cup & Saucer, Morning Glory, Elsmore & Forster	135.00
Cup & Saucer, Square Ridge, Wedgwood	85.00
Cup & Saucer, Straight, Meakin	60.00
Cup Plate, Wilkinson, 3 1/4 In.	50.00
Cup, Handleless, 3 3/4 In.	100.00
Dish, Soap, Liner, Meakin	100.00
Eggcup, Adams	45.00

Gravy Boat, Attached Underplate, Adams	95.00
Gravy Boat, Fishhook, Meakin, 2 3/4 x 8 In.	65.00
Gravy Bowl Set, 4 Piece	32.50
Gravy, Underplate, Meakin	75.00
Ladle, Sauce	265.00
Mug, Shaw	125.00
Oyster Bowl, Meakin	50.00
Pitcher, Bamboo, Meakin, 7 1/2 In.	225.00
Pitcher, Mayer, 7 1/2 In.	65.00
Pitcher, Meakin, 8 1/8 In.	325.00
Pitcher, Meakin, 8 In.	160.00 To 225.00
Plate, 7 3/4 In.	18.00
Plate, 8 In.	75.00
Plate, 9 In.	45.00
Plate, 10 In.	80.00
Plate, Adams, 6 1/8 In.	6.50
Plate, Child's, Cloverleaf Variant, Gold Luster, Bridgewood, 4 5/8 In.	10.00
Plate, Child's, Cloverleaf, Gold Luster, Meakin, 4 5/8 In.	10.00
Plate, Chinese, Shaw, 7 7/8 In.	15.00
Plate, Gold Luster Variant, Buford, 7 1/2 In.	10.00
Plate, Gold Luster, Bridgewood, 7 In.	10.00
Plate, Handle, Oval, Shaw, 12 In.	45.00
Plate, Meakin, 7 In.	10.00
Plate, Meakin, 9 3/4 In.	25.00
Plate, Mellor Taylor, 9 In.	12.00
Plate, Sandwich, Fishhook Handles	65.00
Plate, Wedgwood, 8 1/4 In.	14.00
Plate, Wedgwood, 9 3/4 In.	22.00
Plate, Wedgwood, 9 In.	18.00
Plate, Wheat, Elsmore & Forster, 7 3/4 In.	22.00
Plate, Wilkinson, 8 In.	20.00
Platter, 10 x 14 In.	65.00
Platter, 11 x 16 In.	75.00
Platter, 12 In.	6.00
Platter, 8 Sides, Adams, 11 1/8 x 8 3/4 In.	18.00
Platter, Chinese Shape, Oval, 14 x 10 In.	85.00
Platter, Meakin, 16 x 11 In.	50.00
Platter, Meakin, 1870	70.00
Platter, Meakin, Rectangular, 10 x 14 In.	95.00 To 110.00
Platter, Oval, Wilkinson, 11 In.	40.00
Platter, Ribbed, Rectangular, Wedgwood, 12 In.	55.00
Platter, Ribbed, Wedgwood, 8 x 10 7/8 In.	45.00
Relish, 8 Sides, Adams, 7 3/4 x 6 3/4 In.	18.00
Relish, Wilkinson, 8 1/2 x 4 1/2 In.	45.00
Sauce, Square, Large	45.00
Sauce, Square, Scalloped Gold Luster, Powell & Bishop, 4 1/2 In.	15.00

Tea Leaf Ironstone, Sugar, Cover, Handles,

Wilkinson, 6 3/4 In.

◆ ◆ ◆ ◆ ◆ ◆ ◆ ◆ ◆ ◆ ◆ ◆ ◆ ◆ ◆ ◆ ◆ ◆ ◆

Check the supports on wall-hung shelves once a year. Eventually a heavy load will cause "creep," and the metal brackets will bend.

◆ ◆ ◆ ◆ ◆ ◆ ◆ ◆ ◆ ◆ ◆ ◆ ◆ ◆ ◆ ◆ ◆ ◆ ◆ ◆

Saucer	9.00
Shaving Mug, 12 Sides, A. Shaw	225.00
Shaving Mug, Luster, Alcock	125.00
Shaving Mug, Shaw	110.00
Soap, Dish, Flanged, Meakin, 8 3/4 In.	27.50
Soup, Dish	10.00
Soup, Dish, Meakin, 8 1/2 In.	17.00
Soup, Dish, Meakin, 8 3/4 In.	27.50
Sugar, Cover, Adams Microtex, 5 In.	55.00
Sugar, Cover, Bamboo, Grindley	75.00
Sugar, Cover, Fishhook, Meakin ....85.00 To	125.00
Sugar, Cover, Fishhook, Meakin, 7 In.	135.00
Sugar, Cover, Gold Luster, Bridgewood	45.00
Sugar, Cover, Handles, Wilkinson, 6 3/4 In. ....*Illus*	150.00
Sugar, Meakin	90.00
Sugar, Mellor & Taylor	90.00
Sugar, Oval, Wilkinson	85.00
Sugar, Wedgwood	90.00
Teapot, Adams	115.00
Teapot, Chinese Shape, Shaw	375.00
Teapot, Fishhook, Meakin, 8 1/2 In.	225.00
Teapot, Morning Glory, Elsmore & Forster	395.00
Toothbrush Holder, Meakin, 5 In. ....185.00 To	195.00
Toothbrush Holder, Mellor, Taylor & Co.	165.00
Tray, Service, Pierced Handle, Anthony Shaw	80.00
Tureen, Cover, Sauce, Bamboo, Ladle & Underplate, Meakin	310.00
Tureen, Sauce, Gothic Handles, Square, Burgess	65.00

TECO is the mark used on the art pottery line made by the American Terra Cotta and Ceramic Company of Terra Cotta and Chicago, Illinois. The company was an offshoot of the firm founded by William D. Gates in 1881. The Teco line was first made in 1885 but was not sold commercially until 1902. It continued in production until 1922. Over 500 designs were made in a variety of colors, shapes, and glazes. The company closed in 1930.

Base, Bulbous, Green Glaze, Marked, 5 In.	450.00
Bowl, Green, 6 x 2 In.	395.00
Lamp, Oil, Green, 2 Handles, 5 1/2 x 8 3/4 In.	637.50
Vase, Aventurine, 3–Footed, Bulbous, 3 1/2 x 3 3/4 In.	137.00
Vase, Brown Matte, 4 Square Sides Form Flat Cutout Handles, 9 x 4 In.	1650.00
Vase, Brown, Squatty, 4 In.	325.00
Vase, Bulbous, 4 Buttressed Handles, 4 In.	467.00
Vase, Buttress Handles, 6 In.	995.00
Vase, Crystalline Glaze, 5 1/4 In.	425.00
Vase, Green Glaze, Gourd Shape, 10 1/4 x 7 1/4 In.	1540.00
Vase, Green Glazed, Rolled Rim, 4 Squared Vertical Strap Handles, Floor, 8 5/8 In.	7150.00
Vase, Green Matte Glaze, Leathery Glaze, Stamped, 3 3/4 x 3 In.	245.00
Vase, Green Matte, 2 Buttressed Handles, 5 3/4 x 5 In.	825.00
Vase, Green Matte, 2 Full Length Buttressed Handles, Ovoid, 5 1/4 x 3 In.	495.00
Vase, Green Matte, 4 In.	200.00
Vase, Green Matte, 4 x 4 In.	325.00
Vase, Green Matte, Leathery Glaze, Buttressed Handles, Marked, 7 In.	525.00
Vase, Green Matte, Ribbed, Bulbous, 5 1/2 x 5 1/4 In.	413.00
Vase, Green Matte, Squatty Base, 13 1/4 In.	605.00
Vase, Green, 4 Handles, Hotel Lobby, 21 In.	4250.00
Vase, Green, Projecting Rim & Handles, 12 In.	3300.00
Vase, Leaves & Flowers, Yellow	1200.00
Vase, Mottled Brown Over Yellow Glaze, Flared Neck, Signed, 6 In.	900.00
Vase, Organic, 4 Rounded Buttressed Handles	1660.00
Vase, Square Sectioned Neck, Peaked Rim, Marked, 11 In.	2420.00

TEDDY BEARS were named for a President of the United States. The first teddy bear was a cuddly toy said to be inspired by a hunting trip made by Teddy Roosevelt in 1902. Morris and Rose Michtom started selling their stuffed bears as *teddy bears* and the name stayed. The Michtoms founded the Ideal Novelty and Toy Company. The German version of the teddy bear was made about the same time by the Steiff Company. There are many types of teddy bears and all are collected. The old ones are being reproduced. Other bears are listed in the Toy section.

Amber Plush, Jointed Arms, Legs, Swivel, Black Eyes, Remove Head Bottle, 5 In.	300.00
Bruno, Plush, Checkered Coat, Key Wind, Box	89.00
Cinnamon, Black Footed, Glass Eyes, 1940s, 18 In.	65.00
Dakin, Russian Olympics, 1980	175.00
Hermann, Black, Tags, 5 In.	65.00
Hermann, Golden Mohair, Jointed, Glass Eyes, Black Floss Nose & Mouth, 26 In.	275.00
Mohair, Blond, Jointed, Shoebutton Eyes, Excelsior, Book, England, 1907, 20 In.	330.00
Mohair, Glass Eyes, Felt Mouth, Moving Head, 9 1/2 In.	140.00
Mohair, Gold, Felt Bellhop Suit, 13 1/2 In.	1150.00
Mohair, Gold, Glass Eyes, Black Embroidered Face, Articulated Limbs, 19 In.	175.00
Mohair, Gold, Jointed	495.00
Mohair, Gold, Jointed, Green & Tan Suit, Wicker Armchair, Germany, 10 In.	550.00
Mohair, Gold, Shoebutton Eyes, Jointed, Excelsior, Germany, 1906, 21 In.	2090.00
Mohair, Hump Back, Glass Eyes, Germany, 24 In.	285.00
Mohair, Sand Color, Straw, Jointed, 10 In.	154.00
Mohair, Straw Filled, Jointed, Shoebutton Eyes, c.1915, 14 In.	325.00
Mohair, Yellow & White, Glass Eyes, Jointed, Straw Stuffing, 1926, 11 1/2 In.	245.00
Mohair, Yellow, Jointed, Shoebutton Eyes, Excelsior, Germany, 1906, 16 In.	550.00
Muffy Bears, Yankee Doodle	35.00
Schuco, Gold Mohair, Glass Eyes, Jointed, Scarf, Mitten & Skis, 1920s, 13 1/2 In.	825.00
Steiff, 1905, 9 1/2 In.	700.00
Steiff, Barley	525.00
Steiff, Blond Mohair, Embroidered Snout, 6 In.	845.00
Steiff, Blond Mohair, Embroidered Snout, Jointed, Overalls, 1906, 8 1/2 In.	522.50
Steiff, Bronze Mohair, Jointed, Shoebutton Eyes, Excelsior, 1906, 18 In.	187.00
Steiff, Brown Mohair, 12 In.	400.00
Steiff, Center Seam, 1904, 16 In.	3800.00
Steiff, Gold, 1940, 16 In.	200.00
Steiff, Long Hair, Jointed	2100.00
Steiff, Mama Bear & Baby, Paper, 1981, 2 Piece	400.00
Steiff, Mohair Head, White, Gutta–Percha Nose, Kapok Stuffed, 14 In.	650.00
Steiff, Mohair Plush, Felt Pads, Excelsior, 8 In.	150.00
Steiff, Otto	345.00
Steiff, Papa Bear, Limited Edition, Paper, 1980, Box	500.00
Steiff, Santa Claus, 11 In.	225.00
Steiff, Yellow Mohair, Jointed, Glass Eyes, Excelsior, Ear Button, 1910, 18 In.	990.00

TELEPHONES are wanted by collectors if the phones are old enough or unusual enough. The first telephone may have been made in Havana, Cuba, in 1849, but it was not patented. The first publicly demonstrated phone was used in Frankfurt, Germany, in 1860. The phone made by Alexander Graham Bell was shown at the Centennial Exhibition in Philadelphia in 1876, but it was not until 1877 that the first private phones were installed. Collectors today want all types of old phones, phone parts, and advertising. Even recent figural phones are popular.

Booth, Beveled Glass, Brass Marquee, Walnut	825.00
Booth, Cast Iron, England, 9 Ft.	4250.00
Booth, Oak, Bifold Door, Pressed Tin Interior, 1930s, 32 In x 7 Ft.	2150.00
Continental–Style, Scandinavia	16.50
Crest Sparkle Man, Box	30.00
Darth Vader	125.00
Desk, Brass, Japan, 1969	45.00
Desk, Hand Crank, Complete	20.00
Directory Holder, Bell Pay Telephone, Weatherproof Plastic, Bracket	10.00

Directory, Camp Papago Park, Prisoner of War Camp, Phoenix, Ariz., Early 1940s	7.00
Directory, Reedsburg, Wisc., 1943	3.50
Directory, Weyauwega, Wisc., 1946	3.50
Ericsson, c.1910	185.00
Ericsson, Non–Dial, Cradle, Round Base	85.00
Fyns Kommunale Telefonselskab, Wall, 28 In.	165.00
Kellogg Supply, Wall, Black Bakelite, 1920	75.00
Kellogg, Candlestick	95.00
Kellogg, Separate Oak Box, France	125.00
Kellogg, Wall	105.00
Monarch, Wall	175.00
Northern Electric, Pay Station, 3 Slot, Cash Box	110.00
Pay Station, Baird	500.00
Pizza Inn, Box	50.00
Ringer Box, Cradle	10.00
Sign, Brass Mouth Pieces & Other Parts, Enameled, 2 Sides	55.00
Snoopy	95.00
Snoopy, With Woodstock	90.00
Stromberg Carlson, Double Box, Oak, Wall	145.00
Western Electric, Desk, Wall Box, Oak, 1920s	135.00
Western Electric, Railroad, Scissors Action, Headset	70.00
Western Electric, Trimline, Touchtone, 10 Buttons, Black	25.00
Western Electric, Volt–Ohm–Ammeter, Digital, Leather Case & Strap	75.00
Western Electric, Wall, Wooden, Oak Cabinet	350.00
Wire, Western Electric, Quad, Box, 600 Ft.	10.00

TELEVISION sets are twentieth–century collectibles. Although the first television transmission took place in England in 1925, collectors find few sets which pre–date 1946. The first sets had only five channels, but by 1949 the additional VHF channels were included. The first color television set became available in 1951.

Admiral, Bakelite, 9–In. Screen	75.00
Brown Bakelite, 1940s, 8–In. Screen	175.00
Emerson, Model 1232, 7 In.	35.00
Philco, Predicta, Bracket Mounted Tube On Wooden Cabinet Base, 27 In.	105.00
Sparton, Console, Mirror In Lid	20.00
Westinghouse, Modern Wooden Stand, 13–In. Screen.	10.00

TEPLITZ refers to art pottery manufactured by a number of companies in the Teplitz–Turn area of Bohemia during the late nineteenth and early twentieth centuries. The Amphora Porcelain Works and the Alexandra Works were two of these companies.

Basket, Cobalt, Gold Handles, Raspberries, Amphora, Signed, 8 In.	375.00
Bust, Girl, Flowers On Head, 12 In.	225.00
Bust, Ophelia, Marked, 24 In.	1200.00
Bust, Woman, Bisque, Art Nouveau Style, 18 1/4 In.	1600.00
Centerpiece, Figural, Seminude Boys, Gathering Roses, Amphora, 7 x 13 In.	335.00
Ewer, Iridescent Leaves, Cream & Green Ground, Vine Handles, 1905, 13 3/4 In.	985.00
Ewer, Minstrel Playing Guitar On Horse, Amphora, Marked, c.1891, 14 In.	350.00
Ewer, Water Lilies Become Handle & Spout, Lavender, Gold, Amphora, 12 1/2 In.	695.00
Figurine, Girl, Curly Hair, 11 In.	295.00
Figurine, Mercury, Sea Goddess, Pale Colors, 18 1/2 In., Pair	885.00
Planter, Gilded Lions, Rocky Outcropping, Amphora, 10 1/2 x 11 x 15 In.	550.00
Planter, Wild Duck & Chicks On Nest, 1903, 8 1/2 x 10 In.	625.00
Teapot, Amphora, 7 1/2 In.	82.50
Vase, 4 Handles, Amphora, Royal Dux, 10 1/2 x 9 In.	137.50
Vase, Arabian Steed Held By Nomad, Marked, Brushed Gold, Amphora, 19 In.	1495.00
Vase, Art Nouveau, Floral Encrusted, Iridized, Amphora, 9 In.	295.00
Vase, Art Nouveau, Nymph, Jeweled, Applied Stoneware, Marked, 10 1/2 In.	880.00
Vase, Beige Basket Weave, Green & Purple Grapes, Gold Leaves, 15 In.	495.00
Vase, Blown–Out, Women Working, Landscape, Marked, Amphora, c.1860, 12 In.	395.00
Vase, Butterflies In Flight, Enameled Flowers, Gold Tracery, 14 In.	525.00
Vase, Eggshell Porcelain, Amphora, Samuel Schellink, c.1920	4400.00

Vase, Figural, Climbing Fox, Chickens, Egg Shaped, Amphora, 8 In.	650.00
Vase, Floral, Green & Gray, Gold Edge, Marked	150.00
Vase, Molded Leaf Design, 2 Handles, 6 1/2 In.	120.00
Vase, Overlapping Caladium Leaves, Baluster, Open Handles, Amphora, 1900, 12 In.	715.00
Vase, Poppies & Leaves Extended Into Handles, Footed, Amphora, 11 In.	495.00
Vase, Portrait, Amphora, Signed, 6 1/2 In.	880.00
Vase, Raised Floral, Gold Trim, Green, 12 In.	165.00
Vase, Rooster, Amphora	900.00
Vase, Salamander Handles, Amphora, 10 1/2 In.	275.00
Vase, Scenic, Handles, 6 In.	130.00
Vase, Serpent Handles, Amphora, 10 In.	295.00

TERRA-COTTA is a special type of pottery. It ranges from pale orange to dark reddish-brown in color. The color comes from the clay, which is fired but not always glazed in the finished piece.

Bust, Man, Wooden Stand, 4 In.	605.00
Bust, Woman, Painted Design, Keramos, 12 x 6 1/2 In.	875.00
Bust, Woman, Pajou Regis Sculptor, Marble Social, 25 1/2 In.	3575.00
Candlestick, Blue & Gold Griffins, Enameled Top & Base	225.00
Figurine, Bears, Embracing, China, Late 18th Century, 8 In., Pair	385.00
Figurine, Bulldog, Polychromed, Glass Eyes, 10 In.	150.00
Figurine, Knight, Bearded, Bois Guilbert, 41 In.	220.00
Figurine, Warriors, On Horseback, 15 1/2 In., Pair	275.00
Figurine, Woman, Renaissance Style, Italy, 21 In.	525.00
Jar, Rope Around Base, Stand, 54 In.	415.00
Mask, Art Deco, Allover Painted Design, Keramos, 12 x 8 1/4 In.	650.00
Mask, Art Deco, Keramos, 11 1/2 In.	500.00
Olive Jar, Glazed Yellow Interior, 23 1/4 In.	665.00
Tea Set, Cylindrical Form, Ridged Design, Watcombe, 6 Piece	935.00
Teapot, Locust Trees, House, Engraved, Late 1800s, Signed	95.00
Teapot, Locust Trees, House, Late 1800s, Signed	125.00
Umbrella Stand, Dragons, Oriental, 23 1/2 In.	85.00
Urn, Cherub Heads, Garlands of Fruit, Campagna Form, Pair	198.00
Urn, Loop Handles, Egg Shaped, Greece, 44 In.	550.00
Vase, Geometric, Short Base, Dark Moss Green, 1914, 9 In., Pair	1320.00
Vase, Relief Designs of Dragons, 12 1/4 In.	25.00

TEXTILES listed here include many types of printed fabrics and table and household linens. Some other textiles will be found under Clothing, Coverlet, Rug, Quilt, etc.

Candle drippings can be removed from fabric or furniture with the help of ice cubes. Rub the wax with the ice until the wax hardens. Scrape off the hard wax with a credit card or stiff cardboard. If some wax remains, put a blotter over it, and then iron with a cool iron.

Textile, Drapes, Valance, Aubusson, Signed, 1768, 36 X 100 In.

Altar Cloth, Figures of Saints, Gilt Braid & Trim, Embroidered, Velvet, 31 x 25 In. 410.00
Antimacassar, Crochet, England, Set of 4 .... 65.00
Bag, Handkerchief, Embroidered, Red Lining 35.00
Bedspread, Beige, Double Yo-Yo Border, Twin Size 32.00
Bedspread, Chenille, Peacock, Purple, Double Size 140.00
Bedspread, Chenille, White, Full Size 15.00
Bedspread, Chenille, White, Queen Size 30.00
Bedspread, Chenille, White, Twin Size 12.00
Bedspread, Floral & Diamond Design, Cutout Corners, White, 72 x 84 In. 80.00
Bedspread, Organdy, Large Embroidered & Appliqued Figures, 1920 .... 35.00
Bedspread, Overshot, White On White, Cotton, 2 Piece, 88 x 108 In. 82.00
Bedspread, White On White, Embroidered, Floral, 76 x 88 In. 85.00
Blanket, Camp, Cotton, Cowboy Design, 1950s 10.00
Blanket, Chief Joseph Pattern, Beaver State, Pendleton, 1920 .... 385.00
Blanket, Homespun, Cotton, Wool, Blue, Natural, 2 Piece, 20 x 86 In. 66.00
Blanket, Homespun, Slate Blue, Mustard, Natural, Ecru, 1 Piece, 44 x 91 In. 165.00
Blanket, Saddle, Diamond Pattern, Center Red Stripe, Peru, 4 Ft. 6 In. x 3 Ft. 6 In. 55.00
Blanket, Tapestry, Blue, Red, Tan, Black, Hanging Rings, Mexico, 54 x 82 In. 88.00
Blanket, Woven, Mexico, 50 x 82 In. 200.00
Cloth, Banquet, Cherub Cartouches, Center Putti Strip, 122 x 45 In. 250.00
Cloth, Banquet, Urn & Cherub Rosettes, Ecru, Venetian Lace, c.1915, 132 x 67 In. 360.00
Draperies, Bark Cloth, Lined, 1950s, 77 x 44 In., Pair 65.00
Drapes, Valance, Aubusson, Signed, 1768, 36 x 100 In. ....*Illus* 6600.00
Flag, American, 13 Stars, Moth Holes, 28 x 46 In. 210.00
Flag, American, 13 Stars, Under Glass In Frame 575.00
Flag, American, 37 Stars, Printed Silk, Glass Frame 230.00
Flag, American, 46 Stars, Printed, 1907–1912, 32 x 60 In. 55.00
Flag, American, 48 Stars, Dated 1918, 10 In. 30.00
Flag, American, 48 Stars, Hand Sewn 65.00
Flag, American, 49 Stars, Cotton, 24 x 36 In. 35.00
Handkerchief, Embroidered C, James Cagney, 1 With Mr. Cagney 465.00
Holder, Handkerchief, Satin, Painted Reflective Birds, Floral, 1890s, 11 x 10 In. 34.50
Lap Robe, Buggy, Horsehair, Reversible 350.00
Lap Robe, Natural & Red, Fringed, Hand Carded & Loomed, Ireland 325.00
Napkin, Damask Linen, Occupied Japan Label, 6 Piece 45.00
Napkin, Dinner, Damask, Narrow Greek Key, Large Fleur-De-Lis, 8 Piece 35.00
Panel, Embroidered, Floral Medallion, Cream Linen, Uzbekistan, 5 Ft. 2750.00
Panel, Embroidered, Gold Metallic, Silk Thread, Dragons, Clouds, 41 1/2 x 45 In. 325.00
Panel, Embroidered, Silk, Sand Trellis, Linen, Ottoman, 18th Century, 3 Ft. 2200.00
Panel, Needlepoint, Poem, Parrot & Squirrel, America, 17 x 17 In. 100.00
Panel, Needlework, Frame, 39 1/2 x 39 1/2 In. 275.00
Panel, Needlework, Woman In Garden, Wool, Silk, Gilt Frame, 16 1/4 x 14 1/2 In. 175.00
Panel, Repeating Equestrians, Silk & Metallic Thread Brocade, 1 Ft. 8 In. x 1 Ft. ... 2750.00
Panel, Tapestry, Architectural, Landscape, 19th Century, France, 7 Ft. 4 In. x 4 Ft. 1650.00
Panel, Women, Flowers, Unicorn, Embroidered Filet, 4 Ft. x 18 In. 525.00
Picture, Needlepoint, Musician Serenading Allegorical Females, 14 1/2 x 17 In. 3025.00
Pillow Cover, Painted Christy-Like Woman Center, Leather Fringe, 22 x 22 In. 35.00
Pillow, Hand Embroidered Indian Princess Bust, Cream Ground, c.1920 .... 125.00
Pillowcase, Cherub Lace Edge, 1920–1930 .... 90.00
Pocket, Blue Wool Crewel, White Linen, 18th Century 605.00
Pocket, Polychrome Crewel, Linen, 18th Century, 18 1/2 In. 1072.00
Pocket, Quilted Chintz, Block Print, Plum Tree & Pheasant, 1825, 14 In. 880.00
Pot Holder, Abolitionist, Yarn, Needlepoint, Velvet, Mid-19th Century, 7 1/2 In. 395.00
Runner, Battenburg Lace, Flower Design At Ends, 13 1/2 x 38 In. 165.00
Runner, Embroidered Butterflies, Linen, Richardson, 50 1/2 x 17 In. 66.00
Runner, Table, Linen, Embroidered Pink Flowers, Arts & Crafts, 54 x 18 In. 132.00
Scarf, Battenburg Lace, 20 x 20 In. 35.00
Scarf, Piano, Silk Damask, Hand Knotted Rust & Green Fringe, 6 Ft. x 6 Ft. 4 In. 355.00
Scarf, Silk, Viking Ship Medallions, Blue Ground, Hermes, Box 175.00
Scarf, Table, Damask, Multicolored Flowers & Foliage, Fringed, 5 Ft. 10 In. x 4 Ft. 410.00
Shawl, Black Egyptian Silver Net 95.00
Shawl, Piano, Embroidered Silk, Long Fringe, White 85.00
Sheet, Embroidered, 1920s, Twin Size 55.00

Tablecloth, Battenburg Lace, 10 In. Linen Center Round, 68 In. 165.00
Tablecloth, Concentric Square, Woven Linen, F. L. Wright, Square, 43 In. 525.00
Tablecloth, Crocheted, Filet, Eagle, Flag, Statue of Liberty, Scalloped, 40 x 40 In. ... 50.00
Tablecloth, Crocheted, White, Pinwheels, 70 x 58 In. 60.00
Tablecloth, Irish Linen, Bangor Linen Co., Ireland, 8 Napkins, 68 x 90 In. 125.00
Tablecloth, Off–White, Embroidered & Cutwork, 12 Napkins, 40 x 120 In. 175.00
Tablecloth, White On White, Ireland, 70 x 106 In. 95.00
Tablecloth, Wool, Art Nouveau Embroidered Design 40.00
Tapestry, 2 Children In Forest Setting, Foliate Border, Flemish, 54 x 74 In. 3750.00
Tapestry, Animal & Geometric Design, Egypt, 2 Ft. 3 In. x 6 Ft. 195.00
Tapestry, Aubusson, 5 Drapes, 2 Valances, Overvalance, Dated 1768 .... 6000.00
Tapestry, Aubusson, Figures Playing Croquet, Stylized Landscape, 6 Ft. x 6 Ft. 7150.00
Tapestry, Aubusson, Fish In Woodland Night Landscape, c.1950, 8 Ft. x 4 Ft. 6 In. .. 3300.00
Tapestry, Baby Moses, Landscape Scene, 18th Century, 64 x 86 In. 4950.00
Tapestry, Birds, Mill Amidst Landscape, Floral Border, France, 78 x 110 In. 4180.00
Tapestry, Brocade, Worn Appliqued Crest, 21 x 45 1/2 In. 60.00
Tapestry, Children Playing, Men Carrying Items From Ship, 50 x 103 In. 600.00
Tapestry, Coat of Arms, Les Armes Du Roy, Frame, 19th Century, 40 x 27 In. 385.00
Tapestry, Foxes, Flowering Trees, Birds, 6 Ft. 6 In. x 2 Ft. 6 In., Pair 935.00
Tapestry, Gentleman In Wooded Landscape, France, 92 x 56 In. 2200.00
Tapestry, Machine Woven, Statue of Liberty, Matted, Frame, 14 In. 55.00
Tapestry, Venetian Canal Scene, Ladies, Dogs, Label, 20 x 60 In. 75.00
Tapestry, Whiplashed Tulips, Fringed, Arts & Crafts, Square, 65 In. 440.00
Towel, Show, Homespun, Floral Design, Susanna Denlinger, 1825, 68 x 17 1/2 In. ... 410.00
Towel, Show, Homespun, Flowers, Hounds & Hunters, E. Musser, 1846, 57 x 18 In. 300.00
Towel, Show, Homespun, Flowers, Star, Bird, Cutwork Panels, 53 x 15 In. 330.00
Towel, Show, Linen, Homespun, Floral Embroidery, 5 Colors, 17 x 54 In. 71.00
Towel, Show, Linen, Homespun, Floral, Birds, Cutwork, F. H. 1818, 14 x 55 In. 300.00
Valance, Painted Cloth, Floral, Natural Ground, 110 In. 110.00
Wall Hanging, Musicians & Dancers, Egyptian, c.1910, 35 x 63 In. 95.00

THERMOMETER is a name that comes from the Greek word for heat. The thermometer was invented in 1731 to measure the temperature of either water or air. All kinds of thermometers are collected, but those with advertising messages are the most popular.

7–Up, White, Green, Red & Black, 15 x 16 In. 40.00
B. Fowler Co., Glen Falls, N.Y., Wooden, 3 Ft. 190.00
Black Boy 26.00
Boyce Motor Meter, Brass, Beveled Glass 60.00
Boyes Hardware, Inside Cardboard Ear of Corn, 1930s 15.00
Cook's Goldblume Ale 32.00
Dad's Old Fashioned Root Beer, Tin, 25 1/2 In. 65.00
Dairy, Floating 9.00
Desk, Arts & Crafts, Slag Glass, Tiffany, c.1915, 8 1/4 In. 495.00
Doan's Pills, Wood, 21 In. 225.00
Dr Pepper, Round, Hot–Cold 115.00
Dr Pepper, Rustic Color 18.00
Dr Pepper, Tin 20.00
Drink Bire–Ley's, Gold & Orange, 1950s, 15 1/4 In. 25.00
Drink Double Cola, Round, 12 In. 80.00
Drugstore, Images of Medicine Boxes, Retailer's Name, Round, 9 In. 22.00
Ex–Lax, Wood, Beige, Brown, Black, 15 x 4 In. 110.00
Farmers' Fertilizers, Columbus, Ohio, 3 Ft. 32.00
Ford, Wooden, Weathered, 1918 .... 25.00
Frostie, Round 90.00
H. N. Janney Best Paint–Varnish, Tin, Round, 12 In. 30.00
Hills Brothers Coffee, Porcelain, 1915 .... 300.00
Hire's, Bottle Shape, Tin 195.00
Kitten Picture, Advertising, 1933 .... 7.50
Lone Star Beer, Round, 1958 .... 135.00
Mail Pouch, Porcelain, Blue, White & Yellow, Frame, 18 x 72 In. 357.00
Mail Pouch, Treat Yourself To The Best, Porcelain, 8 x 38 In. 100.00

Man, Woman Picking Grapes, Cobalt Blue, Porcelain, Signed ER, 8 In.	435.00
Maxfield Parrish, Golden House	65.00
Meat & Candy, Betty Furness, Box	14.00
Mission Orange, Tin, 5 x 17 In.	25.00
Moxie, Multiple Image Exterior Building, Tin, 25 1/2 x 9 1/2 In.	605.00
Moxie, Tin, Drink Moxie Good At Any Temperature, Orange, Green	445.00
Nesbitt's Orange, Picture of Bottle	65.00
Old Dutch Root Beer	80.00
Orange Crush, Bottle Shape	95.00
Orange Crush, Round, 12 In.	110.00
Packard Automobiles, Metal, 27 In.	165.00
Packard, 27 In.	17.00
Parodi Cigars, Always First, First All Ways, 6 x 15 In.	75.00
Pepsi–Cola, 1955	60.00
Philip Morris	38.00
Piggily Wiggly, 6 x 2 In.	17.50
Prestone, Porcelain, 36 x 9 In.	45.00
Prestone, Safe & You Know It, Blue, Gray & Red, 36 In.	110.00
Pullman, Cast Brass	65.00
RC Cola, Red	40.00
Royal 400 Gasoline, Stenciled Wood, Red & Green Lettering, 21 In.	187.00
Sealtest Milk Pan	140.00
Sealtest, Round	75.00
Statue of Liberty, Hardware Store, Crossed Corners Frame, 4 5/8 x 5 5/8 In.	28.00
Sterling Salt, Round	50.00
Stork Carrying Baby's Room, 1930s	85.00
Tannhauser Beer, Brass Cased Paper, Logo Image On Front, c.1896, 9 In.	105.00
Taylor Monroe, Glass In Aluminum Tube, Pin On Chain	6.00
Tru–Aide, Round, 12 In. ....80.00 To 100.00	
Tums, Tin Lithograph, 9 In.	34.00
Washer Hardware, Sheldon, Iowa, Wooden Frame	24.00
Winchester	150.00
Winston Cigarettes, Tin	45.00

TIFFANY GLASS was made by Louis Comfort Tiffany, the American glass designer who worked from about 1879 to 1933. His work included iridescent glass, Art Nouveau styles of design, and original contemporary styles. He was also noted for stained glass windows, unusual lamps, bronze work, pottery, and silver. Other types of Tiffany are listed under Tiffany Pottery, Tiffany Silver, or at the end of this category under Tiffany. The famous Tiffany lamps are under Tiffany, Lamp. Reproductions of some types of Tiffany are being made. Tiffany jewelry is listed in the jewelry and wristwatch categories.

Louis C. Tiffany

TIFFANY GLASS, Bonbon, Favrile, Gold Iridescent, Short Pedestal, 2 x 4 3/4 In.	275.00
Bowl, Blue Swirl, Marked, 8 1/4 In.	600.00
Bowl, Favrile, Blue, Slight Ruffled, Silver Highlights Interior, 3 1/2 x 7 In.	850.00
Bowl, Favrile, Gold Iridescent, Flared Ruffle, Ribs, 2 1/2 x 8 1/2 In.	600.00
Bowl, Fawn With Flower Floater, 4 In.	145.00
Bowl, Gold Iridescent, Crinkled Top Rim, 4 x 1 In.	275.00
Bowl, Gold Iridescent, Favrile, Flared, Signed, 2 1/2 x 4 1/2 In.	600.00
Bowl, Gold Iridescent, Uneven Crinkled Rim, 4 1/2 x 1 3/4 In.	275.00
Bowl, Onionskin Brim, Pink Pastel, 9 In.	850.00
Bowl, Optic Ribs, Scalloped Rim, Favrile, Signed, 4 In.	295.00
Bowl, Raised Lily Pads, Long Stems, Signed, 4 x 2 In.	435.00
Bowl, Ruffled, Interior Leaves & Vines, Teardrop Stem, Signed, 6 In.	725.00
Bowl, Underplate, Favrile, Pastel, Stretch, Gold Iridescent, 5 In., 2 Piece	700.00
Candlestick, Favrile, Gold Iridescent, Oval Shaped Top, 3 3/4 In., Pair	2100.00
Candlestick, Gold Iridescent, Oval Top, 4 1/4 x 3 In., Pair	2100.00
Candlestick, Pale Green, Elephant's Foot Base, White Dividers, 11 In.	1500.00
Candy Dish, Cover, Blue Flowers, Orange & Tan	65.00
Cigarette Box, Favrile, Grapevine, Rectangular, 4 5/16 In.	385.00
Compote, Favrile, Gold Iridescent, Ruffled, Footed, 3 x 4 In.	595.00
Compote, Favrile, Gold Iridescent, Ruffled, Pedestal, 2 1/2 In.	450.00

Tiffany Glass, Vase, Favrile,

Gold, Signed, 9 In.

♦♦♦♦♦♦♦♦♦♦♦♦♦♦♦♦♦♦♦♦♦♦♦

Always vacuum your moose from the snout upward and scrub your pheasant with fresh white bread, torn, not sliced. Use the furniture attachment when vacuuming your moose head, and go with, not against, the grain. Rinse the head with water every five years. Careful—too much water will make a mildewed moose.

♦♦♦♦♦♦♦♦♦♦♦♦♦♦♦♦♦♦♦♦♦♦♦

Compote, Favrile, Leaves, Blue Iridescent, Footed, 3 1/4 In.	420.00
Compote, Floriform, Ruffled Lip, Continuous Feathering, c.1903, 5 In.	1650.00
Compote, Laurel Leaves, Clear Stem, Opalescent, Blue–Green, 5 In.	500.00
Compote, Pastel Opalescent Optic Laurel Leaves, Clear Stem, 3 3/4 In.	500.00
Cordial Set, Cut Faceting At Stopper, Neck & Shoulder, c.1899, 9 Piece	3575.00
Cordial, Favrile, Gold Iridescent, Swirl, Stemmed, Signed, 4 1/2 In.	325.00
Dish, Light Green Radiating Loops, Pink Ground, Art Nouveau	1150.00
Finger Bowl, Underplate, Green Bronze, Purple Highlights, 2 Piece	785.00
Flower Bowl, Gold Iridescent, Double–Tiered Flower Frog, Signed, 7 In.	1100.00
Flower Bowl, With Frog, Intaglio Lily Pads, Trailings, c.1919, 10 In.	3575.00
Garniture Set, Favrile, Green Iridescent, Footed, 3 3/4 In., 3 Piece	990.00
Inkwell, Favrile, Vertical Decoration, Iridescent, 1 9/16 In.	495.00
Jar, Cover, Favrile, Gold Iridescent, Intaglio Cut Knob, 8 In.	1500.00
Perfume Bottle, Favrile, Heart–Shaped Leaves, Green, Vines, Stopper, 5 1/2 In.	2300.00
Perfume Bottle, Gold, 1910, Signed	950.00
Perfume Bottle, Russian Pattern, Silver Base, 3 1/2 In.	395.00
Perfume Vial, Silver Cap, Collar & Chain, Vertical Panels, c.1919, 4 9/16 In.	2200.00
Pitcher, Favrile, Blue, Applied Handle, Label, 4 In.	850.00
Plate, Ivory Iridescent Center, Peacock Blue Rim, Gold Band, 7 In.	550.00
Plate, Pastel Green, Favrile, Signed, 8 1/2 In.	310.00
Rose Bowl, Gold, Favrile, Gold Feather Pulls, Signed, 6 In.	2600.00
Salt, Blue Iridescent, Ruffled	585.00
Salt, Blue Iridescent, Ruffled, Signed	585.00
Salt, Favrile, Gold Iridescent, Ruffled, Rainbow Highlights, Pair	400.00
Salt, Gold Iridescent, Favrile, Ribbed, Pedestal, Stand–Up Collar, 1 1/2 In.	275.00
Scarab, Red Iridescent, Favrile, 3/4 In.	125.00
Shade, Domed, Chain Feathering, Golden Amber Iridescent, 1895, 8 In.	2200.00
Shade, Domed, Green Brickwork Tiles, 1899–1928, 10 In.	3300.00
Shade, Favrile, Green Feather, Opalescent, Flared, Bulbous, 4 In., Pair	950.00
Sherbet, Favrile, Gold Iridescent, Blue Highlights, Stemmed, 3 1/2 In.	275.00
Sherbet, Favrile, Gold Iridescent, Curved Stem, 3 1/2 x 3 1/2 In.	275.00
Sherry Glasses, Bell–Form Bowl, Faceted Stem, Amber, 1899–1928, 7 Piece	1875.00
Tile, Stylized Chinese Cloud Center, Mottled Ocher & Green, 4 x 4 In.	330.00
Tumbler, Favrile, Applied Lily Pads, Gold Iridescent, 3 3/8 In.	165.00
Vase, Agate, Tapered	3000.00
Vase, Allover Millefiori White Blossoms, Olive Leaves, 1 3/4 x 2 1/4 In.	1500.00
Vase, Amber Body, Gold Zigzag Medial Design, Gold Lip Wrap, 5 1/2 In.	3300.00
Vase, Amber Iridescent, Ruffled, Onion Form, Floriform, 1910, 13 5/8 In.	2750.00
Vase, Amber Leafage, Striated Trailing, Favrile, c.1906, 1 1/2 In.	2200.00
Vase, Amber Ribbed & Dimpled Conical Body, Gold Surface, 4 3/4 In.	467.50

Vase, Black, Deep Turquoise Cartouches Band, 1921, 7 1/2 In. 3575.00
Vase, Blue, Favrile, Egg Shaped, 1921, 7 1/8 In. 1870.00
Vase, Bud, Amber Spiral Ribbing, c.1904, 5 1/8 In. 990.00
Vase, Bud, Deep Blue Gold Iridescent, Pedestal, Flared, 3 1/4 In. 265.00
Vase, Bud, Pulled Green Feathering At Sides, c.1919, 7 7/8 In. 1100.00
Vase, Bud, Trumpet Form, Amber Pulled Feathers At Side, c.1915, 5 7/8 In. 885.00
Vase, Bulbous 10-Ribbed Amber Body, Orange-Gold Iridescence, 6 In. 825.00
Vase, Bulbous Lip, Pulled Trailings & Lappets, Silvery Blue, c.1900, 3 5/8 In. 2200.00
Vase, Cobalt Blue, 7 In. 325.00
Vase, Cut Flowers & Butterflies, Favrile 2150.00
Vase, Cypriote, Black Glass, Pulled Prunts, Favrile, c.1904, 2 1/8 In. 2750.00
Vase, Cypriote, Tapered, 10 In. 2250.00
Vase, Deep Blue Iridescent, Baluster Shouldered, 1917, 8 1/2 In. 2100.00
Vase, Double Gourd, Blue & Green, Red Interior, 9 In. 4200.00
Vase, Drapery Pattern At Neck, Gold Favrile, Signed, 8 1/2 In. 990.00
Vase, Favrile, Blue, Bronze Cross-Hatched Arranger, Signed, 4 x 6 In. 2500.00
Vase, Favrile, Blue, Ribbed, Flared Lip, Signed, 2 3/8 In. 1800.00
Vase, Favrile, Blue, Stand-Out Ribs All Around, 5 1/2 In. 850.00
Vase, Favrile, Gold Iridescent, Ruffled Edge, Tapered Body, Signed, 4 In. 650.00
Vase, Favrile, Gold Iridescent, Ruffled, Violet Highlights, 4 In. 650.00
Vase, Favrile, Gold, Signed, 9 In. ....*Illus* 4950.00
Vase, Favrile, Golden Yellow, 10 In. 525.00
Vase, Favrile, Peacock Blue Iridescent, Short Pedestal, 2 3/8 In. 1800.00
Vase, Favrile, Trailings & Leaves, Random White Blossoms, c.1902, 2 3/8 In. 2200.00
Vase, Favrile, Trumpet Shape, Bronze Base, Gold Iridescent, 15 In. 495.00
Vase, Favrile, Upright Peacock Feathers, c.1908, 14 5/8 In. 6000.00
Vase, Floriform, Favrile, 1902, Onion Form Cup, Feathering, Rose, Green, 15 In. 825.00
Vase, Floriform, Flared Rim, 8-Ribbed Amber Body, Gold Base, 9 1/4 In. 1300.00
Vase, Floriform, Flared Top, Pedestal Base, Signed, 6 In. 575.00
Vase, Floriform, Gold Iridescent, Domed Foot, Signed, 9 3/4 In. 1250.00
Vase, Floriform, Green Feathering, Amber Domed Foot, Marked, 14 3/8 In. 3575.00
Vase, Floriform, Spring Green Striated Feather, Ruffled, 13 3/4 In. 4400.00
Vase, Floriform, Trumpet Blossom, Honey Amber, Cupped Pedestal Foot, 15 In. 1540.00
Vase, Floriform, Wintergreen Iridescent Striated Feathering, 20 In. 7700.00
Vase, Gold Iridescent, Flared Top & Base, Signed, 2 1/4 In. 265.00
Vase, Gold Iridescent, Signed, 3 In. 229.00
Vase, Green Heart-Shaped Leaves, Scrolling Tendrils, c.1917, 8 7/8 In. 3850.00
Vase, Green To White Body, Applied Gold Collar, Rim, Black Cupped Foot, 8 In. 4950.00
Vase, Hat, Favrile 250.00
Vase, Intaglio-Cut Top, Favrile, Gold, 12 1/2 In. 2420.00
Vase, Iridescent Interior, Gold To Green Ground, Signed, 4 1/2 In. 880.00
Vase, Iridescent Silver & Green, Cobalt Blue Interior, Domed Foot, 4 1/2 In. 192.00
Vase, Jack-In-The-Pulpit, Flaring Rim, Ribbed, Twisted Stem, c.1909, 14 1/8 In. ... 3575.00
Vase, Jack-In-The-Pulpit, Irregular Floriform Neck, Favrile, c.1905, 9 3/4 In. 2750.00
Vase, Jack-In-The-Pulpit, Ruffled Rim, Iridescent, Marked, 11 In. 2200.00
Vase, Lily Pads, Stems, Gold Iridescent, Horizontal Lines, 4 1/2 x 2 In. 435.00
Vase, Lily Trumpet, Pastel, Sticker, 12 In. 1000.00
Vase, Olive Green, Iridescent Amber Blossoms & Trailing, 1896, 3 In. 880.00
Vase, Paperweight, Streaked Carmel & Green, Favrile, Signed, 7 1/2 In. 2640.00
Vase, Peacock Blue Iridescent, Ribbed, Flared, Signed, 2 3/8 In. 1800.00
Vase, Pulled Side Handles, Blue Pulled Feathering, c.1909, 3 1/2 In. 2100.00
Vase, Pulled Side Handles, Flattened Ovoid Form, Favrile, c.1897, 3 3/8 In. 550.00
Vase, Pulled-Out 5-Pointed Rim, Iridescent Gold, Signed, 1905, 3 In. 750.00
Vase, Silver-Blue Pulled Lappets Top, Emerald, Ovoid, 1902, 2 5/8 In. 1650.00
Vase, Tel El Amarna, Inverted Pyriform, Blue Over White, c.1910, 8 1/4 In. 6050.00
Vase, Trailings & Serrated Leaves, Squared Rim, c.1906, 4 1/2 In. 1650.00
Vase, Trumpet, Golden Amber Iridescent Body, Knopped Stem, 10 In. 990.00
Vase, Trumpet, Pale Green, Clear Stem & Foot, Favrile, 1918-1928, 6 1/2 In. 665.00
Whiskey, Favrile, Gold Iridescent, Flared Top, Red Highlights, Signed, 2 In. 225.00
TIFFANY GOLD, Case, Cigarette, 14K 525.00
TIFFANY POTTERY, Jar, Cover, Bee Finial, Shamrock Design 3750.00
Jar, Floral, 1 3/4 x 2 1/4 In. ....*Illus* 3750.00
Lamp, Crystalline Pink, Brown & Purple Flambe, Squat, Marked, 9 1/2 In. 410.00

◆◆◆◆◆◆◆◆◆◆◆◆◆◆◆◆◆◆◆◆◆◆◆

Don't put crazed pottery or porcelain in the dishwasher. It will often break even more.

◆◆◆◆◆◆◆◆◆◆◆◆◆◆◆◆◆◆◆◆◆◆◆

◆◆◆◆◆◆◆◆◆◆◆◆◆◆◆◆◆◆◆◆◆◆◆

Never stack cups or bowls inside each other.

◆◆◆◆◆◆◆◆◆◆◆◆◆◆◆◆◆◆◆◆◆◆

Tiffany Pottery, Jar, Floral, 1 3/4 X 2 1/4 In.

Pitcher, Cat–O'–Nine–Tails Around Body, Handle, Green Interior, 12 1/2 In.	1800.00
Vase, 4–Cluster Stalky Leaves, Matte Olive Green, Cylindrical, 7 1/4 In.	1650.00
Vase, Apple Green Glazed, Overlapping Iris Leaves, Signed, 8 x 7 In.	2500.00
Vase, Bronze, Green Iridescent Ground, Pods, 2 1/4 In.	950.00
Vase, Cluster of Milkweed Pods, Glazed Yellow–Green, 1910, 8 1/4 In.	4400.00
Vase, Flared Cylinder, Mottled Blue & Mustard Glaze, 14 1/2 In.	1870.00
Vase, Glazed, Flared, Light & Dark Green Glaze, Label, 6 In.	950.00
Vase, Glazed, Hanging Pods & Leaves, Blue–Green, Signed, 6 1/2 In.	2000.00
Vase, Grecian Classical Figures Around, Unglazed, Irregular Shape, 4 In.	750.00
Vase, Grecian Dressed Figures, Signed, 4 In.	750.00
Vase, Green Glaze, Horizontal Lines, Flared, 6 x 4 In.	950.00
Vase, Leaves At Collar, Green Glaze Interior, Signed, 4 1/2 In.	750.00
Vase, Raised Blossoms, Pale Yellow–Green Glaze, 2 x 3 In.	1100.00
Vase, Raised Blossoms, Vines, Green Glaze Interior, Signed, 13 1/4 In.	1500.00
Vase, Unglazed, Green Glazed Interior, Carved Leaves, Bulbous, 4 1/2 In.	750.00
TIFFANY SILVER, Blotter Set, Marquis Pattern, 5 In., 4 Piece	485.00
Bowl, Center, Reindeer Handles	1870.00
Bowl, Centerpiece, Chased Edge Design, Floral Border, 14 In.	2310.00
Bowl, Holly, Scalloped Rim, c.1903, 12 In.	850.00
Bowl, Incurved Body, 1920s, 9 In.	1100.00
Bowl, Rectangular Molded Rim, 1907–1938, 11 In.	475.00
Bowl, Repousse, Scalloped, 10 1/2 In.	1650.00
Bowl, Serving, Fluted, 10 In.	385.00
Box, Overall Floral, c.1887, 2 3/4 In.	220.00
Butter Chip, Wave Edge, 12 Piece	45.00
Cake Stand, c.1924, 3 1/2 x 11 In.	550.00
Cheese Scoop, Flemish	125.00
Clock, Travel, Japanese Style, 14K Gold Butterfly, Snail & Flower, 3 1/2 In.	1195.00
Coaster, Wine, Chrysanthemum, Zigzag Interior, c.1885, 6 3/4 In.	3025.00
Cocktail Shaker, Textured Ground, Engraved Designs	935.00
Compote, Ovolo Molded Borders, Putto Handles, 1870–1875, 10 In.	4125.00
Compote, Stag's Head Handles, Monogram, 1875–1891, 9 x 7 In.	1650.00
Compote, Vintage Border, Low Round Form, 1875–1891, 10 5/8 In.	770.00
Cracker Scoop, Chrysanthemum	875.00
Cup, Baby's	95.00
Cup, Wedding, Figural	2430.00
Dinner Knife, Broomcorn	75.00
Dish, Engraved Arabesques, Polychrome Enamel, c.1910, 6 7/8 In.	1980.00
Dish, Nut, Leaf Shape, 3 x 3 In.	95.00
Dish, Petal Form, 6 7/8 In.	247.00

Fish Knife, Wave Edge, 6 Piece 400.00
Fish Set, Renaissance, 2 Piece 750.00
Flask, Etched Knight 1 Side, Squirrel Other, Scrolls & Berries, 7 5/8 In. 220.00
Flask, Japanese Style, Grasshopper & Bee, Screw–On Cap, c.1880, 8 1/4 In. 3575.00
Fork, Dinner, Audubon, Gold Wash, 6 Piece 600.00
Fork, English King, 7 1/2 In., 12 Piece 715.00
Fork, Faneuil, 8 In. 45.00
Fork, Lettuce, Renaissance 160.00
Grape Shears, Chrysanthemum 950.00
Hand Mirror & Brush 175.00
Jigger, Double, Sterling, Marked 90.00
Jug, Tapering Body, Dome Lid, c.1910, 10 In. 522.50
Ladle, Pierced, Stem of Embracing Putti, c.1910, 13 3/8 In. 1760.00
Ladle, Scrolled & Beaded Design, 13 In. 1600.00
Ladle, Soup, Broomcorn, 1890 .... 385.00
Nutcracker, Chrysanthemum 650.00
Salt, Blown–Out Center Band, Square Rim, Signed, 2 3/4 In. 195.00
Salt, Greek Key Border, 3 Hock Supports, 3 In., 6 Piece 880.00
Scissors Holder 70.00
Server, Pancake, Renaissance 500.00
Silent Butler, Hinged Top, Wooden Handle, 10 3/4 In. 135.00
Spoon, Chocolate, Richelieu, Gilt 40.00
Spoon, Salt, English King 35.00
Spoon, Stuffing, English King 675.00
Spoon, Sugar, Palm 65.00
Spoon, Vine, Grapes, Kidney Shape 495.00
String Holder, 3 In. 110.00
Sugar Sifter, Gilded, 1916 .... 245.00
Sugar Sifter, Olympian 275.00
Tablespoon, Audubon 85.00
Tea & Coffee Set, Georgian Style, Oviform, 6–Sided Base, Urn Finial, 5 Piece 3400.00
Tea & Coffee Set, Pear Shape, 9 1/2–In. Coffeepot, 5 Piece 2200.00
Tea Set, Flowers Repousse of Roses, Violets & Peonies, 3 Piece 1760.00
Teaspoon, Audubon 45.00
Teaspoon, Renaissance 35.00
Teaspoon, Wave Edge 25.00
Tongs, Sandwich, Marquise, Bird–Claw & Pierced Ends, 5 1/2 In. 335.00
Tongs, Sugar, Shell Design, Claw Feet, Marked 125.00
Tongs, Sugar, Strawberry 250.00
Tray, Figure of Leaf, 3 In. 36.50
Tray, Footed, Arts & Crafts Style, 12 In. Diam. 1980.00
Tray, Tea, Colonial Revival, 1873–1891 .... 8250.00
Tureen, Cover, Rococo Revival, Cartouche of Florals, Turtle Feet, 15 In. 7975.00
Vase, Loving Cup, 11 In. 650.00
Vase, Pierced Lip of Flowers, Cap Foot, 1930s, 10 In. 990.00
Waffle Server, Chrysanthemum 675.00

TIFFANY objects made from a mixture of materials, such as bronze and
glass boxes, are listed here. Tiffany lamps are included in this category.

TIFFANY, Ashtray, Match Safe, Bronze, American Indian, 6 1/2 x 3 1/4 In. 125.00
Ashtray, Zodiac Center, Curved Line, Gold Dore, Bronze, 4 x 3 In. 135.00
Blotter Ends, Pine Needle, Bronze, 19 x 2 In., Pair 350.00
Blotter Ends, Spider Web, Bronze, 4 Piece 225.00
Blotter Ends, Zodiac, Bronze, 4 Corner, 3 3/4 x 3 3/4 x 5 In. 200.00
Blotter, Hand, Chinese, Knob Handle, 3 x 5 3/4 In. 200.00
Blotter, Hand, Pine Needle, Gold Dore, Amber Glass, Knob Handle, Signed 300.00
Bookends, Abalone, Gold Dore, Bronze, 5 1/2 x 5 1/2 In. 750.00
Bookends, Buddha, Bronze, Gold Dore Finish, Signed, 6 x 5 1/2 In. 650.00
Bookends, Buddha, On Raised Platform, Bronze, Gold Dore, 6 x 5 1/2 In. 650.00
Bookends, Grapevine, Bronze, Gold Dore, Amber Slag Glass, 5 1/2 In., Pair 900.00
Bookends, Oriental, Jeweled, Bronze Gold Dore, Deep Blue, 5 1/2 In., Pair 1200.00
Bookends, Zodiac, Bronze, Gold Dore, 5 x 6 In., Pair 495.00
Bookends, Zodiac, Bronze, Signed 375.00

Bookrack, Abalone, Bronze, Gold Dore, 6 x 5 1/2 In. 1200.00
Bookrack, Grapevine, Gilt–Bronze, Favrile Glass, Expanding, 14 To 23 In. 1650.00
Box, Adam, Bronze, Sunburst Hinged Cover, 4 x 3 1/2 x 1 1/2 In. 350.00
Box, Bronze, Graduate, Gold Dore, Raised Line Border, 3 1/2 x 5 1/2 x 1 1/4 In. 350.00
Box, Cigar, Cedar Lined, Gold Dore, Signed 225.00
Box, Domed Cover, Enameled Beetle On Copper, Round, 3 1/4 In. 3575.00
Box, Enameled Multicolored Star, Purple Ground, Gold Dore, Bronze, 6 x 3 3/4 In. . 650.00
Box, Glove, Grapevine, Bronze, Green Slag Glass, 13 1/4 x 4 1/4 x 3 In. 2700.00
Box, Grapevine, Green Patina, Beaded Edge, Signed 425.00
Box, Hinged Cover, Enameled, Black & Red, Marked, 6 In. 1760.00
Box, Jewel, Grapevine, Bronze, Amber Slag Glass, 2 Section, Hinged Lid, 6 x 4 In. 1200.00
Box, Jewel, Grapevine, Gold Dore, Bronze, Amber Slag Glass, 9 1/2 x 7 x 3 In. 1500.00
Box, Pine Needle Over Green Glass, Bronze, Hinged Cover, Square, 8 x 3 In. 1200.00
Box, Stamp, Indian, Gold Dore, Bronze, Hinged Cover, Compartments, 5 x 3 In. 300.00
Box, Stamp, Pine Needle, Bronze & Glass, 3–Compartment Tray, 4 x 2 1/4 In. 400.00
Box, Stamp, Venetian, Gold Dore, Chest, Minks Border, 3 Compartments, 4 In. 400.00
Box, Stamp, Zodiac, Bronze Marked 275.00
Box, Twine, Grapevine, Bronze, Green Slag Glass, Hexagon Shape, 4 x 3 1/4 In. 1500.00
Box, Utility, Graduate, Bronze 225.00
Box, Zodiac, Gold Dore, Hinged Cover, Signed, 5 1/4 x 3 1/4 x 1 1/4 In. 350.00
Bust, Woodrow Wilson, Bronze, 6 3/4 In. 220.00
Calendar, Daily, Abalone, Gold Dore, Bronze, 6 x 4 3/4 In. 575.00
Candelabrum, 4 Arm, Bronze, Green Glass Blown, Bobeches, 15 x 14 In. 2200.00
Candelabrum, Gilt–Bronze, 2 Arms, Twisted Handle, 1899–1918, 9 1/4 In., Pair 2750.00
Candlestick, Bronze, 2 Arms, Gold Dore, 6 x 9 1/2 In., Pair 2000.00
Candlestick, Bronze, 2 Arms, Oval Base, Leaf Decoration, 6 In., Pair 2000.00
Candlestick, Bronze, 8 In. ....*Illus* 700.00
Candlestick, Bronze, Blown Apple Green Glass, Bobeche, 3 Curved Feet, 8 In. 1800.00
Candlestick, Bronze, Carved Feet, Iridescent Jewels, Tapered Shade, 17 In., Pair 4200.00
Candlestick, Bronze, Favrile, Green Glass, Wild Carrot, 1899–1920, 17 1/2 In., Pair 1350.00
Candlestick, Bronze, Gold Dore, Bobeche, Stick Body, 17 In., Pair 2100.00
Candlestick, Bronze, Gold Iridescent Glass Ball, Favrile, 8 In. 2000.00
Candlestick, Bronze, Green Glass Holder, 3 Curved Feet, Signed, 8 In. 1800.00
Candlestick, Bronze, Griffin, Pair 550.00
Candlestick, Cobra, Bronze Dore, 8 In. 975.00
Candlestick, Crimson Red, Hollow Stem Candleholders, 8 3/4 In., Pair 2200.00
Candlestick, Domed Shade, 15 In. ....*Illus* 1750.00
Candlestick, Favrile, Gold Iridescent, Ruffled & Ribbed Top, 4 1/2 In., Pair 575.00
Canister, Bronze, Dark Patina, Curved Top Cover, Round, 3 1/2 x 3 1/4 In. 225.00
Chamberstick, Enamel, Purple, Gold Dore, Side Loop, 3 1/2 In., Pair 1500.00

◆◆◆◆◆◆◆◆◆◆◆◆◆◆◆◆◆◆◆◆◆◆◆◆◆

To be sure you have a genuine Tiffany lamp, you must find the words "Tiffany and Co." printed on the metal base. The glass shades were also marked "L. C. Tiffany," or just with the letters "L. C. T." According to the records of the Tiffany Company, all these lamps were marked.

◆◆◆◆◆◆◆◆◆◆◆◆◆◆◆◆◆◆◆◆◆◆◆◆◆

Tiffany, Candlestick, Bronze, 8 In.

Tiffany, Candlestick, Domed Shade, 15 In.

Chest, Enamel, Blue, Bronze, Gold Dore, 8 x 3 3/4 x 3 In. 1500.00
Clock, Mantel, Glass Jewels, Portrait On Pendulum, Time, Strike, Bronze, 18 In. 6875.00
Clock, Mantel, Octagonal, Gilt Bronze, 1870, 9 1/2 In. 1320.00
Compote, Bronze, Gold Dore, Sunburst Line Design, 3 x 3 1/2 In. 195.00
Compote, Enamel, Blue, Bronze, Gold Dore, Florets, Pedestal, 8 1/4 In. 425.00
Compote, Flattened Rim, Shell Inserts, Raised Dish, Pedestal Foot, 3 In. 165.00
Compote, Gilt Bronze, Pedestal, Tapered Stem, Raised Rim, 4 In. 165.00
Compote, Ruffled, Gold, Footed, 5 1/2 In. 750.00
Cup & Saucer, Chocolate, Gold, Octagonal, 6 Piece 350.00
Cup, Engineers Club, Gold Bronze, 1907 .... 1750.00
Cup, Gold Bronze, Commemorative, 7 1/2 In. ....*Illus* 1600.00
Desk Set, Abalone, Bookends, Clip, Stamp Box, Etc., 6 Piece 1200.00
Desk Set, Abalone, Gilt Bronze, 1899–1928, 10 Piece 1550.00
Desk Set, American Indian, Pen Tray, Blotter Ends, Bronze Patina 225.00
Desk Set, Grapevine, Beaded Paper Rack, Green Slag Glass, 7 Piece 990.00
Desk Set, Pine Needle, Amber Slag Glass, Gilt Bronze, 12 Piece 2090.00
Desk Set, Pine Needle, Inkwell, Match Holder, Candleholder, Pen Tray, 5 Piece 2200.00
Desk Set, Venetian, Polychrome Enhancements, Medallions, 3 Piece 550.00
Desk Set, Zodiac, 5 Piece 1430.00
Desk Set, Zodiac, Inkwell, Pen Tray, Letter Opener, Blotter, Ashtray, 8 Piece 1400.00
Desk Set, Zodiac, Silver Dore, 5 Piece 950.00
Dish, Gold Dore, Favrile Glass Insert, Signed, 5-In. Diam. 550.00
Frame, Acorns & Oak Leaves, Bronze, Rectangular, 35 1/2 x 27 1/2 In. 605.00
Frame, Etched Metal, Amber Slag Glass, 10 x 8 In. 770.00
Frame, Geometric Line Around, Bronze, Silk Backing, 9 1/2 x 11 1/4 In. 850.00
Frame, Grapevine Etched Metal, Glass Pattern, Green, Oval, 10 In. 1045.00
Frame, Grapevine, Emerald Green Glass, Bronze, 1899–1918, 6 1/4 x 4 3/8 In. 605.00
Frame, Grapevine, Green Glass, Bronze, Double Picture, 7 1/2 x 18 In. 3200.00
Frame, Grapevine, Green Glass, Bronze, Easel, Oval Opening, 9 3/4 x 11 In. 2800.00
Frame, Pine Needle, Amber Slag Glass, Easel, 12 x 14 In. 2800.00
Frame, Pine Needle, Gold Dore, Amber Slag Glass, 6 x 4 In. 300.00
Frame, Pine Needle, Green Slag Glass, Bronze, 7 x 6 1/2 In. 1200.00
Frame, Pine Needle, Oval Opening, Beaded Design, Bronze, c.1915, 10 x 8 In. 990.00
Frame, Scroll, Floral Swag Motif, Gold Dore, 10 1/2 In. 275.00
Frame, Zodiac, Bronze, 1899–1928, 8 3/4 x 7 1/8 In. 880.00
Frame, Zodiac, Gold Dore Finish, Signed, 7 x 8 In. 950.00
Glass, Vase, Favrile Gold Iridescent, Round Body, Narrow Neck, 3 1/2 In. 625.00
Glue Pot, Cover, Brush, Grapevine, Dore 350.00
Humidor, Cover, Bronze, Grapevine, Green Slag Glass, Signed 3200.00
Inkwell, Abalone, Line & Leaf Design, Hinged Cover, Glass Insert, 3 1/2 In. 650.00

Tiffany, Cup, Gold Bronze,
Commemorative, 7 1/2 In.

◆ ◆

Cuckoo clocks sometimes need minor first aid or major repair. For minor problems, try home remedies before calling professional help. If the clock stops, it may be because it is not level, so try shifting the clock a bit. A clock will not run correctly in a draft. Hanging clocks should be flat against the wall. Have clocks oiled every 2 years, cleaned every 4 years. Major repairs should be done by a professional.

◆ ◆

Tiffany, Lamp, Bronze, Leaded Vine
Border, 18-In. Shade

Tiffany, Lamp, Bronze, Lemon
Leaf Shade, 24 1/2 In.

Inkwell, Adam, Oval Shaped, Hinged Lid, Glass Insert, Bronze, Signed, 4 x 3 In.	400.00
Inkwell, Byzantine, Jeweled, Beaded, Bronze, 4 1/2 x 2 3/4 In.	2500.00
Inkwell, Chinese, Pyramid, Octagon Shaped, Bronze, Glass Insert, 5-In. Base	550.00
Inkwell, Crab, Bronze, Hinged Shell, 1899-1918, 8 In.	5225.00
Inkwell, Double, Chinese, Liner	395.00
Inkwell, Grapevine, Green Slag Glass, Bronze, Ball Feet, Square, 4 1/2 In.	600.00
Inkwell, Modeled, Bronze, Greek Key	350.00
Inkwell, Ninth Century, Bronze, Jeweled, Dome-Shaped Cover, Square, 4 In.	750.00
Inkwell, Owl, Rocker Blotter, Bronze, 10 x 7 In.	1200.00
Inkwell, Pine Needle, Green Slag Glass, Bronze, 3 1/2 x 3 In.	400.00
Inkwell, Pine Needle, Green Slag Glass, Square, Ball Feet, Bronze, 4 1/4 x 3 1/2 In.	600.00
Inkwell, Scarab Beetle, Domed Hinged Cover, 1899-1918, 4 1/4 In.	4400.00
Inkwell, Spanish, Gold Dore, Hinged Cover, Knob Handle, 4 1/2 In.	1200.00
Inkwell, Venetian, Treasure Chest Type, 14K Gold Plate, Double, 5 x 3 In.	650.00
Inkwell, Zodiac, Bronze, Octagonal Design, Hinged Cover, 2 x 4 x 4 In.	220.00
Inkwell, Zodiac, Hinged Cover, Hexagonal, Bronze, 6 1/2 x 4 In.	550.00
Lamp, 16-Panel Shade, Frosted Drapery Fold Segments, 18 In.	4125.00
Lamp, 3-Arm, Paw Foot Urn Base, Green Favrile Shade, 15 In.	2750.00
Lamp, Abalone In Circular Design, Bronze, Gold Dore, 9 In.	3200.00
Lamp, Acorn, Bronze, Favrile, Opalescent Green Glass, 1899-1928, 16 In.	3300.00
Lamp, Acorn, Green & White, Bronze, Urn Shape On Platform, 21 In.	5500.00
Lamp, Bamboo, Stick, 3 Curved Arms, Bronze, Favrile Shade, 14 1/2 In.	2200.00
Lamp, Bronze & Glass Desk, Octagon Shade, Adam Pattern, 17 In.	6000.00
Lamp, Bronze Base, Curved Arms, Bell Shaped Glass Shade, 13 In.	2000.00
Lamp, Bronze Counter-Balance, Paneled Glass Shade, Marked, 16 3/4 In.	4950.00
Lamp, Bronze, Adjustable Standard, Silk Shade, Signed, 59 In.	770.00
Lamp, Bronze, Amber Glass Shade, Signed, 15 In.	4500.00
Lamp, Bronze, Leaded Vine Border, 18-In. Shade ....*Illus*	8800.00
Lamp, Bronze, Lemon Leaf Shade, 24 1/2 In. ....*Illus*	7500.00
Lamp, Bronze, Light-Blue Glass Beads Design Shade, Stamped, 28 1/2 In.	6600.00
Lamp, Bronze, Linen Fold Shade, Signed, 16 In.	8250.00
Lamp, Bronze, Quezal Iridescent, Counter-Balance, 1899-1918, 4 Ft. 6 In.	2550.00
Lamp, Bronze, Stick, Cone Shaped Dicroic Shade, 24 In.	5500.00
Lamp, Candle, Gold Iridescent, Brass Lace Shade, Electrified, Swirl Ribbed, 12 In.	675.00
Lamp, Candle, Green Pulled Lappets, Spiral Ribbed Base, Favrile, 13 3/8 In.	1925.00
Lamp, Candle, Honeycomb Ruffled Shade, Twisted Stick, Favrile, 14 1/4 In.	2750.00
Lamp, Candle, Ruffled Shade, Pulled Green Feathers, 12 1/4 In., Pair	5225.00
Lamp, Candlestick, Bronze, Iridescent Jewels, Gold Iridescent Shade, 17 In., Pair	4200.00
Lamp, Candlestick, Gold Favrile Ruffled Shade & Twisted Gold Glass Base	1450.00
Lamp, Candlestick, Iridescent, Peacock Blue, Twisted Rib Body, 14 In.	5000.00

Lamp, Counterweight, Bronze, Curved Arm, Blue, Gold Damascene Shade, 7 In. 6000.00
Lamp, Double Arm, Bronze Base, Stick Body, Diamond Pattern Shades, 21 In. 2500.00
Lamp, Favrile, Diamond Pattern, Gold Iridescent, Bronze, 2 Arms, 21 In. 2500.00
Lamp, Gilt Bronze, Banded Dome Shade, 3–Arm Spider, 14 In. 1430.00
Lamp, Gilt Metal, Favrile, Pulled Green Feathering, 1899–1928, 15 5/8 In. 2200.00
Lamp, Glass & Bronze Acorn Border, Marked, 17 3/4 In. 6600.00
Lamp, Grape Vine, Adjustable Shade, Bracket Arm, Gilt Bronze & Slag, 8 In. 885.00
Lamp, Green & White Geometric Shade, Urn Shape, Bronze, Signed, 23 In. 900.00
Lamp, Green, Gold–Dome Shade, Ribbed Ball Foot, Platform Base, 18 In. 1980.00
Lamp, Hanging, Multicolored Acorns, Orange Ground, Signed, 20 1/2 In. 7750.00
Lamp, Harvard, Bronze, Favrile, Mottled Amber Glass, 8–Sided Shade, 26 In. 5500.00
Lamp, Lily, 3–Light, Floriform Bronze Base, 3–Stem Arms, Ribbed Cup, 16 In. 990.00
Lamp, Lily, 3–Light, No. 305, Telescoping Base, Blossoms, Gold Shades, 22 In. 2100.00
Lamp, Lily, 4–Light, Bronze, Domical Base, 1892–1918, 20 5/8 In. 4400.00
Lamp, Lily, 6–Light, Favrile, Bronze, 1899–1920, 20 1/2 In. 330.00
Lamp, Lily, 6–Light, Signed 5225.00
Lamp, Linen Fold, 12–Sided Shade, Gilt Bronze Base, Marked, 18 1/2 In. 2420.00
Lamp, Mosque, Opalescent, Green Feather Pattern, Gold Iridescent Band, 9 In. 2500.00
Lamp, Nautilus Shell, Bronze, 2 Arms, 13 In. 7500.00
Lamp, Pine Needle, Arms Spread To Hold 2–Piece Shade, Green, 13 In. 2000.00
Lamp, Pine Needle, Green Glass, Blown Out, Bronze Patina 2500.00
Lamp, Pine Needle, Green Glass, Bronze, 13 In. 2000.00
Lamp, Ribbed Stem, Textured Gold–Type Finish, Flowers & Leaves On Shade 3520.00
Lamp, Roman, Olive–Green Patina, Bronze, 28 1/2 In. 4950.00
Lamp, Table, Turtleback, Dome Shade, Amber Segments, 21 In. 8800.00
Letter Holder, American Indian, Bronze, Geometric, 6 1/2 x 2 3/4 x 4 1/2 In. 550.00
Letter Holder, Venetian, Bronze, 14K Gold Plate, Minks On Sides, 4 1/2 x 6 In. 600.00
Letter Opener, Bookmark, Gold Dore, Symbol Both Sides of Handle, 10 1/2 In. 200.00
Letter Opener, Chinese 195.00
Letter Opener, Grapevine, Gold Dore, Amber Slag Glass Handle, 9 In. 275.00
Letter Opener, Pine Needle, Bronze, Gold Dore, Amber Glass Handle, 9 In. 275.00
Letter Opener, Venetian, Gold Dore, Signed, 10 1/2 In. 250.00
Letter Rack, Abalone, Bronze, Discs, Gold Dore, 2 Sections 900.00
Letter Rack, Chinese, Bronze, 2 Section, Chinese Symbol, 9 1/2 x 6 In. 550.00
Letter Rack, Grapevine, Bronze, 3 Section, Green Slag Glass, Signed, 12 1/2 In. 1500.00
Letter Rack, Grapevine, Bronze, Green Slag Glass, Center Divider, 4 1/2 x 6 In. 700.00
Letter Rack, Ninth Century, Bronze, Jeweled, 2 Sections, 10 x 6 In. 900.00
Letter Rack, Pine Needle, Etched Metal, Amber Slag Glass, 3 1/4 x 3 In. 950.00
Letter Rack, Zodiac, 2 Compartments 295.00
Lighter, Byzantine, Gold Dore, Gold Iridescent Discs, Handle, 3 In. 750.00
Lighter, Sealing Wax, Byzantine, Kettle Shape, Handle, Hinged Lid, Signed 750.00
Magnifying Glass, Abalone, Gold Dore, 4–In. Round Glass, 9 In. 750.00
Magnifying Glass, American Indian, Gold Dore, 4–In. Glass, 8 3/4 In. 500.00
Magnifying Glass, Bookmark, Gilt Bronze, 8 3/4 In. 825.00
Magnifying Glass, Bronze & Enamel, Geometric Pattern, Blue, 7 In. 700.00
Magnifying Glass, Zodiac, Gold Dore Finish, Signed, 8 3/4 In. 500.00
Match Safe, Zodiac, Brown 295.00
Ornament, Dragonfly, Bronze, Green Favrile Glass, 1899–1920, 9 7/8 In. 4950.00
Paper Clip, Pine Needle, Gold Dore, Amber Glass, 2 1/2 x 3 3/4 In. 350.00
Paperweight, Bronze, Knob Handle, Dinner, March 1905 Imprinted, 3 1/2 In. 250.00
Paperweight, Bulldog, Sitting, Bronze, Dark Patina, 2 1/4 x 1 1/2 In. 475.00
Paperweight, Grapevine, Green Slag, Bronze, Knob Handle, Round, 3 3/4 In. 400.00
Paperweight, Lioness, Recumbent, Bronze, Gold Dore, 5 x 1 1/2 x 1 1/2 In. 700.00
Paperweight, Owl, Bronze, Dark Patina, 3 x 1 1/4 In. 850.00
Pen Holder, Grapevine Over Green Slag Glass, Bronze, Easel Style, 5 x 4 In. 550.00
Pen Holder, Venetian, Gold Dore, Enameled, 7 1/2 x 4 1/2 x 1 In. 750.00
Pen Tray, Chinese 195.00
Pen Tray, Gilt Bronze, Marked, 9 6/8 In. 66.00
Planter, Bronze Dish, Copper Liner, Marsh Marigold, 3 3/4 In. 3750.00
Planter, Bronze Frame, Pierced Ovals, Green Blown–Out Glass, Marked, 3 1/4 In. 3575.00
Planter, Bronze, Gold Dore Finish, Geometric Design, Separate Liner, 8 1/2 In. 650.00
Planter, Mosaic, Bronze, Favrile Glass, 1899–1920, 12 1/2 In. 9625.00
Plaque, Grecian–Style Women, Plaster Bas Relief, 1897, 16 x 37 In. 950.00

Platter, Bronze, Gold Dore, Deep Center Well, Signed, 9–In. Diam.	95.00
Scale, Grapevine, Gold Dore, Amber Slag Glass	650.00
Scale, Letter, Graduate, Dore & Blue Enamel	300.00
Scale, Letter, Zodiac, Dark Patina, 3 1/4 x 2 3/4 In.	550.00
Scale, Pine Needle, Gold Dore, Amber Slag Glass, Signed	650.00
Scale, Venetian, Gold Dore, Sculptured Mink Border, 1 1/2 x 3 x 3 3/4 In.	675.00
Scale, Zodiac, Dark Patina Finish, Signed	550.00
Tazza, Abalone, Bronze, Circular, 8 1/16 In.	121.00
Tazza, Rim of Flower Heads, Enameled Centers, Gilt Bronze, 1918–1928, 10 In.	660.00
Tray, Bronze, Gold Dore Finish, Enamel Handles, Floral Leaf Pattern, 8 1/4 In.	400.00
Tray, Bronze, Red Jewels, Gold Dore, 10 In.	250.00
Tray, Card, Nude Women On Side, Bronze, 7 1/2 In.	265.00
Tray, Card, Raised Geometric Border, Bronze, Round, 8 In.	150.00
Tray, Gilt Bronze, Dished Round Plate, Applied Ring Foot	165.00
Tray, Gold Dore, Bronze, Raised Rim, Leaves & Berries Border, 6 3/4 In.	125.00
Tray, Pen, Grapevine, Green Glass, Bronze, 3 Section, Ball Feet, 9 1/2 x 2 3/4 In.	250.00
Tray, Red Enamel, Bronze, 3–Leaf Clover, Monogram Center, 9 In.	375.00
Tray, Serving, Bronze, Gold Dore Finish, Raised Border, Signed, 12 x 15 In.	650.00
Trivet, Dragonfly, Bronze, Favrile Glass Mosaic, 1899–1920, 7 1/4 In.	9900.00
Vase, Bronze, Raised Buds, Silver Finish, Green Ground, 2 1/4 x 3 In.	950.00
Vase, Favrile, Bronze, Floriform, Glass Blossom, Green Leaves, 20 1/2 In.	550.00
Vase, Stick, Enameled Base, Bronze, 16 In.	1400.00

TIFFIN Glass Company of Tiffin, Ohio, was a subsidiary of the United States Glass Co. of Pittsburgh, Pennsylvania, in 1892. The U.S. Glass Co. went bankrupt in 1963, and the Tiffin plant employees purchased the building and the inventory. They continued running it from 1963 to 1966, when it was sold to Continental Can Company. In 1969, it was sold to Interpace, and in 1980, it was closed. The black satin glass, made from 1923 to 1926, and the stemware of the last twenty years are the best-known products.

Ashtray, Twilight, 6 In.	125.00
Bonbon, Heart, Twilight, Handle, 7 In.	60.00
Bowl, Desert Red, Handle, 8 1/4 In.	45.00
Bowl, Teardrop, Smoky, Low, 12 In.	75.00
Bulb Box, Crystal Satin Glass, 1920s	95.00
Cake Plate, Rosepoint, Handle, 13 1/2 In.	58.00
Candlestick, Black Satin, 7 3/4 In., Pair	90.00
Candlestick, Frog, Black, Frosted, Pair	250.00
Candy Jar, Footed, Red, 9 1/2 In.	95.00
Champagne, Adam, Pink	30.00
Champagne, Cherokee, Rose	20.00
Champagne, Flanders	16.75
Champagne, Flanders, Crystal	16.00
Champagne, Flanders, Pink	32.00
Champagne, June Night	20.00
Champagne, Persian Pheasant	28.00
Champagne, Princeton	12.00
Champagne, Shawl Dancer	18.00
Cocktail, Cerise	20.00
Cocktail, Cherokee Rose, Crystal	22.50
Cocktail, Fuchsia	18.00
Cocktail, June Night	19.50 To 22.00
Cocktail, Princess, Wide Optic	12.00
Console Set, Vaseline, Flared Out Bowl, 14 1/2 In., 3 Piece	37.00
Cordial, Fuchsia	45.00
Cordial, June Night	45.00
Cordial, Persian Pheasant	48.00
Cordial, Wisteria	45.00
Creamer, Cerice, Footed, Crystal	25.00
Cup & Saucer, Flanders, Crystal	35.00
Dish, Sundae, Flanders, Crystal	14.00
Flower Frog, Twilight, 6 1/2 In.	85.00 To 110.00

Goblet, Byzantine	15.00
Goblet, Cherokee Rose	32.50
Goblet, Cordella, Crystal	18.00
Goblet, Eternally Yours	14.00
Goblet, Flanders, Stemmed, Crystal	20.00
Goblet, Iced Tea, June Night, Footed, 6 1/2 In.	24.00
Goblet, June Night	28.00
Goblet, La Rue, 11 Piece	165.00
Goblet, Rosalind, Pedestal, Yellow, 7 3/8 In.	25.00
Goblet, Water, Byzantine, Plain Stem	16.00
Goblet, Water, Cherokee Rose	20.00
Goblet, Water, Empire	22.00
Goblet, Water, Flanders, Topaz, 8 1/4 In.	32.00
Goblet, Water, Fuchsia, Crystal	25.00
Goblet, Water, June Night, Crystal	22.50
Goblet, Water, June, Bean, 8 1/8 In.	16.00
Goblet, Water, La Fleur, Topaz, 8 1/4 In.	26.00
Goblet, Water, Wisteria	25.00
Jug, Lid, Fontaine, Green	475.00
Lamp, Flower Basket, Black Glass Base	325.00
Lamp, Parrot, Orange–Red, Green Head, 1920s	400.00
Mirror, Blue Beveled, Felt Back, Large	55.00
Oyster Cocktail, Cherokee Rose	16.00
Parfait, Cafe, Rosalind, Yellow, 6 1/4 In.	45.00
Parfait, Cherokee Rose	40.00
Pitcher, Cadena, Yellow	265.00
Plate, Byzantine, Crystal, 10 1/2 In.	35.00
Plate, Cerise, 8 In.	9.00
Plate, Cherokee Rose, 8 In.	18.50
Plate, Dinner, Byzantine	35.00
Plate, Dinner, Julia, Amber	20.00
Plate, Flanders, Yellow, 10 1/2 In.	35.00
Plate, Fontaine, Green, 8 In.	15.00
Plate, Fuchsia, 8 In.	15.00
Plate, Julia, Amber, 8 1/2 In.	10.00
Plate, Julia, Amber, 10 In.	20.00
Plate, June Night, 8 In.	10.00 To 12.00
Plate, La Fleur, Topaz, 8 1/4 In.	14.00
Plate, La Fleur, Yellow, 9 3/4 In	13.00
Plate, Persian Pheasant, Pink, 8 In.	22.75
Punch Set, Williamsburg, 13 Piece	180.00
Sherbet, Cerise, Low	14.00
Sherry, Persian Pheasant, Wide Mouth	18.00
Sugar & Creamer, June Night	50.00
Tray, Stag, Black Satin Glass, Oblong, 1924, 6 In.	50.00
Tumbler, Iced Tea, June Night, Footed, 6 1/2 In.	24.00
Tumbler, Iced Tea, Shawl Dancer, Cone	19.95
Tumbler, Juice, Cherokee Rose	20.00 To 25.00
Tumbler, Juice, Rosalind, Footed, Yellow, 4 In.	35.00
Tumbler, Juice, Wisteria	25.00
Tumbler, Water, Cerise	18.00
Tumbler, Water, Flanders, Yellow	20.00
Tumbler, Water, Shawl Dancer, Cone	16.00
Vase, Bud, Cherokee Rose, 8 In	45.00
Vase, Bud, Cherokee Rose, 10 1/2 In.	45.00
Vase, Bud, June Night, 10 1/2 In.	32.00
Vase, Cornucopia, Blue, 8 1/4 In.	75.00
Vase, Etched, Sterling Silver Base, 11 In.	45.00
Vase, Princess, Crystal, 4 In.	22.50
Vase, Swedish Modern, Morning Glory, Blue	75.00
Vase, Teal & Crystal, 7 3/4 In.	95.00
Vase, Twilight, Daisy, 10 1/4 In.	175.00
Wine, Byzantine, Plain Stem	18.00

Tinware, Figurine, Lamb, Standing, Painted, 6 X 5 In.

Wine, June Night	20.00
Wine, La Rue, 12 Piece	125.00
Wine, Persian Pheasant	15.00

TILES have been used in most countries of the world as a sturdy building material for floors, roofs, fireplace surrounds, and surface toppings. Many of the American tiles are listed in this book under the factory name.

Blue Basket, Flowers, White Ground, Faience, California, Round, 5 1/4 In.	77.00
Bluebirds, Pink & Brown Ground, California, 8 1/2 x 5 1/2 In.	85.00
Calendar, 1898, McDuffee & Stratton Co., Boston, King's Chapel Reverse, 3 x 5 In.	55.00
Calendar, 1916, Jones, McDuffie, Straton	85.00
Calendar, 1917, Jones, McDuffie, Straton	40.00
Classical Portrait Scene, Green Glaze, Impressed Mark, Osborne, 19 x 9 In.	1350.00
Cottage & Stone Bridge Scene, Semimatte Glaze, Richmond, 6 x 12 In.	192.00
Deer, Matte, Mostique Tile, Oakland	35.00
Fireplace, Classical Nudes Dancing, Mountain Ground, Claycroft, 50 x 18 In.	385.00
Gentlemen Fencing, Earthenware, Frame, John Mortlock, 12 x 14 In., 6 Piece	7150.00
Little Bopeep, Beige & Blue, 6 x 6 In.	25.00
Month of December & February, Blue, White, Frame, Wedgwood, 9 3/4 In., Pair	170.00
Multicolor Flowers In Basket, 5 1/4 In.	275.00
Neptune, Blue & White, 19th Century, 12 x 12 In.	195.00
Peacock, Matte Brown, Turquoise Border, California, Round, 5 3/4 In.	110.00
Pottery, Stylized Design, Shaped Square, Spain, 8 x 8 In.	220.00
President Harding, Geo. Cartlidge, Black, White, Frame, 8 1/2 x 5 1/2 In.	396.00
Seashell & Seaweed, Turquoise, Beaver Falls	30.00
Seashell, Harris Strong, Oak Frame, Pair	125.00
Ship, Riding The Waves, Bas–Relief, Dead Matte Glaze, Morasque, 6 In.	77.00
Spanish Galleon, Cloisonne, Faience, Turquoise Glaze, California, 5 3/4 In.	88.00
Tea, Ferris Institute, Big Rapids, Mich., China	50.00
Tea, Niagara Falls, China	50.00
Tea, Pink Roses, Hand Painted	20.00
Woman's Head, Hat, Profile, Caramel Glaze, Frame, Trent, 4 1/4 In.	110.00
Woman's Head, Kerchief, Profile, Blue Glaze, Frame, J. J. G. Low, 5 1/2 In.	165.00
Young Woman, Messenger Dove, Beaver Falls, Isaac Broome, 17 3/4 x 6 In.	1210.00

TINWARE containers for household use have been made in America since the seventeenth century. The first tin utensils were brought from Europe, but by 1798, tin plate was imported and local tinsmiths made the wares. Painted tin is called *tole* and is listed separately. Some tin kitchen items may be found listed under Kitchen. The lithographed tin containers used to hold food and tobacco are listed in the Advertising category under Tin.

Bed Warmer, Brass Trim, Turned Wooden Handle, Black Paint, 42 1/2 In.	83.00
Box, Harlequin Clown Serenading Woman With Fan, Art Deco	27.50
Bucket, Dinner, Trays & Cup Cover	42.00
Candlestick, Hog Scraper, Plume–Like Push–Up Knob, 6 1/2 In.	82.50

Coffeepot, Maxim's Patent Coffeepot, Double Spout 60.00
Coffeepot, Parrot Beak Spout, 10 1/2 In. 440.00
Coffeepot, Removable Drip Top, Black Wooden Handle, Pewter Finial, 9 3/4 In. 71.00
Cover, Food, Dome Top, Platter & Reticulated Base, 12 x 15 In. 27.50
Figurine, Lamb, Standing, Painted, 6 x 5 In. ....*Illus* 32.00
Foot Warmer, Pierced, Wooden, Tray, 5 1/2 x 8 x 9 1/2 In. 99.00
Foot Warmer, Punched Hearts & Circles, Walnut Frame, 6 In. 225.00
Foot Warmer, Punched, Butternut Frame, Turned Posts, 7 1/2 x 9 x 5 3/4 In. 220.00
Foot Warmer, Wooden, For Church Pew 225.00
Holder, Napkin, Amish Woman, Figural 27.50
Lunch Bucket, Miner's, Bail, Wooden Grip, 5 Piece 65.00
Magnet, Acrobat & Horse, Original Card, 1913 .... 25.00
Mold, Candle, 8 Tube 100.00
Mold, Candle, 10 Tube 165.00
Mold, Candle, 12 Tube, 20 In. 130.00
Mold, Candle, 12 Tube, Cherry Frame, A. D. Richmond, New Bedford 1650.00
Mold, Candle, 12 Tube, Round, Handle 1000.00
Mold, Candle, 24 Tube, W. Webb, New York 2650.00
Mold, Candle, Free Standing, c.1830, 10 1/2 In. 125.00
Mold, Chocolate, Santa Claus 165.00
Mold, Chocolate, Santa Claus, 7 1/2 In. 165.00
Mold, Food, Scalloped, Crown, 6 1/2 In. 38.50
Mold, Pudding, 8 Points 50.00
Mold, Sandtorten, Bundt, Germany 45.00
Pitcher, Scrolled Ear Handle, Punched, Tooled Sunburst Design, 11 In. 137.00
Sconce, Candle, Crimped Crest, 9 3/4 In. 150.00
Sconce, Candle, Punched, Primitive, 11 1/4 In. 71.50
Shaving Set, Folding, Red & Black, Milk Glass Dish 105.00
Teapot, Pewter Finial, 8 In. 104.00
Torch, Campaign, 2 Spouts, Bamboo Handle, 48 In. 27.50
Tray, Hessian Office Medallion Center, 19th Century, 20 1/2 x 16 In. 330.00
Urn, Coffee, Brass Spigot, 15 1/4 In. 115.00

TOBACCO CUTTERS may be listed in both the Advertising and the Store categories.

TOBACCO JAR collectors search for those made in odd shapes and colors. Because tobacco needs special conditions of humidity and air, it has been stored in special containers since the eighteenth century.

Bearded Black Man, Seated On Bale of Cotton, Painted Ceramic, 8 1/ 2 In. 1045.00
Black Man's Face, Smoking Cigarette, Avocado Shape, Ceramic, 6 In. 1100.00
Black Woman Emerging From Barrel, Painted Ceramic, 7 1/2 In. 605.00
Blue Boar Inn, Brown Transfer, Gold Ground 65.00
Friar Tuck, Head Is Lid, England, Late 1800s, 5 In. 125.00
Human Skull, Black Eye Sockets, Brown Trim, 5 In. 145.00
Indian Looking Out of Wigwam, Austria, 9 3/4 In. 200.00
Man's Head, Yellow Skin, Black Hair, Germany, 4 3/4 In. 95.00
Wolf's Head, Light Brown Trim, 4 In. 65.00
Young Black Man, Seated On Squash, Painted Ceramic, 8 3/4 In. 935.00

TOBY JUG is the name of a very special form of pitcher. It is shaped like the full figure of a man or woman. A pitcher that shows just the top half of a person is not correctly called a toby. More examples of toby jugs can be found under Royal Doulton and other factory names.

Beethoven, 2 5/8 In. 15.00
Ben Franklin, 9 In. 3080.00
Friar, France, 1920 .... 250.00
MacArthur, Royal Minton, 3 1/2 In. 35.00
Napoleonic Military Officer, Faience, Eiderville, Large 395.00
Old King Cole, England 45.00
Seated Man Holding Stein, Staffordshire 3080.00
Shepherd, With Staff, White, Orange, Black Hat, Germany, 5 In. .... 75.00 To 85.00

TOLE is painted tin. It is sometimes called *japanned ware, pontypool,* or *toleware.* Most nineteenth–century tole is painted with an orange–red or black background and multicolored decorations. Many recent versions of toleware are made and sold. Related items may be listed in the Tin category.

Basket, Directoire, Pierced Everted Rim, Pierced Handles, Oval Base, Red, 6 3/4 In.	4125.00
Box, Apple Shape, Shenandoah Valley Apple Candy, Twine Stem, 4 In.	45.00
Box, Candle, Hinged Lid, Red, Black Striping, Floral Design, 9 In.	71.00
Box, Deed, Brown Japanning, Basket of Fruit Stencil, 9 1/2 In.	45.00
Box, Deed, Brown Japanning, Striping, Yellow, Red & Green Design, 3 In.	330.00
Box, Deed, Brown Japanning, White Band, Foliage, Green, Red, 4 1/4 In.	38.00
Box, Deed, Dome Top, Black Paint, Polychrome Floral, Red, White, Yellow, 9 In.	110.00
Box, Deed, Dome Top, Brown Japanning, Floral Stencil, 9 In.	121.00
Box, Dome Top, Brown & Black Japanning, Floral, 7 In.	192.00
Box, Dome Top, Brown Japanning, White Band, Yellow, Green, Red, 4 1/4 In.	75.00
Box, Shoeshine, Original Black, Gold, Iron Shoe Top	65.00
Box, Spice, 7 Interior Canisters, Gold Striping, Round, 6 3/4 In.	82.00
Box, Wig, Ravenscroft, Law Wig & Robe Maker, London, 19th Century, 23 In.	145.00
Bread Box, Floral, Red Cover, 1950	10.00
Bread Tray, Green Paint, Yellow Striping, Stenciled Bronze Fruit, 8 x 14 In.	55.00
Bucket, Coal, Green Ground, Flowers, Scrolling Handles, Lion's Head Feet, 22 In.	85.00
Cache Pot, Yellow Classical Scenes, Paw Feet, Italy, 9 In.	132.00
Canister, Floral, Black Paint, Resoldered Cap, 8 1/4 In.	115.00
Canister, Tea, Green Paint, Yellow, Red, Green Commas & Stars, 8 In.	33.00
Carrier, Gasoline, Fancy, Handle, Spigot, 10 In.	55.00
Chamberstick, Brown Japanning, Gold Stenciling, Push–Up, 5 In.	55.00
Chandelier, 6–Light, Empire Style, Gilt Stenciled Anthemion, Electrified, 32 In.	880.00
Chandelier, 6–Light, Hexagonal Pagoda, Chinoiserie Scenes, Electrified, 23 In.	2200.00
Cistern, Neoclassical Style, Female Mask At Spigot, 19 In.	1430.00
Coffeepot, Dark Brown Japanning, Floral Design, 10 1/2 In.	3100.00
Coffeepot, Dome Hinged Lid, Flowers & Leaves, 10 3/4 In.	1540.00
Coffeepot, Floral & Leaf Design, American, 19th Century, 10 In.	600.00
Coffeepot, Floral Design, Red Paint, Black, Red, White, 10 1/2 In.	412.00
Coffeepot, Floral, Black Ground, 8 1/2 In.	220.00
Coffeepot, Gooseneck, Black, Design	1842.00
Creamer, Brown Japanning, Floral Design, Red, Yellow, Green, Black, White, 4 In.	165.00
Cuspidor, Smoked White, Red Stripes, Gold Stencil, 8 1/4 In.	14.00
Desk, Black Paint, Gold Trim, Paw Feet, 8 In.	94.00
Egg Warmer, Divided Hinged Top, Removable Stand, Swan Handles, Red, 10 In.	1870.00
Figurine, Country Folk, Woman Carrying Bucket, Man With Walking Staff, 15 In.	1980.00
Foot Warmer, Brown Japanning, Gold Stenciled Lyre, 7 1/2 x 7 1/2 In.	94.00
Humidor, Florals, Black, 1830s, 5 In.	50.00
Lamp, Mustard Yellow, Brown Striping, Green Foliage Design, 8 In., Pair	198.00
Lamp, Peinte, Empire, Swan Handles, Dolphin Terminal, Paw Feet, Red, 23 1/2 In.	990.00
Lantern, 2 Sockets, Black & Gold Paint, Clarke's Astronomical, 12 In.	385.00
Lavabo & Basin, Peinte Faux Marble, France, 16 In.	1210.00
Mug, Japanning, Polychrome Floral & Fruit Design, 4 3/4 In.	605.00
Samovar, Lion's Heads Handles, Dolphin Head Spigot, Lamp Mounted, 30 1/2 In.	880.00
Sconce, 2–Light, Lemon Tree Form	25.00
Shaving Stand, Oval Mirror, 2 Candle Arms, Ball Feet, France, 46 In.	770.00
Spice Box, Black, Design, Nutmeg Grater In Slot In Lid, 6 Cans	135.00
Syrup, Birds, Flowers, Red Repaint, 5 5/8 In.	71.00
Teapot, Oval, Ribbed Handle, Punched Design, Tulip, Wavy Line Border, 5 3/4 In.	220.00
Tray, 2 Men Bartering, Woman Hiding In Trees, Painted, 20 x 27 In.	192.00
Tray, Black Paint, Yellow, Green, Red Design, 8 3/4 x 12 1/2 In.	55.00
Tray, Empire, Laurel Leaf Border, Red, Oval Gallery, 29 1/2 In.	550.00
Tray, Floral & Bird Design, 32 x 24 In.	410.00
Tray, Fruits & Vines, Black Bamboo Stand, 30 1/2 x 24 3/4 In.	440.00
Tray, George III, Painted Domestic Interior, People, Oval, 28 1/2 In.	2530.00
Tray, Gypsy Maiden, Polychrome, Raised Rim	143.00
Tray, Peaceable Kingdom, Birds, Grazing Sheep, Edward Hicks, 23 1/4 x 29 1/2 In.	1650.00

Tray, Regency, Center Medallion, Boy & Girl, Umbrella, Gilt Border, 22 x 29 In. 220.00
Tray, Regency, Hunt Scene, Gilt Border, Lacquered Bamboo Stand, 19 x 30 In. 605.00
Tray, Romantic Scene, 19th Century, 22 3/4 x 17 1/4 In. 715.00

TOM MIX was born in 1880 and died in 1940. He was the hero of over 100 silent movies from 1910 to 1929, and 25 sound films from 1929 to 1935. There was a Ralston Tom Mix radio show from 1933 to 1950, but the original Tom Mix was not in the show. Tom Mix comics were published from 1942 to 1953.

Arrowhead, Lucite 40.00
Book, Comic, No. 5, March 1941 .... 100.00
Book, Comic, No. 20 .... 25.00
Book, Tony & His Pals, 1934 ....75.00 To 125.00
Boots, Box 350.00
Bowl 39.00
Bracelet, ID, Ralston 35.00
Buckle, Belt, Secret Compartment 75.00
Card, Tobacco, Uncut 15.00
Catalog, Premium, 1936 .... 40.00
Catalog, Premium, 1939 .... 30.00 To 40.00
Compass & Magnifier, Glow In The Dark 50.00
Good Luck Spinner 32.00
Knife, Straight Shooters, Pocket 49.00
Knife, Tom & Tony, Pocket 325.00
Manual, Secret, Writing, Ralston, 1944, 3 x 5 1/2 In. ....70.00 To 100.00
Medal, Glow In The Dark, Ribbon 85.00
Neckerchief, Ralston ....125.00 To 145.00
Parachute, Rocket, Box, 1936 .... 100.00
Patch, Ralston 65.00
Periscope, 1939 .... 20.00
Pistol, Moving Chamber 150.00
Pocket Piece, Lucky 125.00
Portrait, Full–Length, Melbourne Spur, 1920s, 13 x 10 In. 550.00
Poster, Movie, 71 x 71 In. 825.00
Program, Life of Tom Mix, 1929 .... 50.00
Ring, Look Around, Original Mailer, Instructions, 1946 .... 125.00
Ring, Magnet 45.00
Ring, Straight Shooters 65.00
Sliding Whistle 65.00
Target, Marlin 245.00
Telescope, Bird Call ....49.00 To 85.00
Telescope, Bullet 75.00
Toy, Rocking Horse, Tony 360.00
Walkie Talkie 125.00
Watch Fob, Gold Ore ....25.00 To 55.00
Wristwatch, Ralston, 1982 .... 300.00

TOOLS of all sorts are listed here, but most are related to industry. Other tools may be found listed under Iron, Kitchen, Tinware, and Wooden.

Adding Machine, Fell & Tarrant 65.00
Anvil, Blacksmith's, 340 Lbs. 750.00
Auger, Carpenter's, Hole, Wooden Beam, T–Handle 5.00
Ax, All Wooden, Repaired Blade, Paint Design, Mohegan Lodge, 34 In. 126.00
Ax, Broad, Goosewing, G. Rohrbach, 3 Touch Marks 1000.00
Ax, Broad, Goosewing, Germany 100.00
Ax, Broad, Goosewing, KF, 11 In. 286.00
Ax, Broad, Goosewing, Marked TM 275.00
Ax, Broad, Shapleigh Hardware 425.00
Ax, Cooper's Side, W. Beatty, 1760 .... 230.00
Ax, Goosewing 350.00
Ax, Ice, Small 105.00
Ax, Keen Kutter, Double Blade 15.00

Ax, Safety, Folding Claw, Marble, No. 2	280.00
Ax, Simmons, 5 In.	20.00
Ax, Tackle Block Maker's, John King, Oakland, Maine	175.00
Battery Tester, W. C. Fields	8.50
Bean Sorter, Treadle Type, Marked B–88	80.00
Bee Skep	295.00
Bee Smoker, To Calm Bees	12.00
Bench Rule, Lufkin, No. 34V, 24 In.	28.00
Bench, Cobbler's, 9 Drawers, Cabinet In Cupboard Section	745.00
Bench, Egg Crate Maker's, With Vise	1250.00
Bench, Harness Maker's, Wooden	60.00
Bevel, Winchester, Sliding T	125.00
Bit Brace, Hawkes, Brass Plated	125.00
Bit Brace, Horton, Bronze	1023.00
Bit Display, Keen Kutter, Wooden, Red Log, Shapleigh Hardware	35.00
Blowtorch, Craftsman, Brass	18.00
Blowtorch, Gasoline, Brass, Lenk, 6 1/2 In.	22.00
Book Press, Wooden Screw, Oak	55.00
Boot Form, Gentleman's, Flat Type	45.00
Boot Pull, Civil War Officer's, Carved Ivory Handle, Cast Iron	110.00
Bootjack, Cow Face, Metal	18.00
Box, Conestoga Wagon, Hand Wrought Hinges & Clasp, Blue–Green Paint	225.00
Box, Oval, Cast Iron, Fits Horse Drawn Cultivator Tongue	4.50
Box, Simmons Hardware, Wooden	25.00
Box, Storage, Wooden, Green Paint, 3 Doors Open From Top, File Cabinet Shape	195.00
Box, Wooden, Lift Top, Blue Paint, Pennsylvania, 60 In.	1600.00
Brace, 6 Bits, M. & K. Works, Lancaster, N.Y. 1890	35.00
Bucket, Kerosene, Wooden, Spout, Large	150.00
Bush Hook, Keen Kutter	40.00
Calf Weaner, Cast Iron	20.00
Caliper Rule, Johnson, No. 46, German Silver, 6 In.	50.00
Caliper, Stanley, No. 136, 4 In.	28.00
Calipers, Human Figure Shape, 5 In.	110.00
Calipers, Jeweler's, Parallel	30.00
Calipers, Rope Gauge, Roebling	95.00
Cap Lamp, Brass Carbide, Justrite, Brass Reflector	45.00
Chest, 5 Drawers, Stained 2–Tone Green, Raised Panel Top, Brass, 25 x 40 In.	245.00
Chest, Carpenter's, Pine, Fitted Mahogany Interior, Hinged Cover, England, 36 In.	385.00
Chest, Machinist's, Beadwork Around Base, Brass Handles, Mahogany	440.00
Chest, Pine, Old Green Paint, Iron Eagle On Lid, 2 Trays, 22 3/4 In.	120.00
Chest, Watchmaker's, 3 Drawers, Wooden, 2450 Crystals For Pocket Watches	220.00
Chest, Watchmaker's, Cotter Pin Hinges, 12 Drawers, Red Paint, 4 x 10 1/2 In.	240.00
Chisel Set, Stanley, No. 110, SW Rollup	210.00
Chisel, Gooseneck, New Handle, 1/2 In.	65.00
Chisel, Hollow Back, Red Oak Handle, Japan, 10 Piece	85.00
Cigar Cutter, Myers–Cox Co., 3 Size Cuts, Lever Type	250.00
Cigarette Maker, Bugle Boy, Metal	28.50
Clamp, Carpenter, All Wood, Large	24.00
Cleaner, Kent's Knife, Cleans & Sharpens Knives, Pat. Nov. 1903	130.00
Compass, Surveyor's, Box	575.00
Compass, Surveyor's, Silvered Dial, Cased, Alex Megarey, 14 1/4 In.	395.00
Cork Press, Apothecary, 1863	95.00
Corker, Wine, 1890	150.00
Corn Dryer, Rodent Guards On Legs, 3 Ft.	165.00
Corn Husker, Hand	90.00
Corn Picker, Hand, Dated 1922	25.00
Corn Planter, Wooden, Hand	30.00
Corn Sheller, Hand Crank	23.00
Corn Sheller, Hand Held, Pat. Nov. 23, 1868, 4 x 6 In.	290.00
Crow Call, Perdew	150.00
Divider's, Cartographer's, Embossed Crest At Joint	375.00
Dowel Machine, Cutter, Stanley, No. 77	350.00
Drafting Set, McCallister, Early 19th Century	176.00

Draftsman's Set, Dietzgen, Velvet Fitted Case 78.00
Draftsman's Set, Ivory, Brass, Shagreen Case, Inscribed T. Blunt, Cornhill, London   975.00
Drawshave, Wedgway, No. 10 .... 10.00
Drill, Brest, Yankee, No. 555, Pat. Dec. 15, 1908, 2 Speed Ratchet 30.00
Drill, M. F. Co., Millers Falls, Mass. 120.00
Duck Stamp, A. E. Crowell, East Harwich, Mass., Rubber Wood, 1 1/2 In. 385.00
Egg Piercer, Fite's Peerless Calculator, c.1900 .... 95.00
Field Binder, Wooden, Salesman Sample 325.00
Flax Comb, Cutout Handles 375.00
Flax Wheel, Double Axle, 1880s 475.00
Fly Net, Horse, Leather, Pair 50.00
Fork, Clover, Wooden 190.00
Fork, Spading, Winchester 90.00
Gauge, Barrel, J. Watts, Charlestown, Mass., Ivory Tipped 675.00
Gauge, Marking, Keen Kutter, Mahogany 28.00
Gauge, Marking, Maple 22.50
Gauge, Mortising, Brass Pistol Grip Handle, Steel, Rosewood & Brass, 6 1/4 In. 25.00
Gauge, Mortising, Geo. Wheatcroft, Rosewood 48.00
Gauge, Wire & Rope, John Roebling & Son, Boxwood & Brass, 5 x 1 3/4 In. 150.00
Gauger Tape, With Reel & Brake, Lufkin, 25 Ft. 65.00
Glove Stretcher, Amethyst Color Stones At Handle, Sterling Silver 200.00
Grinder, Keen Kutter, Pedal Action 25.00
Hammer, Log Marking, E. H. T., 1 1/2 x 3 In. 45.00
Hammer, Silversmith's, Peer, Hanging Hole In Handle 20.00
Handcuffs, Peerless, USA, Leather Case 45.00
Hat Blocker, Man's, Wooden, 2 Piece 25.00
Hat Mold, Wooden, Paramount Hat Block, Some Paint, 6 3/4 x 7 1/2 x 8 In. 110.00
Hatchet & Box Opener, Estwing, Wooden Handles 40.00
Hatchet, Bench, Evansville Tool Works, 5 1/2–In. Blade 35.00
Hatchet, Camp, Winchester, Wooden Handle 75.00
Hatchet, Shingling, Mohaw–Blish, Mize & Silliman Hardware 40.00
Hatchet, Winchester, Sheath .... 50.00 To 55.00
Hedge Trimmer, Iron 65.00
Hinges, Door, Wrought Iron, Pair 220.00
Ice Pick, Winchester, Wooden Handle 65.00
Ice Pick, Wooden Handle, Leather Sheath 22.00
Ice Tongs, Iron 18.00
Ice Tongs, J. G. B. & C, Strasburg, New York, Cast Iron 42.00
Inclinometer, Rufus Porter 385.00
Jig, Doweling, Stanley, No. 59 .... 35.00
Joiner Gauge, Stanley No. 386 .... 70.00
Joiner, Carpenter's Union No. 13 of Wheeling Painted On Side, 1912 .... 330.00
Kit, Berghoff Brewing Co., Leather Case 35.00
Kit, Cut Tire Repair, Goodyear, Flying Shoe Logo 23.50
Kit, To Make Leather Gloves, Dies & Mallets, 8 Piece 180.00
Label Marking System, Monarch, Box 95.00
Lathe, Jeweler's, Brass, 18 In. 250.00
Lathe, Jeweler's, Compound Feed, Tool Rest, Tailstock 700.00
Lathe, W. F. & J. Barnes, 1 Or 2 People Pedal 1400.00
Lathe, Watchmaker's, American Watch Tool Co. 50.00
Level, Carpenter's, Chapin, Wooden, Brass Ends, Pine Meadow, Conn., 1870 .... 75.00
Level, Carpenter's, Dietzen, Tripod, Box, Brass 225.00
Level, Chapin–Stevens, No. 0223, 16 In. Brass Ends & Side Plates, Cherry 28.00
Level, Davis & Cook, Iron, Tapered Ends, 18 In. 375.00
Level, Davis, Pat. Sept. 17, 1867, 7 In. 350.00
Level, Keen Kutter, No. 104, Wooden, Logo Simmons 36.00
Level, Rollis, 12–In. Steel Frame, Brass Adjustable Vial Holders, Pat. 1896 .... 95.00
Level, Stanley No. 21, Brass Bound, 30 In. 110.00
Level, Stanley, No. 1093, Brassbound Mahogany, 18 In. 90.00
Level, Torpedo, Stanley, No. 259 .... 30.00
Loom, Child's, 2 Shuttles, Unpainted Pine, 12 x 15 3/4 x 9 1/2 In. 150.00
Loom, High Tape, Wooden, Dark Paint, On Stand, New England, 38 1/2 In. 1250.00
Loom, Tape, Pine, Dovetailed Box, 2 Ratchet Spindles, 10 x 19 In. 275.00

Measurall Tape, Lufkin, No. 9212, Box 17.50
Measure, Grain, Primitive, Graduated, Set of 3 .... 180.00
Measure, Horse Collar, Everitts, Patent 1873 .... 110.00
Measure, Mileage On Maps 15.00
Micrometer, Bench, Walthan, Patent 1907 .... 65.00
Milk Container, Galvanized, Sidney Wanzer 20.00
Milling Machine, Watchmaker's, Ball Bearing Spindle, Switzerland 850.00
Milling, Shaftru, For Crankshafts On Cars, Atherton–Salter Mfg., Wooden Box, 1920 150.00
Mold, Boot, Wooden Crank, Sections Can Be Added Or Removed For Size 375.00
Mold, Bullet, Winchester 65.00
Mold, Ink Bottle, Hover, Philad., Brass, 2 Handles, Domed, Squatty, 1850 .... 1550.00
Mold, Spoon, Bronze Bottom Half, 8 In. 150.00
Mold, Spoon, Bronze, For Casting In Pewter, 6 1/4 In., 2 Piece 220.00
Mold, Spoon, Iron & Brass 247.00
Mortise, W. F. & J. Barnes, Claw Feet, 1870s 350.00
Nail Pull, Keen Kutter 19.00
Niddy–Noddy, Chip Carved Heart & Pinwheel Design 725.00
Nipper–Pliers, Nipper Swings Down, Pliers Come To Top 75.00
Oiler, Lukenheimer Steam Engine, Alpha, No. 6, Glass, Brass Pump Lever, 1 Pt. 70.00
Padlock, B & E, Fancy Cast Iron 175.00
Padlock, Burn Bingham Best, Brass 150.00
Padlock, J. Gerard, Cast Iron 375.00
Padlock, Skull & Bones, Cast Iron 275.00
Padlock, W. H. Hall, Dock Square, Boston, Key, Brass 875.00
Peg, For Hand Planting Tobacco, Wooden 6.00
Pig Catcher, Iron, 1872 .... 15.00
Pike, Boatman's, Hand Forged, 18th Century, Primitive, 15 In. 55.00
Pitch Fork, Oak, 3 Prong, 60 In. 250.00
Plane & Box, Stanley, No. 55, 30 Chisel Bits 200.00
Plane, Beading, John Basset, Early 18th Century, 10 In. 225.00
Plane, Bed Rock, Stanley, No. 604 .... 55.00
Plane, Chamfer, Stanley, No. 72, 1st Model 260.00
Plane, Circular, Stanley, No. 13, Iron .... 75.00 To 145.00
Plane, Combination, Stanley, No. 50, Rosewood Handle, Cutters, Box 130.00
Plane, Cox & Luckman 225.00
Plane, Door Trim & Router, Stanley, No. 171 .... 300.00 To 310.00
Plane, Floor, Stanley, No. 11 1/2, Japanned 325.00
Plane, Fore, Carved Animal Head On Front, Oak, 20 In. 175.00
Plane, Jack, Record, No. 5, Box 35.00
Plane, Ogee Molding, C. Tobey, Flat Chamfers, Lignum Vitae Boxing, Birch 143.00
Plane, Plow, Albany Tool, Rosewood, Boxwood Screw Arms, Handle 400.00
Plane, Plow, Auburn Tool, Boxwood Nuts 385.00
Plane, Plow, Casey & Co., Wooden 800.00
Plane, Plow, Chelor, Mid–1700s, Box 7000.00
Plane, Plow, Howland, Boxwood Nuts 165.00
Plane, Rabbet, Hosea Edson & C. Tobey, 1 x 10 5/8 In. 100.00
Plane, Rabbet, Scrollwork On Top, Teardrop Pinwheel Inlays On Side 82.50
Plane, Rabbet, Stanley, No. 278, No Fence 130.00
Plane, Rounding, Boat Shape, Chip Carved Allover, Cherry, Inscribed 1615 .... 1402.50
Plane, Sargent, No. 407 .... 150.00
Plane, Scrub, Stanley, No. 40, Rosewood 45.00
Plane, Smoothing, Bailey, No. 1 .... 450.00 To 700.00
Plane, Smoothing, Edward Preston & Sons, Parallel Sides, Rosewood Handle, 9 In. 135.00
Plane, Smoothing, Stanley, No. 122 .... 40.00
Plane, Smoothing, Victor, No. 04, Japanned, Hardwood Handle & Knob 78.00
Plane, Spill, Table Mounted, Beech & Mahogany, 15 In. 175.00
Plane, Stanley, No. 55, With Cutters, Instruction Book 225.00
Plane, Stanley, No. 129, With Fence, 1 Blade 160.00
Plane, Stanley, No. 190, Box 85.00
Plane, Toothing, H. George, Beech, 2–In. James Cam Butter 48.00
Plane, Yankee Plow, D. Hubbard, Chamfered, 9 3/4 In. 1300.00
Pliers, Long Nose, Keen Kutter, 4 3/4 In. 15.00
Pliers, Winchester 35.00

Plumb & Level, Stanley, No. 98, 12 In. 325.00
Plumb Bob, Stanley, No. 2, Pat. Apr. 28, 1874 .... 135.00
Plumb Bob, Stanley, No. 5, Cast Iron 150.00
Press, Bookbinder's, Cast Iron, American 285.00
Printing Press, Chandler & Price, Black, Designs, 1885, 4 x 4 Ft. 675.00
Printing Set, Wooden Stamp, Letters, Numbers, Ruler, Wooden Box, 1896, 78 Piece 55.00
Protractor, Bevel, Union, No. 612, Box 38.00
Pulley, Well, Iron 25.00
Punch Watch 150.00
Quill Winder, Signed John Gilman, Some Missing Parts 225.00
Router, Beech Base, Brass Fittings, England 170.00
Rule, Arch Joint, Stanley, No. 12, 2 Fold 80.00
Rule, Caliper, Stanley, No, 13, 2 Fold, 6 In. 35.00
Rule, Ivory, Stanley, No. 87 .... 430.00
Rule, Lufkin, No. 39, Ivory, Silver Hinges 250.00
Rule, Lufkin, No. 863L, With Level & Protractor 85.00
Rule, Stanley, No. 15 .... 95.00
Rule, Zigzag, Victor, No. L 856, 6 Ft. 30.00
Ruler, Folding, Ivory, Brass Trim, 12 In. 135.00
Ruler, Shoe Size, Belchor 55.00
Ruler, Slide, Ivory, Patent 1900 .... 250.00
Ruler, Stanley, No. 70, 4 Fold, 2 Ft. 80.00
Ruler, Walking, Lufkin, No. 202, Bell, 100 Ft. 15.00
Ruler, With Caliper, Ivory, Silver Trim, 12 In. 145.00
Saw, Jeweler's, Lancaster, Brass, Cotter Pin Blade Holder, 1800s 250.00
Saw, Rip, Crank & Belt Driven, W. F. & J. Barnes, Pat. April 17, 1877 .... 800.00
Saw, Scroll, Pedal Powered, W. F. & J. Barnes, Pat. March 1876 .... 1000.00
Saw, Scroll, Seneca Falls Mfg., Treadle, Empire, 1860s 1025.00
Scale, Log, Lufkin, No. 524 .... 35.00
Scissors, Keen Kutter 10.00
Scissors, Winchester 20.00
Screwdriver, Irwin, Marked Bell System, Black Handle 12.00
Screwdriver, Yankee, No. 131A, Spiral Ratchet 55.00
Scythe, Hand Forged, 18th Century, Primitive, 19 In. 45.00
Sharpener, Ice Skate, Iron 45.00
Shaving Horse, Ax Shaped Head, Cutout Heart Between 2 Boards, Splayed Legs 750.00
Shears, Circular, Tinsmith's, Peck, Snow & Wilcox 500.00
Shell Reducing Cartridge, Pat. 1899 .... 20.00
Shovel, Grain, Walnut, 19th Century, 36 In. 193.00
Shovel, Grain, Winter Scene, Painted 450.00
Shovel, Grain, Wooden, Traces of Gold Paint, 36 In. 138.00
Skein Winder, Hand Turned Spindles, Automatic Counter, 1850–1860 .... 189.00
Splitter, Steer, Hand Forged, 18th Century, Primitive, 29 1/4 In. 45.00
Spoke Shave, E. C. Stearns, Flexible Sole 95.00
Spoke Shave, Universal, Stanley, No. 67 .... 65.00
Spurs, Inlaid Silver Heel Band, Rowel Shank, Garcia Saddlery, Calif. Style, 1930s 2150.00
Square, Lufkin Taylor, Brass Ends 25.00
Stamp, Complete Letters & Numbers, Steel, 1/2 In. 85.00
Stapler, Office, Speed Products, Bakelite, c.1870 .... 15.75
Stone, Sharpening, Winchester 35.00
Strap Hinge, Wrought Iron, Rectangular Plate Pintel, 20 In., 6 Piece 82.50
Swift, Carved Hand & Vines, Red & Blue Paint 2475.00
Swift, Yarn, Table, Clamp, Wooden 55.00
Tape Measure, Stanley, No. 6386n, 6 Ft. 40.00
Tape Shooter, For Packing, Cast Iron, Fancy, Victorian 50.00
Tractor, Walking, Walsh, Gas Powered 125.00
Trammel, Sawtooth, Wrought Iron, 19 1/2 In. 150.00
Trammel, Turned Hook, Single Candle Cup, Adjustable Bobeche, Iron, 27 1/4 In. ... 2525.00
Trammel, Wrought Iron, 12 3/4 In. 95.00
Transit, Brass, Label Frederick W. Lincoln Jr., Boston, Tripod, 19th Century 550.00
Transit, Girlie, Brass, Tripod & Case, c.1860 .... 1375.00
Traveler, Single Bar, Ringed Wooden Handle 45.00

Trencher, Wooden, Arrowhead Shaped Handles, Round	250.00
Truncheon, Police, Oak, Mottled Patina, England, 20 In.	95.00
Twibil, Short Handle, American	350.00
Vacuum Cleaner, Barrnett's Sanitary, Hand Held	40.00
Vacuum Cleaner, Wireless	3.00
Warmer, Mitten, Copper	85.00
Wax Jack, Brass, England, Early 18th Century, 4 In.	220.00
Weatherstrip, Stanley, No. 238, 7 Cutters, Japanning	200.00
Wheelbarrow, Red	385.00
Wheelbarrow, Wooden, Late 19th Century, Large	340.00˙
Work Bench, Maple Top, Dovetailed Vises, Dated 1896, 26 x 84 In.	825.00
Work Bench, Old Blue Paint, Tin Top	550.00
Wrench, Adjustable, Bullard, No. 1, 0–6 In.	65.00
Wrench, Bergman, Queen City, 4–In. S Handle	65.00
Wrench, Horse Carriage, Cast Iron	2.50
Wrench, Pipe, Brass	60.00
Wrench, Socket, Mechanics, T Handle, Iron	2.00
Yardstick, Folding, Wooden, Tupperware	7.00
Yarn Winder, 4 Arms, Turned Spindles, Heart Shape Base, Maple, E. Frost, 44 In.	385.00
Yarn Winder, Reel Type, Pine, Mortised Frame, Green Paint, Iron Handle, 24 In. ...	83.00
Yarn Winder, Shoe Foot, 18th Century	235.00
Yarn Winder, Various Hardwoods, Geared Counter Mechanism, 36 In.	93.00
Yarn Winder, Walnut, America, 19th Century, 40 In.	55.00

TOOTHPICK HOLDERS are sometimes called *toothpicks* by collectors. The variously shaped containers used to hold small wooden toothpicks are made of glass, china, or metal. Most of the toothpick holders are Victorian. Additional items may be found in other categories, such as Bisque, Silver Plate, Slag Glass, etc.

Aluminum, Woman's Rear End	12.00
Atlanta	30.00
Aunt Jemima, Bisque	4.25
Beaded Ovals In Sand, Apple Green	175.00
Beaded Swag, Red Stain, Opalescent	40.00
Beaded Swag, White Opalescent	100.00
Beatty Rib, Blue Opalescent	30.00
Bird Tips Into Box, Spears Toothpick, Metal Beak, Red, Black, 6 1/4 In.	190.00
Blazing Heart	45.00
Bonzo The Dog, White & Orange, Porcelain	35.00
Boy At Fountain, 5 1/2 In.	85.00
Cherub, Bisque, Lavender, Gold Trim, 4 In.	18.00
Cherub, Lavender, Gold Trim, Bisque, 4 In.	35.00
Cut Glass, Fan & Diamond, Footed	40.00
Cuttyhunk Life–Saving Station	35.00
Daisy & Fern	110.00
Diamond Spear, Blue Opalescent	125.00
Diamond Spearhead, Cobalt Blue Opalescent	195.00
Diamond Spearhead, Green Opalescent	115.00
Diamond Spearhead, Vaseline Opalescent	65.00
Diamond Spearhead, Yellow Opalescent	165.00
Dog, Holding Holder	15.00
Fern, White Opalescent	195.00
Gentleman Swirl, Blue Opalescent	185.00
Iris With Meander, Blue Opalescent	100.00 To 110.00
Iris With Meander, Green Opalescent, Gold Trim	55.00 To 65.00
Iris With Meander, Vaseline	125.00
Leaf Mold, Vasa Murrhina	100.00
Little Lobe, Souvenir	50.00
Reverse Swirl, Cranberry Opalescent	225.00
Ribbed Lattice, Cranberry Opalescent	250.00
Ribbed Spiral, Blue Opalescent	70.00
Ruby Glass, 1894	30.00
Skunk, By Tree Trunk	15.00

Souvenir of Ireland, China 20.00
State Fair, 1917, Custard Glass, Ring & Beads 85.00
Swag With Brackets, Green Opalescent 125.00
Victorian, St. Louis Silver, Ornate 125.00
Wild Bouquet, Blue Opalescent 300.00
Wild Bouquet, Custard Glass, Design 850.00
Witch, Blue Milk Glass, Vogelsong Summit 7.00
Woman, Hat, Bisque 50.00
Woodpecker On Log, Metal, Mechanical 12.00
Wreath & Shell, White Opalescent 125.00

TORQUAY is the name given to ceramics by several potteries working near Torquay, England, from 1870 until 1962. Until about 1900, the potteries used local red clay to make classical-style art pottery vases and figurines. Then they turned to making souvenir wares. Items were dipped in colored slip and decorated with painted slip and sgraffito designs. They often had mottoes or proverbs, and scenes of cottages, ships, birds, or flowers. The *Scandy* design was a symmetrical arrangement of brushstrokes and spots done in colored slips. Potteries included Watcombe Pottery (1870–1962); Torquay Terra–Cotta Company (1875–1905); Aller Vale (1881–1924); Torquay Pottery (1908–1940); and Longpark (1883–1957).

TORQUAY

Bowl, Motto Ware, 5 1/4 In. 55.00
Candlestick, Thistles, Marked, 5 1/2 In., Pair 110.00
Coffee Mug & Chocolate Cup, Landscape Scene, 4 Piece 150.00
Coffeepot, Motto Ware, Scandy, 7 1/4 In. 65.00
Cracker Jar, Ruby Glass 295.00
Creamer, Cottage, Motto Ware, 3 In. .... 30.00 To 35.00
Creamer, Fresh From The Dairy, Scandy, 3 In. 35.00
Cup & Saucer, Cottage, Motto Ware 45.00
Cup & Saucer, Cottage, No Wealth But Life, 4 3/4-In. Saucer 40.00
Eggcup, Hose, Verse 28.00
Jam Jar, Cottage, Motto Ware, 4 1/2 In. 45.00
Jam Jar, Underplate, Sea Gull 33.00
Jug, Cottage, Time & Tide Wait For No Man, Square, 3 1/2 In. 55.00
Mug, Cottage, Drop On Dew On Grass Blades, 5 In. 45.00
Mug, Cottage, Motto Ware, 4 3/4 In. 48.00
Pitcher, Cottage, Motto Ware, 4 1/8 In. 45.00
Plate, Motto Ware, 8 In. 18.00
Tray, Pin, Scandy, A Place For Pins, 2 1/2 x 5 In. 28.00
Vase, Diving Kingfisher, Water Lilies, 3 Handles, Marked, 9 3/4 In. 220.00
Vase, Double, Tree Stumps, Bench, Flowers At Base, Majolica, 5 In. 95.00
Vase, Red Fruit, Green Leaves, 3 Handles, 8 In. 65.00
Vase, Rooster, Motto Ware, 2 1/4 In. 60.00
Vase, Sack, Black Cockerel, Motto Ware, 4 x 4 1/2 In. 75.00

TORTOISESHELL GLASS was made during the 1800s and after by the Sandwich Glass Works of Massachusetts and some firms in Germany. Tortoiseshell glass is, of course, named for its resemblance to real shell from a tortoise. It has been reproduced.

Compote, 8 In. 95.00
Pitcher, Collar Base Coming Up Body, 9 In. 150.00

TORTOISESHELL is the shell of the tortoise. It has been used as inlay and to make small decorative objects since the seventeenth century. Some species of tortoise are now on the endangered species list, and objects made from these shells cannot be sold legally.

Box, Serpentine Rectangular Form, Velvet Lined, Ivory Edges, 5 1/2 In. 330.00
Box, Trinket, 3 1/8 In. 275.00
Case, Card, Regency, 4 x 3 In. 165.00
Comb, Folds Out, Carved American Indian Case, 7 In. 395.00
Hairpin, Vine Design, Stones, Midwest, 1850, 3 Piece 30.00

TOY collectors have special clubs, magazines, and shows. Toys are designed to entice children, and today they have attracted new interest among adults who are still children at heart. All types of toys are collected. Tin toys, iron toys, battery operated toys, and many others are collected by specialists. Dolls, Games, Teddy Bears, and Bicycles are listed in their own categories. Other toys may be found under company or celebrity names.

8 Jointed Acrobatic Figures, Wood, Carved, John Scholl, Penna., 1900, 17 3/4 In.	990.00
Acrobat, Boy On Trapeze, Windup, Celluloid, Japan	125.00
Acrobat, Clockwork, Tin Lithograph, Japan, 11 In.	44.00
Acrobats, Wood & Paper Lithograph On Wood, Crandall, Box, 10 x 6 In.	687.00
Adding Machine, Wolverine, Box	14.00 To 30.00
Admiral Peary of The North, Tin, Windup Dog Sled, Martin, 1909, 8 1/2 In.	1250.00
Africa, Ostrich With Cart, Tin, String Wind Drive, Lehmann, 1900, Box, 7 In.	2300.00
Airplane, Air Devil, Windup, Tin, Strauss, 1926, 9 1/2 In. Wingspread	500.00
Airplane, American Airlines, DC7, Battery Operated, Yonezawa, 1960s	515.00
Airplane, Biplane, RAF Marked, Pressed Steel, Kingsbury	495.00
Airplane, Blue Ribbon Flyer, Balsa Wood, Box	12.00
Airplane, Boeing 727, 5 In.	22.00
Airplane, Boeing Strato, Wyandotte, Box	375.00
Airplane, Bomber, Camouflage, Tin, Windup, Marx, 1939, 19 In.	316.00
Airplane, Capitol Airline, Globe Master, Battery Operated, Tin Plate	225.00
Airplane, Cessna 182, Friction, Tin, Plastic Windshield & Prop, 12 In.	125.00
Airplane, Cessna Sky Taxi, Friction, Tin, Spinning Prop., T. T. Co., 1950s	75.00
Airplane, Dual Cannon, Propeller Turns When Cannon Fires, 13 In.	650.00
Airplane, Eastern 727, Japan, 16–In. Wingspan	95.00
Airplane, Fighter, Camouflaged Tin, Cross & Swastika Decals, Heinkel No. 70	215.00
Airplane, Fighter, World War II, Fold Up Wings, Hubley	55.00
Airplane, Fisher–Price, 12–In. Wingspan	25.00
Airplane, Flying Circus Decal, Hubley	50.00
Airplane, Flying Tigers 747, Plastic, Advertising, 14–In. Wingspan, Box	110.00
Airplane, Fokker, Vindex, Cast Iron	550.00
Airplane, Globemaster Troop Carrier, Bandai, Japan, Box, 13 1/4 In.	660.00
Airplane, Gold, Red, Spring Loaded Retractable Landing Gear, Tipp, Box	1435.00
Airplane, Jet Fighter, Shooting Star, Remote Control, Marx, 13–In. Wingspan	110.00
Airplane, Jet, Eagle, Blue, Silver, Tootsietoy, 1979	22.00
Airplane, Learjet, Red, Silver Bottom, Black Jets, Tonka, 1979, 9 x 7 In.	39.00
Airplane, Lockheed Sirus Steelcraft, Pressed Steel, Replace Tail Section, 1930s	1295.00
Airplane, Lufthansa, Marklin, 1930s	6335.00
Airplane, Pan Am, Boeing 747, Plastic, Gray, White, Battery Operated, China, 13 In.	20.00
Airplane, Pan–Am, Battery Operated, Schuco, Tin, 16 In.	445.00
Airplane, Pip–Squeak Airlines, Pilot & Stewardess Dolls, Pull Toy	30.00
Airplane, Silver Eagle, Windup, Aluminum, 13–In. Wingspan	125.00
Airplane, Singer Engine, Wooden Wheels, Pressed Steel	40.00
Airplane, Sky Taxi, Cessna Plane, Japan, 12 In.	145.00
Airplane, Spirit of St. Louis, American National	5500.00
Airplane, Starfire Rocky F949, Tin	185.00
Airplane, Stun, Cox Red Knight, Tool Box, Accessories, 10–In. Wingspan	87.00
Airplane, Sun Rubber, 1920s	50.00
Airplane, TWA Super Jet, Marx, Battery Operated	125.00
Airplane, U.S. Air Force X–15, Friction, Tin, Masuya, Box, 9 1/2 In.	169.00
Airplane, U.S. Army Air Fighter, Friction, Tin, Army Colors, Japan, 8 In.	110.00
Airplane, United Boeing, White Tires, Cast Iron	185.00
Airplane, Viking, Dinky Toy, England	55.00
Airplane, Wyant, 1920s	65.00
Airplane–Go–Round, Airplanes Around Tower, Windup, Painted Steel, 1930s, 12 In.	605.00
Airship, Pull Toy, Original Paint & Decals, Pressed Steel, 27 In.	550.00
Alabama Coon Jigger, Pedestal, Windup, Lehmann, 1912	490.00
Alligator, Open Felt Mouth, Glass Eyes, Mohair, Steiff	225.00
Alligator, Schoenhut	500.00
Alligator, Snapping, Windup, Tin, S & E, 12 In.	149.00

Alligator, Windup, Tin, German, 6 3/4 In.	143.00
Alligator, Windup, Tin, Penny Toy, 7 1/4 In.	220.00
Alphabet High Chair, Paper Lithograph On Wood, Reed, Box	715.00
Ambulance, Lithographed Nurse, Spoked Wheels, Tin, c.1917, 6 In.	175.00
Ambulance, Sturditoy	4950.00
American Theater, Little Red Riding Hood Play, Booklet, McLoughlin, 14 x 12 In.	990.00
Amos & Andy Fresh Air Taxi, Tin Litho, Windup, Marx, 1900, 8 In. ....900.00 To	1400.00
Analglyph Stereo Picture Set, 2 Color Eyeglasses, Redeffer Art Co., Box	220.00
Andy, Knockoff, Derby & Cigar, Wooden, Push Toy, Germany	95.00
Apollo–X Moon Challenger, Battery Operated, Box	200.00
Apple Vendor, Seated Black Man, Pulling Cart, Windup, Tin, Martin & Co.	500.00
Ark, 44 & 12 Matched Pairs Animals, Painted Paper, Germany, 17 x 5 x 7 In.	1375.00
Ark, Paper On Wood, On Wheels, ABC Block Set, 11 x 3 x 6 In.	440.00
Arnold, Walking Seal, Umbrella Moves Up & Down, Windup, Germany	110.00
Astronaut, Battery Operated, Tin, Cragstan, Daiya, Box, 14 In.	2000.00
Astronaut, Blue Rosko, Battery Operated, Tin, Japan, Box, 13 In.	3200.00
Astronaut, Blue, Battery Operated, Tin, Walks, Fires Gun, Flashing Lights, 11 In. ...	585.00
Astronaut, Space Patrol, Step–Over Action, Vinyl Head, Tin, Tomiyama, 5 In.	445.00
B. O. Plenty, Windup, Waddles Around, Hat Bounces, Marx, 1930s .... 100.00 To	175.00
Baby, Crawling, O'Brien, 1893	995.00
Badge, Buck Jones, Horseshoe Club	45.00
Badge, Wyatt Earp, Dated 1957	47.00
Bake Set, Fry, Box, 1930s	325.00
Baker, Roller Skating, Windup, Tin & Cloth, 7 In.	190.00
Balance, Tin Lithograph, Figure Walks Down Platform, 3 1/2 In.	99.00
Balky Mule, Clown Face, Tin, Clockwork, Box, Lehmann, 7 x 5 In. .... 190.00 To	495.00
Balky Mule, Windup, Tin, Marx, Box	300.00
Ballerina, Dancing, Metal Activator, Marx	125.00
Balloon Seller, Tin Lithograph, Windup, Germany, 6 1/2 In.	440.00
Bambi, Steiff	150.00
Banjo Cowboy, Tin, Windup, Linemar, 5 1/2 In.	164.00
Banjo Playing Monkey, Windup, Japan, Box	95.00
Barbie & Ken Little Theater, 3 Double Sided Cardboard, With 18 Tickets	105.00
Barnum's Museum, Educational, 5 Moving Strips, C. C. Shepard, Box, 11 x 10 In.	995.00
Baseball, Batter, Battery Operated, Tin, Hits Balls, Team Litho Base, 5 1/2 In.	835.00
Baseball, Home Run King, Windup, Tin, Sellrite Prod., 1920s	330.00
Bassinet, Doll's, Wicker	85.00
Bat, Steiff	135.00
Bathtub, 2 Color Tin Plate, 1890, Germany	90.00
Battleship, Key Wind, Tin, German Bing	195.00
Battleship, New Mexico, Tin, Gray, Green, Clockwork Motor, Orkin, 25 x 9 1/2 In.	2300.00
Battleship, New York, Orkin, Clockwork, 25 In.	495.00
Battleship, Wooden, Green & Black, 36 1/2 In.	225.00
Be–Bop Jivin', Jigger, Tin Lithograph of Circus Clown, Marx, c.1950, 8 In.	440.00
Bears are also listed in the Teddy Bear category	
Bear, Blowing Balloon, Battery Operated, Alps	195.00
Bear, Brown Plush, Key Wind, Occupied Japan	75.00
Bear, Brown, Windup, Walks, Shaking Head, Stops & Looks Around, Japan	70.00
Bear, Dentist, Battery Operated, Shines Light Up and Down	550.00
Bear, Drinking, Pours Soda Into Glass & Drinks, Windup, Japan	110.00
Bear, Fishing Fish & Hat, Battery Operated, Alps	45.00
Bear, Golfer, Mechanical, Japan, 1950s	395.00
Bear, Housekeeper, Battery Operated, Plush Over Tin, Head Turns, 9 In.	311.00
Bear, Jumping, Windup, White & Brown Fur, Illustrated Box	85.00
Bear, Papa, Smoking Pipe, Battery Operated, Box	120.00
Bear, Playing Golf, Windup, Tin	30.00
Bear, Shoeshine, Battery Operated, Cragston	195.00
Bear, Straw Stuffed, On Wheels	725.00
Bear, Traveler's Suitcase, Battery Operated, Plush Over Tin, Japan, Box, 9 In.	439.00
Bear, Tumbles, Porter, Walks & Somersaults, Battery Operated, Box	105.00
Bear, Walking, Plush Over Tin, Walks On All Fours, Occupied Japan, 5 In.	55.00
Bear, Windup, Turns Pages of Tin Baby Book, Japan	165.00

Bear, With Xylophone, Line Mar 180.00
Beaver, Standing, Frizzy, Light Brown, 5 1/4 In. ....*Illus* 18.00
Bed, Doll's, Carved Mahogany, 4 Poster, 1820, Mattress & Bolster 2250.00
Bed, Doll's, Iron, Salesman's Sample, 1930 Style .... 135.00 To 150.00
Bed, Doll's, Iron, Ticking Mattress, 1920s, 14 In. 65.00
Bed, Doll's, Maple, Spool Turned, Honey Color, 1780 .... 1795.00
Bed, Doll's, Metal, Blue Paint, Wood Casters, Amsco 45.00
Bed, Doll's, Pine & Poplar, Red Repaint, 12 1/2 x 27 In. 65.00
Bed, Doll's, Rope, Ball & Ball Turned Posts, 2 Mattresses & Pillows, 14 3/4 In. 95.00
Bed, Doll's, Rope, Curly Maple, Linens & Crazy Quilt, Small 525.00
Bed, Doll's, Sheets & Round Pillow, Mattress Cover, 7 1/2 x 12 In. 595.00
Bed, Doll's, Turned Walnut Tester, 1830, America, 24 In. 2200.00
Bell, Black Man Riding Log, Pull Toy, Cast Iron, 5 x 6 In. 500.00
Bell, Darkie, No. 56, Victorian, Cast Iron 550.00
Bell, Harold Lloyd, Tin Lithograph, Germany 450.00
Bell, Landing of Columbus, Monochromed Gold, Removable Figure, 7 In. 550.00
Bicycles are listed in their own category
Bicyclist, Clockwork, Tin, Germany, 8 In. 660.00
Billiard Champion, Pool Player, Hits Ball, Repeats, Ki Co., Germany, 1920, 6 In. ... 560.00
Billy Goat, Straw Stuffed, 1940s, 20 In. 40.00
Bird, Mohair, Windup, Vibrates, Metal Eyes & Feet, Orange & Tan 75.00
Bird, Singing, Celluloid, Occupied Japan 50.00
Black Mama, Ramp Walker, Wilson Walker, 1930s, 4 1/2 In. 90.00
Black Man Tap Dances & Swings Arms, Windup, 1950s, 8 In. 325.00
Blocks, Alphabet of Country Scenes, McLoughlin, Hinged Box 1435.00
Blocks, Alphabet, Girls 1 Side, Animals Other Side, Schoenhut 800.00
Blocks, Alphabet, Wood, Embossed, Box, 27 Piece, 2–In. Square 82.00
Blocks, Architectural, Stained Glass Windows, Wooden, Germany, Box, 12 x 10 In. ... 220.00
Blocks, Beasts & Birds, Alphabet & Animal, Circular, Lyman & Whitney, 1874 ...... 745.00
Blocks, Building & Instructo, Crandall, Wood Panels, 8 x 5 In. 176.00
Blocks, Fairyland, ABC, Numbers, 9 Piece 575.00
Blocks, Fairyland, McLoughlin, 1897, 10 x 13 In. 225.00
Blocks, Little Pet's Picture, ABC Picture, McLoughlin, Paper Over Flat Wood, 1884 ... 350.00
Blocks, Nested, Mammoth Story, Crandall, 9 Build 38 In. Tower 360.00
Blocks, Pictorial & Alphabet, Lithographed Wooden Box, McLaughlin, 1884 .... 500.00
Blocks, Picture Builder Series, Puzzle, McLoughlin, 1894, 32 Piece 660.00
Blocks, Picture of Surreal Looking Airship, Reverse Locomotive, McLoughlin 1215.00
Blocks, Santa Claus, Snug In Bed Scroll, Puzzle, McLoughlin, 1889 .... 525.00
Blocks, Santa Claus, The Night Before Christmas, Puzzle, McLoughlin, 1889 .... 2315.00
Blocks, Sawyer Sunday, Biblical, Gast, 1889, 24 Paper Over Wood 300.00
Blocks, Victorian Children In Different Scenes, 6 Lithographed Pictures, 1890s 250.00
Blocks, White Squadron Puzzle, McLoughlin, Warships, 1892, 21 x 11 In. 1595.00
Blocks, Wonder Cubes, Singer, 9 Paper Lithograph Cover Hollow Wood 1650.00
Blocks, Wood, 1936, Colorful Paper Label, Animals, Numbers, Letters 75.00
Blocks, Yankee Doodle ABC, McLoughlin, Paper Over Flat Wood 335.00
Bo Jangle, Black, Wooden Jointed Figure, Tin Arms & Hat, 1940s, Box 275.00

Toy, Beaver, Standing, Frizzy,
Light Brown, 5 1/4 In.

Toy, Bowling Set, Mikado Ten-Pins, 3 Balls,

Box, 1885, 10 1/4 In.

Toy, Onion, Windup, Plastic, 2 3/4 In.

Toy, Cucumber, Mechanical, Key Wind,

Plastic, 3 1/4 In.

Bo Jangle, Jointed, Wooden, Tin Arms & Hat, Mechanical Dances, Box 275.00
Boar, Wheeled Platform Penny Toy, Germany, 2 1/2 In. 373.00
Boat, Blue, Wood & Canvas, 28 In. 95.00
Boat, Carved From 1 Piece of Wood, Brown, Blue Paint, 12 3/4 In. 70.00
Boat, City of Chicago, Wilkens 1750.00
Boat, City of New York, Cast Iron, 15 In. 1540.00
Boat, Great Flying, Friction, Metal, China, Box, 13 In. 39.00
Boat, Gun, Clockwork, Marklin, Repainted, 12 In. 575.00
Boat, Gun, Kasuga, Clockwork, Fires Gun, Turns Rudder, Bing, Steel, 1904, 15 In. 245.00
Boat, Launch, Tin, Clockwork, 9 x 3 1/2 In. 105.00
Boat, Light Green Paint, Gold Trim, Wooden, 14 1/4 In. 95.00
Boat, Passenger Liner, Clockwork, Tin, Germany, 12 1/2 x 4 1/2 In. 335.00
Boat, Speedboat, Battery Operated, Tin, Fleet Line, Box, 13 In. 165.00
Boat, Tug, Battery Operated, Shakes, Whistles, Neptune, Tin, 14 In. 50.00
Boat, Tug, Buddy L 5500.00
Boat, Tug, Neptune, Bump–Go Action, Windup, Engine Noise, Whistle, Tin, 15 In. 135.00
Boat, U.S. Merchant Marine Freighter, Tin, Clockwork, 10 x 5 In. 575.00
Boat, Wood, Lithograph Paper, Sailors In Rowboat, 29 1/2 In. 935.00
Bombo, Acrobatic Monk, Unique Art, Windup 165.00
Boots, G.I. Joe, On Card 225.00
Bow & Arrow Set, Lacquered Stand, 10 Arrows, Hardwood Box 445.00
Bowling Set, Mikado Ten–Pins, 3 Balls, Box, 1885, 10 1/4 In. ....*Illus* 3300.00
Box 'em Sock 'em Robots, Marx, Box, 1960 .... 40.00
Box, Snake Pops Out When Lid Is Open, Wooden, Floral Design, Green Paint, 4 In. 885.00
Boy, At Chalkboard, Tin, Windup 1900.00
Boy, Black, With Mule, Pull Toy, Cast Iron, 1890s .... 800.00 To 885.00
Boy, Fishing, Windup, Tin, Plastic Base, Yone, Box 60.00
Boy, Native, Beats Drum, Windup, Leans Forward and Back, Earrings, Tin, 7 In. 350.00
Boy, On Bicycle, Windup, Ball On Back End, Tin, 1950s, 4 In. 45.00
Boy, On Cycle, Hill Climber, Battery, Hubley, 6 1/2 In. 800.00
Boy, On Tricycle, Celluloid, Windup, Attached Dog, Prewar, 5 1/2 In. 145.00
Boy, On Tricycle, Lithographed Metal, Windup, Marx, 1920s, 9 x 8 In. 225.00
Boy, Swinging On Trapeze, Celluloid, Windup, Japan 140.00
Boy, Trapeze, Celluloid, Windup, Box 140.00
Boy, Walking, Hoop, Penny, Tin Lithograph, Souvenir Universal Theaters, 3 In. 1760.00
Bozo The Clown, Windup, Tin, Plays Drums, Alps, 8 In. 495.00
Bucket, Red, Black Union Stencil, 4 1/2 In. 350.00
Bucking Bronco, Windup, Celluloid, TM, Box 125.00
Buffalo, Carved Head, Leather Horns, Glass Eyes, Schoenhut .... 325.00 To 635.00

Buffalo, Glass Eyes, Schoenhut 1050.00
Buffet, Doll's, Step Back, Wolverine, Tin Lithograph, 6 1/2 x 17 x 20 In. 85.00
Building Set, Girder, Panel, Bridge, & Turnpike, Motorized, Box, Kenner, 1960 ...... 75.00
Building Set, Painted Tin, Interlocking, Indestructible, Pat. 1882, Box, 7 x 3 In. 605.00
Bull, Fighting, Battery Operated, Grows, Nostrils Smoke, Alps, Box 130.00
Bulldozer, Big Bull, Blade, No Tracks, Yellow, Matchbox, 1975 .... 4.75
Bulldozer, Caterpillar, Red Metal, Plastic Yellow Blade, Tootsietoy, 4 1/2 x 3 In. ... 10.00
Bulldozer, Crawler, Orange, Black, Rubber Tracks, Metal, Tonka No. 6, 9 x 6 In. ... 25.00
Bulldozer, Friction, Japan, 1950s, 7 1/2 In. 100.00
Bulldozer, Front End Blade, Light Green, Structo, 12 In. 29.00
Bulldozer, Green, Red & Black Trim, Working Lift, Dinky No. 561 .... 98.00
Bulldozer, Mighty Tonka No. 3907, Yellow, Black, 16 3/4 In. 25.00
Bulldozer, Orange, Tonka, 12 In. 110.00
Bulldozer, Red, Yellow Blade, Black Wheels, Vinyl, 7 In. 10.00
Bulldozer, Robot, Forward, Reverse, Light, United Pioneer Co., 1950s, 8 In. 895.00
Bulldozer, Sparkling Tractor, Driver, Tin, Windup, Box, 1940s 195.00
Bulldozer, Yellow Cab, Red Blade Dual Rear Wheels, Rubber, Auburn, 7 In. 69.00
Bunny Cart, With Bell, NPS, 1938 .... 135.00
Bunny Pull Candy Container Cart, Chicks, Fisher-Price, 1940, 9 In. 45.00
Bunny, Bubble Blowing, Battery Operated, Box 110.00
Burro, Painted Eyes, Schoenhut 350.00
Bus Driver's Outfit, Jackie Gleason, Coin Changer, Puncher, Empire Plastic Corp. 325.00
Bus, Century of Progress, Arcade, 7 In. 225.00
Bus, Century of Progress, Arcade, Box, 10 In. 900.00
Bus, Continental Trailways, Friction, Tin 35.00
Bus, Double Decker, Red, Cream, No Rear Stairs, Dinky Toy 60.00
Bus, Greyhound Lines, New York World's Fair, Arcade, 1 7/8 x 6 3/4 In. 200.00
Bus, Greyhound, New York World's Fair, Arcade, Cast Iron, 8 1/4 In. 165.00
Bus, Greyhound, Scenic, Friction, Box, 13 In. 95.00
Bus, Interstate Double Decker, Strauss, Green, Yellow Striping, 10 1/2 In. ... 450.00 To 995.00
Bus, Jitney, Clockwork, Tin Lithograph, Strauss, 9 1/2 In. 335.00
Bus, London Transportation, Esso Safety Grip Tires, Red, 1970, Dinky No. 289 ...... 15.00
Bus, Public Service, Blue, Original Sample Tag, 4 1/2 x 14 In. 4600.00
Bus, Robot, Clockwork, Bum & Go Action, Tin, Woodhaven, 14 1/2 In. 125.00
Bus, Royal Bus Line, Headlights, Rack, Luggage Compartment, Marx, c.1930, 11 In. 95.00
Bus, School, Orange, Metal, Buddy L, 7 In. 6.00
Bus, Sightseeing, Battery Operated, Tin, Lift Up Lid Windows, Japan, 9 In. 216.00
Bus, Wolverine, Mechanical, 1940s, Box, 14 In. 195.00
Busy Bridge, Marx 325.00
Butterfly, Push Toy, Paper Lithograph, On Tin, Cast Iron Wheels, 9-In. Wingspan 176.00
Buzzy Bee, Fisher-Price 8.00
Cabinet, Doll's, Dish, Oak 185.00
Cable Car, San Francisco, Friction, Bell, Lithographed Metal, Box, 8 1/4 In. 165.00
Cable Car, San Francisco, Tin 95.00
Cable Car, San Francisco, Tin, Gong, 3-D Figures, Japan, 1950s 65.00
Calliope, Elephant, Lion & Driver, Steiff 1200.00
Calliope, Steiff, Box 700.00
Camel, Arabina, Schoenhut 375.00
Cane, Secret Sam, Converts To Rifle, Lion Head Top, Plastic, Topper, 1965, 32 In. 89.00
Cannon, Airplane, Propeller Turns When Cannon Fires, 13 In. 650.00
Cannon, Big Band, Carbide, Iron, Large 60.00
Cannon, Big Boom, 17 In. 60.00
Canoe, Carved From 1 Piece of Wood, Dark Red Paint, 1 Paddle, 9 3/4 In. 65.00
Cap Gun, '49er, Internal Hammer, Revolving Cylinder, Stevens, 1940, 9 In. 350.00
Cap Gun, 49er, Stevens, Box 495.00
Cap Gun, Atomic Disintegrator, Hubley 65.00
Cap Gun, Automatic Repeater, 4 In. 15.00
Cap Gun, Automatic, Hubley 35.00
Cap Gun, Bango-O, Cast Iron, Cowboy, Horsehead, Stevens, 1930s, Box, 7 In. 139.00
Cap Gun, Bat Masterson Set, Cane & Vest, 1958, Gene Barry On Display Box 255.00
Cap Gun, Big Chief 35.00

Cap Gun, Big Horn Six–Shooter, Big Horn Sheep On Handle, Kilgore, 7 In. 40.00
Cap Gun, Bronzo, Kilgore 75.00
Cap Gun, Buffalo Bill, 14 In. 50.00
Cap Gun, Buffalo Bill, Long Barrel, 1890s 350.00
Cap Gun, Bulldozer, Derringer Shape, 6–Shot Cylinder, Cast Iron, 5 In. 110.00
Cap Gun, Chrome, Matched Pair 300.00
Cap Gun, Cowboy, Hubley, Box 175.00
Cap Gun, Daisy 35.00
Cap Gun, Deputy Pistol, Hubley, 1 In. 95.00
Cap Gun, Deputy, Metal, Scrolled, Medallion On Handle, Hubley, Badge, 10 In. 121.00
Cap Gun, Detective Special, Hubley 18.00
Cap Gun, Dixie 85.00
Cap Gun, Fanner 50, Mattel 65.00
Cap Gun, Fanner, Mattel, Box 150.00
Cap Gun, Flintlock, Hubley, 1950s 30.00
Cap Gun, Grizzly, Kilgore 110.00
Cap Gun, Hopalong, Metal Trigger, Leather Holster & Belt 55.00
Cap Gun, Junior Police Chief, Orange Grips, Die Cast 25.00
Cap Gun, Kit Carson 50–Shot Repeater, Metal, Kit On Handle, Kilgore, Box, 8 In. ... 110.00
Cap Gun, Kit Carson, Kilgore, Pair 100.00
Cap Gun, Lugar, Canada 30.00
Cap Gun, Nickel Plated, 5 1/2 In. 20.00
Cap Gun, Pluck, With Holster, Cast Iron 55.00
Cap Gun, Pony Boy, GS, 1950s 30.00
Cap Gun, Punch & Judy 895.00
Cap Gun, Ranger, Kilgore 125.00
Cap Gun, Red Ranger, Metal, Plastic, Box, 9 In. 146.00
Cap Gun, Remington, Nickel Finish, Plastic Grip, Revolving Cylinder, Hubley, 8 In. .. 150.00
Cap Gun, Repeating, Nickel Plated, 1930s, 4 In. 60.00
Cap Gun, Ric–O–Shay, No. 45, Hubley 75.00
Cap Gun, Ricochet, Hubley 55.00
Cap Gun, Rodeo, Amber Handle, Hubley, Box 25.00
Cap Gun, Rodeo, Leather Holster, Hubley, Box 25.00
Cap Gun, Scout, Rifle, Metal Trigger Mechanism, Plastic, Card, Marx, 1950s, 32 In. . 105.00
Cap Gun, Secret Agent, Box 25.00
Cap Gun, Secret Agent, Hamilton, Box 38.00
Cap Gun, Shoo Fly 165.00
Cap Gun, Smoking Texan Jr., Metal, Longhorn Design, Hubley, Box, 9 In. 110.00
Cap Gun, Stallion 45, Mark II, Bullets, Nichols 110.00
Cap Gun, Texan Jr., Hubley, Box .... 25.00 To 40.00
Cap Gun, Texan, Cast Iron, Box 135.00
Cap Gun, Texas Jr., Hubley, Gold Plated 145.00
Cap Gun, Tom Corbett, With Visor 45.00
Cap Gun, Trooper, Hubley .... 16.00 To 35.00
Cap Gun, Victor, 1880 .... 295.00
Cap Gun, Wagon Train, Holster, Double 125.00
Cap Gun, White & Black Steer Handle, Hubley 42.00
Cap Gun, Wyatt Earp 40.00
Cap Gun, ZI Zip 30.00
Cap Gun, Zorro, Holster, Marked 125.00
Capitol Hill Racer, Travels Down Ramp Into Station House & Back, Unique Art 150.00
Captain Blushwell, Battery Operated, Box 175.00
Captain Kangaroo & His Magic Zoo Colorforms Set, Box, 1960 .... 90.00
Captain Sandy Andy, Sand Toy, Wolverine, No. 63C, 1930s, Box 120.00
Car Carrier, 3 Austens, Cast Iron, Williams, 12 In. 1000.00
Car, Ambulance, Friction, Tin, 3 1/2 In. 20.00
Car, AMX Javelin, Black, Matchbox, 1972 .... 8.00
Car, Armored, U.S. Army, Tootsietoy 125.00
Car, Aston Martin, James Bond, Husky, Corgi 9.00
Car, Atom Jet, Yamaichi, Japan 1650.00
Car, Austin Healey, British Green, Matchbox, 1956 .... 17.00
Car, Austin, Mini Van, Austin, Corgi, Green 18.00
Car, Batmobile, Friction, Japan, Tin, 12 In. 250.00

Car, Bucking Bear, Friction, Tin, Japan, 1950s, 5 1/2 In. 150.00
Car, Buick, Convertible, 1940s, Die Cast, Hubley, 7 In. 100.00
Car, Buick, Convertible, Die Cast, Cast Iron Windshield, Hubley, 1940s, 7 In. 100.00
Car, Buick, Corgi, Kojak, Box, 1975 .... 65.00
Car, Buick, Regal, Man In Window, Roof Blinker, Doors Open, Corgi, 6 In. 15.00
Car, Buick, Retractable Top, Line Mark, Friction, 1959, 9 1/2 In. 40.00
Car, Buick, Roadmaster, Cream, Blue, AHI, Japan, 1 7/8 In. 7.00
Car, Buick, Sedan, 1927 Model, Celluloid, Red, Gold, Spare Tire, Arcade, 8 1/4 In. 3500.00
Car, Cadillac, Blue, Lone Star, 1962, 4 1/2 In. 20.00
Car, Cadillac, Convertible, Black, Tin, Friction, Bandai, 11 In. 418.00
Car, Cadillac, Friction, White, Tin, Japan, 12 In. 250.00
Car, Cadillac, Sedan, Tootsietoy, 1927 .... 60.00
Car, Carrier, Transmobile Jr., Wyandotte 85.00
Car, Century of Progress, Yellow, Cast Iron, Arcade, 1933, 6 1/2 In. 2500.00
Car, Chitty Chitty Bang Bang, Corgi 65.00
Car, Citroen CV, Gray, Matchbox, 1957 .... 17.00
Car, Convertible Roadster, Town & Country Car, Wooden, Buddy L 225.00
Car, Convertible Roaster, Removable Top, Tin, Nylint 75.00
Car, Convertible, Black, Silver Sides, Spare Tires, Golden Oldie, 1955 .... 10.00
Car, Convertible, Mesh Grille, Cast Iron, Arcade, 6 3/4 In. 770.00
Car, Corvette, Stingray, Racer, Battery Operated, Box 95.00
Car, Corvette, Stingray, Wire Wheels, Corgi, Silver 22.00
Car, Country Squire, Yellow 6.00
Car, Coupe, Green Paint, Missing Rumble Seat, Cast Iron, Arcade, 5 In. 85.00
Car, Coupe, No. 54, 5 Passenger, Master Deluxe, Blue, London, 6 In. 25.00
Car, Crazy, 2 Drivers, Windup, Tin, 9 In. 350.00
Car, Dodge Challenger, Toymari, Yellow, Matchbox, 1975 .... 5.00
Car, Dodge'M, Battery Operated, Tin, Bump-Go, Noise, Lights, Alps, 10 In. 242.00
Car, Dump Hopper, Buddy L, Outdoor Railroad 2865.00
Car, Dune Buggy, Yellow, Wood Wheels 4.00
Car, Fageol, Safety Coach, Arcade 330.00
Car, Ferrari, Ingap, Chrome, Battery Operated, 1950s, 12 In. 3500.00
Car, Ferrari, Marchesini F 1, Chrome, Windup, 1950s, 10 In. 3700.00
Car, Ferrari, Movosprint, Explosion Engine, 1950s, 12 In. 3950.00
Car, Fire Chief Coupe, Windup Siren & Lights, Red, c.1930s 325.00
Car, Fire Dept. Chief, Tin Lithograph, Red 7 Yellow, Friction, Japan, 4 In. 25.00
Car, Firebird III, Bump-Go, Lights, Noise, Cragstan, Battery Operated, Tin, 11 In. 440.00
Car, Flintstone, Flint Mobile, Ride-On 150.00
Car, Flivver Coupe, Black, Red Spoked Wheels, Buddy L, Label 1375.00
Car, Ford, Anglia, Matchbox 20.00
Car, Ford, Convertible, Lift Trunk, Bandai, 1955, 12 In. 750.00
Car, Ford, Fairlane, 1957, Convertible, Retractable Hard Top, Tin, Battery Operated 150.00
Car, Ford, Model A, Sedan, Arcade 400.00
Car, Ford, Model T Coupe, Cast Iron, Arcade 450.00
Car, Ford, Model T, 1912, Matchbox, Box 15.00
Car, Ford, Model T, Coupe, Woman Driver, Windup, Bing, 6 1/4 In. 302.50
Car, Ford, Model T, Touring, Windup, Tin, Bing, Germany, 6 1/2 In. 552.00
Car, Ford, Roadster, Tootsietoy, 1939 .... 50.00
Car, Ford, Sedan, Rubber Tires, Tootsietoy, 1936 .... 45.00
Car, Ford, Thunderbird, Battery Operated, Cragstan, Box 200.00
Car, Ford, Thunderbird, Convertible, Red, Matchbox, 1955 .... 17.00
Car, Ford, Toronado, Bandai, 1966, 9 In. 35.00
Car, Ford, V8, 1934 Model, Eligor, Box 18.00
Car, Ford, Woody, 1930 Model, Revell, 1974 .... 10.00
Car, German, Tin, Original Paint, 16 In. 895.00
Car, Girard, With Bell 385.00
Car, Graham Sedan, 1939 Model, Tootsietoy 85.00
Car, Grandpa's New, Windup, Lithographed Metal, E. T. C. P., Japan, 5 1/2 In. 110.00
Car, Gremlin, Maroon, Tootsietoy, 1970, 4 In. 5.00
Car, Herbie's Volkswagen, Battery Operated, Box 135.00
Car, Hessmobile, Lavender, 8 In. 1750.00
Car, Hot Rod Racer, Sweet Sue, Goggled Driver, Tin, Windup, Llupor, c.1950, 7 In. 155.00

Car, Hot Rod, Friction, Tin, 1950s Racer, Boy, Japan, 6 In. 100.00
Car, Hot Rod, Rock & Roll, Tin, Battery Operated, Lights, Bump–Go Action, 7 In. 242.00
Car, Huckleberry Hound, Tin, Vinyl Head, Marx, Hanna Barbera, 1962, 4 In. 210.00
Car, Jalopy, Clown, Fisher–Price No. 174 .... 12.00
Car, James Bond 007 Moonraker, Corgi, Box, 1979 .... 65.00
Car, Key Wind, Original Red Paint, 1930s 35.00
Car, La Salle & Trailer, Wyandotte 395.00
Car, Land Warrior, Matchbox, Boltron, Box 40.00
Car, Limousine, Cast Iron, 1900s, 5 In. 225.00
Car, Limousine, Clockwork, Painted Tin, Carrette, 8 1/2 In. 3600.00
Car, Limousine, Tin, Woman Driver, Germany, 3 1/2 In. 465.00
Car, Lincoln Continental, Green, Matchbox 4.00
Car, Luxus, Sedan, Lehmann, 1925 .... 3500.00
Car, Man From U. N. C. L. E., Thrush–Buster, Corgi, 1960s, Box 195.00
Car, Mercedes 300 SE, Chiko, Tin, Friction, Box, 24 In. 475.00
Car, Mercedes Benz 300 SL, Coupe, Battery Operated, Tin, Japan 450.00
Car, Mercer, 1913 Model, Schuco 375.00
Car, Mercer, Raceabout, 1913 Model, Champagne, Matchbox 40.00
Car, Micro Racer, No. 2, Schuco, Yellow 90.00
Car, Micro Racer, No. 7, Schuco, Red 75.00
Car, Mortimer Snerd, Crazy 750.00
Car, Oldsmobile 88, Light Blue, Corgi, England 22.00
Car, Oldsmobile, Starfire, Olive Green, Husky, Corgi 4.00
Car, Plymouth, Century of Progress Sedan, Arcade 650.00
Car, Police, Pontiac, Bonneville, White, 1980 .... 4.00
Car, Police, Red & Black Lithograph, Friction, Lupor, Box 125.00
Car, Police, Siren, Windup, Marx, 1930s 625.00
Car, Porsche Prototype, Asahi, Battery Operated, Tin, Box, 9 In. 550.00
Car, Porsche, Carrera Turbo, Joustra, Tin, Box, 11 1/2 In. 100.00
Car, Porsche, Visible Engine, Remote Control, Bandai, Box 90.00
Car, Racing & Driver, Windup, Marx, Tin, 5 In. 175.00
Car, Racing Set, Tin, Windup, Litho Drivers, 2 Pattern, US Zone Germany 315.00
Car, Racing Set, Yellow, Orange, Blue, S Pattern, US Zone Germany, 6 In. 315.00
Car, Racing, Acor, 10 1/2 In. 75.00
Car, Racing, Aluminum, Wilbur Shaw 195.00
Car, Racing, Corvette Fever, White, Hot Wheels, 1977 .... 6.00
Car, Racing, Datsun Gold Wheels, Yellow, Hot Wheels, 1981 .... 5.00
Car, Racing, Driver, Tin Windup, Marx, No. 4 .... 135.00
Car, Racing, E. R. Bost, Cast Aluminum 37.50
Car, Racing, Ford, Micro, Metal, Clockwork, Schuco, 4 1/2 In. 145.00
Car, Racing, Hare Splitter, Yellow, Hot Wheels, 1978 .... 5.00
Car, Racing, Indy 500, With Driver, Engine Sound, Battery Operated, Box 145.00
Car, Racing, King, Marx, Box 1300.00
Car, Racing, Porsche, Micro, Metal, Clockwork, Schuco, 4 1/4 In. 60.00
Car, Racing, Schuco, No. 7, Red 125.00
Car, Racing, Streamline, Windup, Marx, Box, 16 In. 375.00
Car, Racing, Tin, Friction, Light Blue, Driver, Japan 70.00
Car, Racing, Windup, Marx, 4 1/2 In. 98.00
Car, Racing, Windup, Painted Steel, Yellow Trim, 1930s, 13 In. 180.00
Car, Racing, Windup, Tin Driver, G & K, Germany, 1925, 7 In. 550.00
Car, Racing, With Driver, Penny Toy, c.1920, 2 In. 180.00
Car, Rambler Classic, Green, Silver, Dinky Toy, Box 115.00
Car, Real McCoy, Gas Engine, Aluminum 575.00
Car, Redline, Fire Chief Cruiser, Hot Wheels, On Card 35.00
Car, Remote Control, Plastic, Battery Operated, Box, 10 In. 88.00
Car, Remote Control, Tin, Windup, Occupied Japan, 4 1/2 In. 55.00
Car, Roadster, Clockwork, Metal Wheels, Painted Steel, 1920s, 15 3/4 In. 210.00
Car, Roadster, Convertible, Original Paint, Decal Label, Wooden, 18 3/4 In. 248.00
Car, Roadster, Miss Piggy, Pink Metal, Miss Piggy Waving, 1975 .... 15.00
Car, Roadster, Nickel Plated, Disc Wheels, 2 1/8 x 4 7/8 In. 350.00
Car, Roadster, Porcelain, Yellow & Black, 1920s Design, 1976, 2 In. 10.00
Car, Roadster, Red Painted Steel, Black Top, Rumble Seat, 1930, 18 In. 300.00

Car, Roadster, Rumble Seat, Celluloid, Painted, 5 3/4 In. 60.00
Car, Roadster, Rumble Seat, Yellow, Green, White Rubber Tires, Cast Iron, 5 In 95.00
Car, Roadster, With Rumble Seat, Cast Iron 85.00
Car, Rolls–Royce, Phantom, Dinky Toy 50.00
Car, Rolls–Royce, Silver Shadow, Matchbox 15.00
Car, Rolls–Royce, Windup Motor, England, Wells, 1930s, 14 In. 700.00
Car, Saloon, Rubber Tires, Head Lamps, Tin Litho, Windup, Carette, c.1915, 16 In. 6000.00
Car, Sedan, 6 Tin Lithograph Figures In Windows, Germany, Key 30.00
Car, Sedan, Lithographed Family, Tin, License Plate 1918, Chein, 6 In. 149.00
Car, Sedan, Woman Driver, Cast Iron 450.00
Car, Sheriff Sam, Whoopee, Marx 195.00
Car, SSS Sports, House Trailer, Friction, Box, Japan, 11 In. 247.50
Car, Station Wagon, Courtland, Tin Lithograph, 7 In. 55.00
Car, Station Wagon, Ford, Matchbox 30.00
Car, Studebaker, 4 Door, Windup, 1949, White Tires, Ideal 50.00
Car, Studebaker, Convertible, Green, 3 In. 12.00
Car, Studebaker, Tan, Cream, Dinky Toy 65.00
Car, Stuz Bearcat, 1914 Model, Revell, Box 12.00
Car, Torpedo Coupe, Tootsietoy No. 1017, Jumbo 25.00
Car, Torpedo Duesenberg, 1934 Model, Monogram, Revell 10.00
Car, Touring, 4 Passengers, Tin Lithograph, Friction Flywheel, 4 1/4 In. 1050.00
Car, Touring, Chauffeur, Passenger, Tin Lithograph, Penny Toy, Germany, 3 1/4 In. 300.00
Car, U.S. Army, MP, Tin, Composition Figures, Clockwork, Arnold, 1949, 9 3/4 In. 350.00
Car, Volkswagen, Battery Operated, Taiyo, Instructions, Box 300.00
Car, Volkswagen, No. 1600TL, Black Tires, Matchbox 15.00
Car, Volkswagen, Van, Plastic, Orange, Hot Wheels, 6 3/4 In. 7.00
Car, Volkswagen, Whizz Wheels, Apple Green, 1969, 2 3/4 In. 7.00
Car, Whoopee Crazy, Windup, Cowboy, Laughing Cows On Wheels, Marx, 1920s 475.00
Car, Whoopie Cowboy, Crazy, Box 1150.00
Car, Windup, Tin, Marx, 11 In. 95.00
Car, Winnebago, Tonka, 22 In. 25.00
Car, Winnebago, Tonka, 23 In. 18.00
Car, Wooden, Rumble Seat, Convertible, Handmade, c.1950, 5 1/2 x 19 In. 90.00
Car, Yellow Cab, Sedan, Tootsietoy, No. 4629, 1922 .... 90.00
Carnival Airplane Go Around, Windup, Tin, 3 Airplanes, 8 x 6 In. 200.00
Carousel, 3 Figure, Tin, Clockwork, American Flag, 8 In. 247.00
Carousel, 8 Animals Move On Poles, Animals, 2 To 6 In. 850.00
Carousel, Red Canopy, Tin Lithograph, Figures, Meier, 2 3/4 In. 775.00
Carpet Sweeper, Busy Betty, Tin Lithograph .... 25.00 To 37.50
Carpet Sweeper, Little Queen, Bissell, 1940s .... 40.00 To 45.00
Carpet Sweeper, Musical, Fisher–Price, 1950s 25.00
Carriage, Doll's, Cream Paint, Green Trim, Fringed Top 759.00
Carriage, Doll's, F. A. O. Schwarz, Label, 1896 .... 535.00
Carriage, Doll's, Landau, 2 Horses, Tin Lithograph, Red Wheels, Meier, 5 In. 445.00
Carriage, Doll's, Metal Body, Pink Metal Hood, Wooden Wheels, Miniature 50.00
Carriage, Doll's, Metal Carriage & Frame, Vinyl Hood, France, 10 In. 185.00
Carriage, Doll's, Oilcloth Seat, Canopy, Wooden Frame, Wheels, Rear Spring, 30 In. 425.00
Carriage, Doll's, Orange, Yellow Handles, Tin Lithograph, Fischer, 3 1/4 In. 410.00
Carriage, Doll's, Push, Enclosed, Victorian 850.00
Carriage, Doll's, Reed, Silk Parasol, 28 In. 265.00
Carriage, Doll's, Tin Lithograph, Multicolored, Penny Toy, 3 1/4 In. 1100.00
Carriage, Doll's, Victorian, Upholstered, Top Canopy 1400.00
Carriage, Doll's, Victorian, Wooden Wheels, Bentwood 315.00
Carriage, Doll's, Wicker, Iron & Wood Frame, 36 In. 220.00
Carriage, Doll's, Wicker, Metal Frame, Metal Wheels, 35 x 32 In. 357.00
Carriage, Doll's, Wicker, Wooden, 1900s 165.00
Carriage, Doll's, Wood, Stencil, Oil Cloth Hood, Spoke Wheels, Handle, 21 In. 75.00
Carriage, Doll's, Wood, Axle, Handle, Wooden Spokes, Oilcloth Hood, 21 In. 425.00
Carriage, Doll's, Wooden Wheels, Spokes & Hubs, Late 1800s 390.00
Carriage, Doll's, Wooden, Original Paint, Oilcloth Hood, Fringed, 21 In. 420.00
Carriage, Doll's, Wooden, Painted, Convertible Fabric Top, 19th Century, 36 In. 195.00
Cart, Clown Donkey, Windup, Tin, Lehmann, 7 1/4 In. 75.00

Cart, Coal, Donkey, Driver, Yellow, Black, Red, Blue, 13 1/2 In.	412.00
Cart, Donkey, Penny, Tin Lithograph, 4 In.	187.00
Cash Box, Tin	10.00
Casper, Pull Toy, Ideal, 6 In.	195.00
Castle, Wood, Lithograph Paper, Drawbridge, Fence, 12 1/2 In.	245.00
Cat & Mouse, Attached By Wire, On Reel, Tin, Japan, Box, 6 In.	75.00
Cat, Black Mohair, Green Glass Eyes, Applied Velvet Ears, Steiff, 8 In.	120.00
Cat, Dressed, Schuco, 12 In.	100.00
Cat, Jumping, With Ball, Remote Lever Operated, Linemar, Box	60.00
Cat, Painted Eyes, Schoenhut	1300.00
Cat, Pink Bow, White, Hubley	85.00
Cat, Pussy, Black, Madame Alexander, No. 3140	95.00
Cat, Siamese, Mohair, Jointed, Steiff Tag, 1950	175.00
Cat, Steiff, Button, 15 In.	125.00
Cat, With Ball, Windup, Tin, U.S. Zone Germany	240.00
Cecil The Sea Serpent Disguise Kit, Box	65.00
Cecil The Sea Serpent, Mattel, 1962, Box	80.00
Cement Mixer, Matchbox, No. 3, 1953	30.00
Cement Mixer, Renwal	85.00
Chair, Doll's, Corner, 3 Spindle Back, 3 Legs, Metal Design On Spindle, Wooden	150.00
Chair, Doll's, Ladder Back, Rush Cord Seat, 14 In.	82.00
Chair, Doll's, Ladder Back, Splint Seat, Red, 13 1/4 In.	82.00
Chair, Doll's, Red, Arms, 10 In.	125.00
Chair, Doll's, Rustic, 12 1/4 In.	22.00
Chair, Doll's, Windsor, Bentwood, Dark Paint, Yellow Striping, 16 1/2 In.	350.00
Chalkboard, Easel, Pressed Design, Oak	60.00
Chariot, Clown & Burro, Gilded Pressed Paperboard, Glass Eyes, 14 In.	3750.00
Charleston Trio, Black Man Dances, Boy Plays Violin, Dog Sways, Marx, 1930s	575.00
Charlie Weaver Bartender, Battery Operated, Box ....85.00 To 100.00	
Chemistry Set, Gilbert, 1946	35.00
Chemistry Set, Gilbert, Cardboard Box, 1936	22.00
Chest, Circus Figures, Wooden, Large	40.00
Chest, Doll's, Brown & Mustard Paint, 2 Globe Box Over 3 Drawers, 16 1/2 In.	445.00
Chest, Doll's, Brown, Mustard Paint Design, Porcelain Knobs, 16 x 17 x 8 In.	440.00
Chicken, Clucking, Green	90.00
Chicken, Metal Feet, Red Comb, Germany, Putz	10.00
Child In Stroller, Penny Toy, Girl In Blue Dress, Pinafore, Germany, 3 In.	375.00
Chimp, Musical, Plush, Clockwork, 7 In.	210.00
Chiromagica, Box, Question Discs, Answer Sheets, McLoughlin, 1870, 11 In.	192.50
Choo–Choo, Tom & Jerry, Battery, Cymbal Crashing	175.00
Chug–Chug, No. 161, Fisher–Price	45.00
Church, Musical, Tin, Hand Crank, Chein	125.00
Circus Parade, Elephant, Pulls 3 Clowns, Windup, Tin, TPS, Box, 11 In.	330.00
Circus Ring, 5 Wooden Animals, Fisher–Price	35.00
Circus Wagon, Overland, Kenton, 14 In.	495.00
Circus, Fisher–Price, 9 Wooden Animals, Clown, 1960s	55.00
Circus, Humpty–Dumpty, Paper Flags, Wooden Animals, Cloth Tent, Schoenhut	1200.00
Circus, Train, Engine, 3 Cars, Animals, People, Fisher–Price	45.00
Circus, Train, Steiff, Complete	3900.00
Circus, Truck, Windup, Tin, With Animal Cylinder, Courtland, 9 In.	112.00
Circus, Wagon Set, Driver, Steiff	2200.00
Circus, Wagon, Wood & Metal, 1920, Fabric & Chenille Design, 27 x 46 In.	550.00
Clarabell, Walks, Balancing On Hands, Windup, Tin, Linemar, 5 In.	600.00
Clown & Donkey, Celluloid, Windup, 7 In.	165.00
Clown, Aerial Tightrope, Tin, Cloth, Windup, Japan, Box, 8 In.	366.00
Clown, Bicyclist, Tin, Windup, Technofix, U.S. Zone Germany, 6 In.	775.00
Clown, Bisque, Glass Eyes, Tin, Mechanical, 8 In.	1400.00
Clown, Bozo, Rubber, 9 In.	25.00
Clown, Donkey Cart, Tin, Windup, Lehmann	65.00
Clown, Drum & Cymbals, Windup, Tin	440.00
Clown, Eat At Joe's, Hobo, Tin, Windup	325.00
Clown, Fiddler, Papier–Mache, Mechanical Platform, Wooden	165.00

Clown, Good Time Charlie, Vibrates, Spins Cane, Blows Air, Alps, 10 In.	800.00
Clown, Handstand, Celluloid Head, Cloth Body, Windup, Pre–1940s, Japan, 10 In. ...	212.00
Clown, Happy, Windup, Tin, U.S. Zone Germany, Box, 6 In.	280.00
Clown, Hoop, Windup, Circus Clown, 1950, Japan	285.00
Clown, In Cart, With Donkey, Windup, Lehmann	215.00
Clown, Jalopy, Fisher–Price	10.00
Clown, Juggling Block, Windup, Tin, Wheeled Platform, Pre–1940s, Japan, 8 In.	227.00
Clown, Jumping, Oversized Shoes, Waving Hanky, Windup, Tin, Mikuni, 7 In.	135.00
Clown, Mechanical, Wooden, 1919	66.00
Clown, On Roller Skates, Windup, Tin, Box, Japan, 6 In.	275.00
Clown, On Unicycle, Push Toy On Stick, Wood Patina, 23 1/4 In.	385.00
Clown, Playing Violin, Windup, Schuco, Germany	125.00
Clown, Plays Violin, Windup, Tin & Cloth, Schuco, 4 1/2 In.	335.00
Clown, Roly Poly, Celluloid, Sits On Tin Cylinder, Windup, 7 In.	350.00
Clown, Roly Poly, Cylinder, Windup, Moves Forward, Back, Celluloid, 7 In.	125.00
Clown, Rubber Neck, Dancing, Celluloid, Windup, Pre–1940s, Japan, Box, 5 In.	185.00
Clown, Skating, Twirls In Tight Circle, TPS	220.00
Clown, Squeaky, Pull Toy, Arms Move, Neck Stretches, Fisher–Price, 7 In.	365.00
Clown, Squeeze, Tips Hat, Composition Head, 12 In.	105.00
Clown, Tricycle, Battery Operated, Tin, Bell Rings, Japan, 7 In.	228.00
Clown, Tumbling, Celluloid, Painted, Clockwork, Japan, 6 1/4 In.	125.00
Clown, Violinist, Plaid Pants, Dunce Hat, Schuco, 5 In.	135.00
Clown, Waddler, Tin, Windup, Chein, 1930, 6 In.	400.00
Clown, Windup, Spins & Balances On Balls, Celluloid	55.00
Clown, With Parasol, Painted Tin, Windup, Germany, 6 In.	286.00
Clown, Yo–Yo, Cloth, Tin, S & E, Box, 10 In.	363.00
Coach, Buddy L, Brass Radiator Cap, Headlights, 1927–1932	5700.00
Coach, Coronation, Horse Drawn, Gold, Matchbox, Box	650.00
Coach, Horse Drawn, Cast Iron, Electrical Interior Light, c.1930	150.00
Coach, State, Britains, No. 1470, 1950s	175.00
Coffee–Drinking Man, Windup, TN, Japan, 7 In.	75.00
Concrete Mixer, Buddy L	50.00
Congo Bug, Cap Bomb, Box	1500.00
Construction Set, Bilt–E–Z, Box, Brochure	65.00
Construction Set, Lionel #454	250.00
Cop, Happy Hooligan, Windup, Tin, Chein, 1930	375.00
Corner Grocer, Foldout Tin Grocery Store, Wolverine, 1930s, 12 x 32 In.	225.00
Couple, Dancing, Celluloid, Occupied Japan, Box	95.00
Cow & Milkmaid, Pull Toy, Tin, 10 x 8 In.	3900.00
Cow, Josie, Walking, Battery Operated, Rosko, Original Box	125.00
Cow, Mohair, Brown, White, Glass Eyes, Ear Button, On Wooden Wheels, 21 In.	600.00
Cow, On Wheels, Working Voice Box	395.00
Cow, On Wooden Wheels, Glass Eyes, Brown & White, Steiff, 1925, 21 In.	600.00
Cow, Pull Toy, Brown, Cream Belly, Glass Eyes, Metal Horns, 6 1/2 In.	125.00
Cowboy, Bucking Horse, Lasso, Moving Arm, Tin, Marx, 1941	195.00
Cowboy, On Horse, Slinky	95.00
Cowboy, Range Rider, Swinging Lasso, Windup, Marx, Box, 10 x 11 In.	550.00
Cowboy, Riding, Rotating Lasso, Marx, Box, 1930s	275.00
Cradle, Doll's, Hanging, Swinging, Wood Wrapped With Braided Twine, 21 x 26 In.	60.00
Cradle, Doll's, Pine, Brown Graining, 19 In.	165.00
Cradle, Doll's, Poplar, Brownish Yellow Repaint, Scalloped Headboard, 17 In.	65.00
Cradle, Doll's, Poplar, Original Brown Vinegar Graining, 14 3/4 In.	195.00
Cradle, Doll's, Rocking, Natural Color Wicker	75.00
Cradle, Doll's, Spindle Sides, Painted, 1860	35.00
Cradle, Hooded, Doll's, Floral, Red & White Pinstriping, With 15 x 22 In. Quilt	600.00
Crap Shooter, Battery Operated, Cragston, Box	135.00
Crawler, Lunar, Marx, 1950	125.00
Creepy Crawler, Mattel, Box	45.00
Crib, Doll's, Pine, American, 20 3/4 x 15 1/2 x 11 1/4 In.	45.00
Crying Baby Bess, Key Wind, Alps	45.00
Cucumber, Mechanical, Key Wind, Plastic, 3 1/4 In. ....*Illus*	10.00
Cupboard, Corner, Walnut, 19th Century	300.00
Cupboard, Doll's, Black, Glass Front, 2 Doors, 16 3/4 x 6 In.	85.00

Cupboard, Dollhouse, Furniture, Mustard Grained Paint, 4 Doors & 2 Drawers 1295.00
Cycle, Top–Hat Driver, Black Groom, Umbrella, Tin, Lehmann, 1900, 5 1/4 In. 335.00
Dancers, Ballroom, Black, Tin, Windup, Germany, 6 1/2 x 5 In. 1375.00
Dancers, Wood, Painted Tin Base, Ives, 7 x 4 In. 2750.00
Dancing Couple, Black, Clockwork, Porcelain Heads, Wooden, Ives, 1870s, 10 In. ... 550.00
Dancing Mammy, Dances Around, 1930s, Lindstrom, 8 In. 364.00
Dancing Sam, Tap Dance Noise, Arms & Legs Swing, Black Man, Windup, 9 In. ... 487.00
Dangling Sam, Vaudeville–Dressed Figure, Tap Dancing On Pedestal, Tin, 10 In. ... 175.00
Dapper Dan, Coon Jigger 379.00
Daredevil, Lehmann 420.00
Darth Vader, Head, Flashing Eyes, Store Display, 1977 .... 275.00
Dennis The Menace, Mischief Kit, Dozen Tricks, Boxed, Hasbro, 1955 .... 45.00
Dino The Dinosaur, Tin, Windup, Open–Close Mouth, Hanna Barbera, 1961, 8 In. 391.00
Dinosaur, Friction, Line Mar 40.00
Dinosaur, King Zor, Battery, Ideal, 1962 .... 850.00
Dinosaur, Twistums, Wooden Jointed 175.00
Diorama, Living Room, Bone Fireplace & Mirror, Paintings On Wall, 16 In. 415.00
Diorama, Parlor, Drapes, Bird Portraits, Blue Dress, Wooden Furniture, 22 In. 385.00
Dirigible, Silver Paint, Cast Iron, 1930s, 6 In. 215.00
Distance Finder, Sgt. Preston 65.00
Dog, Beagle, Mohair Plush, Jointed Neck, Sitting, Steiff Ear Button, 4 1/2 In. 60.00
Dog, Bulldog, Button, Tag, Steiff, 1920s, 10 In. 795.00
Dog, Bulldog, Papier–Mache, Pull Toy, Glass Eyes, Growls, 1920s 1200.00
Dog, Candy Loving Canine, Candy Flips To Mouth, Windup, Tin, Japan, Box, 6 In. 237.00
Dog, Cloth, Stuffed, Beige Flannel, Painted Brown Spots, Button Eyes, 12 In. 115.00
Dog, Cloth, Stuffed, Beige, Applied Red, White, Black, Black Embroidery, 18 In. 22.00
Dog, Collie, Tin, Cloth, Windup 65.00
Dog, Flipo The Jumping Dog, See Me Jump, Marx, 1940 .... 150.00
Dog, Frisky Jumping Spaniel, Battery Operated, Box 65.00
Dog, Non–Fall Snoopy, Battery Operated, Box 85.00
Dog, On Skates, Tripper Trapper, Mohair, Pull Toy, Bavaria 135.00
Dog, On Wheels, Glass Eyes, Spotted, Steiff, 1920s, 15 In. 450.00
Dog, Poodle, Clockwork, White Fur, Glass Eyes, Key Wind, Jumps, French, 9 In. ... 500.00
Dog, Poodle, Painted Eyes, Schoenhut 180.00
Dog, Puppy Pippin, Composition Head, Jointed, Grace Drayton, 1911, 12 In. 175.00
Dog, Scotty, Windup, Tin, Marx, c.1939, 5 In. 250.00
Dog, Shaggy, Begging, Gebruder Heubach, 7 In. 450.00
Dog, Skiing, Poles, Friction, Head Pivots, Arms Move, Japan 120.00
Dog, Slinky, Box 95.00
Dog, Space, Jo, Tin, Engine Noise, Ears Go Up & Down, Eyes Spin, Tin, 5 In. 465.00
Dog, St. Bernard, On Cast Iron Wheels, Steiff 450.00
Dog, Strutting, Twirling Cane, Windup, Tin, Alps, Box 90.00
Dog, Terrier, Steiff, 3 3/4 In. 90.00
Dog, Tripel–Trappel, Bing, Metal Tag, 6 In. 250.00
Dog, Twister, Whimsical, Smiling, c.1930 .... 90.00
Dog, Wee Scottie, Windup, Wooden & Tin Wheels, Runs In Circles, Marx 150.00
Dolls are listed in their own category
Dollhouse, 2 Story, Paper Lithograph, Wood Frame, 3 Dormer Windows, 23 In. 3300.00
Dollhouse, Bliss, Lithograph Paper On Wood, Front Opens 330.00
Dollhouse, Bliss, Lithograph, 14 1/2 In. 450.00
Dollhouse, Bliss, Paper Lithograph On Wood, Front Opening, 2 Rooms, 13 In. 510.00
Dollhouse, Blue Paint, Red Trim, Wooden, 19 In. 440.00
Dollhouse, Cottage, 2 Story, Porch, Schoenhut, 1920, 27 x 23 x 23 In. 1045.00
Dollhouse, Cottage, Picket Fence, Working Shutters, Grandpa Russell, 1864 .... 2600.00
Dollhouse, Furniture, 5 Rooms, Accessories, Renwal, Metal Lithograph, c.1938 ...... 110.00
Dollhouse, Furniture, Bathroom Set, Green & White, Tootsietoy, 9 Piece 125.00
Dollhouse, Furniture, Bathroom, Newlyweds, Marx, 1925 .... 170.00
Dollhouse, Furniture, Bathtub, Kilgore, Iron 40.00
Dollhouse, Furniture, Bedroom Set, Metal, Tootsietoy, 3 Piece 30.00
Dollhouse, Furniture, Colonial, 6 Rooms, Attic, Hand Crafted, 1–Inch Scale, 1920s 665.00
Dollhouse, Furniture, Cupboard, Sprays of Flowers, c.1900, 18 x 10 1/2 In. 210.00
Dollhouse, Furniture, Dining Room, Newlyweds, Tin Lithograph, Marx, 1925 .... 165.00
Dollhouse, Furniture, Dining Room, Stenciled People, Renwal, 5 Piece 38.00

Dollhouse, Furniture, Dining Room, Strombecker, Wooden	45.00
Dollhouse, Furniture, Dining Set, Red Cast Iron, Arcade, 5 Piece	300.00
Dollhouse, Furniture, Dining Table, Metal, Tootsietoy, 1920s	25.00
Dollhouse, Furniture, Dresser, Oak, Mirror, 10 x 17 In.	185.00
Dollhouse, Furniture, Dresser, Oak, Mirror, 12 3/4 x 16 In.	495.00
Dollhouse, Furniture, High Chair, Kilgore, Iron	40.00
Dollhouse, Furniture, Hutch, Glass Doors, Wooden, 10 In.	25.00
Dollhouse, Furniture, Kitchen Cabinet, Wolverine	125.00
Dollhouse, Furniture, Kitchen, Strombecker, Wooden, Box	45.00
Dollhouse, Furniture, Kitchen, Wolverine, Tin, Pink	85.00
Dollhouse, Furniture, Library, Newlyweds, Marx, 1925	187.00
Dollhouse, Furniture, Parlor Set, Newlyweds, Marx No. 198, Box	65.00
Dollhouse, Furniture, Refrigerator, Metal, Tootsietoy, 1920s	25.00
Dollhouse, Furniture, Refrigerator, Wolverine	12.00
Dollhouse, Furniture, Sink, Wolverine	12.00
Dollhouse, Furniture, Table & 4 Chairs, Arcade	300.00
Dollhouse, Furniture, Toilet, Metal, Tootsietoy, 1920s	25.00
Dollhouse, Library, 3 Wing Chairs, Grandfather Clock, Marx, 1920s	83.00
Dollhouse, McLoughlin, 4 Open Rooms, Lithograph, Folding, 12 x 12 In.	635.00
Dollhouse, McLoughlin, Folding, Lithograph, Cardboard, 17 x 20 In.	1045.00
Dollhouse, Paper Lithograph On Wood, 2 Floors, 4 Rooms, 26 x 27 In.	1650.00
Dollhouse, Ranch Style, Dolls, Furniture, Metal, Marx, 32 x 16 In.	85.00
Dollhouse, Steps, Railing, Tin, Original Paint, Early 20th Century, 14 x 14/3/4 In.	275.00
Dollhouse, Superior, Tin, With 24 Piece Plastic Furniture	75.00
Dollhouse, Tin, Marx, With Wooden Furniture	55.00
Dolly Bouncing Ball, Windup, T. P. S., Box	150.00
Donkey, Stubborn, Instruction Sheet, Lehmann, Box	650.00
Doughboy, World War I, Windup, Tin, No Hat, Chein	90.00
Dr. Who, K–9 Robot Dog, Battery, Original Box, Palltoy, 1978	115.00
Drawing Set, Sheri Lewis, Electric, 1962	25.00
Dredge, On Treads, Buddy L	6050.00
Drum Major, No. 27, Tin Lithograph, Clockwork, Wolverine, 13 1/2 In.	209.00
Drum Major, Windup, Tin, J. Chein, Box, 9 In.	357.00
Drum Set, Wall Bear Band	49.00
Drum, Noah's Ark, Animals Pictured, Tin	110.00
Drum, Tin Lithograph, Cowboys, Chein, 9 In.	35.00
Drum, Tin Lithograph, Zeppelins, Airplanes, 1930s, 9–In. Diam.	45.00
Drum, Tin, Embossed, Wood Rims, Leather Skin, 2 Sticks, Gold, 7 In.	25.00
Drummer Boy, Windup, Tin, Celluloid Head, Pre–1940s, Box, 6 In.	400.00
Drummer, Soldier, Windup, Tin, Chein, No. 109, Box, 9 In.	235.00
Drummer, Spic Coon, Marx	1500.00 To 1650.00
Drummer, Windup, Open–Close Mouth, Tin Body, Painted Uniform, Marx, 9 In.	185.00
Dry Sink, Doll's, 2 Door, Wooden	125.00
Duck, Long Billed, Windup, Chein, 4 In.	35.00 To 85.00
Duck, Longbill, Windup, Plastic, Rico, 1930s	110.00
Duck, Nodding Head, Papier–Mache, Germany	45.00
Duck, Pull Toy, Papier–Mache, Wooden Base, 4 In.	115.00
Duck, Ramp Walker, Celluloid, 3 In.	28.00
Duck, Walking, Plush, Red Tin Shoes, Celluloid Beak, Waddles, Japan, 5 1/2 In.	95.00
Duck, Walks, Quacks, Flaps Wings, Windup, Japan	50.00
Dune Buggy, Metal, White, Black Trim, Decal, Tonka, 7 x 4 1/2 In.	9.00
Elephant, Carrying Boy On Trunk, Windup, 1930s, Japan	120.00
Elephant, Circus, Plays Xylophone, Pull Toy, American Preschool	50.00
Elephant, Circus, Plush, Windup, Celluloid Native On Trunk, Japan, Box, 7 In.	215.00
Elephant, Jumbo Bubble Blowing, Plush, Tin, Battery Operated, Japan, Box, 8 In.	132.00
Elephant, Leather, Abercrombie & Fitch, 1940s	300.00
Elephant, Mohair, Excelsior Stuffed, Unjointed, 8 In.	70.00
Elephant, Musical, Battery Operated, 1948	120.00
Elevator, Coal, Lionel, Model 77, 1930s	175.00
Elsie The Cow, Dairy Wagon, Fisher–Price	110.00
Elsie, The Cow, Aqua Plush, Vinyl Head, Borden's, 14 In.	40.00
Erector Set, Electric, Red Metal Box, 75 Pieces	65.00
Erector Set, Gilbert, Directions, Plastic Case	35.00

Erector Set, Gilbert, No. 7, 1929 .... 125.00
Erector Set, Gilbert, No. 333, Box, 1947 .... 35.00
Explodarts, Cap–Type, Box 35.00
Fancy Dan The Juggling Man, Windup, Celluloid, Occupied Japan, 6 In. 275.00
Farm Play Set, Auburn Rubber, No. 553 .... 135.00
Farm Set, Tractor, Milk Wagon, Hay Wagon, Cart, Wood, Peter Mar, 1940, 60 In. 225.00
Farm Wagon, 2 Horses, Cast Iron, Arcade, McCormick–Deering, 12 x 4 In. 305.00
Farmer In The Dell, Fisher–Price 10.00
Farmer In The Dell, Mattel, 1950s 45.00
Felix The Cat, Fire Chief, Wooden, Pull Toy 135.00
Felix The Cat, Poseable, Wooden, Pat Sullivan, 7 In. 715.00
Felix The Cat, Pull Toy, Nifty ....*Illus* 6325.00
Felix The Cat, Rubber Head, Wooden Body 285.00
Felix The Cat, Wooden, Ball Shaped Head, 1922, Original Label, 8 In. 400.00
Ferris Wheel, 2 Cars, Riders, Key Wind 400.00
Ferris Wheel, 6 Gondolas, Tin, Germany, 15 3/4 x 12 1/4 In. 410.00
Ferris Wheel, Hercules, Tin, Windup, Chein, Box, 17 In. 380.00
Ferris Wheel, Musical, 4 Little People, 1967 .... 35.00
Ferris Wheel, Steel Frame, Wooden Litho Chairs, Riders, Pull String, N. N. Hill 175.00
Ferris Wheel, Tin Lithograph, Chein, U.S.A. 250.00
Ferris Wheel, Windup, Ohio Art 125.00
Fiddler, Clown, Mechanical, Papier–Mache, Wooden Platform, Pull Toy 300.00
Fido Zilo, Fisher–Price, 1970s .... 30.00 To 65.00
Fighting Knights, Action Play Set, 1950s, Tin Carryall, Marx 250.00
Fingerprint Set, G–Men, Complete, N.Y. Toy & Game, 1937, 11 x 15 In. .....95.00 To 123.00
Fire House & Fire Chief Car, Automatic, Friction, Tin, Marx, Box, 8 In. 470.00
Fire Patrol, 2 Horses, Hubley 350.00
Fire Pumper, Automotive, Cast Iron, Hubley 6820.00
Fire Pumper, Iron and Rubber Wheels, 3 Horses, Fireman, U.S.A., 12 In. 350.00
Fire Pumper, Pair of Horses, Black, Red, Gold Paint, Iron, 14 1/2 In. 93.00
Fire Pumper, Penny Toy, Tin Lithograph, 5 1/2 In. 330.00
Fire Truck, Buddy L, 1950s 165.00
Fire Truck, Buddy L, Water Tower 4400.00
Fire Truck, Cast Aluminum, Metal Ladders, Freeport Toy, 8 In. 75.00
Fire Truck, Celluloid, Painted, Red, Silver Wheels, Driver, Kenton, 8 1/2 In. 160.00
Fire Truck, Friction, Sheet Metal & Cast Iron, Lever Switches, Dayton, 14 3/4 In. 350.00
Fire Truck, Hook & Ladder, 1 Horse, Driver, 13 In. 75.00
Fire Truck, Hook & Ladder, 2 Horses, 30 1/2 In. 2400.00
Fire Truck, Hook & Ladder, Celluloid, Painted, Rubber Tires, Figures, 7 1/2 In. 130.00
Fire Truck, Horse Drawn, Arcade 190.00
Fire Truck, Ladder Lift, Buddy L 375.00
Fire Truck, Ladder Raises, Tin Lithograph, Meier, 3 34/ In. 775.00
Fire Truck, Ladder, Tin, Friction, Republic, 1921, 17 x 6 In. 165.00
Fire Truck, Metal, Renwal, Box 75.00
Fire Truck, Nickel Plated, Balloon Wheels, Bronze Trim, Bell, 6 1/4 x 10 7/8 In. ... 1300.00
Fire Truck, Nylint, No. 6, Extension Ladder, Original Red Finish 100.00

Toy, Felix The Cat, Pull Toy, Nifty; Toy, Krazy
Kat, Pull Toy, On Platform, With Mouse

Fire Truck, Pedal, 1935	600.00
Fire Truck, Pumper, Double Horse Team, 2 Figures, Red, Ives, Iron, 16 In.	480.00
Fire Truck, Pumper, Movable T–Bone Cap, Hubley, 12 In.	475.00
Fire Truck, Red, USA Processed Plastic Co., Red & Black, 8 In.	5.00
Fire Truck, Rossmoyne, Ladder	360.00
Fire Truck, Rubber Wheels, Red, 3 1/4 x 5 In.	150.00
Fire Truck, Siren, Doepke	195.00
Fire Truck, Steelcraft, 1920s	595.00
Fire Truck, Tonka 54	225.00
Fire Truck, Trailer, Red, Ladder Raises To 36 In., Structo, 1949, 30 In.	160.00
Fire Truck, Windup, Tin, Sparks, U.S. Zone Germany, 4 1/2 In.	150.00
Fire Truck, Winky Blinkey, 1954, 1/2 x 1 1/2 In.	75.00
Fire Truck, With Siren, Doepke	195.00
Fire Water Pump, Ohio Art, Tin Lithograph	65.00
Fireball XL–5, Space City Play Set, Multiple Toy, 1964	1000.00
Firebox, Buddy L, 1926	660.00
Fireman, Windup, Climbs Ladder, Tin Lithograph, 22 1/8 In.	270.00
Fish In Fishbowl, Twirls Down Central Spiral Wires, Penny Toy, Japan	45.00
Fish, On Rubber Wheels, Steiff	625.00
Fish, Wood, Metal, Paint, Pull Toy, 5 In.	66.00
Five Jolly Darkies Way Down In Old Virginia, Wooden, Mechanical	770.00
Flashlight, Clown	15.00
Flintstones Magic Eyes 3–D Set, TruVue, 1960s	50.00
Flintstones Play Set, Complete, Figures, Marx, Hanna Barbera	235.00
Flying Floogle, In Whip Flying Airplane, Multiple, Plastic, Box, 1964	32.00
Football Kicker, Mechanical	250.00
Ford, Car, Touring, Cast Iron, 6 In.	475.00
Fort Apache Play Set, Marx, Tin Box	135.00
Fort Sumpter, Target With Cannon, Reed, Wooden Soldiers, 17 In.	2450.00
Fox, Red Stone Button Eyes, Mohair, Move Tail, Head Nods	100.00
Fox, The Magician, Tin, Cloth, Windup, Japan, Box, 6 In.	375.00
Frankenstein In Antique Flivver Auto, Japan, 1960	800.00
Fred & Wilma Flintstone, On Dinosaur, Ramp Walker	125.00
Fred Flintstone & Dino, Tin, Plush, Battery Operated	300.00
Fred Flintstone On Dino, Windup, Tin, Box, 8 In.	685.00
Fright Factory Thingmaker Pak, Mattel, 1965, Box	250.00
Frogman, Battery–Operated, Remco	95.00
Funland Locomotive, Battery Operated, Box	110.00
G.I. Joe & K–9 Pups, Walker, Windup	275.00
G.I. Joe Adventure Team, Hasbro, Box	175.00
G.I. Joe Land Adventurer, Box	90.00
G.I. Joe Space Capsule, Blond Doll, Space Suit, Helmet, Record, Hasbro, 1966	125.00
G.I. Joe, Talking, Jeep, Trailer, 12 In.	125.00
Gambling Man, Roulette, Cragston	250.00
Games are listed in their own category	
Garage & Sedan, Windup, Tin, Lehmann, 1913, 6 x 3 In.	655.00
Garage, Esso, 2 Story, Metal Pumps & Signs, Matchbox	100.00
Gas Pump, Metal, 1930s, 8 In.	85.00
Gaucho Set, Black, Dagger, Mask, Whip, Lariat, Nadel & Sons, On Card, 1950s	48.00
Geese, Feeding, Tin, Turn Crank, Penny Toy, Meier, 2 In.	260.00
Geese, Pull Toy, Spring Legs, Wooden Platform, Cast Iron Wheels, 10 1/4 In.	825.00
Geisha Girl, Pretty Butterfly, Dances Around, Raises Fan & Parasol, Linemar, 9 In.	200.00
Gentleman, Black, Top Hat, Cigar, Head Moves, Cane Spins, Tin, 8 3/4 In.	715.00
George, Drumming Man, Marx, Box	250.00
Gik–Gak, Germany, 1918	750.00
Giraffe, Glass Eyes, Schoenhut	375.00
Giraffe, Jungle, Fisher–Price	75.00
Giraffe, Mohair, Button Ear, Original Tag, Steiff, 1960, 8 Ft.	1595.00
Girl, In Boardwalk Chair, Push, Tin	38.00
Girl, In Stroller, Penny Toy, Germany, 3 In.	363.00
Girl, On Scooter, Bell Rings, Windup, Tin, 7 In.	117.00
Girl, On Swing, Wooden Base, Gibbs No. 5, c.1920, 8 1/2 In.	155.00

Girl, With Umbrella, Black, Cloth Dress, Windup, Tin, France, Prewar, 5 In. 250.00
Glendale Depot Railroad Station, Tin, Steel, 1930s, Marx, 10 x 14 In. Base 326.00
Glockenspiel, Case 18.00
Go–Go Girl, Battery Operated, Box 65.00
Golfer, With Bag of Clubs, Steiff 100.00
Good Time Charlie, Windup, Tin, Composition, Cloth Body, Japan, 11 In. 965.00
Goose, Golden, Pecking, Clockwork, Tin Lithograph, 9 1/2 In. 85.00
Goose, Painted Eyes, Carved Nostrils, Painted Wings, Schoenhut, 5 1/2 In. 335.00
Grader, Motor, Green, Gold Decals, Structo, 18 In. 25.00
Grand Prix Racing, 2 Cars, Drivers, All Tin, English, 1940s 175.00
Grasshopper, Animated, Pull Toy, Wooden, 10 In. 150.00
Grasshopper, Wooden, Hand Made, Legs Move On Wheels, 1900s 50.00
Great Billiard Champion, Tin, Windup, 1920, Ki Co., 6 In. 560.00
Green Hornet Colorforms Set, 1966 .... 130.00
Guitar, Beany & Cecil 50.00
Guitar, Elvis Presley, 1984, Lapin Products 65.00
Guitar, Romper Room, Mr. Do Bee, Box 55.00
Gun & Holster Set, The Texan, Nalco, 1959 .... 110.00
Gun & Holster, Man From U. N. C. L. E., Black Plastic, Ideal, 1965 .... 39.00
Gun & Holster, Maverick, Belt, Metal, James Garner Display Card, Overland, 1950s 45.00
Gun Set, Buffalo Bill Jr., With Belt & Whistle, On Card 20.00
Gun, Air Pistol & Target, Cast Iron, 1905 .... 250.00
Gun, Bonanza, Ben Cartwright, Metal, Cylinder Spins, Spain, Box, 9 In. 69.00
Gun, Buccaneer, Metal, Bakelite Grip, Hubley 60.00
Gun, Cork Bullets, Daisy, Red Ryder, Box 275.00
Gun, Cowhide Holster, Fanner Shootin' Shell, Mattel 250.00
Gun, G–Man, Automatic, Windup 85.00
Gun, Holster & Target, Outdraw The Outlaw, Box 65.00
Gun, Hydrogen Ray, Space Patrol 160.00
Gun, Invader Grenade, Hamilton, Box 85.00
Gun, Junior Burp, Tin, Friction, Japan, 10 In. 25.00
Gun, Machine, Tin Lithograph, Plastic Ammo Belt, 1940s, Japan, 24 In. 235.00
Gun, Paper Shooting, Tin, Pneumatic .... 38.00 To 60.00
Gun, Pistol, Hubley Colt . 45 .... 100.00
Gun, Revolver, Daisy II, Tin Lithograph, Electric, Chatters In Box 395.00
Gun, Rocket Dart, Steel Lithograph, On Card, Daisy, c.1950, 7 In. 135.00
Gun, Snubnose, . 38, Mattel 85.00
Gun, Space, Kaleidoscope, Battery Operated, U.S.A. 65.00
Gun, Space, Repeater, Wyandote, Red Metal 45.00
Gun, Space, X–Ray, Tin, Battery Operated, Noise, Flashing Lights, Box, 17 In. 167.00
Gun, Sparking, Ronson 25.00
Gun, Sparkler, Atomic, Tin, Japan, 9 In. 28.00
Gun, Squirt, Untouchables, Knickerbocker, 1960 .... 40.00
Gun, Tom Corbett Space Cadet, Tin, Click Action, Marx, 1939, Box, 10 In. 319.00
Gun, Water, Daisy, 1917 .... 25.00
Gun/Rifle, Napoleon Solo, Cap, Original Box, Ideal, 1965 .... 900.00
Gunboat, Clockwork, Bing, c.1910, 10 1/4 In. 467.50
Gunboat, Clockwork, Painted Metal, Carette, 1910, Box 1045.00
Ham & Sam, Tin Lithograph, Clockwork, Strauss, 7 In. 550.00
Handcar, Windup, Tin, Linemar 200.00
Hansom Cab, Penny Toy, Tin Lithograph, Germany, 4 1/2 In. 385.00
Happy Clown Puppet Show, Battery, Clown Makes Pinocchio Dance, Japan, 10 In. 435.00
Happy Family Menagerie Wagon, Paper On Wood, Crandall, 16 x 8 x 7 In. 3300.00
Happy Grandpa, Windup, Tin, Yone, Box, 1950s 60.00
Happy Hippo, Japan, Box 150.00
Harmonica, Popeye 65.00
Helicopter Set, Batman, Remco, Box 198.00
Helicopter, Fire Chief, Tin, Plastic Rotors, Battery Operated, Japan, Box, 13 1/2 In. 50.00
Helicopter, Hiller Hornet, Tin, Pilot, Co–Pilot, U.S. Army, 10 In. 144.00
Helicopter, Hubley, Box 125.00
Helicopter, Police Bell, Dinky Toy, Box 30.00
Helicopter, Scorpion, Purple, Yellow, Tootsietoy, 3 In. 3.00
Helicopter, Sikorsky, Westland, Model S–56, Friction Drive, Tin, 1950s 225.00

Toy, Horse, Rocking, Cloth Cover,
Swivel Rocker Base, 30 X 34 In.

Toy, Horse, Rocking, Hide Cover,
Nickolaus Klein, 52 X 46 In.

Toy, Horse, Rocking, Pine, Painted,
America, Mid-19th Century

Helicopter, Whirling Blade, Battery Operated, Marx, Box	85.00
Helmet, Fireman's, Gold Metal Eagle On Top, 1880s	350.00
Helmet, Pilot, Oxygen Mask, Slip–Down Visor, Steve Canyon Decal, Field, 1959	90.00
High Chair, Doll's, Raggedy Ann, Wooden	25.00
Home Run King, Baseball, Key Wind, Sellrite, 1920s	300.00
Hometown Movie Theater, Hand Wind, Rolls & Movie, Marx	125.00
Honeymoon Express, Windup, Marx	95.00
Hoop, Wooden, Green Over Old Red Paint, Tells On Top	423.00
Horse & Cart, Drawn, Key Wind, Germany	110.00
Horse & Cart, Drawn, Matchbox	50.00
Horse & Cart, Dump, Celluloid, Painted, 8 1/2 In.	90.00
Horse & Cart, Dump, Tin, Painted, 7 In.	220.00
Horse & Cart, Pull Toy, Cast Iron Wheels, Red & Silver Paint, 13 1/2 In.	50.00
Horse & Cart, Pull, Green, Yellow, Orange, Black, Tin, 9 1/2 In.	286.00
Horse & Cart, Pull, Wood, Original Varnish, Red Striping, 26 In.	350.00
Horse & Cart, Tin, Key Wind, Germany	121.00
Horse & Rider, Wood, Windup, Japan, c.1930, 4 x 6 In.	375.00
Horse & Wagon, Red Wagon, Yellow Wheels, Rubber, Auburn, 9 In.	69.00
Horse & Wheel, Musical, Tin Lithograph, Multicolored, 10 In.	341.00
Horse Team, Flannel Cover, Mohair Mane, Tail, Wooden Platform, 12 1/2 x 12 In.	770.00
Horse, Black Flocked, Composition, 2 Wheels In Feet, Modern Saddle, 16 In.	65.00
Horse, Burlap Cover, Cast Iron Wheel Base, 25 x 26 In.	427.00
Horse, Cart, 2 Wheel, Cast Iron, Ives, 10 3/8 In.	550.00
Horse, Felt, Glass Eyes, Battery Operated, Germany	95.00
Horse, Gliding, Dapple Gray, Wood, Leather, Felt Saddle, Red Frame, 34 x 38 In.	335.00
Horse, On Iron Wheels, Saddled, Pull Toy, Steiff, Straw Filled	775.00
Horse, On Metal Wheels, Felt, Red Saddle Blanket, Steiff, 1913, 9 In.	385.00
Horse, On Wheels, Brown Rubber, Tan Mane & Tails, Auburn, 3 x 3 x 3 In., Pair	49.00
Horse, Platform, Wood, Stencil, 34 In.	525.00
Horse, Platform, Wooden, 4 Wheels, Dapple Gray, 1900, 26 x 27 In.	295.00

Horse, Platform, Wooden, Mohair Cover, Tin Wheels, 10 1/2 In. 132.00
Horse, Pull Toy, Wood, Cast Iron Wheels, Painted, 19 1/2 In. 190.00
Horse, Pull Toy, Wood, Papier–Mache, Brown Hair Cloth, Wooden Base, 8 In. 192.00
Horse, Riding, Straw Stuffed, Red Wheels 275.00
Horse, Rocking, Cloth Cover, Swivel Rocker Base, 30 x 34 In. ....*Illus* 330.00
Horse, Rocking, Dare, c.1860 .... 2300.00
Horse, Rocking, Glass Eyes, 31 x 57 In. 360.00
Horse, Rocking, Glass Eyes, Hair Mane & Tail, Leather Saddle, Painted, 59 In. 935.00
Horse, Rocking, Hairless & Tailless, Glider Frame, Angular 415.00
Horse, Rocking, Hide Cover, Nickolaus Klein, 52 x 46 In. ....*Illus* 1100.00
Horse, Rocking, Iron, 1880s 345.00
Horse, Rocking, Leather Saddle, Horsehair Mane, Iron Stirrups, 1917, 45 1/2 In. 225.00
Horse, Rocking, Lithograph Paper On Head, Wooden, Germany 525.00
Horse, Rocking, Pedestal, Wood, 33 In. 495.00
Horse, Rocking, Penny Toy, Tin Lithograph, Multicolored, J. P. Meier, 3 In. 511.00
Horse, Rocking, Pine, Painted, America, Mid–19th Century ....*Illus* 1100.00
Horse, Rocking, Pine, Repainted, America, 60 In. 250.00
Horse, Rocking, Real Hair, Blue Saddle 650.00
Horse, Rocking, Swivel Rocker Base, Cloth Covered, Saddle, 30 x 34 In. 335.00
Horse, Rocking, Topper, Hopalong Cassidy 650.00
Horse, Rocking, Wood, Paint, Leather Harness, Saddle, Horsehair Mane, 64 In. 665.00
Horse, Rocking, Wooden Body, Gray Paint, Glass Eyes, Saddle Blanket, 36 In. 425.00
Horse, Rocking, Wooden, Dapple Gray Paint, Blue Rockers, No Mane, 26 In. 900.00
Horse, Shoebutton Eyes, Steiff, 1905 .... 1100.00
Horse, Spark Plug, Leather Ears, Rope Tail, Paper Label, Schoenhut, 9 In. 415.00
Horse, Stuffed Cloth, Pulling Wood & Wicker Sulky, 35 x 54 In. 1155.00
Horse, Stylized Carved, Dappled Gray, Horsehair Mane, Tail, Pull Toy, 31 x 28 In. 1760.00
Horse, Sulky & Driver, Celluloid, Painted, Gold, Red Wheels, 8 1/2 In. 80.00
Horse, Sulky & Driver, Nickel Plated, Celluloid, Painted, Red Wheels, 5 In. 60.00
Horse, Swing, Original Paint, America, 1920, 38 x 34 In. 585.00
Horse, Wagon, With Driver, Pull Toy, Red, Black & Yellow Paint, Tin, 14 1/2 In. 425.00
Hospital Set, Ben Casey MD, Transogram, 1962 .... 150.00
House, Tom Swift, On Wheels 50.00
Hovercraft, Red, White, Yellow, No Propeller, Dinky No. 290, 1970 .... 12.00
Huckleberry Hound, Hanna Barbera, Ceramic, Box, 1961, 6 In. 85.00
Huffy Puffy Engine, NPS, 1951 .... 50.00
Humpty Dumpty Circus, Ringmaster & Performers, Schoenhut, Porcelain Heads 4500.00
Humpty Dumpty, Fisher–Price, 1972, Box 23.00
Hurdy Gurdy, Dancing Monkey, Box 55.00
Ice Cream Vendor, Windup, Tin, Vinyl Head, Box 15.00
Ice Maker, Snoopy 10.00
Ice Skates, Wood & Steel, 15 In. 60.00
Ice Wagon, Horse Drawn, Hubley 200.00
Icebox, Wooden, Tin Plated, 2 Wooden Milk Bottles, 1920, 11 x 12 In. 125.00
Icing Station, Lionel, With Car 200.00
Indian Boy, Rotating Oars Canoe, Tin, Friction, Fronkonia, Box 120.00
Indian Chief, Windup, Chein 80.00
Indian Drummer, Warpath, Battery Operated, Alps, Box 120.00
Indian Joe, Mechanical Indian Drummer 85.00
Indian, In Canoe, Rows, Tin, Arnold, Box 275.00
Indian, Nutty Mad, Marx, Windup, Box 190.00
Iron, 1900 .... 15.00
Iron, 1920 .... 20.00
Iron, Sunny Suzy, Chrome, Electric 18.00
Ironing Board, Little Bopeep, Tin Lithograph, Wolverine 19.00
Ironing Board, Red Metal 25.00
Ironing Board, Snow White, Dwarfs, House On Top, Metal, Wolverine, 27 x 21 In. 135.00
Ironing Board, Wooden, Folding 15.00
Jack, Kicking Donkey, Pull Toy, 1926 .... 90.00
Jack–In–The–Box, Mattel, Snoopy, 1966 .... 15.00
Jack–In–The–Box, Winnie The Pooh, Tin 15.00
Jazzbo Jim, Boy, With Violin, Unique 575.00

Jazzbo Jim, Dancer On Roof 55.00
Jazzbo Jim, Tin Lithograph, Windup, Strauss, Box, 5 x 6 In. 770.00
Jazzbo Jim, Tin Lithograph, Windup, Unique Art, 9 In. .... 450.00 To 725.00
Jeep, Army, 1950s, Tootsietoy, Box 95.00
Jeep, Army, Olive, Buddy L, 4 In. 5.00
Jeep, Black, White Interior, Hood Comes Off, Tonka 3.00
Jeep, Desert Rats, Metal, Buddy L, Box 55.00
Jeep, Gumby, 1966, Plastic 145.00
Jeep, Hi Wheeler, Red With Yellow Roll Bar 6.00
Jeep, Hogan's Heroes, World War II, Plastic 115.00
Jeep, Jouncing, G.I. Joe, Unique Art, 7 In. 465.00
Jeep, Nellybelle, Ideal 85.00
Jeep, Orange & White, Fisher-Price, 2 1/2 In. 5.00
Jeep, Police Patrol, Tin, Battery Operated, Box, 1960s 600.00
Jeep, Radar, Soldier At Wheel Manning Radar Unit, Tin, 11 In. 195.00
Jeep, Red, Silver Steering Wheel & Windshield, Tootsietoy, 6 In. 13.00
Jeep, U.S. Army, Tin, Composition Driver, Clockwork, Arnold, 1949, 6 3/4 In. 100.00
Jeep, Willys, U.S. Armed Forces Radio, Steel, Marx, 2 Soldiers, Accessories, 11 In. 185.00
Jenny, The Balking Mule, Strauss 325.00
J. F. K., Rocking Chair, Music, Windup, Vinyl, Cloth, Kamar, 1963, 11 In. 450.00
Joe Penner & His Duck Goo-Goo, Windup, Tin, Marx, Box, 1930s, 9 In. 1260.00
Jolly Jumper, 1956 .... 40.00
Jolly Santa On Snow, Battery Operated, Alps, Box, 12 In. 274.00
Joy Rider, Windup, Marx, Box 625.00
Jukebox, Junior, Gong Bell Mfg. Co., Box, 1950s 125.00
Jump Rope, Jolly Green Giant's Little Sprout 10.00
Jump Rope, Weatherbird Shoes, Best For Boys & Girls 25.00
Jumpin' Jeep, Forward, Backward, Spins, 4 Soldiers, 1930s, Marx, 6 In. 330.00
Kaiser, Windup, Occupied Japan, 1947 .... 110.00
Kaleidoscope, Wonder Wheel, 1973, 13 In. 75.00
Kangaroo, Baby In Pouch, Knickerbocker 40.00
Kangaroo, Glass Eyes, Schoenhut 1150.00
Kangaroo, Jumping, Tin 50.00
Katy Kackler, Pull Toy, Fisher-Price, Box 16.50
Kermit The Frog, Plush, Eavan, Early 1960s, 21 In. 95.00
Kid Peddles Tricycle, Windup, Tin, Bell Noise, Unique Art, 8 In. 2778.00
Kiddie Car, Painted & Stenciled Wood, S.A. Smith Mfg. Co., 1915, 39 x 18 1/2 In. 3995.00
Kiddy, Cyclist, Tin Lithograph, Clockwork, Unique Art, 8 1/2 In. 176.00
Kitchen, With Corn Husk Doll, Pots, Pans, Pump, Polychrome Paint, 19 In. 300.00
Kite, Green Hornet, Unopened Package, 1950s 35.00
Kitten, Tabby, Gray Mohair Plush, Green Glass Eyes, Steiff, 4 In. 95.00
Knock Out Prizefighters, Tin, Windup, Strauss 475.00
Ko-Ko The Sandwich Man, Cloth, Tin, Vinyl Face, Windup, 8 In. 165.00
Krazy Kat, Pull Toy, On Platform, With Mouse ....Illus 1430.00
Lady Bug, Friction, Metal, 1 In. 25.00
Lamb, On Wheels, Lambskin, Felt Face & Legs, Button, Steiff, c.1913, 13 1/2 In. 725.00
Lanterna Magica, 23 Color Slides, Germany, Box 185.00
Launcher, Guided Missile, Nylint 160.00
Lazy Day Barn, Silo & Livestock, Marx 42.00
Leopard, Reclining, Steiff, 1950, 31 In. 325.00
Leopard, Spotted, Steiff 625.00
Lester The Jester, Windup, Tin, Cloth Clothes, Alps, 9 In. 385.00
Li'l Abner, Dogpatch Band, Windup, Unique Art ....495.00 To 1195.00
Lincoln Logs, No. 4CF, Metal Lid, Design Sheet, 155 Piece 70.00
Lion, Growler On Back, Button, Steiff, 36 x 62 In. 525.00
Little Folks Railway, Nister & Bradley, Cutout Paper Toy, Stand-Ups, 8 x 12 In. ... 250.00
Little Movie Make-Up Kit, Complete With Tins, Instructions, Box, 1937 .... 40.00
Little Orphan Annie, Skipping Rope, Key Wind 550.00
Little Red Riding Hood Set, Lithographed, Ohio Art, 10 Piece 75.00
Log Cabin, Wooden, Metal Doors & Shutters, Pencil Dated 1865, 7 x 9 x 5 In. 209.00
Looky Chug Chug, Fisher-Price, 1949 .... 85.00
Louis Armstrong, Windup, Plays Trumpet, 10 In. ....435.00 To 475.00
Lumber Mill, Lionel, Box 120.00

Mac The Turtle, Battery Operated, Pushes Barrel, Face Lights, Japan, Box, 9 In. 242.00
Machine Gun, Paper Popper, Box 55.00
Maggie & Jiggs Family Squabble, Windup, Nifty–Borgfeldt, 1920–1930 .... 1430.00
Magic Kit, Mandrake, Complete, Transogram, 1949 .... 120.00
Magic Lantern, Plank, 5 Slides, Box, 11 x 8 In. 220.00
Magic Lantern, Royal English Decal, 2 Glass & Kaleidoscope Slides, 6 x 8 x 10 In. 319.00
Magic Mirror, McLoughlin, 10 Anamorphic Views, Wooden Box, 8 x 11 In. 2200.00
Magic Slate, Super Star Barbie, 1977 .... 15.00
Magnastiks, Ohio Art, Box 25.00
Mailbox, Dancing, Windup, Marx 30.00
Mailbox, Plastic, Windup, Marx, 6 In. 18.00
Mallard Duck, Pulls 3 Ducklings In Basket, Tin, Windup, Lehmann, 1903, 7 1/2 In. 360.00
Mammy, Dancing, Tin, Windup, Lindstrom, 1930s, 8 In. 364.00
Man On Horse, Pull Toy, Tin, Berman 2300.00
Man, Black, Plays Bell, Woman, White, Dances, Clockwork, 1870s, 9 x 8 5/8 In. 1325.00
Man, Black, Pushing Cart, Tip Top, Windup, Tin, Straus, 6 1/4 In. 115.00
Man, Walking, Incline, Tin Lithograph, Pat. 1911, Box, 9 x 5 In. 357.00
Manicure Set, Doll's, 4 Piece 35.00
Marionette Theater, Celluloid Ballerina & Clown, Windup, Japan, 10 In. 420.00
Marionette, Flub–A–Dub 275.00
Mary Open Television Car, License Plate 1953, Screen On Dash, Asahitoy, 7 In. 85.00
Mask, Darth Vader, 1977, Don Post Studios 39.00
Masquerade Blocks, Puzzle, Crandall, Humorous Images 522.00
Megaphone, Snoopy, Metal, Chein 12.00
Merry–Go–Round, 3 Horses, Tin, Windup, U.S.A. 175.00
Merry–Go–Round, 4 Flags & 4 Airplanes, Wolverine, 1930s 650.00
Merry–Go–Round, Playland, Chein .... 550.00 To 675.00
Merry–Go–Round, Tin Lithograph, Lever Action, Clockwork Mechanism, 11 1/2 In. 247.00
Merry–Go–Round, Tin, Hand Crank, Mattel, 1950s 90.00
Merrymakers, Mice, Windup, Tin, Marx, 1935, 10 In. ....885.00 To 1225.00
Miami Sea Sled, Strauss 247.00
Microphone Sam, Black Jigger, 1930 .... 1200.00
Microscope, Steel Storage Cabinet, Gilbert 55.00
Midget Climbing Fighting Tank, Windup, Tin, Marx, Box, 1930, 5 In. 240.00
Midget Town Builder Set, 1935 .... 35.00
Mighty Robot, Tin, Windup, Sparkling Chest 95.00
Milk Cart, Pulled By Man In Raincoat, Mechanical, Welso Toys Dairies, 5 3/4 In. .. 110.00
Minnie Mouse, Steiff, 1935, 15 In. 875.00
Mirror, 3–Way Folding 48.00
Miss Friday The Typist, Battery Operated, Box 225.00
Miss Tillie Tinker 85.00
Missile Tank, Remote Control, Darts, Battery Operated, Tin, Daisy, 9 In. 152.00
Mobile Satellite Tracking Station, Cape Canaveral, Battery 575.00
Model Kit, Addams Family, Aurora, 1964, Partially Painted & Assembled, Box 498.00
Model Kit, Airplane, Eldon Match, Unopened, Miniature 8.00
Model Kit, Barnabas Collins, Dark Shadows, MPC, 1968, Box 339.00
Model Kit, Bonanza, Hoss, Ben & Joe, Plastic, Revell, Box, 9 In. 135.00
Model Kit, Bride of Frankenstein, Aurora, 1965, Box 798.00
Model Kit, Car, Duesenberg, Hubley, Unused, Box 85.00
Model Kit, Car, Model A, Roadster, Hubley 11.00
Model Kit, Car, Packard, Sport Phaeton, Hubley, 1930 .... 11.00
Model Kit, Dracula, Assembled, Aurora, 1962 .... 42.00
Model Kit, Frankenstein, Assembled, Aurora, 1961 ....45.00 To 125.00
Model Kit, Get Smart, Sunbeam, 1967 .... 185.00
Model Kit, Godzilla, Motorized 18.00
Model Kit, Goodyear Blimp, Make Your Own Signs, Revell, Box, 1983 .... 25.00
Model Kit, Hunchback of Notre Dame, Aurora, 1964, Box 339.00
Model Kit, Land of The Giants Snake Attack, Aurora, Sealed, 1968 .... 589.00
Model Kit, Lockheed F–4 Starfighter, Stunt Plane, Trim, Tab Controls, 1950s 10.00
Model Kit, Lost In Space, Aurora, 1966 .... 498.00
Model Kit, Paddy Wagon, Flintstone 300.00

Model Kit, Para–Plane, Hop Harrigan	135.00
Model Kit, Phantom of The Opera, Aurora, 1963	379.00
Model Kit, Phantom of The Opera, Glow In The Dark, Aurora, 1972	89.00
Model Kit, Robot, Lost In Space, Aurora, 1968, Box	898.00
Model Kit, Robot, Tsu Kuda Terminator, 1st Issue, 1984	300.00
Model Kit, Star Trek, USS Enterprise, 1966	39.00
Model Kit, Superboy, Sealed, Aurora, 1965	298.00
Model Kit, Tarzan, Aurora, 1967	49.00
Monkey, Bombo, Windup, Unique	25.00
Monkey, Bubble Blowing, Battery Operated, Box	135.00
Monkey, Circus Motorcyclist, Engine Noise, Windup, Balls On Umbrella, 5 1/2 In.	500.00
Monkey, Clancy, Roller Skating, Battery Operated, Ideal	100.00
Monkey, Climbing, Painted Tin, String, Lehmann, Box, 8 In.	187.00
Monkey, Climbing, Penny, Tin Lithograph, Pull String, Lead Weight To Drop, 7 In.	269.00
Monkey, Drinking, Pours, Eyes Light, Tin, Battery Operated, Linemar, 12 In.	150.00
Monkey, Drummer, Battery Operated	150.00
Monkey, Frankie, Roller–Skating, Battery Operated, Unused	150.00
Monkey, In Coconut Tree, Marble, U.S.A., 1930s, 17 In.	275.00
Monkey, Marvel Acrobatic, Windup, Tin, Marx	250.00
Monkey, Mohair, Yes/No, Bellhop, Schuco, 1930	200.00
Monkey, On Picnic, Banana, Juice To Mouth, Tummy Expands, Plush, 10 In.	435.00
Monkey, Playing Violin, Solisto, Schuco, 5 In.	275.00
Monkey, Tuxedo, Tails, Glass Eyes, Norah Wellings	150.00
Monkey, With Field Glass, Vibrates As Tail Spins, Lifts Binoculars, Tin, 6 In.	80.00
Moon City, Cragstan, Box, 1971	45.00
Moon Rocket, Stackup Toy, Wooden, Holgate No. 111, 1940s, Box	40.00
Moon Rocket, Tin, Battery Operated, Pilot & Co–Pilot, 16 In.	650.00
Mortimer Snerd, Windup, Tin, Marx, 9 In.	285.00
Mother Goose, Windup, Head Turns, Pecks, Walks, Japan, Box	55.00
Mother Swan, Followed By Gosling, Windup, Tin, Japan, Box, 8 In.	107.00
Motorcycle Cop, Plastic, Red Cycle, Black Cop, Hubley	55.00
Motorcycle, AA, Decal, Dinky Toy	55.00
Motorcycle, Acrobatic Monkey, Japan, Windup	160.00
Motorcycle, Champion, Cast Iron, 7 In. .... 200.00 To	250.00
Motorcycle, Clown Riding, Performs U–Turn, Tin, Windup, 6 In.	363.00
Motorcycle, Clown, Tin, Hits Object and Breaks Apart, 9 In.	550.00
Motorcycle, Driver & Sidecar, With Rider, Windup, Box	30.00
Motorcycle, Friction, Japan	35.00
Motorcycle, Harley–Davidson, 1950s, Japan, 15 In.	5500.00
Motorcycle, Harley–Davidson, Celluloid, Painted, Nickel Plated Wheels, 5 1/2 In. ...	275.00
Motorcycle, Harley–Davidson, Moving Pistons, Marx	425.00
Motorcycle, Honda, With Trailer, Box, Matchbox	18.00
Motorcycle, Indian, Crash Car, Cast Iron, 6 In.	300.00
Motorcycle, Machine Gunner, Sidecar, Hand Painted Lead, Britains, 1920s, 3 In.	88.00
Motorcycle, Plastic, Suzuki	40.00
Motorcycle, Police Dept., Windup, Tin, Red, 3 Wheels, KO	275.00
Motorcycle, Police Patrol, Jointed Arms, Moves With Clicking Noise, Tin,, 8 In.	275.00
Motorcycle, Police With Sidecar, Tin, Friction, Japan, 1950s, 7 In.	510.00
Motorcycle, Police, Sidecar, Tin Lithograph, Clockwork, Siren, 9 In.	260.00
Motorcycle, Racing, Tin, SFC, France, 1930s, 5 1/2 In.	142.00
Motorcycle, Rider, Blue, White, Friction, Tin, Box	30.00
Motorcycle, Rider, Friction, Tin, Japan, 8 In.	75.00
Motorcycle, Rubber, Orange Wheels, Auburn Rubber, 3 1/2 In.	28.00
Motorcycle, Side Car, 2 Men, Windup, Tin, 6 In.	190.00
Motorcycle, Sidecar, 2 Riders, Hubley, Electric, Cast Iron, Original Bulb	1475.00
Motorcycle, Sidecar, Driver, Balloon Tires, Luggage Rack, France, 6 1/2 In.	310.00
Motorcycle, Sidecar, Policeman, Marx, 1940s, 8 1/2 In.	390.00
Motorcycle, Sidecar, Red, Silver Handlebars, Rider, Hubley, 8 3/4 In.	625.00
Motorcycle, Sidecar, Rubber Tires, Celluloid, Painted, Champion, 6 1/2 In.	190.00
Motorcycle, Speed Boy, Windup, Marx, 4 In.	325.00
Motorcycle, Windup, Turns Over, Metal, 3 1/2 In.	45.00

Motorcyclist, Mac, Windup, Tin, Arnold 1200.00
Motorcyclist, Racing, Balloon Tires, Engine Noise, Tin, Technofix, 7 In. 275.00
Movie Machine, Kinora, 6 Reels, Metal Viewing Hood On Wooden Base, 11 x 5 In. 850.00
Mr. Dan, Coffee Drinking Man, 8 In. 95.00
Mr. Locomotive, Ideal 55.00
Mr. Machine, Ideal 65.00
Mr. Magoo, In Open Air Jalopy, Battery Operated, Tin 375.00
Mr. Potato Head Ice Pops, Plastic, Hassenfeld Bros., Inc., Box, 1950s, 2 Piece 65.00
Mr. Potato Head, Hasbro, Double Set, Box, 1950 .... 65.00
Mrs. Potato Head, Box, 1972 .... 10.00
Music Box, Farmer In The Dell, Mattel, Incomplete 85.00
Music Box, Tin, Mattel, 6 x 8 In. 35.00
Musical Chimes, Wooden Wheels, Fisher-Price, 1951 .... 24.00
Musicians, Black, Tin, Painted, Windup, Gunthermann, 8 x 4 In. 632.00
Mysto Magic Set, Gilbert, With Catalog, 17 x 9 In. 285.00
Native Riding Turtle, Windup, Chein, c.1930 .... 225.00
Native, On Turtle, Chein 95.00
Noah's Ark, 15 Animals & People, Polychrome Paint, Replaced Hinges 700.00
Noah's Ark, Animals, Unpainted 495.00
Noah's Ark, On Custom Built Stand, Late 19th Century, Germany, 120 Animals 7800.00
Noah's Ark, Original Paint, Hinged Roof, Removable Panel, 101 Figures, 18 In. 4800.00
Noah's Ark, Paper & Wood, Animals & People, 21 1/2 In. 495.00
Nodding Goose, Penny-Toy, Tin 121.00
Noisemaker, Tin Clown Face, Clapper, Wooden, M. B. Co., 1910, 4 In. 50.00
Onion, Windup, Plastic, 2 3/4 In. ....*Illus* 10.00
Orange Vendor, Woman Pushing Cart, 10 Cent Orange Sign, Martin & Co. 1000.00
Organ, Cathedral, Chein, Box, 1930s 275.00
Oxen, Pull Toy, Alligatored Brown, Blue Paint, 2 Wheels, Wooden, 11 In. 660.00
Paak Paak, Tin Lithograph, Clockwork, Lehmann, 7 In. 415.00
Paddy & Pig, Painted Tin & Cloth, Lehmann, 6 In. ....525.00 To 1050.00
Pail, 3 Little Pigs, Chein, 3 1/2 In. 25.00
Pail, Atlantic City, Eagle, Stars & Stripes, Tin, Dated 1880-1885 .... 250.00
Pail, Candy, Cover, Felix On 1 Side, Felix Riding Mule Other, Tin Litho, 8 x 7 In. 2750.00
Pail, Children Marching To Water 40.00
Pail, Elsie The Cow, Dairy, Shovel 85.00
Pail, Jack & Jill, Ohio Art 15.00
Pail, Jack & Jill, Square, 4 In. 35.00
Pail, Jungle Book, Shovel, Chein, 1966 .... 22.00
Pail, Kittens, Chein, 3 1/2 In. 25.00
Pail, Pinocchio, Portraits, Tin, Green, 4 1/2 In. 110.00
Pail, Sand, Little Red Riding Hood, Shovel, Ohio Art 50.00
Pail, Snail, Fish, Tin, Ohio Art 12.00
Pail, Three Girls On Beach, Ships, Tin, Green & Black Litho, Handle, 3 1/4 In. 66.00
Pail, Tin Lithograph of Kids On Carnival Rides, Chein, c.1940 .... 45.00
Pail, Tin, Fisher-Price, 4 In. 26.00
Paint Book, Gone With The Wind, Scarlett On Cover, 15 x 10 1/2 In. 135.00
Paint Box, Alice In Wonderland, Tin 30.00
Paint Box, Artists Fine, Deer's Head, Bricks, Our Boy's Color Box, 15 x 9 In. 145.00
Paint Box, Water Color, Rampant Eagle Embossed Bricks, Unused, 8 x 11 In. 415.00
Paint Set, Blondie & Dagwood, Tin, 1952 .... 35.00
Paint Set, Oil, Phantom, 1965, Hasbro 129.00
Paint Set, Reg'lar Fellows 45.00
Panda, Schuco, 3 In. 170.00
Panda, Straw Head, Glass Eyes, Dalon, 1960s, 10 In. 225.00
Parrot, On Perch, Flaps Wings, Noise, Battery Operated, Plush, 11 In. 252.00
Pedal Car, 1950 Buick, Murray 350.00
Pedal Car, 1957 Model Chevy 4000.00
Pedal Car, American General, 1930s 2750.00
Pedal Car, Buick, Torpedo, Pink 1100.00
Pedal Car, Bus, Keystone, Riding Handle 3525.00
Pedal Car, Cannonball Express No. 9, Painted Tin & Steel, 36 In. 310.00
Pedal Car, Casey Jones 245.00
Pedal Car, Chrysler, 1942 .... 750.00

Pedal Car, Fire Chief, 2 Ladders, Bell, Siren, 1930s, 50 In. 2200.00
Pedal Car, Fire Chief, Red, Metal 95.00
Pedal Car, Fire Chief, Steel, Red, AMF, 34 In. 80.00
Pedal Car, Fire Truck, 1960s 125.00
Pedal Car, Fire Truck, Red 675.00
Pedal Car, Garton Hot Rod No. 5, Yellow, Chain Driven 275.00
Pedal Car, Garton, Red Paint, 1927 .... 1300.00
Pedal Car, Gray, Red Wheels 600.00
Pedal Car, Lincoln Zephyr, Steel Craft, 2 Tone Blue, Restored, 1941 .... 2500.00
Pedal Car, Murray Champion, 1952 .... 175.00
Pedal Car, Pacer, Yellow, c.1965 .... 198.00
Pedal Car, Peddle, Packard, Running Board, 50 x 28 x 24 In. 5500.00
Pedal Car, Red, Black & Yellow Trim, Wood, Tin & Steel, 45 In. 350.00
Pedal Car, Station Wagon, Steel, Original Decal, Murray, 1949, 44 1/2 In. 300.00
Pedal Car, Steelcraft, 1949 .... 1500.00
Pedal Car, Supersonic Jet, Steel, Chain Drive, Murray, 1955, 45 In. 170.00
Pedal Car, Tractor, BMC, Red, 1930s 550.00
Pedal Car, Tractor, International 450, With Trailer 850.00
Pedal Car, Trunk Opens, Headlights, Brakes, Radio & Horn 1875.00
Pedal Horse & Sulky, Metal, Movable Legs, Detached Rubber Mane 225.00
Pedal Sulky, Chain–Driven, Pulled By Horse, Red & Yellow, Iron 412.50
Pelican, Windup, Walks, Rubs Along Wings, Chein 50.00
Penguin, Red & Yellow Beak, Green To Gray Back, Tag, 12 In. 300.00
Penguin, Red & Yellow Beak, Light Green To Gray, Steiff Tag, 12 In. 325.00
Penguin, Tin Lithograph, Windup, Red, Yellow & Black, Chein 60.00
Penny, Monkey, On Stick 150.00
Piano, 10 Wooden Keys, Picture On Front Panel, Schoenhut, Wooden, 8 x 11 In. 75.00
Piano, Barbie, With Piano, Bench Fits Around Waist, Sears, Box 27.50
Piano, Bliss, 1910 .... 150.00
Piano, Change–A–Tune, Fisher-Price 35.00
Piano, Grand, Bench, Renwal 65.00
Piano, Grand, Mahogany, Gilt Script, Celluloid Keys, Schoenhut, Small 235.00
Piano, Grand, Schoenhut ....85.00 To 130.00
Piano, Harmony 42.00
Piano, Jay Mar, c.1950 .... 45.00
Piano, Play–A–Way, Baby Grand, Tin, Marx 125.00
Piano, Player, Chein 650.00
Piano, With Player, Tin, Windup, E. M. System, Paris, 6 x 5 1/2 In. 950.00
Piano, Wood Keys, Flowers On Front, Schoenhut 48.00
Piano, Wooden, 10 Wooden Keys, Ornate Picture Front, Schoenhut, 8 In. 75.00

Toy, Picture Cubes, ABC, Baby Bunting, McLoughlin, 1884, 9 Piece

Pianolodeon, Player, 1 Roll 225.00
Picture Cubes, ABC, Baby Bunting, McLoughlin, 1884, 9 Piece ....*Illus* 500.00
Pie Safe, Doll's, 2 Glass Doors 135.00
Pig, Hide Cover, Glass Eyes, Clockwork, De Camps, 9 In. 825.00
Pig, Walking, Windup, Tin, Chein, 3 In. 150.00
Pig, Windup, Dances Around & Around, Chein 50.00
Pig, Windup, Tin, Squeaker Base 104.00
Piggy Cook, Mechanical, Metal, Rubber–Type, Box 89.00
Piggy Cook, Shakes Bacon & Egg In Pan, Lighted Tin Stove, Battery, Japan, 11 In. 240.00
Pinocchio, Walking, Linemar 600.00
Pip-Squeak, Child In Cradle 385.00
Pip-Squeak, Duck, Compress Neck, Bill Opens & Squeaks, 6 1/2 In. 30.00
Pip-Squeak, Hen On Nest 220.00
Pip-Squeak, Horse Drawn Checkerboard Wagon, Ralston Purina 30.00
Pip-Squeak, Mother Cat & Kittens 522.50
Pip-Squeak, Parrot In Cage 577.50
Pip-Squeak, Popeye 85.00
Pip-Squeak, Rooster, Spring Legs, Cage, Pops Out When Door Opens 95.00
Pip-Squeak, Santa Claus, Coat, Fur Beard, Papier–Mache, Germany, 1958, 7 In. 55.00
Pip-Squeak, Santa Claus, Red Coat, Fur Beard, Papier–Mache, Germany, 16 In. 185.00
Pip-Squeak, Sheep, Lamb's Wool Body, Papier–Mache Face, 14 1/2 In. 1300.00
Pip-Squeak, Wagon, Checkerboard, Horse Drawn 25.00
Planet of The Apes, Ramp Walker 15.00
Play Golf, Windup, Tin Lithograph, Strauss, Box, 1920s, 12 1/8 In. 905.00
Play Set, Fort Comanche, Tin, Marx 165.00
Play Set, Lost In Space, Mattel, 1966 .... 1250.00
Play Set, Pioneer Wagon, Marx, Box 45.00
Play Set, Planet of The Apes, Box, 5 Piece 200.00
Play–Doh Fun Factory, 8 Piece Set, 1960 .... 150.00
Play–Doh, Captain Kangaroo, Box 40.00
Playground, Seesaw, Swing, 8 Babies, 1920s, Tin, Friction, Lee Co., Playground 390.00
Playsuit, Rifleman, TV, Flannel & Corduroy, Felt Hat, Pla–Master, 1959, Box 198.00
Polar Bear, Jointed Legs, Steiff 550.00
Pony, Open Felt Mouth, Glass Eyes, Red Saddle, White & Brown, Steiff 95.00
Poodle, Papier–Mache, Mohair, Painted Nose, Glass Eyes, 1910, French, 20 In. 525.00
Pool Player, Tin Lithograph, Clockwork, 6 x 2 1/2 In. 275.00
Pop–Up Kritter, Fisher–Price, Pat. Oct. 5, 1926 ....70.00 To 175.00
Popcorn Popper Jr., Machine, With Corn & Shipping Box, 1940s 425.00
Popgun, Cardboard, Sheffield, Iowa, Clay Products, Dated 1914 .... 20.00
Popgun, Nu–Matic, Box 35.00
Popgun, Single Barrel, Metal, Wood Stock, Wyandotte, 1930s, 22 In. 68.00
Porky Pig, Top Hat, Marx 425.00
Porter, Black, Red Cap, Walks, Windup, Tin, 1930s, 8 In. 1310.00
Porter, Pushing Wagon With Trunk, Tin, Windup, Strauss, 6 1/2 x 6 1/2 In. 225.00
Porter, Red Cap, Windup, Carries Bags As Walks, Marx, Tin, 1930s, 8 In. 450.00
Porter, Red Cap, Windup, Tin, Strauss, 1920, 7 In. 600.00
Porter, Tip Top, Walking, Tin, Windup, Strauss, 1920, 8 In. 1315.00
Pot & Pan Set, Little Miss, Aluminum, Criterion, Original Sticker 59 Cents, 8 Piece ... 60.00
Power–Mite Workshop, Ideal, 1969 .... 150.00
Preacher, Black, Clockwork, Ives, 1880 .... 7500.00
Pretty Village Buildings Set, McLoughlin Bros., Box 80.00
Printing Press, Daisy, Box 75.00
Printing Press, Rubber Type, Box, Superior 25.00
Projector, Give–A–Show, 23 Reels 25.00
Projector, Hand, Movie Comics, 1 Film 55.00
Pumper, Snorkel, Red & White, Tonka 15.00
Punching Bag, Dixie & Pixie, Punch, Inflatable, 1959, 18 In. 29.00
Puppet, Black Minstrel, 27 In. 467.00
Puppet, Hand, Green Hornet, 1966 .... 225.00
Puppet, Hand, Punch & Judy, Pair 550.00
Puppet, Mortimer Snerd 36.00
Quack–Quack, Lehmann, 1910–1935, 7 5/8 In. 600.00
Quacky Doodles, Papier–Mache, Wood, Hinged Beak, Schoenhut, 1902, 8 In., Pair ... 950.00

Queen Busy Bee, Pull Toy, Fisher–Price	15.00
Quick Draw McGraw, Hanna Barbera, Ceramic, Box, 1961, 6 In.	90.00
Rabbit Carriage, Mother Pushes Baby, Parasol, Windup, Celluloid, 7 In.	190.00
Rabbit On Police Motorcycle, Tin, Vinyl Head, Friction, Japan, Box	110.00
Rabbit, Dancing, Mohair, Wood, Metal, Glass Eyes, Schuco, 20th Century, 8 In.	275.00
Rabbit, Mohair, Glass Eyes, Jointed Head, Felt Mouth, Steiff, 9 1/2 In.	140.00
Rabbit, Oswald The Lucy Rabbit, Felt Stuffed, Walker, Clockwork, Tag, 17 In.	1050.00
Rabbit, Pull Toy, Tin Lithograph, Chein, 6 In.	35.00
Rabbit, Pulling Cart, Tin, 8 In.	15.00
Rabbit, Schuco, 12 In.	125.00
Rabbit, White Fur, Glass Eyes, Clockwork, French, 20th Century, 10 In.	395.00
Rabbit, Windup, Tin, Occupied Japan, 4 In.	52.00
Race Track, Figure 8, Windup Cars, Double Track, Marx	182.00
Racer, Speedy, Pull Toy, Black Rubber Tires, Gray & Foster, Box, 5 In.	38.00
Radio Joe, On Tractor, Windup	425.00
Radio, 759, Wooden, Fisher–Price	23.00
Radio, Tom & Jerry, Portable, Marx	35.00
Rail Car, Chimp & Pup, Battery Operated, Bump/Go, Faces Light, Tin, 8 In.	265.00
Range Rider, Pinto Horse, White Outfit, Spins Lasso, Gun, Marx, 1938, 11 In.	651.00
Rattle & Whistle, Gilded Brass, Red Coral Handle, 5 1/8 In.	247.00
Rattle, Child's, Wooden, Hand Painted, Late 1800s	18.00
Record Player, Electric, Case, 1950s	22.00
Red Queen Buzzy Bee, 1956	40.00
Red Riding Hood, Ramp Walker, Wilson, 1930s	60.00
Refrigerator, Mary Lu, Green, Wooden, J. C. Penney, 1930s	65.00
Refrigerator, Wolverine, Tin, Late 1950s, 13 x 8 In.	58.00
Rifle, Lasermatic, Battlestar Galactica, Box	35.00
Rifle, Scope, Cork Ball, Daisy, Box, 1956	350.00
Rifle, Winchester, Rifleman, Hubley	125.00
Ring, Flicker, Display Card, 3 Piece	300.00
Ring, G–Men, Metal, 1930s	15.00
Ring, Sky King, 4 Pictures	225.00
Ring–A–Ling Circus, Tin Lithograph, Clockwork, Marx, 8–In. Diam.	1100.00
Rip Van Winkle Set, New Pretty Village, McLoughlin, 1897, 16 x 11 In.	495.00
Road Grader, Adams Motor, Doepke	275.00
Road Grader, Structo, 17 In.	85.00
Road Race Set, James Bond, Track, Complete, Gilbert, 1965, Box	495.00
Road Race, 3 Windup Cars, Ohio Art, Box, 1940s	125.00
Road Roller, Buddy L	3960.00
Road Sweeper, Green With Red Wheels, 3 1/4 x 8 3/4 In.	4000.00
Road Tug Wrecker, Steel, Baked Enamel Paint, 1966, 12 In.	175.00
Robot With Spark, Tin, Windup, Engine Noise, Spark Action, Box, 7 In.	335.00
Robot, Astronaut, Battery Operated, Tin, Plastic, Horikawa Toy Ind., 11 3/4 In.	160.00
Robot, Aurora, Lost In Space, 1968	1000.00
Robot, Battery Operated, Linemar, Remote Control, Box, 7 3/4 In.	250.00
Robot, Battery Operated, Metal Lithograph, Orchid, Gray & Silver, Japan, 15 In.	2200.00
Robot, Driver Flaps Mouth As Car Moves, Yoshiya	600.00
Robot, Father & Son, Marx, Box	500.00
Robot, Jupiter, Box	6000.00
Robot, Lost In Space, Battery, 1960s, Remco, Box	375.00 To 625.00
Robot, Marvelous Mike, At Controls of Bulldozer, Box	375.00
Robot, Moon Explorer, Battery Operated, Box, 12 In.	75.00
Robot, Mr. Brain, Remco, Box	145.00
Robot, Mr. Mercury, Gold	400.00
Robot, New Astronaut, Pistons On Chest	120.00
Robot, Piston, Taiwan, Box, 1970s	95.00
Robot, Planet Patrol, Blue, Box	1850.00
Robot, Planet, Walks As Light Flashes, Battery Operated, KO, 9 In.	1450.00
Robot, Robert, Box	275.00
Robot, Spaceman, Smokes, Walks, Lights Up	2550.00 To 2750.00
Robot, Swivel–O–Matic, Battery Operated	165.00
Robot, Tractor, Marvelous Mike, Battery Operated	300.00

Robot, Video, Tin, Space Scenes On Big Screen, Box 145.00
Robot, Windup, Gears Spin In Chest, Sparkling Action, Tin, 9 In. 325.00
Robot, Zoomer, Face Lights When Walks, 1950s, Tin, Battery Operated, 8 In. 433.00
Rock–N–Roll Monkey, Battery Operated 160.00
Rocket Express, Windup, Tin, Technofix, No. 286, 1950s, 2–In. Car, 15–In. Track 545.00
Rocket, Moon, Tin Pilot, Space Scene, Red Lights Flash, Battery, 1950s, 16 In. 650.00
Rocking Horse, Black & Red, 27 In. 160.00
Rodeo Joe, Windup, Tin, Unique Art, 1940s 250.00
Roller Coaster, 2 Cars, Chein, 1930s 185.00
Roller Coaster, Coney Island, 2 Cars, Windup, Ohio Art, Box 250.00
Roller Coaster, Double Loop The Loop, McDowell, 1930s, Box 425.00
Roller Coaster, Jet, Windup, Tin, Futuristic Bus, Passengers, Wolverine, 12 In. 227.00
Roller Coaster, Loop The Loop, Wolverine, Box, 1930s 390.00
Roller Coaster, Ohio Art 185.00
Roller Coaster, Windup, Tin, 2 Cars, Chein, 1960, 19 In. 335.00
Roller Skates, Clamp–On, Single Wooden Ball–Shaped Rollers 12.00
Roller Skates, Clamp–On, Union Hardware No. 5, Pair 6.45
Roller Skates, Winchester, No. 10, Box 120.00
Rollo–Chair, Riding Boardwalk, Windup, Strauss ..../................................ 467.00
Roly Poly, Keystone Cop, Blue Suit, Papier–Mache, 5 In. 155.00
Roly Poly, Owl, Celluloid, U.S., 3 3/4 In. 105.00
Roly Poly, Pinocchio, Gund 15.00
Roman Gladiator, 2 Clubs, Clockwork, Lehmann Ajax, Box, 10 In. 2200.00
Rooster, Crowing, Windup, Marx, 9 In. 110.00
Rooster, Pip–Squeak, Papier–Mache, Polychrome Paint, Spring Legs, 7 In. 155.00
Rooster, Tin Cart, Blue, Violet, Windup, Marx, 1930s 75.00
Round–Up Tex, Cowboy Whirls Around On Base, Twirls Lariat, 1950s, 10 In. 115.00
Rower, Key Wind, Unpainted Wood, Automatic Toy Works 3225.00
Sand Loader, Automatic, Wolverine 180.00
Sandy & Merry Miller, Elf, Dog Back & Forth, Tin, Wolverine, 1930s, Box, 13 In. ... 345.00
Saxophone, Brass, Germany, 1939, 12 In. 30.00
Scarab, Windup, Buddy L 195.00
Science Outfit, G–Man, 1936 .... 100.00
Scooter, Kid Flyer, Tin Lithograph, String Pull, Clockwork, B & R, 7 x 3 In. 412.00
Scooter, Platform Seat, 4 Wheels 95.00
Scooter, Ribbed Metal Foot Holder, A. J. G. Rideout, c.1930, 32 x 43 In. 352.00
Sea Wolf Pirate, Peg–Legged, Windup, Tin, Alps, Box, 7 In. 273.00
Seal, Tin, Painted, Clockwork, Lehmann, 7 In. 99.00
Seal, With Ball, Friction Drive, Lehmann, 1930s 120.00
Service Station, 3 Level Revolving Car Lift, 6 Cars, Accessories, Box, 1940s 175.00
Service Station, Tin, Marx 200.00
Seven Dwarfs, Sieberling Tire Co. 465.00
Sewing Machine, Casige, British Zone Germany .... 50.00 To 90.00
Sewing Machine, Gateway, Red Metal, 8 1/2 x 4 1/2 In. 68.00
Sewing Machine, Kay & E Sew Master, Blue, Box 50.00
Sewing Machine, Little Red Riding Hood, Stencil 95.00
Sewing Machine, Meier, Tin, Hand Operated Wheel, Germany, 3 1/4 In. 175.00
Sewing Machine, Pretty Maid, Tin 35.00
Sewing Machine, Red Metal, Wooden Case, Electric 42.00
Sewing Machine, Seam–Master Junior 25.00
Sewing Machine, Singer, Side Wheel, Box 96.00
Sewing Machine, Vulcan, Metal 30.00
Sewing Machine, Wilcox & Gibbs, Gold Trim, Flowers, Black, 9 x 15 In. 250.00
Sheep, Glass Eyes, Ribbon & Bell, Leather Ears, Schoenhut, 7 1/2 In. 745.00
Sheep, Glass Eyes, Straw, Cast Iron Platform and Wheels, 21 In. 295.00
Sheep, Grazing, Mohair, Ear Button, Glass Eyes, Felt & Synthetic Wool, 29 In. 825.00
Sheep, Papier–Mache Face, Lamb's Wool Body, Sound Squeaker 1300.00
Sheep, Papier–Mache Painted Face, Leather Ears, Wool Body, Pegged Feet, 14 In. .. 1400.00
Sheep, Platform, Wool–Covered Wood, Glass Eyes, Leather Bridle, 11 1/4 In. 575.00
Sheep, Pull Toy, Wood, Wool, Papier–Mache, Tin Wheels, 7 1/4 In. 355.00
Sheriff Sam's Car, Windup, 1930s 100.00
Sheriff, 2 Gun, Battery Operated, Cragstan 165.00

Shooting Gallery, Jungle Eyes, Mechanical, Ohio Art, 1950s 75.00
Siam Sue, Composition Head & Body, Wooden Arms, 11 1/4 In. 335.00
Sideboard, Mirror, 23 In. 225.00
Skates, Bugs Bunny 8.00
Ski Boy, Friction, 1930s, Chein 350.00
Ski Ride, Winter Scene Lithograph, Skis On Wheels, Chein 350.00
Skip Rope Animals, Girl, With Dog & Squirrel, Windup, TPS 160.00
Sky Bird Flyer, Marx, Box 450.00
Skydome Set, Stadium, Rookies, Topps 69.00
Sled, Baby's, Wheeled Steering Device, Yellow Flower, Red Ground 665.00
Sled, Blue–Green Paint, Turned Handles, Enclosed, Willimantic, Maine 335.00
Sled, Child's, Wood, Steel, Bentwood Runners, Scrolled Steel Ends, 39 In. 900.00
Sled, Flexible Flyer, Model J 95.00
Sled, Flexible Flyer, No. 47 .... 100.00
Sled, Green, Red Runners, Rosebud In Center, Paris Mfg. Co. 195.00
Sled, Indian Head Stencil, Paris, Red, 29 In. 275.00
Sled, Mickey Mouse, Original Rope & Decals 900.00
Sled, Old Furniture Boards, Spoon Carved 250.00
Sled, Original Stencil, Hand Grips, 1880 .... 325.00
Sled, Painted Floral Pattern, Wooden & Metal, 34 In. 235.00
Sled, Painted Galloping Horse & Rider, Painted Red, J. H. R. 1831, 41 In. 415.50
Sled, Pine, Wrought Iron, Black Pin Striping, Signed Lewis, 8 x 22 In. 600.00
Sled, Pine, Wrought Iron, Yellow Pin Striping, Green Runners, I. J. T., 17 x 37 In. 1650.00
Sled, Push, Spindle Front, Red Velvet Lining 385.00
Sled, South Paris, Stenciled Santa Claus 665.00
Sled, Stenciled Horse, Red With Black, Wooden 595.00
Sled, Swan Head Finials On Front Runners, Victorian, 1870 .... 265.00
Sled, Wooden, Green Paint 175.00
Sled, Yankee Clipper 95.00
Smiling Sam The Carnival Man, Tin, Cloth, Windup, Alps, 9 In. 384.00
Snappy The Dragon, Battery Operated, Japan, 1950s 1870.00
Snoopy Copter, Pull Toy 40.00
Snoopy, Pull Toy, Fisher–Price 29.00
Snorkel Pumper, Tonka, 19 In. 85.00
Snowball, Snow Man, Germany, 5 1/2 In. 38.00
Snowflake Riding Spark Plug, Tin, Nifty–Borgfeldt 935.00
Soldier Set, German Imperial Army, Marching Band, Infantry, 20th Century, 1900 ... 165.00
Soldier, Armistice Day Band, Set, Elastolin, World War I, 10 1/2 In. 300.00
Soldier, Bahama Police Band, Britains 295.00
Soldier, Britains, No. 1720, Scots Greys, Mounted, 7 Piece 154.00
Soldier, Coldstream Band, Britains, Box, 21 In. 1750.00
Soldier, French Army, Horse–Drawn Ambulance, Britains, 1910s 4125.00
Soldier, German, With Trench, Set, Elastolin, 7 In. 350.00
Soldier, Infantry, Lead, Painted, McLoughlin, Box, 11 Piece 242.00
Soldier, Marching, Arms & Legs Move, Tin, Windup, Prewar, 9 In. 650.00
Soldier, Marching, Tin, Windup, Celluloid Head, Pre–1940s, Box, 9 In. 665.00
Soldier, Military Police, Britains, No. 2201, 8 Piece 150.00
Soldier, Mounted Canadian Gov. Guard, Britains, No. 163, 5 Piece 225.00
Soldier, Mounted Egyptian Cavalry, Britains, No. 115, 5 Piece 225.00
Soldier, Paper, With Tents & Stands, Cardboard, McLoughlin, 1891, Box 525.00
Soldier, Queen's Own Cameron Highlanders, Britains, Box, 1983, 12 Piece 1000.00
Soldier, Scots Highlanders, Set, Elastolin, 10 1/2 In. 300.00
Soldier, Scots Highlands, Britains, No. 11, Box, 7 Piece 150.00
Soldier, Welsh Guards Fife & Drum Band, Britains, Box, 1956–1960 .... 1760.00
Soldiers, Infantry, Lead, Painted, McLoughlin, Box, 18 Piece 632.00
Soldiers, With Army Training Center Building, Tin, Marx 65.00
Sonicon Rocket, Box, 1958 .... 250.00
Space Capsule, G.I. Joe, Hasbro, 1966 .... 75.00
Space Car, Sea Hawk, Battery Operated, Astronaut Pilot, Japan, 12 In. 665.00
Space Craft Jupiter, Tin Astronaut, Plastic Bubble, Windup, Japan, Box, 5 In. 95.00
Space Explorer Train, Tin, Battery Operated, Rocket Shape, Tracks, Japan, 21 In. ... 850.00
Space Patrol Top Secret Diplomatic Pouch, Scene, Toys of Tomorrow, 1950 .... 454.00
Space Ship, Tom Corbett, Windup, Spark, Noise, Tin, Marx, 12 In. 1400.00

Space Ship, Whirling Blades, Driver, Friction, ATC, Box 90.00
Space Shuttle & Challenger, NASA, With 747, Battery Operated, Plastic 45.00
Space Station, Battery Operated, Lights Flash, Astronaut Pilot, Japan, 9–In. Diam. 165.00
Space, Lunar Module, Apollo II Eagle, Bump–Go, Lights, Tin, 9 In. 225.00
Spaceship, Polaris, Tom Corbett, Windup 375.00
Spaceship, X–15, Windup, Japan 155.00
Sparkler, Archie, 3–Dimensional, Pull Cord, Eyes Spark, Ronson, 1923, 9 In. 175.00
Sparrow, Chirping, Windup, Tin, Kohler 50.00
Speed Boy Delivery, Windup, Marx 395.00
Spider, Windup, Key, Occupied Japan, 3 In. 24.00
Spreader, Red & White Wheels, Decal, Carter True Scale, 10 1/4 In. 50.00
Sprinkler, Chein, Tin 20.00
Sprinkler, Ohio Art 165.00
Sprinkling Can, Southwestern Design, Ohio Art 45.00
Squirrel In Cage Whistle, Penny Toy, Tin, Germany, 4 1/2 In. 110.00
Station, Girard Whistling, Tin Lithograph, Red Brick, Gray Roof, Marx 30.00
Steam Engine, Aneroide Barometer, Spring Driven, Brass, Marble, France, 14 In. ... 2200.00
Steam Engine, Lunar, Marx, 1950 .... 125.00
Steam Roller, Pressed Steel, Keystone, 1930s 300.00
Steam Shovel, Metal, Blue, Hubley, 11 x 6 In. 45.00
Steam Shovel, On Treads, Buddy L 7150.00
Steam Shovel, Sturdy Construction Co., Tin Lithograph, Wyandotte, 1920s 125.00
Steamboat, Tin Lithograph, Japan, 4 In. 15.00
Steamer, Windup, Painted Steel, Fleishmann, 7 1/2 In. 220.00
Stool, Doll's, Tapestry Cushion, Painted, 1840, 5 1/2 x 5 In. 295.00
Stove, Charter Oak, Cast Iron, Small 750.00
Stove, Eagle 115.00
Stove, Eagle, Warming Oven, 16 In. 200.00
Stove, Electric, Green & Cream, Kingston Products Corp., 10 1/2 x 12 1/2 In. 105.00
Stove, Electric, Metal, 3 Burners, Green Paint, Ivory Figures, Working 85.00
Stove, Great Majestic Jr., 30 x 23 In. 4000.00
Stove, Kenmore Toy Cook Stove, Light Green, 14 x 15 x 7 In. 35.00
Stove, Kitchen Range, Doll's, Cast Iron, Little Eva, 2 Griddles, 9 x 14 x 10 In. 300.00
Stove, Little Chef, Ohio Art, Box 65.00
Stove, Little Lady Range, Electric 30.00
Stove, Little Orphan Annie, Red, 5 In. 40.00
Stove, Magic Cook Oven, Jr. Chef, Electric, Pink, Blue, Ago Ind., 12 x 6 x 12 In. ... 35.00
Stove, Marklin, Pots, Tools, 1890 .... 3000.00
Stove, Nickel–Plated, Ceramic Pulls, 3 Pots, 5 1/2 In. 165.00
Stove, Parlor, Little Fanny, Adams, Peckover & Co. 225.00
Stove, Pots, Pans & Teakettle, Gas Hookup, Graniteware 2000.00
Stove, Queen's, Black Iron 40.00
Stove, Queen's, Cast Iron, Utensils 45.00
Stove, Star Crescent, Iron, Large 125.00
Stove, The Queen, Cast Iron, 6 Utensils, 24 x 22 x 12 In. 1400.00
Stove, Tin, Electric, Hughes 24.00
Stove, Wolverine, Tin, Late 1950s, 15 x 14 In. 68.00
Streamline Speedway, Marx, Box 300.00
Streetcar, Sunny Andy, Pull Toy, Tin, Wolverine, 1935, 13 In. 201.00
Stroller, Doll's, Blondie & Dagwood, Tin Lithograph, 1949 .... 110.00
Stroller, Doll's, Canvas Top 400.00
Stroller, Doll, Tan Wicker, Rickshaw Type 110.00
Submarine Kit, Polaris, Thomas Jefferson 25.00
Submarine, Nautilus No. 108, Light & Diving, Battery Operated, Line Marx, Box ... 200.00
Submarine, Nautilus, 20, 000 Leagues Under The Sea, Tin, Original Box 275.00
Submarine, Nautilus, Windup, Tin, Box 275.00
Submarine, Pressed Steel, Tin Lithograph, Windup, Red, Gray, Wolverine, 13 In. ... 50.00
Submarine, Sea Wolf, Atomic, Windup, Tin, Sutcliffe, England, Box, 10 In. 118.00
Submarine, Windup, Wolverine, Box 150.00
Suitcase, Doll's, Suzy Cute, Vinyl, U.S.A., 1965 .... 8.00
Sulky Racer, Windup, Marx 75.00
Sunday Driver, Smoking, Battery Operated, Box, Japan 125.00

Surrey, 2–Seater, Striped Cloth Top, Pedal Action, 53 In. 300.00
Surrey, Doll's, Wooden, Iron Wheels, Natural Finish, 1800s 150.00
Susie Seal, Fisher–Price, 1961 .... 30.00
Sweeping Mammy, Windup, Swings Broom, Tin, Lindstrom, 8 In., 1930s 275.00
Swimmer, Celluloid, Windup, Tin Arms Whirl Around, 1930s 95.00
Swing, Boy In Boat, Germany, Wooden, 3 In. 18.00
Table & Chairs, Black Table, Yellow Vinyl Chairs, 1960s, 3 Piece 145.00
Table Set, Tin Lithograph, 6 Chairs, 1940–1950 .... 135.00
Table, Chestnut, Collapsible Folded Legs, Metal Ring Connects Legs, Octagon 75.00
Table, Porcelain, Advertising Calumet Baking Powder 225.00
Tailspin Tabby, Fisher–Price, No. 400 .... 85.00
Tank & Sprinkle, Buddy L 5720.00
Tank, Atomic, Battery Operated, Tin, 1950s, 6 In. 76.00
Tank, Battery Operated, Tin, No. 03871, Marx 16.50
Tank, Bulldog, Remco 175.00
Tank, Machine Guns, Twin Gun Turret, Clockwork, Gama 225.00
Tank, Midget Climbing Fighting, World War I, Marx, 5 In. 240.00
Tank, Radar, Space, Battery Operated, Tin, Japan, 8 In. 290.00
Tank, Sparkling, Advances With Sparking Action, Tin, Marx, 1935, 4 In. 133.00
Tank, Sparkling, World War I, Marx 140.00
Tank, Turnover, Tank Does Flips, 1935, Marx, 4 In. 161.00
Tank, U.S. Army M–62, Battery Operated, Missiles From 2 Guns, 1950s, Box 140.00
Tanker Truck, Mobile, Smith Miller 325.00
Tap Dancers, Bears, Flywheel, Tin Lithograph, 7 1/2 x 7 x 3 In. 445.00
Target Game, Wink, Woody Woodpecker, Shooting Cannon, 1959, 7 x 11 In. 36.00
Target Set, Starsky & Hutch Police, Arco, 1977, Unused, Box 49.00
Taxi, Austin London, Black, 1969 .... 15.00
Taxi, Austin, Dublo Dinky Toy 25.00
Taxi, Brown & White, Cast Iron, Arcade, 9 In. 850.00
Taxi, Checker Cab, Red, Black, Tin, License Plate 1924, Chein, 8 In. 520.00
Taxi, Windup, Tin Lithograph, Chein, 1918 .... 110.00
Taxi, Yellow Cab, 1921 Model, Tootsietoy 65.00
Taxi, Yellow Cab, Battery Operated Sign Top, Friction, Tin, Japan, Box, 8 In. 360.00
Taxi, Yellow, Friction, Tin, SSS, Japan, Box, 7 In. 160.00
Tea Set, Child's, Floral, Gold Trim, RS Prussia, 15 Piece 1400.00
Tea Set, China, Japan 42.00
Tea Set, Cow Jumped Over The Moon, Tin, With Tray, Ohio Art 285.00
Tea Set, Doll's, White Paste, Blue Design, Service For 6, Germany, Box 99.00
Tea Set, Enamelware, White, 11 Pieces 75.00
Tea Set, Little Miss Muffet, Pottery, Box, Service For 6 .... 110.00
Tea Set, Little Red Riding Hood, Tin, Ohio Art, 10 Piece .... 150.00 To 210.00
Tea Set, Ohio Art, The Cow Jumped Over The Moon, With Tray 285.00
Tea Set, Punch & Judy, Lithography, 15 Piece 775.00
Tea Set, White Ironstone, Gold Trim, Germany 65.00
Tea Set, White Paste, Gold & Red, Service For 6, Box 247.00
Teddy Bears are also listed in the Teddy Bear category
Teddy Bear, Steiff, Brown Mohair, Glass Eyes, Chain, Pull Toy, 12 In. 850.00
Teddy The Artist, Battery Operated 145.00
Teddy Zilo, Fisher–Price, No. 752, 1964 ....95.00 To 120.00
Telegraph Set, Western Union 18.00
Telegraph Signal Set, Brumberger 20.00
Telephone, Gong Bell, Box 40.00
Telephone, Speaker, Darth Vader, Box 225.00
Television Studio, Admiral Prom, TV, Stage, Lights, Scenery, 1953, 50 Pieces 135.00
Theater, Marionette, Celluloid Clown & Girl, Prewar, Figures 5 In. 850.00
Theater, Punch & Judy 16.50
Threshing Machine, McCormick, Deering, Yellow & Red, Arcade .... 225.00 To 350.00
Tick & Tack Tumbling Clown & Acrobat, Windup, Marx, Box 350.00
Tiger Trike, Windup, Revolving Bell, Tin, Marx, Box 125.00
Tiger, Trophy Head, Plaque, Steiff, 1955, 12 In. 350.00
Time Machine, Color Transfer Set, Buster Brown 15.00
Tinker Toy, Tube, 1915 .... 32.00
Tiny Teddy, Fisher–Price, 1962 .... 35.00

Tip–Cart, Horse & Driver, Tin, Cast Iron, Wilkens No. 165, 1908 .... 1695.00
Tool Box, Interior Lithograph, Tools, Bliss 95.00
Tool Chest, Wooden, 8–Piece Cast Iron Tool Set 85.00
Toonerville Trolley, Clockwork, Red, Yellow & Black, Tin, Fontaine Fox, 5 In. 357.00
Toonerville Trolley, Lift–Off Roof, Painted Steel, 1950s, 43 x 48 In. 880.00
Toonerville Trolley, Station & Figures, Tin Lithograph, Lyle Cain 375.00
Toot Toot Loco, Pull Toy, Fisher-Price 15.00
Top, Wood, Painted, 4 1/2 In. 33.00
Tote Bag, Beanie & Cecil, Vinyl, Matching, 2 Piece 150.00
Tractor Trailer, Allis Chalmers, Arcade, 12 1/2 In. 275.00
Tractor Trailer, Cattle, Chevrolet, Cream, Green, Roll–Up Door, Nylint, 26 In. 49.00
Tractor Trailer, Girard, Restored 250.00
Tractor Trailer, Red, Marx, A & P, Cab Only 40.00
Tractor Trailer, Sturditoy, Green 5500.00
Tractor, Allis–Chalmers, Arcade, 3 1/2 In. 50.00
Tractor, Aveling Bradford, Shovel, Matchbox, 2 3/4 x 1 1/4 In. 9.00
Tractor, Brass Boiler, Live Steam, Cast Iron Wheels,, Weeden, 6 1/2 In. 465.00
Tractor, Cab Over, Red, Tootsietoy, 1970, 3 1/2 In. 4.00
Tractor, Cast Iron, Arcade, 1930s 100.00
Tractor, Cast Iron, Steel Wheels, Orange, Arcadia, 3 In. 65.00
Tractor, Caterpillar, Front End Loader, Green & Yellow, Nylint, 11 In. .... 20.00 To 35.00
Tractor, Caterpillar, Mighty Dump Hydraulic, Repaint Orange, Black, Nylint, 17 In. 59.00
Tractor, Caterpillar, Pull Toy, West Germany, Wooden 8.00
Tractor, Climbing, Driver, Windup, Marx, Box 95.00
Tractor, Climbing, Marx 100.00
Tractor, Cowboy Riding, Windup, Tin, Circle Motion, Marx, 1935, 8 In. 365.00
Tractor, Crawling, Gray, Red Wheels, Woodhaven, Windup,, 1916, 8 In. 175.00
Tractor, Farm, Driver, Windup, Tin Lithograph, Marx, 5 1/4 x 8 1/4 In. 38.50
Tractor, Farm, Plastic Wheels, Yellow, 1967, 3 In. 10.00
Tractor, Ford Industrial, Loader & Back Hoe, Yellow, Ertl 35.00
Tractor, Ford, Blue & Gray, Ertl, 1968 .... 95.00
Tractor, Ford, Blue, Man, Yellow Tires, Allis Chalmers, 1950, 3 1/2 In. 39.00
Tractor, Ford, Green, White, Majorette, 4 1/2 In. 15.00
Tractor, Fordson, Red, Silver Wheels, Hubley 25.00
Tractor, Friction, Red, Yellow & Green, Japan, 5 x 3 1/4 In. 20.00
Tractor, Front End Loader, Carter True Scale 100.00
Tractor, Front Scoop, 4 Plastic Wheels & Tires, Yellow Cast, Hubley 10.00
Tractor, Gray, Cast Iron, Fordson, Driver, Red Wheels, Arcade, 1926 .... 175.00
Tractor, International Harvester, Orange–Red Grill, Decal 40.00
Tractor, International Harvester, Red & Black, Ertl, 2 1/2 In. 7.00
Tractor, John Deere Model A 100.00
Tractor, John Deere, High Lift, Cast Aluminum, 1960 .... 145.00
Tractor, Loader & Back Hoe, Industrial, International, No. 3400 .... 55.00
Tractor, Log Trailer, Red Cast, Black Rubber Tires, 1930s, 5 In. 14.00
Tractor, Manure Spreader, Red, 4 Wheels, Tootsietoy, 1970, 4 In. 10.00
Tractor, Massey–Harris 44, Ruehl 450.00
Tractor, Massey–Harris, Dinky 37.50
Tractor, Massey–Harris, Silk 135.00
Tractor, McCormick Deering, Gray, Gold Trim, Red Wheels, Black Rubber, Arcade 495.00
Tractor, Mechanical, Tin, Windup, Courtland, 6 In. 116.00
Tractor, Milton Berle 250.00
Tractor, Oliver 70, Arcade 360.00
Tractor, Oliver No. 60, Arcade, 1936, 5 1/4 In. 175.00
Tractor, Orange, Plastic Wheels, Tootsietoy, 1967, 3 In. 15.00
Tractor, Pedal, John Deere, Model 730 .... 325.00
Tractor, Pedal, John Deere, Series 10, Eska 200.00
Tractor, Plastic, Orange, Marx, 1956 .... 65.00
Tractor, Power Trac, Minneapolis–Moline, Chain Drive, Red 115.00
Tractor, Red Wagon, Rubber Wheels, Tailgate Opens, International Harvester, 4 In. 5.00
Tractor, Red, Plastic, Bar Rubber Co., 6 1/2 In. 20.00
Tractor, Shovel, Orange, Matchbox, 1977 .... 6.00
Tractor, Sparkling, Climbing, Tin Plow, Tin Driver, 1950s 375.00
Tractor, Sparkling, Driver, Long Trailer, Windup, Tin, Marx, Box 135.00

Tractor, Standard, Driver, Red, Black Rubber Tires, Arcade 175.00
Tractor, Timber Transport Freight Liner, Orange, Blue, Metal, Nylint, 12 x 4 In. 15.00
Tractor, Utility, Yellow, Silver Grill, Carter True Scale, 1967 .... 45.00
Tractor, Weatherill Hydraulic, Yellow, Matchbox, 1959 .... 9.00
Tractor, Wide Front, Green, Orange & Yellow, Gama, Box 45.00
Tractor, Yellow Plastic, Ohio Art Company 8.00
Train & Village, Flintstone, 1979, Box 100.00
Train Car, Caboose, Outdoor Railroad, Buddy L 1650.00
Train Set, American Flyer, Engine & 4 Cars, 1928 .... 550.00
Train Set, American Flyer, No. 282 .... 450.00
Train Set, American Flyer, O Gauge, Red, Brass Trim, 4 Piece 300.00
Train Set, Battery Operated, Engine, Tender, Gondola, Caboose, Tracks, Box 18.00
Train Set, Bing, Locomotive, Baggage, 2 Observation, Tracks, Tin Lithograph 187.50
Train Set, Buddy L, Locomotive, Coal Tender, Flat Car, Box Car, Caboose 5800.00
Train Set, Buddy L, No. 50, Industrial, Gas Engine Locomotive, 1929-1932, 8 Piece 885.00
Train Set, Dorfan, Pre-1940, Box 1100.00
Train Set, Engine & 2 Gondolas, Windup, Courtland No. 9000, Box 160.00
Train Set, Ives, Engine & 2 Passenger Cars, Standard Gauge, 1926 .... 600.00
Train Set, Ives, Yankee, O Gauge, Locomotive, 2 Pullman Cars, Track, Box 475.00
Train Set, Lionel, Engine, Gondola, Caboose, Standard Gauge, 1916 .... 350.00
Train Set, Lionel, No. 256, O Gauge, Station, Tunnel, Track 770.00
Train Set, Lionel, No. 6-13l83, Engine, Box, Complete 125.00
Train Set, Lionel, Standard Gauge Blue Comet, Passenger Car, Box 1760.00
Train Set, Lionel, Standard Gauge, Locomotive, Pullman, Observation 225.00
Train Set, Lionel, Standard, No. 318 Engine, 3 Passenger Cars, Individual Boxes 2250.00
Train Set, Locomotive, Tender, Parlor & Pullman Cars, 0 Gauge, Jep 120.00
Train Set, Louis Marx, Commodore Vanderbilt 140.00
Train Set, Presidential Series, O Gauge, Pullman, Observation, Vista Dome, Box 600.00
Train Set, Santa Fe, N Gauge, Tracks 68.00
Train Station, Schoenhut 350.00
Train, American Flyer, Coach, White Panels, Black Frame & Trim, 4 Wheel 13.00
Train, American Flyer, Coal Loader, Lionel, S Gauge 120.00
Train, American Flyer, Engine, 3 Passenger 400.00
Train, American Flyer, Hopper, No. 716, Side Dump, Red, Black Trim 25.00
Train, American Flyer, Locomotive & Tender, No. 354, Silver Bullet 125.00
Train, American Flyer, Locomotive, Pullman & Tailcar, Aluminum, 1936 .... 395.00
Train, American Flyer, Locomotive, Windup, 8 Spoke Tin Wheels, Black, 1932 .... 70.00
Train, American Flyer, Mail Car, Middle, Tail Car, Windup, Tin, Burlington Zephyr 225.00
Train, American Flyer, Oil Drum Loader, With Controller, S Gauge 155.00
Train, American Flyer, Santa Fe, Engine & Dumpie, 2 Piece 240.00
Train, American Flyer, Town Depot, Brick & White, Green Roof, 6 x 4 x 4 In. 35.00
Train, Auburn Rubber, Locomotive, Western No. 922, Black, Gold, Red, 7 In. 19.00
Train, Bing, Coach, Lithographed & Painted, Pair 852.00
Train, Buddy L, Locomotive, Red Metal, Plastic, White Decal, 4 1/2 In. 10.00
Train, Cars, Circus Flat Cars, Primex, Boxes 110.00
Train, Converse, Coach, Lithographed & Painted 410.00
Train, Cor-Cor, Washington, Ind. 975.00
Train, Dorfan, Locomotive, No. 51, Pullmans, No. 498, Boston & Atlanta 425.00
Train, Dorfan, Locomotive, Steam, No. 55, Black Domes & Boiler, Brass Plates 225.00
Train, Dorfan, New York Central, Box, Hopper, Tank, Caboose, 0 Gauge 120.00
Train, Engine, 1 Car, Pull Toy, Green, Red, Black, 9 1/2 In. 275.00
Train, Engine, 1750 Model, Hudson 773 .... 1400.00
Train, Engine, Lionel, Standard GGI, No. 2360, Carton 1550.00
Train, Engine, Tender, NWJ 746 .... 1000.00
Train, Flintstone, 1979, Empire, Box 60.00
Train, Fulguex, Locomotive, 0 Gauge, Box 1045.00
Train, Ives, Water Tank, Orange 145.00
Train, Joyline, Passenger Coach, No. 3570, Gold Windows & Numbers, Green 25.00
Train, Lionel, Cars, Gondola, Cattle, Caboose, Lumber, Refrigerator, 5 Piece 880.00
Train, Lionel, Cattle Car 175.00
Train, Lionel, Coal Car 75.00

Train, Lionel, Commando Assault, Box	55.00
Train, Lionel, Locomotive & Tender	605.00
Train, Lionel, Locomotive, Tender, Track & Transformer	85.00
Train, Lionel, No. 8 Engine, NYC Passenger Cars & Post Office Car, 1925–1932	575.00
Train, Lionel, No. 90, Locomotive, Electric, 8 Pieces of Track	3850.00
Train, Lionel, No. 117, Caboose, Black Roof, Brown, New York Central	55.00
Train, Lionel, No. 219, Crane Car, Box ....*Illus*	1200.00
Train, Lionel, No. 318, Locomotive, Baggage, Observation, Pullman ....*Illus*	1100.00
Train, Lionel, No. 400E, Blue Comet, Engine & Tender	3000.00
Train, Lionel, No. 408E, Engine, Lime–Green	450.00
Train, Lionel, No. 665, Steam Locomotive, O Gauge, Non–Whistling Tender	85.00
Train, Lionel, No. 746, Engine & Tender	1400.00
Train, Lionel, No. 1030, Transformer, Train, 50 Watt	35.00
Train, Lionel, No. 1035, Locomotive, Cowcatcher, Red Spoke Wheels, Copper	70.00
Train, Lionel, No. 2146ws, Original Box, 1948	2100.00
Train, Lionel, No. 2328, Burlington Gp–9	340.00
Train, Lionel, No. 2343, Santa Fe, 1950	450.00
Train, Lionel, No. 2349, Northern Pacific, Box	450.00
Train, Lionel, No. 2356, Southern	1075.00
Train, Lionel, No. 2579, Box Car, Baby Ruth, 8 Wheel, Automatic Couplers	22.00
Train, Lionel, No. 2755, Sunoco Tank, Gray	60.00
Train, Lionel, No. 3356, Horse Car & Corral, Box	130.00
Train, Lionel, No. 3359, Twin Bin Dump	35.00
Train, Lionel, No. 3424, Wabash Operating Box Car, Signals, 1956	90.00
Train, Lionel, No. 3469, Lionel Lines, Operating Coal Dump	30.00
Train, Lionel, No. 3482, Milk Car & Platform	50.00
Train, Lionel, No. 6015, Sunoco Tanker, Single Dome, Yellow	10.00
Train, Lionel, No. 6464–900, New York Central, Box	110.00
Train, Lionel, No. 6530, Safety & Fire Fighting, Box, 1960	65.00
Train, Lionel, No. 8352, Santa Fe Gp–20, Box	60.00
Train, Lionel, No. 8754, New Haven Rectifier, Box, 1977	150.00
Train, Lionel, No. 9301, U.S. Mail	20.00
Train, Lionel, No. 18402, Lionel Lines Burro Crane, Box	110.00
Train, Lionel, No. 19709, Caboose & Switcher No. 8977	695.00
Train, Lionel, No. 31131, Gondola, Drop Hook Coupler, Yellow, Green, Black	30.00
Train, Lionel, Operating Mail Pick–Up	20.00
Train, Lionel, Operating Saw Mill	85.00
Train, Lionel, Operating Searchlight Tower	30.00
Train, Lionel, Operating Switchman	40.00
Train, Lionel, Piggyback Transporter, Box	175.00

◆ ◆

Do not keep wine and spirits in lead crystal decanters. The lead
will leach out and go into the wine. It is unhealthy to drink liquid
with lead.

◆ ◆

Toy, Train, Lionel, No. 219,
Crane Car, Box

Toy, Train, Lionel, Set No. 318, Locomotive,
Baggage, Observation, Pullman

Train, Lionel, Power Station, Green & Cream	145.00
Train, Lionel, Standard Gauge, Freight Car, 5 Piece	1320.00
Train, Lionel, Station, Green & Brown	150.00
Train, Lionel, Tank Car, Orange	50.00
Train, Lionel, Tender, Ohio–Central, Coal Pile, Handrails, 8–Wheel Coupler	45.00
Train, Locomotive & Passenger Car, New York Central, Aratoga, Chein, 1930	485.00
Train, Locomotive, Clockwork, Stenciled Boss, Painted Tin, Ives, 8 1/2 In.	1100.00
Train, Locomotive, Silver Mountain Express, Battery Operated, Japan, Box, 15 In.	55.00
Train, Marklin, Gondola, Hand Painted	165.00
Train, Marklin, Locomotive & Tender, Boxes	220.00
Train, Marklin, Locomotive, Electric, 3–Part Engine, HO Gauge, 11 1/4 In.	150.00
Train, Marklin, Tin, Germany, With Track, Box, 3 Piece	250.00
Train, Marklin, Track, 1940s, 20 Piece	75.00
Train, Marx, Boxcar, N.Y. Central, Tin	20.00
Train, Marx, Electric, Track, Transformer, 1950, 6 Piece	130.00
Train, Marx, Locomotive, Red, Stamped Steel, Key Wind	80.00
Train, Marx, No. 9100, Union Pacific Freight Car, Metal Tilt Couplers, 3/16th Scale	25.00
Train, Marx, Track, Transformer, 1942, 6 Piece	165.00
Train, McCoy, Locomotive, Standard Gauge, 2–Tone Blue, Box	220.00
Train, Nabisco	300.00
Train, No. 6456, Lehigh Valley Hopper, Black	15.00
Train, Primex, Orient Express, Box	198.00
Train, Signal Tower	12.50
Train, Steiff, Circus, Teddy Clown Drivers	1950.00
Train, Trolley & Trailer, Tin Lithograph, Trix	70.00
Transporter, Eagle, Space 1999, Die Cast, Dinky	45.00
Travel Bag, Twiggy, Vinyl, Psychedelic	75.00
Trestle Set, Lionel, Box	20.00
Tricycle, Iron Fittings, Wood Spoke Wheels, Steel Rims, Red Paint, Wood, 32 In.	575.00
Trolley, Broadway, Red, Green, Tin, 1930s, Chein, 8 In.	310.00
Trolley, City Hall Park, Reversible Seats, Converse, 16 In.	275.00
Trolley, Friction, Dayton, Tin	495.00
Trolley, Gold Wheels, Friction, Tin, 11 1/2 In.	80.00
Trolley, Horse–Drawn, Baltimore Line, Fallow	800.00
Trolley, Pressed Steel, Iron Wheels, 22 In.	225.00
Trolley, Tin Lithograph, Meier, Cam Driven, 3 In.	225.00
Trolley, Toonerville, Fontaine Fox, Box, 1922, 1 1/2 x 1 7/8 In. .... 400.00 To	575.00
Truck Terminal, 3 Trucks, Box Converts To Garage, Structo, 1950s	200.00
Truck, American Express Toys, Steel, Banner, 12 In.	152.00
Truck, Antiaircraft, Windup, Tin, Alps, 5 1/2 In.	139.00
Truck, Armored, Sturditoy	4950.00
Truck, Army, 1939 Model, Tootsietoy	40.00
Truck, Army, Canvas Top, Marx, 1950s	135.00
Truck, Army, Cast, Black Rubber Wheels, Olive, Midgetoy, 1950s, 4 In.	12.00
Truck, Army, Metal Wheels, Canvas Top, Battery Lights, Structo, 1930s, 17 In.	390.00
Truck, Avis, Decal, 1977, Box, 5 In.	12.00
Truck, B. F. Goodrich, Medal Craft, 11 1/4 In.	285.00
Truck, Baby Ruth, Butterfinger, Buddy L, 1949, 29 In.	500.00
Truck, Baggage, Buddy L, Rubber Tires, Headlights, Bumper, 1930–1932	8800.00
Truck, Bakery, Baker Boy Tin Lithograph On Roof, Friction	40.00
Truck, Bedford Evening News Van, Matchbox	40.00
Truck, Bedford Ice Cream, Decals, Matchbox	20.00
Truck, Bekins Nationwide Moving & Storage, White, 1950s	72.00
Truck, Bell Telephone, Hubley, Trailer & Tools, 1940s, 12 1/2 In.	140.00
Truck, Black Diamond Coal, Tin, Windup, Courtland, Box, 1950s, 11 In.	129.00
Truck, Boom, U.S. Hwy. Maintenance, Steel, Orange, Structo	65.00
Truck, Brinks Bank, White, Red, Working Lock, Nylint, 1960s, 16 In.	35.00
Truck, Bubble Yum, Bubble Gum, Buddy L, Box, 5 In.	15.00
Truck, Buddy L, Ice Truck, Yellow, Green, 22 In.	225.00
Truck, Cannon, Army, Battery Operated Gun, Compass, Nylint, 19 In.	150.00
Truck, Cattle, Structo	135.00
Truck, Cement Mixer, Mack, Tootsietoy, 1955	15.00
Truck, Cement Mixer, Matchbox	35.00

Truck, Cement Mixer, Tin, Japan, 7 1/2 In.	65.00
Truck, Chevrolet, Van, Tin, Opening Rear Door, Plastic Windows, 12 In.	98.00
Truck, Coca–Cola, Painted Cases, Marx, 1950s	450.00
Truck, Coca–Cola, See–Through Trailer, Buddy L	250.00
Truck, Concrete, Copper Color, White Tank, Structo, 18 In.	165.00
Truck, Delivery, Tin, Uniform Driver, Screened Panels, Packages, Chein, 8 In.	400.00
Truck, Delivery, Windup, 3 Wheels	275.00
Truck, Digger, Tonka, Box, Unopened	95.00
Truck, Dodge, 6 Wheeler, Metal Dump, Cab Over, Orange, Yellow, Red, 6 In.	10.00
Truck, Driver, International Harvester, Arcade, Paper Labels, Cast Iron	1100.00
Truck, Dump & Scoop, Hydraulic, Marx, Early 1950s, 26 In.	185.00
Truck, Dump, 10 Wheels, Red, Tonka No. 55, 5 x 2 1/4 x 2 1/4 In.	5.00
Truck, Dump, Atlas, Blue & Orange, 1975, Matchbox	5.00
Truck, Dump, Clockwork, Gear Driven, Hand Crank, Steel, Structo, 1920s, 18 In.	515.00
Truck, Dump, Cor–Cor, 1920s, 23 In.	475.00
Truck, Dump, Die Cast, Tin, Windup, London Toy, 7 1/2 In.	35.00
Truck, Dump, Dodge, Metal, 4 White Wheels, Nickel Grill, Tonka, 1960, 14 In.	24.00
Truck, Dump, Front Loader, Roberts, Yellow & Red, Metal, 1930s, 24 In.	65.00
Truck, Dump, Hydraulic, Blue & White, Tonka	35.00
Truck, Dump, Mack, Arcade, Green, 12 In.	2250.00
Truck, Dump, Mack, Nickel Plated, Green, 2 3/4 x 5 1/4 In.	400.00
Truck, Dump, Mack, Red Cab, Green Body, Rubber Tires, Steel Craft, 1933, 25 In.	650.00
Truck, Dump, Polished Aluminum, 2 1/4 x 5 In.	175.00
Truck, Dump, Son–Ny, Detachable Cab, 26 In.	725.00
Truck, Dump, Tin, White Mustang Logo, Wolverine, 13 In.	185.00
Truck, Dump, Tractor Trailer, Girard, 1920s, 12 In., 2 Piece	250.00
Truck, Dump, Wooden Wheels, Wyandotte, 1920s, 6 In.	125.00
Truck, Dump, Wyandotte, 15 In.	225.00
Truck, Dump, Yellow, Matchbox, No. 26	4.00
Truck, Euclid, Gravel, 28 In.	50.00
Truck, Fire, Tonka, 1950s, 17 1/2 In.	85.00
Truck, Flivver, Delivery Truck, Spoke Wheels, Black, Buddy L, 1924, 11 3/4 In.	412.50
Truck, Foden, Open, Type 2, Red Cab, Gray, Dinky Toy	100.00
Truck, Gnome Series, Momentum, Tin, Lehmann, Germany, 4 1/4 In.	75.00
Truck, Gold Star Moving Van, Opening Doors, Farm Animals, Marx, 1950s, 21 In.	165.00
Truck, Grader, Yellow, Mighty Tonka No. 3945, 1972, 24 In.	39.00
Truck, Gravel, Wyandotte, 6 In.	25.00
Truck, Heavy Duty AA Wrecker Service, Tonka, No. 3915, 1971, 17 In.	49.00
Truck, Hydraulic Aerial, Aluminum Tires, Painted Steel, Buddy L, 33 1/2 In.	165.00
Truck, Ice, Red, Arcade	240.00
Truck, Karrier Refuse, Matchbox, Gray	18.00
Truck, Lazy Dairy Farms, Sheet Metal, 3 Bales of Hay, Marx, 17 x 6 In.	165.00
Truck, Loader, On Tracks, Barber & Greene, Doepke	350.00
Truck, Machinery Moving, Hoist Winch, Tin, Marx, Box, 21 In.	600.00
Truck, Mars Candy, Corgi, 1985	12.00
Truck, Michigan Scraper, Yellow, Dinky No. 98, 4 In.	10.00
Truck, Minitown Parcel Post, Wyandotte	175.00
Truck, Mixer, Jaeger, Akenton, Green, 9 In.	1950.00
Truck, Nationwide Van Lines, Tin, Plastic, 4 In.	12.00
Truck, Oil Tanker, Buddy L	1200.00
Truck, Pickup, Apache, Red, 2 3/4 In.	3.00
Truck, Pickup, Commercial, Matchbox	20.00
Truck, Pickup, Ford 50, Black Rubber Tires, Tootsietoy	4.00
Truck, Pickup, Tonka, White, With 5th Wheel Trailer	45.00
Truck, Railway Express Agency, Buddy L, Green Paint, Decals, 23 In.	350.00
Truck, Railway Express, Buddy L, 1928	1500.00
Truck, Ready Mix Concrete, Gray, Orange, Structo, 12 In.	50.00
Truck, Red Baby, Doors Open, Pressed Steel, Buddy L	4650.00
Truck, Refrigerator, GMC, Red, Green, 1967, Matchbox	6.00
Truck, Road Maker, Gray Roller, Yellow, Roscal, 5 x 2 1/2 In.	39.00
Truck, Road Service No. 5, Decals, Red & Green, Tootsietoy, 4 In.	5.00
Truck, Sanitary Service, White & Blue, Tonka, 1967, 9 1/2 x 5 1/2 In.	13.00

Truck, Semi, Sears Allstate, Aluminum, Large	175.00
Truck, Shell Oil, Tootsietoy	65.00
Truck, Sit & Ride, Buddy L, 1930s	175.00
Truck, Stake Bed, Buddy L	535.00
Truck, Stake, Farm, Tonka, 1956	30.00
Truck, Stake, Girard, With Lights, 10 In.	185.00
Truck, Stake, Hubley, Cast Iron	165.00
Truck, Stake, Old MacDonald, Battery Operated	135.00
Truck, Stake, Schieble, 1930s, 19 In.	425.00
Truck, Stake, Shell Motor Oil, Pressed Steel, Metalcraft, 12 1/4 In.	495.00
Truck, State Highway Dept. Dump, Flasher, Tonka No. 975, 13 In.	90.00
Truck, Tank, Mack, American Oil Co., Bronze Trim, 6 x 15 1/2 In.	3600.00
Truck, Tanker, Benzol, Gnome Series, Momentum, Lehmann Germany, 4 1/4 In.	168.00
Truck, Tanker, Tour With Texaco, Plastic, 3 In.	15.00
Truck, Texaco Tanker, Knockoff, Friction, Japan	35.00
Truck, Texaco Tanker, Steel, Buddy L, 26 In.	95.00
Truck, Texaco, Red Paint, 1960s, 3 Ft.	125.00
Truck, Tow, Buddy L, Rubber Tires	6600.00
Truck, Tow, Manoil, Red Paint, White Rubber Tires, 4 1/2 In.	55.00
Truck, Toy Town Express, Momentum, Plastic Cab, Tin Tires, Marx, 1950s	250.00
Truck, Toyland Oil Co. Tanker, Windup, Structo No. 66	210.00
Truck, Tractor–Trailer, Green, Sturditoy	5500.00
Truck, Trash Hauling, Lever Lifts Load, 2nd Lever Loads Conveyor, Friction, Japan	65.00
Truck, U.S. Mail, Buddy L, 5 In.	95.00
Truck, Uniformed Driver At Wheel, Fischer, c.1920, 3 1/2 In.	400.00
Truck, Utility Garbage, City of Toyland No. 7, Red, Orange, Gray, 21 In.	149.00
Truck, Volkswagen Pickup, Blue, Budgie, 3 1/2 In.	65.00
Truck, Wrecker, Crane, Goodrich Silvertown Tires, Metalcraft, 1920s, 11 5/8 In.	247.50
Truck, Wrecker, Rubber Tires, Pressed Steel, Buddy L	6600.00
Truck, Wrecker, Tonka, 1960s	75.00
Truck, Wrecker, White Rubber Tires, Hubley, 7 In.	150.00
Truck, Wrigley Spearmint Gum, Buddy L, Green, 1950s	240.00
Trunk, Doll's, Dome Top, Inside Tray, Painted Wood	230.00
Trunk, Doll's, Dome, Leather Handles, Inside Tray, Metal Trim, Wooden, 16 In.	175.00
Trunk, Doll's, Hump, Insert Tray, Pine	120.00
Trunk, Doll's, Humpback, Tray With Sections, Parasol	200.00
Trunk, Doll's, Lift–Out Tray, Wallpaper Lined, Black Tin, 1800s	55.00
Trunk, Wardrobe, Doll's, 4 Drawers, Hanging Space, Travel Stickers, 19 In.	50.00
Turtle & Ladybug, Penny, Lithograph, Souvenir Universal Theaters, 3 In.	120.00
Turtle, Open Felt Mouth, Glass Eyes, Mohair, Steiff, Large	75.00
Turtle, Timothy, Fisher–Price, 1953	45.00
Typewriter, Berwin	20.00
Typewriter, Dial, Marx	45.00
Typewriter, Simplex, 1930s, Box, 8 x 10 In.	40.00
Typewriter, Simplex, No. 2	23.00
Typewriter, Tom Thumb, 1940s	75.00
Typewriter, Tom Thumb, Metal Cover, 1930s	90.00
Typewriter, Tom Thumb, Model 449e, Western Stamping Co., Box, 1930s	75.00
Typewriter, Unique Art, Box	50.00
U–Turn Caterpillar Bulldozer, Battery, 1960s, 10 In.	295.00
U–Turn Circus Cycle, Tin, Windup, Japan, 6 In.	248.00
Umbrella, Uncle Wiggily	175.00
Uncle Sam, Jigger, On Wooden Base, Crank Handle, 14 In.	385.00
Van & Trailer, Bell System, Gray, Blue & White, Tonka	8.00
Van, Chevrolet, Racing, B. F. Goodrich, White, Matchbox, 4 x 4 In.	6.00
Van, Express, Junior Supply Co., Spoked Wheels, Silver Tires, 7 1/4 x 15 1/2 In.	9000.00
Van, Express, Nickel Plated, Disc Wheels, Mack, 3 1/4 x 6 1/2 In.	550.00
Velocipede, Clockwork, Cotton Clothing, Riding Cast Iron Tricycle, 10 In.	1650.00
Velocipede, Horse Shape, Wood, Metal, Glass Eyes, 31 1/2 x 36 In.	385.00
Viewmaster Set, Mod Squad	28.00
Viewmaster Set, Munsters, 1964	185.00
Viewmaster, Around The World Trip, 3 Reels	125.00
Viewmaster, Godzilla, With Insert, Complete	15.00

Viewmaster, Mighty Mouse Meets Powerful Puss, GAF, Package, 1958 .... 13.00
Village Blacksmith, Paper Steam Accessory, Weeden, Box, 9 x 10 In. 665.00
Violin Player, Tin, Red, White, Blue Tuxedo, Windup, Linemar, 5 1/2 In. ... 164.00 To 188.00
Vulcan Ears, Mr. Spock, From Star Trek, Rubber, 1976 .... 10.00
Waffle Iron, Cast Iron, Arcade 150.00
Waffle Iron, Keen Kutter 300.00
Wagon, Aero–Flyer, Oak, 1930s 100.00
Wagon, American Milk Co., Stenciled, Metal Rimmed Wheels, Wooden, 24 In. 245.00
Wagon, Beer, 4 Horses, Driver, Beer Kegs, Cast Iron, 20 1/2 x 7 x 4 In. 220.00
Wagon, Beer, Marx 140.00
Wagon, Blue Streak, Metal Rings Over Wooden Spoked Wheels 475.00
Wagon, Bluegrass Coaster, Wood, Stencil, Spoked Wheels, Hand Brake, 41 In. 176.00
Wagon, Circus, 2 Horses, Driver, Wood, Sheet Metal, Polychrome, 14 1/2 In. 352.00
Wagon, Coal, Horses, Cast Iron 295.00
Wagon, Coaster, Big Boy, Rubber Wheels 175.00
Wagon, Coaster, Greyhound, Red Metal, 24 In. 45.00
Wagon, Delivery, Clockwork, Trailer, Caterpillar Treads, Structo, Painted Steel 510.00
Wagon, Evening Star, Sunday Morning Edition Painted On Sides 235.00
Wagon, Express, Wood, Metal Spoke Wheels, Stencil, Red, Blue & Black, 35 In. 154.00
Wagon, Globe Aeroflite, Covered Wheels, Metal 425.00
Wagon, Glove Racer, Bumpers & Rails 1000.00
Wagon, Greyhound, Red Dog Logo, Steel 75.00
Wagon, Happy Times 100.00
Wagon, Hot Rod, No. 750, Fisher–Price 100.00
Wagon, Ice, Horse Drawn, Hubley, Cast Iron 250.00
Wagon, Military, Polychromed Horses, Tin Lithograph, Meier, 4 1/2 In. 885.00
Wagon, Milk & Cream, Horse Drawn, Tin Lithograph, 1920s, 11 1/4 In. 325.00
Wagon, Milk, Horse, Tin & Cast Iron, 7 In. 95.00
Wagon, Newspaper The Evening Star, Wooden, 1930s 325.00
Wagon, Pressed Steel, Painted, Stenciled, Wooden Slat Bed, America, 30 In. 252.00
Wagon, Pulled By 2 Oxen, Driver, Cast Iron, 15 In. 225.00
Wagon, Pulled By Horse, Stenciled Borden's Farm Products, 14 In. 800.00
Wagon, Red, Arcade, Small 50.00
Wagon, Roller Bearing Coaster 695.00
Wagon, Streak–O–Lite, World's Fair, 1937 .... 850.00
Wagon, Studebaker Jr, Wood, Stencil, 40 In. 775.00
Wagon, Tin, Wire Wheels, Wooden, Faded Green Paint, 27 In. 265.00
Wagon, Water Tank, Tin, Cast Iron Horse, Working Valve, Water Buckets, 14 In. ... 1045.00
Wagon, Word Dentist Painted On Side, Late 1800s 550.00
Wally Bear Band, Drum Set 48.00
Waltzing Royal Couple, Windup, Irwin, 1950s, Box, 5 In. 116.00
Washboard, Clear Glass, Midget Washer, 8 x 6 In. 28.00
Washboard, Doll's 27.00
Washboard, Starr, Zinc Surface, Wooden Frame 24.00
Washboard, Stoneware, Embossed Pat. Applied For 275.00
Washing Machine, Little Suzie 12.00
Washing Machine, Marx, Blue Tin, Glass 90.00
Washing Machine, Renwal 65.00
Watch, Snoopy, Red 35.00
Watermelon Eater, Animated, Black Sailor, Kobe, Japan, 1880s, 3 1/4 In. 165.00
Whale, Water Spouting, Battery Operated, Moving Tail, Box 225.00
Whale, Windup, Tin, U.S. Zone Germany 65.00
Wheel Barrow, Tip Top, Tin, Painted, Clockwork, Strauss, 7 x 3 In. 209.00
Wheelbarrow, Child's, Wood, Tin, Steel, Brown Paint, Stenciled Design, 31 In. 385.00
Wheelbarrow, Red Paint, Removable Sides, 40 In. 250.00
Wheelbarrow, Wood, Stencil, Horse On Sides, 25 1/2 In. 55.00
Whip, Amusement Park Ride, Tin Lithograph, Windup, Germany, 9 x 9 In. 2310.00
Whistle, Steam, Brass, 9 In. 95.00
Whistling Spooky Tree, Battery Operated, Tin, Plastic, Marx, 15 In. 950.00
Wild West Rodeo, General Electric Promo, 1952, 65 Piece, 15 x 16 In. 95.00
Winnebago, Camper, Light Blue & White, Tootsietoy, 5 x 1 3/4 x 1 1/2 In. 8.00
Winnebago, Motor Home, Tonka, 18 In. 30.00
Wolf, Glass Eyes, No Tail, Schoenhut 1100.00

Wonderscope, Rin Tin Tin	110.00
Woodpecker, Worn Paint, Wood, 4 In.	126.00
Xylophone Player, Man In Tuxedo Plays, Moving Back & Forth, Celluloid, 6 In.	75.00
Xylophone, Pinky Lee, Emenee, Box	125.00
Yellow Kid, In Goat Cart, Cast Iron, Kenton	395.00
Yogi Bear Jellystone National Park Play Set, Marx, 1962	330.00
Zebra, Steiff, 5 1/2 In.	100.00
Zeppelin, Polished Aluminum, 1 1/2 x 5 In.	85.00
Zeppelin, Shenandoah, Windup, Tin, Lehmann	220.00
Zeppelin, Tin, Prop Activated By Wheels, Marx, 1930, 6 In.	293.00
Zeppelin, Windup, Lehmann, Box, 11 1/2 In.	1045.00
Zoetrope, Bardley, 3 Views, 8 x 10 In.	632.00
Zorro, Magic Slate	45.00

TRAMP ART is a form of folk art made since the Civil War. It is usually made from chip–carved cigar boxes. Examples range from small boxes and picture frames to full–sized pieces of furniture.

Box, Drawer & Sliding Lid, 8 In.	137.00
Box, Drawer, Pyramids All Over, Crackled Varnish, 12 x 12 x 18 In.	270.00
Box, Dresser, Mirrored Doors, 2 Drawers, Pink Interior, Sandwich Pull	595.00
Box, Dresser, Picture Frame Top	138.00
Box, Gum, Colored Geometric Designs All Surfaces, 2 5/8 x 2 1/2 x 1 1/4 In.	95.00
Box, Pyramid Top, 1 Drawer, Sawtooth, 7 x 7 In.	95.00
Box, Worn Finish, White Porcelain Buttons, 10 In.	110.00
Chair, 10 In.	265.00
Chest, Alligatored Varnish, Porcelain Pulls, 13 In.	137.00
Chest, Dome, Ornate Carved, 15 x 10 x 9 1/2 In.	295.00
Chest, Incise–Carved All Sides, Corbett Puterbough, 1932, 5 x 9 x 5 1/2 In.	190.00
Chest, Jewelry, Lift Top, 18 1/2 In.	495.00
Clock, Key Wind, 8 Day	1275.00
Cross, Matchstick, Hope, Wall	28.00
Cross, Popsicle Sticks	28.00
Desk, Rolltop, Cigar Box Wood, 10 3/4 x 13 In.	180.00
Desk, Victorian	4675.00
Figure, Soldier Type, Painted, 10 1/2 In.	165.00
Frame, Crown of Thorns	245.00
Frame, Dark Brown Finish, Gold, 6 1/4 x 4 1/2 In.	50.00
Frame, Linear Form, Creamy White Paint, Silver Highlights, Square	450.00
Frame, Mirror, Cork	65.00
Frame, Star Shape, Brown Paint, 10 3/4 In.	330.00
Frame, With Picture of Locomotive No. 3650, Wooden	185.00
Lamp, Fireplace, Popsicle Sticks & Miniature Ceramic Tiles, 1940s	195.00
Lamp, Table, Shade, Hidden Drawer	350.00
Planter, White Paint, 1920s	435.00
Rocker, Made of Cigar Boxes, Late 1920s	190.00
Shelf, Hanging, Carved, Dated 1930	115.00
Washstand, Fish Carvings On Side, Wallpaper Interior, 2 Piece	1200.00

TRAPS for animals may be handmade. One of the most unusual is the mousetrap made so that when the mouse entered the trap, it was hit on the head with a mallet. Other traps were commercially manufactured and often are marked with the name of the manufacturer. Many traps were designed to be as humane as possible, and they would trap the live animal so it could be released in the woods.

Bear, American Fur & Trade Co., 46 In.	325.00
Bear, Hills No. 1796, Hang Forged & Spring Loaded	550.00
Bear, Kodiak, No. 6, 42 In.	275.00
Bear, Mackensie District Fur Co., No. 15, 1886, 36 In.	225.00
Bear, Newhouse, No. 5	450.00
Fly, Blown Glass	45.00
Lobster, Maine	95.00
Mouse, Delusion	35.00
Mouse, Round	15.00

Mouse, Wooden, 4 Hole 10.00
Skeet, Remington Arms Expert, Cast Iron, Single Throw, Portable 87.00
Wolf, Newhouse, No. 4 1/2, Oneida Community, Double Chain, 4 Prong Drag, 1894   300.00

TREEN, see Wooden category

TRENCH ART is a form of folk art made by soldiers. Metal casings from
bullets and mortar shells were cut and decorated to form useful objects,
such as vases.

Letter Opener, Made From Machine Gun Bullet 15.00
Lighter, 20 Mm Brass Bullet, World War II 45.00
Vase, Brass, World War I 45.00

TRIVETS are now used to hold hot dishes. Most trivets of the late
nineteenth and early twentieth centuries were made to hold hot irons. Iron
or brass reproductions are being made of many of the old styles.

Advertising, American Foundry Co., St. Louis, Iron, Flatiron, Legs 9.50
Brass, Pierced, England, Early 19th Century, 7 1/2 x 23 3/4 In. 330.00
Brass, Victorian, England, 19th Century, 12 3/4 In. 137.00
Cutout Hearts, Compass Star Flower, Ram's Horn Handle, Iron, 11 In. 522.00
Double Heart, Shoe Feet, Black Paint, Iron, 4 1/2 In. 165.00
George Washington, Cast Iron, 9 1/4 In. 104.00
Heart Shape, Wrought Iron, Primitive, 9 3/4 In. 303.00
Horseshoe Shaped, 1884 In Center, Cast Iron 65.00
Iron, Wooden Handle, 18th Century, 10 In. 350.00
Manx Cat, Water Wheel, Brass, Marked Isle of Man, Brass 22.00
Parrot Shape, Colorful, Art Deco 350.00
Peened Rivets, Penny Feet, c.1800, 13 1/2 x 13 1/4 In. 245.00
Pierced Design, Cabriole Legs, Brass, 12 x 13 1/2 In. 245.00
Scrolled & Pierced Heart, Iron, 14 1/2 In. 170.00
Star, Cast Iron, 8 1/4 In. 38.00
Tin, Wrought Iron, Peened Rivets, Penny Footed, 1800, 13 x 9 x 13 In. 245.00

TRUNKS of many types were made. The nineteenth–century sea chest was
often handmade of unpainted wood. Brass-fitted camphorwood chests were
brought back from the Orient. Leather–covered trunks were popular from
the late eighteenth to mid–nineteenth centuries. By 1895, trunks were
covered with canvas or decorated sheet metal. Embossed metal coverings
were used from 1870 to 1910. By 1925, trunks were covered with
vulcanized fiber or undecorated metal.

Bar, Traveling, Brass, Leather Handle, Louis Vuitton, 12 x 16 1/2 x 4 1/2 In. 990.00
Bedding, Dome Top, Iron Strapping, Hinges & Handles, Pine, 33 3/4 x 50 1/2 In.   550.00
Case, Hat, Woman's, Fitted, Louis Vuitton, 18 1/2 x 26 x 15 In. 1760.00
Curved Side, Original Tray, 1860, 25 x 12 In. 175.00
Dome Top, Painted Pine, 17 x 33 In. 1760.00
Dome Top, Wallpaper Lined Interior, Original Hide Covering, 36 In. 27.00
Drop Lid, Plinth Base, Elm Wood, 33 In. 220.00
Elm Wood, Georgian, Low, 33 In. 200.00
Hide Cover, England, 1800, 13 x 22 x 13 In. 330.00
Humpback, Original Orange Trays, Small 185.00
I Am Yours, You Are Mine, Floral Painted Panels, Germany, Dated 1866 .... 750.00
Immigrant's, Oak, Wrought Iron Strapping, England, 36 1/4 In. 302.00
Lift Top, Polychrome Design, Brass Studded 660.00
Louis Vuitton XI, Red, Leather, 23 x 22 In. 950.00
Luggage, Tweed, Leather Trim, Hartman, 5 Piece 825.00
Mediterranean, Painted Design, Cedar Lined, 21 x 36 In. 90.00
New England, Dome Top, Wooden, Mustard Paint, 1800s, 24 In. 310.00
Picnic Case, 2 Thermoses, Lidded Box, Fitted, Louis Vuitton 770.00
Pine, Grained, Iron Lock & Handles, Chinese Black Stand, 12 x 24 In. 275.00
Sheet Steel, Tooled Ribbing, Worn Black Paint, Tan Trim, Brass Lock, 22 In. 55.00
Steamer, 6 Drawers, Cloth Partitions For Hanging, Louis Vuitton, 44 x 21 x 22 In.   1650.00
Traveling, Worn, Louis Vuitton 770.00

TUTHILL Cut Glass Company of Middletown, New York, worked from 1902 to 1923. Of special interest are the finely cut pieces of stemware and tableware.

Bowl, Hobstars & Canes, Handles, 11 In.	325.00
Box, Hinged Cover, Round	650.00
Cologne Bottle, Signed	600.00
Decanter, Floral & Leaf Design, Sterling Silver Top & Handle	2700.00
Mayonnaise Set, Underplate, Phlox Pattern	745.00
Powder Jar, Wild Rose, Gorham Cover, 3 x 7 In.	495.00
Vase, Vintage, Intaglio Cut, 8 In.	165.00
Water Set, Blackberry, 5 Piece	850.00

TYPEWRITER collectors divide typewriters into two main classifications: the index machine, which has a pointer and a dial for letter selection, and the keyboard machine, most commonly seen today. The first successful typewriter was made by Sholes and Glidden in 1874.

American Typewriter Co., No. 165267, Index Style, Part of Wooden Case	275.00
American, Black Enameled, Mahogany Base, 11 1/2 x 8 x 3 In.	275.00
Blickensderfer, No. 5, Manual & Accessories, Wooden Case	98.00
Corona No. 3, Folding, Case	55.00
Hammond, Mahogany Base, Ebony Keys, Pat. 1882–1883, 14 x 12 x 6 In.	605.00
Oliver, No. 9, Manual, Accessories	45.00
Simplex, Box	50.00 To 65.00
Smith–Corona, Model 250, Electric	40.00

UHL pottery was made in Evansville, Indiana, in 1854. The pottery moved to Huntingburg, Indiana, in 1908. Stoneware and glazed pottery were made until the mid–1940s.

Bean Pot, Blue	95.00
Bean Pot, Light Yellow	30.00
Crock, Blue, 6 In.	70.00
Jar, 2 Gal.	25.00
Jar, 5 Gal.	50.00
Jar, Cover, Apple Butter, Brown	15.00
Jar, Double Stamped, 3 Gal.	225.00
Jar, Krogman Whiskey, Brown, 2 Handles, 8 Gal.	55.00
Jar, No. 2	25.00
Jug, Baseball, 2 1/2 In.	55.00 To 75.00
Jug, Canteen, Blue	32.00
Jug, Christmas	160.00 To 220.00
Pitcher, Ball, Tan	12.50
Pitcher, Barrel, Rose, 1 Qt.	45.00
Pitcher, Burgundy, Stopper, Marked, 1 Qt.	20.00
Pitcher, Grape, Blue, 2 Qt.	70.00
Vase, Blue, 8 In.	48.00

UMBRELLA collectors like rain or shine. The first known umbrella was owned by King Louis XIII of France in 1637. The earliest umbrellas were sunshades, not designed to be used in the rain. The umbrella was embellished and redesigned many times. In 1852, the fluted steel–rib style was developed and it has remained the most useful style.

Buick Automobile Advertising, Large	60.00
Parasol, Black Lace, White Carved Handle, Edwardian	135.00
Parasol, Child's, Wooden, Brass & Ivory, Taffeta Covered	85.00
Parasol, Collapsible, Ivory Inlay	15.00
Parasol, White Linen, Lace Floral Embroidered, Edwardian	135.00
Uncle Wiggly	200.00

◆◆◆

Beware of fire. Never put a heavy object on top of an extension cord. Never put the cord under a rug.

◆◆◆

UNION PORCELAIN WORKS was established at Greenpoint, New York, in 1848 by Charles Cartlidge. The company went through a series of ownership changes and finally closed in the early 1900s. The company made a fine quality white porcelain that was often decorated in clear, bright colors.

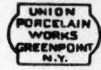

Oyster Plate, Nautical Design	100.00
Pitcher, Card Player, c.1876	4100.00
Vase, Tortoise, c.1879	2500.00

UNIVERSITY OF NORTH DAKOTA, see North Dakota School of Mines

VAL ST. LAMBERT Cristalleries of Belgium was founded by Messieurs Kemlin and Lelievre in 1825. The company is still in operation. All types of table glassware and decorative glassware were made. Pieces were often decorated with cut designs.

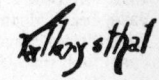

Ashtray, Crystal, Signed	30.00
Bowl, Cobalt Blue, 12 In.	1500.00
Bowl, Crystal, Red Flashed Overlay, Signed, 10 x 4 In.	350.00
Box, Ring Finial, Basketweave, Handle, Blue, 3 3/4 x 4 In.	85.00
Box, Wreath On Cover, Signed, 2 x 1/2 x 3 In.	25.00
Decanter Set, Dance Pattern, 24K Gold Trim, 5 Piece	800.00
Lamp, Boudoir, Jewel Leaves Around Base, Turtle Feet, Brass Fitter	5800.00
Perfume Bottle, Diamond & Arch, Amber & Crystal, 6 1/4 In.	95.00
Vase, Cranberry, Crystal, Signed, 12 1/2 In.	295.00
Vase, Dance, Cobalt Blue, 10 In.	700.00
Vase, Floral, Enameled, 10 1/2 In.	505.00
Vase, Ruby Cut To Clear, Signed, 6 In.	215.00 To 250.00
Wine Bucket, Wavy Design, 9 1/2 In.	250.00

VALLERYSTHAL Glassworks was founded in 1836 in Lorraine, France. In 1854, the firm became Klenglin et Cie. It made table and decorative glass, opaline, cameo, and art glass. A line of covered, pressed glass animal dishes was made in the nineteenth century. The firm is still working.

Bowl, Dolphin Legs, Blue Milk Glass	35.00
Compote, Cover, Tree Trunk Base, White Bowl, 9 In.	150.00
Dish, Hen Cover, Yellow, Green, Brown, 8 In.	360.00
Figurine, Dog On Rug, Blue Milk Glass	145.00

VAN BRIGGLE pottery was made by Artus Van Briggle in Colorado Springs, Colorado, after 1901. Van Briggle had been a decorator at the Rookwood Pottery of Cincinnati, Ohio. He died in 1904. His wares usually had modeled relief decorations and a soft, dull glaze. The pottery is still working and still making some of the original designs.

Bookends, Bears	145.00
Bookends, Peacock, 1920s	150.00
Bowl, Blossoms At Rim, Blue & Purple Glaze, No. 513, 1906, 3 1/2 x 7 In.	470.00
Bowl, Blossoms, Robin's–Egg Blue, Marked, 4 x 4 1/2 In.	330.00
Bowl, Blue, Colorado Springs, 5 In.	25.00
Bowl, Dragonflies, Dated 1920	250.00
Bowl, Heart & Leaf, Ming Blue, Signed, 4 In.	40.00
Bowl, Ming, Turquoise, Curdled Glaze, 7 1/2 In.	145.00
Bowl, Persian Rose, Leaf Pattern, Signed, 8 1/2 In.	125.00
Bowl, Turquoise, 7 In.	40.00
Candleholder, Blue, Double, Pair	95.00
Chamberstick, Shaped Socket On Dish Base, Arched Handle, 1917, 3 1/4 In.	110.00
Conch Shell, Persian Rose, 8 In.	55.00
Console, Flower Frog, Dragonfly, Green, Brown, Colorado Springs, 3 Piece	400.00
Console, Lady of The Lake, Detached Flower Frog, Persian Rose Color	475.00
Cup & Saucer, Blue Demitasse	75.00
Figurine, Deer, Lying Down, 4 In.	40.00
Figurine, Elephant, 3 In.	85.00
Figurine, Elephant, Turquoise	85.00

Figurine, Indian Girl, Kneeling, Grinding Corn, Ivory	125.00
Figurine, Mule, Turquoise, 3 3/4 In.	40.00
Figurine, Nude Girl, Holding Shell, Burmese Red	275.00
Figurine, Starfish, 14 In.	115.00
Flower Frog, Duck, Maroon	58.00
Flower Frog, Figural, 1915	125.00
Head Vase, Black, 11 In.	125.00
Incense Burner, Light & Dark Blue Matte Glaze, 4 1/4 x 4 1/2 In.	345.00
Lamp Base, Woman Carrying Water, 11 In.	195.00
Lamp, Blue, Rebecca At The Well, No Shade, 1950s, 16 1/2 In.	250.00
Lamp, Damsel of Damascus, Shade	225.00
Lamp, Finger, Owl, Plum Color	260.00
Lamp, Girl Kneeling, Urn On Shoulder, Floral Shade, 10 In.	385.00
Lamp, Turquoise, Butterfly Shade	135.00
Lamp, Vase, Mountain Craig, Brown	120.00
Mug, Green–Gray, 5 In.	400.00
Mug, Matte Green Glaze, 1902, 5 x 5 1/2 In.	330.00
Paperweight, Rabbit, 1920s	125.00
Planter, Swan, 7 1/2 In.	88.00
Plaque, Big Buffalo & Little Star, Pair	190.00
Plaque, Indian Head, Persian Rose	110.00
Plate, Embossed Poppy, Blue Glaze, Burgundy Ground, No. 12, 1908, 8 In.	450.00
Salt & Pepper, Persian Rose, Barrel Shape	40.00
Tea Set, Turquoise, Green To Blue, Signed, 4 Piece	150.00
Urn, Burgundy To Wine, 8 3/4 In.	295.00
Urn, Yucca Leaves, Blue & Red Glaze, 2 Handles, Colo. Springs, 14 x 7 In.	330.00
Urn, Yucca Leaves, Mustard To Green Glaze, 1915, 13 1/2 x 6 1/2 In.	990.00
Vase, Aqua Blue, Flared, Molded 6 Long Stemmed Flowers, 9 In.	220.00
Vase, Aqua, Flower, 4 In.	35.00
Vase, Art Deco Style, 12 In.	160.00
Vase, Bears, Mountain Craig Brown, 1926–1932, 13 1/2 In.	1450.00
Vase, Brown, Handle, 9 In.	25.00
Vase, Bud, Blue–Gray Glaze, 4 Buttresses, Long Neck, 1914, 5 x 3 1/2 In.	165.00
Vase, Butterfly, 3 1/2 In.	49.50
Vase, Butterfly, Turquoise, Bowl Type, Dated 1915, 4 In.	285.00
Vase, Conch, 1928	30.00
Vase, Decorative Band, Lavender Glaze, 8 In.	220.00
Vase, Despondency, 1926–1932, 13 1/2 In.	155.00
Vase, Despondency, Matte Blue Finish, 13 In.	605.00
Vase, Despondency, Turquoise Blue, 1920s, 13 1/2 In.	1100.00
Vase, Dragonfly, Mulberry, Dated 1913, 7 In.	485.00
Vase, Feathered Peacock, Blue To Rose Pink Glaze, 1904, 11 x 7 In.	330.00
Vase, Flower & Leaves, Purple & Green, Handles, No. 49, 10 x 7 1/2 In.	1750.00
Vase, Flower Design, 4 In.	25.00
Vase, Glaze Burst, Handles, 13 1/4 In.	99.00
Vase, Green, Blue Highlights, 1913, 10 In.	715.00
Vase, Indian Head, Marked, 1925, 11 1/4 In.	357.00
Vase, Indian Head, Maroon, 11 1/2 In.	495.00
Vase, Indian Head, Rose Matte, 11 1/2 In.	260.00
Vase, Indian Woman With Pot, 8 In.	145.00
Vase, Leaves, Deep Mulberry Glaze, 2 Handles, 1920s, Tall	170.00
Vase, Lorelei, 10 In.	275.00
Vase, Luna Moth, Dark Blue, 1912, 2 3/4 In.	325.00
Vase, Mardi Gras, Matte Ivory, Handles, 9 In.	15.00
Vase, Maroon, Flower, 4 In.	50.00
Vase, Mistletoe, Mottled Turquoise On Cream, 1908, 4 In.	500.00
Vase, Mulberry, Handle, 13 In.	295.00
Vase, Mustard Glaze, 1907–1911, 8 In.	950.00
Vase, Outlined Design, Allover Blue Mottling, 1902, 4 1/2 In.	1400.00
Vase, Peacock–Green Brown–Eyed Susans, Burgundy Ground, 9 1/2 In.	385.00
Vase, Persian Rose, 10 In.	175.00
Vase, Persian Rose, 1926–1932, 7 1/2 In.	88.00
Vase, Persian Rose, Leaf Design, Signed, 3 1/2 x 4 In.	65.00

Vase, Purple Closed Yucca Plants, Light Green Ground, 17 1/4 In. 33.00
Vase, Stick, Turquoise, 9 In. 45.00
Vase, Vegetable Pattern, Blue–Gray Baluster, 7 1/8 In. 715.00
Wall Pocket, Little Red Riding Hood, 9 In. 400.00
Wall Pocket, Mountain Craig, Brown, 10 In. 325.00
Wall Pocket, Persian Rose, 8 In. 195.00
Water Set, Black High Gloss Finish, Ice Lip Pitcher, 9 Piece 300.00

VASA MURRHINA is the name of a glassware made by the Vasa Murrhina
Art Glass Company of Sandwich, Massachusetts, about 1884. The
glassware was transparent and was embedded with small pieces of colored
glass and metallic flakes. The mica flakes were coated with silver, gold,
copper, or nickel. Some of the pieces were cased. The same type of glass
was made in England. Collectors often confuse Vasa Murrhina glass with
aventurine, spatter, or spangle glass. There is uncertainty about what
actually was made by the Vasa Murrhina factory. Related pieces may be
listed under Spangle Glass.

Basket, Applied Clear Thory Handle, Ruffled, 7 In. 135.00
Basket, Stripes of Mica Flakes Outside, White Interior, 8 3/4 In. 195.00
Basket, Turquoise, Handle, Fenton, 11 In. 110.00
Biscuit Jar, Blue, Gold Mica Spatter, Silver Plate Lid & Handle 135.00
Bowl, Berry Prunt On Bottom, Pink Lining, 5 x 5 In. 235.00
Dish, Attached On Brass Base, 8 1/2 In. 65.00
Dish, Burgundy & Gold Flakes, Cranberry, Crimped Rim, 8 In. 85.00
Rose Bowl, 8–Crimp, Pink & Beige Spatter Outside, White Lining, 3 1/4 In. 110.00
Vase, Aventurine Green, Ribbed, 14 In. 95.00
Vase, Gold Flecks, Hand Painted Design, 4 1/2 In. 140.00
Vase, Green & White On Crystal, Experimental 55.00
Vase, Jack–In–The–Pulpit, Spatter, Allover Silver Spangles, 7 In. 85.00
Vase, Mica Flake Design, Clear Handles, Squared Top, 8 1/2 In. 135.00
Vase, Ruffled, Shell Trim, Silver Mica Flaking, Pink, 9 1/4 In. 145.00

VASELINE GLASS is a greenish–yellow glassware resembling petroleum
jelly. Some vaseline glass is still being made in old and new styles. Pressed
glass of the 1870s was often made of vaseline–colored glass. Additional
pieces of vaseline glass may also be listed under Pressed Glass in this book.

Bowl, Gilded Design, Fluted, Footed 25.00
Bowl, Green Opalescent, Open Edge, 5 In. 24.00
Bowl, Ruffled, Opalescent, Fenton, 8 In. 30.00
Chocolate Pot, Imperial Crown China, Vienna, Austria, Battle Scene 100.00
Coffeepot, Floral Design, Small 27.50
Compote, Clark's Teaberry Gum 80.00
Condiment Set, Ranson, 4 Piece 395.00
Daisy & Button, Bowl, 11 In. 95.00
Dish, Hens Cover, Opaque 30.00
Jam Jar, Triangles Within Squares, Metal Lid & Handle, 5 1/2 In. 120.00
Pitcher, Cream, Alaska, Opalescent, Footed 90.00
Pitcher, Hobnail, Clear Handle 27.50
Rose Bowl, Alaska, Opalescent 90.00
Spooner, Iris With Meander, Opalescent, Jefferson Glass, 1903 .... 65.00
Spooner, Wreath & Shell 65.00
Table Set, Columbia, 4 Piece 265.00
Toothpick, Balder 40.00
Tray, Daisy & Button, Triangular, 12 In. 75.00
Tray, Willow Oak, Scalloped Rim, 16 1/2 In. 80.00
Tumbler, Ranson, 5 Piece 200.00
Vase, Asymmetrical Enameled, Japanese Style, 1862, 8 In. 95.00
Vase, Corncob 135.00

VENETIAN GLASS, see Glass–Venetian

VENINI glass was first designed by Paolo Venini, who established his factory in Murano, Italy, in 1925. He is best known for pieces of modern design, including the famous *handkerchief* vase. The company is still working. Other pieces of Italian glass may be found in the Glass–Contemporary, Glass–Midcentury, and Glass–Venetian categories of this book.

Bowl, Clamshell, Gold Flecks, Green & Black Stripes, Signed, 12 x 11 1/2 In.	850.00
Bowl, Riccardo Licata, 15 In.	2970.00
Box, Murrine, Irregular Orange Spirals On Cover, Marked, 6 1/4 In.	660.00
Decanter, Conical Stopper, Yellow & Black Vertical Pattern, Marked, 17 3/4 In.	9350.00
Figurine, Chicken, Opaque White Body, c.1950	8500.00
Figurine, Poodle, Black, White Eyes, Marked, 5 1/2 In.	440.00
Vase, Applied Glass Drops On Lower Part, Signed, Marked, 9 1/4 In.	2640.00
Vase, Clear, 12 In.	1870.00
Vase, Flared Large Trumpet Form, Squares In Red, Blue, Green, Black, 9 In.	5500.00
Vase, Flattened Oval Form, Transparent Amber, Opaque Black Glass, 9 In.	1210.00
Vase, Flattened Sides, Patchwork Pattern, Paper Label, 8 1/2 In.	4620.00
Vase, Handkerchief, Fazzoletto, 11 1/4 In.	1650.00
Vase, Handkerchief, Latticinio Stripes, Marked, 4 3/4 x 9 3/4 In.	495.00
Vase, Handkerchief, White Over Lavender, Signed, 1949, 10 3/4 In.	1650.00
Vase, Mahogany, White Interior, 14 In.	800.00
Vase, Undulating Rim, Patchwork Pattern, Marked, 9 1/4 In.	4180.00
Vase, Vaso A Canne, Striped Design, 5 3/4 In.	660.00

VERLYS glass was made in France after 1931. It was made in the United States from 1935 to 1951. The glass is either blown or molded. The American glass is signed with a diamond–point–scratched name, but the French pieces are marked with a molded signature. The designs resemble those used by Lalique.

Ashtray, Intaglio Butterflies, Beveled Rim, Signed, 4 1/2 x 3 1/2 In.	95.00
Bowl, Birds, Dragonflies, 11 In.	135.00
Bowl, Chinois	37.50
Bowl, Clear & Frosted, Signed, 13 1/2 In.	165.00
Bowl, Tassels, Beige, 12 In.	90.00
Bowl, Water Lily, Amber, 14 In.	375.00
Box, Art Nouveau Floral, Signed	275.00
Charger, Birds & Dragonflies, 12 In.	120.00 To 135.00
Dish, Pinecone, Blue, 7 In.	55.00
Vase, Alpine Thistle, Flashed Tan On Flowers & Leaves, 9 In.	525.00
Vase, Autumn Scene, Signed, 8 1/4 In.	225.00
Vase, Butterflies, 5 In.	225.00
Vase, Mandarin, Crystal, 9 In.	295.00
Vase, Signed, 10 x 8 In.	195.00
Vase, Thistle, Topaz, Signed, 9 1/2 In.	750.00

VERNON KILNS was the name used after 1958 by Vernon Potteries, Ltd. The company, which started in Vernon, California, in 1931, made dinnerware and figurines until it closed in 1958. Collectors search for the brightly colored dinnerware and the pieces designed by Rockwell Kent, Walt Disney, and Don Blanding. For more information, see *Kovels' Depression Glass & American Dinnerware Price List.*

Ashtray, Mission San Rafael	25.00
Ashtray, Statue of Liberty	15.00
Bowl, Disney Winged Nymph, Pink, 12 In.	225.00
Bowl, Homespun, 5 1/2 In.	4.00
Bowl, Ultra California, Aqua, 9 In.	27.00
Bowl, Vegetable, Divided, Homespun	12.00
Bowl, Vegetable, Divided, Tickled Pink	20.00
Bread Plate, Organdy	2.00
Butter, Cover, Casual California, Pink	35.00
Casserole, Cover, Organdie	20.00
Chop Plate, California, 13 In.	25.00

Chop Plate, Lei Lani, 12 In.	135.00
Chop Plate, Native California, Yellow, 14 In.	30.00
Chop Plate, Winchester, 14 In.	195.00
Creamer, Heavenly Days	8.00
Cup & Saucer, Lei Lani	20.00
Mug, Heavenly Days	10.00
Pitcher, Gingham, 2 Qt.	20.00
Pitcher, Lei Lani, Blanding	28.00
Plate, City of Montgomery, Alabama, State Capitol Building, 10 1/2 In.	45.00
Plate, Coral Reef, Brown, 10 1/2 In.	85.00
Plate, Cottage Windows, 10 1/2 In.	18.00
Plate, Homespun, 10 In.	9.00
Plate, Nutcracker, 9 1/2 In.	150.00
Plate, Organdie, 9 1/2 In.	5.00
Plate, Tweed, 9 1/2 In.	6.00
Plate, Ultra California, Pink, 7 1/2 In.	9.00
Plate, Winchester, 10 In.	45.00
Platter, California, Turquoise, 12 In.	18.00
Platter, Heavenly Days, 11 In.	9.00
Platter, Heavenly Days, 13 1/2 In.	10.00
Relish, Tickled Pink	18.00
Salt & Pepper, Anytime, Turquoise	15.00
Salt & Pepper, Fantasia, Hoop Low, Mushroom	145.00
Sauce, Autumn Ballet, Disney	40.00
Soup, Dish, Flat, Organdie	7.00
Soup, Dish, Flat, Tweed	8.00
Soup, Homespun, Lug	9.00
Sugar & Creamer, Winchester	69.50
Sugar, Cover, Organdie	7.00
Teapot, Brown–Eyed Susan	45.00
Tumbler, Frontier Days	48.00
Tumbler, Gingham	8.00

VERRE DE SOIE glass was first made by Frederick Carder at the Steuben Glass Works from about 1905 to 1930. It is an iridescent glass of soft white or very, very pale green. The name means *glass of silk,* and it does resemble silk. Other factories have made verre de soie, and some of the English examples were made of different colors. Verre de soie is an art glass and is not related to the iridescent, pressed, white carnival glass mistakenly called by its name. Related pieces may be found in the Steuben category.

Compote, Cover, Celeste Blue Rim, Green Leaves, 8 x 6 In.	1250.00
Perfume Bottle, Green Iridescence, Numbered	245.00
Rose Bowl, Raised Rib, Steuben	110.00
Sherbet, Rolled–Over Rim, Etched	35.00
Tumbler, Pink Threading, Steuben, 6 In.	302.50
Vase, Engraved Flowers, Steuben, 10 In.	200.00

VIENNA ART plates are round metal serving trays produced at the turn of the century. The designs, copied from Royal Vienna porcelain plates, usually featured a portrait of a woman encircled by a wide, ornate border. Many were used as advertising or promotional items and were produced in Coshocton, Ohio, by J. F. Meeks Tuscarora Advertising Co. and H. D. Beach's Standard Advertising Co.

Kaier's Brewing Co., Tin, 10 In.	82.00
MacNicol's Saloon, Bare Chested Beauty, 10 In.	270.00
Plate, Walker Baker, Girl & Tray, 10 1/4 In.	165.00

VIENNA, see Beehive category

VILLEROY & BOCH Pottery of Mettlach was founded in 1841. The firm made many types of wares, including the famous Mettlach steins. Collectors can be confused because although Villeroy and Boch made most

of its pieces in the city of Mettlach, Germany, they also had factories in other locations. The dating code impressed on the bottom of most pieces makes it possible to determine the age of the piece. Additional items may be found in the Mettlach category.

Bowl, Stick, Spatter, 7 3/4 x 4 1/2 In.	104.00
Charger, Castle Scene, 12 In.	190.00
Ewer, Pewter Lid, Majolica, Art Nouveau Flowers, Olive Ground, 10 In.	350.00
Mug, 4/10 Liter, Mettlach, 1930s	35.00
Mustard, Pedestal, Blue Transfer	30.00
Pitcher, Cover, Red Poppy, Leaves, White, 7 1/2 In.	125.00
Pitcher, Pug, Hunting, 7 In.	185.00
Stein, Man On Horse, Bugle, Raised Floral, Pewter Top, 10 In.	125.00
Stein, No. 1821, Pewter Lid, 13 1/2 In.	247.50
Vase, Bacchus, 13 In.	265.00
Vase, Enameled Flowers, Amethyst, 5 In.	60.00

VOLKMAR pottery was made by Charles Volkmar of New York from 1879 to about 1911. He was associated with several firms, including the Volkmar Ceramic Company, Volkmar and Cory, and Charles Volkmar and Son. Volkmar had been a painter, and his designs often look like oil paintings drawn on pottery.

VOLKMAR
Corona N.Y

Lamp Base, Flambe Glaze, Oil Font, Leaded Glass Shade, Marked, 17 In.	550.00
Vase, Crackled High–Gloss, Pink Glaze, Marked, 3 1/2 In.	220.00

VOLKSTEDT was a soft–paste porcelain factory started in 1760 by Georg Heinrich Macheleid at Volkstedt, Thuringia. Volkstedt–Rudolstadt was a porcelain factory started at Volkstedt–Rudolstadt by Beyer and Bock in 1890. Most pieces seen in shops today are from the later factory.

Candlestick, Man & Woman, Period Costumes, c.1886, 11 In., Pair	695.00
Clock, Mantel, Man & Woman Playing Instruments, c.1886, 9 x 9 In.	295.00
Figurine, Ballerinas, White, Pink Lace Skirts, c.1930, 7 In.	225.00
Figurine, Music Book, 3 Figures, Mandolin, 9 x 9 1/2 In.	1050.00
Figurine, Portrait Painter, Seated Woman & Artist, 7 x 9 In.	550.00
Figurine, Wedding March, 9 x 13 In.	1250.00

WADE pottery is made by the Wade Group of Potteries started in 1810 near Burslem, England. Several potteries merged to become George Wade & Son, Ltd. early in the twentieth century and other potteries have been added through the years. The best known Wade pieces are the small figurines given away with Red Rose Tea and other promotional items. The Disney figures are listed in this book in the Disneyana category.

c. 1936 +

Antique Shop	5.00
Bowl, Barge Posy, Brown	30.00
Bowl, Posy, Log With Squirrel	17.50
Candleholder, Mayfair	10.00
Candleholder, Venetian	9.00
Canisters, Village Stores	240.00
Crocodile, Red Rose Tea	5.00
Dish, Aqua, Angelfish	9.50
Dish, Blue Bird, Oval	25.00
Dish, Cat	35.00
Dish, Chalk & Cheese	70.00
Dish, Crackle, Tan & Gold	20.00
Dish, Log, Fawn	35.00
Dish, Spaniel	40.00
Dish, Starfish	15.00
Mill With Water Wheel	10.00
Polar Bear, 1956	6.00
Posy Holder, Bridge	10.00
Salt, Village Stores	25.00
Teapot, Bramble, 1952	50.00
Tony Weller, Guinness, 1968	85.00
Trinket Box, Crab	30.00

Trinket Box, Hedgehog	30.00
Trinket Box, Romance Range, Rectangular	17.50
Urn, Posy, Green, Brown, White	7.50
Vase, Koala, Tree Trunk	35.00
Whimsy–On–Why Village	88.00

WAHPETON POTTERY, see Rosemeade category

WALLACE NUTTING photographs are listed under Print, Nutting. His reproduction furniture is listed under Furniture.

WALRATH was a potter who worked in New York City, Rochester, New York, and at the Newcomb Pottery in New Orleans, Louisiana. Frederick Walrath died in 1920. Pieces listed here are from his Rochester period.

Mug, Brown	85.00
Paperweight, Scarab, Blue	210.00
Vase, Pine Needles, Cones, 8 In.	1500.00
Vase, Trees Bearing Red Fruit, Lighter Green Ground, 4 3/4 x 4 3/4 In.	1100.00

WALT DISNEY, see Disneyana

WALTER, see A. Walter

WARWICK china was made in Wheeling, West Virginia, in a pottery working from 1887 to 1951. Many pieces were made with hand painted or decal decorations. The most familiar Warwick has a shaded brown background. The name *Warwick* is part of the mark and sometimes the mysterious word *IOGA* is also included.

Ale Set, Dickens Characters, IOGA, 5 Piece	320.00
Beer Set, Monk Pouring Beer On Pitcher, Monk Playing Violin On Cups, 9 Piece ...	395.00
Chocolate Pot, Cherries	55.00
Mug, Poppies, Brown	65.00
Pitcher, Flowers, IOGA	75.00
Pitcher, Flowers, Small	65.00
Pitcher, Monk Pouring Beer, Set of 8 Cups	395.00
Plate, Swimming Fish, 8 1/4 In.	50.00
Tankard, Elks, Square Handle, 10 1/2 In.	175.00
Vase, Narcissus, Seagulls, Ring Handles, White, 10 In.	100.00
Vase, Woman, Drape On Shoulder & Bust, Black Hair, Twig Handles, 10 1/2 In. ...	175.00

WATCH FOBS were worn on watch chains. They were popular during Victorian times and after. Many styles, especially advertising designs, are still made today.

Airship, Bi–Plane, Galleon	30.00
American Legion, Airplane Shape, 1930	14.00
American Old Line Insurance Co., Pictures Indian Head	40.00
Aultman Taylor, Starved Rooster	150.00
Baseball Shape, With Pitcher	45.00
Bobcat Head, Leather Strap, Bakelite	90.00
Brotherhood of Railroad Trainmen, Small Diamond, 10K Gold	35.00
Buffalo Bill, Pawnee Bill	125.00
Chrysler, 1942	15.00
Cincinnati Mfg., Horseshoe Shape	50.00
Coca–Cola, Relieves Fatigue, 1907	125.00
Columbian Exposition, Keystone Watch Case Co., 1893 .... 50.00 To 95.00
Compass, Bloodstone, 15K Gold	200.00
Compliments of Keystone Watch Case Co.	40.00
Cooks Linen, Chefs In Kitchen, St. Louis, Enameled	60.00
Deere Centennial, 1937	85.00
Dodge Brothers	75.00
Elks, Membership Certificate, Sterling Case	50.00
Glad Hand Soap	65.00
Grain Livestock Commission, Cow's Head, Brass, Leather Straps	50.00

Hoard's Dairyman 40.00
Hook Mechanism, Monogram, Sterling Silver, Kalo Shop, 1 5/8 In. 225.00
Intaglio Cut Carnelian, With Hairwork Gold–Filled Watch Chain 175.00
International Harvester 75.00
Ivory, 3–D Horsehead, Horseshoe & Nail Hang From Movable Bit 350.00
J. I. Case, Oval 60.00
Jaguar, Chain 35.00
Jersey Creme Soda 85.00
John Deere, Mother–of–Pearl 150.00
Medal, Tennis, 1916 Singles, Gold Filled 85.00
Mickey Mouse 195.00
Moose, Gold Finish, Stamp Holder 50.00
National Guard Encampment, Nevada, Missouri 75.00
Opening of East River Bridge, New York–Brooklyn 30.00
Panama–Pacific Expo 25.00
Patton Brewing Co., Celluloid On Metal 40.00
Providence, Seal of City, Roger Williams, Brass 25.00
Red Diamond Overalls 75.00
Silver, Holds 2 Coins, Germany 50.00
Star Brand Shoes, St. Louis 50.00
Studebaker, Leather Strap, Brass & Enamel 48.00
Wyandotte Chemical, Indian 50.00
Yellowstone Park, Bear & Waterfall 25.00

WATCH pockets held the pocket watch that was important in Victorian times because it was not until World War I that the wristwatch was used. All types of watches are collected: silver, gold, or plated. Watches are arranged by company name or by style. Pocket watches are listed here; wristwatches are a separate category.

Agassiz, Split Second Chronograph, 20 Jewel, 18K Gold, c.1900 .... 2200.00
American Watch Co., Skeletonized Movement, Open Face, Train On Back Cover 125.00
Audemars, Piquet, Art Deco Platinum & Black Enamel Case 2310.00
Avalon, Lapel, Gold Filled, 1940s 100.00
Brevette, Alarm, Steel Case, Desk Or Pocket, Size 18 .... 500.00
Buder Klumak, Chronograph, Hunting Case, 18K Yellow Gold, 19th Century 2475.00
Character, Lucy of Peanuts Cartoon, Timex, Box, 1970s 45.00
Colsen, Railroad Train On Back Cover, 17 Jewel, 10K Rolled Gold 150.00
Dunlop Tire & Rubber Co., Figural Golf Ball Case, Chain, Silver, Pocket 225.00
E. Jaccard, Hunting Case, Minute Repeater, 18K Gold, 1881 .... 9680.00
Elgin National, Coin Silver Hunting Case, Key Wind, Pocket 225.00
Elgin National, Silver Cased, 17 Jewel 42.50
Elgin, Black & Chrome Dial 85.00
Elgin, Gold Filled, 17 Jewel, c.1903 .... 95.00
Elgin, Gold Filled, Fancy Case 475.00
Elgin, Hunting Case, Gold Filled, Key Wind, Pocket, Wooden Box, 1876 .... 125.00
Elgin, Illinois Gold Case, Engineer, Cut Diamond, Stars, 25 Year 350.00
Elgin, Key Wind, Hunting Case, Coin Silver .... 110.00 To 200.00
Elgin, Key Wind, Hunting Case, Silver 140.00
Elgin, Key Wind, Open Face, Coin Silver, Size 18, c.1874 .... 95.00
Elgin, Man's, Gold Filled, Jeweled Movement, Hand Wind 143.00
Elgin, National, Silver Case 42.00
Elgin, Silver Case 25.00
Elgin, Size 18, Gold 175.00
Elgin, World War II Military Issue, Timer, Size 16 .... 80.00
Emil Eisner, Hunting Case, Jeweled Nickel Movement, Enameled Dial, 18K Gold ... 455.00
English, Fusee, Key Wind & Set, Sterling Silver Case, c.1862 .... 200.00
Girard Perregaux, Cruciform, Rose Cut Diamond Set Bezel, Enamel, c.1900 .... 6600.00
H. R. Ekegren, Double Dial Hunter Case, Visible Movement, c.1900 .... 4400.00
H. Samuel, Silver, Key Wind, Manchester Marked, Victorian 110.00
Hamilton, Gold, Original Box 170.00
Hamilton, Silver Case, Size 16, 1940s 100.00
Hampden, 17 Jewel 245.00
Hampden, John Hancock, Hunting Case, 21 Jewel, c.1900 .... 200.00

Watch, Lapel, Scotty Dog, Marcasite,

Sterling Silver, France, c.1930

◆◆◆◆◆◆◆◆◆◆◆◆◆◆◆◆◆◆◆◆◆◆◆◆

You can list only your phone number and not your street address in the local phone book. Ask your phone company. Good idea for known collectors.

◆◆◆◆◆◆◆◆◆◆◆◆◆◆◆◆◆◆◆◆◆◆◆◆

Hampden, Molly Stark, Open Face, Neck Chain, 1896	150.00
Henry Ducommun, 10K Gold, Key Wind, Huntington Case, Patent Lever	300.00
Howard, 14K Gold, 23 Jewel, c.1910	395.00
Howard, 18K Yellow Gold, White Face, Black Arabic Numerals, 21 Jewel	220.00
Howard, Chronometer, Railroad, Series 11, 21 Jewel	350.00
Illinois, 14K Gold Filled, 1920s	85.00
Illinois, Key Wind, Gold Case	180.00
Illinois, Woman's, 14K Gold Hunting Case, Deer Scene, Jewels, 1887	525.00
Ingraham, Uncle Sam	100.00 To 125.00
Jaeger, Clip, Platinum, Gold, Sapphire & Diamond, 18K Gold, 15 Jewel, c.1925	9350.00
John C. Heppert, Railroad, Lever Set, 21 Ruby Jewels, Large	200.00
John Emery, Diamond Set Fuzee Movement, Key Wind, Wooden Case, Marked	965.00
John Harrison, Open Face, Fusee Movement, Diamond End Stone, 18K Gold	352.00
Lapel, 14K Gold, Seed Pearl, France	525.00
Lapel, Ball Form, Woman's, Art Deco, Fleur–De–Lis Pin, Red & Black	55.00
Lapel, Blue Enameled & Diamonds, 18K Gold	600.00
Lapel, Scotty Dog, Marcasite, Sterling Silver, France, c.1930 ....*Illus*	545.00
Longines, Lapel, Diamond Initials, Enamel Dragonfly Pin Set With Sapphires	605.00
Metal Dial, Seconds Dial, Longines Movement, Tiffany, 18K Yellow Gold	395.00
New Haven, Sports Timer, Football & Basketball, Picture, 1920s	225.00
Omega, Chronograph, Porcelain Dial, 2 Subsidiary Dials, 18K Yellow Gold	1150.00
Open Face, Minute Repeating, Wolf Tooth Wind, 18K Gold, c.1900	2475.00
Patek Philippe, 18K Gold, Leather Case, c.1916	2100.00
Patek Philippe, Arabic Chapters, White Enamel Dial, Signed, 18K Gold	2905.00
Patek Philippe, Gold Filled Case, Pocket	968.00
Patek Philippe, Hunter Case, Regulator, Diamond End Stone, c.1900	6325.00
Patek Philippe, Stainless Steel, 18 Jewel, c.1920	1100.00
Patek Philippe, Woman's, Jeweled Movement, Porcelain Dial, Jeweled Holder	3995.00
Piaget Polo, Quartz Movement, Gold Links & Bars Bracelet, 18K Gold	7150.00
Purse, Movado, Day, Date & Moon Phase, Leather Case, c.1950	550.00
Renfer–Abrecht, Alarm, Luminescent Hands, Sweep Second, Pocket	95.00
Rockford, D. P. Richards, Key Wind	250.00
Rockford, Key Wind, Hunting Case, Coin Silver, 1885	95.00
Rockford, Key Wind, Hunting Case, Silver	150.00
Rockford, Key Wind, Open Face, Stem Wind, Coin Silver, 1891	95.00
Rolex, Gold Bracelet, Lantern Form Case, 17 Jewel, Linked Gold Bracelet, c.1950	4400.00
Rolex, President, Blue Face, Diamond Marks Dial, Seal	7500.00
Strafford, Trans Pacific, 21 Jewel	75.00
Swiss, 18K Open Face, 15–Minute Repeater, Pocket	1595.00
Swiss, Minute Repeater, Size 16	10000.00
Timekeeper, Railway, Pocket	50.00
Turn–of–The–Century Women Golfers, English, Sterling Silver	2900.00
Universal, Enameled Dial, Verso Day, Digital Date & Month, Open Face	725.00
Vacheron & Constantin, Key Wind, Enameled Dial, 18K Gold	485.00
Waltham, Coin Silver, Victorian, Key Wind, Secondary Dial	132.00
Waltham, Engraved 14K Gold Hunter Case, Pocket	605.00

Waltham, Gold Case	35.00
Waltham, Vanguard, 23 Jewel	275.00 To 325.00
Waltham, Woman's, 14K Gold Hunting Case, Ornate Floral	275.00
Waltham, Woman's, Hunting Case, 18K Gold, 1889	550.00
William Hilbert, Second Hand, Separate Dial	50.00

WATERFORD type glass resembles the famous glass made from 1783 to 1851 in the Waterford Glass Works in Ireland. It is a clear glass that was often decorated by cutting. Modern glass is being made again in Waterford, Ireland, and is marketed under the name *Waterford*.

Chess Set, Crystal, Box, 1970	6900.00
Decanter, Stopper, 6 5/8 In.	105.00
Humidor	140.00
Jam Pot, Lid	50.00
Liqueur Set, Decanter & 4 Glasses	110.00
Vase, Foliate, Diamond & Fluted Design, 10 In.	100.00

WATT family members bought the Globe pottery of Crooksville, Ohio, in 1922. They made pottery mixing bowls and dishes of the type made by Globe. In 1935 they changed the production and made the pieces with the freehand decorations that are popular with collectors today. Apple, Starflower, Rooster, Red & Blue Tulip, and Autumn Foliage are the best-known patterns. Apple, the most popular pattern, can be dated from the leaves. Originally, the apples had three leaves; after 1958 two leaves were used. The plant closed in 1965. For more information, see *Kovels' Depression Glass & American Dinnerware Price List.*

Bean Pot, Apple	100.00
Bean Pot, Cover, Apple, No. 76	150.00
Bean Pot, Cover, Peedeeco	15.00
Bean Pot, Teardrop, Red	100.00
Berry Bowl, Starflower, No. 4	15.00
Bowl Set, Mixing, Stack of 5	250.00
Bowl Set, Nested, Size 5, 6 & 7, 3 Piece	50.00
Bowl Set, Pansy, Set of 3	125.00
Bowl, Apple, No. 5	25.00
Bowl, Apple, No. 7	35.00
Bowl, Apple, No. 8	45.00
Bowl, Apple, No. 9	55.00
Bowl, Apple, No. 63	40.00 To 65.00
Bowl, Apple, No. 63, Advertising	60.00
Bowl, Apple, No. 65	50.00
Bowl, Apple, No. 74, 5 1/2 In.	35.00
Bowl, Autumn Foliage, No. 7	17.00
Bowl, Casserole, Cover, Apple, No. 601	50.00
Bowl, Cereal, Mexican	38.00
Bowl, Kitch-N-Queen, No. 14	65.00
Bowl, Kitch-N-Queen, No. 7	30.00
Bowl, Kitch-N-Queen, No. 9	40.00
Bowl, Pansy, No. 5	20.00
Bowl, Salad, Apple, No. 65	55.00
Bowl, Salad, Apple, No. 73	130.00
Bowl, Spaghetti	35.00 To 75.00
Bowl, Spaghetti, Cherry	85.00
Bowl, Starflower, No. 8	40.00
Bowl, Tab Handle, Starflower	22.50
Bowl, Tear Drop, No. 7	45.00
Bowl, Tulip, No. 63	48.00
Box, Mixing, Watt, No. 9	25.00
Canister, Coffee, Apple	325.00
Canister, Flour, Apple	325.00
Casserole, Cover, Apple, No. 96	35.00
Casserole, Cover, Apple, No. 600	175.00
Casserole, Cover, Apple, No. 601	65.00 To 95.00

Casserole, Cover, Pansy 85.00
Casserole, Cover, Rooster 95.00
Casserole, Cover, Starflower 75.00
Casserole, Dutch Tulip, Advertising 145.00
Casserole, Pansy, Handles 69.50
Casserole, Raised Pansy, Stick Handle, Individual 125.00
Casserole, Starflower, No. 18 .... 58.50
Cookie Jar, Basket Weave, No. 101, Blue & White 210.00
Cookie Jar, Cover, Policeman 1550.00
Cookie Jar, Esmond 65.00
Cookie Jar, Pansy 120.00
Cookie Jar, Starflower, No. 21 .... 175.00
Cookie Jar, Tulip, No. 80 .... 325.00
Cracker Jar, Crosshatch Pansy, No. 21 .... 180.00
Creamer, Apple, No. 62 .... 45.00 To 68.00
Creamer, Rooster, No. 62 .... 40.00
Creamer, Starflower, No. 62 .... 60.00
Crock, Cover, Kla–Ham, 1 Handle, Round 30.00
Cup & Saucer, Starflower, Pink, Green Ground 200.00
Dispenser, Iced Tea, Lid 125.00
Ice Bucket, Apple 300.00
Ice Bucket, Kitch–N–Queen 45.00
Jar, Grease, Starflower 60.00
Mixing Bowl, Apple, No. 601 .... 50.00
Mixing Bowl, Kitch–N–Queen, No. 12 .... 65.00
Mixing Bowl, No. 9 .... 25.00
Mug, Apple, No. 121 .... 200.00
Mug, Poinsettia, No. 501 .... 85.00 To 95.00
Mug, Starflower, No. 501 .... 85.00 To 125.00
Pie Plate, Apple, Akron, Iowa 95.00
Pie Plate, No. 33, Advertising 90.00
Pie Plate, Renville, Minn. 70.00
Pie Plate, Starflower, Advertising 90.00
Pitcher, American Bud, Red, No. 15 .... 35.00
Pitcher, Apple, No. 15, Advertising 60.00
Pitcher, Apple, No. 16 .... 60.00 To 70.00
Pitcher, Apple, No. 17 .... 190.00
Pitcher, Apple, No. 17, Ice Lip 220.00
Pitcher, Apple, Refrigerator 350.00
Pitcher, Autumn Foliage, No. 16 .... 30.00
Pitcher, Bleeding Heart, No. 15 .... 35.00
Pitcher, Cherry, No. 15 .... 45.00 To 55.00
Pitcher, Milk, Apple No. 16 .... 48.00
Pitcher, Rooster, No. 15 .... 80.00
Pitcher, Starflower, No. 15 .... 30.00 To 60.00
Pitcher, Starflower, No. 16 .... 100.00
Pitcher, Teardrop, No. 15 .... 55.00
Pitcher, Tulip, Ice Lip, 8 In. 200.00
Pitcher, Tulip, No. 16 .... 105.00
Pitcher, Tulip, No. 17, Ice Lip 95.00
Plate, Pansy, 6 In. 45.00
Salt & Pepper, Black–Eyed Susan 40.00
Salt & Pepper, Starflower, No. 501 .... 95.00 To 140.00
Sugar, Apple 140.00
Sugar, Rooster, Advertising 225.00
Sugar, Starflower, Handles, Advertising 100.00
Tumbler, Starflower 300.00

WAVE CREST glass is a white glassware manufactured by the Pairpoint Manufacturing Company of New Bedford, Massachusetts, and some French factories. It was decorated by the C. F. Monroe Company of Meriden, Connecticut. The glass was painted in pastel colors and decorated with flowers. The name *Wave Crest* was used after 1898.

WAVE CREST WARE

Box, Baroque Shell Design, Enameled Flowers, 7 1/2 In.		625.00
Box, Blown–Out Aster, Hinged Cover, 4 In.		275.00
Box, Blue Floral, Rococo Embossed, Hinged Cover, Blue, Oval, 5 1/2 In.		485.00
Box, Christmas Holly Design, Iridescent Interior, 7 In.		1450.00
Box, Collar & Cuff, Floral Design, Brass Collar, 6 1/2 In.		950.00
Box, Collar & Cuff, Puffy Mold, Ormolu Collar, Enameled Flowers		975.00
Box, Collar, Floral, Brass Collar, Puffy Mold, 6 1/2 In.		950.00
Box, Embossed Rococo Mold, Floral Design, Oval, Marked, 5 1/2 In.		395.00
Box, Glove, Dark Green Ground, 5 1/2 x 10 In.		1750.00
Box, Hinged, Floral Decoration, Helmschmied Swirl, 4 1/2 In.		300.00
Box, Pink Roses, Rococo All Around, Ormolu, Banner Mark, 4 x 3 In.		270.00
Box, Pink, Blue Embossed, Footed, 6 In.		795.00
Box, Swirl, Hand Painted Purple Flowers, 7 In.		525.00
Card Holder, Marked		700.00
Cracker Jar, Floral		360.00
Dish, Trinket, Marked		300.00
Fernery, Blue Flowers On White, Pink Ground, Blown Out, Liner		375.00
Holder, Photo, Opaque White, Egg Crate, Florals, Ornate Metal Rim, 3 x 4 1/2 In.		335.00
Lamp, Farm Scene, With Children, Hanging		1100.00
Letter Holder, Egg Crate, Red Banner		400.00
Match Holder, Pink Floral, 2 In.		225.00
Pin Dish, Small		80.00
Powder Box, Blown–Out Flowers On Lid, Signed, 4 1/2 In.		350.00
Powder Box, Blown–Out Swirls, Pink Flowers, Signed, 3 1/2 In.		350.00
Powder Box, Hand Painted Flowers On Top, Hinged Lid, 4 1/2 In.		495.00
Powder Box, Hinged Cover, Blown–Out Swirls, Pink Flowers, 3 1/2 In.	250.00 To	295.00
Salt & Pepper, Cat Sitting In Foliage, Spider In Web		195.00
Salt & Pepper, Erie Twist, White		85.00
Salt & Pepper, Pillow, Box		300.00
Saltshaker, Erie Twist, Peach & White		70.00
Saltshaker, Swirl Erie Twist, Painted Flowers, 2 1/2 In.		185.00
Spooner, Opaque White, Floral Transfers All Around, Brass Rim, Signed, 4 In.		95.00
Stand, Jewelry, Pedestal, Florals, Ormolu		125.00
Sugar Shaker, Pink Daisies Front & Back, Cylindrical		295.00
Toothpick, Pink & Yellow Flowers		185.00
Vase, Floral Design, Gilt Filigree Foot, Handles & Rim, 7 In.		200.00
Vase, Pink Apple Blossoms, White Dotting, Ormolu Feet, 6 1/2 In.		325.00
Vase, Pink Florals, Opaque White, Gray, Blue, Rococo On Sides, Red Shield, 16 In.		850.00
Vase, Sea Green Florals, Dark Green Lines On White, Green Ground, Signed		525.00
Vase, Shell Design Back & Front, Ormolu Neck & Handles, 3 In.		250.00
Vase, Spray of Mums, Enameled Foliage, Beaded Rim, 10 In.		595.00
Vase, Sprigs of Pink Chrysanthemum Blossoms, Signed, 9 In.		585.00

WEAPONS listed here include instruments of combat other than guns, knives, rifles, or swords. These are listed in their own sections.

Battle Ax, Tubular Haft, Crescent Form, Steel, 29 In.	140.00
Billy Club, Policeman's, Lead Insert	45.00
Halberd, Armorer's Mark, Riveted Base, European, c.1600, 5 Ft.	850.00
Hitting Stick, Knobkerry, Spherical Head Tapered Haft, Zulu, 21 1/2 In.	97.50
Spear, Iron Blade & Socket, Indonesia, 10 1/2 In.	190.00
Spear, Thrusting, Leaf Shaped Head, Rattan Wrapped Socket, Zulu, 47 In.	125.00
Spear, Zulu Assegai, Expanded Butt, Wrapped In Wire, Shaped Blade, 47 1/4 In.	275.00

WEATHER VANES were used in seventeenth–century Boston. The direction of the wind was an indication of coming weather, important to the seafaring and farming communities. By the mid–nineteenth century, commercial weather vanes were made of metal. Today's collectors often consider weather vanes to be examples of folk art, even though they may not have been handmade.

3 Owls On Branch, Sheet Iron	1200.00
Arrow, Gilded, Mounted On Vertical Rod, 37 In.	120.00
Banner, Cutout Letter A, Gilt Iron	365.00
Bird, Balance On Wing Tip, Copper, Hollow Body, Directionals	4800.00

Blacksmith, With Hammer, Polychrome Black, Sheet Metal, 39 In. 665.00
Bull's-Eye Propeller, Sheet Metal & Iron, 6-Bladed Fan, Flat Tail, 33 1/2 In. 120.00
Bull, On Arrow, Zinc 395.00
Canada Goose, Flying, Pine, Black & White Paint, 40 In. 2750.00
Cod Fish, Carved & Gilt, 37 In. 9025.00
Cod Fish, Copper, Gilded, J. W. Fiske & Co., Turned Urn Base, 33 1/2 In. 3300.00
Cow, Copper Body, Iron Head, 27 In. 1550.00
Cow, Pine, Sheet Copper, Painted, Swell Bodied, 15 1/2 In. 2550.00
Directionals, From Howard Johnson's, Marion, Mass. 750.50
Dove, Flying, Sheet Copper, Stylized Silhouette, Metal Base, 15 1/2 In. 775.00
Eagle, Copper & Gilt, 32 1/2 In. 965.00
Eagle, Copper, Reguilding, 28-In. Wingspan 115.00
Eagle, Flying, On Ball, Arrow Molded Copper, Regilded, 17 x 18 In. 445.00
Eagle, Gilt Metal, 27 In. 605.00
Eagle, Tooled Copper, Floor Stand, 72 In. 100.00
Eagle, Tooled Copper, Green Patina, 65 1/2 In. 250.00
Fish, Open Mouth, Sheet Metal Fins, 47 In. 990.00
Fish, Pine, Mounted On Rod, 8 x 35 In. 1980.00
Fish, Zinc, Gilt Traces, 36 In. 1265.00
Gabriel, Pine, Trumpet, Carved & Painted, Stylized, 7 In. 4400.00
Gabriel, Wings Raised, Sheet Iron, Bullet Holes, 26 x 55 In. 5225.00
Gamecock, Copper, Gilded, Swell Bodied, Foliate Wooden Base, 11 In. 1100.00
Goddess of Liberty, Holding Flag, Copper, Molded, 51 1/2 In. 7955.00
Grasshopper, Copper, Green, Marble Eyes, Stylized, Painted, 23 3/4 In. 1980.00
Henry Hudson's Ship Half Moon, Copper, Inscribed, 44 x 45 In. 1870.00
Herring Seagull, Carved & Painted Cedar, Stelfox, 1950 .... 750.00
Horse & Jockey, Parcel Gilt & Painted Metal, 19th Century 4400.00
Horse & Rider, Sheet Metal, 36 x 24 In. 330.00
Horse, Copper, Original Mount 2750.00
Horse, Flying, Zinc, Copper Mane, Sphere, A. L. Jewell, 27 x 36 In. 8250.00
Horse, Hackney, Copper, Full-Bodied, Early 20th Century, 32 x 33 In. 1375.00
Horse, Hollow Body, Copper, Boston 2400.00
Horse, Prancing, Copper, Zinc, Weathered, 27 x 35 In. 2750.00
Horse, Prancing, Sheet Metal, Black Paint, Silhouette, 20 In. 1650.00
Horse, Racing, With Sulky, Patinated, 31 In. 5225.00
Horse, Running, Copper, 19th Century 2750.00
Horse, Running, Copper, Bullet Hole, 43 In. 825.00
Horse, Running, Copper, Cast Zinc, Gilded, Pyramid Base, Sphere, 55 In. 7150.00
Horse, Running, Copper, Zinc, Traces of Gilt, 23 x 43 In. 8250.00
Horse, Running, Full-Figure, Copper, 33 x 22 1/2 In. 2310.00
Horse, Running, Gilt, 1880 .... 2200.00
Horse, Running, Kretzer, St. Louis, Wind Indicator, White, Copper, 15 In. 210.00
Horse, Running, Original Pole, Copper, 19 x 31 In. 880.00
Horse, Running, Sheet Metal, 48 x 30 In. 330.00
Horse, Running, Zinc, Hollow Bodied, Mustard Paint, 44 In. 4500.00
Horse, Sheet Copper & Zinc, 24 In. 1455.00
Horse, Staff & Directionals, c.1900, Miniature 970.00
Horse, Trotting, Gilded Body, Mounted On Rod, 15 1/2 In. 110.00
Hunting Dog, Silhouette, Polychromed White, Green Base, Pine, 42 In. 250.00
Indian, Kneeling, Bow, Arrow, Sheet Metal, Early 20th Century, 34 x 33 In. 2450.00
Locomotive, Carved From 2-In. Plank, Paint Traces, Folk Art, 38 In. 3850.00
Mariner With Spy Glass, Sheet Metal, America, Painted Black 600.00
Merino Sheep, Copper, America, 28 In. 4135.00
Ox, Zinc & Copper, America, 19 x 34 In. 3850.00
Peacock, Copper, Gilded, A. L. Jewell, On Orb, 25 In. 9350.00
Plume Pen, Sheet Copper, Gilded, 32 In. 2750.00
Quill, Copper, Directionals, c.1880 .... 1600.00
Ram, Copper, Zinc, L. W. Cushing & Co., 26 3/4 In. 6600.00
Rochester Horse, Directionals, Cast Iron, 2 Piece 4620.00
Rooster, Cast Iron, Swell Bodied, Molded Feather, 34 3/4 In. 9350.00
Rooster, Copper, Gold & Green Patina, 38 In. 2000.00
Rooster, Flat Pressed, Wrought Iron, Victorian, Delicate Looking 412.00
Rooster, Sheet Iron, Stylized Silhouette, Red Paint, 19th Century, 17 In. 1100.00

Rooster, Sheet Metal, Painted, Pine Base, 20th Century, 20 1/2 In.	3515.00
Rooster, Standing On Arrow, Copper, Gilded, Swell Bodied, 22 3/4 In.	2475.00
Rooster, Stylized, Sheet Iron Silhouette, Black Repaint, 13 In.	150.00
Rooster, Tin, European, 1910s	595.00
Sheep, Molded Copper, Green Patina, 34 In.	4250.00
Ship, 2–Masted Copper & Sheet Metal, 1885	1028.00
Ship, Hermaphrodite Brig, New England, 1930, Wood, Metal, 16 x 25 In.	715.00
Ship, Sailing, Pine, Sheet Metal, Black Base, 13 x 22 In.	990.00
Sign, Scroll Banner, Pfllug & Ackle, Sheet Copper, c.1880, 42 x 59 In.	7425.00
Silhouette of Young Boy With Hoop, Dog, Sheet Iron, c.1930, 44 In.	2000.00
Stag, Leaping, Copper, Gilded, L. W. Cushing & Sons, 37 In.	9350.00
Stag, Leaping, Harris & Co., Copper, Zinc, 30 In.	9900.00
Stag, Leaping, Standard, Gilt, 28 In.	8525.00
Train, Sheet Metal	225.00
Whale, Iron	2200.00
Witch On Broom, Pat. 1930 On Shaft	275.00

WEBB BURMESE is a colored Victorian glass made by Thomas Webb & Sons of Stourbridge, England, from 1886. They also made Webb Peachblow and many other types of art and cameo glass during the Victorian era. The factory is still producing glass.

Bowl, Butterfly Design, Blossoms, 2 1/2 x 4 1/2 In.	485.00
Bowl, Crimped Turned–Down Rim, Marked	1400.00
Lamp, Fairy, Clarke Insert	1100.00
Lamp, Fairy, Ivy Design, Pyramid, Clarke Insert, 5 3/4 In.	1950.00
Rose Bowl, 8–Crimp Top, 5–Petal Flowers, Foliage, 3 1/4 In.	395.00
Rose Bowl, 8–Crimp, 3 1/4 x 3 1/8 In.	225.00
Rose Bowl, 8–Crimp, Salmon To Yellow, Lavender Flowers, 2 3/8 In.	295.00
Rose Bowl, Enameled Flowers, Small	330.00
Toothpick, Crimped Top	675.00
Vase, 6–Sided, 5–Petal Flowers, 3 3/4 In.	325.00
Vase, Ball Shape, Flared Fluted Top, 3 1/2 In.	265.00
Vase, Blue Floral, Salmon Pink To Yellow, Ruffled, 3 3/4 x 2 5/8 In.	295.00
Vase, Collared, 6–Sided Top, 3 1/8 In.	195.00
Vase, Flowering Vines, 2 Birds, Signed, 12 In., Pair	4250.00
Vase, Folded Over Star–Shaped Top, 3 3/8 In.	200.00
Vase, Folded Over Star–Shaped Top, Blue & White Flowers, 3 1/4 In.	295.00
Vase, Green Ivy & Vines, Dot Round Top, Salmon Inside Neck, 7 7/8 In.	695.00
Vase, Orange Berries, Green & Brown Leaves, 8 1/2 In.	750.00
Vase, Red Bud Flowers, Leaves, 8 1/2 In.	695.00
Vase, Ruffled Flared Top, Ball Shape, 3 1/8 In.	200.00
Vase, Ruffled, 5–Petal Flowers, 3 3/4 In.	300.00
Vase, Ruffled, 5–Petal Flowers, Foliage, 4 1/4 In.	385.00
Vase, Ruffled, 5–Petal Flowers, Leaves, Signed, 3 3/4 In.	300.00
Vase, Ruffled, Pedestal Foot, 4 In.	225.00
Vase, Salmon To Yellow, Flower Petal Top, 2 7/8 In.	225.00
Vase, Salmon To Yellow, Lavender Flowers, Ruffled, 3 3/4 x 2 5/8 In.	300.00
Vase, Star–Shaped Top, Blue & White Flowers, Brown Foliage, 3 In.	300.00
Vase, Wide Flared Ruffled Top, 3 In.	200.00

WEBB PEACHBLOW is a colored Victorian glass made by Thomas Webb & Sons of Stourbridge, England, from 1885. The factory is still in business.

Cuspidor, Ruffled, Chinese Type	395.00
Finger Bowl, Gold Flowers & Branches, 5 In.	425.00
Finger Bowl, Ruffled, Off–White Lining, Gold Flowers & Branches	425.00
Vase, Allover Gold Enameled Branches & Leaves, 5 1/4 In.	295.00
Vase, Applied Acorn & Leaf Design, 7 In.	525.00
Vase, Blackthorn Flowers, Frosted Leaves, 5 In.	450.00
Vase, Blackthorn Flowers, Frosted Leaves, Thorny Base, 5 In., Pair	750.00
Vase, Gold Floral, 3 Handles, 6 1/2 In.	300.00
Vase, Gold Prunus & Dragonfly, 5 1/4 In.	295.00
Vase, Raised Gold Bird On Gold Branches, Signed, 6 In.	335.00
Vase, Rose To Creamy Pink, Gold Floral, Leaves, Cream Lining, 7 In.	550.00

♦ ♦ ♦ ♦ ♦ ♦ ♦ ♦ ♦ ♦ ♦ ♦ ♦ ♦ ♦ ♦ ♦ ♦ ♦ ♦

A dating tip for bottle collectors: The words "Federal Law forbids sale or re-use of this bottle" were used on liquor bottles from 1933 to 1964.

♦ ♦ ♦ ♦ ♦ ♦ ♦ ♦ ♦ ♦ ♦ ♦ ♦ ♦ ♦ ♦ ♦ ♦ ♦ ♦

Webb, Perfume Bottle, Red,
Fuchsia Blossoms, Silver Rim, 4 In.

Vase, Vines & Beetle, 6 In. 465.00

Webb glasswares which are not the Burmese or Peachblow listed above are included here.

Bowl, Cameo, Emerald Green Ruffle, Daisies, Blackberry Design, 2 1/2 In. 1650.00
Bowl, Coralene, White Drape Design, Black Spots Interior 100.00
Bowl, Gold Prunus, Brown, Cream Lining, Tricorner Shape, 2 1/2 x 3 In. 295.00
Bride's Bowl, Gold Mother-of-Pearl, Pink Lining, Cupids Pedestal 1950.00
Bride's Bowl, Holder, Opaque White To Deep Fuchsia, Scalloped, 11 1/2 In. 175.00
Candlestick, Daisies & Leaf Design, Numbered, 12 In., Pair 350.00
Compote, Cameo, Cranberry Cut To Frosted White, Signed 125.00
Cup, Rainbow, Frosted Handle, Signed, 2 1/2 In. 40.00
Decanter, Red & White Grape & Vine, 7 1/2 In. 440.00
Ewer, Light Blue, Applied Design, 8 1/2 In. 50.00
Fairy Lamp, Enameled Peachblow Shade, Gold Plated Stand, With Goat, Ornate 1600.00
Perfume Bottle, Blue & White Floral, Butterfly, Lay Down, 3 1/2 In. 1045.00
Perfume Bottle, Cameo, Ball-Form, Red, White, Fuchsia Blossoms, 6 In. 1825.00
Perfume Bottle, Cameo, Dolphin, Yellow Body, Swimming Fish, 4 1/4 In. 4950.00
Perfume Bottle, Cameo, Elongated Lay-Down Bottle, Blossoms, Buds, 11 In. 2300.00
Perfume Bottle, Cameo, Teardrop-Form, Multiblossomed Floral Spray, 4 In. 1750.00
Perfume Bottle, Fish, Diamond Cut Body, Fishtail Cap, 6 1/2 In. 2850.00
Perfume Bottle, Red, Fuchsia Blossoms, Silver Rim, 4 In. ....*Illus* 1650.00
Perfume Bottle, Yellow & White Leaf Design, Butterfly, Lay Down, 10 1/2 In. 2965.00
Pitcher, Water, Light Green To Opalescent, Coralene Birds & Flowers 335.00
Planter Ashtray, Mountain Boys, 8 x 8 In. 175.00
Rose Bowl, Butterfly, White & Yellow, 4 In. 575.00
Rose Bowl, Gold Prunus & Butterfly, Miniature 295.00
Salt, Cut Nude, Blowing Iridescent, Colored Bubbles, Crystal, Signed, 3 x 2 1/2 In. 95.00
Scent Bottle, Cameo, Red Teardrop-Form, Blossoms, Buds, Spring Cap, 3 In. 1055.00
Vase, Blue, White Diamonds, Florals, Signed, 6 In. ....90.00 To 175.00
Vase, Butterflies, Florals & Ferns, Double Handles, 8 In. 3400.00
Vase, Cameo, 2 Exotic Birds, Bamboo Shoots, Leafed Foliage, 9 In. 4400.00
Vase, Cameo, Bright Blue, Oval Body, White Grass, Leaves, Beetles, 7 In. 9350.00
Vase, Cameo, Leafy Vines, Tendrils, Berry Clusters, 7 In. 2750.00
Vase, Fishscale, Gold Band At Top & Bottom, Marked, 4 3/4 In. 475.00
Vase, Flaring Neck, Bronze Glass, 6 1/2 In. 135.00
Vase, Gold & Silver Butterflies, 9 1/2 In. 350.00
Vase, Gold Prunus & Butterfly, Cream Lining, 6 1/2 In. 295.00
Vase, Gold, Silver & White Bird, Yellow Cased, Marked, 9 1/2 In. 415.00
Vase, Ivory Cameo, 3 Medallions, Floral, Bird, Butterfly Design, 8 1/4 In. 3850.00

Vase, Morocco, Blue Daisies, Pale Pink, Yellow	175.00
Vase, Mother-of-Pearl, Quilted Satin, Pink To Fuchsia, Signed, 11 In.	325.00
Vase, Opaque White, Pink & Gold Florals, Brown Leaves & Vines, Signed, 6 x 5 In.	185.00
Vase, Pink To Apricot, Flared, Signed, Bulbous, 11 In.	185.00
Vase, Pink, Satin Glass, Diamond Quilted, Signed, 5 In.	40.00
Vase, Satin Glass, Pink, White Cased, Signed, 7 1/2 In.	85.00
Vase, Tulips, Tapered, Footed, 14 In.	5250.00
Vase, White Clustered Flowers, Tapered, 8 In.	1300.00

WEDGWOOD, one of the world's most successful potteries, was founded by Josiah Wedgwood, who was considered a cripple by his brother and was forbidden to work at the family business. The pottery was established in England in 1759. A large variety of wares has been made, including the well-known jasperware, basalt, creamware, and even a limited amount of porcelain. There are two kinds of jasperware. One is made from two colors of clay, the other is made from one color of clay with a color dip to create the contrast in design. The firm is still in business. Other Wedgwood pieces may be listed under Flow Blue or in other porcelain categories.

WEDGWOOD

Ashtray, West Point, 4 1/4 In.	10.00
Basket, Creamware, Oval Pierced Form, 19th Century, 7 1/2 In.	45.00
Bidet, Creamware, Undecorated, c.1800, 20 In.	220.00
Biscuit Barrel, Horse Design, Bail, Marked, c.1840	400.00
Biscuit Barrel, Tricolor	900.00
Biscuit Jar, Blue Jasperware, White Classical Scenes, Silver Plated Cover, 5 1/2 In.	159.00
Biscuit Jar, Jasperware, Classical Figures, 6 In.	150.00
Biscuit Jar, Jasperware, Silver Plated Top & Base, Marked, 7 In.	225.00
Biscuit Jar, Women, Barrel Shape, Blue & White Jasperware, 6 In.	225.00
Bough Pot, Cover, Pearlware, Green Glaze, c.1780, 12 In.	2100.00
Bowl, Black Jasperware, Dancing Hours, Marked, 9 3/4 In.	660.00
Bowl, Cover, Classical Figurine, Double Handle, Green, 3 3/4 In.	55.00
Bowl, Dancing Maidens, Acanthus Leaf, Black & White, 10 In.	120.00
Bowl, Fairyland Luster, Elves Inside & Out, Marston, c.1925, 3 3/4 In.	885.00
Box, Cobalt Blue, 3 1/2 x 4 1/4 In.	75.00
Box, Jasperware, Green, 2 1/2 x 3 In.	95.00
Box, Royal Wedding, Blue Heart	75.00
Box, Sardine, Blue & Cream	695.00
Bulb Pot, Gilt Floral Orders, Landscape Panel, Marked, 1815, 13 In.	2860.00
Bust, Bearded Man, Black Basalt, Marked, c.1800, 4 1/2 In.	302.50
Bust, Cupid & Psyche, Basalt, c.1820, 8 1/2 In., Pair	3200.00
Bust, Locke, c.1800, 9 In.	1300.00
Bust, Mercury, Black Basalt, Winged Helmet, Basalt Base, Marked, 18 In.	600.00
Bust, Shakespeare, Raised Circular Base, Marked, 13 In.	995.00
Candlestick, Capriware, Terra-Cotta, 8 In., Pair	950.00
Candlestick, Classical Figures, Marked, c.1860, 8 In., Pair	300.00
Chocolate Pot, Classical Figures	295.00
Coffeepot, Cover, Tea Party, Creamware, 19th Century	1870.00
Coffeepot, Tea Party, Black Transfer, Double Entwined Handle, c.1780, 12 1/4 In.	2975.00
Creamer, Basalt, Open Handle, Marked, 18th Century, 3 1/2 In.	77.00
Creamer, Basalt, Souvenir of Quebec, c.1895, 3 In.	95.00
Creamer, Bird & Fan	250.00
Creamer, Classical Figures, White Borders, Marked, c.1860, 6 1/8 In.	250.00
Creamer, Custer's Last Stand	400.00
Crocus Pot, Insert, Blue Jasperware, White Classical Scenes, 7 7/8 In.	170.00
Cup & Saucer, Countryside	8.00
Cup & Saucer, Light Blue	50.00
Cup & Saucer, Terra-Cotta	115.00
Cup, Chocolate, Cover, Floral Finial, Tricolor Diceware, 4 1/2 In.	1760.00
Cup, Stella, Footed, Yellow Luster, Green Scroll, 1925-1935, 4 1/2 In.	110.00
Dish, Cheese, Palm Leaves & Birds Around Dome Cover, Elephant On Top	3400.00
Dish, Luster, Coiling Dragon Center, Square, Marked, c.1925, 8 1/2 In.	357.50
Dish, Moonlight Luster, Shell Shape, Marked, c.1810, 11 1/4 In.	300.00
Dish, Serving, Classical Figures, Marked, c.1860, 9 1/4 In.	225.00
Dish, Yellowware Body, Portrait, Lessore, Oval, c.1865, 7 x 9 In.	1100.00

Figurine, Bulldog, Black Basalt, Glass Eyes, c.1917, Marked, 2 3/4 In. 440.00
Figurine, Cleopatra, Black Basalt, Holding Snake, On Rocky Base, Marked, 8 In. 770.00
Figurine, Duck, Marked, 4 In. 135.00
Figurine, Psyche, Nude, Seated On Rocky Base, Marked, c.1840, 8 In. 825.00
Figurine, Sleeping Boy, Black Basalt, 1890s, 5 In. 1980.00
Figurine, Sleeping Boy, Black Basalt, Head On Basket of Fruit, Marked, 4 7/8 In. ... 2100.00
Figurine, Sleeping Boy, On His Back, Black Basalt, Marked, 4 3/4 In. 1450.00
Garden Seat, Stork 1540.00
Incense Burner, Blue Jasperware, Leafy Garlands, 3 Dolphin Supports, 4 3/4 In. 1045.00
Incense Burner, Drabware, 3 Dolphin Feet, 1830s, 5 1/2 In. 885.00
Jar, White, Applied Lavender, Grayish Green Floral Acanthus Leaf Design, 7 In. 400.00
Jardiniere, Classical, Black, Floral, c.1830, 6 In. ....*Illus* 440.00
Jardiniere, Fox Hunt, Dark Blue, c.1895, 8 3/4 In. ....*Illus* 110.00
Lighter, Cigarette, Light Blue 60.00
Mug, Black Basalt, Silver Mounted Rim, Acorn Leaf Relief, Marked, 3 3/4 In. 665.00
Pin, Butterfly Luster, Medallion, Silver Frame, Marked, c.1923, 1 3/8 x 2 In. 300.00
Pin, Ornate Silver Mount, Marcasites, 2 1/2 In. 85.00
Pitcher, Black & White Transfer of Longfellow, Pottery, 6 5/8 In. 135.00
Pitcher, Blue Jasperware, 1910s, 2 1/2 In. 159.00
Pitcher, Crimson Jasperware, Rope Twist Handle, c.1920, 4 1/8 In. 525.00
Pitcher, Pin Box, Tray & Chamberstick, Hunt Scene, Etruria, 4 Piece 300.00
Pitcher, White Relief, Dark Blue, Jasper Dip, c.1840, 7 1/2 In. ....*Illus* 330.00
Place Setting, Amherst, 5 Piece 65.00
Planter, Jasperware, Raised Lion Head & Garland, Blue Ground, 8 1/2 In. 385.00
Plaque, Fall of Phaeton, Frame, 1977, 11 3/4 x 19 3/4 In. 1045.00
Plaque, Madonna & Child, Wooden Frame, Marked, c.1982, 13 1/4 In. 385.00
Plate, Black Formosa Transfer, Polychrome Enamel, 9 1/2 In. 105.00
Plate, Calendar, 1971 .... 40.00
Plate, Christmas, 1969 .... 75.00

Wedgwood, Vase, Black Classical Figures, Lion Handles, 1820, 6 3/4 In.,
Pair; Wedgwood, Jardiniere, Classical, Black, Floral, c.1830, 6 In.

Wedgwood, Jardiniere, Fox Hunt, Dark Blue, c.1895, 8 3/4 In.; Wedgwood,
Pitcher, White Relief, Dark Blue, Jasper Dip, c.1840, 7 1/2 In.

Wedgwood, Vase, Snakes,
Beachwork Borders, 1780, 14 1/2 In.

Plate, Countryside, 6 In.	3.00
Plate, Countryside, 10 In.	10.00
Plate, Historical, Blue & White, 8 Piece	165.00
Plate, Hoosac Tunnel, Blue	50.00
Plate, Leaf Border, Purple Grapes, Copper Luster Band, 10 1/4 In., 12 Piece	495.00
Plate, Marietta College, Blue, 1960, 10 1/2 In.	18.00
Plate, Trinity Church, Newport, R.I.	100.00
Plate, Water Lily, Etruria, 10 1/4 In.	35.00
Platter, Charwood, 3984, 15 3/4 In.	185.00
Platter, Mandarin, Blue Transfer, Oval, 16 In.	90.00
Relish, Boat Shape, 2 Attached Pots, Fruiting Vines, Creamware, 13 1/4 In.	525.00
Ring Stand, Blue	60.00
Salt Cellar, Open, Solid Blue Jasper, White Jasper Rim, Dancing Hours, 2 1/8 In.	445.00
Shell, Etruria, White, Large	125.00
Strainer, Creamware, Scrolled Floral Design, Rectangular, 18th Century, 12 In.	75.00
Sugar & Creamer, Cover, Salt Glaze, Facial Design, 19th Century	110.00
Sugar & Creamer, Medici	50.00
Sugar, Cover, Sage Green, Classical Figures, Double Handle, 3 3/4 In.	80.00
Syrup, Classical Figures, Shell Design On Lid, Marked, c.1860	250.00
Tea Set, Green Jasperware, 3 Piece	350.00
Tea Set, Muse, Black Basalt, Oval Medallions of Muses, Marked, 3 Piece	825.00
Teapot, Blue Jasperware, White Figures, 5 In.	65.00
Teapot, Button Finial, White Handle & Spout, Marked, 4 3/4 In.	275.00
Teapot, Capri Ware, c.1875	375.00
Teapot, Classical Figures, White Border, Marked, c.1860, 4 In.	250.00
Teapot, Jasperware, Raised White Figures, Marked, 6 1/4 In.	295.00
Teapot, Lion Finial, Basalt, c.1780, 8 In.	375.00
Teapot, Melon, White, Gold & Black, 8 In.	325.00
Teapot, Pearlware, Molded Leaf Border, Swan Finial, c.1800, 9 3/4 In.	165.00
Teapot, Rosso Antico, Square Handle, Marked, c.1870, 9 In.	440.00
Tile, Calendar, 1903	75.00
Tile, Calendar, 1910	75.00
Tile, Calendar, 1911	75.00
Tile, Calendar, 1918	60.00
Tray, Bridge St., Green, 4 Piece	125.00
Tray, City of London, Black, Rosso, 4 1/2 In.	60.00
Tray, Diamond Shape, Lilac	40.00
Tray, Fairyland Luster, Garden of Paradise Scene, c.1920, 11 In.	2300.00
Tray, Heart Shape, Pink	40.00
Tray, Lily, Fairyland Luster	2310.00

Umbrella Stand, Creamware, Fan Shape, Raised Tassels, c.1880, 24 1/2 In. 335.00
Urn, Dancing Horse, Blue & White, c.1820, 7 In. 700.00
Urn, Water & Wine, Black Basalt, 18th Century, Pair 4070.00
Vase, Black Classical Figures, Lion Handles, 1820, 6 3/4 In., Pair ....*Illus* 1870.00
Vase, Classical Figures, 2 Handles, Marked, c.1860, 7 In. 400.00
Vase, Classical Figures, Perforated Insert, Marked, c.1860, 5 In. 350.00
Vase, Cover, Classical Figures, Dark Blue & White, Handles, 1906, 11 In. 950.00
Vase, Cover, Dancing Hours, Jasperware, Black & White, 9 1/2 In., Pair 1950.00
Vase, Cover, Rainbow, Fairyland Luster 1760.00
Vase, Double Portrait, Cobalt Ground, 8 1/4 In. 250.00
Vase, Fairyland Luster, Jeweled Tree, c.1923, 8 In., Pair 4950.00
Vase, Fairyland Luster, Ruby Firbolg, Squared, 8 In. 4200.00
Vase, Potpourri, Caneware, Rosso Antico Grape Vine Banding, c.1800, 7 1/4 In. 412.00
Vase, Queensware, Powder Blue, Grape Relief, 9 In. 80.00
Vase, Snakes, Beachwork Borders, 1780, 14 1/2 In. ....*Illus* 11000.00
Vase, Undraped Figures, Cobalt Blue Jasperware, 1839, 11 1/2 In. 2800.00
Wine Cooler, Cane, Loop Handles, Grapevine Border, Marked, 9 1/2 In. 770.00

WELLER pottery was first made in 1873 in Fultonham, Ohio. The firm
moved to Zanesville, Ohio, in 1882. Art wares were introduced in 1893.
Hundreds of lines of pottery were produced, including Louwelsa, Eocean,
Dickens Ware, and Sicardo, before the pottery closed in 1948.

LOUWELSA
WELLER

Ashtray, Dachshund, 1920s 85.00
Ashtray, Frog, Coppertone .... 150.00 To 195.00
Basket, Cameo, Beige, 7 1/2 In. 30.00
Basket, Copra, Green, Marked 155.00
Basket, Flemish 40.00
Basket, Hanging, Flemish, 8 In. 150.00
Basket, Hanging, Owl, 5 1/2 x 10 In. 325.00
Basket, Ivoris, White, Label 35.00
Basket, Sicardo, Locust, 5 x 4 1/4 In. 49.50
Basket, Silvertone, 13 In. 75.00
Bowl, Blue Drapery, 4 In. 30.00
Bowl, Burnt Wood, 3 1/2 In. 85.00
Bowl, Claywood, Butterflies, 3 In. 12.50
Bowl, Coppertone, Square Block Handles, Metallic Glaze, 9 In. 14.00
Bowl, Flemish, 9 1/2 In. 110.00
Bowl, Hudson, Pastels, 15 In. 285.00
Bowl, Silvertone, Leaf & Drape Design, Footed, 9 x 4 In. 195.00
Bowl, Squirrel, 5 1/2 In. 105.00
Bowl, Woodcraft, 4 1/2 x 8 In. 185.00
Candleholder, Ardsley, 1920s, 3 In. 38.50
Candleholder, Aurelian, Brown & Yellow Floral, Initial K, 4 In. 115.00
Candleholder, Lavonia, Lavender, Ribbed, 5 In. 50.00
Candleholder, Louwelsa, Yellow & Orange Clover, Brown Glaze, 5 In. 115.00
Candleholder, Monochrome, 1903–1904, 14 In. 44.00
Candleholder, Turtle, Pair 350.00
Candlestick, Arcola, Pair 70.00
Candlestick, Birds & Nests, Green Ground, Marked, 2 1/2 In., Pair 135.00
Candlestick, Creamware, Mauve & Green Design 120.00
Candlestick, Hudson, Butterfly, 9 In. 650.00
Candlestick, Klyro, 10 In., Pair 100.00
Candlestick, Lavonia, 4 1/4 In., Pair 70.00
Candlestick, Louwelsa, Blossoming Flowers, Inlay, 14 1/4 In. 165.00
Candlestick, Louwelsa, Yellow & Peach Clover, Brown Glaze, 5 In. 80.00
Cigarette, Holder, Coppertone 75.00
Clock, Nasturtium Design, Artist K, 11 x 10 In. 605.00
Compote, Noval, Cupped Top, 3–Footed, Fruit Design, 6 In. 65.00
Console Set, Lavonia, 5 Piece 200.00
Console, Coppertone, 16 In. 435.00
Cornucopia, Sydonia, 7 1/2 In. 98.00
Cornucopia, Wild Rose, 6 In. 18.00
Creamer, Louwelsa, Orange & Yellow Flower 110.00

Cuspidor, Claywood 125.00
Dish, Feeding, Strutting Duck 45.00
Ewer, Lonhuda, 10 In. 280.00
Ewer, Louwelsa, Carnation, 3 Spouts, 4 x 5 1/4 In. 155.00
Ewer, Roba, Blue, 11 In. 85.00
Figurine, 3–Headed Dog, Turquoise 85.00
Figurine, Dachshund 70.00
Figurine, Dog, Glossy Eyes, 4 In. 495.00
Figurine, Dog, With Bone Ashtray, Glossy White 165.00
Figurine, Frog, Coppertone, 2 In. 155.00
Figurine, Frog, Coppertone, 6 In. .... 500.00 To 650.00
Figurine, Garden Ornament, Squirrel 2450.00
Figurine, Kingfisher, Brighton, 9 In. .... 192.00 To 250.00
Figurine, Nude, Hobart, White 225.00
Figurine, Nude, Lavonia, 11 1/2 In. 375.00
Figurine, Parrot, Brighton 35.00
Figurine, Pheasant, Brighton, 5 x 7 In. 145.00
Figurine, Woodpecker, Hole In Base 135.00
Flower Frog, Brighton, Double Swans 395.00
Flower Frog, Glendale 95.00
Flower Frog, Lorbeek, Lavender, 5 1/2 In. 60.00
Flower Frog, Muskota, Bird Dogs, Green 75.00
Flower Frog, Warwick 135.00
Garden Ornament, Gnome, On Boulder, 17 In. 6050.00
Garden Ornament, Gnome, Peeking Around Leaves & Flowers, 16 In. ... 5225.00
Garden Ornament, Long–Nosed Elf, Orange Coat, Feather, Marked, 14 1/4 In. 2310.00
Garden Ornament, Squirrel, Hangs On Tree, 13 In. 875.00
Ginger Jar, Cover, Golden Glow, 2 Handles, 1920–1933 .... 88.00
Humidor, Dickens Ware, Captain .... 425.00 To 525.00
Humidor, Dickens Ware, Chinaman 495.00
Humidor, Dickens Ware, Irishman .... 500.00 To 525.00
Humidor, Dickens Ware, Turk 425.00
Jar, Evergreen, Handle, 4 In. 35.00
Jardiniere, Baldin, 8 In. 275.00
Jardiniere, Blue Ware, 7 1/2 In. 155.00
Jardiniere, Cameo Jewell, 8 1/2 In. 250.00
Jardiniere, Eocean, 10 In. 300.00
Jardiniere, Eocean, 7 In. 200.00
Jardiniere, Eocean, Roses, 10 In. 300.00
Jardiniere, Forest, 4 1/2 In. 65.00
Jardiniere, Fruitone, 8 In. 195.00
Jardiniere, Lorber, 10 In. 650.00
Jardiniere, Marvo, Brown, 8 In. 195.00
Jardiniere, Pearl, 7 In. 175.00
Jardiniere, Pedestal, Forest, Matte Green, Brown & Yellow, 29 In. 660.00
Jardiniere, Rosemont, Black, Bluebird, 7 In. 370.00
Jardiniere, Woodcraft, Handle, 9 In. 125.00
Jug, Aurelian, Grape Design 195.00
Jug, Gold Full–Blown Rose, Thorny Branches, Signed, 5 1/2 In. 245.00
Jug, Louwelsa, Jolly Monk, Dark Brown & Green Ground, c.1910, 12 In. ... 220.00
Jug, Louwelsa, Yellow & Orange Floral, Brown Glaze, Artist M. L., 5 x 3 In. 155.00
Kitchen Set, Mammy, 6 Piece 8000.00
Lamp Base, Dickens Ware, Deep Blue Floral 600.00
Lamp Base, Louwelsa, Jonquil 175.00
Lamp Base, Peacock On Fountain, Marked, 11 In., Pair 770.00
Lamp, Aurelian, Cavalier, 15 In. 1325.00
Lamp, Dickens Ware, Yellow Roses, Minnie Mitchell, 11 In. 285.00
Lamp, Louwelsa, Floral, Brown Glaze, Orange Globe, W. M. Stemm, 13 x 7 In. 400.00
Mug, Dickens Ware II, Monk Drinking 450.00
Mug, Dickens Ware, Bearded Indian 395.00
Mug, Dickens Ware, Full Figure of Monk 210.00
Mug, Dickens Ware, Indian, Blue Hawk On Side 375.00
Mug, Dickens Ware, White Cavalier, Blue To Green Shading, 6 In. 275.00

Mug, Eocean, Cherries, Gray To Pink Shading, 5 1/4 In. 150.00
Mug, Floretta 120.00
Pitcher, Art Nouveau, 1903–1904, 12 1/2 In. 137.50
Pitcher, Barcelona, 1920s, 10 In. 66.00
Pitcher, Coppertone, Fish Handle, Lily Pad Spout 550.00
Pitcher, Eocean, Floral, 6 1/2 In. 325.00
Pitcher, Etna, Floral Slip Design, 6 In. 150.00
Pitcher, Louwelsa, 1896–1924, 3 x 5 In. 121.00
Pitcher, Milk, Louwelsa, 4 1/2 In. 110.00
Pitcher, Sicard, Locust, Signed, 6 3/4 x 5 1/2 In. 49.50
Pitcher, Zona, Kingfisher, Green 125.00
Pitcher, Zona, Splashing Duck 165.00
Planter, Roma 45.00
Planter, Woodcraft, 1920s, 4 1/2 x 9 1/2 In. 44.00
Plaque, Abraham Lincoln, President, World's Fair 125.00
Plaque, Sicardo, Spider Mum, 10 In. 1200.00
Platter, Dickens Ware, Advertising Dickens Pottery, Scene 3250.00
Platter, Dickens Ware, Pickwick Papers, Glazed, 12 In. 3575.00
Rose Bowl, Woodrose 85.00
Sign, Squeez–Bag Advertising 1800.00
Smoking Stand, Woodcraft, 5 x 8 In. 200.00
Stein, Louwelsa, Compliments of H. Burg Brew Co., Fouts, 7 In. 495.00
Syrup, Mammy .... 300.00 To 650.00
Tankard, Louwelsa, Hand Painted Corn Design, Marge Hurst, c.1904, 13 1/2 In. 725.00
Tankard, Louwelsa, Indian Portrait, Brown Glaze, 13 In. 440.00
Tile, House & Full Moon Carved, 5 Colors, 4 1/2 In. 600.00
Umbrella Stand, Claywood, 21 In. 650.00
Umbrella Stand, Cornish 95.00
Umbrella Stand, Flemish .... 375.00 To 795.00
Umbrella Stand, Forest Scene, Green 605.00
Umbrella Stand, Ivory, 19 1/2 In. 25.00
Umbrella Stand, Louwelsa, Orange Grapes & Leaves, Ruffled, Ferrell, 22 In. 440.00
Umbrella, Marvo, Silver Green, 19 1/2 In. 350.00
Urn, Burntwood, 1910, 7 1/2 In. 143.00
Vase, Ardsley, Fan Shaped, Double, 9 In. 65.00
Vase, Aurelian, Ferrell, 11 1/2 x 7 1/4 In. 660.00
Vase, Aurelian, Lillie Mitchell, 14 In. 900.00
Vase, Aurelian, Orange & Black Berry, Brilliant Painted Ground, 9 In. 275.00
Vase, Baldin, 10 x 12 In. 350.00
Vase, Baldin, 7 In. .... 75.00 To 99.00
Vase, Barcelona, 15 In. 215.00
Vase, Bedford, Green, Pink & Yellow, On White Clay, Majolica Type, 8 In. 120.00
Vase, Besline, Orange, Mirror Glaze, Etched Grapes & Leaves, 11 In. 605.00
Vase, Blossom, Double Handle, Blue, 7 1/2 In. 45.00
Vase, Blossom, Green, 9 1/2 In. 45.00
Vase, Bonito, Blue Daisy, Flared, Artist, 4 In. 95.00
Vase, Bonito, Daisies, Fuchsias, Roses, 9 x 11 In. 300.00
Vase, Burnt Wood, 7 In. 185.00
Vase, Cameo, Green, Bulbous, 7 1/2 In. 38.00
Vase, Cameo, Pink, Cream, 9 In. 15.00
Vase, Chase, Blue, 7 In. 225.00
Vase, Chengtu, 7 In. 50.00
Vase, Chengtu, 16 In. .... 425.00 To 465.00
Vase, Clarmont, Double Loop Handles, 5 In. 45.00
Vase, Claywood, Spider Web Design, 3 1/2 In. 50.00
Vase, Coppertone, 8 1/2 x 5 1/2 In. 180.00
Vase, Copra, 8 In. 120.00
Vase, Cretone, Black Antelopes, Ivory Ground, 5 3/4 In. 440.00
Vase, Dickens Ware, Checkers Game, 4 3/4 In. 325.00
Vase, Dickens Ware, Dutch Lady, 9 In. 165.00
Vase, Dickens Ware, Indian Chief, A. Vaughan, 10 In. 875.00
Vase, Dickens Ware, Indian Portrait, Lean Wolf, 1900–1905, 7 1/2 In. 660.00
Vase, Dickens Ware, Indian Portrait, Yellow, Orange, Green Ground, ELP, 13 In. 715.00

Vase, Dogwood, 8 In. 185.00
Vase, Dogwood, 12 In. 250.00
Vase, Eocean Rose, Dark Gray, White To Pale Pink Ground, McLaughlin, 13 In. ... 605.00
Vase, Eocean Rose, Wild Rose, 5 In. 250.00
Vase, Eocean, Pink Violets, 4 In. 99.00
Vase, Eocean, Purple & Pink Rose, Gray To White Ground, A. Haubrich, 13 In. 1320.00
Vase, Eocean, Raspberries & Vines, Pinks & Beige, Levi Burgess, 14 In. 775.00
Vase, Etna, 5 1/2 In. 115.00
Vase, Etna, Brown To Yellow Daffodils, Gray, White To Lavender, 11 In. 330.00
Vase, Etna, Thistles, 10 In. 175.00
Vase, Etna, Yellow & Gray Floral, Gray, White To Pink Ground, 9 In. 160.00
Vase, Evergreen, 2 Handles, 10 In. 110.00
Vase, Fairfield, 8 In. 110.00
Vase, Fan, Coppertone, 2 Flower Frogs, 8 In. .... 675.00 To 705.00
Vase, Fan, Forest, 8 In. 125.00
Vase, Forest, 8 1/4 In. 350.00
Vase, Geode, White Star & Shooting Star Design, Marked, 7 In. 660.00
Vase, Glendale, 6 In. 350.00
Vase, Glendale, 7 In. 295.00
Vase, Glendale, 9 In. .... 325.00 To 375.00
Vase, Glendale, 10 In. 525.00
Vase, Greora, Bulbous, 6 In. 90.00
Vase, Hudson, Allover Red Blossoms, 9 In. 299.00
Vase, Hudson, Cherry Blossoms, White, Narrow Neck, 10 In. 310.00
Vase, Hudson, Dogwoods, Blue, Signed, MT, 9 1/2 In. 400.00
Vase, Hudson, Floral, 8 In. 325.00
Vase, Hudson, Irises, Blue Ground, H. Pillsbury, Marked, 9 In. 550.00
Vase, Hudson, Lilies–of–The–Valley, Pillsbury, 8 In. .... 575.00 To 625.00
Vase, Hudson, Red Raspberry, Yellow Flowers, 4 1/2 In. 150.00
Vase, Hudson, Scenic, Winter Landscape, S. McLaughlin, 8 1/2 In. 245.00
Vase, Hudson, White, 7 In. 250.00
Vase, Hudson, Yellow & Pink Florals, 5 1/4 In. 145.00
Vase, Hudson, Yellow Flowers, Blue, Signed MT, 7 1/2 In. 335.00
Vase, Hudson–Perfecto, Purple & Pink Rose, Black Outlined, 10 x 9 In. 825.00
Vase, Jap Birdimal, Fish Surrounded By Bubbles, 8 In. 605.00
Vase, Jap Birdimal, White & Yellow Bird In Flight, Green Glaze, 8 In. 327.00
Vase, Jap Birdimal, White Flying Goose, Pink Glaze, 5 In. 250.00
Vase, Jap Birdimal, Yellow Bird, Green Glazed Ground, 8 In. 360.00
Vase, Kenova, 1915, 5 1/2 In. 302.00
Vase, Knifewood, Peacock, 9 In. 360.00
Vase, LaSa, 4 In. 250.00
Vase, LaSa, 6 1/4 In. 299.00
Vase, LaSa, 9 In. 60.00
Vase, Lavonia, 7 1/2 In. 250.00
Vase, Louwelsa, Brown Glaze, Orange Flower, 4 1/2 In. 80.00
Vase, Louwelsa, Concave Sides, 10 In. 195.00
Vase, Louwelsa, Green Leaf Design, 5 In. 90.00
Vase, Louwelsa, Indian Portrait, Artist A. D., 12 In. 990.00
Vase, Louwelsa, Perfecto Matte, 16 1/4 In. 975.00
Vase, Louwelsa, Poppies, 14 In. 295.00
Vase, Louwelsa, Slip Design of Grapes. M. Lybarger, Marked, 14 In. 880.00
Vase, Louwelsa, Spiraled Concave Sides, Floral, 10 In. 265.00
Vase, Marvo, Green, 7 In. 40.00
Vase, Marvo, Green, 10 In. 25.00
Vase, Nile, Green Drip Glaze, Handles, 7 1/2 In. 150.00
Vase, Pearl, 6 In. 125.00
Vase, Pillow, Louwelsa, 4 In. 77.00
Vase, Pillow, Louwelsa, 7 1/2 In. 250.00
Vase, Raceme, Timberlake, Signed, 5 In. 230.00
Vase, Rochelle, Floral, Shaded Pink, White, Yellow & Blue Ground, 9 In. 190.00
Vase, Rochelle, Pink Cherry Design, Light Blue Ground, 6 In. 165.00
Vase, Roma, 9 In. 65.00
Vase, Roma, 10 In. 50.00

Weller, Vase, Sicard, 8 In.

♦ ♦

If you have a battery-operated 1940s toy such as "Smoking Grandpa," you might want to replenish the smoke-maker when it wears out. Just put a few drops of sewing machine oil into the smoking tube. An electric spark in the toy will cause the oil to smoke, and make the toy appear to puff on a cigarette, pipe, or cigar.

♦ ♦

Vase, Sicard, 5 In.	450.00 To 650.00
Vase, Sicard, 6 In.	395.00
Vase, Sicard, 8 In. ....*Illus*	450.00
Vase, Sicard, 12 In.	2200.00
Vase, Sicard, Clover Design, 5 In.	650.00
Vase, Sicard, Dandelion Leaves, 6 In.	550.00
Vase, Sicard, Gold Floral, Red, Purple & Blue Iridescent Glaze, 9 In.	935.00
Vase, Sicard, Gold Peacock Feather, Dark Red Iridescent, 5 In.	375.00
Vase, Sicard, Iridescent Glaze, 5 In.	450.00
Vase, Sicard, Locust, Signed, 6 1/4 x 3 1/2 In.	44.00
Vase, Sicard, Maroon, Silvery Green Flowers, 6 In.	595.00
Vase, Silvertone, 8 In.	135.00
Vase, Silvertone, 9 In.	195.00
Vase, Souevo, Indian Design, Cream, Black & Orange, Brown Interior, 12 In.	255.00
Vase, Stellar, Blue Stars, Ivory, 5 In.	165.00
Vase, Warwick, 10 In.	225.00
Vase, Wild Rose, 6 3/4 In.	30.00
Vase, Wild Rose, 8 In.	40.00
Vase, Woodcraft, Apples, 8 1/2 In.	75.00
Vase, Woodcraft, Owl Peeking Out of Tree Trunk, 13 3/4 In.	440.00
Vase, Woodrose, Cylinder, 7 In.	50.00 To 59.00
Wall Pocket, Fairfield, 10 In.	135.00
Wall Pocket, Glendale, 12 In.	425.00
Wall Pocket, Owl, 10 In.	225.00
Wall Pocket, Sabrinian	300.00
Wall Pocket, Woodcraft, Owl	325.00
Wall Pocket, Woodrose, 5 1/4 In.	80.00

WESTMORELAND GLASS will be found in the milk glass section.

WHEATLEY Pottery was established in 1880. Thomas J. Wheatley had worked in Cincinnati, Ohio, with the founders of the art pottery movement, including M. Louise McLaughlin of the Rookwood Pottery. Wheatley Pottery was purchased by the Cambridge Tile Manufacturing Company in 1927.

Lamp Base, Brass Base, Bulbous, Electrified, 12 In.	400.00
Vase, Dated 1879, 14 In.	100.00
Vase, Matte Green Glaze, Indented Petals, Double Gourd Form, 12 3/4 In.	1050.00

*Willets, Soup, Cream, Floral, 2
Handles, Belleek, 5 1/2 In.*

Never clean marble with vinegar or lemon juice. Either will damage the marble. If someone spills lemonade on your marble-topped table, wipe it up immediately and wash the area with ammonia and water to neutralize the acid.

WHIELDON was an English potter who worked alone and with Josiah Wedgwood in eighteenth–century England. Whieldon made many pieces in natural shapes, like cauliflowers or cabbages.

Cream Jug, Cauliflower, c.1765, 4 1/2 In.	990.00
Creamer, Cow Form, Pink Luster Spots, 18th Century, 7 3/4 x 5 3/4 In.	495.00
Figurine, Cow, 8 In.	550.00
Plate, Feather Edge Rim, Tortoiseshell Glaze, Brown, Black, Green, 9 In.	220.00
Platter, Tortoiseshell Glaze, Embossed Rim, 10 3/8 In.	300.00
Tea Canister, Cauliflower, c.1765, 5 1/4 In.	660.00 To 990.00
Teapot, Cauliflower, c.1765, 5 1/2 In.	4950.00
Teapot, Green Glazed Leaves, Cream Florets, c.1765, 4 In.	935.00

WILLETS Manufacturing Company of Trenton, New Jersey, began work in 1879. The company made belleek in the late 1880s and 1890s in shapes similar to those used by the Irish Belleek factory. They stopped working about 1912. A variety of marks were used, all including the name Willets.

Hatpin Holder, Gold Scrolling, Enameled Dots, Signed	225.00
Salt, Painted Rose, Pedestal, 1 1/4 In.	50.00
Soup, Cream, Floral, 2 Handles, Belleek, 5 1/2 In. ....*Illus*	135.00

WILLOW, see Blue Willow category

WINDOW glass that was stained and beveled was popular for houses during the late nineteenth and early twentieth centuries. The old windows became popular with collectors in the 1970s; today, old and new examples are seen.

Continental, St. Elizabeth, Stained & Leaded, Frame, 22 x 22 In.	185.00
Courting Scene, Leaded, Stained & Painted, c.1920, 40 x 20 In.	885.00
Foliage Framing Center Panel, Fruit Still Life, Leaded, 23 1/2 x 35 3/8 In., Pair	1760.00
Grate, Bronze, c.1900, 36 x 28 In.	625.00
Kling's Beer, Bubble & Flaked Glass, 20 x 28 In.	635.00
Leaded Glass, Blue, Red & Green Stylized Floral, Prairie School, 28 x 13 In., Pair	275.00
Leaded Glass, Frank Lloyd Wright, From Bradley House	6050.00
Leaded Glass, Pabst Beer, Logo, Jewels In Surround, 37 1/2 x 40 In.	7150.00
Louvered, Arched, Old Green Paint	275.00
Stained Glass, Billy Stevens & Fred Higson, Blue & Gold Beer, 152 x 29 In.	3850.00
Stained Glass, Edelweiss Beer, Cabin Amid Mountains, Hyacinths, 33 1/2 x 37 In.	3850.00
Stained Glass, Fairy, 21 1/2 x 32 1/2 In.	100.00
Stained Glass, Geometric, From Jay, Vt. Building, Blue, Red, Pink, Green	400.00

Stained Glass, Lion Brewing Co., Reverse Painted Logo, Lion Inset, 23 x 23 In. 775.00
Stained Glass, Schlitz, Globe, N. Amer. Continent, Slag Glass Trim, 58 x 31 In. 1100.00
Stained Glass, Ulmer Beer, Lettered Rippled & Slag Glass, 3 x 8 Ft. 550.00
Transom, Reverse Painted Lamb's Head, Center Logo, Jewels, 21 1/2 x 64 In. 1320.00

WOOD CARVINGS and wooden pieces are listed separately in this book.
There are also wooden pieces found in other categories, such as Kitchen.

6 Elephants, Ivory Tusks, Inlaid Toes, Teakwood, Stand, 3 x 18 In. 350.00
Alligator, Glass Marble Eyes, 20 1/2 In. 137.00
Alligator, Shell Eyes, 19 In. 190.00
Bald Eagle, Stylized Detail, 30 In. 275.00
Basket of Fruit, Whitewashed 180.00
Bear, 8 In. 71.00
Bird On Nest, Eagle Or Hawk, Natural Finish, 5 3/4 In. 77.00
Bird, Original Polychrome Paint, Button Eyes, 17 In. 220.00
Blue Jay, Original Paint, Tin Feet, 8 1/2 In. 385.00
Bust, Benjamin Franklin, 19th Century, 8 1/2 In. 935.00
Bust, Woman Smiling, 10 In. 355.00
Cherub, Glass Eyes, Plump Torso, Fruitwood, 9 In. 605.00
Dalmatian Dog, 5 In. 28.00
Deer Head, Real Stag Horn Antlers, Pink, Beige Repaint, 17 In. 220.00
Dog's Head, Black Paint, Glass Eyes, 4 1/4 In. 60.00
Dog's Head, Not Free Standing, Made To Be Applied, Signed, 7 In. 49.00
Dog, Walnut, Gold Repaint, 9 In. 55.00
Dog, Walnut, Worn Dark Finish, 9 1/2 In. 94.00
Eagle, Left Wing Raised, Carved & Gilded, 19th Century, 17 In. 2100.00
Eagle, Painted, Peter Libby, 1975, 84 In. 1300.00
Elephant, Trunk Up, Leather Molded Over, India, 1890, 14 In. 225.00
Emperor Penguin, Hollowed Out As A Bank, Charles Hart, 1930, 17 In. 3500.00
Figurehead, 20th Century, 37 1/2 In. 1100.00
Fish, 4 Trout, Hanging, Original Paint, 15 In. 850.00
Head, Wig Or Hat Mannequin, Worn Paint, Wood Base, 10 3/8 In. 1050.00
Horse, Leather Harness, Labeled Silver, 7 3/4 In. 95.00
Lion, Gray Finish, Bottom Label, 6 In. 110.00
Man In Uniform, Full Figure, Painted, 20 1/4 In. 165.00
Mary & Child, Gessoed & Gilded, 17th Century, 19 In. 710.00
Mask, African, Tunnel Shape, Pierced Eyes 200.00
Mask, Folk Play, 1900 ....*Illus* 275.00
Mask, Folk Play, Fenjin Type ....*Illus* 275.00
Mask, Hannya, Sandalwood ....*Illus* 605.00

Wood Carving, Mask, Hannya, Sandalwood; Wood Carving, Mask, Folk Play, 1900; Wood Carving, Mask, Folk Play, Fenjin Type; Wood Carving, Mask, Southwest Asian, 19th Century

Mask, Mexican Dance, Red, 7 1/4 In. 22.00
Mask, Southwest Asian, 19th Century ....*Illus* 110.00
Plaque, Eagle, Spread Wings, In God We Trust, 1930s, 33 x 60 In. 1380.00
Plaque, Profile Bust of A Man, Marked Duke of Wellington, 9 3/8 x 6 3/8 In. 50.00
Punch, Oak, England, 1870 .... 3250.00
Rocky Mountain Goat's Head, J. B. Cook, c.1915 .... 475.00
Saint Francis, Gilt Robe, Holding Bible & Christ, 13 In. 1210.00
Saint Peter, Holding A Key, 40 In. 200.00
Santos, Man With Child, 18 1/2 In. 467.00
Shoe, High Button, Red & Black Painted, 3 In. 295.00
Short Man Embracing Tall Naked Lady, 12 5/8 In. 55.00
Soldier, Painted, Blue, Black, White, Mustard, Red, 17 In. 8250.00
Stand, Plant, Mahogany, Stork Design, 1860, 6 In. 1850.00
Tiger, Painted, 13 In. 192.00
Whippet, Gilt Collar, Seated On Gilt Base, Silver–Gilt, 31 In., Pair 1980.00
Woman, Bathing Suit, Original Dark Varnish, Green Paint, Rhinestones, 6 In. 28.00
Woman, Original Polychrome Paint, Blue Dress, 6 1/8 In. 70.00

WOODEN wares were used in all parts of the home. Wood was used for
many containers and tools. Small wooden pieces are called *treenware* in
England, but the term *woodenware* is more common in the United States.
Additional pieces may be found in the Advertising, Kitchen, and Tool
categories.

Bootjack, Fish Shape, Heart Pierced Handle, 23 1/2 In. 440.00
Bottle Stopper, Kicking Donkey 35.00
Bottle Stopper, Kissing Couple 35.00
Bottle Stopper, Sailor Salutes, Nods When String Pulled 15.00
Bowl, Boat Shaped, Oval, Ends Have Cutout Handles, 6 1/2 In. 4400.00
Bowl, Boat Shaped, Painted, 13 3/4 x 23 1/2 x 4 3/4 In. 575.00
Bowl, Burl, 17–In. Diam. 1200.00
Bowl, Burl, Handles, Oblong, 16 3/4 x 4 1/2 In. 1265.00
Bowl, Burl, Oblong, Cutout Handles, 11 3/4 x 16 1/4 x 4 1/4 In. 880.00
Bowl, Burl, Original Red Paint, Swags of Red & Black, 2 In. 357.00
Bowl, Burl, Soft Finish, 14 x 4 1/2 In. 935.00
Bowl, Burl, Worn Finish, 11 1/2 x 4 3/4 In. 770.00
Bowl, Chopping, Carved, Black Painted Trim, 21 In. 605.00
Bowl, Deep, 30–In. Diam. 100.00
Bowl, End Handles, Patina, 15 x 24 3/4 In. 181.00
Bowl, European, Elongated, Metal End Reinforcement, 14 x 35 In. 100.00
Bowl, Hooked Handle, 1890s, 11 1/4 In. 440.00
Bowl, Oblong, Birch, Brown Paint, Shallow, 1 In. 214.00
Bowl, Oblong, Butternut Grained Wood, Geometric Rim, Base Carving, 2 x 4 In. 82.00
Brush, Clothes, Painted Woman Top 5.00
Bucket, Cover, Green Paint, String Handle, 3 1/4 In. 137.00
Bucket, Iron Bands, Wide Wooden Handles, Orange, Green Paint, 10 3/4 In. 85.00
Bucket, Mincemeat, Tin Bands, Lid 25.00
Bucket, Sap, Staved Pine, Bentwood Lap Bands, Large 42.00
Bucket, Stave Constructed, Iron Bands & Handle, 1 Gallon .... 18.00 To 25.00
Bucket, Sugar, Stave Constructed, Metal Bands, Pink Painted Interior, 11 1/2 In. 130.00
Bucket, Sugar, Stave Constructed, Old Blue Paint, 9 3/4 In. 165.00
Bucket, Sugar, Stave Constructed, Red Repaint, Bands, W. M. P., 9 3/4 In. 65.00
Bucket, Sugar, Swivel Handle, 13 3/4 In. 85.00
Carrier, 2 Lidded, Red & Mustard, Turned, Footed 3300.00
Chest, Rosewood, Brass Bound, Design, 15 & 8 Sections, 18 3/4 x 12 3/4 In. 360.00
Chest, Stagecoach, Handwrought Handles, 2 1/2 Ft. 195.00
Cup, Burl, Hand Carved, 2 In. 120.00
Egg Crate 35.00
Firkin, Blue Milk Paint, Handle, 12 x 12 1/2 In. 395.00
Firkin, Large 195.00
Firkin, Original Green & Brown Paint, 10 In. 150.00
Frame, Beveled, Pine, Red Flame Graining, Design, 20 1/4 In. 135.00
Jar, Cover, Basketry, Woven Curlicue Design, 4 In. 80.00
Jar, Cover, Footed, Wire Bale Handle, 2 3/4 In. 605.00

Worcester, Vase, Dr.Wall, Blue,

White Ground, 15 In., Pair

Although paper is acid, ink fades, and insects and light cause damage, it is still possible to preserve paper antiques. Keep paper dry, cool, sealed away from oxygen and ultraviolet light. Mylar plastic bags are the best. Important papers should be deacidified by an expert. Dirt and other damage can be repaired.

Jar, Footed, Wire Bale Handle, 3 1/2 In.	85.00
Jar, Footed, Wood & Wire Bale Handle, 6 1/2 In.	295.00
Jug, Dog Shape, Removable Head, Holes, Black Spots, 3 5/8 In.	93.00
Noggin, Pitcher, Stamped Initials, Old Finish, 6 1/2 In.	100.00
Plaque, 2 Glass Fish, Oval, Paper Label, 14 1/4 In.	93.00
Post Head, Carved, Man & Woman, Ernst Jantach, 1880, Pair	1475.00
Spoon, Burl, 5 In.	165.00
Spoon, Curly Maple, Long Handle, 17 In.	95.00
Spoon, Engagement, Scratch-Carved Bowl, Joined By Wooden Chain, 22 In.	125.00
Spoon, Treen, Bird Handle, Polychrome, Gilt, Russia, 6 3/4 In.	27.50
Traveling Case, Figured, Brass Corners, Fitted, Cologne Bottles, England, 12 In.	302.00
Trencher, 28 1/2 In.	135.00
Trencher, 8 x 8 5/8 In.	300.00
Trencher, Pine, Barn Red, Large	425.00
Watch Holder, Hanging, Hinged Door, Center Glazed Bull's-Eye, 10 1/2 In.	600.00

WORCESTER porcelains were made in Worcester, England, from 1751. The firm went through many name changes and eventually, in 1862, became The Royal Worcester Porcelain Company Ltd. Collectors often refer to *Dr. Wall, Barr, Flight,* and other names that indicate time periods or artists at the factory. It became part of Royal Worcester Spode Ltd. in 1976. Related pieces may be found in the Royal Worcester category.

Basket, Oval Reticulated, Twig Handles, Yellow Ground, c.1765, 9 1/8 In.	775.00
Biscuit Jar, Hop Flowers, Leaves, Gold Trim, 6 x 7 In.	350.00
Butter, Cover, The Fence, Blue & White, Circular, Scroll Handles, Stand, c.1770	550.00
Candlesnuffer, Heads Molded As Jesters, Marked, c.1885, 3 5/8 In., Pair	1450.00
Cup & Saucer, Japan Pattern, Blue Ground, c.1770	415.50
Dish, Exotic Bird, Scalloped, Free-Form Leaves Border, Marked, c.1810, 11 1/4 In.	385.00
Dish, Lettuce Leaf, Blue & White, Tulip Spray, c.1760, 13 3/4 In.	440.00
Dish, Oval, Basket Mold, Floral Vines, Yellow Ground, c.1765, 11 13/16 In.	7700.00
Mug, Bell Shape, Floral Sprigs, Yellow Ground, c.1758, 4 9/16 In.	5500.00
Plate, Blind Earl, Pair	4125.00
Sugar Shaker, Pineapple Pattern, Silver Plated Top, Marked, 6 In.	75.00
Tea Set, Bacchanal, 3 Piece	45.00
Teapot, Chinoiserie, Chinaman Seated At Table, 1765, 5 5/8 In.	885.00
Teapot, Cover, Prunus Root, Blue & White, Top Knob, c.1754, 4 In.	1650.00
Teapot, Japan Pattern, Bird & Floral Designs, Marked, c.1770, 6 1/4 In.	935.00
Teapot, Sprays & Sprigs of Flowers, 1765, 5 In.	440.00
Teapot, Stand, Sepia, Oval	88.00
Teapot, Urn Finial, Blue & Gilt Border, Fluted, 7 1/2 In.	170.00

Vase, Dr. Wall, Blue, White Ground, 15 In., Pair ....*Illus*   4125.00
Vase, Hand Painted Peacock, Cream Ground, 7 In. 295.00
Vase, Peacock, Cream, Scrolling At Neck, Artist, Locke, 7 In. 350.00
Vase, Triple, Bud, Coral To Yellow, Gold Trim, Locke, c.1895 .... 175.00
Wall Pocket, Shell Form, Conch Shell & Coral, 11 In. 165.00

WORLD WAR I and World War II souvenirs are collected today. Be
careful not to store anything that includes live ammunition. Your local
police will tell you how to dispose of the explosives. See also Gun, Sword,
and Trench Art.

WORLD WAR I, Bank, Doughboy 250.00
    Belt, Cartridge Pouch, Australian Army, Buff Leather 40.00
    Booklet, Food Value of Candy, 4 Pages, 6 x 9 In. 5.00
    Cartridge Belt, Doughboy, Canteen, 2 Medical Packs 35.00
    Field Glasses, German Military, Original Case, Busch 60.00
    Gas Mask, Bag, Doughboy, Marked 307 M. G. Battalion 33.00
    Handkerchief, Silk, Souvenir De France, Embroidered Eagle, Crest 15.00
    Helmet, Crash, Flight, Neck Flap, France 1000.00
    Helmet, Germany, Spiked, Gray Plate, 2 Lions, Crown 110.00
    Helmet, Germany, Steel, Leather Strap 55.00
    Helmet, Germany, Steel, Liner, No Chin Strap 55.00
    Knife, Trench, Pewter Grip, 7 3/4 In. 90.00
    Medal, Iron Cross, 1st Class, Germany, 1914 .... 62.00
    Mirror, Trench, Box 11.00
    Pin, Insignia, U.S. Army Soldier, Brass 3.50
    Poster, Hun Or Home, 20 x 30 In. 110.00
    Poster, I Want You For The U.S. Army, James Montgomery Flagg, 40 x 30 In. 1100.00
    Poster, Soldier of Breton, World War I, C. Trubert, 1917, 41 x 30 In. 250.00
    Poster, Women of America Save Your Country, Buy Bonds, 40 x 30 In. 45.00
    Scarf, Silk, Souvenir of France, Lace Border, Embroidered, 24-In. Square 55.00
    Sea Bag, Navy, United States, Marked Unit 15.00
    Shaving Kit, Mirror, Blade Holder, Khaki 15.00
    Swagger Stick, Doughboy Officer 11.00
    Tunic, Doughboy, Canada 57.00
    Tunic, Dress, Marine 78.00
    Uniform, Doughboy, Summer 85.00
    Uniform, Soldier's Pistol, Bayonet, Canteen 632.50
WORLD WAR II, Badge, Wound, Nazi, Silver 25.00
    Banner, Nazi Youth Corps, Swallow Tail, 16 In. 195.00
    Binoculars, Navy, Bausch & Lomb, 7 x 50 In. 125.00
    Binoculars, Russia, Case 125.00
    Blotter, American Insignias, 1941 .... 7.50
    Book, Crusade In Europe, Eisenhower, 1949 .... 20.00
    Book, History & Rhymes of The Lost Battalion, McCollum, 1939 .... 10.00
    Book, Mein Kampf, Hitler, First English Translation, 1941 .... 95.00
    Book, Nazi Soldier's Song, 77 Pages 30.00
    Book, Ration, Stamps, 1943 .... 5.00
    Bottle Top, Milk, Buy War Bonds, Keep 'em Flying, Cardboard, 3 Airplanes 7.00
    Buckle, Belt, Nazi 20.00
    Button, Hitler & Tojo Picture, Pinback 8.00
    Button, Let's Pull Together, Uncle Sam & Hitler 28.00
    Button, Pack Up Japan The Yanks Are Coming 10.00
    Button, To Hell With Hitler 18.00
    Button, Uncle Sam Hanging Hitler 58.00
    Cap, Flight, Fleece Lined 55.00
    Case, Stationery, U.S. Army Soldiers, Hard Cover, 1942 Calendar 5.00
    Chain Saw, Pioneer, Engineers Montreal Contract, Canada, Leather Case 33.00
    Coat, Uniform 15.00
    Container, Moth Flakes, Red White & Blue, 6 In. 10.00
    Dagger, Nazi Storm Trooper, Hanger 275.00
    Dagger, Nazi, S.A. 125.00
    Dagger, Officer's, Nazi, Dull Aluminum Mount, Leather Scabbard, 19 In. 176.00
    Dart Board, Japan 75.00

Filmstrip, U.S. Military Identification, Aeronautics Flash Projector, Box 299.00
Flag, Battle, Nazi, 3 x 5 Ft. 25.00
Flag, Nazi Youth Corps Headquarters, 5 x 4 Ft. 495.00
Flag, Nazi, 29 x 46 In. 95.00
Flight Goggles, United States 120.00
Game, Battle of The Bulge 18.00
Gas Mask, Nazi, Swastika, No Bag 19.00
Hat, Nazi, Political Leader, Visor 250.00
Hatchet, Bomber Survival, British Air Force 20.00
Helmet, Battle, Japan 150.00
Helmet, Camouflage, Italy 85.00
Helmet, German Army, Liner 45.00
Jacket, Afrika, Germany 245.00
Jacket, Blouse, Olive Wool, T-Brass Buttons, 3rd Rank, Size 39–R 33.00
Jacket, Coveralls, Boots, Air Force, Size 38–40 .... 95.00
Knife, German SS, Officer's Model 595.00
Letter, Dachau Concentration Camp, Stationery, Censor Marks, Stamp 80.00
Medal, Good Conduct, Bronze 15.00
Medal, Iron Cross, Nazi, 2nd Class 35.00
Mug, Etched Recording of Allied Campaign Against Nazis In North Africa 20.00
Pants, Deck, Carrier, Navy, Wool 27.00
Pants, Olive Wool, Size 34–In. Waist, 31–In. Length 15.00
Parka Cover, Reversible, Ski Troops, White, Olive 119.00
Pin, American Red Cross Volunteer, Enameled, 1 In. 12.50
Pin, Nazi, Volkswagen, Swastika 25.00
Poker Chips, Nazi, 20 Piece 30.00
Postage Stamp, Hitler 5.00
Postcard, Saipan Japanese Officer, Remarks By G. I. 25.00
Poster, Because Somebody Talked, Dog In Front, 1944, 20 x 14 In. 75.00
Poster, Care Is Costly, Wounded Soldier, Adolph Treidler, 26 x 8 1/2 In. 50.00
Poster, Do With Less–They'll Have Enough, Rationing, 1943, 22 x 27 In. 37.50
Poster, Flying Instruction 110.00
Poster, Keep 'em Shooting, Norman Rockwell, 1942, 27 In. 225.00
Poster, Next Japan, 6th War Loan, Official U.S. Treasury, 20 x 27 In. 50.00
Poster, They Shall Not Perish, Voke, 1918 .... 140.00
Poster, United We Are Strong, 22 1/2 x 16 In. 45.00
Poster, We've Made A Monkey Out of You, Uncle Sam, Organ Grinder, 15 In. 32.50
Poster, Your War Bonds, Stake In The Future, A. Saalberg, 1943, 10 x 14 In. 12.00
Ribbon, Winston Churchill, Citizen of U.S., Act of Congress, 1963 .... 20.00
Scarf, Flier's, U.S. Army Air Corps Patch, White Silk, 42 In. 25.00
Sheet Music, Do What They Do In The Infantry, 254 Infantry Song 9.00
Shirt, U.S.M.C. Devil Dog, Large Bulldog Patch 75.00
Spade, Entrenching, G. I., Folding, 1944 .... 17.00
Stamp, Hitler, With Nazi 1943 Coin 8.00
Stationery, Official V–Mail, 75 Unused Sheets, Box 10.00
Suit, WAC, Green 55.00
Sword, Japanese Officer's, Fish Skin Grip, 37 In. 450.00
Trench Scope, Japan 135.00
Uniform, 9th Air Force, With Battle Ribbons & Sterling Wings 145.00
Uniform, Captain's, German Waffen S. S., Award Loops, Complete 2500.00

WORLD'S FAIR souvenirs from all of the fairs are collected. The first fair
was the Great Exhibition of 1851 in London. Other important exhibitions
and fairs include Philadelphia, 1876 (Centennial); Chicago, 1893 (World's
Columbian); Buffalo, 1901 (Pan–American); St. Louis, 1904 (Louisiana
Purchase); San Francisco, 1915 (Panama–Pacific); Philadelphia, 1926
(Sesquicentennial); Chicago, 1933 (Century of Progress); Cleveland, 1936
(Great Lakes); San Francisco, 1939 (Golden Gate International); New
York, 1939 (World of Tomorrow); Seattle, 1962; New York, 1964;
Montreal, 1967; New Orleans, 1984; Tsukuba, Japan, 1985; Vancouver,
B.C., 1986; Brisbane, Australia, 1988; Seville, Spain, 1992; and Genoa,
Italy, 1992. Memorabilia of fairs include directories, pictures, fabrics,
ceramics, etc.

Ashtray & Crumb Tray, 1933, Chicago	20.00
Ashtray, 1933, Chicago, Chrysler Building, Copper, 3 x 3 In.	7.50
Ashtray, 1933, Chicago, Sky Ride & Fort Dearborn, Brass, 5 In.	10.00
Ashtray, 1934, Chicago, Brass Plated, Stamped Cuckoo Tower, 5 In.	12.50
Ashtray, 1934, Chicago, Firestone, Rubber Tire, A Century of Progress, 6 In.	45.00
Ashtray, 1934, Chicago, Tarmur Building, Sky Ride, In Lithograph, 4 In.	15.00
Ashtray, 1964, New York, Unisphere, Composition	28.00
Badge, 1893, Chicago, Ferris Wheel, Gold Color	35.00
Bandana, 1892, Chicago, Columbian Expo, Pictures of Buildings, Red	125.00
Bank, 1934, Chicago, Canco, Tin	30.00
Bank, 1939, Block Glass, Watch Your Savings Grow With Esso	40.00
Bank, 1939, San Francisco, Trylon & Perisphere, Book Shape	45.00
Blocks, 1891, Columbian Expo, Johnson Toy Co., 30 Piece	385.00
Book, 1904, The Forest City, St. Louis, Pictures	40.00
Book, 1933, Century of Progress Atlas of The World, 108 Pages, 7 x 10 In.	20.00
Book, 1933, Chicago, Official Guide, Century of Progress, 176 Pages, 9 1/2 In.	15.00
Book, 1933, Chicago, Official Pictures, Kaufmann & Fabry, 64 Pages, 7 x 10 In.	20.00
Book, Souvenir, 1934, Chicago, Copyright Curt Teich, 64 Pages, 6 x 9 In.	22.50
Booklet, 1901, Buffalo, Pan-American Exposition, Color, 10 Pages	15.00
Booklet, 1933, Baltimore & Ohio Railroad, Route Map & Schedule, 20 Pages	12.50
Booklet, 1933, Chicago, Bible	7.00
Booklet, 1939, New Hampshire Exhibit, Parrish	75.00
Brochure & Map, 1937, Paris Exposition, English Writing, 2 Piece	32.00
Brochure, 1933, Chicago, Canada From Sea To Sea, Colorful	2.50
Cake Plate, 1939, New York	85.00
Cane, 1933, Wooden, Century of Progress, Sticker & Dated, 10–12–33	20.00
Cards, Playing, 1933, Chicago, Century of Progress	35.00
Cards, Playing, 1933, Chicago, Sky Ride Back, Arrco Playing Card Co.	20.00
Cards, Playing, 1933, Maroon Backs, Comet Design, Western Playing Card Co.	30.00
Cards, Playing, 1934, Official Souvenir, Red, Green, Henry Fenenbock Co.	25.00
Coaster Set, 1934, Chicago, Wooden, Round Indian Box, 6 Piece	35.00
Comics Page, 1934, Chicago, Reynolds Tobacco, Sunday, Full Page	15.00
Compact, 1933, Chicago, Embossed	20.00
Compact, 1968, San Antonio	10.00
Compact, Century of Progress, Chicago, 1933 .... 17.00 To 35.00	
Creamer, 1904, St. Louis	95.00
Cruet, 1893, Chicago, Mother, Sunken Honeycomb, Ruby Flash, Stopper, Small	95.00
Crumb Tray, 1933, Chicago, With Scraper, Silver Plated	25.00
Cuff Links, 1968, San Antonio	15.00
Cup, 1904, St. Louis, Enameled	65.00
Cup, Peachblow, New England, 1893, 2 1/4 In.	132.00
Decal, Luggage, 1939, New York, Unused, 4 Piece	24.00
Doll, 1904, St. Louis, Bisque, Painted Features, Seashells	55.00
Folder, 1939, New York, Young Henry Ford Went To The Fair	5.00
Game, 1964, New York, Box	30.00
Handkerchief, 1901, Buffalo, Pan-Am Expo, Silk, Electric Tower, 20 x 20 In.	38.00
Holder Identification, 1933, Chicago, James Owen Nurseries, Black	12.00
Ice Pick, 1939, San Francisco, Iron, Wooden Handle	3.75
Jackknife, 1933, Chicago, Marbelized Plastic	20.00
Jug, Water, 1939, New York	35.00
Key Ring, 1964, New York	18.00
Key, 1933, Chicago, To The Fair, Peeling Paint, Box	25.00
Key, 1933, Master Lock Co., Keep Me For Good Luck, 4 Buildings, Metal, 2 In.	12.50
Knife, 1933, Chicago, Mickey Mouse On Handle	200.00
Lamp, 1934, Chicago, Chase Brass	55.00
Letter Opener, 1904, St. Louis	68.00
Letter Opener, 1939, New York, Bakelite	20.00
License Plate, 1939, California	15.00
Map, 1933, Chicago, Map of The World's Fair, V. Price & Co.	5.00
Map, 1934, Chicago, Pure Oil Co.	5.00
Map, 1939, New York, Subway	25.00
Map, 1964, New York	5.00

Map, Directions To 1933 World's Fair, Marshall Field	12.00
Match Cover, 1939, New York, Wrigley's Spearmint Gum	5.00
Match Safe, 1904, St. Louis Exposition	50.00
Matchbook, 1933, Fort Dearborn, Marked Chicago World's Fair, 20 Matches	7.50
Medal, 1934, Chicago, Federal Bldg., Brass, 1 1/4 In.	12.50
Mirror, 1933, Chicago, Auto, Rear View, No Glaze, Box	75.00
Mirror, 1933, Chicago, Pocket	50.00
Mug, 1893, Chicago, Columbus Landing 1 Side, Santa Maria Other	110.00
Mug, 1933, Chicago, Ceramic, Nude Female Handle, Green, 6 1/2 In.	40.00
Mug, 1933, Chicago, Ceramic, Sky Ride, Fort Dearborn, Multicolored, 5 In.	25.00
Napkin Ring, 1934, Comet Logo, Gold Outline, Fair Building, 2 x 2 In.	15.00
Padlock, 1904, St. Louis	695.00
Paperweight, 1893, Chicago, Winged Victory	110.00
Paperweight, 1893, Columbian, 3 3/4 x 2 1/4 In.	15.00
Pass, 1893, Chicago, Columbian Exposition, To Irish Village	40.00
Pass, Workman's, 1904, St. Louis, Mechanical–Electric	35.00
Pastry Server, 1939, Silver Plate	45.00
Pendant, 1968, San Antonio, Hemisphere Logo, Rhinestones	5.00
Pig, With Ring Tail, 1893, Chicago, Columbian Expo, Emblem, Silver, 1 In.	125.00
Pin, 1939, Trylon & Perisphere, Porcelain	45.00
Pitcher, 1892, Portrait of Columbus, Flags, Flowers	175.00
Plaque, 1904, St. Louis, Jasperware, Green & White	25.00
Plate, 1904, St. Louis, Lincoln, Weller, 4 1/2 In.	71.50
Plate, 1909, Seattle, Alaska–Yukon Pacific, 8 3/4 In.	95.00
Plate, 1939, New York, 4 Seasons, Autumn Winter	45.00
Plate, 1964, New York, Unisphere, 8 In.	15.00
Postcard Set, 1934, Chicago, 18 Different Scenes	16.00
Postcard, 1904, St. Louis, Temple of Mirth On The Pike, Rotograph Co.	40.00
Postcard, 1933, Chicago, A Century of Progress, Curt Teich, Electrical Building	10.00
Postcard, 1939, Golden Gate Expo	2.00
Postcard, 1939, New York, Firestone Tires	5.00
Postcard, 1939, New York, Jos. Renier Design	8.00
Poster, 1933, Go Chicago, Century of Progress, Cuneo Press, 13 x 19 In.	27.00
Poster, 1938, New York, Official, Art Deco, Staehle, Matted, 9 x 12 1/2 In.	75.00
Poster, 1939, New York, Night At New York World's Fair	25.00
Poster, 1940, Visit The International Stamp Exhib., British Pavilion, Framed	175.00
Poster, 1964, New York, Dr Pepper	20.00
Poster, 1984, New Orleans, Coca–Cola	20.00
Print, 1893, Chicago, Columbian, Watercolor, C. Graham, 9 x 12 In.	35.00
Print, 1893, The Water Gate, Columbian Expo., Chas. G. Curran, 11 1/2 x 16 In.	12.00
Program, 1939, New York, Aquacade, Weissmuller Centerfold	20.00
Puzzle Blocks, 1876, Philadelphia, 5 Scenes, Paper On Wood, Box, 11 x 22 In.	185.00
Puzzle, 1964, New York, Interlocking	38.00
Salt & Pepper, 1939, New York, Plastic, Blue, Orange Base, 1 Piece	30.00
Scarf, 1892–1893, Red Woven, Fringe Honor To Industry, 38 x 21 In.	40.00
Sea Shell, 1933, Raised Letters Chicago Fair 1933, 3 x 2 In.	15.00
Seat, 1939, New York, Folding, Cane	55.00
Sewing Needle Folder, 1933, Chicago, Century of Progress	9.00
Sheet Music, 1939, New York, Yours For A Song	15.00
Snuffbox, 1965, New York, Metal, With Pincher	35.00
Spoon, 1893, Chicago	18.00
Spoon, 1933, Travel & Transportation Building, Female Head, Wm. A. Rogers	10.00
Tea Infuser, 1934, Chicago, Teapot Shape, Blue Enamel, Medallion Date	15.00
Thermometer, 1933, Chicago, Fair Havoline, Tower	29.00
Thermometer, 1939, Coke, 16 x 7 In.	85.00
Tile, 1933, Chicago, Travel Building, Blue On White, 1833–1933, Square, 6 In.	35.00
Tile, Tea, 1904, St. Louis, China	50.00
Token, 1933, Chicago, Don't Worry Club	12.00
Token, 1939	10.00
Toothpick, 1893, Chicago, Metal Boot	45.00
Toy, Policeman, 1939, Japan, Celluloid, Movable Head, Arms	22.00
Tray, 1933, Chicago, Panoramic View of Fairgrounds, Comet Logo, 10 x 7 In.	45.00
Tray, 1933, Chicago, Skyline, Blimp, Airplane, Silver Color, 7 1/2 x 5 In.	15.00

Tumbler, 1893, Chicago, Mary Gregory Style 70.00
Tumbler, 1904, St. Louis, Engraved Fair Scenes, 5 In. 30.00
Tumbler, 1962, Seattle, All Different, 7 Piece 25.00
Tumbler, 1964, New York, Ringling Big Top Circus 24.00
Umbrella, 1933, Chicago, Sunbeam 20.00
Vase, 1939, New York, Trylon & Perisphere, Royal Art Pottery Label, 7 In. 80.00
Waffler, 1933, Chicago, Sunbeam 25.00
Watch Fob, 1915, San Francisco, Panama Pacific, Brass, Black Leather Strap 75.00

WRISTWATCHES came into use during World War I. Wristwatches are
listed here by manufacturer or as advertising or character watches. Pocket
watches are listed in the Watch category.

Advertising, Charlie The Tuna .... 30.00 To 75.00
Advertising, Ernie, Keebler 35.00
Advertising, Hawaiian Punch, Box 65.00
Advertising, Shoney's, Windert, Big Boy 85.00
Advertising, Swiss Miss 35.00
Audemars Piguet, Man's, 18K Yellow Gold, Thin Case, Leather Strap 770.00
Audemars Piguet, Royal Oak, Moon Face, Gold Numeral Markers, 18K Gold 7700.00
Audemars Piguet, Woman's, 18K Yellow Gold, Diamond 2250.00
Baume & Mercier, Dual Time Zone, 17 Jewel, Oval Dials, 18K Gold 2475.00
Benrus, Teckni, Quartz 75.00
Benrus, Woman's, 10K Gold 45.00
Breguet, No. 2990, Silvered Dial, Constant Seconds, 17 Jewel, 18K Gold 4730.00
Breitling, White Face & Bezel, Quartz Movement, Stainless 770.00
Bucherer, Woman's, Bracelet, Silver & Domed Marcasite Lid, 1890–1900 .... 225.00
Bueche Girod, Elongated Oval, Black Roman Numerals, 18K, c.1960 .... 4500.00
Bulova, 14K Gold, 1944 .... 125.00
Bulova, Acutron Space View 225.00
Bulova, Diamond & Platinum, Narrow, 1920 .... 600.00
Cartier, Art Deco, Diamond 9350.00
Cartier, Ellipse, 17 Jewel, Sapphire Crown, Oblong, Gold, c.1975 .... 1870.00
Cartier, Golfer's, 18K Gold, Sterling Silver, 1927 .... 900.00
Cartier, Santos, White Face, Black Numerals, 18K Yellow Gold 5280.00
Cartier, Square–Cut Frame, Manual Wind, Leather Strap, 18K Gold 2785.00
Cartier, Woman's, 18K Yellow Gold 2200.00
Cartier, Woman's, Yellow Gold, Diamond 2420.00
Character, 3 Stooges, A & M, Hollywood 85.00
Character, Alice In Wonderland, 1950s 40.00
Character, Barbie, Blond Swirl Ponytail, Coral Band, Bradley 85.00
Character, Barbie, Clear Plastic Band, Bradley, 1971 .... 45.00
Character, C3PO, Star Wars 55.00
Character, Cinderella, Animated Hands, Box, 1960s 70.00
Character, Cinderella, Bradley, Box 48.00
Character, E.T., 1982 .... 45.00
Character, G.I. Joe, Gilbert, Box, 1966 .... 175.00
Character, Garfield, Box, 1978 .... 60.00
Character, Girl From U. N. C. L. E. 98.00
Character, Gremlins, Gizmo, Box, 1984 .... 55.00
Character, Hot Wheels, 1970s 45.00
Character, Irish Spring 35.00
Character, J. R. Ewing, From Dallas TV Show, 1980 .... 45.00
Character, Jackie Gleason, Ralph Cramden Face, Criterion, 1986 .... 50.00
Character, James Bond, 007, Gilbert, Box, 1966 .... 175.00
Character, Kermit The Frog, Box 48.00
Character, R2–D2, Star Wars 55.00
Character, Snoopy, 1958 .... 45.00
Character, Snoopy, Hero–Time, Original Card, 1968 .... 200.00
Character, Snow White, 1950s 40.00
Character, Spiro Agnew, Box 60.00
Character, Spiro Agnew, Swiss, Box 80.00
Character, Winnie The Pooh, Missing Stem, 1960s 48.00
Character, Wonder Woman, Timex, Plastic Box 55.00

Coronet, 17 Jewel, Pieced Gold Cover, 14K Yellow Gold 270.00
Corum, Bracelet, Peacock Feather Dial, Oval, 17 Jewel, 18K Gold 1430.00
Corum, Rolls–Royce Shape, Dial Beneath Grill, 18 Jewel, 18K Gold 3575.00
Curvex, 17 Jewel, 14K Pink Gold 500.00
Dueber Hampden, 15 Jewel, Lever Set 125.00
Ebel, Man's, 14K Yellow Gold Case & Band 2860.00
Ebel, Woman's, 18K Yellow Gold, Sterling Silver, Quartz 550.00
Elgin, Art Deco, 17 Jewel, Diamond Case, Diamond Links, Cord Band 725.00
Elgin, Pierced Case, Cushion Shape, Bold Numbers, WW I, 7 Jewel 1300.00
Elgin, Woman's, 14K Gold, 6 Diamonds, 17 Jewel 100.00
Elgin, Woman's, Gold Case, 1891 .... 195.00
Glyane, Single Cut & Baquette Diamonds 22.00
Gruen, Curvex, Gold Filled Case & Band, Black Dial, 17 Jewel 250.00
Gruen, Doctor's Watch, White Dial, Raised Numbers, 10K, 15 Jewel, 1930s 2200.00
Hamilton, 17 Jewel Nickel Movement, Silver Dial, Diamond Set Chapters 785.00
Hamilton, 90 Single, Brilliant & Full Cut Diamonds, 14K White Gold 1210.00
Hamilton, Cord Band, 10K Gold 45.00
Hamilton, Woman's, Platinum Iridium, Square Dial, Diamond Clusters 385.00
Hamilton, Woman's, Platinum, Diamond, Hand Wind, Jeweled, Rectangular Dial 495.00
International, Man's, 18K Yellow Gold, Flexible Gold Bracelet 440.00
Jaeger, Tonneau, Silvered Dial, 18 Jewel, 18K Gold, Gold Buckle, c.1930 .... 5500.00
Jules Jurgensen, Woman's, 20 Diamonds, 14K White Gold 750.00
Juvenia, 20 Dollar Gold Coins, Hand Wind, Leather Strap, 18K Yellow Gold 880.00
LeCoultre, Automatic, Engraved Bezel, Leather Band, 18K Gold 330.00
LeCoultre, Outer Ring Date, Month, 18K Gold, 1945 .... 1210.00
Longines, Lindbergh, Aviator's, Sweep Seconds, Steel, 15 Jewel, c.1930 .... 3850.00
Longines, Man's, 14K Yellow Gold, 1950 .... 475.00
Lord Elgin, 23 Jewel, Adjustable To 6 Positions 250.00
Lucerne, Woman's, Enameled Floral Face, Leopard Skin Band 85.00
Lucien Piccard, 14K Yellow Gold, Pearl, Sapphire, 5–Strand Bracelet 963.00
Martel, Chronograph Calendar, Pulsemeter & Moon Phases, 18K Gold, 1945 .... 1980.00
Movado, 14K Gold, Calendar, Second Hand, 1940s 1000.00
Movado, Calendar, Moon Phases, 17 Jewel, 14K, Gold, 1940 .... 2475.00
Movado, Woman's, 14K Yellow Gold, Quartz, Sapphire Crown, Mesh Bracelet 385.00
Ollendorf, 15 Jewel, Box 75.00
Omega, 18K Gold, Band & Watch 1 Piece 4000.00
Omega, Arabic Chapters At Quarter Hour, 17 Jewel, Inscribed, 14k Yellow Gold 110.00
Omega, Calendar, Moon Phases, 17 Jewel, 18K Gold, c.1945 .... 2420.00
Omega, Chronograph, Register, Tachometer & Telemeter, Single Button, 1945 .... 2200.00
Omega, Chronograph, Registers & Pulsemeter, 14K Gold, c.1955 .... 3740.00
Omega, Man's, Flat Link Bracelet, Gold Filled 77.00
Omega, Rectangular, Silver Dial, Yellow Gold Case, 14K, c.1940s 1800.00
Patek Philippe, 18 Jewel, Blued Matte Dial, Square, 18K White Gold 1650.00
Patek Philippe, Cushion, 8 Adjustments, 18 Jewel, 18K Gold, c.1930 .... 4125.00
Patek Philippe, Man's, 18K Yellow Gold, Hand Wind, Jeweled Movement 4400.00
Patek Philippe, Nickel Movement, Luminescent Hands, Leather Band, 18K Gold 3750.00
Patek Philippe, Silvered Matte Dial, Baton Numerals, Platinum, c.1940 .... 6600.00
Paul Ditisheim, Silver Dial, Diamond Numerals, 10% Platinum, Mesh Band 2860.00
Piaget, 18 Jewel, Square Dial, 18K Yellow Gold 330.00
Piaget, Calendar, Self–Winding, 30 Jewel, 18K Gold, c.1969 .... 1760.00
Piaget, Diamond, Flexible Mesh Bracelet, 18K Yellow Gold 2865.00
Rolex, Coin Edge, Porcelain Dial, Skeleton Hands, c.1918 .... 2200.00
Rolex, Man's, 14K Yellow Gold, Stainless, Perpetual Movement, Jubilee Bracelet 990.00
Rolex, Man's, Oyster Movement, Stainless Steel & 14K Yellow Gold, c 1940 .... 1650.00
Rolex, Oyster, Chronograph, Tachometer & Register, No. 3834, c.1940 .... 3575.00
Rolex, Oyster, Perpetual, Day, Date, Self–Winding, 18K Gold, c.1970 .... 6600.00
Rolex, Oyster, Self–Winding, Baton Numerals, 18K Gold, c.1945 .... 2750.00
Rolex, Precision, 18 Jewel, Silvered Dial, 18K Gold, c.1945 .... 3025.00
Rolex, Woman's, Chronometer, Rose Gold 1500.00
Swatch, American Encaustic Tiling Co., Box, Vivid Orange Glaze 110.00
Swatch, Andromeda 65.00
Swatch, Asetra, Metal Band 150.00
Swatch, Betty Lou 55.00

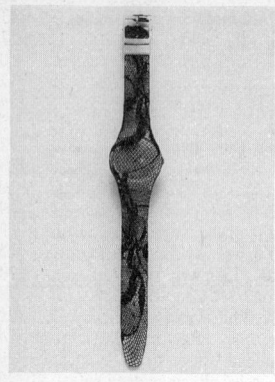

Wristwatch, Swatch,

Velvet Underground, White, Black Stocking

♦ ♦

To clean sleep eyes on a doll, fill an eye dropper with iso-propyl alcohol diluted by half with water. Put the doll on its back and hold the eyes open. Drop the solution into each eye, adding liquid until the eyeball is covered. Open and close the eyelid several times. Turn the doll facedown and let the fluid drain out. Then stand the doll upright, hold a clean cloth against the eyes, and tip the doll until the last of the liquid drains out.

♦ ♦

Swatch, Blade Napkin, Metal Band	75.00
Swatch, Day & Date, 1983	315.00
Swatch, First Series, 1983	790.00
Swatch, Four Flags	1695.00
Swatch, High Moon	225.00
Swatch, High Tech	455.00
Swatch, Johnny Guitar	100.00
Swatch, Keith Haring	357.00
Swatch, Knight of Night, Date	55.00
Swatch, Large Logo, 1983	475.00
Swatch, Ping–Pong, Blue	110.00
Swatch, Tennis Grid, Red, 1985	700.00
Swatch, Ticker Tape	200.00
Swatch, Velvet Underground, White, Black Stocking ....*Illus*	4400.00
Union of Operating Engineers, 25 Jewel, Automatic	125.00
Vacheron & Constantin, 2–Tone Gold Bracelet, 17 Jewel, 18K Gold, 1940	3850.00
Vacheron & Constantin, Square, 17 Jewel, 18K Gold, c.1945	2750.00
Vacheron & Constantin, Subsidiary Seconds, 17 Jewel, 18K Pink Gold, 1945	3300.00
Waltham, Surround of Single–Cut Diamonds, Platinum Bezel, 14K Gold	180.00
Woman's, 14K Yellow Gold, Diamond	220.00
Woman's, Gold, Minute Repeater, Judaic Symbols, Diamond, H. C.	1650.00
Woman's, Lorus, 15th Anniversary, Box	75.00
Woman's, Mido, 4 European–Cut Diamonds, 22 Single–Cut Diamonds	2100.00

YELLOWWARE is a heavy earthenware made of a yellowish clay. It varies in color from light yellow to orange–yellow. Many nineteenth– and twentieth–century kitchen bowls and jugs were made of yellowware. It was made in England and in the United States. Another form of pottery that is sometimes classed as yellowware is listed in this book in the Mocha category.

Bank, Pig	45.00
Batter Bowl, Pouring Lip	26.00
Bed Pan	15.00
Bowl, Cottage Scene, 10 In.	115.00
Bowl, Cup Shaped, White, Blue Seaweed Design, 4 1/4 In.	214.00
Bowl, Molded Rim, Sharpes Warranted Fireproof, 14 x 3 3/4 In.	85.00
Bust, Franklin, Brown Running Glaze, 6 In.	30.00
Canister, 4 Spices & Salt Box, Wheat Pattern	450.00
Chamber Pot, Blue Seaweed, White Bands, Brown Stripes, 1 3/4 In.	190.00
Chamber Pot, White Band With Blue Seaweed Design, Brown Stripes, 9 In.	104.00

Crock, 8 In.	48.00
Custard Mold, Brown Sponge	60.00
Jar, Preserving, 8 1/4 In.	120.00
Jug, Molasses, Dated 1892	125.00
Ladle, 7 1/2 In.	25.00
Lion, Brown Glaze, 6 1/2 In.	72.00
Match Holder, Stag Form, Trimmed In Gold	145.00
Mixing Bowl, Blue Stripes	22.00
Mixing Bowl, Blue Stripes, Set of 4	75.00
Mixing Bowl, Brown & White Stripes, 13 1/2 x 6 1/2 In.	65.00
Mixing Bowl, Cobalt Blue Bands, 11 In.	35.00
Mixing Bowl, White Stripes, 13 1/2 x 5 3/4 In.	55.00
Mixing Bowl, White Stripes, 9 1/2 In.	22.00
Mold, Corn Pattern In Bottom, 7 x 5 1/2 In.	70.00
Mold, Food, Ear of Corn, Phila., 6 1/2 In.	35.00
Mold, Food, Fish, Oval, 7 1/2 In.	65.00
Mold, Food, Grapes	85.00
Mold, Food, Rabbit, 8 1/4 In.	45.00
Mold, Food, Small Sheaf, 5 1/4 In.	35.00
Mold, Grape Cluster, Small	135.00
Mold, Grapes	65.00
Mold, Rabbit	65.00
Mug, 3 Cream Rings	75.00
Mug, Brown Earthworm	750.00
Mug, Seaweed Band, White, Blue, Black, Leaf Handle, 3 3/4 In.	165.00
Mug, White Band, Dark Brown Stripes, 3 3/4 In.	105.00
Pitcher, Blue & White Stripes	385.00
Pitcher, Blue Bands, White & Brown Stripes, Mocha Ground, 7 1/2 In.	440.00
Pitcher, Goddess of Liberty	250.00
Pitcher, Incised Boat, Flowers, Sun, Bird, Bluish Green Glaze, 9 In.	22.00
Pitcher, Man's Head With Tricorn, Cobalt Drip, 5 1/4 In.	60.00
Pitcher, Molded Ribs, Green, Brown Dripping Glaze, 5 5/8 In.	25.00
Pitcher, Stripes & Earthworm Design, Blue, White, Black, 7 5/8 In.	330.00
Rolling Pin	425.00
Salt, Blue Seaweed, Master	400.00
Salt, Brown Seaweed, White Band, Footed, 3 In.	225.00
Saucer, Impressed Design, Square	35.00
Shaker, Stripes In Blue, Brown, White, 4 3/8 In.	385.00
Tankard Set, Buckeye, 7 Piece	300.00
Washboard	795.00

ZANE Pottery was founded in 1921 by Adam Reed and Harry McClelland in South Zanesville, Ohio, at the old Peters and Reed Building. Zane pottery is very similar to Peters and Reed, but it is usually marked. The factory was sold in 1941 to Lawton Gonder.

Basket, Hanging, Moss Aztec	65.00
Vase, Florals, Circles, 5 In.	18.00
Vase, Landsun, 10 In.	170.00

ZANESVILLE Art Pottery was founded in 1900 by David Schmidt in Zanesville, Ohio. The firm made faience umbrella stands, jardinieres, and pedestals. The company closed in 1962. Many pieces are marked with just the words *La Moro*.

LA MORO

Mug, La Moro, Autumn Leaves, 3 Handles, Signed, 5 3/4 In.	150.00
Vase, Bud, Cream Matte Glaze, Brushed Gold Color, Tab Handles, 6 In.	35.00

ZSOLNAY pottery was made in Hungary after 1862 and was characterized by Persian, Art Nouveau, or Hungarian motifs. A series of new Zsolnay figurines with green-gold luster finish is available in many shops today. Early Zsolnay was not marked, but by 1878, the tower trademark was used.

Dish, Flowers & Scroll Forms, Scalloped, 10 1/2 In., Pair	255.00
Figurine, Dog, Weimaraner	70.00

Figurine, Elephant, Green, Miniature 65.00
Jug, Puzzle, 4 Roundels, Castle Mark, 12 x 10 In. 1350.00
Vase, Art Nouveau, Wave Design On Body, Purple & Brown Glaze, 18 1/4 In. 2530.00
Vase, Blue & Silver Iridescent, 1891–1910, 8 1/2 In. 895.00
Vase, Colored Bubbles, Marked, 4 x 3 1/2 In. 440.00
Vase, Double Gourd Shape, 4 Handles, Red & Mustard, Marked, 6 7/8 In. 990.00
Vase, Leaf & Flower, Outlined In Blue & Yellow, 1900, 8 In. 750.00
Vase, Marbelized Blue, Green & Gold, c.1890, 11 1/2 In. 595.00
Vase, Nude, Standing, In Niche, Purple To Green To Copper, Iridescent, 15 7/8 In. 2530.00

This index is computer-generated, making it as complete as possible. References in uppercase type are to category listings. Those in lowercase letters refer to additional pages where the piece can be found. There is also an internal cross-referencing system used in the main part of the book, so, for instance, if you look for a Kewpie doll in the doll category you will be told it is in its own "Kewpie" category. There is additional information at the end of many paragraphs about where to find prices of pieces similar to yours.

THE KOVELS' LIBRARY

KOVELS' Antiques & Collectibles PRICE LIST 1994 Over 50,000 APPROVED PRICES 500 Photographs IN COLOR & BLACK AND WHITE

KOVELS DEPRESSION GLASS & AMERICAN DINNERWARE PRICE LIST

KOVELS' BOTTLES PRICE LIST

DICTIONARY of MARKS — POTTERY and PORCELAIN by Ralph M. and Terry H. Kovel

KOVELS' ANTIQUES & COLLECTIBLES FIX-IT SOURCE BOOK RALPH & TERRY KOVEL

KOVELS' GUIDE TO SELLING YOUR ANTIQUES & COLLECTIBLES RALPH & TERRY KOVEL

KOVELS NEW DICTIONARY OF MARKS POTTERY & PORCELAIN 1850 TO THE PRESENT Ralph & Terry Kovel

KOVELS' KNOW YOUR COLLECTIBLES The comprehensive guide to antiques of the future ••• by America's foremost experts in the field ••• d Terry Kovel UPDATED

KOVELS' KNOW YOUR ANTIQUES The best-selling guide to evaluating, buying, and selling for antiques by America's foremost experts in the field Ralph and Te REVISED

KOVELS' AMERICAN SILVER MARKS 1650 TO THE PRESENT RALPH & TERRY KOVEL

Kovels' AMERICAN ART POTTERY The Collector's Guide to Makers, Marks, and Forgery Histories Ralph and Terry Kovel

Ralph & Terry Kovel AMERICAN COUNTRY FURNITURE 1780-1875 ILLUSTRATED WITH MORE THAN 700 PHOTOGRAPHS

KOVELS' AMERICAN ART POTTERY
The Collector's Guide to Makers, Marks, and Factory Histories

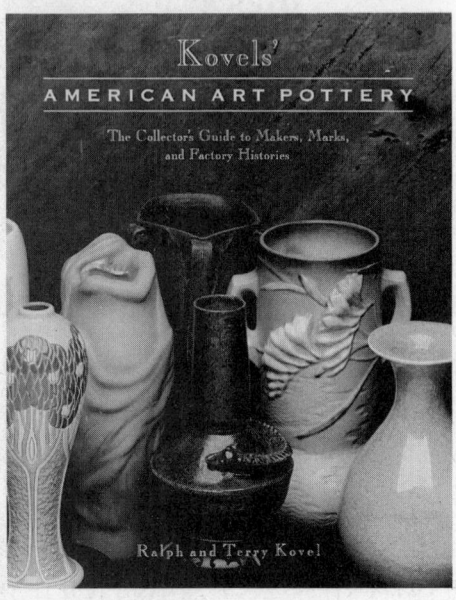

At last! *Kovels' American Art Pottery*, the book you have been waiting for. Here is information on 104 potteries and 95 tile factories. Fabulous color and black-and-white photographs show details of design, lists of makers with the identifying marks, factory marks with dating information, and hundreds of clues to help the collector identify all types of art pottery. More than 700 pictures of art pottery, from the $198,000 green Rookwood "fish" vase to the ordinary Weller bowl worth $50 are included. This is the book for the beginner or serious collector, with extensive history and production information written to aid you in identification of art pottery. Listed here from *A* to *Z* are the major potteries, such as Rookwood, Weller, Ohr, Roseville, Newcomb, Van Briggle, and Dedham, as well as the less well-known works of the North Dakota School of Mines, Arequipa, Avon, Ouachita, Roblin, or Walrath. Also included are tile companies, with marks, pictures, and histories. *Kovels' American Art Pottery* is a beautiful coffee-table color picture book that belongs in every collector's research library.

580128   336 pages / $60.00 hardcover

KOVELS' BOTTLES PRICE LIST
Ninth Edition

Kovels' Bottles Price List is the complete guide to collecting bottles of all types.
More than 10,000 current prices are included in this, the most complete bottle
book available. More than 200 illustrations in full color and black-and-white
aid in identification of bottles. Included are old and new bottles, bitters,
perfumes, figurals, flasks, Avons, Beams, and a host of others. Notes on styles
of manufacturers, lists of bottles magazines and clubs, recommended reading,
and a bibliography for the serious collector make *Kovels' Bottles Price List* the
best listing of current bottle prices available.

589443   240 pages / $14.00 paperback

KOVELS' DEPRESSION GLASS & AMERICAN DINNERWARE PRICE LIST
Fourth Edition

The inexpensive pastel-colored glassware that became popular from 1925 on and the ceramic dinnerware produced during the same period are now attracting collectors in great numbers. Here are the latest and most accurate prices, based on a comprehensive survey of actual sales, shows, catalogs, auctions, and other reliable sources. The more than 6,000 pieces are listed by pattern, along with dates, descriptions, marks, and illustrations. Also included are charts of factories with all the known patterns and their name variations, and a 16-page, full-color quick-reference guide.

584441   256 pages / $13.00 paperback

KOVELS' KNOW YOUR ANTIQUES
Revised & Updated Edition

The best guide in print today for beginning collectors. Learn how to recognize, evaluate, and purchase virtually any type of antique—large or small—like an expert. There is detailed advice about caring for your antiques, identifying fakes, and finding bargains. This best-seller is used by collectors and college classes alike.

578069   368 pages / $15.00 paperback

KOVELS' KNOW YOUR COLLECTIBLES
Updated Edition

The up-to-date illustrated guide to today's most fascinating collecting trends: pottery, porcelain, silver, glass, furniture, toys, and other collectibles made since 1890. These items are not old enough to be officially called "antiques" but are rapidly increasing in value. Included here are more than 1,000 photographs and illustrations, information about marks, value, origin, availability, storage, and buying and selling, plus extensive bibliographies.

588404   416 pages / $15.00 paperback

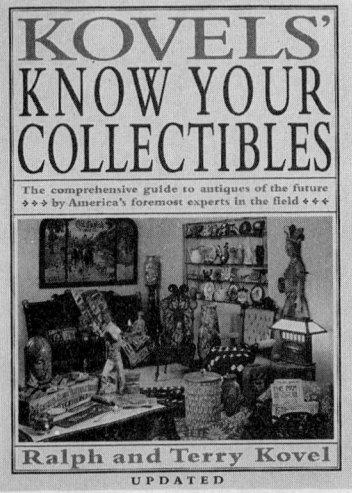

KOVELS' GUIDE TO SELLING YOUR ANTIQUES & COLLECTIBLES
Updated Edition

Learn how to sell your antiques and collectibles for the best possible price. What is the right market for your collection? Should you have your items professionally appraised? Should you sell to a friend? What are the proper procedures for a house sale? How do you rent table space at a flea market? These are just some of the questions that the Kovels answer. There is advice on how to sell more than seventy-five categories of collectibles, from baseball cards, beer cans, carousel figures, decoys, furniture, and glass to music boxes, postcards, radios, toys, and Western art.

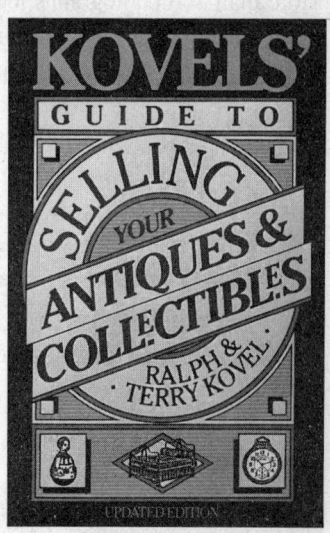

58008X   240 pages / $9.95 paperback

KOVELS' ANTIQUES & COLLECTIBLES FIX-IT SOURCE BOOK

Looking for the parts and services needed to fix your antiques? Want a tail for your carousel horse, a glass liner for the open salt, bellows for the cuckoo clock, or ears for your toy robot? The Kovels list names and addresses of the people and organizations that sell the parts and know how to repair fine antiques and minor collectibles. All sources listed are able to help you by mail or phone.

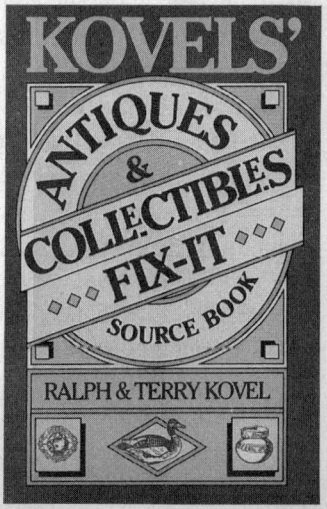

573334   192 pages / $9.95 paperback

K O V E L S

ND ORDERS & INQUIRIES TO: **Crown Publishers, Inc.,
o Random House, 400 Hahn Road
/estminster, MD 21157**
TT: ORDER DEPT.

**SALES & TITLE INFORMATION
1-800-733-3000**

AME _____

DDRESS _____

TY & STATE _____   ZIP _____

LEASE SEND ME THE FOLLOWING BOOKS:

TEM NO.	QTY.	TITLE		PRICE	TOTAL
80652	_____	Kovels' Antiques & Collectibles Price List 26th Edition	PAPER	$14.00	_____
80128	_____	Kovels' American Art Pottery: The Collector's Guide to Makers, Marks, and Factory Histories	HARDCOVER	$60.00	_____
4668X	_____	American Country Furniture 1780–1875	PAPER	$14.95	_____
01411	_____	Dictionary of Marks — Pottery and Porcelain	HARDCOVER	$14.95	_____
59145	_____	Kovels' New Dictionary of Marks	HARDCOVER	$17.95	_____
68829	_____	Kovels' American Silver Marks	HARDCOVER	$40.00	_____
89443	_____	Kovels' Bottles Price List 9th Edition	PAPER	$14.00	_____
84441	_____	Kovels' Depression Glass & American Dinnerware Price List 4th Edition	PAPER	$13.00	_____
78069	_____	Kovels' Know Your Antiques Revised and Updated	PAPER	$15.00	_____
588404	_____	Kovels' Know Your Collectibles Updated	PAPER	$15.00	_____
8008X	_____	Kovels' Guide to Selling Your Antiques & Collectibles Updated Edition	PAPER	$ 9.95	_____
573334	_____	Kovels' Antiques & Collectibles Fix-It Source Book	PAPER	$ 9.95	_____
_____		TOTAL ITEMS	TOTAL RETAIL VALUE		_____

**:HECK OR MONEY ORDER ENCLOSED MADE PAYABLE TO
:ROWN PUBLISHERS, INC.**
r telephone 1-800-733-3000
No cash or stamps, please)

:harge: ☐ MasterCard ☐ Visa ☐ American Express
.ccount Number (include all digits)   Expires MO.   YR.

_____

ignature _____

Thank you for your order.

Shipping & Handling
Charge $2.00 for one book;
50¢ for each additional book.
Please add applicable
sales tax.   _____

TOTAL AMOUNT DUE _____

PRICES SUBJECT TO CHANGE
WITHOUT NOTICE. If a more
recent edition of a price list has
been published at the same price, it
will be sent instead of the old edition.